THE MOTION PICTURE GUIDE

★ ★ ★ ★ ★ ★ ★ ★ ★ ★ ★ ★ ★ ★ ★

1991 ANNUAL
(THE FILMS OF 1990)

WITHDRAWN

BASELINE

New York • Beverly Hills • London • Paris • Toronto • Tokyo

Published by BASELINE II, Inc., 838 Broadway, New York NY 10003

©1991, BASELINE II, Inc.

ISBN: 0-933997-00-0   THE MOTION PICTURE GUIDE (10 Vols.)
ISBN: 0-933997-11-6   THE MOTION PICTURE GUIDE INDEX (2 Vols.)
ISBN: 0-918432-92-8   THE MOTION PICTURE GUIDE
                      1991 ANNUAL (THE FILMS OF 1990)

Printed in the United States
First Edition

1   2   3   4   5   6   7   8   9   10

TABLE OF CONTENTS

INTRODUCTION

The 1991 Motion Picture Annual is the sixth supplement to the *Motion Picture Guide*, bringing you up to date on films released through the end of 1990. This is the first of the *Annuals* to appear under the imprint of BASELINE, which is now publishing and distributing titles formerly associated with CineBooks. We are delighted to incorporate the CineBooks service within our broader operation, and happy that products such as the *Annual* will benefit from access to BASELINE's enormous information resources. For more information about BASELINE, please turn to the end of this book.

It is our goal to provide in *The 1991 Motion Picture Annual*, and subsequent volumes, the most extensive survey of the U.S. film year available. We have covered nearly every film released theatrically in the U.S., as well as numerous straight-to-video titles. Every effort has been made to ensure that our information is as complete and accurate as possible. Given the morass of conflicting source information, however, it is inevitable that mistakes get made; we apologize for any which may have slipped past us, and welcome your comments and suggestions.

One feature we have not carried over from earlier issues of the *Annual* is the CineBooks star rating. This does not mean that we now consider the reviews to be strictly objective; they are, and will continue to be, spiced with entertaining—and informed—opinion. We simply feel that it is reductive, without being particularly useful, to summarize the merits of each film on a numeric scale. If you want to know about the movie, read the review!

The Year in Review

1990 was the year in which the summer "blockbusters"—the mega-budget, action/adventure extravaganzas which had come to dominate annual boxoffice performance—were knocked from their pedestals by surprise, "sleeper" hits such as *Pretty Woman*, *Ghost* and—to the tune of over $270 million*—*Home Alone*. Industry analysts were quick to point out why: While movies about international terrorists, race-car drivers or rogue cops were designed to appeal to the male, 18-to-25-year-old audience (apparently the most movie-hungry section of the population), they were effectively shutting out other demographic groups. The "warm," sentimental qualities of the "smaller" films appealed to a less easily targeted, but broader—and ultimately bigger—audience.

Demographics were not the only reason for the generally poor performance of the summer's "big" films. Several high-budget features suffered from production delays, which led to rushed post-production, which in turn led to shoddily made movies.

Only two of the major summer releases came within reasonable reach of commercial expectations. *Total Recall* combined the talents of Arnold Schwarzenegger, Dutch director Paul Verhoeven, and special-effects wizard Rob Bottin to create a visceral and imaginative science-fiction thriller based on a story by Philip K. Dick; in *Die Hard 2*, Bruce Willis was put through his paces by young Finnish director Renny Harlin, who turned out an entertaining sequel to the smash hit of 1988.

Most of the other sequels which dominated the season, such as *Robocop 2* and *Another 48 Hrs.*, proved poor imitations of their first installments. Warren Beatty's much-awaited—and massively hyped—return as star/director/producer, with the comic-strip-based *Dick Tracy*, generated only lukewarm critical success.

As well as cementing the comeback of Richard Gere, *Pretty Woman* confirmed Julia Roberts as one of the most popular stars of 1990, if not the most bankable actress of the last two decades. Kevin Costner, already a much-liked performer, branched out to reach a wider audience with his smash directorial debut, *Dances With Wolves*. The film won seven Oscars, including Best Picture and Best Director, and proved hugely popular in the international market.

A fair share of the year's prestigious hits came from seasoned directors adding another critical notch to their bows. Martin Scorsese triumphed with *GoodFellas*, a riveting account of life on the edge of the mob featuring superb ensemble performances from Ray Liotta, Lorraine Bracco, Joe Pesci, and Robert De Niro. (De Niro was also effective opposite Robin Williams in Penny Marshall's *Awakenings*, based on the work of Oliver Sacks.) Sidney Lumet returned to the familiar territory of police corruption (*Serpico*, *Prince of the City*) to make *Q&A*, a finely observed account of ethnic tension within the force starring Nick Nolte and Timothy Hutton. Mike Nichols crafted a deftly structured comedy featuring Shirley MacLaine and—in her first *successful* comic role—Meryl Streep, based on Carrie Fisher's semi-autobiographical

Postcards From the Edge. Rob Reiner undertook his second Stephen King adaptation with *Misery*, a well-paced comic horror story which brought James Caan back into the spotlight and earned esteemed stage actress Kathy Bates a Best Actress Oscar.

Several other "old hands" turned in solid, if not ground-breaking, work. Alan Pakula made a rather solemn screen adaptation of Scott Turow's best-selling *Presumed Innocent*, starring Harrison Ford, Bonnie Bedelia, and Greta Scacchi. Woody Allen made a relatively lightweight addition to his *oeuvre* with *Alice*, starring long-time partner Mia Farrow; *Akira Kurosawa's Dreams*, though it contained moments of great beauty, was too uneven and didactic to stand as a summation of his astonishing career. The producing/directing/writing team of Merchant/Ivory/Jhabvala again proved their adeptness at literary adaptations with *Mr. and Mrs. Bridge*, starring the venerable husband-and-wife combination of Paul Newman and Joanne Woodward.

Some of the year's disappointments were also the work of seasoned veterans. Francis Ford Coppola's much-awaited third installment of the "Godfather" saga came off as a passionless pastiche of his earlier triumphs. (Marlon Brando, meanwhile, pastiched his own "capo di tutti i capi" persona in Andrew Bergman's *The Freshman*.) Brian De Palma engineered the most notorious flop of the year, a lifeless, clunking adaptation of Tom Wolfe's *Bonfire of the Vanities*. Peter Bogdanovich failed to recreate the magic of *The Last Picture Show* with his sequel, *Texasville*, which again starred Jeff Bridges and Cybill Shepherd. Bernardo Bertolucci's eagerly anticipated screen version of Paul Bowles's *The Sheltering Sky* took viewers on a long, arid, inconclusive trek across the desert, leaving stars John Malkovich and Debra Winger apparently as puzzled as the rest of us.

1990 also saw the first ripples of what, the following year, would develop into a wave of fresh, provocative movies by black filmmakers. The Hudlin brothers' *House Party* and Charles Burnett's *To Sleep With Anger*—two very different takes on black America—both generated positive critical responses.

Other non-mainstream highlights included two films from the "*wunderkind*" school. Tim "Batman" Burton paid stylish homage to his comic-strip roots and to his childhood idol Vincent Price in the surreal suburban fable, *Edward Scissorhands*; and the Coen brothers made an ambitious, if somewhat *too* self-conscious, attempt to revivify the gangster genre with *Miller's Crossing*. David Lynch's *Wild at Heart*, though not without its moments of high invention, failed to achieve the darkly consistent vision of his earlier *Blue Velvet*. Whit Stillman created a low-budget gem of a social comedy with *Metropolitan*, the hit of the 1990 Sundance Festival.

The independent sector spawned something of a *film noir* revival, particularly with a string of features adapted from the works of newly rediscovered pulp thriller writer, Jim Thompson: Stephen Frears's *The Grifters*, with a stunning performance by Anjelica Huston, and James Foley's *After Dark, My Sweet*, similarly propelled by Jason Patric, stood out. (Dennis Hopper also made an intriguing contribution to the genre, with *The Hot Spot*.)

Among independent directors who attempted to reach a more mainstream market were Kathryn Bigelow, with the stylish thriller *Blue Steel*; John Waters, whose *Cry-Baby* was the first of his films to feature traditional "name" actors (Johnny Depp); and Sam Raimi, whose cartoon-like *Darkman* similarly starred Liam Neeson and Frances McDormand. English *auteur* Peter Greenaway scored his first significant American recognition with the meticulously composed—and X-rated—*The Cook, the Thief, His Wife & Her Lover*.

The producers and/or distributors of two independent films—John McNaughton's *Henry: Portrait of a Serial Killer* and Pedro Almodovar's *Tie Me Up! Tie Me Down!*—were among numerous parties who challenged the Motion Picture Association of America's rating system, contributing in some measure to the introduction of the new "NC-17" category; the first film to benefit from that rating was the Universal release *Henry and June*, Philip Kaufman's account of the relations between Henry and June Miller and Anais Nin.

As in previous years, there were times when it seemed that the artistic quality of a film was in inverse proportion to its commercial success. Barry Levinson's *Avalon*, a poignant account of the immigrant experience followed through several generations, earned less than $15 million at the box-office; *Teenage Mutant Ninja Turtles*, meanwhile, has taken in over $130 million and already spawned its first sequel. *Plus ca change* . . .

* Cumulative figure as of June 1, 1991.

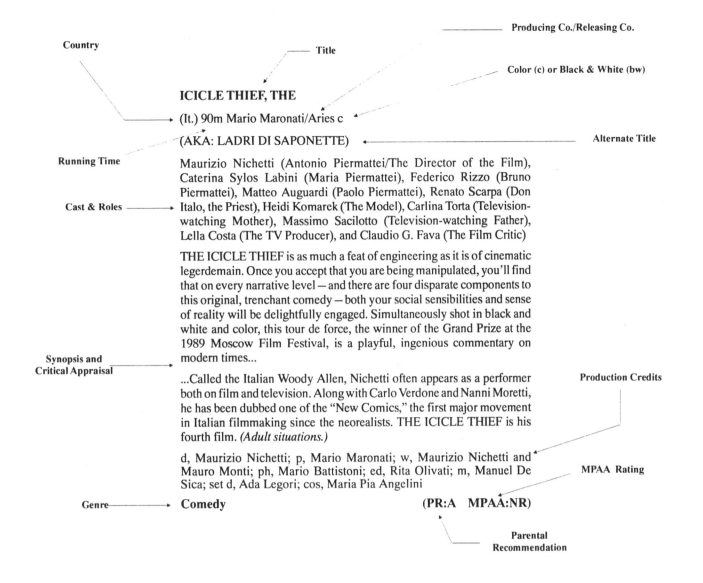

Country ──────────

Title ────── Title

Producing Co./Releasing Co. ──────────

Color (c) or Black & White (bw) ──────────

ICICLE THIEF, THE

(It.) 90m Mario Maronati/Aries c

(AKA: LADRI DI SAPONETTE) ◄──────── Alternate Title

Running Time ──────────

Cast & Roles ──────────► Maurizio Nichetti (Antonio Piermattei/The Director of the Film), Caterina Sylos Labini (Maria Piermattei), Federico Rizzo (Bruno Piermattei), Matteo Auguardi (Paolo Piermattei), Renato Scarpa (Don Italo, the Priest), Heidi Komarek (The Model), Carlina Torta (Television-watching Mother), Massimo Sacilotto (Television-watching Father), Lella Costa (The TV Producer), and Claudio G. Fava (The Film Critic)

THE ICICLE THIEF is as much a feat of engineering as it is of cinematic legerdemain. Once you accept that you are being manipulated, you'll find that on every narrative level — and there are four disparate components to this original, trenchant comedy — both your social sensibilities and sense of reality will be delightfully engaged. Simultaneously shot in black and white and color, this tour de force, the winner of the Grand Prize at the 1989 Moscow Film Festival, is a playful, ingenious commentary on modern times...

Synopsis and Critical Appraisal ──────────►

...Called the Italian Woody Allen, Nichetti often appears as a performer both on film and television. Along with Carlo Verdone and Nanni Moretti, he has been dubbed one of the "New Comics," the first major movement in Italian filmmaking since the neorealists. THE ICICLE THIEF is his fourth film. *(Adult situations.)*

Production Credits

d, Maurizio Nichetti; p, Mario Maronati; w, Maurizio Nichetti and Mauro Monti; ph, Mario Battistoni; ed, Rita Olivati; m, Manuel De Sica; set d, Ada Legori; cos, Maria Pia Angelini

MPAA Rating

Genre ──────────► **Comedy**

(PR:A   MPAA:NR)

Parental Recommendation

INFORMATION KEY

Titles

All entries are arranged alphabetically by title, with articles (A, AN, THE) appearing after the main title. Where appropriate, alternate titles (AKA), Great Britain titles (GB), and foreign-language titles are listed parenthetically.

International Productions

When a film has been produced by a country other than the US, the country is noted in parentheses after the title. Countries are abbreviated as follows: Arg. — Argentina; Aus. — Australia; Aust. — Austria; Bel. — Belgium; Brit. — Great Britain; Can. — Canada; Czech. — Czechoslovakia; Den. — Denmark; E. Ger. — East Germany; Fin. — Finland; Fr. — France; Gr. — Greece; Hung. — Hungary; It. — Italy; Mex. — Mexico; Neth. — Netherlands; Phil. — Phillipines; Pol. — Poland; Rum. — Rumania; Sp. — Spain; Switz. — Switzerland; Thai. — Thailand; USSR — Union of Soviet Socialists Republic; W. Ger. — West Germany; Yugo. — Yugoslavia. Where no country designation appears, the film is a US production.

Producing/Releasing Companies

The film's producing company or companies are listed first, with a slash separarating them from the releasing company or companies.

Production Credits

The credits for the creative and technical personnel of a film include: d (director); p (producer); w (screenwriter, followed by source); ph (cinematographer); ed (editor); m (musical composer); md (musical director); prod d (production designer); art d (art designer); set d (set designer); cos (costumes); spec (special effects); ch (choreographer); makeup; stunts; tech (technical adviser).

Genres

Each film is classified by up to three genres. The genres are: Action, Adventure, Animated, Biography, Children's, Comedy, Crime, Dance, Disaster, Docu-drama, Drama, Fantasy, Historical, Horror, Musical, Mystery, Prison, Religious, Romance, Science Fiction, Sports, Spy, Thriller, War, Western.

Parental Recommendations

The parental recommendations (PR) provide parents with an indication of the film's suitability for children. The recommendations indicate: AA — good for children; A — acceptable for children; C — cautionary, some scenes may be objectionable for children; O — objectionable for children.

Film Reviews

A

ADVENTURES OF FORD FAIRLANE, THE

100m Silver/FOX c

(AKA: FORD FAIRLANE)

Andrew Dice Clay (*Ford Fairlane*), Wayne Newton (*Julian Grendel*), Priscilla Presley (*Colleen Sutton*), Morris Day (*Don Cleveland*), Lauren Holly (*Jazz*), Maddie Corman (*Zuzu Petals*), Gilbert Gottfried (*Johnny Crunch*), David Patrick Kelly (*Sam*), Brandon Call (*The Kid*), Robert Englund (*Smiley*), Ed O'Neill (*Lt. Amos*), Vince Neil (*Bobby Black*), Sheila E. (*Club Singer*), David Arnott, Mark Goldstein (*Club Guys*), Cody Jarrett (*Kyle Troy*), William Shockley, Mark Zuelke (*Punk Gunslingers*), Steve White (*Detective*), Kari Wuhrer (*Melodi*), Delia Sheppard, Kimber Sissons, Monique Mannen, Pamela Segall (*Pussycats*), Hili Park, Gry Park (*Twin Club Girls*), Kurt Loder (*MTV VJ*), Cindy Lehre (*Lydia*), Phil Soussan, Carlos Cavazo, Randy Castillo (*Black Plague Band*), Peter Michael Escovedo, Zina Escovedo, Juan Jose Escovedo, Paul Christopher, J.D. Reilly, Bonnie Boyer (*Club Band*), Consuela Nance, Aurorah Allain, Diane Almeida (*Backup Singers*), Kurt James Stefka (*Bouncer*), Jaz Kaner (*Mixer*), David Bowe, Michael Alan Kahn (*College Boys*), Willie Garson, Ladd Vance (*Frat Boys*), Robert Mangiardi (*Sleazy Guy*), Kristin Pearcey, Lori Pfeiffer, Diana Barrows, Lala (*Sorority Girls*), Lee Lawrence (*Bartender*), Connie Johnson (*Tour Guide*), Jordan Lund (*Amiable Tourist*), Allan Wasserman, Charlie Hawke (*Morticians*), Rita Bland, Kathleen Monica (*Receptionists*), Randy Crenshaw (*Bel Air Party Singer*), John Hammond (*Piano Player*), Tone Loc (*Slam the Rapper*), Hot Tub Johnny West (*Damion Flemm*), Edward DiLorenzo (*Chef*), Sandra Sheeler (*Girl on Ladder*), Edmund E. Villa (*Piano Mover*), Jimmy Zavala, David McLaurin, Lee Thornberg, William "Smitty" Smith, James Dale, John Menzano, and Rick Marotta (*Studio Musicians*)

THE ADVENTURES OF FORD FAIRLANE is a star vehicle for controversial stand-up comedian Andrew Dice Clay, who has risen to fame by adopting a vulgar, homophobic, misogynistic persona—a parody of a Brooklyn Italian ladies' man—and by employing shockingly crude stage methods that appeal to his mostly teenage audience. His humor may not be everyone's cup of tea (indeed, Clay has been banned from MTV, and his appearance as the guest host of "Saturday Night Live" prompted cast member Nora Dunn and musical guest Sinead O'Connor to boycott the show), but it is effective in a base way. In responding negatively to Clay's brand of humor, however, most observers have failed to recognize that the comedian is playing a *character*—an extremely exaggerated parody that could not possibly be taken seriously. The misogynistic attitude and crude language Clay employs are completely over-the-top, and therein lies the humor. Much more disturbing are the attitude and persona adopted by Eddie Murphy, who matches Clay's crudeness with regularity and seems to be sincere in his hatred for women and contempt for homosexuals. Since Clay's audience isn't particularly demanding, adapting his stage persona for the screen wouldn't seem to be a difficult undertaking (just place Clay in the middle of a film with a minimal plot and plenty of women and let him go to town), yet one of the pleasures of FORD FAIRLANE is the surprising amount of care that has gone into its making. Exceptionally well put together by the prodigiously talented Renny Harlin (who also directed DIE HARD 2), and performed and written with style, FORD FAIRLANE is better than it had to be, and it also works as a perfect vehicle for Clay.

A "rock 'n' roll detective," Ford Fairlane (Clay) solves crimes that affect the movers and shakers of the LA music scene. When he's not chasing down perverts obsessed with female rock bands, he's sleeping with as many women as possible. However, Ford's reputation as a rock 'n' roll detective doesn't sit well with him, and he's anything but fond of the adoring teenager (Brandon Call) who hangs out in front of his beach house emulating his every move. Of late, Ford's private detective agency has been faltering: his secretary and former lover, Jazz (Lauren Holly), is unsatisfied with her job and with Ford's treatment of her, his case load is dwindling, and, worst of all, Ford's musician clients pay him in drumsticks and guitar picks instead of money (at one point, Jazz protests that Milli Vanilli have settled their account with a year's supply of bicycle shorts). Nonetheless, Ford's latest case may prove to be his most exciting. After heavy-metal superstar Bobby Black (Vince Neil of the real-life heavy-metal band Motley Crue) is murdered and Ford's old buddy Johnny Crunch (Gilbert Gottfried) is electrocuted, the detective is hired by the mysterious Colleen Sutton (Priscilla Presley) to find a missing girl, Zuzu Petals (Maddie Corman). Although he is initially reluctant, Ford takes the case, convinced that these dramatic events are somehow connected. The clues lead him from the garden parties of rich executives to the bizarre funeral of Bobby Black—where Ford finds Zuzu—and, eventually, to powerful record executive Julian Grendel (Wayne Newton, in a funny turn). Naturally, Ford unlocks the mystery, which involves stolen money, secret stocks, and three coded compact discs that contain all of the answers to the murders.

The film climaxes at a concert where the detective confronts Grendel (who, not very surprisingly, is behind everything) and sets him on fire. In the end, Ford changes his ways and decides to settle down with Jazz and to take responsibility for his teenage buddy.

Strikingly similar to DICK TRACY (all the way down to its "adopted family" ending), FORD FAIRLANE plays as a sort of adult comic book. Based on a character created over 10 years ago by Rex Weiner for a monthly serial that appeared in *New York Rocker* and the *LA Weekly*, the film is essentially a dated detective spoof. The goofy voiceover narration and comic handling of private-eye cliches have been done before, but what sets this film apart from other detective parodies is its attitude. Part star vehicle, part nasty satire, FORD FAIRLANE is a truly schizophrenic film that makes the most of its dual personality. No doubt Clay's participation has much to do with the film's down-and-dirty tone (the nasty portrayal of women and overabundance of foul language are certainly the result of his influence), but the hand of Daniel Waters (HEATHERS), who rewrote James Cappe and David Arnott's original script, is also very much in evidence. Waters' ugly, cynical portrait of LA is the single strongest element of the film. The LA depicted here is populated only by wanton women, empty-headed groupies, greedy power brokers, idiot musicians, and sadistic barbarians (played, in quick cameos, by a swarm of well-known pop icons, including Ed O'Neill of "Married with Children," Robert "Freddy Krueger" Englund, MTV stars Kurt Loder and Kari Wuhrer, and musicians Tone Loc, Morris Day, and Sheila E.). That Andrew Dice Clay is the hero of the film says even more about the morality on display here. Unfortunately, this searing satire of the music business and potent commentary on LA nightlife is marred somewhat by the necessity of adapting Clay's persona for the screen. Tellingly, the film is least successful in the incongruous scenes that attempt to incorporate bits from Clay's stage act into the story.

In the hands of a less assured director, the film's split personality might have been its undoing, but with Harlin behind the camera, the film remains cohesive, sharp, and very funny. Harlin (who reportedly left most of the editing to his crew so he could move on to DIE HARD 2) has once again proven himself to be one of the finest visual stylists in Hollywood. FORD FAIRLANE is only Harlin's fifth film, but he has already defined a style of his own, and his use of the camera is amazingly assured. Full of rich nighttime images and wonderfully lit interiors (shot by DIE HARD 2's cinematographer Oliver Wood), FORD FAIRLANE is a treat for the eyes. Even Clay is photogenic in this movie. The pacing is quick, and the comic-booklike transitions work nicely, but as Harlin proved with DIE HARD 2, his strongest talent is his handling of action sequences. The two best scenes in FORD FAIRLANE are action-oriented. The first is an extended car chase through a graveyard (chock full of necrophilia jokes and rolling corpses), and the second is an outstanding sequence that takes place on the Capitol Records Tower. High above the ground, Ford and Zuzu are pursued down the side of the tower by a group of thugs whom Ford must fight off while trying not to fall. The sequence, which ends with Ford, Zuzu, and the rest of the gang plummeting from the building, involves impressive stunts and imaginative scuffles, and it's all shot in grand style. Harlin utilizes dizzying close-ups of his actors and displays his usual sharp editing style, and the result is a scene that is both deliriously funny and exciting.

FORD FAIRLANE is far from perfect. Long stretches are simply not funny; the misogynistic attitude starts to wear thin after a while; Presley and Englund are terrible; and the plot doesn't really amount to a hill of beans. But there is enough good stuff in the film to make it worth a look. Harlin's direction alone is worth the price of admission, and if you're a Clay fan, you won't be disappointed. Of course, there is something in this movie to offend just about anyone. However, the screenplay does play it safe by eventually backing away from every single "taboo" it *almost* breaks: the corpse Clay jokes about having sex with turns out to be a living woman; a cute Koala bear is found dead, strung up by his neck, only to be brought back later wearing a neck brace. Trying to be both "bad" and "good," the screenplay definitely wants to have its cake and eat it too. THE ADVENTURES OF FORD FAIRLANE is an exceptionally well-made film that is everything you could ever want in an Andrew Dice Clay movie; it's vulgar, tasteless, nasty, cynical, and, at times, very funny. (*Excessive profanity, adult situations, brief nudity, violence.*)

d, Renny Harlin; p, Joel Silver and Steve Perry; w, Daniel Waters, James Cappe, and David Arnott (based on the story by James Cappe, David Arnott and on characters created by Rex Weiner); ph, Oliver Wood; ed, Michael Tronick; m, Yello; prod d, John Vallone; art d, Christiaan Wagener; set d, Charles Breen, Mark Fabus, and Eric Orbom; spec, Chuck Gaspar; stunts, Charles Picerni; cos, Marilyn Vance-Straker; makup, Scott Eddo; chor, Aurorah Allain

Action/Comedy   (PR:O   MPAA:R)

ADVENTURES OF MILO AND OTIS, THE

(Japan) 76m Fuji Television/Columbia c

(KONEKO MONOGATARI)

Dudley Moore (Narrator)

Of all the buddy movies ever made, MILO AND OTIS has one of the most unlikely pairs of friends—a cat and dog that befriend each other on a farm and eventually wander out into the not-so-friendly world. Not a single human being appears on-screen in this delightful live-action entry from Japan. It all starts when the kitten, Milo, decides to take a trip down the river in a box, with his faithful canine chum, Otis, following behind. But soon Otis loses track of his friend, who gets into many adventures. Based on a charming screenplay by Mark Saltzman, this clever children's film contains beautiful nature photography and moments of humor along with many impressive animal stunts. Surely it was no small feat to get bears and dogs, chickens and cats, pigs and cows to work together on-screen. Shot from the animals' point of view and narrated by Dudley Moore, MILO AND OTIS also contains some important messages about friendship and responsibility. The only drawback is that the film tends to drag in spots, but the animal "performances" and the nature scenes are enough to hold anyone's interest, especially that of animal lovers.

d, Masanori Hata; p, Masaru Kakutani and Satoru Ogata; w, Mark Saltzman (based on a story by Masanori Hata); ph, Hideo Fujii and Shinji Tomita; ed, Chizuko Osada; m, Michael Boddicker

Children's   (PR:AA MPAA:G)

AFTER DARK, MY SWEET

114m Avenue c

Jason Patric (Collie), Rachel Ward (Fay), Bruce Dern (Uncle Bud), George Dickerson (Doc Goldman), James Cotton (Charlie), Corey Carrier (Jack), Rocky Giordani (Bert), Jeanie Moore (Nanny), Tom Wagner (Counterman), Burke Byrnes (Cop), Michael G. Hagerty, James E. Bowen Jr. (Truck Drivers), Vincent Joseph Mazzella Jr. (Flashback Fighter), and Napoleon Walls (Boxing Referee)

AFTER DARK, MY SWEET is a would-be new-style film noir involving the intertwined destinies of three boozy lowlifes. Collie (Jason Patric) is a near-psychopathic ex-boxer who left the ring after killing a competitor. He becomes involved with Fay (Rachel Ward), a seductive, alcoholic widow, and Uncle Bud (Bruce Dern), a sleazy former lawman, and is drawn into their scheme to get rich quick by kidnapping the young scion of a wealthy local family. At first confused by Fay's drink-influenced mixed messages, Collie splits the scene for a while. He is taken in by an all-too-interested physician, Doc Goldman (George Dickerson), but soon grows tired of the doctor's attempts to enforce domesticity and returns to Fay. The wheels of the crime are now set in motion, as are the surprising detours and plot twists one expects in the genre. For starters, the kidnap victim proves to be seriously diabetic. A few more monkey wrenches are also thrown in before AFTER DARK, MY SWEET reaches its bloody conclusion.

AFTER DARK, MY SWEET is based on a 1955 novel by the prolific tough-guy novelist Jim Thompson, who worked on the screenplays of THE KILLING and PATHS OF GLORY for Stanley Kubrick, and whose The Grifters and The Kill-Off were also turned into 1990 releases. The film was shot in Indio, California, and the dry purity of the air is almost palpable. Director James Foley (RECKLESS; AT CLOSE RANGE) has the kind of visual style that can lend a glamorous, carefully hued patina to the most mundane suburban settings, and Mark Plummer's fluent cinematography lends the story an ambience of oblique beauty. Groves of palm trees, a lush green golf course set flush against the Sierras, desultory honky-tonks, and tract-house interiors have an atmosphere of enervated complacency that could easily drive one to drink or sin. In one scene, as an aroused Collie charges in search of Fay into her house, the camera snakes after him with virtuoso, one-take urgency, down deserted hallways and into empty rooms.

What a shame, then, that the story itself is so uninvolving. Robert Redlin's screenplay is competent but threadbare, lacking the wit necessary to make the thoroughly unpleasant goings-on entertaining. (The diabetic child is the kind of deadly device it would take genius, and maybe something more, to lift above the level of bad taste.) Also critically absent are dynamic personalities that might flesh out and heat up the proceedings. Though the darkly cherubic Patric, smoldering like a combination of James Dean and Robert De Niro, gives it his all, it's the wrong kind of intensity: Patric makes Collie so unappealing in his wacky demonstrations of violence (ripping phones out of walls, flashing guns) that any sense of identification with the character's basic, hard-won decency is precluded. Ward, looking androgynous and elfin, begins well, tossing off bitter put-downs between sips of drinks, but her characterization wears thin when deeper passion is required. She fails to convey the mysterious radiance essential to the role, and lacks the technique to be a convincing noir bitch; Fay's crying

jags and hysteria are merely embarrassing in Ward's stiff rendering. She and Patric are vital only in a steamy, extended afternoon sex scene—effectively interrupted by blackouts—that has the real sense of danger, perversity, and latent violence the film otherwise lacks. Dern rounds out the unappetizing triangle with an unpleasant performance, proving himself a worthy contender in the Dennis Hopper/Harry Dean Stanton creepstakes. Dickerson tries a naturalistic, underplayed approach to the closeted Doc Goldman, but comes off as smarmily false as the rest. A stirringly romantic or savvy regional score might have helped immeasurably; instead, the ubiquitous Maurice Jarre furnishes his usual uninspired earwax. (Violence, profanity, nudity, sexual situations, adult situations, substance abuse.)

d, James Foley; p, Ric Kidney and Robert Redlin; w, James Foley and Robert Redlin (based on the book by Jim Thompson); ph, Mark Plummer; ed, Howard Smith; m, Maurice Jarre; art d, Kenneth A. Hardy; set d, Margaret Goldsmith; spec, Ken Diaz; stunts, A.J. Nay; makup, Felicity Bowring

Crime   (PR:O MPAA:R)

AFTERSHOCK

90m Bonaire/Overseas—Spectrum c

Jay Roberts Jr. (Willie), Eilizabeth Kitaen (Sabina), Chuck Jeffries (Danny Girard), John Saxon (Oliver Quinn), Christopher Mitchum (John Slater), James Lew (Mr. James), Chris De Rose (Brandt), Russ Tamblyn (Hank Franklin), Michael Standing (Gruber), Richard Lynch (Comdr. Eastern), Michael Berryman (Queen), Claudia Wick (Voice of Big Sister), Matthias Hues, Julie Woodside, Bob Schott, Pat McGroarty, Ron Althoff, and Deanna Olivier

AFTERSHOCK is a clumsy grab-bag of post-apocalyptic action cliches and offbeat touches. Naturally, the setting is the 21st century. Because citizens have stopped questioning their leaders, civilization has collapsed. Paramilitary goons prowl the ruins, exterminating well-scrubbed refugees and dissidents, while the voice of "Big Sister" broadcasts aphorisms like "A clean weapon is a safe weapon." Sabina (Elizabeth Kitaen) suddenly materializes in an abandoned missile site, dressed like a Vogue model and bearing some old photographs. Dragged before a brutal authority figure, Oliver Quinn (John Saxon), she smiles vacantly at his interrogation and is held for observation. When Willie (Jay Roberts, Jr.) and Danny (Chuck Jeffries), two troublemakers who are also being held, stage a breakout, Sabina mindlessly follows them. Danny leads them to a rebel headquarters, where freedom fighters tap into the state computer system and learn that Sabina is not as dumb as she seems. In fact, she's really a superintelligent extraterrestrial. By this point Sabina has learned enough English to haltingly explain: it seems her people intercepted a NASA space probe, and the friendly photos it bore suggested that Earth had developed an "equitable society." Sabina has come to learn the secret of such peace and harmony for her own troubled planet. Oh well. Realizing that she can't survive on Earth, Sabina is determined to get back to the missile site to catch the next "energy cycle" home. As Quinn's forces raid the rebel base, Willie and Sabina set out for the missile site. Alas, she falls into the clutches of a bounty-hunter (Chris De Rose), who hands her over to Quinn. Improbably, the group ends up at the missile site anyway, and after Willie uses his martial-arts skills to dispense with the bad guys, Sabina is set to rendezvous with her probe. "Always Question," reads the rebel graffito in the final shot.

All right. Why does the superintelligent space gal behave like an imbecile even after overcoming the communications barrier? Why does Willie's character change from a smart-mouth rascal to a terse mystic? How does he dodge several point-blank bullets? What's the deal with the smoke that engulfs him during one swordfight? Director Frank Harris doesn't provide answers to any of these questions. And the slipshod action and transitional scenes make it hard to tell who's doing what to whom. However, the film does show unexpected strength in the supporting cast, with B-movie stalwarts Saxon and Christopher Mitchum playing roles a scintilla above the usual cartoon characters. And Jeffries makes a likable and energetic sidekick; regrettably, he disappears halfway through the tale. (Excessive violence, profanity, adult situations.)

d, Frank Harris; p, Roy McAree; w, Michael Standing; ed, Howard Heard; m, Kevin Klingler and Bob Mamet; art d, Brian Densmore; spec, Fred Cramer; cos, Julie Carnahan

Science Fiction   (PR:O MPAA:R)

AGATHA CHRISTIE'S TEN LITTLE INDIANS

(SEE: TEN LITTLE INDIANS)

AIR AMERICA

112m Daniel Melnick—Indieprod—Carolco/Tri-Star c

Mel Gibson *(Gene Ryack)*, Robert Downey Jr. *(Billy Covington)*, Nancy Travis *(Corinne Landreaux)*, Ken Jenkins *(Maj. Donald Lemond)*, David Marshall Grant *(Rob Diehl)*, Lane Smith *(Sen. Davenport)*, Art LeFleur *(Jack Neely)*, Ned Eisenberg *(Pirelli)*, Marshall Bell *(O.V.)*, David Bowe *(Saunders)*, Burt Kwouk *(Gen. Lu Soong)*, Tim Thomerson *(Babo)*, Harvey Jason *(Nino)*, Sinjai Hongthai *(Gene's Wife)*, Natta Nantatanti *(Gene's Daughter)*, Purin Panichpan *(Gene's Son)*, Yani Tramod *(Gene's Brother-in-Law)*, Chanarong Suwanapa *(Kwahn)*, Chet Vimol *(Tribal Warrior)*, Wasan Uttamayodhin, Meesak Naakkarat *(Nightclub Singers)*, Ernie Lively *(Truck Driver)*, Burke Byrnes *(Recruiter)*, Greg Kean *(DJ)*, and Roger Welty *(Ambassador)*

Director Roger Spottiswoode won critical acclaim in 1983 for his topical drama about the war in Nicaragua, UNDER FIRE. But times change. What's more, UNDER FIRE crashed and burned at the box office. With a reported $35-million budget, Spottiswoode's AIR AMERICA comes on like a noisy, overproduced sitcom pilot as it details the zany exploits of kooky flyboys ferrying contraband in Laos during the Vietnam War, circa 1969. Though attempting to mimic the dark, satirical tone of Robert Altman's M*A*S*H, Spottiswoode's most recent effort remains on an inoffensive cartoon level, building to a mock socially conscious telemovie windup. All that is missing is an over-insistent laughtrack. The film's lengthy opening credits sequence includes a scene in which a CIA plane is brought down by a single bullet fired from a musket by a Laotian peasant. It's pretty funny stuff until we see the dead bodies littering the runway back at the Air America base in Vientiane, Laos, where the crippled plane attempted a crash-landing. It's here we first glimpse veteran pilot Gene Ryack (Mel Gibson), photogenically knitting his brow over the carnage, and his Air America boss, Rob Diehl (David Marshall Grant), who now has to find more pilots. Without further mention of the opening air crash, seemingly staged solely to give superstar Gibson a fitting introduction, the film abruptly cuts to Los Angeles, where we're introduced to Billy Covington (Robert Downey, Jr.), who reports on traffic conditions from a helicopter. When we first see this rebel with a cause, wacky Billy is buzzing rush-hour rubberneckers to clear them away from a freeway accident. Recruited by Diehl, Billy is promised exotic adventure in Laos, along with a new flying license out of Taiwan. When Billy arrives at the Air America base, Ryack takes him under his wing. Obviously not a union operation, Air America has no pension plan for its pilots, which leads them to operate scams on the side to build their retirement nest eggs. Ryack's racket happens to be gun-running, though it's not really *gun-running*—he is the hero, after all. What he's actually doing is buying up guns and ammunition with his savings and stashing them along the route he flies so he can resell them when he decides to end his Air America career. Assigned his own route, Billy discovers that, along with pigs and sacks of grain, his cargo includes refined opium, being flown for the commander of the Laotian forces, General Soong (Burt Kwouk, Inspector Clouseau's indestructible manservant in the "Pink Panther" series), in exchange for "protection." At one point, Billy wonders aloud why American planes are flying drugs destined to addict US soldiers in Vietnam, but no one takes him seriously. Meanwhile, Billy proves to be something of a jinx in the air when his first cargo flight crashes. General Soong swoops in, to rescue *not* the downed fliers but his opium, leaving Billy and his crew to dodge bullets from a guerilla ground attack. Ryack appears at the last second to pull Billy out of the line of fire, but the helicopter Ryack is piloting promptly crashes, leading to an extended trek through the jungle during which the pilots are captured by mountain peasants. However, Billy and Ryack are saved when a rainstorm prevents the peasants' antique flintlock rifles from firing, allowing Ryack to negotiate the fliers' release in exchange for some of his modern, waterproof weapons. Back at the base, Billy settles the score with Soong by blowing up the general's opium-processing plant. To placate the enraged Soong, and to impress a visiting senator (Lane Smith) who is on hand to investigate rumors of opium smuggling by Air America pilots, Billy's bosses plot to frame him for drug running. Meanwhile, Ryack decides to bail out of the flying business. With his transport plane loaded with the weapons he has collected, Ryack faces a weighty last-reel decision: Should he dump his load to save a sexy US aid worker (Nancy Travis) and the refugees who are being driven from their encampment by Soong? Without giving away how Billy and Ryack make out, suffice it to say that the movie ends happily in the style Hollywood loves best, laying the groundwork for a sequel—or a TV series.

Notwithstanding this extended synopsis, AIR AMERICA works hard at appearing to have no plot whatsoever. Instead, it breezes along episodically, cutting away from Billy and Ryack to the day-to-day lives of the other fliers, and depicting drunken binges and sessions with B-girls at the flyboys' favorite hangout, Vientiane's White Rose bar; attempts by Air America to recruit civilian pilots for psychological warfare against the Viet Cong forces who are using a pathway through Laos to transport men, arms, and supplies to South Vietnam; and the efforts of the Air America bosses to cover up their involvement in the drug smuggling. Despite occasional stabs at relevance, AIR AMERICA is careful not to push too hard or delve too deeply into any of the implications, political or moral, of its plot. Its tone is apolitical macho nihilism (masquerading in Gibson's

character as Buddhist non-involvement), wrapped up into a neat, shiny, slickly crafted Hollywood package that is entertaining but utterly empty. It used to be that critics took Hollywood to task for not making enough films about the Vietnam War. AIR AMERICA might make you wish Hollywood would stop making them. *(Profanity.)*

d, Roger Spottiswoode; p, Daniel Melnick; w, John Eskow and Richard Rush (based on the book by Christopher Robbins); ph, Roger Deakins; ed, John Bloom and Lois Freeman-Fox; m, Charles Gross; md, Becky Mancuso and Tim Sexton; prod d, Allan Cameron; art d, Steve Spence and Tony Reading; set d, Fred Carter; spec, George Gibbs and Roy Fields; stunts, Vic Armstrong; cos, John Mollo; makeup, Lois Burwell

Comedy/War   (PR:C   MPAA:R)

AKIRA KUROSAWA'S DREAMS

(SEE: DREAMS)

ALICE

106m Rollins-Joffe/Orion c

Mia Farrow *(Alice)*, William Hurt *(Doug)*, Alec Baldwin *(Ed)*, Joe Mantegna *(Joe)*, Cybill Shepherd *(Nancy Brill)*, Blythe Danner *(Dorothy)*, Bernadette Peters *(Muse)*, Gwen Verdon *(Alice's Mother)*, Patrick O'Neal *(Alice's Father)*, Keye Luke *(Dr. Yang)*, Julie Kavner *(Decorator)*, Judy Davis *(Vicki)*, June Squibb *(Hilda)*, Marceline Hugot *(Monica)*, Dylan O'Sullivan Farrow *(Kate)*, Matt Williamson *(Dennis)*, Billy Taylor *(Trainer)*, Holland Taylor *(Helen)*, Michael-Vaughn Sullivan *(Hairstylist)*, Robin Bartlett *(Nina)*, Linda Wallem *(Penny)*, Gina Gallagher *(Joe's Daughter)*, Patience Moore *(School Teacher)*, Diane Cheng *(Dr. Yang's Assistant)*, Kim Chan *(Dr. Yang's Patient)*, Lynda Bridges *(Saleslady)*, Anthony Cortino *(Dog Groomer)*, Katja Schumann *(Circus Equestrian)*, Vanessa Thomas *(Circus Aerialist)*, Kristy Graves *(Alice at 18)*, Laurie Nayber *(Young Dorothy)*, Rachel Miner *(Alice at 12)*, Amy Louis Barrett *(Mrs. Keyes)*, Caroline Aaron *(Sue)*, Alexi Henry *(Kimberly)*, James Toback *(Professor)*, Elle MacPherson *(Model)*, Ira Wheeler, Lisa Marie *(Office Party Guests)*, Diane Salinger *(Carol)*, David Spielberg *(Ken)*, Bob Balaban *(Sid Moscowitz)*, and Peggy Miley *(Dorothy's Maid)*

In her 11th collaboration with companion Woody Allen, Mia Farrow plays Alice Tate, an upscale Manhattan housewife with an uncaring husband (William Hurt) and two children whom she rarely sees. Alice spends most of her time making the rounds at Manhattan boutiques and shops and supervising the staff that keeps her sleek apartment organized and tidy. She seems to have it all, yet she is unsatisfied and troubled. She is attracted to a man named Joe (Joe Mantegna) who picks up his kids at the same nursery school attended by the Tate children. Being a shy, guilt-ridden Catholic, Alice would never think of approaching the man. When she complains of a back pain, she is advised to visit an acupuncturist named Dr. Yang (Keye Luke in his last film appearance). Yang immediately surmises that the problem is not her back. He provides her with a strange herb mixture that, when taken by Alice, helps her overcome her inhibitions, enabling her to make a date with Joe. When the effect of the herbs wears off, however, she breaks the date and retreats into her shell. Later, she returns to Dr. Yang, who hypnotizes her, offers her opium, then makes her invisible. Roaming around unseen, she discovers that her husband is having an affair and that her friends maliciously gossip about her behind her back. When she returns from her invisible state, she begins an affair with Joe and continues to visit Dr. Yang for his mystical aid. She confronts her past, settling an old argument with her sister (Blythe Danner) and encountering the ghost of her first lover (Alec Baldwin). She begins to give in to her artistic impulses (her muse takes on the human form of Bernadette Peters). Eventually, it leads her to dump her husband and to head for Calcutta where she begins working with Mother Teresa—something she has always longed to do. At the fade-out, her friends are seen talking about how Alice "found herself," while Alice frolics in the park with her kids.

ALICE covers many of the recurring themes in Allen's work, with this film playing much like a combination of ANOTHER WOMAN and THE PURPLE ROSE OF CAIRO (Alice's character is strikingly similar the character Farrow played in the latter film). The problem is that as Allen reworks these themes, he offers no new insights into the issues he raises. He is an uncommonly simplistic artist whose work, despite its staunch earnestness, remains trite and contrived. The core messages of ALICE—the life of the rich is hollow and one can obliterate guilt by living impulsively—are so uninspired that even Allen's skill at disguising the banal doesn't work here. In fact, the light tone and the supernatural elements serve to highlight the emptiness of the project. Of course, Allen's increasingly annoying habit of relying on other filmmakers to provide him with his *mise-en-scene* is in full force; this time, it's the work of Fellini, rather than that of Bergman, that is raided, but the results are as dreary as ever.

Although Alice is a typically neurotic Allen protagonist, she is not as pathetic as many previous lead characters in Allen's films. The fact that Allen allows his main character to triumph in the end, rather than being bathed in pathos, is something of a step forward. Still, Alice Tate is yet another variation on the Allen screen persona, the highly moral yet sadly weak character who is surrounded by selfish hypocrites. Further undermining the film is some unpleasant racism. Dr. Yang's stereotypical Oriental is appallingly similar to those commonly found in films of the 30s, and a joke involving a black man who falls in love with Alice at a party leaves a bad aftertaste, particularly since black characters almost never appear in Allen's work. The film does have the polished look which Allen's work invariably displays, and offers a few laughs as the director continues to show that, if nothing else, he knows how to stage a gag. Overall the performances are adequate, though Cybill Shepherd and Gwen Verdon are wasted, and only Baldwin really shines. It's a competent work and those who are fans of Allen will no doubt enjoy it, but even they must be growing weary of seeing him continue to make the same film over and over again. The film earned an Oscar nomination for Best Screenplay Written Directly for the Screen. *(Adult situations, profanity, substance abuse.)*

d, Woody Allen; p, Robert Greenhut; w, Woody Allen; ph, Carlo Di Palma; ed, Susan E. Morse; prod d, Santo Loquasto; art d, Speed Hopkins; set d, Susan Bode

Comedy/Fantasy (PR:A-C MPAA:PG-13)

ALIENATOR

92m Amazing Movies—American Independent—Majestic c

Jan-Michael Vincent *(Commander)*, John Phillip Law *(Sheriff Ward)*, Ross Hagen *(Kol)*, Dyana Ortelli *(Orrie)*, Jesse Dabson *(Benny)*, Dawn Wildsmith *(Caroline)*, P.J. Soles *(Tara)*, Teagen Clive *(Alienator)*, Robert Clarke *(Lund)*, Leo V. Gordon *(Col. Coburn)*, Richard Wiley, Robert Quarry, Fox Harris, Hoke Howell, Jay Richardson, Dan Golden, and Jeffrey C. Hogue

This uninvolving science-fiction drama concerns an outer-space fugitive, Kol (Ross Hagen), who escapes to Earth, tailed by the eponymous Alienator (Teagen Clive). The film opens as Kol, who has led a rebellion that overthrew the Great Tyrant Baal, is captured, taken to a prison planet, and sentenced to die. Prior to his scheduled execution, a pacifist donning monk's clothing (Robert Clarke), appears from out of nowhere and tries to talk the Commander (Jan-Michael Vincent) out of killing the rebel. The plea for clemency fails, but just before he is about to be strapped into the dematerializing chair, Kol somehow manages to elude an entire battalion of men and, dodging an incredible amount of laser fire, escapes the prison planet in a small spaceship. Eventually, he makes it to Earth and crash-lands in a forest, where he is taken in by some teenaged campers and local sheriff Ward (John Phillip Law). But it isn't long before the Commander and his crew also arrive on Earth, and send the indestructible Alienator after Kol. Looking like a punked-out linebacker in drag, the Alienator first meets up with two (highly stereotyped) backwoods inhabitants who, for the moment, manage to avoid the strange alien's wrath. Meanwhile, sheriff Ward, Kol, and the band of campers take refuge in the cabin of retired army colonel Coburn (Leo Gordon). They shoot it out with the robot, which seems unbeatable until a metal net is dropped on it, temporarily demagnetizing the creature. Thinking he's finally safe, Kol takes over one of the human bodies in order to stay on Earth. But the Alienator is not easily fooled and, after getting some much needed beauty sleep, comes back with a vengeance.

Written by Paul Garson, the ALIENATOR is an unsuspenseful, extremely violent film. The dialog is silly, and though the TERMINATOR-like premise is sufficient to support the action, the characters are for the most part undeveloped and unsympathetic. A particularly damaging technical flaw is the low-budget special-efforts work, which is distractingly poor. *(Profanity, graphic violence.)*

d, Fred Olen Ray; p, Jeffrey C. Hogue; w, Paul Garson; ph, Gary Graver; ed, Chris Roth; m, Chuck Cirino; art d, Linda Lauderbaugh; stunts, Bobby Bragg; cos, Jill Conner; makeup, Shelley Fox and Monica Maynor

Science Fiction (PR:C MPAA:R)

ALLIGATOR EYES

101m Castle Hill/J&M—Academy c

Annabelle Larsen *(Pauline)*, Roger Kabler *(Robbie)*, John Mackay *(Peterson)*, Mary McLain *(Marjorie)*, and Allen McCulloch *(Lance)*

This is one of those low-low-budget offerings that critics go out of their way to praise and that festivals go out of their way to honor. Despite flashes of idiosyncratic talent, the movie, the feature debut for documentary filmmaker John Feldman, is a glorified student film that compromises its best ideas and self-destructs before its ludicrous climax. A sort of comic riff on *film noir* mysteries, the film tries to intertwine two different plots. First, it's about the reunion of a lovable drunk, Robbie (Roger Kabler), who can't hold onto a woman, his buddy Lance (Allen McCulloch), and their mutual friend Marjorie (Mary McLain), who once was Lance's lover. Second, it unfolds the bizarre saga of a blind woman, Pauline (Annabelle Larsen), who insinuates herself into their lives (rather too easily). A vacation car trip down south for the trio of friends gets off to a bumpy start after Robbie's latest girl friend dumps him. Concurrently, Lance and Marjorie try to rekindle their affair. Meanwhile, the film flashes back to Pauline's childhood, when she was accidentally blinded by a mystery killer who murdered her parents. Egged on by Peterson (John Mackay), a thoroughly unconventional psychoanalyst, Pauline pursues a misguided revenge plan, and is picked up by the trio as she is hitch-hiking. Less than forthcoming about her motives, Pauline quickly changes the lives of her companions as she entrances Robbie, then seduces Lance.

But "musical beds" is just a sidelight for the conniving Pauline, who persuades the others to head for her destination, promising them a music festival in which she is slated to perform. There is no festival, and Pauline's real goal is to rendezvous with the man she believes killed her parents. When her fellow travelers discover she is carrying a gun, they want to ditch her, but she has asserted a strong psychological hold on them. Arriving at her destination, she heads for her meeting only to learn find that she has been involved in an elaborate charade orchestrated by Peterson, her Svengali-like shrink, in an effort to keep her under his care. Furious, Pauline attacks and kills Peterson. This somehow frees her from her past, and she returns to Robbie, who forgives her for everything—a remarkable act of charity considering she is a killer, chronic liar, manipulator, and sex tease. Obviously, those who survive a childhood trauma are to be forgiven anything.

The initial promise of ALLIGATOR EYES and its pack of quirky characters quickly degenerates into meaningless posturing. Logic quickly falls by the wayside, as does our goodwill toward this alleged *film noir* comedy. On the plus side, Roger Kabler is thoroughly amusing as Robbie, even if he is more of a funny presence than a comic actor, and even if neither he nor Allen McCulloch as Lance has the acting ability to be convincing in their scenes of alleged drunkenness. One can't help but admire the offbeat nature of the film, its air of improvisation, and its spellbinding score by classical composer Sheila Silver, but director John Feldman somehow lets the audience down again and again. There simply is no credibility in the brittle and charmless Pauline's ability to continually dupe this trio of seemingly intelligent characters. Annabelle Larsen has neither the charisma nor the sexuality to make Pauline the *femme fatale* the character needs to be. Despite some attractive visuals, the photography isn't distinctive enough to sustain the air of mystery Feldman obviously wishes to convey. Tentative in presentation and inconsistent in tone, the shakily structured screenplay borrows heavily from such disparate sources as John Cassavetes, Jim Jarmusch, and Jacques Tourneur. Somewhat agreeable as a character comedy-on-wheels, it doesn't make the grade as a meditation on the *film noir* genre. *(Nudity, violence, sexual situations, profanity, alcohol abuse.)*

d, John Feldman; p, Ken Schwenker and John Feldman; w, John Feldman; ph, Todd Crockett; ed, Cynthia Rogers; m, Sheila Silver; art d, Jeff Tandy; spec, Mark Dolson; cos, Jeff Tandy

Comedy/Drama (PR:C MPAA:R)

ALMOST AN ANGEL

96m Paramount c

Paul Hogan *(Terry Dean)*, Linda Kozlowski *(Rose Garner)*, Elias Koteas *(Steve)*, Doreen Lang *(Mrs. Garner)*, Robert Sutton *(Guido)*, Sammy Lee Allen *(Bubba)*, Charlton Heston *(Moses)*, Parley Baer, and Hank Worden

Australia's Paul "Crocodile Dundee" Hogan serves up some heavenly hash in this film, a well-intentioned but (alas) self-defeating comedy about a professional thief named Terry Dean (Hogan) who, having survived a life-threatening accident, convinces himself that God has given him one last opportunity to redeem himself. On the lam following a bank holdup, Terry finds himself performing an uncharacteristically heroic act by saving a life and winding up in the hospital as a result. Believing he has died and gone to purgatory, Terry fantasizes an audience with Moses (Charlton Heston) and becomes convinced he has been returned to earth to serve the Lord. Released from the hospital, Terry goes to a bar where he meets a paraplegic, Steve (Elias Koteas). The two men hit it off and Steve takes Terry home with him to meet his sister, Rose (Linda Kozlowski, Hogan's real-life wife and co-star of his "Dundee" films). Rose has left a good job to devote herself to taking care of her wheelchair-bound brother. During their first meeting, Terry displays a comical and thoroughly unorthodox grasp of Biblical text, which baffles Rose, leading her to take an immediate dislike to this stranger. However, through a series of misadventures during which Terry consistently displays his good-heartedness, Rose is won over by the reformed thief, as is every other character in the film.

While Hogan's messages about brotherly love, peace, and understanding are certainly noble, he lacks the flair and genius to incorporate them into the type of entertaining film created by masters such as Frank Capra and Leo McCarey, filmmakers he obviously wishes to emulate. Those directors knew instinctively how to make sweetness and light work onscreen, giving their pictures enough bite and wit to keep them from becoming corny or saccharine. Hogan gives it the old college try and while the attempt is occasionally admirable, most of his bad-man-turned-good-guy jokes fall flat. Scenes designed to be uplifting sink into preachiness, while much of the film moves at a snail's pace. Hogan does manage to elicit some laughs as he disguises himself as Rod Stewart, Willie Nelson, and others, and he is an appealing performer. Certainly it is commendable that he would attempt to offer an oasis of love, laughter, and compassion in the midst of a contemporary cinematic desert of lust, hate, gore, and graphic violence. Unfortunately, his talents aren't equal to his intents and ALMOST AN ANGEL commits the unpardonable cinematic sin of being largely dull. *(Mild profanity, mild violence.)*

d, John Cornell; p, John Cornell; w, Paul Hogan; ph, Russell Boyd; ed, David Stiven; m, Maurice Jarre; prod d, Henry Bumstead; set d, Dick Goddard; spec, Dave Kelsey; cos, Alice Ferry

Comedy   (PR:A   MPAA:PG)

AMERICAN BOYFRIENDS

(Can.) 90m Telefilm Canada — First Choice — National Film Board of Canada — Canadian Broadcasting — B.C. — Alliance c

Margaret Langrick *(Sandy Wilcox)*, John Wildman *(Butch Wilcox)*, Jason Blicker *(Marty Kaplan)*, Liisa Repo Martell *(Julie La Belle)*, Delia Brett *(Lizzie)*, Michelle Bardeaux *(Thelma)*, Troy Mallory *(Spider)*, Scott Anderson *(Daryl)*, Gordon Currie *(Glider)*, Loren Dunsworth *(Cynthia)*, Terry Moore *(Al Wilcox)*, Jane Mortfee *(Kitty Wilcox)*, and Richard Donat *(Maj. Wilcox)*

In this pleasant but rather lackadaisical follow-up to the modest Canadian sleeper MY AMERICAN COUSIN (1985) set several years later in the 1960s, Sandy Wilcox (Margaret Langrick), the now-almost-grown Canadian heroine of the first film, faces that awkward time of life when all her friends begin marrying. Feeling abandoned, poised between her teenage years and responsible adulthood, she embraces college as the best way to prolong adolescence and postpone joining the white-picket-fence set. At her progressive school, Sandy makes friends with would-be hippie Julie La Belle (Liisa Repo Martell) and tires of her classes quickly. Receiving a wedding invitation from Butch (John Wildman), the American cousin of the previous film, she persuades her hometown pals Lizzie and Thelma (Delia Brett and Michelle Bardeaux) to accompany her and Julie from Canada to Portland. Although Thelma is preparing for her own nuptials, she chauffeurs the other three to the United States. Arriving just in time for the ceremony, the quartet surprises Butch and has a great time contemplating true love during his wedding reception. Lizzie, smitten with best man Daryl (Scott Anderson), abandons her principles and accompanies him to the parking lot, where he both seduces her and informs her that he is about to be sent to Vietnam. Meanwhile, while conversing with her beloved cousin and his new bride, Sandy is stunned when he gives her his red Cadillac. Her plans change immediately, as do Lizzie's. Remaining Stateside, Lizzie moves in with Daryl before he goes overseas, while Sandy and Julie decide to cut loose and explore California (leaving bride-to-be Thelma stuck with going back home by herself). Dreaming of blond surfers, the coeds are disappointed with the Santa Cruz locals, who ignore them, and when they must rescue Berkeley radical Marty (Jason Blicker) and his African-American friend Spider (Troy Mallory) from the very same beach boys they had previously coveted, the young women re-examine their priorities. Sandy pairs off with Spider, who wants to return to his school in LA; Julie grows enamored of anti-war activist Marty, who wants to head for Mexico. Their plans are upset, however, when, Sandy receives (from Lizzie) the tragic news that her cousin Bruce has been killed in an automobile accident, and after dropping Spider off on the highway, the group returns to Portland for the funeral. Afterwards, Sandy and Julie — accompanied by Lizzie, whose romance is on the rocks — survive a close call with border authorities and successfully sneak Marty into Canada so he can dodge the draft. As the film ends, Sandy informs us in a voice-over that Julie and Marty happily settled down on a Canadian island. As for Sandy herself: after making it to Thelma's wedding, she dropped out of school, hitchhiked through Europe, and vowed never to settle down.

AMERICAN BOYFRIENDS plays like the thinking person's WHERE THE BOYS ARE, reset in the Pacific Northwest and Canada. Coasting along sweetly and appealingly, this light drama is more notable for its occasional observations about its 60s milieu than for any insights into the coming-of-age experience. Unfortunately, the script tends to ramble almost as much as the characters do, and one begins to grow impatient with director-writer Sandy Wilson's habit of padding out scenes and letting the actors' slow rhythms set the pace. Though admirable in its understatedness, the story is too diffuse to achieve any dramatic

pay-offs, so that the film's "big moments" (Butch's funeral and Lizzie's seduction) seem like screenplay conveniences, and because the actors are often called upon to make the big dramatic statements that Wilson wants to put across, the proceedings sometimes become static and talky.

AMERICAN BOYFRIENDS works best in its gentle exploration of middle-class attitudes in the 60s. In a sense, the film's ambling nature is as much its charm as it is a drawback, since the off-hand quality lends a certain spontaneity to some of the film's observations. A scene in which the girls are having their hair teased (until they resemble a trio of Marie Antoinettes) while their beauticians argue about military involvement in Vietnam is a comic gem, and the cast of unknowns give sympathetic and winningly low-key performances.

If one can tolerate its meandering quality and ignore a few implausible plot developments, this picaresque film offers enough incidental pleasures to make it rewarding. It's knowing but affectionate, never mean-spirited or parodic — and since there have been so few good coming-of-age films about young women, AMERICAN BOYFRIENDS's airy drollery and deadpan humor make it stand out all the more. Although predictably nostalgic, the film wears its heart on its sleeve with a casual flair. *(Mild profanity, sexual situations.)*

d, Sandy Wilson; p, Sandy Wilson and Steven Denure; w, Sandy Wilson; ph, Brenton Spencer; ed, Lara Mazur; m, Terry Frewer; md, Sam Feldman; prod d, Phillip Schmidt; cos, Jennifer Grossman; chor, Linda Thorslund

Comedy/Drama   (PR:AA   MPAA:PG-13)

AMERICAN EAGLE

92m Triax/Vidmark c

Asher Brauner *(Max Shane)*, Robert F. Lyons *(Rudy Argente)*, Vernon Welles *(Johnny Burke)*, Kai Baker *(Angela Argente)*, Anthony Fridjhon *(Richard Assad)*, Ron Smerczak *(Edward Slovak)*, Robert Whitehead *(Detective Lambert)*, Joe Ribiero *(Manny)*, Reuben Nthodi *(Arthur)*, Diane Appleby *(Lina)*, Lawrence Ginsberg *(Carmello)*, Drummond Marais *(Spencer)*, Al Karaki *(Paco)*, Carrie Glynn *(Juliet)*, Michael Atkinson *(Silverhair)*, Terrence Reis *(Allan)*, Scott Ateah *(Hostage)*, Douglas Lookwhy *(Cashier)*, and Debra Kaye *(Waitress)*

Action movie buffs able to shut off their thought processes for 92 minutes should get a bang out of this exciting but illogical exercise in violence. Spanning the years from the Vietnam War to the present, AMERICAN EAGLE covers a lot of ground as it incorporates terrorism, patriotism, white slavery, and illegal arms sales into its plot. The film opens 20 years ago in Vietnam, with three buddies parting company violently. When Max (Asher Brauner) and Rudy (Robert F. Lyons) prevent their war-loving pal Johnny (Vernon Welles) from murdering a Vietnamese civilian, Johnny carries a grudge for several decades. Although Rudy abandons his warrior role to become a restaurateur, Max and Johnny become soldiers of fortune, meddling in various conflicts around the globe — always on opposite sides. However, Max has begun to question the ethics of his mercenary activities for the US government. Pressured by his girl friend, Angela (Kai Baker), who also happens to be Rudy's sister, Max opts for retirement, without realizing that Uncle Sam, like a Mafia don, expects his employees to remain in his organization for life. Hiring Johnny to reawaken his old friend's warrior instincts, US intelligence tries to re-enlist Max's cooperation. Naturally, Johnny has a secret revenge agenda in mind. Working for Assad (Anthony Fridjhon), a Middle Eastern big cheese with whom the US government wants to maintain friendly relations at any cost, Johnny kidnaps Angela (along with five other gorgeous models) when she visits Rudy in the Ivory Coast. When the cops are slow to respond, Max and Rudy decide to blast the hell out of their enemies. Capturing Johnny's henchman Manny (Joe Ribiero), Max and Rudy nearly drown him in order to learn the whereabouts of the women. Although one of the models is killed during a dispute between Johnny and a lesbian white slaver, Max and Rudy free the others and confront not only Hassad's men but also Max's former boss, Slovak (Ron Smerczak), who has cooperated in this elaborate scheme to bring Max back into the fold. Functioning as a two-man commando team, Max and Rudy wipe out most of Hassad's trained guards. After denouncing Slovak for his involvement in Hassad's plot to assassinate a prominent American politician and to install a new government in a Middle Eastern country, Max prepares for his showdown with the vengeful Johnny. In the brutal hand-to-hand combat that ensues, Johnny is killed when he falls on his own knife. With Angela in tow, Max and Rudy escape, but not before they destroy Hassad's munitions compound and foil his takeover plans. After seeing how low the US government is willing sink to hold on to a valued employee like himself, Max is definitely ready for retirement.

If you overlook several far-fetched plot developments, AMERICAN EAGLE is acceptably gritty action fare. Most notably, it seems implausible that Johnny would carry a grudge for over two decades just because his friends prevented him from carrying out a senseless killing. The desperate recruitment tactics practiced by the US government in this film also seem highly unlikely, but, given the disturbing revelations of the Iran-Contra affair, perhaps anything is possible—even government-instigated assassinations of American citizens. The script is lent added depth by its questioning of US intervention in the affairs of other nations.

Other aspects of AMERICAN EAGLE are more conventional. Most of the villains are stereotypical bad guys, and Welles' characterization of Johnny is right out of FRIDAY THE THIRTEENTH (he's as hard to take seriously as he is to kill). In the leading roles, Brauner (who also wrote the script) is brooding and forceful without being sufficiently charismatic, but Lyons accomplishes the nearly impossible feat of subtly fleshing out a role in a full-throttle action picture. His flashes of sensitivity amidst all the carnage are both credible and moving. For genre fans, grenades are exploded, buildings are blitzed, women are victimized, and the sneering villains are finally punished after the film's death toll has surpassed that of a natural disaster. Unremarkable, but fast and efficient, AMERICAN EAGLE is satisfactory escapism with an edge. (Violence, profanity, nudity, substance abuse, sexual situations.)

d, Robert J. Smawley; p, Lionel Ephraim; w, Asher Brauner; ph, Rod Stewart; ed, Chuck Weiss; m, Robert Schroder; prod d, Hazel Crampton; art d, Ben Horowitz; set d, Erin Miller; stunts, Scott Ateah; cos, Dee Campbell

Action   (PR:C   MPAA:R)

ANDY AND THE AIRWAVE RANGERS

(SEE: ANDY COLBY'S INCREDIBLY AWESOME ADVENTURE)

ANDY COLBY'S INCREDIBLY AWESOME ADVENTURE

88m Fiat Lucre/Concorde c

(AKA: ANDY AND THE AIRWAVE RANGERS)

Randy Josselyn (Andy Colby), Jessica Puscas (Bonnie Colby), Chuck Kovacic (Lord Chroma), Don Sparks (Glitch), Diane Kay (Mrs. Colby), John Franklin (The Gatekeeper), Lara Piper (Bionda), John Bluto (Video Store Clerk), Bo Svenson, Vince Edwards, Luca Bercovici, Patsy Pease, Thom Christopher, and Don Washburn

For those of you keeping score, ANDY COLBY'S INCREDIBLY AWESOME ADVENTURE may be Roger Corman's biggest ripoff yet. It's a soulless, cynical attempt to wring more bucks out of some old New Horizons productions, and it's even more maddening in view of its genuinely charming setup: stuck with the chore of baby-sitting little sister Bonnie (Jessica Puscas), 12-year-old Andy (Randy Josselyn) visits the local video store in search of a tape to make the coming hours pass as painlessly as possible. When Andy finds an unfamiliar cassette labeled "Incredible Video Adventure," a mysterious clerk informs him that it is the only copy of the tape in the world. To watch it, Andy is told, he must make sure not to sit too close to the screen and under no circumstances is he to let go of the remote control. Back home, after starting the tape, Andy has to leave the room to answer the phone. Alone with the TV, Bonnie is suddenly addressed by a strange, dark-cloaked man on the screen who beckons her closer. Andy returns in time to see his sister vanish into the tube. Unfazed, he uses the remote control to rewind the action, but when Bonnie fails to emerge, Andy climbs into the screen. He finds himself in a desert, but using the remote control he changes his surroundings to footage from the Corman production SPACE RAIDERS. Yes, for what seems like hours the kid gawks at the antics of Vince Edwards as the 1983 film unspools. Then Andy enters WIZARDS OF THE LOST KINGDOM (1985), in which he shares some tiresome adventures with affable barbarian Bo Svenson. Sharp-eyed viewers who still give a damn will also recognize scenes from CHOPPING MALL; DEATHSTALKER II; WHEELS OF FIRE; and other Corman productions, as Andy hops from channel to channel. After being stunned by a laser, the boy enters a region of static where a fuzzy, friendly beast named Glitch dwells. Glitch reassures Andy, telling him "It's only a movie," and suggests that Bonnie's abductor might be Lord Chroma (Chuck Kovacic) a resident of the Higher Channels—a zone so rarefied that it's all in black and white, except for the color stolen and hoarded by Chroma. Eluding Chroma's robot cyclists (provided by DEATHSPORT [1978]), Andy penetrates the villain's fortress and finds Chroma about to vacuum the color from his sister. Again using the remote control, Andy freeze-frames Chroma, but the effect is only temporary, and the kids flee back to their point of entry with Chroma in pursuit. Glitch delays Chroma long enough for Andy and Bonnie to climb out of the TV set, just as Mom comes home. Finding the two on the floor, she accuses them of roughhousing and tells them they can't watch TV for a week, much to the children's delight.

Marathon recycling of stock footage is nothing new to Corman. He and then-fledgling director Peter Bogdanovich once cut a Russian sci-fi spectacle, PLANET OF STORMS, into two look-alike cheapies, VOYAGE TO THE PREHISTORIC PLANET and VOYAGE TO THE PLANET OF PREHISTORIC WOMEN. But ANDY COLBY'S INCREDIBLY AWESOME AD-

VENTURE makes those cinematic crimes look like misdemeanors. Director Deborah Brock (SLUMBER PARTY MASSACRE II) lets the leftovers unreel like old home movies, making only a slight attempt to integrate the new characters into the old footage. Still, the original sections that she has shot for the film show some real talent.

The young actors perform capably, and Lord Chroma's castle is a cute bit of surrealistic design. As Chroma, however, Chuck Kovacic seems to be impersonating a kiddie-show host run amok; he cackles, gloats, raps, and performs imitations of Pee-Wee Herman and Carl Sagan—all to little effect.

ANDY COLBY'S INCREDIBLY AWESOME ADVENTURE is obviously aimed at younger viewers, and indeed the stock footage has been cleansed of the usual Corman sleaze. But the death of a crewman in the SPACE RAIDERS segment and Chroma's casual elimination of a youthful slave make the film a questionable time-waster for young children. (Violence.)

d, Deborah Brock; p, Jed Horovitz; w, Jed Horovitz and Deborah Brock; ph, David Sperling; ed, Tim Amix; m, Ernest Troost and James Horner; set d, Rozanne Taucher; cos, Nadine Reimers; makup, Kathleen Vandale

Adventure/Children's/Fantasy   (PR:C   MPAA:PG)

ANGEL TOWN

87m Ellendale Place/Imperial — Taurus c

Olivier Gruner, Theresa Saldana, Frank Aragon, Tony Valentino, Peter Kwong, and Mike Moroff

Following in the bone-breaking footsteps of Jean-Claude Van Damme, kickboxing sensation Olivier Gruner stars in ANGEL TOWN. His woodenness easily matches Van Damme's and, being French, he, like the Belgian Van Damme, also has a thick accent, rendering even his rudimentary line readings unintelligible to all but the most practiced ear. Not that ANGEL TOWN needs much dialog. The splendidly silly prolog (supposedly set in Paris), which explains the French kickboxing champion's presence in East Los Angeles, is about as dramatically complicated as the film ever gets. On his way to the airport, Gruner stops at the grave of his father, explaining that he's going to America to coach a kickboxing team and, while he's at it, to pick up an advanced engineering degree from "Southern California University." Having performed the arduous task of moving their hunk from Paris to LA, writer S.N. Warren and director Eric Karson (THE OCTAGON) now must transport him from the safety of the campus to the wilder (in this case Chicano) side of LA, where he moves in with a widowed mom (Theresa Saldana). Her son (Frank Aragon) reminds Gruner of his own youth (depicted in a series of not-so-splendidly-silly "Paris"-based flashbacks that explain virtually nothing and, thankfully, disappear entirely about halfway through this epic). Of course, the real reason the moviemakers move Gruner into the barrio is to have him kick butt. Gruner's main antagonists are a renegade gang run by Uzzi-wielding Angel (Tony Valentino), a sociopath from the Trinidad Silva school, who is obsessed with forcing Aragon either to join the gang or to die slowly. Valentino becomes even more obsessed with Gruner, who protects Aragon and his mom while urging the lad to take on Valentino by himself, avenging the gang leader's murder of Aragon's father, a kindhearted community activist. Fortunately, virtually all of these fine points of character and plot motivation fall by the wayside as the film's raison d'etre—kickboxing action—becomes apparent. Gruner is even allowed to abandon his classes in a single scene that shows him falling asleep during a quiz—not because he's just had two huge fights, but because he is so much more advanced than either his classmates or his teacher. In his now-ample free time, Gruner begins bashing Chicanos by the carload. He even recruits a friend, an Asian martial-arts teacher (Peter Kwong), and his students to join the fun, allowing for some really big fight scenes. Valentino's madness provides the motivation for some drive-by violence, an attempted bombing of Gruner's expensive sports car, a grisly attempt to frame Gruner for murder, the rape of Saldana, and other assorted mayhem. As always, the purpose of these violent episodes is to make the hero even more irate than he was to begin with. The final, "big" scene has it all, including a semi-paralysed Vietnam vet who uses an M16 rifle to help Aragon and Gruner hold off rampaging hordes of Mexican-Americans. Of course, Aragon and Valentino finally go one-on-one (after Gruner has softened Valentino up).

As the going gets fast and furious near the film's end, ANGEL TOWN almost becomes crazy enough to make you forget how terrible a movie it is, though the sensation is a fleeting one. Even by this genre's standards it is hardly an impressive effort. The fights are badly staged, the action ranges from the rudimentary to the ridiculous, and the props are laughable (in particular, the Uzzi that Valentino wields looks like a toy). Moreover, why bother giving Angel an Uzzi when he never uses it, even after Aragon takes some potshots at him with a shotgun? To the film's credit Valentino has some good, edgy moments as Angel, and Saldana brings some conviction to her role; however, their efforts are totally wasted. (Violence, brief nudity.)

d, Eric Karson; p, Ash R. Shah and Eric Karson; w, S.N. Warren; ph, John Le Blanc; ed, Duane Hartzell; m, Terry Plumeri

Action   (PR:O MPAA:R)

ANIMAL BEHAVIOR

90m Millimeter/Cinestar c

Karen Allen *(Alex Bristow)*, Armand Assante *(Mark Mathias)*, Holly Hunter *(Coral Grable)*, Josh Mostel *(Mel Gorsky)*, Richard Libertini *(Dr. Parrish)*, Alexa Kenin *(Sheila Sandusky)*, Jon Mathews *(Tyler Forbes)*, Nan Martin *(Mrs. Norton)*, and Crystal Buda *(Cleo Grable)*

Though filming began in 1984, ANIMAL BEHAVIOR was not released until 1990 because producers Kjehl Rasmussen and Randolph Clendenen wanted to raise additional funds to boost the budget. Delays forced Rasmussen to finish the project for director Jenny Bowen (the pseudonym H. Anne Riley was used for the director's credit), but the substitution apparently did no harm to this low-key, intelligent romance.

Armand Assante plays Mark Mathias, a cellist and composer from New York who takes a teaching job at Lamont University so he can enjoy some midwestern peace and quiet while working on a new composition. Women are drawn to him irresistibly, but he, being an incurable white knight, is only attracted to damsels in distress. He is smitten immediately by Dr. Alex Bristow (Karen Allen) when he discovers her trying to coax a chimpanzee out of a campus tree. A psychologist experimenting with inter-species communication, Alex is trying to teach Michael, her chimp, sign language. She is considered something of a joke by most of the faculty (referred to as "Our Lady of the Apes" at a cocktail party) and is distraught because her department chairman and former lover, Dr. Parrish (Richard Libertini), is cutting her research budget two months before a visit by the American Science Foundation (ASF), which is considering Alex for a sizeable grant. When Mark tries to woo Alex, he discovers that she has no time for anything but her work. So he decides to learn sign language and become her lab assistant. He also befriends another down-on-her-luck woman, Coral Grable (Holly Hunter), who lives in the apartment below Mark's with her mute daughter, Cleo (Crystal Buda). Watching videotapes of Mark at play with Michael, Alex realizes that she is attracted to the musician and goes to his apartment to tell him. But there she meets Coral and Cleo and mistakes them for Mark's wife and daughter. Without explaining her feelings to Mark, Alex suddenly turns cold toward him. She keeps him around, however, because she needs help in the lab. Frustrated and confused by Alex's change of attitude, Mark is soon unable to concentrate on his work. One day, while baby-sitting Cleo, Mark discovers that she understands sign language—something she must have learned from playing with Michael. Excited, Mark takes Coral and Cleo to the lab and tries to tell Alex. However, Alex, offended because she thinks Mark is flaunting his wife and child, throws them out of the lab. Feeling completely rejected, Mark decides to leave the university and go back to New York. Meanwhile, the ASF people arrive for the site visit and inspect Alex's lab, barely able to conceal their boredom. When Alex tries to put Michael through his paces, he doesn't cooperate, and the ASF members stop paying attention, failing to see Michael ask for milk by forming a new word with sign language—proof that he has acquired language skills and is not merely mimicking Alex. When the committee asks Alex to have Michael repeat the new word, he again refuses to cooperate. As a result, Alex's grant application is turned down, and Parrish commandeers the chimp for one of his own experiments. Parrish straps Michael into a computerized machine that looks like a torture device and the chimp panics. Infuriated, Alex bursts into the lab and releases Michael, who promptly bites Parrish on the nose, then runs away, pursued by Parrish, the ASF committee, Alex, and Mark, who has stopped by to say goodbye. After leading a chase through a maze-like art installation, Michael runs into Cleo and begins talking with her in sign language, demonstrating inter-species communication. The ASF committee is floored by this scientific breakthrough and awards Alex a grant. Learning why Alex has been so distant, Mark explains that he isn't married, and he, Alex, and Michael become happy housemates.

ANIMAL BEHAVIOR was almost entirely overlooked in its token theatrical release, in which it was slipped onto a few screens in major cities at the same time PRETTY WOMAN and TEENAGE MUTANT NINJA TURTLES were cleaning up at the box office. A pity, because this modest little movie deserves to be seen and appreciated. It manages to be intelligent without being pompous or pretentious, and entertaining without resorting to titillation. No one gets killed and no one walks around naked—except the monkey. (To be sure, the nasty Dr. Parrish gets poked in the snoot at the end, but this action falls under the heading of just desserts.) The lack of gratuitous violence and sex is so unusual that the viewer is nearly left with the feeling that something is missing. No rape, no romping, no mayhem. Only quiet, understated interactions among interesting people.

Ostensibly a love story, ANIMAL BEHAVIOR is also a story about how people do their jobs. The film reveals much about its characters by showing them at work: teaching students, planning art exhibits, endlessly reviewing laboratory results. The romance that involves all the main characters is only on the periphery of their lives—an unusual touch that adds a surprising amount of realism to the situation. In keeping with the subtle tone, all of the actors give believable, understated performances. Playing against type, Assante turns in a surprisingly gentle, almost diffident, performance as the soft-hearted musician. And Hunter is also effective in an extended cameo as a downtrodden but spunky young mother in this extraordinary film.

d, Jenny Bowen and Kjehl Rasmussen; p, Kjehl Rasmussen and Randolph Clendenen; w, Susan Rice; ph, David Spellvin; ed, Joseph Weintraub; m, Cliff Eidelman; prod d, Jeannine Oppewall; art d, David Brisbin; set d, Lisa Fischer

Comedy/Romance   (PR:A MPAA:PG)

ANOTHER 48 HRS.

95m Lawrence Gordon-Eddie Murphy/Paramount c

Eddie Murphy *(Reggie Hammond)*, Nick Nolte *(Jack Cates)*, Brion James *(Ben Kehoe)*, Kevin Tighe *(Blake Wilson)*, Ed O'Ross *(Frank Cruise)*, David Anthony Marshall *(Willy Hickok)*, Andrew Divoff *(Cherry Ganz)*, Bernie Casey *(Kirkland Smith)*, Brent Jennings *(Burroughs)*, Ted Markland *(Malcolm Price)*, Tisha Campbell *(Amy Smith)*, Felice Orlandi *(The Warden)*, and Page Leong *(Angel)*

To be fair, ANOTHER 48 HRS. isn't quite a carbon copy of 48 HRS. In the original film, Eddie Murphy's big-screen debut, Nick Nolte's name was above Murphy's in the credits. Now, Murphy takes the top credit and the sequel comes to us "in association with Eddie Murphy Productions." Unfortunately, Murphy's new prominence in the credits is not matched by his work on the screen. The energy and go-for-broke comic creativity that he brought to the first film are only hinted at here. Indeed, he could have phoned in much of his performance. Nolte and director Walter Hill try harder, probably because neither has had as big a hit since 48 HRS. But in the end, they are overwhelmed by what otherwise amounts to a smash-'em-up exercise in cinematic deja vu. Murphy's Reggie Hammond adds James Brown's "I Got the Feeling" to his repertoire, but he also reprises his headphone-*karaoke* performance of the Police hit "Roxanne." While the first film had a scene set in a rundown Chinatown apartment building and a shootout in an upscale hotel-brothel, the sequel has a shootout in a rundown Chinatown hotel-brothel. And while the first film had one barroom brawl, ANOTHER 48 HRS. has three—including one in which Nolte, not Murphy, holds an entire bar at bay. "It's such a cliche," Nolte's Jack Cates says to an ex-con in the bar who had been arrested by Cates and wants to settle the score. "Pretty soon a bottle will be busted over someone's head, punches will be thrown, and someone will break a chair over someone else." Without missing a beat, Cates then busts a bottle over the ex-con's head, punches a second brawler, and breaks a chair over a third. Such moments of wit are tiny oases in a desert of boredom.

Fittingly enough, ANOTHER 48 HRS. begins in a desert, at a roadhouse in the middle of nowhere. There three biker-goons—one of them the brother of Ganz, the psycho-criminal killed by Cates in the original film—meet with a mobster and accept a $100,000 contract to kill Hammond. On their way out, as if to show they are up to the job, the three murder two state troopers and a bartender. The contract on Hammond has been taken out by the Iceman, an elusive master criminal, from whom Hammond and his partner stole the $500,000 in the first film and with whose arrest Cates has been long obsessed. That obsession now lands Cates in big trouble. At a motor-cross racetrack, he watches as a mechanic agrees to back up the bikers on the Hammond hit. But Cates' attempt to make an arrest leads to a shootout, after which the mechanic's gun mysteriously disappears. In the aftermath of the incident, Cates faces both dismissal from the department and criminal charges as a result of the mechanic's death. Nevertheless, Cates picks up on Hammond's connection to the Iceman and intercepts Hammond as he is released from prison. Instead of the six months Hammond had left on his sentence at the end of the first film, he wound up serving five more years on trumped-up additional charges. Hammond and Cates' hate-at-first-sight relationship is pointlessly repeated with the two eventually joining forces, once again, to catch the same criminals for different reasons. The extended male-bonding fistfight from the first film is compressed into a couple of sucker punches here.

What also distinguishes ANOTHER 48 HRS. from its predecessor is its lazier plotting. Not only is the climax, the unmasking of the Iceman, tossed away, but it doesn't even make much sense. Early in the film, Cates identifies the Iceman's agent in the Hammond hit by using a police composite-drawing kit. Later, it emerges that the real reason the Iceman wants Hammond dead is that Hammond knows what he looks like. But rather than having Hammond also use the composite kit, Cates drags him throughout San Francisco (barely distinguishable here from the average neon-bathed backlot soundstage) to look at an Internal

Affairs detective who Cates thinks is the master criminal. It plays as if someone had written the last half of ANOTHER 48 HRS. without reading the first half.

The idea of dropping in on Reggie Hammond and Jack Cates five years later presents some amusing and intriguing possibilities. But little thought or imagination have been devoted to considering how the two characters might have changed over the years. Instead, one of the sequel's better running jokes is that Cates is *exactly* the same now as he was then. He drives the same car and wears the same clothes. He even has the same haircut. Meanwhile, Hammond, the compulsive skirt-chaser from the first film, has somehow evolved into something of a liberal curmudgeon here, scolding a woman for putting up with an abusive boy friend in one scene and lecturing Cates about social justice in another. It's only too bad nobody lectured the producers about creative cowardice. If someone had, ANOTHER 48 HRS. might have been another good movie instead of just another damned sequel. (*Violence, profanity, adult situations, nudity.*)

d, Walter Hill; p, Lawrence Gordon and Robert D. Wachs; w, John Fasano, Jeb Stuart, and Larry Gross (based on a story by Fred Braughton); ph, Matthew F. Leonetti; ed, Freeman Davies, Carmel Davies, and Donn Aron; m, James Horner; prod d, Joseph C. Nemec III; cos, Dan Moore

Action/Comedy/Crime   (PR:O MPAA:R)

ARACHNOPHOBIA

107m Amblin/Hollywood c

Jeff Daniels (*Dr. Ross Jennings*), Harley Jane Kozak (*Molly Jennings*), John Goodman (*Delbert McClintock*), Julian Sands (*Dr. James Atherton*), Stuart Pankin (*Sheriff Parsons*), Brian McNamara (*Chris Collins*), Mark L. Taylor (*Jerry Manley*), Henry Jones (*Dr. Sam Metcalf*), Peter Jason (*Henry Beechwood*), James Handy (*Milton Briggs*), Roy Brocksmith (*Irv Kendall*), Kathy Kinney (*Blaire Kendall*), Mary Carver (*Margaret Hollins*), Garette Patrick Ratliff (*Tommy Jennings*), Marlene Katz (*Shelley Jennings*), Jane Marla Robbins (*Edna Beechwood*), Theo Schwartz (*Bunny Beechwood*), Cori Wellins (*Becky Beechwood*), Chance Boyer (*Bobby Beechwood*), Brandy (*Brandy Beechwood*), Frances Bay (*Evelyn Metcalf*), Lois de Banzie (*Henrietta Manley*), Warren Rice (*Dick Manley*), Robert Frank Telfer (*Mayor Bob*), Michael Steve Jones (*Irv's Assistant*), Fiona Walsh (*Little Girl*), Terese Del Piero (*Mom*), Nathaniel Spitzley (*Todd Miller*), Jay Scorpio (*Mover*), and Mai-Lis Kuniholm (*Girl Friend*)

Arachnophobia is defined here as the deep-rooted fear of spiders, those creepy, crawly insects that give most of us a twinge of anxiety, if not pangs of out-and-out terror. Catering to this prevalent dread, Frank Marshall's directorial debut is a predictable formula film that also panders to yet another basic psychological state, what might be called *phobiaphilia*, the love of being scared. But as Steven Spielberg's longtime partner and executive producer of some of the most popular movies ever made (RAIDERS OF THE LOST ARK; POLTERGEIST; BACK TO THE FUTURE), Marshall has learned a few tricks along the way. Conventional though it may be, ARACHNOPHOBIA is almost flawlessly executed. Cute rather than clever, this self-styled "thrill-omedy" breaks no new ground, but it is fun to watch, beautifully produced, and guaranteed to evoke lighthearted screams along with its share of nervous laughter.

The obligatory prolog (long at 18 minutes) establishes the movie's premise in the remote Venezuelan rain forest. During a scientific expedition to uncover new species of spiders, photographer Jerry Manley (Mark L. Taylor) dies after being bitten by a deadly new breed. (Not the usual sort of friendly daddy longlegs, this large, furry spider has fierce-looking fangs and is as ugly as sin.) Undetected by the expedition's leader, world famous entomologist Dr. James Atherton (Julian Sands), one of these hideous spiders stows away in Manley's casket, which is bound for the photographer's hometown, Canaima, California. Enter Ross Jennings (Jeff Daniels), a yuppie Yalie with a medical degree and a fondness for vintage wine. Battle-scarred from the urban warfare of San Francisco, Ross moves his family (stockbroker wife, two kids, and pet dog) to Canaima—where else?—to take over the small-town medical practice of the retiring local doctor. However, crotchety old Doc Metcalf (Henry Jones) changes his mind and decides to continue his practice, which includes practically everyone in town. Jennings' only patient is his neighbor, Margaret Hollins (Mary Carver). But after she throws a garden party to introduce the young doctor to the locals, Jennings is left patientless when Margaret is found dead, the cause of her death unknown. The audience knows better: the obvious has happened; the film's "star" has escaped from Manley's casket in the town mortuary. Grown to enormous proportions after draining the corpse of blood, the spider has gone in search of its next meal and found Margaret. Jennings, whose reputation is already suffering, is nicknamed "Doctor Death" when a new patient, a member of the high-school football team, dies after a spider crawls unnoticed into his helmet. Jennings' requests for autopsies are rejected by both Metcalf and the simpleton sheriff (Stuart Pankin) until the older physician himself becomes a victim. Lab tests point to minute amounts of an unidentified poison as the cause, and Jennings contacts Atherton, who sends his assistant (Brian McNamara) to investigate.

After the spider "feeds" on the undertaker and his wife—in a bizarre but funny sequence—Atherton himself shows up and pushes the panic button. Engaging in doubletalk about the ecological breakdown of the spiders' natural habitat, Atherton warns that unless their nest is found and destroyed, the spiders will multiply rapidly and kill everyone and everything in their path (a surprising prediction, considering that these spiders lack reproductive organs). The hunt for the nest is on! In no time, Atherton spots a prominently displayed photo that Jennings' wife, Molly (Harley Jane Kozak), has taken of the huge spiderweb in their barn. It becomes immediately obvious that this is where "the General," as the original spider has been dubbed, has set up housekeeping (though it's never made clear how a family of Ivy Leaguers couldn't have made this connection on their own). Atherton rushes into the barn, looks around admiringly at all the dead animals caught in the huge web (a pretty gory sight), and utters a respectful "My, you have been busy." Unfortunately, his next words, "C'mon. Supper's ready," are his last. He's the main course. For the film's grand finale, Jennings, who's had a chronic case of arachnophobia since he was two, escapes with his family from the mass infestation of newborn spiders inside his house. On the attack, the creatures crawl though rooms, atop the TV, under doors, and across the floor; they even corner Jennings in the bathroom. Naturally, he escapes (never for a moment do you doubt it), then heads for the barn. In a battle to the death with "the General," Jennings burns the spider and its nest, using his vintage wine collection for fuel. In the last scene, with San Francisco's skyline in the background and Tony Bennett singing his signature number on the soundtrack, the Jennings celebrate their move back to civilization, happy to be in control of their lives again. However, their short-lived bliss is interrupted by the increasingly loud rumble of an earthquake. (The Moral? There's no escape.)

Big John Goodman doesn't appear until the midpoint of the picture and does little to further the plot. In a very small role as the boob of an exterminator who's hired to rid the Jennings' farmhouse of termites, Goodman is on hand solely to provide comic relief. Swaggering, using his spray cans like six-shooters, and dressed like a one-man posse from the Wild West, he has precious few lines, but is funny even without saying a word. The rest of the cast is perfectly fine, especially Daniels, who suitably underplays the city sophisticate transplanted to the sticks. However, little is demanded from any of the roles.

Considerably more lifelike than any of these caricatures are the spiders. Steven Kutcher, Hollywood's best-known insect specialist, screen-tested dozens of spiders before coming up with a versatile creature from New Zealand, the Delena, which fit the bill perfectly. Wranglers were then hired to keep an eye on the spiders during the filming—which used as many as 200 of the insects in some scenes.

The first release from Disney's new Hollywood Pictures, ARACHNOPHOBIA did boffo business when it opened. Some critics even likened it to Spielberg's JAWS and Hitchcock's THE BIRDS; however, those comparisons are far too generous. Those films are classics; ARACHNOPHOBIA is merely an also-ran. It may be a seamless tongue-in-cheek thriller, but it lacks the superbly developed psychological tension of its illustrious predecessors. Director Marshall's film is nothing more than a diversion, and if you personally have no fear of spiders, you might wonder what all the fuss is about. Nevertheless, parents might want to think twice before bringing small children to this one. (*Violence, gore effects.*)

d, Frank Marshall; p, Kathleen Kennedy and Richard Vane; w, Don Jakoby and Wesley Strick (based on a story by Don Jakoby, Al Williams); ph, Mikael Salomon; ed, Michael Kahn; m, Trevor Jones; prod d, James Bissell; art d, Christopher Burian-Mohr; set d, Carl J. Stensel; spec, Matt Sweeney and Chris Walas; stunts, Chuck Waters; cos, Jennifer L. Parsons; makup, James L. McCoy and David Quashnick; tech, Steven Kutcher, Arnold Peterson, and Chuck Kristensen

Comedy/Horror   (PR:C MPAA:PG-13)

AVALON

126m Baltimore/Tri-Star c

Leo Fuchs (*Hymie Krichinsky*), Eve Gordon (*Dottie Kirk*), Lou Jacobi (*Gabriel Krichinsky*), Armin Mueller-Stahl (*Sam Krichinsky*), Elizabeth Perkins (*Ann Kaye*), Joan Plowright (*Eva Krichinsky*), Kevin Pollak (*Izzy Kirk*), Aidan Quinn (*Jules Kaye*), Israel Rubinek (*Nathan Krichinsky*), Elijah Wood (*Michael Kaye*), Grant Gelt (*Teddy Kirk*), Mindy Loren Isenstein (*Mindy Kirk*), Shifra Lerer (*Nellie Krichinsky*), Mina Bern (*Alice Krichinsky*), Frania Rubinek (*Faye Krichinsky*), Neil Kirk (*Herbie*), Ronald Guttman (*Simka*), Rachel Aviva (*Elka*), Sylvia Weinberg (*Mrs. Parkes*), Ralph Tabakin (*Principal Dunn*), Steve Aronson (*Moving Man*), Miles A. Perman (*Gas Attendant*), Beatrice Yoffe (*Nursing Home Receptionist*), Brian Sher (*Country Club Page*), Frank Tamburo (*Mugger*), Patrick Flynn (*Fire Chief*), Herb Levinson (*Rabbi at Funeral*), Paul Quinn (*K & K Employee*), Kevin Blum (*Young Jules*), Alvin Myerovich (*The Father*), Moishe Rosenfeld (*William as a Young Man*), Michael Krauss (*Sam as a Young Man*), Michael David Edelstein (*Gabriel as a Young Man*), Bernard Hiller

(*Hymie as a Young Man*), Brian Shait (*Nathan as a Young Man*), Dawne Hindle (*Eva as a Young Woman*), Christine Mosere (*Nellie as a Young Woman*), Anna Bergman (*Alice as a Young Woman*), Mary Lechter (*Faye as a Young Woman*), Barbara Morris (*Mollie as a Young Woman*), Tom Wood (*Michael as an Adult*), Christopher James Lekas (*Sam, Michael's Son*), Ava Eileen Quinn (*David as a Baby*), David Thornhill (*David, age 8 Months*), Jordan Young (*David, age 10*), Tammy Walker (*Camera Girl*), David Long (*TV Commercial Director*), Brenda Alford (*Night Club Singer*), Thomas Joy (*Country Club Singer*), James A. Zemarel (*Supper Club Singer*), Jesse Adelman, Judy Bach, Alisa Bernstein, Eva Cohen, Josh Lessner, Samantha Shenk, Patty Sherman, Irv Stein, Thelma Weiner, and Robert Zalkind (*Miscellaneous Family Members*)

Completing writer-director Barry Levinson's "Baltimore trilogy," which began with DINER and TIN MEN, AVALON is the strangely sour chronicle of a family (said to be based upon Levinson's own) that gradually disintegrates as its younger members move from the bustling city to the bleak suburbs. Armin Mueller-Stahl plays patriarch Sam Krichinsky, and Joan Plowright (I LOVE YOU TO DEATH) takes the role of his wife, Eva. Immigrating to Baltimore in 1914, Sam is reunited with his brothers — Gabriel (Lou Jacobi), Hymie (Leo Fuchs), and Nathan (Israel Rubinek) — and drawn into the "family circle," whose members pool their resources to bring relatives like Sam over from the old country. Wallpaper hangers during the week, the brothers are musicians on the weekends, and it is during one of their gigs that Sam meets Eva. But the film's real focus is on Sam's grown son, Jules (Aidan Quinn), who does not follow in his father's footsteps as a manual laborer. Instead he goes into door-to-door sales, sometimes taking along his young son, Michael (Elijah Wood), the character said to be based on Levinson himself. During one of these sales outings, Michael watches in terror as his father is stabbed by a mugger. While recuperating, Jules is given a television set by his family. The only "program" at that time is a nonstop test pattern; nevertheless, Jules glimpses a future in the new invention. Teaming up with his cousin, Izzy (Kevin Pollak), he opens a store that sells only TVs, all of them showing the same test pattern. Business is nonexistent at first, but it quickly picks up some time after "Howdy Doody" abruptly breaks through the test-pattern monotony. Before long, the small TV store has taken over an entire building, growing into a department store guaranteeing the lowest prices in town. Later, the department store expands into a huge discount warehouse by the waterfront. But Izzy, who manages the business's money, skips insurance payments on the warehouse to invest in TV spots promoting the grand opening. Playing in the basement of the warehouse on opening day, Michael indulges in his hobby, building model airplanes, then setting fire to them and blowing them up with firecrackers. Red-hot embers spread throughout the basement nearly causing a fire. That night, when a fire actually does destroy the warehouse, Michael is tortured by guilt, believing that he may have been responsible. Instead, it turns out that an electrical short was the cause of the blaze. Jules' partnership with his cousin becomes the fire's major casualty.

With the business bankrupt after the fire because of Izzy's failure to make the insurance payments, Jules settles down to steady work to support his family. Like Izzy, he also continues his cultural assimilation. Rather than having an Old World wedding, Jules and Izzy wind up opting for a double elopement. At the same time, both Americanize their surnames, Jules shortening his last name to Kaye, while Izzy Krichinsky becomes Izzy Kirk, provoking Sam's momentary anger. When Jules and Izzy move to the suburbs, they break up the family's closeness. Sam's brothers begin to regard his family with anger and suspicion, leading to a rift in the family circle. Meanwhile, the family talks less and less and watches television more and more. By the end, Jules and his wife (Elizabeth Perkins) even eat Thanksgiving dinner in front of the tube. In the film's final scene, a now-grown Michael brings his own son to visit Sam, who now lives alone in a nursing home, spending most of his time watching TV.

Not unlike Martin Scorsese's GOODFELLAS, AVALON is concerned with the perils of sacrificing humaneness for hollow material success, a sort of 90s cinematic hangover from the "go for it" excesses of the 80s. The crucial difference between the approaches taken by these two films is that Scorsese's theme rises naturally from his material while Levinson imposes his themes on his material. Thus, GOODFELLAS's strengths — its strong sense of time, place, character, and mood — become AVALON's weaknesses. Despite the film's meticulously detailed production design, its human details don't ring true. It's hard to imagine even the most alienated of families eating Thanksgiving dinner silently in front of the TV. If Jules' family is really that alienated, how did it become that way? The movie offers no clue beyond the presence of the all-powerful boob tube, which has displaced the extended family that once gathered in the living room, talking, arguing, and telling stories of their immigrant experiences.

Despite a spirited performance by Perkins, Jules' wife, like all the women in AVALON (and, for that matter, in all of Levinson's films), remains only a hazily defined character. Equally vague is Sam, who goes from paperhanging to owning a nightclub, then returns to paperhanging, inexplicably amassing a fortune in the process. The nightclub interlude includes the film's most bizarre scene, in which,

Jules, Izzy, and their wives, after announcing their double wedding, boogie-woogie with Sam and the black clientele in Sam's club. It's bizarre mainly because AVALON has no major African-American characters, which, among other things, leaves unexplained how Sam was able to open a successful jazz club without having any visible connections to the black music scene or the black community. But AVALON is full of loose plot threads; Levinson continually sacrifices narrative sense to clobber his audience with obvious and underdeveloped thematic points. We don't know how Sam built his comfortable retirement from a career as a paperhanger. We don't know what Jules does for a living after dropping out of his retailing partnership with his cousin. More important, Avalon, the neighborhood in which Sam settles his family, never comes alive; it never becomes tangible enough to justify the film being named after it. As a result AVALON never really comes alive as a movie, though the photography by Allen Daviau (E.T.) gives the film a great look. It should also be noted that the cast is quite good, especially Quinn, whose performance holds the story's center. Ultimately, however, Levinson's very personal project never acquires a personality of its own. The film earned Oscar nominations for cinematography, costumes, original score, and screenplay. (*Profanity, violence.*)

d, Barry Levinson; p, Mark Johnson and Barry Levinson; w, Barry Levinson; ph, Allen Daviau; ed, Stu Linder; m, Randy Newman; md, Allan Mason; prod d, Norman Reynolds; art d, Fred Hole and Edward Richardson; set d, Linda DeScenna; spec, Allen L. Hall, Thomas R. Burman, and Bari Dreiband-Burman; stunts, Joel Kramer; cos, Gloria Gresham; makup, Irving Buchman and Paul Gebbia

Drama   (PR:A   MPAA:PG)

AWAKENINGS

121m Colombia c

Robert De Niro (*Leonard Lowe*), Robin Williams (*Dr. Malcolm Sayer*), Julie Kavner (*Eleanor Costello*), Ruth Nelson (*Mrs. Lowe*), John Heard (*Dr. Kaufman*), Penelope Ann Miller (*Paula*), Alice Drummond (*Lucy*), Judith Malina (*Rose*), Barton Heyman (*Bert*), George Martin (*Frank*), Anne Meara (*Miriam*), Richard Libertini (*Sidney*), Laura Esterman (*Lolly*), Dexter Gordon (*Rolando*), Jayne Haynes (*Frances*), Le Chance DuRand (*Magda*), Yusef Bulos (*Joseph*), Steve Randazzon (*Luis*), Gloria Harper (*Dottie*), Gwyllum Evans (*Desmond*), Mary Catherine Wright (*Nurse Beth*), Mary Alice (*Nurse Margaret*), Keith Diamond (*Anthony*), Steve Vinovich (*Ray*), Tiger Haynes (*Janitor*), John Christopher Jones (*Dr. Sullivan*), Bradley Whitford (*Dr. Tyler*), Max Von Sydow (*Dr. Peter Ingham*), Harvey Miller (*Hospital Director*), Tanya Berezin (*Psychiatrist*), Peter Stormare (*Neurochemist*), Shane Fistell (*Man in Hall*), Waheedah Ahmad (*Hysterical Woman*), Charles Keating (*Mr. Kean*), Christina Huertes (*Christina*), Linda Burns (*Fishsticks*), Judy Jacksina (*Hospital Receptionist*), Gary Tacon (*George, Security Guard*), Rico Elias (*1st Orderly*), Mel Gorham (*Nurse Sara*), Chris Carolan (*EEG Technician*), Debra Kovner-Zaks (*Cafeteria Nurse*), Max Rabinowitz (*Orderly, 5th Ward*), Libby Titus (*Club Singer*), Michael Hyde (*Bus Driver*), Tomislav Novakovic (*Bartender*), Adam Bryant (*Librarian*), Anthony J. Nici (*Young Leonard Lowe*), Joan E. MacIntosh (*Teacher*), Oliver Block, Buck Smith (*Leonard's Friends*), Gordon Joseph Weiss, Byron Utley, Anthony McGowen, Paul Montgomery, Leonard Tepper, Vinny Pastore, and Howard Feller (*Patients, 5th Ward*)

This "fictionalization" of a true story strains to draw a conventionally upbeat, feel-good message from a remarkably downbeat story. The film's basis is the work and writings of neurologist Oliver Sacks, whose name is changed to Dr. Malcolm Sayer for the film, which is set in the late 1960s, Robin Williams plays Dr. Sayer, a man so shy and retiring he would rather sit alone and study his reference books than have a cup of coffee with nurse-admirer Eleanor Costello (Julie Kavner). A researcher prior to his assignment at a Bronx psychiatric hospital, Sayer examines the first human patients he has ever had and finds that, despite their seemingly impenetrable state, they have the ability to respond to certain stimuli. Further research reveals a common thread among the patients, each having been a victim of an encephalitis epidemic in the 1920s. Sayer suspects that his patients haven't lost their higher brain functions, though the hospital's chief physician, Dr. Kaufman (John Heard), finds the contention absurd. When Sayer learns that a new drug called L-DOPA has achieved some success in the treatment of victims of Parkinson's disease, he seeks permission to use the drug on his patients. Kaufman resists the proposal, but finally agrees to let Sayer test the drug on one patient, Leonard Lowe (Robert De Niro). Leonard has been a patient since the 1930s and he is visited each day by his mother (Ruth Nelson). At first, the drug has no effect, but when Sayer increases the dosage, Leonard eventually regains consciousness. Sayer then wages a successful campaign to have the entire ward treated with the drug, and the once-silent ward becomes raucously alive as patients come out of their comas eager to live the lives they have missed for so long. At the same time, however, Leonard begins displaying disturbing side effects, beginning with nervous tics and leading to fits of paranoia and violence. Sayer moderates Leonard's L-DOPA dosage, which makes him more manageable, but also reduces him to a spastic who is barely able to walk and talk. Soon, Leonard returns to his catatonic state, as do the other patients. An end title notes that other drugs and therapies have been tried on the patients in the years since without success.

With its RAGTIME-ish Randy Newman score, drab cinematography by Miroslav Ondricek (AMADEUS), and a scenario that more than faintly resembles a much-softened reworking of ONE FLEW OVER THE CUCKOO'S NEST, AWAKENINGS seems nothing so much as a Milos Forman film without, of course, Forman directing. There's nothing wrong with being derivative, but director Penny Marshall (BIG) never seems to have decided precisely what type of film she wanted to make. The film keeps vacillating uncomfortably between straight-on realistic drama and fanciful comedy and romance. The scenario cries out for a more rigorous, unsentimental approach in telling what is essentially a story of the horror of suddenly lucid patients clashing with a society of friends, relatives, and caretakers unable to cope with what should be a joyous occasion for all involved. As it is, the film never feels true for a single moment. Williams attempts to earn dramatic credibility by not doing what he does best. De Niro, deprived of a fully realized character, seems to resort to the kind of tortured, showy mannerisms that usually impress Oscar voters—indeed his performance won him a Best Actor Academy Award nomination. Altogether, AWAKENINGS comes across as little more than a series of big, splashy, hollow moments in a film that needed the skill, intelligence, and discipline of a good neurosurgeon behind and in front of the camera. In addition to De Niro's nomination, the film was nominated for Best Picture and Best Screenplay Based on Material from Another Medium. *(Mild profanity.)*

d, Penny Marshall; p, Walter Parkes and Lawrence Lasker; w, Steve Zaillian (based on the novel by Oliver Sacks); ph, Miroslav Ondricek; ed, Jerry Greenberg, Battle Davis, and Jere Huggins; m, Randy Newman; prod d, Anton Furst; art d, Bill Groom; set d, George DeTitta Jr.; cos, Cynthia Flynt; makup, Bernadette Mazur and Ilona Herman

Drama   (PR:A   MPAA:PG-13)

B

BACK TO BACK

95m Motion Picture Corporation of America/Vertex — Concorde c

Bill Paxton (*Bo Brand*), Todd Field (*Todd Brand*), Apollonia Kotero (*Jessie*), Luke Askew (*Sheriff Wade Duro*), Ben Johnson (*Eli Hix*), David Michael-Standing (*Hank Brand*), Susan Anspach (*Madeline Hix*), Sal Landi (*Deputy Jackson*), Roger Brook (*Manny Duro*), Warner McKay (*Cable Hogue*), Jay Zingler (*Stanislaw*), Henry Kendrick (*Sabatini*), Bill Parker, Tony Gaznick, Terry Marinan, Thom Kahler, Edward Alberty, Steven Kent, and Mildred Brian

BACK TO BACK walks the thin line between the offbeat and the merely ridiculous, eventually tumbling headlong into the latter. The setting is the Superstition Mountains of Arizona, a place long haunted by legends of buried treasure and ill-gotten riches. The story, which unfolds in a confusing shuffle of flashbacks and through Johnson's voiceover narration, begins, more or less, with the robbery of an armored car loaded with $7 million. The bandits and the car vanish completely, leaving one wounded security guard, Hank Brand (David Michael-Standing), as the only survivor. Encouraged by Sheriff Duro (Luke Askew), whose brother, Manny (Roger Brook), was murdered during the heist, the numbskull townspeople blame Hank for orchestrating the crime. A firebombing turns Hank into a scarred invalid, but until his death he continues to search for possible witnesses to clear his name. Stung by the hostility of the townsfolk and the sheriff, Hank's oldest son, Bo (Bill Paxton), a successful LA-based lawyer, takes up his father's search, working from Hank's notes. Hitting the trail, Bo and his younger, mentally impaired brother, Todd (Todd Field), are joined almost immediately by Jessie (Apollonia Kotero), a calculating hitchhiker. Meanwhile, Sheriff Duro follows them; in addition to revenge, he wants the missing cash for himself. Various witnesses help the Brands piece together the truth, and in time it becomes clear that the bandits double-crossed and killed one another after leaving the stolen armored car and money buried in rubble on land owned by Eli Hix (Ben Johnson), a longtime desert resident. When Bo and company finally meet Eli, he is happy to have the bloodstained loot taken off his hands. But as the group finishes digging out the truck, Jessie declares that she is none other than Manny Duro's daughter and that she, and not the sons of the evil Hank Brand, deserves the money. Just then Sheriff Duro and his henchmen show up and a gun battle ensues, during which Jessie finds evidence proving that it was her father and not Hank who was in cahoots with the bandits. How devastatingly ironic. In the ludicrous climax, the sheriff is set on fire, but while shrouded in flames, he manages to shoot an arrow that pierces both Bo and Todd, giving new meaning to the term "male bonding" and providing one interpretation of the movie's title. Naturally, this dual-impalement doesn't injure the Brands seriously, and Todd stays behind with Eli, having at last found his place in the world. The final scene also contains a plot twist concerning Eli's motivations, but it will be lost on anyone unfamiliar with the historical lore of the Superstition Mountains.

That the twist will not be clear to everyone is the least of the film's problems, however. Filmed largely in Apache Junction, Arizona, BACK TO BACK boils down to an ordinary, predictable melodrama, gussied up with a non-linear flashback structure and offering a truly bizarre attempt to duplicate the offbeat brotherly-love motif of RAIN MAN. Streetwise Bo and childlike Todd are deliberately fashioned to recall Tom Cruise's and Dustin Hoffman's RAIN MAN characters; however, the makers of BACK TO BACK are left with a major problem: the Brands just aren't very compelling characters. The initial appearance of Apollonia's Jessie promises some excitement, but her ulterior motive and her father's guilt are telegraphed early on. In the film's other key roles, Askew makes a terribly one-dimensional bad guy, but Johnson's homey appeal helps a little, as does James L. Carter's luminous photography. To its credit, the script contains some almost-memorable B-movie dialog, and a peripheral figure is named after Sam Peckinpah's western character Cable Hogue, but more healthy self-parody would have improved the picture considerably. The soundtrack is spiked with monotonous rock 'n' roll tunes, most of which are on a cassette in Paxton's car stereo, but the music gets better after Field destroys the tape during a temper tantrum. It's only too bad the film doesn't. (*Profanity, violence, adult situations, sexual situations.*)

d, John Kincade; p, Brad Krevoy and Steven Stabler; w, George Frances Skrow (based on a story by George Frances Skrow, Paul E. Stoudemire, Franklin Smith); ph, James L. Carter; ed, Peter Maris and Kevin Michaels; m, Rick Cox; prod d, Don Day; art d, Brian Densmore; set d, Nigel Klinker; spec, Steve Galich; stunts, Cole McKay; cos, Gini Kramer; makeup, Steven Wanzell

Action/Thriller　　　　　　　　　　　　　　　　　　　　　　　　(PR:O　MPAA:R)

BACK TO THE FUTURE PART III

118m Steven Spielberg/Universal c

Michael J. Fox (*Marty McFly/Seamus McFly*), Christopher Lloyd (*Dr. Emmett Brown*), Mary Steenburgen (*Clara Clayton*), Thomas F. Wilson (*Buford "Mad Dog" Tannen/Biff Tannen*), Lea Thompson (*Maggie McFly/Lorraine McFly*), Elisabeth Shue (*Jennifer*), Matt Clark (*Bartender*), Richard Dysart (*Barbed Wire Salesman*), Pat Buttram, Harry Carey Jr., Dub Taylor (*Saloon Old-Timers*), James Tolkan (*Marshal Strickland*), Marc McClure (*Dave McFly*), Wendie Jo Sperber (*Linda McFly*), Jeffrey Weissman (*George McFly*), Christopher Wynne, Sean Gregory Sullivan, Mike Watson (*Buford Tannen's Gang*), Hugh Gillin (*Mayor*), Burton Gilliam (*Colt Gun Salesman*), Bill McKinney (*Engineer*), Donovan Scott (*Deputy*), Flea (*Needles*), J.J. Cohen, Ricky Dean Logan (*Needles' Gang*), Marvin J. McIntyre (*Mortician*), Kaleb Henley (*Strickland's Son*), Todd Cameron Brown (*Jules*), Dannel Evans (*Verne*), Leslie A. Prickett (*Celebration Man*), Dean Cundey (*Photographer*), Jo B. Cummings (*Pie Lady*), Steve McArthur, John Ickes (*Festival Men*), James A. Rammel (*Festival Dance Caller*), Michael Klastorin, Michael John Mills, Kenny Myers (*Townsmen*), Brad McPeters (*Eyepatch*), Phinnaes D. (*Toothless*), Rod Kuehne (*Ticket Agent*), Leno Fletcher (*Conductor*), Joey Newington (*Joey*), Larry Ingold (*Train Fireman*), Tim Konrad (*Barbed Wire Salesman's Companion*), and Glenn Fox (*Boy with Gun*)

Well...uh...let's see. Biff Tannen still hates manure. But his name's not Biff, it's Buford. And it's not 1985 or 1955 or 2015. It's 1885. And Mad Dog Tannen is so named because he drools a lot. Needless to say, he's also another classic Tannen butthead. And Marty McFly, whose name this time out is Clint Eastwood (instead of Calvin Klein), still does a slow, dangerous burn when anyone calls him chicken.

Confused? Don't worry. It's part of the fun in what is allegedly the last installment of the time-bending, mind-bending BACK TO THE FUTURE trilogy. Part III begins at the end of both Part I and Part II and ends roughly one-third of the way into Part II. Part II ended at the end of Part I, with Part II's Doc (Christopher Lloyd) and Marty (Michael J. Fox) trying to avoid significant contact with Part I's Doc and Marty while both Martys and the 1985-vintage Doc were trying to get back to 1985. Although Part I's Marty gets back to 1985, Part II's Marty gets stuck in 1955 when Part II's Doc is sent careening back to 1885 by a thunderbolt. Soooo...Marty runs into town to find Part I's Doc to help him get back to 1985 again. In the meantime a letter arrives from Doc, written in 1885, in which he explains that he was unable to repair the familiar DeLorean time machine and has buried it outside of town.

Are you still with us? While digging up the DeLorean, Marty stumbles over Doc's tombstone, inscribed "With love from Clara," Doc's death having occurred only days after the date of the letter he wrote to Marty in 1885. The 1955 Doc then sends 1985 Marty back to save 1885 Doc from getting killed, which would snuff out Doc's family line, thus preventing Doc's existence in either 1955 or 1985. And, logically, without Doc there could be no BACK TO THE FUTURE in the first place. By the way, who is Clara?

That's right. Among many, many other things, BACK TO THE FUTURE PART III answers the question that has been nagging adult viewers ever since the first film: Where exactly did Doc, whose various incarnations share an aversion to women, come from? With its adult emphasis, PART III is fittingly the one installment in the trilogy that most resembles an old-fashioned movie, from its lovingly evoked western setting (peopled with such erstwhile genre character actors as Dub Taylor, Harry Carey, Jr., and Matt Clark) to its sweet, sentimental mood and its rousing, cliffhanger finale.

Marty intends to bring 1885 Doc back to 1985 to save the scientist from the bullet destined to kill him. But first, Marty has to be rescued by his own forebears, Seamus (Fox again) and Maggie (Lea Thompson, sporting a fetching Irish brogue). Instead of taking his name from his Calvin Klein underwear, as he did in Part I, this time Marty adopts the name of Eastwood (viewers may recall that Clint Eastwood was Biff's favorite actor in Part II). The name not only sticks, but Marty also has to preserve Doc's cherished "space-time continuum" by defending the Eastwood name when Buford "Mad Dog" Tannen (Thomas F. Wilson) calls Marty out after he saves Doc at a town dance celebrating the dedication of the familiar tower clock. Pat Buttram (yes, Mr. Haney from "Green Acres") notes that if Marty doesn't meet Buford's challenge to a showdown, "Everybody, everywhere will see Clint Eastwood is the biggest yellabelly in the West."

In a series as movie-obsessed as this, such an outcome is simply beyond contemplation. Doc, meanwhile, has his hands full. Clara turns out to be Clara Clayton (Mary Steenburgen), the new schoolmarm for budding Hill Valley, whom Doc realizes he is destined to meet and whom he winds up rescuing when the buckboard she rents upon her arrival careens out of control on the road to town. Naturally, it's love at first sight that only grows when Doc finds that Clara also shares his passion for Jules Verne, still a hot new author in 1885.

But Doc still has to get Marty back to 1985. The problem: how to get the DeLorean up to the 88 mph required for the time travel? (When he arrives in 1885, Marty accidentally severs the car's fuel line and is prevented from stopping the gas leak by an ornery bear.) The solution: hijack a steam locomotive and send it, pushing the DeLorean, down an uncompleted spur of the railroad that is straight enough to allow the time machine to get up to the necessary speed. Fortunately, the train is scheduled to arrive just when Marty is to meet Buford. Doc severs his ties with Clara to go back to 1985, but when she learns of his true love for her, she mounts a horse and chases down the locomotive. However, the railroad spur ends in an uncompleted bridge over what is ominously known in 1985 as Clayton Gorge, so named for the schoolteacher who is supposed to have died by throwing herself into it.

The hair-raising chase climax is as old as "The Perils of Pauline" and every bit as delightful. Occurring in 1985, on the day after Marty left Jennifer (Elisabeth Shue) sleeping on her front porch before he returned to 1955 in Part II, the ending ties up a crucial loose end from Part II and manages to fulfill Doc's wish to destroy the DeLorean once and for all. It also leaves the door open for future FUTURE sequels, despite the vows of all involved that Part III is the last installment.

BACK TO THE FUTURE has been one fun-filled ride, a masterpiece of moviemaking ingenuity and virtuoso craft from start to finish. Yet, for all its style and smarts, it has been a remarkably charming, human ride, and never so much as in Part III, which boasts the welcome presence of Mary Steenburgen, playing as sweet and spirited a heroine as has ever crossed a screen. In the final analysis, it would be a shame to see the series come to an end, not so much because it would be fun to see how they'd top Part III (though it would be), but because this is just a darned nice bunch of folks with whom to spend a couple of hours in a dark theater. *(Profanity.)*

d, Robert Zemeckis; p, Bob Gale and Neil Canton; w, Bob Gale (based on a story and characters created by Robert Zemeckis and Bob Gale); ph, Dean Cundey; ed, Arthur Schmidt and Harry Keramidas; m, Alan Silvestri; prod d, Rick Carter; art d, Marjorie Stone McShirley and Jim Teegarden; set d, Martha Johnston, Paul Sonski, Beverli Eagan, Nancy Nickelberry, Joseph G. Pacelli, and Lisa Newman; spec, Ken Ralston, Scott Farrar, and Michael Lantieri; stunts, Walter Scott; cos, Joanna Johnston; makup, Michael Mills and Kenny Myers; chor, Brad Jeffries; tech, Arvo Ojala; anim, Wes Takahashi

Comedy/Science Fiction/Western   (PR:A MPAA:PG)

BACKSTREET DREAMS

104m O'Malley/Vidmark c

Brooke Shields *(Stephanie Bloom)*, Jason O'Malley *(Dean Costello)*, Sherilyn Fenn *(Lucy Costello)*, Tony Fields *(Manny Santana)*, Burt Young *(Luca Garibaldi)*, Anthony Franciosa *(Angelo Carnivale)*, Nick Cassavetes *(Mikey Acosta)*, Ray "Boom Boom" Mancini *(Aldo)*, Joseph Viezzi, John Viezzi *(Shane Costello)*, Meg Register, and Joe Pantoliano

BACKSTREET DREAMS is about a New Jersey street hood, Dean (Jason O'Malley), and his great love and devotion to his autistic son Shane (played by twins Joseph and John Viezzi). The film begins with Dean coming home from another hard day of intimidation and violence. It becomes increasingly obvious that he and his wife Lucy (Sherilyn Fenn of TV's "Twin Peaks") are unable to reach their extremely introverted child. Enter NYU Ph.D. candidate Stephanie Bloom (Brooke Shields), who is bound and determined to get through to Shane. After weeks of seemingly unproductive therapy, Lucy, thinking Stephanie is more interested in her husband than in Shane, tells Stephanie to leave. Soon afterward, Dean catches Lucy in bed with another man, and their marriage breaks up. As one might have predicted, Stephanie reenters the picture and gets Dean involved in a new type of bonding therapy called "forced holding." As the new therapy takes hold, Dean and Stephanie become very close. And it isn't long before Dean contemplates leaving the mob, after his hood idol Luca (Burt Young) is arrested. But Shane then becomes a pawn as the mob seeks revenge.

Despite its interesting story idea, the screenplay by Jason O'Malley is often unbearably predictable, offering only one-dimensional characters. Shields is unconvincing as the concerned psychologist and O'Malley's transformation is undeveloped. With the exception of veteran character actor Young, the other performers are only adequate. However, director Rupert Hitzig exhibits a good visual sense and photographer Stephen M. Katz has successfully captured the dark, tough streets of working class New Jersey neighborhoods. If more time and energy had been devoted to the script and the actors, BACKSTREET DREAMS could have been a believable and involving film. *(Violence, profanity, drug abuse.)*

d, Rupert Hitzig; p, Jason O'Malley and Lance H. Robbins; w, Jason O'Malley; ph, Stephen M. Katz; ed, Robert Gordon; m, Bill Conti; prod d, George Costello; stunts, B.J. Davis; cos, Elisabeth Scott

Drama   (PR:C MPAA:R)

BAD INFLUENCE

99m Epic/Triumph c

Rob Lowe *(Alex)*, James Spader *(Michael Boll)*, Lisa Zane *(Claire)*, Christian Clemenson *(Pismo Boll)*, Kathleen Wilhoite *(Leslie)*, Tony Maggio *(Patterson)*, and Marcia Cross *(Ruth Fielding)*

Curtis Hanson's BAD INFLUENCE is a stylish, sexy, and above all, exceedingly well-made thriller that depicts the framing of an innocent man. Michael Boll (James Spader) is a successful Los Angeles marketing analyst who has it all: a great job, a state-of-the-art apartment, lots of money, and a beautiful fiance. But he is also quiet and timid, allows people to walk all over him, and secretly desires to break off his engagement. What's more he would love to see Patterson (Tony Maggio) a sneaky colleague and rival disappear. These evil wishes begin to come true when Michael begins a strange relationship with Alex (Rob Lowe), a mysterious drifter with a questionable past who brings out Michael's dark side. In addition to helping Michael assert himself, Alex also introduces him to the world of sex, drugs, and crime. Soon, Michael's engagement is called off (after Alex shows the bride-to-be and her family a sex videotape starring Michael) and the problems with his rival stop shortly thereafter, thanks to some violent behavior. Things are going well for Michael until a drunken night of robbing liquor stores climaxes with him and Alex beating Patterson to a pulp. Realizing how corrupt he has become, and how psychologically damaging his relationship with Alex is, Michael kicks his new friend out of his apartment. But this doesn't end Alex's quest to transform Michael from yuppie to psycho, and his efforts include betrayal, deceit, and eventually murder. There is a final confrontation between Michael and Alex, but to describe any of the twists that lead to it would ruin the wonderful surprises in the script.

BAD INFLUENCE is a terrific thriller, jammed with unexpected turns and nail-biting suspense. Hanson, whose last film was the Hitchcock rip-off THE BEDROOM WINDOW, more than proves himself to be an accomplished filmmaker here. Building tension deftly (especially in the fabulous scene in which Michael has to move a dead body), Hanson creates a seductive underworld for Alex to guide Michael through. Employing expressive and innovative visuals (notably, his effective use of repeated shots), Hanson keeps the film moving along at a quick pace. Hanson's direction also makes the most of the shifting point of view and weird morality of David Koepp's screenplay.

A curious mixture of styles that works brilliantly, BAD INFLUENCE is both a Hitchcock homage (particularly its second half) and of a piece with such recent disturbing films as THE HITCHER; AT CLOSE RANGE; and the Koepp-scripted APARTMENT ZERO. The performances are top-notch. Spader, an extraordinary actor, is again terrific, his transition from uptight yuppie drip to despicable criminal a joy to witness. With this picture and MASQUERADE (in which he also played a bad guy), Lowe has definitely found his niche in movies. His sexually menacing presence works in his favor here, and his character is both chilling and funny (at one point he shouts, "Elvis has left the building!" as he leaves Michael's apartment after having beaten a woman to death with a golf club). The chemistry and tension between Lowe and Spader is flawlessly handled. Michael's desire to hang out with the alluring Alex is made perfectly believable, and his shock at Alex's casual discussion of violence subtly conveys to the viewer just how dangerous this drifter really is.

Despite its wide range of influences (a clip from a Godard film is prominently featured), Hanson's movie is made in the style of the best American thrillers and clearly targeted for an American audience. With BAD INFLUENCE the director has definitely come into his own, as has Lowe, whose annoying reliance on his pretty-boy looks is replaced by a stronger, more confident approach that brings depth to his character. Adult, suspenseful, and wildly entertaining, this is simply one of the best thrillers of 1990. *(Violence, profanity, nudity, sexual situations, adult situations, substance abuse.)*

d, Curtis Hanson; p, Steve Tisch; w, David Koepp; ph, Robert Elswit; ed, Bonnie Koehler; m, Trevor Jones; prod d, Ron Foreman; art d, William S. Combs; set d, Leslie Morales

Mystery/Thriller   (PR:O MPAA:R)

BAIL JUMPER

96m Big Buildings/Angelika c

Eszter Balint *(Elaine)*, B.J. Spalding *(Joe)*, Tony Askin *(Dan)*, Bo Brinkman *(Steve)*, Alexandra Auder *(Bambi)*, Joie Lee *(Athena)*, and Ishmael Houston-Jones *(Reed)*

A quirky, charming odyssey through a dusty, disaster-ridden America, BAIL JUMPER restores a sense of exhilaration to the road movie. The determinedly deadpan humor, sudden — albeit harmless — outbursts, strong visuals, and eccentric cast may recall the work of Jim Jarmusch, but director Christian Faber has his own style, which is much livelier and less detached than Jarmusch's approach. Beautifully edited, the film moves along snappily with none of the *longeurs* that have become Jarmusch's signature.

Joe (B.J. Spalding) and Elaine (Eszter Balint) are a pair of endlessly bickering lovers in Murky Springs, Missouri. To describe Joe as an underachiever would be an understatement: his days consist largely of staying in bed, drinking, and shooting at bugs on the ceiling with a hand gun. Elaine has her own manner of aberrant behavior. A chronic K-Mart shoplifter, she has recently jumped bail on an out-of-state arrest for a bank robbery performed with her twin sister. Joe and Elaine decide to skip town and follow their dreams to Manhattan. On the road, they encounter a spiritualist (Joie Lee) who offers a terse but telling interpretation of the couple's relationship: "When the two of you are together, there are tremendous influences." Her words appear to be on target, for their trail is dogged by tornadoes, meteor showers, solar eclipses, and locust plagues. Upon arrival in the Big Apple, they are immediately stranded on Staten Island by a massive tidal wave, but their love is supreme, ensuring their survival.

Faber's off-the-cuff approach makes the most of the behavioral humor of his scenes. His feel for youthful, low-budget amusement is cannily on the money. A desultory summertime bash, a target-practice party, and a motel pool celebration all perfectly capture Midwestern anomie. Faber also deftly intercuts stock footage of various natural disasters, which amount to a stirringly romantic accompaniment to the whacked-out lovers' hegira. Tomasz Magierski's dark-hued cinematography further enhances the film's effectiveness, catching the shadowy ambience of the characters' environs and psyches, and blending almost seamlessly with the disaster footage. (The cataclysms are less natural in Manhattan: Joe is attacked by a group of Wall Street maenads, simply because he reminds them of their old boy friends.) A tinkly, angelic score by Richard Robbins provides just the right glue to hold all of this together, investing the story line with a dreamy resonance (Elaine's mother was a country singer whose song haunts her daughter and the film).

Employing the "just got out of bed" acting style already used to great advantage by Adam Coleman Howard in SLAVES OF NEW YORK and Nicolas Cage in VAMPIRE'S KISS, Spalding has the humorless mannerisms of his psychotic character down pat. He is especially funny delivering his reductive existential manifesto: "You know, those days when everybody looks ugly and you don't know why people look at you strange. I'm better off right here [in bed]." It's to Spalding's credit, however, that despite his character's often juvenile behavior, he is able to convince us of his abiding love for Elaine (making the most of his watery blue eyes in the process). After a six-year absence following her memorable debut in STRANGER THAN PARADISE, the lovely Balint makes a triumphant return to independent cinema. At times she is reminiscent of Tracey Ullman (especially when impersonating her own twin); at other moments she has the wily, secretive look of the quintessential Warhol diva, Andrea Feldman. Her naturalistic acting—which could be described as amateurish but heartfelt—is as strangely compelling as ever, and it tickles the ear to hear what her Hungarian accent makes of simple phrases like "Elk's Lodge" or "alkaline batteries." The image of Balint floating through her new Staten Island home, gun in hand, to the strains of "Pistol Packin' Mama" is unforgettable. Of the supporting performers, Alexandra Auder is sweetly touching as Elaine's friend Bambi, and Tony Askin is the Evil Nerd personified, forever accosting Joe with childhood reminiscences ("Remember third grade?"). Lee (on vacation from brother Spike's heated sphere) has a relaxed ambiguity as the omniscient Athena, and Bo Brinkman is briefly amusing as the hunting-happy Steve, who meets his end by lightning. His funeral, set in a field of daisies, is just one of BAIL JUMPER's utterly disarming moments. *(Violence, profanity, substance abuse, sexual situations.)*

d, Christian Faber; p, Josephine Wallace and Christian Faber; w, Josephine Wallace and Christian Faber (based on a story by Christian Faber); ph, Tomasz Magierski; ed, James Bruce; m, Richard Robbins; prod d, Lynn Ruth Appel; cos, Arianne Phillips; makeup, Erica Rosenast

Comedy　　　　　　　　　　　　　　　　　　　　　　　　**(PR:O　MPAA:NR)**

BASHU, THE LITTLE STRANGER

(Iran) 120m International House c

Susan Taslimi *(Nai)* and Adnan Afravian *(Bashu)*

One of an increasing number of Iranian films arriving in the US in the wake of the Ayatollah Khomeini's demise, this deceptively simple tale of a young boy orphaned by the Iran-Iraq war was made under government sponsorship but banned, presumably for its pacifistic sentiments. BASHU opens with an Iraqi air attack on a village in southern Iran. The imagery is horrifying but intriguingly

double-edged, since it connects the symbols of Iran's fundamentalist religion with destruction and death. A woman burns to death when her veil catches fire; then a praying man disappears through a hole that appears beneath the prayer rug in a living room floor. Later, we learn that the woman and man were the mother and father of 10-year-old Bashu (Adnan Afravian), who, having witnessed the deaths of his entire family, flees his desert village in terror, stowing away in a passing truck. Bashu falls asleep on the truck, and when he wakes up, he can hardly believe his eyes. Instead of his dusty homeland, he is confronted with the lush greenery and quaint country houses of northern Iran. A blast from a nearby construction site again frightens Bashu, who jumps from the truck and runs into a wood, thinking he is once again in the middle of an air raid. When the truck leaves without him, he finds shelter in a rice paddy that belongs to Nai (Susan Taslimi), the mother of two tiny children. (Nai's husband, we learn later, is away "looking for work," though the implication is that he is fighting in the war.) Upon discovering Bashu asleep in a lean-to, Nai's first reaction is to throw a rock at him, in an attempt to drive him off her land. In short order, however, she relents, leaving behind part of her picnic lunch when she and her children go back to the house. Still frightened, Bashu waits until the three have gone before coming out and eating. That night, Nai leaves rice and water outside her front door, luring Bashu out of hiding. After hungrily devouring the rice and slurping down the water, the curious Bashu goes into the barn, where he is trapped by Nai and locked in for the night. The next morning, Bashu wakes up to sunlight streaming through the door, now open. What's more, he finds that Nai simply wants to care for him. However, there is no way Nai can tell Bashu this; though northern and southern Iran have identical written languages, their spoken languages are completely different. As a result, Nai has to communicate her intentions through her actions. She feeds Bashu, washes his clothes, and nurses him when he falls ill, all the while thinking she is just caring for him until his parents show up to claim him. Although Nai doesn't understand that Bashu has "adopted" her family, she doesn't object when he immediately begins pitching in to help with chores and caring for the children. Yet, despite Bashu's model behavior, Nai finds herself forced to defend him constantly to her prejudiced neighbors, who warn Nai that Bashu will steal from her. Like her neighbors, Nai is fair-complected; southerner Bashu, on the other hand, is dark-skinned, and his skin color and odd-seeming habits (such as playing his flute to help the rice grow) earn him the taunts of the neighbor's children. Matters only get worse for Bashu when Nai's husband writes home to instruct his wife to send the boy away. The drama heats up when Nai takes a stick to a group of village kids who have beaten up Bashu, leading to a final confrontation with the villagers over Bashu's presence in the community. All ends well, however, with the appearance of Nai's husband, who has had a change of heart.

With its sunny simplicity and eagerness to coax smiles from the audience, BASHU ends up like an Iranian remake of POLLYANNA. But beneath this simplicity is a surprising wisdom and a richness of emotion. The depictions of life in the village and on Nai's farm are alive with detail, and the characters are vivid and memorable. Much of the credit must go to the cast—from the gifted Taslimi and Afravian to the uniformly capable supporting players. Still, it is the contributions of writer-director Bahram Beizai and cinematographer Firooz Malekzadeh that make BASHU work. Though the film is filled with ravishing images, it is never merely picturesque. Its imagery is so effectively used to tell the story that long stretches of the movie have virtually no dialog at all, which goes a long way in making BASHU a fine film for young children who might normally fidget through two hours of subtitles. (It should be noted, however, that the early war scenes may be too intense for the very young.) BASHU offers eloquent universal messages about racial tolerance and the strength of the family. It also delivers a gentle, realistic portrait of day-to-day life in rural Iran that makes it an eye-opener for adults more used to the media image of Iranians as animated savages bent on world domination. *(Violence.)*

d, Bahram Beizai; p, Ali Reza Zarrin; w, Bahram Beizai; ph, Firooz Malekzadeh; ed, Bahram Beizai

Adventure/Children's　　　　　　　　　　　　**(PR:AA　MPAA:NR)**

BASKETCASE 2

89m Ievins-Henenlotter/Shapiro-Glickenhaus c

Kevin Van Hentenryck *(Duane Bradley)*, Annie Ross *(Granny Ruth)*, Kathryn Meisle *(Marcie Elliott)*, Heather Rattray *(Susan)*, Jason Evers *(Lou)*, Ted Sorel *(Phil)*, and Matt Mitler *(Artie)*

Although at the end of 1982's BASKET CASE the film's stars were left for dead, in BASKET CASE 2 it turns out they were merely injured, and are now ready to start causing trouble all over again. Those who saw the first BASKET CASE will recall Duane and Belial Bradley, who were born Siamese twins. Duane (Kevin Van Hentenryck) is perfectly normal-looking, while Belial (created by special effects) is a small, grotesque mutant — just a slimy head with two slimy arms. A bloody operation in the first movie painfully separated the boys, but Belial did not die as expected, and Duane subsequently carried his brother around in a laundry basket every place he went. Hence the movie's title.

When the brothers "died" in the first film, they were making their escape after having murdered the doctors who separated them. As BASKET CASE 2 begins, we see that the brothers were merely injured by their fall out of a Times Square window. In a guarded hospital room, the two engineer their escape by killing the police officer outside—that is, Belial does the killing, sticking himself to a wall and ripping off his victim's face. Duane just watches and directs. Waiting outside the hospital, very conveniently, are Granny Ruth (jazz singer Annie Ross, of Lambert, Hendricks, and Ross) and her beautiful granddaughter, Susan (Heather Rattray). Granny, a physician, has devoted her life to caring for and protecting freaks. Her Staten Island mansion is a veritable haven for a weirdly fascinating collection of unfortunate individuals born with most unusual defects, the majority with animal- or monster-like oversized heads, many with no bodies, some with giant gills. One resembles a huge hippopotamus; another, a terribly shy female who in a perverse final scene becomes Belial's "mate," remains constantly covered by a blanket. While Duane recovers from his injuries and Belial adapts to life among his own kind, the police hunt for the killer brothers. Much hotter on the trail, however, is a nosy, ambitious reporter, Marcie Elliott (Kathryn Meisle). She actually manages to discover the Bradley boys' whereabouts, but poor Marcie's luck ends at Granny's Staten Island sanctuary, where the freaks make sure the newswoman's biggest scoop is her last. Unfortunately, she is not the only one to leave this world at the mercy of mutants. Her photographer and editor are sacrificed as well, in some of the movie's gorier scenes.

For fans of the macabre and weird, BASKET CASE 2 may be an enjoyable experience. It is not without humor (although this humor is black and somewhat depraved), and there are moments of gruesomeness that will entertain die-hard horror fans (although this is not an excessively bloody film). The makeup and special effects, cleverly executed by Gabe Bartalos, are superb and memorable. Unfortunately, director Frank Henenlotter (who also directed the original BASKETCASE and BRAIN DAMAGE, 1988) did not elicit equally memorable acting from his stars. Granted, the film is weakly plotted to favor visual effects over story and characters, but the actors in "normal" roles could show much more personality and spark; as it is they are bland in comparison to the colorful mutants. Considering these failures, it seems unlikely that the BASKET CASE series will progress much further than this. *(Violence, adult situations.)*

d, Frank Henenlotter; p, Edgar Ievins; w, Frank Henenlotter; ph, Robert M. Baldwin; ed, Kevin Tent; m, Joe Renzetti; spec, Gabe Bartalos

Horror   (PR:C   MPAA:R)

BEDROOM EYES II

87m Distant Horizon—Anant Singh/Vidmark c

Wings Hauser *(Harry Ross)*, Kathy Shower *(Carolyn Ross)*, Linda Blair *(Sophie)*, Jane Hamilton *(JoBeth)*, Joe Giardina *(Vinnie)*, Kevin Thomsen *(Matthew)*, Jennifer Delora *(Gwendolyn)*, Harvey Siegel *(Detective Briar)*, Maraya Chase *(Karen)*, and Kimberly Taylor *(Michelle)*

This sequel to the equally forgettable BEDROOM EYES stars Wings Hauser as Harry Ross, the jogging voyeur who was almost killed in the first film by the insane and evil JoBeth. Harry is now married to Carolyn (Kathy Shower), an art dealer who comforted him after the hit-and-run death of his first wife. Harry and his partner, Vinnie (Joe Giardina), are running a less-than-successful investment firm, but hope to salvage their finances when they gain some potentially very lucrative insider information. Enter JoBeth (Jane Hamilton), recently released from prison, who decides to pay Harry a visit and make some thinly veiled threats. Enter also Sophie (Linda Blair), a young artist who bears a remarkable resemblance to Harry's first wife. When Harry falls prey to his voyeuristic instincts again and watches Carolyn being seduced by one of her young proteges, he decides to use Sophie in a plan to make Carolyn pay for her infidelity, but his scheme backfires when she merely explodes with anger at him, rather than admitting her guilt. As if all this were not enough, Sophie then turns out to be the sister of Harry's dead wife. Blaming Harry for her sibling's death, she plots with JoBeth to drug Harry and tie him up, but JoBeth kills her partner, planning to frame Harry for Sophie's death. Harry escapes from JoBeth, but when he returns the next day, it appears that nothing has happened. After showing signs of taking off, the film now begins to trip over itself as Harry reunites with Carolyn, only to receive a call from Vinnie, who tells him their office has been ransacked and an all-important computer disc has been stolen. Sophie's body is discovered in the trunk of Carolyn's car, and some (badly overacted) cops become convinced that a jealous Carolyn killed the young artist because her husband was having an affair with the girl. Harry, meanwhile, tries to get the police after JoBeth, who is found dead at the home of the artist with whom *Carolyn* was fooling around. It isn't hard to guess that Carolyn has been setting her hubby up all along, with help from the other major characters, but Harry still doesn't see it.

If the plot summary isn't enough to warn you away from BEDROOM EYES II, the film has plenty of additional faults worth considering. The symbolism attached to Harry's voyeurism is overwrought and obvious, and his stupidity seems endless. Low-budget sexploitation producer-director Chuck Vincent shows less flesh than usual in this effort made in 1986 (though there is still enough gratuitous sex to keep his fans happy), but apparently wanted to rip off every mystery thriller he had ever seen, piling on the plot twists when only a few would have been sufficient. The acting is second-rate at best (B-film queen Blair seems pained to be participating), and the ending is thoroughly implausible. It's perhaps unfortunate that BEDROOM EYES II shows enough potential in places to indicate that with a decent director, a good edit of the screenplay, and a few qualified actors it might have been a satisfying Hitchcockian thriller. *(Violence, profanity, nudity, sexual situations.)*

d, Chuck Vincent; p, Chuck Vincent; w, Gerard Ciccoritti; ph, Larry Revene (Agfa Gevaert Color); ed, James Davalos; md, Budd Carr; art d, Todd Rutt; cos, Jeffrey Wallach

Mystery/Thriller   (PR:C   MPAA:R)

BELLY OF AN ARCHITECT, THE

(Brit./It.) 108m Callender/Hemdale c

Brian Dennehy *(Stourley Kracklite)*, Chloe Webb *(Louisa Kracklite)*, Lambert Wilson *(Caspasian Speckler)*, Vanni Corbellini *(Frederico)*, Sergio Fantoni *(Io Speckler)*, Stefania Casini *(Flavia Speckler)*, Alfredo Varelli *(Julio Ficcone)*, Geoffrey Copleston *(Caspetti)*, Francesco Carnelutti *(Pastarri)*, Marino Mase *(Trettorio)*, Marne Maitland *(Battistino)*, Claudio Spadaro *(Mori)*, Rate Furlan *(Violinist)*, Julian Jenkins *(Old Doctor)*, Enrica Maria Scrivano *(Mother)*, Riccardo Ussani *(Little Boy)*, Stefano Gragnani *(The Nose Man)*, Andrea Prodan *(Young Doctor)*, and Fabio Sartor *(Policeman)*

Capturing the glory of Roman architecture, this exquisitely shot film about obsession reaffirmed director Peter Greenaway's reputation as a visually stunning filmmaker. Brian Dennehy stars as Stourley Kracklite, a corpulent Chicago architect of some renown, who travels to Rome with his considerably younger wife Louisa (Chloe Webb) to oversee an exhibition commemorating a little-known 18th-century French architect, Etienne Louis Boullee (an actual historical figure). It has long been Kracklite's dream to mount this tribute to his idol and the exhibition is to be done on a grand scale. A handsome young Italian architect, Caspasian Speckler (Lambert Wilson), is in charge of the project's finances, and he covets both Kracklite's control of the exhibition and Louisa. Like the other Italians working with Kracklite, he has contempt for both the American and Boullee. Upon his arrival in Rome, Kracklite begins to experience terrible abdominal pains. As he notices the interest Speckler is taking in his wife and she in him, he begins to suspect that Louisa is trying to poison him. He visits a doctor and is told he is suffering from dyspepsia and given some medication. As the months of arduous preparation wear on, he becomes totally immersed in the project and increasingly concerned with his stomach problems. Meanwhile, Speckler and Louisa conduct a passionate affair that Kracklite is aware of but does nothing to stop. His obsession with his aching belly leads him to an almost fetishist interest in other stomachs, particularly those of the famous rendered in paintings and statues, of which he makes endless photocopies. But for all his interest in bellies, he fails to notice that Louisa is pregnant. She assures him that it is his child and not Speckler's, but she makes no attempt to hide her affair. Throughout the film, Kracklite has written letters to the long-dead Boullee, and it is these missives that express the true state of his mind. All along Speckler has been skimming funds from the exhibition's budget to finance the restoration of a Mussolini-commissioned structure. As the funds grow tighter and as others become aware that Kracklite is a very sick man, the pressure grows to replace him with Speckler. Desperate to complete the project his way, Kracklite tells his wife he wants to mortgage their home and change his will to come up with the necessary money. She refuses to allow this and tells him that she is leaving him for Speckler. In a short time, Kracklite also loses control of the exhibition to his young Italian rival. He undergoes a more thorough examination and is informed that he has pancreatic cancer and only a few months to live. He does not appear at the exhibition's opening ceremony, but instead watches from a balcony above, and when Louisa cuts the ribbon, he leaps to his death through an open window.

Collaborating with cinematographer Sacha Vierny, who has worked with Bunuel and Resnais and is known for his painstaking lighting and mastery of deep-focus photography, Greenaway presents one beautifully composed image after another. Each densely textured composition is like a painting in its own right. As in Greenaway's past films (THE DRAUGHTSMAN'S CONTRACT, A ZED & TWO NOUGHTS), the director's arrangements of the elements within the shot are triumphs of symmetry, and, perhaps, even more than a cinematic painter, Greenaway can be seen as an architect of images. He sees parallels between the architect's role and the filmmaker's. In an interview in *Sight and Sound* (Summer 1987), he explained that both are accountable to those who have put up the money for a project, to the people who will see the finished product, and to the architect's/filmmaker's need for self-satisfaction and fulfillment of his idea of culture. In this way, THE BELLY OF AN ARCHITECT is somewhat autobiographical and Dennehy can be seen as a surrogate for Greenaway. Yet another autobiographical component is the fact that both of Greenaway's parents died of stomach cancer, and he has said that in some way all of his films deal with loss.

At the center of the film is Dennehy's extraordinary performance. Using his stomach almost like a character itself, he makes his fixation on it and his battle to stage the perfect tribute to Boullee seem like the center of the universe. Both Kracklite's health and his marriage are secondary to staging the tribute to the architect who, like Kracklite, has left few buildings behind to speak for him. Dennehy magnificently conveys the architect's obsessive behavior. As believable as his physical pain is his mental anguish as both his wife and his project slowly slip from his grasp. Webb (SID AND NANCY) is not entirely successful with her role. Her flightiness and boredom with her older husband are plausible prerequisites for her affair, but one is left wondering how she and Kracklite would have ever gotten together in the first place. Wilson is totally convincing as the architect of Kracklite's downfall. Handsome, suave, and completely unprincipled, he is every inch the swine. *(Sexual situations, nudity, profanity, adult situations.).*

d, Peter Greenaway; p, Colin Callender and Walter Donohue; w, Peter Greenaway; ph, Sacha Vierny; ed, John Wilson; m, Wim Mertens and Glenn Branca; art d, Luciana Vedovelli; set d, Giorgio Desideri; cos, Maurizio Millenotti; makup, Franco Corridoni

Drama   (PR:O   MPAA:NR)

BETSY'S WEDDING

97m Silver Screen Partners IV/Touchstone-Buena Vista c

Alan Alda *(Eddie Hopper)*, Joey Bishop *(Eddie's Father)*, Madeline Kahn *(Lola Hopper)*, Anthony LaPaglia *(Stevie Dee)*, Catherine O'Hara *(Gloria Henner)*, Joe Pesci *(Oscar Henner)*, Molly Ringwald *(Betsy Hopper)*, Ally Sheedy *(Connie Hopper)*, Burt Young *(Georgie)*, Julie Bovasso *(Grandma)*, Nicolas Coster *(Henry Lovell)*, Bibi Besch *(Nancy Lovell)*, Dylan Walsh *(Jake Lovell)*, Camille Saviola *(Angelica)*, Allan Rich *(Nate Tobias)*, Sully Boyar *(Morris, Lola's Dad)*, Monica Carr *(Joy)*, Frankie R. Faison *(Zack Monroe)*, Tom Mardirosian *(Dave Delahaas)*, Larry Block *(Barber)*, Helen Hanft *(Fitter)*, J.K. Loftin *(Bandleader)*, Mario Todisco *(Anselmo, the Bodyguard)*, Paul B. Mixon *(Plumber)*, William Duff-Griffin *(Caterer)*, Thomas John Caligiuri *(Man at Wedding)*, Samuel L. Jackson *(Taxi Dispatcher)*, and Janet Pasquale *(Georgie's Companion)*

The most entertaining films are generally made so by virtue of deft direction; a solid screenplay with well-written characters, convincing relationships, and lively dialog; and fine acting all around. A memorable yet unobtrusive score, good camerawork, and tight editing will further enhance the proceedings. Happily, BETSY'S WEDDING fulfills all these requirements. Alan Alda, the film's screenwriter-director-star, delivers his best and most fully realized movie to date with this captivating and humane romantic comedy, the story of a proud father's dogged determination to give his beloved eldest daughter the very best wedding his money *can't* buy.

Combining Runyonesque farce, an updated FATHER OF THE BRIDE and CATERED AFFAIR family milieu, and a plot slightly reminiscent of the more recent comedy THE IN-LAWS, BETSY'S WEDDING revolves around the obsessed attempts of Eddie Hopper (Alda) to give his daughter Betsy (Molly Ringwald) the most memorably spectacular wedding any girl could have. In doing so, he throws all financial considerations to the wind. It becomes apparent to his long-suffering wife, Lola (Madeline Kahn), that Eddie's extravagance is rapidly heading them toward the poorhouse. Moreover, Betsy herself wants just a small, intimate wedding. This situation leads to a number of highly amusing developments as Betsy's wedding turns into a one-man crusade for Eddie, who gets in deeper and deeper with the likes of Lola's brother-in-law, Oscar (Joe Pesci), and Oscar's shady "business partner," Georgie (Burt Young). It's not long before Eddie finds himself being shot at by the henchmen of Georgie's "business" rival, by which time it dawns on Eddie that he's managed to get mixed up with the mob. Unfortunately, getting out of this fix isn't quite as easy as getting in, and Eddie realizes he's not going to extricate himself from his unbearable situation without help. Luckily, help comes in the form of Stevie Dee (Anthony LaPaglia), the Mafia prince who is courting Eddie's daughter Connie (Ally Sheedy), a tough policewoman. The riotous proceedings all climax in a hilariously disastrous wedding reception, involving a rain-soaked tent and sopping, muddy guests.

Produced by Martin Bregman (who was also behind Alda's THE FOUR SEASONS and THE SEDUCTION OF JOE TYNAN, as well as SERPICO; DOG DAY AFTERNOON; and SEA OF LOVE), BETSY'S WEDDING is not

only a fine comedy, but also a film that yields one of moviegoing's most exciting experiences: that of "discovering" an actor, some hitherto unfamiliar face and talent of whom it is immediately evident that he or she is destined to be a genuine screen presence for years to come. BETSY'S WEDDING provides just such a discovery in LaPaglia, a clever actor with a flair for subtle, underplayed comedy characterization. LaPaglia (who bears a startling resemblance to the young Robert De Niro) gives a picture-stealing performance, though this in no way diminishes the solid acting around him. Character actors Pesci, Young, and Catherine O'Hara (who is marvelous as Pesci's shrewd, viper-tongued wife, determined to get even with her husband for his philandering ways) register strongly, as do Alda and Kahn as the bride's parents and Sheedy as her hoydenish younger sister. Also splendid are Ringwald and Dylan Walsh (as the groom), as well as Nicolas Coster and Bibi Besch (as Eddie's in-laws-to-be, who vie with him for the right to finance the wedding). As the ghost of Eddie's father, Joey Bishop pops up from time to time to give his fretting son some sage advice, and Julie Bovasso shines as a plump Italian grandmother who is not afraid to speak her mind.

It's a pity Alda chose to incorporate (in a generally sparkling script) a few four-letter words and one slightly vulgar visual gag, since BETSY'S WEDDING is otherwise both suited for the entire family and of notable quality. In addition, the characters are not uniformly colorful or fleshed-out and there are also a few plot holes. Ultimately, however, Alda is to be commended heartily for successfully pulling together numerous story elements, characters, situations, and subplots into joyous and sharply coherent unity. BETSY'S WEDDING is a thoroughly satisfying movie. *(Profanity, mild violence.)*

d, Alan Alda; p, Martin Bregman and Louis A. Stroller; w, Alan Alda; ph, Kelvin Pike; ed, Michael Polakow; m, Bruce Broughton; prod d, John Jay Moore; art d, Andrew Moore; set d, Barbara Kahn; spec, Greg Hull; stunts, Frank Ferrara and Don Hewitt; cos, Mary Malin; makup, Jeff Goodwin

Comedy   (PR:C   MPAA:R)

BEYOND THE RISING MOON

(SEE: STAR QUEST: BEYOND THE RISING MOON)

BIG BAD JOHN

92m Red River/Magnum c

Jimmy Dean, Jack Elam, Ned Beatty, Romy Windsor, Bo Hopkins, Jeff Osterhage, Ned Vaughn, Buck Taylor, Jerry Potter, Amzie Strickland, Doug English, Red Steagall, and Anne Lockhart

It's hard to believe that the song "Big Bad John" dates back only to 1961, when it stayed at the top of the charts for five weeks. Jimmy Dean's ballad of the big, quiet man with a murderous past who sacrifices himself to save his fellow miners has the mythic quality of a folktale. The movie version, which zipped in and out of theaters prior to appearing on videocassette, is about as memorable as a second feature at a drive-in. Dean himself has a starring role, not as John but as a retired sheriff in the Louisiana swamp country. He is visited by his erstwhile deputy (Jack Elam) and an old nemesis (Ned Beatty), the latter of whom married Dean's ex-wife (now deceased) and raised the sheriff's daughter as his own. Elam and Beatty are the bearers of disturbing news: that "big ol' boy" John Tyler (former Detroit Lion Doug English) has killed a local bully named Mahoney (in self-defense, of course) and fled with Dean's daughter. The local police aren't too concerned, but Dean sets out after English, armed with a monster shotgun and accompanied by Elam. Unknown to our heroes, however, Beatty contacts a psycho ex-con (Hopkins) and the vengeful brother of the dead man, paying them to follow Dean and Elam and to kill English, the ex-lawmen, and Dean's daughter. With his stepdaughter out of the way, Beatty will be able to sell the family estate to interested oil companies (don't bother checking; none of this is in the song). At long last the story turns to English, who, as it happens, is not a bad guy at all. In fact, he's brought Dean's daughter with him to save her from Beatty's beatings. English has kinfolk in Colorado, so he and his lady love travel there and are married. A nearby non-union mining operation is in need of workers, and English signs on. At this point the filmmakers borrow a few bars from Tennessee Ernie Ford; loading his 16 tons, English learns that he does indeed owe his wages to the company store. The action cuts back to Dean and Elam, just arrived in Colorado, hot on the trail. Another of the dead man's brothers shows up and warns Dean of Beatty's treachery. Nevertheless, Dean and Elam walk into Hopkins' ambush, and the ensuing shootout leaves Elam wounded and Hopkins apparently dead. For the sake of phony suspense, the paramedics who arrive on the scene ignore Hopkins, and he recovers and crawls off into the bushes. Later, as Dean reunites with his daughter at her home, Hopkins barges in and must be blasted once and for all. So, let's see, are we forgetting anything? Oh yes. Back in the mine, there's a cave-in. English supports the roof by himself while his comrades scramble to safety, but he is buried when the tunnel collapses. Dean and his daughter go back to the swamp country, run Beatty off "his" land, and care for her newborn, English's son.

The obvious mistake here is overlaying Big John's tragic tale with a silly backwoods melodrama. If the filmmakers' intent was to make Dean the star of the show, they have succeeded, and the project isn't a complete disaster; Dean contributes a more-than-adequate performance.Fans may remember his role in TV's "Daniel Boone" series and his performance in the James Bond adventure DIAMONDS ARE FOREVER. But his character here, a typical folksy good guy, has few interesting features. The film's miscasting, however, is the role of Big Bad John. English's John is a big, protective, teddy-bear of a guy—hardly "bad" at all. The film might have been a tiny bit compelling had a truly fearsome actor taken the part. Believe it or not, Arnold Schwarzenegger was among those considered for the role until the producers met English during a golf game and decided his beefy benevolence suited them best. As Dean's grizzled sidekick, Elam is as comfortable as a favorite pair of old shoes, but heavies Beatty and Hopkins badly overact. As a sort of inside joke, country musician-film producer Red Steagall also appears, playing the nasty owner of the mining company who won't shore up the old timbers.

Director Kennedy has made some notable westerns, including THE WAR WAGON and SUPPORT YOUR LOCAL SHERIFF. Given his background, it's especially odd that BIG BAD JOHN takes place in the present day, putting Dean and Elam on the highway in a drug-dealer's confiscated truck (complete with a digital defense-system). One bow to tradition the movie should have avoided was outfitting Dean with an insufferable performing dog as a companion. It's one of the breed that covers its ears with its paws when somebody says something cute, and it tags along through the entire film just so it can bite Beatty's buttocks at the finish. Despite Dean's prominence here (his line of meat products even featured discount coupons for rentals of the videocassette), he does not perform "Big Bad John" on the country & western soundtrack; that honor falls to the Charlie Daniels Band, with an assist from the Oak Ridge Boys. Other songs include "Little Bits and Pieces" (Shelby Lynne), "Poncho and Lefty" (Willie Nelson, Merle Haggard), "Stay Out of My Arms" (Jim Lauderdale), "Big City" (Haggard), "Redneck Riviera" (Danny Steagall), "Houston" (Larry Gatlin and the Gatlin Brothers Band), "Every Road You Take Will Bring You Home" (Steagall), "Uncle Pen" (Ricky Skaggs), "Life Turned Her That Way" (Ricky van Shelton). (*Profanity, violence, adult situations, substance abuse.*)

d, Burt Kennedy; p, Red Steagall; w, Joseph Berry (based on a story by C.B. Wismar); ph, Ken Lamkin; ed, John W. Wheeler; m, Ken Sutherland

Action   (PR:C   MPAA:PG-13)

BIG DIS, THE

84m Olympia bw

James Haig (*JD*), Kevin Haig (*Kevin*), Monica Sparrow (*Monica*), Allysun Walker (*Allyson*), Gordon Eriksen (*Gordon*), Heather Johnson (*Heather*), Lisa Rivers, and Aratha Johnston

Granted an unexpected 48-hour pass from the Army, 19-year-old JD (James Haig) comes home to Long Island with one thing on his mind: getting lucky before his leave is up. Everyone is sympathetic—particularly his brother, Kevin (Kevin Haig), and his best friend, the newly engaged Gordon (Gordon Eriksen). They set about helping JD find an obliging lady, but things just don't go smoothly. JD's former girl friend won't open the door because JD didn't telephone before coming to visit. On the other hand, Monica (Monica Sparrow) is game and doesn't even back down when she realizes their trysting place is a mattress behind a gas station, though she does suggest they move it somewhere dark, pointing out that the change of lighting will be more romantic. Just when everything is about to fall into place for JD, he realizes that the condoms are in the car and that he has lost the key. "Do I have stupid written on my face?" Monica demands when JD tries to persuade her to proceed anyway. Later, JD and Gordon invite neighborhood fast girls to a party at Gordon's place. Again things are moving right along until Gordon's fiancee, Heather (Heather Johnson), shows up and spoils the fun. Another buddy gives JD some cologne he swears will drive women wild, then fixes him up with an eager babe. But this encounter comes to nought when the woman develops an allergic reaction to the scent. A party in a motel ends with a drunken JD dumped in the shower. Finally, JD meets the willing Allysun (Allysun Walker), only to creep by mistake into her mother's bedroom. JD is a victim of the big dis (disrespect) from the women in his life and, for that matter, from the women in other people's lives as well. Disappointed and fed up with the whole business, he must return to base the next morning. But the sight of a pretty girl at the airport convinces him that there's still hope.

A low-budget, independently produced film, THE BIG DIS was shot in black and white in 1988, completely on location in Long Island. Reviewers have likened coproducer-writer-director-editor-actor Gordon Eriksen to a young John Cassavetes, but it's a spurious comparison, mostly based on the film's technical rawness. Eriksen and his partner, John O'Brien (who also shot the film), have

an altogether lighter touch than Cassavetes; James is frustrated, but there's no hollowness at the core of his life—he's just a middle class kid learning that you don't always get what you want.

THE BIG DIS is distinguished by a distinctly suburban voice—not the disaffected anger of Jonathan Kaplan's OVER THE EDGE, but a more mellow, satisfied sensibility—and by the casual, familiar way it depicts middle-class African-American characters. The problems at the center of THE BIG DIS aren't unique to African-Americans; they're a teenaged guy's problems. James is black and Gordon is white, their acquaintances are black, white, hispanic, and oriental, and their relationships are determined by class and geography, not race.

The picture's grasp of the rhythm of James' life is easy and assured, and the subsidiary characters are remarkably distinct. Tammy, Monica, Nikki, Princess, and Allysun appear only briefly, but each one makes her mark; they aren't faceless bodies solely defined by James' desire for them.

THE BIG DIS is a fresh and funny film, from the opening rap song—in which female rappers ask, "What's the matter with these boys today?" and a male chorus answers, "We just want to get laid"—to the final image of the ever hopeful James, mesmerized by the young woman at the airport. (*Sexual situations, profanity, alcohol abuse.*)

d, Gordon Eriksen and John O'Brien; p, Gordon Eriksen and John O'Brien; w, Gordon Eriksen and John O'Brien; ph, John O'Brien; ed, Gordon Eriksen and John O'Brien; m, Kev Ses & Harry B. and Dr. Cranium and the Big Dis Crew

Comedy   (PR:O   MPAA:NR)

BIKINI GENIE

(SEE: WILDEST DREAMS)

BIRD ON A WIRE

110m Badham-Cohen-Interscope/Universal c

Mel Gibson (*Rick Jarmin*), Goldie Hawn (*Marianne Graves*), David Carradine (*Eugene Sorenson*), Bill Duke (*Albert Diggs*), Stephen Tobolowsky (*Joe Weyburn*), Joan Severance (*Rachel Varney*), Harry Caesar (*Lou Baird*), Alex Bruhanski (*Raun*), John Pyper-Ferguson (*Jamie*), Clyde Kusatsu (*Mr. Takawaki*), Jackson Davies (*Paul Bernard*), Florence Paterson (*Molly Baird*), Tim Healy (*Paul*), Wes Tritter (*Scotty*), Lossen Chambers (*Lossen*), Ken Camroux (*Neff*), Wendy Van Riesen (*Secretary*), Lesley Ewen (*Night Reception-ist*), Robert Metcalfe (*Dex*), Kevin McNulty (*Brad*), Robert Thurston (*Bank Teller*), Brian Torpe (*Bank Vice-President*), Oscar Goncalves (*Bank Guard*), Tim Price (*Beggar*), Oscar Ramos (*Cop at Fire*), Dan Zale (*Fireman*), Blu Mankuma (*Plainclothesman*), Doug Judge (*Cop at Cafe*), Jon Garber (*Nikita Knatz*), Paul Jarrett (*Carl Laemmle*), James Kidnie (*Underworld Boss*), Kim Kondrashoff (*Guard at Gate*), Michel Barbe (*Maitre d'*), Maria Leone (*Sales Clerk*), and Danny Wattley (*Cement Worker*)

Big, dull, and noisy, this comedy-romance has chases galore, but its comedy is flat and its romance is grating and graceless. It also has one of those inane but complicated big-budget plots that huffs, puffs, grunts, and bends over backwards to make sure that its stars do the same. Goldie Hawn starts as big-time wheeler-dealer Marianne Graves, who's looking forward to a dull week of business meetings in Detroit as the film lurches to putative life. Stopping at a gas station, she recognizes the attendant as her former boy friend, Rick Jarmin. We, of course, recognize him as Mel Gibson. But for some reason Jarmin refuses to recognize Graves, insisting that he's a simpleminded redneck mechanic named Billy Ray instead of the dashing left-wing radical who ditched Graves at the altar 15 years previously. She stakes out the station to see if she's right about his identity. Meanwhile, big-time drug dealer Sorenson (David Carradine), who was put away by Jarmin's testimony, is being released from prison. When Sorenson joins his still-at-large partner Diggs (Bill Duke), vengeance is the name of their game. It seems that after testifying against Sorenson and Diggs, Jarmin became part of the Federal Witness Relocation Program, which explains why he refuses to recognize Graves. Nevertheless, Graves has blown Jarmin's cover, and he makes a frantic call to his relocation contact for a new identity. He finds, however, that his old contact has been retired. What's more, his new contact, Joe Weyburn (Stephen Tobolowsky), is in league with Diggs and Sorenson. Just as Graves prepares to confront Jarmin, Sorenson and Diggs show up at the gas station with guns blazing. They kill Jarmin's kindly old boss at the gas station and pin the murder on Jarmin and Graves, who get away, but now have the police as well as drug dealers and rogue FBI agents hot on their trail. While eluding their pursuers, Jarmin and Graves visit old acquaintances of Jarmin's from his various incarnations, primarily tall, sexy Joan Severance as a country veterinarian, and Alex Bruhanski as a hairdresser who used to be Jarmin's boss. Severance sews up the buckshot wound in Jarmin's rear, and Bruhanski returns Jarmin's address book, which contains the home address of Jarmin's former FBI contact. Eventually Jarmin and Graves catch up with the contact, only to find that he's now senile.

While most of the police forces of the Western world close in on the fugitive couple, a final confrontation occurs at a zoo after hours.

There's more plot, but it doesn't get any better. Along the way are plenty of chases—in cars, on motorcycles, and in airplanes. And through it all, Jarmin and Graves blissfully bicker while trudging through the woods, crawling along skyscraper ledges, and staying in cheap motels infested with giant roaches. It's all meant to be zany, wacky and endearing; instead, it's uniformly dull, derivative, and tedious. Though the script by David Seltzer, Louis Venosta, and Eric Lerner is overstuffed with exposition—including the dreaded flashback—the characters remain shrill and annoying. It's impossible to care about the romance between Jarmin and Graves, because it's impossible to care about them as people.

The humor in BIRD ON A WIRE is even less compelling than the film's illogical plot and cardboard characters, consisting mostly of underwear jokes, feeble sex gags about Jarmin's "Mister Wiggly," and stereotypical swishery when Jarmin confronts his hairdresser ex-employer. All of this uninspired slop is wrapped up in a glossy but crude package by John Badham (STAKEOUT), who never seems to have decided just what type of film he was directing. Brutal gunplay gives way to bathroom jokes, which give way to steamy romance, all without the slightest rhyme or reason. From its brainless big-name casting to its sloppy script and its overblown, by-the-numbers direction, BIRD ON A WIRE serves best as a one-film course in everything that's mind-numbingly mediocre in contemporary mainstream American cinema. *(Adult situations, violence, profanity.)*

d, John Badham; p, Rob Cohen; w, David Seltzer, Louis Venosta, and Eric Lerner (based on a story by Venosta, Lerner); ph, Robert Primes; ed, Frank Morriss and Dallas Puett; m, Hans Zimmer; md, Shirley Walker; prod d, Philip Harrison; art d, Richard Hudolin; set d, Rose Marie McSherry; spec, John Thomas; stunts, Mic Rodgers and Betty Thomas; cos, Wayne Finkelman, Eduardo Castro, and Monique Stranan; makup, Sandy Cooper

Comedy/Romance/Thriller   **(PR:C   MPAA:PG-13)**

BLACK RAIN

(Japan) 123m Imamura—Hayashibara—Tohokushinsha/Toei bw

(KUROI AME)

Yoshiko Tanaka *(Yasuko)*, Kazuo Kitamura *(Shigematsu)*, Etsuko Ichihara *(Shigako)*, Shoichi Ozawa *(Shokichi)*, Norihei Miki *(Kotaro)*, and Keisuke Ishida *(Yuichi)*

Shohei Imamura's BLACK RAIN is about the dropping of the atomic bomb on Hiroshima and its after-effects. An estimated 119,000 of the city's total wartime population of 340,000 people were killed instantly in the bombing, 140,000 died within four months afterwards, and an additional 70,000 succumbed to radiation poisoning by 1950. Imamura has taken an intimate approach to his harrowing subject, focusing on the dark destiny of one family that was caught in the holocaust. The film opens with the bombing, showing the blinding flash of light, the shock wave that disintegrates people and buildings, and the black rain falling on young Yasuko (Yoshiko Tanaka), her aunt Shigako (Etsuko Ichihara) and her uncle Shigematsu (Kazuo Kitamura), which exposes them all to radiation poisoning. Five years pass, and the well-to-do family's main problem is now the difficulty of finding a husband for Yasuko. Several suitors have been scared off after learning of her exposure to contamination, and Yasuko feels like a pariah. The entire town lives in daily dread of the consequences of radiation, which they have seen all too clearly: Shigematsu, himself relatively healthy and able-bodied, must watch his dear friends pass away one by one. The townspeople have become used to funeral processions and to the taking of various home remedies, including the cure-all aloe, white peaches for appetite, and carp blood for warmth; Shigako, in her desperation, even turns to a noisy charlatan of a faith healer. Yasuko gradually becomes involved with Yuichi (Keisuke Ishida), a lower-class man whose nerves have been shattered by the war. Shigako becomes sick and dies, and it grows clear that Yasuko's end is near, as well. In the last scene, Shigematsu watches her being taken to the hospital, accompanied by the loving, loyal Yuichi.

Imamura (PIGS AND BATTLESHIPS; THE BALLAD OF NARYAMA) films his story in black and white, but however elegant these images may be in the latter portions of the film, the use of color might have had a less distancing effect. Dramatic elements are also problematic: one is both moved by the characters' horrific plight and somewhat puzzled by the rather soap opera-ish and protracted handling of the subject. Yasuko and her family are all incredibly noble and self-effacing; they accept their fate with a weary, bewildered resignation, never once expressing real rage or sorrow. The importance of an arranged marriage was (and is), of course, a given in Japanese society (where discrimination persists against the survivors of the Hiroshima and Nagasaki fallout, called *hibakusha*), but is somewhat untranslatable here, given the larger horrors at hand. (The traditional humor and absurdity of Japanese formality have worked better in the context of a film like THE MAKIOKA SISTERS.) Also questionable are

the uses to which BLACK RAIN puts the mental disability of Yuichi, who is supposedly driven flamboyantly crazy by the sounds of moving vehicles that remind him of a terrifying battle experience. He acts his explanation out in a calculated theatrical solo that, while effective, throws the film momentarily out of kilter; and at the end, he rides calmly away with Yasuko in a rumbling ambulance, supposedly cured by selfless love. The resolution smacks somewhat of Hollywood, limiting its emotional resonance.

Imamura's restaging of the holocaust itself calls up a mixed response. No one except the actual survivors will ever really know what it was like; one only feels that it was just so much worse than the charred babies and sculptural human remains we are shown (in merciful black and white) here. (There is, however, one breathtaking, you-are-there shot of the escaping townspeople staring back at the looming mushroom cloud.) Similarly, the music is admirably unsentimental, but becomes monotonous.

Kitamura is a handsome, likably dignified presence as Shigematsu, and Tanaka plays Yasuko with the unassuming gentility typical of hundreds of Japanese movie heroines, which also typifies Ichihara's performance as her aunt. More forcefulness on all three actors' parts might have precipitated more audience involvement, and a brief subplot involving a conniving village matchmaker and her wayward daughter (also unmarriageable, but for different reasons than Yasuko) could have been developed further, if only as a respite from the idealized central family unit. Ishida mugs and grovels in time-honored fashion as that dramatist's friend, the village idiot, but in the role of another scenarist's favorite—the senile grandmother—an elf of an old woman is genuinely irresistable. *(Violence, nudity, adult situations, sexual situations.)*

d, Shohei Imamura; p, Hisa Iino; w, Shohei Imamura and Toshiro Ishido (based on a novel by Masuji Ibuse); ph, Takashi Kawamata; ed, Hajime Okayasu; m, Toru Takemitsu; art d, Hisao Inagaki

Drama   **(PR:O   MPAA:NR)**

BLADES

99m Finnegan/Troma c

Robert North *(Roy Kent)*, Jeremy Whelan *(Deke Slade)*, Victoria Scott *(Kelly Lange)*, Holly Stevenson *(Bea Osgood)*, William Towner *(Norm Osgood)*, Peter Wray *(Lyle)*, Charlie Quinn *(Charlie Kimmel)*, Bruce Katlin *(Morgue Attendant)*, Lee Devin *(Squire Evans)*, Bill Kimble *(Sonny Fagan)*, Donald Jackson *(Detective)*, Hank Berkheimer *(Mr. Simpkins)*, Anna Haddad *(Mrs. Simpkins)*, Andy Fertal *(Bert)*, Larry Stromberg *(Don)*, Kara Callahan *(Jenny)*, William Pace *(Earl)*, and Greg Leiner *(Glenn)*

Before BLADES' opening credits roll, two typically oversexed horror-film teenagers are shown making out on the greens of the Tall Grass Country Club, then being mowed down by an unseen monster. What is this menace? A giant lawn mower, of course. That's the premise of this tongue-in-cheek spoof that will strike terror into the hearts of golfers and non-golfers alike.

Something is cutting people to pieces at Tall Grass Country Club, but the owner, Norm Osgood (William Towner), is too preoccupied with an upcoming televised Pro-Am tournament to care. His loyal assistant, Kelly Lange (Victoria Scott), is angry with him because he gave the job of head golf pro to out-of-towner Roy Kent (Robert North), whose first official duty (aside from trying to placate Kelly) is to examine the body parts lying on the greens. In order to keep his job, he also has to score a hole-in-one with the boss's wife (Holly Stevenson). The next day, the body of an amateur golfer is discovered, looking as if it had already undergone an autopsy. At a meeting of concerned citizens, Osgood and police chief Charlie Kimmel (Charlie Quinn) attempt to calm everyone down, but the crowd feels the perpetrator is fired Tall Grass employee Deke Slade (Jeremy Whelan). Deke, however, suggests to Roy that an evil force is responsible for the deaths. When a young caddy gets diced up in front of witnesses, a fairway-wrecking vigilante hunt ensues, after which, holding up a lawn mower like a bagged deer, the townspeople turn in Deke. After Roy and Kelly find an overturned golf cart and then unsuccessfully search the allegedly murderous mower for body parts, however, they realize the true killer is still at large. During the big tournament, Kelly competes against Squire Evans (Lee Devin), an accomplished cheater, while Roy keeps an eye out for missing persons. Then, sweeping across the grass, an enormous metal predator appears to chew up Evans while dragging the golfer away. Deke, his innocence thus established, is released from jail and accompanies Kelly and Roy on a get-the-mower mission in a mega-van fortified with grenades, assault rifles, and bales of hay (for bait). Deke explains that the belligerent blades have assumed a life of their own: when the country club fired his father and replaced the old-fashioned equipment with modern machinery, this antiquated grass-cutter vowed revenge. (Why it has taken so long for the metal demon to start mass murdering is never explained; it killed Deke's dad years ago.) Although the monster mower repeatedly attacks the trio's van, the real trouble starts the following day, when they get a flat tire, after which Roy smashes the van in a getaway attempt. While the malicious mower re-energizes itself, Deke acts as bait and barely escapes the blades by hanging onto Roy, who's on top of the van. He is unable to hold on, however, and falls into the deadly metal. Roy, after dumping some plastic explosive on the monster, tries to detonate it by hitting golf balls at the mad machine. His third drive hits the target and boom! – one less possessed lawn mower in the world.

As ludicrous as the premise sounds, BLADES is moderately exciting drive-in movie fare. At times, however, this horror parody gets mired in a few sand traps of its own. While blessed with some breezy dialog and a zany air, the film includes some cast members who are either amateurish (Towner) or don't seem to be aware of the joke (handsome North, who has presence but lacks comic zest). Although the rampant silliness doesn't need to be overplayed, it could have used a little more acting pizazz. Luckily, Scott's feisty tomboy heroine and Whelan's saturnine blade-hunter are on-target characterizations that keep the spoof humming along.

If you don't scale your expectations too high, BLADES also offers legitimate thrills and references to better-known horror films, particularly JAWS, which it rips off gleefully. But it doesn't quite find the proper balance in dishing out fright-night frissons while simultaneously lampooning the genre. Steering a middle course between the two genres (horror and spoof), it meets the respective requirements of each, without blending the scares and laughs into a coherent, stylish whole. Still, if you enjoy monster-mashes, BLADES offers ample chills, superior mechanical effects, and enough cheeky drollery to keep viewers amused. Enough talent is in evidence in the writing and directing for one to hope the film's creative personnel will reunite. If the sight of a giant, grudge-minded lawn mower chewing up caddies tickles your fancy, then BLADES is an offbeat gore movie spoof you should tee off with. (*Violence, gore effects, profanity, substance abuse.*)

d, Thomas R. Rondinella; p, John P. Finnegan; w, William R. Pace and Thomas R. Rondinella (based on a story by John P. Finnegan); ph, James Hayman; ed, Thomas R. Rondinella; m, John Hodian; prod d, J.C. Svec; spec, Wilfred Caban; makup, Lauren Matenus

Comedy/Horror (PR:C   MPAA:R)

BLIND FURY

86m Interscope Communications/Tri-Star c

Rutger Hauer (*Nick Parker*), Terrance O'Quinn (*Frank Devereaux*), Brandon Call (*Billy Devereaux*), Lisa Blount (*Annie Winchester*), Randall "Tex" Cobb (*Slag*), Noble Willingham (*MacCready*), Meg Foster (*Lynn Devereaux*), and Sho Kosugi (*The Assassin*)

BLIND FURY stars Rutger Hauer as Nick Parker, an American soldier in Vietnam who loses his sight when a bomb explodes in his face during combat. He is rescued by some villagers, who teach him to be a brilliant swordsman, despite his blindness. The story then jumps 20 years forward, and Nick, back Stateside, is now a drifter. Harassed by bullies, he beats them up with his cane (which conceals a large sword). Next, he visits the home of an old Army buddy, Frank Devereaux (Terrance O'Quinn), and finds not Frank, but Frank's ex-wife, Lynn (Meg Foster) and son, Billy (Brandon Call). Suddenly, a group of men pretending to be policemen break into the house, led by Slag (played by boxer-turned-character actor Randall "Tex" Cobb, the Lone Biker from RAISING ARIZONA). Nick slices all of the bad guys except Slag, but not before the ersatz cops have mortally wounded Lynn. Although Billy despises him, Nick takes the boy to Reno to find Frank, who, we learn, is a brilliant scientist whose emotional weakness was responsible for the accident that blinded Nick, and who has become a compulsive gambler. As a result of Frank's gambling, casino owner MacCready (Noble Willingham) has sent Slag and the other killers out to kidnap Billy, in order to force Frank to pay off his enormous debts by making designer drugs. Continually pursued by these baddies, Nick and Billy become closer, the former even revealing that he can't cry any more because his tear ducts were injured in the Vietnam accident. Once they get to Reno, they are instantly abducted, but Nick, Billy, and Frank's girl friend, Annie (Lisa Blount), manage to take over the crooks' van – with Nick driving – leading to a big car chase through downtown Reno traffic. Nick then heads for MacCready's casino, exposes the management as cheaters, and, using his keen sense of hearing and thwarting untold numbers of guards, finds Frank. The two men flee, but upon learning that MacCready has kidnaped Annie and Billy, they go to MacCready's ski resort home. There, Nick kills lots more baddies, including an expert Japanese swordfighter (whom Nick electrocutes in a hot tub), and Slag (who is cut in half and pushed through a window by the blind vet). Now Frank is ready to be a family man, and prepares to set up house with Annie and Billy. Miserable because Nick won't stay, Billy chases him through the streets, SHANE-style, but goes back to his father, as Nick finally sheds a tear and heads off alone.

While BLIND FURY has a good deal to offer, it's ultimately a disappointment. The film's premise, taken from a Japanese serial about a blind samurai, is wonderful. But the hero is neither sympathetic enough (we almost never see him

handicapped by his blindness, so we don't feel his triumph over it) nor sufficiently mysterious and awe-inspiring (unlike, for instance, Mel Gibson's character in LETHAL WEAPON) for us to care what happens to him. Given this lack of development and the absence of truly witty dialog – which might have helped immensely in making the main character more compelling – the film's cast and crew do about as well as they can with the existing material. O'Quinn, so memorable in THE STEPFATHER, creates a marvelous persona of harmful weakness. Hauer, who acts Nick's blindness well, is a terrific fighter and screen presence, but he has yet to find the vehicle that would put him in the top echelon of action stars (Gibson, Clint Eastwood, Arnold Schwarzenegger). His fight scenes are shot more to show off Hauer's swordfighting skills than for dramatic effect – but since one can't really show one actor cutting another's head off, even these scenes begin to drag after a while.

Director Phillip Noyce (BACKROADS; NEWSFRONT) has had an extremely varied career, and is well known in Australia as one of the major forces of that country's cinema. Internationally, he's probably best known for last year's thriller DEAD CALM. BLIND FURY offers him a chance to do a lighter action film with a bit more heart, but the screenplay by Charles Robert Carner fails to provide a worthy showcase for Noyce's talents. In the end, BLIND FURY wastes a potentially terrific idea – to follow the exploits of a blind swordfighter – with a treatment that is slick but uninteresting. (*Adult situations, profanity, violence.*)

d, Phillip Noyce; p, Daniel Grodnik and Tim Matheson; w, Charles Robert Carner; ph, Don Burgess; ed, David Simmons; m, J. Peter Robinson; prod d, Peter Murton; cos, Katherine Dover

Action/Comedy (PR:C   MPAA:R)

BLOOD OF HEROES

(Aus.) 102m Kings Road/Filmpac c

(AKA: SALUTE OF THE JUGGER, THE)

Rutger Hauer (*Sallow*), Joan Chen (*Kidda*), Vincent Phillip D'Onofrio (*Young Gar*), Delroy Lindo (*Mbulu*), Anna Katarina (*Big Cimber*), Gandhi Macintyre (*Gandhi*), Justin Monju (*Dog Boy*), Max Fairchild (*Gonzo*), Hugh Keays-Byrne (*Lord Vile*), Lia Francisa (*Maria*), and Aaron Martin (*Samohin Boy*)

The time: after the Fall. The place: beyond Thunderdome. Civilization has retreated to vast subterranean cities, while barbarism reigns on the barren surface. There, in a scorched, poverty-stricken town where mere survival is a struggle, the ragged inhabitants gather to watch the Jugger Game, a brutal sport whose object (to impale a dog skull on a spike as a sign of victory) is simple, and whose rules – protect your teammates and try not to die – are even simpler. Two five-man teams suit up, disappearing under homemade armor and wielding the vicious tools of a game that's something between prison-yard football and war. There are no rounds or defaults, and only the inexorable thud of stones thrown against metal plate marks the passage of time. The players batter and lacerate one another until a goal is scored or until 100 stones are thrown three times, in which case a tie is declared. Nomadic teams play against locals for honor, money, and such glory as the debased can imagine, then move on to the next town and do it all again. Rutger Hauer plays one such combatant, namely Sallow (think *salaud*, meaning *bastard* in French), who leads his grimly scarred team through the wasteland. As a young man, he was admitted to the elite Jugger League, whose players live in luxury and rub elbows with the effete aristocracy, but he was banished to the desert after he overstepped an invisible line. Sallow and his companions accept their debased existence, until one of them is crippled and his replacement, an ambitious peasant girl named Kidda (Joan Chen), convinces her teammates to challenge the League. Winning isn't the issue – the youthful challenge that won Hauer admittance was over in minutes and left three of his companions dead – but putting up a good fight means getting the chance to leave the harsh life above ground forever. Kidda and Young Gar (Vincent Phillip D'Onofrio) are willing to take the risk, and once they convince Sallow they're right, the others follow. Their challenge accepted, the team fights against impossible odds and triumphs, proving that theirs is indeed the blood of heroes.

Though presumably intended to be futuristic, BLOOD OF HEROES seems to take place in a vague, nowhere place and time, its ambiguity designed to make the story seem a kind of parable for all times and all places. The film derives its imagery and metaphors from a variety of sources – conspicuous among them ROCKY; ROLLERBALL; A BOY AND HIS DOG; the "Mad Max" series and its imitations; and gladiator movies too numerous to name – and has a formulaic, basic story with undeniable appeal: underdog takes on the big guys and wins. However, the film goes wrong by appropriating worn material, then constructing around it a narrative so ruthlessly straightforward it steamrolls over any possibility of dramatic suspense. The new kid wants to shoot for the stars, the old hands hesitate to rock the boat, the man who was once a dreamer recognizes his last chance to grab the brass ring, and so on, as the story proceeds from stereotype to cliche without a single dramatic diversion. The international cast (representing Holland, China, Switzerland, Australia, the US, and Great Britain) can make little of this sketchy material, and are also handicapped by having to work under disfiguring makeup—a few get by with artfully placed scars, but the rest labor beneath latex deformities.

In the end, therefore, BLOOD OF HEROES is just one more ROAD WAR-RIOR clone, noteworthy only for its outstanding, rhythmically complex score by Todd Boekelheide, which hypnotically combines "primitive" and "industrial" effects. *(Violence, profanity, brief nudity, sexual situations.)*

d, David Peoples; p, Charles Roven; w, David Peoples; ph, David Eggby; ed, Richard Francis-Bruce; m, Todd Boekelheide; prod d, John Stoddart; stunts, Guy Norris; makup, Michael Westmore and Bob McCarron

Action/Science Fiction   **(PR:C   MPAA:R)**

BLOOD RED

91m Kettledrum/Hemdale c

Eric Roberts *(Marco Collogero)*, Giancarlo Giannini *(Sebastian Collogero)*, Dennis Hopper *(Berrigan)*, Burt Young *(Andrews)*, Carlin Glynn *(Miss Jeffreys)*, Lara Harris *(Angelica)*, Francesca De Sapio *(Rosa Collogero)*, Julia Roberts *(Maria Collogero)*, Alexandra Masterson *(Anna Collogero)*, Joseph Running Fox *(Samuel Joseph)*, Al Ruscio *(Antonio Segestra)*, Michael Madsen *(Enziio)*, Elias Koteas *(Silvio)*, Marc Lawrence *(Michael Fazio)*, Frank Campanella *(Dr. Scola)*, Aldo Ray *(Fr. Stassio)*, Gary Swanson, Susan Anspach, Charles Dierkop, Horton Foote Jr., and Maurine Logan

Filmed in 1986 and first released (regionally) in 1989, BLOOD RED stars Dennis Hopper as Berrigan, a 19th-century California railroad tycoon used to getting his own way—even if that means laying tracks right through the property of Italian immigrant grape-growers. Having recently been given American citizenship, the Italian vintners have lovingly worked their vineyards after fleeing oppression in their homeland, and believe that the American laws will protect them from capitalist cutthroats. Making sure he has the Railroad Commission in his pocket, Berrigan doesn't give the landowners an opportunity to publicly protest their evictions, which he has masterminded after his purchase offers were refused. When Sebastian Collogero (Giancarlo Giannini) inspires the others to hold onto their land, Berrigan hires thugs (led by Burt Young, in the character of Andrews) to terrorize the wine-pressers into submission. Meanwhile, Sebastian's son, Marco (Eric Roberts), who has been busy sowing his wild oats with an attractive widow (Susan Anspach), falls for his neighbor's convent-bred daughter (Lara Harris) and assumes his rightful place by his combative father's side. One night, while Marco is trysting with his new love, Andrews' men torture and kill Sebastian in full view of his daughter Maria (Julia Roberts, who is also Eric Roberts' sister in real life). When the frightened landowners won't fight back, Marco calls upon his Indian pal Samuel Joseph (Joseph Running Fox) and two cousins to help him start a series of reprisals against Berrigan's empire. With Maria's aid, Marco and his cronies invade a makeshift whorehouse and rub out two of the assassins. Andrews, having disappointed Berrigan and the railroad engineers, vows to save face, but Marco's gang has already blown up a trestle, at which point Miss Jeffreys (Carlin Glynn), an upright citizen in the morally bankrupt local community, joins in the fray by taking photos of the havoc and starting a press campaign against Berrigan. As more hired guns descend on the town, Marco and his gang hide out in the woods, where they are joined by his pregnant girl friend. Backed by a state senator (Gary Swanson), Marco and Miss Jeffreys denounce the Railroad Commission for caving in to Berrigan's greed. Despite some close calls, Andrews' bounty hunters fail to capture Marco, and an official investigation into the illegal vineyard evictions is launched. Marco surfaces to visit his kin and is betrayed by the family retainer (Elias Koteas), but narrowly escapes with the help of his widowed ex-lover (and eventually pays back his betrayer in a tunnel explosion). With negative publicity pressuring him from all sides, Berrigan apparently consents to the senator's request that he hold peace talks with Marco. Luckily, the vintner smells an ambush and circumvents the death-trap laid for him by the railroad baron's henchmen. With his own gang's help, Marco wipes out Berrigan's desperadoes. In the end, the double-dealing tycoon is forced to return the wine-makers' property and to build his railroad around the vineyards at great cost to himself.

Notwithstanding its delayed release, there is nothing incompetent about BLOOD RED; it's simply that little directorial imagination has been brought to bear on filming its representation of Americana. Once again, a veteran cast walks around in beautiful period costumes that look as if they've never seen the light of day, which is also the light of life. Everything *appears* authentic, but there is so little cinematic spark in the movie that it resembles a historical pageant more than it does an engrossing, dynamic drama. While managing to avoid sounding contemporary, the dialog is flat, and the actors must do their best in mouthing cliches. A project like BLOOD RED requires visual sweep in order to make the long-ago live again. Instead, director Peter Masterson (THE TRIP TO BOUN-TIFUL) does such a pedestrian job of framing the action that we're left with a

history lesson, attractively photographed but dry. BLOOD RED unfolds a tale of little guys squeezed out by a reign of terror that merely holds one's attention, without stimulating deep interest in the outcome of the struggle. Competently played but unexcitingly directed, it remains ordinary and commonplace through-out, a would-be epic (whose influence over viewers' emotions is not aided by Carmine Coppola's overinsistent score).

Not as hyperkinetic here as he has been on occasion, Eric Roberts cuts a dashing heroic figure and doesn't seem out of place in this glorified western. In general, the other actors also acquit themselves with honor, although Hopper sabotages his performance with a ludicrous Irish accent. Instead of concentrating on his performance, we're constantly aware of how unconvincing his brogue is. If you are in the mood for a western historical drama, BLOOD RED records the basic circumstances of the coming of the railroad straightforwardly within its fictional framework. What it fails to do is transform this saga of far-reaching greed into a morality play that sweeps viewers along. Without a sense of visual panorama, the history lesson doesn't pulse with energy, becoming academic and remote. *(Violence, profanity, sexual situations.)*

d, Peter Masterson; p, Judd Bernard and Patricia Casey; w, Ron Cutler; ph, Toyomichi Kurita; ed, Randy Thornton; m, Carmine Coppola; prod d, Bruno Rubeo; cos, Ruth Myers

Drama   **(PR:C   MPAA:R)**

BLOOD RELATIONS

(Can.) 90m SC/Miramax c

Jan Rubes *(Dr. Andrea Wells)*, Lydie Denier *(Marie DeSette)*, Kevin Hicks *(Thomas Wells)*, Lynne Adams *(Sharon Hamilton)*, Sam Malkin *(Yuri)*, Stephen Saylor *(Jack Kaplan)*, Carrie Leigh *(Diane Morgan)*, and Ray Walston *(Charles MacLeod)*

A baroque exercise in Grand Guignol horror, BLOOD RELATIONS dresses up its thin, predictable plot with layers of menacing atmosphere. After a period of jet-setting around Europe, young Thomas Wells (Kevin Hicks) returns to the family mansion married to Marie (Lydie Denier), a pretty little gold-digger he picked up in a Monte Carlo casino. At once the couple plots the death of Thomas' father, Andrea (Jan Rubes), whom Thomas claims to hate because he caused the auto accident that left Thomas' late mother paralyzed. Moreover, with Andrea out of the way, Thomas stands to inherit $250 million from his dying grandfather, Charles (Ray Walston). In an effort to cause Andrea to overstrain his heart, Marie and Thomas play sadistic practical jokes on him. But Andrea proves to be in better health than expected; his ticker just keeps ticking, even after vigorous sex. Hmmmm. Coincidentally, father and son are brain surgeons, and together they drug Marie and take extensive cranial measurements. Hmmmm. And when Charles is brought home from the hospital, he has Marie strip and remarks how closely she resembles his poor, dead daughter. Hmmmm. Awakened by shrieks one night, Marie finds Andrea in a basement operating-room, driving steel rods into a girl friend's skull. And Thomas' mother, paralyzed but very much alive, lies in a corner looking on approvingly. Hmmmm. After the family's young attorney tells Marie he believes she's being set up, he winds up strapped to the operating-chair with Charles' brain transplanted into his head. Hmmmm. Having decided that something's going on that might affect her future well-being, Marie flees to the protection of the gentle family caretaker. But he, too, turns out to be a brain-surgery enthusiast, and when last seen Marie looks even more empty-headed than usual as Mother is wheeled into the operating-room.

In the hands of anyone else, BLOOD RELATIONS probably would have been a waste of time. But director Graeme Campbell (whose previous work includes the superior crime thriller MURDER ONE) has a florid, over-the-top style that is well suited to this material. Here he mixes the ghastly with the erotic and utilizes Rhett Morita's moody photography to good effect. In the role of Dr. Andrea Wells, Rubes appears to be employing techniques learned at the Vincent Price School of Dramatic Arts, and he even gets to sing some stirring operatic solos. Denier has the face and body of a high-fashion model, but the amoral character she is asked to play is paper-thin. This shallowness may have been a calculated move to keep viewers from being too disturbed by her fate, but it leaves the film without a sympathetic character in sight. Even Stephen Saylor, who wrote the screenplay, takes on a dim-witted role; he plays the ill-fated young attorney, who, we are told, is more useful as a cadaver than a counselor. Viewers who enjoy the Cinema of Cruelty could do worse than this handsome brain-jug-gling act, but they shouldn't expect much in the way of surprises. *(Sexual situations, adult situations, violence, nudity.)*

d, Graeme Campbell; p, Nicolas Stiliadis; w, Stephen Saylor; ph, Rhett Morita; ed, Michael McMahon; m, Mychael Danna; art d, Gina Hamilton; set d, Theresa Buckley-Ayrea; cos, Sharon Fedoruk and Michael Austin

Horror   **(PR:O   MPAA:R)**

BLOOD SALVAGE

98m Ken C. Sanders — High Five/Paragon Arts — Magnum c

Danny Nelson *(Jake Pruitt)*, Lori Birdsong *(April Evans)*, John Saxon *(Clifford Evans)*, Ray Walston *(Mr. Stone)*, Christian Hesler *(Hiram Pruitt)*, Evander Holyfield *(Himself)*, Ralph Pruitt Vaughn *(Roy Pruitt)*, Laura Whyte *(Pat Evans)*, and Andy Greenway *(Bobby Evans)*

Another entry in the odd but enduring horror sub-genre that pits deep-woods psychos against unwary city slickers, BLOOD SALVAGE achieves a reasonable level of entertainment by mixing the requisite gore with a fair amount of black humor. The plot centers around Jake Pruitt (Danny Nelson), a master mechanic, religious nut, and medical whiz who went permanently around the bend after his wife was denied an organ transplant that might have saved her life. With the help of his two sons, Hiram (Christian Hesler) and Roy (Ralph Pruitt Vaughn), Jake runs tourists off the road and hooks them up to homemade life-support systems in his "body" shop, where he lops off parts and sells them to a traveling organ broker (Ray Walston of "My Favorite Martian"). Things run pretty smoothly until Jake develops a crush on April Evans (Lori Birdsong), a wheelchair-bound teen he spots competing in a local beauty contest. Jake has Hiram sabotage the Evans family RV, which conveniently breaks down in front of the Pruitts' place of business. Jake lures April's little brother (Andy Greenway), mother (Laura Whyte), and father (John Saxon) into his house one-by-one, chloroforms them, and straps them into the spare-parts department. April becomes suspicious and begins registering her complaints with a shotgun. The Pruitts capture her, however, and take her to the room previously occupied by the former Mrs. Pruitt. Jake plans to heal April's spinal injury and make her his bride. He begins the surgery by withdrawing spinal fluid from April's brother (storing it in a mason jar crudely labeled "Boy") then injects it into April. After a couple of aborted escape attempts, the resourceful April bops Roy on the head with a plaster saint and, cured by Jake's ministrations, succeeds in hobbling away, with Jake's pet alligator in pursuit. April, who has a nasty little mean streak of her own, manages to lure the reptile into a trash compactor. But she does not manage to elude Jake, who is miffed when he learns that his intended has clobbered his son and his gator. Accompanied by the misogynistic and therefore delighted Hiram, Jake takes April into the body shop to administer a little pain. When Jake turns his back to heat a scalpel in a kerosene lamp, April kicks the lamp over, setting Jake on fire. Hiram runs after his father, and April searches for her parents. She finds her liverless father pinned to a board and her mother, minus her eyes, in an animal pen. Failing to notice her brother's head floating in a large jar of brine, April is preparing to leave with her parents when Hiram returns. A struggle ensues during which April's father sacrifices himself so that his wife and daughter can escape in the family RV. Hiram chases them in his Torino but is soon run off the road by April, though her mother dies in the process. Just when it seems the threat is over, Jake, severely burned, pops up from under a seat in the RV. April slams on the brakes, pitching Jake through the windshield and onto the highway, where she runs over him a few times for good measure. Soon, Roy appears in the family tow truck and scoops up Jake, promising that he will fix him up as good as new.

BLOOD SALVAGE should qualify as trashy good fun for those who like this sort of thing. The film adds enough twists to the standard formula to keep things interesting, especially in the substition of a tough, resourceful young woman for the usual helpless-bimbo victim. The filmmakers' decision to juice up the threat to the key victim-to-be by making her a paraplegic, however, may strike some viewers as offensive — especially when she is nearly sexually assaulted.

BLOOD SALVAGE does include a good deal of black comedy that keeps things from becoming too grim. In addition to some pretty snappy dialog (after chloroforming one of his victims, Jake rapturously rolls his eyes heavenward and says, "Praise the Lord — another convert"), the film is loaded with sight gags. The broken sign on Jake's salvage yard, for instance, reads "Body and Pain," and one of the unwilling donors in Jake's body shop bears an uncanny resemblance to Elvis Presley. BLOOD SALVAGE is also bolstered by Nelson's gung-ho performance as Jake and Hesler's scenery-chewing turn as Hiram, the ultimate redneck. Despite its apparently low budget (the film was shot primarily in Georgia, using local actors), BLOOD SALVAGE does not look cheap, thanks to the technical proficiency of its crew and first-time director Tucker Johnston, who keeps things moving along at a rapid clip. Boxing fans should note that heavyweight Evander Holyfield, BLOOD SALVAGE's co-executive producer, makes a cameo appearance in the film. *(Gore effects, profanity, sexual situations.)*

d, Tucker Johnston; p, Martin J. Fischer and Ken C. Sanders; w, Tucker Johnston and Ken C. Sanders; ph, Michael Karp; ed, Jacquie Freeman Ross; m, Tim Temple; prod d, Rob Sissman; art d, Rob Sissman; spec, Bill Johnson; cos, D. Jean Hester

Comedy/Horror (PR:O MPAA:R)

BLUE HEAT

(SEE: LAST OF THE FINEST)

BLUE STEEL

102m Lightning — Precision — Mack — Taylor/MGM-UA — Vestron c

Jamie Lee Curtis *(Megan Turner)*, Ron Silver *(Eugene Hunt)*, Clancy Brown *(Nick Mann)*, Elizabeth Pena *(Tracy Perez)*, Louise Fletcher *(Shirley Turner)*, Philip Bosco *(Frank Turner)*, Kevin Dunn *(Assistant Chief Stanley Hoyt)*, Richard Jenkins *(Attorney Mel Dawson)*, Markus Flannagan *(Husband)*, Mary Mara *(Wife)*, Skipp Lynch *(Instructor)*, Mike Hodge *(Police Commissioner)*, Mike Starr *(Superintendent)*, Chris Walker *(Officer Jeff Travers)*, Tom Sizemore *(Wool Cap)*, David Ilku *(Counterman)*, Andrew Hubatsek *(Cashier)*, Joe Jamrog *(Doorman)*, Matt Craven *(Howard)*, Reginald Wells, Heidi Kempf *(TV Announcers)*, Toni Darling *(Prostitute)*, William J. Marshall *(Hood)*, James Shannon *(Maitre D'Hotel)*, Thomas Dorff *(Businessman Victim)*, William Wise *(Internal Affairs Man)*, Lauren Tom *(Reporter)*, Faith Geer *(Lady Bum)*, Doug Barron, Carol Schneider, L. Peter Callender *(Reporters)*, Becky Gelke *(Nurse No. 1)*, Frank Girardeau *(Uniform Cop)*, Larry Silvestri *(Precinct Cop)*, John Capodice *(Trial Commissioner)*, Sam Coppola *(PBA Representative)*, Bellina Logan *(Rookie No. 1)*, Ralph Nieves *(Homicide Detective)*, Al Cerullo *(Helicopter Pilot)*, Michael Philip Del Rio *(John Perez)*, Harley Flannagan, and James Drescher *(Punks)*

In BLUE STEEL, Jamie Lee Curtis plays Megan Turner, a rookie New York cop whose first week on the job is less than pleasurable. In fact, on her first night, she breaks up the robbery of a crowded supermarket and shoots and kills the armed thief, unloading six bullets into the man, whose gun flies into the air and lands in front of a customer, Eugene Hunt (Ron Silver), who is lying on the floor. In the confusion, Hunt takes the gun and quietly leaves the scene. A successful broker on Wall Street, Hunt becomes obsessed with Megan and sees the gun as a way to release the repressed thoughts in his head. After taking the gun home and inscribing Megan's name on the bullets, he begins a killing spree. Meanwhile, Megan has problems of her own: her mother (Louise Fletcher) is being abused by her father (Philip Bosco), she hasn't had a date in months, and she is suspended from the force for shooting an unarmed man (since the supermarket thief's gun was not found at the scene). Enter Hunt, who sweeps the unsuspecting Megan off her feet with fancy dinners and romantic helicopter rides. But soon his first victim is found, and the inscribed bullet casings lead police detective Nick Mann (Clancy Brown) and his department to reinstate Megan (as a detective) in order to keep an eye on her. Hunt, aided by mysterious voices in his head, continues the killing of victims and the courting of Megan, who remains unaware that he is the murderer she is after, until one night when they arrive at Hunt's apartment for a nightcap. After a few passionate kisses, Hunt touches Megan's gun (still in her shoulder holster) and becomes seemingly more aroused by the feel of the gun than the kisses. Soon he makes Megan hold the weapon (in the same way she did when she killed the supermarket thief) and tells her she has become his "radiance." "You didn't blink an eye when you killed him," he says, "you were perfect." He confesses more of his bizarre thoughts, including ideas about them being two halves of the same person. Shaken, and at once realizing that Hunt is the killer, Megan phones for backup and has him arrested. But Hunt's lawyer gets him released on a technicality, and soon Nick and Megan are looking for the freed maniac. Following a few more killings (including that of Megan's best friend) and a surprise visit to Megan's parents' house, Hunt is tracked to Central Park (where he has buried his gun). Nick is nearly killed during a shootout between Hunt and Megan, and Hunt is wounded, but he gets away. The detectives go back to Megan's apartment, where, unknown to them, Hunt is waiting. After shooting Nick, Hunt attacks Megan, who gets to her gun and again shoots Hunt as he escapes through the fire escape. The cops are brought to the hospital and put into guarded rooms, but Megan knocks out her guard, puts on his police uniform, and hits the streets for a final, violent showdown with Hunt, climaxing in a shootout on Wall Street.

Relentless in its intensity, and suspenseful beyond belief, BLUE STEEL is a wonderful piece of filmmaking. Director Kathryn Bigelow (whose first commercial film was the unusual vampire western NEAR DARK) has created a stark battle between good and evil that is photographed and edited with striking proficiency. Certain scenes (such as the amazing opening credits and the wonderful sequence in the police station, filled with criss-crossing shafts of light) startle and surprise with their audacious beauty. But Bigelow's talent is not restricted to visuals; she is also an exceptionally adept action director (whose main influences seem to be Walter Hill and Sam Peckinpah), and she has a sharp eye for the eroticism of violence. NEAR DARK features a highly erotic scene in which a vampire opens her wrist to her blood-lusting lover, while oil wells behind the couple turn and pump in the night. In BLUE STEEL, Bigelow matches the unusual intensity of that scene with the powerful, sexually loaded scene in which Hunt watches Megan hold her gun. The script (cowritten by

Bigelow and her NEAR DARK collaborator Eric Red, who wrote and directed COHEN AND TATE) deals with private and forbidden thoughts, as well as their exorcising. Very similar in theme to most of Red's work (BLUE STEEL is a perfect companion piece to his THE HITCHER), the screenplay is stocked with confrontations between good and evil and right and wrong, and it seems OK for the main character to possess a bit of both.

As cynical as it appears, BLUE STEEL is a sincere work with some interesting ideas weaved into the heart-pounding suspense. In fleshing out these ideas, the performers are uniformly good: Fletcher and Bosco turn in reliably strong portrayals, and Silver cuts completely loose as the psycho, adding real menace and tension to the film. Bigelow's offbeat choice of Brown as a leading man (he is usually cast as a hulking bad guy) is a surprising success, since he's both likable and believable as a cop. But the movie belongs to Curtis, whose incredible range is put to comprehensive use. She's vulnerable one moment and shockingly strong the next, and there is not a false note in her performance. She creates a full, three-dimensional character who is worth caring about and rooting for. Her character's dark thoughts and killer instincts are at the center of the film — repeatedly asked why she became a cop, Megan gives reasons that include her need to commit violent acts — and she doesn't back away from the brutal aspects of the script. Curtis seems to be enjoying herself, and it adds immeasurably to the depth of the film.

Full of unforgettable images (like the blood-soaked Silver screaming on a Manhattan rooftop, or the beams of light shooting through the bullet holes of a paper target), BLUE STEEL is a hardcore thriller, packed with suspense and bold action. With this film and NEAR DARK, Kathryn Bigelow has easily established herself as America's best female director (and one of cinema's best directors in general), whose brave movies make the films of the overrated Susan Seidelman and Amy Heckerling appear all the more weak by contrast. She is a filmmaker of enormous talent whose films transcend their genres and push the boundaries of the art. BLUE STEEL, one of the most wildly intense films in years, will please genre fans and may even knock them for a loop. Quite simply, this is an outstanding film. *(Graphic violence, profanity, adult situations, sexual situations, brief nudity.)*

d, Kathryn Bigelow; p, Edward R. Pressman, Oliver Stone, and Michael Rauch; w, Kathryn Bigelow and Eric Red; ph, Amir Mokri; ed, Lee Percy; m, Brad Fiedel; prod d, Toby Corbett; set d, Susan Kaufman; spec, Steve Kirshoff; stunts, Jery Hewitt; cos, Richard Shissler; makup, Toni Trimble

Thriller (PR:O MPAA:R)

BODY CHEMISTRY

87m Concorde c

Marc Singer (*Dr. Tom Redding*), Lisa Pescia (*Dr. Claire Archer*), Mary Crosby (*Marlee*), David Kagen (*Freddie*), H. Bradley Barneson (*Jason*), Doreen Alderman (*Kim*), Lauren Tuerk (*Wendy*), and Joseph Campanella (*Dr. Pritchard*)

A cautionary tale about the tragic consequences of mixing business and pleasure in the field of psychosexual research, BODY CHEMISTRY refashions FATAL ATTRACTION for the white-lab-coat set. Marc Singer (BEASTMASTER) stars as Dr. Tom Redding, an ambitious thirtysomething sex researcher up for promotion as lab director. His boss instructs him to do everything in his power to please Dr. Claire Archer (Lisa Pescia), a buxom, blonde sex researcher dangling a fat government grant for research into aberrant sexual behavior and violence. Tom gives his all their first night at the lab, after Claire plays him her favorite sicko S & M videotape for him (in the interest of science) and hits him up for some (safe) commitment-free sex. After a night of frenzied field research, Tom wakes up in Claire's apartment and slinks home to his wife and child (Mary Crosby and H. Bradley Barneson). Claire calls him to say she inadvertently left her panties in the lab last night (right next to the empty bottle of champagne), and Tom rushes to the lab to remove the evidence, only to be informed by his boss that Claire has pulled the plug on the grant. Tom then rushes back to Claire's place, where she tells him she assumed he might find it difficult to work with her after their impetuosity of the night before. He proves that nothing could be further from the truth, plunging into another kinky romp with his colleague. Claire awards the grant to the lab and Tom is rewarded with his promotion. Tom's wife decides to celebrate hubby's coup by throwing a party for the whole lab; meanwhile, Claire becomes more and more demanding, even showing up in a van outside Tom's home and demanding sex while his wife and child are unloading groceries in the driveway. Tom decides to break off the liaison, invoking the no-commitments clause in their sexual contract, but Claire reneges. She demands that he show up for an intimate dinner at her apartment, and when he fails to appear, she responds violently, smashing the romantic table settings and two uneaten crab dinners — which she then mails to his ex-lover's home. Now Tom begins to realize that Claire is a tad unstable and refuses to see her or take her phone calls. She responds by sending him a videotape of their fandango in the van, filmed without his knowledge. Tom agrees to meet her at a restaurant,

where she embarrasses everyone within shouting distance by declaring that sex with him was the greatest experience of her life. Tom remains aloof, however, so she steps up her retribution campaign, mailing the van video to his nine-year-old son and showing up at the lab's victory party with his best friend (David Kagen). Mrs. Redding, who has begun to suspect Tom of philandering, overhears a juicy argument between him and Claire and declares dibs on her husband. Claire leaves the party, but returns later with a can of gasoline and torches part of the house. Tom's wife decides enough is enough and leaves with the kid; Tom, enraged, returns to Claire's apartment and flings her around a little until she grabs a gun from a nightstand and shoots him dead. When the police arrive, she tearfully explains that they had been having a love affair at the office and that when she tried to break it off, he became violent — forcing her to act in self-defense.

BODY CHEMISTRY is a tawdry, pointless exercise in sleaze redeemed only by above-average work from director Kristine Peterson and her technical crew. The substance of the film is questionable, to say the least, so Peterson opts for style — and lots of it. The result is a trashy, but watchable and even entertaining, exploitation film graced by flashy edits, an effective score, and surprisingly attractive cinematography. The film's sexual content is its only reason to exist, and Peterson makes it steam: several scenes between the randy researchers, as well as a couple of their lab videos, push the boundaries of the R rating about as far as they will go. This sort of action could have become boring very quickly, after the initial titillation, but Peterson has a visual flair that maintains excitement. She also manages to establish a certain amount of tension within the confines of the film's ludicrous plot. *(Sexual situations, nudity, violence, profanity.)*

d, Kristine Peterson; p, Alida Camp; w, Jackson Barr; ph, Phedon Papamichael; ed, Nina Gilberti; m, Terry Plumeri; prod d, Gary Randall; art d, Ella St. John Blakey; set d, Cee Parker; cos, Sandra Araya Jensen

Drama (PR:O MPAA:R)

BONFIRE OF THE VANITIES

126m De Palma/WB c

Tom Hanks (*Sherman McCoy*), Bruce Willis (*Peter Fallow*), Melanie Griffith (*Maria Ruskin*), Kim Cattrall (*Judy McCoy*), Morgan Freeman (*Judge White*), F. Murray Abraham (*Abe Weiss*), John Hancock (*Reverend Bacon*), Saul Rubinek (*Jed Kramer*), Kevin Dunn (*Thomas Killian*), Alan King (*Arthur Ruskin*), Clifton James (*Albert Fox*), Louis Giambalvo (*Ray Andruitti*), Barton Hayman (*Detective Martin*), Norman Parker (*Detective Goldberg*), Donald Moffat (*Mr. McCoy*), Patrick Malone (*Henry Lamb*), Beth Broderick (*Caroline Heftshank*), Kurt Fuller (*Pollard Browning*), Brian De Palma (*Prison Guard*), Adam LeFevre (*Rawlie Thorpe*), Richard Libertini (*Ed Rifkin*), Andre Gregory (*Aubrey Buffing*), Geraldo Rivera (*Robert Corso*), Mary Alice (*Annie Lamb*), Robert Stephens (*Sir Gerald Moore*), Marjorie Monaghan (*Evelyn Moore*), Rita Wilson (*Public Relations Woman*), Kirsten Dunst (*Campbell McCoy*), Troy Windbush (*Roland Auburn*), Emmanuel Xuereb (*Filippo Chirazzi*), Scotty Bloch (*Sally Rawthrote*), Hansford Rowe (*Leon Bavardage*), Elizabeth Owens (*Inez Bavardage*), Malachy McCourt (*Tony, Doorman*), John Bentley (*Bill, Doorman*), William Clark (*Eddie, Doorman*), Jeff Brooks, T.J. Coan, Don McManus, James Lally, Marcia Mitzman (*Bondsmen*), William Woodson (*Gene Lopwitz*), Nelson Vasquez (*Pimp*), Fanni Green (*Prostitute*), Roy Milton Davis (*Latino*), Shiek Mahmud-Bey (*Lockwood*), Stewart J. Zully (*Court Clerk*), Helen Stenborg (*Mrs. McCoy*), Timothy Jenkins (*Billy Cortez*), Sam Jenkins (*Fox's Assistant*), Vito D'Ambrosio (*Intercom Man*), Paul Bates (*Buck*), Camryn Manheim, J.D. Wyatt, Edye Byrde, David Lipman, George Merritt (*Poe Picketers*), Kirk Taylor (*Aide*), O. Laron Clark (*Cecil Hayden*), Louis P. Lebherz (*"The Commandatori"*), Walker Joyce (*Bobby Shaflet/"Don Giovanni"*), Anatoly Davydov (*Boris Karlevskov*), Nancy McDonald, Ray Iannicelli, Daniel Hagen, Kimberleigh Aarn, Walter Flanagan, Mike Hodge, Ernestine Jackson, Nicholas Levitin, Novella Nelson, Noble Lee Lester (*Media Jackals*), Adina Winston (*Female Guest*), Richard Belzer (*TV Producer*), Cynthia Mason (*Maid*), Ermal Williamson (*Butler*), W.M. Hunt (*Nunally Voyd*), Gian-Carlo Scandiuzzi (*Maitre d'*), Jon Rashad Kamal (*French Waiter*), Channing Chase (*Shocked Woman*), Hal England, Joy Claussen, John Fink, Judith Burke (*French Restaurant Patrons*), Barry Michlin (*Funeral Director*), Connie Sawyer (*Ruskin Family Member*), Johnny Crear (*Manny Leerman*), Sherri Paysinger (*Anchorwoman*), Staci Francis, Barbara Gooding, Kathleen Murphy Palmer, Lorraine Moore, Doris Leggett (*Gospel Singers*), Kathryn Danielle (*Public Relations Assistant*), Oliver Dixon (*Diplomat*), Jennifer Bassey (*Diplomat's Wife*), Katrina Braque (*Diplomat's Daughter*), Richard Gilbert-Hall, Marie Chambers, Virginia Morris, Barry Niekrug (*Aides to Weiss*), George Plimpton, and Susan Forristal (*Well Wishers*)

One of the bona fide box-office and critical bombs of 1990, this adaptation of Tom Wolfe's best-selling novel is a windfall of waste. It's a great-looking film with a great-looking cast, it had some of Hollywood's top talent behind the cameras, and a budget of more than $45 million, but it lacks bite and conviction and utterly failed to strike a single spark, much less catch fire.

Tom Hanks stars as top Wall Street bond trader Sherman McCoy, a self-styled "Master of the Universe" who wheels and deals in hundreds of millions of other people's dollars every day to ever-exploding profits. Besides his great job, he has a prim and proper wife, Judy (Kim Cattrall), a plush Manhattan apartment, and a sexy mistress, Maria (Melanie Griffith). At the height of his wealth and power, Sherman and his world are about to come undone. His descent begins innocently enough when, while walking his dog in the rain, he stops at a pay phone to call Maria. Dialing his home number by mistake, he reaches Judy instead, who reaches the obvious conclusion and heads for a divorce attorney. Still unbowed, Sherman arranges to pick up Maria at the airport, taking a wrong turn on the way back to Manhattan. They wind up in the South Bronx ghetto, and when Sherman finally makes his way to the freeway entry ramp, he finds it blocked with debris. He leaves the car to clear the way, and is approached by two probable muggers. He fights them off while Maria takes the wheel of the car. Sherman returns to the car and as Maria drives off, she hits one of the muggers. As they speed away, he lapses into a coma and is hospitalized. Back at Maria's apartment, she and Sherman argue over reporting the incident to the police. Since Maria was driving, she adamantly refuses to make such a report, and Sherman goes along with her wishes. Both return to their normal lives, while the plight of the comatose mugger, Henry Lamb (Patrick Malone), comes to the attention of a self-interested community activist, Reverend Bacon (John Hancock). Bacon turns the case into a major controversy, demanding that police find the rich white people who callously ran down poor Henry. The reverend's pressure forces district attorney Abe Weiss (an unbilled F. Murray Abraham), who is up for reelection in a predominantly black borough, to upgrade his efforts to catch the guilty party. In the meantime, alcoholic tabloid reporter Peter Fallow (Bruce Willis) sees the story as a chance to revive his sagging career, and with information from Bacon, turns the story into a headline-grabbing blockbuster. The police and media eventually close in on Sherman, who is arrested and charged with the crime. His firm quickly insists that he take an unpaid leave of absence, while Maria runs off to Europe with another lover. She returns to attend the funeral of her wealthy husband (Alan King), who suffered a heart attack while being interviewed by Fallow. Once there, she agrees to meet Sherman at their love nest, and Sherman shows up wearing a recording device provided by his lawyer, Thomas Killian (Kevin Dunn). Maria, intent on making love rather than discussing the case, discovers the wire and repays Sherman's treachery by turning state's witness. But Killian comes up with a last-minute trump card in tapes made by the landlord of the building in which Sherman and Maria enjoyed their affair. It seems the landlord was attempting to gather evidence which would enable him to evict the apartment's lease-holder, who was illegally subletting it to Maria. The tape includes their frank discussion following the accident, in which it is made clear Maria was driving the car. Declaring a miscarriage of justice, Judge White (Morgan Freeman) throws the case out of court, leaving Sherman vindicated but broke and unemployed, Fallow a wealthy best-selling author, and Bacon and Weiss with egg on their faces.

By necessity, screenwriter Michael Cristofer trimmed most of the underpinnings of Wolfe's sprawling novel—itself condensed from the original serialized version which ran in *Rolling Stone* magazine. Reduced to pure plot, the film is not so much the sendup of 1980s greed that the novel was as it is an orgy of banal, juvenile mean-spiritedness. The subtle, cutting irony of Wolfe's book becomes shrill, screaming sarcasm, unpleasant, and, worse, unfunny. But the film's biggest weakness, ironically, is one it shares with the novel in its problematic protagonist. In both book and film, Sherman McCoy is implausibly passive for a Wall Street "Master of the Universe" whose failure to take decisive control of his own fate lasts virtually up to the final scene. Wolfe, an unapologetic elitist, evidently meant McCoy to be taken for an Everyman ground up in the inhuman urban justice system. Yet, it goes without saying, no one with McCoy's wealth and clout could ever be considered average and would hardly be likely to sit idly by while his world is torn to shreds. In Wolfe's case, the plot functions as little more than a pretext for the author to showcase his real gifts as a journalist—his powers of observation and description—which would suffer in any film treatment. Director Brian De Palma has said that he set out to make a modernist version of a Capra-Sturges social satire. He also said he rejected early drafts of the script because it made McCoy too sympathetic. If so, De Palma would do well to go back and watch the films of both directors. He might notice that both consistently demonstrated a respect for the dignity of their deluded dreamers, endowing them with a basic humanist dignity even as they satirized the shallowness of their dreams. De Palma has the shallowness nailed. However, respect and dignity are foreign not only to this film, but to virtually all of the director's work. What one is left with—besides a wincingly bad performance from Willis, though Hanks does as well as could be expected with his deficient character—is a lot of empty gee-whiz camerawork and hollow cinematic bombast that makes for one very long night at the movies. *(Sexual situations, nudity, profanity.)*

d, Brian De Palma; p, Brian De Palma; w, Michael Cristofer (based on the novel by Tom Wolfe); ph, Vilmos Zsigmond; ed, David Ray and Bill Pankow; m, Dave Grusin; prod d, Richard Sylbert

Comedy   (PR:O MPAA:R)

BOYFRIEND SCHOOL, THE

(SEE: DON'T TELL HER IT'S ME)

BRAIN DEAD

85m Julie Corman/Concorde c

Bill Pullman (*Rex Martin*), Bill Paxton (*Jim Reston*), Bud Cort (*Jack Halsey*), Nicholas Pryor (*Conklin/Ramsen*), Patricia Charbonneau (*Dana Martin*), and George Kennedy (*Vance*)

Dr. Rex Martin (Bill Pullman) is a "brain man," a doctor whose research specialty is isolating the physical causes of mental illness. Jim Reston (Bill Paxton) is a sleek corporate Mephistopheles whose shallow, opportunistic career plan depends on the mathematical genius of one Dr. Jack Halsey (Bud Cort). The problem: Halsey has gone mad, murdered his wife and children, and been locked away in a facility for the criminally insane. Halsey is gripped by a dazzling array of paranoid hallucinations, the most persistent of which is that he is being followed by a man in a bloodstained white suit, the man who really murdered his family. Reston and his employers, the executives of the sinister Eunice Corporation, want the equations Halsey was working on before his breakdown. If they can't have them, they want to make sure no one else gets them either; the one thing they *don't* really care about is what happens to Halsey. Reston offers Martin a deal: Eunice Corporation's ongoing financial support and the opportunity to do ground-breaking research on a human subject, in return for a small favor. Martin must perform an experimental surgical procedure on Halsey in the hope that the mathematician can be returned to rationality; if he can't be made sane, however, Reston wants Halsey's memory wiped clean. Martin struggles with the sticky ethics of the situation, and finally agrees to perform the operation. The procedure seems to be a success, but Martin suddenly finds himself haunted by the imaginary man in white. Is he real, or is Martin losing his mind as well? Martin later sees—or thinks he sees—his wife, Dana (Patricia Charbonneau), and Reston making love, then finds them dead and a weapon in his own hand. As the logic of the everyday world seems to unravel, Martin finds himself in a mental institution where the staff insists on calling him Dr. Halsey. After a series of increasingly bizarre encounters in the hospital, Martin wakes up to find himself under the knife; he has, the surgeon explains, been in a serious car accident and is undergoing brain surgery. As Dana and Reston watch from behind glass, Martin dies before the operation is completed.

A low-budget exploitation picture with big ideas, BRAIN DEAD uses the conventions of the horror movie to pull off a cinematic sleight of hand many movies with far more material resources have failed to make work. Its narrative is an embedded one, a tangle of dreams and fantasies and hallucinations forever turning in on themselves until it's impossible to tell at any given moment where the primary narrative is in relation to what's on the screen. This is usually the province of European art films—think of Woiciech Has' THE SARAGOSSA MANUSCRIPT—but BRAIN DEAD stumbles only occasionally as it pitches to a genre audience while treading the thin line between cleverness and being too tricky for its own good. The overall effect is vertiginous but titillating, and first-time director Adam Simon makes the most of the original story by veteran Roger Corman collaborator Charles Beaumont (QUEEN OF OUTER SPACE; LITTLE SHOP OF HORRORS; and many, many others). Catherine Hardwicke's production design delivers some surprisingly high-quality goods on a low budget, and the above-average cast helps position BRAIN DEAD head and shoulders above most exploitation vehicles. Pullman (THE SERPENT AND THE RAINBOW), Paxton (ALIENS; NEAR DARK), Charbonneau (DESERT HEARTS), and cult favorite Bud Cort (HAROLD AND MAUDE) all deliver far better than passable performances, with Paxton the standout as the embodiment of sleek corporate wickedness. BRAIN DEAD provides a strong argument for the existence of exploitation movies: a picture that entertains the lowest-common-denominator viewer while giving more sophisticated moviegoers the thrill of discovering a diamond in the rough. *(Nudity, sexual situations, violence.)*

d, Adam Simon; p, Julie Corman; w, Charles Beaumont and Adam Simon (based on a story by Charles Beaumont); ph, Ronn Schmidt; ed, Carol Oblath; m, Peter Francis Rotter; prod d, Catherine Hardwicke; art d, Gilbert Mercier; set d, Gene Serdena; cos, Catherine Taieb

Horror   (PR:C MPAA:R)

BURNDOWN

87m M.C.E.G.-Virgin c

Peter Firth *(Jake Stern)*, Cathy Moriarty *(Patti Smart)*, Hal Orlandini *(James Manners)*, Michael McCabe *(Doc Roberts)*, Hugh Rouse *(George Blake)*, Victor Melleney *(Warriner)*, Gay Lambert *(Sady)*, Nadia Bilchick *(May Ellen)*, Joanne Ward *(Mugger)*, Alan Granville *(Joe Barnes)*, Owen De Jager *(Terry Coleman)*, Graham Weir *(Freddie)*, Lyndsey Reardon *(Hunter)*, Ron Smerczak *(Mason)*, Tracy Corff, Ashley Hayden, Philippa Vernon *(Victims)*, Ken Marshall *(Mayor)*, John Hussey *(Editor)*, John Whittley *(Doc Freeman)*, Larry Taylor *(Chuck)*, Sam William *(Burt)*, and Adam Gordon *(Attacker)*

Before BURNDOWN self-destructs in its ludicrous finale, it's a potent action thriller that benefits from news-headline immediacy and biting cynicism about small-town corruption. In the opening sequence, a beautiful motorist is tricked into believing she's run over someone on a fog-shrouded roadway near Thorpeville. When she investigates the macadam, she's mauled to death by a taloned creature. While trying to solve this third case in a bizarre murder spree, sheriff Jake Stern (Peter Firth) is informed that all of the dead women have been sexually assaulted. By accident, Jake and Doc Roberts (Michael McCabe), a pathologist, also discover that the most recent victim's corpse is radioactive. Significantly, her body was discovered near a shuttered nuclear power plant that had transformed Thorpeville into a boomtown before small-scale accidents forced the plant's closing. Why does the plant's designer, James Manners (Hal Orlandini), continue to guard the defunct reactor, and why is he so defensive when Jake questions him? Soon Manners even sends Freddie (Graham Weir), a troubled Vietnam vet with a history of mental problems, to spy on Jake. Taken in again by savvy reporter Patti Smart (Cathy Moriarty), who has betrayed Jake before for a story, the sheriff confides details of the radioactive sex crimes to her. When the story appears in print, Manners throws an even thicker smokescreen around the sinister mysteries at the plant. After Doc Roberts informs Jake that the killer is a radioactive mutant, Manners, who has friends in high places, makes it difficult for the sheriff to discover the source of the contamination. When Jake is ordered away on vacation, another woman is raped and killed, but this time Patti's editor nixes her latest scoop. Manners engineers a successful coverup by cremating one of the corpses and stealing Roberts' paperwork; at this point Patti and Jake decide to put an end to the murder spree no matter what it takes. When still more victims are found (a young couple at a drive-in), Manners has Jake reassigned to the case, figuring that a country bumpkin sheriff is easier to manipulate than state or federal law officers. So determined are the plant's guardians to keep Jake from continuing his investigation that they present him with a fall guy, Freddie. When the cops pursue Freddie, the bad guys arrange to eliminate him in a way that will look like an accident. What Manners doesn't know is that Freddie couldn't possibly be the mutated rapist-killer because his testicles were shot away in Vietnam. After exhaustive prying, Patti locates a witness who has kept quiet about the plant accidents for many years—Freddie's uncle, George Blake (Hugh Rouse). Furious that his pathetic nephew has been sacrificed for nothing, George spills the beans: one day, when he wasn't at work, the plant was rocked by a major meltdown. Although George leads Patti and Jake into the plant's top-secret area, Manners has no intention of letting any of them out alive to spread damaging news of the danger of nuclear power. Near the reactor's core, Patti and Jake encounter a small group of employees who have been living underground for over a decade because exposure to the outside world would kill them. The mad rapist (one of these meltdown survivors) has now almost completely deteriorated because of his forays into the outside world. When Patti and Jake attempt to escape, the crazed survivors, who have nothing left to lose, blow up the plant, visiting nuclear destruction upon the entire state of Florida.

For much of its running time, this is a moderately involving anti-nuke thriller. Playing on our worst fears about nuclear energy mishaps, it presents a fanciful but frightening picture of the aftermath of a sort of down-south Three Mile Island accident. Since nuclear disaster is a relatively fresh subject for a horror flick, BURNDOWN gets points for the novelty of its premise. It is also greatly enhanced by the easygoing professionalism of the supporting cast, who convey small-town types effortlessly. In the leading roles, Firth (a Briton employing a flawless American accent) and Moriarty (ten times sexier than Kathleen Turner) exhibit an obvious chemistry, compelling us to care about their mission. Wrapped up in their relationship, we don't question the plot's lapses in logic as scrupulously as we might have.

Although BURNDOWN doesn't simmer with suspense from start to finish, it does create an atmosphere of uneasiness and dread that gives viewers a queasy feeling. In some ways, it even takes shape more as a whodunit than as a conventional horror film. Unfortunately, after devoting much attention to the grotesque array of rape/murders, the film falls apart during its climactic confrontation in the plant. The radioactive waste-scarred victims aren't a very scary lot, and they're forced to deliver pages of exposition about the plant's burndown and the subsequent fallout. While BURNDOWN's plot may end with a bang, the film goes out with a whimper. Couldn't the filmmakers have concocted a better pay-off than the explosion? Although this note of despair may suit the film's cynicism, it's not a satisfying end for the mystery, and the big nuclear ka-boom seems too contrived—too overwhelming a conclusion for what begins as a fun B movie about a loony mutant. *(Nudity, violence, profanity, sexual situations, adult situations.)*

d, James Allen; p, Ed Fredericks and Colin Stewart; w, Anthony Barwick and Colin Stewart (based on the novel by Stuart Collins); ph, Paul Michelson; ed, Leslie Healey; m, Tony Britten; prod d, Michael Fowlie; art d, Michael Fowlie; makup, Anne Taylor

Horror   (PR:C   MPAA:R)

BYE BYE BLUES

(Can./US) 110m Allarcom – True Blue/Circle c

Rebecca Jenkins *(Daisy Cooper)*, Michael Ontkean *(Teddy Cooper)*, Luke Reilly *(Max Gramley)*, Stuart Margolin *(Slim Godfrey)*, Robyn Stevan *(Frances Cooper)*, Kate Reid *(Mary Wright)*, Leslie Yeo *(Arthur Wright)*, Wayne Robson *(Pete)*, Sheila Moore *(Doreen Cooper)*, Susan Wooldridge *(Lady Wilson)*, Leon Pownall *(Bernie Blitzer)*, Kirk Duffee *(Richard Cooper, Age 9)*, Aline Levasseur *(Emma Cooper)*, and Vincent Gale *(Will Wright)*

At first blush, BYE BYE BLUES is almost achingly reminiscent of the exquisitely mounted "Masterpiece Theatre" period pieces you could swear you've seen dozens of times before. It's one of those How She and Her Kids Survived While Her Husband Was Away at the War movies in which the heroine, having changed much in her spouse's absence, not only doesn't know if her husband is still alive but wonders if she will still love him if he returns. Naturally, she also anguishes over whether she should give herself to the other man in her lonely life. No matter. BYE BYE BLUES is a wonderful, old-fashioned romance with a dreamy, sensual tone rarely found in movies nowadays. It is also a sheer pleasure to watch. That it's not mawkish at all is a credit to Canadian filmmaker Anne Wheeler, whose enchanting tale is based on her mother's wartime experiences during the long years her husband was held captive by the Japanese. But BYE BYE BLUES is much more than a tale of survival, more than the story of a young woman suddenly forced to handle adversity and support herself and her two small children. It is a lovingly drawn, mesmerizing account of a woman's struggle to cope with insecurity, to define herself, and to eventually succeed in an altogether unfamiliar world for which she was remarkably unprepared.

It's 1941; Daisy Cooper (Rebecca Jenkins) is the shy young wife of a Canadian army doctor stationed in colonial India. The memsahib's privileged lifestyle ends abruptly when her husband, Teddy (Michael Ontkean), is posted to Singapore; pregnant with their second child, Daisy is to return to Canada to live with her parents. At a farewell fancy-dress ball on the eve of Teddy's departure, Daisy entertains her fellow guests with a song. It's sweetly done, but she's not terribly good. Several months later, after the birth of her daughter, Daisy travels to North America with infant Emma and young son Richard to wait out WW II. She's had no news from Teddy in months (nor will she for four long years); her letters to him have all been returned. All she knows is that Singapore has fallen to the Japanese and that thousands were taken prisoner. In India, she was able to send her parents an allowance, but with the war on, she doesn't even receive support checks from the government for herself. Things are tight. To raise much-needed cash, she sells her fancy Indian silks on consignment, then tries but fails to find work as a salesgirl. However, it takes a small request from her young son—for a pair of running shoes she can't afford to buy him—to get Daisy to appraise her limited assets. There isn't very much she can do. But she can play the piano a little and she can sing after a fashion, so Daisy wangles her way into a job doing both with a small band that caters to soldiers at a local army base. Although her debut performance bombs and she's not asked back, Max (Luke Reilly), a handsome, gifted trombone player, takes an instant liking to Daisy and secretly coaches her. Soon after, in a gutsy move, she walks into the club, sits in with the band, and softly sings a wistful rendition of "Am I Blue." Reminding the soldiers of the girls back home, Daisy becomes an instant hit, and Slim (Stuart Margolin), the group's leader, hires her to perform full-time, for $3 a night. Now assured of a steady income ($3 went a lot further in those days), Daisy rents a house on the edge of town and makes a home for herself and her kids. Meanwhile, the very smitten Max supplies a steady stream of musical advice and encouragement.

Several years pass, and there is still no word from Teddy. Thinking about her husband, Daisy admits that she can't even imagine him anymore. Her closest friend, Teddy's sister Frances (Robyn Stevan), is surprised to learn that even after her brother's long absence, Teddy remains Daisy's only lover. Frances, who married right before her husband went into the army and hasn't heard from him in over a year, thinks nothing of picking up a succession of men to help her while away her lonely nights. "Women," she tells Daisy, "need sex as much as men do." What about Daisy? Should she or shouldn't she? She's fallen hard for Max, and struggles to keep her emotions in check and him at arm's length. For his part,

the gentle, talented Max, a devoted surrogate father to her kids, is deeply in love
and wants to marry Daisy. (Reilly's Max is so entirely credible and appealing
that it is easy to empathize with Daisy's quandary. In the hands of lesser actors,
the plot might have been reduced to banalities. But that is never the case here.)
Another problem arises when Blitzer (Leon Pownall), a club owner and promoter, hires the band for a tour that means much more money for the members
but that will require Daisy to leave her kids for weeks at a time. Either she goes
or she's out of a job. Needing the income, she has little choice. As the band's
popularity and Daisy's proficiency keep growing, she discovers that Slim has
been cheating the other members of the group. Blitzer takes over the band's
management, sponsoring an extended tour with appearances on nationwide radio
broadcasts. While they're away, Max and Daisy hear that Germany has surren-
dered. After a night of celebrating, they finally do some intimate partying of their
own. The camera shows them entering Daisy's hotel room together, then
discreetly cuts to the band's return home. There Daisy finds her children growing
distant, and Frances pregnant by her soldier boy friend, who is away at the front.
The once-puritanical Daisy has grown non-judgmental ("The older I get, the less
I know") and lends her sister-in-law money to move to the city for an abortion
that ultimately isn't performed. With the war in Europe over and the local base
closing down, Blitzer tells the band that it's time to move to the big city. Fame
for the newly named Max Gramley's Band is within reach. They're to have their
own radio show, and if Daisy doesn't go with them, she'll be replaced. Again
Daisy faces an extremely difficult decision, compounded by news that the
A-bomb has been dropped on Hiroshima and the war is over. Now that she's on
the brink of success, but with the possibility Teddy's return still looming, should
she uproot her kids and leave? Should she marry Max? The day before the band
is to depart, a still undecided Daisy gets a telegram informing her that Teddy is
arriving that very night by train. Their first meeting at the station is warm but
understandably strained. Thinner, wearied by his years in prison, Teddy returns
to their home, where a poignant, low-keyed reunion takes place with his son and
the daughter he has never seen. Late that night, Daisy sneaks off to Max's hotel
room. "He's back," she says. But Max already knows. Realizing she's made her
choice, he tells Daisy to go home before her husband misses her. The next
morning, before the band takes off, it makes one last stop to bid farewell to Daisy.
Only Max, unhappy and morose, stays seated inside the bus until it pulls away.

Like the similarly satisfying MY BRILLIANT CAREER, another so-called
"woman's film," BYE BYE BLUES avoids the obvious, refusing to ram its
feminism down anyone's throat. Instead, it chronicles one woman's personal
growth with an unerring sensitivity that's universally appealing. Beautifully
acted and lushly photographed, the film garnered a series of major awards,
including Best Film at the Houston International Film Festival and three Genies
(the Canadian equivalent of the Oscar), Best Actress for Jenkins (an honor also
accorded her at the Seattle Film Festival), Best Supporting Actress for Stevan,
and Best Original Song for composer Bill Henderson's ballad "When I Sing."
(*Brief nudity.*)

d, Anne Wheeler; p, Anne Wheeler and Arvi Liimatainen; w, Anne Wheeler;
ph, Vic Sarin; ed, Christopher Tate; m, George Blondheim; prod d, John
Blackie; art d, Scott Dobbie; cos, Maureen Hiscox

Drama/Romance   (PR:A   MPAA:PG)

C

CADILLAC MAN

95m Donaldson-Roven-Cavallo/Orion c

Robin Williams *(Joey O'Brien)*, Tim Robbins *(Larry)*, Pamela Reed *(Tina O'Brien)*, Fran Drescher *(Joy Munchack)*, Zack Norman *(Harry Munchack)*, Annabella Sciorra *(Donna)*, Lori Petty *(Lila)*, Paul Guilfoyle *(Little Jack Turgeon)*, Bill Nelson *(Big Jack Turgeon)*, Eddie Jones *(Benny)*, Mimi Cecchini *(Ma)*, Tristine Skyler *(Lisa)*, Judith Hoag *(Molly)*, Lauren Tom *(Helen, the Dim Sum Girl)*, Anthony Powers *(Capt. Mason)*, Paul Herman *(Tony Dipino)*, Paul L.Q. Lee *(Henry)*, Jim Bulleit *(Funeral Director)*, Erik King *(Davey)*, Richard Panebianco *(Frankie Dipino)*, Gary H. Klar *(Detective Walters)*, Boris Leskin *(Soviet Husband)*, Elzbieta Czyzewska *(Soviet Wife)*, Ben Lin *(Korean Customer)*, Wai Ching Ho *(Korean Customer's Wife)*, William Hugh Collins *(Hearse Driver)*, Bill Nunn *(Grave Digger)*, Vinnie Capone *(Louie)*, Bill Moor *(Antique Salesman)*, Kim Chan *(Dim Sum Cook)*, Mario Todisco, Max, Kenneth Simmons *(Steel Jaws)*, Bunny Levine *(Woman Customer)*, Carmen A. Mathis *(Police Woman)*, Harlan Cary Poe *(Mason's Aid)*, Jordan Derwin *(Paramedic)*, Philip Moon *(Nightclub Selector)*, Sal Lioni *(Nightclub Customer)*, Brian Sanet *(Paparazzi)*, Merwin Goldsmith *(Showroom Buyer)*, Richard Mark Arnold *(Porsche Buyer)*, Marilyn Dobrin *(Porsche Buyer's Wife)*, David Stepkin *(Maroni)*, Matt Nikko, Keenan Shimizu, Tony Masa, Ken Kensei, Toshio Sato *(Japanese Buyers)*, Chester Drescher *(Chester)*, and Elaine Stritch *(The Widow)*

CADILLAC MAN starts out as a portrait of those smooth-talking, high pressure car salesmen who live to make a deal. However, Joey O'Brien (Robin Williams) hasn't closed too many deals lately at Turgeon Motors, although he loves to sell, as he explains in his asides to the audience. Because he also loves to spend money and fools around with several different women, Joey finds himself in a tight spot. Not only is he in debt to the mob, but his various girl friends are pressuring him for a commitment, and his ex-wife berates him for not paying attention to their teenage daughter, who is now missing. What's more, Joey's job is on the line; he must sell a dozen cars during Turgeon Motors' big sale, or he'll be let go. During the sale, while Joey is trying to placate several disgruntled customers, Larry (Tim Robbins) bursts through the glass wall of the dealership on his motorcycle. Armed and unstable, Larry is ticked off (to put it mildly) because his wife, Donna (Annabella Sciorra), has been having an affair with one of the company's employees. But Larry is not your average psycho: once he breaks in and the police surround the place, Larry is not sure what he wants. He just knows that his wife has been unfaithful and that someone is going to pay for it. While he's deciding what to do next, Larry holds the dealership's employees and customers hostage. Using his carefully honed negotiating skills, Joey confesses that *he* has been having an affair with Donna (a lie), and manages to persuade the all-too-impressionable Larry to free most of the hostages. As the day wears on, Joey has to deal with his mother and various girl friends, while trying to prevent Larry from killing him and the other hostages. Finally, Joey persuades Larry to give himself up, and everyone is saved. Larry is shot by the cops, but looks like he'll survive, Joey is told that his job is his for life, his daughter turns up, and there's even a hint that he may reconcile with his ex-wife.

Like Larry, CADILLAC MAN doesn't know quite what it wants to do. At first the film seems to be a low-key comedy about a small-time hustler, then it becomes a kind of DOG DAY AFTERNOON-style melodrama. Ultimately it is an uneasy mix of the two. Nevertheless, the film does have several things going for it. To begin with, there are the spirited performances by Williams and Robbins, although these roles are hardly a stretch for either actor. Williams manages to draw on his fast-talking stage persona while minimizing the excesses of his anarchic comic approach, and Robbins is both goofy and scary as an extreme example of wounded male pride.

CADILLAC MAN also has some unusual touches and crazy characters that raise it a cut above typical frenzied comedies. There's Lori Petty as Lila, Joey's designer girl friend, who wears outrageous Cyndi Lauper-type outfits and uses Joey's captivity as a publicity opportunity; and Fran Drescher is perfect as Joey's married lover, an archetypal Queens housewife, complete with nasal voice and an obnoxious, snapping Pomeranian dog. Lauren Tom is also funny as a deadpan, wisecracking waitress in a Chinese restaurant.

However, some of the film's other elements are awkward. Notably, Joey's intermittent voice-overs and asides to the camera give the impression that screenwriter Ken Friedman couldn't think of any other way to convey the information they provide. Moreover, the ending is too pat and feels tacked-on. Once the hostage drama starts, the film gets bogged down several times, and for good reason: How much drama can be generated from a hostage situation if the gunman has no demands? Had CADILLAC MAN focused more on Joey's personal and professional life, it might have been an interesting comedic character study; as it is, the film is less a cohesive whole than a collection of amusing moments. *(Violence, excessive profanity, sexual situations.)*

d, Roger Donaldson; p, Charles Roven and Roger Donaldson; w, Ken Friedman; ph, David Gribble; ed, Richard Francis-Bruce; m, J. Peter Robinson; prod d, Gene Rudolf; art d, Patricia Woodbridge; set d, Justin Scoppa Jr.; spec, Connie Brink; stunts, Cliff Cudney; cos, Deborah La Gorce Kramer; makup, Bernadette Mazur

Comedy/Drama   (PR:C   MPAA:R)

CAGED FURY

95m Atlantic/21st Century c

Erik Estrada *(Victor)*, Richie Barathy *(Dirk Ramsey)*, Roxanna Michaels *(Kathie Collins)*, Paul Smith *(Head Guard)*, James Hong *(Detective Stoner)*, Michael Parks *(Mr. Collins)*, Jack Carter *(Mr. Castaglia)*, April Dawn Dollarhide *(Rhonda Wallace)*, Blake Bahner *(Buck Lewis)*, Hugh Farrington *(Detective Elston)*, Elena Sahagun *(Tracy Collins)*, Ty Randolph *(Warden Sybil Thorn)*, Beano *(Tony)*, Greg Cummins *(Spider)*, Ron Jeremy Hyatt *(Pizzaface)*, and Alison LePriol *(Blond Escapee)*

As soon as this women's prison flick cuts from a scene in which a female convict tries to escape a hellhole to a domestic scene in which a virginal young woman informs her dad that she's headed to LA to break into the movies, we know this sheltered cutie is going to end up behind bars. Although this sexist junk can't be judged by standards reserved for most action films, even within the tacky framework of a babes-behind-bars flick, CAGED FURY is a disappointment.

Determined to be an actress, naive Kathie Collins (Roxanna Michaels) leaves behind her father (Michael Parks) and her worldly sister, Tracy (Elena Sahagun), and heads for LaLaLand. Purely by coincidence, she picks up Rhonda (April Dawn Dollarhide), a hitchhiker who's fleeing a fat, horny motorist, and who offers to show Kathie the show biz ropes in the big city. Crashing at the pad of Rhonda's former boy friend Buck (Blake Bahner), a sexy photographer with the instincts of a pimp, the two women jump at the chance for a screen test. During a night on the town, Kathie is nearly gang raped in a biker bar — while Buck is engaged in an impromptu photo session with Rhonda in the ladies' room. Kathie is rescued by Victor (Erik Estrada, who is barely in the movie despite his top billing) and his martial-arts pal, Dirk (Richie Barathy). Before Kathie's new romance with Victor can blossom, she and Rhonda try out for a softcore porn movie. (One of the bigger implausibilities in this illogical screenplay is the gusto that the innocent Kathie brings to her audition.) Not realizing they are being set up by Buck, the two women argue with an obese director, are arrested on trumped-up charges, and are sent to a correctional institute. After being forced to lie over the phone to her father about being cast in a movie in Mexico, Kathie is gradually inducted into the sadomasochism that dominates life in the penitentiary. Refusing to believe her sister's phone call, Tracy visits Buck's apartment to pump him for information, but she, too, is nearly raped. Again Victor and Dirk come to the rescue, then beat Buck into revealing information about the porn ring. When Tracy foolishly goes undercover and is subsequently framed and arrested like her sister, Victor and his multitalented mercenary buddy spring into action. Although Victor is wounded in a shootout at the porn ring's headquarters (and vanishes from the storyline for much of the film's running time), his muscular friend heads for the unusual correctional facility. Reunited in jail, Kathie and Tracy launch a plan. As lesbian Warden Thorn (Ty Randolph) fondles Tracy, and Spider (Greg Cummins), a sadistic guard, tries to get Kathie drunk, Kathie smashes a bottle over the guard's head and makes a dash for the phone. She contacts a dim-witted cop who finally reports the call to Stoner (James Hong), the detective who handled the missing-persons report filed by Tracy. While hiding out in the prison, Kathie discovers the corpses of other women who supposedly have been freed. Then, while Dirk scales the prison walls, we learn that Warden Thorn is busy conducting a slave auction of some of the prisoners for visiting millionaires! It turns out that this arrest-and-imprison operation is an elaborate scam to provide fresh meat for a white slave ring. While Dirk busts assorted heads, Kathie saves her sister and frees some of her penitentiary pals. A bloodbath ensues when Warden Thorn issues orders that none of the girls is to get out alive. During the climax, Dirk kills most of the guards, cops arrive, and Kathie is nearly killed by Spider (whose eye she has mutilated) when she returns from outside the prison to rescue Rhonda. A happy ending is in store for the survivors (Kathie and Victor eventually ride off into the sunset) but not for the sexual slavers.

Credibility may not be an important element in women's prison films, but that's no excuse for the myriad coincidences that underlie the plot of CAGED FURY. Among many unanswered questions in this sloppily made film are: Why would Kathie, who has been given a strict upbringing, audition for a sleazy movie? What happens to the sapphic warden during the riot and why does she insist on shooting even the women who are still safely behind bars? Why would Kathie endanger herself to rescue Rhonda, who is responsible for her being in this mess in the first place? Who were the prisoners whose corpses Kathie finds?

Bargain-basement action flicks are supposed to provide cheap thrills for a male audience, and if this film were a turn-on, none of the above questions would matter. But on every level, this film is a turn-off. For some reason, the titillation sequences are played for laughs, which dissipates the tension of the women's false arrest. What's more, despite liberal amounts of female nudity, CAGED FURY won't send male pulse rates quickening. As for the standard action scenes, when Barathy's Dirk starts kung-fuing bad guys all over the prison, he seems to have wandered in from a Chuck Norris film. Since his character is peripheral to the plot, it's ridiculous to treat him as the hero, even though the film's nominal star, Estrada, is written out of the film until the end. Aside from Bahner, who puts a real leer into his villainy, the cast sinks to the low level of the material. CAGED FURY is a pitiful, disjointed example of the women's prison genre at its trashiest. (Nudity, substance abuse, sexual situations, excessive violence, profanity.)

d, Bill Milling; p, Bill Milling and Bob Gallagher; w, Bill Milling; ph, Kenneth Wiatrak; ed, Matthew Mallinson; m, Joe Delia; stunts, Solly Marx

Prison   (PR:O MPAA:NR)

CAGED IN PARADISO

84m Vidmark c

Irene Cara (Eva), Peter Kowanko (Eric), Joseph Culp (Terrorist), Paula Bond (Queenie), Luis Vera (Jocelito), Wolf Muser (Helmut), Christopher Pennock (McHenry), Laurence Haddon (Sen. Paradiso), Wycliffe Young (Instructor), Big John Studd (Big Man), Beverly Purcell (Rosa), Ji-Tu Cumbuka (Josh), David Dunard (Congressman), Mary Louise Picard (Judith), Michael McCabe (Satellite Officer), Christopher Spensley (Link), and Wayne Wasserman (Button Pusher)

In the not-so-distant future, recidivist criminals and terrorists are being dropped onto a deserted island and forgotten by society at large. Once the convicts parachute into this no-man's-land, it's every creep for himself. The brainchild of one Senator Paradiso (Laurence Haddon), this escape-proof penal colony houses the world's scurviest thieves and killers, including Eric (Peter Kowanko), who is shown assisting in the bombing of a federal building at the start of CAGED IN PARADISO. Apprehended as a member of the Red Hand Brigade, the terrorist group who claimed responsibility for the bombing (in which 60 people were killed), Eric is sentenced to Paradiso Island, which is hemmed in by shark-infested waters and guarded by a deadly laser beam two miles from shore. Vowing to follow her man to the ends of the earth, ingenuous Mexican immigrant Eva (FAME's Irene Cara, whose accent here is hard to place, originating somewhere north of Jamaica and south of Brooklyn) points out that the law allows spouses to accompany their felonious mates to the island hellhole, although she's apparently the first soul to take advantage of this dubious privilege. After parachuting onto Paradiso, anti-imperialist Eric gets separated from Eva. She is nearly raped by some inmates, but rescued by Queenie (Paula Bond), the lesbian leader of the local Amazons, who can't believe Eva's naivete. The island is divided into various contingents, including some old bikers, a group of cannibals, a black-power faction headed by Josh (Ji-Tu Cumbuka), and Queenie's tribal-bead-wearing, feminist-consciousness-raising crew, who teach Eva archery and how to do some nifty body-painting. The film cuts back and forth between Eva's indoctrination and Eric's ongoing struggle to survive; finally, Eric is befriended by kindly peasant Jocelito (Luis Vera), a lifelong resident of the island-turned-penitentiary who nurses Eric back to health in his cabin. When Eric manages a reunion with his wife, he makes anti-gay remarks about her girl friends and persuades her to leave the security of the tribe. The sexist pig then foolishly goes off to play manly food-hunter, leaving Eva alone to fend for herself against an attack by two men—which she does, killing the brutes. Later—after not-so-nice political activist Eric has cruelly forced old Jocelito out of his cabin in order to move in with Eva—Helmut (Wolf Muser), head of the Red Hand Brigade, arrives with his convict troops and insists that Eric join in his efforts to "civilize" the island. Helmut's attempts at improving life on Paradiso include having his henchman challenge black-power leader Josh to a fair fight, then stabbing him when his back is turned. Realizing that this bunch of macho pigs plans to attack the lovely Amazons and sexually subjugate them, Eva decides she wants no part of hubby's activities and warns her pals by sounding a conch shell given to her by the mystical Jocelito, enabling the women to plan for the attack. Disillusioned with her man, Eva decides to end her life by sailing into the laser, but the monitoring officer identifies her by computer and allows the Coast Guard to pick her up. Her Paradiso playmates believe that the big beam got her, however.

Will Eva sail off to write a best-seller about prison conditions when she returns to America? Most viewers won't bother to ask, but will merely bid her good riddance. After a taut opening sequence, CAGED IN PARADISO rapidly disintegrates. Admittedly, the central premise is no more ludicrous than that of the infinitely superior action fantasy ESCAPE FROM NEW YORK (in which

all of Manhattan is turned into a penal colony), but that film offered rapid pacing and tongue-in-cheek delivery. CAGED IN PARADISO, by contrast, is an almost languorous action film—a contradiction in terms—that is further marred by its uniformly abysmal acting. (Cara must be singled out for special censure, however; her accent is so slippery, she practically gives a world tour of dialects.) Since the film takes itself seriously, it can only be appreciated as a gut-wrenching action movie, which it clearly is not, or as unintentional camp. Unfortunately, CAGED IN PARADISO isn't outrageous enough to be an entertainingly bad movie. It's worthless, all right, but in an uninvolving, enervated way.

Even if one overlooks the central implausibility of Eva's deciding to accompany her husband to Paradiso, the film suffers from technical sloppiness and impoverished scripting throughout. The ridiculous structuring of the first half, in which the filmmakers cut back and forth between Eva's athletic training and Eric's attempts to stay alive, serves no function other than to pad this dull prison movie out to feature length. The direction is hack work and the editing lackadaisical; worse, the film completely lacks any sense of menace. No one on Paradiso seems like a killer—the cast behaves more as if they were on a wilderness weekend that features encounter group therapy and psychological prison games. Bond, clad in her native togs, looks like a third-place finisher in a Josephine Baker lookalike contest, while the male cutthroats seem about as tough as Captain Hook's merry men. Unless you're an inveterate fan of babes-behind-bars films or an aficionado of truly bad movies, avoid CAGED IN PARADISO. Viewing it is a sentence to boredom in itself. (Violence, nudity, profanity, sexual situations.)

d, Mike Snyder; p, John G. Thomas; w, Michele Thyne; ph, James Rosenthal; m, Bob Mamet and Kevin Klingler; art d, Brian Densmore; spec, Marcus Drury and Polycom

Action/Prison   (PR:O MPAA:R)

C'EST LA VIE

(Fr.) 110m Samuel Goldwyn c

Nathalie Baye (Lena), Richard Berry (Michel), Zabou (Bella), Jean-Pierre Bacri (Leon), Vincent Lindon (Jean-Claude), Valeria Bruni-Tedeschi (Odette), Didier Benureau (Ruffier), Julie Bataille (Frederique), Candice Lefranc (Sophie), Alexis Derlon (Daniel), Emmanuelle Boidron (Suzanne), Maxime Boidron (Rene), and Benjamin Sacks (Titi)

Set in 1958, C'EST LA VIE is something of a follow-up to Diane Kurys' immensely popular ENTRE NOUS. Having decided to divorce her husband Michel (Richard Berry), the beautiful Lena (Nathalie Baye) puts her two daughters, Frederique (Julie Bataille), who narrates much of the tale, and Sophie (Candice Lefranc), on a train in Lyon. Accompanying the girls is their nanny, Odette (Valeria Bruni-Tedeschi), who is taking them to La Buale Les Pins for a seaside vacation with the family of her best friend, Bella Mandel (Zabou). The summer proves an eventful one, with the girls and their brood of "cousins" learning all manner of lessons in living. Lena eventually joins her daughters and engages in what she thinks is a secret affair with a young artist, Leon (Jean-Pierre Bacri), though the children observe her dashing off into the night to meet him. The tranquility of their idyll is shattered by the arrival of Michel. Still in love with Lena, Michel finds out about Leon, and a vicious fight, witnessed by Frederique, ensues. The summer draws to a close with the family forever parted.

No one can accuse Kurys of any real depth here; her strength as a director lies primarily in her sense of detail and in her ability to convey a nostalgic atmosphere. In its indolent sensuality and wealth of everyday observation, Kurys' work resembles some of the lighter, summery short stories of Colette. C'EST LA VIE is the merest trifle, but, given its sun-soaked ambience, the film is utterly painless and enjoyable. It has been exquisitely photographed by Gui Feppe Lanci, who skillfully captures the calm prosperity of postwar resort life in images that are the understated equal of any in Visconti's DEATH IN VENICE. The cabanas filled with bustling families and the buoyant sound of American pop songs on transistor radios, the dinner dances at roadside inns, the gloriously rosy light of sunset on the water, and the warm night air are all palpably seductive. Philippe Sarde's restrained but evocative music supports the mood.

Although Kurys has repeatedly extolled her love of working with children, the adults here are most impressive, all of them sophisticated and attractive. The director has imbued their sketchily written characters with personality plus. Never more glamorous, Baye communicates a slightly neurotic, Jennifer Jones-like quality and makes an appealingly complex heroine. The scene where she first sees her lover on the beach and snakes her way through the cabanas to meet him is dizzyingly romantic, abetted by the fluid tracking camera and Baye's potent star quality. Zabou gives an ingratiating and intelligent performance as the hugely pregnant Bella, and Lindon, as Bella's rakish spouse (a dream uncle to the kids), is every bit as charming as Zabou. Bacri is properly sexy as Lena's lover, upon whom Frederique develops an immediate crush, and Berry exudes the right amount of pained anguish as Michel.

Somehow the shallowness of the screenplay works. Unanswered questions and unexplained motives help cloak the adults in a mysterious sexiness that is perfectly suited to the film's child's-eye point of view. However, Kurys' use of Frederique's diary to tell the story is a tired, underdeveloped device, and the director falls back on it whenever inspiration fails her. Like Truffaut, Kurys has a precious, idealized view of children. They're all angelic, brilliant little paragons. The girls have a woman-in-a-child's-body beauty that is as much of a Gallic cliche as their huskily precocious voices are; the boys are budding artistic geniuses. Still, all of this sweetness and light leaves the viewer yearning for the youthful raunch and anarchy of a film like LIFE IS A LONG QUIET RIVER. (Adult situations, brief nudity).

d, Diane Kurys; p, Alexander Arcady and Diane Kurys; w, Diane Kurys and Alain Le Henry; ph, Gui Feppe Lanci; m, Philippe Sarde

Drama   (PR:C   MPAA:NR)

CHATTAHOOCHEE

98m John Daly-Derek Gibson/Hemdale c

Gary Oldman (*Emmett Foley*), Dennis Hopper (*Walker Benson*), Frances McDormand (*Mae Foley*), Pamela Reed (*Earlene*), Ned Beatty (*Dr. Harwood*), M. Emmet Walsh (*Morris*), William De Acutis (*Missy*), Lee Wilkof (*Vernon*), Matt Craven (*Lonny*), Gary Klar (*Clarence*), Timothy Scott (*Harley*), Richard Portnow (*Dr. Debner*), William Newman (*Jonathan*), Whitey Hughes (*Mr. Johnson*), Wilbur Fitzgerald (*Duane*), Yvonne Denise Mason (*Ella*), Ralph Pace (*Leonard*), Wesley Mann, Tim Monich (*Cops*), Laurens Moore (*Pa Foley*), Mary Moore (*Ma Foley*), Peggy Beasley (*Mae's Mother*), F. Drucilla Brookshire, Dorothy L. Grissom Hardin (*Women on Street*), David Fitzsimmons (*Ambulance Driver*), Gary Bullock (*Sadistic Attendant*), David Dwyer (*Goading Attendant*), Robert Gravel (*Lucas*), Marc Clement (*Theo*), John Brasington (*Dr. Towney*), Jim E. Quick (*Dr. Everly*), C.K. Bibby (*Baker*), Bob Hannah (*Earl*), George Nannerello (*Patient Without Shoes*), Ed Grady (*Stream of Conciousness Man*), Kevin Barber (*Upside-down Inmate*), James "Fred" Culclasure (*Hymn-singing Inmate*), Shane Baily (*Ozell*), Kevin Campbell (*Inmate in Cesspool*), E. Pat Hall (*Inmate in Movie Theater*), Jerry Campbell (*Inmate in Tunnel*), Roger Jackson (*Inmate*), Suzi Bass (*Harwood's Secretary*), Jill Rankin (*Governor's Secretary*), F. Douglas McDaniel (*Jimbob*), Chris Robertson, Bill Collins, Bud Davis, Michael Easler (*Attendants*), Randy Randolph (*Miami Guard*), Kathryn Cobb (*Miami Nurse*), Jim Gloster (*Miami Attendant*), Charles Lawler, Traber Burns (*Miami Cops*), Kristi Frankenheimer (*Weather Girl*), Perry Simpson, Joe Loy (*Quincy Cops*), Wallace Merck (*Patrolman*), Don Wayne Bass (*First Guard*), Mykel Mariette (*Male Nurse*), Raul Apartella (*First Man at Investigation*), and B.J. Koonce (*Woman at Investigation*)

More remarkable for what it isn't than for what it is, CHATTAHOOCHEE stars Gary Oldman as Emmett Foley, a Korean War veteran who, in the mid-1950s, pretends to have a breakdown and begins firing potshots at his neighbors from his yard. He really wants to be killed by the police, so that his life insurance money can help his struggling family survive. When the police prove to be abysmally bad shots, Foley tries to commit suicide, intending to make it look as though the police had killed him. Unfortunately for him he survives, only to be declared insane wrongly and sent to the title Florida state mental institution. There, instead of getting treatment, he is warehoused with other residents, sane and insane, under inhuman conditions and bullied by sadistic guards. It takes Foley five grueling years to draw attention to his plight and the scandalous conditions at Chattahoochee. When he brings legal action over the state's failure to provide treatment, the facility's doctor (Ned Beatty) gives him shock treatment and tranquilizers to keep him quiet. Later Foley is put into solitary, where he is forced to sit straight and still in a growing pile of his own waste. But all along, Foley meticulously records every specific instance of abuse and questionable death in the margins of a Bible, which he passes to his sister (Pamela Reed), who passes it on to the authorities. An end title tells us that Foley and his friend Walker Benson (Dennis Hopper) were released from custody, and that Foley's efforts led to reforms in Florida's mental health system.

What's different about CHATTAHOOCHEE is the style British telefilm director Mick Jackson brings to its story — a story that recalls ONE FLEW OVER THE CUCKOO'S NEST; COOL HAND LUKE; FRANCES; THE SNAKE PIT; and numerous other prison/psychiatric nightmare tales. Jackson strives to resist the dramatic cliches of those films by unfolding CHATTAHOOCHEE in a series of distanced, elliptical, almost random scenes, freely alternating among Foley's setbacks, tiny steps forward, brutal defeats, and small victories. Some of these scenes are paradoxical, if not inexplicable. When Walker and Foley literally walk away from Chattahoochee, using a key Foley obtained by blackmailing one of the guards, Foley pleads exhaustion and meekly returns to the hospital (while Walker makes good his escape) to accept a grotesque punishment. Why Foley does so — in confrontations with guards he seems fit enough — is never convincingly explained. In general we know only a little more about him by the end of

the film than we did at the beginning. In a voice-over at the end, Foley admits he had no idea why he did what he did.

Therein lies CHATTAHOOCHEE's main problem. Jackson doesn't want audiences standing up and cheering at the end of the film, but instead means them to contemplate scene after scene emphasizing humankind's limitless capacity for cruelty towards the weak and our utter helplessness in the face of fate. Foley's triumph is presented almost as an accident. The authorities at the institution could just as easily have deprived him of paper and prevented him from writing, and had Foley failed to pass the Bible to his sister, he could just as easily have died in Chattahoochee. Jackson and screenwriter James Hicks ultimately fail to find the key to unlock their enigmatic main character, who alternates between Christ-like passivity (accompanied by obvious, ill-advised Christian imagery) and a fierce defense of his fellow inmates' dignity and of his own sanity. Although the story is based on the real-life case of Korean War veteran Chris Calhoun, Jackson and Hicks are unable to make Foley's motivations manifest, and consequently never realize the character. Oldman makes Foley as compelling as possible under the circumstances, but is defeated by the character's contradictions. His performance is at once technically flawless and curiously lifeless. However, Jackson, Hicks, and Oldman do succeed in their concerted effort to present Foley's experiences as realistically as possible on the surface level, powerfully conveying the tedium, anguish, and despair of Foley's plight. But the film seems sheepish, if not embarrassed, about showing his ultimate triumph over overwhelming odds.

Despite its flaws, CHATTAHOOCHEE is worthwhile viewing because of its solid cast (which also includes Frances McDormand and M. Emmet Walsh) and for its attempt to tell a familiar story in an original way. On the strength of this film and his television work ("Threads," "The Race for the Double Helix," "A Very British Coup"), Jackson is a director to watch. CHATTAHOOCHEE fails overall, but remains a promising big-screen debut. (Violence, adult situations, profanity.)

d, Mick Jackson; p, Aaron Schwab and Faye Schwab; w, James Hicks; ph, Andrew Dunn; ed, Don Fairservice; m, John Keane; prod d, Joseph T. Garrity; art d, Patrick Tagliaferro; set d, Celeste Lee; spec, Richard O. Helmer; stunts, Bud Davis; cos, Karen Patch; makup, Gandhi Bob Arrollo

Drama   (PR:O   MPAA:R)

CHICAGO JOE AND THE SHOWGIRL

(Brit.) 103m Polygram — Working Title/New Line c

Emily Lloyd (*Elizabeth Maud Jones/"Georgina Grayson"*), Kiefer Sutherland (*Karl Hulten/"Ricky Allen"*), Patsy Kensit (*Joyce Cook*), Keith Allen (*Lenny Bexley*), Liz Fraser (*Mrs. Evans*), Alexandra Pigg (*Violet*), Ralph Nossek (*Inspector Tansil*), Colin Bruce (*Robert DeMott*), Roger Ashton-Griffiths (*Inspector Tarr*), Harry Fowler (*Morry*), John Junkin (*George Heath*), John Lahr (*Radio Commentator*), Angela Morant (*Customer*), John Surman (*Mr. Cook*), Janet Dale (*Mrs. Cook*), John Dair (*John*), Stephen Hancock (*Doctor*), Hugh Millais (*US Colonel*), Harry Jones (*Taxi Driver*), Gerard Horan (*John Wilkins*), Richard Ireson, Malcolm Terris, Gary Parker, Karen Gledhill, and Niven Boyd (*Reporters*)

CHICAGO JOE AND THE SHOWGIRL is based on a true story, the "Cleft Chin Murder," which dominated British headlines for a time in 1944. A teenaged showgirl, Georgina Grayson (Emily Lloyd), meets an American serviceman, Ricky Allen (Kiefer Sutherland), and the two embark on a wild affair. Movie-mad Georgina envisions herself as a glamorous gun moll to Ricky's imagined mobster kingpin. She goads him to commit one crime after another for her. The fun of appropriating an Army truck and stealing a fur coat escalates nightmarishly into the murders of a lady hitchhiker (Alexandra Pigg) and a cabbie (John Junkin). The pair are found out and tried. The lovers come to discover each other's duplicity: he is an Army deserter named Karl Hulten, while she is, in reality, Elizabeth Maud Jones, a stripper. Although she is eventually granted a reprieve, he is found guilty and becomes the only American serviceman ever to be executed by the British.

According to producer Tim Bevan, there was very little fictionalization in the film. It covers the six-day crime spree that took place after the couple's chance meeting in a Hammersmith cafe. Bevan and screenwriter David Yallop have, however, taken wild license with the motivational aspects of the story. They have chosen the rather heavy-handed device of showing Ricky and Georgina at regular intervals in their fantasy roles as mobster and moll. London turns into Chicago, the stolen truck becomes a snazzy roadster, Ricky's fatigues metamorphose into a flashy zoot suit, and Georgina appears as Veronica Lake, blonde bangs and all, while Benny Goodman's "Sing Sing Sing" booms on the soundtrack. Unfortunately, this too-literal interpretation of their fantasies serves only to distance the viewer from the carefully developed wartime atmosphere. The heedlessness of youth, Georgina's basic shallowness and acquisitiveness, and the alienation Ricky feels as a none-too-admired Yank in wartime London might instead have been further developed in the interests of credibility. Ricky and Georgina come off as marginally attractive ciphers; it's hard to believe they'd commit such dastardly deeds. Indeed, the moonlit scene of the woman's murder is so harrowing that it throws the entire film off kilter. Gemma Jackson's art direction also seems wrong. She gets the gritty filth of wartime London down all right, but goes overboard with matte and process shot effects — notably, the nocturnal trysting place set amid the rubble, and a very pictorial *Luftwaffe* — that resemble something of a Vincent Minnelli film or DICK TRACY, at least. The framing device of Georgina's fantasy appearance at her own premiere is also unnecessary. A more documentary approach to the subject, as in Mike Newell's DANCE WITH A STRANGER, would have been preferable.

With such sketchily developed characters, real stars were needed to make a go of this. Try as they might, Sutherland and Lloyd merely come across as baby-faced innocents. He is stalwart enough, but rather dull, failing to suggest either the implicit danger in Ricky or a thwarted romantic quality that would have made the character more involving. Lloyd's imperishable life spirit makes her one of the most naturally ingratiating young actresses on the screen, but she lacks the range to play a properly heartless *noir* bitch. The fatalistic opacity of evil that made Barbara Stanwyck's performance in DOUBLE INDEMNITY and Rita Hayworth's in LADY FROM SHANGHAI so mesmerizingly sexy is beyond Lloyd. She gives Georgina's eleventh hour betrayal of Ricky a brave try, but nothing we have seen previous to this prepares us for her snivelling actions. On the other hand, Patsy Kensit, who has a small role as Ricky's jilted fiancee, manages to hint at more complexity in her character than is scripted. (The film might have been more successful had she and Lloyd exchanged parts.) The best performance is actually delivered by Pigg, whose lifelike portrayal of the hapless Violet blasts right through the labored artifice. *(Violence, adult situations, sexual situations, alcohol abuse, profanity.)*

d, Bernard Rose; p, Tim Bevan; w, David Yallop; ph, Mike Southon; ed, Dan Rae; m, Hans Zimmer and Shirley Walker; md, Gerry Butler; prod d, Gemma Jackson; art d, Peter Russell and Richard Holland; set d, Lia Cramer; stunts, Gareth Milne; cos, Bob Ringwood; makup, Alan Boyle; chor, Warren Heyes

Drama   **(PR:O   MPAA:R)**

CHILD'S PLAY 2

95m David Kirschner/Universal c

Alex Vincent *(Andy Barclay)*, Jenny Agutter *(Joanne Simpson)*, Gerrit Graham *(Phil Simpson)*, Christine Elise *(Kyle)*, Brad Dourif *(Voice of Chucky)*, Grace Zabriskie *(Grace Poole)*, Peter Haskell *(Sullivan)*, Beth Grant *(Miss Kettlewell)*, Greg German *(Mattson)*, Raymond Singer *(Social Worker)*, Charles Meshack *(Van Driver)*, Stuart Mabray *(Homicide Investigator)*, Matt Roe *(Policeman in Car)*, Herb Braha *(Liquor Store Clerk)*, Edan Gross *(Voice of Tommy Doll)*, Adam Ryen *(Rick Spires)*, Adam Wylie *(Sammy)*, Bill Stevenson *(Adam)*, Don Pugsley, Ed Krieger, and Vince Melocchi *(Technicians)*

This sequel to the surprise 1988 hit is a slicker and ultimately more disturbing film than the first. In the original, the evil Chucky Doll, a toy possessed with the spirit of a psycho killer, killed a slew of people while trying to steal the soul of a little boy named Andy (Alex Vincent). In the end, the doll was destroyed, but since the film made more than $40 million it was inevitable that Chucky would be back. As part two opens, Chucky is being reconstructed by a group of technicians at the Good Guy Toy Company, creators of the doll. During the reassembly process, a bolt of lightning surges through the doll, sending a technician flying through a window — Chucky's back. Meanwhile, little Andy is separated from his mother (who has been institutionalized) and lives with foster parents, the Simpsons (Gerrit Graham and Jenny Agutter) and another foster child, 16-year-old Kyle (Christine Elise). Kyle is an orphan, and at first she and Andy don't get along. Back at the toy company, Chucky has escaped and heads out to find Andy, still determined to steal the kid's soul before his spirit becomes forever trapped in the doll. Taking the place of a look-alike doll already in the house, Chucky again threatens Andy. When Andy realizes Chucky is back, he tries to tell his foster parents of the danger, but they refuse to believe his story. When Chucky ties Andy to a bed and begins casting a voodoo spell that will enable him to take the boy's soul, Kyle bursts in and thwarts the doll's plan. When the Simpsons stumble upon the scene, they believe Kyle has tied Andy to the bed and ignore Andy's claims to the contrary. Soon thereafter, a teacher and then the Simpsons are murdered, and Kyle teams with Andy to stop Chucky, setting up a climatic battle with the killer doll in the toy factory.

Much like 1990's biggest hit, HOME ALONE, the true subjects of this film are child abuse and revenge. The horror elements don't really work (the suspense is heavy-handed and the doll just isn't all that scary), but the film's delicate subtext is most unnerving. Director John Lafia (THE BLUE IGUANA) shoots the film almost entirely from the child's viewpoint, employing low camera angles and a wild use of fish-eye lenses to create a surreal atmosphere. This style serves to make the film's violence all the more unsettling. For most of the film,

Andy is treated as a sociopath and dismissed in a variety of cruel ways. The Simpsons are unsympathetic, and the rest of the adults are abusive, evil caricatures who eventually "get theirs" at the hands of the doll. It's the ultimate revenge for an abused child. The fact that Chucky is controlled by an adult (Brad Dourif again supplies the voice) adds another interesting dimension to the film. When Chucky attacks an adult, the action is depicted in an almost comedic manner. But when the doll goes after Andy or Kyle, the action is more frightening as Chucky seems to be an overpowering adult. Ultimately, Chucky is not the villain here. The adults are. While the film is certainly not for children, its climactic battle in the toy factory plays almost like a disturbing, adult version of WILLY WONKA AND THE CHOCOLATE FACTORY. With its elaborate conveyor belts, primary colored machinery, and mounds of plastic doll parts, the setting is a surrealistic playground in which Andy and Kyle take their revenge, not just on the doll, but on the entire adult world. The climax also includes allusions to THE 5,000 FINGERS OF DR. T, the classic surrealist children's film from 1953, while the entire film is rich in theme's from children's literature. When Kyle and Andy stagger out of the factory, they are alone, with no family and nowhere to go. Yet Lafia handles this is an upbeat ending. This is unsettling material, and while the film may lack thrills, it has an undeniably powerful effect that makes it an interesting and finally compelling horror film. *(Extreme violence, gore effects, profanity, adult situations.)*

d, John Lafia; p, David Kirschner; w, Don Mancini (based on the characters he created); ph, Stefan Czapsky; ed, Edward Warschilka; m, Graeme Revell; md, Shirley Walker; prod d, Ivo Cristante; art d, Donald Maskovich; set d, Rance Barela; spec, Kevin Yagher, Image Engineering, and Apogee Productions; stunts, Dick Warlock; cos, Pamela Skaist; makup, Deborah Larsen; anim, Harry Moreau

Horror   **(PR:O   MPAA:R)**

CINEMA PARADISO

(It./Fr.) 123m Ariane — Cristaldifilm — TFI — RAI — TRE — Forum/Miramax c

(NUOVO CINEMA PARADISO)

Jacques Perrin *(Toto as an Adult)*, Salvatore Cascio *(Toto as a Child)*, Marco Leonardi *(Toto as a Teenager)*, Philippe Noiret *(Alfredo)*, Nino Terzo *(Peppino's Father)*, Roberta Lena *(Lia)*, Nicolo di Pinto *(Madman)*, Pupella Maggio *(Older Maria)*, Leopoldo Trieste *(Fr. Adelfio)*, Enzo Cannavale *(Spaccafico)*, Agnese Nano *(Elena)*, Antonella Attili *(Young Maria)*, Isa Danielli *(Anna)*, Leo Gullotta *(Bill Sticker)*, and Tano Cimarosa *(Blacksmith)*

For 30 years Salvatore has turned his back on the past. Not once has he returned to the Sicily of his youth, not once has he visited his dear, aging mother, who has to call collect if she wants to get a word out of her big-shot movie director son. Not once has he caved in to sentiment, to the seductions of his roots, and all because of the advice given him years ago by kindly old Alfredo (role model, mentor, substitute father): Forget about us and go to Rome. Make a life for yourself. And never come back to the town of your birth, because if you do I'll pretend I never knew you and you won't be welcome in my house. Thus a talented young man has met his fate, forsaking his humble origins to make his way in the world alone, and leaving the audience to wallow in nostalgia for a mythic moviegoing past that CINEMA PARADISO serves up in self-infatuated gobs. What one hand gives the other takes away, and no one's supposed to notice because it all comes from the heart.

No, they don't make movies like they used to anymore, and this Oscar-winning Italian-French coproduction (Best Foreign Film) spends the better part of three hours proving it. Actually it's more on the order of two hours, since CINEMA PARADISO has been cut by almost a third for US consumption. Salvatore (played by Jacques Perrin as an adult), a successful film director, goes back to the Sicilian village where he grew up to attend the funeral of an old friend. In extended flashback he reviews his postwar childhood and his relationship with the friend — Alfredo (Philippe Noiret), projectionist at the town's only theater, the Cinema Paradiso. As a prankish altar boy, Salvatore or Toto for short (played as a boy by Salvatore Cascio, chosen from 300 Sicilian boys director Giuseppe Tornatore had photographed for consideration for the part), follows the local priest to a private screening at the Paradiso. The priest doubles as the town censor, and as he registers disapproval of the films that flicker past (it's the kissing scenes that invariably arouse his ire), Alfredo snips out the offending footage, much to the amusement of Salvatore, who badgers the projectionist into giving him a strip of discarded celluloid. At first Alfredo considers the boy a pest, but a bond soon grows between them, despite the objections of Salvatore's mother (Antonella Attili), a war widow pining for her lost husband. The whole town, of course, has been affected by the war, and for many the Paradiso has become a refuge from the impoverishment and indignity that surrounds them. "It's like you're the one who makes them laugh," Alfredo says in summing up his occupational philosophy, and his young protege is soon learning the tricks of the trade himself. On a night of spillover crowds (the popular comedian Toto is on the bill), Alfredo moves the program out of doors (the walls of the town square become a giant movie screen), but disaster strikes when the theater projection booth catches fire. Salvatore rescues Alfredo from the flames, but the Paradiso is destroyed and Alfredo permanently blinded. When a new theater finally rises from the ashes (built from the proceeds of a lottery), Salvatore is installed as the projectionist. It's now the mid-50s, the old priest censor is nowhere to be found, and Brigitte Bardot's backside is beginning to appear onscreen. Life has also taken an erotic turn for Salvatore, now a young man in his teens (Marco Leonardi). He longs unrequitedly for the girl of his dreams, Elena (Agnese Nano), shoots movies of her in his spare time, and even surprises her in a church confessional. The blind Alfredo spurs him on with inadvertent profundities, and during an improbable screening at the Paradiso in the wee hours of New Year's Day, Salvatore and Elena finally come together. But their happiness is short-lived. Salvatore is called up for military duty, and when he returns home on leave, Elena is nowhere to be found. However, Alfredo has more avuncular advice to peddle. Leave friends and family behind you, we can only hold you back, Alfredo tells him, and Salvatore complies. Wave good-bye to Mamma, say hello to Rome. Now, 30 years later, the successful son (Perrin again) is back to lay his friend to rest. The Paradiso is about to be demolished (paradise lost for good), but a gift of spliced-together footage Alfredo saved for years brings all Salvatore's memories flooding back. Kiss, kiss, kiss, the old forbidden images flicker on the screen, and it's handkerchief time for all.

Some repertory house, that Paradiso. There's Fritz Lang's FURY, Renoir's LOWER DEPTHS, Visconti's LA TERRA TREMA, and enough Anna Magnani classics for a month of screenings at the Museum of Modern Art, but for the folks in this backwater hamlet it's just ordinary weekend fare. And why not, when it's the moviegoer's attitude that's at the heart of the story? Going to the movies is like staking out the pews in church, a reverential act, as anyone gazing on these rows of spellbound faces can tell. They laugh, they cry, they bliss out on cue: was there ever anything so simple, yet so profound? Director Tornatore (IL CAMORRISTA) pushes every sentimental button that comes within his reach — some Felliniesque, some marginally personal, but none that hasn't been pushed a dozen times before. And the ingratiating Noiret runs through his avuncular routine yet another time, dispensing platitudes like wadded-up candy wrappers. Once a formidable actor, Noiret is running out of credit fast. Preaching self-fulfillment while doting on community nostalgia, CINEMA PARADISO is the perfect pacifier. The film's censor priest might well approve of the carefully tailored sentimentality, but the less easily co-opted can just say no. Still, Tornatore's film — shot on location in the director's hometown of Bagheria, Sicily — won a number of film festival accolades, including the Grand Jury prize at Cannes in 1989. *(Adult situations, nudity.)*

d, Giuseppe Tornatore; p, Franco Cristaldi; w, Giuseppe Tornatore; ph, Blasco Giurato; ed, Mario Mora; m, Ennio Morricone and Andrea Morricone; prod d, Andrea Crisanti; cos, Beatrice Bordone; makup, Maurizio Trani

Comedy/Drama (PR:C MPAA:NR)

CIRCUITRY MAN

87m IRS/Skouras c

Jim Metzler *(Danner)*, Dana Wheeler-Nicholson *(Lori)*, Lu Leonard *(Juice)*, Vernon Wells *(Plughead)*, Barbara Alyn Woods *(Yoyo)*, and Dennis Christopher *(Leech)*

This film is worth seeing, or, more precisely, hearing, for the music of Deborah Holland. The sleek, cool, and stylish composer, songwriter, and lead singer for the musical group Animal Logic is listed as the film's soundtrack composer, singing four of her own songs and making a brief appearance as a lounge singer. Her contribution aside, this is yet another tired rehashing of BLADE RUNNER, with touches of MAD MAX (including the casting of ROAD WARRIOR villain Vernon Wells as the heavy). Stop us if you've heard this one before: the film is set in the not-too-distant future, long after the Earth's surface has become uninhabitable. The ozone layer is but a fond memory and the destruction of the ecology has led to a contaminated atmosphere virtually devoid of oxygen. Cities are now underground, and in subterranean Los Angeles, Dana Wheeler-Nicholson (perhaps best remembered as the towel-clad damsel in distress opposite Chevy Chase in FLETCH) plays Lori, the film's hard-bitten "Mad Max" stand-in. She's an ex-bodyguard trying to launch a career as a fashion designer. Her plans are sidetracked when her old gangster boss, Juice (Lu Leonard), forces her out of retirement for that ever-popular "one last job." Juice has a briefcase filled with computer chips and she needs them to be delivered to New York in a hurry. Juice has a dangerous partner in Plughead (Wells), a gruesome humanoid whose bald head is mottled with various outlets he uses to tap into human emotions, especially pain, to give himself drug-like rushes. Juice brings Lori along as muscle for a meeting with Plughead, but things go awry when a couple of inept cops try to crash the meeting. In the chaos, Lori escapes with the chips and decides to carry out her mission, heading for New York, with male android

pleasure unit Danner (Jim Metzler) along for company. Along the way, they get help from underground dweller Leech (Dennis Christopher), and love develops between Lori and Danner.

This could have been a fairly entertaining film. The cast is solid (especially Leonard, who offers a funny, well-tuned performance as Juice), the special effects are imaginative and technically above par, and Jamie Thompson's expressive cinematography makes good use of the California desert locations. But Steven Lovy's direction, along with the script he co-wrote with his brother, Robert, are tired and uninvolving. The film lacks narrative coherence and is filled with gaping plot holes — the most troubling being that it never bothers to explain just why the chips Lori is toting are so valuable. At every chance, CIRCUITRY MAN opts for the banal and the conventional. Its action scenes lack drive and conviction, as though the filmmakers were too cool to condescend to providing simple popcorn movie entertainment. In the final analysis, CIRCUITRY MAN's greatest failing may be that it is just too smart for its own good. *(Violence, profanity, adult situations.)*

d, Steven Lovy; p, Steven Reich and John Schouweiler; w, Steven Lovy and Robert Lovy; ph, Jamie Thompson; ed, Jonas Thaler; m, Deborah Holland; prod d, Robert Lovy

Action/Science Fiction (PR:C MPAA:R)

CLASS OF 1999

98m Lightning — Original/Taurus c

Bradley Gregg *(Cody Culp)*, Traci Lin *(Christine Langford)*, Malcom McDowell *(Dr. Miles Langford)*, Stacy Keach *(Dr. Bob Forrest)*, Patrick Kilpatrick *(Mr. Bryles)*, Pam Grier *(Ms. Connors)*, John P. Ryan *(Mr. Hardin)*, Darren E. Burrows *(Sonny)*, Joshua Miller *(Angel)*, Sharon Wyatt *(Janice Culp)*, Jimmy Medina Taggert *(Hector)*, Jason Oliver *(Curt)*, Brent Fraser *(Flavio)*, Jill Gatsby *(Dawn)*, Sean Haggerty *(Reedy)*, Sean Gregory Sullivan *(Mohawk)*, David Wasman *(Guard)*, Landon Wine *(Noser)*, Barbara Coffin *(Matron)*, Linda Burden-Williams *(Secretary)*, Lanny Rees *(Desk Sergeant)*, Barry M. Press *(Gould)*, James McIntire, and Lee Arenberg *(Technicians)*

In 1982, Mark Lester directed a bland, punk-rock, blood-and-guts update of THE BLACKBOARD JUNGLE called CLASS OF 1984. Inexplicably, the film received a fair amount of critical praise, paving the way for this lame follow-up. Not so much a sequel as a reworking of old nonsense, CLASS OF 1999 is a thuddingly dull B movie that borrows its few thrills from other, more satisfying films. The movie opens with a prolog that is shamelessly stolen, almost graphic for graphic, from John Carpenter's far superior ESCAPE FROM NEW YORK, telling of the wild developments that will take place in the future, setting up its version of 1999 America. There are no laws in certain parts of the country and youth gang activity has virtually closed down the nation's schools. In response, the government comes up with a plan to start educating the students and controlling the violence, an experimental approach that will be tested at Kennedy High, located in a virtual war-zone of gang activity in Seattle. The school will re-open with three newly employed androids as teachers, and the whole operation will be overseen by the mad Dr. Bob Forrest (Stacy Keach, sporting wild white hair and red contact lenses). At first the experiment seems to be going fine, but then the robot teachers (who were programmed by the military) begin to discipline their charges with too much vigor. One of the students is Cody Culp (Bradley Gregg), a paroled gang leader who is trying to clean up his act. Disgusted by his family (his father is missing, his mother and brother are both dope fiends) and tired of gang warfare, Cody makes it clear he wants to change. He becomes friends with Christine (Traci Lin), the daughter of the school principal (Malcolm McDowell), and refuses to participate in gang activities, thus becoming an outcast. Not surprisingly, no one believes Cody when he claims that the teachers are killer robots and charges them with having started the raging gang warfare. Soon, however, the gangs unite in all-out war against the three cyborgs, and it all climaxes in the school with a final showdown between Cody and the battle-crazed Dr. Forrest, who holds Christine at gunpoint. Forrest is killed by one of the deranged robots, Christine gets free, and, eventually, Cody destroys the android. The film ends with Cody and Christine walking off into the sunrise, while the school burns down.

Apparently, Lester's point is to put a twist on the dynamics in CLASS OF 1984. This time it's not the punks who are portrayed as the bad guys, but the teachers. It's a novel idea, but the whole robot aspect ruins it all. Why can't these teachers just be crazed humans? This is the unanswered question that dogs the entire film. Lester also misses the boat concerning his story's possible political implications. The screenplay is ripe with possibilities in this regard, but Lester chooses to ignore subtext in favor of brainless thrills — which would be an acceptable strategy if the film *were* thrilling, but it isn't.

In addition to these conceptual problems, the picture is utterly unoriginal. After a while one begins to count how many ideas are stolen from other films. There's the setting from ESCAPE FROM NEW YORK, the vehicles from THE ROAD

WARRIOR, the silver sphere-like weapon from PHANTASM, and countless references to THE TERMINATOR. In fact, CLASS OF 1999 resembles THE TERMINATOR so much (especially during the final reel) that there might be grounds for a lawsuit here. Lester handles these cinematic "references" without any flair or imagination, resulting not in homage, but in outright thievery. While not a particularly talented filmmaker, Lester has in the past injected a certain raw energy into his work (which has varied from broad comedies like ARMED AND DANGEROUS [1986] to action flicks like COMMANDO [1985], probably his best film), that has made it tolerable viewing. Oddly, CLASS OF 1999 contains little of that energy. It is a maddeningly stiff film, full of boring action sequences and rusty performances. The cast would seem perfect for the story, but they are put to minimal use. Only Keach (whose outrageous appearance calls far too much attention to itself) seems to be awake, while veteran B-movie actors like John P. Ryan, McDowell (who was the ultimate futuristic punk in A CLOCK-WORK ORANGE, which Lester obviously tries to copy), Joshua Miller, and (most disappointingly) Pam Grier sleepwalk through the entire movie. Lester seems to be trying much too hard, and the screenplay is full of forced and unfunny dialog, including the hero's standard Schwarzenegger-like quips after each killing (this is a tired trend in action films that should be eliminated as soon as possible), delivered by Gregg with the finesse of a sledgehammer.

This kind of film (the science-fiction B-movie actioner, if you will) can be fun when it's done with a sense of humor and style, as can be seen in the movies CLASS OF 1999 so desperately rips off. Unfortunately, CLASS OF 1999 fails on so many simple and essential levels that even the most die-hard fan of the genre will be bored. Except for some neat special effects (and a funny line concerning Ann Beattie's novels), CLASS OF 1999 is a waste of time. (Violence, gore effects, profanity, brief nudity, adult situations, substance abuse.)

d, Mark L. Lester; p, Mark L. Lester; w, C. Courtney Joyner (based on a story by Mark L. Lester); ph, Mark Irwin; ed, Scott Conrad; m, Michael Hoenig; md, Derek Power and Seth Kaplan; spec, Eric Allard and Rick Stratton; stunts, Paul Baxley; cos, Leslie Ballard

Action/Science Fiction (PR:O MPAA:R)

COLD FEET

91m Avenue c

Keith Carradine (*Monte Latham*), Sally Kirkland (*Maureen*), Tom Waits (*Kenny*), Bill Pullman (*Buck Latham*), Rip Torn (*Sheriff*), Kathleen York (*Laura*), Macon McCalman (*Store Owner*), Robert L. Mendelsohn (*Airline Passenger*), Vincent Schiavelli (*Vet*), Amber Bauer (*Rosemary Latham*), Tom McGuane, Jim Harrison (*Cowboys in Bar*), Jeff Bridges (*Bartender*), Iris R. Burchett (*Secretary*), Joe Bourque (*Airline Official*), Joseph Mangiantini (*Airline Employee*), Gary D. Rogers (*Bob*), Pete Clark (*Duane*), Shaun Lee Case (*Clerk*), and Mark Phelan (*Border Cop*)

In this leisurely directed, deplorably scripted folk comedy/black farce, colorful characters foist their eccentricities on the audience for what seems an eternity. The entire project is off-center from its opening sequence in which a horse is surgically vented, stuffed with emeralds, and sewn back up so it can serve as a hiding place for stolen gems. In a movie rife with miscalculations, the scene only makes the viewers feel sorry for the animal and undermines any sympathy the film attempts to cultivate for its gang of larcenous misfits—Monte (Keith Carradine), the saturnine leader; his girl friend Maureen (Sally Kirkland), a voracious eater and hopeless romantic; and Kenny (Tom Waits), a mother-fixated hit man. The surgery takes place in Mexico, and the plan is for the three thieves to make their separate ways to Tucson where they will cut up the horse (which is to be taken there by Monte) and divvy up the spoils. Kenny complicates matters by senselessly killing the vet who inserted the jewels in the stallion, and the thieves quickly flee. En route to Tucson, Monte has a change of heart and decides to go straight (sort of). He heads for the Montana ranch of his brother Buck (Bill Pullman) where he plans to let the stallion mate with some brood mares. Furious when Monte doesn't show up in Tucson, Kenny and Maureen stalk Monte's daughter Rosemary (Amber Bauer), hoping she will lead them to Monte and the gems. When Monte sends for Rosemary, Kenny and Maureen follow her to Montana where they confront Monte in a bar. However, Monte is able to evade the bungling duo, though that night they track him down at Buck's ranch. Even more bungling follows as the film careens toward its unfunny conclusion.

COLD FEET tries to be laid-back and hyperactive at the same time. Sort of a leaden Southwestern omelette, the film assaults the viewer with folksiness while the contrived storyline grows steadily more sour. The tasteless plottings undermine the film's happy-go-lucky mood, and the effort is further hampered by Pullman's flavorless reading of the narration. The pacing is so sluggish that the energy of the actors seems out of whack. Carradine, who remains aloof and underplays effectively, is the only performer who manages to maintain some semblance of dignity. Pullman, the poor man's Jeff Daniels, registers as a slightly sexier, younger version of Gabby Hayes; Waits strangles his lines and

demonstrates no comprehension of how to maintain character consistency; while Kirkland merely makes a spectacle of herself. Australian director Robert Dornhelm (ECHO PARK) is clearly out of his element here, and COLD FEET is a completely misguided effort that should be avoided at any cost. (*Adult situations, violence, profanity.*)

d, Robert Dornhelm; p, Cassian Elwes and Mary McLaglen; w, Tom McGuane and Jim Harrison; ph, Bryan Duggan; ed, David Rawlins and Debra McDermott; m, Tom Bahler; prod d, Bernt Capra; art d, Corey Kaplan; cos, Carol Wood

Comedy (PR:C MPAA:R)

COME SEE THE PARADISE

138m Alan Parker — Dirty Hands/FOX c

Dennis Quaid (*Jack McGurn*), Tamlyn Tomita (*Lily Kawamura*), Sab Shimono (*Mr. Kawamura*), Shizuko Hoshi (*Mrs. Kawamura*), Stan Egi (*Charlie Kawamura*), Ronald Yamamoto (*Harry Kawamura*), Akemi Nishino (*Dulcie Kawamura*), Naomi Nakano (*Joyce Kawamura*), Brady Tsurutani (*Frankie Kawamura*), Elizabeth Gilliam (*Young Mini*), Shyree Mezick (*Middle Mini*), Caroline Junko King (*Older Mini*), Pruitt Taylor Vince (*Augie Farrell*), Colm Meaney (*Gerry McGurn*), Becky Ann Baker (*Marge McGurn*), John Finnegan (*Brennan*), Takumaro Ikeguchi (*Mr. Fujioka*), Danny Kamekona (*Mr. Nishikawa*), Yoshimi Imai (*Mr. Yamanaka*), Lenny Imamura (*Japanese Actor*), Goh Misawa (*Acting Troupe Manager*), Sanae Hosaka (*Social Club Singer*), Shuko Akune (*Reiko Sakoda*), Keenan Shimuzu (*Master of Ceremonies*), Dale Ishimoto (*Mr. Ogata*), Shinko Isobe (*Mrs. Ogata*), Mariko Fujinaka (*Fumiko*), Fred Irinaga (*Mr. Matsui*), Tad Horino (*Mr. Noji*), George P. Wilbur, Allan Graf (*Theatre Men*), Frank Trocha, Tricia L. Campbell, Kelsy White (*McGurn Children*), Cynthia Aso, Emi Endo (*Japanese Girls*), Marian Mukogawa (*Fujioka's Mother*), Fran Lucci (*Dance Hall Singer*), John Jensen, John Mazzocco, Joe Heinemann, Michael York (*Dance Hall Band Members*), Mark Earley (*Wedding Singer*), Paul A. DiCocco Jr. (*Eddie*), Joe Lisi (*Detective*), David MacIntyre (*Santa*), Doug MacHugh (*Store Manager*), Howard French (*Draft Clerk*), Gigi Toya (*Kindergarten Teacher*), Don Adler (*Race Track Soldier*), Teri Eiko Koide, Jumi Emizawa (*Camp Singers*), Ian Woolf (*Basic Training Sergeant*), Ben Slack (*Farmer*), Bill M. Ryusaki (*Issei Gentleman*), Ken Katsumoto (*Kenji*), Kim Robillard (*Road Block Soldier*), George Buck, Kevin McDermott (*Administrators*), Harunobu Yoshida (*Demonstration Leader*), David Carpenter (*Army Captain*), Ben DiGregorio (*FBI Agent*), Saachiko (*Woman in Uniform*), Robert F. Colesberry (*Truck Driver*), Richard Iwamoto (*Committee Chairman*), Douglas Kato, Ken Y. Mayeno, Makio Sasaki (*Hecklers*), Tommy Allen, and John McColpin (*MP Soldiers*)

British screenwriter/director Alan Parker (MIDNIGHT EXPRESS, MISSISSIPPI BURNING) here offers a depiction of the Japanese internment camps that were established in the US in the early 1940s following Japan's attack on Pearl Harbor. Leisurely paced, the film opens by detailing the background of union organizer Jack McGurn (Dennis Quaid). McGurn stirs up political unrest in New York in the mid-1930s, then flees to California to escape prosecution for some of his activities. In Los Angeles, Jack is hired by Japanese immigrant Hiroshi Kawamura (Sab Shimono) to run the projector at his cinema located in the city's "Little Tokyo" section. Jack and Kawamura's teenage daughter Lily (Tamlyn Tomita) soon fall in love, a relationship Lily's father fiercely opposes. Since California law at the time prohibits interracial marriage, Jack and Lily run off to Seattle where they are married. Years pass as Jack takes on factory work and Lily gives birth to a daughter, Mini. When Jack resumes his union activity, Lily takes their child and returns to her parents' home. By now, the US has entered WW II and Lily finds her family in turmoil. Her father has been arrested by the FBI and the rest of the family is about to be sent to an internment camp. Kawamura is eventually released and returns to his family in the camp. In the meantime, Jack reconciles with his wife, then enters the Army. He goes AWOL to visit Lily and Mini in the internment camp, and during the reunion he is able to finally gain acceptance from his father-in-law, who persuades him to return to his unit. Jack ships out to Europe, but hardship continues to befall the Kawamura family. A son is deported to Japan and another is killed in action while serving in the US Army. Despondent, and haunted by accusations that he is a collaborator with the enemy, Kawamura commits suicide. At the war's end, Jack serves a prison term for having gone AWOL, and it is not until 1948 that he is able to rejoin his wife and child, who support themselves as strawberry pickers in a California farming community.

Parker's intent seems to be to offer a traditional love story with the social and political turmoil of the 1930s and 40s serving merely as a backdrop, but the numerous issues he raises make it impossible for the film to function as an old-fashioned romance. The despair of the Japanese-Americans as they find their lives so ruthlessly torn apart and the almost maniacal prosecution of union activitists by authorities in the 1930s are forcefully portrayed, but to the detriment of the main story. In short, the film suffers from too many characters and subplots, so that the project probably would have been better served had it been made as a six-hour TV mini-series.

The performances, however, are first-rate. Quaid (THE RIGHT STUFF, D.O.A., INNERSPACE), in a role he seems born to play, is splendid, far outshining his previous work. Tomita (THE KARATE KID, PART II) is also memorable. The Japanese-Americans who fill the numerous roles in the Kawamura family and the internment camp are uniformly excellent. Production values are high, with special mention going to Randy Edelman's terrific score, Geoffrey Kirkland's enviable production design, and authentic period costumes provided by Molly Maginnis. *(Profanity, adult situations, violence.)*

d, Alan Parker; p, Robert F. Colesberry; w, Alan Parker; ph, Michael Seresin; ed, Gerry Hambling; m, Randy Edelman; prod d, Geoffrey Kirkland; art d, John Willitt; set d, Jim Erickson; cos, Molly Maginnis

Historical/Romance   (PR:C-O   MPAA:R)

COMMENT FAIRE L'AMOUR AVEC UN NEGRE SANS SE FATIGUER

(Can./Fr.) (SEE: HOW TO MAKE LOVE TO A NEGRO WITHOUT GETTING TIRED)

COOK, THE THIEF, HIS WIFE & HER LOVER, THE

(Brit./Fr.) 124m Allarts Cooks — Erato — Films Inc./Recorded c

Richard Bohringer *(Richard Borst, the Cook)*, Michael Gambon *(Albert Spica, the Thief)*, Helen Mirren *(Georgina Spica, the Wife)*, Alan Howard *(Michael, the Lover)*, Tim Roth *(Mitchel)*, Ciaran Hinds *(Cory)*, Gary Olsen *(Spangler)*, Ewan Stewart *(Harris)*, Roger Ashton Griffiths *(Turpin)*, Ron Cook *(Mews)*, Liz Smith *(Grace)*, Emer Gillespie *(Patricia)*, Janet Henfrey *(Alice)*, Arnie Breevelt *(Eden)*, Tony Alleff *(Troy)*, Paul Russell *(Pup)*, Alex Kingston *(Adele)*, Ian Sears *(Phillipe)*, Willie Ross *(Roy)*, Ian Dury *(Terry Fitch)*, Diane Langton *(May Fitch)*, Prudence Oliver *(Corelle Fitch)*, Roger Lloyd Pack *(Geoff)*, Bob Goody *(Starkie)*, Peter Rush *(Melter)*, Pauline Mayer *(Fish Girl)*, Ben Stoneham *(Meat Boy)*, Andy Wilson, John Mullis *(Diners)*, Brenda Edwards, Sophie Goodchild *(Dancers)*, Alex Fraser, Michael Clark, Gary Logan, Tim Geary, Saffron Rainey, Hywel Williams Ellis, Michael Maguire, Patricia Walters, Sue Maund, Nick Brozovic, and Karrie Pagano *(Waiters/Kitchen Staff)*

Peter Greenaway's sixth film, THE COOK, THE THIEF, HIS WIFE & HER LOVER, is his most commercially successful since THE DRAUGHTSMAN'S CONTRACT (1982), probably because of its potent mix of sex, violence, and artistic respectability — a paradox for this most vociferously intellectual of filmmakers.

Gambon is the thief, a crude gangster who holds court every night at the chic restaurant he owns. Mirren is his wife. Abused, humiliated, but quiet and sensitive, she alone among Gambon and his pack of obsequious henchmen appreciates the gourmet meals prepared by Bohringer, a dignified French chef. Mirren notices Howard sitting alone, reading at a nearby table; later they make love silently in the ladies' bathroom, barely escaping detection by the suspicious Gambon. The next night, with Bohringer's connivance, they make love again in one of the kitchen's storerooms. The third night, Saturday, Gambon drags Howard over to their table on a whim. At last Howard and Mirren exchange words, and learn each other's names. When they next resume their affair the two are spotted by the moll of one of Gambon's henchmen, and when Gambon insults her the following night (Monday), the moll spills the beans. In a rage, Gambon vows that he will kill and eat Howard, but Bohringer helps the naked couple escape to the library, where Howard is engaged in cataloging works on the French Revolution. Gambon tracks them down after torturing the kitchen boy who delivers food to the lovers. While Mirren visits the boy in the hospital, Gambon and his men stuff Howard with pages from his books until he is dead. Mirren returns to find the corpse, spends the night beside him, and in the morning tells him about her life with her husband. She then persuades Bohringer to cook Howard. Gambon finds himself "the guest of honor" at the restaurant when his bodyguard is disarmed, and he is confronted by his many past victims while Mirren presents him the cooked body of her lover. She orders Gambon to eat, and as he takes his first bite, she shoots him.

Peter Greenaway describes the impulses behind his work as "technical and aesthetic and cerebral and academic." His films have not been developed according to the demands of narrative ("Cinema is much too important to be left to the storytellers," says Greenaway), but by equally deterministic formulas of the director's own devising: formalism, structural symmetry, recurring patterns and symbols, puns and conceits. THE COOK, THE THIEF, HIS WIFE & HER LOVER is built around the four characters of the title, the divisions of the restaurant (each room perhaps representing its own historical epoch), the tradition of table painting (a huge Frans Hals reproduction dominates the dining

room), and the central metaphysical conceit linking mouth with anus, food with feces, and sex with death.

Greenaway reportedly identifies with the cook: he watches, maintains a dignified distance, but acts decisively on behalf of the lovers. Michael Gambon's Thief and Alan Howard's Lover are diametrical opposites, the one boorish, crude, and ignorant, the other calm, gentle, and cultured. Gambon never stops talking but has little to say; Howard, on the other hand, remains silent for the first 20 minutes of the film but proves thoughtful and wise. Setting out to create an irredeemable monster, Greenaway takes his film to the very limits of screen permissiveness, from graphic torture to cannibalism. The film has been seen as a vitriolic condemnation of contemporary consumerism and greed, but for all the brutality and physical savagery Greenaway depicts, one suspects his contempt is really aimed at the *nouveau riche* who do not appreciate the gourmet dishes they pay for but whose names they cannot pronounce. If there is a connection between this philistine lack of sophistication and Howard's study of the French Revolution, then Gambon is surely representative of the peasants and the Terror — in his resolutely one-dimensional role he embodies every snob or aesthete's nightmare villain. Not surprisingly, his ranting soon becomes repetitive and boring. Greenaway's dialog cannot sustain our interest, and his lack of humor is the film's biggest drawback. For a lover of games, the director is never remotely playful.

Despite Greenaway's formalist protestations to the contrary, this is fundamentally a moral film. When the cook takes a positive role in the action — putting himself at risk to save the lovers — Greenaway follows suit, abandoning formalities and escaping the confines he has set for himself. The theatrical unities so meticulously established (the restaurant set, the time structure of consecutive nights) fall by the wayside. Mirren's speech to Howard's corpse — part confession, part eulogy — is not another word game or modernist disavowal, but emotional and psychological, everything Greenaway purports to reject. Be this a momentary aberration or a positive sign of the filmmaker acknowledging his humanity, it may be relevant here to note that this dispassionate intellectual has returned surprisingly often to a narrative pattern in which sexually exploited women turn against, and finally dispose of, the men in their lives. The film's *coup de grace*, Gambon eating the corpse he has stuffed, marks Greenaway's return to cinematic game playing. The ultimate metaphor for consumerism is cannibalism, and this last bit of business is poetic justice and symmetrical to boot.

THE COOK, THE THIEF, HIS WIFE & HER LOVER boasts neither formal perfection nor unmitigated pleasure, but it does exert a macabre fascination. It is an avant-garde ballet for hooligans and vulgarians, and an exploitation movie for aesthetes and connoisseurs. All the hallmarks of Greenaway's to-date extraordinary oeuvre — Sacha Vierny's ravishing cinematography, Michael Nyman's forceful score, Greenaway's own elegant compositions — are in evidence here in spades. *(Graphic violence, profanity, sexual situations, adult situations.)*

d, Peter Greenaway; p, Kees Kasander; w, Peter Greenaway; ph, Sacha Vierny; ed, John Wilson; m, Michael Nyman; md, Michael Nyman; prod d, Ben Van Os and Jan Roelfs; set d, Constance de Vos; cos, Jean-Paul Gaultier; makup, Sara Meerman and Sjoerd Didden

Drama   (PR:O   MPAA:NR)

COUPE DE VILLE

98m Morgan Creek/Universal c

Patrick Dempsey *(Bobby Libner)*, Arye Gross *(Buddy Libner)*, Daniel Stern *(Marvin Libner)*, Annabeth Gish *(Tammy)*, Rita Taggart *(Betty Libner)*, Joseph Bologna *(Uncle Phil)*, Alan Arkin *(Fred Libner)*, James Gammon *(Doc Sturgeon)*, Ray Lykins *(Rick)*, Chris Lombardi *(Raymond)*, Josh Segal *(Billy)*, John Considine *(Kloppner)*, Steve Boles, Don Tilley *(Cops)*, Terry Loughlin, Reid "Pete" Shook *(Gas Station Attendants)*, Rod Swift *(Finkelstein)*, Fred Ornstein *(Barney)*, Don Sheldon *(Fishing Buddy)*, Boots Crowder *(Waitress)*, Edan Gross *(Young Bobby)*, Michael Weiner *(Young Buddy)*, and Dean Jacobson *(Young Marvin)*

Yet another road movie about male bonding, COUPE DE VILLE follows three brothers as they deliver the classic car of the title to Florida for their mother's birthday in 1963. The boys' father, Fred (Alan Arkin), an inventor of special fishing poles and indestructible stop signs, has instructed oldest son Marvin (Daniel Stern) to pick up the car in Detroit. There, Marvin learns that his brothers, Buddy (Arye Gross) and Bobby (Patrick Dempsey), will be making the journey south with him. It's immediately apparent that the Libner boys have little rapport. What's more, Bobby is picked up from a reform school, which has obviously made little dent in his rebellious nature. The brothers spend most of the time en route annoying one another, but during a lull in their bickering we learn that Fred is dying (cue the soft music), and that he has given instructions to deliver the car in perfect condition, which, of course, doesn't occur. When Buddy falls asleep at the wheel, the car crashes. If this isn't trouble enough, an encounter with some southern cops wipes out the boys' savings. Somehow the Libners make it to Florida, where they stop to visit Buddy's sweetheart, Tammy (Annabeth Gish), whom he's planning to marry. She, unfortunately, doesn't have the same plans, and the brothers find her with another guy—who gives Buddy a trouncing, to boot. As for fixing the car, their uncle (Joseph Bologna), a high-rolling gambler, has no cash to help them out, but gives them a hot tip on a dog race. The tip pays off, and after collecting the money, the boys find a kindly but eccentric mechanic, whom they help to magically restore the car to its original state—in what seems like only a day or two. Meanwhile, Marvin finds time to go off on his own and clobber Tammy's new boy friend. Presumably, this retribution for the thrashing of Buddy is intended to demonstrate that Marvin is really a caring, devoted brother after all. (Or maybe he just likes beating people up.) With the car fixed, the boys arrive at their parents' house, where Fred lets Marvin in on the real reason for their journey: to reunite his sons. A final voice-over then explains that Fred dies that night, secure in the knowledge that his sons have gotten back together, certain they won't forget the importance of staying close as a family.

With some imagination and a spin or two on its well-worn plot, COUPE DE VILLE could have been enjoyable; instead it's depressingly familiar and, worse, unfunny. The brothers have very little of importance to say to one another, and spend so much of the film screaming and fighting that the ending is ludicrous. We're asked to believe that these three young men, who've spent practically the entire trip at odds, become close merely because of their father's admonition that they get together. Each of the brothers is little more than a stereotype: Marvin is dominating and humorless; Buddy, sensitive and lovesick; and Bobby, messed-up but basically good. To his credit, Dempsey does manage to bring some life to his Bobby, and his performance is one of the few bright spots in the movie.

What is perhaps most puzzling about this "road movie" is that it spends so little time on the road: few memorable incidents occur, few interesting characters are encountered along the way, and the boys seem to reach Florida in record time (in fact, the second half of the film takes place after they have more or less reached their destination). The filmmakers' half-hearted approach to their material is evident as early as the opening sequences where the car is shown going over a series of long bridges that certainly look *like* they're in Florida, although the story begins in Detroit.

One of the genuinely funny moments in the film is an argument about the lyrics to the 1960s rock classic "Louie Louie." Naturally, Bobby thinks the song is about sex, Buddy believes it's about dancing, and Marvin says it's a sea shanty. People have debated the nearly unintelligible lyrics of "Louie Louie" for years, but seeing the brothers revive the debate onscreen is COUPE DE VILLE's one unexpected delight. If the script had provided a few more original moments like this, COUPE DE VILLE might not have been such a formulaic, forgettable movie. *(Profanity, violence, sexual situations.)*

d, Joe Roth; p, Larry Brezner and Paul Schiff; w, Mike Binder; ph, Reynaldo Villalobos; ed, Paul Hirsch; m, James Newton Howard; md, Joel Sill; prod d, Angelo Graham; art d, James J. Murakami; set d, Don Ivey; spec, Greg Hull; stunts, Mickey Gilbert; cos, Deborah Scott; makup, Elizabeth Lambert

Comedy/Drama   (PR:C   MPAA:PG-13)

COURAGE MOUNTAIN

98m Epic — Stone Group — France/Triumph c

Juliette Caton *(Heidi)*, Joanna Clarke *(Ursula)*, Nicola Stapleton *(Ilsa)*, Charlie Sheen *(Peter)*, Jan Rubes *(Grandfather)*, Leslie Caron *(Jane Hillary)*, Jade Magri *(Clarissa)*, Kathyrn Ludlow *(Gudrun)*, Yorgo Voyagis *(Signor Bonelli)*, and Laura Betti *(Signora Bonelli)*

Made famous in films by Shirley Temple, who played her in 1937, and re-played many times since, Johanna Spyri's spunky Swiss heroine, Heidi, returns yet again to face more perils in COURAGE MOUNTAIN. Unfortunately, mixed in with the usual array of villains and catastrophes this time is a bit of bizarre, crucial miscasting and a sloppy, mediocre script.

Well-cast, at least, are Juliette Caton (who played the angel of temptation in THE LAST TEMPTATION OF CHRIST) as Heidi and Jan Rubes as her grandfather. Set on the eve of WW I, the story picks up with Heidi in a quandary over whether or not to use some inheritance money to attend a ritzy finishing school in northern Italy. Just why anyone would want to leave neutral Switzerland for Italy just as the latter is about to be invaded is never made clear. But before that implausibility can register, any remaining suspension of disbelief is blown out of the water when none other than Charlie Sheen, Mr. WALL STREET himself, pops up as Heidi's mountain pal Peter. Sheen is hardly anyone's idea of a strapping Swiss lad. Besides that, he's...well, he's a mite *old* to be frolicking in the fields with the barely-adolescent Caton. Though barely-adolescent girls in the audience might find the prospect pleasant, adults are bound to be made queasy, especially at the end, which fades out on the two in a romantic (though chaste) embrace. Luckily, however, no sooner is Peter introduced than he joins the army and leaves the film, returning only to save the day for Heidi and her

friends toward the end. And even then, Sheen's stunt double does most of the work. Since there wouldn't be much of a movie if she had done otherwise, Heidi chooses to overlook the gathering clouds of war on the horizon and heads off to Italy. There she enrolls in the school, which is run by none other than Leslie Caron as the very civilized Jane Hillary, whose curriculum seems to consist of highly partisan history lessons that, at least, fill in the backdrop for the story. There are also sessions of Isadora Duncan-style dance exercises to Stravinsky's "Rites of Spring" droning out of a Victrola. At every turn, Heidi is tormented for her country bumpkin ways. Buffeted by Miss Hillary in class for not being able to dance to Stravinsky or to find her homeland on a map, she is further taunted out of class, particularly by the snooty Ursula (Joanna Clarke). These halcyon days abruptly end when the Italian army requisitions the school as a command post, sending the youngsters packing. Those unable to return home easily, including Heidi and Ursula, are bundled off to an orphanage, run by the evil Signor Bonelli and his wife (Yorgo Voyagis, Laura Betti). There they endure Dickensian abuse and squalor while being forced to make and package fine soap for resale, and when Miss Hillary's attempts to reclaim her charges fail, Heidi and her pals decide to escape, make their way back across the Alps into Switzerland, and hide out with Heidi's granddad until this war thing blows over. Somehow, Miss Hillary manages to get ahead of Heidi to alert Gramps (perhaps she was able to use the tuition money left over from her shortened semester). Gramps sends Peter to intercept Heidi, who is being pursued by Bonelli, who intends to do away with Heidi to stop her from blowing the whistle on his orphan-abuse racket.

Virtually none of this makes any more sense than Heidi's original decision to risk death so she can dance like Isadora. But some parts of it are easier to swallow than others. For example, it's easy to accept that Peter, though a new Army recruit, seems free to abandon his post and go searching for lost little girls in the mountains. After all, if it weren't for their swell pocket knives, most of us wouldn't even know there *was* a Swiss army. On the other hand, since Bonelli was only able to get his mitts on Heidi because he had a cozily corrupt relationship with the governor of his province in the first place, why he should care that Heidi is about to expose what everybody seems to know already is, like so much else, never made clear. And we're still wondering how Miss Hillary got to Grandpa's place so much sooner than Heidi did and why, having gone through all the trouble to get there, the writers didn't give Caron and Rubes, easily the best actors in the film, more scenes together.

It may seem like quibbling to point out these lapses in what is essentially a kids' adventure. But kids aren't dumb. They may not know the hows and whys, but they instinctively know when adults are selling them a bill of goods. And that's exactly what the makers of this film are doing from the start, when they top-bill Charlie Sheen, who's barely in the film. They also promise adventure, then deliver a lot of trudging through the Alps with a few ski stunts near the end. Worst of all, they advertise a film with a good, engaging story and deliver a mixture of the dreary and the dreadful, barely held together by a script so half-baked it's an insult to the intelligence of kids the world over. The actors mostly give better performances than the material deserves (with the exception of Sheen, who doesn't make much of an effort to overcome his miscasting), but COURAGE MOUNTAIN is recommended only for parents who have trouble getting their kids to sleep. It's a great movie sedative for adults, too.

d, Christopher Leitch; p, Stephen Ujlaki; w, Weaver Webb (based on a story by Fred Brogger and Mark Brogger); ph, Jacques Steyn; ed, Martin Walsh; m, Sylvester Levay; prod d, Robb Wilson King

Adventure/Children's   (PR:A   MPAA:PG)

CRAZY PEOPLE

92m Paramount c

Dudley Moore *(Emory Leeson)*, Daryl Hannah *(Kathy Burgess)*, Paul Reiser *(Stephen Bachman)*, Mercedes Ruehl *(Dr. Elizabeth Baylor)*, J.T. Walsh *(Charles F. Drucker)*, Ben Hammer *(Dr. Horace Koch)*, Dick Cusack *(Mort Powell)*, Alan North *(Judge)*, David Paymer *(George Cartelli)*, Danton Stone *(Saabs)*, Doug Yasuda *(Hsu)*, Bill Smitrovich *(Bruce Concannon)*, Paul Bates *(Manuel Robles)*, and Floyd Vivino *(Eddie Avis)*

Emory Leeson (Dudley Moore) lies for a living. A top advertising executive, he gets fed up with writing dishonest ad copy and decides to tell the truth, coming up with such candid ads as, "Volvos: they're boxy but good" and "Metamucil: it makes you go to the toilet." His boss, Charles Drucker (J.T. Walsh), is so incensed by the unorthodox ads that he not only fires Emory, but also has him committed. The sanitarium to which Emory is sent is populated with the usual movie-variety crazies, along with a token female patient, Kathy Burgess (Daryl Hannah), who conveniently develops a hankering for Emory. Lonely and confused, she is obsessed with her brother, who, she claims, is coming to get her when his tour of duty in the Army is over. While Emory is "away," his "honest" ads are accidentally sent to papers and magazines all over the country. However, the plain-talking, sometimes crude ads are a surprise hit, and Drucker, seeing the errors of his ways, rehires Emory. Meanwhile, Emory has been teaching his fellow residents to write ads, and they start a makeshift agency in the sanitarium. The facility's director doesn't take kindly to this idea, but after learning of the money to be made from the venture, he teams with Drucker to exploit the patients' copywriting abilities. When Emory objects, he is again dismissed, both from the sanitarium and from the agency. The patients are lost without him, and Kathy gets more depressed; then, miraculously, her brother and Emory arrive in an Army helicopter to rescue her and the other kooky copywriters.

CRAZY PEOPLE is an example of "high concept" filmmaking at its worst, for all that the film has going for it is its concept. The idea of revolutionizing advertising by telling the truth and by using mental patients to do the telling is amusing; however, it is introduced in the first third of the movie, with no other innovative ingredients added to the mix. Random plot devices—the romance between Emory and Kathy, Drucker's corporate greed—are thrown in to pad the film, but CRAZY PEOPLE never seems to know what it's about or what its tone should be. Although presented with enough comic exaggeration to be a farce, the film lacks the energy that the genre requires; moreover, it's neither well-written nor biting enough to be a satire. The script also suffers from an infuriating disregard for logic, comic or otherwise. Notably, Kathy tells Emory of her fear of open spaces as she walks calmly in a large open space, and Emory's ads magically appear on billboards and in print without anyone so much as bothering to check the copy. The ads, which are frequently amusing, are not always wholly "honest," either. Although many are more truthful than conventional advertising, the script equates honesty with explicitness. An ad for Jaguar, for example, implies that beautiful women will provide sexual favors for the man who drives one in terms that are merely plainer than usual. (The ads in the movie are for real products, except for the cigarette ad that bluntly states the product's taste is worth the cancer risk. Apparently no tobacco company was hungry enough for free publicity to associate its name with that claim.)

As for the performances, Moore doesn't bring anything special to his role, but Hannah's slightly awkward and befuddled demeanor works to her advantage, since she's playing someone with a tenuous grip on reality. The other performers are generally left adrift by the simpleminded, juvenile script, which, devoid of comic inspiration, resorts to gratuitous profanity and crude sex jokes. *(Profanity, sexual situations.)*

d, Tony Bill; p, Tom Barad; w, Mitch Markowitz; ph, Victor J. Kemper; ed, Mia Goldman; m, Cliff Eidelman; md, Cliff Eidelman; prod d, John J. Lloyd; cos, Mary Vogt

Comedy   (PR:C MPAA:R)

CRY-BABY

85m Imagine/Universal c

Johnny Depp *(Cry-Baby)*, Amy Locane *(Allison)*, Susan Tyrrell *(Ramona)*, Polly Bergen *(Mrs. Vernon-Williams)*, Iggy Pop *(Belvedere)*, Ricki Lake *(Pepper)*, Traci Lords *(Wanda)*, Kim McGuire *(Hatchet-Face)*, Darren E. Burrows *(Milton)*, Stephen Mailer *(Baldwin)*, Kim Webb *(Lenora)*, Alan J. Wendl *(Toe-Joe)*, Troy Donahue *(Hatchet's Father)*, Mink Stole *(Hatchet's Mother)*, Joe Dallesandro *(Milton's Father)*, Joey Heatherton *(Milton's Mother)*, David Nelson *(Wanda's Father)*, Patricia Hearst *(Wanda's Mother)*, Willem Dafoe *(Hateful Guard)*, Jonathan Benya *(Snare-Drum)*, Jessica Raskin *(Susie-Q)*, Robert Tyree *(Dupree)*, Angie Levroney *(Dupree's Girl Friend)*, Drew Ebersole, Kenny Curtis, Scott Neilson *(Wiffles)*, Robert Walsh *(Judge)*, Jeni Blong *(Inga)*, Craig Wallace, Phillip Broussard, Reggie Davis, Nick Fleming, Robbie Jones *(Conks)*, Vivienne Shub *(Mrs. Tadlock)*, Robert Marbury *(Angelic Boy Friend)*, Skip Spencer, Holter Graham *(Strip Pokers)*, Susan Lowe *(Night Court Parent)*, Dan Griffiths *(Snake-eyed Hood)*, Kirk McEwen, Eric Lucas, Frank Maldonado, Patrick Mitchell *(Convicts)*, Mary Vivian Pearce *(Picnic Mother)*, Steve Aronson *(Mean Guard)*, and Kelly Goldberg *(Pepper's Baby)*

With CRY-BABY, John Waters finally joins the big league as a truly savvy, comedic director. Though Waters has already covered some of this film's specific terrain in its predecessor, 1988's HAIRSPRAY (set in Baltimore in the early 60s, while CRY-BABY takes place in Baltimore in the mid-50s), his latest effort is a delight, seamlessly integrating his usual elements of nostalgia, corn, sex, and perversity into a breathlessly paced and stylish entertainment. Leave it to this dementedly gifted impresario to mine gold from the juvenile delinquent film, one of cinema's most negligible genres. Waters finds just the right satiric tone here, and the film provides a thumping good time.

The year is 1954 and Baltimore is torn apart by the rivalry between the "Drapes" and the "Squares" (Baltimore slang of the era, roughly translating into biker-greasers and jocks). The Drapes are led by the bad and beautiful Cry-Baby Walker (Johnny Depp), a rebel with a cause—specifically, avenging his parents, who were wrongfully sent to the electric chair by the father of the Squares' leader, Baldwin (Stephen Mailer). Cry-Baby has fallen in love with Baldwin's girl,

Allison (Amy Locane), the daughter of Mrs. Vernon-Williams (Polly Bergen), proprietress of the town's leading charm school. All the upright citizens of Baltimore are aghast at Allison's new romance, but Cry-Baby really wows and offends the good townspeople after he enters the local talent show and puts on a rockabilly show that causes a sensation. Many a rumble, game of chicken, and musical number later, he is pardoned by the judge for his rebel ways and happily united with his beloved.

The intense, kitsch-loving fervor Waters brings to the treatment of the period is enough to make WEST SIDE STORY or GREASE pale by comparison. This is more than mere nostalgia for Baltimore native Waters; to his film's benefit, he seems to have never left the era of his youth, revelling in its lost innocence and pettiness. He knows the sweaty, dirty, teenage impulses that lurk beneath the pristine Peter Pan collars and freshly pressed chinos. Excruciatingly familiar songs like "Sh Boom," "Mister Sandman," and "A Teenage Prayer" are actually given pleasurable new life through the clever, heartfelt staging and vividly realized context in which they appear. CRY-BABY lacks the gratuitous gross-out effects of Waters' early cult hits (PINK FLAMINGOS; FEMALE TROUBLE), as well as the queasily sentimental politicizing of HAIRSPRAY (sadly, it also lacks Divine, Waters' favorite star). Retained, however, is the director's genius for casting (his discoveries including Divine, Ricki Lake, and the essential Edith Massey), and this time Waters uses his ultra-eclectic assemblage of personae as never before. All contribute seriously to the fun, beyond the shock value of their names and faces.

As the eponymous juvenile delinquent, Depp ("21 Jump Street") is iconic; with a glycerine or tattooed tear forever coursing from his left eye, he's the first conventionally beautiful lead Waters has ever used. Waters' star-making machinery proves to be as effective here as it was for the late, lamented Divine, and Depp repays his director's loving attention with a performance that's like the young Elvis on Spanish Fly. It's the funniest, sexiest performance since Matt Dillon in DRUGSTORE COWBOY. Depp is fully attuned to the satiric and romantic resonances of his overripe dialog, and never more so than when instructing Allison on how to French-kiss. (Waters follows this with a shot of a forestful of similar amorously involved couples that's a wildly funny extension of Antonioni's famous image in ZABRISKIE POINT.) Although Depp's singing, like Locane's, is expertly lip-synced (he by James Intveld, she by Rachel Sweet), never has it mattered less, so exuberantly physical are his bad-boy-glamorous gyrations. Locane (LOST ANGELS) is pertly right as the marshmallow-sweet Allison ("I'm so tired of being good," she mutters, eyeing Cry-Baby), though more might have been made of her big turnabout entrance as a "Drapette." The fetishistic use both teen lovers make of the tears they shed is a good example of the new, revitalized Waters touch.

Among the other performers, the horrifically leering Kim McGuire is in the cherished Grand Guignol/Tod Browning tradition of Waters' grotesque finds. (The scene in which she terrifies an entire theater full of convicts watching CREATURE FROM THE BLACK LAGOON is hilarious.) Ever-frosty, perfectly cast Polly Bergen displays a hitherto unsuspected comic talent as Mrs. Vernon-Williams; Patty Hearst sparkles in her brief scenes as an archetypal suburban mother, obsessed with crosswalk safety tips; and former porn star Traci Lords (as a Drapette) is very funny in the virtuoso opening polio vaccination scene, grimacing lasciviously as the needle finds its mark. ("We use our breasts as weapons!" she declares in the midst of a rumble, and proceeds to demonstrate her point.) HAIRSPRAY star Lake isn't given much to do here, but brings her uncanny, angelic sweetness to the role of Cry-Baby's pregnant sister. Joey Heatherton (now rather ferocious-looking) has a scary moment or two as a holy roller who speaks in tongues, while David Nelson and Troy Donahue bring period authenticity to their dear old Dad roles. Add to the mix Susan Tyrrell (as Cry-Baby's biker grandma), Iggy Pop (as her scraggly inamorato), Waters veteran Mink Stole, Joe Dallesandro, and Willem Dafoe, and you have a real mugger's paradise.

The Kodak home-movie color, stylized framing, and whirling camera movement from director of photography David Insley satisfyingly call up images from Douglas Sirk or Vincente Minnelli's SOME CAME RUNNING, especially in the big rumble scene. The costumes by Van Smith (the designer responsible for Divine's most memorable outrages) have a witty flair, and Christine Mason's hairstyles are, of course, as important to the action as the script. The soundtrack mixes well-known oldies, forgotten classics of the era, and new original compositions. *(Adult situations, sexual situations, profanity.)*

d, John Waters; p, Rachel Talalay; w, John Waters; ph, David Insley; ed, Janice Hampton; m, Patrick Williams; md, Becky Mancuso and Tim Sexton; prod d, Vincent Peranio; art d, Dolores Deluxe; set d, Chester Overlock III and Virginia Nichols; spec, Steve Kirshoff; stunts, Jery Hewitt; cos, Van Smith; makeup, Van Smith; chor, Lori Eastside

Comedy/Musical   (PR:O MPAA:PG-13)

CYRANO DE BERGERAC

(Fr.) 135m Union Generale – Hachette Premiere/Orion Classics c

Gerard Depardieu *(Cyrano de Bergerac)*, Anne Brochet *(Roxane)*, Vincent Perez *(Christian de Neuvillette)*, Jacques Weber *(Count DeGuiche)*, Roland Bertin *(Ragueneau)*, Philippe Morier-Genoud *(Le Bret)*, Pierre Maguelon *(Carbon de Castel-Jaloux)*, Josiane Stoleru *(Roxane's Handmaid)*, Anatole Delalande *(The Child)*, Ludivine Sagnier *(The Little Sister)*, Alain Rimoux *(The Father)*, Philippe Volter *(Viscount of Valvert)*, Jean-Marie Winling *(Ligiere)*, Louis Lavarre *(Le Facheux)*, Gabriel Monnet *(Montfleury)*, Francois Marie *(Bellerose)*, Pierre Triboulet *(Jodelet)*, Jacques Pater *(Le Tire-laine)*, Lucien Pascal *(Academy Member)*, Jean-Damien Barbin *(Young Snob)*, Nicole Felix *(Matron)*, Philippe Girard *(Officer De Guiche)*, Quentin Ogier *(The Cook)*, Catherine Ferran *(Lise Ragueneau)*, Christiane Culerier *(Uranie)*, Cecile Camp *(Gremoine)*, Benoit Vergne *(Lysimon)*, Madeleine Marion *(Mother Superior)*, Amelie Gonin *(Sister Marthe)*, Sandrine Kimberlain *(Sister Colette)*, Isabelle Gruault *(Sister Claire)*, Claudine Gabay *(Naughty Sister)*, Baptiste Roussillon, Christian Roy *(Military Officers)*, Pierre Aussedat, Yves Aubert *(Marquises)*, Christian Loustau, Alain Perez, Franck Jazede, Eric Bernard, Franck Ramon, Alain Dumas, and Herve Pauchon *(Cadets)*

Gerard Depardieu's Cyrano is nothing short of magnificent. In this version of Edmond Rostand's classic drama of unrequited love, his Cyrano is less physical caricature, more flesh and blood, and a markedly younger, more virile nobleman than the usually avuncular ones of the past. It is a virtuoso performance that earned him a Best Actor Oscar nomination as it had for Jose Ferrer, who won the award for the same role in 1950. Dealing as it does with universals—that beauty is both in the eye of the beholder and only skin deep—this slightly abbreviated adaptation by director Jean-Paul Rappeneau and Jean-Claude Carriere retains both the panache and poignancy of its source.

Because of his disfiguring nose, Cyrano (Depardieu), a master swordsman and articulate man of letters, is unable to admit his deep affection for his beautiful cousin Roxane (Anne Brochet). She, in turn, is in love with Christian (Vincent Perez), a handsome young soldier who is similarly smitten but has nothing going for him except his good looks. Admitting that he is a "brainless fool," he asks Cyrano, his mentor, for help in wooing Roxane. Cyrano gives him a love letter he has written to Roxane, but never sent, and Christian passes it off as his own. Impressed by its passion, Roxane is delighted when her admirer appears under her balcony one night. She is anxious to hear more of his heartfelt declarations, but Christian is tongue-tied, and Cyrano, who is hiding in the shadows, provides him with the words he needs. The ruse is a success, and creates an enduring bond between the young lovers. Cyrano is heartbroken, but tries to accustom himself to being a lover-by-proxy. Even when it's apparent that Roxane has not so much fallen in love with Christian as with the tenderness and sensitivity that is really Cyrano's, Cyrano remains silent.

When the French forces—Cyrano and Christian among them—go into battle against the Spanish, Cyrano continues to write Christian's letters to Roxane. When Christian is killed in battle, Roxane goes into mourning, retreating into a convent. Fifteen years pass, and once a week during that period Cyrano has visited Roxane, regaling her with stories of the outside world, while she speaks only of her love for Christian. Then, one week he is late for the first time. En route, he has been ambushed by one of his enemies, and mortally wounded. Arriving at dusk and hiding his pain, he carries on in a typically witty fashion. Roxane, as usual, speaking of her devotion to her lost love, gives him Christian's last letter to read, which, of course, Cyrano has written. Near death and with the light fading, Cyrano recites the letter from memory, shocking Roxane. At long last, just before he dies in a tear-inducing scene, Roxane realizes it was not Christian but the soul of her cousin that she really loved.

As in the play, the film opens in a theater where the lovers first meet and where Cyrano has come to jeer at his enemy, the ham Montfleury (Gabriel Monnet). Cyrano is heard before he is seen, and his voice practically bellows with resonant majesty. When he finally appears, in profile, his nose immediately draws attention. What is interesting here is, unlike other productions where the nose stops just short of Pinocchio's and makes an obvious freak of the character, the producers have gone to pains to see that this Cyrano is not grotesque. It is Depardieu's normal nose in shape, only extended, and by making the character less of a freak, the filmmakers also succeed in making his pain all the more poignant.

The extraordinarily talented Depardieu, who has appeared in more than 70 films, gives his Cyrano a winning combination of grace and gusto, and is a commanding presence, both literally and figuratively. He's unexpectedly fleet of foot during the dueling scenes, recalling Douglas Fairbanks or Burt Lancaster. He brings a welcome vibrancy to the role, which won him the Best Actor award at the Cannes Film Festival. Brochet's Roxane is not shallow, as she is often portrayed, but much a product of her times, impressed with the literary conceits of poseurs of her generation. With its masterful acting, exquisitely muted cinematography, vast complement of extras, extravagant props and scenery,

CYRANO DE BERGERAC was, at $20 million, France's most expensive movie production. Though filmed on a grand scale, it does not lose the emotional impact of the play, which had its premiere in Paris in 1898, and has been a mainstay of the legitimate theater ever since. One quibble with the film is that it presents something of a problem for those who don't speak French because the English subtitles often flash on and off the screen in staccato fashion to suit the rapid action. That aside, this is a welcome addition to the catalog of film classics. The film was nominated for Academy Awards for Best Foreign Film, Best Actor, makeup, and art direction, and won an Oscar for its costumes.

d, Jean-Paul Rappeneau; p, Rene Cleitman and Michel Seydoux; w, Jean-Claude Carriere and Jean-Paul Rappeneau (based on the play by Edmond Rostand); ph, Pierre Lhomme; ed, Noelle Boisson; m, Jean-Claude Petit; art d, Ezio Frigerio; cos, Franca Squarciapino; makup, Jean-Pierre Eychenne and Michele Burke (nose)

Romance/Drama   (PR:A   MPAA:PG)

D

DADDY'S DYIN'...WHO'S GOT THE WILL?

95m Propaganda/MGM-UA c

Beau Bridges (*Orville*), Beverly D'Angelo (*Evalita*), Tess Harper (*Sara Lee*), Judge Reinhold (*Harmony*), Amy Wright (*Lurlene*), Patrika Darbo (*Marlene*), Molly McClure (*Mama Wheelis*), Bert Remsen (*Daddy*), and Keith Carradine (*Clarence*)

As the energy and lucidity seep away from the aging Daddy (Bert Remsen), he and his mother-in-law, Mama Wheelis (Molly McClure), are joined at his Texas farmhouse by his four children: Sara Lee (Tess Harper), bragging of her recent engagement to Clarence (Keith Carradine), a local urban cowboy; Lurlene (Amy Wright), an uptight and judgmental born-again Christian; Evalita (Beverly D'Angelo), the rebel of the family, who brings her sixth husband, Harmony (Judge Reinhold), a hippie musician; and, finally, Orville (Beau Bridges), who bullies and berates his sweet, overweight wife, Marlene (Patrika Darbo). Daddy is still in possession of his will, which starts a family argument, mostly about Evalita's failings. She storms out and heads to a nearby bar, rejecting even Harmony's comfort, and meets up with Clarence, who gets her to sing along with the band. Back at the house, Orville searches for the will while Harmony, Lurlene, Marlene, and Mama Wheelis sing a hymn at the piano. Daddy comes in and watches them, but thinks he's watching his family as children. Meanwhile, Harmony heads over to the honky-tonk, thrilling the patrons with his guitar playing; however, Evalita rebuffs him and stays with Clarence. The next morning, as the family continues to complain about Evalita, Lurlene finds Daddy out cold. Later, in the hospital, he admits that he can't find the will, and that he's "made a mistake." That evening, Orville and Evalita search the whole place for the will, to no avail, starting another family argument. Evalita leaves again, and Sara Lee follows her to the bar to confess to Clarence that she's faked the engagement. Stoned, Harmony and Marlene gigglingly gorge food and speak of their mutual attraction. Harmony then nearly seduces Marlene, but Orville walks in, chastising his wife for eating. Later, Mama Wheelis remembers a strongbox where they find the will, which gives nothing to Lurlene or Orville. Sara Lee agrees to share her part, but Evalita refuses. Harmony leaves Evalita, and Marlene leaves Orville to start a new life with Harmony. When Daddy's funeral comes around, Orville and Evalita refuse to attend—he out of resentment over the will, and she because she doesn't have appropriate clothes. But when the others rehearse a hymn at the piano, Evalita and Orville slowly join in, pleasing Daddy's smiling ghost.

The script for DADDY'S DYIN'...WHO'S GOT THE WILL? has a number of problems, among them too many coincidences, too pat an ending, and too many loose ends. Perhaps if the makers had decided more clearly whether the film was drama, a black comedy, or a character study, the structure would have held together better. Also, as so often happens with movies based on plays (especially when the screenplay is written by the playwright), this film suffers from betraying its stage origins throughout. The comic timing and acting are often too broad for cinema, and the majority of the action is confined to a single set. But the most telltale sign of the film's stage origins is that people talk much more than they act.

These problems aside, however, the movie has a good deal to offer, particularly in its performances. D'Angelo earns the top acting honors, delivering an energetic, sexy, and sad performance, as well as a number of songs. Harper, Wright, and McClure also do fairly well with characters the script ought to have fleshed out more. The inspired casting of terminal good guy Bridges as a detestable character adds depth to the role of Orville (his family and the audience know he's nice deep down). As the hippie Harmony, Reinhold takes some getting used to, but ultimately he carries the role well, and he and Darbo add much-needed warmth to this otherwise often cruel film. And Remsen gives a wonderful, nuanced performance, delicately making us feel his confusion and pain, as well as his deluded joy.

With all its flaws, DADDY'S DYIN' does succeed as a film, if only because it manages to reveal certain truths about families that other movies shy away from or sentimentalize. (*Profanity, drug abuse, adult situations.*)

d, Jack Fisk; p, Sigurjon Sighvatsson, Steve Golin, and Monty Montgomery; w, Del Shores (based on his play); ph, Paul Elliott; ed, Edward Warschilka Jr.; m, David McHugh; prod d, Michelle Minch; set d, Susan Eschelbach; cos, Elizabeth Warner Nankin

Comedy/Drama   (PR:C   MPAA:PG-13)

DAMNED RIVER

96m River Enterprises/Silver Lion—CBS-FOX c

Stephen Shellen (*Ray*), John Terlesky (*Carl*), Lisa Aliff (*Anne*), Marc Poppel (*Luke*), Bradford Bancroft (*Jerry*), Louis Van Niekerk (*Van Honnegin*), Leslie Mongezi (*Movuso*), Moses Neube, Mtcheso Neube, Maita Sibanda, and Boniface Chivurenga

Filmed under the title DEVIL'S ODDS, DAMNED RIVER is an unmemorable tale of man against nature, man against man, man against a lousy script. In search of, like, white-water action, dude, some young river-rafting enthusiasts travel from the US to Africa for a trip down Zimbabwe's treacherous Zambezi River. The group consists of Carl (John Terlesky), an aspiring lawyer, his leggy girl friend, Anne (Lisa Aliff), Luke (Marc Poppel), a novelist, and overweight party animal Jerry (Bradford Bancroft). They engage Ray (Stephen Shellen), a moody American, as their guide. Before the group embarks, Ray has a tense confrontation with Van Honnegin (Louis Van Niekerk), a local bigwig. Ray later claims that Van Honnegin represents rival tour operators who want to put the guide out of business. As the little band journeys downstream, Ray grows increasingly domineering and paranoid, insisting that they're being followed. He's right, and he proves it by emerging from the bushes with Van Honnegin's severed head as a trophy. Ray, it seems, is a psycho ex-soldier with notions of making the Zambezi his private domain, and he picks this point in the proceedings to go completely insane, raping Anne while keeping the others covered with his AK-47. Carl tries to go for help, but Ray tracks him down and mortally wounds him. Meanwhile, the others in the group try to escape down the river, but the rapids capsize their raft and deposit survivors Luke and Anne at Ray's feet. Later, while Ray is busy ambushing Zimbabwean authorities, Luke recovers a pistol and gets the drop on Ray at last, forcing him to row the raft. But ahead lies the impassible network of waterfalls known as Devil's Odds. Babbling about "a soldier's grave,"Ray steers the raft toward the deathtrap. In the ensuing struggle, the raft overturns, leaving the trio grappling on a small beach above the falls, into which Anne knocks Ray with a well-placed swing of an oar.

"Now we're just like you," Anne murmurs after dispatching Ray, making clear to latecomers that the whole affair has pretty much been a remake of DELIVERANCE, with the African setting adding little to the familiar story. One raging cataract looks very much like another, although the raft stunts here are fairly impressive. The youthful actors—all of whom look like *GQ* cover models—are burdened with dumb dialog and stock roles that range from unbelievable to aggravating. As if Bancroft's one-note slob weren't annoying enough, he is given an inordinate share of the dialog early on. Not a moment passes without his boorish comments, usually dealing with the breasts of native women or his unquenchable thirst for "brewskies." Ray's hostility toward Bancroft's Jerry is supposed to signify the guide's murderous psychosis, but because Jerry comes off as such a reprehensible jerk, viewers find themselves on the madman's side.

The only time the narrative stirs up any real emotion occurs with Ray's brutal assault on Anne. It's a raw, savage scene with a lot more impact than the silly slow-motion shootouts that follow. Because Carl is too frightened to intervene, his ill-fated character takes on tragic dimensions. However, it's a desperate film indeed that is forced rely on so vicious a sexual attack to stir itself from torpor. DAMNED RIVER is, on the whole, a trip that can be avoided. After an extremely limited theatrical run, the film was released on a videocassette double bill with another wilderness thriller, SURVIVAL QUEST. (*Profanity, sexual situations, violence, nudity.*)

d, John Crowther and Michael Schroeder; p, Lance Hool; w, Bayard Johnson; ph, George Tirl; ed, Mark Conte; m, James Wesley Stemple; art d, Carol Fenton-Wells; stunts, Paul Connoly; cos, Poppy Cannon; makeup, Tracy Crystal

Adventure   (PR:O   MPAA:R)

DANCES WITH WOLVES

183m TIG/Orion c

Kevin Costner (*Lt. John W. Dunbar*), Mary McDonnell (*Stands with a Fist*), Graham Greene (*Kicking Bird*), Rodney A. Grant (*Wind in his Hair*), Floyd Red Crow Westerman (*Chief Ten Bears*), Tantoo Cardinal (*Black Shawl*), Robert Pastorelli (*Timmons*), Charles Rocket (*Lt. Elgin*), Maury Chaykin (*Maj. Fambrough*), Jimmy Herman (*Stone Calf*), Nathan Lee Chasing His Horse (*Smiles a Lot*), Michael Spears (*Otter*), Jason R. Lone Hill (*Worm*), Tony Pierce (*Spivey*), Doris Leader Charge (*Pretty Shield*), Tom Everett (*Sgt. Pepper*), Larry Joshua (*Sgt. Bauer*), Kirk Baltz (*Edwards*), Wayne Grace (*Major*), Donald Hotton (*Gen. Tide*), Annie Costner (*Christine*), Conor Duffy (*Willie*), Elisa Daniel (*Christine's Mother*), Percy White Plume (*Big Warrior*), John Tail (*Escort Warrior*), Steve Reevis, Sheldon Wolfchild (*Sioux Warriors*), Wes Studi (*Toughest Pawnee*), Buffalo Child, Clayton Big Eagle, Richard Leader Charge (*Pawnees*), Redwing Ted Nez, Marvin Holy (*Sioux Warriors*), Raymond Newholy (*Sioux Courier*), David J. Fuller (*Kicking Bird's Son*), Ryan White Bull (*Kicking Bird's Eldest Son*), Otakuye Conroy (*Kicking Bird's Daughter*), Maretta Big Crow (*Village Mother*), Steve Chambers (*Guard*), William H. Burton (*General's Aide*), Bill W. Curry (*Confederate Cavalryman*), Nick Thompson,

Carter Hanner (*Confederate Soldiers*), Kent Hays (*Wagon Driver*), Robert Goldman (*Union Soldier*), Frank P. Costanza (*Tucker*), James A. Mitchell (*Ray*), and R.L. Curtin (*Ambush Wagon Driver*)

The plodding personal project of star, director, and co-producer Kevin Costner, this three-hour-plus revisionist western, much of it in subtitled Sioux language, shocked movie-industry observers by becoming one of the year's biggest hits and garnering 12 Oscar nominations, winning seven, including Best Picture and Best Director. The Sioux gave the film their own rave review by admitting Costner as a full tribal member.

Costner plays the title role, though we first meet him as Lt. John W. Dunbar, a depressed Union officer during the Civil War who, trying to commit suicide, instead becomes a hero and is rewarded with his choice of post. He chooses to go as far away as he can and still be in the Army, selecting a remote post in South Dakota where he is to wait, alone, for reinforcements. The cavalry is exceedingly slow in coming because Dunbar's commanding officer has himself committed suicide after dispatching Dunbar as his final official act. The "Heart of Darkness" mood continues as Dunbar, accompanied by a half-mad trader (Robert Pastorelli of television's "Murphy Brown"), arrives at the post to find it deserted, its previous commander apparently having retreated to an earthen dugout some distance away before disappearing. Dunbar finds the post water supply intentionally fouled by dead elk carcasses thrown into the pond next to the post. These and other signs Dunbar finds everywhere warn white men to either go away or go crazy and die. Still seeking his own private oblivion, Dunbar is well-pleased. The mood becomes more ominous as the trader is attacked and murdered by Pawnees—the film's "bad" Indians—on his way back to civilization. Instead of crossing paths with the Pawnee, however, Dunbar meets the "good" Indians, the Lakota Sioux, who have not yet learned to hate white men. He becomes close to the tribe's holy man, Kicking Bird (Graham Greene), the warrior Wind in his Hair (Rodney A. Grant), and, particularly, Stands with a Fist (Mary McDonnell), a white woman adopted by the tribe after her family was killed by Pawnees when she was a girl. She becomes a convenient interpreter for Dunbar. Dunbar's other prairie "friends" include his loyal horse Cisco, who twice outfoxes Sioux attempts to steal him, and a mangy lone wolf he names "Two Socks" for his two white feet. It is Dunbar's antics with the wolf that earns him his Lakota name, Dances with Wolves. As Dunbar comes to earn the trust and respect of the Sioux, he finds his dark outlook turned around and invigorated by the Lakota's rich culture and down-to-earth lifestyle. His increasingly passionate involvement with Stands with a Fist doesn't hurt his mood either. Eventually he abandons his post and his uniform, trading it in bits and pieces to build his own snappy Sioux ensemble. He is given a lodge in the Lakota camp, admitted into the tribe, and takes Stands with a Fist as his wife. He is allowed to participate in a buffalo hunt and witnesses the desecration of the wilderness by his fellow white men, who kill the buffalo for their pelts and tongues, leaving the carcasses to rot. He also helps the Sioux in their fight against the Pawnee by giving them rifles and ammunition he had stored at his outpost. Preparing to leave with the tribe for its winter camp, Dunbar makes one last trip to his outpost to retrieve his journal. By then, however, the cavalry has arrived and Dunbar is taken prisoner. When he refuses to lead the soldiers to the Sioux, he is ordered transported back to the fort where he will be hanged for insubordination. A Sioux party sent to find out what was delaying Dunbar frees him while he is in transit, killing his captors. Dunbar returns to the Sioux, but fearing the Army will continue to search for him and his friends will suffer reprisals, he and his wife ride off into the wilderness.

Not a great film by any standard, this is a western for people who don't like westerns, at its heart little more than a *Boy's Life* adventure fantasy blown up to a lumbering epic. Costner's direction is barely competent and frequently clumsy. Michael Blake's script, adapted from his novel, is loose and disconnected, rambling about with no real story holding it together, beyond the imminent arrival of the white bad guys to spoil Dunbar's frontier fantasy paradise. For all its attention to surface details of day-to-day Sioux life, the film shows no genuine curiosity about the larger designs of the Sioux culture, missing opportunities to deepen and widen its viewpoint. The only reason we know Kicking Bird is a holy man is because Stands with a Fist tells us he is. We see little of tribal life through Sioux eyes, and come away having learned nothing at all about Sioux spirituality. Instead, the film renders the Sioux as just average folks. The overall attitude of the film toward the Indians has the easy, false chumminess of a TV series, its insistent shallowness only occasionally disturbed by movie moments of grisly violence and a few dashes of sex.

For all of that, the film proves once again that conviction and sincerity are about all that is really needed to make a compelling movie. Costner, with longtime associates Blake and co-producer Jim Wilson, virtually willed the film into existence. Unable to sell it to an American studio, despite Costner's box-office clout, they finally had to secure foreign financing to make the film. Thus, whatever else it may be, DANCES WITH WOLVES is not a cynical exercise in commercial moviemaking that rolled off a studio assembly line. If Costner's vision of the West is not a great one, it is his own. That doesn't make

the film any easier to sit through, but it does make it an impossible film to wholeheartedly hate. In addition to the Best Picture and Best Director Oscars the film won, it also won Academy Awards for its screenplay, editing, score, cinematography, and sound, and earned nominations for Best Actor (Costner), Best Supporting Actor and Actress (Greene and McDonnell), makeup, and costumes. (*Violence, adult situations, profanity.*)

d, Kevin Costner; p, Jim Wilson and Kevin Costner; w, Michael Blake (based on his novel); ph, Dean Semler; ed, Neil Travis; m, John Barry; md, John Barry; prod d, Jeffrey Beecroft; art d, William L. Skinner; set d, Lisa Dean; spec, Robbie Knott; stunts, Norman L. Howell; cos, Elsa Zamparelli; makeup, Frank Carrisosa

Western   (PR:C   MPAA:PG-13)

DARK ANGEL

(SEE: I COME IN PEACE)

DARK SIDE OF THE MOON

96m Wild Street/Vidmark c

Robert Sampson (*Capt. Flynn*), Will Bledsoe (*Giles*), Joe Turkel (*Paxton*), Camilla More (*Lesli*), John Diehl (*Jennings*), Wendy MacDonald (*Alex*), Alan Blumenfeld (*Dreyfuss*), and Kenneth Lesco (*Michael Gotier*)

In 2022, a maintenance spacecraft is headed for the dark side of the moon—and death. That's the premise of this well-done ALIEN rip-off, in which a veteran crew on a routine mission encounters the ultimate evil shortly after losing contact with Houston Space Control. As the sparks literally fly and the lights go out, the space travellers discover they have only 24 hours of power left. While the temperature drops and the air thins, the crew accuse one another of responsibility for the disaster, then notice a large spaceship floating towards them. The mission's resident android (Camilla More) fails to provide any answers as to the other ship's origins, and it appears not to be issuing any signal, so Captain Flynn (Robert Sampson) boards the drifting vehicle, which turns out to be a ship from the old US Discovery program. Despite his crew's misgivings, Flynn hooks his spacecraft into the floating mystery ship in order to draw upon the latter's power. In the process, the mission members find the cut-open corpse of an astronaut on the old ship and bring the body on board their own craft for testing, although crew member Giles (Will Bledsoe) is fearful that alien contamination will result. Investigating the matter with the assistance of the android, Giles learns that the floating ship is actually a spaceship that was lost in the Bermuda Triangle, that the body of the deceased astronaut was never recovered from the ocean, and that the trajectory of the splashdown runs in a direct line from the Bermuda Triangle to the dark side of the moon. Soon the corpse proves less dead than everyone thought and rises from the medical examiner's table, its stomach producing a grotesque head that attempts to possess Alex (Wendy MacDonald). When she goes into convulsions, Giles theorizes that something has literally gotten into her, but the other crew members are skeptical. Meanwhile, Flynn reboards the mystery ship, planning to retrieve relays that will repower their ship and enable them to break free of the abandoned spacecraft. Dreyfuss (Alan Blumenfeld) and Giles follow him, but are separated; eventually Flynn, like the previous mysterious corpse, turns up as a carved-up cadaver. Coming out of her fit, Alex is visited by a fellow crew member—apparently Jennings (John Diehl)—with whom she has sex. With Flynn dead and time running out, Giles decides to risk his life and go back for the relays on the ghost ship, ordering his crewmates to blow up the Discovery spacecraft if he doesn't return soon. All hell breaks loose: Jennings tries to cut Giles' time short, but Dreyfuss manages to rescue him, and the possessed Paxton (Joe Turkel) menaces Jennings, who shoots him. Jennings, in turn, is killed (by Dreyfuss) when he attacks the safely returned Giles. In a surprise twist, it is now revealed that the monstrous force did not jump to Jennings from Paxton (who was Alex's *real* visitor), but has actually taken over Dreyfuss. While Giles conceals his suspicions, the evil presence (still residing in Dreyfuss) turns out to be Satan, who feeds on the energy of souls he transports from the Bermuda Triangle to the dark side of the moon. Luckily, the noble Giles cleverly blows up the spaceship, losing his life but not his eternal soul, and foiling Satan for the time being.

DARK SIDE OF THE MOON owes much to ALIEN, but if one forgets its derivativeness it can be appreciated as a rousingly good B movie. The screenwriters know when to withhold information (although the twist obscuring whether Paxton or Jennings has been possessed is overly puzzling), and deserve points for concocting the original premise of Satan's soul route from the moon to the Bermuda Triangle. Combining the occult and stranded-in-space genres, this far-fetched but intriguing setup actually makes a lot more sense than more conventional thrillers about body-snatching extraterrestrials. And while the game of musical bodies becomes more confusing than scary towards the film's climax, DARK SIDE OF THE MOON dishes out its red herrings with aplomb.

Boasting resourceful special effects and a solid cast, this spine-tingling space adventure will keep audiences off-guard for most of its running time.

D.J. Webster's direction makes particularly ingenious use of gliding camerawork to suggest disorientation. We're cast adrift like the unfortunate space voyagers trapped on their damaged vessel; unsettled and frightened, we float without knowing where the journey into darkness will lead us. Drawing on various subcategories of the horror and sci-fi genres, DARK SIDE OF THE MOON is an effective shocker that travels familiar space terrain in an inventive and accomplished way. *(Graphic violence, profanity, sexual situations.)*

d, D.J. Webster; p, Keith Walley; w, Carey Hayes and Chad Hayes; ph, Russ T. Alsobrook; ed, Peter Teschner and John O'Connor; m, Mark Ryder and Phil Davies; prod d, Michelle Minch; art d, Janna Sheehan; spec, John Fante, Christopher Biggs, and Art and Magic; cos, Barbara Inglehart

Science Fiction   **(PR:C   MPAA:R)**

DARKMAN

96m Robert Tapert/Universal c

Liam Neeson *(Peyton Westlake/Darkman)*, Frances McDormand *(Julie Hastings)*, Colin Friels *(Louis Strack, Jr.)*, Larry Drake *(Robert G. Durant)*, Nelson Mashita *(Yakitito)*, Jesse Lawrence Ferguson *(Eddie Black)*, Rafael H. Robledo *(Rudy Guzman)*, Danny Hicks *(Skip)*, Theodore Raimi *(Rick)*, Dan Bell *(Smiley)*, Nicholas Worth *(Pauly)*, Aaron Lustig *(Martin Katz)*, Arsenio "Sonny" Trinidad *(Hung Fat)*, Said Faraj *(Convenience Store Clerk)*, Nathan Jung, Toru Tanaka *(Chinese Warriors)*, John Lisbon Wood *(Carnival Booth Attendant)*, Frank Noon *(Side Show Barker)*, William Dear *(Limo Driver)*, Julius Harris *(Gravedigger)*, Bridget Hoffman *(Computer Voice)*, Philip A. Gillis *(Priest)*, Maggie Moore *(Nurse)*, Carl Bresk, Sean Daniel *(Policemen)*, John Landis *(Physician)*, Carrie Hall *(Screaming Woman)*, John Cameron *(Bartender)*, Craig Hosking *(Helicopter Pilot)*, Karl Wickman, Cliff Fleming *(Police Helicopter Pilots)*, Andy Bale, Neal McDonough, Stuart Cornfeld, William Lustig, Scott Spiegel, Cary Tyler *(Dockworkers)*, Charles W. Young *(Dockworker with Bullet in Forehead)*, and Bruce Campbell *(Final Shemp)*

While the press doted on David Lynch in 1990, another cutting-edge independent filmmaker, Sam Raimi, creator of the brilliant, nightmarish "Evil Dead" movies, came to Hollywood with a relative lack of fanfare to make this ambitious, hallucinatory, comic-book-inspired epic that never quite takes off despite its cinematic virtuosity. DARKMAN's major weakness is its disjointed screenplay. Having virtually nothing to do with the rest of the film, the pre-credit sequence establishes not the hero but the movie's second-rate villain, Durant (Larry Drake). In a pitched gun battle, Durant and his truly scary henchmen wipe out a rival gang without breaking a sweat, stopping only so that Durant can indulge his hobby—cutting off the fingers of his enemies with his cigar guillotine, to "stuff" and add them to his collection. After an introduction like that, the hero can't help but seem dull, and Peyton (Liam Neeson) seems duller than most. A "scientist," he is working furiously on a formula for artificial skin, but though his state-of-the-art lab is full of really neat, expensive-looking stuff, we never learn who is funding the project. Peyton's major problem is that the pseudo-skin doesn't last long enough; after 99 minutes the cells decompose and the skin turns into bubbling goo. During a power failure, however, Peyton discovers that the skin lives much longer in the dark—a neat angle that gives immediate meaning to the film's title, but which Raimi fails to capitalize on further. Meanwhile, Peyton's girl friend, Julie (Frances McDormand), a lawyer working for crooked developer Strack (Colin Friels), finds herself in an ethical quandary when she stumbles on a memo showing illegal payoffs to members of the city council. It turns out that Strack is trying to push through permits for a massive waterfront development. (What kind of bonehead writes memos about illegal payoffs?) Hardly a jolly Donald Trump clone, Strack is a full-time, foaming-at-the-mouth urban megalomaniac bent on taking over the city. With Durant as his muscle, it looks as though Strack will easily succeed in achieving his nefarious ends. Failing to persuade Julie to hand over the incriminating memo, Strack sends Durant to visit Peyton's lab, where Julie has spent the preceding evening. As we have already seen, Durant is no gentle persuader. His thugs murder Peyton's assistant, take his fingers, then bash, burn, and finally blow up Peyton and his lab. Presumed dead by Julie—who, strangely, begins dating Strack almost immediately—and taken for a bum by those who find him, Peyton is cared for by an odd "doctor" (the uncredited Jenny Agutter) and her assistants (including director John Landis). Trying out a radical new therapy on her anonymous patient, the doctor severs Peyton's nerves to prevent pain messages from the burns from reaching his brain. As an unfortunate side effect, Peyton turns into a raving, adrenaline-pumped, superhuman schizophrenic—a comic-bookish anti-hero who makes Michael Keaton's tormented Batman look like a regular guy. Recovering consciousness, Peyton slips out of the hospital and re-creates his artificial skin lab in an abandoned factory. From there, he plots his revenge and

works on winning back Julie. An assortment of "masks" allows him to infiltrate Durant's gang and to hide his gruesome disfigurement from Julie.

DARKMAN has much going for it, but, ultimately, it doesn't quite work. Riddled with annoying inconsistencies, the script—credited to five writers, including Raimi, who also receives solo credit for the story—is clearly an example of too many cooks spoiling the broth. And what dramatic energy the film does have is often misdirected. Running just over 90 minutes, DARKMAN finds it necessary to show us Peyton inventing artificial skin not once but twice. But a deeper problem lies with the title character himself. An obvious attempt to capitalize on the success of BATMAN, which took many in the film industry by surprise, DARKMAN has the right look, even the right sound, owing to another thundering, mock-operatic score by BATMAN composer Danny Elfman. However, Raimi's film never strikes the right emotional chords. Aiming at nothing less than turning the comic-adventure genre inside-out, Raimi has created a hero for whom conventional notions of good and evil have no meaning. Peyton's motivations have nothing to do with idealism and everything to do with bloodlust, revenge, and the severed circuits in his brain. At the film's climax, the villain, Strack, rightfully asks who the real monster is. But it's a question the film never convincingly answers.

As antiheroes go, Darkman remains too "anti" for a film that barely gives its characters a chance to breathe, much less an opportunity to grow and develop. (Even the film's villains aren't particularly well-defined. Tellingly, it's not disclosed until about halfway through the film that Durant works for Strack.) Like any good comic-book adventure film, DARKMAN is visually riveting, offering bigger-than-life villains, an intriguingly flawed hero, and a tough, appealing heroine—all portrayed by terrific actors. But in attempting to bring dark, ambiguous depth to a fast-moving, no-nonsense adventure, the film tries, and fails, to have it both ways. While delivering the action goods in spades, DARKMAN offers only pseudo-substance beneath all its pyrotechnics. *(Extreme violence, profanity, adult situations.)*

d, Sam Raimi; p, Robert Tapert; w, Chuck Pfarrer, Sam Raimi, Ivan Raimi, Daniel Goldin, and Joshua Goldin (based on a story by Sam Raimi); ph, Bill Pope; ed, Bud Smith, Scott Smith, and David Stiven; m, Danny Elfman; prod d, Randy Ser; art d, Phil Dagort; set d, George Suhayda and Ginni Barr; spec, Introvision Systems International, FourWard Productions, Tony Gardner, and Larry Hamlin; stunts, Chris Doyle; cos, Grania Preston; makup, Deborah Larsen; anim, Chiodo Brothers Productions, Kevin Kutchaver, and Jammie Friday

Action/Science Fiction   **(PR:O   MPAA:R)**

DAYS OF THUNDER

106m Simpson-Bruckheimer/Paramount c

Tom Cruise *(Cole Trickle)*, Robert Duvall *(Harry Hogge)*, Randy Quaid *(Tim Daland)*, Nicole Kidman *(Dr. Claire Lewicki)*, Cary Elwes *(Russ Wheeler)*, Michael Rooker *(Rowdy Burns)*, John C. Reilly *(Buck Bretherton)*, Don Simpson *(Aldo Benedetti)*, Stephen Michael Ayers *(Jack Man, Cole's Crew)*, Donna Wilson *(Darlene)*, Chris Ellis *(Harlan Hoogerhyde)*, Peter Appel *(Tire Carrier, Cole's Crew)*, Mike Slattery *(Front Tire Changer, Cole's Crew)*, Fred Dalton Thompson *(Big John)*, and J.C. Quinn *(Waddell)*

Tim Daland (Randy Quaid) owns a used car dealership but dreams of making his name on the stock car circuit. He persuades racing veteran Harry Hogge (Robert Duvall) to build him a car, on the condition that the car dealer find a suitable driver. Daland's discovery, Cole Trickle (Tom Cruise), makes his entrance on a motorcycle in a nimbus of golden dust and is unsuitable in almost every way. A California pretty boy with no experience in stock-car racing, Trickle doesn't even know much about cars. But he wants to drive, wants to win, and is a natural behind the wheel. After a rocky start, Trickle begins winning races and earns the good-natured enmity of champion Rowdy Burns (Michael Rooker), a good old boy with a dream: to stop racing and work the farm he's bought for his family. Trickle's dark night of the soul comes in the form of a near-fatal accident. He and Burns wind up at the same hospital under the care of Dr. Claire Lewicki (Nicole Kidman). Trickle's recovery is aided by his affair with the delectable doctor, but when he returns to the track, he has lost his edge. Worse still, the driver who replaced him while he was injured, hotshot Russ Wheeler (Cary Elwes), has stayed on as Daland's second driver and now competes against Trickle. Burns, meanwhile, is sidelined with cranial bleeding, a diagnosis he refuses to accept. In a fit of temper, Trickle demolishes his car, then persuades Burns to undergo brain surgery that will save his life but that will keep him from driving in the big race at Daytona. The stage is set for a showdown; Trickle must conquer his fear of driving and compete against Wheeler at Daytona in Burns' car. Naturally, Trickle triumphs. DAYS OF THUNDER reunites the key players responsible for the hit TOP GUN—flamboyant producers Don Simpson and Jerry Bruckheimer, director Tony Scott, and star Cruise—and it should comes as no surprise that the movie was referred to as "Top Car" during its making. No one really expects an action movie to resonate with profound meaning, but the shallowness of DAYS OF THUNDER is extraordinary even by genre standards. Written by Robert Towne, one of the most highly respected screenwriters in Hollywood and the author of CHINATOWN, it oozes cynicism and contempt for its audience. Designed as a summer date machine, DAYS OF THUNDER delivers only the bare essentials. Boys, the reasoning seems to go, will be lured into the theater by the siren call of gasoline and super-charged engines, while their girl friends will tag along to get a look at Cruise in tight jeans.

Beyond that, there's no story to speak of, and the much-ballyhooed racing footage, shot on real tracks during real races, isn't tremendously compelling. Viewers didn't need to be interested in flying to be seduced by TOP GUN's aerial sequences; the vicious grace of needle-nosed fighter planes piercing the fabric of the sky was a cheap thrill, but a thrill nonetheless. Stock cars, by contrast, are just cars — clunky, beat-up cars covered with logos, racing around in circles. TOP GUN turned ordinary young men into demigods, fighter pilots ennobled by contact with amazing machines. DAYS OF THUNDER, on the other hand, is dragged down by the white trash reputation of stock-car racing, which the film does nothing to alleviate.

To call the characters here underdeveloped does them the favor of suggesting they're developed at all. Imagine casting the leads with unknowns and the problem leaps into focus. Only the presence of actors with strong identities (Duvall, Cruise) and larger-than-life faces (Quaid, Rooker) differentiates one character from another. Even their names sound like faintly smutty in-jokes; what else is one to make of a hero named Cole Trickle? DAYS OF THUNDER embodies the worst tendencies of current Hollywood filmmaking. Bloated and expensive — with little of the money on the screen — it reflects no glory on anyone involved. The film earned an Oscar nomination for Best Sound. *(Sexual situations.)*

d, Tony Scott; p, Don Simpson and Jerry Bruckheimer; w, Robert Towne (based on a story by Robert Towne, Tom Cruise); ph, Ward Russell; ed, Billy Weber and Chris Lebenzon; m, Hans Zimmer; art d, Benjamin Fernandez; cos, Susan Becker; tech, Rick Hendrick and Greg Sacks.

Sports (PR:A MPAA:PG-13)

DEAD AIM

88m Double Helix c

Ed Marinaro *(Mace Douglas)*, Darrell Larson *(Mark Cain)*, Cassandra Gavas *(Amber)*, John Hancock *(Talbot)*, William Sanderson *(Brennan)*, Corbin Bernsen *(Webster)*, William Windom *(Mc Whorter)*, Harry Goz *(Androsov)*, Terry Beaver *(Agent Johnson)*, Lynn Whitfield *(Sheila Freeman)*, Donna Briscoe *(Denise Long)*, Mike Russo *(Alvarez)*, Rick Washburn *(Epi Flexner)*, Randal Patrick *(Stephens)*, Sandi Brannon *(Misty)*, Diana Brittan *(Candi)*, Carol Chambers *(Nicole)*, Shirlene Foss *(B.J.)*, Marisu Werhenberg *(Bunny)*, and Ted Henning *(Bloomington)*

This above-average action escapist fare may seem a bit dated as the Berlin Wall comes tumbling down, but its attempt to meld a cold-war thriller with a cop drama isn't totally behind the times. Paranoia about US governmental meddling in world affairs and the questionable ethics of such exclusive boys' clubs as the CIA, the FBI, and the KGB can never be considered out of fashion. Cold wars may end, but international conspiracies and screw-ups like the one portrayed in DEAD AIM will probably always be with us.

Why are so many topless dancers dying of drug overdoses, and what do these untimely deaths have to do with the latest case for maverick cop Mace Douglas (Ed Marinaro)? How will the surveillance team (headed by Corbin Bernsen and William Windom) that's conducting an undercover investigation of prostitution rings fit into this mystery? Demoted from the police force's homicide division, Mace is a streetwise cop with an unfortunate habit of killing perpetrators before they can be turned over to the courts. As punishment, he's assigned to work with Mark Cain (Darrell Larson), a college-trained procedure fiend with a high arrest record. Interwoven into the story line are Bulgarian diplomat Androsov (Harry Goz) and his pet hit man, Epi Flexner (Rick Washburn), as well as a drug pusher with ties to Androsov and a planned Third World revolution. In pursuit of drug dealer Alvarez (Mike Russo), Mace finds an empty diplomatic pouch from Bulgaria and the body of a man just shot by Alvarez (later revealed to have been a spy), and discovers that the film in his surveillance camera has been confiscated. Meanwhile, independent of Mace's investigation, Mark has obtained the name of a hooker who knew some of the deceased strippers from news reporter Sheila Freeman (Lynn Whitfield). When this prostitute is found dead of an overdose shortly after questioning, Mace and Mark pool resources and team up in their investigation. Meanwhile, Androsov has asked his hit man to eliminate all the exotic dancers that attended a wild party with him and the dead spy, and a drug dealer associate of Androsov plots to assassinate a prominent drug lord. After the cops discover that a fingerprint on Mace's camera belongs to KGB hit

man Flexner, Mace goes undercover as a bouncer and befriends topless talent Amber (Cassandra Gavas). Although she gives him important information about the party (whose guest list now resembles an obituary column), the investigation is set back when the FBI arrives and pulls rank on the local cops. After another stripper is killed in an explosion, Amber arranges to meet Mace (in defiance of FBI requests), but is run over by Flexner en route to the rendezvous. Surreptitiously, Mace removes a cleaner's receipt from the dead girl's hand, but his chief is forced to suspend him for butting into the FBI's jurisdiction. As the international espionage hits the fan, Androsov's pal puts the hit out on the drug lord but fails to get the big man. Mace obtains Amber's dress from the cleaners, finds inside it a photo of the party that shows Androsov in attendance, and discovers that the Bulgarian is not only a diplomat but probably a KGB plant. Unfortunately, Mace's vice-squad pals are investigating a hooker on the party list and are wiped out by Flexner, who also attempts to garrote Mark. Back on the case, Mace intercepts Androsov as the latter attempts a getaway. After killing Flexner and the chauffeur, Mace drives his car into the escape plane. While Androsov cries "Diplomatic immunity!" Mace blows him away, and shows little remorse when he learns that Androsov was a double agent for the FBI who has badly bungled this entire secret mission.

While DEAD AIM's script is cleverly conceived, it doesn't maximize suspense by tying up its numerous loose ends. The film fails to juggle its various subplots with enough skill to keep them all up in the air at the same time — not every payoff hits the audience with as much impact as it should. On the other hand, DEAD AIM deserves credit for refurbishing the buddy-cop formula, jazzing it up with foreign intrigue. The police work itself is depicted engrossingly — though one laments the standard sexism of the " pretty young things getting dispatched in various states of undress" story line and the generic casting of the actresses in these roles (each looks as if she has the designation *typical victim* sewn into the sequins on her G-string). The film's most glaring weakness, however, is its utter failure to integrate the drug-world plotline into the central story. These scenes seem extraneous — as if they were filmed at another time and place and inserted into the film as an afterthought.

Nonetheless, the film sometimes hits the mark in making all its intricate investigative twists and turns; the manner in which the vice-squad surveillance team's activities are woven into the central story line is especially surprising and exciting. Capably directed by William Van Der Kloot and persuasively acted by its leads, DEAD AIM is gut-grabbing action moviemaking. It lacks polish, but it's not that inferior to such big-budget celebrations of machismo as RED HEAT or TANGO AND CASH. If you're an action aficionado, DEAD AIM delivers the goods often enough to make it good police-work escapism that niftily reworks genre expectations. *(Substance abuse, profanity, nudity, violence, sexual situations.)*

d, William Van Der Kloot; p, Michael A. Simpson and William Van Der Kloot; w, Michael A. Simpson; ph, John Davis; ed, William Van Der Kloot; m, James Oliverio; art d, Lynn Wolverton; spec, Spectacular Effects Intl.

Action/Thriller (PR:O MPAA:R)

DEAD PIT

95m Cornerstone c

Jeremy Slate *(Dr. Gerald Swan)*, Cheryl Lawson *(Jane Doe/Sara)*, Steffen Gregory Foster *(Christian Meyers)*, Danny Gochnauer *(Dr. Colin Ramzi)*, Geha Gertz *(Sister Clair)*, Joan Bechtel *(Nurse Kygar)*, Michael Jacobs *(Bud Higgins)*, Mara Everett *(Nurse Robbins)*, Randy Fontana *(Orderly Jimmy)*, Jack Sunseri *(Head Orderly Jimmy)*, Frederick Dodge *(First Patient)*, Nettie Heffner *(Night Nurse)*, Luana Speelman *(Day Nurse)*, and Rorey Edelman *(Little Sara)*

In the prolog to this better-than-average gore flick, Dr. Gerald Swan (Jeremy Slate), the head of a psychiatric institute, stops his crazed partner, Colin Ramzi (Danny Gochnauer), from indulging in nonregulation experiments. When Ramzi is through lobotomizing and formaldehyding his patients, he dumps them into a pit (hence the film's title). After giving the Frankenstein-like doctor a taste of his own medicine, Swan bricks him up behind cement walls and seals off the dead pit, but Ramzi vows to return with a vengeance. Flash forward 20 years: beautiful amnesiac Jane Doe (Cheryl Lawson) is admitted to Swan's asylum, whose occupants include deranged nun Clair (Geha Gertz), gentle neurotic Bud Higgins (Michael Jacobs), and overzealous demolitions expert Christian Meyers (Steffen Gregory Foster). During an earthquake (or a psychic rumbling), the sealed pit gets a considerable shaking. As it turns out, the upheaval is actually a response to the new patient, who claims her memory has been surgically removed, and who seems to be in psychic communication with the entombed Ramzi. (Later, during hypnotherapy, Jane remembers details from her childhood, including her mother's determination to keep her away from her father — guess who turns out to be the mystery papa.) On the loose once more, the mad Ramzi, with his satanic, glow-in-the-dark red eyes, has become a zombie master who feeds off Jane's energy and who can't wait to let his ghouls run amok through his former partner's institution. His first victim is a kindly nurse (Mara Everett), who is killed and made into one of the living dead. Shortly after her disappearance, the joint starts jumping: the normally pacific Bud attacks a male nurse and is locked in a padded cell, then is discovered to be mysteriously missing from this room. An orderly (Randy Fontana) trails Bud to the abandoned building housing the dead pit, where he finds the AWOL patient with a dental drill shoved into his eye socket, trips over the body of the nurse, and is bumped off by the red-eyed demon doctor. Under hypnosis, Jane reveals to Swan that Ramzi is indeed roaming around in an undead homicidal state; later, she enlists Christian's aid in a plan to visit the abandoned building and destroy the zombie shrink. Christian is caught by the staff, however, and Ramzi proceeds to chase Jane around the eerie medical facility, intending to make her his nurse. Meanwhile, as the patients grow restless at the loony bin, Christian escapes and rushes to rescue Jane. Ramzi, however, stares with his traffic-light eyes and raises the dead, who crawl out of the pit and begin their mission of mass murder on the institution's grounds, where, although the head nurse (Joan Bechtel) and several others get zombied to death, Christian manages to fight off a pack of the rather resourceful ghouls. Hiding out, Swan encounters Jane and Christian, relates his ex-partner's grisly past in flashback, and vows to personally rub Ramzi out for eternity. Nonetheless, it's Jane and Christian—having noticed that one zombie is terrified of the insane nun and that the good sister puts holy water to good use in zombie-elimination—who manage to rig a nearby water tower (after it's blessed by the nun) with explosives and spritz the dead pit. Although Swan is captured and killed by Ramzi and Christian gets blown up, the strategy essentially works. Afterwards, however, Jane makes the mistake of putting on the ring of her late, late father. Naturally, she gets that familiar, evil red look in her eyes.

As zombie-ramas go, DEAD PIT delivers the goods for gorehounds and manages to keep traditional horror buffs entertained, too. Unfortunately, while the lighting adds to the atmosphere of oozing evil and while the locations are used very well, the reactivated ghouls are too run-of-the-mill to terrify. Resembling fugitives from the colorized NIGHT OF THE LIVING DEAD, they amble along without creating any shudders—though there is some compensation in the fact that they move faster than your garden-variety zombie, and are an enterprising bunch capable of removing distributor caps from cars. More damaging, the cast leaves much to be desired. Slate's professionalism is reassuring and Gochnauer is hammily nasty as the resurrected surgeon-psychiatrist, but the other performers exhibit little panache. In the key role of the heroine, Lawson screams well, acts indifferently, and scowls petulantly whenever she is required to express terror. The supporting cast underplays or overplays, but never in any consistent ensemble style.

On the plus side, DEAD PIT is competently directed, unfolding with relative coherence and delivering its psychiatric horrors more or less straightforwardly (though there are also some welcome flashes of humor). What's missing is the intensity of suspense that might have given viewers the creepy crawlies; the film plays more as a series of funhouse thrills than a truly terrifying experience. Moreover, as in most contemporary horror movies, the screenplay sloppily leaves several questions unanswered. (For example, how did Ramzi remove Jane's memory surgically? Did he actually leave the dead pit to do it or did he perform some sort of psychic lobotomy?) Despite such flaws, however, DEAD PIT is wildly imaginative, particularly in its outrageous holy water tower denouement. With better structuring of the screenplay and some more inspired acting, it could have been first-rate; as it is, DEAD PIT is a moderately spine-tingling zombie shocker with enough ghoul attacks and gore to satisfy genre fans. (*Graphic violence, gore effects, profanity.*)

d, Brett Leonard; p, Gimel Everett and Dan Wyman; w, Brett Leonard and Gimel Everett; ph, Marty Collins; ed, Brett Leonard and Gimel Everett; art d, Ransom Rideout; spec, Ed Martinez

Horror   (PR:O   MPAA:R)

DEATH WARRANT

90m Mark DiSalle/MGM-UA c

Jean-Claude Van Damme *(Louis Burke)*, Robert Guillaume *(Hawkins)*, Cynthia Gibb *(Amanda Beckett)*, George Dickerson *(Attorney General Tom Vogler)*, Art LaFleur *(Sgt. DeGraff)*, Patrick Kilpatrick *(Christian Naylor, "The Sandman")*, Joshua Miller *(Douglas Tisdale)*, Hank Woessner *(Romaker)*, George Jenesky *(Konefke)*, Jack Bannon *(Ben Keane)*, and Abdul Salaam El Razzac *(Priest)*

In many respects, DEATH WARRANT, starring Jean-Claude Van Damme, resembles any number of "I've just fought 100 guys single-handedly and I'm still standing" action movies. Nevertheless, screenwriter David S. Goyer and director Deran Sarafian have produced an often suspenseful film. It opens with Detective Louis Burke (Van Damme) confronting a maniac called "the Sandman" (Patrick Kilpatrick) in an abandoned house. Although the Sandman nearly kills Burke, the detective manages to stop him with a bullet. Sixteen months later, Burke joins a task force put together by the governor to investigate a number of

murders that have occurred at the Harrison Penitentiary. While Burke poses as an inmate, attorney Amanda Beckett (Cynthia Gibb) acts the role of his wife. Like many screen couples, Burke and Beckett don't care for each other much in the beginning. In the penitentiary, Burke is forced to survive in an environment so dismal and filthy that it makes a public restroom in a New York City subway look like the Hilton. But though he is surrounded by hostility and suspicion, the undercover cop succeeds in befriending a few of the inmates, including Hawkins (Robert Guillaume) and Priest (Abdul Salaam El Razzac), who help him with the investigation. Meanwhile, more inmates are mysteriously murdered. Before you can say kick-boxing, Burke's cellmate is killed, and stone-faced prison guard DeGraff (Art LeFleur) puts Burke in solitary confinement, where he's interrogated and beaten. As if the insult and injury Burke endures were not enough, the Sandman ends up at Harrison. Several fight scenes later, it's revealed that prisoners are being murdered for their body organs. Back on the outside, Beckett attends a party given by Vogler (George Dickerson), the state's attorney general. Just as she's preparing to tell him about the slayings at the prison, Beckett receives a call from her computer whiz kid assistant, who identifies Vogler's henchman Keane (Jack Bannon) as the man behind the murders. The assistant's suspicions are confirmed when Vogler tries to kill Beckett. Meanwhile, Burke begins his great escape from the penitentiary, pursued by the Sandman and hundreds of angry inmates who have been set free and armed with the knowledge that Burke is a cop. As expected, Burke and the Sandman have a final, brutal showdown. Guess who wins and guess who ends up with Beckett in his arms.

Although DEATH WARRANT resorts to several familiar plot devices, its storyline is a little more complex than those of most films of this genre. Moreover, secondary characters like Hawkins and Priest are believable and likable enough that we care what happens to them. The film also offers some interesting visual effects. In particular, some skillful photography serves to emphasize the contrast between Beckett's life on the outside and Burke's dismal existence in prison. (*Excessive violence, profanity, adult situations.*)

d, Deran Sarafian; p, Mark DiSalle; w, David S. Goyer; ph, Russell Carpenter; ed, G. Gregg McLaughlin and John A. Barton; m, Gary Chang; prod d, Curtis Schnell; art d, Robert E. Lee; cos, Joseph Porro

Action   (PR:O   MPAA:R)

DEBT, THE

(Arg./Brit.) (SEE: VERONICO CRUZ)

DEF BY TEMPTATION

95m Bonded Filmworks-Orpheus/Troma c

James Bond III *(Joel)*, Kadeem Hardison *(K)*, Bill Nunn *(Dougy)*, Cynthia Bond *(Temptress)*, Minnie Gentry *(Grandma)*, Melba Moore *(Madam Sonya)*, Samuel L. Jackson, Rony Clanton, John Canada Terrell, Freddie Jackson, and Najee

A handsome bartender strikes up a conversation with a beautiful customer (Cynthia Bond); to his delight, she invites him to her place. The look of her apartment—candle-lit, dominated by a huge bed shrouded with gauzy curtains—leads him to expect an evening of exotic delights. Exotic it is: as they shower together the water suddenly turns to blood, and soon the bartender has been slashed to ribbons by his sexy date. Referred to only as the Temptress, this stunning beauty is an incarnation of pure evil. Resuming her place at the bar, she focuses her seductive charms on a succession of unwitting victims. More than anything, however, she wants to corrupt and destroy Joel (James Bond III), an aspiring minister. An orphan raised by his pious grandmother (Minnie Gentry), Joel doesn't realize that his father's death, many years earlier, was the result of a confrontation with the Temptress, and that it is his destiny to destroy her. The Temptress's depredations have not gone entirely unnoticed. Dougy (Bill Nunn), a renegade police detective, is on to her and plots her destruction, enlisting the aid of K (Kadeem Hardison), an actor who nearly succumbed to the charms of the Temptress. K is also Joel's best friend. Together, Dougy and K visit a psychic (Melba Moore), who explains that the Temptress is a supernatural being. Dougy and K then try to poison the demon with holy water but fail; though she writhes and drools, her powers remain intact. Dougy flees, only to find himself in a taxi with an unearthly creature; K is devoured by his television set. Meanwhile, the Temptress's determination to seduce and destroy Joel intensifies. She lures him to her lair, and it seems he will not be strong enough to fight her off. But the last minute appearance of his grandmother saves the day. Joel's and grandma's combined faith reduces the Temptress to a pool of slime.

Produced, written, and directed by first-time filmmaker James Bond III, who also stars as Joel, DEF BY TEMPTATION is a promising film. Its story is conventional and there are problems with the pacing—the whole business drags on far too long—but the accomplished visuals (cinematographer Ernest Dickerson's credits include Spike Lee's equally low-budget SHE'S GOTTA HAVE IT) and sure performances suggest that Bond is genuinely talented. Like many young filmmakers, he's at his best when depicting extreme situations; the Temptress's fatal seductions and the horrifying vision of a bar filled with her victims play flawlessly. However, Bond's expositional passages and those scenes intended to develop his characters are more uneven.

What may be most interesting about DEF BY TEMPTATION is that while Bond and his entire cast are African-Americans, the film resolutely avoids addressing the "Black Experience." It's just a horror picture: the menace is the Devil, not the devil of white oppression embodied in drug addicts and pushers, welfare mothers, pimps, and doomed youngsters trying to escape the claws of the ghetto—the only claws here are the Temptress's long, golden fingernails. While it may not be a virtue in and of itself that a young African-American filmmaker can make a film that is as shallow and commercially oriented as this one, DEF BY TEMPTATION does suggest Bond has the same chance of making it in the marketplace as any young filmmaker. *(Violence, profanity, sexual situations.)*

d, James Bond III; p, James Bond III; w, James Bond III; ph, Ernest Dickerson; ed, Li-Shin Yu; m, Paul Laurence; prod d, David Carrington; art d, Marc Henry Johnson; spec, Rob Benevides

Horror   (PR:C   MPAA:R)

DELTA FORCE 2

106m Globus-Pearce/MGM-UA c

Chuck Norris *(Col. Scott McCoy)*, Billy Drago *(Ramon Cota)*, John P. Ryan *(Gen. Taylor)*, Richard Jaeckel *(John Page)*, Begonia Plaza *(Quinquina)*, Paul Perri *(Maj. Bobby Chavez)*, Hector Mercado *(Miguel)*, Mark Margolis *(Gen. Olmedo)*, and Mateo Gomez

What would America do without enemies? Or, more to the point, what would American movies do without enemies? For one thing, the five people killed in a helicopter crash during the making of DELTA FORCE 2 might still be alive (the crash also seriously injured costars John Ryan and Mateo Gomez). After a flurry of lawsuits and amid depressingly familiar accusations of inadequate safety on the set, the film's stunt coordinator, Dean Ferrandini, was voted out of the International Stunt Association. And what was it all for? To present theaters and video stores with yet another boneheaded action epic noteworthy mostly for its shift of American right-wing political paranoia away from the Soviet Union and on to the Third World. Battles that were once fought over ideology are now fought over drugs. It's a tricky maneuver. Nobody ever had to convince American moviegoers that communism was bad. The Berlin Wall, after all, wasn't built to keep people out. But now the Wall is history, and the communist world is busily taking on a capitalist sheen. Illicit drugs are a different matter. Here is a commodity on which billions of American dollars are spent every year without so much as a nickel being allocated for promotion or advertising. Thus, it surely can be said of the drug war that we have met the enemy and they are us.

DELTA FORCE 2 doesn't ignore this irony. Its script merely soft-pedals it by putting this terse assessment of the drug problem into the mouth of the corrupt defense minister of the fictional South American country of San Carlos, where most of the action takes place. DELTA FORCE 2 actually opens in Argentina—not a fictional country, but one with a US extradition treaty—where DEA agents led by John Page (Richard Jaeckel) are trying to arrest San Carlos drug kingpin Ramon Cota (Billy Drago, best known for his portrayal of Frank Nitti in THE UNTOUCHABLES) during a Mardi Gras celebration. Of course, the agents arrest the wrong guy (after all, the opening credits still haven't ended). Cota's goons, meanwhile, ambush the DEA command post, killing everyone inside. Back in the States, the Delta Force, the elite Army squad formed (as shown in the first film) to combat Middle Eastern terrorism, is activated to arrest Cota in mid-air while a jet in which he is a passenger briefly enters American air space. Leading the Force is Chuck Norris, reprising his role as Col. Scott McCoy, who, along with best buddy Bobby Chavez (Paul Perri), carries off the arrest without a hitch. Freed on one of those all-purpose action-movie legal technicalities, Cota stays in the US just long enough to kill the wife and son of Chavez, Chavez having impulsively punched out Cota in the courtroom. In a blind fury, Chavez follows Cota back to San Carlos to kill him, only to be stopped within yards of his quarry by fellow agents, including Page, who are then captured by Cota's men. Not only does Cota torture and kill Chavez in an effort to obtain the name of the spy in Cota's midst who informed the Americans of his flight plans, but the drug kingpin also videotapes the whole grisly business to send to Chavez's Delta Force pals back in the US. They react by invading San Carlos to rescue Page and to destroy the country's cocaine industry. It's at this point that DELTA FORCE 2 gets into high gear. The actual rescue is handled by Norris—singlehandedly, of course—who scales a sheer cliff to get to Cota's compound, where the agents are being held. Meanwhile, Ryan, as Delta Force's General Taylor, and Gomez, as a hectoring San Carlos official, wing around the country in the ill-fated helicopter, blowing up rural villages that harbor cocaine refineries.

Under the direction of Aaron Norris (yes, Chuck's brother), the performances are largely superfluous to the boom-boom, stand-tall heroics. And that's a good thing. Chuck Norris' acting skills have not noticeably improved. He still has the dull, sullen screen presence of a baked potato. Oddly, he also disappears from the action for long stretches. But even performers who should know better and who are given more screentime offer little in the way of performances. Drago, especially, vamps his way through the film looking somewhat like Emo Phillips on a bad night. As if any more irony were needed, most of the best acting is done by Ryan and Gomez, who have an unexpected comic chemistry in their scenes together. To Aaron Norris' credit, the action moves along at a ferocious pace, never letting the plot's pile of implausibilities get in the way of well-staged battles and rescues. But despite these mitigating factors DELTA FORCE 2 remains yet another entry in a tiresome, retrograde genre, made even harder to watch by the realization that people died getting this tedious warmongering crud on the screen. *(Violence, profanity.)*

d, Aaron Norris; p, Yoram Globus and Christopher Pearce; w, Lee Reynolds (based on characters created by James Bruner, Menahem Golan); ph, Joao Fernandes; ed, Michael J. Duthie; m, Frederic Talgorn; prod d, Ladislav Wilheim; stunts, Dean Ferrandini; cos, Kady Dover

Action   (PR:C   MPAA:R)

DEMON WIND

97m Demon Wind—United Filmmakers/Prism c

Eric Larson *(Cory Harmon)*, Francine LaPensee *(Elaine)*, Mark David Fritsche *(Jack)*, Bobby Johnston *(Del)*, Jack Vogel *(Stacey)*, Lynn Clark *(Teri)*, Steven Quadros *(Chuck)*, Rufus Norris *(Harcourt)*, Richard Gabai *(Willie)*, Kym Sawtelle *(Harriet)*, Sherry Bendorf, Mia Ruiz, Stella Kastner, and Jake Jacobson

A direct-to-video gore carnival, DEMON WIND starts off with a couple of carloads of young adults driving to the country at the behest of their friend Cory (Eric Larson). It seems that most of his family vanished from their homestead in 1931, and when Cory's father investigated the disappearance a while back, he ended up an insane alcoholic. The kids arrive at the skeleton-strewn homestead and find it unnaturally preserved. Inside, one of the group (who obviously hasn't seen EVIL DEAD) reads aloud a bit of Satanic graffiti. That does it; a strange fog hems in the young visitors, and as night descends the landscape crawls with overacting zombies. Cory's girl friend, Elaine (Francine LaPensee), finds a diary that reveals that one of the area's original settlers was a devil worshiper, engaged in efforts to bring the Evil One to Earth. Although the settlers lynched the Satanist, demonic forces appeared and transformed the dead man's neighbors into zombies. Cory's grandmother, a good witch of some sort, was the last holdout; even now her residual spells hold back the zombies for a time, but they eventually *zombify* all the young interlopers except Cory and Elaine. At this point Satan (or his son; it's unclear) shows up, ready to rule the world. When this bald, misshapen geek confronts Cory, our hero turns into an odd-looking alien (reminiscent of a Skinhead from MONSTER HIGH's Planet Polyester). Cory punishes the Evil One for his crimes against humanity by kicking him in the groin. However, the Devil responds by making life more than miserable for Cory and Elaine before they read the last spell in the diary and incinerate their tormentor.

The major problem with DEMON WIND, apart from its existence in the first place, is its elimination of the only interesting characters early on. Jack Vogel and Steven Quadros play a pair of kung-fu-fighting, wise-cracking professional magicians who've come along on the expedition to use their mastery of illusion to fend off Satan. In the film's best scene, the two look out a window, see a topless showgirl beckoning them into the night, and, turning to each, announce in unison, "Demon." Alas, they go outside anyway, get slaughtered, and show up later among the horde of putty-faced walking dead, snarling tiresome one-liners a la Freddy Krueger. The rest of the cast includes the usual bunch of jocks, nerds, and banal types well-suited to be zombie chow.

Writer-director Charles Philip Moore shows some imagination, but in the end, the story simply gets away from him. What exactly is the creature that Cory becomes? Why didn't his grandmother's super-spell save her back in 1931? How many times can the protagonists die before it starts to affect their health? After a while the unanswered questions become to much to take. Moreover, while the makeup effects by Lance Anderson (THE SERPENT AND THE RAINBOW) emphasize decay, the actors overplay their evil zombies to an almost comical degree, dissipating the film's shock value. *(Profanity, nudity, excessive violence.)*

d, Charles Philip Moore; p, Michael Bennett and Paul Hunt; w, Charles Philip Moore; ph, Thomas Callaway; ed, Chris Roth; m, Bruce Wallenstein; prod d, Don Day; cos, Jan Rowton; makeup, Lance Anderson

Horror   (PR:O   MPAA:R)

DEMONSTONE

(Aus.) 93m International Film/Fries c

(AKA: HEARTSTONE)

R. Lee Ermey *(Maj. Joe Haines)*, Jan-Michael Vincent *(Andrew Buck)*, Nancy Everhard *(Sharon Gale)*, Pat Skipper *(Tony McKee)*, Peter Brown *(Admiral)*, Joonee Gamboa *(Sen. Belfardo/Chief Pirate)*, Rolando Tinio *(Prof. Olmeda)*, Noel Colet *(Esteban Belfardo)*, Edgar Santiago *(Nonoy Belfardo)*, Rey Malte-Cruz *(Roberto Belfardo)*, Monsour Del Rosario *(Pablo Belfardo)*, Jose Mari Avellana *(Han Chin)*, Rina Reyes *(Madeleine)*, Marilyn Bautista *(Julie)*, Crispin Medina *(Gen. Santos)*, Fred Bailey *(Navy Doctor)*, and Symon Soler *(R.J. Belfardo)*

A number of worthwhile plot elements are thrown haphazardly at the screen in DEMONSTONE, and few of them stick. At the center is the traditional horror-movie curse, cast 500 years before the main action of the story begins and depicted in flashback. A Filipino warlord played by Joonee Gamboa oversees the massacre of a cult headed by Chinese mystic Han Chin (Jose Mari Avellana), who swears with his dying breath that the warlord's clan will be wiped out. Flash forward to the present. Gamboa now portrays Senator Belfardo, a powerful Filipino gangster-politician whose high-placed relatives are being ritualistically murdered, their foreheads branded with the demonstone, a symbol of revenge. Belfardo suspects the rival Hong Kong underworld, but when a young US Marine, Tony McKee (Pat Skipper), is found at the scene of one slaughter, the corrupt senator sets him up as a scapegoat. Ex-Marine Andrew Buck (Jan-Michael Vincent), bounced out of the service for prying into Belfardo's crooked affairs, thinks McKee is innocent; so do viewers, who know that Buck's girl friend, TV reporter Sharon Gale (Nancy Everhard), is now possessed by the spirit of Han Chin. When McKee escapes from custody during an anti-American demonstration, Buck and base commander Maj. Joe Haines (R. Lee Ermey) try to find him. Meanwhile, the killings continue. Seized by Belfardo and his minions, the leathernecks are threatened with hideous death unless they produce the real murderer. But just when our heroes look like goners, Hong Kong mobsters attack, and during the ensuing gun battle, Buck and Haines escape, only to be pursued by a ruthless Filipino general. Needless to say, he, too, is related to Belfardo. In short order, a scream draws Buck and Haines to the general's bloody corpse, from which Gale, identified by McKee as the murderer, flees. That night Gale bursts into Belfardo's heavily defended mansion. Bullets barely affect her as she slays the rest of his clan, finally skewering the tyrant Belfardo with an ancient ceremonial sword. Only the senator's youngest son, a mere child, remains alive. When Buck appears on the grizzly scene, he pleads with Gale to spare the boy. She relents and exorcises the spirit of Han Chin the only way that she can, by killing herself.

DEMONSTONE might have worked better had it eschewed the supernatural stuff altogether and remained a straight action-thriller. Unlike a lot of potboilers shot in the Philippines, this one incorporates the volatile political climate of the country into the story. Hoping to parlay Filipino opposition to the US military presence into election to the presidency, Belfardo whips up anti-American sentiment among his countrymen by claiming that the Marines are harboring a Filipino-killing psycho. Meanwhile, he traffics in guns filched from the Yanks, and his underhanded dealings with the Pentagon brass make it possible for him to get away with everything. This potent premise is all the more powerful because, as Australians, the film's creators have no conspicuous patriotic axe to grind. But after the riot scene (highlighted by Haines's pep talk to the Marine defenders), the plot lapses into chases, gun battles, and enactments of Han Chin's revenge. Tellingly, John Trayne's original script was rewritten to deemphasize the oriental mysticism, which explains why the possessed Gale makes like Rambo, donning camouflage fatigues and automatic weapons—hardly the style one would expect from an ancient Eastern wraith.

Delicately pretty, Everhard is an unconventional avenger, but her character is so poorly drawn that it's frequently unclear when she is possessed and when she isn't. Ermey (who received an Oscar nomination for his performance in FULL METAL JACKET) and Vincent make a good ultra-macho team, although Ermey's tough-guy narration merely states the obvious. Newcomer Skipper makes the most of his supporting role and may be an actor to reckon with in the future.

Veteran film editor Andrew Prowse took over the project's directing chores when Brian Trenchard-Smith fell ill, but Prowse's considerable cutting-room experience doesn't appear to have helped him much with DEMONSTONE's plentiful action scenes, which leave something to be desired. The gun-toting heroes never miss, the bad guys never aim, and it's generally hard to tell what's going on, even during a basic fistfight.

Domestically, DEMONSTONE had a limited run in Nashville movie theaters before going the home-video route. It's likely, however, that the film will enjoy more success overseas, where Vincent is a major star due to his "Airwolf" TV series. *(Profanity, violence, adult situations, sexual situations.)*

d, Andrew J. Prowse; p, Antony I. Ginnane; w, John Trayne, David Phillips, and Frederick Bailey; ph, Kevan Lind; ed, Michael Thibault; m, Gary Stockdale; art d, Sammy Aranzamendez; set d, Fergus Martin; spec, Die-Aktion and Starr Jones; stunts, Pat Statham; makeup, Violy Puzon

Action/Horror   (PR:O   MPAA:R)

DESPERATE HOURS

106m Dino DeLaurentiis/MGM-UA c

Mickey Rourke *(Michael Bosworth)*, Anthony Hopkins *(Tim Cornell)*, Mimi Rogers *(Nora Cornell)*, Lindsay Crouse *(Chandler)*, Kelly Lynch *(Nancy Breyers)*, Elias Koteas *(Wally Bosworth)*, Mike Nussbaum *(Mr. Nelson)*, David Morse *(Albert)*, Shawnee Smith *(May Cornell)*, Danny Gerard *(Zack Cornell)*, Gerry Bamman *(Ed Tallent)*, Matt McGrath *(Kyle)*, John Christopher Jones *(Neff)*, Dean Norris *(Maddox)*, John Finn *(Lexington)*, Christopher Curry *(Chabon)*, Stanley White *(Devereaux)*, Peter Crombie *(Connelly)*, Ellen Parker *(Kate)*, Elizabeth Ruscio *(Judge)*, Kenneth Bass *(Repairman)*, Ellen McElduff *(Bank Teller)*, Brittney Lewis, Lise Wilburn *(College Girls)*, Ron Bird, Alexis Fernandez, Bob Evans *(Reporters)*, James Rebhorn *(Prosecutor)*, Michael Flynn *(Ornitz)*, Jeff Olson *(Coogan)*, Robert Condor *(Trooper)*, George Sullivan, Robert Rowe *(Snipers)*, Daniel Cussiter, Gary Flender, Richard Hernandez, Gary Parker, James Thornton *(SWAT Team)*, Bradley Leatham *(Police Detective)*, Brian James Anderson *(Coroner)*, and Matthew Rangi Brown *(Security Guard at Bank)*

This remake of the 1955 Humphrey Bogart thriller DESPERATE HOURS reunites director Michael Cimino and star Mickey Rourke, who last worked together on the so-bad-it's-good YEAR OF THE DRAGON. This time out, the result of their collaboration is merely bad, despite rich, painterly cinematography by Doug Milsome (FULL METAL JACKET), a driving score by David Mansfield, and a terrific cast. Regrettably, what that cast is called upon to do here is often downright embarrassing, especially for Kelly Lynch, Matt Dillon's alluring love interest in DRUGSTORE COWBOY, here haplessly cast as Rourke's "abuse" interest. Lynch plays Nancy Breyers, a lawyer who is inexplicably in love with client Michael Bosworth (Rourke), a simpering, sociopathic convict. During a parole hearing, Nancy sneaks a gun to Bosworth (because she has the weapon strapped to her thigh, Cimino has a chance to show Bosworth groping under her skirt—in close-up, of course). After Bosworth snaps a guard's neck (which provides the movie's first big laugh, considering the combatants' relative sizes), lawyer and client slip away down a fire escape, pausing only for Bosworth to rip open Nancy's blouse—again in close-up. (That bit of chivalry forces Nancy to wear her coat backwards when she hits the street. And since the street happens to be in Salt Lake City, one would think that a woman wearing her coat backwards would be conspicuous. But this is a Cimino film, so nobody bats an eye.) Only a friend of Nancy's impedes the escape, when she literally bumps into the lovesick lawyer, knocking her off her ultra-high heels, so that Bosworth has to leave Nancy behind. Joining his brother, Wally (Elias Koteas), and their partner, the hulking, half-witted Albert (David Morse), Bosworth goes screeching off into the sunset. Needing a hideout until Nancy can catch up with them, the three settle on the home of Tim (Anthony Hopkins) and Nora (Mimi Rogers) Cornell, who have a young son, Zack (Danny Gerard), and nubile daughter, May (Shawnee Smith). Bosworth is attracted to the house because the "For Sale" sign out front indicates to him a home in trouble. He's right; Tim and Nora are in the process of getting a divorce, but why that makes them desirable victims is never made clear. However, it's hard to quibble with the gimmick that brings Rogers and Hopkins into the film, since their performances come close to redeeming this dismal fiasco. Rogers succeeds in the tougher assignment, making Nora compelling even though she is yet another basically brainless Cimino female. But Hopkins steals the movie, putting a venomous spin on each line of his typically boneheaded Ciminoesque dialog (credited, in part, to Lawrence Konner and Mark Rosenthal, who reportedly quit the film's production over "creative differences" with Cimino).

While Bosworth and his buddies are fooling around with the Cornells, FBI agent Chandler (Lindsay Crouse) takes charge of the manhunt. She's the only woman in the film who can think and walk at the same time, so, this being a Cimino film, she's made to look like a wig-wearing man and is given dialog that would be more at home in SMOKEY AND THE BANDIT. Crouse, nonetheless, manages to have some fun with her wily backwoods character, babbling about "goin' tactical," which means that she lets her gung-ho underlings use the Cornell house for target practice. This being a Cimino film, Bosworth eventually becomes the bull's eye.

DESPERATE HOURS is silly from start to finish, but its biggest laugh comes during the end credits, which list an entire staff of credibility consultants. Of course, the joke is that DESPERATE HOURS isn't credible for a single second. Despite the involvement of a "hostage negotiations" consultant, the film's negotiations consist solely of Bosworth screaming into a phone for 10 seconds to demand a car, a plane, and a bag of money. Didn't he ever see DOG DAY

AFTERNOON? More to the point, has Cimino ever seen it? In DESPERATE HOURS credibility gives way to contrivance. Instead of negotiating further, Chandler sends Nancy into the Cornell house to lure Bosworth and his brother out (Albert has already bitten more than his share of bullets while trying to escape). Neither a professional at this sort of thing nor very stable emotionally at the moment, Nancy seems like an unlikely candidate for this assignment. But, this being a Cimino film, it's numbingly obvious that the sole reason Nancy is reintroduced into the action is so that Bosworth can again rip her blouse open.

After so many years and so many bad films, it has become clear that Cimino is simply in over his head, that perhaps he would be better off as a second-unit director. As in other Cimino films, individual scenes throughout DESPERATE HOURS are well-staged, especially the chases and stuntwork. But, taken as a whole, the film is dragged down by the same old incoherent plotting and characters, driven by the same old half-baked machismo and mealy-mouthed misogyny that have come to define Cimino the *auteur*. As a result, and despite the efforts of Rogers and Hopkins, DESPERATE HOURS is more than a title; it's a description of a movie-going experience. *(Profanity, violence, sexual violence, adult situations.)*

d, Michael Cimino; p, Dino DeLaurentiis and Michael Cimino; w, Lawrence Konner, Mark Rosenthal, and Joseph Hayes (based on the novel, screenplay, and stage play by Hayes); ph, Doug Milsome; ed, Peter Hunt; m, David Mansfield; prod d, Victoria Paul; art d, Patricia Klawonn; set d, Tom Lindblom; spec, Make Up & Effects Labs, Inc., Allan A. Apone, and Thomas L. Fisher; stunts, Billy Burton; cos, Charles DeCaro; makup, Ed Ternes, Alberto Fava, and Robert James Mills; tech, Stanley White, Ray Birge, Oksana Bihum, and Harvey Giss

Thriller   (PR:O   MPAA:R)

DETECTIVE KID, THE

(SEE: GUMSHOE KID, THE)

DICK TRACY

103m Silver Screen Partners IV/Touchstone-Buena Vista c

Warren Beatty *(Dick Tracy)*, Charlie Korsmo *(Kid)*, Glenne Headly *(Tess Trueheart)*, Madonna *(Breathless Mahoney)*, Al Pacino *(Big Boy Caprice)*, Dustin Hoffman *(Mumbles)*, William Forsythe *(Flattop)*, Charles Durning *(Chief Brandon)*, Mandy Patinkin *(88 Keys)*, Paul Sorvino *(Lips Manlis)*, R.G. Armstrong *(Pruneface)*, Dick Van Dyke *(DA Fletcher)*, Seymour Cassel *(Sam Catchem)*, James Keane *(Pat Patton)*, Allen Garfield, John Schuck, Charles Fleischer *(Reporters)*, James Tolkan *(Numbers)*, Kathy Bates *(Mrs. Green)*, Catherine O'Hara *(Texie Garcia)*, Henry Silva *(Influence)*, James Caan *(Spaldoni)*, Bert Remsen *(Bartender)*, Frank Campanella *(Judge Harper)*, Michael J. Pollard *(Bug Bailey)*, Estelle Parsons *(Mrs. Trueheart)*, Mary Woronov *(Welfare Person)*, Henry Jones *(Night Clerk)*, Mike Mazurki *(Old Man at Hotel)*, Michael Donovan O'Donnell *(McGillicuddy)*, Jim Wilkey *(Stooge)*, Stig Eldred *(Shoulders)*, Neil Summers *(The Rodent)*, Chuck Hicks *(The Brow)*, Lawrence Steven Meyers *(Little Face)*, Ed O'Ross *(Itchy)*, Marvelee Cariaga *(Soprano)*, Michael Gallup *(Baritone)*, Robert Costanzo *(Lips' Bodyguard)*, Jack Kehoe *(Customer at Raid)*, Marshall Bell *(Lips' Cop)*, Michael G. Hagerty *(Doorman)*, Lew Horn *(Lefty Moriarty)*, Arthur Malet *(Diner Patron)*, Tom Signorelli *(Mike)*, Tony Epper *(Steve, the Tramp)*, Jack Goode Jr., Ray Stoddard *(Lab Technicians)*, Hamilton Camp *(Store Clerk)*, Ed McCready, Colm Meaney *(Cops at Tess')*, Robert Beecher *(Ribs Mocca)*, Sharmagne Leland-St. John, Bing Russell *(Club Ritz Patrons)*, Tom Finnegan *(Uniform Cop at Ritz)*, Billy Clevenger *(Newspaper Vendor)*, Ned Claflin, John Moschitta Jr., Neil Ross, Walker Edmiston *(Radio Announcers)*, Ian Wolfe *(Forger)*, Rita Bland, Lada Boder, Dee Hengstler, Liz Imperio, Michelle Johnston, Karyne Ortega, and Karen Russell *(Dancers)*

The most publicized film of 1989 (perhaps of all time) was easily BATMAN. You couldn't go into a store or walk down the street without seeing some form of BATMAN merchandise—T-shirts, bedsheets, mugs, bumperstickers, and the like; the BATMAN logo was everywhere. In 1990, it seemed the DICK TRACY logo was everywhere. Once again, coffee cups and hats were dedicated to the selling of the film, but to add to the merchandising, and in lieu of BATMAN's built-in audience, DICK TRACY also had the always controversial and mysterious (at least to the press) Warren Beatty as its creator and star. And so the push began, fueled by Beatty's persona. The film was touted as Beatty's "comeback" after the disastrous ISHTAR, its budget was rumored to change practically every day, it featured mystery stars who would make cameos under heavy make-up, and, of course, the film was to costar Madonna—whose album *I'm Breathless* was released to coincide with the movie's release, and who was not only the most popular music star in the world, but, to pique interest, was reportedly the latest of Beatty's many romantic conquests. Comic-book aficionados could hardly wait; Beatty fans were excited (and Beatty-haters were rooting for another flop);

and Disney executives, unsure of the outcome, held their breath. Although the merchandising and publicity were relatively tame compared with the BATMAN onslaught—with the exception of one ingenious nationwide publicity stunt that required patrons to purchase a DICK TRACY T-shirt in order to be admitted to a sneak preview of the film, a great example of killing two birds with one stone—DICK TRACY remained the most highly touted, eagerly awaited movie of 1990.

All this hype and press surrounding the release of the film was absolutely necessary, considering the content of the movie itself. Although DICK TRACY is visually breathtaking, it's never very thrilling, suspenseful, or exciting, and it's surprisingly cold. Despite its mass-culture origins, it is a weirdly personal film, which plays more like a character study than a comic-book adventure. However, nothing less should have been expected from Beatty, who continues to make films for personal reasons, films that are not necessarily conceived as "entertainments"—a commendable choice that may not please studios, but is quite refreshing. Here, in adapting the Chester Gould comic-book character, Beatty has removed all personality from Tracy and surrounded him with supporting characters who are much more flamboyant, but just as soulless. The result is a film that, like much of Beatty's other work, is about people searching for identity and stability, about imposed reputations and expected behavior. In other words, it's about Warren Beatty.

The story, which is told with wild changes in tone and pace, takes place in a strikingly stylized comic-book city of the 30s. Handsome, hardworking detective Dick Tracy is hot on the trail of bad guy Big Boy Caprice (played with astonishing energy by Al Pacino), who has taken the entire underworld syndicate of the city away from Lips Manlis (Paul Sorvino). After killing Lips, taking over his nightclub, and stealing his girl friend, Breathless Mahoney (Madonna), Big Boy comes up with the idea of uniting all the villains in town under his leadership, thereby running the city. This idea doesn't sit well with Tracy, who, having gotten so close to nabbing Big Boy in the past, won't let him get away this time. With the help of his trusty two-way wristwatch radio and of his police department, Tracy puts his counterplan into action. But while Tracy flourishes professionally (after planting a microphone in Big Boy's office, he successfully raids Big Boy's businesses and arrests several culprits), his personal life is a shambles. "Adopting" a young orphan known only as the Kid (Charlie Korsmo, who was so good in MEN DON'T LEAVE) burdens the bachelor with unneeded responsibilities, and though Tracy and his girl friend, Tess Trueheart (Glenne Headly), love each other very much, his dedication to duty prevents them from settling down and getting married. To complicate things further, Breathless has been tempting Dick with lustful come-ons that not only jeopardize his relationship with Tess, but threaten his life as well. Tracy becomes torn between the fervent advances of Breathless and the stability represented by the Kid and Tess. It's not long before Big Boy (who himself is being manipulated by a mysterious villain with no face, called the Blank) puts into effect a plan to frame Tracy for murder, resulting in Dick's being thrown in jail. Meanwhile, the Blank kidnaps Tess and brings her to Big Boy's club with the intent of framing Big Boy. When Dick (who has been released by his coworkers) and the police arrive, Big Boy, who has no knowledge of the abduction, appears to be the kidnaper. Panic-stricken, Big Boy flees with Tess and is pursued by Dick and the Kid to a bridge, where a final confrontation involving Dick, Big Boy, and the faceless villain takes place. The film ends with Tracy and his "family" (the Kid has taken the name Dick Tracy, Jr.) eating dinner in a restaurant. Just as Tracy is about to ask Tess to marry him, he receives a summons on his trusty wrist-radio and is off to work once more. However, as he and Dick, Jr., leave, the detective-hero tosses an engagement ring to Tess, who accepts it and his offer of marriage.

Never less than astounding visually, and impeccably edited and mounted, Beatty's DICK TRACY is an exceedingly well-made film, but it lacks life and dimension; it seems to search for a tone and personality, while the audience is left unable to identify with or care about the characters. However, this seems to be Beatty's desired effect. DICK TRACY is a film *about* soullessness, about having no identity and searching for stability, and it's natural for Beatty's *mise-en-scene* to reflect the theme. From the opening shot of the famous fedora and badge to the wildly extravagant long sweeps of the matte-painted comic-book city, DICK TRACY has a disturbingly hollow look. It's the first film to transfer successfully the look of a comic book to the screen (kudos to Vittorio Storaro, whose striking photography makes wonderful use of primary colors) in an entirely cinematic way (Beatty's use of montage is particularly brilliant).

The movie's shifting mood is matched by the weird array of characters, all of whom are hopelessly confused. The inhabitants of Beatty's world seem a procession of psychological case studies. Tracy is a boring shell of a man, never once excited, scared, or nervous, who robotically operates only to stop "bad guys" and has no time for anyone else, not even himself. The Kid, who remains otherwise nameless for most of the film, is a homeless drifter whose only purpose seems to be chasing after Tracy. Tess, too, drifts aimlessly between a life dominated by her mother (Estelle Parsons) and a life dictated by Tracy's career. The villains—played by actors in grotesque make-up—are even more dysfunctional. Big Boy is a hunchbacked outcast desperately trying to earn respect and, as played by Pacino, a character whose constant quotes from Nietzsche, Thomas Jefferson, and others reveal his search for something to say—and he usually gets the quotes wrong. Madonna's Breathless Mahoney (whose musical numbers provide the film's only major distractions) is probably the most interesting character, a woman who's locked into a nasty life and an unwanted reputation. The remaining members of this gallery of the grim include Mumbles (Dustin Hoffman), a timid creature who can't even talk; 88 Keys (Mandy Patinkin), a cabaret pianist whose loyalties shift nightly; DA Fletcher (refreshingly played by Dick Van Dyke), a corrupt government official; and various other outcasts and weirdos. But perhaps the most striking element of the film is the Blank, a character so devoid of personality that he operates in the shadows, without a natural voice and without a face. This soulless being—a nonentity whose defeat clears the way for the evolution of Tracy's own personality—becomes the film's ultimate visual image.

The only common feature among all of these characters is a strange, almost obsessive love for food—which is photographed with wild delight. Whether it's a close-up of a can of chili or a perfectly composed long shot of a tray of muffins, food seems to be DICK TRACY's main leitmotif (during one montage, the phrase "When do we eat?" is essentially used as a repeated plea from the Kid for love), and it proves the only way to tell one character from another. (Mumbles has a yen for water, Lips likes oysters, and Big Boy loves walnuts: "They're good for the liver!") But food is a biological need, not an emotion, and it's emotion that these characters truly crave.

The performances are all fairly interesting. Hoffman's cameo is creepy and surprisingly funny, Headly and Korsmo are terrific, and Beatty is mesmerizingly hollow. The true star of this film, however, is Pacino, who provides the only true "entertainment" in the movie with his wildly over-the-top performance as Big Boy—in many ways he out-Jokers Jack Nicholson's Joker in BATMAN. Ranting and raving like a lunatic (the scene in which he discovers the audio bug in his office is priceless) and creating a thoroughly fascinating villain, Pacino is excellent and earned a Best Supporting Oscar nomination for his work.

Instead of concentrating on the action of the story, or even the possibility of some lively, flamboyant performances, Beatty scales things down to personal conflict. Tracy wants to settle down in marriage and domesticity with Tess, with the Kid completing the family unit, but he must first acquire his own identity by destroying the symbolic Blank, and that is the true focus of the film. Unfortunately, this focus—too abstract a confrontation to interest youngsters and never handled with enough flair to hide the lack of action—is too "interesting" to be lively. Ultimately, DICK TRACY is a bold, personal, and incredibly beautiful film that is likely to infuriate many of its viewers. It's not entertaining in the usual sense, but it's a truly original vision, that of a headstrong director-star who intelligently studies his own persona and confidently displays his conclusions with $30-million vigor. In addition to Pacino's Academy Award nomination, the film won Oscars for its makeup and the song "Sooner or Later (I Always Get My Man)" (Stephen Sondheim), and earned nominations for its art direction, cinematography, costumes, and sound. (Mild violence, adult situations.)

d, Warren Beatty; p, Warren Beatty; w, Jim Cash and Jack Epps Jr. (based on characters created by Chester Gould); ph, Vittorio Storaro; ed, Richard Marks; m, Danny Elfman; prod d, Richard Sylbert; art d, Harold Michelson; set d, Rick Simpson, James J. Murakami, Eric Orbom, and Henry Alberti; spec, Buena Vista Visual Effects Group, John Caglione Jr., and Doug Drexler; stunts, Billy Burton; cos, Milena Canonero; makeup, Cheri Minns and Kevin Haney; chor, Jeffrey Hornaday; anim, Allen Gonzales and Sanuel Recinos

Adventure/Comedy   (PR:A-C   MPAA:PG)

DIE HARD 2

124m Gordon-Silver/FOX c

(AKA: DIE HARDER)

Bruce Willis *(John McClane)*, Bonnie Bedelia *(Holly McClane)*, William Atherton *(Dick Thornberg)*, Reginald VelJohnson *(Al Powell)*, Franco Nero *(Gen. Ramon Esperanza)*, William Sadler *(Col. Stuart)*, John Amos *(Capt. Grant)*, Dennis Franz *(Carmine Lorenzo)*, Art Evans *(Barnes)*, Fred Dalton Thompson *(Trudeau)*, Tom Bower *(Marvin)*, Sheila McCarthy *(Samantha Copeland)*, Don Harvey *(Garber)*, Tony Ganios *(Baker)*, Peter Nelson *(Thompson)*, Robert Patrick *(O'Reilly)*, Michael Cunningham *(Sheldon)*, John Leguizamo *(Burke)*, Tom Verica *(Kahn)*, John Costelloe *(Cochrane)*, Vondi Curtis Hall *(Miller)*, Mark Boone Junior *(Shockley)*, Ken Baldwin *(Mulkey)*, Danny Weselis, Gregg Kovan, Don Charles McGovern, Vincent Joseph Mazzella Jr., Jeff Langton, Danial Donai, Bob "Rocky" Cheli, Dale Jacoby *(Blue Light Team)*, Pat O'Neal *(Cpl. Telford)*, Ben Lemon *(Sergeant)*, Jason Ross-Azikiwe *(Second Sergeant)*, Anthony Droz *(Soldier)*, Michael Francis Clarke *(Northeast Plane Pilot)*, Steve Pershing *(Northeast Plane Copilot)*, Tom Everett *(Northeast Plane Navigator)*, Sherry Bilsing, Karla Tamburrelli *(Northeast Plane Stewardesses)*, Jeanne Bates *(Older Woman)*, Colm Meaney *(Windsor Plane Pilot)*, Steffen

Gregory Foster *(Windsor Plane Copilot)*, James Lancaster *(Windsor Plane Navigator)*, Amanda Hillwood, Felicity Waterman *(Windsor Plane Stewardesses)*, Alan Berger *(Windsor Plane Passenger)*, Jessica Gardner *(Little Girl)*, Vance Valencia *(Foreign Military Plane Pilot)*, Gilbert Garcia *(Foreign Military Plane Copilot)*, Julian Reyes *(Young Corporal)*, Richard Domeier *(TV Cameraman)*, David Katz *(TV Soundman)*, Robert Lipton *(Chopper Pilot)*, Robert Steinberg *(Victor)*, Paul Abascal *(TV Director)*, John Rubinow *(TV Producer)*, Bob Braun, Dominque Jennings, Carol Barbee *(TV Newscasters)*, Jerry E. Parrott, Robert Sacchi, Edward Gero, Robert J. Bennett, Jim Hudson, Thomas Tofel, Wynn Irwin, Ken Smolka, Martin Lowery, Dick McGarvin, Stafford Morgan, Nick Angotti, Tom Finnegan, Earl Bullock, Rande Scott *(Engineers)*, Robert Costanzo *(Vito Lorenzo)*, Lauren Letherer *(Rent-A-Car Girl)*, Connie Lillo-Thieman *(Information Booth Girl)*, Ed DeFusco *(Morgue Worker)*, Charles Lanyer *(Justice Man)*, Bill Smillie *(Custodian)*, Dwayne Hargray *(Luggage Worker)*, John Cade *(Lobby Cop)*, Paul Bollen, Joseph Roth *(Airport Cops)*, and David Willis Sr. *(Tow Truck Driver)*

It's always nice to discover a filmmaker who comes out of nowhere, whose work is unexpectedly good, and whose future seems bright. One such discovery is Finnish director Renny Harlin, who burst onto the scene in 1988 with A NIGHTMARE ON ELM STREET PART 4: THE DREAM MASTER, which turned out to be not only the most imaginative entry of the series, but also the most profitable. Although it was already Harlin's third film (following the bleak actioner BORN AMERICAN [1986] and the terrific B chiller PRISON [1987]), he became known as a hot "newcomer" after NIGHTMARE 4's release, and was barraged with offers and scripts as Hollywood's latest young "genius" director: quite a step up for a man who came to America in 1984 with only 20 rough minutes of BORN AMERICAN in tow, hoping to find financing to finish the picture. Producers liked the fact that he could make a quality film on a low budget, and make it good enough to turn a profit. One of the impressed big shots was Joel Silver, the powerful producer of such popular action films as LETHAL WEAPON; 48 HRS.; and ROADHOUSE, who offered Harlin a lucrative deal devised to turn Harlin into a new Walter Hill (director of such action classics as THE WARRIORS; THE DRIVER; and 48 HRS.). Under that deal, the first film to be directed by Harlin was the Andrew Dice Clay vehicle, THE ADVENTURES OF FORD FAIRLANE, to be followed by the sequel to one of Silver's most successful films, DIE HARD.

To make a sequel to a low-budget slasher film is one thing, but to direct the follow-up to a massively successful, big-budget blockbuster like DIE HARD is another, and some, feeling that the director from Helsinki was just a fluke, believed Harlin was simply not up to the task. After seeing the amount of craftsmanship on display in DIE HARD 2, however, no one should question Harlin's talent again. DIE HARD 2 is not only better than the original, it is simply one of the most exciting action films in years, spectacularly put together. Renny Harlin is no fluke. He may very well be the new Walter Hill after all.

Picking up a year after the terrorist high-rise takeover in DIE HARD, DIE HARD 2 takes place at Dulles International Airport outside of Washington, DC. It is Christmas Eve, and in addition to the usual holiday crowds, the airport is also expecting a "guest" from another country: a South American dictator named Esperanza (Franco Nero) who has been accused of drug smuggling and is being brought to America for trial. Reporters are everywhere, but security seems light for such a busy evening, making things easier for the unit of terrorists who are planning to virtually shut down the airport, intercept the dictator's incoming flight, and free him. Led by maniacal former US military colonel Stuart (William Sadler), the group puts its plan into effect. First they take over an old church near the airport runways and set up headquarters there. Next, they cut the power at the airport's control tower and intercept all radio transmissions to and from the planes. Now the air traffic is incredibly heavy (the sky full of circling planes with nowhere to land and dwindling fuel supplies, pilots kept in the dark about what is happening on the ground), the weather conditions are dangerous, and the terrorists are the air traffic controllers. Their demands are simple: let Esperanza's plane land safely and allow the dictator and terrorist group to leave the country on a fully fueled 747. If these demands are not met (and if the airport tries to make radio contact with the planes overhead), the terrorists will pick a circling plane at random and direct it to "land"—into the ground. The situation looks hopeless and the plan looks like it might even work, but there's one factor the terrorists didn't expect: John McClane (Bruce Willis). McClane, you'll recall, was the smart-ass New York cop who saved his estranged wife and other hostages from a group of terrorists who took over the Nakatomi high-rise in Los Angeles. Since then he has reunited with his wife, Holly (Bonnie Bedelia), and moved to LA, where he is a successful cop. As it happens, McClane is now at Dulles, waiting for Holly's flight. It's already been a busy night: in addition to having had his car towed and having been recognized by the press (as "the Nakatomi hero"), McClane has noticed some strange things going on in the airport. After following two suspicious-looking men into the baggage loading area, he finds himself in the middle of a shootout and winds up killing one man. Lambasted by Lorenzo (the terrific Dennis Franz), the airport police captain, and nearly kicked out of the airport, McClane launches his own investigation. With the help of a strange little custodian (Tom Bower), a FAX machine, and his partner back in LA (Reginald Veljohnson), McClane discovers the identity of one of the men in the shootout and deduces that he is part of a terrorist organization. No one listens to McClane until it's too late, however, and the terrorists take control and prove their sincerity by crashing a plane full of people. Now it's up to McClane and the rest of the authorities (among them Fred Dalton Thompson and Art Evans as air traffic controllers and John Amos as the leader of a counter-terrorist unit) to stop the terrorists and save the rest of the circling planes—including the one Holly is on—before they run out of fuel and/or crash. This unlikely situation again has McClane squeezing his way through air ducts and sliding down poles, as well as blazing around on a snowmobile, hanging from the wing of a moving 747, and, in one incredible sequence, flying through the air in an ejector seat catapulting away from an exploding plane. He has again become the reluctant hero.

Although DIE HARD 2, like the original, suffers from a weak script, it succeeds in every other aspect. DIE HARD was extremely well-made and supremely exciting, but it couldn't disguise its nasty core—the film was full of blatant stereotypes (the dumb authority figures and wicked foreigners) and had a shallow subtext (blaming Holly's professional success for the failure of the McClanes' marriage and portraying technology as simply mindless). However, John McTiernan (THE HUNT FOR RED OCTOBER) directed DIE HARD with such a strong hand that these cliches were not only forgivable, they became enjoyable. DIE HARD 2's script (by Steven de Souza, who cowrote the original, and Doug Richardson), while not as narrow in tone and attitude as DIE HARD, tries so desperately to duplicate that film's style that it creates a forced, entirely familiar atmosphere that threatens to plunge DIE HARD 2 into pure formula. The sequel features the same idiotic authorities (represented this time by Franz, Amos, and, repeating his idiot duties from the first film, William Atherton as a heartless reporter), reprised key plot developments (all the way down to the discovery of a walkie-talkie), and duplicated sequences from the first film. All of this rehashing is accompanied by dialog acknowledging the repetition (Willis arrives in a steamy boiler room to complain, "Another elevator, another base-ment...How can the same shit happen to the same guy twice?!"). It's a gimmick that's initially amusing, but quickly becomes tedious.

However, what de Souza and Richardson lack in story and character invention, they more than make up for in imaginative action situations. By setting the film at an airport (but not confining it to that single location) they have created endless possibilities for great set pieces and exciting scenes. The script is jammed with creatively thought-out action sequences that, as directed by Harlin, range from terrific to absolutely breathtaking in their effectiveness. Keeping Willis' tenden-cies toward annoying smugness under control and handling the special effects with ease, Harlin displays enormous confidence and a tremendously natural filmmaking technique. With exquisite framing and a sharp cutting style, Harlin is a director of remarkable assurance—which makes for some incredibly exciting footage. DIE HARD 2 is jam-packed with wonderful moments, especially the standout sequence in which a SWAT team is ambushed by terrorists in a partially constructed hallway. At the center of the hallway is a long moving sidewalk with ladders and scaffolds on either side. The SWAT team rides the moving conveyor belt into the ambush and a huge shootout ensues. McClane arrives on the scene—via an air duct, in the first film's style—and the sequence ends with McClane, about to be shot by the last terrorist, reaching for his gun as it moves toward him on the conveyor belt. This sequence alone is worth the price of admission; Harlin makes use of every object in the scene (the belt, the scaffolds, the bullet casings, even the grating of the air duct) and shoots and cuts it all together with amazing skill. Combining a wonderful use of slow motion (as when Willis rolls across the floor firing his weapon, or when a terrorist is shot and crashes through a sheet of glass) and a potent use of long takes with minimal cutting (Harlin's action sequences contain seemingly fewer edits than his dra-matic setups), the scene is a visceral masterpiece that stands as one of the finest bits of gunplay ever filmed. (Richard Donner, the director of the wildly overrated LETHAL WEAPON and its sequel, should study it frame by frame.)

From beginning to end DIE HARD 2 is a pleasure to watch, triumphing over its script's weaknesses with fun performances (especially from Franz and Amos), with Oliver Wood's richly dark photography, reminiscent of BORN AMERI-CAN, and with lightning pace. Fans of the original DIE HARD will not be disappointed, and although admirers of Willis should note that his performance here is much more subdued, with considerably fewer wisecracks, the sequel is often quite humorous. DIE HARD 2 is a knockout action film, a brainless good time, and solid Hollywood entertainment. That it is also one of the most technically proficient films of the year makes its achievement all the more impressive, if not astounding. Harlin has displayed talent in the past, but none of his films has come close to the quality of DIE HARD 2, in which his love of the medium shines in every frame. His style has matured, although he has not disowned his other, less high-profile films; indeed, he incorporates direct refer-ences to both NIGHTMARE 4 and BORN AMERICAN into his setting here. DIE HARD 2 may not earn Harlin respect among more "serious" viewers (even

though the filmmaking skill on display here would never be found in a Woody Allen film, for example), but it is nonetheless a brilliantly done movie that action fans will eat up, and cinemaphiles will adore. *(Excessive violence, profanity, adult situations, brief nudity.)*

d, Renny Harlin; p, Lawrence Gordon, Joel Silver, and Charles Gordon; w, Steven E. de Souza and Doug Richardson (based on the novel *58 Minutes* by Walter Wager and on original characters by Roderick Thorp); ph, Oliver Wood; ed, Stuart Baird and Robert A. Ferretti; m, Michael Kamen; md, Michael Kamen; prod d, John Vallone; art d, Christiaan Wagener; set d, Eric Orbom, Sally Thorton, Nick Navarro, Paul McKenzie, and Carol Bentley; spec, Al DiSarro, Industrial Light & Magic, Tom Burman, and Bari Dreiband-Burman; stunts, Charles Picerni; cos, Marilyn Vance-Straker; makup, Scott H. Eddo; tech, Jerry Parrott

Action   **(PR:O   MPAA:R)**

DISTURBANCE, THE

81m Cerasuola—Deibele—House—AFT/VidAmerica c

Timothy Greeson *(Clay Moyer)*, Lisa Geoffrion *(Susan)*, Ken Ceresne *(Frank Moyer)*, Carole Garlin *(Maureen Moyer)*, Jerry Disson *(Dr. Dressler)*, John George *(Detective Redus)*, Nina Mazey *(Head Nurse)*, Jackie Sparke, Frank Pena, Ken Mullinix, Cindy Million, Kim Woodruff, Shane Anderson, and Joel Jacob

Imagine, somewhere out there in the universe, a roving swarm of horror-movie special effects in search of a plot—any plot, no matter how insubstantial. This plot opens on a beach, where Susan (Lisa Geoffrion), a pretty waitress, unac-countably falls for Clay (Timothy Greeson), a young man intently building sand castles. Actually Clay is a 27-year-old mental hospital outpatient living with his parents, and even great sex with Susan fails to cure him of his affliction: recurring visions of a demon and of himself murdering submissive women. As Clay's behavior becomes more aberrant, he alienates Susan. After losing his menial job, Clay staggers home to find he has run out of Thorazine, allowing the filmmakers to indulge in loads of is-this-a-dream-or-is-it-real? sequences as Clay is over-whelmed by macabre delusions. When Clay begs Susan to return to him, she refuses. Nevertheless, Clay tells his folks to expect his girl friend for dinner that night. Instead the police appear to arrest Clay for Susan's murder. After slitting his wrists, Clay is taken to the hospital, from which he escapes—pursued by the cops, the demon, and visions of bloody, naked women. In Susan's apartment, where Clay seeks refuge, he is haunted by a hallucination of Susan's mutilated corpse. Forced to remember that he stabbed her after she rejected him, Clay also apparently realizes that he has killed the other women in his visions. The tormented wretch then rushes toward a squad of police, leaving them no option but to shoot him. As the viewer ponders the horror, the misery, the insanity of it all, a final credit appears onscreen: "Filmed Entirely on Location in Sunny South Florida."

While filmmaking in the Sunshine State has progressed technically since the days of DEATH CURSE OF TARTU (1968), there is still room for improvement if this film is any indication. There's no real theme, no hint of characterization, and only the faintest excuse for a plot. Did Clay really kill the other women? Is some supernatural agency at work? Whence comes the demon? At least the last question can be partly answered: the demon came from the makeup lab of effects artist Barry Anderson (DAY OF THE DEAD; THE UNHOLY), who uses the film's slim story as an excuse to display a profusion of ghastly wounds. Director Cliff Guest has gained some notoriety for his music videos, notably for Madonna's "True Blue," which bears little resemblance to this film. Still, Guest doesn't hesitate to provide THE DISTURBANCE with a number of good-time tunes, including "Baby, Won't You Be My Baby" (by Stark Naked), "Baby, Can You Rock Me" "Spark in My Heart,"and "Caught up in Your Love" (Joel Jacob and Paul Pettit). *(Profanity, graphic violence, excessive nudity, sexual situa-tions.)*

d, Cliff Guest; p, Ron Cerasuola and Cliff Guest; w, Laura Radford (based on a story by David Benjamin, Ron Cerasuola); ph, Angel Gracia; ed, Nicholas Tsiotsias; m, Joel Jacob and Paul Pettit; art d, Nick Farentello; spec, Gary Roberts; makup, Barry Anderson

Horror   **(PR:O   MPAA:NR)**

DR. CALIGARI

80m Joseph F. Robinson/Steiner c

Madeleine Reynal *(Dr. Caligari)*, Fox Harris *(Dr. Avol)*, Laura Albert *(Mrs. Van Houten)*, Jennifer Balgobin *(Ramona Lodger)*, John Durbin *(Gus Pratt)*, Gene Zerna *(Mr. Van Houten)*, David Parry *(Dr. Lodger)*, Barry Phillips *(Cesare)*, Magie Song *(Patient in Straitjacket)*, Jennifer Miro *(Miss Koonce)*, Stephen Quadros *(Scarecrow)*, Carol Albright *(Screaming Patient)*, Catherine Case *(Pa-*

tient with Extra Hormones), Debra Deliso *(Grace Butter),* Lori Chacko, Marjean Holden *(Patients in Bed),* Vera Butler *(Human Lamp),* Salvador R. Espinoza *(Spanish Patient/Baby-Man),* Joseph Baratelli *(Shoe Salesman on TV),* April Hartz *(Shoe Customer on TV),* Anthony Robertson *(Patient in Doorway),* and Tequila Mockingbird *(Door Tongue)*

The Caligari Insane Asylum (CIA, to those in the know) is an unusual place. Built on a festering toxic waste dump, its strangely two-dimensional towers rise darkly against the night sky in an expressionistic wriggle of impossible angles. It's no surprise that the patients are a strange bunch, but their keepers are little better. There's leering Dr. Avol (Fox Harris), and Dr. and Nurse Lodger (David Parry and Jennifer Balgobin), a peculiar couple who do everything—smoke, speak, move—in tandem. Strangest of all is Dr. Caligari (Madeleine Reynal) herself, a statuesque beauty whose professional interests have a distinctly lurid cast. Years of research into the function of the hypothalamus have convinced her that she can use the preserved brain juice of her famous grandfather to absorb his intellect. But before she goes sticking long, nasty needles into her own forehead, she perfects the process through experimentation on her patients. Dr. Avol sanctions her investigations by looking the other way, but the Lodgers disapprove strongly. They're willing to resort to drastic measures to see Caligari stopped, but are no match for the ravishing degenerate and her unholy obsessions. Justice nevertheless prevails, as Caligari's brain-fluid switching goes awry and leads to a terminal confusion of personalities.

This basic plot summary doesn't begin to convey the mannered style of DR. CALIGARI's goings-on. The film opens with shots of CIA patients in primary-colored hospital gowns, melting out of the shadows in eerily lit compositions. Barely dressed, Mrs. Van Houten (Laura Albert) watches television in the middle of the barren dump. The television speaks to her, and she escapes through a freestanding door that rises in splendid isolation. Once inside, she is terrorized by a doll-faced man who gets up from a bathtub, straight razor in hand. And so it goes. DR. CALIGARI presents a succession of sometimes startling, sometimes beautiful, sometimes grotesque, but always carefully composed images that are undeniably striking. While they don't ultimately constitute a movie in any conventional sense of the word, they are something to behold.

DR. CALIGARI's relationship with THE CABINET OF DR. CALIGARI, a classic of German Expressionist filmmaking, is tenuous. Though the opening credits include a series of stills from that silent film, once DR. CALIGARI gets started the similarity between the two movies is primarily a matter of attitude. But this is *some* attitude: DR. CALIGARI is 78 minutes of sinister "voguing" with dialog. Caligari poses with the accessories of her profession: hypodermic needles, an electroshock apparatus that looks more like an electric chair than any therapeutic device, and a hot pink lab dress fit to raise the comatose if not the dead. Mrs. Van Houten—usually semi-clad—postures and pretends, while the Lodgers take their stylized duet to its outer limits. Holding up the verbal end, John Durbin, as a loquacious cannibal killer, delivers a nonstop monolog loaded with mordant wit.

On the self-conscious hipness meter, DR. CALIGARI is off the dial. But it's ultimately less interesting than director-cowriter-designer Stephen Sayadian's first film, the pornographic CAFE FLESH, directed under the pseudonym "Rinse Dream." CAFE FLESH crosses adult movie conventions with post-nuclear science-fiction cliches by way of CABARET, and the result is legitimately novel. DR. CALIGARI is an exercise in MTV/performance art/postmodern mannerisms, successful and stylish enough as such things go, but no ground breaker. *(Nudity, sexual situations, violence.)*

d, Stephen Sayadian; p, Joseph F. Robertson; w, Jerry Stahl and Stephen Sayadian; ph, Ladi von Jansky; ed, G. Martin Steiner; m, Mitchell Froom; prod d, Stephen Sayadian; spec, Ken Diaz; cos, Belinda Williams-Sayadian; makeup, Sheri Short

Comedy/Horror   **(PR:O   MPAA:NR)**

DOG TAGS

100m Arthur Schweitzer—Krishna Shah—Daars/Cinevest c

Clive Wood *(Alan "Cecil" Hart),* Baird Stafford *(Roy Hope),* Robert Haufrecht *(Willy Cross),* Mike Monty *(Capt. Newport),* Chris Hilton *(Himself),* Jericho Ondevilla *(Tannoy Patoura Janty),* Peter Erlich, and Gigi Doenas

DOG TAGS is about exploitation—at least that's what its director, Romano Scavolini (NIGHTMARE, 1981), tells us in the film's last frame, when we learn that the US government was not only aware of black marketeering during the Vietnam War, but, presumably, also knew of the involvement of military personnel in the movement of goods. If you haven't figured out that that's what the film's about after the first half-hour, however, you're not alone.

The problem with DOG TAGS is that it has no dramatic structure. Loosely summarizing, then, the plot concerns Al (Clive Wood) and Roy (Baird Stafford), commandos who free a group of POWs from a Vietcong cage, then have to take the GIs along on their "special mission." Unfortunately, since the film is half

over before we understand the nature of this mission, we could care less about *what* they are doing. Moreover, since the cutting between the men and commanding officer Captain Newport (Mike Monty) at headquarters is badly paced and doesn't create the least bit of tension, it takes awhile to realize that the CO is actually working *against* the men in the jungle. Along the way, none of the characters appear to have any motivation beyond surviving the war—and they don't even do that very well. (One soldier goes crazy and walks over a land mine; another is shot by Roy after failing to kill a Vietcong woman.) Newport, as acted by Monty, is a cipher, and it's hard to know what to make of Scavolini's bizarre lighting in his scenes. Although it eventually becomes apparent that Al and Roy have been tricked into retrieving an illegal shipment, we don't feel any sense of betrayal, since we've had no opportunity to get to know these characters in the first place. The whole story has supposedly been recounted by a Vietnamese boy, now grown, whom the soldiers picked up along the way, but not only are his flashbacks amazingly detailed, the film contains incidents he could not have witnessed in the first place. To complicate matters, the now-grown boy tells his story to a writer, who in turn narrates the first half of the film in voice-over. And if that weren't bad enough, the writer's monolog, sounding like a bad translation from Italian, adds an especially amateurish and fabricated touch to DOG TAGS.

Scavolini has no idea where to place the camera, and editor Nicholas Pollock doesn't know how to cut in a way that moves the plot along or creates suspense. As a result, scenes that could have been dramatic are merely tedious. In the sequence in which Al and Roy must use a badly constructed bridge to retrieve a box from a downed helicopter, for instance, we know that the helicopter is sitting in a lagoon near a waterfall. A close-up reveals that there are also sticks of dynamite under a bridge, but we don't know where, because Scavolini's camera doesn't give us that information. Moreover, since we don't know how close they are to the dynamite at any given moment, the cutting between the explosives and the men generates no feelings of apprehension.

If you've seen some of Hollywood's best WW II movies, you've probably also seen some of the rip-off B movies that followed on their heels, the ones that turned all the big moments into boring cliches. DOG TAGS is like that—a Vietnam War B film.

d, Romano Scavolini; p, Alain Adam and Dalu Jones; w, Romano Scavolini; ph, John McCallum; ed, Nicholas Pollock; m, John Scott; prod d, Art Nicdao; art d, Mon Nicdao; makup, Medy Alpa

War   **(PR:O   MPAA:R)**

DON'T TELL HER IT'S ME

101m John Daly—Derek Gibson/Hemdale c

(AKA: BOYFRIEND SCHOOL, THE)

Steve Guttenberg *(Gus Kubicek),* Jami Gertz *(Emily Pear),* Shelley Long *(Lizzie Potts),* Kyle MacLachlan *(Trout),* Kevin Scannell *(Mitchell Potts),* Beth Grant *(Babette),* Madchen Amick *(Mandy),* Caroline Lund, and Sally Lund *(Annabelle Potts)*

By now everyone has heard of New Age music. Many record stores even have special sections set aside for it; tapes and CDs with titles like "Sun Song" offer noodling acoustic instrumentals that go on forever and sound like the musicians are making it up as they go along. A whole side of one of the these tapes might be taken up with something called "Manifesto" that you've never gotten to the end of because you always fall asleep halfway through it. If you've had this experience, it's a good bet that you'll start yawning during the opening credits of DON'T TELL HER IT'S ME, a sort of New Age romantic comedy complete with noodling performances and a script that plays like the actors are making it up as they go along. Even the music, credited to Michael Gore, sounds like someone left the radio tuned to the local soft-jazz station. Under the wavering direction of Malcolm Mowbray (guiding his first film since the well-received A PRIVATE FUNCTION), DON'T TELL HER IT'S ME starts out with satirical promise but quickly turns into drivel distinguished only by its cynicism and insensitivity.

Steve Guttenberg stars as cartoonist Gus Kubicek, whose body is hairless and swollen after undergoing chemotherapy treatment for Hodgkin's Disease. Too eager to get him back into the swing of things, his romance-novelist sister, Lizzie (Shelley Long), sets Gus up with Emily Pear (Jami Gertz), a pretty reporter who's writing a story on Lizzie. Emily's romance with her handsome editor, Trout (Kyle MacLachlan), is on the rocks, and she tells Lizzie that looks aren't important to her anymore; what she wants is a man with integrity. For her part, Lizzie desperately wants to believe that women don't really go for the musclebound hunks she writes about in her novels. She is, of course, mistaken. A quiet dinner, to be cooked by Lizzie's ditzy husband, Mitchell (Kevin Scannell), is arranged. However, the affair is a disaster. The food is unpalatable, and Emily is neither fooled by Gus' lounge-lizard toupee nor moved by his cuddly chemistry with dogs and Lizzie's cute daughter, Annabelle (played by twins Caroline and Sally Lund). Determined to help her brother win Emily's favor, Lizzie decides to make over Gus in the image of the most virile, irresistible romantic hero her fertile imagination can conjure up. Not only does a strict workout regimen bring tone to Gus' body, but hair begins growing on his head again (leaving him looking more and more like the Steve Guttenberg of yore). But Lizzie isn't content with these changes; she wants to redesign her brother, right down to his undershorts. Soon, Gus is tooling around town on a Harley, looking and talking like an extra from a "Mad Max" film. "Mad Gus" first encounters Emily at a gas station-convenience store where, very conveniently, an armed robbery is taking place, giving Gus an opportunity for some off-the-cuff heroics with a coffee pot (a la FAST TIMES AT RIDGEMONT HIGH). Emily, of course, is smitten, and Gus is faced with the movie's non-dilemma: Will Emily still love him once the masquerade is over. Displaying little of the integrity Emily claims to desire, Gus withholds his true identity until after they spend a night together, leading to some 11th-hour fireworks that don't delay the predictable ending by more than a couple of minutes.

Fairly cynical at heart (with its implication that only the young, healthy, and attractive are eligible for romance), DON'T TELL HER IT'S ME nonetheless tries to come across as a full-frontal attack of cute kittens and fuzzy bunny rabbits, which, in the end, makes it seem even more cynical than it really is. Guttenberg is less whiny than usual, but how likable can a character be who deceives a woman to get her into bed? Though Gertz is warmer than usual, her character's stupidity seems bottomless. How did she ever get to be a reporter? At a romance writers' convention, she doesn't even recognize Lizzie when the author is standing next to a life-size cardboard cutout of herself. As Lizzie, Long is less grating than usual, but that might only be because she's not at the center of the action most of the time. Neither is MacLachlan, who, along with costar Madchen Amick, must have been splitting his time between this film and "Twin Peaks." Either you'll wish you could follow them back to the mad, mad world of David Lynch, or, if you're lucky, you'll drift off into calm, untroubled slumber to the strains of the inanely noodling actors. (Adult situations.)

d, Malcolm Mowbray; p, George G. Braunstein and Ron Hamady; w, Sarah Bird (based on her novel The Boyfriend School); ph, Reed Smoot; ed, Marshall Harvey; m, Michael Gore; prod d, Linda Pearl; set d, Debra Schutt; cos, Carol Wood

Comedy/Romance   (PR:C MPAA:PG-13)

DOWN THE DRAIN

106m Ronnie Hadar/Trans World c

Andrew Stevens (Vic Scalia), Teri Copley (Kathy Miller), Don Stroud (Dick Rogers), Nick DeMauro (Dino Carpatti), Ken Foree (Buckley), John Matuszak (Jed Stuart), Barry Niekrug (Tom Dart), Dominic Barto (Louie Girardo), Sal Lopez (Chico), Marco Fiorini (Boris), Mickey Morton (Jay), Joseph Campanella (Don Santiago), Irwin Keyes (Patrick), Stella Stevens (Sophia), Jerry Mathers (Desk Sergeant), Margot Hope, Benny "The Jet" Urquidez, Leon Martell, Pedro Gonzalez-Gonzalez, Buddy Daniels, Lee Benton, and Alexander Tabrizi

DOWN THE DRAIN begins like a scrappy, diverting caper comedy in the tradition of A FISH CALLED WANDA; unfortunately, it falls flat at the halfway point. Andrew Stevens plays Vic Scalia, a Los Angeles criminal defense attorney with a 90-percent success rate in winning acquittals for his clients. Actually, Scalia is also a criminal mastermind who organizes heists on demand for underworld customers, employing the same crooks he defends in court. Dick Rogers (Don Stroud) commissions Scalia to break into a bank's safety-deposit vault and nab the entire contents; as long as nothing is missing, Scalia and his crew will get $20 million. Scalia and his motley band of specialists enter the vault through the drain system and empty the place with ease; the tough part is keeping the greedy band from filching trinkets for themselves, jeopardizing the whole contract. Finally, Scalia transfers the booty, in several suitcases, to his safe (located, by the way, in a warehouse filled with schlock-movie posters). Scalia goes to finalize the deal with Rogers, but the villain attempts to double-cross him. After a gun battle, Scalia's car plunges over a cliff. News of Scalia's death reaches the crooks who assisted in the job, and they converge on the warehouse to seize the loot. A free-for-all ensues, and the thieves end up killing one another off. Only Kathy Miller (Teri Copley), Scalia's cute but avaricious moll, is left with the suitcases, and guess what — Scalia shows up. It turns out that he managed to jump free of the car wreck; however, Rogers and his goons are right behind him, and the movie turns into a tiresome series of chases involving the suitcases. In time, it is revealed that the traitorous Rogers is really after a piece of microfilm hidden somewhere amongst the vault contents. Naturally, that microfilm details the special features of a top-secret American jet fighter, vital to national security, etc. "I may be a lawyer, and I may be a thief — I don't know what's worse — but there are some things I will not do," announces Scalia, as he risks life and limb to keep the microfilm.

Scalia's patriotic declaration is about the only insight the script offers into his character. He's really a void in the midst of the warped outlaw types who populate

this picture. In fact, the real fun in DOWN THE DRAIN stops once the vault raiders have neatly disposed of one another. Up to that point, the film is an entertaining, if vulgar, farce of dishonor among thieves, with a crew of lowlifes who take every opportunity to harass, betray, and ultimately eliminate their comrades with undisguised glee. In one of his last films before his death, football-player-turned-actor John Matuszak makes a strong impression as a crazed demolitions expert. And veteran actress Stella Stevens, Andrew's mother, flaunts her durable beauty by portraying the sexy wife of the hood played by Nick DeMauro. The filmmakers try to make Rogers and his gang into an equally eccentric bunch; one lug constantly checks his blood pressure and whines about his health, and Rogers himself is so obsessed with his Rubik's cube that Scalia chokes him with it in the end. But by the time that moment rolls around the plot has run down into tedium, with all sorts of clumsy devices employed to keep the lackluster chase scenes rolling. At various points Scalia tries to turn in the suitcases to the cops, but he is never able to get past an argumentative desk sergeant played by Jerry Mathers (of "Leave It to Beaver" fame). In one mystifying scene, two zombie-like street people inexplicably transform into kung-fu fighting machines to keep the suitcases out of the wrong hands. All this merely prolongs the narrative well beyond its natural life. If DOWN THE DRAIN had kept up the drive and cleverness of its early reels, the production wouldn't deserve its all-too-apt title. (Nudity, profanity, violence, sexual situations.)

d, Robert C. Hughes; p, Ronnie Hadar; w, Moshe Hadar; ph, James Mathers; ed, Michael Ruscio; m, Rick Krizman; prod d, Yuda Ako; art d, Zeev Tankus and Ginni Barr; spec, Kevin McCarthy; stunts, Gunter Simon, Solly Mark, and Ellie A. Mite; cos, Linda Stein; chor, Isaac Florentine

Comedy/Crime   (PR:O MPAA:R)

DOWNTOWN

96m Gale Anne Hurd/FOX c

Anthony Edwards (Alex Kearney), Forest Whitaker (Dennis Curren), Penelope Ann Miller (Lori Mitchell), Joe Pantoliano (White), David Clennon (Jerome Sweet), Art Evans (Henry Coleman), Kimberly Scott (Christine Curren), Rick Aiello (Mickey Witlin), Roger Aaron Brown (Lt. Sam Parral), Ron Canada (Lowell Harris), Wanda De Jesus (Luisa Diaz), and Frank McCarthy (Inspector Ben Glass)

Amiable if undistinguished, DOWNTOWN faithfully follows the buddy-buddy, bang-bang cop movie formula that audiences have memorized from 48 HOURS; LETHAL WEAPON; and far too many other recent films. Anthony Edwards plays Alex Kearney, a uniformed cop with a cushy beat in a yuppiefied suburb of Philadelphia (appearing, cameo-style, in a few exterior shots; the bulk of the action was all too obviously filmed in and around LA). When Kearney stops the wrong rich guy for speeding, he quickly finds himself transferred to the city's toughest precinct, on Diamond Street, downtown. There, in a bit of seriocomic symbolism, Kearney and his car are promptly stripped, leaving him to enter his new world naked. To the film's credit, that is about as heavy-handed as Kearney's rude awakening gets, and in no time he seems to make friends with everybody in the precinct — the significant exception being the very first person he meets on Diamond Street, his partner, the gruff, hard-bitten loner Dennis Curren (Forest Whitaker). Curren goes out of his way to have nothing to do with Kearney, but, as most viewers will recognize, his standoffishness is little more than the buddy-cop equivalent of love at first sight. Just as we know that within the next 90 minutes we'll see several cars get destroyed, we also know that before too long the partnered cops (after their obligatory male-bonding fistfight) will become the best of friends, and will break a big case together. We'll also find out that, deep down inside, Curren is just a big softie who is really keeping Kearney at arm's length because his last partner, also his best friend, died in his arms in the line of duty. Along the way, Kearney will avenge the death of his old partner and friend (Rick Aiello), and will also get back at the snide yuppie who caused him to be sent to Diamond Street in the first place.

Strangely, the main reason that DOWNTOWN is entertaining, rather than tiresome, is that the film makes no pretensions to either artistic or blockbuster status. Executive producer Gale Anne Hurd — best known for her collaborations with her ex-husband, director James Cameron, on films like TERMINATOR; ALIENS; and THE ABYSS — has demonstrated a respect for genres and a dedication to basic filmmaking craft in her past efforts, and her talents are evident here in DOWNTOWN's sturdy B-movie virtues. Director Richard Benjamin (MY FAVORITE YEAR; RACING WITH THE MOON; LITTLE NIKITA) does a good job of balancing the tone between melodrama and tongue-in-cheek comedy, while keeping the pace fast and the narrative sharply focused. Benjamin is helped by the tight, neat plotting of the action as scripted by Nat Mauldin, a TV writer ("Barney Miller," "Night Court") who makes his screenwriting debut here.

The performances by the two leads keep all the formula and action functioning on a human level. Both Edwards (TOP GUN; REVENGE OF THE NERDS; MIRACLE MILE) and Whitaker (BIRD; GOOD MORNING VIETNAM) seem to enjoy playing fast and loose as big-city flatfoots, and give well-realized portrayals. Whitaker, especially, brings more depth to his character than is customary in the genre, although the filmmakers make the mistake of taking him out of the action for the climactic scene, a strange choice that looks suspiciously like the result of a scheduling conflict.

In tune with the lead performances, DOWNTOWN feels relaxed, taking the time to poke genial fun at itself. The film's best scenes have an element of parody, as when, in the opening credits, a squad car is seen tearing up and down suburban streets while frantic reports of an armed robbery crackle on its radio, only to arrive at the scene of the "crime" and find two kids fighting over money stolen from a lemonade stand. The film's wittiest sequence in its "urban" section is also its first, in which Kearney arrives at Diamond Street to find himself in the middle of open warfare in the precinct house itself and meets his new partner during a hostage crisis.

Also lending DOWNTOWN likability is its strong supporting cast, including Penelope Ann Miller (BILOXI BLUES) as Kearney's sweet, sharp, sexy, and loyal girl friend, and Art Evans (THE MIGHTY QUINN; A SOLDIER'S STORY) as the diminutive, apoplectic Diamond Street precinct captain. Other notables include Kimberly Scott, as Curren's strong-willed wife, and Joe Pantoliano and David Clennon as the refined, ruthless villains. In all, DOWNTOWN could hardly be considered a must-see — too much of it has already been seen too many times. But it's a solid, respectable bit of genre filmmaking. *(Profanity, violence, adult situations.)*

d, Richard Benjamin; p, Charles H. Maguire; w, Nat Mauldin; ph, Richard H. Kline; ed, Jacqueline Cambas and Brian Chambers; m, Alan Silvestri; prod d, Charles Rosen; art d, Gregory Pickrell; set d, Don Remacle; stunts, Terry Leonard; cos, Daniel Paredes

Action/Comedy   (PR:C   MPAA:R)

DREAMS

(Japan/US) 119m Akira Kurosawa USA/WB c

(AKA: AKIRA KUROSAWA'S DREAMS)

Akira Terao *("I")*, SUNSHINE THROUGH THE RAIN: Mitsuko Baisho *(Mother of "I")*, Toshihiko Nakano *("I" as a Young Child)*, THE PEACH ORCHARD: Mitsunori Isaki *("I" as a Boy)*, Mie Suzuki *("I's" Sister)*, THE BLIZZARD: Mieko Harada *(The Snow Fairy)*, Masayuki Yui, Shu Nakajima, Sakae Kimura *(Members of the Climbing Team)*, THE TUNNEL: Yoshitaka Zushi *(Pvt. Noguchi)*, CROWS: Martin Scorsese *(Vincent Van Gogh)*, MT. FUJI IN RED: Toshie Negishi *(Child-carrying Mother)*, Hisashi Igawa *(Power Station Worker)*, THE WEEPING DEMON: Chosuke Ikariya *(The Demon)*, VILLAGE OF THE WATERMILLS: Chishu Ryu *(103-year-old Man)*, Tessho Yamashita, Misato Tate, Catherine Cadou, Mugita Endo, Ryujiro Oki, Masaru Sakurai, Masaaki Sasaki, Keiki Takenouchi, Kento Toriki, Tokuju Masuda, Masou Amada, Shogo Tomomori, Ryo Nagasawa, Akisato Yamada, Tetsu Watanabe, Ken Takemura, Tetsuya Ito, Shoichiro Sakata, Naoto Shigemizu, Hiroshi Miyasaka, Yasuhiro Kajimoto, Makoto Hasegawa, Nagamitsu Satake, Satoshi Hara, Yasushige Turuoka, Shigeru Edaki, Hideharu Takeda, Katsumi Naito, Masaaki Enomoto, Nori Takei, Eiji Iida, Koji Kanda, Hideto Aota, Kazue Nakanishi, Rika Miyazawa, Mika Edaki, Mayumi Kamimura, Sayuri Yoshioka, Teruko Nakayama, Toshiya Ito, Takashi Ito, Motoyuki Higashimura, Yasuhito Yamanaka, Haruka Sugata, Noriko Hayami, Ayaka Takahashi, Yuko Ishiwa, Sachiko Oguri, Masayo Mochida, Miki Kado, Mika Ikeya, Sakiko Yamamoto, Mayumi Ono, Yumiko Miyata, Aya Ikaida, Megumi Hata, Asako Hirano, Chika Nishio, Yuko Harada, Tomomi Yoshizawa, Kumiko Ishizuka, Masumi Yoda, Hatsue Nishi, Michiko Kawada, Machiko Ichihashi, Yumi Ezaki, Chika Yamabe, Mayuko Akashi, Fujio Tokita, Michio Kida, Ayako Honma, Haruko Togo, Reiko Nanao, Shin Tonomura, Junpei Natsuki, Shigeo Kato, Saburo Kadowaki, Goichi Nagatani, Shizuko Azuma, Yoshle Kihira, Yukie Shimura, Setsuko Kawaguchi, Kumeko Otowa, Machiko Terada, Umiko Takahashi, Harumi Fujii, Hiroko Okuno, Mon Ota, Akitoku Inaba, Kou Ishikawa, Tatsunori Tokuhashi, Yoshiko Maki, Hiroko Maki, Ryoko Kawai, Miyako Kawana, Miyuki Egawa, Megumi Sakai, Yoko Hayashi, Yuko Matsumura, Takashi Odajima, Mitsuru Shibuya, Koichi Imamura, Wasuke Izumi, Sachio Sakai, Torauemon Utazawa, Yukimasa Natori, Tadashi Okumura, Kenzo Shirahama, Masato Goto, Sumimaro Yochimi, Junichi Kubozono, Masam Ozeki, Yasuyuki Iwanaga, Akira Tashiro, Koichi Kase, Kenji Fujita, Hiroto Tamura, Osamu Yayama, Yuji Sawayama, Mitsuji Tsuwako, Masatoshi Miya, Maiko Okamoto, Nana Yamakawa, Yuka Kojima, Shizuka Isami, Mai Watanabe, and Sayuri Kobayashi

Coming from virtually any other director on Earth, DREAMS might have been unwatchable, overflowing as it is with over-the-top message mongering on topics ranging from ecology to pacifism. On the surface, this is the film director

as Dutch uncle, scolding his audience for their wanton ways from an insufferably privileged position. Even coming from a master like Akira Kurosawa, DREAMS is a triumph of style over content. But as it is with any filmmaker of Kurosawa's high caliber, the style, finally, is the content. And what style! With his artistic powers undiminished as he enters his 80s, Kurosawa remains a genius of cinematic form, virtually without peer in the 1990s, which says as much about the impoverishment of contemporary screen art as it does about Kurosawa's durability. Best-known as the director's director of epic action dramas, Kurosawa has seen his THE SEVEN SAMURAI; YOJIMBO; and, most famously, THE HIDDEN FORTRESS all be adapted by westerners, as THE MAGNIFICENT SEVEN; A FISTFUL OF DOLLARS; and STAR WARS, respectively.

DREAMS has its own moments of spectacle. However, it is more deeply rooted in the side of Kurosawa that produced IKIRU; DODES'KA-DEN; THE MOST BEAUTIFUL; and other films with which American audiences are less familiar and which lack the presence of Toshiro Mifune or samurai swordplay. These are intimate dramas focusing on everyday people searching, no less than Kurosawa's samurai warriors on their grander canvas, for the right path to follow in life. If the samurai epics are Kurosawa's "Western" films, his dramas are more recognizably Japanese in their concern with man's relationships to his social and natural environments, placing Kurosawa in the contemplative company of fellow countrymen such as Ozu and Mizoguchi, directors who, with exquisite subtlety and delicacy, pursued similar themes throughout their careers. Reflecting Kurosawa's "high-low" eclecticism, one somber shot in DREAMS is lifted almost directly from Bergman's THE SEVENTH SEAL, and it follows what amounts to an antic tribute to GODZILLA. (In the latter, Kurosawa is undoubtedly also paying tribute to Ishiro Honda, a longtime collaborator. Credited on DREAMS as creative advisor, Honda, during his own directorial career, virtually created Godzilla, as well as Rodan, Mothra, and a host of other Japanese movie monsters.) But the most stunning moments and images in DREAMS owe nothing to anybody else.

Beginning with a wedding that looks more like a funeral and ending with a funeral that seems more like a wedding, DREAMS is made up of eight vignettes, thematically united by their concern with Man's relationship to nature, mystery and his fellow man. In "Sunshine Through the Rain," a little boy disobeys his mother, running into a forest during a sunlit rainstorm to witness a gravely magical wedding procession of foxes (played by mime actors in makeup). Because the boy has glimpsed the forbidden ceremony, his mother hands him a hara-kiri knife and locks him out of the house until he either obtains the forgiveness of the foxes or takes his own life. "The Peach Orchard" focuses on a boy who is made to understand what his parents have lost by cutting down a peach orchard on their property when the spirits of the downed trees appear to him. In "The Blizzard," the weary leader of a mountain expedition is tempted by death in the form of a beautiful snow demoness. "The Tunnel" concerns a military officer who is tormented by the ghosts of the soldiers who were killed in combat under his command. In "Crows," an aspiring artist enters a Vincent Van Gogh painting to learn the artist's secrets from the painter himself (played with appropriate intensity by director Martin Scorsese). In "Mt. Fuji in Red," Japan's most famous landmark is destroyed in a nuclear power-plant meltdown. Inspired as much by Bergman as by Hieronymus Bosch and set following a nuclear war, "The Weeping Demon" shows the torture of the damned following a conflagration that has left the earth a scorched ruin. Concluding the film is "Village of the Watermills," in which a traveller, passing through the title village, joins a 99-year-old man as he buries his 103-year-old "sweetheart" who never returned his love.

None of the vignettes have much narrative beyond their rudimentary premises. And when they do, as with "Sunshine," they are left eerily unresolved — Kurosawa closes the opening episode with the youngster returning to the forest in search of the foxes; he never shows us if the boy finds them, or if he makes use of the knife. As the plot of the first episode also indicates, DREAMS is not without its nightmarish moments. Though the snowstorm in "The Blizzard" is frankly unrealistic and obviously studio-bound, the action is staged in stylized, excruciating slow motion, giving a haunting conviction to the agonized exhaustion of the explorers. The lush visual romanticism of "Crows" is given an edge by the obsessed Van Gogh as its center. Fresh from a stay in a mental asylum, he matter-of-factly tells his would-be protege that he couldn't get the ear just right while painting his self-portrait, so, rather than fudging the painting, he cut off his ear, giving the younger man obvious pause about just how committed *he* is to his art.

But as "Crows" also reveals, DREAMS is not without moments of wry humor, which often come when least expected. "Mt. Fuji in Red" is staged in darkly satirical fashion like a classic Godzilla attack, complete with a hysterical mob of fleeing movie extras and a bespectacled concerned scientist who soberly (and conveniently) explains what is going on. The difference, of course, is that the monster here is Man, and the horrific rendering of the destruction of Mt. Fuji, courtesy of George Lucas' Industrial Light and Magic special-effects workshop, is bound to remind Godzilla fans that the rubber-suit movie monster was only a symbol to begin with, a fire-breathing physicalization of the traumatic nuclear destruction Japan suffered during the war.

At other times, DREAMS is almost dismayingly mundane, especially in its scripting. The old man's wisdom imparted to the traveller in "Waterfalls" may have been meant to sound profound, but it plays like an overlong fiber-cereal commercial. Yet, just as the old man is about to bring the film to a groaning halt, the funeral procession of the sweetheart who had forsaken him happens along, led by a brass band and alive with exuberant synchronized acrobatics and spirited song, an inspirational blaze of color, beauty, and energy. In a similar fashion, lulls come to be as important to DREAMS as climaxes, neither having meaning without its opposite, formally elaborating the film's greater concern with balance in life and nature. But, at its heart, there is something more deeply inexplicable about DREAMS; that so many simple yet disparate ingredients can be blended and finally transformed with apparent ease into a cumulative cinematic experience that is so unexpectedly overpowering is the mark of a master. Amid its diverse influences, DREAMS finally recalls nothing so much as the observation attributed to another master filmmaker, Luis Bunuel, that the greatest films possess a core of impenetrable mystery. DREAMS preaches respect for nature, but it also teaches awe. And that, in any language, is the strongest stuff of all.

d, Akira Kurosawa; p, Hisao Kurosawa and Mike Y. Inoue; w, Akira Kurosawa; ph, Takao Saito and Masahuro Ueda; ed, Tome Minami; m, Shinichiro Ikebe; art d, Yoshiro Muraki and Akira Sakuragi; set d, Koichi Hamamura; spec, Industrial Light & Magic; cos, Emi Wada; makup, Shoshichiro Ueda, Tameyuki Aimi, and Norio Sano; chor, Michiyo Hata

Fantasy   (PR:A   MPAA:NR)

DUCKTALES: THE MOVIE – TREASURE OF THE LOST LAMP

73m Walt Disney Animation-S.A./Disney Movietoons – Buena Vista c

VOICES OF: Alan Young *(Scrooge McDuck)*, Terence McGovern *(Launchpad McQuack)*, Russi Taylor *(Huey/Duey/Louie/Webby)*, Richard Libertini *(Dijon)*, Christopher Lloyd *(Merlock)*, June Foray *(Mrs. Featherby)*, Chuck McCann *(Duckworth)*, Joan Gerber *(Mrs. Beakley)*, and Rip Taylor *(Genie)*

Scrooge McDuck, the fabulously wealthy character featured in a series of popular comic books in the 50s and 60s, made his film debut here in the first offering of the Disney Movietoons company. The story opens in Scrooge's hometown of Duckburg, where the "jillionaire" isn't sure that his three cubic acres of money is quite enough. He longs for the hidden treasure of the legendary Arabian thief Collie Baba, and decides to head off to search for it. Along for the adventure are his nephews, Huey, Duey, and Louie, their female friend Webby, and the wildly adventurous pilot Launchpad McQuack. In the Middle East, Scrooge discovers the location of the treasure, but his efforts to acquire it are thwarted by Merlock, a mysterious figure with magical powers who very nearly spells the end for the band of adventurers. They escape without the treasure, returning to Duckburg with only an old lamp to show for their efforts. However, Huey, Duey, and Louie soon discover that the lamp is the home for a genie who can grant their every wish, and the three ducklings are soon enjoying a wish extravaganza. Unfortunately, Merlock is intent on getting the lamp back and it isn't long before he shows up in Duckburg intent on retrieving the magical possession.

Inspired by the very successful "Duck Tales" television program, this expanded adventure is a reasonably pleasing children's effort, with enough fantasy elements to keep the kids interested. The animation is just a cut above standard TV quality, but the voices are all good, especially comedian Rip Taylor as the genie.

d, Bob Hathcock; p, Bob Hathcock; w, Alan Burnett; ed, Charles King; m, David Newman; prod d, Skip Morgan; art d, Karen Silva; spec, Serge Conchonnet; anim, Paul Brizzi, Gaetan Brizzi, Clive Pallant, Mattias Marcos Rodric, and Vincent Woodcock

Animated/Children's   (PR:AA   MPAA:G)

DUE OCCHI DIBOLICI

(US/It.) (SEE: TWO EVIL EYES)

E

EAT A BOWL OF TEA

102m American Playhouse/Columbia c

Cora Miao (*Mei Oi*), Russell Wong (*Ben Loy*), Victor Wong (*Wah Gay*), Lee Sau Kee (*Bok Fat*), Eric Tsiang Chi Wai (*Ah Song*), Law Lan (*Aunt Gim*), and Lau Siu Ming (*Lee Gong*)

This engaging romantic comedy-drama set in New York's Chinatown examines an intriguing post-WW II American phenomenon: after years of strict immigration laws and forced separation of husbands and wives, Chinese immigrants were finally able to bring their spouses to the US. For longtime residents of Chinatown, it was too late to effect conjugal reunions, but an older generation of Chinese-American men wanted their sons to provide them with grandchildren by finding brides in China.

Although eager to meet his mother in China, Ben Loy (Russell Wong) has to be badgered by his father, Wah Gay (Victor Wong), to marry a native Chinese girl. He quickly changes his mind when he spots Meo Oi (Cora Miao) in his family's ancestral village. Once the local matchmakers have approved the couple's horoscopes, Ben blissfully returns to America with his new bride, who's eager to become acquainted with Bok Fat (Lee Sau Kee), the father she's never met. Despite Ben and Meo's storybook courtship and marriage, and their love for each other, their period of adjustment is a difficult one in the New World. Not only must Meo become acclimatized to a foreign culture, but she and Ben also have to deal with the constant interference of their fathers and the neighborhood elders, who try to run the couple's lives as if they had a personal stake in the young twosome's future. The pressure put on Meo to have a child immediately is enormous. While Ben works day and night as a restaurant manager, Meo broods at home. And as Ben becomes burdened by the feeling that everyone is charting their procreative progress, the young couple's lovemaking begins to slacken. Ben and Meo escape for a brief vacation, but when he receives a visit from an old flame, Meo feels threatened and insecure. In time, she is seduced by a roguish card sharp who lavishes her with the kind of attention the preoccupied Ben doesn't have time to provide. During the funeral of a family friend, she announces that she is pregnant; however, this happy event is marred by the increasing gossip about her extra-marital affair. When rumors flare, Ben and Meo are banished to New Jersey, where he's stuck in a degrading job as a fortune cookie maker; their fathers are shamed. Embittered by this dishonor, the couple battles, with Meo proving to be anything but the shy, retiring wife Ben expected her to be. When Meo's seducer, who doesn't realize that the ostracized couple have been forced to move, arrives at their old apartment, he finds Wah Gay waiting with a meat cleaver. With divorce imminent, Ben is surprised to find himself suspected of the attempted murder of his wife's lover. (Meanwhile, the real assailant, Wah Gay, who has bid a sad farewell to Bok Fat, flees to the Caribbean.) After obtaining some oriental tea that is believed to have the power to revive a marriage, Meo asks her husband for a second chance, and he agrees. The film then flashes forward a few years to San Francisco to show the happy couple (with a child on the way) reunited with their fathers, who are thrilled with the grandchildren they have dreamed of for so long.

In this smoothly crafted, clever comedy-drama, director Wayne Wang (CHAN IS MISSING; DIM SUM: A LITTLE BIT OF HEART) and screenwriter Judith Rascoe have fashioned a graceful movie powered by deliciously eccentric characters. Enriched by local color and exotic customs, this is no ersatz orientalism like FLOWER DRUM SONG, but an authentic slice of American life most of us are unfamiliar with. Steeped in foreign rituals and customs, EAT A BOWL OF TEA nonetheless conveys universal truths. Although several scenes run too long and some material is repetitive, there's no denying the movie's life-affirming spirit and charm. Working miracles with his talented cast, Wang shows how the interaction of an insular community affects the fortunes of a couple who only wish to live their own way. In the large ensemble, even the bit parts are acted to perfection. Fortunately, the romantic leads, Russell Wong and Cora Miao, aren't the usual attractive but vapid stick figures; they're fleshed-out characters with passion and thwarted desires.

Peppered with keen observations about the human condition, EAT A BOWL OF TEA transforms cliches with oriental spice. Abounding in magical moments (like the scene in which Ben and Meo fall in love in front of an outdoor screen on which LOST HORIZON is playing), the film cleverly equates the difficulties of adjusting to a foreign culture with those of adjusting to a new marriage. While Wang might have shaped some of the scenes more dynamically and clarified his focus with sharper editing, the film is nonetheless a delight, a piquant fairy tale in which the happily-ever-after ending is postponed by the meddling Chinatown's fairy godfathers. Finding humor and drama in the dislocation experienced by all immigrants and in the particular history of Chinese-Americans, Wang has fashioned a film that is both a perceptive historical document

and a captivating love story. (*Violence, sexual situations, adult situations, profanity.*)

d, Wayne Wang; p, Tom Sternberg; w, Judith Rascoe (based on the novel by Louis Chu); ph, Amir Mokri; ed, Richard Candib; m, Mark Adler; prod d, Bob Ziembicki; art d, Timmy Yip; set d, Lisa Dean; cos, Marit Allen; makeup, Nancie Marsalis and Yam Chan Hoi

Romance   (PR:C   MPAA:PG-13)

EDGAR ALLAN POE'S MASQUE OF THE RED DEATH

(SEE: MASQUE OF THE RED DEATH)

EDWARD SCISSORHANDS

100m FOX c

Johnny Depp (*Edward Scissorhands*), Winona Ryder (*Kim Boggs*), Dianne Wiest (*Peg Boggs*), Anthony Michael Hall (*Jim*), Kathy Baker (*Joyce*), Robert Oliveri (*Kevin*), Conchata Ferrell (*Helen*), Caroline Aaron (*Marge*), Dick Anthony Williams (*Officer Allen*), O-Lan Jones (*Esmeralda*), Vincent Price (*The Inventor*), Alan Arkin (*Bill*), Susan J. Blommaert (*Bill*), Linda Perry (*Cissy*), John Davidson (*TV Host*), Biff Yeager (*George*), Marti Greenberg (*Suzanne*), Bryan Larkin (*Max*), John McMahon (*Denny*), Victoria Price (*TV Newswoman*), Stuart Lancaster (*Retired Man*), Gina Gallagher (*Granddaughter*), Aaron Lustig (*Psychologist*), Alan Fudge (*Loan Officer*), Steven Brill (*Dishwasher Man*), Peter Palmer (*Editor*), Marc Macaulay, Carmen J. Alexander, Brett Rice (*Reporters*), Andrew Clark (*Beefy Man*), Andrew Crofton (*Pink Girl*), Linda Hess Hess (*Older Woman, TV*), Rosalyn Thomson (*Young Woman, TV*), Lee Ralls (*Red-Haired Woman, TV*), Eileen Meurer (*Teenage Girl, TV*), Bea Albano (*Rich Widow, TV*), Donna Pieroni (*Blonde, TV*), Tricia Lloyd (*Other Teen*), Kathy Dombo (*Police Sergeant*), Sherry Ferguson (*Max's Mother*), Tabetha Thomas (*Little Girl on Bike*), Ken DeVaul, Michael Gaughan (*Policemen*), Tammy Boalo, Jackie Carson, Carol Crumrine, Suzanne Chrosniak, Ellin Dennis, Kathy Fleming, Jalaine Gallion, Miriam Goodspeed, Dianne L. Green, Mary Jane Heath, Carol D. Klasek, Laura Nader, Doyle Anderson, Harvey Bellman, Michael Brown, Gary Clark, Roland Douville, Russell Green, Cecil Hawkins, Jack W. Kapfhamer, Bill Klein, Phil Olson, Joe Sheldon, and James Spicer (*Neighborhood Extras*)

With movies such as PEE-WEE'S BIG ADVENTURE, BEETLEJUICE, and BATMAN, Tim Burton established himself as a distinctive and unique American filmmaker. The title characters of those films were outsiders or weirdos, but none was as strange as the title character in this film. Edward (Johnny Depp) is the creation of an inventor who lived in a large gothic mansion overlooking a quiet suburb filled with pastel-colored homes. The inventor (Vincent Price) died before he could finish his creation, leaving Edward incomplete and alone. Edward has a heart, a brain, and a covering of skin, but instead of hands, pointy metal shards hang at the ends of his arms. For years Edward has lived in isolation in the deserted mansion, creating elaborate topiaries from the hedges that surround the mansion. His isolation is shattered one day when Avon Lady Peg (Dianne Wiest) comes calling at the mansion. Peg is fascinated by Edward and she takes him to her home down below to show him what life is like. Edward is terrified at first (after all, one of his gestures could be lethal), but he soon gains acceptance with his unique talents for hedge trimming and his newfound abilities as a hair stylist. Edward is attracted to Peg's beautiful daughter Kim (Winona Ryder, barely recognizable as a blonde). Kim finds Edward a little too strange for her tastes, preferring the company of her brutish boy friend Jim (Anthony Michael Hall). As Edward's celebrity grows, a promiscuous housewife (Kathy Baker) tries to seduce him; Peg's husband (a wonderful Alan Arkin) encourages Edward to use his bizarre skills on home maintenance; and a local TV show does an hour-long feature on him. Even Kim starts to grow fond of him, but Edward's newfound happiness is soon threatened when the suburban residents mistakenly come to believe he is guilty of a crime.

Drawing upon influences that range from FRANKENSTEIN to BEING THERE, Burton creates a poignant, strikingly personal fairy tale that is both funny and deeply moving. The first half of the film is potent satire that succeeds in skewering suburbia while respectfully creating a wide variety of well-rounded characters. Bo Welch's sharp production design and Stefan Czapsky's beautiful photography help bring Burton's wild and wonderful vision to life. The film opens with an overhead shot sweeping above the imaginary suburb (the shot echoing the opening of BEETLEJUICE) to finally settle on the mansion. The opening presents the visual realization of the film's central theme: that just beyond the edge of apparent normalcy lies the truly bizarre. In addition to the unique visual approach, the screenplay is rich with emotion and personality. The story works as both allegory and satire while achieving the magic of a fairy tale. It also seems to be the story of Burton's struggles in Hollywood. (The fact that Edward resembles Burton is no coincidence.) Like Edward, Burton is a fiercely creative force, but one who is an outsider in Hollywood. That Vincent Price (whose films have had a major influence on Burton) plays the inventor who creates Edward is the film's most nuanced element. In addition to being a revealing portrait of an artist, EDWARD SCISSORHANDS offers a powerful and positive message. Edward is a pure innocent, uncorrupted by the outside world and filled with curiosity and wonder. His art is his way of expressing love since his touch can only bring pain. When he creates a beautiful figure from a slab of ice as Kim dances in the flakes of shaved ice, the effect is enormously moving.

The performances add to the film's rich emotion. Depp is a revelation whose performance easily surpasses his work in CRY-BABY and TV's "21 Jump Street." He gives a subtle performance that effectively conveys Edward's wonder and his tenderness. Using facial expressions and double takes, and employing a distinctive walk and expressive body movements, Depp makes Edward an unforgettable character. Ryder (MERMAIDS, HEATHERS), a remarkably natural actress, is perfect, bringing a much-needed gravity to a role that could have been one-dimensional. Arkin (HAVANA, THE IN-LAWS) is hilarious, Weist (HANNAH AND HER SISTERS, PARENTHOOD) is bubbly, Baker (CLEAN AND SOBER, DAD) is weirdly amusing, and Hall (SIXTEEN CANDLES, JOHNNY BE GOOD) is unforgettable. Price's cameo is inspired and concludes with a close-up that makes him look angelic; it is the film's most memorable image. The combination of the performances, script, and direction make this a marvelous cinematic experience. The film earned an Oscar nomination for its makeup. *(Adult situations, violence.)*

d, Tim Burton; p, Tim Burton and Denise DiNovi; w, Caroline Thompson and Tim Burton; ph, Stefan Czapsky; ed, Richard Halsey; m, Danny Elfman; prod d, Bo Welch; art d, Tom Duffield; set d, Rick Heinrichs, Paul Sonski, and Ann Harris; spec, Stan Winston and Michael Wood; cos, Colleen Atwood

Fantasy/Romance   (PR:C   MPAA:PG-13)

ELLIOT FAUMAN, PH.D.

86m Ventcap – Double Helix/Taurus c

Randy Dreyfuss *(Elliot Fauman)*, Jean Kasem *(Meredith Dashley)*, Tamara Williams *(Stella)*, Shelley Berman *(Stromberg)*, Bryan Michael McGuire *(Denton)*, and John Canada Terrell *(Gene)*

Jean Kasem and Randy Dreyfuss star in this slow-moving comedy about a psychologist who is studying human sexuality. The life and work of Dr. Elliot Fauman (Dreyfuss) become as confused as this film's implausible plot when Stella (Tamara Williams), a local hooker, and Meredith Dashley (Kasem), a famous actress, enter on the scene. As the film opens, Elliot asks Stella to fill out a questionnaire. However, Stella, who finds academic types irresistible, is interested in much more than Elliot's intellect and insists he sleep with her. Although this is good for the psychology professor's ego, it's not exactly the research he had in mind. So Elliot decides to drive Stella to her place of employment, Dweezil's Escort Service, to collect more data. En route, his car breaks down, right in front of a theater where Meredith is starring in a play. Just as Elliot manages to fix his car, Meredith storms out of the theater after a frustrating rehearsal. She talks Elliot into giving her a lift, and the three continue to Dweezil's, where the prostitutes, who are fed up with Dweezil, elect Elliot as their new boss. Further confusing the story line, Meredith's CPA eventually becomes the escort service's business manager. In the meantime, someone is following Elliot around with a video camera. The following week, when Elliot presents a research proposal to his colleagues in the psychology department at the university, they are less than impressed. In fact, they're already thinking of giving the grant Elliot has applied for to his competitor. With a deadline looming over his head, Elliot continues his research, still tailed by the mystery man with the JVC equipment, who turns out to be Elliot's faculty rival. From this point on there aren't many surprises: Elliot gets the grant and the girl (Meredith), and the escort service is a big success.

The premise of ELLIOT FAUMAN, PH.D., is limited at best, and, not surprisingly, fails to work on any level. The screenplay, by Ric Klass, lacks any real wit, and the actors sleepwalk through their stereotyped roles. Kasem's Meredith is identical to the bimbo she played on the short-lived TV series "The Tortellis," but while the ditzy character was well suited to that show, it doesn't work here. Regrettably, Dreyfuss' portrayal of the uptight college professor isn't very convincing or interesting either. In fact, none of the characters in this movie are sufficiently developed or original. Besides the beautiful shots of Mt. Vernon College and the surrounding Maryland countryside, and one amusing scene at a pimp convention, there is little here to hold the viewer's attention. *(Nudity, profanity.)*

d, Ric Klass; p, Ric Klass; w, Ric Klass; ph, Erich Roland; ed, Judith Herbert; m, Roger Trefousse; prod d, Henry Shaffer; art d, Tony Cisek; cos, Sheri Dunn

Comedy   (PR:C   MPAA:PG-13)

ERNEST GOES TO JAIL

81m Silver Screen Partners-Touchstone/Buena Vista c

Jim Varney *(Ernest P. Worrell/Felix Nash/Auntie Nelda)*, Gailard Sartain *(Chuck)*, Bill Byrge *(Bobby)*, Barbara Bush *(Charlotte Sparrow)*, Barry Scott *(Rubin Bartlett)*, Randall "Tex" Cobb *(Lyle)*, Dan Leegant *(Oscar Pendlesmythe)*, Charles Napier *(Warden)*, Jim Conrad *(Eddie)*, Jackie Welch *(Judge)*, Melanie Wheeler *(Prosecutor)*, Buck Ford *(Defense Attorney)*, Daniel Butler *(Waiter)*, Charlie Lamb, Mac Bennett *(Cons)*, Rick Shulman *(Mean Guard)*, Bruce Arntson *(Juror)*, Andrew Stahl *(Jerry)*, Myke Mueller *(Vinnie)*, Bob Babbitt *(Washing Con)*, John Davis *(Other Guard)*, Michael Montgomery *(Warden's Assistant)*, and Mike Hutchinson *(Gate Guard)*

Director John Cherry knows it doesn't take much to entertain a 12-year-old, and he has no trouble meeting the expectations of that target audience with ERNEST GOES TO JAIL, the third film to star Jim Varney as Ernest P. Worrell, the character he made famous in television commercials. In this installment, Ernest thinks it is a great honor to be chosen for jury duty. However, he is the spitting image of incarcerated crime boss Felix Nash (also played by Varney), and, naturally, when the jury is taken to visit the jail, a switch is made. While Ernest tries to survive prison (with the help of boxer-turned-actor Randall "Tex" Cobb), Nash plots the robbery of the bank where Ernest, two bungling security men, and beautiful assistant bank supervisor Charlotte Sparrow (Barbara Bush) work. Still, Ernest has a few things going for him: he is so stupid he often does the right thing accidentally and he seemingly has the ability to absorb massive amounts of electricity without any great harm coming to him. Nash, on the other hand, is forced to deal with Ernest's reputation for stupidity and incompetence.

Strictly slapstick juvenile humor, ERNEST GOES TO JAIL is simply not very good. But then neither were the first two "Ernest" films, and they both made substantial amounts of money. There must be a segment of the moviegoing public that thinks Ernest is funny, or maybe there are just a lot of 12-year-olds with disposable incomes. To his credit, Varney actually displays some fine acting ability in his multiple roles (he also plays Auntie Nelda), and Gailard Sartain and Bill Byrge are also good as the security guards. Something is wrong with a movie, though, when the director has to take the funniest scene and repeat it at the end of the film just for the sake of a few laughs. This is the kind of film most of us don't really want to admit we've seen, let alone laughed at. Nevertheless, ERNEST GOES TO JAIL gives Varney fans more or less what they expect, and they keep coming back for more. Ernest may not be pretty but he has been profitable.

d, John Cherry; p, Stacy Williams; w, Charlie Cohen; ph, Peter Stein; ed, Sharyn L. Ross; m, Bruce Arntson and Kirby Shelstad; prod d, Chris August; art d, Mark Ragland; set d, Connie Gray; spec, Tim McHugh and William H. Schirmer; stunts, Chuck Waters; cos, Shawn Barry; makeup, June Rudley Brickman; anim, Allen Gonzales

Comedy   (PR:A   MPAA:PG)

EVERYBODY WINS

97m Orion c

Debra Winger *(Angela Crispini)*, Nick Nolte *(Tom O'Toole)*, Will Patton *(Jerry)*, Judith Ivey *(Connie)*, Kathleen Wilhoite *(Amy)*, Jack Warden *(Judge Harry Murdoch)*, Frank Converse *(Charlie Haggerty)*, Frank Military *(Felix)*, Steven Skybell *(Fr. Mancini)*, Mary Louise Wilson *(Jean)*, Mert Hatfield *(Bellanca)*, Peter Appel *(Sonny)*, Sean Weil *(Montana)*, Timothy D. Wright *(Defense Attorney)*, Elizabeth Ann Klein, T.M. Nelson George *(Judges)*, James Parisi *(Reporter)*, and R.M. Haley *(Driver)*

The 1990 film year started on a less than promising note when the first major American release, EVERYBODY WINS, didn't even rate a press screening. Starring Nick Nolte and Debra Winger (who last appeared together, inauspiciously, in CANNERY ROW), directed by Karel Reisz (whose credits include one of Nolte's best films to date, WHO'LL STOP THE RAIN), and produced by Jeremy Thomas (THE LAST EMPEROR), this murky mystery also features Arthur Miller's first screenplay since 1961's THE MISFITS. Regrettably, despite this stellar lineup, the studio's reticence in promoting the film was well justified. EVERYBODY WINS is no treasure, buried or otherwise.

The film's basic problem can be summed up in the script's most repeated verb: *talk* – as in too much. Responding to a phone request, private eye Tom O'Toole (Nolte) arrives in a small Connecticut town and *talks* to Angela Crispini (Winger), who wants him to investigate the case of Felix (Frank Military), who, she says, has been wrongly imprisoned for the murder of his pillar-of-the-community uncle. She sends O'Toole to *talk* to a simple-minded backwoods woman (Kathleen Wilhoite), who leads O'Toole to *talk* to Jerry (Will Patton), a deranged biker who worships a dead Civil War hero and who may or may not be the real killer. Not much comes of O'Toole and Jerry's conversation; instead of a tense, psychological cat-and-mouse game, their meeting digresses into rambling mumbo-jumbo. At home, O'Toole *talks* to his sister (Judith Ivey) and gets interrupted by phone calls urging him to *talk* to other people who may know something. As for the none-too-stable Crispini, she turns out to be a prostitute plagued by multiple personalities, ranging from a truck-stop whore to the classy mistress of the prosecutor (Frank Converse), an old nemesis of O'Toole's, who put away Felix. A gladhander readying for a run at the Senate, the prosecutor smacks Crispini around and wrecks her apartment looking for their old love letters after O'Toole serves notice that Crispini has convinced him to investigate the murder case.

There are so many unstable characters here that EVERYBODY WINS might have been better titled "Everybody's Insane." Actually, Miller's original title ("Two-Way Mirror") conveys all too well the film's lack of thematic subtlety. An innocent motivated by the idealistic pursuit of justice, O'Toole winds up being manipulated into setting right what seems to have been essentially a murder contract gone sour. Putting Felix behind bars wasn't supposed to have been part of the deal, so O'Toole is brought in to help force the hand of the powers that be (his investigation into a previous case led to a reversal of a verdict won by the prosecutor). But who killed whom and why is only hazily explained, and when it is, it doesn't make a whole lot of sense dramatically or logically. Miller has a higher purpose in mind than merely presenting a competently crafted story: he is bent on nothing less than exposing the casual corruption of our diseased modern age.

Rarely, however, has corruption been depicted as lifelessly as it is here. Rather than being propelled from one clue to the next, Nolte's O'Toole, smitten with Winger's Crispini, seems to wander around in a befuddled haze (shared by the audience) until someone pulls him aside and tells him to go talk to someone else. Missing is anything resembling dramatic conflict—an odd weakness in a script credited to one of the century's leading playwrights. The real villain, as it turns out, is dead before the action of the film even begins. O'Toole thus finds himself striking out at shadows with the vague objective of bringing down a corrupt state power structure and dealing another defeat to the despised prosecutor.

EVERYBODY WINS is finally a series of sketches for potentially intriguing characters and a potentially interesting plot that plays like an overwritten treatment. What little there is of interest comes from the efforts of Reisz and his cast to breathe life into Miller's DOA scenario. Notably, Reisz creates a nightmarish aura of dread and unease with a stark, elliptical narrative style accented by complex, deep-focus visual compositions. Nolte has little to do as the one-dimensional good guy; as always, however, he does what he does very well. Nevertheless, this is unquestionably Winger's show, and her performance is all the more persuasive because it is so artfully subdued. Changing personalities within a single scene just by a slight alteration in her line reading and body language, Winger makes herself one of those irresistibly seductive and downright scary. It's easy to sympathize with O'Toole for thinking—as he puts it—"with his dingus." But the only real mystery in EVERYBODY WINS is, what was Miller thinking with when he wrote this windy, uncinematic screenplay? *(Sexual situations, nudity, profanity, violence.)*

d, Karel Reisz; p, Jeremy Thomas; w, Arthur Miller; ph, Ian Blake; ed, John Bloom; m, Mark Isham and Leon Redbone; md, Ray Williams; prod d, Peter Larkin; art d, Charley Beal; set d, Hilton Rosemarin; stunts, David Ellis; cos, Ann Roth; makeup, Leonard Engelman and Ed Henriques

Drama/Mystery   (PR:O   MPAA:R)

EXORCIST III, THE

110m Morgan Creek/FOX c

George C. Scott *(Lt. Kinderman)*, Ed Flanders *(Fr. Dyer)*, Brad Dourif *(James Venamon, "The Gemini Killer")*, Jason Miller *(Patient X)*, Nicol Williamson *(Fr. Morning)*, Scott Wilson *(Dr. Temple)*, Nancy Fish *(Nurse Allerton)*, George DiCenzo *(Stedman)*, Don Gordon *(Sgt. Ryan)*, Lee Richardson *(University President)*, Grand L. Bush *(Sgt. Atkins)*, Mary Jackson *(Mrs. Clelia)*, Viveca Lindfors *(Nurse X)*, Ken Lerner *(Dr. Freedman)*, Tracy Thorne *(Nurse Keating)*, Barbara Baxley *(Shirley)*, Zohra Lampert *(Mary Kinderman)*, Harry Carey Jr. *(Fr. Kanavan)*, Sherrie Wills *(Julie Kinderman)*, Edward Lynch *(Patient A)*, Clifford David *(Dr. Bruno)*, Alexander Zuckerman *(Korner Boy)*, Lois Foraker *(Nurse Merrin)*, Tyra Ferrell *(Nurse Blaine)*, James Burgess *(Thomas Kintry)*, Kevin Corrigan *(Altar Boy)*, Peggy Alston *(Mrs. Kintry)*, Fr. John Durkin *(Elderly Jesuit)*, Bobby Deren *(Nurse Bierce)*, Jan Neuberger *(Alice)*, Alexis Chieffet *(Counter Attendant)*, Debra Port *(Waitress)*, Walt MacPherson *(Police Sergeant)*, David Dwyer *(2nd Police Officer)*, Daniel Epper *(Police Driver)*, William Preston *(Old Man in Wheelchair)*, Chuck Kinlaw *(Attendant)*, Demetrios Pappageorge *(Casperelli)*, Nina Hansen *(Little Old Lady)*, Shane Wexel, Ryan Paul Amick *(Dream Boys)*, John A. Coe *(Old Man in Dream)*, Jodi Long, Kathy Gerber *(Dream Women)*, Samuel L. Jackson *(Dream Blind Man)*, Jan Smook *(Radio Man)*, Amelia Campbell *(Young Girl in Dream)*, Cherie Baron *(Nurse)*, Larry King *(Himself)*, C. Everett Koop *(Himself)*, and Patrick Ewing *(Angel of Death)*

Fifteen years have passed since young Regan McNeil was possessed by the Devil, fifteen years since doubting Fr. Damien Karras died at the foot of that long flight of stairs while performing the exorcism that set Regan free. Karras' best friends, smart-mouthed Father Dyer (Ed Flanders) and weary police lieutenant Kinderman (George C. Scott) have carried on with their lives, making certain they're together on the anniversary of Karras' death, each rationalizing that he's doing it to cheer up the other. But this year things are more somber than usual. The grisly mutilation murder of a young boy has Kinderman in despair over the casual brutality of modern life, while Dyer hides the troubling signs of illness. Soon, a priest is murdered in his confessional. Then Dyer is killed in his hospital bed and mysteriously drained of blood. The crimes, Kinderman notes, are reminiscent of the so-called "Gemini" murders of the mid-70s, down to the smallest detail. But this line of reasoning appears to be a dead end: "the Gemini Killer," James Venamun (Brad Dourif), was caught, convicted, and executed in the electric chair 15 years previously. Kinderman's investigation centers on the hospital's staff and patients, including a large population of mental patients, ranging from elderly Alzheimer's sufferers to the criminally insane. Nervous, chain-smoking Dr. Temple (Scott Wilson) seems to be hiding something, but Kinderman is more interested in an anonymous man in a maximum security cell. An amnesiac brought to the hospital 15 years earlier, this mystery man sometimes looks exactly like Father Karras (Jason Miller); at other moments he is a ringer for Venamun. Indeed, the patient tells Kinderman that he *is* the Gemini Killer, that during his execution his spirit possessed the body of the dying Father Karras, and that he continues to kill from within the hospital walls. Kinderman reluctantly comes to believe him. Independently, Father Morning (Nicol Williamson), a grave, ascetic priest, realizes something evil is afoot and attempts an exorcism in the madman's cell. However, when Father Morning is overpowered, Kinderman finds himself face to face with the Devil in the flesh. Ultimately, Kinderman prevails, setting free Karras' tormented soul and stopping the Gemini Killer for good.

Written and directed by William Peter Blatty, on whose novel William Friedkin's taboo-busting EXORCIST was based, THE EXORCIST III avoids the two most obvious sequel traps into which it could have plunged. First, it abandons the Regan McNeil story entirely, rather than attempting a follow-up that would have only led to embarrassment. There isn't room enough in the world for Linda Blair in an "Exorcist" spoof (REPOSSESSED) and in a serious "Exorcist" sequel; never mind that people are still laughing at EXORCIST II. Second, EXORCIST III doesn't succumb to the temptation to go hog wild with state-of-the-art special effects. In 1973, THE EXORCIST's effects blew moviegoers away, but in the can-you-top-this atmosphere of current horror movies, the law of diminishing returns is fast coming into play; if EXORCIST III had tried to be as profoundly shocking as THE EXORCIST, it would only have failed.

Though the notion of yet another "Exorcist" sequel reeks of bottom-line money grubbing, what's most surprising about EXORCIST III is how clearly it's a writer's movie, not the product of communal thought. Blatty relies on dialog to carry the film to an astonishing degree, and if the banter between Kinderman and Dyer lets him down, Venamun's nonstop rants are electrifying; Dourif's performance alone makes EXORCIST III worth seeing.

Moreover, Blatty brings breathtaking skill to his staging of the suspenseful scene in which a nurse investigates a suspicious noise in a deserted ward. The setup is pure genre cliche—a by-the-numbers progression from false relief to unwarranted jump—but the payoff is so flawlessly executed it makes you gasp. Trusting viewers to pay attention to the background, Blatty uses long, deep focus takes, and the sense of sick dread that the scene generates is palpable. Much of the rest of the film is less than interesting, but it doesn't really matter; EXORCIST III gives viewers more than they had any reason to expect. *(Violence, profanity.)*

d, William Peter Blatty; p, Carter DeHaven; w, William Peter Blatty (based on the book *Legion* by William Peter Blatty); ph, Gerry Fisher; ed, Todd Ramsay and Peter Lee-Thompson; m, Barry DeVorzon; prod d, Leslie Dilley; art d, Robert Goldstein and Henry Shaffer; set d, Hugh Scaife; spec, Bill Purcell and Greg Cannom; stunts, Paul Baxley; cos, Dana Lyman; makeup, Paul Stanhope; tech, Fr. George Murray

Horror   (PR:C   MPAA:R)

F

FACE OF THE ENEMY

92m Tri-Culture c

Rosana DeSoto *(Neiloufar)*, George DiCenzo *(James Wald)*, and Cindy Cryer *(Darya)*

Two very able actors, better known for their supporting work elsewhere, step forward in this two-character psychological drama that is remarkably subtle and engrossing despite its contrived premise. George DiCenzo plays James Wald, a former CIA agent whose life has been on a steady slide since his extended captivity as a hostage in an unnamed country in the Middle East. Despite steady physical and psychological torture, Wald didn't reveal any secrets, but the ordeal has left him an emotional invalid. With his once-promising career down the drain, Wald is now head of security at a chemical plant. His picture-perfect wife and kids have deserted him; even his rambling Long Beach, California, house has a "condemned" sign out front. Wald's former government employers have been next to no help. Indeed, they have him in their computer files under the heading of "annoying loony," to be humored when he does call, or, better yet, ignored entirely. When Wald reports that he has spotted a woman whom he recognizes as one of his former captors, the sighting is all but dismissed in light of the "paranoid" label in Wald's file. An FBI agent does show up at his door, but only to warn him that, due to a political agreement, blanket amnesty has been granted to all former terrorists from the Middle Eastern country where Wald was held hostage. Deprived even of the satisfaction of bringing his tormentor to justice, Wald takes matters into his own hands, kidnaping the woman in question, who goes by the name of Nell Neal (Rosana DeSoto), and locking her in his basement. What he intends to do with her is never quite clear. He tells her he will kill her, but from the outset, that doesn't seem likely. Wald seems vaguely intent on subjecting her to some of the same tortures he suffered, but even in this pursuit he seems only halfhearted. At first, he keeps her bound hand-and-foot and blindfolded. But before long, though he still keeps her locked in the basement, he unties her and allows her to wander at will. When she insists on taking a shower, Wald has her strip down to submit to the same humiliating body search he was subjected to during his captivity. But, again, he hasn't the heart to go through with it. Amid all this, Nell is anything but a terrified victim. She constantly probes for Wald's vulnerabilities in search of a means of escape, not so much to save herself, but to protect her young daughter from Wald's possible wrath.

What emerges is a taut, fascinating battle of wills. Just as Nell is more than a victim, so Wald is more than a standard-issue slobbering psycho. DiCenzo plays him as a man who seems to be dead but just doesn't know it yet. His kidnaping of Nell has none of the heat of real vengeance; rather it appears to be the last futile gesture of a man whose entire life has been a masterpiece of futility. It's his one last attempt to exert some control over a life that has been resolutely slipping through his fingers since the first time he awoke in a cell with a veiled woman—who may or may not be in his basement—standing over him.

It would be easy to overstate the modest virtues of a film like this, especially since it's difficult to recall a two-character political-psychological drama that isn't just plain painful to sit through. But in this case, the premise works. And the lion's share of credit has to go to the actors. Although DiCenzo's most prominent role to date remains the role of prosecutor Vincent Bugliosi in "Helter Skelter," the TV miniseries about Charles Manson, most of his roles have been on the fringes of A movies (he was Lea Thompson's dad in BACK TO THE FUTURE) and as villains in series television and B movies. His work here is masterful. While FACE OF THE ENEMY is largely his show, DeSoto, best known for playing nurturing roles in LA BAMBA and STAND AND DELIVER, also gives a skilled and emotionally sharp performance.

The skill of the performances is carried throughout the production. Iranian-American director Hassan Ildari never lets the action lag, keeping his main theme—how the inhumanity of high-stakes international politics cripples and crushes individual lives—in focus without belaboring it. The script, adapted by Philip Alderton from a story by Ildari, and the cinematography, by Peter Indergand, are similarly noteworthy for their richness and understatement. FACE OF THE ENEMY is a rare example of a low-budget movie that manages to make virtues of its limitations. *(Profanity, adult situations, violence.)*

d, Hassan Ildari; p, Behrouz Gueramian, Elizabeth Lynch Brown, and Catherine Rocca; w, Philip Alderton (based on a story by Hassan Ildari); ph, Peter Indergand; ed, Toby Brown; m, Esfandiar Monfaredzadeh; prod d, Marina Kieser and Pierluca DeCarlo; art d, John Allen; cos, Sylvia Vasquez

Drama   (PR:C   MPAA:NR)

FALSE IDENTITY

95m Pavilion/RKO c

Stacy Keach *(Ben Driscoll/Harlan Erickkson)*, Genevieve Bujold *(Rachel Roux)*, Tobin Bell *(Marshall Erickkson)*, Veronica Cartwright *(Vera Erickkson)*, and Mike Champion *(Luther)*

As any long-suffering film critic will tell you, most bad movies contain at least one flashback. FALSE IDENTITY begins with one. It is 1973 in San Diego, California. A young US Navy intelligence agent, Harlan Erickkson, makes the not-very-intelligent move of getting out of his car late at night on an abandoned pier and hollering the name of the person he is supposed to meet there, Driscoll. Driscoll does appear, and then some, caving in Erickkson's head with a lead pipe, bashing in his face with a plank, and finally burning off his fingerprints with acid. After changing clothes with his victim, Driscoll tries to make his getaway, only to have his car explode in a flurry of skyrockets, as if it were carrying a trunkload of fireworks.

It turns out that the skullduggery at the root of this violent meeting has something to do with top-secret weaponry stolen by Driscoll. It also turns out that, amazingly, Erickkson lives, though his memory is gone, and he believes he is Driscoll. Unfortunately, so do the authorities, who throw him into prison for the next 17 years. Those thinking, at this point, that FALSE IDENTITY will be about Erickkson's efforts to see justice done by exposing the real culprits and putting his life back together are only half-right. The wrong half. In fact, what really happened on the pier that night is never very central to IDENTITY'S concerns. In time we learn that it was a gimmick calculated to give Erickkson amnesia without really giving him amnesia (bad movies lean on flashbacks; really terrible movies lean on flashbacks plus amnesia). Getting out of prison, and still thinking he's Driscoll, Erickkson (now played by Stacy Keach) heads to the fictional California town of Lexington, which also happens to be the home of the rest of the Erickkson clan. However, Erickkson heads there simply because the town gives him a funny feeling. Besides, IDENTITY would pretty much come to a grinding halt if he went to some other Lexington, say Lexington, Kentucky, or Lexington, Ohio.

Actually, that wouldn't have been a half-bad idea considering what does happen. In Lexington, Harlan finds himself hip-deep in southern fried gothic weirdness magically transplanted to the West Coast. Erickkson's brother, Marshall (Tobin Bell), the head of the clan, grows oranges instead of tobacco or cotton. He also happens to be a bug-eyed psychotic bully who likes to beat up women and whose sadistic henchmen help to keep the town in his iron grip. Marshall's leading victim is his wife, Vera (Veronica Cartwright), who, quite understandably, is a babbling, neurotic alcoholic. It only makes sense, somehow, that this nest of corn-pone craziness should also include a dippy radio deejay (Genevieve Bujold), a transplanted French-Canadian who calls herself Coyote on the air and Rochelle Roux in "real life." Her investigations into Erickkson's life, part of her radio series on local heroes, trigger the amnesiac's memories, cause Vera to switch from vodka to coffee as her morning beverage of choice, and, most important, turn Marshall red with sputtering rage, leading him to order his henchmen to bump off what seems to be half the town's population. If you haven't already guessed—or if you've never read any Tennessee Williams or William Faulkner—this is a family hiding a terrible secret. And Erickkson's return, along with Rochelle's radio show, threatens to blow the lid off.

Unfortunately, the only ones still sputtering with rage at the end of this film are those who've sat through it. Besides being resolutely unoriginal, Sandra K. Bailey's script is also slow-moving, convoluted, and smothered in talk, much of it so embarrassing that the actors, at times, seem visibly confounded by some of the things the script forces them to say with straight faces. The direction by James Keach (Stacy's brother) is awash in TV-style clunkiness further burdened by an apparent attempt to include as much footage as possible of Stacy riding around town on his Harley-Davidson. The only compensation offered by this misguided effort is Bernard Auroux's cinematography, which gives the film a style and moodiness it never deserves.

The title, at least, has a backhanded kind of honesty to it. FALSE IDENTITY tries to palm itself off as a suspense drama. In reality, it's a big snooze. *(Violence, profanity, adult situations.)*

d, James Keach; p, James Shavick; w, Sandra K. Bailey; ph, Bernard Auroux; ed, Nancy Frazen; m, Barry Goldberg; md, Steve Bedell; prod d, Kevin Ryan; art d, Trey Scott; set d, Ron Lombard

Thriller   (PR:C   MPAA:PG-13)

FAR OUT MAN

85m Paul Hertzberg-Lisa Hansen/CineTel c

Tommy Chong *(Far Out Man)*, C. Thomas Howell *(Himself)*, Rae Dawn Chong *(Herself)*, Shelby Chong *(Tree)*, Paris Chong *(Kyle)*, Martin Mull *(Psychiatrist)*, Bobby Taylor *(Bobby)*, Reynaldo Rey *(Lou)*, Peggy F. Sands *(Misty)*, Al Mancini

(Fresno Detective), Judd Nelson *(Himself)*, Cheech Marin *(Himself)*, Michael Winslow *(Airport Cop)*, Rae Allen *(Holly)*, Paul Bartel *(Weebee Cool)*, Mr. Bill *(Mr. Bill, the Dog)*, Patrick Campbell *(Clerk)*, Alina Cenal *(Maid)*, Carlos Cervantes *(Mexican)*, Buddy Daniels *(Gang Leader)*, Lewis Dix Jr. *(Airport Guard)*, Tina Fava *(Woman with Lou)*, Peter Ferrara *(Rae Dawn's Director)*, Paul Hertzberg *(Drunk Man with Wine)*, K. Theodore Howard *(Desk Sergeant)*, Myra J. *(Young Lady)*, Henri Kingi *(Mean Indian)*, Terence Kirkland *(Hitchhiker)*, Paul Murray *(Redneck in Cafe)*, Penelope Jane Reed *(Stewardess)*, Lisa M. Hansen *(Police Radio Dispatcher)*, Don Dokken, Paul Monroe, John Norum *(Rock Group)*, Robbi Chong *(Dancer)*, Ronnie Tanksley *(Nurse)*, Patricia Van Santen *(Truck Stop Waitress)*, John Welsh *(Driver)*, Glen Wilder *(Security Cop)*, Guitar Shorty *(Himself)*, and Floyd Sneed *(Drummer in Band)*

After years of success as part of the comedy team Cheech and Chong, Tommy Chong goes it alone with this film, and as bad as FAR OUT MAN is cinematically, it's still not entirely unwatchable. Chong is a tremendously untalented filmmaker, but at least he knows that's the case (indeed the opening credit reads "A Tommy Chong Attempt"), and his first solo project is charmingly unpretentious. All those involved with the project (the cast seems to include the entire Chong family) are seemingly unaware that they are making a major film, and the result is a sloppy but oddly refreshing movie.

FAR OUT MAN tells the story of a hippie (played by Chong) who, although incredibly rich, is lost in today's society. He still smokes pot, talks about karma, and uses phrases like "Far out, man," while wandering through his broken-down amusement park, once known as Hippie Land. Deserted by his second wife after he threw her out of their rock band, Far Out Man repeatedly embarrasses his daughter, actress Rae Dawn Chong (Chong's real-life daughter, playing herself), by making unannounced visits to her movie sets. Lamenting the loss of his wife, Tree (Chong's real-life wife, Shelby), longing for the days when life was simpler (and marijuana was cheaper), Far Out Man is a total mess. But when Rae Dawn calls in a psychiatrist (Martin Mull), her father's life begins to change. Under hypnosis he comes to believe that he is once again in his youth, doing what he loves most—acting as a roadie for rock bands. Far Out Man's adventures on the road lead to a reunion with Tree, who has been living with actor C. Thomas Howell (played, of course, by C. Thomas Howell), and to a meeting with the aging roadie's estranged teenage son (Paris Chong). The film ends with a rock concert featuring the entire Chong clan, the ultimate family activity.

Needless to say, plot is nowhere to be found in this mess, and many of the scenes seem to have been improvised. Moreover, the direction is flat (at times nonexistent), the photography dull, and the editing atrocious. In fact, the technical quality of the film is so bad that occasionally FAR OUT MAN threatens to disappear from the screen. Still, this badly made movie is not entirely without merit.

First of all, it's funny. Sometimes the humor is crude, other times it is unintentional, but the film *is* funny. The performers are so likable and relaxed that the worst jokes remain amusing (even lighting farts with a match gets a laugh), and only Tommy Chong could make a funny bit out of a drug overdose. Part of the charm of Cheech and Chong's extremely successful 1980s movies was the same lack of organization on display in FAR OUT MAN (oddly, Chong demonstrated more personality as a director in those films than he does here). Of course, it didn't hurt that Cheech and Chong are also two very funny guys.

Essentially, FAR OUT MAN plays like a Cheech and Chong movie without Cheech, who makes only a cameo appearance. But it is also a strikingly personal film in which Chong admits that his worldview is outdated and acknowledges that his former partner has gone on to much greater success than he has. (Cheech directed and starred in the well-received BORN IN EAST L.A., a sharper, more amusing film than this one. In fact, during Cheech's weird cameo in FAR OUT MAN, he looks directly at the camera and says, "Why am I doing this? I got development deals all over town!") But despite the personal nature of the film, Chong wanders aimlessly from one gag to the next without contemplating any of them.

The performances are uniformly funny. Tommy, Shelby, Paris, and Rae Dawn all have some nice moments, but they are upstaged in their own "home movie!" by the supporting players. Bobby Taylor, Reynaldo Rey, and Mull are all very amusing. However, this movie is stolen by Howell, who plays a screamingly funny parody of himself. His image as a "Brat Packer" is demolished in some of the funniest moments of the film year. Sporting a goofy-looking goatee and ridiculously fancy clothes, he egotistically rants and raves about not getting a part that was promised to him, and later has a wonderfully funny scene with Judd Nelson (as himself) in which Howell names all of the films he has appeared in, hoping that Nelson will recognize him. And when Nelson—who still doesn't know who Howell is—recognizes Tree from a cheap slasher movie, Howell castigates Nelson for having seen that movie but not RED DAWN. This is truly funny stuff. A strange little movie, FAR OUT MAN is a must-see for Cheech and Chong fans. *(Profanity, brief nudity, substance abuse.)*

d, Tommy Chong; p, Lisa M. Hansen; w, Tommy Chong; ph, Greg Gardiner and Eric Woster; ed, Stephen Myers and Gilberto Costa Nunes; m, Jay

Chattaway; md, Barry Levine; art d, David B. Miller; set d, T.K. Kirkpatrick; spec, Thomas L. Bellissimo; stunts, Leon Delaney; cos, Dennis Michael Bansmer and James Gutierrez; makup, Donna Lou Henderson

Comedy   (PR:C-O   MPAA:R)

FEUD, THE

96m Feud/Castle Hill c

Rene Auberjonois *(Reverton)*, Ron McLarty *(Dolf Beeler)*, Joe Grifasi *(Bud Bullard)*, Scott Allegrucci *(Tony Beeler)*, Gale Mayron *(Bernice Beeler)*, David Strathairn *(The Stranger)*, Stanley Tucci *(Harvey Yelton)*, Lynne Killmeyer *(Eva Bullard)*, Kathleen Doyle *(Frieda Bullard)*, Libby George *(Bobby Beeler)*, Rob Vanderberry *(Junior Bullard)*, Mert Hatfield *(Clive Shell)*, James Eric *(Walt Huff)*, Don Hartman *(Ernie)*, Joshua Bo Lozoff *(Dickie Herkimer)*, Rick Warner *(Ray Dooley)*, John Bennes *(Ivan)*, Kay Shrider *(Ingrid)*, Michael Stanton Kennedy *(Curly)*, Lynda Clark *(Marie)*, Roger Black *(Bartender)*, George Earl Lee *(Doc Stevens)*, David Dwyer *(Coach)*, Tom Davis *(Teammate)*, Howard Kivett *(Relative)*, Red Suydam *(Red Sedan)*, and Allen Kelman *(Man at Counter)*

Dolf Beeler (Ron McLarty) and Bud Bullard (Joe Grifasi) are just two ordinary, everyday Americans living in neighboring small towns. Beeler works in a factory, Bullard owns a hardware store. Each man has a pretty wife, an attractive home, and a loving family. But all that is about to change. Things begin simply enough, when Beeler tries to buy a can of paint thinner from Bullard's sullen son, Junior (Rob Vanderberry), who takes disrespectful exception to Beeler's unlit cigar, spitefully citing the store's "No Smoking" policy. Beeler gets all hot under the collar and gives the boy a piece of his mind, only to find himself looking down the business end of a pistol held by Bullard's cousin, Reverton (Rene Auberjonois), a black-clad railroad detective with a few screws loose. Bullard tries to mediate the dispute, alternately scolding and supporting his son, apologizing to Beeler while suggesting Beeler was in the wrong, and encouraging Reverton to keep things in perspective, but the damage is done. Everyone's feeling offended and wronged, and no one quite knows what to do about it. There's no feud yet, but the stage is set, leaving Beeler fretting and Bullard fuming. However, it takes two unfortunate coincidences to get the fires really burning—quite literally, as it happens. The next morning, Bullard awakens to find his store in ashes. Later that day, Beeler's car explodes. Both men leap to the natural (though, as it happens, incorrect) conclusions, and the battle is on. To complicate matters, Beeler's son (Scott Allegrucci) and Bullard's daughter (Lynne Killmeyer) are deeply in puppy love, Beeler's daughter (Gale Mayron) is pregnant and determined to convince the local chief of police (Stanley Tucci) that he's the father, and Junior jumps tracks when Reverton lends him his gun, turning into a wanton juvenile delinquent faster than you can say "rebel without a cause." What a muddle! And we haven't even mentioned the sleek stranger who says he's a bowling-ball salesman but seems to have bigger things on his mind, the neighborhood techno-nerd whose sole aim in life is to blow things up, or the relentlessly optimistic Mrs. Bullard, who faces everything—from her husband's attempted suicide to his mad conviction that he's a gorilla—with an apparently endless supply of cheerful bromides.

Once the action is set in motion, THE FEUD concerns itself less with the feud itself—the Beelers and the Bullards aren't, after all, shotgun-blasting Hatfields and McCoys—than with the quirky personalities populating two superficially ordinary small towns. Director Bill D'Elia (in his feature debut) and writer Robert Uricola, who adapted the screenplay from the novel by Thomas Berger (whose *Little Big Man* and *Neighbors* were also filmed), aren't interested in madcap farce. Instead, they've constructed a deceptively low-key and surprisingly macabre comedy, rooted in the notion that madness lies just below the surface of everyday life and it only takes a single wrong turn, one careless whisper, to unleash the chaos. That's not to say THE FEUD is unrelentingly dark. In fact, the film's costumes, production design, and cinematography are all aggressively sunny, evoking an archetypal, early 60s suburban America, and the characters, though quirky, owe more to "Father Knows Best" than to the psychopaths of David Lynch's BLUE VELVET. But there's an unmistakable edge to things, and THE FEUD plays for keeps. Characters die and lives are destroyed, the all's-well-that-ends-well denouement notwithstanding.

THE FEUD also features a stylized graphic titles sequence in which names are folded, spindled, mutilated, and eventually incinerated by a twisting, turning fuse. Its anachronistic look seems at first excessively mannered, but ultimately fits right in with the movie's winking, self-referential tone. *(Violence.)*

d, Bill D'Elia; p, Bill D'Elia and Carole Kivett; w, Bill D'Elia and Robert Uricola (based on the book by Thomas Berger); ph, John Beymer; ed, Bill Johnson; m, Brian Eddolls; prod d, Charles Lagola; cos, Ron Leamon

Comedy   (PR:A   MPAA:NR)

FIELD, THE

(Ireland) 110m Granada — Treesdale/Avenue c

Richard Harris *(Bull McCabe)*, Sean Bean *(Tadgh McCabe)*, Tom Berenger *(Peter the American)*, Frances Tomelty *(The Widow)*, Brenda Fricker *(Maggie McCabe)*, John Hurt *(The Bird)*, Joan Sheehy, Ruth McCabe *(Tinker Women)*, Jer O'Leary *(Tinker Girl's Father)*, Noel O'Donovan *(Tomas)*, John Cowley *(Flanagan)*, Ronan Wilmot *(Tinker)*, Jenny Conroy *(Tinker Girl)*, Sean McGinley *(Father Doran)*, Malachy McCourt *(Sergeant)*, Eamon Keane *(Dan Paddy Andy)*, Sara Jane Scaife *(McRoarty Girl)*, David Wilmot *(Boy at Dance)*, Rachel Dowling, Sarah Cronin *(Girls at Dance)*, Peadar Lamb *(Paddy Joe O'Reilly)*, Aine Ni Mhuire *(Priest's Housekeeper)*, Frank McDonald, Brendan Gleeson *(Quarrymen)*, Mairtin Jaimsie, Tom Jordan, Johnny Choil Mhike, and Bina McLoughlin

Bull McCabe (Richard Harris) is a man of the land, a farmer whose reverence for nature far exceeds his tolerance for human frailty. McCabe and his wife Maggie (Brenda Fricker) haven't spoken for 18 years, their relationship poisoned by the suicide of their 13-year-old son. McCabe's friend Bird O'Donnell (John Hurt) is in awe of his strength, and his surviving son, Tadgh (Sean Bean), lives in sullen fear of his father's disapproval. The remote Irish village where McCabe holds sway has scarcely changed over the centuries; even the local priest, Father Doran (Sean McGinley), concedes that the veneer of Christianity — let alone respect for the laws of men, especially outsiders — is thin. But change threatens the community in the form of a field McCabe has worked for years. Its lush fertility, the product of his labor, stands in stark contrast to the harshness of the surrounding landscape. The owner, a widow (Frances Tomelty) whom the community has never accepted, decides to sell the field and return to her own people. McCabe is the natural buyer until the arrival of Peter (Tom Berenger), a wealthy American. Peter's plans for the field are commercial. He wants to pave it over and provide access to the limestone-rich hills beyond, and he has far more money than McCabe could ever hope to scrape together.

McCabe's world begins to crumble. Tadgh falls in love with Katie (Jenny Conroy), a gypsy girl whom McCabe despises because he feels gypsies are rootless and alienated from the land. Peter wins Father Doran's support for his plans by pointing out the economic benefits it will have for the community, only confirming McCabe's contempt for the clergy ("No priest died during the potato famine," he spits). Finally, McCabe and his son follow Peter to a deserted lake area and hope to frighten him so badly he will return to America. Things get out of hand and Peter is killed, father and son sinking the body in the lake. The way is now clear for McCabe to buy the field, which he does, but he takes no pleasure in his victory as it soon leads to more violence and tragedy.

THE FIELD was director Jim Sheridan's much-anticipated follow-up to his surprisingly successful MY LEFT FOOT, and, as that film did, it focusses on the strength of human will in the face of overwhelming adversity. But while MY LEFT FOOT was ferociously personal, chronicling one man's valiant efforts to live a full life despite his crippled body, THE FIELD is heavily allegorical. Bull McCabe is a modern-day Antaeus, a man whose strength comes from the earth; he and his friend Bird, who shares his complicity with nature, don't even go by human names. Peter (who's listed in the credits simply as "The American") embodies the decadence of urban living. From his shiny black car to his camel hair coat, there's not a thing about him that blends into the landscape. The point is articulated early and often: the land and those who live in harmony with it are good; everyone else is corrupt, unnatural, and just plain evil. While it's often oppressively heavy-handed, the film is exceptionally well-photographed. Ireland's terrible beauty — simultaneously harsh and verdant — isn't sentimentalized. The performance by Harris earned him an Oscar nomination, and it certainly is a real scene-stealer, though if he isn't over the top, he's quite close to it. Ray McAnally, who played the father in MY LEFT FOOT (opposite Brenda Fricker who won a Best Supporting Actress for her performance in that film) was being considered for the role of Bull McCabe at the time of his death in 1989. It's also worth noting that in a year of unpleasant dental appliances, John Hurt's easily matches the one worn by Willem Dafoe in WILD AT HEART. *(Violence.)*

d, Jim Sheridan; p, Noel Pearson; w, Jim Sheridan (based on the play by John B. Keane); ph, Jack Conroy; ed, J. Patrick Duffner; m, Elmer Bernstein; md, Audrey Collins; prod d, Frank Conway; art d, Frank Hallinan Flood; set d, Josie MacAvin; cos, Joan Bergin; makup, Tommie Manderson

Drama   (PR:C   MPAA:PG-13)

FILOFAX

(SEE: TAKING CARE OF BUSINESS)

FIRE BIRDS

85m Nova — -Keith Barish — Arnold Kopelson/Touchstone — Buena Vista c

(AKA: WINGS OF THE APACHE)

Nicolas Cage *(Jake Preston)*, Tommy Lee Jones *(Brad Little)*, Sean Young *(Billie Lee Guthrie)*, Bryan Kestner *(Breaker)*, Dale Dye *(A.K. McNeil)*, Mary Ellen Trainor *(Janet Little)*, J.A. Preston *(Gen. Olcott)*, Peter Onorati *(Rice)*, Charles Lanyer *(Darren Phillips)*, Illana Shoshan *(Sharon Geller)*, Marshall Teague *(Doug Daniels)*, Cylk Cozart *(Dewar Proctor)*, Charles Kahlenberg *(Oscar DeMarco)*, Gregory Vahanian *(Tom Davis)*, Robert Lujan *(Steward Rives)*, Scott Williamson *(Scott Buzz)*, Mickey Yablans *(Butch Tippet)*, Bert Rhine *(Stoller)*, Peter Michaels *(Lt. Steve Dobbs)*, Richard Soto *(Capt. Tejada)*, Samuel Hernandez *(Latino Pilot)*, Kristin Wynn *(Jesse Little)*, Kristin Nicole Barnes *(Sam Little)*, Phillip Troy *(Dance Partner)*, Harrison Le Duke *(Broker)*, Garth Le Master *(Waiter)*, and Judson Spence *(Singer)*

If TOP GUN is a war movie for the MTV generation, then FIRE BIRDS is TOP GUN for the FULL METAL JACKET generation. Whenever foreign directors take on an American subject, chances are that they will either get it completely wrong (Norman Jewison's IN COUNTRY) or they'll tell us more about ourselves than we perhaps care to know (virtually all of Alfred Hitchcock's American films). Directed by Britain's David Green, FIRE BIRDS falls solidly into the latter category. It's not so much a war film as a film at war with itself.

FIRE BIRDS opens with a quote from a policy speech given by US President George Bush in September, 1989, in which he pledged armed American aid to friendly governments anywhere in the world doing battle against narco-terrorists, primarily the wealthy and powerful South American cocaine cartels. In a real-world context, the implications are chilling, conjuring up images of WW III as a battle between the world's superpowers and privately financed, well-equipped mercenary armies. In such a war there would be no holds barred, including the use of nuclear weapons.

But FIRE BIRDS doesn't dwell on these messy complexities, except by implication. That is, from the second Nicolas Cage comes on-screen as hot-shot flier Jake Preston, you don't need no stinking nukes. On an observer mission in South America, Preston witnesses the shooting-down of two South American military helicopters by narco-terrorist ace Stoler (Bert Rhine), the movie's Red Baron, in his fast-flying Scorpion attack copter. Returning home, Preston gives his report and urges retaliation. Alarmed by Preston's account, the military and DEA brass brush aside the sticky political complications (underscoring the movie's fantasy element) and authorize the training of an elite team to fly the Apache helicopters — combining the speed and maneuverability of a copter with the firepower of a small destroyer — to support a raid on a high-echelon meeting of "The Cartel." With blinding speed the elite force is whipped into shape by tough old flier Brad (Tommy Lee Jones), the John Wayne-like character whose dilemma is that he is so good that the commanders refuse to let him risk his life in actual combat. Preston quickly becomes Brad's star student, along with Billie Lee (Sean Young), who, very conveniently, is also Preston's former girlfriend. Along the way, Preston has to win back Billie Lee and contend with an "eye-dominance thing" that threatens to scrub him from the team. For a while, it seems as if Brad is intentionally pushing Preston to wash out so the veteran can take the rookie's place. But, Brad's patriotism overriding his thirst for combat, he confesses that he had the same problem in training and shows Preston how to overcome it. Naturally, the cure involves Preston careening around the base in a jeep with red panties tied over his head. Winning his place on the team also wins Preston a new place in Billie Lee's heart (or was it the panties over his head?), and even Brad wins a place on the team at the last minute.

With so many happy endings falling into place, the climactic battle might almost seem to be beside the point. And, in a way, it is. What makes FIRE BIRDS truly riveting entertainment is the not conflict between good and bad guys, but the conflict between the film's apparent intent and the loony subversiveness of its performances. Hardly routine actors, Cage, Jones, and Young are cast in what amounts to a routine B programmer (albeit on an A budget) seemingly intended to serve as Disney's shameless public service contribution to the war on drugs. And this cast gives anything but routine performances. Cage brings an almost frightening ferocity to Preston's cockiness, giving even the most ordinary scenes — especially a training session in a computerized flight simulator — a deeply disturbing edge. As Cage's performance makes clear, Preston's idea of walking tall and going for the gusto teeters on the edge of psychosis. As a result, Preston winds up having far more in common with FULL METAL JACKET's Pyle (Vincent D'Onofrio) than he does with TOP GUN's Maverick (Tom Cruise). Jones, meanwhile, plays Brad as a likable old geezer with a thousand-yard stare. His drill-sergeant's tirades, recited by rote, have the sound of a voice from beyond the grave. Rather than taking cocky young Preston and turning him into a cold-blooded killer, it's more as if Brad were refining what is already a dangerous weapon that happens to walk like a man. Young and Mary Ellen Trainor (as Brad's wife) bring an earthy blue-collar grit to their roles, charging them with a heady dose of erotic energy. However, both of these female characters suffer from script underdevelopment in the face of their men's testosterone-charged death obsessions, against which even the well-staged balletic duel to the death with the dreaded Stoler seems like just so much filler. FIRE BIRDS is one odd movie. But it's the kind of odd that could pass for brilliance. *(Violence, adult situations, profanity.)*

d, David Green; p, William Badalato; w, Nick Thiel and Paul F. Edwards (based on a story by Step Tyner, John K. Swensson, Dale Dye); ph, Tony Imi; ed, Jon Poll, Norman Buckley, and Dennis O'Connor; m, David Newman; md, Peter Afterman; prod d, Joseph T. Garrity; art d, Pat Tagliaferro; set d, Bill Rea; spec, Pat Tagliaferro; stunts, Dennis Madalone; cos, Ellis Cohen; makup, Michael Hancock; tech, Christopher G. Chalko

War   (PR:C   MPAA:PG-13)

FIRE IN EDEN

(SEE: TUSKS)

FIRST POWER, THE

99m Nelson-Interscope/Orion c

Lou Diamond Phillips *(Russell Logan)*, Tracy Griffith *(Tess Seaton)*, Jeff Kober *(Patrick Channing)*, Mykel T. Williamson *(Detective Oliver Franklin)*, Elizabeth Arlen *(Sister Marguerite)*, Dennis Lipscomb *(Commander Perkins)*, Carmen Argenziano *(Lieutenant Grimes)*, Julianna McCarthy *(Grandmother)*, Nada Despotovich *(Bag Lady)*, Sue Giosa *(Carmen)*, Clayton Landey *(Mazza)*, Hansford Rowe *(Father Brian)*, Philip Abbott *(Cardinal)*, David Gale *(Monsignor)*, J. Patrick McNamara *(Priest)*, Lisa Specht *(Anchorwoman)*, Mark Bringelson *(Driver in Alley)*, William Fair *(Detective #2)*, Brian Libby *(Bum/Detective)*, Michael McNab *(Uniform)*, David Partington *(Detective)*, Dan Tullis Jr. *(Cop at Arrest)*, Michael Wise *(Cop at Tenement)*, Andrew Amador, Paula McClure, Tiiu Leek *(Reporters)*, Mitch Carter, Jeff Mooring *(Uniform Cops)*, Todd Jeffries *(Cop)*, Grand L. Bush *(Resevoir Worker)*, Gokul *(Street Vendor)*, David Katims *(Man In Parking Structure)*, Lynn Marta *(Nun)*, Charles Raymond, Scott Lawrence *(Gang Members)*, Bill Moseley *(Bartender)*, Melanie Shatner *(Shopgirl)*, R. David Stephens *(Desk Clerk)*, Oz Tortora *(Antonio)*, Robert Colaizzi *(Driver)*, and Ron J. Goodman *(Bum in Hotel)*

Original ideas are hard to come by in mainstream Hollywood. If it's not a father and son switching bodies, it's a group of scientists battling monsters underwater. The latest trend (in horror films at least) seems to be the resurrection of condemned psycho-killers who can enter people's bodies at will—not a particularly brilliant plot device, but one that resurfaced in at least two films during 1989 (SHOCKER and THE HORROR SHOW), and that now returns again in THE FIRST POWER. This time out, Lou Diamond Phillips plays Russell Logan, a police detective with a reputation for nailing serial killers. Presently, Logan is hard at work on the case of the "Pentagram Killer" (Jeff Kober), a madman who ritualistically murders his victims and carves inverted pentagrams (the mark of the devil) on their chests. After receiving an anonymous tip concerning the killer's whereabouts, Logan and his partner, Oliver Franklin (Mykel T. Williamson), go to a park and confront the killer, who is about to murder an undercover policewoman (Sue Giosa). After a long chase on foot, Logan catches the killer and is stabbed in the ensuing fight. Reinforcements arrive and take the killer away, while Logan is taken to the hospital. Time passes and the killer (whose name, we now find out, is Patrick Channing) is brought to court. Logan wants him to get the death penalty, even though the detective was ominously warned by his mystery informant not to let Channing die. After the psycho is sentenced to the gas chamber, Logan gets a call from the informant telling him the problems with the killer are just beginning. Channing is executed, and faster than you can say "apparition from beyond the grave," he begins showing up in the visions of Logan and of Tess Seaton (Tracy Griffith), a psychic who has been following the case. Tess meets with Logan to discuss her weird visions and, in addition to admitting that she was his informant, tells him that Channing is a being with "The First Power." This power, apparently granted by Satan himself, gives Channing the ability to come back from the dead and enter the body of any innocent victim he chooses (though drug addicts and street people seem to be the most susceptible. "His body may be dead, but his spirit is released," Tess tells Logan. Needless to say, Logan is a bit skeptical, but he soon changes his mind when Detective Franklin is trampled by a horse-drawn carriage, and the escaping driver of the carriage jumps from the roof of a 10-story building and strolls away. After several more such possessions and killings, Logan and Tess enlist the aide of Sister Marguerite (Elizabeth Arlen), a nun who has been following these events with apocalyptic vigor. It seems the only way to stop this satanically empowered being is to stab him with a powerful bladed crucifix, which the sister just happens to have access to. The film climaxes with a battle between Logan and Channing (whose original body has fully materialized for some obscure reason) that ends with Logan stabbing Channing and then

being shot by the police. In the final scene, as Tess visits the hospitalized Logan, Channing makes another appearance that may or may not be a dream.

Religious mumbo-jumbo and psychic-power nonsense have always been a part of the supernatural horror genre, but it is becoming increasingly hard to suspend one's disbelief when the *same* mumbo-jumbo is repeated in countless movies. THE FIRST POWER not only resembles THE HORROR SHOW and SHOCKER (which in turn resembled THE HIDDEN), but there are snatches of THE SEVENTH SIGN, elements of THE EXORCIST, and heaping portions of THE OMEN (from which the climax is stolen outright, almost shot for shot) present throughout the film. Admittedly, THE FIRST POWER is entertaining and the action is nicely filmed, but the overall lack of originality and the downright silliness of the plot finally sink it. Aided by good work from cinematographer Theo Van de Sande (CROSSING DELANCEY), writer-director Robert Resnikoff exhibits a flair for visuals in his feature-film debut, but his handling of the suspense sequences is weak, as is the film's whole horror angle. THE FIRST POWER's script is essentially a combination of two genres: the occult-horror film and the cop-action movie. Clearly, Resnikoff prefers the latter; his direction exhibits the most conviction in the action sequences. Resnikoff has also found a fine action lead in Phillips, a strong screen presence and very capable physical actor who is convincing in his hard-guy cop persona. True, Phillips isn't given much to do, but the little that is required of him is done in grand style. By contrast, the other performances seem bland: Griffith fails to impress, and Kober, although he has a wonderfully evil face, seems a wee bit tired and uninterested, lacking true menace.

But for all its problems and flaws (and it has many), THE FIRST POWER remains a very entertaining movie. The religious hokum and crazy plot twists get so wild that they soon become fun, and when Phillips and Griffith are attacked by a possessed bag lady (Nada Despotovich), things get downright hilarious. Wacky moments like the heroes' visit to the killer's grandmother's house (which ends with the grandmother raving like a lunatic) are terrifically off-the-wall, while certain images, such as that of a nun crawling through a sewer armed with a deadly crucifix, have got to be seen to be believed. Strange dialog and unusual actions abound, and the pacing is so fast you may not be able to catch your breath. After a while, Resnikoff starts throwing everything at the viewer, some of which sticks and some of which doesn't. Unfortunately, most of this fun appears to be unintentional, since Resnikoff (who was inspired to write the script by real-life convicted killer Gary Gilmore's belief that he would be reincarnated after his execution) surely wants it to be taken seriously. He has supplied countless reasons for everything that happens in the film and, at least for the first 40 minutes, it's all delivered with a straight face. But regardless of his true intentions, Resnikoff has made a screwy horror movie that, despite itself, is fun to watch. *(Violence, profanity, adult situations.)*

d, Robert Resnikoff; p, David Madden; w, Robert Resnikoff; ph, Theo Van de Sande; ed, Michael Bloecher; m, Stewart Copeland; prod d, Joseph T. Garrity; art d, Pat Tagliaferro; set d, Bill Rea and Wendy Guidery; spec, Edward French; stunts, John Moio; cos, Tim D'Arcy; makup, Sheri Short, Debbie Zoller, and Camille Calvet

Horror   (PR:C-O   MPAA:R)

FLAME IN MY HEART, A

(Fr./Switz.) 110m Roxie bw

(UNE FLAME DANS MON COEUR)

Myriam Mezieres *(Mercedes)*, Benoit Regent *(Pierre)*, Aziz Kabouche *(Johnny)*, Biana *(Friend)*, Jean-Yves Berthelot *(Partner)*, Andre Marcon *(Etienne)*, Anne Rucki *(The Pianist)*, and Jean-Gabriel Nordmann *(Director)*

Obsessive love of the most terrifying kind is the subject of A FLAME IN MY HEART, the latest film from Alain Tanner, the Swiss director of JONAH — WHO WILL BE 25 IN THE YEAR 2000 (1976) and THE MIDDLE OF THE WORLD (1974). Myriam Mezieres, whose screenplay was adapted by Tanner, stars as Mercedes, a Parisian actress who, as the film opens, is attempting to break off with Johnny (Aziz Kabouche), her Arab lover. He cannot accept this, however, and dogs her continually. One day on the Metro she picks up the journalist Pierre (Benoit Regent), and falls desperately in love with him after a single tryst. Luckily for Mercedes, he's receptive to her sudden adoration; unluckily for both, he soon finds it necessary to leave town on business. This precipitates a major breakdown for clinging-vine Mercedes, who walks out on the play she's been rehearsing and holes up in Pierre's flat, where she spends her days hanging around nude, watching TV, masturbating, and living on cereal. He returns to find his place in a shambles, the phone cut off, and the besotted actress in an irrational and near-infantile state. After Mercedes finds employment in a sex establishment, performing a striptease for the delectation of an audience of needy men, the unbelievably forbearing Pierre agrees to take her with him to Cairo, where he is to work on an assignment. They make love on the banks of the Nile, after which she disappears. She is last seen sitting in a rubble-heap, completely out of her mind and staring at some poor children who are playing near her.

A FLAME IN MY HEART was shot in 16 millimeter black and white, then blown up to 35 millimeter for the big screen, lending the film a grainy, unappetizing look that Tanner evidently thought appropriate for this most unromantic of love stories. The tone of the film is similarly alienating: the director seems completely detached, observing his heroine's torturous peregrinations like some half-interested, pitiless God. At the same time, there is an undeniable sureness in his handling of the scenes of rough sex between Mercedes and Johnny, and especially in the long, bravura sequence showing Mercedes' subway seduction of Pierre, largely a matter of come-hither-and-be-quick-about-it facial expression. The editing is masterfully smooth and watchful.

Although the film depicts extremes of degradation and mania that compare with the obsessive loves in such diverse European films as LAST TANGO IN PARIS; THE STORY OF ADELE H.; THAT OBSCURE OBJECT OF DESIRE; and BETTY BLUE (American films, with the garish exceptions of FATAL ATTRACTION and 9 1/2 WEEKS, customarily veer away from the serious treatment of the topic), Mercedes' descent into madness seems too predictable, in part because we've seen it before in the films just named. No explanation is given for the character's apparent need to attach herself to some man, and the film begins to play like a sick comedy, with Mezieres happily acting out every cliche of lovelorn womanhood imaginable. Mezieres—resembling, with her ravaged, libidinous face, a down-at-the-mouth Rita Moreno—gets to run the gamut of obsessive nuttiness; abased in scene after scene, she weeps great black streams of mascara, munches mountains of breakfast snacks, wanders forlornly along a highway carrying her shoes (bare feet being *de rigeur* in such *amours fou*), and even, at one point, attacks Pierre with a huge kitchen knife. After a while one watches just to see what behavioral atrocity will follow next, while wondering just how much of this was intended to be comic. In particular, Mezieres' extended sex dance with a stuffed gorilla could go down in movie history as a classically bad moment (though it's still not a patch on Dietrich's original simian sarabande in BLONDE VENUS). What could Tanner have intended by this scene? Or does it represent simply another excuse for Mezieres to show off her trim figure?

Clearly, A FLAME IN MY HEART is Mezieres' film in more ways than one, but Kabouche is convincingly intense, bestial, and sexy as Johnny, and has the best-observed scene in the film when Johnny destroys the clothes he gave to Mercedes, while she looks on. Regent is amusingly square as the thickheaded, solemn Pierre, whose conversation with Mercedes about the relative merits of journalism is so deadeningly high-minded it's almost a comic high point. *(Nudity, sexual situations, violence, profanity, adult situations.)*

d, Alain Tanner; p, Paulo Branco; w, Myriam Mezieres and Alain Tanner; ph, Acacio de Almeida; ed, Laurent Uhler; m, J.S. Bach

Drama   **(PR:O MPAA:NR)**

FLASHBACK

108m Marvin Worth/Paramount c

Dennis Hopper *(Huey Walker)*, Kiefer Sutherland *(John Buckner)*, Carol Kane *(Maggie)*, Cliff De Young *(Sheriff Hightower)*, Michael McKean *(Hal)*, Richard Masur *(Barry)*, Paul Dooley *(Donald R. Stark, FBI Director)*, Kathleen York *(Sparkle)*, Tom O'Brien *(Phil Prager)*, Eric Lorentz, Jan Van Sickle *(Prison Guards)*, Jack Casperson *(Man in Dining Car)*, Dwayne Carrington *(Waiter in Dining Car)*, David Underwood, Bobby Price, Timothy G. Riley *(Deputies)*, Liz Jury *(Barmaid)*, Kelli Van Londersele *(Girl in Bar)*, Allan Graf *(Studie)*, Kenneth Jensen Bryan *(Buckner's Father)*, Donna McMullen *(Buckner's Mother)*, Adam Seils *(Young Buckner)*, Alan August *(Hal's Son)*, Jason Iselin *(Barry's Son)*, Norm Silver *(Conductor)*, Jason Campbell *(Kid on Train)*, Wendelin Harston *(Woman on Train)*, Steve Spencer *(Man on Train)*, and Delbert Highlands *(Loomis)*

Never as funny or as satirically sharp as it wants to be, this generation-gap comedy succeeds only as a vehicle for Dennis Hopper. It's only too bad that it's such a flimsy vehicle. Hopper plays legendary 60s radical Huey Walker—a fictional blend of Abbie Hoffman and Jerry Rubin—who has come out of hiding after 20 years to face charges of endangering the life of Nixon-era Vice-President Spiro Agnew, whose train car Walker unhitched during a whistle-stop tour in 1969. Sent cross-country from Washington, DC, to bring Walker to trial is yuppieish FBI agent John Buckner (Kiefer Sutherland). We know from the start that Buckner is not as tough as he appears to be when he giggles while reading Walker's file and questions his superior (Paul Dooley) about the purpose of using Bureau time, money, and manpower to arrest Walker. Nevertheless, Buckner dutifully heads off to the Pacific Northwest, where Walker has been captured. Because bad weather has closed the airport, Buckner takes his prisoner aboard a train for the long, slow trip to the site of the trial. (An obvious gimmick to allow Buckner and Walker to develop a relationship, this screenwriter's device man-

ages to work, and it's only when Buckner and Walker get off the train that FLASHBACK gets into trouble.) Once on the train, Walker tricks Buckner into getting drunk so he can switch clothes with him. During a stopover, Buckner is mistaken for the legendary radical, and abused and brutalized by Hightower (Cliff De Young), the local sheriff who also happens to be running for Congress. Meanwhile, the identity switch backfires when a pair of aging would-be hippies (Richard Masur, Michael McKean) take Walker hostage, believing him to be an FBI man, and offer him in exchange for Buckner, whom they think is their countercultural hero. The sheriff, fearful that Buckner will expose his brutality and cost him the election, decides it would be just as easy to kill both Buckner and Walker during the hostage exchange. When Buckner manages to outwit Hightower and save Walker, the sheriff has more of an excuse than ever to go after Buckner, who is now aiding and abetting the escape of a prisoner. Arriving on the scene, Buckner's boss, for reasons of his own, is none too convinced that Buckner has turned outlaw. Naturally, Buckner has a few surprises of his own up his sleeve. Firstly, he's not quite who he appears to be, as he reveals during a visit to a commune-turned-60s-relic watched over by Maggie (Carol Kane). As it happens Buckner was born and raised on this commune; joining the FBI has been his own unique version of rebelling against his parents. After sitting through some scratchy home movies of himself and his parents, Buckner decides that he will help Walker escape across the border into Canada. And having taken a liking to Buckner, Walker becomes just as determined that he will help the young agent save his career by making sure Buckner brings him in for trial.

While FLASHBACK has plenty of comic potential and enough plot for two movies, the film rarely rises to the occasion. The script is too flat and contrived most of the time, with its changes in direction mostly a matter of convenience rather than arising from the characters or situations. (How is it, for example, that Buckner has been able to hide his hippie background from the FBI?) The film is finally slowed to a crawl by its heavy cargo subplots.

In his American debut, Italian director Franco Amurri does a mediocre job at best in orchestrating the action. At its worst, FLASHBACK has the tinny shrillness of a mediocre made-for-TV movie. But had this been produced for the small screen it would probably have been made without the participation of Sutherland and Hopper, and the R-rated invectives that Hopper so frequently offers up would certainly have been absent.

While Sutherland contributes as a capable performance as the embattled Buckner, it is Hopper who justifies FLASHBACK's existence. The genuine article, he brings the authority of his experience to the role. In his best scenes, Sutherland is wise enough to step back and let Hopper work what turns into a kind of magic despite the lackluster script and direction. In the process—and before he, too, begins showing the strains of making the plot's dull contrivances believable—Hopper provides glimpses of the kind of madly grand entertainment FLASHBACK could have been but, sadly, is not. Buried in the cloying soundtrack of 60s hits are superior renditions by Natalie Merchant of "Walk on the Wild Side" by Edie Brickell, and of "People Get Ready" by Bob Dylan. *(Profanity, adult situations.)*

d, Franco Amurri; p, Marvin Worth and David Loughery; w, David Loughery; ph, Stefan Czapsky; ed, C. Timothy O'Meara; m, Barry Goldberg; md, Jody Taylor Worth; prod d, Vincent Cresciman; art d, James Terry Welden; set d, Cecilia Rodarte; spec, Dennis Dion; cos, Eileen Kennedy; makup, Charles Balasz

Action/Comedy   **(PR:C MPAA:R)**

FLATLINERS

111m Stonebridge/Columbia c

Kiefer Sutherland *(Nelson Wright)*, Julia Roberts *(Rachel Mannus)*, Kevin Bacon *(David Labraccio)*, William Baldwin *(Joe Hurley)*, Oliver Platt *(Randy Steckle)*, Kimberly Scott *(Winnie Hicks)*, Joshua Rudoy *(Billy Mahoney)*, Benjamin Mouton *(Rachel's Father)*, Aeryk Egan *(Young Nelson)*, Kesha Reed *(Young Winnie)*, Hope Davis *(Anne)*, Jim Ortlieb *(Uncle Dave)*, John Joseph Duda *(Young Labraccio)*, Megan Stewart, Tressa Thomas, Gonzo Gonzalez *(Playground Kids)*, Afram Bill Williams *(Ben Hicks)*, Deborah Thompson *(Terry)*, Elinore O'Connell *(Rachel's Mother)*, Marilyn Dodds Frank *(Bag Lady)*, Sanna Vraa *(Bridget)*, Nicole Niblack, Cynthia Bassham, Sarabeth Tucek, Ilona Margolis, Julie Warner, Iilana B'Tiste, Deborah Torchio, Deborah Goomas, Michelle McKee, Nancy Moran, Dede Latinopoulos *(Joe's Women)*, Patricia Belcher *(Edna, the Ward Nurse)*, Susan French *(Terminal Woman)*, Beth Grant *(Housewife)*, Cage S. Johnson *(Near-Death Patient)*, Jared Milmeister, Patrick Gleeson *(Young Nelson's Friends)*, John Benjamin Martin *(Man on Crack)*, Lynda Odums *(Nurse)*, John Fink, Angela Paton *(Doctors)*, Evelina Fernandez *(Latin Woman)*, Miguel Delgado *(Latin Husband)*, Ingrid Oliu *(Latin Wife)*, Raymond Hanis *(Latin Orderly)*, Zoaunne LeRoy *(Waitress)*, Tom Kurlander *(Medical Student)*, Nili Levi *(Little Girl)*, Anne James *(Beth)*, K.K. Dodds *(Jill)*, and Natsuko Ohama *(Professor)*

Medical students Rachel Mannus (Julia Roberts), Nelson Wright (Keifer Sutherland), David Labraccio (Kevin Bacon), Joe Hurley (William Baldwin) and Randy Steckle (Oliver Platt) are friends and future colleagues. Nelson, the wild dreamer in the group, concocts an outrageous plan and presents it to the others. They're all interested in the nature of death, he reasons; they wouldn't want to be doctors if they weren't. So why don't they do a little first-hand research? Nelson suggests they kill themselves one by one—not in some gory orgy of self-destruction, but coolly, rationally, scientifically. After experiencing clinical death when the brainwave line of the EKG monitor goes flat (hence "Flatliners"), they'll be brought back through CPR. Each member of the group has reservations. Serious Rachel worries about brain damage. Egocentric Steckle—whose favorite pastime is imagining the title of his best-selling autobiography—is afraid that getting involved in such a wacko project might ruin his career. Ladies' man Joe, a little lacking in the brains department, doesn't believe the scheme will work. And New Age nonconformist David thinks it's a dangerous exercise in futility. Nevertheless, they all agree to give it a try. Nelson goes first and soars through a vision of children laughing and playing in a field of flowers. He returns shaken but intact and tells the others it was a beautiful experience. What he fails to share is that as he was coming back the vision became dark and ominous. Worse still, he soon discovers—and keeps to himself—that he's brought back something from the other side. Unaware of the danger, Joe goes next, only to find himself haunted by images of the many women he has seduced and betrayed. David brings back the memory of a small girl he and his classmates taunted relentlessly in the schoolyard, and Rachel is tormented by the image of her father, who committed suicide when she was a child. Steckle never goes under; by now it's clear that they've all stirred up the demons from their past and must somehow make peace with them if they're to go on with their lives. David tracks down his former classmate and apologizes. Joe's fiancee learns of his relentless womanizing and leaves him; by hurting him as he has hurt others, she inadvertently pays off his psychic debt. Rachel realizes that her father came home from war a drug addict and killed himself in despair, not because of her. Nelson has the toughest time of all. Responsible for the death of another child, he convinces himself that the only way to settle up is to die. But his friends come to his rescue and everything works out all right in the end.

FLATLINERS is nothing if not easy on the eyes. Director Joel Schumacher (THE LOST BOYS) goes for broke visually, setting the story in a world of BLADE RUNNER images drenched in MTV glossiness, leaving the viewer to wonder why the characters would ever crave altered states. The look is overpowering enough to delay—though not forever—examination of the plot, which has to pull a fast one at every turn to keep moving and which eventually makes a mockery of plausibility.

The premise is ludicrous but potentially interesting; however, the inconsistency of what the Flatliners bring back from their trips to the other side soon becomes a problem. Nelson talks about sins, but Rachel is blameless. Joe's career as a Don Juan is part of his adult life, while the rest of the Flatliners are haunted by childhood experiences. Moreover, since they're middle-class medical students, time and circumstance work against the likelihood that any of them have done anything really awful. Taunting another child at school isn't nice, but it's not the kind of action on which to hang a tale of retribution.

In order to coast on atmosphere, a movie must be seamless enough that inconsistencies like these don't come to the viewer's attention. Once they do, the questions they raise distract mightily from the film's ambience. Here we are faced with a raft of perplexing questions: How did Nelson and his friends manage to get all that expensive medical equipment to the ornate building where they conduct their experiments, and why doesn't anyone miss it? How come they have so much free time—isn't medical school a killer? Where did they find those huge, fabulous designer apartments draped with gauze and who's paying for them? What is that artfully arranged rack of rubber gloves?

There aren't any answers, of course. In the final analysis FLATLINERS is eye candy, full of hopped-up jolts and knee-jerk emotional effects that fade away without a trace. The film earned an Oscar nomination for sound effects editing. *(Violence, profanity.)*

d, Joel Schumacher; p, Michael Douglas and Rick Bieber; w, Peter Filardi; ph, Jan De Bont; ed, Robert Brown; m, James Newton Howard; md, Dick Rudolph; prod d, Eugenio Zanetti; art d, Jim Dultz; set d, Stephen Homsy and Paul Sonski; spec, Phil Cory and Hans Metz; stunts, Bill Erickson; makup, Ve Neill

Horror   **(PR:C   MPAA:R)**

FOOLS OF FORTUNE

(Brit.) 104m Polygram—Working Title—Film Four—Palace/New Line c

Mary Elizabeth Mastrantonio *(Marianne)*, Iain Glen *(Willie Quinton)*, Julie Christie *(Mrs. Quinton)*, Michael Kitchen *(Mr. Quinton)*, Sean T. McClory *(Young Willie Quinton)*, Frankie McCafferty *(Tim Paddy)*, Niamii Cusack *(Josephine)*, Neil Dudgeon *(Sergeant Rudkin)*, and Catherine McFadden *(Imelda)*

This is a tragic tale of the troubled Ireland, specifically how the troubles ruined one family. It begins shortly after WW I at Kilneagh, the estate belonging to the Quintons. In this dream of aristocratic life, Mr. Quinton (Michael Kitchen), his wife, Evie (Julie Christie), and their three beautiful children enjoy all the benefits of the landed gentry. The idyll is shattered when a worker's body is found hanging from a tree, his tongue cut out. He was rumored to have been an informer to the Black and Tan, the despised paramilitary force the British have sent to quell Irish rebellion. An orgy of revenge is then released upon the Quintons by the Black and Tans. Led by one Sgt. Rudkin (Neal Dudgeon), they set fire to the house one night and shoot Quinton, as well as a couple of unfortunate witnesses. Young Willie Quinton (Sean T. McClory) survives, but his sisters perish in the flames and his mother will never be the same. Years pass with Evie becoming a hopeless alcoholic, tended to by their faithful servant Josephine (Niamh Cusack). A cousin, Marianne (Mary Elizabeth Mastrantonio) comes to visit, and she and Willie (now played by Iain Glen) fall in love. After Marianne departs, Evie kills herself and Willie, unable to bear the guilt and fury over the past any longer, seeks out Rudkin and kills him. Meanwhile, Marianne discovers she is pregnant and fruitlessly tries to discover Willie's whereabouts. She is eventually taken in at Kilneagh by Willie's aunts. Later, her daughter, Imelda, is born. Willie is eventually reunited with his wife and child, but by then, the girl, haunted by all that has gone before, is hopelessly mad.

Pat O'Connor's film follows William Trevor's acclaimed book closely, and is at its best in the first half as it lovingly creates the atmosphere at Kilneagh before "the troubles." After the unfortunate STARS AND BARS and JANUARY MAN, O'Connor is back on more congenial territory, and the strong sense of period he showed in A MONTH IN THE COUNTRY again is in evidence. He is immensely abetted by the glowing work of his camera and design teams, as well as the floridly symphonic score by Hans Zimmer. The nostalgic grandeur of the early scenes makes the destruction of this life all the more heart-breaking. The performances in this section are especially good: Kitchen is the perfect gallant country squire, somewhat addled, but fiercely proud of all he owns, and McClory is a cherubic delight as young Willie. O'Connor stages the fire massacre magnificently, showing it through Willie's eyes, making the horror of it excruciating. It is in the second half that the film tails off, lacking the romantically Gothic aura of dashed hopes and ruined lives that permeated such films as William Wyler's WUTHERING HEIGHTS, Orson Welles' THE MAGNIFICENT AMBERSONS, or John Huston's THE DEAD. The political background is too sketchy and events are somewhat confusing. The numerous employees of Kilneagh are insufficiently delineated and therefore lack the resonance their recurring mention and presence would deem. Iain Glen is too pallidly the sufferer to make the grown Willie an effectively stirring hero. Mastrantonio also seems too tentative a presence. Her performance is too similarly scaled to the more lyrical aspects of Julie Christie's; there's not enough contrast, and it's hard to believe she could possess the forceful will to have a child out of wedlock and trail all over the British Isles in search of its father. Catherine McFadden is darkly lovely as Imelda, but the madness theme is unconvincing.

Christie is a major reason to see this flawed film. It's about time to claim her as a rarity: one of the screen's great, heart-stopping beauties, who is, as well, a fine actress. She's a radiant embodiment of the Edwardian classical ideal in the early sequences and rivetingly unsparing of herself later on. Her chilling performance is a delicate, uncanny mixture of Vivien Leigh and Una O'Connor. *(Violence, adult situations, substance abuse.)*

d, Pat O'Connor; p, Sarah Radclyffe; w, Michael Hirst (based on the novel by William Trevor); ph, Jerzy Zielinski; ed, Michael Bradsell; m, Hans Zimmer; prod d, Jamie Leonard; cos, Judy Moorcroft

Drama   **(PR:C   MPAA:NR)**

FOR BETTER OF FOR WORSE

(SEE: HONEYMOON ACADEMY)

FORBIDDEN DANCE, THE

94m 21st Century—Menahem Golan/Columbia c

Laura Herring *(Nisa)*, Jeff James *(Jason)*, Sid Haig *(Joa)*, Richard Lynch *(Benjamin Maxwell)*, Barbra Brighton *(Ashley)*, Angela Moya *(Carmen)*, Miranda Garrison *(Mickey)*, Shannon Farnon *(Katherine Anderson)*, Linden Chiles *(Bradley Anderson)*, Ruben Moreno *(The King)*, Gene Mitchell *(Cutter)*, Kenny Johnson *(Dave)*, Connie Woods *(Trish)*, Tom Alexander *(Kurt)*, Steven Lloyd Williams *(Weed)*, Sabrina Mance *(Cami)*, Pilar Del Rey *(The Queen)*, Robert Apisa *(Security Guard No. 2)*, Greg Niebel, Kenny Scott Carrie *(Jail Cops)*, Remy O'Neill *(Robin)*, Charles Meshack *(Eddie)*, John Rice *(Mr. Gaines)*, and Kid Creole & The Coconuts

One of a number of recent dance films capitalizing on the lambada craze, THE FORBIDDEN DANCE stands out by throwing social and political commentary in with its dirty dancing. Laura Herring plays Nisa, the princess of a Brazilian tribe, who comes to Los Angeles to stop an American corporation from destroying her rain forest home. With her is tribal shaman Joa (Sid Haig), who uses black magic to get past the company guards and see the chairman (one method not employed in ROGER AND ME), resulting in his arrest. Nisa flees and, left to find her way in LA alone, finds work in a Beverly Hills mansion as the servant of an uptight couple whose son, Jason (Jeff James), lives only to dance. After spying on Nisa as she dances provocatively in her bedroom, Jason takes her out to a club. She's rejected by Jason's friends, he's berated by his parents for dating the help, and Nisa runs away and gets a job at Xtasy, a sleazy dance joint/brothel, as a dance partner for mauling male customers. Jason visits the club with his chums, looking for sex, but Nisa rebuffs him. He becomes morose, turns away from his buddies and his girl friend (Barbra Brighton), and returns to Xtasy to try to take Nisa out of the place. A bouncer beats the would-be rescuer up and prepares to deflower Nisa, but fortunately Joa walks in and magically stuns the attacker, which clears the place. The shaman then heads back to the tribe, while Nisa and Jason — now in love — prepare for a dance contest, hoping to speak out about the plight of the rain forest when they're showcased on TV. They win the contest, but the multinational's head stooge (Richard Lynch) kidnaps Nisa afterwards. Jason finds them and helps Nisa escape, but twists his ankle, ruining their chances of performing on the TV show. Luckily, *deus ex machina* Joa shows up backstage and heals Jason's wound, and the dance goes ahead as planned. The crowd loves 'em, they start a boycott against the forest-rapers, and everyone gets into the lambada.

There are some painfully obvious drawbacks to THE FORBIDDEN DANCE (whose title refers to the Brazilian government having banned the lambada some 50 years ago for being too sexy, though there is some dispute as to whether this actually happened or is just a marketing ploy). The story relies on one absurd coincidence after another, the acting is pedestrian, and the screenplay is often unintentionally laughable. However, although overlong, the film is consistently entertaining, primarily due to Greydon Clark's efficient direction and the attractive players. One nice aspect of these low-budget musicals is that they can't afford to hire dance-doubles for the leads (as in FLASHDANCE and FOOT-LOOSE), so the dance sequences are shown in a more respectful style, letting the moves play instead of just quickly intercutting body parts. Luckily James, Brighton, and especially Herring, a former Miss USA, are good enough dancers to merit this restraint (ironically, the one exception to this style is the contest sequence, when it's most important that we see Herring and James as accomplished dancers). There's also a great deal of fun in seeing how many current issues this well-intentioned film can fit in — these include not only the despoiling of rain forests, but also homelessness, racism, safe sex, and drunken driving among young people, along with the main story line's focus on the difficulties faced in the US by immigrants from south of the border. Then, too, Clark (whose 1990 credits also include the terrible SKINHEADS) was smart enough to let the camera linger on Herring's delightful smile and Kid Creole and the Coconuts' dance-contest stage show, to leave the acting chores to the entertaining Haig and reptilian Klaus Kinski lookalike Lynch, and to keep the story moving, logic be damned. THE FORBIDDEN DANCE once again gives proof that a low-budget quickie can still be fun, given the virtues of charming performers and a heart in the right place. The soundtrack includes music by Kid Creole and the Coconuts and Kaoma's single "Lambada." *(Adult situations, brief nudity, violence.)*

d, Greydon Clark; p, Marc S. Fischer and Richard L. Albert; w, Roy Langsdon and John Platt (based on a story by Joseph Goldman); ph, R. Michael Stringer; ed, Robert Edwards and Earl Watson; m, Vladimir Horunzhy; md, Jackie Krost and Joe LaMont; prod d, Don Day; art d, Frank Bertolino; set d, Shirley Starks; cos, Susan Bertram; chor, Miranda Garrison and Felix Chavez

Dance (PR:C MPAA:PG-13)

FORCE OF CIRCUMSTANCE

89m Ad Hoc/Upfront c

Boris Major *(Mouallem)*, Jessica Stutchbury *(Katrina)*, Tom Wright *(Hans)*, Eric Mitchell *(The Envoy)*, Glenn O'Brien *(Charles Floris)*, Mark Boone Jr. *(Herman)*, Kathleen Anderson *(Hortensia)*, Steve Buscemi *(Virgil)*, Filip Pagowski, Evan Lurie, Rockets Redglare, and Pam Osowski

Mouallem (Boris Major), a young Moroccan girl living in a dismal shantytown, is elected to undertake a dangerous mission for the revolutionary underground. She must travel to the United States carrying papers that document government abuses of the Moroccan people and deliver them to Katrina (Jessica Sutchbury), a Washington-based journalist whose aristocratic heritage belies her sympathy for the downtrodden. Meanwhile, the corrupt king of Morocco has sent an envoy (Eric Mitchell) to the States to purchase a mansion to which the king can flee when his own country — bled dry by the excesses of his regime — finally becomes too inhospitable. The mansion he selects belongs to Hans (Tom Wright), Katrina's boy friend, a major, if low key, player in international politics.

The envoy also pays a visit to a munitions dealer whose ignorance of the geography of the Middle East is equalled only by her enthusiasm to sell weapons to its inhabitants. Mouallem is thwarted in her efforts to get to Katrina, primarily because the journalist appears to ignore her phone messages. A sinister man with a camera seems to be following Mouallem, though he never does anything. In the meantime, Hans' family gives him a hard time about selling the ancestral estate, particularly to a foreigner in a fez. Katrina, already angry because her editor isn't interested in the story she wants to write about Moroccan politics, is infuriated by Hans' refusal to recognize the political implications of the sale of the mansion. He, in turn, is annoyed by what he perceives as her naive liberalism. Mouallem and Katrina finally connect, and Hans decides not to sell the house. The king's envoy is quietly furious, and the film ends as he tells Hans ominously that choice is a Western concept.

FORCE OF CIRCUMSTANCE perches uneasily on the borderline between commercial and non-commercial filmmaking. Its form is essentially conventional, while its emphases are not. Elements common to mainstream political thrillers provide the film's building blocks: revolution in an exotic locale, individuals swept away by the tide of history, high-level conspiracies to preserve the status quo, a responsible reporter frustrated by the system. But producer-director-cowriter Liza Bear paces her narrative with an elliptical grandeur worthy of avant-garde filmmaker Stan Brakhage. If its tempo were picked up and its talkiness reduced, FORCE OF CIRCUMSTANCE might appeal to an ordinary moviegoer, so it seems willfully perverse that Bear — clearly far more interested in politics than in thrills — has chosen to tell what she considers to be an important story about America's relationship with the developing world in such an off-putting way. Movies are, after all, a mass medium, and such filmmakers as Costa Gavras (Z; STATE OF SIEGE; MISSING) and Oliver Stone (especially in SALVADOR) have managed to present complex, unpleasant political realities in films that are both informative and accessible. If Bear is not interested in reaching a wide audience, then why spend the money needed to make a film? There are far less expensive ways to be obscure.

FORCE OF CIRCUMSTANCE's production values are surprisingly good, given its obviously low budget. The Moroccan shantytown, constructed on an abandoned lot in New York's East Village, is utterly convincing, and other locations are used to good effect. But the quality of the cast is conspicuously variable, ranging from such Downtown personalities as Rockets Redglare and filmmaker Mitchell to professional actors — notably Steve Buscemi, in a small role as a pig farmer — and non-professionals. The stiffness of certain key performances is exacerbated by the stilted dialog, and the budget limitations are often apparent in static camera placement and long takes that are uninterrupted by close-ups. These could also be stylistic conceits, reflective of the Brechtian approach common in avant garde cinema, but, given the essentially naturalistic model followed by the rest of the film, it seems unlikely. FORCE OF CIRCUM-STANCE is a serious and well-intentioned film, but ultimately its limitations obscure its message. *(Sexual situations.)*

d, Liza Bear; p, Liza Bear; w, Craig Gholson and Liza Bear; ph, Zoran Hochstatter; ed, J.P. Roland-Levy and Liza Bear; m, M. Mader

Political/Thriller (PR:A MPAA:NR)

FORCED MARCH

104m A-Pix/Shapiro Glickenhaus c

Chris Sarandon *(Kline/Miklos Radnoti)*, Renee Soutendijk *(Myra)*, John Seitz *(Hardy)*, and Josef Sommer *(Father)*

Despite capable performances and good direction by Rick King (HARD CHOICES), this behind-the-scenes drama suffers from an excess of thematic baggage in its attempts to come to grips with the Holocaust's meaning to its victims and their descendants. The film stars Chris Sarandon as Ben Kline, a Jew of Hungarian descent who is the star of a hit TV series. Ben's father, Richard (Josef Sommer), is a Holocaust survivor who has always refused to speak of his experiences and, especially, of the suffering of Ben's mother, a Catholic who was persecuted and died while Ben was still an infant. Ben has always been especially troubled by his father's silence, and also by the question of why his father and other victims didn't fight back against their own slaughter by the Nazis. Wanting to understand the Holocaust on his own terms, and over his father's protests, Ben quits his series to star in a low-budget docu-drama about Hungarian Jewish poet Miklos Radnoti, who was murdered by the Nazis as the war in Europe was ending. While the director of the film, Walter Hardy (John Seitz), is grateful to Ben — whose agreement to star as Radnoti has helped Hardy raise the production money — he is nonetheless a tyrant on the set, clashing sharply and frequently with Ben over the portrayal of his character. Hardy insists on sticking strictly to the historical record, according to which Radnoti kept out of trouble, even as Jews were being arrested in the street in front of his apartment building to be carted off to death camps, expressing his anguish and anger only in his poetry. Ben, meanwhile, leans towards portraying Radnoti in conventionally heroic, though historically inaccurate, terms. Radnoti's story, as related by the film-within-a-film, runs thus: Radnoti was imprisoned in a forced-labor camp, but freed when his publisher mounted a petition drive to have him released. Despite that support and the conversion of Radnoti and his wife to Catholicism, he was afterwards still forced to do periodic stints in labor camps, a form of civilian draft, to aid the Nazi war effort. The last of these stints, in Yugoslavia, occurred as the defeat of the Nazis was imminent. In the face of the Allied advance, Radnoti's camp was abandoned and the prisoners forced to march back to Hungary. During the march, Radnoti, exhausted and unable to continue, was killed by his captors, as were many others along the way. To play Radnoti, Ben enlists the help of an advisor, who helps the actor trace his own family's history. Ben also has an affair with his feisty costar, Mira (Renee Soutendijk), who plays Radnoti's wife and urges Ben on in his clashes with Hardy. As the action shifts to the labor camp, Hardy challenges Ben to probe his character's consciousness more deeply. Ben responds by forcing himself to endure as much as possible the suffering and privation Radnoti underwent, carrying realism to an unhealthy extreme that lands him on the cover of *People* magazine, but is clearly leading to an emotional breakdown. Both Mira (with whom Ben had a falling out when she ended their affair after her role in the film was completed) and Ben's father, disturbed by the *People* story, come to the set and try to shake Ben out of his obsession with Radnoti. Finally, during filming of Radnoti's death scene, Ben has a sudden revelation that leads him to understand the full horror of the Holocaust, and why his father refuses to talk about it. Finishing the film, Ben returns to California a changed man, though FORCED MARCH leaves open the question of whether it is a change for the better.

There are plenty of good reasons to see FORCED MARCH. The performances are uniformly excellent in their low-key realism, and King's direction is similarly effective and straightforward. The film's depiction of life on a movie set, with its creative personalities engaging in daily clashes, alliances, and love affairs, has a sharply observed, insider's feel that almost, but not quite, compensates for the triteness of the script. As a character, Ben is never sufficiently developed to make his dilemma in any way comparable to that of the character he is playing. Also — and despite Seitz's best efforts — Hardy, with his nonstop rants and raves about Art and Truth, quickly becomes a windy bore. FORCED MARCH's film-within-the-film is so much more compelling than its framing story that, every time the camera pans to show Hardy yelling "Cut!" and jumping up to bawl out his actors, home viewers may well be tempted to hit the fast-forward button on their VCR remotes, speeding ahead to the next "movie" scene. Perhaps King has done his job too well: FORCED MARCH makes its best case for Miklos Radnoti's story getting a movie all its own — though with Chris Sarandon, not Ben Kline, as Radnoti. *(Profanity, adult situations, brief nudity, violence.)*

d, Rick King; p, Dick Atkins; w, Dick Atkins and Charles K. Bardosh; ph, Ivan Mark; ed, Evan Lottman; prod d, Laszlo Rajk

Drama   (PR:C   MPAA:NR)

FORD FAIRLANE

(SEE: ADVENTURES OF FORD FAIRLANE)

FOURTH WAR, THE

95m Kodiak/Cannon c

Roy Scheider *(Col. Jack Knowles)*, Jurgen Prochnow *(Col. N.A. Valachev)*, Tim Reid *(Lt. Col. Timothy Clark)*, Lara Harris *(Elena Novotna)*, Harry Dean Stanton *(Gen. Hackworth)*, Dale Dye *(Sergeant Major)*, Bill MacDonald *(MP Corporal)*, David Palffy *(Gawky Soldier)*, Neil Grahn *(Needle-Nose Soldier)*, Ernie Jackson *(Knowles' Driver)*, Ron Campbell *(Young US Soldier)*, John Dodds *(Defector)*, Richard Durven *(Young Soldier)*, Harold Hecht Jr. *(Dwayne)*, Alice Pesta *(Hannelore)*, Gregory A. Gale *(Communications Corporal)*, Henry Kope *(Mayor)*, Garry Galinsky, Ed Soibelman, Gary Spivak *(Red Army Privates)*, Yefim Korduner, Brent Woolsey *(Red Army Majors)*, Kent McNeill *(US Private)*, Brian Warren, Guy Buller *(MP and Wide Soldier)*, Roman Podhora, Joseph Vrba *(Czech Guards)*, George Scholl *(Innkeeper)*, Gordon Signer *(Bavarian Wife)*, Lilo Bahr *(Innkeeper's Wife)*, Claus Diedrich *(Frontier Police Captain)*, Kyle Maschmeyer, Kurt Darmohray *(Villagers)*, Igor Burstyn *(Czech Tower Guard)*, Matus Ginzberg *(Puppeteer)*, Boris Novogrudsky *(Aide to Valachev)*, and Tom Kelly *(Sports Announcer)*

With the advent of *glasnost* and the crumbling of the Berlin Wall, films with Cold War themes seem a bit out of style. It is simply a case of bad timing for filmmakers, a notable case being John McTiernan, whose ridiculously paranoid THE HUNT FOR RED OCTOBER feels like a relic of the 50s. Its politics are dated, but more importantly, its thrills are few. Just as dated, but much more thrilling, is John Frankenheimer's Cold War drama THE FOURTH WAR, an effective, tightly constructed thriller that packs an emotional punch in the end, when even its politics are compelling.

Roy Scheider plays Col. Jack Knowles, a born soldier and embittered Vietnam veteran who fights wars even during peacetime. He is the Army's loose cannon, a troublemaker who, after a string of unsuccessful commands, has been stationed at an unimportant and generally quiet post where it is hoped he will stay out of trouble. Knowles has gotten the job thanks to his friend and commanding officer, General Hackworth (Harry Dean Stanton), who has fought beside Knowles in many a battle. The post is located at the West German-Czechoslovakian border (marked with red posts on the Soviet troops' side, blue on the Americans'). Positioned across the way is Colonel Valachev (Jurgen Prochnow), Knowles' Soviet opposite number. Like Knowles, Valachev is an embittered fighting machine, and it's not too long before these two have a confrontation. While patrolling with his men, Knowles witnesses the shooting of a defector who was trying to cross the border. Infuriated, Knowles (who is forbidden to use real ammunition) hurls a snowball at Valachev, who promptly returns the favor. This seemingly innocuous exchange soon escalates into a obsessive and quite treacherous battle, in which the weapons become much more dangerous than snowballs. Knowles sneaks over the border one night and forces, at gunpoint, a group of Czech soldiers to sing "Happy Birthday" to him; Valachev responds by blowing up Knowles' jeep as the latter surveys the border the next day. This weird, private battle attracts the attention of Knowles' second-in-command, Lt. Col. Timothy Clark (Tim Reid), who files a report with Hackworth. Hackworth, after a few more exchanges between the opposing loose cannons, is forced to travel to the post and warn Knowles to stop before he gets court-martialed. But Knowles (who has by now agreed to help a young woman [Lara Harris] get across the border) won't stop, and the game soon becomes an all-out war, with the climax taking place between the borders as Valachev and Knowles (who have exhausted all of their weapons) fight and claw at each other on a frozen lake. Surrounded by soldiers on either side, the two heroes stop fighting and look around to survey the situation. With guns aimed directly at them and tension filling the air, the men realize how frightening and ridiculous the situation has become and silently call a truce. Distressed, and yet somehow enlightened, Knowles makes a snowball and meekly tosses it over his shoulder, and both men sit quietly contemplating the future. The film ends with a voice-over of Hackworth, quoting Einstein, who, when asked what weapons would be used in World War III, replied that he didn't know, but prophesied, "The fourth war will be fought with stones."

Although it has its share of problems — outdated politics, an unnecessary subplot, failure to develop one major character — THE FOURTH WAR is still a successful thriller, providing plenty of excitement and, by the end, a strong message. Frankenheimer (whose work has ranged from the exceptional [THE MANCHURIAN CANDIDATE] to the ridiculous [PROPHECY]), here seems to hark back to his days of directing 50s television. THE FOURTH WAR is done in a surprisingly straightforward, non-flashy style, with the exposition introduced nicely and the action building strongly. This is a very professional piece of work from Frankenheimer, who has lately become a king of low-budget thrillers, creating some very sharp films on a shoestring (including 52 PICK-UP, which also starred Scheider). THE FOURTH WAR is no exception to this trend. Frankenheimer always seems to be able to get strong performances out of weak players (such as Don Johnson, in 1989's DEAD BANG), and does so again here. Reid is very effective, and even Harris (who was terrible in 1987's NO MAN'S LAND) does well. The two central performances are terrific. Scheider, who has done some of his best work of late with Frankenheimer, is fiery and powerful as Knowles, creating a character full of quirks and almost-unlikable attributes. This is a man who knows nothing but war and soldiering, who will never fit in as a civilian (this is wonderfully conveyed in an early scene in which Knowles speaks to his son over the phone). Prochnow is also fine, though he falls victim to a vastly underdeveloped role. While it is clear that his character parallels Scheider's in circumstance and spirit, one wishes Frankenheimer had dedicated more screen time to Prochnow's Valachev, so that we could understand his motivations as well as we do Knowles'. Unfortunately, the film's failure to concentrate more on the Soviet sometimes turns his character into a standard evil Russkie.

Stanton's General Hackworth, on the other hand, is both perfectly realized and wonderfully performed. In what is easily his best performance since REPO MAN, Stanton steals every sequence he is in, and Hackworth's reprimanding of Knowles is the film's best scene. Becoming an intergral part of the film (indeed, the entire movie is told from his point of view, in a voice-over flashback), he is an absolute joy to watch. THE FOURTH WAR's strongest element, however, is its potent ending, which is startlingly effective in its simplicity, conveying a feeling both of overwhelming sadness and of peace. It's an exceptional accomplishment for a little thriller, and quite a step for Frankenheimer. THE FOURTH WAR is a nice example of low-budget American filmmaking and a strong, exciting story to boot. *(Violence, profanity.)*

d, John Frankenheimer; p, Wolf Schmidt; w, Stephen Peters and Kenneth Ross (based on the novel by Stephen Peters); ph, Gerry Fischer; ed, Robert F. Shugrue; m, Bill Conti; prod d, Alan Manzer; art d, Rick Roberts; set d, Janice

Blackie; spec, Grant Burdette; stunts, Allan Graf and Brent Woolsey; cos, Ray Summers; makup, Louis Lazzara and Al Magallon; tech, Capt. Dale Dye

Thriller/War (PR:C MPAA:R)

FRANKENHOOKER

90m Ievins-Henenlotter/Shapiro Glickenhaus c

James Lorinz *(Jeffrey Franken)*, Patty Mullen *(Elizabeth)*, Charlotte Helmkamp *(Honey)*, Shirley Stoler *(Spike)*, Louise Lasser *(Jeffrey's Mom)*, Joseph Gonzalez *(Zorro)*, Lia Chang *(Crystal)*, Jennifer Delora *(Angel)*, Vicki Darnell *(Sugar)*, Kimberly Taylor *(Amber)*, Heather Hunter *(Chartreuse)*, Sandy Colisimo *(Monkey)*, Stephanie Ryan *(Anise)*, and Paul-Felix Montez *(Goldie)*

The latest film from the current king of the midnight movie, writer-director Frank Henenlotter, is his best yet—a witty, stylish, if extremely gross, black comedy boasting surprisingly effective performances from its unknown leads. Grossness is a Henenlotter hallmark—his BASKET CASE is still a stomach-turning favorite on the midnight screening circuit almost a decade after its 1982 release—but microscopic budgets and compromise casting have kept style and wit in short supply in his films. Until now, Henenlotter's ideas have tended to be better than his execution. But in FRANKENHOOKER he hits his stride, blending B-movie anything-for-a-gasp outrageousness with A-movie craftsmanship. In short, with FRANKENHOOKER, Frank Henenlotter has arrived.

Combining elements of sex, horror, and fantasy with a twisted, but strangely valid moral, the film's scenario (like that of any midnight movie worth its salt) resembles a rejected "Twilight Zone" script sprung from the fevered brain of an adolescent who hasn't left his room since hitting puberty. Jeffrey Franken (James Lorinz), of Hohokus, New Jersey, is a power-plant worker and part-time mad scientist. As the film opens, he is conducting a weird experiment on his mother's kitchen table while a birthday party is going full tilt in the back yard. A single eye peers out from the center of the brain Jeff has grown in a petri dish. To get the eye to respond, Jeff has decided to perform impromptu sugery with a hammer and scalpel. However, he is soon interrupted by his pretty but plump fiancee, Elizabeth (Patty Mullen), who prevails upon Jeff to join the party so her mother can use the table to make her famous cole slaw. Festiveness gives way to tragedy, though, when Elizabeth runs herself over with the remote-control lawnmower Jeff has built. Elizabeth rests in bloody pieces all over the lawn, but Jeff manages to save her head, with which he dines by candlelight from time-to-time while working on his master plan: providing his fiancee with the sexiest new body he can find on 42nd Street. After using a power drill to stimulate his own brain centers, Jeff concocts some "super crack" that will cause its users to explode. All he has to do is find the right set of victims, give them the crack, sew the most appealing body parts back together, attach Elizabeth's head, and wait for a thunderstorm. While auditioning a roomful of hookers, Jeff finds that he can't go through with his plan, despite the fact that he has become, as he himself puts it, "dangerously amoral." But it's too late. Once the hookers get hold of the crack, Jeff is left with a dazzling array of spare parts to choose from in reconstructing his beloved. And it isn't long before "Frankenhooker" is staggering up 42nd Street, wreaking late-night havoc and frying johns with her lethal high-voltage love.

In almost any other hands, this material would have become another unwatchable exercise in cinematic idiocy. Instead, Henenlotter, who cowrote the script with Robert Martin, makes you wonder whether Preston Sturges might have wound up making midnight movies if he were alive today. Indeed, Lorinz's acting style—as wildly funny as it is wanly low-key—eerily recalls Sturges-stalwart Eddie Bracken's whiny plaintiveness filtered through a Jersey drawl. Lorinz's performance is more than matched by former *Penthouse* Pet of the Year Mullen. A genuine find as Frankenhooker, Mullen pays fond, funny tribute to Elsa Lanchester's BRIDE OF FRANKENSTEIN with her remarkably refined comic performance.

Of course, the usual disclaimers also apply. FRANKENHOOKER is obviously not for all tastes and is out of the question for kids (drive-in movie critic Joe Bob Briggs reported that the MPAA ratings board found FRANKENHOOKER so patently offensive that it offered to refund the film's screening fee). Nevertheless, moviegoers with a sense of adventure, or even a sense of humor, may find themselves indecently amused by this hilarious exercise in Hohokus Gothic. *(Violence, gore effects, nudity, sexual situations, drug abuse.)*

d, Frank Henenlotter; p, Edgar Ievins; w, Robert Martin and Frank Henenlotter; ph, Robert M. Baldwin; ed, Kevin Tent; m, Joe Renzetti; spec, Gabe Bartalos

Comedy/Horror (PR:O MPAA:NR)

FRANKENSTEIN UNBOUND

85m Byron—Mount—Concorde/FOX c

(AKA: ROGER CORMAN'S FRANKENSTEIN UNBOUND)

John Hurt *(Dr. Joseph Buchanan)*, Raul Julia *(Baron Frankenstein)*, Bridget Fonda *(Mary Godwin)*, Jason Patric *(Lord Byron)*, Michael Hutchence *(Percy Bysshe Shelley)*, Nick Brimble *(The Monster)*, Catherine Rabett *(Elizabeth)*, Catherine Corman *(Justine)*, Mickey Knox *(General)*, and Terri Treas *(Voice of Car)*

Somewhere, sometime in the future, Dr. Joseph Buchanan (John Hurt) has developed a revolutionary weapon that will change the way wars are fought. But during the testing of his new super weapon, something unexpected has happened: somehow a hole has opened up in the time/space continuum, creating a "timeslip," a gateway into the past. Buchanan and his state-of-the-art computerized car are sucked into the hole, ending up in 1818. Shocked but ever adaptable, Buchanan hides the car—he might, after all, be able to explain his clothing, but the car would be bound to cause a problem. He makes his way to the nearest town, barters for a meal and finds himself in the company of the arrogant Baron Frankenstein (Raul Julia). Within days he's also met free-thinking Mary Godwin (Bridget Fonda), soon to be the author of *Frankenstein*. Through Mary he meets her lover, poet Percy Bysshe Shelley (singer Michael Hutchence of the group INXS), and his friend, the mad, bad, and dangerous-to-know Lord Byron (Jason Patric). All are ensconced in Bohemian rhapsody at a nearby villa. Understandably puzzled by this confluence of fact and fiction and desperate to find a way back to his own time, Buchanan discovers that Frankenstein is carrying out the experiments that will be described in Mary's novel. He has created a misshapen but intelligent creature (Nick Brimble) who is driven by frustration to maim and murder. Frankenstein tries to enlist Buchanan's aid in his ghastly plan to build a monster mate, but Buchanan double-crosses him and they are all projected into a frozen future. Frankenstein and the creatures die, leaving Buchanan alone in the ruins of a sophisticated research facility, pondering the meaning of it all.

This was Roger Corman's first directorial effort since 1970 when he did VON RICHTOFEN AND BROWN, and the film is a curious anachronism, resolutely old-fashioned, almost stuffy. This is surprising since Corman, as a producer with Concorde/New Horizons, managed to keep his finger on the pulse of the exploitation industry, turning out low-budget films such as GALAXY OF TERROR (1981), CHOPPING MALL (1986), and NIGHTFALL (1988) that appealed to contemporary audiences. If this film starred unknowns (or has-beens) rather than the surprisingly distinguished cast Corman assembled, it would be easy to imagine that it was made in the late 60s. Though this could make for a pleasantly nostalgic film, the two intervening decades have been crucial ones for horror films. Elaborate special effects have bred a technically sophisticated audience, the link between sex and horror has become increasingly complex, and mordant self-consciousness is evident in all but the crudest films. To watch FRANKENSTEIN UNBOUND is to feel as though none of that has happened, a feeling that ultimately undermines the picture. On the plus side, the performances are generally above average. Newcomer Hutchence and Patric (THE LOST BOYS) are fey as the unconventional poets and as Mary, Fonda (SCANDAL, SHAG) has what may be the film's most memorable line. Seducing Buchanan, she saucily declares, "Percy and Byron preach free love...I practice it." The European locations are beautiful and wonderfully photographed, and the overall production values are high—only the monster is disappointing. *(Sexual situations, violence.)*

d, Roger Corman; w, F.X. Feeney and Roger Corman (based on the novel by Brian Aldiss); ph, Armando Nannuzzi; ed, Jay Cassidy and Mary Bauer; m, Carl Davis; prod d, Enrico Tovaglieri; set d, Ennio Michettoni; spec, Illusion Arts; makup, Nick Dudman

Horror/Science Fiction (PR:C MPAA:R)

FREEZE—DIE—COME TO LIFE

(USSR) 105m Lenfilm/International Film Exchange bw

(ZAMRI OUMI VOSKRESNI)

Dinara Drukarova *(Galiya)*, Pavel Nazarov *(Valerka)*, Yelena Popova *(Valerka's Mother)*, Vyacheslav Bambushek *(Vitka)*, and Vadim Ermolayev *(School Principal)*

Vitaly Kanevski's FREEZE-DIE-COME TO LIFE is a grim, wrenching, beautifully realized story of a trouble-prone boy growing up in a postwar gulag town in Soviet Asia. Valerka (Pavel Nazarov) lives in a decrepit block of flats with his mother (Yelena Popova), a prostitute and dance-hall bartender who is struggling to build some sort of future for her son. But Valerka just can't keep his nose clean, and he is responsible for all kinds of clever pranks, such as putting yeast in the school sewage system, which creates a major mess in the schoolyard. The school officials, however, refuse to let this mess stop marching practice, and, praising Stalin in song, the children march through the river of human waste. It becomes clear that these antics provide Valerka with a much-needed release from the dreary reality of his existence; it is his street-smarts and wit that keep him from becoming one of the walking dead that inhabit his town. Indeed his fellow citizens do not seem to fare much better than the political prisoners and Japanese POWs in the nearby gulag. Valerka is also enterprising, and he goes into competition with his friend Galiya (Dinara Drukarova) as a tea seller. In a sly depiction of capitalism in action, Valerka tries to scare away Galiya's customers by claiming that her water is rusty and that her kettle has very recently been a home to cockroaches. He also makes false claims about his own tea, boasting that it is made with fresh spring water. These attempts to whip up customers are not entirely successful, but Valerka earns enough money to buy a pair of ice skates, which are soon stolen by some older boys. At first Valerka's mother is incensed that her son would insult her efforts to provide for him by working, but they reach a temporary truce, and she buys him a pig that sleeps in his bed, an arrangement that Galiya threatens to expose whenever the two friends get into an argument. Valerka and Galiya are never protected from the harsh realities of the adult world. At one point, they encounter a young woman prisoner who desperately attempts to convince a soldier to grant her freedom in return for sexual favors. In his apartment block, Valerka discovers an old woman drowning kittens so that they can be eaten. A crazy, destitute man, given a handful of flour by a sympathetic housewife, uses it to make mud pies that he eats, surrounded by a crowd of taunting children. Eventually, Valerka's mother finds out about his yeast-in-sewer prank, and she does the honorable thing, reporting her son to the school. Then, while playing with a slingshot by a railroad track, Valerka pushes the switching lever, causing a train to derail after its sudden, unexpected turn. When the police investigate the crash, Valerka runs away to his grandmother's town, and falls in with a gang of thieves. After helping them in one of their heists and witnessing a murder in the process, Valerka is found by Galiya, but their escape from the gang results in tragedy.

Shot in black-and-white photography that adds to the feeling of a world of perpetual grays, FREEZE-DIE-COME TO LIFE is a moving document that recalls the best of Neo-Realism. The film has an undeniable aura of authenticity and movingly captures the indomitability of Valerka's and Galiya's spirits, even under the most hopeless circumstances. The performances, particularly by Nazarov and Drukarova as the children who will not let life beat them down, are compelling and spontaneous. Kanevski's direction is impressive, and his script unsparing and touched with humor, though too often he sets up a situation that is hard to follow and then has one of his characters explain what has just occurred. Kanevski effectively uses a naturalistic style that is confusingly contradicted by a highly symbolic last scene in which the filmmaker seems to be overreaching his sensibilities, offering a final, unexpectedly false note in this otherwise beautifully crafted but brutal film. (*Profanity, nudity, violence.*)

d, Vitaly Kanevski; p, Valentina Tarasova; w, Vitaly Kanevski; ph, Vladimir Brylyakov; ed, Galina Kornilova; m, Sergei Banevich; cos, Tatyana Kochergina and Natalya Milliant

Drama   (PR:C MPAA:NR)

FRESHMAN, THE

102m Lobell-Bergman/Tri-Star c

Marlon Brando (*Carmine Sabatini*), Matthew Broderick (*Clark Kellogg*), Bruno Kirby (*Victor Ray*), Penelope Ann Miller (*Tina Sabatini*), Frank Whaley (*Steve Bushak*), Jon Polito (*Chuck Greenwald*), Paul Benedict (*Arthur Fleeber*), Richard Gant (*Lloyd Simpson*), Kenneth Welsh (*Dwight Armstrong*), Pamela Payton-Wright (*Liz Armstrong*), B.D. Wong (*Edward*), Maximilian Schell (*Larry London*), Bert Parks (*Himself*), Tex Konig (*Leo*), Leo Cimino (*Lorenzo*), Gianni Russo (*Maitre D', Gourmet Club*), Warren Davis (*Fr. Frank*), Vera Lockwood (*Aunt Angelina*), Jefferson Mappin (*Hunter*), Daniel Dion (*Gas Attendant*), Marnie Edwards (*Mall Mother*), Doug Silberstein (*Mr. Glassman*), J.H. Millington (*FBI Man*), Drake Arden, David Stratton, Geraldine Quinn, Derek Mitchell (*Students in Fleeber Classroom*), Joe Ingoldsby (*Waiter in Resturant*), Adrienne Howe, Patricia Andrews, Edward Roy, Amanda Smith, Andrew Airlie, Daniel DeSanto, Wendy Dickson, Christina Trivett (*Mall Patrons*), and Fifi Donahue (*Grand Central Station Booth Lady*)

An advertising campaign once asked, What becomes a legend most? That question is implicit in every review of every film in which Marlon Brando now appears. Audiences have loved, hated, and jeered him, but one point is beyond dispute: Brando is in a class by himself, arguably the very last of the true stars, whose very presence, for better or worse, transforms and reshapes the films in which he appears. Brando's larger-than-life charisma has been fueled by the fierce loyalty to friends and family that he has maintained despite potential costs to his career. This, after all, is the man who used Oscar night to call attention to the plight of native Americans by sending Sacheen Littlefeather to accept the star's Best Actor award for THE GODFATHER. The abiding sense of loyalty that we have come to associate with Brando has also been a key ingredient in many of his best film roles, a point not lost on writer-director Andrew Bergman (THE IN-LAWS; SO FINE) when he conceived THE FRESHMAN, which features Brando's first true starring role since 1980's THE FORMULA. In the

end, it is the unflagging fidelity again embodied by Brando that holds together this amiable, though rambling shaggy-lizard farce that, almost against its will, becomes a poignant meditation on the price of betrayal.

Matthew Broderick stars as Clark Kellogg, the title character, down from Vermont to study film at New York University under Arthur Fleeber (a scene-stealing turn by Paul Benedict), whose course requirements include the memorization of every shot and line of dialog from THE GODFATHER PART II and the purchase of $700-worth of the professor's publications. Kellogg, however, is broke, having been robbed almost immediately after arriving in New York by Victor Ray (Bruno Kirby, whose filmography includes the role young Clemenza in GODFATHER II). Kellogg eventually tracks Victor down, but instead of returning the young man's property, Victor offers to introduce the freshman to his Uncle Carmine (Brando), an "importer-exporter" who can provide Kellogg with a high-paying, "totally legitimate" job. Soon, Kellogg is deeper than he could ever have imagined in farcical, sometimes labored, complications. In short order, the lad from Vermont transports an illegally imported Komodo dragon to be filleted and served up at a "gourmet club," is chased by crooked Federal agents, and finds himself engaged, against his will, to Carmine's volatile daughter, Tina (Penelope Ann Miller). Behind all these occurrences is an elaborate con game designed not only to extricate Carmine from the endangered-species-peddling business but also to rid him forever of the deadly pursuit of the crooked agents, whose real boss is a rival gangster. Kellogg is recruited to play a role in the scam solely because his stepfather (Kenneth Welsh) is a radical animal-rights activist — a hunter of hunters. The success of the Carmine's scheme depends upon the certainty of Kellogg's betrayal by his stepfather, which brings the crooked agents into the open to be nailed by upstanding FBI agents.

If anything, the plot — which also involves the elaborate scam that is the gourmet club — is even more unwieldy than it sounds. In fact, virtually nothing in THE FRESHMAN is quite what it appears to be, except for Kellogg, who becomes the perfect tool for everybody else in the film. He eventually becomes a willing participant in the con, but by that point you'll need a program to keep track of who's conning whom and why. And that seems to be Bergman's whole point. Life, as portrayed here, is little more than one con after another, a theme with a long and noble history in a medium that is itself one big con.

By far the best chuckles in the film come from Brando's resurrection of his landmark role in THE GODFATHER, Don Vito Corleone. Yet having Brando reprise the famous don for laughs is anything but an arbitrary choice. Without Brando's presence, THE FRESHMAN would be so slight it would float off the screen. Instead, Brando galvanizes the action by symbolizing the virtues of loyalty for Broderick's Kellogg, who rejects his duplicitous stepfather for having betrayed him to the authorities.

Ultimately, it is a belief in loyalty that links THE FRESHMAN and THE GODFATHER. Both films convey the same message: in a world full of thieves, back-stabbers, and deranged idealists (like Kellogg's father), who value things, ideas, and even movies (as evidenced by the movie-mad Fleeber), over people, loyalty is our only hope. Movies become an especially important part of Kellogg's education, with Carmine's family playing movie-style roles to seduce the freshman into what Fleeber describes as a *film noir* caper ("shot in grainy black and white, with a KISS ME DEADLY feel to it"). This particular filmlike caper comes complete with a criminal mastermind who turns out to be an importer-exporter with a misguided fondness for rare animals, and also includes a *femme fatale* who is really an average all-Italian-American girl. It is a measure of Kellogg's new maturity that he is relieved to find out that neither Carmine nor Tina are what they appeared to be.

It's hard not to wish that THE FRESHMAN were a better film. Both its plot and characters could have been sharper, and its pacing more precise. As it is, the film stumbles as often as it soars, and its self-conscious stabs at seriousness and complexity tend to distract from the action, rather than deepen it. Still, whether as a result of Bergman's rising to the occasion or because Brando has transformed its shape and texture, THE FRESHMAN finally does service to the legend at its core more often than it doesn't. And if Bergman isn't quite adept with the overall mechanics, no film that puts Brando on ice skates, that has Bert Parks deliver a rousing rendition of Bob Dylan's "Maggie's Farm," or that so wonderfully spoofs film-school pedantry can be dismissed out of hand. THE FRESHMAN could have been much better than it is, but it could have been much worse. (*Profanity.*)

d, Andrew Bergman; p, Mike Lobell; w, Andrew Bergman; ph, William A. Fraker; ed, Barry Malkin; m, David Newman; md, Harlan Goodman; prod d, Ken Adam; art d, Alicia Keywan; set d, Gordon Sim; spec, Neil Tifunovich; stunts, David Ellis; cos, Julie Weiss; makeup, Patricia Green; tech, Rocco Musacchia

Comedy   (PR:C MPAA:PG)

FRIGHT HOUSE

110m Studio c

FRIGHT HOUSE (Part One): Paul Borgese (*Les Moran*), Jennifer Delora (*Dr. Sedgwick*), Al Lewis (*Capt. Levi*), Kit Jones (*Darlissa*), ABADON (Part Two): Duane Jones (*Charles Harmon*), Orly Benyair (*Ione*), Kit Jones (*Young Abadon*), Jackie James (*Madeline*), John Bly (*Mike*), Robin Michaels (*Debbie*), Jett Julien (*George*), Thomas Belgrey (*Frank*), Laura Quisenberry (*Rose*), Dennis Meyera (*Leo Fuller*), Joey Haber (*Anthony*), Thomas Ostuni (*Gary*), Vicki Richardson (*Helen*), Karen Nielsen (*Tracy*), Lawrence Norikoff (*Wes*), Branden Marlowe (*Evangelist*), and Ryan Daniels (*Peter*)

In episode one ("Fright House") of this creepy-crawly two-parter, devil worshippers try to get away with murder by making it look like suicide. Police detective Les Moran (Paul Borgese) discovers he has a personal stake in the case when his brother—an occult buff who suspects the gates of hell may soon be added to the local tourist attractions—becomes the latest pawn in Satan's master plan. Beginning to see a pattern in a recent rash of college student suicides, Moran wonders why the patients of psychological counselor Dr. Sedgwick (Jennifer DeLora) have had such a high mortality rate. Included among the dead is the son of police captain Levi (Al Lewis), Moran's superior. Meanwhile, the college campus is buzzing with news of a spooky mansion that's been donated for use as a fraternity house—little do the jocks and cheerleaders know what initiation rites await them. As for Moran, not only is his fiancee temporarily possessed during a visit to the fright house, but his female partner is slain while investigating. Although the somewhat untrustworthy Levi advises him to give up the case, Moran is soon tripping over lots of dead, dismembered college kids on the eerie mansion's premises. While Dr. Sedgwick conducts brutal sacrifices, Moran teams up with another young woman and encounters the ancient owner of the house, who dispenses vital information on how to defeat the devilish fiends with a powerful crystal. Soon Satan himself is about to surface, but Moran saves the day and sends the cult to a warmer climate—permanently, although apparently not in time to reclaim the spirit of his fiancee.

Episode two ("Abadon") concerns the beautiful, ageless Madeline (Jackie James), who has benefitted from her late scientist-husband's experiments with retardation of the aging process, and who now presides over a posh school at her own sinister-looking mansion. When drilling for reconstruction begins, something evil in the bowels of the mansion is awakened. At this point, students start mysteriously disappearing, and the film intercuts between the mansion's old custodian, who warns Jackie to destroy the malevolence afoot, and Charles Harmon (Duane Jones), who decides to head for this den of iniquity and for Jackie, his old flame. Arriving in the college community, Harmon—a tarot card reader and occultist—immediately feels a kinship with coed Debbie (Robin Michaels). A part-time vampire, Harmon wants to mend his immortality-seeking ways, even if it means shriveling like a prune and upsetting Jackie, who's enjoyed decades of good looks without benefit of plastic surgery or trips to Elizabeth Arden. A flashback reveals that the two were lovers 75 years earlier in Paris. Now Jackie, in her lust for a wrinkle-free existence, is robbing young students of their lives, and the evil schemes of her late husband are spinning out of control. Although Debbie has discovered some vital scientific data (about energy polarization, which has allowed Jackie and Harmon to stay young) in the house's basement, she finds herself in danger of being energy-sucked by Jackie. When Harmon arrives in the nick of time, Debbie discovers that the energy vampires are actually her long-lost parents. In minutes, she gets to see them grow very old and gray together. In a coda, we realize that she has inherited her mother and father's vampire ways.

This nifty fright-night package offers two times the thrills of most horror movies and exemplifies low-budget filmmaking at its most resourceful. Making excellent use of creepy locales, FRIGHT HOUSE's two short tales convey a sense of evil most effectively. The title episode suffers from cut-aways that pad out its length while compiling an overabundance of collegiate victims, and, after their initial impact, the scenes of Dr. Sedgwick's savage rituals lose their suspenseful impact. When it zeroes in on its main characters, however, "Fright House" has maximum impact, and also offers an intriguing glimpse at devil worship while touching on the contemporary issue of suicide among young people—it's ROSEMARY'S BABY meets HEATHERS. In a successful change of pace, Lewis (Grandpa on "The Munsters") is convincing as a cop who deserves to go to hell. Borgese exhibits strength and no-nonsense charisma, and DeLora looks fetching enough in her witch's robe to build enrollment in satanic cults nationwide.

Part two's better-structured script helps flesh out its elegant supernatural tale, enhanced by eerily gliding camerawork, a pounding rock score, and vibrant color photography that recall Dario Argento's horror classic SUSPIRIA (1977). Although desperate efforts to maintain immortality are a science-fiction stock-intrade, "Abadon" is a refreshing dip in the fountain of youth, neatly cross-breeding its mad scientist and vampire motifs. Jones gives a polished, authoritative performance, investing the film with credibility. Drawing strength from the

precept that unseen terror is more shattering than overt gore, "Abadon" scores some of its most suspenseful moments in an oblique manner, particularly in the shuddery scene in which two students are sucked from a bedroom caress into the embrace of the unknown.

With plenty of thrills and chills (and enough gratuitous nudity to satisfy those who like a little prurience in their horror films), FRIGHT HOUSE delivers the scary goods—a perfect excuse for grabbing onto your date on a Saturday night. After seeing FRIGHT HOUSE, you'll think twice about venturing into basements of creepy mansions, where you're always a footstep away from death. (*Nudity, violence, sexual situations, profanity.*)

d, Len Anthony; p, Len Anthony; w, Len Anthony and James Harrigan (based on a story by Len Anthony); ph, Larry Revine and Ernest Dickerson; ed, Len Anthony and Damian Begley; m, Chris Burke, Tony Bongiovi, and Marty Dunayer; cos, Claudia Berman and Gail Bartley

Horror   (PR:O   MPAA:R)

FULL FATHOM FIVE

80m Concorde c

Michael Moriarty (*McKenzie*), Maria Rangel (*Justine*), Daniel Faraldo (*Santillo*), John LaFayette (*Lasovic*), Diego Bertie (*Miguel*), German Gonzales (*Sebastian*), Ramsay Ross (*Mishkin*), Michael Cavanaugh (*Garver*), Todd Field (*Johnson*), and Orlando Sacha (*Barrista*)

FULL FATHOM FIVE is an action-adventure film with neither action nor adventure. Michael Moriarty stars as McKenzie, the commander of an American nuclear submarine on the eve of the Panama Invasion. During a mission to save the head of a Panamanian revolutionary group, he meets the rebel's sister, Justine (Maria Rangel), who hates Americans. Guess what? She likes this one. To prevent the invasion, the Panamanian military gathers a group of Cubans to hijack a Russian nuclear sub, which the Panamanians will use to threaten the US. The Cubans have ideas of their own, however, and threaten to destroy Houston unless *their* demands are met. (Miami is actually the crew's preferred target, but the captain's cousin lives there; besides he had a particularly bad time when he visited Houston.) As luck would have it, when all of this happens, McKenzie's sub is Johnny-on-the-spot, but the commander is on leave, busily seducing Justine. In a blatant attempt to inject some kind of suspense into the film, the screenplay calls for McKenzie to take a mini-sub into a deep underwater trench to find his sub so he can deal with the blackmailers.

Moriarty, who appears to be heavily sedated throughout this gratefully short film, sleepwalks through every scene except for the obligatory sexual encounter, which isn't very exciting either. Equally disappointing is the screenplay's failure to explain why the Cubans are attempting to blackmail the US government and how they plan to succeed. There is simply nothing in FULL FATHOM FIVE that is even remotely plausible. The Russian sub is captured without a fight; McKenzie has little or no trouble finding his own sub, despite the fact that it is sitting silently on the bottom of the ocean, hundreds of miles from port; and the revolutionary leader forgoes an easy opportunity to prevent plans for the American invasion from being leaked. Moreover, the film's subplots are either poorly conceived or left unresolved. Undeniably, the film's climactic battle scene is engaging, but before it begins, viewers must endure 70 minutes of tedium. DAS BOOT this isn't. (*Adult situations, violence.*)

d, Carl Franklin; p, Luis Llosa; w, Bart Davis (based on the novel by Brad Davis); ed, Karen Horn

Action   (PR:A   MPAA:PG)

FUNLAND

86m Double Helix—Hyacinth/RMC—Vestron Video c

David L. Lander (*Bruce Burger/Neal Stickney*), Bruce Mahler (*Mike Spencer*), William Windom (*Angus Perry*), Mike McManus (*T.J. Hurley*), Robert Sacchi (*Mario DiMaurio/Bogie*), Clark Brandon (*Doug Sutterfield*), Mary McDonough (*Kristen Cumming*), Richard Reiner (*Larry DiMaurio*), Terry Beaver (*Carlo DiMaurio*), Lane Davies (*Chad Peller*), Randal Patrick (*Chip Cox*), Jan Hooks (*Shelly Willingham/Orientation Lady*), Bonnie Turner (*Darlene Dorker*), Andy Werhenberg (*Steve Murphy*), Muriel Moore (*Mrs. Perry*), Randi Layne (*Janna McMartin*), Ron Culbreth (*Bertram Joseph*), Marisu Werhenberg (*Ruth Anne*), Dan Jacobs, Shirlene Foss, Elliott Street, Gene Murrell, Jeff Benninghofen, Leslie Winston, Marla Maples, Michael Bologna, Dawn Stone, and Crystal Mercer

After its 1987 premiere at Cannes, FUNLAND received only a few theatrical screenings, and was released on videocassette in 1990. Its striking package artwork, featuring a frenzied sniper in whiteface, might lead potential cassette renters to assume the film is a thriller. Wrong. FUNLAND is a haphazard black comedy, with a good concept but bland (or absent) punch lines.

It's the start of a new season at Funland, a second-rate amusement park that helps promote a nationwide fast-food chain, Brewster's Pizzeria Palaces. This year, however, there are rumors that Funland is to be sold. "The day that they take the park away from me, it will have to be over my dead body!" declares owner-operator Angus Perry (William Windom). In the next scene, Perry's corpse is carted off. Apparently he has killed himself. His widow sells out to a corporation controlled by the DiMaurios, organized crime bigwigs. The DiMaurios have big plans for Funland, including the introduction of Las Vegas showgirls and ghoulish midway rides. But they also announce salary cuts for all employees, and evict Funland's "goodwill ambassador," an unstable clown called Bruce Burger (David Lander, playing a sort of pizza-pushing equivalent of Ronald McDonald), from his dressing room. Taking up residence in the shuttered wax museum, he begins to sink into madness, his descent hastened by the arrival of the "real" Bruce Burger, Chad Peller (Lane Davies), the clown who does the national commercials for Brewster's Pizzeria Palaces. One day in the employee cafeteria, the dejected Funland clown encounters the moldering ghost of Perry, who denies his death was a suicide. Revealing that he was murdered by Larry DiMaurio (Richard Reiner), Perry explains the mobsters plan to close Funland and exploit its real estate. Meanwhile, the DiMaurios find that they do not yet own controlling stock in the park. Funland's original accountant, one Neal Stickney, has that honor, and he seems to have vanished. As it happens, crazy old Bruce Burger is really Neal Stickney. The accountant put on the greasepaint after an earlier mental breakdown, and now, totally insane, he has taken to shooting at the other Bruce Burger from Funland's clock tower. Larry DiMaurio is sent to kill Stickney, but Stickney plugs the mobster first. In the ironic, TAXI DRIVER-style epilog, Stickney is hailed as the heroic rescuer of Bruce Burger. Now the owner-operator of Funland, Stickney is back to normal. Or is he?

FUNLAND tries desperately to be an adroit dark satire like THE HOSPITAL or SMILE (appropriating a running gag from the latter). Certainly the setting is rich in comic possibilities; every county seems to have its own little Coney Island (the park used here is actually Six Flags Over Georgia). But the film proves to be a weak, disorganized cavalcade of grotesques, lacking in real wit. Cowriters Bonnie and Terry Turner have contributed to the scripts of "Saturday Night Live," which may explain why FUNLAND fails to maintain any of its themes for any longer than an average blackout sketch. The satire of corporate greed turns into a tired burlesque of mafia types, with Robert Sacchi as an elderly don, complete with grossly distended cheeks. And since Sacchi is best known for his uncanny Humphrey Bogart impression, he turns up in the wax museum in Bogie's CASABLANCA suit as one of Bruce Burger's delusions. Subplots involving gay choreographers, rascally teens, and visiting celebrities are introduced, then dumped. The main storyline, revolving around Stickney's torment, is well-conceived but ill-executed.

Lander, fated to be forever remembered as Squiggy from TV's "Laverne and Shirley," works hard at the role of Stickney (remaining in clown makeup until his final scene), but his character lacks pathos. For one thing, he's already crazy as the picture begins, so there's not much dramatic progression involved in his decline. At no point is he actually shown enjoying his work as Funland's "goodwill ambassador," so his loss of the position carries little impact. The script also botches the portrait of the other Bruce Burger; a classically trained actor who hates dressing up as a wedge of pizza to entertain brats, he's never shown in character as the clown. The film's best role goes to Windom as the fatherly boss from beyond the grave, but mention should also be made of the contribution of comedienne Jan Hooks ("Saturday Night Live"), who plays an office sex object and adds an unbilled appearance as a frumpy coworker. And if you pay close attention you'll catch a glimpse of actress-model Marla Maples, best-known for her relationship with financier Donald Trump. *(Profanity, violence, adult situations.)*

d, Michael A. Simpson; p, Michael A. Simpson and William Van Der Kloot; w, Michael A. Simpson, Bonnie Turner, and Terry Turner; ph, William Van Der Kloot; ed, William Van Der Kloot and Wade Williams; m, James Oliverio; set d, Lynn Wolverten; cos, Linda Brenick; makup, Harriett Landau

Comedy   **(PR:O   MPAA:PG-13)**

FUNNY ABOUT LOVE

101m Jon Avnet — Jordan Kerner/Paramount c

Gene Wilder *(Duffy Bergman)*, Christine Lahti *(Meg Lloyd)*, Mary Stuart Masterson *(Daphne Delillo)*, Stephen Tobolowsky *(Dr. Hugo Blatt)*, Robert Prosky *(Emil T. Bergman)*, Susan Ruttan *(Claire Raskin)*, Anne Jackson *(Adele Bergman)*, Jean De Baer *(Vivian)*, David Margulies *(Dr. Benjamin)*, and Tara Shannon *(Redhead)*

Gene Wilder and Christine Lahti try very hard to breathe life into this disappointing dramedy-romance that is marred by a lackluster and sometimes miscalculated screenplay by Norman Steinberg and David Frankel. Wilder is

Duffy Bergman, a liberal political cartoonist patterned after Gary Trudeau. When he first meets Lahti's Meg Lloyd at a book-signing, she is working as a caterer's assistant. Duffy approaches the counter to register a complaint about the coffee, only to end up complimenting the coffee-maker once he gets a gander at Meg. Within a few minutes of screen time, Duffy and Meg are married (the second time around for each), yet they remain ambitious career-oriented people. Despite Meg's blossoming career as a chef at a swanky restaurant, the newlyweds decide it's time to start a family. (Naturally, their respective biological clocks are ticking loudly.) That decision is followed by a tedious, overly clinical, sometimes vulgar, and almost totally unfunny 25-minute stretch of plot dealing with Duffy and Meg's efforts to alter his sperm count and to do whatever else is necessary for them to have a baby. Both Meg and Duffy try hard, but she is unable to conceive. Three years pass, and Meg, now at the top of her profession, is growing weary of Duffy's increasingly obnoxious persistence about trying to have a child. When she finally says no, they separate, and Duffy has a fling with Daphne (Mary Stuart Masterson), a foul-mouthed sorority leader who ends up pregnant with Duffy's baby. After Daphne miscarries, Duffy decides to leave her to try and patch things up with Meg. It requires real effort, but Duffy succeeds, and he and Meg (who by now owns her own plush restaurant) live happily ever after, complete with an adopted baby.

Directed unevenly by Leonard Nimoy, FUNNY ABOUT LOVE never quite seems to know where it's headed or what—precisely—it is trying to say. Everything about this film is tentative, and as a result, the viewer is made to feel like Jimmy Durante when he asked the musical question: "Did you ever have the feeling that you wanted to go...but you wanted to stay...still you wanted to go?" Clearly, the filmmakers hoped to involve the audience in the plight of Duffy and Meg, whose situation has the makings of a hilarious comedy; unfortunately, Nimoy and company fail to come up with a consistent style with which to tell their story. Should they relate this tale with unabashed sentimentality, as in 1941's Cary Grant-Irene Dunne classic PENNY SERENADE, the story of a couple who decide to adopt a child once they know they can never have one of their own? Or should they opt for a FISH CALLED WANDA-style black comedy. (Reminiscent of the scene in that film in which a large safe, dropped from an upstairs window, sends a pair of pet dogs to their ultimate reward, FUNNY ABOUT LOVE plays for laughs an otherwise tragic scene in which a falling stove crushes Anne Jackson, who portrays Wilder's mother.) Is FUNNY ABOUT LOVE another in the genre of cutesy baby comedies like THREE MEN AND A BABY; LOOK WHO'S TALKING; and BABY BOOM, or is it intended in part as a clinical study of the methods of improving a would-be father's sperm count?

Though all of these questions remain unanswered, Wilder, Lahti, and Masterson still manage to acquit themselves well, and Jackson, Robert Prosky, and Susan Ruttan offer adequate if uninspired support. Fred Murphy provides the film with truly impressive photography, and Miles Goodman serves up a charmingly well-blended background score. *(Sexual situations, profanity.)*

d, Leonard Nimoy; p, Jon Avnet and Jordan Kerner; w, Norman Steinberg and David Frankel (based on the article "Convention of the Love Goddesses" by Bob Greene); ph, Fred Murphy; ed, Peter Berger; m, Miles Goodman; prod d, Stephen Storer; art d, Nathan Haas; cos, Albert Wolsky

Comedy/Romance   **(PR:C   MPAA:PG-13)**

G

GAME, THE

116m Curtis/Visual Perspectives c

Curtis Brown (*Leon Hunter*), Richard Lee Ross (*Jason McNair*), Vanessa Shaw (*Silvia Yearwood*), Billy Williams (*Vail Yearwood*), Charles Timm (*Ben Egan*), Michael P. Murphy (*George Paturzo*), Dick Biel (*Carl Rydell*), Carolina Beaumont (*Gloria*), Bruce Grossberg (*Norman*), Damon Clark (*Arrington*), Erick Shawn, Erick Coleman, Joanna Wahl, Rick Siler, Claire Waters, and Jerome King

As THE GAME opens, a tough New York mayoral campaign is about to get tougher: Leon Hunter (Curtis Brown), an ambitious black executive in a public relations firm, is hired to act as campaign manager for Carl Rydell (Dick Biel), a white candidate with little more than his looks and a gift for glib rhetoric to recommend him. Rydell's chief opponent is Bill Arrington (Damon Clark), an intelligent, committed politician who bills himself as the candidate for all people and looks to be a shoo-in as New York's first black mayor. Hunter knows Rydell can't beat Arrington on the real issues, so he looks for something he can engineer to his vapid candidate's advantage. Hunter finds his opportunity after a racist police officer, Ben Egan (Charles Timm), and his liberal partner, Jason McNair (Richard Lee Ross), arrest black bicycle messenger Vail Yearwood (Billy Williams) for suspected robbery. In a fit of anger, Egan shoots the unarmed man. A hospital mix-up allows Hunter to fake Yearwood's death, and Rydell takes to the airwaves, denouncing police brutality and swearing his administration will halt such abuses of the public trust. Hunter also pressures Yearwood's articulate wife (Vanessa Shaw)—who thinks she is a widow—to speak out against the injustice of her husband's death, and she does so persuasively. Egan goes to trial and is convicted on McNair's testimony; despite pressure from the police department, McNair's conscience won't allow him to cover up for his partner. Arrington drops in the polls and Rydell rises to win the election. Hunter basks in the satisfaction of having won and proved his mettle, even as he makes sure to secure a compromising videotape of Rydell for future use to his own advantage.

Produced, directed, and cowritten by star Brown, THE GAME is a movie you could almost mistake for a 1970s "blaxploitation" picture—gritty, angry, and obviously produced on a painfully low budget, the inadequacies of which undermine the production's effectiveness. But THE GAME is also informed by a despairing cynicism masquerading as cool rationality that could only be the legacy of the 80s. A paranoid expression of a conspiracy theory in which the world is run by conniving cabals and the little guy always gets the short end of the stick, it uses chess as its principal metaphor. Hunter is a master at chess, and employs a similarly detached, calculating skill to manipulate the "game" of politics and real life.

At the same time, attitudes are carefully balanced: for every racist pig who wants to kill all blacks or ship them back to Africa, the film provides a liberal to point out that blacks have as much right to a piece of the American dream as any other immigrant group (mentioning for good measure that unlike others they were brought here in chains). In a flashback, a Black Panther's violent denunciation of white oppression is balanced by another Panther's observation that if all whites really had it so good, there wouldn't be any of them eating out of garbage cans. Egan is a racist, but he's also a devoted family man demoralized by his job; the devoutly religious McNair wavers between loyalty to the police department and his Christian principles before he comes down on the side of justice. The character of Hunter, a scheming manipulator and opportunist determined to bring down the system from within, is balanced by that of Silvia Yearwood, an advertising executive who believes she can work with the system to bring about social change. Brown pays scrupulous attention to the population of every scene: women and men, blacks, whites, Hispanics, and Asians mingle in hospitals, courtrooms, offices, and streets.

But in the end, everything still comes up ashes. A shallow media operator is elected over an honest man, the reunited Yearwoods are forced to go into exile, and Hunter learns that "once you get rid of the ethics, everything else is a piece of cake." THE GAME is a bleak and pessimistic movie, and without the high-tech trimmings of INTERNAL AFFAIRS, it's a bitter pill to swallow. (*Sexual situations, adult situations.*)

d, Curtis Brown; p, Curtis Brown; w, Julia Wilson and Curtis Brown (based on a story by Brown); ph, Paul Gibson; ed, Gloria Whittemore; m, Julia Wilson; prod d, Walter Jorgenson

Political   (PR:C   MPAA:NR)

GHOST

128m Howard W. Koch/Paramount c

Patrick Swayze (*Sam Wheat*), Demi Moore (*Molly Jensen*), Whoopi Goldberg (*Oda Mae Brown*), Tony Goldwyn (*Carl Brunner*), Rick Aviles (*Willie Lopez*), Gail Boggs (*Louise Brown*), Armelia McQueen (*Clara Brown*), and Vincent Schiavelli (*Subway Ghost*)

The lure of the spirit world has been irresistible in Hollywood during the last year or so. This spooky mystery-thriller-comedy-fantasy-romance-melodrama followed Spielberg's ALWAYS into theaters by just a few months; and during its theatrical run, it was possible to buy a ticket to GHOST at a multiplex and wind up being steered into Bill Cosby and Sidney Poitier's GHOST DAD instead. All three films focus on loved ones dying suddenly only to linger in spirit form, helping the mortals they have left behind. These tales have been known to turn sour in the past—as Norman Bates, unable to shake the specter of his late mother in PSYCHO, could well testify—but in the feel-good present, they have become yet another cinematic way for us to have our cake and eat it too.

In Demi Moore's second supernatural foray (following the solemn silliness of THE SEVENTH SIGN), she and hunky Patrick Swayze costar as Molly Jensen and Sam Wheat, a yuppie couple newly transplanted to a stylish Manhattan loft. While Sam is at his high-powered banking job, Molly stays home and works at ceramic art, though she never seems to get very far. However, planted before her potter's wheel in a sheer, slightly damp shirt, she inspires Sam to amorously push the boundaries of the film's PG-13 rating. So much for artistic struggles. At the office, Sam's coworker and best buddy, Carl Brunner (Tony Goldwyn), demonstrates an overeager interest in the computer access codes Sam holds to the bank's major accounts. One night, returning home from the theater, Sam and Molly are attacked by mugger Willie Lopez (Rick Aviles). As Sam and Willie struggle over Willie's gun, a shot rings out, and Willie runs off, with Sam in hot pursuit. Sam loses Willie, but when he returns to see if Molly is all right, Molly can't see or hear Sam. More disturbing than that, Sam sees himself in Molly's arms, dying of a gunshot wound at the same time he's standing over her. Only at the hospital does it dawn on Sam that he's now a ghost—and it takes another ghost to explain it to him. As the film progresses, it becomes apparent that Sam is generally a little slow on the uptake, and it takes him an indecently long time even to suspect what we've pretty much known all along—that good old Carl is, in fact, a lowdown rat in cahoots with Willie. Later, Willie breaks into the loft while Molly is busy in the bedroom, but Sam manages to scare off his murderer before Willie can do any harm to Molly. Leaving the loft, Sam follows Willie home so he can have Molly turn his killer in. However, still unable to communicate with Molly, Sam calls in heretofore phony spiritualist Oda Mae Brown (Whoopi Goldberg), who can hear but not see Sam. When Sam persuades Oda to seek out his wife, Molly contacts Carl. Sam then follows Carl to Willie's apartment, fearing that Carl is going to confront the murderer. Instead, Sam watches as Carl bawls out Willie for killing Sam when he was only supposed to get his wallet with the access codes Carl needed to carry out a money-laundering scheme. Following Carl, Sam discovers that the laundered money has been deposited in the account of a fictional Rita Miller. Sam convinces Oda to masquerade as Miller and empty the account before Carl, who has stolen the codes from Sam's loft while putting the make on Molly, can transfer the funds to his dirty-money client's offshore bank. Carl, who's a little brighter than Sam, figures out the ruse Oda has pulled off. Then, recognizing Sam's spirit state, Carl threatens to kill Molly unless Sam gets Oda to return the money. This brings about the climax, which features, among too many other things, Sam caressing Molly by taking temporary possession of Oda's body. This scene isn't as weird as it sounds—we see Oda as Sam—but it's weird enough.

What's even weirder is that GHOST manages to work despite the constant distractions of writer Bruce Joel Rubin's mishmash script and Jerry Zucker's uneven direction. Zucker makes his solo debut here after codirecting AIRPLANE!; TOP SECRET; and RUTHLESS PEOPLE with brother David Zucker and Jim Abrahams. His work here isn't the embarrassment that often results when a comedy director turns serious; on the contrary, Zucker shows great potential. But instead of packing GHOST with every possible gag—the hallmark of his comedy collaborations—he fills it with an array of clashing movie styles that never harmonize into a compelling whole. Oddly, the comedy interludes with Goldberg fall flattest, though, as has been the case before, the failure is due more to the weakness of the material than to a lack of talent on Goldberg's part.

GHOST might have been far more interesting had the filmmakers cast a male in Goldberg's role and explored the possibilities of having him fall for Moore while helping to solve Sam's murder. But, in keeping with mainstream cinema's current mores, Molly remains monogamous even after Sam's death, not to mention chastely uncorrupted by the need to make a living in the urban shark pool. As Sam rides off on heavenly moonbeams, it's hard not to wonder what Molly's going to do with no mate, a non-existent career, and rent due on that stylish loft. Still, viewers will find it hard not to reach for their hankies at the million-dollar moment when Sam finally reveals himself in spirit form to Molly, proving that, however cluttered by extraneous characters and subplots, the theme of romantic love reaching beyond the grave, and into eternity, remains potent and pure as a cinematic conceit. Or maybe what makes this movie so appealing are all of those romantic notions *plus* a shirtless Patrick Swayze and a nude Demi Moore. Surprisingly, the film earned an Oscar nomination for Best Picture, no doubt a tribute more to its box-office performance than to its quality — although HOME ALONE's success carried over into 1991 making it the Number One money-maker among 1990 releases, GHOST had the highest box-office receipts in 1990. Goldberg won an Oscar for Best Supporting Actress, and the film was nominated for Academy Awards for its editing, score, and screenplay. *(Violence, adult situations, profanity.)*

d, Jerry Zucker; p, Lisa Weinstein; w, Bruce Joel Rubin; ph, Adam Greenberg; ed, Walter Murch; m, Maurice Jarre; prod d, Jane Musky; spec, Industrial Light & Magic and Richard Edlund; cos, Ruth Morley

Fantasy/Romance   (PR:C   MPAA:PG-13)

GHOST DAD

84m SAH/Universal c

Bill Cosby *(Elliot Hopper)*, Kimberly Russell *(Diane Hopper)*, Denise Nicholas *(Joan)*, Ian Bannen *(Sir Edith Moser)*, Christine Ebersole *(Carol)*, Barry Corbin *(Mr. Collins)*, Salim Grant *(Danny Hopper)*, Brooke Fontaine *(Amanda Hopper)*, Dakin Matthews *(Mr. Seymour)*, Dana Ashbrook *(Tony Ricker)*, Omar Gooding *(Stuart)*, Raynor Scheine *(Cabbie)*, Arnold Stang *(Mr. Cohen)*, Brian Mitchell *(Teacher)*, Lisa Mene Nemacheck *(Jonelle)*, Donzaleigh Abernathy *(ER Nurse)*, George Ganz *(Mr. Nero)*, Cyndi James Gossett *(ER Doctor)*, Joseph Hajduk, Kevin Lee, Becky Katzen, Bryant Edwards, Trenton Teigen *(Students)*, Mary Munday, Norman Merrill, Ted Hayden, Raymond E. Foti, Frank Biro *(Executives)*, Amy Hill, Patrika Darbo *(Nurses)*, Kenny Ford Jr, Adam Jeffries, Austin Garrett *(Buddies)*, Douglas Johnson *(Lab Technician)*, James McIntire *(Sheriff)*, Eric Menyuk *(Clinic Doctor)*, Rita Vassallo, Jeanne Mori *(ICU Nurses)*, Jizelle Morris *(Screaming Girl)*, Pamela Poitier *(Nurse Satler)*, Robin Pearson Rose *(Hospital Administrator)*, Becky Sweet *(Classmate)*, Robert Covarrubias *(Man in Waiting Room)*, Meredith Gordon *(Woman in Taxi)*, and Cedric Scott *(Announcer)*

Bill Cosby stars as a widowed executive trying to raise his kids and, at the same time, make a big business deal that will get him a promotion, which includes life insurance benefits. After narrowly avoiding a number of life-threatening accidents, Elliot Hopper (Cosby) takes a cab that speeds off a high bridge. Although he escapes the accident, Elliot discovers that people can't see or hear him; he's a ghost. However, when he returns home, Elliot learns that he can be seen if there is no bright light around, and that he can be heard and take on a corporeal solidity if he concentrates. What's more, because of some screw-ups in Heaven, Elliot still has some time left on Earth — long enough, he hopes, to wind up his big deal. The next day, after cleverly passing a physical exam for the life insurance policy, Elliot rides to school with eldest daughter, Diane (Kimberly Russell). There he tosses Tony (Dana Ashbrook), the object of Diane's romantic dreams, out of the car. Mortified by her ghostly father's actions, Diane argues with Elliot all the way home, catching the eye of Stuart (Omar Gooding), an evil yuppie neighbor. All at once, Elliot is forced to deal with an array of new problems. Not only do his girl friend, Joan (Nicholas), and his business partners and kids feel neglected, but Gooding hatches a blackmail scheme. As if all of this weren't enough, Tony telephones repeatedly to complain about being tossed from the car. The next morning, Elliot leaves a major business meeting to save his son, Danny (Salim Grant), from an embarrassing situation at school. Of course, Elliot is fired, but that night he realizes that his body is still alive; if he can just find it in time, he can return to life. While everyone is searching for Elliot's body, Diane has a bad accident. In the emergency room, Diane's spirit leaves her body. However, she thoroughly enjoys the freedom of her new state, despite Elliot's orders to get back into her body. But while flying away from her father, Diane discovers his body, to which Elliot returns. When Diane's spirit and body are reunited, the whole family is together again.

Take TV's favorite father, add Hollywood's recent affection for special-effects comedy, and the result is a film whose attempt to capitalize on two good things is embarrassingly blatant. Had the makers of GHOST DAD taken the film's premise a bit farther — perhaps emphasizing that a father who's never home is pretty ghostlike to begin with — this might have been a charming, clever little movie. Instead, screenwriters Chris Reese, Brent Maddock, and S.S. Wilson and director Sidney Poitier have ended up with a bland, fairly empty exercise in professionalism. To be sure, there are lots of clever ideas in the movie, and the performances are uniformly excellent, but GHOST DAD is too unfocused for us to really care about any of it. Even Elliot's ghostly state is never satisfactorily explained (Why, for example, does he have a problem with blinking on and off near the end of the film?).

Rather than undertake any kind of exploration of the difficulties encountered by African-American executives in white-run corporations, GHOST DAD is content to trade in silly political jokes and toilet humor, a feeble attempt to woo an older crowd that succeeds only in sullying an otherwise squeaky-clean movie. In his television shows, his books, and his many records, Cosby has always evinced a core sincerity that has lifted his work above that of other comedians who mine similarly G-rated material. However, on the big screen Cosby's heartfelt decency continues to come across as blandness.

In a sense, Poitier is an even greater disappointment. Here, as in the other films he has directed (including UPTOWN SATURDAY NIGHT; LET'S DO IT AGAIN; STIR CRAZY), he shows himself to be a most competent director. But when are his directorial efforts going to demonstrate the passion that has made his work as an actor so brilliant? There's nothing really wrong with GHOST DAD. It just seems that two of the most important African-American entertainers of the last half-century could have come up with something a little more exciting.

d, Sidney Poitier; p, Terry Nelson; w, Chris Reese, Brent Maddock, and S.S. Wilson (based on a story by Maddock, Wilson); ph, Andrew Laszlo; ed, Pembroke Herring; m, Henry Mancini; prod d, Henry Bumstead; art d, Bernie Cutler; set d, John Cartwright; spec, Richard O. Helmer, Apogee Productions, The Chandler Group, and R/Greenburg Associates; stunts, Alan Oliney; cos, Winnie D. Brown; makup, Stephanie R. Cozart; tech, Malcolm Atterbury Jr.

Comedy/Fantasy   (PR:A   MPAA:PG)

GODFATHER PART III, THE

161m Zoetrope/Paramount c

Al Pacino *(Michael Corleone)*, Diane Keaton *(Kay Adams)*, Talia Shire *(Connie Corleone)*, Andy Garcia *(Vincent Mancini)*, Eli Wallach *(Don Altobello)*, Joe Mantegna *(Joey Zasa)*, George Hamilton *(B.J. Harrison)*, Bridget Fonda *(Grace Hamilton)*, Sofia Coppola *(Mary Corleone)*, Raf Vallone *(Cardinal Lamberto)*, Franc D'Ambrosio *(Tony Corleone)*, Donal Donnelly *(Archbishop Gilday)*, Richard Bright *(Al Neri)*, Helmut Berger *(Frederick Keinszig)*, Don Novello *(Dominic Abbandando)*, John Savage *(Andrew Hagen)*, Franco Citti *(Calo)*, Mario Donatone *(Mosca)*, Vittorio Duse *(Don Tommasino)*, Enzo Robutti *(Licio Lucchesi)*, Michele Russo *(Spara)*, Al Martino *(Johnny Fontane)*, Robert Cicchini *(Lou Pennino)*, Rogerio Miranda *(Armand, Twin Bodyguard)*, Carlos Miranda *(Francesco, Twin Bodyguard)*, Vito Antuofermo *(Anthony "The Ant" Squigliaro)*, Robert Vento *(Father John)*, Willy Brown *(Party Politician)*, Jeannie Linero *(Lucy Mancini)*, Remo Remotti *(Camerlengo Cardinal)*, Jeanne Savarino Pesch *(Francesca Corleone)*, Janet Savarino Smith *(Kathryn Corleone)*, Tere L. Baker *(Teresa Hagen)*, Carmine Caridi *(Albert Volpe)*, Don Costello *(Frank Romano)*, Al Ruscio *(Leo Cuneo)*, Mickey Knox *(Matty Parisi)*, Rick Aviles, Michael Bowen *(Masks)*, Brett Halsey *(Douglas Michelson)*, Gabriele Torrei *(Enzo the Baker)*, Abineri John *(Hamilton Banker)*, Brian Freilino *(Stockholder)*, Gregory Corso *(Unruly Stockholder)*, Marino Mase *(Lupo)*, Dado Ruspoli *(Vanni)*, Valeria Sabel *(Sister Vincenza)*, Luigi Laezza, Beppe Pianviti *(Keinszig Killers)*, Santo Indelicato *(Guardia del Corpo)*, Francesco Paolo Bellante *(Autista di Don Tommasino)*, Paco Reconti *(Gesu)*, Mimmo Cuticchio *(Puppet Narrator)*, Richard Honigman *(Party Reporter)*, Nicky Blair *(Nicky the Casino Host)*, Anthony Guidera *(Anthony, the Bodyguard)*, Frank Tarsia *(Frankie, the Bodyguard)*, Diane Agostini *(Woman with Child at Street Fair)*, Jessica DiCicco *(Child)*, Catherine Scorsese, Isa Bernardini *(Women in Cafe)*, Joseph Drago *(Party Security)*, David Hume Kennerly *(Party Photographer)*, James D. Damiano *(Son Playing Soccer)*, and Michael Boccio *(Father of Soccer Player)*

It was the sequel that was never meant to be. It was also, of course, the sequel no one could refuse.

Well, almost no one. Robert Duvall, who figured prominently in the first two films, stayed away when the producers reportedly refused equal billing and equal money with Al Pacino. The intended newcomer co-star — with Andy Garcia — Winona Ryder almost made it. But coming off starring roles in three other major 1990 releases (WELCOME HOME, ROXY CARMICHAEL, MERMAIDS, EDWARD SCISSORHANDS), she reportedly wasn't up to the rigors of playing Michael Corleone's daughter. She never got beyond a Rome hotel room where a doctor was said to have looked at her and sent her home following a diagnosis of complete mental and physical exhaustion.

Meanwhile, all of the familiar Coppola stories surfaced over the course of the production. Budget excesses, creative clashes, last-second rewrites, a breakneck pace to meet a December release, and cast dissension over the director's decision to cast his daughter, Sofia, as Michael's daughter, all were reported to have plagued the project. Out of the confusion came one of the most perplexing films of 1990, an epic without an epic scope, a muted, strained, unnatural affair that never comes into strong dramatic focus. Its storylines wander and fail to come to life due to laborious, sometimes pointless, recycling of themes, elements, and even individual scenes from the first two films, while striving to tell its own difficult, complex story and introducing a platoon of new characters. Yet, for all its weaknesses, it stands as proof that, though his greatest films may be behind (or ahead) of him, Coppola is incapable of making an unoriginal film that is without genuine emotion.

The most compelling argument against the sequel was that the first two films formed a closed, complete narrative tracing criminal heir Michael Corleone's (Pacino) rise and fall, purely and simply, needing no elaboration. Nonetheless, Coppola's wisest move in PART III was to not try to take the Corleone saga into a radically different direction. Instead, the third part becomes an extended coda to the ending of PART II, as Michael continues to fulfill his tragic legacy as a man who tries to do his best for his family, only to destroy it in the process.

Establishing its connection to the second film, as well as its tone, the film, set in 1979, begins with a elegiac montage of the Corleone Lake Tahoe complex, where much of PART II was set, now in ruins. The montage gives way to Michael writing a letter to his children (who now live with his ex-wife, Kay), inviting them to a ceremony in New York, where he now lives. He is to be honored by the Catholic church for his charitable works through a foundation, named in honor of his father, Vito Corleone. He prevails upon the children to convince Kay (Diane Keaton) to accompany them. The party afterwards, mirroring the parties that opened the other two films, introduces the major players and conflicts.

Having sold off all his major criminal and legitimate gambling enterprises (presumably at a monstrous profit; a highlight of the party is Michael donating $100 million to the foundation), Michael still maintains his influential role in "The Commission," the governing body of the nation's organized crime operation. Crashing the party are Joey Zasa (Joe Mantegna), a flamboyant gang leader who had been awarded the Corleone's New York territory with Michael's support, and Vincent (Andy Garcia), the illegitimate son of Michael's late brother Sonny. At the urging of Michael's sister Connie (Talia Shire), Michael allows Vincent to be present at a meeting with Zasa where Zasa is airing his complaints about Vincent. Michael's attempt to make peace between the two is violently rebuffed when Vincent bites off a chunk of Zasa's ear during a "conciliatory" embrace. While Michael warns Vincent to steer clear of Zasa, he also decides to take the young hothead under his wing, again at Connie's urging, in an effort to make him an enforcer for the family. Returning to the party, Vincent is vamped by Michael's daughter Mary (Sofia Coppola), who is also honorary chairman of the Corleone Foundation. Kay has elected to attend the party, but Michael's reunion with her is only marginally more successful than his aborted attempt to reconcile Vincent and Zasa. With his children grown and his health failing, Michael would like to rekindle his relationship with Kay, but she has built a life of her own and is not interested in a reconciliation. She has only attended the party to implore Michael to let their son Anthony (Franc D'Ambrosio) drop out of law school and pursue a career as an opera singer. Michael desperately wants Anthony to continue his education and eventually assume a prominent position in the family business, but he's no longer the stubbornly intractable man he once was, and he gives in to the wishes of Kay and Anthony.

Following the party, Michael tries to build on his Papal honors by approaching Archbishop Gilday (Donal Donnelly), head of the Vatican Bank who presided over the ceremony, with an offer to buy controlling interest in Immobiliare, the Vatican's vast European conglomerate run by some of the continent's most powerful business leaders. (No "Godfather" film would be complete without a far-ranging conspiracy to destroy the family.) The archbishop is somewhat interested in Michael's offer, but first extorts $600 million from him to cover an embarrassing deficit at the Vatican Bank. Later, when Pope Paul IV dies, dissident members of the Immobiliare board attempt to squeeze Michael ever further by blocking his appointment to the board, a move that must be ratified by the Pope. Back in the US, even uglier doings are afoot. Michael has arranged a meeting of The Commission at a rooftop garden in Las Vegas where he intends to resign his position. The meeting turns into a bloodbath when it is attacked by a heavily armed helicopter (a tongue-in-cheek reference to Coppola's APOCALYPSE NOW). Many of The Commission members are killed, though Michael escapes with the assistance of Vincent, who is certain the massacre was engineered by Zasa. Michael, however, knows Zasa hasn't the resources, ambition, or brains to stage such an audacious attack. Looking instead at his Immobiliare deal, Michael finds traitors at every level, up to and including the Vatican itself. He begins staging his revenge, again mirroring the first two films, which will culminate during Anthony's starring operatic debut in Palermo, Sicily.

The film's major subplots include Michael's ongoing attempts at reconciliation with Kay and Vincent's courting of his cousin Mary, both significant personal failings. Kay continues to be repulsed by "the Sicilian thing," while Michael forces Vincent to give up Mary in exchange for admission to the family since, as head of the Corleone Foundation, Mary must remain untainted by Vincent's criminal involvement. Connie, meanwhile, emerges as the family's Lucretia Borgia, using a box of poisoned canolis against the close associate of Michael (Eli Wallach) who has betrayed him.

Despite a running time closing in on three hours, THE GODFATHER PART III is narratively choppy. A victim of its own ambitions, it tries to cover too much thematic ground. Rather than using organized crime as a metaphor for predatory capitalism, as the first two films did, this movie reverses itself, using legitimate business as a metaphor for organized crime. However, there are few subjects as inherently uncinematic as the world of high finance, a point evidently not lost on the public who stayed away in droves after a record-setting turnout on the film's opening day. Vincent's clash with Zasa, the only real gangster plot in the film, is really a truncated subplot, too obviously added to liven up the slow-moving main plot. Michael's attempts to win back Kay have little emotional immediacy. Too often, their scenes together play like high-school debates on morality, power, and corruption.

What finally does hold PART III together is what film scholars and buffs will be arguing about for years to come: the casting of Sofia Coppola as Mary Corleone. Through all the plots, subplots, sideplots, digressions, and diversions, the only element that comes to bear on everything is Michael's love for his daughter and his determination to have her be the standard-bearer for the next generation of Corleones. The "anti" argument is that for such a pivotal role Coppola should have chosen a professional actress (Sofia's voice, in fact, was dubbed for the movie). But Mary is not as important for her own sake as for what she symbolizes to Michael as the first Corleone to have grown up without having experienced the violent Corleone family legacy. That is why it becomes so important for Michael to get Mary away from Vincent and why Vincent, as he matures, comes to see Michael's wisdom, that the best way to love her is to set her free. As she is outside and above Michael's and Vincent's world, it makes a kind of sense that she be somehow outside and above the acting ensemble. Coppola doesn't so much direct her as create a cinematic context for her as the ethereal presence who drives the film through Michael's and Vincent's ambitions for her. Coppola makes her lack of acting experience register as openness and guilelessness that comes to imbue her with an aching poignancy, making the film's climax almost unexpectedly devastating. In contract to the career acting professionals around her, she gives the honest impression of someone doing a favor for her father, unaware of its importance, to get on with her life, a hope undoubtedly shared by Coppola himself, who has said in many interviews that he never much liked gangster movies to begin with. (*Violence, profanity, adult situations.*)

d, Francis Ford Coppola; p, Gray Frederickson, Fred Roos, Francis Ford Coppola, and Charles Mulvehill; w, Mario Puzo and Francis Ford Coppola; ph, Gordon Willis; ed, Barry Malkin, Lisa Fruchtman, and Walter Murch; m, Carmine Coppola and Nino Rota; md, Carmine Coppola; prod d, Dean Tavoularis; art d, Alex Tavoularis; set d, Gary Fettis and Franco Fumagalli; spec, Lawrence James Cavanaugh and R. Bruce Steinheimer; stunts, Buddy Joe Hooker; cos, Milena Canonero; makup, Fabrizio Sforza and Tom Lucas

Crime   (PR:C   MPAA:R)

GODS MUST BE CRAZY II, THE

97m Weintraub/Columbia c

N!Xau (*Xixo*), Lena Farugia (*Dr. Ann Taylor*), Hans Strydom (*Dr. Stephen Marshall*), Eiros (*Xiri*), Nadies (*Xisa*), Erick Bowen (*Mateo*), Treasure Tshabalala (*Timi*), Pierre Van Pletzen (*George*), Lourens Swanepoel (*Brenner*), Richard Loring (*Jack*), Lesley Fox (*Ann's Secretary*), Simon Sabela (*General*), Ken Marshall (*Convener*), Peter Tunstall (*Chief Game Warden*), Andrew Dibb (*Computer Operator*), and Shimane Mpepela (*Man on Bike*)

This sequel to South African filmmaker Jamie Uys' worldwide hit THE GODS MUST BE CRAZY (1981), which earned a surprising $13 million in rentals during its 1984 North American release, covers the same ground as its predecessor with similarly pleasant results—though the naive charm seems a bit forced this time around. Part two opens in the Kalahari Desert, where N!Xau, the Kalahari Bushman who starred in the first film, is preparing to go on a foraging expedition with his nine-year-old daughter (Nadies) and five-year-old son (Eiros). An offscreen narrator sets the scene for any viewers who might have missed the first installment. The Bushmen are an isolated people who live in an area of the desert considered uninhabitable by modern man. They are therefore completely unaware of the modern world and live in a state of primitive innocence, completely in harmony with their environment. The Bushmen also have no concept of machinery, ownership, work, or war—screened as they are from civilization by the buffer of the harsh Kalahari. While hunting, N!Xau is separated from his children when they explore what they construe as a very strange animal: the parked truck of a pair of hapless elephant poachers (Pierre Van Pletzen and Lourens Swanepoel). Unaware of their inquisitive passengers, the poachers drive off with the children, forcing N!Xau to pursue the truck, following its tracks in the sand. Meanwhile, the film's other principal characters arrive in the same remote region of the desert via separate subplots. Lena Farugia, playing New York attorney Dr. Ann Taylor, and Hans Strydom, playing ranger-zoologist Dr. Stephen Marshall, have been blown off course by a freak storm that lodges their ultra-light airplane in the branches of a Baobab tree. Farugia, a high-powered lawyer in the Big City, is helpless and panic-stricken in the wilds of the Kalahari—leaping six feet in the air and onto the shoulders of Strydom every time she sees a lizard or some equally exotic animal. Despite initial mutual disdain, they come to rely on each other until they are separated after a disastrous attempt to take off Flintstones-style in the airplane: Strydom tries to compensate for a flat tire by running with his feet through a hole in the cockpit floor, but Farugia pulls back too suddenly on the controls and flies away, leaving him to wander after her in the desert. While all of this has been taking place, two soldiers (Erick Bowen and Treasure Tshabalala), separated from armies engaged in a nearby border war, have been playing a deadly game of tag—taking turns making each other a prisoner. N!Xau happens upon their tracks and goes to greet them, explaining that he does not have time to play with them because he is searching for his children. Farugia also stumbles upon the soldiers after parachuting to earth with her plane and attempting to walk back to Strydom, who is by now near collapse from lack of water and the effect of a scorpion bite. Farugia manages to take both soldiers prisoner with a purse filled with rocks and forces them to drive her toward Strydom. N!Xau, as it happens, has also run across Strydom's faltering tracks and has taken time from his search (he has been running two nights and three days) to save the stricken man. He then finds Farugia and her captives and leads them to Strydom before resuming his mission. By this time, both children have escaped from the truck, one by accident, the other purposely when the poachers stopped to get their bearings. Separately, they follow the truck's tire tracks in an attempt to return to their father. Swanepoel, the evil poacher, discovers that Van Pletzen, his kindhearted but incompetent assistant, has been driving in the wrong direction. They double back along their tracks, almost running over both children and then N!Xau, whom they capture after he sees their truckload of tusks. The poachers also capture Farugia, Strydom, Bowen, and Tshabalala by using N!Xau as a hostage. Swanepoel drives off to contact his boss, leaving the prisoners with Van Pletzen. Van Pletzen manages to shoot himself in the foot after dropping his pistol in his waistband and the prisoners escape. Swanepoel returns and sets fire to the underbrush to kill them all, but N!Xau saves them by making a circular firebreak. They return and capture Swanepoel, who is now being held at bay on top of his truck by a pride of lions forced out of the veldt by his fire. Van Pletzen tells N!Xau where he last saw the lost children. The two soldiers part as friends, one taking the poachers to justice, after helping Strydom and Farugia repair their airplane. Strydom and Farugia return to the hotel where she is scheduled to represent a corporate client at an important meeting. As their airplane glides to earth, they attempt to kiss, but Farugia slips through the hole in the cockpit floorboard, dangling precariously with her dress pulled over her head. Corporate and government officials who have been supervising her rescue search gawk at her underwear. Finally, N!Xau is reunited with Nadies and Eiros, who joined forces just in time to save the little boy from a hyena attack, and the family embraces for a tearful happy ending.

Considered outside of its political context—THE GODS MUST BE CRAZY II and its predecessor were financed and shot entirely in South Africa and many anti-apartheid sympathizers have condemned both films—this film provides many simple pleasures. Uys has a fine sense of the absurd and the settings for both of these films, which throw the civilized world into sharp contrast with the primitive, provide him with abundant comic opportunities. The almost-mythical story line of the first film—N!Xau's heroic journey to return an empty Coke bottle, tossed from an airplane, to the Land of the Gods after it brings the evils of ownership, jealously, and violence to his people—is missing from this installment. Even so, the underlying idea that sustained the first film is still effective and involving. The audience is able to see itself through the eyes of a man to whom the most serious "civilized" activity, such as two soldiers desperately trying to gun each other down, is mysterious and ridiculous. In Uys' skillful hands, even the animals seem to look bemusedly at the silly behavior of modern man.

Yet Uys never preaches. He is out for laughs, not revelations about the human condition. His approach is always whimsical and gentle—even in the frequent slapstick sequences that he gooses along with a little fast-motion filmwork a la Benny Hill. Despite a few dull spots and a certain amount of predictability, THE GODS MUST BE CRAZY II delivers enough laughs and does it with enough charm to be worthwhile viewing, especially for fans of the first film. In addition, this film qualifies as entertainment genuinely suitable for the entire family. It manages to be wholesome, intelligent, and amusing without succumbing to smarminess. The comedy that appeals to children in this film will also, no-doubt, appeal to adults—a rare accomplishment.

The political controversy that hangs over these films is unfortunate, given Uys' obvious love of the Kalahari and its people. Uys has spent years living among the Bushmen, seeking the ideal actors and locations for his films, and seems genuinely fascinated by juxtaposing their ways with those of the civilized world. It seems clear that these films arise from his admiration of these people. Nonetheless, it is understandable how these films could be offensive to viewers with sensitive political antennae. Financed, created, and distributed by white South Africans, THE GODS MUST BE CRAZY and its sequel could easily be viewed as a condescending pat on the heads of the cute little Bushmen by the culture that has usurped their land.

d, Jamie Uys; p, Boet Troskie; w, Jamie Uys; ph, Buster Reynolds; ed, Renee Engelbrecht and Ivan Hall; m, Charles Fox; set d, Joi Design; stunts, Buster Reynolds; makup, Rose Bruins

Comedy   (PR:AA   MPAA:PG)

GOKIBURI

(Japan) (SEE: TWILIGHT OF THE COCKROACHES)

GOODFELLAS

148m Irwin Winkler/WB c

Robert De Niro *(James Conway)*, Ray Liotta *(Henry Hill)*, Joe Pesci *(Tommy DeVito)*, Lorraine Bracco *(Karen Hill)*, Paul Sorvino *(Paul Cicero)*, Frank Sivero *(Frankie Carbone)*, Tony Darrow *(Sonny Bunz)*, Mike Starr *(Frenchy)*, Frank Vincent *(Billy Batts)*, Chuck Low *(Morris Kessler)*, Frank DiLeo *(Tuddy Cicero)*, Henny Youngman *(Himself)*, Gina Mastrogiacomo *(Janice Rossi)*, Catherine Scorsese *(Tommy's Mother)*, Charles Scorsese *(Vinnie)*, Suzanne Shepherd *(Karen's Mother)*, Debi Mazar *(Sandy)*, Margo Winkler *(Belle Kessler)*, Welker White *(Lois Byrd)*, Jerry Vale *(Himself)*, Julie Garfield *(Mickey Conway)*, Christopher Serrone *(Young Henry)*, Elaine Kagan *(Henry's Mother)*, Beau Starr *(Henry's Father)*, Kevin Corrigan *(Michael Hill)*, Michael Imperioli *(Spider)*, Robbie Vinton *(Bobby Vinton)*, John Williams *(Johnny Roastbeef)*, Daniel P. Conte *(Dr. Dan)*, Tony Conforti *(Tony)*, Frank Pellegrino *(Johnny Dio)*, Ronald Maccone *(Ronnie)*, Tony Sirico *(Tony Stacks)*, Joseph D'Onofrio *(Young Tommy)*, Steve Forleo, Richard Dioguardi *(City Detectives)*, Frank Adonis *(Anthony Stabile)*, John Manca *(Nickey Eyes)*, Joseph Bono *(Mikey Franzese)*, Katherine Wallach *(Diane)*, Mark Evan Jacobs *(Bruce)*, Angela Pietropinto *(Cicero's Wife)*, Marianne Leone *(Tuddy's Wife)*, Marie Michaels *(Mrs. Carbone)*, Lo Nardo *(Frenchy's Wife)*, Melissa Prophet *(Angie)*, Illeana Douglas *(Rosie)*, Susan Varon *(Susan)*, Elizabeth Whitcraft *(Tommy's Girl Friend at Copa)*, Clem Caserta *(Joe Buddha)*, Samuel L. Jackson *(Stacks Edwards)*, Fran McGee *(Johnny Roastbeef's Wife)*, Paul Herman *(Dealer)*, Edward McDonald *(Himself)*, Edward Hayes *(Defense Attorney)*, Daniela Barbosa, Gina Mattia *(Young Henry's Sisters)*, Joel Calendrillo *(Young Henry's Older Brother)*, Anthony Valentin *(Young Michael)*, Edward D. Murphy, Michael Citriniti *(Liquor Cops)*, Peter Hock *(Mailman)*, Erasmus C. Alfano *(Barbeque Wiseguy)*, John DiBenedetto *(Bleeding Man)*, Manny Alfaro *(Gambling Doorman)*, Thomas Lowry *(Hijacked Driver)*, Margaret Smith *(School Guard)*, Richard Mullally *(Cop No. 1)*, Frank Albanese *(Mob Lawyer)*, Paul McIssac *(Judge, 1956)*, Bob Golub *(Truck Driver at Diner)*, Louis Eppolito *(Fat Andy)*, Tony Lip *(Frankie the Wop)*, Mikey Black *(Freddy No Nose)*, Peter Cicale *(Pete the Killer)*, Anthony Powers *(Jimmy Two Times)*, Vinny Pastore *(Man with Coatrack)*, Anthony Alessandro, Victor Colicchio *(Henry's 60s Crew)*, Mike Contessa, Philip Suriano *(Cicero's 60s Crew)*, Paul Mougey *(Terrorized Waiter)*, Norman Barbera *(Bouncer)*, Anthony Polemeni *(Copa Captain)*, James Quattrochi, Lawrence Sacco, Dino Laudicina *(Henry's Greeters)*, Thomas E. Camuti, Andrew Scudiero *(Mr. Tony's Hoods)*, Irving Welzer *(Copa Announcer)*, Jesse Kirtzman *(Beach Club Waiter)*, Russell Halley, Spencer Bradley *(Bruce's Brothers)*, Bob Altman *(Karen's Dad)*, Joanna Bennett *(Marie No. 1)*, Gayle Lewis *(Marie No. 2)*, Gaetano Lisi *(Paul No. 3)*, Luke Walter *(Truck Driver)*, Ed Deacy *(Detective Deacy)*, Larry Silvestri *(Detective Silvestri)*, Johnny Cha Cha Ciarcia *(Batt's Crew No. 1)*, Vito Picone *(Vito)*, Janis Corsair *(Vito's Girl Friend)*, Frank Aquilino *(Batt's Crew No. 2)*, Lisa Dapolito *(Lisa)*, Michael Calandrino *(Godfather at Table)*, Vito Antuofermo *(Prizefighter)*, Vito Balsamo, Peter Fain, Vinnie Gallo, Gaetano LoGiudice, Garry Blackwood *(Henry's 70s Crew)*, Nicole Burdette *(Carbone's Girl Friend)*, Stella Kietel *(Henry's Older Child, Judy)*, Dominque DeVito *(Henry's Baby, Ruth)*, Michaelangelo Graziano *(Bar Patron)*, Paula Gallo, Nadine Kay *(Janice's Girl Friends)*, Tony Ellis *(Bridal Shop Owner)*, Peter Onorati *(Florida Bookie)*, Jamie DeRoy *(Bookie's Sister)*, Joel Blake *(Judge, 1971)*, H. Clay Dear *(Security Guard with Lobsters)*, Thomas Hewson *(Drug Buyer)*, Gene Canfield *(Prison Guard in Booth)*, Margaux Guerard *(Judy Hill, Age 10)*, Violet Gaynor *(Ruth Hill, Age 8)*, Tobin Bell *(Parole Officer)*, Berlinda Tolbert *(Stacks' Girl Friend)*, Nancy Ellen Cassaro *(Joe Buddha's Wife)*, Adam Wandt *(Kid)*, Joseph P. Gioco *(Garbage Man)*, Isiah Whitlock Jr. *(Doctor)*, Alyson Jones *(Judy Hill, Age 13)*, Ruby Gaynor *(Ruth Hill, Age 11)*, and Richard "Bo" Dietl *(Arresting Narc)*

Much as he did a decade ago in RAGING BULL, Martin Scorsese delves into the lives of people you don't even want to know in GOODFELLAS. Yet, this film, like RAGING BULL, offers a unique and fascinating vision of America and American lives. It is at once an extremely personal film and one that is so in tune with its characters and setting that it has the comic yet horrifying impact of an epic Marcel Ophuls documentary—despite the famous actors sprinkled throughout. Critics voted RAGING BULL the most important film of the 80s. While it may be premature to predict a similar status for GOODFELLAS in the 90s, it is certainly not too soon to recognize it as one of the most important films of 1990.

Based on journalist Nicholas Pileggi's nonfiction book *Wiseguy* (the film's original title, changed to avoid confusion with the TV series of the same name), GOODFELLAS revolves around the career of low-level gangster Henry Hill (Ray Liotta), who became part of the federal witness protection program after testifying against his erstwhile partners in crime. At the center of the book is Hill's insider's account of the $6 million robbery of a Lufthansa cargo facility at New York's Idlewild Airport. As might be expected of the director of TAXI DRIVER, GOODFELLAS doesn't even show the robbery. Instead it focuses on the bloody aftermath of the heist, in which all the participants are brutally murdered by Henry's partners, the lethally paranoid Jimmy Conway (Robert De Niro) and the psychotic Tommy DeVito (Joe Pesci). Generally, GOODFELLAS is concerned with Tommy and Jimmy's climb up the mob ladder and its effects on Henry, but Scorsese's rich tapestry is both broader in scope and more detailed than a mere recounting of the events in the trio's life of crime. Because Scorsese is equally concerned with the minutiae of his main characters' world (most of which is provided by Pileggi's book) and with the grand design that appears to underlie that world (the director's contribution), the downfall of Henry and his associates seems fated.

As the film begins, Henry is a youngster (Christopher Serrone). His family lives across the street from a taxi stand that doubles as the local mob headquarters. Admiring the criminals' wealth and clout in the community, Henry begins hustling odd jobs from them, parking their Cadillacs during card games and running numbers. Selling untaxed cigarettes out of the trunk of a car results in Henry's first arrest, during which he maintains the mob code of silence. He is rewarded by being put on a Mafia "career track" under the direction of Jimmy, who, like Henry, is part Irish and therefore barred from ever becoming a member of the Mafia inner circle. A full Sicilian, Tommy begins working with Henry while both are still in their teens. But, owing to Tommy's homicidal temper, it emerges that his career outlook is also limited. All three work for local mob overlord Paul Cicero (Paul Sorvino), a cold, manipulative bully who has little of the redemptive grace of THE GODFATHER's Don Corleone. The difference between THE GODFATHER and GOODFELLAS can be summed up in their catch phrases: "Make him an offer he can't refuse" is replaced by GOODFELLAS' "Fuck you! Pay me!" The brutality of this latter demand is usually enforced with the thud of a pistol whip to the head of some poor schnook unfortunate enough to be somehow beholden to Cicero.

GOODFELLAS encompasses so much that to adequately describe it would virtually require a transcription of the entire film. Many of the seemingly peripheral subplots are showstoppers. Focusing on the one-woman war Henry's wife, Karen (wonderfully played by Lorraine Bracco), fights against his mistress, Henry's homelife functions as a raucous parody of the domineering husbands and quiet wives of THE GODFATHER. But what is perhaps the most remarkable accomplishment of GOODFELLAS is the way in which it radically rethinks the epic cinematic form. In traditional epics a long, complicated, linear narrative unfolds over an extended period of time, serving to draw the audience into the world of its characters, causing viewers to have an emotional stake in the joys, pains, triumphs, and tragedies of the people on the screen. In GOODFELLAS, neither the characters develop nor does any audience empathy for them. The narrative is even more fragmented than it is in Pileggi's book — resembling bits and pieces of home movies spliced together rather than a traditional movie plot. Characters continually appear, disappear, and change drastically, usually without much explanation. Karen, so fiercely self-possessed early in the film, is cowed and exhausted by the movie's hellish climax, during which Henry has gone from a trim, fit, mob dandy to a wired, coked-up, misshapen mess in little more than a jump cut (Scorsese borrows much from Truffaut's and Goddard's bag of cinematic tricks in the film). Henry's cocaine courier, Lois (Welker White), is not so much introduced as dropped into the action. He goes on to bring about Henry's arrest and induction into the witness protection program, leading to the film's final and most disturbing image — a suburbanized Henry appearing at the front door of his expensive new tract home to bring in the morning paper. At just under two and a half hours, GOODFELLAS manages to feel as if it were cut from an even greater length. Moving with dizzying speed, it packs in so much information and observation, and so many New Wave-style "privileged moments" on so many levels that if virtually any other filmmaker had made it, the film would probably have run about twice as long.

An Italian-American who grew up in New York's Little Italy, Scorsese has to this point resisted the obvious career move of making a gangster movie, notwithstanding MEAN STREETS, which, while taking place against a mob backdrop, was not a gangster film in the strict sense of the genre. GOODFELLAS is Scorsese's essay on why the Mafia subject is artistically uninteresting to him. In the end, what most decisively damns Henry is also what makes him most accessible to the audience (in addition to Liotta's excellent performance). Despite being at the center of the film, he's often on the edges of the its most

horrible events. He doesn't even participate directly in the Lufthansa heist. The only real violence we see him commit comes in revenge for an attack on Karen. Nonetheless, he's no hero because he has no commitment, finally, except to himself. From the director who fulfilled a career obsession by bringing THE LAST TEMPTATION OF CHRIST to the screen, that lack of commitment is the only unforgivable sin. In GOODFELLAS Scorsese denies the gangster the single characteristic that has made him a viable screen subject practically from the dawn of cinema, his false tragic stature. Instead of growing over the course of the film, Henry shrinks under Scorsese's scrutiny into a spineless louse surrounded by violent sociopaths, fit neither for sorrow nor pity. It is thus ironic that, as religious fundamentalists did with LAST TEMPTATION, Italian-American advocacy groups publicly condemned GOODFELLAS upon its theatrical release. However, even this condemnation is powerful testimony to Scorsese's artistry. A mediocre filmmaker can upset people, but it takes a real artist to get them hopping mad. Pesci won an Oscar for Best Supporting Actor for his performance, and the film earned nominations for Best Picture, Best Director, Best Supporting Actress (Bracco), Best Editing, and Best Screenplay Based on Material from Another Medium. *(Violence, profanity, adult situations, drug abuse.)*

d, Martin Scorsese; p, Irwin Winkler; w, Nicholas Pileggi and Martin Scorsese (based on the book *Wiseguy* by Pileggi); ph, Michael Ballhaus; ed, Thelma Schoonmaker; prod d, Kristi Zea; art d, Maher Ahmad; set d, Les Bloom; spec, Connie Brink; stunts, Michael Russo; cos, Susan O'Donnell and Thomas Lee Keller; makup, Allen Weisinger and Carl Fullerton; tech, John Manca

Crime/Drama   (PR:O MPAA:R)

GRAFFITI BRIDGE

90m Paisley Park/WB c

Prince *(The Kid)*, Morris Day *(Morris)*, Jerome Benton *(Jerome)*, Ingrid Chavez *(Aura)*, Mavis Staples *(Melody Cool)*, T.C. Ellis *(T.C.)*, Robin Power *(Robin)*, Levi Seacer Jr., Rosie Gaines, Miko Weaver *(The Kid's Band)*, Kirk Johnson, Tony Mosley, Damon Dickson *(The Game Boyz)*, George Clinton, Jill Jones, and Tevin Campbell

Something of a sequel to PURPLE RAIN (1984), GRAFFITI BRIDGE stars Prince as The Kid, the owner of Glam Slam, a dance club where he plays his own brand of spiritual funk. The Kid is struggling to keep his place from the clutches of Morris (Morris Day) and his musical gang, The Times, who own every other joint in town. Meanwhile, he is pursuing a beautiful angel, Aura (Ingrid Chavez), who shows up in reality and in his dreams, often giving him spiritual pep talks in front of a strange stone bridge covered in grafitti, where the sky changes color with every edit. Eventually Morris and his top aide Jerome (Jerome Benton) find Aura and take her to one of their clubs, not realizing she's on a soul-saving mission, even though she informs them that she is seeking "a spiritual substitute for sex." Morris gives her a drug which knocks her out and which has the power to cause her to fall in love with the first person she sees upon awakening. Hearing of the abduction, The Kid searches for Aura and finds her just as she regains consciusness, thereby becoming her heart's desire. They share a romantic dream, then she tries to heighten The Kid's spiritualism while he continues to battle Morris. He challenges his rival to a performance match and does a tough number ("Tick Tick Bang") with fireworks. The Times top him with a rendition of "Shake," and The Kid loses his club. While speeding away in a car, one of The Times hits and kills Aura. The Kid sings a poem Aura had given him, "Grafitti Bridge," which proves to be so inspirational that Morris is humbled and makes peace with The Kid.

Rock musicals have generally succeeded when they are built around strong existing personas, such as Elvis Presley in JAILHOUSE ROCK or The Beatles in A HARD DAY'S NIGHT. With his enormous popularity and his unique personality, Prince would seen ideally suited to create such a musical. Yet in this, his third narrative film, his ego and his bizarre philosophies about life conspire to undermine his movie potential. The musings about spirituality which permeate the film are puzzling, if not silly. Moreover, the film is technically inept. He has improved as a filmmaker since UNDER THE CHERRY MOON (1986) — which is not saying much — largely because he holds his ego a little more in check. The performances are, however, the real death of the film (how many films are there were the *extras* are noticeably bad?). The music is quite good and will certainly appeal to Prince fans, but it is buried under so much tedious pretention that even the performer's most devoted fans will find it difficult to sit through the film. In addition to Prince and the Times, the film features entertaining performances by funk star George Clinton, Gospel queen Mavis Staples, and rising star Tevin Campbell. When Prince really performs on screen, he's terrific. If he'd take some acting lessons and team with a competent scriptwriter and director, he might be capable of creating a first-rate musical.

d, Prince; p, Arnold Stiefel and Randy Phillips; w, Prince; ph, Bill Butler; ed, Rebecca Ross; m, Prince; md, Prince; prod d, Vance Lorenzini; cos, Helen Horatio and Jim Shearon; chor, Otis Sallid

Musical   (PR:C   MPAA:PG-13)

GRAVEYARD SHIFT

90m Larry Sugar/PAR c

(AKA: STEPHEN KING'S GRAVEYARD SHIFT)

David Andrews *(John Hall)*, Kelly Wolf *(Jane Wisconsky)*, Stephen Macht *(Warwick)*, Brad Dourif *(Tucker Cleveland)*, Andrew Divoff *(Danson)*, Vic Polizos *(Brogan)*, Robert Alan Beuth *(Ippetson)*, and Jimmy Woodard *(Carmichael)*

The Bachman Textile Mill (in-joke alert: Richard Bachman is a pseudonym for Stephen King) is plagued with rats, making on-the-job conditions unpleasant...particularly on the graveyard shift. That's when worker Jason Reed (Jonathan Emerson) has a nasty accident: something gives him such a fright that he tumbles into a mechanical picking machine's vicious teeth and is killed; there's hardly enough left to bury. An exterminator, eccentric Tucker Cleveland (Brad Dourif), is hired to eliminate the rats, but his efforts are fruitless. To make matters worse, a safety inspector has threatened to have the place shut down. Though a bribe buys the plant's loathsome foreman Warwick (Stephen Macht) some time, the basement has to be thoroughly cleaned as soon as possible. It's an undesirable job, to say the least, and Warwick assembles a cleaning crew from the mill's financially strapped work force. Crew members include college-educated drifter Hall (David Anderson), "tough girl with a heart of gold" Jane (Kelly Wolf), bullies Danson and Brogan (Andrew Divoff and Vic Polizos), class clown Ippetson (Robert Alan Beuth) and new guy Carmichael (Jimmy Woodard). They're a mismatched bunch, and less than thrilled at the prospect of having to work together under such unappealing and potentially dangerous circumstances. Needless to say, they find more in the lower depths than broken furniture and moldering financial records. Not only is the basement rat infested, it's home to a mutant monster (a kind of giant, hairless rat-bat) that begins killing off the crew members one-by-one.

For a multi-million dollar best-selling author who rates his name in the title, Stephen King has had very little luck on film. Though close to two dozen of his works have been made into movies, most have ranged from tolerable to dismal. The few exceptions have been Brian De Palma's CARRIE, Stanley Kubrick's THE SHINING, Mary Lambert's PET SEMATARY, and Rob Reiner's STAND BY ME and MISERY. GRAVEYARD SHIFT, unfortunately, doesn't rate with that company, rising no higher than tepid King adaptations such as CUJO, CHILDREN OF THE CORN, and CAT'S EYE. It's difficult to say what the problem is. King isn't a literary writer whose work is carried by its prose; most of his books read like outlines (if exceptionally long ones) for movies anyway. But the qualities that makes King's work so popular in print seldom translate to the screen. Adapting short stories to feature-length is particularly tricky, and this film falls prey to the usual pitfalls—there just isn't story to go around. Consequently, for the first two-thirds of the movie the characters are forced to muddle through various forms of small-town unpleasantness to fill up time. Overall the cast does well with the material, and Macht (GALAXINA, THE MONSTER SQUAD) is a standout as the vile, despicable boss. Dourif (BLUE VELVET, CHILD'S PLAY) strikes some sparks as the Vietnam-veteran-turned-exterminator (not one of your baby-killing flashback freaks like Bruce Dern plays, he assures Hall), but he's killed halfway through the film. Released at Halloween, the film had the calculated feel of a movie made simply because the title was guaranteed to pull in audiences on opening weekend. Sadly, it's the kind of effort that gives horror films a bad name. *(Violence, profanity.)*

d, Ralph S. Singleton; p, William J. Dunn and Ralph S. Singleton; w, John Esposito (based on the short story by Stephen King); ph, Peter Stein; ed, Jim Gross and Randy Jon Morgan; m, Anthony Marinelli and Brian Banks; prod d, Gary Wissner

Horror   (PR:C   MPAA:R)

GREEN CARD

(Aus./Fr.) 108m Touchstone — Green Card/Buena Vista c

Gerard Depardieu *(George Faure)*, Andie MacDowell *(Bronte Parrish)*, Gregg Edelman *(Phil)*, Bebe Neuwirth *(Lauren)*, Robert Prosky *(Bronte's Lawyer)*, Jessie Keosian *(Mrs. Bird)*, Ethan Phillips *(Gorsky)*, Mary Louise Wilson *(Mrs. Sheehan)*, Lois Smith *(Bronte's Mother)*, Conrad McLaren *(Bronte's Father)*, Ronald Guttman *(Anton)*, Danny Dennis *(Oscar)*, Stephen Pearlman *(Mr. Adler)*, Victoria Boothby *(Mrs. Adler)*, John Spencer *(Harry)*, Ann Dowd *(Peggy)*, Novella Nelson *(Marriage Celebrant)*, Vasek Simek *(Maitre d')*, Ernesto Gallo *(Butler)*, Chris Odo *(Immigration Supervisor)*, Michele Nevirs *(Immigration*

Clerk), Rick Aviles *(Vincent)*, Abdoulaye N'Gom *(Street Beggar)*, Clint Chin *(Flower Seller)*, Larry Wright *(Drummer)*, John Scanlan, Arthur Anderson *(House Committee)*, Christian Mulot, Francois Dumaurier *(Waiters)*, Jeb Handwerger, Michael David Tanney *(Oscar's Boys)*, Conrad Roberts, Ed Feldman *(Taxi Drivers)*, Ann Wedgeworth, Stefan Schnabel, Anne Shropshire, Simon Jones, Malachy McCourt, and Emily Cho *(Party Guests)*

After making a name for himself in his native Australia with films such as THE LAST WAVE and THE YEAR OF LIVING DANGEROUSLY, director Peter Weir found success in the US with productions such as WITNESS and DEAD POET'S SOCIETY. Here he attempts to add an international flavor to his American work with the casting of French superstar Gerard Depardieu in his US film debut. Depardieu plays George Faure, a French alien who desperately wants to remain in the US. Andie MacDowell is Bronte Parrish, a quiet horticulturist who also has a desperate desire—she wants to rent an exclusive Manhattan apartment complete with a greenhouse. Trouble is, building management will only rent to married couples. Through a mutual friend, George and Bronte meet and strike a deal—they'll get married so that George can get his green card and Bronte can get her apartment. They marry in a quick legal ceremony, then part company. Bronte's life seems to go smoothly for a time thereafter as she adores her apartment and dates a co-worker (Gregg Edelman). She tells no one of her marriage of convenience (her landlords think her husband is on an expedition in Africa). However, things get tense when immigration officials start snooping around, an investigation that threatens Bronte's lifestyle and George's visa. As a result, George and Bronte must get to know each other so they can convince investigators that they have been in love for years. Naturally these efforts are complicated because the two are so different—he's big and boisterous, she's small and shy; he smokes constantly, she despises cigarettes; and so on. To make matters worse, Bronte's best friend Lauren (Bebe Neuwirth) falls for George and Bronte's boy friend learns of her secret marriage. Needless to say, the main characters have a lot to sort out in the final reel.

The film's fine photography and effective use of music make GREEN CARD one of the few Disney films that doesn't seem like a made-for-TV film, but the threadbare screenplay and Weir's weak direction are barely able to hold the film together. Much of the dialog is insipid, and the action is driven by absurd coincidence and unmotivated behavior to the point that one can only feel exasperated by it all. For the most part, it's a screenplay that seems better suited to a TV sitcom. Fortunately, the film is salvaged by its performances, with Depardieu stealing the show and single-handedly making the film worth watching. The actor (who earned a Best Actor nomination for another 1990 release, CYRANO DE BERGERAC) displays wonderful physical capabilities and a remarkable talent for creating winning characters. Using a wide range of vocal inflections, facial expressions, and movement, the huge Depardieu makes George a truly memorable guy. He's funny and smart and devastatingly wry. MacDowell (SEX, LIES AND VIDEOTAPE) is absolutely convincing as the uptight prude whose eyes are opened by this gregarious Frenchman, while Neuwirth (TV's "Cheers") and Edelman (CRIES AND MISDEMEANORS) provide solid support. Peter Weir's talent, so evident in his Australian films, remained dormant here, but Depardieu's lively performance is a good reason to see this film. The movie earned an Oscar nomination for its screenplay. *(Mild profanity, adult situations.)*

d, Peter Weir; p, Peter Weir, Duncan Henderson, and Jean Gontier; w, Peter Weir; ph, Geoffrey Simpson; ed, William Anderson; m, Hans Zimmer; prod d, Wendy Stites; art d, Christopher Nowak; set d, John Anderson and Ted Glass; cos, Marilyn Matthews; makup, Sharon Ilson and Marie-France Vassel

Comedy/Romance   (PR:C   MPAA:PG-13)

GREMLINS 2 THE NEW BATCH

105m Mike Finnell — Amblin/WB c

Zach Galligan *(Billy Peltzer)*, Phoebe Cates *(Kate Beringer)*, John Glover *(Daniel Clamp)*, Robert Prosky *(Grandpa Fred)*, Howie Mandel *(Voice of Gizmo)*, Tony Randall *(Voice of "Brain" Gremlin)*, Robert Picardo *(Forster)*, Christopher Lee *(Dr. Catheter)*, Haviland Morris *(Marla Bloodstone)*, Dick Miller *(Murray Futterman)*, Jackie Joseph *(Sheila Futterman)*, Keye Luke *(Mr. Wing)*, Gedde Watanabe *(Katsuji)*, Kathleen Freeman *(Microwave Marge)*, Don Stanton *(Martin)*, Dan Stanton *(Lewis)*, Shawn Nelson *(Wally)*, Archie Hahn, Leslie Neale, Ron Fassler, Time Winters *(Forster's Technicians)*, Heather Haase, Jason Presson *(Yogurt Jerks)*, Lisa Mende, Patrika Darbo, Jerry Goldsmith *(Yogurt Customers)*, Rick Ducommun *(Security Guard)*, John Capodice *(Fire Chief)*, Belinda Balaski *(Movie Theater Mom)*, Nicky Rose *(Movie Theater Kid)*, Paul Bartel *(Theater Manager)*, Kenneth Tobey *(Projectionist)*, Heidi Kemp, Eric Shawn, Michael Salort *(TV Reporters)*, Frank P. Ryan *(Cop)*, Diane Sainte-Marie *(TV Reporter at Wing's)*, Kristi Witker *(TV Anchor in Bar)*, Sarah Lilly *(Reporter in Lobby)*, Vladimir Bibic *(Taxi Driver)*, Page Hannah, Liz Pryor *(Tour Guides)*, Raymond Cruz *(Messenger)*, Julia Sweeney *(Lab Receptionist)*, Jeff

Swanson *(Forster's Assistant)*, Charlie Haas *(Casper)*, Dale Swann *(Surveillance Supervisor)*, Gray Daniels *(TV Cameraman)*, Stephanie Menuez *(Clamp's Secretary)*, Jacque Lynn Colton *(Lady at Elevator)*, May Quigley, Anthony Winters *(Hallway Employees)*, Isiah Whitlock Jr. *(Fireman)*, Dean Norris *(SWAT Team Leader)*, Saachiko *(Newsstand Lady)*, John Astin *(Janitor)*, Henry Gibson *(Fired Employee)*, Leonard Maltin, Hulk Hogan, Dick Butkus, Bubba Smith *(Themselves)*, Frank Welker *(Voice of Mohawk)*, Kirk Thatcher, Mark Dodson *(Voices of Gremlins)*, Neil Ross *(Voice of Announcer)*, and Jeff Bergman *(Voices of Bugs Bunny and Daffy Duck)*

"The horror...The horror...The breakage!"

Any movie that can reduce British horror star Christopher Lee to muttering incoherence is not a movie to be trifled with. As Dr. Catheter, head researcher of Splice of Life Designer Genes, Lee is moved to the utterance quoted above after the title creatures have trashed his lab. But the mayhem is anything but mindless; for all its impressive destruction, done on a reported $30-million budget, GREMLINS 2: THE NEW BATCH is surprisingly sympathetic towards the title menace and surprisingly thought-provoking in its use of the gremlins to make an extended commentary on modern life and morality.

That the monsters should wind up the tragically ill-fated good guys should come as no surprise to those familiar with the first film, or with any of the films by director Joe Dante, whose idiosyncratic output ranges from THE HOWLING to THE 'BURBS and both "Gremlins" movies. Dante is an enthusiastic fan of classic Hollywood kitsch, especially those monster movies, from KING KONG to THE BEAST FROM 20,000 FATHOMS (quoted in GREMLINS 2), in which the saddest scene is the one in which the monster dies. But Dante is up to more than looting Hollywood's movie heritage. In fact, he quotes constantly, if not obsessively, from all aspects of pop culture, old and new—and this is just one element in the work of a director who has pretty much become a genre unto himself, deftly incorporating his sincere affection for science-fiction, horror, and special effects with equal parts parody, satire, farce, and homespun Capraesque comedy (and with random bits and pieces inspired by everyone from Buster Keaton to Frank Tashlin) into his distinctive output. Yet Dante's films are held together by a basic decency and instinctively populist nonconformism, which provide emotional, intellectual, and historical continuity between the director's contemporary sensibility and his fondness for past movie masters.

Dante's films are also, in all probability, clinically insane, or at least certifiably schizophrenic. They constantly double back, contradicting and satirizing themselves while letting no sticky, if heartfelt, sentiment pass without zinging retort. Though Dante's movies have had an unusually high sequel quotient (his PIRANHA; THE HOWLING; and HOLLYWOOD BOULEVARD have all spawned sequels, with PIRANHA II directed by no less than THE TERMINATOR's James Cameron), he himself has until now avoided succumbing to sequel-itis. Having taken the plunge in GREMLINS 2, however, Dante has come up with what may be his best film yet—a dizzying, no-holds-barred satirical spectacle that will please fans of the original GREMLINS and anyone else lucky enough to drop by.

As GREMLINS 2 begins, Mr. Wing (Keye Luke)—the owner of the trinket shop where the "good" gremlin-mogwai Gizmo was purchased in the first film—turns down an offer to sell his shop to Daniel Clamp, who wants to raze Chinatown to build "Clamp's Chinatown Center: Where business gets oriented." An obvious amalgamated spoof of developer Donald Trump and cable-TV-mogul/movie-colorizer Ted Turner, Clamp (John Glover) doesn't even make the offer in person; instead he sends his emissary (Robert Picardo) with a VCR and TV to play a videotape of Clamp making his final offer. Wing is able to resist Clamp, but cannot withstand old age. When he dies six weeks later, the demolition equipment moves in—causing Gizmo to flee the shop. Captured in an alley by an employee of Dr. Catheter, Gizmo is brought back to Catheter's lab on the top floor of Clamp's midtown office center, where GREMLINS holdovers Kate (Phoebe Cates) and Billy (Zach Galligan) now work for Clamp, she as a tour guide and he as a draftsman working on the Chinatown Center. Up at Splice of Life, Catheter has nothing but dire designs on Gizmo, planning to run tests and then dissect him for further study. A messenger passing through the lab hears Gizmo humming his plaintive signature "song," and later hums it to himself as he passes Billy's office cubicle. After recognizing the song and interrogating the messenger, Billy masquerades as a copier repairman to rescue Gizmo from Catheter's clutches. But, of course, that's only the beginning. Before he can get Gizmo out of the building, Billy is distracted by his power-hungry boss, Marla Bloodstone (Haviland Morris), who has her own designs on Billy after his work receives favorable notice from Clamp. To prevent Marla from seeing Gizmo, Billy agrees to a dinner date with her. It's up to Kate, now worried about the seemingly straying Billy, to fetch Gizmo from Billy's office and bring him back to their apartment. By then, however, it's too late. What follows will be familiar to anyone who saw the first film, particularly those who remember the apocalyptic consequences of violating the three rules of proper mogwai care—never expose them to bright light, never get them wet, and never, *ever*, feed them after midnight. Soon the scaly, lizard-like spawn of Gizmo's soaking

and post-midnight feeding are overrunning the high-rise Center, from the kiosk shops to the penthouse lab, where they ingest Catheter's genetic cocktails and metamorphose into diverse creatures, including an erudite William F. Buckleyish commentator-gremlin (voiced hilariously by Tony Randall) and a giant spider-gremlin (undoubtedly an advance plug for executive producer Steven Spielberg's later summer release, ARACHNOPHOBIA).

What may not be familiar to fans of the first film is the precision and depth of Dante's work here, aided by the Charlie Haas (RIVER'S EDGE) script. This is no lifeless retread, even though every big scene from the first film has its equivalent in GREMLINS 2. (Dante still seems especially concerned about the safe use of microwave ovens.) And even if the filmmakers' apparent intent was to make a movie that feels wildly out of control, GREMLINS 2 rarely loses sight of its objectives. Almost every plot twist, stunt, and sight gag elaborates the movie's basic theme: the metaphysical price paid for plundering a rich human past to build a dubious, impoverished, and inhumane future, of which the gremlins are merely an unnatural byproduct. The theme is mainly suggested by Clamp's urgency in tearing up New York's heritage (such as Chinatown), to construct cold, high-tech, soulless structures in their place, but it is echoed everywhere—from the Splice of Life lab, dedicated to developing new and "improved" life forms, to the romantic subplot, in which Billy is tempted to throw away his long-term romance with Kate to further his career with Clamp. Even the throwaway jokes get into the act, as when a public-address announcement hypes a "new, improved CASABLANCA, in color and with a happier ending."

At the same time, no one who makes movies as thoroughly modernist and as full of high-tech special effects (by Rick Baker, who also coproduced and who is credited with the Splice of Life subplot) as Dante does can ever make a sincere claim to yearning for gentler, simpler times. As a result, the film exhibits an oddly compelling ambivalence toward the gremlins throughout. Moreover, Clamp winds up articulating much of the movie's thematic thrust, despite his status as villain. Not only does he have the last, best word on Gizmo ("He reminds me of dolls hanging from suction cups staring out from behind car windows"), he also sums up the gremlins themselves. Eulogizing his idiotically high-tech high-rise, he notes, "We didn't make a place for people, we made a place for things. And when you make a place for things, things come." Of course, this doesn't stop Clamp, at the fadeout, from spotting Billy's sketch of his Kingston Falls hometown and becoming instantly inspired to plan the "biggest, most sensational small, quiet town development the world has ever seen." It also doesn't stop us from feeling a little sad for the gremlins after they meet their sticky end. They may be nasty, but they know how to party, particularly when they spontaneously mount a lavish musical number inspired by the Kander and Ebb classic "New York, New York."

It doesn't necessarily take a great moviemaker to produce feature-length, bellicose screen belches against modern excess. But it certainly takes an exceptional one to bend a conventional entertainment to such unconventional ends. At its heart, GREMLINS 2 is no less than a sober, multifaceted consideration of the interaction between humankind and its self-created environments, from bleak physical cityscapes to the cultural wasteland of cable television and colorized movies. Notwithstanding his stunning talents as a film craftsman, it is that lively, penetrating, and playful intelligence that makes Dante one of the most important directors working in Hollywood today—and that makes GREMLINS 2 one of the best films of the year. *(Violence.)*

d, Joe Dante; p, Michael Finnell; w, Charlie Haas (based on characters created by Chris Columbus); ph, John Hora; ed, Kent Beyda; m, Jerry Goldsmith; prod d, James Spencer; art d, Joe Lucky; set d, John Berger, Greg Papalia, and Dawn Snyder; spec, Rick Baker; stunts, Mike McGaughy; cos, Rosanna Norton; makup, Michael Germain; anim, Chuck Jones

Comedy/Horror   **(PR:C   MPAA:PG-13)**

GRIFTERS, THE

113m Martin Scorsese/Cineplex Odeon-Miramax c

John Cusack *(Roy Dillon)*, Anjelica Huston *(Lilly Dillon)*, Annette Bening *(Myra Langtry)*, Pat Hingle *(Bobo Justus)*, J.T. Walsh *(Langtry)*, Henry Jones *(Desk Clerk)*, Gailard Sartain *(Myra's Landlord)*, and Jeremy Piven

THE GRIFTERS has the mastery and hallucinatory, all-involving feel of an instant classic. Stephen Frears (THE HIT, MY BEAUTIFUL LAUNDRETTE), a fearlessly diverse director, has immersed himself in the Los Angeles world of *film noir* and emerged with a movie that can easily stand alongside such classics of the genre as THE MALTESE FALCON, THE BIG SLEEP, OUT OF THE PAST, and PRIZZI'S HONOR. Adapted from modish tough-guy writer Jim Thompson's novel, Donald Westlake's script has the right combination of vivid characters, mordant wit, and avaricious savagery which have marked the best works of this type. The characters speak in a faintly disconcerting 1950s argot right out of the book, adding an authentic flavor to the simmeringly suggestive stew Frears has concocted.

The tale is spun of three "grifters," con artists forever on the lookout for an easy hustle. Lily (Anjelica Huston) is an ultra-experienced pro who specializes in racetrack odds altering. Her son, Roy (John Cusack), is basically small-time, hustling sailors and bartenders with loaded dice and sleight-of-the-hand tricks. His inamorata, Myra (Annette Bening), likes corporate action, a field she is easily able to ply with her siren's body and wardrobe of Chanel suits. Lily had Roy when she was but a girl herself, and the two have mostly gone their separate ways. They meet up again in California, where Lily takes an immediate dislike to Myra. Her ill feeling is met and matched by Roy, who has never resolved his filial feelings for her, as well as by Myra, who, having been wholly rebuffed by Lily, resolves to take her down. Lily's got troubles of her own, what with her boss, mobster Bobo Justus (Pat Hingle), suspecting her of gypping him. In a scene that bristles with implied and delivered terror, he makes her pay a painful price for her suspected duplicity. Myra gets into face as well and the climax, involving Lily and Roy, is swift, ugly, cathartic, and ultimately elegiac all at once.

Huston has again done the impossible — she surpasses herself. Her Lily is a slightly older, but equally funny and laconic version of her treasurable Maerose in PRIZZI'S HONOR. She's the ultimate *noir* woman, with something operatic thrown in — this toughest and most dignified of babes could even throw a scare into Barbara Stanwyck's Phyllis Dietrichson in DOUBLE INDEMNITY. The whole film resonates with her presence. In her steely way, she's believably maternal as well, ever ready to take care of Roy's bills and wanting him to get off the grift (although her slammingly derisive approach doesn't help her case much). Huston and Bening must have two of the best figures on the screen and face each other down entertainingly — Huston's body language in a parking lot scene is particularly expressive. Bening is a fabulous sexpot, her piquant face naughtily alive with the pleasure she takes in her scams. She also possesses the greatest jello-on-springs wiggle since Marilyn Monroe. Draped on a bed for some afternoon trade, she looks painted on velvet and incarnates every drugstore dime novel fantasy cover ever seen. It's to Cusack's great credit that he isn't completely overshadowed by these two formidable femmes. He is a very good actor who is able to make a style out of recessiveness. He does the minimal, but it's always dead on target emotionally — it's in his eyes. He gets a lot of humorous mileage out of his asides, delivered with a mixture of rue and boy-next-door-gone-wrong sarcasm. The final, horrifying confrontation with Lily works in large part to his ingenious attitudinizing and opaque, flickering nervous expression.

The sadly underrated and too infrequently seen Pat Hingle is a standout in the supporting cast as the monstrously menacing, ridiculously named Bobo. He has just one scene, but every second of it is packed with threatening terror. As a hotel clerk, gabby character actor Henry Jones is an affectionate reminder of 1950s Hollywood.

Oliver Stapleton's photography turns the City of Angels into both a dream and a nightmare. Orange is the dominant hue, the orange of cruddy, toxic-looking sunsets, low-slung lamps in motel rooms, Myra's dress, and the fruit Lily fears. Seductive afternoons in seedy apartment complexes, solitary meals in diners, Roy's ultra-beat room, the whispery halls of the hotel in which he and Myra retreat, Lily's roadside pitstop, are all filmed in lushly moody, yet unforced, artistry. It's nice to see the old split screen used effectively in the opening establishing shots of the characters. Elmer Bernstein's hyperactive, propulsive music adds another layer of mood. Richard Hornung has garbed the women in a memorable succession of skin-tight, short-skirted ensembles, confident heels, and the best come-hither array of earrings in screen history. "Beauty's where you find it," goes the popular song, and Frears has managed to come up with the grungiest, most glamorous film of the year. (*Nudity, violence, profanity, adult situations, sexual situations.*)

d, Stephen Frears; p, Martin Scorsese, Robert Harris, and James Painten; w, Donald E. Westlake (based on the novel by Jim Thompson); ph, Oliver Stapleton; ed, Mick Audsley; m, Elmer Bernstein; prod d, Leslie McDonald; art d, Leslie McDonald

Crime   (PR:O   MPAA:R)

GRIM PRAIRIE TALES

94m East-West/Coe Hahn c

James Earl Jones (*Morrison*), Brad Dourif (*Farley*), Will Hare (*Lee*), Marc McClure (*Tom*), Michelle Joyner (*Jenny*), William Atherton (*Arthur*), Lisa Eichhorn (*Maureen*), Wendy Cooke (*Eva*), Scott Paulin (*Martin*), and Bruce Fischer (*Colochez*)

Farley (Brad Dourif), a mild-mannered city fella, is heading east across the frontier to visit his wife. One cold and lonely night, his campsite is invaded by Morrison (James Earl Jones), a wild mountain man with a corpse slung over his pack horse. Initially antagonistic, the two men slowly develop a rapport as they tell each other stories to pass the time. Morrison relates the tale of a man (Will Hare) who desecrates an Indian burial ground, only to find himself interred alive

by a tribe of phantoms. When Farley seems entertained by the story, Morrison tells another, this one concerning a traveler (Marc McClure) who encounters a pregnant woman (Michelle Joyner) wandering in the wilderness. He takes her under his wing, but during the night discovers she is not what she seems. No longer pregnant, she entices him to make love to her, then absorbs him into her own body. Farley, an aspiring writer, is horrified by this gratuitously shocking ending. Taking his turn, he tells a story with a moral. A southern family moves west to start a new life, but one family member, Arthur (William Atherton), is unable to leave behind the prejudice and violence that have played so large a role in his upbringing. Morrison retorts with the saga of a fastidious gunslinger (Scott Paulin) who's driven mad when he kills a man with particular brutality. The sun comes up and the two men part company, each enriched by the experience.

Written and directed by first-time filmmaker Wayne Coe, this compendium horror movie is grounded in the culture and imagery of the Old West. Its framing story is neatly reflexive, offering two men who, like the film's audience, sit in the dark delighting in horror stories. As a whole, however, GRIM PRAIRIE TALES doesn't work. It may be that there is something about the sun-baked prairie that doesn't lend itself to tales of horror, but whatever the reason, these stories just aren't very interesting. It doesn't help matters that Jones overacts outrageously as Morrison. Playing opposite Jones' relentless display of spitting, drooling, scratching, and quivering, the always twitchy Dourif is a model of composure.

It's tough to make a horror movie that breaks new ground; the genre's popularity insures that all kinds of filmmakers — from rank beginners to seasoned veterans — have tried their hand. With GRIM PRAIRIE TALES, Coe tries to put an unusual spin on genre conventions; regrettably, he isn't up to the challenge. (*Violence, sexual situations.*)

d, Wayne Coe; p, Richard Hahn; w, Wayne Coe; ph, Janusz Minski; ed, Earl Ghaffari; m, Steve Dancz; prod d, Anthony Zierhut; art d, Angela Levy; set d, Shirley Starks; cos, American Costume, Ron Tolsky, and Sylvia Vasquez

Horror/Western   (PR:C   MPAA:R)

GUARDIAN, THE

98m Joe Wizan/Universal c

Jenny Seagrove (*Camilla*), Dwier Brown (*Phil*), Carey Lowell (*Kate*), Brad Hall (*Ned Runcie*), Miguel Ferrer (*Ralph Hess*), Natalia Nogulich (*Molly Sheridan*), Pamela Brull (*Gail Krasno*), Gary Swanson (*Allan Sheridan*), Jack David Walker, Willy Parsons, Frank Noon (*Punks*), Theresa Randle (*Arlene Russell*), Xander Berkeley (*Detective*), Ray Reinhardt (*Dr. Klein*), Jacob Gelman (*Scotty*), Iris Bath (*Mrs. Horniman*), Rita Gomez (*Rosaria*), Dr. Berry Herman (*Doctor at Birth*), Bonnie Snyder (*Older Woman*), Chris Nemeth, Craig Nemeth, Aaron Fischman, and Josh Fischman (*Baby Jake*)

Taking the most unlikely bits and pieces of fairy tales, myths, and legends — from Druidic tree worship to Hansel and Gretel — director William Friedkin has fashioned a well-tooled little scream machine of a movie that leaves behind logic and coherence to go straight for the jugular. THE GUARDIAN doesn't work on the grandiloquent scale of Friedkin's past horror classic, THE EXORCIST. It's smaller and much closer to home, involving not a pitched battle between good and evil but a battle between parents and a nanny who feeds newborns to a gnarled old tree in the forest. THE GUARDIAN is a completely irrational movie that works because fear is an irrational emotion — a survival reaction to an illogical world in which the best we can hope to do is avoid the things that can harm us. Of course, it's a battle we ultimately lose. But Friedkin proves again that his movies don't have to make sense to make audiences shudder.

THE GUARDIAN takes place in one of the most idyllic fairy-tale settings imaginable, Canyon Country, a rustic wilderness only minutes from Los Angeles, where the wealthy and successful pay millions to live in splendid isolation. Moving there from Chicago are Phil (Dwier Brown) and Kate (Carey Lowell). An advertising artist, Phil has given up his creative independence to make big money with a large LA firm. In one of the film's many funny low-key scenes, Phil is shown at his job interview boldly asserting his contempt for the idea of losing his independence in the corporate advertising world. Without missing a beat, he accepts immediately once he is offered the job. At first, it looks as though Phil has made the right move. He's working on important assignments. The new house is beautiful. The neighbors are nice. The architect who designed their house, Ned Runcie (Brad Hall), lives just up the street. And Kate is just about to give birth to a beautiful baby boy. The young couple begins to interview prospective nannies. Most seem personable, capable, and qualified. However, the interviewing stops with Camilla (Jenny Seagrove), not for any practical reason, but because Camilla agrees with Kate that she should continue breast-feeding her infant even though her doctor has told her that her breast milk is too thin and watery to nourish him. Camilla is hired, and life at home begins looking even more copacetic, especially from Phil's point of view when he happens upon Camilla taking a late-night bath with the baby. Camilla makes it quite clear she isn't bothered in the least by Phil looking at her in the nude. While Phil mulls over this fact (and has the strangest dreams about it), distraught mother Molly Sheridan (Natalia Nogulich) is trying desperately to contact Phil and Kate. It seems a nanny very much like Camilla disappeared from the Sheridan home one night, taking Molly's baby with her. Neither the nanny nor the baby were ever seen again. Attempts to track down the nanny have proved futile. It's as if she had never existed. Ned, meanwhile, has developed an attraction to Camilla, which leads him to make the grievous mistake of following her into the woods on her night off. He's rewarded by being torn to pieces by a pack of angry coyotes (which is nevertheless a far kinder fate than that which befalls the trio of would-be rapists who cross paths with Camilla earlier in the film). But Ned manages to leave a message on Phil's answering machine, warning him about Camilla's strange side. And it's a side that only gets stranger as THE GUARDIAN lurches towards its gory climax. Phil orders Camilla out of the house. But Camilla, with her tree and pack of coyotes, is not about to go without a fight.

Nobody goes to a Friedkin film expecting an uplifting experience. In a filmography ranging from THE EXORCIST to THE FRENCH CONNECTION; CRUISING; and TO LIVE AND DIE IN L.A.; Friedkin has emerged as a poet of social decay and chaos whose protagonists tend to be losing their grip on reality. In THE GUARDIAN, where nice, boring yuppies innocently coexist with baby-eating trees and crazed, bloodthirsty governesses, Phil's own enraged exorcism is performed with a chain saw after all civilized remedies have failed.

It's not a nice movie; like THE EXORCIST, it is ugly, cynical, and mean-spirited. Yet it's also rendered with the same gripping, unholy conviction that has been Friedkin's "saving grace" throughout his career. THE GUARDIAN is a movie that may make you laugh, but, like a particularly nasty nightmare, it's not one you'll easily forget. And that, after all, is what a real horror film is supposed to be about. *(Violence, adult situations, nudity.)*

d, William Friedkin; p, Joe Wizan; w, Stephen Volk, Dan Greenburg, and William Friedkin (based on the book *The Nanny*, by Dan Greenburg); ph, John A. Alonzo; ed, Seth Flaum; m, Jack Hues; prod d, Gregg Fonseca; art d, Bruce Miller; set d, Sarah Burdick; spec, Phil Cory and Matthew Mungle; stunts, Buddy Joe Hooker; cos, Renee Alaina Sacks; makup, Teresa M. Austin

Horror   **(PR:O   MPAA:R)**

GUMSHOE KID, THE

98m Pacific—Skouras/Argus—Academy c

(AKA: DETECTIVE KID, THE)

Jay Underwood *(Jeff Sherman)*, Tracy Scoggins *(Rita Benson)*, Vince Edwards *(Ben Sherman)*, Arlene Golonka *(Gracie Sherman)*, Pamela Springsteen *(Mona)*, Miguel Sandoval *(Carl Ortega)*, Amy Lynne *(Emily Sherman)*, Gino Conforti *(Meester)*, Xander Berkeley *(Monty Griswold)*, Biff Yeager *(Billings)*, David Dunard *(Fitzgerald)*, Michael Alaimo *(Sergio)*, Charles Lucia *(Glenn Devlin)*, Tim Haideman, Steve Whitaker, Don Pugsley, Leslie Rivers, and Janet Rotblatt

At intervals, the young hero of this film dons a hat and turns to the camera to either grimace inanely or comment on the action in the style of a hard-bitten detective. Only once does he say anything useful. During a soliloquy on stakeouts he declares, "You keep asking yourself: 'Am I wasting my time?'" It is an experience that is all too familiar to anyone who sits through this dumb farce. Jay Underwood plays teenager Jeff Sherman, who idolizes Humphrey Bogart and other 1940s movie private eyes. What a lucky break, then, that his financially troubled family is part owner of a detective agency. To earn some vital cash, Jeff angles a job with the agency, which is run by his Uncle Ben (Vince Edwards). At first, Ben assigns his nephew only the most menial of chores, but when a racketeer needs someone to spy on his cheating fiancee, Rita Benson (Tracy Scoggins), Jeff is put on the case. Hiding in a hotel closet, Jeff photographs a tryst between the dishy Rita and her lover, Glenn Devlin (Lucia). Suddenly goons burst in, pump Devlin full of tranquilizer bullets, and carry him off. When Jeff accidentally falls out of the closet, Rita latches on to him and flees from the distracted thugs. Rita and Jeff go to the police, but when Rita notices the cops conferring with the kidnapers, she and Jeff sneak off. With the police and hoods after the pair, the movie becomes a tedious series of scams and strategies employed by the fugitives to elude their pursuers. After modeling an array of wacky disguises and eventually sharing some passionate sex, Rita and Jeff are captured by the kidnapers, who turn out to be CIA agents. It seems Devlin was an important Russian spy, and Rita was being used to set him up. "Why didn't you just tell us?" Rita demands. Good question.

Nothing in THE GUMSHOE KID is particularly funny, not even the self-conscious reference to Scoggins' role on TV's "Dynasty." Nonchalant about Jeff's spying, virtually unshaken by the kidnaping, never even bothering to speculate about her pursuers' motives, Scoggins walks through her vampish role with bland detachment. The only time Scoggins' Rita shows any enthusiasm is when she is trying on new clothes. Underwood's portrayal of the teenage sleuth is equally lacking in viewer appeal. Once the chases start, Underwood drops most of the

Bogart shtick (which has provided only the most feeble amusement anyway) and behaves like any dumb movie teen, failing to become the charming lead the film so desperately needs. The only members who make an impression are Pamela Springsteen, as a sassy secretary, and Miguel Sandoval, whose exasperated demeanor wins immediate audience acceptance. Adding to the general banality of the film is a cartoonish score that toot-toots relentlessly, even during the leads' slow-motion love scene in a shower. Composer Peter Matz and lyricist Pamela Phillips Oland do contribute the pleasant "Why Can't I?" (performed by Deborah Davis), but that, too, wears thin by its third reprise. *(Profanity, nudity, sexual situations, substance abuse.)*

d, Joseph Manduke; p, Joseph Manduke; w, Victor Bardack; ph, Harvey Genkins; ed, Richard Haines; m, Peter Matz; prod d, Batia Grafka; set d, Don Diers; stunts, Spiro Razatos; cos, Ron Talsky; makup, Sher Flowers

Comedy   **(PR:O   MPAA:R)**

H

HAMLET

(Brit./Fr./Sp.) 135m Marquis/WB c

Mel Gibson *(Hamlet)*, Glenn Close *(Gertrude)*, Alan Bates *(King Claudius)*, Paul Scofield *(THe Ghost)*, Ian Holm *(Polonius)*, Helena Bonham Carter *(Ophelia)*, Stephan Dillan *(Horatio)*, Nathaniel Parker *(Laertes)*, Sean Murray *(Guildenstern)*, Michael Maloney *(Rosencrantz)*, Trevor Peacock *(Gravedigger)*, John McEnery *(Osric)*, Richard Warwick *(Bernardo)*, Christien Anholt *(Marcellus)*, Dave Duffy *(Francisco)*, Vernon Dobtcheff *(Reynaldo)*, Pete Postlewaite *(Player King)*, Christopher Fairbank *(Player Queen)*, Sarah Phillips, Ned Mendez, Roy York, Marjorie Bell, Justin Case, Roger Low, Pamela Sinclair, Baby Simon Sinclair, and Roy Evans *(Players)*

Director Franco Zeffirelli's third adaptation of the works of William Shakespeare (following ROMEO AND JULIET in 1968 and the opera OTELLO in 1986) more than anything else shows that Mel Gibson, macho action hero of the "Mad Max" and "Lethal Weapon" films, can act. With his Prince Valiant haircut, he even looks the part, and he really *can* speak the Queen's English. Two months of intensive work with a voice coach enabled him to eliminate his Australian accent, and his years of dramatic training in classical theater are much in evidence. But don't expect overwhelming tragedy here. Zeffirelli's production is neither high art nor lowbrow pandering, but something in between. This is "Hamlet for the 90s," according to the director, and it is an especially entertaining, accessible version. With much of the text pruned, the pace quickened, and the action streamlined, the film offers what amounts to an introduction to Shakespeare's classic, without losing any of the play's psychological complexities. Like *nouvelle cuisine* there's not as much on the plate, but what's there looks good.

With a melodramatic scenario fit for a soap opera, the film is filled with soupcons of sex (adultery and hints of incest), cunning deception, and wanton murder. But the artistry of Shakespeare's words and philosophy elevate the work far beyond those basic underpinnings. Returning to his native Denmark after going to school in Germany, young Prince Hamlet (Gibson) finds his uncle, Claudius (Alan Bates), now sits on the throne of the family castle, Elsinore. Claudius has married Hamlet's mother, Queen Gertrude (Glenn Close), a scant few weeks after the death of Hamlet's beloved father, the king. Hamlet is visited by the ghost of his father (Paul Scofield), who tells him he was poisoned by Claudius, and commands his son to avenge his murder. The troubled prince is plagued with doubts about the truth of what the ghost has spoken and determines to find out what really happened. He feigns madness to disguise his intentions and when a troupe of players visits Elsinore, he invites them to reenact a scene that closely duplicates his father's murder. His plan is to observe the reactions of Claudius in the hope it will help him determine if his uncle is guilty. The ploy works only too well. Claudius is so unnerved that he leaves before the performance ends, and plots to have Hamlet killed. This, in turn, precipitates unexpected havoc. Polonius (Ian Holm), a garrulous old courtier, is killed in error by Hamlet, who mistakes him for Claudius, while Ophelia (Helena Bonham-Carter), Polonius' daughter and Hamlet's one-time lover, goes mad and drowns herself. During the course of a supposedly friendly duel, the queen accidentally drinks from a goblet laced with poison intended for her son, and Hamlet and Claudius are done in by a poisoned-tipped sword.

Unlike the cerebrally tormented, noble protagonist presented in most versions of "Hamlet," including Laurence Olivier's 1948 Oscar winner for Best Picture, Zeffirelli's film gives us a more simple central character. Gibson's Hamlet doesn't soar; his speeches are uttered in a straightforward manner defined by action rather than poetry, yet Gibson is in total control of the role. If his Hamlet is less introspective, he is also more physical and boyish. Nevertheless, the performance is moving as Gibson makes his fidgety Hamlet a lost sheep in the midst of a pack of wolves. Zeffirelli's seemingly unorthodox choice of superstar Gibson for the role turned out to be a casting coup as Gibson's charm and likability are decided assets to the film — he immediately has the audience rooting for him. Zeffirelli doesn't merely settle for altering the main character however; he also lessens the importance of the role to some degree, allowing the work to become much more of an ensemble piece than it normally is. Around Gibson, the director has gathered a stellar international cast, packed with Oscar winners and nominees, who, for better or worse, have added a new perspective to the play. The ghost of Hamlet's father appears on stage rather than as simply a voiceover, and he is powerfully portrayed by Paul Scofield, who won a Best Actor Oscar in 1966 for A MAN FOR ALL SEASONS. While it might seem a bit awkward for 43-year-old Close to play the mother of 35-year-old Gibson, Close pulls it off beautifully. Hers is a wonderful performance as she offers a more radiant, girlish, and sexy Gertrude. Finally, Bates brings strength and subtle venality to the villainous Claudius. Less successful, however, are Holm and Bonham-Carter. Holm makes Polonius a tiresome bore, while Bonham-Carter's

performance has no shadings — she seems mad from the start and simply stays that way.

Zeffirelli's massive cuts, which enabled him to get what is normally a four-hour production down to just over two hours, make for a more linear, clearly understood course of events. Of course, this wholesale pruning results in the loss of many of the play's most famous speeches, but overall the director's instincts seemed to have been correct. The film earned Oscar nominations for its art direction and its costume design.

d, Franco Zeffirelli; p, Lovell Dyson; w, Franco Zeffirelli and Christopher DeVore (based on the play by William Shakespeare); ph, David Watkin; ed, Richard Marden; m, Ennio Morricone; prod d, Dante Ferretti; art d, Michael Lamont; set d, Francesca LoSchiavo

Drama   (PR:A   MPAA:PG)

HANDMAID'S TALE, THE

109m Danny Wilson — Bioskop — Cinetudes — Odyssey/Cinecom c

Natasha Richardson *(Kate)*, Robert Duvall *(Commander)*, Faye Dunaway *(Serena Joy)*, Aidan Quinn *(Nick)*, Elizabeth McGovern *(Moira)*, Victoria Tennant *(Aunt Lydia)*, Blanche Baker *(Ofglen)*, Traci Lind *(Ofwarren/Janine)*, David Dukes *(Doctor)*, Zoey Wilson *(Aunt Helena)*, Kathryn Doby *(Aunt Elizabeth)*, and Lucile McIntyre *(Rita)*

Director Volker Schlondorff and screenwriter Harold Pinter have adapted Margaret Atwood's much-admired feminist novel about the status of women in the not-so-distant future with little subtlety. Heavy-handed and literal-minded, THE HANDMAID'S TALE spins serious themes all over the screen without managing to create engrossing drama from them. As the film opens, Kate (Natasha Richardson), with her husband and child, is trying to escape a totalitarian state by crossing its heavily guarded border. The trio are spotted by the police, the husband is shot, the child is left to wander, and Kate is sent to a government facility. In the film's polluted, war-devastated future, few women are capable of bearing children — thus, Kate's fertility is both a reprieve from death and a sentence to sexual slavery. At the state indoctrination center, women are brainwashed with almost religious fervor into accepting their new lot in life as docile "handmaids." Under these grim circumstances, Kate is befriended by Moira (Elizabeth McGovern), a self-deprecating lesbian who constantly plans her escape, and who finally pulls it off by feigning a fainting spell. After an interview with Serena Joy (Faye Dunaway), the ultrareligious wife of a high-ranking government official known as the Commander (Robert Duvall), Kate becomes a sexually indentured slave in the couple's home. Each month, while Serena Joy holds her down, Kate is forced to endure loveless intercourse with the Commander for the purpose of procreation. If she conceives, the child will be handed over to her masters. Learning of the existence of an underground resistance movement from a fellow handmaid (Blanche Baker), Kate begins to harbor hope of flight, and when she is temporarily reassigned to the center, she risks her life to help the recaptured Moira decoy and subdue the facility's watchdog matron (Victoria Tennant), allowing Moira to flee again. Already playing psychological games with her master, who orders her to a secret rendezvous (a violation of the law), Kate is stunned when Serena Joy suggests that she have sex with Nick (Aidan Quinn), the household's chauffeur, because Serena Joy fears the Commander is sterile. A surrogate child is this society's No. 1 status symbol, and Serena Joy wants one badly. To encourage Kate's cooperation, Serena Joy promises to bring the handmaid news of her missing daughter, who may have been adopted by a prominent family. Back at the center, masters and servants attend a public execution where a handmaid who had illicit sex is hanged and an alleged rapist — later revealed to have been a political prisoner — is torn apart by the crowd. The Commander, infatuated with his pretty slave, spirits Kate away to a top-secret nightclub/brothel where the elite power structure can hypocritically indulge in pleasures prohibited elsewhere, and where Kate is briefly reunited with Moira, who admits she prefers prostitution to the life of a handmaid. Increasingly desperate, Kate doesn't want to give up the child she has conceived with Nick, whom she has come to love, and when the Commander summons her to his quarters with the intention of dismissing her (Serena Joy having found out about the love affair), Kate stabs him to death. Arrested by state police, she mistakenly believes she's been betrayed by her lover; then, relieved to learn that the men who've apprehended her are actually revolutionaries, Kate begins a new life in the rebel-held mountains, awaiting reunion with Nick and better times.

One cannot disparage the loving care with which Atwood's fable has been brought to the screen, but despite the film's splendid production values and air of importance, *The Handmaid's Tale* has been handled rather clumsily. Faithfulness to a literary source is moot when the material is re-created with so little cinematic inventiveness and so little dramatic vitality that points are blunted and the impact is diminished. An uneven filmmaker, Schlondorff brought "Death of a Salesman" (in Dustin Hoffman's TV version) and *The Tin Drum* to life on the screen, but failed in the Proust adaptation SWANN'S WAY and now with THE HANDMAID'S TALE. Set pieces lifted from the novel fall with a thud here, and the film's tone seems off-kilter from its outset. Instead of presenting a harsh, forbidding, and effectively chilling environment, Schlondorff gives us a sometimes laughably heavy-handed portrait of oppressive forces. Also damaging is the performance of Tennant, whose thin, whiny delivery botches the key role of the soulless mother hen who shepherds the handmaids through their training. The combination of Tennant's toothless acting, some amateurish performances among the ensemble of handmaids, and Schlondorff's ham-fisted direction fashion a future feminist nightmare that seems as frightening as forced cheerleading tryouts for high-school rebels.

Having failed to terrify or astonish us with Atwood's bleak premise, the film slips further and further out of the director's control. We're never moved, merely enervated by the accumulation of future-shock horrors. With the exception of Duvall, who humanizes the powerful Commander, and McGovern, who gives the performance of her career as the rebellious lesbian, no one in the cast commands our attention as they should. Still exhibiting traces of her MOMMIE DEAREST impersonation, Dunaway seems mannered and almost campy, while Richardson gives a phlegmatic performance. Schlondorff's sensibility can work brilliantly when a project is attuned to his forceful, dogged touch, but Atwood's material needed to be approached more elliptically and with more restraint. Also implicated in the film's failure is playwright Pinter (whose screenplays include ACCIDENT and THE SERVANT). Pinter's adaptation is uninspired, and this half-heartedness, combined with Schlondorff's heavy-handedness, serves to crush Atwood's feminist concerns through overkill and to turn a provocative novel into a screen polemic that invites no discussion. This isn't filmmaking; it's haranguing by celluloid. *(Violence, sexual situations, profanity.)*

d, Volker Schlondorff; p, Danny Wilson; w, Harold Pinter (based on the novel by Margaret Atwood); ph, Igor Luther; ed, David Ray; m, Ryuichi Sakamoto; prod d, Tom Walsh; art d, Gregory Melton; set d, Jan Pascale; cos, Colleen Atwood

Drama (PR:O MPAA:R)

HAPPILY EVER AFTER

74m Lou Scheimer/Kel-Air c

VOICES OF: Irene Cara *(Snow White)*, Edward Asner *(Scowl)*, Carol Channing *(Muddy)*, Dom DeLuise *(Looking Glass)*, Phyllis Diller *(Mother Nature)*, Zsa Zsa Gabor *(Blossom)*, Linda Gary *(Critterina/Marina)*, Jonathan Harris *(Sunflower)*, Michael Horton *(Prince)*, Sally Kellerman *(Sunburn)*, Malcolm McDowell *(Lord Maliss)*, Tracey Ullman *(Moonbeam/Thunderella)*, and Frank Welker *(Batso)*

Just what happens to Snow White and Prince Charming once the official story ends, when we are told they lived "happily ever after"? In this animated feature from Filmation, a kind of sequel to Disney's SNOW WHITE AND THE SEVEN DWARFS, the loving pair head back into the woods to invite the dwarfs to their wedding. Problems begin when the Wicked Witch's brother, Lord Maliss (voiced by Malcolm McDowell), finds out his sister has been killed by the Prince and vows revenge. He finds the Prince (Michael Horton) and Snow White (Irene Cara) on their way to the dwarfs' cottage and captures the Prince, but allows Snow White to escape. Coming to the cottage, she finds not the dwarfs but the dwarfelles — seven tiny ladies, each with special powers that have been bestowed by Mother Nature (Phyllis Diller). Snow White and her female helpers venture into the realm of doom to save the Prince and prove to Mother Nature that the dwarfelles are deserving of their powers; though Lord Maliss tricks Snow White and her cohorts, sending his evil creatures to menace them, in the end, of course, they prove their mettle and everyone gets to live happily ever after again.

HAPPILY EVER AFTER is a respectable animated feature, distinguished mainly by the voice acting of Sally Kellerman, Carol Channing, Tracey Ullman, and Zsa Zsa Gabor as dwarfelles; Cara as Snow White; Diller as Mother Nature; Ed Asner as a mean owl; and Dom DeLuise as the magic mirror and narrator. The actors lend some creativity and humor to the otherwise standard proceedings, adding interest in the way each manages to bring his or her own personality to an animated character. Channing and Ullman (as Muddy and as the slightly incompetent Thunderella, respectively) stand out, and Gabor (as Blossom) has a great scene with DeLuise's mirror, but the real star is Mother Nature Diller, though she is in the film for only two scenes. To think that this lady is in charge of the elements is not only funny, but a bit frightening.

The film's musical numbers are superfluous, and its darker moments may scare young children. Overall, however, the kids will overlook its flaws and find it enjoyable viewing, while the voice acting will make HAPPILY EVER AFTER tolerable for adults. *(Violence.)*

d, John Howley; p, Lou Scheimer; w, Robby London and Martha Moran; ph, Fred Ziegler; ed, Jeffrey C. Patch and Joe Gall; m, Frank W. Becker; art d, John Grusd; spec, Bruce Heller

Animated/Children's (PR:A MPAA:G)

HAPPY TOGETHER

98m Apollo c

Patrick Dempsey *(Chris Wooden)*, Helen Slater *(Alex Paige)*, Dan Schneider *(Stan)*, Marius Weyers *(Drama Professor)*, Barbara Babcock, and Kevin Hardesty *(Slash)*

Not much happens in this sweet-tempered, small-scale romantic comedy — college boy meets, loses, and wins back college girl — yet the film is surprisingly touching and amusing, almost in spite of itself. As the film opens, Chris (Patrick Dempsey) leaves his Chicago home for an unnamed Los Angeles university (the exteriors resemble USC), where he is to study playwrighting. Arriving on campus, he finds that roommate Alex has moved in six days previously, decorating their room in pastel plastic backyard kitsch, complete with an inflatable wading pool. The reason for the wading pool soon becomes obvious when Alex turns out to be Alexandra (Helen Slater), who uses the pool in lieu of the showers in the otherwise all-male dormitory. An over-the-top cross between Auntie Mame and Holly Golightly, Alex is an aspiring actress who turns everything in her life into high drama, causing her to clash immediately with Chris, whose only interest is in quietly burying himself in his books and writing. Chris immediately applies for a room change, but during the three weeks required to make the change, he is won over by Alex's high spirits, not to mention her boudoir wardrobe, which has been heavily influenced by Frederick's of Hollywood. When his replacement roommate arrives, Chris puts on a dress, which sends the new guy packing. Yet the romantic road is anything but smooth for Chris and Alex. Chris learns firsthand the problems that come with being in love with a sexy, provocative woman like Alex. When she wears a fetching strapless gown out to dinner with Chris, every man in the restaurant buys her drinks. Later, Alex earns $3,000 at a charity kissing booth, along with an unsavory reputation, which further alienates Chris. Still, Chris comes to Alex's rescue when budding rock star Slash (Kevin Hardesty, a dead ringer for Sal Mineo), to whom Alex frivolously became engaged before he took off for an extended working trip to Europe, returns to claim her hand. The rocker relinquishes Alex's hand, but not before breaking Chris' arm. Alex and Chris' relationship reaches its climactic crisis when Chris' convalescence interrupts his studies, forcing him to cheat on a final exam. When the cheating is discovered, Chris is suspended. Will Alex drop out to support him while he struggles to start his writing career in New York City? Do bears sleep in the woods?

HAPPY TOGETHER continually teeters toward cliches that threaten to (but never quite) deflate the story, most of them, like the standard-issue hard-drinking, macho playwrighting instructor (THE GODS MUST BE CRAZY's Marius Weyers) and the no-nonsense acting teacher (Barbara Babcock), drawn from the drama school setting. The best that can be said about these cliched characters is that they serve primarily to keep the plot going. Weyers' writing-instructor character shocks Chris out of his bookishness by giving him D minuses until the young would-be playwright goes out and lives life. Meanwhile, Babcock's stern taskmaster conveniently highlights Alex's character flaw — "acting" her feelings rather than "feeling" them. The art-as-therapy theme is as bogus here as it has ever been, but the acting talents of Weyers and Babcock at least make their characters far less irritating than they might have been.

HAPPY TOGETHER succeeds generally because of the skill and conviction of its cast, especially that of Dempsey and Slater. Slater takes an initially grating, annoying character and, without drawing undue attention to her transformation, gradually gives Alex a depth and poignancy that seduce the audience as much as Chris. Faced with the flamboyance of Slater's Alex, Dempsey has little to do much of the time but be her straight man. Nevertheless, he manages to find a basic reality in his character that gives Chris, no less than Alex, an unexpected depth.

Credit also Craig J. Nevius' script for avoiding the obvious most of the time. A less inspired writer would have gotten far more snickering mileage out of Alex's residency in an all-male dorm. Here it merely illustrates Alex's individualism. Also credit Mel Damski's brisk, breezy direction, which makes its points without pounding them too hard. The funny supporting work from Hardesty and Dan Schneider also helps make HAPPY TOGETHER a frothy confection that may not change the history of cinema as we know it, but that does provide a couple of easygoing hours of old-fashioned, screwball entertainment. *(Adult situations.)*

d, Mel Damski; p, Jere Henshaw; w, Craig J. Nevius; ph, Joe Pennella; ed, O. Nicholas Brown; m, Robert Folk; prod d, Marcia Hinds; chor, Jeffrey Calhoun

Comedy/Romance (PR:C MPAA:PG-13)

HARD TO KILL

95m Adelson-Todman-Simon/WB c

Steven Seagal *(Mason Storm)*, Kelley Le Brock *(Andy Stewart)*, William Sadler *(Vernon Trent)*, Frederick Coffin *(O'Malley)*, Bonnie Burroughs *(Mrs. Storm)*, Zachary Rosencrantz *(Sonny Storm)*, and Branscombe Richmond *(Quintero)*

Said to be Warner Brothers' choice to fill the studio's in-house he-man gap—which has been steadily widening as Clint Eastwood edges toward retirement age—Steven Seagal, in 1988's ABOVE THE LAW and now in HARD TO KILL, has played characters that make Eastwood's Dirty Harry look like a poetry-loving peacenik. Moreover, while Harry Callahan battles criminals as an upstanding (if overzealous) employee of the San Francisco police department, Seagal's enemies tend to be authority figures gone bad. In ABOVE THE LAW, he was up against CIA covert action. In HARD TO KILL, the villains are badge-carrying members of the Los Angeles Police Department (the LAPD's image has taken a beating in 1990, between HARD TO KILL and INTERNAL AFFAIRS), led by a senator who gained office by having his opponent murdered by the mob.

The politician, Vernon Trent (Bill Sadler), is running a high-profile re-election campaign, using a catchphrase in his television commercials—"You can take that to the bank"—that becomes crucial to the film's primitive plot. "I'm gonna take you to the bank," Seagal mumbles back to one of Trent's TV ads, "I'm gonna take you to the blood bank." And who can blame him? HARD TO KILL begins on Oscar night, 1983. (Steven McKay's script, which is not without its moments of wit, includes a character cheering Ben Kingsley's Best Actor award for GANDHI.) LA cop Mason Storm (Seagal) is having a busy evening himself. On undercover surveillance, he videotapes the meeting during which the murder contract is made. When his cover is blown, he gets away temporarily, but he is overheard calling in his report by corrupt cops working for Trent. On his way home, Storm stops at a liquor store to pick up some champagne to celebrate his undercover coup with his wife (Bonnie Burroughs) and son. Right on cue, five gun-wielding thugs come into the store and blow away the cashier. Storm goes into action, quickly crippling three of the thugs (HARD TO KILL boasts a fitting visual motif in its repeated closeups of Storm breaking arms, legs and necks with his bare hands). Says Thug 4 to Thug 5, "He's just a punk! Take him!" Famous last words, of course; with his hair barely mussed, Storm heads home, the five thugs safely incarcerated at the city morgue. Tucking in his son, he opens the champagne and begins a session of passionate lovemaking with his wife—stamina is evidently this man's middle name—but before you can say "coitus interruptus," the dirty cops who overheard Storm's report are at the bedroom door, guns blazing. Storm's wife is killed. His son is missing, presumed dead. Storm himself, declared dead at the hospital, revives only to remain in a coma. A clean cop, O'Malley (Frederick Coffin), enlists the help of a doctor to keep Storm's survival secret until he can recuperate and give information on his assailants. Cut ahead seven years, to 1990: O'Malley has been forced off the force, with Trent's dirty crew now running the show. Storm, in a coma center under the wily alias of "John Doe," is cared for by goofy nurse Andrea (Kelly Le Brock, Seagal's offscreen spouse), who passes the time admiring Storm's manly attributes ("Puh-lease wake up," she moans while peering under his sheets) and giving him a goofy Fu-Manchu beard and mustache. Of course, since this *is* an action movie, Storm soon recovers and proceeds to aid his assailants in making their corpuscular contributions to the Red Cross.

Luckily, HARD TO KILL doesn't make too much of its by-the-numbers plot. Writer McKay also doesn't make the common action-movie mistake of making his bad guys incredibly stupid to make the hero look smarter. Instead, McKay keeps the goons on top of Storm every step of the way, using the "How's he gonna get out of this one?" principle to keep the action in high gear. Director Bruce Malmuth—formerly most famous for enraging the citizens of New York's Roosevelt Island by tying up their cable tramway to film his 1981 contribution to the Sylvester Stallone legend, NIGHTHAWKS—demonstrates a masterful facility for staging the mayhem and maintaining a rooting interest in his limb-twisting hero. He also has a talent for sly in-jokes, such as pinning the plot on Storm's ability to get the incriminating videotape to Los Angeles newscaster Jerry Dunphy, best known to those in the know as the real-life model for TV's air-headed "Mary Tyler Moore" anchorman Ted Baxter. As an actor, Seagal shows improvement in refining his low-key persona and gravelly, soft-spoken delivery, which owes more than a little to the man he is meant to replace in the Warners star firmament. In fact, Seagal may be no more than a film or two from filling Eastwood's shoes outright. As it is, HARD TO KILL has just enough going for it between the explosions and bone-crunching fight scenes to qualify as two hours of solid, high-decibel action entertainment. *(Graphic violence, profanity, adult situations.)*

d, Bruce Malmuth; p, Gary Adelson, Joel Simon, and Bill Todman Jr.; w, Steven McKay; ph, Matthew F. Leonetti; ed, John F. Link; m, David Michael Frank; prod d, Robb Wilson King; art d, Louis Mann; stunts, Buddy Joe Hooker; chor, Steven Seagal

Action/Thriller (PR:O MPAA:R)

HARDWARE

(Brit.) 91m Wicked/Miramax c

Dylan McDermott *(Mo)*, Stacey Travis *(Jill)*, John Lynch *(Shades)*, William Hootkins *(Lincoln)*, Iggy Pop *(Angry Bob)*, and Mark Northover *(Alvy)*

Although billed as a sci-fi film, HARDWARE is unquestionably a horror. In his calculated enthusiasm to shock, first-time writer-director Richard Stanley has filled the screen with gratuitous violence and psychosexual perversion but failed to present a plausible, reasonably coherent plot. Like other movies of its genre (TERMINATOR, MILLENNIUM, etc.), HARDWARE is set in an oppressive, post-apocalyptic future world dominated by debris and clunky hardware. Because the environment is contaminated, human life is confined to overcrowded, claustrophobic dwellings. Synthetic nutrients have replaced now-inedible real food, and an emerging mutant population is growing at such an accelerated rate that the government has enacted the diabolical "Population Control Bill," creating a killer cyborg force, the MARK 13, to destroy violators of birth control laws. Mo (STEEL MAGNOLIAS' Dylan McDermott) is a "zone tripper," a scavenger who dares to venture outdoors, collecting fragments of machinery that might have some value on the black market. An easygoing guy, he wanders the earth's parched surface in a protective suit and mask that shield him from the radiation polluting the landscape. In desert sands, Mo finds the head and hand of an android, which he gives to his girl friend, Jill (Stacey Travis), a sculptress who spends her days in a fortresslike apartment, welding metal scraps into works of art. Mo's present should come in handy; instead it proves to be the remnants of a MARK 13 cyborg, which latches onto the power supply in Jill's building, systematically reconstructs itself, and goes on a murderous rampage, fulfilling its programmed mission to "spare no flesh." Almost everyone in the small cast is killed, including Mo's black market fence, the dwarf Alvy (Mark Northover). Jill's neighbor, Lincoln (William Hootkins), a particularly disgusting, sexually repressed peeping tom, is also dispatched, and in one of the film's most disturbing scenes, a security guard is severed at the waist by a steel door. Finally, to the background strains of an angelic choir, Mo himself bites the dust in an equally discomfiting manner as MARK 13 injects him with a deadly poison. The robot, a Robocop II lookalike, is ultimately destroyed by Jill, who survives, no doubt, to continue her work with metallic sculpture. As the film closes, the shrill singing voice of former Sex Pistols frontman John Lydon repeatedly intones, "This is what you want...This is what you get."

HARDWARE's imaginative, splendidly effective sets are unquestionably the film's most laudable attribute, lending the movie a look that belies its small ($1.5 million) budget and brief (8-week) shooting schedule at the Camden Roadhouse and Spiller's Wharf in London. Considering the stilted screenplay they've been handed, the actors also give competent performances. But, regrettably, Stanley's emphasis on design and visual effects fatally undermines the content of this "cyberpunk" thriller. In the production notes for HARDWARE, the 25-year-old film school graduate credits, with great specificity, his cinematic influences (the gothic atmosphere of the Hammer horror movies of the 50s and 60s; the lighting of Italian horror master Dario Argento; German Expressionist classics; the little-known Danish Film ELEMENTS OF CRIME; a Tibetan film, THE HORSE THIEF; Luc Besson's costumes; and the climax of Sam Peckinpah's THE OSTERMAN WEEKEND). But in Stanley's eagerness to emulate his influences, he's made a vice of their virtues. By tossing everything he's ever admired into the same pot, Stanley has homogenized the distinguishing filmmaking methods he values most, doing both himself and his mentors a disservice. *(Gore effects, sexual situations.)*

d, Richard Stanley; p, Joanne Sellar and Paul Trybits; w, Richard Stanley; ph, Steven Chivers; ed, Derek Trigg; m, Simon Boswell; prod d, Joseph Bennett; spec, Image Animation

Science Fiction (PR:O MPAA:NR)

HAUNTING OF MORELLA, THE

87m Concorde c

David McCallum *(Gideon)*, Nicole Eggert *(Morella/Lenora)*, Christopher Halsted *(Guy Chapman)*, Lana Clarkson *(Miss. Deveroux)*, Maria Ford *(Diane)*, Jonathan Farwell *(Dr. Gault)*, Brewster Gould *(Miles Archer)*, Gail Harris *(Ilsa)*, Clement Von Franckenstein *(Judge)*, R.J. Robertson *(Rev. Ward)*, and Debbie Dutch *(Serving Girl)*

Loosely based upon the Edgar Allan Poe story of the same name, THE HAUNTING OF MORELLA becomes nothing more than an excuse for its female characters to take off their clothes and kill each other. As the story begins,

Morella (Nicole Eggert, playing both Morella and her daughter, Lenora) is crucified by the local priest and townspeople for practicing witchcraft. Prior to having her eyes put out, she pledges to return to haunt the body of her newborn. Her husband, Gideon (David McCallum), hides behind a tree, meekly watching the crucifixion with baby Lenora in his arms. Seventeen years later, we find him living as a recluse, and blind. Lenora has grown into a striking young woman, but is kept at home, where she is instructed by the mysterious Miss Deveroux (Lana Clarkson). Miss Deveroux and the serving girl (who are having an affair) place Gideon's diary on Lenora's bed, leading to an inevitable flashback in which it is revealed that shortly after Lenora's birth Morella discovered witchcraft and began to seek immortality, helped by an unknown accomplice. She had killed a serving girl and was about to kill Lenora when Gideon stopped her and the townspeople took their revenge. It's not hard to guess that Miss Deveroux was Morella's accomplice, especially since her every line is accompanied by a sidelong glance, quick exit, and burst of foreboding music. She spends most of the film using her witchcraft to bring Morella back to life; meanwhile, Guy Chapman (Christopher Halsted), a young lawyer from a nearby town, arrives to inform Gideon that Morella's family has set up a trust for Lenora, to be handed over on her 18th birthday. He is dismissed by Gideon, but the sinister governess sets up a meeting between the lawyer and her charge. The young couple fall in love, but Chapman's presence is nothing more than an excuse to stage an energetic love scene between him and Lenora, who has been possessed by Morella. A dramatic lightning bolt flashes throughout the film whenever witchcraft is being practiced, and it appears to be a tenet that witchcraft must be practiced without clothing.

Rated R, but apparently designed to pique the interest of high schoolers by displaying plenty of flesh and hinting at a number of lesbian relationships, THE HAUNTING OF MORELLA contains the important message that healthy people should stay away from corpses that seem to be coming back to life. It seems that women would particularly benefit from this moral, since, although one young man is killed in the effort to bring Morella back to life, women are the victims throughout THE HAUNTING OF MORELLA. Eggert shows some depth in her portrayal of the wholly innocent Lenora and the equally wicked Morella, and one wonders how she got herself into this softcore horror film to begin with. The brightest star in the film's ensemble, however, is the ubiquitous lightning bolt, which not only appears throughout the film but also dramatically concludes it. Sadly, this dreck was produced by Roger Corman, whose Poe adaptations of the 1960s (especially THE MASQUE OF THE RED DEATH and THE TOMB OF LIGEIA, both from 1964) are horror classics. But Poe is less than ill-served here, and while the thought of Poe's rolling over in his grave is an intriguing one and fittingly macabre, it's disturbing to think that a film as poor as this might elicit even that much interest. *(Violence, nudity, sexual situations.)*

d, Jim Wynorski; p, Roger Corman; w, R.J. Robertson (based on the story by Edgar Allan Poe); ph, Zoran Hochstatter; ed, Diane Fingado; m, Fredric Nesign Teetsel and Chuck Cirino; prod d, Gary Randall

Horror   (PR:O   MPAA:R)

HAVANA

145m Mirage/Universal c

Robert Redford *(Jack Weil)*, Lena Olin *(Bobby Duran)*, Raul Julia *(Arturo Duran)*, Alan Arkin *(Joe Volpi)*, Thomas Milian *(Menocal)*, Daniel Davis *(Marion Chigwell)*, Tony Plana *(Julio Ramos)*, Betsy Brantley *(Diane)*, Lise Cutter *(Patty)*, Richard Farnsworth *(Professor)*, Mark Rydell *(Meyer Lansky)*, Vasek Simek *(Willy)*, Fred Asparagus *(Baby Hernandez)*, Richard Portnow *(Mike MacClaney)*, Dion Andreson *(Roy Forbes)*, Carmine Caridi *(Capt. Potts)*, James Medina *(Corporal)*, Joe Lala *(Cuban Businessman)*, Salvadore Levy *(Menocal's Lieutenant)*, Bernie Pollack *(Hotel Man)*, Owen Roizman *(Santos)*, Victor Rivers, Alex Ganster *(Young Cubans)*, Rene Monclova, Miguel Angel Suarez *(Sims)*, Segundo Tarrau *(Ricardo)*, Felix German *(Tomas)*, Giovanna Bonnelly *(Monica)*, David Jose Rodriguez *(Bufano)*, Franklin Rodriguez *(Jose)*, Hugh Kelly *(Carlos)*, Terri Hendrickson, Karen Russell *(Dancers)*, David Gibson *(Sailor)*, Adriano Gonzalez *(Rebel Captain)*, Raul Rosado *(Roadblock Sergeant)*, Mildred I. Ventura *(Woman at Burning Building)*, Pepito Guerra *(Floridita Manager)*, Anthony Bayarri *(Modest Casino Cuban)*, Alfredo Vorshim *(Modest Casino Tuxedo)*, Bonita Marco, Sharon Velez, Darlene Wynn *(Strippers)*, Miguel Bucarelly *(Gomez)*, Carlos Miranda, Enrique Chao Barros *(Inspectors)*, Daniel Vasquez *(Kid at Finca)*, and Carmen De Franco *(Monica's Grandmother)*

The seventh teaming of Robert Redford and director Sydney Pollack, and the first since 1985's Best Picture Oscar winner OUT OF AFRICA, opens late in 1958 with gambler Jack Weil (Redford) sailing for the then wide-open city of Havana. On board, he meets the lovely Bobby Duran (Lena Olin) and immediately falls for her. Bobby is somehow involved with the revolution which is taking place in Cuba, siding with the rebel forces led by Fidel Castro against

the incumbent government under the rule of Fulgencio Batista. Though Jack is not the least bit political, he chivalrously agrees to help her do some smuggling to aid the rebels. Once in Havana, they go their separate ways, with Jack heading off to visit his old friend, mob-connected casino operator Joe Volpi (Alan Arkin). Jack's ready for a big score, he tells Volpi, asking his friend to approach gang kingpin Meyer Lansky (Mark Rydell) with the idea of backing Jack in a high-stakes game against some high rollers. The philosophical Volpi has little enthisiasm for the propositon, but reluctantly agrees to do his friend's bidding.

Later, Jack goes out on the town with another friend, Cuban journalist Julio Ramos (Tony Plana). In a restaurant, Jack spots Bobby, who is accompanied by her husband Arturo (Raul Julia). Though he is from a wealthy, politically well-connected family, Arturo, too, supports the rebel cause. When he meets Jack, he thanks him for helping Bobby, and asks if he would care to continue his involvement with the "cause." Jack declines, and he and Ramos continue on their way, picking up a couple of female American tourists (Betsy Brantley and Lise Cutter) who are looking for the "real" Havana. When Ramos gets drunk and passes out, Jack takes the girls to a club that features live sex shows, then heads back to their hotel room where the three engage in a live sex show of their own. The next morning, newspapers report that Arturo has been killed by government forces. Meanwhile, Vopli has arranged for Jack to get in on the big game he seeks, but Jack instead engages in a more exciting game as he attempts to protect Bobby from the dangers posed by the Battista forces.

HAVANA's greatest achievement is in its stunning production design. Unable to get permission from the US government to film in Cuba, Pollack and his crew evaluated alternate sites throughout the Caribbean, finally settling on the Dominican Republic. There a replica of Havana of the 1950s was stunningly recreated, a quarter-mile long stretch complete with hotels, casinos, nightclubs, and restaurants which included exact replicas of the Floridita Bar, the department store El Encanto, and the offices of the newspaper *El Pais*. Teaming with cars, locals, and tourists, the set successfully evokes a Havana that was, at the time, considered to be the sexiest and most corrupt city in the world.

Unfortunately, against that impressive backdrop, Pollack mounts a film that is lifeless and slow-moving, offering neither a compelling love story nor a tense tale of a city in turmoil. Part of the problem is that Redford simply isn't right for the part of the somewhat seedy professional gambler. Sure, the lines of age are visible on his face, he sports a tattoo (lingered over by the camera during a card game, lest anyone miss it), and he engages in sordid sex with adventurous tourists, but he's still pretty boy, erstwhile romantic leading man Robert Redford. To work, Jack needs to have an edge of cynicism that Redford just isn't able to supply. Olin, who won an Oscar nomination for her steamy performance in ENEMIES, A LOVE STORY, is certainly a lovely woman, but here she is so reserved that it is difficult to believe that she possesses the fiery passion that would lead her to pick up the rebel cause. She and Redford have no chemistry together so that their love affair is sadly lacking in the immediacy it needs. In fact, all the performances are so subdued that the film never captures the tumult, excitement, and peril that engulfed Havana as Castro's forces closed in on the city. A much better account of the same period can be seen in Richard Lester's little-seen CUBA (1979), a darkly comic film starring Sean Connery. The previous efforts of Pollack and Redford, including OUT OF AFRICA, THREE DAYS OF THE CONDOR, and THE WAY WE WERE, generally were well-received by audiences, but HAVANA enjoyed no such success, disappearing from theaters quickly after its release. The film earned an Oscar nomination for its score.

d, Sydney Pollack; p, Sydney Pollack and Richard Roth; w, Judith Rascoe and David Rayfiel (based on the story by Rascoe); ph, Owen Roizman; ed, Fredric Steinkamp and William Steinkamp; m, Dave Grusin; prod d, Terence Marsh; art d, George Richardson; set d, Michael Seirton; cos, Bernie Pollack; makup, Gary Liddiard; chor, Vincent Paterson

Drama   (PR:C   MPAA:R)

HEART CONDITION

100m Steve Tisch—James D. Parriott/New Line c

Robert Apisa *(Teller)*, Jeffrey Meek *(Graham)*, Frank R. Roach *(Sen. James Marquand)*, Kieran Mulroney *(Dillnick)*, Lisa Stahl *(Annie)*, Bob Hoskins *(Jack Moony)*, Ray Baker *(Harry Zara)*, Denzel Washington *(Napoleon Stone)*, Eva LaRue *(Peisha)*, Chloe Webb *(Crystal Gerrity)*, Roger E. Mosley *(Capt. Wendt)*, Alan Rachins *(Dr. Posner)*, Clayton Landey *(Dr. Posner's Assistant)*, Julie Silverman *(Staff Member)*, Phyllis Hamlin *(TV Announcer)*, Jeff MacGregor *(Dating Game Host)*, George Kyle, Bill Applebaum *(Dancing Cops)*, Mary Catherine Wright *(Nurse)*, Kenneth J. Martinez, Johnny Walker *(Cops in Precinct)*, Diane Civita *(Terri)*, Ja'net Dubois *(Mrs. Stone)*, Monte Landis *(Beverly Palm Hotel Waiter)*, Anthony "Wink" Atkinson, Deidre Harris *(Rap Singers)*, Ron Taylor *(Bubba)*, Kendall McCarthy *(Archimedes)*, Theresa Randle *(Ciao Chow Club Maitre D')*, Mark Lowenthal *(Ciao Chow Club Waiter)*, Billy Oscar *(Man in Bathroom)*, Dasanea Johnson, Johquache Johnson, Shauntae Johnson

(*Baby Leon*), Leontine Guilliard (*Duty Nurse*), Johnnie Johnson (*Resident*), Rick Marzan (*Irate Cop*), Dean Wein, Bobby Bass, Greg Barnett, Tom Huff (*Armed Men*), Gary Sax (*Usher Cop*), and Felix the Cat (*Chuck*)

Too often, movies tackle social issues and make you wish they hadn't. A case in point is this lame crime comedy (from the producer of the forgettable SOUL MAN) that is almost made watchable by the chemistry between its two stars, Bob Hoskins and Denzel Washington, who spend most of the film fighting an uphill battle against a awful script. Los Angeles cop Jack Moony (Hoskins) and dapper lawyer Napoleon Stone (Washington) are forced to see the world through each other's eyes when Moony receives Stone's heart in a transplant operation. Prior to the operation, both lead dangerous lives: Moony boozes while on duty, chasing grease-dripping burgers with cans of beer and swigs of bourbon; Stone provides legal services for the high-priced hookers controlled by Graham (Jeffrey Meek), an evil pimp. In the elaborate setup, Crystal (Chloe Webb), a hooker once involved with Moony and now involved with Stone, takes photos of a session between a crusading politician and fellow hooker Peisha (Eva LaRue). Conveniently, the politician also smokes a crack pipe for the camera. But inconveniently for Crystal, the politician drops dead of an overdose. While her pimp cleans up the mess, Crystal and Peisha slip away with Stone's help. In no time, however, Moony, who hates Stone for having stolen Crystal from him, is in pursuit of the lawyer, chasing him on foot through Westwood. Although Moony catches Stone, the lawyer is released and the cop is brought up on harassment charges. What's more, the chase leaves the out-of-shape Moony a candidate for the emergency room, and when he gets home, he collapses with a heart attack. Stone, on the other hand, doesn't even make it back home, becoming the victim of a car accident rigged by Graham to remove him as a witness to the politician's death. When the dying cop and the dead lawyer arrive at the hospital at virtually the same time, the former needs a heart and the latter has one to give. Back at work, Moony is given less strenuous desk duty by his precinct captain (Roger E. Mosley). However, since we are only about a reel into the film at this point, the story obviously isn't over. Ignoring his doctor's orders, Moony heads for his favorite burger joint, but as he prepares to commit suicide with beef and brew, Stone appears, returning from the spirit world to prod the cop into solving his murder. Stone also undertakes a makeover of Moony, transforming the incorrigible slob into a stylish character so that he can move more easily in Graham's world. But, of course, what we're really talking about here is male bonding with a message: Moony must overcome his racial prejudice in order to work with Stone to save Crystal.

Notwithstanding its strong performances, HEART CONDITION is a disaster. As a plea for racial harmony, the film fails completely, offering nothing in the way of motivation for Moony's change of heart. Instead of raising the racist cop's consciousness, Stone leads Moony to a cache of cash that allows him to buy new suits and a car to impress Crystal. Moreover, Stone is saddled with ridiculous dialog about how Moony is jealous of him because he's slick, wealthy, black, and hung "like a Shetland pony." For most of the film, Crystal is nothing more than a plot device to bring Moony and Stone together, but late in the proceedings, it is revealed that she has given birth to Stone's son, though apparently the lawyer has no idea how her pregnancy came about. Evidently, writer-director James D. Parriott expects viewers to believe that the stork still brings babies, which is hardly more farfetched than the notion that a new suit is enough to change the mind of a racist.

It is a mystery how performers of the stature of Hoskins, Washington, and Webb ever became involved in this mess. But if HEART CONDITION is tolerable at all, it is as a result of their presence. Because Moony is the only one who can see Stone when he returns as a spirit, Hoskins is often forced to act opposite a void when the camera point of view isn't Moony's, a feat not unlike the fine British actor's performance in WHO FRAMED ROGER RABBIT? As he did in that film, Hoskins brings off this tricky bit of acting with great panache, leading to some of the film's funniest scenes. Providing a "cool" foil for the blustering Hoskins, Washington manages to rise above most of the cliches heaped on his character by the script. Similarly, Webb invests her Crystal with more credibility than she deserves, giving a poignant portrayal of a ritzy call girl who hasn't quite left behind her working-class roots. Indeed, the three actors are good enough together that it is possible to imagine HEART CONDITION as a good movie, were it not for its confused attempt at social commentary and its weak, implausible plot. (*Profanity, adult situations, violence.*)

d, James D. Parriott; p, Steve Tisch; w, James D. Parriott; ph, Arthur Albert; ed, David Finfer; m, Patrick Leonard; prod d, John Muto; cos, Louise Frogley

Comedy/Crime (PR:O   MPAA:R)

HEARTSTONE

(SEE: DEMONSTONE)

HEAVEN AND EARTH

(Japan) 106m Haruki Kadokawa/Triton c

Takai Enoki (*Kenshin Uefugi*), Masahiko Tsugawa (*Takeda*), Atsuko Asano (*Nami*), Tsunehiko Watase (*Usami*), Naomi Zaizen (*Yae*), Binpachi Ito (*Kakizaki*), Isao Natsuyagi (*Kansuke*), Akira Hamada (*Naoe*), Masataka Naruse (*Okuma*), Osamu Yayama (*Irobe*), Takeshi Obayashi (*Murakami*), Masayuki Sudo (*Onikojima*), Kaitaro Nozaki (*Naya*), Tatsuhiko Tomoi (*Sone*), Takuya Goto (*Tokura*), Satoshi Sadanaga (*Akiyama*), Hironobu Nomura (*Taro*), Hideo Murota (*Obu*), Taro Ishida (*Tenkyu*), Hiroyuki Okita (*Kosaka*), Akisato Yamada (*Hajikano*), Morio Kazama (*Imperial Messenger*), Masuto Ibu (*Shoda*), Yuki Kazamatsuri (*Shoda's Wife*), Kyoko Kishida (*Servant*), Hideji Otaki (*Rifle Merchant*), and Stuart Whitman (*Narration*)

In this stunning-looking clone of an Akira Kurosawa epic set in 16th century Japan, two rival warlords gobble up neighboring kingdoms with different priorities in mind, mercilessly wage battle against each other, and eventually reach a stalemate after much pictorially presented carnage. For Takeda (Masahiko Tsugawa) and his Lady Macbeth-like mistress Yae (Naomi Zaizen), total domination of Japan and the molding of his empire into a world power are the interlocking goals. For Uefugi (Takai Enoki) the desire to maintain the status quo of his dominion while ruthlessly crushing acquisitive invaders is the driving force.

Sumptuously photographed, HEAVEN AND EARTH's screenplay is designed like a military chess game between two keen minds who try to check each other's moves throughout the film. Complicating Uefugi's plight is his spiritual nature which has prompted him to make a vow of celibacy to ensure the cooperation of his gods. Torn by his love of Nami (Atsuko Asano), the daughter of his ally Usami (Tsunehiko Watase), Uefugi has doubts about his worthiness as a ruler. Although he will later act cruelly when he shoots Yae as she rides toward his camp spewing taunts and challenges, he is indecisive when expected to issue orders to execute the family of a turncoat. Shaken, he flees his kingdom but is intercepted by loyal followers who inform him of the defection of Usami. Escaping a close call in the forest when Takeda and entourage ride by, he returns to power and gives up all hope of marrying Nami after he engages her father in a duel on horseback and slays him. Uefugi then launches an all-out assault on Takeda, who pushes his power base to the borders of Uefugi's kingdom. In a climactic series of battles, the warlords try to outmaneuver each other. Aided by fog, Uefugi gains the upper hand and surrounds his rival's troops. However, neither warrior-king is slain and with an impasse reached, the narrator intones that both rulers lived for many years, but respectfully avoided future conflicts.

While this handsome production manages to pique historical curiosity, it never engages the emotions. Playing like an endless dress rehearsal for "Shogun — The Musical," the film offers thousands of extras parading across the screen in beautifully detailed costumes. Take away the wide-screen presentation and the drama that is left barely attains the level of interest of a TV mini-series. The narration provided by Stuart Whitman sounds as though it was taken from a grade-school textbook on the history of Japan, reducing the entire effort to an elaborate history lesson. The film's power is limited by the reduction of its protagonists to puppet status. The best historical epics are careful to see that events don't dwarf the main characters, but here no such care has been taken. On technical grounds, the film cannot be faulted, but as drama it is strictly pedestrian. (*Extreme violence.*)

d, Haruki Kadokawa; p, Yutaka Okada; w, Toshio Kamata, Isao Yoshihara, and Haruki Kadokawa (based on the novel by Chogoro Kaionji); ph, Yonezo Maeda; ed, Akira Suziki and Robert C. Jones; m, Tetsuya Komuro; prod d, Hiroshi Tokuda; art d, Kazuhiko Fujiwara; spec, Stewart Bradley; stunts, John Scott and Brent Woolsey; cos, Yoko Tashiro and Wendy Partridge; makup, Shigeo Tamura; chor, Hiroshi Kuze and Jean-Pierre Fournier

Historical (PR:C   MPAA:PG-13)

HENRY AND JUNE

136m Walrus & Associates/Universal c

Fred Ward (*Henry Miller*), Uma Thurman (*June Miller*), Maria de Medeiros (*Anais Nin*), Richard E. Grant (*Hugo*), Kevin Spacey (*Osborn*), Jean-Philippe Ecoffey (*Eduardo*), Bruce Myers (*Jack*), Jean-Louis Bunuel (*Editor-Publisher*), Feodor Atkine (*Spanish Dance Instructor*), Sylvie Huguel (*Emilia*), Artus de Penguern (*Brassai*), Pierre Etaix (*Friend*), Pierre Edernac, Gaetan Bloom (*Magicians*), Alexandre de Gall (*Clown*), Karine Couvelard (*Osborn's Girl Friend*), Louis Bessicres (*Accordionist*), Erika Maury-Lascoux, Claire Joubert (*Contortionists*), Annie Fratellini (*The Patronne*), Brigitte Lahaie (*Henry's Whore*),

Maite Maille (*Frail Prostitute*), Frank Heiler (*Steamship Agent*), Stephanie Leboulanger (*Prostitute Brushing Long Hair*), Suzy Palatin (*Bal Negre* Performer), Samuel Ateba (*Black Musician for Quat'z Arts* Ball), Marc Maury (*Man in Silent Film*), Annie Vincent (*Fat Prostitute*), Maurice Escargot (*Pop*), and Liz Hasse (*Jean*)

Philip Kaufman's latest excursion into literary erotica isn't the earnest bore that THE UNBEARABLE LIGHTNESS OF BEING was, but it still stumbles more than it sizzles. HENRY AND JUNE is noteworthy for being the first film to be released with the MPAA's NC-17 rating, created in 1990 to replace the X rating. The introduction of the new rating and the film carrying it met with picketing by parental and religious groups at some theaters. HENRY AND JUNE also made headlines by being banned from a theater in suburban Boston by local government officials. And all of this hubbub was created by a movie in which the only violence is inflicted on a kitchen sink during a domestic argument.

Henry Miller, the Henry of the title, would undoubtedly have been delighted had he lived to see the furor. Though published in 1934, Miller's first novel, *Tropic of Cancer*, could not be legally distributed in the US or in most other English-speaking countries until 1961. HENRY AND JUNE is concerned with the writing of that book, which Miller worked on while living in Paris in 1931-32. At the beginning of the film, Henry (played by Fred Ward) has been sent to France by his wife, June (Uma Thurman), a former taxi dancer who has been supporting his career on her earnings as another man's mistress. The purpose of the trip is twofold: 1) to get Henry away from distractions in New York so he can finish the novel, 2) to allow June, a bisexual, more freedom to frolic with a new girl friend. The film actually opens not with Henry or June, but with Miller's lover, lifelong friend, and literary advocate Anais Nin (Maria de Medeiros), upon whose diaries the script (by Kaufman and his wife, Rose) is based. An aspiring literary critic working on her own first book, a study of D.H. Lawrence, Anais is given to erotic flights of fancy. When a college professor stiffly kisses and fondles her during a meeting, she transforms the light indiscretion into a full-blown seduction in her diary, in which she scribbles each night before retiring with her bland but likable middle-class husband, Hugo (Richard E. Grant). Anais generally chafes at her mundane existence and yearns for a more bohemian social life and, especially, for a big, swarthy lover. Enter big and swarthy Henry, brought to Anais' house by her husband, who is friends with Henry's eccentric roommate (Kevin Spacey). Initially, Anais and Henry are tentative friends, providing each other with support for their respective writing projects. And though Anais has polite erotic palpitations when she is around the earthy but cultured Henry, it is June, briefly in Paris to check up on Henry, who brings Anais' passions to a furious boil. Sensing Anais' attraction to Henry, June begins a flirtation with her that is left unconsummated when June must return to New York, but not before she asks Anais to "take care" of Henry for her. And take care of Henry she does, seducing him and spending the bulk of the movie exploring other facets of her new sexual awareness, which has been awakened by her contact with June. Besides her affair with Henry, Anais begins reaching new sensual heights with her husband by introducing fantasy scenarios into their lovemaking and even seduces her cousin (Jean-Philippe Ecoffey), who has lusted after her since they were children. For Anais, however, all of this is mere preparation for the climactic return of June late in the film, which turns out not only to be anti-climatic, but also upends the movie. Without giving the ending away, suffice it to say that June comes out the "hero." As the film's postscript notes, both Nin and Miller were destined to spend the rest of their careers writing books about her, while June abandoned them both for a career as a social worker.

HENRY AND JUNE earns its NC-17 rating. Its couplings are about as explicit as any to be found in mainstream cinema. However, much of the sex here is mild when compared to films by Almodovar, Bertolucci, Imamura, Oshima, and many others, proving only that while few national cinemas can match Hollywood's painfully realistic depictions of graphic violence, when it comes to sex, the American film industry is still stuck somewhere back in the Victorian era. Even Kaufman adopts an air of professorial sobriety to give the eroticism an aura of legitimacy. But his approach is still far less stultifying than it was in THE INCREDIBLE LIGHTNESS OF BEING, one of those erotic "art" films that manages to make sex seem dull. At times, HENRY AND JUNE is downright lively, largely because of Ward and Thurman. Ward's performance here is his best yet, a multi-layered portrait of a multi-layered man that succeeds by conveying all the contradictions of Miller's character. Thurman is even better with a character defined only by her mercurialness. Without straining, she makes June easily credible as the object of the heated obsessions of both Henry and Anais, her influence felt on the action even during her lengthy absences.

Indeed, HENRY AND JUNE bogs down when both Ward and Thurman are offscreen for long stretches to allow the action to center on Anais. Despite having more on-screen sex than anyone else in the film, de Medeiros' Anais remains the least interesting and involving member of the trio. She seems fully engaged only when she is acting with her costars, whether during a playful moment with Henry or while being tantalizingly trifled with by June when they dance together in a lesbian cafe. Otherwise, de Medeiros goes through the film sporting the expres-

sion of a slightly pained Pekingese, which, however true to her character, is never particularly compelling and tends to take the heat out of her dizzying string of seductions.

It's too hard to tell whether Kaufman has genuinely improved as a writer-director since THE INCREDIBLE LIGHTNESS OF BEING or whether his stifling tendency towards leaden self-seriousness is merely being subverted here by Ward's and Thurman's freewheeling performances. But in the long run, it probably doesn't matter. HENRY AND JUNE is no LAST TANGO IN PARIS. However, as adult erotic cinema retreats from rising tides of censorship, even flawed efforts merit some praise. And HENRY AND JUNE is a well-acted, reasonably spicy alternative to half-baked snoozers like WILD ORCHID and to the hard-core gynecologist-training videos that pass for "adult cinema." The film earned an Oscar nomination for its score. (*Sexual situations, adult themes, nudity, profanity.*)

d, Philip Kaufman; p, Peter Kaufman; w, Philip Kaufman and Rose Kaufman (based on the diaries of Anais Nin); ph, Philippe Rousselot; ed, Vivien Hillgrove, William S. Scharf, and Dede Allen; md, Alan Splet, Rose Kaufman, and Philip Kaufman; prod d, Guy-Claude Francois; art d, Georges Glon; set d, Thierry Francois; cos, Yvonne Sassinot de Nesle; makup, Didier Lavergne; chor, Nathalie Erlbaum

Drama   (PR:O   MPAA:NC-17)

HENRY: PORTRAIT OF A SERIAL KILLER

83m Maljack/Greycat c

Michael Rooker (*Henry*), Tom Towles (*Otis*), and Tracy Arnold

HENRY: PORTRAIT OF A SERIAL KILLER surely ranks as one of the most frightening and disturbing films ever made. An angry and raw independent feature that received limited release after becoming a cult favorite in Chicago (where it was filmed), four years after its 1986 completion, HENRY begins with a creepy montage of shots of dead bodies. The corpses are the victims of Henry (Michael Rooker), a low-life drifter who looks for victims while driving around in his green Impala. Rooker murders with knives, guns, rope, even his hands—he has no preferred method or pattern. Rooker lives with Towles, a degenerate he met while in prison (for killing his mother) and who now works in a gas station and sells drugs on the side. When Towles' sister (Arnold) comes to Chicago, she stays with Towles and Rooker while she looks for a job; meanwhile, Rooker, who works as a bug sprayer, continues to kill. Arnold becomes interested in him, and (after hearing a few things from Towles) asks some very personal questions, including "Did you really kill your momma?" Rooker proceeds to tell her how his mother would force him to watch her have sex with strangers and sometimes made him wear a dress. He says he killed his mother on his 14th birthday, although he's not sure how (after so many murders you lose track of individual details). None of this seems to shock Arnold (a victim of paternal incest herself), who still seems interested in Rooker. Towles takes no notice; he wants to seduce her himself. (At one point, Towles grabs Arnold and kisses her, whereupon Rooker threatens him, saying, "It's not right; she's your sister.") One night, Towles and Rooker pick up a couple of hookers and park their car in an alley. Moments later, Rooker snaps the women's necks and dumps the bodies—an action that at first shocks Towles, but once he and Rooker get something to eat he seems fine. Soon, Towles joins Rooker in his killing spree. When he and Rooker visit a fat, sleazy TV repairman who operates out of a garage, Rooker stabs the repairman, smashes a TV over his head, and instructs Towles to plug the set in. Though he has become a murderer, Towles feels no remorse, having gotten a video camera out of the deal. Afterwards, they go home and have fun with the camera, filming Rooker and Arnold as they dance and Towles as he jumps around. The next day, Towles reports to his parole officer, a shockingly quick and meaningless meeting. He continues to sell marijuana—to teenage boys, coming on to them while he's at it and saying offhandedly, after one of the kids punches him, that he'd like to kill someone. Replies Rooker, "Let's me and you take a ride," and the two wind up on the shoulder of Chicago's Lower Wacker Drive, where they pop their car's hood and flag down a car. When a driver stops to see if they need help, Rooker laughs, Towles shoots the man dead, and they get back in the car and drive off, both feeling much better.

Towles and Rooker continue to murder people at random, videotaping every detail, until they start to get on each other's nerves. When Rooker can no longer stand Towles' stupidity and sloppiness, the two argue; meanwhile, Arnold quits her job in a hair salon and asks Rooker to move away with her. After Arnold and Rooker go out for dinner one night, they return home to find Towles (who likes to watch the videotaped murders, viewing them repeatedly and in slow motion) passed out on the couch. Arnold brings Rooker into the bedroom, but Towles wakes up and interrupts them. Feeling uncomfortable, Rooker goes out for cigarettes and—after passing up an opportunity to kill another person—returns home to find Towles raping his sister. Towles and Rooker fight, Arnold stabs her brother in the eye, and Rooker finishes him off with a screwdriver in the stomach.

Arnold is hysterical; Rooker calmly chops his ex-roommate into pieces, which he deposits in garbage bags. After packing their suitcases, Rooker and Arnold drive to a bridge, from which Rooker drops the garbage bags. He and Arnold then declare their love, talk of a future together, and drive to a motel. The next day, Rooker departs alone in his car. Stopping, he opens the trunk, removes a large, heavy suitcase, and drops it by the side of the road. Having left Arnold's body behind, Rooker drives off, free to continue murdering.

A stunning feature debut from director John McNaughton, HENRY tells its horrible story with chilling straightforwardness. Presenting his sick characters nonjudgmentally and without shrinking from gory details, McNaughton creates a world in which there is no good to counterbalance evil, where incest and rape are permitted and murder is an acceptable way to relieve tension. Providing no "good" characters to identify with — not even a cop to offer us hope — and ending on a bitter, ugly note, HENRY leaves viewers emotionally drained and deeply, deeply disturbed. Mainstream audiences are so used to faceless killers who get their comeuppance in the end (or are at least temporarily defeated) that HENRY may simply be too much for most to take. (The film's distributors rejected an X rating from the MPAA.) McNaughton succeeds in showing just how vulnerable anyone can be to someone like Henry, a frightening reality few will want to contemplate. HENRY forces one to think about such things, however.

In addition to its brave, raw screenplay by McNaughton and Richard Fire, HENRY benefits from some extraordinary performances. Michael Rooker is absolutely chilling as Henry, a deeply deranged character who — unlike the killers in most horror films — is a multifaceted man with a bizarre set of "morals." Although never a sympathetic character, he is not an evil stereotype either, but ultimately both sick and sad. Tom Towles is brilliant in his role, making Otis a monster who is, at times, even more frightening than Henry (as when he gleefully snaps the neck of one woman and attempts to rape her corpse). There is not one false note in his terrifying performance.

HENRY even benefits from the constraints of its $120,000 budget, which lends the film a moody edge. McNaughton uses his Chicago locations impeccably, creating a dark, at times surrealistic atmosphere (some Chicagoans may want to move after seeing this picture). The film is well-paced and intelligently constructed: it begins quietly, then builds in perversity and intensity until it reaches its shattering climax.

No film in recent memory has tapped into primal, visceral fear like HENRY does, with its vision of a depraved world that seems at once too horrible to exist and too realistic to be denied. Hard to watch (though at times it's bizarrely and blackly funny) and definitely not for the squeamish, HENRY will prove unforgettable for the brave souls who do see it. A major achievement in independent filmmaking, HENRY: PORTRAIT OF A SERIAL KILLER is a horror masterpiece. (*Graphic violence, nudity, adult situations, profanity, sexual situations.*)

d, John McNaughton; p, Lisa Dedmond and Steven A. Jones; w, Richard Fire and John McNaughton; ph, Charlie Lieberman; ed, Elena Maganini; md, Robert McNaughton; makup, Berndt Rantscheff

Crime/Horror　　　　　　　　　　　　　　　　　　　　　(PR:O　MPAA:NR)

HIDDEN AGENDA

(Brit.) 108m Hemdale — Initial Film & Television/Hemdale c

Frances McDormand (*Ingrid Jessner*), Brian Cox (*Peter Kerrigan*), Brad Dourif (*Paul Sullivan*), Mai Zetterling (*Moa*), Bernard Bloch (*Henri*), John Benfield (*Maxwell*), Jim Norton (*Brodie*), Patrick Kavanaugh (*Alec Nevin*), Bernard Archard (*Sir Robert Neil*), Michelle Fairley (*Teresa Doyle*), Maurice Roeves (*Harris*), Oliver Maguire (*Supt. Fraser*), Robert Patterson (*Ian Logan*), George Staines (*Tall Man*), Brian McCann (*Molloy*), Des McAleer (*Sgt. Kennedy*), Mandy McIlwaine (*RUC Policewoman*), Ivan Little (*TV Reporter*), Llew Gardner (*TV Announcer*), John McDonnell (*Labour MP*), Kate Smith (*News Reporter*), Victoria D'Angelo (*Journalist*), John Keegan (*Detective Sergeant Hughts*), Ian McElhinney (*Jack Cunningham*), Maureen Bell (*Mrs. Molloy*), Stephen Brigden (*Army Major*), Kym Dyson (*Carol*), Jim McAllister (*Liam Philbin*), Gerry Fearon (*Taxi Driver*), Ron Kavana, and Terry Woods (*Musicians*)

Director Ken Loach (POOR COW, THE GAMEKEEPER) here offers a plot-heavy thriller to which his naturalistic approach is inappropriate and ineffective. As propaganda, the film is intelligently presented and scary in its implications, but as suspenseful entertainment, it is cramped and poorly paced. The film is set in a hopelessly divided Northern Ireland where British forces continually scour cities and towns in search of IRA members. Paranoia is so rampant that the police have adopted a "shoot to kill" policy. In a land where the entire country seems to be under house arrest, a panel of lawyers, working under the auspices of an international amnesty group, is investigating charges of prisoner mistreatment. American attorney Paul Sullivan (Brad Dourif) is drawn into the fray when he is informed of the existence of a tape that proves there is a conspiracy among supporters of British Prime Minister Margaret Thatcher. Telling his plans to no one, including his girl friend and fellow panel member

Ingrid Jessner (Frances McDormand), Paul agrees to a secret meeting with Harris (Maurice Roeves), a British secret service turncoat who has a copy of the tape. Paul is killed by a squad of secret police and the tape confiscated. Embarrassed over the death of an American, the British government dispatches a police unit to investigate the incident. The unit is led by the dogged and honest Inspector Kerrigan (Brian Cox). As Kerrigan sifts through the clues, with Ingrid's assistance, he soon learns the truth, but finds that a coverup has been engineered to hide the facts of the case, and that involvement in the coverup reaches high in the Thatcher government. Despite interference from authorities, the two continue the investigation, and Ingrid meets with the mysterious Harris, who tells her that the tape contains evidence of a CIA-backed English plot to unseat former Prime Minister Harold Wilson. Ingrid eventually succeeds in securing a copy of the tape, but Harris is slain by British forces, and Kerrigan gives in to pressure from high-ranking British politicians, abandoning the investigation, leaving Ingrid to attempt to reveal the conspiracy with no official support.

Well-intentioned, but rather murky, HIDDEN AGENDA chokes on its own righteous anger. The documentary approach employed by Loach doesn't work here as the film needs a leaner shaping and a deeper focus on its characters. Instead of sweeping the audience from one startling discovery to the next, the film moves slowly along, intriguing the viewer, but never gripping him. While the sordid plottings depicted in the film do engender outrage, the film never really penetrates the ugly vortex of British policies in Northern Ireland, leaving the viewer to almost casually observe the scheming from the outside. (*Extreme violence, profanity.*)

d, Kenneth Loach; p, Eric Fellner; w, Jim Allen; ph, Clive Tickner; ed, Jonathan Morris; m, Stewart Copeland; prod d, Martin Johnson; art d, Nigel Phelps; spec, Vendetta Effects; cos, Daphne Dare; makup, Louise Fisher

Political/Thriller　　　　　　　　　　　　　　　　　　(PR:C　MPAA:R)

HIDDEN VISION

(SEE: NIGHT EYES)

HIGH DESERT KILL

120m MCA — Lehigh/MCA-Universal c

Anthony Geary (*Dr. Jim Cole*), Marc Singer (*Brad Mueller*), Chuck Connors (*Stan Brown*), Micah Grant (*Ray Bettencamp*), Vaughn Armstrong (*Paul Bettencamp/The Alien*), Lori Birdsong (*Terry*), and Deborah Anne Mansy (*Kathleen*)

Though this is clearly a rip-off of PREDATOR, it is a well-crafted film that succeeds in surpassing its source material. Strange things are happening in the craggy rocks above an isolated campsite in New Mexico. Before the opening credits, an Indian brave is shown turning his knife against an elder after falling under the influence of — what? An evil spirit? A demon possessor? An alien being? The story then picks up as a trio of hunters is preparing for a trip to the site in honor of their friend, Paul (Vaughn Armstrong), who was electrocuted the year before. The group includes Paul's nephew Ray (Micah Grant); Jim (Anthony Geary), a research scientist; and Brad (Marc Singer), a macho gym operator. At the site, they encounter Stan (Chuck Connors), a grizzled hunter who informs them that something in the area has spooked the animals. Stan camps with the others, and that night, while the men sleep, an unseen force reads their minds, probing for frailties. The following day, hostilities arise among the campers, and Jim elects to go off on his own. In his absence female campers Terry (Lori Birdsong) and Kathleen (Deborah Anne Mansy) arrive at the site, creating even more tension among the men. The following morning, the women are gone and when Jim returns, his companions have only a sketchy recollection of what happened the night before. Soon each of the men is visited by the spirit of the dead Paul, and their behavior becomes increasingly bizarre. Brad goes off to search for the women, and later stumbles upon the others, who have killed a bear and are eating the meat raw. Briefly returning to their senses, all four men realize they had better return to civilization, but when they try to they find their vehicle won't start. They seek shelter in an Indian lodge, then find Stan's pack animals dead, each operated on with surgical precision. Kathleen is found in the woods, sobbing hysterically. Terrified, she recounts how a powerful force possessed her mind and soul. As the terror mounts, Jim comes to the conclusion that he and his fellow campers are all the victims of an experiment being conducted by alien beings, and he determines to find a way to defeat the powerful foe.

As far-fetched as its premise is, HIGH DESERT KILL is a taut, no-frills shocker that is potent enough to enable the audience to suspend its disbelief. Thirty years ago, it would have been considered a B movie, but today it's a neglected little gem that ends up collecting dust on the video shelves. With antagonisms simmering among the main characters, the film sets off in three different directions — it's an action/adventure; it's a psychological games thriller;

and it's a space invader film. Succeeding in all three categories, the film surpasses expectations with enough plot twists to keep the viewer off-guard and interested. The film neatly explores the downside of machismo, while also touching on the morality of animal experimentation. It features a finely realized villain, a creature that seems to be the horrific monster from ALIEN with an advanced degree in psychology. Despite some shortcomings in the acting department, this film provides some joltingly good science-fiction escapism. (*Adult situations, violence.*)

d, Harry Falk; p, G. Warren Smith; w, Tom S. Cook; ph, Michel Hugo; m, Dana Kaproff; prod d, Roger Holzberg; set d, Joanie Montoya; spec, Jack Faggard and Steve Faggard; cos, Lynn Bernay; makeup, Melanie Hughes

Adventure/Science Fiction

HIT LIST

87m Cinetel/New Line c

Jan-Michael Vincent (*Jack Collins*), Leo Rossi (*Frank DeSalvo*), Lance Henriksen (*Chris Caleek*), Charles Napier (*Tom Mitchum*), Rip Torn (*Vic Luca*), Jere Burns (*Jared Riley*), Ken Lerner (*Gravenstein*), Harriet Hall (*Sandi Collins*), Junior Richard (*Kenny Collins*), Jack Andreozzi (*Abe Fazio*), and Harold Sylvester (*Brian Armstrong*)

Mafia hits, grand jury hearings, and the exigencies of witness protection form the basis of this above-average crime thriller. As the movie opens, two FBI agents bust up a funeral at which some mob members have hidden drugs inside the corpse of a priest. Spiriting away lowlifes Gravenstein (Ken Lerner) and DeSalvo (Leo Rossi), the federal agents, Tom Mitchum (Charles Napier) and Jared Riley (Jere Burns), launch plans for the two crooks to testify against Vic Luca (Rip Torn), a slimy underworld kingpin. Although he informs reporters that he is merely a harassed businessman, Luca is secretly planning to eliminate any potential witnesses to his illegal activities. For added protection, he instructs his lawyer to buy off the judge. For the present, Chris Caleek (Lance Henriksen), a part-time shoe clerk *and* part-time hit man, accepts Luca's offer to rub out Gravenstein, who's being held in a prison facility. That night, Caleek sneaks into the hoosegow, slays several guards, and prevents Gravenstein from testifying— permanently. The other potential witness, DeSalvo, and his son are being guarded by Mitchum and Riley in a suburban house across the street from the home of Jack Collins (Jan-Michael Vincent), his wife Sandi (Harriet Hall), and son Kenny (Junior Richard). While DeSalvo is being grilled and steadfastly refuses to cooperate, the Collinses are enjoying a barbecue with Brian (Harold Sylvester), a family friend. Meanwhile, Luca has ordered Caleek to eliminate DeSalvo and has given him the address. Unfortunately, when Jack leaves on an errand, Brian slams the front door so hard that the final nine in the address is shaken loose from its nail and changes into a six. Accordingly, instead of stalking the house where DeSalvo is sequestered, Caleek enters the Collins home. After knocking out Sandi, the hit man gets into a knock-down-drag-out fight with Brian and shoots him. Caleek then grabs young Kenny in the mistaken belief that he's kidnaping DeSalvo's kid (thereby ensuring that DeSalvo won't testify before the grand jury). When Jack returns and discovers his wife unconscious and his son missing, he is understandably miffed. But he becomes even more furious when the FBI decides to perpetuate the illusion that it is DeSalvo's son who has been nabbed. Learning DeSalvo's whereabouts, Jack sneaks off to the hideaway and springs the prize witness. Although Jack wants to be led to his son immediately, DeSalvo gets him to cool down; however, DeSalvo becomes equally enraged when he learns that his own father has been killed by Luca's thugs. When DeSalvo and Jack are spotted by two of Luca's men, they become embroiled in a shootout that builds to a climax in a nightclub. After obtaining vital information from a wounded thug (whom DeSalvo subsequently kills), DeSalvo and Jack set off to nab Caleek, who cleverly leads them into a trap, from which they are rescued by the FBI. Finally, DeSalvo agrees to testify if the authorities release Jack, who immediately pursues Caleek. After the grand jury, influenced by the judge, dismisses the charges against Luca, DeSalvo rushes off to team up with Jack. Together, they finally manage to kill the elusive Caleek. Disgusted with the legal system (and taking into account his own terminal illness), Federal Agent Mitchum turns vigilante and blasts Luca outside the court building.

Competently directed, HIT LIST is a Feds vs. the Mafia adventure with enough professional gloss to lift it out of the ordinary. Boasting expert second-unit work, HIT LIST is crammed with enough edge-of-seat car chases and assassination gambits to satisfy hardcore action fans. The film's problem lies in its script, which is more ambitious than those of most action movies, yet fails to develop the potential of its best ideas. A parallel is drawn between the reprobate DeSalvo's love for his kid and good citizen Jack's feelings for his son. Lending additional depth to the standard cops-and-robbers formula, this intriguing comparison transforms the film into an offbeat buddy movie. But there are too many different plot strands and not enough time is available to allow a substantial

relationship to develop between DeSalvo and Jack. As a result their unusual relationship becomes an interesting sidebar rather than the core of the film.

Other plot details are left dangling. When the judge blows the case with a prejudicial statement, it is left to the viewer to make the less-than-clear connection between this action and Luca's original plan to bribe the judge. Moreover, the key courtroom scenes are weakened by the director's failure to cross-cut pointedly between Jack's mission and DeSalvo's attempts to drag out the proceedings. As scripted, the climax is mired in a static Perry-Mason-Revisited treatment. At this point, the film leaves all logic behind and careens out of control, presenting Caleek as an unstoppable, HALLOWEEN-style killer. With its interest in male bonding and father-son relationships, HIT LIST could have been engrossing without resorting to this kind of annoying manipulation.

Yet for all its failure to follow through, HIT LIST rates high on the excitement scale. Several polished performances bring some meaty characters to life: most notably Rossi's complex dishonorable criminal/honorable father and Napier's dying fed, who's driven to ignore the law he's dedicated himself to upholding. Are the FBI's methods that dissimilar from the mob's? HIT LIST serves up slam-bang entertainment with more than enough zest to compensate for its shortcomings. (*Violence, profanity, drugs, adult situations.*)

d, William Lustig; p, Paul Hertzberg and Jef Richard; w, John Goff and Peter Brosnan (based on a story by Aubrey K. Rattan); ph, James Lemmo; ed, David Kern; m, Gary Schyman; prod d, Pamela Marcotte; art d, Pamela Marcotte; set d, Michael Warga; stunts, Spiro Razatos; cos, Elizabeth Gower-Grudzinski

Action/Thriller   (PR:O MPAA:R)

HOLLYWOOD HOT TUBS II: EDUCATING CRYSTAL

100m Alimar/LIVE c

Jewel Shepard (*Crystal Landers*), Patrick Day (*Jason Bizmark*), David Tiefen (*Gary Mathers*), Remy O'Neill (*Pamela Landers*), Bart Braverman (*Prince Ahmet*), Phil Diskin (*Nahbib*), J.P. Bumstead (*Mr. Darby*), Michael Pataki (*Professor Drewdon*), Rob Garrison (*Billy Dare*), Dayna Danika (*Sandy*), Martina Castle (*Hardy Mathers*), Tally Chanel (*Mindy Wright*), Spice Williams, Greg Finley, and Patty Toy

Those who remember the original HOLLYWOOD HOT TUBS (1984) — or who have vainly tried to forget it — may recall that Crystal Landers was a grotesquely caricatured Valley Girl, the daughter of a spa owner. In this installment of the epic saga, mom Pamela (Remy O'Neill) enrolls Crystal (Jewel Shepard, repeating her role from the first film) in a night-school business course, where she meets Jason (Patrick Day), a glib yuppie-in-training who tries to educate the comely lass in the proper diction and attire for the financial world. Meanwhile, Pamela's heart is stolen by an oily Arab prince; naturally, the desert scoundrel's chauffeur, Gary (David Tiefen), falls for Crystal. When he overhears Prince Ahmet (Bart Braverman) plotting a hostile takeover of the Landers' hot-tub business, Gary warns Crystal, and they set out to prevent Pamela's wedding to Ahmet by photographing the lusty prince with a bikinied babe. There's also a subplot about a middle-aged hot-tub repairman who turns out to be a legendary rock 'n' roll guitarist — the guy who taught Pete Townsend and Jimi Hendrix. All this and a pie fight too.

Ostensibly a comedy, HOLLYWOOD HOT TUBS II doesn't provide a single laugh. The pacing is tortuously slow, and the Arab portrayals are embarrassingly racist. Even if you are able to find some amusement in Crystal and her, like, mannerisms, she's only on-screen for about a third of the running time. Under better circumstances, Day's fast-talking capitalist boy wonder would have been fun, but here he's just part of the inanity. Tiefen's stuck with a character gimmick that wore out ages ago; he's an aspiring pulp novelist who continually dictates hardboiled narration to himself. There are also numerous topless scenes, none of which involve the principal actors, despite a home-video ad campaign featuring a scantily clad Shepard. The film also offers a bawdy closing theme, "Educating Crystal Rap" (Kirkman Ridd, Patrick "Sore Throat" Day, Sammy "The Beach" Klien, performed by Whitey Got No Soul). (*Nudity, sexual situations, profanity, adult situations.*)

d, Ken Raich; p, Mark Borde and Ken Raich; w, Brent V. Friedman; ph, Areni Milo; ed, Michael Hoggan; m, John Lombardo and Bill Bodine; prod d, Thomas Cost; art d, Jack Licursi; stunts, Eddie Braun

Comedy   (PR:O MPAA:R)

HOME ALONE

98m Hughes/FOX c

Macaulay Culkin (*Kevin McCallister*), Joe Pesci (*Harry*), Daniel Stern (*Marv*), John Heard (*Peter*), Roberts Blossom (*Marley*), Catherine O'Hara (*Kate*), Angela Goethals (*Linnie*), Devin Rattray (*Buzz*), Gerry Bamman (*Uncle Frank*), Hillary Wolf (*Megan*), John Candy (*Gus Polinski*), Larry Hankin (*Officer

Balzak), Michael C. Maronna *(Jeff)*, Kristen Minter *(Heather)*, Campeanu Daiana *(Sondra)*, Jedediah Cohen *(Rod)*, Kieran Culkin *(Fuller)*, Senta Moses *(Tracy)*, Anna Slotky *(Brook)*, Terrie Snell *(Aunt Leslie)*, Jeffrey Wiseman *(Mitch Murphy)*, Virginia Smith *(Georgette)*, Matt Doherty *(Steffan)*, Ralph Foody *(Johnny, 1st Gangster)*, Michael Guido *(Snakes, 2nd Gangster)*, Ray Toler *(Uncle Rod)*, Billie Bird *(Woman at Airport)*, Bill Erwin *(Man at Airport)*, Clarke Devereux *(Officer Devereux)*, Dan Charles Zulcoski *(Pizza Boy)*, Lynn Mansbach *(French Woman)*, Peter Siragusa *(Lineman)*, Alan Wilder *(Scranton Ticket Agent)*, Hope Davis *(French Ticket Agent)*, Dianne B. Shaw *(Airline Counter Person)*, Tracy Connor *(Check Out Girl)*, Jim Ryan *(Stock Boy)*, Kenneth Hudson Campbell *(Santa Claus)*, Sandra Macat *(Santa's Elf)*, Mark Beltzman *(Stosh)*, Ann Whitney *(Drugstore Clerk)*, Richard J. Firfer *(Store Manager)*, Jim Ortlieb *(Herb, Drugstore Clerk)*, Kate Johnson *(Police Operator)*, Jean-Claude Sciore *(French Gate Agent)*, Monica Devereux *(Flight Attendant)*, Gerry Becker, Victor Cole *(Officers)*, Porscha Radcliffe, Brittany Radcliffe *(Cousins)*, Michael Hansen, Peter Pantaleo *(Airport Drivers)*, Edward Bruzan, Frank R. Cernugel, John Hardy, Eddie Korosa, Robert Okrzesik, Leo Perion, and Vince Waidzulis *(Polka Band Members)*

With its box-office receipts carrying over strongly into 1991, HOME ALONE was not only the most successful 1990 release but the highest grossing comedy of all time. It also made a star out of a ten-year-old kid named Macaulay Culkin. As usual for a John Hughes film, the movie is set in north-suburban Chicago, opening with a huge gathering at the McCallister household on the eve of the family's departure for a Christmas vacation in Europe. Eight-year-old Kevin McCallister (Culkin) is the object of everyone's scorn (he's constantly referred to as a "dweeb" or a "jerk") and even gets mistakenly blamed for a disastrous spill in the kitchen. Exiled to his room by his mother (Catherine O'Hara), Kevin fatefully wishes that his family would "all disappear." The next morning, he awakens to find himself all alone in the house, and, filled with guilt that he may have wished his family members away, he runs to his parents' room where he cowers under the covers of their bed. In truth, the rest of the McCallister clan is on a plane heading for Europe, unaware that Kevin has been left behind. When Kevin's mother finally realizes he's missing, she frantically begins making arrangements to get back to him. Kevin, however, is starting to adapt to his solitude and begins to do things he could never get away with if his parents were home. Soon the responsibilities of being alone in an adult world start to take their toll, and Kevin must learn to shop, cook, and clean the house. He starts to enjoy his responsibilities, taking pride in his daily accomplishments and becoming as much of an adult as an eight-year-old who is still afraid of the basement furnace can be. The imaginary threat posed by the furnace soon gives way to a very real danger when a pair of bumbling burglars (Joe Pesci and Daniel Stern) set their sights on breaking into the McCallister residence. In defending the homestead, Kevin proves to be an extraordinarily clever and resourceful little fellow as he arranges an elaborate system of booby traps that successfully thwarts the thieves.

The first half of HOME ALONE features the sugar-coated sentimentality that can usually be found in a Hughes film, while the second half is full of unanticipated sadism. There is nothing funny about watching two men being systematically tortured and maimed for 20 minutes (a close-up of Stern's bare foot slipping slowly down a six-inch nail is the film's most ghastly image). As directed by Chris Columbus (HEARTBREAK HOTEL), the film's slapstick falls flat and only the pain remains. Yet the film's message seems even more disturbing than its violence. This could be the first comedy — it's certainly the first holiday film — which focuses on child abuse. HOME ALONE is essentially about a kid who is systematically abused by a thoughtless family. He takes out his anger on the two closest representations of adulthood, the thieves (who also represent the evil city dwellers who pose a threat to the serene suburbs, a theme often found in the work of Hughes, as well as in Columbus' ADVENTURES IN BABYSITTING). As Kevin shoots pellets into the intruders and takes a blowtorch to their heads, he is directing the hostility he feels toward his parents at these two guys. It seems that in addition to the other responsibilities he has to assume as he tries to function in the adult world, he must also become abusive — it's all part of growing.

Aside from the film's disturbing subtext, it simply isn't all that funny. The jokes are stiff and familiar (*must* John Candy appear in all of John Hughes' productions, and *must* he always play the same guy?). The dialog is crude and the acting ranges from fair (O'Hara) to pitiful (Pesci and Stern). The only really likable thing about the film is Culkin (UNCLE BUCK, JACOB'S LADDER). He is an uncommonly natural child actor, but even he doesn't always survive the tiresome gags (him shaving once is funny; three times is tedious). The film earned two Oscar nominations, for its score by John Williams and for the song "Somewhere in My Memory" by Williams and Leslie Bricusse. *(Violence, profanity.)*

d, Chris Columbus; p, John Hughes; w, John Hughes; ph, Julio Macat; ed, Raja Gosnell; m, John Williams; prod d, John Muto; art d, Dan Webster; set d, Bill

Fosser and Karen Fletcher-Trujillo; spec, Bill Purcell; stunts, Freddie Hice; cos, Jay Hurley; makeup, Kim Phillips and Kenny Myers

Comedy   (PR:C   MPAA:PG)

HOMER & EDDIE

99m Kings Road — Borman-Cady/Skouras c

James Belushi *(Homer Lanza)*, Whoopi Goldberg *(Edwina "Eddie" Cervi)*, Karen Black *(Belle)*, Nancy Parsons *(Maid)*, Anne Ramsey *(Edna)*, Beah Richards *(Linda Cervi)*, Vincent Schiavelli *(Priest)*, Tracey Walter *(Tommy Dearly)*, Ernestine McClendon *(Esther)*, Angelyne *(Blonde)*, John Waters *(Robber)*, Robert Glaudini, Jim Mapp, James Thiel, Jeffrey Thiel, Andy Jarrel, and Wayne Grace

The fate of Andrei Konchalovsky's once brilliant and visionary HOMER & EDDIE is one of the saddest stories of the 1990 film year. The picture's original releasing company, Kings Road, went out of business during the movie's post-production. As a result the film sat on the shelf for a year, waiting for a distributor. Eventually it was picked up by Cineplex Odeon Films, but before the company agreed to release the picture, several changes were demanded: an appalling score was added, scenes were cut, and, most upsetting of all, the ending was made "more upbeat." But even after these changes were made, Cineplex Odeon dropped HOMER & EDDIE. Finally, the film was picked up by Skouras Pictures and given an extremely limited release (shown for a week in one theater in two cities) before it was added to the endless list of straight-to-video releases. This movie definitely deserved a better fate.

Beginning in Arizona, the story of HOMER & EDDIE centers on the relationship between two misfits: Homer Lanza (James Belushi), an innocent, mentally retarded dishwasher in his mid-30s, and Eddie Cervi (Whoopi Goldberg), a recently escaped mental patient, given to fits of rage that sometimes turn violent. The two become traveling companions after Homer, trying to hitchhike to Oregon to visit his dying father, whom he hasn't seen in 20 years, is robbed by a pair of criminals (one of whom is played by director John Waters). Coming across Homer in a junkyard, Eddie decides to help him get to Oregon. Homer is thrilled to acquire this new friend, but soon Eddie's unstable mental condition begins to take its toll. After using a stolen credit card to pay for a meal, Eddie leaves Homer to explain things to a meat-cleaver-wielding cook; when Eddie realizes that Homer has never been with a woman, she promptly robs a convenience store to pay for a night in a brothel for her companion. The two argue about the existence of God (Homer believes; Eddie doesn't) and the importance of honesty, but these arguments eventually precipitate seizures for Eddie, who has a brain tumor. It has been 10 years since Eddie has seen *her* mother, and Homer convinces his friend that they should stop in Oakland to visit her. However, the reunion is a painful one. Eddie's mother (Beah Richards) proves a depressed soul; obsessed with her impending death, she spends most of her time in a cemetery, waiting beside her own tombstone. Leaving Eddie's mother, the two continue their trek to Oregon, but along the way Eddie kills a gas station attendant, prompting the panicked Homer to contemplate going it alone. Only after Eddie reveals that she has but a month to live does Homer forgive her, insisting that she go to church and confess her sins. When the priest (Vincent Schiavelli) suggests that Eddie turn herself in, she gives up on religion once and for all. Homer and Eddie finally make it to Oregon, where Homer discovers that his father has died two days before their arrival. It soon becomes clear that Homer was never meant to come home; he has been all but forgotten by his embarrassed family. Realizing that he has been abandoned by his parents, Homer breaks down at the funeral home and confronts his mother. That night, during a town festival, Homer and Eddie become separated. When an old friend offers him a job, Homer decides to make his home again in Oregon. Meanwhile, Eddie (who has had strange visions of a man wearing a robe, dragging a cross through the streets) is compelled to rip off yet another convenience store, but this time the results are fatal, separating the two friends forever.

Although the core of HOMER & EDDIE remains more or less intact, many of Konchalovsky's stronger ideas are lost in the edited version. (The original was publicly screened at a handful of film festivals.) Most notably, the powerful religious subtext of the original is completely missing from the release version (in the stunning final moments of the uncut film, the dying Eddie's sins are forgiven by a madman dressed like Christ). What's more, many of the film's most powerful scenes are either marred by the horrendous music or eliminated. Still, HOMER & EDDIE, like all of Konchalovsky's work (including the brain-numbing actioner TANGO AND CASH), is worth seeing. Full of rich insights into weirdly compelling, unfamiliar characters, this film is yet another example of Konchalovsky's growing adeptness at depicting an America few people know, and in this way recalls the work of Jonathan Demme and David Lynch. It is also beautifully photographed (by Lajos Koltai) and sharply edited (by Henry Richardson). And although Patrick Cirillo's screenplay sometimes becomes predictable, the sheer intensity and conviction of Konchalovsky's direction give it a fresh feel. Soviet-born Konchalovsky (whose impressive filmography includes such brilliant American productions as MARIA'S LOV-ERS, RUNAWAY TRAIN, and SHY PEOPLE, as well as the Russian master-piece SIBERIADE) is a director with fierce vision and a bold style. Offering unique characters in complex situations, his movies are anchored by a strong point of view and loads of interesting subtext. HOMER & EDDIE is no exception, and although most of the emotional power of Konchalovsky's original version is gone, the director's intensions are still evident.

Those intentions are kept alive in HOMER & EDDIE's exceptional perfor-mances. Konchalovsky has always been a terrific director of actors, and here he coaxes some extraordinary work from what appears at first glance to be a limited cast. Goldberg is mesmerizing, creating a well-rounded, profoundly emotional character whose convincing fits of rage are both scary and sad. Richards, Karen Black (as the madam of the brothel), and Schiavelli are all terrific, but the real surprise here is Belushi, whose performance is nothing less than great. Normally considered a comedic actor, Belushi plays Homer with just the right combination of pathos (the confrontation scene with his mother is spellbinding) and humor (Homer's fabricated accounts of his boxing glory are wonderful). Belushi and Goldberg, both products of improvisational training, work together like a well-oiled machine, and the result is an extraordinarily poignant and powerful onscreen relationship. That Belushi and Goldberg have made two inherently strange and potentially unlikable characters warm and human is in itself no mean achievement.

Despite the film's radical editing, a number of individual scenes still hold up wonderfully—notably, the scene in which Homer dances with Eddie on a pier, the creepy moments between Eddie and her mother, and Eddie's trauma when she hears planes flying overhead. Unfortunately, by changing the ending, the film's distributors have greatly diminished the power of HOMER & EDDIE, and the potent scenes that remain appear random and disconnected. Why all of these changes had to be made is still a mystery (especially since Cineplex Odeon ultimately didn't release the film). But the upshot is that a near masterpiece has been transformed into an only partly successful, too formulaic "buddy" film. Nevertheless, as the work of Konchalovsky, HOMER & EDDIE, even in its present form, contains moments of genius. What happened to this film should be against the law. (Violence, brief nudity, profanity, adult situations.)

d, Andrei Konchalovsky; p, Moritz Borman and James Cady; w, Patrick Cirillo; ph, Lajos Koltai; ed, Henry Richardson; m, Eduard Artemyev; md, David Chackler; prod d, Michel Levesque; art d, P. Michael Johnson; cos, Katherine Kady Dover

Drama   (PR:C-O MPAA:R)

HONEYMOON ACADEMY

94m Trans World—Sarlui—Diamant—Fidelity—Paul Maslansky/Triumph c

(AKA: FOR BETTER OR FOR WORSE)

Kim Cattrall (Chris), Robert Hays (Sean McDonald), Leigh Taylor-Young (Doris Kent), Charles Rocket (Alex), Lance Kinsey (Lance), Christopher Lee (Lazos), Jonathan Banks (Pitt), Jerry Lazarus, and Max Alexander

HONEYMOON ACADEMY brings a diverse group of talented actors and comedians into a third-rate spy spoof. Simple minded and badly written, HON-EYMOON ACADEMY stars Robert Hays (AIRPLANE!) as Sean, a rather dim-witted intellectual who falls in love at first sight with Chris (Kim Cattrall). Though his beloved is actually employed by the State Department, working as a courier who pays off blackmailers, Sean believes her cover as a travel agent. The two are married within six weeks, and given a European vacation as a wedding present by Chris' boss. She apparently isn't much smarter than her new husband, and doesn't realize the "gift" is a scheme to get her to do one last job. International crook Lazos (Christopher Lee, who is completely wasted in his cameo role) has made a set of perfect counterfeit $20 bill plates that he wants to sell to the US government and Chris, of course, is the only go-between he trusts. She can't tell Sean about any of this, making for humorous complications when her old spy friends show up, as do a group of enemy agents who try to keep her from getting the plates. When Chris' meeting with Lazos goes sour and he is shot, Lazos—in a scene reminiscent of Hitchcock's THE MAN WHO KNEW TOO MUCH—hands Sean a clue to the whereabouts of the plates and whispers into the bookworm's ear before dying. A series of car chases involving Chris, Sean, and a whole slew of spies, a totally ridiculous escape, and a not-so-sur-prising plot twist ensue before a funny ending rounds out this disjointed film.

It's hard to tell what director-cowriter Gene Quintano wanted to accomplish with HONEYMOON ACADEMY. Each time the film begins to show some evidence of creativity, Quintano moves it in another direction. The slapstick-based comedy of Chris and Sean's honeymoon (which, unknown to Sean, is really a spy mission) ends with Lazos' entrance, moving into Hitchcockian spoof. Quintano fails to follow through with that spoof, however; instead, he gives us a car chase and the Three Stooges of spying. Genuinely creative and funny, the apparent conclusion follows, only to be ruined by a poor plot twist. Then

Quintano comes up with another genuinely humorous moment at the film's very end.

Perhaps Quintano meant HONEYMOON ACADEMY to be more than just a cute little spy comedy. But if he wanted to impress us with clever cinematic references, he should have followed through in his take-offs of older movies; and if he wanted to make an action film, he needn't have cast romantic leads Hays and Cattrall. As it is, HONEYMOON ACADEMY fails even as a caper comedy, because its reach so far exceeds its grasp. It's a very disappointing film. (Violence.)

d, Gene Quintano; p, Tony Anthony; w, Gene Quintano and Jerry Lazarus (based on a story by Gene Quintano); ph, John Cabrera; ed, Hubert C. de la Bouillerie; m, Robert Folk; stunts, Alain Petit

Comedy/Spy   (PR:C MPAA:PG-13)

HOSTILE TAKEOVER

93m Overland/SC c

(AKA: OFFICE PARTY)

David Warner (Eugene Bracken), Kate Vernon (Sally Ladd), Jayne Eastwood (Mrs. Talmadge), John Vernon (Mayor), Will Lyman (Police Chief), Michael Ironside (Larry Gaylord), Graeme Campbell (Sergeant), and Anthony Sherwood

Set in Canada and based on Michael A. Gilbert's novel Office Party, HOS-TILE TAKEOVER is too slackly directed to take full advantage of some promisingly bizarre situations. Nonetheless, HOSTILE TAKEOVER manages to keep its grip on viewers through a solid basic plot. Eugene Bracken (David Warner), a milquetoast office worker, plans a surprise for the Saturday overtime shift he's working with domineering boss Larry Gaylord (Michael Ironside), hot-to-trot coworker Sally Ladd (Kate Vernon), and outwardly placid secretary Mrs. Talmadge (Jayne Eastwood). Although nice-guy Eugene has never pre-viously shown any noticeable symptoms of psychosis, he has decided to take over the office and hold his coworkers hostage. Eugene is motivated not by politics, nor by monetary gain, nor grievances against the company, but simply wants to call the shots himself for a few choice days. Flashbacks reveal that he has suffered at the hands of an abusive, militaristic father, and before this harrowing weekend is over, his captive coworkers will reveal some secrets of their own as a result of the pressure. While civic and police forces outside try to placate him, Eugene enjoys being in charge. Unfortunately, the town's mayor (John Vernon) opposes a plan by the police chief (Will Lyman) to appease the hostage-taker, and instead instructs a SWAT team leader to blow Eugene away if given a chance to do so. As tension builds in this Canadian version of a Mexican stand off, Eugene angrily shoots Larry's chair out from under him and then humiliates Mrs. Talmadge, forcing the secretary—who has slapped his face in her emotional distress—to strip to her underwear. After this incident, the captives realize that Eugene's the boss, even as they consider escape possibilities. Constantly muttering that "the circle is closing," Eugene is enraged when a radio report brands him a maniac. As the weekend continues, it is revealed that Sally has had sexual relations with a company big-wig and resents having been passed over for the position given to Larry. While Eugene stymies any police move to end his siege, the women hostages discuss office politics and sexism, Mrs. Talmadge confiding to Sally that she had an abortion as a teenager. When the secretary remains in the ladies room too long, Eugene bursts inside the restroom's door, but the other hostages don't have time to grab the weapon he leaves behind. Picking up clues from their phone conversations, the police chief realizes that Eugene has been making references to T.S. Eliot's "The Hollow Men"; inside, as the hostages attempt to get their poetry-quoting captor intoxicated, the "office party" shifts into high gear, with drinking and wild dancing. Tempers flare when Sally hints that Larry makes his wife sleep with other executives to facilitate his corporate rise; she even threatens to castrate him with scissors, but stops when Mrs. Talmadge vomits all over the intended victim. Angered by her accusations, Larry becomes unhinged after watching Sally seduce Eugene. Going off the deep end, he attacks Sally, and is shot to death by Eugene. Crazed by her ordeal and this killing, Mrs. Talmadge believes she is back in high school and somersaults out of the window. Realizing that his power has slipped away from him, Eugene stands at the window and allows himself to be shot. The office party is over, and three people are dead.

HOSTILE TAKEOVER's intriguing central situation and complex psycho-logical power games might have resulted in a top-notch thriller if George Mihalka's direction weren't so plodding. It's also obvious that Gilbert and Stephen Zoller, the screenwriters, would have liked to squeeze in more material concerning the characters' pasts as a means of fleshing out the frustration that links the captives and their captor, a tactic that both enhances and detracts from the film's effectiveness. Although the flashbacks and surreal dream sequences are easily the most arresting passages in the film, HOSTILE TAKEOVER generally captures the hard feelings that exist in the competitive corporate world—the rampant sexism, the buzz of white-collar drones worked to death and then replaced, and the screw-or-be-screwed office politics, with their sexual implications. But the film fails to build momentum and create a sufficient level of suspense because it bogs down in plot exposition and character background, cutting away for character revelations when it should be detailing escape attempts or showing more concrete evidence of Eugene's obsession. Thrillers often give short shrift to developing motivation, but HOSTILE TAKEOVER errs in correcting this oversight by failing to provide the requisite thriller tautness. Especially damaging is the filmmakers' habit of cutting away from the hostages to show the infighting and problems of the cops and city officials handling the crisis. The cross-cutting is not sufficiently acute to build much tension, and distracts from the crescendo of violence brewing in the office, which is the real source of the film's suspense.

Only in fits and starts does HOSTILE TAKEOVER succeed. While Warner is only adequate as the power-hungry terrorist, Ironside, Eastwood, and Kate Vernon are exemplary as the walking wounded who are taken hostage. As these three actors bait one other or break down in confessions, we glimpse the powerhouse movie this misfired thriller might have been. Potentially powerful subject matter—with its subtext of contemporary violence and worker alienation—comes to life in spurts. Though sporadic, the emotional excitement in HOSTILE TAKEOVER makes this flawed film far from negligible. *(Sexual situations, violence, substance abuse, profanity, nudity, adult situations.)*

d, George Mihalka; p, George Flak; w, Stephen Zoller and Michael A. Gilbert (based on the novel *Office Party* by Michael A. Gilbert); ph, Ludek Bogner; ed, Stan Cole; m, Aaron Davis and Billy Bryans; prod d, John Meighan; art d, Bora Bulajic

Thriller   (PR:O MPAA:R)

HOT SPOT, THE

130m Paul Lewis/Orion c

Don Johnson *(Harry Madox)*, Virginia Madsen *(Dolly Harshaw)*, Jennifer Connelly *(Gloria Harper)*, Charles Martin Smith *(Lon Gulik)*, William Sadler *(Frank Sutton)*, Jerry Hardin *(George Harshaw)*, Barry Corbin *(Sheriff)*, Leon Rippy *(Deputy Tate)*, Jack Nance *(Julian Ward)*, Virgil Frye *(Deputy Buck)*, John Hawker *(Uncle Mort)*, Margaret Bowman *(Woman at Gas Station)*, Debra Cole *(Irene Davey)*, Karen Culley *(Cowgirl)*, Cody Haynes *(Cowboy)*, George Haynes *(Mr. Haynes)*, James Harrell *(Elderly Man)*, Edith Mills *(Elderly Woman)*, Shannon Quinlan *(Table Dancer)*, and Roosevelt Williams *(Grey Ghost)*

Harry Madox (Don Johnson) is a man with a past, a feckless past of drifting and scamming. He usually manages to get out of town just before things blow up on him, then heads out in search of a new town where he can start the sorry business all over again. A town like hot, dusty Taylor, Texas, for example. It's not much more than a strip joint, a used car lot, and a few tired houses baking in the sun; little to catch a man's eye, you might think, but that would depend on what the man wanted. Madox is a classic pulp hero, the kind of man who blows through stories by James M. Cain and Jim Thompson, David Goodis and Charles Williams, on whose novel *(Hell Hath No Fury)* THE HOT SPOT was based. He's a hustler and a grifter who's got all the angles covered. He figures all women are whores and all men are dupes, and he's just waiting for that one big score that will change his life. Madox cons his way into a job at Harshaw's Used Car Lot, figuring it's the best deal in town, and soon runs up against the two women who will drive his every thought and action.

First, there's Dolly Harshaw (Virginia Madsen), a blonde bombshell in a pink convertible who was put on earth for the express purpose of making men sweat and squirm. That Madox works for her husband (naturally he's *much* older than she) only adds to her appeal, and the way she fondles the gearshift and rubs her thighs together sends a message it would take a blind man to miss. The town may be hot, but Dolly is hotter. Then there is Gloria Harper (Jennifer Connelly), a long drink of water with a virginal smile that seems to hide some secret sorrow; she's Harshaw's bookkeeper and the sight of her patiently typing and filing, that evasive, slightly sad look on her face, is too much for Madox to resist. Soon he's involved with both women and working out what seems to be a foolproof plan to rob the local bank. Needless to say, things don't go exactly right for Madox, largely because Dolly proves to be every bit the conniver she is.

Director Dennis Hopper's terminally cool sensibilities ought to be the perfect match for such ludicrously overheated material, and sometimes THE HOT SPOT comes very close to making it all work. Rather than playing the *film noir* cliches for revisionist irony, Hopper lays them on the line as though they were brand new, and his faith in the power of repressed eroticism and violence is bracing. The streets shimmer, the cars reflect lethal shards of sunlight, everybody sweats and the thermometer inches past the 100-degree mark. This is the same overheated territory David Lynch explored in WILD AT HEART, delivered without a self-conscious smirk. But THE HOT SPOT doesn't quite come together. Part of the problem is its length; at two hours and ten minutes it meanders rather than building up a head of steam and barreling straight through logic and plausibility

on the way to Hell. And part of the problem is Don Johnson; though he turns in a perfectly respectable performance, he doesn't have the right kind of sleaze for the role. In a movie that cries out for a rangy, weathered loner whose sex appeal lies in his apparent indifference—Scott Glenn or Lance Henriksen, for example—Johnson is salon-tanned and smarmy. It's difficult to get past his smooth, pampered flesh to the brutalized soul of Harry Madox. In addition, the madonna/whore dichotomy looks particularly dated—Dolly is such an over-the-top slut and Gloria such an untouchable virgin that it plays like a porno movie convention, bringing out the impulse to nudge and snicker. THE HOT SPOT is stylish enough to get away with it all for awhile, but in the end it's dragged down by the sheer weight of flesh and sweat. *(Nudity, sexual situations, profanity.)*

d, Dennis Hopper; p, Paul Lewis; w, Nona Tyson and Charles Williams (based on the novel *Hell Hath No Fury* by Williams); ph, Ueli Steiger; ed, Wende Phifer Mate; m, Jack Nitzsche; md, Michael Hoenig; prod d, Cary White; art d, John Frick and Michael Sullivan; spec, Dennis Dion; stunts, Eddy Donno; cos, Mary Kay Stolz; makeup, Charles Balazs

Thriller   (PR:O MPAA:R)

HOUSE PARTY

100m New Line c

Christopher Reid *(Kid)*, Robin Harris *(Pop)*, Christopher Martin *(Play)*, Martin Lawrence *(Bilal)*, Tisha Campbell *(Sidney)*, A.J. Johnson *(Sharane)*, Paul Anthony *(Stab)*, Bowlegged Lou *(Pee-Wee)*, B. Fine *(Zilla)*, Edith Fields *(Principal)*, Kelly Jo Minter *(La Donna)*, Clifton Powell *(Older Brother)*, Verda Bridges *(Sharane's Sister)*, Desi Arnez Hines III *(Peanut)*, Lou D. Washington *(Uncle Otis)*, Kimi Sung *(Sunni)*, Barry Diamond, Michael Pniewski *(Cops)*, Diana Mendoza, Randy Harris *(Lovers)*, Barry Wiggins *(Waiter)*, George Clinton *(D.J.)*, Ellaraino *(Sidney's Mom)*, J. Jay Saunders *(Sidney's Dad)*, Myra J. *(Guest)*, Norma Donaldson *(Mildred)*, Eugene Allen *(Groove)*, Darryl Mitchell *(Chill)*, Belal Miller *(Herman)*, Shaun Baker *(Clint)*, Leah Aldridge *(Benita)*, Val Gamble *(La Shay)*, John Witherspoon *(Mr. Strickland)*, Bebe Drake-Massey *(Mrs. Strickland)*, Richard McGregor *(Evrette)*, Anthony Johnson *(E.Z.E.)*, Ronn Riser *(Guy)*, D-Zire *(Girl No. 1)*, Bentley Evans *(Tall Teen)*, Reginald Hudlin, Warrington Hudlin *(Crooks)*, George Logan *(Pimp)*, Rodney Hill *(Albert)*, Cliff Frazier *(Brutus)*, Cederick Hardman *(Rock)*, Stan Haze *(Hatchett)*, Chino Williams *(Fats)*, Jaime Cardriche *(Tattoo)*, and Alexander Folk *(Guard)*

In recent years, several black filmmakers have caught the attention of critics and have begun surmounting the ridiculous obstacles set in their way by Hollywood and society in general. This growing force of directors includes major talents like Keenen Ivory Wayans (whose hilarious I'M GONNA GIT YOU SUCKA made more money than anyone expected), Robert Townsend, and, of course, Spike Lee. They have paved the way for more filmmakers to make movies by blacks, for blacks, and about blacks. No longer are African-Americans forced to make films cleverly structured around the stereotypical characters of pimps and vigilante cops (although the "blaxploitation" genre of the 70s, in which these characters had currency, was a vital and serious movement in the history of cinema that produced terrific movies like SHAFT; TRUCK TURNER; and the stunning BLACK CAESAR). Without being labeled "renegades"—as was Melvin Van Peebles (WATERMELON MAN; SWEET SWEETBACK'S BAADASSSSS SONG), for example—black filmmakers can now make films dealing with serious subjects, containing strong messages and covering a variety of styles and subjects, maybe even styles and subjects that (gasp!) whites won't understand. It took a long time for this creative freedom to be achieved and the current batch of directors are taking full advantage of it. (A notable exception is Eddie Murphy, who continues to make sloppy and narrow films, filled with appalling stereotypes and nastiness.) Two new members of this current batch are Reginald and Warrington Hudlin, a team of brothers out of East St. Louis, Illinois. With Reggie directing and Warrington producing, the Hudlins have collaborated to expand Reggie's Harvard thesis film from a short into a feature, and the result is HOUSE PARTY, a low-budget comedy that is a seriously funny look at a night in the lives of some black teenagers.

The film is more of a portrait than a story. Kid (Christopher Reid, one half of the rap duo Kid N' Play) is dying to go to a party hosted by his buddy Play (Christopher Martin, the other half). Unfortunately, Kid has gotten into some trouble with the local bullies (played by three members of the hiphop band Full Force) at school and, after a note from the principal's office arrives at home, he is grounded by his strict father (the late, great Robin Harris; see Obituaries). Determined to go to Play's party, especially since two of the prettiest girls in school are going to be there, Kid risks life and limb to sneak out of the house while Pop sleeps in front of the TV, which is playing the blaxploitation classic DOLEMITE (the audio of which provides one of the films bigger laughs). He makes it to the party and gets to know the girls, one of whom has a crush on him, while dancing up a storm. The evening is not without its problems, though. Kid is pursued constantly by the aforementioned thugs, a pair of obnoxious white cops hassle him for no reason, and his hot-under-the-collar dad shows up at the party looking for him. By the time the night is over—after rap duels, chase scenes, and kissing sessions — Kid has been beaten up, locked in a refrigerator, thrown in jail, and nearly gang-raped by a group of convicts. Morning finally comes, and he sneaks into his room, thinking that he has successfully fooled Pop and that his travails are over. But his dad appears with belt in hand, telling Kid, "Don't go to bed yet. Your ass is mine!"

Deceptively simple on the surface, HOUSE PARTY is a realistic depiction of black teenagers. Though its main purpose is obviously to provoke laughter—which it does, very often—it also provokes thought by dealing honestly, and never heavy-handedly, with a variety of subjects, including safe sex, teen drinking, class prejudice, and, in a roundabout way, racism. Reginald Hudlin has given his wide assortment of characters a great deal of intelligence, much more than usual for this kind of film, allowing each room to breathe and establish a personality. The secondary characters are painted in such uniquely funny strokes that they too come to life, particularly John Witherspoon's hilarious next-door neighbor, who complains about the music by saying, "Don't be playing that Public Enema stuff!" The female characters are treated with respect and grace (something Eddie Murphy should try); as wonderfully portrayed by A.J. Johnson, Tisha Campbell, and Kelly Jo Minter, they are shown to be intelligent and thoughtful young women, shown in most scenes to be smarter than the men. Stars Kid N' Play make a strong film debut, creating a fun, light image for themselves without sacrificing the edge of their music; their rap-duel scene is fast and funky. Kid, with his foot-high fade haircut (one character refers to him as "Eraserhead") and freckle-faced grin, handles the duties of "leading man" extremely well, giving a supremely likable performance. His nice turn is matched by his supporting players. Martin Lawrence, who was so good in DO THE RIGHT THING, is hilarious as the DJ of the party, particularly as he becomes increasingly upset when an obnoxious guest repeatedly bumps the table on which he is spinning records. (One of his favorite movies is BREAKIN', a joke which inspires the film's biggest laugh.) The Full Force bullies are uniformly funny (although Bowlegged Lou's high-pitched voice becomes quite tiresome), and Robin Harris is terrific, just as he was in DO THE RIGHT THING. Harris, whose best scene in the film was improvised, was a major talent who will be sorely missed. Rap and hiphop fans will also note the inspirational presence of Parliament-Funkadelic pioneer George Clinton in the cast.

Aside from its likable performances and message, HOUSE PARTY is a film that *moves* in every way possible. From the opening dream sequence to the final sight gag, the film sways to a funky contagious rhythm that will have most viewers rocking in their seats. The dance sequences are directed with such lively timing and slick camera movements that one can't help but bounce along. Reginald Hudlin is a terrific filmmaker who has a wonderfully assured feel for the camera. With cinematographer Peter Deming (who did impressive work in EVIL DEAD 2), he creates a high-energy visual playground that is never less than alive—at one point the camera even assumes a toilet's-eye view—and whose low budget is not evident on screen. The lively *mise-en-scene* enhances the comedy, complementing the jokes and running gags, which include the repeated showing of an obnoxious TV commercial and the endless supply of Dick Gregory diet drinks. With HOUSE PARTY, Hudlin has created one of the flat-out funniest films in a long time.

Nonetheless, HOUSE PARTY is not without flaws. Some jokes are flat, and the final sight gag doesn't work. Most disturbing, however, is Kid's jailhouse rap, performed when he is almost gang-raped by a group of convicts. It is homophobic and cruel, and completely out of character with the rest of the film. Kid's parting shot to his would-be attackers when he leaves the jail is a crotch-grabbing profanity, a strange ending to a strange scene. Why Hudlin chose to include this shockingly crude sequence is a mystery, because it is in no way essential to the film.

Aside from this glaring failure, HOUSE PARTY is topnotch all the way. Reggie Hudlin has burst onto the scene as a filmmaking force to be reckoned with. *(Profanity, adult situations.)*

d, Reginald Hudlin; p, Warrington Hudlin; w, Reginald Hudlin; ph, Peter Deming; ed, Earl Watson; m, Marcus Miller; prod d, Bryan Jones; art d, Susan Richardson; set d, Molly Flanegin; stunts, Eddie Smith; cos, Harold Evans; makup, Laini Thompson; chor, A.J. Johnson, Kid 'N Play, and Tisha Campbell

Comedy   (PR:C-O MPAA:R)

HOW TO MAKE LOVE TO A NEGRO WITHOUT GETTING TIRED

(Can./Fr.) 97m Stock — Molecule/Aska c

(COMMENT FAIRE L'AMOUR AVEC UN NEGRE SANS SE FATIGUER)

Issach de Bankole *(Man)*, Maka Kotto *(Bouba)*, Roberta Bizeau *(Miz Literature)*, Miriam Cyr *(Miz Suicide)*, Marie-Josee Gauthier *(Miz Mystic)*, Susan Almgren

(Miz Duras), Alexandra Innes *(Miz Oh My God)*, Nathalie Coupal *(Miz Disillusioned)*, Isabelle L'Ecuyer *(Miz Redhead)*, and Patricia Tulasne *(Miz Feminist)*

The Negro in question, called simply "Man" (Issach de Bankole), is a handsome writer who has recently moved to Montreal in the hope of finding fun, fortune, and fame—not necessarily in that order. He finds a roommate in the studious Bouba (Maka Kotto), an afficionado of tea, jazz, and Freud, and their cramped apartment quickly becomes the hub of an ever-expanding network of friends and lovers. Armed with an ancient portable typewriter rumored to have belonged to Chester Himes, Man spends the summer days polishing his come-ons and his summer nights sleeping with white women who can't wait to find out whether all the smutty rumors they've heard about black men are true. In his spare time he writes a book called, of course, *How to Make Love to a Negro Without Getting Tired*. Man's women don't have real names either, but—in contrast to his own aggressively nonjudgmental, all-encompassing moniker—they have designations. His main squeeze is Miz Literature (Roberta Bizeau) a wealthy, educated girl. She's mortified when her upper-class friends snigger about her sex life, but she's drawn to the exotic thrill of Man's blackness. The parade of other conquests includes Miz Suicide (Miriam Cyr) a reformed junkie in love with the idea of killing herself, or at least in love with talking about it; Miz Mystic (Marie-Josee Gauthier) who spent too much time in the ashram; Miz Duras (Susan Almgren), who wants to talk literature; and Miz Oh My God (Alexandra Innes), who talks dirty while she and Man have sex on the kitchen table. Then there's Miz Redhead (Isabelle L'Ecuyer), who resists being picked up while she waits in an endless line and Miz Feminist (Patricia Tulasne), who seizes the opportunity to denounce the patriarchal oppression inherent in cruising. Each holds dear a different cliche about black men: they're brutes, they're erotic athletes, they're happy all the time, they have insatiable carnal appetites, they're helpless victims of white subjugation, they're in touch with their jungle natures, they're gods in human form. Oh, la la! Man eventually finds time to finish his novel, nearly loses it in a fire set by jealous lowlifes, and triumphs in the end.

Based on the novel of the same title by Haitian writer Dany Laferriere, HOW TO MAKE LOVE TO A NEGRO WITHOUT GETTING TIRED is informed by the contemporary notion that the personal—and specifically the sexual—is political, and intends its observations to be trenchant, witty, and irreverent. But in the hands of Canadian director Jacques W. Benoit, all they amount to is another set of cliches: black men are feckless and oversexed, white women can't resist the lure of black flesh, and white men are stupid, effete, and viciously jealous. Black *women* don't even enter the picture, except in Man's barroom explanation of the hierarchy of sexual subservience, which begins with the premise that white men are on top, so everyone has to service them. White women come next, so they naturally look down the ladder to dominate black men. Black women are at the bottom of the heap, so they have to service everyone. The film itself, shapeless and shallow, neither supports nor undermines this model. In fact, its naivete is both puzzling and disturbingly disingenuous; though it purports to explore racial and sexual stereotypes, it merely perpetuates them with an ingratiating smile.

Shown with little fuss in Europe and Canada, HOW TO MAKE LOVE TO A NEGRO WITHOUT GETTING TIRED's titilating title and advertising materials (the poster shows a black man under a sheet that appears to cover an impossibly prodigious erection) generated some controversy in the US. Some theaters refused to book it, many newspapers (including the *New York Times*) refused to run its ads without copy changes, and the NAACP made a formal request that the distributor change the movie's name. *(Profanity, nudity, sexual situations.)*

d, Jacques W. Benoit; p, Richard Sadler, Ann Burke, and Henry Lange; w, Dany Laferriere and Richard Sadler (based on the novel by Dany Laferriere); ph, John Berrie; ed, Dominique Roy; m, Manu Dibango

Drama   (PR:C-O MPAA:NR)

HUNT FOR RED OCTOBER, THE

134m Mace Neufeld-Jerry Sherlock/Paramount c

Sean Connery *(Capt. Marko Ramius)*, Alec Baldwin *(Jack Ryan)*, Scott Glenn *(Capt. Bart Mancuso)*, Sam Neill *(Capt. Vasily Borodin)*, James Earl Jones *(Admiral James Greer)*, Joss Ackland *(Andrei Lysenko)*, Richard Jordan *(Jeffrey Pelt)*, Peter Firth *(Ivan Putin)*, Tim Curry *(Dr. Petrov)*, Courtney B. Vance *(Seaman Jones)*, Stellan Skarsgard *(Capt. Tupolev)*, Jeffrey Jones *(Skip Tyler)*, Timothy Carhart *(Bill Steiner)*, Larry Ferguson *(Chief of the Boat)*, Fred Dalton Thompson *(Admiral Painter)*, Daniel Davis *(Capt. Davenport)*, Tomas Arana *(Loginov)*, Ned Vaughn *(Seaman Beaumont)*, Anthony Peck *(Lt. Comdr. Thompson)*, Mark Draxton, Tom Fisher, Pete Antico *(Dallas Seamen)*, Ronald Guttman *(Lt. Melekhin)*, Michael George Benko *(Ivan)*, Anatoly Davydov, Ivan G'Vera *(Officers)*, Artur Cybulski *(Diving Officer)*, Sven-Ole Thorsen *(Russian COB)*, Michael Welden *(Kamarov)*, Boris Krutonog *(Slavin)*, Kenton Kovell, Radu

Gavor, Ivan Ivanov, Ping Wu, Herman Sinitzyn *(Red October Seamen)*, Christopher Janczar *(Andrei Bonovia)*, Vlado Benden, George Winston *(Konovalov Seamen)*, Don Oscar Smith *(Helicopter Pilot)*, Rick Ducommun *(Navigator C-2A)*, George H. Billy *(DSRV Officer)*, Reed Popovich *(Lt. Jim Curry)*, Andrew Divoff *(Andrei Amalric)*, Peter Zinner *(Adm. Padorin)*, Tony Veneto *(Padorin's Orderly)*, Ben Hartigan, Robert Buckingham *(Admirals at Briefing)*, Ray Reinhardt *(Jodge Moore at Briefing)*, F.J. O'Neil *(General at Briefing)*, A.C. Lyles, John McTiernan Sr. *(Advisors)*, David Sederholm *(Sunglasses)*, John Shepherd *(Foxtrot Pilot)*, William Bell Sullivan *(Lt. Cmdr. Mike Hewitt)*, Gates McFadden *(Caroline Ryan)*, Louise Borras *(Sally Ryan)*, and Denise E. James *(Stewardess)*

In spite of the high level of talent on board and at the helm, THE HUNT FOR RED OCTOBER is surprising mostly as a disappointment. It's not that RED OCTOBER is a terrible film, but it's not really a successful one, either. The film revolves around Marko Ramius (Sean Connery), a veteran Soviet sub commander who is guiding the new, super-advanced *Red October* submarine on its maiden mission as the story begins. Abruptly, Ramius murders the onboard political officer and burns his orders. *Red October* is supposed to participate in war games meant to showcase its ability to evade sonar detection and deliver a full load of nuclear missiles to major American targets. Ramius instead tells his crew that they will approach the US coastline to embarrass the American military. In fact, he has something very different in mind. When Ramius goes off course, factions within the US military and government suspect a sneak attack. The Soviets, who assume Ramius is defecting with their most advanced weaponry, float a cover story that Ramius has had a mental breakdown and intends to attack the US coast singlehandedly. Guided by CIA analyst Dr. Jack Ryan (Alec Baldwin), who happens to be an expert on Ramius, the American security brain trust has to decide whether the Russians are telling the truth. Then they must choose the appropriate response — either helping the Russians sink *Red October* (the FAIL SAFE scenario) or helping Ramius defect — as Ramius seeks to evade a search that appears to involve the entire Soviet navy, and that is spearheaded by a protege of Ramius who knows the commander at least as well as Ryan does.

It sounds pretty exciting and undoubtedly was exciting in Tom Clancy's best-seller, which served as the basis for the film. But on the screen, RED OCTOBER suffers from a bad case of bloated scenario. Perhaps in an effort to please the book's fans, the film tries to preserve the intricacies of the high-level maneuvering between the superpowers. It also keeps Clancy's hero, Dr. Ryan, at the forefront, as he decodes the strategic importance of Ramius' defection. Moreover, in an effort to engage action junkies (the audience that made RED OCTOBER director John McTiernan's DIE HARD and PREDATOR into box-office megahits), the film attempts to play up the underwater maneuvers, as Ramius outfoxes both the American and Russian submarines hovering in his wake.

In Aristotelian terms, RED OCTOBER lacks unities of place and action. In simpler terms, it should have stayed put, either above the surface or in the briny depths. Instead, the two major plots — two different movies, really — wind up neutralizing each other. Each time McTiernan cuts from one setting to the other, he's forced to start from scratch in rebuilding tension and involvement. Over the course of two hours-plus, the strain takes its toll on the film and on the audience. It doesn't help that the characters in the adaptation by Larry Ferguson (who appears as an officer on the American sub) and Donald Stewart are irritatingly thin. Ramius wants to defect so he can go fishing. His first officer (Sam Neill) wants to cruise around the US in an RV. They don't have lakes in Russia? But at least these characters have some motivation. Ryan is so lacking in substance viewers may find it hard to remember that he is the movie's hero.

The actors do what they can, but it's a losing battle. As for McTiernan, if PREDATOR and DIE HARD revealed him to be an outstanding craftsman and a superb technician, RED OCTOBER highlights his limitations. The film comes alive only in its most generic moments, which is another way of saying that the three submarines — *Red October* and the Russian and American subs pursuing it — wind up stealing the show, along with the torpedoes that zoom at Ramius' vessel from time to time. If only somebody had directed a few torpedoes at RED OCTOBER's slow-moving, gridlocked script. The film earned an Oscar for its sound effects editing, and nominations for its editing and sound. *(Violence.)*

d, John McTiernan; p, Mace Neufeld; w, Larry Ferguson and Donald Stewart (based on the book by Tom Clancy); ph, Jan De Bont; ed, Dennis Virkler and John Wright; m, Basil Poledouris; prod d, Terence Marsh; art d, Dianne Wager, Donald Woodruff, and William Cruse; set d, Mickey S. Michaels; spec, Scott Squires; stunts, Charles Picerni Jr.; cos, James Tyson; makup, Wes Dawn and James R. Kail; tech, Michael T. Sherman; anim, Eric Swenson, Christopher Dierdorff, Pat Meyers, and Charlie Canfield

Thriller   (PR:C   MPAA:PG)

HYPERSPACE

82m Earl Owensby c

Paula Poundstone, Chris Elliott, Robert Bloodworth, and Alan Marx

Reportedly on the shelf for five years, this lame space spoof might easily have stayed on hold forever had Los Angeles' Vagabond movie theater not staged an ambitious 3-D festival in 1990, complete with a traditional dual-projector system and programs ranging from KISS ME KATE and DIAL M FOR MURDER to THE STEWARDESSES and HYPERSPACE, which had its "world premiere" at the Vagabond festival. However, whether intended or not, the biggest joke in HYPERSPACE is that there are virtually no scenes that take advantage of the film's Stereovision 3-D process, which uses polarized glasses (rather than the red and blue lenses of 50s-vintage 3-D) to achieve its effect. Hence, HYPERSPACE's distinctions are two: Audiences get to see comedian Paula Poundstone in her underwear, and they have to wear funny glasses to do it.

A spoof aimed directly at STAR WARS — this in itself indicates how long the film has been languishing, probably in the garage of Southern fried B-movie mogul Earl Owensby, the film's producer — HYPERSPACE explains in a long, rolling crawl that it is, in fact, "Episode IV: The Last Resort." The bad guys — black-hooded smurfs led by the Darth Vadar-ish Buckethead (Robert Bloodworth) — are in pursuit of Princess Serina, a rebel forces leader who has absconded with valuable radio transmissions. Using their hyperspace drive, they overshoot their destination and land in a sleepy redneck town on Earth. There, one of the smurf-soldiers scares two kids and their parents before winding up locked in the truck of a pest exterminator (Alan Marx). Meanwhile, the helpful locals send Bloodworth and his crew to a local auto repair shop in their quest for the lost *transmissions*. It is there they confront Poundstone and take her captive to interrogate her. Meanwhile, the smurf escapes the truck, with exterminator Marx in hot pursuit to retrieve his work schedule, which the smurf has stolen. The smurf leads the exterminator back to Bloodworth and brings him together with Poundstone. Together, Marx and Poundstone escape from Bloodworth; meanwhile the town authorities have called in UFO scientist Chris Elliott to help them investigate the spacy invaders.

Owensby favors chase movies (his GONE IN 60 SECONDS boasts a 40-minute chase), and HYPERSPACE lumbers from one tedious pursuit to another in lieu of a plot. The most imaginative of these sequences, and the only one that exploits the 3-D format, involves flying shopping carts in a supermarket. But the thrills are negated by the cheap special effects, which wind up looking even cheaper in 3-D. There is an endless rescue in which Marx rushes up and down hallways in the spaceship while Poundstone, in the aforementioned underwear, lies trussed up on a table while the smurfs poke and prod her, conducting tests of the type reported in tabloid accounts of alien abduction. In the climactic showdown between the nefarious Bloodworth and the human race, the Earth army is led by Elliott, who rushes onto the field of battle to bluster at Bloodworth when his death ray sputters out and then rushes cravenly back to the barricades when the weapon's power is restored. Marx eventually rescues Poundstone and the fed-up smurfs boot Bloodworth off the spaceship before taking off, allowing Bloodworth to menace Marx and Poundstone one last time before the "surprise" ending.

The surprise ending is nothing compared to the shock of seeing Elliott and Poundstone, both regulars on TV's utterly urban "Late Night with David Letterman," involved in a film that looks like it was otherwise cast from Owensby's relatives, friends, neighbors, and creditors, along with any other good old boys who happened to be hanging around the set. Elliott and Poundstone both turn in credible enough performances under the circumstances, but neither is able to overcome the "Late Night" meets "Hee Haw" effect. In his Mark Hamill role, Marx is inoffensive but undistinguished — an evaluation that can also be applied to HYPERSPACE as a whole. For what it's worth, writer-director Todd Durham has a sure sense of pacing and his script occasionally conveys the impression that HYPERSPACE is genuinely funny. That may be higher praise that it sounds, since no less than Mel Brooks took on the same STAR WARS-spoof premise in SPACEBALLS with only slightly more entertaining results, despite a considerably higher production budget. But that doesn't mean HYPERSPACE is a good movie. A more likely conclusion is that spoofing STAR WARS is the kind of dumb idea that is all but guaranteed to result in dumb movies.

d, Todd Durham; p, Earl Owensby; w, Todd Durham

Comedy/Science Fiction   (PR:A   MPAA:NR)

I

I COME IN PEACE

91m Damon-Saunders — Vision/Epic — Triumph c

(AKA: DARK ANGEL)

Dolph Lundgren *(Jack Caine)*, Brian Benben *(Lawrence Smith)*, Betsy Brantley *(Diane Pollon)*, Matthias Hues *(Talec, the Bad Alien)*, David Ackroyd *(Switzer)*, Jim Haynie *(Capt. Malone)*, Kevin Page, Robert Prentiss *(White Boys)*, Michael J. Pollard *(Boner)*, Jesse Vint *(Man in Mercedes)*, Jay Bilas *(Azeck, the Good Alien)*, Sherman Howard *(Victor Manning)*, Sam Anderson *(Warren)*, Mark Lowenthal *(Bruce, the Scientist)*, Alex Morris *(Ray Turner)*, Nik Hagler *(Bail Bondsman)*, Tony Brubaker *(Garage Sweeper)*, Mimi Cochran *(Female Mechanic)*, Matthew Posey, Alexander Johnston *(Psychos)*, Jack Willis *(Liquor Store Owner)*, Albert Leong *(Luggage Salesman)*, Brandon Smith *(Market Clerk)*, Wayne Dehart *(Market Customer)*, Kevin Howard *(Security Guard)*, Woody Watson *(Federal Agent)*, Luis Lemus *(Sgt. Hawkins)*, Chris Kinkade *(Detective)*, Steve Chizmadia, Sebastian White, Dean Kinkel, David Poynter, Folkert Schmidt, Gary Baxley *(Other White Boys)*, Tom Campitelli *(Patrolman)*, Kristin Baxley *(Girl on Phone)*, Suzanne Savoy *(Patrolwoman)*, Howard French *(Federal Clerk)*, Willie Minor *(Pool Hustler)*, Arienne Battiste *(Malone's Secretary)*, Jack Verbois *(Man Hostage)*, Stacey Cortez *(Lady Hostage)*, and Nino Candido *(Frank)*

Renegade cop Jack Caine (Dolph Lundgren) isn't about to let the rules of police procedure prevent him from single-handedly wiping out the White Boys, yuppie drug dealers who killed his partner and stole a ton of heroin from the Houston Police Department, bringing down the wrath of the DEA on Caine's head. But Caine's headstrong ways are creating friction on every front. His superiors want him to lie low; his coroner girl friend, Diane (Betsy Brantley), wants him to make a commitment to their relationship; and his new by-the-book partner, Smith (Brian Benben), brought in to investigate the drug theft and the subsequent murder of several key White Boys, wants him to shape up and toe the line, pronto. Caine's instincts tell him there's more to this matter than meets the eye, and he's right. The first clue is the murder weapon used in the White Boys' massacre — a vibrating disk like nothing Caine or Smith has ever seen. The second is a series of drug-related killings that have Diane — and everyone else — very puzzled. The corpses are full of heroin, but the cause of death isn't overdose. As you might guess, Caine and Smith don't follow the department manual in their pursuit of answers. Before you know it, they are hot on the trail of a vicious drug dealer from outer space, a giant blond alien who shoots his victims full of dope, then uses otherworldly technology to extract endorphins from their brains, synthesizing them into a substance to be peddled to addicts on his home planet. The alien pusher is, in turn, being pursued by an alien cop, who warns Caine and Smith that if their quarry isn't stopped, he'll pave the way for thousands of intergalactic drug thugs to come to earth and slaughter its population. Putting their differences aside, Smith and Caine team up to confront the alien dealer with their version of the "Just Say No" campaign.

Above all else, I COME IN PEACE (originally titled DARK ANGEL) is a stupid movie whose premise recalls both 1983's precious LIQUID SKY (in which aliens get high from human endorphins) and the more recent HIDDEN (in which an alien cop and criminal get mixed up in human crimes). Moreover, the deadly disk that plays a central role in I COME IN PEACE appears to have been inspired by PHANTASM's flying ball and by the alien weapon in 1980's low-rent WITHOUT WARNING (which itself is greatly indebted to PREDATOR). This isn't to say that I COME IN PEACE is any more derivative than the average exploitation film — only that its influences are painfully obvious. General dumbness aside, I COME IN PEACE benefits from better-than-average production values (in particular, the cinematography is unusually rich and evocatively lit) and taut direction by former stuntman Craig Baxley, who made his directing debut with the neo-blaxploitation picture ACTION JACKSON. To Baxley's credit, the narrative moves at such a quick clip that the threadbare story has little time to grate on the nerves, and the onscreen stunts belie the film's limited budget. *(Violence, profanity, drug abuse.)*

d, Craig R. Baxley; p, Jeff Young; w, Jonathan Tydor and Leonard Maas Jr.; ph, Mark Irwin; ed, Mark Helfrich; m, Jan Hammer; prod d, Phillip M. Leonard; art d, Nino Candido; set d, Phillip M. Leonard; spec, Bruno Van Zeebroeck, Tony Gardner, and Larry Hamlin; stunts, Paul R. Baxley Jr.; cos, Joseph Porro; makeup, Ron Clark and Suzanne Bell; anim, Jay Johnson

Action/Science Fiction   (PR:C MPAA:R)

I LOVE YOU TO DEATH

96m Chestnut Hill/Tri-Star c

Kevin Kline *(Joey Boca)*, Tracey Ullman *(Rosalie Boca)*, Joan Plowright *(Nadja)*, River Phoenix *(Devo Nod)*, William Hurt *(Harlan James)*, Keanu Reeves *(Marlon James)*, James Gammon *(Lt. Schooner)*, Jack Kehler *(Wiley)*, Victoria Jackson *(Lacey)*, Miriam Margolyes *(Joey's Mother)*, Alisan Porter *(Carla Boca)*, Jon Kasdan *(Dominic Boca)*, Heather Graham *(Bridget)*, Michelle Joyner *(Donna Joy)*, John Kostmayer *(Benny)*, Kathleen York *(Dewey Brown)*, John Billingsley *(Jailhouse Informant)*, Samantha Kostmayer *(Waitress)*, Michael Chieffo *(Blue Light Bartender)*, Robert Radonich *(Java Jive Bartender)*, Jeff Klein *(Young Man with Bat)*, G. Valmont Thomas *(Cabbie)*, Art Cahn *(Priest)*, Audrey Rapoport *(Librarian)*, Shiri Appleby *(Millie)*, Luke Rossi *(Sammy)*, Henry Beckman *(Wendel Carter)*, Susan Chin, Tony Romano, Johnny Willis *(Reporters)*, Joe Lando *(Pizza Guy)*, William R. Breyette *(Biker)*, and Phoebe Cates

Having tried his hand at a wide range of films, from the *noir* flourishes of BODY HEAT, to the revisionist western SILVERADO, to the thirtysomething yuppie angst of THE BIG CHILL, director Lawrence Kasdan undertakes a dark, blue-collar screwball comedy in I LOVE YOU TO DEATH. The result is a one-joke movie. Granted, the joke is pretty good and, when it comes, is well-executed. But it's not enough to sustain a full-length feature that is further hindered by surprisingly weak performances from its leading players.

I LOVE YOU TO DEATH (henceforth referred to as ILYTD) is based on a true story, which may be its biggest single problem. In attempting to maintain a nodding acquaintance with the facts, Kasdan and writer John Kostmayer (for the first time Kasdan isn't working from his own script) may have been prevented from fully exploring the comic possibilities of the genuinely funny and offbeat cast of characters they've assembled here, played by some of the screen's most gifted actors. Kevin Kline leads the ensemble as Joey Boca, the married owner of an apartment building and a pizza shop, who "suffers" from a prolific case of Don Juanism. Many of his conquests, like Lacey ("Saturday Night Live's" Victoria Jackson), are tenants whose "plumbing" is in constant need of attention. But Joey is also active on the disco scene, where one of his pickups is played, without credit, by Kline's offscreen wife, Phoebe Cates. Another fertile hunting ground is the local library, where Joey is finally spied in *flagrante delicto* in the stacks by his trusting, frumpish wife, Rosalie (Tracey Ullman). Furious at her husband's betrayal, Rosalie impulsively decides to murder Joey. But he proves amazingly impervious to her attempts at doing him in, first with the help of a bat-wielding family friend, then with a car bomb. Rosalie's weapons in the film's key scene are an overdose of sleeping pills mixed into Joey's spaghetti sauce, and a gun. The gun is first used by Devo (River Phoenix), the cleanup worker at the pizza shop, who has a crush on Rosalie, then by hired-killer cousins Harlan and Marlon (William Hurt, Keanu Reeves). Each time, Joey rises, FRIDAY THE 13TH-style, complaining first of stomach discomfort, and then, after being shot in the head, of a splitting headache. The murder plot proves so inept that dimwitted police detectives Schooner and Wiley (James Gammon, Jack Kehler) manage to bring the would-be killers to justice before the evening is out.

Its tone set by the presence of comedians Ullman and Jackson (though both are oddly unfunny and subdued here), ILYTD emerges as little more than a series of blackout sketches, fragments of funny ideas, and inside jokes (in addition to Cates' presence, Kasdan himself provides one of the film's funnier moments as Devo's lawyer). The early scenes function as little more than set-ups for ILYTD's single funniest scene, Joey's repeated resurrection, and the ending is less a resolution than an attempt to find a fuzzy, feel-good moral as the film races to fadeout on a clinch between Joey and Rosalie.

In the real-life case of Tony and Frances Toto, Tony lay in bed for four days after being drugged and shot. The film shows Rosalie being released the next day after Joey refuses to press charges; Frances Toto spent four years in prison after pleading guilty to criminal solicitation to commit murder. But wavering somewhat from the facts isn't the main problem here. Despite Joey's evident success as a pizza maker, ILYTD is half-baked. For Kasdan, a director whose best films — THE BIG CHILL and THE ACCIDENTAL TOURIST — are set among the middle-class, the blue-collar setting may have been just too much of a stretch. The characters in ILYTD have no real dimension, remaining caricatures who, while sometimes funny, are finally too thin to sustain a feature-length film. Generally, the cast can't be faulted. As in A FISH CALLED WANDA, Kline displays a gift for physical comedy in his big scenes. But he fails to make Joey come alive in the small moments, falling back instead on crude ethnic stereotyping. Ullman, meanwhile, brings little energy to the action. The deficit is made up by supporting players — Hurt, Reeves, Phoenix, Joan Plowright (as Rosalie's murderous mom), Gammon, Kehler, and Miriam Margolyes, as Joey's own outraged mother — who all have their moments. But their efforts only make ILYTD that much more exasperating for its failure to give them anything more to do than random mugging and a few muted pratfalls. As a video rental, ILYTD has enough chuckles in it to liven up a dull evening; as a big-screen offering, it's strictly small potatoes. *(Adult situations, violence.)*

d, Lawrence Kasdan; p, Jeffrey Lurie and Ron Moler; w, John Kostmayer; ph, Owen Roizman; ed, Anne V. Coates; m, James Horner; prod d, Lilly Kilvert; art d, Jon Hutman; set d, Cricket Rowland; spec, Roy Arbogast; cos, Aggie Guerard Rodgers; makup, Ben Nye Jr.; chor, Tad Tadloch; tech, Clara Quisenberry

Comedy   (PR:O   MPAA:R)

ICH UND ER

(W. Ger.) (SEE: ME AND HIM)

ICICLE THIEF, THE

(It.) 90m Mario Maronati/Aries c

(LADRI DI SAPONETTE)

Maurizio Nichetti *(Antonio Piermattei/The Director of the Film)*, Caterina Sylos Labini *(Maria Piermattei)*, Federico Rizzo *(Bruno Piermattei)*, Matteo Auguardi *(Paolo Piermattei)*, Renato Scarpa *(Don Italo, the Priest)*, Heidi Komarek *(The Model)*, Carlina Torta *(Television-watching Mother)*, Massimo Sacilotto *(Television-watching Father)*, Lella Costa *(The TV Producer)*, and Claudio G. Fava *(The Film Critic)*

THE ICICLE THIEF is as much a feat of engineering as it is of cinematic legerdemain. Once you accept that you are being manipulated, you'll find that on every narrative level—and there are four disparate components to this original, trenchant comedy—both your social sensibilities and sense of reality will be delightfully engaged. Simultaneously shot in black and white and color, this tour de force, the winner of the Grand Prize at the 1989 Moscow Film Festival, is a playful, ingenious commentary on modern times. That writer-director Maurizio Nichetti (who appears as the film's dual anti-heroes) brings it off at all is nothing short of amazing. The convoluted film-within-a-film structure of his tightly plotted, complex movie, would seem to require the expert touch of a master architect and a skilled logician. Nichetti proves himself both. On the film's first level, filmed in color, Nichetti is seen as the fictitious Maurizio Nichetti, a noted director. His latest movie (not so coincidentally titled "The Icicle Thief") is being shown as a last minute substitution on a highbrow Italian TV program dealing with cinema. In the Charlie Chaplin-Buster Keaton tradition, the waiflike, klutzy Nichetti, a short, bushy-haired man with unkempt mustache and dark, round spectacles, is continually put upon by the show's unprepared host, an arrogant film critic (Claudio G. Fava). To Nichetti's growing frustration, his neorealistic black-and-white masterpiece (a facile parody of De Sica's THE BICYCLE THIEF), is repeatedly interrupted at its most sensitive moments by crass commercials in color. On the film's second level, Nichetti plays the lead in that tragic film-within-the-film, the poor, unemployed Antonio Piermattei, who is desperate for work. (Without his glasses and mustache, Nichetti is barely recognizable in this role.) To make ends meet, Antonio's wife, Maria (Caterina Sylos Labini), sings in a trio, his young son, Bruno (Federico Rizzo), works diligently at the church doing odd jobs; and his infant, Paolo (Mattio Auguardi), doesn't do much except get into everything, creating a continual comic hazard to life and limb. Aghast when he mistakenly thinks Antonio plans to go into the black market, the local priest, Don Italo (Renato Scarpa), helps him find work at the local chandelier factory, bringing joy to the Piermattei household. Now they'll be able to afford more than boiled cabbage. Besides, Maria has always dreamed of one day having a chandelier in her home—they remind her of icicles—and Antonio secretly steals a fixture to carry home to her on his bicycle. The film's third level (also shot in color) is the reality of a bourgeois household moored in front of their TV set, passively watching both the movie and the recurrent commercials. However, only the pregnant mother is paying any attention at all to Nichetti's film. The father just ogles the buxom bathing beauties in the colorful commercials, and the pampered son, mainly interested in playing with his enormous collection of Lego toys, keeps switching channels with the remote control. The commercials, which punctuate the telecast, represent the film's fourth and final narrative level.

During the program, there's a momentary power failure at the TV studio. When the current is restored and the film resumes, fiction and reality merge, as if by magic. The neorealistic movie switches from a black-and-white tragedy to a screwball fantasy in living color. We see Antonio riding home on his bike, the chandelier tied to his handlebars. When he hears a cry for help by a lake, he stops and runs to save the victim, the gorgeous swimsuit-clad American model Heidi (Heidi Komarek), whom we've been seeing in the TV commercials. Antonio and the surroundings are still in black and white, but not Heidi; she's in color. And they're both together in the same frame. When Antonio drags Heidi out of the water and dries her off, he also wipes off her color in the process—an effect that's fascinating to watch—whereupon Heidi becomes an integral part of the black-

and-white drama. Antonio brings her home, but his wife, who has made a special celebration dinner to welcome him after his first day at work, misunderstands the situation. One look at the sexy model and she's convinced that Antonio is two-timing her. Because he's left the crystal fixture at the lake, he brings Maria to the site of the rescue to prove he's been telling her the truth. But the chandelier is gone, and Maria walks into the water and disappears, presumably drowned. When Antonio is charged with his wife's murder and jailed, the fictitious Nichetti, back at the TV studio, is horrified to see the plot of his film so drastically changed. (In his original movie, the father eventually becomes paralyzed, the mother becomes a prostitute, and the two small children are sent off to an orphanage.) From this point, THE ICICLE THIEF erupts into farce. Nichetti jumps into the TV screen, emerges as a black-and-white character in his own movie, and returns to Antonio's village by train to emend his film's structure. Nichetti eventually makes things right, or at least sees to it that Antonio is released and his family reunited, but not before all the movie-within-the-movie characters appear in the color commercials. Still, everyone lives happily ever after; that is, except for director Nichetti. He's stuck in a black-and-white never-never land on the bourgeois family's television screen, and he disappears when they turn the set off and go to bed for the night.

If this all seems crazy, it is. For 90 minutes, as the film quick cuts from one narrative level to another, combining them in a farcical melange, you'll have a wonderful time. It is only later on that you'll find yourself thinking about the film's universal implications. In its seriocomic way, THE ICICLE THIEF says as much about the passivity of people who casually watch TV at home as it does about the indiscriminate, often odious incursion of TV commercials. Here, clearly, the medium is the message. The real-life Nichetti seems to imply that television is nothing more than a distraction in most homes, with viewers unable to differentiate among the accumulated images or to "remember if a face is from a film, a commercial, or the news."

With counterfeit commercials an integral part of his film, Nichetti reputedly savors the irony of eventually seeing the film aired on television. However, whether THE ICICLE THIEF will be intruded upon by any real commercials on TV in the director's native country remains to be seen; in 1989, the Italian parliament introduced an amendment prohibiting private television networks from interrupting a film with commercials, but in the fall of 1990 the amendment was dropped.

Nichetti's multifaceted background—he studied architecture, mime, and acting, wrote screenplays and advertising copy, and worked as a circus clown—obviously has proved invaluable to his highly creative approach to THE ICICLE THIEF. While this tightly edited film might seem anarchic, it was painstakingly constructed by Nichetti, frame by frame on a storyboard. No computers were used for his special effects; everything was done on film. (The 20-second bit where Nichetti dries the color off the model took three months to do.) Even the near-perfect simulation of the look of a 1940s movie was the result of processing the film to make it appear older, then re-filming it a second time in black and white to give it the necessary texture.

Called the Italian Woody Allen, Nichetti often appears as a performer both on film and television. Along with Carlo Verdone and Nanni Moretti, he has been dubbed one of the "New Comics," the first major movement in Italian filmmaking since the neorealists. THE ICICLE THIEF is his fourth film. *(Adult situations.)*

d, Maurizio Nichetti; p, Mario Maronati; w, Maurizio Nichetti and Mauro Monti; ph, Mario Battistoni; ed, Rita Olivati; m, Manuel De Sica; set d, Ada Legori; cos, Maria Pia Angelini

Comedy   (PR:A   MPAA:NR)

IMPORTED BRIDEGROOM, THE

90m Lara Classics c

Gene Troobnick *(Asriel Stroon)*, Avi Hoffman *(Shaya)*, Greta Cowan *(Flora)*, Annette Miller *(Mrs. Birnbaum)*, Miriam Varon, Andreas Teuber, Ted Jacobs, Ira Solet, Ira Goldenberg, Barry Karas, Helene Lantry, Moshe Waldocks, and Seth Yorra

Set in turn-of-the-century Boston, THE IMPORTED BRIDEGROOM is a quaint but slow-paced film that suffers from the obvious constraints of a small budget. Asriel Stroon (Gene Troobnick) is a grouchy, widowed landlord who emigrated from Poland as a young man and made his fortune in America. When he tries to raise the rent on an unemployed tenant, the tenant's wife reminds Stroon that the landlord has not done much to insure his entry into Heaven. Returning to his well-appointed town house, Stroon announces to his daughter, Flora (Greta Cowan), and his housekeeper, Mrs. Birnbaum (Annette Miller), that he is going to go back to the town of his birth, to try to rediscover the purity of spirit that he feels has been lost on his road to success in America. Back in Poland, Stroon provokes the jealousy of the rich men in his village, whose combined fortunes are not the equal of his own. To get back at them for cheating him out of the prayer reading that he has bid for in the temple, Stroon sets his sights on persuading Shaya (Avi Hoffman), a brilliant young scholar, to be his daughter's husband. Unfortunately, this will not sit well with Flora, who is determined to marry only a cultured American doctor. When Stroon returns to Boston with the shy young scholar, the headstrong Flora balks at the suggestion of marriage. Put off but not defeated by Flora's lack of enthusiasm for Shaya, Stroon is determined to see his daughter married to the pious young man, who will spend the rest of his days studying sacred texts, thereby winning Stroon a place in Heaven for bringing his daughter such a "treasure." To help Shaya cope with his new country, Stroon hires a tutor to improve Shaya's broken English. The tutor lets Shaya read books on many different subjects, opening his eyes to the world outside religious literature. Shaya begins to sneak these forbidden books into the house, but Stroon catches him, and tells the tutor not to come back. Meanwhile, Flora has begun to warm to Shaya, and she takes charge of his education after the tutor is fired. An idea takes hold of her: what if Shaya were to become a doctor? Flora and Shaya conspire to continue his non-religious education, and the two find a common bond in their enthusiasm for learning. Soon, however, Stroon grows suspicious of Shaya's claim that he goes out every afternoon to pray at different temples around the city. Following Shaya one afternoon, Stroon is shocked to witness the young scholar meeting with the fired tutor, going to the public library, and even eating in a non-kosher restaurant. In the restaurant, Stroon confronts Shaya, vowing that he will never allow Shaya to marry Flora. But by this point, Shaya and Flora are in love, and they elope and have a civil wedding. When Stroon hears about this, he has no choice but to approve of the marriage; however, he insists that they have a religious ceremony as soon as possible. With all of his carefully laid plans in disarray, Stroon throws caution to the wind and proposes to Mrs. Birnbaum, asking her to emigrate with him to the Holy Land, where he hopes to find the salvation that has eluded him. The couples are married in a double wedding, and Stroon seems to have found some peace of mind.

A well-intentioned but slightly deficient dramatization of a simple story, THE IMPORTED BRIDEGROOM suffers greatly from a lack of dramatic conflict, yet it succeeds in finding much humor in the clashes of will in Stroon's household. Director-writer Pamela Berger effectively re-creates the atmosphere of turn-of-the-century Boston despite low-budget production values that are best exemplified by Shaya's pasted-on beard. While all the performances are good, particularly Cowan's portrayal of Flora, the film feels underpopulated; additional well-developed characters are needed to enrich the story. Uneven editing also works against the film's success. Overall, THE IMPORTED BRIDEGROOM never quite reaches the level of charm to which it apparently aspires. *(Adult situations.)*

d, Pamela Berger; p, Pamela Berger; w, Pamela Berger (based on a story by Abraham Cahan); ph, Brian Heffron; ed, Amy Summer; m, Bevan Manson and Rosalie Gerut; prod d, Martha Seely

Drama (PR:C MPAA:NR)

IMPROMPTU

(Brit.) 107m Governor—Ariane/Hemdale c

Judy Davis (*George Sand*), Hugh Grant (*Frederic Chopin*), Mandy Patinkin (*Alfred DeMusset*), Bernadette Peters (*Marie d'Agoult*), Julian Sands (*Franz Liszt*), Ralph Brown (*Eugene Delacroix*), Georges Corraface (*Felicien Mallefille*), Anton Rodgers (*Duke d'Antan*), Emma Thompson (*Duchess d'Antan*), Anna Massey (*George Sand's Mother*), Jezabelle Amato (*Inn Keeper's Wife*), Claude Berthy (*Chopin's Valet*), David Birkin (*Maurice*), Georges Bruce (*Doctor*), Andre Chaumeau (*Priest*), Jean-Michel Dagory (*Inn Keeper*), Nicholas Hawtrey (*Philosopher*), Isabelle Guiard (*Princess*), Fernand Guiot (*Butler*), Sylvie Herbert (*Sophie*), Francois Lalande (*Local Doctor*), Ian Marshall DeGarnier (*Editor*), Annette Milsom (*Ursule*), Nimer Rashed (*Didiar*), John Savident (*Buloz*), Stuart Seide (*Clerk*), Lucy Speed (*Aurore*), Elizabeth Spriggs (*Baroness Laginsky*), and Fiona Vincente (*Solange*)

Within its historical setting, the life and many loves of French novelist George Sand (1804-67) as depicted in James Lapine's IMPROMPTU, has the feel of a contemporary romantic comedy. The feature-film debut for Pulitzer Prize-winning stage director Lapine ("Sunday in the Park with George") is distinguished by a fine cast, including Judy Davis as the truly liberated Sand, a woman whose vacillation with respect to men is exceeded only by her passion for them. The author, whose romantic novels were enormously popular in her own time, lived life to the fullest, casting aside convention and socializing with the most celebrated authors of her day. Her love affairs made for titillating gossip, if not envy. The film introduces viewers to Sand's circle of friends, including the painter Eugene Delacroix (Ralph Brown), poet and one-time lover Alfred DeMusset (Mandy Patinkin), and composers Franz Liszt (Julian Sands) and Frederic Chopin (Hugh Grant). It is Chopin who captures Sand's heart and is the object of her determined affection throughout the film. An unassuming man, in continual ill-health, Chopin first encounters the brazen Sand when she steals into

his room, hides under his piano, and revels in his music. This takes place during the summer of 1835 at the country estate of the Duke and Duchess d'Antan (Anton Rodgers and Emma Thompson), where Chopin, Liszt, Delacroix, and DeMusset have been invited to enrich the lives of their culture-starved hosts. Sand has quite candidly invited herself and her two young children. The gathering also includes Liszt's mistress, Marie d'Agoult (Bernadette Peters), and Sand's newly jilted lover, Felicien Mallefille (Georges Corraface), her children's tutor. Consumed with jealousy, Mallefille spends his time threatening any man who looks at Sand, and instigating a duel with DeMusset. Sand, meanwhile, enlists Marie's help in delivering a note to Chopin. Envious of Sand and feeling neglected by Liszt, Marie passes on the note, but not before removing Sand's name and substituting her own. While nothing comes of the matter, Delacroix seduces the duchess just before the guests crown their visit by staging a play that resoundingly patronizes their hosts. Chopin is embarrassed by the effort, and denounces the others as the fortnight holiday comes to an end. Sand, having had no luck in corrupting Chopin, departs with her children and Mallefille. Throughout the following winter, Sand regularly travels from her home in Nantes to Paris to visit her aged mother and to try to sway Chopin. Thanks to Marie's conniving, Chopin remains convinced that Sand is a deplorable creature. Only after Chopin learns of Marie's chicanery involving the note does he take an interest in Sand. In no time at all, the two become lovers as Sand encourages the frail composer to partake of her considerable strength.

Favored by Sarah Kernochan's character-driven screenplay and its elegant French locations, IMPROMPTU gives its actors ample room in which to play. Davis shines as Sand, balancing her decided independence with her desire for heady companionship. Grant's Chopin is a bit overplayed, making him seem too prudish. Patinkin is credible as the volatile DeMusset, as are Sands as Liszt, Brown as Delacroix, and Corraface as Mallefille. Peters is well-cast as the manipulative, ever-pregnant, Marie, and Thompson is hilarious as the duchess—a woman with far too much free time. Those performances, along with the fine music and costumes, help to make this an appealingly offbeat period piece. *(Adult situations.)*

d, James Lapine; p, Stuart Oken and Daniel A. Sherkow; w, Sarah Kernochan; ph, Bruno de Keyzer; ed, Michael Ellis; m, Frederic Chopin and Franz Liszt; md, John Strauss; art d, Gerard Daoudal; set d, Alain Pitrel; spec, Gilbert Pieri; stunts, Mario Luraschi; cos, Jenny Beavan; makup, Jean-Luc Russier, Dominique Plez, and Cedric Gerard

Biography/Romance (PR:C MPAA:PG-13)

IMPULSE

108m Ruddy Morgan/WB c

Theresa Russell (*Lottie Mason*), Jeff Fahey (*Stan Harris*), George Dzundza (*Joe Morgan*), Alan Rosenberg (*Charley Katz*), Nicholas Mele (*Rossi*), Eli Danker (*Dimarjian*), Charles McCaughan (*Frank Munoff*), Lynne Thigpen (*Dr. Gardner*), Shawn Elliott (*Tony Peron*), Angelo Tiffe (*Luke*), Christopher Lawford (*Steve*), Nick Savage (*Edge*), Dan Bell (*Anson*), Tom Dahlgren (*District Attorney*), Daniel Quinn (*Ted Gates*), David Crowley (*Trick in Car*), Mark Rolston (*Man in Bar*), Russell Curry (*Bartender, Mills*), Pete Antico (*Vice Cop in Bar*), Karl Anthony Smith (*Gas Station Attendant*), Paul Acerno (*Junkie in Apartment*), Maria Rangel (*Maria*), Don Ruffin, Cliff McLaughlin (*Munoff's Bodyguards*), Paul A. Calabria (*Man with Dog*), Valente Rodriguez (*Doorman*), Ronald L. Colby (*Liquor Store Clerk*), Robert Phalen (*Coroner*), Douglas Rowe (*Criminologist*), Wendy Gordon (*TV Reporter*), Jerry Dunphy (*TV Anchorman*), Jerry Martinez, Peder Melhuse (*Vice Cops at Motel*), Sorin Serebe Priscopie, Thomas Rosales Jr. (*Colombian Drug Dealers*), Elaine Kagan (*Stan's Receptionist*), Michael McCleery (*Punk Delivering Flowers*), and James Edgcomb (*Cop Behind Safe House*)

IMPULSE, directed by Sondra Locke, is an involving and suspenseful story of a Los Angeles undercover cop. The film stars Theresa Russell as Lottie Mason, a tough but vulnerable police decoy, working for both the vice and narcotics divisions, who becomes so immersed in and affected by her dangerous work that she fantasizes about really becoming the dodgy characters she impersonates. As the story opens, a drug deal is going down in New York. Several people are killed, but it is uncertain whether drug kingpin Tony Peron (Shawn Elliott) has come out of the fracas alive. Word of these developments gets back to California, making an already nervous government witness against Peron even more nervous, despite the reassurances of Assistant DA Stan Harris (Jeff Fahey). Lottie and Stan end up working together on the Peron case and eventually become romantically involved. However, Lt. Joe Morgan (George Dzundza), a police officer of questionable character and Lottie's former boy friend, is not exactly thrilled about this last development. Meanwhile, Lottie puts her life on the line almost daily, often posing as a hooker or drug addict. During one bust, the operation goes awry and she barely gets out alive. Exhausted and shaken, she gets into her car and rushes home. But on the way, a tire goes flat, and Lottie kills time in a bar while it is being repaired. While she's nursing a drink, a handsome stranger flashing a lot of money manages to charm her into accompanying him to his home. There, Lottie goes upstairs to freshen up, and only moments later the wealthy stranger is murdered. She manages to hide until the killer leaves, then takes an airport locker key out of the victim's coat pocket, and reports the crime anonymously. Soon it emerges that the victim was Peron. Morgan eventually figures out that Lottie was at the crime scene and tips off Stan, who in turn confronts Lottie. It's then leaked to the press that there was an "eyewitness" to Peron's death. Hoping to catch the killer, the police stake out Lottie's house. That evening, a man carrying a long case (we later find out he's a floral deliveryman) pulls up in front of her home, and the cops all converge on him. Meanwhile, the real killer is still at Lottie's. Alone and terrified, she shoots her would-be assassin in the dark. The wounded stalker turns out to be the government witness, who confesses to murdering Peron. The next day, Lottie resigns and makes plans to leave town. Stopping at the airport to get the money in Peron's locker, she's accosted by Morgan, who struggles with her for the briefcase in the locker. It falls open, but only stuffing falls out. Soon Stan appears on the scene and breaks up the fight. In the closing scene, he gives Lottie the keys to his car, which contains the drug money in the trunk. As she's about to drive away, Lottie has a change of heart and decides to stay with Stan.

Locke, Clint Eastwood's former on- and off-screen costar, who previously directed RATBOY (1986), has made a suspenseful film with interesting psychological insights. Lit in classic *film noir* style, IMPULSE provides the necessary action and thrills of that genre, but at the same time examines the temptations and the excitement of living on the edge on a more intimate level. We feel as if we really know something about what makes the characters tick, and their motivations are made all the more compelling and believable through the work of the talented cast. *(Violence, profanity, nudity, adult situations, sexual situations.)*

d, Sondra Locke; p, Albert S. Ruddy and Andre Morgan; w, John De Marco and Leigh Chapman (based on a story by John De Marco); ph, Dean Semler; ed, John W. Wheeler; m, Michel Colombier; md, Joe Isgro; prod d, William A. Elliott; set d, Adolph Salas; spec, Richard Ratliff and Mike Del Gino; stunts, David Ellis and Fred Hice; cos, Deborah Hopper; makup, Michael Hancock

Thriller   (PR:O MPAA:R)

IN THE SPIRIT

93m Running River/Castle Hill c

Elaine May *(Marianne Flan)*, Marlo Thomas *(Reva Prosky)*, Jeannie Berlin *(Crystal)*, Olympia Dukakis *(Sue)*, Peter Falk *(Roger Flan)*, Melanie Griffith *(Lureen)*, Chad Burton *(Lt. Kelly)*, Thurn Hoffman *(Detective Pete Weber)*, Laurie Jones, Michael Emil, Hope Cameron, Rockets Redglare, Danny Davin, and Christopher Durang

In this flaky but engaging female buddy movie, the lives of three vastly different women (Marlo Thomas, Elaine May, and Jeannie Berlin—May's real-life daughter) intersect. Are they ruled by the stars or is it just coincidence that they meet? An advocate of New Age philosophies, healing crystals, and vegetarianism, New Yorker Reva Prosky (Thomas) is one of those pushy do-gooders who can't help "improving" the lifestyle of everyone she meets—including neighbor Crystal (Berlin), who's trying to leave prostitution for a career in bartending. Meanwhile, on the West Coast, the wealthy Roger (Peter Falk) and Marianne Flan (May) nervously endure his recent firing. After deciding to start anew in Manhattan, Marianne makes the fateful decision to allow Jill-of-all-trades Reva to redecorate her co-op apartment. After all, Reva has been recommended by a trusted friend, Sue (Olympia Dukakis), the sister-in-law of the widowed Reva. Disaster strikes when the renovation, guaranteed to last only a few days, drags out into a snafu-ridden six-month debacle. Persuaded to move in with the kooky Reva, Marianne has to contend with her depressed husband, whose futile job search has made him an ice cream addict. Marianne and Roger are slowly driven crazy by Reva's friends (believers in reincarnation, Shirley MacLaine groupies, and Crystal, the reforming hooker). One day, Crystal wanders in, expresses interest in a newspaper article on the Mafia, then leaves without her datebook. Shortly thereafter, she is found murdered in her apartment. At the same time, Roger leaves Marianne for his former wife. Angrily blaming Reva for all her woes, Marianne storms out and moves into her uninhabitable apartment. When both Marianne's and Reva's apartments are broken into, however, the two women begin to form a bond. Trying to figure out how the break-ins are related to Crystal's death, they decide that the killer wants Crystal's appointment book. In an attempt to break its code, the two visit prostitute Lureen (Melanie Griffith), a former associate of Crystal's. Still reeling from a recent attempt on their lives, Marianne and Reva are further horrified when Lureen is run down by a hit-and-run killer. Realizing that the police don't take them seriously and that their lives are in danger, the women grab some quick cash from Sue, who is reluctant to become involved, and hit the road as fugitives. Heading

for a New Age retreat, they arm themselves, leaving a trail of credit card purchases for the murderer to follow. Peace-loving Reva plans to get the desperate killer before he can get them, but Marianne just wants to defend herself. At their hideout, Reva and Marianne grow closer as they rig booby traps and place the coveted datebook in an ice cooler that will electrocute anyone who grabs for the book. When the police manage to locate their whereabouts, the women realize a cop is the culprit; however, they suspect the wrong policeman. Later, after avoiding most of their traps, the killer corners Marianne and Reva, and confides that he would be tops on a Mafia hit list if the datebook were handed over to authorities. But when he sticks his hand in the ice chest, he's electrocuted. Not wanting any involvement with grand jury hearings about the Mafia, now-devoted pals Reva and Marianne concoct a story about the cop having a heart attack and face their husbandless futures together.

For all its shortcomings, this raggedly amusing farce offers more laughs than most smoothly crafted Hollywood assembly line comedies. The basic problem with the script is its failure to follow through with its amusing premise and clever structure. After setting up a wonderful satire of the New Age set and framing it with telling narration, the film then abandons both and becomes a conventional buddy movie. The screenplay is chock-full of good ideas, but they tumble out helter skelter, and director Sandra Seacat (heretofore best known as the acting coach of such stars as Jessica Lange, Mickey Rourke, Faye Dunaway, and Michelle Pfieffer) isn't always able to milk them for maximum impact. We expect, for example, that Berlin's key character will reappear in the fanciful story line as a ghost and not just in flashbacks. Moreover, the scene in which Sue refuses to help the fleeing duo should have been infused with humor. Although the scene's point is to show that Reva and Marianne have only each other to rely on, there is no need to portray Sue as unfeeling. However, notwithstanding the numerous comic payoffs that might have been a little sharper, the film remains an irresistible exercise in silliness seemingly possessed by the spirit of the Marx Brothers or at least by that of their mother, Minnie. It's like a Mel Brooks movie without the crudity.

In the tradition of other uneven wacky comedies like BIG TROUBLE and FINDERS KEEPERS, the strength of IN THE SPIRIT lies in rich comic material that recalls the glory days of revue humor and performers like Barbara Harris and Alan Arkin, who were trained in the improvisational style that enhances this film. Berlin (who cowrote the screenplay) isn't onscreen long enough, but Thomas makes a bewitching straight woman. And Falk and May are side-splittingly funny; everything they do is so on target you laugh as if you're seeing their shtick for the first time. In fact, May's performance as the downwardly mobile executive's wife is one of the most outrageously funny exhibitions of comic acting in years. Because of the script's adventurousness and the cast's sparkle, IN THE SPIRIT emerges as an off-the-wall surprise. If reincarnation is a reality, then it's just possible that the spirit of screwball comedy lives again in IN THE SPIRIT. *(Violence, sexual situations, profanity.)*

d, Sandra Seacat; p, Julian Schlossberg and Beverly Irby; w, Jeannie Berlin and Laurie Jones; ph, Dick Quinlan; ed, Brad Fuller; m, Patrick Williams; prod d, Michael C. Smith; art d, Jaqueline Jacobson; cos, Carrie Robbins

Comedy   (PR:C MPAA:R)

INHERITOR

83m Inheritor/Film World—VidAmerica c

Lisa McGuire *(Alison/Marybeth)*, Barnaby Spring *(Simon Proctor)*, John Rice *(Sgt. Mark Deacon)*, Dan Haggerty *(Dr. Berquist)*, Daniel Stephen *(Minotaur)*, Jonathon Russo *(Rev. Proctor)*, Catherine Curtin *(Mrs. Proctor)*, Vincent Rosselli, Jacki Prentice, and Russell Otto

Filmed in Wisconsin, INHERITOR is a confused, unrewarding horror yarn with some notable names improbably involved. Director Brian Kendal-Savegar was one of a quartet who shared a 1986 Academy Award for Best Art Direction/Set Decoration in the prestige production A ROOM WITH A VIEW. Executive producers Alexander W. Kogan, Jr., and Barry Tucker received credits for the "Hellraiser" films and the terrific dark comedy HEATHERS (1989). And the musical score is attributed to Atticus Finch, who was a character in TO KILL A MOCKINGBIRD. But INHERITOR won't enhance any of their resumes, and it sat on the shelf for a few years before its unheralded release to video. It opens with chaotic flashback scenes in which nasty Puritan settlers bury a woman alive in the crypt of a church. Flash ahead to the present, where young Alison (Lisa McGuire) learns that her twin sister has been found dead, spread-eagled nude on the floor of a rural house that stands on the spot once occupied by the Puritan church. Alison travels out to the boondocks to identify the body and elects to stay at the house (what the heck, the rent's paid). Soon she is approached by the owner, Simon (Barnaby Spring), an unsavory writer who eventually reveals that he is a descendant of the Puritan minister seen in the flashback. The minister offended the local Indians in some way and was cursed; his wife mated with a spirit beast, gave birth to an inhuman offspring, and was punished with premature burial. The curse has brought torment to Simon's family down through the years, and Alison's sister, who had psychic abilities, died in a ritualistic attempt to remove it. Simon now wants to make a second try, using Alison. She traces the vibes down to a network of Indian caves beneath the house, where she is separated from Simon. In one chamber, Alison meets the buffalo-headed being who (ahem) compromised the minister's wife all those years ago. The boyish-looking creature resembles a satyr, is labeled in the credits as a minotaur, and was probably meant to be a wendigo; in any case, he's horny in more ways than one and commences lovemaking with a very willing Alison. Just as they finish, Simon appears and shoots the creature to death. "You are the inheritor," he says to Alison. But if Simon thinks he's escaped the curse, he's fatally mistaken. The puzzling final scene finds Alison, happily pregnant herself, apparently joined by a reincarnation of the minister's wife for a tour of the homestead.

This plot is so full of holes that it's hard to tell if the filmmakers are merely inattentive or deliberately out to confound the viewer. In one scene, a police officer scans Simon's record and finds something that sends him to warn Alison immediately. What has he discovered? It's never revealed, and the cop gets killed shortly thereafter. Early in the story, a glowing *something* starts to burst up through the floorboards of the old house, but Alison orders it back below. What is this all about? The actors' overly melodramatic posing seems to indicate that all these characters know more than they're telling. And Spring—who creeps around in a trench coat even Dick Tracy wouldn't touch—has a particularly ill-conceived role (it seems he must defeat the curse or face...writer's cramp!). The photography is the best element of the film, helping at times to recall, distantly, that Australian masterpiece of aboriginal terror THE LAST WAVE, but that's about it. The great American minotaur movie remains to be made. *(Nudity, profanity, sexual situations.)*

d, Brian Kendal-Savegar; p, Christopher Webster and Cheryl Webster; w, Julian Weaver (based on an original idea by Brian Kendal-Savegar); ph, Joseph Friedman; ed, Amy Sumner; m, Atticus Finch; art d, William McCrow; spec, Michael A. Pearce; cos, Donna McCrow

Horror (PR:O MPAA:R)

INNOCENT VICTIM

(Brit.) 90m Greenpoint — Grenada/Castle Hill — Academy c

(AKA: TREE OF HANDS, THE)

Helen Shaver *(Benet Archdale)*, Paul McGann *(Barry)*, Lauren Bacall *(Marsha Archdale)*, Malcolm Stoddard *(Ian Raeburn)*, Kate Hardie *(Carol Stratford)*, Barnaby Brown *(Jason)*, Peter Firth *(Terrance)*, Tony Haygarth *(Kostas)*, David Schofield *(Leatham)*, Charles Pountney *(James)*, Phyllida Law, Amanda Dickinson, Simon Prebble, and Elvi Hale

London-based novelist Benet Archdale (Helen Shaver) has just written a best-seller attacking traditional family structures. Not surprisingly, she lives alone with her young son, born out of wedlock. Benet's mother, Marsha (Lauren Bacall), visiting from the States, is mildly disapproving. But she's also a manic-depressive, prone to psychotic episodes. When Benet's child perishes after a sudden illness, Marsha goes into town and snatches a boy of the same age as a replacement. Benet is horrified by her mother's action, and public furor over the missing child grows, but the novelist doesn't want Marsha committed to an institution. Moreover, the kidnaped child has apparently been savagely beaten by his parents. While Marsha takes the next flight back to the US, Benet uses her writer's credentials to visit the boy's mother, Carol (Kate Hardie), a tawdry lounge singer with a moody live-in lover, Barry (Paul McGann). Having grown fond of the boy, Benet can't imagine sending him back to this pair, but while she deliberates, events inexorably spin out of control. The police, the public, and even Carol believe Barry has murdered the boy. Meanwhile, Terrance (Peter Firth), a greedy servant, learns that Benet has the missing boy, leading to a blackmail plot. In the end, Terrance, Carol, and Barry perish in a grim murder-suicide fiasco, and Benet keeps the boy, passing him off as her own son.

If a filmmaker with the sensibilities of Hitchcock or DePalma had handled INNOCENT VICTIM, it could have been a classic suspense film. Based on Ruth Rendell's novel *The Tree of Hands*, the film sets up a chillingly insoluble moral dilemma. But director Giles Foster, whose previous film was the anti-establishment farce CONSUMING PASSIONS, barely touches on the issues of guilt and responsibility. Instead he presents the tale in a straightforward, oddly nonjudgmental fashion. Benet runs a gamut of emotions, from bereavement to murderous rage, and by the end of the film her indecision has caused three deaths, yet her character undergoes little change. The final freeze-frame of Benet and "son" romping joyfully in a meadow carries none of the ironic weight it should have. Nevertheless the acting is expert, right down to little Barnaby Brown as the abused, kidnaped child. He evolves from a quiet, withdrawn figure to a happy, chatty toddler under Benet's maternal care. Even Marsha's psychosis is soft-pedaled; it's a relief that legendary actress Bacall isn't typed as a raving loony as Bette Davis and Joan Crawford were at the end of their careers. In the most

overtly villainous role, Firth chews the scenery as the classic English cad—all he lacks is a hooked nose and a black mustache to twirl. He's a bit much, but one wishes INNOCENT VICTIM had taken as many chances as Firth does with his performance—it might have made more compelling viewing. *(Profanity, violence, adult situations, sexual situations, nudity.)*

d, Giles Foster; p, Ann Scott; w, Gordon Williams (based on the novel *The Tree of Hands* by Ruth Rendell); ph, Kenneth McMillan; ed, David Martin; m, Richard Hartley; prod d, Adrian Smith; art d, Henry Harris and Alison Stewart-Richardson; stunts, Gareth Milne and Andy Bradford; cos, Barbara Kidd; makup, Jenny Shircore

Thriller (PR:C MPAA:R)

INTERNAL AFFAIRS

115m Frank Mancuso, Jr. — Pierre David/Paramount c

Richard Gere *(Dennis Peck)*, Andy Garcia *(Sgt. Raymond Avila)*, Nancy Travis *(Kathleen Avila)*, Laurie Metcalf *(Sgt. Amy Wallace)*, Richard Bradford *(Lt. Sgt. Grieb)*, William Baldwin *(Van Stretch)*, Michael Beach *(Dorian)*, Ron Vawter *(Comdr. Oakes)*, John Getz *(Teeters)*, Faye Grant *(Penny Stretch)*, Anabella Sciorra *(Heather Peck)*, Susan Forristal *(Lolly)*, Lew Hopson *(Buster)*, Julio Oscar Mechoso *(Gregory)*, and Allan Havey

How many ridiculous movies can an actor's career endure? Richard Gere continues to put that question with his appearance in this solemnly silly police thriller directed by Michael Figgis. For Figgis—in the follow-up to his critically successful debut, STORMY MONDAY, a low-key, *noir*ish melodrama that reveled in its larger-than-life characters and dreamlike tale of love and corruption—INTERNAL AFFAIRS also represents a professional stumble. Figgis again goes for a moody tone here, but there are so many other clashing tones clamoring for attention in INTERNAL AFFAIRS that the resulting movie is a noisy mishmash. Barely held together by a patchwork plot, it plays as if it were being made up by the actors and director as it goes along, despite a script credited to debuting writer Henry Bean.

Gere plays Dennis Peck, a star cop in one of the ritzier precincts of LA's San Fernando Valley. In his spare time, Peck is also a master criminal, running a vast empire of corruption out of that notorious breeding ground for vice, the Sherman Oaks Galleria shopping mall. Previously best known to moviegoers as the central setting of Amy Heckerling's FAST TIMES AT RIDGEMONT HIGH, the Galleria here serves as Peck's pork barrel, from which he draws high-paying, cushy part-time jobs for his loyal friends on the police force. Taking a bribery cut out of seemingly all the vice in the Valley, Peck launders his ill-gotten fortunes through his four ex-wives, making them all tycoons on paper, though they seem to spend all of their time making breakfast and doing laundry for Peck and his passel of kids. Peck also has a unique method of keeping his criminal operatives under control: he turns their wives into his pliant sex slaves by introducing the women to the joys of kinky love making during his free afternoons—of which he seems to have quite a few for a rich, powerful crime entrepreneur cum cop. In fact, we rarely see Peck doing anything so mundane and legit as actually arresting people; nonetheless, when LAPD internal affairs investigator Raymond Avila (Andy Garcia) tries to unravel Peck's web of corruption, he meets a wall of resistance from his superiors for going after one of the force's most "productive" cops. Instead, Avila is called in to investigate Peck's partner, Van Stretch (William Baldwin), an old friend of Avila's who has apparently been stretched to the breaking point as Peck's right-hand man. It seems that Stretch has developed an unseemly habit of punching out everyone within striking distance, from criminal suspects to his wife (Faye Grant)—with whom, of course, Peck is dallying in the Valley. From her, Peck learns that Stretch is about to blow the lid on Peck's enterprises to save his own hide. Accordingly, he has his partner killed, giving Avila a personal motive to continue his pursuit of Peck. However, Peck's own colorful habit of reverting to kill-crazy psychosis during tense moments proves to be his undoing, specifically when an elaborate (and credibility-straining) murder-for-money plot goes awry. Meanwhile, Peck manages to throw Avila off his scent by taunting him with suggestions that Avila's neglected wife, Kathleen (Nancy Travis), has become Peck's latest love conquest, driving the Internal Affairs investigator into a surprisingly stereotyped frenzy of offended Latino machismo, complete with giggle-inducing, tequila-induced fantasies of Kathleen and Peck in a hot and sweaty clinch.

Although INTERNAL AFFAIRS, unlike STORMY MONDAY, was not scripted by director Figgis, the films are similar in that both involve an idealistic outsider who must navigate a corrupt world of power-crazed men and their hard-bitten, wanton women. In STORMY MONDAY, however, Figgis was working with a much smaller setting (the depressed industrial town of Newcastle, England) in which he could more easily take liberties with realism and plot logic for the sake of mood and atmosphere. Anyone who knows LA, on the other hand, knows that just getting from here to there in that city can turn into a full-time job, and the idea of Peck carrying on demanding dual careers as a cop and master criminal while stoking the fires of half the women in the Valley is, to say the least, a rather tough sell as plot premises go. It doesn't help that the plot itself is so mindlessly complex, with little room left to develop any kind of consistent mood, much less to develop characters beyond the sum of their cliches. Moreover, as LETHAL WEAPON and its spin-offs have indicated, today's high-impact cop thriller is no place for subtlety anyway. When in doubt, LETHAL WEAPON damned the critics to plunge full-speed ahead into boom-boom cartoon action, giving audiences a wild roller-coaster movie ride in lieu of compelling drama. Figgis tries to have it both ways, creating an ersatz aura of worldly cynicism for the art-house crowd, while providing plenty of sleazy sex and blood-pellet violence for those in the cheaper seats. The result is yet another goofy credit in Gere's already overloaded resume of embarrassment (KING DAVID; BREATHLESS)—although some may consider this one of those movies that's so silly it's good, a rarity in big-budget studio productions. Like Figgis' debut film, INTERNAL AFFAIRS has moments of quirky, purpose-fully incongruous humor, but too many of its laughs are unintended. This is one cop thriller that should have stayed undercover. (*Sexual situations, nudity, violence, profanity.*)

d, Michael Figgis; p, Frank Mancuso Jr. and Pierre David; w, Henry Bean; ph, John A. Alonzo; ed, Robert Estrin; m, Michael Figgis, Anthony Marinelli, and Brian Banks; prod d, Waldemar Kalinowski; set d, Florence Fellman

Crime/Thriller   **(PR:O   MPAA:R)**

INTERROGATION, THE

(Pol.) 158m Unit X – Zespoly c

(PRZESLUCHANIE)

Krystyna Janda (*Antonia Dziwisz*), Janusz Gajos (*Zawada*), Adam Ferency (*Morawsky*), Agnieszka Holland (*Witowska*), Anna Romantowska, Bozena Dykiel, and Olgiard Lukaszewicz

Relentlessly depressing and over-emphatic, THE INTERROGATION is a grueling marathon of political oppression, sadistic inquisitions, and survival in prison. Filmed in 1982, this Polish import was banned in its homeland until recently. Intended as a paean to the human spirit, the 158-minute long movie becomes an endurance test for both protagonist and audience. A popular cabaret performer, Antonia (Krystyna Janda) is a flighty, high-strung woman who takes her pleasure where she finds it (sometimes with military officers). Ironically, it is her hedonism—seen here as a metaphor for her strongly individualized will—that causes her arrest yet proves to be her salvation. Tricked into accompanying two government agents on a drunken spree, she's dumped off at headquarters, arrested, and subjected to Kafka-esque questioning. No matter what the head investigator or his gung-ho associates do to her, however, they cannot turn Antonia into one of the sheeplike convicts that inhabit the over-crowded last stop for political prisoners. Tortured into a near-stupor, she almost confesses in writing that she was politically involved with a major with whom she had sex. Innocent pranks that the reckless but apolitical Antonia instigated while entertaining the troops are now interpreted as acts of treason by a regime that equates sexual indiscriminateness with betrayal of country. While the other women prisoners submit to the system by turning informer or by succumbing to brainwashing that convinces them of their own guilt, Antonia maintains her defiance even after being starved, tortured, and tossed into solitary. The only time she truly despairs is after the visit of her husband, who has accepted the official party interpretation of her indiscretions and denounces her. Failing to commit suicide, Antonia recovers her strong sense of self-worth and eventually attracts the admiration and then the passion of the interrogator who risks his career by making love with her. Sparing him the disgrace of revealing their affair when she becomes pregnant, Antonia bears her child in prison. When the authorities take the baby to an orphanage, the interrogator is unable to bear the pain and kills himself. Many years later, Antonia is finally released from prison. Reunited uneasily with her husband and child, she picks up the pieces of her shattered life.

Filmed in a style that shoves every horror into the viewer's face, THE INTERROGATION is a worthwhile, very political film that has more than a little visceral power. Directorial restraint might have resulted in an even more disturbing condemnation of officially sanctioned evil. So insistent is director Ryszard Bugajski's style that, at times, the film's brutality seems to be assaulting viewers in 3-D. But even given the charged emotions at the core of the film, a long shot here or there would have provided a welcome relief from the film's nonstop intensity. Only so much torture can be watched close-up. Ultimately, this expose of governmental intolerance and bureaucratic viciousness is only sporadically gripping and never really enlightening.

Nevertheless, Janda is brilliant as the framed entertainer whose pleasure-loving instincts belie a matchless inner strength. Despite some shrillness in the opening scenes—in which she overdoes the wild abandon with which Antonia lives—Janda creates a moving portrait of a woman's painful journey to self-re-

alization. The Best Actress citation that she won at last year's Cannes Film Festival was richly deserved. Unfortunately, the other cast members are all too willing to accommodate the director's penchant for heavily underscoring every emotion. THE INTERROGATION's noble intentions do not justify its all-too-apparent excesses. A more detached style and coolly ironic tone might have lent this film some much needed balance and made the filmmaker's message clearer and more memorable. (*Adult situations, profanity, nudity, sexual situations.*)

d, Ryszard Bugajski; p, Tadeuz Drewno; w, Ryszard Bugajski and Janusz Dymek; ph, Jacek Petrycki; ed, Katarzyna Maciejko; prod d, Janusz Sosnowski

Drama/Political   **(PR:O   MPAA:NR)**

ISTANBUL, KEEP YOUR EYES OPEN

(Sweden) 88m Omega/Cori – Magnum c

(AKA: ISTANBUL)

Timothy Bottoms (*Frank Collins*), Emma Kihlberg (*Mia Collins*), Twiggy (*Maud*), Lena Endre (*Ingrid*), Celal Khoshrowshahi (*Ali*), Robert Morley (*Mr. Atkins*), Sverre Anker Ousdal (*Consul*), David Gartenkraut (*Bill*), Engin Inal (*Uncle*), Nuvit Ozdogru, Merden Taner, and Zeki Goker

The plot mechanics of this would-be thriller creak like a rusty box spring, and the characters are shallow and unbelievable. Frank Collins (Timothy Bottoms), an American reporter living in Sweden, suffers a near-fatal heart attack during the opening credits. Although this occurrence has little to do with the rest of the film, it sets the tone for the jumpy editing and confusing dialog that follow. Collins' young stepson receives a videocassette from his real father, a Turk. While the cassette appears to be home movies of the clan in Istanbul, it's accompanied by a dire warning to Collins not to lose the tape. Curious, Collins journeys to Istanbul to see what's up, but, fearing impending danger, he leaves his stepson behind. Nevertheless, Collins brings his adolescent daughter with him. Naturally, much mystery does indeed await them; anonymous letters, stealthy searches, phantom intruders, and dead bodies are all in the offing. Turkish officials are unwilling to talk about the people who appear the videocassette, but Collins strikes up a warm relationship with Maud (Twiggy), another guest at the hotel at which he and his daughter are staying. With Maud's assistance, Collins finds his way to Atkins (Robert Morley), who is in the process of spilling the beans about a weapons-smuggling racket when thugs burst in and knock Collins unconscious. He awakens to find his daughter missing, Atkins murdered, and the hotel staff pretending Maud never existed. It's all because of the tape, of course, which holds evidence of an assassination. After a number of chases, the film ends in an unsatisfying, downbeat muddle.

A Swedish production for the international market, ISTANBUL is a sort of low-rent version of Polanski's FRANTIC or Hitchcock's THE MAN WHO KNEW TOO MUCH, though there is no danger of mistaking Bottoms' Frank Collins for a man who knows too much about anything. He's a clownish dullard as the movie begins and a terrified dullard when it ends, having spent most of the intervening time running through the streets of Istanbul calling his daughter's name—even before she is kidnaped. "Why can't you be like normal people?" Collins' daughter asks at one point. "Because I'm not like normal people!" Collins replies, balancing precariously on a hotel balcony. No kidding. It's suggested that a mid-life crisis has induced his annoying behavior, but whatever his motivation, Collins is a pretty hopeless hero. Morley and Twiggy, eminently watchable performers, have been shortchanged by the script. There are revealing views of Istanbul's back streets and markets, but its people are reduced to sinister-dark-foreigner cliches. Needless to say, there are better ways to spend your time and money than on this less-than-thrilling thriller. (*Violence, adult situations.*)

d, Mats Arehn; p, Peter Kropenin; w, Bo Sigvard Nilsson, Mats Arehn, and Thomas Samuelson; ph, Erling Thurmann Andersen; ed, Thomas Samuelson; m, Tomas Ledin; prod d, Eric Johnson; cos, Hedwig Ander; makup, Bibi Dawe and Zubeyde Erden

Thriller   **(PR:C   MPAA:PG-13)**

JK

JACOB'S LADDER

115m Carolco/Tri-Star c

Tim Robbins (*Jacob Singer*), Elizabeth Pena (*Jezzie*), Danny Aiello (*Louis*), Matt Craven (*Michael*), Pruitt Taylor Vince (*Paul*), Jason Alexander (*Geary*), Patricia Kalember (*Sarah*), Eriq La Salle (*Frank*), Ving Rhames (*George*), Brian Tarantina (*Doug*), Anthony Alessandro (*Rod*), Brent Hinkley (*Jerry*), S. Epatha Merkerson (*Elsa*), Suzanne Shepherd (*Hospital Receptionist*), Doug Barron (*Group Leader*), Jan Saint (*Santa*), Kisha Skinner, Dion Simmons (*Street Singers*), Sam Coppola (*Taxi Driver*), Patty Rosborough (*Drunk*), Evan O'Meara (*Sam*), Kyle Gass (*Tony*), Gloria Irizarry (*Mrs. Carmichael*), Lewis Black (*Jacob's Doctor*), Raymond Anthony Thomas (*Policeman*), Christopher Fields, Jaime Perry (*Field Medics*), Michael Tomlinson, A.M. Marxuach (*Field Doctors*), Antonia Rey (*Woman on Subway*), John Capodice, John Patrick McLaughlin (*Army Officers*), Bellina Logan (*Emergency Ward Nurse*), Scott Cohen (*Resident Doctor*), Davidson Thomson (*Evil Doctor*), Bryan Larkin (*Jed*), B.J. Donaldson (*Eli*), Thomas A. Carlin (*Doorman*), Carol Schneider, Becky Ann Baker, Diane Kagan (*Nurses*), Billie Neal (*Della*), Mike Stokie (*Field Sergeant*), James Ellis Reynolds (*EMT Bearer*), Dennis Green (*Attendant*), Brad Hamler, Byron Keith Minns (*Orderlies*), Reggie McFadden, Stephanie Berry, Chris Murphy, John-Martin Green (*Partygoers*), Arleigh Richards (*Paul's Wife*), Ann Pearl Gary, Barbara Gruen (*Mourners*), Joe Quintero (*Street Kid*), John Louis Fischer (*Machine Gunner*), Alva Williams (*Masked Man*), Elizabeth Abassi, Nora Burns, Alison Gordy, Jessica Roberts, Holly Kennedy, Blanche Irwin Stuart (*Hospital Patients*), Perry Lang (*Jacob's Assailant*), and Macaulay Culkin (*Gabe*)

Director Adrian Lyne follows his smash hit FATAL ATTRACTION (1987) with this overly flashy, but profoundly moving drama written with great skill by Bruce Joel Rubin (GHOST). JACOB'S LADDER stars Tim Robbins as Jacob, a divorced Vietnam veteran who lives in New York with his girl friend Jezzie (a smoldering Elizabeth Pena) and works as a mailman. Jacob is haunted by the painful memories of his dead son (a mysteriously unbilled Macaulay Culkin, star of 1990's monster hit HOME ALONE) and of his Vietnam experience when he was nearly killed by a soldier with a bayonet. As the film progresses, Jacob also begins to see weird creatures and startling visions. Suddenly, there are monsters roaming through the streets of New York; closed subway stations take on a creepy life of their own; a crowded party turns into a room full of winged demons; a train full of strangers look as though they have sprouted tails and horns. Are these the visions of a madman or have demons actually come to get Jacob Singer? While trying desperately to cling to his sanity, Jacob enlists the help of his ex-wife (Patricia Kalember), a mysterious stranger (Matt Craven) and an angelic chiropractor (Danny Aiello) to help solve the mystery. After almost causing the break-up of his relationship with Jezzie, and nearly dying from a severe fever, Jacob meets another Vietnam vet, Paul (Pruitt Taylor Vince), who has also been seeing demons. Both men discuss their nightmares about Vietnam (Jacob's visions all revolve around how he received the near-fatal bayonet wound), their feeling of dread and paranoia, and their shared hallucinations of demons. When Paul is mysteriously blown up in his car, Jacob is reunited with more of his veteran friends. They soon come to the conclusion that during the war, their platoon was used to test a strange experimental drug invented by the government, the side effects of which are now manifesting themselves in these wild visions. Jacob, along with the surviving members of his platoon, decides to expose the conspiracy. But hidden behind the surface is something much more profound and mysterious, something Jacob must face alone. Without his friends or family, Jacob learns the truth in a surprising and thought-provoking outcome that combines the past with the future, twists fantasy into reality and ultimately leaves Jacob's mind and soul at peace.

The much-touted script for JACOB'S LADDER had been circulating in Hollywood for almost a decade, and in a 1983 *American Film* article, Rubin's screenplay was listed among the ten best unproduced scripts. All of the praise and hype surrounding the script is absolutely deserved. JACOB'S LADDER is a complexly structured and intelligently written film, rich with ideas and potent horror. Even a questionable talent like Lyne (his forgettable credits include FLASHDANCE, 9 1/2 WEEKS and FOXES), a director who works best as a visual stylist, can't ruin the uncommon sincerity and intelligence of the script. Rubin's interest in the supernatural and the metaphysical (an interest that has been a part of every script he has written, including GHOST and BRAIN-STORM) never seems forced or ridiculous. Even when the proceedings become hard to swallow in JACOB'S LADDER, there is a feeling of such genuine concern for the characters, and such an overwhelmingly sure sense of the unearthly, that the most bizarre things in the film become believable. It is also to the film's benefit that Robbins has been cast in the lead. Known primarily as a comedic actor (ERIK THE VIKING, THE SURE THING, BULL DURHAM),

Robbins is simply outstanding as Jacob, bringing a conviction to the role that allows him to make the audience both identify with his plight and want to follow him anywhere. Although his character's reason for being in Vietnam remains a mystery (why would he enlist, and if he didn't enlist, since when do they draft married doctors of psychology?) there is never a question as to his motivations or his beliefs. Robbins brings a remarkable amount of sincerity to Jacob, which makes the horrifying aspects of the film more potent. When, for instance, Jacob hallucinates that he is strapped to a gurney being wheeled through bloody corridors populated with deformed monsters leading to a dark operating room, the effect is terrifying. Robbins completely understands the vision of Rubin and brings a personal and unique light to the character.

Unfortunately, Lyne seems determined to undermine the considerable accomplishments of Robbins and Rubin by handling it all with a stylized distance. Lyne's concerns are strictly visual—Is there enough smoke? Can the camera be placed at a lower angle? Is the pavement wet enough?—and his lack of understanding nearly sinks the film (when, about halfway through the running time, he almost turns the film into a conventional consripiracy thriller it completely goes off track). Luckily, Robbins keeps things real, and the sharp intelligence of the script rises above Lyne's hollow excesses (although Lyne *does* deserve some credit for personally adding Aiello's wonderful character to the story, and changing the original design of the script's demons from medieval-looking creatures to the much creepier nearly human monsters).

On the simplest of levels the film is a good thriller that's full of mystery and suspense. The special effects are good, the photography and editing are top-notch and it is well-acted; in addition to Robbins' incredible performance, Craven, Vince and Jason Alexander all are strong. Aiello and Pena are outstanding, and provide wonderful support for Robbins. JACOB'S LADDER is a powerful piece of work. (*Violence, gore effects, profanity, nudity*)

d, Adrian Lyne; p, Alan Marshall; w, Bruce Joel Rubin; ph, Jeffrey Kimball; ed, Tom Rolf; m, Maurice Jarre; prod d, Brian Morris; art d, Jeremy Conway; set d, Kathleen Dolan; spec, FXSMITH Inc., Gordon J. Smith, Connie Brink, Steven Dewey, and Musikwerks; stunts, Phil Nelson; cos, Ellen Mirojnick; makeup, Richard Dean; tech, Dale Dye

Horror   (PR:O MPAA:R)

JESUS OF MONTREAL

(Can./Fr.) 120m Max — Gerard Mital/National Film Board of Canada c

(JESUS DE MONTREAL)

Lothaire Bluteau (*Daniel*), Catherine Wilkening (*Mireille*), Johanne-Marie Tremblay (*Constance*), Remy Girard (*Martin*), Robert Lepage (*Rene*), Gilles Pelletier (*Fr. Leclerc*), Yves Jacques (*Richard Cardinal*), and Denys Arcand (*The Judge*)

Denys Arcand's JESUS OF MONTREAL is a modern Passion Play that takes aim at the superficial values of our media-saturated society, yet finds ultimate salvation in technology. If all of this sounds too academic, it pinpoints the main weakness of an otherwise strong, provocative film.

The story begins as Daniel (Lothaire Bluteau), a long-haired young actor, is hired to stage the annual Summer Passion Play in a park overlooking the skyline of Montreal. From the start, Daniel's production—which he is to direct, as well as to star in as Jesus—is not entirely conventional. Daniel's ensemble cast comprises fellow actor friends forced to make a living with such jobs as dubbing porn movies and modeling for sexy commercials glorifying materialism. Mireille (Catherine Wilkening) is the Passion Play's (as well as the film's) Mary Magdalene. At the beginning of the film she is adrift in the loose morality of the modern world, having an affair with the priest who hired Daniel to stage the play. But as the film goes on, she finds meaning in her life through her devotion to Daniel and the play. Daniel becomes fascinated with some of the more unorthodox theories that he encounters in his research of Jesus' life, including questions of Jesus' true parentage, and these details go into the play. When the play is finally ready to be performed, it has been transformed into a kind of avant-garde performance piece, with audiences ushered to the various installations representing the events in Jesus' life. The resulting drama may not adhere to standard biblical interpretations, but it truly moves and inspires the audience, and the revisionist Passion Play, its cast, and particularly Daniel become the toast of the town, cooed over by critics and culture vultures. Soon, life begins to imitate art, as church officials decide to discontinue the play because of questions about its possibly blasphemous content. The actors are cast out, just as the Disciples were, and the group looks to Daniel for guidance and inspiration. When Mireille goes on a cattle call for a commercial and is asked to take her shirt off in front of a room full of people and cameras, Daniel, like Jesus in the Temple, damns the purveyors of decadence and wrecks their instruments of destruction—the cameras. Later that night, during the final performance of the play, Daniel is arrested for destruction of property. A series of tragic events unfolds, and Daniel is "crucified" by the forces of mainstream society. However, hope is not completely lost; Daniel is "resurrected" in a tribute to the real miracles of modern medicine and science.

Arcand's excellent screenplay invests his vision of this spiritual parable with scathing satire and social commentary. And he brings his script to life with a superb cast and top production values. Particularly good are Bluteau as Daniel, his quiet brooding erupting into indignant rage; Remy Girard as Martin, the most down-to-earth character in the film; and Wilkening as Mireille, who represents the modern-day lost soul's search for meaning. However, in drawing parallels between Daniel and Jesus, Arcand paints himself into a corner. The too-literal quality of these comparisons, as well as the sometimes over-scholarly (rather than dramatic) tone, diminishes the film's overall impact. The final resurrection sequence should be extraordinarily powerful; instead it is cold and clinical. But despite these weaknesses, JESUS OF MONTREAL remains fresh, intelligent, and at times fascinating. *(Adult situations, nudity, profanity.)*

d, Denys Arcand; p, Roger Frappier; w, Denys Arcand; ph, Guy Dufaux; ed, Isabelle Dedieu; m, Yves Laferriere; prod d, Francois Seguin.

Drama   **(PR:O   MPAA:R)**

JETSONS: THE MOVIE

82m Hanna-Barbera/Universal c

VOICES OF: George O'Hanlon *(George Jetson)*, Mel Blanc *(Mr. Spacely)*, Penny Singleton *(Jane Jetson)*, Tiffany *(Judy Jetson)*, Patric Zimmerman *(Elroy Jetson)*, Don Messick *(Astro)*, Jean Vanderpyl *(Rosie the Robot)*, Ronnie Schell *(Rudy 2)*, Patti Deutsch *(Lucy 2)*, Dana Hill *(Teddy 2)*, Russi Taylor *(Fergie Furbelow)*, Paul Kreppel *(Apollo Blue)*, and Rick Dees *(Rocket Rick)*

JETSONS: THE MOVIE allows those who grew up with the successful TV cartoon series not only to visit again their favorite futuristic family, but also to introduce their own children to the Jetsons. However, it's a bit doubtful that 1990s children, brought up on a diet of "The Simpsons," will find the Jetson family as enjoyable as their parents did when *they* were kids in the 1960s. Regrettably, JETSONS also serves as a sad reminder of the loss of two of Hollywood's top comedy talents, Mel Blanc and George O'Hanlon, both of whom died shortly after completing their vocal chores on this picture. Will anyone ever forget the wonderful voices Blanc provided for Bugs Bunny or Daffy Duck? And older filmgoers may remember the delightful "Behind the 8-Ball" short subjects O'Hanlon (who contributes the voice for George Jetson) made for Warner Bros. four decades ago. Still another well-loved voiceover artist, Daws Butler, didn't live long enough to re-create the voice for Elroy, the Jetsons' son. But, fortunately for producers William Hanna and Joseph Barbera (veterans of so many glorious MGM "Tom and Jerry" cartoons of the 1940s and 50s), Patric Zimmerman proves to be an able replacement for Butler. Besides Elroy, the only other regular Jetson character not voiced by the original actor is Judy Jetson. In an effort to attract a teen audience, the producers chose to hire pop star Tiffany to replace Janet Waldo, whose long list of credits includes a stint as the star of radio's "Corliss Archer" in the late 1940s. Much to the film's credit, however, Waldo contributes other smaller vocal characterizations to JETSONS. The voice of George Jetsons's faithful housewife, Jane, is once again provided by Penny Singleton, another veteran of the Hollywood's Golden Era, best-known for her continuing role as Blondie in both the film series and TV program named for her character. Other noteworthy vocal contributions include Don Messick as Astro, the Jetsons' talking dog; Ronnie Schell as Rudy 2; Dana Hill as Teddy 2; Patti Deutsch as Lucy 2; and Jean Vanderpyl, who is very funny as the Jetsons' automated maid, Rosie the Robot.

Though by no means a great animated feature, JETSONS does offer unqualified family entertainment, and it even includes a socially responsive message. While the film is neither brilliant nor hilariously funny, it is frequently quite enjoyable, and fans of the Jetsons will not be disappointed. The producers have sensibly updated all the futuristic gimmicks and gadgets the Jetsons have at their disposal; however, feminists may find that the characters of mother Jane and daughter Judy are badly in need of a makeover, having lost little of their 60s flightiness. It seems both would still rather go shopping than undertake anything of galaxy-shattering importance, though Jane is now at least involved in a community recycling program.

There's nothing taxing about the plot. The only difference between the story here and that of a typical Jetsons TV episode is the film's inclusion of a few relevant comments about ecology during the Jetsons' attempt to save a community of cuddly little creatures known as Grungies. Moreover, the major change in the Jetsons' lifestyle is that the family has moved their home from Earth to a garden estate somewhere in the galaxy. George's boss, Mr Spacely (Mel Blanc), has had trouble finding a permanent vice-president for his problem-ridden sprockets factory. Someone or something is sabotaging the plant, and it is up to George to keep the plant running smoothly, thereby providing Mr. Spacely with his coveted one-millionth money-making sprocket. Either George is successful or, like the last four vice-presidents before him, he gets the axe. Eventually,

George discovers that it's the Grungies who are fouling up the machinery, but that they are acting in self-defense. When he stumbles upon a way both to preserve the Grungies' home and to see that the one-millionth Spacely sprocket is produced, George becomes everyone's hero. *(Violence.)*

d, William Hanna and Joseph Barbera; p, William Hanna and Joseph Barbera; w, Dennis Marks; ed, Pat Foley, Terry W. Moore, and Larry C. Cowan; m, John Debney; md, George Tobin; prod d, Al Gmuer; tech, Gerald Mills; anim, Ray Patterson

Animated/Children's/Science Fiction   **(PR:AA   MPAA:G)**

JEZEBEL'S KISS

97m Film Warriors/RCA-Columbia c

Katherine Barrese *(Jezebel)*, Meredith Baxter-Birney *(Virginia DeLeo)*, Meg Foster *(Amanda Faberson)*, Brent Fraser *(Hunt Faberson)*, Malcolm McDowell *(Ben Faberson)*, Elizabeth Ruscio *(Margie DeLeo)*, Bert Remsen *(Dr. Whatley)*, Everett McGill *(Dan Riley)*, Ernestine Mercer, and Stacey Renee Greenberg

Watching this film one can only wonder how they found the money to finance it and why the actors couldn't have appeared in a dinner-theatre production to better occupy their time. Stultifyingly dull, it seems like an adaptation of a bad, anti-establishment fiction of the 1960s, offering the heart of a hippie protestor and the mind of a sieve. Zooming into town on her motorcycle, Jezebel (Katherine Barrese) immediately captivates the locals. However, black-and-white flashbacks inform us that Jezebel has been here before. Could she be the granddaughter of the venerable old Indian whom years before refused to sell his land to bigtime developer Ben Faberson (Malcolm McDowell)? After Faberson's dopey son (Brent Fraser) crashes into her on the highway, Jezebel accepts a position as a waitress in the bar/restaurant run by Virginia DeLeo (Meredith Baxter-Birney), who occasionally sleeps with the town's sleazy sheriff, and who is burdened with a crippled sister, Margie (Elizabeth Ruscio). It seems all the town's residents have secrets to hide, and all of the men want to sleep with Jezebel. Slowly it develops that Jezebel is, in fact, the granddaughter of the Indian, who died of a heart attack as a result of the brutal harassment he suffered at the hands of Faberson and others in the town. She had extracted some measure of revenge by getting a job with the state coastal commission, thwarting Faberson's efforts to develop the land he acquired after her grandfather's death. However, Jezebel wants an even greater measure of revenge, and she has returned to the town to viciously vamp granddad's tormentors. She soon sets in motions a chain of events carefully planned to make all pay for the suffering they caused her grandfather.

Unconvincing in its depiction of a sexually-heated atmosphere and deficient in exploring the psychological underpinnings of revenge, JEZEBEL'S KISS is a thoroughly lackluster film. Slow-moving and sloppy, the film also drives home its points about the rape of the environment with sledgehammer subtlety. It would take a lot more than black-and-white flashbacks to draw the viewer into this silly saga of how bad karma catches up with a real estate mogul, yet the film offers little beyond those segments. Further, the most obvious nutcase in the film is its alleged heroine. Full of lip and long of face, Barrese seems to practice pouting as a second career. As the film fizzles instead of sizzles, one is left to ponder the movie's subtext—the correlation between sexual frustration and unscrupulous land acquisition. If her grandfather had lived, would Jezebel have simply become the town slut and made everyone happy while pleasuring them on her sacrosanct property? An intriguing movie could be made about the use of sex as a weapon, but this movie isn't it. *(Nudity, profanity, violence, adult situations.)*

d, Harvey Keith; p, Eric F. Scheffer; w, Harvey Keith; ph, Brian Reynolds; ed, Mort Fallick; m, Mitchel Forman; art d, Alan Baron

Drama   **(PR:O   MPAA:R)**

JOE VERSUS THE VOLCANO

94m Amblin/WB c

Tom Hanks *(Joe Banks)*, Meg Ryan *(Patricia/Angelica/DeDe)*, Lloyd Bridges *(Graynamore)*, Robert Stack *(Dr. Ellison)*, Abe Vigoda *(Chief of the Waponis)*, Dan Hedaya *(Waturi)*, Barry McGovern *(Luggage Salesman)*, Ossie Davis *(Marshall)*, and Amanda Plummer *(Dagmar)*

JOE VERSUS THE VOLCANO is a thoroughly captivating romantic adventure in the grand tradition of the screwball comedies of the 1930s and 40s. With a plot flavored with elements from such classics as the Carole Lombard-Fredric March romp NOTHING SACRED and Frank Capra's delightful masterpiece YOU CAN'T TAKE IT WITH YOU, this Tom Hanks-Meg Ryan outing is writer-director John Patrick Shanley's gift to moviegoers who are tired of films distinctive only for their excessive violence, sex, gutter language, or a combination of all three. What this picture may lack in depth of characterization or substance, it more than makes up for in the sheer joy of watching Hanks and

Ryan at work. Like a young Tracy and Hepburn, Hanks and Ryan exude that certain special, unexplainable, but magical quality that spells success for a screen pair. Both are in top form here, and both are scene stealers, with Ryan, perhaps, having the edge—but only because she plays three entirely different characters (all delicious) to Hanks' one, the gray young hypochondriac Joe. As enjoyable as Hanks is during his every moment of screen time, Ryan melts one's heart with her triple-threat performance: first as Joe's mousey, bespectacled coworker at the medical supply manufacturing plant where he feels trapped in a life of constant drudgery; then as a snappy pair of half-sisters, who enter Joe's drab—but soon-to-be-changed—life in a most unusual way. Someone has decided to take full advantage of Joe's hypochondria, and the half-sisters, red-haired Angelica and blonde Patricia, play a significant, though unwitting, part in this elaborate ploy. Joe, whose boring lifestyle and confining job are enough to do anyone in, decides to visit the company doctor (Robert Stack). Joe is told he has a "brain-cloud," a rare malady that leaves people feeling great until they suddenly die. Since Joe assumes he has only a few months to live, he's ripe for the proposition made to him by Graynamore (Lloyd Bridges), the billionaire who shows up at Joe's bachelor flat the following morning. Joe accepts Graynamore's offer of instant wealth (via unlimited use of credit cards) and a few days of all-stops-out fun and frolic in exchange for his life. Graynamore's continued affluence depends upon a rare mineral found only on the Pacific Island of Waponi Woo, but this source will soon dry up if the natives aren't appeased by some volunteer willing to leap into their active volcano as a sacrifice to save the island. Since he is going to kick the bucket soon anyway, Joe reasons, why not make the end more meaningful by doing Graynamore this one little favor? The adventure begins with Angelica, the redhead, who looks and sounds like a bubbly 1960s flower child. She introduces Joe to Patricia, the brave and daring skipper of a charming little schooner. While the film gets off to a slow start, once the high seas adventure begins, it's fullsail entertainment, with the gloriously expansive Pacific seascapes provided by cinematographer Stephen Goldblatt nearly as engaging as Hanks' and Ryan's performances.

A visually beautiful endeavor further enhanced by production designer Bo Welch's imaginative South Sea island setting and by a heartwarming score from Georges Delerue, the film ultimately becomes an odyssey of faith, hope, and courage, culminating in a completely sincere portrayal of the love and devotion that blossoms between Joe and Patricia. Screenwriter John Patrick Shanley (MOONSTRUCK; FOUR CORNERS; THE JANUARY MAN) makes an impressive directorial bow, proving himself to be a director with a flair for telling a fanciful yarn in pure cinematic terms—no mean trick. It's one thing to shoot a down-to-earth cop movie set amidst the gritty realism of a major American metropolis, but to be able to captivate an audience with a work of pure wit and unadulterated fantasy is nothing short of genius. Despite some unevenness in Shanley's direction, especially during the early sequences at the medical supply company, his overall work—both as director and screenwriter—deserves applause. In particular, some of his dialog is extremely touching.

Hanks and Ryan are well supported by the likes of Stack, Bridges, Abe Vigoda (in a funny cameo as a native chieftain), Dan Hedaya, Barry McGovern, and Ossie Davis (as a sly limo driver). The filmmakers also make clever use of four large trunks that Joe innovatively straps together to make a life raft. Whats more, Hanks' impromptu "funky chicken" dance routine while standing atop this raft is hilarious. Ryan's delectable, but all too brief, appearance as the spunky Angelica is also especially memorable. Fortunately, we get to see even more of Ryan's wonderful turn as Patricia. (Profanity.)

d, John Patrick Shanley; p, Teri Schwartz; w, John Patrick Shanley; ph, Stephen Goldblatt; ed, Richard Halsey; m, Georges Delerue; prod d, Bo Welch; spec, Industrial Light & Magic; cos, Colleen Atwood

Adventure/Comedy   **(PR:A   MPAA:PG)**

KILL ME AGAIN

94m MGM-UA c

Joanne Whalley-Kilmer *(Fay Forrester)*, Val Kilmer *(Jack Andrews)*, Michael Madsen *(Vince Miller)*, Jonathan Gries *(Alan Swayze)*, and Michael Greene *(Cop)*

Well-crafted and competently acted, KILL ME AGAIN is anything but a terrible film; however, like so many other films that have struggled mightily to pay homage to the great *films noir* of the past, it fails to come to life on its own terms.

The story opens promisingly, with thrill-hungry cutie Fay (Joanne Whalley-Kilmer) and her handsome but half-witted boy friend, Vince (Michael Madsen), staging a robbery of a roadhouse-casino that escalates into a bloody shootout, resulting in the death of a mob collection man. In a rare moment of sanity, Vince plans for the couple to hide out in the heartland until the heat dies down, but Fay, ill-suited to the pastoral life, demands her share of the loot, intent on heading for Nevada. When Vince testily disagrees, Fay settles the argument by applying a

large rock to the back of his head, then takes off for Reno. After glimpsing a tabloid headline about her criminal exploits, Fay offers down-and-out private eye Jack (Val Kilmer, Whalley-Kilmer's real-life spouse) $10,000—the amount he owes some very mean loan sharks—to fabricate evidence of her death so that she can create a new identity and make good her escape. Rechristened Vera Billings, Fay ditches Jack, having paid him only half of what she owes him and having thoughtfully left behind evidence implicating Jack in her "murder." For the rest of the film, Jack chases Fay while the police, the mob, and Vince chase Jack.

If nothing else, KILL ME looks and sounds great. Jacques Steyn's cinematography brings a harsh, surreal beauty to the forgotten corners of Nevada where the action is set, and William Olvis' score is rich, romantic, and foreboding in the *noir* tradition. But the film suffers throughout because of a clash between the old-fashioned style of the storytelling and the contemporary morality of the script. It doesn't help matters much that the film's "hero by default," Jack, is thinly conceived. All that is really revealed about him is that he's a loser; having lost both his wife and his business (which he doesn't seem to have been very good at in the first place), Jack doesn't want anything beyond the money Fay owes him. Even his short-lived affair with her lacks passion, despite Whalley-Kilmer's incendiary good looks.

High on technique but low on idiosyncratic artistry, the performances are generally disappointing. Although a capable actor, Kilmer is unconvincing here as a gumshoe on the skids—too healthy for the part, with bland, boy-next-door good looks. His energetic presence was perfect for his roles in the underrated comedies TOP SECRET! and REAL GENIUS, but here Kilmer just looks out of place, seemingly incapable of suggesting the grubby desperation his character requires. The kittenish Whalley-Kilmer also fails to convince as KILL ME AGAIN's wanton woman, with the problem again being too much technique and not enough genuine heat. Similarly, Madsen is effective as the violent bully, but without ever conveying the kind of inspired craziness that would place him among the ranks of truly scary movie villains.

Though the script by director John Dahl and coproducer David W. Warfield is more imaginative than those of most similar genre efforts, it lacks urgency, playing out more like cleverly constructed clockwork than as an edge-of-the-seat thriller. KILL ME AGAIN marks the feature debuts of both Dahl and Warfield, and both show some promise; however, their debut too nearly resembles a film-school project. Full of witty references to other films, it will keep hardcore movie buffs searching their memories through multiple viewings, but more casual viewers may find it a slow-moving, mannered dud. (*Sexual situations, violence, profanity.*)

d, John Dahl; p, David W. Warfield, Sigurjon Sighvatsson, and Steve Golin; w, John Dahl and David W. Warfield; ph, Jacques Steyn; ed, Frank Jimenez, Jonathan Shaw, and Eric Beason; m, William Olvis; prod d, Michelle Minch

Crime/Thriller   **(PR:O   MPAA:R)**

KILL-OFF, THE

100m Filmworld/Cabriolet c

Loretta Gross *(Luanne)*, Jackson Sims *(Pete)*, Steve Monroe *(Ralph)*, Cathy Haase *(Danny Lee)*, Andrew Lee Barrett *(Bobbie)*, Jorjan Fox *(Myra)*, William Russell *(Rags)*, Sean O'Sullivan *(Doctor)*, Ellen Kelly *(Lily)*, Ralph Graff *(Lily's Brother)*, Jim Woyt, Cesar Pares, Mike Towstik *(Bar Regulars)*, Bill Busto *(Policeman)*, and Spencer Neyland *(Dancing Drums)*

The place: a small resort town on the Jersey shore. The time: off-season. The hottest spot in town is the Pavilion, a bar that's seen better days. Pete (Jackson Sims), the owner, is desperate to drum up some business. Though his only employees are his daughter Myra (Jorjan Fox), bartender Rags (William Russell), and part-time janitor Ralph (Steve Monroe), the bar can't turn a profit when the summer people aren't in town. He hires a stripper, Danny Lee (Cathy Haase), and when she falls in love with the handsome but slow-witted Ralph, the trouble really starts. The trouble being Ralph's wife, Luanne (Loretta Gross). The woman is twenty years his senior, bedridden (though the doctor says there's nothing wrong with her), and possessed of the nastiest tongue on the eastern seaboard. She holds the entire town in her thrall as her relentless and all-too accurate gossip causes misery, ruins lives, and has even driven people to suicide. Her curious relationship with Ralph is disrupted by his affair with Danny Lee—she doesn't mind if he sleeps with other women, but the thought that he might be in love with one of them drives her mad with jealousy. She lashes out by doing what she does best—spreading gossip. She spreads the word that Bobbie (Andrew Lee Barrett), the son of her doctor, is dealing drugs out of the Pavilion; that Myra—Bobbie's girl—is a junkie; that Rags killed his family in a car accident; and that Pete once raped his own daughter. Everyone in town has good reason to kill the woman, but when somebody does, it marks only the beginning of a series of violent acts.

The film was adapted from the novel by pulp cult novelist Jim Thompson who died in 1977, but whose work experienced a renaissance in 1990. His novels had been adapted for such films as Sam Peckinpah's THE GETAWAY (1972), Burt Kennedy's THE KILLER INSIDE ME (1976), and Bertrand Tavernier's COUP DE TORCHON (1981), but in 1990, THE KILL-OFF was one of three films to be based on Thompson novels, following AFTER DARK, MY SWEET and THE GRIFTERS. This was the lowest budgeted of the three, and its dark, claustrophobic atmosphere is certainly true to the source material. First-time director/screenwriter Maggie Greenwald, however, made a number of changes in adapting the material, the most important one being that in the novel, the identity of Luanne's killer is never revealed. Greenwald's decision makes cinematic sense, giving the story structure and dramatic arc, but it undermines Thompson's characterization of Luanne as a malevolent cloud of metaphorical ugliness; in the film, she's simply a nasty old woman with some grudges to settle. That aside, within the limitations of the budget, Greenwald has made the best of her material. Perhaps her cleverest notion is to cut in frequent shots of telephone lines abuzz with audible but incomprehensible chatter. Luanne's hurtful words seem embodied in the whip-like wires. The locations are appropriately weathered and run-down, and the photography relentlessly grim. The cast, mainly composed of New York stage actors, captures the hopeless meanness of the characters with exceptional conviction, and the score is hauntingly sleazy. While THE KILL-OFF couldn't really compete with the higher-powered Thompson adaptations of 1990, in its small way it makes a solid contribution to the roster of the author's books that have been brought to the screen. (*Adult situations, nudity, violence, alcohol and drug abuse, profanity.*)

d, Maggie Greenwald; p, Lydia Dean Pilcher; w, Maggie Greenwald (based on the novel by Jim Thompson); ph, Declan Quinn; ed, James Y. Kwei; m, Evan Lurie; prod d, Pamela Woodbridge; stunts, Andy Kahan; cos, Daryl Kerrigan

Crime   (PR:C MPAA:R)

KINDERGARTEN COP

111m Universal c

Arnold Schwarzenegger (*Kimble*), Penelope Ann Miller (*Joyce*), Pamela Reed (*Phoebe*), Linda Hunt (*Miss Schlowski*), Richard Tyson (*Crisp*), Carroll Baker (*Eleanor Crisp*), Christian Cousins, Joseph Cousins (*Dominic*), Cathy Moriarty (*Sylvester's Mother*), Park Overall (*Samantha's Mother*), Jayne Brook (*Zach's Mother*), Richard Portnow (*Capt. Salazar*), Tom Kurlander (*Danny*), Alix Koromzay (*Cindy*), Betty Lou Henson (*Keisha's Mother*), Heidi Swedberg (*Joshua's Mother*), Justin Page (*Zach*), Peter Rakow (*Joshua*), Sarah Rose Karr (*Emma*), Marissa Rosen (*Samantha*), Ben McCreary (*Lowell*), Miko Hughes (*Joseph*), Robert Cave (*John*), Ben Diskin (*Sylvester*), Tameka Runnels (*Keisha*), Medha Garg (*Latiana*), Brian Wagner (*William*), John Christian Graas (*Kevin*), Jim Jim Jackson (*Sedgewinn*), Ian Baumer (*Sam*), Amy Wald (*Sarah*), Tiffany Materas (*Tina*), Krystle Materas (*Rina*), James Chance (*Matthew*), Adam Wylie (*Larry*), Nicole Nagorsky (*Heather*), Ross Malinger (*Harvey*), Amber Reaves (*Mary*), Odette Yustman (*Rosa*), Tina Hart (*Dorothy*), Emily Ann Lloyd (*Jennifer*), Haley Urman (*Courtney*), Bethany Jaye Allyn (*Catherine*), Zachary March (*Nick*), Anthony Wong (*Tom*), Remone Bradley (*Erwin*), Stephen Root (*Sheriff*), Robert Nelson (*Henry*), Molly Cleator (*Schlowski's Assistant*), Gary Hollis (*Superintendent Rice*), Susan Burns (*Waitress*), Tom Dugan (*Crisp's Lawyer*), Roma (*Manicurist*), Jason Stuart (*Male Hairstylist*), Kim Delgado, Ray Glanzman, Ed Crick (*Security Guards*), John Hammil (*Zach's Father*), Rick Jones (*Samantha's Father*), Tiffany Reaves (*Tiffany*), and Jason Reitman (*Jason*)

Following his blood-soaked megahit TOTAL RECALL, Arnold Schwarzenegger successfully swung for a second time from "Arnold the Killer" in the summer to "Arnold the Cuddly" at Christmas. The first time was with TWINS in 1988, which followed that summer's RED HEAT. In both cases, Arnold helped the career of director Ivan Reitman (STRIPES, GHOSTBUSTERS), who was on the ropes in '88 following his big-budget flop LEGAL EAGLES and in disrepute in '90 due to the failure of GHOSTBUSTERS II the previous year.

COP didn't quite repeat the success of TWINS. Like virtually every other 1990 Christmas release, it lost a good chunk of its audience to HOME ALONE. Further, it suffered from a mild media controversy over its awkward splicing of family humor and cop violence. Still, the film was no slouch and continued to play in theatres long after higher-profile offerings such as HAVANA and BONFIRE OF THE VANITIES had disappeared. Unlike some of its woeful competition, KINDERGARTEN COP is abundantly entertaining, buoyed by Schwarzenegger's self-deprecating charm and easy chemistry, both with the hammiest bunch of tykes ever assembled for a movie and his very capable co-star, Pamela Reed.

Indeed, this is a smartly cast film from top to bottom as it also includes exceptional villains in Richard Tyson (he was one of the moons in the steamy sex drama TWO MOON JUNCTION) as Crisp, an Oedipal psychopath, and

Carroll Baker as his cold-blooded mom, Eleanor. Long sought by LA cop Kimble (Schwarzenegger), the pair is hunting down Crisp's wife and son, who have fled to Oregon. Kimble teams with fellow cop Phoebe (Reed), a former schoolteacher, to go undercover in an Oregon elementary school to find the woman and child and bring them back to LA to testify against Crisp and his mother. The gimmick is that unlike the villains, Kimble and Phoebe have no idea what the wife and son look like.

It sounds more complicated than it plays. In fact, the film's plot at heart has an elemental simplicity, borrowed from classic westerns, with Kimble serving as the sheriff who brings order to the frontier while gallantly rescuing sweet-schoolmarm-in-distress Joyce (Penelope Ann Miller)—owner of the cutest shoulders in Hollywood, displayed here to good advantage in a succession of off-the-shoulder outfits. It matters hardly at all that the tough-but-tender sheriff (besides having a cute, frisky pet ferret, a book of A.A. Milne poems causes him to tear up) is at heart another burnt-out LA cop; the frontier is a picture-postcard town in Oregon overrun with sexy, lonely single mothers; the rabble is a mob of pint-sized unruly over-actors and the justice is dealt to a ponytailed mama's boy who cops his act from Steven Seagal.

What counts is that it works, often in spite of itself. Reitman remains one of Hollywood's most hamhanded directors. His handling of the film's female characters reveals little sensitivity either to the talents he's assembled or the chemistry of the leads. Something weirdly erotic happens throughout the film whenever Reed and Schwarzenegger are on screen together. Starting out as the standard bickering mismatched cop partners, Reed plays her part as if she were working toward a randy seduction of Schwarzenegger, making the early parts of the film livelier and spicier than they deserve to be, since her performance is obviously at odds with the script. The film takes the pairing nowhere and Reed is taken out of the script in a particularly inane and tasteless manner. Meanwhile, the blossoming romance between Miller and Schwarzenegger plays like a contrived, superfluous afterthought. Similar misdirection around the fringes includes the pet ferret getting more screen time than capable supporting players such as Cathy Moriarty and Linda Hunt.

Yet KINDERGARTEN COP proves to be doggedly director-proof in the long run. Schwarzenegger tames his kindergarten class by having them do calisthenics, thus shamelessly using his role to promote his offscreen position as chairman of the President's Council on Physical Fitness—and therefore the political ambitions he constantly denies having. But his scenes with the kids can't help but amuse as they effectively sendup Schwarzenegger's super-hero image. (*Violence, profanity, adult situations.*)

d, Ivan Reitman and Brian Grazer; p, Ivan Reitman; w, Murray Salem, Herschel Weingrod, and Timothy Harris (based on a story by Salem); ph, Michael Chapman; ed, Sheldon Kahn; m, Randy Edelman; art d, Richard Mays; set d, Anne D. McCulley; stunts, Joel Kramer; cos, Gloria Gresham; makup, Jeff Dawn and Ken Chase

Action/Comedy   (PR:A-C MPAA:PG-13)

KING OF NEW YORK

(It./US) 103m Augusto Caminito/New Line c

Christopher Walken (*Frank White*), David Caruso (*Dennis Gilley*), Larry Fishburne (*Jimmy Jump*), Victor Argo (*Roy Bishop*), Wesley Snipes (*Thomas Flannigan*), Janet Julian (*Jennifer Poe*), Joey Chin (*Larry Wong*), Giancarlo Esposito (*Lance*), Paul Calderon (*Joey Dalesio*), Steve Buscemi, Theresa Randle, Leonard Lee Thomas, Roger Guenver Smith, Carrie Nygren, Freddie Jackson, Sari Chang, Ariane Koizumi, Vanessa Angel, Phoebe Legere, and Pete Hamill

Frank White (Christopher Walken), a middle-aged drug lord, is released from prison to find that the streets of New York are just a little bit tougher and less forgiving than they were when he went in. Still, his gang remains loyal, and his enemies—police and thieves alike—are as hostile as ever. Everything is pretty much the same...except Frank White, who's decided it's time to make some reparations. The streets have made him rich and powerful, and he figures there's nothing to stop a motivated man from making his mark on society. However, countless hurdles stand in the way of White's civic-minded ambitions, which revolve around raising the $16 million needed to keep open a public hospital in a poverty-stricken neighborhood. For starters, he has made a bad name for himself in virtually every ethnic enclave in New York. Nevertheless, White decides to raise the money by teaming with Lance Wong (Joey Chin), a young dealer who operates in Chinatown and who has a huge shipment of drugs to move. Wong's lack of altruism ("If I wanted socialized medicine, I'd have stayed in the Peking province") is a problem, as is the hostility of the Mafia, which is horrified by White's interracial operation. Further complicating White's efforts are some frustrated Brooklyn cops who are willing to use any means necessary to put an end to White's scheme. The cops' commanding officer, Roy Bishop (Victor Argo), tries to keep them within the bounds of the law, but hot-headed

Dennis Gilley (David Caruso) persuades his fellow officers that the system favors the criminal and that if anything is to be done about White, it won't be done by the book. Doomed from the start, White's plan precipitates a wave of violence. He declares war on the Italian and Chinese mobs, only to be betrayed by one of his own subordinates, who helps the rogue cops raid White's headquarters in the guise of yet another gang. White and right-hand man Jimmy Jump (Larry Fishburne) escape, but only White makes it until morning, when he confronts Bishop, who fatally wounds him. White dies, alone, trapped in a taxi in a Time Square traffic jam.

Widely accused of racism and of glamorizing drug dealing, KING OF NEW YORK is an extraordinary, incisive investigation of race, class, and power in New York. Writer-director team Nicholas St. John and Abel Ferrara, both native New Yorkers, are responsible for a series of tough, stylish films—including MS. 45 and CHINA GIRL—and KING OF NEW YORK is easily their best effort to date. It is the film Sidney Lumet's Q&A claimed to be, managing to address issues that make most filmmakers and audiences cringe, without ever stooping to didacticism.

Ferrara and St. John's vision of New York is jittery, complex, and defined by juxtapositions of wealth and poverty, legal and illegal commerce, politics and crime, business and recreation that are so extreme as to verge on the ludicrous. Their New York is the biggest, glossiest, most high-tech banana republic conceivable, a jungle of steel and concrete animated by atavistic rhythms and primitive, clannish conceptions of place, loyalty, and interdependence. St. John's screenplay isn't subtle, but it's apt and brutally direct; there's no beating around the bush, no coyness in his depiction of the mechanics of manipulation, intimidation, and exclusion of one group by another.

Ferrara's great gift as a director is his ferocious sense of place: New York's boroughs, ethnic neighborhoods, subways, hotels, landmarks, bars, and fast-food joints are all convincingly rendered here. Like the characters who inhabit and are defined by them, these places couldn't be anywhere but in New York. Ferrara's KING OF NEW YORK cast is uniformly excellent. Along with Fishburne (TV's "Pee Wee's Playhouse") and Caruso ("Crime Story"), the cast includes Giancarlo Esposito (SCHOOL DAZE), Wesley Snipes (MO' BETTER BLUES), Steve Buscemi (MILLER'S CROSSING), and, of course, Walken, who delivers a high wire performance that stops just this side of an on-screen nervous breakdown.

In a year defined by epic, prestige gangster films—including Joel and Ethan Coen's MILLER'S CROSSING, Martin Scorsese's GOODFELLAS, Phil Joanou's STATE OF GRACE, and Francis Ford Coppola's GODFATHER III—Ferrara and St. John managed to make a film that holds its own with the best of its big-budget competition. However, despite their evident gifts, Ferrara and St. John remain marginal filmmakers by virtue of their vicious subject matter and uncompromising approach. (*Violence, profanity, drug abuse, nudity.*)

d, Abel Ferrara; p, Mary Kane; w, Nicholas St. John; ph, Bojan Bazelli; ed, Anthony Redman; m, Joe Delia; prod d, Alex Tavoularis; art d, Stephanie Ziemer; set d, Sonja Roth; spec, Matt Vogel; stunts, Phil Neilson; cos, Carol Ramsey

Crime   (PR:C MPAA:R)

KONEKO MONGATARI

(Japan) (SEE: ADVENTURES OF MILO AND OTIS, THE)

KRAYS, THE

(Brit.) 119m Fugitive—Parkfield/Miramax c

Billie Whitelaw (*Violet Kray*), Gary Kemp (*Ronald Kray*), Martin Kemp (*Reginald Kray*), Susan Fleetwood (*Rose*), Charlotte Cornwell (*May*), Jimmy Jewel (*Cannonball Lee*), Avis Bunnage (*Helen*), Kate Hardie (*Frances*), Alfred Lynch (*Charlie Kray, Sr.*), Tom Bell (*Jack "The Hat" McVitie*), Steven Berkoff (*George Cornell*), Gary Love (*Steve*), Victor Spinetti (*Mr. Lawson*), Barbara Ferris (*Mrs. Lawson*), Julia Migenes (*Judy, Singer in Club*), Roger Monk (*Charlie Kray, Jr.*), John-Paul White (*Ronald Kray, Age 3*), Michael White (*Reginald Kray, Age 3*), Harlon Haveland (*Ronald Kray, Age 8*), Sam Haveland (*Reginald Kray, Age 8*), Jason Bennett (*Ronald Kray, Age 10*), Jamie Bennett (*Reginald Kray, Age 10*), John McEnery (*Charlie Pelham*), and Patti Love (*Iris*)

THE KRAYS begins after identical twins Ronald and Reginald Kray (Gary and Martin Kemp) are born in a working-class slum in London's East End. They are raised amidst the hardship and deprivation of WW II, in a world of women and children—the men being either in the army or draft dodgers like the twins' own father. Brought up by their strong-willed mother, Violet (Billie Whitelaw), and her equally commanding mother and sisters, the boys grow up fiercely devoted to each other and to the women who raised them, admiring strength and cunning and contemptuous of weakness and of the law. Bullies as children, the Krays turn into criminals hardened by stints in prison and the army. Vicious,

fearless, and highly conscious of the figure they cut as twins, they begin to build an illegal empire based on gambling and protection rackets. But as their businesses expand, the twins begin to grow apart. Ron (who is homosexual) begins to show signs of mental instability, is prone to fits of irrational violence, and is also determined to dominate his brother. Reg tries to escape Ron's influence by getting married, but his high-strung bride can't take the strain of living as a gangster's wife and commits suicide. After her death, the twins are closer than ever; however, Ron's arrogant savagery eventually brings them down. Paranoid and furious at Reg's cautious approach to their criminal competitors, he decides that Jack the Hat (Tom Bell), a small-time member of their own organization, and George Cornell (Steven Berkoff), a member of the rival Richardson gang, must die. Ron kills Cornell, shooting him in a crowded pub. He goads Reg into dealing with Jack the Hat, a murder that takes on unexpectedly gruesome proportions when Reg's gun misfires and he's forced to finish the job with a knife. The Krays are arrested and incarcerated, Reg in prison and Ron in a maximum security mental hospital. They are reunited only once, briefly, at their mother's funeral.

Although the real-life Krays—called the "Kings of Crime" during their heyday in the London underworld in the 60s—are genuine celebrities in the UK (where they are still serving time), they're all but unknown elsewhere. THE KRAYS isn't compelling enough to explain the brothers' enduring notoriety to outsiders. The key to their appeal isn't that they were criminal masterminds (they weren't, not by any stretch of the imagination), but that they were *performers*, flash lower-class icons who mixed with celebrities and aristocrats, carefully cultivating their own myth. Twins, they dressed identically, travelled in tandem, and finished each other's thoughts. One homosexual and one heterosexual; one mad and one sane; both simultaneously brutal and stylish, the Krays were bound by an intricate web of loyalty and love. You couldn't make them up without being charged with lurid sensationalism.

On the other hand, no one could accuse screenwriter Philip Ridley or director Peter Medak of exploiting the story. They've stuck close to the facts of the Krays' lives, but rendered the inherently bizarre material almost lifeless. In concentrating on locating the Krays in a socioeconomic and historical context, Ridley winds up with a script top-heavy with scenes of the twins as children, when they weren't doing anything very interesting. Medak (A DAY IN THE DEATH OF JOE EGG; THE RULING CLASS) vacillates between theatrical stylization and cheerless realism, but the styles don't mesh and neither has any real punch. Nicolas Roeg and Donald Cammell's overwrought PERFORMANCE (1970), which isn't overtly about the Krays at all, captures better the studied decadence of their short, brutal turn in the limelight.

THE KRAYS' one unequivocal asset is the Kemps—brothers, former child actors, and members of the Spandau Ballet—who are extraordinary as the twins. Many rock singers have tried to make the transition to acting, few of them triumphantly. Even such superstars as Mick Jagger (the star of PERFORMANCE), David Bowie, and Madonna have achieved only limited success on the screen. But the Kemps use what they've learned about stage presence and channelled it into characterizations. They've got the charismatic performers in the Krays down pat, and they play off one another with authoritative ease. (Even the fact that they aren't twins works for them, since, as adults, Ron and Reg looked significantly different.) The Kemps make THE KRAYS worth watching. (*Violence, sexual situations.*)

d, Peter Medak; p, Dominic Anciano and Ray Burdis; w, Philip Ridley; ph, Alex Thomson; ed, Martin Walsh; m, Michael Kamen; prod d, Michael Pickwoad; spec, Aaron Sherman and Maralyn Sherman; stunts, Stuart St. Paul; cos, Lindy Hemming; makup, Jenny Boost; tech, Charlie Kray

Crime   (PR:C MPAA:R)

KUROI AME

(Japan) (SEE: BLACK RAIN)

L

LA DUEDA INTERNA
(Arg./Brit.) (SEE: VERONICO CRUZ)

LA VIE EST RIEN D'AUTRE
(Fr.) (SEE: LIFE AND NOTHING BUT)

LABYRINTH OF PASSION
(Sp.) 100m Alphaville/Cinevista c

(LABERINTO DE PASION)

Cecilia Roth (Sexilia), Luis Ciges (Her Father), Imanol Arias (Riza Niro), Antonio Banderas (Sadeq), Helga Line (Toraya), Marta Fernandez-Muro (Queti), Angel Alcazar (Eusebio), Agustin Almodovar (Hassan), and Pedro Almodovar (Performer)

Made in 1982, but released generally in the US in 1990 after the success of his WOMEN ON THE VERGE OF A NERVOUS BREAKDOWN (1988), Pedro Almodovar's LABYRINTH OF PASSION is a screwball sex comedy set in a world of unorthodox and baroquely intertwined personal relationships in Madrid. Predicated on mistaken identity and misinterpreted motives, the plot is a tangle that defies simple summary. Among the some 50 characters is Sexilia (Cecilia Roth), "Sexi" for short, a carefree, heliophobic nymphomaniac whose father (Luis Ciges) is a repressed, world-famous fertility specialist. Hoping to exorcise her fear of sunlight (sexual insatiability is not, in her estimation, a problem), Sexi consults a therapist, who announces that Sexi's trouble is incestuous attraction to her father. The therapist then confesses her own determination to seduce the fertility expert, whose patients include the manipulative, aristocratic Toraya (Helga Line). Toraya, in turn, has designs on Riza Niro (Imanol Arias), the homosexual son of the deposed ruler of the Arab nation of Tyran. Riza, who just wants to cruise the Spanish bars and docks incognito, has difficulty maintaining a low profile. Scandal sheets speculate about his activities, revolutionary student terrorists hope to kidnap him, and Toraya is determined to find and seduce him as part of a plot to avenge herself on her father. Blithely unaware of these goings-on, Riza meets Sexi in a discotheque, and they fall head over heels for one another. Needless to say, the course of their love—true though it is—does not run smooth. Riza, confused by his attraction to a woman, leaves with another man; Sexi goes off to an orgy, but realizes she wants only the young Arab. There follows a slew of complications: Riza hesitates to tell Sexi of his real identity and sexual past; she worries that he thinks she's a slut. Sexi's therapist fails to seduce Sexi's father—who admits he's never been interested in sex—and Sexi's new best friend, Queti (Marta Fernandez-Muro), confesses that she wants to leave home because she finds her father's sexual demands distasteful. These and many other matters are resolved in a last minute flurry of unlikely invention and flamboyant circumstance: Queti undergoes plastic surgery that makes her Sexi's double, then moves into Sexi's life and the fertility specialist's bed. The terrorists kidnap Toraya, and Sexi and Riza flee the country, consummating their relationship on the plane that will bear them away to a new life.

Spanish writer-director Almodovar is noted for the slyly subversive power with which he infuses his stylized comedies of sexual error, and this early effort from the director of MATADOR and WHAT HAVE I DONE TO DESERVE THIS? is no exception. Its outlandish plot—which includes such absurdist touches as a cageful of identical test-tube parakeets who refuse to sing and a terrorist who tracks people through his sense of smell—pokes good-natured fun at more traditional romantic comedies even as it's driven by the same fundamental idea: that in the end, love truly conquers all. What gives the film its revolutionary twist is the breadth of its definition of love. LABYRINTH OF PASSION's sexual landscape is a virtual catalog of erotic possibility, a pop paean to a multiplicity of forms and desires. Old and young, fat and thin, beautiful and homely pair off and break up according to the whims of outrageous fortune, paying little, if any, attention to conventional notions of appropriate coupling. And in the end, all's well that ends well—an optimistic message delivered with sophisticated bite. (Nudity, sexual situations, adult situations.)

d, Pedro Almodovar; w, Pedro Almodovar; ph, Angel L. Fernandez; ed, Jose Salcedo; prod d, Pedro Almodovar

Comedy   (PR:O MPAA:NR)

LADRI DI SAPONETTE
(It.) (SEE: ICICLE THIEF, THE)

LAMBADA
98m Cannon/WB c

J. Eddie Peck (Kevin Laird), Melora Hardin (Sandy), Shabba-Doo (Ramone), Ricky Paull Goldin (Dean), Basil Hoffman (Superintendent Leland), Dennis Burkley (Uncle Big), and Keene Curtis (Principal Singleton)

It's Lambada time—time to celebrate the amatory movements that come as close to dance-floor sexual intercourse as any two-step can get without prompting a police raid. In LAMBADA, our principal dance instructor is sexy Kevin (J. Eddie Peck), whose shapely buns (no doubt the result of his nightly participation in Lambada competitions) attract the lustful attention of all the women in the film, including his high-school students. By day, Kevin is a clean-cut math teacher at an exclusive Beverly Hills high school. But by night, he sheds his suit and his respectability and slithers down to the barrio where his Latino side emerges. Cutting loose as his alter ego, "Blade," at an East LA disco called No Man's Land, Kevin leads a double life so he can dance his way into the hearts of local high-school dropouts. Each night, after grinding his groin into a female pelvis or two, he instructs the dancing dropouts in a back room with textbooks he's taken from his school without permission. Appointed head of the math department by starchy principal Singleton (Keene Curtis), Kevin enjoys the best of both worlds until Sandy (Melora Hardin), his horniest pupil, spots Kevin at No Man's Land after she's had an argument with her jock boy friend, Dean (Ricky Paull Goldin). Kevin, who is devoted to his unusually understanding wife, and who explains to his young son that he dresses in leather and earrings as part of a tutoring project for the underprivileged, was raised in the barrio, and later adopted by Anglos who inspired him to give up street fighting and get a decent education. Now he returns to his old community as a not-quite-white knight. But problems arise when tough teen Ramone (Shabba-Doo) resents the teacher's meddling because Kevin uses mathematical theories to beat him at a game of pool, and when Sandy begins frequenting the club, hoping that the pounding Latino beat will loosen up the upright Kevin. Although the school superintendent (Basil Hoffman) is impressed by Kevin's progress with the spoiled Beverly Hills students, it isn't long before the two worlds that Kevin lives in collide. While Kevin loads his barrio entourage onto a school bus headed for the computer room at the posh Beverly Hills school, Ramone lies to Sandy about Kevin's nocturnal activities with his female pupils. When Dean shows up at the disco to drag Sandy away, Ramone spills the beans about Kevin's excursion to Beverly Hills. Later, however, No Man's Land's owner, Uncle Big (Dennis Burkley), makes Ramone realize that he has been a jerk to wreck the GED plans of his friends. Outside the school, Dean and his snooty pals rumble with the barrio kids until the cops show up. The next day, Kevin is fired. Responding to a petition by the reformed Sandy (who has since learned that Kevin really is an upstanding family man), the superintendent agrees to hold a math competition pitting the privileged brats against the barrio crowd. Naturally, Kevin's job is on the line. When the poor students beat the bluebloods, Kevin is reinstated, thus paving the way for an all-dancing finale in which upper and lower classes forget their differences and lambada the night away.

There may be a more ridiculously plotted musical, but it is hard to imagine one as silly as LAMBADA. Scads of illogical developments make it difficult for the average viewer to take this exercise in escapism seriously. Most notably, all the high-school kids look like college graduates, and the supposedly mature Kevin looks every bit as young as his students.

Nearly as annoying as the film's lapses in logic is its failure to deliver on its promise of steamy romance. Without any real release for the libido, the film is little more than an unsatisfying tease. After being privy to Sandy's fantasy of dancing with Kevin, we almost wish he would begin an adulterous relationship with her. Why was it necessary to have Kevin married? Couldn't Hardin have played another teacher instead of one of Kevin's pupils? The film's credibility is further damaged by its failure to live up to its avowed pro-ethnicity stance. If LAMBADA is supposed to make a statement about ethnic pride, then why does Kevin use his adoptive Anglo parents' name at work? Why is he so reluctant to call attention to his Mexican heritage?

Admittedly, the lambada beat is catchy and the choreography is sensual enough to compensate for the lamebrain plot much of the time. If only they had teamed up this sexy South American dance with a more workable storyline. (Violence, profanity, substance abuse, sexual situations.)

d, Joel Silberg; p, Peter Shepherd; w, Sheldon Renan and Joel Silberg (based on a story by Joel Silberg); ph, Roberto D'Ettorre Piazzoli; ed, Marcus Manton; m, Greg DeBelles; prod d, Bill Cornford; chor, Shabba-Doo

Drama/Musical   (PR:C MPAA:PG)

LANDSCAPE IN THE MIST

(It./Fr./Gr.) 126m Angelopoulos — Paradis — Greek Film Center — Greek Television — Basicinematografica c

Michalis Zeke *(Alexander)*, Tania Palaiologou *(Voula)*, Stratos Tzortzoglou *(Orestes)*, Eva Kotamanidou, Aliki Georgouli, Vassilis Kolovos, Vassilis Bouyouklakis, Ilias Logothetis, Vangelis Kazan, Stratos Pachis, Michalis Yannatos, Kyr. Katrivanos, Grigoris Evangelatos, Yannis Firios, N. Kouros, Nadia Mourouzi, Vasia Panagopoulou, Toula Stathopoulou, N. Papazafiropoulou, Chr. Nezer, T. Skiadaressis, S. Alafouzos, D. Kamberidis, T. Palatsidis, P. Botinis, Th. Vouyoukas, and A. Varouchas

LANDSCAPE IN THE MIST weighs in with a slew of international awards and critical raves, including a 1988 Venice Film Festival Silver Lion and the 1989 European Felix for Best Picture. The film's director, Theo Angelopoulos, was also honored with a retrospective showing of his work at the Museum of Modern Art. This film tells the simple story of two children, Voula (Tania Palaiologou) and Alexander (Michalis Zeke), who are on the run in northern Greece, trying to make it to Germany to find their father (who may or may not be there). This odyssey is by turns heartwarming and harrowing. En route, the children encounter an indifferent uncle, a traveling troupe of actors, a truck driver who rapes Voula, and, most important, the kindly Orestes (Stratos Tzortzoglou, handsome and natural in his role), a young man on a motorcycle who is about to go into military service, and who takes a generous interest in the pair. By the skin of their teeth and a few minor miracles, the kids finally make it to Germany, their "landscape in the mist."

Though visually stunning, the film somehow manages never to rely on the travel-poster images of Greece or the famed Grecian light that featured so prominently in the recent HIGH SEASON and SHIRLEY VALENTINE. Instead, LANDSCAPE IN THE MIST's action occurs on a succession of uniformly overcast days and in drab locales — bleak roadside cafes and truck stops, desolate villages, uninviting beaches. Greece has surely never more resembled New Jersey than in this film by one of its foremost directors. Yet, Giorgos Arvanitis' cinematography imbues these unprepossessing setups with a somber beauty that is the film's most compelling aspect. Angelopoulos likes to keep things in longshot, evoking a sense of alienation and emphasizing the obliqueness of the story. He is also fond of overhead angles suggestive of a godlike point of view. These stylistic decisions work most powerfully in the rape scene, which is handled with an almost unbearable Brechtian objectivity. Unfortunately, Angelopoulos' other set pieces are less successful, including a sub-Fellini tableaux of people on a street, frozen like statues in wonder at a sudden snowfall; the agonizing death of a horse; yellow-clad railroad workers pumping a handcar in and out of scenes like some mute Greek chorus; and a violinist's abrupt, melancholy entrance into a restaurant. (The film is at its most absurd when an immense, sculpted hand bobs up from the sea and is hoisted aloft by a helicopter right out of LA DOLCE VITA.) Angelopoulos hangs onto his scenes for what seems like forever, as if the extra beats alone are sufficient to make the images indelible. The effect is at first provocative, then affected and annoying (to suggest ennui in a disco, Angelopoulos employs a funereally tracking camera that is so relentlessly subjective it's punishing.) In keeping with this style, the film's characters are impressively taciturn, but when they do speak, their words can be disconcertingly high-flown, as when one speaks the first line of Rilke's *Duino Elegies* (translated by the subtitles as "If I were to shout, who would hear me out of the armies of angels"). Ponderous and self-conscious, LANDSCAPE IN THE MIST would have benefitted from having an indulgent half-hour or so of footage excised.

Although they are mere pawns in Angelopoulos' directorial game, the actors serve the filmmaker well. Palaiologou, with her preternaturally adult face, conveys a steely survivor's determination that almost convinces you of the improbable attainment of her quest. Tiny Zeke has an amusing, naturally grave demeanor; his actions could be those of a courtly, elderly statesman. Unfortunately, Angelopoulos' conceptual grip is so vise-like that these two never seem to break out into anything resembling the spontaneous behavior of kids. (When the eerie violinist makes his entrance, for example, Alexander immediately takes a seat to listen respectfully.) Instead, they are used to convey the director's banal notion of children as beings of mysterious, unfathomable beauty. *(Sexual situations, adult situations, violence.)*

d, Theo Angelopoulos; p, Theo Angelopoulos; w, Theo Angelopoulos, Tonino Guerra, and Thanassis Valtinos (based on a story by Angelopoulos); ph, Giorgos Arvanitis; ed, Yannis Tsitsopoulos; m, Eleni Karaindrou; art d, Mikes Karapiperis; cos, Anatasia Arseni

Drama   **(PR:O   MPAA:NR)**

LASER MAN, THE

92m Peter Wang — Hong Kong Film Workshop c

Marc Hayashi *(Arthur Weiss)*, Maryann Urbano *(Jane Cosby)*, Tony Ka-Fei Leung *(Joey Chung)*, Peter Wang *(Lt. Lu)*, Joan Copeland *(Ruth Weiss)*, George Bartenieff *(Hanson)*, David Chang *(Jimmy Weiss)*, Sally Yeh *(Susu)*, and Neva Small *(Martha Weiss Chung)*

Another low budget independent film from Peter Wang, the director of A GREAT WALL (1986), THE LASER MAN pokes fun at everything from cultural identity to the military-industrial complex in highly quirky fashion. Disjointed and rambling, the essentially plotless movie is set in the near future (political posters saying "Reelect Ollie for President" can be seen) and focuses on Hayashi, a somewhat nerdy, apolitical young New York City laser researcher, half-Chinese, half-Jewish, who accidentally kills his assistant during an experiment. Blackballed from the laser industry because of the accident, the divorced Hayashi spends his time trying to find other work, eating his Jewish mother's horrible Chinese meals, hanging out with his small-time hood brother-in-law (Leung), taking his son to the park, and falling in love with Urbano, a Caucasian woman obsessed with things oriental. Director Wang himself plays an NYC police detective and Hayashi family friend who narrates the film and keeps tabs on the young laser scientist and his crooked brother-in-law. Hayashi finally does land a job in laser research, but he is hired by a very mysterious corporation that wants the laser scientist to build them a powerful weapon. As it turns out, the men are working for the government and Hayashi is unknowingly helping to develop the Strategic Defense Initiative (SDI), aka Star Wars. His invention, a small, light, and very lethal laser gun, is to be tested on the noggin of his crooked brother-in-law, who has sold Hayashi's employers some bad merchandise and made them angry. After years of blithely doing weapons research without even considering the practical implications, Hayashi suddenly realizes the horrible nature of his work and decides to fight back. By now, however, it's too late and Leung apparently is killed by the laser. In a decidedly goofy climax, Hayashi finally takes some personal responsibility and fights back. With the help of his family, girl friend, brother-in-law (who isn't dead after all), and detective Wang, Hayashi is able to double-cross his employers and frustrate their plans for Star Wars.

A character comedy with political and societal overtones, THE LASER MAN is almost too idiosyncratic for its own good. For every telling and relevant moment, there are half a dozen comic or dramatic bits that fall very flat. Director Wang's satiric eye is everywhere, commenting on race relations, family life, dating, sex, marriage, politics, religion, New York City, crime, defense, New Age, the generation gap, modern technology, etc., etc. While Wang's fervent approach is indeed spirited, the film is too scattershot to be truly engaging. Wang seems to have much on his mind, but he fails to present it in a persuasive, coherent way. Part of the problem is his comedic approach, which borders on the sophomoric. One must wonder if the flip, and sometimes even crude, humor is tongue-in-cheek and supposed to be viewed ironically, or if Wang does indeed have a very indifferent attitude toward his subject matter. Although the movie seems to be a plea for the populace to wake up and become politically and socially committed, its humor is far from biting and Wang fails to persuade the viewer that anything important is at stake.

While he bobbles the bigger issues, Wang does succeed in creating some vivid characters. Although Hayashi himself remains a bit vague by the end of the film, the supporting cast is wonderful. Joan Copeland, as the quintessential Jewish mother who has "a Chinese soul," is hilarious, as is Maryann Urbano as the white woman searching for fulfillment through Eastern culture. Director Wang is also memorable as the eccentric police detective. When one considers that the film was shot by Spike Lee's cinematographer, Ernest Dickerson (whose work is better here than in Lee's SCHOOL DAZE), it would seem to indicate that once again a small group of socially and politically committed independent filmmakers is on the rise in New York City. Although they have shown promise, their cinematic skills have yet to attain a truly strong and graceful authority. Perhaps their best work is yet to come. THE LASER MAN premiered at film festivals in the US in 1988, but was not in general release until 1990. *(Adult situations, sexual situations, violence, nudity, profanity.)*

d, Peter Wang; p, Peter Wang; w, Peter Wang; ph, Ernest Dickerson; ed, Grahame Weinbren; m, Mason Daring; prod d, Lester Cohen; cos, Barbara Weis

Comedy   **(PR:O   MPAA:NR)**

LAST EXIT TO BROOKLYN

(W. Ger.) 102m Neue Constantin/Cinecom c

Stephen Lang *(Harry Black)*, Jennifer Jason Leigh *(Tralala)*, Burt Young *(Big Joe)*, Peter Dobson *(Vinnie)*, Jerry Orbach *(Boyce)*, Stephen Baldwin *(Sal)*, Jason Andrews *(Tony)*, James Lorenz *(Freddy)*, Maia Danziger *(Mary Black)*, Cameron Johann *(Spook)*, Ricki Lake *(Donna)*, Zette *(Regina)*, Alexis Arquette *(Georgette)*, John Costelloe *(Tommy)*, Hubert Selby Jr. *(Hit-Run Driver)*, Christopher Murney *(Paulie)*, Frank Military *(Steve)*, and Sam Rockwell *(Al)*

Red Hook, Brooklyn, 1952: Korea-bound conscripts, sadistic teenage gangs, and despondent strikers eke out their desolate existences amidst a frenzied mixture of prostitutes, transvestites, psychos, winos, and junkies. Based on a collection of short stories by Hubert Selby Jr., which unleashed a storm of controversy upon their publication in 1964, German director Uli Edel's film is a relentlessly bleak account of life in the neighborhood during a brief period in the summer of '52. The stories of a cross-section of characters is recounted in episodic fashion. Tralala (Jennifer Jason Leigh) is a prostitute who picks up tricks in sleazy bars and lures them to rubble-strewn vacant lots where they are mugged by ex-convict Vinnie (Peter Dobson) and his gang of thugs. Harry (Stephen Lang) is in charge of the local strike office, enjoying his position of power, but troubled by his awakening homosexuality. Georgette (Alexis Arquette) is an effeminate, tormented gay who lusts after Vinnie. Big Joe (Burt Young) is a striking worker who is upset over the pregnancy of his unmarried daughter Donna (Ricki Lake), while his motorcycle-obsessed son Spook (Cameron Johann) pines for Tralala. Tralala, tired of being short-changed by Vinnie, takes up with a handsome soldier (Frank Military), hoping it will lead to a big payoff. But when he ships out, he leaves her with nothing but a love letter, sending her back to her sordid life in Red Hook. During a party, Harry meets transvestite Regina (Zette), and spends the night with him, causing him to be late the next morning when scabs break through factory picket lines. Fired by union boss Boyce (Jerry Ohrbach), Harry is also rejected by Regina, and his world begins to completely unravel. Unable to win the affections of Vinnie, Georgette, high on heroin late one night, charges into the street and is run down and killed by a cab (driven by author Selby). Tommy (John Costelloe), father of Donna's unborn child, agrees to marry her, somewhat mollifying the emotional Big Joe, while Spook's love for Tralala only leads to pain.

In blending the personal worlds of these characters into a complete cosmology of the abyss, director Uli Edel (CHRISTIANE F.) and scriptwriter Desmond Nakano have demonstrated great skill. They have taken the episodic nature of Selby's book and transformed it into an aesthetic whole that is greater than the sum of its parts. Moreover, Edel's and Nakano's efforts are just part of what was clearly the engaged teamwork of a group of gifted people committed to doing justice to Selby's uncompromising artistic vision. Producer Bernd Eichinger's LAST EXIT TO BROOKLYN is one of the first great films of the 1990s. An apocalyptic vision packed with soul-shuddering violence and brutality, it is even more successful on all levels than Eichinger's last production, THE NAME OF THE ROSE, and marks his coming of age as an international filmmaker. *(Graphic violence, excessive profanity, nudity, sexual situations, substance abuse, adult situations.)*

d, Uli Edel; p, Bernd Eichinger; w, Desmond Nakano (based on the novel by Hubert Selby Jr.); ph, Stefan Czapsky; ed, Peter Przygodda; m, Mark Knopfler; art d, Mark Haack; cos, Carol Oditz; makup, Kathryn Bihr

Drama   (PR:O   MPAA:NR)

LAST OF THE FINEST, THE

106m Davis Entertainment/Orion c

(AKA: STREET LEGAL; GBTI: BLUE HEAT)

Brian Dennehy *(Frank Daly)*, Joe Pantoliano *(Wayne Gross)*, Jeff Fahey *(Ricky Rodriguez)*, Bill Paxton *(Howard "Hojo" Jones)*, Michael C. Gwynne *(Anthony Reece)*, Henry Stolow *(Stant)*, Guy Boyd *(R.J. Norringer)*, Henry Darrow *(Capt. Joe Torres)*, J. Kenneth Campbell *(Calvert)*, Deborra-Lee Furness *(Linda Daly)*, Lisa Jane Persky *(Hariett Gross)*, Patricia Clipper *(Rose)*, Michelle Little *(Anita)*, Susannah Kelly, Sheila Kelly *(Daly Baby)*, Micah Rowe *(Justin Daly)*, Joey Wright *(Jimmy Gross)*, Georgie Paul *(Myrna)*, John Finnegan *(Tommy Grogan)*, Ron Canada *(Cregan)*, Michael Strasser *(McCade)*, Xander Berkeley *(Fast Eddie)*, Pam Gidley *(Haley)*, Burke Byrnes *(Comdr. Orsini)*, Tom Nolan *(Travers)*, Jason Ross *(Braden)*, Kathleen Dennehy *(Lab Technician)*, Patricia Stack *(Press Officer)*, Larry Carroll *(Newsman)*, Jeanne Mori *(Female Journalist)*, Kimble Jemison *(Scared Dealer)*, Michael Simpson *(Disc Jockey)*, James Delesandro, Ray Vegas, Joe Minjares, Victor Contreras, Ramon Angeloni *(Contras)*, David Allen Young *(Paramedic)*, Chenoa Ellis *(Arresting Officer)*, Frank V. Trevino *(Clerk)*, Charles Chiquette, Rudy F. Morrison, Robert Figg *(Guests)*, John D. Johnston III *(Referee)*, Robert Lee Jarvis *(Armorer)*, and James W. Gavin *(Pilot)*

THE LAST OF THE FINEST is a cop actioner featuring four of the finest character actors working in American films today. Brian Dennehy, Joe Pantoliano, Jeff Fahey, and Bill Paxton play Frank Daly, Wayne Gross, Ricky Rodriguez, and Howard "Hojo" Jones, the four members of an elite unit of the Los Angeles Police Department, assigned to crack the cases no one else can

solve. As the film opens, they are close to breaking up a large drug ring operating out of a meat-packing company. Led by Daly (who, according to police records, is a marginal personality: an obsessive near-alcoholic who stops at nothing to get his man), the group raids the meat-packing company and comes up virtually empty. Scolded by their superiors for neither waiting for proper backup nor informing the FBI, the cops are put on suspension, and begin their own, private investigations. The close-knit group (whose families also socialize) stumbles upon more and more startling information, involving rich businessmen, dirty FBI agents, and corrupt government officials. After the cops question a hooker to get information on a businessman they have been trailing, she is beaten up and hides in a hotel. Daly and his group go to the hotel, discover her corpse, and see the murderer fleeing from the scene. Jones pursues the killer by car and follows him to a remote canyon. There, Jones is attacked from behind and killed. The rest of the unit arrives too late to catch the killer, and the LAPD's internal affairs division is brought in to investigate the affair, since the men were on suspension when the incident occurred. Eventually, Daly, Rodriguez, and Gross turn in their badges and continue their battle as vigilantes. After trailing a businessman to a government meeting on sending arms to Central America, they videotape him (without sound) making a deal with a government official, then use the expertise of an old retired cop to figure out what is being said on the tape, giving them further leads on the drug ring. Later, they raid a warehouse where the drugs are stored and the money is laundered, and inadvertently steal a truck full of money ($22.5 million, to be exact). They contemplate keeping this money for themselves, until threats against their families' lives drive them to compromise. The men have uncovered a conspiracy that involves the US government in a possible weapons-for-drugs deal with parties in Central America. With their families in hiding, Daly and gang decide to strike a deal with the crooks (who include the once trusted, but now corrupt, lieutenant of their department). They will turn over the money, provided Daly can come face to face with the man behind it all, a certain R.J. Norringer (Guy Boyd). A meeting is set, and the film climaxes with a huge shootout that results in Norringer's death and the unit's reinstatement in the LAPD. In the end, a family park is dedicated in the fallen Jones' name and the group is finally happy. But a televised statement from the White House (by an aide who was involved in the deal) denies any knowledge of the mysterious conspiracy and implies a solid future for arms deals with Central America. It seems the story is not over.

Impeccably photographed by the highly talented Juan Ruiz-Anchia (HOUSE OF GAMES) and professionally put together, THE LAST OF THE FINEST is a solid action yarn that moves along at an agreeable pace. Director John Mackenzie (THE LONG GOOD FRIDAY) handles the complicated and, unfortunately, predictable script strongly, making up for the huge plot holes and annoying inconsistencies. Guessing who the bad guys are (though it's very easy here) seems to be half the fun, and watching the performers is a pleasure. Dennehy is, as usual, a strong presence, but his part is underdeveloped and misleading. The darker side of Daly's personality — his drinking and obsessiveness — is never really brought into play effectively, and his relationship with his wife (SHAME's Deborra-Lee Furness) is not entirely convincing. As the remaining three squad members, Paxton (NEAR DARK; ALIENS), Pantoliano (MIDNIGHT RUN), and Fahey (WHITE HUNTER, BLACK HEART) fare better, their characters entailing less development and more pure personality, allowing these three exceptional character actors to do what they do best, though Paxton's role is regrettably small. As a group, they establish a sense of male camaraderie among the cops that adds to the picture's plausibility and provides plenty of laughs.

The film's action sequences are routine — if not bland at times — but always watchable, the plot developments are handled with the right buildup and pay-off, and the climax is exciting. It's all by-the-numbers and predictably executed, but what sets this picture apart from other cop films (besides the truly extraordinary cinematography) is its surprisingly strong political stance. The final minutes, featuring the White House speech, present a striking and unusually venomous cynicism concerning "trustworthy" government. It's an odd viewpoint in this genre, and though the politics in THE LAST OF THE FINEST seem as confused as the politics of John Carpenter's brilliant satire THEY LIVE, the film's final note of doubt is effective and undeniably refreshing. Overall, THE LAST OF THE FINEST is a serviceable thriller that's worth a look. *(Violence, profanity, adult situations, substance abuse.)*

d, John Mackenzie; p, John A. Davis; w, Jere Cunningham, Thomas Lee Wright, and George Armitage (based on a story by Jere Cunningham); ph, Juan Ruiz-Anchia; ed, Graham Walker; m, Jack Nitzsche and Michael Hoenig; prod d, Lawrence G. Paull; art d, Geoff Hubbard; set d, John Thomas Walker; spec, Dale L. Martin; stunts, David Ellis; cos, Marilyn Vance-Straker; makup, John M. Norin and Mel Berns Jr.; tech, William C. Jordan

Action/Thriller   (PR:O   MPAA:R)

LEATHERFACE: THE TEXAS CHAINSAW MASSACRE III

87m New Line c

R.A. Mihailoff (*Leatherface*), Kate Hodge (*Michelle*), William Butler (*Ryan*), Ken Foree (*Benny*), Viggo Mortensen (*Tex*), Jennifer Banko (*Little Girl*), Ron Brooks (*TV Newsman*), Miriam Byrd-Nethery (*Mama*), David Cloud (*Scott*), Beth Depatie (*Gina*), Tom Everett (*Alfredo*), Toni Hudson (*Sara*), Joe Unger (*Tinker*), Dwayne Whitaker (*Kim*), and Michael Shamus Wiles (*Checkpoint Officer*)

A feuding couple—Michelle (Kate Hodge) and Ryan (William Butler)—are driving from California to Florida. In Texas they pass the floodlit site of a grisly discovery: a slimy pit from which body after body is being removed by workers cocooned in eerie airtight suits. Told by a state trooper to keep moving ("Don't stop for nothing or nobody," he says ominously), they pull into the rundown Last Chance Gas Station. A rangy stranger (Viggo Mortensen) looking for a lift directs them to a shortcut, but they're reluctant to give him a ride. An awkward situation becomes terrifying when the gas station's crazy owner threatens them with a shotgun and the stranger fights him off, allowing them to escape. They take his detour, hoping to find help. Out of the darkness a Land Rover with hunting lights appears and tries to run them off the road. When they stop to survey the damage, a chainsaw-wielding maniac appears out of the night like a bad dream.

From this point on, LEATHERFACE is on familiar ground. Michelle and Ryan try to flee, joining forces with the most useful guy you could run into on a dark road crawling with homicidal sociopaths, a weekend survivalist (Ken Foree) with a trunkful of serious weapons. But the dark, tangled forest in which they're trapped is more than Texas topography; it's the horror movie version of a fairy-tale's wicked woods, and in the center lies a haunted house aglow with golden light. Inside there's more of what made THE TEXAS CHAINSAW MASSACRE great: vertebrae and teeth, feathers and femurs, ribs and skulls fashioned into furniture and scattered across the floor in sublime disarray. And while there's no witch lurking here, a cannibal family holds court: the eponymous Leatherface (R.A. Mihailoff), his crippled mother, and three lethal siblings. Ryan is strung up and butchered like a calf, Michelle is nailed to a chair, and everyone's looking forward to dinner. The big question, of course, is who gets out alive? And what will be left of them?

If LEATHERFACE weren't the second sequel to THE TEXAS CHAINSAW MASSACRE, audiences probably wouldn't ask such questions. Taken as a separate entity, this is a competently packaged horror movie that plays by the rules and delivers what the title promises: sadistic killers, whimpering victims, and chainsaws. But the hope that something really scary is in the offing springs from the memory of THE TEXAS CHAINSAW MASSACRE, which came out of nowhere and sucker-punched into near-catatonia audiences who thought they were watching just another horror movie. You've got to go back to George Romero's taboo-busting NIGHT OF THE LIVING DEAD to find a film that's even in the same ballpark. LEATHERFACE can't compete with that memory, but unlike TEXAS CHAINSAW MASSACRE II—which used the original's theme as the starting point for a macabre joke about consumerism and dog-eat-dog yuppie mores—it takes itself very seriously while it tries. Splatterpunk novelist-turned-screenwriter David Schow and director Jeff Burr take the material back to its roots, re-creating the minimal plotting and alternately muddy and washed-out look of the original. In deference to contemporary tastes, LEATHERFACE pulls as few gory punches as prevailing standards permit (TEXAS CHAINSAW MASSACRE only *seemed* unbearably graphic) and underscores the mayhem with an abrasive speed metal soundtrack. It builds considerable momentum in the opening scenes, playing on urban unease about the sparsely populated heartland, but once Hodge, Butler, and Foree are set loose in the woods, there's a numbing sameness to the action: it's all running and screaming, and we've seen it all before. There is roadkill all over Texas, as traumatized survivor Hodge asserts, and LEATHERFACE affords a close-up look that falters when the traffic accident appeal wears off. (*Gore effects.*)

d, Jeff Burr; p, Robert Engelman; w, David J. Schow (based on characters created by Kim Hendel, Tobe Hooper); ph, James L. Carter; m, Jim Manzie and Pat Regan; prod d, Mick Strawn; stunts, Kane Hodder; cos, Joan Hunter; makeup, Kurtzman Nicotero & Berger EFX Group and Suzanne Sanders

Horror   (PR:C-O MPAA:R)

LEMON SISTERS, THE

92m Miramax c

Diane Keaton (*Eloise Hamer*), Carol Kane (*Franki D'Angelo*), Kathryn Grody (*Nola Frank*), Elliott Gould (*Fred Frank*), Ruben Blades (*C.W.*), Aidan Quinn (*Frankie McGuinness*), Estelle Parsons (*Mrs. Kupchak*), Richard Libertini (*Nicholas Panas*), Sully Boyar (*Baxter O'Neil*), Bill Boggs (*MC on TV Quiz Show*), Emily A. Rose (*Sadie Frank*), Ashley Peldon (*Sarah Frank*), Nicky Bronson (*Scotty Willard*), Francine Fargo (*Charlene*), Joe Milazzo (*Vinnie*), Neil Miller (*Stage Manager*), Nathan Lane (*Charlie Sorrel*), Joanne Bradley (*Real Estate Agent*), Joel S. Fogel (*Man at Bacchanal Room*), Julius Clifton Webb (*Doorman*), Kourtney Donohue (*Young Eloise*), Rachel Hillman (*Young Nola*), Rachel Aviva (*Young Franki*), Sal Domani (*Hawker*), Maggie Burke (*Teacher*), Tany Taylor Powers (*Marilyn Fogelman*), Paulette Attie (*Nola's Mother*), Peter Costa (*Edward*), Ben Lin (*Bellhop*), Tony Devon (*Booker*), Scheryll Anderson (*Waitress*), J. Mark Danley, Nina Hodoruk (*Yuppie House Buyers*), Nicole Weinstein (*Daddy's Girl Voice*), Murray Weinstock (*Piano Player*), Monique Nichole Alterman (*Taffy Girl*), Ashley Walls, Lauren Walls, Melissa Walls (*Baby*), and Matthew Modine (*Eloise's Father*)

There's a word for movies like this. The word is painful. Of recent films, only ISHTAR engendered the kind of accusations of big-star self-indulgence that greeted THE LEMON SISTERS, which brings a condescending, heavy-handed cuteness to its portrayal of three amateur musicians of negligible talent. Although many critics found similar fault with ISHTAR, at least Elaine May's film had a plot. THE LEMON SISTERS doesn't. Instead it cuts back and forth between half-baked, vaguely related vignettes set in the present and jury-rigged flashbacks tacked on to give the other scenes some illusory semblance of order and logic. Like the film in general, this structure is an exercise in futility.

What plot there is revolves around three friends who grew up together in Atlantic City—hence the flashbacks, which, despite having little or nothing to do with the present action, are generally more entertaining than the rest of the film. Franki (Carol Kane) is "the dreamer." Eloise (Diane Keaton) is "the kooky asthmatic schizophrenic," a character whose presence indicates immediately that there's trouble afoot. Rounding out the trio is Nola (Kathryn Grody), "the sensible one," who marries and raises a family—though marrying an even-more-annoying-than-usual Elliott Gould may seem less than sensible to many viewers. Since Franki is "the dreamer," it's her idea that the three form a singing group. But this would-be plot gets scuttled almost before the movie gets underway, when the married couple who own the supper club where the trio performs decide to sell out and move to Florida. In an abortive attempt to keep the group together, Franki takes their pooled earnings—all of $675—gambles part of it away in slot machines, buys some losing lottery tickets, and invests the rest in "Plan X." "Franki always had a Plan X," chirps Nola, who, for no discernible reason, narrates the transitions between the present action and the flashbacks. In one flashback, "Plan X" is a jar of breast development cream Franki has swiped from her aunt and which the three friends decide to try, though we never see the outcome of their experiment. Back in the present, Franki's newest "Plan X" calls for Eloise to make a jerk of herself on an inane, anachronistic 50s-style quiz show. Mercifully sparing us from more of Franki's moneymaking schemes, a real estate agent abruptly offers Eloise and Nola big bucks for their boardwalk businesses: Eloise operates a musty TV museum started by her father (played by an uncredited Matthew Modine in the flashbacks), and Nola is the owner of a failing salt-water taffy shop that was started by her mother. Franki tries to talk her friends into using their money to buy another supper club; Eloise and Nola quite sensibly tell her to forget it. Then, not so sensibly, Eloise develops a fixation on Atlantic City Greco-Roman kitsch—mostly fiberglass statues of naked men. In an extended, morosely unfunny sexual sight gag, we see her schlepping one of these statues back to her place from a casino. Eventually, Eloise fritters away her money on a home museum of sculpted hands and male genitalia. Nola's husband, certain that his nauseating "Taffit" taffy rabbits will make a fortune, convinces his wife to use the money from the sale of their old failing taffy store to buy a new failing taffy store. Miffed because her friends won't help finance her harebrained idea, Franki stomps off to launch a solo singing career under the dubious management of her new boy friend, also named Frankie (Aidan Quinn), a would-be sharpie who wears luminescent suits and advises his client to fondle herself while singing "Wild Thing." The trouble is Franki, who actually sounds pretty good when singing with the Lemons, for unexplained reasons sounds suddenly wheezy and awful on her own. Eloise, who supposedly suffers from debilitating asthma, doesn't sound wheezy at all, yet she has an attack that lands her in the hospital. After getting out, she has a schizoid fit when her friends stage a surprise coming-home party for her. In the process, Eloise alienates her sometime boy friend, C.W. (Ruben Blades in a role that is almost as superfluous as his gangster character in THE TWO JAKES), Nola, and both Frankies. (What kind of friends walk out on someone in obvious turmoil?) Because of Franki's and Eloise's tantrums, the Lemons spend a lot of screen time apart from one another in a film supposedly about lifelong friendship. But that doesn't stop the three from posing picturesquely on the beach at the end, Nola having gone broke and moved her family into her sister's place in Philadelphia, Franki having inexplicably landed a gig at Caesar's, and Eloise having probably slipped more deeply into genteel madness.

If curdled whimsy could kill, THE LEMON SISTERS would make a neat murder weapon. It wants to be a deep, warmhearted comedy about three complex women, but its characters are thin, undeveloped, and unpleasant. As a result the film winds up resembling something like MC TEAGUE played for laughs, with top Hollywood stars cast as appallingly moronic, possibly disturbed characters meant to pass for touching everyday people. This film could serve as yet more damning evidence of the sad state of roles for women in male-dominated Hollywood; however, THE LEMON SISTERS was the pet project of the three lead actresses, who spent years bringing it to the screen. But by the time the film was completed, Keaton had her producer's credit removed and did nothing to promote the movie during its theatrical run. Even the releasing company kept the film on the shelf for about a year. On the whole, everyone would have been better off had the film not been released at all. It is tempting, of course, to belabor the obvious by labelling THE LEMON SISTERS a lemon of a movie, but that would be an insult to what is, after all, a perfectly fine fruit. *(Adult situations.)*

d, Joyce Chopra; p, Joe Kelly; w, Jeremy Pikser; ph, Bobby Byrne; ed, Edward H. Glass, Joseph Weintraub, and Michael R. Miller; m, Dick Hyman; md, Paul Shaffer; prod d, Patrizia Von Brandenstein; stunts, Danny Aiello III, Jery Hewitt, and Sandy Richman; cos, Susan Becker; chor, Anita Mann

Comedy   **(PR:C   MPAA:PG)**

L'ETAT SAUVAGE

(Fr.) 111m Films 66 — Gaumont/Interama c

Marie-Christine Barrault *(Laurence)*, Claude Brasseur *(Gravenoire)*, Jaques Dutronc *(Avit)*, Doura Mane *(Patrice Doumbe)*, Michel Piccoli *(Orlaville)*, Baaron *(Modimbo)*, Umban U'kset *(Kotoko)*, Jean-Baptiste Tiemele *(Gohanda)*, Rudiger Vogler *(Tristan)*, Peter Bachelier *(Renard)*, Philippe Brizard *(Paul)*, Pierre Walker *(Swiss Minister)*, Marblum Jequier *(Minister's Wife)*, Celia *(Irene)*, Sidiki Bakaba *(Cornac)*, Akonio Dolo *(Boy Elie)*, Joseph Mono *(Boy Raoul)*, Jaques Sereys *(Prime Minister)*, Assane Falle *(Minister of Children's Affairs)*, Cheik Doukoure *(Industrial Minister)*, Alphonse Beni *(Minister One)*, and Lazare Kenmegne *(Guard)*

SAVAGE STATE is one of the most lunatic botches ever perpetrated on a movie audience. It is impossible to come up with a single reason why it was necessary to re-release this cinematic blight from 1978. The mere depiction of the nightmare of racial prejudice, here recorded with almost obscene relish, seldom provides the necessary insight into the problem.

In 1963, a time of de-colonization in French Africa, Laurence (Marie-Christine Barrault) is the center of a storm of societal disapproval for being the lover of a black man, Patrice Doumbe (Doura Mane), the Minister of Health. Prior to this, she was married to a neglectful UNESCO official, Avit (Jaques Dutronc), whom she left for Gravenoire (Claude Brasseur), an adventurer who has gotten rich exploiting the local population. Avit has come to Africa on business, as well as to search for his wife. Almost immediately, he encounters Gravenoire, who, outraged that his mistress has deserted him for a black, is only too willing to reunite the two. Upon meeting with her husband, Laurence is conciliatory, but Avit resists her overtures of friendship. Meanwhile, the black population has become incensed that their adored political leader, Doumbe, has "betrayed" them with his affair with Laurence. They turn against him, and, at the end of a long night in which he is arrested and beaten to a pulp, Doumbe is killed. In grave danger, Laurence attempts to escape from the country with a now-resigned Avit. They seem to have the entire population — black and white — against them, but finally make it to the airport, and, presumably, to a calmer life.

"Sex is an enormous problem here. The climate drives women's hormones mad," a character says at one point; that is as much of an explanation as is provided for the nonsensical events that are spun out here. The Georges Conchon novel on which the film is based won the prestigious Prix Goncourt prize in France, and, reportedly, several filmmakers were interested in the material. As a parable of the universality of racism and man's inhumanity to man, the story undoubtedly played better on the printed page. Director-cowriter Francis Girod's work has an archaic feel to it: events take place with an obscure, primitive abruptness; nothing is gauged dramatically, and there is a feeble music score intermittently laid over the action like an afterthought.

THE SAVAGE STATE resembles the climax of DO THE RIGHT THING, extended for an unconscionable length. Girod overloads it with so many unblinkingly gruesome effects — the mob's attack on Doumbe, a truckload piled with black corpses (victims of the nightly violence), bigoted whites goading young blacks into raping Laurence — that whatever moral point he is trying to make is nullified. The viewer simply becomes numb, waiting for the next outrage to top the one just witnessed. How is one to respond, for example, to the scene in which the African cabinet ministers mock Doumbe with jungle-drum rhythms while wearing Savile Row suits?

The characters, for the most part, are unsympathetic, and, apart from Barrault and Mane, the performers have zero rapport with each other. They all seem to be playing some form of ideological monster, but the performances lack creative zest. People are despicable, racism inevitable, Girod trumpets, as if struck by a miraculous revelation.

As glacially imperial as Grace Kelly, Barrault still evinces some passion in her boudoir scenes with Mane, but her actions become increasingly inscrutable

as the tensions mount around her. Her flight in a car from her villa, surrounded by menacing natives at every point, lacks the real terror it should be invested with, due to Barrault's opacity and the lax direction. Brasseur gives an inexhaustibly offensive and cliched performance that reaches absurd heights in the final moments, during which he records Laurence's and Avit's attempts at escape with a movie camera. The ultimate viewer ordeal, this last sequence, is staged as if the beleaguered couple were on their way to Golgotha. (Like the obtuse families in horror movies that find themselves in demonically possessed houses, they should have gotten out a hell of lot sooner.) Dutronc is so passive in even the most trying circumstances that he's almost funny (especially when he and Barrault snipe at each other like Lucy and Desi while fleeing for their lives); Leslie Howard was a tornado of dynamism by comparison. The handsome, elegantly lithe Mane is the only person who commands any respect or compassion; naturally, he is soon disposed of in relentlessly brutal fashion. Michel Piccoli also appears, doing his cynically resigned, knowing specialty as Orlaville, a police chief, who serves as something of a Greek chorus. Affecting an Ernest Hemingway-ish grizzled, Great White Hunter guise, Orlaville spends his free time typing up unpublished novels, whom one suspects are as witless as this film. *(Excessive violence, nudity, sexual situations, adult situations, profanity.)*

d, Francis Girod; w, Georges Conchon and Francis Girod; ph, Pierre Lhomme; ed, Genevieve Winding; md, Pierre Jansen; set d, Jean-Jacques Caziot; cos, Jacques Fonteray, Corinne Jorry, and Francoise Monico; makup, Eric Muller

Drama   **(PR:O   MPAA:R)**

LIFE AND NOTHING BUT

(Fr.) 135m Hachette Premiere — Little Bear — A2/UGC c

(LA VIE EST RIEN D'AUTRE)

Philippe Noiret *(Maj. Dellaplanne)*, Sabine Azema *(Irene de Courtil)*, Pascale Vignal *(Alice)*, Maurice Barrier *(Mercadot)*, Francois Perrot *(Perrin)*, Jean-Pol Dubois *(Andre)*, Daniel Russo *(Lt. Trevise)*, Michel Duchaussoy *(Gen. Villerieux)*, Arlette Gilbert *(Valentine)*, Louis Lyonnet *(Valentin)*, Charlotte Maury *(Cora Mabel)*, Francois Caron *(Julien)*, Thierry Gimenez *(Engineers' Adjutant)*, Frederique Meninger *(Mme. Lebegue)*, Pierre Trabaud *(Eugene Dilatoire)*, Jean-Roger Milo *(Mons. Lebegue)*, Catherine Verlor *(Nun on Beach)*, Jean-Christophe Lebert *(Amnesiac)*, Bruno Therasse *(Rougeaud)*, Philippe Uchan *(Legless Man)*, Marion Loran *(Solange de Boissancourt)*, Charlotte Kadi *(Nun in Hospital)*, Gabriel Cattand *(Prof. Mortier)*, Christophe Odent *(Poirleau)*, Jean Champion *(Lagrange)*, Philippe Deplanche *(Lecordier)*, Michel Cassagne *(Abel Mascle)*, Frederic Pierrot *(Marcel)*, Francois Domange *(Georges)*, Jean-Paul Comart *(Fagot)*, Patrick Massieu *(Cemetery Warden)*, Didier Harlmann *(One-armed Man)*, Pascal Elso *(Blind Man)*, Odile Cointepas *(Mme. Hannesson)*, Louba Guertchikoff *(Blue-eyed Woman)*, Jean-Claude Calon *(Sgt. Zele)*, Jean-Yves Gautier *(Corporal)*, Gilles Janeyrand *(NCO)*, Nicolas Tronc *(Soldier Lefevre)*, Jerome Frossard *(Messenger)*, Michele Gleizer *(Farmer)*, Daniel Langlet *(Mons. Ichac)*, Adrienne Bonnet *(Mme. Ichac)*, Marcel Zanini *(Leo)*, Marc Perrone *(Pochin)*, Georges Staquet *(Priest)*, Alain Frerot *(Pelat)*, Francois Dyrek *(Vergnes)*, Oswald d'Andrea *(Cora Mabel, Pianist)*, Mickey Baker *(Banjo Player)*, Sangoma Everett *(Drummer)*, Stephen Potts *(Saxophonist)*, Mike Zwerin *(Jennings)*, Bruno Raffaelli *(Maginot)*, and Eric Dufay *(Soldier Thain)*

LIFE AND NOTHING BUT, the latest film from Bertrand Tavernier (ROUND MIDNIGHT [1986]; COUP DE TORCHON [1982]; A SUNDAY IN THE COUNTRY [1984]), is a compelling successor to such antiwar movies as Stanley Kubrick's PATHS OF GLORY (1957) and Lewis Milestone's ALL QUIET ON THE WESTERN FRONT (1930), focusing, like Kubrick's and Milestone's films, on WWI. Instead of detailing the ongoing carnage and cannon fire of life in the trenches, however, Tavernier paints a harrowing portrait of devastation after the fact. The year is 1920 (almost two years after the Armistice), and the massive task of counting corpses and identifying the missing among the French soldiers remains. Supervising these efforts is Major Dellaplane (Noiret), a career soldier obsessed with logic and detail who turns his responsibility into a personal crusade to justify the sacrifice made by the dead men, believing that by naming the unidentified and humanizing the grim statistics, he can somehow make sense of the horror that has occurred. Noiret's quest to tie up the loose ends of war in peacetime is interwoven with the story of another officer's mission to locate one suitable unknown soldier for ceremonial enshrinement in the Arc de Triomphe, and with vignettes concerning families seeking information about the fate of their relatives. Among those vying for Noiret's attention are Vignal, a young working-class woman looking for her fiance, and Azema, a senator's daughter-in-law traveling throughout Europe in search of her missing husband. Although he locks horns with the latter, a proud aristocrat who's tired of getting the bureaucratic runaround, Noiret also falls in love with her, and the fitful progress of their incongruous affair is played out on the former battlefields. In one scene, during a visit to a body identification center where family members sift through medals and personal belongings in the hope of locating loved ones, the travelers pause from their heart-rending task to picnic on the grass, and an explosion rocks a tunnel where the dead are stored pending identification. It's as if the war's appetite can never be satisfied. When Noiret discovers that Vignal's fiance and Azema's husband are the same man, the knowledge frees each woman to go on with her life. The unknown soldier is interred and the war is officially laid to rest, but it will never be over for Noiret. Allowing Azema to slip out of his life, he can only proclaim his love in letters, after she's moved to America.

Cowritten by Tavernier and Jean Cosmos (a playwright and TV scenarist making his screenwriting debut), LIFE AND NOTHING BUT is a muted, carefully wrought drama about the emotionally shell-shocked survivors of WW I. Somber, handsome, exquisitely produced, and featuring a towering lead performance by Philippe Noiret in what is reportedly his 100th screen role, Tavernier's elegy strikes no false notes. With an extraordinary talent for conveying the bustle of life amidst the stasis of death, Tavernier employs his sweeping camera and his skill in relating characters to their widescreen environment to create an unforgettable *mise-en-scene*. Despite its brilliant technical accomplishment and its seamless blend of gallows humor and intriguing drama, however, Tavernier's examination of lives held in check by the fortunes of war lacks the full-throttle emotionalism that might have made it a classic pacifist epic. Visually, it couldn't be improved upon (Tavernier's cinematographer, once again, is the superb Bruno de Keyzer), but one does wish it were a little less calculated, a little more reckless. The *chagrin d'amour* of Noiret's unconsummated affair with Azema palls in comparison with Tavernier's moving depiction of war and loss on a larger scale. Somehow the intimate love story fails to move us as much as some of the vignettes, such as the darkly humorous scene in which town officials plead for re-zoning because they don't have any dead war heroes in their district. Even more haunting is the last shot, in which Noiret walks through a cemetery that appears to stretch on forever — remarking that the French victory parade lasted three hours, but a march by all the dead would have taken eleven days. *(Violence, adult situations, profanity.)*

d, Bertrand Tavernier; p, Rene Cleitman and Albert Prevost; w, Bertrand Tavernier and Jean Cosmos; ph, Bruno de Keyzer; ed, Armand Psenny; m, Oswald d'Andrea; prod d, Guy-Claude Francois; set d, Pierre Fontaine; cos, Jacqueline Moreau; makup, Eric Muller

Drama   **(PR:O   MPAA:PG)**

LIFE IS CHEAP...BUT TOILET PAPER IS EXPENSIVE

89m Far East Stars/Silver Light c

Spencer Nakasako *(The Man with No Name)*, Cora Miao *(Money)*, Victor Wong *(Blind Man)*, John K. Chan *(The Anthropologist)*, Chan Kim Wan *(The Duck Killer)*, Cheng Kwan Min *(Uncle Cheng)*, Allen Fong *(Taxi Driver)*, Cinda Hui *(Kitty)*, Lam Chung *(The Red Guard)*, Lo Wai *(The Big Boss)*, Kai-Bong Chau *(Himself)*, Mrs. Kai-Bong Chau *(Herself)*, Gary Kong, Rocky Ho, Lo Lieh, Bonnie Ngai, Wu Kin Man, and Yu Chien

Hong Kong 1990, last frontier in the Wild, Wild East, where life is cheap, but toilet paper is expensive. Arriving from San Francisco's Chinatown to deliver a locked briefcase to the Big Boss (Lo Wai) is the Man with No Name (Spencer Nakasako, who wrote the screenplay and codirects). He is in love with the idea of Hong Kong, but the reality of the place is something else. For one thing, no one seems to take his courier mission as seriously as he expected. First, he has to rendezvous with eccentric Uncle Cheng (Cheng Kwan Min), who seems far more interested in demonstrating his song-and-dance skills and dispensing hokey advice than in acting as a liaison for our nameless protagonist. Next, No Name makes his way to the Big Boss's office, where the Boss's right hand man (Lam Chung) gives him the runaround. Depending on whom No Name talks to, the Big Boss is either sick, dying, on vacation, consolidating his power in anticipation of a gang war, or dead. No Name meanders around the city, trying to have a good time and meeting a weird assortment of characters in the process. A drunken taxi driver cheats him and calls him a foreign devil. A man who slaughters ducks (Chan Kim Wan) philosophizes. Kitty (Cinda Hui), a prostitute, delivers a perplexing monolog about the services she does and doesn't offer. Eventually, the briefcase is stolen by street punks and can't be recovered. No Name befriends the Big Boss's mistress, Money (Cora Miao), and learns she's having a lesbian affair with the Boss's daughter. When he is threatened and humiliated by the Boss, No Name finally accepts that Hong Kong is a more complex and alien place than he imagined.

Director Wayne Wang gained notoriety with his low-budget feature CHAN IS MISSING, then followed it with SLAMDANCE and EAT A BOWL OF TEA. Asian-American filmmakers are few and far between, and by making and distributing four feature films — three of which explicitly examine aspects of Asian-American culture — Wang has accomplished something significant. LIFE IS CHEAP is doubly noteworthy because it was released with a self-imposed A (Adult) rating after receiving an X from the MPAA. The film is neither pornographic nor exploitative, and its X rating seemed arbitrary. With the MPAA

coming under increasing criticism for its rating system, Wang's A rating may have played a significant role in prompting the MPAA to institute its less-than-revolutionary NC-17 classification.

LIFE IS CHEAP is, however, a tedious and pretentious film with little to recommend it to the mainstream moviegoer. Character development isn't an issue: the Man with No Name, Money, the Big Boss, and a host of lesser characters are two-dimensional figures meant to recall classic gangster types. Likewise, the story is of secondary importance. LIFE IS CHEAP strings together a series of incidents, again recalling traditional crime films, but fails to develop them into anything resembling a real plot. This isn't to say that LIFE IS CHEAP is incompetently made; these apparent deficiencies are part of a deliberate strategy. Indeed, Wang also employs a host of distancing devices to remind the viewer that film is a mannered and artificial medium, just as Hong Kong is a mannered, artificial city. Disjunctive editing, direct address to the camera, voice-over narration, and cryptic visual inserts regularly bring the narrative to a standstill. There's an academic argument to be made for this exercise: LIFE IS CHEAP is a meditation on racial and cultural stereotypes, filtered through a cinematic prism. But what's the point? It ultimately reveals nothing, and it's certainly no fun to watch. *(Violence, adult situations.)*

d, Wayne Wang and Spencer Nakasako; p, Winnie Fredriksz; w, Spencer Nakasako; ph, Amir M. Mokri; ed, Chris Sanderson and Sandy Nervig; m, Mark Alder; art d, Collete Koo

Comedy/Thriller   **(PR:O   MPAA:NR)**

LIFE IS A LONG QUIET RIVER

(Fr.) 95m MK2/USA c

Benoit Magimel *(Momo)*, Helene Vincent *(Marielle Le Quesnoy)*, Andre Wilms *(Jean Le Quesnoy)*, Christine Pignet *(Mme. Groseille)*, Maurice Mons *(M. Groseille)*, Catherine Hiegel *(Josette)*, Catherine Jacob *(Marie-Therese)*, and Daniel Gelin *(Dr. Louis Mavial)*

At least on film, the renowned Gallic wit appears to be in serious decline. Nowhere is this more evident than in LIFE IS A LONG QUIET RIVER, the first feature by Etienne Chatiliez, currently France's hottest new filmmaker. More dull than droll, this tepid foray into social satire has about as much fizz and sparkle as flat Perrier. A spinoff of Mark Twain's "Pudd'nhead Wilson," with hints of "The Prince and the Pauper" (not to mention BIG BUSINESS and TWINS) thrown in, LIFE IS A LONG QUIET RIVER features a nature vs. nurture plot that contains all the elements for good farce or parody, but fails to deliver. When her lover opts to spend Christmas with his wife, Josette (Catherine Hiegel), the longtime mistress of Dr. Mavial (Daniel Gelin) and a nurse at his private maternity clinic, switches a pair of newborns in an act of spite. Young Momo (Benoit Magimel) is unwittingly raised as their son by the Groseilles, a family of lowlife miscreants and prostitutes. Conversely, Bernadette (Valerie Lalande), the Groseilles' real daughter, is reared by the bourgeois, pretentious Le Quesnoys in their rigidly formal, conservative household. Momo becomes a likable petty thief; Bernadette is rather charmless and self-indulgent. Their lives couldn't be more different, and living as they do at opposite ends of town and society, they never have occasion to meet. Twelve years after the switch, however, Mavial's wife dies. He refuses to marry his long-suffering paramour, so she exacts revenge (before leaving his employ) by writing to both families and to the doctor, informing them of her misdeed. Voila! the *merde* hits the fan, and life will never be the same again. The flustered Le Quesnoys take in Momo, though they pretend he is their adoptive son and call him Maurice. Without telling Bernadette of her true lineage, they also pay off her real parents in order to keep her where she is. The sleazy Groseilles are only too happy with this arrangement, viewing it purely as a means to extract ever-increasing amounts of money from the Le Quesnoys, who, in typical bourgeois fashion, always try to do the right and proper thing. This leads to an almost humorless sequence of events. Momo can neither believe his good fortune nor give up his larcenous habits, so he steals the family silver and introduces his new sisters and brothers to the loose ways of the Groseilles, with whom he still maintains close contact. Under his influence, life at the Le Quesnoys generally goes to pot. The virginal housekeeper gets pregnant, one of Momo's Le Quesnoy brothers starts dating a Groseille daughter (a world-class teenage whore), and the rest of the bourgeois brood, straining at the bit after years of rigidly enforced standards of behavior, end up sniffing glue and eating ketchup sandwiches. Mme. Le Quesnoy (Helene Vincent), a doting eternal mother who previously would have felt guilty over not making enough placemats for the local church play, now ends up sitting around the house in sunglasses and boozing all day. The stern and once severely repressed M. Le Quesnoy (Andre Wilms) now gets turned on by his wife's inebriation — much to her horror. Only Josette, the cause of it all, gets exactly what she wanted. Forced to close down his clinic in disgrace, Dr. Mavial ends up in her house at the seashore, an almost unwilling captive of Josette's love, and in the final scene, he sits at her side, speechless and morose. Throughout all this, the Groseilles—whose name, incidentally, has become synonymous in France with the English *yahoo*—are consistently objects of ridicule and derision. The fat, slovenly mother (Christine Pignet) does nothing but dye her hair and yell, while unemployed Dad (Maurice Mons) just sits and watches TV. The kids, in turn, are lewd, rude, and crude.

Although there are occasional, briefly funny moments—most notably those between the doctor and his nurse and those featuring a grinning local priest (Patrick Bouchitey), who fancies himself a rock singer—the film generally offers unconnected, fleeting visual impressions instead of well-developed characters. Most of the roles are glossed over, including that of Bernadette. Her tribulations are, in fact, almost entirely ignored in the unfolding tale, and the void is significant. In general, we're left with a film that realizes virtually none of its potential.

In this age of prefabrication and instant, inconsequential humor, it was just a matter of time before French cinema picked up on American-style sitcom sensibilities. Director Chatiliez, 38, formerly a prominent maker of French TV commercials, has adapted his skills from that medium to the big screen with commercial success: LIFE IS A LONG QUIET RIVER has been a hit in Paris since its release there in 1987. But in a country that once produced such filmmakers as Rene Clair, Jacques Tati, and Eric Rohmer—or even the more recent work of Bertrand Blier, Jean-Charles Tacchella (COUSIN, COUSINE), Francis Veber (LES COMPERES), and Coline Serreau (THREE MEN AND A CRADLE)—Chatiliez's film bodes ill for the continued vigor of France's remarkable tradition of cinematic satire and farce. LIFE IS A LONG QUIET RIVER is a major disappointment. *(Adult situations.)*

d, Etienne Chatiliez; p, Charles Gassot; w, Etienne Chatiliez and Florence Quentin; ph, Pascal Lebegue; ed, Chantal Dalattre; m, Gerard Kawczynski

Comedy   **(PR:C   MPAA:NR)**

LIONHEART

105m Taliafilm II—Jack Schwartzman/WB c

Eric Stoltz (*Robert Nerra*), Gabriel Byrne (*The Black Prince*), Nicola Cowper (*Blanche*), Dexter Fletcher (*Michael*), Deborah Barrymore (*Mathilda*), Nicholas Clay (*Charles De Montfort*), Bruce Purchase (*Simon Nerra*), Neil Dickson (*King Richard*), Penny Downie (*Madelaine*), Nadim Sawalha (*Selim*), John Franklin-Robbins (*The Abbot*), Chris Pitt (*Odo*), Matthew Sim (*Hugo*), Paul Ryhs (*Mayor of the Underground City*), Sammi Davis (*Baptista*), Wayne Goddard (*Louis*), Courtney Roper-Knight (*David*), Michel Sundin (*Bertram*), Louise Seacombe (*Girl from Plague Village*), Patrick Durkin (*Fat Peasant*), Haluk Bilginer (*Merchant*), Ralph Michael (*William Nerra*), Barry Stanton (*Duke de Bar*), Jan Waters (*Duchess de Bar*), and Ann Firbank (*Cataonic Woman*)

LIONHEART is one of the last films from the late Franklin Schaffner, a director whose enviable track record (PAPILLON; PLANET OF THE APES) lacked a solid success since 1978's THE BOYS FROM BRAZIL. Unfortunately, this film received a shamefully brief theatrical release through Orion Pictures in 1987, then languished until it made a quiet home-video debut in 1990. A return to the epic filmmaking for which Schaffner is best known, LIONHEART is set in a 12th-century France that is ravaged by plague, poverty, and petty territorial wars. Eric Stoltz plays Robert Nerra, a young nobleman who, rather than following King Richard the Lionhearted on his latest Crusade, suits up for battle against a rival landowner. Robert is knighted for the occasion, but during the bloody combat he panics and runs. As he wanders the landscape, the disconsolate Robert is mistaken for a valiant Crusader, and he's joined by numerous orphaned and abandoned children. The kids want protection against the slave traders who prey on homeless youths; of these villains none is more feared than the Black Prince (Gabriel Byrne), a Crusader-gone-bad who sells children to the same Arabs he once fought. Seeing Robert as the embodiment of virtue and innocence, the Black Prince vows to destroy him. As the ever-growing retinue of children march across France in search of King Richard, the Black Prince follows. When the children reach the sea, they find a castle flying King Richard's banner. Alas, it's a trap set by the Black Prince, whose forces round up the little ones to make slaves of them. But Robert challenges the Black Prince to one-on-one combat and manages to kill the fiend. At this point King Richard himself rides in with a troop of Crusaders. Now a loyal Crusader, Robert reunites with his father. Various youthful romantic entanglements are also happily sorted out, and all, in King Richard's words, go off to follow their destinies.

LIONHEART was to have been the first installment in a Crusades trilogy from screenwriter Menno Meyjes (THE COLOR PURPLE). Reportedly, the second entry would have dealt with Arab leader Saladin and might have balanced out the portrayal of black-hearted Saracens seen here. Then again, in LIONHEART, historical accuracy takes a back seat to standard movie histrionics. There actually were children's crusades during the period covered in the film—naive expeditions of youths who believed their purity would liberate Jerusalem, though the armies of Europe had failed—but it's unlikely that any of these crusades ended

as rosily as the one in this film. There also really was a Black Prince, the son of the British monarch Edward III; however, his ominous nickname referred to his taste in clothing rather than his morality.

Conspicuously aimed at families and younger viewers (the action stays safely within the confines of the film's PG rating), LIONHEART too often serves up the sort of medieval kitsch that the Monty Python troupe effectively trampled in their HOLY GRAIL satire. Burdened with literally every urchin in Paris, Stoltz's Robert transforms the unruly kids into a well-organized unit with one brief speech. Equally implausible is his rapid metamorphosis from frightened deserter to fierce warrior. The other cast members (Britishers all; there doesn't seem to be a Frenchman in the picture) resemble a chorus from "Oliver!"—too modern in their dialog and attitude for the period. Look closely, though, and you'll see an early appearance by Sammi Davis, who later went on to showier roles in Ken Russell's LAIR OF THE WHITE WORM and THE RAINBOW. The film also marks the debut of Deborah Barrymore, the daughter of Roger Moore, but she's stuck with the utterly thankless role of a spirited tomboy who wants to be a Crusader. Barrymore approaches this I-can-lick-any-knight-in-the-castle stuff with enthusiasm, but to no avail. The most intriguing and forceful presence onscreen is Byrne as the Black Prince. A tortured soul, this once-zealous knight has lost faith in the Crusades and now commits heinous acts as his personal vengeance against God. With his unnatural pallor and black garb, Byrne resembles Olivier's Richard III, and his malice approaches supernatural proportions. It's not unusual in movies for a villain to be more interesting than the hero, but seldom does the gap seem so wide; often it seems Stoltz's colorless Robert isn't worth the Black Prince's evil attentions.

LIONHEART was filmed in Hungary and Portugal, and whenever possible, the company made use of existing medieval castles and fortifications. Extras were recruited from two state orphanages, as well as from the Hungarian Circus Arts Institute, which provided jugglers and street performers. Although the most visually impressive scenes of this handsome film are the result of well-designed interiors—like the subterranean "city" of orphans—LIONHEART lacks sweeping spectacle.

Film buffs might remember that Schaffner made another medieval epic, THE WAR LORD, early in his directorial career. A further connection with Schaffner's filmmaking past is the participation of Francis Ford Coppola (author of the script for Schaffner's Oscar-winning PATTON), who is credited as executive producer here. In fact, LIONHEART originated with Coppola's ill-fated Zoetrope production company. The property was then purchased by producer Jack Schwartzman, husband of Coppola's sister, actress Talia Shire, who served as a coproducer on the film. LIONHEART deserves more recognition than it has received, if only for the names connected with it. *(Violence.)*

d, Franklin J. Schaffner; p, Stanley O'Toole and Talia Shire; w, Menno Meyjes and Richard Outten (based on a story by Meyjes); ph, Alec Mills; ed, David Bretherton and Richard Haines; m, Jerry Goldsmith; prod d, Gil Parrondo; art d, Cliff Robinson; set d, Josie MacAvin; spec, Michael White; stunts, Peter Diamond; cos, Nana Cecchi; makup, Pat Hay and Yvonne Coppard; chor, Anthony Van Laast

Adventure   **(PR:A   MPAA:PG)**

LISA

93m Yablans/MGM-UA c

Cheryl Ladd (*Katherine*), D.W. Moffett (*Richard*), Staci Keanan (*Lisa*), Tanya Fenmore (*Wendy*), Jeffrey Tambor (*Mr. Marks*), Edan Gross (*Ralph*), Julie Cobb (*Mrs. Marks*), Michael Ayr (*Scott*), Lisa Moncure (*Sarah*), Tom Dugan (*Mr. Adams*), Frankie Thorn (*Judy*), John Hawker (*Mr. Howard*), Drew Pillsbury (*Don*), Elizabeth Gracen (*Mary*), Dennis Bowen (*Alison's Boy Friend*), Tom Burke (*Maitre 'D*), Tom Nolan (*Waiter*), Hildy Brooks (*Alison's Landlady*), Bob Roitblat (*Porsche Driver*), Sharon Clark (*Porsche Passenger*), and David Niven Jr. (*Flower Shop Patron*)

"Mothers don't lock up your daughters" might be the message of this satisfying, well-crafted tongue-in-cheek thriller from director Gary Sherman, whose previous films include DEAD AND BURIED; VICE SQUAD; WANTED: DEAD OR ALIVE; and POLTERGEIST 3. LISA stars Staci Keanan, the essence of cute perkiness from the TV sitcom "My Two Dads," as its spunky 14-year-old title character, whose first, tentative adolescent stirrings are being thwarted by her mom, Katherine (Cheryl Ladd). A perhaps uniquely Californian (the film is set in Los Angeles), contradictory mix of laid-back liberalism and paranoid repression, Katherine insists that Lisa call her by her first name and share everything with her, while allowing Lisa to lead an "independent" life except in one respect: she is not allowed to date until she turns 16. This restriction is prompted by Katherine's own past experience as a young, unwed mom disowned by her parents and abandoned by Lisa's father. Through a lot of hard work and sacrifice, Katherine has been able both to build a thriving flower business and maintain close ties with her daughter. But her siege mentality concerning men

(Katherine herself resists romantic involvements for fear of subjecting Lisa to emotional trauma) has had some odd effects on her daughter. Left out of the teenage mainstream as a result of her mom's dating prohibition, Lisa has withdrawn into a romantic fantasy world. Not only does she harbor the usual crushes on rock stars, she also follows strange men, takes photos of them, tracks them down through their car license plates, and then makes enticing phone calls to them. This being California, it isn't too long before Lisa latches onto the wrong guy, namely suave restaurant manager Richard (D.W. Moffett), who, in his spare time, is the notorious Candlelight Killer. Like Lisa, Richard tracks down his female victims through their license plates and taunts them with insinuating calls (all of which he records for his private collection). Eventually, he sneaks into their apartments and forcibly wines and dines them by candlelight before killing them (in deference to the film's PG-13 rating, most of the violence takes place off-screen). After Lisa's best friend (Tanya Fenmore) suggests that Mom's own social life could use a little improvement, Lisa tries to set Katherine up with Richard, bringing about the film's climax.

Though the actors in LISA do effective work, the film's true stars are its answering machines and telephones—all sleek, sexy designer models seen in constant, admiring closeup. And that's as it should be, since LISA does for these devices what SEX, LIES AND VIDEOTAPE did for the camcorder and VCR. Through Lisa's and (later) Richard's "antics," they are seen from the start as tools of fantasy and sexual gratification. Though intended for communication, they are also instruments of deception, allowing both Lisa and Richard to obtain a sexual power they lack in their real lives, through the assumption of seductive and dangerous alter egos. Lisa is especially accomplished at this game, affecting a husky, bedroom drawl that transforms her, with disturbing quickness, from a plaid-skirted schoolgirl into a stalker of helpless men. Once Lisa and Richard connect, the film comes alive as a high-stakes game of tense, telephonic cat-and-mouse. The two characters are clearly differentiated, however, in that Sherman (who cowrote LISA's script with Karen Clark) portrays Lisa's phone games as, at worst, a healthy reaction to the unhealthy repressiveness of her mother, whose own motivations the film views sympathetically. That Richard uses Lisa's MO to stalk his own victims says more about Richard's murderously arrested emotional development than it does about Lisa's psychological makeup.

Astute viewers will recognize more than a little Hitchcockian influence in LISA's plot and characters. Lisa's relationship with Katherine is a much-softened reworking of Norman Bates' relationship with his "mother" in PSYCHO, while Lisa's relationship with Richard recalls that between Teresa Wright's character and Joseph Cotten's Merry Widow Murderer in SHADOW OF A DOUBT. But LISA is no mindless run-of-the-mill ripoff. Closer to a true homage, it has a style and wit all its own in the hands of Sherman, who, after a decade of turning out such minor genre gems, continues his career as one of Hollywood's most underrated directors. *(Violence.)*

d, Gary Sherman; p, Frank Yablans; w, Gary Sherman and Karen Clark; ph, Alex Nepomniaschy; ed, Ross Albert; m, Joe Renzetti; prod d, Patricia Van Ryker; set d, Nancy Patton; spec, Guy Faria; stunts, Ben Scott; cos, Shari Feldman; makeup, June Haymore

Thriller   **(PR:C   MPAA:PG-13)**

LONELY WOMAN SEEKS LIFE COMPANION

(USSR) 91m Kiev/International Film Exchange c

Irina Kupchenko *(Klavdia)*, Alexander Zbruyev *(Valentin)*, Elena Solovei *(Neighbor)*, Marianna Vertinskaya *(Anya)*, and Valery Sheptekita *(Kasianov)*

Despite its billing as the first *glasnost*-era Soviet comedy, LONELY WOMAN SEEKS LIFETIME COMPANION has no characters who loudly demand more democracy and freedom, and offers no digressions on what a bad guy that Joe Stalin really was. In fact, there is little in LONELY WOMAN to indicate any particular political epoch, which is its strength. Its bleak look at single life achieves a depressing universality. The film's view of day-to-day Soviet life may even baffle viewers used to conventional media images of gray lumps living a dozen to a room and standing in line for hours to purchase a couple of rotten potatoes. Though not wealthy, the characters, like their American "thirtysomething" counterparts, have the time and energy to worry about finding the right mates, and sometimes resort to desperate measures to do so.

LONELY WOMAN opens with Klavdia (Irina Kupchenko) venturing out during a driving evening rainstorm with the notice that gives the film its title. She posts the notice, which even includes her home address, in a number of public places; and she winds up with pretty much the kind of character one would expect—a gruff, dirty, bedraggled hobo, Valentin (Alexander Zbruyev), who barges into her apartment that same night demanding money. Hardly a delicate flower, Klavdia reacts by bashing Valentin over the head with an ironing board. So begins the oddball relationship that occupies the center of this light, low-key romantic comedy. When Valentin comes to, he protests that the whole thing was just a joke, but his sense of humor doesn't prevent Klavdia from kicking him out

of her apartment. However, Valentin manages to keep finding excuses to show up on her doorstep. After a number of invasions, Klavdia develops a hesitant affection for the homeless Valentin, and eventually she gives him an apartment key so he will have a place to rest during the day while he hunts for a job. She even buys him a suit, as much to make him presentable when they go out together as to help him in his job search. At first mystifying, Klavdia's attraction to Valentin becomes more understandable as the film delves into her dreary daytime existence as a seamstress, work she's forced to bring home with her at night to help make ends meet. Imbued with some of the rebellious spirit that led Klavdia to post her lonelyhearts notice in the first place, her friendship with Valentin (they never do become lovers) provides a dash of color in her otherwise drab existence and gives fleeting expression to her individuality. When a friend from work, horrified at the relationship, offers to set Klavdia up with more suitable partners, Klavdia impetuously unleashes what are undoubtedly years of pent-up frustration over her life. Yet she isn't quite spirited enough to make a complete break with her dreary past, leading to the film's bittersweet, though sadly plausible, ending.

LONELY WOMAN isn't WHEN HARRY MET SALLY . . . , or even a DOWN AND OUT IN BEVERLY HILLS; Klava and Valentin are too real to fit comfortably into either of those Hollywood fantasies, both of which the film superficially resembles. Unlike their Hollywood counterparts, Klavdia and Valentin eke out their existence as best they can. And they live in real places. Klavdia may live alone, but her apartment looks like a cramped afterthought, crudely carved out of what may once have been a one-bedroom "palace." What's more, the pair's yearnings are more rooted in the soul than in the bedroom. There is no attempt, as there is in DOWN AND OUT, to propose a hearty tumble in the hay as a surefire solution to the characters' problems. What Klava and Valentin are involved with is a midlife crisis. Becoming more aware of their mortality, both look back on lives now closer to their end than their beginning, and inevitably they find precious little to show for their efforts to achieve some measure of happiness. Ultimately, it is a shared existential inquiry that, more than any physical or emotional attraction, becomes the basis for their tentative relationship.

LONELY WOMAN is hardly a breakthrough film. Too often, it plays like an audition showcase for its two excellent leading players. Moreover, its script is perhaps a bit too flimsy to sustain a feature-length film; even at just over 90 minutes it feels slow-moving. But it is nevertheless a film with enough sensitivity and poignancy to linger in the heart long after it has gone from the screen. *(Adult situations, sexual situations.)*

d, Viacheslav Krishtofovich; w, Viktor Merezhko; ph, Vasily Trutkovsky; m, Vadim Khrapachev; art d, Alexei Levchenko

Comedy/Romance   **(PR:A   MPAA:NR)**

LONGTIME COMPANION

96m American Playhouse/Samuel Goldwyn c

Bruce Davison *(David)*, Campbell Scott *(Willy)*, Stephen Caffrey *(Fuzzy)*, Mark Lamos *(Sean)*, Patrick Cassidy *(Howard)*, Mary-Louise Parker *(Lisa)*, John Dossett *(Paul)*, Brian Cousins *(Bob)*, Dermot Mulroney *(John)*, Brad O'Hara *(Alec)*, and Michael Schoeffling *(Michael)*

An American Playhouse production, LONGTIME COMPANION is one of the few mainstream feature films to deal directly and seriously with the subject of AIDS and its specific impact on the gay community. As such, its intentions and message are largely unimpeachable. Artistically, however, it leaves something to be desired.

The film opens on July 3, 1981, the day the *New York Times* first reported of the existence of a "cancer" that was killing off a number of homosexual men. The news is shared in Manhattan and Fire Island by a group of six men and a woman, all linked to each other in various ways. It ends eight years later, with the devastating prophecy of the news item fulfilled. AIDS has taken its toll on victims and survivors. The early and later scenes contrast markedly—the invincibly youthful, hedonistic pleasure of dancing and drugging at summer discos has been replaced by fear and an endless round of memorial services, doctor's appointments, and volunteer work. The film's surviving friends can only hope to see the day when a cure is found.

The serious presentation of terminal illness is always problematical on the screen. Filmmakers must simultaneously educate, move, and, yes, entertain the audience by achieving a highly delicate balance. LONGTIME COMPANION is distinguished by some good, sincere acting, but unfortunately, as written by Craig Lucas and directed by Norman Rene, it falls too often into soap opera and the cliches implicit in such undertakings. The protagonists are uniformly white and upper-class, possessed of such appealing vocations as health club manager (Campbell Scott), the heir to wealth (Bruce Davison), entertainment lawyer (Stephen Caffrey), soap-opera writer (Mark Lamos), and successful actor (Patrick Cassidy), the last three being conveniently and rather simplistically connected. The only minority characters (both male) are stereotypes: an understanding black housekeeper who cleans up the emotional and physical messes of his employers, and a bitchy Hispanic PWA (Person With AIDS) who refuses to cope with his illness in the blandly noble way of the main protagonists. (He is put straight by one of them, though.) There are also the now almost-requisite scenes of men warily feeling their lymph glands, searching for clues, and lying fearfully awake at night. On the other hand, the film's treatment of New Age advocates' holistic remedies just borders on satire.

In the film PARTING GLANCES, Steve Buscemi played a PWA who was a true original—scabrously witty and poignant, and, to date, the best filmed handling of the subject. LONGTIME COMPANION, by contrast, although it (barely) manages to avoid the out-and-out mawkishness of such television productions as "An Early Frost" and Terence McNally's more recent "Andre's Mother," never really seems to pierce the emotional surface of its characters. It all seems too dramatically tidy. These well-heeled men are antiseptically upright and forebearing as they face illness and death, and the movie's ending—a fantasy sequence in which the dead return to reunite the living—is an idea that was perhaps best left on writer Lucas' personal computer screen. Through the years covered, certain characters don't seem to change or develop so much as grow or shave off facial hair. The efforts at humor are heavy-handed, sharing that in-joke glibness that made Lucas' BLUE WINDOW so discomfiting at times. (You may laugh, but self-consciously, and only because the actors seem to be having such an uproarious time.) These include a recollection of a deceased friend's drag antics at his sister's wedding, the lawyer's suddenly breaking into a lip-synced song from Michael Bennett's "Dreamgirls," and a scene in which a string ensemble dolefully plays the Village People's 70s anthem "YMCA" at a benefit. Another flaw is the cliched character of Lisa (Mary-Louise Parker): benevolent heterosexual Earth Mother to the guys, who doles out healing portions of support and humor, the first to do volunteer work, blessed with an understanding boy friend.

Davison is a standout in the cast (he earned an Best Supporting Actor Oscar nomination), giving a simple, affecting performance. The scene in which he must deal with his dying lover, Sean (Lamos), and Sean's producer over the phone is excruciatingly, nerve-wrackingly funny and sad, and the film's best moment. Davison is beautifully focused, as well, in a later death scene. The other actors fill their roles capably and, for the most part, attractively. Dermot Mulroney is especially effective and touching as an archetypal party boy, the first to die.

At a budget of under $2 million, the film looks good and has been capably photographed by Tony Jannelli. The film makes striking use of popular songs like Debbie Harry's "The Tide Is High" and the late Sylvester's "Do You Wanna Funk" to capture the dizzying high of the pre-AIDS years, but a depressingly middle-of-the-road jazz score by Lia Vollack is obtrusive. *(Sexual situations, adult situations, profanity.)*

d, Norman Rene; p, Stan Wlodkowski; w, Craig Lucas; ph, Tony Jannelli; ed, Katherine Wenning; md, Lia Vollack; prod d, Andrew Javnoss; art d, Ruth Ammon; set d, Kate Conklin; cos, Walter Hicklin

Drama   (PR:O   MPAA:NR)

LOOK WHO'S TALKING TOO

81m Big Mouth—Tri-Star/Tri-Star c

John Travolta *(James)*, Kirstie Alley *(Mollie)*, Olympia Dukakis *(Rosie)*, Elias Koteas *(Stuart)*, Twink Caplan *(Rona)*, Bruce Willis *(Voice of Mikey)*, Roseanne Barr *(Voice of Julie)*, Damon Wayans *(Voice of Eddie)*, Mel Brooks *(Voice of Mr. Toilet Man)*, Gilbert Gottfried *(Joey)*, Lorne Sussman *(Mikey)*, Megan Milner *(Julie, as a 1-year-old)*, Georgia Keithley *(Julie, as a 4-month-old)*, Nikki Graham *(Julie, as a Newborn)*, Danny Pringle *(Eddie)*, Louis Heckerling *(Lou)*, Neal Israel *(Mr. Ross)*, Lesley Ewen *(Debbie)*, Noelle Parker *(Woman Client)*, Douglas Warhit *(Man Client)*, Terry David Mulligan *(IRS Inspector)*, Paul Shaffer *(Taxi Businessman)*, Don S. Davis *(Dr. Fleischer)*, Morris Panych *(Arrogant Businessman)*, Alex Bruhanski *(Needle Doctor)*, Dorothy Fehr *(Blonde)*, Heather Lea Gerdes *(Hot Babe on Fire Escape)*, Robin Trapp *(Cool Chick)*, Rick Avery *(Burglar)*, Steven Dimopoulos *(Fire Chief)*, James Galeota *(Punk Baby)*, Frank Totino *(Candy Man)*, Coleman Lumley *(Blonde Baby)*, Constance Barnes McCansh *(Sexy Dancer)*, Janet Munro *(Businessman's Babe)*, Mollie Israel *(Mikey's Dream Friend)*, and Alicia Mizel *(Slob Child)*

The rigors of potty training may be fine as a source of amusement for, maybe, five minutes, but toilet turmoil alone cannot carry an 81-minute movie to the peak of hilarity. Yet there are moments when it seems that is exactly what co-writer (with husband Neal Israel) and director Amy Heckerling is attempting to do with this lackluster sequel to the surprise 1989 hit LOOK WHO'S TALKING. Potty training doesn't really take up all the movie (maybe just half of it), but the filmmakers' incredible preoccupation with the bathroom humor can only be seen as a desperate attempt to cover up a dearth of original concepts. It's a pity because the idea of several talking babies is a delightful one which

could have offered a captivating opportunity to explore modern human foibles through the eyes of toddlers.

As the film opens, James (John Travolta) is trying to provide for his wife Mollie (Kirstie Alley) and their child Mikey (voiced by Bruce Willis) by driving a cab in New York, though he still dreams of becoming an airline pilot. Mollie is still an overworked accountant who confides her problems to her best friend Rona (Twink Caplan). James and Mollie seem to bicker over just about everything until Mollie learns she's pregnant again. She gives birth to a daughter, Julie (voiced by Roseanne Barr), leaving Mikey to have to contend with this invader in his home, while also taking on the challenge of dealing with Mr. Toilet (voiced by Mel Brooks). Mikey discusses his problems with his baby pal Eddie (voiced by Damon Wayans), watches dad do an Elvis Presley impersonation, listens to his Mom whine and his grandmother (Olympia Dukakis) bitch, while his relationship with Julie develops.

If one can get by Vancouver standing in for New York, this film is generally well-produced, with decent photography, editing and scoring. But the decidedly weak material gives the actors little to work with, with Dukakis suffering the most as she is completely wasted in a thankless role. Willis, Barr, and Wayans manage to generate a few laughs with their baby talk, but overall this is a mostly unfunny effort that, even for a sequel, is decidedly deplorable. *(Excessive profanity, adult and sexual situations.)*

d, Amy Heckerling; p, Jonathan D. Krane and Bob Gray; w, Amy Heckerling and Neal Israel; ph, Thomas Del Ruth; ed, Debra Chiate; m, David Kitay; md, Maureen Crowe; prod d, Reuben Freed; art d, Richard Wilcox; set d, Barry W. Brolly; spec, Al Benjamin and Chris Walas, Inc.; stunts, Rick Avery and Bill Ferguson; cos, Molly Maginnis; makup, Todd McIntosh

Comedy   (PR:C   MPAA:PG-13)

LOOSE CANNONS

94m Aaron Spelling-Alan Greisman/Tri-Star c

Gene Hackman *(Mac Stern)*, Dan Aykroyd *(Ellis Fielding)*, Dom DeLuise *(Harry "The Hippo" Gutterman)*, Ronny Cox *(Bob Smiley)*, Nancy Travis *(Riva)*, Robert Prosky *(Curt Von Metz)*, Paul Koslo *(Grimmer)*, Dick O'Neill *(Capt. Doggett)*, Jan Triska *(Steckler)*, Leon Rippy *(Weskit)*, Robert Elliott *(Monseigneur)*, Herb Armstrong *(Cheshire Cat)*, Robert Dickman *(White Rabbit)*, David Alan Grier *(Drummond)*, S. Epatha Merkerson *(Rachel)*, Christopher Murney *(Stan)*, Kay Joyner *(Stan's wife)*, Reg E. Cathey *(Willie)*, Alex Hyde-White *(Moderator)*, Tobin Bell *(Gerber)*, Thomas Kopache *(TV Station Man)*, Susan Peretz *(Lady Tenant)*, Al Mancini *(Man Tenant)*, Kevin McClarnon *(Oaf)*, Debbee Hinchcliffe *(Oaf's Sweetie)*, Jay Ingram *(Patrolman)*, Arthur French *(Bus Driver)*, Clem Moorman *(Train Driver)*, Brad Greenquist *(Embassy Officer)*, Ira Lewis *(Hitler)*, Margaret Klenck *(Eva Braun)*, John Bolger *(Young Von Metz)*, Bill Fagerbakke *(Giant)*, Robert Pentz *(Guy at Bar)*, Erik Cord, George P. Wilbur, Gene LeBell, Danny Aiello III *(Grimmer's Men)*, Billy Anagnos, Gary Tacon *(Israeli Agents)*, Dean Mumford *(Guy in Baths)*, John Finn *(Cop)*, Adrienne Hampton *(Security Guard)*, Dutch Miller *(Jacuzzi Guy)*, Gregory Goossen *(Marsh Policeman)*, Chris S. MacGregor *(Military Policeman)*, Ralph Redpath *(Train Engineer)*, Nancy Parsons *(Nurse)*, David Correia *(Orderly)*, Jennifer Roach *(Little Girl)*, and Philip Shafran *(Little Boy)*

In LOOSE CANNONS, Gene Hackman plays Mac, a Washington, DC, police detective teamed with a new partner, Ellis (Dan Aykroyd), to break open a case that involves the FBI, Nazis, Israelis, and pornographers. In addition to this dangerous and complicated case, each man has his own set of problems. Mac—for reasons the script keeps unclear—is homeless; living out of his "woody" station wagon, he is full of disdain for his ex-wife and for his life in general. Ellis, who is fresh out of a psychiatric institution, is a virtual genius of deduction, but having been made a detective (thanks to his uncle), he can't handle the violent aspects of the job. Whenever something dangerous or difficult seems about to happen, Ellis changes into one of the many strange alternate personalities he harbors in his head. As different as the two cops are, they must work together and overcome these obstacles to catch the criminals. Sound familiar? Exactly how many buddy-cop movies can be made before people stop going to see them? Though Andrei Konchalovsky's extravagantly weird TANGO AND CASH seemed to be the most appropriate wrap-up for the tired concept, Hollywood failed to take the hint of that film's self-parody, and now comes LOOSE CANNONS, with its boring gimmick and moronic plot.

Briefly, this plot involves the fight for the possession of a pornographic film starring Hitler and a prominent German politician. Various people want to get their hands on this hot property, including sadistic neo-Nazi Grimmer (Paul Koslo), 350-pound porno dealer Gutterman (the wildly miscast Dom DeLuise), a group of Israeli spies, a corrupt FBI agent (Ronny Cox), and the many, many personalities of Ellis. After several convoluted chase scenes and ridiculous plot twists, the whole thing climaxes in New York's Grand Central Station. Mac finds the film, and is chased by Grimmer into an enclosed billboard high above the crowd in the station. Cornered at gunpoint, Mac flings the film through the billboard, where it falls into the waiting hands of the Israelis. Grimmer is then shot by Ellis (who has survived various tortures) and falls to his death. Later, the Hitler footage is shown at a debate (the porno film has now become a suicide film, but that's beside the point), exposing the German politician as a Nazi. Ellis and Mac recover in the hospital, and upon release are recruited to work for Israeli intelligence.

To put it bluntly, LOOSE CANNONS is garbage. It contains not one original idea or funny gag, not even a remotely entertaining moment. It's a painfully bad "comedy" that is full of the trademarks of director Bob Clark. Clark, whose credits include such gems as RHINESTONE; PORKY'S; and TURK 182!, fills his movies with startlingly crass elements. Crude themes, loud performances, and hammer-me-over-the-head comedy abound in his films, and LOOSE CANNONS is no exception. After a confusing and ineptly handled boat chase, the movie opens, in typical Clark fashion, with a group of characters eavesdropping on a couple having sex. This bit of comic inspiration is followed by some condom jokes, "dick" jokes, and fat jokes, culminating in Aykroyd and Hackman's first meeting, with Aykroyd vomiting. This sets the tone for what follows, including a scene at an S&M bar (easily Aykroyd's most embarrassing moment on celluloid) and several ridiculous chases. The gags are painfully flat and the plot is needlessly complicated.

Moreover, Clark seems to have no idea of how to handle his actors. DeLuise is horrible playing a sleaze who bizarrely ends up as a lovable goof and who is "so great with kids"; Hackman seems lost and completely disinterested, relying on his charm to get him through this mess; and Aykroyd is neither funny nor sympathetic in his obnoxious, overbearing character. Ellis' sudden personality changes are forced excuses for him to do bad impersonations (if your idea of comedy is Dan Aykroyd doing Pee-Wee Herman, then LOOSE CANNONS is for you), and his performance occasionally goes *beyond* over-the-top.

The mix of violence and comedy (which also marred DOWNTOWN, another 1990 buddy-cop film) is unsettling here. Beheadings are smoothly followed by slapstick, and torture is used for comedic purposes. LOOSE CANNONS also wastes the talents of attractive newcomer Nancy Travis, who was so good in Mike Figgis' INTERNAL AFFAIRS. Playing the leader of the Israelis, Travis is essentially used to model tight-fitting, loosely-buttoned sweaters, but she's still the reason for the generous one-star rating. LOOSE CANNONS is a horrible movie, and as such a fitting entry on Bob Clark's resume. *(Profanity, violence, brief nudity, adult situations.)*

d, Bob Clark; p, Aaron Spelling and Alan Greisman; w, Richard Christian Matheson, Richard Matheson, and Bob Clark; ph, Reginald H. Morris; ed, Stan Cole; m, Paul Zaza; prod d, Harry Pottle; art d, William J. Durrell Jr.; set d, Timothy J. Eckel; spec, Roy Arbogast; stunts, Glenn Randall Jr.; cos, Clifford Capone; makup, Michael R. Thomas

Comedy   (PR:O MPAA:R)

LORD OF THE FLIES

90m Jack's Camp – Signal Hill – Castle Rock/Columbia c

Balthazar Getty *(Ralph)*, Chris Furrh *(Jack)*, Danuel Pipoly *(Piggy)*, Badgett Dale *(Simon)*, Edward Taft, Andrew Taft *(The Twins)*, Gary Rule *(Roger)*, Terry Wells *(Andy)*, Braden MacDonald *(Larry)*, Angus Burgin *(Greg)*, Martin Zentz *(Sheraton)*, Brian Jacobs *(Peter)*, Vincent Amabile *(Patterson)*, David Weinstein *(Mikey)*, Chuck Bell *(Steve)*, Everado Elizondo *(Pablo)*, James Hamm *(John)*, Charles Newmark *(Will)*, Brian Matthews *(Tony)*, Shawn Skie *(Rapper)*, Judson McCune *(Luke)*, Zane Rockenbaugh *(Tex)*, Robert Shea *(Billy)*, Gordon Elder *(Rusty)*, Bob Peck *(Marine Officer)*, Bill Schoppert *(Marine Petty Officer)*, and Michael Greene *(The Pilot)*

Near a lush tropical island, a small plane carrying young military school cadets crashes into the ocean. In a stunning prolog, we see the cadets fall helplessly into the waves while the camera shoots them treading water, from below. But after its arresting, almost surreal opening sequence, this unnecessary remake of William Golding's much-read allegory becomes an exercise in futility.

Making their way to a tropical Garden of Eden (with one seriously wounded grown-up), the children are left to fend for themselves without a social structure. Civilization quickly starts to unravel. Although Ralph (Balthazar Getty), a born leader, establishes rules and encourages cooperation, Jack (Chris Furrh), a rotten apple, seductively appeals to the boys' anarchic spirit. Even though his classmates ridicule the portly Piggy (Danuel Pipoly), his physical limitations become advantageuos when Ralph realizes that Piggy's spectacles can be used to start a fire. Guards are appointed, and a signal fire is kept burning. Meanwhile, Simon (Badgett Dale), the most sensitive of the lads, clings to the hope that the adult will recover. Innocently at first, cruel children's games are instituted and duties are shirked. Flexing his leadership muscles, Jack persuades the others to track down wild boar. Racked with fear, the surviving grown-up wanders from camp; the boys assume he drowns. When Jack leads another pig hunt, the youngsters

allow the fire to go out and miss an opportunity to signal a passing plane. At this point, the cadets split into factions, Jack's renegade group attracting more followers once a storm has wrecked the camp. When one boy wanders into a dark cave and stabs what he thinks is a sleeping monster, Jack consolidates his power by frightening the others with tales of a fiend he can protect them from. Reverting to savagery, Jack's faction paint their bodies with blood, dance around the fire, and steal from the other boys. Then Simon discovers that the slain monster was actually their missing teacher; that same night, Simon himself is attacked and killed by a mob that has been stirred up by the increasingly brutal Jack. Ralph and Piggy try to reason with the hooligans on several occasions (and attempt to retrieve Piggy's glasses, which have been stolen), but their former friends jeer at them. The most bloodthirsty of the tribe, Roger (Gary Rule), crushes Piggy with a boulder. Having secured the allegiance of everyone but Ralph, Jack initiates a hunt to eliminate his only rival for leadership. But, just as the boys smoke Ralph out and close in for the kill, marines arrive on the island.

This pointless remake is a Classic Comics' version of Golding's beautifully structured masterwork. Filmed in 1963, Peter Brook's intriguing but disappointing original screen adaptation of the novel was enhanced by stark black-and-white photography and some haunting performances. This version begins excitingly and goes steadily downhill. Neither Brook's film nor this one adds anything new to Golding's vision; they merely iterate themes better conveyed in literary form. For a film version of Golding's tale to succeed, it would have to reshape the material into a cold-blooded adventure story (a black comedy SWISS FAMILY ROBINSON without adults) or a spine-tingling horror yarn (an island full of Bad Seeds wiping out the noble student-council types). No rethinking has been attempted save except for the abbreviation of Piggy's murder, which was a highlight of the earlier version.

Several problems compound the failure of imagination on display. Filmed in gorgeous color, the movie unfolds like postcards from a Junior Club Med. While black-and-white cinematography may be out of fashion, it worked for the previous stab at capturing Golding. Here, instead of counterpointing the terror, the movie's pretty look diminishes the sinister atmosphere. Moreover, the over-elaborate score comes on like a relentless town gossip prattling on about everything that's happening on-screen. In the process of this ear-bending, the score deprives the viewer of the opportunity to experience the story for himself. Shifting the nationality of the boys from English to American is also problematic: the behavior of English youngsters is governed by centuries of tradition, whereas their American counterparts seem always to do what they please (often in the classroom). Indifferently presented by the script and blandly portrayed by the actors, the protagonists are like children of the shopping malls; their fall from grace is neither unexpected nor moving. Instead of conveying innocence, the fresh-faced cast of amateurs distance us with their inability to act. A lovely-to-look-at photo album treatment of Golding's heart of darkness pessimism, this movie misses the point and mood of *Lord of the Flies* completely. *(Violence, profanity.)*

d, Harry Hook; p, Ross Milloy; w, Sara Schiff (based on the novel by William Golding); ph, Martin Fuhrer; ed, Harry Hook; m, Philippe Sarde; md, Harry Rabinowitz; prod d, Jamie Leonard; art d, Jennifer Chang; spec, Giorgio Ferrari, John-Peter Dabdoub, Roland Vickers, Errol Dias, Clovis Nelson, Warren Dunn, Albert McTaggert, Terry Frazee, Logan Frazee, Andy Miller, Michael Meinardus, and Frank Edge; stunts, Jerry Gatlin; cos, Doreen Watkinson; makup, Sarah Monzani

Action/Adventure   (PR:O MPAA:R)

LORDS OF MAGICK, THE

98m Marsh International/American Cinema – Prism c

Jarrett Parker *(Michael Redglen)*, Mark Gauthier *(Ulric Redglen)*, David Snow *(Thomas)*, Ruth Zackerian *(Princess Luna)*, Brendan Dillon Jr. *(Salatin)*, Candace Galvane *(Ellen)*, John Clark *(King)*, Dolores Nascar *(Mme. Esmeralda)*, Renee St. Peter *(Prostitute)*, Clement St. George *(Edgar)*, Robert Ankers *(Merlin)*, Laura Piening, Richard Rifkin, Robert Hopper, Debbie Davis, Robert Axelrod, Gary Wayton, Debra Young, Ron Jeremy Hyatt, Ken Ronzal, and Tom Corvell

Credit THE LORDS OF MAGICK with this much: an unheralded low-budget fantasy, released directly to home video, it's just as entertaining (if not more so) than recent overproduced fairy stories (like KRULL) whose failure at the box office have left the sword-and-sorcery genre in a comatose state. Most movie fantasies suffer from what could be called "Dragon Burnout Syndrome," a numbing familiarity with stock characters and plots. No matter how lavish the sets, how incendiary the special effects, or how flamboyant the performances, one unicorn is very much like another. THE LORDS OF MAGICK at least manages a few original touches. Ulric (Mark Gauthier) and Michael (Jarrett Parker) are brothers, a pair of young "Merlinite" wizards sowing their magical oats in England in the year 988. Dragged before the king on a charge of necromancy (they resurrected an ungrateful nobleman, murdered by thieves), the pair plead for a chance to redeem themselves. Remembering the pre-credit sequence in which his daughter was abducted by Salatin (Brendan Dillon, Jr.), "the most evil and feared sorcerer of black magic," the king orders the two brothers to retrieve Princess Luna (Ruth Zackarian) and kill her captor. Michael is doubtful, but the older, bolder Ulric warms to the task; Salatin has fed the souls of many a kindred wizard to the Dark Powers in his plan to rule the Universe. The brothers find Salatin's altar, and the spectral villain challenges them to follow him a thousand years into the future, where he has hidden the princess. Because of the gap between the centuries, only one of the brothers will be under the personal protection of Merlin, but they depart anyway, landing in modern Los Angeles. The expected culture-shock incidents ensue (including a scuffle with a stage company of "The Princess and the Pea"), but magic bails the brothers out. However, during a fight with a street gang, Ulric forgets the escape spell until it's shouted at him by an onlooker, Thomas (David Snow). A college student steeped in magical lore, he joins the wizards in their quest. Directly, the trio is attacked by a driverless car, which Thomas traces to a rural farm where the heroes do indeed find Salatin and Princess Luna, both in a trance-like state. When our heroes take the princess, Salatin awakens and his taunts pursue the group (via car radio) back to Thomas' neighborhood, where they must again battle the street gang, now transformed into sword-wielding zombies. Clearly, Salatin must be eliminated, and Thomas and Michael look for guidance in a university archives. A medieval manuscript indicates that Michael will prevail (thanks a lot; there goes the suspense element), but it gives no hint of Ulric's fate. Meanwhile, Ulric, dallying with an LA prostitute, is corrupted by Salatin. With the princess in his clutches, Ulric telephones Michael and tells him Salatin can be found at a certain warehouse. There, Michael challenges the fiend, but his magic is ineffective; Ulric, hiding out of sight, deflects his brother's every spell. However, Thomas has learned some wizardry of his own by now, and he grapples with Ulric while Michael and Salatin magically duke it out in a sequence strongly reminiscent of the Boris Karloff-Vincent Price spellfest in THE RAVEN. Thomas purges Ulric with the standard movie exorcism routine, and the elder wizard steps in front of his brother to take a death blow from Salatin. His rage unleashed, Michael reduces the evil sorcerer to a blackened skeleton, then takes Princess Luna and his brother's body back to medieval England, where the grateful king grants Michael permission to raise Ulric from the dead. He also makes the heroic wizard a nobleman, opening the possibility of marriage to the princess, who has fallen in love with the younger wizard. As the pair embrace, Michael decides Ulric can remain safely dead until after the wedding. The wearily cliched final shot shows Salatin reappearing.

THE LORDS OF MAGICK is a mixed bag, but it becomes fairly diverting at times. The rather tired time-travel gimmick — no compelling reason is given for Salatin's excursion into 1988, unless it's just to get far away from Merlin — gives the plot some verve, and it saves money on medieval scenery. The computer-generated special effects endow the film with the look of a video game. Dillon resembles a Marvel Comics super-villain in his cape, skullcap, and cowl, but he makes an adequate menace. Looking far too old for a college kid, Snow's Thomas is hardly a memorable character, but his presence provides an excuse for the wizards to explain a bit about their magical realm. Producer-director-cowriter Marsh does well with some of the details, like the cute spell Michael uses to open any lock and an interlude with a storefront gypsy fortuneteller who considers time-travelling wizards to be minor league. Of greatest interest is the relationship between the two heroes; despite his good humor and bravado Ulric will never be as powerful a wizard as his younger brother and he knows it. His secret resentment is what really gives Salatin control over him. It's this sort of archetypal conflict that makes good fantasy, and it endows these characters with an added layer of meaning. Even with its cheesy production values and low-rent acting, THE LORDS OF MAGICK should please now-desperate fans of the genre who bother to hunt it up at the video store. *(Violence, profanity, substance abuse, adult situations.)*

d, David Marsh; p, David Marsh; w, David Marsh and Sherman Hirsch; ph, Bruce Burnside; ed, David Marsh; m, George Stewart and Ken Bilderbeck; prod d, Mike Rennekamp; spec, Tom Shouse and David Marsh; stunts, Gary Wayton; cos, John Bowen; makeup, Nina Craft

Fantasy   (PR:C   MPAA:PG-13)

LOSER TAKE ALL

(SEE: STRIKE IT RICH)

LOVE AT LARGE

97m Orion c

Tom Berenger *(Harry Dobbs)*, Elizabeth Perkins *(Stella Wynkowski)*, Anne Archer *(Miss Dolan)*, Ted Levine *(Frederick King/James McGraw)*, Annette O'Toole *(Mrs. King)*, Kate Capshaw *(Mrs. Ellen McGraw)*, Ann Magnuson *(Doris)*, Barry Miller *(Marty)*, Kevin J. O'Connor *(Art, Farmhand)*, Neil Young *(Rick)*, Ruby Dee *(Corrine Dart)*, Meegan Lee Ochs *(Bellhop)*, Gailard Sartain *(Taxi Driver)*, Robert Gould *(Tavern Bartender)*, Dirk Blocker *(Hiram Culver, Used-Car Salesman)*, Bob Terhune *(Harley, Rick's Bodyguard)*, Ariana Lamon-Anderson *(Missy McGraw)*, Michael Wilson *(Maitre D', Blue Danube)*, Debra Dusay *(Blue Danube Waitress)*, Sunshine Parker *(Ranch Foreman)*, Billy Silva *(Motel Manager)*, Pamela Abas-Ross *(Nanny)*, Laura Kenny *(Tavern Waitress)*, Leticia Keith *(Rick's Girl Friend)*, Andrew Barr, Jessica Boegel *(King Children)*, Stan Asis *(Counterperson)*, Holly Morrison *(Stewardess)*, Ileane Meltzer *(Angry Neighbor)*, Jeffrey Calvin *(Mario)*, William Lee *(Chinese Man)*, Evelyn Ching *(Chinese Woman)*, Susan Medak *(Neighbor Mom)*, Kate Suzanne Medak *(Neighbor Child)*, Greg Murphy, Shawnee Rad *(Valets)*, Paul Till *(McGraw Taxi Driver)*, and Stephen Kimberley *(Man on Train)*

When you walk into an Alan Rudolph film, you can be pretty sure of what you are going to see: a dreamy, misty romance — cool but sexy and long on mood. LOVE AT LARGE, a soft-boiled, tongue-in-cheek detective fantasy, is no different. Tom Berenger plays Harry Dobbs, a down-at-heel private eye with a maniacally jealous girl friend (Ann Magnuson). Just as the two are about to have a racy reconciliation after their latest fight, Dobbs receives a call from the mysterious Miss Dolan (Anne Archer), who offers him a case. Mistaking the call for a romantic rendezvous, Doris (Magnuson) gives Dobbs a less-than-loving send-off as he goes out to interview for the job. Miss Dolan, as it turns out, wants her boy friend, Rick (Neil Young), put under surveillance. He has threatened her life and she, quite reasonably, wants to know where he is so she can make sure to keep out of his way. Working with a sketchy description, Dobbs finds himself trailing the wrong man, Frederick King (Ted Levine), who, as it happens, has some interesting secrets of his own. The "real" Rick, a bad egg with a short temper, doesn't come to dominate the film as he might in a more conventional *film noir*-style gumshoe melodrama. Instead, Rudolph keeps Dobbs on King's trail through most of the film. Dobbs reports to Dolan that, to all appearances, King is a boring business executive with a devoted, picture-perfect wife (Annette O'Toole) and kids. Then comes the day when King loads his luggage into a waiting cab while his wife tearfully bids him farewell. Dobbs follows King to the "north" (Rudolph's films are rarely set in real places), where, Dobbs discovers, King keeps a large ranch under an alias, complete with another wife (Kate Capshaw) and daughter. Through all of this, Dobbs himself is being followed, none too inconspicuously, by another private eye, Stella (Elizabeth Perkins), hired by Dobbs' girl friend to get the goods on Dobbs and Dolan. When Dobbs and Stella are brought together by car trouble, Doris suspects Stella of fooling around with Dobbs, which gets her fired by her detective agency (run by, of all people, Ruby Dee). Dobbs and Stella begin working together on King, finding out, almost too late, Dobbs' mistake, all of which leads to a frantic climax.

Though complicated, the plot outcome is fairly predictable. All who deserve it get their comeuppances and the right couplings occur. But those familiar with past Rudolph films know that plot is of secondary importance in the director's work. Mostly, it's an excuse to get the characters into evocative settings. At the weird, lavish Blue Danube nightclub, where Dobbs and Dolan meet to discuss the case, everybody moves in a slow, deliberate, dreamlike manner. Fittingly, Dolan is herself a creature of gossamer fantasy, living only for love and romance (and to break into song at the oddest moments). The "north," meanwhile, exists mostly as a stark netherland in which Dobbs and Stella come together as two lost souls starved for emotional sustenance.

Beyond its serious moments, LOVE AT LARGE has an appealing playfulness that has been missing in Rudolph's other recent efforts TROUBLE IN MIND and, especially, MADE IN HEAVEN (THE MODERNS, on the other hand, was entirely too fatuous). There is also a looser, more freewheeling flavor to the performances, reminiscent of CHOOSE ME, still Rudolph's best film. Both a visual director and an actor's director, Rudolph has great sympathy for his male performers. Rarely has it been as much fun to watch and listen to Berenger as it is here. But Rudolph also loves his female players. His camera is enchanted by them, zeroing in with a fetishist's fervor on such details as Archer's full, sensuous lips, O'Toole's knees, Perkins' alabaster skin, and Magnuson's severe, masklike face. On the whole, Rudolph might benefit from a good, tough-minded collaborator to sharpen up his plots and characters. Still, even for those uninitiated to Rudolph's sometimes fragile charms, LOVE AT LARGE is a much better than average place to park your eyes for a while. *(Adult situations.)*

d, Alan Rudolph; p, David Blocker; w, Alan Rudolph; ph, Elliot Davis; ed, Lisa Churgin; m, Mark Isham; prod d, Steven Legler; art d, Steve Karatzas; set d, Susan Mina Eschelbach; spec, Frank Ceglia; stunts, Greg Walker; cos, Ingrid Ferrin; makeup, Cynthia Barr

Comedy/Romance   (PR:C   MPAA:R)

M

MACK THE KNIFE

120m Menahem Golan/21st Century c

(AKA: THREEPENNY OPERA, THE)

Raul Julia *(MacHeath)*, Richard Harris *(Mr. Peachum)*, Julia Migenes *(Jenny Diver)*, Roger Daltrey *(Street Singer)*, Julie Walters *(Mrs. Peachum)*, Rachel Robertson *(Polly Peachum)*, Clive Revill *(Money Matthew)*, Bill Nighy *(Tiger Brown)*, Erin Donovan *(Lucy Brown)*, Julie T. Wallace *(Coaxer)*, Louise Plowright *(Dolly)*, Elizabeth Seal *(Molly)*, Chrissie Kendall *(Betty)*, Miranda Garrison *(Esmerelda)*, Mark Northover *(Jimmy Jewels)*, Roy Holder *(Wally the Weeper)*, Clive Mantle *(Johnny Ladder)*, Russel Gold *(Hookfinger Jake)*, John Woodnut *(Reverend Kimball)*, Peter Rutherford *(Warden)*, Iain Rogerson *(Filch)*, Steven Law *(Sergeant Smith)*, Dong Ji Hong *(Sukey Tawdry)*, and Sandor Kaposi *(Organ Grinder)*

MACK THE KNIFE, the new film version of Bertholt Brecht and Kurt Weill's "The Threepenny Opera," could serve as a textbook example of why film producers generally don't direct. Menaham Golan, of the Cannon Films Golan-Globus production team, has taken what may be the greatest musical play of them all and made an unequivocal botch of it. For those unfamiliar with the play, the story goes something like this: at the time of Queen Victoria's coronation, the streets of London are infested with crime and licentiousness. Polly (Rachel Robertson), the daughter of the Peachums (Richard Harris and Julie Walters), has engaged herself to marry MacHeath (Raul Julia), the dread King of the Underworld. Her parents strenuously object to this and set about to plan the lawful entrapment of the elusive MacHeath. Besides Tiger Brown (Bill Nighy), the chief of police, who has a friendly, shared past with MacHeath, Mr. Peachum enlists the help of his sometime inamorata, Jenny Diver (Julia Migenes), an unscrupulous whore. The net closes in on MacHeath with the revelation that he has also had marital relations with Brown's daughter, Lucy (Erin Donovan), and with a Chinese tart, Sukey Tawdry (Dong Ji Hong). The noose is just about to tighten around his neck when a highly Brechtian turn of events saves the day.

The film's production is visually dead—a murky blight seems to have permanently settled over the lens—with interpolated surrealistic and dream effects that are downright tacky. It's nearly impossible to enjoy Kurt Weill's acrid, seductive music as a compensation for the lack of exciting images, however, given the Las Vegas/Percy Faith arrangements of the truncated score. Golan has chosen to set his production in a set that looks like a leftover from a bus-and-truck OLIVER, and indeed, the whole film seems infected more with the spirit of Dickens than that of Brecht—whose original, bitter, and ruefully humorous commentary on social hypocrisy and injustice has been converted into rambunctious jollity, a mere excuse for the cast to dance about in the streets with an ain't-the-low-life-grand insouciance. (The choreography is nightmarishly bad, though luckily obscured by the MTV-ish editing.) In a miserable attempt to open things up (as well as to provide the now-requisite chase scene), director-screenwriter Golan even includes a madcap, Keystone Kops pursuit of MacHeath towards the finale that only manages to add insult to injury. The famous ending is utterly devoid of wit or surprise, leaving the actors rather pitiably stranded.

The entire thing comes off about on the level of a high-school production—one hopes the actors' parents, at least, will enjoy it. Some of them may not, however, since the performances vary wildly in conception and execution. The one who emerges from the farrago with the most honor is Roger Daltrey—who, though a bit too Cockney as the Street Singer, displays an easy professionalism and charm, while managing not to be too jarringly modern. It's a pity Daltrey didn't play the lead here. Julia's MacHeath was striking a decade ago in Richard Foreman's brilliant, avant-garde 1976 Broadway staging of "The Threepenny Opera," in which his somewhat bland (though Tony-winning) conception of the role and toneless singing were augmented by the battery of expressionistic effects and spirited performances with which Foreman surrounded him. Unfortunately, Julia's performance here is so enervated that it almost seems redundant to worry about his execution in the last scene—MacHeath was dead on arrival. Strutting about in feather boas and striking dance-hall girl poses, Migenes is an adequate, but very conventional, Jenny; one misses the wondrous eccentricity and dazzle of Lotte Lenya (in G.W. Pabst's 1930 German film version) or Ellen Greene (in the Foreman production), two diseuses who really knew how to pack a wallop. Migenes gives her big "Pirate Jenny" number a brave try, but is undone by Golan's cross-cutting and a too-literal image of a toy galleon surmounted by skeletons.

Robertson, however, is something of a find, possessed of a pre-Raphaelite beauty, ingenue acting ability, and a lovely, ethereal voice. Her duet with Daltrey is the film's high point. By contrast, Donovan (as Lucy Brown) is a yowling nuisance whose catfight/duet with Robertson seems calculated to please the

kinkier members of the audience. Harris is a bore as Peachum, falling back on drunken slapstick effects with a bottle and a floppy nightcap, and Nighy is even less than that as MacHeath's buddy-nemesis, Tiger Brown (especially since he and Julia lack chemistry). Walters, however, gets the biggest booby prize as Mrs. Peachum, whom she plays with an incessant leer and over-the-top line readings. *(Profanity, adult situations, sexual situations.)*

d, Menahem Golan; p, Stanley Chase; w, Menaham Golan (based on "The Threepenny Opera" by Bertolt Brecht and Kurt Weill); ph, Elemer Ragalyi; ed, Alain Jakubowicz; m, Kurt Weill; md, Dov Seltzer; prod d, Tivadar Bertalan; set d, Miklos Hajdu; stunts, Tamas Pinter; cos, John Bloomfield; makeup, Christine Allsopp; chor, David Toguri

Musical   (PR:A MPAA:PG-13)

MADHOUSE

90m Boy of the Year/Orion c

John Larroquette *(Mark Bannister)*, Kirstie Alley *(Jessie Bannister)*, Alison LaPlaca *(Claudia)*, John Diehl *(Fred)*, Jessica Lundy *(Bernice)*, Bradley Gregg *(Jonathan)*, Dennis Miller *(Wes)*, Robert Ginty *(Dale)*, Wayne Tippit *(Grindle)*, Paul Eiding *(Stark)*, Aeryk Egan *(C.K.)*, Deborah Otto *(Katy)*, Mark Bringelson *(Prick Automaton Cop)*, Karen Kronwell *(Female Cop)*, Heather McNair *(Karen Kelly)*, Mark Manning *(Russell Fenn)*, Bob Sorenson *(Field Reporter)*, Rob Camilletti *(Shady Character Outside Strip Joint)*, Elizabeth Lang *(Mark's Secretary)*, Peppi Sanders *(Receptionist)*, Jay Bernard *(Kaminsky)*, Frank Dworsky *(Mailroom Employee)*, Rene L. Moreno *(Mailroom Runner)*, JESSIE'S INTER-VIEWEES: Deborah Swartz *("Chloroform")*, Lisa Rubin *("Tom Cruise" Girl Fan)*, Hart Throb *("Tom Cruise" Boy Fan)*, Aaron Berger *("Space People Eat my Mom and Dad")*, Elaine Moe *("Fistful of Valium")*, Loy Burns *("Get Drunk")*, Jack Edward *("Polka Man")*, Pat Willoughby *("Polka Lady")*, Dick Alexander *("Bust Somebody")*, Francis Brooks *("Pump Iron")*, Marlon Darton *("Meditation")*, Freida Smith *("Sex")*, Jon Proudstar *("Shoot 'Em")*, Mel Coleman *("Strangle 'Em")*, Kimberly Steuter *("Cook 'Em in the Oven")*, Elizabeth Kneeland *("Hide His Medication")*, Ed Peterson *("Her Ancient Husband")*, Grant Moran *("Kindness")*, Michael Waltman *("Insulin")*, Darwin Hall *("Hammer")*, Karen Deconcini *("Bean Dip")*, Earl Smith *("Shiv")*, Kevin Wadowski *("Hit 'N' Run")*, Ethan Aronson *("His Car")*, Michael Zand *(Voice of Kaddir)*, and Dr. Jack Penix *(Voice of Dr. Jack Penix)*

John Larroquette and Kirstie Alley play Mark and Jessie Bannister, a yuppie couple who have just moved into their first home: a small but comfortable "starter house" near the ocean that is about to be invaded by houseguests from hell. It all begins when Mark's cousin Fred (John Diehl) and his pregnant wife, Bernice (Jessica Lundy), come to visit. They are an obnoxious pair of goofs from New Jersey, who greet the Bannisters with offhanded remarks about plastic surgery and who have brought along an ugly cat that vomits all over their car. It doesn't take long before Fred and Bernice move into the master bedroom, lose their travelers checks, and completely disrupt their hosts' love life. To make matters worse, Jessie's money-hungry sister, Claudia (Alison LaPlaca), walks out on her rich husband and also comes to stay with the Bannisters, taking over the rest of the house. Now Mark and Jessie have no privacy or peace, but that's only the beginning. After five long days, Fred and Bernice prepare to leave, but when the pregnant Bernice slips and falls flat on her back, Jessie is informed by a doctor—to her horror—that Bernice must remain in the nearest bed for the rest of her pregnancy. Accordingly, she is brought back to the Bannisters' master bedroom, where a harness is constructed that will enable her to be suspended comfortably, over the bed. Just when it looks as though things couldn't possibly get any worse, the next door's neighbors' house is burned down (thanks to Mark) and the entire family is forced to move in with the Bannisters. The little "starter house" has become a madhouse, full of obnoxious, demanding, and unwanted guests who have literally taken over. Eventually, Fred leaves to "find himself," Bernice's pregnancy is discovered to be false, Jessie has a nervous breakdown, Mark becomes a fugitive drug dealer, and the particularly hard-to-kill cat loses out its nine lives. Pushed over the edge, Mark and Jessie kick everyone out (destroying the house in the process), and are eventually rewarded with better jobs and a bigger home. The film ends with a title telling us that the Bannisters lived happily ever after—until their parents came to visit.

Strikingly similar to NATIONAL LAMPOON'S CHRISTMAS VACATION (all the way down to the unwanted houseguests and dead cat jokes), except with fewer laughs, MADHOUSE is a badly executed slapstick comedy with little redeeming value. Debuting director-writer Tom Ropelewski's flat-footed style suffocates all potential humor and creates a thoroughly tedious mood. He leaves jokes dangling in the air, waiting for a much needed punch that never comes, and the characters are never developed into more than one-joke stereotypes. Alley ("Cheers") and Larroquette (of "Night Court," for which Ropelewski has written) are strong TV personalities, but they practically disappear in this big-screen outing, despite MADHOUSE's transparent, TV-movie feel. There is no chemistry between them, nor are they interesting individually (it's only when Alley runs around in a lace bra that she becomes watchable, and that's hardly a point of recommendation, especially after her work in 1989's surprise hit LOOK WHO'S TALKING). The gags range from exploding toilets to runaway elephants, and the funny moments involve the cat—considering how many times they "kill" it off during the picture, it's bound to get at least one laugh, and its vomit scene is particularly amusing. Everything else is flat and badly timed.

Admittedly, no one who goes to MADHOUSE will expect edification in the first place. But though the material in MADHOUSE is intentionally sophomoric, though slapstick comedies can be funny, and though there's nothing wrong with a bit of good silliness, assured, deftly paced direction and adroit, lively performances are necessary to pull such broad comic romps off. MADHOUSE fails to deliver on both these crucial counts. *(Profanity, adult situations, sexual situations.)*

d, Tom Ropelewski; p, Leslie Dixon and Donald C. Klune; w, Tom Ropelewski; ph, Denis Lewiston; ed, Michael Jablow; m, David Newman; prod d, Dan Leigh; art d, C.J. Simpson; set d, Leslie Rollins; spec, Cliff Wenger; stunts, Brad Bovee; cos, Jim Lapidus; makup, Todd Andrews; chor, Chrissy Bocchino

Comedy   **(PR:C   MPAA:PG-13)**

MAGDALENE

89m Theumer-Goetz/Prism c

Steve Bond *(Fr. Joseph Mohr)*, Nastassja Kinski *(Magdalene)*, David Warner *(Von Seidl)*, Gunter Meisner *(The Prior)*, Cyrus Elias *(Franz Gruber)*, Franco Nero *(Janza)*, Ferdy Mayne *(Archbishop)*, Katharina Bohm *(Helga)*, Anthony Quayle *(Fr. Nossler)*, William Hickey *(Rudolf)*, Janet Agren *(Anna)*, Max Tidof *(Robert)*, Karina Szulc *(Elisabeth)*, Ralf Weikinger *(Baader)*, Ulrich Gunther *(Hans)*, Armin Kraft *(Konrad)*, and Francesca Ferre *(Sophia)*

In this sluggish historical romance, former "General Hospital" star Steve Bond plays a selfless priest who not only finds time to be tempted by laundress/slut Nastassja Kinski but also manages to pen the lyrics to the Christmas hymn "Silent Night." All is not well in Germany. Rogues wander the roads, terrorizing wayfarers; Catholic Church officials keep a stranglehold on local politics and land values. Into this maelstrom of intrigue and religious hypocrisy comes Father Mohr (Bond). While the emperor is busy repressing a radical student movement, the Church is making crooked deals with swinish politicians like von Seidl (David Warner), who fears Father Mohr's incorruptible presence. Immediately, the new priest makes waves by mingling with the riff-raff at the local tavern and catching the eye of Magdalene (Kinski), a barmaid who (we later learn) has been sexually abused by von Seidl since childhood. While the prelate and the tavern wench grapple with their mutual attraction, (1) the bandit Janza (Franco Nero) pursues both his reluctant fiancee, Magdalene, and a life of crime, (2) von Seidl and the Prior (Gunter Meisner) discuss plans to eliminate Mohr, (3) von Seidl meets secretly with Magdalene and tries to force her to sign a confession falsely accusing Father Mohr of being her lover. During a struggle, von Seidl stabs Magdalene accidentally, but she is rescued by Janza and nursed back to health by the priest. Although Magdalene starts a new unsullied life as a laundress, the Prior tries to entangle her in his evil web and even attempts her abduction. Redeemed by their impossible love, Magdalene and Father Mohr are reunited, but nothing carnal transpires between them, except in his dreams. In the meantime, none of the Church power-brokers take notice of the Prior's insinuations, and Janza is wounded but escapes from soldiers and confesses his life of crime. Reassigned to another parish, Father Mohr takes time out from his soul-searching and his busy schedule of saving the souls of bandits and barmaids and writes "Silent Night" with town musician Franz Gruber. With a hit song added to his resume, the priest's religious stock rises; suddenly he finds it easier to remain celibate and love Magdalene platonically. God has won his heart.

Playing fast and loose with several historical events (all of which are reduced to the level of background for a Harlequin romance), MAGDALENE is a tepid love story that emits no heat and evinces no passion. What can you say about a movie whose hunky leading man, best-known as a beefcake poster boy, is clothed up to his adam's apple in priestly garb throughout. It's like casting Steve Reeves as Truman Capote or Jayne Mansfield as Maria von Trapp. What we are left with is a clammy sex tease about a priest who doesn't succumb to the temptation of the flesh. Since all the historical-political details are handled in mediocre fashion, our attention continually returns to the stalled central romance. Had the conniving of the church officials and the political upheaval been better handled, this might have added up to a more interesting movie. Fashioned like a cut-rate mini-series, MAGDALENE never evokes a sense of the period or location. We know it's supposed to be taking place in the Europe of long ago, but the cast members could be portraying members of a modern folk dance group who've been stranded at a cultural festival in 1990. Nothing about MAGDALENE is convincing except for Kinski, who brings surprising radiance and conviction to

a standard fallen woman role; she should be getting the parts that are going to her clone, Isabella Rossellini. Although Mayne and Quayle comport themselves with dignity, bad guys Warner and Meisner seem to have studied the fine art of hammy menace at an acting seminar held by Donald Pleasence and Jack Palance. Worse yet is the stiff Bond, whose idea of holiness is to stare straight ahead without blinking. Watching Bond piously spurn Kinski, viewers will yearn for "The Thornbirds." You will end up so bored with unrequited love that you will want Magdalene to slip the priest a Mickey Finn and get it over with. If you are a sucker for historical fiction, you may find some enjoyment in this period piece, but true romantics will feel short-changed. Despite Kinski's allure, MAGDALENE creates no sexual sparks. If this movie is to be believed, writing a hit song like "Silent Night" must be more fulfilling than a mad affair with a voluptuous barmaid. *(Violence, adult situations.)*

d, Monica Teuber; w, Monica Teuber; ph, Armando Nannuzzi; ed, Silvana Zafosnik; m, Cliff Eidelman; md, Cliff Eidelman; prod d, Gianni Quaranta; art d, Vlastimil Gavric and Luigi Marchione; set d, Stefano Paltrinieri; spec, Elio Terribili; cos, Fabrizio Caracciolo

Romance   **(PR:A   MPAA:NR)**

MAHABHARATA, THE

(Brit./Fr./US) 171m Les Prods. du 3eme Etage/Reiner Moritz c

Robert Langton-Lloyd *(Vyasa)*, Antonin Stahly-Vishwanadan *(Boy)*, Bruce Myers *(Ganesha/Krishna)*, Vittorio Mezzogiorno *(Arjuna)*, Andrzej Seweryn *(Yudhishthira)*, Mamadou Dioume *(Bhima)*, Jean-Paul Denizon *(Nakula)*, Mahmoud Tabrizi-Zadeh *(Sahadeva)*, Miriam Goldschmidt *(Kunti)*, Mallika Sarabhar *(Draupadi)*, Erica Alexander *(Madri/Hidimbi)*, Nolan Hemmings *(Abhimanyu)*, Ryszard Cieslak *(Dhritharashtra)*, Helene Patarot *(Gandhari)*, Urs Bihler *(Dushassana)*, Jeffrey Kissoon *(Karna)*, Sotigui Kouyate *(Bishma/Parashurama)*, Yoshi Oida *(Drona)*, Tuncel Kurtiz *(Shakuni)*, Georges Corraface, Tapa Sudana, Bakary Sangare, Corrine Jaber, Clement Masdongar, Ken Higelin, Joseph Kurian, Myriam Tadesse, and Hapsarif Hardjito

In adapting the 100,000-stanza Sanskrit poem that is roughly the equivalent of India's Bible, renowned stage director Peter Brook has created a work that is more filmed theater than fluid moviemaking. In fact, Brook first tackled this material in a nine-hour stage production. The resultant play was then condensed into a six-hour miniseries for American Public Television and a five-hour feature for theatrical release in India. The version reviewed here, an adaptation thrice removed, runs just under three hours. In spite of all this cutting and pasting, THE MAHABHARATA manages to be both overlong—a byproduct both of its staginess and of its emphasis on talk over action—and underdeveloped. Yet the cumulative power of this 2,000-year-old tale is undeniable, and Brook's approach, if debatable on an artistic level, is nevertheless respectful without being overly reverential.

In its broadest outline, THE MAHABHARATA is the story of two warring families, the Pandavas, descendants of King Pandu (Tapa Sudana), and the Kaurava family, the offspring of Pandu's blind brother, Dhritharashtra (Ryszard Cieslak). As the film begins, Pandu violates traditional law by killing a gazelle while it is mating, and as a result of this action, the king is forced to relinquish his throne to his brother. Although he is forbidden to have children of his own, Pandu is lucky enough to have married Kunti (Miriam Goldschmidt), who is able to mate with the gods while remaining a virgin. Even before becoming Pandu's wife, Kunti gave birth to one child, Karna (Jeffrey Kissoon), the offspring of the Sun; however, youthful fear and ignorance prompted her to give up this child. But while married to Pandu, Kunti becomes a mother many times over, giving life to Yudhishthira (Andrzej Seweryn), the son of Dharma, the god of earthly harmony; mighty Bhima (Mamadou Dioume), the son of Vayu, god of the wind; and Arjuna (Vittorio Mezzogiorno), son of Indra, the king of the gods. Kunti shares her power with Pandu's second wife, Madri (Erica Alexander), who gives birth to Nakula (Jean-Paul Denizon) and Sahadeva (Mahmoud Tabrizi-Zadeh), twin sons of the gods of patience and wisdom. Meanwhile, Dhritharashtra has married Gandhari (Helene Patarot), whose two-year pregnancy yields what looks like a cannonball, which is broken up and cultivated to produce 100 children. Included in this brood are the greedy, vindictive Duryodhana (Georges Corraface) and Dushassana (Urs Bihler). Raised together, the offspring of Pandu and the blind king constantly fight with one another and form alliances that become crucial as the story develops. Unable to control the cousins, their first teacher, Bishma (Sotigui Kouyate), is replaced by Drona (Yoshi Oida), a strict disciplinarian and expert in martial arts. Bhishma, a fearsome warrior with the power to choose the day of his death, aligns himself with Duryodhana. After being rejected by his half-brother Arjuna because of his "low birth," Karna also takes sides with Duryodhana. Meanwhile, Arjuna marries the proud and beautiful Draupadi (Mallika Sarabhai), whom he shares with his other four brothers, as his mother has commanded. Determined to win Draupadi from his cousins—along with everything else they own—Duryodhana challenges Yudhishthira to a dice game without telling him that his adversary will be Shakuni (Tuncel Kurtiz), an expert gambler who has never lost. The Pandavas are defeated and driven into exile, though Duryodhana is thwarted in his attempt to possess Draupadi. A war follows when the Kauravas refuse to grant the exiled Pandavas a role in the kingdom. Both sides boast an array of magical weapons and allies that serve only to assure an extended, bloody conflict. The prospect of a victor emerges only when the god Krishna (Bruce Myers), seeking to right the injustice, assumes human form and sides with the Pandavas, empowering Arjuna by teaching him the meaning of life.

That the above synopsis covers only a small part of what actually occurs in THE MAHABHARATA is indicative of the film's main problem, the over-complexity of its plot. It takes a tremendous effort just to follow the story, let alone to savor its subtleties. Moreover, the talky script—co-authored by Brook, Jean-Claude Carriere, Marie-Helene Estienne—and staginess of the action are added distractions. Nonetheless, what Brook, his collaborators, and the uniformly excellent cast are able to accomplish in THE MAHABHARATA far outweighs the film's weaknesses. Brook manages to emphasize what is uniquely Indian in the epic poem that provides the film's basis without neglecting its points of contact with other enduring works of spiritual enlightenment. As much as possible, the international cast, many of whom appeared in the stage version, also labor to give the characters a human realism, imbuing the tale with a poignant intimacy to match its epic sweep. Though filmed at minimal cost, THE MAHABHARATA is a story for the ages. *(Violence)*

d, Peter Brook; p, Michel Propper; w, Jean-Claude Carriere, Peter Brook, and Marie-Helene Estienne; ph, William Lubtchansky; ed, Nicolas Gaster; m, Djamchid Chemirani, Toshi Tsuchitori, Kudsi Erguner, Kim Menzer, and Mahmoud Tabrizi-Zadeh; prod d, Chloe Obolensky; art d, Emmanuel de Chauvigny and Raul Gomez; cos, Pippa Cleator; makup, Josee de Luca

Historical   (PR:A MPAA:NR)

MAMA, THERE'S A MAN IN YOUR BED

(Fr.) 110m Cinea/Miramax c

Daniel Auteuil *(Romuald)*, Firmine Richard *(Juliette)*, Pierre Vernier *(Blache)*, Maxime Leroux *(Cloquet)*, Gilles Privat *(Paulin)*, Muriel Combeau *(Nicole)*, Catherine Salviat *(Francoise)*, Nicolas Serreau *(Housing Department Deputy)*, Alain Tretout *(Vidal)*, Alain Fromager *(Marton)*, Jacques Poitrenaud *(Civil Servant)*, Caroline Jaquin *(New Secretary)*, Gilles Cohen *(Driver)*, Alexandre Basse *(Benjamin)*, Aissatou Bah *(Felicite)*, Mamadou Bah *(Desire)*, Marina M'boa Ngong *(Claire)*, Sambou Tati *(Aime)*, Isabelle Carre *(Valerie)*, and Jean-Christophe Itier *(Patrick)*

Try to overlook the heinous title; this film by Coline Serreau is a stylishly done puff pastry that has a feel-good, modern fairy-tale aura reminiscent of those Capra pictures in which little guys take on big business baddies and triumph. Romuald (Daniel Auteuil) is the CEO of a powerhouse Paris yogurt factory. His job barely leaves him enough time to spend with his wife and children. Juliette (Firmine Richard) is the woman who cleans his office at night. She lives with her five children in a small, cramped apartment and struggles to make ends meet and to keep the kids on the right path. Although Romuald is unaware of it, his company is rife with internecine conspiracies, largely the work of two executives whom he has passed over for promotion. A shipment of yogurt is contaminated, the firm is on the brink of disaster, and Romuald is the victim of malevolently manipulated circumstances. His enemies have not counted on Juliette, however, who, in the course of emptying wastebaskets and clearing desks, really uncovers the dirt. Taking matters into her capable hands, she saves her boss and eventually becomes the unwilling recipient of his sudden romantic interest.

Serreau's last film, THREE MEN AND A CRADLE (remade in the US as THREE MEN AND A BABY), was a hugely successful bit of calculated Gallic yuppie whimsy, the shenanigans of its three ultra-puckish bachelors and endlessly incontinent infant having all the freshness of curdled milk. Like that film, MAMA is set in an unreal, Disneyesque world, but its interracial romance and the down-to-earth grittiness of Juliette's side of the story give it much-needed weight. Significantly, the property has already been optioned for development by US producers, and it's telling that Hollywood has to look to Europe to find scripts containing intelligent roles for African-Americans.

Jean-Noel Ferragut's photography here has a pleasing, deep-toned look that undercuts the glossy plot developments, and Serreau keeps things spinning so fast the improbabilities barely have time to register. The evocative music the film employs is also a real boon: Memphis Slim, T. Bone Walker, and Duke Ellington's "On the Sunny Side of the Street" spice up the farcical action, and wonderful, bluesy guitar work by Stevie Ray Vaughn underscores the darker moments.

It is always satisfying when tables are turned and an underling controls the destinies of mandarins, and in MAMA, Serreau's leading lady, Richard, makes this reversal particularly enjoyable. In her film debut, Richard is a majestic

wonder of natural poise and charismatic authority. Her Antilles-accented French registers soothingly, and she brings an authenticity to her role that no amount of formal training could impart. Her Juliette is the unscarred veteran of five marriages, and the birthday party she throws for her children and their fathers is a genuine "bright" spot, replete with tropical colors and lively music. Romuald, who has been blithely piggish in his condescending acceptance of her help, overhears her charming refusal of one of her ex-husbands' entreaties, and later spies Juliette sleeping in the nude. She has the opulent sensuality of a Matisse odalisque, and Romuald's adoration of her is palpable. Auteuil also is appealing in what is becoming his specialty: the frantic Everyman, Jack Lemmon sans neutering tics. The playing-out of the romance between Romuald and Juliette is overextended, however, complete with an insistently cheerful wedding scene. Regrettably, the pat, perfect sealing of so many characters' fates—happy families as far as the eye can see—becomes cloying. *(Adult situations, nudity.)*

d, Coline Serreau; p, Jean-Louis Piel and Philippe Carcassonne; w, Coline Serreau; ph, Jean-Noel Ferragut; ed, Catherine Renault; m, Jerome Reese; prod d, Michelle Plaa; set d, Jean-Marc Stehle; spec, Jerome Levy; cos, Monique Perrot; makup, Michel Deruelle

Comedy   (PR:A MPAA:NR)

MAN INSIDE, THE

93m Philippe Diaz/New Line c

Jurgen Prochnow *(Gunter Wallraff)*, Peter Coyote *(Henry Tobel)*, Nathalie Baye *(Christine)*, Dieter Laser *(Leonard Schroeter)*, Monique Van de Ven *(Tina Wallraff)*, Philip Anglim *(Rolf Gruel)*, Sylvie Granotier *(Kathy Heller)*, Henry G. Sanders *(Evans)*, and James Laurenson *(Mueller)*

While in 1990 the return of *film noir* was touted in such films as THE HOT SPOT, THE GRIFTERS, and AFTER DARK, MY SWEET, this unheralded offering from executive producer-writer-director Bobby Roth (THE HEART-BREAKERS) came closer than most to recreating the eerie menace of genre classics such as DETOUR and THE BIG HEAT, charged with the rawness of a Sam Fuller (SHOCK CORRIDOR) in its free-swinging, muckraking vitality.

It seems fitting that THE MAN INSIDE is set in Germany, where *film noir* was born. The film tells the story of lone-wolf investigative journalist Gunter Wallraff (Jurgen Prochnow), who infiltrates West Germany's leading right-wing newspaper—a politicized *National Enquirer* with the circulation clout of a *USA Today*—to write an expose about how the paper manufactures news to serve propagandistic ends. Wallraff, whose book *Lead Story* served as the film's basis and who is credited as a consultant, is shown exposing a 1975 military coup in Portugal as the film begins. Along the way, he uncovers a connection between extremist right-wing political forces in Portugal and West Germany. When the German newspaper, *The Standard* (the thinly disguised real-life *Bild Zeitung*), runs a hysterical, distorted "expose" on Wallraff, the journalist suspects a further link between the paper and the government and decides to go undercover to test his theory.

Using a dissident ex-staffer as his introduction, Wallraff obtains an interview with managing editor Leonard Schroeter (Dieter Laser). Having changed his identity and appearance, and fabricated a model background for a *Standard* reporter, Wallraff manages to get hired immediately, even as the paper and the country's security police are searching for him on charges related to his Portugal expose. Wallraff is befriended by star reporter Henry Tobel (Peter Coyote), who gives Wallraff a crash course on the paper's style of "journalism." On its surface, their first assignment is a fairly bland human interest story about a company president and a truck driver who switch places for a day. From that, Tobel emerges with the paper's trademark mixture of propaganda and titillation (the driver is photographed with the president's pretty secretary sitting on his lap), calculated to assure working-class readers that the life of the wealthy capitalist is not to be envied. Trying his own hand, Wallraff profiles an attractive female martial arts expert, another harmless story that is transformed into a frothing anti-feminist diatribe in rewrite. As a result of the story, Wallraff quickly rises at *The Standard*, as the subject's life is turned into a living hell of sexual harassment. By comparison to other *Standard* subjects, she gets off easy as the paper's stories often lead to murder and/or suicide. Clearly, this is not a nice place to work, yet Wallraff thrives on the pressure of being so close to those who are after him, and revels somewhat in being the paper's new star reporter. After years of low-paying assignments with alternative papers, Wallraff can't help but be thrilled with his words now reaching more than 11 million readers. For a while it appears that he may follow in the footsteps of the self-loathing Tobel, but shocking events soon intervene.

The very existence of this film, along with Wallraff's participation in its production, testifies to the success of the reporter's expose, in turn dictating a nominally "happy" ending. However, that success only comes after extended court battles waged by the newspaper in an effort to suppress Wallraff's book. The film details the toll the whole affair took on Wallraff's life, covering a broken marriage, the harassment of his ex-wife and children, and a disintegrating relationship with his partner (Nathalie Baye). By turns queasy, disturbing, and terrifying, THE MAN INSIDE benefits from Roth's straightforward writing and direction and the rich, vivid work of the cast. Giving a low-key performance, Prochnow becomes the film's moral compass, around which revolve such enjoyably out-sized performances as that by Coyote (star of Roth's HEART-BREAKERS and BAJA OKLAHOMA), as the worm who turns late in the film. Laser, meanwhile, almost steals the film as the surrealistically hard-driving editor. Overall, Roth's brutally direct style is well-suited to the sordid subject matter and THE MAN INSIDE is just as nasty as it should be. *(Adult situations.)*

d, Bobby Roth; p, Philippe Diaz; w, Bobby Roth (based on selected writings by Gunter Wallraff); ph, Ricardo Aronovitch; ed, Luce Grunewaldt; m, Tangerine Dream; art d, Didier Naert; cos, Brigitte Nierhaus

Docu-drama   **(PR:C   MPAA:PG)**

MARKED FOR DEATH

93m Victor & Grais-Steamroller/FOX c

(AKA: SCREWFACE)

Steven Seagal *(John Hatcher)*, Basil Wallace *(Screwface)*, Keith David *(Max)*, Tom Wright *(Charles)*, Joanna Pacula *(Leslie)*, Elizabeth Gracen *(Melissa)*, Bette Ford *(Kate Hatcher)*, Danielle Harris *(Tracey)*, Al Israel *(Tito)*, Arlen Dean Synder *(Duvall)*, Victor Romero Evans *(Nesta)*, Michael Ralph *(Monkey)*, Jeffrey Anderson-Gunter *(Nago)*, Tony DiBenedetto *(Jimmy Fingers)*, Kevin Dunn *(Roselli)*, Peter Jason *(Pete Stone)*, Danny Trejo *(Hector)*, Richard Delmonte *(Chico)*, Elana Sahagun *(Carmen)*, Tom Dugan *(Paco)*, Rita Verreos *(Marta)*, Joe Renteria *(Raoul)*, Carlos Cervantes *(Little Richard)*, Wayne Montanio *(Mexican Bouncer)*, Nick Corello *(Nicky)*, Grant Gelt *(Tommy)*, Justin Murphy *(Freddy)*, Earl Boen *(Dr. Stein)*, Stanley White *(Sheriff O'Dwyer)*, Matt Levin, Philip Tanzini *(Boys)*, Leslie Danon, Terri Ivens *(Girls)*, Dale Harimoto *(News Reporter)*, Tracey Burch, Teri Weigel *(Sexy Girls)*, Robert Ashiya Ganta Strickland *(Arms Dealer)*, Noel L. Walcott III *(Posse Leader)*, Prince Ital Joe *(Dread with Hostage)*, Andria Martel *(Young Stripper)*, Nick Celozzi *(Man in High Hart Bar)*, Debby Shively *(Barmaid)*, Craig Pinkard *(Bartender)*, Matt O'Toole *(Yuppie Dealer)*, Linus Huffman *(DEA Agent)*, Kerrie Cullen *(Department Store Hostage)*, Roger Romero Godbout, Harry John Leamy, John Endeveri, Christopher Allen Goss *(Band at McGilly's)*, Libert Steer, Philip Chen, Rock Deadrick, Einstein Brown, Eric Bernard, Haile Maskel *(Reggae Band)*, and Jimmy Cliff *(Himself)*

As DEA soldier John Hatcher (Steve Seagal) heads undercover into a meeting of drug dealers, his frightened co-worker, Chico (Richard Delmonte) asks him, "Since when did anyone accuse me of being sane?" It's unlikely anyone ever did make that accusation, as Hatcher goes about his business with an obsessive vengeance that is anything but sane. His cover is blown during the meeting, leading to a violent bloodbath, which horrifies even Hatcher. He retires to his boyhood home in Chicago, feeling that he's lost his moral center and that the war against drugs is a lost cause. He visits his old friend Max (Keith David) and they go to a bar, where a gun battle breaks out between local drug dealers and a new "posse" (a fanatic group of Jamaicans who engage in drug dealing for religious and political reasons). Hatcher battles a few from both sides before the riot is quelled. The next day, some Jamaicans shoot up his home as they drive by, and Hatcher quickly abandons retirement to join Max in a battle against the villains. As Hatcher learns the Jamaicans would rather die than squeal, the evil leader of the posse, Screwface (Basil Wallace), breaks into the Hatcher home and is about to murder Hatcher's sister Kate (Bette Ford), but flees with Hatcher's arrival. Hatcher now realizes that the only way to stop the posse is to kill Screwface. Teaming with Jamaican cop Charles (Tom Wright), who has been trailing Screwface for years, Hatcher and Max head for Kingston and a battle with Screwface, a duel Hatcher seems to have won...but Screwface proves to be a cunning adversary.

While there are many problems with the film, including predictable plotting, second-rate dialog, and a deplorable depiction of Jamaicans, as a showcase for the martial arts skills of Seagal the film is quite entertaining. If anything, he's almost an even less verbal caricature of some of Clint Eastwood's violent heroes. His odd multi-racial looks (he could easily play a European, a Japanese, or a Latin American), and his ponytail atop a football player's frame, give him an odd star power, and that power works to good advantage in MARKED FOR DEATH. His bone-breaking fight scenes are better handled than they were in his HARD TO KILL, but here Seagal is something of a moralist as well, though his mild moralizing is quickly countered by the film's overall reactionary tone. Those bothered by crunching violence and plot lapses won't find much here to enjoy, but action fans will find it delivers just about all they want from a film. *(Excessive violence, profanity, nudity, drug abuse, sexual situations, adult situations.)*

d, Dwight H. Little; p, Michael Grais, Mark Victor, and Steven Seagal; w, Michael Grais and Mark Victor; ph, Ric Waite; ed, O. Nicholas Brown; m, James Newton Howard; prod d, Robb Wilson King; art d, James Burkhart; set d, Gilbert Wong; spec, Dale Martin and John Blake; stunts, Conrad E. Palmisano; cos, Isabella Van Soest Chubb; makup, Jef Simons and Bob Arrollo; chor, Dorian Gursman; tech, Manny Mata

Action   **(PR:O   MPAA:R)**

MARTIANS GO HOME!

87m Edward R. Pressman/Taurus c

Randy Quaid *(Mark Devereaux)*, Margaret Colin *(Sara Brody)*, Anita Morris *(Dr. Jane Buchanan)*, John Philbin *(Donny)*, Ronny Cox *(The President)*, Gerrit Graham *(Stan Garrett)*, Barry Sobel, and Vic Dunlop *(Main Martians)*

Mark Devereaux (Randy Quaid) is living the good life, Los Angeles-style. A musician waiting for his big break, he's making good money composing music for television programs; pals around with his shallow but amiable buddy Stan Garrett (Gerrit Graham), a game show producer; and lives in domestic bliss with his pretty girl friend, Sara Brody (Margaret Colin). Sara paints large pictures of sushi and works as an on-air producer for honey-voiced therapist Dr. Jane Buchanan (Anita Morris), who dispenses sexual advice to radio listeners. Meanwhile, Mark's future looks brighter than ever when he is offered the chance to compose the score of a science-fiction feature by the hottest movie director in town. All he has to do is prove himself to the wunderkind by writing an acceptable symphonic greeting for the benign aliens who arrive (as in Spielberg's CLOSE ENCOUNTERS OF THE THIRD KIND) at the film's conclusion. Sequestered in his isolated cabin, Mark comes up with the tune he thinks will do the trick and calls Sara at work to play the melody to her on the phone. Unfortunately, fate intervenes in the form of a psychotic fan who arrives at the station demanding to speak to the radio Love Doctor. In the ensuing confusion, Mark's composition goes out over the airwaves and its message of welcome is heard on Mars. Next stop: Hell. The Martian invasion isn't what you'd expect—there are no death rays, no sinister experiments, no bug-eyed monsters. The men from Mars (there don't seem to be many women, which may be why they're so eager to travel) are green, it's true, and their taste in clothes (green again) is pretty poor, but they have no plans to subjugate the Earthlings. Far from it, in fact; they just want to have fun. Problem is, their idea of fun involves playing the accordion, appearing and disappearing without warning at all hours of the day and night, reciting execrable jokes, and, worst of all, blurting out people's most embarrassing secrets in public. And they just won't leave. Instead, they invade the airwaves, turning the news into an incomprehensible muddle of snide remarks. They horse around on the floor of the stock exchange, paralyzing markets all over the world. They invade couples' bedrooms and set up bleachers, calling out advice and encouragement. Exhibitionists like Dr. Buchanan adapt pretty well to life with these intrusive aliens, but Mark decides something must be done. With Sara's assistance, he designs a satellite link and broadcasts a reversed version of his composition, driving the not-so-little green men back where they came from.

Adapted from a novel by the versatile Frederic Brown *(The Screaming Mimi)*, MARTIANS GO HOME is a broad, good-natured comedy whose one-joke welcome quickly wears thin. Yes, the Martians in their green Hawaiian shirts, lurex jackets, and warm-up suits are the ultimate loathsome tourists. And yes, the idea of abrasive Borscht Belt comedians from space is enough to trigger an involuntary smile. But it doesn't seem to be a notion well-suited to the feature-length movie format, either because there's nowhere for it to go or because first-time director David Odell and screenwriter Charles Haas weren't the guys to take it anywhere. The joke doesn't get better with repetition. It only gets tired.

MARTIANS GO HOME plays less like a movie than an attenuated television skit, an impression supported by the (perhaps deliberately) cheesy photography and production design. The movie seems to have some pretensions to social satire, but they're supremely unconvincing. Admittedly, Garrett's idea for a game show in which newlyweds have to crawl through pools of mud and slime is stupefyingly venal, and the hot director's inflated vision of his dumb science-fiction movie as an important statement about universal brotherhood is breathtakingly trivial. But Quaid's new composition, supposedly the best thing he's ever written, is equally banal—and if your protagonist is no better than the shallow jerks who surround him, where's the difference by which all meaning is produced? MARTIANS GO HOME is a gag in search of a movie, destined to jockey for shelf space with other science-fiction parodies like EARTH GIRLS ARE EASY; SPACED INVADERS; and MORONS FROM SPACE. *(Sexual situations.)*

d, David Odell; p, Michael D. Pariser; w, Charlie Haas (based on a book by Frederic Brown); ph, Peter Deming; ed, M. Kathryn Campbell; m, Allan Zavod; prod d, Catherine Hardwicke and Don Day; art d, Tom Cortese; set d, Gene Serdena; cos, Robyn Reichek

Comedy/Science Fiction   **(PR:A   MPAA:PG-13)**

MASQUE OF THE RED DEATH

85m Concorde c

(AKA: EDGAR ALLAN POE'S MASQUE OF THE RED DEATH)

Patrick Macnee *(Machiavel)*, Adrian Paul *(Prospero)*, Clare Hoak *(Julietta)*, Jeff Osterhage *(Claudio)*, and Tracy Reiner *(Lucrecia)*

Although produced by Roger Corman and released through his company, Concorde Pictures, MASQUE OF THE RED DEATH is not a remake of his 1964 masterwork, but simply a cheaply made retelling of the Edgar Allan Poe story the earlier film was based on. The tale of 12th-century Prince Prospero (Adrian Paul) and his reign over a small village ravaged by plague, MASQUE OF THE RED DEATH is a miserable failure. Haunted by dreams of death and punishment, Prospero has completely ignored the teachings of his peaceful childhood tutor (Patrick Macnee), and has ruled his people cruelly (as his sadistic father did). An undeniably nasty fellow, Prospero has married his sister, lived decadently, and tortured his best friend, Claudio (Jeff Osterhage), for disobeying him. When the "Red Death" spreads from village to village, Prospero orders his men to round up "clean" females and to seal the gates of the castle. It seems the prince intends to beat death and his nightmares by simply barring them from his domain. In time, Prospero falls for one of the village women (Clare Hoak), and requests her to be at his side during his masquerade ball. Meanwhile, a mysterious figure in a red cloak rides through the countryside, leaving plague-ridden corpses in his wake. Arriving at the castle, the mysterious rider is allowed to pass through the gates after presenting an invitation to the ball. When he enters the ballroom, Prospero threatens the stranger with death for wearing the outlawed color of red and removes the intruder's mask, revealing him to be Prospero's childhood tutor. The prince is pleased to see his old friend, and the dance continues; however, after removing his gloves, the tutor touches several of the guests, causing them to drop with the plague. He soon pursues Prospero into the dungeon, where the prince is forced to become either a victim of the plague or of suicide. Prospero chooses suicide, allowing the village girl and Claudio to escape the death-filled castle and return to the countryside and to the survivors of the Red Death.

Director Larry Brand's version of the story can't compare with Corman's lyrical, haunting original. There are vast differences in style, tone, and interpretation (the major difference being in the character of Prospero, a devil-worshipping sadist in Corman's film, a misunderstood soul in Brand's). Corman's subtle use of color and the director's homages to Bergman made the original MASQUE one of the "King of the Bs"' more memorable Poe adaptations (THE TOMB OF LIGEIA remains the masterpiece of the series); Brand's film, on the other hand, goes nowhere, constricted by a low budget and poor craftsmanship. Although Brand and Daryl Haney's screenplay comes very close to capturing the spirit of Poe's original story, the characters are strangely underdeveloped and the poetry of Poe's language has given way to stale line readings and limp visuals. What's more, the acting is uniformly bad. Paul is especially dull (in a role to which Vincent Price brought tremendous vigor in 1964); looking ridiculous in a cheap "Star Trek"-like costume, he wearily mumbles his dialog, apparently confused as to his motivation.

Ultimately, it's this drastic change in the nature of Prospero's character that sinks the film, although the typically cheap production values don't help: the sets are obviously sets (apparently the same ones that were used in another Concorde bomb, TIME TRACKERS), and the photography is painfully flat and grainy. In addition, the pacing is slow and the climax comes without sufficient development; as a result, the final 10 minutes seem rushed and out of place. Brand's tedious shooting style and botched rhythms also prevent the film from developing any suspense, and before long the whole affair becomes a tiring experience.

MASQUE OF THE RED DEATH, although better than most of the junk Corman has been producing lately, is still terribly heavy-handed (Macnee's final speech seems to have been written for those who may have fallen asleep and missed the film's moral). Plagued by an annoying cheapness that obscures any directorial personality that might have been injected, the film will bore horror fans, disappoint lovers of Poe, and anger admirers of Corman's wonderful original version, which has stood the test of time and remains a definitive interpretation of the Poe work. *(Brief nudity, violence, adult situations.)*

d, Larry Brand; p, Roger Corman; w, Daryl Haney and Larry Brand (based on the story by Edgar Allan Poe); ph, Edward Pei; ed, Stephen Mark; m, Mark Governor; art d, Troy Meyers; cos, Sania M. Hays

Horror   (PR:C-O MPAA:R)

MAY FOOLS

(Fr.) 108m Nouvelles – TF 1 – Ellepi/Orion Classics c

(MILOU EN MAI)

Michel Piccoli *(Milou)*, Miou-Miou *(Camille)*, Michel Duchaussoy *(Georges)*, Dominique Blanc *(Claire)*, Harriet Walter *(Lily)*, Bruno Carette *(Grimaldi)*, Francois Berleand *(Daniel)*, Martine Gautier *(Adele)*, Paulette Dubost *(Mme. Vieuzac)*, Rozenn Le Tallec *(Marie-Laure)*, Renaud Danner *(Pierre-Alain)*, Jeanne Herry-Leclerc *(Francoise)*, Benjamin Prieur, Nicolas Prieur *(The Twins)*, Marcel Bories *(Leonce)*, Etienne Draber *(Mr. Boutelleau)*, Valerie Lemercier *(Mrs. Boutelleau)*, Hubert Saint-Macary *(Paul)*, Bernard Brocas *(The Priest)*, Georges Vaur *(Delmas)*, Jacqueline Staup, Anne-Marie Bonange *(Neighbors)*, Denise Juskiewenski *(Mme. Abel)*, Stephane Broquedis *(Young Man)*, and Serge Angeloff *(Adele's Fiance)*

Louis Malle's latest film, MAY FOOLS, is a radical, comic departure from the somber intensity of his last, AU REVOIR LES ENFANTS. Would that it were as successful and moving a work as AU REVOIR (or his ATLANTIC CITY; LACOMBE LUCIEN; or even MY DINNER WITH ANDRE), but, unfortunately, MAY FOOLS is cloying and precious in the annoying way that French films (and some people) have when convinced too mightily of their own charm.

The action is set in May 1968, at the time of the student uprisings in Paris. Mme. Vieuzac (Paulette Dubost), the feisty matriarch of an aristocratic family, suddenly dies of a heart attack, provoking the one good line in the film, "Death must have surprised her; she was a planner." The family, which gathers from all over France for her funeral, includes her sons, Milou (Michel Piccoli) and Georges (Michel Duchaussoy); Milou's daughter, Camille (Miou-Miou); her neglectful husband and three children; and Claire (Dominique Blanc), an orphaned lesbian granddaughter. Meals are shared, property is squabbled over, ancient resentments are voiced, and unlikely romance blooms while the radio proclaims the latest unsettling news from Paris. As the student unrest reaches a boiling point, the family decides to flee to the hills, fearing an encore of the bloody revolution in which aristocrats paid for their wealth with their lives. Roughing it brings out the best and the worst in the family; then a faintly enigmatic closing shot ties things up neatly.

Malle and his frighteningly prolific cowriter, Jean-Claude Carriere, seem to be attempting a repeat of Jean Renoir's superb RULES OF THE GAME, with the frivolous antics of the landed gentry juxtaposed against the backdrop of world-shaking events. This is pointed up by the presence of Dubost, who played the maid in Renoir's film and remains a disarming beauty. However, with its cartoonish characters, improbable plot developments, and general air of empty-headedness, MAY FOOLS seems more akin to the fluffy inconsequentiality of COUSIN COUSINE or Woody Allen's various odes to WASP family order. Malle has already worked dry the familiar territory of his own aristocratic upbringing (in parts of AU REVOIR LES ENFANTS and in the overrated MURMUR OF THE HEART). And there's an unseemly complacency about his nostalgia-tinged treatment of the privileged; not one of his blueblooded characters displays the wit, personality, or charm to justify this beneficence. Georges is a pompous international journalist, who drops supposedly uproarious English phrases into his conversation. His British wife, Lily (Harriet Walter), is a hippie sometime-actress, with a caftan and reefer always within easy reach. Naturally, she is also an advocate of free love, and stages a family orgy that proves distressingly dull for both the participants and the audience (a shoddy excuse to throw a little naughty T&A into the "family entertainment" that leaves the viewer feeling humiliated for the exposed actresses.) Adele (Martine Gautier), the maid, is a typically idealized servant, whose easy virtue accommodates Milou's needs and is eventually rewarded in Mme. Vieuzac's will (*quel* surprise).

Malle is at his most ham-handed with the character of Claire. A physical and emotional cripple, she stalks about with mournful cow-eyes and downturned mouth like a Gothic caricature of a grieving Jeanne Moreau. She despised her grandmother for forcing her to practice the piano, and proves this by thundering the keys with angst befitting a soapy Warners diva of the 40s. Claire blooms, however, under the practiced touch of a virile truck driver. Earlier, Malle has Camille's darling imp of a daughter (Jeanne Herry-Leclerc) discover Claire's lesbian lover, Marie-Laure (Rozenn Le Tallec), in bed, nude and bound to the bedpost – even kinky sex is deodorized and made cute here. Marie-Laure herself takes up with one of those obnoxiously gabby young radicals no film like this can afford to be without. For good measure, there are also a darling pair of twin boys and a lovable cat. The viewer's patience, already wearing thin, gives out, finally and completely, with the whole hoary back-to-nature episode, which is both unbelievable and unfunny.

Apart from Dubost, the two players who manage to occasionally transcend the film's banality are Piccoli and Miou-Miou. He has a rich, handsome presence as a Mama's boy who can't let go of the past and who pursues every fleshly pleasure available to him. The best scene in the film takes place with Piccoli's Milou in bed, suddenly giving in to his grief when a white owl with an alarmingly human face flies into the room. (The shot of him peeping up his granddaughter's pinafore could have been eliminated, though.) Miou-Miou, a marvelous comedienne, again displays her elegantly impressive range, portraying the epitome of *haut-bourgeois* avariciousness, forever preparing perfect meals, with occasional breaks to raid Grandma's jewelry box.

MAY FOOLS is visually undistinguished in a generically handsome way, and Stephane Grappelli has provided some original muzak that adds further gloss to the winsomeness. (Nudity, adult situations, sexual situations.)

d, Louis Malle; w, Louis Malle and Jean-Claude Carriere; ph, Renato Berta; ed, Emmanuelle Castro; m, Stephane Grappelli; makup, Joel Lavau and Francoise Chapuis

Comedy   (PR:O   MPAA:NR)

ME AND HIM

(W. Ger.) 90m Neue Constantin/Columbia c

(ICH UND ER)

Griffin Dunne (Bert Uttanzi), Ellen Greene (Annette Uttanzi), Mark Linn-Baker (Him), Craig T. Nelson (Peter Karamis), Kelly Bishop (Eleanor Karamis), Carey Lowell (Janet Landerson), Kara Glover (Juliette), Kim Flowers (Corazon), Robert LaSardo (Tony), Nancy Giles (Martella), Rocco Sisto (Art Strong), David Alan Grier (Peter Conklin), Bill Raymond (Humphrey), Jodie Markell (Eileen), Darryl Fong (Chinese Deliveryman), Jarrod Scott Gormick (Bert, Jr.), Samuel E. Wright, Leslie Ayvasian (Paramedics), James Lally (Clerk), Michael Earl Reid, Dan Moran (Homeless Men), Rene Rivera (Jose, Mrs. Karamis' Limo Driver), Toukie Smith (Deli-Delilah), Justin Williams (David), James A. Baffico (Stu Gazzo), Frederick Newman (Priest), Jolie Bennett (Blonde in Church), Connie Baker (Art Strong's Wife), William DeAcutis (Elliot), Tyler York (Stu Gazzo's Wife), Lisbeth Bartlett (Female Reporter), Mary Bergman (Pretty Woman), Laura Esterman (Bag Lady), John Sacco (Architect), Deborah Arters (Architect's Wife), Cortland Jessup (Humphrey's Wife), Barbara Allen, Carol Clements, Kim Flowers, Alison Fraser, Alisa Gyse, Mary Ann Kellogg, Gretchen MacLane, Kathi Moss, Karen Shallo, Jana Schneider, Christine Uchida, Rita-Jo Westfall, Lillias White, Charlaine Woodard, and Nora York (Singing Secretaries)

It's difficult to describe the extraordinary wrong-headedness of this failed comedy about a man whose genitals start talking to him and equally difficult to fathom how this film could be based on a work by celebrated author Alberto Moravia. Something must have been lost in the translation from the Italian original. Best described as LOOK WHO'S TALKING for salacious grown-ups (with a wisecracking penis replacing the loquacious baby), ME AND HIM is stupefying from start to finish.

Bert Uttanzi (Griffin Dunne), a workaholic architect and stalwart family man, reaches a turning point in his harried existence when his penis begins speaking to him on the eve of an important architectural project. Urging him to go out and live it up, the meddlesome organ puts Bert in a quandary: Should he pursue domestic bliss or hedonistic pleasure? After fainting from shock and being revived by paramedics, Bert is ill-prepared for his project presentation before his coworkers, his boss, Peter (Craig T. Nelson), and his boss's wife, Eleanor (Kelly Bishop). Somehow, Bert's penis manages to talk him through the meeting and even helps him submit a well-received proposal for a building called "Venice on the Marina." Capitulating to the demands his penis later makes, Bert angers his allegedly loveable but rather shrewish wife, Annette (Ellen Greene), when he temporarily moves into the apartment of a coworker who's been transferred. Bert claims he needs to work without distraction in order to win the coveted job of project manager, but his penis has other plans for him, involving extra-marital fun. After seducing a woman he picks up at his health club, Bert is beset by a number of complications, including (a) his wife, who's growing increasingly suspicious, (b) a beautiful coworker, Janet (Carey Lowell), who's having a fling with Peter, and (c) Eleanor, who's willing to use her influence to get Bert the job if he goes to bed with her. After engaging in some ridiculous fantasies, Bert refuses to sleep his way to the top, strikes out with the two-timing Janet, and upsets his wife when he visits home. He also eagerly has sex with another office worker when he's supposed to go to an important meeting with his boss and a political figure. Following some advice about controlling his talking "thing" with a voodoo ritual involving burning a snapshot, Bert manages to silence his penis for awhile. Telling the luscious Janet (who's suddenly aroused by him) that he now only thinks of her platonically, Bert returns to Annette, but mistakenly believes that she has become unfaithful. After being replaced as temporary project manager by Janet, Bert later blows his last big opportunity by refusing to have bizarre sex with Eleanor at a party. His penis is suddenly talking again, and when everyone's genitals begin conversing at the party, Bert is fired. Janet gets the project manager's job, but Bert gets his wife and family back. Two years later, Bert has become a major architect; however, he is still tempted by the taunts of his talking penis.

The premise of this film easily provokes nervous laughter, and one can only imagine what the "high-concept" meetings for the project were like. It's hard to believe that Doris Dorrie, who created the sprightly German comedy MEN, could have contributed such lackluster direction. Poorly paced, ME AND HIM offers a steady stream of smutty jokes and sexual innuendo. Although it aims to

be something different, Dorrie's teasing film is full of unerotic shots of clothed body parts and turns some attractive comic actors into clods.

After choosing to appear in this film and WHO'S THAT GIRL?, Dunne is in need of career guidance. He and most of the players ham it up to compensate for the script's lack of wit, but to little avail. Mark Linn-Baker is the essence of cloying cuteness as the voice of the penis. And the badly misdirected Greene—an actress always in need of a tight rein—is utterly unappealing, tearing into every paper-thin comic scene as if she were performing Ibsen.

Conveying little humor, this satirical battle of the sexes meanders from dirty joke to dirty joke until the smutty sit-com proceedings begin to wear down the viewer. As Bert's penis cajoles him, we watch in disbelief as the film presents a vision of the penis as Auntie Mame. Tasteless and unfunny, this feeble farce has so little comic identity that its climax is a song-and-dance number by female office workers—from stag movie to musical comedy is quite a leap. (Sexual situations, profanity.)

d, Doris Dorrie; p, Bernd Eichinger; w, Warren D. Leight, Michael Juncker, and Doris Dorrie (based on the novel Lo E Lui by Alberto Moravia); ph, Helge Weindler; ed, Raimund Barthelmes; m, Klaus Doldinger; prod d, Suzanne Cavedon; set d, Gretchen Rau; cos, Eugenie Bafaloukas; makup, Kathryn Bihr; chor, Barbara Allen

Comedy   (PR:O   MPAA:R)

MEMPHIS BELLE

106m Enigma/WB c

Matthew Modine (Dennis Dearborn), John Lithgow (Col. Bruce Derringer), Eric Stoltz (Danny Daly), Sean Astin (Richard "Rascal" Moore), Harry Connick Jr. (Clay Busby), Reed Edward Diamond (Virgil), Tate Donovan (Luke Sinclair), D.B. Sweeney (Phil Rosenthal), Billy Zane (Val Kozlowski), Courtney Gains (Eugene McVey), Neil Giuntoli (Jack Bocci), David Strathairn (The Commanding Officer), Jane Horrocks (Faith), Mac McDonald (Les), Jodie Wilson (Singer), Keith Edwards ("S-2"), Steven MacKintosh (Stan, the Rookie), Greg Charles (Adjutant), Bradley Lavell (Sergeant), Ben Browder (Rookie Captain), Mitch Webb (Group Navigator), Paul Birchard (Lieutenant), Bill Cullum (Farmer), Eric Loren (Cook), Morag Siller, Cathy Murphy (Jitterbuggers), Steve Elm, Jason Salkey, and Martin McDougal (Footballers)

To a post-Vietnam War generation put off by militarism, David Puttnam's moving MEMPHIS BELLE may seem hopelessly dated, but older viewers are likely to find much to enjoy in the film. Ironically, this inspiring story of the final and most harrowing WW II mission of the B-17 bomber The Memphis Belle is surprisingly timely, given the US military's recent involvement in the Middle East. Produced by Puttnam and Catherine Wyler (whose father, legendary filmmaker William Wyler, made a much-acclaimed wartime documentary about The Memphis Belle) and directed by Michael Caton-Jones (SCANDAL), MEM-PHIS BELLE is a grand reminder of an era when American ideals were less tarnished and when Americans seemed somehow nobler than today. Though flawed (especially during its ponderous beginning), the film blossoms into a deeply involving, visually stunning powerhouse of a movie.

As a result of Caton-Jones' assured direction, no single actor stands out as the film's star; every performance is on target. John Lithgow's Col. Bruce Derringer is perhaps the film's most colorful character, but it may be that more attention is drawn to him because he is the only major character who is not a member of the crew of The Memphis Belle. Instead, he is excellent as the Army PR officer who is less concerned with the outcome of the bomber's final mission than he is with the Stateside impact of the young heroes he has helped to create. Quietly effective are the 10 young actors who portray the crew of The Memphis Belle. Because their deceptively subtle ensemble performances are so seamless, it is the suspense of the dangerous mission rather than any one character that captivates the audience. Matthew Modine is Dennis Dearborn, the Belle's pilot; Tate Donovan is co-pilot Luke Sinclair, who is more concerned with challenging Dearborn's decisions than he is with performing his own job. Eric Stoltz is radio operator Danny Daly, a likable redhead who almost loses his life over Germany. When Danny is seriously wounded, the self-avowed medical wizardry of Billy Zane's bombardier is put to a pressure-filled test. Courtney Gains and Neil Giuntoli provide some of the film's most wrenching moments as a pair of waist gunners, one a religious zealot, the other a cynical atheist. Equally impressive are Sean Astin and Harry Connick, Jr., as the ball-turret gunner and tail gunner, respectively. Rounding out the Belle's crew are Reed Edward Diamond as flight engineer Virgil and D.B. Sweeney as Phil Rosenthal, the navigator. David Strathairn, as the sqaudron's commanding officer, also has a memorable moment at the climax when his voice is heard over the closing credits reading the names of the men who didn't make it back.

Much credit must be given to Richard Conway's dazzling special aerial effects, to David Watkin's breathtaking aerial photography, and George Fenton's evocative score. Jim Clark's editing also deserves mention, though his abrupt cutting between action scenes on the ground is not nearly as effective as his skillful handling of the suspenseful final mission. Caton-Jones does a craftsman-like job of enlivening the Monte Merrick screenplay, deftly drawing the audience into the events unfolding for the crew of *The Memphis Belle*. Viewed out of context, some of the film's scenes might appear to be suffused in cliche-ridden Hollywood sentimentalism, but when taken as a whole MEMPHIS BELLE is an extremely touching film. Only by allowing the film to develop as a whole will viewers be able to appreciate the sincerity of such scenes as the charming encounter between a young airman and a local farmer. Although he is terribly anxious about the dangerous upcoming mission, the farmboy-turned-flyboy spends his last hours on the ground unselfishly repairing the farmer's harvester. It is quiet moments like this one, as well the thrilling final mission, that make MEMPHIS BELLE a very special film indeed. *(Profanity, adult situations, violence.)*

d, Michael Caton-Jones; p, David Puttnam and Catherine Wyler; w, Monte Merrick; ph, David Watkin; ed, Jim Clark; m, George Fenton; prod d, Stuart Craig; art d, John King and Alan Tomkins; set d, Ian Giladjian; spec, Richard Conway; cos, Jane Robinson; makeup, Joan Hills; chor, David Toguri; tech, Roger Freeman, Tommy Garcia, and Bruce Orriss

War   (PR:C   MPAA:PG-13)

MEN AT WORK

98m Epic — Elwes — Euphoria/Triumph c

Charlie Sheen *(Carl Taylor)*, Emilio Estevez *(James St. James)*, Leslie Hope *(Susan Wilkins)*, Keith David *(Louis Fedders)*, Dean Cameron *(Pizza Man)*, John Getz *(Maxwell Potterdam III)*, Hawk Wolinki *(Biff)*, John Lavachielli *(Mario)*, Geoffrey Blake *(Frost)*, Cameron Dye *(Luzinski)*, John Putch *(Mike)*, Tommy Hinckley *(Jeff)*, Darrell Larson *(Jack Berger)*, Sy Richardson *(Walt Richardson)*, Kari Whitman *(Judy)*, Troy Evans *(Capt. Dalton)*, Brad Wyman, Matthew Robinson *(Rent-A-Cops)*, Bob Brown, Erik Stabenau, Bobby Burns, and Eddie Braun *(Henchmen)*

Begin with a dash of WEEKEND AT BERNIE'S; add one scoop of REAR WINDOW, two dumb cops who couldn't have made the grade in POLICE ACADEMY, and a jigger of third-rate Laurel & Hardy; shake well and what you have is MEN AT WORK, an action comedy of sorts from writer-director-costar Emilio Estevez. The plot concerns two fun-loving garbagemen, longtime friends whose major ambition is to earn enough money collecting trash to open a store that caters to surfers. Clowning their way through their daily grind, Carl Taylor (Charlie Sheen, Estevez's real-life brother) and James St. James (Estevez) get their kicks by harassing a pair of bicycle-riding beach-front policemen who are anxious to pin something on the boys—any misdemeanor will do, just as long as it gives the cops an excuse to haul our heroes to the slammer. Neither Carl nor James is very popular with their boss, who, fed up with their on-the-job antics, assigns his brother-in-law, Louis Fedders (Keith David), a Vietnam vet, to ride along with the boys as their supervisor. What should pop up in one of the large trash cans but the body of Jack Berger (Darrell Larson), a corrupt city councilman and mayoral candidate who made the mistake of double-crossing an even more corrupt corporate bigwig (John Getz). Unknowingly, James has contributed to the politician's death. The previous evening, from the rear window of his apartment, James witnessed Berger's physical abuse of his attractive campaign manager (a badly miscast Leslie Hope) and responded by shooting the councilman in his rear end with a pellet gun. However, that is the last James is to see of his "victim" until Berger's corpse is discovered in the trash, whereupon the film turns into a game of hide-and-seek, with James, Carl, and Louis trying to keep the cops from finding the body while the trio tries to solve the murder.

At its best, MEN AT WORK is charming nonsense for undiscriminating audiences, yet it would be unfair to dismiss the film as a waste of time and energy. Its pacing is excellent, and though its lowbrow entertainment values are of questionable merit, filmmaker Estevez nevertheless demonstrates a flair for comedy. Someday he's going to be a director to be reckoned with; regrettably, that day hasn't arrived. Despite its ample flaws, MEN AT WORK is never boring and often is a lot of fun; however, it would have benefitted from the pruning of a few of its misfired visual gags, particularly those involving excrement. And don't expect any profound messages about toxic waste or our polluted environment—they've all been lost in the shuffle in this would-be high-level farce. That Stewart Copeland's above-average score provides many of MEN AT WORK's most enjoyable moments is indicative of the downward slide the film takes after the discovery of the politician's body. *(Profanity, violence, adult situations.)*

d, Emilio Estevez; p, Cassian Elwes; w, Emilio Estevez; ph, Tim Suhrstedt; ed, Craig Bassett; m, Stewart Copeland; md, Jonathan Scott Bogner; prod d, Dins Danielsen; art d, Patricia Klawonn; set d, Will Combs; spec, Thomas F. Sindicich; stunts, Bud Davis; cos, Keith Lewis; makeup, Jeanne Van Phue

Comedy   (PR:C   MPAA:PG-13)

MEN DON'T LEAVE

115m Paul Brickman-Jon Avnet — Geffen/WB c

Jessica Lange *(Beth Macauley)*, Chris O'Donnell *(Chris Macauley)*, Charlie Korsmo *(Matt Macauley)*, Arliss Howard *(Charles Simon)*, Tom Mason *(John Macauley)*, Joan Cusack *(Jody)*, Kathy Bates *(Lisa Coleman)*, Corey Carrier *(Winston Buckley)*, Jim Haynie *(Mr. Buckley)*, Belita Moreno *(Mrs. Buckley)*, Shannon Moffett *(Dale Buckley)*, Kevin Corrigan *(Mike)*, David Cale *(Fred)*, Constance Shulman *(Carly)*, Mark Hardwick *(Ian)*, Ernesto D. Borges Jr. *(Officer)*, Lora Zane *(Nina Simon)*, Rick Rubin *(Craig)*, Tom Towles *(Evan Taylor)*, Richard Wharton *(Nick)*, Rosemary Knower *(Nurse)*, Jane Morris *(Laura)*, Annabel Armour *(Susan)*, Deanna Dunagan *(Fay)*, Tom Irwin *(Gary)*, Stacey Guastaferro *(Julia)*, Jesse James *(Blues Artist)*, Richard Burton Brown *(Sam Burrows)*, Mary Seibel *(Real Estate Agent)*, Robert D. North *(Moving Man)*, Stesha Merle *(Girl Student)*, William DeAcutis *(Mark)*, Ann McDonough *(Female Customer)*, Theresa Wozniak *(Female Polka Dancer)*, Sandra V. Watters *(Bureaucrat)*, Zaid Farid *(Store Clerk)*, Wandachristine *(School Teacher)*, Richard DeAngelis *(Tailor)*, Peter Miller *(Chris' Friend)*, Gerry Becker *(Uncle Hugh)*, Dick Sasso *(Lottery Winner)*, Chuck McLennan *(Lottery Announcer)*, Seka, Tanl, Brad Michael *(Adult Film Stars)*, Eddie Korosa *(Polka Band Leader)*, and Antonio M. Calderon *(Joey)*

MEN DON'T LEAVE is an unabashed, four-hanky family melodrama. But it's also an unexpectedly poignant slice of life, the best film of its type since THE ACCIDENTAL TOURIST. Jessica Lange plays Beth Macauley, who is widowed as the film begins by an accident that claims the life of her construction contractor husband. Besieged by leftover debts from his last unfinished project, she is forced to sell the family home, over the loud objections of her teenage son, Chris (Chris O'Donnell). To cut expenses, she relocates her family, which also includes younger son Matt (Charlie Korsmo), to an apartment in Baltimore. There, she takes a job as assistant manager of a gourmet food market run by the acerbic Lisa (Kathy Bates, star of Rob Reiner's film adaptation of Stephen King's *Misery*).

Despite its familiar premise, reminiscent of films like PLACES IN THE HEART and Lange's own COUNTRY, MEN DON'T LEAVE is not just another tale about a strong mother holding her family together through hardships and calamities. Its characters are more believably flawed and frail than those generally found in films of this ilk, and therefore more interesting. Through much of the film it seems as if Beth's family is dissolving around her. Chris almost immediately becomes involved with an "older" woman, Jody (Joan Cusack), a twentysomething X-ray technician who lives in the same building as the Macauleys. Matt, meanwhile, takes up with Winston (Corey Carrier), a pint-sized, knife-carrying schoolyard terror who makes money on the side by stealing VCRs and selling them to a video porno freak. More important to Matt, Winston comes from a solid upper-middle-class family, complete with a dad who becomes a surrogate father for Matt. Only Beth is unable to adjust to her new life. Her budding relationship with likable musician Charles (Arliss Howard) falls victim to her preoccupation with supporting her family. Then, a show of temper costs her job. Finding herself in an empty apartment and feeling all but abandoned by her wandering brood, Beth plunges into a depression and winds up falling back on the kindnesses of strangers to pull herself back together.

Notwithstanding Beth's breakdown, MEN, like THE ACCIDENTAL TOURIST, isn't really about its big crises. Instead, it's about how people live from one day to the next, and the hard choices and compromises they make to survive. Beth swallows her pride to get her job back at Lisa's store and tentatively revives her relationship with Charles. Chris also continues his involvement with Jody, though he stops wearing the laughably garish, country club clothes she buys for him. Nevertheless, the film ends with Jody and Charles left waiting on shore while Beth, Chris, and Matt enjoy a "family day" boat ride, alone and together. While the crises, especially those faced by Beth and Matt, give MEN DON'T LEAVE its dramatic shape, it is in its small, beautifully observed details that the film really comes to life. A fine screenplay by Barbara Benedek is painstakingly directed by Paul Brickman, who elicits meticulous ensemble performances from his cast. As she did in her scripts for THE BIG CHILL and IMMEDIATE FAMILY, Benedek compellingly examines how average people cope with extraordinary changes in their lives. Once again she demonstrates a rare talent for writing characters that eloquently express her themes yet remain utterly believable people. Brickman—directing his first film since his remarkable debut, RISKY BUSINESS (1983)—deftly maintains a precarious emotional balance between the script's joys and heartaches and laughter and tears. Visually, MEN DON'T LEAVE is as expressive as any film in recent years, its subtle shifts from light to darkness richly conveying the inner states and outer realities of its characters.

Lange complained in interviews at the time of MEN's release that Brickman kept pushing her to give a more comic performance despite what she saw as the script's straight dramatic focus. However, it is clear that what Brickman was after wasn't out-and-out comedy, but a feeling of unpredictability in the performances that proves to be one of the film's greatest assets. Newcomers O'Donnell and Korsmo struggle to establish their authority as actors just as their characters struggle for identity. The rest of the more experienced cast play interestingly against type. As the secure mom suddenly thrust into an insecure world, Lange seems to have been allowed to give a "dramatic" performance, but the slight uncertainty in her acting helps to convey the uncertainty of her character. Similarly, Howard, best known for more physical roles in films like FULL METAL JACKET, and Cusack, who added ditzy comic relief to BROADCAST NEWS; WORKING GIRL; and SAY ANYTHING, find themselves in unfamiliar territory — he as a sensitive, intelligent artist, and she as a woman of depth and compassion — but turn this unfamiliarity to their advantage. The overall result is a film that is refreshingly realistic and spontaneous, a work of consummate craft from all involved. MEN DON'T LEAVE is a rare film that can be equally savored as rich, offbeat entertainment and admired for its sheer artistry. *(Adult situations, mild profanity.)*

d, Paul Brickman; p, Jon Avnet; w, Barbara Benedek (based on the film LA VIE CONTINUE written by Moshe Mizrahi); ph, Bruce Surtees; ed, Richard Chew; m, Thomas Newman; prod d, Barbara Ling; art d, John Mark Harrington; set d, William Arnold; spec, John E. Gray; stunts, Rick LeFevour; cos, J. Allen Highfill and Susan Becker; makeup, Susan Mayer and Bob Mills

Drama   **(PR:A   MPAA:PG-13)**

MEN IN LOVE

87m Tantric/Movie Visions c

Doug Self *(Steven)*, Joe Tolbe *(Peter)*, Emerald Starr *(Robert)*, Kutira Decosterd *(Christiana)*, Vincent Schwickert *(B.S.)*, James A. Taylor *(Jonathan)*, Carlo Incerto *(Rocco)*, Jaiia *(Herself)*, Scott Catamas *(Victor)*, Renee DePalma *(Laurel)*, Lulu *(Herself)*, Steve Warren, Maura Nolan, Joe Capetta, Lily Gurk, and Toni Maher

The use of New Age philosophy to combat the emotional impact AIDS has on victims' loved ones is explored in this low-budget, independent, and largely unsuccessful film. Steven (Doug Self) is a sensitive young man living in San Francisco who has just lost his lover, Victor, to AIDS. Steven holds a "send-off" ceremony at which Victor's friends gather to share memories of him; it ends with each person releasing a red balloon into the sky as a symbol of Victor's freedom from the mortal world. Steven follows Victor's request to take his ashes to Maui, where Victor's former lover, Robert (Emerald Starr), has founded a New Age community. While Robert occupies himself with preparing for various ceremonies, Steven is left to deal with the loss of Victor. Soon, Steven loses his patience with the evasive Robert and admonishes him for failing to visit Victor during the end of their friend's life. Steven also angrily reminds Robert that he never had to deal with the day-to-day problems of taking care of an AIDS patient. Steven's misgivings about Robert and skepticism about the New Age philosophy are partly diverted by his growing relationship with Peter (Joe Tolbe), the Hawaiian gardener at the community. Peter seems to be the only one who is willing to help Steven deal with his grief on a human level, setting aside all of the ethereal rhetoric. Their closeness grows until the two are ready to consummate their relationship, but there are some hitches. The main problem is that Steven has never taken an AIDS test and does not know if he is infected. Peter shows Steven how one couple has dealt with a similar situation: Rocco (Carlo Incerto) has decided to stay with Jonathan (James A. Taylor) and have a full physical relationship with him, even though Jonathan is HIV positive. Peter decides that he is willing to accept the consequences if Steven is found to be infected. After a few weeks at the community, Steven starts to get along better with Robert, who admits that he is terrified of death, which is why he, too, has never had the AIDS test and why he has built the cloistered community where death never shows its face. Receiving the news that one of his friends in San Francisco has just died, Steven must decide whether to stay on the island with Peter or go back to the mainland and pick up the pieces of his life. After a night of meditation and some primal screaming in a cave, Steven decides to return to San Francisco. Robert is then seen having a blood test, and there is another brief ceremony before Steven scatters Victor's ashes off a cliff.

MEN IN LOVE has an interesting premise; however, the production is bogged down by a poorly written script, undefined characters, and unconvincing performances by a cast made up primarily of nonprofessional actors. We never learn anything about Steven aside from his relationships with the other characters; we don't really know what his life was like in San Francisco, so his dilemma in choosing whether or not to leave Maui lacks impact. Moreover, Peter's decision to consummate his relationship with Steven does not seem to be as painstakingly thought out as it ought to be under the circumstances. Perhaps because MEN IN LOVE was originally shot on video and then transferred to film, the supposedly paradisiacal location looks relatively bleak and uninviting. While the main purpose here seems to be to inspire the audience, the film is regrettably not up

to the task and provokes more unintended laughs than spiritual awareness. *(Adult situations, nudity, sexual situations.)*

d, Marc Huestis; p, Scott Catamas; w, Scott Catamas and Emerald Starr; ph, Fawn Yacker and Marsha Kahm; ed, Frank Christopher; m, Donald James Regal; art d, Vola Ruben

Drama   **(PR:O   MPAA:NR)**

MERMAIDS

110m Nicita-Lloyd-Palmer/Orion c

Cher *(Mrs. Flax)*, Bob Hoskins *(Lou Landsky)*, Winona Ryder *(Charlotte Flax)*, Michael Schoeffling *(Joe)*, Christina Ricci *(Kate Flax)*, Caroline McWilliams *(Carrie)*, Jan Miner *(Mother Superior)*, Betsey Townsend *(Mary O'Brien)*, Richard McElvain *(Mr. Crain)*, Paula Plum *(Mrs. Crain)*, Dossy Peabody *(Coach Parker)*, William Paul Steele *(Boss in Oklahoma)*, Rex Trailer *(Dr. Reynolds)*, Pete Kovner *(Perfect Family Father)*, Patricia Madden *(Perfect Family Mother)*, Justin Marchisio *(Perfect Family Boy)*, Caitlin Marie Bottomley *(Perfect Family Girl)*, Amy Gollnick, Seacia Pavao *(Girls in Bathroom)*, Merle Perkins *(Nurse)*, Baxter Harris *(Boss in Massachusetts)*, Carol Moss *(Boss's Fiancee)*, Denise Cormier *(Pretty Girl in Shoe Store)*, Al Hodgkins *(Crying Man in Street)*, Tamasin Scarlet Johnson *(Young Nun)*, Sandra Shipley *(Crying Nun)*, Russell Jones *(Judge at Swim Meet)*, Shawna Sullivan *(Charlotte, 5 years old)*, Bob Rogerson *(Charlotte's Dad)*, and Tom Kemp *(Carrie's Husband)*

This is yet another coming-of-age story, the title referring to the three central characters (a mother and her two daughters) who float like flotsam and jetsam between two worlds as opposed to being anchored in one place. Mrs. Flax (Cher) is a true eccentric; a free-spirited and often irritatingly independent woman who lost any sort of stable homelife when her husband walked out on her and her children years before. She has drifted from man to man and place to place and her latest move to the small Massachusetts coastal town of East Port in 1963 marks her 18th. Not only must Mrs. Flax cope with her own immaturity, she also must try to deal with the problems of her daughters, teenaged Charlotte (Winona Ryder), and nine-year-old Kate (Christina Ricci), a swimming champ who is obsessed with the water. The family relationships are further complicated by the fact that Mrs. Flax is so wrapped up in her latest romance with Lou (Bob Hoskins) that she virtually ignores her children. In the meantime, Charlotte lusts after young Joe (Michael Schoeffling), the groundskeeper at a nearby convent. At the same time, she wrestles with her strong religious convictions — she wants to become a nun, even though she is Jewish. Torn between her conflicting feelings, Charlotte is close to a nervous breakdown, while Kate suffers a near-fatal accident. The inability of her mother to come to grips with any of these realities further enrages and confuses Charlotte, and the relationship between mother and daughter grows steadily more strained. With the help of Lou, the members of the unconventional family try to overcome their difficulties and to reach some sort of a tenuous understanding.

This is an intermittently entertaining human relationship story, it's strongest points being its actors. Cher, Ryder, and Ricci combine their ample talents to deliver a uniformly bang-up job of delineating the vagabond mom and her two at-loose-ends daughters. Since Ryder has the most complicated role she tends to steal all the scenes in which she appears. Hoskins is fine as Mrs. Flax's shoe salesman love interest, while young Schoeffling is quite impressive. Actor-turned-director Richard Benjamin (MY FAVORITE YEAR, MY STEP-MOTHER IS AN ALIEN), however, struggles with story structure, allowing the film to meander along at a too-leisurely pace. Character motivation is sometimes muddled, and Benjamin never seems to decide whose story he is telling. Moreover, the film features many mood swings (melancholy, comic, pathos, sweet), but the swings are so abrupt that it gives an uneven feel to the overall effort. Still, the picture's strong characters and acting carry it to at least a partial success. Sadly, the film had all the elements to be a very captivating experience, but it fails to bring those elements together into a strong whole. *(Adult situations, sexual situations, profanity.)*

d, Richard Benjamin; p, Lauren Lloyd, Wallis Nicita, and Patrick Palmer; w, June Roberts (based on the novel by Patty Dann); ph, Howard Atherton; ed, Jacqueline Cambas; m, Jack Nitzsche; prod d, Stuart Wurtzel; art d, Steve Saklad and Evelyn Sakash; set d, Deborah Kanter and Philip Messina; stunts, Brian Ricci; cos, Marit Allen

Romance/Comedy   **(PR:C   MPAA:PG-13)**

METROPOLITAN

98m Westerly/New Line c

Carolyn Farina *(Audrey Rouget)*, Edward Clements *(Tom Townsend)*, Christopher Eigeman *(Nick Smith)*, Taylor Nichols *(Charlie Black)*, Allison Rutledge-Parisi *(Jane Clarke)*, Dylan Hundley *(Sally Fowler)*, Isabel Gillies *(Cynthia*

McClean), Bryan Leder (*Fred Neff*), Will Kempe (*Rick Von Sloneker*), Elizabeth Thompson (*Serena Slocum*), Stephen Uys (*Victor Lemley*), Roget W. Kirby (*Man at Bar*), Alice Connorton (*Mrs. Townsend*), Linda Gillies (*Mrs. Rouget*), John Lynch (*Allen Green*), Donald Lardner Ward (*North Greenwich Preppie*), Tom Voth (*Cab Driver*), Caroline Bennett (*Sabina*), Frank Creighton (*Cadet Frawley*), Joel S. Schreiber (*A.T. Harris*), Catherine Atzen (*Herself*), J. Harden Rose (*TV Voice of Debutante Ball*), Victoria Chickering, Blayne Perry, Kevin Schack, Tina Thornton, Hank Foley, and Andrew Lyle (*SFRP Friends*)

METROPOLITAN is a film about a strata of the young and privileged it would be easy to despise. Yet as a result of terse direction, urbane writing, and beguiling performances by a number of new actors, the young, privileged characters at the heart of this film are surprisingly disarming. It's the Christmas season in Manhattan and the rush is on. The rush, in this case, refers to the heady round of debutante balls and get-togethers that are the highlight of the social season for an Upper East Side bunch still in the thrall of arcane rituals. This determinedly proper crew, the self-dubbed SFRP (Sally Fowler Rat Pack), includes Nick (Christopher Eigeman), its arrogantly dissolute leader; Audrey (Carolyn Farina), a sweet young thing trying to uphold the ideals of Jane Austen in an increasingly unkind world; Charlie (Taylor Nichols), an uptight stutterer paralyzed by his love for Audrey; Cynthia (Isabel Gillies), a *femme fatale*-in-training; and pudgy, narcoleptic Fred (Bryan Leder). One snowy eve, Tom Townsend (Edward Clements), a proletarian radical, stumbles into their exalted midst from truly alien territory—the West Side. With Nick as his Mephistophelian guide, Tom gradually becomes caught up in such life-and-death matters as whether to buy his tux from Brooks Brothers or Paul Stuart. Although Audrey is infatuated with Tom, he is still weathering the after-effects of a fatal crush on the notorious heartbreaker Serena Slocum (Elizabeth Thompson). Also threatening the welfare and happiness of the clique is Nick's special enemy, Rick von Sloneker (Will Kempe), a meretricious, pony-tailed Lothario over whom an alarming number of debs have committed suicide. The film climaxes with a pursuit and rescue of virtue in Southampton, and ends on a sweet note of comradeship.

Exhibiting a prodigy's control over his cleverly devised material, Whit Stillman has made an updated drawing-room comedy that takes place largely at deb-party postmortems, with the SFRP endlessly jawing about honor and position. Only occasionally does METROPOLITAN indulge in more earthy pursuits involving Truth games, mescaline, and strip poker. Yet, surprisingly, the film is so adroitly written and played that there is nothing claustrophobic about the proceedings—who wants to leave the room with such stimulating talk going on?

METROPOLITAN is a party-night dream vision of New York, with roots in Astaire-Rogers musicals, screwball comedies, and Woody Allen films. But most notably, it brings to mind George Cukor's elegant masterpiece, HOLIDAY. Like Cary Grant's outsider in that film, Tom wins the heart of an aristocratic rebel, and Christopher Eigeman invests his Nick with some of the pixilated omniscience of Lew Ayres' character in the 1938 film. In the process, Nick emerges as the most engaging of METROPOLITAN's characters, with his easy hypocrisy in carnal matters and propensity for spreading scandalous stories about his rivals. "When you are an egotist, none of the harm you do is intentional...I'm about to go upstate to a stepmother of untrammeled malevolence," he explains, with aplomb worthy of Clifton Webb or George Sanders. Epigrams like these and visual touches like the silly Lester Lanin hats the boys wear in one scene should give some idea of the real joy of METROPOLITAN. Stillman is a careful observer with an obvious love of language, and his wonderful, fresh cast handles the script with ease, conveying just the right measure of deadpan, *jejune* super-seriousness.

The limited budget obviously precluded any actual footage of deb balls; instead, Stillman provides graceful suggestions of these *fetes* with montages outside the Plaza Hotel. John Thomas' mellow cinematography captures a magical, wintry Manhattan in all its landmark glory and is especially alert to the beautifully detailed interiors. (The filmmakers managed to get a serendipitous shot of a holiday window display of *The Collected Works of Jane Austen* in the legendary Scribner's Bookstore.) The choice of music is also skillful, Philadelphia Soul ballads alternating with cha-chas and melancholy themes.

Clements is amusingly sobersided as the opinionated Tom, who carries on weighty conversations about books although he only reads criticism of them. He makes his seduction by high society both convincing and touchingly desperate, a portrayal that is reminiscent of *The Great Gatsby*'s Nick Carraway, but with less angst. As a would-be sophisticate, Farina has an appealing, demure ruefulness, like a brainier Molly Ringwald. She can say a line like, "There's something dubious about Tom," and get away with it. In just a few scenes, Alice Connorton, as Tom's mother, completely and emphatically captures the character of a slightly harried single parent. Nichols is very funny as the intense Charlie, whose smug beliefs are forever being shattered. The scene in which he gracefully bows out, leaving the field romantically open for Tom and Audrey in the finale, is far superior to similar scenes in most other farces dealing with romantic triangles; utterly devoid of malice, this scene provides METROPOLITAN with a lovely,

perfect ending. The film earned an Oscar nomination for its screenplay. (*Adult situations, substance abuse, profanity.*)

d, Whit Stillman; p, Whit Stillman, Brian Greenbaum, and Peter Wentworth; w, Whit Stillman; ph, John Thomas; ed, Chris Tellefsen; m, Mark Suozzo; cos, Mary Jane Fort

Comedy   **(PR:C   MPAA:NR)**

MIAMI BLUES

97m Tristes Tropiques/Orion c

Fred Ward (*Sgt. Hoke Moseley*), Alec Baldwin (*Frederick J. "Junior" Frenger*), Jennifer Jason Leigh (*Susie "Pepper" Waggoner*), Nora Dunn (*Ellita Sanchez*), Obba Babatunde (*Blink Willie*), Charles Napier (*Sgt. Bill Henderson*), Shirley Stoler (*Edie Wulgemuth*), Paul Gleason (*Sgt. Frank Lackley*), Gary Goetzman (*Hotel Desk Manager*), Ron Bozman (*Senor Lerner*), Edward Saxon (*Ravindra*), and Kenneth Utt (*Ram Ba*)

Frederick Frenger, Jr. (Alec Baldwin), an amoral con man and killer fresh out of prison, arrives in Miami with a dead man's wallet and a powerful, if impractical, urge to remake his life along more prosaic lines. In the airport he is annoyed by a Hare Krishna, whose finger he breaks out of instinctive viciousness, shocking the weak-hearted religious zealot to death. When Frenger checks into a hotel, he sends for a hooker. Pepper (Jennifer Jason Leigh), the naive, not particularly smart young woman who answers the summons, harbors a secret wish to be an ordinary housewife. And the two see in each other an opportunity to live out their fantasies of conventionality. Detective Hoke Moseley (Fred Ward) is called in to investigate the death of the Hare Krishna and quickly catches up with Frenger. A grizzled, pragmatic loner, Moseley recognizes Frenger as real trouble and tries to persuade the guileless Pepper to turn him in. Despite his promise to Pepper to abandon his criminal ways, Frenger breaks into Moseley's hotel room, beats him, and steals his badge, gun, and as a spiteful afterthought, his false teeth. With Moseley hospitalized, Frenger and Pepper move to Coral Gables and play house: she trades in her high heels for housewear, while he, equipped with Moseley's gun and badge, becomes a one-man crime wave. Battered and angry, Moseley tracks Frenger, facing off with him during the aborted robbery of a pawn shop, after the store's owner (Shirley Stoler) chops off Frenger's fingers with a machete she keeps behind the cash register. Pepper, who now knows Frenger has broken his promise to her, abandons him. Moseley then trails Frenger home and kills him.

Adapted from a novel by Charles Willeford, MIAMI BLUES toys with hard-boiled crime-film cliches and keeps the viewer constantly off balance. Its plot is minimal and straightforward, and no attempt is made to explain the psychology of the sociopath who murders casually and yet yearns for the security of a middle-class life. But the movie's details are fascinating and often surprising. Director George Armitage, a Roger Corman protege, exposes a collection of idiosyncratic characters to Florida's hot sun and the effect is startling.

Unlike the television series MIAMI VICE, Armitage's film does not portray Florida's largest city as a surreal, neon wonderland of high-stakes depravity; instead, it focuses on pastel seediness and petty criminality. Even the character of Frenger lacks psychotic grandeur; he is a dangerous cipher with some endearing quirks (after his death, Pepper observes wistfully that there were good things about him: he never hit her and always ate everything she cooked).

MIAMI BLUES suffers from a number of basic structural problems. Awkwardly paced, it alternates sharp, compact scenes with aimless ones that neither advance the plot nor illuminate the characters. Time passes erratically, without logic and without any visual cues to keep the viewer clear on the story's development. Moreover, the characters never deviate far from their initial notes: Frenger is crazy, Pepper is dumb, and Moseley has seen it all. In a slam-bang action picture in which something is blown up every 10 minutes, these would be minor complaints, but MIAMI BLUES' overt quirkiness promises more without delivering. Often on the verge of wearing out its welcome, MIAMI BLUES is nevertheless redeemed by its offbeat sensibility and sporadic, intense set pieces. (*Violence, drug use, nudity, sexual situations.*)

d, George Armitage; p, Jonathan Demme and Gary Goetzman; w, George Armitage (based on the novel *Miami Blues* by Charles Willeford); ph, Tak Fujimoto; ed, Craig McKay; prod d, Maher Ahmad

Crime   **(PR:C   MPAA:R)**

MILLER'S CROSSING

115m Circle—Ben Berenholtz—Ted and Jim Pedas—Bill Durkin/FOX c

Gabriel Byrne (*Tom Reagan*), Marcia Gay Harden (*Verna*), John Turturro (*Bernie Bernbaum*), Jon Polito (*Johnny Caspar*), J.E. Freeman (*Eddie Dane*), Albert Finney (*Leo*), Mike Starr (*Frankie*), Al Mancini (*Tic-Tac*), Richard Woods (*Mayor Dale Levander*), Thomas Toner (*O'Doole*), Steve Buscemi (*Mink*),

Mario Todisco (*Clarence "Drop" Johnson*), Olek Krupa (*Tad*), Michael Jeter (*Adolph*), Lanny Flaherty (*Terry*), Jeanette Kontomitras (*Mrs. Caspar*), Louis Charles Mounicou III (*Johnny Caspar Jr.*), John McConnell (*Brian, a Cop*), Danny Aiello III (*Delahanty, a Cop*), Helen Jolly (*Screaming Lady*), Hilda McLean (*Landlady*), Monte Starr, Don Picard (*Gunmen in Leo's House*), Salvatore H. Tornabene (*Rug Daniels*), Kevin Dearie (*Street Urchin*), Michael Badalucco (*Caspar's Driver*), Charles Ferrara (*Caspar's Butler*), Esteban Fernandez, George Fernandez (*Caspar's Cousins*), Charles Gunning (*Hitman at Verna's*), Dave Drinkx (*Hitman No. 2*), David Darlow (*Lazarre's Messenger*), Robert LaBrosse, Carl Rooney (*Lazarre's Toughs*), Jack David Harris (*Man with Pipe Bomb*), Jery Hewitt (*Son of Erin*), Sam Raimi (*Snickering Gunman*), John Schnauder Jr. (*Cop with Bullhorn*), Zolly Levin (*Rabbi*), Joey Ancona, Bill Raye (*Boxers*), and VOICE OF: William Preston Robertson

A gang war is brewing. The Irish run the town (what town? Anytown, USA), led by tough but sentimental Leo (Albert Finney) and his acerbic right-hand man, Tom (Gabriel Byrne). The Italians are the new kids on the block, and they're sensitive about it. Johnny Caspar (Jon Polito) is particularly thin-skinned, and he's mad as hell because small-time chiseler Bernie Bernbaum (John Turturro) is cutting in on his gambling action ("It's getting so a man can't trust a fixed fight anymore," Caspar complains). He wants Bernie killed, but Leo—who, by all rights, should acquiesce to keep the peace—won't hear of it because he's promised Bernie's tough-as-nails sister, Verna (Marcia Gay Harden), that he'll look out for her brother. Verna is the love of Leo's life, but she's also sleeping with Tom. It's a volatile situation, to say the least. Caspar's chief lieutenant, the sociopathic Eddie Dane (J.E. Freeman), is itching for a fight. Meanwhile, Tom, a drinker and gambler, is deeply in debt to his bookie, who's putting the screws to him. When Leo and Tom have a falling out over Verna, Tom offers his services to Caspar. Forced to prove his loyalty by killing Bernie, Tom fakes the murder, only to have Bernie prove himself to be the scum of the earth by turning around and trying to blackmail Tom. A full-scale war erupts, Leo is toppled, and double crosses are the order of the day. It all comes out more or less right in the end: Tom engineers Bernie's and Caspar's deaths, Leo is returned to power and Verna goes back to him, peace and order are restored.

The plot isn't the main event in MILLER'S CROSSING; it's clever enough, but this ground has been covered before. Gangs, guns, booze, and broads—they are all gangster film cliches. But MILLER'S CROSSING is anything but cliched. The newest film by brothers Joel and Ethan Coen (Joel directs, Ethan produces, they both write) is a remarkable advance over their first two efforts, BLOOD SIMPLE and RAISING ARIZONA. Though the nature of their style changes from film to film, the Coens are consistently stylish: BLOOD SIMPLE was *noirer* than *noir*; RAISING ARIZONA gave new meaning to the term larger than life. MILLER'S CROSSING is no exception. Richly colored and painstakingly composed (the film was shot by Barry Sonnenfeld), its images are punchy without being cartoonish.

What differentiates MILLER'S CROSSING from the Coens' first two films is its astonishing emotional complexity. Neither less witty nor less ironic than the Coens' earlier films, it resonates long after the novelty of its presentation has worn off. MILLER'S CROSSING tackles big issues—the nature of love, loyalty, friendship, and responsibility—without putting any of them in the foreground. Never does the film resort to didacticism. Still more surprising, the Coens resisted the Hollywood dictum that the protagonist must be sympathetic (that is, better than the rest of us—no messy moral complexities allowed).

Byrne's Tom is a man of principles, smart, loyal, and willing to gratify his own ambitions through Leo. But he's also a drunk, and he gambles compulsively. What's more, he sleeps with Verna and murders her brother. Tom has his reasons, and they're eminently reasonable, but what's remarkable is that the Coens trust their audience to understand him. They also assume moviegoers can follow a fairly convoluted plot devoid of deadening expository interludes designed to bring everyone up to speed, and they proceed from a position of absolute confidence in the evocative power of language. After opening in the woods, with a man's fedora swirling in the breeze, the film cuts to a lengthy scene in which Caspar propounds his self-serving theory of ethics. A study in contrast—between silence and sound, light-filled woods and darkened rooms, action and verbiage—these two scenes introduce the film's major themes with an economy and style that the Coens maintain throughout the film. MILLER'S CROSSING takes place in an artificial world constructed largely from the mythology of other movies, but its internal structure is so seamless that the film possess its own veracity.

Several contemporary filmmakers are capable of constructing a movie this well—Martin Scorsese, Francis Ford Coppola, Jonathan Demme, and Terrence Malick come to mind—but none of them can do it better. And the Coens have so far proved consistent as well. As they continue to make films, it is almost inevitable that their string of triumphs will be broken, but for now they are three for three. (*Violence, sexual situations, adult situations.*)

d, Joel Coen; p, Ethan Coen; w, Joel Coen and Ethan Coen; ph, Barry Sonnenfeld; ed, Michael R. Miller; m, Carter Burwell; prod d, Dennis Gassner; art d, Leslie McDonald; set d, Kathleen McKernin; spec, Image Engineering

and Peter Chesney; stunts, Jery Hewitt; cos, Richard Hornung; makup, Kathrine James

Crime   (PR:C   MPAA:R)

MILOU EN MAI

(SEE: MAY FOOLS)

MISADVENTURES OF MR. WILT, THE

(Brit.) 93m London Weekend TV—Picture Partnership—Talkback/Rank c

(GBTI: WILT)

Griff Rhys Jones (*Henry Wilt*), Mel Smith (*Inspector Flint*), Alison Steadman (*Eva Wilt*), Diana Quick (*Sally*), Jeremy Clyde (*Hugh*), Roger Allam (*Dave*), David Ryall (*Rev. Froude*), Roger Lloyd Pack (*Dr. Pittman*), Mermot Crowley (*Braintree*), John Normington (*Treadaway*), Tony Mathews (*Gladden*), Charles Lawson (*Cranham*), Gabrielle Blunt (*Mrs. Bulstrode*), Edward Clayton (*Mossop*), Geoffrey Chiswick (*Macari*), Julia McCarthy (*Mrs. McClaren*), Geoffrey McGivern (*Mr. Yeo*), Ling Tai (*Manageress*), Christopher Saul (*Vice-Principal*), Barbara Hicks (*Ms. Clinch*), Adam Bareham (*Board*), Ian Barritt (*Science Teacher*), Togo Igawa (*Japanese Visitor*), Fergus McLarnon (*Jessell*), Mark Monero (*Figgis*), Sam Smart (*Gilmore*), Christopher Priest (*Student*), Josephine Tewson (*Miss Leuchars*), Ken Drury (*Chief Inspector Farmiloe*), David Quilter (*Boffin*), Debra Hearst (*WPC Longman*), Beccy Wright (*WPC Duncan*), Dan Hildebrand (*Constable*), Don Williams (*Adam*), Billy Gerachty (*DJ*), Imogen Claire, Peter Gluckstein, Gina McKee, Neville Phillips, Ann Queensbury (*Party Guests*), Jim Dunk (*Urwin*), Sidney Livingstone (*Barney*), Stewart Harwood (*Driver*), and John Melainey (*Reporter*)

The second big-screen outing for British TV comedians Griff Rhys Jones and Mel Smith (the first was the disastrous MORONS FROM OUTER SPACE), casts the duo from "Not the Nine O'Clock News" in a quintessentially English farce based on a novel by Tom Sharpe. Jones takes the title role, that of polytechnic lecturer Henry Wilt. As his name suggests, he's an English weed just waiting to be trampled by anyone and everyone—by his domineering wife (Steadman), by her aggressive best friend (Quick), by his bosses and colleagues, even by his students. Steadman is a class-conscious, trendy "new woman," into karate and karma; Jones, by contrast, is resolutely unfashionable and unpretentious. While out walking the dog one night, Jones stumbles across a mugging in progress. He knocks the gun-brandishing assailant unconscious and allows the victim to escape, only to discover that the "mugger" is in fact a police inspector (Smith) who was making a drug bust. Three weeks later: construction workers on a site near the college where Jones teaches spot what looks like a woman's body just before they cover it with cement. Investigating, policeman Smith inquires about an abandoned car nearby. Of course it belongs to Jones, whose wife, it transpires, has disappeared. In explanation, Jones claims that he accompanied Steadman to a party at Quick's opulent mansion. There, having rejected his hostess' advances and subsequently watched her flirt with his wife, he confronted Quick, only to wake up naked and strapped to an inflatable sex doll. Unable to free himself, he hopped into the midst of the party. Mortified, Steadman turned to Quick for comfort, and the hapless Jones left in disgrace, still tied to the doll. When his attempts to puncture it proved ineffectual (but produced a "murder" witness), he ditched it at the construction site. Smith refuses to believe this story, and remains convinced he has unmasked a murderer—perhaps even the infamous "Swaffam Strangler"—but when the site is excavated the "corpse" is indeed a doll. Checking out Jones' story, the police learn that not only Steadman, but also Quick and her husband, have not been seen since the night of the party. Exhausted, Jones confesses he murdered all three with a chainsaw and disposed of the bodies at a local meat packing factory. Smith swallows this blatant invention, but Jones is released on orders from higher up, and upon returning home answers a phone call from Steadman. She tells Jones that she has been marooned for days on a boat with Quick and Quick's husband, that she escaped on a dinghy once she understood her friend's true nature, and that she is now phoning from a country vicarage and wants Jones to pick her up. This he does, just in time to save her from the vicar—the Swaffam Strangler himself. Smith, who has tailed his suspect, bungles again, and in despair takes himself into custody on the charge of false arrest.

Since humor, like music, is a universal language, THE MISADVENTURES OF MR. WILT's failure to be funny cannot be blamed on its Englishness; if anything, the film is even more limited in its style, which is reminiscent of TV sitcoms at their most small-scale and parochial. True wit is in painfully short supply here. Jokes like "I'm about to nab the biggest drug ring this side of Bury St. Edmonds" may make more sense to Brits than others, but still will not raise more than a titter outside of that particular town. The larger-than-life creations of Tom Sharpe's best-selling book are reduced by the film to mean-spirited stereotypes: acquisitive Japanese entrepreneurs; lazy, stupid students; and (most offensively) Alison Steadman's nagging, foolish, Eva Wilt and Diana Quick's predatory lesbian, both of them misogynist characterizations.

The part of the dull-witted inspector Flint presents rather less than a challenge to Smith, being restricted to linguistic and logical goofs, the occasional slow burn, and plenty of egg on the face. Smith—who is physically the Hardy to Jones' Laurel—directed Jeff Goldblum and Rowan Atkinson in THE TALL GUY, and has played a number of minor parts (both straight and comic) in feature films, most memorably the albino jailer in Rob Reiner's THE PRINCESS BRIDE. Here, in something of a vacuum, Smith plays broad—and the results are not good. Jones has more going for him as Wilt, who may be a hapless, mumbling weakling, but is still the only likable character in the movie. He is intelligent and witty in his own quiet way, and we sympathize with his Billy Liar-type fantasies (mostly concerned with disposing of his wife), knowing that he is actually harmless. Jones fits the part to a tee, and milks the only truly funny sequence, when he struggles, naked, with the inflatable doll in the midst of a large party. This scene is the only point at which the story's farcical elements take on a life of their own, and the only remotely "outrageous" moment in a film that manages to anesthetize adultery, stabbings, and multiple murders. Think of what fun Pedro Almodovar might have made of this material! Instead, we get flat, gross direction by Michael Tuchner that only accentuates the script's shortcomings. In the long middle section, comprising Smith's interrogation of Jones and flashbacks detailing the latter's story, the structure becomes complicated to the point that Smith himself pops up in Jones' narrative—for no reason, since the two of them are miles apart in the flashback. This slack and careless approach is sadly typical of MR. WILT, a movie that shows dishearteningly few signs of having been thought through as a story at all, let alone reconceived for the cinema. *(Nudity, profanity, sexual situations.)*

d, Michael Tuchner; p, Brian Eastman; w, Andrew Marshall and David Renwick (based on the novel by Tom Sharpe); ph, Norman Langley; ed, Chris Blunden; m, Anne Dudley; prod d, Leo Austin; set d, Steve Hedinger; stunts, Gareth Milne; cos, Liz Waller; makup, Morag Ross

Comedy (PR:O MPAA:NR)

MISERY

107m Castle Rock—Nelson/Columbia c

James Caan *(Paul Sheldon)*, Kathy Bates *(Annie Wilkes)*, Richard Farnsworth *(Buster, Sheriff)*, Frances Sternhagen *(Virginia)*, Lauren Bacall *(Marcia Sindell)*, Graham Jarvis *(Libby)*, Jerry Potter *(Pete)*, Tom Brunelle *(Anchorman)*, June Christopher *(Anchorwoman)*, Wendy Bowers *(Waitress)*, Julie Payne, Archie Hahn III, Gregory Snegoff *(Reporters)*, and Misery the Pig

In the "Kill the Bitch" tradition of FATAL ATTRACTION, this adaptation of Stephen King's misogynist fable about a "serious" (male) author trapped by his own "frivolous" (female) commercial creation isn't quite satisfying either as a flat-out horror screamer or a psychological thriller. Curiously, it derails itself on a combination of a lack of conviction behind the camera and a show-stopping performance in front of the camera.

It's doubtful anyone but the most diehard fans would actually want to read a "serious" novel by King. But King, when writing from his own solid-gold bondage in the horror genre, retains his genius for physicalizing subconscious fears. And Paul Sheldon (James Caan) has a fan in Annie Wilkes (Kathy Bates) who is willing to die hard for him. Trouble is, she wants to take him with her. At first, Wilkes is an angel of mercy, rescuing Sheldon from a car wreck in the midst of a Colorado blizzard. Sheldon, the creator of the fabulously successful romance-novel heroine Misery Chastain, has just killed her off in the final book of the series and gone on to complete his first serious novel, which he is delivering to his agent when his car runs off a remote mountain road. Severely injured, with both legs broken, he becomes Wilkes' unwilling, though not uncomfortable guest. Wilkes is a former nurse who expertly splints his legs while stroking his ego with her worshipful admiration for the man and his work. In return, Sheldon lets her sneak a peak at his newest book. And that's where the trouble starts. Annie has an extreme reaction, bordering on hysteria, to the gutter language in Sheldon's new work, an autobiographical novel about the gritty lives of ghetto street kids. And much worse is yet to come when Annie gets through her just-published copy of the latest and last "Misery" novel. Having lived vicariously through the character since her invention, Annie becomes livid at the tragic ending of the new installment. She, or rather, God decides, "speaking" directly to Annie, to help Sheldon purge himself of his unhealthy impulse to turn serious novelist and to set him back on the course of his true calling. After forcing Sheldon to put the match to his new manuscript, she sits him at a table with his assignment from above to resurrect Misery Chastain and write a new final chapter that has the heroine finding happiness. What gradually becomes apparent to Sheldon is that Misery's final chapter will also be his. Sheldon confirms his suspicions when, getting out of his room when Annie is away from the house, he discovers that she is a serial killer of some repute, and more than a match for

Sheldon's anxious agent (Lauren Bacall) and the wily local sheriff (Richard Farnsworth) who bring the state police in on the search for the missing author.

Not surprisingly for the director of the comedies THIS IS SPINAL TAP, THE SURE THING, and WHEN HARRY MET SALLY, as well as an earlier, non-horror, King adaptation, STAND BY ME, Rob Reiner is clearly more comfortable with the humor and humanity than the gory horror in King's grisly tale. The script by William Goldman (BUTCH CASSIDY AND THE SUNDANCE KID, ALL THE PRESIDENT'S MEN) is also at its strongest early on when Sheldon faces off in a test of artistic mettle against the toughest editor of his life in Wilkes. As a result, when the horror comes, it feels forced, unoriginal, and unconvincing. In part, the lack of originality comes from the source work. The plot element of the writer driven into a murderous rage is derived from King's *The Shining* (and was much better handled in Stanley Kubrick's filming of that work). The climactic battle between Sheldon and Annie degenerates into yet another recycling of the unkillable killer movie gimmick of "Friday the 13th" ilk.

However, what is most ironic is the effectiveness of Bates' Oscar-winning performance in rendering MISERY ineffective as a horror tale. Her work is a subtle mixture of wit, energy, psychological realism, and, most of all, a weird empathy which winds up all but upending the possibility of a pat, bloodthirsty resolution. In the end, it is Caan's Sheldon who becomes the monster, a civilized man of words who allows himself to be driven to barbaric violence in response to a woman whose real offense in relation to Sheldon was to believe what he had written. King, Reiner, Goldman, and Caan don't demonstrate much interest in exploring Sheldon's culpability in creating his own predicament. Yet, Bates' performance demands it. As a result, MISERY is about as entertaining as any film made from King's work as far as it goes. But its ending leaves a sour taste. As a result, instead of succeeding as a "Kill the Bitch" movie, it works best as an inadvertent critique of horror-movie misogyny, which, on the whole, comes as a welcome relief from the real thing. *(Violence, profanity.)*

d, Rob Reiner; p, Rob Reiner, Andrew Scheinman, Steve Nicolaides, and Jeffrey Stott; w, William Goldman (based on the novel by Stephen King); ph, Barry Sonnenfeld; ed, Robert Leighton; m, Marc Shaiman; prod d, Norman Garwood; art d, Mark Mansbridge; set d, Stan Tropp; spec, Phil Cory and KNB EFX Group; stunts, David Ellis; cos, Gloria Gresham; makup, John Elliott and Margaret Elliott

Horror (PR:O MPAA:R)

MR. AND MRS. BRIDGE

124m Merchant Ivory-Robert Halmi/Miramax c

Paul Newman *(Walter Bridge)*, Joanne Woodward *(India Bridge)*, Robert Sean Leonard *(Douglas Bridge)*, Margaret Welsh *(Carolyn Bridge)*, Kyra Sedgwick *(Ruth Bridge)*, Blythe Danner *(Grace)*, Simon Callow *(Dr. Sauer)*, Malachy McCourt *(Dr. Forster)*, Austin Pendleton *(Mr. Gadbury)*, Diane Kagan *(Julia)*, Saundra McClain *(Harriet)*, Gale Garnett *(Mabel Ong)*, Marcus Giamatti *(Gil Davis)*, and Remak Ramsey *(Virgil Barron)*

Everything's up-to-date in Kansas City, but then the clock stops, circa the early 40s for Walter and India Bridge, the leads of this gem of a period piece and finely wrought drama of an American marriage. Actually, life for the provincial upper middle class couple—played brilliantly by the long-married Paul Newman and Joanne Woodward—hasn't stopped or even settled in. More precisely, it has congealed. As if frozen in time, their stolidly conservative, predictable existence is clearly stultifying. Still, boring lives don't necessarily make for boring films, and the cumulative impact onscreen is anything but. The main characters are indelibly set in their ways with an almost foolish consistency. *He* is a prosperous lawyer who is hopelessly intractable. Archly self-satisfied and authoritarian, he patronizes his wife (*all* women, for that matter), votes straight Republican, and confines his actions to the very narrow channels he deems acceptable. *She* is a relic of Victorian sensibilities, a living embodiment of the antique aphorism, "children should be seen, not heard" grown to maturity. So hungry for affection and desperate to please, she has long since lost any individual identity and emerges as a mass of repression.

So what happens? Not much. But then that's just the point of the film, derived almost literally from both of Evan S. Connell's best-selling novels (*Mrs. Bridge* was written in 1959; *Mr. Bridge* in 1967). What fills the screen is not heightened melodrama, but a series of stark, sometimes painfully poignant vignettes that reflect the oppressive stasis of their lives. The events depicted are episodic in nature. India is rebuffed by her son when he refuses to kiss her at a Boy Scout ceremony. One daughter, the rebellious, sexually charged Ruth (Kyra Sedgwick), opts for the arty, Bohemian life in New York, and is tolerantly bankrolled by her father. Her younger, more conventional sister, Carolyn (Margaret Welsh) makes an impulsive marriage to a college beau. Mrs. Bridge is ordered by her husband to ignore tornado warnings during a dinner at their club, and despite entreaties from fellow members and the staff that she head for shelter, fearfully obeys him until the storm subsides. Her best friend Grace (Blythe Danner), a banker's wife (and closet heretic), conforms to the ultraconservative codes expected of her until the strain grows too much to bear. Another friend, Mabel (Gale Garnett), who fancies herself a rebel, turns to a psychoanalyst for help. Mr. Bridge ignores the feelings of his secretary of 20 years, a spinster who has long been in love with him. And so on. Everything leads up to the final scene, which seems to synthesize the very essence of the film. One ordinary winter day, India dresses for a trip to town, gets into her car and starts backing out of the garage when the motor conks out. The garage is too narrow for her to open the car door and get out, so she is trapped, and sits waiting for her husband to come home and rescue her.

As India Bridge, Woodward (who earned a Best Actress Oscar nomination for her performance) eloquently recreates an emotional dishrag that's been squeezed dry. She perceptively portrays a naive, totally guileless mother of three, a suburban matron and country club member whose inner dreams have been put on permanent hold. Her utterly respectable, lackluster life remains defined by what everyone else—especially her husband—expects of her. She wouldn't think of making a decision without his input. Though Newman does an excellent job as Mr. Bridge—his low-keyed interpretation of the highly controlled, highly controlling patriarch is a powerful example of emotional restraint—-the kudos must go to his wife. But to both their credit, they play the parts with enough humor and compassion to avoid reducing their roles to caricatures. You might not quite exactly like them as individuals, but as a film, you will. This was another entertaining collaboration from the long-time producing/directing/writing team of Ismail Merchant, James Ivory, and Ruth Prawer Jhabvala, whose previous efforts have included THE BOSTONIANS, A ROOM WITH A VIEW, and MAURICE.

d, James Ivory; p, Ismail Merchant; w, Ruth Prawer Jhabvala (based on the novels *Mrs. Bridge* and *Mr. Bridge*, by Evan S. Connell); ph, Tony Pierce-Roberts; ed, Humphrey Dixon; m, Richard Robbins; prod d, David Gropman; cos, Carol Ramsey

Drama   (PR:A   MPAA:PG-13)

MR. DESTINY

110m Silver Screen Partners IV—Orr—Cruickshank—Laurence Mark/Buena Vista c

James Belushi (*Larry Burrows*), Linda Hamilton (*Ellen Burrows*), Michael Caine (*Mike*), Jon Lovitz (*Clip Metzler*), Hart Bochner (*Niles Pender*), Bill McCutcheon (*Leo Hansen*), Rene Russo (*Cindy Jo*), Jay O. Sanders (*Jackie Earle*), Maury Chaykin (*Guzelman*), Pat Corley (*Harry Burrows*), Douglas Seale (*Boswell*), Courteney Cox (*Jewel Jagger*), Doug Barron (*Lewis Flick*), Jeff Weiss (*Ludwig*), Tony Longo (*Huge Guy*), Kathy Ireland (*Gina*), Andrew Stahl (*Jerry Haskins*), Bryan Buffinton (*Boy*), Sari Caine (*Girl*), Martin Thompson (*Guest Stilton*), Michael Genevie, Howard Kingkade (*Guests*), Osamu Sakabe (*Nakamura*), Eddita Hill (*Juanita*), Collin Bernsen (*Tom Robertson*), William Griffis (*Maitre D'*), John Garver (*Waiter*), Terry Loughlin (*Wine Steward*), Adam Eichhorst (*Teenager*), Jeffrey Pillars (*Truck Driver*), Richie Devaney (*Young Larry*), Bruce Evers (*Team Coach*), Whit Edwards (*Young Jerry*), Sky Berdahl (*Young Clip*), Raymond L. Anderson (*Umpire*), Heather Lynch (*Young Ellen*), James Douglas (*Mr. Ripley*), Chris Stacy (*Teammate*), and Jesse J. Donnelly (*The Cop*)

In MR. DESTINY, James Belushi plays Larry Burrows, an average hardworking guy who is not very happy with his life. He has an unsatisfying office job with Liberty, a company that manufactures sporting goods. There he is surrounded by bosses with nicknames like "Cement Head" and by sexy female coworkers for whom he lusts. Larry is married to Ellen (Linda Hamilton of TV's "Beauty and the Beast"), a beautiful woman who doesn't seem to have time for him in between her overtime hours at Liberty (where she works on the assembly line) and her union meetings. His best friend, a goof named Clip (Jon Lovitz), likes to play practical jokes on Larry and kiss him on the head. Rounding out Larry's life are a family dog with a weak bladder, a mound of mud that his lazy contractor calls a driveway, and a car that consistantly breaks down. Worst of all, everyone, including Ellen, seems to have forgotten Larry's 35th birthday (everyone except Clip, who gifts his pal with some fake vomit). All of this bad luck, according to Larry, can be traced to the worst day of his life—his fifteenth birthday, when in the bottom of the ninth with two out and a man on, he struck out to blow his high school's chance of winning the state baseball championship. If he had hit that last pitch, his life would be different now; Larry is sure of it. After being fired for uncovering a scandal that his boss wants hushed up, Larry goes to a bar for a drink. There he meets a mysterious bartender (Michael Caine), who listens as Larry laments his sorry state, then makes the put-upon patron a magical drink. When Larry downs this concoction and walks out of the bar, he steps into MR. DESTINY's version of "The Twilight Zone." It seems that history has been altered, that Larry *didn't* strike out during his infamous turn at bat; in

fact, he hit the game-winning home run, and that golden moment changed the course of his life. Now the town hero, Larry is about to discover what it's like to live like a king.

For starters, Larry is married to his boss's gorgeous daughter Cindy Jo (Rene Russo), and lives with her and their two children in a mansion. Naturally, he has loads of money. He also has several fancy cars, a mistress (Courteney Cox), the biggest office at Liberty, and power beyond his wildest imaginings. But he doesn't have Ellen, who is married to someone else. Moreover, judging by the general dislike most people seem to have for Larry, success has made him a heartless jerk. For a while he lives out this new life as best he can (with periodic help from the bartender, Mr. Destiny), but soon his longing for Ellen and for friendship forces him to alter his life in ways that Mr. Destiny has warned him against. Set up by his jealous coworkers (lead by Hart Bochner, in a wonderfully wicked performance), Larry is caught with Ellen (in effect cheating on his wife with his wife). Eventually, he is even wanted for murder. A fugitive, he is pursued by the police into a dead end, and when he asks for help from Mr. Destiny, Larry finds himself back in the bar, safe and sound. After thanking Mr. Destiny for helping him realize that his life isn't so bad after all, Larry goes to a high-powered Liberty board meeting to expose his boss's hidden scandal. He then returns home to discover that dozens of his friends have thrown him a surprise birthday party. They haven't forgotten his birthday after all. What's more, Larry is rehired by Liberty and given a high-paying job.

MR. DESTINY obviously owes a great deal to Frank Capra's twinkling fantasy classic IT'S A WONDERFUL LIFE, from which it borrows the bare bones of its plot. But times have changed, and, judging by this Disney release, so have values. While IT'S A WONDERFUL LIFE emphasizes the importance of family, MR. DESTINY emphasizes the importance of money and sex. Even though Larry realizes that his "real" life is more fulfilling than his "new and improved" one, he still ends up with a high-paying job and a Mercedes. In IT'S A WONDERFUL LIFE, James Stewart's George Bailey desperately *needs* the gifts of money that come his way in the film's final scene, but Larry Burrows doesn't *need* a Mercedes; it's just cool for him to have one. It would appear that in the age of psuedo-fairy-tales like PRETTY WOMAN (also a Disney release), happy endings are not really happy unless the protagonist receives some kind of monetary reward (as if filmmakers are saying to their characters *and* to the audience, "You've learned your lesson, now you can keep all of the neat stuff!").

Essentially the story of a man who takes a vacation from his responsibilities by going to a bar and reveling in his secret fantasies, MR. DESTINY also perversely caters to the fantasies of male viewers. Larry drives fancy cars, is waited on by servants, and sleeps with a woman that he has lusted after for years. When he returns to his marriage, not only are all of his problems solved, but he receives a nice fat reward. Although this hardly qualifies as a morally uplifting message, the film tries to pass itself off as an innocent fantasy. In reality, MR. DESTINY is little more than a role-reversed version of PRETTY WOMAN, although it does not begin to rival that film's reprehensible treatment of women and absurd glorification of consumerism.

MR. DESTINY also fails as whimsical fantasy; director Orr handles the supernatural elements in such a flat-footed manner that he never evokes the necessary magical atmosphere, and though Caine tries desperately to be charming and fairylike, he is no Henry Travers (IT'S A WONDERFUL LIFE's unforgettable angel, Clarence). In fact, most of the time Caine simply looks distracted. The rest of the supporting cast either embarrass themselves (Lovitz and Cox) or look as if they wish they were somewhere else (Hamilton and Bochner).

When all is said and done, MR. DESTINY remains watchable and at times even becomes entertaining only because of Belushi's presence. Just as he did with the tepid TAKING CARE OF BUSINESS (yet another Disney release with a consumerist bent), Belushi redeems almost every scene he's in with his supremely winning charm. His performance here establishes him as one of the most likable comedic actors of his generation (he has also proved himself a terrific dramatic actor in THE PRINCIPAL; SALVADOR; and Andrei Konchalovsky's HOMER & EDDIE), and perhaps he will begin to get some of the Cary Grant-like roles that always seem to go Tom Hanks' way.

MR. DESTINY is by no means a good movie, but James Belushi is unquestionably a good actor, and his portrayal of Larry Burrows almost makes the film worth watching. *(Profanity, adult situations.)*

d, James Orr; p, James Orr and Jim Cruickshank; w, James Orr and Jim Cruickshank; ph, Alex Thomson; ed, Michael R. Miller; m, David Newman; prod d, Michael Seymour; art d, Catherine Hardwicke; set d, Kathleen McKernin; spec, Peter Donen, Apogee Productions, Richard C. Huggins, and Ray Bivins; stunts, Monty Cox; cos, Jane Greenwood; makup, Charles Balazs; anim, Available Light Ltd., Katherine Kean, and John T. Van Vliet

Fantasy   (PR:A-C   MPAA:PG-13)

MR. FROST

(Brit./Fr.) 104m Selena — Hugo — AAA-Overseas/Triumph c

Jeff Goldblum *(Mr. Frost)*, Alan Bates *(Inspector Detweiler)*, Kathy Baker *(Dr. Sarah Day)*, Roland Giraud *(Raymond Reynhardt)*, Francois Negret *(Christophe Kovac)*, Jean-Pierre Cassel *(L'Inspector Correlli)*, Maxime Leroux *(Francis Larcher)*, Daniel Gelin *(Simon Scolari)*, Catherine Allegret *(Dr. Corbin)*, Boris Bergman *(Victor Sabowsky)*, Henri Serre *(Andre Kovac)*, Mike Marshall *(Patrick Hollander)*, Charlie Boorman *(Thief)*, Herve Laudiere *(Joseph)*, Aina Walle *(Carole)*, Patrice Melennec *(Phil)*, Jo Sheridan *(Jogger)*, Raymond Aquilon *(Elias)*, Catherine Cyler *(Christie)*, Elisabeth Forgo *(Patient)*, Herve Laglois *(Racket)*, Louise Vincent *(Louise)*, Steve Gadler *(Archer)*, and Philippe Polet *(Roland)*

This is an extremely silly horror movie starring Jeff Goldblum in a role some might think he was born to play — Satan. Set In England, the film begins as police inspector Detweiler (Alan Bates) pays a visit to Mr. Frost (Goldblum) at his estate. Frost knows the reason for the visit — he's suspected of murder. When the inspector arrives, Frost is the midst of burying one of the many corpses lying about the grounds. Frost is arrested and Detweiler retires, then nearly goes mad. Years pass and Frost (who has remained silent since his arrest) is taken to St. Claire's Hospital where he breaks his silence by speaking to Dr. Sarah Day (Kathy Baker). He tells her that he is Satan...and he loves to cook. Detweiler shows up at the hospital as if he were Donald Pleasence in a "Halloween" movie, babbling about how dangerous Frost is. Frost continues to talk only to the doubting Sarah, then proves he is Satan by possessing a quiet patient and turning him into a psychotic killer. Sarah's convinced and she and Detweiler then team in an effort to thwart Frost's dirty deeds.

Muddled is the perfect word to describe this mess. As directed by Philippe Setbon, the film plays like a parody, but was clearly meant to be taken seriously. The somber tone is hammered home by the blaring musical score and the heavy-handed imagery. The film isn't suspenseful, nor is it scary. It never succeeds in creating the aura of mystery for which it so desperately strives. There are numerous "shock" cuts and phony tension-relieving moments that inspire laughs instead of chills. Moreover, there's enough fog to fill all of Freddy Krueger's movies. All this film has going for it is the performances. Bates is riotously over-the-top as the mad detective, injecting life into the somber proceedings. Baker (CLEAN AND SOBER, EDWARD SCISSORHANDS) turns in another delightful performance, making her character the only one in the film with any depth. But it is Goldblum with his wild eyes and jaunty air who seems to be having the most fun. There has always been something creepy about him and he plays that for all it's worth here. Of course, Goldblum's hair makes a big impression, leading one to speculate that perhaps his weird hair deserves an acting credit of its own. *(Violence, profanity, adult situations, sexual situations, brief nudity.)*

d, Philippe Setbon; w, Philippe Setbon and Brad Lynch; ph, Dominique Brenguier; ed, Ray Lovejoy; m, Steven Levine; art d, Max Berto; set d, Patrick Weibel

Horror   (PR:O   MPAA:NR)

MO' BETTER BLUES

127m 40 Acres and a Mule/Universal c

Denzel Washington *(Bleek Gilliam)*, Spike Lee *(Giant)*, Wesley Snipes *(Shadow Henderson)*, Giancarlo Esposito *(Left Hand Lacey)*, Robin Harris *(Butterbean Jones)*, Joie Lee *(Indigo Downes)*, Bill Nunn *(Bottom Hammer)*, John Turturro *(Moe Flatbush)*, Dick Anthony Williams *(Big Stop Gilliam)*, Cynda Williams *(Clarke Bentancourt)*, Nicholas Turturro *(Josh Flatbush)*, Jeff "Tain" Watts *(Rhythm Jones)*, Samuel L. Jackson *(Madlock)*, Leonard Thomas *(Rod)*, Charles Q. Murphy *(Eggy)*, Steve White *(Born Knowledge)*, Ruben Blades *(Petey)*, Abbey Lincoln *(Lillian Gilliam)*, Linda Hawkins *(Jeanne)*, Raye Dowell *(Rita)*, Angela Hall *(Cora)*, Coati Mundi *(Roberto)*, Zakee L. Howze *(Young Bleek/Miles)*, Deon Richmond *(Tyrone)*, Anaysha Figueroa *(Shanika)*, Raymond Thomas *(Joe)*, Sheldon Turnipseed *(Benny)*, Christopher Skeffrey *(Louis)*, Terrence Williams *(Sam)*, Darryl M. Wonge Jr. *(Miles at Birth)*, Jelani Asar Snipes *(Miles, Age 1)*, Glenn Williams III *(Miles, Age 3)*, Arnold Cromer *(Miles, Age 5)*, Leon Addison Brown *(Smith)*, Scot Anthony Robinson *(Cooley)*, Herbert Daughtry *(Minister)*, Bill Lee *(Father of the Bride)*, Branford Marsalis *(Party Guest)*, Douglas Bourne *(Jimmy the Busboy)*, Tracy Camilla Johns, John Canada Terrell, Monty Ross, Carol M. Wiggins, Isabella, Mamie Louis Anderson *(Club Patrons)*, Joe Seneca *(Big Stop's Friend)*, John Sobestanovich *(Taxi Driver)*, and Flavor Flav *(Impatient Movie Patron)*

After making the powerful and important DO THE RIGHT THING, Spike Lee took a break from controversial social issues and brought a quieter, more introspective work to the screen in MO' BETTER BLUES, a funny, moody jazz picture that focuses more on relationships and character. This does not represent

a step backward for Lee: DO THE RIGHT THING may have had greater social relevance, but MO' BETTER BLUES is a sharper, more controlled film. An exceptionally well-made movie that shows Lee's considerable technical maturation, MO' BETTER BLUES is also his first film to incorporate several obvious homages to other directors, and scenes that reveal the filmmaker's visual influences. The most prominent of these influences is Martin Scorsese, whose work seems to have given Lee virtually his entire *mise-en-scene* here. With scenes recalling moments from RAGING BULL; WHO'S THAT KNOCKING AT MY DOOR; and especially MEAN STREETS, MO' BETTER BLUES plays like a jazz film as directed by Scorsese — NEW YORK, NEW YORK done right, perhaps. This is not to say that Lee's own personality is missing from the film, however. Quite the contrary: from the music to the locations to the attitude, MO' BETTER BLUES is a true "Spike Lee Joint" in all respects.

MO' BETTER BLUES is the story of Bleek Gilliam (Denzel Washington), a popular and talented jazz trumpeter whose life — both personally and professionally — is about to come to a turning point. An intensely self-centered artist whose single-minded concentration on his music (forced on him by a domineering mother) begins to alienate the people in his life, Bleek is nonetheless a charismatic figure, and his quintet fills the Beneath the Underdog club every night. But there is turmoil within the band. The over-ambitious saxophonist, Shadow Henderson (Wesley Snipes), hogs the spotlight and extends his solos to ridiculous lengths. Egos clash, disagreements abound, and everyone — including Bleek — wants more money. Unfortunately, the group is managed by Giant (Spike Lee), a childhood friend of Bleek's and a habitual gambler. Giant has trapped Bleek's boys into a low-paying, nonnegotiable contract with the Underdog's owners (John and Nicholas Turturro), and he spends more time with his bookie (Ruben Blades) than he does with the musicians. Everyone tells Bleek to get rid of Giant, but Bleek feels obligated to keep his old friend on. As if problems in the band weren't enough, Bleek is having problems in his bed as well (*mo' better* is a slang euphemism for sex). Juggling two very different women is starting to become tiresome for him, while his flippant attitude and lack of commitment are beginning to bother the ladies (in this respect, the film is a kind of role-reversed SHE'S GOTTA HAVE IT). The two women in Bleek's life are Indigo (Joie Lee, the director's sister), a schoolteacher who genuinely loves Bleek and feels a great need for stability in their relationship, and Clarke (newcomer Cynda Williams), an aspiring singer who also cares for Bleek a great deal and who wants to be included in his band. Needless to say, Bleek won't even consider Clarke's talents, and he refuses to commit to Indigo. He tells Clarke that "everything else [in life] is secondary" to his music, and this single-mindedness eventually costs him the love of both women. Meanwhile, Giant's gambling debts become dangerously high and (after two of Giant's fingers are broken by thugs) Bleek fires him as his manager, though the jazzman agrees to help Giant pay off his bookie. The band is still not satisfied with the money situation, and Shadow is moving in on Clarke, just as he moved in on Bleek's stage time. Upon discovering Clarke's relationship with Shadow, Bleek kicks the saxophonist out of the band and plays a gig without him. During the performance, Giant is grabbed by two thugs to whom he owes money, taken outside, and beaten to a pulp. Bleek finally comes on the scene to lend a hand, and winds up getting his jaw broken and his lips mangled. The film then picks up a year later, as Bleek returns to the stage, sitting in with the now successful Shadow Henderson Quartet — consisting of Bleek's old players and with Clarke on vocals — at a club where Giant is a lowly doorman. Discovering, to his horror, that he can no longer play, Bleek gives his horn to Giant — who promises not to sell it — and leaves the club, knowing he will never perform again. He heads over to Indigo's house and begs her to forgive his past mistakes and "save [his] life." After initial resistance, Indigo gives in and accepts Bleek back into her life. They are soon married and settled down. Bleek teaches their child how to play the trumpet.

Generally assessed, MO' BETTER BLUES is a very entertaining film. Full of wonderful music, grand visuals, and involving melodramatic plot twists, the movie is laced with very funny moments, as well as interesting insights into the world of jazz and the plight of the dedicated musician. A lot goes on in the plot, but the pacing is agreeably quick and the characters are fleshed out in enthrallingly complex fashion. Lee has again created a fun film to watch that is also an insightful presentation of a specifically African-American milieu (in this case the jazz world).

But what makes MO' BETTER BLUES particularly notable is its startlingly assured style. Lee has never been better behind the camera; except for two shaky scenes, MO' BETTER BLUES is flawlessly directed. The camera glides fluidly and Ernest Dickerson's photography is astounding. Lee's gift for expressive camera angles has developed, and he establishes visual themes quite confidently (the opening credit sequence, reminiscent of the opening credits of Kathryn Bigelow's brilliant BLUE STEEL, has the camera lingering over the curves of a trumpet and the curves of a woman's body in a coolly seductive manner, establishing the film's thematic focus and creating a strong visual metaphor). He has become a true filmmaker, and like all true filmmakers he has influences, which he acknowledges regularly here. Most notably, Scorsese's style and themes are present in seemingly every frame of MO' BETTER BLUES. The central relationship, between the irresponsible Giant and the ever-patient Bleek, echoes that of Robert De Niro's Johnny Boy and Harvey Keitel's Charlie in MEAN STREETS, and many of MO' BETTER's improvised male-banter sequences also recall that film. The scene in which Giant is beaten up is an obvious homage to RAGING BULL—all the way down to the use of slow motion and bizarre sound effects—while the cutting style, camera placement, and use of music in certain scenes recall early Scorsese efforts like WHO'S THAT KNOCKING AT MY DOOR. Moreover, the film's narrative structure (with its frantic, time-jumping montage ending) recalls THE LAST TEMPTATION OF CHRIST. These similarities never feel like theft, but like homage in its truest form.

Though MO' BETTER BLUES is never as powerful as DO THE RIGHT THING and certainly doesn't have that film's potential to generate argument, it doesn't need to. With less explosive subject matter and much more personal issues at hand—for the first time Lee doesn't overcrowd his screenplay with social issues, although the mainstream's under-appreciation of black music and the exploitation of black artists is touched upon here—Lee has come up with his most tightly constructed film. This newfound technical bravado should make his work all the more powerful in the future; had Lee shown this much assurance with DO THE RIGHT THING it would have been a masterpiece.

The performances are uniformly terrific. Lee himself (playing another irresponsible character, after DO THE RIGHT THING's Mookie and SHE'S GOTTA HAVE IT's Mars) is, as always, tremendously appealing and quite convincing as the gambling manager. Joie Lee shines with intelligence and sensuality, as does newcomer Williams, who's got a terrific singing voice. (However, a nagging problem within all of Lee's films, including this one, is his presentation of under-developed female characters.) Giancarlo Esposito, Bill Nunn, the Turturros, and the other Spike Lee "regulars" are all in fine form, while the late Robin Harris (Pop in HOUSE PARTY; Sweet Dick Willie in DO THE RIGHT THING) is absolutely hilarious as Butterbean, the nightclub's standup comic. Lee includes wonderfully long takes of Butterbean's routine, and a side-splitting party sequence in which he refers to Washington's Bleek as a goof who "looks like a question mark." This film, Harris' last, is dedicated to his memory.

After his Oscar-winning work in GLORY, Washington has turned in another impressive performance. It's a portrayal that sneaks up on you, that seems effortless as you watch the film—but after MO' BETTER BLUES has ended, the true power of Washington's execution is revealed in recollection, his gestures and looks lingering so that Bleek's power over people (and music) becomes all the more plausible. But the nicest surprise among the actors is Snipes (STREETS OF GOLD; MAJOR LEAGUE), whose performance as Shadow Henderson is absolutely arresting. Shadow (a part originally meant for Branford Marsalis until an extensive concert tour forced him to decline) is both unlikably sly and undeniably cool, and Snipes plays him perfectly. Ambitious, talented, and determined, Shadow is in many ways like Bleek, but Snipes' acting approach is entirely different from Washington's. It's a showier performance, but an equally effective one.

Lee has successfully brought a jazz "feel" to the screen in MO' BETTER BLUES, which contains wall-to-wall music (sometimes too much of it) and some very fine songs performed and written by the likes of Branford Marsalis, Terence Blanchard, and the director's father, Bill Lee, who also wrote the score. (The elder Lee has scored all his son's films.) The film also features performances by salsa crossover star Blades (CROSSOVER DREAMS; THE MILAGRO BEANFIELD WAR) and jazz singer-actress Abbey Lincoln (NOTHING BUT A MAN; FOR THE LOVE OF IVY). Dickerson's photography is sharper and more experimental than the usual smoky greens and browns of jazz films, and the set design and costumes combine the style of the be-bop era with a modern look. Not only is MO' BETTER BLUES entertaining and accomplished, it's truly original in its look and feel. While MO' BETTER BLUES is not the ground-breaking film that DO THE RIGHT THING was, it is fun, insightful, and well acted, and it will provide the viewer with two hours of genuine entertainment. Musical selections include "Say Hey," "Beneath the Underdog," "Knocked out the Box" (Branford Marsalis, performed by the Branford Marsalis Quartet), "All Blues" (Miles Davis, performed by Davis), "Pop Top 40" (Marsalis, Spike Lee, performed by Denzel Washington, Wesley Snipes, and the Branford Marsalis Quartet), "Tunji," "Mr. Knight," "A Love Supreme" (John Coltrane, performed by Coltrane), "Rescue Me" (Gary Jackson, Carl Smith, Raynard Miner, performed by Fontella Bass), "Mercy, Mercy, Mercy" (Josef Zawinul, performed by Cannonball Adderly), "Footprints" (Wayne Shorter, performed by Davis), "Mo' Better Blues," "Again Never" (Bill Lee, performed by the Branford Marsalis Quartet), "Sing Soweto" (Terence Blanchard, performed by Blanchard), "Goodbye Pork Pie Hat (Theme for Lester Young)" (Charles Mingus, performed by Mingus), "Harlem Blues" (W.C. Handy, performed by the Branford Marsalis Quartet), "Lonely Woman" (Ornette Coleman, performed by the Branford Marsalis Quartet), "Jazz Thing" (Marsalis, Christopher Martin, Keith Elam, Almo Irving, Lolis Eric Elie, performed by Gangstarr). *(Profanity, brief nudity, adult situations, sexual situations, violence.)*

d, Spike Lee; p, Spike Lee; w, Spike Lee; ph, Ernest Dickerson; ed, Sam Pollard; m, Bill Lee; md, Bill Lee; prod d, Wynn Thomas; art d, Pam E. Stephens; set d, Ted Glass; spec, Tom Newton and Tom Brumberger; stunts, Jeff Ward; cos, Ruth E. Carter; makup, Matiki Anoff; tech, Terence Blanchard, Michael Max Fleming, and Donald Harrison

Comedy/Drama   (PR:O   MPAA:R)

MODERN LOVE

109m SVS — Lyric — Soisson — Murphey/Triumph c

Robby Benson *(Greg)*, Karla DeVito *(Billie)*, Rue McClanahan *(Evelyn)*, Burt Reynolds *(Col. Parker)*, Frankie Valli *(Mr. Hoskins)*, Louise Lasser *(Greg's Mom)*, Kaye Ballard *(Receptionist)*, Lou Kaplan *(Greg's Dad)*, Cliff Bemis *(Dirk)*, and Lyric Benson *(Chloe)*

A nonstop annoyance in the form of a movie, this romantic comedy is irritating enough to serve as an advertisement for singleness, celibacy, and childlessness. To be fair, young costar Lyric Benson is cuter than a bug's ear and a natural as an actress. It's a good thing, too. If her dad, star-writer-director Robby Benson, makes too many more movies like this, it may be up to her to bring home the bacon for the entire Benson clan.

Robby Benson plays Greg, a public relations flack in Columbia, South Carolina, whose life changes when he meets Billie (Karla DeVito, formerly Meat Loaf's backup singer, now Benson's offscreen wife). A full-time urologist and part-time standup comedienne, Billie occasionally confuses the two occupations, telling bad jokes during examinations and wearing her lab coat and stethoscope for club dates. After a mercifully short montage of hand-holding and puppy-love cuteness, Greg and Billie get married and have a baby. In most movies of this type, the couple would go on to share laughter, tears, heartache, and joy. Here, they experience one bummer after another. Almost as soon as Billie gets pregnant, Greg goes into a whining fit that doesn't end until the movie does. First, the baby won't bond with him, crying every time Greg comes near her. Then baby clothes are too expensive. In the meantime, Greg's boss (Frankie Valli) makes him the publicist-cum-babysitter for Dirk (Cliff Bemis), a brain-dead, overweight TV series star. (One of the few funny running gags that MODERN LOVE has to offer hangs on the reaction of Greg's family to Dirk; although they have seen him only on TV, they are convinced Dirk is a terrific actor and an all-around nice guy, which leaves Greg continually choking back the truth and sorely tests his mettle as a publicist.) However, Greg's boss isn't about to allow the young family man to go on vacation. Matters go from bad to worse when Greg's daughter finally bonds with him, only to drive Greg crazy with her constant need for attention. As if that weren't enough, Greg's Catholic mother-in-law (Rue McClanahan) tries to baptize the baby—more than a small bother for Greg, who is Jewish. Then Billie, who has remained plump and unsexy long after giving birth, compounds that "offense" by returning to her practice and to the comedy stage while trying to care for the baby. Billie and Greg are finally reconciled when he recalls an emotional moment from their wedding. The problem is that moment wasn't part of the original wedding scene; in other words, it is a flashback to something that didn't happen in the first place.

Aside from Greg's virtually nonstop tantrums—his baby is a model of maturity by comparison—MODERN LOVE is virtually without a plot. Instead, the movie repeatedly introduces story lines and characters only to drop them so that Greg's next outburst can be shown. During the prolog, Greg tells his life story via narrated flashbacks that portray him as a hopeless romantic always falling in love with beautiful, blond heartbreakers, which does little to explain why he has ended up with Billie, a brunette who is as faithful as the day is long. Billie's father (played by Benson's buddy Burt Reynolds in an extended cameo) is an Army colonel who first threatens to break Greg into 10,000 pieces, then kisses him. Although this little culture clash results in what is certainly the first time Reynolds has kissed a leading man, MODERN LOVE never really explores the potential conflict between Greg's Jewish background and Billie's ultra-Gentile upbringing. Equally underdeveloped are Greg's relationships with his boss and with his client.

MODERN LOVE is a movie that has been turned inside out. The scenes that might have made it work all seem to take place offscreen, while the bulk of the film's running time, aside from Greg's incessant whining, is devoted to the screenplay's worst, most derivative ideas. Lame confessional voiceovers are copped from Woody Allen, tasteless baby's point-of-view shots are borrowed from LOOK WHO'S TALKING, laborious expeditions into family farce are inspired by PARENTHOOD, and addled exaggerations of domestic crises are even more unfunny here than they were in John Hughes' SHE'S HAVING A BABY. Besides involving most of his family and friends in the production, Benson made the film as a class project while teaching a course at South Carolina State University. Benson deserves credit for giving his students professional experience it might have taken them years to gain otherwise, but it should be noted that even in this endeavour Benson is following in the footsteps of Brian

DePalma, whose HOME MOVIES grew out of a class he taught at New York's Sarah Lawrence University. *(Adult situations, profanity.)*

d, Robby Benson; p, Robby Benson; w, Robby Benson; ph, Christpher G. Tufty; ed, Gib Jaffe; m, Don Peake; prod d, Carl E. Copeland; art d, Nancy Harvin; cos, Robin Lewis

Comedy/Romance   **(PR:C   MPAA:R)**

MONSIEUR HIRE

(Fr.) 81m Cinea — Hachette — FR3/UGC — Orion c

(M. HIRE)

Michel Blanc *(M. Hire)*, Sandrine Bonnaire *(Alice)*, Luc Thuillier *(Emile)*, and Andre Wilms *(Inspector)*

A superb thriller containing the ugliest portrait of French provincialism since Henri-Georges Clouzot's LE CORBEAU (1943), Patrice Leconte's MON-SIEUR HIRE is set in a Parisian suburb in which conformity reigns supreme, and anyone who doesn't behave like everyone else is apt to be viewed suspiciously. Based on *Les Fiancailles de Monsieur Hire*, the Georges Simenon novel that also inspired Julien Duvivier's PANIQUE (1946), MONSIEUR HIRE is a penetrating psychological portrait of a warped, love-starved outsider who, by the film's end, arouses the audience's protective instincts. When a lovely young girl is murdered, a dogged police investigator (Wilms) immediately suspects Blanc, a loner distrusted and hated by his neighbors. Tormented by children who play vicious pranks and singled out for suspicion by his neighbors, Blanc is hounded mercilessly by the detective. Blanc resembles his tormenter in that he is an ever-vigilant soul, if in a less acceptable form — for the outcast is a voyeur who spies on Bonnaire, the country-fresh girl who has moved in across the way, when he is not toiling away joylessly at his tailor's shop. Watching Bonnaire — whose innocent look recalls that of the murdered girl — as she undresses or as she makes love to her handsome, ne'er-do-well boy friend (Thuillier), Blanc becomes infatuated with her. Eventually, she spots her secret admirer and, surprisingly, pays him a visit rather than reporting him to the police. An uninhibited free spirit, she is drawn to Blanc and allows him to share the simple pleasures of his life with her. Despite continual harassment from Wilms, Blanc even makes plans to move to Switzerland with Bonnaire — who, despite her apparent attraction to the rabbitlike Blanc, remains loyal to Thuillier, no matter how much he may take her for granted or what he may have done. It would destroy the film's suspenseful climax to reveal further plot developments, but the denouement provides a heart-rending exploration of duplicity and betrayal, with a particularly effective freeze-frame halting the action just before it flows into the twist ending.

Rather than jazz up the suspense through the conventional device of cross-cutting, director Leconte works within the frame to create a sense of inexorable doom. MONSIEUR HIRE doesn't move at a fast clip; instead, it involves the viewer in a downward spiral by making us covoyeurs with the title character, whose life has been a study in self-protective detachment. The audience is implicated in this point of view, eyeing Bonnaire hungrily through her window as Leconte's camera pulls back to an over-the-shoulder shot of Blanc doing the same. In another dazzling, sexually provocative sequence that puts the same motif to very different purposes, the film cuts from an over-the-shoulder shot of Bonnaire watching Thuillier as he enjoys a brutal boxing match to a shot of Blanc fondling her sensually — connecting Blanc and Bonnaire at last, and irrevocably.

Anchored by a haunting performance from Michel Blanc (Gerard Depardieu's diminutive lover in Bertrand Blier's MENAGE [1986]) as the Peeping Tom who throws years of self-control to the winds, MONSIEUR HIRE is a study of blindness on two levels: that of prejudice and that of love. As a result of this blindness, both the deceiver and the deceived become victims of fate in this icily compelling film. *(Violence, sexual situations, adult situations.)*

d, Patrice Leconte; p, Philippe Carcassonne and Rene Cleitman; w, Patrice Leconte and Patrick Dewolf (based on the novel *Les Fiancailles de Monsieur Hire* by Georges Simenon); ph, Denis Lenoir; ed, Joelle Hache; m, Michael Nyman

Thriller   **(PR:O   MPAA:NR)**

MONSTER HIGH

84m Catapult/Lightyear c

David Marriott *(Mr. Armageddon)*, Dean Iandoli *(Norm Median)*, Diana Frank *(Candice Cain)*, Kevin Dominguez *(Paul Smith)*, David Fuhrer *(Mel Anoma)*, D.J. Kerzner *(Orson "O.D." Davis)*, Robert M. Lind *(Dume)*, Sean Haines *(Glume)*, Troy Fromin *(Eggbert Hoser)*, Colin Reynolds *(Robert Gigo)*, Henry Young *(Coach Otto Parts)*, David Bloch *(Todd Uppington Smythe III)*, Bob Cady *(Jon Doe/Monster-in-Charge)*, Margy Stein *(Voice of Slisa Bealzeberg)*, Julie McPherson *(Beatrice Beldam)*, Susan Smeltzer *(Anna Thorpe)*, Denisa Willhite

(Camelia Carver), Kim Jones *(Mummy)*, Seth Weinstein *(Art, the Gargoyle)*, Chad Michaels *(Game Announcer)*, Mark Spear, Donald Hightower, Missy Rayl, Anne Whatu, David Lewis, Jeff Rubens, Andrew Husmann, Randall Frederick, Lori "Chacko" Davies, Paula Young, and Rhonda Grey

Set just a couple of blocks past "the farthest point in the universe," MONSTER HIGH begins in the office of Monster-in-Charge Syridium Damianus Hectophantasmigona, a faceless being with gangster mannerisms. Checking a list of planets scheduled for destruction, he finds Earth's demise has been mysteriously postponed. A video reveals that Mr. Armageddon, who had responsibility for the Earth project, was being punished for his incompetence when two "skinheads" from the planet Polyester nabbed him, believing him to be a secret weapon. Landing on Earth outside Montgomery-Sterling High School at night, the pair inadvertently release Armageddon (David Marriott), who turns out to be a foppish demon in a purple lame jacket — a combination of George Sanders, Shadoe Stevens, and Satan. The next day Armageddon works his evil mischief among the stereotypical high schoolers, suffocating the class stud inside a condom, merging a computer nerd with his PC, and chasing the skirt of French exchange student Candice Cain (Diana Frank). "He's not only ending the world, he's hitting on girls!" exclaims average teen Norm Median (Dean Iandoli), selected by Armageddon as the official prophet of doom. Soon night falls ("Clunk" goes the soundtrack), and, with time running out for planet Earth, Norm tries a desperate gambit: he challenges the forces of evil to a basketball game, to decide the fate of the planet in a sporting fashion. Armageddon accepts, and the "Game of the Millennium" begins. Representing the Earth are the high school's undefeated hoopsters, the Blue Demons, while the "visitors" comprise Armageddon, the skinheads, and assorted zombies and fiends. It's a close game, with the monsters maintaining a steady lead but being ejected one by one every time they kill and/or mutilate a Blue Demon. Finally, the game boils down to a one-on-one contest between Norm and Armageddon. As time runs out, the teen snatches the ball and takes a long shot that hovers on the rim for such an absurdly long time that it almost makes up for the bad jokes that have preceded it. At last it drops in. The Earth is safe; Norm gets another shot, this time with the lovely Candice; and the Monster-in-Charge obliterates Armageddon, concluding, "Never hire a relative!".

When MONSTER HIGH concentrates on parodying horror films, it delivers some inspired spoofing (one character sits bolt upright in bed again and again in a neat burlesque of the cheap it-was-only-a-nightmare motif). Regrettably, the bulk of the film isn't that focused. Instead, it is a vulgar hodgepodge that too often relies on dimwitted teen-comedy formulas, with the usual cast of jocks, slobs, potheads, and preppies, and a plethora of ethnic slurs. Director Rudiger Poe overloads the soundtrack with rap music, flashes bare breasts on the screen, and even quotes Dylan Thomas, and the result is indulgent goonery — none of which is very funny. Presented with one-dimensional characters, the actors are able to do little more than pose. So electronically modulated is Marriott's voice that one hardly comprehends his Mr. Armageddon; however, the other special effects are adequate, and often clever. The film's musical selections are also typically loopy, as you might guess from titles like "Monster High Theme Song" ("Heads are lopping/But we're all bopping") and "You're So Glam It Hurts." *(Graphic violence, profanity, nudity, sexual situations, substance abuse.)*

d, Rudiger Poe; p, Eric Bernt; w, Roy Langsdon and John Platt; ph, Eric Goldstein; ed, Warren Chadwick; m, Richard Lyons; prod d, Gigi Lorick; spec, Matthew Mungle, David Domeyer, Howard St. James, Bryan Goetz, and Special Effects Unlimited; cos, Robin Lewis

Comedy/Fantasy/Horror   **(PR:O   MPAA:R)**

MORGEN GRAUEN

(US/Aust.) (SEE: TIME TROOPERS)

MORNING TERROR

(US/Aust.) (SEE: TIME TROOPERS)

MOUNTAINS OF THE MOON

135m Carolco/Tri-Star c

Patrick Bergin *(Capt. Richard Francis Burton)*, Iain Glen *(Lt. John Hanning Speke)*, Richard E. Grant *(Laurence Oliphant)*, Fiona Shaw *(Isabel Arundell Burton)*, John Savident *(Lord Murchison)*, James Villiers *(Lord Oliphant)*, Adrian Rawlins *(Edward)*, Peter Vaughan *(Lord Houghton)*, Delroy Lindo *(Mabruki)*, Bernard Hill *(Dr. David Livingstone)*, Matthew Marsh *(William)*, Richard Caldicot *(Lord Russell)*, Christopher Fulford *(Herne)*, Garry Cooper *(Stroyan)*, Roshan Seth *(Ben Amir)*, Jimmy Gardner *(Jarvis)*, Doreen Mantle *(Mrs. Speke)*, Anna Massey *(Mrs. Arundell)*, Peter Eyre *(Norton Shaw)*, Leslie Phillips *(Mr. Arundell)*, Frances Cuka *(Lady Houghton)*, Roger Ashton-Griffiths *(Lord Cowley)*, Craig Crosbie *(Swinburne)*, Paul Onsongo *(Sidi Bombay)*,

Leonard Juma *(Jemadar)*, Bheki Tonto Ngema *(Ngola)*, Martin Okello *(Veldu)*, Philip Voss *(Col. Rigby)*, Pip Torrens *(Lt. Hesketh)*, Esther Njiru *(Lema)*, Alison Limerick *(Sorceress)*, Asiba Asiba *(Nubian Servant)*, Ian Vincent *(Lt. Allen)*, Ralph Nossek *(Doctor)*, Stewart Harwood *(Attendant)*, George Malpas *(Lead Actor)*, Robert Whelan, Bill Croasdale, Renny Krupinkski *(Reporters)*, Rod Woodruff *(Fencer)*, Fikile Mdleleni, Martin Ocham, Wilson Ng'Ong'A, Rocks Nhlapo, Patrick Letladi, Konga Mbandu, Michael Otieno *(Bearers)*, Fatima Said, Zam Zam Issa, Norta Muhammed, Pineniece Joshua *(Somali Girls)*, and Roger Rees *(Edgar Papworth)*

A long-cherished project for director Bob Rafelson, this fact-based adventure does not take as long to sit through as it took its central characters, 19th-century British adventurers Richard Burton and John Hanning Speke, to discover the source of the Nile. It only seems that way.

The Rafelson in the director's chair here is less the filmmaker justly famed for movies like FIVE EASY PIECES; THE KING OF MARVIN GARDENS; and BLACK WIDOW than he is the Rafelson who managed to make a dreary, snooze-inducing melodrama out of THE POSTMAN ALWAYS RINGS TWICE, with Jessica Lange as the lust-crazed, greasy-spoon waitress driven to murder after thrashing in the flour with Jack Nicholson. MOUNTAINS also cools off a hot-blooded character in Burton, who ran afoul of Victorian prudery with his graphic studies of sex practices around the world and such bedside classics as his translation of the Arabic erotic text *The Perfumed Garden*.

Unfortunately, that Burton barely exists in this film. The action starts in 1854 Kenya, with the first meeting between the refined dilettante Speke (Iain Glen) and Burton (Patrick Bergin), the earthy explorer and writer fluent in 23 languages and a dizzying array of scientific disciplines. On leave from the British Army, Speke (who the film obliquely suggests is a repressed homosexual attracted to Burton) joins one of Burton's expeditions in order to do some big-game hunting. The two become friends after a battle with restless natives, during which each gets a chance to save the other's life. Back home in England, Speke resumes his training to become a physician, while Burton courts — or, more accurately, is pursued by — the high-born Isabel Arundell (Fiona Shaw of MY LEFT FOOT, who has one marvelous moment here when Isabel secretly peruses *The Perfumed Garden* by candlelight, with a deliciously naughty gleam in her eye). There is eventually a lovemaking scene between Burton and Arundell that, like so much else in the film, is staged with more silly solemnity than heated abandon, but — unfortunately for the film and for Burton — Isabel gets left behind once the boys are off again, this time to find the Nile's source, under the auspices of the Royal Geographic Society. Back in Africa, the two face many trials. Speke gets a bug in his ear. Burton's legs swell up. The explorers also get captured by another group of natives, who hold Burton hostage and torture him while Speke is allowed to continue — eventually, it seems, stumbling onto the Nile's source at Lake Victoria. When he returns to England, Speke is turned against Burton by his backbiting publisher, who tells Speke that Burton intends to ridicule Speke's contributions in his own book about the expedition. Why Speke would accept this at face value without confronting Burton is never explained. But it sets the stage for the film's anticlimactic climax, a Royal Geographic Society debate in which Burton goes head-to-head with Speke over who really has the right scientific stuff.

Through all this, Rafelson and cowriter William Harrison, upon whose book about Burton and Speke the film is partly based, utterly fail to bring any sense of excitement to the quest, mainly because they fail to bring their central characters to life. There is undoubtedly a basic fidelity to facts — few writers outside of the Monty Python gang would *contrive* to present a bug crawling into somebody's ear as a crucial scene in an adventure drama. But Rafelson seems to have been unable to get beneath the surface to communicate whatever it was about this real-life story that excited him enough to bring it to the screen in the first place. For all its blood, sweat, and conflict, and despite a handsome, painstaking production filmed mostly on the locations where the events actually occurred, MOUNTAINS remains curiously uninvolving, seemingly endless, and not helped at all by the colorless casting of Bergin and Glen in the lead roles. Only Shaw manages to cut through the overwrought, Hemingway-esque machismo with which Rafelson has otherwise smothered what should have been a ripping good true-life adventure yarn. *(Violence, adult situations, nudity.)*

d, Bob Rafelson; p, Daniel Melnick; w, Bob Rafelson and William Harrison (based on his book and on original journals by Richard Burton and John Hanning Speke); ph, Roger Deakins; ed, Thom Noble; m, Michael Small; prod d, Norman Reynolds; art d, Maurice Fowler and Fred Hole; set d, Harry Cordwell; spec, David Harris; stunts, Alf Joint; cos, Jenny Beavan and John Bright; makup, Christine Beveridge; chor, Eleanor Fazan

Adventure/Historical   **(PR:C   MPAA:R)**

MURDER BY NUMBERS

91m Burnhill/Cobra — Magnum c

Sam Behrens *(Lee Bolger)*, Shari Belafonte *(Lisa)*, Ronee Blakley *(Faith)*, Stanley Kamel *(George)*, Jayne Meadows *(Pamela)*, Debra Sandlund *(Leslie)*, Dick Sargent *(Patrick Crain)*, Cleavon Little *(David Shelby)*, Robert Hosea *(Richard Parrish)*, Brian Bradley *(Marion)*, Alison Jane Frazer *(Anne)*, Richard Roat *(Jim Thomson)*, Christina Schulze *(Nurse)*, Bel Sandre *(Alice Griffin)*, James Anjelico *(Masseur)*, Mel Johnson Jr. *(Mayor's Assistant)*, Mark Atha *(Man at Bar)*, Wlad Cembrowicz *(Walter)*, and Thomas Ryan *(The Sergeant)*

MURDER BY NUMBERS is intriguing enough to make one weep at the missed opportunities and carelessness in the movie's execution. Exceedingly well acted, it is that rare mystery whose solution is almost impossible to guess. There are so many possible suspects that suspense fans will be trying to unravel the mystery right up to the last minute. When Walter (Wlad Cembrowicz), a wealthy homosexual, disappears, his sister, Leslie (Debra Sandlund), inveigles her former husband, Lee Bolger (Sam Behrens), a lawyer, into investigating the case. Why has realestate broker Patrick Crain (Dick Sargent), who discovered Walter's body in his bathtub, removed the corpse and hidden it? How does Walter's demise/vanishing act affect his weak-willed brother, George (Stanley Kamei), and his homophobic mother, Pamela (Jayne Meadows)? Are the apparent motives of Walter's heirs just a smokescreen for the plans of the actual murderer? In order to secure a desperately needed commission, Crain persuades Walter's lover, Richard (Robert Hosea), and his faithful assistant, Lisa (Shari Belafonte), to help him forge a transfer deed on a building. However, Crain doesn't reveal that Walter is dead, a small detail that would prohibit the transfer of the $30-million deed. Convinced that he was dying of AIDS and determined to prevent his family from contesting his will and cheating Richard out of the inheritance, Walter arranged his financial affairs to prohibit just such a transfer. When Walter's body is discovered, the police buy a suicide theory, but Bolger suspects that one of Walter's in-laws killed him. Working with David Shelby (Cleavon Little), an ex-con with a talent for breaking and entering, Bolger finds his way through a labyrinth of cross-purposes and hidden motives, surviving a few blows on the head from Crain in the process. But most of Bolger's theories are blown out of the water when Richard turns up dead and the police declare his death a suicide. Questioning the doctor who treated her late brother, Leslie learns that Walter did not have AIDS. Then why did he kill himself? If greed was the murder motive, which one of his intimates bumped Walter off? Using a hidden tape recorder, Bolger is able to trick a confession out of the killer, though it isn't quite as easy as it sounds.

Managing skillfully to camouflage the killer's identity, MURDER BY NUMBERS glides smoothly along, full of irony. It excels in delineating colorful characters who exhibit human frailty and idiosyncratic behavior. In the lead role, Behrens is most convincing as the amateur detective who's hung up on his ex-wife; Little exudes silken confidence as the cynical ex-con; Kamel brings layers of meaning to his portrayal of the sexually confused sibling; and Meadows is icily brilliant in her few scenes as the domineering matron. The smallest parts are cast to perfection.

Why, then, does this movie, which is so full of surprises, fail to satisfy? Why does this sleek suspenser featuring Belafonte's best screen work to date fall short of the mark? Certainly one answer is writer-director Paul Leder's failure to introduce key bits of information at the most effective moments and thereby to provide a maximum of suspense. Rather than falling neatly into place, the movie works in fits and starts. An out-of-control quality permeates MURDER BY NUMBERS, as if the film's creators had lost a grip on their story. Continuity problems abound, and the editing is slipshod. When the film cuts to a scene in which the principal characters are suddenly in different outfits, disoriented viewers may have the impression that they are witnessing a flashback. Haven't the makers of this film ever heard of using dissolves to link scenes? It is this kind of sloppiness that drags a potentially first-rate suspense film down to the level of a moderately enjoyable made-for-TV mystery. With more fluid scene transitions and keener direction, this crisply acted, always-keeps-you-guessing whodunit might even have been a classic. Still, if you lower your expectations a bit, there's plenty of entertainment to be found in this nifty suspense film. *(Violence, sexual situations, profanity.)*

d, Paul Leder; p, Ralph Tornberg and Paul Leder; w, Paul Leder; ph, Francis Grumman; ed, Paul Leder; m, Bob Summers; set d, Robert Holcombe; cos, Ewa Zbroniec; makup, Carol Collini

Mystery   **(PR:C   MPAA:PG-13)**

MY BLUE HEAVEN

97m Hawn-Sylbert/WB c

Steve Martin (*Vinnie Antonelli*), Rick Moranis (*Barney Coopersmith*), Joan Cusack (*Hannah Stubbs*), Melanie Mayron (*Crystal Rybak*), Carol Kane (*Shaldeen*), Bill Irwin (*Kirby*), William Hickey (*Billy Sparrow*), and Daniel Stern

As we zoom in on this so-perfect-it-must-be-a-set vision of suburbia, we see an unlikely new neighbor: gangster Vincent Antonelli (Steve Martin). Vinnie, with his spiky black hair, shiny suits and New York accent, is not here by choice; he's a mob informant who's been plunked down in this land of barbecue grills and picket fences as part of the government's witness relocation program. FBI agent Barney Coopersmith (Rick Moranis) is in charge of Vinnie, and must ensure that the gangster stays out of trouble until he can testify at two important mob trials in New York. But Vinnie still can't resist swiping the occasional car or ripping off a supermarket here and there, which brings him to the attention of District Attorney Hannah Stubbs (Joan Cusack). Hannah refuses to be won over by the charming though conniving Vinnie and is even less amused when Barney informs her that as a government-protected witness Vinnie cannot be prosecuted for his crimes. To further complicate matters, Vinnie has also encountered a number of his old Mafia pals, all of whom are apparently living in the same suburb under assumed names. Naturally, this gang plans a new crime spree. But thanks to his quick thinking and cunning, Vinnie outwits both Stubbs and the gunmen who are after him, and by the time the film ends he's a local hero, with a Little League stadium named after him, and a couple of wives and girl friends to boot.

For a film with as many missed plot opportunities as this one, MY BLUE HEAVEN is actually fairly amusing. The notion of a gangster adjusting to anonymity in suburbia is funny, but the film pays scant attention to this idea; instead, MY BLUE HEAVEN is really about Vinnie and Barney and their differing ideas of law and order. Still, the film manages to work about two-thirds of the time, largely due to the efforts of the cast. Moranis is well-suited to his role as the repressed Barney, and Cusack, like a high-school teacher from hell, with her pulled-back hair and stern, unflinching demeanor is wonderful as Hannah. (She's also one of the few actresses whose look can change from goofy to striking within a single film.) As Moranis' partner, performance artist Bill Irwin gets to show off his unique dance style; however, Carol Kane is wasted, given only about five lines as a woman Vinnie picks up in a supermarket and marries a few scenes later. As for Martin, he may not be the most likely actor for the part of Vinnie, but his exaggerated mannerisms aren't that out of place in a film that's basically an extended sketch. Although the script seems to lose track of the story in the second half of the film, when the plot is stretched a little thin, for the most part, this is an amiable comedy with some unexpected laughs. (*Violence, profanity.*)

d, Herbert Ross; p, Herbert Ross and Anthea Sylbert; w, Nora Ephron; ph, John Bailey; ed, Stephen A. Rotter; m, Ira Newborn; prod d, Charles Rosen; art d, Richard Berger; set d, Jim Bayliss, Robert Maddy, and Nick Navarro; cos, Joseph G. Aulisi; chor, Lynne Taylor-Corbett

Comedy/Crime   (PR:C   MPAA:PG-13)

MY 20TH CENTURY

(Hung./Can.) 104m Friedlander — Mafilm — ICAIC/Aries bw

Dorotha Segda (*Dora/Lili/Mother*), Oleg Jankowski (*Z*), Peter Andorai (*Thomas Alva Edison*), Gabor Mathe (*X*), Paulus Manker (*Weininger*), Gyula Kery, Andrei Schwartz, Sandor Tery, Sandor Czvetko, Endre Koronszi, Agnes Kovacs, and Eszter Kovacs

Filmed in shimmering black and white that suggests a fairy tale, this film is so breathtakingly lovely to look at it makes one mourn the fact that black-and-white cinematography has fallen into disfavor. This is a dazzling celebration of feminism, mechanical progress, unbreakable familial ties, and the early history of the 20th century. Despite some occasionally slack pacing, it is a magical achievement that creates its own universe.

Taking the form of a fable, the film outlines a world of unlimited possibilities. In Hungary in 1880, identical twin girls are separated while selling matches. The different paths of the girls, Lili and Dora (both played by Dorotha Segda) are then followed over many years before they serendipitously cross once more. Aglow with revolutionary fervor, Lili has become a radical determined to free the masses and willing to employ a bomb to get her point across. Accustomed to trading her favors to support her lifestyle, Dora leans toward the pleasures of the flesh. To his total confusion, a man known as Z (Oleg Jankowski) meets both women while traveling on the Orient Express, believing them to be one fascinating creature. Intercut with this dual romance are depictions of technological breakthroughs of the time, including the tale of a laboratory dog who outsmarts his scientist keepers, and commentary by Thomas Alva Edison (Peter Andorai). Somehow the fanciful comedy of errors which forms the film's basic plotline

seems to be a logical extension of the progress-driven world in the early 1900s; the characters exist in a shining new world where anything can happen. Since creativity charges the air, the ingenuity of the characters in getting themselves out of scrapes seems only natural. At the film's climax, Lili (en route to eliminate the minister of the interior) encounters her long-lost sister in a hall of mirrors where the women are held rapt by their endless reflections. Abandoning her revolutionary goals, Lili links up with Dora, who casts off her need to be protected by men. Freed of their dependencies, both women dump Z. Blending an intellectual political bent with a sexual nature, the women combine their best qualities and find they are now free to be themselves.

In his directorial debut, Ildiko Enyedi dexterously unfolds a fanciful tale layered with whimsical and historical segments that touch tangentially on the main storyline. Never tied to a linear structure, it is full of delightful asides, such as the story of the monkey whose naivete about human beings lands him in captivity. In this enchanting fairy tale, the narrative doesn't proceed as expected, but all the side roads link up with Enyedi's destination. The best way to enjoy MY 20TH CENTURY is to approach it as a fantastic cavalcade in which human truths are revealed by accident. Despite the fact that the characters wander through a technological wonderland, the most magical proposition of the film lies not in inventiveness but in the capacity of the spirit to reinvent itself. At the end of the fairy tale the little match girls find a happy ending for themselves, rather than waiting around for a man to impose his idea of a happy ending on them. Watching the film is a liberating experience and a joyful occasion for movie lovers in search of a fresh filmmaking visionary. (*Sexual situation, nudity.*)

d, Ildiko Enyedi; w, Ildiko Enyedi; ph, Tibor Mathe; ed, Maria Rigo; m, Laszlo Vidovszky; prod d, Zoltan Labas; cos, Agnes Gyarmathy

Comedy/Drama

MY UNCLE'S LEGACY

(Yugo.) 107m Urania — Avala — Stassen c

(ZIVOT SA STRICEM)

Alma Prica and Davor Janic

It would seem, from the recent Yugoslavian productions that have received any form of international attention, that a major interest of the Yugoslavian people today is the 1950s, a period of political confusion during which Tito's isolationist policies had some very strong effects on personal lives. The filmmakers who grew up during this period have now had the chance to put their experiences on film and are doing just that, making entertaining and thoughtful films in a country primarily known for animation. Like Emir Kusturica's award-winning DO YOU REMEMBER DOLLY BELL? and WHEN FATHER WAS AWAY ON BUSINESS and like Jovan Actin's HEY BABU RIBA, Krsto Papic's MY UNCLE'S LEGACY concentrates on young people and the effect the political climate of the 1950s had on their lives. As the film opens, an old man (the actor is very badly made up), dressed only in pajamas and robe, walks through the busy section of a city. This is Uncle Stephan, who has disconnected his life-support system at the hospital and left his bed to ask forgiveness from his nephew, Martin. As Martin himself ponders events that have had a profound effect upon his life, the narrative lapses 36 years into the past. The year is 1952; Martin is a student at a state school and Uncle Stephan an important party dignitary and prime advocate of a collectivist policy of shared wealth and the abolishment of individual enterprise. Martin's grandfather, who raised him after his father died on a small farm in the North, thinks the new policies ridiculous and refuses to join the commune his son has formed. With these two men's conflicting influences, an indication of the dilemma that exists for Martin is established immediately, and brought into the public arena at school, where he is one of the brightest students and a devoted member of the Party's youth faction. However, Martin also likes to draw satiric caricatures, which he then displays on the school walls. This gets him into trouble when two of his prime targets, an attractive but dumb blonde and an ignorant oaf who are also youth party leaders, join forces with a teacher — a slimy sort who has been sleeping with the blonde and is interested in advancing himself politically — to make life miserable for Martin. Their first efforts fail after Uncle Stephan intervenes to reveal the ridiculousness of the charges they bring against his nephew. But when Martin writes his uncle a letter telling him that there are elements at the school who are destructive to Party ideals and not worthy of the positions they occupy, Stephan in turn writes to the local police inspector, telling him he feels Martin has shown signs of a growing independence and needs to be taught a lesson. The inspector brings Martin in for questioning and has him spend a night in jail. No real harm is done to Martin until the inspector shows the uncle's letter, in confidence, to the teacher, who uses this to have Martin expelled from both the Party and the school. In a humiliating inquiry, the letter is read in front of the entire school, Martin's head is shaved, and he is tarred and feathered. In the excitement, the oaf takes out a shotgun and fires at Martin as he leaves the school. A bullet ricochets off a rock and strikes Martin in the genitals. Martin is castrated, and this is his uncle's "legacy." Back in the present, the mature Martin, now a successful writer and social critic, indicates that it is the memories of this time—when he was in love with a girl at the school who fled to Italy after witnessing his humiliation, never to return to Yugoslavia—that has kept him going and provided the motivation for all his writings.

Notwithstanding its concentration upon political issues, MY UNCLE'S LEGACY is also filled with lively and likable (as well as not-so-likable) characters, whose personalities are woven together realistically and entertainingly. It is the people who become important and not the politics—itself a political statement. Harm is done only through blind allegiance to empty, symbolic slogans that hide other ills, and by opportunists who use them to protect and further their own self-interests. In this respect, the film is a powerful critique of the Yugoslavian political system of the 1950s. MY UNCLE'S LEGACY was a multiple winner at the Pula Festival of Yugoslavian Films and earned Davor Janic the Best Actor award at the Montreal Film Festival. (In Yugoslavian; English subtitles.) *(Sexual situations, profanity, brief nudity.)*

d, Krsto Papic; w, Krsto Papic

Historical   (PR:C   MPAA:NR)

N

NARROW MARGIN

97m Carolco—Jonathan A. Zimbert/Tri-Star c

Gene Hackman *(Robert Caulfield)*, Anne Archer *(Carol Hunnicut)*, James B. Sikking *(Nelson)*, J.T. Walsh *(Michael Tarlow)*, M. Emmet Walsh *(Sgt. Dominick Benti)*, Susan Hogan *(Kathryn Weller)*, Nigel Bennett *(Jack Wootton)*, J.A. Preston *(Martin Larner)*, B.A. "Smitty" Smith *(Keller)*, Codie Lucas Wilbee *(Nicholas)*, Barbara E. Russell *(Nicholas' Mother)*, Antony Holland *(Elderly Man)*, Doreen Ramos *(Elderly Woman)*, Kevin McNulty *(James Dahlbeck)*, Andrew Rhodes *(Nigro)*, Lon Katzman *(Loughlin)*, Dana Still *(Bellman with Message)*, Lesley Ewen *(Larner's Secretary)*, Barney O'Sullivan *(Ticket Agent)*, Natino Bellantoni *(Bartender)*, Ted Stidder, Tom McBeath *(Conductors)*, Lindsay Bourne *(Club Car Waiter)*, Robert Rozen *(Dining Car Waiter)*, Ron Cummins *(Hotel Valet)*, and Harris Yulin *(Leo Watts)*

As long as actors like Gene Hackman can haul themselves around atop moving trains without looking silly, there will probably always be meat-and-potatoes thrillers like this one for them to star in. Hackman's record has been spotty of late—from the overrated THE PACKAGE to underrated efforts like BAT 21—but as commercial thrillers go, those in which he has starred have more decency, class, and civility than most. NARROW MARGIN, Hackman's most recent genre effort, provides solid entertainment, offering a leaner plot and more engaging characters than THE PACKAGE, over which it is a notable improvement. Mostly, NARROW MARGIN has an old-fashioned feel for cliff-hanging adventure.

Hackman stars as Los Angles Deputy District Attorney Robert Caulfield, who would like nothing more than to put white-collar gangster Leo Watts (the dependably slimy Harris Yulin) away for a long, long time. But Caulfield is convinced that his past efforts have been sabotaged by his boss, Martin Larner (J.A. Preston). Determined to have nothing go wrong this time, Caulfield himself takes charge of bringing in an eyewitness to a recent murder committed by Watts. The witness, Carol Hunnicut (Anne Archer), was on a blind date with the victim (J.T. Walsh) when he was killed. Although she saw the whole thing, neither Watts nor his hitman-partner saw Hunnicut, who was hiding in another room of the victim's hotel suite. Forgoing a call to 911, Hunnicut instead wisely scrams out of LA, planning to hide out in her brother's cabin, deep in the Canadian wilderness, until things cool down. With the help of police Sgt. Dominick Benti (M. Emmet Walsh), however, Caulfield has tracked Hunnicut down and hops a helicopter to the remote cabin to convince her to come back and testify against Watts. Unfortunately, the bad guys have also tracked her down and shoot the cabin to bits, leaving Caulfield and Hunnicut unscathed but costing Benti his life. Nelson (James B. Sikking), the dapper hired killer who has come in search of Hunnicut, also grounds the helicopter that brought Caulfield, leaving Hunnicut's jeep-wagon the only means of escape. After a decent chase scene, Hunnicut and Caulfield manage to board a train, followed by Nelson. A game of cat-and-mouse ensues aboard the train, with Nelson trying to catch Hunnicut, whom he still has not seen, by sticking close to Caulfield. Nelson even offers Caulfield a bribe to turn the witness over to him but meets with the expected results (hasn't this guy ever seen THE FRENCH CONNECTION?). Not surprisingly, there are a few more twists and turns as the train winds its way to the end of NARROW MARGIN's perilous journey. Not only must Caulfield evade Nelson and keep Hunnicut hidden, but he also has to contend with an attractive divorcee (Susan Hogan) and ferret out the traitor in the DA's office who's tipping Watts to Caulfield's movements. Just for the heck of it, the crackerjack finale takes place on top of the train with the principal actors trying hard not to look terrified.

To his credit, writer-cinematographer-director Peter Hyams (RUNNING SCARED) doesn't pretend he's reinventing the wheel here, as director Andy Davis seemed to be doing with THE PACKAGE. Hyams just sees to it that all the pieces are in place and that there aren't too many opportunities for the premise to trip over its own implausibilities, of which there are more than a few. In short, NARROW MARGIN is no lightning bolt of cinematic genius, but it wasn't meant to be one. It's more the kind of movie a viewer slips into like a hot bath, escaping the cares of the world for a couple of hours, leaving it feeling relaxed and refreshed. In this respect, NARROW MARGIN succeeds, due largely to the sure hands and cool heads in front of and behind the cameras. The banter, bickering, and verbal byplay in Hyams' script are less than inspired, but they do the job. The actors also do their jobs, and the Canadian wilderness has rarely looked better. With a relatively low body count, a shortage of gore, and not even a single acrobatic sex scene, NARROW MARGIN relies on old-fashioned movie virtues, which makes sense since it's a remake of a 1952 film of the same name. *(Violence.)*

d, Peter Hyams; p, Jonathan A. Zimbert; w, Peter Hyams (based on the screenplay by Earl Fenton, from a story by Martin Goldsmith, Jack Leonard);

ph, Peter Hyams; ed, James Mitchell; m, Bruce Broughton; prod d, Joel Schiller; art d, David Willson, Kim Mooney, and Eric Orbom; set d, Kim MacKenzie; spec, Stan Parks; stunts, Glenn Wilder; cos, Ellen Mirojnick; makup, Margaret Solomon and Pat Gerhardt

Thriller   (PR:C   MPAA:R)

NASTY GIRL, THE

(W. Ger.) 93m Sentana/Miramax c

Lena Stolze *(Sonja)*, Monika Baumgartner *(Maria)*, Michael Garr *(Paul Rosenberger)*, Fred Stillkrauth *(Uncle)*, Elisabeth Bertram *(Grandmother)*, Robert Giggenbach *(Martin)*, Michael Guillaume *(Robert)*, Karin Thaler *(Nina)*, Hans-Reinhard Muller *(Dr. Juckenack)*, Barbara Gallauner *(Miss Juckenack)*, Willi Schultes *(Father Brummel)*, Richard Susmeier *(Burgomaster)*, Udo Thmer *(Schulz)*, Ludwig Wuhr *(Mergenthaler)*, Herbert Lehnert *(Dr. Fasching)*, Irmgard Henning-Beyrhammer *(Mrs. Stangl)*, Ossi Eckmuller *(Retired Man)*, and Hermann Hummel *(Roeder)*

From Germany comes THE NASTY GIRL, a parodistic account of the uproar caused when a precocious female student, Sonja (Lena Stolze), enters a writing competition. That in itself is not the cause of the commotion; rather, it is her chosen topic, which is the extent to which her supposedly benignly innocent hometown collaborated with the Nazis. In the course of her research, she encounters an escalating, impenetrable front of evasion, lies, bureaucratic impediments, and even personal danger.

The subject is, of course, endlessly fascinating: one of the century's great "enigmas." Unfortunately, the film's conception is too lightweight to be really involving. It's the reverse of Stanley Kramer's weighty JUDGEMENT AT NUREMBERG and errs likewise in its equally extreme, if more whimsical, handling. It captures the attention, but only fitfully, inspiring mild interest in the midst of all the scripted and directorial distractions, rather than the emphatic involvement of the great detective story it could have been. The biographical sections which focus on the heroine play too glibly, like rapid-fire vaudeville or sitcom sketches, telling little about her while remaining extraneous to the main theme. We see her school days and early sexual experimentation and, through it all, she remains a rather unappealing, perky smart-ass. Sonja comes on with teeth-chattering shrillness, dons Heidi costumes for not-too-subtle ironic effect, is relentlessly self-righteous and seems devoid of the intellectual conviction that would keep her so resolutely on her course. A bomb explodes in her own home, but the Brechtian staging of the scene (which holds true for the entire film), combined with Stolze's off-putting performance, has the viewer watching dispassionately and unmoved. The film might have worked better with, say, the beneficently orb-like Marianne Sagebrecht (BAGHDAD CAFE) working her comic yet always intelligent wiles in the role.

With all the theatrical use of rear-projected, gigantic photographic blowups of settings, director Michael Verhoeven's effort is certainly stylish. But the overload of flourishes becomes oppressive, so many effects merely cancel one another out and the result is alienating and too precious by far. The only really striking conceit brought off by Verhoeven is of Sonja's family being interviewed sitting in a mockup of their living room on a truck which wheels through city streets to the *cinema verite* astonishment of the townspeople they glide by.

With the exception of the funny, feisty grandmother (Elisabeth Bertram), easily the most sensible person in the film, the other characters are complacent stereotypes. The men are mostly thick-headed chauvinists, although Robert Giggenbach as Sonja's husband is a feminist-fantasy nurturing teddy bear. There is, naturally, a surfeit of hostile, red-faced, beady-eyed, beer-guzzling villagers who seem culled from a Hollywood WW II propaganda film. Verhoeven is undeniably unsparing of his own people, but that is about the best that can be said about this too clever film. *(Nudity, adult situations, sexual situations.)*

d, Michael Verhoeven; p, Michael Verhoeven and Michael Senftleben; w, Michael Verhoeven; ph, Axel DeRoche; ed, Barbara Hennings; m, Mike Hertung and Elmar Schloter; prod d, Hubert Popp; cos, Ute Truthmann; makup, Helga Sander and Cordula Aspock

Drama   (PR:O   MPAA:PG-13)

NAVY SEALS

104m Brenda Feigen/Orion c

Charlie Sheen *(Lt. Dale Hawkins)*, Michael Biehn *(Lt. James Curran)*, Joanne Whalley-Kilmer *(Claire Verens)*, Rick Rossovich *(Leary)*, Cyril O'Reilly *(Rexer)*, Bill Paxton *(Dane)*, Dennis Haysbert *(Graham)*, Paul Sanchez *(Ramos)*, Nicholas Kadi *(Ben Shaheed)*, Ron Joseph *(Capt. Dunne)*, S. Epatha Merkerson *(Jolena)*, Greg McKinney, Rob Moran *(US Helicopter Pilots)*, Richard Venture *(Adm. Colker)*, Mark Carlton *(Jim Elmore)*, Ira Wheeler *(Warren Stinson)*, Ron Faber *(Gen. Mateen)*, Bill Cort *(Elliott West)*, Randy Hall *(Navy Seal No. 8)*, Duncan Smith *(EOD Officer)*, William Knight *(Submarine Captain)*, Nehme

Fadlallah *(Ali)*, Marc Zuber *(Villa Hostage)*, Vic Tablian *(Terrorist)*, Adam Hussein *(Latanya Captain)*, George Jackos *(Druze Fighter)*, Ian Tyler *(Shepherd)*, Michael Halphie, Ezra Abraham *(Israeli Intelligence)*, John Pruitt *(Local TV Announcer)*, Tom Sean Foley *(Crewman C130)*, William Roberts, Michael Fitzpatrick *(Aircraft Carrier Officers)*, Cathryn De Prume *(Bartender)*, and Titus Welliver *(Redneck in Bar)*

Charlie Sheen and Michael Biehn star in this visually engaging, fast-paced action film about an elite anti-terrorist unit of the US Navy. Unfortunately, an uneven script and undeveloped characters weaken the dramatic content of the story. The film opens at the wedding of one of the Seals, but just as Dane (Bill Paxton) is about to walk down the aisle, he and his aquatic comrades are called to duty. The team is sent to the Middle East to rescue hostages from a ship. The mission is successful, but during the Seals' retreat, Hawkins (Sheen) discovers some stolen weapons and wants to remain behind to destroy the "Stingers" (hand-launched missiles). However, the team's leader, Curran (Biehn), orders a quick escape. Within days, the Seals are sent to Syria, where the Stingers are now believed to be on a merchant ship. Despite a skillful surprise attack, the Seals find no Stingers aboard the ship. Enter journalist and would-be love interest Claire (Joanne Whalley-Kilmer), a half-Lebanese woman who is believed to have Middle Eastern military contacts. Curran's attempts to use his good looks and charm to gain information from Claire fail, but after the terrorists start using civilian airplanes for target practice, the stubborn journalist is more willing to talk. In Cyprus, the Seals kidnap an FBI informant, but lose Dane in the process. Eventually, the informant reveals the location of the much-sought-after Stingers, and in short order, our aquatic heroes find themselves in Beirut. In the climactic final scene, two more Seals die and Curran is wounded, but the Stingers are finally destroyed.

Lewis Teague has directed an often suspenseful and visually arresting film. Obviously, much time and attention have been given to the look of the picture, which was shot by gifted cinematographer John A. Alonzo. However, despite the great set design by Guy J. Comtois and Veronica Hadfield and strong aerial photography and special effects, the film lacks dramatic consistency and impact. We never really get to know any of the main characters or why they're Navy Seals. Tellingly, even the relationship between Curran and Claire is not adequately developed. It is also difficult to understand why so much time is spent lamenting Dane's death when two more Seals die in the last scene and hardly an eye is blinked. This failure to explore the motivations of the characters, coupled with only competent performances, serves to undermine many potentially dramatic scenes. Given the filmmakers' apparent lack of interest in their main characters, it comes as no surprise that the film's Middle Easterners are faceless and completely expendable, making easier the macho glorification of violence found throughout the movie. Add an upbeat musical score by Sylvester Levay to this less-than-involving mix and you have what amounts to a less-than-involving two-hour commercial for the Navy. *(Excessive violence, profanity, alcohol abuse.)*

d, Lewis Teague; p, Brenda Feigen and Bernard Williams; w, Chuck Pfarrer and Gary Goldman; ph, John A. Alonzo; ed, Don Zimmerman; m, Sylvester Levay; md, Michael Dilbeck; prod d, Guy J. Comtois and Veronica Hadfield; art d, Ed Williams and Vaughn Edwards; set d, Malcolm Stone and Debra Schutt; spec, John Stears and Matthew Mungle; stunts, Bud Davis; cos, Brad Loman; makup, Lynne Eagan; tech, Chuck Pfarrer, Christopher Lindsay, Steve Fraser, Duncan Smith, Tom Harbrecht, Mark Steffanich, Dan Jessee, Keith Woulard, and Frank Leslie

Action   (PR:C   MPAA:R)

NEVER CRY DEVIL

(SEE: NIGHT VISITOR)

NIGHT ANGEL

90m Paragon Arts c

Isa Andersen *(Lilith)*, Karen Black *(Rita)*, Linden Ashby *(Craig)*, Debra Feuer *(Kirstie)*, Helen Martin *(Sadie)*, Doug Jones *(Ken)*, Gary Hudson *(Rod)*, Sam Hennings *(Mr. Crenshaw)*, Tedra Gabriel *(Mrs. Crenshaw)*, Ben Ganger *(Tommy Crenshaw)*, Twink Caplan *(Jenny)*, and Celia Xavier *(Koko)*

Not more than a month separated the release of two 1990 films dealing with the Lilith legend of Jewish folklore—Troma's DEF BY TEMPTATION and this film, NIGHT ANGEL. Although traditionally portrayed as the murderous, demonic incarnation of pure lust, Lilith is a deadly bore this time around. As NIGHT ANGEL opens, Lilith (Isa Andersen) slithers out of a grave while an off screen voice explains that the demon has plagued mankind since the dawn of history. The scene shifts suddenly to the offices of *Siren* magazine, where employees are working feverishly to finish an overdue cover design. Craig (Linden Ashby), the art director, is feeling a bit ragged because of the strange

dreams he's been having in which a woman slithers out of a grave at night (get it?). Hoping that widespread exposure to her image will plunge the world into chaos, Lilith makes several attempts to get on the cover of *Siren*. First, she dates the owner of the magazine (Sam Hennings), but when he balks at making her a cover girl, Lilith suddenly appears in his bedroom to seduce and slaughter him, slicing up his wife and son for kicks. After a mourning period of about 30 seconds, the *Siren* gang proceeds with plans for a big party to impress a client. In the process, Craig falls in love with Kirstie (Debra Feuer), sister of Rita (Karen Black), who has just inherited the magazine. Lilith makes a grand entrance at the party, demonstrates her sensuality by licking the foam off the neck of a beer bottle, then jumps to the nearest pole for a writhing, pelvis-thrusting dance number. As you might guess, she makes a big impression on all the men in the crowd, particularly on Rod (Gary Hudson), an editor, and Ken (Doug Jones), the perpetually horny office boy. Rod steals Lilith from Ken and takes her home to his swinging bachelor pad; however, she puts a damper on his plans by shoving him down an elevator shaft to be impaled on a giant spring. Ken, who followed them to Rod's place, is so upset by this gruesome scene that he pounds on the glass security door, shattering it and apparently losing an arm in the process (though the arm reappears in his next scene). When Lilith shifts her attentions to the new owner of *Siren*, she has more luck; in no time Rita announces that Lilith will be on the cover of the upcoming issue. This upsets Craig, who is vexed because Lilith has no resume. She responds to this criticism by attempting to cause a heavy light to drop on his head. Nearly done in by this "accident," Craig rushes off for a date with Kirstie, pausing only to brush off the strange old lady (Helen Martin) who has been trying to warn him that his life is in danger. While romping in the sack with Kirstie, Craig hallucinates that she is actually Lilith. A jewelry designer by trade, Kirstie gives Craig an amulet containing a stone that she claims has spiritual powers. Back at the *Siren* offices, the staff has been engaging in a nonstop orgy since taking a gander at Lilith's cover spread. Meanwhile, Kirstie calls Craig and asks him to pick her up at a neighborhood bar. When Craig enters the bar, it is suddenly transformed into a little corner of hell, with a dozen or so grotesque scenes of torment and degradation on view. Lilith appears and comes close to plucking out Craig's heart but is thwarted by his amethyst amulet, whereupon the bar suddenly returns to normal and Kirstie drags Craig home. Kirstie, it seems, has become buddies with Sadie, the crazy old lady who has been trying to warn Craig and who happens to be a witch doctor with a longstanding grudge against Lilith. Brandishing a foot-long knife, Sadie explains that the only way to kill Lilith is by piercing her heart. Setting out to do just that, Sadie, Craig, and Kirstie proceed directly to the *Siren* offices for a little slow-motion violence. Ken, who by this point has been transformed into one of Lilith's minions, hits Craig with a baseball bat, then drives off to the graveyard with Kirstie in tow, prepared to offer her to Lilith. But, shoving a tire iron through the cast on Ken's leg, Kirstie escapes and is later joined by Craig and Sadie. Lilith shows her displeasure with Ken by ripping his heart out, a procedure he seems to enjoy. During the confused scrambling that follows in the graveyard, Sadie appears to have a heart attack, and Craig again comes near to having his heart plucked out by Lilith, who has reverted to her disgusting demonic form. At the last moment, Sadie comes to the rescue, skewering Lilith who dies, wings spread, in a spectacular explosion of meaty demon bits. In the obligatory capper scene, Craig is in bed with Kirstie when the *Siren* cover photo suddenly seems to come to life, almost causing him to choke himself to death with his own hands. At the last minute, he wakes up and finds that it was only a nightmare...or was it?

Despite plenty of grotesque sex and violence, NIGHT ANGEL is a remarkably tedious film, with an unengaging plot that unfolds at a sluggish pace. Its characters are bland, and its action is cliched and confusing. The only remarkable thing about this tepid horror film is Lilith's preferred method of dispatching her victims; she uses "killer" fingernails to slash throats and to administer direct heart massage. NIGHT ANGEL's biggest disappointment is its complete waste of exploitation stalwart Black in a dull, colorless role. Nevertheless, the film does feature some fairly impressive effects by Steve Johnson, including a slimy, rubber-suited monster vaguely reminiscent of Paul Blaisdell's title beast in SHE CREATURE (1956). *(Excessive violence, nudity, sexual situations.)*

d, Dominique Othenin-Girard; p, Joe Augustyn and Jeff Geoffray; w, Joe Augustyn and Walter Josten; ph, David Lewis; ed, Jerry Brady; m, Cory Lerios; prod d, Ken Aichele; spec, Steve Johnson, XFX Group, and K.N.B. EFX Group; stunts, Shane Dixon; cos, Renee Johnston; makup, Teresa Austin; chor, Joanne DeVito

Horror   (PR:O   MPAA:R)

NIGHT EYES

98m Amritraj—Baldwin/Paramount—Prism c

(AKA: HIDDEN VISION)

Andrew Stevens *(Will Griffith)*, Tanya Roberts *(Nikki Walker)*, Warwick Sims *(Brian Walker)*, Cooper Huckabee *(Ernie Griffith)*, Karen Elise Baldwin *(Ellen)*, Veronica Henson-Phillips *(Lauretta)*, Paul Carr *(Michaelson)*, Stephen Burks *(Tom Clemmons)*, Yvette Buchanan *("Baby Doll")*, Chick Vennera *(Adam Shapiro)*, Stephen Meadows *(Michael Vincent)*, Robb Weller *(Reporter)*, Barbara Ann Klein, James Cohen, Dena Drotar, Larry Poindexter, Dana Dellinger, and Kevin Hynes

A well-acted erotic thriller, NIGHT EYES almost succeeds but gives away the game too early, making it fairly easy to tell who's setting up whom. Andrew Stevens, the hardest-working man in direct-to-video show business, helped write the script and portrays Will Griffith, the co-owner of a Los Angeles security agency. Griffith is hired to monitor the house of glamorous Nikki Walker (Tanya Roberts), who is going through a messy divorce with her rock star husband, Brian (Warwick Sims). After rigging up security cameras and high-tech alarms, Griffith learns that his job isn't to protect Nikki but rather to videotape the beautiful woman with her lovers. Brian and his lawyer plan to use the footage in divorce court to obtain a favorable settlement. Griffith takes a liking to the vulnerable beauty, however, and when the security cameras catch her having kinky sex with an actor friend, Griffith conceals the tape. Griffith's attraction to Nikki grows, and, sensing this, the jealous Brian clashes with the pair in public. Later, an intruder resembling Brian attacks Nikki in the house. Griffith chases off the intruder, and the security guard's attempts to comfort Nikki result in their making love. Nikki entices Griffith into joining her for regular sessions of sado-masochistic sex, until one night a frantic Brian breaks in brandishing a gun. Griffith shoots him, but the subsequent murder investigation reveals that Brian had been summoned to the house by a phone caller who claimed that Nikki was in danger. What's more, not only is Nikki reluctant to defend Griffith, but also the rough bedroom antics between her and Griffith were recorded by the security cameras; on the tape Griffith appears to be raping her. At this point, it's clear to Griffith and the viewer that he's been framed, but the story plods along until Nikki's accomplice is unmasked.

Within its limited horizons, NIGHT EYES does an admirable job of conjuring a moody, devious atmosphere (far superior to director Jag Mundhra's earlier effort, the slasher film OPEN HOUSE). Stevens manages to come across as likable and intelligent, even as he's obviously being played for a chump. Roberts is alluring as the object of his desires, although her character proves to be disappointingly shallow once her scheme is revealed (she's a snob, basically). The love scenes are especially intense (if there are children in the room, warn them that the technique with the molten wax poses a fire hazard). In fact, the film was released on video in both an R-rated version and a steamier unrated version. Anyone who needs to be warned of approaching sex scenes should simply listen for the rather overdone saxophone solos that precede the heavy-breathing stuff with monotonous regularity. *(Violence, profanity, nudity, sexual situations, adult situations.)*

d, Jag Mundhra; p, Amrok Amritraj; w, Tom Citrano and Andrew Stevens; ph, James Mathers; ed, David H. Lloyd; m, Richard Glasser; prod d, Brian McCabe; set d, Erzibet Frank; cos, Ha Nguyen; makup, Cindy F. Adams

Thriller   **(PR:O   MPAA:R)**

NIGHT OF THE LIVING DEAD

96m John Russo-21st Century/COL c

Tony Todd *(Ben)*, Patricia Tallman *(Barbara)*, Tom Towles *(Harry Cooper)*, McKee Anderson *(Helen Cooper)*, William Butler *(Tom)*, Katie Finnerman *(Judy Rose)*, Bill Mosley *(Johnnie)*, Heather Mazur *(Sarah)*, David Butler *(Hondo)*, Zachary Mott *(Bulldog)*, Pat Reese *(The Mourner)*, William Cameron *(The Newsman)*, Pat Logan *(Uncle Rege)*, Berle Ellis *(The Flaming Zombie)*, Bill "Chilly Billy" Cardille *(TV Interviewer)*, Greg Funk *(Cemetary Zombie)*, Tim Carrier *(Autopsy Zombie)*, John Hamilton *(Crowbar Zombie)*, Dyrk Ashton *(Truck Zombie)*, Jordan Berlant *(Porch Zombie)*, Albert Shellhammer *(Cousin Satchel)*, Jay McDowell *(Front Door Zombie)*, Walter Berry *(McGruder)*, Kendal Kraft *(Bob Evans Zombie)*, David Grace *(Policeman Zombie)*, Stacie Foster *(Doll's Mom Zombie)*, and Charles Crawley *(Window Zombie)*

The 1990 version of this 1968 George Romero production begins almost exactly as its predecessor: with a shot of a car driving along a winding, deserted road. An extended voiceover offers one of the original film's most memorable lines — "They're coming to get you, Barbara." — and establishes Barbara (Patricia Tallman) and Johnnie (Bill Mosley) as the squabbling siblings on their way to visit their mother's grave in an isolated cemetery. It all seems like an elaborate homage to Romero's very low-budget, very creepy original, but it's not...not exactly. Directed by makeup artist Tom Savini, a longtime Romero collaborator who created the ground-breaking splatter effects for several Romero films, this NIGHT OF THE LIVING DEAD is virtually a shot-by-shot recreation of the first film.

Barbara and Johnnie are attacked by men who behave very oddly. Johnnie is killed, and Barbara escapes to a nearby farmhouse, where she teams with Ben (Tony Todd), who tells her the dead are rising from their graves as cannibal zombies. After seeing some of the walking dead up close, she realizes he is right. They discover other people hiding in the cellar: bossy Harry (Tom Towles), his wife (McKee Anderson) and sick daughter (Heather Mazur), and a teenaged couple, Tom (William Butler) and Judy Rose (Katie Finnerman). One by one, zombies gather outside as the besieged argue over the best way to proceed; Harry wants them to barricade themselves in the basement, while Ben favors staying upstairs, where they'll have a chance to run for it if the zombies break in. Tom and Judy are killed in an abortive attempt to get gasoline from a nearby pump; Harry's child dies, becomes a zombie and kills her mother; Ben and Harry shoot one another and Barbara strikes out to look for help. When she returns in the morning with a posse of locals, Ben has died of his wounds and returned as one of the living dead. Harry has survived through the night, but Barbara shoots him dead.

The primary difference between the original and the remake is that the latter is in color, though a deliberately subdued color. In addition, the zombies created by Everett Burrell and John Vulich, are far more elaborate than those in the first film. Finally, an attempt has been made to add some depth to the characters, with Barbara undergoing the greatest transformation. In the original film the shock of seeing her brother killed leaves her almost catatonic, while in the remake she becomes the strongest of the characters trapped in the farmhouse. In most other respects, the 1990 version is so similar to the 1968 release as to be uncanny. As such, it is an often chilling effort, but hardly the breakthrough film the initial work was.

Given that the 1968 film was an enormously popular and influential film, the natural question is, why did Romero bother to produce a virtual remake? The answer is largely one of economics. When he created the first film, Romero was a Pittsburgh advertising executive who was quite naive with respect to the movie business. He and his fellow investors neglected to properly copyright the property, so that the film could be copied and sold without permission, and without any of the profits going to the investors. Moreover, it led to two films, Dan O'Bannon's RETURN OF THE LIVING DEAD (1985) and Ken Widerhorn's RETURN OF THE LIVING DEAD PART 2 (1987), which cashed in on the title, but in which Romero had no involvement. Romero did, however, create his own sequels, DAWN OF THE DEAD (1979) and DAY OF THE DEAD (1985). He has said he saw the 1990 remake as a way of compensating investors in the original film who missed out on the profits that movie has generated over the years. The film marked Romero's first collaboration in years with original investors John Russo (co-writer of the 1968 film), and Russell Streiner (Johnnie in the '68 movie). Romero wrote the new screenplay and served as executive producer while Russo and Streiner were given producer credits. Given the reasons behind its production, it's hard to fault the second NIGHT OF THE LIVING DEAD for being what it is. Perhaps audiences who hate black and white will find it even more appealing than the original. *(Violence.)*

d, Tom Savini; p, John A. Russo and Russ Streiner; w, George Romero (based on the screenplay by Romero, Russo); ph, Frank Prinzi; ed, Tom Dubensky; m, Paul McCollough; md, Chris Pangikas; prod d, Cletus Anderson; art d, James Feng; set d, Brian J. Stonestreet; spec, Matt Vogel, John Vulich, and Everett Burrell; stunts, Phil Neilson; cos, Barbara Anderson; makup, Jeanne Josefczyk; anim, Kensington Falls Animation

Horror   **(PR:C   MPAA:R)**

NIGHT OF THE SHARKS

87m RAI/Italian International Films-Rauino c

Treat Williams *(David Ziegler)*, Christopher Connelly *(Fr. Mattia)*, Antonio Fargas, Janet Agren, Steven Elliott, Ergidio Termine, Charles Mucary, Nina Soldano, Sal Borgese, John Steiner, Ivano Silveri, Rinaldo Zamperla, and Ferdinando Tomassini

When this forgettable JAWS rip-off commences, a shark bites off a diver's leg with all the pent-up fury of a guppy munching on its Hartz Mountain fish food. Unfortunately, this is as high as the film's energy quotient ever gets. Lacklusterly directed and pedestrianly photographed, NIGHT OF THE SHARKS is just one more international production in the action genre destined for oblivion on video store shelves.

On the eve of a local festival (the "Night of the Sharks") on an island in scenic Mexico, Williams discovers that he cannot put aside his former life as a James Bond-type adventurer and just pal around with buddy Fargas. Hoping to retire as a millionaire, his irresponsible brother has gotten involved with a multinational corporation run by scoundrels just as bloodthirsty as the sea creatures of the title. Purloining an incriminating CD disk, Williams' brother mails the hot data to priest Connelly (friend to both siblings) and then proceeds to blackmail the corporation's depraved CEO. When he demands a fortune in diamonds to keep what he knows secret, the company acquiesces, but secretly tails him, catching up with him when he flees to Mexico to enlist Williams' aid. After the nefarious corporate henchmen blow up his brother, Williams finally gets his dander up and strikes back. Being a reasonable felon, the corporate tycoon decides that his company doesn't need more bloodshed and employs less overt methods to get the disk back. Playing on her sympathies, he persuades Williams' ex-wife to pay a visit to her former spouse's bedroom in order to appropriate the disk, but she gets eaten by an ever-hungry local shark during an attempt on Williams' life. Having lost two family members, Williams wants revenge. First he sinks the box of diamonds he had gotten from his brother down to the ocean floor; then he allows his nemesis, the shark, to swallow the blackmail disk for safekeeping. (This leaves the film's corporate man-eaters in the unenviable position of having to negotiate with a real shark.) Despite the company chief's desire to get his tape and to have Williams "brought back alive," a rather dim-witted hit man has his own ideas about handling the situation. Assorted corporate thugs are sent out to eliminate Williams, but while stalking their prey on the island, these company employees fail to reckon with the ingenuity of Williams and faithful sidekick Fargas, who've booby-trapped the entire area. Even though the bad guys kidnap Connelly and Williams' girl friend, Fargas and Williams prevail and, succumbing to one trap after another, the villains bite the dust. Ever-resourceful Williams puts a hole in the boat of the main hit man and places his own wounded arm in the water to attract Mr. Shark, who soon takes the bait and swallows the head honcho and most of his dinghy. Having rescued his girl friend and the padre, Williams digs up the diamonds and has his last fateful encounter with the finny fiend. Led to believe that Williams has died in this shark attack, the company CEO retrieves his disc, and decides to leave the local village in peace after Connelly informs him that everyone there knows the contents of the disk. To make the community's happiness complete, Williams resurfaces and plans to live out his days playing Crusoe to Fargas' Friday and to act as a father figure for the island's many orphans.

Devoid of anything remotely resembling inventiveness, this derivative seaside adventure meanders on its weary way as if its creative personnel had fallen asleep under the tropical sun. The script seems to have been pieced together from various word processors plugged into different action hits. In fact, all that NIGHT OF THE SHARKS has going for it is the easy-going camaraderie of Williams and Fargas as they crack jokes while rigging death-traps. Even undiscriminating action fans will be dismayed by the low level of the thrills on tap. Contributing to the torpor is the haphazard presentation of key plot devices. (Are there two disks? Is the one mailed to Connelly the same that Williams feeds to the shark? Which one did Williams' wife put in the hotel safe? For that matter, how do we know the acid in the shark's stomach wouldn't destroy the evidence, and why is everyone so concerned about the diamonds? Maybe they could be used to pay for the installation of shark alerts!)

Perhaps we're not meant to question all these poorly inserted plot devices. If that was the plan, then this water-logged adventure should have delivered more nonstop thrills, more flashy stuntwork, and more dynamic suspense. The plot is hard to keep track of; the supporting cast is riddled with hammy players; the editing is a beat off during all the gang assaults and shark attacks. In this sluggish yarn, even the poor shark looks asleep in the deep. It's a toothless fish story with little to recommend it. *(Violence, profanity, sexual situations.)*

d, Anthony Richmond; p, Fulvio Vicisuno; w, Tito Carpi (based on a story by Tonino Ricci); ph, Giovanni Bergamini; ed, Gianfranco Amicucci; m, Stelvio Cipriani; spec, Paolo Ricci

Action (PR:C MPAA:R)

NIGHT VISITOR

93m Premiere/MGM-UA c

(AKA: NEVER CRY DEVIL)

Elliott Gould *(Ron Devereaux)*, Richard Roundtree *(Capt. Crane)*, Allen Garfield *(Zachary Willard)*, Michael J. Pollard *(Stanley Willard)*, Derek Rydall *(Billy Colton)*, Teresa Van Der Woude *(Kelly Fremont)*, Shannon Tweed *(Lisa Grace)*, Brooke Bundy *(Mrs. Coulton)*, Kathleen Bailey *(Detective Dolan)*, and Henry Gibson *(Dr. Lawrence)*

Although sometimes genuinely scary, this boy-who-cried-wolf thriller is done in by script implausibilities that weaken a promising premise and transform NIGHT VISITOR into an all-too-typical, teen-in-trouble suspense flick. As the film opens, prostitutes are disappearing from the streets (and not because they're being solicited for sexual purposes). Meanwhile Billy Colton (Derek Rydall), who is known for stretching the truth to the breaking point, gets into trouble with his petulant history teacher Zachary Willard (Allen Garfield), an overweight asthmatic with contempt for his high school students. Promising his hard-working mom he'll stay out of trouble, Billy dreams that his best pal, Kelly (Teresa Van Der Woude), will become his girl friend. However, when the seductive Lisa Grace (Shannon Tweed) moves in next door, Billy becomes fascinated by her,

spying on her with his telescope and discovering that she is a whore. Billy invites Kelly and another friend over to sneak a peek at Lisa's activities; unfortunately, she takes the night off, and Billy's friends think he's fibbing as usual. Determined to prove his suspicions, Billy climbs onto Lisa's roof one night with a camera and stumbles onto the scene of her murder. What's more, the man in the satanic mask who is stabbing Lisa turns out to be Zachary Willard, his teacher! When police detective Crane (Richard Roundtree) investigates, he takes Billy's camera, but doesn't buy the kid's story. Although the cops interrogate Willard and his retarded brother, Stanley (Michael J. Pollard), noting the duo's weirdness, they can't find any incriminating evidence. After the cops depart, Stanley goes down to the brothers' cellar to inspect their newest piece of "furniture" — the demented siblings' nickname for the whores they have chained in the basement for purposes of torture and eventual sacrifice to Beelzebub. Frustrated after learning he forgot to remove the lens cap from his camera, Billy visits Ron Devereaux (Elliott Gould), a friend of his late father and a former policeman who is leery of coming out of retirement to involve himself in this far-fetched case about a demonic high-school killer. Zachary threatens Billy on the phone, challenging the young fibber with his lack of credibility as a witness. In the death house, Stanley leads his victim upstairs, to a sacrificial chamber where Zachary bloodily offers her body to Satan. Later, after Zachary toys with Billy after class one day, Billy and Kelly take matters into their own hands and are nearly run down by Stanley while snooping around at the den of devil worshippers. Reconsidering his decision to stay off the case, Devereaux meets up with Billy and agrees to help him search the Willards' house for evidence. Unfortunately, Kelly, unable to contact Billy, sneaks over to the crazed brothers' house and gets nabbed by Stanley. Trusting him to get rid of the interloper, Zachary goes to school, but becomes suspicious when Billy doesn't attend class. Meanwhile, Billy and the ex-cop search the schoolteacher's house and stumble upon the sacrifice room. Devereaux — who now admits that he was never a detective, merely a forensics worker — having heard Kelly's screams in the cellar, battles the chainsaw-wielding Stanley and manages to shoot him. Zachary shows up, and he and Billy scuffle. Falling into the basement, the teacher grabs a gun, but Billy manages to kick him against a hook in the wall. Only after Billy and Devereaux have saved the day do the police arrive.

Overlooking its derivative nature, one could have had a passably good time watching NIGHT VISITOR, largely because of its talented cast of pros and agreeable newcomers. Unfortunately, the film's good points get swallowed up in a plethora of implausibilities and convenient happenstance. Although the boy-who-cried-wolf plotline dovetails nicely with the prostitute murders and satanism, the screenwriters throw in unbelievable turns of events simply to pump up suspense. Wouldn't the cops have been a little more sympathetic to Billy's eyewitness account of the slaying, given the recent string of prostitute killings? How could Billy's mother allow him to continue going to Willard's classes if her son was terrified of him? Why would the boy place himself in such a situation without requesting a transfer? And what teenage girl, aware that serial murders of women are occurring, would go poking around the suspect's strange house by herself? Another liability is Michael J. Pollard, whose patented loony act turns into unnecessary comic relief and dissipates tension. On the plus side, Rydall is a promising young actor who holds the screen authoritatively, able to project the teen's outer cockiness and inner terror simultaneously.

Managing to keep us on the edge of our seats, the suspense scenes are well-directed set-pieces, particularly Billy's close-up view of his neighbor's murder as his camera snaps away. Easily the most disturbing scene is the eerie prelude to the prostitute's sacrifice, in which Pollard's Stanley lures his unwary victim to her death while pretending to help her escape. As a depiction of the sadistic dementia of serial killers, several of the scenes with Garfield and Pollard in the death house are unsettling. They might have been truly frightening if Pollard had not succumbed to his usual cutesy, crackpot-characterization tricks. By contrast, Garfield's portrayal of a mass murderer is at times so powerful it overcomes the conventionality of the rest of the film. NIGHT VISITOR is a disappointment, but shuddery enough on occasion to make you wonder about your own high-school teachers' hobbies. *(Violence, nudity, profanity.)*

d, Rupert Hitzig; p, Alain Silver; w, Randal Visovich; ph, Peter Jansen; ed, Glenn Erickson; m, Parmer Fuller; prod d, Jon Rothschild

Thriller (PR:O MPAA:R)

NIGHTBREED

102m FOX c

Craig Sheffer *(Boone)*, Anne Bobby *(Lori)*, David Cronenberg *(Decker)*, Charles Haid *(Capt. Eigerman)*, Hugh Quarshie *(Detective Joyce)*, Hugh Ross *(Narcisse)*, Doug Bradley *(Lylesberg)*, and Catherine Chevalier *(Rachel)*

If Stephen King is to be trusted on the subject of literary horror, then Clive Barker is a force to be reckoned with. The British author has already been dubbed nothing less than the genre's future by its best-known brand name in the States.

But film is a different ball game, as the thoroughly unwatchable, King-written and-directed MAXIMUM OVERDRIVE can readily attest. On the evidence of Barker's own second film as a writer-director, NIGHTBREED (his first, HELLRAISER, stretched the makings of a decent "Tales from the Darkside" episode to a distended feature length), the Future of Horror adds his own new ingredient to the genre: incoherent, slack-jawed boredom.

Craig Sheffer plays Boone, a young man in Calgary, Canada, who dreams about monsters chasing him through a field near an imaginary place called Midian. That's a step up, since he *had* been dreaming about mass murders that had a nasty habit of also occurring in real life. But we're hardly reassured about Boone's prognosis when we find out that his psychiatrist is none other than David Cronenberg, the real-life director of THE FLY and DEAD RINGERS (who, let's say it now, could make a better film than NIGHTBREED before breakfast). Playing the devious Dr. Decker, Cronenberg gives Boone some little pills that will "calm him down." Instead, Boone is found wandering in traffic and babbling incoherently. At the hospital, a doctor casually informs him that Decker's medicine is actually a strong hallucinogenic. Meanwhile, yet another mass murder Boone described to Decker has occurred, and Decker is busying himself with violating patient-doctor confidence by prodding the police into arresting Boone. If, by this point, you've grasped the obvious and figured out who is actually committing the murders, then feel free to stop reading and rest assured: you're already too smart for this movie. Besides, NIGHTBREED goes steadily downhill from there anyway. It turns out that Midian actually exists, and prior to ripping off his face on-camera, a fellow patient conveniently reveals to Boone its location, just a short scenic drive from Calgary. Escaping from the hospital, Boone heads there. The police follow him, kill him, and bring his body back. But—for no discernible reason except that this is a horror film—Boone rises from the dead and hightails it back to Midian, where he is welcomed by the title's beasts, who are actually shape-shifters, as one of them solemnly explains. Back in Calgary, Lori (Anne Bobby), Boone's girl friend, becomes obsessed with seeing the place where her honey bit the bullets. So she sets out for Midian—followed, again, by Decker, who is himself obsessed with destroying the night breeders. To aid him in his crusade, Decker enlists a geeky redneck sheriff (Charles Haid), helping to turn NIGHTBREED into a touching allegory about intolerance along the way. Eventually, Boone gets to have his big confrontation with Decker before chucking him off a cliff. But—to the surprise of absolutely no one—Barker thoughtfully takes the time to lay the groundwork for the theoretical NIGHTBREED 2.

In portraying his monsters, Barker himself has a hard time keeping straight what they can and cannot do. The shape-shifters rarely shift shapes, but we keep wishing they would. Their repulsive appearance is matched only by their need to natter on endlessly about their deep significance to the film's largely nonexistent plot. It is also solemnly intoned that it takes all kinds of methods to kill a shape-shifting night breeder (and, while we're on the subject, we never see them breeding at night; in fact, we never see them breeding at all, which, considering their appearance, is probably a good thing). It is even specifically stated that bullets won't necessarily work against them. Yet, in the film's big, noisy climax, Haid and his blood-crazed cops demonstrate that bullets, and lots of them, in fact work very well.

As it runs considerably longer, the actual movie is even harder to get through than its synopsis. But the synopsis serves as a critique of the movie. To put it less politely, is the Future of Horror really someone badly in need of a beginner's course in story construction? Besides a lot of scenic driving in and around Calgary, NIGHTBREED does have its fair share of sound and fury, not to mention blood and entrails. But it plays as if Barker were making it up as he went along, despite the film's having been based on his own novel *Cabal*.

The acting is mostly routine. Haid, once again, is stuck with a character he doesn't deserve. Sheffer is OK, nothing more. Bobby lends loads of appealing spunk and charm to her character, which, as written, needs all the help she can get. The only real surprise is "Dr." Cronenberg, who actually turns out to be a pretty good actor, coming on here a little like a malignant Raymond Massey—although, probably at Barker's bidding, he swallows most of his lines.

In fact, we are reluctant to praise Cronenberg's performance too highly, lest he reconsider his career as Cronenberg the director. Despite a multitude of missteps, Barker's approach to horror does have an unmistakable stamp of originality. But until he acquires considerably more skill behind the camera, the future of horror, in films at least, is best left in the hands of the "Doctor." *(Graphic violence, profanity, adult situations.)*

d, Clive Barker; p, Gabriella Martinelli; w, Clive Barker (based on the novel "Cabal" by Barker); ph, Robin Vidgeon; ed, Richard Marden and Mark Goldblatt; m, Danny Elfman; prod d, Steve Hardie; makeup, Image Animation

Horror   (PR:O   MPAA:R)

NOBODY'S PERFECT

89m Panorama — Steve Ader/Moviestore c

Chad Lowe *(Stephen/Stephanie)*, Gail O'Grady *(Shelly)*, Patrick Breen *(Andy)*, Kim Flowers *(Jackie)*, Todd Schaefer *(Brad)*, Robert Vaughn *(Dr. Duncan)*, and Vitas Gerulaitis

The title NOBODY'S PERFECT might qualify as truth in movie advertising, since it certainly applies to the makers of this lame, misogynist cross-dressing farce. However, the aptness of the film's moniker goes beyond that. By taking its title from Joe E. Brown's famous fadeout line in SOME LIKE IT HOT, this film makes you wish you were watching that Billy Wilder classic or just about anything else. Chad Lowe plays frisky college freshman Stephen Parker, who enrolls at one of those free-spirited California universities where the most prominent faculty member is the tennis coach, here played by a hapless Vitas Gerulaitis. (Real-life former tennis star Gerulaitis is joined in the cast by an even more hapless Robert Vaughn, who mutters his way through an absolutely painful scene as the school gynecologist.) Stephen, seemingly majoring in tennis, has trouble concentrating on his backhand because his attention is focused on the women's court and blonde, blue-eyed, well-endowed Shelly (Gail O'Grady). Stephen's inattention earns him the ire of his coach, who cuts Stephen from the tennis team, eliminating his easy access to Shelly. Enter Stephen's best buddy, the campus con man, Andy (Patrick Breen), who suggests a "simple" solution, advising Stephen to create an alternate female identity ("Stephanie") and go out for the women's tennis team. Of course, Andy has an ulterior motive. With Stephen on the women's team as a ringer, Andy bets the ranch on them to win the league championship. Needless to say, laboriously zany, wacky complications ensue, all of them easily predicted by the few viewers who don't slip deep into dreamland long before Stephen slips on his wig. Along with stumbling "her" way through the expected women's locker room scene (thereby pushing the film's PG-13 envelope), Stephanie winds up as Shelly's roommate and doubles partner. The film takes a strangely somber turn when Stephanie gets some firsthand experience of the sort of pain and humiliation that women go through to make themselves attractive to men. The somberness deepens when Shelly confides to Stephanie that her dates with her handsome boy friend are usually little more than date rapes.

The obvious intent here is to invest NOBODY'S PERFECT with a TOOTSIE-like sensitivity for the plight of women, seen, of course, through the eyes of a man. O'Grady does her best to give her character some genuine feeling. For that reason, the date-rape confession almost works, until you begin to wonder why someone with her looks and supposed intelligence couldn't do better than endure weekend maulings by the campus goon. But by this point in the film, we have to assume her character is brain dead; after all, she still has not noticed that the girl she's been living with in extremely close quarters for weeks is actually a guy.

Fully functioning brains were evidently in short supply throughout the production of this lower-than-lowbrow comedy. Tellingly, instead of suggesting that Shelly find herself a guy who will treat her like a human being, Stephanie advises her to find one who will kiss her all over her body. Later, when Stephen's ruse is revealed to Shelly, he justifies it by saying that enduring the "degradation" of being a woman to be near her is proof of his love. To O'Grady's credit, she reacts to this soliloquy with the slack-jawed amazement it deserves. But she can't change a script that has her falling for Stephen anyway. She also can't stop Stephen from masquerading as Stephanie one more time to win the tennis championship so Andy can collect on his bets. Neither, it seems, can the school administration, since the championship is played while Stephanie is under academic probation for plagiarizing one of Stephen's term papers.

A patriotic American can't help but suspect an organized foreign conspiracy in a movie so deliberately subhuman as this. There are people in the credits with names like Lars, Claus, and Just, and the production company is something called Panorama Film International; however, an investigation would not be worth the effort. NOBODY'S PERFECT finally isn't even bad enough to be seriously offensive, though it is plenty bad enough to be a good remedy for insomnia. *(Profanity, adult situations, nudity.)*

d, Robert Kaylor; p, Benni Korzen; w, Annie Korzen and Joel Block; ph, Claus Loof; ed, Robert Gordon; m, Robert Randles

Comedy   (PR:O   MPAA:PG-13)

NUNS ON THE RUN

(Brit.) 90m Handmade/FOX c

Eric Idle *(Brian Hope)*, Robbie Coltrane *(Charlie McManus)*, Camille Coduri *(Faith)*, Janet Suzman *(Sister Superior)*, Doris Hare *(Sister Mary of the Sacred Heart)*, Lila Kaye *(Sister Mary of the Annuciation)*, Robert Patterson *("Case" Casey)*, Robert Morgan *(Abbott)*, Winston Dennis *(Morley)*, Tom Hickey *(Father Seamus)*, Colin Campbell *(Norm)*, Richard Simpson *(Mr. Norris)*, Nicholas

Hewetson (*Louis*), Gary Tang (*Ronnie Chang*), David Forman (*Henry Ho*), Nigel Fan (*Dwayne Lee*), Ozzie Yue (*Ernie Wong*), Tatiana Strauss (*Michelle*), Wabei Siyolwe (*Julie*), Helen Fitzgerald (*Tracey*), Stewart Harwood (*Faith's Father*), Peter Geeves (*Faith's Brother*), Irene Marot (*Hysterical Bank Manager*), Louis Mellis (*Bank Security Guard*), Craig Crosbie (*Policeman in Car Park*), Fred Haggerty (*Gatekeeper*), Michael Beint (*Bewildered Policeman*), Tex Fuller (*Taxi Driver*), Lee Simpson (*Policeman with Radio*), Oliver Parker (*Doctor*), Julie Graham (*Casino Waitress*), Dan Hildebrand (*Casino Manager*), Joanne Campbell (*Ward Nurse*), Gedren Heller (*Chemist Shop Assistant*), Britt Morrow (*Hospital Receptionist*), David Becalick (*Police Sergeant*), Aran Bell (*Police Constable*), Francine Walker, Shirley Anne Selby (*Tied-up Nurses*), Jennifer Hall (*Airport Ticket Girl*), and John Pythian (*Airport Policeman*)

NUNS ON THE RUN reunites three of England's most prominent entertainment figures—Monty Python's Eric Idle, writer-director Jonathan Lynn (best known outside Britain for the ubiquitous BBC satire series "Yes Minister" and "Yes Prime Minister"), and stage/screen/TV producer Michael White (MONTY PYTHON AND THE HOLY GRAIL; THE ROCKY HORROR SHOW; MY DINNER WITH ANDRE)—for the first time since 1963. That year White transferred "Cambridge Circus," a student show involving Idle and Lynn, from Cambridge University to London's West End for a successful run, followed by a stint on Broadway. Unfortunately, this bland and ultimately banal comedy is nowhere near as auspicious a collaboration. Idle plays Brian Hope, a mild-mannered, middle-aged gangster who yearns for the good old nonviolent days of robbery, before drug money brought in a new breed of vicious criminals like his own boss, "Case" Casey (Robert Patterson). Along with his partner, Charlie McManus (Robbie Coltrane), Brian plans to abscond with a large cache of cash they have been assigned to steal from a drug-dealing Hong Kong gang, the Triads, and to use the money to go straight. Brian takes leave of his new girl friend, Faith (Camille Coduri), and, with Charlie, manages to steal a million pounds from the Triads and Casey's gang. Unfortunately, while the boys are making their escape, their car runs out of gas—in front of a convent. With their former cohorts and the Triads in close pursuit, Brian and Charlie duck into the convent and disguise themselves as nuns. The only witness to their escape into the cloister is Faith, who had learned of Casey's plan to kill his two underlings after the heist and had gone to the scene of the crime to warn Brian of the danger. Inside the convent, Charlie (a lapsed Catholic) and Brian pass themselves off as visiting sisters from a different order, on temporary assignment prior to leaving the country for missionary work. They are required to teach theology to the convent's students—comprised entirely of beautiful 18-year-old girls—and to supervise them in gym and showers. Faith, slightly wounded during the theft and nearly blind after losing her glasses, follows the cons into the establishment and asks the crafty Sister Superior (Janet Suzman) for permission to look around the premises, pretending to be a teaching applicant. Sister Superior, who sees through Faith's deception, treats her bullet wound after the girl faints, whereupon Brian looks after Faith in his nun's guise, then changes into his own clothes to break up with her for her own safety. The shattered girl leaves the convent and is promptly kidnaped by the Triads, who release her when they learn she knows nothing. In a hospital, she is watched over by her father and brother, who vow to punish the gangster who has broken her heart. Brian, meanwhile, realizes he loves her and goes to visit her in the hospital with Charlie, the two still disguised as nuns. On their return to the convent, they are spotted as men by an alcoholic sister who recently embezzled 50,000 pounds from the convent's drug clinic and lost it by betting on horses. They escape detection that night, but are caught by Sister Superior the following morning when they break into a locked cupboard to retrieve their suitcases containing the stolen money. Escaping with the loot, Brian and Charlie head for the airport, followed by the nuns, the Triads, and their own gang. At the last minute, Brian forces Charlie to go to the hospital to pick up Faith, who slaps Brian repeatedly as he explains his actions. She forgives him just as the nuns, the gangsters, and the police (newly added to the chase) are closing in, and the trio elude their pursuers by posing as nurses wheeling a patient on a gurney, losing one of the cash-filled suitcases in the process. The lost luggage falls into the hands of Sister Superior, who proclaims it a miracle and plans to use the drug money to expand her convent's drug clinic tenfold. Casey is arrested while Faith, Brian, and Charlie, still sought by the gangsters and the police, board a plane to Rio—the men disguised as stewardesses.

NUNS ON THE RUN might seem, on the surface, to be more than vaguely blasphemous, but it is far too mild to offend the religious on that score; in fact, the comedy might have gained needed piquancy if it had been more daring in that respect. Except for a few gentle zingers—such as this line from a discussion of the nature of the Holy Trinity: "If it made sense, it wouldn't have to be a religion, would it?"—the Catholic setting is given short shrift. The basic comedic idea at work here is that cross-dressing is inherently funny. It is a venerable premise that has given good service to practitioners ranging from William Shakespeare to Billy Wilder—essentially, NUNS ON THE RUN is SOME LIKE IT HOT re-dressed in habits—and the film's few genuinely amusing moments arise directly from this age-old principle. But the fun of putting men in drag is

not enough to carry an entire film. NUNS ON THE RUN strives mightily to supplement its transvestite humor with shootouts, chases, and romance, but those distractions fail to satisfy, having little to do with the film's central comedic opportunity.

The humor in this film should have arisen from absurd contrasts in the predicament of the main characters. A man wearing a dress is reasonably amusing, but a man forced to impersonate a sexy or eligible woman is much funnier. That is the main difference, laugh-wise, between NUNS ON THE RUN and SOME LIKE IT HOT. Since nuns are relatively asexual figures, the gender-bending humor should have been heightened by emphasizing the type of man being forced to wear a habit—a gangster constrained by religious surroundings. Coltrane and Idle are not terribly funny as nuns because, though they are ostensibly tough guys, they behave more like mischievous choirboys throughout the film. Donning nun's robes hardly makes them seem out of character. NUNS ON THE RUN seems about to get on the right track when Coltrane's Charlie occasionally forgets himself and starts to curse or throw a punch, but those moments are never developed. Instead, the audience is expected to laugh at little more than the sight of erstwhile thugs pursing their lips, speaking in high-pitched voices, and not quite remembering the stations of the cross. That is settling for very little, considering the potential richness of this situation and the fact that Idle and Coltrane make a very effective team. Their pairing is especially interesting because they represent two generations of cutting-edge British comic actors, Coltrane having come to prominence as part of "The Comic Strip," an alternative comedy troupe producing television projects for the BBC similar in outrageous spirit to "Monty Python's Flying Circus." (*Violence, adult situations, alcohol abuse.*)

d, Jonathan Lynn; p, Michael White; w, Jonathan Lynn; ph, Michael Garfath; ed, David Martin; m, Yello and Hidden Faces; md, Frank Fitzpatrick; prod d, Simon Holland; art d, Clinton Cavers; set d, Michael Seirton; spec, John Evans; stunts, Martin Grace; cos, Susan Yelland; makeup, Pat Hay

Comedy   (PR:A-C   MPAA:PG-13)

NUOVO CINEMA PARADISO

(Fr./It.) (SEE: CINEMA PARADISO)

NUTCRACKER PRINCE, THE

(Can.) 75m Hinton Animation—Lacewood/WB c

VOICES OF : Peter O'Toole (*Pantaloon*), Kiefer Sutherland (*Nutcracker/Hans*), Megan Follows (*Clara*), Michael MacDonald (*Mouseking*), Noam Zylberman (*Fritz*), Diane Stapley (*Mr. Stahlbaum*), Peter Boretski (*Uncle Drosselmeier*), George Merner (*Dr. Stahlbaum*), Stephanie Morgenstern (*Louise*), Christopher Owens (*Erik*), Lynne Gorman (*Trudy*), Teresa Sears (*Queen*), Mona Wasserman (*Princess Perlipat*), and Phyllis Diller (*Mouse Queen*)

Regrettably, this animated film is an unabashed bore, and that's a shame because the glorious Tchaikovsky ballet has been loved and admired by generations of stage, film, and television viewers of all ages. Why Warner Bros. selected this Canadian-produced independent feature as its Christmas 1990 family attraction is puzzling, given the lackluster quality of the production. For the record, the film tells the story of Clara (voiced by Megan Follows), a sweet young girl who finds an enchanted nutcracker in the shape of a prince under her Christmas tree. The Prince (Kiefer Sutherland) is under a spell that has transformed him into a toy. Clara helps break the spell, is taken on a tour of Toyland, and returns to find a charming young man named Hans (Sutherland again), who has a startling resemblance to the Nutcracker Prince. Uncle Drosselmeier (Peter Boretski) is on hand to tell Clara the story of the Mouseking (Michael MacDonald). The main trouble here is that the story doesn't go anywhere. In Tchaikovsky's original ballet, most of the enchantment (aside from the immortal score) lies in the bright and beautiful Christmas set decorations, costumes, and energetic dancing. Though animation offers limitless possibilities, here it simply cannot capture the glory of a staging of "The Nutcracker" featuring *live* performers. Still, the film might have worked had the animators provided the audience with the same awesomely mounted artwork seen in Walt Disney classics. Instead, the picture spotlights thoroughly amateurish animation, not even equal to that seen on Saturday morning television shows. The backgrounds are flat and colorless, while the readings supplied by the actors are every bit as washed out as the animation. The film's only asset is its score, performed by the London Symphony Orchestra and featuring some clever arrangements by Victor Davies. That's not nearly enough to save the picture, however, and the film deservedly disappeared from theatres shortly after its release.

d, Paul Schibli; p, Kevin Gillis; w, Patricia Watson and E.T.A. Hoffman; md, Boris Brott; art d, Peter Moehrle

Animated/Children's   (PR:AA   MPAA:G)

OPQ

OFFICE PARTY

(SEE: HOSTILE TAKEOVER)

OPPONENT, THE

(It.) 102m Medusa/Dania c

Daniel Greene (*Bob Mulligan*), Julian Gemma (*Martin Durant*), Ernest Borgnine (*Victor*), Mary Stavin (*Gilda*), Kelly Shaye Smith (*Anne*), A.J. Duhe (*Baby*), Dwight Sauls (*Slim*), Bill Wohrman (*Larry*), James Warring (*Eddy*), Federico Pavani (*Bookmaker*), Lenny Moore (*Duncan*), Jose Nino Ribalta (*Lance*), Ruben Rabasa (*Ollie*), Scott Gallin (*Pappy*), Mark McCraken (*Don*), Edgar Allan Poe IV, Gregg Todd Davis, Reggie Pierre (*Punks*), Rocky Golio (*Rocky*), Paola Padovani (*Kathy*), and Raquel Herring (*Singer*)

The world does not really need another yarn about a contender who rises to the top of the boxing racket despite the machinations of corrupt promoters. But if you're determined to step inside the ropes with another fight film, THE OPPONENT is a reasonably entertaining jab at a little guy vs. the establishment drama.

Impatient to get his shot at the big time, Bob Mulligan (Daniel Greene) is tired of sparring with loudmouthed Eddy (James Warring), whose favorite pastimes are throwing fights and sending goons to harass Mulligan. Angry with his manager, Larry (Bill Wohrman), for giving his shot at a fight to Eddy, Mulligan calms down when he learns the fight has been fixed by tycoon Martin Durant (Julian Gemma), who controls the local boxing game. Mulligan's love life is also on hold because Victor (Ernest Borgnine), father of Anne (Kelly Shaye Smith), the woman Mulligan loves, has a seemingly irrational hatred of prizefighters. While trying to interest Durant in his career, Mulligan twice rescues the big shot's alcoholic mistress, Gilda (Mary Stavin), and is forced to defend himself against Durant's thugs. Refusing to accede to Anne's wishes that he retire from the ring so they can wed, Mulligan breaks up with her, and finally gets his chance to fight. Due to complaints from fans, Durant is forced to clean up the fight game temporarily. When he goes looking for a potential champ, the obvious choice is Mulligan, who has not only proved himself against Durant's bodyguards but also flattened Eddy. Despite Larry's warnings about Durant, Mulligan trains hard and punches his way to the top. But with fair-play triumph just out of reach, Mulligan allows himself to be seduced by Durant's mistress, Gilda. Unfortunately, their tryst is witnessed by Eddy, who snitches to Durant. Not one to share, Durant dumps Mulligan for the pliant Eddy, and orders Mulligan to throw his next fight or else. When hard-headed Mulligan wins the match anyway, Durant commands his henchmen to cripple Mulligan's famous right hand. Mulligan looks to be on the road to Palookaville, but Larry nurses him back to health and reunites him with Anne—Victor having finally accepted Mulligan once he realized that his daughter's suitor doesn't throw fights. Despite a negative prognosis, Mulligan subjects his hand to intensive therapy. As part of the regimen, he nearly drowns Durant, who retaliates by drowning Larry. Instead of throwing in the towel, Mulligan challenges Durant to match him against the reigning champ. To ensure victory, Durant kidnaps Anne and confidently places heavy bets on his fighter. However, while Mulligan takes heavy punishment in the ring, Gilda shows her true colors, kayoing Anne's guard and helping her escape. The women hightail it to the arena, where Gilda gets her revenge against Durant when Mulligan spots Anne and pounds his way to the world championship. Pushed to the limit, Durant kidnaps Gilda, Victor, Mulligan, and Anne after the fight, planning to give them cement overshoes. But Mulligan saves the day during a warehouse gun battle, dispatching Durant and his goons, though the ever-helpful Gilda is fatally shot and Victor is wounded.

This average punch-a-thon does its job with reasonable skill but little inspiration. In the lead role, Greene fills out his trunks nicely and exudes he-man charisma, receiving strong support from the rest of the cast. Borgnine turns in a thoughtful performance as the father tortured by secrets of corruption in his own past; Stavin is a standout as the good-time girl who drowns her scruples in booze; and Gemma humanizes his villain by showing us the seductiveness of power and Durant's hang-ups about Gilda.

Unfortunately, there's nothing exceptional about either the script or the way it is realized by director Sergio Martino. Every fight movie cliche is in evidence, and there isn't one plot development that isn't telegraphed several scenes in advance. With no real suspense to stiffen its spine, THE OPPONENT often seems to be an out-of-shape contender, not flabby, but hardly championship material. Although the lackluster musical score doesn't help matters, the film is edited with uncommon precision. If you're a die-hard fan of the "Rocky" series, you might want to go a few rounds with THE OPPONENT (if nothing else, Greene is a more attractive and articulate hero than Stallone). But if you're not a fight film fan, THE OPPONENT is a routine action movie that shadow boxes

in a familiar arena. (*Violence, nudity, profanity, sexual situations, substance abuse.*)

d, Sergio Martino; w, Sauro Scavolini, Sergio Martino, Maria Perrone Cupano, and Robert Brodie Booth (based on a story by Luciano Martino); ph, Giancarlo Ferrando; ed, Eugenio Alabiso; m, Luciano Michelini; art d, Federico Padovan; cos, Valentina Di Palma; makup, Stefano Fava

Sports   (PR:C   MPAA:R)

OPPORTUNITY KNOCKS

105m Imagine Entertainment/Universal c

Dana Carvey (*Eddie Farrell*), Robert Loggia (*Milt Malkin*), Todd Graff (*Lou Pasquino*), Julia Campbell (*Annie Malkin*), Milo O'Shea (*Max*), James Tolkan (*Sal Nichols*), Doris Belack (*Mona*), Sally Gracie (*Connie*), Mike Bacarella (*Pinkie*), John M. Watson Sr. (*Harold Monroe*), Beatrice Fredman (*Bubbie*), Thomas McElroy (*Men's Room Attendant*), Jack McLaughlin-Gray (*Wine Steward*), Gene Honda (*Japanese Businessman*), Del Close (*Williamson*), Michael Oppenheimer (*Chase*), Paul Greatbatch (*Driver*), Sarajane Avidon (*Commissioner's Secretary*), Mindy Suzanne Bell, Richard Steven Mann (*Executives*), Ron Max, Kent Logsdon (*Sales Associates*), Jed Mills (*Club MC*), Michelle Johnston (*Club Singer*), Bill Bradshaw (*David*), John Cothran Jr. (*Building Commissioner*), Tal Galomb (*Bar Mitzvah Boy*), James Hassett (*Vendor*), Mark Hutter (*Stan*), Joshua Livingstone (*Nathan*), Jill Shellabarger (*Ginger*), Adam Jason Weiss (*Myron*), Lorna Raver Johnson (*Eddie's Secretary*), Michelle Quigley (*Woman at Accident*), Judith Scott (*Milt's Secretary*), Mark Ross (*Jonathan*), Rebecca Cagen, Don Cagen, Paul Dallas, Randy Harrah, Peter Hennes, Pennington McGee, and Steven Zoloto (*Bar Mitzvah Band*)

Dana Carvey, of TV's "Saturday Night Live," follows other "SNL" players to a starring role in the movies with OPPORTUNITY KNOCKS, in which he plays a small-time Chicago con man who gets involved in a very complicated scam. Unfortunately, despite some funny moments, Carvey's big-screen bid is for the most part dull and predictable. Eddie (Carvey) is a likable (but unlikely) thief who, along with his roommate and partner, Lou (Todd Graff), also bilks people for a living. The pair are first seen together when Lou is "hit" by a car. While Lou complains of alleged injuries and lost work, Eddie talks the driver into giving Lou some money to avoid a lawsuit. Next, they attempt to rob a house by dressing up as gas company repairmen, but are unsuccessful. Frustrated by this failure, Eddie and Lou do some old-fashioned breaking and entering. While they're in the midst of cleaning out a house, the phone rings, triggering the answering machine. The recording announces that the homeowner will be away on business for many weeks, after which the caller leaves a message saying he won't be able to house-sit. It's a crook's dream come true, and the booty they reap from the abandoned domicile allows the thieves to pay money owed to hefty hood Pinkie (Mike Bacarella). After settling up, Eddie wins part of the loot back in a bet. However, Pinkie reneges on the wager and tosses the two out of a pool hall. Angry and humiliated, they take Pinkie's car for a joy ride and eventually ditch the vehicle, but not before taking $60,000 left in the trunk—money belonging to mobster Sal (James Tolkan). This precipitates an unpleasant visit from some thugs who come to shake down the pair, although Eddie for some reason attempts to ward them off by using a Japanese accent. Needless to say, this doesn't work. But the implausibilities don't stop here: after a chase, Eddie and Lou split up, the former repairing to the house they robbed earlier, where he literally makes himself at home. The next morning, the owner's parents, Milt and Mona Malkin (Robert Loggia and Doris Belack), drop by unexpectedly. Assuming that Eddie is their son's house-sitter—whom they have conveniently never met even though he and their son are close friends—the Malkins promptly give Eddie $300, the housekeys, and their son's car. They also invite him to lunch, where he meets their attractive daughter, Annie (Julia Campbell), and learns that Milt is a wealthy vendor of bathroom appliances. However, although he's quick on his feet, Eddie is unable to come up with a clever business scam to fleece Milt. Anxious and confused about the fix he's gotten himself into, Eddie consults with his mentor, veteran con artist Max (Milo O'Shea). Max advises him to get close to Annie, counsel Eddie follows, and it isn't long before romance is developing between Eddie and Annie. To top it off, the gracious Milt gives Eddie a job as an ad executive. Later, Eddie returns home to find Sal and his buddies using Lou as a punching bag. The gangsters want their money, and Eddie promises to get them $180,000 stored in Milt's office safe. In the uninvolving scenes that follow, Eddie gives Sal the $180,000 and gets him to participate in an elaborate wrecking scam masterminded by Max and his partner, Connie (Sally Gracie). On the evening the illegal demolition deal is to be finalized, the Malkins once again show up at the house unexpectedly. While Eddie thinks up false identities for Max and Connie, the Malkins' son makes his way home from the airport, threatening to blow Eddie's cover for good. The con artists manage to make it to their rendezvous with Sal in time to deliver the gangster a bogus contract in exchange for enough money for them all to retire, but Eddie suddenly has an attack of conscience, returns to the house, and confesses to the Malkin family. At the film's end, Sal is arrested and Eddie and Annie reunite.

Despite a talented cast and some good production values (in particular the cinematography), OPPORTUNITY KNOCKS is a disappointing feature and an unremarkable vehicle for Carvey. Mitchel Katlin and Nat Bernstein's screenplay is tailor-made for Carvey's familiar accents and impressions, but none of these are integrated into the feeble plot and, except for providing a few chuckles, they don't sustain the film on their own. Carvey is obviously a talented comedian, but his lack of big-screen presence here makes him unconvincing as either a likable con artist or a love interest. (Profanity.)

d, Donald Petrie; p, Mark R. Gordon and Christopher Meledandri; w, Mitchel Katlin and Nat Bernstein; ph, Steven Poster; ed, Marion Rothman; m, Miles Goodman; md, Becky Mancuso and Tim Sexton; prod d, David Chapman; art d, Leslie A. Pope; set d, Derek Hill; spec, Sam Barkan; stunts, Ernie Orsatti; cos, Nan Cibula; makeup, Rodger Jacobs; chor, Jeffrey Hornaday

Comedy   (PR:A-C   MPAA:PG-13)

OVER EXPOSED

80m Concorde c

Catherine Oxenberg (*Kristen*), David Naughton (*Phillip*), Jennifer Edwards (*Helen*), John Patrick Reger (*Terrance*), William Bumiller (*Hank*), Larry Brand (*Morrison*), and Karen Black (*Mrs. Towbridge*)

In the time-honored tradition of exploitation films, OVER EXPOSED attempts to deliver a few cheap thrills by capitalizing on a genuinely disturbing trend—in this case, the danger posed to celebrities by obsessed, homicidal fans. Catherine Oxenberg ("Dynasty") is the psycho-bait in this tame thriller, playing Kristen, an actress featured in the vixen role of a sleazy prime-time soap opera. Kristen has been receiving death threats in the mail, and now finds one taped to her dressing-room mirror. When she leaves the TV studio, she is besieged by a gaggle of frenzied fans, among them Karen Black as Mrs. Towbridge, a brain-damaged victim of the 60s who calls the actress a "whore of the airwaves" and attempts to attack her with a *TV Guide*. Soon Kristen is spacing out to a soft-focus shot of a knife slicing into a cake, playing with matches, and flashing back to a birthday party at which a childhood friend accidentally set her own hair on fire. Not surprisingly, her wimpy doctor boy friend, Phillip (David Naughton of AN AMERICAN WEREWOLF IN LONDON), begins to worry about her mental health. One night, Kristen finds a nasty note from the psycho taped to her front door and decides to go for a walk through the mean streets of her suburban neighborhood. She is nearly molested by a group of transplanted street toughs, but saved by Hank (William Bumiller), a mysterious beach-bum ceramicist with a king-sized German shepherd. Next day at the studio, she discovers the body of one of her fellow actresses, propped up in a closet with her face peeled off. However, by the time she can summon security guards, the body has vanished, and she is driven home by the show's makeup artist, Helen (Jennifer Edwards), who tells her she shouldn't blame people for being fascinated with her because she is so rich, famous, and beautiful. Kristen begins to think she is cracking up, and Phillip suggests that she see a psychiatrist, which lands him in the doghouse. Back at the studio, Kristen, accosted once more by Mrs. Towbridge, runs her tormentor over with a car then jumps out to check the damage. Mrs. Towbridge attacks her, whereupon Morrison (the suspicious-looking character played by director Larry Brand) who has been trailing Kristen, jumps into the fray and decks the nutty woman. Morrison, it turns out, is an undercover policeman. He arrests Mrs. Towbridge, interrogates her, and decides that she probably isn't the psycho in question—though she does confess to having murdered her husband years ago. Meanwhile, another member of the soap's cast puts on some cold cream in his dressing room. His face melts off, and he dies as he crawls to the door. Kristen seeks consolation for her romantic troubles with Hank, and almost puts her hand in some powerful acid he keeps around the house to etch ceramics. After a quick roll in the hay, Kristen discovers that Hank has photos of her tacked up all over the house, decides he's the psycho, and sneaks away. Hank calls to explain that he is merely obsessed with her beauty, then goes over to her house, where he is arrested by Morrison for murder, the police having discovered the missing body of Kristen's actress colleague. Back at work, Kristen opens up another closet and finds the melted remains of the cold-cream victim. Hank is released for lack of evidence, but trailed by the cops; meanwhile, makeup artist Helen gives Kristen another lift home and reveals herself to be the killer, peeling off a mask and wig to reveal her hideously burned face and head. After conking Kristen with an ashtray, Helen explains it was she who burned herself at Kristen's birthday party years ago and that she has been nursing a desire for revenge against Kristen and all the world's beautiful people ever since. Outside the house, Morrison jumps Hank, who was attempting to reach Kristen. While the men duke it out, Helen threatens to peel Kristen's lovely face off. The actress runs downstairs, where she discovers Phillip dead in an armchair with a pair of scissors stuck in his neck, killed while watching TV. Borrowing the scissors,

Kristen runs upstairs to fight with Helen. They grapple, and Helen falls down the staircase, becoming impaled on the scissors just as Morrison and Hank burst into the house.

With its grotesque twist ending, OVER EXPOSED perks up considerably in the final 10 minutes, but otherwise it's basically a snoozer, with a few disgusting makeup effects and a little nudity tossed in here and there to pique the viewer's interest. The most noteworthy thing about this loser is its unpleasant basis in real-life tragedy: the film recalls the 1989 murder of actress Rebecca Schaeffer by an obsessive fan—particularly since Naughton costarred with Schaeffer and Pam Dawber in the CBS sitcom "My Sister Sam." His presence here reflects poorly on the casting director.

On the other hand, the film's writers (director Brand and Rebecca Reynolds) slip enough red herrings into the absurd plot to provide a certain amount of suspense for those viewers who care enough for the vapid Kristen to worry about who is trying to kill her in the first place. OVER EXPOSED is also graced by an enjoyably wacko performance by Black as Mrs. Towbridge, who believes Kristen should be punished for her soap-opera sins. (*Graphic violence, nudity, sexual situations, profanity.*)

d, Larry Brand; p, Roger Corman; w, Larry Brand and Rebecca Reynolds; ph, David Sperling; ed, Patrick Rand; m, Mark Governor; prod d, Robert Franklin

Thriller   (PR:O   MPAA:R)

PACIFIC HEIGHTS

107m James G. Robinson—Morgan Creek/FOX c

Melanie Griffith (*Patty Palmer*), Matthew Modine (*Drake Goodman*), Michael Keaton (*Carter Hayes*), Mako (*Toshio Watanabe*), Nobu McCarthy (*Mira Watanabe*), Laurie Metcalf (*Stephanie MacDonald*), Carl Lumbly (*Lou Baker*), Dorian Harewood (*Dennis Reed*), Luca Bercovici (*Greg*), Tippi Hedren (*Florence Peters*), Sheila McCarthy (*Liz Hamilton*), Guy Boyd (*Warning Cop*), Jerry Hardin (*Bennett Fidlow*), Dan Hedaya (*Loan Officer*), James Staley (*District Attorney*), Miriam Margolyes (*Realtor*), Luis Oropeza (*Revilla*), F. William Parker (*Judge*), Nicholas Pryor (*Hotel Manager*), Tony Simotes (*Desk Clerk*), O-Lan Jones (*Hotel Maid*), Seth Isler (*Sergeant*), Dabbs Greer (*Mr. Thayer*), Florence Sundstrom (*Mrs. Thayer*), Noel Evangelisti (*Mr. Smith*), Nicolas Rutherford (*Child*), Tim Pulice (*Younger Man*), Ray Hanis (*Older Man*), Takayo Fischer (*Bank Teller*), Tom Nolan (*Al*), Daniel MacDonald (*George*), J.P. Bumstead, Hal Landon Jr. (*Assistant Deputies*), Hy Anzell (*Locksmith*), Tracey Walter (*Exterminator*), William Patterson (*Mr. Hill*), D.W. Moffett (*Bill*), Barbara Bush (*Amy*), John Diaz (*Shoe Shine*), Roger Bearde (*Arresting Cop*), Ed Hodson (*Other Cop*), Frank Di Elsi (*Precinct Cop*), Michael J. Parker (*Man at Police Station*), Maggy Myers Davidson (*Diamond Lady*), Buddy Ekins, Danny Wynands (*Thugs*), David Lloyd Wilson (*Television Host*), Matthew Flint, Scott Freeman, Alice Barden, Danny Kovacs, Wat Takeshita, Frank Maruoka, Tohoru Masamune, Aida Anderson, Linda Austin (*Neighbors*), and Beverly D'Angelo (*Carter's Lover*)

Call it "Rental Attraction" or "Fatal Tenant"; it was not for nothing that the ad campaign for this thriller featured a critical blurb comparing it to Adrian Lyne's classic of middle-class paranoia FATAL ATTRACTION. In both films, basically bland yuppie couples are driven to murderous rage by sociopathic barbarians at the gates of their castles. Both films also have a common fault: if you stop to think about them for more than a minute, their plots dissolve before your eyes. Yet, if PACIFIC HEIGHTS is a trifle, under the direction of veteran filmmaker John Schlesinger (MIDNIGHT COWBOY; DAY OF THE LOCUST; MARATHON MAN), it is an uncommonly tasty one, a nerve-jangling Hitchcockian thriller that rises above the usual plundering of the Master of Suspense as a well-crafted homage.

PACIFIC HEIGHTS' basic plot fits easily in a nutshell: After buying a multi-unit house they can't afford, Patty Palmer (Melanie Griffith) and Drake Goodman (Matthew Modine) are toyed with and tormented by tenant-from-hell Carter Hayes (Michael Keaton), a man of many aliases who has made a career out of pillaging real-estate properties for profit. Daniel Pyne's story, reportedly based on his own experiences as a beleaguered landlord, unfolds like a 90s amorality play. As the film opens, Hayes and a blonde woman (Beverly D'Angelo) are wrapped in each others arms, but their lovemaking is interrupted by the appearance of Hayes' latest victims, two angry rednecks who pound a passive Hayes to a bloody pulp. The action shifts to San Francisco, where Patty, who teaches horseback riding, and Drake, an entrepreneur who owns a kite factory, fall in love with a house in the prestigious but pricey Pacific Heights neighborhood. It will cost them all their savings to make a down payment and stretch their credit to the limit to move in. Naturally, their best friend (Dorian Harewood) advises them against the purchase. Nevertheless, after lying on their application ("It's expected," says Patty), the two get their loan. In no time, they also get their first tenants for the house's two rental units. A Japanese-American couple (Mako and Nobu McCarthy) take the one-bedroom apartment, and the studio is claimed by Lou Baker (Carl Lumbly), an African-American who balks at filling out a credit report. He's dismissed as a "minority scam artist" by Drake, who thinks he knows about such things. It's clear from the outset, however, that Patty is the real brains of the couple. She has misgivings when Drake dismisses Baker only to abruptly forgo a credit report when he rents the studio to Hayes after the prospective tenant flashes a wad of hundreds, makes up a cockamamie story about why he can't fill out the report, and promises to have six months' rent wired to Drake's account from his own bank. It comes as little surprise to Patty, then, that Hayes' money keeps getting "delayed" and that the personal references he provides fail to check out. In the house for barely a month, Drake and Patty are already in danger of defaulting on their mortgage due to the delinquency of Hayes' payment. Still, Hayes moves in, changes the locks, and boards up the windows, hammering and drilling at all hours, to the consternation of the other tenants. Hoping to drive Hayes out by turning off his utilities, Drake instead winds up in court, where he is ordered to lower Hayes' rent for violating eviction laws. Then a plague of roaches, spilling over from Hayes' apartment, drives the Japanese-American couple out of the building. With frustration overtaking his already-minimal common sense, Drake attacks Hayes and is rewarded with a restraining order that bars him from his own house. Adding insult to injury, Hayes files a civil lawsuit calculated to force Drake to give up the property. But the tables are turned when Patty learns the rules of Hayes' game, giving him a heavy dose of his own medicine, precipitating the film's climax.

John Schlesinger brings a corrosive view of middle-class mores to his movies that is unequalled by contemporary mainstream directors. That view, more than anything else, is what distinguishes PACIFIC HEIGHTS from other, less successful attempts to emulate Hitchcock, who was never much of a proponent of standard middle-class values. Like Hitchcock's thrillers, PACIFIC HEIGHTS depends on a number of implausibilities to keep its plot moving. It also leaves Keaton's character confusingly underdeveloped, marring the climax slightly. But, as they do in Hitchcock's films, the flaws and implausibilities serve as means to an end. Innocent and ignorant at the beginning of their tenure as landlords, Drake and Patty are transformed by experience, and by the end of the film, they are as shrewd and manipulative as Hayes is. As a result, not only do Drake and Patty survive Hayes' onslaught, but at the fadeout, it appears likely they will sell their house for a tidy profit. By that point, few would argue that they haven't earned their little reward.

Fewer still would argue that PACIFIC HEIGHTS is anything but a crafty, unusually complex thriller, acted with skill and conviction by a uniformly strong cast. It's also just plain nail-biting fun. Schlesinger, unlike Adrian Lyne, conceives movies as extended narratives, rather than as three-minute, music-video-style segments filled with smoke and lingerie. Beyond its canny deployment of Hitchcockian themes—primarily its ambivalent view of the heroes, Hitchcock's celebrated "exchange of guilt"—PACIFIC HEIGHTS also has plenty of in-jokes for fans of the master. First and foremost, there is the charged casting of Griffith alongside her mother, Tippi Hedren (star of Hitchcock's THE BIRDS); then there is Schlesinger's own Hitchcock-style cameo (as the guy who sticks his hand in the elevator door). Alternately grim, playful, and gripping, PACIFIC HEIGHTS breathes new life into what was becoming a moribund genre. *(Profanity, violence, adult situations, brief nudity.)*

d, John Schlesinger; p, Scott Rudin and William Sackheim; w, Daniel Pyne; ph, Amir Mokri; ed, Mark Warner; m, Hans Zimmer; md, Shirley Walker; prod d, Neil Spisak; art d, Gershon Ginsburg and Sharon Seymour; set d, Clay A. Griffith and Debra Shutt; spec, Image Engineering, Peter M. Chesney, and J.D. Streett; stunts, Bobby Foxworth; cos, Ann Roth and Bridget Kelly; makup, Valli O'Reilly; tech, J.P. Pomposello

Thriller   (PR:C MPAA:R)

PAINT IT BLACK

102m Vestron c

Rick Rossovich *(Johnathan Dunbar)*, Doug Savant *(Eric Kinsley)*, Julie Carmen *(Gina Hayworth)*, Sally Kirkland *(Marion Easton)*, Peter Frechette *(Gregory Paul)*, Jason Bernard *(Lt. Wilder)*, Martin Landau *(Daniel Lambert)*, Frances Chaney *(Mrs. Russell)*, Lang Yun *(Mrs. Lee)*, John Fujioka *(Mr. Lee)*, Monique Van de Ven *(Kyla Leif)*, Andy Romano *(Mark Caniff)*, Marion Eaton *(Leonore Kinsley)*, Claudia Robinson *(Claudia Wilder)*, Mike Kimmel, and Leonard Pollack

Produced by the ill-fated Vestron Pictures, PAINT IT BLACK quickly ended up on videocassette; in fact, it was one of the last Vestron Video titles out before the pioneering home entertainment company folded. Among the factors in Vestron's demise were losses in its neophyte motion picture division, but a wide theatrical release for PAINT IT BLACK would probably not have turned the tide. It's a retrograde attempt to revive the Alfred Hitchcock thrillers of yore (especially STRANGERS ON A TRAIN), with an unfortunate emphasis on artifice and contrivance. One wonders if misty black-and-white cinematography

would have served this material better. Johnathan Dunbar (Rick Rossovich) is a struggling Santa Barbara artist in commercial and sexual bondage to slinky gallery owner Marion Easton (Sally Kirkland). Their contract gives her sole rights to his work, and she lures him into her bed with elusive promises of a one-man show. By chance Johnathan meets Eric Kinsley (Doug Savant), a wealthy but psychotic art collector who is responsible for a series of burglaries and assaults. Eric goes crazy (literally) over Johnathan's creations and murders Marion in order to help his idol. Of course, Johnathan becomes the prime suspect in the crime. He looks even more guilty when it is revealed that he broke into Marion's office on the night of her murder and scrutinized her ledgers to confirm that she'd been cheating him. Marion's slimy associate, Gregory Paul (Peter Frechette), has an incriminating business card Johnathan dropped during his break-in, and he successfully blackmails the artist with it; that is, until Eric knocks Gregory off, too. In the meantime, art-broker Daniel Lambert (Martin Landau) takes a serious interest in Johnathan and sells one of his sculptures to a business magnate. The furious Eric, who wanted the piece for himself, tries to kill Lambert, but Johnathan foils the murder attempt. Knowing now that Eric is guilty but fearing the killer will frame him with the incriminating business card, Jonathan doesn't go to the police. Instead, he and his girl friend, Gina Hayworth (Julie Carmen), go to Eric's mansion-of-horrors to look for the card. The protracted finale appears to be an homage either to the climax of NORTH BY NORTHWEST or to the Three Stooges; Carmen and Eric dangle off the side of the worst-looking cliff since the days of Jungle Jim, at opposite ends of a rope desperately held by Johnathan.

Mannered phoniness runs throughout PAINT IT BLACK: the exterior shots are unnaturally lit, resembling studio sets, and the characters and dialog seem to spring from Late Show reruns. Eric's mania, for instance, is attributed to a wobbly metal plate in his head. "Anything can be a work of art," he declares, "Sometimes you've got to kill to create." And so he does, using death-masks of Marion and Gregory in a subplot more suited to a horror tale set in a wax museum. Kirkland's sultry performance goes way over the top, but since that's appropriate for the material, the viewer really misses her when she's gone (Kirkland suffers a particularly gruesome death). Rossovich isn't given much to work with as the working man's artist who fixed auto bodies before turning his welding tools to cultural pursuits. Moreover, his easy submission to blackmail goes against his rebel hero pose.

PAINT IT BLACK had a rather troubled production history. Original director Roger Holzberg departed and was replaced by Tim Hunter, straight from his acclaimed work on 1987's THE RIVER'S EDGE. The script was revised so much by Holzberg and Hunter that the original writers, Tim Harris and Herschel Weingrod, asked for pseudonymous credits. Despite having so many cooks, the film has a fairly consistent tone; however, when all is said and done, it's just a superficial exercise in style without much innovation. Even the musical score quotes Hitchcock, using Bernard Herrman's "Fanfare for 'Torn Curtain'," as well as Strauss' "Voices of Spring" and "Bach Bouree." *(Violence, profanity, nudity, sexual situations, adult situations.)*

d, Tim Hunter; p, Anne Kimmel and Mark Forstater; w, Tim Harris and Herschel Weingrod; ph, Mark Irwin; ed, Curtiss Clayton; m, Jurgen Knieper; prod d, Steven Legler; set d, Steven Karatzas; spec, Larz Anderson; stunts, A.J. Nay; cos, Leonard Pollack; makup, Bridget Bergman

Thriller   (PR:O MPAA:R)

PATHFINDER

(Fin.) 155m International Film Exchange c

Mikkel Gaup *(Aigin)*, Ingvald Guttorm *(Father)*, Ellen Anne Buljo *(Mother)*, Inger Utsi *(Sister)*, Svein Scharffenberg *(Tchude Chief)*, Helgi Skulason *(Tchude with Scar)*, Knut Walle *(Tchude Interpreter)*, John S. Kristensen *(Tchude Strongman)*, Nils-Aslek Valkeapaa *(Siida-Isit)*, Nils Utsi *(Raste the Noaidi)*, Sara Marit Gaup *(Save)*, Anne-Marja Blind *(Varia)*, Henrik H. Buljo *(Dorakas)*, Svein Birger Olsen *(Diemis)*, Sverre Porsanger *(Sierge)*, Amund Johnskareng *(Heina)*, and Aliu Gaup *(Orbes)*

Nominated for an Oscar as Best Foreign-Language film in 1987, PATHFINDER provides a rousingly old-fashioned good time. Norwegian director Nils Gaup has a real talent for straightforward, soul-stirring action, a gift that has already landed him employment at Disney Studios. In the 10th century, on the frozen plains of Lapland, in the northernmost part of Norway, a peaceful tribe of families is menaced by nomadic savages called the Tchude. Sixteen-year-old Aigin (Mikkel Gaup) returns from a solo hunting trip to witness his parents and little sister being murdered by this savage band. He is wounded by a Tchude crossbow, but manages to escape on a single ski to a neighboring tribe. He warns this tribe of the oncoming savagery of the Tchude, and the camp is split between those who want to stay and fight and others who choose to flee to a safer haven on the northern coast. Aigin stays back at the campsite with the braver element and is captured by the Tchude, who slaughter all of the other remaining men.

The Tchude then force Aigin to lead them to those who fled. When all seems most hopeless, however, Aigin concocts an eleventh-hour scheme that places him in deadly peril but that eventually saves the day.

PATHFINDER is based on an ancient Lapp legend and is the first film to be shot in the Lapp language. It is also the first Scandinavian film to be made in wide-screen 70-millimeter Panavision and recorded in Dolby six-track stereo, and these two technical processes give vital dimension to the tale. Indeed, if there is any one true star of the piece, it is Erling Thurmann-Andersen's awe-inspiring cinematography, which captures the icy, bleak terrain of the Arctic with sublime power. The plot unfolds slowly, but gathers force as it reaches its exhilarating, death-defying climax. It behooves the viewer to set aside all expectations of immediate slam-bang gratification and merely revel in the invigorating, unfamiliar locale — the world of Scandinavian folklore. Animals figure prominently in this milieu, adding their own aura of mythic depth.

The acting is as artless as is required. Mikkel Gaup, besides being a whiz on skis, is angelic and determined; Nils Utsi as Raste, Aigin's spiritual leader, is saturnine and self-sacrificing; and the Tchude themselves ooze evil, with Svein Scharffenberg a terrifying standout as their leader. It should be noted that the Lapp tribeswomen are presented as intelligent, strong presences, every bit the survivalist equals of their men. (*Violence, brief nudity.*)

d, Nils Gaup; p, John M. Jacobsen; w, Nils Gaup; ph, Erling Thurmann-Andersen; ed, Niels Pagh Andersen; m, Nils-Aslak Valkeapaa, Marius Muller, and Kjetil Bjerkestrand; prod d, Harald Egede-Nissen; stunts, Martin Grace; cos, Eva Schjolberg and Marit Sofie Holmestrand; makup, Siw Jarbyn and Par Hjorth

Adventure   (PR:C   MPAA:NR)

PEACEMAKER

90m Crawford-Lane/Fries c

Robert Forster (*Yates*), Lance Edwards (*Townsend*), Hilary Shepard (*Dori Caisson*), Robert Davi (*Sgt. Frank Ramos*), Bert Remsen (*Doc*), John Denos (*Reeger*), Wally Taylor (*Moses*), Kyra Stemple, and Garth LeMaster (*Couple at Beach*)

A slam-bang action film with science-fiction underpinnings, PEACEMAKER sets itself apart from other features of its type, particularly those made on low budgets, by effectively blending suspense, romance, and comedy. The action begins when an interplanetary space rover crashes into the Pacific Ocean, frightening a young couple on a beach. The alien pilot, Townsend (Lance Edwards), who looks like a normal man, heads into Los Angeles and antagonizes some police officers by trying to steal a shotgun from their squad car and sending one them flying about 30 feet with a casual blow. More police arrive and pursue Townsend through back alleys and tenements, shooting him several times with little effect. Finally Townsend is surrounded and felled by a fusillade from the desperate cops. At the city morgue, Assistant Medical Examiner Dori Caisson (Hilary Shepard) is working on the bullet-riddled corpse when it suddenly heals itself and returns to life. Caisson runs away, but Townsend captures her and tries to force her to help him escape in her car. Meanwhile, Yates (Robert Forster), another alien, hears news accounts of the mysterious crash-landing and the police battle and, putting two and two together, proceeds to the morgue. When Yates spots Townsend and Caisson, he immediately tries to kill them. After a spectacular car-and-gun duel, Townsend succeeds in knocking Yates off the roof of a parking garage. Townsend forces Caisson to take him to her home, where he ties her up and teaches himself English overnight by scanning radio and TV broadcasts. The next day, Townsend explains that he is a peacemaker, a lawman from another planet, and that Yates is a dangerous criminal he has been assigned to capture. He also explains his miraculous rejuvenation, saying that his race can only be destroyed by massive damage to the brain. Meanwhile, Sgt. Frank Ramos (Robert Davi), a Los Angeles cop with a romantic interest in Caisson, worries when she fails to show up at work and decides to check for her at home. He arrives there shortly after Yates appears minus one hand, the result of his own encounter with the LAPD. Ramos' arrival interrupts a vicious battle between the two aliens. Despite being shot in the stomach, Townsend pursues Yates on foot, then on motorcycle when Yates steals a pickup truck. After a lengthy chase, Townsend jumps onto the truck and, while struggling with Yates, forces it off the road into a dynamite shack, resulting in a tremendous explosion. Caisson tries to tell Ramos that the two men were aliens, but he refuses to believe her. Naturally, everyone assumes the explosion killed Townsend and Yates, that is, until Yates, severely burned but mostly intact, turns up at Caisson's house. He ties her up, rejuvenates, then convinces her that he, not Townsend, is the peacemaker and that Townsend is actually an extremely clever and dangerous criminal. He says she is in danger because Townsend will probably return to make her help find the key to his space rover, which was lost during his first confrontation with the police. In no time, Townsend returns and attempts to kill Yates. But Caisson helps the severely wounded Yates escape, returning him to

his room in a run-down hotel. She goes to retrieve the missing key from Townsend's clothes at the morgue, intending to bring it to Yates. However, Townsend captures her again and manages to convince her that despite what Yates has told her, he, not Yates, is truly the peacemaker. After some inter-species hanky-panky in a motel room, Caisson gives Townsend the key, sends him out to buy some clothes, and calls Ramos to let him know she is safe. However, Ramos informs Caisson that she is anything but safe, since her boss at the morgue was tortured to death the previous night, apparently by Townsend, who was searching for the missing key. Ramos quickly drives to the motel with an army of police and attempts to capture Townsend, only to find that the alien has fled with Caisson. Caisson then manages to escape from Townsend herself, running over him in a pickup truck and returning to Yates' hotel. There she discovers that Yates had been lying to her after all — that he is the criminal and Townsend is the peacemaker. Townsend shows up, badly wounded from clinging to the undercarriage of Caisson's truck, and surrenders his weapon when Yates threatens to kill Caisson, whereupon she distracts Yates long enough for Townsend to attack bare-handed. After a desperate battle, Townsend reaches into a gash in his stomach, pulls out a handgun he has hidden there, and shoots Yates between the eyes. Caisson returns Townsend's key and takes him to his space ship so he can return to his home.

PEACEMAKER is an unexpected gem, a thriller that actually thrills, delivering the goods with a surprising amount of intelligence and style. Fans of sci-fi action films accustomed to dull knockoffs with one or two memorable moments at best will undoubtedly be impressed by director-screenwriter Kevin Tenney's verve and inventiveness. PEACEMAKER is lots of fun — the highest compliment you can pay a film of this type.

The film is also technically impressive, boasting rich nighttime cinematography by Thomas Jewett and elaborate but convincing makeup effects by John Blake. With the exception of a few scenes that show that the shooting and post-production of the film were probably rushed, PEACEMAKER looks like a big-budget effort throughout. Take a close look, for instance, at Yates' now-you-see-it, now-you-don't severed hand in the motorcycle-pickup truck chase scene. However, quibbles about continuity and poor timing in a few chase scenes seem petty when compared to all that this film has to offer.

For one thing, PEACEMAKER is a stunt extravaganza, packed from beginning to end with some truly spectacular and imaginative action sequences. It also manages to build genuine suspense by keeping the audience guessing as to which alien is the bad guy. Tenney even scores reasonably often in his attempts at humor, usually with throwaway lines such as Davi's contemptuous reference to Townsend as "Mork."

The acting by the entire cast is more than adequate to carry the film along. Forster (DELTA FORCE; THE BLACK HOLE) turns in a very strong performance as the impassive alien who may or may not be a murderer, and newcomer Edwards is equally effective as his foil. Davi, who usually plays the heavy (LICENCE TO KILL), is also interesting, despite his apparent discomfort in this good-guy role. (*Excessive violence, adult situations, nudity.*)

d, Kevin S. Tenney; p, Wayne Crawford and Andrew Lane; w, Kevin S. Tenney; ph, Thomas Jewett; ed, Dan Duncin; prod d, Rob Sissman; art d, Tucker Johnston; spec, John Carter, Bob Tiller, John D. Egget, and Special Effects Shop; stunts, B.J. Davis; makup, John Blake

Action/Science Fiction   (PR:O   MPAA:R)

PERFECT MURDER, THE

(India) 93m Merchant Ivory/Perfect Movie c

Naseeruddin Shah (*Inspector Ghote*), Madhur Jaffrey (*Mrs. Lal*), Stellan Skarsgard (*Axel Svensson*), Amjad Khan (*Lala Heera Lal*), Ratna Pathakshah (*Pratima Ghote*), and Sakin Jaffrey (*Neena Lal*)

Light, lively, and good fun, this English-language mystery-comedy set in India could be called a LETHAL WEAPON for movie lovers who relish witty wordplay over gunplay. Indeed, not a single shot is fired throughout the film, and the eponymous murder isn't even a murder. It's also far from perfect, in the generally understood sense of the "perfect crime." It seems that one Mr. Perfect, personal secretary to a jolly, fat, punning construction contractor named Lala (Amjad Khan), has been assaulted in his employer's Bombay home. Because there is no sign of forced entry, the list of suspects is a short one, consisting of Lala himself, his wife, his two sons, and his daughter-in-law. The case should be a piece of cake for Inspector Ghote (Naseeruddin Shah) — but if it were, of course, there wouldn't be much of a movie. If fact, Ghote is juggling not one, but four "top-priority" matters the day after Mr. Perfect's imperfect murder. Before that crime even occurred, Ghote had been trying, with no success, to crack a diamond-smuggling ring. A ring of another kind figures in a third case: a piece of costume jewelry with special sentimental value to the Minister of Justice, given to him by dazzling Bombay movie starlet Miss Twinkle, is now missing from his office desk drawer. Last, but not least, Ghote is assigned to escort a visitor from Sweden, criminologist Axel Svensson (Stellan Skarsgard), who's on hand to observe Bombay investigative procedures, and who becomes a mildly klutzy Mel Gibson to Ghote's East Indian Danny Glover. From the start of his investigation into the assault on Mr. Perfect, Ghote is hampered not by a shortage of clues or suspects, but by Indian social mores that dictate a degree of decorum in interrogation that even Svensson finally finds intolerably exasperating. Ghote's questioning of the upper-class Lala family is permitted only until they become annoyed, which happens with blinding suddenness whenever he broaches the matter of where each family member was when the unfortunate Perfect got clobbered with a candlestick. Meanwhile, Svensson keeps tripping over Ghote's diamond-smuggling investigation. Stepping off his plane, Svensson is accosted by a stranger who sidles up to inform him that "Krishna has stolen the butter" and who then attempts to wrest a large coffee-table book about the Hindu god from the Swede, who is carrying it with him. The real smuggler escapes, the diamonds concealed in a book identical to Svensson's. Later the smugglers, still convinced that Svensson is carrying the jewels and determined to force the truth from him, kidnap him by tickling him into submission. The quick-thinking Ghote, lacking police backup, diverts an anti-pornography demonstration to the smugglers' hideout to distract them, allowing him to free Svensson. Then, Ghote's too-diligent investigation of the missing Twinkle ring is brought to an abrupt end by the Minister of Justice's confession that he had the ring all along, and called for the investigation only to test Ghote's mettle. The plot continues to thicken, its solution coming, magically and literally, with the onset of the monsoon, which simultaneously speeds Mr. Perfect's recovery and gives Ghote the information he needs to tie up all his outstanding cases—which, from the Twinkle ring to the smuggling ring, turn out to be parts of one and the same case.

The clever symmetry and logic of THE PERFECT MURDER's mystery plot can be attributed to its basis in an acclaimed novel by H.R.F. Keating, who cowrote the script with director Zafar Hai. But, as in most good whodunits, getting to the solution is only half the fun. Incidental pleasures also abound in this Merchant Ivory production, starting with winning performances from lead actors Shah and Skarsgard and able supporting performances. Hai's direction is brisk, straightforward, and adroit, as well as unpretentiously sensitive and observant (perhaps a legacy of Hai's background in documentary filmmaking). Though frothy to a fault, THE PERFECT MURDER has a strong, realistic sense of place and character that somehow makes it even more richly amusing. Keating has authored an entire series of mysteries featuring Inspector Ghote; it is to be hoped that THE PERFECT MURDER won't be the last to reach the screen. *(Profanity.)*

d, Zafir Hai; p, Wahid Chohan; w, H.R.F. Keating and Zafar Hai (based on the book by Keating); ph, Walter Lassally; m, Richard Robbins; prod d, Kiran Patki and Sartaj Noorani; art d, Ram Yedekar; cos, Sally Turner

Comedy/Mystery   (PR:A MPAA:NR)

PLOT AGAINST HARRY, THE

81m New Yorker bw

Martin Priest *(Harry Plotnick)*, Ben Lang *(Leo)*, Maxine Woods *(Kay)*, Henry Nemo *(Max)*, Jacques Taylor *(Jack)*, Jean Leslie *(Irene)*, Ellen Herbert *(Mae)*, and Sandra Kazan *(Margie)*

Released 20 years after it was made, this hilarious tale of a small-time hood who can't get a break stars Martin Priest as the infamous Harry Plotnick, whose bad luck starts the moment he is freed after a nine-month prison term, when Max (Henry Nemo), his faithful driver and not-too-bright sidekick, is late meeting him. On the way home, they have an car accident, not just with anyone, but with Harry's ex-brother-in-law, Leo (Ben Lang), whose passengers include Harry's ex-wife, Kay (Maxine Woods), and the grown daughter Harry didn't know he had. Just as Harry is starting to settle into life on the outside, he becomes ill, prompting visits from his overprotective sister, Mae (Ellen Herbert), and an entourage of assorted relatives bearing fruit baskets and vaporizers. While reporting to his parole officer, Harry faints from anxiety and is taken to the hospital, where he learns he has an enlarged heart. His woes continue when he checks out of the hospital and returns to his hotel only to discover that there has been a fire, set by Max, who, panicking over an impending IRS audit, torched Harry's accounting books. Naturally, everybody—including Max—contends that Harry put the driver up to the dirty deed. To complicate matters further, Harry's daughter becomes pregnant, and Kay informs Harry's parole officer about one of her ex-husband's parole violations. Later, Harry is invited to the Heart Foundation's "Have a Heart" marathon, during which he becomes drunk, walks onto the set, and has a heart attack on national television. Thinking he's not long for this world, Harry pledges $20,000 to the Heart Foundation, and claims that he did, in fact, tell Max to burn "the books." Eventually, Harry ends up where he began, in prison.

Michael Roemer and his talented cast have created an extremely funny film, which, unlike Woody Allen's overtly neurotic comedies, conveys the problems and anxieties of its characters with great subtlety. As interesting as this well-crafted film is, the story behind its long-delayed release is even more fascinating. After garnering critical praise for their low-budget feature NOTHING BUT A MAN (1965), Roemer, a professor of Film and American Studies at Yale, and former Harvard classmate Robert Young (director of the acclaimed SHORT EYES) received financing from the Seattle-based King Screen Productions to make another film. Made on a budget of $680,000, written and directed by Roemer with Young again acting as the cinematographer, that film, THE PLOT AGAINST HARRY, was completed in 1969; however, Roemer was unable to find a distributor. Shelving THE PLOT AGAINST HARRY, Roemer continued to teach and made a number of documentaries and features, mostly for public television, the best-known being the fiction film "Haunted," which was aired on PBS's "American Playhouse" series in 1984. Twenty years after his original attempt to distribute THE PLOT AGAINST HARRY, Roemer decided to transfer the film to videotape so that, as he explained to the *New York Times*, his kids could see it. In the process of reworking the soundtrack, he decided to make new 35 mm prints of the film and sent them off to the New York and Toronto film festivals, where THE PLOT AGAINST HARRY was extremely well received, leading to the film's general release.

A period film that was not intended to be a period film, THE PLOT AGAINST HARRY is a wonderful document of the sights and sounds of the late 1960s. Well-acted, deftly written and directed, and expertly shot by Young, this darkly comic tale of a hapless small-time gangster is an engaging cinematic artifact that remains as fresh today as the day it was made. *(Adult situations.)*

d, Michael Roemer; p, Michael Roemer and Robert Young; w, Michael Roemer; ph, Robert Young; ed, Terry Lewis and Georges Klotz; m, Frank Lewin; art d, Howard Mandel; cos, Lily Partridge

Comedy   (PR:A-C MPAA:NR)

POSTCARDS FROM THE EDGE

101m Columbia c

Meryl Streep *(Suzanne Vale)*, Shirley MacLaine *(Doris Mann)*, Dennis Quaid *(Jack Falkner)*, Gene Hackman *(Lowell)*, Richard Dreyfuss *(Dr. Frankenthal)*, Rob Reiner *(Joe Pierce)*, Mary Wickes *(Grandma)*, Conrad Bain *(Grandpa)*, Annette Bening *(Evelyn Ames)*, Simon Callow *(Simon Asquith)*, Gary Morton *(Marty Wiener)*, C.C.H. Pounder *(Julie Marsden)*, Sidney Armus *(Sid Roth)*, Robin Bartlett *(Aretha)*, Barbara Garrick *(Carol)*, Anthony Heald *(George Lazan)*, Dana Ivey *(Wardrobe Mistress)*, Oliver Platt *(Neil Bleene)*, Michael Ontkean *(Robert Munch)*, Pepe Serna *(Raoul)*, Mark Lowenthal *(Bart)*, Michael Byers *(Allen)*, J.D. Souther *(Ted)*, George Wallace *(Carl)*, Peter Onorati *(Cameraman)*, Roy Helland *(Makeup Man)*, Douglas Roberts *(Soundman)*, R.M. Haley *(Assistant Director No. 1)*, Kathleen Gray *(Cindy)*, Gloria Crayton *(Maid at Party)*, Gary Matanky, Marc Tubert *(Sound Editors)*, John Verea *(Young Intern)*, Rene Assa *(Passport Official)*, Natalia Nogulich, Susan Forristal *(Friends at Airport)*, Evelina Fernandez *(Airline Employee)*, Neil Machlis *(Rob Sonnenfeld)*, Gary Jones *(Fan at Party)*, Jane Galloway *(Nurse)*, Steven Brill *(Assistant Director No. 2)*, Jason Tomlins *(Officer)*, Shelley Kirk *(First Lady)*, Jessica Z. Diamond *(Script Supervisor)*, Scott Frankel *(Pianist at Party)*, Sheridan Leatherbury *(Stand-in)*, Ken Gutstein *(Director of Photography)*, James Deeth, Robert Marshall *(Helicopter Pilots)*, Jim Cuddy, Greg Keelor, Bazil Donovan, Mark French, and Bob Weiseman *(Blue Rodeo Band)*

Adapted by Carrie Fisher from her first novel, POSTCARDS FROM THE EDGE is yet more proof that Hollywood makes its best films about what it knows best—making films in Hollywood. But while POSTCARDS is entertaining and observant of the world of moviemaking—with a casual command of mood, character, and *mise en scene*—too much of its running time is taken up with the predictable, cliched mother-daughter drama at the film's center. Continuing in the dark comedy vein she began with SHE DEVIL, Meryl Streep, playing actress Suzanne Vale, starts at rock bottom. While working on a film, Suzanne is so addled by a cocaine habit that her director, Lowell (Gene Hackman), finds it necessary to threaten her life just to get her focused. When she then overdoses on sedatives while in the bed of Jack Falkner (Dennis Quaid), the womanizing producer anonymously wheels her into a hospital emergency room. There her stomach is pumped by a doctor (Richard Dreyfuss) who sends her a card and flowers and asks her out on a date. During her rehabilitation, Suzanne must contend with a therapist (C.C.H. Pounder of BAGDAD CAFE fame) whose grab-bag of what Suzanne calls "bumper-sticker" self-help slogans is enough to drive a patient back to drugs. Upon completing her clinical rehab, Suzanne finds her career in need of resuscitation. She has developed a "reputation" and is only able to find work on a mediocre B-grade cop movie. As a stipulation of her employment on even this lowly project, Suzanne must submit to random drug testing. During the production she is also required to live with her domineering, alcoholic, entertainer-mom, Doris (Shirley MacLaine), the too-obvious cause of Suzanne's problems. Suzanne can't open her mouth without finding herself in a battle of oneupmanship with Doris, who matches her daughter's tales of drug addiction with fondly overwrought reminiscences of her own nervous breakdown and who responds to Suzanne's anguish with adroit guilt-mongering. Even a casual singing performance at a party becomes a show-biz battle-to-the-death between mother and daughter. Suzanne finds that being drug-free poses new challenges on other fronts as well. On the set, she is forced to sit still for her hack producers' unsolicited advice on her performance. She also listens in secrecy while her director (Simon Callow) and wardrobe mistress (Dana Ivey) casually discuss how they will shoot around Suzanne's weight gain in close-up love scenes—which actually makes no sense, since Streep, notwithstanding the can of cola and bag of corn chips permanently grafted to her hands, looks as trim as ever. Then Suzanne has to endure the return of Falkner, who professes his love for her, though his main interest is in adding notches to his "gun."

However, the film never resolves its on-the-set subplot, letting it fall by the wayside as MacLaine's Doris bulldozes into the action, finally appearing, sans wig and balding, in a hospital room after wrapping her Mercedes around a tree and getting cited for driving under the influence. Talk about upstaging! Ultimately, Hackman's bullying director makes a climactic reappearance to give Suzanne permission to break away from her mom and build her own life. Beyond its sexist implications and the fact that it deprives Suzanne of a victory that is solely her own, this is scene is just plain implausible. How exactly has Hackman's Lowell, who has been absent since the beginning of the film, come into all this intimate knowledge of Suzanne's personal crises? While there is no easy answer to that question, Lowell's dispensation and Suzanne's response do echo Mike Nichols' previous film, WORKING GIRL, in which Melanie Griffith's strong heroine irrationally requires the endorsement of Harrison Ford's hunky hero to be complete.

If the foreground action is predictable, Nichols and Fisher nevertheless manage to slip a few provocative ideas into the background, much as Nichols did with WORKING GIRL. Notably, Suzanne's return to sobriety is anything but rewarding; instead it provides her with a new sensitivity to the callousness and treachery of agents, producers, directors, lovers, and, most importantly, of her mother. Suzanne's personal struggle is also contrasted throughout with Doris' nonstop, unrepentant boozing. On her way to a dubbing session for the film she made with Lowell, Suzanne finally backslides, popping enough tranquilizers to make her woozy. Although she pulls over to throw up along the way, the point is made that sedation is not an unreasonable response to a life as grueling and crazy as the one Suzanne leads. Because she is caught up in a world of constant role-playing, events that happen off the set seem even less "real" than those enacted before the cameras. The movie winds up with Suzanne's triumphant country-and-western singing debut, but Nichols gives her success a double edge; behind the crowd of madly cheering extras is a less-than-enthusiastic "real" audience, the moviemaking crew—bored grips and gaffers marking time until lunch.

If for no other reason, POSTCARDS deserves praise for giving movie audiences their first real exposure to Streep's singing voice, much lauded by those familiar with her stage work. Her performance here isn't riveting, but she does a good job of belting out a tune. The performance earned her a Best Actress Oscar nomination, while the song, "I'm Checking Out" (Shel Silverstein), also was nominated. What sabotages POSTCARDS are the extended screaming scenes between Streep and MacLaine, who seem to be acting in two different films—MacLaine in some sort of MOMMIE DEAREST-like show-business horror story and Streep in a far more delicate modern comedy of bad manners, LA-style (which is more in keeping with Fisher's largely plotless novel). Instead of sending off either dramatic or comedic sparks, they wind up highlighting each others' weaknesses, with MacLaine's scene-gobbling stridency steamrolling Streep's technical polish and emotional reserve.

In the final analysis, POSTCARDS is a mixed bag. There are a number of entertaining moments; however, potentially interesting characters and situations wither from lack of development for the sake of the central relationship, which is never wholly convincing—the idea of MacLaine mothering Streep never gets past its initial bizarreness. While Fisher shows some potential as a screenwriter, her script here is mostly an exercise in technique, its pieces fitting neatly together. But though no Screenwriting 101 teacher could fail to give her an A, the script never comes to life under Nichols' direction, which remains irritatingly self-conscious; again he has carefully and condescendingly packaged sophistication for a mass audience. If anything holds the film together, it is Streep's comic flair. But she's almost as stranded here as she was in SHE DEVIL, with material that rarely allows her to call upon her strengths as an actress. She deserves better, and so does the audience. (*Adult situations, substance abuse, profanity.*)

d, Mike Nichols; p, Mike Nichols and John Calley; w, Carrie Fisher (based on her novel); ph, Michael Ballhaus; ed, Sam O'Steen; m, Carly Simon; md,

Howard Shore; prod d, Patrizia Von Brandenstein; art d, Kandy Stern; set d, Chris A. Butler; cos, Ann Roth; makup, J. Roy Helland

Comedy/Drama   **(PR:C   MPAA:R)**

PREDATOR 2

108m Silver—Davis—Gordon/FOX c

Danny Glover (*Mike Harrigan*), Gary Busey (*Peter Keyes*), Ruben Blades (*Danny Archuletta*), Maria Conchita Alonso (*Leona Cantrell*), Bill Paxton (*Jerry Lambert*), Robert Davi (*Heinemann*), Adam Baldwin (*Garber*), Kent McCord (*Captain Pilgrim*), Morton Downey Jr. (*Pope*), Calvin Lockhart (*King Willie*), Steve Kahan (*Sergeant*), Henry Kingi (*El Scorpio*), Corey Rand (*Ramon Vega*), Elpidia Carrillo (*Anna*), Lilyan Chauvin (*Irene Edwards*), Michael Mark Edmondson (*Gold Tooth*), Teri Weigel (*Colombian Girl*), Louis Eppolito (*Patrolman*), Charlie Haugk (*Charlie*), Sylvia Kauders (*Ruth*), Charles David Richards (*Commuter*), Julian Reyes (*Juan Beltran*), DeLynn Binzel (*Hooker*), Carl Pistilli (*Cop on Phone*), Vonte Sweet (*Sweet*), Ron Moss (*Jerome*), Brian Levinson (*Anthony*), Diana James (*Leona's Friend*), Beth Kanar (*Woman Officer*), William R. Perry (*Subway Gang Leader*), Alex Chapman, Gerard G. Williams, John Cann, Michael Papajohn (*Subway Gang Members*), Casey Sander, Pat Skipper, Carmine Zozzora (*Federal Team Members*), Valerie Karasek, Chuck Boyd, David Starwalt, Abraham Alvarez, Jim Ishida, George Christy, Lucinda Weist (*Reporters*), Richard Anthony Crenna, Billy "Sly" Williams (*Paramedics*), Paolo Tocha, Nick Corri (*Detectives*), Tom Finnegan, Patience Moore (*Officers*), Kashka, Jeffrey Reed (*Jamaicans*), Paul Abascal, and Michael Wiseman (*Cops*)

This sequel to the popular 1987 film starring Arnold Schwarzenegger takes place in 1997 with the setting changed from the jungles of South America to the urban jungles of Los Angeles. The ozone layer has been further depleted, the smog is worse than ever, and LA is in the midst of its worst heat wave in history. As if environmental problems weren't enough, drug lords have taken over the streets, turning the city into a war zone. Trying desperately to control the criminal elements is Det. Mike Harrigan (Danny Glover), who is aided by an elite group of cops including his right-hand man, Danny Archuletta (Ruben Blades); a tough Venezuelan, Leona Cantrell (Maria Conchita Alonso); and a newcomer, Jerry Lambert (Bill Paxton). The cops are soon baffled when someone or something uses incredible strength and strange weaponry to brutally dispense with gang members. It isn't long before the mysterious killer also starts murdering the cops. As Harrigan and his men hunt for the killer, a task force headed by government agent Peter Keyes (Gary Busey) conducts its own investigation. Keyes orders Harrigan to get off the case, but after Archuletta and Lambert are killed and Cantrell is injured, Harrigan (much as Schwarzenegger did in the original film) resolves to become a one-man gang and battle the creature his way.

The screenplay for this film is every bit as silly as it was for the 1987 film, the only difference being that this time there are none of Schwarzenegger's inane asides. However, director Stephen Hopkins' sharp, stylish work overcomes many of the script's flaws. Hopkins is a graduate of the "Nightmare on Elm Street" school of filmmaking, having directed the fifth entry in that series. He does a terrific job of keeping things moving and the film features some distinctive camerawork and editing. The action sequences are taut and the atmosphere memorably tense. The creature itself (created by Stan Winston and played again by Kevin Peter Hall) is a bit too reminiscent of ALIEN (in fact, late in the movie there is an in-joke reference to that movie monster), but is a frightening adversary. Busey (who gives a wonderfully hammy speech about the Predator's behavior), Blades, Alonso, and Paxton are all solid, and it's refreshing to see a black action hero (Glover) in a major motion picture. There are also a number of delightful cameos, from such performers as Kent McCord (TV's "Adam 12"), Adam Baldwin (FULL METAL JACKET), Robert Davi (DIE HARD), Calvin Lockhart (WILD AT HEART), and Morton Downey, Jr., of course playing a slimy reporter. The cast members seem to be having fun and it shows in the good-natured humor running through the film.

PREDATOR 2 is not without its problems, however. There is an extended subway scene that goes on too long and is ineptly staged. Further, this was the second 1990 film (following MARKED FOR DEATH) which featured an unfortunate anti-Jamaican sentiment—every Jamaican in the film is a wild-eyed drug addict. Naturally, the film has its share of misogynist ingredients—in fact, there are numerous hints that the monster may be female. Still, the film's energy and style are enough to recommend it. Lovers of the original should be pleased with this effort, as should most fans of the genre. (*Violence, gore effects, profanity, adult situations, substance abuse, nudity.*)

d, Stephen Hopkins; p, Lawrence Gordon, Joel Silver, and John A. Davis; w, James E. Thomas and John C. Thomas; ph, Peter Levy; ed, Mark Goldblatt and Bert Lovitt; m, Alan Silvestri; prod d, Lawrence G. Paull; art d, Geoff Hubbard; set d, Alan Manzer, Richard Mays, Louis Mann, and Sally Thornton; spec, Stan

Winston, Joel Hynek, and Ken Pepiot; stunts, Gary Davis; cos, Marilyn Vance-Straker; makup, Scott H. Eddo, Michael Mills, and Kevin Westmore

Action/Horror   (PR:O   MPAA:R)

PRESUMED INNOCENT

127m Mirage/WB c

Harrison Ford (*Rusty Sabich*), Brian Dennehy (*Raymond Horgan*), Raul Julia (*Sandy Stern*), Bonnie Bedelia (*Barbara Sabich*), Paul Winfield (*Judge Larren Lyttle*), Greta Scacchi (*Carolyn Polhemus*), John Spencer (*Detective Lipranzer*), Joe Grifasi (*Tommy Molto*), Tom Mardirosian (*Nico Della Guardia*), Anna Maria Horsford (*Eugenia*), Sab Shimono (*"Painless" Kumagai*), Bradley Whitford (*Jamie Kemp*), Christine Estabrook (*Lydia "Mac" MacDougall*), Michael Tolan (*Mr. Polhemus*), Madison Arnold (*Sgt. Lionel Kenneally*), Ron Frazier (*Stew Dubinsky*), Jesse Bradford (*Nat Sabich*), Joseph Mazzello (*Wendell McGaffney*), Tucker Smallwood (*Detective Harold Greer*), Leland Gantt (*Leon Wells*), Teodorina Bello (*Ernestine*), David Wohl (*Morrie Dickerman*), John Michael Bennett (*Guerasch*), Bo Rucker (*Mike Duke*), Peter Appel (*Glendenning*), John Ottavino (*Chet*), Robert Katims (*Cody*), Joseph Carberry (*Mr. McGaffney*), John Seitz (*Balestrieri*), Bill Winkler (*Tom*), John Vennema (*Judge Mumphrey*), Michael Genet (*Court Clerk*), Richard L. Newcomb (*Undercover Cop*), Ed Wheeler (*Jim, Arresting Detective*), Miles Watson (*Arresting Detective*), DeAnn Mears (*Loretta*), Julia Meade (*Moderator*), Thom Cagle (*Camp Counselor*), Ricky Rosa (*Camper*), Allison Field, Janis Corsair, Bill Corsair, Carla Goff (*Reporters*), Rick DeFuria, Victor Truro, Elizabeth Williams, Jeffrey Wright, Ted Neustadt, and Kimberleigh Aarn (*Prosecuting Attorneys*)

If they gave an Oscar for the year's most claustrophobic film, PRESUMED INNOCENT could win it in a walk. Everything about this film is as cramped, clenched, and constricted as Harrison Ford's face, which looks like a tightly balled-up fist here. Even in his love scenes he manages to look more like he's withdrawing than advancing, kissing with his lips pressed tightly together against both the dazzling Greta Scacchi and the exquisite Bonnie Bedelia. However, Ford's perpetually coiled-up state also makes him the perfect murder suspect in this adaptation of attorney Scott Turow's best-selling novel, which presents a perversely fascinating view of the beleaguered American criminal justice system and the flawed people who run it. Finishing the novel, the reader wonders how anything of merit is accomplished amid the crosscurrents of ambition, greed, and lust that fill the courtrooms of mythical Kindle County. Coming away from the movie, the viewer is likely to feel as drained as Gordon Willis' trademark monochromatic cinematography and Ford's desiccated performance.

Ford plays prosecuting attorney Rusty Sabich, the quintessential good soldier right down to his absurd Roman Centurion haircut. But Sabich serves a degraded master, District Attorney Raymond Horgan (Brian Dennehy), a soured idealist whose principles have been compromised by years of deals made to keep the wheels of justice from grinding to a halt. As the film begins, Horgan is making a halfhearted run at re-election, but his campaign is fatally rocked by the sordid rape-murder of his star prosecutor in the sex-crimes division, the brilliant, beautiful, and ambitious Carolyn Polhemus (Scacchi). Initially, the list of suspects is extensive, a grim tribute to Polhemus' enviable conviction rate, if not her rapacious sex life. But that list narrows to a single name when Sabich's fingerprints are found on a beer glass five feet from Polhemus' body and when tests reveal that the killer's blood type also matches that of Sabich, who had an affair with Polhemus that ended messily. That affair damaged but failed to destroy Sabich's marriage to his wife Barbara (Bedelia), a frustrated academic. Now it has come back to haunt his career. Ever the good soldier, and despite a clear conflict of interest, Sabich takes charge of the investigation after being practically begged to do so by Horgan, who is himself one of Polhemus' former lovers. Not content with having driven Horgan from office in disgrace and embarrassment, the newly elected county DA, Nico Della Guardia (Mardirosian), seizes upon the Sabich case, which he handles personally, in an effort to thoroughly discredit Horgan's tenure. To save his new career in private practice, Horgan is content to shift the blame to Sabich. Furious because Sabich failed to disclose his tryst with Polhemus to him, Horgan is even willing to commit perjury on the witness stand. As the film progresses it becomes clear that truth and justice are the real victims here. Seeing that justice is done is not the object—winning a case is. To that end, Sabich engages top defense lawyer Sandy Stern (Raul Julia), whose stock strategy is to weave a web of doubt around seemingly expert and unimpeachable witnesses. (Stern was the real hero of Turow's novel, a character so rich and vivid that the author placed him at the center of *The Burden of Proof*, his follow-up to *Presumed Innocent*.) While the other characters, including Sabich, scramble to conceal and confuse, Stern succeeds by exposing human frailty and remorseless self-interest in the cold light of the courtroom. So thorough is his demolition of the prosecution that he never has to present anything so mundane as a defense. The case is dismissed by the judge (Paul Winfield) before Stern can place any of his own witnesses on the stand. And a

good thing, too. As it turns out, his first witness was fully prepared to confess to the crime.

The solution to this whodunit will hardly surprise any of the millions who have read Turow's novel. However, neither the book nor the movie hinges on the killer's disclosure. Instead the mystery serves to pull readers and viewers deeply into the world of characters whose lives and careers are taken up by the endlessly fascinating business of placing inhuman acts in a human perspective for their evaluation and punishment. In these characters—who have one foot planted outside society and one within—the most civilized ideals mix freely with the most base instincts and motivations.

Despite Turow's contributions, the controlling sensibilities behind the film are those of director Alan J. Pakula, who cowrote the script, and cinematographer Willis. Sabich is repeatedly and implausibly seen poring over legal documents in near-complete darkness for the sake of an expressive photographic effect from Willis, known for his artful use of shadows and darkness in films like THE GODFATHER and its sequels. Meanwhile, Pakula at times seems overly attuned to the weary, overstressed quality that dominated the characters in Turow's book. Forget the dashing, physical Ford of STAR WARS and Indiana Jones fame. Here, we rarely see him walk, much less crack whips or punch out bad guys. Mostly—almost too often—we see him sitting and moping.

However, in the end, along with its strong basic story line, there are simply too many powerful themes, ideas, and characters in PRESUMED INNOCENT to make it anything less than absolutely engrossing whatever its incidental flaws. Though Pakula and company have abridged Turow's work, they wisely haven't altered it in any important way. Turow's familiarity with the world of the law and its personalities cannot be disputed. But, like any lawyer, he also knows how to weave the "physical evidence" into a persuasive narrative rich with nuance. And those qualities carry over easily into PRESUMED INNOCENT, aided by a uniformly fine cast and Pakula's best work since he turned out Oscar winners such as KLUTE; SOPHIE'S CHOICE; and ALL THE PRESIDENT'S MEN. (*Adult situations, sexual situations, nudity, profanity.*)

d, Alan J. Pakula; p, Sydney Pollack and Mark Rosenberg; w, Frank Pierson and Alan J. Pakula (based on the novel by Scott Turow); ph, Gordon Willis; ed, Evan Lottman; m, John Williams; prod d, George Jenkins; art d, Bob Guerra; set d, Carol Joffe; spec, C5, Inc.; cos, John Boxer; makup, Fern Buchner; tech, William N. Fordes

Crime/Mystery   (PR:C   MPAA:R)

PRETTY WOMAN

119m Silver Screen Partners—Touchstone/Buena Vista c

Richard Gere (*Edward Lewis*), Julia Roberts (*Vivian Ward*), Ralph Bellamy (*James Morse*), Jason Alexander (*Philip Stuckey*), Laura San Giacomo (*Kit De Luca*), Alex Hyde-White (*David Morse*), Amy Yasbeck (*Elizabeth Stuckey*), Elinor Donahue (*Bridget*), Hector Elizondo (*Hotel Manager*), Judith Baldwin (*Susan*), Jason Randal (*Magician*), Bill Applebaum (*Howard*), Tracy Bjork, Gary Greene (*Guests*), William Gallo (*Carlos*), Abdul Salaam El Razzac (*Happy Man*), Hank Azaria (*Detective*), Larry Hankin (*Landlord*), Julie Paris (*Rachel*), Rhonda Hansome (*Bermuda*), Harvey Keenan (*Man in Car*), Marty Nadler, Lynda Goodfriend (*Tourists*), Reed Anthony (*Cruiser*), Frank Campanella (*Pops*), Jacqueline Woolsey (*Artist*), Cheri Caspari (*Angel*), Scott A. Marshall (*Skateboard Kid*), Patrick Richwood (*Night Elevator Operator Dennis*), Kathi Marshall (*Day Desk Clerk*), Laurelle Brooks (*Night Desk Clerk*), Don Feldstein (*Desk Clerk*), Marvin Braverman (*Room Service Waiter*), Alex Statler (*Night Doorman*), Jeff Michalski (*Day Doorman*), Patrick D. Stuart (*Day Bellhop*), Lloyd T. Williams (*Bellhop*), R. Darrell Hunter (*Darryl, The Limo Driver*), James Patrick Dunne (*Lounge Pianist*), Valorie Armstrong (*Woman in Lobby*), Steve Restivo (*Italian Businessman*), Rodney Kageyama (*Japanese Businessman*), Douglas Stitzel (*American Businessman*), Larry Miller (*Mr. Hollister*), Dey Young (*Snobby Saleswoman*), Shane Ross (*Marie*), Carol Williard, Minda Burr, Robyn Peterson, Mariann Aalda (*Saleswomen*), RC Everbeck (*Tie Salesman*), Michael French (*Maitre d'*), Allan Kent (*Waiter*), Stacy Keach Sr. (*Sen. Adams*), Lucinda Sue Crosby, Nancy Locke (*Olsen Sisters*), Calvin Remsberg (*Sodstomping Announcer*), Lloyd Nelson (*Game Announcer*), Norman Large (*Polite Husband*), Tracy Reiner (*Woman at Car*), Tom Nolan (*Vance*), John David Carson (*Mark*), Daniel Bardol (*Jake*), Karin Calabro (*"Violetta"*), Bruce Eckstut (*"Alfredo"*), Amzie Strickland (*Matron*), and Mychael Bates (*Usher*)

Director Garry Marshall tips his hand in this lackluster film when he shows Julia Roberts, as Hollywood hooker Vivian Ward, gleefully watching Audrey Hepburn and Cary Grant kissing at the end of a Stanley Donen romantic comedy. Though the man who gave the world "Laverne and Shirley" strives in PRETTY WOMAN for a sophistication that is beyond his grasp, he is right about one thing: Roberts radiates a sprightly, Hepburnish star quality that goes a long way towards making PRETTY WOMAN tolerable entertainment. She is a nonstop delight to watch and demonstrates an astounding maturity in her performance here.

Richard Gere costars as Roberts' love interest, hard-driving corporate takeover specialist Edward Lewis, who, as the film begins, is at a high-powered Holly-wood Hills party. But he is without his girl friend, who is in the process of moving out of their New York apartment. Leaving the party to head back to his Beverly Hills hotel, Lewis winds up in Hollywood instead. Meanwhile, Vivian is getting ready to hit the streets because her roommate, Kit (SEX, LIES AND VIDEOTAPE's Laura San Giacomo), has spent the household nest egg and the rent is due. On the street, Vivian meets the lost Lewis, who pays her $20 for directions back to Beverly Hills, and even lets her drive his car. On an impulse, he invites her up to his penthouse suite to spend the night—harboring only the purest of intentions, of course. Stripping down to her silky lingerie, however, Vivian manages to loosen up the staid Lewis. The next morning, saying he needs a social partner during his week in LA, Lewis hires Vivian to fill the role. This being a romantic comedy, emotions and nature then take their course.

While only some viewers may find it unlikely that a hooker would be named Vivian, most will agree that the chances are considerably slimmer that two cover girl knockouts like Roberts and San Giacomo would be plying their trade on the boulevard. All right, so PRETTY WOMAN is supposed to be a fairy tale. But whose? It's hard to tell, because the script fails to make the film the street-smart "Pygmalion" it wants to be. Vivian is hardly more than a stereotype, little more than a pneumatic fantasy whore. It's never even completely clear why Lewis hires her, because most of his working week is taken up with business meetings with James Morse (Ralph Bellamy), whose company Lewis is bidding to take over (since when do you bring dates to business meetings?). Between meetings, Lewis seems to have a lot of time on his hands, and he spends it hanging out with Vivian while his evil lawyer, Stuckey (Jason Alexander), plays hardball with Morse. Not many lawyers try to rape their clients' girl friends, but so many illogical events occur in this film that Stuckey's attempted rape of Vivian becomes just one more bizarre development in a script full of implausibilities.

Still, if Marshall knows anything, it's how to cast a film. Roberts is on the screen most of the time because she deserves to be there (and needs to be there, to provide a distraction from the script and ham-handed direction). Her perfor-mance earned a Best Actress Oscar nomination. Yet surprisingly, most of the overt sexual titillation is contributed by Gere, whose physique is on display more than that of Roberts or San Giacomo. Although Gere seems to have phoned in his performance, he nevertheless displays a potential flair for comedy (though that potential may never be realized unless Gere works with a director who finds the key to waking him up). San Giacomo, on the other hand, gives the film's funniest performance in her brief role as the gum-cracking Kit. The other actors comprise a solid ensemble. Alexander, Bellamy, and Marshall regular Hector Elizondo, as the hotel's indulgent manager, all contribute fine performances. Had the producers just been able to lure Stanley Donen out of retirement—and George Bernard Shaw back from the dead—they might have had a good movie on their hands. *(Adult situations, profanity.)*

d, Garry Marshall; p, Arnon Milchan and Steven Reuther; w, J.F. Lawton; ph, Charles Minsky; ed, Priscilla Nedd; m, James Newton Howard; prod d, Albert Brenner; art d, David M. Haber; set d, Garrett Lewis; spec, Gary Zink; stunts, Rick Avery; cos, Marilyn Vance-Straker; makup, Bob Mills

Comedy/Romance   **(PR:O   MPAA:R)**

PRIMAL RAGE

(It.) 91m Laguna—Elpico/Lorimar—Warner Home Video c

Bo Svenson *(Dr. Etheridge)*, Patrick Lowe *(Sam Nash)*, Mitch Watson *(Frank Duffy)*, Cheryl Arutt *(Lauren Daly)*, Sarah Buxton *(Debbie)*, and Doug Sloan

This inane Italian-produced gorefest is set on a college campus in Florida where Sam Nash (Patrick Lowe) and Frank Duffy (Mitch Watson) are reporters on the school newspaper. Campus researcher Dr. Etheridge (Bo Svenson) is conducting research on a monkey in an attempt to find a method for revitalizing damaged brain cells and, during one of his experiments, an injection causes the monkey to become ferocious to the point that the doctor is almost unable to control it. That night, Duffy, who is certain Etheridge is up to no good, breaks into the lab and starts taking photographs of the monkey, who goes berserk, escapes from its cage, and bites Duffy on the arm before crashing through a window. As Duffy beats a hasty retreat, the monkey is run down by a police car. The next day, Duffy feels feverish, but he agrees to go out with Sam, his new girl friend Lauren (Cheryl Arutt) and her recently arrived roommate Debbie (Sarah Buxton). At the end of the night, Duffy and Debbie begin kissing when he bites her neck, drawing blood, but she doesn't seem to mind much. Of course, the next day, she feels deathly ill, as does Duffy, who soon embarks on a violent rampage, brutally killing anyone who crosses his path. When a trio of slobbering frat boys tries to rape Debbie, she responds by biting each one before finally escaping. Now there are all sorts of potential murderous fiends wandering around campus, as well as the demented Dr. Etheridge, and it's up to Sam and Lauren

to straighten the whole mess out, which they try to do during the big Halloween dance that serves as the film's climax.

There's nothing here that could possibly be of interest to anyone but the most undiscriminating gorehounds. There are some extremely weak attempts at humor in the dialog and in the wacky costumes prevalent at the climactic Halloween ball, but mostly this is simply an excuse to string together a bunch of grisly deaths. Victims have their scalp ripped off, veins torn from their necks, their eyes gouged out, and their mouths scratched to shreds, to name but a few choice methods of death. The acting ranges from barely competent to inept, while the soundtrack features an array of irritatingly pounding rock and rap songs. But, if explosions of blood, vital organs, and flesh are to your liking, by all means give this one a look. *(Gore effects, profanity, sexual situations.)*

d, Vittoria Rambaldi; w, Harry Kirkpatrick; ph, Antonio Climati; spec, Carlo Rambaldi

Horror   **(PR:O   MPAA:R)**

PRIMARY TARGET

85m Isabel Sumayao/MGM-UA c

John Calvin *(Cromwell)*, Miki Kim *(Pao)*, Joey Aresco *(Frank Rosi)*, Chip Lucia *(Jack Sturges)*, John Ericson *(Phil Karlson)*, Colleen Casey *(Mrs. Karlson)*, Henry Strzkowski *(Joe Lewis)*, Fred Bailey *(Nyby)*, Leo Martinez *(Gen. Swai)*, Anabelle Roa *(Mrs. Swai)*, Joonee Gamboa *(Head Opium Smuggler)*, Ben Medina *(Camp Director)*, Bernard Canaberal *(Pirate Leader)*, and Manny Roxas *(Hmong Lieutenant)*

In a roundabout way, PRIMARY TARGET is reminiscent of the famous horror film FRANKENSTEIN in that its creators have pieced together the remains of a number of action films to concoct a monstrous Vietnam adventure movie. The cinematic graveyard that has been robbed here includes the desiccated corpses of MISSING IN ACTION; RAMBO; COMMANDO; and BAT 21, to name but a few. However, the derivative action genre elements in PRIMARY TARGET stubbornly refuse to come to life. Ugly American government official Karlson (John Ericson) calls upon a trio of spirited misfits when his spouse is kidnaped by a renegade soldier, Sturges (Chip Lucia), who is allegedly looking for loot to finance his drug trafficking. Our heroes are rock solid Cromwell (John Calvin), once married to a Cambodian who was murdered by the Viet Cong; steadfast marksman Lewis (Henry Strzkowski), who, we realize immediately, is doomed to sacrifice his life for his buddies because he's not as attractive as they are; and Rosi (Joey Aresco), a madcap womanizer who is jailed—though later sprung by his friends—when he's caught with a Vietnamese official's lover. When Karlson offers them amnesty for their misdemeanors, lots of cash, and a chance to relive their Vietnam glory days, the three leap at the chance to rescue the abducted American woman and to stop Sturges, their former war buddy, from collecting the ransom. With the assistance of Pao (Miki Kim), a feisty refugee who serves as a jungle guide, Cromwell, Lewis, and Rosi manage to make their way through the dense foliage, to prevail over river pirates, and to arrive at the compound where Mrs. Karlson (Colleen Casey) is being held. A few surprises are in store for them but not for action buffs, who will have figured out the plot in the first scene. The film intends to dupe us into believing Mrs. Karlson is actually a Jezebel who's betrayed her hubby and Uncle Sam in order to fatten the wallet of her lover, Sturges. Seeing through this transparent plot device, the audience will not be knocked for a loop when the falsely accused adulteress/traitor reveals that it is her husband who is the real drug runner. Yes, the kidnaping has been faked, but it was engineered to provide Sturges with the wherewithal to fight communist oppression. It is also no surprise that the selfless Lewis is wounded and dies; nor is it any surprise that Cromwell finally puts two and two together and realizes that Sturges and Mrs. Karlson are fighting on the side of the angels. Moreover, viewers will hardly be stunned when the helicopter that is supposed to pick up our heroes has room only for Mrs. Karlson, whose evil husband never had any intention of paying the soldiers of fortune. However, Karlson has messed with the wrong mercenaries. After besieging Karlson's home and slaying all of his bodyguards, Cromwell and Rosi collect their salaries (most of which they donate to Sturges' struggle for a free Cambodia). When Karlson tries to shoot Sturges, Mrs. Karlson blows her husband away. Reunited with Pao, Cromwell learns to love again; Rosi is free to tour Vietnamese hot spots; and the war in Vietnam goes on and on.

In films like this, Vietnam is reduced to one of those recreational "warrior weekends" that allow macho types to test their mettle. In this contrived tale, the bullets are supposed to be real, but the conflicts are so phony that you can't buy either the pumped-up excitement or the characters' interaction. No premise is too far-fetched for action movie hucksters to use as an excuse to re-open the war in Vietnam. Confusing the political issues and reducing moral dilemmas to confrontations between good guys and bad guys, PRIMARY TARGET lacks conviction, energy, and even visceral action. Burdened with the sort of intrusive score that is *de rigueur* for the genre, this movie has little to recommend it. Fans of 50s cinema will note, however, that former matinee idol Ericson has made a graceful transition to character roles. Calvin also fills out his hero fatigues with sufficient leading-man swagger, but aside from the assured performances of these two actors, this dull film tests one's patience. Plodding and predictable, PRIMARY TARGET leaves viewers with the impression that they've already suffered through the film before. (Violence, profanity.)

d, Clark Henderson; p, Isabel Sumayao; w, Clark Henderson; ph, Austin McKinney; ed, Marc Tarnate and Joseph Zucchero; m, Jeff Mar; md, Tony Marcus; art d, Ricky Yu; set d, Mar De Guzman; cos, Ronni Martinez and Lino Dalay

Action   (PR:C   MPAA:R)

PROBLEM CHILD

81m Imagine/Universal c

John Ritter (Ben Healy), Jack Warden (Big Ben Healy Sr.), Michael Oliver (Junior), Gilbert Gottfried (Mr. Igor Peabody), Amy Yasbeck (Flo Healy), Michael Richards (Martin Beck), Peter Jurasik (Roy), Charlotte Akin (Lorraine), Anna Marie Allred (Kid No. 3), Adam Anderly (Catcher), Robert A. Anderson (Boy in Chair), Cody Beard (Second Baseman), Jordan Burton (Kid No. 1), Eli Cummins (Umpire), John S. Davies (Paramedic), Vince Davis (Clown), Dennis Dugan (All-American Dad), Justin Elledge (Freddy), Eric Elterman (All-American Boy), Ward Emling (Mr. Henderson), John William Galt (Warden), Corki Grazer (Sister Mary), Vernon Grote (Guard No. 2), Garland Hampton (Serious Boy), Helena Humann (Mother Superior), Philip Jhin (Mr. Yangita), Judy Jones (Anchorperson), Melody Jones (Sister Abigail), Danny Kamekona (Mr. Hirohito), Eiichi Edward Kawanabe (Mr. Mitsui), Colby Kline (Lucy), Joseph Kolb (Kid No. 5), Hugh Lampman (Master of Ceremonies), Ellen Locy (Nun No. 2), Kristen Lowman (Mrs. Henderson), Joshua Martin (Shortstop), Melissa Martin (Friend No. 2), Julie Mayfield (Harriet), Andrea McCall (Rich Lady), Willie Minor (Guard No. 1), Ron Miranda (Juan), Shepler Mobley (Friendly Woman), S. "Monty" Moncibais (Prisoner), Norma Moore (Sister Samantha), Abby Newman (Friend No. 1), John O'Connell (Psychiatrist), Kristy Lynne Patrick (Kid No. 2), Eric Poppick (Dr. Strauss), John Rainone (Circus Clown), Martin Rayner (Ringmaster), Dennis Redfield (Cameraman), Symone Redwine (Friend No. 3), Lico Reyes (Pedro), Florence Shauffler (Mrs. Perkins), Shaun Shimoda (Kinjo Hirohito), Garry Smith (Angry Little Person), Josh Stoppelwerth (Kid No. 4), Al Trejo (Policeman), Alex Utroska (Kid in Dugout), Kerry Von Erich (Neo Natzi), Jack Willis (Regular Joe), Ed Yeager (Jim O'Conner), and Jessica Zucha (Serious Girl)

When it comes to comedy, 1990 will go down in history as the year of the ill-mannered slob. Ed O'Neill won rating points for "Married with Children" by scratching his crotch, Andrew Dice Clay and Roseanne Barr got plenty of media attention for grabbing theirs, and Bart Simpson T-shirts were everywhere. However, PROBLEM CHILD, Hollywood's attempt to re-enact THE BAD SEED for laughs, proved that no mere standup comic or series TV star—cartoon or human—could hope to match the crassness of a major-studio feature. Michael Oliver stars as Junior, an orphan who, as the movie starts, is shuttled from doorstep to doorstep, steadily working his way down the social ladder. The reason for the lad's continual relocation becomes apparent when Junior, left at a mansion by his mother, promptly urinates in the face of his wealthy new "foster" mother. The opening sequence ends (though, sadly, the movie does not) with Junior being dumped in an orphanage run by draconian nuns. There, Junior's "antics" range from throwing his food and swinging a nun by a rope outside the window to striking up a pen-pal correspondence with serial killer Martin Beck (Michael Richards), the "Bow Tie Killer." Emulating his hero, Junior begins wearing a bow tie, which makes him deceptively appealing to Ben and Flo (John Ritter and Amy Yasbeck), a childless suburban couple. A sad-sack slug, Ben is browbeaten by both his battle-ax wife and his monstrous father, Big Ben (Jack Warden). An ultrapatriotic sporting-goods retailer, Big Ben has secretly sold out to the Japanese so he can run an "America First" campaign for mayor of his appropriately named hometown, Cold River. Ben takes to Junior immediately, even though the boy continues his rampage—setting fire to his bedroom, throwing a cat into Big Ben's face, demolishing a neighbor's birthday party, ruining a camping trip by luring a bear into the campsite, and reducing a little-league baseball game to chaos by bludgeoning members of the opposing team with his bat. The plot thickens when the Bow Tie Killer escapes from prison and finds his way to Junior's new home. Meanwhile, Ben struggles with whether or not to return Junior to the crooked child-welfare agent (Gilbert Gottfried) who engineered the adoption. When the killer kidnaps Junior and Flo, demanding a $100,000 ransom, Ben is initially ecstatic. But, rifling through Junior's bedroom, Ben finds evidence that Junior loves him as much as he loves Junior. He rushes off to see Big Ben, hoping to raise the ransom money. Ben's appeal is unsuccessful, but he effectively short-circuits his father's mayoral campaign by turning a live TV camera on Big Ben just as he is dropping his trousers. Ben then hurries

to the ransom site, a circus, hoping to bluff the kidnaper. Naturally, this leads to more grotesque "antics." At the fadeout, Flo ends up with a pig's posterior pressed to her face, while Ben and Junior are happily reunited.

To call PROBLEM CHILD a comedy remake of THE BAD SEED does a terrible disservice to Mervyn LeRoy's chilling little film. Indeed, the gardener's monolog in THE BAD SEED, in which he explains that there are little pink and blue electric chairs for bad girls and boys, is far funnier than anything to be found in this film. There is some evidence that PROBLEM CHILD might have been conceived as a satire of yuppie consumerism and suburban class prejudice. However, there are also indications that the filmmakers may have intended the film to be any one of a half-dozen or so other types of movies. Whatever the moviemakers' intentions, the result of their labor is a humorless mess. TV veteran Dennis Dugan, directing his first feature film, has managed to completely waste a talented comic cast. Here is a movie so thoroughly inept it's hard to know where to begin. Jokes and sight gags alike are stale and unfunny; executed without any awareness of the rudiments of staging and pacing, this "humor" exhibits a total disregard for human decency. The film is further marred by choppy editing, indicating what was probably a last-ditch attempt to save the film with the scissors. It's too bad the editors of PROBLEM CHILD couldn't have saved time and money by just putting the whole film through a shredder. (Profanity, adult situations.)

d, Dennis Dugan; p, Robert Simonds; w, Scott Alexander and Larry Karaszewski; ph, Peter Lyons Collister; ed, Daniel Hanley and Michael Hill; m, Miles Goodman; prod d, George Costello; art d, Michael Bingham; set d, Denise Pizzini; spec, Jack Bennett; stunts, Mickey Gilbert; cos, Eileen Kennedy; makeup, Nena Smarz

Comedy   (PR:O   MPAA:PG)

PRZESLUCHANIE

(Pol.) (SEE: INTERROGATION, THE)

PUMP UP THE VOLUME

(Can./US) 105m New Line c

Christian Slater (Mark Hunter), Samantha Mathis (Nora), Ellen Greene (Jan Emerson), Scott Paulin (Keith Hunter), Cheryl Pollak (Paige), Andy Romano (Murdock), Mimi Kennedy (Martha Hunter), Annie Ross (Mrs. Cresswood), Mark Ballou, Jill Jarres, Lala, Ahmet Zappa, Dan Eisenstein, Nigel Gibbs, Seth Green, James Hampton, and Clayton Landey

Bad teen films can be one of life's more heinous experiences. The effort to exploit simultaneously youthful vulnerability and hip, contemporary humor is particularly excruciating when, devoid of wit or freshness, it fails. The few such films that have succeeded—SIXTEEN CANDLES; FAST TIMES AT RIDGEMONT HIGH; HEATHERS; HOUSE PARTY—have a savvy tartness and satiric eye for detail that are both exhilarating and affecting. PUMP UP THE VOLUME would desperately like to be in that league but falls way short through sheer muddleheadedness, unbelievability, and a dire lack of originality. It mixes elements from HANDLE WITH CARE; NETWORK; and HEATHERS into a messy hodgepodge that proves off-putting to adults and adolescents alike.

Alienated Mark Hunter (Christian Slater) is a legend in his Arizona hometown as a result of a ham-operated pirate radio program he broadcasts each night. Calling himself "Hard Harry," Mark entertains his listeners by aurally simulating masturbation. In between orgasms, he serves as a kind of combination Dr. Joyce Brothers/Timothy Leary to classmates oppressed by burgeoning gonads and the crazed machinations of their ruthless principal, Mrs. Cresswood (Annie Ross). She is hell-bent on maintaining her school's high SAT scores and ridding it of under-achievers and nonconformists. Mark's activities are unknown to his father, who happens to be the school commissioner and who is eternally mystified by his son's anti-social behavior. Among the characters—all of them stock—who see Mark as a saviour are Paige (Cheryl Pollak), the perfect Ivy League-bound princess, and Nora (Samantha Mathis), the misfit soul mate of our deejay hero. Mark's inflammatory broadcasts send the entire burg into an uproar that becomes a media circus. The police and FCC arrive on the scene to quell the student protests that erupt when the program is yanked from the air. Roused to non-anonymous action by Nora ("You can't just shout fire in a theatre and walk out!"), Mark exhorts his fellows to "Steal the air! Talk hard! Find your voice!"

PUMP UP THE VOLUME is every bit as tiresome as its synopsis indicates. The humor is entirely forced, the sensitivity even more so. Its message may appeal to a few alienated pre-teens, but phoniness informs nearly every frame. It has a smarmy, laboriously "with it" aura that is testament to its creators' misguided approach. (The title alone bespeaks strained hipness.) Moreover, Mark's improbable sermons are hysterical, empty rants that pander to narcissistic teenage anomie, and the homosexual's suicide is wrung shamelessly for cheap pathos. The view of adults here is right out of EAST OF EDEN, presenting them as monstrous villains or fools. When Mark's ultra-nerd father discovers his son in bed with Nora, Dad's unbelievable, relieved comment is a smirking, "That little lech." The big climax — in which police helicopters buzz overhead, Mark gives his final broadcast from a careening jeep commandeered by Nora, and the student body is pitted against the authorities — is hopelessly ludicrous. Walt Lloyd's photography puts an MTV gloss over everything, as does the uninspired rock music score. Any visual rhythm that might have transpired from the use of songs by Bad Brains, Cowboy Junkies, Henry Rollins, Peter Murphy, or the Pixies is shattered by Mark's constant, abrupt interruption of the music to pontificate.

Slater's performance is a slightly less psychopathic extension of his work in HEATHERS. The charm of his methodical, whiny delivery and chronic case of the smirks remains elusive. At one point, he ceremoniously removes his shirt, as if to clinch the surefire appeal-deal he's supposedly made with the audience. As for Mathis, simply put, she is no Winona Ryder. (The filmmakers have cited Patti Smith as their inspiration for Nora; Mathis doesn't even suggest Patty Duke.) As the one sympathetic teacher, Ellen Greene is a brief oasis of sanity in the film. *(Profanity, adult situations, sexual situations, nudity, substance abuse.)*

d, Allan Moyle; p, Rupert Harvey and Sandy Stern; w, Allan Moyle; ph, Walt Lloyd; ed, Wendy Bricmont, Ric Keeley, and Kurt Hathaway; md, Nicole Freegard; prod d, Bruce Bolander; cos, Michael Abbot

Drama (PR:O MPAA:R)

Q&A

134m Regency International — Odyssey/Tri-Star c

Nick Nolte *(Lt. Mike Brennan)*, Timothy Hutton *(Al Reilly)*, Armand Assante *(Bobby Texador)*, Patrick O'Neal *(Kevin Quinn)*, Lee Richardson *(Leo Bloomenfeld)*, Luis Guzman *(Detective Luis Valentin)*, Charles Dutton *(Detective Sam Chapman)*, Jenny Lumet *(Nancy Bosch)*, Paul Calderon *(Roger Montalvo)*, International Chrysis *(Jose Malpica)*, Dominick Chianese *(Larry Pesch)*, Leonard Cimino *(Nick Petrone)*, Fyvush Finkel *(Preston Pearlstein)*, Gustavo Brens *(Alfonse Segal)*, Martin E. Brens *(Armand Segal)*, Maurice Schell *(Detective Zucker)*, Tommy A. Ford *(Lubin)*, John Capodice *(Hank Mastroangelo)*, Frederick Rolf *(District Attorney)*, Hal Lehrman *(Altshul)*, Gloria Irizarry *(Mrs. Bosch)*, Brian Neill *(Sylvester/Sophia)*, Susan Mitchell *(Flo)*, Drew Eliot *(Magnus)*, Frank Raiter *(Seabury)*, Harry Madsen *(Tony Vasquez)*, Jerry Ciauri *(Bruno Valli)*, George Kodisch *(Inspector Flynn)*, Burtt Harris *(Phil)*, Michael A. Joseph *(Pimp)*, Cynthia O'Neal *(Agnes Quinn)*, Victor Colicchio *("After Hours" Alvarado)*, Anibal Lleras, Jose Rafel Arango *("After Hours" Patrons)*, David Dill *(Bartender)*, Alex Ruiz *(Danny)*, Richard Solchik *(Phillie)*, Edward Rogers III *(Jose's Apartment Detective)*, Junior Perez *(Nancy Captain)*, Javier Rios *(Boat Lover)*, June Stein *(ADA)*, Rod Rodriquez *(Carlo)*, Sonny Vito *(Gino)*, Olga Merediz *(Mrs. Valentin)*, Peter Gumeny *(Guard)*, Edward Rowan *(Ed)*, Danny Darrow *(Phone Investigator)*, and Jose Collazo *(Fisherman)*

Director Sidney Lumet has depicted the world of the New York City policeman in two very successful films, SERPICO and PRINCE OF THE CITY. Forceful exposes that delve into the dark and complex world of police corruption, they remain two of the director's finest works. After a string of commercially and artistically unsuccessful efforts, Lumet returns to SERPICO's terrain with Q&A, but the results are not nearly as good; in fact, they're pretty bad. Widespread corruption of body and soul (and its effect on the judicial system and police force of New York City) are again at the center of Lumet's film. The embodiment of that corruption is Lt. Mike Brennan (Nick Nolte), hailed by his peers as one of the finest cops in New York. "The first through any door, window, or skylight," he has taken a bullet for a fellow officer on several occasions. But, unknown to most, Brennan is also one of the dirtiest cops on the force. In the film's opening scene, he kills an unarmed Latino drug dealer in cold blood, then plants a gun on him. When more officers arrive on the scene, it appears that Brennan simply shot the dealer in self-defense. Still, this incident requires an investigation by the DA's office, and ex-cop turned assistant DA Al Reilly (Timothy Hutton) is assigned to the case. This being Reilly's first investigation, chief of homicide Kevin Quinn (Patrick O'Neal) briefs him on how to go about it: Reilly will ask questions regarding the incident, a stenographer will record Brennan's answers (the Q&A of the title), and after a few interviews with some witnesses, the whole matter will be neatly cleared up. In their initial meeting, Brennan explains his side of the story in suspiciously thorough detail; then Reilly learns his own former girl friend, Nancy (Jenny Lumet, the director's daughter), is now romantically involved with Bobby Texador (Armand Assante), a drug dealer who is also a witness. The young assistant DA decides to launch a full investigation of this seemingly simple matter and events take a dangerous turn. The trail of corruption leads from drug dealers to Brennan and ultimately directly to Quinn's office. Assisted by an African-American cop (Charles Dutton), a Hispanic officer (Luis Guzman), and Jewish district attorney and mentor Leo

Bloomenfeld (Lee Richardson), Reilly discovers plenty of dirt on Brennan and Quinn. In the process, Reilly makes enemies of both Brennan and Texador, the latter failing to appreciate Reilly's attempt to win back Nancy's love. While Brennan is killing all those who might incriminate him (most of whom are homosexuals), Reilly struggles with the truth about the system and about himself. Tellingly, we learn that Nancy broke up with him after his negative reaction upon learning that her father is African-American. As the film moves to its close, big questions remain to be answered. Is the system that corrupt? (With Reilly's case on the rocks, Brennan and all the witnesses dead, and Quinn's freedom imminent, Reilly asks Leo if it is really possible to cover up something so big. "Bigger," Leo responds.) Is Reilly truly a racist? Will he ever get Nancy back? By the closing credits we know that the investigation has been aborted, and that Reilly catches up with Nancy on an island, announces that he is a changed man, and declares his love for her. What we don't learn is whether she will take him back.

The true subject of this film seems to be the nature of corruption and racism, both very real problems within the police community. Unquestionably, there are many racist policeman, but in Q&A *every* character has notable racist tendencies (the words "spic," "nigger," and "guinea" are used regularly). While it is clear that the film's dramatic conflict centers on Reilly's coming to terms with his prejudice, Q&A is neither enlightening nor sure of its message. Lumet, whose recent FAMILY BUSINESS is also loaded with racial stereotypes and slurs, has mistaken the trading of racial insults for camaraderie, and stereotypes for atmosphere (straining for a "melting pot" ambiance, he creates the least authentic New York in recent memory). The result is an uncomfortably nasty picture. The disturbing subtext of Lumet's last two pictures is especially surprising coming from this director. Lumet was once married to an African-American woman, Lena Horne's daughter (Jenny is one of their two children), and it is odd that he fails to demonstrate a greater awareness of the sensitive nature of his subject matter. Instead the screenplay abounds with overtones of bigotry. It is unfathomable why any director would choose to have a hispanic character tell a black character to "quit eating watermelons" in what is supposedly a friendly exchange. In addition to racist slurs, the film is jam-packed with insulting depictions of homosexuals and with gay-bashing scenes. Brennan strangles two transvestites and nearly emasculates another; gay characters are referred to as "fags" and Lumet photographs them in the most unflattering ways possible.

All of this could be forgiven had the film followed through on its ideas. But while trying to create a dark, seedy world (which the film's glossy photography works against), Lumet overstuffs Q&A with plot. Providing little or no character motivation, he reduces the film's central concerns (racism and corruption) to an offensive subplot. Clearly, Lumet wanted to present a serious look at racism, but his naive and superficial treatment of his subject both prevents him from making a good film and insults the viewer. The film's shifting point of view doesn't help matters, either. Is this Reilly's story or Brennan's? Is it a police expose or a character study? This lack of focus goes a long way toward sinking the film. In addition, although Lumet's strongest talent has always been his handling of actors, Q&A is full of below-par performances. Nolte is particularly bad, giving a performance that is as weak as his turn in FAREWELL TO THE KING. Completely out of his element as the hulking Irish cop, he overplays his hand on several occasions. And it doesn't help that his character's motivation is a complete mystery (notably, there are unanswered questions concerning his drinking and possible latent homosexuality). Hutton, complete with a shaky Brooklyn accent, is too restrained and flat-out boring to be the central character of the film. Making her film debut, Jenny Lumet is absolutely terrible; she fails to convince in any of the three emotionally challenging scenes in which she appears. Not surprisingly, O'Neal and Richardson ham it up tirelessly. Although at times he, too, is painfully over-the-top, Assante at least adds life to the proceedings. Despite his homophobia and racism, Assante's Bobby Texador is the only character in the film that is almost likable.

Even on the technical level Q&A is a disappointment, its screenplay forgettable, its music ridiculous (at the most inappropriate moments, the film's lame theme song comes thudding over the soundtrack). Lumet's boring editing style and immobile camera are more appropriate for television than the big screen. Moreover, his obsession with introducing plot twists reaches absurd heights when the film *ends* with a new plot development. But the main problem with the movie is its lack of likable characters. In PRINCE OF THE CITY and SERPICO, Lumet's focus was on one tortured character, and the effect in both films was powerful. In Q&A, Reilly is too transparent and Brennan too repellent to hold the viewer's interest. Aside from two or three effective scenes (all of which include Assante), the film is a tremendous disappointment. *(Violence, excessive profanity, adult situations, sexual situations, brief nudity.)*

d, Sidney Lumet; p, Arnon Milchan and Burtt Harris; w, Sidney Lumet (based on the book by Edwin Torres); ph, Andrzej Bartkowiak; ed, Richard Cirincione; m, Ruben Blades; md, Carlos Franzetti; prod d, Philip Rosenberg; art d, Beth Kuhn; set d, Gary Brink; cos, Ann Roth and Neil Spisak; makup, Joe Cranzano

Crime/Drama (PR:O MPAA:R)

QUICK CHANGE

88m Devoted/WB c

Bill Murray *(Grimm)*, Dale Grand *(Street Barker)*, Bob Elliott *(Bank Teller)*, Geena Davis *(Phyllis)*, Randy Quaid *(Loomis)*, Kimberleigh Aarn *(Bank Teller)*, Ron Ryan *(Bank Customer)*, Brian McConnachie *(Bank Manager)*, Jack Gilpin *(Yuppie Hostage)*, Jordan Cael, Rhe DeVille, Marya Dornya, Barbara Flynn, Elizabeth A. Griffin, Connie Ivie, Skipp Lynch, J.D. Montalbo, Suzen Murakoshi, Anthony T. Paige, Jane Simms, Wendell Sweda, Angel Vargas *(Hostages)*, Jason Robards Jr. *(Chief Rotzinger)*, Richard Joseph Paul *(Lt. Jameson)*, Reg E. Cathey *(Sound Analyst)*, William Sturgis *(Forensic Detective)*, Sam Ayers *(Esu Commander)*, Joe Pentangelo, Bill Raymond *(Policemen)*, Randle Mell *(TV Reporter)*, Jamey Sheridan *(Mugger)*, Anthony Bishop, Larry Joshua *(Street Sign Workers)*, Michelle Lucien *(Shut-Up Lady)*, Tim Halligan, Deborah Lee Johnson, Lucia Vincent *(Reporters)*, Elliot Santiago, Manny Siverio *(Bicycle Jousters)*, Bobby Harrigan *(Fat Person)*, Phil Hartman *(Mr. Edison)*, Kathryn Grody *(Mrs. Edison)*, Tony Shalhoub *(Cab Driver)*, Gary Goodrow *(Radio DJ)*, Frank Maldonado, Ryan Mitchel *(Kids at Grocery)*, Steve Park *(Grocery Cashier)*, Alfa-Betty Olsen *(Customer)*, Jim Ward *(Police Artist)*, Davenia McFadden *(Policewoman)*, Michael Chapman, Michael C. Mahon *(Policemen at Grocery)*, Stanley Tucci *(Johnny)*, Victor Argo *(Skelton)*, Philip Bosco *(Bus Driver)*, Gary Klar *(Mario)*, Paul Herman *(Interrogating Policeman)*, Stuart Rudin *(Bus Rider with Guitar)*, Teodorino Bello *(Flower Lady)*, Barton Heyman *(Airport Security Chief)*, Justin Ross *(Airline Clerk)*, Kurtwood Smith *(Lombino/"Russ Crane")*, Susannah Bianchi *(Lombino/"Mrs. Russ Crane")*, Ira Wheeler *(Businessman In Men's Room)*, and Margo Skinner *(Flight Attendant)*

It's another routine day in New York City. A man wearing a clown suit and makeup walks into a bank, pulls a gun, and announces that a robbery is about to take place. (Actually, he has to fire his gun at the ceiling before anyone pays attention to him.) Grabbing several bags of cash, the clown herds the customers and an elderly guard into the bank vault. When Police Chief Rotzinger (Jason Robards) and his men show up, the robber demands that a "monster" truck and a city bus be delivered to the bank before he will release any of the hostages. As Rotzinger begins to comply with the clown's outrageous demands, three hostages are freed. What the police chief doesn't realize is that the three released hostages are also the perpetrators of the crime: Grimm (Bill Murray), who has now taken off his clown get-up; Phyllis, his girl friend (Geena Davis); and Loomis, Grimm's dimwitted, adoring sidekick (Randy Quaid). The three escape the area around the bank with ease, and we learn that Grimm is a city planner. Fed up with New York, he hatched the robbery plot with his friends in order to escape to a more hospitable environment. At this point in the proceedings, however, their getaway begins to go awry. Grimm and company get totally lost while trying to get to the airport, and when they pull over to ask for directions, a friendly-looking motorist robs them of some of their loot. Returning to Phyllis's apartment, the three leave their car by a fire hydrant, only to watch the vehicle be destroyed by the Fire Department when a nearby building goes up in flames. Eventually, the trio is able to corral a cab; however, the driver doesn't understand a word of English, and Loomis, panicking, bolts from the moving cab and is knocked unconscious. Rotzinger, meanwhile, has begun to catch on to the plot and is in hot pursuit of Grimm and his friends. Through an incredible series of lucky breaks and misunderstandings, including a hilarious visit to a mob hideout, the three make it to the airport, though the threat of capture doesn't end until the film's final moments.

QUICK CHANGE provides many laughs, especially for New Yorkers. The mishaps that befall Grimm, Phyllis, and Loomis will be familiar to anyone who's spent time in the Big Apple; non-English-speaking cabbies, by-the-book bus drivers, interminable supermarket lines, and unmarked highways are all part of the New York experience. Indeed, the three robbers are nearly done in not so much by their own ineptitude as by the inefficiency and myriad inconveniences of life in New York City.

Murray's usual deadpan, sarcastic style works perfectly here, since he's playing a character who is used to the absurdities of city life; Davis is both convincingly exasperated and loving as the girl friend who can't decide whether Grimm is the right guy for her. The supporting performances are also on target, including the wonderful portrayal of the bank guard by Bob Elliott (of Bob and Ray), and Philip Bosco's bus driver, whose unflagging adherence to MTA policy causes Grimm to dub him "Ralph Kramden's evil twin."

Codirected by Murray (with screenwriter Howard Franklin), QUICK CHANGE unfolds cleverly, keeping the audience in the dark on the robbery plot throughout the film's opening reel. After piquing our curiosity, Murray and Franklin skillfully let us in on the scheme and slowly reveal the nature of the three characters at the center of it. Although the ending is a bit unbelievable, the excellent performances and unexpected plot twists make QUICK CHANGE a very entertaining film. *(Profanity.)*

d, Howard Franklin and Bill Murray; p, Robert Greenhut and Bill Murray; w, Howard Franklin (based on the book by Jay Cronley); ph, Michael Chapman; ed, Alan Heim; m, Randy Edelman and Howard Shore; art d, Speed Hopkins; set d, Dave Weinman and Susan Bode; stunts, Frank Ferrara; cos, Donna Zakowska; makup, Peter Montagna

Comedy/Crime   (PR:C   MPAA:R)

QUIGLEY DOWN UNDER

120m Pathe/MGM-UA c

Tom Selleck *(Matthew Quigley)*, Laura San Giacomo *(Crazy Cora)*, Alan Rickman *(Elliott Marston)*, Chris Haywood *(Maj. Pitt)*, Ron Haddrick *(Grimmelman)*, Tony Bonner *(Dobkin)*, Jerome Ehlers *(Coogan)*, Conor McDermottroe *(Hobb)*, Roger Ward *(Brophy)*, and Ben Mendelsohn *(O'Flynn)*

Another failed attempt to make Tom Selleck a movie star, this is a handsomely mounted but vapid western that lumbers across the screen for two hours, providing little entertainment. Selleck is Matthew Quigley, a 19th century sharpshooter from Wyoming who is summoned to Australia by rancher Elliott Marston (Alan Rickman). Fresh off the boat, Quigley saves an American prostitute named Crazy Cora (Laura San Giacomo) from a group of ruffians who turn out to be employees of Marston. They take Quigley—and Cora—to Marston's ranch. When Quigley learns that he's been hired to kill aborigines, he throws Marston out a window, which prompts the rancher to order his men to drag Quigley and Cora out into the desert where they will be left to die. Of course, Quigley and Cora, with the help of some aborigines, survive the ordeal, and Quigley sets out to get revenge against the evil Marston.

Coupling the thoroughly predictable story with the inept direction of Simon Wincer (THE LIGHTHORSEMEN), the film becomes a stultifying experience. Wincer has a nice flair for scenery and stages a few competent action sequences, but he exhibits no understanding of the western genre. Quigley is a completely one-dimensional character who is heroic to the point of absurdity. As played by Selleck, his only function seems to be to model some really neat-looking leather chaps. The film also flows uneasily between light comedy and violence. Then there is the strange handling of San Giacomo's character. The character's mental instability seems to have been included here only to add some sort of psychological depth to the film, but instead it merely leads to some bizarre and wholly unnecessary scenes. Much of the dialog has to be heard to be disbelieved. At one point, Selleck, watching a hungry baby eating, wryly observes, "That little feller's eatin' like his belly button's been rubbin' a blister on his backbone." Other than some lovely scenery, the only thing this film has going for it is a lively performance by Rickman, who plays a variation on the villain he so richly portrayed in DIE HARD. That, however, is not nearly enough to recommend this thoroughly contrived, confused, and ultimately tedious effort. *(Violence, profanity, adult situations.)*

d, Simon Wincer; p, Stanley O'Toole and Alexandra Rose; w, John Hill; ph, David Eggby; ed, Adrian Carr; m, Basil Poledouris; prod d, Ross Major; art d, Ian Gracie; stunts, Guy Norris; cos, Ross Major and Wayne Finkelman

Western   (PR:C   MPAA:PG-13)

R

RAGGEDY RAWNEY, THE

(Brit.) 102m Handmade/Island c

Bob Hoskins *(Darky)*, Dexter Fletcher *(Tom)*, Zoe Nathenson *(Jessie)*, Dave Hill *(Lamb)*, Ian Dury *(Weasel)*, Zoe Wanamaker *(Elle)*, J.G. Devlin *(Jake)*, and Perry Fenwick *(Victor)*

While Bob Hoskins the actor was getting all the attention for his charming performance in WHO FRAMED ROGER RABBIT, Bob Hoskins the director (same guy) was making his feature film debut with this picture—shown at Cannes in 1988, but not released to the general public until 1990—based on stories told him by his gypsy grandmother. Filmed in Czechoslovakia, with a Czech and British cast, but set in an unnamed country bearing a striking resemblance to WW II England, this fantasy drama revolves around a band of Gypsies and the misfortune that befalls them when they take in an army deserter. Tom (Dexter Fletcher, best known for his work in THE RACHEL PAPERS and CARAVAGGIO) is a trembling young recruit in an army that roams the countryside bullying and robbing the citizens while searching for undefined "enemy units." During a campfire chat, an older recruit advises Tom that he shouldn't even think of deserting, that his fellow soldiers will hunt down and kill him and anyone who has anything to do with him. Yet desert Tom does, just moments later, during a mortar attack. After the older soldier, intending to pull the terrified Tom to safety, is blown to bits, Tom tries to flee, but is stopped by his stern, slightly maniacal commanding officer. Panicking, Tom slashes the officer in the face with a jagged piece of shrapnel and continues his flight. Stumbling on the band of Gypsies led by Darky (Hoskins), Tom is comforted during the night by beautiful young Jessie (Zoe Nathenson), who warms him with her blanket and her body after he goes into shock and is unable to speak. But the next morning her caravan moves on and Tom is left alone again. Wandering the countryside, Tom comes upon a farm where a little girl plays cheerfully with her mother's clothes and makeup in the barn. Giving Tom a fashion makeover, the girl paints his face and cloaks him in one of her mother's dresses. She then leads him to "meet" her parents; killed for helping their deserter son, they now hang next to his bloody corpse in the courtyard. Once again Tom runs off into the woods, where he encounters Darky, who's fallen asleep by a stream while fishing. Still mute, and still wearing the makeup and dress, Tom leads Darky to a better fishing spot, and the Gypsy becomes convinced that the deserter is a madman with magical powers. Thinking Tom will bring more luck, Darky allows him to travel with the caravan. This arrangement suits Tom fine, not only because it will help him evade his revenge-seeking commander, but also because Jessie happens to be Darky's daughter. Tom does bring luck to Darky and his caravan, almost all of it bad. As the film ends, Tom is fleeing again, with Jessie and a truckload of women and children, leaving Darky and his friends behind to face certain death from the army, more bloodthirsty than ever after Tom's killing of the commander.

THE RAGGEDY RAWNEY is not a great film, but it's not quite like any other film, either. Its downwardly spiraling plot has a nightmarish logic recalling Edgar G. Ulmer films like THE BLACK CAT and DETOUR, yet its tone is almost coolly oblivious, lacking Ulmer's horrific angst and hysteria. Hoskins' painstakingly detailed direction creates a world that is almost completely artificial in a film that is at once passionately moralistic and sullenly amoral, naturalistic and fatalistic, realistic and romantic, prosaic and poetic. Whatever it may or may not be, THE RAGGEDY RAWNEY is never less than engrossing. At times its imagery is hauntingly powerful. It's also uniformly well-acted. Its script, cowritten by Hoskins and Nicole De Wilde, is tight and briskly paced, full of colorful and intriguing characters. However, the script never makes clear how we're to view Tom, whether he is magical and heroic or just cowardly and opportunistic. It's also unclear whether the film itself is meant to be a universal antiwar tract, a bitter indictment of British army brutalization of the Gypsies during the war, or none or all of the above. And, anyway, who are these "Gypsies" who tell not a single fortune and who play bagpipes at weddings instead of tambourines? Consistency may be the hobgoblin of tiny minds, but without a consistent point of view, THE RAGGEDY RAWNEY is finally too insubstantial to make much of a lasting impact, and its ambiguity too often resembles evasiveness. At the same time, it is a film loaded with potential, making Hoskins undeniably a director to watch. *(Violence, adult situations, nudity, profanity.)*

d, Bob Hoskins; p, Bob Weis; w, Bob Hoskins and Nicole De Wilde; ph, Frank Tidy; ed, Alan Jones; m, Michael Kamen; prod d, Jiri Matolin; cos, Theodor Pistek

Drama   (PR:C MPAA:NR)

REAL BULLETS

87m Vidmark c

John Gazarian, Darlene Landau, Merritt Yohnka, C. Justin Campbell, Jim Poslof, Patrick Lloyd, Martin Landau, Bob Rochelle, Claudia Stenke, Wolfgang Linkman, Samir Mamouni, Damita Jo Fox, Dianne Wolston, Sue Benson, Roy Hill, and Dayna Quinn

This dreary, abysmally acted, and poorly photographed action flick is little more than a vanity production. A troupe of professional stunt people (with higher aspirations) banded together to create this amateurish exercise in escapism, and it can only be hoped that they all kept their steady jobs.

After several dull introductory scenes, we are finally able to sort out the many members of a stunt class taught by John Gazarian. An inseparable bunch, they even take their vacations together, and when they embark on one such holiday the plot complications begin. While the All-American stunt folks ride the road to recreation, drug lord Martin Landau is masterminding a major drug deal near their vacation site at Vasquez Rocks. As Gazarian and Merritt Yohnka reminisce about tooling around in the local hills, they encounter a grizzled old-timer, Roy Hill, whom they used to know. He's been laying low in some abandoned park property that's become the headquarters for Landau's drug operation. As the stuntmen and stuntwomen look for campsites, Landau's men are busy weeding out disloyal employees. At a local dive, the stuntpeople get into an altercation with some of the drug thugs, and an interminable brawl breaks out. Back at the off-limits area where the stunt folks have chosen to camp, two of the more bimbolike stuntwomen are kidnaped by the nefarious pushers while visiting the ladies' room. When Landau is informed of the interlopers' presence, he pronounces a death sentence by phone. However, the stunt crew takes the offensive. While one of the stunt people infiltrates the drug plant in pursuit of the missing women, Claudia Stenke leaves on horseback for help (though she is forced to dismount when the bad guys shoot at her). In the meantime, the other stuntpeople set off diversionary explosions and put various guards out of commission as they sneak into the plant. Although Dianne Wolston dies, the stunt folks rescue the heavily drugged Damita Jo Fox and set off more explosions as they make their getaway. Hiding out in a dead-end canyon, they await help that may be a long time in coming, since Stenke hasn't been able to elude her pursuers. The ingenious stuntpeople are able to survive the seige by Landau's lackeys until the drug lord calls in professional killers. Gazarian's friends begin dropping like flies, but Gazarian continues to shoot deadly arrows at the villains, although the chief henchman (Jim Poslof) eludes his marksmanship. Reunited with her horse, Stenke finally manages to make it to the sheriff's office. But by the time the sheriff arrives at the canyon, it's too late for most of the stuntpeople. When sadistic Poslof tries to knife Gazarian's girl friend, Darlene Landau, Gazarian finally manages to dispatch the creep with William Tell-like finesse. At the fade-out, only Gazarian, Darlene Landau, Stenke, and Yohnka are left alive.

The many featured performers of REAL BULLETS may be very capable stuntpeople but they exhibit only rudimentary acting skills here. Moreover, director Lance Lindsay allows the plot to unfold as if it were an unwelcome interruption of the stunts—and thus not worthy of his or our full attention. Still, there's something endearingly inept about this attempt to make a movie; it's as if Mickey Rooney and Judy Garland had brought their "Let's put on a show!" approach to staging stunts. But while this collection of catchy stunts might make a terrific audition reel, it hardly adds up to exciting entertainment. Padded-out footage, tedious cutaways to Martin Landau (whose part was too obviously filmed at another place and time, then clumsily inserted into the movie), cheesy photography, and awful editing add up to a miserable adventure flick.

Only Poslof, as the sadistic heavy, shows any flair for acting; the other performers more or less play themselves, and their personalities don't exactly leap off the screen. Had the filmmakers introduced fewer characters—instead of overcrowding the screen with half of the stuntpeople in Hollywood—it might be easier to identify with the vacationing group's plight. On every level, this macho mayhem fizzles, but it will make a fine video for the cast to play years from now when they're in the Stuntmen's Wing of the Motion Picture Retirement Home. *(Violence, profanity, drugs, sexual situations.)*

d, Lance Lindsay; p, John Gazarian and Lance Lindsay; w, Lance Lindsay and John Gazarian; ph, Bob Caramico, Bob Hayes, and Gary Graver; ed, Fred Roth; m, Ron Jones

Action   (PR:C MPAA:R)

RED SURF

105m Greg H. Sims/Arrowhead c

George Clooney *(Mark Remar)*, Doug Savant *(Attila)*, Dedee Pfeiffer *(Rebecca)*, Gene Simmons *(Doc)*, Philip McKeon *(True Blue)*, and Rick Najera *(Calavera)*

A sort of poor man's TEQUILA SUNRISE, RED SURF is strictly cinema for the brain dead. Or maybe for surfers. Suffused in warmed-over, whiny southern California angst, and revolving around a former champion surfer who has turned to drug running, RED SURF is a self-consciously significant beach movie in which the usual shrill, high-decibel rambunctiousness alternates with tinny, overwrought drama. Watching it can give you a headache, making you wonder if surfers ever just talk to each other, rather than screaming, flapping their arms, and yanking each other around by the lapels as they do here. RED SURF's characters also have dopey nicknames, like Attila and True Blue, that seem to have come from a Wrestlemania fight card. And, of course, they all look like Hollywood stars.

But whoa! Wait! These *are* Hollywood stars. Well, sort of. While George Clooney's name is anything but familiar, he looks enough like a David Naughton for the 90s to qualify as a promising newcomer. Doug Savant is best remembered as the would-be killer in MASQUERADE. And Dedee Pfeiffer, Michelle's little sister, is one of the better answers to the question, "Are there any more like you at home?" Other familiar names in the cast include Philip McKeon (from TV's "Alice") as True Blue, and Gene Simmons, onetime member of the rock band Kiss, apparently old enough now to play characters named "Doc."

The B-movie plot features Clooney as ex-surf champ Mark Remar (as the hero of the piece, he is spared having to tote around a silly nickname), who has turned to drug-running after an injury put a stop to his surfing "career." When his long-suffering, sleek, blonde, and pregnant girl friend, Rebecca (Pfeiffer, naturally; aside from her sister, and maybe Meg Ryan, there are few blonder or sleeker), threatens to leave him and take their baby-to-be to Portland to make a fresh, drug-free start, Mark decides to reform. But before he quits, he wants to make one last big score.

If that were the whole plot, RED SURF might have stood a chance of being a sharp little low-budget crime melodrama. But its script and story, credited to four different people including debuting director H. Gordon Boos, is so over-stuffed with subplots and peripheral characters that the film winds up an overlong, annoying, and confusing mess. The most garrulous subplot revolves around True Blue, a goofy-but-likable screw-up who gets busted and, after spending a few nights in a cell with a transvestite, either does or does not sell out drug lord Calavera (Rick Najera), a character seemingly sprung from the pages of the Marquis de Sade, complete with a gloomy run-down mansion and a pack of hungry wolf-dogs that dispose of people he doesn't like. Calavera threatens to call off the big deal, but Remar is already being prevented from participating in it by Attila (Savant), who has moved in on Remar's action.

While all this less-than-interesting extracurricular activity is going on, a number of basic questions go unanswered—chiefly, how, exactly, do Remar and Attila make a living? Periodically they are shown riding jet skis—not the most inconspicuous mode of travel—out to a buoy late at night to pick up a brick of cocaine someone (we are never told who) has conveniently left there for them to deliver to Calavera. The film's climax includes Calavera ambushing Remar and Attila at the buoy, which leaves us wondering why Calavera hasn't dispensed with their services entirely by going out to get the damned coke himself.

Even more of a problem then these plot holes are RED SURF's uninvolving characters. What is one to make of a movie in which drug running is the only viable career option to surfing? Whatever happened to skateboarding, or managing a tanning parlor or fitness spa? Despite its pretensions (RED SURF's ad copy proclaimed it an EASY RIDER for the 90s), the film finally boils down to just another retrograde, sunbaked "youth" movie about a rad California white dude who outwits and kills a bunch of dumb, hotheaded ethnics, then rides off into the sunset with a cool, foxy babe. When you add the film's view of drug running and revenge murder as little more than high-spirited youthful high jinks, you are left with a movie that is much less this decade's answer to EASY RIDER than it is a humorless PORKY'S for the 90s—an insult to that film, which almost looks like a classy piece of filmmaking by comparison. *(Profanity, violence, adult situations, substance abuse.)*

d, H. Gordon Boos; p, Richard C. Weinman; w, Vincent Robert (based on a story by Brian Gamble, Jason Hoffs, Vincent Robert and additional material by H. Gordon Boos); ph, John Schwartzman; ed, Dennis Dolan; m, Sasha Matson; prod d, Lynda Burbank

Action/Crime   **(PR:O MPAA:R)**

REINCARNATION OF GOLDEN LOTUS, THE

(Hong Kong) 99m Golden Harvest c

Joi Wong *(Lotus)*, Eric Tsang *(Wu Dai)*, Lam Chun Yen *(Wu-long)*, and Sin Lap Man *(Simon)*

There are easily enough ideas and plot in this overpacked combination of history, drama, romance, and literary revisionism to fill three films. But the makers of THE REINCARNATION OF GOLDEN LOTUS have settled for making just one film, and it fails to find a dramatic focus until its final, frenzied

minutes. At the center of the movie is Lotus, Chinese literature's infamous "slut of all time." During the 10th-century Sung dynasty, Lotus was the central character of a classic Chinese pornographic novel about a beautiful woman who is abused, raped, sold, and murdered by the men in her life. The film's prolog finds Lotus (Joi Wong) beheaded and awaiting admission at the gates of Hell. Given a chance to be reincarnated, she vows to take revenge on the male sex. The film then flashes forward to the People's Republic of China in 1968, at the height of the Cultural Revolution. Lotus is now a ballet student. After fending off the advances of a Communist party official who offers to help her career in exchange for sexual favors, Lotus is denounced as a counter-revolutionary by the official and as a slut by her female teachers and fellow students. Expelled from the arts academy, she is forced to work in a garment-making sweatshop. There she becomes attracted to fellow worker Wu-long (Lam Chun Yen), who's also the star of the sweatshop's basketball team. Saving her meager wages, Lotus buys him a new pair of sneakers. But when her past catches up with her, Lotus is once again branded a traitor, accused of stealing the sneakers, and then condemned for squandering the people's money on the "frivolity" of new sneakers when she denies the theft. To make Lotus' humiliation complete, Wu-long is forced to take a leading role in her public censure. Exiled to a village that caters to tourists, Lotus works as a fruit seller and prostitute until a Hong Kong businessman (Eric Tsang) proposes marriage. But after moving to Hong Kong, Lotus finds that her new husband's brother, chauffeur, and confidant is none other than Wu-long. Soon, Lotus is tormented by visions of her past life, and her personality splits. As the modern Lotus, she taunts Wu-long for his cowardice, but as the ancient Lotus, she brazenly tries to seduce him. Consumed by her old desires, Lotus ventures to a high-class Hong Kong sex club, where she abandons herself to a night of pleasure with sensualist Simon (Sin Lap Man). However, she leaves behind a sheet of paper with her home address and phone number written on it, and Simon begins phoning Lotus, threatening to reveal their affair to her husband. A professional photographer, Simon then contacts Lotus' husband directly, inquiring about renting the family estate for a photo shoot. In a scene reminiscent of Glenn Close's surprise home visit to Anne Archer in FATAL ATTRACTION, Simon even dares to show up in Lotus' living room. At this point, Lotus, still unconscious of her notorious past life, finally stumbles upon a copy of the original *Golden Lotus* novel. Skipping to the end, she finds that the story climaxes with the murder of the heroine's husband by her lover, followed by the murder of the lover and the heroine by her enraged brother-in-law. In short order, Lotus is put in the position of trying to prevent this literary bloodshed from being repeated.

Hong Kong-born, British-educated director Clara Law shows great promise in what is only her third full-length film (and second commercial feature). GOLDEN LOTUS demonstrates a dizzying directorial range, incorporating aspects of feminist drama, romantic comedy, and melodrama, with a flurry of martial-arts action thrown in for good measure in the film's absolutely riveting finale. While this mix never quite gels, and the film proceeds in fits and starts, by the time the picture finally does kick into gear, the wait is more than worthwhile. Even when it isn't quite working, GOLDEN LOTUS is engrossing, benefitting from strong performances and Law's stylish, whirlwind-paced direction.

Law's biggest mistake is that GOLDEN LOTUS bites off more than most audiences can chew in one sitting. Nonetheless, it is rare to find a film from any nation that can boast as many tasty morsels as this one can. *(Violence, sexual situations, nudity, substance abuse.)*

d, Clara Law; p, Teddy Robins; w, Lee Pik Wah; ph, Ma Chor Shing; ed, Hamilton Yu; m, Teddy Robins and Richard Lo; art d, Lee King Man, Yuen Ching Yeung, Tang Wei Ling, and Chan Yiu Wing

Drama/Thriller   **(PR:O MPAA:NR)**

REPOSSESSED

84m Seven Arts/New Line c

Linda Blair *(Nancy Agler)*, Ned Beatty *(Ernest Weller)*, Leslie Nielsen *(Fr. Mayii)*, Anthony Starke *(Fr. Brophy)*, Melissa Moore *(Bimbo)*, Lana Schwab, and Thom J. Sharp

There have been so many movies like this one lately that it might be time to consider them a new genre, what might be called *film Pinot Noir*, movies whose ideas and casting look good on paper but that end up looking as if they were made by drunks. REPOSSESSED is a prime example. As ideas go, the one behind this film is better than average: Sign up Linda Blair, star of THE EXORCIST, and place her at the center of a sequel spoof in which she plays a sweet suburban housewife who is possessed by the Devil. Is it any surprise that Blair was game? Since vomiting pea soup, twisting her head around, and talking like Mercedes McCambridge in the 1973 William Friedkin shocker, she has starred in a string of B movies ranging in quality from mediocre to dismal. A starring role in a clever satire of the movie in which she made her name would seem to be just the ticket to get Blair back into the moviemaking big leagues. Toss in Leslie Nielsen as a costar, add veteran Ned Beatty in support, and it would appear that Blair finally had another winner on her hands, right? Wrong. With REPOSSESSED Blair's luck remains unchanged. At least the awfulness of the film isn't the fault of the actors; however, those who worked behind the camera on this one deserve to do some heavy penance.

What plot there is concerns suburban *housefrau* Nancy Agler (Blair), a grown-up version of THE EXORCIST's Regan. One night, while watching a pair of Jim-and-Tammy-like evangelists (Beatty, Lana Schwab) on TV, Nancy is again possessed by her old nemesis, the Devil. From the safety of a classroom podium, Nielsen, as Father Mayii, recounts much of the mayhem that ensues, allowing for plenty of laboriously wacky reactions shots. Father Brophy (Anthony Starke, playing the Jason Miller role to Nielsen's Max Von Sydow) tries to convince his superiors to sanction another exorcism, then stands by helplessly while Ernest Weller (Beatty) undertakes the exorcism as part of a live TV broadcast. An extended sequence in a health spa follows, featuring a cameo appearance by exercise-guru-cum-sitcom-star Jake Steinfeld and plenty of leering closeups of skimpily clad cuties who work out and then hop in the shower — all of which is, of course, integral to the plot. We are told that Father Mayii has come to the spa to get in shape for the exorcism, but then he ends up watching it on television. Even more indispensable to the storyline is a sequence in which various religious leaders chase Nancy around the TV studio. While this sequence clearly provided some work for the Pope John Paul II and Dalai Lama lookalikes who appear in it, it has, like so many of the film's sequences, little to do with anything else that transpires in the film. Actually, by about the movie's halfway point, most viewers won't care what's happening on the screen. Needless to say, Good wins out.

Everybody else loses, especially the audience. Through it all, Blair still twists her head with aplomb, and her satanic leer and McCambridge growl haven't diminished with age. But what's most remarkable is the professional poise she maintains as the movie sinks around her. And she needs all the poise she can muster in a film that doesn't provide a single good laugh in its entire 90-minute running time. Even the makeup is horrendously cheap-looking.

Having somehow coerced Nielsen into participating in the project, writer-director Bob Logan attempted to fashion REPOSSESSED into an AIRPLANE!-style farce. What he ended up with is a mess. To say that his work isn't on par with that of the Zucker-Abrahams-Zucker team that made the films that he is desperately trying to imitate is a colossal understatement. The only really good thing that can be said about REPOSSESSED is that it makes EXORCIST II look like a classic. To hell with it. *(Profanity, brief nudity, adult situations.)*

d, Bob Logan; p, Steven Wizan; w, Bob Logan; ph, Michael Margulies; ed, Jeff Freeman; m, Charles Fox; prod d, Shay Austin; art d, Gae Buckley; set d, Lee Cunningham; cos, Tim D'Arcy

Comedy/Horror   (PR:O   MPAA:PG-13)

RESCUERS DOWN UNDER, THE

109m Silver Screen Partners IV — Walt Disney/Buena Vista c

VOICES OF: Bob Newhart *(Bernard)*, Eva Gabor *(Miss Bianca)*, John Candy *(Wilbur)*, Tristan Rogers *(Jake)*, Adam Ryen *(Cody)*, Wayne Robson *(Frank)*, George C. Scott *(McLeach)*, Douglas Seale *(Krebbs)*, Frank Welker *(Joanna)*, Bernard Fox *(Chairmouse/Doctor)*, Peter Firth *(Red)*, Billy Barty *(Baitmouse)*, Ed Gilbert *(Francoise)*, Carla Meyer *(Faloo/Mother)*, and Russi Taylor *(Nurse Mouse)*

As the title implies, this sequel to the 1977 hit THE RESCUERS is set in Australia where young Cody (voiced by Adam Ryen), a fatherless boy, leads his own band of animal rescuers against evil poacher McLeach (George C. Scott). Barely after bounding out of bed in the morning (and skipping breakfast — some role model!), Cody comes to the rescue of McLeach's latest quarry, a giant, majestic golden eagle whose mate was already victimized by the poacher. With Cody's help, the eagle escapes McLeach's trap and Cody is rewarded with a soaring flight on the eagle's back, ending in her nest where she shows him three eggs which are about to hatch. While returning home, Cody falls into one of McLeach's traps and is captured by the villain. Finding one of the eagle's feathers on the boy, McLeach attempts to force him to reveal the location of the nest. Word of McLeach's misdeeds soon gets back to the International Rescue Aid Society in New York, where the original film's mouse hero and heroine, Bernard (Bob Newhart) and Miss Bianca (Eva Gabor), are once again pressed into service. They get down under with the help of goofy albatross Wilbur (John Candy). Once there, they acquire a Crocodile Dundee-type mouse guide (soap opera star Tristan Rogers) who has an eye for Miss Bianca, to whom Bernard was about to propose marriage before they got swept up in their new adventure. It isn't long before the mouse trio finds itself deep in trouble as they attempt to foil McLeach's foul plan.

Not a great hit with audiences (it didn't even sell as many tickets as Disney's low-budget 1990 television knockoff DUCKTALES: THE MOVIE — THE TREASURE OF THE LOST LAMP), the problems with the film begin with its title. Three years in the making, it was obviously conceived during the height of this country's fascination with Australia, brought on by Paul Hogan's fabulously successful CROCODILE DUNDEE. By 1990, the mania had long since subsided, and this film's Australian setting did nothing to enhance its box office appeal. Further, the film doesn't make particularly imaginative use of the location. Take away the accents and the obligatory kangaroos and koalas, and the story could have taken place anywhere. Another problem is that "the rescuers" themselves don't even enter the action until a third of the film has passed. And when they do appear, they don't have much to do with the main plot until near the film's end. The characters seem grafted on to a story that probably would have been more successful without them. Finally, the film suffers from some action and plotting that is questionable in a children's film. The villain is far too malignant, the young vigilante hero seems to be a kiddie "Rambo," and some of the action is quite violent, if not tasteless.

Still, whatever else it is, this is a Disney cartoon. And, as those that went before it, it sets the standard for animated spectacle with some truly stupendous sequences — the eagle in flight is the obvious highlight — that will keep kids on the edges of their seats. Appearing with this film during its theatrical run was an animated short, THE PRINCE AND THE PAUPER, featuring Mickey Mouse. It actually could have been a nifty feature of its own, but for some inexplicable reason, the Disney studio decided to adapt the Mark Twain classic as a brutally abrupt 30-minute short subject. Mickey Mouse plays both title roles in the story of a prince who trades places with a lookalike peasant. Pluto, the amazing dog who wears human dentures, is as manically frisky as ever as the pauper's faithful pooch, with Goofy as goofy as ever as the pauper's roommate and best friend. Donald Duck, alas, only consented to a cameo appearance. If anything, the quality of the animation in this short is even better than the feature it precedes, but the truncated script comes close to ruining a terrific story.

d, Hendel Butoy and Michael Gabriel; p, Thomas C. Schumacher; w, Jim Cox, Karey Kirkpatrick, Byron Simpson, and Joe Ranft; ed, Michael Kelly; m, Bruce Broughton; art d, Maurice Hunt; spec, Randy Fullmer; anim, Glen Keane, Mark Henn, Russ Edmonds, David Cutler, Ruben A. Aquino, Nik Ranieri, Ed Gombert, Anthony DeRosa, Kathy Zielinski, Duncan Marjoribanks, and Lisa Keene

Animated/Children's   (PR:A-C   MPAA:G)

RETURN OF SUPERFLY, THE

95m Littoral — Crash/Triton — Vidmark c

Nathan Purdee *(Superfly)*, Margaret Avery *(Francine)*, Sam Jackson *(Nate Cabot)*, Leonard Thomas *(Joey)*, Kirk Taylor *(Renaldo)*, Carlos Carrasco *(Hector)*, Tico Wells *(Willy Green)*, Luis Ramos *(Manuel)*, Christopher Curry *(Tom Perkins)*, David Groh *(Wolinski)*, John Gabriel *(Joyner)*, David Weinberg *(DEA Officer)*, Jack Lotz *(Customs Marshal)*, Rony Clanton *(Eddie Baker)*, Lisa Joliff *(Eddie's Girl)*, Arnold Mazur *(Marty Ryan)*, Patrice Ablack *(Irene Gates)*, Marie O'Malley *(Receptionist)*, Douglas Wade, Randy Frazier *(Bartenders)*, Gerald M. Kline *(Sergeant)*, John Canada Terrell *(Detective Loomey)*, Bill Corsair *(Inspector Kinsella)*, Timothy Stickney *(Rasta)*, Maxine Harrison *(Marla Cabot)*, Ruthanna Graves *(Jasmine Jackson)*, Eric Payne *(Security Guard)*, Sonia Hensley *(Martha Nixon)*, Marc Webster *(Waiter)*, O.L. Duke *(Cashier)*, Oscar Colon *(Pop)*, Kevin Rock *(Yuppie Man)*, Toni Ann Johnson *(Yuppie Woman)*, Rynel Johnson *(Homeboy)*, Rafton Trew *(Old Man)*, Juanita Fleming *(Angry Woman)*, John Patrick Hayden, Joe Spataro, Ken Threet *(Cops)*, Eric Griffin, Gregory Cook, and Tye Pierson *(Drug Dealers)*

In this belated sequel to SUPERFLY (1972), Superfly (Nathan Purdee) is back, and he's caught between a rock and a hard place. Having gone straight for the past two decades in Paris, the expatriate makes the mistake of returning to the US. A retired drug dealer who always dreamed of having enough cash to quit the business, Superfly is being coerced into putting out the word that he wants to be a pusher once more. As the film begins, one of Superfly's former colleagues Eddie Baker (Rony Clanton) is blown away by ruthless drug dealers who are infinitely more vicious than those who ruled the trade in Superfly's heyday. Hector (Carlos Carrasco), a cop turned crook, and his righthand man Joey (Leonard Thomas) control the area's drug traffic, and they suspect Superfly is working with the government when he returns to the scene. Even if he's not, Hector isn't about to let him cut in on his business. Warned by Nate (Sam Jackson), an old friend, of just how dangerous the times are, Superfly contemplates a return to Europe, but the cops tell him he will be arrested on long-standing drug charges if he doesn't play ball. After he's severely beaten by Hector's men and a female friend is cut down by bullets meant for him, Superfly gets good and mad, and decides to go after Hector and his thugs his own way. Aided by the beautiful Francine (Margaret Avery), Superfly enlists the aid of explosives expert Willy (Tico Wells) in his plan to bring Hector down. Hector's men kill Nate and rape Francine, prompting Superfly to retaliate by kidnapping Eddie, forcing him to reveal the location of Hector's stash. Superfly then laces the dope with a substance guaranteed to make users sick, and soon drug users all over the city are complaining that Hector's drugs are no good. Hector's problems mount as Willy detonates explosives at all of his drug-manufacturing labs, and the drug kingpin realizes that he's got to destroy Superfly in order to protect his standard of living.

At the height of the popularity of blaxploitation films in the early 1970s, SUPERFLY, starring Ron O'Neal and directed by Gordon Parks, Jr., was attacked on the grounds of its dubious morality — its hero, after all, was a drug pusher. Similar condemnations aren't likely to be leveled at this film, which manages to be both up-to-the-minute and out-of-date. What gave the original film its punch was its strong anti-establishment tone. Here, the anti-hero comes across like Eliot Ness after kicking a drug habit. As portrayed by newcomer Purdee, he's a squeaky clean graduate of the Billy Dee Williams School for Leading Men. For all its current street jive and rap songs, the film is a stolid action movie, an urban drama that could have been produced years ago. Setting the film even further apart from its predecessor, race isn't even an integral issue here — change a few lines and the main character could have been played by Dolph Lundgren or Michael Dudikoff. But what's most unfortunate about the film is its lack of vitality. The filmmakers have changed Superfly into an acceptable role model for these anti-drug times, but they haven't made him an exciting hero. Director Sig Shore (THE ACT, SUDDEN DEATH) injects little life into the film, so that it plays like a hybrid of a public service announcement against substance abuse and a K-Tel commercial for romantic soul music. It seems obvious that the Superfly character would have been better served by remaining a memory from a more ambiguous, more exciting era. (*Violence, sexual situations, nudity, profanity, drug abuse.*)

d, Sig Shore; p, Sig Shore and Anthony Wisdom; w, Anthony Wisdom; ph, Anghel Decca; ed, John Mullen; m, Curtis Mayfield; art d, Jeremie Frank; set d, Charlotte Snyder; spec, Willy Caban and Rick Washburn; cos, Ida Gearon and Varcra Russal; makup, Lauren Matonis

Action   (PR:O   MPAA:R)

REVENGE

124m Rastar/Columbia — New World c

Kevin Costner (*Cochran*), Anthony Quinn (*Tiburon "Tibey" Mendes*), Madeleine Stowe (*Miryea Mendes*), Tomas Milian (*Cesar*), Joaquin Martinez (*Mauro*), James Gammon (*Texan*), Jesse Corti (*Madero*), Sally Kirkland (*Rock Star*), Luis De Icaza (*Ramon*), Gerardo Zepeda (*Elefante*), Miguel Ferrer (*Amador*), John Leguizamo (*Ignacio*), Joe Santos (*Ibarra*), Christofer De Oni (*Diaz*), Daniel Rojo (*Vaquero*), Edna Bolkan (*Roxanne*), Pia Karina (*Rochelle*), Monica Hernandez (*Neli*), Julian Pastor (*Quinones*), Claudio Brook (*Barone*), Trini Rodriguez (*La Vieja*), Mauricio Ruby (*Resabio*), Gilberto Compan (*Roberto*), Karmin Murcelo (*Madam*), Alfredo Cienfuegos (*Antonio*), Salvador Garcini (*Doctor*), Kathleen Hughes (*Mother Superior*), Rosa Radjune, Julieta Egurrola (*Nuns*), and Jorge Pascual Rubio (*Mendoza*)

Deferential machismo. From THE UNTOUCHABLES through NO WAY OUT, BULL DURHAM, and even the sentimental FIELD OF DREAMS, it's been the core of Kevin Costner's screen persona: quiet, sensitive, enigmatically distracted, and — most of all — passive. Apparently drawn to his inertia, the women in Costner's films wrap themselves around him at the slightest provocation (actually, at *no* provocation, in keeping with the basic premise of Costner's passive innocence), though most of the time you get the feeling he'd rather be playing frisbee with his dog. He's a peace-loving sort who never courts trouble, but somehow trouble usually manages to find him and to drag him down into the human muck and mire, into passion and violence and the life of an action hero. He's a man seduced by circumstance, by the devil at the heart of things. And the devil, more often than not in this myth of the innocent male, is a woman.

REVENGE brings all these elements together with (natch) a vengeance. Costner plays Cochran, a retiring Navy pilot invited to visit his old friend Tiburon (Anthony Quinn), called "Tibey," in Mexico. Tibey proves to be a baronial cliche: rich, powerful, and corrupt, with a young wife, Miryea (Madeleine Stowe), whose beauty causes the visiting American's unwilling head to turn. But Tibey's thugs are everywhere, his estate is a nest of prying eyes, and, besides, the old *senor* displays a nasty temper — killing off a pair of flunkies before breakfast, tossing one of his guard dogs in the swimming pool, etc. Disinclined to tempt fate, our safety-first hero settles in for a round of tennis. But Miryea — drawn by Cochran's inertia, his winning way with dogs, and so on — has other ideas, leading to a walk along the sea, a beach-house rendezvous, Cochran's squeezing limes while she presses ever closer . . . This seduction is cut short, only to be resumed at an evening party, where, after herculean efforts to resist her, Cochran finally succumbs to Miryea's all-too-palpable charms. But have

they been seen, and will the jealous Tibey uncover their indiscretion? Cochran plays coy, while Tibey remains a puzzle, dropping ambiguous remarks and casting pained glances at his guest. Finally, the lovers decide on a getaway fling, obscuring their intentions with lies as they repair to a mountain hideaway. But Latin hothead Tibey and his goons soon burst in on their adulterous coupling, blow away Cochran's faithful dog, and beat the pilot to a bloody pulp while putting Miryea's fair features to the knife. The hideaway is torched and Cochran is dumped off on the road to die, a feast for the fire ants and buzzards. With Miryea packed off to a brothel and shot up with smack at regular intervals, Tibey's revenge is now complete; Cochran's, however, has yet to begin. Saved from a grisly end and nursed back to health by a kindly *campesino*, he resolves to settle scores with his former friend and to find out what's happened to Miryea. A sickly horse trader (James Gammon) offers him companionship and a ride, and hardly lifts an eyebrow when Cochran knifes one of Tibey's henchmen in the back of a seedy bar. But the new friend's days are numbered, and Cochran soon finds himself heir to a battered pickup and on the road alone. Next, an over-the-hill rock star (Sally Kirkland, in a thankless cameo) provides him with temporary solace and a cover, and another of Tibey's enemies (Miguel Ferrer) teams up with Cochran, but the search for Miryea among the bawds and lowlifes comes up frustratingly empty. Their only hope of finding her is to get to Tibey, and when Cochran and company track him down at last (out on the hardscrabble hills, bodyguards in tow), the fate of the faithless wife is finally revealed. After sufficient blood is spilled, an uneasy truce is struck (vengeance is always honorable) and Cochran rushes off to the convent where Miryea lies comatose. The outcome is all but inevitable — the price of corrupted male innocence being the death of the seducer — but real men don't shed tears, and neither will the audience.

If films were medieval paintings, director Tony Scott would be known as the Master of the Billowing Draperies. Give him an open window and a bit of breeze and no swatch of fabric is safe from his attention. Scott's decorative agenda differs from executive producer-star Costner's macho one, though their purposes don't so much clash as wander off on separate tracks. Scott seems eager to distance himself from the sleek, reflecting surfaces of his last two films (TOP GUN and BEVERLY HILLS COP II, although he does include an overt opening *hommage* to the former) in REVENGE. The ambience here is sultry, primitive, and decidedly low-tech, as thick and humid as the cloister (or the brothel apartment) Miryea winds up in. REVENGE gets off to an indifferent start, with too many talking heads too closely cropped, but by the time the hero has been plunged headlong into corruption, Scott's operating at something like full throttle. Fancy lighting, sweaty colors, lurid amber filters — it's the best work he's ever done, and for a few delirious stretches the film blossoms like a desert plant after a healthy rain.

None of which has much to do with the macho conceits of the screenplay, adapted from scenarist Jim Harrison's own novella, or with the performances — there aren't any to speak of, since Costner and Stowe merely fill in the blanks to enact *ideas* of characters rather than the real thing, while Quinn seems badly used. Still, for all the violence and cliched plotting, REVENGE still has enough stylistic personality and hothouse panache to make it worth enduring. (*Violence, profanity, nudity, adult situations.*)

d, Tony Scott; p, Hunt Lowry and Stanley Rubin; w, Jim Harrison and Jeffrey Fiskin (based on the novella "Revenge" by Jim Harrison); ph, Jeffrey Kimball; ed, Chris Lebenzon; m, Jack Nitzsche; prod d, Michael Seymour and Benjamin Fernandez; art d, Tom Sanders and Jorge Sainz; set d, Crispian Sallis and Fernando Solorio; spec, Jesus Duran; stunts, Terry Leonard; cos, Aude Bronson-Howard; makup, Ellen Wong, Ester Oropeza, and Frank Carrisosa

Adventure/Drama   (PR:O   MPAA:R)

REVERSAL OF FORTUNE

120m Edward R. Pressman — Shochiku Fuji — Sovereign/WB c

Jeremy Irons (*Claus von Bulow*), Glenn Close (*Sunny von Bulow*), Ron Silver (*Alan M. Dershowitz*), Anabella Sciorra (*Carol*), Uta Hagen (*Maria*), Fisher Stevens (*David Marriott*), Christine Baranski (*Andrea Reynolds*), Mano Singh, Felicity Huffman, Alan Pottinger, Julie Hagerty, Sarah Fearon, and Jad Mager

Having plunged into the lower depths of humanity with BARFLY, director Barbet Schroeder now explores the very upper strata of Newport society with this cool, quirky adaptation of lawyer Alan Dershowitz's book about his successful appeal of Claus von Bulow's conviction for the attempted murder of his wife, Martha "Sunny" von Bulow. Neither docudrama nor out-and-out fiction, REVERSAL OF FORTUNE is, in the words of screenwriter and co-producer Nicholas Kazan "some kind of fiction based on fact." It is also, as all good courtroom dramas should be, a drama about the clash between absolutes of truth, justice, and judgement and the ambiguity of the human animal. As a result, it is one of the best and most intriguing films of its kind since Otto Preminger's classic of the genre, ANATOMY OF A MURDER.

As in BARFLY, Schroeder reveals himself as a director as interested in extremes as he is disinterested in the middle ground. The film begins with its most extreme character of all, Sunny (Glenn Close), who becomes the film's narrator from the vantage point of her "persistent vegetative state," not too unlike William Holden's narration of SUNSET BOULEVARD from the vantage point of being face-down dead in a swimming pool. She supplies a quick summary of Claus's (Jeremy Irons) first trial, which ended in his sentencing to a 30-year term and his release on $1 million bail. FORTUNE really begins with Claus approaching Dershowitz (Ron Silver) to file his appeal. Dershowitz is reluctant to accept Claus as a client at first. Claus displays a tinge of anti-semitism, and, as an arrogant, elitist, decadent multi-millionaire, he generally represents everything Dershowitz hates. Yet, the lawyer finally accepts on the basis of his recurring "Hitler dream," in which Hitler approaches Dershowitz to defend him. Instead of making a choice between acquitting him or killing him, Dershowitz decides to first acquit him then kill him. Dershowitz has no special desire to kill Claus von Bulow, but, as he would be with Hitler, he is stimulated by the challenge of defending the indefensible.

The remainder of FORTUNE becomes a review of the evidence, from depositions to the characters of Claus and Sunny themselves. In the process, Dershowitz, working with what amounts to an army recruited from his classes at Harvard Law School, manages to pretty much demolish the prosecution case, which had Claus injecting Sunny with enough insulin to bring about her coma. Yet, Dershowitz can't supply a theory of what really happened until he comes to see Claus as an average man instead of a symbol, like most average people, neither completely culpable nor entirely innocent. His chastening comes about in one of the film's more intriguing subplots, in which Dershowitz personally involves himself in the investigation of a witness (Fisher Stevens) who, it turns out, is aiming to destroy Dershowitz and his case. Dershowitz is taken in by the witness because he is the only one in the film who fully confirms his contemptuous view of the rich, seducing him by telling him what he wants to hear.

But it is Irons's performance that dominates the film and Claus's character that seems to have captivated Schroeder's camera. Claus is finally the odd man out. Too old world and old money to make a comfortable fit with Dershowitz's world view, he's also out of place in his own milieu, even his own family. Sunny calls him a "prince of perversion" not for the obvious reasons but because he wants to work as a member of a class that simply does not work. In the face of Sunny's tirades and neuroses, Claus reacts with an odd devotion. He is unabashedly adulterous, but when Sunny insists on sleeping with the windows wide-open in the middle of winter, Claus simply wears heavy clothes and a ski hat to bed without complaint. We believe him when he tells Dershowitz that he loves her as he loves all the women in his life, though of the two mistresses we see, one is a traitor and the other seems more concerned with getting back Claus's million-dollar bail than seeing him exonerated. With Sunny's children from her first marriage, he has to compete with Burt Lancaster and THE CRIMSON PIRATE on television while trying to tell them of the likelihood of their own divorce. Irons's plays the role with a frankness and a quiet dignity rather than with melodramatic villainy. Schroeder's camera virtually always frames him in isolation to convey his dramatic bleakness and isolation. As a result he remains enigmatic. The single trait that finally stands out most in him is a kind of willful, self-destructive childishness that drives him to revel in his naughty public image but that also drives him to childish extremes of devotion and loyalty. Sunny's millions become his solace, rather than his motivation for a crime.

Whether any of this has anything to do with the real people portrayed is finally anybody's guess. But, in essence, that is the whole point. The movie finally "guesses" that Claus neither meant to kill Sunny nor that Sunny necessarily meant to commit suicide. The truth, like so much else in REVERSAL OF FORTUNE, is somewhere in-between. Schroeder is finally not nearly the visually expressive director that Preminger was, and FORTUNE suffers for it. His sensitivity to the von Bulows seems at times too insistent. The telemovie visual flatness with which he treats Dershowitz's bright-eyed, bushy-tailed legal forces keeps threatening to edge over into under-served derision. But what saves FORTUNE is what is usually fatal to good filmmaking— Schroeder's own honest indecision about his plot and his characters. He doesn't seem sure of who is right and who is wrong, whether he was making a film about the banality of evil or the evil of banality. It finally doesn't make for as luridly flashy drama as FORTUNE easily could have been, but it does make for a fascinating one, a strange and compelling tragicomedy of ill manners. Irons won the Best Actor Oscar, and the film earned nominations for its director and its screenplay. *(Profanity, adult situations.)*

d, Barbet Schroeder; p, Edward R. Pressman and Oliver Stone; w, Nicholas Kazan (based on the book by Alan Dershowitz); ph, Luciano Tovoli; ed, Lee Percy; m, Mark Isham; prod d, Mel Bourne; cos, Judianna Makovsky and Milena Canonero

Drama   (PR:C   MPAA:R)

RIVER OF DEATH

103m Breton/Cannon c

Michael Dudikoff *(John)*, Robert Vaughn *(Wolfgang Manteuifil)*, Donald Pleasence *(Heinrich Spaatz)*, Herbert Lom *(Col. Diaz)*, Cynthia Erland *(Maria)*, Sarah Maur Thorp *(Anna)*, L.Q. Jones *(Hiller)*, Foziah Davidson *(Dalia)*, Victor Melleney *(Blakeley)*, Gordon Mulholland *(Fanjul)*, Alain Woolf *(Serrano)*, Lindsey Reardon *(Kellner)*, Goliath Davids *(Shamen)*, Crispin De Nuys *(Schuster)*, Ian Yule *(Long John Silver)*, Gail McQuillun *(Young Maria)*, James White *(Pilot)*, Elzabe Zeitsman *(Cabaret Artiste)*, and Norman Aintsey *(Tracy)*

The time is WW II; the place is a concentration camp laboratory, an evil playground for Wolfgang Manteuifil (Robert Vaughn), a Nazi fiend who enjoys playing God. Unmoved by a Nazi officer's demand that he abandon his inhuman experimentation, the mad scientist murders the officer while the officer's small daughter, Maria (Gail McQuillun), hides under a table and witnesses the slaying. When another SS bigwig, Heinrich Spaatz (Donald Pleasence), arrives, he and Manteuifil discuss the imminent collapse of the Third Reich, their booming sideline in art smuggling, and their possible escape to South America. Later, while waiting in a getaway plane, Manteuifil cunningly shoots Spaatz in the knee so that he can't flee with him; then Manteuifil flies to South America to continue his medical depravity.

Twenty years later, John (Michael Dudikoff), a rugged jungle guide, accompanies a doctor and his daughter, Anna (Sarah Maur Thorp), on a mission to save natives by discovering the source of a fatal disease. Hundreds of miles from civilization, the party is attacked by natives who shoot the doctor and kidnap Anna; only John escapes. Guilt-stricken, John regains his health at a jungle outpost on the Amazon and vows to rescue the girl he left behind. When John reveals his expedition plans to local authorities, police chief Diaz (Herbert Lom) tries to discourage John from making the trip and warns that he doesn't want any native treasures disappearing (in reality, Diaz is an agent for the Nazis and neo-Nazis hiding in the jungle.) Accompanied by his mercenary partner, Hiller (L.Q. Jones), John commences his journey only to find that his expedition has attracted a representative of Diaz, two Nazi hunters, the duplicitous Spaatz, his mistress, and a henchman. Posing as a politically neutral tycoon, Spaatz actually wants to locate Manteuifil for revenge; what he doesn't realize is that his lovely girl friend, Maria (now played by Cynthia Erland), is the young German girl who witnessed Manteuifil's brutal killing of her father. Double-crossed by a pilot who lands their helicopter directly in the path of river pirates and then takes off alone, the explorers fight for their lives during a gun battle, sabotage the pirates' headquarters, and maneuver their way out of a river ambush by natives. Another copter pilot, known as Long John Silver (Ian Yule), a friend of John's, was supposed to meet the jungle travellers, but he is discovered dead. After Spaatz kills one mutineer who is wary of the increasingly dangerous trip, John orders Hiller to remain with Long John's copter. While guarding it, Hiller is shot by Diaz, who hesitates to finish the job only when he realizes he needs a pilot. After the remaining adventurers are captured by flesh-eating natives who kill three of them, Diaz and Hiller show up and rescue Spaatz, John, and Maria. In the Lost City of the Nazis, John re-encounters Anna, who has contracted the deadly disease perpetuated by Manteuifil. Although Spaatz exacts revenge from Manteuifil, an accident occurs when Maria tries to kill Manteuifil. Mortally wounded, she fires her gun, precipitating an explosion that engulfs Spaatz and Manteuifil in flames. Knowing he has helped rid the world of assorted Nazis, John gets out alive.

Although based on an Alistair MacLean thriller, RIVER OF DEATH is a convoluted journey burdened with too many plot twists and too much exposition. How much mileage do suspense moviemakers believe they can still coax from the Nazi menace? Even though the subplot about John's initial mercy mission strengthens his character's motivation for returning to the jungle, the film could have handled this entire excursion as a flashback or with an interior monolog. Rather than whet our appetite for thrills with disparate plot strands, the film fails to tie everything together and instead stumbles over its too-complicated heart-of-darkness story line. Since it's quite easy to figure out that Diaz is a Nazi aide and that Maria is the little girl we saw traumatized by her father's murder, the film ruins two more opportunities for mining suspense.

RIVER OF DEATH is also xenophobic and racist in its attitudes, delivering a wide variety of brown-skinned menaces willing to kill at the drop of a poisoned spear; it's as if we're back on the set of Johnny Weissmuller's Tarzan flicks. Brutal and viscerally frightening, the attacks by these savages do have an undeniable impact, but this movie is too realistic in its intentions and tone for us to excuse its unflattering portrait of the South American Indians as an exercise in good old-fashioned Kiplingesque storytelling. Among the actors, Dudikoff makes an attractive hero, but none of the other actors matches his performance. Pleasence continues to pick up paychecks for walking through underwritten roles; Vaughn hams it up as if he were auditioning for the life of Vincent Price in his Dr. Phibes period.

A sluggish jungle adventure complete with plagues, ritual sacrifices, and retrograde Nazis, RIVER OF DEATH simply fails to make the grade as a suspense thriller. Nonetheless, it may contain sufficient excitement to satisfy adventure genre fans who don't quibble about weak story structuring. *(Violence, profanity, substance abuse, adult situations.)*

d, Steve Carver; p, Harry Alan Towers and Avi Lerner; w, Edward Simpson and Andrew Deutsch (based on the novel by Alistair MacLean); ph, Avi Karpick; ed, Ken Bornstein; m, Sasha Matson; art d, John Rosewarne; set d, Dankert Guillaume; spec, Joe Quinlivan; cos, Robyn Smith; makup, Debbie Christiani

Adventure   (PR:O MPAA:R)

RIVERBEND

106m Vandale/Prism c

Steve James *(Samuel Quentin)*, Tony Frank *(Sheriff Jake)*, Julius Tennon *(Tony Marx)*, Margaret Avery *(Bell Coleman)*, Alex Morris *(Butch Turner)*, Keith Kirk *(Mike)*, Vanessa Tate *(Pauline)*, Al Evans *(Mayor)*, Linwood Walker *(Fatman)*, Troy Dale *(Cook)*, John Norman *(Marcus Coleman)*, Tyrees Allen *(Gus)*, Michael Ballard *(Stone)*, T.J. Kennedy *(Sgt. Monroe)*, Norm Colvin *(Hugo)*, Doug Sivod, Derrell Craddock, Jim Harrell, Frank Bates, John Evans, and Bill McGhee

Hollywood has no problem with rewriting the Vietnam War according to changing standards of audience bloodlust. Why should the civil rights movement of the 1960s remain immune? Even the prestige production MISSISSIPPI BURNING ran into charges of factual distortion. Perhaps it was inevitable, then, that someone would apply RAMBO's bare-chests-and-automatic-weapons formula to the civil rights struggle. It's 1966, and three African-American Army officers are being escorted through Georgia to a court-martial (their crime: refusing a direct order to massacre Vietnamese women and children). The soldiers manage to escape their MP guards and seek shelter in the home of widow Bell Coleman (Margaret Avery) in the isolated little town of Riverbend. Local blacks have been terrorized by Sheriff Jake (Tony Frank), a raping, murdering, name-calling mega-racist, and the lawman's abuse of power stirs the anger of Samuel Quentin (Steve James), the leader of the trio of vets. With the reluctant help of his fellow escapees, Quentin sets up a clandestine boot camp in the woods and trains the town's able-bodied African-American men in armed combat. Then, one night, Quentin directs a paramilitary takeover of Riverbend. Sheriff Jake, his deputies, and the mayor are locked in the jailhouse, while the remainder of the white population is herded into the church. Black citizens take up positions on the periphery of town and blockade the roads. Quentin demands media attention and an investigation into the sheriff's crimes, warning that the church and its occupants will go up in smoke if the authorities try any tricks. Once they stop laughing, the cops on the outside dig in for a siege. Back in Riverbend, Quentin has his hands full with volatile Tony Marx (Julius Tennon), another of the vets, who forces Sheriff Jake and the mayor into a knife duel. The sheriff wins, of course, and both he and Marx have to be beaten into obedience by Quentin. Meanwhile, the authorities send commandoes to infiltrate Riverbend by night. The invaders get as far as the town square before encountering Marx, who has just robbed the bank and is making his getaway. The resulting firefight leads to heavy casualties, but when the victorious African-Americans add the surviving white soldiers to the prisoners in the church, the authorities give in to Quentin's demands. As the siege is lifted, the media arrives, and a wounded Sheriff Jake expires. Quentin has all of Riverbend's people assemble in the town square, where blacks and whites join hands in friendship. Yeah, right.

Filmed in Texas, RIVERBEND represents an attempt by TV producer Samuel Vance ("The New Odd Couple") and wife Valerie to start a Houston-based film industry. The stars and the director, action specialist Sam Firstenberg (AVENGING FORCE, the "American Ninja" series), were imported from Hollywood, but local talent filled out the cast and crew. The sharp-looking project was completed for under $2.3 million, but was beset with post-production delays and disputes with co-financiers before receiving a limited theatrical lease. Alluding to the film's rather subdued home-video release in 1990, Valerie Vance reportedly expressed the belief that major distributors were afraid the movie was too inflammatory. That's a Texas-sized understatement.

Clearly, RIVERBEND intends to convey the message that African-Americans should control their own destinies, defend themselves if need be, and not wait for white liberals to take up their cause. However, despite its intentions, the film plays like a racial revenge fantasy, implying that the only way for African-Americans to win respect from whites is through armed insurrection ("It ain't your town and it never will be...unless you take it over by force!" declares Quentin). As the black rebels shepherd the townsfolk to the church, a white liberal steps forward and protests that this action is unnecessary; he himself has compiled evidence of Sheriff Jake's atrocities and was planning to submit it to a circuit court that very day. "You're a good man, Mr. Cook, but you're white. Right now that's a problem," replies a black acquaintance of the liberal.

At no time does the screenplay question the takeover: moreover, Quentin is portrayed only as a straight-arrow hero, possessed of impeccable judgement and brilliant leadership abilities. The negative aspects of terrorism are instead embodied in Marx, who, incidentally, is the only character to initially oppose the takeover. Still, even Marx manages to blast a white invader before snuffing it; in fact, almost none of the rebels fall in battle without first killing several whites.

RIVERBEND is set in 1966, but the struggle for equality in America continues today; however, any film advocating guerilla warfare as the way to racial harmony ought to leave a bad taste in anyone's mouth. In fairness, it should be noted that RIVERBEND fulfills one of Samuel Vance's stated goals by giving black actors roles that are different from the usual pimps and street scum of more conventional action movies. *(Violence, profanity, adult situations.)*

d, Sam Firstenberg; p, Samuel Vance and Valerie Vance; w, Samuel Vance; ph, Ken Lamkin; ed, Marcus Manton; m, Paul Loomis; art d, Jack Marty; set d, Rob Edelson; cos, Janet Lucas Lawler; makup, Jeanne D'Iorio

Action/Political   (PR:O MPAA:R)

ROBOCOP 2

118m Jon Davison/Orion c

John Glover *(Magnavolt Salesman)*, Mario Machado *(Casey Wong)*, Leeza Gibbons *(Jess Perkins)*, John Ingle *(Surgeon General)*, Tom Noonan *(Cain)*, Roger Aaron Brown *(Whittaker)*, Mark Rolston *(Stef)*, Willard Pugh *(Mayor Kuzak)*, Phil Rubenstein *(Poulos)*, Felton Perry *(Donald Johnson)*, Jeff McCarthy *(Holzgang)*, Daniel O'Herlihy *(Old Man)*, Lila Finn *(Old Woman)*, John Hateley *(Purse Snatcher)*, Gage Tarrant *(Hooker)*, Tommy Rosales *(Chet)*, Brandon Smith *(Flint)*, Wallace Merck *(Gun Shop Owner)*, Peter Weller *(Robocop)*, Michael Medeiros *(Catzo)*, Gabriel Damon *(Hob)*, Galyn Gorg *(Angie)*, Linda Thompson *(Mother with Baby)*, Lily Chen *(Desperate Woman)*, Nancy Allen *(Anne Lewis)*, Clinton Austin Shirley *(Jimmy Murphy)*, Robert DoQui *(Sgt. Reed)*, Stephen Lee *(Duffy)*, Jimmy Pickens *(Mesnick)*, Eric Glenn *(Injured Cop)*, Richard Reyes, Charles Bailey, Jo Perkins, Erik Cord *(Angry Citizens)*, Martin Casella *(Yuppie)*, Belinda Bauer *(Dr. Juliette Faxx)*, John Doolittle *(Schenk)*, George Cheung *(Gillette)*, Wanda De Jesus *(Estevez)*, Tzi Ma *(Tak Akita)*, Gary Bullock *(Hack Doctor)*, Bill Bolender *(Cabbie)*, Wayne De Hart *(Vendor)*, Fabiana Udenio *(Sunblock Woman)*, Ken Lerner *(Delaney)*, Yogi Baird *(Contortionist)*, Jerry Nelson *(Darren Thomas)*, Michael Weller, Woody Watson *(OCP Security)*, Rutherford Cravens, Christpher Quinten *(Reporters)*, Ed Geldhart *(Electronic Store Owner)*, David Dwyer *(Little League Coach)*, Adam Faraizl *(Little League Kid)*, James McQueens *(Dr. Weltman)*, Cynthia Mackey *(Surgeon)*, and Justin Seidner *(Brat)*

Something of an old-fashioned allegorical sci-fi drama, ROBOCOP 2 appears to be aimed at those moviegoers who stayed away from the original ROBOCOP because they were turned off by its futuristic nihilism. But that doesn't mean Robocop has gone completely soft in the sequel, which not only offers a plot that is all but a clone of its predecessor, but also features most of the original cast. However, it's the style and tone imposed on the film by director Irvin Kershner that most distinguish the sequel from the Paul Verhoeven-directed original. The shift in tone also has much to do with the Frank Miller-Walon Green script. Comic-book writer Miller's "Batman: The Dark Knight Returns" was a key inspiration for BATMAN, and screen veteran Green's long list of credits includes such genre classics as THE WILD BUNCH and THE HELLSTROM CHRONICLES. The result of this collaboration between old-timers and young Turks is an offbeat but engaging effort that brings a little unruly personality to what could easily have been just another noisy, by-the-numbers retread.

A sly, self-mocking sense of humor is apparent even in ROBOCOP 2's title, which identifies both the film's sequel status and its hero. And what a fantastic nightmare creation Robocop 2 is. Controlled by the drug-addled brain of a master criminal, it is a hulking, mechanized killer that packs the firepower of a small army. Stuffed with enough subplots and characters for three normal movies, the film is almost as feverishly whacked out as its title character. Until its climax — a thundering battle royal between Robocops 1 and 2 — the plot is structured like an old-fashioned action-adventure serial, which may reflect Miller's comic-book sensibilities. Elegantly punctuated by what is probably Green's hardboiled dialog, cliffhanger endings segue each "episode" into the next. As a result of this serial-like structure, the film plays like three sequels in one. Unfortunately, ROBOCOP 2 staggers rather than builds to its climax; however, the film's structure accommodates intriguing detours and digressions that deepen its characters and mood.

As in the first film, Robocop is still patrolling the streets of Detroit for a police force that is under the control of Omni Consumer Products (OCP). That business conglomerate's CEO (Daniel O'Herlihy) commissioned the building of Robocop from the remains of murdered Detroit patrolman Alex Murphy in the first film after OCP's first attempt to build a robot policeman failed because of the prototype's lack of humanness. Now, OCP finds their present model hampered by memories of his human past, and the conglomerate's brain trust decides that a "new, improved" model must be more efficient and controllable. The problem is that psychologist Juliette Faxx (Belinda Bauer), who is assigned to build the new Robocop, is herself on the unstable side. She turns to Death Row to find a human heart for Robocop 2 on the theory that condemned inmates will kill more readily than cops and will be more inclined to follow orders out of gratitude for the chance to live forever. On the streets, the original Robocop has become a one-android army waging a war against a super-addictive illicit drug, Nuke, whose marketing, manufacture, and distribution are controlled by master criminal Cain. In time, Robocop manages to destroy a Nuke factory and stage a raid on Cain's headquarters, which looks like the same abandoned chemical plant that was master criminal Boddicker's HQ in the first film. However, like Murphy in the first film, Robocop is captured, tortured, and dismembered by Cain and his gang, which includes 12-year-old second-in-command Hob (Gabriel Damon). OCP reluctantly renovates Robocop. But, in response to community pressure, Faxx overloads Robocop's memory with so many "socially conscious" directives that he is unable to fight crime effectively. In the wake of a police strike and Robocop's failure to get the job done, a cry goes up for the new, more ruthless robot that is in the works at OCP. Sensing his problem, Robocop plugs himself into a handy fuse box, frying the extraneous programming. He then leads a contingent of striking cops in an attack on Cain's headquarters. Cain is captured by Robocop but injured in the process, and Faxx decides that the maniacal drug addict is the perfect choice to provide the "soul" for Robocop 2. The new robot proves his murderous mettle by breaking up a meeting between the Detroit mayor and Cain's old gang, now run by Hob. Only the mayor escapes with his life to identify Robocop 2 as the killer, setting the stage for the battle between Robocops 1 and 2.

Director Kershner is no stranger to sequels. His past works include THE EMPIRE STRIKES BACK and the RETURN OF A MAN CALLED HORSE. Yet Kershner's filmmaking roots are in the 50s, when socially responsible themes were as important as plots and characters. Verhoeven, by contrast, didn't begin working on feature films until a decade or so after Kershner got his start. Though ROBOCOP and ROBOCOP 2 share a bleak vision of the future, there is a distinct difference in the films' underlying attitudes that is the result of a cinematic generation gap between Kershner and Verhoeven. Tellingly, the bloodshed in the sequel is more horrifying than that in the original because of Kershner's more empathetic approach to his characters. He makes us care about everyone in the film, so that when they are destroyed, we feel their loss. On the other hand, even Verhoeven's main players are caricatures. The only fully human characters in the original film are Murphy—whose murder was recut to fend off a dreaded MPAA X rating—and his partner, Lewis (Nancy Allen), who is present in the sequel, though underutilized. While Verhoeven may have a firmer grip on what audiences want to see today, as evidenced by his 1990 box-office triumph TOTAL RECALL, it is reassuring to know that angry old men like Kershner are still around and employable. We may learn something from them yet. And if Verhoeven's work is in any way a harbinger of movies to come, we had damn well better. *(Extreme violence, profanity.)*

d, Irvin Kershner; p, Jon Davison; w, Frank Miller and Walon Green (based on a story by Miller and on characters created by Edward Neumeier, Michael Miner); ph, Mark Irwin; ed, William Anderson; m, Leonard Rosenman; md, Leonard Rosenman; prod d, Peter Jamison; art d, Pam Marcotte; set d, Colin Irwin; spec, Rob Bottin, Peter Kuran, and VCE, Inc; stunts, Dick Hancock; cos, Rosanna Norton; makup, Cheri Montesanto-Medcalf; anim, Phil Tippett

Action/Science Fiction   (PR:O   MPAA:R)

ROBOT JOX

96m Epic-Empire/Triumph c

Gary Graham *(Achilles)*, Anne-Marie Johnson *(Athena)*, Paul Koslo *(Alexander)*, Robert Sampson *(Commissioner Jameson)*, Danny Kamekona *(Dr. Matsumoto)*, Hilary Mason *(Prof. Laplace)*, and Michael Alldredge *(Tex Conway)*

This is a loving tribute to those joyously bad science fiction films churned out by Japan in the 1960s and 70s. The film takes place in a distant future when all global disagreements are settled in an arena. A combatant (known as a "jock") from each warring nation inhabits a heavily armed robot and battles representatives of other nations to the death. As the film opens, the US is about to do battle with the Soviet Union. As the combatants battle, the US robot is hit and falls into a viewing stand, killing thousands of spectators. The US jock, Achilles (Gary Graham), is injured and taken to a hospital to recover, while the government begins developing cyborgs to serve as robot jox. When the Soviets demand a rematch, a female cyborg, Athena (Anne-Marie Johnson) is chosen to serve as the Americans' robot jock. The battle begins and is not going well for the American's, until Achilles arrives and decides to take control of the struggle.

While this is not as well made as director Stuart Gordon's previous films such as RE-ANIMATOR and FROM BEYOND, it is still an entertaining movie. It seems to have been made to appeal to those who enjoy "Godzilla" movies and the "Transformer" TV series. The battle sequences feature many of the same elements and cheesy special effects found in those Japanese efforts. Huge robots stomp across the desert wiping out machinery and firing missiles from their arms, while super-imposed spectators cheer from the stands. The film is great for kids since it's not very violent and evokes a spirit of innocence. The performers all ham it up, the pacing is sharp, and the music appropriately corny. Though Gordon is obviously coasting here, it's all in fun and those who have a fondness for Godzilla, Mothra, Ghidrah, and the other Japanese monster superstars might find this to be enjoyable mindless fun. *(Profanity, violence.)*

d, Stuart Gordon; p, Charles Band and Albert Band; w, Joe Haldeman (based on a story by Stuart Gordon); ph, Mac Ahlberg; ed, Ted Nicolaou and Lori Ball; m, Frederic Talgorn; prod d, Giovanni Natalucci; spec, David Allen Productions

Science Fiction   (PR:A-C   MPAA:PG)

ROCKY V

104m Star Partners III — MGM-UA — Chartoff-Winkler/MGM-UA c

Sylvester Stallone *(Rocky Balboa)*, Talia Shire *(Adrian Balboa)*, Burt Young *(Paulie)*, Sage Stallone *(Rocky Balboa, Jr.)*, Burgess Meredith *(Mickey)*, Tommy "Duke" Morrison *(Tommy Gunn)*, Richard Gant *(George Washington Duke)*, Tony Burton *(Tony)*, James Gambina *(Jimmy)*, Delia Sheppard *(Karen)*, Michael Sheehan *(Merlin Sheets)*, Michael Williams *(Union Cane)*, Kevin Connolly *(Chickie)*, Elisebeth Peters *(Jewel)*, Hayes Swope *(Chickie's Pal)*, Nicky Blair *(Fight Promoter)*, Jodi Letizia *(Marie)*, Don Sherman *(Andy)*, James Binns *(Himself)*, Meade Martin *(Las Vegas Announcer)*, Michael Buffer *(Fight Announcer, 3rd Fight)*, Albert J. Myles *(Benson)*, Jane Marla Robbins *(Gloria)*, Ben Geraci *(Cab Driver)*, Clifford C. Coleman *(Motorcycle Mechanic)*, Patrick Cronin *(Dr. Rimlan)*, Leroy Neiman *(Fight Announcer)*, Michael Pataki *(Nicolai Koloff)*, Bob Giovane *(Timmy)*, Carol A. Ready *(Russian Woman)*, Katherine Margiotta *(Woman in Dressing Room)*, Chris Avildsen, Jonathan Avildsen *(Druggies)*, Stu Nahan, Al Bernstein *(Fight Commentators)*, Lou Filippo, Frank Cappuccino *(Referees)*, Lauren K. Woods, Robert Seltzer, Albert S. Meltzer, John P. Clark, Stanley R. Hochman, Elmer Smith *(Conference Reporters)*, Henry D. Tillman, Stan Ward *(Contenders)*, Brian Phelps, Mark Thompson, Paul Cain, Kent H. Johnson, Cindy Roberts *(Reporters)*, Helena Carroll, Tony Munafo, Bob Vazquez, Richard "Dub" Wright, Susan Parsily, Lloyd Kaufman, Gary Compton, John J. Cahill *(Drinkers)*, Jennifer Flavin, Tricia Flavin, and Julie Flavin *(Delivery Girls)*

A special facet of all the "Rocky" films is that they give Sylvester Stallone, a frequently underrated screen personality, a magnificent opportunity to perform at his very best—for if ever an actor was meant for a part, Stallone was born to play Rocky Balboa. Even the weakest of the films provides an uplifting experience, an experience seldom equalled in other films of the generation. It is even conceivable that this film, along with the first and third entries in the series, will go down in film history as classics of the genre; and rightfully so.

The film picks up where ROCKY IV ended, with Rocky (Stallone) returning to Philadelphia from the Soviet Union after defeating his huge Russian challenger in a brutal bout. Rocky has little time to bask in his glory, however. He quickly learns that his boxing career has left him with irreparable brain damage and his fortune, which he had entrusted to his dimwitted brother-in-law Paulie (Burt Young), has been squandered by an incompetent accountant. Deeply in debt to the Internal Revenue Service, Rocky is forced to sell all his possessions, including his mansion. Rocky, his wife Adrian (Talia Shire), and son Rocky, Jr. (Stallone's real-life son Sage), move back to his old neighborhood in seedy South Philadelphia. Adjustment to the dramatically different lifestyle proves to be most difficult for Rocky, Jr., who quickly becomes involved with a bad crowd. Meanwhile, financially desperate Rocky is tempted to re-enter the ring when shady, flamboyant promoter George Washington Duke (Richard Gant) offers him a huge sum of money to defend his title. Adrian, however, is adamant that Rocky not risk his life by returning to the ring. Rocky's future looks bleak until he is approached by a young boxer named Tommy Gunn (Tommy Morrison), who idolizes the champ and begs him to help him train. Rocky agrees to the arrangement, which puts a further strain on his relationship with his son, who believes Rocky is neglecting him in favor of his protege. The boy becomes even more deeply involved with the bad company he keeps. Events turn when Gunn dumps Rocky and winds up in promoter Duke's camp. While this gives father and son a chance to reconcile, it also poses a threat to Rocky as the increasingly more arrogant Gunn continually challenges his former mentor, soon leaving Rocky no choice but to take on his star pupil.

Reportedly the last of the "Rocky" films, this was, despite its poor box-office performance, one of the best. John G. Avildsen returned to direct this film, his first since helming the original film in 1976, and he once again gives the story the gritty emotion and realism that made the first film so successful. This movie brings the saga full cycle, tracing Rocky from his humble beginnings through his many triumphs and ultimately his return to hard times. ROCKY V seems an appropriate finale to the series, providing a logical climax to the story. Stallone is splendid, as are cast regulars Shire and Young. Though his character was killed off in the third film, Burgess Meredith returns here as a spiritual guide seen only in Rocky's mind, and he is again very effective as the wily fight manager. For fans of the series, these characters have become old friends and it will be with much regret, no doubt, that they will part with them. For the most part, the "Rocky" pictures have been outstanding entertainments, beautifully crafted and executed, and ROCKY V is an important and worthwhile addition to the series. *(Violence, adult situations, mild profanity.)*

d, John G. Avildsen; p, Irwin Winkler and Robert Chartoff; w, Sylvester Stallone; ph, Steven Poster and Victor Hammer; ed, John G. Avildsen and Michael N. Knue; m, Bill Conti; prod d, William J. Cassidy; art d, William Durrell Jr.; set d, John Dwyer; spec, Joe Digaetano III; makup, Michael Westmore

Sports   (PR:C MPAA:PG-13)

ROGER CORMAN'S FRANKENSTEIN UNBOUND

(SEE: FRANKENSTEIN UNBOUND)

ROOKIE, THE

121m Malpaso/WB c

Clint Eastwood *(Nick Pulovski)*, Charlie Sheen *(David Ackerman)*, Raul Julia *(Strom)*, Sonia Braga *(Liesel)*, Tom Skerritt *(Eugene Ackerman)*, Lara-Flynn Boyle *(Sarah)*, Pepe Serna *(Lieut. Ray Garcia)*, Marco Rodriguez *(Loco)*, Pete Randall *(Cruz)*, Donna Mitchell *(Laura Ackerman)*, Xander Berkeley *(Blackwell)*, Tony Plana *(Morales)*, David Sherrill *(Max)*, Hal Williams *(Powell)*, Lloyd Nelson *(Freeway Motorist)*, Matt McKenzie *(Wang)*, Joel Polis *(Lance)*, Roger LaRue *(Maitre 'd)*, Robert Dubac *(Waiter)*, Anthony Charnota *(Romano)*, Jordan Lund *(Bartender)*, Paul Ben-Victor *(Little Felix)*, Jeanne Mori *(Connie Ling)*, Anthony Alexander *(Alphonse)*, Paul Butler *(Capt. Hargate)*, Seth Allen *(David, as a Child)*, Coleby Lombardo *(David's Brother)*, Roberta Vasquez *(Heather Torres)*, Joe Farago *(Anchorman)*, Robert Harvey *(Whalen)*, Nick Ballo *(Vito)*, Jay Boryea *(Sal)*, Mary Lou Kenworthy *(Receptionist)*, and George Orrison

When he made this film, Clint Eastwood had worked with Warner Bros. for 21 years as an actor and director. Over the years, an unwritten deal had developed between the actor and the studio — in return for starring in a commercial vehicle for Warner Bros., he would have the chance to direct a more "personal" film. In 1988, he resurrected his "Dirty Harry" character in THE DEAD POOL so that he was allowed to direct BIRD, the biography of Charlie Parker. In 1990, he directed and starred in the noncommercial WHITE HUNTER, BLACK HEART, and THE ROOKIE was his payback. It features Charlie Sheen as David Ackerman, a recently promoted plain-clothes detective who's lugging around a lot of emotional baggage. He's estranged from his wealthy father (Tom Skerritt) because of his career choice and he's having troubles with his live-in girl friend (Lara-Flynn Boyle of TV's "Twin Peaks"). David's most upsetting trauma, however, is a result of the accidental death of his brother, an accident for which David was responsible. David has chosen to work in the auto theft division, believing it offers a chance for quick promotion, and ends up as a partner to Nick Pulovski (Eastwood), a former auto race driver who is now a grizzled, mean-spirited veteran cop. The two couldn't be more dissimilar — David always keeps his emotions in check while the hard-drinking Nick can explode at the least provocation. For their first assignment, David and Nick must team to break up a massive auto theft operation run by Strom (Raul Julia) and his partner Liesel (Sonia Braga). Coincidentally, Strom just happens to be the man who murdered Nick's former partner, and Nick is determined to bring him down. As the policemen stake out their quarry, their hatred for one another slowly dissipates and David begins to see he can learn something about police work from Nick. When Nick is kidnapped by the gang, David has to rescue him and he relies heavily on the crude techniques taught to him by his partner, ripping Los Angeles apart in the process. Meanwhile, Nick is being held in a warehouse where he is brutalized by Strom and Liesel. The villains are able to get away when David arrives on the scene, then the cops must make a harrowing escape as the warehouse explodes around them. A team again, Nick and David head out on a final violent quest for their quarry.

There is little that is new in THE ROOKIE as the tired formula old cop/young cop story has been done countless times. This *is* a Clint Eastwood film, however, and the quality of the filmmaking is extremely high. In fact, this is Eastwood's most elaborately staged and spectacularly executed film, surpassing THE GAUNTLET on both counts. It is jammed with explosive stunts, wild chases, and powerful pyrotechnics. Eastwood is known for the unusually small scale of

his action pictures, but THE ROOKIE (though it was made for a relatively small amount of money) is a frantic departure. The film opens with a spectacular chase scene in which Eastwood pursues a car transporter truck as luxury sports cars are set careening across a crowded freeway. It climaxes with the staggering collision of two airplanes. Those scenes make it seem as though Eastwood was making a blatant attempt at being commercial. The film also contains one of the most expensive "cheap" jokes in film history. The scene involving the exploding warehouse contains a very funny line — it's a sight gag of phenomenal proportion. The film is, in fact, filled with a lot of humor, particularly in the dialog which features numerous crude one-liners and weird references to other films.

The performances are all topnotch. Julia, inexplicably playing a German, has fun with his ever-changing accent, and Braga is both scary and sexy as his partner. The scene in which she sexually violates Eastwood (a scene that is certain to offend some) is the strangest scene in an Eastwood film since he was oiled up and handcuffed in 1984's TIGHTROPE. Sheen gives his best performance since PLATOON, expertly playing off of Eastwood and nicely handling the physically demanding scenes. But it's Eastwood's movie all the way and his Nick Pulovski is a great character, filled with flaws and hidden desires. As a result, the film works as a character study exploring many of the themes of the director's previous efforts. The only glaring problem with the film is its questionable moral stance. The film offers some disturbingly misogynist elements as well as a healthy dose of crushing violence. Still, those quibbles aside, this is a fun movie and a must-see for Eastwood fans. *(Extreme violence, profanity, sexual situations.)*

d, Clint Eastwood; p, David Valdes, Howard Kazanjian, and Steven Siebert; w, Boaz Yakin and Scott Spiegel; ph, Jack N. Green; ed, Joel Cox; m, Lennie Niehaus; prod d, Judy Cammer; art d, Ed Verreaux; set d, John Berger and Dawn Snyder; spec, John Frazier; stunts, Terry Leonard; cos, Glenn Wright and Deborah Hopper; makup, Michael Hancock and Ralph Gulko

Action/Comedy   (PR:C-O MPAA:R)

ROSALIE GOES SHOPPING

(W. Ger.) 94m Pelemele/Weltvertrieb des Autoren c

Marianne Sagebrecht *(Rosalie)*, Brad Davis *(Liebling Ray)*, Judge Reinhold *(Priest)*, Willy Harlander *(Rosalie's Father)*, Erika Blumberger *(Rosalie's Mother)*, Patricia Zehentmayr *(Barbara)*, John Hawkes *(Schnuki)*, Alex Winter *(Schatzi)*, Courtney Kraus *(April)*, David Denney, Lisa Fitzhugh, Lori Fitzhugh, Dina Chandel, Bill Butler, Ed Geldhart, and John William Galt

The third (and final) part in Percy Adlon's "Marianne" trilogy, ROSALIE GOES SHOPPING is a respectable attempt to maintain the runaway success of Adlon's last feature, BAGDAD CAFE. It's always hard to follow a hit, but Adlon certainly hasn't missed the mark this time. Marianne Sagebrecht, as chubbily charming as ever, stars as Rosalie, a German peacetime bride residing in her GI husband's hometown of Stuttgart, Arkansas. Although she has lived in Arkansas many years and raised her ridiculously harmonious family there, she still yearns for Bavaria, for Bad Tolz, and — even more — to spend, spend, spend...but not her own money. With her collection of 37 credit cards, skill at fraud and forgery, and her ability to wheedle husband Davis' pay packet from his boss weeks before it's due, Sagebrecht indulges all her own and her family's whims and fancies. Each time she commits another act of embezzlement, she rushes off to confession to clear her soul of guilt. The day Sagebrecht gives a megacomputer to her daughter is the day her life changes for good, the stakes becoming much higher. As a bold, canny computer hacker, Sagebrecht begins to shuffle stocks around the markets and to move cash around bank accounts. One day, her friendly postman gives her a tip — "If you owe the bank $100,000, it's your problem; if you owe them a million, it's theirs" — and from that point on she never looks back.

Adlon's film plays off its cute love-hate relationship with materialism, in which Sagebrecht's practical Bavarian acquisitiveness meets childlike American consumer decadence. This satiric marriage is a happy one — a fantasy in which the client rips off the bank and not vice versa.

d, Percy Adlon; p, Percy Adlon and Eleonore Adlon; w, Eleonore Adlon, Christopher Doherty, and Percy Adlon; ph, Bernd Heinl; ed, Heiko Hindkers; m, Bob Telson; cos, Elizabeth Warner Nonkin; makup, N. Christine Chadwick

Comedy   (PR:C-O MPAA:PG-13)

ROUGE

(Hong Kong) 98m Golden Way/Golden Harvest c

(YANZHI KOU)

Anita Mui *(Fleur)*, Leslie Cheung *(Chan)*, Alex Man, Emily Chu, and Leung Man Chi

The runaway success of GHOST probably had much to do with the art-house release of this supernatural romance from Hong Kong received in the Fall of 1990 (it was made in 1987). Audiences that were lucky or smart enough to find their way to ROUGE were enchanted by this poignant, entertaining film. Fleur (Anita Mui), a high-priced prostitute (she claims a man once paid $500 just to stroke her neck), commits suicide in 1934 so that she can join her lover, Chan (Leslie Cheung, like Mui, a pop star), in the spirit world. Chan is the scion of a prosperous business family who won't allow him to see Fleur, so the lovers have opted for a dual suicide. But something has gone wrong. Chan is missing (as it were), and the ghostly Fleur has been wandering alone in the netherworld between Earth and Heaven for more than 50 years, waiting to be reunited with her love. In desperation, she returns to the natural world, asking a clerk at a newspaper (Leung Man Chi) to place a missing person ad for her. Fleur also takes up residence in the clerk's apartment while waiting for Chan to respond to her ad, which greatly irritates the clerk's girl friend (Emily Chu), a spunky reporter. But after being convinced that Fleur is who she says she is, the couple embrace her cause, joining their spectral visitor nightly at the location Fleur has designated for her reunion with Chan. Meanwhile, Fleur tells her star-crossed love story to her new friends. However, her time is running short; the corporeal world is wearing her down, threatening to kill her spirit.

Without giving away the ending, suffice to say it is tragic, ironic, and utterly true to the characters, a heartbreaking acknowledgement of human frailty in the face of a grand obsession that endures beyond the grave. Throughout the film, Fleur's epic passion is contrasted with the fastidious relationship of her modern host couple. The contemporary couple wonder if they could kill themselves for love, as Fleur did, reaching the honest conclusion that they couldn't. Director Stanley Kwan drenches the slow-moving flashbacks in warm sensuous color, while the modern story has a cooler look and moves crisply. Still, Kwan invests both of his love stories with vibrant emotions that keep the film lively and engrossing. Fleur and Chan's romance has an idealized dreaminess; the love between their modern counterparts is more like the chirpy sparking of a television sitcom couple. But as the film goes on, the contemporary twosome becomes more engaging. Their honesty and rational determination to experience their relationship one day at a time prove very winning. In ROUGE romantic obsession exacts a bitter price. But ROUGE wouldn't be much of a movie without it. *(Substance abuse, adult situations.)*

d, Stanley Kwan; w, Li Pak-wah

Fantasy/Romance   (PR:C MPAA:NR)

RUSSIA HOUSE, THE

123m Pathe/MGM-UA c

Sean Connery *(Barley Blair)*, Michelle Pfeiffer *(Katya)*, Roy Scheider *(Russell)*, James Fox *(Ned)*, John Mahoney *(Brady)*, Klaus Maria Brandauer *(Dante)*, Ken Russell *(Walter)*, J.T. Walsh *(Quinn)*, Michael Kitchen *(Clive)*, David Threlfall *(Wicklow)*, Mac McDonald *(Bob)*, Nicholas Woodeson *(Niki Landau)*, Martin Clunes *(Brock)*, Ian McNeice *(Merrydew)*, Colin Stinton *(Henziger)*, Denys Hawthorne *(Paddy)*, George Roth *(Cy)*, Peter Mariner *(US Scientist)*, Ellen Hurst *(Anna)*, Peter Knupffer *(Sergey)*, Nikolair Pastukhov *(Uncle Matvey)*, Jason Salkey *(Johnny)*, Eric Anzumonyin *(Nasayan)*, Daniel Wozniak *(Zapadny)*, Georgi Andzhaparidze *(Yuri)*, Vladek Nikiforov *(Tout)*, Christopher Lawford *(Larry)*, Mark LaMura *(Todd)*, Blu Mankuma *(Merv)*, Tuck Milligan *(Stanley)*, Jay Benedict *(Spikey)*, David Timson *(George)*, Elena Stroyeva *(Anastasia)*, Fyodor Smirnov, Pavel Sirotin *(Watchers)*, Paul Jutkevich *(Mischa)*, Margot Pinvidic *(Woman Interpreter)*, David Henry *(Junior Minister)*, Martin Wenner *(Scientist)*, Paul Rattee *(Army Officer)*, Simon Templeman *(Psychoanalyst)*, Gina Nikiforov, Raisa Ryazanova *(Russian Guests)*, Kate Lock *(Jacky)*, Charlotte Cornwell *(Charlotte)*, Craig Crosbie *(Technician)*, Keith Edwards, Michael Fitzpatrick, Bob Freeman *(Hoover)*, Gennady Venov *(Katya's Father)*, Vladimir Sidirov, Nikolai Nikitin *(Leningrad Police Officers)*, Sasha Yatsko *(Russian Writer)*, Vladimir Zunetov *(Dan)*, Jack Raymond *(Lev)*, David Ryall *(Colonial Type)*, Alexei Jawdokimov *(Arkady)*, Constantin Gregory *(KGB Interviewer)*, Sergei Reusenko *(KGB Man)*, and Yegueshe Tsturvan *(Flute Player)*

The so-called "adult audience" inexplicably stayed away from this finely crafted, thoroughly absorbing, and beautifully acted adaptation of John le Carre's glasnost-era espionage novel, making it an undeserving victim of the HOME ALONE juggernaut, as that film crushed all its competition in the latter part of 1990. A movie as good as this will certainly find new life on video and cable, but audiences will still be the losers. This is an epic of the heart that demands to be seen in a theater. Directing on an expansive, wide-screen canvas, Fred Schepisi (PLENTY, ROXANNE) and his regular cinematographer Ian Baker constantly startle and enrapture the eye, making expressive use of their settings in the first entirely US-produced film to be substantially filmed on-location in the Soviet Union, primarily Moscow and Leningrad. Indeed, if THE RUSSIA HOUSE has a fault, it is that it needs to be seen twice, once to be overwhelmed by the scenery and once to appreciate the outstanding work of the cast and the rich intricacies of the plot, which Schepisi and screenwriter Tom Stoppard keep in constant motion through the two-hour plus running time.

The film opens at a Moscow audio-book fair where a furtive Russian woman, Katya (Michelle Pfeiffer) is seeking a British publisher named Barley Blair. Katya has an important manuscript she wishes to deliver to Blair, but he has elected not to attend the fair. Desperate, she enlists the aid of another exhibitor at the fair, Niki Landau (Nicholas Woodeson), imploring him to help her by smuggling the manuscript out of Moscow and giving it to Blair in London. Landau agrees to help, but when he arrives in London, he turns the manuscript over to British intelligence. A cover letter, though signed by Katya, was clearly written by an unidentified Soviet scientist who indicates he has met Blair and urges him to publish the manuscript, which contains a detailed analysis of Russian defense systems. Naturally, intelligence authorities want to know more about the entire matter, and they search for Blair (Sean Connery), finding him in his apartment in Lisbon, where he indulges in his favorite activities: drinking and playing the saxophone in seedy jazz clubs. Cynical and weary, Blair has little interest in being involved in espionage games, but he does reveal that he met the author, whom he knew only as "Dante" (Klaus Maria Brandauer) at a writers' retreat in the Soviet Union months earlier. British intelligence agents Ned (James Fox) and Walter (played with expected flamboyance by director Ken Russell) want Blair to become involved in a plan to establish the identity of the author and, thereby, the credibility of the manuscript, but Blair is unwilling to cooperate. That is, until he sees a photograph of Katya and is quickly smitten with her. Blair then agrees to become a pawn in the scheme, which grows more sticky when the British reveal the entire affair to the American intelligence community. Led by CIA agent Russell (Roy Scheider), the Americans run roughshod over Ned's delicate operation. While bickering among themselves, both the British and Americans wind up underestimating Blair, who turns out to have an agenda of his own that is entirely unrelated to the sordid matters of international politics.

With the onset of glasnost and the fall of the Berlin Wall, there was a great deal of doubt as to whether a spy film such as this would have any audience appeal at the time of its release. Yet what is remarkable is how perceptively and poetically Stoppard and Schepisi have honed in on some of the potential problems facing the West's reconciliation with the USSR. THE RUSSIA HOUSE is a profound study in miscommunication and misinterpretation, contrasting a jaded West, made complacent by its long history of freedom, and the East, passionate and sincere as it tests the bounds of that same freedom it is only beginning to taste. What sets the action in motion is Dante's initial mistake in accepting Barley's drunken ramblings at the writers' retreat as a genuine expression of his ideals and intentions to act. Katya inserts Dante's key phrases in the cover letter to Barley to remind him of Dante's identity, which is misconstrued by Ned as a straight love letter to Blair. Ned takes to and trusts Blair immediately, while being suspicious of Dante, when, as the plot revolves, it's apparent he should have done the opposite. Then, when the Americans jump into the fray, they suspect a homosexual affair between Blair and Dante. And so it goes throughout the film. All these plot turns and diversions are superbly handled by the excellent cast. Connery is in top form as the apparent cynic who at his heart is a true romantic, while Pfeiffer is thoroughly credible as the idealistic Katya. Brandauer makes good use of his limited screen time, Fox is excellent as the intelligence professional who is wise enough to recognize the foibles of the game, and Scheider convincing as the CIA man who is as much a politician as he is an expert on international intrigue.

A good thriller puts its characters in physical peril and has them use their intelligence and stealth to survive. A great thriller also puts its characters in spiritual peril, drawing its thrills from the makeup of the characters and the extent to which they act, or fail to act, on their ideals. On that criteria, THE RUSSIA HOUSE has to be judged as a great thriller and one of the year's best films. *(Mild profanity.)*

d, Fred Schepisi; p, Fred Schepisi and Paul Maslansky; w, Tom Stoppard (based on the novel by John le Carre); ph, Ian Baker; ed, Peter Honess; m, Jerry Goldsmith; prod d, Richard MacDonald; set d, Simon Wakefield; cos, Ruth Myers

Romance/Spy   (PR:C MPAA:R)

S

SALUTE OF THE JUGGER, THE

(Aus.) (SEE: BLOOD OF HEROES)

SANTA SANGRE

(It./Sp.) 124m Expanded c

Axel Jodorowsky *(Fenix, Age 20)*, Blanca Guerra *(Concha)*, Guy Stockwell *(Orgo)*, Adan Jodorowsky *(Fenix, Age 8)*, Thelma Tixou *(Tattooed Woman)*, Sabrina Dennison *(Alma)*, and Faviola Elenka Tapia *(Young Alma)*

Alejandro Jodorowsky's first film in 10 years and only his third since his notorious 1971 debut, the surrealist western EL TOPO, SANTA SANGRE is nearly a decade out of step. Despite the film's surrealist trappings, parody is at the heart of this effort. Unfortunately, Jodorowsky chooses to parody oedipal slasher films, which long ago slipped into the realm of self-parody (especially the latter installments in the FRIDAY THE 13TH series), if, indeed, they were ever intended to be taken seriously. SANTA SANGRE begins with a brief scene involving a Christ-like nude perched on a tree limb in what appears to be the cell of a sanitarium. A doctor and nurses arrive with food—a conventional dinner and a plate of raw fish. It's the fish, of course, that brings the man down from his perch. While the doctor and nurses coax him into overalls, an elaborate tattoo of an eagle is revealed on the young man's chest. The film promptly flashes back to tell the story behind the tattoo as well as the story behind the young man's present state. As a youngster, Fenix (played as a child by Jodorowsky's son Adan, then as an adult by his elder son, Axel) is billed as the world's youngest magician. He performs his act for the Circus del Gringo, run by his womanizing father, Orgo (Guy Stockwell), and his mother, Concha (Blanca Guerra), a crazed religious fanatic. Fenix is assisted in his act by an ethereal deaf-mute girl, who always wears white-face makeup, and with whom he is falling in puppy love. To initiate Fenix into manhood his father painstakingly (and painfully) carves the eagle tattoo into Fenix's chest. But Fenix's life takes an even more traumatic turn when Concha, enraged by her husband's latest infidelity (with the circus's curvaceous tattooed lady, the deaf-mute's mother), interrupts the adulterers in bed, and attacks Orgo's genitals with acid. Orgo, a knife thrower, retaliates with the tools of his trade, slicing off Concha's arms before slitting his own throat. Having been locked in his trailer by Concha, Fenix must then watch helplessly as the tattooed lady and her daughter disappear into the night following the bloodbath. Back in the present, Fenix, on a field trip with his fellow patients, spots the tattooed lady, now a drunken prostitute, and is consumed with rage. Coaxed into escaping from the sanitarium by the armless Concha, Fenix becomes her vengeful "hands," both in a bizarre nightclub act and in an orgy of murder that only begins with his skewering of the tattooed lady. Fenix's later victims include a hardened, drug-addicted stripper who becomes a virginal, coquettish schoolgirl onstage, and a wrestler, the "world's strongest woman," who fights off a small army of male wrestlers in her act. The film's climax is brought about by the reappearance of the deaf-mute girl, now grown up (played by deaf actress Sabrina Dennison). Fenix is stirred to revolt when Concha orders him to kill this beautiful young woman, his former love, just as he has killed all the other women who have brought confusion into his life.

SANTA SANGRE could hardly be described as boring. Moreover, gorgeously photographed and crammed with the startling imagery for which Jodorowsky is justly famed, the film is never less than beautiful visually. It also boasts a splendidly effective cast, even if Axel Jodorowsky is a dead ringer—both in looks and acting style—for Bronson Pinchot. Yet the film can't help but remain stubbornly earthbound because of its derivative, pedestrian scenario, too-obviously bearing the influence of its producer, Claudio Argento, the younger brother of splashy Italian horror specialist Dario Argento. Whether SANTA SANGRE would have been a better film had it been more purely Jodorowsky's work is debatable. The surrealist interludes here recall Bunuel, but never attain an identity of their own. If anything, they come across as calculated and intellectualized in a way that is almost the antithesis of Bunuel's instinctual approach. Still, if Jodorowsky is not yet worthy of inclusion in the pantheon with Bunuel and Hitchcock (the latter can be either credited with or blamed for starting the oedipal-slasher trend with PSYCHO), he is, nonetheless, in a class by himself. Although obviously not for every taste, SANTA SANGRE is a film that no adventurous moviegoer can afford to miss. *(Violence, sexual situations, nudity, profanity.)*

d, Alejandro Jodorowsky; p, Claudio Argento; w, Alejandro Jodorowsky, Roberto Leoni, and Claudio Argento (based on a story by Alejandro Jodorowsky); ph, Daniele Nannunzi; ed, Mauro Bonanni; m, Simon Boswell; prod d, Alejandro Luna; cos, Tolita Figueroa; makup, Lamberto Marini

Horror/Thriller   (PR:O MPAA:R)

SAVAGE BEACH

95m Malibu Bay/RCA-Columbia c

Hope Marie Carlton *(Taryn)*, Dona Speir *(Donna Hamilton)*, John Aprea *(Capt. John Andreas)*, Bruce Penhall *(Bruce Christian)*, Rodrigo Obregon *(Rodrigo Martinez)*, Al Leong *(Fu)*, Eric Chen *(Erik)*, Michael Mikasa *(Warrior)*, Teri Weigel *(Angelica)*, Michael Shane *(Shane Abilene)*, Patty Duffek *(Pattycakes)*, Lisa London *(Rocky)*, Roy Summersett *(Paul Michaels)*, Dann Seki *(Admrl. Kenji Inada)*, Maxine Wasa, Casey Kono, Robert Ogata, Jim Brunner, James Lew, and Nicole Aprea

Andy Sidaris, an Emmy-award winning sports director for ABC-TV, has made a series of distinctive action/exploitation films that wallow unashamedly in babes, beefcake and bullets. They feature a regular company of well-sculpted males and Playboy-centerfold females as swinging young Drug Enforcement Agency operatives in Hawaii, who have sex and save the world from narco-terrorists, in that order of priority. Admittedly, Sidaris's writing and direction have improved a bit over the years, and the previous installment, PICASSO TRIGGER, boasted a tricky quasi-Bond plot in between all the erotic acrobatics. SAVAGE BEACH, which played a few theater screens before washing up on home video, has less to offer on both counts. This time the story focuses on lookalike blond bombshell adventuresses Taryn (Hope Marie Carlton) and Donna (Dona Speir). After delivering needed medical supplies to a settlement in the Marshall Islands, their plane is forced down by bad weather on a remote speck of land. Following the obligatory nude swim, the heroines discover they're not alone. A Japanese holdout from WW II (Mikasa, in mummy makeup) still creeps around the jungle, guarding a fortune in gold looted from the Philippines by the Imperial Japanese Navy. Coincidentally, the location of the treasure has just been divulged, and an assortment of armed factions land on the island. There's a rogue US Navy officer, a CIA hunk, Filipino communist guerrillas and some freelance mercenaries. Taryn and Donna happen to have a small arsenal on board their plane, and they dispose of the bad guys, with unexpected help from the Japanese warrior. Wounded in the end, he explains (in a ludicrously protracted death scene) that he recognized Taryn from her baby picture; it seems he killed her castaway GI father during the war and has been agonizing over it ever since. Let's see, that means the twentysomething Taryn is portraying a character in her late forties—maybe she spends all that time in the hot tub for arthritis relief.

Compared to Sidaris's previous cinematic efforts, the explicit stuff in SAVAGE BEACH is fairly brief. The supporting cast of oversexed undercover agents are left behind this time while the two girls struggle to survive and find excuses to take off their tops. Against all odds, Carlton and Speir are somewhat better actresses than this dumbness deserves, at least enough so for Speir to be credible when she bristles at being called a bimbo. But the plot is idiotic, the action unexceptional (even though there's an overemphasis on sheer bloodletting). Weigel plays an absurd Marxist rebel with a taste for leather bikinis. Shane's role as the stud DEA team leader is part of a joke throughout the series; he's the latest in a set of brothers who have had the job, and he speaks in leering double-entendres: "I want you to see this special equipment I have for you...Are you comfortable with a big gun?...Once loaded and cocked, all you need is a steady hand on the barrel." He's not involved enough to spring the best running gag, that none of the Abilene boys can shoot accurately with anything smaller than a grenade launcher. Sidaris and his crew have shown panache in the past, but SAVAGE BEACH is just all wet. *(Nudity, excessive violence, sexual situations, profanity.)*

d, Andy Sidaris; p, Arlene Sidaris; w, Andy Sidaris; ph, Howard Wexler; ed, Michael Haight; m, Gary Stockdale; prod d, Jimmy Hadder; spec, Hayley Cecile, Steve Lombardi, and Gary Bentley; chor, Robert Aoyagi

Action   (PR:O MPAA:R)

SCREWFACE

(SEE: MARKED FOR DEATH)

SHADOW OF THE RAVEN, THE

(Iceland/Sweden) 108m LW Blair c

Renir Brynolfsson *(Trausti)*, Tinna Gunnlaugsdottir *(Isold)*, Egil Olafsson *(Hjorleif)*, and Sune Mangs *(The Bishop)*

This saga, an Icelandic-Swedish co-production, has epic sweep, rousing adventure, engrossing drama, and a beautiful heroine. It is also unusually intelligent and sometimes wildly funny—a film with something for anyone who doesn't mind reading subtitles.

"You said Iceland was a peaceful land," cries the artist "Leonardo" as the film begins. The artist is being brought to Iceland's craggy coast from Norway in the year 1077 by the story's hero, Trausti (Renir Brynolfsson), to paint an altarpiece for his mother's Christian chapel. The chapel is dedicated to Trausti's dead father, interred in a Viking temple built to honor the Norse god Odin. The apparent religious contradiction introduces the film's historical subject — the tumultuous introduction of "modern" Christianity to the ancient pagan Icelandic culture. In truth, the country is anything but peaceful. Like Moses returning from the mountain, Trausti returns from Norway to find his country slipping back into barbarism. He lands in the middle of a pitched battle over the carcass of a whale beached on the shore. The battle pits Trausti's family against that of Eric, and soon Eric's forces retreat, but not before mortally wounding Trausti's mother. Trausti and his lieutenant, Grim, pursue Eric, Trausti to negotiate a Christian peace, Grim to extract revenge. Grim gets to Eric first and slays him, an act which Isold (Tinna Gunnlaugsdottir), Eric's beautiful daughter, believes was committed by Trausti. She swears revenge, but has a change of heart when Hjorlief (Egil Olafsson), her betrothed, challenges Trausti to a duel to avenge the death of Eric. Trausti wins the duel, but refuses to kill Hjorlief, an act of Christian benevolence that wins the heart of Isold. A wedding is arranged between Trausti and Isold, but more violence looms ahead as Hjorlief still craves revenge and Grim, disgusted by what he perceives to be Trausti's cowardice, switches his allegiance to Trausti's rivals.

This is one wild Viking ride, a variation on the "Tristan and Isolde" saga, that is filled with burning, pillaging, and looting, not to mention a lot of spitting, the way in which Icelanders show contempt for their enemies. But for all that, and for assembling a truly ugly cast, THE SHADOW OF THE RAVEN at heart is an absorbing, intelligent film, combining epic sweep and gritty realism with a strong storyline and vividly drawn characters. Though tersely written and forcefully directed by Hrafn Gunnlaugsson, what really gives the film its dramatic spine is its effective use of historical movement as the motivator of its action, recalling the classic American westerns of John Ford and Howard Hawks. The film has a kinship to the work of Ford most obviously in its expressive use of landscapes and settings as Iceland's cliffs, glaciers, and rocky shorelines become mute, unforgiving supporting players in the elemental human drama. This is a rare action epic made all the more entertaining by its depth and intelligence, a classically styled popcorn programmer with a flair for the outrageous and sublime. (*Violence, adult situations.*)

d, Hrafn Gunnlaugsson; w, Hrafn Gunnlaugsson; ph, Esa Vuorinen; m, Hans-Erik Philip

Drama/Historical   (PR:C   MPAA:NR)

SHADOWZONE

88m Full Moon/Paramount c

David Beecroft (*Capt. Hickock*), Louise Fletcher (*Dr. Erhardt*), James Hong (*Dr. Van Fleet*), Frederick Flynn (*Tommy Shivers*), Lu Leonard (*Mrs. Cutter*), Miguel Nunez (*Wiley*), Shawn Weatherly (*Dr. Kidwell*), Maureen Flaherty, and David Hicks

Independent producer Charles Band scored with the critics and at the box office with the H.P. Lovecraft adaptations REANIMATOR and FROM BEYOND. Band's SHAWDOWZONE (for which Band served as executive producer) aspires to be a high-tech variation of Lovecraftian cosmic horror but ends up a weak sci-fi chiller, obviously influenced by ALIEN. It's set in a remote, underground NASA laboratory, where scientists put human subjects through the prolonged periods of deep sleep necessary for long space voyages. When one subject dies, the NASA administration sends Capt. Hickock (David Beecroft) to investigate. The project's director, Dr. Van Fleet (James Hong), claims that no cause could be found for the subject's death (although a clumsy autopsy has left the corpse completely gutted — for your viewing pleasure), so Hickock requests that one of the two remaining deep sleepers be put through the same procedure the deceased underwent. Sure enough, Dr. Van Fleet has been withholding crucial information about the experiments. It seems that at a certain level of human unconsciousness a gateway to another dimension opens briefly, whereupon the sleeper explodes, and a super-intelligent, shape-changing entity enters this world. Like most super-intelligent, shape-changing entities in movies, this one shreds everyone it meets, until only Hickock and Dr. Erhardt (Louise Fletcher), another scientist, remain. Using a computer, they manage to communicate with the creature, which calls itself John Doe and says it cannot survive long in the lab's environment. The creature promises to spare Hickock and Erhardt if they return it to its home dimension, so the humans wheel out the last sleeper and tune in the dimensional interface. Before stepping through the shimmering border to its own world, the creature assumes its natural form (which resembles a bug-eyed skeleton made out of meatloaf). When Erhardt can't resist looking into Doe's world, the creature snatches the scientist and brings her with it. Having seen enough, Hickock initiates an emergency shutdown of the lab, smashing the equipment himself.

Notwithstanding its gratuitous nudity and gore, SHADOWZONE progresses adequately up to a point. But once John Doe starts hunting the humans, the plot resorts to the usual stalk-and-slash cliches. It's irksome to see rocket scientists fall prey to typical FRIDAY THE 13TH doomed-teen setups; exploring dark passageways, looking for a lost pet, breaking away from the group on the most trivial of excuses, they are torn apart by the ravenous fiend they all know waits in the dark. The characters are drawn in broad strokes, with Beecroft substituting repeated use of the universal "gag me" gesture for character development. Only Fletcher makes her role believable. Other notables in the cast include Lu Leonard and Frederick Flynn as a pair of grotesque sure-to-die menials. Onetime Miss USA Shawn Weatherly also appears, but the film's cheap sexual thrills are provided not by her but by the naked, young male and female sleepers encased in brightly lit, transparent capsules. Director J.S. Cardone and production designer Don Day do a nice job of conveying the claustrophobic atmosphere of the sealed lab. One particularly memorable sequence cleverly enforces the story's geographical context; after a 360-degree pan shot of the desert, the camera dives through the ground to the carnage-strewn corridors of the subterranean lab. Richard Band's musical score is lush as always, though it is little more than a pastiche of his earlier themes. SHADOWZONE played some New York theaters before its videocassette release, which includes ads for Charles Band's movie-related merchandise. (*Profanity, nudity, violence.*)

d, J.S. Cardone; p, Carol Kottenbrook; w, J.S. Cardone; ph, Karen Grossman; ed, Thomas Meshelski; m, Richard Band; prod d, Don Day; set d, Ginnie Durden; spec, Perpetual Motion Pictures, Inc. and Mark Shostrum; stunts, Paul M. Lane and J. Suzanne Rampe; cos, Virginia Kramer

Horror/Science Fiction   (PR:O   MPAA:R)

SHELTERING SKY, THE

(It./Brit.) 135m Shochiku-Fuji — Sahara — WB — Recorded Picture — Glinwood/WB c

John Malkovich (*Port Moresby*), Debra Winger (*Kit Morseby*), Campbell Scott (*Turner*), Eric Vu-An (*Belqassim*), Jill Bennett (*Mrs. Lyle*), and Timothy Spall (*Eric Lyle*)

Director Bernardo Bertolucci's impenetrable film follows the spiritual/romantic travels of three Americans as they try to find themselves in North Africa. Based on a minor classic by Paul Bowles that has intrigued filmmakers for years, this failed attempt to adapt existential angst for the big screen is photographed with a golden, burnished glow and exquisitely scored using musical instruments from the region in which it was filmed. However, Bertolucci has built the foundation of his film on shifting sands, and, for all its technical mastery, the movie never succeeds in capturing the true natures of its characters.

Tired of their careers and social lives, married couple Kit (Debra Winger) and Port (John Malkovich) visit North Africa not simply as tourists but as travelers eager to experience the hot, primitive locale in hopes it will rekindle their dying love for one another. Accompanying them is Turner (Campbell Scott), a superficial dandy who accommodates Kit in bed to alleviate her boredom. In North Africa, Port sleeps with a prostitute who robs him, prompting him to merely taunt her rather than to seek the return of his money. He then makes unusual travel plans, journeying into the interior with a bigoted travel writer (Jill Bennett) and her alcoholic son (Timothy Spall), who steals Port's passport. When Port is reunited with Kit and Turner, he insists they take a bus trip, during which they are attacked by a horde of flies. Slipping away from Turner, Kit and Port attempt a reconciliation, but Port then comes down with a severe case of chills and fever. After Port dies at a foreign legion post, Kit becomes unhinged, wandering into the desert, her suitcase in hand. She is abducted by a sheik who takes her to his oasis where he repeatedly rapes her then locks her in a room. She is eventually freed by one of the sheik's jealous wives. She returns to civilization, presumably a changed woman who will write a book about her experiences and the indomitability of the human spirit.

Watching this seemingly endless major studio production, one's impatience rises to the breaking point as question after question goes unanswered. Who are these superficial bores who are so intent on putting down all those around them? Why couldn't they have simply gone to a marriage counselor and spent their vacation in a remote part of Long Island? Does Bertolucci really think he suggests emotional turmoil by having Winger stare off into the blinding sun? Rarely has a movie been so crippled by an unfocused lead performance. Winger's acting doesn't suggest neurotic restlessness as much as it does a woman's desire to win a staring contest. At least Malkovich is bad in an energetic way, but when his character dies all the juice flows out of the film. We're left with a metaphysical Yvonne de Carlo costume epic. In short, the viewer never really has any reason to care about the smug, self-satisfied bores who are this film's subjects, and can only wonder why Bertolucci has lavished so much time on them. Brimming with obscure meaning and devoid of drive and fervor, the film dries up in that symbolic desert sun, the victim of its own pretensions and a casualty of trying to film something best suited to the realm of cult literature. (*Violence, nudity, profanity, adult situations.*)

d, Bernardo Bertolucci; p, Jeremy Thomas; w, Bernardo Bertolucci and Mark Peploe (based on the novel by Paul Bowles); ph, Vittorio Storaro; ed, Gabriella Cristiani; m, Richard Horowitz and Ryuichi Sakamoto; md, Ray Williams; prod d, Gianni Silvestri and Ferdinando Scarfiotti; art d, Andrew Sanders; spec, Renato Agostini; cos, James Acheson; makeup, Paul Engelen

Drama   (PR:O   MPAA:R)

SHOCK TO THE SYSTEM, A

91m Corsair c

Michael Caine (*Graham Marshall*), Elizabeth McGovern (*Stella Anderson*), Peter Riegert (*Robert Benham*), Swoosie Kurtz (*Leslie Marshall*), Will Patton (*Lt. Laker*), Jenny Wright (*Melanie O'Connor*), John McMartin (*George Brewster*), Barbara Baxley (*Lillian*), Haviland Morris (*Tara Liston*), Philip Moon (*Henry Park*), Kent Broadhurst, Zach Grenier, David Schramm (*Executives*), Sam Schacht (*David Jones*), Christopher Durang (*Convention Speaker*), Mia Dillon (*Graham's Secretary*), Alice Haining (*Benham's Secretary*), Patience Moore (*Wanda Maas*), Darrell Wilks (*Mailroom Boy*), Scotty Bloch, Kim Staunton, Alicia Hoge (*Secretaries*), Mike Cicchetti (*Beggar in Subway*), Rick Petrucelli (*Beggar*), Victor Truro, Rik Colitti, Mike Starr (*Bums*), Michael Perez (*Transit Cop*), John Finn (*Motorman*), Tyrone Jackson (*Messenger*), Marie Sylvia (*Waitress/Dazzles*), Samuel L. Jackson (*Ulysses*), Jonathan Freeman (*Decorator*), Elizabeth Morin (*Partygoer*), Joe Zaloom (*Hot Dog Vendor*), Socorro Santiago (*Rental Car Attendant*), Welker White (*Kennel Driver*), Frank Ferrara (*Cab Driver*), and Sheila Stainback (*News Anchor Woman*)

An entertaining satire in its own right, this dark tale of a corporate climber offers yet another opportunity to raise a glass to Michael Caine. Despite winning an Oscar for HANNAH AND HER SISTERS and being the recipient of almost constant and universal acclaim, Caine has yet to succumb to the big-star syndrome of limiting himself to increasingly pompous film roles. In typical Caine style, he was unable to pick up his Oscar because he was tied up in the Caribbean re-filming sequences for the ignominious JAWS: THE REVENGE. His every role may not be a gem, but there's something heartening about an actor who puts his work first, come hell or high water.

In A SHOCK TO THE SYSTEM, Caine plays Graham Marshall, an aging ad executive (how many first-rank stars are willing to play an aging anything?) who is brimming with confidence over an upcoming promotion, the reward for his long tenure in the salt mines. Graham's associates wine and dine him, and his social-climbing wife, Leslie (Swoosie Kurtz), has already spent his raise. However, when the superior whose job Graham is to take over is nudged into early retirement rather than promoted, it becomes clear that the company has decided to go with a youth movement, and that Graham is one of its casualties. Not only is he passed over for promotion, but his nemesis within the department, the contemptible Bob Benham (Peter Riegert), is made his new boss. Graham is already undergoing a mid-life crisis, and this professional setback sends him over the edge. But rather than suffering in silence or swallowing his pride, he takes matters into his own hands, determined to show the world just how bloodthirsty a shark he can be.

Once SHOCK puts its premise in place, there are few surprises as Graham — with a hilarious wave of his hand and a "Bippity, boppity, boo" — murderously removes one obstacle after another in his quest for success. Moreover, the film's venomous satire of corporate life is diluted by the hint of moral uplift in its resolution. But that doesn't dampen the delights of SHOCK, which lie not so much in the tale itself as in its telling.

A true writer's movie, SHOCK was associate produced by SILKWOOD cowriter Alice Arlen. Its clever script, adapted by Andrew Klavan from Simon Brett's novel, is a model of economical storytelling, and anyone who has ever been passed over, put down, or otherwise humiliated professionally is bound to wince with recognition at the intricate power politics beautifully observed in SHOCK's script. Rather than filling holes in a sloppy scenario, Caine's voice-over narration serves to fill out his character and to give the story a wry edge, paralleling Graham's descent into madness with his ascent into corporate heaven. Director Jan Egleson, in his feature debut, does a commendable job of confining the film's point of view to Graham's perspective, aided by cinematographer Paul Goldsmith, whose fluid camerawork conveys both Graham's paranoid worldview and his madman's exhilaration at the discovery that a true "killer instinct" can be very useful in today's business world. Gary Chang's jazzy score also helps by providing a cool, syncopated counterpoint to the action.

But it's the fine ensemble performances that really make SHOCK a hearty dose of mean-spirited fun. Caine is as subtly superb as he's ever been. Although he hasn't won any awards for his succession of memorable psychotic leads in DRESSED TO KILL; THE HAND; DEATHTRAP, and this film, they may be among the best performances he's given. And the supporting cast simply couldn't be any better. In addition to Riegert and Kurtz, who are viciously perfect as Graham's antagonists, Elizabeth McGovern is at once earthy and ethereal as his

mistress (following Leslie's "untimely death") and unwitting coconspirator. Though relegated to lesser roles, Will Patton, Jenny Wright, John McMartin (as Caine's hapless ex-boss), Barbara Baxley, Haviland Morris, and Philip Moon also shine. Taken together, these performances make A SHOCK TO THE SYSTEM the first "feel good" movie for anyone who's ever wanted to see yuppies burned, blown up, or dropped from the sky. (*Profanity, adult situations.*)

d, Jan Egleson; p, Patrick McCormick; w, Andrew Klavan (based on the novel by Simon Brett); ph, Paul Goldsmith; ed, Peter C. Frank and William Anderson; m, Gary Chang; prod d, Howard Cummings; art d, Robert K. Shaw Jr.; set d, Robert J. Franco; spec, Randall Balsmeyer; stunts, Frank Ferrara; cos, John Dunn; makeup, Kathryn Bihr and Toni Trimble

Comedy/Drama   (PR:O   MPAA:R)

SHORT TIME

97m Joe Wizan-Gladden/FOX c

Dabney Coleman (*Burt Simpson*), Matt Frewer (*Ernie Dills*), Teri Garr (*Carolyn Simpson*), Barry Corbin (*Captain*), Joe Pantoliano (*Scalese*), Xander Berkeley (*Stark*), Rob Roy (*Dan Miller*), Kaj-Erik Eriksen (*Dougie Simpson*), Tony Pantages (*Vito*), Sam Malkin (*Hostage*), Wes Tritter (*Coffin Salesman*), Kim Kondrashoff (*Michael Lutz*), Paul Jarrett (*Jonas Lutz*), Deejay Jackson (*Spivak*), Paul Batten (*Dr. Goldman*), Kevin McNulty (*Dr. Drexler*), Shawn Clements (*Older Dougie*), Betty Phillips (*Clerk*), Jack Ammon (*Elderly Man*), Enid Saunders (*Elderly Woman*), Dwight Koss (*Car Salesman*), Russell J. Roberts (*Waiter*), Meredith Bain Woodward (*Psychiatrist*), Brenda Crichlow, Gillian Barber (*Nurses*), J. McRee Elrod (*Priest*), Tony Morelli, Gene Heck (*Stark's Cohorts*), Jack Bastow (*Sidewalk Preacher*), Beverley Henry (*Soap Opera Policewoman*), Peter Yunker (*Soap Opera Man*), Kimelly Anne Warren (*Soap Opera Woman*), Jack Little (*Hospital Cop*), Steven J. Wright (*Helicopter Pilot*), Jay Brazeau, Gordon Doerkson, Jerry Wasserman, Alvin Sanders, Fred Perron, and David Symons (*Cops*)

It's old news that the urban cop thriller has taken the place of the western as the pre-eminent movie and television genre. From the big screen's LETHAL WEAPON to the small screen's "21 Jump Street," it seems that audiences just can't get their fill of car chases, cop banter, high-caliber shootouts, and screaming precinct captains. The problem is that there are only so many story lines that will accommodate the stock cop-movie set pieces. As a result, writers and directors are straining to find new twists on the same old story. Signs of that strain certainly show in SHORT TIME, a fairly routine cop opera that stars Dabney Coleman and Teri Garr, two of Hollywood's best but most consistently ill-used comic actors. Here Coleman and Garr are trapped in a bland, family-oriented, feel-good comedy-drama that is periodically interrupted by the usual chases, shootouts, buddy-buddy byplay (Matt Frewer, amazingly billed *above* Garr, does the buddy duty with Coleman), and precinct screaming sessions (with Barry Corbin, looking understandably apathetic, as the captain). The ensemble is completed by Joe Pantoliano, who contributes virtually the same performance he gave in DOWNTOWN, again playing a refined but ruthless villain, this time negotiating to buy a load of stolen experimental weapons from a street hood (Xander Berkeley).

The unusually tortured premise finds Coleman in the role of Seattle police detective Burt Simpson, who is one week away from retirement (hence the title). When Burt undergoes a physical examination for his life insurance policy, a bus driver switches his blood and urine samples with Burt's. The driver is afraid that detection of marijuana in his samples will lead to his firing. What the driver doesn't know is that he also has a fatal disease, and, naturally, when the samples are switched, it appears that Burt is ready to kick the bucket. Checking his insurance policy, Burt learns that insurance benefits from death in the line of duty would put his young son, Dougie (Kaj-Erik Eriksen), through college and support his ex-wife, Carolyn (Garr), well into the foreseeable future. Since he's going to die anyway, Burt decides to go out of his way to become the target for a bad guy's bullet. Since there wouldn't be much of a movie otherwise, it turns out that Burt has a charmed life; his line-of-duty suicide attempts repeatedly turn into acts of heroism, leading to some of the film's funnier scenes, in which Burt's incredulous Captain (Corbin) pins medals on a visibly distracted and irritated Burt. Of course, Burt learns the truth about his good health at the very moment that it looks as though his death wish will be fulfilled. Predictably, along the way Burt also finds time to re-establish his emotional bonds with his ex-wife and son.

There is probably a good movie floating around somewhere in SHORT TIME, but only hints of it are to be found in John Blumenthal and Michael Berry's illogical script. Early in the film, before the misdiagnosis, Burt keeps his partner from chasing a suspect because of his desire to play it safe so close to his retirement. For his timidity Burt is publicly lambasted by his captain. Later, however, the captain inexplicably tries to calm Burt down, putting him behind a desk as a response to Burt's life-risking heroism. If there is anything in the film that justifies its existence, it is the scenes between Coleman and Garr, who bring a tender romanticism to their reconciliation. Yet, even here, the script's sloppiness is apparent, since Blumenthal and Berry make no attempt to explain how these two decent, perfectly compatible people could have broken up in the first place.

A second unit director for John Badham on STAKEOUT; BLUE THUNDER; and WAR GAMES, and the son of choreographer Gower Champion, director Gregg Champion obviously knows his way around a car chase. Unfortunately, the extended sequence in which Champion playfully and effectively spoofs the great car chases in THE FRENCH CONNECTION and BULLITT looks like it belongs in another film. What's more, in the quieter scenes, Champion reverts to a flat television style that emphasizes the meandering incoherence of the script. Coleman and Garr come close to finding the good film that is buried in SHORT TIME—but not close enough. As it is, SHORT TIME could have been a lot shorter. *(Violence, profanity, adult situations.)*

d, Gregg Champion; p, Todd Black; w, John Blumenthal and Michael Berry; ph, John Connor; ed, Frank Morriss; m, Ira Newborn; md, Derek Power; prod d, Michael Bolton; art d, Eric Fraser; set d, Gwendolyn Margetson; spec, Rory Cutler; stunts, Conrad E. Palmisano; cos, Christopher Ryan; makeup, Jayne Dancose

Comedy/Drama   (PR:C   MPAA:PG-13)

SHOW OF FORCE, A

93m John Strong-Golden Harvest/Paramount c

Amy Irving *(Kate Ryan de Melendez)*, Andy Garcia *(Luis Angel Mora)*, Lou Diamond Phillips *(Jesus Fuentes)*, Robert Duvall *(Howard Baslin)*, Kevin Spacey *(Frank Curtin)*, and Erik Estrada

Drawn from recent conflicts between Puerto Rican *independistas* and Americans who are intent on statehood for the island colony, Paramount's A SHOW OF FORCE makes a radical-chic botch of a potentially interesting dramatic situation. Jesus Fuentes (Lou Diamond Phillips), an undercover cop working for renegade FBI agent Frank Curtin (Kevin Spacey), sets student activists up for a fall by prompting a strike on a TV tower. Curtin's intent is to fabricate evidence of an attempted terrorist bombing, but in the course of the arrests, Curtin murders the students and intimidates into silence the taxi driver who witnesses the killings. Amy Irving plays Kate Melendez, the semi-competent *gringa* TV journalist who investigates the murders and subsequent cover-up; she persists in trying to unravel the various accounts of the incident although her boss (Robert Duvall) insists that the FBI's version is the *only* version. Meanwhile, further intimidation comes from the incumbent governor's re-election campaign committee. Eventually, on the strength of the taxi driver's testimony, Senate hearings are convened, with the prosecution headed by Luis Angel Mora (Andy Garcia, hidden under a full beard in his extended cameo). Ultimately, Mora uses a hidden camera to capture Curtin admitting that he is behind the entire violent episode.

Extremely choppy and contrived, this try at a Caribbean Z winds up a near-total failure. While cinematographer James Glennon's saturated browns and greens are gorgeous, the overall effect of the visuals is akin to watching a deck of postcards being shuffled—stagy, set-bound conversations alternated with the picturesque squalor of slums, bars, and cockfights. Moreover, the characterization is dopey throughout. Irving's Kate Melendez is frequently lauded for her reporting skills, yet she continually misses pertinent details. Her videotaped report from the murder site may contain a major clue, but it has to be pointed out to her. Kate's response? "Gee! I hadn't noticed." That the clue even made it onto the tape is something of a miracle, since Kate's inept camera crew invariably points the camera in the wrong direction, shooting useless cover footage while neglecting interviews.

The Nancy Drew-like tone that Irving brings to the proceedings persists in the portrayals and stilted banter of other characters: "Hey!" Diamond Phillips announces to the startled cab driver, "We're revolutionaries!" Bruno Barreto, best known as a director of softcore art movies like DONA FLOR AND HER TWO HUSBANDS, makes a mess of this film on almost every level, though his cameras are most certainly in focus for his leering shots of Irving's deeply tanned body. Even the romantic rumble of Georges Delerue's music isn't up to his excellent work in SALVADOR, but it's a fine try.

The crowning touch of this goofy melodrama is the astounding disclaimer that follows the final shot: while much of the story is based on fact, we're told, some characters, particularly the renegade FBI agent, are invented. In other words, it's all true except for the story. Condescending and lackluster, A SHOW OF FORCE is almost instantly forgettable. *(Violence, adult situations, profanity.)*

d, Bruno Barreto; p, John Strong; w, Evan Jones and John Strong (based on the book *Murder Under Two Flags* by Anne Nelson); ph, James Glennon; ed, Henry Richardson; m, Georges Delerue; prod d, William J. Cassidy

Political   (PR:C   MPAA:R)

SHRIMP ON THE BARBIE, THE

86m Unity c

Cheech Marin *(Carlos Munoz)*, Emma Samms *(Alex Hobart)*, Vernon Wells *(Bruce Woodley)*, Terence Cooper *(Ian Hobart)*, Jeanette Cronin *(Maggie)*, Carole Davis *(Dominique)*, and Bruce Spence *(Wayne)*

A one-sentence synopsis alone could serve as the review for this film: Cheech Marin goes down under and finds romance with madcap heiress Emma Samms. THE SHRIMP ON THE BARBIE is an odd mixture of flavors of the month. Unfortunately, the month for which they were chosen passed years before this movie limped into theaters. At the time the film was made Marin was a hot comedy commodity, Samms ruled the primetime TV soap-opera roost, and television viewers were just starting to get tired of Paul "Crocodile Dundee" Hogan wishing them g'day. However, it is not as if civilization progressed much in the interim. By 1990 Andrew Dice Clay had become a comedy star largely by bashing minority groups, and primetime TV was overrun with home videos showing people's pants falling down. Nonetheless, BARBIE remains particularly dated, insubstantial fare. Not only have the film's pop icons become instant anachronisms, but its tired plot was abandoned by Hollywood some time around 1935. Samms plays Alex Hobart, the rebellious daughter of a really rich Australian (Terence Cooper) who refuses to approve of her impending marriage to a fat-slob ex-rugby star, Bruce Woodley (Vernon Wells), who is apparently looking to marry into money because his endorsement contract with a beer company is about to run out. To rid his family of Bruce, Daddy promises to give the green light to Alex's next prospective husband, whoever he may be. Hoping that she will upset her father so much that he will relent and allow her to marry Bruce, Alex recruits an inept Mexican waiter, Carlos Munoz (Marin), for a weekend gig as her latest fiance. Naturally, Daddy winds up liking Carlos, especially after overhearing the Mexican and Alex argue over their bargain, to which Carlos agreed selflessly, determined to earn enough money to help his friend and employer (Bruce Spence) keep his ramshackle eatery open. Daddy formally welcomes Carlos into the family; Alex cancels the deal and sends her "fiance" packing off to Sydney while she prepares to meet Bruce at a resort hotel. But when their car breaks down en route to the station, Carlos misses his bus and Alex is late for her rendezvous, providing Bruce with enough time for a close encounter with Alex's sexy best friend, Dominique (Carole Davis), whose accent changes from scene to scene, but whose physical assets are always in sharp focus. It's also long enough for a private eye, hired by Daddy, to record Bruce's indiscretion on film. Arriving at the hotel the next day, Carlos is punched out by Bruce, who is bent on keeping the Mexican from telling Alex that he saw Bruce with Dominique. Having finally made his bus, Carlos is headed for a plane that will carry him to the States when Alex is presented with the incriminating photos. After Alex sees the light and dumps Bruce, her father uses his influence to stop the plane on which Carlos is a passenger, and the film ends with a clinch between Alex and Carlos.

Yes, Cheech gets the girl. But that's about as subversive as BARBIE gets. Though Marin gets top billing, BARBIE was obviously conceived as a vehicle for Samms, meaning that most of its running time is devoted to boring romantic pseudo-problems of rich, stupid white people. Samms looks great in tight, short dresses and form-fitting designer jeans, but her performance has the overwrought earnestness of, well, a primetime soap star trying to prove she can *really act*. With her costar proving a less than adequate comic foil, Marin has a hard time generating any kind of warmth or energy in his scenes with Samms. Nevertheless, he manages almost singlehandedly to provide what bright moments BARBIE offers. Regrettably, a talented, largely Australian supporting cast never quite rises above the comatose material.

BARBIE's direction is credited to "Allen Smithee," the Directors Guild of America's fictional pseudonym for real-life directors who want their names taken off a film. BARBIE is too innocuous to be *that* bad, but it ain't too good either, mate. For those who will watch Cheech Marin in just about anything and for connoisseurs of lithe beauties shoe-horned into tight, revealing outfits, BARBIE will not be a disappointment. But those viewers who are interested in laughs might do better to look elsewhere. *(Adult situations, brief nudity, profanity.)*

d, Allen Smithee; p, R. Ben Efraim; w, Grant Morris, Ron House, and Alan Shearman; ed, Fred Chulack

Comedy   (PR:C   MPAA:PG-13)

SIBLING RIVALRY

88m Castle Rock/Columbia c

Kirstie Alley *(Marjorie Turner)*, Jami Gertz *(Jeanine)*, Bill Pullman *(Nick)*, Carrie Fisher *(Iris)*, Scott Bakula *(Harry Turner)*, Sam Elliott *(Charles Turner)*, Ed O'Neill *(Wilbur Meany)*, Frances Sternhagen *(Mrs. Turner)*, John Randolph

(Mr. Turner), Bill Macy *(Pat)*, Matthew Laurance *(Mr. Hunter)*, and Paul Benedict *(Dr. Plotner)*

Perfect wife Marjorie Turner (Kirstie Alley) is neglected by her husband Harry, a doctor who's married to his career and devoted to his family (each and every relative a doctor). Marjorie also has a troubled relationship with her hellraiser sister, Jeanine (Jami Gertz). Marjorie has always been a model of decorum, but when she does cut loose, it is with fatal results. Dismayed by her in-laws casual disregard and egged on by her sister, Marjorie has a brief affair with a handsome stranger (Sam Elliott), whom she meets while helping him write a note to accompany a gift basket of fruit he's sending to a party he wishes he didn't have to attend. (He gets his wish.) Meanwhile, policeman Wilbur Meany (Ed O'Neill) is afraid that his brother Nick (Bill Pullman), a bumbling Levelor blind salesman, may do something to hurt his chances of a major promotion. His relationship with Nick is counterpointed with Marjorie's sibling rivalry with her sister—soon these lives are going to intersect. Nick breaks into a hotel room (that's just been vacated by Marjorie) in order to hang some blinds he hopes to show to the hotel manager. What he doesn't realize is that Marjorie's extra-marital affair has resulted in her lover's death due to a heart ailment. Having panicked and fled to a dinner party she's throwing for a brother-in-law she's never met, Marjorie abandons her bedmate's corpse. While hanging his blinds, Nick backs them into the bed and mistakenly believes he's slain the man in bed. Once, he finds Marjorie's phone number in the purse left behind in her hasty exit, the complications grow and multiply swiftly.

In this raucous, knockabout comedy, Carl Reiner is in top form—recalling the glory days of WHERE'S POPPA. Deftly balancing the dual stories of over-achieving/underachieving brothers and sisters, SIBLING RIVALRY delves into the psychology of familial relationships while remaining true to the precepts of wacky farce. Although some of the supporting roles aren't cast felicitously (the ever-mugging Pullman, the unappealingly abrasive Fisher), the film generates enough belly laughs to coast over these over-played spots and emerge with its hilarity intact. Whether the twists and turns of this complicated game of "what to do with the body" would work as ingeniously well without Kirstie Alley is open to question. She's the comedy's heart and soul. In the wrong hands, her character could have seemed like a whiny neurotic, but Alley's ace timing, understated delivery, and verve result in a flawless comic creation—a goody two shoes who liberates herself from playing the constricting role that her in-laws and her own inhibitions prescribe. Her scenes with short-term lothario Sam Elliott are so charming you hate to see him killed off. As the comic misconceptions and mistaken identities escalate, and the tangy one-liners whiz by, SIB-LING RIVALRY snowballs into side-splitting escapism. Too good-natured for true black comedy, the film is offbeat, but upbeat, fun that garners laughs out of grim situations while underlining some basic truths about human frailty aggravated by family pressures. Despite some rough patches when the heavy plotting threatens to overwhelm the proceedings, SIBLING RIVALRY is brash, madcap entertainment. The film might have worked even better if Alley's in-laws had been written and played more as eccentrics than as outright pompous villains and if more screen time were allotted to juxtaposing the sibling relationships mentioned in the film's title. Those quibbles aside, SIBLING RIVALRY is outrageous entertainment for lovers of farce and for anyone who's ever felt that their parents favored another sibling over them. *(Adult situations, profanity.)*

d, Carl Reiner; p, David Lester, Don Miller, and Liz Glotzer; w, Martha Goldhirsh; ph, Reynaldo Villalobos; ed, Bud Molin; m, Jack Elliott; prod d, Jeannine Claudia Oppewall; set d, Lisa Fischer; cos, Durinda Wood

Comedy   **(PR:C   MPAA:PG-13)**

SIDE OUT

100m Jay Weston—Aurora—Then/Tri-Star c

C. Thomas Howell *(Monroe Clark)*, Peter Horton *(Zack Barnes)*, Courtney Thorne-Smith *(Samantha)*, Harley Jane Kozak *(Kate Jacobs)*, Christopher Rydell *(Wiley Hunter)*, Terry Kiser *(Uncle Max)*, and Randy Stoklos *(Rollo Vincent)*

SIDE OUT stars C. Thomas Howell as Monroe Clark, a pre-law student from Milwaukee who comes to Los Angeles for the summer to work for his wealthy uncle (Terry Kiser, the corpse in WEEKEND AT BERNIE'S), a sleazy real-estate lawyer. When not distributing Pay-or-Quit notices to insolvent tenants for his uncle, Monroe hangs out with his old buddy Wiley Hunter (Christopher Rydell), who teaches him the joys of playing volleyball on the beach. Coincidentally, one of the tenants to whom Monroe has served notice is volleyball coach Zack Barnes (Peter Horton, of "thirtysomething"), a onetime champion of the beach now washed-up and badly in debt. While chasing down Zack, Monroe meets a pretty marine biology student, Samantha (Courtney Thorne-Smith). She likes him, but is disgusted by "rich boys slumming," and rejects him when she learns about his uncle. Seeing that she's attracted to volleyballers, Monroe works hard on his game. While he and Wiley are playing abysmally in a match, Zack

sees them and offers to coach them in return for Monroe's keeping the rental case out of court. The guys immediately start improving under Zack's tutelage, despite the taunts of the obnoxious current champion, Rollo (Randy Stoklos), who bets Zack that he and another pal can beat the newcomers. On the day of the match, Zack doesn't show up, since he's busy being seduced by his former girl friend, Kate (Harley Jane Kozak). Monroe and Wiley lose, the latter breaking his arm due to their lack of teamwork. Furious at Zack, Monroe threatens to punish him at the rental trial. However, when the day of the trial comes and Zack seems certain to face a ruling against him, Monroe speaks out and presents evidence that makes Zack the winner. Zack now decides to become Monroe's teammate for the Volleyball Classic. During their preparations, Samantha warms up to Monroe, figuring he's her type (his uncle has fired him), and it is revealed that Zack's career went down the tubes because Kate once talked him into throwing a championship. At the Classic, Zack and Monroe surprise the crowd with the excellence of their play, making it to the finals against Rollo and his pal. Of course, this year Kate has bet everything on Rollo, and she persuades Zack to blow the match for her again. He plays badly, until Monroe convinces him to do the right thing. The underdogs win, Monroe decides to go to UCLA and stay with Samantha, and all the good guys end up happy.

Ever since the success of ROCKY, Hollywood has tried to use every possible sport in the already hoary good-guy-wins-big-match-and-redeems-himself story line (the nearly countless examples range from ONE ON ONE and VISION QUEST to CADDYSHACK and BREAKING AWAY). So it shouldn't come as much of a surprise to see volleyball made the vehicle for the familiar plot. One can almost imagine the producers discussing how to stretch the volleyball scene in TOP GUN into two hours—and they could have done worse, but not much. Most of the movie's faults lie with the script: the characters aren't captivating or believable, the dialog is inane, and the story is routine. Moreover, though Howell (YOUNG TOSCANINI) and Thorne-Smith (sometimes seen on "L.A. Law") are attractive and do their best with what they've got, and though Horton is actually pretty good, the supporting players are generally awful (Rydell is an exception). Even the requisite pop soundtrack doesn't create any excitement.

Still, SIDE OUT's saddest failure is that most of the volleyball sequences are simply dull. These scenes are edited to try to make the game sexy—with plenty of intercut bikinied T & A—but showcase only the editing itself, not the volleyball players or beach bunnies. Admittedly, the Volleyball Classic that climaxes the picture offers some appreciation of the sport, but by then it's too late. Made with the assistance of the Association of Volleyball Professionals and featuring real-life champs of the sport (bad guy Stoklos among them), SIDE OUT might interest a few beach bums, volleyball fans, and product-placement buffs, but otherwise it has limited appeal. *(Brief nudity, adult situations.)*

d, Peter Israelson; p, Gary Foster; w, David Thoreau; ph, Ron Garcia; ed, Conrad Buff; m, Jeff Lorber; prod d, Dan Lomino; art d, Bruce Crone; set d, Cloudia

Sports   **(PR:C   MPAA:PG-13)**

SKI PATROL

91m Epic—Sarlui-Diamant—Paul Maslansky/Triumph c

Roger Rose *(Jerry)*, Yvette Nipar *(Ellen)*, T.K. Carter *(Iceman)*, Leslie Jordan *(Murray)*, Paul Feig *(Stanley)*, Sean Gregory Sullivan *(Suicide)*, Tess *(Tiana)*, George Lopez *(Eddie)*, Corby Timbrook *(Lance)*, Stephen Hytner *(Myron)*, Ray Walston *(Pops)*, Martin Mull *(Maris)*, Rascal *(Dumpster)*, Deborah Rose *(Ski Inspector Crabitz)*, Beirne Chisolm *(Ian)*, Jim Allman *(Troy)*, Wink Roberts, Faith Minton *(Skiing Couple)*, Lachlen French *(Photographer)*, Margaret Aoki *(Lady in Car)*, Michelle Smoot-Hyde *(Santa's Elf)*, James Alt *(Young Father)*, John Garrison *(Elder Skier)*, Kiyo Hamada *(Japanese Lady)*, Nancy Ann Nahra *(Girl at Party)*, Geoffrey Bennett *(Ski Schooler)*, Michelle Minailo *(Party MC)*, Carole Taylor *(Mayor Biard)*, Eric Hart *(Man on Table)*, Brittney Lewis *(Contact Lens Girl)*, Mark Alston *(Contact Lens Guy)*, Jennifer Rahr *(Chair Lift Rider)*, Bernie Ben Garcia *(Hispanic Boy)*, Michelle Rohl *(Singer)*, Brad Goode *(Talent Show MC)*, David Nowell *(Sound Technician)*, Jason Johnson *(Brat)*, Robert Conder, and Susan Dolan *(Brat's Parents)*

SKI PATROL is the latest entry in the seemingly endless list of brainless slapstick comedies that include PORKY'S and POLICE ACADEMY (which shares this film's producer). Set at the Snowy Peaks ski lodge and its surrounding slopes, SKI PATROL follows the zany adventures of the bunch of lovable misfits that patrol the area. Led by the charismatic Jerry (Roger Rose), the group is all set to celebrate Snowy Peaks' 40th anniversary when trouble rears its ugly head in the form of evil real estate baron Maris (Martin Mull). It seems that Maris wants to take Snowy Peaks away from lovable old Pops (Ray Walston), the resort's owner, and that he will use any devious means necessary to attain this objective. These include hiring the evil Lance (Corby Timbrook) and his friends—sworn enemies of the ski patrol—to sabotage the slopes and make the patrol look bad in an effort to force Snowy Peaks to close. The ski patrol has other worries, though, like passing the difficult tests (which include tortuous maneuvering through caves and down elaborate slopes) required to earn their badges as patrolmen. The gang must also keep an eye out for a schizophrenic daredevil named Suicide (Sean Gregory Sullivan), who flies down the slopes on one ski. And, of course, they have to find the time for those all-important practical jokes. Other patrol antics include the efforts of Stanley (Paul Feig) to overcome his clumsiness and impress an attractive foreign exchange student, while Jerry tries to rekindle a romance with Pop's niece (Yvette Nipar) and two other squad members enter a talent contest to get yet another patrolman out of jail. Meanwhile, the bad guys sabotage snowmobiles and drop mice on people, which eventually forces Pops to sell his property to Maris. Never fear, however; our wacky heroes come through with flying skis in the end.

SKI PATROL is lame-brained entertainment stuffed with tired gags and stale slapstick. Scraping the bottom of the barrel for its desperate laughs, the film serves up fat jokes, short jokes (one of which is stolen from "The Brady Bunch," of all places), breast jokes, nerd jokes, and dog jokes—as well as countless pratfalls and stumbles. All the characters exhibit the kind of idiocy it takes to inhabit the genre, and the plot is recycled from every formula comedy of the past 10 years (in fact, it's a virtual remake of CADDYSHACK). This would not be so bad if some of the gags were even remotely funny, but none of them are. The stupidest moments include a short man tripping over a slobbering bulldog (the same bulldog is also used in a joke blatantly stolen from USED CARS), a woman being thrown into a cake, and another character being soaked in hot dog condiments. There are also slaps, punches, and crashes, several chase scenes, and, of course, the requisite man in drag. Director Richard Correll's timing is appalling; so many sight gags are mishandled that after a while it becomes depressing. Executive produced by Paul Maslansky, the self-crowned King of Slapstick responsible for all six "Police Academy" outings, SKI PATROL fits well into the "Police Academy" numbskull mold; even its star, Rose, follows in the Steve Guttenberg tradition of unbearable smugness and shallowness. Let's just hope that SKI PATROL doesn't follow too thoroughly in the footsteps of Maslansky's other films, or we might be in for a SKI PATROL 2. *(Profanity, adult situations.)*

d, Richard Correll; p, Phillip B. Goldfine and Donald L. West; w, Steven Long Mitchell and Craig W. Van Sickle (based on a story by Steven Long Mitchell, Craig W. Van Sickle, Wink Roberts); ph, John Stephens; ed, Scott Wallace; m, Bruce Miller; prod d, Fred Weiler; art d, Seven L. Nielsen; set d, Steven A. Lee; spec, Pioneer FX, Inc.; stunts, Lane Parrish and Tony Jefferson; cos, Angee Beckett; makup, Barbara Page; chor, Jeff J. Adkins

Comedy   (PR:C   MPAA:PG)

SKINHEADS—THE SECOND COMING OF HATE

93m Amazing Movies/Greydon Clark c

Chuck Connors *(Mr. Huston)*, Barbara Bain *(Martha)*, Jason Culp *(Jeff)*, Brian Brophy *(Damon)*, Elizabeth Sagal *(Amy)*, Bill Kohne *(Jeff)*, Lynna Hopwood *(Liz)*, Gene Mitchell *(Frank)*, Frank Noon *(Walt)*, Dennis Ott *(Brains)*, James A. Stunden *(Randy)*, Michael Fox *(Saul)*, Bunny Summers *(Bessie)*, Cynthia Cheston *(Carla)*, Jadili Johnson *(Willie)*, Duane Davis *(Tiny)*, and Clark Corkum *(Paul)*

In this low-grade exploitation flick, pesky neo-Nazis shatter the peace and quiet of Nevada. Sadly, one almost pities the scruffy skinheads on display here, since even the worst racist scum deserves better than this rabble-rousing indictment. Brought to us by Greydon Clark, the creator of the immortal SATAN'S CHEERLEADERS (which exposed the then-prevalent scourge of demonic possession among half-time entertainers at high-school sporting events), SKINHEADS is bad enough to discourage any interest in white supremacy groups. Maybe it will do some public service after all.

After beating up the Jewish proprietors of a convenience store and rumbling with a gang of African-American street toughs, the shaved-head crowd takes to the open road with mischief on their minds. Prior to departure, they adopt Randy (James A. Stunden), a naive young man who's just been fired and is easy prey for their crazed theories about the survival of the white-est. Rude and rowdy, the gang—which, in addition to Randy, includes vicious leader Damon (Brian Brophy), mean-tempered alcoholic Frank (Gene Mitchell), chicken-hearted Jeff (Bill Kohne), token main squeeze Liz (Lynna Hopwood), and two brain-damaged hulks, Brains and Walt (Dennis Ott and Frank Noon)—takes off on a terror spree. When rugged outdoorsman Huston (Chuck Connors) bids goodbye to his restaurateur girl friend, Martha (Barbara Bain), he doesn't realize that his cozy cabin-in-the-woods existence will be shattered forever by the gang's rampage. Invading Martha's diner, the outlaw bigots knock out Berkeley student Jeff (Jason Culp), molest and kill coed Carla (Cynthia Cheston), murder Jeff's pals (Duane Davis and Clark Corkum), and make the big mistake of rubbing out Martha, too. When Jeff revives and rescues his sole fellow survivor, Amy (Elizabeth Sagal), the chase is on. Reminding them that they must eliminate any

witnesses to their rampage, Damon vetoes the gang's plan to split to Mexico. As the film becomes a standard escape-and-pursuit picture, the collegiate good guys collapse in Huston's cabin after a near-miss with the skinheads. Entering his domain only to be informed by Jeff and Amy that Hitler enthusiasts are stinking up his weeds, Huston recalls WW II and prepares for battle. The skinheads intercept our trio with a roadblock and badly wound Huston (who later retaliates by snuffing out Walt), then, using the crybaby skinhead (also named Jeff) as a shield, the ersatz stormtroopers lay siege to the cabin, resulting in a stand-off. When Randy annoys him by weakening in his resolve, Damon murders his new disciple, and also finishes off Huston. Jeff and Amy—after setting off a small gunpowder explosion and after the Berkeley student's neo-Nazi namesake gets caught in an animal trap—flee into the woods. Not considered gung-ho enough, skinhead Jeff is nailed to the cabin's exterior, where he becomes a grizzly bear's dinner; meanwhile, good-guy Jeff manages to choke Frank to death and throw a rattlesnake on Brains. Unfortunately, Damon rapes Amy in the meantime, much to gang moll Liz's chagrin. After lunatic Damon further decimates the skinhead population by murdering Liz, he tries to run down Amy and Jeff on the road. As Jeff and Damon fight to the death, Amy grabs a gun and pumps the budding Hitler full of lead.

Certainly, a coherent thriller could be made out of the frightening premise of neo-Naziism's popularity in America's heartland. Instead, filmmakers have pounced on this provocative material in the tawdriest tabloid manner possible. From Costa-Gavras' BETRAYED to cable TV's "Into the Homeland" to SKINHEADS, each blast at white supremacists has further trivialized important issues. SKINHEADS treats racists as garden-variety comic-book villains; its biker riffraff are cut from the same cloth as misguided punks from 50s juvenile-delinquent movies, leaving the particular nature of their insidiousness unexplored. Moreover, SKINHEADS fails to deliver the visceral goods even as exploitation filmmaking. There's no sense of danger and no building of suspense; every naughty Nazi incident is telegraphed in advance, and most of the film consists of padded-out hide-and-seek escapades in the woods. Through these noticeably sluggish proceedings, the cast stumbles around in a daze. As the lone survivors of the diner massacre, Sagal and Culp seem more concerned about the protocol of sharing a sleeping bag than being wracked with grief over the loss of their friends or fearful for their own lives. Veterans Bain and Connors sleepwalk through their roles, while Mitchell overacts to the nth degree, as if trying to give off enough energy for a cast of 12 in his single performance.

With no socially redeeming substance, weak in characterization, short on plot logic, and amazingly low on energy, SKINHEADS is a poorly structured newspaper-headline horror movie. Lacking sufficient punch to interest even those action buffs who might overlook meaninglessness and incoherence if enough cheap thrills were provided, the lethargic SKINHEADS fails on every level. *(Violence, nudity, adult situations, sexual situations, profanity.)*

d, Greydon Clark; p, Greydon Clark; w, David Reskin and Greydon Clark; ph, Nicholas Von Sternberg; ed, Travis Clark; m, Dan Slider; art d, Doug Abrahamson; set d, Chris McCann; cos, Leslie Yarmo

Action   (PR:O   MPAA:R)

SLEEPING CAR, THE

87m Vidmark/Triax c

David Naughton *(Jason)*, Judie Aronson *(Kim)*, Kevin McCarthy *(Vincent Tuttle)*, Jeff Conaway *(Bud Sorenson)*, Dani Minnick *(Joanne)*, John Carl Buechler *(Mr. Erickson)*, Ernestine Mercer *(Mrs. Erickson)*, Steve Lundquist *(Dwight)*, Bill Stevenson *(Kerry)*, David Coburn *(Harris)*, Nicole Hanson *(Clarice)*, and Sandra Margot *(19-year-old Girl)*

The American rail system gains a whole new set of troubles in this weird horror thriller. The story is set in motion by past events: 10 years ago, officious train conductor Erickson (played by special-effects man John Carl Buechler)—called "the Mister"—admonished his horny assistant to stop fooling around with the woman he had stashed away on board and to pay attention to railroad business. When the fledgling failed to carry out his duties, a devastating train wreck resulted, and when the smash-up was blamed on the Mister, the conductor was totally derailed mentally. Ten years later, some time after the Mister's death, divorced college returnee Jason (David Naughton) is looking for cheap digs. After examining the sleeping car inhabited by the Mister after his (and the car's) retirement, Jason pays his widow, Mrs. Erickson (Ernestine Mercer), the rent and moves in. Little does he realize the terror that awaits him and his next-door neighbor, spirtualist Vincent Tuttle (Kevin McCarthy). Jason's reception at school is a little rocky, since his professor, Bud Sorenson (Jeff Conaway)—another refugee from the real world—is constantly razzing him, and fellow student Kim (Judie Aronson) comes across as a bit of a bitchy tease. After having a nightmare in which he's visited by his ferocious ex-wife (Dani Minnick), Jason is surprised by Sorenson and Kim, who drop by with a house-warming gift. It's a tape of railroad noises, which mysteriously turn into a replay of the sounds from the night of the Mister's infamous train wreck. When jock Dwight (Steve Lundquist), who's jealous of Jason's relationship with Kim, breaks into the sleeping car with mischief on his mind, he awakens the spirit of the ever-vengeful Mister, who kills Dwight and dumps the body in a ravine behind the sleeping car. As things start to go bump in the night, Jason is informed by his sleeping-car-mate, Vincent, that their abode is haunted, and (after some harassment by Dwight's pals) Jason and Kim stop bickering long enough to become lovers. When professor Sorenson drunkenly stops by for a chat, he becomes the Mister's next victim. Wires pin him to the sleeper cushions, cutting into him before the bed folds up and crushes him to death. Kim herself is later possessed by the Mister's spirit while she is making out with Jason, and starts choking her lover. Jason now begins to believe Vincent's ghost-obsessed ramblings, and the men force their landlady to reveal the truth about the evil sleeping car. They discover that after the Mister was fired, Mrs. Erickson made him move out of their house and into the sleeping car — where he used to bring nubile bimbos, then slay them. Vincent claims that the Mister is feeding off Jason's energy, and he and Jason hatch plans for an exorcism on the Super Chief, assisted by Kim. While the trio try to de-Misterize the place, Jason's ex-wife returns to become the latest victim. As all hell breaks loose and lightning streaks through the car, Vincent starts chanting and the Mister unleashes his full fury. Mrs. Erickson intercedes, only to be slain with her own hatchet. Following Vincent's mystical advice, Jason forgives the Mister for the train wreck and, as the fateful crash is replayed, the conductor's spirit is freed and finds eternal peace.

Likeable mainly due to Naughton's amiable charm and McCarthy's pleasantly nutty performance, THE SLEEPING CAR is imaginative fright-night fun, but flawed on several counts. First of all, setting the film in a sleeping car (that just happened to be preserved for the Mister to live in and then haunt) seems overly contrived. Even if you buy the bizarre premise of the haunted car, however, the film proves a shaky ride in other respects. Conaway for example, registers less as a jocular, comic relief wiseguy than as a complete motor. He's so constantly in motion, you begin to believe he's been possessed by an entire set of Lionel trains rather than the Mister's spirit — it's as hammy a performance as you're likely to see. Lundquist's Dwight is extraneous to the plot and makes an uninteresting victim; in general, our involvement with the film would have been intensified if the initial victims were people Jason really cared about. Later on, when Jason's nasty ex-wife gets her fatal comeuppance, it's more satisfying than when characters are simply introduced to be slaughtered.

On the plus side, the special effects cannot be faulted. They pump sorely needed energy into the movie whenever the story line starts to sag. THE SLEEPING CAR is also enjoyable for its steady stream of clever one-liners, although the constant joking mitigates the terror somewhat. The film settles into combining laughs and goosebumps in equal amounts, and without moving into all-out parody, it's a fairly funny spook show. The essential elements of the physical production — including the score, visual effects, and sound effects, are all exemplary. Although they don't camouflage the film's scripting and casting flaws, they help provide chiller fans with sufficient shocks and surprises. Reasonably amusing and creepily effective on occasion, THE SLEEPING CAR gives us a scary train ride to terror, with a conductor who probably rides the rails with Freddy Krueger in hell. (*Violence, sexual situations, nudity, substance abuse, profanity.*)

d, Douglas Curtis; p, Douglas Curtis; w, Greg O'Neill; ph, David Lewis; ed, Allan Holzman and Betty Cohen; m, Ray Colcord; prod d, Robert Benedict; spec, Max W. Anderson and John Carl Buechler

Horror   (PR:C   MPAA:R)

SLIPSTREAM

92m M.C.E.G./Virgin c

Mark Hamill (*Tasker*), Kitty Aldridge (*Belitski*), Bill Paxton (*Matt Owen*), Tony Allen (*Bartender*), Susan Leong (*Abigail*), Rita Wolf (*Maya*), Eleanor David (*Ariel*), Deborah Leng (*Girl on Swing*), Bob Peck (*Byron*), F. Murray Abraham (*Cornelius*), and Ben Kingsley (*Avatar*)

Sometime and somewhere in a desolate future made bleak by man's abuse of the environment, a fugitive, Byron (Bob Peck), is apprehended by Tasker (Mark Hamill), a gung-ho cop, and his partner, Belitski (Kitty Aldridge). When Matt (Bill Paxton), a roving jack-of-all-trades, learns that there's a price on the wanted man's head, he tricks the police and spirits the prisoner away in his rickety plane. Before Matt makes his getaway, Tasker shoots him with a poison dart tracking device, then Matt flies into the dangerous slipstream (an area blasted by harsh winds that are treated as gods by superstitious locals). While Tasker is busy playing Dirty Harry and eliminating some of Matt's smuggler pals, Matt literally lands in trouble and is tied up by members of a battle-scarred religious cult, who mistrust Byron because he has demonstrated healing powers. The cultists attach Byron to a giant wind-borne kite to determine whether he's a friendly spirit. When Tasker and Belitski encounter the trussed-up Matt, they free him only after

he agrees to help them retrieve the up-in-the-clouds Byron. Mistrusting Matt's intentions as he sails upwards, Belitski likewise flies heavenward; as Matt tries to free Byron (who we learn is actually an android), Belitski tries to circumvent the double-cross, but the violent wind nearly tosses all three into oblivion, and Tasker is nearly crushed by debris from the oversized kite. After the selfless Byron manages to rescue everyone, a visiting cave-dweller (Eleanor David) who's not a member of the wind religion insists that Matt and Byron accompany her to her homeland, where Matt can obtain an antidote for the poison now coursing through his veins, as well as supplies. Leaving Belitski behind to look for Tasker, the three journey to an elitist settlement dedicated to sensual pleasure and high culture. While the android explores humankind with his hostess, Matt beds down with a beautiful blonde. After a swinging party (during which Byron entertains with a Fred Astaire impression), Tasker and his partner arrive and shoot their way in, demanding the return of Byron. (Belitski eventually provides Matt with an antidote, but she remains loyal to Tasker for the time being.) During a gun battle, Matt is wounded and Byron's girl friend is killed. Although Matt has revealed to the android that he now considers him a friend and couldn't betray him, Tasker has no compunction about turning Byron over to the authorities and collecting the reward. Crazed by the death of his lover and the end of his plans to improve life in the utopian society, Byron jumps onto Tasker's plane after Tasker tries to run him down with it. Tearing the motor apart, the android succeeds in crashing the plane into a mountain and Tasker is killed — leaving Matt free to pair up with Belitski, and Byron free to pursue his dream of locating the land of the androids.

If you can cut through all the mystical mumbo-jumbo about wind-worship and if you can stifle a yawn over the too-familiar post-apocalyptic setting, you may enjoy this mildly diverting action flick. Playing like a western set on the lawless frontier of an environmentally damaged future-world, SLIPSTREAM unfolds its derivative plotline with some ingenuity. The problem is that the metaphysics and philosophizing keep slowing the action down. And one sometimes grows tired of the saintly android turning the other cheek while gazing soulfully past the camera with his other-worldly baby blues. Trying for something different, the movie should have integrated its pseudo-religious gobbledygook more smoothly into the rough-and-tumble adventure or cut back sharply on the pontificating.

It is surprising that SLIPSTREAM's producers were able to persuade Ben Kingsley and F. Murray Abraham to accept thankless roles in what is basically a Saturday matinee feature gussied up with variations on the theme of man's inhumanity to man and robot. Sloppy camerawork and jagged editing mar several sequences, including the one in which Peck performs the Fred Astaire number. Hamill is convincingly cast against type as a police-state villain, and Paxton makes a ruggedly attractive self-mocking hero. As the angelic android, Peck has an unusual presence and makes some of the gooey religiosity palatable. SLIPSTREAM is an offbeat adventure, somewhat awkward in its transitions from scene to scene, but just intriguing enough to hold the attention of jaded action fans. (*Violence, profanity, sexual situations, nudity, substance abuse.*)

d, Steven Lisberger; p, Gary Kurtz; w, Tony Kayden, Charles Pogue, and Steven Lisberger (based on a story by Bill Bauer); ph, Frank Tidy; ed, Terry Rawlings; m, Elmer Bernstein; prod d, Andrew McAlpine; art d, Malcolm Stone; spec, Brian Johnson; cos, Catherine Cook; makup, Aileen Deaton

Adventure/Science Fiction   (PR:C   MPAA:PG-13)

SONNY BOY

98m Brouwersgracht — Trans World/Triumph c

David Carradine (*Pearl*), Paul L. Smith (*Slue*), Brad Dourif (*Weasel*), Conrad Janis (*Dr. Bender*), Sydney Lassick (*Charlie*), Savina Gersak (*Sandy*), Alexandra Powers (*Rose*), Steve Carlisle (*Sheriff*), and Michael Griffin (*Sonny Boy*)

This nightmare-drama set in New Mexico, was filmed in 1987 and features POPEYE's Bluto as the head of a twisted "family," consisting of David Carradine in a dress, a killer cannibal "son," and, of course, Brad Dourif.

Beefy Paul L. Smith, who played Bluto opposite Robin Williams' Popeye in Robert Altman's 1980 film (as well as the sadistic prison guard in MIDNIGHT EXPRESS in 1978), looks none the worse for the passing years as he plays Slue, lord and master of the little town of Harmony, New Mexico. He apparently supports himself and his dependents by stealing and reselling television sets that he stores in a wood-and-canvas pyramid. In his spare time he is a munitions expert — he has his own field howitzer — and a surrealist painter. The film opens in 1970 when Weasel (Dourif), a member of Slue's gang, is stalking a couple settling in for the night at the town's motel. Weasel plans to steal their vintage red Lincoln Continental, but things get a little messy. Weasel has to kill the couple, then escapes with their car and their belongings, only to discover an infant son among the booty. Back at Slue's headquarters, Pearl (the cross-dressing Carradine) takes a liking to the baby, saving him from Slue, who wants to feed him to his hogs. Slue gives in to Pearl's pleadings and decides to raise the boy as his own. As Sonny Boy (Michael Griffin) grows, Slue toughens him up by dragging him around behind his car and tying him to a stake, then setting him afire. Slue helps Sonny Boy develop a taste for blood by keeping him locked in an old water tank with an access chute into which Slue drops live chickens at mealtime. Finally, Slue decides to put his creation to use when the mayor of the town starts taking his job too seriously to suit Slue. He loads Sonny Boy into the back of an ice-cream truck, drives to the mayor's house, and lets the kid loose. Loping more like an animal than a human, Sonny Boy bursts into the mayor's house and kills him by biting his neck. Pleased with the results, Slue looks for ways to expand his empire, using Sonny Boy as his secret weapon. Little comes of his efforts, and later, he stops at a bar and leaves Sonny Boy alone long enough to meet sexy blonde Sandy (Savina Gersak). Sonny is attracted to her, but can't communicate with her since Slue, fearing the boy might one day be apprehended by the police, has cut his tongue out. When Slue leaves town on business, Sonny Boy is taken on a job by Weasel and another partner Charlie (Sydney Lassick, who, along with Dourif played one of the mental patients in the 1975 hit ONE FLEW OVER THE CUCKOO'S NEST). They have Sonny Boy kill a prospector so that they can steal his gold, an act that outrages the town, leading to a FRANKENSTEIN-style climax in which the citizens massacre the "family," although Sonny Boy survives. He is reunited with Sandy, who teaches him a less destructive form of necking, and tended to by a disgraced doctor (Conrad Janis), who solves Sonny Boy's speech problems. (Put it this way—if there were a sequel it would probably be called "Monkey Tongue.")

Director Robert Martin Carroll reportedly had SONNY BOY taken from his control and re-edited by the producers (among them Ovidio G. Assonitis, who directed the similarly strange TENTACLES). That may account for its choppy, disjointed narrative. That aside, SONNY BOY is an oddly compelling study of family pathology in the tradition of Wes Craven's THE HILLS HAVE EYES and Tobe Hooper's THE TEXAS CHAINSAW MASSACRE. Carroll's main accomplishment in adapting Graham Whiffler's original screenplay is to tell the story from Sonny Boy's viewpoint, which translates Slue's every act of cruelty towards him as a twisted expression of paternal love. As reflected by Sonny Boy, Slue acquires a comprehensible humanity. Perhaps too obviously, Sonny Boy is portrayed as a Christ figure with unlimited charity toward Slue. Also helping to humanize this very bizarre tale is the strong work of the ensemble cast, especially Griffin, who is uncommonly convincing as the title savage innocent. Carradine and Smith make an unexpectedly engaging couple, and the supporting work is all strong. SONNY BOY is a heady, offbeat mix of myth, social drama, and psychological thriller that is added testimony to the creative vitality to be found in the B-movie fringe. (*Violence, profanity, adult situations.*)

d, Robert Martin Carroll; p, Ovidio G. Assonitis and Peter Shepherd; w, Graham Whiffler; ph, Roberto D'Ettorre Piazzoli; ed, Claudio Cutry; m, Claudio Mario Cordio; prod d, Mario Molli

Horror   (PR:O   MPAA:R)

SPACE 2074

(SEE: STAR QUEST: BEYOND THE RISING MOON)

SPACED INVADERS

102m Silver Screen Partners IV—Smart Egg—Luigi Cingolani/Touchstone—Buena Vista c

Douglas Barr (*Sheriff Sam Hoxly*), Royal Dano (*Old Man Wrenchmuller*), Arianna Richards (*Kathy Hoxly*), J.J. Anderson (*Brian "Duck"*), Gregg Berger (*Steve W. Klembecker*), Wayne Alexander (*Vern*), Fred Applegate (*Russell Pillsbury*), Patrika Darbo (*Mrs. Vanderspool*), Tonya Lee Williams (*Ernestine*), Ryan Todd (*Sid Ghost*), Barry O'Neill (*Clown Kid*), Adam Hansley (*Pig Kid*), Casey Sander (*Radio Announcer*), Rose Parenti (*Old Wife*), Glen Vernon, Hal Riddle (*Old Guys*), William Holmes, Kent Minault (*Dumb Guys*), Jim Eusterman (*Clown*), Justine L. Henry (*Dody*), Kevin Thompson (*Blaznee/Voice of Blaznee*), Jimmy Briscoe (*Capt. Bipto*), Tony Cox (*Pez*), Debbie Lee Carrington (*Dr. Ziplock*), Tommy Madden (*Giggywig*), Jeff Winklis (*Voice of Capt. Bipto*), Bruce Lanoil (*Voice of Pez*), Joe Alaskey (*Voice of Dr. Ziplock*), Tony Pope (*Voice of Giggywig*), Patrick Johnson (*Voices of Commander and Enforcer Drone*), and Kirk Thatcher (*Voice of Spiff*)

While there is nothing Earth-shattering about director Patrick Read Johnson's first film, it is often quite entertaining. SPACED INVADERS makes fun of just about every outer space film ever made, and throws in some Three Stooges-like mayhem for good measure. The simple yet creative story line concerns a small group of Martians (short green creatures with heads that look like watermelons) who believe they are supposed to invade Earth. Led by a captain who wears aviator glasses and a leather flying jacket, and whose voice bears a remarkable resemblance to Jack Nicholson's, the Martians pick up a rebroadcast of Orson Welles' "War of the Worlds" and assume they are late for the invasion. Their

broken-down spacecraft lands near Big Bean, Illinois, on Halloween night. Sam (Douglas Barr), the town's new sheriff, and his daughter, Kathy (played wonderfully by Ariana Richards), join with Brian (J.J. Anderson, a child dressed as a duck) to help the Martians avoid the townspeople who want to kill them. "Prepare to die Earth scum," one Martian repeatedly tells the townsfolk, but the captain just wants to get home in one piece. The ensuing action allows for jokes that are variously dumb, mildly funny, or hilarious.

SPACED INVADERS is ET meets Monty Python, with a little subtle Hollywood humor thrown in. And it is not as bad as it sounds. This is a film that children can watch without parents having to worry about rough language or adult situations—no mean recommendation given the current dearth of suitable entertainment for young children. Richards takes on her role as the new kid in town with a joyful mixture of innocence and precociousness. "They're not bad, just stupid," she says of the Martians, and her father can't help but believe her. SPACED INVADERS could have been a fantastic spoof of alien films *and* a fine comedy were it not for its unevenness and lazy writing. It appears as if no one challenged the writers to undertake a rewrite to perfect the silliness; presumably they assumed their target audience to be 10-to 12-year-olds and wrote accordingly. SPACED INVADERS has all the elements of a very good film; regrettably, it is something less than that.

d, Patrick Read Johnson; p, Luigi Cingolani; w, Patrick Read Johnson and Scott Alexander; ph, James L. Carter; ed, Seth Gaven and Daniel Gross; m, David Russo; md, David Russo; prod d, Tony Tremblay; art d, Scott Alexander; set d, Chava Danielson; spec, Criswell and Johnson Effects, Frank Ceglia, John Knoll, and Whiz-Bang Effects; stunts, Spiro Razatos; cos, Sanja Milkovic Hays; makup, Suzanne Sanders; anim, Perpetual Motion Pictures

Comedy/Science Fiction   (PR:AA   MPAA:PG)

SPONTANEOUS COMBUSTION

88m Taurus c

Brad Dourif (*David*), Jon Cypher (*Dr. Marsh*), Cynthia Bain, William Prince, Melinda Dillon, and John Landis

Horror director Tobe Hooper's latest fiasco is a work of nonsense called SPONTANEOUS COMBUSTION. Clumsy, confusing, and forgettable, the film tells the story of David (played as an adult by the ever-demented Brad Dourif), a man with an unwanted ability to make himself and others catch fire. Beginning in Nevada, during the hydrogen-bomb testing of the 50s, and ending in the present day with the start-up of a nuclear power plant, SPONTANEOUS COMBUSTION has a science-fiction plot: as the film opens, a typical 50s couple is being used in government experiments involving a serum that may or may not immunize the human body against the effects of radiation. The couple is exposed to an explosion, then monitored to observe the effects of the drug. It seems to have worked, and—except for one complication (the woman has become pregnant)—the experiment is called a success. After the child is born (named David, and bearing a odd birthmark on his hand), things start to get strange. The baby appears normal until he is brought to his mother, whereupon she catches fire and burns to death, as does the father. The deaths—in which a mysterious man named Olander seems to be involved—are declared the result of spontaneous human combustion. The film then jumps to the present, when the now-adult David is a teacher and anti-nuclear activist. A new nuclear power plant is about to open in the area, and David, his girl friend (Cynthia Bain), and many others are opposed to it. David is an unusual fellow: his body temperature is always 100 degrees, and his life seems to be dominated by the decrepit old grandfather of his ex-wife. Things get even weirder when a woman David has argued with is found burned to death. He begins having bizarre visions of his unknown parents, and worst of all, his arm becomes a kind of flame thrower. As David tries to survive and to uncover the conspiracy-obscured truth of the 50s experiments, charred bodies drop like flies; policemen, doctors, radio station engineers, and security guards are among David's blackened victims as he helplessly rampages through the streets of California. In hot pursuit is the mysterious Dr. Marsh (Jon Cypher), who desperately tries to inject David with a phosphorescent serum that will destroy him. Finally, David discovers that his "gift" is a side effect of the experiments, for which his ex's grandfather is responsible. (He also discovers that his girl friend possesses the same talent for torching things.) In a final confrontation (as the new nuclear plant goes online), David uses his unfortunate power to engulf himself and the old man in flames, but his work is not finished, and he virtually comes back from the grave to save his girl friend from Dr. Marsh and from his ex-wife. Before disintegrating into a puddle of glowing liquid, David saps his girl friend's fire, relieving her of the "gift" of spontaneous combustion.

As complicated and confusing as all this is, the synopsis above represents only half the story. The film features several twists and subplots that are impossible to fully explain, as well as moments of such sheer stupidity that no explanation would suffice. Hooper (POLTERGEIST; THE TEXAS CHAINSAW MASSA-

CRE) seems to be going for the old mad-scientist and government-experiment-gone-awry plot lines, but has little success with either. The film's opening is relatively strong, with some very nicely re-created 50s "newsreel" footage, and some early scenes that evoke a pleasantly satirical mood. But once Hooper unleashes the story fully, the film disintegrates like one of David's victims. Badly edited and shot with no apparent rhythm or pace, SPONTANEOUS COMBUSTION becomes increasingly hard to watch. Characters wander around for no reason; major plot developments are handled with quick fixes of badly written dialog. The special effects are shoddy (David's fake fire-spewing arm is particularly bad), and the tedium of watching one flaming body after another is matched in dullness by the incessant melodramatics.

Still, Dourif is fun to watch (he is a brilliantly weird actor, whose strongest work can be seen in ONE FLEW OVER THE CUCKOO'S NEST and in John Huston's underrated gem WISE BLOOD), and there is one death scene — the spontaneous combustion of a radio engineer played by filmmaker John Landis — that's worth viewing. To see one of the most undeservedly successful directors in Hollywood blow up before your very eyes is a perverse treat for film fans. As for Hooper, his talent has remained dormant since 1973, when he made THE TEXAS CHAINSAW MASSACRE. That film, a raw horror masterpiece, seems to have been a fluke, and SPONTANEOUS COMBUSTION continues Hooper's downward slide. Missing the strong opportunity presented by the story's political subtext, as well as many possibilities for some good suspense, Hooper has again slapped together the kind of horror film that gives the genre a bad name, and it's clear that he should no longer be mentioned in the company of such horror masters as John Carpenter, George Romero, or David Cronenberg. Hooper is simply not a good filmmaker, and SPONTANEOUS COMBUSTION is a bust. *(Excessive violence, profanity, adult situations, substance abuse.)*

d, Tobe Hooper; p, Jim Rogers; w, Tobe Hooper and Howard Goldberg (based on a story by Tobe Hooper); ph, Levie Isaacks; ed, David Kern; m, Graeme Revell; spec, Stephen Brooks

Horror   (PR:O   MPAA:R)

STANLEY AND IRIS

104m Lantana/MGM-UA c

Jane Fonda *(Iris King)*, Robert De Niro *(Stanley Everett Cox)*, Swoosie Kurtz *(Sharon)*, Martha Plimpton *(Kelly King)*, Harley Cross *(Richard King)*, Jamey Sheridan *(Joe)*, Feodor Chaliapin Jr. *(Leonides Cox)*, Zohra Lampert *(Elaine)*, Loretta Devine *(Bertha)*, Julie Garfield *(Belinda)*, Karen Ludwig *(Melissa)*, Kathy Kinney *(Bernice)*, Laurel Lyle *(Muriel)*, Mary Testa *(Joanne)*, Katherine Cortez *(Jan)*, Stephen Root *(Mr. Hentley)*, Eddie Jones *(Mr. Hagen)*, Fred J. Scollay *(Mr. Delancey)*, Dortha Duckworth *(Librarian)*, Jack Gill *(The Pursesnatcher)*, Bob Aaron *(Bakery Foreman)*, Gordon Masten *(Oscar Roebuck)*, Richard Blackburn *(Park Ranger)*, B.J. Reed *(Nurse)*, Conrad Bergschneider *(Apple Picker Foreman)*, Guy Sanvido *(Man in Car)*, Michael Blackburn, Paul Horruzey *(Kids)*, and Gerry Quigley *(Bellhop)*

STANLEY AND IRIS takes place in a small industrial town in New England. Iris King (Jane Fonda), a working-class mother of two, is riding home on the bus when her purse is stolen. After unsuccessfully attempting to recover the purse, she meets Stanley Cox (Robert De Niro), who offers to walk her home. Stanley and Iris discover that they work at the same large bakery (she on the production line, he in the canteen) and strike up a friendship. Times are tough for both of them. Eight months a widow, Iris still grieves for her husband, but that is hardly the extent of her troubles. Her teenage daughter Kelly (Martha Plimpton) is pregnant, and her unemployed sister, Sharon (Swoosie Kurtz), and Sharon's contentious husband, Joe (Jamey Sheridan), have taken up residence in Iris' home. For his part, Stanley devotedly cares for his 89-year-old father, Leonides (Feodor Chaliapin), and is determined to work hard and honestly to keep him happy. However, there is one problem: Stanley can't read or write. Iris discovers Stanley's handicap when she goes to the canteen one day in search of aspirin. Looking into a medicine cabinet stocked with dozens of bottles he can't read, Stanley hands Iris the wrong bottles one by one. Recognizing Stanley's problem, Iris tells his boss, who responds by firing Stanley ("You can't tell sugar from roach powder...you're dangerous," says his boss). Matters only get worse for Stanley and Iris, as she tries in vain to keep her family together, while he is forced to put his father in a home. When Leonides dies, Stanley finally asks Iris to teach him to read, and slowly they begin to build a strong friendship. After several triumphs (like writing the word "bird") and failures (like not being able to read directions and find his way home), Stanley succeeds in overcoming his problem, eventually securing a patent for a machine he has invented that cools hot pastry. In the process, Iris stops grieving over her husband and finds love again. What's more, Kelly has a baby girl, whom she names after Iris. After moving to Detroit and finding success there, Stanley returns to New England for Iris and her family. As they prepare to go to the Motor City as husband and wife, Iris asks Stanley

if he thinks he can handle the problems of her family, to which Stanley replies, "Anything is possible."

STANLEY AND IRIS is a difficult film to assess, since it deals sincerely with a serious subject yet disturbingly oversimplifies the real and complicated issue of illiteracy. Husband-and-wife screenwriting team Harriet Frank, Jr., and Irving Ravetch (who cowrote NORMA RAE) have crammed their story with a number of shallow melodramatic subplots (Plimpton's pregnancy, Chaliapin's death, etc.) and have dealt with illiteracy in the same superficial manner. Regrettably, Martin Ritt's bland, uninvolving direction doesn't help matters, leaving the actors alone to struggle with the inanities of the script. Supporting characters wander through the film with little apparent purpose (Kurtz and Sheridan are particularly wasted), and there are several moments of surprising heavy-handedness (like Plimpton's appearance on the production line after having quit school). Also working against the film's success is an uninvolving "single-mother-raising-her-kids" subplot that is filled with all of the wrong cliches (similar ground is covered much more skillfully in Paul Brickman's masterful MEN DON'T LEAVE). Unfolding in a choppy style, the film's main plot also never becomes compelling, despite noble attempts by the actors.

Fonda gives a steady performance as Iris, and though it's hard to believe she has ever seen the inside of a factory, she has some nice moments. De Niro is much better. His quirky but natural mannerisms are a joy to watch, and as always it's difficult to take your eyes off of him (especially during his wonderful drunk scene, and the library scene in which he demonstrates his newfound reading ability.) But even De Niro's brilliant performance isn't enough to save what is essentially a soap opera with high aspirations.

While some of the sloppy filmmaking can be forgiven, the film's core message cannot. If you cannot read you are a non-person, the film tells us. And if you learn how to read (which is a surprisingly simple task in this movie) your reward is lots of money! — all of which is a little misleading to say the least. It might have worked better by concentrating more on its eponymous main characters and less on the countless subplots. Over the years Ritt has demonstrated a sensitivity to the problems of the American working class in films like NORMA RAE and CONRACK, but by employing illiteracy as a cheap form of audience manipulation (and having all the rewards for his protagonist's struggle be monetary), the director shows that he has definitely lost touch. *(Profanity, adult situations, substance abuse.)*

d, Martin Ritt; p, Arlene Sellers and Alex Winitsky; w, Harriet Frank Jr. and Irving Ravetch; ph, Donald McAlpine; ed, Sidney Levin; m, John Williams; prod d, Joel Schiller; art d, Alicia Keywan and Eric Orbom; set d, Steve Shewchuk and Les Bloom; spec, Neil Trifunovich and Connie Brink; stunts, Jack Gill; cos, Theoni V. Aldredge; makup, Suzanne Benoit and Mickey Scott

Drama   (PR:C   MPAA:PG-13)

STAR QUEST: BEYOND THE RISING MOON

85m Pentan — Common Man/Films Around the World — VidAmerica c

(AKA: BEYOND THE RISING MOON; SPACE 2074)

Tracy Davis *(Pentan)*, Hans Bachmann *(Harold Brickman)*, Michael Mack *(John Moesby)*, Ron Ikejiri *(Takashi Kuriyama)*, Rick Foucheux *(Robert Thorton)*, James Hild *(Kyle)*, Reggie Vaughn *(George)*, Judith Miller *(Promethian Captain)*, Charles Lunsford *(Mr. Beaufusse)*, Rick Sabatini *(Tebrook)*, Norman Gagnon *(Promethian Helmsman/Trooper)*, Philip Fidandis *(Trooper/Interworld Courier)*, Michael Genebach *(Norwegian Interworld Courier)*, Richard Lee Rutherford *(Sparring Partner)*, Gary Cooper *(Trooper)*, Angela Judy *(Rachel)*, Jon Trapnell *(Ian Borge)*, Victoria Eves *(Kuriyama's Computer)*, Wayne Keyser *(Spaceport Announcer)*, and John Ellis *(Col. Kruger)*

Although STAR QUEST: BEYOND THE RISING MOON amounts to one small step for the science-fiction genre, it's one giant leap for low-budget, independent filmmaking. This imaginative outer-space tale traverses the galaxy, offering three different planetary environments, aerial dogfights, and a climactic duel with atomic warheads, all on a production budget of about $175,000 — which could buy about half a minute's worth of screen time in TOTAL RECALL. The story begins with a dizzying amount of exposition efficiently presented. By the middle of the next century mankind has made fantastic technological progress due to the discovery of a derelict alien spacecraft, the only known remnant of the vanished "Tesseran" culture. Thanks to the scientific knowledge gleaned from the oddly shaped hulk, humans routinely travel between the stars. Then comes word that another Tesseran ship has been found by a Norwegian space expedition. The explorer who staked the salvage claim dies in an accident, leaving ownership of the priceless relic in a legal limbo. Enter Kuriyama (Ron Ikejiri), a ruthless tycoon with his own paramilitary force and a giant interstellar dreadnought, the *Promethian*. But for this hostile takeover Kuriyama calls upon "the most subtle and effective tool of corporate warfare," a woman called Pentan (Tracy Davis). Although she is normal in appearance, Pentan isn't your average woman; endowed by her "creators" with enhanced mental and physical abilities, she knows all forms of combat. Dispatched to the North African spaceport of Star City, Pentan ambushes the returning Norwegians. But, fed up with her job as a professional killer and recognizing the alien vessel as her ticket to wealth and independence, she records the much-sought-after data relating to the Tesseran ship in her brain and takes flight. For this disobedience Pentan's masters activate a "stroker" device in her head that will kill her in 72 hours unless she surrenders. Pentan latches onto Brickman (Hans Bachmann), a Han Solo-type star pilot, who reluctantly agrees to take her to the only person who can save her, Thorton (Rick Foucheux), Pentan's "designer," another ex-Kuriyama employee, who now resides on the planet Inisfree. After a skirmish with Kuriyama's "Tulwar" fighter craft, the heroes get to Inisfree in time for Thorton to remove the stroker. Using Thorton's computers to retrieve and decode the Norwegian data from her brain, Pentan learns that the Tesseran ship is now located on the barren planet Elyseum. She and Brickman head for Elyseum, with the *Promethian* in pursuit. Along the way Brickman declares his love for Pentan, but she disappoints him by stating (during sex, no less) that she was given only rudimentary emotions required for deception; she really feels nothing for him. Upon arriving at the abandoned Tesseran ship, Pentan and Brickman are surrounded by Kuriyama's soldiers. Pentan coolly rejoins Kuriyama, leaving Brickman to his doom, but—surprise—she's only fooling. Commandeering a Tulwar fighter at the first opportunity, she handily blasts the enemy fighters and soon threatens the orbiting *Promethian* itself. As a last resort, Kuriyama sends out Tulwars armed with thermonuclear bombs, but Pentan survives their first salvo and chases them back to the *Promethian*. The villains on board panic and fire a missile that accidentally detonates a Tulwar's bomb; the resulting holocaust appears to envelop all the combatants. Back on Elyseum, a disconsolate Brickman is left with the Tesseran treasure. Suddenly Pentan lands, safe after all, and embraces him warmly—a double miracle even Geppetto might have trouble explaining.

Most of this intriguing film was shot inside a warehouse near Alexandria, Virginia, with but few forays to exterior locations. A farmer's field became the plain of Elyseum, and an access tunnel near the Pentagon was used for a portion of Star City. Working with 16mm stock, the filmmakers, whose backgrounds are in music-videos and commercial graphics, accomplished the movie's 270 special-effects shots using basic camera techniques almost as old as moving pictures themselves—double exposures, matte split-screens, semi-reflective mirrors, and stop-motion animation. Director-effects artist Philip Cook carefully selected studio lighting techniques, set designs, and color schemes to ensure that the best image quality would be maintained in the anticipated blowup to 35mm. But BEYOND THE RISING MOON, as the film was originally titled, received only scattered festival screenings before going to video with a title change.

Though Cook's visuals lack the hypergloss of modern George Lucas-scale space epics, they're usually convincing and often striking (indeed, only the panoramic sprawl of Star City looks like the table-top model it was; ironically, it was also the most expensive effect in the production). With its design inspired by the Fiero sportscar, Brickman's bright red spaceship looks sleek enough for the parking lot of some cosmic Spago's, and Kuriyama's headquarters, a slender structure towering over an iridescent sea, lingers long in the mind.

Much thought went into the film's smallest details, including the naming of the characters, planets, and space hardware. The planets Elyseum and Inisfree were named, respectively, after a mythical paradise for the soul of warriors and the hero's ancestral home in John Ford's THE QUIET MAN. "Tulwar" is an old Persian word for a sword. According to producer John Ellis, the evil Kuriyama was conceived not to bring Japan-bashing into the 21st century, but to invest the film with the feudal pageantry of his banner-waving, samurai-armored troops. Such internationalized touches disguise the film's regional origins.

Ron Ikejiri's stoic demeanor is well-suited to the part of Kuriyama, but the film's standout performance is by Michael Mack, who brings humor and charm to his role as the villain's strategist and chief henchman. On the other hand, Bachmann is stuck with a stock science-fiction character that was old even when Harrison Ford made it his own, and as Pentan, Davis struggles with a part that uneasily combines "Star Trek's" Mr. Spock with "The Avengers" Mrs. Peel. Furthermore, her martial-arts skills appear to be minimal; like a lot of B-movie action heroines, Pentan unconvincingly snaps spines with the merest brush of her fingertips. Finally, Davis' Pentan is simply too cold and aloof to be really engaging.

The plot generally falters in the second half of the film, falling back on chases and battles instead developing in an innovative fashion. Tellingly, nothing whatever is learned about the mysterious Tesserans. A peek inside the alien vessel reveals only that, like the Monolith in 2001, it's full of stars. So despite the proliferation of nukes at its climax, STAR QUEST: BEYOND THE RISING MOON ends with less of a bang than it should have. Still, it provides a number of thrills, and neither the filmmakers nor viewers can say they didn't get their money's worth. (*Violence, adult situations, sexual situations.*)

d, Philip Cook; p, John Ellis; w, Philip Cook; ph, Philip Cook; ed, Philip Cook; m, David Bartley; prod d, John Poreda; art d, John Ellis; set d, Dale Alan Hoyt; spec, Philip Cook; stunts, Kevin Bedgood; cos, Nancy Handwork and Helen Cook; makup, Charles Lunsford

Adventure/Science Fiction   (PR:C   MPAA:PG)

STATE OF GRACE

134m Cinehaus/Orion c

Sean Penn (*Terry Noonan*), Ed Harris (*Tommy Flannery*), Gary Oldman (*Jackie Flannery*), Robin Wright (*Kathleen Flannery*), John Turturro (*Nick*), John C. Reilly (*Stevie*), R.D. Call (*Nicholson*), Joe Viterelli (*Borelli*), Burgess Meredith (*Finn*), Deirdre O'Connell (*Irene*), Marco St. John (*Cavello*), Thomas G. Waites, Brian Burke, Michael Cumpsty, Michael Cunningham, Daniel O'Shea, Thomas F. Duffy (*Frankie's Men*), Jaime Tirelli (*Alvarez*), Sandra Beall (*Stevie's Date*), Vincent Guastaferro, John Anthony Williams, John Roselius, Louis Eppolito (*Borelli's Men*), Mo Gaffney (*Maureen*), John Mackay (*Raferty*), John Ottavino (*Raferty's Son*), Tim Gallin, Timothy D. Klein (*Bar Customers*), Jack Wallace (*Matty's Bartender*), Frank Girardeau, Michael P. Moran, Frank Coletta (*Bartenders*), Paul-Felix Montez (*Pool Hall Manager*), Freddi Chandler (*Waitress*), Tommy Sullivan (*Police Detective*), Ben Fine (*Hotel Doorman*), Saasha Costello, and Catherine Stewart (*Frankie's Children*)

STATE OF GRACE, directed by Phil Joanou, is a violent, tortuous melodrama that labors mightily to be an Irish MEAN STREETS or a latter-day WILD BUNCH. Sean Penn plays Terry Noonan, an undercover cop who returns unannounced to New York's Hell's Kitchen, "dropped off by the angels," according to Jackie Flannery (Gary Oldman), his childhood best friend. Noonan's task is to infiltrate the gang led by Jackie's brother, Tommy (Ed Harris). In the process, Noonan discovers he is still in love with his childhood sweetheart, Jackie and Tommy's sister, Kathleen (Robin Wright). Noonan is torn: Can he abjure loyalties to old friends or does he return to the habits of his youth? A series of insanely self-defeating betrayals and double-crosses leads to a vengeful bloodbath set against the backdrop of a St. Patrick's Day parade.

STATE OF GRACE is a long movie, yet its historical context remains unclear. Is it set today or in the 1970s, when the Westies gang perpetrated their futile crimes? One thing that is clear is that the film is drenched in religious imagery. Jackie's drunken confession in a cathedral, recurring references to angels and saints, and a final shootout right out of THE WILD BUNCH during the parade strain for significance, but they are a far cry from the powerful cross-cutting between the murders and the confirmation ceremony at the end of THE GODFATHER. There are some wonderful scenes in the film, however, including a 100-yard dash through sheets of flame during an arson, and the reunion between Kathleen and Noonan, during which she looks into his eyes and says in the most bluntly sexual way, "C'mon Terry no one forgets their first love, you know that."

The performances are uniformly good. Oldman's drunken psycho-greaser, a descendant of Robert DeNiro's Charlie-Boy in MEAN STREETS; Harris' gang leader; R.D. Call's fish-faced, malicious thug; and Burgess Meredith's tremulous cameo as Finn are all wonderful. But while based in part on the actions of the Westies, the behavior of most of the characters is so impenetrably stupid that it's ultimately difficult to care about them. There's no insight into what drives them, unless you count throwaway dialog like, "I'm Irish, we drink, we shoot people..."

For the most part, however, the dialog is very good. The screenplay, written by playwrights Dennis McIntyre and David Rabe (the latter uncredited), possesses the verve of writing for the stage. While the movie may be unconvincing scene by scene, the juicy language of the drunken, semiliterate characters holds our attention. In technical terms, STATE OF GRACE is impeccable, a great leap beyond Joanou's earlier work (THREE O'CLOCK HIGH; U2: RATTLE & HUM). Cameraman Jordan Cronenweth's camera movements and crisp photography of New York are assured; editor Claire Simpson's cutting is swift and razor sharp. Visually, STATE OF GRACE joins MILLER'S CROSSING as one of the best-looking movies in ages. But, as it nears its bloody ending, the film just gets dumber and dumber. (*Graphic violence, excessive profanity, nudity, substance abuse.*)

d, Phil Joanou; p, Ned Dowd, Randy Ostrow, and Ron Rotholz; w, Dennis McIntyre and David Rabe (Uncredited); ph, Jordan Cronenweth; ed, Claire Simpson; m, Ennio Morricone; md, Ennio Morricone; prod d, Patrizia Von Brandenstein and Doug Kraner; art d, Shawn Hausman and Timothy Galvin; set d, George DeTitta; spec, Al Griswold and William Traynor; stunts, Jery Hewitt; cos, Aude Bronson-Howard; makup, Bob Laden; tech, Tommy Sullivan

Crime   (PR:O   MPAA:R)

STEEL AND LACE

93m Cinema Home Video/Fries c

Clare Wren (*Gaily*), Bruce Davison (*Albert*), Stacy Haiduk (*Allison*), David Naughton (*Detective Dunn*), Michael Cerveris (*Daniel Emerson*), Scott

Burkholder *(Tobby)*, Paul Lieber *(Oscar)*, Brian Backer *(Norman)*, John J. York *(Craig)*, Nick Tate *(Duncan)*, David L. Lander *(Schumann)*, John DeMita, Brenda Swanson, Cindy Brooks, Hank Garrett, Beverly Mickins, William Prince, Mary Boucher, and Dave Edison

In this unlikely and largely unsuccessful B-movie marriage between ROBOCOP and THE ACCUSED, Clare Wren stars as the victim of a gang rape who commits suicide when her five attackers are freed, only to come back as an android to dispense her own form of robo-justice. Movie confusion from the film's porous script sets in almost from the fade-in, at the rape trial of real estate developer Danny Emerson (Micahel Cerveris). He is the only one on trial for raping Gaily (Wren), even though the flashbacks to the attack show four business partners participating in the brutal act. At the trial, the partners who inexplicably avoided being charged provide Danny with his alibi. Danny is acquitted, and Gaily, accompanied by her brother, Albert (Bruce Davison), a NASA scientist, exits the courtroom. Facing a crush of reporters, Gaily ducks into a stairwell while Albert tries to fend off the media representatives. Alone, Gaily climbs to the roof of the building, then jumps off as the late-arriving Albert looks on in horror. Five years later, Danny and his partners begin dying horrible deaths at the hands of the new, improved robo-Gaily created by Albert. Gaily's disembowelments, decapitations, and castrations are recorded on a self-contained video device to be played back for Albert. When not viewing his grisly handi-work, Albert occupies himself by trying to rebuild his career as a concert pianist. Problems arise for Albert when Dunn (David Naughton), the investigating officer on Gaily's rape case, and Allison (Stacy Haiduk), a sketch artist who covered Danny's trial, are reunited, become romantically involved, and begin to put together some clues which make it hot for Albert.

The special effects are pretty much the whole show here. Besides her arsenal of imaginative weapons, Gaily is also capable of completely changing her appearance, an ability that enables her to get close to her victims. But the film never really focuses on Gaily who, abused by males when she was alive, finds herself abused by another male, her own brother, after her death. Since Gaily is portrayed by several other actors and actresses over the course of the film, Wren is simply required to drift through her few appearances, looking sullen, de-pressed, and put-upon. Davison, who was nominated for a Best Supporting Actor Oscar in 1990 for LONGTIME COMPANION, is able to get surprising mileage out of his underwritten character, however, a role that faintly recalls his title role as the ruler of the rat kingdom in WILLARD. It's largely due to his work that the climax is more poignant than it deserves to be. On the strength of his performance and its thematic potential, however unrealized, STEEL AND LACE escapes complete movie oblivion, though not by much. *(Extreme violence, profanity, adult situations, nudity.)*

d, Ernest Farino; p, John Schouweiler and David DeCoteau; w, Joseph Dougherty and Dave Edison; ph, Thomas L. Callaway and Howard Wexler; ed, Chris Roth; m, John Massari; prod d, Blair Martin; spec, Jerry Macaluso and Roy Rnyrim; stunts, Chuck Borden; cos, Maria Aguilar; makup, Lorelei Loverde

Horror/Science Fiction   (PR:O MPAA:R)

STELLA

106m John Erman — Touchstone — Samuel Goldwyn/Buena Vista c

Bette Midler *(Stella Claire)*, John Goodman *(Ed Munn)*, Trini Alvarado *(Jenny Claire)*, Stephen Collins *(Dr. Stephen Dallas)*, Marsha Mason *(Janice Morrison)*, Eileen Brennan *(Mrs. Wilkerson)*, Linda Hart *(Debbie Whitman)*, Ben Stiller *(Jim Uptegrove)*, William McNamara *(Pat Robbins)*, John Bell *(Bob Morrison)*, Ashley Peldon *(Jenny, Age 3)*, Alisan Porter *(Jenny, Age 8)*, Kenneth Kimmins *(Security Guard)*, Bob Gerchen *(Bartender)*, Willie Rosario *(Dancing Waiter)*, Rex Robbins *(Minister)*, Ron White *(Tony De Banza)*, Matthew Cowles *(Sid)*, Justin Louis *(Cocaine Dealer)*, Peter MacNeill *(Bobby)*, Michael Hogan *(Billy)*, George Buza *(George)*, Eric Keenleyside *(Wendell)*, Catherine Robbin *(Leider Singer)*, Rob McClure *(Stephen's Friend)*, Sam Malkin *(Man in Theatre)*, Jayne Eastwood *(Nurse)*, Charles Gray *(Parent at PTA)*, Jon Kozak *(Mr. Wilkerson)*, Terrence Langevin *(Bingo Announcer)*, Elva Mai Hoover *(Mrs. Hough)*, Glynis Davies *(Mrs. Douglas)*, Philip Akin *(Police Officer)*, Jayne Rager, Megan Gallivan *(Preppy Girls)*, Todd Louiso, Jeff Nichols *(Preppy Boys)*, Christian Hoover, Philip Astor *(Bar Customers)*, Eve Crawford *(Janice's Secretary)*, Elizabeth Lennie *(Airline Reservation Clerk)*, Dwayne McLean *(Tom)*, Tedd Dillon *(Freddie)*, Jane Dingle *(Bingo Winner)*, and Jamie Shannon *(Teenage Heckler)*

The first question that this remake of the 1937 Barbara Stanwyck vehicle STELLA DALLAS brings to mind is: Why bother? Stanwyck's definitive version (which, along with THE LADY EVE and DOUBLE INDEMNITY, represented a career peak for her), directed by King Vidor, was already a remake of a 1925 silent that itself contained a legendary performance by Belle Bennett. Moreover, even back in 1937 the critics questioned the shameless hokum of this

bathetic tale of motherly sacrifice, although they were happy to succumb to Stanwyck's daringly extreme, gut-wrenching portrayal. Actresses possess nothing if not healthy egos, however, and Bette Midler seems to have had no trepidations in re-entering this well-trod ground with STELLA. Unfortunately, the filmmakers here seem to lack any notion of how to create a well-crafted vehicle, and the whole thing comes off as an uncertain, shoddy attempt to wring box-office dollars from sniffling audiences.

The story opens in 1969 (a favorite year in recent movie scripts), when Stella Claire (Midler) is a waitress in a small-town, upstate New York bar. While performing a rambunctious striptease parody for the patrons, she attracts the eye of Stephen Dallas (Stephen Collins), a handsome pre-med student. Despite her initial misgivings — the guy has "out of her league" written all over him — a night of love ensues and she soon finds herself pregnant. Not being one to take the easy road, she turns down Stephen's rather lackadaisical marriage proposal, deciding to raise the child on her own, and, through the years, baby Jenny (Trini Alvarado) grows up as Mama's pride and somewhat overprotected joy. Determined to keep her daughter away from the neighborhood riff-raff, Stella is happy to pack the young woman's bags for a vacation at Stephen's tony Manhattan domicile, now shared with his wife (Marsha Mason) and her son by a previous marriage. There, Jenny meets the scion of an upper-crust family (William McNamara), and she returns home dazzled with high-flown romantic possibilities. Stella sees the change in her and, after some parlor *Sturm und Drang*, makes the ultimate sacrifice, deciding to give Jenny up for good. As these things go, everyone concerned is incredibly understanding of the working-class Stella's desire to hold on to her kid — she has so little, after all — but Mother knows best, and Stella achieves final, complete maternal fulfillment when she lurks outside the Tavern on the Green restaurant, watching Jenny marry her rather fey prince.

Aside from some pseudofeminist sentiments voiced by the pregnant Stella early in the film (wherein she bewails the excess of unappetizing choices offered her as an unmarried mother, from abortion to adoption), screenwriter Robert Getchell has made little attempt to update the material. The best filmed soap operas — including Bette Davis' DARK VICTORY (1939), Margaret Sullavan's BACK STREET (1941), Olivia de Havilland's TO EACH HIS OWN (1946), and Stanwyck's STELLA DALLAS — were cannily engineered to have a night-marish inevitability, each masochistic effect carefully inserted for maximum tear-jerking potential. STELLA plays like a warped record, with artificially bravura moments springing out of nowhere, while the calmer sequences are suffused by a treacly, bathetic sentimentality. The camera continually lingers a beat too long on the aftermaths of big dramatic scenes, followed by even slower fades. This inadvertently gives the audience too much time to anticipate (and dread) the next feeble emotional assault. Even the familiar story's famous birthday party scene is robbed of whatever pathetic delicacy it might have, because of a gratuitous shot of some boys mooning Stella and Jenny.

Midler gives a sloppy, inattentive performance, worse than any of her previous screen appearances. Can this possibly be the same woman who shook the heavens in THE ROSE and could knock you out of your seat in live performance? Midler's acting here makes even her work in BEACHES seem a miracle of freshness. As Stella, she employs a wispy, little-girl voice that every now and then remembers to assume some kind of regional accent — presumably meant to sound working-class (four dialect coaches are listed in the credits). In her tearfully sacrificial exchanges with Alvarado, she comes perilously close to Joan Crawford-style grimacing, and her feigned insensitivity in the big get-outta-my-life scene with her daughter is facile, one-level acting devoid of subtext. (The scene is further falsified when, incredibly, Stella hurls a bottle that just misses Jenny's head.) Stanwyck set the tone for her characterization in the very first scenes; her Stella was flashily ambitious and vulgar and completely un-apologetic, which made her eventual self-realization all the more heartbreaking. Midler, once motherhood takes hold, is a mousy, puritanical drag, forever alone and stitching at something in the dark. Her brassier moments — the striptease, her telling off a young thug who has come to woo Jenny, and, especially, her psychedelically attired cavorting in Florida that horrifies her daughter's set (and plays like a rejected number from her stage act) — are totally out of character. Such mixed signals are, of course, partly the fault of the slovenly filmmaking (in which even Stella's famed penchant for gaudy outfits is confused: a Christmas reunion with Stephen has her suddenly appearing in perfect, matronly elegance, after having rid her dress of an obstreperous spangle), but Midler also seems curiously hesitant to go all the way with the role — the only way it could possibly work — and her final scene is a pale imitation of Stanwyck's indelible hankie-chewing, ecstatic image.

Alvarado, a dark beauty, does what she can with the basically impossible part of the daughter, who, in all versions, is scripted as a blindly insensitive princess who gets it all in the end. Collins is far more attractive than the gruesomely complacent John Boles was in 1937, but is undone by his repeated, smarmy exhortations to Alvarado to "put [her] head right here" (pointing to his shoulder). Marsha Mason lacks the languid hauteur of Alice Joyce (1925) and Barbara O'Neil (1937) that would make her an effective contrast to Stella, and is predictable in a predictable part, while the near-ubiquitous John Goodman — appearing in Alan Hale's old role as Stella's vulgarian friend—is particularly demeaned by the film. Ben Stiller (son of Stiller and Meara) brings some menacing life to his punk role in a ludicrous "just-say-no" drug episode involving a momentarily confused Jenny, but Eileen Brennan, in a bit part as a disapproving snob, disappears from the film after Midler gets to insult her with a patented bitchy remark. *(Profanity, substance abuse, adult situations, sexual situations.)*

d, John Erman; p, Samuel Goldwyn Jr.; w, Robert Getchell (based on the novel *Stella Dallas* by Olive Higgins Prouty); ph, Billy Williams; ed, Jerrold L. Ludwig; m, John Morris; prod d, James Hulsey; art d, Jeffrey Ginn; set d, Steve Shewchuk; spec, Doug Graham; stunts, Jack Gill; cos, Theodora Van Runkle; makeup, Suzanne Benoit, Richard Blair, and Bob Mills; chor, Pat Birch

Drama (PR:C MPAA:PG-13)

STEPHEN KING'S GRAVEYARD SHIFT

(SEE: GRAVEYARD SHIFT)

STRAPLESS

(Brit.) 97m Granada—Film Four/Gavin c

Blair Brown *(Dr. Lillian Hempel)*, Bruno Ganz *(Raymond Forbes)*, Bridget Fonda *(Amy Hempel)*, Alan Howard *(Mr. Cooper)*, Michael Gough *(Douglas Brodie)*, Hugh Laurie *(Colin)*, Suzanne Burden *(Romaine Salmon)*, Camille Coduri *(Mrs. Clark)*, Gary O'Brien *(Mr. Clark)*, Julian Bunster *(Carlos)*, Imogen Annesley *(Imogen)*, Ann Firbank *(Daphne Brodie)*, Rohan McCullough *(Annie Rice)*, Joe Hare *(Richard Forbes)*, and Alexandra Pigg *(Helen)*

From the writer of PLENTY and writer-director of WETHERBY, British playwright David Hare, comes yet another decidedly odd but utterly irresistible study of isolation, loneliness, and strength. Blair Brown, Hare's longtime companion, stars as a slightly less neurotic, though considerably more successful, variation of the character she portrays in the critically acclaimed TV series "Days and Nights of Molly Dodd." A cancer specialist and expatriate American, Dr. Lillian Hempel (Brown) is unstinting in her care and support of her patients at the government-run British hospital where she works. But her emotional life is constricted and repressed. A long-term visit from her younger sister (Bridget Fonda) is turning into a comedy of horrors as Lillian's fastidiousness clashes hard and often with the free, easy, and sloppy ways of her sister. As the film begins, Lillian is on vacation, visiting "every church in Europe" by herself, when she drops a handkerchief that is retrieved by Raymond Forbes. Wonderfully portrayed by Bruno Ganz, Raymond is like a character from bad romantic pulp fiction. Shady and shadowy, he is an unabashed romantic who, he tells Lillian, lives for the anticipation of love, freely given. Lillian is enchanted but cautious, accepting Raymond's invitation to tour the church and have lunch with him. But she balks at a later rendezvous at his hotel and returns to England without giving him her address. Back home and back at work, Lillian must cope with a young, robust patient laid low by a tumor on his spine. She gently urges him to accept radiation and chemotherapy, explaining that, while the tumor is malignant and incurable, the therapy will ease his suffering. The patient becomes less cooperative, however, as the traumatic side-effects of the treatment reduce him to a wan shadow of his former self. Lillian's other problems include coping with severe cutbacks at her hospital and with her fellow doctors, who are urging her to lead a public protest against the cutbacks; at home, Lillian's sister has turned the apartment into a fashion photo studio while tentatively considering a career in dress designing. Soon Raymond abruptly shows up on Lillian's doorstep, having obtained her home address from a hotel where she stayed. He has brought with him a most unusual gift, a horse. (Lillian spoke about her love of riding during their conversation on the Continent.) Raymond begins courting Lillian in earnest, but when he proposes marriage, Lillian again balks, though she agrees to move in with him. Raymond's idea of playing house turns out to be an extended stay at a casino-hotel that ends on an ominous note when he bounces a check in attempting to cover his betting losses. Lillian makes good on Raymond's bad check and returns home. There she finds messes in her apartment and in the personal life of her sister, who is pregnant by an Argentine designer who has since deserted her and gone home. In the face of the mounting chaos in her life, Lillian suffers a minor breakdown. She chastises her sister for daring to bring a baby into the world when she can't even keep an apartment clean. She also impulsively agrees to marry Raymond, who carries over his romantic excesses into their domestic life. When Lillian protests, Raymond goes out for a walk and never returns. It later turns out that Raymond has bought all the gifts he's given Lillian on credit, and Lillian is forced to empty her bank account to pay off the debts. Now it's her sister's turn to chastise Lillian, for giving her heart to a scoundrel. Lillian attempts to track down Raymond, only to find out that she is not the first to have fallen under Raymond's spell. But she also discovers a lack of regret, both within herself and in Raymond's other "victims." Raymond, she is told by one of them, "truly loves women, and that's rare in a man." Lillian

returns to England, takes her young patient off therapy so he can die with dignity and agrees to lead a campaign against the government cutbacks. At home, meanwhile, she finds that her sister has somewhat ironically put her life in order for the sake of her baby. At the same time, she is launching a promising line of strapless gowns. "I don't know what holds them up," she says. "But they do stay up."

That sentiment is evidently meant to apply to Lillian's life and the lives of women in general. STRAPLESS is an ode to both independence and interdependence. While Lillian's repression and forced isolation lead her to be seduced by Raymond's romanticism, her independent strength allows her to take the experience on its own terms and use it to enrich her own life. That strength leads her to break out of her shell and become a participant in the lives around her. At the same time, her sister learns from Lillian the need to pull back and tend to her inner needs to make a proper environment for her new baby.

In spite of its dreamy allegorical tone and terse political overtones, STRAPLESS is anything but dour and preachy. Instead it is alive with feeling, empathy, and outright wonder for its characters and their world. Though beautifully controlled under Hare's direction, STRAPLESS is full of poignant, human moments of precise observation, gentle comedy and penetrating drama. It's also full of exquisite performances, especially from Brown, Ganz, and Fonda, who make the most of the rich roles Hare has written for them. They all help to make STRAPLESS a quietly quirky and deliciously heartwarming piece of filmmaking. *(Adult situations.)*

d, David Hare; p, Rick McCallum; w, David Hare; ph, Andrew Dunn; ed, Edward Marnier; m, Nick Bicat; prod d, Roger Hall

Drama (PR:C MPAA:R)

STREET ASYLUM

94m Metropolis-Hit/Magnum c

Wings Hauser *(Sgt. Arliss Ryder)*, Alex Cord *(Capt. Bill Quinton)*, Roberta Vasquez *(Kristin)*, G. Gordon Liddy *(Jim Miller)*, Marie Chambers *(Dr. Weaver Cane)*, Sy Richardson *(Sgt. Tatum)*, Jess Doran *(Det. Stoddard)*, Jesse Aragon *(Rosie Raton Lopez)*, Brion James *(Reverend Mony)*, Lisa Robbins *(Burney)*, Lisa Marlowe, Galen Yuen, James Bershad, William Shockley, and Harry Harte-Browne

STREET ASYLUM stirred up a bit of interest when convicted Watergate conspirator G. Gordon Liddy, a supporting actor in the film, refused to help publicize the picture. Supposedly the finished film offended Liddy's right-wing sensibilities. In any case, the brouhaha made news nationwide, Liddy later reportedly withdrew his opposition, STREET ASYLUM extended its theatrical run before coming out on video, and the film's publicists probably ended up buying each other drinks in celebration. But what of STREET ASYLUM itself? Well, let's just say Liddy's sensibilities aren't the only ones that will be offended by this offering from director Greggory Brown.

Liddy plays Los Angeles Police Chief Jim Miller, a man with totalitarian political ambitions and a taste for sado-masochism. Most of the time he sits in his whip-and-chain festooned lair and beholds the action unfolding on video monitors. Tough cop Arliss Ryder (Wings Hauser) cruises the mean streets, and during a "routine" call (a runaway billed as "Teen Jesus" has crucified himself on a rooftop TV antenna), he is shot and wounded by Miller's henchmen. Ryder wakes up in a police-run clinic, where surgeon Weaver Cane (Marie Chambers) has treated Ryder's injury as a pretext for attaching something to his spine. Subsequently, Ryder is invited to join Miller's pet project, the Strike SQUAD (Scum Quelling Urban Assault Division), an elite force of policemen, all recently wounded, all treated at that clinic, all raving psychotics. Ryder's fellow SQUAD members run amok, killing suspects and innocent bystanders, before dying themselves under suspicious circumstances. Ryder feels his own personality gravitating toward violence (yet the numbskull continues to return to Cane for mysterious regular treatments), and the very evident changes in his demeanor repel his kickboxing girl friend, Kristin (Roberta Vasquez). Overcome by these violent urges, Ryder rapes a prostitute, but in the process he learns that Miller may be behind the SQUAD's high mortality rate. Sneaking into the chief's office, Ryder finds X-rays revealing the electronic spinal implants, which (as you have probably already guessed) turn ordinary cops into ultraviolent vigilantes. Ryder has Kristin cut the implant out of his spine; then the cop fakes a suicide to throw off Miller's spies. Meanwhile, the outraged citizens have rioted against the brutal police, and the SQUAD is out conducting massacres in response. As a result the police station is nearly deserted when Ryder and Kristin infiltrate it. The sequence that follows is hilarious; Ryder knows of Miller's fondness for bondage, so he has the faithful Kristin dress up as a dominatrix and approach the villain. Kristin takes a whip to Miller, much to his delight, though he's considerably less pleased when Ryder appears. The two battle and Miller winds up electrocuted inside a satellite dish. However, an epilog states that SQUADs are being prepared in several other states.

Director Brown and producer Walter Gernert are perhaps better known as "the Dark Brothers," the evocative sobriquet they used as the makers of adult film and videos. But with STREET ASYLUM and their previous mainstream effort, DEAN MAN WALKING (which also starred Wings Hauser), Brown and Gernert have successfully tapped into a subgenre of violent sci-fi action films that revel in the cynical mistrust of authority. "Don't go knockin' off da middle class...or else," foams a SQUAD cop, and after Liddy's snub, the filmmakers announced that some box-office receipts would be donated to the American Civil Liberties Union. But whatever political fires STREET ASYLUM was meant to light, they're soon extinguished in a miasma of sleaze.

It doesn't help that Hauser's character is terribly slow to figure out what's going on; he has to watch not one, but two successive partners go berserk and die before he suspects something's wrong about that clinic. Still, the filmmakers manage to create an appropriately lurid atmosphere, greatly aided by Paul Desatoff's vivid city-after-dark photography and a special "sound design" by Leonard Marcel that offers a continuous undercurrent of low-level, almost subliminal noise, including garbled music and news broadcasts detailing grotesque crimes (one of which involves a kid who says he chopped up his grandmother at the behest of Mr. Ed the Talking Horse). Though these effects are evidently intended to depict Ryder's descent into madness, an hour of this stuff will make any viewer wish he had a *Playboy* Playmate girl friend with a knack for kitchen-table neurosurgery. Another audio gimmick bookends the story, a radio phone-in show on which Miller's spokesman defends the chief's policies while citizens of diverse political and sexual orientations call up to spew their hatred. Maybe for their next production Gernert and Brown can recruit Henry Kissinger. (*Excessive violence, profanity, nudity, adult situations, sexual situations.*)

d, Greggory Brown; p, Walter D. Gernert; w, John Powers (based on a story by Greggory Brown); ph, Paul Desatoff; ed, Kert Vander Meulen; m, Leonard Marcel; prod d, Robert Fox; cos, Dorothy Amos; makup, Angela Levin

Science Fiction   **(PR:O   MPAA:NR)**

STREET LEGAL

(SEE: LAST OF THE FINEST)

STREETS

83m Concorde c

Christina Applegate (*Dawn*), David Mendenhall (*Sy*), Eb Lottimer (*Lumley*), Patrick Richwood (*Bob*), Kady Tran (*Dawn's Blonde Roommate*), Starr Andreeff (*Policewoman on Horse*), Julie Jay (*Dawn's Tatooed Roommate*), Mel Castelo (*Elf*), Alan Stock (*Allen*), Rhetta Green (*Paramedic*), and Kay Lenz (*Lieutenant*)

Director Katt Shea Ruben's string of B movies—STREETS is her fourth—for producer Roger Corman continue to herald a major talent in the making. Christina Applegate—almost unrecognizable here to those who know her as the curvaceous Kelly on the Fox sitcom "Married with Children"—plays Dawn, a heroin-addicted LA teenage hooker who meets up with Sy (David Mendenhall), a fresh-scrubbed suburban teen who's ridden down from Santa Barbara (on his bike!) for the weekend with the vague idea of becoming a Hollywood rock star. His dreams begin turning to disillusionment pretty much from the start, when he begins his LA visit by saving Dawn from a gun-toting trick who takes violent exception when Dawn refuses to deliver as much as he thinks he's paid for. Having been marked by some nasty fingernail scratches, the trick spends the rest of the film hunting Dawn to get murderous revenge. While they evade the killer, Dawn gives Sy a hellish tour of LA street life. And it's no place for kids, to say the least. Dawn lives in a drainage pipe with some friends, including a hardened 11-year-old she tries vainly to keep off the streets. News of another girl's murder in a motel room inspires not mourning, but a fast trip to the motel to recover whatever usable belongings might have been left behind. It's at the motel that Sy learns of Dawn's addiction, "inherited" from her streetwalker mother, who has abandoned Dawn. After taking what she needs, Dawn delivers the remainder of the cache to the "troglodytes," a group of younger kids living in another drain pipe, who, like Dawn, are sometimes protected by Bob (Patrick Richwood, outstanding here—as he was playing the elevator operator in PRETTY WOMAN), another goofy street kid. As the killer closes in on the young couple, Sy is mugged, losing his wallet and his bike. In the meantime, Dawn is distracted by a trick who inadvertently puts her in danger from the killer, who has been eliminating her friends one by one in gruesome fashion while hunting for her.

In her first three films—STRIPPED TO KILL 1 and 2 and DANCE OF THE DAMNED—Ruben, along with her writer-producer husband, Andy Ruben, effectively mixed stylish genre storytelling with a realistic, sympathetic look at the world of bar dancers, a world rarely treated with either realism or sympathy in mainstream American films. Here she turns her distincive attention to runaway and abandoned street kids, with equally effective results. Ruben's approach is

an odd, but undeniably original, mixture of hardboiled toughness and streetwise humaneness. Her films have the style and feeling of moviemaking on the run. Never quite polished or neatly resolved, they are intriguing and memorable precisely because they do not resort to heavyhanded, editorial-page moralizing. Open-ended and ambiguous, they are alive in ways that exploitation films rarely are.

A weakness of STREETS is that its thriller and realistic subplots are a somewhat uneasy mix. The motivation for the killer's pursuit of Dawn and Sy is simply a given based on scenes showing the killer to be some kind of sadomasochistic psycho. Ironically, in a less ambitious film, this might have been enough. But here, Ruben etches such compelling, multidimensional supporting characters in the street kids that it's hard not to feel a little frustrated by the sketchiness of the killer, especially since the real perils these kids face every moment would have been more than enough to make for a compelling drama. The kids' street life here resembles nothing so much as a kind of latter-day THE GRAPES OF WRATH, in which these sorry descendants of the Joads are cast adrift in a craven new world of hard drugs, hard sex, and harder violence. Part of nobody's idea of a kinder and gentler nation, it's a subculture whose very existence should shame us all. Ruben doesn't point a finger, though; what comes across more strongly is the resilience of her characters' hard-edged humanity in a world not fit for animals. The Rubens may never get the call from Spielberg to write and direct ET 2; their vision are too tough and uncompromising to suit big-budget urban cartoons like LETHAL WEAPON. But they are genuine cinematic street poets, and, as such, are in a class by themselves. (*Violence, profanity, adult situations.*)

d, Katt Shea Ruben; p, Andy Ruben; w, Katt Shea Ruben and Andy Ruben; ph, Phedon Papamichael; ed, Stephen Mark; m, Aaron Davis; prod d, Virginia Lee; art d, Johan Le Tenoux; set d, Abigail Scheuer; cos, Fionn

Thriller   **(PR:O   MPAA:R)**

STRIKE IT RICH

87m British Screen—BBC—Ideal—Flamingo/Millimeter c

(AKA: LOSER TAKE ALL)

Molly Ringwald (*Cary Porter*), Robert Lindsay (*Ian Bertram*), John Gielgud (*Herbert Dreuther*), Max Wall (*Bowles*), Simon de la Brosse (*Philippe*), Margi Clarke (*Bowles' Nurse*), Vladek Sheybal (*Kinski*), Michel Blanc (*Hotel Manager*), Frances De La Tour (*Mrs. De Vere*), Gerard Dimiglio (*Henri*), Stephen Marlowe (*Head Waiter*), Nadio Fortune (*Wine Waiter*), Yves Aubert (*Waiter*), Terence Beesley (*Croupier*), John C.P. Mattocks (*Fat Man*), Lawrence Davidson (*Receptionist*), Su Yong (*Chinese Woman*), Claude LeSache (*Man with Chips*), Patrick Holt (*Man with Wink*), Stephen Gressieux (*Casino Attendant*), Margaret Clifton (*Old Lady*), Jack Raymond (*Cashier at Casino*), Marius Goring (*Blixon*), Richenda Carey (*Miss Bullen*), Godfrey Talbot (*Naismith*), Tim Seely (*Arnold*), Victoria Wicks (*Jane Truefitt*), John Otway (*Harry Truefitt*), Nicolas Mead (*Barman in Hotel*), Jeffrey Robert (*Bus Conductor*), David Marrick (*Hotel Waiter*), Marianne Price (*Bus Conductor*), Al Fiorentini (*Lift Man at Hotel*), Willie Ross (*Man at Theater*), Joseph Arton (*Small Boy*), Ben Feitelson (*Man with Gold Bracelet*), Mark Tandy (*Mat at Sitra*), Harriet Reynolds (*Telephonist at Sitra*), John Serret (*Ticket Clerk*), Anthony Collin (*Man of Odd Couple*), and Christine Hewett (*Lady of Odd Couple*)

Set in 1956, STRIKE IT RICH is the story of Ian Bertram (Robert Lindsay), a bored accountant with the huge London firm of Sitra, and his relationship with Cary Porter (Molly Ringwald), a British-born American. After several chance meetings, Ian and Cary decide to marry, planning a quiet ceremony in the small town of Bournemouth. Before his vacation, however, Ian is called into Sitra's dreaded Room 10, the office of his boss, Herbert Dreuther (John Gielgud). After correcting a mathematical problem (Ian is a whiz at numbers) and making a strong first impression (he and Dreuther have the same tastes in poetry), Ian is invited to have his marriage ceremony at Dreuther's expense in Monte Carlo, and afterwards to honeymoon aboard Dreuther's large yacht. Ian and Cary accept this generous invitation, of course, and head off to Monte Carlo. After the wedding (which Dreuther seems to have forgotten to attend) they laze about in the lap of luxury at the Hotel de Paris. While Cary eats rolls and sightsees, Ian spends his time at the roulette tables, and when the couple discovers that—thanks to Dreuther's having abandoned them—they have run out of money, Ian decides to devise the perfect mathematical system to win at roulette. He soon wins more money than he ever dreamed of, but in the process he has become an arrogant, vengeful jerk. Blinded by greed, he sets out to tip the scales of power at Sitra by buying all of the stock owned by a key shareholder (Max Wall), then to fire Dreuther. Appalled, Cary leaves him for a quiet Frenchman (Simon de la Brosse) she met in the casino. Ian wins her back, but only after he throws away all of his new wealth, after which the pair sails off on Dreuther's yacht.

STRIKE IT RICH is stupefying and tedious in every way. The film's message (money corrupts, and can't buy happiness) has been done to death, its central relationship is boring (Lindsay and Ringwald display absolutely no chemistry), and the direction by James Scott, full of soft-focus shots and stock footage, is stiff. (Scott also wrote the screenplay, adapted from Graham Greene's *Loser Takes All*.) The pacing is leaden: major events (including Ian and Cary's courtship, their marriage, and the trip to Monte Carlo) fly by in the first few minutes, while the final half is devoted to repetitive gambling sequences and slow plot developments. Reaching desperately for a romantic, lush tone, director Scott never gets past the artificial gloss of the cheap sets and painfully bright photography (though, inexplicably, the opening five minutes are in black and white). The tone ranges from strained romance to strained comedy (sometimes unnecessarily cruel comedy) and none of the elements seem to connect in a true romantic comedy. Scott cut his teeth in documentary filmmaking, and STRIKE IT RICH, at times, feels like a documentary; with its useless voice-overs and travelog footage, the film has no cohesive narrative structure and simply provides a stream of boring data.

The actors seem completely lost in all of this, especially Ringwald, whose sweet-sixteen mannerisms have become increasingly annoying. She gives a stilted performance, sorely lacking in the alluring sexuality needed for her character. Lindsay fares better, and although he is essentially playing Jonathan Pryce's character from BRAZIL (which seems to have been a major influence on Scott), he manages to add a few genuine quirks of his own. Nonetheless, his work is overwhelmed by the script's cliched dialog and thin character development. Gielgud appears to be in it for the paycheck, while the supporting performances of Wall and de la Brosse are simply impenetrable. Boring and repetitive, STRIKE IT RICH is a messy piece of filmmaking that can be added to the increasing and varied list of Ringwald's duds. *(Adult situations, profanity.)*

d, James Scott; p, Christine Oestreicher and Graham Easton; w, James Scott (based on the novel *Loser Takes All* by Graham Greene); ph, Robert Paynter; ed, Thomas Schwalm; prod d, Christopher Hobbs; art d, Mike Buchanan; set d, Christopher Hobbs; cos, Tom Rand; makeup, Paul Hay

Comedy/Romance (PR:C MPAA:PG)

STUFF STEPHANIE IN THE INCINERATOR

97m Troma/Allied c

Catherine Dee *(Stephanie/Casey)*, Willian Dame *(Paul/Jared)*, M.R. Murphy *(Roberta/Robert)*, Dennis Cunningham *(Nick/Rory)*, Paul Nielsen *(Henchman/Butler)*, Andy Milk *(Henchman/Chauffeur)*, Phil Vincent *(Bad-Tempered Man)*, Paula Lee Gangemi *(Instructor)*, Nicola Kerwin *(Woman Holding Photos)*, Judy St. James *(Woman With Nail File)*, Neil McHarry *(Cyclist)*, and Karen A. Santos *(Woman With Towel)*

STUFF STEPHANIE IN THE INCINERATOR is such a complex Chinese puzzle box of a movie it's difficult to summarize the plot with clarity. A weird little item, STEPHANIE is a horror film within a black comedy within a satire of the actor's psyche. As the film opens, William Dame, an airplane mechanic, is kidnaped by two men and brought to a strange, sealed house, where he's paired with Catherine Dee, a demure girl kept under the watchful eye of her repressed female guardian, Murphy. Much to his apparent shock, Dame becomes a pawn in a psychosexual game in which Murphy—who is able to monitor the entire house—hopes to watch him have sex with the young maiden. During an escape attempt, Dame and Dee actually do make love, never realizing that Murphy has been watching all along. (Since it's apparent that a male actor, Murphy, is playing the female voyeur, the viewer is kept disquietingly off-guard throughout these proceedings.) Peeping Thomasina threatens to kill Dee if Dame doesn't go to bed with the girl; however, at this point, we learn that Dame and Dee are *really* an eccentric rich couple who have hired Murphy as an actor in their perverse sexual charade. Driving to the small local airport to drop off the actor, the couple stops at a gas station, where Dee makes a play for attendant Dennis Cunningham. Later, with all the outside players paid off, the isolated, jaded couple bickers at home. Dee is weary of her hubby's masquerades and doesn't want to dress up as Beethoven's wench; unfortunately, Dame holds all the purse strings, and she complies. That night, a prowler enters—it's Murphy. Informed by Dee that everything of value is stashed away, he is drawn into Dee's newly hatched plot to ice her mate, and soon the unscrupulous Murphy launches his own counterplan, enlisting the aid of Vincent—who owns a van and can help him transport the couple's furniture out of their mansion—to carry out his scheme. While Dame dreams of his new theatrical game, to be based on *Robinson Crusoe*, Dee awaits Murphy's return. Together, the conspirators enter the master bedroom and viciously club a body sleeping under the blanket. Without looking underneath the comforter, the adulterous killers drag the corpse away. Some shocks are in store for them, however, since (1) the body in the blanket is garage mechanic Cunningham, whom Dee seduced earlier, (2) Murphy had planned not only to bump off Dame, but also to stuff Dee in the incinerator, and (3) the wily Dame is about to take a cue from THE MOST DANGEROUS GAME and give his wife and her lover a taste of their own lethal medicine. Now the film launches

into a simultaneously funny and chilling flight pattern, as the would-be assassins scramble for cover and tentatively join forces to outwit Dame. At the climax, Murphy is stabbed in the back, Dame heads menacingly for Dee, Murphy revives and forces Dame into an Iron Maiden intended for Dee, Dee is crushed to death by a household elevator, and Murphy collapses. At least, that's what we *think* has happened . . . until we realize that the trio of protagonists are actually fanatical acting buffs who have staged all the preceding theatricals for their own twisted amusement. Props are dismantled and carted away, points of the "game" are discussed, and fond farewells are exchanged. In a final twist, Dame and Cunningham drive off together—apparently they are the lovers, not Dee and Dame, as we have been led to believe throughout.

Outlandish and unremittingly clever, this film-within-a-film-within-another-film is stylized, theatrical fun in the tradition of DEATHTRAP and SLEUTH. The movie fails to explore the deeper psychological question of why its characters are driven to play roles in the first place (as in the truly disturbing NEGATIVES), but it does succeed in gleefully fooling its audience as it indulges in a marathon of staged murder and mayhem. Although the cinematography lacks the Hollywood sparkle upon which this kind of escapism thrives, and although the direction doesn't maximize the potential of the screenplay in the opening scenes, STEPHANIE manages the difficult feat of being both suspenseful and maliciously funny. Witty lines abound in this oddball journey into the actor's obsessive psyche, while the structure of the movie is particularly admirable as it folds in upon itself, shifting our expectations at every turn. Especially smashing is the film's metamorphosis, from a sick black comedy about the murderous upper classes into a mischievous spoof that lampoons mystery movies and deftly satirizes the mystique of acting. Called upon to enact this send-up of their vocation, several minor players ham it up a bit, but the three principals are splendid. Dee is convincingly ethereal or cunningly seductive as required, Dame conveys both macho authority and daffy derangement, and Murphy spans the sexes with aplomb as both the two-timing killer and the sinister spinster Roberta.

Though comedy-mysteries sometimes cheat their audiences by deliberately planting red herrings, this tale of the Games People Play works by simply showing us "everything," without correcting our false impression of what is being shown. At its most enjoyable, STUFF STEPHANIE IN THE INCINERATOR allows the viewer to enter into its sense of make-believe and to enjoy being hoodwinked. It's equal parts Grand Guignol about the perils of unfaithfulness, comedy of manners among the wacky rich, and spiky satire of the actor's lust to lose his or her identity. Sheer nastiness has never been so much fun. *(Profanity, violence, sexual situations.)*

d, Don Nardo; p, Don Nardo; w, Don Nardo and Peter Jones; ph, Herb Fuller; ed, James Napoli; cos, Iris Klesert and Kay Traywick

Comedy/Horror/Mystery (PR:C MPAA:PG-13)

SUMMER VACATION: 1999

(Japan) 90m New Century/CBS-SONY c

(1999—NEN NO NATSU YASUMI)

Eri Miyajima *(Yu/Kaoru)*, Tomoko Otakara *(Kazuhiko)*, Miyuki Nakano *(Naoto)*, and Rie Mizuhara *(Norio)*

An idyllic countryside provides the picturesque backdrop for this psychosexual Japanese drama concerning four teenage boys left alone for the summer at a boarding school. The boys, all orphans with no one to go home to during their vacation, are at the height of the androgynous, sexually ambiguous stage with which adolescence begins—a murky territory made even more so by the casting of teenage girls in the roles of the boys.

The film begins with a dramatic nighttime sequence in which Yu (Eri Miyajima), in the throes of unrequited love, dives off a cliff into the rippling waters of the lake below. This fall to death has its desired effect: Kazuhiko (Tomoko Otakara) the object of his affection, can never again ignore Yu, nor the urgency of Yu's feelings for him. As Kazuhiko says, now Yu will always have a place in his heart. The remaining three boys spend their time in front of their homemade computers, doing endless mathematical problems, and take turns cooking for each other (using such state-of-the-art equipment as a machine that cracks eggs and separates the insides). This serene, if slightly sterile, world is disturbed by the arrival of Kaoru (also played by Eri Miyajima) the spitting image of Yu. The other boys are understandably upset by the look-alike newcomer, who claims he has arrived early in preparation for the next term. Kaoru's arrival serves to unearth the layers of forbidden passion and deceit among the boys, who feel that the new boy's presence in the physical form of Yu—though his personality is clearly more outgoing and confident than that of their former schoolmate— must be a form of intervention by some higher power. It is as if Yu's spirit cannot rest until all of the repressed sexuality and shackled emotions are freed. Slowly, the boys get used to Kaoru. When Kaoru rushes home upon hearing the news of his mother's death, Kazuhiko, by now smitten, follows Kaoru and spends the night comforting him. However, one of the other boys had already caught Kaoru faking phone calls to his "mother." Kaoru finally admits that he is indeed Yu, and, threatened by a jealous rival for Kazuhiko's affections, makes a lovers' leap with his friend off the cliff. This time, Yu/Kaoru does not survive, though the other boys manage to rescue Kazuhiko. The film ends as another incarnation of Yu arrives at the school, in a frame-by-frame reenactment of Kaoru's arrival. This time, the boys smile knowingly at this boy who looks like Yu, who grins right back at them.

Director Shusuke Kaneko has created a visually stylish film, set in a boarding school that, except for the futuristic gadgetry, seems locked in the Victorian era. This sterile, indoor environment is juxtaposed with beautiful photography of the Japanese countryside. But while technically accomplished, SUMMER VACATION: 1999 lacks the spark that would raise it above the level of a curio. The film seems to be striving for the combined effect of Peter Brook's LORD OF THE FLIES and Peter Weir's PICNIC AT HANGING ROCK, but doesn't achieve the power of either of these films. The casting of teenage girls in the roles of boys initially pays off, but loses some of its clever charm as the story proceeds, when viewers may feel that Kaneko is winking at his audience too much. *(Sexual situations.)*

d, Shusuke Kaneko; p, Naoya Narita and Mitsuhisa Hida; w, Rio Kishida; ph, Kenji Takama; ed, Isao Tomita; m, Yuriko Nakamura; art d, Shu Yamaguchi

Drama   (PR:O   MPAA:NR)

SURVIVAL QUEST

90m Starway/MGM-UA c

Lance Henriksen *(Hank Chambers)*, Dermot Mulroney *(Gray Atkinson)*, Traci Lin *(Olivia)*, Mark Rolston *(Jake Cannon)*, Ben Hammer *(Hal)*, Catharine Keener *(Cheryl)*, Steve Antin *(Raider)*, Paul Provenza *(Joey)*, Dominic Hoffman *(Jeff)*, Ken Daley *(Checker)*, Michael Allen Ryder *(Harper)*, Reggie Bannister *(Pilot)*, Brooke Bundy, and Carol Kottenbrook

SURVIVAL QUEST earned its only superlative when a critic called it "one of the least visible movies ever to bear the fabled MGM logo." After the briefest of theatrical releases, it came out on videocassette in a double bill with another forgettable wilderness adventure, DAMNED RIVER. SURVIVAL QUEST follows two sets of campers into California's Sierra Madre Mountain. One group is the Blue Legion, a gun-happy squad of teenaged boys under the command of tyrannical survivalist Jake Cannon (Mark Rolston). The other bunch, Survival Quest, is a sort of backpacking self-help group led by humane mountain man Hank Chambers (Lance Henriksen). The beneficiaries of Hank's wisdom include smart-aleck Joey (Paul Provenza), Cheryl (Catharine Keener), a fragile divorcee, and Gray (Dermot Mulroney), an alienated convict. Through various exercises and object lessons beneath the sheltering pines, firm-but-gentle Hank teaches this crew to "strive as one and not to yield." Meanwhile, Jake has made harassment of the Survival Questers part of his curriculum, but when one ill-mannered junior storm trooper called Raider (Steve Antin) ends up shooting Hank, this breach of discipline annoys Jake to no end. He starts to beat his overzealous charge, but Raider responds by "fragging" his commander and blaming the murder on the Survival Questers. Now led by Raider, the Blue Legion aims to kill the rival campers (first executing the few Blue Legionnaires who want to negotiate a truce). The Survival Quest gang, with Cheryl in charge, hang together and race over the river and through the woods to get to the nearest airstrip. There, Gray tricks the bloodthirsty Legionnaires into coming near an inflammable fuel tank, and as the odor of fried fascists rises on the breeze, a plane appears. On board is Hank, who managed to overcome his grievous wound and signal for help.

Written and directed by B-movie maven Don Coscarelli (creator of the "Phantasm" series), SURVIVAL QUEST is a dim but passable diversion. The notion of a mismatched bunch learning to cooperate and surmount terrible obstacles is an old formula, but it still works, even though these characters are pretty flat—their stereotyped introductions recalling a 1970s disaster movie. Fortunately, the very capable Henriksen is around to add flavor. With his leathery voice and larger-than-life warmth, he's the best thing in the picture. Regrettably, Rolston, another strong personality (who teamed with Henriksen in ALIENS), is permitted to display only the very least of his acting abilities; his character is basically a walking cartoon. Watching Hank's cooperative crew triumph over Jake's psycho platoon should be satisfying, but the film actually starts to lose interest once the bloodshed begins, mainly because Henriksen and Rolston are out of the picture. The action scenes are nothing special, and one stunt involving a log teetering on the edge of the waterfall looks like a playground ride. SURVIVAL QUEST was filmed in 1986, but Coscarelli took a hiatus from the post-production work when the chance arose to work on PHANTASM II (1988). *(Profanity, violence, adult situations.)*

d, Don Coscarelli; p, Roberto Quezada; w, Don Coscarelli; ph, Daryn Okada; ed, Don Coscarelli; m, Fred Myrow and Christopher L. Stone; prod d, Andrew Siegal; set d, Robb Bradshaw and Scott Bruza; stunts, John Stewart; cos, Carla Gibbons; makup, Melanie Kay and Ed Wada

Adventure   (PR:O   MPAA:R)

T

TAKING CARE OF BUSINESS

108m Silver Screen Partners IV/Hollywood-Buena Vista c

(AKA: FILOFAX)

James Belushi (*Jimmy Dworski*), Charles Grodin (*Spencer Barnes*), Anne DeSalvo (*Debbie*), Loryn Locklin (*Jewel*), Stephen Elliott (*Walter Bentley*), Hector Elizondo (*Warden*), Veronica Hamel (*Elizabeth Barnes*), Mako (*Sakamoto*), Gates McFadden (*Diane*), John de Lancie (*Ted*), Thom Sharp (*Mike*), Ken Foree (*J.B.*), J.J. (*LeBradford*), Andre Rosey Brown (*Heavy G*), Terrence E. McNally (*Hamilton*), Lenny Hicks, Joe Bratcher (*Mediators*), Burke Byrnes, Tony Auer (*Prison Guards*), Marte Boyle Slout (*Brenda*), John P. Menese (*Chauffeur*), Stanley DeSantis (*Car Rental Man*), Tommy Morgan, Buddy Daniels (*Gang Members*), Chris Barnes (*Luggage Boy*), Jill Johnson (*Tennis Court Girl*), Tom Nolan (*Mr. Wright*), Marjorie Bransfield (*Tennis Club Receptionist*), Selma Archerd (*Woman in Pro Shop*), Joe Lerer (*Ira Breen*), Howie Guma (*Sakamoto's Assistant*), Elisabeth Barrett (*Diane's Assistant*), Tom Taglang (*Waiter*), Michele Harrell (*High Quality Receptionist*), Stu Nahan (*Radio Reporter*), Andrew Amador, Sandra Eng (*Prison Reporters*), Louisa Abernathy (*Guard*), Michael McNab (*Main Gate Guard*), Michael Kinney (*Malibu Jail Guard*), Leslie Suzan (*Malibu Jail Woman*), Janet Julian (*Woman on Plane*), Dan Kern (*Snooty Man*), David Ruprecht (*Yuppie Dad*), Whitby Hertford (*Yuppie Son*), Baldo Dal Ponte (*National Anthem Singer*), Joe Torre, Mark Grace, Bert Blyleven (*Themselves*), T. Rodgers (*Stadium Guard*), Hank Robinson (*Umpire*), Michael Blue, Ron Chenier (*Beach House Cops*), Darlene J. Hall (*Jeep Driver*), Jaqueline Alexandra Citron, and Kristen Amber Citron (*Twins*)

Right from the start, it's easy to tell that TAKING CARE OF BUSINESS is pure fantasy. Its premise includes a World Series pitting the perennially frustrated California Angels and Chicago Cubs against each other. Like its baseball matchup, the main plot of TAKING CARE OF BUSINESS also involves underdogs having their day in the sun. James Belushi plays Jimmy Dworski, a likable convict and diehard Cubs fan who's about to be released from prison, though not soon enough to collect the tickets to the deciding Series game he has won in a radio contest. When the warden (Hector Elizondo) rejects Jimmy's pleas for an early release, Jimmy's fellow convicts, who universally adore him, stage a riot, taking Jimmy "hostage" and allowing him to slip away undetected to the airport, where he is to rendezvous with his radio hosts. Flying in at the same time is advertising whiz Spencer Barnes (Charles Grodin). Risking his marriage by postponing a weekend getaway with his wife (Veronica Hamel), he's in Los Angeles to pitch a potential new client, Japanese food mogul Sakamoto (Mako). Spencer leaves his filofax (the wallet-datebook that provides the film with its alternate title) at a phone booth, where it is picked up by Jimmy, who intends to track down its owner and collect a promised $1,000 reward for its return. The hunt takes Jimmy to a high-tech, high-security Malibu mansion belonging to Spencer's boss, Walter (Stephen Elliott). It also puts Jimmy on Spencer's fast-track itinerary, setting in motion the predictable mistaken-identity plot. Unwisely, Jimmy beats Sakamoto at tennis in straight sets; then he outrages the CEO of Sakamoto's American operations by shooting from the hip in the crucial pitch-meeting over dinner that evening. Jimmy also ends up in a hot tub, and later in bed, with the boss's sleek, sexy, blonde daughter (Loryn Locklin). Meanwhile, the real Spencer drives a beat-up clunker rental car and gets stuffed into a garbage dumpster by a standard movie multi-ethnic gang of muggers. He has to con the accountant at the tennis club because he doesn't know his own boss's address. He then has to wheedle a lovelorn high-school acquaintance (Anne DeSalvo) into chauffeuring him all over town and takes a side trip to jail after getting arrested for breaking into the mansion. Finally cornering Jimmy, Spencer drags him to Sakamoto's office to explain the mix-up. There Spencer watches his firm lose the account and is fired when he rebels against Walter. After Jimmy and Spencer stomp out of the office, Sakamoto fires his American CEO for being too rude and obnoxious. In the meantime, Jimmy and Spencer make it to the big game and sort things out at the prison, while the boss's daughter and Spencer's wife sort things out at the mansion. And, of course, in no time Sakamoto offers jobs to Jimmy and Spencer.

The average viewer will be able to grasp the entire plot of this movie no more than 10 minutes after it begins. Aside from its if-you-can't-beat-'em, work-for-'em attitude, there's precious little here that hasn't already been done in a multitude of other films, and usually done better. The real problem with TAKING CARE OF BUSINESS is that it doesn't even get much mileage out of what it does have going for it. Grodin and Belushi have both done their best work in buddy-buddy pairings (MIDNIGHT RUN and RED HEAT, respectively), but while the two demonstrate some comedy chemistry here, they aren't brought together onscreen until the film is virtually over. Until that point, both actors

amble from one uninspired situation to another without being given much to sink their teeth into under Arthur Hiller's lackadaisical direction.

Something of a family affair, TAKING CARE OF BUSINESS was executive produced by veteran filmmaker Paul Mazursky (HARRY AND TONTO; DOWN AND OUT IN BEVERLY HILLS) and cowritten by his daughter, Jill. It's not quite a home movie. But it's not quite a movie, either. (*Profanity, adult situations.*)

d, Arthur Hiller; p, Geoffrey Taylor; w, Jill Mazursky and Jeffrey Abrams; ph, David M. Walsh; ed, William Reynolds; m, Stewart Copeland; prod d, Jon Hutman; set d, Charles William Breen; spec, Richard Ratliff; stunts, Joe Dunne; cos, Marilyn Matthews; makup, Richard Arrington

Comedy   (PR:C   MPAA:R)

TALES FROM THE DARKSIDE: THE MOVIE

93m Richard P. Rubinstein/Paramount c

Deborah Harry (*Betty*), Christian Slater (*Andy Smith*), David Johansen (*Halston*), William Hickey (*Drogan*), James Remar (*Preston*), Rae Dawn Chong (*Carola*), Matthew Lawrence (*Timmy*), Robert Sedgwick (*Lee*), Steve Buscemi (*Edward Bellingham*), Julianne Moore (*Susan*), and Robert Klein (*Wyatt*)

Since completing his "Living Dead" horror-movie trilogy, director George A. Romero has developed a lucrative sideline as the guiding light of the syndicated television series "Tales from the Darkside" and "Monsters." Both are unpretentious surprises featuring capable, underemployed character actors in sly, witty little horror tales often directed by some of New York's finest fringe and avant-garde filmmakers. Neither series could be called a landmark, but both are executed with enough care, craft, and off-network irreverence to provide smart diversions from the usual simpleminded syndicated fare. Transferred to the big screen, however, the modest virtues of these shows all but vanish. Consisting of three dull, derivative tales held together by an amusing "wraparound" story, TALES FROM THE DARKSIDE: THE MOVIE is a disappointment, no matter how you cut (or slash) it.

In Romero's signature satirical fashion, the wraparound story hints at the unspeakable horrors that often lie just beneath the surface banality of middle-class life. Deborah Harry, the glamorous punk rocker who fronted the celebrated late 1970s band Blondie, plays Betty, a prim suburban matron so outwardly innocuous that she makes the opening of DARKSIDE resemble a commercial for a perfectly wholesome product no environmentally conscious yuppie home should be without. We find her out and about in a picturesque small town, shopping for only the freshest fruits and vegetables for a dinner party. Naturally, we soon learn that the main course is to be a small boy (Matthew Lawrence), who is kept in a cell adjoining Betty's spotless gourmet kitchen. Having taken over a friend's paper route for a day, the youngster made the mistake of trying to collect payment from Betty. To delay his date with her oven, he now begins telling her stories, Scheherazade-style, from the *Tales from the Darkside* book that Betty has given him. The resolution of this connecting story, which comes at the film's end, is too funny and too ingenious to give away. If only the same could be said of the three stories-within-a-story.

In the first story, "Lot 249," a collegiate nerd (Steve Buscemi) gets his revenge against a preppy tormentor (Christian Slater), using an ancient incantation that brings a murderous mummy to life. In "Cat from Hell," a pharmaceutical magnate (William Hickey) hires a mob hit man (David Johansen) to rid his mansion of the killer feline that has already claimed three victims. And in the final tale, "Lover's Vow," an artist (James Remar) pays a deadly price for breaking his romantic promise to his wife (Rae Dawn Chong).

It doesn't do anyone much of a service to give away "surprise" endings, but the tales in DARKSIDE are distinguished by their plodding predictability. In "Lot 249" Slater says, "Well, that takes care of that," while burning the mummy's head, but we know that it most certainly doesn't. From the moment Johansen accepts a $50,000 blood retainer from Hickey in "Cat from Hell," we can rest assured that the cat will claim a fourth victim before too long. And anyone who's truly surprised by the gory conclusion of "Lover's Vow"—featuring a killer gargoyle that looks remarkably like a moonlighting creature from GREMLINS 2—probably makes a habit out of staying away from this type of movie anyway.

Fans of the horror genre have come to expect more from Romero, who scripted "Cat from Hell" from a Stephen King story. But director John Harrison, a longtime associate of Romero's making his feature debut after working on the "Darkside" series, betrays little understanding of either cinematic suspense or horror. Instead, DARKSIDE is overrun with flashy camerawork and *film noir* stylistic flourishes that pad, rather than propel, the already weak stories offered. All that DARKSIDE really has going for it is its clever cast, most of them also alumni of the series. Harry and Lawrence all but steal the show. In the "body" of the movie, top honors go to Buscemi, whose offbeat, low-key portrayal of a stereotypical nerd is more original than anything the script gives him to do. The ensemble in general is fun to watch; unfortunately, they succeed mainly in making DARKSIDE one of those movies that looks as though it were more fun to make than to sit through. *(Extreme violence, gore, profanity, adult situations.)*

d, John Harrison; p, Richard P. Rubinstein and Mitchell Galin; w, Michael McDowell and George Romero (based on stories by Arthur Conan Doyle, Stephen King, Michael McDowell); ph, Robert Draper; ed, Harry B. Miller III; m, John Harrison, Donald A. Rubinstein, Jim Manzie, Pat Regan, and Chaz Jankel; prod d, Ruth Ammon; spec, Dick Smith and K.N.B. EFX Group; cos, Ida Gearon

Comedy/Horror   **(PR:O   MPAA:R)**

TALL GUY, THE

(Brit.) 92m LWT — Virgin Vision — A Working Title/Virgin Vision c

Jeff Goldblum *(Dexter King)*, Emma Thompson *(Kate Lemon)*, Rowan Atkinson *(Ron Anderson)*, Geraldine James *(Carmen)*, Emil Wolk *(Cyprus Charlie)*, Kim Thompson *(Cheryl)*, Harold Innocent *(Timothy)*, Anna Massey *(Mary)*, Joanna Kanska *(Tamara)*, Peter Kelly *(Gavin)*, Timothy Barlow *(Mr. Morrow)*, Hugh Thomas *(Dr. Karabekian)*, Angus Deayton, Robin Driscoll *(Actors in Agent's Office)*, Harriet Keevil *(Mary's Secretary)*, Tony Forsyth, Stephen Marchant *(Berkoff Actors)*, Ian Lindsay *(TV Director)*, Kate Duchene, Angela Meredith *(Old Girl Friends)*, Fred Bryant *(Dying Old Man)*, Susan Field *(Dr. Freud)*, Michael Fitzgerald *(Vacuum Cleaner Man)*, Jason Isaacs, Martin Sadler *(Doctors)*, Francis Johnson *(Male Nurse)*, Charles Lamb *(Old Man in Wheelchair)*, Thomas Lockyer *(Michael)*, Kate Lonergan *(Stage Manager/Rubberface)*, Declan Mulholland *(Rubberface Doorman)*, Anthony Woodruff *(Elephant Doorman)*, Simon Bell *("After Dark" Presenter)*, Susan Beresford *(Woman Police Constable)*, Sarah-Jane Fenton *(Actress at Awards Show)*, Piers Fletcher *(Himself)*, Neil Hamilton *(Naked George)*, Peter Brewis *(Freddy)*, Joola Cappelman *(Costume Designer)*, and John Waldon *(Company Stage Manager)*

Another British film with its roots in television, THE TALL GUY was partly financed by LWT, scripted by Richard Curtis (best known for the "Blackadder" TV series), and directed by Mel Smith—who first came to prominence in the UK as partner to Rowan Atkinson, Griff Rhys Jones, and Pamela Stephenson in the hit show "Not The Nine O'Clock News." Despite the presence of Hollywood star Jeff Goldblum, this is *not* A FISH CALLED WANDA. Goldblum is straight man to egotistical comedy star Atkinson in his long-running stage show, "Rubberface Revue." Depressed by the work and his miserable luck with women, Goldblum is further handicapped by violent hayfever and chronic allergies. To cure the latter he undergoes a series of injections and ends up out of work—but in love with nurse Thompson. After the usual fumbles and false starts, a date is fixed up, and soon the couple are starring in a romantic montage of the type so brilliantly parodied in THE NAKED GUN, set to the song "It Must Be Love." Goldblum's agent sends him to audition for the chorus in the Royal Shakespeare Company's new production, "Elephant!" a musical version of "The Elephant Man," and to everyone's surprise he lands the title role. The show is a big hit, but Thompson moves out on opening night, aware that Goldblum has slept with his leading lady. He is shattered and humiliated when he spots Thompson at Atkinson's side as Atkinson collects an award on television for "Rubberface Revue." In a fury, the "Elephant Man" pedals across London to take his revenge on Atkinson, then tackles Thompson at the hospital and pledges his love before a cheering ward of patients.

Although Curtis' screenplay and Smith's direction clearly aspire to more than a straight gag comedy, focussing on the central romance in a bid for emotional depth, THE TALL GUY never attains the authenticity nor the momentum it needs so badly. Jeff Goldblum is distinctly ill at ease in a part Curtis based on himself; the smart trading on transatlantic experience John Cleese exploited so expertly in WANDA is by-passed completely here, with only a couple of passing references to the character's nationality. Goldblum is a likable actor, but the character's insecurity, especially sexual insecurity, seems peculiarly English, and his portrayal is pitched all over the place. Likewise Thompson's prim, matter-of-fact, essentially Home Counties Nurse Lemon is an unlikely inspiration for romantic obsession, the outrageous sex scene notwithstanding.

The movie only sparkles in its second half, when it neatly satirizes the London theatrical scene: Steven Berkoff, Andrew Lloyd Webber and the RSC's crass commercial efforts. The musical "Elephant!" is an inspired and wicked swipe at the Company's dismal staging of a musical "Carrie" (and predates their forthcoming production of "A Clockwork Orange" with music by U2's the Edge). Some of these sequences are priceless (a chorusline of tap-dancing elephants; John Merrick's death-bed rising up to heaven), and finally Smith seems to get the measure of his material. Although THE TALL GUY cannot stand comparison with the likes of WANDA or WITHNAIL AND I, it does have its moments, bolstered by good support from Anna Massey as Goldblum's agent and Rowan Atkinson, very much in his element snarling lines like "If you ever do anything funny in my show again, you're out, you elongated droplet of dung!" Songs include "Heartbreak Hotel" (M. Axton, T. Durdon, Elvis, performed by Sam

Williams), "Breaking Up Is Hard to Do" (Neil Sedaka, Howard Greenfield), "Crying in the Rain" (Carole King, Howard Greenfield, performed by Philip Greenfield). *(Nudity, sexual situations, profanity.)*

d, Mel Smith; p, Tim Bevan; w, Richard Curtis; ph, Adrian Biddle; ed, Dan Rae; m, Peter Brewis; prod d, Grant Hicks; stunts, Jim Dowdall; cos, Denise Simmons; makeup, Morag Ross and Daniel Parker; chor, Charles Augins

Comedy   **(PR:C   MPAA:NR)**

TAX SEASON

93m Movidex/Prism c

Fritz Bronner *(Allen Mills)*, James Hong *(Tagasaki)*, Jana Grant *(Susan Quinn)*, Toru Tanaka *(Moto)*, Dorie Krum *(Mary Ann)*, Kathryn Knotts *(Cinnamon Star)*, Jorge Gil *(Jorge Horhay)*, Kerry Ruff *(T. William Douglas III)*, Al Schecter *(Eli)*, Patti Karr *(Dorothy Mills)*, Arte Johnson *(Lionel Goldberg)*, Zara Karen *(Lana LaTour)*, Ken Letner *(Detective Jensen)*, Tony C. *(Sal)*, Beano *(Tony)*, Jim "Bonk" Branca *(Larry)*, Chuck Lacey, Rob Slyker, Debra Fares, Barry Cooper, Clive Rosengren, Bunny Summers, Ray Nieman, Don Hinson, Chad Taylor, Larry Canova, and Richard Lee Sung

Released direct to home video a few weeks before the April 15 tax deadline, TAX SEASON was sent to retailers accompanied by a cassette (produced in association with the firm Laventhol and Horwath) explaining the latest IRS rulings on the depreciation of tapes. Decide for yourself if that sounds more entertaining than the movie's story, in which Allen Mills (Fritz Bronner) is a milquetoast accountant from Cleveland who dreams of glory when he purchases the Hollywood Tax Service, sight unseen, from loony Lionel Goldberg (Arte Johnson). As it happens, the storefront bookkeeping firm is actually a cover for gambling and prostitution operations, leading to various merry mixups when Mills shows up in Hollywood to take control. But that's actually a subplot; the real action is set in motion when local fortune-cookie magnate Tagasaki (James Hong) hires the Hollywood Tax Service to look over his books, then mistakenly sends Mills the records of his cocaine smuggling enterprise, rather than those of his legitimate cookie business. Tagasaki steals the books back before the accountant can show them to the skeptical police, and—to keep the plot lurching ahead—orders a hit on the honest Clevelander. Luckily, Mills has an ally in Susan Quinn (Jana Grant), the villain's cuddly secretary, who warns him of her boss's intentions and, after a few chases, helps him break into Tagasaki's computer files. The smuggler has been concealing the cocaine in extra-large fortune cookies, so Mills reroutes a shipment of the cookies to a public banquet in Tagasaki's honor. At the fete, Tagasaki tries to gather up all the incriminating snacks before anyone can discover the real nature of the fortune concealed therein, but one powder-filled cookie escapes. It's dramatically broken open before the shocked dignitaries, and justice triumphs at last.

Had TAX SEASON stuck with the eccentric goings-on at the Hollywood Tax Service it might have been faintly amusing. But once the lame coke-smuggling story line takes over for good the film is a lost cause, even though the actors (especially Hong) work hard to energize the material. It doesn't help that the anti-drug posturings contradict an earlier scene in which a doddering janitor suddenly becomes a hip dude after smoking generous amounts of reefer.

TAX SEASON is laudable mainly in that writer-director Tom Law avoids profanity and nudity, despite lots of jiggling female flesh early on. And although there is a plethora of Los Angeles area location shots, the filmmakers manfully refrain from including the magic words "Beverly Hills" in the title. *(Adult situations, sexual situations, substance abuse.)*

d, Tom Law; p, Thomas Davis Jr.; stunts, Jeff Popick, John Williamette, and Tom Frantz

Comedy   **(PR:C   MPAA:PG-13)**

TAXI BLUES

(Fr./USSR) 110m Lenfilm — ASK Eurofilm — La Sept/MK2 Diffusion c

Piotr Mamonov *(Lyosha)*, Piotr Zaitchenko *(Schlikov)*, Vladimir Kachpur *(Old Man)*, Natalia Koliakanova *(Christina)*, Hal Singer, Elena Safonova, and Sergei Gazarov

Mother Russia is a crone and her dissolute, deprived children seem hell-bent on self-destruction. In a very strange buddy film, TAXI BLUES blatantly shows Moscow with all its warts in stunning profusion. The film's unblinking realism, impeccable acting, and tightly paced scenario combined to help first-time director Pavel Lounguine win the Best Director prize at the Cannes Film Festival. In the film, Lounguine shows a grim Russia of overt anti-Semitism, black markets, rampant alcoholism, and internalized rage and resentment that have only recently been allowed to publicly surface. It's a foray into oppressive squalor, dank apartments, and sordid back alleys that somehow succeeds in maintaining a sense of humor. It's a black comedy in which the deprived populace displays pin-ups of fancy autos rather than voluptuous models.

Vanya Schlikov (Piotr Zaitchenko), a simple, vaguely bigoted taxi driver, is stiffed on a 70-ruble fare by the Jewish Lyosha (Piotr Mamonov, one of the Soviet Union's most popular rock musicians), a saxophone player. Lyosha is a drunk and a human wreck who is unable to make personal commitments. Vanya wants his money and tracks the musician to a rehearsal studio where he first seeks the saxophone in lieu of payment, then takes Lyosha himself back to his apartment, intent on reforming him. What follows is an uneasy friendship between two lost souls. Lyosha, ugly, gangly, and missing teeth, turns out to be a major talent, but he's also a liar, a cheat, and a sponge. Stripped of his clothes and left alone in the flat, he does extensive damage by flooding the building during a drunken binge. Furious, Vanya has him jailed, then softens and drops the charges. He takes Lyosha's passport as collateral then subjects him to indentured servitude, demanding that the musician do menial work around the apartment.

Lyosha eventually persuades Vanya to return his passport and his saxophone so he can attempt to earn some money. At a recording studio, he is "discovered" by American musicians and joins them on tour, first going to Leningrad, then the US where he becomes something of a celebrity. Vanya learns of Lyosha's success when he sees him performing on television. Hearing his friend is returning to Moscow, Vanya arranges an extravagant welcome home party for him. Lyosha shows up with his troupe, very late and very drunk. Lyosha bestows gifts on Vanya, then abruptly leaves in a "don't call me, I'll call you," manner. Vanya is both heartsick and angry that he has been shut out of Lyosha's new life and good times.

The characters in this film all seem to be filled with a frantic sense of loneliness and need. The only legitimate expression of feeling is Vanya's peculiar love-hate relationship with the decadent Lyosha — in a way typifying the clash of the old, more soulful Russia versus the country's new hedonism. Yet both men are emotionally crippled. The film's greatest failing is that its characters are so unappealing. Nobody changes, nobody grows, there's no one to admire. Yet as difficult as that makes it to enjoy this picture, its no-holds-barred examination of present-day Russia makes it a truly important effort. To say it explores the *seamy* side of Gorbachev's Soviet Union would not be precise since that seems to be the *only* side of the country. The film's grim perspective, unencumbered by censorship, reveals a throroughly depressed economic state, baring its citizens' cynical views on the corrupt vestiges of communism. It's amazing the film, denounced in the Soviet Union as "immoral," was even made.

When casting for the film, director Lounguine intially felt the kind of actor he needed to play Lyosha (a sort of "Dustin Hoffman full of humor, charm, and egotism") didn't exist in his country. Then he saw Mamonov, Russia's oldest rock star, on television. Mamonov is a mythical figure in the Soviet Union who is well known for his "wild lifestyle, his excesses, and his permanent temptation for self destruction." Lounguine decided he would be the ideal Lyosha, and when he showed Mamonov the script, the musician said, "But how could you write that? It's me!" Zaitchenko, who does a wonderful job as the beleaguered Vanya, was appearing in only his second film. Technically, the film is first-rate, at least partly because it was a French/Soviet co-production which gave Lounguine access to state-of-the-art equipment. *(Adult situations, brief nudity, profanity.)*

d, Pavel Lounguine; p, Marin Karmitz; w, Pavel Lounguine; ph, Denis Evstigneev; ed, Elisabeth Guido; m, Vladimir Chekassine; art d, Valeri Yurkevich

Drama   **(PR:C   MPAA:NR)**

TEENAGE MUTANT NINJA TURTLES

93m Golden Harvest-Limelight/New Line c

Judith Hoag *(April O'Neil)*, Elias Koteas *(Casey Jones)*, Josh Pais *(Raphael/Passenger in Cab/Voice of Raphael)*, Michelan Sisti *(Michelangelo/Pizza Man)*, Leif Tilden *(Donatello/Foot Messenger)*, David Forman *(Leonardo/Gang Member)*, Michael Turney *(Danny Pennington)*, Jay Patterson *(Charles Pennington)*, Raymond Serra *(Chief Sterns)*, James Saito *(The Shredder)*, Toshishiro Obata *(Tatsu)*, Sam Rockwell *(Head Thug)*, Kitty Fitzgibbon *(June)*, Louis Cantarini *(Cab Driver)*, Joseph D'Onofrio, John D. Ward *(Movie Hoodlums)*, Ju Yu *(Shinsho)*, Cassandra Ward-Freeman *(Charles' Secretary)*, Mark Jeffrey Miller *(Technician)*, John Rogers *(New Recruit)*, Tae Pak, Kenn Troum *(Talkative Foots)*, Robert Haskell *(Tall Teen)*, Joshua Bo Lozoff *(Beaten Teen)*, Winston Hemingway, Joe Inscoe *(Police Officers)*, Robbie Rist *(Voice of Michaelangelo)*, Kevin Clash *(Voice of Splinter)*, Brian Tochi *(Voice of Leonardo)*, David McCharen *(Voice of The Shredder)*, Michael McConnohie *(Voice of Tatsu)*, and Corey Feldman *(Voice of Donatello)*

New York is being terrorized by a series of crimes perpetrated by the youthful members of a ninja gang called the Foot. Their leader: the awesome Shredder (James Saito), whose face is concealed behind a mask that owes as much to traditional Japanese armor as to Darth Vader's helmet. Television reporter April

O'Neil (Judith Hoag) is on the case, demanding investigation by the complacent police force and making herself the target of the gang's fury. What no one knows is that New York's citizens include four rather unusual individuals who aren't afraid to take on the teenage shadow warriors on their own ground: Michelangelo, Donatello, Leonardo and Raphael, the smart-talking, sewer-dwelling, pizza-eating Teenage Mutant Ninja Turtles. With the help of their martial-arts master — a one-eared rat named Splinter (voiced by Kevin Clash) — and the childlike vigilante Casey Jones (Elias Koteas), the Turtles team up with April to get to the bottom of matters. Complications arise when April's boss is blackmailed into firing her, Splinter is kidnaped, and Raphael is seriously injured by marauding gang members. April, Casey, and the Turtles escape New York and recuperate in an isolated farm house, then return to the city and confront the ninja gang, prevailing in a drawn-out battle that tests the limits of their abilities. April is rehired, Casey declares his love for her, and Splinter and the Turtles are reunited.

One might ask why anyone would want to make a live action movie about life-size talking turtles and their martial-arts adventures. The answer, of course, is that the Teenage Mutant Ninja Turtles — who started life as comic-book characters, then moved into cartoons and an awesome array of merchandising opportunities — have a tremendous pre-teen following that could be counted on to fill theaters, on their own and in the company of parents and baby-sitters. But, unlike THE GARBAGE PAIL KIDS MOVIE or other films inspired by existing marketing concepts, TEENAGE MUTANT NINJA TURTLES is entertaining enough to gloss over the crassness of its underpinnings. Brought to life by state-of-the-art special effects techniques that combine performers in full-body suits with radio-controlled animation, the Turtles and their mentor emerge as genuine characters rather than larger-than-life advertising come-ons. In addition, the relationships that motivate Splinter, the Turtles, and the movie's human characters are positive without being cloying. The notion of family looms large in the story. Saito's ninja teens fall under his influence because they feel rejected by their own relatives. The gang's headquarters is a kid's dream (24-hour pool tables, skateboard tracks, video games, cigarettes, and junk food), but the real draw is that it offers a sense of belonging and camaraderie. When the gang members realize they're just being used, their loyalty to Saito evaporates. Splinter, by contrast, is a positive paternal figure, teaching the Turtles that their real strength lies not in kung fu fighting but in their love and respect for one another. Offset by the Turtles' Val-speak sarcasm and by action sequences staged with a hip nod to years of martial-arts movie conventions, the message goes down pretty smoothly. And while many reviewers were put off by Splinter's rheumy-eyed philosophizing and the Turtles' ninja antics, the movie's youthful target audience squealed with delight.

A conspicuous flaw in the Teenage Mutant Ninja Turtle universe is the uniformly dark cinematography. *Noir* aesthetics notwithstanding, this imagery often becomes distracting. The flashback to the genesis of the Turtles — little green pet store terrapins exposed to radioactive waste — and their meeting with Splinter, once the pet of a ninja master, is so underlit that without the rat's voice-over narration it would be difficult to follow. This may be corrected in the further Turtle adventures likely to come. *(Violence.)*

d, Steve Barron; p, Kim Dawson, Simon Fields, and David Chan; w, Todd W. Langen and Bobby Herbeck (based on a story by Bobby Herbeck, and characters created by Kevin Eastman, Peter Laird); ph, Mike Brewster; m, John Du Prez; art d, Gary Wissner; set d, Jerry Hall; spec, Special Effects, Unlimited and Joey DiGaetano; stunts, Pat Johnson; cos, Alonzo Wilson; makup, Jeff Goodwin; chor, Pat Johnson

Action/Fantasy   **(PR:A   MPAA:PG)**

TEN LITTLE INDIANS

98m Breton/Cannon c

(AKA: AGATHA CHRISTIE'S TEN LITTLE INDIANS)

Donald Pleasence *(Justice Wargrave)*, Frank Stallone *(Capt. Philip Lombard)*, Sarah Maur Thorp *(Vera Claythorne)*, Herbert Lom *(Gen. Romensky)*, Brenda Vaccaro *(Marion Marshall)*, Warren Berlinger *(Detective Blore)*, Yehuda Efroni *(Dr. Hans Werner)*, Paul L. Smith *(Elmo Rodgers)*, Moira Lister *(Ethel Rodgers)*, and Neil McCarthy *(Anthony Marston)*

Whoever had the not-so-bright idea of setting this remake of Agatha Christie's perennial thriller smack dab in the middle of an African safari really struck out. Perhaps the filmmakers got a good deal on location shooting in Africa, because there's no other discernible reason for redoing this Old Dark House thriller in the sunny veldt. Instead of winding staircases and locked doors, we get swinging rope bridges and open tent flaps.

After de-training, the cast begins a safari led by Capt. Philip Lombard (Frank Stallone). Sponsored by a mysterious benefactor, this dream vacation almost immediately goes awry. After making a perilous crossing of a gorge, the travelers are trapped in "dangerous" surroundings (what looks like a Lion Country Safari picnic area) when Africans slice the ropes to the basket used for the crossing. As the wayfarers reveal how they came to be invited on the trip, the familiar Christie plot unfurls. Among the honored guests are: Elmo Rodgers (Paul L. Smith), an obese cook; his jittery wife, Ethel (Moira Lister); Romensky (Herbert Lom), a general; Marion Marshall (Brenda Vaccaro), an actress; Wargrave (Donald Pleasence), a hanging judge; former nanny Vera Claythorne (Sarah Maur Thorp); gentleman dandy Anthony Marston (Neil McCarthy); Hans Werner (Yehuda Efroni), an alcoholic doctor; and Blore (Warren Berlinger), a veteran detective. Bwana Lombard, we later learn, is actually taking the trip in place of a friend. Following instructions left by the absent host, Elmo plays a phonograph record that lists the host's death sentence for each of his invitees, as well as the crimes he claims they have committed with impunity. For example, Vera wasn't able to save a young charge from drowning, and a patient died under the shaky scalpel of Dr. Werner. Whoever he is (and he may actually be one of those assembled), the host intends to pick off his guests one by one. Ethel dies after taking sedatives Dr. Werner had given her to calm her nerves when she saw Marston take a fatal drink. Each time one of the guests is killed, the head of a little doll (one of ten dolls—to coincide with the nursery rhyme "Ten Little Indians") is removed. After Romensky takes a deadly fall from a cliff, the others pass the time by trying to deduce the killer's identity. Tempers flare as Wargrave starts dredging up details of everyone's hidden past, and in short order he is found shot (we later learn that his "death" has been faked, part of an attempt by Wargrave and Werner to flush out their tormentor). Repairing a badly damaged radio transmitter, Lombard secretly signals for a rescue plane, but the guests may not last the night. While Lombard and Vera are busy falling in love, the surly Elmo, who has seemed the most likely suspect up to this point, gets a hatchet planted in his noggin. In time, Marion gets stung with a hypo, Blore is stabbed, and Werner also turns up dead. Terrified and mistrustful, Vera shoots Lombard, believing him to be the only survivor besides herself. To her amazement, Wargrave reappears, alive but deranged. It seems that when he learned he had a terminal illness, Wargrave concocted this nightmarish vacation. He quaffs poison, but still forces Vera to hang herself. In the nick of time, however, Lombard recovers and saves her, as we hear the rescue plane humming in the background.

Although Christie's story was brilliantly filmed by Rene Clair (AND THEN THERE WERE NONE), filmmakers the world over have been unable to resist ripping off or remaking this property. None of the subsequent updates has equaled the wry black comic tone of Clair's film, but this version is the weakest. The casting is particularly uninspired: Lom, Berlinger, Vaccaro, and Pleasence are so overweight, they seem in danger of expiring just from walking in the jungle heat. Moreover, the charismaless Stallone fails to lend his character the necessary heroic stature. As for Pleasence, he's the same in every movie—pointing a paranoid finger at the audience here as if he were still on the lookout for HALLOWEEN's Michael Myers.

Even if the casting were brilliant, the film couldn't overcome two more serious obstacles. Surely, by now, everyone has either read Christie's novel or is familiar with the plot; unimaginatively, these re-makers haven't altered one iota of the story line. Worse yet is their decision to transfer this creepy tale (about travelers transformed into sitting ducks) from a sinister mansion to sun-drenched Africa. A mansion can have hidden stairways, sliding panels, and cobwebs. What can one do in the jungle—hide behind a bush? Because the intricacies of Christie's ingenious plot are not given their proper showcase, her deadly parlor game becomes perfunctory. Torpid direction and extremely sloppy editing further diminish the suspense. Stagnant and convictionless, this slapdash film casts an unflattering light on its cast of seasoned pros and does a disservice to one of the cleverest crime thrillers of this century. (Violence, profanity, adult situations, substance abuse.)

d, Alan Birkinshaw; p, Harry Alan Towers; w, Jackson Hunsicker and Gerry O'Hara (based on the play by Agatha Christie); ph, Arthur Lavis; ed, Penelope Shaw; m, George S. Clinton; prod d, Roger Orpen; art d, George Canes; set d, Anita Fraser; spec, Johan Laas, Tony de Groote, Wilson Mbuyawzwe, and Rubin Malematsha; stunts, Chris Olley; cos, Dianna Villiers; makup, Annie Bartels

Mystery   (PR:C   MPAA:PG)

TEXASVILLE

123m Cine-Source — Nelson/Columbia c

Jeff Bridges (*Duane Jackson*), Cybill Shepherd (*Jacy Farrow*), Annie Potts (*Karla Jackson*), Timothy Bottoms (*Sonny Crawford*), Cloris Leachman (*Ruth Popper*), Randy Quaid (*Lester Marlow*), Eileen Brennan (*Genevieve*), William McNamara (*Dickie Jackson*), Angie Bolling (*Marylou Marlow*), Katherine Bongfeldt (*Nellie*), Romy Snyder (*Julie*), Jimmy Howell (*Jack*), Kay Pering, Gina Sleete, Su Hyatt, Earl Poole Ball, Allison Marich, Lavelle Bates, Lloyd Catlett, Pearl Jones, Harvey Christiansen, Leiland Jaynes, Sharon Ullrick, Barclay Doyle, Gordon Hurst, Ty Chambers, and Adam Englund

The ads called it the long-awaited sequel to THE LAST PICTURE SHOW, but it's doubtful there were many clamoring to find out what happened to the cross-section of losers in the godforsaken Texas town that first came to the screen in 1971. But in Hollywood today, whole movie seasons can pass with nothing but familiar titles followed by numbers. As long as there's a buck to be made, nothing and nobody is safe from the cinematic deja vu syndrome. Still, writer-director Peter Bogdanovich, working from novelist Larry McMurtry's literary sequel and reuniting most of the major cast members from the original, has come up with a surprisingly smart, funny, and heartfelt mood piece, despite a muddled, overstuffed plot.

Set in 1954, THE LAST PICTURE SHOW explored how its characters suffered under the repressive, hypocritical morality of the era in a small Texas town. TEXASVILLE, set in the same town 30 years later, looks at how the same characters have fared in the age of personal liberation. Are they having fun yet? Hint: If they were, there wouldn't be much reason for making a movie about them. TEXASVILLE is told from the point of view of Duane Jackson (Jeff Bridges), whose mood swings between exhaustion and depression. A part-time oil wildcatter in THE LAST PICTURE SHOW, Duane now has an oil-drilling business that has made him rich. However, since the year is 1984, OPEC has lifted its embargo and declared its intention to flood the world market with crude oil to bring prices back to their pre-embargo level. This couldn't come at a worse time for Duane, who is $12 million in debt to Lester Marlow (Randy Quaid), the dorky rich kid who hosted the skinny-dipping party in the first film, and who is now the dorky president of the local bank. Life is not much better on the home front for Duane. His penchant for infidelity has created a major rift between him and his waspish but essentially loving wife, Karla (Annie Potts). Son Dickie (William McNamara) is fast following in his father's footsteps, creating problems at home for his fiancee (Allison Marich) and for others all around town because of his special enthusiasm for wandering wives, including Lester's missus, whom Dickie has gotten pregnant. Meanwhile, Duane's voluptuous daughter (Katherine Bongfeldt) breaks engagements as easily as Hollywood agents cancel lunch dates, and his youngest kids, a twin boy and girl, scandalize the town with their precociously bawdy antics. Also troubling Duane is the quiet return of his old flame, Jacy Farrow (Cybill Shepherd). An eccentric recluse frazzled by three decades of starring in B movies in Italy, she is in mourning over the recent death of her son. Equally reclusive and eccentric is Duane's erstwhile rival for Jacy, Sonny Crawford (Timothy Bottoms), who is slowly slipping into insanity. Sonny has more or less taken over the role Ben Johnson's Sam the Lion played in the life of the town in THE LAST PICTURE SHOW. In addition to owning several storefront businesses, Sonny also holds the deed to the burned-out old movie theater that was so central to the first film, and he can still be found there from time to time, watching imaginary movies playing in the sky. Sonny's secret lover in the original film, Ruth Popper (Cloris Leachman), who now works as Duane's office manager, has becomes something of a mother to Sonny, taking care of him and trying to keep him out of danger. The plot, such as it is, primarily concerns the impending celebration of the county's centennial and Jacy's deepening involvement in the lives of everyone in Duane's family but Duane himself. At the film's climax, with the centennial celebration descending into chaos, Jacy is about to spirit Duane's entire family away to her house in Italy.

TEXASVILLE's main flaw is that it comprises two incompatible films uncomfortably rolled into one. Comical couplings and their farcical repercussions are at the center of the film that culminates in the town celebration. The other film, concerning Duane's attempts to make peace with the past when confronted with Jacy, leads to his last-ditch effort to keep his family from slipping away from him. For the most part, the drama tends to deflate the comedy, and the comedy tends to derail the drama. Also working against the film is an overall choppiness, the apparent product of editing-room tampering. Character relationships become so confused that you may feel you need a program to keep track of who's sleeping with whom; major plot points sneak by in single, often-mumbled snippets of dialog.

Very much on the plus side, the cast is as inspired an ensemble now as it was in 1971, with newcomer Potts bringing a welcome jolt of comic energy, though Quaid, gobbling analgesics while anguishing over his collapsing financial "empire," winds up getting the movie's biggest laughs. Bridges turns in his usual skillfully laid-back performance in the lead, though he's hampered by his two-note, inarticulate character. Shepherd, as in her past efforts for Bogdanovich, is effectively cast here more for type than for talent, inhabiting her role rather than acting it. But though her performance doesn't have the finesse of a Streep outing, it is, nevertheless, realistic and convincing. The big surprise, however, is Bottoms, who reportedly was reluctant to join the project, but who provides the movie's emotional core as the quietly crumbling Sonny.

Although Bogdanovich never seems to have decided exactly what type of movie he was making, his work here is never less than competent, and it is inspired just often enough to keep the film compelling. At its best, TEXAS-VILLE is a member of an increasingly rare Hollywood breed, movies that are made by adults, about adults, and for adults. It's about and for people who have been around the block a few times, who have had to surrender some of their dreams while looking for ways to pay the bills, and who have tried to find some measure of happiness with the onset of diminishing expectations. As movies go, it's far from perfect, but it's always human. (*Profanity, adult situations, substance abuse.*)

d, Peter Bogdanovich; p, Barry Spikings and Peter Bogdanovich; w, Peter Bogdanovich (based on the novel by Larry McMurtry); ph, Nicholas von Sternberg; ed, Richard Fields; prod d, Phedon Papamichael; set d, Daniel Boxer; cos, Rita Riggs

Comedy/Drama (PR:C MPAA:R)

THREE MEN AND A LITTLE LADY

100m Interscope — Touchstone/Buena Vista c

Tom Selleck (*Peter Mitchell*), Steve Guttenberg (*Michael Kellam*), Ted Danson (*Jack Holden*), Nancy Travis (*Sylvia*), Robin Weisman (*Mary Bennington*), Christopher Cazenove (*Edward*), Sheila Hancock (*Vera*), Fiona Shaw (*Miss Lomax*), Jonanthan Boswall (*Barrow, Butler*), Jonathan Lynn (*Vicar Hewitt*), Sidney Walsh (*Laurie*), Lynne Marta (*Morgan School Teacher*), Everett Wong (*1st Boy*), Edwina Moore (*Dr. Robinson*), Patricia Gaul (*Mrs. Walker*), Edith Fields (*Mrs. Heard*), Darcy Pulliam (*Waitress*), Rosalind Allen (*Pretty Girl*), Lucia Neal (*Party Lady*), Bryan Pringle (*Old Englishman*), Neil Hunt (*Wilfred Blair*), Ian Redford (*English Farmer*), Charles David Richards (*Stagehand*), Steven L. Vaughn (*Usher*), and Melissa Hurley (*Dancing Girl at Party*)

This sequel to the 1987 blockbuster film picks up five years after the first film and reintroduces the three bachelors from the original — architect Peter (Tom Selleck), cartoonist Michael (Steve Guttenberg), and amorous would-be actor Jack (Ted Danson). The baby they struggled to care for in the original is now a five-year-old charmer, Mary (Robin Weisman). Mary's mom, Sylvia (Nancy Travis), is also back and as the film opens, all are part of a happy extended family. Trouble brews, however, when Sylvia, also an aspiring actress, announces that she is taking Mary with her to England, where she is to star in a play directed by her current boy friend, Edward (Christopher Cazenove). The three bachelor-papas are upset by the prospect of the breakup of the "family," and then Sylvia gives them even worse news: she has accepted Edward's marriage proposal. While Jack, Mary's biological father, isn't in love with Sylvia, he's despondent over the thought of his daughter leaving. Peter also has a special reason to be opposed to Sylvia's move — he's long been secretly in love with her. At first the bachelors stoically accept Sylvia's decision, but once mother and daughter depart for the United Kingdom, despair sets in, and the three decide to head for London. Once there, Peter realizes how deeply he loves Sylvia, but he's burned before, and fears making another commitment. However, when he learns that, after they are married, Edward plans to pack Mary off to a rigid boarding school, he is moved to action. There follows a series of misadventures, which only serve to delay the inevitable happy ending in which mother, daughter, and the three bachelors all seem to get what they want.

While it's not a top-drawer romantic comedy, this is certainly a worthy sequel to THREE MEN AND A BABY. Selleck, Guttenberg, and Danson share a nice chemistry that smoothly blends the elements of comedy, romance, and pathos...and this comfortable balance makes for an enjoyable film. Travis and little Weisman lend fine support, but the actress who steals every scene she's in is Fiona Shaw, who plays the sex-starved head of the boarding school Mary is slated to attend. Cazenove is appropriately insincere, and Jonathan Boswall has a few choice moments as a batty butler. Director Emile Ardolino (DIRTY DANCING, CHANCES ARE) keeps the action lively and the pace quick, and all the technical credits are first-rate. (*Adult situations, mild profanity.*)

d, Emile Ardolino; p, Robert W. Cort and Ted Field; w, Charlie Peters; ph, Adam Greenberg; ed, Michael A. Stevenson; m, James Newton Howard; md, Marty Paich; prod d, Stuart Wurtzel; art d, David M. Haber; set d, Antoinette Gordon; spec, Richard Ratliff; cos, Louise Frogley; makeup, John Caglione Jr. and Doug Drexler

Comedy/Romance (PR:A MPAA:PG)

THREEPENNY OPERA, THE

(SEE: MACK THE KNIFE)

TIE ME UP! TIE ME DOWN!

(Sp.) 101m El Deseo/Miramax c

Victoria Abril (*Marina*), Antonio Banderas (*Ricky*), Francisco Rabal (*Maximo Espejo*), Loles Leon (*Lola*), Julieta Serrano (*Alma*), Maria Barranco, and Rossy De Palma

This outrageous title is a tad deceiving. Pedro Almodovar's latest film, while not without his patented kinky touches and outre humor, is really a pure

contemplation of *amour fou* and a change of pace for the director. Campy, boisterous hilarity has been replaced by anguished, albeit offbeat, romantic heterosexual yearning.

Ricky (Antonio Banderas), a young inmate in a mental institution, is one day deemed fit for society and released. He has no hesitation as to what his plan of action will be. On a previous escape from the hospital, he met and made love to Marina (Victoria Abril), a junkie and former porn star. Besotted by the memory of her, he determines to seek her out again and win her love. He finds her on the set of a legitimate film, working under the direction of the aged Maximo Espejo (Francisco Rabal), who is also obsessed with her. Marina has no recollection of Ricky when she sees him, but he trails her home and kidnaps her. Tying her up in her own apartment, he makes her a "captive" audience for his desperate romantic overtures. She is at first fiercely resistant to him, but gradually succumbs, especially when he returns to her bruised and bloodied from attempting to score drugs for her. Eventually, Marina's frantic sister, Lola (Loles Leon), comes to the rescue, but by that time, Marina's fate is happily sealed.

The shock effects of Almodovar's earlier work were considerably diluted in his Lubitschian crazy-love roundelay, WOMEN ON THE VERGE OF A NERVOUS BREAKDOWN, and TIE ME UP! TIE ME DOWN!, despite its bondage theme and lightly sadomasochistic overtones, makes a similar attempt to enter the mainstream. In fact, the film recalls Hitchcock's THE 39 STEPS, with its bickering handcuffed lovers, as well as the sweeping romantic intensity of Douglas Sirk trash-fests of the 50s. Ennio Morricone's ubiquitous, expensive-sounding music contributes to this attempt to explore the traditions of classic cinema, but it lacks the savvy, finger-popping verve of the more street-smart scores of other Almodovar films. Moreover, Morricone's score has an off-putting miasmic texture, far from the lyrical accompaniment the material could have really used.

Taking a respite from the carnival streets of Madrid, Almodovar largely relegates the action to Marina's bedroom. Though the setting is claustrophobic, the director's technique is very assured and owes much to Jose Luis Alcaine's fluid photography, which revels in the physical charms of the leads, with huge closeups that bring to mind the gargantuan, gorgeous shots of Elizabeth Taylor and Montgomery Clift in A PLACE IN THE SUN. At one point the camera feasts lovingly, Caravaggio-like, on the sleeping Banderas, and there's a delectably piquant scene involving Abril and a wind-up toy in her bathtub.

"It's an August weekend, everyone's gone and handcuffs are no problem," Ricky happily tells Marina as they go for an evening stroll, and the direction captures the balmy atmosphere to perfection. Almodovar also creates a wonderful film-within-a-film sequence that ends with Abril dangling pendulum-like from a balcony, an image that ignites her dying director's imagination. More might have been made of Maximo Espejo's side of the story, however, as Rabal gives a richly suggestive performance in those few scenes he is in (a portrayal that can be seen as a tribute to Bunuel, in whose films Rabal performed so brilliantly). This might have given the film more balance and depth; as good as they are, Abril and Banderas have the callowness of youth, and, as scripted, their characterizations don't go much beyond "junkie" and "loony." The screenplay focuses relentlessly on them, and is devoid of the frantic multitude of characters that have typified Almodovar's work. The non-sequiturs and comic asides we have come to expect in his films are also kept to a minimum, apart from a recipe for pesto and a gangrene remedy. Staying with TIE ME UP! TIE ME DOWN! demands a bit of patience, but the director's timing doesn't fail him, and he brings things to a close on an upbeat note.

Almodovar is fortunate, indeed, that he has such wonderful natural camera subjects in his leads; a script and acting talent almost seem beside the point with lookers like these. The two actors are embattled, romantic troupers in every sense. At age 29, Banderas has embodied a range of characters for Almodovar — the dim-witted, would-be terrorist with an uncanny sense of smell in LABYRINTH OF PASSION, the failed-matador fantasist in MATADOR, the gay murderer in LAW OF DESIRE, and the handsome, Clark Kentish nerd in WOMEN ON THE VERGE. Each of these characters has been something of a bumbler — a hipper, more dangerously amorous version of the boob Eddie Bracken used to play for Preston Sturges. Ricky is the kind of humorless but beguiling one-note crazy that can drain an actor's resources, but Banderas goes deep inside this man-child's psyche and makes the character work. He's both deadly earnest and funny when he asks the struggling, bound-and-gagged Marina, "Can't you try to be a little less selfish and think of others?" When she insults him, it's like a blow to the stomach, and he staggers out of the room, crying in the adolescent, stifled way on which James Dean built a career.

Abril, Spain's biggest box-office star and already the veteran of over 40 films, draws on that experience to make Marina a touching compendium of fragility and survivalist strength. She makes the moment when she finally yields, willingly saying to Ricky, "Tie me up," a real romantic epiphany. Leon, who sings a charming song at Espejo's wrap party, does much to put over the final scene, during which, in typical Almodovar-style, a popular tune on a car radio makes everything all right. Almodovar's unlikeliest muse, the wonderfully hatchet-faced Rossy De Palma, makes the best bad bike-girl since Mercedes

McCambridge growled, "I wanna watch," to a helplessly writhing Janet Leigh in TOUCH OF EVIL. *(Violence, nudity, substance abuse, sexual situations, adult situations.).*

d, Pedro Almodovar; p, Agustin Almodovar; w, Pedro Almodovar; ph, Jose Luis Alcaine; ed, Jose Salcedo; m, Ennio Morricone; prod d, Esther Garcia

Comedy/Romance   (PR:O   MPAA:NR)

TIME GUARDIAN, THE

(Aus.) 89m International Film Management — Chateau/Hemdale — Nelson c

Tom Burlinson *(Ballard)*, Nikki Coghill *(Annie Lassiter)*, Carrie Fisher *(Petra)*, Dean Stockwell *(Boss)*, Damon Sanders *(Smith)*, Tim Robertson *(Ernie McCarthy)*, Wan Thye Liew *(Dr. Sun-Wah)*, Roy Rafferty *(Jim Holt)*, Peter Merrill *(Zuryk)*, Terry Crawford *(Tucker)*, Kirk Alexander *(Narrator)*, Adrian Shirley, Tom Karpanny, Henry Salter, Michaele D. Read, and Peter Healy

Set in 4039, in the wake of the last great neutron war, THE TIME GUARDIAN concerns the earth's last remaining city. Outfitted for time travel, the city jumps from eon to eon in an attempt to escape the Jen-Diki, a once-human race of evil cyborgs who seek to wipe out mankind. When the Jen-Diki penetrate the city's defenses during one especially brutal battle, a portion of the city must be blown up to repel the invaders. As the crippled city careens through time, its leaders dispatch Ballard (Tom Burlinson), a military man, and Petra (Carrie Fisher), a historian, to the Australian outback circa 1988, to ready a site for the city's imminent repair stop. The two materialize safely down under, but the Jen-Diki have traced their route and open up a time portal of their own. Fortunately, the Jen-Diki are thwarted when a 20th-century truck smashes into a cyborg's downlink terminal (unwisely placed in the middle of a highway). Ballard finds an ally in Annie Lassiter (Nikki Coghill), the area's resident sexy geologist, but she and the time travelers are thrown in jail by corrupt local lawmen. By fiddling with Ballard's bracelet, the sheriff unwittingly gives the Jen-Diki a new fix on Ballard and Petra's location, prompting the appearance of a whole army of Jen-Diki enforcers just as Ballard busts out of jail. Fortunately, the city also picks this moment to materialize, and a showdown ensues. The Jen-Diki appear to be winning; then Ballard gets an idea. Stepping into the mighty control room of the city, he emerges with what looks like a giant glowing crayon, which he uses to zap the dreaded Jen-Diki.

Visually lavish but otherwise lackluster, THE TIME GUARDIAN was partly written by John Baxter, an Australian science-fiction writer. Not surprisingly, the film is a pastiche of various sci-fi elements, and the real fun comes from identifying the source material. The domed, nomadic metropolis is straight out of James Blish's "Cities in Flight" novels, while the Jen-Diki (resembling armored samurai soldiers) are a variant of the Cybermen fought by TV time-traveler Doctor Who. It's even suggested that Ballard is a grown-up version of the feral child from THE ROAD WARRIOR, which director-cowriter Brian Hannant helped script.

In THE TIME GUARDIAN, Hannant demonstrates a talent for arresting special effects; however, his inattentiveness to story details mars the film. Viewers are expected to believe that the city-dwellers have no idea what the Jen-Diki are or why they're so nasty; that is, until the extremely clever Ballard thinks to do an autopsy on one of the baddies. What's more, Ballard's mission to the 20th century is just this side of pointless: all he has to do to ready a repair site for the city is create a mound of dirt on which it can land — roughly the equivalent of setting up cinderblocks in the garage. Fisher's Petra, made out to be the city's foremost authority on 20th-century customs, is given virtually nothing to do but camp by a billabong and die heroically. Coghill, the film's romantic interest, plays the kind of unbelievable character who exists only in science-fiction B movies — an aggressive woman scientist who walks around scantily clad despite ever-present danger from deadly androids and threatening humans. The subplot about the backwater Aussie town and its bullying cops is less than enthralling; more intriguing (and barely explored) is the notion that the local aborigines have had contact with the city since ancient times.

Reportedly, THE TIME GUARDIAN experienced much post-production tinkering, with additional scenes hastily shot under the direction of editor Andrew Prowse. This might explain the narrative's choppiness. In any case, this picture is only a minor morsel for genre fans. *(Violence, profanity, nudity, sexual situations.)*

d, Brian Hannant; p, Norman Wilkinson and Robert Lagettie; w, John Baxter and Brian Hannant; ph, Geoff Burton; ed, Andrew J. Prowse; m, Allan Zavod; prod d, George Liddle; art d, Tony Raes and Andrew Blaxland; set d, Christopher Webster and Vicki Niehus; spec, Andrew Mason and Mirage Effects; cos, Jean Turnbull; makup, Jane Surrich and Beverly Freeman

Science Fiction   (PR:C   MPAA:PG)

TIME OF THE GYPSIES

(Yugo.) 142m Forum — Sarajevo/Columbia c

Davor Dujmovic *(Perhan)*, Bora Todorovic *(Ahmed)*, Ljubica Adzovic *(Grandmother)*, Elvira Sali *(Danira)*, Sinolicka Trpkova *(Azra)*, and Husnija Hasimovic *(Merdzan)*

The third film from the Yugoslavian director of the acclaimed WHEN FATHER WAS AWAY ON BUSINESS is an extraordinary epic filled with love, hate, lust, laughter, tears, violence, magic, and much more. But like all good epics, its premise has an elemental simplicity. A kindhearted Gypsy teenager, Perhan (Davor Dujmovic, who costarred in WHEN FATHER WAS AWAY), is forced to leave his ramshackle home in the Skopje ghetto to accompany his young sister Danira (Elvira Sali) on a journey to a hospital where she is to undergo an operation on her bad leg, courtesy of Ahmed (Bora Todorovic), the richest man in the ghetto. Danira and Perhan become separated, and he spends the rest of the film trying to find her so that he can return home and marry Azra (Sinolicka Trpkova), the girl of his dreams. During his odyssey Perhan loses his innocence and learns the way of the world. He becomes involved with Ahmed when his grandmother (Ljubica Adzovic), a magical healer, cures Ahmed's infant son of an illness (Perhan himself has inherited the power to move metal objects through mental telepathy). In return, Ahmed promises to take care of Danira's leg, which is beyond the grandmother's powers. During their journey, Perhan and Danira learn that Ahmed is a ruthless criminal whose wealth has come from exploiting youngsters. Along the way, Ahmed makes stops to pick up children who will work for him as beggars, a young girl who is to become a prostitute, and babies who are to be sold across the border in Italy. Perhan and Danira reassure each other that Ahmed would never cheat them. They also dream that the spirit of their dead mother is with them, her wedding veil trailing in the wind behind Ahmed's car. Of course, their hopes are dashed. Reaching the hospital, Ahmed convinces Perhan to leave his sister in the care of the doctors and to accompany him to Milan to make his fortune. It sounds glamorous until Perhan arrives at Ahmed's squalid headquarters — a collection of rundown house trailers under a freeway. There the child beggars are brutally beaten when they don't bring in enough money, and the girl is "taught her trade" during a gang rape by all the men in the encampment except for Perhan, who refuses to have anything to do with Ahmed and his activities. That soon changes after Perhan himself is beaten and Ahmed threatens to have his sister discharged from the hospital. Perhan's specialty becomes home burglaries, and though he turns over most of his booty to Ahmed, Perhan manages to keep a cut for himself, which he hides in a stone wall. He hopes to accumulate a fortune of his own to take back to his grandmother and bride-to-be, whom he dreams of marrying in a ceremony that will be part Gypsy celebration and part Dorothy Lamour island adventure. As Perhan's criminal career blossoms the homely, gangly teenager becomes a dapper, smooth operator in the Milan underworld. But he never loses sight of his goals. When Ahmed suffers a stroke, he is betrayed by his brothers, who steal his army of Gypsy beggars. Ahmed makes Perhan the new head of the organization and immediately sends him out to find new recruits, warning him, however, to stay away from his home village and his sister's hospital to evade the authorities. Of course, Perhan ignores Ahmed. He finds his sister missing, never even having been admitted to the hospital. Back home, he learns that Azra is pregnant by his womanizing uncle and that the house Ahmed had promised to build for him as a reward for his loyalty doesn't exist. It's a measure of how Perhan has changed that he agrees to marry Azra only on the condition that he can sell her baby as soon as it's born. Born out of wedlock himself, Perhan declares he will not bring up a "bastard" as his own. Returning to Milan, he confronts Ahmed, who dodges Perhan's questions and then slips away. For awhile, Perhan lives the high life with the army of beggars he has brought back for Ahmed, but that ends when Perhan, without Ahmed's protection, loses his organization to a new crime lord who moves onto Ahmed's abandoned turf. Going back to the stone wall, Perhan finds the area flooded, his "fortune" lost. He is left with nothing but the search for his sister and the revenge he has vowed against Ahmed, who has emerged more powerful and prosperous than ever.

Besides having more than enough plot to fill its two-and-a-half hour running time, TIME OF THE GYPSIES has the scale, deep emotions, and rich textures that make its characters and their world come vividly and vitally alive. Director Emir Kusturica has said that his style in this film is a mixture of Ford and Bunuel, and GYPSIES has telling echoes of both. But a more useful comparison may be to Francis Coppola's GODFATHER films — in GYPSIES' operatic tone and tragic vision, as well as the more obvious similarities in both films' treatment of a criminal ethnic subculture (and in the striking resemblance between Ahmed after his stroke and Brando's Don Corleone in decline). Yet, Kusturica also conveys a genuine sense of wonder at the Gypsies' ability to live, love, and dream amid the squalor. But while he displays a master storyteller's eye for detail, GYPSIES is not quite a masterpiece. In its latter stages the film's transitions are a bit abrupt and some of Kusturica's attempts at Bunuelian surrealism are more distracting than compelling. But THE TIME OF THE GYPSIES is certainly a major work and offers the promise that Kusturica may yet produce masterpieces that will require no comparison to other filmmakers' work. (*Violence, nudity, adult situations.*)

d, Emir Kusturica; p, Mirza Pasic; w, Emir Kusturica and Gordan Mihic; ph, Vilko Filac; m, Goran Bregovic

Drama   **(PR:C MPAA:R)**

TIME TROOPERS

(Aust./US) 90m Heritage – Arion – Austrian TV/Prism c

(MORGEN GRAUEN; AKA: MORNING TERROR)

Albert Fortell (*Lenn Varta*), Hannelore Elsner (*Sara Fischer*), Hans Georg Panczak (*Jakob*), Barbara Rudnick (*Rena*), Wolfgang Gasser, Dietrich Siegl, Renee Felden, and Wolfgang Mullner

This film's pedigree is worth noting: it played to crowds in its native Austria in 1984 under the title MORGEN GRAUEN (which can be translated either as "Morning Mist" or "Tomorrow's Cruelty"), then a redubbed, re-edited version appeared bearing a 1986 copyright with the moniker MORNING TERROR. Finally, in 1990, Americans got a look at it on home video under the wholly misleading name TIME TROOPERS (which, however, dispenses with the ambiguity inherent in the German title). As it turns out, TIME TROOPERS is basically a low-key variation on the main premise of LOGAN'S RUN: in the future, after "nuclear fire" has devastated the Earth, one city-state manages to rebuild a modern society. In order to maintain the status quo, the authorities issue every citizen of a certain age an "energy chip," which is a sort of all-purpose credit card. Used carefully, an energy chip should last a person a lifetime. It had better, since those who let their energy credits expire too soon must die – either by their own hands or with the aid of "exit-men." Lenn Varta (Albert Fortell) is the best of these elite assassins, quick and efficient. Jakob (Hans Georg Panczak) is No. 2, and so gung-ho to compete with Lenn he's even acquired Lenn's former lover, Rena (Barbara Rudnick), in a standard two-year state marriage contract. Lenn is a good guy at heart who really loves his current companion, Sara Fischer (Hannelore Elsner), so when the state's top killer discovers that his lover is in touch with the rebel underground (she had to smuggle her aged father out when his energy credits ran low), he protects her. The government finds this out and sends Jakob to execute the pair. He gets Sara, but Venn tracks him back to his apartment for a routine shootout that ends, predictably, with Venn and Rena reunited, facing an uncertain but free future in the wastelands beyond the government's reach.

TIME TROOPERS is more of a think piece than an action film or futuristic spectacle. The bland visuals rely primarily on a block of gray skyscrapers to convey the Orwellian ambience, and the main characters are not particularly interesting (a typical hazard in this genre), with the more memorable dialog provided by the hero's back-talking computer. The best scenes belong to the several victims of the exit-men; one doomed bohemian type, who has burned through his credit in the pursuit of luxuries and good times, throws a "going-away party" with music, rich food, and all his friends present to watch Lenn rub him out. The energy-chip concept is a clever idea of dystopian social control, although explanations of how the scheme works are unfortunately obscured by a haze of futurespeak in the film's early moments. Whatever name you choose to call it, TIME TROOPERS is not terribly exciting. Still, it's not without interest, especially for science-fiction buffs who might want to compare it to the glitzy but shallow LOGAN'S RUN. (*Violence, nudity, sexual situations.*)

d, Peter Samann and L.E. Neiman; p, Knut Ogris, Veit Heidusehka, L.E. Neiman, and Robert Steloff; w, Hans Bachmann, James Wager, James Becket, and Byrd Ehlman; ph, Hanus Polak; ed, Ingrid Koller and Ron Brody; m, Willi Resetarits, Georg Herrnstadt, and Michael Bishop; cos, Evelyn Luef

Science Fiction   **(PR:O MPAA:R)**

TO SLEEP WITH ANGER

95m Edward R. Pressman-SVS/Samuel Goldwyn c

Danny Glover (*Harry Mention*), Richard Brooks (*Babe Brother*), Paul Butler (*Gideon*), Mary Alice (*Suzie*), Carl Lumbly (*Junior*), Sheryl Lee Ralph (*Linda*), Vonetta McGee (*Pat*), Wonderful Smith (*Preacher*), and Ethel Ayler (*Hattie*)

Writer-director Charles Burnett received a lot of attention as a new, major black filmmaker in 1990, even though he had been making films for more than a decade. As a look at black life, TO SLEEP WITH ANGER is indeed notable for its honest, naturalistic presentation. But the film is more than a movie with its heart in the right place; by any standards it is one of the best films of the year, full of strong performances and with a rich script and expressive direction.

Human-scaled movies of any kind about day-to-day family life are rare today, regardless of the race, nationality, or religion of the family members. In this era,

small-scale dramas have beeb relegated to television, and this film itself began as a project for the Public Broadcasting System. But the disappearance of this sort of production from movie theatres is also largely due to the fact that Hollywood simply doesn't do them very well. Whatever entertainment value it may have had, few would argue that PARENTHOOD, as an example, was not as generic a movie as its title indicated, intentionally so to reach the widest possible audience.

But TO SLEEP WITH ANGER grows from its small scale – dictated by its small budget – into a work as full of universal feeling as it is detailed and observant. Danny Glover, like much of the first-rank cast, agreed to appear in the film for a fraction of his usual fee and helped to raise production money as an executive producer. He plays Harry Mention, a hard-bitten drifter who could be a direct descendant of Mister, the cruel husband Glover played opposite Whoopi Goldberg in THE COLOR PURPLE. Harry thoroughly disrupts the lives of a middle-class family in modern-day Los Angeles, and Burnett uses that simple plot as a pretext to examine a surprisingly wide range of human experiences and emotions. Harry shows up one day on the doorstep of Gideon (Paul Butler) and his wife Suzie (Mary Alice). He is an old friend who grew up with the couple in the South. At the time, Gideon's household is filled with tension, much of it created by son Samuel (Richard Brooks), who has kept his nickname, "Babe Brother," into adulthood, largely because he's never grown up. His wife Linda (Sheryl Lee Ralph) is a successful real estate agent. Samuel harbors deep resentment against his older brother, Junior (Carl Lumbly). Junior is hard-working and successful, and Samuel feels that he has always been the favored brother. Junior, meanwhile, resents what he sees to be the way his parents dote on Samuel, despite the fact that Junior does all the heavy work around the house while supporting his pregnant wife, Pat (Vonetta McGee).

Briefly, Harry's arrival adds some excitement to the family life as he helps his citified friends rediscover their rural roots. But Harry begins to develop an insidious edge. He starts bringing old friends into the house, blues singers and hustlers who drink heavily and have vaguely violent pasts. It's indicated that Harry himself may have been involved with a couple of murders. Pat, who does charity work in her spare time, is treated to Harry's folksy dissertation on the values of selfishness, while Samuel's indolence is encouraged by the intruder. When Gideon is disabled by a stroke, Harry assumes control of the household with bleak results, exploiting the family's weaknesses and tensions.

While the drama focuses on the battle for Samuel's soul, there's little in the way of fiery, overwrought confrontation. There aren't even any clearcut delineations of good and evil. The family members, while basically decent, are often selfish and petty, while Harry's seedy friends aren't depicted as completely bad people. Even Harry isn't so much diabolical as he is limited by a life he never chose but tries to live as best he can. Burnett maintains a rigorously even-handed approach to his story, while bringing a wholly original lyricism to his direction. The ensemble cast is inspired, with all handling their characters with assurance. But what really sticks out in TO SLEEP WITH ANGER is its richness of imagery. Burnett photographs Harry as a character who is alternately reassuring and disturbing, going from a placid shot of Harry sleeping on the floor, to a smiling Harry sitting at the kitchen table calmly cleaning his fingernails with the largest pocket knife anyone has ever seen. Other memorable images include shots of the kid next door struggling to play a trumpet, undercutting the stereotypes about blacks and music; Harry cutting his toenails in Gideon's favorite chair as Gideon lies stricken upstairs; and the poignant montage showing the deterioration of Gideon's beloved garden in the wake of his illness. Individually, these scenes could appear in any film, but it is their context that gives them there power here, marking Burnett as a filmmaker with a vital and important vision.

d, Charles Burnett; p, Caldecot Chubb, Thomas S. Byrnes, and Darin Scott; w, Charles Burnett; ph, Walt Lloyd; ed, Nancy Richardson; m, Stephen James Taylor; md, Budd Carr; prod d, Penny Barrett; art d, Troy Myers; cos, Gaye Shannon-Burnett

Drama   **(PR:A MPAA:PG)**

TOO BEAUTIFUL FOR YOU

(Fr.) 91m Cine Valse – D.D. – Orly – S.E.D.I.F. – T.F.1/Orion Classics c

(TROP BELLE POUR TOI)

Gerard Depardieu (*Bernard Barthelemy*), Josiane Balasko (*Colette Chevassu*), Carole Bouquet (*Florence Barthelemy/Neighbor*), Roland Blanche (*Marcello*), Francois Cluzet (*Pascal Chevassu*), Didier Benureau (*Leonce*), Philippe Loffredo (*Tanguy*), Sylvie Orcier (*Marie-Catherine*), Myriam Boyer (*Genevieve*), Flavien Lebarbe (*The Son*), Juana Marques (*The Daughter*), Denise Chalem (*Lorene*), Jean-Louis Cordina (*Gaby*), Stephane Auberghen (*Paula*), Philippe Faure (*Colette's Husband*), Jean-Paul Farre (*Pianist*), Richard Martin (*Man on the Tram*), and Sylvie Simon (*Receptionist*)

Bertrand Blier's wry serio-comedy TOO BEAUTIFUL FOR YOU is a love triangle with some unexpected angles. Depardieu, a stolid bourgeois, has made a success of his life, with a thriving business, two bright children, and a surpassingly beautiful, upper-class wife (Bouquet). Into this life comes a stout and no longer young secretary (Balasko) with whom he falls recklessly in love. Electrified with passion, he finds himself in a continual state of sexual excitement in which the woman who should be his wife is his mistress and vice versa. Starting from this topsy-turvy turn of events, Blier (director of GOING PLACES; GET OUT YOUR HANDKERCHIEFS; and the irresistibly wacky MENAGE) fashions a droll and often surreal comedy of manners. TOO BEAUTIFUL FOR YOU is a bedroom farce played in slow motion, however; there is a melancholy undertone to the ironic adultery taking place beneath the bedsheets.

The early scenes, establishing the growing attraction between the beefy boss and his plump secretary-seductress, are the film's most successful. Although Depardieu and his stunning spouse are the envy of their friends, the picture-perfect Bouquet senses trouble in paradise. Dropping by Depardieu's office unexpectedly, Bouquet is relieved to discover that her husband's office temp is a nonthreatening frump. Depardieu, however, is unable to curb his animal lust and begins absenting himself from hearth and home often enough to reawaken Bouquet's suspicion, a reversal that is also the impetus of a fantasy sequence in which Bouquet appears as Balasko's bedraggled neighbor, who has been abandoned by her husband. In another comic high point, Balasko wanders around a subway station full of men, sharing the afterglow of her love-making with these strangers as if she were the town crier of sexual satisfaction. When presenting such slyly exaggerated versions of reality, director-writer Blier sends our spirits soaring. Unfortunately, as the affair unravels, so does the film—though not before a brilliant set-piece that foreshadows the unhappy ending: through subtle camera movement and costume changes, a dinner party is transformed from a feast for the long-married couple into their wedding celebration, then into yet another party that is crashed by Balasko. By the time Depardieu comes to his senses, his wife has lost all but proprietary interest in him, while Balasko (in flash forwards) settles into a comfortable domestic life with another man. Depardieu is no longer torn between wife and mistress, but abandoned by both.

Since the conceptual interest of Blier's wife-mistress role reversal can only energize his film partially, TOO BEAUTIFUL FOR YOU derives much of its energy from such cinematic devices as flash forwards and internal monologs that express the characters' thoughts. But Blier's narrative freedom and fluid camera cannot provide enough *elan* to preserve the farcically upbeat tone. With no rapprochement in the battle of the sexes, the comedy turns sour as Blier explores his theme, apparently concluding that sexual passion and marital love cannot exist in the same relationship. Blier fails, however, to bring much depth to his observations of how people make their own beds but refuse to lie in them, relying on his considerable technical skills to take the place of insight. Having been led to expect a comedy, one feels betrayed when the film's message turns out to be not only bleak but unedifying. Though TOO BEAUTIFUL FOR YOU remains prodigiously clever, and individual sequences continue to impress, this film about the impossibility of sustaining love is a failure of sustentation in itself. Instead of informing our sadness, Blier's comedic sequences only make it more painful. Musical selections include: Impromptus, Op. 90, Nos. 2 and 3; Andantino, Sonata in D Major, D.959 (performed by Odette Garentlaub); "Rosamunde," D.797, Entr'acte No. 2 (performed by Elly Ameling, Kurt Masur); String Quartet in D Minor, D.810, No. 14 ("Death and the Maiden") (performed by the Melos Quartet); "Wiegenlied," D.498 (performed by Ameling, Dalton Baldwin); Sonata for Piano and Arpeggione, D.821 (performed by Mstislav Rostropovitch, Benjamin Britten); "Fierabras," D.796, Overture (performed by Paul Angerer); Serenade (performed by Doris Soffel, Roland Keller, Marinus Voorberg); "Deutsche Messe," D.872 ("The Lord's Prayer") (performed by the Tolzer Knabenchor, Gerhard Schmidt-Gaden); "German Dance," D.90, No. 1 (performed by Horst Stein, the Bamberger Symphony); "Zwischenaktmusik," Op. 26, No. 3 (performed by Stein, the Bamberger Symphony); Mass in E-flat Major, D.950 ("Sanctus") (performed by Sawallisch, Donath, Popp, Fassbaender, Schreier, Araiza, Dallapozza, Fischer-Dieskau); Waltz, D.779, No. 18 (performed by Alice Ader), all by Franz Schubert; "Love Story" (Francis Lai). (*Adult situations, profanity, nudity, sexual situations.*)

d, Bertrand Blier; w, Bertrand Blier; ph, Philippe Rousselot; ed, Claudine Merlin; m, Franz Schubert; prod d, Theobald Meurisse; cos, Michele Mermande-Cerf; makup, Joel Lavau

Comedy   (PR:O   MPAA:R)

TORN APART

95m Castle Hill c

Adrian Pasdar (*Ben Arnon*), Cecilia Peck (*Laila Malek*), Machram Huri (*Mahmoud Malek*), Amon Zadok (*Prof. Ibrahim Mansour*), Margrit Polak (*Ilana Arnon*), Michael Morim (*Moustapha*), Amos Lavi (*Fawzi*), Hanna Azulai (*Jamilah*), and Barry Primus (*Arie Arnon*)

Gentle-hearted and intermittently effective, TORN APART is an Israeli-Arab version of "Romeo and Juliet" that could be called "West Bank Story." Although prettily photographed in pastels and for the most part savvily cast, the film is one of those well-intentioned, narrative-heavy movies that show little evidence of cinematic intelligence, concentrating all of its energy on presenting a romantic drama with lots of medium shots and cutaways to sunsets. As the film begins, an Israeli soldier, Ben Arnon (Adrian Pasdar), retrieves a letter from a rocky childhood hiding place. He examines the letter, leading to a flashback detailing his boyhood friendship with an Arab girl. Though their parents are unconventional enough not to discourage the children's feelings, Israeli-Arab friendships are not socially acceptable. While the girl's family is away on vacation, the boy and his family move to America, and the children are separated, presumably forever. Years pass, and the Arabs become an occupied people under Israeli rule. The story picks up in 1973, when Ben, returning home with idealistic fervor, has become a soldier in the Israeli army. While inspecting Arabs at a West Bank checkpoint, he encounters his childhood sweetheart, Laila Malek (Cecilia Peck), who is very reluctant to resume their acquaintance. Foolishly, Ben won't take no for an answer, even though Laila's family disapproves of their association. Agreeing to meet Ben, Laila pours out her resentment of Israelis and takes him to see her professor (Arnon Zadok), who educates Ben about the Arab side of the ongoing conflict. Torn between love and duty, Ben realizes his puppy love has blossomed into the real thing—deep but forbidden. Despite some idyllic moments (when the two work together at a kibbutz) the couple cannot get their families to accept their friendship, let alone their burgeoning passion. When Ben temporarily deserts his post, his gun is stolen and some Israeli soldiers are wounded—an occurrence that lands him in serious trouble—but while his moral dilemma grows more complicated, his love cannot be denied. While Ben is admonished by comrades to end the affair, Laila is warned by her family that she might actually be killed for her indiscretion. Eventually Ben's father (Barry Primus) is killed by a mine during the 1973 fighting, causing Ben to turn away from Laila for a time. But he can't suppress his love, and the star-crossed duo make plans to flee the country. Rejecting his patriotic duty, Ben steals a jeep and picks up Laila, who has nearly been seized by her former suitor, an Arab patriot. The lovers run away, and Laila's professor is brutally slain by her ex-admirer—who, in turn, is killed by Israeli soldiers. Unfortunately, Ben and Laila's flight is prevented. Separated from Ben the next day—when the funerals of the slain Arabs turn into a melee—Laila is fatally shot by someone in the rioting crowd. Clasping her body to him, Ben carries her into the Arab settlement. The film ends as it began, with Ben reading the letter he hid in the rocks when he and his Arab love were childhood friends.

Brimming with goodwill toward all mankind, TORN APART has an interesting story to relate, but does so with little urgency. The result is an overly familiar love triangle, the three points being girl, boy, and ideology. Despite all the love-versus-duty conflicts brewing in the story, the film emerges as a rather placid romance, without the necessary vitality to pump life into its pedestrian dramaturgy. Director Jack Fisher, an acclaimed documentary filmmaker (A GENERATION APART) making his feature debut here, obviously cares deeply for the message implicit in the movie's screenplay, but the script offers neither memorable dialog nor revelation. You can predict all the plot developments practically from the opening credits, and the movie's sluggish pacing doesn't drive the film forward.

Though pleasant to look at and cast with two attractive leads, TORN APART's preponderance of talking-heads political scenes becomes tiresome, leaving viewers with nothing to do but wonder about the lovers' foolhardiness. No longer swept along by the lovers' passion and frenzy, one begins to ask some simple questions. Couldn't less drastic travel plans for leaving the country have been arranged? Why does Ben constantly jeopardize his beloved's life—isn't his grand amour a little selfish? Why isn't he jailed for going AWOL? What happens to him after Laila's death? And why is it almost always the woman who bites the dust at the end of all these ill-fated romance films? (WEST SIDE STORY is an exception.)

Among the large cast, Primus is a standout as the hero's nationalistic father, and Peck (Gregory's daughter, in her film debut) is striking, although the purple passions she is required to enact sometimes threaten to overwhelm her characterization. Charismatic and darkly sensual, Pasdar (NEAR DARK; VITAL SIGNS) seems headed for major movie stardom; he holds this unexceptional movie together with his magnetic presence. (*Sexual situations, profanity, violence, nudity, adult situations.*)

d, Jack Fisher; p, Danny Fisher and Jerry Menkin; w, Marc Kristal (based on the book *A Forbidden Love* by Chayym Zeldis); ph, Barry Markowitz; ed, Michael Garvey; m, Peter Arnow

Drama/Romance   (PR:C   MPAA:R)

TORRENTS OF SPRING

(Fr./It.) 101m Erre — Reteitalia — Ariane/Millimeter c

Timothy Hutton (*Dimitri Sanin*), Nastassja Kinski (*Maria Nikolaevna Polozov*), Valeria Golino (*Gemma Rosselli*), William Forsythe (*Polozov*), Urbano Barberini (*Von Doenhof*), Francesca De Sapio (*Signora Rosselli*), Jacques Herlin (*Pantaleone*), Antonio Cantafora (*Richter*), Christopher Janczar (*Kluber*), Christian Dottorini (*Emilio*), Alexia Korda (*Frau Stoltz*), Marinella Anaclerio (*Luisa*), Pietro Bontempo (*Man With Glasses*), Thierry Langerak (*The Moon*), Xavier Maly (*Pulcinella*), Anna Piccioni, Massimo Sarchielli (*Gypsies*), Serge Spira (*Doctor*), Elena Schapova, Antonella Ponziani (*Maids*), and Jerzy Skolimowski (*Victor Victorovich*)

For those who were wondering, TORRENTS OF SPRING answers the question of whatever happened to Timothy Hutton and Nastassja Kinski. But it also signals a strong return for director Jerzy Skolimowski, whose last major work was 1982's MOONLIGHTING, and who adapted the film from Ivan Turgenev's novel *Torrents of Spring*.

On the negative side, Skolimowski's version has most of the earmarks of a mishmash multinational production — including bad dubbing, cheap cinematography, and a cheesy, dentist-office music score. But, for all of that, it is also beguiling, mesmerizing, and memorable. In TORRENTS, a Russian nobleman, Sanin (Hutton), returning home from a tour of Europe, stops off in Mainz, Germany, where he is smitten with a pastry cook, Gemma (Valeria Golino, who played Tom Cruise's girl friend in RAINMAN). He steals her away from her foppish, haberdasher fiance and even fights a duel with an Army officer who insults her in public. Having proposed marriage, Sanin decides to sell his Russian estate, freeing his serfs, and invest in Gemma's family business. However, noblemen do not become humble pastry shop proprietors overnight, and before too long, Sanin is smitten again, this time with Maria (Kinski), the wanton wife of his blueblooded childhood friend Polozov (William Forsythe), who emerges as a buyer for Sanin's Russian holdings. Herself the illegitimate daughter of a Russian nobleman, Maria has used her wits, along with beauty, to put together a fortune of her own. Sanin offers the estate at a bargain-basement price, with the freeing of the serfs as a prerequisite for the sale, and to expedite the deal, Maria gives Sanin a literal tumble in the hay — with predictable, though logical, results for all involved.

What gives TORRENTS its unexpected power is the ironic distance Skolimowski maintains from all these 19th-century heaving bosoms and fevered brows. The characters are finally not so much enslaved to their passions as they are to history — not too unlike the Polish foreman Jeremy Irons played in MOONLIGHTING, stranded in London during the rise of Solidarity and the imposition of martial law in his homeland. Sanin is defined by his utter fecklessness (making the terminally boyish Hutton a perfect casting choice for the role). He's vaguely aware that he and his kind are teetering on the verge of extinction, but he has no real idea of how he is to fit into the new society about to be created by the rise of the middle class. He makes a tentative move in the right direction with Gemma, and with his decision to free his serfs, at the time a radical idea. Yet he remains tragically vulnerable to Maria's world of leisure, luxury, and romantic intrigue (and with Kinski as tantalizing as ever as Maria, who can blame him?). Gemma, guided by her hardheaded mother, is motivated by ruthless practicality, sensing in Sanin (much more than in her former suitor) the opportunity to expand her business, with the prospect of becoming a noblewoman by marriage providing an added bonus. Maria, meanwhile, is just plain ruthless, a self-made woman who would be a formidable match for any of today's Wall Street sharks, shrewdly using her connections to nobility and her sexual prowess to build her personal fortune — buying low (estates in decline from the likes of Sanin) and selling high (her charms, also to the likes of Sanin).

There is neither a misty nostalgia for a noble age gone by nor a knowing anticipation of modernism in Skolimowski's treatment, which makes the film eminently faithful to Turgenev, whose novel was published in 1872. Rather, the director keeps linking the movements of his characters to the rhythms of nature. One result of this is that TORRENTS may have more animal actors in it than THE BEAR: Skolimowski fills the frame with horses, geese, dogs, cats, and pigs, often in humorously witty, attention-getting contexts, as if the key image, for him, were the kitten stranded in a tree that first brings Sanin and Gemma together. As we later discover, the kitten has more in common with Sanin than it does with Gemma. Thus, what happens to Sanin is neither tragic nor absurd — though it has both tragic and absurd elements — but instead emblematic of the historical passage from an age of stratified noble rot to a free-enterprise social Darwinism.

For all its cerebral complexity, however, TORRENTS moves along at almost torrential speed, clocking in at just over 100 minutes. Once again, Skolimowski's talent for crafting a taut, compelling narrative rich in ideas is evident. His is a cinema of intelligence, vitality, and feeling — attributes rarely found together in movies nowadays. It can only be hoped that it doesn't take another eight years before we hear decisively from him again. (*Adult situations.*)

d, Jerzy Skolimowski; p, Angello Rizzoli; w, Jerzy Skolimowski and Arcangelo Bonaccorso (based on the novel by Ivan Turgenev); ph, Dante Spinotti and Witold Sobocinski; ed, Cesare D'Amico and Andrzej Kostenko; m, Stanley Myers; prod d, Francesco Bronzi; set d, Nello Giorgetti; stunts, Franco Fantasia; cos, Theodor Pistek and Sibylle Ulsamer; makup, Guiseppe Banchelli

Drama/Romance   (PR:C   MPAA:PG-13)

TOTAL RECALL

109m Mario Kassar — Andrew Vajna — Carolco — Ronald Shusett/Tri-Star c

Arnold Schwarzenegger (*Doug Quaid*), Rachel Ticotin (*Melina*), Sharon Stone (*Lori Quaid*), Ronny Cox (*Cohaagen*), Michael Ironside (*Richter*), Marshall Bell (*George/Kuato*), Mel Johnson Jr. (*Benny*), Michael Champion (*Helm*), Roy Brocksmith (*Dr. Edgemar*), Ray Baker (*McClane*), Rosemary Dunsmore (*Dr. Lull*), David Knell (*Ernie*), Alexia Robinson (*Tiffany*), Dean Norris (*Tony*), Mark Carlton (*Bartender*), Debbie Lee Carrington (*Thumbelina*), Lycia Naff (*Mary*), Robert Costanzo (*Harry*), Michael LaGuardia (*Stevens*), Pricilla Allen (*Fat Lady*), Ken Strausbaugh (*Immigration Officer*), Marc Alaimo (*Everett*), Michael Gregory (*Rebel Lieutenant*), Ken Gilden (*Hotel Clerk*), Mickey Jones (*Burly Miner*), Parker Whitman (*Martian Husband*), Ellen Gollas (*Martian Wife*), Gloria Dorson (*Woman in Phone Booth*), Erika Carlson (*Miss Lonelyhearts*), Benny Corral (*Punk Cabbie*), Bob Tzudiker (*Doctor*), Erik Cord (*Lab Assistant*), Frank Kopyc (*Technician*), Chuck Sloan, Dave Nicolson (*Scientists*), Paula McClure (*Newscaster*), Rebecca Ruth (*Reporter*), Milt Tarver (*Commercial Announcer*), Roger Cudney (*Agent*), Monica Steuer (*Mutant Mother*), Sasha Rionda (*Mutant Child*), Linda Howell (*Tennis Pro*), and Robert Picardo (*Voice of Johnnycab*)

TOTAL RECALL is a prime example of a Hollywood movie run amok. Overloaded with special effects and action, flooded with wall-to-wall music, and dominated by a larger-than-life star, the film drowns in its own excesses. What starts out as an interesting and possibly engrossing story quickly degenerates into a horribly violent, idiotic vehicle for Arnold Schwarzenegger. Having become a sub-genre unto himself — complete with certain script requirements and a mandatory directorial style — Schwarzenegger has once again managed to stifle the talents of a good director (as he did to John Irvin with RAW DEAL). In this case the victim is Dutch filmmaker Paul Verhoeven, an extremely talented director who has created some first-class work, including SPETTERS; THE FOURTH MAN; FLESH AND BLOOD (probably the best of the sword and sorcery films of the 80s); and his breakthrough film, ROBOCOP. But little of Verhoeven's personality is able to penetrate the walls of the rampant Schwarzenegger persona in TOTAL RECALL, and the results are numbing.

Set in the year 2084, TOTAL RECALL tells the story of Doug Quaid (Schwarzenegger), a construction worker with a beautiful wife (played with overwhelming seductiveness by Sharon Stone) and a nice home. The future has brought Quaid a pretty wonderful life on earth, and it has also brought the colonization of the planet Mars. Quaid has never been to Mars, but he dreams of it every night (and of a mysterious woman he has never met). Determined to find out what these dreams mean, Quaid decides to visit Rekall Inc., a travel service that specializes in implanting *memories* of vacations into its customers' brains. For a small fee, Quaid buys a memory trip to Mars. Included in the package is Rekall's special Ego Trip, which allows the customer to take his memory trip as another person. Quaid chooses to make his trip as a secret agent. When the doctors begin the implant, something goes terribly wrong. Even before the memory is implanted, Quaid becomes crazed, claiming that he *is* a secret agent from Mars. Eventually, the doctors subdue Quaid and erase the entire episode from his brain. Later, Quaid is attacked by coworkers and nearly killed by his wife, who confirms that he really was an agent (a part of his life that has been erased from his memory). She also explains that she is not really his wife, but another agent assigned to watch him. After fighting off would-be killers and learning more about his past (with the help of a pre-recorded message from himself), Quaid escapes to Mars to unlock the rest of the mystery. But he is hotly pursued by members of the agency that is headed by the evil Cohaagen (scenery-chewing Ronny Cox), a politician who rides roughshod over the colonies on Mars. So tyrannical is Cohaagen's rule that he provides nothing for Mars' inhabitants (most of whom are mutant criminals), allowing the planet to become a kind of outer-space version of Beirut, where a war is raging between Cohaagen's troops and rebels led by the mysterious Kuato when Quaid arrives. Hooking up with a group of rebel mutants, Quaid meets the girl from his dreams (Rachel Ticotin), who, it turns out, knew him when he was an agent. Many twists and turns (and *plenty* of deaths, including that of Quaid's "wife") later, Quaid discovers the truth of his past. The film climaxes with a battle between Cohaagen and Quaid over an ancient alien conductor capable of providing the colonists with air (Mars' atmosphere is too pressurized to live in, and Cohaagen has refused to supply the confined denizens with air). In the end Quaid saves the planet, kills

Cohaagen, and gets the girl—just the way the salesman at Rekall promised Quaid's vacation would turn out.

Based on a story by Phillip K. Dick, TOTAL RECALL has an interesting subtext (the search for identity, a theme prominent in much of Dick's work) and for the first half-hour, the film is quite intriguing. But it doesn't take long before Schwarzenegger's bulging muscles and Rob Bottin's exploding bodies take over completely. Regrettably, Verhoeven is not accomplished enough as an action director to keep these flashy elements in check, even though his previous work (most of which was also very violent) has been uncommonly intelligent. In the past Verhoeven has explored the psyches of his characters and provided much food for thought. He would seem a natural choice to direct a version of a Dick story (ROBOCOP's themes are strikingly familiar to those explored by the writer). However, Verhoeven is simply unable to tame the spectacle of TOTAL RECALL.

Verhoeven's ROBOCOP is weakest in its action sequences; directed with little personality and too much emphasis on wild camera movements, they are heartless and too crowd-pleasing, marring what could have been a classic film. Luckily, there is much more to ROBOCOP than just action. Unfortunately, the same can't be said for TOTAL RECALL. ROBOCOP works for all the reasons TOTAL RECALL doesn't. ROBOCOP has resonance, TOTAL RECALL doesn't. ROBOCOP has terrific performances, TOTAL RECALL doesn't. Most important, ROBOCOP has heart, a virtue that is totally lacking in TOTAL RECALL. In fact, TOTAL RECALL is a strikingly hollow film that owes its lifelessness to Schwarzenegger, whose features are cold, by-the-numbers work-outs despite the talents of his collaborators. (Tellingly, director Ridley Scott, normally a cold visualist, did a better job with the Schwarzenegger-less BLADE RUNNER, based on another Dick story, than the more talented Verhoeven has done here.) Reportedly budgeted between $60 and $73 million, TOTAL RE-CALL is a disappointment even in its production values. Although Bottin's special effects are quite impressive and some of the sets are striking, the overall effect is routine. The matte paintings are weak and the design is rather cheesy looking (with some shots even resembling Dino De Laurentiis' FLASH GOR-DON [1980]), begging the question, where did all the money go?

Failing to hide the flaws of the effects, TOTAL RECALL's lamebrained, derivative script (which Verhoeven claims went through some 20 revisions) appears to have been the director's greatest obstacle. Owing a great debt to BLADE RUNNER; OUTLAND; THE THING; THE DARK CRYSTAL; and even the low-budget horror film BASKETCASE, TOTAL RECALL reeks of desperation. The story is told in huge expository chunks, intercut with massive action sequences, and none of it holds together.

Schwarzenegger performs the usual Schwarzenegger shtick (fortunately he's limited to only two or three of his patented "witty" quips) as he lumbers around looking confused—which is essentially all that the script requires of him. The villains, on the other hand, steal the show. Cox (who also performed bad guy duties in ROBOCOP) has plenty of fun and, near the end, delivers the film's best line. And Michael Ironside (a terrific character actor whose best work can be seen in SCANNERS and VISITING HOURS) is wonderful as the agency's top pursuer. The other performers don't fare as well: Stone, although very sexy, is wasted, and Ticotin is nothing but window dressing.

Of course, a film of this genre wouldn't be complete without the all-important misogyny, and TOTAL RECALL has plenty of it. Women are punched, slapped, insulted, and, at one point, ordered up on a menu. Obviously the inclusion of these misogynistic elements is disturbing, but what is even more reprehensible is that they have become de rigueur in films like TOTAL RECALL.

Another disturbing element of the film is its incredible violence. In a year in which controversy has surrounded the X ratings for THE COOK, THE THIEF, HIS WIFE AND HER LOVER and the low-budget sci-fi thriller HARDWARE, nothing has been said about the extraordinary blood-letting in TOTAL RECALL (heads are blown off, arms are ripped from bodies, people are drilled, punctured, and broken in two—not to mention the exploding heads and bulging eyes). Maybe if Schwarzenegger had starred in HARDWARE and its budget had been $70 million, the MPAA would have thought differently. The fact remains that TOTAL RECALL is an ultra-violent film that may be too much for some to take. Despite a strong opening third (with some really funny moments that recall the wit of ROBOCOP) and ace technical credits, TOTAL RECALL is a major disappointment, yet another idiotic musclefest that adds to the increasing volume of Schwarzenegger turkeys. The film earned Oscar nominations for its sound and its sound effects editing. (Gore effects, profanity, adult situations, nudity, sexual situations.)

d, Paul Verhoeven; p, Buzz Feitshans and Ronald Shusett; w, Ronald Shusett, Dan O'Bannon, and Gary Goldman (based on a story by Ronald Shusett, Dan O'Bannon, Jon Povill, from the short story "We Can Remember It for You Wholesale" by Phillip K. Dick); ph, Jost Vacano; ed, Frank J. Urioste; m, Jerry Goldsmith; prod d, William Sandell; art d, James Tocci and Jose Rodriguez Granada; set d, Marco Trentini, Miguel Chang, and Carlos Echeverria; spec, Rob Bottin, Thomas L. Fisher, and Eric Brevig; stunts, Vic Armstrong and Joel

Kramer; cos, Erica Edell Phillips; makup, Jefferson Dawn, Craig Berkeley, and Robin Weiss; anim, Jeff Burks

Action/Science Fiction   (PR:O   MPAA:R)

TOUCH OF A STRANGER

87m Raven-Star c

Shelley Winters *(Lily)*, Anthony Nocerino *(Jet)*, Danny Capri *(Finny)*, and Haley Taylor-Block *(Grocery Girl)*

Too tasteful to be a true camp classic but too nutty to be viewed as anything but camp, this maudlin melodrama plays a little like SUNSET BOULEVARD—were that great film to have been written and directed by its tragic heroine, Norma Desmond. Certainly there is none of Billy Wilder's trademark irony in this straight-faced tale of a lonely old woman and the brooding, hunky young cop killer (Stallone-clone Anthony Nocerino in his film debut) who invades her home—and seemingly touches her heart. Actually, it's not clear exactly what the old woman's reaction is to the intruder, since Shelley Winters, as Lily, gives one of her more daft performances-from-another-planet, acting in a movie playing only in her head. During the opening credits, Lily engages in what seems to be her sole daytime activity, sitting on a bench in the walled-in backyard of her Middletown tract home and staring into space. That night, fate rears its ugly head and deposits the plot of the film on her doorstep in the form of the young thug, Jet (Norcerino). Sporting a nasty-looking bullet wound in his side, Jet, who has allegedly killed a cop, needs a place to stay for the night; he's leaving the next day for South America. Why he's going and how he'll get there is never explained. But that doesn't matter. What does matter (and this is the true horror) is that Jet is a Method-acting houseguest who won't leave. (That's right, we're in another installment of "It Came from Actor's Studio!") Lily splashes a little gin on the bullet wound, applies a few bandages, and Jet is back to normal. In fact, the very next morning he demonstrates his usual violent nature when he gets into a snarling match with Lily about putting tomatoes in his omelette. "I don't open my door in decades! And when I do, I let in a maniac!" complains Lily. But she gets back at her visitor soon enough, first with a seemingly endless a cappella croaking of an ancient Johnny Mercer tune, then by hiding Jet's gun. Jet responds with another fit of sub-Brando moping, mumbling, and Methodizing. Lily counters by talking into linen closets, conversing with her reflection in the dinnerware, and becoming upset when Jet begins playing with an electric train that belonged to someone who was very important to Lily, though we never learn who. However, it is apparent these two lonely people have something in common (in addition to the ferocious inarticulateness of the actors portraying them), though, again, what they have in common never becomes clear. Apparently, virtually all of the scenes dealing with Lily's character were either cut or went unfilmed when the production money ran out. Lily does tend to go into voiceover mode before she drifts off to sleep at night, but these voiceovers explain nothing. Nonsensical flashbacks, introduced by rippling-water effects, aren't much help either. One reveals that Jet's little buddy, Finny (Danny Capri), was run over by a Mercedes after trying to steal nails from a hardware store; another demonstrates that Jet did indeed shoot a cop, who was trying to roust him out of the city park at closing time.

Naturally, a grudging affection develops between Lily and Jet. Soon the misunderstood hunk is happily tinkering in the garage—fixing broken furniture and trying to get Lily's ancient sedan running again. He doesn't really finish either project, but his involvement with them sets the stage for the affectionate scenes between Lily and Jet that make up the bulk of TOUCH OF A STRANGER's running time. Sliding into the immobile car, the two fall asleep in each other's arms. The next morning, Jet and Lily cryptically refer to something that happened the previous night that has apparently put their relationship on a new plane. Jet begins wearing old clothes and smoking cigars that belonged to Lily's husband, son, or maybe the last maniac she let into the house. Tragically, an evil girl scout blows the whistle on Lily and Jet's cozy little arrangement. In no time, the cops arrive. Actually, we don't see any police as such, but sirens and mouthy extras are heard on the soundtrack and weird lights come through Lily's windows. As Jet, hands on his head, mopes off to meet his fate, Lily yells at the mouthy extras, "Whatsamatter? Haven't you ever seen a woman before?" Then she slams her door for the next couple of decades.

Wacky, weird, zany—TOUCH OF A STRANGER is all of those things and more. Unfortunately, it doesn't appear that the film was intended to embody any of those characteristics. What it wants to be is one of those intense, overwrought talking-heads dramas—last in vogue during the late 50s and early 60s—in which a couple of characters sit in a room and bare their souls to each other for what seems like an eternity. In truth, there's something admirable about Winters' refusal to go gently into dignified show-business dotage; instead, she insists on going hysterically over the top in movies like this. Her offbeat rebellion is a breath of fresh air in today's sterilized, corporate moviemaking environment. That doesn't make TOUCH OF A STRANGER a good movie, but there is nevertheless something strangely reassuring about the fact that it was made at all. (*Profanity.*)

d, Brad Gilbert; p, Hakon Gundersen and Andre Stone Guttfreund; w, Joslyn Barnes and Brad Gilbert; ph, Michael Negrin; ed, William Goldenberg; m, Jack Alan Goga; prod d, Richard Sherman; cos, Sharon Lynch

Drama   (PR:C   MPAA:R)

TREE OF HANDS, THE

(SEE: INNOCENT VICTIM)

TREMORS

96m No Frills — Wilson-Maddock/Universal c

Kevin Bacon (*Valentine McKee*), Fred Ward (*Earl Basset*), Finn Carter (*Rhonda LeBeck*), Michael Gross (*Burt Gummer*), Reba McEntire (*Heather Gummer*), Bobby Jacoby (*Melvin Plug*), Charlotte Stewart (*Nancy*), Tony Genaro (*Miguel*), Ariana Richards (*Minday*), Richard Marcus (*Nestor*), Victor Wong (*Walter Chang*), Sunshine Parker (*Edgar*), Michael Dan Wagner (*Old Fred*), Conrad Bachmann (*Jim*), Bibi Besch (*Megan*), John Goodwin (*Howard*), and John Pappas (*Carmine*)

Since they appeared in theaters at about the same time, early in 1990, TREMORS and DOWNTOWN would make a good double feature. The executive producer on both was Gale Anne Hurd (TERMINATOR; ALIENS; THE ABYSS), and it's no coincidence that both are also entertaining, well-crafted B movies. Demonstrating the approach that she learned from her Roger Corman roots, Hurd now arguably out-Cormans Corman, who continues pumping out B movies that seldom make it to theater screens before shuffling off into home video limbo.

Although this is only the third film Hurd has made without the collaboration of her ex-husband, director James Cameron, she has been able to persuade a major studio to release all three. Her success is somewhat unlikely, however; her films go against the grain of Hollywood's high-concept fixation, offering instead relatively well-known stars in modest genre efforts. One explanation may be that, in time-honored B-movie tradition, the films are made so cheaply (at least by studio standards) that the studio can sink a considerable amount of money into a weekend of frenzied promotion and still wind up ahead once sales to video and cable outlets are exploited.

This isn't to complain; if anything, it's a relief that studios still find space in their megabuck production schedules to put out modest, quirky entertainment. Much has been made of the fact that TREMORS fondly recalls monster movies of the 50s, but since the majority of today's moviegoers were born in the 70s, most will barely remember whence Freddy Krueger sprang, much less such films as Howard Hawks's THE THING, one of many sci-fi creature features TREMORS fondly quotes. Thus, TREMORS draws on a genre so old that it's new (a departure from Hurd's BAD DREAMS, a gory psycho-horror epic scored by heavy-metal rockers Guns N' Roses, and her LETHAL WEAPON clone DOWNTOWN). As a result, the script, cowritten by director Ron Underwood and producers S.S. Wilson and Brent Maddock (Wilson and Maddock wrote SHORT CIRCUIT and its sequel and cowrote BATTERIES NOT INCLUDED), wisely treads a middle path between knowing sendup and cannily crafted chiller.

Trying to escape their dead-end life in the desert town of Perfection (population 14), handymen Val (Kevin Bacon) and Earl (Fred Ward) find themselves sidetracked when corpses mysteriously begin piling up around them, the causes of death ranging from the strange (an old drunk is found halfway up an electrical tower dead from dehydration) to the unknown. When the handymen have a run-in with some creepy tentacled creatures that have apparently made lunch out of a road crew, they realize they are in deep trouble and retreat to the town to spread some hysteria and prepare for Mankind's last stand against a really disgusting menace: giant, foul-smelling, flesh-eating, mutant maggots. Although these maggots are not the intellectual equals of THE THING's thinking carrot, their mental powers are still mind-boggling. Detecting a human morsel hiding in a car, the maggots dig under the vehicle, causing it to sink into the earth. When the survivors think they have outwitted the wily worms by taking refuge atop the roofs of buildings, the beasts merely destroy the buildings' foundations. The maggots are quick learners when it comes to stalking their prey, and the humans must be continually on their toes if they are to keep from becoming worm food while they try desperately to find a more permanent way to defeat the monsters.

TREMORS bends its movie cliches just enough to keep the action interesting and entertaining. One of the most fondly held conventions of 50s horror films was to withhold a straight-on view of the monsters until late in the picture; in TREMORS the beasts emerge early in the action, which, in another departure from convention, takes place almost entirely in broad daylight. The special effects are first-rate, with the maggots easily withstanding extended camera scrutiny. Another upended convention places a female scientist (Finn Carter) in the thick of the action, although she contributes little to our knowledge of the beasts and, before long, becomes irritated by the questions of the excited townsfolk. It turns out that the dumbest guys in the movie, Val and Earl, contribute the most towards eradicating the big bugs, with their prime motivation being to get the job done so they can continue their rudely interrupted journey out of Perfection.

You don't have to be a perennial late-night movie vidiot to get a kick out of TREMORS. It's fast-moving fun for kids of all ages who harbor a secret delight in movies starring gooey, smelly monsters. It's also very well cast, with Ward and Bacon proving affable and enjoyable comedy leads. Carter also has an offbeat appeal as the irritable woman of science, while Michael Gross and country star Reba McEntire, in a most unlikely film debut (she also wrote and sings the end-credit song, "Why Not Tonight?"), provide solid support as a survivalist couple who dispatch one of the creatures in a hail of bullets. It may not top anyone's 10-best list, but TREMORS is nevertheless solid meat 'n' potatoes (and maggots) entertainment. (*Violence, profanity.*)

d, Ron Underwood; p, Brent Maddock and S.S. Wilson; w, S.S. Wilson and Brent Maddock (based on a story by S.S. Wilson, Brent Maddock, and Ron Underwood); ph, Alexander Gruszynski; ed, O. Nicholas Brown; m, Ernest Troost; md, Ernest Troost; prod d, Ivo Cristante; art d, Donald Maskovich; set d, Debra Combs; spec, Gene Warren Jr.; stunts, Gary Jensen; makeup, The Flying Fabrizi Sisters

Comedy/Horror   (PR:C   MPAA:PG-13)

TROP BELLE POUR TOI

(Fr.) (SEE: TOO BEAUTIFUL FOR YOU)

TUNE IN TOMORROW

108m Polar/Cinecom c

Barbara Hershey (*Aunt Julia*), Keanu Reeves (*Martin Loader*), Peter Falk (*Pedro Carmichael*), Bill McCutcheon (*Puddler*), Patricia Clarkson (*Aunt Olga*), Jerome Dempsey (*Sam/Sid*), Peter Gallagher (*Richard Quince*), Dan Hedaya (*Robert Quince*), Buck Henry (*Fr. Serafim*), Hope Lange (*Margaret Quince*), John Larroquette (*Dr. Albert Quince*), Elizabeth McGovern (*Elena Quince*), Robert Sedgwick (*Elmore Dubuque*), Henry Gibson (*Big John Coot*), Richard B. Schull, and Joel Fabiani

TUNE IN TOMORROW, the screen adaptation of Mario Vargas Llosa's acclaimed novel *Aunt Julia and the Scriptwriter*, is an amiable comedy that overcomes its faults with the sheer charm of its performers and the talent of its director, Jon Amiel. The film, which takes place in 1951, stars Barbara Hershey as Aunt Julia, a 36-year-old divorcee who comes to New Orleans in search of a new husband (preferably a rich old one with a heart condition), but instead begins a secret romance with her 21-year-old nephew—by marriage—Martin (Keanu Reeves), who is a newswriter at a local radio station. Another new arrival to town is eccentric scriptwriter Pedro Carmichael (Peter Falk), a self-proclaimed "artist" who likes to dress up in outlandish costumes and live out the lives of his characters. He is hired by Martin's bosses at WXBU to raise their sagging ratings by writing a new radio soap opera called "Kings of the Garden District." On their first meeting, Martin and Pedro nearly kill each other fighting over a typewriter, but soon they become friends. Pedro turns into a mentor for Martin, who has aspirations of becoming a real writer himself. Dedicated to turning Martin into a "true artist," Pedro begins manipulating Aunt Julia and Martin's relationship, as well as using their actual exchanges as dialog for his radio show. The soap opera becomes a huge success (Amiel presents the radio show on two levels; scenes of the older, plain-looking actors reading their lines in the studio are intercut with a full and extravagantly realized unfolding of the drama, complete with a cast of unbilled well-known actors—including Buck Henry, Elizabeth McGovern and Peter Gallagher—hamming it up riotously), but there is some backlash; Pedro has laced the show with offensive ethnic wise-cracks about Albanians, causing protesters to picket the station and threaten the well-being of all those involved. In addition to the "Albanian problem," Pedro's meddling has infuriated Martin and caused the breakup of his love affair with Julia (an affair which is now well-known to the family, thanks to Pedro). The film climaxes as Pedro, alone in the studio, performs the last episode of "Kings of the Garden District" while angry Albanians assault the station. Meanwhile, Martin tries to win back the love of Julia and prove to her that their relationship can last. Martin and Julia finally get back together and, needless to say, Pedro's tampering has provided some valuable lessons for Martin, who can now become a true "artist." The film ends with Pedro—in one of his many disguises—being pursued by angry Albanians and infuriated station managers, as he drives off to a new town; while Martin and Aunt Julia decide to get married and live in Paris.

Amiel would seem to be the perfect choice to direct TUNE IN TOMORROW. The story-within-the-story construction of the film echoes the style of "The

Singing Detective," the brilliant mini-series that Amiel directed for British TV, and the overall sentimental tone of the script matches the feel of Amiel's terrific 1989 release QUEEN OF HEARTS. But the director fails to successfully bring these two styles together. Although extremely funny, the outrageous melodrama of the soap opera feels like an intrusion on the relationships of the real characters. The drama that unfolds between Reeves and Hershey (which remains the most interesting thing in the film) always seems to get shortchanged in favor of a cheap laugh or kooky sight-gag. The film does work, despite the wildly uneven screenplay, mainly due to the performances. Falk is absolutely hilarious (especially funny is the inspiring speech he gives his radio actors before they go on the air), Hershey, as usual, is wonderful and the cast of players acting out the "Kings of the Garden District" are quite amusing (with Henry, Gallagher and Dan Hedaya as the standouts); only Reeves seems to be struggling, and his forced southern accent is a bit distracting (much more distracting are moments in the film when he looks *exactly* like Jerry Lewis). The technical credits are all impressive: Robert Stevens' photography is terrific, Jim Clay's production design is strikingly authentic and Wynton Marsalis' score is easily one of the best of the year; the opening credits—which are *read* by Henry Gibson and not shown—are wonderfully original. TUNE IN TOMORROW's structure and tone may be a bit of a mess, but the film is never boring and it's often quite funny (the Albanian jokes—which are so ridiculous that they could never be considered offensive—standout as the film's biggest laughs); it provides 105 minutes of light, goofball entertainment, but, one still wishes that Amiel would have chosen something with a bit more resonance as his followup to QUEEN OF HEARTS. (*Adult situations, profanity.*)

d, Jon Amiel; p, John Fiedler and Mark Tarlov; w, William Boyd (based on the novel *Aunt Julia and the Scriptwriter* by Mario Vargas Llosa); ph, Robert Stevens; ed, Peter Boyle; m, Wynton Marsalis; prod d, Jim Clay; cos, Betsy Heiman; chor, Quinny Sacks

Comedy/Romance   (PR:A-C   MPAA:PG-13)

TUSKS

99m Elephant's Child/Magnum c

(AKA: FIRE IN EDEN)

John Rhys-Davies *(Roger Singh)*, Lucy Gutteridge *(Micah Hill)*, Andrew Stevens *(Mark Smith)*, Julian Glover *(Ian Taylor)*, Wendy Clifford *(Jane Taylor)*, David Phetoe *(Watson)*, Victor Melleney *(Fred Johnson)*, John Rixey Moore, James Coburn Jr., Sekai Sadza, Tembi, Kathy Kuleyz, Godfrey Majonga, Sam Williams, Oliver Tengende, and David Guwaza

Filmed several years ago in Zimbabwe under the title FIRE IN EDEN, this movie underwent delays and postproduction surgery before limping into the 1990 home-video marketplace as TUSKS. An unsure blend of wildlife conservation drama and revenge thriller, the film features Lucy Gutteridge as Micah Hill, a famous artist invited to an African nature preserve by park ranger Ian Taylor (Julian Glover). He wants her visit to bring attention to the plight of the elephant herds, which are under constant threat from poachers. Micah imprudently speaks out against Roger Singh (John Rhys-Davies), a notorious ivory hunter. Fresh out of prison, Singh nurses a grudge against his former partner, Mark Smith (Andrew Stevens), who testified against Singh in court and who is now a park ranger. On the trail of an elephant herd that has strayed from the nature preserve, Singh, Mark, and Micah collide, and considerable unpleasantness results. Singh kidnaps Micah to force a showdown with Mark, who's fallen in love with her. After some tedious chase scenes in the veldt, Singh gets flattened by a jeep, but before dying he exacts his revenge in the brutal conclusion. However, the film's final images are of elephants strolling safely as happy music plays and the credits roll.

TUSKS suffers from general sloppiness that is somewhat understandable given the circumstances of the film's production. It was conceived by Tara Hawkins Moore, a Maryland-based wildlife artist, onetime fashion model, and documentarian. Making a film in the wilds of southern Africa proved a more difficult undertaking than Moore ever imagined. Reportedly, not only was she faced with uncooperative actors whose ad-libbing ruined the continuity of the story, but also, when half the project's funding disappeared after a pullout by fickle South African investors, some members of the cast and crew responded with work stoppages and other mischief. In one instance cameras were locked up at a critical juncture in the shooting. Nevertheless, Moore managed to raise the needed funds and brought the film in for less than $2 million. But she then found distributors unwilling to get behind a nature film that wasn't intended for a youthful audience. Eventually, TUSKS was exhibited overseas, but its US run consisted mainly of a benefit screening for the Baltimore Zoo.

Considering all the obstacles encountered by Moore, it should come as no surprise that TUSKS fails to hang together. But though it lacks a consistent point of view, there are moments when a more cohesive film can be glimpsed lurking in the underbrush. To Moore's credit, there is much about the main characters

that is unexpected and interesting. Micah is a strident city-dweller who doesn't know as much about wildlife conservation as she thinks she does, and Glover turns out to be a twitching fanatic who places Micah in jeopardy so that her martyrdom will rally international opinion against poachers. But perhaps the most intriguing character is Singh, whom cowriter Rhys-Davies invests with subtle emotional shading. It's suggested that self-loathing over his mixed parentage has molded Singh's violent persona, but once this motivation is established, the plot does little with it. Likewise the screenplay fails to take advantage of other promising set-ups; notably, Micah's prolonged captivity with Singh leads only to stale dialog and a surfeit of stock footage, including real-life scenes of elephants being killed and butchered during a government-sanctioned "thinning" of the herds. Reportedly, Zimbabwean authorities, wary of bad publicity over these scenes, compelled Moore to set the story in the fictitious nation of "Sekomo." In any case, the end credits proclaim that no animals were killed, maimed, or harmed in making the picture. On a completely different note, fans of James Coburn may want to pay close attention to the opening of TUSKS for a look at James Coburn, Jr., who greatly resembles his father. (*Profanity, violence, nudity, adult situations, sexual situations.*)

d, Tara Hawkins Moore; p, Keith C. Jones; w, Tara Hawkins Moore and John Rhys-Davies; ph, Jerry Pantzer; ed, Brian O'Hara; m, Tom Alonso; prod d, Syd Cain; art d, Don Mingate; set d, Nick St. Clair; stunts, Reo Ruiters; cos, Robyn Smith; makup, Anne Taylor; tech, Vivian Bristow

Adventure   (PR:O   MPAA:R)

TWILIGHT OF THE COCKROACHES

(Japan) 105m TYO/Streamline c

(GOKIBURI)

VOICES OF: Kaoru Kobayashi and Setsuko Karamsumarau

The plot is a staple of children's classics from BAMBI to WATERSHIP DOWN: cute, little anthropomorphic animal creatures band together for survival when they are threatened by oafish humans. There is a difference, though. In this case, it is quite forgivable to root for a "sad" ending. As the title implies, the cute little creatures this time around are cockroaches, those greedy, scurrying little insects who foul your food and infest your kitchen. They carry diseases. They have made many a city apartment uninhabitable. And they're the heroes? Go figure.

Naomi is the spunky roach-heroine who has grown up living the easy life with her colony in the apartment of slovenly single guy Saito (Kaoru Kobayashi), who almost never does his dishes and eats only half his meals, leaving the rest for the roaches to feast on. And feast they do. We also see them dancing and generally whooping it up nightly, converting Saito's kitchen table into a swinging dinner club. Naomi is betrothed to Ichiro, a feckless young dreamer who has grown soft on the good life at Saito's. As the movie begins the colony is about to celebrate its earlier "victory" over the humans, accomplished only after thousands of cockroach comrades perished in insecticide attacks by the apartment's previous tenants. But a damper is put on the celebration by the arrival of Hans, the movie's dashing hero, a broad-shouldered flying roach from the colony "across the field," which has the misfortune of inhabiting the apartment of a woman (Setsuko Karamsumaru) who is more fastidious than Saito. In fact, she despises roaches and smashes, poisons, and sets sticky traps for them. (This is tragic?) The plot thickens when Naomi falls in love with Hans while he stays with Naomi and her aged father to recuperate from the battle wounds that led him to seek refuge with her colony. When Hans returns home, Naomi risks her life by following him across the "vast" field. Losing her way after a sudden rainstorm, she is saved by a pile of talking doggie doo-doo (no kidding) that puts her back on course. Still trusting humans, Naomi confronts the woman apartment dweller directly, innocently asking where she can find Hans. When her request is met by a rolled-up newspaper, Naomi barely escapes with her life. Rescued and wooed by Hans, she sees firsthand the carnage, as well as the efforts of Hans and his friends to combat the human menace (their strategy consisting mainly of flying, en masse, into the woman's face). As Ichiro pines away back in Saito's apartment, the story becomes even more complex when Saito and the woman roach-killer begin a liaison. Saito's new girl friend immediately busies herself with cleaning and roach-proofing his apartment. During the all-out war that follows, the colony is decimated. But don't yet cheer. Naomi, the sole survivor, is told—by a talking toy rabbit, no less—that she is, in fact, the first of a new breed of poison-resistant roaches destined to keep her species alive and numerous. Having been impregnated by Hans, she is shown in a still, blue-line drawing in the end—the film's animation budget apparently having run out—happily surrounded by hundreds of little baby super-roaches.

Somebody please get that rolled-up newspaper and smack Japanese writer-director Hiroaki Yoshida in the head with it. COCKROACHES doesn't even qualify as a camp classic. Besides being thoroughly deranged, it's also slow, dull, and numbingly mediocre. The painstaking efforts to maintain the roach-eye view in the live action are negated by smeared, discolored cinematography. Moreover, the animation itself is stilted and lifeless. WHO FRAMED ROGER RABBIT it ain't. Indeed, it isn't even ASTRO BOY. Besides being too dumb for adults, COCKROACHES may set a new kid-movie precedent by being equally unacceptable for children. What parents want their youngsters digging through the garbage in search of "pets" after sitting through this nonsense? Yoshida has allegedly described COCKROACHES as an allegory about the fear, suspicion, and hatred with which the Japanese are currently regarded in other parts of the world, including the US, proving patriotism to be the final refuge of bad filmmakers as well as scoundrels. (Violence, adult situations.)

d, Hiroaki Yoshida; p, Hiroaki Yoshida and Hidenori Taga; w, Hiroaki Yoshida; ph, Kenji Misumi; m, Morgan Fisher; art d, Kiichi Ichida; anim, Hiroshi Kurogane

Animated (PR:O MPAA:NR)

TWISTED JUSTICE

90m Hero/Borde c

David Heavener (*James Tucker*), Erik Estrada (*Cmdr. Gage*), Jim Brown (*Morris*), James Van Patten (*Kelsey*), Shannon Tweed (*Hinkle*), Don Stroud (*Pantelli*), Karen Black (*Mrs. Granger*), David Campbell (*Steelmore*), Lauri Warren, and Julia Austin

A film only the NRA could love, TWISTED JUSTICE is set in the year 2020, which looks not a whole lot different from the near future depicted in the considerably bigger-budgeted (and ideologically antithetical) THE HANDMAID'S TALE. Guns are illegal for everyone, especially the police, who now wear goofy-looking, chrome-armor-plated vests and subdue criminals with little toylike dart-guns. Of course, the film's cop hero, James Tucker (writer-producer-director David Heavener), will have none of this armor. He also carries an illegal holster cannon, which is put to use early in the film to blow away a ranting, bomb-toting psycho who's impervious to both darts and fists. Tucker's specialty, it turns out, is hunting psychos of every stripe, from the bomb thrower to the serial killer that his police commander, Gage (Erik Estrada), assigns him to track down. Tucker's investigation uncovers a mad scientist, Steelmore (David Campbell), who blackmails a pharmaceutical corporation into supplying him with the ingredients for a street drug that turns its users, like the psycho bomber, into super-beings with ultrahigh IQs, tremendous strength, and a seeming imperviousness to pain. To keep his suppliers in line, Steelmore gets into the habit of murdering wives, ex-wives, and mistresses of the executives and scientists with the pharmaceutical company—these are the serial killings that put Tucker on his case. Along the way, Tucker has to convert one of those pesky female civil-libertarian types (Julia Austin) to his pro-gun cause, and must also endure Morris and Kelsey (Jim Brown and James Van Patten), two dunderheaded fellow cops who drop by his apartment occasionally and tear the place up in search of his illegal weapon (which is disassembled when not in use, its parts converted into common bathroom items). There are also the routine bawlings-out by Gage, the standard quota of desultory car chases, and a few pitched, blood-pellet gun battles. Virtually the film's only original touch is a lame running joke in which a seemingly gay male radio dispatcher spends the film flirting with Tucker; "he" turns out to be played by none other than ex-Hugh Hefner main squeeze Shannon Tweed, the mix-up occurring because her voice is distorted over Tucker's radio.

Most of TWISTED JUSTICE's funniest moments are purely unintentional, however. There's Tucker's pet rat, seen in close-up at the beginning of one scene only to appear inexplicably, several shots later, in Tucker's medicine cabinet during one of the police searches of his apartment. There's a brief scene of Steelmore talking into his cellular car phone, precisely filmed and lit in such a way as to show clouds of the actor's spittle spraying into the air as he barks into the receiver. Later, Steelmore takes a bullet square in the chest from Tucker's revolver, but continues scampering through the film's climactic gunfight as if he's barely been nicked. The topper is the anticlimactic scene in which Gage chirpily addresses the camera, telling us about his hope that the glorious day will come soon when the police, once again, will be allowed to carry guns. All that's missing is a superimposed American flag fluttering in the breeze and the "Star Spangled Banner" on the soundtrack.

Such moments of unintended amusement aside (there's also an *intentionally* funny cameo by Karen Black as one of Steelmore's victims), much of TWISTED JUSTICE, like many another budget-basement action thriller, plays like a grown-up version of children's cops-and-robbers games in the backyard, with the dart guns and silly outfits heightening the effect. The main difference—besides the huge chunks of klutzy expository dialog that deaden the film's already snail-like pacing—is that, judging by what can be had at most toy stores nowadays, the kids probably have more realistic props. (Violence, profanity, adult situations, nudity.)

d, David Heavener; p, David Heavener; w, David Heavener; ph, David Hue; ed, Gregory Schorer; art d, Dian Skinner; stunts, Warren Stevens; cos, Kevin Ackerman

Crime/Thriller (PR:O MPAA:R)

TWISTED OBSESSION

107m IVE c

Jeff Goldblum (*Dan Gillis*), Miranda Richardson (*Marilyn*), Anemone (*Marianne*), Dexter Fletcher (*Malcolm*), Daniel Ceccaldi (*Legrand*), Liza Walker (*Jenny*), Jerome Natali (*Danny*), Arielle Dombasle (*Marion Derain*), and Asuncion Blaguer (*Juana*)

A queasy, unpleasant psychological sex drama somewhat redeemed by a solid cast, this English-language debut by Spanish director Fernando Trueba starts murkily and turns progressively more dark, turgid, and confusing, almost negating the efforts of its actors. Jeff Goldblum stars as Dan Gillis, an expatriate American screenwriter living in Paris on occasional commercial-feature assignments from a French pal, producer Legrand (Daniel Ceccaldi). As the film begins, Dan's wife, Marianne (Anemone), is leaving him and their young son, Danny (Jerome Natali), for unspecified reasons. Distracting Dan from his dismal homelife, Legrand calls the writer in to pitch a change-of-pace art film inspired by a line in PETER PAN that also inspired Dan's sole, out-of-print novel. But Dan is unimpressed when he meets the director, an intense, chain-smoking British *wunderkind* named Malcolm (Dexter Fletcher), whose meager claims to fame include an award-winning short film and a handful of music videos. Dan is ready to chalk up Legrand's unwarranted enthusiasm to an artistic mid-life crisis, but he reserves judgement when Malcolm reveals that it was his own enthusiasm for Dan's novel that has led him to seek out the writer's services. A screening is arranged of Malcolm's short, a Warholian exercise with a commercial gloss, consisting solely of a head-and-shoulders shot of a disturbingly youthful girl, played by Malcolm's sister, Jenny (Liza Walker), in an unmistakable state of adult sexual ecstasy. The short leaves Legrand transfixed in a way peculiar to producers. "I don't know what it means," he declares. "But this is a work of art!" Now embarrassed as well as unimpressed, Dan meets with his agent, Marilyn (Miranda Richardson), who compounds his misgivings with her own vague warnings not to get involved with Malcolm and Jenny. Finally, agent and client decide to offer Dan's services, but for twice his normal fee. In a series of messages on his answering machine, Dan learns that Legrand is outraged by his friend's high-priced offer and that Marilyn is apologetic for souring her client's relations with the producer. Those messages are followed by a mysterious call from Malcolm assuring Dan that everything will work out. Sure enough, almost magically, everything does work out, though Marilyn persists in her dire warnings. Visiting Malcolm's loft residence for a working session, Dan discovers that Malcolm is even flakier than he first appeared. But Dan's inclination to leave disappears once he lays eyes on the nymphet star of Malcolm's short, who lives with her brother. As Dan's involvement with Malcolm's film deepens, so, too, does the writer's obsession with Jenny. That obsession is brought to a boil when Dan, reaching a creative impasse with Malcolm, is seduced by Jenny. However, the episode arouses Dan's suspicions as well as his libido. After Legrand reads Dan and Malcolm's screenplay and declares it unfilmable—the clear implication being that Dan and Malcolm have written a kiddie-porn epic—Dan lingers outside Legrand's office. Within an hour, his festering suspicions are confirmed when Jenny, dressed to thrill, shows up at the office. Shortly thereafter, the project is back on track. Confronted by Dan, Jenny confesses that she has been bestowing her favors on both Dan and Legrand to keep the film going. Dan later discovers that, far from being Jenny's pimp, Malcolm is his sister's pawn. Behind his hip facade, Malcolm is a feckless drug addict, utterly helpless without Jenny. But these disclosures hardly matter. By this point, Dan and Legrand have been reduced to craven submission by Jenny's sexual manipulation. Rather than abandoning the project, they use their influence to involve a major star (Arielle Dombasle), assuring backing for the film that, Dan confesses in TWISTED OBSESSION's very first moments, should never have been made. Matters go from bad to worse when Jenny disappears, presumed dead, and Dan's suspicions turn to Marilyn's shadowy role.

Despite its provocative subject, TWISTED OBSESSION is finally too cool for its own good. Smart, stylish, and gorgeously photographed (by Jose Luis Alcaine, whose credits include Almodovar's WOMEN ON THE VERGE OF A NERVOUS BREAKDOWN), it nevertheless fails to build to any compelling climax. Instead, the film resorts to a frenzied tying up of loose plot ends. Most notably, Dan spends a hellish evening in the basement morgue of a medical school, where he has come in search of Jenny's remains.

Walker is sufficiently beguiling and beautiful as Jenny, but she is not well-served by the script (cowritten by Trueba and Manolo Matji from Christopher Frank's novel *The Mad Monkey*). Jenny seems to control everything and everybody in the film, even after her disappearance, yet the script almost perversely keeps her away from any direct involvement in the action. As a result Walker's performance is a void at the film's center rather than the driving force that it should be. It is left, then, to Goldblum to convey the power and pathos of Jenny through his complex reactions to her. In his best-known performance, in David Cronenberg's THE FLY, Goldblum revealed a dramatic flair for giving a fantastic premise recognizably human credibility, and he continues to exhibit that talent here. Through his eyes, we come to see the remnants of the child in Jenny that have been stifled and hardened by her too-early submersion in adult sexuality, giving the film an emotional clarity and substance it otherwise lacks. The other cast members give similarly accomplished performances, with the ubiquitous Fletcher standing out along with Richardson, Ceccaldi, and the leads. It's unfortunate that the film never quite fulfills the expectations these performers raise. *(Adult situations, sexual situations, profanity.)*

d, Fernando Trueba; p, Andres Vicente Gomez; w, Fernando Trueba and Manolo Matji; ph, Jose Luis Alcaine; ed, Carmen Frias; m, Antoine Duhamel; art d, Pierre-Louis Thevenet; cos, Ivette Frank

Drama (PR:O MPAA:R)

TWO EVIL EYES

(It./US) 105m Gruppo Bema—ADC/Taurus c

(DUE OCCHI DIABOLICI)

Adrienne Barbeau *(Jessica Valdemar)*, E.G. Marshall *(Steven Pike)*, Harvey Keitel *(Rod Usher)*, Madeleine Potter *(Annabel)*, Ramy Zada *(Dr. Robert Hoffman)*, Bingo O'Malley *(Ernest Valdemar)*, Martin Balsam *(Mr. Bee)*, Kim Hunter *(Mrs. Bee)*, and Sally Kirkland *(Eleonora)*

Directed by George Romero (NIGHT OF THE LIVING DEAD) and Dario Argento (SUSPIRIA), TWO EVIL EYES consists of two short adaptations of tales by Edgar Allan Poe, with no connecting story. The first segment, Romero's, is based on "The Facts in the Case of M. Valdemar," while Argento's contribution was inspired by "The Black Cat." In the first story, rich old Ernest Valdemar (Bingo O'Malley) is dying. His much younger wife, Jessica (Adrienne Barbeau), and his private physician, Dr. Hoffman (Ramy Zada), are lovers and have concocted a plan to liquidate Valdemar's assets so that when he dies they will be free to live it up without having to wait for his will to be probated. Using a metronome, Hoffman, a mesmerist, hypnotizes Valdemar and compels him to sign over his estate to Jessica, bit by bit. Valdemar's lawyer (E.G. Marshall) is suspicious but can prove nothing. Only Valdemar's premature death could spoil the crafty couple's set up; naturally, the old man dies. Jessica and Hoffman decide to conceal Valdemar's body in a freezer and forge his signature on additional documents, but the gruesome task unnerves Jessica. Even more problematic, Valdemar died while under hypnosis, and though his body is dead, his soul is suspended between life and death. Able to speak to Hoffman, he makes alarming references to "others" who are with him, spirits who intend to use his body to seek revenge in the world of the living. The lovers' plan starts to unravel. When Jessica begins drinking too much, she and Hoffman find themselves growing farther apart. Finally, the terrified Jessica comes face to face with the spirits and kills herself. Hoffman flees, but the malevolent spirits follow him to his hotel, and as he lies in an auto-hypnotic slumber, they plunge the metronome into his chest.

In the second tale, crime photographer Rod Usher (Harvey Keitel) revels in the ugly, the violent, and the bizarre. His photographs of crime scenes have made him notorious, and his new book, *Metropolitan Horrors*, is about to be published. Things are going well until his girl friend, Annabel (Madeleine Potter), a violinist, brings home a black cat. She adores the creature, but it irritates Usher. Finally, in a fit of temper, he kills the cat. When Annabel finds out and becomes upset, Usher kills her, too, then walls up her body behind the bookcase. What he doesn't realize is that he has walled up his lover's corpse with a cat that looks exactly like the one he killed. Despite Usher's careful attempts to explain Annabel's disappearance, the neighbors are suspicious and call the police, who find the corpse—half-eaten by the litter of kittens born behind the wall. With his back against the wall (so to speak), Usher kills the two policemen, then is hanged in a freak accident.

Highly respected in Europe, though less well known in the US, Argento is widely considered Italy's finest horror director. Romero, a native of Pittsburgh (where TWO EVIL EYES was shot), revolutionized American horror movies with his bleak, nihilistic zombie films. The two worked together in 1979, when Argento coproduced Romero's DAWN OF THE DEAD, and their collaboration on TWO EVIL EYES sounded like a can't-miss proposition: a pair of contemporary masters of the horror film coming together to make a movie inspired by America's first—and some say greatest—horror writer. The mix was sweetened with the addition of a fairly strong cast and special-effects wizard Tom Savini, who was responsible for the gut-crunching gags in DAWN OF THE DEAD and DAY OF THE DEAD. However, though technically impressive, TWO EVIL EYES amounts to less than the sum of its parts.

Each director wrote his own screenplay (Argento with Franco Ferrini), but both had problems fleshing out the source material; Poe's stories tend to be very short, and many are little more than mood pieces. Romero's segment is largely concerned with the mechanics of Jessica and Hoffman's scheme—all new material with no basis in Poe's story—and its eye-for-an-eye ending is logical but unsurprising. Argento's installment is packed with allusions to Poe stories ranging from "The Pit and the Pendulum" to the little known "Berenice," but again, Usher's dilemma is conventional: he kills his girl friend, tries to get away, and can't escape poetic justice. Argento's trademark visual flamboyance is nowhere in evidence. While far from the worst adaptation of Poe's work (there are so many candidates for that dubious honor it's hard to know where to start), TWO EVIL EYES breaks no new ground. *(Violence, profanity.)*

d, Dario Argento and George Romero; p, Achille Manzotti and Dario Argento; w, George Romero, Dario Argento, and Franco Ferrini (based on stories by Edgar Allen Poe); ph, Peter Reniers; ed, Pat Buba; m, Pino Donaggio; art d, Cletus Anderson; spec, Tom Savini; cos, Barbara Anderson

Horror (PR:C MPAA:R)

TWO JAKES, THE

138m Robert Evans-Harold Schneider/Paramount c

Jack Nicholson *(Jake Gittes)*, Harvey Keitel *(Jake Berman)*, Meg Tilly *(Kitty Berman)*, Madeleine Stowe *(Lillian Bodine)*, Eli Wallach *(Cotton Weinberger)*, Ruben Blades *(Mickey Nice)*, Frederic Forrest *(Newty)*, David Keith *(Loach)*, Richard Farnsworth *(Earl Rawley)*, Tracey Walter *(Tyrone Otley)*, Joe Mantell *(Walsh)*, James Hong *(Khan)*, Perry Lopez *(Capt. Escobar)*, Jeff Morris *(Tilton)*, Rebecca Broussard, Paul A. DiCocco Jr., John Hackett, Rosie Vela, Allan Warnick, Susan Forristal, Will Tynan, Van Dyke Parks, William Duffy, and Sue Carlton

It may have been expecting too much for THE TWO JAKES to have been a film on the high order of its predecessor, CHINATOWN. But this sequel has more going against it than having to follow in the footsteps of that brilliant film—surely one of the best movies of the past 20 years, possibly one of the finest films of all time. Where the original had the impeccable structure and fearsome momentum of a classical tragedy, the sequel is a loose, meandering, and murky affair that isn't even particularly good on its own, comparatively modest terms. Set in post-WW II Los Angeles, THE TWO JAKES begins, as CHINATOWN did, in the office of Jake Gittes (Jack Nicholson), a private eye who specializes in divorce cases. Gittes is busy coaching a client, the title's other Jake, Jake Berman (Harvey Keitel). Having gathered evidence that Berman's wife, Kitty (Meg Tilly), is having an affair, Gittes instructs Berman to walk in on his wife and her lover during one of their afternoon motel trysts. In the next room, Gittes records the staged confrontation. But the operation goes horribly wrong when Berman, in an apparent jealous rage, deviates from Gittes' "script" by killing his wife's lover. It seems to be an open-and-shut case of temporary insanity, but as was the case in CHINATOWN, nothing is quite what it seems here. Kitty's lover is also Berman's partner in a housing development in the San Fernando Valley. For business reasons, the partner's will excludes his wife, Lillian (Madeleine Stowe), and names Berman the sole beneficiary. Gittes, it seems, has been used again (as he was in the original film), this time as an unwitting accomplice in a carefully planned murder-for-profit scheme. While exposing the scheme would violate Gittes' confidential relationship with his client, the detective's alternative is to have his career ruined by Lillian, who has hired a hotshot lawyer (Frederic Forrest) to turn Gittes' life into litigation hell. Gittes tries to negotiate a compromise by having Berman pay off Lillian with her late husband's share of their partnership. However, the plot develops yet another layer of betrayal, involving a grab for mineral rights to the oil-rich land by none other than Katherine Mulwray, the daughter-sister of CHINATOWN'S ill-fated, incestuous heroine, Evelyn Mulwray (Faye Dunaway). Katherine is the original owner of the orange grove upon which Berman and his late partner were building their development. An important clue in the increasingly convoluted mystery comes from a reference to Katherine on the motel-room wire recording, leading Gittes to conduct an extended and obsessive investigation into her present whereabouts. Through the various plot twists, leading up to a not-too-surprising surprise revelation (Kitty turns out to be Katherine), Gittes is finally forced to decide whether or not to tamper with evidence and perjure himself to protect the daughter of the woman he was unable to protect in the first film.

Unquestionably, THE TWO JAKES has the look of CHINATOWN. What it lacks are the dramatic underpinnings and emotional core that made the original film an engrossing mystery as well as a cinema classic. As a sequel, it falls somewhere between a by-the-numbers retread and an original work in its own right. Groping for originality, it's filled with pointless scenes set for no discernible reason in exotic 40s LA locations. THE TWO JAKES also reprises characters from its predecessor, along with the actors who originally played them, without integrating those characters into the action in any meaningful way.

Where characters can't return for the sequel, THE TWO JAKES awkwardly offers "stand-ins" — like Richard Farnsworth's flinty oil tycoon for John Huston's Noah Cross — that have even less to do with the main action than the returning characters.

THE TWO JAKES is also more self-indulgent and mean-spirited than the original. Perhaps in deference to the sequel's star-director Nicholson, Gittes is the hero here, though he wasn't in the original. If CHINATOWN has a hero, it is Evelyn Mulwray who, alone among the major characters, cares about someone else (her daughter) more than she does about herself. Acting out of love, rather than self-interest, Evelyn is destroyed. THE TWO JAKES has no corresponding tragic hero at its core to propel the action. As a result, it rambles through its distended running time rather than being driven to a catharsis of horror and fear as the original is. Worse, the sequel tries substituting melodrama for tragedy, relying on a fatal disease — of all things — and Gittes' promise to protect Kitty to absolve both a cold-blooded murder and its subsequent coverup. The film's mean-spiritedness comes through primarily in the grotesque portrayal of Lillian, who's not only a drunk, but also a pill popper, a neurotic, and an off-the-wall nymphomaniac — all of which serves only to make her somehow more deserving of the treachery Gittes inflicts upon her to protect Kitty. Despite having used her own sexuality to lure a man to his death, Kitty manages to appear chastely ephemeral throughout the film and therefore somehow more deserving of Gittes' protection. Even more gratuitous is the inclusion of the character played by David Keith. The son of the policeman who killed Evelyn Mulwray in the original film, Keith's character exists solely to allow Gittes to humiliate him as a weird form of cross-generational revenge.

Through it all, what makes THE TWO JAKES most disappointing is the degree to which Nicholson and writer Robert Towne seem to have failed to understand their own creation. The seasoned, classical sensibility of CHINATOWN's director, Roman Polanski, is sorely missed. Nicholson doesn't appear to have so much directed THE TWO JAKES as supervised it. Generally, he has done a better job directing the other actors than he has directing himself. Most of the performers have at least one memorable moment, while Nicholson, despite being in virtually every shot of the film, never makes much of an impression. However, lacking a strong plot with which to work, even the ensemble seems to be acting in a dramatic void. Towne's typically rich dialog is similarly disconnected, anchored in nothing but the author's own verbal virtuosity. The script contains ideas that should have been interesting (such as Gittes' injury in a natural-gas explosion in the early going, which causes him to wander through the film in a concussed stupor) but that aren't developed, much less exploited, in Nicholson's direction or performance. The historical framework, which lent such resonance to CHINATOWN, is so inadequately explained here that it ultimately works against the plot's resolution.

The film's overall lack of inspiration may in part be due to its tortured production history. THE TWO JAKES originally went before the cameras in 1985, only to be shut down days later amid a bitter feud sparked by then-director Towne's firing of then-costar and producer Robert Evans, originally cast in the role of Jake Berman. Whatever the causes, the magic is simply gone from this star-crossed sequel. The best that can be said about THE TWO JAKES is that it provides a means to more deeply appreciate the film that came before it. *(Profanity, adult situations, violence.)*

d, Jack Nicholson; p, Robert Evans and Harold Schneider; w, Robert Towne; ph, Vilmos Zsigmond; ed, Anne Goursaud; m, Van Dyke Parks; prod d, Jeremy Railton and Richard Sawyer; art d, Richard Schreiber; set d, Jerry Wunderlich; cos, Wayne Finkelman

Crime   **(PR:C MPAA:R)**

UV

UNBELIEVABLE TRUTH, THE

90m Action/Miramax c

Adrienne Shelly (*Audry Hugo*), Robert Burke (*Josh Hutton*), Christopher Cooke (*Vic Hugo*), Julia Mueller (*Pearl*), Mark Bailey (*Mike*), Gary Sauer (*Emmet*), Katherine Mayfield (*Liz Hugo*), David Healy (*Todd Whitbread*), Matt Malloy (*Otis*), Edie Falco (*Jane, the Waitress*), Jeff Howard (*Irate Driver*), Kelly Reichardt (*Irate Driver's Wife*), Ross Turner (*Irate Driver's Son*), Paul Schultze (*Bill*), Mike Brady (*Bob*), Bill Sage (*Gus*), Tom Thon (*News Vendor*), and Mary Sue Flynn (*Girl at Counter*)

THE UNBELIEVABLE TRUTH is a promising feature-film debut for writer-director Hal Hartley, who shows some talent in this black comedy that manages to be original if not particularly fresh. In the vein of Jim Jarmusch's STRANGER THAN PARADISE and the work of David Lynch, THE UNBELIEVABLE TRUTH searches for the unexpected, bizarre, and magical essence of prosaic American locales. For director Hartley, Lindenhurst, Long Island, packs the allure of Lynch's Twin Peaks. Everyone has a secret or knows a secret they're dying to tell, and the hero's quirky odyssey sets the stage for self-revelation among the inhabitants and visitors of the town. Lindenhurst is the hometown of Josh Hutton (Robert Burke), a paroled convict who, as the film opens, returns to the area (where everyone remembers the details of his crime differently) because he has nowhere else to go. Haunted by a past that includes the manslaughter of his sweetheart and a prison stretch for killing her grieving father in an argument about her death, Hutton is too shell-shocked to begin his life anew until he meets Audry Hugo (Adrienne Shelly), a high-school student with an obsessive fear of nuclear attack. When Audry's father, garage owner Vic (Christopher Cooke), agrees to hire Josh for his exceptional mechanical skills, Audry and Josh can't fight off their growing attraction. Worried by his daughter's involvement with this shady character, Vic promotes Audry's fledgling modeling career, with the help of a photographer who secures her work out of town. Complicating matters is Audry's best friend, Pearl (Julia Mueller), the sister of the girl Josh killed. After a hectic climax in which everyone converges on Josh's house and clashes at cross-purposes, the unbelievable truth is revealed and sets up a happy ending for Audry and Josh, clearing Josh's name.

Hartley exhibits a born filmmaker's eye for composition and camera placement in this offbeat, dryly humorous film. His screenwriting skills are less solid, however, and the film is further damaged by the uneven quality of its cast, which weakens the already delicate balance in this black comedy. Although Burke (a combination of Christopher Walken and Michael Weller) makes the ideal loner hero providing the center for Hartley's crazy universe, Shelly is saddled with a role that's more a collection of nonconformist attitudes than a true character, and although she projects a distinct personality, she isn't resourceful enough as an actress to make Audry believable. More damaging is the casting of Cooke, whose delineation of the harried middle-class father is almost amateurish. David Healy, by contrast, does a refreshing turn as a girl-crazy photographer who uses his camera as an aphrodisiac, with poor results.

Despite these flaws, THE UNBELIEVABLE TRUTH captivates with its committedly off-center vision of suburban angst. Long Island becomes a world of identity crises, serendipitous occurrences, and genuinely surprising contrivances. It's an impressive, if not always cogent, attempt to mine humor out of tragic circumstances, and it manages to send up small-town life without being condescending—no mean feat. Unfortunately, in making his central character a passive victim of fate, Hartley condemns his film to a low energy level throughout. What seems promisingly wacky at first eventually flattens out and becomes repetitive. Instead of deepening our understanding of the characters and lifting the story toward its redemptive conclusion, the film fails to sustain its inventiveness.

Within its limits, however, THE UNBELIEVABLE TRUTH provides moments of splendid weirdness and several memorably zany characters. It is a zippy vision of everyone's hometown, relocated to a twilight zone in which all the boredom one left behind has acquired a retrospective fascination. The film challenges our perceptions and prejudices about small-town life, finding mystery in the mundane. Hartley is clearly a filmmaker to keep watching. (*Mild violence, profanity, adult situations, sexual situations.*)

d, Hal Hartley; p, Bruce Weiss and Hal Hartley; w, Hal Hartley; ph, Michael Spiller; ed, Hal Hartley; m, Jim Coleman, Wild Blue Yonder, and The Brothers Kendall; prod d, Carla Gerona; set d, Sarah Stollman; cos, Kelly Reichardt; makup, Judy Chin

Comedy/Drama   (PR:O MPAA:R)

UNDER THE BOARDWALK

102m Chanin-Blackwell/New World c

Keith Coogan (*Andy*), Danielle Von Zerneck (*Allie*), Richard Joseph Paul (*Nick Rainwood*), Hunter Von Leer (*Midas*), Tracey Walter (*Bum*), Steve Monarque (*Reef*), Brian Wimmer (*Cage*), Roxana Zal (*Gitch*), Stuart Fratkin (*Lepps*), Christopher Rydell (*Tripper*), Brett Marx (*Maroni*), Megan Gallivan (*Joan*), Wally Ward (*Backwash*), Greta Blackburn (*Mrs. Vorpin*), Elizabeth Kaitan (*Donna*), Dick Miller (*Official*), Sonny Bono (*Ancient Two*), Corkey Carroll (*Ancient One*), and Brian Avery (*Hap Jordan*)

Full of silly, juvenile high jinks on the beach, UNDER THE BOARDWALK might easily have starred Frankie and Annette in their prime, especially if its unnecessary sex and profanity had been swept out on the waves. Despite the idiocy of its post-apocalyptic framing device, UNDER THE BOARDWALK is likable in its dumb-bunny way, offering special appeal to adolescents prone to crushes that change daily, surfing freaks, or sociologists fixated on southern Californian dating rituals.

Floating in the debris-filled sludge of the Pacific Ocean of the future, a bearded surf maven relates the legend of Nick Rainwood (Richard Joseph Paul), the most radical wave warrior of all time. As the flashbacks unfold (we return to the future framing scene and its surfing narrator several times), we revisit California before its ocean became a floating junkyard—a time when tanned teen manhood was tested on surfboards. However, the heroic Nick is torn between pursuing a lifetime of surfing with older buddy Midas (Hunter Von Leer) or accepting a college scholarship and entering mainstream society. Meanwhile, far from this soul-searching in the San Fernando Valley, the Vorpin family faces its own crises. Self-centered wave champ Reef (Steve Monarque) mistreats his sister, Allie (Danielle Von Zerneck), pays no heed to his mom, and dumps on Andy (Keith Coogan), his visiting cousin, who idolizes him. After dipping into his mother's marijuana stash, Reef and his pals drive off in pursuit of surf babes before an upcoming surfing competition, leaving Allie to escort the awkward Andy to a beach party, where they encounter various specimens of surfers, including tough-talking Gitch (Roxana Zal). Busy fornicating on the beach, Reef's buddy Tripper (Christopher Rydell) doesn't realize that his friend's dope has been swept out to sea. Reef, noticing that Nick and his Valley contingent have arrived, blames Nick for stealing his dope, and a miniversion of "Romeo and Juliet" erupts when Reef insists on rumbling and Nick and Allie can barely contain their starry-eyed romantic inclinations. During the ensuing melee, only Andy and Gitch get arrested, and she tries to loosen up the little geek. As for Nick, despite Midas' warnings of the dire consequences of a Valley boy dating an LA chick, he can't forget Allie's wholesome blondness. After the surfing preliminaries (where both Reef and Nick are approached by a former surf champ who wants them to model a line of sportswear—would this be selling out the ideals of surferhood?), Nick's friend breaks his arm in an accident caused by Reef, and a hardcore rumble is planned as things get more Capulet and Montague-ish. Abandoning true-blue Allie at a super-cool party, Nick tries to prevent the fighting, but ends up joining the fracas, much to his girl's displeasure. A few more repetitive plot developments ensue, then comes the day of the big meet, when Nick lets the ultimate Big Wave pass him by—thus making a statement about good sportsmanship, commitment to college scholarships, and pressure from pushy girl friends who don't approve of surfing. Just as victory seems to be in creepy Reef's reach, however, Gitch unexpectedly grabs the wave and rides it to victory, a humbling experience for the sexist teen villain. Meanwhile, true love blossoms for Nick and Allie, and in the future scene to which the film again flashes forward, it is revealed that the veteran surfer who has been relating this water-logged fable is none other than former landlubber Andy.

For a while, as the large, often indistinguishable cast of young actors mouth their surf lingo, you may feel as if you've wandered into a foreign film that no one's bothered to subtitle, and you may begin to wish you'd prepared yourself with a cassette of ENDLESS SUMMER or BIG WEDNESDAY before attempting to navigate the intricacies of language here. Viewers of UNDER THE BOARDWALK will have to wade through both the secret terminology of the new generation and some slangy surf lingo only a diehard board-waxer could dig. This may be a blessing in disguise, since much of the dialog is on the level of "See Dick surf. See Jane ogle Dick." Moreover, anyone who's ever read the Cliff Notes for "Romeo and Juliet" can figure out the major subplot, allowing one to forget the story line and enjoy some spectacular surf footage, attractive scenery (both the beach topography and the half-clad bodies of male and female sun-worshippers), and a swinging soundtrack.

In UNDER THE BOARDWALK, life isn't a cabaret so much as it's a mindless beach party, but despite the flimsy plotting and pedestrian direction, the film isn't a total wipeout, especially if you are young and able to fit into a form-fitting bathing suit, or can imagine yourself as such. And though older audiences might enjoy this sand-and-surf nonsense more if an identification figure from their past (e.g., Fabian or Sandra Dee, although Sonny Bono does put in a cameo) had been added to the cast, the various rock 'n' roll classics on the soundtrack will soften the hearts of the most inveterate surfing-phobes around. *(Substance abuse, profanity, violence, sexual situations.)*

d, Fritz Kiersh; p, Steven H. Charnin and Gregory S. Blackwell; w, Robert King (based on a story by Matthew Irmas and Robert King); ph, Don Burgess; ed, Daniel Gross; m, David Kitay; prod d, Maxine Shepard; art d, Corey Kaplan; set d, Gina Scoppitici; stunts, Gary Jensen; cos, Cindy Bergstrom

Comedy   (PR:C   MPAA:R)

UNE FLAME DANS MON COEUR

(Fr./Switz.) (SEE: FLAME IN MY HEART, A)

VAMPIRE'S KISS

105m Hemdale c

Nicolas Cage *(Peter Loew)*, Maria Conchita Alonso *(Alva Restrepo)*, Jennifer Beals *(Rachel)*, Elizabeth Ashley *(Dr. Glaser)*, Kasi Lemmons *(Jackie)*, Bob Lujan *(Emilio)*, and Sol Echeverria

Peter Loew (Nicolas Cage) is an affected, self-centered literary agent living in New York, and his life is the usual mess. In therapy because he doesn't understand why his love life—a series of one-night stands—isn't making him happy, he takes out his frustration on his high-strung secretary, Alva (Maria Conchita Alonso). Full of spite, Loew assigns Alva a pointless, time-consuming project, then berates her mercilessly for her failure to complete it quickly. But Loew's petty problems come to an abrupt halt when he picks up Rachel (Jennifer Beals), a beguiling beauty who just may be a vampire. After he has been bitten by Rachel, Loew becomes convinced he is turning into a blood drinker. His smokey-voiced therapist (Elizabeth Ashley) thinks Peter is just projecting, but Alva—reduced to quivering terror whenever Loew comes into the office—isn't so sure. She confides her fears to her brother and tries to stay home from work, but her practical mother will have none of it; work is just one of those things you have to deal with, Mom reasons, and bad bosses go with the territory. But Alva is convinced that even if he isn't a vampire, Peter Loew is the true Boss from Hell. Loew's behavior degenerates rapidly: he eats bugs and pigeons, blacks out his windows, wears sunglasses day and night, indoors and out, constructs a makeshift coffin for himself, and dreams of the exotic Rachel. Tortured by the need to know for sure if he's a vampire and aware that Alva carries a gun, Loew tries to prompt his secretary to shoot him; he threatens to rape her, and Alva fires at him point blank. Since Loew doesn't feel a thing, he's now convinced of his vampirism. Making his way to a trendy club, he selects his first victim. After tearing out her throat and drinking her blood, he returns home bloodied and bedraggled, ignored by jaded passers-by. But surprise: Alva's brother is waiting, and dispatches Loew with a stake through the heart.

Written by Joe Minion (AFTER HOURS) and directed by Robert Bierman, VAMPIRE'S KISS is a terminally hip black comedy that carefully dodges the key question to the very last, never committing to Loew's vampirism or indicating unequivocally that it's all the delusion of a selfish, unbalanced young man. The seductive Rachel seems to be the real thing, but perhaps that's just Loew's imagination trying to turn a superficial, unsatisfying sexual encounter into an outre erotic thrill. It's true that Alva's gun is loaded with blanks, so her shooting of him didn't prove anything. And a stake through the heart, well, that will dispatch mortal flesh and blood as easily as one of the undead. It's a tough balancing act, one VAMPIRE'S KISS manages with surprising skill.

But what truly distinguishes the movie is Cage's performance, which is so off the wall that even if you don't like it you have to watch in awe. With his voice a strangled, nasal whine, his hair combed straight back, and clothes just the wrong side of casual perfection, Cage's Loew is a thoroughly artificial creation, a man who's made himself over according to an ideal so obscure that it eludes everyone but him. Who better to be a vampire's victim than such a studied misfit? Loew's abuse of the cowering Alva generates the movie's funniest moments, even as it veers dangerously close to the humiliating truth of many workplace relationships (Sigourney Weaver's monster boss in WORKING GIRL has nothing on Loew). Hurling himself across his desk shrieking, "Alva! Am I getting through to you?" or gleefully chanting, "Too late, too late, too late..." when Alva finally completes the loathsome task she's been assigned, Cage's Loew is a grotesque whose outrageous whims and psychotic mood swings are risible and painful to watch in equal degrees. And you don't have to read reports that Cage really ate that cockroach to start squirming the moment it scuttles across the stove top; from the glint in his eye to the crunchy punchline, the scene is flawlessly verisimilar. If Peter Loew would chow down on a giant roach, wiggling legs and all, then why should Nicolas Cage flinch?

At a time when the vampire has all but vanished from movies except as a figure of fun, VAMPIRE'S KISS makes use of its traditions with skill and insight. Its tone is brittle and sly, and viewers willing to go with it will find much to amuse and admire. VAMPIRE'S KISS had a very limited theatrical release in 1989 and is here reviewed as a 1990 video release. *(Sexual situations, violence, adult situations.)*

d, Robert Bierman; p, Barbara Zitwer and Barry Shils; w, Joseph Minion; ph, Stefan Czapsky; ed, Angus Newton; m, Colin Towns; prod d, Christopher Nowak; cos, Irene Albright

Comedy/Horror   (PR:C   MPAA:R)

VERONICO CRUZ

(Arg./Brit.) 100m Yacoraite — Mainframe/British Film Institute c

(LA DEUDA INTERNA; AKA: DEBT, THE)

Juan Jose Camero *(Lehrer)*, Gonzalo Morales *(Veronico Cruz)*, Juanita Caceres *(Juanita)*, Anna Maria Gonzales *(Grandmother)*, Guillermo Delgado *(Policeman)*, Rene Olaguivel *(Beamter)*, Titina Gaspar *(Veronico's Mother)*, Raul Calles *(Officer)*, Leo Salgado *(Police Officer)*, Luis Uceda, Juan Carlos Ocampo *(Soldiers)*, and Adolfo Blois

VERONICO CRUZ is the impressive feature film debut of Argentine director Miguel Pereira, who graduated from the London Film School on the day Argentine troops invaded the Falklands (Malvinas) Islands, precipitating the 1982 war between Argentina and the United Kingdom. Filmed in Argentina and postproduced in London on funds from the British Film Institute and Channel 4, VERONICO CRUZ would be remarkable for this collaboration even if it were not the fine film it is. Set in the province of Jujuy in Argentina's mountainous extreme northwest, the film tells the story of Veronico (Gonzalo Morales), a little boy born in 1964 in the isolated village of Chorcan. His mother does not survive his birth and his father, desperately poor, leaves the village to seek work and never returns, leaving Veronico in his grandmother's care. Much of the film concentrates on his lonely childhood in the austerely beautiful, arid, rocky, and windswept region, where he herds his grandmother's sheep and helps her with subsistence farming. One day a schoolteacher, Lehrer (Juan Jose Camero), comes to Chorcan, bearing such exotic items as eyeglasses, a transistor radio, and some historical comic books that he gives to the illiterate Veronico. The boy becomes fascinated with the comics' strange images of pirates, "Uniforms of the Royal Navy," ships, and the sea. He associates the sea with a huge nearby salt flat, the vastest thing he can think of, where shells can be found in the salt and where Veronico hears the sound of waves as he looks over the white expanse. When a puma kills their sheep, Veronico's grandmother finally allows him to attend the village school. There, "Maestro" Lehrer teaches Argentine history and introduces aspects of 20th-century civilization to the children, while he himself becomes entranced with its indigenous culture. In the meantime, "civilization" makes more violent inroads after the 1975 military coup; soldiers come to Chorcan to depose the mayor and put the town constable (a likable, slow man who needs Maestro's help to pick out the "political" books he has been ordered to seize from the teacher's library) in charge. After Veronico's grandmother dies, Maestro takes him in, and the two live happily until the teacher receives a letter from Veronico's father, imploring Maestro to teach the boy to stay in Chorcan rather than leaving for the troubled south. When Maestro and Veronico embark on an expedition to find the boy's father in the provincial capital, the boy gawks at the statue of General Belgrano and the Flag Room in the capital building, while the teacher is interrogated by the police and learns that Veronico's leftist father has "disappeared" as a result of his activity in labor disputes. The two go home, Veronico filled with technological visions of urban life and Maestro filled with dread for his country. Shortly thereafter (1978), Maestro is transferred to a post in the city. The film then shifts entirely to his perspective, picking up in 1982 as he views the beginning of the Falklands-Malvinas War and the sinking of the battleship *Belgrano*. When Veronico doesn't respond to his letters, Maestro visits Chorcan and learns from an old friend (whose radio has broken, cutting him off from national events) that Veronico has left town. He shows Maestro a picture of the 18-year-old, smiling Veronico with two companions in Navy garb, captioned "The Lads from the *Belgrano*."

VERONICO CRUZ is not about the Falklands-Malvinas War, but about the individual's relationship to historical processes. While Pereira has been criticized for his leisurely, "artsy" portrayal of Veronico's childhood, as opposed to the telescoped narration of the last half-hour, the film's structure and the understatement of its climax mimic the manner in which a single, distinct life is swallowed in the larger movements of the state. The irony of Veronico's story—that the teacher's appearance in Chorcan opened up a world to him that both fueled his dreams and proved his undoing—is one instance of a national tragedy, in which a naive schoolbook patriotism and dreams of glory led many to simply accept military rule and warmongering. Pereira underscores this point with parallel images, first of the flag-waving, chanting fervor of Chorcan's residents as they cheer for Argentina during the radio broadcast of a World Cup soccer match, later of the flag-waving, chanting fervor of city residents (in TV footage) in support of the taking of the Malvinas. Pereira also parallels the lives of Veronico and his father; both leave their culturally "backward" environment and disappear as a consequence of "civilized" state decisions. Moreover, Pereira establishes a strong link between mass culture—from historical comics and textbooks to national icons such as Belgrano, to radio broadcasts of sports events—and nationalism, indicating what powerful instruments such apparently innocuous and discrete phenomena can be in the workings of history and in the hands of a totalitarian regime. As the people of Jujuy slowly lose their regional distinctness and gain in educational opportunity, they are robbed of their natural defense against partaking in a national destiny. The inevitability of this process is also suggested in the steady shift of emphasis from Veronico's story to the more sophisticated, sadder point of view of Maestro.

The scenes of life in Chorcan are very beautiful indeed, with impressive images from Pereira and cinematographer Gerry Feeny of the spare but majestic landscape, the changing light of the high skies, and the vast, white salt flat that comes to symbolize the bitter end of Veronico's seafaring dreams. The acting is uniformly fine, with just the right balance of naivete and dignity in the performances and in the dialog by Pereira and cowriter Eduardo Leiva Muller. (In Spanish; English subtitles.) *(Adult situations.)*

d, Miguel Pereira; p, Julio Lencina and Sasha Menocki; w, Miguel Pereira and Eduardo Leiva Muller (based on a book by Fortunato Ramos); ph, Gerry Feeny; ed, Gerry Feeny; m, Jaime Torres; prod d, Kiki Aguiar; cos, Rene Olaguivel

Drama (PR:A MPAA:NR)

VINCENT AND THEO

(Brit./Fr./US) 138m Belbo—Central—La Sept—Telepool—RAI Uno—Vara—Sofica Valor/Hemdale c

Tim Roth *(Vincent van Gogh)*, Paul Rhys *(Theodore van Gogh)*, Jip Wijngaarden *(Sien Hoornik)*, Johanna Ter Steege *(Jo Bonger)*, Wladimir Yordanoff *(Paul Gauguin)*, Jean-Pierre Cassel *(Dr. Paul Gachet)*, Bernadette Giraud *(Marguerite Gachet)*, Adrian Brine *(Uncle Cent)*, Jean-Francois Perrier *(Leon Bouscod)*, Vincent Vallier *(Rene Valadon)*, Hans Kesting *(Andries Bonger)*, and Anne Canovas *(Marie)*

Director Robert Altman has tackled the monumental story of Vincent van Gogh and his brother Theo and, for the most part, comes up a winner. Really fine films about painters are rare, with Charles Laughton's REMBRANDT, Martin Scorsese's contribution to NEW YORK STORIES, and shards of THE HORSE'S MOUTH being among the worthy attempts. Generally, the films are excruciating efforts such as THE AGONY AND THE ECSTASY, MOULIN ROUGE, THE NAKED MAJA, or LUST FOR LIFE. Altman, working from a minimalist script by Julian Mitchell, offers a stripped-to-the-bones rendition of this saga. The actors he uses—Tim Roth as Vincent and Paul Rhys as Theo—are resolutely British, but the overall tone of the film is the kind of Americanese only Altman can pull off in so many myriad contexts of time and place. At one point, Vincent rebuffs the remonstrations of a pompous, conventional painter by announcing, "I'm a working man!" That statement is the key to Altman's vision.

The film's beginning is the director's most audacious conceit. We see actual footage of the painting "Sunflowers" as it is being auctioned off at Christie's, and Altman, one of the keenest users of sound in all cinema, sustains the soundtrack of the bidding during his opening, staged scene between Vincent and Theo. As the brothers argue over the money their rich uncle sends each month to Vincent to sustain his creative, if uncommercial, journey, the point is clearly made about the often arbitrary elusiveness of artistic success. Familiar ground is subsequently covered, including Vincent's fascination with prostitutes and disastrous relations with them, and Theo's syphilitic torment. The film could have easily veered into pure cliche of soap opera, but Altman's visceral, straightforward, warts-and-all conception, coupled with the behavioral naturalness of his cast, avoids such pitfalls. The story line continues through Vincent's uneasy friendship with Gauguin, his encroaching mental instability, Theo's personal financial struggles as a gallery owner with aesthetic standards, and his troubled courtship and marriage to Jo Bonger (Johanna Ter Steege), Vincent's suicide, and Theo's descent into madness and death shortly thereafter.

As photographed by Jean Lepine, the film is visually stunning. This should come as no surprise from Altman, whose MCCABE AND MRS. MILLER, THE LONG GOODBYE, and THIEVES LIKE US all showed thick, wondrously appropriate, painterly influences. He and Lepine—both true artists themselves—scrupulously avoid the literal-mindedness of Vincente Minnelli's let's-restage-the-painting-cost-be damned approach in LUST FOR LIFE. VINCENT AND THEO is brimful of the pictorial splendors of nature and the human form, but they are captured fleetingly, in an off-the-cuff kind of way that captures the finely attuned peripheral vision, the febrile antennae, of an artist. The early scene of Vincent observing and rapidly sketching the whore as she takes a break from posing, stretches, looks through the window at the moon, and even relieves herself, comes as close to depicting the actual creative process of painting as anything ever filmed. The creation of the sunflower paintings is aptly expressed in the silent, sketchy takes of him out in the fields, experiencing quick frustration

more than anything else, with the end result a terse, panning shot of his room in Arles, filled with his finished efforts glowing from the walls. His suicide is likewise breathtaking: unexpected, rending, almost comic, and as abrupt as the flock of crows which suddenly flies up to the sky from the wheat field at the sound of the gunshot.

Unfortunately, the film's energy flags somewhat in its final quarter. The laconic conception of the van Gogh brothers, while dramatically and aesthetically pretty sound, is insufficient to the final, nihilistic tragedies of their lives. That ultimate rarity—a deeply researched and felt script by a writer of near-genius—would be necessary to answer some if not all the questions engendered in the viewer's mind. The film becomes too much a surface exercise—shots of Vincent screaming before a mirror, menacing Gauguin or Theo, surrounded by his impoverished wife and child, or, finally, in an asylum, nude and crouching like a Fuseli creature lit by the moon, are just not enough.

Roth plays Vincent in the great tradition of mumbling, shambling Altman heroes such as Warren Beatty's McCabe or Elliott Gould's Philip Marlowe. His asides are often amusing and he convincingly conveys the artist's recessive nature, along with an accessible quality akin to the more raffish silent movie clowns. Rhys as Theo seems to be enjoying a real turn. If Vincent is the boho tramp of nature, then Rhys' Theo is the epitome of the over-civilized, bloodless urbanite. His performance is riddled with nervous tics, darting, piercing glances, sudden little snits, and abrupt explosions of laughter. It's an oddball performance, mostly repellant, but intermittently redeemed by its little, hard-won payoffs of humor. Wladimir Yordanoff as Gauguin has an intriguing ambivalence, a faint duplicity beneath the sublime "artist as great liver and prince among men" pose. The women are all unusual, gratifyingly strong presences. Anne Canovas as the prostitute, with her harsh accented voice, looks like a garret-bred Jennifer Grey and has an immediately dominating, almost frightening forceful presence. Ter Steege is lovely in an Old World, slightly bovine way, like one of Reubens' cream, rose, and gold beauties. She bides her time, waiting for Theo to woo her, and wins handily. It's just a shame that the screenwriter had her character dissolve into a screeching harpy by the end. *(Nudity, violence, adult situations, sexual situations, substance abuse.)*

d, Robert Altman; p, Ludi Boeken; w, Julian Mitchell; ph, Jean Lepine; ed, Francois Coispeau and Geraldine Peroni; m, Gabriel Yared; prod d, Stephen Altman; art d, Dominique Douret, Ben Van, and Jan Roelfs; set d, Pierre Siore; cos, Scott Bushnell

Biography (PR:O MPAA:R)

VITAL SIGNS

103m FOX c

Adrian Pasdar *(Michael Chatham)*, Diane Lane *(Gina Wyler)*, Jack Gwaltney *(Kenny Rose)*, Laura San Giacomo *(Lauren Rose)*, Jane Adams *(Suzanne Maloney)*, Tim Ransom *(Bobby Hayes)*, Bradley Whitford *(Dr. Ballentine)*, Lisa Jane Persky *(Bobby)*, William Devane *(Dr. Chatham)*, Norma Aleandro *(Henrietta)*, Jimmy Smits *(Dr. David Redding)*, Wallace Langham *(Gant)*, James Karen *(Dean of Students)*, Leigh C. Kim *(Dr. Chen)*, Enid Kent *(Vivian)*, Telma Hopkins *(Dr. Kennan)*, Daniel Ziskie *(Dr. Kelly)*, Rob Neukirch *(Rita's Resident)*, Grant Heslov *(Rick)*, Karen Fineman *(Julie)*, Laurie Souza *(Mother)*, Stanley DeSantis *(Loan Officer)*, Kenia *(Rita)*, Steve Bean *(OB/GYN Intern)*, Claudia Harrington *(Pregnant Woman)*, Seth Isler *(Male Resident)*, Jay Arlen Jones *(Paramedic)*, Donna Lynn Leavy *(Cynthia)*, Matt Thompson *(Billy)*, Jeanne Mori *(Billy's Nurse)*, Gigo Vorgan *(Nell)*, Angelo Tiffe *(George)*, Christine Avila *(Non-Clown Nurse)*, Mary Pat Gleason *(Rotunda Woman)*, Perla Walter *(Hispanic Woman)*, Paul Carlton Bryant *(Pharmacist)*, Ellaraino *(Phone Nurse)*, Rose Weaver *(Henrietta's Night Nurse)*, Myra Turley *(Henrietta's IV Nurse)*, Lou Saint James *(Redding's Paramedic)*, Joan Newlin *(ER Nurse)*, Vicki Winters *(Hospital Employee)*, Doug Robinson *(Competing Swimmer)*, Charlie Hawke, Billy Bacon *(Swimmers)*, and Craig Hosking *(Helicopter Pilot)*

Is third-year medical school as difficult as they say it is? VITAL SIGNS, starring Diane Lane and Adrian Pasdar, answers this question with a resounding "yes." But despite its success at portraying the trials and tribulations of this critical year, the film is slow-paced and for the most part predictable. VITAL SIGNS' six main characters, Gina (Lane), Michael (Pasdar), Kenny (Jack Gwaltney), Suzanne (Jane Adams), Bobby Hayes (Tim Ransom), and another, female Bobby (Lisa Jane Persky), are all friends and student doctors at a major California university who face the toughest year of their education together. This pack of masochists is led by Dean of Third Year Studies and Chief of Surgery Dr. David Redding (Jimmy Smits). The movie's main focus is on the rivalry between Michael and Kenny. The two compete for honors rotation and surgical internship, Redding's approval, and virtually everything else. But towards the film's end, a crisis arises with one of Michael's patients and it's Kenny who bails his colleague out. Another rivalry involves surgical resident Dr. Ballentine (Bradley Whitford), who instructs Michael to give a cancer patient (Norma

Aleandro) a certain treatment that Michael knows in his heart is wrong. Going against Ballentine's orders and university rules, he cares for the patient his own way. Outraged, Dr. Redding calls a hearing and suspends Michael. But Kenny manages to clear him by informing Dr. Redding that Ballentine was jealous over losing Gina to Michael, and consequently sought to jeopardize the life of one of Michael's patients in an effort to make Michael look bad. Meanwhile, Kenny's marriage to Lauren (Laura San Giacomo) is suffering from the stress of medical school, and they eventually separate. But, like most of the problems in this film, their conflict is eventually resolved, and everybody ends up interning at the hospital of his or her choice.

VITAL SIGNS is believably acted, and well directed by Marisa Silver (PERMANENT RECORD). What damages the film most is its flawed script by Jeb Stuart (best known for action films such as DIE HARD and LOCK UP) and Larry Ketron (who cowrote PERMANENT RECORD with Silver and adapted his own play for the atrocious FRESH HORSES). The story is predictable, and the film conspicuously fails to create interesting female characters. The women students in VITAL SIGNS for the most part serve only as love interests and objects of competition. Although there is one harrowing scene in which Gina loses a pediatric patient, more time is spent examining the complications that arise when she leaves Ballentine for Michael than on her struggles as a medical student. And it would be refreshing to see Adams' Suzanne in the operating room at least once, rather than just in bed with Ransom's Bobby Hayes. *(Nudity, sexual situations, profanity.)*

d, Marisa Silver; p, Laurie Perlman and Cathlen Summers; w, Larry Ketron and Jeb Stuart (based on a story by Larry Ketron); ph, John Lindley; ed, Robert Brown and Danford B. Greene; m, Miles Goodman; prod d, Todd Hallowell; art d, Dan Maltese; set d, Keith Burns; stunts, Charles Picerni Jr.; cos, Deborah Everton; makeup, Bruce Hutchinson and Susan Cabral; tech, Linda Klein

Drama   (PR:C MPAA:R)

WEDDING BAND

82m IRS Media c

William Katt *(Marshall Roman)*, Joyce Hyser *(Karla Thompson)*, Tino Insana *(Hugh Bowmont)*, Lance Kinsey *(Ritchie)*, David Bowe *(Max)*, Pauly Shore *(Nicky)*, Fran Drescher *(Veronica)*, and David Rasche *(Sloane Vaughn)*

Someone must have called in a lot of favors to bring about WEDDING BAND's parade of celebrity cameos (including appearances by Joe Flaherty of "SCTV," Tim Kazurinsky of "Saturday Night Live," director Penelope Spheeris, and, in an uncredited role as an Amish minister, Jim Belushi). But well-known faces are not enough to enliven this tired comedy about a small-time musical combo. William Katt (BUTCH AND SUNDANCE: THE EARLY YEARS; HOUSE) stars as the leader of the Shakers, an ersatz rock group eking out a living at an endless round of wedding receptions. Katt's long-suffering girl friend (Joyce Hyser) stirs things up when she encourages him to drop wedding performances and concentrate on his own music. Katt, however, is proud of his band and its ability to play any request. He feels that the Shakers, in their own small way, are making people happy. Hyser increases the pressure by proposing marriage to Katt during a romantic dinner. With unvoiced misgivings, Katt accepts, and Hyser, a professional bridal consultant, prepares for her dream wedding — including a staggering bridal registry. Katt faces impending wedlock with growing anxiety and is relieved when his agent (Tino Insana) arranges the Shakers' first tour, forcing postponement of the wedding ceremony. Hyser is outraged and demands that Katt choose between her and the Shakers. Naturally, Katt picks the Shakers and is promptly given the heave-ho by Hyser. The band's tour proves to be a jarring disappointment, however, with each gig more miserable than the last. Meanwhile, Hyser finds a new boy friend (David Rasche of "Sledge Hammer") and goes through the motions of her spectacular wedding shower (the breakup having occurred too late to cancel the party), though she gets no satisfaction from her booty. When Katt leaves a message on Hyser's answering machine, she seizes upon it as an opportunity for a reconciliation. She arrives at the last wedding on the Shaker's tour, and Katt plays an original love song for her. Needless to say, the next wedding the Shakers play is Katt and Hyser's.

The best thing that can be said about WEDDING BAND is that it is essentially pleasant. It unreels its goofy gags and romantic conflict with good cheer, unencumbered by nastiness or bitterness. Unfortunately, the film isn't funny, and its many attempts at humor all fall flat. One of the most predictable of these attempts comes during a bridal-wear fashion show, when a near-sighted model walks off the runway and falls into the audience. Equally humorless is a sight gag featuring a maternity wedding dress with the word *baby* embroidered over an arrow pointing downward. At an Amish wedding, the participants decline to dance on religious grounds, but are unable to prevent themselves from boogeying to the Shakers' pseudo-rock 'n' roll. Not only is this joke silly and familiar, it is also slightly offensive. Predictability is WEDDING BAND's major flaw, along with flat execution by Daniel Raskov, directing his first film after making commercials and music videos. Even the Shakers' music is flat. A collection of bland covers of bland pop songs like Paul Fishman's "Politics of Dancing," these tunes sound as if they are being heard through a transistor radio. This failure is especially disappointing and surprising, not only because music is so central to the film, but because WEDDING BAND was produced and distributed theatrically by IRS Media, a wing of IRS records. When a record company cannot put together a listenable soundtrack, something has obviously gone seriously wrong. *(Adult situations, profanity.)*

d, Daniel Raskov; p, John Schouweiler and Tino Insana; w, Tino Insana; ph, Christian Sebaldt; ed, Jonas Thaler; m, Steve Hunter; prod d, Tori Nourafchan; art d, Michael Thomas; set d, Lucie Munoz; cos, Rozanne Taucher

Comedy   (PR:A-C MPAA:R)

WELCOME HOME, ROXY CARMICHAEL

98m ITC/Paramount c

Winona Ryder *(Dinky Bossetti)*, Jeff Daniels *(Denton Webb)*, Laila Robins *(Elizabeth Zaks)*, Thomas Wilson Brown *(Gerald Howells)*, Frances Fisher *(Roshelle Bossetti)*, Graham Beckel *(Leo Bossetti)*, Dinah Manoff *(Evelyn Whittacher)*, Ava Fabian *(Roxy Carmichael)*, Joan McMurtrey *(Barbara Webb)*, Robby Kiger *(Beannie)*, Sachi Parker *(Libby)*, and Stephen Tobolowsky *(Bill Klepler)*

WELCOME HOME ROXY CARMICHAEL is less a movie than it is an example of what the studios refer to as "product," the kind of toothless comedy that features big stars in frenetic and forgettable farces. As he did with his solo

directing debut, BIG BUSINESS, Jim Abrahams (one-third of the AIRPLANE! directing troika that includes David and Jerry Zucker) seems intent on reviving the Preston Sturges style of screen comedy. However, Abrahams's work recalls Sturges without recapturing what made him unique — his anarchic spirit. When movies become "product," true anarchy has no place. While BIG BUSINESS, with its twin couples and a plot hinging on love and money, vaguely echoes THE PALM BEACH STORY, Abrahams dusts off HAIL THE CONQUERING HERO. In ROXY, a small town is driven into lunacy by the triumphant return of the title character, who has come home to dedicate the institute of drama and cosmetology that is to bear her name. HERO focuses on the dilemma of a phony war hero (played by Eddie Bracken) who is about to be celebrated by his hometown; ROXY shrouds its eponymous heroine ("played" by onetime *Playboy* centerfold Ava Fabian) in mystery. Although we get a lingering look at Roxy's bare bottom during a skinny-dip, we never do see her face. Instead ROXY puts at its center what was the sideshow in Sturges's classic, the town — in this case Clyde, Ohio.

As Roxy's arrival approaches, the women of the town drive the local beauty shop and dressmakers to distraction, vying to make a competitive showing with the returning beauty. The men are mostly compelled to recall her "reputation." Roxy's arrival also provokes bittersweet memories, particularly for Denton Webb (Jeff Daniels), Roxy's former sweetheart, with whom she had a baby. Another ex-lover, a woman (Dinah Manoff), is similarly affected. But the film's real center is town misfit Dinky Bossetti (Winona Ryder), the adopted daughter of a local carpet mogul, who becomes convinced that Roxy is her real mother. An outcast at her high school — the kids sit far away from her in the cafeteria and pelt her with food — Dinky writes overwrought romantic poetry hoping to win the love of a bland classmate (Thomas Wilson Brown, a Sean Penn lookalike who seems a little old to be cruising around town on his skateboard). She also keeps her own "ark," a wrecked cabin cruiser that is home to a pig Dinky has saved from slaughter, a goat, a tortoise, and a cute Benji-like dog with a bandaged forepaw. Given Dinky's bohemian-rustic nature, it's a little hard to fathom her worship of Roxy. Though Roxy is a misfit herself, her fame stems mainly from having had a love song (performed by Melissa Etheridge on the soundtrack) written about her. Presumably, Roxy's songwriter-lover has also signed the royalty rights over to her, giving her ample wealth and leisure time for her languorous nude swims.

Thus ROXY would have us believe that sensitive, intelligent, and creative small-town girls want nothing more than to grow up to be Hollywood bimbos. In this pursuit, Dinky even has a mentor, her drop-dead gorgeous guidance counselor (Laila Robins), who carts Dinky off to Cleveland to get her some grown-up clothes and to reassure her about her breast development. All of this nonsense is especially odd for a movie whose writer (Karen Leigh Hopkins) and producer (Penney Finkelman Cox) are women. But the nonsense doesn't end there; Denton's shrewish wife angrily abandons him, not because he resumes his affair with Roxy (DOES HE?), but because he parks his truck outside her house. What's more, not much is made of Dinky's stepfather's sexual indiscretion with his sales assistant. Dinky catches Dad in the act, but he is apparently able to buy her silence by — what else? — recarpeting Dinky's bedroom in her favorite color, black.

WELCOME HOME, ROXY CARMICHAEL tries to imitate Sturges, but it obviously misses the point. Sturges loved the same small-town characters that the makers of this film treat with cynical derision. Sturges gave these characters an understated nobility in their deluded pursuit of the American Dream — not to mention some of his best dialog. The makers of ROXY give them little more than the simpleminded cravings of stale sitcom grotesques. What real soul ROXY has is provided by Ryder's performance. Her poignant yearning, compulsive generosity, and infinite capacity for forgiveness are the only elements in ROXY that would be at home in a Sturges film. In transcending the general crassness and inanity of ROXY, Ryder reminds the viewer of the transcendent spirit of great movies like those by Sturges. It can only be hoped that today's Hollywood will be able to rise to her challenge. *(Nudity, adult situations.)*

d, Jim Abrahams; p, Penney Finkelman Cox; w, Karen Leigh Hopkins; ph, Paul Elliott; ed, Bruce Green; m, Thomas Newman; prod d, Dena Roth; art d, John Myhre, Rosemary Brandenburg, and Nina Ruscio; set d, Richard G. Huston and James A. Gelarden; cos, Mali Finn

Comedy   (PR:C MPAA:PG-13)

WHERE THE HEART IS

94m Touchstone — Silver Screen Partners IV/Buena Vista c

Dabney Coleman *(Stewart McBain)*, Uma Thurman *(Daphne McBain)*, Joanna Cassidy *(Jean McBain)*, Crispin Glover *(Lionel)*, Suzy Amis *(Chloe McBain)*, Christopher Plummer *(Homeless Gent)*, David Hewlett *(Jimmy McBain)*, Dylan Walsh *(Tom)*, Sheila Kelley *(Sheryl)*, Maury Chaykin *(Harry)*, Ken Pogue *(Hamilton)*, Michael Kirby *(Lionel's Father)*, Dennis Strong *(Marvin X)*, Timothy Stickney *(Marcus)*, Emma Woollard *(Olivia)*, Paulina Gillis *(Secretary)*,

Gary Krawford (*Presidential Aide*), Albert Scultz (*Edgar*), Sandi Ross (*Woman Speaking in Tongues*), George Seremba (*Preacher*), Ralph Small (*Eviction Man*), Ann-Marie MacDonald, Frances Flanagan (*TV Reporters*), Najma Uddin (*Porna*), Prabha Gandhi (*Mya*), Juan Sanchez (*Jose*), Ida Carnevali (*Mrs. Jose*), Philip Williams (*Man with Writ*), and Howard Lende (*Wall Street Man*)

Vilified by critics upon its release, John Boorman's farcical rumination on modern families disappeared quickly from theatres, but this is a film that deserves the second chance video stores now offer. Dabney Coleman stars as Stewart McBain, the prosperous owner of a demolition company who lives in New York with his wife Jean (Joanna Cassidy), and their three children, Chloe (Suzy Amis), Jimmy (David Hewlett), and Daphne (Uma Thurman), all in their early twenties. As the film opens, Stewart's plans to destroy the buildings on a block to make way for a new development are thwarted when a community group succeeds in getting landmark status for a structure on the block known as the Dutch House. Things aren't much better for Stewart on the homefront where his spoiled children seem inclined to allow the old man to support them while they find ways to keep themselves amused. Stewart has finally had enough of their irresponsible ways and decrees, over the objections of his far-less demanding wife, that they be banished from his household and forced to live in the abandoned and dilapidated Dutch House. The kids are horrified at the prospect, with Daphne exclaiming, "You can't spoil us for all these years and then just throw us out," but Stewart is adamant.

The kids move into the Dutch House with no means of support. Jimmy dabbles in creating computer games and Daphne simply dabbles, while Chloe is an artist who creates "living" camouflage paintings in which human bodies are painted to blend in with surreal backgrounds she creates. Chloe has a contract to create a calendar for an insurance company, but her work takes time, and to get some income the kids decide to take in boarders. Among them are aspiring dress designer Lionel (Cripsin Glover); Jimmy's friend Tom (Dylan Walsh), a stockbroker who is in love with Chloe; and a homeless bum (a barely recognizable Christopher Plummer). As the Dutch House gang strives to survive, Stewart's fortunes fade. A corporate raider tries to take over his company and Stewart goes deeply into debt to acquire the corporate stock to fend off the raider—losing everything when the stock falls. Now he and his wife are homeless, and they too move into Dutch House while trying to figure a way to recoup their losses.

As a followup to his highly successful autobiographical film HOPE AND GLORY, Boorman here continued to work in a comical vein, after years of creating violent adventures such as DELIVERANCE, POINT BLANK, and EXCALIBUR. He was quoted as saying that in his later years he wants to amuse, rather than abuse, his audience, and he succeeds here with a film that is often beautiful and entertaining. Continuing to utilize the persona he developed on television as the title character in "Buffalo Bill," Coleman is ideally suited to playing Stewart McBain, the gruff, defiant entrepreneur who is at odds with and baffled by current society. As portrayed by Coleman, Stewart is neither sympathetic nor villainous—he's just a guy who has always been successful doing things his own way and who doesn't let fears or doubts get in his way. Cassidy (who played opposite Coleman on "Buffalo Bill") does an acceptable job as the supportive wife who doesn't always understand her husband, while Plummer is a delight as the philosphical bum whose bathroom habits earn him the nickname of "Shitty." The rest of the cast is generally competent and the screenplay, which Boorman co-wrote with his daughter Telsche, offers a fresh story that's filled with humor and neat twists.

Enhancing the appeal of the film is the *trompe l'oeil* art which Amis's character supposedly creates, but which was actually provided by artist Timna Woollard. Each of the film's main characters gets a chance to appear in one of the camouflage paintings, in which naked bodies merge into and emerge from backgrounds of fantastic scenery. The images Woollard created for the film are often stunning and thoroughly inventive. Though WHERE THE HEART IS failed to generate much interest upon its release, it is a unique and entertaining film that is well worth a look. (*Profanity, brief nudity.*)

d, John Boorman; p, John Boorman; w, John Boorman and Telsche Boorman; ph, Peter Suschitzky; ed, Ian Crafford; m, Peter Martin; prod d, Carol Spier; art d, James McAterr and Susan Kaufman; cos, Linda Matheson; chor, Richard Murphy

Comedy/Drama   (PR:C   MPAA:R)

WHITE GIRL, THE

94m Tony Brown c

Troy Beyer (*Kim*), Taimak (*Bob*), Teresa Yvon Farley (*Vanessa*), Dianne B. Shaw (*Debbie*), O.L. Duke (*Nicky*), Petronia Paley (*Dr. McCullough*), Donald Craig (*Mr. W.*), Michael Duerloo (*Charles*), Don Hannah (*Karl*), Sherry Williams (*Mrs. Barnes*), Twila Wolfe (*Tracy*), and Kevin Campbell (*Roger*)

Pretty Kim (Troy Beyer), a middle-class, African-American high-school student, seems to have the world at her feet. Her parents love and indulge her,

she gets excellent grades and intends to become a lawyer, and her clothes and accessories are infinite in number and variety. But something goes terribly wrong when she gets to college: she becomes a cocaine addict, and her grades drop so precipitously that she's placed on academic probation. A sympathetic campus counsellor tries to help, but her advice falls on deaf ears. Efforts to persuade Kim—who protests that she doesn't see colors, only people—to join the Black Student Union are more successful, however, and through the Union she meets Bob (Taimak), a handsome, hard-working pre-med student. Bob proves a positive influence; he even suggests that they study together, as a means of helping Kim to make up work she has missed and be able to graduate with the rest of her class. He is Kim's first black boyfriend, and his supportiveness and acceptance helps her admit her drug problem. It appears that Kim has a chance at recovery, until the arrival of her new roommate—seductive, ruthless, manipulative Vanessa (Teresa Farley), who is determined to become a television anchorwoman, sees people solely in terms of what they can do for her, and is willing to sleep with anyone she thinks can further her cause. She is also a hard-core coke addict, and eventually tempts Kim to go back on the stuff, after which Kim abandons the antidrug Bob. Vanessa also promises one well-connected TV executive that she will persuade Kim to sleep with him, and agrees to participate in a humiliating sexual charade with another man, all in the name of advancing her career. In time, Vanessa's involvement with a vicious, drug-dealing pimp has fatal consequences for her, and Kim is nearly killed as well. Bob—who has always hoped that Kim would see the error of her ways and return to him—arrives in time to get her to the hospital. Awakening from her drug-induced coma, Kim realizes she truly loves him, and the two begin planning a new life together.

The "white girl" of the title is cocaine. It is also, however, an indication of Kim's self-destructive desire to be assimilated by white society without acknowledging her African-American roots. Her warped self-image is made painfully literal in the opening scene, through a lingering tracking shot of the white Barbie doll surmounting her birthday cake. Written, produced and directed by African-American TV journalist Tony Brown (host of public television's "Tony Brown's Journal"), THE WHITE GIRL is a message movie of the most heavy-handed kind. While its messages are reasonable enough—drug abuse is dangerous, pride in one's ethnic heritage is healthy, the power of love can help ease the pain of living—they are driven home at the expense of plot, characterization, and other cinematic virtues by Brown, a newcomer to feature filmmaking. One striking scene shows the face of Vanessa, wearing eerie blue contact lenses emblematic of her rejection of her racial identity, appearing in Kim's mirror like some irrepressible demon from the subconscious, but such effective moments are the exception rather than the rule in this generally clumsy film.

It's bad enough that THE WHITE GIRL is didactic. Unfortunately, like last year's THE BOOST (which also addressed the perils of cocaine dependency), it is also frequently ludicrous, a modern-day REEFER MADNESS. Audiences reduced to laughter by stilted, preachy dialog and inept plot development are unlikely to pay much heed to a movie's moral lessons. And while THE BOOST, for all it flaws, was vitalized by a riveting James Woods performance, THE WHITE GIRL's cast is clearly too inexperienced to keep the stereotyped nature of their characters from standing out in high relief. THE WHITE GIRL's "just say no" theme is well-intentioned, but the delivery falls flat. (*Violence, drug use, adult situations.*)

d, Tony Brown; p, James Cannady; w, Tony Brown; ph, Joseph M. Wilcots; ed, Joseph M. Wilcots and Tony Vigna; m, George Porter Martin and Jimmy Lee Brown; prod d, Brent Owens; set d, Bill Webb; cos, Paul Simmons

Drama   (PR:C   MPAA:PG-13)

WHITE HUNTER, BLACK HEART

112m Malpaso-Rastar/WB c

Clint Eastwood (*John Wilson*), Jeff Fahey (*Pete Verrill*), Charlotte Cornwell (*Miss Wilding*), Norman Lumsden (*Butler George*), George Dzundza (*Paul Landers*), Edward Tudor Pole (*Reissar*), Roddy Maude-Roxby (*Thompson*), Richard Warwick (*Basil Fields*), John Rapley (*Gun Shop Salesman*), Catherine Neilson (*Irene Saunders*), Marisa Berenson (*Kay Gibson*), Richard Vanstone (*Phil Duncan*), Jamie Koss (*Mrs. Duncan*), Anne Dunkley (*Scarf Girl*), David Danns (*Bongo Man*), Myles Freeman (*Ape Man*), Geoffrey Hutchings (*Alec Laing*), Christopher Fairbank (*Tom Harrison*), Alun Armstrong (*Ralph Lockhart*), Clive Mantle (*Harry*), Mel Martin (*Mrs. MacGregor*), Martin Jacobs (*Dickie Marlowe*), Norman Malunga (*Desk Clerk*), Timothy Spall (*Hodkins*), Alex Norton (*Zibelinsky*), Eleanor David (*Dorshka*), Boy Mathias Chuma (*Kivu*), Andrew Whalley (*Photographer*), and Conrad Asquith (*Ogilvy*)

Based on Peter Viertel's *roman a clef*, WHITE HUNTER, BLACK HEART uses the making of another classic film, THE AFRICAN QUEEN, to explore arrogance and the artistic process. It's also the story of one enigmatic film director as told by another. Star-director Clint Eastwood plays a thinly disguised

John Huston, here called John Wilson. Eastwood even invests Wilson with a touch of Huston's distinctive gravelly voice. Set in 1951, the film begins as Wilson has summoned an old friend, writer Pete Verrill (Jeff Fahey, Viertel's surrogate in the story), to his Irish estate to recruit him for his latest project — the title of which he never can remember — about a salty, hard-drinking boat captain and a prissy schoolmarm who take on the German navy in Africa during WW II. All Wilson really cares about is that the film will give him a fast infusion of cash to put a dent in personal debts totalling a quarter of a million dollars. Even more important, it will provide him with an all-expenses-paid opportunity to fulfill his longtime dream of going big-game hunting. Meetings with producer Paul Landers (George Dzundza, playing a role modeled on real-life producer Sam Spiegel) and potential backers put the production on track, and Wilson and Verrill begin work on the script. But a major dispute arises over the fate of the leading characters, who, in Wilson's version, are killed, while Verrill insists they should live as the fair reward for their extraordinary heroism. Even after Wilson and Verrill's arrival in Africa, the film continues to take a back seat to the director's planned safari to kill an elephant. Meanwhile, at the hotel where Wilson and Verrill stay, the filmmaker insults an anti-Semitic woman and then loses a fistfight with the openly racist hotel manager. Soon thereafter, Wilson and his cowriter travel to the wilderness hunting lodge where, Wilson has decided, the cast and crew will be housed during the making of the film. Naturally, with the lodge as his base of operations, the director will have a chance to hunt his elephant. On Wilson's very first expedition, a bull elephant whose tusks nearly touch the ground is sighted, but the conditions for making the kill are not ideal. Wilson restrains himself but, having had his quarry in his rifle sights, he becomes even more obsessed. By the time the cast, crew and Landers arrive in Africa, Wilson is somewhere out in the bush with a native tracker, having sent back word that he intends to film in the tracker's village for authenticity. This news, along with troubling reports Landers has been receiving from the production manager, have made the producer apprehensive. Landers' anxiety is heightened when he meets Verrill, who has quit the project in disgust to return to Europe, convinced that Wilson will never make the film. Landers prevails on Verrill to remain, which he does after learning that the final draft of the script never reached Landers. Wilson has the only copy of the script, so to fulfill his contractual obligation, Verrill agrees to help find Wilson, get the script, and deliver it to Landers. Arriving at the hunting lodge, Landers and Verrill find a tuxedoed and gracious Wilson hosting a lavish welcoming dinner. But their delight at Wilson's seeming return to sanity evaporates when he declares that he will take his elephant whatever the cost to the film. While preparing to shoot the first scene, Wilson, true to his word, keeps a Land Rover idling and ready to rush him into the bush at a moment's notice. Finally, that notice comes and Wilson sets out, but tragedy results when his native guide is killed while saving the director's life. Wilson returns to make his film, humbled and accepting of Verrill's upbeat ending for the script.

At first glace, Eastwood seems about the least likely person to bring WHITE HUNTER, BLACK HEART to the screen. As filmmakers and as people, Huston and Eastwood could not be more different. As Viertel (who cowrote WHITE HUNTER's screenplay and served as the production's advisor) noted in an *LA Times* interview, "[Huston] didn't give a damn about the schedule or what kind of hell he was putting the investors through. At the time, John was just interested in his experiences. Clint is a very responsible filmmaker, very concerned with the schedule and the budget." Yet, as Eastwood noted in the same article, "The irony of it is that with everything that happened, [Huston] landed on his feet and made a good movie."

While it is by no means clear what Eastwood was actually hoping to accomplish in WHITE HUNTER — and this lack of clarity is the film's major weakness — the linking of Huston's experiences with the "good movie" that made them possible makes WHITE HUNTER a more intriguing film overall than the sum of its parts, a trait shared by many of Eastwood's projects as an independent filmmaker and star, from DIRTY HARRY to BIRD. The personification of the post-Hemingway action hero, Eastwood initially looks and sounds uncomfortable filling Huston's decidedly Hemingwayesque shoes. As the action shifts to Africa, Eastwood seems inordinately laid-back as his character's obsession grows. He can't quite get a hold on the first predominantly unsympathetic character he's played since TIGHTROPE, and Wilson's early nobility in the face of the racism at the African hotel gives way to the macho arrogance of a dilettante risking lives in his quest for a hunting trophy.

The end of WHITE HUNTER can't help but hit close to home for those in the film community facing the question of whether putting people at serious risk is a fair price to pay for making a movie. In well-publicized cases, such as TWILIGHT ZONE: THE MOVIE, where lives were lost, the onscreen results were notable only for their mocking mediocrity. But what if, as WHITE HUNTER asks, the result is a screen classic? Eastwood implies his own answer by failing to supply a post script explaining the fate of Wilson's film and, more tellingly, through the words that follow the end credits: "This is a work of fiction." Thus the film ends with Wilson essentially unredeemed, if not a figure of outright contempt.

In truth, as a director Eastwood has yet to pose much of a threat to Huston. As entertainment, WHITE HUNTER, like other Eastwood-directed films, lacks precisely the clear, lean narrative approach that characterizes Huston's best work (including THE AFRICAN QUEEN) or even that of Eastwood's mentor, director Don Siegel (DIRTY HARRY; ESCAPE FROM ALCATRAZ). At this point, in fact, it has to be considered a coup that Eastwood was able to keep WHITE HUNTER's running time under two hours. Still, Eastwood's body of work constitutes a uniquely personal, compelling consideration of the role of the black-and-white action hero in a modern society full of shades of gray. At this point, Eastwood may not have all the answers, either to the dilemmas of filmmaking or the moral dilemmas faced by his protagonists, but he is asking the right questions with a sensitivity and seriousness that is otherwise virtually absent from American commercial cinema. *(Adult situations, profanity, violence.)*

d, Clint Eastwood; p, Clint Eastwood; w, Peter Viertel, James Bridges, and Burt Kennedy (based on the novel by Peter Viertel); ph, Jack N. Green; ed, Joel Cox; m, Lennie Niehaus; prod d, John Graysmark; art d, Tony Reading; set d, Peter Howitt; spec, John Evans and Roy Field; stunts, George Orrison; cos, John Mollo; makup, Paul Engelen; chor, Arlene Phillips

Adventure/Drama   (PR:C   MPAA:PG)

WHITE PALACE

103m Mirage — Double Play/UNIV c

Susan Sarandon *(Nora Baker)*, James Spader *(Max Baron)*, Jason Alexander *(Neil Horowitz)*, Kathy Bates *(Rosemary Powers)*, Eileen Brennan *(Judy)*, Steven Hill *(Sol Horowitz)*, Rachel Levin *(Rachel Horowitz)*, Corey Parker *(Larry Klugman)*, Renee Taylor *(Edith Baron)*, Jonathan Penner *(Marv Miller)*, Barbara Howard *(Sheri Klugman)*, Hildy Brooks *(Ella Horowitz)*, Mitzi McCall *(Sophie Rosen)*, Cathy "K.C." Carr *(Stripper)*, Glenn Savan *(White Palace Customer)*, Fannie Belle Lebby *(Marcia)*, Vernon Dudas *(Jimmy, The Bartender)*, Maryann Kopperman *(Reba Pasker)*, Maria Pitillo *(Janey)*, Jeremy Piven *(Kahn)*, Robert Bourgeois, Lance Harshbarger, Jordan Stone *(Bachelor Party Men)*, William Oberbeck *(Eddie Lobodiak)*, John Flack *(Advertising Executive)*, Wilma Myracle *(Helen)*, Joseph Rosenblum *(Rabbi)*, Michael Arnett *(Country Western Singer)*, Kim Meyers *(Heidi Solomon)*, Robert Plunket *(Director)*, and Janet Lofton *(Supermarket Checker)*

Having displayed his yuppie sexual angst in 1989 in SEX, LIES, AND VIDEOTAPE and BAD INFLUENCE, James Spader continues to suffer as his inability to put a personal tragedy behind him leads him to a cheap bar and then to Susan Sarandon's bed in WHITE PALACE. Sarandon plays Nora, a waitress in the title's greasy St. Louis burger joint. She lives in a rundown area called "Dogtown," while Spader, as Max, dwells amid the upwardly mobile Jewish middle class. Max spends his working days in a towering downtown highrise, where he seems to have the same job many movie yuppies do, earning large sums of cash for gazing wistfully at the spectacular view outside his tastefully furnished, high-tech office. But Max's real occupation is his preoccupation with his late wife. Since her death in a car accident, Max has been obsessed with order and control in every aspect of his life. He can't even loosen up at a bachelor party for his buddy Neil (Jason Alexander). While his friends get smashed and ogle the obligatory exotic dancer, Max leaves to return to the White Palace, where he had earlier purchased burgers for the bash. It seems some of the burgers are missing, and the righteously indignant Max is determined to get a refund. After a terse exchange with Nora, the waitress, Max gets his money and returns to the party just as it is winding down. Needled by Neil for his button-down existence, Max stops at a sleazy bar on the way home, and there finds Nora, relaxing after her shift. Though Nora's attempts at friendly banter are initially rebuffed, a couple of scotches take their toll on Max and he begins to warm up to her, especially when she reveals her own tragedy — the death of her son. She takes the wobbly Max home and tucks him in the sofa-bed, later to treat him to a steamy wakeup call. Soon Max is spending all his free time, and then some, with Nora, deep in the heart of Dogtown. Curiosity quickly builds among his friends about his "mystery woman," while Nora chafes at being Max's backstreet girl, even as she dreads the impact exposure might have on their relationship. Nora's fears prove well-based when Max invites her to accompany him and his mother (Renee Taylor) to a Thanksgiving feast. Nora downs vodkas and tells everybody where to get off, finally forcing a hasty retreat. Nora then leaves town, moving to New York to live with her eccentric, Tarot-reading sister (Eileen Brennan), leaving behind a note urging Max to forget about her. Fat chance.

Sarandon is at her best playing a diamond in the rough, but here she is merely rough. She keeps the filthiest house on the planet and is rarely seen without a butt hanging out of the corner of her mouth. These quirks register as arbitrary traits, imposed rather than growing out of the character. WHITE PALACE works best when it's just being an offbeat romantic comedy. Spader seems properly worshipful, though his ardor seems more directed at Sarandon herself than the character she is playing. But the film hobbles itself with its insistence on wringing big statements out of a little romance, as if a simple younger man, older woman love story is inadequate for a feature-length film. Nora can't merely be older than Max. She also has to be crude, lewd, and tattooed. Max can't merely be shy and retiring, he has to be monstrously neurotic. And both have to have a haunting tragedy in their pasts. Under the direction of Luis Mandoki (GABY, A TRUE STORY), the film is simultaneously overplotted and underdeveloped, with the deep, dark secrets registering as annoying clutter rather than character exploration. When a movie needs a psychic to unravel its exposition, as WHITE PALACE does, it can't help but signal deep trouble in the script department. Sarandon, as she has been in so many other indifferent films, becomes the main reason to see WHITE PALACE. There is something uncanny about her ability to effortlessly dominate a film by taking a character, even one as sketchy as Nora, and transform her into a vital creation. She winds up holding together a film that is otherwise too knotted up to ever decide quite what it wants to be. *(Sexual situations, nudity, profanity.)*

d, Luis Mandoki; p, Mark Rosenberg, Amy Robinson, and Griffin Dunne; w, Ted Tally and Alvin Sargent (based on the novel by Glenn Savan); ph, Lajos Koltai; ed, Carol Littleton; m, George Fenton; prod d, Jeannine Claudia Oppewall; art d, John Wright Stevens; set d, Lisa Fischer; spec, Mack Chapman; stunts, Gary Hymes, Jerry Spicer, and Ike Mizen; cos, Lisa Jenson; makeup, Ron Specter

Comedy/Drama/Romance   **(PR:O   MPAA:R)**

WHY ME?

88m Epic/Triumph c

Christopher Lambert *(Gus Cardinale)*, Christopher Lloyd *(Bruno)*, Kim Greist *(June Cardinale)*, J.T. Walsh *(Inspector Mahoney)*, Michael J. Pollard *(Ralph)*, Tony Plana *(Benjy)*, John Hancock *(Tiny)*, Lawrence Tierney, Wendel Meldrum, Rene Assam, Gregory Millar, Jill Terashita, and Thomas Callaway

In this lame-brained but painless caper comedy, various factions battle over the Byzantine Fire, a priceless ruby. The jewel is in the possession of the Republic of Turkey until Armenian terrorists grab it. A few plot contrivances later, the gem has fallen into the hands of a gang of inept thieves, led by Gus Cardinale (Christopher Lambert). The Turkish government, members of the Armenian Liberation Army, the CIA, and agents of other nations all want the gem, which puts Gus in a sticky situation. When Gus and his father-in-law, Bruno Daley (Christopher Lloyd), pay a visit to their fence, Ralph (Michael J. Pollard), they are amazed when police burst in and confiscate their stolen property. It seems the cops are cracking down on all criminal activity in their search for the gem, and the local federation of crooks asks Gus to track down the missing gem. Gus is also grilled by the CIA, offered a deal by Turkish authorities, and threatened by crude cop Mahoney (J.T. Walsh). Gus makes a deal with Mahoney by which he will hand over the ruby if the jewels he has stolen are returned. However, Bruno has made a deal with the Turkish government in which he will get cash for the return of the jewel. Both plans are jeopardized when they learn Gus's wife, June (Kim Greist), has put the jewel in a bank safe deposit box. Since it's the weekend and the jewel is needed immediately, Gus and Bruno have to break into the bank to get the ruby, while also figuring a way out of the fine mess they've gotten themselves in.

Aiming for a cross between the Keystone Kops and TOPKAPI, this flat effort fails on all but the most rudimentary level of escapism. As a time-waster, it provides the pleasure of an ingenious bank heist, but bungles its climax in which dozens of bird-brained characters fumble about. Complicated without being clever, the film lacks suspense and is sluggishly paced. Although the dialog is another debit, the major drawback here is Lambert, an attractive male model who was much better when all he had to do was grunt as Tarzan in GREYSTOKE— THE LEGEND OF TARZAN, LORD OF THE APES. Required to deliver allegedly snappy patter, he can't hold the screen. All the zany supporting characters whirl around the deadpan Lambert to no avail. Although expensive demolitions, car chases, and slapstick shenanigans are momentarily distracting, they can't overcome the film's numerous shortcomings. *(Violence, profanity.)*

d, Gene Quintano; w, Donald E. Westlake and Leonard Mass Jr. (based on the novel by Westlake); ph, Peter Deming; ed, Alan Blesam; m, Basil Poledouris; prod d, Woody Grocker

Comedy   **(PR:C   MPAA:R)**

WILD AT HEART

126m Polygram—Propaganda/Samuel Goldwyn c

Nicolas Cage *(Sailor Ripley)*, Laura Dern *(Lula Pace Fortune)*, Diane Ladd *(Marietta Pace)*, Willem Dafoe *(Bobby Peru)*, Isabella Rossellini *(Perdita Durango)*, Harry Dean Stanton *(Johnnie Farragut)*, Crispin Glover *(Dell)*, Grace

Zabriskie *(Juana)*, J.E. Freeman *(Marcello Santos)*, W. Morgan Sheppard *(Mr. Reindeer)*, Calvin Lockhart *(Reginald Sula)*, David Patrick Kelly *(Drop Shadow)*, Marvin Kaplan *(Uncle Pooch)*, Bellina Logan, Glenn Walker Harris Jr., Gregg Danddridge, Freddie Jones, Charlie Spradling, Eddie Dixon, Brent Fraser, John Lurie, Jack Nance, Tommy G. Kendrick, Scott Coffey, Sherilyn Fenn, and Sheryl Lee

Anyone familiar with the work of director David Lynch realizes that he is an original, one of the few American directors whose films possess not only a signature but true vision. When you watch a film by Lynch you are sharing his dream. Although DUNE bombed at the box office and was mauled by the critics, Lynch's next film, his visionary masterpiece BLUE VELVET (1986), more than confirmed the filmmaker's prodigious talents. Before BLUE VELVET, Lynch had only a small cult following that had discovered and loved the extraordinary ERASERHEAD (1978)—still the director's best work. An audacious exercise in excess, this dark, deeply disturbing portrait of repressed sexuality is constructed in dreamlike fashion, without a plot and lacking real, identifiable characters. With each of his subsequent films, however, Lynch has lost a bit of the brazenness of ERASERHEAD; at the same time, his work has become more commercial and accessible (this is especially true of his foray into primetime TV, "Twin Peaks," which, terrific as it is, is watered-down Lynch). This is not to say that the quality of Lynch's work has deteriorated; he has simply adjusted his vision for wider acceptance (THE ELEPHANT MAN, his weakest and least personal work, is the only film to suffer from this adjustment). Following up BLUE VELVET is no easy task. Admirers of that film are adamant about their love for it, and many will find Lynch's most recent effort, WILD AT HEART, a major disappointment simply because it's *not* BLUE VELVET. Indeed, WILD AT HEART is so far removed from that film that at times it seems to be the work of a different director. Gone is the threateningly repressed sexuality found in BLUE VELVET (and in most of Lynch's work for that matter); in its place is a wildly unhinged energy that propels WILD AT HEART through a series of episodes that transpire in a passionate, sexy, but surprisingly upbeat environment. Lynch's view of the world is still askew, but it is much healthier. This change in approach is not only admirable, but in many ways it has been necessary for Lynch to grow as an artist. And grown he has: WILD AT HEART is not only one of the very best films of 1990; it is a masterpiece.

Based on the novel by Barry Gifford, this winner of the Cannes Film Festival's Palme d'Or is the story of love on the run. Sailor Ripley (Nicolas Cage) is a rebellious, 23-year-old Elvis acolyte who has just served 22 months and 18 days in the Pee Dee correctional facility for manslaughter. Waiting for him on the outside is Lula Fortune (Laura Dern), a 20-year-old, gum-popping, sex-loving cyclone of a gal who picks him up from prison the day of his release. They are in love and spend most of their time smoking (their philosophical conversations about cigarettes echo the similar conversations about beer in BLUE VELVET), dancing, and having sex. Embarking on a journey that takes them from the Carolinas to Texas, they encounter nightmarish accidents and outrageously evil characters, all the while trying to keep one step ahead of Lula's murderous, witchlike mother, Marietta (Diane Ladd, Dern's real-life mother). Sailor's arrest and imprisonment were actually Marietta's doing. After failing to seduce him in a bathroom stall at a ballroom dance, Marietta paid a man to attack Sailor (who, in addition to spurning Marietta's advances, may also know a little too much about the mysterious death of her husband). When Sailor beat his assailant to death, he was thrown in prison. Even now, after Sailor's release, Marietta harbors a bizarre hatred for the young man, and hires her private-detective boy friend, Johnnie Farragut (Harry Dean Stanton), to find her daughter and get her away from the rebellious Sailor. Marietta is so determined to separate Sailor and Lula that she also asks ex-lover Marcello Santos (J.E. Freeman), a mobster, to find Sailor and kill him. Meanwhile, Lula and Sailor drive, smoke, dance, and have lots of sex. Lula tells Sailor about her past (she was raped at 13 by an uncle), her relatives (Crispin Glover plays a weirdo cousin who wears a Santa Claus suit and puts cockroaches in his underwear), and her fantasies (obsessed with THE WIZARD OF OZ, she has visions of the Wicked Witch during the trip's scariest moments). Like Lula, Sailor wishes he were "over the rainbow," and his fate seems to be controlled by the Wicked Witch (the lowest points in his life are shown through a crystal ball as a black-nailed hand passes over it). Sailor and Lula's love is strong and pure (though this doesn't prevent their sex from being hot), but it is put to the test as they cross the country, finally arriving in Big Tuna, Texas, where they encounter Bobby Peru (Willem Dafoe), a psychotic former Marine with rotten teeth and a nasty disposition. After attempting to seduce Lula (in the film's most powerful scene), Peru talks Sailor into participating in a hold-up. Sailor agrees because Lula is pregnant and the young lovers are broke. The catch is that Peru has been hired by Santos to kill Sailor, which Peru plans to do during the robbery. When the stick-up goes badly, Peru ends up dead and Sailor is sent back to prison. After serving six more years, Sailor is released and reunited with Lula and their son. Convinced that he is no good for Lula, and that true love cannot survive in an evil world, Sailor leaves his family. While walking down an alley, Sailor is ambushed by a group of punks. After being knocked unconscious, Sailor has a vision: in a bright floating bubble, Glenda the Good Witch (Sheryl Lee of "Twin Peaks") appears and gives him some truly valuable advice. Sailor awakens, apologizes to his attackers, and runs back to be reunited with his family.

WILD AT HEART is brilliant. A thoroughly involving and utterly spellbinding love story, it is as beautiful as an abstract painting and as intelligent as a classic novel. Alternating between jolting violence and manic comedy, the film has a thoroughly original tone. Moreover, Lynch packs WILD AT HEART with striking visuals. The film's recurring visual motif, a flame raging out of control, not only offers a perfect metaphor for the film's philosophical concerns but also reflects its controlling style. Yet this film differs from Lynch's other projects in almost every conceivable way. From the editing (featuring surprisingly quick cuts), to the use of sound (always a strong quality in Lynch's work), to the color scheme (here orange and yellow replace the dominant blue and green of BLUE VELVET), the filmmaking approach of WILD AT HEART is a clear departure from Lynch's norm.

But though the style Lynch employs here may be different, some of the themes are familiar. WILD AT HEART, like BLUE VELVET and "Twin Peaks," is essentially about the evil underbelly of America. It is also about good triumphing over evil. In addition to his seemingly customary Oedipal obsessions (Marietta's desire to seduce Sailor), Lynch throws in a bunch of the kind of offbeat characters that we've come to expect from his work. Besides Glover's Cousin Dell and Dafoe's Bobby Peru, the parade of Lynchian weirdos includes W. Morgan Sheppard as Mr. Reindeer, a mysterious crime lord who is constantly surrounded by topless hookers; Freddie Jones as a bar patron with a mangled voice; Isabella Rossellini as Perdita, Peru's bleach-blond girl friend; Jack Nance, John Lurie, and Scott Coffey as three of the many eccentrics that populate Big Tuna, Texas; and David Patrick Kelly, Calvin Lockhart, and Grace Zabriskie as a trio of psycho killers. At the center of this wild hodge-podge are Cage and Dern, who turn in outstanding performances. Dern is particularly impressive, creating a character that is different from anything she has ever done before (miles from the innocent Sandy of BLUE VELVET). Her Lula is both deliciously sexy and sweetly innocent, a character whose basic needs are simple and whose personality is unique and likable. Cage is, as always, outstanding in a role he was born to play. Sailor, like Lula, is both good and bad. Despite the fact that he has killed a man, Sailor is something of an innocent, and his heartfelt renditions of Elvis' "Love Me" and "Love Me Tender" are unforgettable. What's more, it's hard not to like a guy who wears an outlandish snakeskin jacket because it represents his "belief in personal freedom and individuality." Together, Cage and Dern ignite the screen, creating a thoroughly believable couple in a thoroughly unbelievable world. They are particularly strong in the exceptional scene in which Lula, appalled by the nonstop reports of murder and mayhem she hears on the radio, pulls off the road, demanding that Sailor find some music on the radio. Tuning past the hideous newscasts, Sailor finds a loud punk-rock tune, to which the couple dance ferociously. It's a terrifically funny scene, and it's one of the most telling moments in the film. The rest of the actors are also impressive, with Dafoe (creating an incredibly creepy representation of evil) and Ladd (completely and wonderfully over-the-top) the stand-outs. She earned an Oscar nomination for Best Supporting Actress for her performance.

There are many unforgettable moments in WILD AT HEART, like the frighteningly funny Jacobean-like scene in which Marietta paints her entire face with blood red lipstick, and the horrifying sequence in which Johnnie Farragut is murdered by the ritual killers (Lynch's use of sound in this sequence is astounding). There is also the moment that almost got WILD AT HEART an X rating: Bobby Peru's infamous decapitation via a shotgun. However, the most haunting scene of all is the one in which Lula and Sailor investigate a car accident. Wandering in the night among bloody bodies and the twisted pieces of the car is a severely injured girl (Sherilyn Fenn, star of "Twin Peaks"). Hallucinating, she fears that her mother is going to "kill her" because she has lost her wallet; meanwhile Lula and Sailor try to get her into their car. What starts out as a weirdly funny scene ("What are we going to do?" asks Lula; to which Sailor replies, "I don't know, but this girl's gonna bleed all over the car.") quickly becomes horrifying when the girl dies in the couple's arms. Lynch brilliantly parallels Lula's fears with those of the dead girl, and the scene plays like a portentous nightmare.

Notwithstanding its hypnotic intensity and style, the real power of WILD AT HEART lies in its surprisingly rich emotion. Unlike most of Lynch's work (with the exception of THE ELEPHANT MAN), WILD AT HEART is moving and sincere. Although Lynch still seems to be making fun of his characters—as he does in most of his films—this time the teasing gives way to genuine care and concern for his characters' plight. Throughout WILD AT HEART Lynch performs a subtle balancing act between parody (the wacky but effective references to THE WIZARD OF OZ) and earnestness (the touching subplot concerning Johnnie Farragut's love for Marietta), and between the outrageous (Grace Zabriskie's clubfooted murderess) and the real (Lula's flashback to an abortion). In the end, when Sailor serenades Lula with "Love Me Tender," and their love

finally triumphs over evil, the film's sincerity wins out over its silliness, and the effect is absolutely exhilarating.

Beautifully photographed by Frederick Elmes (who also shot BLUE VEL-VET), and featuring a memorable score by Angelo Badalamenti, WILD AT HEART may not be for everyone (perhaps not even for some Lynch fans); nonetheless, it is a flamboyantly original work that is undeniably entertaining and remarkably assured—the most fearlessly original American film since BLUE VELVET. A startling alternative to the stale and gutless work of many American directors, WILD AT HEART proves once again that David Lynch is one of the most exciting and talented filmmakers alive. (Extreme violence, nudity, profanity, sexual situations, adult situations.)

d, David Lynch; p, Monty Montgomery, Steve Golin, and Joni Sighvatsson; w, David Lynch (based on the novel by Barry Gifford); ph, Frederick Elmes; ed, Duwayne Dunham; m, Angelo Badalamenti; prod d, Patricia Norris; spec, David B. Miller, Louis Lazara, and David Domeyer; cos, Patricia Norris

Comedy/Drama/Romance   (PR:O   MPAA:R)

WILD ORCHID

100m Damon-Saunders/Vision c

Mickey Rourke (James Wheeler), Jacqueline Bisset (Claudia Lirones), Carre Otis (Emily Reed), Assumpta Serna (Hanna Minch), Bruce Greenwood (Jerome MacFarland), Oleg Vidov (Otto Minch), Milton Goncalves (Flavio), Jens Peter (Volleyball Player), Antonio Mario Da Silva (Rambo), Paul Land (Big Sailor), Michael Villella (Elliot), Bernardo Jablonsky (Roberto), Luiz Lobo (Juan), Lester Berman, Steven Kaminsky (Interviewers), Hollister Whitworth, Franco Pisano (Bodyguards), Carlinhos Jesus (Conga Line Leader), Veluma (Manuella), Anya Sartor (Woman in Old Hotel), Joao Carlos Dos Santos (Workman in Old Hotel), Antonio Agusto Do Carmo (Construction Foreman), David Rudder (Himself), Simone Moreno (Herself), Kathleen Kaminsky (Emily's Mother), Mato Chi (Mr. Chin), Yomiko Ribeiro (Chinese Lady), Omi Raia (Black Angel), Daniel Anibal Blasco (Man in Airport), Antonio Onofre, Marco Onofre, Marcelo Mandonca Pereira, Lucila Carvalho Medeiros, Solange Dantas Dos Santos (Conga Line), Geronimo (Dance Hall Singer), Silvia Gomez Torres (Slave Quarter Singer), Kim Donaldson, Gilmar Sampaio, and Marina Salomao (Dancers)

You know you're in trouble when even Jacqueline Bisset can't save a film.

Not that there's much of her to be seen in this inane eroto-drama. In fact Bisset, as the character Claudia, has just enough time to make an entrance before she takes off for Buenos Aires, where she winds up at a wedding—drinking, dancing, and threatening to put a leash on some rich old guy who couldn't be happier about it. Unfortunately, while Bisset is off having all the fun, we're stuck watching a makeup-encrusted, earringed Mickey Rourke, as Wheeler, introducing Carre Otis (playing Emily) to the world of sex and sensuality during Carnival in Rio. If only this were as steamy as it sounds.

In fact, aside from some snippets of stock footage, there's not much more to be seen of Carnival than there is of Bisset. The plot, or what little there is of it, begins as bright-eyed, innocent young Emily bids her family a tearful goodbye upon leaving Kansas to pursue a career in international law in big, bad New York. After seeming to sleepwalk through her interview, she is hired on the spot, apparently because she is able to leave for Rio the next day. She hooks up with fellow lawyer Claudia, whom she is to assist in closing a deal with some Chinese investors to save a floundering Rio resort development, while easing out the original developer, who caused the floundering. None of this has much of anything to do with anything except to interrupt the scenes between Otis and Rourke, though what the latter's character actually has to do with the plot is anybody's guess. For what it's worth, Claudia, upon arriving in Rio, finds that the developer has fled for Buenos Aires, and leaves Emily in the care of Wheeler, with whom Claudia has been inexplicably obsessed. Wheeler (as in wheeler-dealer) is an uneducated street kid who overcame a stutter and became wealthy by buying and selling real estate. He steps in, late in the film, to muddy the deal with the Chinese by buying an old hotel that is part of the property of the proposed resort. His price for relinquishing the lease turns out to be a hot minute with Emily in the film's doubly controversial climax. (The scene was reportedly trimmed to win the film an R rating, and actors Otis and Rourke were rumored to have actually had sex on camera. That's entertainment?) But, again, all of this is merely filler for what Preston Sturges, in a much wittier age long past, referred to as Topic A. Wheeler, to entertain sweet young Emily, takes her to places where people wear masks and have photogenic sex at the drop of a G-string. For the most part, we're spared the spectacle of Rourke/Wheeler au naturel since, like BEING THERE's Chauncey Gardner (from a wittier age not all that long ago), Wheeler likes to watch. It's left to Emily to give him something to watch. Going to one of these masked-sex places, she allows herself to be used as a whore by an American while Wheeler looks on. And isn't her face red when the American turns out to be her adversary in the negotiations to remove the developer from the resort?

Well, actually it isn't. That would imply acting skill. Otis, a fashion model making her movie debut, was cast after original choice Brooke Shields reportedly balked at the role's copious nudity. Here Otis shows little evidence of any skills beyond the ability to look good wearing nothing but a sheen of sweat. To be fair, she doesn't get much help from director Zalman King or from the screenplay—cowritten by King and Patricia Louisianna Knop, who in the past have helped put the boredom back into big-screen sex with SIESTA; TWO MOON JUNCTION; and the immortal 9 1/2 WEEKS, also starring Rourke. It would be charitable to describe WILD ORCHID's script and direction as dreary; downright deadly would be a more accurate assessment.

Emily seems not so much fresh from law school as from day-care. Her eyes pop in wonder that people actually do these kinds of things with their clothes off—as if they didn't have sex in Kansas, let alone law school. And, needless to say, there is precious little lawyering going on. In fact, it's somewhat difficult to figure out what it is that Emily does for a living when she isn't running around with Wheeler all night and sleeping in until noon. That's just as well, since Otis doesn't resemble a lawyer any more than she resembles an actress. Her main accomplishment is that she almost manages to make Rourke—who still reads dialog as if his lips were glued together—look good. Rourke's inflections may be for the best, actually, since the idiotic dialog rolls off the tongue like congealed gobs of peanut butter. Even Bisset has to struggle to keep from looking embarrassed. Sadly, despite these numerous flaws, WILD ORCHID isn't even bad enough to be good. (*Nudity, sexual situations.*)

d, Zalman King; p, Mark Damon and Tony Anthony; w, Patricia Louisianna Knop and Zalman King; ph, Gale Tattersall; ed, Marc Grossman and Glenn A. Morgan; m, Geoff MacCormack and Simon Goldenberg; prod d, Carlos Conti; art d, Alexandre Meyer, Yeda Lewinsohn, and Jane Cavedon; set d, Leonardo Haertling; spec, Edu Paumgartten; stunts, Webster Whinery; cos, Marlene Stewart, Ileane Meltzer, and Luciano Soprani; makup, Hiram Ortiz; chor, Morleigh Steinberg

Drama   (PR:O   MPAA:R)

WILDEST DREAMS

80m Platinum/Vestron c

(AKA: BIKINI GENIE)

James Davies (*Bobby Delaney*), Deborah Blaisdell (*Joan Peabody*), Heidi Paine (*Dancee*), Ruth Collins (*Stella*), Jill Johnson (*Rachel Richards*), Jeanne Marie (*Isabelle*), Murray Pilch (*Professor Foley*), Angela Nicholas (*Betty*), Harvey Seigal (*Mr. Delaney*), Jane Hamilton (*Mrs. Delaney*), Scott Baker (*Dexter*), Daniel Capman (*Louie*), Brouke Franklin, Michael Zezima, Donna Harris, and John Altamura

Filmmaker Chuck Vincent's softcore sex films occasionally enjoy crossover appeal, and indeed there are times when this one comes within a few city blocks of being likable. That's an achievement considering the circumstances: Left in charge of the family antique shop while his parents take a trip, lovelorn Manhattan teen Bobby Delaney (James Davies) receives a shipment of ancient pottery containing a mysterious bottle. When Bobby rubs the bottle, he frees Dancee (Heidi Paine) a sexy genie whose 2,000 years of captivity have not inhibited her use of four-letter words. Bobby rapidly expends his obligatory three wishes, requesting that Dancee: (1) clean the house, (2) get into a skimpy bikini, and (3) help him find that one special girl, "the kind of love that will last a lifetime." This last wish proves to be tricky. Bobby gets to try out an assortment of women—a party-going bimbo, a servile housewife, an aggressive movie star, and a shrewd businesswoman—as the genie makes each of them instantly infatuated with him. But while each of the lovelies disrobes with enthusiasm, Bobby finds fault with all of them (the housewife is already married, the movie queen is a bondage freak, and so on). Worse, Dancee can't remember how to "unzap" the females, and Bobby is pursued throughout the Big Apple by his obsessed harem. Even more troublesome, a crazed professor learns of Dancee's existence, and learns too that if he can kill Bobby before the third wish is fulfilled the genie will be his to command. But all ends happily after a big catfight: Dancee remembers the spell (which sounds like a verse from a greeting card); the bewitched girls come to their senses and depart, snarling; the professor is imprisoned in the bottle; and Bobby finds his perfect love after all—the pretty student who has been working side by side with him at the shop all along (surprise, surprise). In the finale, the two sweethearts embrace before the sunset, their love so pure that the girl doesn't even take off her top (more than a little ironic since the actress, billed here as Deborah Blaisdell, is better known to adult film viewers as Tracey Adams).

It is perhaps a backhanded compliment to the film that acting and not lewd sexual depiction is its biggest problem. Everyone but Blaisdell mugs atrociously. The smut, on the other hand, is largely a matter of talk and mime, plus some

rather brief topless scenes. In fact, Bobby's quest for blissful monogamy is an endearing departure from the plague of PORKY'S-inspired teen-lust marathons ("The more the merrier, I always say," Dancee asserts; "Well, that's not what I say!" Bobby responds). Although the jokes are mostly puerile, director Vincent does achieve a comic rhythm by cutting between Bobby's various female tormentors as they attempt to seduce him. Trivia buffs can try to spot John Altamura, one of the actors who played the Toxic Avenger, in a bit part as a gladiator dallying with Dancee. WILDEST DREAMS was filmed in 1987 but received wide release only with its videocassette debut in 1990. (*Excessive profanity, nudity, adult situations, substance abuse.*)

d, Chuck Vincent; p, Chuck Vincent; w, Craig Horrall (based on a story by Chuck Vincent); ph, Larry Revene; ed, James Davalos; m, Joey Mennonna; art d, Mark Hammond; cos, Jeffrey Wallach

Comedy/Fantasy   (PR:O   MPAA:R)

WILT

(Brit.) (SEE: MISADVENTURES OF MR. WILT, THE)

WINGS OF THE APACHE

(SEE: FIRE BIRDS)

WITCHES, THE

(Brit./US) 91m Jim Henson—Lorimar/WB c

Anjelica Huston (*Mrs. Ernst/Grand High Witch*), Mai Zetterling (*Helga*), Jasen Fisher (*Luke*), Rowan Atkinson (*Mr. Stringer*), Bill Paterson (*Mr. Jenkins*), Brenda Blethyn (*Mrs. Jenkins*), Charlie Potter (*Bruno Jenkins*), Anna Lambton (*Woman in Black*), Jane Horrocks (*Miss Irvine*), Sukie Smith (*Marlene*), Rose English (*Dora*), Jenny Runacre (*Elsie*), Annabel Brooks (*Nicola*), Emma Relph (*Millie*), Nora Connolly (*Beatrice*), Rosamud Greenwood (*Janice*), Anjelique Rockas (*Henrietta*), Ann Tirard, Leila Hoffman (*Ladies*), Jim Carter (*Head Chef*), Roberta Taylor (*Witch Chef*), Brian Hawksley (*Elderly Waiter*), Debra Gillett (*Waitress*), Darcy Flynn (*Luke's Mother*), Vincent Marzello (*Luke's Father*), Serena Harragin (*Doctor*), Greta Nordra (*Norwegian Witch*), Elsie Eide (*Erica*), Kirstin Steinsland (*Child Helga*), Merete Armand (*Erica's Mother*), Ola Otnes (*Erica's Father*), Johan Sverre, Arvid Ones, and Sverre Rossummoen (*Policemen*)

Never known for the accessibility of his films, director Nicolas Roeg (DON'T LOOK NOW, THE MAN WHO FELL TO EARTH, INSIGNIFICANCE) here has created a wildly entertaining fairy tale. The film begins in Germany where a little boy named Luke (Jasen Fisher) listens to bedtime stories read by his grandmother Helga (Mai Zetterling). Helga tells Luke that she has had experience with witchcraft, adding that it cost her a finger on her left hand. She wants to prepare the boy to protect himself against the witches in the world, who are constantly plotting to kill children. She gives him tips on how to spot a witch, noting that they have a purple tinge to their eyes, wear squared shoes because they have no toes, and always wear gloves to hide their hideous hands. They also have a keen sense of smell which enables them to locate children. Helga relates the story of a girl who was captured by witches and thought to be gone forever until she suddenly appeared as an image in a painting owned by her parents. Over the years, the image aged from that of a little girl to that of an old lady, until finally the image disappeared. After the story-telling session, Luke's parents are killed in a car accident, leaving the boy and his grandmother alone. They travel to England where Helga buys a pair of mice as pets for Luke. When she is stricken with a mild attack of diabetes, they head for a seaside resort while Helga recovers. Coincidentally, all the witches in England arrive at the resort, summoned there by Mrs. Ernst (Anjelica Huston) for seminars on how to capture British children. The witches pose as conventioneers who are members of the fictional Royal Commission for the Prevention of Cruelty to Children. While exploring the hotel, Luke stumbles upon a meeting of the witches. He watches from a hiding place and is stunned to see Mrs. Ernst, as she removes her disguise, transform herself into the frightening Grand High Witch. The head witch says she is disappointed in efforts to wipe out the children of England, and has developed a magic potion that turns children into mice. When the witches' smelling abilities lead them to discover Luke, he is forced to drink some of the potion and is quickly turned into a mouse. It's now up to Luke to thwart the heinous plan concocted by Mrs. Ernst, a difficult task for a mouse, and one which requires the assistance of the wily Helga.

The first 30 minutes of this film are genuinely eerie, depicting Helga's witch stories and the death of Luke's parents. Roeg successfully creates a bedtime story atmosphere that is often downright creepy. Based on a story by Roald Dahl (source author of WILLY WONKA AND THE CHOCOLATE FACTORY, and author of the screenplay for CHITTY CHITTY BANG BANG), the film explores many childhood fears (the loss of a parent, strangers, and unfamiliar surroundings), weaving those fears within the entertaining action. THE WITCHES is a fairy tale that does what any good fairy tale should do—provide entertainment, a few scares, and a moral. Roeg directs with his usual visual flair, notably excelling during the wondrous mouse point-of-view scenes. These exciting sequences feature mice puppets designed by the late Jim Henson, who served as the film's executive producer, the last film in which he was involved before his death in 1990. In addition to the lively visuals, THE WITCHES features sharp art direction and beautiful locations. The actors seem to be having a good time, particularly Huston, who gives a wonderfully over-the-top performance as the Grand High Witch. From her exaggerated German accent to her ominous cackle, Huston makes her character a memorably menacing witch. Zetterling, making her first appearance in a US release since THE MAN WHO FINALLY DIED in 1967, is impressive, turning in a performance that is both rich and comic, and giving the film its emotional center. Newcomer Fisher proves to be quite capable, and his voiceovers during the mouse scenes are particularly effective. The supporting players provide many of the film's funnier moments. Rowan Atkinson as the bumbling hotel manager, Charlie Potter as a young victim of the witches, and Bill Paterson (COMFORT AND JOY) as the boy's baffled father, all are notable. The film is expertly paced and the tone, which shifts from somber to goofy, matches the frantic shifts of the action. The movie has its faults—some of the comic subplots seem unnecessary, there are more than a few loose ends, and it all ends with a rather obvious setup for a sequel—but it is a family movie that is neither condescending or corny. While it may be frightening for the younger children, older kids and their parents are certain to be entertained by the movie.

d, Nicolas Roeg; p, Mark Shivas; w, Allan Scott (based on the book by Roald Dahl); ph, Harvey Harrison; ed, Tony Lawson; m, Stanley Myers; md, Christopher Palmer; prod d, Andrew Sanders; art d, Norman Dorme; set d, Robin Tarsnane; spec, Jim Henson's Creature Shop, Steve Norrington, Nigel Booth, and John Stephenson; cos, Marit Allen; makup, Christine Beveridge

Fantasy   (PR:A   MPAA:PG)

WITHOUT YOU, I'M NOTHING

89m Jonathan D. Krane-Nicolas Roeg/M.C.E.G. c

Sandra Bernhard *(Herself)*, John Doe *(Himself)*, Steve Antin *(Himself)*, Lu Leonard *(Sandra's Manager)*, Ken Foree *(Emcee)*, Cynthia Bailey *(Roxanne)*, Grace Broughton, Kimberli Williams, Axel Vera, Estuardo M. Volty, Kevin Dorsey, Arnold McCuller, Oren Waters *(Backup Singers)*, Vonte Sweet, Tonya Natalie Townsend, Jeff Wiener *(Children Carolers)*, Stephanie Clark, Indrani DeSouza, Hardy Keith, Sebastian Russell, Ellen Sims, Carlton Wilborn *(Ballet Dancers)*, Joe DiGiandomenico, Felix Montano, David Stuart Rodgers *(Go Go Dancers)*, Paul Thorpe *(Apollo)*, Denise Vlasis *(Shoshanna)*, Djimon Hounson *(Ex-Boy Friend)*, Roxanne Reese, Ludie C. Washington *(Hecklers)*, Stephanie Albers, Robin Antin, and Annie Livingstone *(Hippie Girls)*

The ferocious-faced Sandra Bernhard has come up with a film of her one-woman off-Broadway show, "Without You I'm Nothing," that's like a direct assault upon the audience. Bernhard is peerless in interviews—whether in print or on TV, as in her near-legendary appearances with David Letterman. When assailing the very latest in ephemeral cultural phenomena (from this week's MTV sensation to the neo-postmodern decor of her home in the Valley), Bernhard can dispense more sarcasm than George Sanders, Clifton Webb, or Eve Arden ever dreamed of. (Her approach is the essence of brainy, bitchy chic—throwaway but irresistibly funny.)

She has bizarrely chosen a nightclub populated with middle-class blacks as the setting for her filmed show. The frequent cuts to the unresponsive, somewhat hostile audience are funny at first, but with repetition have the deadening, too-cute effect of acts involving unresponsive dogs and desperate trainers. Bernhard has explained that she has chosen this format as a response to those "performance" movies in which over-responsive audiences are an excruciating embarrassment. However, in performing for a passive audience, she robs herself of an essential part of her act—her blindingly fast interaction with the audience. Much of what she does here is either so multilayered with meaning or so incomprehensible that moviegoers will be just as stupefied as the audience in the film is.

In the rich tradition of such entertaining Jewish performers as Fannie Brice, Sophie Tucker, Barbra Streisand, and Bette Midler, Bernhard is possessed of killer wit as well as a deeply affecting singing voice. Many of Bernhard's set-pieces begin with her soulfully crooning a pop standard and interrupting it with some campy oration. (Her voice is lullingly appealing on ballads but evinces strain in the many funkier, black-influenced paces it's put through.) A Diana Ross impersonation segues into a Warren Beatty putdown, Laura Nyro's quaveringly heartfelt "I Never Meant to Hurt You" becomes a hysterical rant against a neglectful lover, thoughts about Andy Warhol's auction are offset by a country ballad, and so on. After a time, however, these *tours-de-force* become repetitive

and exhausting. And there's more: Bernhard gives us not one but two shattering climaxes. The first is an intense, screamed berating of the Moral Majority. This is followed by a striptease before a now-emptied room, with the star left clad in the tiniest of American flag G-strings, that suggests the heavy price a performer pays in loneliness and self-exploitation. Or is it just an excuse to flaunt an admirably svelte, leggy figure? This last act of outrage is prefaced by a clothed Bernhard delivering an out-of-context monolog about wanting to drop the "fame" stuff. Before you've recovered from these exhibitionistic displays (which are as self-indulgent and overlong as they were on the stage), the last can-we-end-the-show-now fillip is in full swing.

At regular intervals, the live performance is interrupted by shots of a mysterious black woman prowling around Los Angeles and by interview footage of various characters purporting to having known Bernhard "back when." These interviews are alternately amusing (a pompously butch personal manager) and tiresome (a nattering boy toy). A Madonna impersonator is intermittently introduced as the real star of the show, perhaps in response to overblown media curiosity about Bernhard's relationship with the singer-actress. There's also a shot of Bernhard making love with a black man. Whether this is meant to answer any questions regarding her much-publicized sexuality is something known only to her and—one supposes—her director, John Boskovich, who seems to have served more in the capacity of supportive, appreciative on-set family member than as a controlling hand.

These serious considerations aside, it cannot be denied that La Bernhard is one powerfully funny lady. The best moment in the film is her volcanically absurd first appearance; outfitted as a capacious African (though not in black-face), she wails Nina Simone's hilariously overblown "Four Women." A second later she moves on to Israeli folk songs. Bernhard is a cool master of period storytelling, and her childhood reminiscences of the 1965 World's Fair are replete with piquant images of pavilions, Sandy Dennis, and Streisand in her unparalleled Nefertiti mode. Her riffs on a WASP-fantasy Christmas and a 60s-style executive secretary stoned under the influence of Burt Bacharach are pretty much hilariously intact from the stage show. When she sits enthroned in Vegas-like plastic finery wailing "This house became a home, wow!" with go-go boys gyrating around her, it's hard for anyone not to crack a smile. Bernhard also performs her audacious, pre-AIDS gay disco homage.

The film is technically very accomplished, with velvety photography by Joseph Yacoe and a capable, eclectic score by Patrice Rushen. Diva that she is, Bernhard revels in a bewildering array of *haute couture* gowns and wigs. The troupe of dancers, for the most part, add unnecessary frosting. Ultimately, the film is a celebration of narcissism and will undoubtedly prove something of a turn-off to those who are less than enchanted with Bernhard. But for those predisposed to like her ultra-hip, campier-than-thou brand of humor, WITHOUT YOU, I'M NOTHING will be a treat. *(Profanity, nudity, sexual situations, adult situations.)*

d, John Boskovich; p, Jonathan D. Krane; w, Sandra Bernhard and John Boskovich; ph, Joseph Yacoe; ed, Pamela Malouf-Cundy; m, Patrice Rushen; md, Morgan Ames; prod d, Kevin Rupnik; art d, Kevin Adams; set d, Douglas A. Mowat; spec, Jeff Jackson; cos, Raymond Lee; makup, Alfonso Noe; chor, Karole Armitage

Comedy   (PR:O   MPAA:R)

XYZ

YANZHI KOU

(Hong Kong) (SEE: ROUGE)

YOUNG GUNS II

104m James G. Robinson-Morgan Creek/FOX c

Emilio Estevez *(William H. Bonney)*, Kiefer Sutherland *(Doc Scurlock)*, Lou Diamond Phillips *(Jose Chavez Y Chavez)*, Christian Slater *(Arkansas Dave Rudabaugh)*, William Petersen *(Pat Garrett)*, Alan Ruck *(Hendry French)*, R.D. Call *(D.A. Ryerson)*, James Coburn *(John Chisum)*, Balthazar Getty *(Tom O'Folliard)*, Jack Kehoe *(Ashmun Upson)*, Robert Knepper *(Deputy Carlyle)*, Tom Kurlander *(J.W. Bell)*, Viggo Mortensen *(John W. Poe)*, Leon Rippy *(Bob Ollinger)*, Tracey Walter *(Beever Smith)*, Bradley Whitford *(Charles Phalen)*, Scott Wilson *(Gov. Lew Wallace)*, Jenny Wright *(Jane Greathouse)*, John Hammil *(Pendleton)*, William Fisher *(2nd Aide)*, Carlotta Garcia *(Deluvina Maxwell)*, Joy Bouton *(Juanita)*, Albert Trujillo *(Jesus Silva)*, Alina Arenal *(Sonia)*, John Alderson *(Guano Miner)*, Lee De Broux, Sixto Joost, Rudy Sena, Adam Taylor *(Bounty Hunters)*, Redmond Gleeson *(Murphy Man)*, David Paul Needles *(Cutter)*, Jerry Gardner *(Sheriff Kimbel)*, Domingo Ambriz, Sonny Skyhawk *(Vaqueros)*, Richard Schiff *(Rat Bag)*, Stephan Kraus *(Pietro)*, Nicholas Sean Gomez *(Fernando)*, Mark Bustamante *(Ignio)*, Airen Balen *(Student)*, Don Simpson *(Pinkerton Man)*, Holt Parker *(Sumner Priest)*, Tony Frank *(Judge Bristol)*, Frank Fierro Jr., Rene L. Moreno *(Villagers)*, Chief Buddy Redbow *(Chief Victorio)*, Danielle Blanchard *(Tom's Dove)*, Joey Joe Hamlin *(Chivato's Pal)*, Alexis Alexander, Ginger Lynn Allen *(Doves)*, Iris Pappas *(Barmaid)*, Ed Adams, Mark Silverstein, Boots Southerland, Bud Stout, Howie Young *(Poe Posse)*, John Fusco *(Branded Man)*, Walter Feldbusch, Bo Gray, Tom Byrd, Donald Guideau, Jon Bon Jovi *(Pit Inmates)*, Robert Harvey *(Townsman)*, Ted Kairys *(Town Dweller)*, William Upchurch *(Drunken Idiot)*, and Michael Eiland *(Shopkeeper)*

Besides featuring some of the same actors in the same roles, what this six-gun sequel has in common with YOUNG GUNS is that it is wholly unmemorable. Watching this film brings to mind the old cliche about Chinese food: 10 minutes after the film is over, you're hungry all over again. The difference is that Chinese cuisine provides good nourishment. YOUNG GUNS II, like its predecessor, is the cinematic equivalent of sugary, high-fat junk food. Somehow the script of YOUNG GUNS II manages to be both plot-heavy and underplotted. The film opens with a prolog set in 1950, in which a journalist meets with an ancient sagebrush character, "Brushy Bill" Roberts (Emilio Estevez, under piles of latex), who claims to be Billy the Kid, having survived sheriff Pat Garrett's "attempt" to murder him on the night of July 14, 1881 in Fort Sumner, New Mexico. Brushy Bill wants the journalist to approach the current governor of New Mexico to win a pardon for the Kid, who is reputed to have killed 21 men during his career. (While there really was a Brushy Bill, including him in this story is an obvious attempt to lay the groundwork for yet another YOUNG GUNS sequel. If Garrett didn't kill Billy, in theory, the "Young Guns" series could continue, like James Bond, into infinity.) However, Billy would hardly qualify for a pardon based on the story he tells here, depicted in flashback. As in the first film, he is presented as bloodthirsty and sadistic, but though he still kills without remorse, this time around Billy is not as outright crazy as he was in Estevez' original portrayal. The main action picks up roughly where YOUNG GUNS left off. In the aftermath of the Lincoln County War in 1878, Gen. Lew Wallace (Scott Wilson), the newly appointed governor of New Mexico, begins a crusade to clean up his territory. Among the outlaws he endeavors to bring to justice are Billy and what's left of his gang—Doc Scurlock (Kiefer Sutherland) and Jose Chavez y Chavez (Lou Diamond Phillips), who are captured and thrown in prison. It's not long before Billy and his latest riding companions, Arkansas Dave Rudabaugh (Christian Slater) and Pat Garrett (William Peterson), come to the rescue. Disguised as a lynch mob, Billy and company ride into town and free Jose and Doc from the clutches of evil lawmen. Reunited, the gang heads for Mexico, except for Garrett, who chooses to stay behind to pursue a more settled life. Two new riders, Hendry French (Alan Ruck) and Tom O'Folliard (Balthazar Getty), join Billy and the boys in their adventures. Eventually Billy is captured and offered a deal by General Wallace: if Billy volunteers his eyewitness testimony to an unsolved murder, all charges against him will be dropped. Billy agrees, only to be betrayed and nearly sent to the gallows before he successfully escapes. However, Wallace isn't the only one who betrays Billy (actually, according to authoritative accounts, Wallace did not so much betray Billy as simply neglect him; it is speculated that at the time Wallace was preoccupied with completing *Ben Hur*, his literary claim to fame). Old friend Pat Garrett, a newly-elected sheriff, now pursues Billy, backed by Wallace and major ranchers like John Chisum (James Coburn, who played Garrett in Peckinpah's PAT GARRETT

AND BILLY THE KID), with whom Billy had a longstanding feud over wages he claimed Chisum owed him for fighting on Chisum's behalf during the war. A series of chases and gun battles leads to the fateful night when Billy either did or did not meet his end.

Though occasionally bending the truth, the "Young Guns" series' portrayal of the life of Billy the Kid is probably more faithful to the historical record than most movies about the famous outlaw have been. Doc Scurlock did exist, and he was a good friend of Billy's; Jose Chavez y Chavez was also a real person, and he fought at Billy's side in the Lincoln County War. However, despite its attempts at historical authenticity, YOUNG GUNS II, like YOUNG GUNS I, utterly fails to bring its rich story to life. Instead, under the direction of New Zealander Geoff Murphy (UTU), YOUNG GUNS II is engineered to not let more than three minutes pass between long, noisy gunfights. Garrett's shooting of Billy, the closest the film comes to a dramatic climax, is thoroughly muddled. If you blink you'll miss it, and even if you don't, you'll still feel like you missed it. Though Petersen makes an effort to give Garrett some depth, he receives scant support from John Fusco's disjointed script. Mostly, Petersen seems to be fighting off a justified temptation to sleepwalk through the part. Regrettably, Coburn is given even less chance to demonstrate his talent. He has one good scene with Billy and his gang, in which the conflict among Billy and his fellow outlaws is established, but the film promptly, and amazingly, drops this subplot without any further mention. In fact, wasting talent is about the closest GUNS II comes to having a unifying motif. Also woefully underused are Ruck and Slater (the latter steals every scene in which he has any dialog whatsoever) as Billy's sidekicks. Meanwhile, the focus of Jenny Wright's performance is her bare derriere. Playing the madam of a brothel where Billy and his gang hide out, she makes a diversionary Lady Godiva-like ride out of town that has to be seen to be disbelieved. The leads, on the other hand, are barely in character, looking most of the time as if they're about to break up at any moment. More than a century after his death (sorry guys, Garrett *did* kill him), Billy the Kid continues to fascinate storytellers, readers, and moviegoers, though neither of these two sloppy, shallow films provides the slightest clue as to why. The film earned an Oscar nomination for the forgettable song "Blaze of Glory" (Jon Bon Jovi). *(Violence, profanity, adult situations, brief nudity.)*

d, Geoff Murphy; p, Irby Smith and Paul Schiff; w, John Fusco (based on characters created by John Fusco); ph, Dean Semler; ed, Bruce Green; m, Alan Silvestri; prod d, Gene Rudolf; art d, Christa Munro; set d, Andy Bernard; spec, Image Engineering, Peter Chesney, and David Anderson; stunts, Mickey Gilbert; cos, Judy Ruskin; makup, Jeanne Van Phue

Western   (PR:C   MPAA:R)

ZAMRI OUMI VOSKRESNI

(USSR) (SEE: FREEZE—DIE—COME TO LIFE)

ZIVOT SA STRICEM

(Yugo.) (SEE: MY UNCLE'S LEGACY)

OSCARS

63rd AWARDS OF THE ACADEMY OF MOTION PICTURE ARTS AND SCIENCES
(Listings in italics indicate winners)

Best Picture

Walter F Parkes, Lawrence Lasker, AWAKENINGS
Jim Wilson, Kevin Costner, DANCES WITH WOLVES
Lisa Weinstein, GHOST
Francis Ford Coppola, THE GODFATHER PART III
Irwin Winkler, GOODFELLAS

Best Actor

Kevin Costner, DANCES WITH WOLVES
Robert De Niro, AWAKENINGS
Gerard Depardieu, CYRANO DE BERGERAC
Richard Harris, THE FIELD
Jeremy Irons, REVERSAL OF FORTUNE

Best Actress

Kathy Bates, MISERY
Anjelica Huston, THE GRIFTERS
Julia Roberts, PRETTY WOMAN
Joanne Woodward, MR. & MRS. BRIDGE
Meryl Streep, POSTCARDS FROM THE EDGE

Best Supporting Actor

Bruce Davison, LONGTIME COMPANION
Andy Garcia, THE GODFATHER PART III
Graham Greene, DANCES WITH WOLVES
Joe Pesci, GOODFELLAS
Al Pacino, DICK TRACY

Best Supporting Actress

Annette Bening, THE GRIFTERS
Lorraine Bracco, GOODFELLAS
Diane Ladd, WILD AT HEART
Mary McDonnell, DANCES WITH WOLVES
Whoopi Goldberg, GHOST

Best Director

Kevin Costner, DANCES WITH WOLVES
Francis Ford Coppola, THE GODFATHER PART III
Martin Scorsese, GOODFELLAS
Stephen Frears, THE GRIFTERS
Barbet Schroeder, REVERSAL OF FORTUNE

Best Original Screenplay

Woody Allen, ALICE
Barry Levinson, AVALON
Bruce Joel Rubin, GHOST
Peter Weir, GREEN CARD
Whit Stillman, METROPOLITAN

Best Adapted Screenplay

Steven Zaillian, AWAKENINGS
Michael Blake, DANCES WITH WOLVES
Nicholas Pileggi, Martin Scorsese, GOODFELLAS
Donald E Westlake, THE GRIFTERS
Nicholas Kazan, REVERSAL OF FORTUNE

Best Foreign Film

CYRANO DE BERGERAC
JOURNEY OF HOPE
JU DOU
THE NASTY GIRL
PORTE APERTE/OPEN DOORS

Best Art Direction/Production Design

Ezio Frigerio (Art Director), Jacques Rouxel (Set Decorator),
    CYRANO DE BERGERAC
Jeffrey Beecroft (Art Director), Lisa Dean (Set Decorator), DANCES
    WITH WOLVES
*Richard Sylbert (Art Director), Rick Simpson (Set Decorator), DICK
    TRACY*
Dean Tavoularis (Art Director), Gary Fettis (Set Decorator), THE
    GODFATHER PART III
Dante Ferretti (Art Director), Francesca Lo Schiavo (Set Decorator),
    HAMLET

Best Cinematography

Allen Daviau, AVALON
Dean Semler, DANCES WITH WOLVES
Vittorio Storaro, DICK TRACY
Gordon Willis, THE GODFATHER PART III
Philippe Rousselot, HENRY & JUNE

Best Costume Design

Gloria Gresham, AVALON
Franca Squarciapino, CYRANO DE BERGERAC
Elsa Zamparelli, DANCES WITH WOLVES
Milena Canonero, DICK TRACY
Maurizio Millenotti, HAMLET

Best Documentary Feature

Arthur Cohn, Barbara Kopple, AMERICAN DREAM
Mark Kitchell, BERKELEY IN THE SIXTIES
Susan Robinson, Mark Mori, BUILDING BOMBS
Judith Montell, FOREVER ACTIVISTS: STORIES FROM THE
    VETERANS OF THE ABRAHAM LINCOLN BRIGADE
Robert Hillmann, WALDO SALT: A SCREENWRITER'S JOURNEY

Best Documentary Short Subject

Kit Thomas, BURNING DOWN TOMORROW
Karen Goodman, Kirk Simon, CHIMPS: SO LIKE US
Steven Okazaki, DAYS OF WAITING
Derek Bromhall, JOURNEY INTO LIFE: THE WORLD OF THE
    UNBORN
Freida Lee Mock, Terry Sanders, ROSE KENNEDY: A LIFE TO RE-
    MEMBER

Best Film Editing

Neil Travis, DANCES WITH WOLVES
Walter Murch, GHOST
Barry Malkin, Lisa Fruchtman, Walter Murch, THE GODFATHER
    PART III
Thelma Schoonmaker, GOODFELLAS
Dennis Virkler, John Wright, THE HUNT FOR RED OCTOBER

Best Makeup

Michele Burke, Jean-Pierre Eychenne, CYRANO DE BERGERAC
John Caglione Jr, Doug Drexler, DICK TRACY
Ve Neill, Stan Winston, EDWARD SCISSORHANDS

Best Original Score

Randy Newman, AVALON
John Barry, DANCES WITH WOLVES
Maurice Jarre, GHOST
David Grusin, HAVANA
John Williams, HOME ALONE

Best Original Song

Jon Bon Jovi (music and lyrics), "Blaze of Glory" from YOUNG GUNS II

Shel Silverstein (music and lyrics), "I'm Checkin' Out" from POST-CARDS FROM THE EDGE

Carmine Coppola (music), John Bettis (lyrics), "Promise Me You'll Remember" from THE GODFATHER PART III

John Williams (music), Leslie Bricusse (lyrics), "Somewhere in My Memory" from HOME ALONE

Stephen Sondheim (music and lyrics), "Sooner or Later (I Always Get My Man)" from DICK TRACY

Best Animated Short Film

Nick Park, CREATURE COMFORTS

Nick Park, A GRAND DAY OUT

Bruno Bozzetto, CAVALLETTE/GRASSHOPPERS

Best Live Action Short Film

Raymond DeFelitta, Matthew Gross, BRONX CHEERS

Peter Cattaneo, Barnaby Thompson, DEAR ROSIE

Adam Davidson, THE LUNCH DATE

Bernard Joffa, Anthony E Nicholas, SENZENI NA?/WHAT HAVE WE DONE?

Hillary Ripps, Jonathan Heap, 12:01 PM

Best Sound

Russell Williams II, Jeffrey Perkins, Bill W Benton, Greg Watkins, DANCES WITH WOLVES

Charles Wilborn, Donald O Mitchell, Rick Kline, Kevin O'Connell, DAYS OF THUNDER

Thomas Causey, Chris Jenkins, David E Campbell, D M Hemphill, DICK TRACY

Richard Bryce Goodman, Richard Overton, Kevin F Cleary, Don Bassman, THE HUNT FOR RED OCTOBER

Nelson Stoll, Michael J Kohut, Carlos DeLarios, Aaron Rochin, TOTAL RECALL

Best Sound Effects Editing

Charles L Campbell, Richard Franklin, FLATLINERS

Cecelia Hall, George Watters II, THE HUNT FOR RED OCTOBER

Stephen H Flick, TOTAL RECALL

Special Achievement Award for Visual Effects

Eric Brevig, Rob Bottin, Tim McGovern, Alex Funke, TOTAL RECALL

Honorary Awards

Sophia Loren

Myrna Loy

Irving G. Thalberg Award

Richard D Zanuck, David Brown

Master List

MASTER LIST

The following is an alphabetical listing of the titles for all sound films reviewed in the MOTION PICTURE GUIDE (1927-1984) and its annuals (1985-1990). The entries include the title, year of release, producing country or countries (if other than the US), and parental recommendation (AA: good for children; A: acceptable for children; C: cautionary, some scenes may be unacceptable for children; O: objectionable for children). Titles in *italic* indicate those films which are available on videocassette. Reviews for films released in the years 1927-1983 are arranged alphabetically in volumes I-IX of the MOTION PICTURE GUIDE. Reviews for later films are arranged as follows:

1984: Volume IX of the MOTION PICTURE GUIDE
1985: 1986 MOTION PICTURE GUIDE ANNUAL
1986: 1987 MOTION PICTURE GUIDE ANNUAL
1987: 1988 MOTION PICTURE GUIDE ANNUAL
1988: 1989 MOTION PICTURE GUIDE ANNUAL
1989: 1990 MOTION PICTURE GUIDE ANNUAL

A

A BOUT DE SOUFFLE (SEE: BREATHLESS) (1959, Fr.)
A CIASCUNO IL SUO (SEE: WE STILL KILL THE OLD WAY) (1967, It.)
A COR DO SEU DESTINO (SEE: COLOR OF DESTINY, THE) (1988, Braz.)
A CORPS PERDU (SEE: STRAIGHT TO THE HEART) (1988, Can./Switz.)
A HORA DA ESTRELA (SEE: HOUR OF THE STAR) (1986, Braz.)
A L'ITALIENNE (SEE: MADE IN ITALY) (1967, Fr./It.)
A LA FRANCAISE (SEE: IN THE FRENCH STYLE) (1963, US/Fr.)
A MEZZANOTTE VA LA RONDA DEL PIACERE (SEE: MIDNIGHT PLEASURES) (1975, It.)
A NAGY GENERACIO (SEE: GREAT GENERATION, THE) (1986, Hung.)
A NOS AMOURS (1983, Fr.) PR:O
. . . A PATY JEZDEC JE STRACH (SEE: FIFTH HORSE-MAN IS FEAR, THE) (1968, Czech.)
A PIED, A CHEVAL ET EN SPOUTNIK (SEE: SPUTNIK) (1958, Fr.)
A PROPOSITO LUCIANO (SEE: RE: LUCKY LUCIANO) (1974, US/Fr./It.)
A TOUT PRENDRE (SEE: TAKE IT ALL) (1966, Can.)
A NOUS LA LIBERTE (1931, Fr.) PR:A
AA, KAIGUN (SEE: GATEWAY TO GLORY) (1970, Jap.)
AARON LOVES ANGELA (1975) PR:O
AARON SLICK FROM PUNKIN CRICK (1952) PR:AA
ABANDON SHIP! (1957, Brit.) PR:C-O
ABANDONED (1949) PR:C
ABANDONED WOMAN (SEE: ABANDONED) (1949)
ABARE GOEMON (SEE: RISE AGAINST THE SWORD) (1966, Jap.)
ABBOTT AND COSTELLO GO TO MARS (1953) PR:A
ABBOTT AND COSTELLO IN HOLLYWOOD (1945) PR:AA
ABBOTT AND COSTELLO IN THE FOREIGN LEGION (1950) PR:A
ABBOTT AND COSTELLO IN THE NAVY (1941) PR:AA
ABBOTT AND COSTELLO LOST IN ALASKA (1952) PR:AA
ABBOTT AND COSTELLO MEET CAPTAIN KIDD (1952) PR:A
ABBOTT AND COSTELLO MEET DR. JEKYLL AND MR. HYDE (1954) PR:A
ABBOTT AND COSTELLO MEET FRANKENSTEIN (1948) PR:A
ABBOTT AND COSTELLO MEET THE GHOSTS (SEE: ABBOTT AND COSTELLO MEET FRANKENSTEIN) (1948)
ABBOTT AND COSTELLO MEET THE INVISIBLE MAN (1951) PR:A
ABBOTT AND COSTELLO MEET THE KEYSTONE KOPS (1955) PR:A
ABBOTT AND COSTELLO MEET THE KILLER, BORIS KARLOFF (1949) PR:A
ABBOTT AND COSTELLO MEET THE MUMMY (1955) PR:A
ABBY (1974) PR:O
ABC MURDERS, THE (SEE: ALPHABET MURDERS, THE) (1966, Brit.)
ABDICATION, THE (1974, Brit.) PR:C-O
ABDUCTION (1975) PR:O
ABDUCTORS, THE (1957) PR:A
ABDUL THE DAMNED (1935, Brit.) PR:C
ABDULLA THE GREAT (SEE: ABDULLAH'S HAREM) (1956, Brit./Egypt)
ABDULLAH'S HAREM (1956, Brit./Egypt.) PR:O
ABE LINCOLN IN ILLINOIS (1940) PR:AA
ABIE'S IRISH ROSE (1928) PR:A
ABIE'S IRISH ROSE (1946) PR:C
ABILENE TOWN (1946) PR:A
ABILENE TRAIL (1951) PR:A

ABISMOS DE PASION (SEE: WUTHERING HEIGHTS) (1953, Mex.)
ABNORMAL (SEE: HENTAI) (1966, Jap.)
ABOMINABLE DR. PHIBES, THE (1971, US/Brit.) PR:O
ABOMINABLE SNOWMAN OF THE HIMALAYAS, THE (1957, Brit.) PR:A
ABOUT FACE (1952) PR:A
ABOUT LAST NIGHT (1986) PR:O
ABOUT MRS. LESLIE (1954) PR:A
ABOVE ALL LAWS (SEE: ADVENTURES IN SILVERADO) (1948)
ABOVE AND BEYOND (1953) PR:A
ABOVE SUSPICION (1943) PR:A
ABOVE THE CLOUDS (1934) PR:A
ABOVE THE LAW (1988) PR:O
ABOVE US THE WAVES (1956, Brit.) PR:A
ABRAHAM LINCOLN (1930) PR:AA
ABROAD WITH TWO YANKS (1944) PR:A
ABSENCE OF MALICE (1981) PR:O
ABSENT-MINDED PROFESSOR, THE (1961) PR:AA
ABSINTHE (SEE: MADAME X) (1929)
ABSOLUTE QUIET (1936) PR:C
ABSOLUTE BEGINNERS (1986, Brit.) PR:C
ABSOLUTION (1981, Brit./Panama) PR:O
ABUS DE CONFIANCE (SEE: ABUSED CONFIDENCE) (1938, Fr.)
ABUSED CONFIDENCE (1938, Fr.) PR:C-O
ABYSS, THE (1989) PR:C
ACAPULCO GOLD (1978) PR:O
ACCA (SEE: ASSA) (1988, USSR)
ACCATTONE! (1961, It.) PR:O
ACCENT ON LOVE (1941) PR:A
ACCENT ON YOUTH (1935) PR:A
ACCEPTABLE LEVELS (1983, Brit.) PR:C
ACCIDENT (1967, Brit.) PR:O
ACCIDENTAL DEATH (1963, Brit.) PR:C
ACCIDENTAL SPY (SEE: MR. STRINGFELLOW SAYS NO) (1937, Brit.)
ACCIDENTAL TOURIST, THE (1988) PR:C-O
ACCIDENTS WANTED (SEE: NUISANCE, THE) (1933)
ACCIDENTS WILL HAPPEN (1938) PR:A
ACCOMPLICE (1946) PR:A
ACCORDING TO MRS. HOYLE (1951) PR:A
ACCOUNT RENDERED (1957, Brit.) PR:A
ACCURSED, THE (1958, Brit.) PR:A
ACCUSED (1936, Brit.) PR:A
ACCUSED, THE (1949) PR:C
ACCUSED (SEE: MARK OF THE HAWK) (1958)
ACCUSED, THE (1988) PR:O
ACCUSED OF MURDER (1956) PR:A
ACCUSED — STAND UP (1930, Fr.) PR:A
ACCUSEE LEVEZ VOUS (SEE: ACCUSED — STAND UP!) (1930, Fr.)
ACCUSING FINGER, THE (1936) PR:A
ACE, THE (SEE: GREAT SANTINI, THE) (1979)
ACE ELI AND RODGER OF THE SKIES (1973) PR:A
ACE HIGH (1969, It.) PR:O
ACE IN THE HOLE (SEE: BIG CARNIVAL, THE) (1951)
ACE OF ACES (1933) PR:C
ACE OF ACES (1982, Fr./W. Ger.) PR:O
ACE OF SPADES, THE (1935, Brit.) PR:A
ACES AND EIGHTS (1936) PR:A
ACES HIGH (1977, Brit.) PR:C
ACES WILD (1937) PR:A
ACHALGAZRDA KOMPOZITORIS MOGZAUROBA (SEE: YOUNG COMPOSER'S ODYSSEY) (1986, USSR)
ACHT MAEDLES IM BOOT (SEE: EIGHT GIRLS IN A BOAT) (1932, Ger.)
ACQUA E SAPONE (1985, It.) PR:C
ACQUITTED (1929) PR:C
ACROSS 110TH STREET (1972) PR:O
ACROSS THE BADLANDS (1950) PR:A
ACROSS THE BRIDGE (1957, Brit.) PR:C
ACROSS THE GREAT DIVIDE (1976) PR:AA
ACROSS THE PACIFIC (1942) PR:A

ACROSS THE PLAINS (1939) PR:A
ACROSS THE RIO GRANDE (1949) PR:A
ACROSS THE RIVER (1965) PR:C
ACROSS THE SIERRAS (1941) PR:A
ACROSS THE WIDE MISSOURI (1951) PR:A
ACT, THE (1984) PR:O
ACT OF LOVE (1953) PR:C
ACT OF MURDER, AN (1948) PR:C
ACT OF MURDER (1965, Brit.) PR:C
ACT OF THE HEART, THE (1970, Can.) PR:O
ACT OF VENGEANCE (1974) PR:O
ACT OF VIOLENCE (1949) PR:C
ACT ONE (1964) PR:A
ACTION FOR SLANDER (1937, Brit.) PR:A
ACTION IN ARABIA (1944) PR:A
ACTION IN THE NORTH ATLANTIC (1943) PR:A
ACTION JACKSON (1988) PR:O
ACTION MAN (SEE: LEATHER AND NYLON) (1969, Fr./It.)
ACTION OF THE TIGER (1957, Brit.) PR:A
ACTION STATIONS (1959, Brit.) PR:A-C
ACTORS AND SIN (1952) PR:C
ACTOR'S REVENGE, AN (1963, Jap.) PR:O
ACTRESS, THE (1953) PR:A
ADA (1961) PR:C
ADALEN RIOTS (SEE: ADALEN 31) (1969, Swed.)
ADALEN 31 (1969, Swed.) PR:C
ADAM AND EVE (1958, Mex.) PR:O
ADAM AND EVELYNE (1950, Brit.) PR:A
ADAM AT 6 A.M. (1970) PR:O
ADAM HAD FOUR SONS (1941) PR:A
ADAM'S RIB (1949) PR:A
ADAM'S WOMAN (1972, Aus.) PR:C
ADDING MACHINE, THE (1969, US/Brit.) PR:C
ADDIO, FRATELLO CRUDELE (SEE: 'TIS PITY SHE'S A WHORE) (1973, It.)
ADDRESS UNKNOWN (1944) PR:A
ADELAIDE (SEE: FINO A FARTI MALE) (1969, Fr./It.)
ADELE HASN'T HAD HER SUPPER YET (1978, Czech.) PR:C
ADERYN PAPUR (1984, Brit.) PR:A-C
ADIEU L'AMI (SEE: FAREWELL, FRIEND) (1968, Fr./It.)
ADIEU PHILLIPINE (1962, Fr./It.) PR:C
ADIEU POULET (SEE: FRENCH DETECTIVE, THE) (1975, Fr.)
ADIOS AMIGO (1975) PR:C
ADIOS GRINGO (1967, It./Fr./Sp.) PR:A
ADIOS, SABATA (1971, It./Sp.) PR:A
ADMIRABLE CRICHTON, THE (1957, Brit.) PR:A
ADMIRAL NAKHIMOV (1948, USSR) PR:C
ADMIRAL WAS A LADY, THE (1950) PR:A
ADMIRALS ALL (1935, Brit.) PR:A
ADMIRAL'S SECRET, THE (1934, Brit.) PR:A
ADOLESCENT, THE (1978, Fr./W.Ger.) PR:C
ADOLESCENTS, THE (1967, Can./It./Fr./Jap.) PR:C
ADOLF HITLER — MY PART IN HIS DOWNFALL (1973, Brit.) PR:A
ADOPTED FATHER, THE (SEE: WORKING MAN, THE) (1933)
ADOPTION, THE (1978, Fr.) PR:O
ADORABLE (1933) PR:A
ADORABLE CREATURES (1956, Fr.) PR:O
ADORABLE JULIA (1964, Fr./Aust.) PR:C
ADORABLE LIAR (1962, Fr.) PR:C
ADORABLE MENTEUSE (SEE: ADORABLE LIAR) (1962, Fr.)
ADRIFT (1971, Czech.) PR:O
ADUA E LE COMPAGNE (SEE: LOVE A LA CARTE) (1965, It.)
ADUEFUE (1988, Fr./Ivory Coast) PR:C
ADULT EDUCATION (SEE: HIDING OUT) (1987)
ADULTERESS, THE (1959, Fr.) PR:O
ADULTEROUS AFFAIR (1966, Can.) PR:A
ADVANCE TO THE REAR (1964) PR:A
ADVENTURE (1945) PR:A
ADVENTURE FOR TWO (1945, Brit.) PR:A

ADVENTURE IN BALTIMORE (1949) PR:AA
ADVENTURE IN BLACKMAIL (1943, Brit.) PR:A
ADVENTURE IN DIAMONDS (1940) PR:A
ADVENTURE IN MANHATTAN (1936) PR:A
ADVENTURE IN ODESSA (1954, USSR) PR:C
ADVENTURE IN SAHARA (1938) PR:A
ADVENTURE IN THE HOPFIELDS (1954, Brit.) PR:AA
ADVENTURE IN WASHINGTON (1941) PR:C
ADVENTURE ISLAND (1947) PR:A
ADVENTURE LIMITED (1934, Brit.) PR:A
ADVENTURE OF LYLE SWANN, THE (SEE: TIMERI-
   DER) (1983)
*ADVENTURE OF SALVATOR ROSA, AN (1940, It.) PR:A
*ADVENTURE OF SHERLOCK HOLMES' SMARTER
   BROTHER, THE* (1975, Brit.) PR:A-A
ADVENTURERS, THE (1951, Brit.) PR:C
ADVENTURERS, THE (1970) PR:O
ADVENTURES AT RUGBY (SEE: TOM BROWN'S
   SCHOOL DAYS) (1940)
ADVENTURE'S END (1937) PR:A
ADVENTURES IN BABYSITTING (1987) PR:C
ADVENTURES IN IRAQ (1943) PR:A
ADVENTURES IN SILVERADO (1948) PR:A
ADVENTURES OF A ROOKIE (1943) PR:A
ADVENTURES OF A YOUNG MAN (1962) PR:A
ADVENTURES OF ARSENE LUPIN (1956, Fr./It.) PR:A
ADVENTURES OF BARON MUNCHAUSEN, THE (1989,
   Brit./W. Ger.) PR:A-C
ADVENTURES OF BARRY MC KENZIE (1972, Aus.)
   PR:C-O
*ADVENTURES OF BUCKAROO BANZAI: ACROSS THE
   8TH DIMENSION, THE* (1984) PR:C-O
ADVENTURES OF BULLWHIP GRIFFIN, THE (1967)
   PR:AA
ADVENTURES OF CAPTAIN FABIAN (1951) PR:A
ADVENTURES OF CASANOVA (1948) PR:A
ADVENTURES OF DON COYOTE, THE (1947) PR:A
ADVENTURES OF DON JUAN (1949) PR:A
ADVENTURES OF FRONTIER FREMONT, THE (1976)
   PR:AA
ADVENTURES OF GALLANT BESS (1948) PR:AA
ADVENTURES OF GERARD, THE (1970, Brit.) PR:A
ADVENTURES OF HAJJI BABA, THE (1954) PR:C
ADVENTURES OF HAL 5, THE (1958, Brit.) PR:A
ADVENTURES OF HERCULES (SEE: HERCULES II)
   (1985)
ADVENTURES OF HUCKLEBERRY FINN (SEE: HUCK-
   LEBERRY FINN) (1939)
ADVENTURES OF HUCKLEBERRY FINN, THE (1960)
   PR:AA
ADVENTURES OF ICHABOD AND MR. TOAD (1949)
   PR:AA
ADVENTURES OF JACK LONDON (SEE: JACK LON-
   DON) (1943)
ADVENTURES OF JANE, THE (1949, Brit.) PR:A
ADVENTURES OF JANE ARDEN, THE (1939) PR:A
ADVENTURES OF KITTY O'DAY (1944) PR:A
ADVENTURES OF MARCO POLO, THE (1938) PR:A
ADVENTURES OF MARK TWAIN, THE (1944) PR:AA
ADVENTURES OF MARK TWAIN, THE (1985) PR:AA
ADVENTURES OF MARTIN EDEN, THE (1942) PR:A
ADVENTURES OF MICHAEL STROGOFF (SEE: SOL-
   DIER AND THE LADY, THE) (1937)
ADVENTURES OF PC 49, THE (1949, Brit.) PR:A
ADVENTURES OF PICASSO, THE (1980, Swed.) PR:O
ADVENTURES OF QUENTIN DURWARD, THE (SEE:
   QUENTIN DURWARD) (1955)
ADVENTURES OF RABBI JACOB, THE (1973, Fr.) PR:C
ADVENTURES OF ROBIN HOOD, THE (1938) PR:AA
*ADVENTURES OF ROBINSON CRUSOE, THE (1952,
   Mex.) PR:A-C
ADVENTURES OF RUSTY (1945) PR:A
ADVENTURES OF SADIE, THE (1955, Brit.) PR:A
ADVENTURES OF SCARAMOUCHE, THE (1964,
   Fr./It./Sp.) PR:C
ADVENTURES OF SHERLOCK HOLMES, THE (1939)
   PR:A
ADVENTURES OF TARTU, THE (1943, Brit.) PR:A
ADVENTURES OF THE AMERICAN RABBIT, THE (1986)
   PR:AA
ADVENTURES OF THE PRINCE AND THE PAUPER,
   THE (SEE: PRINCE AND THE PAUPER, THE) (1969)
ADVENTURES OF THE WILDERNESS FAMILY, THE
   (1975) PR:AA
ADVENTURES OF TOM SAWYER, THE (1938) PR:AA
ADVENTURES OF TORCHY BLANE, THE (SEE: FLY-
   AWAY BABY) (1937)
ADVENTURESS, THE (1946, Brit.) PR:A
ADVENTUROUS BLONDE, THE (1937) PR:A
ADVERSARY, THE (1973, India) PR:A
ADVICE TO THE LOVELORN (1933) PR:A
ADVISE AND CONSENT (1962) PR:C
AERIAL GUNNER (1943) PR:A
AEROBICIDE (SEE: KILLER WORKOUT) (1987)
AFFAIR AT AKITSU (1980, Jap.) PR:O
AFFAIR AT THE VILLA FIORITA (SEE: BATTLE OF
   THE VILLA FIORITA) (1965, Brit.)
AFFAIR BLUM, THE (1949, W. Ger.) PR:C

AFFAIR IN HAVANA (1957) PR:O
AFFAIR IN MONTE CARLO (1953, Brit.) PR:A
AFFAIR IN RENO (1957) PR:A
AFFAIR IN TRINIDAD (1952) PR:C
AFFAIR LAFONT (SEE: CONFLICT) (1939, Fr.)
AFFAIR OF SUSAN, THE (1935) PR:A
AFFAIR OF THE HEART, AN (SEE: BODY AND SOUL)
   (1947)
AFFAIR OF THE HEART, AN (SEE: LOVE AFFAIR; OR
   THE CASE OF THE MISSING SWITCHBOARD OP-
   ERATOR) (1967, Yugo.)
AFFAIR OF THE SKIN, AN (1964) PR:O
AFFAIR TO REMEMBER, AN (1957) PR:A
AFFAIR WITH A STRANGER (1953) PR:A
AFFAIR, THE (SEE: THERE'S ALWAYS VANILLA)
   (1972)
AFFAIRS IN VERSAILLES (SEE: ROYAL AFFAIRS IN
   VERSAILLES) (1957, Fr.)
AFFAIRS OF A GENTLEMAN (1934) PR:A
AFFAIRS OF A MODEL (1952, Swed.) PR:O
AFFAIRS OF A ROGUE, THE (1949, Brit.) PR:A
AFFAIRS OF ADELAIDE (1949, US/Brit.) PR:C
AFFAIRS OF ANNABEL, THE (1938) PR:A
AFFAIRS OF CAPPY RICKS (1937) PR:A
AFFAIRS OF CELLINI, THE (1934) PR:C
AFFAIRS OF DOBIE GILLIS, THE (1953) PR:A
AFFAIRS OF DR. HOLL (1954, W. Ger.) PR:A
AFFAIRS OF GERALDINE (1946) PR:A
AFFAIRS OF JULIE, THE (1958, W. Ger.) PR:C
AFFAIRS OF MARTHA, THE (1942) PR:A
AFFAIRS OF MAUPASSANT (1938, Aust.) PR:A
AFFAIRS OF MESSALINA, THE (1954, It.) PR:O
AFFAIRS OF SALLY, THE (SEE: FULLER BRUSH
   GIRL, THE) (1950)
AFFAIRS OF SUSAN, THE (1945) PR:A
AFFECTIONATELY YOURS (1941) PR:A
AFRAID TO TALK (1932) PR:C
AFRICA EROTICA (SEE: KAREN, THE LOVEMAKER)
   (1970)
AFRICA SCREAMS (1949) PR:AA
AFRICA —TEXAS STYLE! (1967, US/Brit.) PR:AA
AFRICAN, THE (1983, Fr.) PR:O
AFRICAN FURY (SEE: CRY THE BELOVED COUN-
   TRY) (1952, Brit.)
AFRICAN MANHUNT (1955) PR:A
AFRICAN QUEEN, THE (1951, US/Brit.) PR:A
AFRICAN STORY, THE (SEE: HATARI!) (1962)
AFRICAN TREASURE (1952) PR:A
AFTER EIGHT HOURS (SEE: SOCIETY DOCTOR)
   (1935)
AFTER HOURS (1985) PR:O
AFTER MIDNIGHT (1989) PR:O
AFTER MIDNIGHT WITH BOSTON BLACKIE (1943)
   PR:A
AFTER OFFICE HOURS (1932, Brit.) PR:A
AFTER OFFICE HOURS (1935) PR:A
AFTER SCHOOL (1989) PR:O
AFTER THE BALL (1932, Brit.) PR:C
AFTER THE BALL (1957, Brit.) PR:A
AFTER THE DANCE (1935) PR:A
AFTER THE FALL OF NEW YORK (1984, It./Fr.) PR:O
AFTER THE FOX (1966, US/Brit./It.) PR:A
AFTER THE REHEARSAL (1984, Swed.) PR:C-O
AFTER TOMORROW (1932) PR:A
AFTER TONIGHT (1933) PR:A
AFTER YOU, COMRADE (1967, South Africa) PR:A
AFTERWARDS (SEE: THEIR BIG MOMENT) (1934)
AGAINST A CROOKED SKY (1975) PR:C
AGAINST ALL FLAGS (1952) PR:A
AGAINST ALL ODDS (1984) PR:C-O
AGAINST THE LAW (1934) PR:C
AGAINST THE TIDE (1937, Brit.) PR:A
AGAINST THE WIND (1948, Brit.) PR:A
AGATHA (1979, Brit.) PR:C
AGATHA CHRISTIE'S ENDLESS NIGHT (SEE: END-
   LESS NIGHT) (1971)
AGE FOR LOVE, THE (1931) PR:A
AGE OF CONSENT, THE (1932) PR:C
AGE OF CONSENT (1969, Aus.) PR:O
AGE OF GOLD (SEE: L'AGE D'OR) (1930, Fr.)
AGE OF ILLUSIONS (1967, Hung.) PR:O
AGE OF INDISCRETION (1935) PR:C
AGE OF INFIDELITY (1958, Sp.) PR:O
AGE OF INNOCENCE, THE (1934) PR:C
AGE OF INNOCENCE (1977, Can.) PR:A
AGE OF THE MEDICI, THE (1979, It.) PR:C
AGENCY (1981, Can.) PR:O
AGENT 38-24-36 (SEE: RAVISHING IDIOT, A) (1966,
   Fr./It.)
AGENT 8 3/4 (1963, Brit.) PR:C
AGENT FOR H.A.R.M. (1966) PR:C
AGENT ON ICE (1986) PR:O
AGENTI SEGRETISSIMI (SEE: 00-2 MOST SECRET
   AGENTS) (1965, It.)
AGGIE APPLEBY, MAKER OF MEN (1933) PR:A

AGGUATO A TANGERI (SEE: TRAPPED IN TANGI-
   ERS) (1960, It./Sp.)
AGITATOR, THE (1949, Brit.) PR:A
AGNES OF GOD (1985) PR:C
AGONIYA (SEE: RASPUTIN) (1981, USSR)
AGONY AND THE ECSTASY, THE (1965) PR:A
AGUIRRE, THE WRATH OF GOD (1973, W. Ger.) PR:O
AH, WILDERNESS! (1935) PR:AA
AH YING (1984, Hong Kong) PR:A
A-HAUNTING WE WILL GO (1942) PR:AA
AI NO KAWAKI (SEE: LONGING FOR LOVE) (1966,
   Jap.)
AIDA (1954, It.) PR:A
AIMEZ-VOUS BRAHMS (SEE: GOODBYE AGAIN)
   (1961)
AIN'T MISBEHAVIN' (1955) PR:A
AIR CADET (1951) PR:A
AIR CIRCUS, THE (1928) PR:A
AIR DEVILS (1938) PR:A
AIR EAGLES (1932) PR:C
AIR FORCE (1943) PR:A
AIR HAWKS (1935) PR:A
AIR HOSTESS (1933) PR:A
AIR HOSTESS (1949) PR:A
AIR MAIL (1932) PR:A
AIR PATROL (1962) PR:C
AIR POLICE (1931) PR:A
AIR RAID WARDENS (1943) PR:AA
AIR STRIKE (1955) PR:A
AIRBORNE (1962) PR:A
AIRCHAUFFEUR (SEE: TAXI TO HEAVEN) (1944,
   USSR)
AIRPLANE! (1980) PR:C
AIRPLANE II: THE SEQUEL (1982) PR:C
AIRPORT (1970) PR:A
AIRPORT 1975 (1974) PR:C
AIRPORT '77 (1977) PR:C
AIRPORT '79 (SEE: CONCORDE, THE – AIRPORT '79)
   (1979)
AKAGE (SEE: RED LION) (1971, Jap.)
AKAHIGE (SEE: RED BEARD) (1965, Jap.)
AKE AND HIS WORLD (1985, Swed.) PR:O
AKIBIYORI (SEE: LATE AUTUMN) (1973, Jap.)
AKOGARE (SEE: ONCE A RAINY DAY) (1968, Jap.)
AL CAPONE (1959) PR:C-O
AL DI LA DELLA LEGGE (SEE: BEYOND THE LAW)
   (1967, It.)
AL JENNINGS OF OKLAHOMA (1951) PR:A
AL-RISALAH (SEE: MOHAMMAD, MESSENGER OF
   GOD) (1977)
ALADDIN (1987, It.) PR:A
ALADDIN AND HIS LAMP (1952) PR:AA
ALAKAZAM THE GREAT (1961, Jap.) PR:AA
ALAMBRISTA! (1977) PR:C
ALAMO, THE (1960) PR:AA
ALAMO BAY (1985) PR:O
ALASKA (1944) PR:A
ALASKA HIGHWAY (1943) PR:A
ALASKA PASSAGE (1959) PR:A
ALASKA PATROL (1949) PR:A
ALASKA SEAS (1954) PR:A
ALBERT, R.N. (1953, Brit.) PR:A
ALBUQUERQUE (1948) PR:A
ALCATRAZ ISLAND (1937) PR:A
ALERT IN THE SOUTH (1954, Fr.) PR:A
ALERTE AU SUD (SEE: ALERT IN THE SOUTH) (1954,
   Fr.)
ALEX AND THE GYPSY (1976) PR:C
ALEX IN WONDERLAND (1970) PR:C
ALEXA (1989) PR:O
ALEXANDER GRAHAM BELL (SEE: STORY OF ALEX-
   ANDER GRAHAM BELL, THE) (1939)
ALEXANDER HAMILTON (1931) PR:A
ALEXANDER NEVSKY (1938, USSR) PR:C
ALEXANDER THE GREAT (1956) PR:A
ALEXANDER'S RAGTIME BAND (1938) PR:AA
ALF 'N' FAMILY (1968, Brit.) PR:C
ALFIE (1966, Brit.) PR:O
ALFIE DARLING (1975, Brit.) PR:O
ALFRED THE GREAT (1969, Brit.) PR:C
ALFREDO, ALFREDO (1973, It.) PR:O
ALF'S BABY (1953, Brit.) PR:A
ALF'S BUTTON (1930, Brit.) PR:AA
ALF'S BUTTON AFLOAT (1938, Brit.) PR:A
ALF'S CARPET (1929, Brit.) PR:A
ALGIERS (1938) PR:C
ALI BABA (1954, Fr.) PR:A
ALI BABA AND THE FORTY THIEVES (1944) PR:AA
ALI BABA GOES TO TOWN (1937) PR:AA
ALI — FEAR EATS THE SOUL (SEE: FEAR EATS THE
   SOUL) (1974, W. Ger.)
ALIAS A GENTLEMAN (1948) PR:A
ALIAS BIG SHOT (1962, Arg.) PR:C
ALIAS BILLY THE KID (1946) PR:AA
ALIAS BOSTON BLACKIE (1942) PR:A
ALIAS BULLDOG DRUMMOND (1935, Brit.) PR:A
ALIAS FRENCH GERTIE (1930) PR:A

ALIAS JESSE JAMES (1959) PR:A
ALIAS JIMMY VALENTINE (1928) PR:A
ALIAS JOHN LAW (1935) PR:A
ALIAS JOHN PRESTON (1956, Brit.) PR:A
ALIAS MARY DOW (1935) PR:A
ALIAS MARY SMITH (1932) PR:A
ALIAS NICK BEAL (1949) PR:A
ALIAS THE BAD MAN (1931) PR:A
ALIAS THE CHAMP (1949) PR:A
ALIAS THE DEACON (1940) PR:A
ALIAS THE DOCTOR (1932) PR:A
ALIBI (1929) PR:C
ALIBI (1931, Brit.) PR:A
ALIBI BREAKER (SEE: DOUBLE EXPOSURES) (1937, Brit.)
ALIBI, THE (1939, Fr.) PR:C
ALIBI, THE (1943, Brit.) PR:C
ALIBI FOR MURDER (1936) PR:A
ALIBI IKE (1935) PR:AA
ALIBI INN (1935, Brit.) PR:A
ALICE (1988, Switz./Brit./W. Ger.) PR:O
ALICE ADAMS (1935) PR:A
ALICE DOESN'T LIVE HERE ANYMORE (1975) PR:O
ALICE IN THE CITIES (1974, W. Ger.) PR:A
ALICE IN WONDERLAND (1933) PR:AA
ALICE IN WONDERLAND (1951) PR:AA
ALICE IN WONDERLAND (1951, Fr.) PR:A
ALICE, OR THE LAST ESCAPADE (1977, Fr.) PR:C
ALICE, SWEET ALICE (1978) PR:O
ALICE'S ADVENTURES IN WONDERLAND (1972, Brit.) PR:A
ALICE'S RESTAURANT (1969) PR:O
ALIEN (1979) PR:O
ALIEN CONTAMINATION (1982, It.) PR:O
ALIEN DEAD (SEE: IT FELL FROM THE SKY) (1980)
ALIEN FACTOR, THE (1984) PR:C
ALIEN FROM L.A. (1988) PR:NR
ALIEN NATION (1988) PR:O
ALIEN PREDATOR (1987) PR:O
ALIEN THUNDER (1975, US/Can.) PR:C
ALIENS (1986) PR:O
ALIMONY (1949) PR:C
ALIMONY MADNESS (1933) PR:C
ALIVE AND KICKING (1962, Brit.) PR:AA
ALIVE ON SATURDAY (1957, Brit.) PR:A
ALL ABOUT EVE (1950) PR:A
ALL-AMERICAN, THE (1932) PR:A
ALL-AMERICAN, THE (1953) PR:A
ALL-AMERICAN BOY, THE (1973) PR:O
ALL-AMERICAN CHUMP (1936) PR:A
ALL-AMERICAN CO-ED (1941) PR:A
ALL-AMERICAN SWEETHEART (1937) PR:A
ALL-AROUND REDUCED PERSONALITY – OUT-TAKES, THE (1978, W. Ger.) PR:A
ALL ASHORE (1953) PR:AA
ALL AT SEA (1935, Brit.) PR:A
ALL AT SEA (1939, Brit.) PR:A
ALL AT SEA (1958, Brit.) PR:A
ALL AT SEA (1970, Brit.) PR:A
ALL BY MYSELF (1943) PR:A
ALL CREATURES GREAT AND SMALL (1975, Brit.) PR:AA
ALL DOGS GO TO HEAVEN (1989) PR:A
ALL FALL DOWN (1962) PR:C
ALL FOR MARY (1956, Brit.) PR:A
ALL HANDS ON DECK (1961) PR:A
ALL I DESIRE (1953) PR:A
ALL IN (1936, Brit.) PR:A
ALL IN A NIGHT'S WORK (1961) PR:C
ALL IN PLACE, NOTHING IN ORDER (SEE: ALL SCREWED UP) (1976, It.)
ALL MEN ARE ENEMIES (1934) PR:A
ALL MINE TO GIVE (1957) PR:AA
ALL MY SONS (1948) PR:C
ALL NEAT IN BLACK STOCKINGS (1969, Brit.) PR:C
ALL NIGHT LONG (1961, Brit.) PR:C
ALL NIGHT LONG (1981) PR:C
ALL NUDITY SHALL BE PUNISHED (1974, Braz.) PR:O
ALL OF ME (1934) PR:C
ALL OF ME (1984) PR:A-C
ALL OVER THE TOWN (1949, Brit.) PR:AA
ALL OVER TOWN (1937) PR:A
ALL QUIET ON THE WESTERN FRONT (1930) PR:C
ALL RIGHT, MY FRIEND (1983, Jap.) PR:A
ALL SCREWED UP (1976, It.) PR:O
ALL THAT GLITTERS (1936, Brit.) PR:A
ALL THAT HEAVEN ALLOWS (1955) PR:A
ALL THAT JAZZ (1979) PR:O
ALL THAT MONEY CAN BUY (SEE: DEVIL AND DANIEL WEBSTER, THE) (1941)
ALL THE BROTHERS WERE VALIANT (1953) PR:A
ALL THE FINE YOUNG CANNIBALS (1960) PR:C
ALL THE KING'S HORSES (1935) PR:A
ALL THE KING'S MEN (1949) PR:C
ALL THE LOVIN' KINFOLK (SEE: KINFOLK) (1970)
... ALL THE MARBLES (1981) PR:C
ALL THE OTHER GIRLS DO! (1967, Fr./It.) PR:A
ALL THE PRESIDENT'S MEN (1976) PR:C

ALL THE RIGHT MOVES (1983) PR:C
ALL THE RIGHT NOISES (1973, Brit.) PR:O
ALL THE WAY (SEE: JOKER IS WILD, THE) (1957)
ALL THE WAY, BOYS (1973, It.) PR:C
ALL THE WAY HOME (1963) PR:A
ALL THE WAY UP (1970, Brit.) PR:A
ALL THE YOUNG MEN (1960) PR:A
ALL THESE WOMEN (1964, Swed.) PR:O
ALL THINGS BRIGHT AND BEAUTIFUL (1979, Brit.) PR:AA
ALL THIS AND GLAMOUR TOO (SEE: VOGUES OF 1938) (1937)
ALL THIS AND HEAVEN TOO (1940) PR:A
ALL THROUGH THE NIGHT (1942) PR:A
ALL WOMAN (1958) PR:O
ALL WOMEN HAVE SECRETS (1939) PR:A
ALLA RICERCA DI GREGORY (SEE: IN SEARCH OF GREGORY) (1970, Brit./It.)
ALLAN QUATERMAIN AND THE LOST CITY OF GOLD (1987) PR:A-C
ALLEGHENY UPRISING (1939) PR:A
ALLEGRO NON TROPPO (1977, It.) PR:A
ALLERGIC TO LOVE (1943) PR:A
ALLEY CAT (1984) PR:O
ALLEY OF NIGHTMARES (SEE: MAN WHO WAS SHERLOCK HOLMES, THE) (1937, Ger.)
ALLEZ FRANCE (SEE: COUNTERFEIT CONSTABLE, THE) (1966, Fr.)
ALLIGATOR (1980) PR:O
ALLIGATOR NAMED DAISY, AN (1957, Brit.) PR:A
ALLIGATOR PEOPLE, THE (1959) PR:C
ALLNIGHTER, THE (1987) PR:C-O
ALLONSANFAN (1985, It.) PR:C
ALLOTMENT WIVES (1945) PR:A
ALLURING GOAL, THE (1930, Ger.) PR:A
ALMOST A BRIDE (SEE: KISS FOR CORLISS, A) (1949)
ALMOST A DIVORCE (1931, Brit.) PR:A
ALMOST A GENTLEMAN (1938, Brit.) PR:A
ALMOST A GENTLEMAN (1939) PR:A
ALMOST A HONEYMOON (1930, Brit.) PR:A
ALMOST A HONEYMOON (1938, Brit.) PR:A
ALMOST ANGELS (1962) PR:AA
ALMOST HUMAN (1974, It.) PR:O
ALMOST MARRIED (1932) PR:C
ALMOST MARRIED (1942) PR:A
ALMOST PERFECT AFFAIR, AN (1979) PR:C
ALMOST SUMMER (1978) PR:A
ALMOST TRANSPARENT BLUE (1980, Jap.) PR:O
ALMOST YOU (1984) PR:C
ALOHA (1931) PR:A
ALOHA, BOBBY AND ROSE (1975) PR:C
ALOHA SUMMER (1988) PR:C
ALOMA OF THE SOUTH SEAS (1941) PR:A
ALONE AGAINST ROME (1963, It.) PR:C
ALONE IN THE DARK (1982) PR:O
ALONE IN THE STREETS (1956, It.) PR:C
ALONE ON THE PACIFIC (1964, Jap.) PR:AA
ALONG CAME JONES (1945) PR:A
ALONG CAME LOVE (1937) PR:A
ALONG CAME SALLY (1934, Brit.) PR:A
ALONG CAME YOUTH (1931) PR:A
ALONG THE GREAT DIVIDE (1951) PR:C
ALONG THE NAVAJO TRAIL (1945) PR:A
ALONG THE OREGON TRAIL (1947) PR:A
ALONG THE RIO GRANDE (1941) PR:A
ALPHA BETA (1973, Brit.) PR:C
ALPHABET CITY (1984) PR:O
ALPHABET MURDERS, THE (1966, Brit.) PR:A
ALPHAVILLE, A STRANGE CASE OF LEMMY CAUTION (1965, Fr./It.) PR:A
ALRAUNE (SEE: DAUGHTER OF EVIL) (1930, Ger.)
ALRAUNE (1952, W. Ger.) PR:A
ALSINO AND THE CONDOR (1982, Cuba/Mex./Costa Rica/Nicaragua) PR:C
ALSKANDE PAR (SEE: LOVING COUPLES) (1966, Swed.)
ALSKAR INNAN (SEE: SWEDISH MISTRESS, THE) (1964, Swed.)
ALTA INFEDELTA (SEE: HIGH INFIDELITY) (1965, Fr./It.)
ALTERED STATES (1980) PR:O
ALTRI TEMPI (SEE: TIMES GONE BY) (1953, It.)
ALVAREZ KELLY (1966) PR:A
ALVIN PURPLE (1974, Aus.) PR:C
ALVIN RIDES AGAIN (1974, Aus.) PR:O
ALWAYS (1985) PR:O
ALWAYS (1989) PR:A-C
ALWAYS A BRIDE (1940) PR:A
ALWAYS A BRIDE (1954, Brit.) PR:A
ALWAYS A BRIDESMAID (1943) PR:A
ALWAYS ANOTHER DAWN (1948, Aus.) PR:A
ALWAYS GOODBYE (1931) PR:A
ALWAYS GOODBYE (1938) PR:A
ALWAYS IN MY HEART (1942) PR:AA
ALWAYS IN TROUBLE (1938) PR:AA
ALWAYS LEAVE THEM LAUGHING (1949) PR:A
ALWAYS TOGETHER (1947) PR:A

ALWAYS TOMORROW (SEE: THERE'S ALWAYS TO-MORROW) (1934)
ALWAYS VICTORIOUS (1960, It.) PR:A
AM ANFANG WAR ES SUNDE (SEE: GREH) (1962, W. Ger./Yugo.)
AM I GUILTY? (1940) PR:A
AMADEUS (1984) PR:C
AMANTI (SEE: PLACE FOR LOVERS, A) (1969, It./Fr.)
AMARCORD (1974, It./Fr.) PR:O
AMATEUR, THE (1982, Can.) PR:C
AMATEUR CROOK (1937) PR:A
AMATEUR DADDY (1932) PR:A
AMATEUR GENTLEMAN, THE (1936, Brit.) PR:A
AMAZING ADVENTURE, THE (SEE: ROMANCE AND RICHES) (1937, Brit.)
AMAZING COLOSSAL MAN, THE (1957) PR:A
AMAZING DOBERMANS, THE (1976) PR:AA
AMAZING DR. CLITTERHOUSE, THE (1938) PR:C
AMAZING GRACE (1974) PR:A
AMAZING GRACE AND CHUCK (1987) PR:A-C
AMAZING MR. BEECHAM, THE (1949, Brit.) PR:A
AMAZING MR. BLUNDEN, THE (1973, Brit.) PR:C
AMAZING MR. FORREST, THE (1943, Brit.) PR:A
AMAZING MR. WILLIAMS, THE (1939) PR:A
AMAZING MR. X, THE (SEE: SPIRITUALIST, THE) (1948)
AMAZING MONSIEUR FABRE, THE (1952, Fr.) PR:A
AMAZING MRS. HOLLIDAY, THE (1943) PR:AA
AMAZING QUEST OF ERNEST BLISS, THE (SEE: ROMANCE AND RICHES) (1937, Brit.)
AMAZING TRANSPARENT MAN, THE (1960) PR:C
AMAZON QUEST (1949) PR:A
AMAZON WOMEN ON THE MOON (1987) PR:O
AMAZONIA – THE CATHERINE MILES STORY (SEE: WHITE SLAVE) (1986, It.)
AMAZONS (1987) PR:O
AMBASSADOR, THE (1984) PR:C
AMBASSADOR BILL (1931) PR:A
AMBASSADOR'S DAUGHTER, THE (1956) PR:A
AMBULANCE CHASER (SEE: NUISANCE, THE) (1933)
AMBUSH (1939) PR:A
AMBUSH (1950) PR:A
AMBUSH AT CIMARRON PASS (1958) PR:A
AMBUSH AT TOMAHAWK GAP (1953) PR:C
AMBUSH BAY (1966) PR:C
AMBUSH IN LEOPARD STREET (1962, Brit.) PR:C
AMBUSH TRAIL (1946) PR:A
AMBUSH VALLEY (1936) PR:A
AMBUSHERS, THE (1967) PR:A
AMELIE OR THE TIME TO LOVE (1961, Fr.) PR:A
AMERE VICTOIRE (SEE: BITTER VICTORY) (1958, US/Fr.)
AMERICA, AMERICA (1963) PR:A
AMERICA 3000 (1986) PR:C
AMERICAN ANTHEM (1986) PR:C
AMERICAN AUTOBAHN (1989, W. Ger.) PR:A-C
AMERICAN COMMANDOS (1986) PR:O
AMERICAN DREAM, AN (1966) PR:O
AMERICAN DREAMER (1984) PR:A-C
AMERICAN EMPIRE (1942) PR:A
AMERICAN FLYERS (1985) PR:C
AMERICAN FRIEND, THE (1977, W. Ger.) PR:C
AMERICAN GIGOLO (1980) PR:O
AMERICAN GOTHIC (1988, Brit./Can.) PR:O
AMERICAN GRAFFITI (1973) PR:C
AMERICAN GUERRILLA IN THE PHILIPPINES, AN (1950) PR:A
AMERICAN HOT WAX (1978) PR:A
AMERICAN IN PARIS, AN (1951) PR:AA
AMERICAN JUSTICE (1986) PR:O
AMERICAN LOVE (1932, Fr.) PR:A
AMERICAN LOVE THING, THE (SEE: TOM) (1973)
AMERICAN MADNESS (1932) PR:A
AMERICAN NIGHTMARE (1984) PR:O
AMERICAN NIGHTMARES (SEE: COMBAT SHOCK) (1986)
AMERICAN NINJA (1985) PR:O
AMERICAN NINJA 2: THE CONFRONTATION (1987) PR:C-O
AMERICAN NINJA 3: BLOOD HUNT (1989) PR:C
AMERICAN POP (1981) PR:O
AMERICAN PRISONER, THE (1929, Brit.) PR:A
AMERICAN ROMANCE, AN (1944) PR:A
AMERICAN SOLDIER, THE (1970, W. Ger.) PR:C
AMERICAN SUCCESS COMPANY, THE (1980) PR:C
AMERICAN TABOO (1984) PR:O
AMERICAN TAIL, AN (1986) PR:AA
AMERICAN TRAGEDY, AN (1931) PR:C
AMERICAN WAY, THE (SEE: RIDERS OF THE STORM) (1988)
AMERICAN WEREWOLF IN LONDON, AN (1981) PR:O
AMERICAN WIFE, AN (SEE: RUN FOR YOUR WIFE) (1966, Fr./It.)
AMERICANA (1981) PR:C
AMERICANIZATION OF EMILY, THE (1964) PR:C
AMERICANO, THE (1955) PR:A
AMERICATHON (1979) PR:C

AMICI PER LA PELLE (SEE: FRIENDS FOR LIFE)
   (1964, It.)
AMIGOS (1986) PR:C
AMIN — THE RISE AND FALL (1982, Kenya) PR:O
AMITYVILLE HORROR, THE (1979) PR:O
AMITYVILLE II: THE POSSESSION (1982) PR:O
AMITYVILLE 3-D (1983) PR:O
AMOK (SEE: MORO THE WITCH DOCTOR) (1964,
   US/Phil.)
AMOK (SEE: SCHIZO) (1977, Brit.)
AMONG HUMAN WOLVES (1940, Brit.) PR:A
AMONG PEOPLE (SEE: ON HIS OWN) (1939, USSR)
AMONG THE CINDERS (1985, New Zealand/W. Ger.)
   PR:O
AMONG THE LIVING (1941) PR:C
AMONG THE MISSING (1934) PR:A
AMONG VULTURES (SEE: FRONTIER HELLCAT)
   (1966, Fr./W. Ger./It./Yugo.)
AMOROUS ADVENTURES OF MOLL FLANDERS,
   THE (1965, Brit.) PR:C
AMOROUS GENERAL, THE (SEE: WALTZ OF THE TO-
   READORS) (1962, Brit.)
AMOROUS MR. PRAWN, THE (1965, Brit.) PR:A
AMOROUS SEX, THE (SEE: SWEET BEAT) (1962, Brit.)
AMOS 'N' ANDY (1930) PR:A
AMOUR A L'AMERICAINE (SEE: AMERICAN LOVE)
   (1932, Fr.)
AMOUR, AMOUR (1937, Fr.) PR:A
AMPHIBIOUS MAN, THE (1961, USSR) PR:AA
AMPHITRYON (1937, Ger.) PR:A
AMSTERDAM AFFAIR, THE (1968, Brit.) PR:C
AMSTERDAM KILL, THE (1978, Hong Kong) PR:O
AMY (1981) PR:AA
ANA (1985, Portugal) PR:C
ANAPARASTASSIS (SEE: RECONSTRUCTION OF A
   CRIME) (1970, Gr.)
ANASTASIA (1956) PR:A
ANATAHAN (1953, Jap.) PR:C
ANATOLIAN SMILE, THE (SEE: AMERICA, AMER-
   ICA) (1963)
ANATOMIST, THE (1961, Brit.) PR:C
ANATOMY OF A MARRIAGE (MY DAYS WITH JEAN-
   MARC AND MY NIGHTS WITH FRANCOISE) (1964,
   Fr.) PR:O
ANATOMY OF A MURDER (1959) PR:C
ANATOMY OF A PSYCHO (1961) PR:C
ANATOMY OF A SYNDICATE (SEE: BIG OPERATOR,
   THE) (1959)
ANATOMY OF LOVE (1959, It.) PR:C
ANCHOR, THE (SEE: PIONEERS OF THE FRONTIER)
   (1940)
ANCHORS AWEIGH (1945) PR:AA
AND BABY MAKES THREE (1949) PR:A
AND COMES THE DAWN. . . BUT COLORED RED
   (SEE: WEB OF THE SPIDER) (1972, Fr./It./W. Ger.)
AND GOD CREATED WOMAN (1956, Fr.) PR:O
AND GOD CREATED WOMAN (1988) PR:O
AND HOPE TO DIE (1972, Fr/US) PR:C
AND JENNY MAKES THREE (SEE: JENNY) (1969)
. . . *AND JUSTICE FOR ALL* (1979) PR:O
. . . AND MILLIONS WILL DIE! (1973) PR:C
AND NOTHING BUT THE TRUTH (SEE: GIRO CITY)
   (1982, Brit.)
*AND NOW FOR SOMETHING COMPLETELY DIFFER-
   ENT* (1972, Brit.) PR:A
. . . AND NOW MIGUEL (1966) PR:AA
AND NOW MY LOVE (1974, Fr.) PR:C
AND NOW THE SCREAMING STARTS (1973, Brit.) PR:O
AND NOW TOMORROW (1944) PR:A
AND ONCE UPON A LOVE (SEE: FANTASIES) (1981)
AND ONE WAS BEAUTIFUL (1940) PR:A
. . . AND PIGS MIGHT FLY (SEE: ADERYN PAPUR)
   (1984, Brit.)
AND QUIET FLOWS THE DON (1960, USSR) PR:A
AND SO THEY WERE MARRIED (1936) PR:AA
AND SO THEY WERE MARRIED (SEE: JOHNNY
   DOESN'T LIVE HERE ANYMORE) (1944)
AND SO TO BED (1965, W. Ger.) PR:O
AND SOON THE DARKNESS (1970, Brit.) PR:O
AND SUDDEN DEATH (1936) PR:A
. . . AND SUDDENLY IT'S MURDER! (1964, It./Fr.) PR:C
AND THE ANGELS SING (1944) PR:A
AND THE SAME TO YOU (1960, Brit.) PR:A
AND THE SHIP SAILS ON (1983, It./Fr.) PR:A
AND THE WILD, WILD WOMEN (1961, It.) PR:C-O
AND THEN THERE WERE NONE (1945) PR:A
AND THEN THERE WERE NONE (SEE: TEN LITTLE
   INDIANS) (1965, Brit.)
AND THEN THERE WERE NONE (SEE: TEN LITTLE
   INDIANS) (1975, Fr./It./Sp./W. Ger.)
AND THERE CAME A MAN (1968, Fr./It.) PR:AA
AND WOMAN. . . WAS CREATED (SEE: AND GOD
   CREATED WOMAN) (1956, Fr.)
AND WOMEN SHALL WEEP (1960, Brit.) PR:C
ANDERSON TAPES, THE (1971) PR:C-O
ANDERSON'S ANGELS (SEE: CHESTY ANDERSON,
   U.S. NAVY) (1976)
ANDREI ROUBLOV (1973, USSR) PR:A

ANDREW'S RAIDERS (SEE: GREAT LOCOMOTIVE
   CHASE, THE) (1956)
ANDROCLES AND THE LION (1952) PR:A
ANDROID (1982) PR:O
ANDROMEDA STRAIN, THE (1971) PR:A
ANDY (1965) PR:A
ANDY HARDY COMES HOME (1958) PR:AA
ANDY HARDY GETS SPRING FEVER (1939) PR:AA
ANDY HARDY MEETS DEBUTANTE (1940) PR:AA
ANDY HARDY'S BLONDE TROUBLE (1944) PR:AA
ANDY HARDY'S DOUBLE LIFE (1942) PR:AA
ANDY HARDY'S PRIVATE SECRETARY (1941) PR:AA
ANDY WARHOL'S DRACULA (1974, Fr./It.) PR:O
ANDY WARHOL'S FRANKENSTEIN (1974, Fr./It.) PR:O
ANGEL (1937) PR:C
ANGEL (1982, Ireland) PR:C
ANGEL (1984) PR:O
ANGEL AND SINNER (1947, Fr.) PR:C
ANGEL AND THE BADMAN (1947) PR:A
ANGEL, ANGEL, DOWN WE GO (1969) PR:O
ANGEL BABY (1961) PR:C
ANGEL COMES TO BROOKLYN, AN (1945) PR:AA
ANGEL FACE (1953) PR:C
ANGEL FROM TEXAS, AN (1940) PR:A
ANGEL HEART (1987) PR:O
ANGEL IN EXILE (1948) PR:A
ANGEL IN MY POCKET (1969) PR:AA
ANGEL LEVINE, THE (1970) PR:A
ANGEL OF H.E.A.T. (SEE: PROTECTORS, BOOK 1,
   THE) (1981)
ANGEL OF VIOLENCE (SEE: MS. 45) (1981)
ANGEL ON MY SHOULDER (1946) PR:A
ANGEL ON THE AMAZON (1948) PR:A
ANGEL PASSED OVER BROOKLYN, AN (SEE: MAN
   WHO WAGGED HIS TAIL, THE) (1957, Sp./It.)
ANGEL RIVER (1986, US/Mex.) PR:O
ANGEL STREET (SEE: GASLIGHT) (1940)
ANGEL 3: THE FINAL CHAPTER (1988) PR:O
ANGEL UNCHAINED (1970) PR:C
ANGEL WHO PAWNED HER HARP, THE (1956, Brit.)
   PR:A
ANGEL WITH THE TRUMPET, THE (1950, Brit.) PR:C
ANGEL WORE RED, THE (1960) PR:A
ANGELA (1955, It.) PR:A
ANGELA (1977, Can.) PR:O
ANGELE (1934, Fr.) PR:C
ANGELIKA (SEE: AFFAIRS OF DR. HOLL) (1954)
ANGELINA (1948, It.) PR:C
ANGELO (1951, It.) PR:C
ANGELO IN THE CROWD (1952, It.) PR:A
ANGELO, MY LOVE (1983) PR:O
ANGELS ALLEY (1948) PR:A
ANGELS AND THE PIRATES (SEE: ANGELS IN THE
   OUTFIELD) (1951)
ANGELS BRIGADE (1980) PR:O
ANGELS DIE HARD! (1970) PR:O
ANGELS FOR KICKS (SEE: WILD RIDERS) (1971)
ANGELS FROM HELL (1968) PR:O
ANGELS HARD AS THEY COME (1971) PR:O
ANGEL'S HOLIDAY (1937) PR:A
ANGELS IN DISGUISE (1949) PR:A
ANGELS IN THE OUTFIELD (1951) PR:AA
ANGELS OF DARKNESS (1956, It.) PR:O
ANGELS OF THE STREETS (1950, Fr.) PR:C
ANGELS ONE FIVE (1954, Brit.) PR:A
ANGELS OVER BROADWAY (1940) PR:A
ANGELS WASH THEIR FACES (1939) PR:A
ANGELS WITH BROKEN WINGS (1941) PR:A
ANGELS WITH DIRTY FACES (1938) PR:C
ANGELUS, THE (SEE: WHO KILLED FEN MARK-
   HAM?) (1937, Brit.)
ANGI VERA (1980, Hung.) PR:C
ANGKOR-CAMBODIA EXPRESS (1986, Thai./It.) PR:O
ANGLAR, FINNS DOM? (SEE: LOVE MATES) (1967,
   Swed.)
ANGRY BREED, THE (1969) PR:O
ANGRY HILLS, THE (1959, Brit.) PR:A
ANGRY ISLAND (1960, Jap.) PR:A
ANGRY MAN, THE (1979, Fr./Can.) PR:C
ANGRY RED PLANET, THE (1959) PR:A
ANGRY SILENCE, THE (1960, Brit.) PR:C
ANGUISH (1988, Sp.) PR:O
ANGUSTIA (SEE: ANGUISH) (1988, Sp.)
ANIMAL CRACKERS (1930) PR:AA
ANIMAL FARM (1955, Brit.) PR:A
ANIMAL HOUSE (SEE: NATIONAL LAMPOON'S ANI-
   MAL HOUSE) (1978)
ANIMAL KINGDOM, THE (1932) PR:A
ANIMALS, THE (1971) PR:O
ANIMAS TRUJANO (SEE: IMPORTANT MAN, THE)
   (1961, Mex.)
ANITA — DANCES OF VICE (1987, W. Ger.) PR:O
ANITA GARIBALDI (1954, It.) PR:C
ANJOS DA NOITE (SEE: NIGHT ANGELS) (1987, Braz.)
ANN CARVER'S PROFESSION (1933) PR:A
ANN VICKERS (1933) PR:A
ANNA (1951, It.) PR:C-O
ANNA (1981, Fr./Hung.) PR:A

ANNA (1987) PR:NR
ANNA AND THE KING OF SIAM (1946) PR:A
ANNA CHRISTIE (1930) PR:C
ANNA CROSS, THE (1954, USSR) PR:A
ANNA KARENINA (1935) PR:A
ANNA KARENINA (1948, Brit.) PR:A
ANNA LUCASTA (1949) PR:C
ANNA LUCASTA (1958) PR:C
ANNA OF BROOKLYN (1958, It.) PR:C
ANNA OF RHODES (1950, Gr.) PR:A
ANNABEL TAKES A TOUR (1938) PR:A
ANNABELLE'S AFFAIRS (1931) PR:A
ANNAPOLIS FAREWELL (1935) PR:A
ANNAPOLIS SALUTE (1937) PR:A
ANNAPOLIS STORY, AN (1955) PR:A
ANNE AND MURIEL (SEE: TWO ENGLISH GIRLS)
   (1972, Fr.)
ANNE DEVLIN (1984, Ireland) PR:C
ANNE-MARIE (1936, Fr.) PR:A
ANNE OF GREEN GABLES (1934) PR:A
ANNE OF THE INDIES (1951) PR:A
ANNE OF THE THOUSAND DAYS (1969, Brit.) PR:C-O
ANNE OF WINDY POPLARS (1940) PR:A
ANNE ONE HUNDRED (1933, Brit.) PR:A
ANNE TRISTER (1986, Can.) PR:O
ANNIE (1982) PR:AA
ANNIE GET YOUR GUN (1950) PR:AA
ANNIE HALL (1977) PR:C-O
ANNIE LAURIE (1936, Brit.) PR:A
ANNIE, LEAVE THE ROOM (1935, Brit.) PR:A
ANNIE OAKLEY (1935) PR:AA
ANNIE'S COMING OUT (1985, Aus.) PR:C
ANNIHILATORS, THE (1985) PR:O
ANNIVERSARY, THE (1968, Brit.) PR:O
ANNO UNO (SEE: YEAR ONE) (1974, It.)
ANONYMOUS VENETIAN, THE (1971, It.) PR:C
ANOTHER CHANCE (SEE: TWILIGHT WOMEN) (1952,
   Brit.)
ANOTHER COUNTRY (1984, Brit.) PR:C
ANOTHER DAWN (1937) PR:A
ANOTHER DAY (SEE: QUARTIERE) (1987, It.)
ANOTHER FACE (1935) PR:A
ANOTHER LANGUAGE (1933) PR:A
ANOTHER LOVE STORY (1986, Arg.) PR:O
ANOTHER MAN, ANOTHER CHANCE (1977, Fr./US)
   PR:C-O
ANOTHER MAN'S POISON (1952, Brit.) PR:C
ANOTHER PART OF THE FOREST (1948) PR:C
ANOTHER SHORE (1948, Brit.) PR:A
ANOTHER SKY (1960, Brit.) PR:A
ANOTHER THIN MAN (1939) PR:A
ANOTHER TIME, ANOTHER PLACE (1958, Brit.) PR:A
ANOTHER TIME, ANOTHER PLACE (1984, Brit.) PR:O
ANOTHER WOMAN (1988) PR:C
ANSIKTET (SEE: MAGICIAN, THE) (1958, Swed.)
ANTARCTICA (1984, Jap.) PR:A
ANTHONY ADVERSE (1936) PR:A
ANTHONY OF PADUA (1952, It.) PR:O
ANTHROPOPHAGOUS (SEE: GRIM REAPER, THE)
   (1981, It.)
ANTI-CLOCK (1980) PR:C-O
ANTICRISTO (SEE: TEMPTER, THE) (1978, It.)
ANTIGONE (1962, Gr.) PR:A
ANTOINE ET ANTOINETTE (1947, Fr.) PR:A
ANTONIO DAS MORTES (1970, Braz.) PR:C-O
ANTONY AND CLEOPATRA (1973, Brit.) PR:A
ANTS IN HIS PANTS (1940, Aus.) PR:AA
ANXIOUS YEARS, THE (SEE: DARK JOURNEY) (1937,
   Brit.)
ANY GUN CAN PLAY (1968, It./Sp.) PR:C
ANY MAN'S WIFE (1936) PR:A
ANY NUMBER CAN PLAY (1949) PR:A
ANY NUMBER CAN WIN (1963, Fr.) PR:A
ANY WEDNESDAY (1966) PR:C-O
ANY WHICH WAY YOU CAN (1980) PR:C
ANYBODY'S BLONDE (1931) PR:A
ANYBODY'S WAR (1930) PR:A
ANYBODY'S WOMAN (1930) PR:A
ANYONE CAN PLAY (1968, It.) PR:O
ANYONE FOR VENICE? (SEE: HONEY POT, THE)
   (1967)
ANYTHING CAN HAPPEN (1952) PR:A
ANYTHING FOR A SONG (1947, It.) PR:A
ANYTHING FOR A THRILL (1937) PR:A
ANYTHING FOR LOVE (SEE: 11 HARROWHOUSE)
   (1974, Brit.)
ANYTHING GOES (1936) PR:A
ANYTHING GOES (1956) PR:A
ANYTHING MIGHT HAPPEN (1935, Brit.) PR:A
ANYTHING TO DECLARE? (1939, Brit.) PR:A
ANZIO (1968, It.) PR:A
AOBE KA MONOGATARI (SEE: THIS MADDING
   CROWD) (1964, Jap.)
APA (SEE: FATHER) (1966, Hung.)
APACHE (1954) PR:A
APACHE AMBUSH (1955) PR:A
APACHE CHIEF (1949) PR:A
APACHE COUNTRY (1952) PR:A

APACHE DRUMS (1951) PR:A
APACHE GOLD (1965, Fr./It./W. Ger./Yugo.) PR:A
APACHE KID, THE (1941) PR:A
APACHE RIFLES (1964) PR:A
APACHE ROSE (1947) PR:A
APACHE TERRITORY (1958) PR:A
APACHE TRAIL (1942) PR:A
APACHE UPRISING (1966) PR:A
APACHE WAR SMOKE (1952) PR:A
APACHE WARRIOR (1957) PR:A
APACHE WOMAN (1955) PR:A
APARAJITO (1959, India) PR:A
APARTMENT, THE (1960) PR:C-O
APARTMENT FOR PEGGY (1948) PR:A
APARTMENT ZERO (1989) PR:O
APE, THE (1940) PR:C
APE MAN, THE (1943) PR:C
APE WOMAN, THE (1964, It.) PR:C
APHRODITE (1982, Fr.) PR:O
APOCALYPSE NOW (1979) PR:O
APOLLO GOES ON HOLIDAY (1968, Gr./Swed.) PR:A
APOLOGY FOR MURDER (1945) PR:A
APPALOOSA, THE (1966) PR:C
APPLAUSE (1929) PR:A
APPLE, THE (1980, US/W. Ger.) PR:C-O
APPLE DUMPLING GANG, THE (1975) PR:AA
APPLE DUMPLING GANG RIDES AGAIN, THE (1979)
  PR:AA
APPOINTMENT, THE (1969) PR:O
APPOINTMENT FOR LOVE (1941) PR:A
APPOINTMENT FOR MURDER (1954, It.) PR:C
APPOINTMENT IN BERLIN (1943) PR:A
APPOINTMENT IN HONDURAS (1953) PR:A
APPOINTMENT IN LONDON (1953, Brit.) PR:A
APPOINTMENT WITH A SHADOW (1958) PR:A
APPOINTMENT WITH CRIME (1945, Brit.) PR:A
APPOINTMENT WITH DANGER (1951) PR:A
APPOINTMENT WITH DEATH (1988) PR:A-C
APPOINTMENT WITH FEAR (1985) PR:O
APPOINTMENT WITH MURDER (1948) PR:A
APPOINTMENT WITH VENUS (SEE: ISLAND RES-
  CUE) (1952)
APPRENTICE TO MURDER (1988) PR:C
APPRENTICESHIP OF DUDDY KRAVITZ, THE (1974,
  Can.) PR:A
APRES L'AMOUR (1948, Fr.) PR:O
APRIL BLOSSOMS (1937, Brit.) PR:A
APRIL FOOLS, THE (1969) PR:C
APRIL FOOL'S DAY (1986) PR:O
APRIL IN PARIS (1953) PR:A
APRIL LOVE (1957) PR:AA
APRIL 1, 2000 (1953, Aust.) PR:A
APRIL ROMANCE (SEE: APRIL BLOSSOMS) (1937,
  Brit.)
APRIL SHOWERS (1948) PR:A
APUR SANSAR (SEE: WORLD OF APU, THE) (1959,
  India)
AQUELLA CASA EN LAS AFUERAS (SEE: THAT
  HOUSE IN THE OUTSKIRTS) (1980, Sp.)
ARABELLA (1969, US/It.) PR:A
ARABESQUE (1966, US/Brit.) PR:C
ARABIAN ADVENTURE (1979, Brit.) PR:AA
ARABIAN NIGHTS (1942) PR:A
ARABIAN NIGHTS (1980, It./Fr.) PR:O
ARASHI NO NAKA NO OTOKO (SEE: MAN IN THE
  STORM, THE) (1969, Jap.)
ARCH OF TRIUMPH (1948) PR:C
ARCTIC FLIGHT (1952) PR:A
ARCTIC FURY (1949) PR:AA
ARCTIC HEAT (SEE: BORN AMERICAN) (1986, US/Fin.)
ARCTIC MANHUNT (1949) PR:A
ARE HUSBANDS NECESSARY? (1942) PR:A
ARE THESE OUR CHILDREN? (1931) PR:A
ARE THESE OUR PARENTS? (1944) PR:A
ARE WE CIVILIZED? (1934) PR:A
ARE YOU A MASON? (1934, Brit.) PR:A
ARE YOU LISTENING? (1932) PR:A
ARE YOU THERE? (1930) PR:AA
ARE YOU WITH IT? (1948) PR:AA
ARENA (1953) PR:A
ARENA, THE (1973) PR:O
AREN'T MEN BEASTS? (1937, Brit.) PR:A
AREN'T WE ALL? (1932, Brit.) PR:A
AREN'T WE WONDERFUL? (1959, W. Ger.) PR:A
ARGENTINE NIGHTS (1940) PR:AA
ARGYLE CASE, THE (1929) PR:A
ARGYLE SECRETS, THE (1948) PR:A
ARIA (1987, US/Brit.) PR:O
ARIANE (1931, Ger.) PR:A
ARIANE, RUSSIAN MAID (1932, Fr.) PR:A
ARISE, MY LOVE (1940) PR:A
ARISTOCATS, THE (1970) PR:AA
ARIZONA (SEE: MEN ARE LIKE THAT) (1931)
ARIZONA (1940) PR:A
ARIZONA BADMAN (1935) PR:A
ARIZONA BOUND (1941) PR:A
ARIZONA BUSHWHACKERS (1968) PR:A

ARIZONA COLT (1965, It./Fr./Sp.) PR:C
ARIZONA COWBOY, THE (1950) PR:A
ARIZONA CYCLONE (1934) PR:A
ARIZONA CYCLONE (1941) PR:A
ARIZONA DAYS (1937) PR:A
ARIZONA FRONTIER (1940) PR:A
ARIZONA GANGBUSTERS (1940) PR:A
ARIZONA GUNFIGHTER, THE (1937) PR:A
ARIZONA KID, THE (1930) PR:A
ARIZONA KID, THE (1939) PR:A
ARIZONA LEGION (1939) PR:A
ARIZONA MAHONEY (1936) PR:A
ARIZONA MANHUNT (1951) PR:A
ARIZONA MISSION (SEE: GUN THE MAN DOWN)
  (1956)
ARIZONA NIGHTS (1934) PR:A
ARIZONA RAIDERS, THE (1936) PR:A
ARIZONA RAIDERS (1965) PR:A
ARIZONA RANGER, THE (1948) PR:A
ARIZONA ROUNDUP (1942) PR:A
ARIZONA STAGECOACH (1942) PR:A
ARIZONA TERRITORY (1950) PR:A
ARIZONA TERROR (1931) PR:A
ARIZONA TERRORS (1942) PR:A
ARIZONA TO BROADWAY (1933) PR:A
ARIZONA TRAIL (1943) PR:A
ARIZONA TRAILS (1935) PR:A
ARIZONA WHIRLWIND (1944) PR:A
ARIZONA WILDCAT (1938) PR:AA
ARIZONIAN, THE (1935) PR:A
ARKANSAS JUDGE (1941) PR:A
ARKANSAS TRAVELER, THE (1938) PR:A
ARM OF THE LAW (1932) PR:A
ARMCHAIR DETECTIVE, THE (1952, Brit.) PR:A
ARMED AND DANGEROUS (1977, USSR) PR:A
ARMED AND DANGEROUS (1986) PR:C
ARMED RESPONSE (1986) PR:O
ARMORED ATTACK (SEE: NORTH STAR, THE) (1943)
ARMORED CAR (1937) PR:A
ARMORED CAR ROBBERY (1950) PR:A
ARMORED COMMAND (1961) PR:C
ARMS AND THE GIRL (SEE: RED SALUTE) (1935)
ARMS AND THE MAN (1932, Brit.) PR:A
ARMS AND THE MAN (1962, W. Ger.) PR:A
ARMS AND THE WOMAN (SEE: MR. WINKLE GOES
  TO WAR) (1944)
ARMY BOUND (1952) PR:A
ARMY CAPERS (SEE: WAC FROM WALLA WALLA,
  THE) (1952)
ARMY GAME, THE (1963, Fr.) PR:C-O
ARMY GIRL (1938) PR:A
ARMY OF SHADOWS, THE (SEE: L'ARMEE DES OM-
  BRES) (1969, Fr./It.)
ARMY SURGEON (1942) PR:A
ARMY WIVES (1944) PR:A
ARNELO AFFAIR, THE (1947) PR:A
ARNOLD (1973) PR:C
AROUND THE TOWN (1938, Brit.) PR:A
AROUND THE WORLD (1943) PR:A
AROUND THE WORLD IN 80 DAYS (1956) PR:AA
AROUND THE WORLD IN EIGHTY WAYS (1987, Aus.)
  PR:A-C
AROUND THE WORLD UNDER THE SEA (1966) PR:A
AROUSE AND BEWARE (SEE: MAN FROM DAKOTA,
  THE) (1940)
AROUSERS, THE (1970) PR:O
ARRANGEMENT, THE (1969) PR:O
ARREST BULLDOG DRUMMOND (1939) PR:A
ARRIVEDERCI, BABY! (1966, Brit.) PR:C-O
ARROW IN THE DUST (1954) PR:A
ARROWHEAD (1953) PR:C
ARROWSMITH (1931) PR:A
ARSENAL STADIUM MYSTERY, THE (1939, Brit.) PR:A
ARSENE LUPIN (1932) PR:A
ARSENE LUPIN RETURNS (1938) PR:A
ARSENIC AND OLD LACE (1944) PR:A
ARSON FOR HIRE (1959) PR:A
ARSON GANG BUSTERS (1938) PR:A
ARSON, INC. (1949) PR:A
ARSON RACKET SQUAD (SEE: ARSON GANG BUST-
  ERS) (1938)
ARSON SQUAD (1945) PR:A
ART OF LOVE, THE (1965) PR:A
ARTHUR (1931, Fr.) PR:C
ARTHUR (1981) PR:C
ARTHUR TAKES OVER (1948) PR:A
ARTHUR 2 ON THE ROCKS (1988) PR:C
ARTHUR'S HALLOWED GROUND (1986, Brit.) PR:C
ARTISTS AND MODELS (1937) PR:AA
ARTISTS AND MODELS (1955) PR:A
ARTISTS AND MODELS ABROAD (1938) PR:A
ARTURO'S ISLAND (1963, It.) PR:C
ARU SONAN (SEE: DEATH ON THE MOUNTAIN)
  (1961, Jap.)
ARUPUSU NO WAKADAISHO (SEE: IT STARTED IN
  THE ALPS) (1966, Jap.)
AS GOOD AS MARRIED (1937) PR:A
AS HUSBANDS GO (1934) PR:A

AS LONG AS THEY'RE HAPPY (1957, Brit.) PR:A
AS LONG AS YOU'RE NEAR ME (1956, W. Ger.) PR:A
AS THE DEVIL COMMANDS (1933) PR:A
AS THE EARTH TURNS (1934) PR:A
AS THE SEA RAGES (1960, W. Ger.) PR:A
AS WE FORGIVE (SEE: BREAKERS AHEAD) (1938,
  Brit.)
AS YOU DESIRE ME (1932) PR:A
AS YOU LIKE IT (1936, Brit.) PR:A
AS YOU WERE! (1951) PR:A
AS YOUNG AS WE ARE (1958) PR:C
AS YOUNG AS YOU FEEL (1951) PR:A
ASCENDANCY (1983, Brit.) PR:C
ASCENSEUR POUR L'ECHAFAUD (SEE: FRANTIC)
  (1958, Fr.)
ASCENT TO HEAVEN (SEE: MEXICAN BUS RIDE)
  (1951)
ASFALTO SELVAGEM (SEE: LOLLIPOP) (1966, Braz.)
ASH WEDNESDAY (1973) PR:C
ASHANTI (1979, Switz.) PR:O
ASHES AND DIAMONDS (1958, Pol.) PR:C
ASHITA ARU KAGIRI (SEE: TILL TOMORROW
  COMES) (1962, Jap.)
ASHIYA KARA NO HIKO (SEE: FLIGHT FROM AS-
  HIYA) (1964, US/Jap.)
ASK A POLICEMAN (1939, Brit.) PR:A
ASK ANY GIRL (1959) PR:A
ASK BECCLES (1933, Brit.) PR:A
ASKING FOR TROUBLE (1942, Brit.) PR:A
ASPHALT JUNGLE, THE (1950) PR:C
ASPHYX, THE (1972, Brit.) PR:C
ASSA (1988, USSR) PR:C
ASSALTO AO TREM PAGADOR; TIAO MEDONHO
  (SEE: TRAIN ROBBERY CONFIDENTIAL) (1965,
  Braz.)
ASSAM GARDEN, THE (1985, Brit.) PR:A-C
ASSASSIN (1973, Brit.) PR:C
ASSASSIN, THE (1953, Brit.) PR:A
ASSASSIN, THE (1965, It./Fr.) PR:O
ASSASSIN FOR HIRE (1951, Brit.) PR:C
ASSASSINATION (1987) PR:A-C
ASSASSINATION BUREAU, THE (1969, Brit.) PR:O
ASSASSINATION OF TROTSKY, THE (1972, Fr./It.) PR:O
ASSAULT, THE (1986, Neth.) PR:C
ASSAULT (1971, Brit.) PR:O
ASSAULT FORCE (SEE: FFOLKES) (1979, Brit.)
ASSAULT OF THE KILLER BIMBOS (1988) PR:O
ASSAULT OF THE REBEL GIRLS (1959) PR:A
ASSAULT ON A QUEEN (1966) PR:A
ASSAULT ON AGATHON (1976, Brit./Gr.) PR:O
ASSAULT ON PRECINCT 13 (1976) PR:O
ASSIGNED TO DANGER (1948) PR:A
ASSIGNMENT IN BRITTANY (1943) PR:A
ASSIGNMENT: ISTANBUL (SEE: CASTLE OF FU MAN-
  CHU, THE) (1968, Brit./It./Sp./W. Ger.)
ASSIGNMENT K (1968, Brit.) PR:A
ASSIGNMENT: KILL CASTRO (SEE: CUBA CROSS-
  ING) (1980)
ASSIGNMENT OUTER SPACE (1960, It.) PR:C
ASSIGNMENT—PARIS (1952) PR:A
ASSIGNMENT REDHEAD (SEE: MILLION DOLLAR
  MANHUNT) (1956, Brit.)
ASSIGNMENT TERROR (1970, Sp./It./W. Ger.) PR:C-O
ASSIGNMENT TO KILL (1968) PR:C
ASSISI UNDERGROUND, THE (1985) PR:C
ASSISTANT, THE (1982, Czech.) PR:C
ASSOCIATE, THE (1982, Fr./W. Ger.) PR:A
ASTERO (1960, Gr.) PR:A
ASTONISHED HEART, THE (1950, Brit.) PR:C
ASTOUNDING SHE-MONSTER, THE (1958) PR:C
ASTRO-ZOMBIES, THE (1969) PR:C
ASYA'S HAPPINESS (1988, USSR) PR:A-C
ASYLUM (1972, Brit.) PR:O
ASYLUM EROTICA (SEE: SLAUGHTER HOTEL)
  (1971, It.)
ASYLUM OF THE INSANE (SEE: FLESH AND BLOOD
  SHOW, THE) (1974, Brit.)
AT (SEE: HORSE, THE) (1984, Turk.)
AT CLOSE RANGE (1986) PR:O
AT DAWN WE DIE (1943, Brit.) PR:A
AT GOOD OLD SIWASH (SEE: THOSE WERE THE
  DAYS) (1940)
AT GUNPOINT (1955) PR:A
AT LONG LAST LOVE (1975) PR:A
AT MIDDLE AGE (1985, Chi.) PR:C
AT SWORD'S POINT (1951) PR:A
AT THE CIRCUS (1939) PR:AA
AT THE EARTH'S CORE (1976, Brit.) PR:C
AT THE RIDGE (1931) PR:A
AT THE STROKE OF NINE (1957, Brit.) PR:A
AT WAR WITH THE ARMY (1950) PR:A
ATALIA (1985, Israel) PR:C
ATHENA (1954) PR:A
ATLANTIC (1929, Brit.) PR:A
ATLANTIC ADVENTURE (1935) PR:A
ATLANTIC CITY (1944) PR:A
ATLANTIC CITY (1981, US/Can.) PR:C-O
ATLANTIC CONVOY (1942) PR:A

ATLANTIC EPISODE (SEE: CATCH AS CATCH CAN)
(1937, Brit.)
ATLANTIC FERRY (1941, Brit.) PR:A
ATLANTIC FLIGHT (1937) PR:A
ATLANTIS, THE LOST CONTINENT (1961) PR:A
ATLAS (1960) PR:C-O
ATLAS AGAINST THE CYCLOPS (1963, It.) PR:A
ATLAS AGAINST THE CZAR (1964, It.) PR:A
ATOLL K (SEE: UTOPIA) (1950, Fr./It.)
ATOM AGE VAMPIRE (1963, It.) PR:C
ATOMIC AGENT (SEE: NATHALIE, AGENT SECRET)
(1960, Fr.)
ATOMIC BRAIN, THE (1964) PR:O
ATOMIC CITY, THE (1952) PR:A
ATOMIC KID, THE (1954) PR:A
ATOMIC MAN, THE (1955, Brit.) PR:A
ATOMIC MONSTER, THE (SEE: MAN MADE MON-
STER) (1941)
ATOMIC ROCKETSHIP (SEE: FLASH GORDON) (1936)
ATOMIC SUBMARINE, THE (1960) PR:A
ATRAGON (1965, Jap.) PR:A
ATT ALSKA (SEE: TO LOVE) (1964, Swed.)
ATTACK! (1956) PR:O
ATTACK AND RETREAT (SEE: ITALIANO BRAVA
GENTE) (1965, It./USSR)
ATTACK OF THE CRAB MONSTERS (1957) PR:A
ATTACK OF THE 50 FOOT WOMAN (1958) PR:A
ATTACK OF THE GIANT LEECHES (1959) PR:C-O
ATTACK OF THE KILLER TOMATOES (1978) PR:C
ATTACK OF THE MAYAN MUMMY (1963, US/Mex.)
PR:C
ATTACK OF THE MUSHROOM PEOPLE (1964, Jap.)
PR:A
ATTACK OF THE PUPPET PEOPLE (1958) PR:A
ATTACK OF THE ROBOTS (1967, Fr./Sp.) PR:C
ATTACK ON THE IRON COAST (1968, US/Brit.) PR:A
ATTEMPT TO KILL (1961, Brit.) PR:A
ATTENTION, THE KIDS ARE WATCHING (1978, Fr.)
PR:C
ATTENTION! UNE FEMME PEUT EN CACHER UNE
AUTRE (SEE: MY OTHER HUSBAND) (1983, Fr.)
ATTIC, THE (1979) PR:C-O
ATTILA (1958, It.) PR:C
ATTORNEY FOR THE DEFENSE (1932) PR:A
AU BOUT DU BANC (SEE: MAKE ROOM FOR TO-
MORROW) (1979, Fr.)
AU HASARD, BALTHAZAR (1970, Fr.) PR:C-O
AU REVOIR LES ENFANTS (1988, Fr.) PR:A-C
AUDELA DELA PEUR (SEE: BEYOND FEAR) (1977, Fr.)
AUDELA DES GRILLES (SEE: WALLS OF
MALAPAGA) (1950, Fr./It.)
AUDREY ROSE (1977) PR:C
AUGUST WEEK-END (1936) PR:A
AUGUSTINE OF HIPPO (1973, It.) PR:A
AULD LANG SYNE (1929, Brit.) PR:A
AULD LANG SYNE (1937, Brit.) PR:A
AUNT CLARA (1954, Brit.) PR:A
AUNT FROM CHICAGO (1960, Gr.) PR:C
AUNT SALLY (SEE: ALONG CAME SALLY) (1934,
Brit.)
AUNTIE MAME (1958) PR:A
AURORA (SEE: QUALCOSA DI BIONDO) (1985, It.)
AURORA ENCOUNTER, THE (1985) PR:C
AUS DEM LEBEN DES MARIONETTEN (SEE: FROM
THE LIFE OF THE MARIONETTES) (1980, W. Ger.)
AUSTERLITZ (1960, Fr./It./Yugo.) PR:A
AUTHOR! AUTHOR! (1982) PR:A
AUTOMAT NA PRANI (SEE: WISHING MACHINE)
(1971, Czech./Fr.)
AUTUMN (1974, USSR) PR:C
AUTUMN CROCUS (1934, Brit.) PR:A
AUTUMN LEAVES (1956) PR:C
AUTUMN MARATHON (1982, USSR) PR:A
AUTUMN SONATA (1978, Swed.) PR:O
AVALANCHE (1946) PR:A
AVALANCHE (1978) PR:O
AVALANCHE EXPRESS (1979) PR:C
AVANTI! (1972) PR:C
AVE MARIA (1984, Fr.) PR:O
AVEC LE SOURIRE (SEE: WITH A SMILE) (1939, Fr.)
AVENGER, THE (1931) PR:A
AVENGER, THE (1933) PR:A
AVENGER, THE (1964, Fr./It.) PR:C
AVENGER, THE (1966, It.) PR:C
AVENGERS, THE (1942, Brit.) PR:A
AVENGERS, THE (1950) PR:A
AVENGING ANGEL (1985) PR:O
AVENGING FORCE (1986) PR:O
AVENGING HAND, THE (1936, Brit.) PR:A
AVENGING RIDER, THE (1943) PR:A
AVENGING WATERS (1936) PR:A
AVIATOR, THE (1929) PR:A
AVIATOR, THE (1985) PR:A-C
AVIATOR'S WIFE, THE (1981, Fr.) PR:O
AVOCATE D'AMOUR (SEE: COUNSEL FOR RO-
MANCE) (1938, Fr.)
AWAKENING, THE (1938, Brit.) PR:A
AWAKENING, THE (1958, It.) PR:AA

AWAKENING, THE (1980) PR:O
AWAKENING OF JIM BURKE (1935) PR:A
AWAY ALL BOATS (1956) PR:A
AWFUL DR. ORLOFF, THE (1964, Sp./Fr.) PR:O
AWFUL TRUTH, THE (1929) PR:A
AWFUL TRUTH, THE (1937) PR:A
AZ EROD (SEE: FORTRESS, THE) (1979, Hung.)
AZAIS (1931, Fr.) PR:A
AZTEC MUMMY, THE (1957, Mex.) PR:O
AZURE EXPRESS (1938, Hung.) PR:A

B

B.F.'S DAUGHTER (1948) PR:A
B.O.R.N. (1989) PR:O
B.S. I LOVE YOU (1971) PR:O
BABAR: THE MOVIE (1989) PR:A
BABBITT (1934) PR:A
BABE RUTH STORY, THE (1948) PR:AA
BABES IN ARMS (1939) PR:AA
BABES IN BAGDAD (1952) PR:A
BABES IN TOYLAND (1934) PR:AA
BABES IN TOYLAND (1961) PR:AA
BABES ON BROADWAY (1941) PR:AA
BABES ON SWING STREET (1944) PR:A
BABETTE GOES TO WAR (1960, Fr.) PR:C
BABETTE'S FEAST (1987, Den.) PR:A
BABIES FOR SALE (1940) PR:C
BABY, THE (1973) PR:C-O
BABY AND THE BATTLESHIP, THE (1957, Brit.) PR:A
BABY BE GOOD (SEE: BROTHER RAT AND A BABY)
(1940)
BABY BLUE MARINE (1976) PR:C
BABY BOOM (1987) PR:A
BABY DOLL (1956) PR:O
BABY FACE (1933) PR:O
BABY FACE HARRINGTON (1935) PR:A
BABY FACE MORGAN (1942) PR:A
BABY FACE NELSON (1957) PR:O
BABY, IT'S YOU (1983) PR:C-O
BABY LOVE (1969, Brit.) PR:O
BABY MAKER, THE (1970) PR:O
BABY: SECRET OF A LOST LEGEND (1985) PR:C
BABY, TAKE A BOW (1934) PR:AA
BABY, THE RAIN MUST FALL (1965) PR:C
BABY VANISHES, THE (SEE: BROADWAY LIMITED)
(1941)
BABYLON (1980, Brit.) PR:O
BABYSITTER (SEE: LA BABY SITTER) (1975, Fr./It./W.
Ger.)
BACCHANTES, THE (1963, Fr./It.) PR:A
BACHELOR AND THE BOBBY-SOXER, THE (1947)
PR:AA
BACHELOR APARTMENT (1931) PR:C
BACHELOR BAIT (1934) PR:A
BACHELOR BAIT (SEE: ADVENTURE IN BALTI-
MORE) (1949)
BACHELOR DADDY (1941) PR:A
BACHELOR FATHER, THE (1931) PR:A
BACHELOR FLAT (1962) PR:A
BACHELOR GIRL APARTMENT (SEE: ANY WEDNES-
DAY) (1966)
BACHELOR GIRL, THE (1929) PR:A
BACHELOR GIRLS (SEE: BACHELOR'S DAUGH-
TERS) (1946)
BACHELOR IN PARADISE (1961) PR:A
BACHELOR IN PARIS (1953, Brit.) PR:A
BACHELOR KNIGHT (SEE: BACHELOR AND THE
BOBBY SOXER, THE) (1947)
BACHELOR MOTHER (1933) PR:C
BACHELOR MOTHER (1939) PR:A
BACHELOR OF ARTS (1935) PR:A
BACHELOR OF HEARTS (1958, Brit.) PR:A
BACHELOR PARTY, THE (1957) PR:C
BACHELOR PARTY (1984) PR:O
BACHELOR'S AFFAIRS (1932) PR:A
BACHELOR'S BABY (1932, Brit.) PR:C
BACHELOR'S DAUGHTERS, THE (1946) PR:A
BACHELOR'S FOLLY (1931, Brit.) PR:A
BACK AT THE FRONT (1952) PR:A
BACK DOOR TO HEAVEN (1939) PR:A
BACK DOOR TO HELL (1964, US/Phil.) PR:A
BACK FROM ETERNITY (1956) PR:C
BACK FROM THE DEAD (1957) PR:C-O
BACK IN CIRCULATION (1937) PR:A
BACK IN THE SADDLE (1941) PR:A
BACK PAY (1930) PR:A
BACK ROADS (1981) PR:O
BACK ROOM BOY (1942, Brit.) PR:A
BACK STREET (1932) PR:A
BACK STREET (1941) PR:A
BACK STREET (1961) PR:A
BACK STREETS OF PARIS (1962, Fr.) PR:C-O
BACK TO BATAAN (1945) PR:A
BACK TO GOD'S COUNTRY (1953) PR:A
BACK TO NATURE (1936) PR:A
BACK TO SCHOOL (1986) PR:C
BACK TO THE BEACH (1987) PR:C
BACK TO THE FUTURE (1985) PR:C

BACK TO THE FUTURE PART II (1989) PR:A
BACK TO THE WALL (1959, Fr.) PR:O
BACK TRAIL (1948) PR:A
BACKFIRE (1950) PR:A
BACKFIRE! (1961, Brit.) PR:C
BACKFIRE (1965, Fr.) PR:C
BACKFIRE (1989) PR:O
BACKGROUND (1953, Brit.) PR:C
BACKGROUND TO DANGER (1943) PR:A
BACKLASH (1947) PR:A
BACKLASH (1956) PR:A
BACKLASH (1986, Aus.) PR:O
BACKSTAGE (1937, Brit.) PR:A
BACKSTAGE MYSTERY (SEE: CURTAIN AT EIGHT)
(1934)
BACKTRACK (1969) PR:A
BAD AND THE BEAUTIFUL, THE (1952) PR:C
BAD BASCOMB (1946) PR:AA
BAD BLONDE (1953, Brit.) PR:C
BAD BLOOD (SEE: FIRST OFFENCE) (1936, Brit.)
BAD BLOOD (1987, Fr.) PR:A-C
BAD BOY (1935) PR:A
BAD BOY (1938, Brit.) PR:A
BAD BOY (1939) PR:A
BAD BOY (1949) PR:A
BAD BOYS (1983) PR:O
BAD CHARLESTON CHARLIE (1973) PR:A
BAD COMPANY (1931) PR:A
BAD COMPANY (1972) PR:A
BAD COMPANY (1986, Arg.) PR:O
BAD DAY AT BLACK ROCK (1955) PR:A
BAD DREAMS (1988) PR:O
BAD FOR EACH OTHER (1954) PR:A
BAD GIRL (1931) PR:C
BAD GIRL (SEE: TEENAGE BAD GIRL) (1959, Brit.)
BAD GIRLS (SEE: SLASHER, THE) (1975)
BAD GIRLS, THE (SEE: LES BICHES) (1968, Fr./It.)
BAD GUY (1937) PR:A
BAD GUYS (1986) PR:C-O
BAD LANDS (1939) PR:A
BAD LITTLE ANGEL (1939) PR:AA
BAD LORD BYRON, THE (1949, Brit.) PR:A
BAD MAN, THE (1930) PR:A
BAD MAN, THE (1941) PR:A
BAD MAN FROM RED BUTTE (1940) PR:A
BAD MAN OF BRIMSTONE, THE (1938) PR:A
BAD MAN OF DEADWOOD (1941) PR:A
BAD MAN OF HARLEM (SEE: HARLEM ON THE
PRAIRIE) (1938)
BAD MAN OF WYOMING (SEE: WYOMING) (1940)
BAD MANNERS (1984) PR:C
BAD MAN'S RIVER (1972, Sp.) PR:A
BAD MEDICINE (1985) PR:C
BAD MEN OF MISSOURI (1941) PR:A
BAD MEN OF THE BORDER (1945) PR:A
BAD MEN OF THE HILLS (1942) PR:A
BAD MEN OF THUNDER GAP (1943) PR:A
BAD MEN OF TOMBSTONE (1949) PR:C
BAD NEWS BEARS, THE (1976) PR:A
BAD NEWS BEARS GO TO JAPAN, THE (1978) PR:C
BAD NEWS BEARS IN BREAKING TRAINING, THE
(1977) PR:C
BAD ONE, THE (1930) PR:C
BAD ONE, THE (SEE: SORORITY GIRL) (1957)
BAD SEED, THE (1956) PR:C
BAD SISTER (1931) PR:A
BAD SISTER (1947, Brit.) PR:A
BAD SLEEP WELL, THE (1960, Jap.) PR:C
BAD TASTE (1988, New Zealand) PR:O
BADGE OF HONOR (1934) PR:A
BADGE OF MARSHAL BRENNAN, THE (1957) PR:A
BADGE 373 (1973) PR:O
BADGER'S GREEN (1934, Brit.) PR:A
BADGER'S GREEN (1949, Brit.) PR:A
BADLANDERS, THE (1958) PR:A
BADLANDS (1974) PR:O
BADLANDS OF DAKOTA (1941) PR:A
BADLANDS OF MONTANA (1957) PR:A
BADMAN'S COUNTRY (1958) PR:A
BADMAN'S GOLD (1951) PR:A
BADMAN'S TERRITORY (1946) PR:A
BAGDAD (1949) PR:A
BAGDAD CAFE (1987, W. Ger.) PR:C-O
BAHAMA PASSAGE (1941) PR:A
BAILIFF, THE (SEE: SANSHO THE BAILIFF) (1954,
Jap.)
BAILOUT AT 43,000 (1957) PR:A
BAISERS VOLES (SEE: STOLEN KISSES) (1968, Fr.)
BAIT (1950, Brit.) PR:A
BAIT (1954) PR:C
BAITED TRAP, THE (SEE: TRAP, THE) (1959)
BAKER'S HAWK (1976) PR:A
BAKER'S WIFE, THE (1938, Fr.) PR:C
BAL NA VODI (SEE: HEY BABU RIBA) (1987, Yugo.)
BAL TABARIN (1952) PR:A
BALALAIKA (1939) PR:A
BALBOA (1986) PR:O
BALCONY, THE (1963) PR:O

BALL AT SAVOY (1936, Brit.) PR:A
BALL AT THE CASTLE (1939, It.) PR:A
BALL OF FIRE (1941) PR:A
BALLAD IN BLUE (SEE: BLUES FOR LOVERS) (1966, Brit.)
BALLAD OF A GUNFIGHTER (1964) PR:A
BALLAD OF A HUSSAR (1963, USSR) PR:A
BALLAD OF A SOLDIER (1959, USSR) PR:A
BALLAD OF CABLE HOGUE, THE (1970) PR:C
BALLAD OF COSSACK GLOOTA (1938, USSR) PR:A
BALLAD OF GAVILAN (SEE: GAVILAN) (1968)
BALLAD OF GREGORIO CORTEZ, THE (1983) PR:C-O
BALLAD OF JOSIE, THE (1968) PR:A
BALLAD OF NARAYAMA (1961, Jap.) PR:C
BALLAD OF NARAYAMA, THE (1983, Jap.) PR:C
BALLERINA (1950, Fr.) PR:A
BALLO AL CASTELLO (SEE: BALL AT THE CASTLE) (1939, It.)
BALLOON GOES UP, THE (1942, Brit.) PR:A
BALTHAZAR (SEE: AU HASARD BALTHAZAR) (1970)
BALTIC DEPUTY (1937, USSR) PR:A
BALTIMORE BULLET, THE (1980) PR:C
BAMBI (1942) PR:AA
BAMBOLE! (1965, It.) PR:C
BAMBOO BLONDE, THE (1946) PR:A
BAMBOO PRISON, THE (1955) PR:A
BAMBOO SAUCER, THE (1968) PR:A
BAMSE (SEE: MY FATHER'S MISTRESS) (1970, Swed.)
BANANA MONSTER, THE (SEE: SCHLOCK) (1971)
BANANA PEEL (1965, Fr./It.) PR:C
BANANA RIDGE (1941, Brit.) PR:A
BANANAS (1971) PR:C
BANANAS BOAT (SEE: WHAT CHANGED CHARLEY FARTHING?) (1976, Brit./Sp.)
BANCO A BANGKOK POUR OSS 117 (SEE: SHADOW OF EVIL) (1967, Fr./It.)
BAND OF ANGELS (1957) PR:A
BAND OF ASSASSINS (1971, Jap.) PR:C
BAND OF GOLD (SEE: HOW TO SAVE A MARRIAGE— AND RUIN YOUR LIFE) (1968)
BAND OF OUTSIDERS (1964, Fr.) PR:C-O
BAND OF THE HAND (1986) PR:O
BAND OF THIEVES (1962, Brit.) PR:A
BAND PLAYS ON, THE (1934) PR:A
BAND WAGGON (1940, Brit.) PR:A
BAND WAGON, THE (1953) PR:A
BANDE A PART (SEE: BAND OF OUTSIDERS) (1964, Fr.)
BANDIDO (1956) PR:A
BANDIDOS (1967, It.) PR:C
BANDIT, THE (1949, It.) PR:A
BANDIT GENERAL (SEE: TORCH, THE) (1950)
BANDIT KING OF TEXAS (1949) PR:A
BANDIT OF SHERWOOD FOREST, THE (1946) PR:AA
BANDIT OF ZHOBE, THE (1959, Brit.) PR:A
BANDIT QUEEN (1950) PR:A
BANDIT RANGER (1942) PR:A
BANDIT TRAIL, THE (1941) PR:A
BANDITI A ORGOSOLO (SEE: BANDITS OF OR-GOSOLO) (1964, It.)
BANDITS (1988, Fr.) PR:C
BANDITS OF CORSICA, THE (1953) PR:A
BANDITS OF DARK CANYON (1947) PR:A
BANDITS OF EL DORADO (1951) PR:A
BANDITS OF ORGOSOLO (1964, It.) PR:A
BANDITS OF THE BADLANDS (1945) PR:A
BANDITS OF THE WEST (1953) PR:A
BANDITS ON THE WIND (1962, Jap.) PR:A
BANDOLERO! (1968) PR:A
BANG BANG KID, THE (1968, US/Sp./It.) PR:A
BANG! BANG! YOU'RE DEAD (1966, Brit.) PR:A
BANG THE DRUM SLOWLY (1973) PR:A
BANG! YOU'RE DEAD (1954, Brit.) PR:C
BANISHED (1978, Jap.) PR:C
BANJO (1947) PR:AA
BANJO ON MY KNEE (1936) PR:A
BANK ALARM (1937) PR:A
BANK DICK, THE (1940) PR:A
BANK HOLIDAY (1938, Brit.) PR:C
BANK MESSENGER MYSTERY, THE (1936, Brit.) PR:A
BANK RAIDERS, THE (1958, Brit.) PR:A
BANK ROBBERY (SEE: RENEGADES OF THE RIO GRANDE) (1945)
BANK SHOT (1974) PR:A
BANKOKKU NO YORU (SEE: NIGHT IN BANGKOK) (1966, Jap.)
BANNER IN THE SKY (SEE: THIRD MAN ON THE MOUNTAIN) (1959)
BANNERLINE (1951) PR:A
BANNING (1967) PR:C
BANZAI (1983, Fr.) PR:C-O
BANZAI RUNNER (1987) PR:C
BAR ESPERANZA (1983, Braz.) PR:O
BAR 51 – SISTER OF LOVE (1986, Israel) PR:O
BAR L RANCH (1930) PR:A
BAR SINISTER (1955) PR:A
BAR 20 (1943) PR:A
BAR 20 JUSTICE (1938) PR:A

BAR 20 RIDES AGAIN (1936) PR:A
BAR Z BAD MEN (1937) PR:A
BAR, THE (SEE: SOME OF MY BEST FRIENDS ARE. . .) (1971)
BARABBAS (1962, It.) PR:C
BARBADOS QUEST (SEE: MURDER ON APPROVAL) (1956, Brit.)
BARBARELLA (1968, Fr./It.) PR:O
BARBARIAN, THE (1933) PR:C
BARBARIAN AND THE GEISHA, THE (1958) PR:A
BARBARIAN QUEEN (1985) PR:O
BARBARIANS, THE (1987, US/It.) PR:O
BARBARIC BEAST OF BOGGY CREEK PART II, THE (SEE: BOGGY CREEK II) (1985)
BARBAROSA (1982) PR:C
BARBARY COAST (1935) PR:A
BARBARY COAST GENT (1944) PR:A
BARBARY PIRATE (1949) PR:A
BARBED WIRE (1952) PR:A
BARBER OF SEVILLE, THE (1947, It.) PR:A
BARBER OF SEVILLE (1949, Fr.) PR:A
BARBER OF SEVILLE, THE (1973, Fr./W. Ger.) PR:A
BARBER OF STAMFORD HILL, THE (1963, Brit.) PR:AA
BARBERINA (1932, Ger.) PR:A
BARCAROLE (1935, Ger.) PR:A
BARE KNUCKLES (1978) PR:O
BAREFOOT BATTALION, THE (1954, Gr.) PR:A
BAREFOOT BOY (1938) PR:A
BAREFOOT CONTESSA, THE (1954) PR:A
BAREFOOT EXECUTIVE, THE (1971) PR:AA
BAREFOOT IN THE PARK (1967) PR:A
BAREFOOT MAILMAN, THE (1951) PR:A
BAREFOOT SAVAGE (SEE: SENSUALITA) (1954, It.)
BARFLY (1987) PR:O
BARGAIN, THE (1931) PR:A
BARGAIN BASEMENT (SEE: DEPARTMENT STORE) (1935, Brit.)
BARGEE, THE (1964, Brit.) PR:C
BARKER, THE (1928) PR:A
BARKLEYS OF BROADWAY, THE (1949) PR:A
BARN OF THE NAKED DEAD (1976) PR:O
BARNACLE BILL (1935, Brit.) PR:A
BARNACLE BILL (1941) PR:A
BARNACLE BILL (SEE: ALL AT SEA) (1958, Brit.)
BARNUM WAS RIGHT (1929) PR:A
BARNYARD FOLLIES (1940) PR:A
BAROCCO (1976, Fr.) PR:O
BARON BLOOD (1972, It.) PR:C
BARON MUNCHAUSEN (1962, Czech.) PR:A
BARON OF ARIZONA, THE (1950) PR:A
BARONESS AND THE BUTLER, THE (1938) PR:A
BARQUERO (1970) PR:O
BARRACUDA (1978) PR:C
BARRANCO (1932, Fr.) PR:A
BARRETTS OF WIMPOLE STREET, THE (1934) PR:A
BARRETTS OF WIMPOLE STREET, THE (1957, Brit.) PR:A
BARRICADE (1939) PR:A
BARRICADE (1950) PR:A
BARRIER, THE (1937) PR:A
BARRIER (1966, Pol.) PR:A
BARRY LYNDON (1975, Brit.) PR:C-O
BARRY MC KENZIE HOLDS HIS OWN (1975, Aus.) PR:C
BARS OF HATE (1936) PR:A
BARTLEBY (1970, Brit.) PR:A
BARTON MYSTERY, THE (1932, Brit.) PR:A
BASHFUL BACHELOR, THE (1942) PR:A
BASHFUL ELEPHANT, THE (1962, Aust.) PR:A
BASIC TRAINING (1985) PR:O
BASILEUS QUARTET (1984, It.) PR:O
BASKET CASE (1982) PR:O
BASKETBALL FIX, THE (1951) PR:A
BASTILLE (1985, Neth.) PR:C-O
BAT, THE (1959) PR:C
BAT PEOPLE, THE (1974) PR:C
BAT 21 (1988) PR:O
BAT WHISPERS, THE (1930) PR:A
BATAAN (1943) PR:C
BATHING BEAUTY (1944) PR:A
BATMAN (1966) PR:AA
BATMAN (1989) PR:A-C
BATMEN OF AFRICA (SEE: DARKEST AFRICA) (1936)
BATTERIES NOT INCLUDED (1987) PR:AA
BATTLE, THE (1934, Fr.) PR:A
BATTLE AT APACHE PASS, THE (1952) PR:A
BATTLE AT BLOODY BEACH (1961) PR:A
BATTLE BENEATH THE EARTH (1968, Brit.) PR:A
BATTLE BEYOND THE STARS (1980) PR:C
BATTLE BEYOND THE STARS (SEE: GREEN SLIME, THE) (1969, US/Jap.)
BATTLE BEYOND THE SUN (1963, USSR) PR:O
BATTLE CIRCUS (1953) PR:A
BATTLE CRY (1955) PR:A
BATTLE FLAME (1959) PR:A
BATTLE FOR MUSIC (1943, Brit.) PR:A
BATTLE FOR THE PLANET OF THE APES (1973) PR:A
BATTLE HELL (1957, Brit.) PR:A
BATTLE HYMN (1957) PR:A

BATTLE IN OUTER SPACE (1960, Jap.) PR:A
BATTLE OF ALGIERS, THE (1966, It./Algeria) PR:C
BATTLE OF AUSTERLITZ (SEE: AUSTERLITZ) (1960, Fr./Yugo.)
BATTLE OF BLOOD ISLAND (1960) PR:A
BATTLE OF BRITAIN (1969, Brit.) PR:A
BATTLE OF BROADWAY (1938) PR:A
BATTLE OF GALLIPOLI (1931, Brit.) PR:A
BATTLE OF GREED (1934) PR:A
BATTLE OF LOVE'S RETURN, THE (1971) PR:A
BATTLE OF NERETVA (1969, US/Yugo./It./W. Ger.) PR:A
BATTLE OF PARIS, THE (1929) PR:A
BATTLE OF POWDER RIVER (SEE: TOMAHAWK) (1951)
BATTLE OF ROGUE RIVER (1954) PR:A
BATTLE OF THE AMAZONS (1973, It./Sp.) PR:A
BATTLE OF THE BULGE (1965) PR:A
BATTLE OF THE CORAL SEA (1959) PR:A
BATTLE OF THE RAILS (1949, Fr.) PR:A
BATTLE OF THE RIVER PLATE, THE (SEE: PURSUIT OF THE GRAF SPEE) (1957, Brit.)
BATTLE OF THE SEXES, THE (1960, Brit.) PR:A
BATTLE OF THE VILLA FIORITA, THE (1965, Brit.) PR:A
BATTLE OF THE V1 (SEE: MISSILE FROM HELL) (1958, Brit.)
BATTLE OF THE WORLDS (1961, It.) PR:A
BATTLE STATIONS (1956) PR:A
BATTLE STRIPE (SEE: MEN, THE) (1950)
BATTLE TAXI (1955) PR:A
BATTLE ZONE (1952) PR:A
BATTLEAXE, THE (1962, Brit.) PR:A
BATTLEGROUND (1949) PR:A
BATTLES OF CHIEF PONTIAC (1952) PR:A
BATTLESTAR GALACTICA (1979) PR:A
BATTLETRUCK (1982) PR:C
BATTLING BELLHOP, THE (SEE: KID GALAHAD) (1937)
BATTLING BUCKAROO (1932) PR:A
BATTLING HOOFER (SEE: SOMETHING TO SING ABOUT) (1937)
BATTLING MARSHAL (1950) PR:A
BAWDY ADVENTURES OF TOM JONES, THE (1976, Brit.) PR:O
BAXTER (1973, Brit.) PR:C
BAXTER MILLIONS, THE (SEE: THREE KIDS AND A QUEEN) (1935)
BAXTER'S MILLIONS (SEE: LITTLE MISS BIG) (1946)
BAY BOY, THE (1984, Can.) PR:C
BAY OF ANGELS (1964, Fr.) PR:C
BAY OF SAINT MICHEL, THE (1963, Brit.) PR:A
BAYAN KO (1984, Phil./Fr.) PR:O
BAYOU (1957) PR:A
BE CAREFUL MR. SMITH (SEE: SINGING THROUGH) (1935, Brit.)
BE MINE TONIGHT (1933, Brit.) PR:A
BE MY GUEST (1965, Brit.) PR:A
BE MY VALENTINE, OR ELSE. . . (SEE: HOSPITAL MASSACRE) (1984)
BE YOURSELF (1930) PR:A
BEACH BALL (1965) PR:A
BEACH BALLS (1988) PR:O
BEACH BLANKET BINGO (1965) PR:A
BEACH GIRLS (1982) PR:C-O
BEACH GIRLS AND THE MONSTER, THE (1965) PR:C
BEACH HOUSE PARTY (SEE: WILD ON THE BEACH) (1965)
BEACH PARTY (1963) PR:A
BEACH PARTY, ITALIAN STYLE (SEE: EIGHTEEN IN THE SUN) (1964, It.)
BEACH RED (1967) PR:A
BEACHCOMBER, THE (1938, Brit.) PR:A
BEACHCOMBER (1955, Brit.) PR:A
BEACHES (1988) PR:C
BEACHHEAD (1954) PR:C
BEADS OF ONE ROSARY, THE (1982, Pol.) PR:A
BEAR, THE (1963, Fr./It.) PR:AA
BEAR, THE (1984) PR:C
BEAR, THE (1989, Fr.) PR:A-C
BEAR ISLAND (1980, Brit./Can.) PR:C
BEARS AND I, THE (1974) PR:C
BEAST, THE (1975, Fr.) PR:O
BEAST, THE (1988) PR:O
BEAST FROM THE HAUNTED CAVE (1960) PR:C
BEAST FROM 20,000 FATHOMS, THE (1953) PR:C
BEAST IN THE CELLAR, THE (1971, Brit.) PR:C
BEAST MUST DIE, THE (1974, Brit.) PR:A
BEAST OF BABYLON AGAINST THE SON OF HERCULES (SEE: HERO OF BABYLON) (1963, It.)
BEAST OF BLOOD (1970, US/Phil.) PR:C-O
BEAST OF BUDAPEST, THE (1958) PR:C
BEAST OF HOLLOW MOUNTAIN, THE (1956, US/Mex.) PR:A
BEAST OF MOROCCO (SEE: HAND OF NIGHT, THE) (1967)
BEAST OF PARADISE ISLAND (SEE: PORT SINISTER) (1953)
BEAST OF THE CITY, THE (1932) PR:C-O

BEAST OF THE DEAD (SEE: BEAST OF BLOOD) (1970, Phil.)
BEAST OF YUCCA FLATS, THE (1961) PR:C
BEAST WITH A MILLION EYES, THE (1956) PR:A
BEAST WITH FIVE FINGERS, THE (1946) PR:C
BEAST WITHIN, THE (1982) PR:O
BEASTMASTER, THE (1982) PR:C
BEASTS OF BERLIN (1939) PR:C
BEASTS OF MARSEILLES, THE (1959, Brit.) PR:C
BEAT, THE (1988) PR:C-O
BEAT GENERATION, THE (1959) PR:C
BEAT GIRL (1962, Brit.) PR:O
BEAT STREET (1984) PR:A-C
BEAT THE BAND (1947) PR:A
BEAT THE DEVIL (1953) PR:A
BEATNIKS, THE (1960) PR:O
BEATRICE (1988, Fr./It.) PR:O
BEATSVILLE (SEE: REBEL SET, THE) (1959)
BEAU BANDIT (1930) PR:A
BEAU BRUMMELL (1954, Brit.) PR:A
BEAU GESTE (1939) PR:A
BEAU GESTE (1966) PR:A
BEAU IDEAL (1931) PR:A
BEAU JAMES (1957) PR:A
BEAU PERE (1981, Fr.) PR:O
BEAUTIES OF THE NIGHT (SEE: LES BELLES-DE-NUIT) (1952, Fr.)
BEAUTIFUL ADVENTURE (1932, Ger.) PR:A
BEAUTIFUL BLONDE FROM BASHFUL BEND, THE (1949) PR:A
BEAUTIFUL BUT BROKE (1944) PR:A
BEAUTIFUL BUT DEADLY (SEE: DON IS DEAD, THE) (1973)
BEAUTIFUL CHEAT, THE (1946) PR:A
BEAUTIFUL PRISONER, THE (1983, Fr.) PR:C
BEAUTIFUL STRANGER (1954, Brit.) PR:C
BEAUTIFUL SWINDLERS, THE (1967, Fr./It./Jap./Neth.) PR:O
BEAUTY (SEE: BEAUTY FOR SALE) (1933)
BEAUTY AND THE BANDIT (1946) PR:A
BEAUTY AND THE BARGE (1937, Brit.) PR:A
BEAUTY AND THE BEAST (1946) Fr.) PR:A
BEAUTY AND THE BEAST (1963) PR:C
BEAUTY AND THE BOSS (1932) PR:A
BEAUTY AND THE DEVIL (1952, Fr./It.) PR:A
BEAUTY AND THE ROBOT (SEE: SEX KITTENS GO TO COLLEGE) (1960)
BEAUTY FOR SALE (1933) PR:A
BEAUTY FOR THE ASKING (1939) PR:A
BEAUTY JUNGLE, THE (1966, Brit.) PR:C
BEAUTY ON PARADE (1950) PR:A
BEAUTY PARLOR (1932) PR:A
BEBO'S GIRL (1964, It./Fr.) PR:A
BECAUSE I LOVED YOU (1930, Ger.) PR:C
BECAUSE OF EVE (1948) PR:C-O
BECAUSE OF HIM (1946) PR:A
BECAUSE OF YOU (1952) PR:A
BECAUSE THEY'RE YOUNG (1960) PR:C
BECAUSE YOU'RE MINE (1952) PR:AA
BECKET (1964, Brit.) PR:A-C
BECKY SHARP (1935) PR:C
BED AND BOARD (1971, Fr./It.) PR:C
BED AND BREAKFAST (1930, Brit.) PR:A
BED AND BREAKFAST (1936, Brit.) PR:A
BED OF ROSES (1933) PR:A
BED SITTING ROOM, THE (1969, Brit.) PR:C
BEDAZZLED (1967, Brit.) PR:C
BEDELIA (1946, Brit.) PR:A
BEDEVILLED (1955) PR:C
BEDFORD INCIDENT, THE (1965, Brit.) PR:C
BEDKNOBS AND BROOMSTICKS (1971) PR:AA
BEDLAM (1946) PR:C
BEDROOM EYES (1984, Can.) PR:O
BEDROOM VENDETTA (SEE: GREEN MARE, THE) (1961, Fr./It.)
BEDROOM WINDOW, THE (1987) PR:O
BEDSIDE (1934) PR:A
BEDSIDE MANNER (1945) PR:A
BEDTIME FOR BONZO (1951) PR:AA
BEDTIME STORY, A (1933) PR:A
BEDTIME STORY (1938, Brit.) PR:AA
BEDTIME STORY (1942) PR:A
BEDTIME STORY (1964) PR:A-C
BEEN DOWN SO LONG IT LOOKS LIKE UP TO ME (1971) PR:A
BEER (1986) PR:O
BEES, THE (1978) PR:C
BEES IN PARADISE (1944, Brit.) PR:A
BEETLEJUICE (1988) PR:C
BEFORE AND AFTER (1985) PR:C
BEFORE DAWN (1933) PR:A
BEFORE HIM ALL ROME TREMBLED (1947, It.) PR:A
BEFORE I HANG (1940) PR:A
BEFORE I WAKE (SEE: SHADOW OF FEAR) (1956, Brit.)
BEFORE MIDNIGHT (1934) PR:A
BEFORE MORNING (1933) PR:A
BEFORE THE REVOLUTION (1964, It.) PR:C

BEFORE WINTER COMES (1969, Brit.) PR:C
BEG, BORROW OR STEAL (1937) PR:A
BEGGAR STUDENT, THE (1931, Brit.) PR:A
BEGGAR STUDENT, THE (1958, W. Ger.) PR:A
BEGGARS IN ERMINE (1934) PR:A
BEGGARS OF LIFE (1928) PR:A-C
BEGGAR'S OPERA, THE (1953, Brit.) PR:C
BEGGARS' OPERA (SEE: THREEPENNY OPERA, THE) (1931, US/Ger.)
BEGINNER'S LUCK (SEE: TWO DOLLAR BETTOR) (1951)
BEGINNER'S LUCK (1986) PR:O
BEGINNERS THREE, THE (SEE: FIRST TIME, THE) (1969)
BEGINNING OF THE END (1957) PR:C
BEGINNING OR THE END, THE (1947) PR:A
BEGINNING WAS SIN, THE (SEE: GREH) (1962, W. Ger./Yugo.)
BEGUILED, THE (1971) PR:O
BEHAVE YOURSELF (1951) PR:A
BEHEMOTH, THE SEA MONSTER (1959, Brit.) PR:A
BEHIND CITY LIGHTS (1945) PR:A
BEHIND CLOSED DOORS (SEE: ONE MYSTERIOUS NIGHT) (1944)
BEHIND CLOSED SHUTTERS (1952, It.) PR:O
BEHIND GREEN LIGHTS (1935) PR:A
BEHIND GREEN LIGHTS (1946) PR:A
BEHIND JURY DOORS (1933) PR:A
BEHIND LOCKED DOORS (1948) PR:A
BEHIND LOCKED DOORS (1976, South Africa) PR:O
BEHIND OFFICE DOORS (1931) PR:A
BEHIND PRISON GATES (1939) PR:A
BEHIND PRISON WALLS (1943) PR:A
BEHIND STONE WALLS (1932) PR:A
BEHIND THAT CURTAIN (1929) PR:A
BEHIND THE DOOR (SEE: MAN WITH NINE LIVES, THE) (1940)
BEHIND THE EIGHT BALL (1942) PR:A
BEHIND THE EVIDENCE (1935) PR:A
BEHIND THE HEADLINES (1937) PR:A
BEHIND THE HEADLINES (1956, Brit.) PR:A
BEHIND THE HIGH WALL (1956) PR:C
BEHIND THE IRON CURTAIN (SEE: IRON CURTAIN, THE) (1948)
BEHIND THE IRON MASK (1977, Aust.) PR:C
BEHIND THE MAKEUP (1930) PR:C
BEHIND THE MASK (1932) PR:C
BEHIND THE MASK (1946) PR:A
BEHIND THE MASK (1958, Brit.) PR:C
BEHIND THE MIKE (1937) PR:A
BEHIND THE NEWS (1940) PR:A
BEHIND THE RISING SUN (1943) PR:C
BEHIND THE SHUTTERS (SEE: CORRUPTION OF CHRIS MILLER, THE) (1979, Sp.)
BEHIND YOUR BACK (1937, Brit.) PR:A
BEHOLD A PALE HORSE (1964) PR:C
BEHOLD MY WIFE (1935) PR:C
BEHOLD WE LIVE (SEE: IF I WERE FREE) (1933)
BEING, THE (1983) PR:C
BEING THERE (1979) PR:C
BELA LUGOSI MEETS A BROOKLYN GORILLA (1952) PR:A
BELIEVE IN ME (1971) PR:O
BELIEVERS, THE (1987) PR:O
BELIZAIRE THE CAJUN (1986) PR:C
BELL' ANTONIO (1962, Fr./It.) PR:C-O
BELL, BOOK AND CANDLE (1958) PR:A
BELL-BOTTOM GEORGE (1943, Brit.) PR:A
BELL DIAMOND (1987) PR:C
BELL FOR ADANO, A (1945) PR:A
BELL JAR, THE (1979) PR:O
BELLA DONNA (1934, Brit.) PR:A
BELLA DONNA (1983, W. Ger.) PR:C
BELLAMY TRIAL (1929) PR:C
BELLBOY, THE (1960) PR:AA
BELLE DE JOUR (1968, Fr.) PR:O
BELLE LE GRAND (1951) PR:A
BELLE OF NEW YORK, THE (1952) PR:A
BELLE OF OLD MEXICO (1950) PR:A
BELLE OF THE NINETIES (1934) PR:A
BELLE OF THE YUKON (1944) PR:A
BELLE STARR (1941) PR:A
BELLE STARR'S DAUGHTER (1947) PR:A
BELLES OF ST. CLEMENTS, THE (1936, Brit.) PR:A
BELLES OF ST. TRINIAN'S, THE (1954, Brit.) PR:AA
BELLES ON THEIR TOES (1952) PR:AA
BELLISSIMA (1951, It.) PR:C
BELLMAN, THE (1947, Fr.) PR:C
BELLS, THE (1931, Brit.) PR:C
BELLS (1981, Can.) PR:O
BELLS ARE RINGING (1960) PR:AA
BELLS GO DOWN, THE (1943, Brit.) PR:A
BELLS OF CAPISTRANO (1942) PR:A
BELLS OF CORONADO (1950) PR:AA
BELLS OF ROSARITA (1945) PR:AA
BELLS OF ST. MARY'S, THE (1945) PR:AA
BELLS OF SAN ANGELO (1947) PR:A
BELLS OF SAN FERNANDO (1947) PR:A

BELLY OF AN ARCHITECT, THE (1987, Brit./It.) PR:O
BELOVED (1934) PR:A
BELOVED BACHELOR, THE (1931) PR:A
BELOVED BRAT (1938) PR:A
BELOVED ENEMY (1936) PR:A
BELOVED IMPOSTER (1936, Brit.) PR:A
BELOVED INFIDEL (1959) PR:A
BELOVED VAGABOND, THE (1936, Brit.) PR:A
BELOW THE BELT (1980) PR:C
BELOW THE BORDER (1942) PR:A
BELOW THE DEADLINE (1936) PR:A
BELOW THE DEADLINE (1946) PR:A
BELOW THE SEA (1933) PR:A
BELSTONE FOX, THE (1976, Brit.) PR:AA
BEN (1972) PR:A
BEN HUR (1959) PR:A
BEND OF THE RIVER (1952) PR:C
BENEATH THE PLANET OF THE APES (1970) PR:AA
BENEATH THE 12-MILE REEF (1953) PR:A
BENEATH WESTERN SKIES (1944) PR:A
BENGAL BRIGADE (1954) PR:A
BENGAL TIGER (1936) PR:A
BENGAZI (1955) PR:A-C
BENGELCHEN LIEBT KRUEZ UND QUER (SEE: 24-HOUR LOVER) (1970, W. Ger.)
BENJAMIN (1968, Fr.) PR:O
BENJAMIN (1973, W. Ger.) PR:AA
BENJAMIN OU LES MEMOIRES D'UN PUCEAU (SEE: BENJAMIN) (1968, Fr.)
BENJI (1974) PR:AA
BENJI THE HUNTED (1987) PR:AA
BENNY GOODMAN STORY, THE (1956) PR:AA
BENSON MURDER CASE, THE (1930) PR:A
BENVENUTA (1983, Fr.) PR:C
BEQUEST TO THE NATION (SEE: NELSON AFFAIR, THE) (1973, Brit.)
BERKELEY SQUARE (1933) PR:A
BERLIN AFFAIR, THE (1985, It./W. Ger.) PR:O
BERLIN ALEXANDERPLATZ (1933, Ger.) PR:A
BERLIN ALEXANDERPLATZ (1979, W. Ger.) PR:O
BERLIN CORRESPONDENT (1942) PR:A
BERLIN EXPRESS (1948) PR:C
BERLIN, APPOINTMENT FOR THE SPIES (SEE: SPY IN YOUR EYE) (1966, It.)
BERMONDSEY KID, THE (1933, Brit.) PR:A
BERMUDA AFFAIR (1956, Brit.) PR:A
BERMUDA MYSTERY (1944) PR:A
BERNADETTE OF LOURDES (1962, Fr.) PR:A
BERNARDINE (1957) PR:AA
BERRY GORDY'S THE LAST DRAGON (SEE: LAST DRAGON, THE) (1985)
BERSERK (1967, Brit.) PR:O
BERSERKER (1988) PR:O
BERT RIGBY, YOU'RE A FOOL (1989) PR:O
BEST DEFENSE (1984) PR:O
BEST FOOT FORWARD (1943) PR:A
BEST FRIENDS (1975) PR:O
BEST FRIENDS (1982) PR:A
BEST HOUSE IN LONDON, THE (1969, Brit.) PR:A
BEST LITTLE WHOREHOUSE IN TEXAS, THE (1982) PR:O
BEST MAN, THE (1964) PR:C
BEST MAN WINS, THE (1948) PR:AA
BEST MAN WINS, THE (1935) PR:A
BEST OF ENEMIES (1933) PR:A
BEST OF ENEMIES, THE (1962, Brit./It.) PR:A
BEST OF EVERYTHING, THE (1959) PR:C-O
BEST OF THE BADMEN (1951) PR:A
BEST OF THE BEST (1989) PR:C
BEST OF TIMES, THE (1986) PR:O
BEST SELLER (1987) PR:O
BEST THINGS IN LIFE ARE FREE, THE (1956) PR:AA
BEST WAY, THE (1978, Fr.) PR:C
BEST YEARS OF OUR LIVES, THE (1946) PR:A
BETRAYAL (1932, Brit.) PR:A
BETRAYAL (1939, Fr.) PR:A
BETRAYAL, THE (1948) PR:A
BETRAYAL, THE (1958, Brit.) PR:A
BETRAYAL (1983, Brit.) PR:O
BETRAYAL, THE (SEE: KAMILLA) (1984, Norway)
BETRAYAL FROM THE EAST (1945) PR:AA
BETRAYED (SEE: WHEN STANGERS MARRY) (1944)
BETRAYED (1954) PR:C
BETRAYED (1988) PR:O
BETRAYED WOMEN (1955) PR:C
BETSY, THE (1978) PR:C
BETTER A WIDOW (1969, Fr./It.) PR:O
BETTER LATE THAN NEVER (1983) PR:C
BETTER OFF DEAD (1985) PR:O
BETTER TOMORROW, A (1987, Hong Kong) PR:O
BETTY BLUE (1986, Fr.) PR:O
BETTY CO-ED (1946) PR:A
BETWEEN FIGHTING MEN (1932) PR:A
BETWEEN HEAVEN AND HELL (1956) PR:A
BETWEEN MEN (1935) PR:A
BETWEEN MIDNIGHT AND DAWN (1950) PR:C
BETWEEN THE LINES (1977) PR:C
BETWEEN TIME AND ETERNITY (1960, W. Ger.) PR:A

BETWEEN TWO WOMEN (1937) PR:A-C
BETWEEN TWO WOMEN (1944) PR:A
BETWEEN TWO WORLDS (1944) PR:A
BETWEEN US GIRLS (1942) PR:C
BEVERLY HILLS BRATS (1989) PR:C
BEVERLY HILLS COP (1984) PR:O
BEVERLY HILLS COP II (1987) PR:O
BEWARE (1946) PR:A
BEWARE, MY LOVELY (1952) PR:C
BEWARE OF BLONDIE (1950) PR:AA
BEWARE OF CHILDREN (1961, Brit.) PR:A
BEWARE OF LADIES (1937) PR:A
BEWARE OF PITY (1946, Brit.) PR:A
BEWARE SPOOKS (1939) PR:A
BEWARE! THE BLOB (1972) PR:A
BEWITCHED (1945) PR:C
BEYOND A REASONABLE DOUBT (1956) PR:C
BEYOND AND BACK (1978) PR:A
BEYOND ATLANTIS (1973, Phil.) PR:O
BEYOND EVIL (1980) PR:A
BEYOND FEAR (1977, Fr.) PR:C
BEYOND GLORY (1948) PR:A
BEYOND GOOD AND EVIL (1984, It./Fr./W. Ger.) PR:O
BEYOND MOMBASA (1957, Brit.) PR:A-C
BEYOND REASONABLE DOUBT (1980, New Zealand) PR:C
BEYOND THE BLUE HORIZON (1942) PR:A
BEYOND THE CITIES (1930, Brit.) PR:A
BEYOND THE CURTAIN (1960, Brit.) PR:A
BEYOND THE DOOR (1975, It./US) PR:O
BEYOND THE DOOR II (1979, It.) PR:O
BEYOND THE FOG (1981, Brit.) PR:O
BEYOND THE FOREST (1949) PR:C
BEYOND THE GATE (SEE: HUMAN EXPERIMENTS) (1980)
BEYOND THE LAST FRONTIER (1943) PR:A
BEYOND THE LAW (1934) PR:A
BEYOND THE LAW (1967, It.) PR:C
BEYOND THE LAW (1968) PR:C
BEYOND THE LIMIT (1983) PR:C
BEYOND THE LIVING (SEE: NURSE SHERRI) (1978)
BEYOND THE PECOS (1945) PR:A
BEYOND THE POSEIDON ADVENTURE (1979) PR:A-C
BEYOND THE PURPLE HILLS (1950) PR:A
BEYOND THE REEF (1981) PR:C
BEYOND THE RIO GRANDE (1930) PR:A
BEYOND THE RIVER (SEE: BOTTOM OF THE BOTTLE, THE) (1956)
BEYOND THE ROCKIES (1932) PR:A
BEYOND THE SACRAMENTO (1941) PR:A
BEYOND THE TIME BARRIER (1960) PR:C
BEYOND THE WALLS (1985, Israel) PR:O
BEYOND THERAPY (1987) PR:O
BEYOND THIS PLACE (SEE: WEB OF EVIDENCE) (1959, Brit.)
BEYOND TOMORROW (1940) PR:A
BEYOND VICTORY (1931) PR:C
BHOWANI JUNCTION (1956, Brit.) PR:C
BIANCO, ROSSO E. . . (SEE: WHITE SISTER) (1973, Fr./It./Sp.)
BIBLE. . . IN THE BEGINNING, THE (1966, US/It.) PR:AA
BICYCLE THIEF, THE (1948, It.) PR:A-C
BIDDY (1983, Brit.) PR:A
BIG (1988) PR:A-C
BIG AND THE BAD, THE (1971, It./Fr./Sp.) PR:C
BIG BAD MAMA (1974) PR:O
BIG BAD MAMA II (1987) PR:O
BIG BEAT, THE (1958) PR:A
BIG BIRD CAGE, THE (1972) PR:O
BIG BLOCKADE, THE (1942, Brit.) PR:A
BIG BLUE, THE (1988, Fr.) PR:A
BIG BLUE, THE (1989) PR:C
BIG BLUFF, THE (1933) PR:A
BIG BLUFF, THE (1955) PR:C
BIG BONANZA, THE (1944) PR:C
BIG BOODLE, THE (1957) PR:C
BIG BOSS, THE (1941) PR:A
BIG BOUNCE, THE (1969) PR:O
BIG BOY (1930) PR:A
BIG BRAIN, THE (1933) PR:A
BIG BRAWL, THE (1980) PR:C
BIG BROADCAST, THE (1932) PR:AA
BIG BROADCAST OF 1936, THE (1935) PR:AA
BIG BROADCAST OF 1937, THE (1936) PR:AA
BIG BROADCAST OF 1938, THE (1937) PR:AA
BIG BROWN EYES (1936) PR:A
BIG BUS, THE (1976) PR:A
BIG BUSINESS (1930, Brit.) PR:A
BIG BUSINESS (1934, Brit.) PR:A
BIG BUSINESS (1937) PR:A
BIG BUSINESS (1988) PR:C
BIG BUSINESS GIRL (1931) PR:A
BIG CAGE, THE (1933) PR:A
BIG CAPER, THE (1957) PR:C
BIG CARNIVAL, THE (1951) PR:O
BIG CAT, THE (1949) PR:C
BIG CATCH, THE (1968, Brit.) PR:A
BIG CHANCE, THE (1933) PR:A

BIG CHANCE, THE (1957, Brit.) PR:A
BIG CHASE, THE (1954) PR:A
BIG CHIEF, THE (1960, Fr.) PR:AA
BIG CHILL, THE (1983) PR:C
BIG CIRCUS, THE (1959) PR:A
BIG CITY (1937) PR:A
BIG CITY (1948) PR:AA
BIG CITY, THE (1963, India) PR:A
BIG CITY BLUES (1932) PR:C
BIG CLOCK, THE (1948) PR:C
BIG COMBO, THE (1955) PR:O
BIG COUNTRY, THE (1958) PR:A
BIG CUBE, THE (1969) PR:O
BIG DADDY (1969) PR:O
BIG DAY, THE (1960, Brit.) PR:A-C
BIG DEAL AT DODGE CITY (SEE: BIG HAND FOR THE LITTLE LADY, A) (1966)
BIG DEAL ON MADONNA STREET, THE (1958, It.) PR:A
BIG DOLL HOUSE, THE (1971) PR:O
BIG EASY, THE (1987) PR:O
BIG ENOUGH AND OLD ENOUGH (SEE: SABAGES FROM HELL) (1968)
BIG EXECUTIVE (1933) PR:A
BIG FELLA (1937, Brit.) PR:A
BIG FISHERMAN, THE (1959) PR:A-C
BIG FIX, THE (1947) PR:A
BIG FIX, THE (1978) PR:C
BIG FOOT (1973) PR:O
BIG FRAME, THE (1953, Brit.) PR:A
BIG GAMBLE, THE (1931) PR:A
BIG GAMBLE, THE (1961) PR:A
BIG GAME, THE (1936) PR:A
BIG GAME, THE (SEE: FLESH AND THE WOMAN) (1954, Fr./It.)
BIG GAME, THE (1972) PR:C
BIG GUNDOWN, THE (1968, It.) PR:A
BIG GUNS (SEE: NO WAY OUT) (1972, Fr./It.)
BIG GUSHER, THE (1951) PR:A
BIG GUY, THE (1939) PR:A
BIG HAND FOR THE LITTLE LADY, A (1966) PR:A
BIG HANGOVER, THE (1950) PR:A-C
BIG HEART, THE (SEE: MIRACLE ON 34TH STREET) (1947)
BIG HEARTED HERBERT (1934) PR:A
BIG HEAT, THE (1953) PR:C
BIG HOUSE, THE (1930) PR:C
BIG HOUSE, U.S.A. (1955) PR:O
BIG JACK (1949) PR:C
BIG JAKE (1971) PR:O
BIG JIM MC LAIN (1952) PR:C
BIG JOB, THE (1965, Brit.) PR:A
BIG KNIFE, THE (1955) PR:O
BIG LAND, THE (1957) PR:A
BIG LEAGUER, THE (1953) PR:A
BIG LIFT, THE (1950) PR:A-C
BIG MEAT EATER (1984, Can.) PR:O
BIG MO (SEE: MAURIE) (1973)
BIG MONEY (1930) PR:A
BIG MONEY, THE (1962, Brit.) PR:A
BIG MOUTH, THE (1967) PR:AA
BIG NEWS (1929) PR:A
BIG NIGHT, THE (1951) PR:C
BIG NIGHT, THE (1960) PR:C
BIG NOISE, THE (1936) PR:A
BIG NOISE, THE (1936, Brit.) PR:A
BIG NOISE, THE (1944) PR:AA
BIG NORTH, THE (SEE: WILD NORTH, THE) (1952)
BIG OPERATOR, THE (1959) PR:O
BIG PARADE, THE (1987, Chi.) PR:A-C
BIG PARTY, THE (1930) PR:A
BIG PAYOFF, THE (1933) PR:A
BIG PICTURE, THE (1989) PR:C
BIG POND, THE (1930) PR:A
BIG PUNCH, THE (1948) PR:A
BIG RACE, THE (1934) PR:AA
BIG RED (1962) PR:AA
BIG RED ONE, THE (1980) PR:C
BIG SCORE, THE (1983) PR:C
BIG SEARCH, THE (SEE: EAST OF KILIMANJARO) (1957)
BIG SHAKEDOWN, THE (1934) PR:A
BIG SHOT, THE (1931) PR:A
BIG SHOT, THE (1937) PR:A
BIG SHOT, THE (1942) PR:A
BIG SHOTS (1987) PR:C
BIG SHOW, THE (1937) PR:A
BIG SHOW, THE (1961) PR:A
BIG SHOW-OFF, THE (1945) PR:C
BIG SKY, THE (1952) PR:A
BIG SLEEP, THE (1946) PR:C
BIG SLEEP, THE (1978, Brit.) PR:C
BIG SOMBRERO, THE (1949) PR:A
BIG SPLASH, THE (1935, Brit.) PR:A
BIG STAMPEDE, THE (1932) PR:A
BIG STEAL, THE (1949) PR:C
BIG STORE, THE (1941) PR:AA
BIG STREET, THE (1942) PR:A
BIG SWITCH, THE (1970, Brit.) PR:O

BIG TIMBER (1950) PR:A-C
BIG TIME (1929) PR:A
BIG TIME OPERATORS (SEE: SMALLEST SHOW ON EARTH, THE) (1957, Brit.)
BIG TIME OR BUST (1934) PR:A
BIG TIP OFF, THE (1955) PR:C
BIG TOP PEE-WEE (1988) PR:A
BIG TOWN (1932) PR:C
BIG TOWN (1947) PR:AA
BIG TOWN, THE (1987) PR:O
BIG TOWN AFTER DARK (1947) PR:AA
BIG TOWN CZAR (1939) PR:C
BIG TOWN GIRL (1937) PR:A
BIG TOWN SCANDAL (1948) PR:AA
BIG TRAIL, THE (1930) PR:A
BIG TREES, THE (1952) PR:A-C
BIG TROUBLE (1986) PR:C
BIG TROUBLE IN LITTLE CHINA (1986) PR:C-O
BIG WEDNESDAY (1978) PR:A-C
BIG WHEEL, THE (1949) PR:A-C
BIGAMIST, THE (1953) PR:C
BIGGER SPLASH, A (1984) PR:O
BIGGER THAN LIFE (1956) PR:C
BIGGEST BUNDLE OF THEM ALL, THE (1968) PR:A
BIKINI BEACH (1964) PR:A
BIKINI SHOP, THE (SEE: MALIBU BIKINI SHOP) (1987)
BILA NEMOC (SEE: SKELETON ON HORSEBACK) (1940, Czech.)
BILL AND COO (1947) PR:AA
BILL & TED'S EXCELLENT ADVENTURE (1989) PR:A
BILL CRACKS DOWN (1937) PR:A
BILL OF DIVORCEMENT, A (1932) PR:A-C
BILL OF DIVORCEMENT, A (1940) PR:C
BILLIE (1965) PR:A
BILLION DOLLAR BRAIN (1967, Brit.) PR:C
BILLION DOLLAR HOBO, THE (1977) PR:A
BILLION DOLLAR SCANDAL (1932) PR:A
BILL'S LEGACY (1931, Brit.) PR:A
BILLY BUDD (1962, Brit.) PR:A
BILLY IN THE LOWLANDS (1979) PR:A-C
BILLY JACK (1971) PR:O
BILLY JACK GOES TO WASHINGTON (1977) PR:C
BILLY LIAR (1963, Brit.) PR:A-C
BILLY ROSE'S DIAMOND HORSESHOE (SEE: DIAMOND HORSESHOE) (1945)
BILLY ROSE'S JUMBO (SEE: JUMBO) (1962)
BILLY THE KID (1930) PR:A
BILLY THE KID (1941) PR:A
BILLY THE KID IN SANTA FE (1941) PR:A
BILLY THE KID RETURNS (1938) PR:A
BILLY THE KID TRAPPED (1942) PR:A
BILLY THE KID VS. DRACULA (1966) PR:A-C
BILLY THE KID WANTED (1941) PR:A
BILLY THE KID, SHERIFF OF SAGE VALLEY (SEE: SHERIFF OF SAGE VALLEY) (1942)
BILLY THE KID'S FIGHTING PALS (1941) PR:A
BILLY THE KID'S RANGE WAR (1941) PR:A
BILLY THE KID'S ROUNDUP (1941) PR:A
BILLY TWO HATS (1973, Brit.) PR:O
BILOXI BLUES (1988) PR:C-O
BIMBO THE GREAT (1961, W. Ger.) PR:A
BINGO BONGO (1983, It.) PR:AA
BINGO LONG TRAVELING ALL-STARS AND MOTOR KINGS, THE (1976) PR:A-C
BIOGRAPHY OF A BACHELOR GIRL (1935) PR:A
BIONIC BOY, THE (1977, Hong Kong/Phil.) PR:O
BIQUEFARRE (1983, Fr.) PR:A
BIRCH INTERVAL (1976) PR:A
BIRD (1988) PR:C-O
BIRD OF PARADISE (1932) PR:C
BIRD OF PARADISE (1951) PR:C
BIRD WATCH, THE (1983, Fr.) PR:C
BIRD WITH THE CRYSTAL PLUMAGE, THE (1969, It./W. Ger.) PR:C
BIRDMAN OF ALCATRAZ (1962) PR:C
BIRDS, THE (1963) PR:C
BIRDS AND THE BEES, THE (1956) PR:A
BIRDS AND THE BEES, THE (SEE: THREE DARLING DAUGHTERS) (1948)
BIRDS COME TO DIE IN PERU (1968, Fr.) PR:C
BIRDS DO IT (1966) PR:A
BIRDS OF A FEATHER (1931, Brit.) PR:AA
BIRDS OF A FEATHER (1935, Brit.) PR:A
BIRDS OF PREY (SEE: PERFECT ALIBI, THE) (1931, Brit.)
BIRDS OF PREY (1987, Can.) PR:C-O
BIRDS OF PREY (1988, Phil.) PR:C
BIRDS, THE BEES, AND THE ITALIANS, THE (1967, Fr./It.) PR:O
BIRDY (1984) PR:O
BIRTH OF A BABY, THE (1938) PR:C
BIRTH OF THE BLUES (1941) PR:A
BIRTHDAY PARTY, THE (1968, Brit.) PR:C
BIRTHDAY PRESENT, THE (1957, Brit.) PR:C
BIRUMA NO TATEGOTO (SEE: BURMESE HARP, THE) (1985, Jap.)
BIRUMANO TATEGOTO (SEE: HARP OF BURMA) (1956, Jap.)

BIS ZUM ENDE ALLER TAGE (SEE: GIRL FROM HONG KING) (1966, W. Ger.)
BISCUIT EATER, THE (1940) PR:AA
BISCUIT EATER, THE (1972) PR:AA
BISHOP MISBEHAVES, THE (1933) PR:AA
BISHOP MURDER CASE, THE (1930) PR:A
BISHOP'S MISADVENTURES, THE (SEE: BISHOP MISBEHAVES, THE) (1933)
BISHOP'S WIFE, THE (1947) PR:A
BITE THE BULLET (1975) PR:C
BITKA NA NERETVI (SEE: BATTLE OF NERETVA) (1969, US/W. Ger./Yugo.)
BITTER CREEK (1954) PR:A
BITTER HARVEST (1963, Brit.) PR:C
BITTER RICE (1950, It.) PR:O
BITTER SPRINGS (1950, Aus.) PR:A
BITTER SWEET (1933, Brit.) PR:A
BITTER SWEET (1940) PR:A
BITTER TEA OF GENERAL YEN, THE (1933) PR:C
BITTER TEARS OF PETRA VON KANT, THE (1972, W. Ger.) PR:O
BITTER VICTORY (1958, US/Fr.) PR:C
BITTERSWEET LOVE (1976) PR:C
BIZALOM (SEE: CONFIDENCE) (1980, Hung.)
BIZARRE BIZARRE (1939, Fr.) PR:A
BIZET'S CARMEN (1984, Fr./It.) PR:A-C
BLACK ABBOT, THE (1934, Brit.) PR:A
BLACK ACES (1937) PR:A
BLACK AND WHITE (1986, Fr.) PR:O
BLACK AND WHITE IN COLOR (1976, Fr.) PR:C
BLACK ANGEL, THE (1946) PR:A
BLACK ANGELS, THE (1970) PR:O
BLACK ARROW, THE (1948) PR:A
BLACK BANDIT, THE (1938) PR:A
BLACK BART (1948) PR:C
BLACK BEAUTY (1933) PR:AA
BLACK BEAUTY (1946) PR:AA
BLACK BEAUTY (1971, Brit./Sp./W. Ger.) PR:AA
BLACK BELLY OF THE TARANTULA, THE (1972, It./Fr.) PR:O
BLACK BELT JONES (1974) PR:O
BLACK BIRD, THE (1975) PR:A-C
BLACK BOOK, THE (1949) PR:A
BLACK CAESAR (1973) PR:O
BLACK CAMEL, THE (1931) PR:A
BLACK CASTLE, THE (1952) PR:C
BLACK CAT, THE (1934) PR:C
BLACK CAT, THE (1941) PR:A
BLACK CAT, THE (1966) PR:O
BLACK CAT, THE (SEE: KURONEKO) (1968, Jap.)
BLACK CAT, THE (1984, It./Brit.) PR:O
BLACK CAULDRON, THE (1985) PR:A-C
BLACK CHRISTMAS (1974, Can.) PR:O
BLACK COFFEE (1931, Brit.) PR:A
BLACK CREAM (SEE: TOGETHER FOR DAYS) (1972)
BLACK DAKOTAS, THE (1954) PR:A-C
BLACK DEVILS OF KALI, THE (SEE: MYSTERY OF THE BLACK JUNGLE) (1955)
BLACK DIAMONDS (1932, Brit.) PR:A
BLACK DIAMONDS (1940) PR:A
BLACK DOLL, THE (1938) PR:A
BLACK DRAGONS (1942) PR:A
BLACK EAGLE (1948) PR:A
BLACK EYE (1974) PR:O
BLACK EYES (1939, Brit.) PR:A
BLACK FLOWERS FOR THE BRIDE (SEE: SOMETHING FOR EVERYONE) (1970)
BLACK FRANKENSTEIN (SEE: BLACKENSTEIN) (1973)
BLACK FRIDAY (1940) PR:A
BLACK FURY (1935) PR:C
BLACK GESTAPO, THE (1975) PR:O
BLACK GIRL (1972) PR:O
BLACK GLOVE (1954, Brit.) PR:A
BLACK GOLD (1947) PR:A
BLACK GOLD (1963) PR:A-C
BLACK GUNN (1972) PR:O
BLACK HAND, THE (1950) PR:C
BLACK HAND GANG, THE (1930, Brit.) PR:A
BLACK HILLS (1948) PR:A
BLACK HILLS AMBUSH (1952) PR:A-C
BLACK HILLS EXPRESS (1943) PR:A
BLACK HOLE, THE (1979) PR:A-C
BLACK HORSE CANYON (1954) PR:A
BLACK ICE, THE (1957, Brit.) PR:A
BLACK JACK (SEE: CAPTAIN BLACK JACK) (1952, US/Fr.)
BLACK JACK (1973) PR:C
BLACK JACK (1979, Brit.) PR:AA
BLACK JOY (1977, Brit.) PR:O
BLACK KING (1932) PR:A
BLACK KLANSMAN, THE (1966) PR:O
BLACK KNIGHT, THE (1954, Brit.) PR:A-C
BLACK LASH, THE (1952) PR:A
BLACK LEGION (1937) PR:C
BLACK LIKE ME (1964) PR:C
BLACK LIMELIGHT (1938, Brit.) PR:A
BLACK MAGIC (1949) PR:C

BLACK MAMA, WHITE MAMA (1973) PR:O
BLACK MARBLE, THE (1980) PR:C-O
BLACK MARKET BABIES (1946) PR:A
BLACK MARKET RUSTLERS (1943) PR:A
BLACK MASK (1935, Brit.) PR:A
BLACK MEMORY (1947, Brit.) PR:A
BLACK MIDNIGHT (1949) PR:AA
BLACK MOON (1934) PR:C
BLACK MOON (1975, Fr.) PR:C
BLACK MOON RISING (1986) PR:O
BLACK NARCISSUS (1947, Brit.) PR:A-C
BLACK OAK CONSPIRACY (1977) PR:C
BLACK ORCHID, THE (1959) PR:C
BLACK ORPHEUS (1959, Fr./It./Braz.) PR:C
BLACK PANTHER, THE (1977, Brit.) PR:O
BLACK PARACHUTE, THE (1944) PR:A
BLACK PATCH (1957) PR:C
BLACK PIRATES, THE (1954, Mex.) PR:C
BLACK PIT OF DOCTOR M (1958, Mex.) PR:O
BLACK RAIN (1989) PR:O
BLACK RAVEN, THE (1943) PR:A
BLACK RIDER, THE (1954, Brit.) PR:A
BLACK ROOM, THE (1935) PR:C
BLACK ROOM, THE (1984) PR:O
BLACK ROSE, THE (1950) PR:A
BLACK ROSES (1936, Ger.) PR:A
BLACK ROSES (1989) PR:O
BLACK SABBATH (1963, US/It./Fr.) PR:O
BLACK SAMSON (1974) PR:O
BLACK SCORPION, THE (1957) PR:C
BLACK SHAMPOO (1976) PR:O
BLACK SHEEP (1935) PR:A
BLACK SHEEP OF WHITEHALL, THE (1941, Brit.) PR:A
BLACK SHIELD OF FALWORTH, THE (1954) PR:A-C
BLACK SIX, THE (1974) PR:C
BLACK SLEEP, THE (1956) PR:C
BLACK SPIDER, THE (1983, Switz.) PR:O
BLACK SPURS (1965) PR:A
BLACK STALLION, THE (1979) PR:AA
BLACK STALLION (SEE: RETURN OF WILDFIRE, THE) (1948)
BLACK STALLION RETURNS, THE (1983) PR:A-C
BLACK SUN, THE (1979, Czech.) PR:A
BLACK SUNDAY (1961, It.) PR:O
BLACK SUNDAY (1977) PR:C
BLACK SWAN, THE (1942) PR:A
BLACK TENT, THE (1956, Brit.) PR:A
BLACK 13 (1954, Brit.) PR:A
BLACK TIDE (SEE: STORMY CROSSING) (1956, Brit.)
BLACK TIGHTS (1962, Fr.) PR:A
BLACK TORMENT, THE (1965, Brit.) PR:A
BLACK TUESDAY (1955) PR:C
BLACK TULIP, THE (1937, Brit.) PR:A
BLACK VEIL FOR LISA, A (1969, It./W. Ger.) PR:C
BLACK WATCH, THE (1929) PR:C
BLACK WATERS (1929) PR:A
BLACK WHIP, THE (1956) PR:A
BLACK WIDOW (1951, Brit.) PR:A
BLACK WIDOW (1954) PR:C
BLACK WIDOW (1987) PR:O
BLACK WINDMILL, THE (1974, Brit.) PR:C
BLACK ZOO (1963) PR:C
BLACKBEARD THE PIRATE (1952) PR:A-C
BLACKBEARD'S GHOST (1968) PR:AA
BLACKBOARD JUNGLE, THE (1955) PR:C
BLACKENSTEIN (1973) PR:O
BLACKIE AND THE LAW (SEE: BOSTON BLACKIE AND THE LAW) (1946)
BLACKIE BOOKED ON SUSPICION (SEE: BOSTON BLACKIE BOOKED ON SUSPICION) (1945)
BLACKIE GOES TO HOLLYWOOD (SEE: BOSTON BLACKIE GOES TO HOLLYWOOD) (1942)
BLACKIE'S RENDEZVOUS (SEE: BOSTON BLACKIE'S RENDEZVOUS) (1945)
BLACKJACK KETCHUM, DESPERADO (1956) PR:A
BLACKMAIL (1929, Brit.) PR:A
BLACKMAIL (1939) PR:A
BLACKMAIL (1947) PR:A
BLACKMAILED (1951, Brit.) PR:A
BLACKMAILER (1936) PR:A
BLACKOUT (1940, Brit.) PR:A
BLACKOUT (1950, Brit.) PR:A
BLACKOUT (1954, Brit.) PR:A-C
BLACKOUT (1978, Fr./Can.) PR:A-C
BLACKOUT (1988) PR:O
BLACKSNAKE (SEE: SWEET SUZY) (1973)
BLACKWELL'S ISLAND (1939) PR:A
BLACULA (1972) PR:O
BLADE (1973) PR:O
BLADE IN THE DARK, A (1986, It.) PR:O
BLADE RUNNER (1982) PR:O
BLADES OF THE MUSKETEERS (1953) PR:A
BLAME IT ON RIO (1984) PR:O
BLAME IT ON THE NIGHT (1984) PR:C
BLAME THE WOMAN (1932, Brit.) PR:A
BLANCHE (1971, Fr.) PR:C
BLANCHE FURY (1948, Brit.) PR:A-C

BLARNEY (SEE: IRELAND'S BORDER LINE) (1939, Ireland)
BLARNEY KISS (1933, Brit.) PR:A
BLARNEY STONE, THE (SEE: BLARNEY KISS) (1933, Brit.)
BLAST OF SILENCE (1961) PR:C
BLAST-OFF (SEE: THOSE FANTASTIC FLYING FOOLS) (1967, Brit.)
BLASTFIGHTER (1985, It.) PR:O
BLAZE (1989) PR:O
BLAZE O' GLORY (1930) PR:A
BLAZE OF GLORY (1963, Brit.) PR:A-C
BLAZE OF NOON (1947) PR:A-C
BLAZING ARROWS (SEE: FIGHTING CARAVANS) (1931)
BLAZING BARRIERS (1937) PR:A
BLAZING FOREST, THE (1952) PR:A-C
BLAZING FRONTIER (1944) PR:A
BLAZING GUNS (1943) PR:A
BLAZING SADDLES (1974) PR:C-O
BLAZING SIX SHOOTERS (1940) PR:A
BLAZING SIXES (1937) PR:A
BLAZING SUN, THE (1950) PR:A
BLAZING TRAIL, THE (1949) PR:A
BLEAK MOMENTS (1972, Brit.) PR:C
BLESS 'EM ALL (1949, Brit.) PR:A
BLESS 'EM ALL (SEE: ACT, THE) (1984)
BLESS THE BEASTS AND CHILDREN (1971) PR:A-C
BLESS THEIR LITTLE HEARTS (1984) PR:O
BLESSED EVENT (1932) PR:A-C
BLIND ADVENTURE (1933) PR:A
BLIND ALIBI (1938) PR:A
BLIND ALLEY (1939) PR:C
BLIND ALLEY (SEE: PERFECT STRANGERS) (1984)
BLIND CHANCE (1982, Pol.) PR:O
BLIND CORNER (SEE: MAN IN THE DARK) (1963, Brit.)
BLIND DATE (1934) PR:A
BLIND DATE (SEE: CHANCE MEETING) (1960, Brit.)
BLIND DATE (1984) PR:O
BLIND DATE (1987) PR:C
BLIND DEAD, THE (1972, Sp.) PR:O
BLIND DESIRE (1948, Fr.) PR:A
BLIND DIRECTOR, THE (1986, W. Ger.) PR:O
BLIND FOLLY (1939, Brit.) PR:A
BLIND GODDESS, THE (1948, Brit.) PR:A
BLIND JUSTICE (1934, Brit.) PR:A
BLIND MAN'S BLUFF (1936, Brit.) PR:AA
BLIND MAN'S BLUFF (1952, Brit.) PR:A
BLIND MAN'S BLUFF (SEE: CAULDRON OF BLOOD) (1967, US/Sp.)
BLIND SPOT (1932, Brit.) PR:A
BLIND SPOT (1958, Brit.) PR:A
BLIND TERROR (SEE: SEE NO EVIL) (1971, Brit.)
BLIND TRUST (SEE: INTIMATE POWER) (1986, Can.)
BLIND WIVES (SEE: LADY SURRENDERS, A) (1930)
BLINDFOLD (1966) PR:A
BLINDMAN (1972, US/It.) PR:O
BLISS (1985, Aus.) PR:O
BLISS OF MRS. BLOSSOM, THE (1968, Brit.) PR:C
BLITHE SPIRIT (1945, Brit.) PR:A
BLOB, THE (1958) PR:A-C
BLOB, THE (1988) PR:O
BLOCK BUSTERS (1944) PR:A
BLOCK NOTES-DIE UN REGISTA-APPUNTI (SEE: INTERVISTA) (1987, It.)
BLOCKADE (1928, Brit.) PR:A
BLOCKADE (1929) PR:A
BLOCKADE (1938) PR:A
BLOCKHEADS (1938) PR:AA
BLOCKHOUSE, THE (1974, Brit.) PR:A
BLOND CHEAT (1938) PR:A
BLONDE ALIBI (1946) PR:A
BLONDE BAIT (1956, US/Brit.) PR:A
BLONDE BANDIT, THE (1950) PR:A-C
BLONDE BLACKMAILER (1955, Brit.) PR:A
BLONDE BOMBSHELL (SEE: BOMBSHELL) (1933)
BLONDE COMET (1941) PR:A
BLONDE CRAZY (1931) PR:A
BLONDE DYNAMITE (1950) PR:A
BLONDE FEVER (1944) PR:A
BLONDE FOR A DAY (1946) PR:A
BLONDE FOR DANGER (SEE: FLAMINGO AFFAIR, THE) (1948, Brit.)
BLONDE FROM BROOKLYN (1945) PR:A
BLONDE FROM PEKING, THE (1968, It./W. Ger./Fr.) PR:A
BLONDE FROM SINGAPORE, THE (1941) PR:A
BLONDE ICE (1949) PR:C
BLONDE IN A WHITE CAR (SEE: NUDE IN A WHITE CAR) (1960, Fr.)
BLONDE IN LOVE, A (SEE: LOVES OF A BLONDE) (1965, Czech.)
BLONDE INSPIRATION (1941) PR:A
BLONDE NIGHTINGALE (1931, Ger.) PR:A
BLONDE PICKUP (1955) PR:A
BLONDE RANSOM (1945) PR:A
BLONDE REPORTER, THE (SEE: SOB SISTER) (1931)

BLONDE SAVAGE (1947) PR:A
BLONDE SINNER (1956, Brit.) PR:C
BLONDE TROUBLE (1937) PR:A
BLONDE VENUS (1932) PR:C-O
BLONDE WIFE, THE (SEE: KISS THE OTHER SHEIK) (1968, Fr./It.)
BLONDES AT WORK (1938) PR:A
BLONDES FOR DANGER (1938, Brit.) PR:A
BLONDIE (1938) PR:AA
BLONDIE BRINGS UP BABY (1939) PR:AA
BLONDIE FOR VICTORY (1942) PR:A
BLONDIE GOES LATIN (1941) PR:AA
BLONDIE GOES TO COLLEGE (1942) PR:AA
BLONDIE HAS SERVANT TROUBLE (1940) PR:AA
BLONDIE HITS THE JACKPOT (1949) PR:AA
BLONDIE IN SOCIETY (1941) PR:AA
BLONDIE IN THE DOUGH (1947) PR:AA
BLONDIE JOHNSON (1933) PR:A
BLONDIE KNOWS BEST (1946) PR:AA
BLONDIE MEETS THE BOSS (1939) PR:AA
BLONDIE OF THE FOLLIES (1932) PR:A-C
BLONDIE ON A BUDGET (1940) PR:AA
BLONDIE PLAYS CUPID (1940) PR:AA
BLONDIE TAKES A VACATION (1939) PR:AA
BLONDIE'S ANNIVERSARY (1947) PR:AA
BLONDIE'S BIG DEAL (1949) PR:AA
BLONDIE'S BIG MOMENT (1947) PR:AA
BLONDIE'S BLESSED EVENT (1942) PR:AA
BLONDIE'S HERO (1950) PR:AA
BLONDIE'S HOLIDAY (1947) PR:AA
BLONDIE'S LUCKY DAY (1946) PR:AA
BLONDIE'S REWARD (1948) PR:AA
BLONDIE'S SECRET (1948) PR:AA
BLOOD (1974, Brit.) PR:C
BLOOD ALLEY (1955) PR:A-C
BLOOD AND BLACK LACE (1965, It.) PR:O
BLOOD AND GUTS (1978, Can.) PR:O
BLOOD AND LACE (1971) PR:O
BLOOD AND ROSES (1961, Fr./It.) PR:C-O
BLOOD AND SAND (1941) PR:C
BLOOD AND STEEL (1959) PR:A
BLOOD ARROW (1958) PR:A-C
BLOOD BATH (1966) PR:C
BLOOD BATH (1976) PR:O
BLOOD BEACH (1981) PR:C
BLOOD BEAST FROM OUTER SPACE (1965, Brit.) PR:C
BLOOD BEAST TERROR, THE (1969, Brit.) PR:C
BLOOD BRIDES (SEE: HATCHET FOR A HONEY-MOON) (1969, It./Sp.)
BLOOD BROTHER, THE (SEE: TEXAS PIONEERS) (1932)
BLOOD BROTHERS (SEE: BROTHERS) (1930)
BLOOD CEREMONY (SEE: FEMALE BUTCHER, THE) (1972, It./Sp.)
BLOOD COUPLE (SEE: GANJA AND HESS) (1973)
BLOOD CREATURE (SEE: TERROR IS A MAN) (1959)
BLOOD CROWD, THE (SEE: MC MASTERS, THE) (1970)
BLOOD DEMON, THE (1967, W. Ger.) PR:O
BLOOD DINER (1987) PR:O
BLOOD DRINKERS, THE (1966, US/Phil.) PR:O
BLOOD FEAST (1963) PR:O
BLOOD FEAST (1976, It.) PR:O
BLOOD FEUD (1979, It.) PR:O
BLOOD FIEND (SEE: THEATRE OF DEATH) (1967, Brit.)
BLOOD FOR DRACULA (SEE: ANDY WARHOL'S DRACULA) (1974, Fr./It.)
BLOOD FROM THE MUMMY'S TOMB (1972, Brit.) PR:O
BLOOD IN THE STREETS (1975, It./Fr.) PR:C
BLOOD IS MY HERITAGE (SEE: BLOOD OF DRACULA) (1957)
BLOOD LEGACY (SEE: LEGACY OF BLOOD) (1971)
BLOOD MAD (SEE: GLOVE, THE) (1980)
BLOOD MANIA (1971) PR:O
BLOOD MONEY (1933) PR:C
BLOOD MONEY (1974, US/Hong Kong/It./Sp.) PR:O
BLOOD OF A POET, THE (1930, Fr.) PR:C
BLOOD OF DRACULA (1957) PR:O
BLOOD OF DRACULA'S CASTLE (1967) PR:O
BLOOD OF FRANKENSTEIN (1970) PR:O
BLOOD OF FU MANCHU, THE (1968, US/Brit./Sp./W. Ger.) PR:O
BLOOD OF GHASTLY HORROR (SEE: PSYCHO A GO-GO!) (1965)
BLOOD OF THE UNDEAD (SEE: SCHIZO) (1977, Brit.)
BLOOD OF THE VAMPIRE (1958, Brit.) PR:O
BLOOD ON MY HANDS (SEE: KISS THE BLOOD OFF MY HANDS) (1948)
BLOOD ON SATAN'S CLAW, THE (1970, Brit.) PR:O
BLOOD ON THE ARROW (1964) PR:C
BLOOD ON THE MOON (1948) PR:A
BLOOD ON THE MOON (SEE: COP) (1988)
BLOOD ON THE SUN (1945) PR:C
BLOOD ORANGE (1953, Brit.) PR:A
BLOOD ORGY OF THE SHE-DEVILS (1973) PR:O

BLOOD QUEEN (SEE: LITTLE MOTHER) (1973, US/W. Ger./Yugo.)
BLOOD RELATIVES (1978, Fr./Can.) PR:O
BLOOD ROSE, THE (1970, Fr.) PR:O
BLOOD SEEKERS, THE (SEE: CAIN'S WAY) (1970)
BLOOD SIMPLE (1984) PR:O
BLOOD SISTERS (SEE: SISTERS) (1973)
BLOOD SISTERS (1987) PR:O
BLOOD SPATTERED BRIDE, THE (1974, Sp.) PR:O
BLOOD SUCKERS (SEE: DR. TERROR'S GALLERY OF HORRORS) (1967)
BLOOD, SWEAT AND FEAR (1975, It.) PR:C-O
BLOOD TIDE (1982) PR:O
BLOOD WATERS OF DOCTOR Z (1982) PR:O
BLOOD WEDDING (1981, Sp.) PR:A
BLOODBATH AT THE HOUSE OF DEATH (1984, Brit.) PR:C-O
BLOODBROTHERS (1978) PR:O
BLOODEATERS (1980) PR:C
BLOODFIST (1989) PR:O
BLOODHOUNDS OF BROADWAY (1952) PR:A
BLOODHOUNDS OF BROADWAY (1989) PR:C
BLOODLINE (1979) PR:O
BLOODLUST (1959) PR:O
BLOODSPORT (1988) PR:O
BLOODSUCKERS (SEE: INCENSE FOR THE DAMNED) (1971)
BLOODSUCKERS FROM OUTER SPACE (1987) PR:O
BLOODSUCKING FREAKS (1982) PR:O
BLOODTHIRSTY BUTCHERS (1970) PR:O
BLOODTHIRSTY EYES (SEE: LAKE OF DRACULA) (1973, Jap.)
BLOODY BIRTHDAY (1986) PR:O
BLOODY BROOD, THE (1959, Can.) PR:O
BLOODY BUSHIDO BLADE, THE (SEE: BUSHIDO BLADE, THE) (1982, US/Brit.)
BLOODY KIDS (1983, Brit.) PR:O
BLOODY MAMA (1970) PR:O
BLOODY PIT OF HORROR, THE (1965, US/It.) PR:O
BLOODY POM POMS (1988) PR:NR
BLOODY WEDNESDAY (1987) PR:O
BLOOMFIELD (1971, Brit./Israel) PR:C
BLOSSOM TIME (SEE: APRIL BLOSSOMS) (1937, Brit.)
BLOSSOMS IN THE DUST (1941) PR:A
BLOSSOMS ON BROADWAY (1937) PR:A
BLOW OUT (1981) PR:O
BLOW TO THE HEART (1983, It.) PR:O
BLOW-UP (1966, Brit.) PR:O
BLOW YOUR OWN TRUMPET (1958, Brit.) PR:A
BLOWING WILD (1953) PR:C
BLU ELETTRICO (SEE: ELECTRIC BLUE) (1988, It.)
BLUE (1968) PR:C
BLUE AND THE GOLD, THE (SEE: ANNAPOLIS STORY, AN) (1955)
BLUE ANGEL, THE (1930, Ger.) PR:O
BLUE ANGEL, THE (1959) PR:O
BLUE BIRD, THE (1940) PR:AA
BLUE BIRD, THE (1976, US/USSR) PR:AA
BLUE BLOOD (1951) PR:AA
BLUE BLOOD (1973, Brit.) PR:C
BLUE CANADIAN ROCKIES (1952) PR:A
BLUE CITY (1986) PR:O
BLUE CLAY (SEE: SON OF DAVY CROCKETT, THE) (1941)
BLUE COLLAR (1978) PR:O
BLUE COUNTRY, THE (1977, Fr.) PR:C-O
BLUE DAHLIA, THE (1946) PR:C
BLUE DANUBE (1932, Brit.) PR:A
BLUE DEMON VERSUS THE INFERNAL BRAINS (1967, Mex.) PR:O
BLUE DENIM (1959) PR:C-O
BLUE FIN (1978, Aus.) PR:A
BLUE GARDENIA, THE (1953) PR:C
BLUE GRASS OF KENTUCKY (1950) PR:AA
BLUE HAWAII (1961) PR:A
BLUE HEAVEN (1985) PR:O
BLUE IDOL, THE (1931, Hung.) PR:A
BLUE IGUANA, THE (1988) PR:O
BLUE JEAN COP (SEE: SHAKEDOWN) (1988)
BLUE JEANS (SEE: BLUE DENIM) (1959)
BLUE LAGOON, THE (1949, Brit.) PR:A-C
BLUE LAGOON, THE (1980) PR:O
BLUE LAMP, THE (1950, Brit.) PR:C
BLUE LIGHT, THE (1932, Ger.) PR:A
BLUE MAX, THE (1966) PR:C
BLUE MONKEY (1988) PR:O
BLUE MONTANA SKIES (1939) PR:AA
BLUE MURDER AT ST. TRINIAN'S (1958, Brit.) PR:AA
BLUE PARROT, THE (1953, Brit.) PR:A
BLUE PETER, THE (SEE: NAVY HEROES) (1955, Brit.)
BLUE SCAR (1949, Brit.) PR:A
BLUE SIERRA (SEE: COURAGE OF LASSIE) (1946)
BLUE SKIES (1946) PR:AA
BLUE SKIES AGAIN (1983) PR:A
BLUE SMOKE (1935, Brit.) PR:A
BLUE SQUADRON, THE (1934, Brit.) PR:A
BLUE STEEL (1934) PR:A
BLUE SUNSHINE (1978) PR:A

BLUE THUNDER (1983) PR:C
BLUE VEIL, THE (1947, Fr.) PR:A
BLUE VEIL, THE (1951) PR:A
BLUE VELVET (1986) PR:O
BLUE, WHITE, AND PERFECT (1941) PR:A
BLUEBEARD (1944) PR:A
BLUEBEARD (SEE: LANDRU) (1963, Fr./It.)
BLUEBEARD (1972, Fr./It./W. Ger.) PR:O
BLUEBEARD'S EIGHTH WIFE (1938) PR:A-C
BLUEBEARD'S TEN HONEYMOONS (1960, Brit.) PR:A-C
BLUEPRINT FOR DANGER (SEE: WALLET, THE) (1952, Brit.)
BLUEPRINT FOR MURDER, A (1953) PR:A-C
BLUEPRINT FOR ROBBERY (1961) PR:A
BLUES BROTHERS, THE (1980) PR:C-O
BLUES BUSTERS (1950) PR:AA
BLUES FOR LOVERS (1966, Brit.) PR:A
BLUES IN THE NIGHT (1941) PR:A
BLUES LA-CHOFESH HAGODOL (SEE: LATE SUMMER BLUES) (1988, Israel)
BLUME IN LOVE (1973) PR:O
BLUMEN FUER DEN MANN IM MOND (SEE: FLOWERS FOR THE MAN IN THE MOON) (1975, E. Ger.)
BMX BANDITS (1983, Aus.) PR:AA
BOARDWALK (1979) PR:C-O
BOAT, THE (1981, W. Ger.) PR:C-O
BOAT FROM SHANGHAI (1931, Brit.) PR:A
BOATNIKS, THE (1970) PR:AA
BOB AND CAROL AND TED AND ALICE (1969) PR:O
BOB LE FLAMBEUR (1955, Fr.) PR:C
BOB MATHIAS STORY, THE (1954) PR:AA
BOB, SON OF BATTLE (1947) PR:AA
BOBBIE JO AND THE OUTLAW (1976) PR:C-O
BOBBIKINS (1959, Brit.) PR:A
BOBBY DEERFIELD (1977) PR:C
BOBBY WARE IS MISSING (1955) PR:A
BOBO JACCO (SEE: JACKO AND LISE) (1979, Bel./Fr./Tahiti)
BOBO, THE (1967, Brit.) PR:A-C
BOB'S YOUR UNCLE (1941, Brit.) PR:A
BOCCACCIO (1936, Ger.) PR:A
BOCCACCIO '70 (1962, Fr./It.) PR:O
BODY AND SOUL (1931) PR:A
BODY AND SOUL (1947) PR:C
BODY AND SOUL (1981) PR:C
BODY DISAPPEARS, THE (1941) PR:A
BODY DOUBLE (1984) PR:O
BODY HEAT (1981) PR:O
BODY ROCK (1984) PR:C
BODY SAID NO!, THE (1950, Brit.) PR:AA
BODY SNATCHER, THE (1945) PR:A
BODY STEALERS, THE (1969, US/Brit.) PR:A
BODYGUARD (1948) PR:A
BODYHOLD (1950) PR:A
BOEFJE (1939, Ger.) PR:AA
BOEING BOEING (1965) PR:C
BOFORS GUN, THE (1968, Brit.) PR:A-C
BOGGY CREEK II (1985) PR:C
BOHEMIAN GIRL, THE (1936) PR:A
BOHEMIAN RAPTURE (1948, Czech.) PR:A
BOILING POINT, THE (1932) PR:C
BOKUTO KIDAN (SEE: TWIN SISTERS OF KYOTO) (1964, Jap.)
BOLD AND THE BRAVE, THE (1956) PR:A
BOLD CABALLERO, THE (1936) PR:A
BOLD CAVALIER, THE (SEE: BOLD CABALLERO, THE) (1936)
BOLD FRONTIERSMAN, THE (1948) PR:A
BOLDEST JOB IN THE WEST, THE (1971, It.) PR:A-C
BOLERO (1934) PR:A-C
BOLERO (1982, Fr.) PR:A
BOLERO (1984) PR:O
BOMB IN THE HIGH STREET (1961, Brit.) PR:A
BOMBA AND THE ELEPHANT STAMPEDE (SEE: ELEPHANT STAMPEDE) (1951)
BOMBA AND THE HIDDEN CITY (1950) PR:A
BOMBA AND THE JUNGLE GIRL (1952) PR:A
BOMBA AND THE LION HUNTERS (SEE: LION HUNTERS, THE) (1951)
BOMBA AND THE SAFARI DRUMS (SEE: SAFARI DRUMS) (1953)
BOMBA ON PANTHER ISLAND (1949) PR:A
BOMBA THE JUNGLE BOY (1949) PR:A
BOMBARDIER (1943) PR:A
BOMBARDMENT OF MONTE CARLO, THE (1931, Ger.) PR:A
BOMBAY CLIPPER (1942) PR:A
BOMBAY MAIL (1934) PR:A
BOMBAY TALKIE (1970, India) PR:C
BOMBEN AUF MONTE CARLO (SEE: BOMBARDMENT OF MONTE CARLO, THE) (1931, Ger.)
BOMBERS B-52 (1957) PR:A
BOMBER'S MOON (1943) PR:A
BOMBS OVER BURMA (1942) PR:A
BOMBS OVER CHINA (SEE: HONG KONG) (1951)
BOMBS OVER LONDON (1937, Brit.) PR:A
BOMBSHELL (1933) PR:A-C

BOMBSIGHT STOLEN (1941, Brit.) PR:A
BON VOYAGE (1962) PR:AA
BON VOYAGE, CHARLIE BROWN (AND DON'T COME BACK) (1980) PR:AA
BONA (1984, Phil.) PR:O
BONANZA TOWN (1951) PR:A
BONAVENTURE (SEE: THUNDER ON THE HILL) (1951)
BOND OF FEAR (1956, Brit.) PR:A
BOND STREET (1948, Brit.) PR:A
BONDAGE (1933) PR:C
BONDS OF HONOUR (SEE: NO RANSOM) (1935)
BONITINHA MAS ORDINARIA (SEE: PRETTY BUT WICKED) (1965, Braz.)
BONJOUR TRISTESSE (1958, Brit.) PR:C-O
BONNE CHANCE (1935, Fr.) PR:A
BONNIE AND CLYDE (1967) PR:O
BONNIE PARKER STORY, THE (1958) PR:O
BONNIE PRINCE CHARLIE (1948, Brit.) PR:A
BONNIE SCOTLAND (1935) PR:AA
BONZO GOES TO COLLEGE (1952) PR:AA
BOOBY TRAP (1957, Brit.) PR:A
BOOGENS, THE (1982) PR:A
BOOGEYMAN, THE (1980) PR:O
BOOGEYMAN II (1983) PR:O
BOOGIE MAN WILL GET YOU, THE (1942) PR:C
BOOK OF NUMBERS (1973) PR:O
BOOLOO (1938) PR:A
BOOM! (1968, US/Brit.) PR:O
BOOM TOWN (1940) PR:A
BOOM TOWN BADMEN (SEE: ROARING WESTWARD) (1949)
BOOMERANG (1934, Brit.) PR:A
BOOMERANG (1947) PR:C
BOOMERANG (1960, W. Ger.) PR:A-C
BOOST, THE (1988) PR:O
BOOT HILL (1969, It.) PR:A
BOOTHILL BRIGADE (1937) PR:A
BOOTLEGGERS (1974) PR:A-C
BOOTS AND SADDLES (1937) PR:A
BOOTS! BOOTS! (1934, Brit.) PR:A
BOOTS MALONE (1952) PR:A
BOOTS OF DESTINY (1937) PR:A
BOP GIRL GOES CALYPSO (1957) PR:A
BORDER, THE (1982) PR:O
BORDER BADMEN (1945) PR:A
BORDER BANDITS (1946) PR:A
BORDER BRIGANDS (1935) PR:A
BORDER BUCKAROOS (1943) PR:A
BORDER CABALLERO (1936) PR:A
BORDER CAFE (1937) PR:A
BORDER DEVILS (1932) PR:A
BORDER FEUD (1947) PR:A
BORDER FLIGHT (1936) PR:A
BORDER G-MAN (1938) PR:A
BORDER HEAT (1988) PR:O
BORDER INCIDENT (1949) PR:C
BORDER LAW (1931) PR:A
BORDER LEGION, THE (1930) PR:A
BORDER LEGION, THE (1940) PR:A
BORDER OUTLAWS (1950) PR:A
BORDER PATROL (SEE: LAWLESS BORDER) (1935)
BORDER PATROL (1943) PR:A
BORDER PATROLMAN, THE (1936) PR:A
BORDER PHANTOM (1937) PR:A
BORDER RANGERS (1950) PR:A
BORDER RIVER (1954) PR:A
BORDER ROMANCE (1930) PR:A
BORDER SADDLEMATES (1952) PR:A
BORDER STREET (1950, Pol.) PR:A
BORDER TREASURE (1950) PR:A
BORDER VIGILANTES (1941) PR:A
BORDER WOLVES (1938) PR:A
BORDERLAND (1937) PR:A
BORDERLINE (1950) PR:A
BORDERLINE (1980) PR:A
BORDERLINES (SEE: CARETAKERS, THE) (1963)
BORDERTOWN (1935) PR:C
BORDERTOWN GUNFIGHTERS (1943) PR:A
BORIS GODUNOV (1959, USSR) PR:A
BORN AGAIN (1978) PR:A
BORN AMERICAN (1986, US/Fin.) PR:O
BORN FOR GLORY (1935, Brit.) PR:A
BORN FOR TROUBLE (SEE: MURDER IN THE BIG HOUSE) (1942)
BORN FREE (1966, Brit.) PR:AA
BORN IN EAST L.A. (1987) PR:O
BORN IN FLAMES (1983) PR:O
BORN LOSERS, THE (1967) PR:O
BORN LUCKY (1932, Brit.) PR:A
BORN OF FIRE (1987, Brit.) PR:O
BORN ON THE FOURTH OF JULY (1989) PR:O
BORN RECKLESS (1930) PR:C
BORN RECKLESS (1937) PR:A
BORN RECKLESS (1959) PR:A
BORN THAT WAY (1937, Brit.) PR:A
BORN TO BE BAD (1934) PR:A
BORN TO BE BAD (1950) PR:A

BORN TO BE LOVED (1959) PR:A
BORN TO BE WILD (1938) PR:A
BORN TO DANCE (1936) PR:A
BORN TO FIGHT (1938) PR:A
BORN TO GAMBLE (1935) PR:A
BORN TO KILL (1947) PR:A
BORN TO KILL (1975) PR:O
BORN TO LOVE (1931) PR:A
BORN TO SING (1942) PR:A
BORN TO SPEED (1947) PR:A
BORN TO THE SADDLE (1953) PR:A
BORN TO THE WEST (1937) PR:A
BORN TO WIN (1971) PR:C
BORN WILD (1968) PR:C
BORN YESTERDAY (1951) PR:A
BORROW A MILLION (1934, Brit.) PR:A
BORROWED CLOTHES (1934, Brit.) PR:A
BORROWED HERO (1941) PR:A
BORROWED TROUBLE (1948) PR:A
BORROWED WIVES (1930) PR:A
BORROWING TROUBLE (1937) PR:A
BORSALINO (1970, Fr./It.) PR:O
BORSALINO AND CO. (1974, Fr.) PR:O
BOSAMBO (SEE: SANDERS OF THE RIVER) (1935, Brit.)
BOSS, THE (1956) PR:A
BOSS NIGGER (1974) PR:C
BOSS OF BIG TOWN (1943) PR:A
BOSS OF BULLION CITY (1941) PR:A
BOSS OF HANGTOWN MESA (1942) PR:A
BOSS OF LONELY VALLEY (1937) PR:A
BOSS OF RAWHIDE (1944) PR:A
BOSS RIDER OF GUN CREEK (1936) PR:A
BOSS' WIFE, THE (1986) PR:C-O
BOSS'S SON, THE (1978) PR:A
BOSTON BLACKIE AND THE LAW (1946) PR:A
BOSTON BLACKIE BOOKED ON SUSPICION (1945) PR:A
BOSTON BLACKIE GOES HOLLYWOOD (1942) PR:A
BOSTON BLACKIE'S CHINESE VENTURE (1949) PR:A
BOSTON BLACKIE'S RENDEZVOUS (1945) PR:A
BOSTON STRANGLER, THE (1968) PR:O
BOSTONIANS, THE (1984, Brit.) PR:A-C
BOTANY BAY (1953) PR:C
BOTH ENDS OF THE CANDLE (SEE: HELEN MORGAN STORY, THE) (1957)
BOTH SIDES OF THE LAW (1953, Brit.) PR:A
BOTTOM OF THE BOTTLE, THE (1956) PR:A
BOTTOMS UP (1934) PR:A
BOTTOMS UP (1960, Brit.) PR:A
BOUDOIR DIPLOMAT, THE (1930) PR:C
BOUDU SAVED FROM DROWNING (1932, Fr.) PR:C
BOUGHT (1931) PR:A-C
BOULDER DAM (1936) PR:A
BOULE DE SUIF (SEE: ANGEL AND THE SINNER, THE) (1947, Fr.)
BOULEVARD NIGHTS (1979) PR:O
BOUND FOR GLORY (1976) PR:A-C
BOUNTIFUL SUMMER (1951, USSR) PR:A
BOUNTY, THE (1984, Brit.) PR:O
BOUNTY HUNTER, THE (1954) PR:A
BOUNTY HUNTERS, THE (1970, It.) PR:A-C
BOUNTY KILLER, THE (1965) PR:A-C
BOUNTY KILLERS, THE (SEE: UGLY ONES, THE) (1968, It./Sp.)
BOURBON STREET (SEE: PASSION STREET, U.S.A.) (1964)
BOWERY, THE (1933) PR:A
BOWERY AT MIDNIGHT (1942) PR:A
BOWERY BATTALION (1951) PR:A
BOWERY BLITZKRIEG (1941) PR:A
BOWERY BOMBSHELL (1946) PR:A
BOWERY BOY (1940) PR:A
BOWERY BOYS MEET THE MONSTERS, THE (1954) PR:A
BOWERY BUCKAROOS (1947) PR:A
BOWERY CHAMPS (1944) PR:A
BOWERY TO BAGDAD (1955) PR:A
BOWERY TO BROADWAY (1944) PR:A
BOXCAR BERTHA (1972) PR:O
BOXER (1971, Pol.) PR:A
BOXER, THE (SEE: RIPPED-OFF) (1971, It.)
BOXOFFICE (1982) PR:C-O
BOY. . . A GIRL, A (1969) PR:O
BOY, A GIRL AND A BIKE, A (1949, Brit.) PR:A
BOY, A GIRL, AND A DOG, A (1946) PR:A
BOY AND HIS DOG, A (1975) PR:O
BOY AND THE BRIDGE, THE (1959, Brit.) PR:A
BOY AND THE PIRATES, THE (1960) PR:AA
BOY CRIED MURDER, THE (1966, Brit./W. Ger./Yugo.) PR:C-O
BOY, DID I GET A WRONG NUMBER! (1966) PR:AA
BOY FRIEND (1939) PR:A
BOY FRIEND, THE (1971, Brit.) PR:A
BOY FROM INDIANA (1950) PR:A
BOY FROM OKLAHOMA, THE (1954) PR:A
BOY IN BLUE, THE (1986, Can.) PR:C-O
BOY MEETS GIRL (1938) PR:A

BOY MEETS GIRL (1985, Fr.) PR:O
BOY NAMED CHARLIE BROWN, A (1969) PR:AA
BOY NEXT DOOR, THE (SEE: TO FIND A MAN) (1972)
BOY OF THE STREETS (1937) PR:A
BOY OF TWO WORLDS (SEE: LURE OF THE JUNGLE, THE) (1970, Den.)
BOY ON A DOLPHIN (1957) PR:C
BOY RENTS GIRL (SEE: CAN'T BUY ME LOVE) (1987)
BOY SLAVES (1938) PR:A
BOY SOLDIER (1987, Wales) PR:C-O
BOY TEN FEET TALL, A (1965, Brit.) PR:AA
BOY TROUBLE (1939) PR:A
BOY! WHAT A GIRL (1947) PR:A
BOY WHO CAUGHT A CROOK (1961) PR:AA
BOY WHO COULD FLY, THE (1986) PR:A
BOY WHO CRIED WEREWOLF, THE (1973) PR:A-C
BOY WHO STOLE A MILLION, THE (1960, Brit.) PR:AA
BOY WHO TURNED YELLOW, THE (1972, Brit.) PR:AA
BOY WITH THE GREEN HAIR, THE (1949) PR:AA
BOYD'S SHOP (1960, Brit.) PR:A
BOYFRIENDS AND GIRLFRIENDS (1988, Fr.) PR:A
BOYICHI AND THE SUPERMONSTER (SEE: GAMERA VERSUS GAOS) (1967, Jap.)
BOYS, THE (1962, Brit.) PR:C
BOYS FROM BRAZIL, THE (1978, US/Brit.) PR:C-O
BOYS FROM BROOKLYN, THE (SEE: BELA LUGOSI MEETS A BROOKLYN GORILLA) (1952)
BOYS FROM SYRACUSE, THE (1940) PR:A
BOYS IN BROWN (1949, Brit.) PR:A
BOYS IN COMPANY C, THE (1978, US/Hong Kong) PR:O
BOYS IN THE BAND, THE (1970) PR:O
BOYS NEXT DOOR, THE (1985) PR:O
BOYS' NIGHT OUT (1962) PR:C
BOYS OF PAUL STREET, THE (1969, Hung./US) PR:A
BOYS OF THE CITY (1940) PR:A
BOYS' RANCH (1946) PR:A
BOY'S REFORMATORY (1939) PR:A
BOYS TOWN (1938) PR:AA
BOYS WILL BE BOYS (1936, Brit.) PR:A
BOYS WILL BE GIRLS (1937, Brit.) PR:AA
BRACELETS (1931, Brit.) PR:A
BRADDOCK: MISSING IN ACTION III (1988) PR:O
BRADY'S ESCAPE (1984, US/Hung.) PR:C
BRAIN, THE (1965, Brit./W. Ger.) PR:A
BRAIN, THE (1969, Fr./US) PR:A
BRAIN, THE (1989, Can.) PR:O
BRAIN DAMAGE (1988) PR:O
BRAIN EATERS, THE (1958) PR:C
BRAIN FROM PLANET AROUS, THE (1958) PR:C
BRAIN MACHINE, THE (1955, Brit.) PR:A
BRAIN OF BLOOD (1971, US/Phil.) PR:C
BRAIN THAT WOULDN'T DIE, THE (1959) PR:O
BRAINSNATCHERS, THE (SEE: MAN WHO LIVED AGAIN, THE) (1936, Brit.)
BRAINSTORM (1965) PR:C
BRAINSTORM (1983) PR:C-O
BRAINWASHED (1961, W. Ger.) PR:A-C
BRAINWAVES (1983) PR:O
BRAMBLE BUSH, THE (1960) PR:O
BRAND OF FEAR (1949) PR:A
BRAND OF THE DEVIL (1944) PR:A
BRANDED (1931) PR:A
BRANDED (1951) PR:A
BRANDED (SEE: BAD BOY) (1938, Brit.)
BRANDED A COWARD (1935) PR:A
BRANDED MEN (1931) PR:A
BRANDY ASHORE (SEE: GREEN GROW THE RUSHES) (1951, Brit.)
BRANDY FOR THE PARSON (1952, Brit.) PR:A
BRANNIGAN (1975, Brit.) PR:A-C
BRASHER DOUBLOON, THE (1947) PR:A
BRASIL ANNO 2,000 (1968, Braz.) PR:A
BRASS BOTTLE, THE (1964) PR:A
BRASS LEGEND, THE (1956) PR:A
BRASS MONKEY (SEE: LUCKY MASCOT, THE) (1951, Brit.)
BRASS TARGET (1978) PR:A-C
BRAT, THE (1930, Brit.) PR:A
BRAT, THE (1931) PR:A
BRAT, THE (SEE: SONS OF NEW MEXICO) (1949)
BRAVADOS, THE (1958) PR:C
BRAVE AND THE BEAUTIFUL, THE (SEE: MAGNIFICENT MATADOR, THE) (1955)
BRAVE BULLS, THE (1951) PR:A
BRAVE DON'T CRY, THE (1952, Brit.) PR:A
BRAVE ONE, THE (1956) PR:AA
BRAVE WARRIOR (1952) PR:A
BRAVESTARR (1988) PR:A
BRAZIL (1944) PR:A
BRAZIL (1985, Brit.) PR:O
BREACH OF PROMISE (1932) PR:A
BREACH OF PROMISE (SEE: ADVENTURE IN BLACKMAIL) (1943, Brit.)
BREAD AND CHOCOLATE (1978, It.) PR:A
BREAD, LOVE AND DREAMS (1953, It.) PR:O
BREAD OF LOVE, THE (1954, Swed.) PR:A
BREAK, THE (1962, Brit.) PR:A
BREAK IN THE CIRCLE, THE (1957, Brit.) PR:A

BREAK LOOSE (SEE: PARADES) (1972)
BREAK OF DAY (1977, Aus.) PR:A
BREAK OF HEARTS (1935) PR:A
BREAK THE NEWS (1938, Brit.) PR:A
BREAK TO FREEDOM (SEE: ALBERT, R.N) (1955)
BREAKAWAY (1956, Brit.) PR:A
BREAKDANCE (SEE: BREAKIN') (1984)
BREAKDOWN (1953) PR:A
BREAKER! BREAKER! (1977) PR:C
BREAKER MORANT (1980, Aus.) PR:A-C
BREAKERS AHEAD (1935, Brit.) PR:A
BREAKERS AHEAD (1938, Brit.) PR:A
BREAKFAST AT MANCHESTER MORGUE (SEE:
    DON'T OPEN THE WINDOW) (1974, It./Sp.)
BREAKFAST AT TIFFANY'S (1961) PR:A
BREAKFAST CLUB, THE (1985) PR:O
BREAKFAST FOR TWO (1937) PR:A
BREAKFAST IN BED (1978) PR:C
BREAKFAST IN HOLLYWOOD (1946) PR:A
BREAKHEART PASS (1976) PR:C
BREAKIN' (1984) PR:A-C
BREAKIN' 2: ELECTRIC BOOGALOO (1984) PR:A-C
BREAKING ALL THE RULES (1985, Can.) PR:O
BREAKING AWAY (1979) PR:C-O
BREAKING GLASS (1980, Brit.) PR:C-O
BREAKING IN (1989) PR:C
BREAKING POINT, THE (1950) PR:A
BREAKING POINT, THE (SEE: GREAT ARMORED
    CAR SWINDLE, THE) (1964, Brit.)
BREAKING POINT (1976) PR:C-O
BREAKING THE ICE (1938) PR:A
BREAKING THE SOUND BARRIER (1952, Brit.) PR:A
BREAKOUT (1960, Brit.) PR:A
BREAKOUT (1975) PR:C
BREAKTHROUGH (1950) PR:A
BREAKTHROUGH (1978, W. Ger.) PR:C
BREATH OF LIFE (1962, Brit.) PR:A
BREATH OF SCANDAL (SEE: HIS GLORIOUS NIGHT)
    (1929)
BREATH OF SCANDAL, A (1960) PR:A
BREATHLESS (1959, Fr.) PR:O
BREATHLESS (1983) PR:O
BREED APART, A (1984) PR:A-C
BREED OF THE BORDER (1933) PR:A
BREEDERS (1986) PR:O
BREEZING HOME (1937) PR:A
BREEZY (1973) PR:O
BREWSTER MC CLOUD (1970) PR:C
BREWSTER'S MILLIONS (1935, Brit.) PR:A
BREWSTER'S MILLIONS (1945) PR:A
BREWSTER'S MILLIONS (1985) PR:O
BRIBE, THE (1949) PR:C
BRIDAL PATH, THE (1959, Brit.) PR:A
BRIDAL SUITE (1939) PR:A
BRIDE, THE (1973) PR:C-O
BRIDE, THE (1985) PR:C
BRIDE BY MISTAKE (1944) PR:A
BRIDE CAME C.O.D., THE (1941) PR:A
BRIDE COMES HOME, THE (1936) PR:A
BRIDE COMES TO YELLOW SKY, THE (SEE: FACE TO
    FACE) (1952)
BRIDE FOR HENRY, A (1937) PR:A
BRIDE FOR SALE (1949) PR:A
BRIDE GOES WILD, THE (1948) PR:A
BRIDE IS MUCH TOO BEAUTIFUL, THE (1958, Fr.)
    PR:O
BRIDE OF FRANKENSTEIN, THE (1935) PR:C
BRIDE OF THE DESERT (1929) PR:A
BRIDE OF THE GORILLA (1951) PR:A
BRIDE OF THE LAKE (1934, Brit.) PR:A
BRIDE OF THE MONSTER (1955) PR:A
BRIDE OF THE REGIMENT (1930) PR:A
BRIDE OF VENGEANCE (1949) PR:A
BRIDE WALKS OUT, THE (1936) PR:A
BRIDE WASN'T WILLING, THE (SEE: FRONTIER
    GAL) (1945)
BRIDE WITH A DOWRY (1954, USSR) PR:A
BRIDE WORE BLACK, THE (1968, Fr./It.) PR:C
BRIDE WORE BOOTS, THE (1946) PR:A
BRIDE WORE CRUTCHES, THE (1940) PR:A
BRIDE WORE RED, THE (1937) PR:A
BRIDEGROOM FOR TWO (1932, Brit.) PR:A
BRIDES ARE LIKE THAT (1936) PR:A
BRIDES OF BLOOD (1968, US/Phil.) PR:A
BRIDES OF DRACULA, THE (1960, Brit.) PR:O
BRIDES OF FU MANCHU, THE (1966, Brit.) PR:A
BRIDES TO BE (1934, Brit.) PR:A
BRIDGE, THE (1961, W. Ger.) PR:A
BRIDGE AT REMAGEN, THE (1969) PR:C
BRIDGE OF SAN LUIS REY, THE (1929) PR:A
BRIDGE OF SAN LUIS REY, THE (1944) PR:A
BRIDGE OF SIGHS (1936) PR:A
BRIDGE ON THE RIVER KWAI, THE (1957) PR:C
BRIDGE TO THE SUN (1961, US/Fr.) PR:A
BRIDGE TOO FAR, A (1977, Brit.) PR:C
BRIDGES AT TOKO-RI, THE (1954) PR:A
BRIEF ECSTASY (1937, Brit.) PR:A

BRIEF ENCOUNTER (1945, Brit.) PR:A
BRIEF MOMENT (1933) PR:A
BRIEF RAPTURE (1952, It.) PR:C
BRIEF VACATION, A (1975, It.) PR:C
BRIGADOON (1954) PR:A
BRIGAND, THE (1952) PR:A
BRIGAND OF KANDAHAR, THE (1965, Brit.) PR:A
BRIGGS FAMILY, THE (1940, Brit.) PR:A
BRIGHAM YOUNG – FRONTIERSMAN (1940) PR:A
BRIGHT EYES (1934) PR:AA
BRIGHT LEAF (1950) PR:A
BRIGHT LIGHTS (1931) PR:A
BRIGHT LIGHTS (1935) PR:A
BRIGHT LIGHTS, BIG CITY (1988) PR:O
BRIGHT ROAD (1953) PR:A
BRIGHT VICTORY (1951) PR:A
BRIGHTNESS (1988, Mali) PR:O
BRIGHTON BEACH MEMOIRS (1986) PR:C
BRIGHTON ROCK (1947, Brit.) PR:C
BRIGHTON STRANGLER, THE (1945) PR:AA
BRIGHTY OF THE GRAND CANYON (1967) PR:A
BRILLIANT MARRIAGE (1936) PR:A
BRIMSTONE (1949) PR:A
BRIMSTONE AND TREACLE (1982, Brit.) PR:C
BRING ME THE HEAD OF ALFREDO GARCIA (1974)
    PR:O
BRING ON THE GIRLS (1945) PR:A
BRING YOUR SMILE ALONG (1955) PR:A
BRINGING UP BABY (1938) PR:A
BRINGING UP FATHER (1946) PR:A
BRINK OF HELL (SEE: TOWARD THE UNKNOWN)
    (1956)
BRINK OF LIFE (1960, Swed.) PR:C-O
BRINK'S JOB, THE (1978) PR:A-C
BRITANNIA MEWS (SEE: AFFAIRS OF ADELAIDE)
    (1949, US/Brit.)
BRITANNIA OF BILLINGSGATE (1933, Brit.) PR:A
BRITISH AGENT (1934) PR:A
BRITISH INTELLIGENCE (1940) PR:A
BRITTANIA HOSPITAL (1982, Brit.) PR:C
BROADCAST NEWS (1987) PR:C-O
BROADMINDED (1931) PR:A
BROADWAY (1929) PR:A
BROADWAY (1942) PR:A
BROADWAY AHEAD (SEE: SWEETHEART OF THE
    CAMPUS) (1941)
BROADWAY BABIES (1929) PR:A
BROADWAY BAD (1933) PR:A
BROADWAY BIG SHOT (1942) PR:A
BROADWAY BILL (1934) PR:A
BROADWAY DANNY ROSE (1984) PR:A-C
BROADWAY GONDOLIER (1935) PR:A
BROADWAY HOOFER, THE (1929) PR:A
BROADWAY HOSTESS (1935) PR:A
BROADWAY LIMITED (1941) PR:A
BROADWAY MELODY, THE (1929) PR:A
BROADWAY MELODY OF 1936 (1935) PR:A
BROADWAY MELODY OF '38 (1937) PR:A
BROADWAY MELODY OF 1940 (1940) PR:A
BROADWAY MUSKETEERS (1938) PR:A
BROADWAY RHYTHM (1944) PR:A
BROADWAY SCANDALS (1929) PR:A
BROADWAY SERENADE (1939) PR:A
BROADWAY SINGER (SEE: TORCH SINGER) (1933)
BROADWAY THROUGH A KEYHOLE (1933) PR:A
BROADWAY TO CHEYENNE (1932) PR:A
BROADWAY TO HOLLYWOOD (1933) PR:A
BROKEN ARROW (1950) PR:A
BROKEN BLOSSOMS (1936, Brit.) PR:A
BROKEN DISHES (SEE: TOO YOUNG TO MARRY)
    (1931)
BROKEN DREAMS (1933) PR:A
BROKEN ENGLISH (1981) PR:O
BROKEN HEARTS AND NOSES (SEE: CRIMEWAVE)
    (1985)
BROKEN HORSESHOE, THE (1953, Brit.) PR:A
BROKEN JOURNEY (1948, Brit.) PR:A
BROKEN LANCE (1954) PR:A
BROKEN LAND, THE (1962) PR:A
BROKEN LINKS (SEE: LEFTOVER LADIES) (1931)
BROKEN LOVE (1946, It.) PR:A
BROKEN LULLABY (1932) PR:A
BROKEN MELODY, THE (1934, Brit.) PR:A
BROKEN MELODY (1938, Aus.) PR:A
BROKEN MIRRORS (1985, Neth.) PR:O
BROKEN ROSARY, THE (1934, Brit.) PR:A
BROKEN STAR, THE (1956) PR:A
BROKEN WING, THE (1932) PR:A
BROLLOPSBESVAR (SEE: SWEDISH WEDDING
    NIGHT) (1965, Swed.)
BRONCO BILLY (1980) PR:C
BRONCO BULLFROG (1972, Brit.) PR:A
BRONCO BUSTER (1952) PR:A
BRONTE SISTERS, THE (1979, Fr.) PR:A
BRONX WARRIORS (SEE: 1990: THE BRONX WAR-
    RIORS) (1983, It.)
BRONZE BUCKAROO, THE (1939) PR:A
BROOD, THE (1979, Can.) PR:C

BROOKLYN ORCHID (1942) PR:A
BROTH OF A BOY (1959, Brit.) PR:A
BROTHER ALFRED (1932, Brit.) PR:A
BROTHER FROM ANOTHER PLANET, THE (1984) PR:O
BROTHER JOHN (1971) PR:A
BROTHER ORCHID (1940) PR:A
BROTHER RAT (1938) PR:A
BROTHER RAT AND A BABY (1940) PR:A
BROTHER SUN, SISTER MOON (1973, Brit./It.) PR:A
BROTHERHOOD, THE (1968) PR:C
BROTHERHOOD OF SATAN, THE (1971) PR:C-O
BROTHERHOOD OF THE YAKUZA (SEE: YAKUZA,
    THE) (1975)
BROTHERLY LOVE (1970, Brit.) PR:O
BROTHERS (1930) PR:A
BROTHERS, THE (1948, Brit.) PR:A
BROTHERS (1977) PR:C
BROTHERS (1984, Aus.) PR:O
BROTHERS AND SISTERS (1980, Brit.) PR:A
BROTHERS IN LAW (1957, Brit.) PR:A
BROTHERS IN THE SADDLE (1949) PR:A
BROTHERS KARAMAZOV, THE (SEE: KARAMAZOV)
    (1931, Ger.)
BROTHERS KARAMAZOV, THE (1958) PR:C-O
BROTHERS OF THE WEST (1938) PR:A
BROTHERS O'TOOLE, THE (1973) PR:A
BROTHERS RICO, THE (1957) PR:C
BROWN ON RESOLUTION (SEE: BORN FOR GLORY)
    (1935, Brit.)
BROWN SUGAR (1931, Brit.) PR:A
BROWN WALLET, THE (1936, Brit.) PR:A
BROWNIE (SEE: DARING YOUNG MAN, THE) (1942)
BROWNING VERSION, THE (1951, Brit.) PR:A
BRUBAKER (1980) PR:C-O
BRUCE LEE AND I (1976, Chi.) PR:C-O
BRUCE LEE – TRUE STORY (1976, Chi.) PR:C-O
BRUCIA, RAGAZZO, BRUCIA (SEE: WOMAN ON
    FIRE, A) (1970, It.)
BRUSHFIRE! (1962) PR:A
BRUTE, THE (1952, Mex.) PR:A-C
BRUTE AND THE BEAST, THE (1968, It.) PR:C
BRUTE FORCE (1947) PR:C
BRUTE MAN, THE (1946) PR:A
BRUTTI, SPORCHI E CATTIVI (SEE: DOWN AND
    DIRTY) (1976, It.)
BUBBLE, THE (1967) PR:A
BUCCANEER, THE (1938) PR:A
BUCCANEER, THE (1958) PR:A
BUCCANEER'S GIRL (1950) PR:A
BUCHAMUKURE DAIHAKKEN (SEE: COMPUTER
    FREE-FOR-ALL) (1969, Jap.)
BUCHANAN RIDES ALONE (1958) PR:A
BUCK AND THE PREACHER (1972) PR:C
BUCK BENNY RIDES AGAIN (1940) PR:A
BUCK PRIVATES (1941) PR:AA
BUCK PRIVATES COME HOME (1947) PR:AA
BUCK ROGERS IN THE 25TH CENTURY (1979) PR:A-C
BUCKAROO BANZAI (SEE: ADVENTURES OF
    BUCAKAROO BANZAI: ACROSS THE 8TH DIMEN-
    SION, THE) (1984)
BUCKAROO FROM POWDER RIVER (1948) PR:A
BUCKAROO SHERIFF OF TEXAS (1951) PR:A
BUCKET OF BLOOD (1934, Brit.) PR:O
BUCKET OF BLOOD, A (1959) PR:A
BUCKSKIN (1968) PR:A
BUCKSKIN FRONTIER (1943) PR:A
BUCKSKIN LADY, THE (1957) PR:A
BUCKSTONE COUNTY PRISON (SEE: SEABO) (1978)
BUCKTOWN (1975) PR:C
BUDDHA (1965, Jap.) PR:C
BUDDIES (1983, Aus.) PR:A
BUDDIES (1985) PR:O
BUDDY BUDDY (1981) PR:C
BUDDY HOLLY STORY, THE (1978) PR:A-C
BUDDY SYSTEM, THE (1984) PR:A-C
BUFFALO BILL (1944) PR:A
*BUFFALO BILL AND THE INDIANS, OR SITTING
    BULL'S HISTORY LESSON* (1976) PR:C
BUFFALO BILL, HERO OF THE FAR WEST (1962, It.)
    PR:A
BUFFALO BILL IN TOMAHAWK TERRITORY (1952)
    PR:A
BUFFALO BILL RIDES AGAIN (1947) PR:A
BUFFALO GUN (1961) PR:A
BUG (1975) PR:A-C
BUGLE SOUNDS, THE (1941) PR:A
BUGLES IN THE AFTERNOON (1952) PR:A
BUGS BUNNY/ROAD-RUNNER MOVIE, THE (SEE:
    GREAT AMERICAN BUGS BUNNY-ROAD RUNNER
    CHASE) (1979)
BUGS BUNNY, SUPERSTAR (1975) PR:A
BUGS BUNNY'S THIRD MOVIE – 1001 RABBIT TALES
    (1982) PR:AA
BUGSY MALONE (1976, Brit.) PR:AA
BUILD MY GALLOWS HIGH (SEE: OUT OF THE
    PAST) (1947)
BULL DURHAM (1988) PR:O
BULLDOG BREED, THE (1960, Brit.) PR:A

BULLDOG DRUMMOND (1929) PR:A
BULLDOG DRUMMOND AT BAY (1937, Brit.) PR:A
BULLDOG DRUMMOND COMES BACK (1937) PR:A
BULLDOG DRUMMOND ESCAPES (1937) PR:A
BULLDOG DRUMMOND IN AFRICA (1938) PR:A
BULLDOG DRUMMOND STRIKES BACK (1934) PR:A
BULLDOG DRUMMOND'S BRIDE (1939) PR:A
BULLDOG DRUMMOND'S PERIL (1938) PR:A
BULLDOG DRUMMOND'S REVENGE (1937) PR:A
BULLDOG DRUMMOND'S SECRET POLICE (1939) PR:A
BULLDOG EDITION (1936) PR:A
BULLDOG JACK (SEE: ALIAS BULLDOG DRUM-
    MOND) (1935, Brit.)
BULLDOG SEES IT THROUGH (1940, Brit.) PR:A
BULLET CODE (1940) PR:A
BULLET FOR A BADMAN (1964) PR:A
BULLET FOR JOEY, A (1955) PR:A
BULLET FOR PRETTY BOY, A (1970) PR:C
BULLET FOR SANDOVAL, A (1970, It./Sp.) PR:C
BULLET FOR STEFANO (1950, It.) PR:A
BULLET FOR THE GENERAL, A (1967, It.) PR:C
BULLET IS WAITING, A (1954) PR:A
BULLET SCARS (1942) PR:A
BULLETPROOF (1988) PR:O
BULLETS FOR O'HARA (1941) PR:A
BULLETS FOR RUSTLERS (1940) PR:A
BULLETS OR BALLOTS (1936) PR:A
BULLFIGHTER AND THE LADY (1951) PR:A
BULLFIGHTERS, THE (1945) PR:A
BULLIES (1986, Can.) PR:O
BULLITT (1968) PR:C
BULLSHOT (1983) PR:A-C
BULLWHIP (1958) PR:A
BUMP IN THE NIGHT (SEE: FINAL TERROR, THE)
    (1983)
BUNCO SQUAD (1950) PR:A
BUNDLE OF JOY (1956) PR:A
BUNDLE OF TROUBLE (SEE: BLONDIE'S BIG MO-
    MENT) (1947)
BUNGALOW 13 (1948) PR:A
BUNKER BEAN (1936) PR:A
BUNNY LAKE IS MISSING (1965, Brit.) PR:C
BUNNY O'HARE (1971) PR:C
BUONA SERA, MRS. CAMPBELL (1968, It.) PR:C
BURAIKAN (SEE: SCANDALOUS ADVENTURES OF
    BURAIKAN, THE) (1970, Jap.)
BURARI BURABURA MONOGATARI (SEE: MY
    HOBO) (1963, Jap.)
'BURBS, THE (1989) PR:A-C
BUREAU OF MISSING PERSONS (1933) PR:A
BURG THEATRE (1936, Ger.) PR:A
BURGLAR, THE (1956) PR:A
BURGLAR (1987) PR:O
BURGLARS, THE (1972, Fr./It.) PR:C
BURIED ALIVE (1939) PR:A
BURIED ALIVE (1951, It.) PR:C
BURIED ALIVE (1984, It.) PR:O
BURKE AND HARE (1972, Brit.) PR:O
BURKE & WILLS (1985, Aus.) PR:A-C
BURMA CONVOY (1941) PR:A
BURMESE HARP, THE (1985, Jap.) PR:O
BURMESE HARP (SEE: HARP OF BURMA) (1956, Jap.)
BURMESE HARP, THE (1956, Jap.) PR:C-O
BURN! (1969, Fr./It.) PR:A
BURN 'EM UP O'CONNOR (1939) PR:A
BURN OUT (SEE: JOURNEY INTO FEAR) (1976, Can.)
BURN, WITCH, BURN! (1962, Brit.) PR:O
BURNING, THE (1981) PR:O
BURNING AN ILLUSION (1982, Brit.) PR:C
BURNING CROSS, THE (1947) PR:C
BURNING GOLD (1936) PR:A
BURNING HEARTS (SEE: KOLBERG) (1945, Ger.)
BURNING HILLS, THE (1956) PR:A
BURNING QUESTION, THE (SEE: REEFER MADNESS)
    (1936)
BURNING SECRET (1988, US/Brit./W. Ger.) PR:C
BURNING UP (1930) PR:A
BURNING YEARS, THE (1979, It.) PR:O
BURNT EVIDENCE (1954, Brit.) PR:A
BURNT OFFERING (SEE: PASSPORT TO HELL) (1932)
BURNT OFFERINGS (1976) PR:C-O
BURY ME AN ANGEL (1972) PR:O
BURY ME DEAD (1947) PR:C
BURY ME NOT ON THE LONE PRAIRIE (1941) PR:A
BUS IS COMING, THE (1971) PR:C-O
BUS RILEY'S BACK IN TOWN (1965) PR:A
BUS STOP (1956) PR:A
BUSH CHRISTMAS (1947, Aus.) PR:AA
BUSH CHRISTMAS (1983, Aus.) PR:AA
BUSHBABY, THE (1970. Brit.) PR:AA
BUSHIDO BLADE, THE (1982, US/Brit.) PR:O
BUSHWHACKERS, THE (1952) PR:A
BUSINESS AND PLEASURE (1932) PR:A
BUSINESSMAN'S LUNCH, THE (SEE: MID-DAY MIS-
    TRESS) (1968)
BUSMAN'S HOLIDAY (1936, Brit.) PR:A
BUSMAN'S HONEYMOON (1940, Brit.) PR:A
BUSSES ROAR (1942) PR:A

BUSTED UP (1986, Can.) PR:O
BUSTER (1988, Brit.) PR:C-O
BUSTER AND BILLIE (1973) PR:C
BUSTER KEATON STORY, THE (1957) PR:A
BUSTIN' LOOSE (1981) PR:O
BUSTING (1974) PR:C
BUSYBODY, THE (SEE: KIBITZER, THE) (1929)
BUSYBODY, THE (1967) PR:A
BUT NOT FOR ME (1959) PR:A
BUT NOT IN VAIN (1948, Brit.) PR:A
BUT THE FLESH IS WEAK (1932) PR:A
BUTCH AND SUNDANCE: THE EARLY DAYS (1979)
    PR:C
BUTCH CASSIDY AND THE SUNDANCE KID (1969)
    PR:A
BUTCH MINDS THE BABY (1942) PR:A
BUTCHER, THE (SEE: LE BOUCHER) (1971, Fr.)
BUTCHER BAKER (NIGHTMARE MAKER) (1982) PR:O
BUTLER'S DILEMMA, THE (1943, Brit.) PR:A
BUTLEY (1974, Brit.) PR:O
BUTTERCUP CHAIN, THE (1971, Brit.) PR:O
BUTTERFIELD 8 (1960) PR:C
BUTTERFLIES ARE FREE (1972) PR:A
BUTTERFLY (1982) PR:O
BUTTERFLY AFFAIR, THE (SEE: POPSY POP) (1971,
    Fr.)
BUTTERFLY ON THE SHOULDER, A (1978, Fr.) PR:C-O
BUY & CELL (1989) PR:C
BUY ME THAT TOWN (1941) PR:A
BWANA DEVIL (1953) PR:A
BY APPOINTMENT ONLY (1933) PR:A
BY CANDLELIGHT (1934) PR:A
BY DESIGN (1982) PR:O
BY HOOK OR BY CROOK (SEE: I DOOD IT) (1943)
BY LOVE POSSESSED (1961) PR:O
BY THE LIGHT OF THE SILVERY MOON (1953) PR:A
BY WHOSE HAND? (1932) PR:A
BY YOUR LEAVE (1935) PR:A
BYAKUYA NO YOJO (SEE: TEMPTRESS AND THE
    MONK, THE) (1963, Jap.)
BYE BYE BABY (1989, It.) PR:O
BYE BYE BARBARA (1969, Fr.) PR:A
BYE BYE BIRDIE (1963) PR:A
BYE BYE BRAVERMAN (1968) PR:A
BYE-BYE BRAZIL (1980, Braz.) PR:C-O
BYE BYE MONKEY (1978, It./Fr.) PR:O
BYGONES (1988, Neth.) PR:C
BYPASS TO HAPPINESS (1934, Brit.) PR:A

C

C-MAN (1949) PR:A
C.H.U.D. (1984) PR:O
CA N'ARRIVE QU'AUX AUTRES (SEE: IT ONLY HAP-
    PENS TO OTHERS) (1971, Fr./It.)
CA S'EST PASSE A ROME (SEE: FROM A ROMAN
    BALCONY) (1961, Fr./It.)
CABARET (1972) PR:C
CABIN IN THE COTTON, THE (1932) PR:A-C
CABIN IN THE SKY (1943) PR:AA
CABINET OF CALIGARI, THE (1962) PR:A
CABIRIA (SEE: NIGHTS OF CABIRIA) (1957)
CABOBLANCO (1981) PR:C
CABRIOLA (SEE: EVERY DAY IS A HOLIDAY) (1966,
    Sp.)
CACTUS (1986, Aus.) PR:C
CACTUS FLOWER (1969) PR:C
CACTUS IN THE SNOW (1972) PR:A
CACTUS JACK (SEE: VILLAIN, THE) (1979)
CADDIE (1976, Aus.) PR:C
CADDY, THE (1953) PR:A
CADDYSHACK (1980) PR:C-O
CADDYSHACK II (1988) PR:C
CADET GIRL (1941) PR:A
CADET-ROUSSELLE (1954, Fr.) PR:A
CAESAR AND CLEOPATRA (1946, Brit.) PR:A
CAESAR THE CONQUEROR (1963, It.) PR:C
CAFE COLETTE (1937, Brit.) PR:A
CAFE DE PARIS (1938, Fr.) PR:A
CAFE EXPRESS (1980, It.) PR:C
CAFE HOSTESS (1940) PR:A
CAFE MASCOT (1936, Brit.) PR:A
CAFE METROPOLE (1937) PR:A-C
CAFE OF THE SEVEN SINNERS (SEE: SEVEN SIN-
    NERS) (1940)
CAFE SOCIETY (1939) PR:A
CAFFE ITALIA (1985, Can.) PR:C-O
CAGE (1989) PR:O
CAGE OF DOOM (SEE: TERROR FROM THE YEAR
    5000) (1958)
CAGE OF EVIL (1960) PR:A-C
CAGE OF GOLD (1950, Brit.) PR:A
CAGE OF NIGHTINGALES, A (1947, Fr.) PR:A
CAGED (1950) PR:O
CAGED FURY (1948) PR:A
CAGED FURY (1984, Phil.) PR:O
CAGED HEAT (SEE: RENEGADE GIRLS) (1974)
CAGED WOMEN (1984, It./Fr.) PR:O
CAGLIOSTRO (1975, It.) PR:C

CAHILL, US MARSHAL (1973) PR:C
CAIN AND MABEL (1936) PR:A
CAINE MUTINY, THE (1954) PR:A
CAIN'S WAY (1970) PR:O
CAIRO (1942) PR:A
CAIRO (1963, US/Brit.) PR:A
CAIRO ROAD (1950, Brit.) PR:A
CAL (1984, Ireland) PR:O
CALABUCH (1956, Sp./It.) PR:A
CALAMITY JANE (1953) PR:AA
CALAMITY JANE AND SAM BASS (1949) PR:A
CALAMITY THE COW (1967, Brit.) PR:AA
CALCULATED RISK (1963, Brit.) PR:A
CALCUTTA (1947) PR:A
CALENDAR, THE (SEE: BACHELOR'S FOLLY) (1931,
    Brit.)
CALENDAR, THE (1948, Brit.) PR:A
CALENDAR GIRL (1947) PR:A
CALIFORNIA (1946) PR:A
CALIFORNIA (1963) PR:A
CALIFORNIA CONQUEST (1952) PR:A
CALIFORNIA DOLLS (SEE: ... ALL THE MARBLES)
    (1981)
CALIFORNIA DREAMING (1979) PR:C
CALIFORNIA FIREBRAND (1948) PR:A
CALIFORNIA FRONTIER (1938) PR:A
CALIFORNIA GIRLS (1984) PR:O
CALIFORNIA HOLIDAY (SEE: SPINOUT) (1966)
CALIFORNIA IN 1878 (SEE: FIGHTING THRU) (1931)
CALIFORNIA JOE (1944) PR:A
CALIFORNIA MAIL, THE (1937) PR:A
CALIFORNIA PASSAGE (1950) PR:A
CALIFORNIA SPLIT (1974) PR:C
CALIFORNIA STRAIGHT AHEAD (1937) PR:A
CALIFORNIA SUITE (1978) PR:A-C
CALIFORNIA TRAIL, THE (1933) PR:A
CALIFORNIAN, THE (1937) PR:A
CALL, THE (1938, Fr.) PR:A
CALL A MESSENGER (1939) PR:A
CALL HARRY CROWN (SEE: 99 AND 44/100% DEAD)
    (1974)
CALL HER SAVAGE (1932) PR:A
CALL HIM MR. SHATTER (1976, Brit./Hong Kong) PR:O
CALL IT A DAY (1937) PR:A
CALL IT LUCK (1934) PR:A
CALL IT MURDER (SEE: MIDNIGHT) (1934)
CALL ME (1988) PR:O
CALL ME A CAB (SEE: CARRY ON CABBY) (1963,
    Brit.)
CALL ME BWANA (1963, Brit.) PR:A
CALL ME GENIUS (1961, Brit.) PR:A
CALL ME MADAM (1953) PR:A
CALL ME MAME (1933, Brit.) PR:A
CALL ME MISTER (1951) PR:A
CALL NORTHSIDE 777 (1948) PR:A
CALL OF THE BLOOD (1948, Brit.) PR:A
CALL OF THE CANYON (1942) PR:A
CALL OF THE CIRCUS (1930) PR:A
CALL OF THE FLESH (1930) PR:A
CALL OF THE JUNGLE (1944) PR:A
CALL OF THE KLONDIKE (1950) PR:A
CALL OF THE PRAIRIE (1936) PR:A
CALL OF THE ROCKIES (1938) PR:A
CALL OF THE SEA, THE (1930, Brit.) PR:A
CALL OF THE SOUTH SEAS (1944) PR:A
CALL OF THE WILD (1935) PR:AA
CALL OF THE WILD (1972, Sp./It./Fr./W. Ger.) PR:A
CALL OF THE YUKON (1938) PR:A
CALL OUT THE MARINES (1942) PR:A
CALL SURFTIDE 77 (SEE: SURFTIDE 77) (1962)
CALL THE MESQUITEERS (1938) PR:A
CALLAN (1975, Brit.) PR:C
CALLAWAY WENT THATAWAY (1951) PR:AA
CALLBOX MYSTERY, THE (1932, Brit.) PR:A
CALLED BACK (1933, Brit.) PR:A
CALLING, THE (SEE: BELLS) (1981)
CALLING ALL CROOKS (1938, Brit.) PR:A
CALLING ALL G-MEN (SEE: YOU MAY BE NEXT!)
    (1936)
CALLING ALL HUSBANDS (1940) PR:A
CALLING ALL MARINES (1939) PR:A
CALLING BULLDOG DRUMMOND (1951, Brit.) PR:A-C
CALLING DR. DEATH (1943) PR:A
CALLING DR. GILLESPIE (1942) PR:A
CALLING DR. KILDARE (1939) PR:A
CALLING HOMICIDE (1956) PR:A-C
CALLING NORTHSIDE 777 (SEE: CALL NORTHSIDE
    777) (1948)
CALLING OF DAN MATTHEWS, THE (SEE: DAN MAT-
    THEWS) (1936)
CALLING PAUL TEMPLE (1948, Brit.) PR:A
CALLING PHILO VANCE (1940) PR:A
CALLING THE TUNE (1936, Brit.) PR:A
CALLING WILD BILL ELLIOTT (1943) PR:A
CALM YOURSELF (1935) PR:A
CALTIKI, THE IMMORTAL MONSTER (1959, It.) PR:C
CALYPSO (1959, Fr./It.) PR:A-C
CALYPSO HEAT WAVE (1957) PR:A

CALYPSO JOE (1957) PR:A
CAME A HOT FRIDAY (1985, New Zealand) PR:C
CAMEL BOY, THE (1984, Aus.) PR:AA
CAMELOT (1967) PR:A-C
CAMELS ARE COMING, THE (1934, Brit.) PR:A
CAMEO KIRBY (1930) PR:A
CAMERA BUFF (1983, Pol.) PR:A
CAMERON'S CLOSET (1989) PR:O
CAMICIE ROSSE (SEE: ANITA GARIBALDI) (1954, It.)
CAMILA (1984, Arg./Sp.) PR:O
CAMILLE (1937) PR:A-C
CAMILLE CLAUDEL (1989, Fr.) PR:O
CAMILLE 2000 (1969) PR:O
CAMMINA CAMMINA (1983, It.) PR:AA
CAMORRA (1986, It.) PR:O
CAMP ON BLOOD ISLAND, THE (1958, Brit.) PR:O
CAMPANE A MARTELLO (SEE: CHILDREN OF
    CHANCE) (1950, It.)
CAMPBELL'S KINGDOM (1957, Brit.) PR:A
CAMPSITE MASSACRE (SEE: FINAL TERROR, THE)
    (1983)
CAMPUS CONFESSIONS (1938) PR:A
CAMPUS HONEYMOON (1948) PR:A
CAMPUS MAN (1987) PR:C
CAMPUS RHYTHM (1943) PR:A
CAMPUS SLEUTH (1948) PR:A
CAN-CAN (1960) PR:A-C
CAN SHE BAKE A CHERRY PIE? (1983) PR:C
CAN THIS BE DIXIE? (1936) PR:A
CAN YOU HEAR ME MOTHER? (1935, Brit.) PR:A
CAN'T BUY ME LOVE (1987) PR:C
CANADIAN MOUNTIES VS. ATOMIC INVADERS
    (SEE: MISSILE BASE AT TANIAK) (1953)
CANADIAN PACIFIC (1949) PR:A
CANADIANS, THE (1961, US/Can./Brit.) PR:A
CANAL ZONE (1942) PR:A
CANARIES SOMETIMES SING (1930, Brit.) PR:A
CANARIS (1955, W. Ger.) PR:C
CANARY MURDER CASE, THE (1929) PR:A
CANCEL MY RESERVATION (1972) PR:A
CANDIDATE, THE (1964) PR:C
CANDIDATE, THE (1972) PR:A-C
CANDIDATE FOR MURDER (1966, Brit.) PR:A
CANDIDE (1962, Fr.) PR:A
CANDLELIGHT IN ALGERIA (1944, Brit.) PR:A
CANDLES AT NINE (1944, Brit.) PR:A
CANDLESHOE (1978, Brit.) PR:AA
CANDY (1968, It./Fr.) PR:O
CANDY MAN, THE (1969) PR:O
CANDY MOUNTAIN (1988, Switz./Can./Fr.) PR:C
CANDY WEB, THE (SEE: THIRTEEN FRIGHTENED
    GIRLS) (1963)
CANICULE (SEE: DOG DAY) (1984, Fr.)
CANNABIS (1970, Fr.) PR:O
CANNERY ROW (1982) PR:C-O
CANNIBAL ATTACK (1954) PR:A
CANNIBAL GIRLS (1973, Can.) PR:C
*CANNIBAL WOMEN IN THE AVOCADO JUNGLE OF
    DEATH* (1989) PR:C
CANNIBALISTIC HUMANOID UNDERGROUND
    DWELLERS (SEE: C.H.U.D.) (1984)
CANNIBALS, THE (1970, It.) PR:C-O
CANNIBALS IN THE STREETS (1982, It./Sp.) PR:O
CANNON AND THE NIGHTINGALE, THE (1969, Gr.)
    PR:A
CANNON FOR CORDOBA (1970) PR:C-O
CANNONBALL (1976, US/Hong Kong) PR:C
CANNONBALL EXPRESS, THE (1932) PR:A
CANNONBALL RUN, THE (1981) PR:A
CANNONBALL RUN II (1984) PR:O
CANON CITY (1948) PR:A
CAN'T HELP SINGING (1944) PR:A
CAN'T STOP THE MUSIC (1980) PR:C
CANTERBURY TALE, A (1944, Brit.) PR:A
CANTERVILLE GHOST, THE (1944) PR:AA
CANTOR'S SON, THE (1937) PR:A
CANYON AMBUSH (1952) PR:A
CANYON CITY (1943) PR:A
CANYON CROSSROADS (1955) PR:A
CANYON HAWKS (1930) PR:A
CANYON OF MISSING MEN, THE (1930) PR:A
CANYON PASS (SEE: RATON PASS) (1951)
CANYON PASSAGE (1946) PR:A
CANYON RAIDERS (1951) PR:A
CANYON RIVER (1956) PR:A
CAPE CANAVERAL MONSTERS (1960) PR:A
CAPE FEAR (1962) PR:O
CAPE FORLORN (SEE: LOVE STORM) (1931, Brit.)
CAPER OF THE GOLDEN BULLS, THE (1967) PR:A
CAPETOWN AFFAIR (1967, US/South Africa) PR:C
CAPONE (1975) PR:O
CAPPY RICKS RETURNS (1935) PR:A
CAPRICE (1967) PR:A
CAPRICIOUS SUMMER (1968, Czech.) PR:C
CAPRICORN ONE (1978) PR:C
CAPTAIN APACHE (1971, Brit.) PR:C
CAPTAIN APPLEJACK (1931) PR:A
CAPTAIN BILL (1935, Brit.) PR:A

CAPTAIN BLACK JACK (1952, US/Fr.) PR:A
CAPTAIN BLOOD (1935) PR:A
CAPTAIN BLOOD, FUGITIVE (SEE: CAPTAIN PIRATE)
    (1952)
CAPTAIN BOYCOTT (1947, Brit.) PR:A
CAPTAIN CALAMITY (1936) PR:A
CAPTAIN CAREY, U.S.A. (1950) PR:A
CAPTAIN CAUTION (1940) PR:A
CAPTAIN CHINA (1949) PR:A
CAPTAIN CLEGG (SEE: NIGHT CREATURES) (1962,
    Brit.)
CAPTAIN EDDIE (1945) PR:AA
CAPTAIN FROM CASTILE (1947) PR:C-O
CAPTAIN FROM KOEPENICK (1933, Ger.) PR:A
CAPTAIN FROM KOEPENICK, THE (1956, W. Ger.)
    PR:A
CAPTAIN FURY (1939) PR:A
CAPTAIN GRANT'S CHILDREN (1939, USSR) PR:AA
CAPTAIN HATES THE SEA, THE (1934) PR:A
CAPTAIN HORATIO HORNBLOWER (1951, Brit.) PR:A
CAPTAIN HURRICANE (1935) PR:A
CAPTAIN IS A LADY, THE (1940) PR:A
CAPTAIN JANUARY (1935) PR:AA
CAPTAIN JOHN SMITH AND POCAHONTAS (1953)
    PR:A
CAPTAIN KIDD (1945) PR:A
CAPTAIN KIDD AND THE SLAVE GIRL (1954) PR:A
CAPTAIN KRONOS: VAMPIRE HUNTER (1974, Brit.)
    PR:O
CAPTAIN LIGHTFOOT (1955) PR:A
CAPTAIN MIDNIGHT (SEE: ON THE AIR LIVE WITH
    CAPTAIN MIDNIGHT) (1979)
CAPTAIN MILKSHAKE (1971) PR:O
CAPTAIN MOONLIGHT (1940, Brit.) PR:A
CAPTAIN NEMO AND THE UNDERWATER CITY
    (1969, Brit.) PR:A
CAPTAIN NEWMAN, M.D. (1963) PR:C
CAPTAIN OF THE GUARD (1930) PR:A
CAPTAIN PIRATE (1952) PR:A
CAPTAIN SCARLETT (1953) PR:A
CAPTAIN SINDBAD (1963) PR:A
CAPTAIN SIROCCO (SEE: PIRATES OF CAPRI) (1949)
CAPTAIN THUNDER (1931) PR:A
CAPTAIN TUGBOAT ANNIE (1945) PR:A
CAPTAINS COURAGEOUS (1937) PR:AA
CAPTAIN'S KID, THE (1937) PR:A
CAPTAINS OF THE CLOUDS (1942) PR:A-C
CAPTAIN'S ORDERS (1937, Brit.) PR:A
CAPTAIN'S PARADISE, THE (1953, Brit.) PR:A
CAPTAIN'S TABLE, THE (1936, Brit.) PR:A
CAPTAIN'S TABLE, THE (1960, Brit.) PR:A
CAPTIVATION (1931, Brit.) PR:A
CAPTIVE (SEE: TWO) (1975)
CAPTIVE CITY, THE (1952) PR:A
CAPTIVE CITY, THE (SEE: CONQUERED CITY) (1966,
    It.)
CAPTIVE GIRL (1950) PR:A
CAPTIVE HEART, THE (1948, Brit.) PR:C
CAPTIVE HEARTS (1988) PR:C
CAPTIVE OF BILLY THE KID (1952) PR:A
CAPTIVE RAGE (1988) PR:NR
CAPTIVE WILD WOMAN (1943) PR:A
CAPTIVE WOMEN (1952) PR:A
CAPTIVES, THE (SEE: ESCAPE TO BERLIN) (1962,
    US/Switz./W. Ger.)
CAPTURE, THE (1950) PR:A
CAPTURE THAT CAPSULE (1961) PR:C
CAPTURED (1933) PR:A
CAR, THE (1977) PR:C
CAR 99 (1935) PR:A
CAR OF DREAMS (1935, Brit.) PR:A
CAR WASH (1976) PR:C
CARAVAGGIO (1986, Brit.) PR:O
CARAVAN (1934) PR:A
CARAVAN (1946, Brit.) PR:A
CARAVAN TO VACCARES (1974, Brit./Fr.) PR:C
CARAVAN TRAIL, THE (1946) PR:A
CARAVANS (1978, US/Iranian) PR:C
CARAVANS WEST (SEE: WAGON WHEELS) (1934)
CARBINE WILLIAMS (1952) PR:A
CARBON COPY (1981) PR:C
CARD, THE (SEE: PROMOTER, THE) (1952, Brit.)
CARDBOARD CAVALIER (1949, Brit.) PR:A
CARDIAC ARREST (1980) PR:O
CARDIGAN'S LAST CASE (SEE: STATE'S ATTORNEY)
    (1932)
CARDINAL, THE (1936, Brit.) PR:A
CARDINAL, THE (1963) PR:C
CARDINAL RICHELIEU (1935) PR:A
CARE BEARS ADVENTURE IN WONDERLAND, THE
    (1987, Can.) PR:AA
CARE BEARS MOVIE, THE (1985, Can.) PR:AA
CARE BEARS MOVIE II: A NEW GENERATION (1986)
    PR:AA
CAREER (1939) PR:A
CAREER (1959) PR:C
CAREER GIRL (1944) PR:A
CAREER GIRL (1960) PR:C

CAREER WOMAN (1936) PR:A
CAREERS (1929) PR:A
CAREFREE (1938) PR:A
CAREFUL, HE MIGHT HEAR YOU (1984, Aus.) PR:A-C
CAREFUL, SOFT SHOULDERS (1942) PR:A
CARELESS AGE, THE (1929) PR:A
CARELESS LADY (1932) PR:A
CARELESS YEARS, THE (1957) PR:A
CARESSED (SEE: SWEET SUBSTITUTE) (1964, Can.)
CARETAKER, THE (SEE: GUEST, THE) (1963, Brit.)
CARETAKERS, THE (1963) PR:C
CARETAKER'S DAUGHTER, THE (1952, Brit.) PR:A
CAREY TREATMENT, THE (1972) PR:C
CARGO OF INNOCENTS (SEE: STAND BY FOR AC-
    TION) (1942)
CARGO TO CAPETOWN (1950) PR:A
CARIBBEAN (1952) PR:A
CARIBBEAN GOLD (SEE: CARIBBEAN) (1952)
CARIBBEAN MYSTERY, THE (1945) PR:A
CARIBOO TRAIL, THE (1950) PR:A
CARLTON-BROWNE OF THE F.O. (SEE: MAN IN A
    COCKED HAT) (1960, Brit.)
CARMELA (1949, It.) PR:A
CARMEN (1931, Brit.) PR:A
CARMEN (1946, It.) PR:A
CARMEN (1949, Sp.) PR:A
CARMEN (1983, Sp.) PR:C
CARMEN (SEE: BIZET'S CARMEN) (1984, Fr.)
CARMEN, BABY (1967, Yugo./W. Ger.) PR:O
CARMEN JONES (1954) PR:C
CARMEN, LA DE RONDA (SEE: DEVIL MADE A
    WOMAN, THE) (1959, Sp.)
CARNABY, M.D. (1967, Brit.) PR:C
CARNAGE (1986) PR:C
CARNAL KNOWLEDGE (1971) PR:O
CARNATION KID, THE (1929) PR:A
CARNE PER FRANKENSTEIN (SEE: ANDY
    WARHOL'S FRANKENSTEIN) (1974, Fr./It.)
CARNEGIE HALL (1947) PR:A
CARNIVAL (1931, Brit.) PR:A
CARNIVAL (1935) PR:A
CARNIVAL (1946, Brit.) PR:A
CARNIVAL (1953, Fr.) PR:A
CARNIVAL BOAT (1932) PR:A
CARNIVAL IN COSTA RICA (1947) PR:A
CARNIVAL IN FLANDERS (1935, Fr.) PR:A
CARNIVAL LADY (1933) PR:A
CARNIVAL OF BLOOD (1976) PR:C
CARNIVAL OF SINNERS (1947, Fr.) PR:A
CARNIVAL OF SOULS (1962) PR:C
CARNIVAL OF THIEVES (SEE: CAPER OF THE
    GOLDEN BULLS, THE) (1967)
CARNIVAL QUEEN (1937) PR:A
CARNIVAL ROCK (1957) PR:A
CARNIVAL STORY (1954) PR:A
CARNY (1980) PR:O
CAROLINA (1934) PR:A
CAROLINA BLUES (1944) PR:A
CAROLINA CANNONBALL (1955) PR:A
CAROLINA MOON (1940) PR:A
CAROLINE CHERIE (1968, Fr.) PR:C
CAROLLIE CHERIE (1951, Fr.) PR:A
CAROSELLO NAPOLETANO (SEE: NEAPOLITAN
    CAROUSEL) (1961, It.)
CAROUSEL (1956) PR:A
CARPENTER, THE (1989, Can.) PR:O
CARPETBAGGERS, THE (1964) PR:C
CARQUAKE (SEE: CANNONBALL) (1976, US/Hong
    Kong)
CARREFOUR (SEE: CROSSRAODS) (1938, Fr.)
CARRIE (1952) PR:C
CARRIE (1976) PR:O
CARRINGTON V.C. (SEE: COURT MARTIAL) (1954,
    Brit.)
CARRY ON ADMIRAL (1957, Brit.) PR:A
CARRY ON AGAIN, DOCTOR (1969, Brit.) PR:C
CARRY ON CABBY (1963, Brit.) PR:C
CARRY ON CAMPING (1969, Brit.) PR:C
CARRY ON CLEO (1964, Brit.) PR:C
CARRY ON CONSTABLE (1960, Brit.) PR:C
CARRY ON COWBOY (1966, Brit.) PR:A
CARRY ON CRUISING (1962, Brit.) PR:C
CARRY ON DOCTOR (1968, Brit.) PR:C
CARRY ON EMMANUELLE (1978, Brit.) PR:O
CARRY ON ENGLAND (1976, Brit.) PR:A
CARRY ON HENRY VIII (1970, Brit.) PR:O
CARRY ON JACK (1963, Brit.) PR:A
CARRY ON LOVING (1970, Brit.) PR:C-O
CARRY ON REGARDLESS (1961, Brit.) PR:C
CARRY ON SCREAMING (1966, Brit.) PR:A
CARRY ON SPYING (1964, Brit.) PR:A
CARRY ON TEACHER (1962, Brit.) PR:A
CARRY ON TV (SEE: GET ON WITH IT) (1963, Brit.)
CARRY ON UP THE JUNGLE (1970, Brit.) PR:A
CARRY ON, UP THE KHYBER (1968, Brit.) PR:A
CARRY ON VENUS (SEE: CARRY ON JACK) (1963,
    Brit.)
CARRY ON, NURSE (1959, Brit.) PR:A

CARRY ON, SERGEANT (1959, Brit.) PR:A
CARS THAT ATE PARIS, THE (1974, Aus.) PR:O
CARSON CITY (1952) PR:A
CARSON CITY CYCLONE (1943) PR:A
CARSON CITY KID, THE (1940) PR:AA
CARSON CITY RAIDERS (1948) PR:A
CARTAGINE IN FIAMME (SEE: CARTHAGE IN FLAMES) (1961, Fr./It.)
CARTER CASE, THE (1947) PR:A
CARTES SUR TABLE (SEE: ATTACK OF THE RO-BOTS) (1967, Fr./Sp.)
CARTHAGE IN FLAMES (1961, Fr./It.) PR:C-O
CARTOUCHE (1957, It./US) PR:A
CARTOUCHE (1962, Fr./It.) PR:A
CARVE HER NAME WITH PRIDE (1958, Brit.) PR:A
CARYL OF THE MOUNTAINS (1936) PR:AA
CASA MANANA (1951) PR:A
CASA RICORDI (SEE: HOUSE OF RICORDI) (1956, It./Fr.)
CASABLANCA (1942) PR:A
CASANOVA (1976, It.) PR:O
CASANOVA AND COMPANY (SEE: SOME LIKE IT COOL) (1977, Fr./It./W. Ger.)
CASANOVA BROWN (1944) PR:A
CASANOVA IN BURLESQUE (1944) PR:A
CASANOVA '70 (1965, Fr./It.) PR:O
CASANOVA'S BIG NIGHT (1954) PR:A
CASBAH (1948) PR:C
CASCARRABIAS (SEE: GRUMPY) (1930)
CASE AGAINST BROOKLYN, THE (1958) PR:A
CASE AGAINST FERRO, THE (1980, Fr.) PR:C
CASE AGAINST MRS. AMES, THE (1936) PR:A
CASE FOR PC 49, A (1951, Brit.) PR:A
CASE FOR THE CROWN, THE (1934, Brit.) PR:A
CASE OF CHARLES PEACE, THE (1949, Brit.) PR:A
CASE OF CLARA DEANE, THE (SEE: STRANGE CASE OF CLARA DEANE, THE) (1932)
CASE OF DR. LAURENT (1958, Fr.) PR:C
CASE OF GABRIEL PERRY, THE (1935, Brit.) PR:A
CASE OF MRS. LORING (SEE: QUESTION OF ADUL-TERY, A) (1959, Brit.)
CASE OF PATTY SMITH, THE (1962) PR:C-O
CASE OF SERGEANT GRISCHA, THE (1930) PR:A
CASE OF THE BLACK CAT, THE (1936) PR:A
CASE OF THE BLACK PARROT, THE (1941) PR:A
CASE OF THE CURIOUS BRIDE, THE (1935) PR:A
CASE OF THE 44'S, THE (1964, Brit./Den.) PR:A
CASE OF THE FRIGHTENED LADY, THE (1940, Brit.) PR:C
CASE OF THE HOWLING DOG, THE (1934) PR:A
CASE OF THE LUCKY LEGS, THE (1935) PR:A
CASE OF THE MISSING BLONDE (SEE: LADY IN THE MORGUE) (1938)
CASE OF THE MISSING MAN, THE (1935) PR:A
CASE OF THE RED MONKEY (1955, Brit.) PR:A
CASE OF THE STUTTERING BISHOP, THE (1937) PR:A
CASE OF THE VELVET CLAWS, THE (1936) PR:A
CASE VAN GELDERN (1932, Ger.) PR:C
CASEY'S SHADOW (1978) PR:A
CASH (SEE: FOR LOVE OR MONEY) (1934, Brit.)
CASH MC CALL (1960) PR:C
CASH ON DELIVERY (1956, Brit.) PR:A
CASH ON DEMAND (1962, Brit.) PR:C
CASINO DE PARIS (1957, Fr./W. Ger.) PR:C
CASINO MURDER CASE, THE (1935) PR:A
CASINO ROYALE (1967, Brit.) PR:A
CASQUE D'OR (1952, Fr.) PR:C
CASS TIMBERLANE (1947) PR:C
CASSANDRA CROSSING, THE (1977, Brit./It./W. Ger.) PR:C
CASSIDY OF BAR 20 (1938) PR:A
CAST A DARK SHADOW (1958, Brit.) PR:A
CAST A GIANT SHADOW (1966) PR:A-C
CAST A LONG SHADOW (1959) PR:C
CASTA DIVA (SEE: DIVINE SPARK, THE) (1935, Brit./It.)
CASTAWAY COWBOY, THE (1974) PR:AA
CASTAWAY, THE (SEE: CHEATERS, THE) (1945)
CASTE (1930, Brit.) PR:A
CASTILIAN, THE (1963, US/Sp.) PR:C
CASTLE, THE (1969, Switz./W. Ger.) PR:C
CASTLE IN THE AIR (1952, Brit.) PR:A
CASTLE IN THE DESERT (1942) PR:A
CASTLE KEEP (1969) PR:C
CASTLE OF BLOOD (1964, Fr./It.) PR:O
CASTLE OF CRIMES (1940, Brit.) PR:A
CASTLE OF DOOM (SEE: VAMPYR) (1932, Fr./Ger.)
CASTLE OF EVIL (1967) PR:C
CASTLE OF FU MANCHU, THE (1968, Sp./It./Brit./W. Ger.) PR:C
CASTLE OF PURITY (1974, Mex.) PR:C-O
CASTLE OF TERROR (SEE: CASTLE OF BLOOD) (1964, Fr./It.)
CASTLE OF THE LIVING DEAD (1964, Fr./It.) PR:C
CASTLE OF THE MONSTERS (1958, Mex.) PR:A
CASTLE OF THE SPIDER'S WEB, THE (SEE: THRONE OF BLOOD) (1957, Jap.)
CASTLE ON THE HUDSON (1940) PR:C

CASTLE SINISTER (1932, Brit.) PR:C
CASUAL SEX? (1988) PR:O
CASUALTIES OF WAR (1989) PR:C
CAT, THE (1959, Fr.) PR:C
CAT, THE (1966) PR:AA
CAT, THE (1971, Fr.) PR:C
CAT AND MOUSE (1958, Brit.) PR:C
CAT AND MOUSE (SEE: MOUSEY) (1974)
CAT AND MOUSE (1975, Fr.) PR:A-C
CAT AND THE CANARY, THE (1939) PR:A
CAT AND THE CANARY, THE (1979, Brit.) PR:A
CAT AND THE FIDDLE, THE (1934) PR:A
CAT ATE THE PARAKEET, THE (1972) PR:A
CAT BALLOU (1965) PR:A-C
CAT BURGLAR, THE (1961) PR:C
CAT CREEPS, THE (1930) PR:AA
CAT CREEPS, THE (1946) PR:A
CAT FROM OUTER SPACE, THE (1978) PR:AA
CAT GANG, THE (1959, Brit.) PR:AA
CAT GIRL (1957, Brit.) PR:C
CAT IN THE SACK, THE (1967, Can.) PR:C
CAT MURKIL AND THE SILKS (1976) PR:O
CAT ON A HOT TIN ROOF (1958) PR:C
CAT O'NINE TAILS (1971, It./Fr./W. Ger.) PR:O
CAT PEOPLE (1942) PR:C
CAT PEOPLE (1982) PR:O
CAT WOMEN OF THE MOON (1953) PR:A
CATACOMBS (SEE: WOMAN WHO WOULDN'T DIE, THE) (1965, Brit.)
CATALINA CAPER (1967) PR:A
CATAMOUNT KILLING, THE (1975, W. Ger.) PR:C
CATCH AS CATCH CAN (1937, Brit.) PR:A
CATCH AS CATCH CAN (1968, It.) PR:C
CATCH ME A SPY (1971, Brit./Fr.) PR:A-C
CATCH MY SOUL (1974) PR:O
CATCH THE HEAT (1987) PR:C
CATCH-22 (1970) PR:O
CATCH US IF YOU CAN (SEE: HAVING A WILD WEEKEND) (1965, Brit.)
CATERED AFFAIR, THE (1956) PR:A
CATHERINE & CO. (1976, Fr.) PR:O
CATHERINE THE GREAT (1934, Brit.) PR:C
CATHOLIC BOYS (SEE: HEAVEN HELP US) (1985)
CATHY'S CHILD (1979, Aus.) PR:C
CATHY'S CURSE (1977, Can.) PR:O
CATLOW (1971, Sp.) PR:C
CATMAN OF PARIS, THE (1946) PR:A
CAT'S EYE (1985) PR:C
CAT'S PAW, THE (1934) PR:A
CATSKILL HONEYMOON (1950) PR:A
CATSPAW MURDER MYSTERY (SEE: SCATTERGOOD SURVIVES A MURDER) (1942)
CATTLE ANNIE AND LITTLE BRITCHES (1981) PR:C
CATTLE DRIVE (1951) PR:AA
CATTLE EMPIRE (1958) PR:A
CATTLE KING (1963) PR:A
CATTLE QUEEN (1951) PR:A
CATTLE QUEEN OF MONTANA (1954) PR:A
CATTLE RAIDERS (1938) PR:A
CATTLE STAMPEDE (1943) PR:A
CATTLE THIEF, THE (1936) PR:A
CATTLE TOWN (1952) PR:A
CAUCHEMARES (SEE: CATHY'S CURSE) (1977, Can.)
CAUGHT (1931) PR:A
CAUGHT (1949) PR:C
CAUGHT (1987) PR:A
CAUGHT CHEATING (1931) PR:A
CAUGHT IN THE ACT (1941) PR:A
CAUGHT IN THE DRAFT (1941) PR:AA
CAUGHT IN THE FOG (1928) PR:A
CAUGHT IN THE NET (1960, Brit.) PR:AA
CAUGHT PLASTERED (1931) PR:A
CAUGHT SHORT (1930) PR:A
CAULDRON OF BLOOD (1967, US/Sp.) PR:C
CAULDRON OF DEATH, THE (1979, It.) PR:O
CAUSE FOR ALARM (1951) PR:C
CAVALCADE (1933) PR:A
CAVALCADE OF THE WEST (1936) PR:A
CAVALIER, THE (1928) PR:A
CAVALIER OF THE GOLDEN STAR (SEE: DREAM OF A COSSACK) (1982, USSR)
CAVALIER OF THE STREETS, THE (1937, Brit.) PR:A
CAVALIER OF THE WEST (1931) PR:A
CAVALLERIA COMMANDOS (SEE: CAVALRY COM-MAND) (1963, US/Phil.)
CAVALLERIA RUSTICANA (SEE: FATAL DESIRE) (1952, It.)
CAVALRY (1936) PR:A
CAVALRY COMMAND (1963, US/Phil.) PR:A
CAVALRY SCOUT (1951) PR:A
CAVE OF OUTLAWS (1951) PR:A
CAVE OF THE LIVING DEAD (1966, W. Ger./Yugo.) PR:A
CAVEGIRL (1985) PR:O
CAVEMAN (1981) PR:O
CAVERN, THE (1965, It./W. Ger.) PR:A
CAYMAN TRIANGLE, THE (1977) PR:C-O
C. C. AND COMPANY (1971) PR:O

CE SACRE GRANDPERE (SEE: MARRIAGE CAME TUMBLING DOWN, THE) (1968, Fr.)
CE SOIR LES JUPONS V OLENT (SEE: TONIGHT THE SKIRTS FLY) (1956, Fr.)
CEASE FIRE (1985) PR:C
CEDDO (1978, Nigeria) PR:C
CEILING ZERO (1935) PR:A
CELESTE (1982, W. Ger.) PR:A
CELIA (1949, Brit.) PR:A
CELINE AND JULIE GO BOATING (1974, Fr.) PR:C
CELL 2455, DEATH ROW (1955) PR:C
CELLAR DWELLER (1988) PR:O
CEMENTERIO DEL TERROR (1985, Mex.) PR:O
CEMETERY GIRLS (SEE: VELVET VAMPIRE, THE) (1971)
CENSUS TAKER, THE (1984) PR:O
CENT BRIQUES ET DES TUILES (SEE: HOW NOT TO ROB A DEPARTMENT STORE) (1965, Fr./It.)
CENTENNIAL SUMMER (1946) PR:AA
CENTO ANNI D'AMORE (1954, It.) PR:C
CENTRAL AIRPORT (1933) PR:A
CENTRAL PARK (1932) PR:A
CENTURION, THE (1962, Fr./It.) PR:A
CEREBROS DIABOLICOS (1966, Mex.) PR:A
CEREBROS INFERNAL (SEE: BLUE DEMON VERSUS THE INFERNAL BRAINS) (1967, Mex.)
CEREMONIA SANGRIENTA (SEE: FEMALE BUTCHER, THE) (1972, It./Sp.)
CEREMONY, THE (1963, US/Sp.) PR:C
CERNE SLUNCE (SEE: BLACK SUN, THE) (1979, Czech.)
CERTAIN FURY (1985) PR:O
CERTAIN SMILE, A (1958) PR:C-O
CERTAIN, VERY CERTAIN, AS A MATTER OF FACT. . . PROBABLE (1970, It.) PR:O
CERVANTES (SEE: YOUNG REBEL, THE) (1967, Fr./It./Sp.)
CESAR (1936, Fr.) PR:A
CESAR AND ROSALIE (1972, Fr./It./W. Ger.) PR:C
C'EST ARRIVE A PARIS (SEE: IT HAPPENED IN PARIS) (1953, Fr.)
CET OBSCUR OBJECT DU DESIR (SEE: THAT OB-SCURE OBJECT OF DESIRE) (1977, Fr./Sp.)
CHA-CHA-CHA BOOM (1956) PR:A
CHAFED ELBOWS (1967) PR:C-O
CHAIN, THE (1985, Brit.) PR:C
CHAIN GANG (1950) PR:C
CHAIN GANG (1985) PR:O
CHAIN LETTERS (1985) PR:O
CHAIN LIGHTNING (1950) PR:A
CHAIN OF CIRCUMSTANCE (1951) PR:A
CHAIN OF EVENTS (1958, Brit.) PR:A-C
CHAIN OF EVIDENCE (1957) PR:A
CHAIN REACTION (1980, Aus.) PR:C
CHAINED (1934) PR:C
CHAINED FOR LIFE (1950) PR:C
CHAINED HEAT (1983, US/W. Ger.) PR:O
CHAINGANG GIRLS (SEE: SWEET SUGAR) (1970)
CHAINSAW HOOKERS (SEE: HOLLYWOOD CHAINSAW HOOKERS) (1988)
CHAIR, THE (1989) PR:O
CHAIRMAN, THE (1969, Brit.) PR:A-C
CHALEURS D'ETE (SEE: HEAT OF SUMMER) (1961, Fr.)
CHALK GARDEN, THE (1964, Brit.) PR:A
CHALLENGE, THE (SEE: WOMAN HUNGRY) (1931)
CHALLENGE, THE (1939, Brit.) PR:A
CHALLENGE, THE (1948) PR:A
CHALLENGE, THE (SEE: IT TAKES A THIEF) (1960, Brit.)
CHALLENGE (1974) PR:O
CHALLENGE, THE (1982) PR:C
CHALLENGE FOR ROBIN HOOD, A (1968, Brit.) PR:A
CHALLENGE OF THE RANGE (1949) PR:A
CHALLENGE THE WILD (1954) PR:AA
CHALLENGE TO BE FREE (1976) PR:A
CHALLENGE TO LASSIE (1949) PR:AA
CHAMBER OF HORRORS (1941, Brit.) PR:A
CHAMBER OF HORRORS (1966) PR:O
CHAMELEON (1978) PR:C
CHAMP, THE (1931) PR:AA
CHAMP, THE (1979) PR:AA
CHAMP FOR A DAY (1953) PR:A
CHAMPAGNE CHARLIE (1936) PR:A
CHAMPAGNE CHARLIE (1944, Brit.) PR:A
CHAMPAGNE FOR BREAKFAST (1935) PR:A
CHAMPAGNE FOR CAESAR (1950) PR:AA
CHAMPAGNE MURDERS, THE (1968, Fr.) PR:C
CHAMPAGNE WALTZ (1937) PR:A
CHAMPION (1949) PR:C
CHAMPIONS (1984, Brit.) PR:C
CHAN IS MISSING (1982) PR:C
CHANCE AT HEAVEN (1933) PR:A
CHANCE MEETING (1954, Brit.) PR:A
CHANCE MEETING (1960, Brit.) PR:C
CHANCE OF A LIFETIME, THE (1943) PR:A
CHANCE OF A LIFETIME (1950, Brit.) PR:A

CHANCE OF A NIGHT-TIME, THE (1931, Brit.) PR:A
CHANCES (1931) PR:A
CHANCES ARE (1989) PR:A
CHANDLER (1971) PR:A
CHANDU THE MAGICIAN (1932) PR:A
CHANEL SOLITAIRE (1981, US/Fr.) PR:C
CHANGE FOR A SOVEREIGN (1937, Brit.) PR:A
CHANGE OF HABIT (1969) PR:C-O
CHANGE OF HEART (1934) PR:A
CHANGE OF HEART (1938) PR:A
CHANGE OF HEART (SEE: HIT PARADE OF 1943)
   (1943)
CHANGE OF HEART, A (SEE: TWO AND TWO MAKE
   SIX) (1962, Brit.)
CHANGE OF MIND (1969) PR:C
CHANGE OF SEASONS, A (1980) PR:C-O
CHANGE PARTNERS (1965, Brit.) PR:C
CHANGELING, THE (1980, Can.) PR:O
CHANGES (1969) PR:O
CHANNEL CROSSING (1934, Brit.) PR:A
CHANT OF JIMMIE BLACKSMITH, THE (1980, Aus.)
   PR:O
CHAPMAN REPORT, THE (1962) PR:O
CHAPPAQUA (1967) PR:O
CHAPTER TWO (1979) PR:C
CHARADE (1953) PR:A
CHARADE (1963) PR:A-C
CHARGE AT FEATHER RIVER, THE (1953) PR:C
CHARGE IS MURDER, THE (SEE: TWILIGHT OF
   HONOR) (1963)
CHARGE OF THE LANCERS (1953) PR:A
CHARGE OF THE LIGHT BRIGADE, THE (1936) PR:A
CHARGE OF THE LIGHT BRIGADE, THE (1968, Brit.)
   PR:C
CHARGE OF THE MODEL-T'S (1979) PR:AA
CHARING CROSS ROAD (1935, Brit.) PR:A
CHARIOTS OF FIRE (1981, Brit.) PR:AA
CHARLATAN, THE (1929) PR:A
CHARLES AND LUCIE (1982, Fr.) PR:A
CHARLES, DEAD OR ALIVE (1972, Switz.) PR:C
CHARLESTON (1978, It.) PR:A
CHARLEY AND THE ANGEL (1973) PR:AA
CHARLEY MOON (1956, Brit.) PR:A
CHARLEY-ONE-EYE (1973, Brit.) PR:C
CHARLEY VARRICK (1973) PR:C
CHARLEY'S AUNT (1930) PR:A
CHARLEY'S AUNT (1941) PR:AA
CHARLEY'S (BIG-HEARTED) AUNT (1940, Brit.) PR:A
CHARLIE BUBBLES (1968, Brit.) PR:C
*CHARLIE CHAN AND THE CURSE OF THE DRAGON
   QUEEN* (1981) PR:A
CHARLIE CHAN AT MONTE CARLO (1937) PR:A
CHARLIE CHAN AT THE CIRCUS (1936) PR:A
CHARLIE CHAN AT THE OLYMPICS (1937) PR:A
CHARLIE CHAN AT THE OPERA (1936) PR:A
CHARLIE CHAN AT THE RACE TRACK (1936) PR:A
CHARLIE CHAN AT THE WAX MUSEUM (1940) PR:A
CHARLIE CHAN AT TREASURE ISLAND (1939) PR:A
CHARLIE CHAN CARRIES ON (1931) PR:A
CHARLIE CHAN IN BLACK MAGIC (1944) PR:A
CHARLIE CHAN IN EGYPT (1935) PR:A
CHARLIE CHAN IN HONOLULU (1938) PR:A
CHARLIE CHAN IN LONDON (1934) PR:A
CHARLIE CHAN IN PANAMA (1940) PR:A
CHARLIE CHAN IN PARIS (1935) PR:A
CHARLIE CHAN IN RENO (1939) PR:A
CHARLIE CHAN IN RIO (1941) PR:A
CHARLIE CHAN IN SHANGHAI (1935) PR:A
CHARLIE CHAN IN THE CITY OF DARKNESS (1939)
   PR:A
CHARLIE CHAN IN THE SECRET SERVICE (1944)
   PR:A
CHARLIE CHAN ON BROADWAY (1937) PR:A
CHARLIE CHAN'S CHANCE (1932) PR:A
CHARLIE CHAN'S COURAGE (1934) PR:A
CHARLIE CHAN'S GREATEST CASE (1933) PR:A
CHARLIE CHAN'S MURDER CRUISE (1940) PR:A
CHARLIE CHAN'S SECRET (1936) PR:A
CHARLIE MC CARTHY, DETECTIVE (1939) PR:AA
CHARLIE, THE LONESOME COUGAR (1967) PR:AA
CHARLOTTE'S WEB (1973) PR:AA
CHARLTON-BROWN OF THE F.O. (SEE: MAN IN A
   COCKED HAT) (1959, Brit.)
CHARLY (1968) PR:A-C
CHARM SCHOOL, THE (SEE: COLLEGIATE) (1936)
CHARMING DECEIVER, THE (1933, Brit.) PR:A
CHARMING SINNERS (1929) PR:A
CHARRO! (1969) PR:A
CHARTER PILOT (1940) PR:A
CHARTROOSE CABOOSE (1960) PR:A
CHASE, THE (1946) PR:A
CHASE, THE (1966) PR:O
CHASE A CROOKED SHADOW (1958, Brit.) PR:A
CHASE FOR THE GOLDEN NEEDLES (SEE: GOLDEN
   NEEDLES) (1974)
CHASER, THE (SEE: NUISANCE, THE) (1933)
CHASER, THE (1938) PR:A
CHASERS, THE (SEE: GIRL HUNTERS, THE) (1960)

CHASING DANGER (1939) PR:A
CHASING DREAMS (1989) PR:A
CHASING RAINBOWS (1930) PR:A
CHASING TROUBLE (1940) PR:A
CHASING YESTERDAY (1935) PR:A
CHASTITY (1969) PR:C
CHASTITY BELT, THE (1969, US/It.) PR:C
CHATEAU EN SUEDE (SEE: NUTTY, NAUGHTY CHA-
   TEAU) (1964, Fr./It.)
CHATO'S LAND (1972, Brit.) PR:O
CHATTANOOGA CHOO CHOO (1984) PR:A-C
CHATTERBOX (1936) PR:A
CHATTERBOX (1943) PR:A
CHAUTAUQUA, THE (SEE: TROUBLE WITH GIRLS
   (AND HOW TO GET INTO IT), THE) (1969)
CHE! (1969) PR:C
CHE? (SEE: DIARY OF FORBIDDEN DREAMS) (1972,
   It./Fr./W. Ger.)
CHEAP DETECTIVE, THE (1978) PR:C
CHEAPER BY THE DOZEN (1950) PR:AA
CHEAPER TO KEEP HER (1980) PR:O
CHEAT, THE (1931) PR:C-O
CHEAT, THE (SEE: LONE HAND TEXAN, THE) (1947)
CHEAT, THE (1950, Fr.) PR:C-O
CHEATERS (1934) PR:A
CHEATERS, THE (1945) PR:A
CHEATERS, THE (1961, Fr./It.) PR:O
CHEATERS AT PLAY (1932) PR:A
CHEATING BLONDES (1933) PR:A
CHEATING CHEATERS (1934) PR:A
CHECK AND DOUBLE CHECK (SEE: AMOS 'N'
   ANDY) (1930)
CHECK IS IN THE MAIL, THE (1986) PR:C-O
CHECK YOUR GUNS (1948) PR:A
CHECKER PLAYER, THE (SEE: DEVIL IS AN EM-
   PRESS, THE) (1939, Fr.)
CHECKERBOARD (1959, Fr./It.) PR:O
CHECKERED COAT, THE (1948) PR:A
CHECKERED FLAG, THE (1963) PR:C
CHECKERED FLAG OR CRASH (1978) PR:C
CHECKERS (1937) PR:A
CHECKING OUT (1989) PR:O
CHECKMATE (1935, Brit.) PR:A
CHECKMATE (1973) PR:O
CHECKPOINT (1957, Brit.) PR:A
CHEECH AND CHONG'S NEXT MOVIE (1980) PR:O
CHEECH AND CHONG'S NICE DREAMS (1981) PR:O
CHEECH AND CHONG'S STILL SMOKIN' (SEE: STILL
   SMOKIN') (1983)
CHEECH AND CHONG'S THE CORSICAN BROTHERS
   (1984) PR:O
CHEER BOYS CHEER (1939, Brit.) PR:A
CHEER THE BRAVE (1951, Brit.) PR:A
CHEER UP! (1936, Brit.) PR:A
CHEER UP AND SMILE (1930) PR:A
CHEERLEADER CAMP (SEE: BLOODY POM POMS)
   (1988)
CHEERS FOR MISS BISHOP (1941) PR:A
CHEERS OF THE CROWD (1936) PR:A
CHEETAH (1989) PR:AA
CHELSEA GIRLS, THE (1966) PR:O
CHELSEA LIFE (1933, Brit.) PR:A
CHELSEA STORY (1951, Brit.) PR:A
CHEREZ TERNII K SVEZDAM (1981, USSR) PR:A
CHEROKEE FLASH, THE (1945) PR:A
CHEROKEE STRIP, THE (1937) PR:A
CHEROKEE STRIP (1940) PR:A
CHEROKEE UPRISING (1950) PR:A
CHERRY 2000 (1985) PR:C
CHERYOMUSHKI (SEE: SONG OVER MOSCOW)
   (1964, USSR)
CHESS PLAYER, THE (SEE: DEVIL IS AN EMPRESS,
   THE) (1939, Fr.)
CHESS PLAYERS, THE (1978, India) PR:C
CHESTY ANDERSON, U.S. NAVY (1976) PR:O
CHETNIKS (1943) PR:A
CHEYENNE (1947) PR:A
CHEYENNE AUTUMN (1964) PR:A
CHEYENNE CYCLONE, THE (1932) PR:A
CHEYENNE KID, THE (1930) PR:A
CHEYENNE KID, THE (1933) PR:A
CHEYENNE KID, THE (1940) PR:A
CHEYENNE RIDES AGAIN (1937) PR:A
CHEYENNE ROUNDUP (1943) PR:A
CHEYENNE SOCIAL CLUB, THE (1970) PR:C
CHEYENNE TAKES OVER (1947) PR:A
CHEYENNE TORNADO (1935) PR:A
CHEYENNE WILDCAT (1944) PR:A
CHI O SUU ME (SEE: LAKE OF DRACULA) (1973, Jap.)
CHI TO SUNA (SEE: FORT GRAVEYARD) (1966, Jap.)
CHICAGO CALLING (1951) PR:A
CHICAGO CONFIDENTIAL (1957) PR:A
CHICAGO DEADLINE (1949) PR:A
CHICAGO KID, THE (1945) PR:A
CHICAGO MASQUERADE (SEE: LITTLE EGYPT)
   (1951)
CHICAGO 70 (1970) PR:C
CHICAGO SYNDICATE (1955) PR:A

CHICAGO, CHICAGO (SEE: GAILY, GAILY) (1969)
CHICHI TO KO (SEE: OUR SILENT LOVE) (1969, Jap.)
CHICK (1936, Brit.) PR:A
CHICKEN CHRONICLES, THE (1977) PR:C
CHICKEN EVERY SUNDAY (1948) PR:A
CHICKEN WAGON FAMILY (1939) PR:A
CHIDAMBARAM (1986, India) PR:O
CHIEF, THE (1933) PR:A
CHIEF CRAZY HORSE (1955) PR:A
CHIEF WANTS NO SURVIVORS, THE (SEE: NO SURVI-
   VORS, PLEASE!) (1963, W. Ger.)
CHIKUMAGAWA ZESSHO (SEE: RIVER OF FOREVER)
   (1967, Jap.)
CHIKYU BOELGUN (SEE: MYSTERIANS, THE) (1959,
   Jap.)
CHILD, THE (1977) PR:O
CHILD AND THE KILLER, THE (1959, Brit.) PR:C
CHILD IN THE HOUSE (1956, Brit.) PR:A
CHILD IS A WILD YOUNG THING, A (1976) PR:O
CHILD IS BORN, A (1940) PR:A
CHILD IS WAITING, A (1963) PR:A
CHILD OF DIVORCE (1946) PR:A
CHILD OF MANHATTAN (1933) PR:C
CHILD UNDER A LEAF (1975, Can.) PR:O
CHILDHOOD OF MAXIM GORKY (1938, USSR) PR:A
CHILDREN, THE (1969) PR:O
CHILDREN, THE (1949, Swed.) PR:AA
CHILDREN, THE (1980) PR:O
CHILDREN ARE WATCHING US, THE (SEE: LITTLE
   MARTYR, THE) (1947, It.)
CHILDREN GALORE (1954, Brit.) PR:A
CHILDREN OF A LESSER GOD (1986) PR:C-O
CHILDREN OF BABYLON (1980, Jamaica) PR:O
CHILDREN OF CHANCE (1930, Brit.) PR:A
CHILDREN OF CHANCE (1949, Brit.) PR:A
CHILDREN OF CHANCE (1950, It.) PR:A
CHILDREN OF CHAOS (1950, Fr.) PR:C
CHILDREN OF DREAMS (1931) PR:A
CHILDREN OF GOD'S EARTH (1983, Norway) PR:C
CHILDREN OF HIROSHIMA (1952, Jap.) PR:C-O
CHILDREN OF MONTMARTRE (SEE: LA
   MATERNELLE) (1933, Fr.)
CHILDREN OF PARADISE (1945, Fr.) PR:C
CHILDREN OF PLEASURE (1930) PR:A
CHILDREN OF RAGE (1975, Brit./Israeli) PR:O
CHILDREN OF SANCHEZ, THE (1978, US/Mex.) PR:O
CHILDREN OF THE CORN (1984) PR:C-O
CHILDREN OF THE DAMNED (1963, Brit.) PR:O
CHILDREN OF THE FOG (1935, Brit.) PR:A
CHILDREN OF THE WILD (SEE: KILLERS OF THE
   WILD) (1949)
CHILDREN SHOULDN'T PLAY WITH DEAD THINGS
   (1972) PR:O
CHILDREN'S GAMES (1969) PR:C-O
CHILDREN'S HOUR, THE (1961) PR:C
CHILD'S PLAY (1954, Brit.) PR:A
CHILD'S PLAY (1972) PR:A-C
CHILD'S PLAY (1988) PR:O
CHILLY SCENES OF WINTER (1979) PR:C
CHILTERN HUNDREDS, THE (SEE: AMAZING MR.
   BEECHAM, THE) (1949, Brit.)
CHIMES AT MIDNIGHT (1967, Sp./Switz.) PR:C
CHIN CHIN CHINAMAN (SEE: BOAT FROM SHANG-
   HAI) (1931, Brit.)
CHIN NU YU HUN (SEE: ENCHANTING SHADOW,
   THE) (1965, Hong Kong)
CHINA (1943) PR:C
CHINA CARAVAN (SEE: YANK ON THE BURMA
   ROAD, A) (1942)
CHINA CLIPPER (1936) PR:A
CHINA CORSAIR (1951) PR:C
CHINA DOLL (1958) PR:C
CHINA GATE (1957) PR:C
CHINA GIRL (1942) PR:A
CHINA GIRL (1987) PR:O
CHINA IS NEAR (1968, It.) PR:C-O
CHINA 9, LIBERTY 37 (1978, It.) PR:O
CHINA PASSAGE (1937) PR:A
CHINA SEAS (1935) PR:A
CHINA SKY (1945) PR:C
CHINA SYNDROME, THE (1979) PR:A
CHINA VENTURE (1953) PR:C
CHINA'S LITTLE DEVILS (1945) PR:C
CHINATOWN (1974) PR:O
CHINATOWN AFTER DARK (1931) PR:A
CHINATOWN AT MIDNIGHT (1949) PR:C
CHINATOWN NIGHTS (1929) PR:A
CHINATOWN NIGHTS (1938, Brit.) PR:A
CHINATOWN SQUAD (1935) PR:A
CHINCERO (SEE: LAST MOVIE, THE) (1971)
CHINESE BOXES (1984, Brit./W. Ger.) PR:O
CHINESE BUNGALOW, THE (1930, Brit.) PR:A
CHINESE CAT, THE (1944) PR:A
CHINESE DEN, THE (1940, Brit.) PR:A
CHINESE PUZZLE, THE (1932, Brit.) PR:A
CHINESE RING, THE (1947) PR:A
CHINESE ROULETTE (1977, W. Ger.) PR:O
CHINO (1976, It./Sp./Fr.) PR:A-C

CHINTAO YOSAI BAKUGEKI MEIR EI (SEE: SIEGE OF FORT BISMARK) (1968, Jap.)
CHIP OF THE FLYING U (1940) PR:A
CHIP OFF THE OLD BLOCK (1944) PR:A
CHIPMUNK ADVENTURE, THE (1987) PR:AA
CHIPS (1938, Brit.) PR:A
CHIPS ARE DOWN, THE (SEE: LES JEUX SONT FAITS) (1947, Fr.)
CHIQUTTO PERO PICOSO (1967, Mex.) PR:A
CHISUM (1970) PR:A
CHIVATO (1961) PR:A-C
CHITTY CHITTY BANG BANG (1968, Brit.) PR:AA
CHLOE IN THE AFTERNOON (1972, Fr.) PR:O
CHOCOLATE SOLDIER, THE (1941) PR:A
CHOCOLATE WAR, THE (1988) PR:C
CHOICE OF ARMS (1981, Fr.) PR:C
CHOIRBOYS, THE (1977) PR:O
CHOKE CANYON (1986) PR:A
CHOLPON — UTRENNYAYA ZVEZDA (SEE: MORNING STAR) (1962, USSR)
C.H.O.M.P.S. (1979) PR:AA
CHOOSE ME (1984) PR:O
CHOOSE YOUR PARTNERS (SEE: TWO GIRLS ON BROADWAY) (1940)
CHOPPERS, THE (1961) PR:C-O
CHOPPING MALL (1986) PR:O
CHORUS LINE, A (1985) PR:C
CHORUS OF DISAPPROVAL, A (1989, Brit.) PR:A-C
CHOSEN, THE (1978, Brit./It.) PR:O
CHOSEN, THE (1982) PR:A
CHOSEN SURVIVORS (1974, US/Mex.) PR:C
CHRIST STOPPED AT EBOLI (1979, It./Fr.) PR:A
CHRISTIAN LICORICE STORE, THE (1971) PR:C
CHRISTIAN THE LION (1976, Brit.) PR:AA
CHRISTINA (1929) PR:A
CHRISTINA (1974, Can.) PR:C
CHRISTINE (1959, Fr.) PR:C
CHRISTINE (1983) PR:C-O
CHRISTINE JORGENSEN STORY, THE (1970) PR:O
CHRISTINE KEELER AFFAIR, THE (1964, Brit.) PR:O
CHRISTMAS CAROL, A (1938) PR:AA
CHRISTMAS CAROL, A (1951, Brit.) PR:AA
CHRISTMAS EVE (1947) PR:A
CHRISTMAS EVIL (SEE: YOU BETTER WATCH OUT) (1980)
CHRISTMAS HOLIDAY (1944) PR:A
CHRISTMAS IN CONNECTICUT (1945) PR:AA
CHRISTMAS IN JULY (1940) PR:A
CHRISTMAS KID, THE (1968, US/Sp.) PR:C
CHRISTMAS STORY, A (1983) PR:A
CHRISTMAS THAT ALMOST WASN'T, THE (1966, It.) PR:A
CHRISTMAS TREE, THE (1966. Brit.) PR:AA
CHRISTMAS TREE, THE (1969, Fr.) PR:A
CHRISTOPHER BEAN (1933) PR:A
CHRISTOPHER COLUMBUS (1949, Brit.) PR:A
CHRISTOPHER STRONG (1933) PR:C
CHROME AND HOT LEATHER (1971) PR:O
CHRONICLE OF A DEATH FORETOLD (1987, Fr./It.) PR:NR
CHRONICLE OF ANNA MAGDALENA BACH (1968, It./W. Ger.) PR:A-C
CHRONOPOLIS (1982, Fr.) PR:A-C
CHU CHIN CHOW (1934, Brit.) PR:A
CHU CHU AND THE PHILLY FLASH (1981) PR:A
CHUBASCO (1968) PR:A
C.H.U.D. II: BUD THE C.H.U.D. (1989) PR:C
CHUKA (1967) PR:C
CHUMP AT OXFORD, A (1940) PR:A
CHURCH MOUSE, THE (1934, Brit.) PR:A
CHUSHINGURA (1963, Jap.) PR:C
CIAO! MANHATTAN (1973) PR:O
CIGARETTE GIRL (1947) PR:A
CIMARRON (1931) PR:A
CIMARRON (1960) PR:A
CIMARRON KID, THE (1951) PR:A
CINCINNATI KID, THE (1965) PR:A-C
CINDERELLA (1937, Fr.) PR:A
CINDERELLA (1950) PR:AA
CINDERELLA JONES (1946) PR:AA
CINDERELLA LIBERTY (1973) PR:C-O
CINDERELLA SWINGS IT (1942) PR:A
CINDERFELLA (1960) PR:A
CINQ FILLES EN FURIE (SEE: FIVE WILD GIRLS) (1966, Fr.)
CINQUE TOMBE PER UN MEDIUM (SEE: TERROR-CREATURS FROM THE GRAVE) (1967, US/It.)
CIPHER BUREAU (1938) PR:A
CIRCLE, THE (SEE: STRICTLY UNCONVENTIONAL) (1930)
CIRCLE, THE (1959, Brit.) PR:C
CIRCLE CANYON (1934) PR:A
CIRCLE OF DANGER (1951, Brit.) PR:C
CIRCLE OF DEATH (1935) PR:A
CIRCLE OF DECEIT (1982, Fr./W. Ger.) PR:O
CIRCLE OF DECEPTON (1961, Brit.) PR:C
CIRCLE OF IRON (1979, Brit.) PR:O
CIRCLE OF LOVE (1965, Fr.) PR:C-O

CIRCLE OF POWER (SEE: MYSTIQUE) (1981)
CIRCLE OF TWO (1980, Can.) PR:O
CIRCUMSTANTIAL EVIDENCE (1935) PR:A
CIRCUMSTANTIAL EVIDENCE (1945) PR:C
CIRCUMSTANTIAL EVIDENCE (1954, Brit.) PR:C
CIRCUS (SEE: INVITATION TO THE DANCE) (1956)
CIRCUS BOY (1947, Brit.) PR:AA
CIRCUS CLOWN, THE (1934) PR:A
CIRCUS FRIENDS (1962, Brit.) PR:AA
CIRCUS GIRL (1937) PR:A
CIRCUS KID, THE (1928) PR:A
CIRCUS OF FEAR (SEE: PSYCHO-CIRCUS) (1967)
CIRCUS OF HORRORS (1960, Brit.) PR:O
CIRCUS OF LOVE (1958, W. Ger.) PR:C
CIRCUS QUEEN MURDER, THE (1933) PR:C
CIRCUS WORLD (1964) PR:A
CISARUV SLAVIK (SEE: EMPEROR AND THE NIGHT-INGALE) (1949, Czech.)
CISCO KID (1931) PR:AA
CISCO KID AND THE LADY, THE (1939) PR:A
CISCO KID RETURNS, THE (1945) PR:A
CISCO PIKE (1971) PR:O
CITADEL, THE (1938, Brit.) PR:A
CITADEL OF CRIME (1941) PR:C
CITADEL OF CRIME (SEE: MAN BETRAYED, A) (1941)
CITIZEN KANE (1941) PR:A
CITIZEN SAINT (1947) PR:AA
CITIZENS BAND (1977) PR:C
CITY ACROSS THE RIVER (1949) PR:C
CITY AFTER MIDNIGHT (1957, Brit.) PR:C
CITY AND THE DOGS, THE (1985, Peru) PR:O
CITY BENEATH THE SEA (1953) PR:C
CITY FOR CONQUEST (1940) PR:A
CITY GIRL (1930) PR:A
CITY GIRL (1938) PR:C
CITY GIRL, THE (1984) PR:O
CITY HEAT (1984) PR:O
CITY IN DARKNESS (SEE: CHARLIE CHAN IN THE CITY OF DARKNESS) (1939)
CITY IS DARK, THE (SEE: CRIME WAVE) (1954)
CITY LIMITS (1934) PR:A
CITY LIMITS (1985) PR:O
CITY LOVERS (1982, South Africa) PR:C
CITY NEWS (1983) PR:C
CITY OF BAD MEN (1953) PR:A
CITY OF BEAUTIFUL NONSENSE, THE (1935, Brit.) PR:A
CITY OF BLOOD (1988, South Africa) PR:O
CITY OF CHANCE (1940) PR:C
CITY OF FEAR (1959) PR:C
CITY OF FEAR (1965, Brit.) PR:C
CITY OF MISSING GIRLS (1941) PR:Aa
CITY OF PAIN (1951, It.) PR:C
CITY OF PLAY (1929, Brit.) PR:A
CITY OF SECRETS (1963, W. Ger.) PR:O
CITY OF SHADOWS (1955) PR:A
CITY OF SILENT MEN (1942) PR:C
CITY OF SIN (SEE: SCAVENGERS, THE) (1959, US/Phil.)
CITY OF SONG (SEE: FAREWELL TO LOVE) (1931, Brit.)
CITY OF SONGS (SEE: VIENNA, CITY OF SONGS) (1931, Ger.)
CITY OF THE DEAD (SEE: HORROR HOTEL) (1960, Brit.)
CITY OF THE WALKING DEAD (1983, Sp./It.) PR:O
CITY OF TORMENT (1950, W. Ger.) PR:C
CITY OF WOMEN (1980, It./Fr.) PR:O
CITY OF YOUTH (1938, USSR) PR:C
CITY ON A HUNT (SEE: NO ESCAPE) (1953)
CITY ON FIRE (1979, Can.) PR:O
CITY PARK (1934) PR:A
CITY SENTINEL (SEE: BEAST OF THE CITY, THE) (1932)
CITY STORY (1954) PR:C
CITY STREETS (1931) PR:A
CITY STREETS (1938) PR:A
CITY THAT NEVER SLEEPS (1953) PR:A
CITY UNDER THE SEA (1965, US/Brit.) PR:A
CITY WITHOUT MEN (1943) PR:A
CLAIR DE FEMME (SEE: WOMANLIGHT) (1979, Fr.)
CLAIRE'S KNEE (1970, Fr.) PR:C-O
CLAIRVOYANT, THE (1935, Brit.) PR:A
CLAMBAKE (1967) PR:AA
CLAN OF THE CAVE BEAR, THE (1986) PR:O
CLANCY IN WALL STREET (1930) PR:A
CLANCY STREET BOYS (1943) PR:A
CLANDESTINE (1948, Fr.) PR:C
CLANDESTINOS (SEE: LIVING DANGEROUSLY) (1988, Cuba)
CLARA'S HEART (1988) PR:C
CLARENCE (1937) PR:A
CLARENCE AND ANGEL (1981) PR:C
CLARENCE, THE CROSS-EYED LION (1965) PR:AA
CLARETTA AND BEN (1983, It./Fr.) PR:O
CLASH BY NIGHT (1952) PR:C
CLASH BY NIGHT (SEE: ESCAPE BY NIGHT) (1965, Brit.)

CLASH OF THE TITANS (1981, Brit.) PR:AA
CLASS (1983) PR:O
CLASS ENEMY (1984, W. Ger.) PR:O
CLASS OF '44 (1973) PR:C
CLASS OF MISS MAC MICHAEL, THE (1978, Brit./US) PR:O
CLASS OF 1984 (1982, Can.) PR:O
CLASS OF NUKE 'EM HIGH (1986) PR:O
CLASS RELATIONS (1986, W. Ger.) PR:A-C
CLAUDELLE INGLISH (1961) PR:C-O
CLAUDIA (1943) PR:A
CLAUDIA AND DAVID (1946) PR:AA
CLAUDINE (1974) PR:A
CLAY (1964, Aus.) PR:C-O
CLAY PIGEON, THE (1949) PR:A
CLAY PIGEON (1971) PR:O
CLAYDON TREASURE MYSTERY, THE (1938, Brit.) PR:A
CLEAN AND SOBER (1988) PR:O
CLEAN SLATE (SEE: COUP DE TORCHON) (1981, Fr.)
CLEANING UP (1933, Brit.) PR:A
CLEAR ALL WIRES (1933) PR:A
CLEAR SKIES (1963, USSR) PR:A-C
CLEAR THE DECKS (1929) PR:A
CLEARING THE RANGE (1931) PR:A
CLEGG (1969, Brit.) PR:O
CLEO FROM 5 TO 7 (1961, Fr.) PR:C
CLEOPATRA (1934) PR:C
CLEOPATRA (1963) PR:A-C
CLEOPATRA JONES (1973) PR:O
CLEOPATRA JONES AND THE CASINO OF GOLD (1975, US/Hong Kong) PR:O
CLEOPATRA'S DAUGHTER (1963, Fr./It.) PR:C
CLICKETYCLACK (SEE: DODES 'KA-DEN) (1970, Jap.)
CLIMAX, THE (1930) PR:A
CLIMAX, THE (1944) PR:A
CLIMAX, THE (1967, Fr./It.) PR:C-O
CLIMBING HIGH (1938, Brit.) PR:A
CLINIC, THE (1983, Aus.) PR:O
CLIO DE CINQ A SEPT (SEE: CLEO FROM 5 TO 7) (1961, Fr.)
CLIPPED WINGS (1938) PR:A
CLIPPED WINGS (1953) PR:A
CLIVE OF INDIA (1935) PR:A
CLOAK AND DAGGER (1946) PR:A
CLOAK AND DAGGER (1984) PR:C
CLOAK WITHOUT DAGGER (SEE: OPERATION CON-SPIRACY) (1957, Brit.)
CLOCK, THE (1945) PR:A
CLOCKMAKER, THE (1974, Fr.) PR:O
CLOCKWISE (1986, Brit.) PR:A
CLOCKWORK ORANGE, A (1971, Brit.) PR:O
CLONES, THE (1973) PR:A
CLONUS HORROR, THE (1979) PR:O
CLOPORTES (1966, Fr./It.) PR:C-O
CLOSE CALL FOR BOSTON BLACKIE, A (1946) PR:A
CLOSE CALL FOR ELLERY QUEEN, A (1942) PR:A
CLOSE ENCOUNTERS OF THE THIRD KIND (1977) PR:A
CLOSE HARMONY (1929) PR:A
CLOSE TO MY HEART (1951) PR:A
CLOSE-UP (1948) PR:A
CLOSELY WATCHED TRAINS (1966, Czech.) PR:C
CLOSEST OF KIN, THE (SEE: KINFOLK) (1970)
CLOTHES AND THE WOMAN (1937, Brit.) PR:A
CLOUD DANCER (1980) PR:A
CLOUDBURST (1952, Brit.) PR:A
CLOUDED CRYSTAL, THE (1948, Brit.) PR:A
CLOUDED YELLOW, THE (1950, Brit.) PR:A
CLOUDS OVER EUROPE (1939, Brit.) PR:A
CLOUDS OVER ISRAEL (1966, Israel) PR:C-O
CLOWN, THE (1953) PR:A
CLOWN AND THE KID, THE (1961) PR:A
CLOWN AND THE KIDS, THE (1968, US/Bulgaria) PR:AA
CLOWN MURDERS, THE (1976, Can.) PR:C
CLOWN MUST LAUGH, A (1936, Brit.) PR:A
CLUB, THE (1980, Aus.) PR:C
CLUB EARTH (SEE: GALACTIC GIGOLO) (1988)
CLUB HAVANA (1946) PR:A
CLUB LIFE (1987) PR:O
CLUB PARADISE (1986) PR:C
CLUE (1985) PR:O
CLUE OF THE MISSING APE, THE (1953, Brit.) PR:AA
CLUE OF THE NEW PIN, THE (1929, Brit.) PR:A
CLUE OF THE NEW PIN, THE (1961, Brit.) PR:A-C
CLUE OF THE SILVER KEY, THE (1961, Brit.) PR:A-C
CLUE OF THE TWISTED CANDLE (1968, Brit.) PR:A
CLUNY BROWN (1946) PR:A
C'MON, LET'S LIVE A LITTLE (1967) PR:A
COACH (1978) PR:C-O
COAL MINER'S DAUGHTER (1980) PR:A-C
COAST GUARD (1939) PR:A
COAST OF SKELETONS (1965, Brit.) PR:A
COAST TO COAST (1980) PR:A
COASTWATCHER (SEE: LAST WARRIOR, THE) (1989, Brit.)
COBRA, THE (1968, It./Sp.) PR:A

COBRA (1986) PR:O
COBRA STRIKES, THE (1948) PR:A
COBRA WOMAN (1944) PR:A
COBWEB, THE (1955) PR:A
COBWEB CASTLE (SEE: THRONE OF BLOOD) (1957, Jap.)
COCA-COLA KID, THE (1985, Aus.) PR:O
COCAINE COWBOYS (1979) PR:O
COCAINE WARS (1986) PR:O
COCK-EYED WORLD, THE (1929) PR:C
COCK O' THE NORTH (1935, Brit.) PR:A
COCK O' THE WALK (1930) PR:A
COCK OF THE AIR (1932) PR:A
COCKEYED CAVALIERS (1934) PR:A
COCKEYED COWBOYS OF CALICO COUNTY, THE (1970) PR:AA
COCKEYED MIRACLE, THE (1946) PR:AA
COCKFIGHTER (SEE: BORN TO KILL) (1975)
COCKLESHELL HEROES, THE (1955, Brit.) PR:A
COCKTAIL (1988) PR:O
COCKTAIL HOUR (1933) PR:C
COCKTAIL MOLOTOV (1980, Fr.) PR:A
COCKTAILS IN THE KITCHEN (SEE: FOR BETTTER, FOR WORSE) (1954, Brit.)
COCOANUT GROVE (1938) PR:AA
COCOANUTS, THE (1929) PR:A
COCOON (1985) PR:C
COCOON: THE RETURN (1988) PR:A
C.O.D. (1932, Brit.) PR:A
CODE NAME: EMERALD (1985) PR:C
CODE NAME: THE SOLDIER (SEE: SOLDEIR, THE) (1982)
CODE NAME TRIXIE (SEE: CRAZIES, THE) (1973)
CODE NAME VENGEANCE (1989) PR:C
CODE NAME ZEBRA (1987) PR:O
CODE OF HONOR (1930) PR:A
CODE OF SCOTLAND YARD (1948, Brit.) PR:C-O
CODE OF SILENCE (1960) PR:C
CODE OF SILENCE (1985) PR:O
CODE OF THE CACTUS (1939) PR:A
CODE OF THE FEARLESS (1939) PR:A
CODE OF THE LAWLESS (1945) PR:A
CODE OF THE MOUNTED (1935) PR:A
CODE OF THE OUTLAW (1942) PR:A
CODE OF THE PRAIRIE (1944) PR:A
CODE OF THE RANGE (1937) PR:A
CODE OF THE RANGERS (1938) PR:A
CODE OF THE SADDLE (1947) PR:A
CODE OF THE SECRET SERVICE (1939) PR:A
CODE OF THE SILVER SAGE (1950) PR:A
CODE OF THE STREETS (1939) PR:A
CODE OF THE WEST (1947) PR:A
CODE 7, VICTIM 5! (1964, Brit.) PR:A
CODE TWO (1953) PR:A
CODICE PRIVATO (SEE: PRIVAE ACCESS) (1988, It.)
COFFEE FORTUNE TELLER, THE (SEE: FORTUNE TELLER, THE) (1961, Gr.)
COFFY (1973) PR:O
COGNASSE (1932, Fr.) PR:A
COHEN AND TATE (1989) PR:O
COHENS AND KELLYS IN AFRICA, THE (1930) PR:A
COHENS AND KELLYS IN ATLANTIC CITY, THE (1929) PR:A
COHENS AND KELLYS IN HOLLYWOOD, THE (1932) PR:A
COHENS AND KELLYS IN SCOTLAND, THE (1930) PR:A
COHENS AND KELLYS IN TROUBLE, THE (1933) PR:A
COIFFURE POUR DAMES (SEE: FRENCH TOUCH, THE) (1954, Fr.)
COL FERRO E COL FUOCO (SEE: INVASION 1700) (1965, Fr./It./Yugo.)
COLD FEET (1984) PR:C
COLD JOURNEY (1975, Can.) PR:C
COLD RIVER (1982) PR:O
COLD STEEL (1987) PR:NR
COLD SWEAT (1974, It./Fr.) PR:O
COLD TURKEY (1971) PR:A
COLD WIND IN AUGUST, A (1961) PR:O
COLDITZ STORY, THE (1955, Brit.) PR:A
COLE YOUNGER, GUNFIGHTER (1958) PR:A
COLLECTOR, THE (1965, Brit.) PR:C
COLLEEN (1936) PR:A
COLLEGE COACH (1933) PR:A
COLLEGE CONFIDENTIAL (1960) PR:C
COLLEGE COQUETTE, THE (1929) PR:A
COLLEGE HOLIDAY (1936) PR:A
COLLEGE HUMOR (1933) PR:A
COLLEGE LOVE (1929) PR:A
COLLEGE LOVERS (1930) PR:A
COLLEGE RHYTHM (1934) PR:A
COLLEGE SCANDAL (1935) PR:A
COLLEGE SWEETHEARTS (1942) PR:A
COLLEGE SWING (1938) PR:A
COLLEGIATE (1936) PR:A
COLLISION (1932, Brit.) PR:A
COLLISION COURSE (SEE: BAMBOO SAUCER, THE) (1968)

COLONEL BLIMP (SEE: LIFE AND DEATH OF COLONEL BLIMP, THE) (1945, Brit.)
COLONEL BLOOD (1934, Brit.) PR:A
COLONEL BOGEY (1948, Brit.) PR:A
COLONEL CHABERT (1947, Fr.) PR:A
COLONEL EFFINGHAM'S RAID (1945) PR:A
COLONEL MARCH INVESTIGATES (1952, Brit.) PR:A
COLONEL REDL (1985, Hung./Aust./W. Ger.) PR:O
COLOR ME BLOOD RED (1965) PR:O
COLOR ME DEAD (1969, Aus.) PR:C
COLOR OF DESTINY, THE (1988, Braz.) PR:C-O
COLOR OF MONEY, THE (1986) PR:C-O
COLOR OF POMEGRANATES, THE (1980, USSR) PR:C-O
COLOR PURPLE, THE (1985) PR:A-C
COLORADO (1940) PR:A
COLORADO AMBUSH (1951) PR:A
COLORADO KID, THE (1938) PR:A
COLORADO PIONEERS (1945) PR:A
COLORADO RANGER (1950) PR:A
COLORADO SERENADE (1946) PR:A
COLORADO SUNDOWN (1952) PR:A
COLORADO SUNSET (1939) PR:A
COLORADO TERRITORY (1949) PR:A
COLORADO TRAIL (1938) PR:A
COLORS (1988) PR:O
COLOSSUS OF NEW YORK, THE (1958) PR:A
COLOSSUS OF RHODES, THE (1961, It./Fr./Sp.) PR:A
COLOSSUS: THE FORBIN PROJECT (1970) PR:A
COLPO GROSSO A GALATA: BRIDGE (SEE: THAT MAN IN ISTANBUL) (1966, Fr./It./Sp.)
COLPO GROSSO A PARIGI (SEE: HOW NOT TO ROB A DEPARTMENT STORE) (1965, Fr./It.)
COLT COMRADES (1943) PR:A
COLT .45 (1950) PR:A
COLUMN SOUTH (1953) PR:A
COMA (1978) PR:A
COMANCHE (1956) PR:A
COMANCHE STATION (1960) PR:A
COMANCHE TERRITORY (1950) PR:A
COMANCHEROS, THE (1961) PR:A
COMBAT SHOCK (1986) PR:O
COMBAT SQUAD (1953) PR:A
COME ACROSS (1929) PR:A
COME AND GET IT (1936) PR:A
COME AND SEE (1986, USSR) PR:O
COME BACK BABY (1968) PR:O
COME BACK CHARLESTON BLUE (1972) PR:O
COME BACK, LITTLE SHEBA (1952) PR:A-C
COME BACK PETER (1952, Brit.) PR:A
COME BACK PETER (1971, Brit.) PR:C
COME BACK TO ME (SEE: DOLL FACE) (1945)
COME BACK TO THE 5 & DIME, JIMMY DEAN, JIMMY DEAN (1982) PR:O
COME BLOW YOUR HORN (1963) PR:A-C
COME CLOSER, FOLKS (1936) PR:A
COME DANCE WITH ME (1950, Brit.) PR:A
COME DANCE WITH ME! (1960, Fr.) PR:C-O
COME FILL THE CUP (1951) PR:C
COME FLY WITH ME (1963, US/Brit.) PR:A
COME LIVE WITH ME (1941) PR:A
COME 'N' GET IT (SEE: LUNCH WAGON) (1980)
COME NEXT SPRING (1956) PR:AA
COME ON, THE (1956) PR:A
COME ON, COWBOYS (1937) PR:A
COME ON DANGER! (1932) PR:A
COME ON DANGER (1942) PR:A
COME ON GEORGE (1939, Brit.) PR:A
COME ON, LEATHERNECKS (1938) PR:A
COME ON, MARINES (1934) PR:A
COME ON RANGERS (1939) PR:A
COME ON TARZAN (1933) PR:A
COME OUT FIGHTING (1945) PR:A
COME OUT OF THE PANTRY (1935, Brit.) PR:AA
COME SEPTEMBER (1961) PR:A
COME SPY WITH ME (1967) PR:A
COME TO THE STABLE (1949) PR:AA
COME UP SMILING (SEE: SING ME A LOVE SONG) (1936)
COMEBACK, THE (1982, Brit.) PR:C
COMEBACK TRAIL, THE (1982) PR:O
COMEDIANS, THE (1967, US/Fr.) PR:C
COMEDIE! (SEE: COMEDY!) (1987, Fr.)
COMEDY! (1987, Fr.) PR:C-O
COMEDY MAN, THE (1964, Brit.) PR:A
COMEDY OF HORRORS, THE (1964) PR:A
COMEDY OF TERRORS, THE (SEE: COMEDY OF HORRORS, THE) (1964)
COMES A HORSEMAN (1978) PR:A-C
COMET OVER BROADWAY (1938) PR:A
COMETOGETHER (1971, US/It.) PR:O
COMFORT AND JOY (1984, Brit.) PR:A-C
COMIC, THE (1969) PR:A
COMIC MAGAZINE (1986, Jap.) PR:O
COMIN' AT YA! (1981, It.) PR:O
COMIN' ROUND THE MOUNTAIN (1936) PR:AA
COMIN' ROUND THE MOUNTAIN (1940) PR:AA
COMIN' ROUND THE MOUNTAIN (1951) PR:AA

COMIN' THRO THE RYE (1947, Brit.) PR:A
COMING ATTRACTIONS (SEE: LOOSE SHOES) (1980)
COMING HOME (1978) PR:C-O
COMING OF AGE (1938, Brit.) PR:A
COMING OUT PARTY (1934) PR:A
COMING-OUT PARTY, A (1962, Brit.) PR:A-C
COMING TO AMERICA (1988) PR:O
COMING UP ROSES (1986, Brit.) PR:A
COMMAND, THE (1954) PR:A
COMMAND DECISION (1948) PR:A
COMMAND PERFORMANCE, THE (1931) PR:A
COMMAND PERFORMANCE (1937, Brit.) PR:A
COMMANDO (1962, It./Sp./Bel./W. Ger.) PR:C
COMMANDO (1985) PR:O
COMMANDO SQUAD (1987) PR:C
COMMANDOS STRIKE AT DAWN, THE (1942) PR:A
COMMISSIONAIRE (1933, Brit.) PR:A
COMMITMENT, THE (1976) PR:C
COMMITTEE, THE (1968, Brit.) PR:C
COMMON CLAY (1930) PR:A
COMMON LAW, THE (1931) PR:C
COMMON LAW WIFE (1963) PR:O
COMMON TOUCH, THE (1941, Brit.) PR:A
COMMUNION (SEE: ALICE, SWEET ALICE) (1977)
COMMUNION (1989) PR:C
COMPANEROS (1970, It./Sp./W. Ger.) PR:C
COMPANIONS IN CRIME (1954, Brit.) PR:A
COMPANY OF COWARDS (SEE: ADVANCE TO THE REAR) (1964)
COMPANY OF KILLERS (1970) PR:A
COMPANY OF WOLVES, THE (1985, Brit.) PR:O
COMPANY SHE KEEPS, THE (1950) PR:C
COMPARTIMENT TUEURS (SEE: SLEEPING CAR MURDER) (1966, Fr.)
COMPELLED (1960, Brit.) PR:A-C
COMPETITION, THE (1980) PR:C
COMPLIMENTS OF MR. FLOW (1941, Fr.) PR:A
COMPROMISED (1931) PR:A
COMPROMISED! (1931, Brit.) PR:A
COMPROMISED DAPHINE (SEE: COMPROMISED!) (1931, Brit.)
COMPROMISING POSITIONS (1985) PR:C-O
COMPULSION (1959) PR:C-O
COMPULSORY HUSBAND, THE (1930, Brit.) PR:A
COMPULSORY WIFE, THE (1937, Brit.) PR:A
COMPUTER FREE-FOR-ALL (1969, Jap.) PR:C
COMPUTER KILLERS (SEE: HORROR HOSPITAL) (1973, Brit.)
COMPUTER WORE TENNIS SHOES, THE (1970) PR:AA
COMRADE X (1940) PR:A
COMRADES (1987, Brit.) PR:C
COMRADESHIP (SEE: KAMERADSCHAFT) (1931, Ger.)
CON ARTISTS, THE (1981, It.) PR:O
CON MEN, THE (1973, It./Sp.) PR:A
CONAN THE BARBARIAN (1982) PR:C-O
CONAN THE DESTROYER (1984) PR:C
CONCEALMENT (SEE: SECRET BRIDE) (1939)
CONCENTRATIN' KID, THE (1930) PR:A
CONCENTRATION CAMP (1939, USSR) PR:A
CONCERNING MR. MARTIN (1937, Brit.) PR:A
CONCERTO (SEE: I'VE ALWAYS LOVED YOU) (1946)
CONCERTO PER PISTOLA SOLISTA (SEE: WEEKEND MURDERS, THE) (1972, It.)
CONCORDE, THE —AIRPORT '79 (1979) PR:A-C
CONCRETE ANGELS (1987, Can.) PR:C-O
CONCRETE JUNGLE, THE (1962, Brit.) PR:C
CONCRETE JUNGLE, THE (1982) PR:O
CONDEMNED (1929) PR:C
CONDEMNED OF ALTONA, THE (1963, Fr./It.) PR:O
CONDEMNED TO DEATH (1932, Brit.) PR:A
CONDEMNED TO LIFE (SEE: WALK IN THE SHADOW) (1962, Brit.)
CONDEMNED TO LIVE (1935) PR:A
CONDEMNED WOMEN (1938) PR:A
CONDORMAN (1981) PR:AA
CONDUCT UNBECOMING (1975, Brit.) PR:A-C
CONDUCTOR, THE (1981, Pol.) PR:A-C
CONE OF SILENCE (SEE: TROUBLE IN THE SKY) (1960)
CONEY ISLAND (1943) PR:A
CONFESS DR. CORDA (1960, W. Ger.) PR:C
CONFESSION (1937) PR:A
CONFESSION (SEE: DEADLIEST SIN, THE) (1955)
CONFESSION, THE (1970, Fr./It.) PR:C
CONFESSION, THE (SEE: QUICK, LET'S GET MARRIED) (1965)
CONFESSIONAL, THE (1977, Brit.) PR:O
CONFESSIONS FROM A HOLIDAY CAMP (1977, Brit.) PR:A
CONFESSIONS OF A CO-ED (1931) PR:A
CONFESSIONS OF A COUNTERSPY (SEE: MAN ON A STRING) (1960)
CONFESSIONS OF A NAZI SPY (1939) PR:C
CONFESSIONS OF A NEWLYWED (1941, Fr.) PR:A
CONFESSIONS OF A POLICE CAPTAIN (1971, It.) PR:A
CONFESSIONS OF A POP PERFORMER (1975, Brit.) PR:O
CONFESSIONS OF A ROGUE (1948, Fr.) PR:A

CONFESSIONS OF A SORORITY GIRL (SEE: SORORITY GIRL) (1957)
CONFESSIONS OF A WINDOW CLEANER (1974, Brit.) PR:O
CONFESSIONS OF AMANS, THE (1977) PR:C-O
CONFESSIONS OF AN OPIUM EATER (1962) PR:C
CONFESSIONS OF BOSTON BLACKIE (1941) PR:A
CONFESSIONS OF FELIX KRULL, THE (1957, W. Ger.) PR:C-O
CONFESSOR (1973) PR:A
CONFIDENCE (1980, Hung.) PR:C-O
CONFIDENCE GIRL (1952) PR:A
CONFIDENTIAL (1935) PR:A
CONFIDENTIAL AGENT (1945) PR:C
CONFIDENTIAL LADY (1939, Brit.) PR:A
CONFIDENTIAL REPORT (SEE: MR. ARKADIN) (1955, Brit./Fr./Sp.)
CONFIDENTIALLY CONNIE (1953) PR:A
CONFIDENTIALLY YOURS! (1983, Fr.) PR:A-C
CONFIRM OR DENY (1941) PR:A
CONFLAGRATION (SEE: ENJO) (1958, Jap.)
CONFLICT (SEE: SWEET MAMA) (1930)
CONFLICT (1937) PR:A
CONFLICT (1939, Fr.) PR:O
CONFLICT (1945) PR:A
CONFLICT OF WINGS (SEE: FUSS OVER FEATHERS) (1954, Brit.)
CONFORMIST, THE (1970, It./Fr./W. Ger.) PR:C
CONGO CROSSING (1956) PR:A
CONGO MAISIE (1940) PR:A
CONGO SWING (SEE: BLONDIE GOES LATIN) (1941)
CONGRESS DANCES (1932, Ger.) PR:A
CONGRESS DANCES (1957, W. Ger.) PR:A
CONJUGAL BED, THE (1963, Fr./It.) PR:O
CONNECTICUT YANKEE, A (1931) PR:A
CONNECTICUT YANKEE IN KING ARTHUR'S COURT, A (1949) PR:AA
CONNECTING ROOMS (1971, Brit.) PR:A
CONNECTION, THE (1962) PR:O
CONQUERED CITY (1966, It.) PR:C
CONQUERING HORDE, THE (1931) PR:A
CONQUEROR, THE (1956) PR:C-A
CONQUEROR OF CORINTH (SEE: CENTURION, THE) (1962, Fr./It.)
CONQUEROR WORM, THE (1968, Brit.) PR:O
CONQUERORS, THE (1932) PR:A
CONQUEST (1929) PR:C
CONQUEST (1937) PR:C
CONQUEST (1984, It./Sp./Mex.) PR:O
CONQUEST OF CHEYENNE (1946) PR:A
CONQUEST OF COCHISE (1953) PR:A
CONQUEST OF MYCENE (1965, It./Fr.) PR:A-C
CONQUEST OF SPACE (1955) PR:A
CONQUEST OF THE AIR (1940, Brit.) PR:A
CONQUEST OF THE EARTH (1980) PR:A
CONQUEST OF THE PLANET OF THE APES (1972) PR:A
CONRACK (1974) PR:A
CONSCIENCE BAY (1960, Brit.) PR:C
CONSEIL DE FAMILLE (SEE: FAMILY BUSINESS) (1987)
CONSOLATION MARRIAGE (1931) PR:A
CONSPIRACY (1930) PR:A
CONSPIRACY (1939) PR:A
CONSPIRACY IN TEHERAN (1948, Brit.) PR:A
CONSPIRACY OF HEARTS (1960, Brit.) PR:AA
CONSPIRATOR (1949, Brit.) PR:A-C
CONSPIRATORS, THE (1944) PR:A
CONSTANCE (1984, New Zealand) PR:O
CONSTANT FACTOR, THE (1980, Pol.) PR:C-O
CONSTANT HUSBAND, THE (1955, Brit.) PR:C
CONSTANT NYMPH, THE (1933, Brit.) PR:A
CONSTANT NYMPH, THE (1943) PR:A
CONSTANTINE AND THE CROSS (1962, It.) PR:C-O
CONSUMING PASSIONS (1988, US/Brit.) PR:O
CONTACT MAN, THE (SEE: ALIAS NICK BEAL) (1949)
CONTACTO CHICANO (1986, Mex.) PR:O
CONTAR HASTA TEN (1986, Arg.) PR:O
CONTEMPT (1963, Fr./It.) PR:C-O
CONTENDER, THE (1944) PR:A
CONTEST GIRL (SEE: BEAUTY JUNGLE, THE) (1966, Brit.)
CONTINENTAL DIVIDE (1981) PR:A-C
CONTINENTAL EXPRESS (1939, Brit.) PR:A
CONTINENTAL TWIST, THE (SEE: TWIST ALL NIGHT) (1961)
CONTINUAVANO A CHIAMARLO TRINITA (SEE: TRINITY IS STILL MY NAME) (1971, It.)
CONTRABAND (SEE: BLACKOUT) (1940, Brit.)
CONTRABAND LOVE (1931, Brit.) PR:A
CONTRABAND SPAIN (1955, Brit.) PR:A
CONTRACT, THE (1982, Pol.) PR:A
CONVENTION CITY (1933) PR:A
CONVENTION GIRL (1935) PR:A
CONVERSATION, THE (1974) PR:A-C
CONVERSATION PIECE (1976, It./Fr.) PR:C
CONVICT 99 (1938, Brit.) PR:A
CONVICT STAGE (1965) PR:A
CONVICTED (1931) PR:A

CONVICTED (1938) PR:A
CONVICTED (1950) PR:A
CONVICTED WOMAN (1940) PR:A
CONVICTS AT LARGE (1938) PR:A
CONVICT'S CODE, THE (1930) PR:A
CONVICT'S CODE (1939) PR:A
CONVICTS FOUR (1962) PR:A
CONVOY (1940, Brit.) PR:A
CONVOY (1978) PR:C
COOGAN'S BLUFF (1968) PR:C-O
COOKIE (1989) PR:C
COOL AND THE CRAZY, THE (1958) PR:C-O
COOL BREEZE (1972) PR:C
COOL HAND LUKE (1967) PR:C
COOL IT, CAROL! (1970, Brit.) PR:O
COOL MIKADO, THE (1963, Brit.) PR:A
COOL ONES, THE (1967) PR:A
COOL WORLD, THE (1963) PR:C-O
COOLEY HIGH (1975) PR:C
COONSKIN (1975) PR:O
COP, A (1973, Fr.) PR:O
COP (1988) PR:O
COP AND THE GIRL, THE (1985, Aust./W. Ger.) PR:C-O
COP HATER (1958) PR:C
COP-OUT (1967, Brit.) PR:C-O
COPACABANA (1947) PR:A
COPLAN FX 18 CASSE TOUT (SEE: EXTERMINATORS, THE) (1965, Fr.)
COPPER, THE (1930, Brit./Ger.) PR:A
COPPER CANYON (1950) PR:A
COPPER SKY (1957) PR:A
COPS AND ROBBERS (1973) PR:A
COQUETTE (1929) PR:C
CORDELIA (1980, France/Can.) PR:C-O
CORDILLERA (SEE: FLIGHT TO FURY) (1966, US/Phil.)
CORKY (1972) PR:A-C
CORKY OF GASOLINE ALLEY (1951) PR:AA
CORN IS GREEN, THE (1945) PR:A
CORNBREAD, EARL AND ME (1975) PR:C
CORNERED (1932) PR:A
CORNERED (1945) PR:C
CORONADO (1935) PR:A
CORONER CREEK (1948) PR:C
CORPSE CAME C.O.D., THE (1947) PR:A
CORPSE GRINDERS, THE (1972) PR:O
CORPSE IN THE MORGUE (SEE: LADY IN THE MORGUE) (1938)
CORPSE OF BEVERLY HILLS, THE (1965, W. Ger.) PR:O
CORPSE VANISHES, THE (1942) PR:C
CORPUS CHRISTI BANDITS (1945) PR:A
CORREGIDOR (1943) PR:C
CORRIDOR OF MIRRORS (1948, Brit.) PR:A
CORRIDORS OF BLOOD (1962, Brit.) PR:C-O
CORRUPT (1984, It.) PR:O
CORRUPTION (1933) PR:A
CORRUPTION (1968, Brit.) PR:O
CORRUPTION OF CHRIS MILLER, THE (1979, Sp.) PR:O
CORSAIR (1931) PR:C
CORSICAN BROTHERS, THE (1941) PR:A
CORVETTE K-225 (1943) PR:A
CORVETTE SUMMER (1978) PR:C-O
COSH BOY (SEE: SLASHER, THE) (1953, Brit.)
COSMIC EYE, THE (1986) PR:AA
COSMIC MAN, THE (1959) PR:A
COSMIC MONSTERS (1958, Brit.) PR:A
COSMIC VOYAGE, THE (SEE: SPACE SHIP, THE) (1935, USSR)
COSSACKS, THE (1960, It.) PR:A
COSSACKS IN EXILE (1939, USSR) PR:A
COSSACKS OF THE DON (1932, USSR) PR:A
COSTELLO CASE, THE (1930) PR:A
COTTAGE ON DARTMOOR (SEE: ESCAPED FROM DARTMOOR) (1929, Brit.)
COTTAGE TO LET (SEE: BOMBSIGHT STOLEN) (1941, Brit.)
COTTON CLUB, THE (1984) PR:O
COTTON COMES TO HARLEM (1970) PR:O
COTTON QUEEN (1937, Brit.) PR:A
COTTONPICKIN' CHICKENPICKERS (1967) PR:C
COUCH, THE (1962) PR:C-O
COUCH TRIP, THE (1988) PR:O
COUNSEL FOR CRIME (1937) PR:A
COUNSEL FOR ROMANCE (1938, Fr.) PR:A
COUNSELLOR-AT-LAW (1933) PR:A
COUNSEL'S OPINION (1933, Brit.) PR:A
COUNT DRACULA (1971, Sp./It./Brit./W. Ger.) PR:C-O
COUNT DRACULA AND HIS VAMPIRE BRIDE (1978, Brit.) PR:C-O
COUNT FIVE AND DIE (1958, Brit.) PR:A
COUNT OF MONTE CRISTO, THE (1934) PR:AA
COUNT OF MONTE-CRISTO (1955, Fr./It.) PR:A
COUNT OF MONTE CRISTO, THE (1976, Brit.) PR:A
COUNT OF THE MONK'S BRIDGE, THE (1934, Swed.) PR:A
COUNT OF TWELVE (1955, Brit.) PR:A
COUNT THE HOURS (1953) PR:A

COUNT THREE AND PRAY (1955) PR:A
COUNT YORGA, VAMPIRE (1970) PR:O
COUNT YOUR BLESSINGS (1959) PR:A-C
COUNT YOUR BULLETS (1972) PR:O
COUNTDOWN (1968) PR:A
COUNTDOWN (1985, Hung.) PR:C
COUNTDOWN AT KUSINI (1976, Nigeria) PR:C
COUNTDOWN TO DANGER (1967, Brit.) PR:AA
COUNTER-ATTACK (1945) PR:A
COUNTER-ESPIONAGE (1942) PR:A
COUNTER TENORS, THE (SEE: WHITE VOICES, THE) (1964, Fr./It.)
COUNTERBLAST (SEE: DEVIL'S PLOT, THE) (1948, Brit.)
COUNTERFEIT (1936) PR:A
COUNTERFEIT COMMANDOS (1978, It.) PR:O
COUNTERFEIT CONSTABLE, THE (1966, Fr.) PR:A-C
COUNTERFEIT KILLER, THE (1968) PR:A
COUNTERFEIT LADY (1937) PR:A
COUNTERFEIT PLAN, THE (1957, Brit.) PR:A
COUNTERFEIT TRAITOR, THE (1962) PR:A-C
COUNTERFEITERS, THE (1948) PR:A
COUNTERFEITERS, THE (1953, It.) PR:A
COUNTERFEITERS OF PARIS, THE (1962, Fr./It.) PR:C
COUNTERPLOT (1959) PR:A
COUNTERPOINT (1967) PR:A-C
COUNTERSPY (SEE: UNDERCOVER AGENT) (1953, Brit.)
COUNTERSPY MEETS SCOTLAND YARD (1950) PR:A
COUNTESS DRACULA (1972, Brit.) PR:O
COUNTESS FROM HONG KONG, A (1967, Brit.) PR:C
COUNTESS OF MONTE CRISTO, THE (1934) PR:A
COUNTESS OF MONTE CRISTO, THE (1948) PR:A
COUNTRY (1984) PR:C
COUNTRY BEYOND, THE (1936) PR:A
COUNTRY BOY (1966) PR:A
COUNTRY BRIDE (1938, USSR) PR:A
COUNTRY DANCE (SEE: BROTHERLY LOVE) (1970, Brit.)
COUNTRY DOCTOR, THE (1936) PR:A
COUNTRY DOCTOR, THE (1963, Portugal) PR:A
COUNTRY FAIR (1941) PR:A
COUNTRY GENTLEMEN (1937) PR:A
COUNTRY GIRL, THE (1954) PR:A-C
COUNTRY MUSIC HOLIDAY (1958) PR:A
COUNTRY MUSIC, U.S.A. (SEE: LAS VEGAS HILLBILLYS) (1966)
COUNTRYMAN (1982, Jamaica) PR:C
COUNTY CHAIRMAN, THE (1935) PR:A
COUNTY FAIR, THE (1932) PR:A
COUNTY FAIR (1933, Brit.) PR:A
COUNTY FAIR (1937) PR:A
COUNTY FAIR (1950) PR:A
COUP DE FOUDRE (SEE: ENTRE NOUS) (1983, Fr.)
COUP DE GRACE (1976, Fr./W. Ger.) PR:C
COUP DE TORCHON (1981, Fr.) PR:O
COURAGE (1930) PR:A
COURAGE (SEE: RAW COURAGE) (1984)
COURAGE OF BLACK BEAUTY (1957) PR:AA
COURAGE OF LASSIE (1946) PR:AA
COURAGE OF THE WEST (1937) PR:A
COURAGEOUS AVENGER, THE (1935) PR:A
COURAGEOUS DR. CHRISTIAN, THE (1940) PR:A
COURAGEOUS MR. PENN, THE (1941, Brit.) PR:A
COURIER OF LYONS (1938, Fr.) PR:A
COURRIER SUD (1937, Fr.) PR:A
COURT CONCERT, THE (1936, Ger.) PR:A
COURT JESTER, THE (1956) PR:AA
COURT MARTIAL (1954, Brit.) PR:A
COURT MARTIAL (1962, W. Ger.) PR:A-C
COURT-MARTIAL OF BILLY MITCHELL, THE (1955) PR:A
COURT MARTIAL OF MAJOR KELLER, THE (1961, Brit.) PR:A-C
COURT OF THE PHARAOH, THE (1985, Sp.) PR:C
COURTIN' TROUBLE (1948) PR:A
COURTIN' WILDCATS (1929) PR:A
COURTNEY AFFAIR, THE (1947, Brit.) PR:A
COURTNEYS OF CURZON STREET, THE (SEE: COURTNEY AFFAIR, THE) (1947, Brit.)
COURTSHIP OF ANDY HARDY, THE (1942) PR:A
COURTSHIP OF EDDY'S FATHER, THE (1963) PR:AA
COUSIN, COUSINE (1976, Fr.) PR:O
COUSINS, THE (1959, Fr.) PR:C-O
COUSINS (1989) PR:A
COUSINS IN LOVE (1982) PR:O
COVENANT WITH DEATH, A (1966) PR:C
COVER GIRL (1944) PR:AA
COVER GIRL KILLER (1960, Brit.) PR:C-O
COVER ME BABE (1970) PR:O
COVER-UP (1949) PR:A
COVERED TRAILER, THE (1939) PR:AA
COVERED WAGON DAYS (1940) PR:A
COVERED WAGON RAID (1950) PR:A
COVERED WAGON TRAILS (1930) PR:A
COVERED WAGON TRAILS (1940) PR:A
COVERGIRL (1984, Can.) PR:O
COVERT ACTION (1980, It.) PR:O

COW AND I, THE (1961, Fr./It./W. Ger.) PR:A
COW COUNTRY (1953) PR:A
COW TOWN (1950) PR:A
COWARDS (1970) PR:C-O
COWBOY (1958) PR:A
COWBOY AND THE BANDIT, THE (1935) PR:A
COWBOY AND THE BLONDE, THE (1941) PR:A
COWBOY AND THE INDIANS, THE (1949) PR:A
COWBOY AND THE KID, THE (1936) PR:A
COWBOY AND THE LADY, THE (1938) PR:A
COWBOY AND THE PRIZEFIGHTER (1950) PR:A
COWBOY AND THE SENORITA (1944) PR:A
COWBOY BLUES (1946) PR:A
COWBOY CANTEEN (1944) PR:A
COWBOY CAVALIER (1948) PR:A
COWBOY COMMANDOS (1943) PR:A
COWBOY COUNSELOR, THE (1933) PR:A
COWBOY FROM BROOKLYN (1938) PR:A
COWBOY FROM LONESOME RIVER (1944) PR:A
COWBOY FROM SUNDOWN (1940) PR:A
COWBOY HOLIDAY (1934) PR:A
COWBOY IN AFRICA (SEE: AFRICA – TEXAS STYLE!) (1967)
COWBOY IN MANHATTTAN (1943) PR:A
COWBOY IN THE CLOUDS (1943) PR:A
COWBOY MILLIONAIRE, THE (1935) PR:A
COWBOY QUARTERBACK, THE (1939) PR:A
COWBOY ROUNDUP (SEE: RIDE 'EM COWBOY) (1936)
COWBOY SERENADE (1942) PR:A
COWBOY STAR, THE (1936) PR:A
COWBOYS, THE (1972) PR:A-C
COWBOYS FROM TEXAS (1939) PR:A
COYOTE TRAILS (1935) PR:A
COZ TAKHLE DAT SI SPENAT (SEE: WHAT WOULD YOU SAY TO SOME SPINACH?) (1976, Czech.)
CRACK HOUSE (1989) PR:O
CRACK IN THE MIRROR (1960) PR:C
CRACK IN THE WORLD (1965) PR:A
CRACK-UP, THE (1937) PR:A
CRACK-UP (1946) PR:A
CRACKED NUTS (1931) PR:AA
CRACKED NUTS (1941) PR:A
CRACKERJACK (SEE: MAN WITH 100 FACES, THE) (1938, Brit.)
CRACKERS (1984) PR:A-C
CRACKING UP (1977) PR:O
CRACKING UP (SEE: SMORGASBORD) (1983)
CRACKSMAN, THE (1963, Brit.) PR:A
CRADLE OF CRIME (SEE: DEAD END) (1937)
CRADLE SONG (1933) PR:A
CRAIG'S WIFE (1936) PR:A-C
CRANES ARE FLYING, THE (1957, USSR) PR:A
CRASH, THE (1932) PR:A
CRASH (1977) PR:C-O
CRASH DIVE (1943) PR:A
CRASH DONOVAN (1936) PR:A
CRASH DRIVE (1959, Brit.) PR:A-C
CRASH LANDING (1958) PR:A
CRASH OF SILENCE (1952, Brit.) PR:A
CRASHIN' THRU DANGER (1938) PR:A
CRASHING BROADWAY (1933) PR:A
CRASHING HOLLYWOOD (1937) PR:A
CRASHING LAS VEGAS (1956) PR:A
CRASHING THRU (1939) PR:A
CRASHING THRU (1949) PR:A
CRASHOUT (1955) PR:C
CRATER LAKE MONSTER, THE (1977) PR:A
CRAWLING EYE, THE (1958, Brit.) PR:C
CRAWLING HAND, THE (1963) PR:A
CRAWLING MONSTER, THE (SEE: CREEPING TERROR, THE) (1964)
CRAWLSPACE (1986) PR:O
CRAZE (1974, Brit.) PR:C
CRAZIES, THE (1973) PR:O
CRAZY BOYS (1987, W. Ger.) PR:O
CRAZY DESIRE (1964, It.) PR:C
CRAZY FAMILY, THE (1986, Jap.) PR:O
CRAZY FOR LOVE (1960, Fr.) PR:C-O
CRAZY HOUSE (1943) PR:A
CRAZY HOUSE (1973, Brit.) PR:C
CRAZY JACK AND THE BOY (SEE: SILENCE) (1974)
CRAZY JOE (1974) PR:O
CRAZY KNIGHTS (1944) PR:A
CRAZY LOVE (SEE: LOVE IS A DOG FROM HELL) (1987, Bel.)
CRAZY MAMA (1975) PR:O
CRAZY OVER HORSES (1951) PR:A
CRAZY PARADISE (1965, Den.) PR:O
CRAZY PEOPLE (1934, Brit.) PR:A
CRAZY QUILT (1966) PR:A
CRAZY THAT WAY (1930) PR:A
CRAZY TO KILL (SEE: DR. GILLESPIE'S CRIMINAL CASE) (1943)
CRAZY WORLD OF JULIUS VROODER, THE (1974) PR:C-O
CRAZYLEGS, ALL-AMERICAN (1953) PR:AA
CREATION OF THE HUMANOIDS, THE (1962) PR:C

CREATOR (1985) PR:O
CREATURE (1985) PR:O
CREATURE CALLED MAN, THE (1970, Jap.) PR:C
CREATURE FROM BLACK LAKE, THE (1976) PR:C
CREATURE FROM THE BLACK LAGOON (1954) PR:A
CREATURE FROM THE HAUNTED SEA (1961) PR:C
CREATURE OF THE WALKING DEAD (1960, Mex.) PR:C
CREATURE WALKS AMONG US, THE (1956) PR:A
CREATURE WASN'T NICE, THE (1981) PR:A
CREATURE WITH THE ATOM BRAIN (1955) PR:O
CREATURE WITH THE BLUE HAND (1971, W. Ger.) PR:O
CREATURES FROM BEYOND THE GRAVE (SEE: FROM BEYOND THE GRAVE) (1973, Brit.)
CREATURES OF EVIL (SEE: CURSE OF THE VAMPIRES) (1970, US/Phil.)
CREATURES OF THE PREHISTORIC PLANET (SEE: HORROR OF THE BLOOD MONSTERS) (1970, US/Phil.)
CREATURE'S REVENGE, THE (SEE: BRAIN OF BLOOD) (1971, US/Phil.)
CREATURES THE WORLD FORGOT (1971, Brit.) PR:O
CREEPER, THE (1948) PR:O
CREEPER, THE (1978, Can.) PR:O
CREEPERS (1985, It.) PR:O
CREEPERS, THE (SEE: ISLAND OF TERROR) (1967, Brit.)
CREEPING FLESH, THE (1973, Brit.) PR:O
CREEPING TERROR, THE (1964) PR:C
CREEPING UNKNOWN, THE (1956, Brit.) PR:C
CREEPOZOIDS (1987) PR:NR
CREEPS (SEE: SHIVERS) (1984, Pol.)
CREEPSHOW (1982) PR:O
CREEPSHOW 2 (1987) PR:C-O
CREMATOR, THE (1973, Czech.) PR:O
CREMATORS, THE (1972) PR:C
CRESCENDO (1972, Brit.) PR:A
CREST OF THE WAVE (1954, Brit.) PR:A
CRIA! (1975, Sp.) PR:C
CRICKET, THE (1979, It.) PR:O
CRIES AND WHISPERS (1972, Swed.) PR:C
CRIES IN THE NIGHT (SEE: AWFUL DR. ORLOFF, THE) (1964, Fr./Sp.)
CRIES IN THE NIGHT (SEE: FUNERAL HOME) (1982, Can.)
CRIME AFLOAT (1937) PR:A
CRIME AGAINST JOE (1956) PR:C
CRIME AND PASSION (1976, US/W. Ger.) PR:C-O
CRIME AND PUNISHMENT (1935, Fr.) PR:A
CRIME AND PUNISHMENT (1935) PR:C
CRIME AND PUNISHMENT (1948, Swed.) PR:A
CRIME AND PUNISHMENT (1975, USSR) PR:A
CRIME AND PUNISHMENT, U.S.A. (1959) PR:A
CRIME AT BLOSSOMS, THE (1933, Brit.) PR:A
CRIME AT PORTA ROMANA (1980, It.) PR:O
CRIME AU CONCERT MAYOL (SEE: PALACE OF NUDES) (1961, Fr./It.)
CRIME BOSS (1976, It.) PR:C
CRIME BY NIGHT (1944) PR:A
CRIME DOCTOR, THE (1934) PR:A
CRIME DOCTOR (1943) PR:A
CRIME DOCTOR'S COURAGE, THE (1945) PR:A
CRIME DOCTOR'S DIARY, THE (1949) PR:A
CRIME DOCTOR'S GAMBLE (1947) PR:A
CRIME DOCTOR'S MAN HUNT (1946) PR:A
CRIME DOCTOR'S STRANGEST CASE, THE (1943) PR:A
CRIME DOCTOR'S WARNING (1945) PR:A
CRIME DOES NOT PAY (1962, Fr./It.) PR:C-O
CRIME ET CHATIMENT (SEE: CRIME AND PUNISHMENT) (1935, Fr.)
CRIME GIVES ORDERS (SEE: HUNTED MEN) (1938)
CRIME IN THE STREETS (1956) PR:C-O
CRIME, INC. (1945) PR:A
CRIME NOBODY SAW, THE (1937) PR:A
CRIME OF DR. CRESPI, THE (1936) PR:C
CRIME OF DR. FORBES, THE (1936) PR:A
CRIME OF DR. HALLET, THE (1938) PR:A
CRIME OF HELEN STANLEY, THE (1934) PR:A
CRIME OF HONOR (1987) PR:O
CRIME OF MONSIEUR LANGE, THE (1936, Fr.) PR:C-O
CRIME OF PASSION (1957) PR:C
CRIME OF PETER FRAME, THE (1938, Brit.) PR:A
CRIME OF THE CENTURY, THE (1933) PR:A
CRIME OF THE CENTURY (1946) PR:A
CRIME OF THE CENTURY, THE (SEE: WALK EAST ON BEACON) (1952)
CRIME ON THE HILL (1933, Brit.) PR:A
CRIME OVER LONDON (1936, Brit.) PR:A
CRIME PATROL, THE (1936) PR:A
CRIME RING (1938) PR:A
CRIME SCHOOL (1938) PR:AA
CRIME TAKES A HOLIDAY (1938) PR:A
CRIME UNLIMITED (1935, Brit.) PR:A
CRIME WAVE (1954) PR:A-C
CRIME WITHOUT PASSION (1934) PR:A
CRIME ZONE (1989) PR:O
CRIMES AND MISDEMEANORS (1989) PR:A-C

CRIMES AT THE DARK HOUSE (1940, Brit.) PR:A-C
CRIMES OF DR. MABUSE, THE (SEE: TESTAMENT OF DR. MABUSE, THE) (1933, Ger.)
CRIMES OF PASSION (1984) PR:O
CRIMES OF STEPHEN HAWKE, THE (1936, Brit.) PR:A-C
CRIMES OF THE FUTURE (1969, Can.) PR:O
CRIMES OF THE HEART (1986) PR:C-O
CRIMEWAVE (1985) PR:C
CRIMINAL, THE (SEE: CONCRETE JUNGLE, THE) (1962, Brit.)
CRIMINAL AT LARGE (1932, Brit.) PR:A
CRIMINAL CODE, THE (1931) PR:A
CRIMINAL CONVERSATION (1980, Ireland) PR:C
CRIMINAL COURT (1946) PR:A
CRIMINAL LAW (1989) PR:O
CRIMINAL LAWYER (1937) PR:A
CRIMINAL LAWYER (1951) PR:A
CRIMINAL LIFE OF ARCHIBALDO DE LA CRUZ, THE (1955, Mex.) PR:O
CRIMINALS OF THE AIR (1937) PR:A
CRIMINALS OF THE GALAXY, THE (SEE: WILD, WILD PLANET, THE) (1967, It.)
CRIMINALS WITHIN (1941) PR:A
CRIMSON ALTAR, THE (SEE: CRIMSON CULT, THE) (1970, Brit.)
CRIMSON BLADE, THE (1964, Brit.) PR:A
CRIMSON CANARY, THE (1945) PR:A
CRIMSON CANDLE, THE (1934, Brit.) PR:A-C
CRIMSON CIRCLE, THE (1930, Brit.) PR:A
CRIMSON CIRCLE, THE (1936, Brit.) PR:A
CRIMSON CULT, THE (1970, Brit.) PR:O
CRIMSON EXECUTIONER, THE (SEE: BLOODY PIT OF HORROR, THE) (1965, US/It.)
CRIMSON GHOST, THE (SEE: CYCLOTRODE X) (1946)
CRIMSON KEY, THE (1947) PR:A
CRIMSON KIMONO, THE (1959) PR:A-C
CRIMSON PIRATE, THE (1952, Brit.) PR:A
CRIMSON ROMANCE (1934) PR:A
CRIMSON TRAIL, THE (1935) PR:AA
CRIPPLE CREEK (1952) PR:A
CRISIS (1950) PR:A
CRISS CROSS (1949) PR:C
CRISTO SI E FERMATO A EBOLI (SEE: CHRIST STOPPED AT EBOLI) (1979, Fr./It.)
CRITICAL CONDITION (1987) PR:C
CRITIC'S CHOICE (1963) PR:A
CRITTERS (1986) PR:C-O
CRITTERS 2: THE MAIN COURSE (1988) PR:C
CROCODILE (1979, Thai./Hong Kong) PR:O
"CROCODILE" DUNDEE (1986, Aus.) PR:A-C
"CROCODILE" DUNDEE II (1988) PR:C
CROISIERES SIDERALES (1941, Fr.) PR:A
CROMWELL (1970, Brit.) PR:A
CRONACA DI UNA MORTE ANNUNCIIATA (SEE: CHRONICLE OF A DEATH FORETOLD) (1987, Fr./It.)
CRONACA FAMILIARE (SEE: FAMILY DIARY) (1963, It.)
CRONACHE DI UN CONVENTO (SEE: RELUCTANT SAINT, THE) (1962, US/It.)
CROOK, THE (1971, Fr.) PR:A
CROOKED BILLET, THE (1930, Brit.) PR:A
CROOKED CIRCLE, THE (1932) PR:A
CROOKED CIRCLE, THE (1958) PR:A-C
CROOKED LADY, THE (1932, Brit.) PR:A
CROOKED RIVER (1950) PR:A
CROOKED ROAD, THE (1940) PR:A
CROOKED ROAD, THE (1965, Brit./Yugo.) PR:C
CROOKED SKY, THE (1957, Brit.) PR:A
CROOKED TRAIL, THE (1936) PR:A
CROOKED WAY, THE (1949) PR:A-C
CROOKED WEB, THE (1955) PR:A
CROOKS AND CORONETS (SEE: SOPHIE'S PLACE) (1970)
CROOKS ANONYMOUS (1963, Brit.) PR:A-C
CROOKS IN CLOISTERS (1964, Brit.) PR:A
CROOKS IN CLOVER (SEE: PENTHOUSE) (1933)
CROOKS TOUR (1940, Brit.) PR:A
CROONER (1932) PR:A
CROSBY CASE, THE (1934) PR:A
CROSS AND THE SWITCHBLADE, THE (1970) PR:A
CROSS CHANNEL (1955, Brit.) PR:A-C
CROSS COUNTRY (1983, Can.) PR:O
CROSS COUNTRY CRUISE (1934) PR:A-C
CROSS COUNTRY ROMANCE (1940) PR:A
CROSS CREEK (1983) PR:C
CROSS CURRENTS (1935, Brit.) PR:A
CROSS-EXAMINATION (1932) PR:A
CROSS MY HEART (1937, Brit.) PR:A
CROSS MY HEART (1946) PR:A
CROSS MY HEART (1987) PR:O
CROSS OF IRON (1977, Brit./W. Ger.) PR:O
CROSS OF LORRAINE, THE (1943) PR:C-O
CROSS OF THE LIVING (1963, Fr.) PR:C-O
CROSS ROADS (1930, Brit.) PR:A
CROSS STREETS (1934) PR:A
CROSS-UP (1958, Brit.) PR:A
CROSSED SWORDS (1954, US/It.) PR:A
CROSSED SWORDS (1978, Panama) PR:A

CROSSED TRAILS (1948) PR:A
CROSSFIRE (1933) PR:A
CROSSFIRE (1947) PR:C
CROSSING DELANCEY (1988) PR:C
CROSSOVER DREAMS (1985) PR:C-O
CROSSPLOT (1969, Brit.) PR:A
CROSSROADS (1938, Fr.) PR:A
CROSSROADS (1942) PR:A
CROSSROADS (1986) PR:C-O
CROSSROADS OF PASSION (1951, Fr.) PR:A
CROSSROADS TO CRIME (1960, Brit.) PR:C
CROSSTALK (1982, Aus.) PR:A
CROSSTRAP (1962, Brit.) PR:C
CROSSWINDS (1951) PR:A
CROUCHING BEAST, THE (1936, US/Brit.) PR:A
CROW HOLLOW (1952, Brit.) PR:A-C
CROWD FOR LISETTE, A (SEE: LISETTE) (1963)
CROWD INSIDE, THE (1971, Can.) PR:C
CROWD ROARS, THE (1932, Brit.) PR:A-C
CROWD ROARS, THE (1938) PR:A
CROWDED DAY, THE (1954, Brit.) PR:A
CROWDED PARADISE (1956) PR:C
CROWDED SKY, THE (1960) PR:A
CROWN CAPER, THE (SEE: THOMAS CROWN AF-
   FAIR, THE) (1968)
CROWN VS STEVENS (1936, Brit.) PR:A
CROWNING EXPERIENCE, THE (1960) PR:A
CROWNING GIFT, THE (1967, Brit.) PR:A
CROWNING TOUCH, THE (1959, Brit.) PR:A
CRUCIBLE OF HORROR (1971, Brit.) PR:C
CRUCIBLE OF TERROR (1971, Brit.) PR:O
CRUCIFIX, THE (1934, Brit.) PR:A
CRUEL SEA, THE (1953, Brit.) PR:A
CRUEL SWAMP (SEE: SWAMP WOMEN) (1955)
CRUEL TOWER, THE (1956) PR:A
CRUISER EMDEN (1932, Ger.) PR:A
CRUISIN' DOWN THE RIVER (1953) PR:A
CRUISING (1980) PR:O
CRUISING CASANOVAS (SEE: GOBS AND GALS)
   (1952)
CRUNCH (SEE: 24-HOUR LOVER) (1970, W. Ger.)
CRUSADE AGAINST RACKETS (1937) PR:A
CRUSADER, THE (1932) PR:A
CRUSADES, THE (1935) PR:A
CRUSOE (1989) PR:C
CRY BABY KILLER, THE (1958) PR:C
CRY BLOOD, APACHE (1970) PR:O
CRY DANGER (1951) PR:A
CRY DR. CHICAGO (1971) PR:C
CRY DOUBLE CROSS (SEE: BOOMERANG) (1960, W.
   Ger.)
CRY FOR HAPPY (1961) PR:C
CRY FOR ME, BILLY (SEE: COUNT YOUR BULLETS)
   (1972)
CRY FREEDOM (1961, Phil.) PR:A
CRY FREEDOM (1987, Brit.) PR:C
CRY FROM THE STREETS, A (1959, Brit.) PR:AA
CRY HAVOC (1943) PR:A
CRY IN THE DARK, A (1988) PR:C
CRY IN THE NIGHT, A (1956) PR:C
CRY MURDER (1950) PR:A
CRY OF BATTLE (1963, US/Phil.) PR:A
CRY OF THE BANSHEE (1970, Brit.) PR:O
CRY OF THE BEWITCHED (SEE: YOUNG AND EVIL)
   (1957, Mex.)
CRY OF THE CITY (1948) PR:C
CRY OF THE HUNTED (1953) PR:A
CRY OF THE PENGUINS (1972, Brit.) PR:A
CRY OF THE WEREWOLF (1944) PR:C-O
CRY, THE BELOVED COUNTRY (1952, Brit.) PR:A
CRY TOUGH (1959) PR:A
CRY VENGEANCE (1954) PR:A
CRY WILDERNESS (1987) PR:C
CRY WOLF (1947) PR:A
CRY WOLF (1968, Brit.) PR:AA
CRYING OUT LOUD (SEE: COTTON QUEEN (1937,
   Brit.)
CRYPT, THE (SEE: HEARTS OF HUMANITY) (1936,
   Brit.)
CRYPT OF DARK SECRETS (SEE: MARDI GRAS MAS-
   SACRE) (1978)
CRYPT OF THE LIVING DEAD (1973) PR:C
CRYSTAL BALL, THE (1943) PR:A
CRYSTAL HEART (1987) PR:C-O
CUBA (1979) PR:C
CUBA CROSSING (1980) PR:O
CUBAN FIREBALL (1951) PR:A
CUBAN LOVE SONG, THE (1931) PR:A
CUBAN PETE (1946) PR:A
CUBAN REBEL GIRLS (SEE: ASSAULT OF THE
   REBEL GIRLS) (1959)
CUCKOO CLOCK, THE (1938, It.) PR:A
CUCKOO IN THE NEST, THE (1933, Brit.) PR:A-C
CUCKOO PATROL (1965, Brit.) PR:A
CUCKOOS, THE (1930) PR:AA
CUJO (1983) PR:O
CUL-DE-SAC (1966, Brit.) PR:C-O

CULPEPPER CATTLE CO., THE (1972) PR:C
CULT OF THE COBRA (1955) PR:A-C
CULT OF THE DAMNED (SEE: ANGEL, ANGEL,
   DOWN WE GO) (1969)
CUP FEVER (1965, Brit.) PR:AA
CUP OF KINDNESS, A (1934, Brit.) PR:A
CUP-TIE HONEYMOON (1948, Brit.) PR:A
CUPID IN THE ROUGH (SEE: AGGIE APPLEBY,
   MAKER OF MEN) (1933)
CUPS OF SAN SEBASTIAN, THE (SEE: FICKLE FIN-
   GER OF FATE, THE) (1967, US/Sp.)
CURE FOR LOVE, THE (1950, Brit.) PR:A
CURFEW (1989) PR:O
CURFEW BREAKERS (1957) PR:C
CURIOUS DR. HUMPP (1967, Arg.) PR:O
CURIOUS FEMALE, THE (1969) PR:O
CURLY TOP (1935) PR:AA
CURSE, THE (1987) PR:O
CURSE OF BIGFOOT, THE (1972) PR:C
CURSE OF DARK SHADOWS (SEE: NIGHT OF DARK
   SHADOWS) (1971)
CURSE OF DRACULA, THE (SEE: RETURN OF
   DRACULA, THE) (1958)
CURSE OF FRANKENSTEIN, THE (1957, Brit.) PR:O
CURSE OF MELISSA, THE (SEE: TOUCH OF SATAN,
   THE) (1971)
CURSE OF SIMBA (SEE: CURSE OF THE VOODOO)
   (1965, Brit.)
CURSE OF THE AZTEC MUMMY, THE (1965, Mex.)
   PR:A-C
CURSE OF THE BLOOD GHOULS (1969, It.) PR:O
CURSE OF THE CAT PEOPLE, THE (1944) PR:C-O
CURSE OF THE CRIMSON ALTAR (SEE: CRIMSON
   CULT, THE) (1970, Brit.)
CURSE OF THE CRYING WOMAN, THE (1969, Mex.)
   PR:C
CURSE OF THE DEMON (1958, Brit.) PR:O
CURSE OF THE DEVIL (1973, Mex./Sp.) PR:O
CURSE OF THE DOLL PEOPLE, THE (1968, Mex.) PR:C-
   O
CURSE OF THE FACELESS MAN (1958) PR:C
CURSE OF THE FLY (1965, Brit.) PR:C
CURSE OF THE GOLEM (SEE: IT!) (1967, Brit.)
CURSE OF THE LIVING CORPSE, THE (1964) PR:O
CURSE OF THE MUMMY'S TOMB, THE (1965, Brit.)
   PR:C
CURSE OF THE MUSHROOM PEOPLE (SEE: ATTACK
   OF THE MUSHROOM PEOPLE) (1964)
CURSE OF THE PINK PANTHER (1983, Brit.) PR:A
CURSE OF THE STONE HAND (1965, Mex./Chile) PR:C
CURSE OF THE SWAMP CREATURE (1966) PR:C
CURSE OF THE UNDEAD (1959) PR:C
CURSE OF THE VAMPIRE (SEE: PLAYGIRLS AND
   THE VAMPIRE, THE) (1963, It.)
CURSE OF THE VAMPIRES (1970, Phil./US) PR:O
CURSE OF THE VOODOO (1965, Brit.) PR:O
CURSE OF THE WEREWOLF, THE (1961, Brit.) PR:O
CURSE OF THE WRAYDONS, THE (1946, Brit.) PR:A-C
CURSED MEDALLION, THE (SEE: NIGHT CHILD)
   (1975, Brit./It.)
CURSES OF THE GHOULS (SEE: CURSE OF THE
   BLOOD GHOULS) (1969, It.)
CURTAIN AT EIGHT (1934) PR:A
CURTAIN CALL (1940) PR:A
CURTAIN CALL AT CACTUS CREEK (1950) PR:AA
CURTAIN FALLS, THE (1935) PR:A
CURTAIN RISES, THE (1939, Fr.) PR:A
CURTAIN UP (1952, Brit.) PR:A
CURTAINS (1983, Can.) PR:O
CURUCU, BEAST OF THE AMAZON (1956) PR:C
CUSTER MASSACRE, THE (SEE: GREAT SIOUX MAS-
   SACRE, THE) (1965)
CUSTER OF THE WEST (1968, US/Sp.) PR:C
CUSTOMS AGENT (1950) PR:A
CUT AND RUN (1986, It.) PR:O
CUTTER AND BONE (1981) PR:O
CUTTING CLASS (1989) PR:O
CYBORG (1989) PR:O
CYBORG 2087 (1966) PR:A
CYCLE, THE (1979, Iran) PR:A-C
CYCLE SAVAGES, THE (1969) PR:O
CYCLONE (1987) PR:C
CYCLONE FURY (1951) PR:A
CYCLONE KID, THE (1943) PR:A
CYCLONE KID, THE (1942) PR:A
CYCLONE OF THE SADDLE (1935) PR:A
CYCLONE ON HORSEBACK (1941) PR:A
CYCLONE PRAIRIE RANGERS (1944) PR:A
CYCLONE RANGER (1935) PR:A
CYCLOPS (1957) PR:C-O
CYCLOTRODE X (1946) PR:A
CYNARA (1932) PR:A-C
CYNTHIA (1947) PR:AA
CYNTHIA'S SECRET (SEE: DARK DELUSION) (1947)
CYRANO DE BERGERAC (1950) PR:AA
CZAR OF BROADWAY, THE (1930) PR:A
CZAR OF THE SLOT MACHINES (SEE: KING OF GAM-
   BLERS) (1937)

CZAR WANTS TO SLEEP (1934, US/USSR) PR:A
CZARINA (SEE: ROYAL SCANDAL, A) (1945)
CZLOWIEK Z MARMURU (SEE: MAN OF MARBLE)
   (1979, Pol.)
CZLOWIEK Z ZELAZA (SEE: MAN OF IRON) (1981,
   Pol.)

D

D-DAY, THE SIXTH OF JUNE (1956) PR:A
D.C. CAB (1983) PR:C
D.I., THE (1957) PR:A
D.O.A. (1950) PR:A
D.O.A. (1988) PR:C-O
DA (1988) PR:A-C
DA BANCARELLA A BANCAROTTA (SEE: PEDDLIN'
   IN SOCIETY) (1949, It.)
DA DUNKERQUE ALLA VITTORIA (SEE: FROM HELL
   TO VICTORY) (1979, Fr./It./Sp.)
DA YUE BING (SEE: BIG PARADE, THE) (1987, Chi.)
DABLOVA PAST (SEE: DEVIL'S TRAP, THE) (1964,
   Czech.)
DAD (1989) PR:C
DAD AND DAVE COME TO TOWN (1938, Aus.) PR:A
DADDY LONG LEGS (1931) PR:AA
DADDY LONG LEGS (1955) PR:AA
DADDY-O (1959) PR:C
DADDY'S DEADLY DARLING (1984) PR:O
DADDY'S BOYS (1988) PR:O
DADDY'S GIRL (SEE: DADDY'S DEADLY DARLING)
   (1984)
DADDY'S GONE A-HUNTING (1969) PR:C
DAD'S ARMY (1971, Brit.) PR:A
DAFFODIL KILLER (SEE: DEVIL'S DAFFODIL, THE)
   (1967, Brit./W. Ger.)
DAFFY DUCK'S MOVIE: FANTASTIC ISLAND (1983)
   PR:AA
DAGGERS OF BLOOD (SEE: INVASION 1700) (1965,
   Fr./It./Yugo.)
DAGORA THE SPACE MONSTER (1964, Jap.) PR:A
DAI SANJI SEKAI TAISEN (SEE: FINAL WAR, THE)
   (1960, Jap.)
DAIBOKEN (SEE: DON'T CALL ME A CON MAN)
   (1966, Jap.)
DAIBOSATSU TOGE (SEE: SWORD OF SOOM, THE)
   (1966, Jap.)
DAIKAIJU GAMERA (SEE: GAMERA THE INVINCI-
   BLE) (1966, Jap.)
DAIKANBU (SEE: GANGSTER VIP, THE) (1968, Jap.)
DAIKYOJU GAPPA (SEE: GAPPA THE TRIFIBIAN
   MONSTER) (1967, Jap.)
DAISIES (1967, Czech.) PR:C-O
DAISY KENYON (1947) PR:A-C
DAISY MILLER (1974) PR:C-O
DAKOTA (1945) PR:A
DAKOTA INCIDENT (1956) PR:A
DAKOTA KID, THE (1951) PR:AA
DAKOTA LIL (1950) PR:A
DALEKA CESTA (SEE: DISTANT JOURNEY) (1950,
   Czech.)
DALEKS — INVASION EARTH 2150 A.D. (1966, Brit.) PR:A
DALLAS (1950) PR:A
DALTON GANG, THE (1949) PR:A
DALTON GIRLS, THE (1957) PR:A
DALTON THAT GOT AWAY (1960) PR:A
DALTONS RIDE AGAIN, THE (1945) PR:A
DALTONS' WOMEN, THE (1950) PR:A
DAM BUSTERS, THE (1955, Brit.) PR:A
DAMA NA KOLEJICH (SEE: LADY ON THE TRACKS,
   THE) (1968, Czech.)
DAMA S SOBACHKOY (SEE: LADY WITH THE DOG,
   THE) (1962, USSR)
DAMAGED GOODS (1937) PR:C
DAMAGED GOODS (SEE: V.D.) (1961)
DAMAGED LIVES (1937) PR:C
DAMAGED LOVE (1931) PR:C
DAMES (1934) PR:AA
DAMES AHOY (1930) PR:AA
DAMIEN — OMEN II (1978) PR:O
DAMN CITIZEN (1958) PR:A
DAMN THE DEFIANT! (1962, Brit.) PR:A
DAMN YANKEES (1958) PR:A
DAMNATION (1988, Hung.) PR:O
DAMNATION ALLEY (1977) PR:C
DAMNED, THE (1969, It./W. Ger.) PR:O
DAMNED, THE (1948, Fr.) PR:C
DAMNED, THE (SEE: THESE ARE THE DAMNED)
   (1965, Brit.)
DAMNED DON'T CRY, THE (1950) PR:A-C
DAMON AND PYTHIAS (1962, US/It.) PR:A
DAMSEL IN DISTRESS, A (1937) PR:A
DAN CANDY'S LAW (SEE: ALIEN THUNDER) (1975,
   US/Can.)
DAN MATTHEWS (1936) PR:A
DANCE BAND (1935, Brit.) PR:A
DANCE, CHARLIE, DANCE (1937) PR:A
DANCE, FOOLS, DANCE (1931) PR:A-C
DANCE, GIRL, DANCE (1933) PR:A

DANCE, GIRL, DANCE (1940) PR:A
DANCE HALL (1929) PR:A
DANCE HALL (1941) PR:AA
DANCE HALL (1950, Brit.) PR:A
DANCE HALL HOSTESS (1933) PR:A
DANCE LITTLE LADY (1954, Brit.) PR:A
DANCE OF DEATH, THE (1938, Brit.) PR:A
DANCE OF DEATH, THE (1971, Brit.) PR:C
DANCE OF LIFE, THE (1929) PR:A
DANCE OF THE DAMNED (1989) PR:O
DANCE OF THE DWARFS (1983, US/Phil.) PR:C
DANCE OF THE VAMPIRES (SEE: FEARLESS VAM-
    PIRE KILLER, OR PARDON ME BUT YOUR TEETH
    ARE IN MY NECK) (1967, US/Brit.)
DANCE PRETTY LADY (1932, Brit.) PR:A
DANCE TEAM (1932) PR:AA
DANCE WITH A STRANGER (1985, Brit.) PR:C-O
DANCE WITH ME, HENRY (1956) PR:A
DANCERS, THE (1930) PR:A
DANCERS (1987) PR:A
DANCERS IN THE DARK (1932) PR:A
DANCING CO-ED (1939) PR:A
DANCING DYNAMITE (1931) PR:A
DANCING FEET (1936) PR:A
DANCING FOOL, THE (SEE: HAROLD TEEN) (1934)
DANCING HEART, THE (1959, W. Ger.) PR:A
DANCING IN MANHATTAN (1945) PR:A
DANCING IN THE DARK (1949) PR:A
DANCING IN THE DARK (1986, Can.) PR:C
DANCING LADY (1933) PR:A
DANCING MAN (1934) PR:A
DANCING MASTERS, THE (1943) PR:A
DANCING ON A DIME (1940) PR:A
DANCING PIRATE (1936) PR:A
DANCING SWEETIES (1930) PR:A
DANCING WITH CRIME (1947, Brit.) PR:A
DANCING YEARS, THE (1950, Brit.) PR:AA
DANDY DICK (1935, Brit.) PR:A
DANDY IN ASPIC, A (1968, Brit.) PR:A
DANDY, THE ALL AMERICAN GIRL (1976) PR:A
DANGER AHEAD (1935) PR:A
DANGER AHEAD (1940) PR:A
DANGER BY MY SIDE (1962, Brit.) PR:A-C
DANGER: DIABOLIK (1968, It./Fr.) PR:A
DANGER FLIGHT (1939) PR:AA
DANGER IN PARIS (SEE: CAFE COLETTE) (1937, Brit.)
DANGER IN THE PACIFIC (1942) PR:A
DANGER IS A WOMAN (1952, Fr.) PR:C-O
DANGER ISLAND (SEE: MR. MOTO IN DANGER IS-
    LAND) (1939)
DANGER LIGHTS (1930) PR:AA
DANGER – LOVE AT WORK (1937) PR:A
DANGER ON THE AIR (1938) PR:A
DANGER ON WHEELS (1940) PR:A
DANGER PATROL (1937) PR:A
DANGER RIDES THE RANGE (SEE: THREE TEXAS
    STEERS) (1939)
DANGER ROUTE (1968, Brit.) PR:A
DANGER SIGNAL (1945) PR:A
DANGER STREET (1947) PR:A
DANGER TOMORROW (1960, Brit.) PR:A-C
DANGER TRAILS (1935) PR:A
DANGER VALLEY (1938) PR:AA
DANGER WITHIN (SEE: BREAKOUT) (1960, Brit.)
DANGER WOMAN (1946) PR:A
DANGER! WOMEN AT WORK (1943) PR:A
DANGER ZONE (1951) PR:C
DANGER ZONE, THE (1987) PR:O
DANGER ZONE II: REAPER'S REVENGE (1989) PR:O
DANGEROUS (1936) PR:A-C
DANGEROUS ADVENTURE, A (1937) PR:A
DANGEROUS AFFAIR, A (1931) PR:A
DANGEROUS AFTERNOON (1961, Brit.) PR:A-C
DANGEROUS AGE (SEE: WILD BOYS OF THE ROAD)
    (1933)
DANGEROUS AGE, A (SEE: BELOVED BRAT) (1938)
DANGEROUS AGE, A (1960, Can.) PR:A
DANGEROUS ASSIGNMENT (1950, Brit.) PR:A-C
DANGEROUS BLONDES (1943) PR:A
DANGEROUS BUSINESS (1946) PR:A
DANGEROUS CARGO (1939. Brit.) PR:A
DANGEROUS CARGO (1954, Brit.) PR:C
DANGEROUS CHARTER (1962) PR:A
DANGEROUS CHARTER (SEE: CREEPING TERROR,
    THE) (1964)
DANGEROUS CORNER (1935) PR:A
DANGEROUS CROSSING (1953) PR:A
DANGEROUS CURVES (1929) PR:AA
DANGEROUS DAVIES – THE LAST DETECTIVE (1981,
    Brit.) PR:A
DANGEROUS EXILE (1958, Brit.) PR:A
DANGEROUS FEMALE (SEE: MALTESE FALCON,
    THE) (1931)
DANGEROUS FINGERS (SEE: WANTED BY SCOT-
    LAND YARD) (1939, Brit.)
DANGEROUS FRIEND, A (SEE: TODD KILLINGS,
    THE) (1971)
DANGEROUS GAME, A (1941) PR:A

DANGEROUS GROUND (1934, Brit.) PR:A
DANGEROUS HOLIDAY (1937) PR:AA
DANGEROUS INTRIGUE (1936) PR:A
DANGEROUS INTRUDER (1945) PR:A
DANGEROUS KISS, THE (1961, Jap.) PR:A
DANGEROUS LADY (1941) PR:A
DANGEROUS LOVE AFFAIR (SEE: LES LIASONS
    DANGEREUSES) (1961, Fr./Ital.)
DANGEROUS MEDICINE (1938, Brit.) PR:A
DANGEROUS MILLIONS (1946) PR:A
DANGEROUS MISSION (1954) PR:A-C
DANGEROUS MONEY (1946) PR:A
DANGEROUS MOONLIGHT (SEE: SUICIDE SQUAD-
    RON) (1942, Brit.)
DANGEROUS MOVES (1984, Switz.) PR:C
DANGEROUS NAN MC GREW (1930) PR:A
DANGEROUS NUMBER (1937) PR:A
DANGEROUS PARADISE (1930) PR:A
DANGEROUS PARTNERS (1945) PR:A
DANGEROUS PASSAGE (1944) PR:A
DANGEROUS PROFESSION, A (1949) PR:A
DANGEROUS SEAS (1931, Brit.) PR:A
DANGEROUS SECRETS (1938, Brit.) PR:A
DANGEROUS TO KNOW (1938) PR:A
DANGEROUS VENTURE (1947) PR:A
DANGEROUS VOYAGE (SEE: TERROR SHIP) (1954,
    Brit.)
DANGEROUS WATERS (1936) PR:A
DANGEROUS WHEN WET (1953) PR:A
DANGEROUS WOMAN, A (1929) PR:A
DANGEROUS YEARS (1947) PR:A
DANGEROUS YOUTH (1958, Brit.) PR:A
DANGEROUSLY CLOSE (1986) PR:O
DANGEROUSLY THEY LIVE (1942) PR:A
DANGEROUSLY YOURS (1933) PR:A
DANGEROUSLY YOURS (1937) PR:A
DANIEL (1983) PR:C
DANIEL BOONE (1936) PR:AA
DANIEL BOONE, TRAIL BLAZER (1957) PR:AA
DANIELLA BY NIGHT (1962, Fr/W. Ger.) PR:C
DANNY BOY (1934, Brit.) PR:A
DANNY BOY (1941, Brit.) PR:A
DANNY BOY (1946) PR:AA
DANNY TRAVIS (SEE: LAST WORD, THE) (1979)
DANS LA VILLE BLANCHE (SEE: IN THE WHITE
    CITY) (1983, Portugal/Switz.)
DANS LES GRIFFES DU MANIAQUE (SEE: DIABOLI-
    CAL DR. Z, THE) (1967, Fr./Sp.)
DAN'S MOTEL (1982) PR:O
DANSE MACABRE (SEE: CASTLE OF BLOOD) (1964,
    Fr./It.)
DANTE'S INFERNO (1935) PR:A
DANTON (1931, Ger.) PR:A
DANTON (1983, Fr./Pol.) PR:O
DANZA MACABRA (SEE: CASTLE OF BLOOD) (1964,
    Fr./It.)
DAO MA DAN (SEE: PEKING OPERA BLUES) (1986,
    Hong Kong)
DAPHNE, THE (1967, Jap.) PR:A-C
DARBY AND JOAN (1937, Brit.) PR:A
DARBY O'GILL AND THE LITTLE PEOPLE (1959) PR:AA
DARBY'S RANGERS (1958) PR:A
DAREDEVIL, THE (1971) PR:C
DAREDEVIL DICK (SEE: YANKEE DON) (1931)
DAREDEVIL DRIVERS (1938) PR:A
DAREDEVIL IN THE CASTLE (1961, Jap.) PR:A
DAREDEVILS OF EARTH (SEE: MONEY FOR SPEED)
    (1933, Brit.)
DAREDEVILS OF THE CLOUDS (1948) PR:A
DARING CABALLERO, THE (1949) PR:A
DARING DANGER (1932) PR:A
DARING DAUGHTERS (1933) PR:A
DARING DOBERMANS, THE (1973) PR:AA
DARING GAME (1968) PR:A
DARING YOUNG MAN, THE (1935) PR:A
DARING YOUNG MAN, THE (1942) PR:A
DARK, THE (SEE: HORROR HOUSE) (1970, Brit.)
DARK, THE (1979) PR:O
DARK ALIBI (1946) PR:A
DARK ANGEL, THE (1935) PR:A
DARK AT THE TOP OF THE STAIRS, THE (1960) PR:C
DARK AVENGER, THE (SEE: WARRIORS, THE) (1955,
    Brit.)
DARK CITY (1950) PR:A
DARK COMMAND (1940) PR:A
DARK CORNER, THE (1946) PR:C
DARK CRYSTAL, THE (1982, Brit.) PR:A
DARK DELUSION (1947) PR:A
DARK END OF THE STREET, THE (1981) PR:O
DARK ENEMY (1984, Brit.) PR:A
DARK EYES (1938, Fr.) PR:O
DARK EYES (1987, It.) PR:A-C
DARK EYES OF LONDON (SEE: HUMAN MONSTER,
    THE) (1940, Brit.)
DARK EYES OF LONDON (1961, W. Ger.) PR:A
DARK HAZARD (1934) PR:A
DARK HORSE, THE (1932) PR:A

DARK HORSE, THE (1946) PR:A
DARK HOUR, THE (1936) PR:A
DARK INTERVAL (1950, Brit.) PR:C
DARK INTRUDER (1965) PR:C
DARK IS THE NIGHT (1946, USSR) PR:C-O
DARK JOURNEY (1937, Brit.) PR:A
DARK LIGHT, THE (1951, Brit.) PR:C
DARK MAN, THE (1951, Brit.) PR:A
DARK MANHATTAN (1937) PR:C
DARK MIRROR, THE (1946) PR:C
DARK MOUNTAIN (1944) PR:A
DARK ODYSSEY (1961) PR:C
DARK OF THE SUN (1968, Brit.) PR:A
DARK PAGE, THE (SEE: SCANDAL SHEET) (1931)
DARK PASSAGE (1947) PR:A
DARK PAST, THE (1948) PR:A
DARK PLACES (1974, Brit.) PR:A
DARK PURPOSE (1964, US/Fr./It.) PR:C
DARK RED ROSES (1930, Brit.) PR:A
DARK RIVER (1956, Arg.) PR:O
DARK ROAD, THE (1948, Brit.) PR:O
DARK SANDS (1938, Brit.) PR:AA
DARK SECRET (1949, Brit.) PR:A
DARK SHADOWS (SEE: HOUSE OF DARK SHAD-
    OWS) (1970)
DARK SIDE OF TOMORROW, THE (1970) PR:O
DARK SKIES (SEE: DARKENED SKIES) (1930)
DARK STAIRWAY, THE (1938, Brit.) PR:A
DARK STAR (1975) PR:C
DARK STREETS (1929) PR:A
DARK STREETS OF CAIRO (1940) PR:A
DARK TOWER, THE (1943, Brit.) PR:A
DARK TOWER (1989) PR:C
DARK VENTURE (1956) PR:A
DARK VICTORY (1939) PR:A
DARK WATERS (1944) PR:A
DARK WORLD (1935, Brit.) PR:A
DARKENED ROOMS (1929) PR:A
DARKENED SKIES (1930) PR:A
DARKER THAN AMBER (1970) PR:O
DARKEST AFRICA (1936) PR:A
DARKEST HOUR, THE (SEE: HELL ON FRISCO BAY)
    (1956)
DARKTOWN STRUTTERS (1975) PR:C
DARLING (1965, Brit.) PR:O
DARLING, HOW COULD YOU! (1951) PR:A
DARLING LILI (1970) PR:C
DARTS ARE TRUMPS (1938, Brit.) PR:A
DARWIN ADVENTURE, THE (1972, Brit.) PR:A
D.A.R.Y.L. (1985) PR:AA
DAS AUSSCHWEIFENDE LEBEN DES MARQUIS DE
    SADE (SEE: DE SADE) (1969, US/W. Ger.)
DAS BOOT (SEE: BOAT, THE) (1981, W. Ger.)
DAS HAUS AM FLUSS (1986, E. Ger./W. Ger.) PR:O
DAS HOFKONZERT (SEE: COURT CONCERT, THE)
    (1936, Ger.)
DAS INDISCHE GRABMAL (SEE: JOURNEY TO THE
    LOST CITY) (1959, Fr./It./W. Ger.)
DAS LETZTE GEHEIMNIS (1959, W. Ger.) PR:C
DAS LIED VOM LEBEN (SEE: SONG OF LIFE, THE)
    (1931, Ger.)
DAS MADCHEN VON MOORHOF (SEE: GIRL FROM
    THE MARSH CROFT, THE) (1935, Ger.)
DAS NACHTLOKAL ZUM SILBERMOND (SEE: 5 SIN-
    NERS) (1961, W. Ger.)
DAS PHANTOM VON SOHO (SEE: PHANTOM OF
    SOHO, THE) (1967, W. Ger.)
DAS SCHLANGENEI (SEE: SERPENT'S EGG, THE)
    (1977, US/W. Ger.)
DAS SCHLOSS (SEE: CASTLE, THE) (1969, Switz./W.
    Ger.)
DAS SCHWEIGEN DES DICHTERS (SEE: POET'S SI-
    LENCE, THE) (1987, W. Ger.)
DAS TANZENDE HERZ (SEE: DANCING HEART, THE)
    (1959, W. Ger.)
DAS TESTAMENT DES DR. MABUSE (SEE: TESTA-
    MENT OF DR. MABUSE, THE) (1933, Ger.)
DAS VERRUECKTESTE AUTO DER WELT (SEE: MAD-
    DEST CAR IN THE WORLD, THE) (1974, W. Ger.)
DATE AT MIDNIGHT (1960, Brit.) PR:A-C
DATE BAIT (1960) PR:O
DATE WITH A DREAM, A (1948, Brit.) PR:A
DATE WITH A LONELY GIRL (SEE: T.R. BASKIN)
    (1971)
DATE WITH AN ANGEL (1987) PR:A-C
DATE WITH DEATH, A (1959) PR:A
DATE WITH DESTINY, A (SEE: MAD DOCTOR, THE)
    (1941)
DATE WITH DISASTER (1957, Brit.) PR:C
DATE WITH JUDY, A (1948) PR:AA
DATE WITH THE FALCON, A (1941) PR:A
DATELINE DIAMONDS (1966, Brit.) PR:A
DAUGHTER OF CLEOPATRA (SEE: CLEOPATRA'S
    DAUGHTER) (1960, It.)
DAUGHTER OF DARKNESS (1948, Brit.) PR:O
DAUGHTER OF DECEIT (1977, Mex.) PR:A-C
DAUGHTER OF DR. JEKYLL (1957) PR:A
DAUGHTER OF EVIL (1930, Ger.) PR:O

DAUGHTER OF FRANKENSTEIN, THE (SEE: SANTO CONTRA LA HIJA DE FRANKENSTEIN) (1971, Mex.)
DAUGHTER OF LUXURY (SEE: FIVE AND TEN) (1931)
DAUGHTER OF MATA HARI (SEE: MATA HARI'S DAUGHTER) (1954, Fr./It.)
DAUGHTER OF ROSIE O'GRADY, THE (1950) PR:AA
DAUGHTER OF SHANGHAI (1937) PR:A
DAUGHTER OF THE DRAGON (1931) PR:A
DAUGHTER OF THE JUNGLE (1949) PR:A
DAUGHTER OF THE NILE (1988, Taiwan) PR:C
DAUGHTER OF THE SANDS (1952) PR:C-O
DAUGHTER OF THE SUN GOD (1962) PR:A
DAUGHTER OF THE TONG (1939) PR:A
DAUGHTER OF THE WEST (1949) PR:A
DAUGHTERS COURAGEOUS (1939) PR:A
DAUGHTERS OF DARKNESS (1971, Bel./Fr./It./W. Ger.) PR:O
DAUGHTERS OF DESTINY (1953, Fr./It.) PR:C
DAUGHTERS OF SATAN (1972) PR:C
DAUGHTERS OF TODAY (1933, Brit.) PR:A
DAVID (1979, W. Ger.) PR:C
DAVID AND BATHSHEBA (1951) PR:C
DAVID AND GOLIATH (1961, It.) PR:A
DAVID AND LISA (1962) PR:A-C
DAVID COPPERFIELD (1935) PR:A
DAVID COPPERFIELD (1970, Brit.) PR:A
DAVID GOLDER (1932, Fr.) PR:A
DAVID HARDING, COUNTERSPY (1950) PR:A
DAVID HARUM (1934) PR:A
DAVID HOLZMAN'S DIARY (1968) PR:C-O
DAVID LIVINGSTONE (1936, Brit.) PR:A
DAVY (1958, Brit.) PR:A
DAVY CROCKETT AND THE RIVER PIRATES (1956) PR:AA
DAVY CROCKETT, INDIAN SCOUT (1950) PR:AA
DAVY CROCKETT, KING OF THE WILD FRONTIER (1955) PR:AA
DAWN, THE (SEE: DAWN OVER IRELAND) (1936, Brit.)
DAWN (1979, Aus.) PR:C
DAWN AT SOCORRO (1954) PR:A
DAWN EXPRESS, THE (1942) PR:A
DAWN OF THE DEAD (1979) PR:O
DAWN ON THE GREAT DIVIDE (1942) PR:A
DAWN OVER IRELAND (1938, Ireland) PR:A
DAWN PATROL, THE (1930) PR:A
DAWN PATROL, THE (1938) PR:C
DAWN RIDER (1935) PR:A
DAWN TRAIL, THE (1931) PR:A
DAY AFTER, THE (SEE: UP FROM THE BEACH) (1965)
DAY AFTER HALLOWEEN, THE (1981, Aus.) PR:O
DAY AFTER THE DIVORCE, THE (1940, Ger.) PR:A
DAY AFTER TOMORROW, THE (SEE: STRANGE HOLIDAY) (1945)
DAY AND THE HOUR, THE (1963, Fr./It.) PR:A
DAY AT THE BEACH, A (1970) PR:O
DAY AT THE RACES, A (1937) PR:AA
DAY FOR NIGHT (1973, Fr.) PR:A-C
DAY IN COURT, A (1965, It.) PR:O
DAY IN THE DEATH OF JOE EGG, A (1972, Brit.) PR:O
DAY MARS INVADED EARTH, THE (1963) PR:C
DAY OF ANGER (1970, It./W. Ger.) PR:O
DAY OF FURY, A (1956) PR:A
DAY OF RECKONING (1933) PR:O
DAY OF THE ANIMALS (1977) PR:C
DAY OF THE BAD MAN (1958) PR:A
DAY OF THE COBRA, THE (1985, It.) PR:O
DAY OF THE DEAD (1985) PR:O
DAY OF THE DOLPHIN, THE (1973) PR:A
DAY OF THE EVIL GUN (1968) PR:A
DAY OF THE HANGING, THE (SEE: LAW OF THE LAWLESS) (1964)
DAY OF THE JACKAL, THE (1973, Brit./Fr.) PR:C
DAY OF THE LANDGRABBERS (SEE: LAND RAIDERS) (1970)
DAY OF THE LOCUST, THE (1975) PR:C-O
DAY OF THE NIGHTMARE (1965) PR:C
DAY OF THE OUTLAW (1959) PR:A
DAY OF THE OWL, THE (1968, Fr./It.) PR:C
DAY OF THE TRIFFIDS, THE (1963) PR:C
DAY OF THE WOLVES (1973) PR:A-C
DAY OF THE WOMAN (SEE: I SPIT ON YOUR GRAVE) (1983)
DAY OF TRIUMPH (1954) PR:A
DAY OF WRATH (1943, Den.) PR:C
DAY THE BOOKIES WEPT, THE (1939) PR:A
DAY THE EARTH CAUGHT FIRE, THE (1961, Brit.) PR:A
DAY THE EARTH FROZE, THE (1959, USSR/Fin.) PR:AA
DAY THE EARTH STOOD STILL, THE (1951) PR:A
DAY THE FISH CAME OUT, THE (1967, Brit./Gr.) PR:C
DAY THE HOTLINE GOT HOT, THE (1968, Fr./Sp.) PR:A
DAY THE SCREAMING STOPPED, THE (SEE: COMEBACK, THE) (1982, Brit.)
DAY THE SKY EXPLODED, THE (1958, Fr./It.) PR:A
DAY THE SUN ROSE, THE (1969, Jap.) PR:A
DAY THE WAR ENDED, THE (1961, USSR) PR:A-C

DAY THE WORLD CHANGED HANDS, THE (SEE: COLOSSUS: THE FORBIN PROJECT, THE) (1970)
DAY THE WORLD ENDED, THE (1956) PR:A
DAY THEY GAVE BABIES AWAY, THE (SEE: ALL MINE TO GIVE) (1957)
DAY THEY ROBBED THE BANK OF ENGLAND, THE (1960, Brit.) PR:A
DAY TIME ENDED, THE (1980, Sp.) PR:A
DAY-TIME WIFE (1939) PR:A-C
DAY TO REMEMBER, A (1953, Brit.) PR:A
DAY WILL COME, A (1960, W. Ger.) PR:A
DAY WILL DAWN, THE (SEE: AVENGERS, THE) (1942, Brit.)
DAY YOU LOVE ME, THE (1988, Colombia/Venezuela) PR:A
DAYBREAK (1931) PR:A
DAYBREAK (1939, Fr.) PR:A
DAYBREAK (1948, Brit.) PR:C-O
DAYDREAMER, THE (1966) PR:AA
DAYDREAMER, THE (1975, Fr.) PR:A
DAYLIGHT ROBBERY (1964, Brit.) PR:AA
DAYS AND NIGHTS (1946, USSR) PR:C
DAYS OF BUFFALO BILL (1946) PR:A
DAYS OF GLORY (1944) PR:A
DAYS OF HEAVEN (1978) PR:A
DAYS OF OLD CHEYENNE (1943) PR:A
DAYS OF 36 (1972, Gr.) PR:C
DAYS OF WINE AND ROSES (1962) PR:C
DAYTONA BEACH WEEKEND (1965) PR:A-C
DAYTON'S DEVILS (1968) PR:A
DE BRUIT ET DE FUREUR (SEE: SOUND AND FURY) (1988, Fr.)
DE L'AMOUR (1968, Fr./It.) PR:C
DE MISLUKKING (SEE: FAILURE, THE) (1986, Neth.)
DE SABLE ET DE SANG (SEE: SAND AND BLOOD) (1989, Fr.)
DE SADE (1969, US/W. Ger.) PR:O
DE SISTA STEGEN (SEE: MATTER OF MORALS, A) (1961, US/Swed.)
DE STILTE ROND CHRISTINE M. . . (SEE: QUESTION OF SILENCE, A) (1983, Neth.)
DE VLASCHAARD (SEE: FLAXFIELD, THE) (1985, Bel./Neth.)
DEAD, THE (1987) PR:A
DEAD AND BURIED (1981) PR:O
DEAD ARE ALIVE, THE (1972, Yugo./It./W. Ger.) PR:O
DEAD-BANG (1989) PR:O
DEAD CALM (1989, Aus.) PR:O
DEAD DON'T DREAM, THE (1948) PR:A
DEAD END (1937) PR:C
DEAD-END DRIVE-IN (1986, Aus.) PR:O
DEAD END KIDS (1986) PR:C-O
DEAD END KIDS ON DRESS PARADE (1939) PR:A
DEAD EYES OF LONDON (SEE: DARK EYES OF LONDON) (1961, W. Ger.)
DEAD HEAT (1988) PR:O
DEAD HEAT ON A MERRY-GO-ROUND (1966) PR:A
DEAD IMAGE (SEE: DEAD RINGER) (1964)
DEAD KIDS (1981, Aus./New Zealand) PR:O
DEAD LUCKY (1960, Brit.) PR:A
DEAD MAN WALKING (1988) PR:O
DEAD MAN'S CHEST (1965, Brit.) PR:A-C
DEAD MAN'S EVIDENCE (1962, Brit.) PR:A-C
DEAD MAN'S EYES (1944) PR:A
DEAD MAN'S FLOAT (1980, Aus.) PR:C
DEAD MAN'S GOLD (1948) PR:A
DEAD MAN'S GULCH (1943) PR:A
DEAD MAN'S SHOES (1939, Brit.) PR:A
DEAD MAN'S TRAIL (1952) PR:A
DEAD MARCH, THE (1937) PR:C
DEAD MATE (1989) PR:O
DEAD MELODY (1938, Ger.) PR:C
DEAD MEN ARE DANGEROUS (1939, Brit.) PR:A
DEAD MEN DON'T WEAR PLAID (1982) PR:C
DEAD MEN TELL (1941) PR:A
DEAD MEN TELL NO TALES (1939, Brit.) PR:A
DEAD MEN WALK (1943) PR:A
DEAD MOUNTAINEER HOTEL, THE (1979, USSR) PR:C
DEAD OF NIGHT (1946, Brit.) PR:O
DEAD OF SUMMER (1970, It./Fr.) PR:C-O
DEAD OF WINTER (1987) PR:O
DEAD ON COURSE (1952, Brit.) PR:A-C
DEAD ONE, THE (1961) PR:O
DEAD OR ALIVE (1944) PR:A
DEAD OR ALIVE (SEE: MINUTE TO PRAY, A SECOND TO DIE, A) (1968, US/It.)
DEAD PEOPLE (1974) PR:O
DEAD PIGEON ON BEETHOVEN STREET (1972, W. Ger.) PR:C
DEAD POETS SOCIETY (1989) PR:A
DEAD POOL, THE (1988) PR:O
DEAD RECKONING (1947) PR:C
DEAD RINGER (1964) PR:C
DEAD RINGERS (1988, Can.) PR:O
DEAD RUN (1967, Fr./It./W. Ger.) PR:C

DEAD TO THE WORLD (1961) PR:A
DEAD WOMAN'S KISS, A (1951, It.) PR:A
DEAD ZONE, THE (1983) PR:O
DEADFALL (1968, Brit.) PR:O
DEADHEAD MILES (1982) PR:A-C
DEADLIER THAN THE MALE (1957, Fr.) PR:C
DEADLIER THAN THE MALE (1967, Brit.) PR:C
DEADLIEST SIN, THE (1956, Brit.) PR:A
DEADLINE, THE (1932) PR:A
DEADLINE (1948) PR:A
DEADLINE (1987, Brit./Israel/W. Ger.) PR:O
DEADLINE AT DAWN (1946) PR:A
DEADLINE FOR MURDER (1946) PR:A
DEADLINE MIDNIGHT (SEE: −30−) (1959)
DEADLINE −U.S.A. (1952) PR:A
DEADLOCK (1931, Brit.) PR:A
DEADLOCK (1943, Brit.) PR:A
DEADLOCK (SEE: MAN-TRAP) (1961)
DEADLY AFFAIR, THE (1967, Brit.) PR:A-C
DEADLY BEES, THE (1967, Brit.) PR:C
DEADLY BLESSING (1981) PR:O
DEADLY CHINA DOLL (1973, Hong Kong) PR:O
DEADLY CIRCLE, THE (SEE: HONEYMOON OF HORROR) (1964)
DEADLY COMPANION (SEE: DOUBLE NEGATIVE) (1980, Can.)
DEADLY COMPANIONS, THE (1961) PR:C
DEADLY DECISION (SEE: CANARIS) (1958)
DEADLY DECOYS, THE (1962, Fr.) PR:A-C
DEADLY DREAMS (1988) PR:O
DEADLY DUO (1962) PR:A
DEADLY EYES (1982) PR:O
DEADLY FEMALES, THE (1976, Brit.) PR:O
DEADLY FORCE (1983) PR:O
DEADLY FRIEND (1986) PR:O
DEADLY GAME, THE (1941) PR:A
DEADLY GAME, THE (1955, Brit.) PR:A
DEADLY HERO (1976) PR:O
DEADLY ILLUSION (1987) PR:NR
DEADLY IS THE FEMALE (SEE: GUN CRAZY) (1949)
DEADLY MANTIS, THE (1957) PR:A
DEADLY NIGHTSHADE (1953, Brit.) PR:A
DEADLY OBSESSION (1989) PR:O
DEADLY PASSION (1985, South Africa) PR:O
DEADLY POSSESSION (1989) PR:O
DEADLY PREY (1987) PR:NR
DEADLY PURSUIT (SEE: SHOOT TO KILL) (1988)
DEADLY RECORD (1959, Brit.) PR:A
DEADLY SILENCE (SEE: TARZAN'S DEADLY SILENCE) (1970)
DEADLY SPAWN, THE (1983) PR:O
DEADLY STRANGERS (1974, Brit.) PR:C
DEADLY STRANGERS (SEE: BORDER HEAT) (1988)
DEADLY TRACKERS, THE (1973) PR:O
DEADLY TRAP, THE (1972, Fr./It.) PR:C
DEADLY TWINS (1988) PR:O
DEADTIME STORIES (1987) PR:O
DEADWOOD PASS (1933) PR:A
DEADWOOD '76 (1965) PR:C
DEAF SMITH AND JOHNNY EARS (1973, It.) PR:C
DEAL OF THE CENTURY (1983) PR:C
DEALERS (1989, Brit.) PR:O
DEALING: OR THE BERKELEY TO BOSTON FORTY-BRICK LOST-BAG BLUES (1971) PR:O
DEAR BRAT (1951) PR:A
DEAR BRIGITTE (1965) PR:A
DEAR, DEAD DELILAH (1972) PR:O
DEAR DETECTIVE (1978, Fr.) PR:C
DEAR HEART (1964) PR:A
DEAR INSPECTOR (SEE: DEAR DETECTIVE) (1978, Fr.)
DEAR JOHN (1966, Swed.) PR:C
DEAR MARTHA (SEE: HONEYMOON KILLERS, THE) (1969)
DEAR MR. PROHACK (1949, Brit.) PR:A
DEAR MR. WONDERFUL (1983, W. Ger.) PR:C
DEAR MURDERER (1947, Brit.) PR:C
DEAR OCTOPUS (SEE: RANDOLPH FAMILY, THE) (1945, Brit.)
DEAR RUTH (1947) PR:A
DEAR WIFE (1949) PR:AA
DEATH AND THE GREEN SLIME (SEE: GREEN SLIME, THE) (1969, US/Jap.)
DEATH AT A BROADCAST (1934, Brit.) PR:A
DEATH AT BROADCASTING HOUSE (SEE: DEATH AT A BROADCAST) (1934, Brit.)
DEATH BEFORE DISHONOR (1987) PR:C
DEATH BITE (SEE: SPASMS) (1983, Can.)
DEATH COLLECTOR (1976) PR:O
DEATH CORDS (SEE: SHOCK WAVES) (1977)
DEATH CROONS THE BLUES (1937, Brit.) PR:A
DEATH CURSE OF TARTU (1967) PR:C-O
DEATH DRIVES THROUGH (1935, Brit.) PR:A
DEATH DRUMS ALONG THE RIVER (SEE: SANDERS) (1963, Brit.)
DEATH FLIES EAST (1935) PR:A
DEATH FROM A DISTANCE (1936) PR:A

DEATH FROM OUTER SPACE (SEE: DAY THE SKY EX-
PLODED, THE) (1958, Fr./It.)
DEATH GAME (1977) PR:O
DEATH GOES NORTH (1939) PR:A
DEATH GOES TO SCHOOL (1953, Brit.) PR:A
DEATH HOUSE (SEE: SILENT NIGHT, BLOODY
NIGHT) (1972)
DEATH HUNT (1981) PR:C
DEATH IN SMALL DOSES (1957) PR:C
DEATH IN THE GARDEN (1956, Fr./Mex.) PR:O
DEATH IN THE SKY (1937) PR:C
DEATH IN VENICE (1971, It./Fr.) PR:C
DEATH IS A NUMBER (1951, Brit.) PR:A-C
DEATH IS A WOMAN (SEE: LOVE IS A WOMAN)
(1967, Brit.)
DEATH IS CALLED ENGELCHEN (1963, Czech.) PR:C
DEATH KISS, THE (1933) PR:A
DEATH MACHINES (1976) PR:O
DEATH OF A BUREAUCRAT (1979, Cuba) PR:A-C
DEATH OF A CHAMPION (1939) PR:A
DEATH OF A CYCLIST (SEE: AGE OF INFIDELITY)
(1955)
DEATH OF A GUNFIGHTER (1969) PR:C
DEATH OF A HOOKER (SEE: WHO KILLED MARY
WHAT'SER NAME?) (1971)
DEATH OF A JEW (SEE: SABRA) (1970, Fr./It.)
DEATH OF A SALESMAN (1952) PR:O
DEATH OF A SCOUNDREL (1956) PR:C
DEATH OF A SOLDIER (1986, Aus.) PR:O
DEATH OF AN ANGEL (1952, Brit.) PR:A
DEATH OF AN ANGEL (1985) PR:C
DEATH OF EMPEDOCLES, THE (1986, Fr./W. Ger.) PR:A
DEATH OF HER INNOCENCE (SEE: OUR TIME) (1974)
DEATH OF MARIO RICCI, THE (1985, Fr./Switz.) PR:C
DEATH OF MICHAEL TURBIN, THE (1954, Brit.) PR:A
DEATH OF NIGHT (SEE: DEATHDREAM) (1972, Can.)
DEATH OF TARZAN, THE (1968, Czech.) PR:C
DEATH OF THE APEMAN (SEE: DEATH OF TARZAN,
THE) (1968, Czech.)
DEATH ON THE DIAMOND (1934) PR:A
DEATH ON THE MOUNTAIN (1961, Jap.) PR:O
DEATH ON THE NILE (1978, Brit.) PR:C
DEATH ON THE SET (SEE: MURDER ON THE SET)
(1936, Brit.)
DEATH OVER MY SHOULDER (1958, Brit.) PR:A-C
DEATH PLAY (1976) PR:C
DEATH RACE (1978, It.) PR:C-O
DEATH RACE 2000 (1975) PR:O
DEATH RIDES A HORSE (1969, It.) PR:O
DEATH RIDES THE PLAINS (1944) PR:A
DEATH RIDES THE RANGE (1940) PR:A
DEATH SENTENCE (1967, It.) PR:O
DEATH SENTENCE (1986, Pol.) PR:O
DEATH SHIP (1980, Can.) PR:O
DEATH TAKES A HOLIDAY (1934) PR:C
DEATH TOOK PLACE LAST NIGHT (1970, It./W. Ger.)
PR:O
DEATH TRAP (1962, Brit.) PR:C
DEATH TRAP (SEE: TAKE HER BY SURPRISE) (1967,
Can.)
DEATH TRAP (SEE: EATEN ALIVE!) (1976)
DEATH VALLEY (1946) PR:A
DEATH VALLEY (1982) PR:O
DEATH VALLEY GUNFIGHTER (1949) PR:A
DEATH VALLEY MANHUNT (1943) PR:A
DEATH VALLEY OUTLAWS (1941) PR:A
DEATH VALLEY RANGERS (1944) PR:A
DEATH VENGEANCE (1982) PR:O
DEATH WATCH (1979, Fr./W. Ger.) PR:O
DEATH WEEKEND (SEE: HOUSE BY THE LAKE, THE)
(1977, Can.)
DEATH WHEELERS, THE (SEE: PSYCHOMANIA)
(1974, Brit.)
DEATH WISH (1974) PR:O
DEATH WISH II (1982) PR:O
DEATH WISH 3 (1985) PR:O
DEATH WISH 4: THE CRACKDOWN (1987) PR:O
DEATHCHEATERS (1976, Aus.) PR:C
DEATHDREAM (1972, Can.) PR:O
DEATHLINE (1973. Brit.) PR:O
DEATHMASTER, THE (1972) PR:O
DEATHROW GAMESHOW (1987) PR:O
DEATHSHEAD VAMPIRE (SEE: BLOOD BEAST TER-
ROR, THE) (1969, Brit.)
DEATHSPORT (1978) PR:O
DEATHSTALKER (1984) PR:O
DEATHSTALKER AND THE WARRIORS FROM HELL
(1989) PR:C
DEATHTRAP (1982) PR:C
DEATHWATCH (1966) PR:O
DEBT OF HONOR (1936, Brit.) PR:A
DECAMERON NIGHTS (1953, Brit.) PR:A
DECEIVER, THE (1931) PR:A
DECEIVERS, THE (1988, Brit./India) PR:O
DECEIVERS, THE (SEE: INTIMACY) (1966)
DECEPTION (1933) PR:A
DECEPTION (1946) PR:A-C
DECISION AGAINST TIME (1957, Brit.) PR:A

DECISION AT SUNDOWN (1957) PR:C
DECISION BEFORE DAWN (1951) PR:A
DECISION OF CHRISTOPHER BLAKE, THE (1948)
PR:A
DECKS RAN RED, THE (1958) PR:A-C
DECLINE AND FALL. . . OF A BIRD WATCHER (1969,
Brit.) PR:C
DECLINE OF THE AMERICAN EMPIRE, THE (1986,
Can.) PR:O
DECOY (1946) PR:C-O
DECOY (SEE: MYSTERY SUBMARINE) (1963)
DEDEE (1949, Fr.) PR:C
DEEP, THE (1977) PR:O
DEEP BLUE SEA, THE (1955, Brit.) PR:C
DEEP DESIRE OF GODS (SEE: KURAGEJIMA – LEG-
ENDS FROM A SOUTHERN ISLAND) (1970, Jap.)
DEEP END (1970, US/W. Ger.) PR:O
DEEP IN MY HEART (1954) PR:AA
DEEP IN THE HEART (1983, Brit.) PR:O
DEEP IN THE HEART OF TEXAS (1942) PR:A
DEEP RED (1976, It.) PR:O
DEEP SIX, THE (1958) PR:A
DEEP THRUST – THE HAND OF DEATH (1973, Hong
Kong) PR:O
DEEP VALLEY (1947) PR:C
DEEP WATERS (1948) PR:A
DEEPSTAR SIX (1989) PR:C
DEER HUNTER, THE (1978) PR:O
DEERSLAYER (1943) PR:A
DEERSLAYER, THE (1957) PR:A
DEF-CON 4 (1985) PR:O
DEFEAT OF HANNIBAL, THE (1937, It.) PR:C
DEFECTOR, THE (1966, Fr./W. Ger.) PR:C
DEFENCE OF THE REALM (1985, Brit.) PR:C-O
DEFEND MY LOVE (1956, It.) PR:A-C
DEFENDERS OF THE LAW (1931) PR:A
DEFENSE OF VOLOTCHAYEVSK, THE (1938, USSR)
PR:A
DEFENSE RESTS, THE (1934) PR:A
DEFIANCE (1980) PR:C
DEFIANT DAUGHTERS (SEE: SHADOWS GROW
LONGER, THE) (1962, Switz./W. Ger.)
DEFIANT ONES, THE (1958) PR:C
DEGREE OF MURDER, A (1969, W. Ger.) PR:O
DEJA VU (1985, Brit.) PR:O
DELAVINE AFFAIR, THE (1954, Brit.) PR:A
DELAY IN MARIENBORN (SEE: STOP TRAIN 349)
(1963. W. Ger.)
DELAYED ACTION (1954, Brit.) PR:A
DELICATE BALANCE, A (1973) PR:C
DELICATE DELINQUENT, THE (1957) PR:A
DELICIOUS (1931) PR:A
DELIGHTFUL ROGUE, THE (1929) PR:A
DELIGHTFULLY DANGEROUS (1945) PR:A
DELINQUENT DAUGHTERS (1944) PR:C
DELINQUENT PARENTS (1938) PR:A
DELINQUENTS, THE (1957) PR:C
DELIRIUM (1979) PR:O
DELITTO A PORTA ROMANA (SEE: CRIME AT PORTA
ROMANA) (1980, It.)
DELIVERANCE (1972) PR:O
DELIVERY BOYS (1984) PR:O
DELOS ADVENTURE, THE (1987) PR:C-O
DELTA FACTOR, THE (1970) PR:C
DELTA FORCE, THE (1986) PR:O
DELTA FOX (1979) PR:O
DELUGE (1933) PR:A
DELUSION (SEE: HOUSE WHERE DEATH LIVES,
THE) (1984)
DELUSIONS OF GRANDEUR (1971, Fr.) PR:C
DEMANTY NOCI (SEE: DIAMONDS OF THE NIGHT)
(1964, Czech.)
DEMENTED (1980) PR:O
DEMENTIA (1955) PR:O
DEMENTIA 13 (1963) PR:C
DEMETRIUS AND THE GLADIATORS (1954) PR:C
DEMI-PARADISE, THE (SEE: ADVENTURE FOR TWO)
(1945, Brit.)
DEMOBBED (1944, Brit.) PR:A
DEMON (SEE: GOD TOLD ME TO) (1976)
DEMON, THE (SEE: ONIBABA) (1965, Jap.)
DEMON, THE (1981, South Africa) PR:O
DEMON BARBER OF FLEET STREET, THE (1939, Brit.)
PR:O
DEMON FOR TROUBLE, A (1934) PR:A
DEMON FROM DEVIL'S LAKE, THE (1964) PR:A
DEMON LOVER, THE (1977) PR:O
DEMON PLANET, THE (SEE: PLANET OF THE VAM-
PIRES) (1965, US/It./Sp.)
DEMON POND (1980, Jap.) PR:C
DEMON SEED (1977) PR:O
DEMON WITCH CHILD (1974, Sp.) PR:O
DEMONI 2 – L'INCUBO RITORNA (SEE: DEMONS 2 –
THE NIGHTMARE RETURNS) (1986, It.)
DEMONIAQUE (1958, Fr.) PR:C-O
DEMONOID (1981) PR:O
DEMONS (1985, It.) PR:O

DEMONS (1987, Swed.) PR:O
DEMONS IN THE GARDEN (1984, Sp.) PR:O
DEMONS OF LUDLOW, THE (1983) PR:O
DEMONS OF THE MIND (1972, Brit.) PR:O
DEMONS 2: THE NIGHTMARE RETURNS (1986, It.) PR:O
DEMONSTRATOR (1971, Aus.) PR:O
DEN OF DOOM (SEE: GLASS CAGE, THE) (1964)
DENKI KURAGE (SEE: PLAY IT COOL) (1970, Jap.)
DENTIST IN THE CHAIR (1960, Brit.) PR:A
DENTIST ON THE JOB (SEE: GET ON WITH IT) (1963,
Brit.)
DENVER AND RIO GRANDE, THE (1952) PR:A
DENVER KID, THE (1948) PR:A
DEPARTMENT STORE (1935, Brit.) PR:A
DEPORTED (1950) PR:A
DEPRAVED, THE (1957, Brit.) PR:A-C
DEPTH CHARGE (1960, Brit.) PR:A
DEPUTY DRUMMER, THE (1935, Brit.) PR:A
DEPUTY MARSHAL (1949) PR:A
DER AMERIKANISCHE SOLDAT (SEE: AMERICAN
SOLDIER) (1970, W. Ger.)
DER BLAUE ENGEL (SEE: BLUE ANGEL, THE) (1930,
Ger.)
DER BLAUE LICHT (SEE: BLUE LIGHT, THE) (1932,
Ger.)
DER BULLE UND DAS MAEDCHEN (SEE: COP AND
THE GIRL, THE) (1985, Aust./W. Ger.)
DER CHEF WUENSCHT KEINE ZEUGEN (SEE: NO
SURVIVORS, PLEASE!) (1963, W. Ger.)
DER FANGSCHUSS (SEE: COUP DE GRACE) (1976,
Fr./W. Ger.)
DER FLIEGER (SEE: FLYER, THE) (1987, W. Ger.)
DER FLUCH DER GRUENEN AUGEN (SEE: CAVE OF
THE LIVING DEAD) (1966, W. Ger./Yugo.)
DER FREISCHUTZ (1970, W. Ger.) PR:A
DER FUSSGANGER (SEE: PEDESTRIAN, THE) (1974,
W. Ger.)
DER GLASERNE TURM (SEE: GLASS TOWER, THE)
(1959, W. Ger.)
DER GREIFER (SEE: COPPER, THE) (1930, Brit./Ger.)
DER HAUPTMANN VON KOEPENICK (SEE: CAPTAIN
FROM KOEPENICK, THE) (1956, W. Ger.)
DER HERR DER WELT (SEE: MASTER OF THE
WORLD) (1935, Ger.)
DER HIMMEL UBER BERLIN (SEE: WINGS OF DE-
SIRE) (1987, Fr./W. Ger.)
DER IDEALE UNTERMIETER (SEE: IDEAL LODGER,
THE) (1957, W. Ger.)
DER JOKER (SEE: LETHAL OBSESSION) (1988, W.
Ger.)
DER JUNGE MOENCH (SEE: YOUNG MONK, THE)
(1978, W. Ger.)
DER JUNGE TORLESS (SEE: YOUNG TORLESS) (1968,
Fr./W. Ger.)
DER KOM EN SOLDAT (SEE: SCANDAL IN DEN-
MARK) (1970, Den.)
DER KONGRESS TANZT (SEE: CONGRESS DANCES)
(1932, Ger.)
DER LIFT (SEE: LIFT, THE) (1983, Neth.)
DER MARTYRER (SEE: MARTYR, THE) (1976, Is-
rael/W. Ger.)
DER MORDER DIMITRI KARAMASOFF (SEE:
KARAMAZOV) (1931, Ger.)
DER PFARRER VON ST. PAULI (SEE: PRIEST OF ST.
PAULI, THE) (1970, W. Ger.)
DER PROZESS (SEE: TRIAL, THE) (1948, Aust.)
DER ROSENKONIG (1986, W. Ger.) PR:O
DER TAG NACH DER SCHEIDUNG (SEE: DAY AFTER
THE DIVORCE, THE) (1940, Ger.)
DER TIGER VON ESCHNAPUR (SEE: JOURNEY TO
THE LOST CITY) (1959, Fr./It./W. Ger.)
DER TOD DES EMPEDOKLES (SEE: DEATH OF
EMPEDOCLES, THE) (1988, Fr./W. Ger.)
DER TRAUMENDE MUND (SEE: DREAMING LIPS)
(1958, W. Ger.)
DER UNSTERBLICHE LUMP (SEE: IMMORTAL VAGA-
BOND) (1931, Ger.)
DER VERLORENE (SEE: LOST ONE, THE) (1951, W.
Ger.)
DER WEISSE DAMON (SEE: WHITE DEMON, THE)
(1932, Ger.)
DERANGED (1974, Can.) PR:O
DERBY DAY (SEE: FOUR AGAINST FATE) (1952, Brit.)
DERELICT (1930) PR:A
DERELICT, THE (1937, Brit.) PR:A
DERSU UZALA (1975, Jap./USSR) PR:A
DES TEUFEL'S GENERAL (SEE: DEVIL'S GENERAL,
THE) (1957, W. Ger.)
DESCENDANT OF THE SNOW LEOPARD, THE (1986,
USSR) PR:AA
DESERT ATTACK (1958, Brit.) PR:A
DESERT BANDIT (1941) PR:A
DESERT BLOOM (1986) PR:A-C
DESERT DESPERADOES (1959, It.) PR:A
DESERT FOX, THE (1951) PR:A
DESERT FURY (1947) PR:C
DESERT GOLD (1936) PR:A
DESERT GUNS (1936) PR:A

DESERT HAWK, THE (1950) PR:A
DESERT HEARTS (1985) PR:O
DESERT HELL (1958) PR:A
DESERT HORSEMAN, THE (1946) PR:A
DESERT JUSTICE (1936) PR:A
DESERT LEGION (1953) PR:A
DESERT MESA (1935) PR:A
DESERT MICE (1960, Brit.) PR:A
DESERT ODYSSEY (SEE: HAREM BUNCH; OR WAR
   AND PIECE, THE) (1969)
DESERT OF LOST MEN (1951) PR:A
DESERT OF THE TARTARS, THE (1976, Fr./It./Iranian)
   PR:C
DESERT PASSAGE (1952) PR:A
DESERT PATROL (1938) PR:A
DESERT PATROL (1962, Brit.) PR:C
DESERT PHANTOM (1937) PR:A
DESERT PURSUIT (1952) PR:A
DESERT RATS, THE (1953) PR:A
DESERT RAVEN, THE (1965) PR:A
DESERT SANDS (1955) PR:A
DESERT SONG, THE (1929) PR:A
DESERT SONG, THE (1944) PR:A
DESERT SONG, THE (1953) PR:A
DESERT TRAIL (1935) PR:A
DESERT VENGEANCE (1931) PR:A
DESERT VIGILANTE (1949) PR:A
DESERT WARRIOR (1961, It./Sp.) PR:A
DESERT WARRIOR (1985) PR:O
DESERTER (1934, USSR) PR:A
DESERTER, THE (1971, US/It./Yugo.) PR:O
DESERTER AND THE NOMADS, THE (1969, Czech./It.)
   PR:O
DESERTERS (1983, Can.) PR:C
DESIGN FOR LIVING (1933) PR:A
DESIGN FOR LOVING (1962, Brit.) PR:A
DESIGN FOR MURDER (1940, Brit.) PR:C
DESIGN FOR SCANDAL (1941) PR:A
DESIGNING WOMAN (1957) PR:A
DESIGNING WOMEN (1934, Brit.) PR:A
DESIRABLE (1934) PR:A
DESIRE (1936) PR:A
DESIRE IN THE DUST (1960) PR:C
DESIRE ME (1947) PR:A
DESIRE, THE INTERIOR LIFE (1980, It./W. Ger.) PR:O
DESIRE UNDER THE ELMS (1958) PR:O
DESIREE (1954) PR:A
DESIREE (1984, Neth.) PR:O
DESK SET (1957) PR:A
DESPAIR (1977, W. Ger.) PR:O
DESPERADO, THE (1954) PR:A
DESPERADO TRAIL, THE (1965, Fr./It./W. Ger./Yugo.)
   PR:A
DESPERADOES, THE (1943) PR:A
DESPERADOES ARE IN TOWN, THE (1956) PR:A
DESPERADOES OF DODGE CITY (1948) PR:A
DESPERADOES OUTPOST (1952) PR:A
DESPERADOS, THE (1969) PR:O
DESPERATE (1947) PR:C
DESPERATE ADVENTURE, A (1938) PR:A
DESPERATE CARGO (1941) PR:A
DESPERATE CHANCE FOR ELLERY QUEEN, A (1942)
   PR:A
DESPERATE CHARACTERS (1971) PR:A-C
DESPERATE DECISION (1954, Fr.) PR:O
DESPERATE HOURS, THE (1955) PR:C
DESPERATE JOURNEY (1942) PR:A
DESPERATE MAN, THE (1959, Brit.) PR:A-C
DESPERATE MEN, THE (SEE: CAT AND MOUSE)
   (1958)
DESPERATE MOMENT (1953, Brit.) PR:A
DESPERATE MOVES (1986, It.) PR:C-O
DESPERATE ONES, THE (1968, US/Sp.) PR:C
DESPERATE SEARCH (1952) PR:A
DESPERATE SIEGE (SEE: RAWHIDE) (1951)
DESPERATE TRAILS (1939) PR:A
DESPERATE WOMEN, THE (1954) PR:O
DESPERATELY SEEKING SUSAN (1985) PR:O
DESTINATION BIG HOUSE (1950) PR:A
DESTINATION GOBI (1953) PR:A
DESTINATION INNER SPACE (1966) PR:A
DESTINATION MILAN (1954, Brit.) PR:A
DESTINATION MOON (1950) PR:A
DESTINATION MURDER (1950) PR:C
DESTINATION 60,000 (1957) PR:A
DESTINATION TOKYO (1943) PR:A
DESTINATION UNKNOWN (1933) PR:A
DESTINATION UNKNOWN (1942) PR:A
DESTINEES (SEE: DAUGHTERS OF DESTINY) (1953,
   Fr./It.)
DESTINY (1938, It.) PR:A
DESTINY (1944) PR:A
DESTINY (SEE: TIME OF DESTINY, A) (1988)
DESTINY OF A MAN (1961, USSR) PR:A
DESTROY ALL MONSTERS (1969, Jap.) PR:A
DESTROY ALL PLANETS (SEE: GAMERA VERSUS
   VIRAS) (1968, Jap.)
DESTROY, SHE SAID (1969, Fr.) PR:O

DESTROYER (1943) PR:A
DESTRUCTION TEST (SEE: CIRCLE OF DECEPTION)
   (1961, Brit.)
DESTRUCTION TEST (SEE: CIRCLE OF DECEPTION)
   (1961, Brit.)
DESTRUCTORS, THE (1968) PR:C
DESTRUCTORS, THE (1974, Brit.) PR:C
DESTRY (1954) PR:A
DESTRY RIDES AGAIN (1932) PR:A
DESTRY RIDES AGAIN (1939) PR:A
DET SJUNDE INSEGLET (SEE: SEVENTH SEAL, THE)
   (1956, Swed.)
DET STORA AVENTYRET (SEE: GREAT ADVENTURE,
   THE) (1955, Swed.)
DET TOSSEDE PARADIS (SEE: CRAZY PARADISE)
   (1965, Den.)
DETECTIVE, THE (1954, Brit.) PR:A
DETECTIVE, THE (1968) PR:C
DETECTIVE BELLI (1970, It.) PR:O
DETECTIVE (1985, Fr./Switz.) PR:A
DETECTIVE KITTY O'DAY (1944) PR:A
DETECTIVE SCHOOL DROPOUTS (1986) PR:A-C
DETECTIVE STORY (1951) PR:C
DETOUR (1945) PR:O
DETOUR, THE (1968, Bulgaria) PR:A
DETOURNEMENT DE MINEURES (SEE: PRICE OF
   FLESH) (1962, Fr.)
DETRAS DE ESA PUERTA (SEE: POLITICAL ASY-
   LUM) (1975, Mex.)
DETROIT 9000 (1973) PR:O
DETRUITE, DIT-ELLE (SEE: DESTROY, SHE SAID)
   (1969, Fr.)
DEUTSCHLAND IM HERBST (SEE: GERMANY IN AU-
   TUMN) (1978, W. Ger.)
DEUX HOMMES DANS LA VILLE (SEE: TWO MEN IN
   TOWN) (1973, Fr.)
DEUX OU TROIS CHOSES QUE JE SAIS D'ELLE (SEE:
   TWO OR THREE THINGS I KNOW ABOUT HER)
   (1970, Fr.)
DEUX SUPER FLICS (SEE: TWO SUPER COPS) (1978,
   It.)
DEUXIEME BUREAU (SEE: SECOND BUREAU) (1936,
   Fr.)
DEVETI KRUG (SEE: NINTH CIRCLE, THE) (1961,
   Yugo.)
DEVI (SEE: GODDESS, THE) (1962, India)
DEVICHYA VESNA (SEE: SPRINGTIME ON THE
   VOLGA) (1961, USSR)
DEVIL, THE (1963, It.) PR:A
DEVIL AND DANIEL WEBSTER, THE (1941) PR:A
DEVIL AND DR. FRANKENSTEIN, THE (SEE: ANDY
   WARHOL'S FRANKENSTEIN) (1974, Fr./It.)
DEVIL AND MAX DEVLIN, THE (1981) PR:A
DEVIL AND MISS JONES, THE (1941) PR:A
DEVIL AND THE DEEP (1932) PR:C
DEVIL AND THE TEN COMMANDMENTS, THE (1962,
   Fr./It.) PR:C
DEVIL AT FOUR O'CLOCK, THE (1961) PR:A
DEVIL BAT, THE (1941) PR:A
DEVIL BAT'S DAUGHTER, THE (1946) PR:A
DEVIL BY THE TAIL, THE (1969, Fr./It.) PR:C
DEVIL COMMANDS, THE (1941) PR:C
DEVIL DOGS OF THE AIR (1935) PR:A
DEVIL DOLL, THE (1936) PR:C
DEVIL DOLL (1964, US/Brit.) PR:C
DEVIL GIRL FROM MARS (1954, Brit.) PR:A
DEVIL GODDESS (1955) PR:A
DEVIL GOT ANGRY, THE (SEE: MAJIN) (1968, Jap.)
DEVIL IN LOVE, THE (1968, It.) PR:C
DEVIL IN SILK (1968, W. Ger.) PR:C
DEVIL IN THE CASTLE (SEE: DAREDEVIL IN THE
   CASTLE) (1961, Jap.)
DEVIL IN THE FLESH, THE (1947, Fr.) PR:C
DEVIL IN THE FLESH (1986, It./Fr.) PR:O
DEVIL INSIDE, THE (SEE: OFFBEAT) (1961, Brit.)
DEVIL IS A SISSY, THE (1936) PR:A
DEVIL IS A WOMAN, THE (1935) PR:C
DEVIL IS A WOMAN, THE (1975, Brit./It.) PR:O
DEVIL IS AN EMPRESS, THE (1939, Fr.) PR:A
DEVIL IS DRIVING, THE (1932) PR:A
DEVIL IS DRIVING, THE (1937) PR:A
DEVIL MADE A WOMAN, THE (1959, Sp.) PR:A
DEVIL MAKES THREE, THE (1952) PR:A-C
DEVIL MAY CARE (1929) PR:A
DEVIL NEVER SLEEPS, THE (SEE: SATAN NEVER
   SLEEPS) (1962, US/Brit.)
DEVIL ON HORSEBACK, THE (1936) PR:A
DEVIL ON HORSEBACK (1954, Brit.) PR:A
DEVIL ON WHEELS (SEE: INDIANAPOLIS SPEED-
   WAY) (1939)
DEVIL ON WHEELS, THE (1947) PR:A
DEVIL PAYS, THE (1932) PR:A
DEVIL PAYS OFF, THE (1941) PR:A
DEVIL PROBABLY, THE (1977, FR.) PR:C
DEVIL RIDERS (1944) PR:A
DEVIL RIDES OUT, THE (SEE: DEVIL'S BRIDE, THE)
   (1968, Brit.)
DEVIL SHIP (1947) PR:A

DEVIL-SHIP PIRATES, THE (1964, Brit.) PR:C
DEVIL STRIKES AT NIGHT, THE (1959, W. Ger.) PR:C
DEVIL TAKES THE COUNT, THE (SEE: DEVIL IS A
   SISSY, THE) (1936)
DEVIL THUMBS A RIDE, THE (1947) PR:A
DEVIL TIGER (1934) PR:A
DEVIL TIMES FIVE (1974) PR:C
DEVIL TO PAY, THE (1930) PR:A
DEVIL WITH WOMEN, A (1930) PR:A
DEVIL WITHIN HER, THE (1976, Brit.) PR:O
DEVIL WOMAN (SEE: ONIBABA) (1965, Jap.)
DEVIL WOMAN (1976, Phil.) PR:O
DEVIL'S CAMERA (SEE: SCUM OF THE EARTH!)
   (1963)
DEVILMAN STORY (SEE: DEVIL'S MAN, THE) (1967,
   It.)
DEVIL'S AGENT, THE (1962, Brit.) PR:C
DEVIL'S ANGELS (1967) PR:O
DEVIL'S BAIT (1959, Brit.) PR:A
DEVIL'S BEDROOM, THE (1964) PR:O
DEVIL'S BRIDE, THE (1968, Brit.) PR:O
DEVIL'S BRIGADE, THE (1968) PR:C
DEVIL'S BROTHER, THE (1933) PR:AA
DEVIL'S CANYON (1953) PR:A
DEVIL'S CARGO, THE (1948) PR:A
DEVIL'S COMMANDMENT, THE (1956, It.) PR:O
DEVIL'S DAFFODIL, THE (1961, Brit./W. Ger.) PR:A
DEVIL'S DAUGHTER, THE (SEE: POCOMANIA) (1939)
DEVIL'S DAUGHTER (1949, Fr.) PR:A
DEVIL'S DISCIPLE, THE (1959, Brit.) PR:A
DEVIL'S DOLL (SEE: DEVIL'S HAND, THE) (1961)
DEVIL'S DOORWAY (1950) PR:A
DEVIL'S 8, THE (1969) PR:C
DEVIL'S ENVOYS, THE (1947, Fr.) PR:A
DEVIL'S EXPRESS (1975) PR:O
DEVIL'S EYE, THE (1960, Swed.) PR:C
DEVIL'S GENERAL, THE (1957, W. Ger.) PR:A-C
DEVIL'S GODMOTHER, THE (1938, Mex.) PR:A
DEVIL'S HAIRPIN, THE (1957) PR:A
DEVIL'S HAND, THE (SEE: CARNIVAL OF SINNERS)
   (1947)
DEVIL'S HAND, THE (1961) PR:C
DEVIL'S HARBOR (1954, Brit.) PR:C
DEVIL'S HENCHMEN, THE (1949) PR:A
DEVIL'S HOLIDAY, THE (1930) PR:A
DEVIL'S IMPOSTER, THE (SEE: POPE JOAN) (1972,
   Brit.)
DEVIL'S IN LOVE, THE (1933) PR:A
DEVIL'S ISLAND (1940) PR:C
DEVIL'S JEST, THE (1954, Brit.) PR:A
DEVIL'S LOTTERY (1932) PR:A
DEVIL'S MAN, THE (1967, It.) PR:C
DEVIL'S MASK, THE (1946) PR:A
DEVIL'S MATE (1933) PR:A
DEVIL'S MAZE, THE (1929, Brit.) PR:A-C
DEVIL'S MEN, THE (SEE: LAND OF THE MINOTAUR)
   (1976, US/Brit.)
DEVIL'S MESSENGER, THE (1962, US/Swed.) PR:C
DEVIL'S MISTRESS, THE (1968) PR:O
DEVIL'S NIGHTMARE, THE (1971, Bel./It.) PR:O
DEVIL'S ODDS (SEE: WILD PAIR, THE) (1987)
DEVILS OF DARKNESS, THE (1965, Brit.) PR:C
DEVIL'S OWN, THE (1967, Brit.) PR:C
DEVIL'S PARTNER, THE (1958) PR:C-O
DEVIL'S PARTY, THE (1938) PR:A
DEVIL'S PASS, THE (1957, Brit.) PR:AA
DEVIL'S PIPELINE, THE (1940) PR:A
DEVIL'S PITCHFORK, THE (SEE: ANATAHAN) (1953, Jap.)
DEVIL'S PLAYGROUND (1937) PR:A
DEVIL'S PLAYGROUND, THE (1946) PR:A
DEVIL'S PLAYGROUND, THE (1976, Aus.) PR:A
DEVIL'S PLOT, THE (1948, Brit.) PR:C
DEVIL'S POINT (SEE: DEVIL'S HARBOR) (1954, Brit.)
DEVIL'S RAIN, THE (1975, US/Mex.) PR:O
DEVIL'S ROCK (1938, Brit.) PR:A
DEVIL'S SADDLE LEGION, THE (1937) PR:A
DEVIL'S SISTERS, THE (1966) PR:O
DEVIL'S SLEEP, THE (1951) PR:A
DEVIL'S SQUADRON (1936) PR:A
DEVIL'S TEMPLE (1969, Jap.) PR:C-O
DEVIL'S TRAIL, THE (1942) PR:A
DEVIL'S TRAP, THE (1964, Czech.) PR:A-C
DEVIL'S WANTON, THE (1959, Swed.) PR:C
DEVIL'S WEDDING NIGHT, THE (1973, It.) PR:O
DEVIL'S WIDOW, THE (1972, Brit.) PR:O
DEVIL'S WOMAN, THE (SEE: EVA) (1962, Fr./It.)
DEVONSVILLE TERROR, THE (1983) PR:O
DEVOTION (1931) PR:A
DEVOTION (1946) PR:A
DEVOTION (1953, It.) PR:C-O
DEVOTION (1955, USSR) PR:A
DEVYAT DNEY ODNOGO GODA (SEE: NINE DAYS
   OF ONE YEAR) (1964, USSR)
DIABOLICAL DR. MABUSE, THE (SEE: THOUSAND
   EYES OF DR. MABUSE, THE) (1960, Fr./It./W. Ger.)
DIABOLICAL DR. Z, THE (1966, Sp./Fr.) PR:O
DIABOLICALLY YOURS (1968, Fr.) PR:C
DIABOLIK (SEE: DANGER: DIABOLIK) (1968, Fr./It.)

DIABOLIQUE (1955, Fr.) PR:O
DIABOLIQUEMENT VOTRE (SEE: DIABOLICALLY
  YOURS) (1968, Fr.)
DIABOLO MENTHE (SEE: PEPPERMINT SODA) (1979,
  Fr.)
DIADIA VANYA (SEE: UNCLE VANYA) (1972, USSR)
DIAGNOSIS: MURDER (1974, Brit.) PR:C
DIAL M FOR MURDER (1954) PR:A-C
DIAL 999 (SEE: WAY OUT, THE) (1955, Brit.)
DIAL 1119 (1950) PR:C
DIAL RED O (1955) PR:C
DIALOGUE (1967, Hung.) PR:A
DIAMOND, THE (SEE: DIAMOND WIZARD, THE)
  (1954, Brit.)
DIAMOND CITY (1949, Brit.) PR:A
DIAMOND COUNTRY (SEE: RUN LIKE A THIEF)
  (1967, US/Sp.)
DIAMOND CUT DIAMOND (SEE: BLAME THE
  WOMAN) (1932, Brit.)
DIAMOND EARRINGS (SEE: EARRINGS OF MA-
  DAME DE. . ., THE) (1953, Fr./It.)
DIAMOND FRONTIER (1940) PR:A
DIAMOND HEAD (1962) PR:C
DIAMOND HORSESHOE (1945) PR:A
DIAMOND HUNTERS (SEE: RUN LIKE A THIEF)
  (1967, US/Sp.)
DIAMOND JIM (1935) PR:A
DIAMOND MERCENARIES, THE (SEE: KILLER
  FORCE) (1975, Ireland/Switz.)
DIAMOND QUEEN, THE (1953) PR:A
DIAMOND SAFARI (1958) PR:A
DIAMOND STUD (1970) PR:C
DIAMOND TRAIL (1933) PR:A
DIAMOND WIZARD, THE (1954, Brit.) PR:A
DIAMONDS (1975, US/Israel) PR:C
DIAMONDS AND CRIME (SEE: HI, DIDDLE DIDDLE)
  (1943)
DIAMONDS ARE FOREVER (1971, Brit.) PR:C
DIAMONDS FOR BREAKFAST (1968, Brit.) PR:C
DIAMONDS OF THE NIGHT (1964, Czech.) PR:C
DIANE (1955) PR:A-C
DIANE'S BODY (1969, Fr./Czech.) PR:A
DIARIO DI UN ITALIANO (SEE: DIARY OF AN ITAL-
  IAN) (1971, It.)
DIARIO SEGRETO DI UN CARCERE FEMMINELE
  (SEE: WOMEN IN CELL BLOCK 7) (1977, US/It.)
DIARY FOR MY CHILDREN (1984, Hung.) PR:O
DIARY OF A BACHELOR (1964) PR:O
DIARY OF A BAD GIRL (1958, Fr.) PR:C
DIARY OF A BRIDE (SEE: I, JANE DOE) (1948)
DIARY OF A CHAMBERMAID (1946) PR:A
DIARY OF A CHAMBERMAID (1964, Fr./It.) PR:O
DIARY OF A CLOISTERED NUN (1973, It./Fr./W. Ger.)
  PR:O
DIARY OF A COUNTRY PRIEST (1950, Fr.) PR:A
DIARY OF A HIGH SCHOOL BRIDE (1959) PR:C-O
DIARY OF A MAD HOUSEWIFE (1970) PR:C-O
DIARY OF A MADMAN (1963) PR:C-O
DIARY OF A NAZI (1943, USSR) PR:C
DIARY OF A REVOLUTIONIST (1932, USSR) PR:A
DIARY OF A SCHIZOPHRENIC GIRL (1970, It.) PR:A
DIARY OF A SHINJUKU BURGLAR (1969, Jap.) PR:O
DIARY OF AN INNOCENT BOY, THE (SEE: BENJA-
  MIN) (1968, Fr.)
DIARY OF AN ITALIAN (1972, It.) PR:C
DIARY OF ANNE FRANK, THE (1959) PR:A
DIARY OF FORBIDDEN DREAMS (1972, It./Fr./W. Ger.)
  PR:O
DIARY OF MAJOR THOMPSON, THE (SEE: FRENCH,
  THEY ARE A FUNNY RACE, THE) (1956, Fr.)
DIARY OF OHARU (SEE: LIFE OF OHARU, THE)
  (1952, Jap.)
DICH HAB ICH GELIEBT (SEE: BECAUSE I LOVED
  YOU) (1930, Ger.)
DICK BARTON AT BAY (1950, Brit.) PR:A
DICK BARTON—SPECIAL AGENT (1948, Brit.) PR:A
DICK BARTON STRIKES BACK (1949, Brit.) PR:A
DICK TRACY (1945) PR:A-C
DICK TRACY MEETS GRUESOME (1947) PR:A-C
DICK TRACY VS. CUEBALL (1946) PR:C
DICK TRACY'S DILEMMA (1947) PR:C
DICK TURPIN (1933, Brit.) PR:A
DICTATOR, THE (1935, Brit./Ger.) PR:A
DID I BETRAY? (SEE: BLACK ROSES) (1936, Ger.)
DID YOU HEAR THE ONE ABOUT THE TRAVELING
  SALESLADY? (1968) PR:A-C
DIE 4 GESELLEN (SEE: FOUR COMPANIONS, THE)
  (1938, Ger.)
DIE ANGST (SEE: FEAR) (1954, It./W. Ger.)
DIE ANGST DES TORMANNS BEIM ELFMETER (SEE:
  GOALIE'S ANXIETY AT THE PENALTY KICK, THE)
  (1971, W. Ger.)
DIE BITTEREN TRAENEN DER PETRA VON KANT
  (SEE: BITTER TEARS OF PETRA VON KANT, THE)
  (1972, W. Ger.)
DIE BLECHTROMMEL (SEE: TIN DRUM, THE) (1979,
  Fr./Pol./W. Ger./Yugo.)

DIE BLEIERNE ZEIT (SEE: GERMAN SISTERS, THE)
  (1982, W. Ger.)
DIE BLUMENFRAU VON LINDENAU (SEE: STORM IN
  A WATER GLASS) (1931, Aust.)
DIE! DIE! MY DARLING (1965, Brit.) PR:O
DIE DREIGROSCHENOPER (SEE: THREEPENNY
  OPERA, THE) (1931, US/Ger.)
DIE EHE DER MARIA BRAUN (SEE: MARRIAGE OF
  MARIA BRAUN, THE) (1979, W. Ger.)
DIE ENDLOSE NACHT (SEE: ENDLESS NIGHT, THE)
  (1963, W. Ger.)
DIE ENTE KLINGELT UM 1/2 7 (SEE: DUCK RINGS AT
  HALF PAST SEVEN, THE) (1969, It./W. Ger.)
DIE FASTNACHTSBEICHTE (1962, W. Ger.) PR:A
DIE FLAMBIERTE FRAU (SEE: WOMAN IN FLAMES,
  A) (1983, W. Ger.)
DIE FLEDERMAUS (1964, Aust.) PR:A
DIE FOLTERKAMMER DES DR. FU MANCHU (SEE:
  CASTLE OF FU MANCHU, THE) (1968, Brit./It./Sp./W.
  Ger.)
DIE GANS VON SEDAN (1962, Fr/W. Ger.) PR:A
DIE GROSSE SEHNSUCHT (SEE: GREAT YEARNING,
  THE) (1930, Ger.)
DIE HAMBURGER KRANKHEIT (1979, Fr./W. Ger.)
  PR:C
DIE HARD (1988) PR:O
DIE HERRIN VON ATLANTIS (SEE: MISTRESS OF AT-
  LANTIS, THE) (1932, Ger.)
DIE HOCHZEIT DES FIGARO (SEE: MARRIAGE OF
  FIGARO, THE) (1970, W. Ger.)
DIE HOLLE VON MACAO (SEE: CORRUPT ONES,
  THE) (1967, Fr./It./W. Ger.)
DIE KAMELIENDAME (SEE: LADY OF THE CAME-
  LIAS) (1987, W. Ger.)
DIE KOFFER DES HERRN O.F. (SEE: TRUNKS OF MR.
  O.F., THE) (1932, Ger.)
DIE LAUGHING (1980) PR:O
DIE LETZTE BRUECKE (SEE: LAST BRIDGE, THE)
  (1957, Aust.)
DIE MANNER UM LUCIE (1931, Fr./Ger.) PR:A
DIE MITLAUFER (SEE: FOLLOWING THE FUHRER)
  (1986, W. Ger.)
DIE, MONSTER, DIE! (1965, US/Brit.) PR:C
DIE NACKTE UND DER SATAN (SEE: HEAD, THE)
  (1969, W. Ger.)
DIE RATTEN (SEE: RATS, THE) (1955, W. Ger.)
DIE REISE (SEE: JOURNEY, THE) (1986, Switz./W. Ger.)
DIE SCHWARZE SPINNE (SEE: BLACK SPIDER, THE)
  (1983, Switz.)
DIE SCREAMING, MARIANNE (1970, Brit.) PR:O
DIE SEHNS UCHT DER VERONIKA VOSS (SEE: VER-
  ONIKA VOSS) (1982, W. Ger.)
DIE SIBEN MANNER DER SU-MARU (SEE: RIO 70)
  (1970, US/Sp./W. Ger.)
DIE TODESSTRAHLEN DES DR. MABUSE (SEE: DR.
  MABUSE'S RAYS OF DEATH) (1964, Fr./It./W. Ger.)
DIE UNENDLICHE GESCHICHTE (SEE: NEVEREND-
  ING STORY, THE) (1984, W. Ger.)
DIE VERLORENE EHRE DER KATHARINA BLUM
  (SEE: LOST HONOR OF KATHARINA BLUM, THE)
  (1975, W. Ger.)
DIE VIER IM JEEP (SEE: FOUR IN A JEEP) (1951, Switz.)
DIE WANNSEEKONFERENZ (SEE: WANNSEE CON-
  FERENCE, THE) (1987, Aust./W. Ger.)
DIE WELT OHNE MASKE (SEE: WORLD WITHOUT A
  MASK) (1934, Ger.)
DIE WILDENTE (SEE: WILD DUCK, THE) (1977,
  Aust./W. Ger.)
DIFENDO IL MIO AMORE (SEE: DEFEND MY LOVE)
  (1956, It.)
DIFFERENT SONS (1962, Jap.) PR:O
DIFFERENT STORY, A (1978) PR:O
DIFFICULT LOVE, A (SEE: CLOSELY WATCHED
  TRAINS) (1966, Czech.)
DIFFICULT YEARS (1950, It.) PR:C
DIG THAT JULIET (SEE: ROMANOFF AND JULIET)
  (1961)
DIG THAT URANIUM (1956) PR:A
DIGBY, THE BIGGEST DOG IN THE WORLD (1974, Brit.)
  PR:AA
DILLINGER (1945) PR:C-O
DILLINGER (1973) PR:O
DILLINGER IS DEAD (1969, It.) PR:O
DIM SUM: A LITTLE BIT OF HEART (1985) PR:A
DIMBOOLA (1979, Aus.) PR:O
DIME WITH A HALO (1963) PR:A
DIMENSION 5 (1966) PR:A
DIMKA (1964, USSR) PR:AA
DIMPLES (1936) PR:AA
DINER (1982) PR:C-O
DING DONG WILLIAMS (1946) PR:A
DINGAKA (1965, South Africa) PR:A
DINKY (1935) PR:A
DINNER AT EIGHT (1933) PR:C
DINNER AT THE RITZ (1937, Brit.) PR:A
DINNER FOR ADELE (SEE: ADELE HASN'T HAD HER
  SUPPER YET) (1978, Czech.)
DINO (1957) PR:A

DINOSAURUS! (1960) PR:AA
DIO MIO, COME SONO CADUTA IN BASSO (SEE:
  TILL MARRIAGE DO US PART) (1974, It.)
DION BROTHERS, THE (SEE: GRAVY TRAIN, THE)
  (1974)
DIPLOMANIACS (1933) PR:A
DIPLOMAT'S MANSION, THE (1961, Jap.) PR:C
DIPLOMATIC CORPSE, THE (1958, Brit.) PR:A
DIPLOMATIC COURIER (1952) PR:A
DIPLOMATIC LOVER, THE (1934, Brit.) PR:A
DIPLOMATIC PASSPORT (1954, Brit.) PR:A
DIRIGIBLE (1931) PR:A
DIRT BIKE KID, THE (1986) PR:A
DIRT GANG, THE (1972) PR:O
DIRTY DANCING (1987) PR:C
DIRTY DISHES (1978, Fr.) PR:O
DIRTY DOZEN, THE (1967, Brit.) PR:C-O
DIRTY GAME, THE (1966, Fr./It./W. Ger.) PR:C
DIRTY HANDS (1976, Fr/It./W. Ger.) PR:O
DIRTY HARRY (1971) PR:O
DIRTY HEROES (1971, It./Fr./W. Ger.) PR:A
DIRTY KNIGHT'S WORK (1976, Brit.) PR:C
DIRTY LAUNDRY (1987) PR:A-C
DIRTY LITTLE BILLY (1972) PR:C-O
DIRTY MARY (SEE: VERY CURIOUS GIRL, A) (1969,
  Fr.)
DIRTY MARY, CRAZY LARRY (1974) PR:O
DIRTY MONEY (SEE: COP, A) (1973, Fr.)
DIRTY O'NEIL (1974) PR:O
DIRTY OUTLAWS, THE (1971, It.) PR:O
DIRTY ROTTEN SCOUNDRELS (1988) PR:C
DIRTY TRICKS (1981, Can.) PR:C
DIRTY WORK (1934, Brit.) PR:A
DIRTYMOUTH (1970) PR:O
DISAPPEARANCE, THE (1981, Brit./Can.) PR:C
DISASTER (1948) PR:A
DISBARRED (1939) PR:A
DISC JOCKEY (1951) PR:A
DISC JOCKEY JAMBOREE (SEE: JAMBOREE) (1957)
DISCARDED LOVERS (1932) PR:A
DISCIPLE OF DEATH (1972, Brit.) PR:O
DISCORD (1933, Brit.) PR:A
DISCOVERIES (1939, Brit.) PR:A
DISCREET CHARM OF THE BOURGEOISIE, THE (1972,
  Fr./It./Sp.) PR:C
DISEMBODIED, THE (1957) PR:C
DISGRACED (1933) PR:A
DISHONOR BRIGHT (1936, Brit.) PR:A
DISHONORED (1931) PR:C
DISHONORED (1950, It.) PR:A
DISHONORED LADY (1947) PR:C
DISILLUSION (1949, It.) PR:A
DISOBEDIENT (1953, Brit.) PR:O
DISORDER (1964, Fr./It.) PR:A
DISORDER AND EARLY TORMENT (1977, W. Ger.)
  PR:A
DISORDERLIES (1987) PR:A-C
DISORDERLY CONDUCT (1932) PR:A
DISORDERLY ORDERLY, THE (1964) PR:A
DISORGANIZED CRIME (1989) PR:C
DISPATCH FROM REUTERS, A (1940) PR:A
DISPUTED PASSAGE (1939) PR:A
DISQUE 413 (SEE: RECORD 413) (1936, Fr.)
DISRAELI (1929) PR:A
DISTANCE (1975) PR:O
DISTANT DRUMS (1951) PR:A
DISTANT JOURNEY (1950, Czech.) PR:C
DISTANT THUNDER (1988, US/Can.) PR:O
DISTANT TRUMPET (1952, Brit.) PR:A
DISTANT TRUMPET, A (1964) PR:A
DISTANT VOICES, STILL LIVES (1989, Brit.) PR:C
DITES 33 (SEE: LADY DOCTOR, THE) (1963, Fr./It./Sp.)
DIVA (1981, Fr.) PR:C
DIVE BOMBER (1941) PR:A-C
DIVIDED HEART, THE (1955, Brit.) PR:A
DIVINA CREATURA (SEE: DIVINE NYMPH, THE)
  (1976, It.)
DIVINE EMMA, THE (1983, Czech.) PR:A
DIVINE MR. J., THE (1974) PR:O
DIVINE NYMPH, THE (1976, It.) PR:O
DIVINE SPARK, THE (1935, Brit./It.) PR:A
DIVING GIRLS' ISLAND, THE (SEE: VIOLATED PARA-
  DISE) (1963, It./Jap.)
DIVING GIRLS OF JAPAN (SEE: VIOLATED PARA-
  DISE) (1963, It./Jap.)
DIVKA S TREMI VELBLOUDY (SEE: GIRL WITH
  THREE CAMELS, THE) (1968, Czech.)
DIVORCE (1945) PR:C
DIVORCE AMERICAN STYLE (1967) PR:C
DIVORCE AMONG FRIENDS (1931) PR:C
DIVORCE IN THE FAMILY (1932) PR:A
DIVORCE, ITALIAN STYLE (1962, It.) PR:A
DIVORCE OF LADY X, THE (1938, Brit.) PR:A
DIVORCEE, THE (1930) PR:C
DIVORZIO ALL'ITALIANA (SEE: DIVORCE, ITALIAN
  STYLE) (1962, It.)
DIXIANA (1930) PR:A

DIXIE (1943) PR:A
DIXIE DUGAN (1943) PR:A
DIXIE DYNAMITE (1976) PR:C
DIXIE JAMBOREE (1945) PR:A
DIXIELAND DAIMYO (1986, Jap.) PR:A
DIZZY DAMES (1936) PR:A
DJANGO (1966, It./Sp.) PR:O
DJANGO IL BASTARDO (SEE: STRANGER'S GUNDOWN, THE) (1974, It.)
DJANGO KILL (1967, It./Sp.) PR:O
DJANGO SPARA PER PRIMO (SEE: HE WHO SHOOTS FIRST) (1966, It.)
DJAVULENS OGA (SEE: DEVIL'S EYE, THE) (1960, Swed.)
DNI I NOCHI (SEE: DAYS AND NIGHTS) (1946, USSR)
DO NOT DISTURB (1965) PR:A
DO NOT THROW CUSHIONS INTO THE RING (1970) PR:O
DO THE RIGHT THING (1989) PR:O
DO YOU KEEP A LION AT HOME? (1966, Czech.) PR:AA
DO YOU LIKE WOMEN? (SEE: TASTE FOR WOMEN, A) (1964, Fr./It.)
DO YOU LOVE ME? (1946) PR:A
DO YOU REMEMBER DOLLY BELL? (1981, Yugo.) PR:O
DOBERMAN GANG, THE (1972) PR:C
DOBRO POZHALOVAT (SEE: WELCOME KOSTYA!) (1965, USSR)
DOBUNEZUMI SAKUSEN (SEE: OPERATION X) (1963, Jap.)
DOC (1971) PR:O
DOC SAVAGE. . . THE MAN OF BRONZE (1975) PR:A
DOCK BRIEF, THE (SEE: TRIAL AND ERROR) (1962, Brit.)
DOCKS OF NEW ORLEANS (1948) PR:A
DOCKS OF NEW YORK (1945) PR:A
DOCKS OF SAN FRANCISCO (1932) PR:A
DOCTEUR FRANCOISE GAILLAND (SEE: NO TIME FOR BREAKFAST) (1978, Fr.)
DOCTEUR JEKYLL ET LES FEMMES (SEE: DR. JEKYLL) (1985, Fr.)
DOCTEUR LAENNEC (1949, Fr.) PR:A
DOCTEUR POPAUL (1972, Fr.) PR:O
DR. ALIEN (1989) PR:O
DOCTOR AND THE DEVILS, THE (1985, Brit.) PR:O
DOCTOR AND THE GIRL, THE (1949) PR:C
DOCTOR AT LARGE (1957, Brit.) PR:A
DOCTOR AT SEA (1955, Brit.) PR:A
DOCTOR BEWARE (1951, It.) PR:A
DR. BLACK, MR. HYDE (1976) PR:O
DOCTOR BLOOD'S COFFIN (1961, Brit.) PR:O
DR. BROADWAY (1942) PR:C
DR. BULL (1933) PR:A
DR. BUTCHER, M.D. (1982, It.) PR:O
DR. CHRISTIAN MEETS THE WOMEN (1940) PR:A
DR. COPPELIUS (1968, US/Sp.) PR:AA
DOCTOR CRIMEN (1953, Mex.) PR:C
DR. CRIPPEN (1963, Brit.) PR:C
DR. CYCLOPS (1940) PR:A
DOCTOR DEATH: SEEKER OF SOULS (1973) PR:O
DOCTOR DETROIT (1983) PR:O
DOCTOR DOLITTLE (1967) PR:AA
DR. EHRLICH'S MAGIC BULLET (1940) PR:A
DOCTOR FAUSTUS (1967, Brit.) PR:C
DR. FRANKENSTEIN ON CAMPUS (1970, Can.) PR:O
DOCTOR FROM SEVEN DIALS, THE (SEE: CORRIDORS OF BLOOD) (1963, Brit.)
DR. GILLESPIE'S CRIMINAL CASE (1943) PR:A
DR. GILLESPIE'S NEW ASSISTANT (1942) PR:A
DR. GOLDFOOT AND THE BIKINI MACHINE (1965) PR:C
DR. GOLDFOOT AND THE GIRL BOMBS (1966, US/It.) PR:O
DR. HACKENSTEIN (1989) PR:C
DR. HECKYL AND MR. HYPE (1980) PR:O
DOCTOR IN CLOVER (SEE: CARNABY, M.D.) (1967, Brit.)
DOCTOR IN DISTRESS (1963, Brit.) PR:A
DOCTOR IN LOVE (1960, Brit.) PR:A
DOCTOR IN THE HOUSE (1954, Brit.) PR:A
DOCTOR IN TROUBLE (1970, Brit.) PR:A
DR. JEKYLL (1985, Fr.) PR:O
DR. JEKYLL AND MR. HYDE (1932) PR:O
DR. JEKYLL AND MR. HYDE (1941) PR:C-O
DR. JEKYLL AND SISTER HYDE (1971, Brit.) PR:A
DR. JEKYLL AND THE WOLFMAN (1971, Sp.) PR:O
DR. JEKYLL'S DUNGEON OF DEATH (1982) PR:O
DR. JOSSER KC (1931, Brit.) PR:A
DR. KILDARE GOES HOME (1940) PR:A
DR. KILDARE'S CRISIS (1940) PR:A
DR. KILDARE'S STRANGE CASE (1940) PR:A
DR. KILDARE'S VICTORY (1941) PR:A
DR. KILDARE'S WEDDING DAY (1941) PR:A
DR. KNOCK (1936, Fr.) PR:A
DR. KNOCK (SEE: KNOCK) (1955, Fr.)
DR. MABUSE'S RAYS OF DEATH (1964, Fr./It./W. Ger.) PR:A

DR. MANIAC (SEE: MAN WHO LIVED AGAIN, THE) (1936, Brit.)
DOCTOR MANIAC (SEE: HOUSE OF THE LIVING DEAD) (1973, South Africa)
DR. MINX (1975) PR:O
DOCTOR MONICA (1934) PR:A
DR. MORELLE—THE CASE OF THE MISSING HEIRESS (1949, Brit.) PR:A
DR. NO (1962, Brit.) PR:C
DR. O'DOWD (1940, Brit.) PR:A
DOCTOR OF DOOM (1962, Mex.) PR:O
DOCTOR OF ST. PAUL, THE (1969, W. Ger.) PR:C
DR. OTTO AND THE RIDDLE OF THE GLOOM BEAM (1986) PR:A
DR. PHIBES RISES AGAIN (1972, Brit.) PR:C-O
DR. RENAULT'S SECRET (1942) PR:C
DR. RHYTHM (1938) PR:AA
DR. SIN FANG (1937, Brit.) PR:A
DR. SOCRATES (1935) PR:A-C
DR. STRANGELOVE: OR HOW I LEARNED TO STOP WORRYING AND LOVE THE BOMB (1964, Brit.) PR:C
DOCTOR SYN (1937, Brit.) PR:A
DR. SYN, ALIAS THE SCARECROW (1975, Brit.) PR:AA
DOCTOR TAKES A WIFE, THE (1940) PR:AA
DR. TARR'S TORTURE DUNGEON (1972, Mex.) PR:O
DR. TERROR'S GALLERY OF HORRORS (1967) PR:O
DR. TERROR'S HOUSE OF HORRORS (1965, US/Brit.) PR:O
DR. WHO AND THE DALEKS (1965, Brit.) PR:A
DOCTOR X (1932) PR:A
DOCTOR, YOU'VE GOT TO BE KIDDING (1967) PR:A
DOCTOR ZHIVAGO (1965) PR:A-C
DOCTOR'S ALIBI (SEE: MEDICO OF PAINTED SPRINGS, THE) (1941)
DOCTORS, THE (1956, Fr.) PR:A
DOCTOR'S DIARY, A (1937) PR:A
DOCTOR'S DILEMMA, THE (1958, Brit.) PR:A
DOCTORS DON'T TELL (1941) PR:A
DOCTOR'S ORDERS (1934, Brit.) PR:A
DOCTOR'S SECRET, THE (1929) PR:A
DOCTORS WEAR SCARLET (SEE: INCENSE FOR THE DAMNED) (1970, Brit.)
DOCTORS' WIVES (1931) PR:C
DOCTORS' WIVES (1971) PR:O
DODES 'KA-DEN (1970, Jap.) PR:C
DODGE CITY (1939) PR:A
DODGE CITY TRAIL (1937) PR:A
DODGING THE DOLE (1936, Brit.) PR:A
DODSWORTH (1936) PR:A
DOES, THE (SEE: LES BICHES) (1968, Fr./It.)
DOG, A MOUSE AND A SPUTNIK, A (SEE: SPUTNIK) (1958, Fr.)
DOG AND THE DIAMONDS, THE (1962, Brit.) PR:AA
DOG DAY (1984, Fr.) PR:O
DOG DAY AFTERNOON (1975) PR:O
DOG EAT DOG (1963, US/It./W. Ger.) PR:A
DOG OF FLANDERS, A (1935) PR:AA
DOG OF FLANDERS, A (1959) PR:AA
DOGADJAJ (SEE: EVENT, AN) (1970, Yugo.)
DOGPOUND SHUFFLE (1975, Can.) PR:A
DOGS (1976) PR:O
DOG'S BEST FRIEND, A (1960) PR:AA
DOGS OF HELL (SEE: ROTWEILER: DOGS OF HELL) (1984)
DOGS OF WAR, THE (1980, Brit.) PR:O
DOIN' TIME (1985) PR:O
DOIN' TIME ON PLANET EARTH (1989) PR:C
DOING TIME (1979, Brit.) PR:A
DOKURITSU KIKANJUTAI IMADA SHAGEKICHU (SEE: OUTPOST OF HELL) (1966, Jap.)
DOLEMITE (1975) PR:O
DOLL, THE (1962, Fr.) PR:A
DOLL, THE (1964, Swed.) PR:C
DOLL FACE (1945) PR:A
DOLL SQUAD, THE (1973) PR:O
DOLL THAT TOOK THE TOWN, THE (1965, It.) PR:A
DOLLAR (1938, Swed.) PR:A
$ (DOLLARS) (1971) PR:O
DOLLS (1987) PR:O
DOLLS, THE (SEE: BAMBOLE!) (1965, It.)
DOLL'S HOUSE, A (1973) PR:A
DOLL'S HOUSE, A (1973, Brit.) PR:A
DOLLY GETS AHEAD (1931, Ger.) PR:A
DOLLY MACHT KARRIERE (SEE: DOLLY GETS AHEAD) (1931, Ger.)
DOLLY SISTERS, THE (1945) PR:AA
DOLORES (1949, Sp.) PR:A
DOLWYN (SEE: LAST DAYS OF DOLWYN, THE) (1949)
DOM S MEZONINOM (SEE: HOUSE WITH AN ATTIC, THE) (1964, USSR)
DOMANI E TROPPO TARDI (1950, It.) PR:C
DOMENICA D'AGOSTO (SEE: SUNDAY IN AUGUST) (1949, It.)
DOMINANT SEX, THE (1937, Brit.) PR:A
DOMINICK AND EUGENE (1988) PR:C
DOMINIQUE (1978, Brit.) PR:C
DOMINO KID (1957) PR:A
DOMINO PRINCIPLE, THE (1977) PR:O

DON CHICAGO (1945, Brit.) PR:A
DON GIOVANNI (1955, Brit.) PR:A
DON GIOVANNI (1979, Fr./It./W. Ger.) PR:A
DON IS DEAD, THE (1973) PR:O
DON JUAN (SEE: PRIVATE LIFE OF DON JUAN, THE) (1934, Brit.)
DON JUAN (1956, Aust.) PR:A
DON JUAN QUILLIGAN (1945) PR:A
DON QUIXOTE (1935, Brit./Fr.) PR:A
DON QUIXOTE (1961, USSR) PR:A
DON QUIXOTE (1973, Aus.) PR:A
DON RICARDO RETURNS (1946) PR:A
DON-KIKHOT (SEE: DON QUIXOTE) (1961, USSR)
DONA FLOR AND HER TWO HUSBANDS (1977, Braz.) PR:O
DONA HERLINDA AND HER SON (1986, Mex.) PR:O
DONATELLA (1956, It.) PR:A
DONDI (1961) PR:AA
DONKEY SKIN (1975, Fr.) PR:C-O
DONNA DI VITA (SEE: LOLA) (1961, Fr./It.)
DONNEZ-MOI MA CHANCE (SEE: GIVE ME MY CHANCE) (1958, Fr.)
DONOVAN AFFAIR, THE (1929) PR:A
DONOVAN'S BRAIN (1953) PR:C
DONOVAN'S REEF (1963) PR:A
DON'S PARTY (1976, Aus.) PR:C-O
DON'T ANSWER THE PHONE (1980) PR:O
DON'T BE A DUMMY (1932, Brit.) PR:A
DON'T BET ON BLONDES (1935) PR:A
DON'T BET ON LOVE (1933) PR:A
DON'T BET ON WOMEN (1931) PR:A
DON'T BLAME THE STORK (1954, Brit.) PR:A
DON'T BOTHER TO KNOCK (1952) PR:O
DON'T BOTHER TO KNOCK (SEE: WHY BOTHER TO KNOCK) (1964, Brit.)
DON'T CALL ME A CON MAN (1966, Jap.) PR:A
DON'T CRY, IT'S ONLY THUNDER (1982) PR:O
DON'T CRY WITH YOUR MOUTH FULL (1974, Fr.) PR:A
DON'T DRINK THE WATER (1969) PR:A
DON'T EVER LEAVE ME (1949, Brit.) PR:A
DON'T FENCE ME IN (1945) PR:A
DON'T GAMBLE WITH LOVE (1936) PR:A
DON'T GAMBLE WITH STRANGERS (1946) PR:A
DON'T GET ME WRONG (1937, Brit.) PR:A
DON'T GET PERSONAL (1936) PR:A
DON'T GET PERSONAL (1941) PR:A
DON'T GIVE UP THE SHIP (1959) PR:A
DON'T GO IN THE HOUSE (1980) PR:O
DON'T GO NEAR THE WATER (1957) PR:A
DON'T JUST LIE THERE, SAY SOMETHING! (1973, Brit.) PR:O
DON'T JUST STAND THERE (1968) PR:A
DON'T KNOCK THE ROCK (1956) PR:A
DON'T KNOCK THE TWIST (1962) PR:A
DON'T LET THE ANGELS FALL (1969, Can.) PR:A
DON'T LOOK IN THE BASEMENT (1973) PR:O
DON'T LOOK NOW (1969, Brit./Fr.) PR:A
DON'T LOOK NOW (1973, Brit./It.) PR:O
DON'T LOSE YOUR HEAD (1967, Brit.) PR:C
DON'T MAKE WAVES (1967) PR:A
DON'T OPEN THE WINDOW (1974, It.) PR:O
DON'T OPEN TILL CHRISTMAS (1984, Brit.) PR:O
DON'T PANIC CHAPS! (1959, Brit.) PR:A
DON'T PLAY WITH MARTIANS (1967, Fr.) PR:A
DON'T RAISE THE BRIDGE, LOWER THE RIVER (1968, Brit.) PR:A
DON'T RUSH ME (1936, Brit.) PR:A
DON'T SAY DIE (1950, Brit.) PR:A
DON'T SCREAM, DORIS MAYS! (SEE: DAY OF THE NIGHTMARE) (1965)
DON'T TAKE IT TO HEART (1944, Brit.) PR:A
DON'T TALK TO STRANGE MEN (1962, Brit.) PR:C
DON'T TELL THE WIFE (1937) PR:A
DON'T TEMPT THE DEVIL (1964, Fr./It.) PR:A
DON'T TOUCH MY SISTER (SEE: GLASS CAGE, THE) (1964)
DON'T TOUCH THE LOOT (SEE: GRISBI) (1953, Fr.)
DON'T TOUCH WHITE WOMEN! (1974, Fr.) PR:C
DON'T TRUST YOUR HUSBAND (1948) PR:C
DON'T TURN 'EM LOOSE (1936) PR:A
DON'T TURN THE OTHER CHEEK (1974, It./Sp./W. Ger.) PR:C
DON'T WORRY, WE'LL THINK OF A TITLE (1966) PR:A
DON'T YOU CRY (SEE: MY LOVER, MY SON) (1970, US/Brit.)
DONZOKO (SEE: LOWER DEPTHS, THE) (1957, Jap.)
DOOLINS OF OKLAHOMA, THE (1949) PR:A
DOOMED AT SUNDOWN (1937) PR:AA
DOOMED BATTALION, THE (1932) PR:A
DOOMED CARAVAN (1941) PR:A
DOOMED CARGO (1936, Brit.) PR:A
DOOMED TO DIE (1940) PR:A
DOOMED TO DIE (1985, It.) PR:O
DOOMED, LIVING (SEE: IKIRU) (1952, Jap.)
DOOMSDAY AT ELEVEN (1963, Brit.) PR:A-C
DOOMSDAY MACHINE (1967) PR:A

DOOMSDAY VOYAGE (1972) PR:O
DOOMWATCH (1972, Brit.) PR:C
DOOR TO DOOR (1984) PR:C
DOOR-TO-DOOR MANIAC (SEE: FIVE MINUTES TO LIVE) (1961)
DOOR WITH SEVEN LOCKS, THE (SEE: CHAMBER OF HORRORS) (1941, Brit.)
DOPE ADDICT (SEE: REEFER MADNESS) (1936)
DOPED YOUTH (SEE: REEFER MADNESS) (1936)
DOPPELGANGER (SEE: JOURNEY TO THE FAR SIDE OF THE SUN) (1969, Brit.)
DORIAN GRAY (1970, It./W. Ger./Liechtenstein) PR:O
DORM THAT DRIPPED BLOOD, THE (1983) PR:O
DORMIRE (1985, W. Ger.) PR:C
DORNROSCHEN (SEE: SLEEPING BEAUTY) (1965, W. Ger.)
DORO NO KAWA (SEE: MUDDY RIVER) (1982, Jap.)
DOS COSMONAUTAS A LA FUERZA (1967, Sp./It.) PR:A
DOSS HOUSE (1933, Brit.) PR:A-C
DOT AND THE BUNNY (1983, Aus.) PR:AA
DOT AND THE KOALA (1985, Aus.) PR:AA
DOTO ICHIMAN KAIRI (SEE: MAD ATLANTIC, THE) (1967, Jap.)
DOUBLE, THE (1963, Brit.) PR:A
DOUBLE AFFAIR, THE (SEE: SPY WITH MY FACE, THE) (1966)
DOUBLE AGENTS, THE (SEE: NIGHT ENCOUNTER) (1959, Fr./It.)
DOUBLE ALIBI (1940) PR:A
DOUBLE-BARRELLED DETECTIVE STORY, THE (1965) PR:A
DOUBLE BED, THE (1965, Fr./It.) PR:C
DOUBLE BUNK (1961, Brit.) PR:A
DOUBLE CON, THE (SEE: TRICK BABY) (1973)
DOUBLE CONFESSION (1953, Brit.) PR:C
DOUBLE CRIME IN THE MAGINOT LINE (1939, Fr.) PR:A
DOUBLE CROSS (1941) PR:A
DOUBLE CROSS (1956, Brit.) PR:A-C
DOUBLE CROSS ROADS (1930) PR:A
DOUBLE CROSSBONES (1950) PR:AA
DOUBLE DANGER (1938) PR:AA
DOUBLE DARING (SEE: FIXER DUGAN) (1939)
DOUBLE DATE (1941) PR:AA
DOUBLE DEAL (1950) PR:A
DOUBLE DECEPTION (1963, Fr.) PR:A-C
DOUBLE DOOR (1934) PR:C-O
DOUBLE DOWN (SEE: STACY'S KNIGHTS) (1983)
DOUBLE DYNAMITE (1951) PR:A
DOUBLE EVENT, THE (1934, Brit.) PR:A
DOUBLE EXPOSURE (1944) PR:A
DOUBLE EXPOSURE (1954, Brit.) PR:A-C
DOUBLE EXPOSURE (1982) PR:O
DOUBLE EXPOSURES (1937, Brit.) PR:A
DOUBLE HARNESS (1933) PR:A-C
DOUBLE INDEMNITY (1944) PR:C
DOUBLE JEOPARDY (1955) PR:A
DOUBLE LIFE, A (1947) PR:C-O
DOUBLE MAN, THE (1967, Brit.) PR:C
DOUBLE MC GUFFIN, THE (1979) PR:A
DOUBLE NEGATIVE (1980, Can.) PR:O
DOUBLE NICKELS (1977) PR:C
DOUBLE OR NOTHING (1937) PR:A
DOUBLE OR QUITS (1938, Brit.) PR:A
DOUBLE POSSESSION (SEE: GANJA AND HESS) (1973)
DOUBLE-STOP (1968) PR:C
DOUBLE SUICIDE (1969, Jap.) PR:O
DOUBLE TROUBLE (1941) PR:A
DOUBLE TROUBLE (SEE: SWINGIN' ALONG) (1962)
DOUBLE TROUBLE (1967) PR:A
DOUBLE WEDDING (1937) PR:A
DOUBLES (1978) PR:C
DOUBTING THOMAS (1935) PR:A
DOUCE (SEE: LOVE STORY) (1949, Fr.)
DOUGH BOYS (1930) PR:AA
DOUGHBOYS IN IRELAND (1943) PR:A
DOUGHGIRLS, THE (1944) PR:A
DOUGHNUTS AND SOCIETY (1936) PR:A
DOULOS – THE FINGERMAN (SEE: FINGERMAN, THE) (1963, Fr.)
DOVE, THE (1974, Brit.) PR:AA
DOVE, THE (SEE: GIRL OF RIO, THE) (1932)
DOVER ROAD, THE (SEE: WHERE SINNERS MEET) (1934)
DOWN AMONG THE SHELTERING PALMS (1953) PR:A
DOWN AMONG THE Z MEN (1952, Brit.) PR:A
DOWN AND DIRTY (1976, It.) PR:O
DOWN AND OUT IN BEVERLY HILLS (1986) PR:C-O
DOWN ARGENTINE WAY (1940) PR:AA
DOWN BY LAW (1986) PR:O
DOWN CUBAN WAY (SEE: CUBAN PETE) (1946)
DOWN DAKOTA WAY (1949) PR:A
DOWN IN ARKANSAW (1938) PR:A
DOWN IN SAN DIEGO (1941) PR:A
DOWN LAREDO WAY (1953) PR:A

DOWN MEMORY LANE (1949) PR:A
DOWN MEXICO WAY (1941) PR:A
DOWN MISSOURI WAY (1946) PR:A
DOWN ON THE FARM (1938) PR:A
DOWN OUR ALLEY (1939, Brit.) PR:A
DOWN OUR STREET (1932, Brit.) PR:A
DOWN RIO GRANDE WAY (1942) PR:A
DOWN RIVER (1931, Brit.) PR:A
DOWN TEXAS WAY (1942) PR:A
DOWN THE ANCIENT STAIRCASE (1975, It.) PR:O
DOWN THE STRETCH (1936) PR:A
DOWN THE WYOMING TRAIL (1939) PR:A
DOWN THREE DARK STREETS (1954) PR:C
DOWN TO EARTH (1932) PR:A
DOWN TO EARTH (1947) PR:A
DOWN TO THE SEA (1936) PR:A
DOWN TO THE SEA IN SHIPS (SEE: LAST ADVENTURERS, THE) (1937, Brit.)
DOWN TO THE SEA IN SHIPS (1949) PR:AA
DOWN TO THEIR LAST YACHT (1934) PR:A
DOWN TWISTED (1989) PR:O
DOWN UNDER THE SEA (SEE: DOWN TO THE SEA) (1936)
DOWN WENT MC GINTY (SEE: GREAT MC GINTY, THE) (1940)
DOWNFALL (1964, Brit.) PR:C
DOWNHILL RACER (1969) PR:C
DOWNSTAIRS (1932) PR:A
DOZENS, THE (1981) PR:C
DOZNANIYE PILOTA PIRKSA (SEE: TEST OF PILOT PIRX, THE) (1978, Pol./USSR)
DRACHENFUTTER (SEE: DRAGON'S FOOD) (1988, Switz./W. Ger.)
DRACULA (1931) PR:C-O
DRACULA (SEE: HORROR OF DRACULA) (1958)
DRACULA (1979) PR:C
DRACULA A.D. 1972 (1972, Brit.) PR:O
DRACULA AND SON (1976, Fr.) PR:C
DRACULA AND THE SEVEN GOLDEN VAMPIRES (1974, Brit./Chi.) PR:O
DRACULA CERCA SANGUE DI VERGINE E. . . MORI DI SETE (SEE: ANDY WARHOL'S DRACULA) (1974, Fr./It.)
DRACULA HAS RISEN FROM THE GRAVE (1968, Brit.) PR:O
DRACULA – PRINCE OF DARKNESS (1966, Brit.) PR:O
DRACULA (THE DIRTY OLD MAN) (1969) PR:O
DRACULA TODAY (SEE: DRACULA A.D. 1972) (1972)
DRACULA VERSUS FRANKENSTEIN (1972, Sp.) PR:O
DRACULA VUOLE VIVERE: CERCA SANGUE DI VERGINA (SEE: ANDY WARHOL'S DRACULA) (1974, Fr./It.)
DRACULA'S LUST FOR BLOOD (SEE: LAKE OF DRACULA) (1973, Jap.)
DRACULA'S DAUGHTER (1936) PR:O
DRACULA'S DOG (1978) PR:O
DRACULA'S GREAT LOVE (1972, Sp.) PR:O
DRACULA'S LAST RITES (SEE: LAST RITES) (1980)
DRACULA'S WIDOW (1988) PR:O
DRAEGERMAN COURAGE (1937) PR:A
DRAG (1929) PR:A
DRAGNET (1947) PR:A
DRAGNET (1954) PR:A
DRAGNET (1987) PR:C
DRAGNET NIGHT (1931, Fr.) PR:A
DRAGNET PATROL (1932) PR:A
DRAGON FLIES, THE (SEE: MAN FROM HONG KONG, THE) (1975, Aus./Chin.)
DRAGON INN (1968, Chi.) PR:C
DRAGON MASTER (SEE: CANNON FOR CORDOBA) (1970)
DRAGON MURDER CASE, THE (1934) PR:A
DRAGON OF PENDRAGON CASTLE, THE (1950, Brit.) PR:AA
DRAGON SEED (1944) PR:A
DRAGON SKY (1964, Fr.) PR:A
DRAGONFLY, THE (1955, USSR) PR:A
DRAGONFLY (SEE: ONE SUMMER LOVE) (1976)
DRAGONFLY SQUADRON (1953) PR:A
DRAGON'S FOOD (1988, W. Ger./Switz.) PR:C
DRAGON'S GOLD (1954) PR:A
DRAGONSLAYER (1981) PR:C-O
DRAGONWYCK (1946) PR:A
DRAGOON WELLS MASSACRE (1957) PR:A
DRAGSTRIP GIRL (1957) PR:A
DRAGSTRIP RIOT (1958) PR:C
DRAKE CASE, THE (1929) PR:A
DRAKE THE PIRATE (1935, Brit.) PR:A
DRAMA OF JEALOUSY [AND OTHER THINGS], A (SEE: PIZZA TRIANGLE, THE) (1970, It./Sp.)
DRAMA OF THE RICH (1975, It./Fr.) PR:A-C
DRAMATIC SCHOOL (1938) PR:A-C
DRAMMA DELLA GELOSIA – TUTTI I PARTICOLARI IN CRONACA (SEE: PIZZA TRIANGLE, THE) (1970, It./Sp.)
DRANGO (1957) PR:A
DRAUGHTSMAN'S CONTRACT, THE (1983, Brit.) PR:O

DREADED PERSUASION, THE (SEE: NARCOTICS STORY, THE) (1958)
DREAM A LITTLE DREAM (1989) PR:C
DREAM COME TRUE, A (1963, USSR) PR:A
DREAM GIRL (1947) PR:A
DREAM LOVER (1986) PR:C
DREAM MAKER, THE (1963, Brit.) PR:A
DREAM NO MORE (1950, Palestine) PR:A
DREAM OF A COSSACK (1982, USSR) PR:A
DREAM OF BUTTERFLY, THE (1941, It.) PR:A
DREAM OF KINGS, A (1969) PR:C
DREAM OF LIFE (SEE: LIFE BEGINS) (1932)
DREAM OF OLWEN, THE (SEE: WHILE I LIVE) (1947, Brit.)
DREAM OF PASSION, A (1978, Gr.) PR:C
DREAM OF SCHONBRUNN (1933, Aust.) PR:A
DREAM OF THE RED CHAMBER, THE (1966, Chi.) PR:A
DREAM ON (1981) PR:O
DREAM ONE (1984, Brit./Fr.) PR:A
DREAM TEAM, THE (1989) PR:C
DREAM TOWN (1973, W. Ger.) PR:C
DREAM WIFE (1953) PR:A
DREAM WORLD OF HARRISON MARKS, THE (SEE: NAKED WORLD OF HARRISON MARKS, THE) (1967, Brit.)
DREAMANIAC (1987) PR:O
DREAMBOAT (1952) PR:AA
DREAMCHILD (1985, Brit.) PR:A
DREAMER, THE (1936, Ger.) PR:A
DREAMER, THE (1970, US/Israel) PR:O
DREAMER (1979) PR:A
DREAMING (1944, Brit.) PR:A
DREAMING LIPS (1937, Brit.) PR:C
DREAMING LIPS (1958, W. Ger.) PR:C
DREAMING OUT LOUD (1940) PR:A
DREAMS (1955, Swed.) PR:C
DREAMS COME TRUE (1936, Brit.) PR:A
DREAMS IN A DRAWER (1957, Fr./It.) PR:A
DREAMS OF GLASS (1969) PR:C
DREAMS THAT MONEY CAN BUY (1948) PR:C
DREAMSCAPE (1984) PR:C-O
DREAMWORLD (SEE: COVERGIRL) (1984, Can.)
DREI GEGEN DREI (1985, W. Ger.) PR:C
DRESSED TO KILL (1941) PR:A
DRESSED TO KILL (1946) PR:A
DRESSED TO KILL (1980) PR:O
DRESSED TO THRILL (1935) PR:A
DRESSER, THE (1983, Brit.) PR:C
DREYFUS (SEE: DREYFUS CASE, THE) (1931, Brit.)
DREYFUS CASE, THE (1931, Brit.) PR:A
DREYFUS CASE, THE (1940, Ger.) PR:A
DRIFT FENCE (1936) PR:A
DRIFTER, THE (1932) PR:A
DRIFTER, THE (1944) PR:A
DRIFTER, THE (1966) PR:C
DRIFTER (1975) PR:O
DRIFTER, THE (1988) PR:O
DRIFTERS, THE (SEE: HALLUCINATION GENERATION) (1966)
DRIFTIN' KID, THE (1941) PR:A
DRIFTIN' RIVER (1946) PR:A
DRIFTING (1932) PR:A
DRIFTING (1983, Israel) PR:O
DRIFTING ALONG (1946) PR:A
DRIFTING WEEDS (SEE: FLOATING WEEDS) (1959, Jap.)
DRIFTING WESTWARD (1939) PR:A
DRIFTWOOD (1947) PR:A
DRILLER KILLER (1979) PR:O
DRIPPING DEEP RED (SEE: DEEP RED) (1976, It.)
DRIVE A CROOKED ROAD (1954) PR:C
DRIVE, HE SAID (1971) PR:O
DRIVE-IN (1976) PR:O
DRIVE-IN MASSACRE (1976) PR:O
DRIVER, THE (1978) PR:O
DRIVER'S SEAT, THE (1975, It.) PR:O
DRIVERS TO HELL (SEE: WILD ONES ON WHEELS) (1967)
DRIVING MISS DAISY (1989) PR:A
DROLE DE DRAME (SEE: BIZARRE BIZARRE) (1939, Fr.)
DROP DEAD, DARLING (SEE: ARRIVEDERCI, BABY!) (1966, Brit.)
DROP DEAD, MY LOVE (1968, It.) PR:C
DROP THEM OR I'LL SHOOT (1969, Fr./Sp./W. Ger.) PR:O
DROWNING BY NUMBERS (1988, Brit.) PR:O
DROWNING POOL, THE (1975) PR:C
DRUGSTORE COWBOY (1989) PR:O
DRUM (1976) PR:O
DRUM, THE (SEE: DRUMS) (1938, Brit.)
DRUM BEAT (1954) PR:A
DRUM CRAZY (SEE: GENE KRUPA STORY, THE) (1959)
DRUM TAPS (1933) PR:A
DRUMMER OF VENGEANCE (1974, Brit./It.) PR:O
DRUMS (1938, Brit.) PR:A

DRUMS ACROSS THE RIVER (1954) PR:A
DRUMS ALONG THE AMAZON (SEE: ANGEL ON THE AMAZON) (1948)
DRUMS ALONG THE MOHAWK (1939) PR:AA
DRUMS IN THE DEEP SOUTH (1951) PR:A
DRUMS O' VOODOO (1934) PR:A
DRUMS OF AFRICA (1963) PR:A
DRUMS OF DESTINY (1937) PR:A
DRUMS OF FU MANCHU (1943) PR:A
DRUMS OF JEOPARDY, THE (1931) PR:A
DRUMS OF TABU, THE (1967, It./Sp.) PR:A
DRUMS OF TAHITI (1954) PR:A
DRUMS OF THE CONGO (1942) PR:A
DRUMS OF THE DESERT (1940) PR:A
DRUNKEN ANGEL (1948, Jap.) PR:C
DRY ROT (1956, Brit.) PR:A
DRY SUMMER (1967, Turk.) PR:A
DRY WHITE SEASON, A (1989) PR:C
DRYLANDERS (1963, Can.) PR:A
DSCHINGIS KHAN (SEE: GENGHIS KHAN) (1965, US/Brit./W. Ger./Yugo.)
DU BARRY WAS A LADY (1943) PR:A
DU BARRY, WOMAN OF PASSION (1930) PR:A-C
DU HAUT EN BAS (SEE: FROM TOP TO BOTTOM) (1933, Fr.)
DU MICH AUCH (SEE: SAME TO YOU) (1987, Switz./W. Ger.)
DU RIFIFI CHEZ DES HOMMES (SEE: RIFIFI) (1955, Fr.)
DUAL ALIBI (1947, Brit.) PR:A
DUBEAT-E-O (1984) PR:O
DUBLIN NIGHTMARE (1958, Brit.) PR:A-C
DUCHESS AND THE DIRTWATER FOX, THE (1976) PR:C
DUCHESS OF BROADWAY (SEE: TALK ABOUT A LADY) (1946)
DUCHESS OF IDAHO, THE (1950) PR:A
DUCK IN ORANGE SAUCE (1976, It.) PR:C
DUCK RINGS AT HALF PAST SEVEN, THE (1969, It./W. Ger.) PR:O
DUCK SOUP (1933) PR:AA
DUCK, YOU SUCKER! (1972, It.) PR:C
DUCKWEED STORY, THE (SEE: FLOATING WEEDS) (1959, Jap.)
DUDE BANDIT, THE (1933) PR:A
DUDE COWBOY (1941) PR:A
DUDE GOES WEST, THE (1948) PR:A
DUDE RANCH (1931) PR:A
DUDE RANGER, THE (1934) PR:A
DUDE WRANGLER, THE (1930) PR:A
DUDES (1988) PR:O
DUE FRATELLI IN UN POSTO CHIAMATO TRINITA (SEE: JESSE AND LESTER, TWO BROTHERS IN A PLACE CALLED TRINITY) (1972, It.)
DUE NOTTI CON CLEOPATRA (SEE: TWO NIGHTS WITH CLEOPATRA) (1953, It.)
DUE SOLDI DI SPERANZA (SEE: TWO PENNIES WORTH OF HOPE) (1952, It.)
DUEL, THE (1964, USSR) PR:A
DUEL AT APACHE WELLS (1957) PR:A
DUEL AT DIABLO (1966) PR:A
DUEL AT EZO (1970, Jap.) PR:C
DUEL AT SILVER CREEK, THE (1952) PR:A
DUEL IN DURANGO (SEE: GUN DUEL IN DURANGO) (1957)
DUEL IN THE JUNGLE (1954, Brit.) PR:A
DUEL IN THE SUN (1946) PR:C-O
DUEL OF CHAMPIONS (1964, It./Sp.) PR:A
DUEL OF THE TITANS (1963, It.) PR:A
DUEL ON THE MISSISSIPPI (1955) PR:A
DUEL WITHOUT HONOR (1953, It.) PR:A
DUELLISTS, THE (1977, Brit.) PR:C
DUET FOR CANNIBALS (1969, Swed.) PR:O
DUET FOR FOUR (1982, Aus.) PR:C
DUET FOR ONE (1986) PR:O
DUFFY (1968, Brit.) PR:C
DUFFY OF SAN QUENTIN (1954) PR:A
DUFFY'S TAVERN (1945) PR:A
DUGAN OF THE BAD LANDS (1931) PR:A
DUGI BRODOVI (SEE: LONG SHIPS, THE) (1964, Brit./Yugo.)
DUKE COMES BACK, THE (1937) PR:A
DUKE IS THE TOPS, THE (1938) PR:A
DUKE OF CHICAGO (1949) PR:A
DUKE OF THE NAVY (1942) PR:A
DUKE OF WEST POINT, THE (1938) PR:A
DUKE WORE JEANS, THE (1958, Brit.) PR:A
DULCIMA (1971, Brit.) PR:A
DULCIMER STREET (1948, Brit.) PR:A
DULCINEA (1962, Sp.) PR:C
DULCY (1940) PR:A
DUMB DICKS (SEE: DETECTIVE SCHOOL DROP-OUTS) (1986)
DUMBBELLS IN ERMINE (1930) PR:A
DUMBO (1941) PR:AA
DUMMY, THE (1929) PR:A-C
DUMMY TALKS, THE (1943, Brit.) PR:A
DUNE (1984) PR:C-O
DUNGEONMASTER (1985) PR:C-O

DUNGEONS OF HARROW (1964) PR:O
DUNKIRK (1958, Brit.) PR:A
DUNWICH HORROR, THE (1970) PR:C
DURANGO KID, THE (1940) PR:A
DURANGO VALLEY RAIDERS (1938) PR:A
DURANT AFFAIR, THE (1962, Brit.) PR:A-C
DURING ONE NIGHT (1962, Brit.) PR:A
DUST (1985, Fr./Bel.) PR:O
DUST BE MY DESTINY (1939) PR:A
DUSTY AND SWEETS MCGEE (1971) PR:O
DUSTY ERMINE (SEE: HIDEOUT IN THE ALPS) (1936, Brit.)
DUTCH TREAT (1987) PR:C-O
DUTCHMAN (1966, Brit.) PR:C
DUVAR (SEE: WALL, THE) (1983, Fr.)
DYBBUK, THE (1938, Pol.) PR:A
DYNAMITE (1930) PR:A
DYNAMITE (1948) PR:A
DYNAMITE CANYON (1941) PR:A
DYNAMITE DELANEY (1938) PR:A
DYNAMITE DENNY (1932) PR:A
DYNAMITE JACK (1961, Fr.) PR:A
DYNAMITE JOHNSON (1978, Phil.) PR:A
DYNAMITE MAN FROM GLORY JAIL (SEE: FOOLS' PARADE) (1971)
DYNAMITE PASS (1950) PR:A
DYNAMITE RANCH (1932) PR:A
DYNAMITE WOMEN (SEE: GREAT TEXAS DYNA-MITE CHASE, THE) (1976)
DYNAMITERS, THE (1956, Brit.) PR:A
DYRYGENT (SEE: CONDUCTOR, THE) (1981, Pol.)
DZINGIS-KAN (SEE: GENGHIS KHAN) (1965, US/Brit./W. Ger./Yugo.)

E

E DIVENNE IL PIU SPIETATO BANDITO DEL SUD (SEE: FEW BULLETS MORE, A) (1968, It./Sp.)
E LA NAVE VA (SEE: AND THE SHIP SAILS ON) (1983, Fr./It.)
E.T. THE EXTRA-TERRESTRIAL (1982) PR:AA
EACH DAWN I DIE (1939) PR:A
EACH MAN FOR HIMSELF (SEE: RUTHLESS FOUR, THE) (1969)
EADIE WAS A LADY (1945) PR:A
EAGER BEAVERS (SEE: SWINGING BARMAIDS, THE) (1975)
EAGLE AND THE HAWK, THE (1933) PR:C
EAGLE AND THE HAWK, THE (1950) PR:A
EAGLE HAS LANDED, THE (1976, Brit.) PR:C
EAGLE IN A CAGE (1971, US/Yugo.) PR:A
EAGLE OVER LONDON (1973, It.) PR:C
EAGLE ROCK (1964, Brit.) PR:A
EAGLE SQUADRON (1942) PR:A
EAGLE WITH TWO HEADS (1948, Fr.) PR:A
EAGLE'S BROOD, THE (1936) PR:A
EAGLE'S WING (1979, Brit.) PR:A
EARL CARROLL SKETCHBOOK (1946) PR:A
EARL CARROLL'S VANITIES (1945) PR:A
EARL OF CHICAGO, THE (1940) PR:A
EARL OF PUDDLESTONE (1940) PR:A
EARLY AUTUMN (1962, Jap.) PR:C
EARLY BIRD, THE (1936, Brit.) PR:A
EARLY BIRD, THE (1965, Brit.) PR:A
EARLY TO BED (1933, Brit./Ger.) PR:A
EARLY TO BED (1936) PR:A
EARLY WORKS (1970, Yugo.) PR:O
EARRINGS OF MADAME DE..., THE (1953, Fr./It.) PR:A
EARTH CRIES OUT, THE (1949, It.) PR:A
EARTH DEFENSE FORCES (SEE: MYSTERIANS, THE) (1959, Jap.)
EARTH DIES SCREAMING, THE (1964, Brit.) PR:A
EARTH ENTRANCED (1970, Braz.) PR:C
EARTH GIRLS ARE EASY (1989) PR:C
EARTH VS. THE FLYING SAUCERS (1956) PR:A
EARTH VS. THE SPIDER (SEE: SPIDER, THE) (1958)
EARTHBOUND (1940) PR:A
EARTHBOUND (1981) PR:C
EARTHLING, THE (1980) PR:C
EARTHQUAKE (1974) PR:A
EARTHWORM TRACTORS (1936) PR:A
EASIEST WAY, THE (1931) PR:A
EAST CHINA SEA (1969, Jap.) PR:C
EAST END CHANT (SEE: LIMEHOUSE BLUES) (1934)
EAST IS WEST (1930) PR:C
EAST LYNNE (1931) PR:A
EAST LYNNE ON THE WESTERN FRONT (1931, Brit.) PR:A
EAST MEETS WEST (1936, Brit.) PR:A
EAST OF BORNEO (1931) PR:A
EAST OF EDEN (1955) PR:C-O
EAST OF ELEPHANT ROCK (1976, Brit.) PR:O
EAST OF FIFTH AVE. (1933) PR:C
EAST OF JAVA (1935) PR:A
EAST OF KILIMANJARO (1959, Brit./It.) PR:A
EAST OF PICADILLY (SEE: STRANGLER, THE) (1941, Brit.)
EAST OF SHANGHAI (SEE: RICH AND STRANGE) (1932, Brit.)

EAST OF SUDAN (1964, Brit.) PR:A
EAST OF SUMATRA (1953) PR:A
EAST OF THE BOWERY (SEE: FOLLOW THE LEADER) (1944)
EAST OF THE RISING SUN (SEE: MALAYA) (1950)
EAST OF THE RIVER (1940) PR:A
EAST OF THE WALL (1986, W. Ger.) PR:C
EAST SIDE KIDS (1940) PR:A
EAST SIDE KIDS MEET BELA LUGOSI, THE (SEE: GHOSTS ON THE LOOSE) (1943)
EAST SIDE OF HEAVEN (1939) PR:A
EAST SIDE SADIE (1929) PR:A
EAST SIDE, WEST SIDE (1949) PR:A-C
EASTER PARADE (1948) PR:AA
EASTER SUNDAY (SEE: BEING, THE) (1983)
EASY COME, EASY GO (1947) PR:A
EASY COME, EASY GO (1967) PR:A
EASY GO (SEE: FREE AND EASY) (1930)
EASY LIFE, THE (1963, It.) PR:C
EASY LIFE, THE (1971, Fr.) PR:C
EASY LIVING (1937) PR:A
EASY LIVING (1949) PR:A
EASY MILLIONS (1933) PR:A
EASY MONEY (1934, Brit.) PR:A
EASY MONEY (1936) PR:A
EASY MONEY (1948, Brit.) PR:A
EASY MONEY (1983) PR:C-O
EASY RICHES (1938, Brit.) PR:A
EASY RIDER (1969) PR:O
EASY TO LOOK AT (1945) PR:A
EASY TO LOVE (1934) PR:A
EASY TO LOVE (1953) PR:A
EASY TO TAKE (1936) PR:A
EASY TO WED (1946) PR:A
EASY WAY (SEE: ROOM FOR ONE MORE) (1952)
EASY WHEELS (1989) PR:O
EAT AND RUN (1986) PR:O
EAT MY DUST! (1976) PR:A
EAT THE PEACH (1987, Brit.) PR:A-C
EATEN ALIVE! (1976) PR:O
EATING RAOUL (1982) PR:O
EAVESDROPPER, THE (1966, US/Arg.) PR:C
EBB TIDE (1932, Brit.) PR:A
EBB TIDE (1937) PR:A
EBIRAH, HORROR OF THE DEEP (SEE: GODZILLA VS THE SEA MONSTER) (1966, Jap.)
EBOLI (SEE: CHRIST STOPPED AT EBOLI) (1979, Fr./It.)
ECHO, THE (1964, Pol.) PR:C
ECHO MURDERS, THE (1945, Brit.) PR:A
ECHO OF A DREAM (1930, Ger.) PR:A-C
ECHO OF BARBARA (1961, Brit.) PR:C
ECHO OF DIANA (1963, Brit.) PR:A-C
ECHO PARK (1986, Aust.) PR:O
ECHOES (1983) PR:O
ECHOES OF A SUMMER (1976) PR:A
ECHOES OF PARADISE (1989, Aus.) PR:C
ECHOES OF SILENCE (1966) PR:C
ECLIPSE (1962, Fr./It.) PR:C
ECSTACY OF YOUNG LOVE (1936, Czech.) PR:A
ECSTASY (1933, Czech.) PR:O
EDDIE AND THE CRUISERS (1983) PR:C
EDDIE AND THE CRUISERS II: EDDIE LIVES! (1989) PR:A
EDDIE CANTOR STORY, THE (1953) PR:AA
EDDIE MACON'S RUN (1983) PR:A-C
EDDY DUCHIN STORY, THE (1956) PR:A
EDEN CRIED (1967) PR:A
EDES MOSTOSHA (SEE: KIND STEPMOTHER) (1936, Hung.)
EDGAR ALLAN POE'S CASTLE OF BLOOD (SEE: CASTLE OF BLOOD) (1964, Fr./It.)
EDGAR ALLAN POE'S CONQUEROR WORM (SEE: CONQUEROR WORM, THE) (1968, Brit.)
EDGAR ALLAN POE'S "THE OBLONG BOX" (SEE: OBLONG BOX, THE) (1969, Brit.)
EDGE, THE (1968) PR:C
EDGE OF DARKNESS (1943) PR:A
EDGE OF DIVORCE (SEE: BACKGROUND) (1953, Brit.)
EDGE OF DOOM (1950) PR:C
EDGE OF ETERNITY (1959) PR:A
EDGE OF FURY (1958) PR:O
EDGE OF HELL (1956) PR:A
EDGE OF HELL, THE (SEE: ROCK 'N' ROLL NIGHT-MARE) (1987, Can.)
EDGE OF SANITY (1989, Brit.) PR:O
EDGE OF THE CITY (1957) PR:A
EDGE OF THE WORLD, THE (1937, Brit.) PR:A
EDISON, THE MAN (1940) PR:AA
EDITH AND MARCEL (1983, Fr.) PR:A
EDUCATED EVANS (1936, Brit.) PR:A
EDUCATING FATHER (1936) PR:A
EDUCATING RITA (1983, Brit.) PR:A
EDUCATION OF SONNY CARSON, THE (1974) PR:C
EDVARD MUNCH (1976, Norway/Swed.) PR:C
EDWARD AND CAROLINE (1952, Fr.) PR:A
EDWARD, MY SON (1949, US/Brit.) PR:C
EEGAH! (1962) PR:C

EERIE MIDNIGHT HORROR SHOW, THE (SEE: TORMENTED, THE) (1978, It.)
EERIE WORLD OF DR. JORDAN, THE (SEE: SOMETHING WEIRD) (1967)
EFFECT OF GAMMA RAYS ON MAN-IN-THE-MOON MARIGOLDS, THE (1972) PR:C
EFFECTS (1980) PR:O
EFFI BRIEST (1974, W. Ger.) PR:O
EGG AND I, THE (1947) PR:AA
EGGHEAD'S ROBOT (1970, Brit.) PR:A
EGLANTINE (1972, Fr.) PR:A
EGON SCHIELE—EXCESS AND PUNISHMENT (1981, W. Ger.) PR:O
EGYPT BY THREE (1953) PR:A
EGYPTIAN, THE (1954) PR:A-C
EHI, A MICO. . .C'E SABATA, HAI CHIUSO (SEE: SABATA) (1969, It.)
EIGER SANCTION, THE (1975) PR:C
8 1/2 (1963, It.) PR:C
EIGHT ARMS TO HOLD YOU (SEE: HELP!) (1965)
EIGHT BELLS (1935) PR:A
EIGHT GIRLS IN A BOAT (1932, Ger.) PR:A
EIGHT GIRLS IN A BOAT (1934) PR:C
EIGHT IRON MEN (1952) PR:C
EIGHT MEN OUT (1988) PR:C-O
EIGHT O'CLOCK WALK (1954, Brit.) PR:A
EIGHT ON THE LAM (1967) PR:A
18 AGAIN! (1988) PR:C
EIGHTEEN AND ANXIOUS (1957) PR:C
EIGHTEEN IN THE SUN (1964, It.) PR:C
18 MINUTES (1935, Brit.) PR:A
1812 (1944, USSR) PR:A
EIGHTH DAY OF THE WEEK, THE (1959, Pol./W. Ger.) PR:C-O
84 CHARING CROSS ROAD (1987) PR:A-C
84 CHARLIE MOPIC (1989) PR:O
80 STEPS TO JONAH (1969) PR:A
80,000 SUSPECTS (1963, Brit.) PR:C
EILO ENO KUROHYO (SEE: FIGHT FOR THE GLORY) (1970, Jap.)
EIN BLICK—UND DIE LIEBE BRICHT AUS (1986, W. Ger.) PR:O
EIN BLONDER TRAUM (SEE: HAPPY EVER AFTER) (1932, Brit./Ger.)
EIN MANN WIE EVA (SEE: MAN LIKE EVA, A) (1985, W. Ger.)
EIN STEINREICHER MANN (SEE: TREMENDOUSLY RICH MAN) (1932, Ger.)
EIN TOTER HING IM NETZ (SEE: IT'S HOT IN PARADISE) (1959, W. Ger./Yugo.)
EIN VIRUS KENNT KEINE MORAL (SEE: VIRUS KNOWS NO MORALS, A) (1986, W. Ger.)
EINE LIEBE IN DEUTSCHLAND (SEE: LOVE IN GERMANY, A) (1984, Fr./W. Ger.)
EINE NACHT IN LONDON (SEE: KNIGHT IN LONDON, A) (1930, Brit./Ger.)
EINER FRISST DEN ANDEREN (SEE: DOG EAT DOG) (1963, US/It./W. Ger.)
EL (1952, Mex.) PR:C-O
EL ALAMEIN (1954) PR:A-C
EL AMOR BRUJO (1986, Sp.) PR:A
EL AMOR ES UNA MUJER GORDA (SEE: LOVE IS A FAT WOMAN) (1988, Arg.)
EL ANGEL EXTERMINADOR (SEE: EXTERMINATING ANGEL, THE) (1967, Mex.)
EL ANO DE LAS LUCES (SEE: YEAR OF AWAKENING, THE) (1987, Sp.)
EL ATAUD DEL VAMPIRO (SEE: VAMPIRE'S COFFIN, THE) (1958, Mex.)
EL BRUTO (SEE: BRUTE, THE) (1952, Mex.)
EL BUQUE MALDITO (SEE: HORROR OF THE ZOMBIES, THE) (1974, Sp.)
EL CASTELLO DELL'ORRORE (SEE: HOUSE OF FREAKS) (1973, It.)
EL CASTILLO DE LOS MONSTROUS (SEE: CASTLE OF THE MONSTERS) (1958, Mex.)
EL CID (1961, US/It.) PR:A
EL COLECCIONISTA DE CADAVERES (SEE: CAULDRON OF BLOOD) (1967, US/Sp.)
EL CONDOR (1970) PR:O
EL DEDO DEL DESTINO (SEE: FICKLE FINGER OF FATE, THE) (1967, US/Sp.)
EL DEDO EN EL GATILLO (SEE: FINGER ON THE TRIGGER) (1965, US/Sp.)
EL DESCUARTIZADOR DE BINBROOK (SEE: GRAVEYARD OF HORROR) (1971, Sp.)
EL DESPERADO (SEE: DIRTY OUTLAWS, THE) (1971, It.)
EL DIABLO RIDES (1939) PR:A
EL DIPUTADO (1978, Sp.) PR:O
EL DORADO (1967) PR:A-C
EL DORADO PASS (1949) PR:A
EL ESPIRITU DE LA COLMENA (SEE: SPIRIT OF THE BEEHIVE, THE) (1976, Sp.)
EL FANTASTICO MUNDO DEL DR. COPPELIUS (SEE: DR. COPPELIUS) (1968, US/Sp.)
EL GRECO (1966, It./Fr.) PR:A

EL HOMBRE DE LOS HONGOS (SEE: MUSHROOM EATER, THE) (1976, Mex.)
EL HOMBRE INVISIBLE (SEE: INVISIBLE MAN, THE) (1958, Mex.)
EL HOMBRE QUE MATO A BILLY EL NINO (SEE: FEW BULLETS MORE, A) (1968, It./Sp.)
EL HOMBRE QUE VINO DEL UMMO (SEE: ASSIGNMENT TERROR) (1970, It./Sp./W. Ger.)
EL HOMBRE Y EL MONSTRUO (SEE: MAN AND THE MONSTER, THE) (1958, Mex.)
EL HOMBRE Y LA BESTIA (SEE: MAN AND BEAST, THE) (1951, Arg.)
EL IMPERIO DE LA FORTUNA (SEE: REALM OF FORTUNE, THE) (1987, Mex.)
EL JARDIN DE LAS DELICIAS (SEE: GARDEN OF DELIGHTS, THE) (1970, Sp.)
EL JORBADO DE LA MORGUE (SEE: HUNCHBACK OF THE MORGUE, THE) (1972, Sp.)
EL MAL (SEE: RAGE) (1966, US/Mex.)
EL MAS FABULOSI GOLPE DEL FAR WEST (SEE: BOLDEST JOB IN THE WEST, THE) (1971, It.)
EL MONSTRUO RESUCITADO (SEE: DOCTOR CRIMEN) (1953, Mex.)
EL MUERTO (1975, Arg./Sp.) PR:C
EL NIDO (SEE: NEST, THE) (1980, Sp.)
EL NORTE (1983) PR:O
EL OJO DE LA CERRADURA (SEE: EAVESDROPPER, THE) (1966, US/Arg.)
EL PASO (1949) PR:A
EL PASO KID, THE (1946) PR:A
EL PASO STAMPEDE (1953) PR:A
EL RETORNO DE LA WALPURGIS (SEE: CURSE OF THE DEVIL) (1973, Mex./Sp.)
EL SONIDO DE LA MUERTE (SEE: SOUND OF HORROR) (1966, Sp.)
EL TESORO DEL AMAZONES (SEE: TREASURE OF THE AMAZON, THE) (1985, Mex.)
EL TESTAMENTO DE MADIGAN (SEE: MADIGAN'S MILLIONS) (1970, It./Sp.)
EL TOPO (1971, Mex.) PR:O
ELDER BROTHER, THE (1937, Brit.) PR:A
ELECTRA (1962, Gr.) PR:A
ELECTRA GLIDE IN BLUE (1973) PR:C
ELECTRIC BLUE (1988, It.) PR:A-C
ELECTRIC BOOGALOO: BREAKIN' 2 (SEE: BREAKIN' 2: ELECTRIC BOOGALOO) (1984)
ELECTRIC DREAMS (1984) PR:A-C
ELECTRIC HORSEMAN, THE (1979) PR:A-C
ELECTRIC MAN, THE (SEE: MAN MADE MONSTER) (1941)
ELECTRONIC MONSTER, THE (1960, Brit.) PR:C
ELEMENT OF CRIME, THE (1984, Den.) PR:O
ELENA AND HER MEN (1956, Fr./It.) PR:A
ELENI (1985) PR:A-C
ELEPHANT BOY (1937, Brit.) PR:AA
ELEPHANT CALLED SLOWLY, AN (1970, Brit.) PR:A
ELEPHANT GUN (1959, Brit.) PR:A
ELEPHANT MAN, THE (1980, Brit.) PR:A-C
ELEPHANT STAMPEDE (1951) PR:A
ELEPHANT WALK (1954) PR:A
ELEPHANTS NEVER FORGET (SEE: ZENOBIA) (1939)
11 HARROWHOUSE (1974, Brit.) PR:C
ELEVENTH COMMANDMENT, THE (1933) PR:A
ELI ELI (1940) PR:A
ELIMINATOR, THE (SEE: DANGER ROUTE) (1968)
ELIMINATORS (1986) PR:A-C
ELINOR NORTON (1935) PR:A
ELISABETH OF AUSTRIA (1931, Ger.) PR:A
ELISABETH VON OESTERREICH (SEE: ELISABETH OF AUSTRIA) (1931, Ger.)
ELIZA COMES TO STAY (1936, Brit.) PR:A
ELIZA FRASER (1976, Aus.) PR:C
ELIZABETH OF ENGLAND (SEE: DRAKE THE PIRATE) (1935, Brit.)
ELIZABETH OF LADYMEAD (1949, Brit.) PR:A
ELIZABETH THE QUEEN (SEE: PRIVATE LIVES OF ELIZABETH AND ESSEX, THE) (1939)
ELIZA'S HOROSCOPE (1975, Can.) PR:O
ELLA (SEE: MONKEY SHINES: AN EXPERIMENT IN FEAR) (1988)
ELLERY QUEEN AND THE MURDER RING (1941) PR:A
ELLERY QUEEN AND THE PERFECT CRIME (1941) PR:A
ELLERY QUEEN, MASTER DETECTIVE (1940) PR:A
ELLERY QUEEN'S PENTHOUSE MYSTERY (1941) PR:A
ELLIE (1984) PR:O
ELMER AND ELSIE (1934) PR:A
ELMER GANTRY (1960) PR:C
ELMER THE GREAT (1933) PR:A
ELNOK KISASSZONY (SEE: MISS PRESIDENT) (1935, Hung.)
ELOPEMENT (1951) PR:A
ELSA MAXWELL'S HOTEL FOR WOMEN (SEE: HOTEL FOR WOMEN) (1939)
ELUSIVE CORPORAL, THE (1962, Fr.) PR:A

ELUSIVE PIMPERNEL, THE (SEE: FIGHTING PIMPERNEL, THE) (1950, Brit.)
ELVIRA MADIGAN (1967, Swed.) PR:A-C
ELVIRA: MISTRESS OF THE DARK (1988) PR:C
ELVIS! ELVIS! (1977, Swed.) PR:A
EMANON (1987) PR:A-C
EMBALMER, THE (1966, It.) PR:C
EMBARRASSING MOMENTS (1930) PR:A
EMBARRASSING MOMENTS (1934) PR:A
EMBASSY (1972, Brit.) PR:C
EMBEZZLED HEAVEN (1959, W. Ger.) PR:A
EMBEZZLER, THE (1954, Brit.) PR:A
EMBRACEABLE YOU (1948) PR:A
EMBRACERS, THE (1966) PR:C
EMBRYO (1976) PR:C
EMBRYOS (1985, Hung.) PR:O
EMERALD FOREST, THE (1985, Brit.) PR:C-O
EMERGENCY! (SEE: HUNDRED HOUR HUNT) (1953)
EMERGENCY (1962, Brit.) PR:A
EMERGENCY CALL (1933) PR:A
EMERGENCY CALL (SEE: HUNDRED HOUR HUNT) (1953)
EMERGENCY HOSPITAL (1956) PR:A
EMERGENCY LANDING (1941) PR:A
EMERGENCY SQUAD (1940) PR:A
EMERGENCY WARD (SEE: CAREY TREATMENT, THE) (1972)
EMERGENCY WEDDING (1950) PR:A
EMIGRANTS, THE (1972, Swed.) PR:A
EMIL (1935, Brit.) PR:AA
EMIL AND THE DETECTIVE (1931, Ger.) PR:AA
EMIL AND THE DETECTIVES (SEE: EMIL) (1938, Brit.)
EMIL AND THE DETECTIVES (1964) PR:AA
EMIL UND DIE DETEKTIVE (SEE: EMIL AND THE DETECTIVE) (1931, Ger.)
EMILY (1976, Brit.) PR:O
EMILY (SEE: AMERICANIZATION OF EMILY, THE) (1964)
EMMA (1932) PR:A
EMMA MAE (1976) PR:O
EMMANUELLE (1974, Fr.) PR:O
EMMANUELLE 5 (1987, Fr.) PR:O
EMPEROR AND A GENERAL, THE (1968, Jap.) PR:O
EMPEROR AND THE GOLEM, THE (1955, Czech.) PR:A
EMPEROR AND THE NIGHTINGALE, THE (1949, Czech.) PR:AA
EMPEROR JONES, THE (1933) PR:C
EMPEROR OF PERU (SEE: ODYSSEY IN THE PACIFIC) (1981, Can./Fr.)
EMPEROR OF THE NORTH POLE (1973) PR:C
EMPEROR WALTZ, THE (1948) PR:AA
EMPEROR'S CANDLESTICKS, THE (1937) PR:A
EMPIRE OF NIGHT, THE (1963, Fr.) PR:C
EMPIRE OF THE ANTS (1977) PR:C
EMPIRE OF THE SUN (1987) PR:A
EMPIRE STRIKES BACK, THE (1980) PR:A
EMPLOYEES' ENTRANCE (1933) PR:A
EMPRESS AND I, THE (1933, Ger.) PR:A
EMPRESS WU (1965, Hong Kong) PR:A
EMPTY CANVAS, THE (1964, Fr./It.) PR:O
EMPTY HOLSTERS (1937) PR:A
EMPTY SADDLES (1937) PR:A
EMPTY STAR, THE (1962, Mex.) PR:A
EN ENDA NATT (SEE: ONLY ONE NIGHT) (1942, Swed.)
EN FREMMED BANKER PA (SEE: STRANGER KNOCKS, A) (1963, Den.)
EN KVINNAS ANSIKTE (SEE: WOMAN'S FACE, A) (1939, Swed.)
EN LEKITON I KARLEK (SEE: LESSON IN LOVE, A) (1954, Swed.)
EN PASSION (SEE: PASSION OF ANNA, THE) (1969, Swed.)
ENCHANTED APRIL (1935) PR:A
ENCHANTED COTTAGE, THE (1945) PR:A
ENCHANTED FOREST, THE (1945) PR:AA
ENCHANTED ISLAND (1958) PR:A
ENCHANTED VALLEY, THE (1948) PR:A
ENCHANTING SHADOW, THE (1965, Hong Kong) PR:A
ENCHANTMENT (1948) PR:A
ENCORE (1951, Brit.) PR:A
ENCOUNTER (SEE: STRANGERS ON THE PROWL) (1953, It.)
ENCOUNTER WITH THE UNKNOWN (1973) PR:C
ENCOUNTERS IN SALZBURG (1964, W. Ger.) PR:C
END, THE (1978) PR:O
END AS A MAN (SEE: STRANGE ONE, THE) (1957)
END OF A DAY, THE (1939, Fr.) PR:A
END OF A PRIEST (1970, Czech.) PR:C
END OF AUGUST, THE (1982) PR:O
END OF AUGUST AT THE HOTEL OZONE, THE (1967, Czech.) PR:C
END OF BELLE, THE (SEE: PASSION OF SLOW FIRE, THE) (1962, Fr.)
END OF DESIRE (1962, Fr./It.) PR:A
END OF INNOCENCE (1960, Arg.) PR:O
END OF MRS. CHENEY (1963, W. Ger.) PR:A
END OF SUMMER, THE (SEE: EARLY AUTUMN) (1962, Jap.)

END OF THE AFFAIR, THE (1955, Brit.) PR:A
END OF THE GAME (1976, It./W. Ger.) PR:C-O
END OF THE LINE, THE (1959, Brit.) PR:A-C
END OF THE LINE (1988) PR:A-C
END OF THE RAINBOW (SEE: NORTHWEST OUT-
  POST) (1947)
END OF THE RIVER, THE (1947, Brit.) PR:A
END OF THE ROAD, THE (1936, Brit.) PR:A
END OF THE ROAD (1944) PR:A
END OF THE ROAD, THE (1954, Brit.) PR:A
END OF THE ROAD (1970) PR:O
END OF THE TRAIL (1932) PR:A
END OF THE TRAIL (1936) PR:A
END OF THE WORLD, THE (1930, Fr.) PR:A
END OF THE WORLD, THE (SEE: PANIC IN YEAR
  ZERO!) (1962)
END OF THE WORLD (1977) PR:C
END OF THE WORLD (IN OUR USUAL BED IN A
  NIGHT FULL OF RAIN), THE (1978, It.) PR:C
END PLAY (1975, Aus.) PR:C
ENDANGERED SPECIES (1982) PR:O
ENDLESS LOVE (1981) PR:O
ENDLESS NIGHT, THE (1963, W. Ger.) PR:C
ENDLESS NIGHT (1971, Brit.) PR:C
ENDSTATION 13 SAHARA (SEE: STATION SIX-SA-
  HARA) (1964, Brit./W. Ger.)
ENEMIES, A LOVE STORY (1989) PR:C
ENEMIES OF PROGRESS (1934, USSR) PR:A
ENEMIES OF SOCIETY (SEE: BIG BRAIN, THE) (1933)
ENEMIES OF THE LAW (1931) PR:A
ENEMIES OF THE PUBLIC (SEE: PUBLIC ENEMY)
  (1931)
ENEMY, THE (SEE: HELL IN THE PACIFIC) (1968)
ENEMY AGENT (1940) PR:A
ENEMY AGENTS MEET ELLERY QUEEN (1942) PR:A
ENEMY BELOW, THE (1957) PR:A
ENEMY FROM SPACE (1957, Brit.) PR:A
ENEMY GENERAL, THE (1960) PR:A
ENEMY MINE (1985) PR:A-C
ENEMY OF THE LAW (1945) PR:A
ENEMY OF THE PEOPLE, AN (1978) PR:A
ENEMY OF THE POLICE (1933, Brit.) PR:A
ENEMY OF WOMEN (1944) PR:C
ENEMY TERRITORY (1987) PR:NR
ENEMY, THE SEA, THE (SEE: ALONE ON THE PA-
  CIFIC) (1964, Jap.)
ENFORCER, THE (1951) PR:C
ENFORCER, THE (1976) PR:O
ENGAGEMENT ITALIANO (1966, Fr./It.) PR:A
ENGLAND MADE ME (1973, Brit.) PR:C
ENGLISH WITHOUT TEARS (SEE: HER MAN
  GILBEY) (1949, Brit.)
ENGLISHMAN'S HOME, AN (SEE: MADMEN OF EU-
  ROPE) (1940, Brit.)
ENIGMA (1983, Brit./Fr.) PR:C
ENJO (1958, Jap.) PR:O
ENLIGHTEN THY DAUGHTER (1934) PR:A
ENORMOUS CHANGES AT THE LAST MINUTE (1985)
  PR:A
ENOUGH ROPE (1966, Fr./It./W. Ger.) PR:A
ENRICO IV (SEE: HENRY IV) (1985, It.)
ENSAYO DE UN CRIMEN (SEE: CRIMINAL LIFE OF
  ARCHIBALDO DE LA CRUZ, THE) (1955, Mex.)
ENSIGN PULVER (1964) PR:A
ENTEBBE: OPERATION THUNDERBOLT (SEE: OPER-
  ATION THUNDERBOLT) (1978, Israel)
ENTENTE CORDIALE (1939, Fr.) PR:A
ENTER ARSENE LUPIN (1944) PR:A
ENTER INSPECTOR DUVAL (1961, Brit.) PR:A-C
ENTER LAUGHING (1967) PR:A
ENTER MADAME (1935) PR:A
ENTER THE DRAGON (1973) PR:O
ENTER THE NINJA (1982) PR:O
ENTERTAINER, THE (1960, Brit.) PR:A
ENTERTAINER, THE (1975) PR:A-C
ENTERTAINING MR. SLOANE (1970, Brit.) PR:O
ENTFUHRUNG INS GLUCK (SEE: WONDER BOY)
  (1951, Brit./Aust.)
ENTITY, THE (1982) PR:O
ENTRE NOUS (1983, Fr.) PR:C
EPILOGUE (1967, Den.) PR:A
EPISODE (1937, Aust.) PR:A
EQUALIZER 2000 (1987) PR:O
EQUINOX (1970) PR:C-O
EQUUS (1977, Brit.) PR:C-O
ERASERHEAD (1978) PR:O
ERASMUS WITH FRECKLES (SEE: DEAR BRIGITTE)
  (1965)
ERCOLE CONTRO I FIGLI DEL SOLE (SEE:
  HERCULES AGAINST THE SONS OF THE SUN)
  (1964, It./Sp.)
ERCOLE CONTRO MOLOCK (SEE: CONQUEST OF
  MYCENE) (1963)
EREDITA FERRAMONTI (SEE: INHERITANCE, THE)
  (1976, It.)
ERENDIRA (1983, Mex./Fr./W. Ger.) PR:O
ERIC SOYA'S "17" (1967, Den.) PR:O
ERIK THE CONQUEROR (1963, Fr./It.) PR:C

ERIK THE VIKING (1989, Brit.) PR:AA
ERNEST GOES TO CAMP (1987) PR:A-C
ERNEST HEMINGWAY'S ADVENTURES OF A YOUNG
  MAN (SEE: ADVENTURES OF A YOUNG MAN)
  (1962)
ERNEST HEMINGWAY'S THE KILLERS (SEE: KILL-
  ERS, THE) (1964)
ERNEST SAVES CHRISTMAS (1988) PR:A
ERNESTO (1979, It.) PR:O
EROICA (1966, Pol.) PR:C
EROTIQUE (1969, Fr.) PR:C
ERRAND BOY, THE (1961) PR:A
ERSTE LIEBE (SEE: FIRST LOVE) (1970, Switz./W. Ger.)
ES GESHAH AM HELLICHTEN TAG (SEE: IT HAP-
  PENED IN BROAD DAYLIGHT) (1960, Switz./W. Ger.)
ES KOMMT EIN TAG (SEE: DAY WILL COME, A)
  (1960, W. Ger.)
ESCAPADE (1932) PR:A
ESCAPADE (1935) PR:A
ESCAPADE (1955, Brit.) PR:A
ESCAPADE IN JAPAN (1957) PR:A
ESCAPE (1930, Brit.) PR:A
ESCAPE, THE (1939) PR:A
ESCAPE (1940) PR:A
ESCAPE (1948, Brit.) PR:A
ESCAPE ARTIST, THE (1982) PR:C
ESCAPE BY NIGHT (1937) PR:A
ESCAPE BY NIGHT (1954, Brit.) PR:A-C
ESCAPE BY NIGHT (1965, Brit.) PR:C
ESCAPE DANGEROUS (1947, Brit.) PR:A
ESCAPE FROM ALCATRAZ (1979) PR:C
ESCAPE FROM CRIME (1942) PR:A
ESCAPE FROM DEVIL'S ISLAND (1935) PR:A
ESCAPE FROM EAST BERLIN (1962, US/W. Ger.) PR:A
ESCAPE FROM FORT BRAVO (1953) PR:A
ESCAPE FROM HELL ISLAND (SEE: MAN IN THE
  WATER, THE) (1964)
ESCAPE FROM HONG KONG (1942) PR:A
ESCAPE FROM NEW YORK (1981) PR:O
ESCAPE FROM RED ROCK (1958) PR:A
ESCAPE FROM SAN QUENTIN (1957) PR:A
ESCAPE FROM SEGOVIA (1984, Sp.) PR:C
ESCAPE FROM TERROR (1960) PR:A
ESCAPE FROM THE BRONX (1985, It.) PR:O
ESCAPE FROM THE DARK (SEE: LITTLEST HORSE
  THIEVES) (1977)
ESCAPE FROM THE PLANET OF THE APES (1971) PR:C
ESCAPE FROM THE SEA (1968, Brit.) PR:AA
ESCAPE FROM YESTERDAY (1939, Fr.) PR:A
ESCAPE FROM ZAHRAIN (1962) PR:A
ESCAPE IF YOU CAN (SEE: ST. BENNY THE DIP)
  (1951)
ESCAPE IN THE DESERT (1945) PR:A
ESCAPE IN THE FOG (1945) PR:A
ESCAPE IN THE SUN (1956, Brit.) PR:A
ESCAPE LIBRE (SEE: BACKFIRE) (1965, Fr.)
ESCAPE ME NEVER (1935, Brit.) PR:A
ESCAPE ME NEVER (1947) PR:A
ESCAPE OF PRINCESS CHARMING, THE (SEE: PRIN-
  CESS CHARMING) (1935, Brit.)
ESCAPE ROUTE (SEE: I'LL GET YOU) (1952, Brit.)
ESCAPE TO ATHENA (1979, Brit.) PR:C
ESCAPE TO BERLIN (1962, US/Switz./W. Ger.) PR:A
ESCAPE TO BURMA (1955) PR:A
ESCAPE TO DANGER (1943, Brit.) PR:A
ESCAPE TO GLORY (1940) PR:A
ESCAPE TO PARADISE (1939) PR:A
ESCAPE TO THE SUN (1972, Fr./Israel/W. Ger.) PR:C
ESCAPE TO VICTORY (SEE: VICTORY) (1981)
ESCAPE TO WITCH MOUNTAIN (1975) PR:AA
ESCAPE 2000 (1983, Aus.) PR:O
ESCAPED FROM DARTMOOR (1930, Brit.) PR:C
ESCAPEMENT (SEE: ELECTRONIC MONSTER, THE)
  (1960, Brit.)
ESCAPES (1987, Brit.) PR:A
ESCORT FOR HIRE (1960, Brit.) PR:A-C
ESCORT GIRL (SEE: HALF MOON STREET) (1986)
ESCORT WEST (1959) PR:A
ESPERAME EN EL CIELO (SEE: WAIT FOR ME IN
  HEAVEN) (1988, Sp.)
ESPIONAGE (1937) PR:A
ESPIONAGE AGENT (1939) PR:A
ESPIONS A L'AFFUT (SEE: HEAT OF MIDNIGHT)
  (1966, Fr.)
ESPIRITISMO (SEE: SPIRITISM) (1965, Mex.)
ESTAMBUL 65 (SEE: THAT MAN IN ISTANBUL) (1966,
  Fr./It./Sp.)
ESTHER AND THE KING (1960, US/It.) PR:A
ESTHER WATERS (1948, Brit.) PR:C
ET MOURIR DE PLAISIR (SEE: BLOOD AND ROSES)
  (1961, Fr./It.)
ETAT DE SIEGE (SEE: STATE OF SIEGE) (1972,
  US/Fr./It./W. Ger.)
ETERNAL FEMININE, THE (1931, Brit.) PR:A
ETERNAL HUSBAND, THE (1946, Fr.) PR:C
ETERNAL LOVE (1960, W. Ger.) PR:A
ETERNAL MASK, THE (1937, Switz.) PR:A-C
ETERNAL MELODIES (1948, It.) PR:A

ETERNAL RETURN, THE (1943, Fr.) PR:A
ETERNAL SEA, THE (1955) PR:A
ETERNAL SUMMER (1961) PR:A
ETERNAL WALTZ, THE (1959, W. Ger.) PR:A
ETERNALLY YOURS (1939) PR:A
ETERNITY OF LOVE (1961, Jap.) PR:C
E'TORNATO SABATA (SEE: RETURN OF SABATA)
  (1972, Fr./It./W. Ger.)
ETSURAKU (SEE: PLEASURES OF THE FLESH, THE)
  (1965, Jap.)
EUREKA (1983, Brit.) PR:O
EUREKA STOCKADE (SEE: MASSACRE HILL) (1949,
  Brit.)
EUROPE 51 (SEE: GREATEST LOVE, THE) (1951, It.)
EUROPEANS, THE (1979, Brit.) PR:A
EVA (1962, Fr./It.) PR:O
EVANGELINE (1929) PR:A
EVE (1968, US/Brit./Sp.) PR:A
EVE KNEW HER APPLES (1945) PR:A
EVE OF ST. MARK, THE (1944) PR:A-C
EVE WANTS TO SLEEP (1961, Pol.) PR:A
EVEL KNIEVEL (1971) PR:A
EVELYN PRENTICE (1934) PR:C
EVENINGS FOR SALE (1932) PR:A
EVENSONG (1934, Brit.) PR:A
EVENT, AN (1970, Yugo.) PR:C
EVENTS (1970) PR:O
EVER IN MY HEART (1933) PR:C
EVER SINCE EVE (1934) PR:A
EVER SINCE EVE (1937) PR:A
EVER SINCE VENUS (1944) PR:A
EVERGREEN (1934, Brit.) PR:A
EVERY BASTARD A KING (1968, Israel) PR:C
EVERY DAY IS A HOLIDAY (1966, Sp.) PR:A
EVERY DAY'S A HOLIDAY (1938) PR:A
EVERY DAY'S A HOLIDAY (SEE: GOLD OF NAPLES)
  (1954, It.)
EVERY DAY'S A HOLIDAY (SEE: SEASIDE SWING-
  ERS) (1965, Brit.)
EVERY GIRL SHOULD BE MARRIED (1948) PR:A
EVERY HOME SHOULD HAVE ONE (SEE: THINK
  DIRTY) (1970, Brit.)
EVERY LITTLE CROOK AND NANNY (1972) PR:C
EVERY MAN A KING (SEE: EVERY BASTARD A
  KING) (1968, Israel)
EVERY MAN FOR HIMSELF (1980, Fr.) PR:O
EVERY MAN FOR HIMSELF AND GOD AGAINST ALL
  (1975, W. Ger.) PR:A
EVERY MAN'S WOMAN (SEE: ROSE FOR EVERY-
  ONE, A) (1967, It.)
EVERY MINUTE COUNTS (SEE: COUNT THE HOURS)
  (1953)
EVERY NIGHT AT EIGHT (1935) PR:A
EVERY OTHER INCH A LADY (SEE: DANCING CO-
  ED) (1939)
EVERY PICTURE TELLS A STORY (1984, Brit.) PR:C
EVERY SATURDAY NIGHT (1936) PR:A
EVERY SPARROW MUST FALL (1964) PR:C
EVERY TIME WE SAY GOODBYE (1986) PR:C
EVERY WHICH WAY BUT LOOSE (1978) PR:C
EVERY WOMAN'S MAN (SEE: PRIZEFIGHTER AND
  THE LADY, THE) (1933)
EVERYBODY DANCE (1936, Brit.) PR:A
EVERYBODY DOES IT (1949) PR:A
EVERYBODY GO HOME! (1962, Fr./It.) PR:A
EVERYBODY SING (1938) PR:A
EVERYBODY'S CHEERING (SEE: TAKE ME OUT TO
  THE BALLGAME) (1949)
EVERYBODY'S ALL-AMERICAN (1988) PR:C-O
EVERYBODY'S BABY (1939) PR:A
EVERYBODY'S DANCIN' (1950) PR:A
EVERYBODY'S DOING IT (1938) PR:A
EVERYBODY'S HOBBY (1939) PR:A
EVERYBODY'S OLD MAN (1936) PR:A
EVERYMAN'S LAW (1936) PR:A
EVERYTHING BUT THE TRUTH (1956) PR:AA
EVERYTHING HAPPENS AT NIGHT (1939) PR:A
EVERYTHING HAPPENS TO ME (1938, Brit.) PR:A
EVERYTHING HAPPENS TO US (SEE: HI 'YA, CHUM)
  (1943)
EVERYTHING I HAVE IS YOURS (1952) PR:A
EVERYTHING IN LIFE (1936, Brit.) PR:A
EVERYTHING IS RHYTHM (1940, Brit.) PR:A
EVERYTHING IS THUNDER (1936, Brit.) PR:A
EVERYTHING OKAY (1936, Brit.) PR:A
*EVERYTHING YOU ALWAYS WANTED TO KNOW
  ABOUT SEX BUT WERE AFRAID TO ASK* (1972) PR:O
EVERYTHING'S DUCKY (1961) PR:A
EVERYTHING'S ON ICE (1939) PR:A
EVERYTHING'S ROSIE (1931) PR:A
EVICTORS, THE (1979) PR:O
EVIDENCE (1929) PR:A
EVIDENCE IN CAMERA (SEE: HEADLINE SHOOTER)
  (1933)
EVIL, THE (1978) PR:O
EVIL COME, EVIL GO (SEE: YELLOW CANARY, THE)
  (1963)
EVIL DEAD, THE (1983) PR:O

EVIL DEAD 2: DEAD BY DAWN (1987) PR:O
EVIL EYE (1964, It.) PR:A
EVIL FORCE, THE (SEE: 4D MAN) (1959)
EVIL GUN (SEE: DAY OF THE EVIL GUN) (1968)
EVIL IN THE DEEP (SEE: TREASURE OF JAMAICA REEF, THE) (1974)
EVIL MIND (SEE: CLAIRVOYANT, THE) (1935, Brit.)
EVIL OF FRANKENSTEIN, THE (1964, Brit.) PR:A
EVIL THAT MEN DO, THE (1984) PR:O
EVIL UNDER THE SUN (1982, Brit.) PR:A
EVILS OF THE NIGHT (1985) PR:O
EVILSPEAK (1982) PR:O
EWA CHCE SPAC (SEE: EVE WANTS TO SLEEP) (1961, Pol.)
EX-BAD BOY (1931) PR:A
EX-CHAMP (1939) PR:A
EX-FLAME (1931) PR:A
EX-LADY (1933) PR:A
EX-MRS. BRADFORD, THE (1936) PR:A
EXCALIBUR (1981) PR:C-O
EXCESS BAGGAGE (1933, Brit.) PR:A
EXCLUSIVE (1937) PR:A
EXCLUSIVE STORY (1936) PR:A
EXCUSE ME, MY NAME IS ROCCO PAPALEO (SEE: ROCCO PAPALEO) (1971, It./Fr.)
EXCUSE MY DUST (1951) PR:AA
EXCUSE MY GLOVE (1936, Brit.) PR:A
EXECUTIONER, THE (1970, Brit.) PR:C
EXECUTIONER PART II, THE (1984) PR:O
EXECUTIVE ACTION (1973) PR:C
EXECUTIVE SUITE (1954) PR:A
EXILE, THE (1931) PR:C-O
EXILE, THE (1947) PR:A
EXILE EXPRESS (1939) PR:A
EXILED TO SHANGHAI (1937) PR:A
EXILES, THE (1966) PR:C
EXIT THE DRAGON, ENTER THE TIGER (1977, Hong Kong) PR:O
EXODUS (1960) PR:C
EXORCISM AT MIDNIGHT (1966, Brit./US) PR:C-O
EXORCISM'S DAUGHTER (1974, Sp.) PR:O
EXORCIST, THE (1973) PR:O
EXORCIST II: THE HERETIC (1977) PR:O
EXOTIC ONES, THE (1968) PR:O
EXPEDITION MOON (SEE: ROCKETSHIP X-M) (1950)
EXPENSIVE HUSBANDS (1937) PR:A
EXPENSIVE WOMEN (1931) PR:C
EXPERIENCE PREFERRED. . . BUT NOT ESSENTIAL (1983, Brit.) PR:C
EXPERIMENT ALCATRAZ (1950) PR:A
EXPERIMENT IN TERROR (1962) PR:C
EXPERIMENT PERILOUS (1944) PR:A
EXPERT, THE (1932) PR:A
EXPERTS, THE (1989) PR:C
EXPERT'S OPINION (1935, Brit.) PR:A
EXPLORERS (1985) PR:C
EXPLOSION (1969, Can.) PR:O
EXPLOSIVE GENERATION, THE (1961) PR:C
EXPOSED (1932) PR:A
EXPOSED (1938) PR:A
EXPOSED (1947) PR:A
EXPOSED (1983) PR:O
EXPRESSO BONGO (1959, Brit.) PR:C
EXTASE (SEE: ECSTASY) (1933, Czech.)
EXTERMINATING ANGEL, THE (1967, Mex.) PR:O
EXTERMINATOR, THE (1980) PR:O
EXTERMINATOR II (1984) PR:O
EXTERMINATORS, THE (1965, Fr.) PR:A-C
EXTERMINATORS OF THE YEAR 3000, THE (1985, It./Sp.) PR:O
EXTORTION (1938) PR:A
EXTRA DAY, THE (1956, Brit.) PR:A
EXTRAORDINARY SEAMAN, THE (1969) PR:A
EXTRAVAGANCE (1930) PR:A
EXTREME PREJUDICE (1987) PR:O
EXTREMITIES (1986) PR:O
EYE CREATURES, THE (1965) PR:A-C
EYE FOR AN EYE, AN (1966) PR:C
EYE FOR AN EYE, AN (SEE: PSYCHOPATH, THE) (1973)
EYE FOR AN EYE, AN (1981) PR:O
EYE OF THE CAT (1969) PR:C
EYE OF THE DEVIL (1967, Brit.) PR:C
EYE OF THE NEEDLE, THE (1965, It./Fr.) PR:C
EYE OF THE NEEDLE (1981, Brit.) PR:C-O
EYE OF THE TIGER (1986) PR:O
EYE WITNESS (1950, Brit.) PR:A-C
EYEBALL (1978, It.) PR:O
EYES IN THE NIGHT (1942) PR:A
EYES OF A STRANGER (1980) PR:O
EYES OF ANNIE JONES, THE (1963, Brit.) PR:A
EYES OF FATE (1933, Brit.) PR:A
EYES OF FIRE (1984) PR:O
EYES OF HELL (SEE: MASK, THE) (1961, US/Can.)
EYES OF LAURA MARS (1978) PR:O
EYES OF TEXAS (1948) PR:A
EYES OF THE AMARYLLIS, THE (1982) PR:A-C
EYES OF THE UNDERWORLD (1943) PR:A

EYES OF THE WORLD, THE (1930) PR:C
EYES THAT KILL (1947, Brit.) PR:A
EYES, THE MOUTH, THE (1982, It./Fr.) PR:O
EYES, THE SEA AND A BALL (1968, Jap.) PR:A
EYES WITHOUT A FACE (SEE: HORROR CHAMBER OF DR. FAUSTUS, THE) (1959, Fr./It.)
EYEWITNESS (1956, Brit.) PR:A
EYEWITNESS (SEE: SUDDEN TERROR) (1970, Brit.)
EYEWITNESS (1981) PR:O
EZO YAKATA NO KETTO (SEE: DUEL AT EZO) (1970, Jap.)

F

F-MAN (1936) PR:A
F.I.S.T. (1978) PR:A-C
F.J. HOLDEN, THE (1977, Aus.) PR:O
F.P. 1 (1933, Brit.) PR:A
F.P. 1 ANTWORTET NICHT (SEE: F.P. 1 DOESN'T ANSWER) (1933, Ger.)
F.P. 1 DOESN'T ANSWER (1933, Ger.) PR:A
FABIAN OF THE YARD (1954, Brit.) PR:A
FABIOLA (1951, It.) PR:A-C
FABLE, A (1971) PR:O
FABULOUS ADVENTURES OF MARCO POLO, THE (SEE: MARCO THE MAGNIFICENT) (1966, Afghanistan/Egypt/Fr./It./Yugo.)
FABULOUS BAKER BOYS, THE (1989) PR:C-O
FABULOUS BARON MUNCHAUSEN, THE (SEE: BARON MUNCHAUSEN) (1962, Czech.)
FABULOUS DORSEYS, THE (1947) PR:A
FABULOUS SENORITA, THE (1952) PR:A
FABULOUS SUZANNE, THE (1946) PR:A
FABULOUS TEXAN, THE (1947) PR:A
FABULOUS WORLD OF JULES VERNE, THE (1958, Czech.) PR:AA
FACCIA A FACCIA (SEE: FACE TO FACE) (1967, It.)
FACE, THE (SEE: MAGICIAN, THE) (1958, Swed.)
FACE AT THE WINDOW, THE (1932, Brit.) PR:C
FACE AT THE WINDOW, THE (1939, Brit.) PR:C
FACE BEHIND THE MASK, THE (1941) PR:C
FACE BEHIND THE SCAR (1937, Brit.) PR:A
FACE IN THE CROWD, A (1957) PR:C
FACE IN THE FOG, A (1936) PR:A
FACE IN THE NIGHT (SEE: MENACE IN THE NIGHT) (1956, Brit.)
FACE IN THE RAIN, A (1963) PR:A
FACE IN THE SKY, THE (1933) PR:A
FACE OF A FUGITIVE (1959) PR:A
FACE OF A STRANGER (1964, Brit.) PR:A-C
FACE OF ANOTHER, THE (1967, Jap.) PR:O
FACE OF EVE, THE (SEE: EVE) (1968, US/Brit./Sp.)
FACE OF EVIL (SEE: DOCTOR BLOOD'S COFFIN) (1961, Brit.)
FACE OF FEAR (SEE: PEEPING TOM) (1960, Brit.)
FACE OF FEAR (SEE: FACE OF TERROR) (1964, Sp.)
FACE OF FIRE (1959, US/Brit.) PR:A
FACE OF FU MANCHU, THE (1965, Brit.) PR:O
FACE OF MARBLE, THE (1946) PR:A
FACE OF TERROR (1964, Sp.) PR:C
FACE OF THE SCREAMING WEREWOLF (1959, Mex.) PR:A
FACE ON THE BARROOM FLOOR, THE (1932) PR:A
FACE THE MUSIC (SEE: BLACK GLOVE) (1954, Brit.)
FACE TO FACE (1952) PR:A
FACE TO FACE (1967, It.) PR:O
FACE TO FACE (1976, Swed.) PR:O
FACE TO THE WIND (SEE: COUNT YOUR BULLETS) (1972)
FACELESS MAN, THE (SEE: COUNTERFEIT KILLER, THE) (1968)
FACELESS MEN, THE (SEE: INCIDENT AT PHANTOM HILL) (1966)
FACELESS MONSTERS (SEE: NIGHTMARE CASTLE) (1966, It.)
FACES (1934, Brit.) PR:A
FACES (1968) PR:O
FACES IN THE DARK (1960, Brit.) PR:A
FACES IN THE FOG (1944) PR:A
FACING THE MUSIC (1933, Brit.) PR:A
FACING THE MUSIC (1941, Brit.) PR:A
FACTS OF LIFE, THE (SEE: QUARTET) (1949, Brit.)
FACTS OF LIFE, THE (1960) PR:A
FACTS OF LOVE (1945, Brit.) PR:A
FACTS OF MURDER, THE (1965, It.) PR:O
FADE TO BLACK (1980) PR:O
FAHRENHEIT 451 (1966, Brit.) PR:C
FAIL SAFE (1964) PR:C
FAILURE, THE (1986, Neth.) PR:O
FAIR EXCHANGE (1936, Brit.) PR:A
FAIR GAME (1985) PR:O
FAIR GAME (1986, Aus.) PR:O
FAIR WARNING (1931) PR:A
FAIR WARNING (1937) PR:A
FAIR WIND TO JAVA (1953) PR:A
FAITHFUL (1936, Brit.) PR:A
FAITHFUL CITY (1952, Israel) PR:A
FAITHFUL HEARTS (1933, Brit.) PR:A
FAITHFUL IN MY FASHION (1946) PR:A

FAITHLESS (1932) PR:A
FAKE, THE (1953, Brit.) PR:A
FAKERS, THE (SEE: HELL'S BLOODY DEVILS) (1970)
FAKE'S PROGRESS (1950, Brit.) PR:A
FALCON AND THE CO-EDS, THE (1943) PR:A
FALCON AND THE SNOWMAN, THE (1985) PR:O
FALCON FIGHTERS, THE (1970, Jap.) PR:C
FALCON IN DANGER, THE (1943) PR:A
FALCON IN HOLLYWOOD, THE (1944) PR:A
FALCON IN MEXICO, THE (1944) PR:A
FALCON IN SAN FRANCISCO, THE (1945) PR:A
FALCON OUT WEST, THE (1944) PR:A
FALCON STRIKES BACK, THE (1943) PR:A
FALCON TAKES OVER, THE (1942) PR:A
FALCON'S ADVENTURE, THE (1946) PR:A
FALCON'S ALIBI, THE (1946) PR:A
FALCON'S BROTHER, THE (1942) PR:A
FALL GIRL, THE (SEE: LISETTE) (1963)
FALL GUY, THE (1930) PR:A
FALL GUY (1947) PR:C
FALL GUY, THE (SEE: FALLGUY) (1962)
FALL GUY (1982, Jap.) PR:C
FALL OF EVE, THE (1929) PR:A
FALL OF LOLA MONTES, THE (SEE: LOLA MONTES) (1955, Fr./W. Ger.)
FALL OF ROME, THE (1963, It.) PR:C
FALL OF THE HOUSE OF USHER, THE (1952, Brit.) PR:C
FALL OF THE HOUSE OF USHER, THE (SEE: HOUSE OF USHER) (1960)
FALL OF THE HOUSE OF USHER, THE (1980) PR:O
FALL OF THE ROMAN EMPIRE, THE (1964) PR:O
FALLEN ANGEL (1945) PR:A
FALLEN IDOL, THE (1949, Brit.) PR:A
FALLEN SPARROW, THE (1943) PR:C
FALLGUY (1962) PR:A
FALLING, THE (SEE: ALIEN PREDATOR) (1987)
FALLING FOR YOU (1933, Brit.) PR:A
FALLING IN LOVE (SEE: TROUBLE AHEAD) (1936, Brit.)
FALLING IN LOVE (1984) PR:C
FALLING IN LOVE AGAIN (1980) PR:C
FALSCHE BEWEGUNG (SEE: WRONG MOVE) (1975, W. Ger.)
FALSE COLORS (1943) PR:A
FALSE EVIDENCE (1937, Brit.) PR:A-C
FALSE FACE (SEE: SCALPEL) (1976)
FALSE FACES (1932) PR:A
FALSE FACES (SEE: LET 'EM HAVE IT) (1935)
FALSE FACES (1943) PR:A
FALSE MADONNA, THE (1932) PR:A
FALSE PARADISE (1948) PR:A
FALSE PRETENSES (1935) PR:A
FALSE RAPTURE (1941) PR:A
FALSE WITNESS (SEE: ZIGZAG) (1970)
FALSE WITNESS (SEE: CIRCLE OF DECEIT) (1982, Fr./W. Ger.)
FALSTAFF (SEE: CHIMES AT MIDNIGHT) (1967, Sp./Switz.)
FAME (1936, Brit.) PR:A
FAME (1980) PR:C
FAME IS THE SPUR (1947, Brit.) PR:A
FAME STREET (1932) PR:A
FAMILY, THE (1970, Fr./It.) PR:O
FAMILY, THE (1987, It./Fr.) PR:A
FAMILY AFFAIR, A (1937) PR:AA
FAMILY AFFAIR (1954, Brit.) PR:A
FAMILY BUSINESS (1987, Fr.) PR:C
FAMILY BUSINESS (1989) PR:C
FAMILY DIARY (1963, It.) PR:A
FAMILY DOCTOR (SEE: RX MURDER) (1958, Brit.)
FAMILY ENFORCER (SEE: DEATH COLLECTOR) (1976)
FAMILY GAME, THE (1984, Jap.) PR:C
FAMILY HONEYMOON (1948) PR:A
FAMILY HONOR (1973) PR:O
FAMILY JEWELS, THE (1965) PR:A
FAMILY LIFE (1971, Brit.) PR:O
FAMILY NEXT DOOR, THE (1939) PR:A
FAMILY PLOT (1976) PR:C
FAMILY SECRET, THE (1951) PR:A
FAMILY WAY, THE (1966, Brit.) PR:O
FAMOUS FERGUSON CASE, THE (1932) PR:A
FAN, THE (1949) PR:A
FAN, THE (1981) PR:C-O
FANATIC (SEE: DIE! DIE! MY DARLING) (1965, Brit.)
FANATIC, THE (SEE: LAST HORROR FILM, THE) (1984)
FANCY BAGGAGE (1929) PR:A
FANCY PANTS (1950) PR:A
FANDANGO (1970) PR:O
FANDANGO (1985) PR:C
FANFAN THE TULIP (1952, Fr.) PR:A
FANGELSE (SEE: DEVIL'S WANTON, THE) (1959, Swed.)
FANGS OF THE ARCTIC (1953) PR:A
FANGS OF THE WILD (1954) PR:A
FANNY (1932, Fr.) PR:A-C

FANNY (1961) PR:A-C
FANNY AND ALEXANDER (1982, Swed./Fr./W. Ger.) PR:C-O
FANNY BY GASLIGHT (SEE: MAN OF EVIL) (1944, Brit.)
FANNY FOLEY HERSELF (1931) PR:A
FANNY HILL: MEMOIRS OF A WOMAN OF PLEASURE (1965, US/W. Ger.) PR:C
FAN'S NOTES, A (1972, Can.) PR:C
FANTASIA (1940) PR:AA
FANTASIES (1981) PR:O
FANTASM (1976, Aus.) PR:O
FANTASTIC COMEDY, A (1975, Rum.) PR:C
FANTASTIC INVASION OF THE PLANET EARTH, THE (SEE: BUBBLE, THE) (1967)
FANTASTIC INVENTION, THE (SEE: FABULOUS WORLD OF JULES VERNE, THE) (1958, Czech.)
FANTASTIC PLANET (1973, Fr./Czech.) PR:A
FANTASTIC THREE, THE (1967, Fr./It./W. Ger./Yugo.) PR:A
FANTASTIC VOYAGE (1966) PR:A
FANTASTICA (1980, Can./Fr.) PR:C-O
FANTASY MAN (1984, Aus.) PR:C
FANTOMAS (1966, Fr./It.) PR:AA
FANTOMAS STRIKES BACK (1965, Fr./It.) PR:A
FAR COUNTRY, THE (1955) PR:A
FAR FROM DALLAS (1972, Fr.) PR:C
FAR FROM HOME (1989) PR:O
FAR FROM POLAND (1984) PR:O
FAR FROM THE MADDING CROWD (1967, Brit.) PR:A
FAR FRONTIER, THE (1949) PR:A
FAR HORIZONS, THE (1955) PR:A
FAR NORTH (1988) PR:C
FAR SHORE, THE (1976, Can.) PR:O
FARARUV KONEC (SEE: END OF A PRIEST) (1970, Czech.)
FAREWELL AGAIN (SEE: TROOPSHIP) (1938, Brit.)
FAREWELL, DOVES (1962, USSR) PR:A
FAREWELL, FRIEND (1968, Fr./It.) PR:O
FAREWELL, MY BELOVED (1969, Jap.) PR:O
FAREWELL, MY LOVELY (SEE: MURDER, MY SWEET) (1945)
FAREWELL, MY LOVELY (1975) PR:C-O
FAREWELL PERFORMANCE (1963, Brit.) PR:A-C
FAREWELL TO ARMS, A (1932) PR:A
FAREWELL TO ARMS, A (1957) PR:C
FAREWELL TO CINDERELLA (1937, Brit.) PR:A
FAREWELL TO LOVE (1931, Brit.) PR:A
FAREWELL TO THE KING (1989) PR:C
FARGO (1952) PR:A
FARGO (SEE: WILD SEED) (1964)
FARGO EXPRESS (1933) PR:A
FARGO KID, THE (1941) PR:A
FARM, THE (SEE: CURSE, THE) (1987)
FARM GIRL (SEE: FARMER'S OTHER DAUGHTER, THE) (1965)
FARM OF THE YEAR (SEE: MILES FROM HOME) (1988)
FARMER, THE (1977) PR:O
FARMER IN THE DELL, THE (1936) PR:A
FARMER TAKES A WIFE, THE (1935) PR:A
FARMER TAKES A WIFE, THE (1953) PR:C
FARMER'S DAUGHTER, THE (1940) PR:A
FARMER'S DAUGHTER, THE (1947) PR:AA
FARMER'S OTHER DAUGHTER, THE (1965) PR:A
FARMER'S WIFE, THE (1941, Brit.) PR:A
FASCINATION (1931, Brit.) PR:A
FASCIST, THE (1965, It.) PR:A
FASHION HOUSE OF DEATH (SEE: BLOOD AND BLACK LACE) (1965, Fr./It./W. Ger.)
FASHION MODEL (1945) PR:A
FASHIONS (SEE: FASHIONS OF 1934) (1934)
FASHIONS IN LOVE (1929) PR:A-C
FASHIONS OF 1934 (1934) PR:A
FAST AND FURIOUS (1939) PR:A
FAST AND LOOSE (1930) PR:A
FAST AND LOOSE (1939) PR:A
FAST AND LOOSE (1954, Brit.) PR:A
FAST AND SEXY (1960, Fr./It.) PR:A
FAST AND THE FURIOUS, THE (1954) PR:A
FAST BREAK (1979) PR:A
FAST BULLETS (1936) PR:A
FAST CHARLIE. . . THE MOONBEAM RIDER (1979) PR:C
FAST COMPANIONS (1932) PR:A
FAST COMPANY (1929) PR:A
FAST COMPANY (1938) PR:A
FAST COMPANY (1953) PR:A
FAST FOOD (1989) PR:C
FAST FORWARD (1985) PR:A-C
FAST LADY, THE (1963, Brit.) PR:A
FAST LIFE (1929) PR:A
FAST LIFE (1932) PR:A
FAST ON THE DRAW (1950) PR:A
FAST TIMES AT RIDGEMONT HIGH (1982) PR:O
FAST-WALKING (1982) PR:O
FAST WORKERS (1933) PR:A
FASTEST GUITAR ALIVE, THE (1967)

FASTEST GUN, THE (SEE: QUICK GUN, THE) (1964)
FASTEST GUN ALIVE (1956) PR:A
FAT ANGELS (1980, US/Sp.) PR:C
FAT CHANCE (SEE: PEEPER) (1975)
FAT CITY (1972) PR:C
FAT GUY GOES NUTZOID!! (1986) PR:O
FAT MAN, THE (1951) PR:A
FAT MAN AND LITTLE BOY (1989) PR:C
FAT SPY, THE (1966) PR:A
FATAL ATTRACTION (1987) PR:O
FATAL BEAUTY (1987) PR:O
FATAL DESIRE (1953, It.) PR:C
FATAL HOUR, THE (1937, Brit.) PR:A
FATAL HOUR, THE (1940) PR:A
FATAL LADY (1936) PR:A
FATAL NIGHT, THE (1948, Brit.) PR:A
FATAL WITNESS, THE (1945) PR:A
FATE IS THE HUNTER (1964) PR:A
FATE TAKES A HAND (1962, Brit.) PR:A
FATHER (1966, Hung.) PR:A
FATHER AND SON (1929) PR:A
FATHER BROWN (SEE: DETECTIVE, THE) (1954, Brit.)
FATHER BROWN, DETECTIVE (1935) PR:A
FATHER CAME TOO (1964, Brit.) PR:A
FATHER GOOSE (1964) PR:AA
FATHER IS A BACHELOR (1950) PR:A
FATHER IS A PRINCE (1940) PR:A
FATHER MAKES GOOD (1950) PR:A
FATHER OF A SOLDIER (1966, USSR) PR:C
FATHER OF THE BRIDE (1950) PR:A
FATHER O'FLYNN (1938, Ireland) PR:A
FATHER STEPS OUT (1937, Brit.) PR:A
FATHER TAKES A WIFE (1941) PR:A
FATHER TAKES THE AIR (1951) PR:A
FATHER WAS A FULLBACK (1949) PR:A
FATHERS AND SONS (1960, USSR) PR:A
FATHER'S DAY (SEE: SINS OF THE CHILDREN) (1930)
FATHER'S DILEMMA (1952, It.) PR:A
FATHER'S DOING FINE (1952, Brit.) PR:A
FATHER'S LITTLE DIVIDEND (1951) PR:AA
FATHER'S ON A BUSINESS TRIP (SEE: WHEN FATHER WAS AWAY ON BUSINES) (1985, Yugo.)
FATHER'S SON (1931) PR:A
FATHER'S SON (1941) PR:A
FATHER'S WILD GAME (1950) PR:A
FATHOM (1967, Brit.) PR:A
FATSO (1980) PR:A
FATTI DI GENTE PERBENE (SEE: DRAMA OF THE RICH) (1975, Fr./It.)
FATTY FINN (1980, Aus.) PR:A-C
FAUSSES INGENUES (SEE: RED LIPS) (1964, Fr./It.)
FAUST (1963, W. Ger.) PR:A
FAUST (1964) PR:A
FAVORITES OF THE MOON (1985, Fr./It.) PR:C
FBI CODE 98 (1964) PR:A
FBI CONTRO DR. MABUSE (SEE: RETURN OF DR. MABUSE, THE) (1961, Fr./It./W. Ger.)
FBI GIRL (1951) PR:A
FBI STORY, THE (1959) PR:C
FEAR (1946) PR:C
FEAR (1954, It./W. Ger.) PR:A
FEAR, THE (1967, Gr.) PR:O
FEAR (1989) PR:O
FEAR AND DESIRE (1953) PR:C
FEAR, ANXIETY AND DEPRESSION (1989) PR:C
FEAR CHAMBER, THE (1968, US/Mex.) PR:C
FEAR CITY (1984) PR:O
FEAR EATS THE SOUL (1974, W. Ger.) PR:O
FEAR IN THE CITY OF THE LIVING DEAD (SEE: GATES OF HELL, THE) (1983, US/It.)
FEAR IN THE NIGHT (1947) PR:C-O
FEAR IN THE NIGHT (1972, Brit.) PR:C
FEAR IS THE KEY (1973, Brit.) PR:C
FEAR NO EVIL (1981) PR:O
FEAR NO MORE (1961) PR:C
FEAR SHIP, THE (1933, Brit.) PR:A
FEAR STRIKES OUT (1957) PR:C
FEARLESS FAGAN (1952) PR:AA
FEARLESS FRANK (1967) PR:A-C
FEARLESS VAMPIRE KILLERS, OR PARDON ME BUT YOUR TEETH ARE IN MY NECK, THE (1967, US/Brit.) PR:C
FEARMAKERS, THE (1958) PR:A
FEAST OF FLESH (SEE: NIGHT OF THE LIVING DEAD) (1968)
FEAST OF FLESH (SEE: BLOOD FEAST) (1976, It.)
FEATHER, THE (1929, Brit.) PR:A
FEATHER IN HER HAT, A (1935) PR:A
FEATHER YOUR NEST (1937, Brit.) PR:A
FEATHERED SERPENT, THE (1934, Brit.) PR:A
FEATHERED SERPENT, THE (1948) PR:A
FEDERAL AGENT (1936) PR:A
FEDERAL AGENT AT LARGE (1950) PR:A
FEDERAL BULLETS (1937) PR:A
FEDERAL FUGITIVES (1941) PR:A
FEDERAL MAN (1950) PR:A
FEDERAL MAN-HUNT (1939) PR:A
FEDERICO FELLINI'S 8 1/2 (SEE: 8 1/2) (1963, It.)

FEDERICO FELLINI'S INTERVISTA (SEE: INTERVISTA) (1987, It.)
FEDORA (1946, It.) PR:A
FEDORA (1978, Fr./W. Ger.) PR:C
FEDS (1988) PR:NR
FEEDBACK (1979) PR:C
FEEL THE HEAT (SEE: CATCH THE HEAT) (1987)
FEELIN' GOOD (1966) PR:A
FEET FIRST (1930) PR:A
FEET OF CLAY (1960, Brit.) PR:A
FELDMANN CASE, THE (1987, Norway) PR:O
FELLINI SATYRICON (1969, Fr./It.) PR:C-O
FELLINI'S CASANOVA (SEE: CASANOVA) (1976, It.)
FELLINI'S ROMA (SEE: ROMA) (1972, It.)
FEMALE (1933) PR:A
FEMALE, THE (1960, Fr.) PR:C
FEMALE (SEE: VIOLENT YEARS, THE) (1956)
FEMALE AND THE FLESH, THE (SEE: LIGHT ACROSS THE STREET, THE) (1957, Fr.)
FEMALE ANIMAL, THE (1958) PR:A
FEMALE BUNCH, THE (1969) PR:O
FEMALE BUTCHER, THE (1972, It./Sp.) PR:O
FEMALE FIENDS (1958, Brit.) PR:A
FEMALE FUGITIVE (1938) PR:A
FEMALE JUNGLE, THE (1955) PR:C
FEMALE ON THE BEACH (1955) PR:A-C
FEMALE PRINCE, THE (1966, Hong Kong) PR:C
FEMALE PRISONER, THE (SEE: LA PRISONNIERE) (1968, Fr.)
FEMALE RESPONSE, THE (1972) PR:O
FEMALE TRAP, THE (SEE: NAME OF THE GAME IS KILL, THE) (1968)
FEMALE TROUBLE (1975) PR:O
FEMININE TOUCH, THE (1941, Brit.) PR:A
FEMININE TOUCH, THE (SEE: GENTLE TOUCH, THE) (1956, Brit.)
FEMMES DE PARIS (SEE: PEEK-A-BOO) (1954, Fr.)
FEMMES DE PERSONNE (1984, Fr.) PR:O
FEMMES D'UN ETE (SEE: LOVE ON THE RIVIERA) (1964, Fr./It.)
FEMMINA (1968, Fr./It./W. Ger.) PR:C
FEMMINE DI LUSSO (SEE: LOVE, THE ITALIAN WAY) (1964, It.)
FENCE RIDERS (1950) PR:A
FERNANDEL THE DRESSMAKER (1957, Fr.) PR:A
FEROCIOUS FEMALE FREEDOM FIGHTERS (1989, Indonesia) PR:O
FEROCIOUS PAL (1934) PR:AA
FERRIS BUELLER'S DAY OFF (1986) PR:C
FERRY ACROSS THE MERSEY (1964, Brit.) PR:A
FERRY TO HONG KONG (1959, Brit.) PR:A
FEUD MAKER, THE (1938) PR:A
FEUD OF THE RANGE (1939) PR:A
FEUD OF THE TRAIL (1938) PR:A
FEUD OF THE WEST (1936) PR:A
FEUDIN' FOOLS (1952) PR:A
FEUDIN', FUSSIN' AND A-FIGHTIN' (1948) PR:A
FEVER HEAT (1968) PR:A
FEVER IN THE BLOOD, A (1961) PR:A
FEVER PITCH (1985) PR:C-O
FEW BULLETS MORE, A (1968, It./Sp.) PR:A
FEW DAYS WITH ME, A (1989, Fr.) PR:C
FFOLKES (1979, Brit.) PR:C
FIANCES, THE (1964, It.) PR:A
FIASCO IN MILAN (1963, Fr./It.) PR:A
FICKLE FINGER OF FATE, THE (1967, US/Sp.) PR:A
FIDDLER ON THE ROOF (1971) PR:AA
FIDDLERS THREE (1944, Brit.) PR:A
FIDDLIN' BUCKAROO, THE (1934) PR:A
FIDELIO (1961, Aust.) PR:A
FIDELIO (1970, W. Ger.) PR:A
FIELD OF DREAMS (1989) PR:A
FIELDER'S FIELD (SEE: GIRLS CAN PLAY) (1937)
FIELDS OF HONOR (SEE: SHENANDOAH) (1965)
FIEND (1980) PR:O
FIEND OF DOPE ISLAND (1961) PR:C
FIEND WHO WALKED THE WEST, THE (1958) PR:O
FIEND WITH THE ELECTRIC BRAIN, THE (SEE: PSYCHO A GO-GO!) (1965)
FIEND WITHOUT A FACE (1958, Brit.) PR:C-O
FIENDISH GHOULS, THE (SEE: MANIA) (1960, Brit.)
FIENDISH PLOT OF DR. FU MANCHU, THE (1980) PR:C
FIENDS, THE (SEE: DIABOLIQUE) (1955, Fr.)
FIERCEST HEART, THE (1961) PR:A
FIERY SPUR (SEE: HOT SPUR) (1968)
FIESTA (1947) PR:A
15 FROM ROM (SEE: OPIATE '67) (1967, Fr./It.)
15 MAIDEN LANE (1936) PR:A
FIFTEEN WIVES (1934) PR:A
FIFTH AVENUE GIRL (1939) PR:A
FIFTH CHAIR, THE (SEE: IT'S IN THE BAG) (1945)
FIFTH FLOOR, THE (1980) PR:O
FIFTH HORSEMAN IS FEAR, THE (1968, Czech.) PR:C
FIFTH MUSKETEER, THE (SEE: BEHIND THE IRON MASK) (1977, Aust.)
FIFTY FATHOMS DEEP (1931) PR:A
55 DAYS AT PEKING (1963) PR:A
FIFTY MILLION FRENCHMEN (1931) PR:AA

FIFTY ROADS TO TOWN (1937) PR:A
52ND STREET (1937) PR:A
FIFTY-SHILLING BOXER (1937, Brit.) PR:A
50,000 B.C. (BEFORE CLOTHING) (1963) PR:O
52 MILES TO MIDNIGHT (SEE: HOT RODS TO HELL) (1967)
52 MILES TO TERROR (SEE: HOT RODS TO HELL) (1967)
52 PICK-UP (1986) PR:O
FIGHT FOR ROME (1969, Rum./W. Ger.) PR:A
FIGHT FOR THE GLORY (1970, Jap.) PR:C
FIGHT FOR YOUR LADY (1937) PR:A
FIGHT FOR YOUR LIFE (1977) PR:O
FIGHT TO THE FINISH, A (1937) PR:A
FIGHT TO THE LAST (1938, Chi.) PR:C
FIGHTER, THE (1952) PR:A
FIGHTER ATTACK (1953) PR:A
FIGHTER SQUADRON (1948) PR:A
FIGHTING BACK (1948) PR:A
FIGHTING BACK (SEE: DEATH VENGEANCE) (1982)
FIGHTING BACK (1983, Brit.) PR:C
FIGHTING BILL CARSON (1945) PR:A
FIGHTING BILL FARGO (1942) PR:A
FIGHTING BUCKAROO, THE (1943) PR:A
FIGHTING CABALLERO (1935) PR:A
FIGHTING CARAVANS (1931) PR:A
FIGHTING CHAMP (1933) PR:A
FIGHTING CHANCE, THE (1955) PR:A
FIGHTING COAST GUARD (1951) PR:A
FIGHTING CODE, THE (1934) PR:A
FIGHTING COMMAND (SEE: WE'VE NEVER BEEN LICKED) (1943)
FIGHTING COWBOY (1933) PR:A
FIGHTING DEPUTY, THE (1937) PR:A
FIGHTING FATHER DUNNE (1948) PR:A
FIGHTING FOOL, THE (1932) PR:A
FIGHTING FOOLS (1949) PR:A
FIGHTING FRONTIER (1943) PR:AA
FIGHTING GENTLEMAN, THE (1932) PR:A
FIGHTING GRINGO, THE (1939) PR:A
FIGHTING GUARDSMAN, THE (1945) PR:A
FIGHTING HERO (1934) PR:A
FIGHTING KENTUCKIAN, THE (1949) PR:A
FIGHTING LAWMAN, THE (1953) PR:A
FIGHTING LEGION, THE (1930) PR:A
FIGHTING MAD (1939) PR:A
FIGHTING MAD (1948) PR:A
FIGHTING MAD (1957, Brit.) PR:A-C
FIGHTING MAD (1976) PR:C
FIGHTING MAN OF THE PLAINS (1949) PR:A
FIGHTING MARSHAL, THE (1932) PR:AA
FIGHTING O'FLYNN, THE (1949) PR:A
FIGHTING PARSON, THE (1933) PR:A
FIGHTING PHANTOM, THE (SEE: MYSTERIOUS RIDER, THE) (1933)
FIGHTING PIMPERNEL, THE (1950, Brit.) PR:A
FIGHTING PIONEERS (1935) PR:A
FIGHTING PLAYBOY (1937) PR:A
FIGHTING PRINCE OF DONEGAL, THE (1966, Brit.) PR:AA
FIGHTING RANGER, THE (1934) PR:A
FIGHTING RANGER, THE (1948) PR:A
FIGHTING REDHEAD, THE (1950) PR:A
FIGHTING RENEGADE (1939) PR:AA
FIGHTING ROOKIE, THE (1934) PR:A
FIGHTING SEABEES, THE (1944) PR:A
FIGHTING SEVENTH, THE (SEE: LITTLE BIG HORN) (1951)
FIGHTING SHADOWS (1935) PR:A
FIGHTING SHERIFF, THE (1931) PR:A
FIGHTING 69TH, THE (1940) PR:A
FIGHTING STALLION, THE (1950) PR:A
FIGHTING STOCK (1935, Brit.) PR:A
FIGHTING SULLIVANS, THE (SEE: SULLIVANS, THE) (1944)
FIGHTING TEXAN (1937) PR:A
FIGHTING TEXANS, THE (1933) PR:A
FIGHTING THOROUGHBREDS (1939) PR:A
FIGHTING THRU (1931) PR:A
FIGHTING TROOPER, THE (1935) PR:A
FIGHTING TROUBLE (1956) PR:A
FIGHTING VALLEY (1943) PR:A
FIGHTING VIGILANTES, THE (1947) PR:A
FIGHTING WESTERNER, THE (SEE: ROCKY MOUN-TAIN MYSTERY) (1935)
FIGHTING WILDCATS, THE (1957, Brit.) PR:A-C
FIGHTING YOUTH (1935) PR:A
FIGURES IN A LANDSCAPE (1970, Brit.) PR:C
FILE OF THE GOLDEN GOOSE, THE (1969, Brit.) PR:C
FILE ON THELMA JORDON, THE (1950) PR:A-C
FILE 113 (1932) PR:A
FILES FROM SCOTLAND YARD (1951, Brit.) PR:A
FILM D'AMORE E D'ANARCHIA (SEE: LOVE AND ANARCHY) (1973, It.)
FILM WITHOUT A NAME (1950, W. Ger.) PR:A
FINAL APPOINTMENT (1954, Brit.) PR:A
FINAL ASSIGNMENT (1980, Can.) PR:C
FINAL CHAPTER—WALKING TALL (1977) PR:O

FINAL CHORD, THE (1936, Ger.) PR:C
FINAL COLUMN, THE (1955, Brit.) PR:A
FINAL COMEDOWN, THE (1972) PR:O
FINAL CONFLICT, THE (1981) PR:O
FINAL COUNTDOWN, THE (1980) PR:C
FINAL CRASH, THE (SEE: STEELYARD BLUES) (1973)
FINAL CUT, THE (1980, Aus.) PR:O
FINAL EDITION (1932) PR:A
FINAL EXAM (1981) PR:O
FINAL EXECUTIONER, THE (1986, It.) PR:O
FINAL HOUR, THE (1936) PR:A
FINAL JUSTICE (1985) PR:O
FINAL OPTION, THE (1982, Brit.) PR:O
FINAL PROGRAMME, THE (SEE: LAST DAYS OF MAN ON EARTH, THE) (1973, Brit.)
FINAL RECKONING, THE (1932, Brit.) PR:A
FINAL TAKE: THE GOLDEN AGE OF MOVIES (1986, Jap.) PR:A
FINAL TERROR, THE (1983) PR:O
FINAL TEST, THE (1953, Brit.) PR:A
FINAL WAR, THE (1960, Jap.) PR:C
FINALLY SUNDAY (SEE: CONFIDENTIALLY YOURS!) (1983, Fr.)
FINCHE DURA LA TEMPESTA (SEE: TORPEDO BAY) (1963, Fr.)
FIND THE BLACKMAILER (1943) PR:A
FIND THE LADY (1936, Brit.) PR:A
FIND THE LADY (1956, Brit.) PR:A
FIND THE WITNESS (1937) PR:A
FINDERS KEEPERS (1928) PR:AA
FINDERS KEEPERS (1966, Brit.) PR:A
FINDERS KEEPERS (1984) PR:C-O
FINDERS KEEPERS, LOVERS WEEPERS (1968) PR:O
FINE AND DANDY (SEE: WEST POINT STORY, THE) (1950)
FINE FEATHERS (1937, Brit.) PR:A
FINE MADNESS, A (1966) PR:C
FINE MESS, A (1986) PR:A-C
FINE PAIR, A (1969, It.) PR:C
FINGER MAN (1955) PR:A
FINGER OF GUILT (1956, Brit.) PR:A
FINGER ON THE TRIGGER (1965, US/Sp.) PR:A
FINGER POINTS, THE (1931) PR:C
FINGERMAN, THE (1963, Fr.) PR:C
FINGERPRINTS DON'T LIE (1951) PR:A
FINGERS (1940, Brit.) PR:A
FINGERS (1978) PR:O
FINGERS AT THE WINDOW (1942) PR:C
FINIAN'S RAINBOW (1968) PR:A
FINISHING SCHOOL (1934) PR:A
FINN AND HATTIE (1931) PR:A
FINNEGANS WAKE (1965) PR:A
FINNEY (1969) PR:A
FINO A FARTI MALE (1969, Fr./It.) PR:O
FIRE AND ICE (1983) PR:C
FIRE AND ICE (1987) PR:A
FIRE DOWN BELOW (1957, US/Brit.) PR:C
FIRE FESTIVAL (SEE: HIMATSURI) (1985, Jap.)
FIRE HAS BEEN ARRANGED, A (1935, Brit.) PR:A
FIRE IN THE FLESH (1964, Fr.) PR:A
FIRE IN THE NIGHT (1986) PR:O
FIRE IN THE STONE, THE (1983, Aus.) PR:AA
FIRE IN THE STRAW (1943, Fr.) PR:A
FIRE MAIDENS FROM OUTER SPACE (1956, Brit.) PR:A
FIRE OVER AFRICA (1954, Brit.) PR:A
FIRE OVER ENGLAND (1937, Brit.) PR:A
FIRE RAISERS, THE (1933, Brit.) PR:A
FIRE SALE (1977) PR:A-C
FIRE WITH FIRE (1986) PR:O
FIRE WITHIN, THE (1964, Fr./It.) PR:O
FIREBALL, THE (1950) PR:A
FIREBALL 500 (1966) PR:A
FIREBALL JUNGLE (1968) PR:C
FIREBIRD, THE (1934) PR:A
FIREBIRD 2015 AD (1981) PR:O
FIREBRAND, THE (1962) PR:C
FIREBRAND JORDAN (1930) PR:A
FIREBRANDS OF ARIZONA (1944) PR:A
FIRECHASERS, THE (1970, Brit.) PR:C
FIRECRACKER (1981, Phil.) PR:O
FIRECREEK (1968) PR:C
FIRED WIFE (1943) PR:A
FIREFLY, THE (1937) PR:A
FIREFOX (1982) PR:C
FIREHOUSE (1987) PR:O
FIREMAN, SAVE MY CHILD (1932) PR:A
FIREMAN SAVE MY CHILD (1954) PR:A
FIREMAN'S BALL, THE (1967, Czech.) PR:C
FIREPOWER (1979, Brit.) PR:O
FIRES OF FATE (1932, Brit.) PR:A
FIRES OF YOUTH (SEE: UP FOR MURDER) (1931)
FIRES ON THE PLAIN (1959, Jap.) PR:O
FIRESTARTER (1984) PR:O
FIRE TRAP, THE (1935) PR:A
FIREWALKER (1986) PR:A
FIRM MAN, THE (1975, Aus.) PR:C
FIRST A GIRL (1935, Brit.) PR:A

FIRST AID (1931) PR:A
FIRST AND THE LAST, THE (SEE: TWENTY-ONE DAYS TOGETHER) (1940, Brit.)
FIRST BABY, THE (1936) PR:A
FIRST BLOOD (1982) PR:O
FIRST COMES COURAGE (1943) PR:A
FIRST DEADLY SIN, THE (1980) PR:O
FIRST FAMILY (1980) PR:O
FIRST GENTLEMAN, THE (SEE: AFFAIRS OF A ROGUE, THE) (1949, Brit.)
FIRST GREAT TRAIN ROBBERY, THE (SEE: GREAT TRAIN ROBBERY) (1978, Brit.)
FIRST HELLO, THE (SEE: HIGH COUNTRY, THE) (1981, Can.)
FIRST HUNDRED YEARS, THE (1938) PR:A
FIRST LADY (1937) PR:A
FIRST LEGION, THE (1951) PR:A
FIRST LOVE (1939) PR:A
FIRST LOVE (1970, Switz./W. Ger.) PR:C-O
FIRST LOVE (1977) PR:O
FIRST MAN INTO SPACE (1959, Brit.) PR:A
FIRST MARINES (SEE: TRIPOLI) (1950)
FIRST MEN IN THE MOON (1964, Brit.) PR:A
FIRST MONDAY IN OCTOBER (1981) PR:O
FIRST MRS. FRASER, THE (1932, Brit.) PR:A
FIRST NAME: CARMEN (1984, Fr.) PR:O
FIRST NIGHT (1937, Brit.) PR:A
FIRST NUDIE MUSICAL, THE (1976) PR:O
FIRST OF THE FEW, THE (SEE: SPITFIRE) (1942, Brit.)
FIRST OFFENCE (1936, Brit.) PR:A
FIRST OFFENDERS (1939) PR:A
FIRST REBEL, THE (SEE: ALLEGHENY UPRISING) (1939)
FIRST SPACESHIP ON VENUS (1960, E. Ger./Pol.) PR:A
FIRST START (1953, Pol.) PR:A
FIRST TASTE OF LOVE (1962, Fr.) PR:C
FIRST TEXAN, THE (1956) PR:A
FIRST TIME, THE (1952) PR:A
FIRST TIME, THE (1969) PR:C
FIRST TIME, THE (1978, Fr.) PR:O
FIRST TIME, THE (1983) PR:O
FIRST TO FIGHT (1967) PR:C
FIRST TRAVELING SALESLADY, THE (1956) PR:A
FIRST TURN-ON!, THE (1984) PR:O
FIRST WIFE (SEE: WIVES AND LOVERS) (1963)
FIRST YANK INTO TOKYO (1945) PR:C
FIRST YEAR, THE (1932) PR:A
FIRSTBORN (1984) PR:C
FISH CALLED WANDA, A (1988) PR:C-O
FISH HAWK (1981, Can.) PR:AA
FISH THAT SAVED PITTSBURGH, THE (1979) PR:AA
FISHERMAN'S WHARF (1939) PR:AA
FIST FIGHTER (1989) PR:O
FIST IN HIS POCKET (1968, It.) PR:O
FIST OF FEAR, TOUCH OF DEATH (1980) PR:O
FIST OF FURY (SEE: FISTS OF FURY) (1973, Chi.)
FISTFUL OF CHOPSTICKS, A (SEE: THEY CALL ME BRUCE) (1982)
FISTFUL OF DOLLARS, A (1964, It./Sp./W. Ger.) PR:C
FISTFUL OF DYNAMITE, A (SEE: DUCK, YOU SUCKER!) (1972, It.)
FISTS OF FURY (1973, Chi.) PR:O
FIT FOR A KING (1937) PR:A
FITZCARRALDO (1982, W. Ger.) PR:C
FITZWILLY (1967) PR:C
FIVE (1951) PR:C
FIVE AGAINST THE HOUSE (1955) PR:C
FIVE AND TEN (1931) PR:A
FIVE ANGLES ON MURDER (1950, Brit.) PR:A
FIVE ASHORE IN SINGAPORE (SEE: SINGAPORE, SINGAPORE) (1968)
FIVE BLOODY GRAVES (SEE: GUN RIDERS, THE) (1969)
FIVE BOLD WOMEN (1960) PR:A
FIVE BRANDED WOMEN (1960) PR:C
FIVE CAME BACK (1939) PR:A
FIVE CARD STUD (1968) PR:C
FIVE CORNERS (1988, US/Brit.) PR:O
FIVE DAY LOVER (SEE: TIME OUT FOR LOVE) (1963, Fr./It.)
FIVE DAYS (SEE: PAID TO KILL) (1954, Brit.)
FIVE DAYS FROM HOME (1978) PR:C
FIVE DAYS HOME (SEE: WELCOME HOME, SOLDIER BOYS) (1972)
FIVE DAYS ONE SUMMER (1982) PR:A
FIVE EASY PIECES (1970) PR:C-O
FIVE FINGER EXERCISE (1962) PR:A
FIVE FINGERS (1952) PR:A
FIVE FINGERS OF DEATH (1973, Hong Kong) PR:O
FIVE GATES TO HELL (1959) PR:O
FIVE GIANTS FROM TEXAS (1966, It./Sp.) PR:C
FIVE GOLDEN DRAGONS (1967, Brit.) PR:O
FIVE GOLDEN HOURS (1961, Brit.) PR:A
FIVE GRAVES TO CAIRO (1943) PR:A
FIVE GUNS TO TOMBSTONE (1961) PR:A
FIVE GUNS WEST (1955) PR:A
FIVE LITTLE PEPPERS AND HOW THEY GREW (1939) PR:AA

FIVE LITTLE PEPPERS AT HOME (1940) PR:AA
FIVE LITTLE PEPPERS IN TROUBLE (1940) PR:A
FIVE MAN ARMY, THE (1970, It.) PR:C
FIVE MILES TO MIDNIGHT (1963, US/Fr./It.) PR:O
FIVE MILLION YEARS TO EARTH (1968, Brit.) PR:A
FIVE MINUTES TO LIVE (1961) PR:C
5 MINUTES TO LOVE (SEE: ROTTEN APPLE, THE)
   (1963)
FIVE OF A KIND (1938) PR:AA
FIVE OF THE JAZZBAND (SEE: JAZZBAND FIVE)
   (1932)
FIVE ON THE BLACK HAND SIDE (1973) PR:A
FIVE PENNIES, THE (1959) PR:A
FIVE POUND MAN, THE (1937, Brit.) PR:C
5 SINNERS (1961, W. Ger.) PR:C-O
FIVE STAR FINAL (1931) PR:C
FIVE STEPS TO DANGER (1957) PR:A
FIVE THE HARD WAY (1969) PR:O
5,000 FINGERS OF DR. T., THE (1953) PR:AA
FIVE TO ONE (1963, Brit.) PR:C
FIVE WEEKS IN A BALLOON (1962) PR:A
FIVE WILD GIRLS (1966, Fr.) PR:O
FIX, THE (1985) PR:C-O
FIXATION (SEE: SHE MAN, THE) (1967)
FIXED BAYONETS (1951) PR:A
FIXER, THE (1968) PR:O
FIXER DUGAN (1939) PR:A
FLAG LIEUTENANT, THE (1932, Brit.) PR:A
FLAME, THE (1948) PR:A
FLAME (1975, Brit.) PR:C
FLAME AND THE ARROW, THE (1950) PR:A
FLAME AND THE FLESH (1954) PR:C
FLAME BARRIER, THE (1958) PR:C
FLAME IN THE HEATHER (1935, Brit.) PR:A
FLAME IN THE STREETS (1961, Brit.) PR:A
FLAME OF ARABY (1951) PR:A
FLAME OF CALCUTTA (1953) PR:A
FLAME OF LOVE, THE (1930, Brit.) PR:A
FLAME OF NEW ORLEANS, THE (1941) PR:A-C
FLAME OF SACRAMENTO (SEE: IN OLD SACRA-
   MENTO) (1946)
FLAME OF STAMBOUL (1951) PR:A
FLAME OF THE BARBARY COAST (1945) PR:A
FLAME OF THE ISLANDS (1955) PR:A
FLAME OF THE WEST (1945) PR:A
FLAME OF TORMENT (SEE: ENJO) (1958, Jap.)
FLAME OF YOUTH (1949) PR:A
FLAME OVER INDIA (1960, Brit.) PR:A
FLAME OVER VIETNAM (1967, Sp./W. Ger.) PR:A
FLAME WITHIN, THE (1935) PR:C
FLAMES (1932) PR:A
FLAMING BULLETS (1945) PR:A
FLAMING DESIRE (SEE: SMALL HOURS, THE) (1962)
FLAMING FEATHER (1951) PR:A
FLAMING FRONTIER (SEE: FLAME OF THE WEST)
   (1945)
FLAMING FRONTIER (1958, Can.) PR:A
FLAMING FRONTIER (1968, Fr./It./W. Ger./Yugo.) PR:A
FLAMING FURY (1949) PR:A
FLAMING GOLD (1934) PR:A
FLAMING GUNS (1933) PR:A
FLAMING LEAD (1939) PR:A
FLAMING SIGNAL (1933) PR:A
FLAMING STAR (1960) PR:C-O
FLAMING TEEN-AGE, THE (1956) PR:A
FLAMINGO AFFAIR, THE (1948, Brit.) PR:A
FLAMINGO KID, THE (1984) PR:C
FLAMINGO ROAD (1949) PR:C
FLANAGAN (1985) PR:O
FLANAGAN BOY, THE (SEE: BAD BLONDE) (1953,
   Brit.)
FLANNELFOOT (1953, Brit.) PR:A
FLAP (1970) PR:A
FLAREUP (1969) PR:O
FLASH AND THE FIRECAT (1976) PR:C
FLASH GORDON (1936) PR:AA
FLASH GORDON (1980, Brit.) PR:AA
FLASH OF GREEN, A (1984) PR:A-C
FLASH THE SHEEPDOG (1967, Brit.) PR:AA
FLASHDANCE (1983) PR:O
FLASHING GUNS (1947) PR:A
FLASHPOINT (1984) PR:O
FLAT TOP (1952) PR:A
FLAT TWO (1962, Brit.) PR:A-C
FLAVOR OF GREEN TEA OVER RICE, THE (SEE: TEA
   AND RICE) (1964, Jap.)
FLAW, THE (1933, Brit.) PR:A
FLAW, THE (1955, Brit.) PR:A
FLAXFIELD, THE (1985, Bel./Neth.) PR:O
FLAXY MARTIN (1949) PR:A
FLEA IN HER EAR, A (1968, US/Fr.) PR:C
FLEDGLINGS (1965, Brit.) PR:O
FLEET'S IN, THE (1942) PR:AA
FLEMISH FARM, THE (1943, Brit.) PR:A
FLESH (1932) PR:C
FLESH AND BLOOD (1951, Brit.) PR:C
FLESH AND BLOOD (1985) PR:O
FLESH AND BLOOD SHOW, THE (1974, Brit.) PR:O

FLESH AND FANTASY (1943) PR:A-C
FLESH AND FLAME (SEE: NIGHT OF THE QUARTER
   MOON) (1959)
FLESH AND FURY (1952) PR:A
FLESH AND THE FIENDS, THE (SEE: MANIA) (1959,
   Brit.)
FLESH AND THE SPUR (1957) PR:C
FLESH AND THE WOMAN (1954, Fr./It.) PR:O
FLESH EATERS, THE (1964) PR:O
FLESH FEAST (1970) PR:O
FLESH FOR FRANKENSTEIN (SEE: ANDY WARHOL'S
   FRANKENSTEIN) (1974, Fr./It.)
FLESH IS WEAK, THE (1957, Brit.) PR:O
FLESH MERCHANT, THE (1956) PR:O
FLESHBURN (1984) PR:O
FLETCH (1984) PR:C
FLETCH LIVES (1989) PR:C
FLICK (SEE: DR. FRANKENSTEIN ON CAMPUS)
   (1970. Can.)
FLICKORNA (SEE: GIRLS, THE) (1972, Swed.)
FLICKS (1987) PR:O
FLIGHT (1929) PR:A
FLIGHT (1960) PR:C
FLIGHT ANGELS (1940) PR:A
FLIGHT AT MIDNIGHT (1939) PR:A
FLIGHT COMMAND (1940) PR:A
FLIGHT FOR FREEDOM (1943) PR:A
FLIGHT FROM ASHIYA (1964, US/Jap.) PR:A
FLIGHT FROM DESTINY (1941) PR:A
FLIGHT FROM FOLLY (1945, Brit.) PR:A
FLIGHT FROM GLORY (1937) PR:A
FLIGHT FROM SINGAPORE (1962, Brit.) PR:A
FLIGHT FROM TERROR (SEE: SATAN NEVER
   SLEEPS) (1962)
FLIGHT FROM VIENNA (1956, Brit.) PR:A
FLIGHT INTO NOWHERE (1938) PR:A
FLIGHT LIEUTENANT (1942) PR:A
FLIGHT NURSE (1953) PR:A
FLIGHT OF THE DOVES (1971, Brit.) PR:AA
FLIGHT OF THE EAGLE (1982, Swed./Norway/W. Ger.)
   PR:A-C
FLIGHT OF THE LOST BALLOON (1961) PR:C
FLIGHT OF THE NAVIGATOR (1986) PR:A
FLIGHT OF THE PHOENIX, THE (1965) PR:C
FLIGHT OF THE SANDPIPER, THE (SEE: SANDPIPER,
   THE) (1965)
FLIGHT OF THE WHITE STALLIONS, THE (SEE: MIR-
   ACLE OF THE WHITE STALLIONS, THE) (1963)
FLIGHT THAT DISAPPEARED, THE (1961) PR:A
FLIGHT TO BERLIN (1984, Brit./W. Ger.) PR:O
FLIGHT TO FAME (1938) PR:A
FLIGHT TO FURY (1966, US/Phil.) PR:C
FLIGHT TO HONG KONG (1956) PR:C
FLIGHT TO MARS (1951) PR:A
FLIGHT TO NOWHERE (1946) PR:C
FLIGHT TO TANGIER (1953) PR:A
FLIM-FLAM MAN, THE (1967) PR:A
FLIPPER (1963) PR:AA
FLIPPER'S NEW ADVENTURE (1964) PR:AA
FLIRTATION WALK (1934) PR:AA
FLIRTING WIDOW, THE (1930) PR:A
FLIRTING WITH DANGER (1935) PR:A
FLIRTING WITH FATE (1938) PR:A
FLIRTING WIVES (SEE: UNEASY VIRTUE) (1931, Brit.)
FLITTERWOCHEN IN DER HOLLE (SEE: ISLE OF SIN)
   (1963, W. Ger.)
FLOATING DUTCHMAN, THE (1953, Brit.) PR:A
FLOATING WEEDS (1959, Jap.) PR:A
FLOOD, THE (1931) PR:A
FLOOD, THE (1963, Brit.) PR:AA
FLOOD TIDE (1935, Brit.) PR:A
FLOOD TIDE (1958) PR:C
FLOODS OF FEAR (1958, Brit.) PR:A
FLOODTIDE (1949, Brit.) PR:A
FLORENTINE DAGGER, THE (1935) PR:A
FLORIAN (1940) PR:AA
FLORIDA SPECIAL (1936) PR:A
FLORODORA GIRL, THE (1930) PR:A
FLOWER DRUM SONG (1961) PR:A
FLOWER THIEF, THE (1962) PR:O
FLOWER WOMAN OF LINDENAU (SEE: STORM IN A
   WATER GLASS) (1931, Aust.)
FLOWERS FOR THE MAN IN THE MOON (1975, E.
   Ger.) PR:A
FLOWERS IN THE ATTIC (1987) PR:C-O
FLOWERS OF ST. FRANCIS, THE (1950. It.) PR:A
FLOWING GOLD (1940) PR:A
FLUCHT NACH BERLIN (SEE: ESCAPE TO BERLIN)
   (1962. US/Switz./W. Ger.)
FLUFFY (1965) PR:AA
FLY, THE (1958) PR:O
FLY, THE (1986) PR:O
FLY-AWAY BABY (1937) PR:A
FLY AWAY PETER (1948, Brit.) PR:A
FLY BY NIGHT (1942) PR:A
FLY NOW, PAY LATER (1969) PR:O
FLY, RAVEN, FLY (SEE: DESERT RAVEN, THE) (1965)
FLY II, THE (1989) PR:O

FLYER, THE (1987, W. Ger.) PR:O
FLYING BLIND (1941) PR:A
FLYING CADETS (1941) PR:A
FLYING CIRCUS, THE (SEE: FLYING DEVILS) (1933)
FLYING DEUCES, THE (1939) PR:AA
FLYING DEVILS (1933) PR:A
FLYING DOCTOR, THE (1936, Aus.) PR:A
FLYING DOWN TO RIO (1933) PR:A
FLYING EYE, THE (1955, Brit.) PR:AA
FLYING FIFTY-FIVE (1939, Brit.) PR:A
FLYING FISTS, THE (1938) PR:A
FLYING FONTAINES, THE (1959) PR:A
FLYING FOOL, THE (1929) PR:A
FLYING FOOL, THE (1931, Brit.) PR:A
FLYING FORTRESS (1942, Brit.) PR:A
FLYING GUILLOTINE, THE (1975, Chi.) PR:O-C
FLYING HIGH (1931) PR:A
FLYING HOSTESS (1936) PR:A
FLYING IRISHMAN, THE (1939) PR:A
FLYING LEATHERNECKS (1951) PR:C
FLYING MARINE, THE (1929) PR:A
FLYING MATCHMAKER, THE (1970, Israel) PR:A
FLYING MISSILE, THE (1950) PR:A
FLYING SAUCER, THE (1950) PR:A
FLYING SAUCER, THE (1964, It.) PR:A
FLYING SCOT, THE (SEE: MAILBAG ROBBERY)
   (1957, Brit.)
FLYING SCOTSMAN, THE (1929, Brit.) PR:A
FLYING SERPENT, THE (1946) PR:C
FLYING SORCERER, THE (1974, Brit.) PR:A
FLYING SQUAD, THE (1932, Brit.) PR:A
FLYING SQUAD, THE (1940, Brit.) PR:A
FLYING TIGERS (1942) PR:C
FLYING WILD (1941) PR:A
FLYING WITH MUSIC (1942) PR:A
FM (1978) PR:C
FOES (1977) PR:C
FOG (1934) PR:A
FOG (SEE: STUDY IN TERROR, A) (1966, Brit./W. Ger.)
FOG, THE (1980) PR:C-O
FOG FOR A KILLER (SEE: OUT OF THE FOG) (1962,
   Brit.)
FOG ISLAND (1945) PR:A
FOG OVER FRISCO (1934) PR:A
FOLIES BERGERE (1935) PR:A
FOLIES BERGERE (1958, Fr.) PR:C
FOLKS AT THE RED WOLF INN, THE (SEE: TERROR
   HOUSE) (1972)
FOLLIES GIRL (1943) PR:A
FOLLOW A STAR (1959, Brit.) PR:A
FOLLOW ME (SEE: PUBLIC EYE, THE) (1972, Brit.)
FOLLOW ME, BOYS! (1966) PR:AA
FOLLOW ME QUIETLY (1949) PR:C
FOLLOW THAT CAMEL (1967, Brit.) PR:A
FOLLOW THAT DREAM (1962) PR:A
FOLLOW THAT HORSE! (1960, Brit.) PR:A
FOLLOW THAT MAN (1961, Brit.) PR:A
FOLLOW THAT WOMAN (1945) PR:A
FOLLOW THE BAND (1943) PR:A
FOLLOW THE BOYS (1944) PR:AA
FOLLOW THE BOYS (1963) PR:A
FOLLOW THE FLEET (1936) PR:AA
FOLLOW THE HUNTER (SEE: FANGS OF THE WILD)
   (1954)
FOLLOW THE LEADER (1930) PR:A
FOLLOW THE LEADER (1944) PR:A
FOLLOW THE SUN (1951) PR:A
FOLLOW THRU (1930) PR:A
FOLLOW YOUR HEART (1936) PR:A
FOLLOW YOUR STAR (1938, Brit.) PR:A
FOLLOWING THE FUHRER (1984, W. Ger.) PR:C
FOLLY TO BE WISE (1953, Brit.) PR:A
FOMA GORDEYEV (SEE: GORDEYEV FAMILY, THE)
   (1961, USSR)
FOND MEMORIES (1982, Can.) PR:C
FONTANE EFFI BRIEST (SEE: EFFI BRIEST) (1974, W.
   Ger.)
FOOD OF THE GODS, THE (1976) PR:O
FOOD OF THE GODS II (SEE: GNAW: FOOD OF THE
   GODS II) (1989, Can.)
FOOL AND THE PRINCESS, THE (1948, Brit.) PR:A
FOOL FOR LOVE (1985) PR:O
FOOL KILLER, THE (1965) PR:O
FOOLIN' AROUND (1980) PR:C
FOOLISH HUSBANDS (1948, Fr.) PR:C
FOOLS (1970) PR:O
FOOLS FOR SCANDAL (1938) PR:A
FOOL'S GOLD (1946) PR:A
FOOLS OF DESIRE (1941) PR:C
FOOLS' PARADE (1971) PR:C
FOOLS RUSH IN (1949, Brit.) PR:A
FOOTBALL COACH (SEE: COLLEGE COACH) (1933)
FOOTLIGHT FEVER (1941) PR:A
FOOTLIGHT GLAMOUR (1943) PR:A
FOOTLIGHT PARADE (1933) PR:A
FOOTLIGHT SERENADE (1942) PR:A
FOOTLIGHTS AND FOOLS (1929) PR:A
FOOTLOOSE (1984) PR:A-C

FOOTLOOSE HEIRESS, THE (1937) PR:A
FOOTSTEPS IN THE DARK (1941) PR:A
FOOTSTEPS IN THE FOG (1955, Brit.) PR:A
FOOTSTEPS IN THE NIGHT (1932, Brit.) PR:A
FOOTSTEPS IN THE NIGHT (1957) PR:A
FOR A DOLLAR IN THE TEETH (SEE: STRANGER IN TOWN, A) (1968, It.)
FOR A FEW BULLETS MORE (SEE: ANY GUN CAN PLAY) (1968, It./Sp.)
FOR A FEW DOLLARS MORE (1967, It./Sp./W. Ger.) PR:C
FOR A FISTFUL OF DOLLARS (SEE: FISTFUL OF DOLLARS, A) (1964, It./Sp./W. Ger.)
FOR A NIGHT OF LOVE (SEE: MANIFESTO) (1988)
FOR ATT INTE TALA OM ALLA DESSA KVINNOR (SEE: ALL THESE WOMEN) (1964, Swed.)
FOR BEAUTY'S SAKE (1941) PR:A
FOR BETTER, FOR WORSE (1954, Brit.) PR:A
FOR BETTER FOR WORSE (SEE: ZANDY'S BRIDE) (1974)
FOR FREEDOM (1940, Brit.) PR:A
FOR HE'S A JOLLY BAD FELLOW (SEE: JOLLY BAD FELLOW, A) (1964, Brit.)
FOR HEAVEN'S SAKE (1950) PR:A
FOR KEEPS (1988) PR:A-C
FOR LOVE & MONEY (1967) PR:O
FOR LOVE OF IVY (1968) PR:A
FOR LOVE OF MONEY (SEE: FOR LOVE & MONEY) (1967)
FOR LOVE OF YOU (1933, Brit.) PR:A
FOR LOVE OR MONEY (1934, Brit.) PR:A
FOR LOVE OR MONEY (1939) PR:A
FOR LOVE OR MONEY (1963) PR:A
FOR ME AND MY GAL (1942) PR:A
FOR MEN ONLY (1952) PR:A
FOR PETE'S SAKE! (1966) PR:A
FOR PETE'S SAKE (1977) PR:C
FOR QUEEN AND COUNTRY (1989, Brit.) PR:O
FOR SINGLES ONLY (1968) PR:O
FOR THE DEFENSE (1930) PR:A-C
FOR THE FIRST TIME (1959, US/It./W. Ger.) PR:A
FOR THE LOVE OF BENJI (1977) PR:AA
FOR THE LOVE OF MARY (1948) PR:A
FOR THE LOVE OF MIKE (1933, Brit.) PR:A
FOR THE LOVE OF MIKE (1960) PR:AA
FOR THE LOVE OF RUSTY (1947) PR:AA
FOR THE LOVE O'LIL (1930) PR:A
FOR THE SERVICE (1936) PR:A
FOR THEM THAT TRESPASS (1949, Brit.) PR:A
FOR THOSE IN PERIL (1944, Brit.) PR:A
FOR THOSE WHO DARE (SEE: LUST FOR GOLD) (1949)
FOR THOSE WHO THINK YOUNG (1964) PR:A
FOR VALOR (1937, Brit.) PR:A
FOR WHOM THE BELL TOLLS (1943) PR:C
FOR YOU ALONE (1945, Brit.) PR:A
FOR YOU I DIE (1947) PR:A
FOR YOUR EYES ONLY (1981, Brit.) PR:A
FORBIDDEN (1932) PR:A-C
FORBIDDEN (1949, Brit.) PR:A-C
FORBIDDEN (1953) PR:A
FORBIDDEN ADVENTURE (SEE: NEWLY RICH) (1931)
FORBIDDEN ALLIANCE (SEE: BARRETTS OF WIMPOLE STREET, THE) (1934)
FORBIDDEN CARGO (1954, Brit.) PR:A
FORBIDDEN CHRIST, THE (SEE: STRANGE DECEPTION) (1953, It.)
FORBIDDEN COMPANY (1932) PR:A
FORBIDDEN FRUIT (1959, Fr.) PR:C
FORBIDDEN GAMES (1953, Fr.) PR:C
FORBIDDEN HEAVEN (1936) PR:A
FORBIDDEN ISLAND (1959) PR:C
FORBIDDEN JOURNEY (1950, Can.) PR:A
FORBIDDEN JUNGLE (1950) PR:A
FORBIDDEN LOVE (SEE: FREAKS) (1932)
FORBIDDEN LOVE AFFAIR (SEE: FOREVER YOUNG, FOREVER FREE) (1976, South Africa)
FORBIDDEN LOVE AFFAIR (SEE: LOLLIPOP) (1966, Braz.)
FORBIDDEN MUSIC (1936, Brit.) PR:A
FORBIDDEN PARADISE (SEE: HURRICANE) (1979)
FORBIDDEN PLANET (1956) PR:C
FORBIDDEN RELATIONS (1983, Hung.) PR:O
FORBIDDEN STREET, THE (SEE: AFFAIRS OF ADELAIDE) (1949, US/Brit.)
FORBIDDEN SUN (1989, Brit.) PR:C
FORBIDDEN TERRITORY (1938, Brit.) PR:A
FORBIDDEN TRAIL (1932) PR:A
FORBIDDEN TRAILS (1941) PR:A
FORBIDDEN VALLEY (1938) PR:AA
FORBIDDEN WORLD (1982) PR:O
FORBIDDEN ZONE (1980) PR:C
FORBIN PROJECT, THE (SEE: COLOSSUS, THE FORBIN PROJECT) (1969)
FORBRYDELSENS ELEMENT (SEE: ELEMENT OF CRIME, THE) (1984, Den.)
FORCE BEYOND, THE (1978) PR:C
FORCE: FIVE (1981) PR:O
FORCE OF ARMS (1951) PR:A

FORCE OF EVIL (1948) PR:C
FORCE OF IMPULSE (1961) PR:A
FORCE OF ONE, A (1979) PR:C-O
FORCE 10 FROM NAVARONE (1978, Brit.) PR:A-C
FORCED ENTRY (1975) PR:O
FORCED LANDING (1935) PR:A
FORCED LANDING (1941) PR:A
FORCED VENGEANCE (1982) PR:O
FORCES' SWEETHEART (1953, Brit.) PR:A
FOREIGN AFFAIR, A (1948) PR:C
FOREIGN AFFAIRES (1935, Brit.) PR:A
FOREIGN AGENT (1942) PR:A
FOREIGN BODY (1986, Brit.) PR:C-O
FOREIGN CITY, A (1988, Fr.) PR:C
FOREIGN CORRESPONDENT (1940) PR:A
FOREIGN INTRIGUE (1956) PR:C
FOREIGNER, THE (1978) PR:C
FOREMAN WENT TO FRANCE, THE (SEE: SOMEWHERE IN FRANCE) (1943, Brit.)
FOREPLAY (1975) PR:O
FOREST, THE (1983) PR:O
FOREST OF FEAR (SEE: BLOODEATERS) (1980)
FOREST RANGERS, THE (1942) PR:A
FOREVER AMBER (1947) PR:C-O
FOREVER AND A DAY (1943) PR:A
FOREVER DARLING (1956) PR:A
FOREVER ENGLAND (SEE: BORN FOR GLORY) (1935, Brit.)
FOREVER FEMALE (1953) PR:A
FOREVER IN LOVE (SEE: PRIDE OF THE MARINES) (1945)
FOREVER MY HEART (1954, Brit.) PR:C
FOREVER MY LOVE (1962, Aust.) PR:A
FOREVER YOUNG (1984, Brit.) PR:C
FOREVER YOUNG, FOREVER FREE (1976, South Africa) PR:AA
FOREVER YOURS (1937, Brit.) PR:A
FOREVER YOURS (1945) PR:A
FORGED PASSPORT (1939) PR:A
FORGET ME NOT (SEE: FOREVER YOURS) (1937, Brit.)
FORGET MOZART! (1985, Czech./W. Ger.) PR:A
FORGOTTEN (1933) PR:A
FORGOTTEN COMMANDMENTS (1932) PR:A
FORGOTTEN FACES (1936) PR:A
FORGOTTEN GIRLS (1940) PR:A
FORGOTTEN WOMAN, THE (1939) PR:A
FORGOTTEN WOMEN (1932) PR:A
FORGOTTEN WOMEN (1949) PR:A
FORGOTTEN WOMEN (SEE: MAD PARADE, THE) (1931)
FORLORN RIVER (1937) PR:AA
FORMULA, THE (1980) PR:C
FORSAKEN GARDEN, THE (SEE: OF LOVE AND DESIRE) (1963)
FORSAKING ALL OTHERS (1935) PR:A
FORSYTE SAGA, THE (SEE: THAT FORSYTE WOMAN) (1949)
FORT ALGIERS (1953) PR:A
FORT APACHE (1948) PR:A
FORT APACHE, THE BRONX (1981) PR:O
FORT BOWIE (1958) PR:A
FORT COURAGEOUS (1965) PR:A
FORT DEFIANCE (1951) PR:A
FORT DOBBS (1958) PR:A
FORT DODGE STAMPEDE (1951) PR:AA
FORT GRAVEYARD (1966, Jap.) PR:C
FORT MASSACRE (1958) PR:C
FORT OSAGE (1952) PR:A
FORT SAVAGE RAIDERS (1951) PR:A
FORT TI (1953) PR:AA
FORT UTAH (1967) PR:A
FORT VENGEANCE (1953) PR:A
FORT WORTH (1951) PR:A
FORT YUMA (1955) PR:A
FORTRESS, THE (1979, Hung.) PR:C
FORTUNATE FOOL, THE (1933, Brit.) PR:A
FORTUNE, THE (1975) PR:C
FORTUNE AND MEN'S EYES (1971, US/Can.) PR:O
FORTUNE COOKIE, THE (1966) PR:A
FORTUNE IN DIAMONDS (SEE: ADVENTURERS, THE) (1951, Brit.)
FORTUNE IS A WOMAN (SEE: SHE PLAYED WITH FIRE) (1956, Brit.)
FORTUNE LANE (1947, Brit.) PR:AA
FORTUNE TELLER, THE (1961, Gr.) PR:A-C
FORTUNES OF CAPTAIN BLOOD (1950) PR:A
FORTY ACRE FEUD (1965) PR:A
FORTY CARATS (1973) PR:A-C
FORTY DEUCE (1982) PR:O
48 HOURS (1944, Brit.) PR:A
48 HRS. (1982) PR:O
48 HOURS TO ACAPULCO (1968, W. Ger.) PR:C
48 HOURS TO LIVE (1960, Brit./Swed.) PR:A
45 FATHERS (1937) PR:AA
40 GRAVES FOR 40 GUNS (SEE: MACHISMO—40 GRAVES FOR 40 GUNS) (1970)
FORTY GUNS (1957) PR:A-C
40 GUNS TO APACHE PASS (1967) PR:A

FORTY LITTLE MOTHERS (1940) PR:A
FORTY NAUGHTY GIRLS (1937) PR:A
FORTY-NINE DAYS (1964, USSR) PR:A
FORTY-NINERS, THE (1954) PR:A
FORTY-NINERS, THE (1932) PR:A
49TH MAN, THE (1953) PR:A
FORTY NINTH PARALLEL (SEE: INVADERS, THE) (1941, Brit.)
FORTY POUNDS OF TROUBLE (1962) PR:AA
42ND STREET (1933) PR:A
47 RONIN, THE (PARTS I & II) (1941, Jap.) PR:C
47 SAMURAI (SEE: CHUSHINGURA) (1963, Jap.)
FORTY SQUARE METERS OF GERMANY (1986, W. Ger.) PR:A
FORTY THIEVES (1944) PR:A
FORTY THOUSAND HORSEMEN (1941, Aus.) PR:A
FORWARD MARCH (SEE: DOUGH BOYS) (1930)
FORWARD PASS, THE (1929) PR:A
FOUETTE (1986, USSR) PR:O
FOUL PLAY (1978) PR:A-C
FOUND ALIVE (1934) PR:A
FOUNTAIN, THE (1934) PR:A
FOUNTAIN OF LOVE, THE (1968, Aust.) PR:C
FOUNTAINHEAD, THE (1949) PR:A
FOUR AGAINST FATE (1952, Brit.) PR:A
FOUR BAGS FULL (1956, Fr./It.) PR:A-C
FOUR BOYS AND A GUN (1957) PR:C
FOUR COMPANIONS, THE (1938, Ger.) PR:A
FOUR CORNERED TRIANGLE (SEE: SCREAM OF THE BUTTERFLY) (1965)
4D MAN (1959) PR:A
FOUR DARK HOURS (SEE: GREEN COCKATOO, THE) (1947, Brit.)
FOUR DAUGHTERS (1938) PR:A
FOUR DAYS (1951, Brit.) PR:A
FOUR DAYS IN JULY (1984, Brit.) PR:C-O
FOUR DAYS LEAVE (1950, Switz.) PR:A
FOUR DAYS OF NAPLES, THE (1963, US/It.) PR:A
FOUR DAYS' WONDER (1936) PR:AA
FOUR DESPERATE MEN (1960, Brit.) PR:C
FOUR DEUCES, THE (1976) PR:O
FOUR DEVILS (1929) PR:A
FOUR FACES WEST (1948) PR:A
FOUR FAST GUNS (1959) PR:A
FOUR FEATHERS, THE (1939, Brit.) PR:A
FOUR FLIES ON GREY VELVET (1972, Fr./It.) PR:C
4 FOR TEXAS (1963) PR:C
FOUR FOR THE MORGUE (1962) PR:C
FOUR FRIENDS (1981) PR:O
FOUR FRIGHTENED PEOPLE (1934) PR:C
FOUR GIRLS IN TOWN (1956) PR:A
FOUR GIRLS IN WHITE (1939) PR:A
FOUR GUNS TO THE BORDER (1954) PR:A
FOUR HORSEMEN OF THE APOCALYPSE, THE (1962) PR:A
FOUR HOURS TO KILL (1935) PR:A
FOUR HUNDRED BLOWS, THE (1959, Fr.) PR:A-C
FOUR IN A JEEP (1951, Switz.) PR:A
FOUR IN THE MORNING (1965, Brit.) PR:C
FOUR JACKS AND A JILL (1941) PR:A
FOUR JILLS IN A JEEP (1944) PR:A
FOUR JUST MEN, THE (SEE: SECRET FOUR, THE) (1940, Brit.)
FOUR KINDS OF LOVE (SEE: BAMBOLE!) (1965, It.)
FOUR MASKED MEN (1934, Brit.) PR:A
FOUR MEN AND A PRAYER (1938) PR:A
FOUR MOTHERS (1941) PR:A
FOUR MUSKETEERS, THE (1975) PR:A-C
FOUR NIGHTS OF A DREAMER (1972, Fr.) PR:O
FOUR POSTER, THE (1952) PR:A
FOUR RODE OUT (1969, US/Sp.) PR:O
FOUR SEASONS, THE (1981) PR:C
FOUR-SIDED TRIANGLE (1953, Brit.) PR:C
FOUR SKULLS OF JONATHAN DRAKE, THE (1959) PR:C-O
FOUR SONS (1940) PR:A
FOUR WAYS OUT (1954, It.) PR:C
FOUR WIVES (1939) PR:A
FOUR'S A CROWD (1938) PR:A
FOURTEEN, THE (1973, Brit.) PR:A
FOURTEEN HOURS (1951) PR:C
FOURTH ALARM, THE (1930) PR:A
FOURTH FOR MARRIAGE, A (SEE: WHAT'S UP FRONT) (1964)
FOURTH HORSEMAN, THE (1933) PR:AA
FOURTH MAN, THE (1983, Neth.) PR:O
FOURTH PROTOCOL, THE (1987, Brit.) PR:C
FOURTH SQUARE, THE (1961, Brit.) PR:A-C
FOX, THE (1967) PR:O
FOX AND HIS FRIENDS (1976, W. Ger.) PR:O
FOX AND THE HOUND, THE (1981) PR:AA
FOX MOVIETONE FOLLIES (1929) PR:A
FOX MOVIETONE FOLLIES OF 1930 (1930) PR:A
FOX WITH NINE TAILS, THE (1969, Jap.) PR:AA
FOXES (1980) PR:O
FOXES OF HARROW, THE (1947) PR:A
FOXFIRE (1955) PR:C
FOXHOLE IN CAIRO (1960, Brit.) PR:A

FOXIEST GIRL IN PARIS (SEE: NATHALIE) (1958, Fr.)
FOXTROT (1977, Mex./Switz.) PR:C-O
FOXY BROWN (1974) PR:O
FOXY LADY (1971, Can.) PR:A
FRA DIAVOLO (SEE: DEVIL'S BROTHER, THE) (1933)
FRAGE 7 (SEE: QUESTION 7) (1961, W. Ger.)
FRAGMENT OF FEAR (1971, Brit.) PR:C-O
FRAGRANCE OF WILD FLOWERS, THE (1979, Yugo.)
    PR:C
FRAIL WOMEN (1932, Brit.) PR:C
FRAME-UP, THE (1937) PR:A
FRAMED (1930) PR:A
FRAMED (1940) PR:A
FRAMED (1947) PR:C
FRAMED (1975) PR:O
FRANCES (1982) PR:O
FRANCESCA (1987, W. Ger.) PR:O
FRANCESCO, GIULLARE DI DIO (SEE: FLOWERS OF
    ST. FRANCIS, THE) (1950, It.)
FRANCHETTE; LES INTRIGUES (1969) PR:O
FRANCHISE AFFAIR, THE (1952, Brit.) PR:A
FRANCIS (1949) PR:AA
FRANCIS COVERS THE BIG TOWN (1953) PR:AA
FRANCIS GOES TO THE RACES (1951) PR:AA
FRANCIS GOES TO WEST POINT (1952) PR:AA
FRANCIS IN THE HAUNTED HOUSE (1956) PR:AA
FRANCIS IN THE NAVY (1955) PR:AA
FRANCIS JOINS THE WACS (1954) PR:AA
FRANCIS OF ASSISI (1961) PR:A
FRANCOISE (SEE: ANATOMY OF A MARRIAGE (MY
    DAYS WITH JEAN-MARC AND MY NIGHTS WITH
    FRANCOISE)) (1964, Fr.)
FRANKENSTEIN (1931) PR:C-O
FRANKENSTEIN AND THE MONSTER FROM HELL
    (1974, Brit.) PR:O
FRANKENSTEIN CONQUERS THE WORLD (1964,
    US/Jap.) PR:C
FRANKENSTEIN CREATED WOMAN (1965, Brit.) PR:O
FRANKENSTEIN EXPERIMENT, THE (SEE: ANDY
    WARHOL'S FRANKENSTEIN) (1974, Fr./It.)
FRANKENSTEIN GENERAL HOSPITAL (1988) PR:O
FRANKENSTEIN—ITALIAN STYLE (1977, It.) PR:O
FRANKENSTEIN MEETS THE SPACE MONSTER (1965)
    PR:C
FRANKENSTEIN MEETS THE WOLF MAN (1943) PR:C
FRANKENSTEIN MUST BE DESTROYED! (1969, Brit.)
    PR:C-O
FRANKENSTEIN 1970 (1958) PR:C
FRANKENSTEIN, THE VAMPIRE AND CO. (1961,
    Mex.) PR:C
FRANKENSTEIN VS. THE GIANT DEVILFISH (SEE:
    FRANKENSTEIN CONQUERS THE WORLD) (1964,
    US/Jap.)
FRANKENSTEIN'S BLOODY TERROR (1968, Sp.) PR:C
FRANKENSTEIN'S CASTLE OF FREAKS (SEE:
    HOUSE OF FREAKS) (1973, It.)
FRANKENSTEIN'S DAUGHTER (1958) PR:C-O
FRANKIE AND JOHNNY (1936) PR:A-C
FRANKIE AND JOHNNY (1966) PR:A
FRANK'S GREATEST ADVENTURE (SEE: FEARLESS
    FRANK) (1967)
FRANTIC (1958, Fr.) PR:C
FRANTIC (1988) PR:A-C
FRASIER, THE SENSUOUS LION (1973) PR:AA
FRATERNALLY YOURS (SEE: SONS OF THE DESERT)
    (1933)
FRATERNITY ROW (1977) PR:O
FRATERNITY VACATION (1985) PR:C
FRAU CHENEY'S ENDE (SEE: END OF MRS.
    CHENEY) (1963, W. Ger.)
FRAUEN UM DEN SONNENKOENIG (SEE: PRIVATE
    LIFE OF LOUIS XIV) (1936, Ger.)
FRAULEIN (1958) PR:C
FRAULEIN DOKTOR (1969, It./Yugo.) PR:C-O
FREAK FROM SUCKWEASEL MOUNTAIN, THE (SEE:
    GEEK MAGGOT BINGO) (1983)
FREAKS (1932) PR:O
FREAKS! (SEE: SHE FREAK) (1966)
FREAKY FRIDAY (1976) PR:AA
FRECKLES (1935) PR:A
FRECKLES (1960) PR:A
FRECKLES COMES HOME (1942) PR:A
FREDDIE STEPS OUT (1946) PR:A
FREDDY UNTER FREMDEN STERNEN (1962, W. Ger.)
    PR:A
FREE AND EASY (1930) PR:A
FREE AND EASY (1941) PR:A
FREE, BLONDE AND 21 (1940) PR:A
FREE FOR ALL (1949) PR:A
FREE GRASS (1969) PR:O
FREE LOVE (1930) PR:C
FREE RIDE (1986) PR:O
FREE SOUL, A (1931) PR:C
FREE SPIRIT (SEE: BELSTONE FOX) (1973, Brit.)
FREE TO LIVE (SEE: HOLIDAY) (1938)
FREE, WHITE AND 21 (1963) PR:C
FREEBIE AND THE BEAN (1974) PR:O

FREEDOM FIGHTERS (SEE: MERCENARY FIGHT-
    ERS) (1988)
FREEDOM FOR US (SEE: A NOUS LA LIBERTE) (1931,
    Fr.)
FREEDOM OF THE SEAS (1934, Brit.) PR:A
FREEDOM RADIO (SEE: VOICE IN THE NIGHT, A)
    (1941, Brit.)
FREEDOM TO DIE (1962, Brit.) PR:A
FREEWAY MANIAC, THE (1989) PR:C
FREEWHEELIN' (1976) PR:A
FREIGHTERS OF DESTINY (1932) PR:A
FRENCH CANCAN (1955, Fr.) PR:A
FRENCH CONNECTION, THE (1971) PR:O
FRENCH CONNECTION II (1975) PR:O
FRENCH CONSPIRACY, THE (1973, Fr.) PR:A
FRENCH DETECTIVE, THE (1975, Fr.) PR:C-O
FRENCH DRESSING (1964, Brit.) PR:A
FRENCH GAME, THE (1963, Fr.) PR:C
FRENCH KEY, THE (1946) PR:A
FRENCH LEAVE (1931, Brit.) PR:A
FRENCH LEAVE (1937, Brit.) PR:A
FRENCH LEAVE (1948) PR:A
FRENCH LESSON (1986, Brit.) PR:C
FRENCH LIEUTENANT'S WOMAN, THE (1981, Brit.)
    PR:O
FRENCH LINE, THE (1954) PR:C
FRENCH MISTRESS (1960, Brit.) PR:A
FRENCH POSTCARDS (1979) PR:A-C
FRENCH QUARTER (1978) PR:O
FRENCH, THEY ARE A FUNNY RACE, THE (1956, Fr.)
    PR:A
FRENCH TOUCH, THE (1954, Fr.) PR:A
FRENCH WAY, THE (1952, Fr.) PR:A
FRENCH WAY, THE (1975, Fr.) PR:O
FRENCH WITHOUT TEARS (1939, Brit.) PR:A
FRENCHIE (1950) PR:A
FRENCHMAN'S CREEK (1944) PR:A
FRENZY (1946, Brit.) PR:A
FRENZY (SEE: TORMENT) (1944, Swed.)
FRENZY (1972, Brit.) PR:C-O
FRESH FROM PARIS (1955) PR:A
FRESH HORSES (1988) PR:C
FRESHMAN, THE (SEE: BACHELOR OF HEARTS)
    (1958, Brit.)
FRESHMAN LOVE (1936) PR:A
FRESHMAN YEAR (1938) PR:A
FREUD (1962) PR:A-C
FRIC FRAC (1939, FR.) PR:A
FRIDAY FOSTER (1975) PR:O
FRIDAY THE 13TH (1934, Brit.) PR:A
FRIDAY THE 13TH (1980) PR:O
FRIDAY THE 13TH PART II (1981) PR:O
FRIDAY THE 13TH PART III (1982) PR:O
FRIDAY THE 13TH—THE FINAL CHAPTER (1984) PR:O
FRIDAY THE 13TH, PART V—A NEW BEGINNING (1985)
    PR:O
FRIDAY THE 13TH PART VI: JASON LIVES (1986) PR:O
FRIDAY THE 13TH PART VII—THE NEW BLOOD (1988)
    PR:O
*FRIDAY THE 13TH PART VIII—JASON TAKES MANHAT-
    TAN* (1989) PR:O
FRIDAY THE 13TH. . . THE ORPHAN (1979) PR:O
FRIEDA (1947, Brit.) PR:A
FRIEND OF THE FAMILY (1965, Fr./It.) PR:A
FRIEND WILL COME TONIGHT, A (1948, Fr.) PR:A
FRIENDLIEST GIRLS IN THE WORLD, THE (SEE:
    COME FLY WITH ME) (1963, US/Brit.)
FRIENDLY ENEMIES (1942) PR:A
FRIENDLY KILLER, THE (1970, Jap.) PR:C-O
FRIENDLY NEIGHBORS (1940) PR:A
FRIENDLY PERSUASION (1956) PR:A
FRIENDS (1971, Brit.) PR:O
FRIENDS AND HUSBANDS (SEE: SHEER MADNESS)
    (1983, W. Ger.)
FRIENDS AND LOVERS (1931) PR:A
FRIENDS AND LOVERS (SEE: VIXENS, THE) (1969)
FRIENDS AND NEIGHBORS (1963, Brit.) PR:A
FRIENDS FOR LIFE (1964, It.) PR:A
FRIENDS, LOVERS AND LUNATICS (1989, Can.) PR:C
FRIENDS OF EDDIE COYLE, THE (1973) PR:O
FRIENDS OF MR. SWEENEY (1934) PR:A
FRIENDSHIP'S DEATH (1988, Brit.) PR:A
FRIGHT (SEE: SPELL OF THE HYPNOTIST) (1956)
FRIGHT (1971, Brit.) PR:O
FRIGHT, THE (SEE: VISITING HOURS) (1982, Can.)
FRIGHT NIGHT (1985) PR:O
FRIGHT NIGHT—PART 2 (1989) PR:O
FRIGHTENED BRIDE, THE (1952, Brit.) PR:A
FRIGHTENED CITY, THE (1961, Brit.) PR:A
FRIGHTENED LADY, THE (SEE: CRIMINAL AT
    LARGE) (1932, Brit.)
FRIGHTENED LADY (SEE: CASE OF THE FRIGHT-
    ENED LADY, THE) (1940, Brit.)
FRIGHTENED MAN, THE (1952, Brit.) PR:A
FRIGHTMARE (1974, Brit.) PR:O
FRIGHTMARE (1983) PR:O
FRIGID WIFE (SEE: MODERN MARRIAGE, A) (1950)
FRINGE DWELLERS, THE (1986, Aus.) PR:A-C

FRISCO JENNY (1933) PR:A
FRISCO KID (1935) PR:A
FRISCO KID, THE (1979) PR:C
FRISCO LIL (1942) PR:A
FRISCO SAL (1945) PR:A
FRISCO TORNADO (1950) PR:A
FRISCO WATERFRONT (1935) PR:A
FRISKY (1955, It.) PR:A
FRISSONS (SEE: THEY CAME FROM WITHIN) (1976,
    Can.)
FROG PRINCE, THE (SEE: FRENCH LESSON) (1986,
    Brit.)
FROG, THE (1937, Brit.) PR:A
FROGMEN, THE (1951) PR:A
FROGS (1972) PR:C
FROM A ROMAN BALCONY (1961, Fr./It.) PR:C
FROM A WHISPER TO A SCREAM (SEE: OFFSPRING,
    THE) (1987)
FROM BEYOND (1986) PR:O
FROM BEYOND THE GRAVE (1974, Brit.) PR:C
FROM BROADWAY TO CHEYENNE (SEE: BROAD-
    WAY TO CHEYENNE) (1932)
FROM HEADQUARTERS (1929) PR:A
FROM HEADQUARTERS (1933) PR:A
FROM HELL IT CAME (1957) PR:C
FROM HELL TO HEAVEN (1933) PR:C
FROM HELL TO TEXAS (1958) PR:C
FROM HELL TO VICTORY (1979, Fr./It./Sp.) PR:C
FROM HERE TO ETERNITY (1953) PR:C
FROM HOLLYWOOD TO DEADWOOD (1989) PR:C
FROM NASHVILLE WITH MUSIC (1969) PR:AA
FROM NOON TILL THREE (1976) PR:C
FROM RUSSIA WITH LOVE (1963, Brit.) PR:A
FROM THE EARTH TO THE MOON (1958) PR:A
FROM THE HIP (1987) PR:C
FROM THE LIFE OF THE MARIONETTES (1980, W.
    Ger.) PR:O
FROM THE MIXED-UP FILES OF MRS. BASIL E.
    FRANKWEILER (1973) PR:AA
FROM THE TERRACE (1960) PR:C
FROM THIS DAY FORWARD (1946) PR:A
FROM TOP TO BOTTOM (1933, Fr.) PR:A
FRONT, THE (1976) PR:C
FRONT LINE KIDS (1942, Brit.) PR:AA
FRONT PAGE, THE (1931) PR:A
FRONT PAGE, THE (1974) PR:C-O
FRONT PAGE STORY (1954, Brit.) PR:A
FRONT PAGE WOMAN (1935) PR:A
FRONTIER AGENT (1948) PR:A
FRONTIER BADMEN (1943) PR:A
FRONTIER CRUSADER (1940) PR:A
FRONTIER DAYS (1934) PR:A
FRONTIER FEUD (1945) PR:A
FRONTIER FUGITIVES (1945) PR:A
FRONTIER FURY (1943) PR:A
FRONTIER GAL (1945) PR:A
FRONTIER GAMBLER (1956) PR:A
FRONTIER GUN (1958) PR:A
FRONTIER HELLCAT (1966, Fr./It./W. Ger./Yugo.) PR:A
FRONTIER HORIZON (SEE: NEW FRONTIER) (1939)
FRONTIER INVESTIGATOR (1949) PR:A
FRONTIER JUSTICE (1936) PR:A
FRONTIER LAW (1943) PR:A
FRONTIER MARSHAL (1934) PR:A
FRONTIER MARSHAL (1939) PR:A
FRONTIER MARSHAL IN PRAIRIE PALS (SEE: PRAI-
    RIE PALS) (1942)
FRONTIER OUTLAWS (1944) PR:A
FRONTIER OUTPOST (1950) PR:A
FRONTIER PHANTOM, THE (1952) PR:A
FRONTIER PONY EXPRESS (1939) PR:A
FRONTIER REVENGE (1948) PR:A
FRONTIER SCOUT (1939) PR:A
FRONTIER TOWN (1938) PR:A
FRONTIER UPRISING (1961) PR:A
FRONTIER VENGEANCE (1939) PR:A
FRONTIERS OF '49 (1939) PR:A
FRONTIERSMAN, THE (1938) PR:A
FRONTIERSMAN, THE (SEE: BUCKSKIN) (1968)
FROU-FROU (1955, Fr.) PR:A
FROZEN ALIVE (1964, Brit./W. Ger.) PR:A
FROZEN DEAD, THE (1967, Brit.) PR:C
FROZEN GHOST, THE (1945) PR:C
FROZEN JUSTICE (1929) PR:A
FROZEN LIMITS, THE (1939, Brit.) PR:A
FROZEN RIVER (1929) PR:A
FRUHLINGSSINFONIE (SEE: SPRING SYMPHONY)
    (1983, E. Ger./W. Ger.)
FRUIT IS RIPE, THE (1961, Fr./It.) PR:C
FRUIT MACHINE, THE (SEE: WONDERLAND) (1988,
    Brit.)
FRUSTRATIONS (1967, Fr./It.) PR:O
FUEGO (SEE: PYRO) (1964, US/Sp.)
FUGITIVE, THE (1933) PR:A
FUGITIVE, THE (1940, Brit.) PR:A
FUGITIVE, THE (1947) PR:C
FUGITIVE AT LARGE (1939) PR:A
FUGITIVE FROM A PRISON CAMP (1940) PR:A

FUGITIVE FROM JUSTICE, A (1940) PR:A
FUGITIVE FROM SONORA (1943) PR:A
FUGITIVE IN THE SKY (1937) PR:A
FUGITIVE KIND, THE (1960) PR:C
FUGITIVE LADY (1934) PR:C
FUGITIVE LADY (1951) PR:O
FUGITIVE LOVERS (1934) PR:A
FUGITIVE ROAD (1934) PR:A
FUGITIVE SHERIFF, THE (1936) PR:A
FUGITIVE VALLEY (1941) PR:A
FUGITIVES FOR A NIGHT (1938) PR:C
FUHARANKENSHUTAIN TAI BARAGON (SEE:
  FRANKENSTEIN CONQUERS THE WORLD) (1964,
  US/Jap.)
FUKKATSU NO HI (SEE: VIRUS) (1980, Jap.)
FUKUSHU SURUWA WARE NI ARI (SEE: VEN-
  GEANCE IS MINE) (1980, Jap.)
FULL CIRCLE (1935, Brit.) PR:A
FULL CIRCLE (SEE: HAUNTING OF JULIA, THE)
  (1981, Brit./Can.)
FULL CONFESSION (1939) PR:C
FULL HOUSE (SEE: O. HENRY'S FULL HOUSE) (1952)
FULL METAL JACKET (1987, Brit.) PR:O
FULL MOON (SEE: MOONCHILD) (1972)
FULL MOON HIGH (1982) PR:A-C
FULL MOON IN BLUE WATER (1988) PR:O
FULL MOON IN PARIS (1984, Fr.) PR:O
FULL OF LIFE (1956) PR:A
FULL SPEED AHEAD (1936, Brit.) PR:A
FULL SPEED AHEAD (1939, Brit.) PR:A
FULL TREATMENT, THE (SEE: STOP ME BEFORE I
  KILL!) (1961)
FULLER BRUSH GIRL, THE (1950) PR:AA
FULLER BRUSH MAN, THE (1948) PR:AA
FUN AND FANCY FREE (1947) PR:AA
FUN AND GAMES (SEE: 1,000 CONVICTS AND A
  WOMAN) (1971, Brit.)
FUN AT ST. FANNY'S (1956, Brit.) PR:AA
FUN GIRLS (SEE: TOWING) (1978)
FUN IN ACAPULCO (1963) PR:A
FUN LOVING (SEE: QUACKSER FORTUNE HAS A
  COUSIN IN THE BRONX) (1970, Ireland)
FUN ON A WEEKEND (1947) PR:AA
FUN WITH DICK AND JANE (1977) PR:C-O
FUNDOSHI ISHA (SEE: LIFE OF A COUNTRY DOC-
  TOR) (1961, Jap.)
FUNERAL, THE (1984, Jap.) PR:O
FUNERAL FOR AN ASSASSIN (1977) PR:A
FUNERAL HOME (1982, Can.) PR:O
FUNERAL IN BERLIN (1966, Brit.) PR:C
FUNHOUSE, THE (1981) PR:O
FUNNY, DIRTY LITTLE WAR, A (1983, Arg.) PR:O
FUNNY FACE (1957) PR:AA
FUNNY FARM, THE (1982, Can.) PR:C
FUNNY FARM (1988) PR:C
FUNNY GIRL (1968) PR:A
FUNNY LADY (1975) PR:A
FUNNY MONEY (1983, Brit.) PR:O
FUNNY PARISHIONER, THE (SEE: THANK HEAVEN
  FOR SMALL FAVORS) (1965, Fr.)
*FUNNY THING HAPPENED ON THE WAY TO THE
  FORUM, A* (1966) PR:C
FUNNYMAN (1967) PR:C
FUOCO FATUO (SEE: FIRE WITHIN, THE) (1964, Fr./It.)
FUR COLLAR, THE (1962, Brit.) PR:A
FURESSHUMAN WAKADISHO (SEE: YOUNG GUY
  GRADUATES) (1969, Jap.)
FURIA (1947, It.) PR:A
FURIA A BAHIA POUR OSS 117 (SEE: OSS 117 – MIS-
  SION FOR A KILLER) (1966, Fr./It.)
FURIES, THE (1930) PR:A
FURIES, THE (1950) PR:C
FURIN KAZAN (SEE: UNDER THE BANNER OF SAM-
  URAI) (1969, Jap.)
FURTHER ADVENTURES OF TENNESSEE BUCK, THE
  (1988) PR:O
FURTHER ADVENTURES OF THE WILDERNESS FAM-
  ILY – PART TWO (1978) PR:AA
FURTHER UP THE CREEK! (1958, Brit.) PR:AA
FURY (1936) PR:C
FURY, THE (1978) PR:O
FURY AND THE WOMAN (1937) PR:A
FURY AT FURNACE CREEK (1948) PR:A
FURY AT GUNSIGHT PASS (1956) PR:O
FURY AT SHOWDOWN (1957) PR:O
FURY AT SMUGGLERS BAY (1963, Brit.) PR:A
FURY BELOW (1938) PR:A
FURY IN PARADISE (1955, US/Mex.) PR:A
FURY OF HERCULES, THE (1961, It.) PR:A
FURY OF THE CONGO (1951) PR:AA
FURY OF THE JUNGLE (1934) PR:O
FURY OF THE PAGANS (1963, It.) PR:A
FURY OF THE SUCCUBUS (SEE: SATAN'S MISTRESS)
  (1982)
FURY OF THE VIKINGS (SEE: ERIK THE CON-
  QUEROR) (1961, It.)
FURY UNLEASHED (SEE: HOT ROD GANG) (1958)
FUSS OVER FEATHERS (1954, Brit.) PR:AA

FUTARI NO MUSUCKO (SEE: DIFFERENT SONS)
  (1962, Jap.)
FUTURE COP (SEE: TRANCERS) (1985)
FUTURE-KILL (1985) PR:O
FUTUREWORLD (1976) PR:C
FUZZ (1972) PR:O
FUZZY PINK NIGHTGOWN, THE (1957) PR:A
FUZZY SETTLES DOWN (1944) PR:A
F/X (1986) PR:C-O

G

G-MAN'S WIFE (SEE: PUBLIC ENEMY'S WIFE) (1936)
G-MEN (1935) PR:A
G.I. BLUES (1960) PR:A
G.I. EXECUTIONER, THE (1985) PR:O
G.I. HONEYMOON (1945) PR:A
G.I. JANE (1951) PR:A
G.I. WAR BRIDES (1946) PR:A
GABLE AND LOMBARD (1976) PR:O
GABLES MYSTERY, THE (1931, Brit.) PR:A
GABLES MYSTERY, THE (1938, Brit.) PR:A
GABRIEL OVER THE WHITE HOUSE (1933) PR:C
GABRIELA (1983, Braz.) PR:O
GABY (1956) PR:A
GABY – A TRUE STORY (1987) PR:C
GAIETY GEORGE (SEE: SHOWTIME) (1948, Brit.)
GAIETY GIRLS, THE (1938, Brit.) PR:A
GAILY, GAILY (1969) PR:C-O
GAL WHO TOOK THE WEST, THE (1949) PR:A
GAL YOUNG 'UN (1979) PR:C
GALACTIC GIGOLO (1988) PR:O
GALAXINA (1980) PR:O
GALAXY EXPRESS (1982, Jap.) PR:A
GALAXY OF TERROR (1981) PR:O
GALIA (1966, Fr./It.) PR:C
GALILEO (1968, It./Bulgaria) PR:A
GALILEO (1975, Brit.) PR:A
GALLANT BESS (1946) PR:A
GALLANT BLADE, THE (1948) PR:A
GALLANT DEFENDER (1935) PR:A
GALLANT FOOL, THE (1933) PR:A
GALLANT HOURS, THE (1960) PR:A
GALLANT JOURNEY (1946) PR:A
GALLANT LADY (1934) PR:A
GALLANT LADY (1942) PR:A
GALLANT LEGION, THE (1948) PR:A
GALLANT ONE, THE (1964, US/Peru) PR:A
GALLANT SONS (1940) PR:A
GALLERY OF HORRORS (SEE: DR. TERROR'S GAL-
  LERY OF HORRORS) (1967)
GALLIPOLI (1981, Aus.) PR:A-C
GALLOPING DYNAMITE (1937) PR:A
GALLOPING MAJOR, THE (1951, Brit.) PR:A
GALLOPING ROMEO (1933) PR:A
GALLOPING THRU (1932) PR:A
GALS, INCORPORATED (1943) PR:A
GAMBIT (1966) PR:A-C
GAMBLER, THE (1958, Fr.) PR:C
GAMBLER, THE (1974) PR:O
GAMBLER AND THE LADY, THE (1952, Brit.) PR:A
GAMBLER FROM NATCHEZ, THE (1954) PR:A
GAMBLER WORE A GUN, THE (1961) PR:A
GAMBLERS, THE (1929) PR:A
GAMBLERS, THE (SEE: JUDGE, THE) (1949)
GAMBLERS, THE (1969) PR:A
GAMBLER'S CHOICE (1944) PR:A
GAMBLING (1934) PR:A
GAMBLING DAUGHTERS (1941) PR:A
GAMBLING HELL (SEE: MASK OF KOREA) (1950, Fr.)
GAMBLING HOUSE (1950) PR:A
GAMBLING LADY (1934) PR:A
GAMBLING ON THE HIGH SEAS (1940) PR:A
GAMBLING SAMURAI, THE (1966, Jap.) PR:C
GAMBLING SEX (1932) PR:A
GAMBLING SHIP (1933) PR:A
GAMBLING SHIP (1939) PR:A
GAMBLING TERROR, THE (1937) PR:A
GAME FOR SIX LOVERS, A (1962, Fr.) PR:A
GAME FOR THREE LOSERS (1965, Brit.) PR:A
GAME FOR VULTURES, A (1980, Brit.) PR:O
GAME IS OVER, THE (1967, Fr./It.) PR:O
GAME OF CHANCE, A (1932, Brit.) PR:A
GAME OF DANGER (SEE: BANG! YOU'RE DEAD)
  (1954, Brit.)
GAME OF DEATH, A (1945) PR:A
GAME OF DEATH, THE (1979) PR:O
GAME OF LOVE, THE (1954, Fr.) PR:C
GAME OF TRUTH, THE (1961, Fr.) PR:C
GAME THAT KILLS, THE (1937) PR:A
GAMEKEEPER, THE (1980, Brit.) PR:A
GAMERA THE INVINCIBLE (1966, Jap.) PR:A
GAMERA VERSUS BARUGON (1966, Jap./US) PR:A
GAMERA VERSUS GAOS (1967, Jap.) PR:A
GAMERA VERSUS GUIRON (1969, Jap.) PR:A
GAMERA VERSUS MONSTER K (1970, Jap.) PR:A
GAMERA VERSUS VIRAS (1968, Jap.) PR:A
GAMERA VERSUS ZIGRA (1971, Jap.) PR:A
GAMES (1967) PR:O

GAMES, THE (1970, Brit.) PR:A
GAMES MEN PLAY, THE (1968, Arg.) PR:O
GAMES THAT LOVERS PLAY (1971, Brit.) PR:O
GAMLET (SEE: HAMLET) (1964, USSR)
GAMMA PEOPLE, THE (1956, Brit.) PR:A
GAMMA SANGO UCHU DAISAKUSEN (SEE: GREEN
  SLIME, THE) (1969, US/Jap.)
GANDAHAR (SEE: LIGHT YEARS) (1988)
GANDHI (1982, Brit./India) PR:A
GANG, THE (1938, Brit.) PR:A
GANG (SEE: WALK PROUD) (1979)
GANG BULLETS (1938) PR:A
GANG BUSTER, THE (1931) PR:A
GANG BUSTERS (1955) PR:A
GANG MADE GOOD, THE (SEE: TUXEDO JUNCTION)
  (1941)
GANG OF FOUR, THE (1989, Fr.) PR:C
GANG SHOW (SEE: DOWN OUR ALLEY) (1939, Brit.)
GANG SHOW, THE (SEE: GANG, THE) (1938, Brit.)
GANG THAT COULDN'T SHOOT STRAIGHT, THE
  (1971) PR:A-C
GANG WAR (1928) PR:A
GANG WAR (1940) PR:C
GANG WAR (SEE: ODD MAN OUT) (1947, Brit.)
GANG WAR (1958) PR:C-O
GANG WAR (1962, Brit.) PR:A
GANG WARS (SEE: DEVIL'S EXPRESS) (1975)
GANGA (SEE: RIVER, THE) (1961, India)
GANGLAND (SEE: VERNE MILLER) (1988)
GANG'S ALL HERE (1941) PR:A
GANG'S ALL HERE, THE (1943) PR:A
GANG'S ALL HERE, THE (SEE: AMAZING MR. FOR-
  REST, THE) (1943, Brit.)
GANGS, INC. (SEE: PAPER BULLETS) (1941)
GANGS OF CHICAGO (1940) PR:A
GANGS OF NEW YORK (1938) PR:A
GANGS OF SONORA (1941) PR:A
GANGS OF THE WATERFRONT (1945) PR:A
GANGSTER, THE (1947) PR:C
GANGSTER STORY (1959) PR:A
GANGSTER VIP, THE (1968, Jap.) PR:C
GANGSTER'S BOY (1938) PR:A
GANGSTER'S BRIDE, THE (SEE: SECRET VALLEY)
  (1937)
GANGSTER'S ENEMY NO. 1 (SEE: TRAIL OF TER-
  ROR) (1935)
GANGSTERS OF THE FRONTIER (1944) PR:A
GANGSTERS OF THE SEA (SEE: OUT OF SINGA-
  PORE) (1932)
GANGSTER'S REVENGE (SEE: GET OUTTA TOWN)
  (1960)
GANGWAY (1937, Brit.) PR:A
GANGWAY FOR TOMORROW (1943) PR:A
GANJA AND HESS (1973) PR:O
GAOL BIRDS (SEE: PARDON US) (1931)
GAOL BREAK (1936, Brit.) PR:A
GAOLBREAK (1962, Brit.) PR:A
GAP, THE (SEE: JOE) (1970)
GAPPA THE TRIFIBIAN MONSTER (1967, Jap.) PR:A
GARAKUTA (SEE: RABBLE, THE) (1965)
GARBAGE MAN, THE (1963) PR:C
GARBAGE PAIL KIDS MOVIE, THE (1987) PR:C
GARBO TALKS (1984) PR:C
GARCON! (1985, Fr.) PR:C
GARDE A VUE (SEE: INQUISITOR, THE) (1982, Fr.)
GARDEN MURDER CASE, THE (1936) PR:A
GARDEN OF ALLAH, THE (1936) PR:C
GARDEN OF DELIGHTS, THE (1970, Sp.) PR:C
GARDEN OF EDEN (1954) PR:O
GARDEN OF EVIL (1954) PR:C
GARDEN OF THE DEAD (1972) PR:O
GARDEN OF THE FINZI-CONTINIS, THE (1971, It./W.
  Ger.) PR:C
GARDEN OF THE MOON (1938) PR:A
GARDENER, THE (SEE: SEEDS OF EVIL) (1972)
GARMENT JUNGLE, THE (1957) PR:A
GARNET BRACELET, THE (1966, USSR) PR:A
GARRISON FOLLIES (1940, Brit.) PR:A
GARU, THE MAD MONK (SEE: GURU, THE MAD
  MONK) (1970)
GAS (1981, Can.) PR:O
GAS HOUSE KIDS (1946) PR:A
GAS HOUSE KIDS GO WEST (1947) PR:A
GAS HOUSE KIDS IN HOLLYWOOD (1947) PR:A
GASBAGS (1940, Brit.) PR:A
GASLIGHT (1940, Brit.) PR:C
GASLIGHT (1944) PR:C
GASOLINE ALLEY (1951) PR:AA
GAS-S-S-S! (1970) PR:O
GASU NINGEN DAIICHIGO (SEE: HUMAN VAPOR,
  THE) (1964, Jap.)
GATE, THE (1987, Can.) PR:C
GATE OF FLESH (1964, Jap.) PR:O
GATE OF HELL (1953, Jap.) PR:C
GATES OF HELL, THE (1983, US/It.) PR:O
GATES OF PARIS (1958, Fr./It.) PR:C
GATES OF THE NIGHT (1950, Fr.) PR:C-O

GATES TO PARADISE (1968, Brit./W. Ger.) PR:C
GATEWAY (1938) PR:A
GATEWAY TO GLORY (1970, Jap.) PR:C
GATHERING OF EAGLES, A (1963) PR:A
GATLING GUN, THE (1972) PR:C
GATOR (1976) PR:C
GATOR BAIT (1974) PR:O
GATOR BAIT II: CAJUN JUSTICE (1989) PR:O
GATTO ROSSI IN UN LABIRINTO DO VETRO (SEE: EYEBALL) (1978, It.)
GAUCHO SERENADE (1940) PR:A
GAUCHOS OF EL DORADO (1941) PR:A
GAUNT STRANGER, THE (SEE: RINGER, THE) (1932, Brit.)
GAUNT STRANGER, THE (SEE: PHANTOM STRIKES, THE) (1939, Brit.)
GAUNTLET, THE (1977) PR:O
GAVILAN (1968) PR:C
GAWAIN AND THE GREEN KNIGHT (1973, Brit.) PR:C-O
GAY ADVENTURE, THE (1936, Brit.) PR:A
GAY ADVENTURE, THE (1953, Brit.) PR:A
GAY AMIGO, THE (1949) PR:A
GAY BLADES (1946) PR:A
GAY BRIDE, THE (1934) PR:A-C
GAY BUCKAROO, THE (1932) PR:A
GAY CABALLERO, THE (1932) PR:A
GAY CABALLERO, THE (1940) PR:A
GAY CITY, THE (SEE: LAS VEGAS NIGHTS) (1941)
GAY DECEIVERS, THE (1969) PR:O
GAY DECEPTION, THE (1935) PR:A
GAY DESPERADO, THE (1936) PR:A
GAY DIPLOMAT, THE (1931) PR:A
GAY DIVORCEE, THE (1934) PR:AA
GAY DOG, THE (1954, Brit.) PR:A
GAY DUELIST, THE (SEE: MEET ME AT DAWN) (1947, Brit.)
GAY FALCON, THE (1941) PR:A
GAY IMPOSTERS, THE (SEE: GOLD DIGGERS IN PARIS) (1938)
GAY INTRUDERS, THE (1946, Brit.) PR:A
GAY INTRUDERS, THE (1948) PR:A
GAY LADY, THE (SEE: LADY TUBBS) (1935)
GAY LADY, THE (1949, Brit.) PR:A
GAY LOVE (1936, Brit.) PR:A
GAY MRS. TREXEL, THE (SEE: SUSAN AND GOD) (1940)
GAY NINETIES (SEE: FLORODORA GIRL, THE) (1930)
GAY OLD DOG (1936, Brit.) PR:A
GAY PURR-EE (1962) PR:AA
GAY RANCHERO, THE (1948) PR:A
GAY SENORITA, THE (1945) PR:A
GAY SISTERS, THE (1942) PR:A-C
GAY VAGABOND, THE (1941) PR:A
GAZEBO, THE (1959) PR:A
GEBROKEN SPIEGELS (SEE: BROKEN MIRRORS) (1985, Neth.)
GEEK MAGGOT BINGO (1983) PR:O
GEHEIMINISSE IN GOLDEN NYLONS (SEE: DEAD RUN) (1969, Fr./It./W. Ger.)
GEISHA, A (1978, Jap.) PR:A
GEISHA BOY, THE (1958) PR:A
GEISHA GIRL (1952) PR:A
GELD AUF DER STRASSE (SEE: MONEY ON THE STREET) (1930, Aust.)
GELIEBTE BESTIE (SEE: HIPPODROME) (1961, W. Ger.)
GELIGNITE GANG (SEE: DYNAMITERS, THE) (1956, Brit.)
GEN TO FUDO-MYOH (SEE: YOUTH AND HIS AMULET, THE) (1963)
GENDARME OF ST. TROPEZ, THE (1966, Fr./It.) PR:O
GENE AUTRY AND THE MOUNTIES (1951) PR:A
GENE KRUPA STORY, THE (1959) PR:A-C
GENERAL CRACK (1929) PR:A-C
GENERAL DELLA ROVERE (1959, It./Fr.) PR:C
GENERAL DIED AT DAWN, THE (1936) PR:C
GENERAL JOHN REGAN (1933, Brit.) PR:A
GENERAL MASSACRE (1973, US/Bel.) PR:O
GENERAL SPANKY (1936) PR:AA
GENERAL SUVOROV (1941, USSR) PR:A
GENERALS OF TOMORROW (SEE: TOUCHDOWN, ARMY) (1938)
GENERALS WITHOUT BUTTONS (1938, Fr.) PR:A
GENERATION (1969) PR:C
GENEVIEVE (1953, Brit.) PR:A
GENGHIS KHAN (1965, US/Brit./Yugo./W. Ger.) PR:C
GENIE, THE (1953, Brit.) PR:A
GENIUS, THE (1976, It./Fr./W. Ger.) PR:C
GENIUS AT WORK (1946) PR:A
GENIUS IN THE FAMILY, A (SEE: SO GOES MY LOVE) (1946)
GENROKU CHUSHINGURA (SEE: 47 RONIN, THE (PARTS I & II)) (1941, Jap.)
GENTLE ANNIE (1944) PR:A
GENTLE ART OF MURDER (SEE: CRIME DOES NOT PAY) (1962, Fr.)
GENTLE CREATURE, A (1971, Fr.) PR:C

GENTLE GANGSTER, A (1943) PR:A
GENTLE GIANT (1967) PR:AA
GENTLE GUNMAN, THE (1952, Brit.) PR:C
GENTLE JULIA (1936) PR:A
GENTLE PEOPLE AND THE QUIET LAND, THE (1972) PR:A
GENTLE RAIN, THE (1966, US/Braz.) PR:O
GENTLE SERGEANT, THE (SEE: THREE STRIPES IN THE SUN) (1955)
GENTLE SEX, THE (1943, Brit.) PR:A
GENTLE TERROR, THE (1962, Brit.) PR:A
GENTLE TOUCH, THE (1956, Brit.) PR:A
GENTLE TRAP, THE (1960, Brit.) PR:A
GENTLEMAN AFTER DARK, A (1942) PR:A
GENTLEMAN AT HEART, A (1942) PR:A
GENTLEMAN CHAUFFEUR (SEE: WHAT A MAN) (1930)
GENTLEMAN FOR A DAY (SEE: UNION DEPOT) (1932)
GENTLEMAN FROM ARIZONA, THE (1940) PR:A
GENTLEMAN FROM CALIFORNIA, THE (SEE: CALIFORNIAN, THE) (1937)
GENTLEMAN FROM DIXIE (1941) PR:A
GENTLEMAN FROM LOUISIANA, THE (1936) PR:A
GENTLEMAN FROM NOWHERE, THE (1948) PR:A
GENTLEMAN FROM TEXAS (1946) PR:A
GENTLEMAN JIM (1942) PR:A
GENTLEMAN JOE PALOOKA (SEE: JOE PALOOKA, CHAMP) (1946)
GENTLEMAN MISBEHAVES, THE (1946) PR:A
GENTLEMAN OF PARIS, A (1931, Brit.) PR:A
GENTLEMAN OF VENTURE (SEE: IT HAPPENED TO ONE MAN) (1941, Brit.)
GENTLEMAN'S AGREEMENT (1935, Brit.) PR:A
GENTLEMAN'S AGREEMENT (1947) PR:A
GENTLEMAN'S FATE (1931) PR:C
GENTLEMAN'S GENTLEMAN, A (1939, Brit.) PR:A
GENTLEMEN ARE BORN (1934) PR:A
GENTLEMEN MARRY BRUNETTES (1955) PR:A
GENTLEMEN OF THE NAVY (SEE: ANNAPOLIS FAREWELL) (1935)
GENTLEMEN OF THE PRESS (1929) PR:A
GENTLEMEN PREFER BLONDES (1953) PR:A
GENTLEMEN WITH GUNS (1946) PR:A
GEORDIE (SEE: WEE GEORDIE) (1955, Brit.)
GEORG (1964) PR:C
GEORGE (1973, US/Switz.) PR:A
GEORGE AND MARGARET (1940, Brit.) PR:A
GEORGE AND MILDRED (1980, Brit.) PR:A-C
GEORGE IN CIVVY STREET (1946, Brit.) PR:A
GEORGE RAFT STORY, THE (1961) PR:A
GEORGE TAKES THE AIR (SEE: IT'S IN THE AIR) (1940, Brit.)
GEORGE WASHINGTON CARVER (1940) PR:A
GEORGE WASHINGTON SLEPT HERE (1942) PR:A
GEORGE WHITE'S 1935 SCANDALS (1935) PR:A
GEORGE WHITE'S SCANDALS (1934) PR:AA
GEORGE WHITE'S SCANDALS (1945) PR:A
GEORGIA, GEORGIA (1972) PR:O
GEORGIA'S FRIENDS (SEE: FOUR FRIENDS) (1981)
GEORGY GIRL (1966, Brit.) PR:A-C
GERALDINE (1929) PR:A
GERALDINE (1953) PR:A
GERMAN SISTERS, THE (1982, W. Ger.) PR:C-O
GERMANY IN AUTUMN (1978, W. Ger.) PR:O
GERMANY PALE MOTHER (1984, W. Ger.) PR:O
GERMANY, YEAR ZERO (1947, It./Fr./W. Ger.) PR:C
GERMINAL (1963, Fr.) PR:A
GERONIMO (1939) PR:C
GERONIMO (1962) PR:C
GERT AND DAISY CLEAN UP (1942, Brit.) PR:A
GERT AND DAISY'S WEEKEND (1941, Brit.) PR:A
GERTRUD (1964, Den.) PR:A
GERVAISE (1956, Fr.) PR:C
GESTAPO (SEE: NIGHT TRAIN) (1940, Brit.)
GET-AWAY, THE (1941) PR:C
GET BACK (1973, Can.) PR:C
GET CARTER (1971, Brit.) PR:O
GET CHARLIE TULLY (1972, Brit.) PR:C
GET CRACKING (1943, Brit.) PR:A
GET CRAZY (1983) PR:O
GET DOWN AND BOOGIE (SEE: DARKTOWN STRUTTERS) (1975)
GET GOING (1943) PR:A
GET HEP TO LOVE (1942) PR:A
GET MEAN (1976, It.) PR:C
GET OFF MY BACK (SEE: SYNANON) (1965)
GET OFF MY FOOT (1935, Brit.) PR:A
GET ON WITH IT (1963, Brit.) PR:A
GET OUT OF TOWN (SEE: GET OUTTA TOWN) (1960)
GET OUT YOUR HANDKERCHIEFS (1977, Fr./Bel.) PR:O
GET OUTTA TOWN (1960) PR:C
GET-RICH-QUICK WALLINGFORD (SEE: NEW ADVENTURES OF GET-RICH-QUICK WALLINGFORD, THE) (1931)
GET THAT GIRL (1932) PR:C
GET THAT GIRL (SEE: CARYL OF THE MOUNTAINS) (1936)
GET THAT MAN (1935) PR:A

GET TO KNOW YOUR RABBIT (1972) PR:O
GET WELL SOON (SEE: VISITING HOURS) (1982, Can.)
GET YOUR MAN (1934, Brit.) PR:A
GET YOURSELF A COLLEGE GIRL (1964) PR:A
GETAWAY, THE (1972) PR:O
GETTING AWAY WITH MUROER (SEE: END OF THE GAME) (1976, It./W. Ger.)
GETTING EVEN (1981) PR:C
GETTING EVEN (1986) PR:O
GETTING GERTIE'S GARTER (1945) PR:A
GETTING IT RIGHT (1989) PR:O
GETTING OF WISDOM, THE (1977, Aus.) PR:C
GETTING OVER (1981) PR:A-C
GETTING STRAIGHT (1970) PR:C-O
GETTING TOGETHER (1976) PR:O
GHARBAR (SEE: HOUSEHOLDER, THE) (1963, US/India)
GHARE BAIRE (SEE: HOME AND THE WORLD, THE) (1984, India)
GHASTLY ONES, THE (1968) PR:O
GHETTO FREAKS (SEE: SIGN OF AQUARIUS) (1970)
GHETTOBLASTER (1989) PR:O
GHIDRAH, THE THREE-HEADED MONSTER (1965, Jap.) PR:A
GHOST, THE (1965, It.) PR:O
GHOST AND MR. CHICKEN, THE (1966) PR:A
GHOST AND MRS. MUIR, THE (1947) PR:A
GHOST AND THE GUEST, THE (1943) PR:A
GHOST BREAKERS, THE (1940) PR:A
GHOST CAMERA, THE (1933, Brit.) PR:A
GHOST CATCHERS (1944) PR:A
GHOST CHASERS (1951) PR:A
GHOST CITY (1932) PR:A
GHOST COMES HOME, THE (1940) PR:A
GHOST CRAZY (SEE: CRAZY KNIGHTS) (1944)
GHOST CREEPS, THE (SEE: BOYS OF THE CITY) (1940)
GHOST DANCE (1984, Brit.) PR:O
GHOST DIVER (1957) PR:A
GHOST FEVER (1987) PR:C
GHOST GOES WEST, THE (1936, Brit.) PR:A
GHOST GOES WILD, THE (1947) PR:A
GHOST GUNS (1944) PR:A
GHOST IN THE INVISIBLE BIKINI (1966) PR:C
GHOST OF DRAGSTRIP HOLLOW, THE (1959) PR:C
GHOST OF FRANKENSTEIN, THE (1942) PR:C
GHOST OF HIDDEN VALLEY (1946) PR:A
GHOST OF JOHN HOLLING (SEE: MYSTERY LINER) (1934)
GHOST OF RASHMON HALL, THE (SEE: NIGHT COMES TOO SOON) (1948, Brit.)
GHOST OF ST. MICHAEL'S, THE (1941, Brit.) PR:A
GHOST OF THE CHINA SEA (1958) PR:A
GHOST OF ZORRO (1959) PR:A
GHOST PATROL (1936) PR:A
GHOST RIDER, THE (1935) PR:A
GHOST SHIP (1953, Brit.) PR:A
GHOST SHIP, THE (1943) PR:C
GHOST STEPS OUT, THE (SEE: TIME OF THEIR LIVES, THE) (1946)
GHOST STORIES (SEE: KWAIDAN) (1965, Jap.)
GHOST STORY (1974, Brit.) PR:C
GHOST STORY (1981) PR:O
GHOST TALKS, THE (1929) PR:A
GHOST THAT WALKS ALONE, THE (1944) PR:A
GHOST TOWN (1937) PR:A
GHOST TOWN (1956) PR:A
GHOST TOWN (1988) PR:C-O
GHOST TOWN GOLD (1937) PR:A
GHOST TOWN LAW (1942) PR:C
GHOST TOWN RENEGADES (1947) PR:A
GHOST TOWN RIDERS (1938) PR:A
GHOST TRAIN, THE (1933, Brit.) PR:A
GHOST TRAIN, THE (1941, Brit.) PR:A
GHOST VALLEY (1932) PR:A
GHOST VALLEY RAIDERS (1940) PR:A
GHOST WALKS, THE (1935) PR:A
GHOSTBUSTERS (1984) PR:A-C
GHOSTBUSTERS II (1989) PR:A
GHOSTS IN THE NIGHT (SEE: GHOSTS ON THE LOOSE) (1943)
GHOSTS, ITALIAN STYLE (1969, It./Fr.) PR:C
GHOSTS OF BERKELEY SQUARE, THE (1947, Brit.) PR:A
GHOSTS ON THE LOOSE (1943) PR:A
GHOSTS ON THE LOOSE (SEE: SPOOKS RUN WILD) (1941)
GHOUL, THE (1934, Brit.) PR:C
GHOUL, THE (1975, Brit.) PR:O
GHOUL IN SCHOOL, THE (SEE: WEREWOLF IN A GIRLS' DORMITORY) (1963, Aust./It.)
GHOULIES (1985) PR:O
GHOULIES II (1988) PR:C-O
GIANT (1956) PR:A
GIANT BEHEMOTH, THE (SEE: BEHEMOTH, THE SEA MONSTER) (1959, Brit.)
GIANT CLAW, THE (1957) PR:A
GIANT FROM THE UNKNOWN (1958) PR:C

GIANT GILA MONSTER, THE (1959) PR:A
GIANT LEECHES, THE (SEE: ATTACK OF THE GIANT LEECHES) (1959)
GIANT MONSTER (SEE: NIGHT THEY KILLED RAS-PUTIN, THE) (1962, Fr./It.)
GIANT OF MARATHON, THE (1960, It.) PR:O
GIANT OF METROPOLIS, THE (1963, It.) PR:A
GIANT SPIDER INVASION, THE (1975) PR:A
GIANTS A' FIRE (SEE: ROYAL MOUNTED PATROL, THE) (1941)
GIBRALTAR (SEE: IT HAPPENED IN GIBRALTAR) (1943, Fr.)
GIBRALTAR ADVENTURE (SEE: CLUE OF THE MISS-ING APE, THE) (1953)
GIDEON OF SCOTLAND YARD (1959, Brit.) PR:A
GIDEON'S DAY (SEE: GIDEON OF SCOTLAND YARD) (1958, Brit.)
GIDGET (1959) PR:A
GIDGET GOES HAWAIIAN (1961) PR:A
GIDGET GOES TO ROME (1963) PR:A
GIFT (SEE: VENOM) (1968, Den./Swed.)
GIFT, THE (1982, Fr./It.) PR:O
GIFT HORSE, THE (SEE: GLORY AT SEA) (1952, Brit.)
GIFT OF GAB (1934) PR:A
GIFT OF LOVE, THE (1958) PR:A
GIG, THE (1985) PR:A-C
GIGANTES PLANETARIOS (1965, Mex.) PR:A
GIGANTIS (1959, Jap./US) PR:A
GIGI (1958) PR:A
GIGOLETTE (1935) PR:A-C
GIGOLETTES OF PARIS (1933) PR:A
GIGOT (1962) PR:A
GILBERT AND SULLIVAN (SEE: GREAT GILBERT AND SULLIVAN, THE) (1953, Brit.)
GILDA (1946) PR:C
GILDED CAGE, THE (1954, Brit.) PR:A
GILDED LILY, THE (1935) PR:AA
GILDERSLEEVE ON BROADWAY (1943) PR:A
GILDERSLEEVE'S BAD DAY (1943) PR:A
GILDERSLEEVE'S GHOST (1944) PR:A
GILSODOM (1986, S.K.) PR:O
GIMME AN 'F' (1984) PR:O
GINA (SEE: DEATH IN THE GARDEN) (1956, Fr./Mex.)
GINGER (1935) PR:A
GINGER (1947) PR:A
GINGER & FRED (1986, It./Fr./W. Ger.) PR:A-C
GINGER IN THE MORNING (1973) PR:A
GION MATSURI (SEE: DAY THE SUN ROSE, THE) (1969, Jap.)
GION NO SHIMAI (SEE: SISTERS OF GION) (1936, Jap.)
GIONBAYASHI (SEE: GEISHA, A) (1978, Jap.)
GIORDANO BRUNO (1973, It.) PR:O
GIORNI DI FUOCO (SEE: LAST OF THE RENEGADES) (1966, Fr./It./W. Ger./Yugo.)
GIOVANI MARITI (SEE: YOUNG HUSBANDS) (1958, It./Fr.)
GIOVANNA D'ARCO AL ROGO (SEE: JOAN AT THE STAKE) (1954, It./Fr.)
GIPERBOLOID INGENERA GARINA (SEE: HYPERBOLOID OF ENGINEER GARIN, THE) (1965, USSR)
GIPSY BLOOD (SEE: CARMEN) (1931, Brit.)
GIRARA (1967, Jap.) PR:A
GIRDLE OF GOLD (1952, Brit.) PR:A
GIRL, THE (1987, Brit.) PR:O
GIRL, A GUY, AND A GOB, A (1941) PR:A
GIRL AGAINST NAPOLEON, A (SEE: DEVIL MADE A WOMAN, THE) (1959, Sp.)
GIRL AND THE BUGLER, THE (1967, USSR) PR:AA
GIRL AND THE GAMBLER, THE (1939) PR:A
GIRL AND THE GENERAL, THE (1967, Fr./It.) PR:C
GIRL AND THE LEGEND, THE (1966, W. Ger.) PR:A
GIRL AND THE PALIO, THE (SEE: LOVE SPECIALIST, THE) (1958, It.)
GIRL CAN'T HELP IT, THE (1956) PR:C
GIRL CAN'T STOP, THE (1966, Fr./Gr.) PR:C
GIRL CRAZY (1932) PR:A
GIRL CRAZY (1943) PR:AA
GIRL CRAZY (SEE: WHEN THE BOYS MEET THE GIRLS) (1965)
GIRL DOWNSTAIRS, THE (1938) PR:A
GIRL FEVER (1961) PR:A
GIRL FOR JOE, A (SEE: FORCE OF ARMS) (1951)
GIRL FRIEND, THE (1935) PR:A
GIRL FRIENDS, THE (SEE: LE AMICHE) (1962, Fr.)
GIRL FROM 5000 A.D., THE (SEE: TERROR FROM THE YEAR 5000) (1958)
GIRL FROM ALASKA, THE (1942) PR:A
GIRL FROM AVENUE A (1940) PR:A
GIRL FROM CALGARY, THE (1932) PR:A
GIRL FROM CHINA, THE (SEE: SHANGHAI LADY) (1929)
GIRL FROM GOD'S COUNTRY (1940) PR:A
GIRL FROM HAMBURG, THE (SEE: PORT OF DESIRE) (1960, Fr.)
GIRL FROM HAVANA, THE (1929) PR:A
GIRL FROM HAVANA (1940) PR:A
GIRL FROM HONG KONG (1966, W. Ger.) PR:A

GIRL FROM IRELAND (SEE: KATHLEEN MAVOUR-NEEN) (1930)
GIRL FROM JONES BEACH, THE (1949) PR:AA
GIRL FROM LORRAINE, THE (1982, Fr./Switz.) PR:O
GIRL FROM MANDALAY, THE (1936) PR:A
GIRL FROM MANHATTAN (1948) PR:A
GIRL FROM MAXIM'S, THE (1936, Brit.) PR:A
GIRL FROM MEXICO (SEE: MEXICALI ROSE) (1929)
GIRL FROM MEXICO, THE (1939) PR:A
GIRL FROM MISSOURI, THE (1934) PR:A-C
GIRL FROM MONTEREY, THE (1943) PR:A
GIRL FROM PARIS, THE (SEE: THAT GIRL FROM PARIS) (1937)
GIRL FROM PETROVKA, THE (1974) PR:A
GIRL FROM POLTAVA (1937) PR:A
GIRL FROM RIO, THE (1939) PR:A
GIRL FROM SAN LORENZO, THE (1950) PR:A
GIRL FROM SCOTLAND YARD, THE (1937) PR:A
GIRL FROM STARSHIP VENUS, THE (1975, Brit.) PR:O
GIRL FROM STATE STREET, THE (SEE: STATE STREET SADIE) (1928)
GIRL FROM TENTH AVENUE, THE (1935) PR:A
GIRL FROM TEXAS, THE (SEE: TEXAS, BROOKLYN AND HEAVEN) (1948)
GIRL FROM THE MARSH CROFT, THE (1935, Ger.) PR:A
GIRL FROM TRIESTE, THE (1983, It.) PR:C
GIRL FROM VALLADOLID, THE (1958, Sp.) PR:A
GIRL FROM WOOLWORTH'S, THE (1929) PR:A
GIRL GAME (1968, Braz./Fr./It.) PR:C
GIRL GETTERS, THE (1966, Brit.) PR:C
GIRL GRABBERS, THE (1968) PR:O
GIRL HABIT, THE (1931) PR:A
GIRL HAPPY (1965) PR:A
GIRL HE LEFT BEHIND, THE (1956) PR:A
GIRL HUNTERS, THE (1963, Brit.) PR:C-O
GIRL I ABANDONED, THE (1970, Jap.) PR:C-O
GIRL I MADE, THE (SEE: MADE ON BROADWAY) (1933)
GIRL IN A MILLION, A (1946, Brit.) PR:A
GIRL IN A SWING, THE (1989, Brit./US) PR:O
GIRL IN BLACK STOCKINGS, THE (1957) PR:C
GIRL IN DANGER (1934) PR:A
GIRL IN DISTRESS (1941, Brit.) PR:A
GIRL IN EVERY PORT, A (1952) PR:A
GIRL IN 419, THE (1933) PR:A
GIRL IN GOLD BOOTS (1968) PR:O
GIRL IN HIS POCKET (SEE: NUDE IN HIS POCKET) (1962, Fr.)
GIRL IN LOVER'S LANE, THE (1960) PR:A
GIRL IN OVERALLS, THE (SEE: SWING SHIFT MAISIE) (1943)
GIRL IN PAWN (SEE: LITTLE MISS MARKER) (1934)
GIRL IN POSSESSION (1934, Brit.) PR:A
GIRL IN ROOM 17, THE (SEE: VICE SQUAD) (1953)
GIRL IN ROOM 13 (1961, US/Braz.) PR:A
GIRL IN THE BIKINI, THE (1958, Fr.) PR:C
GIRL IN THE CASE (1944) PR:A
GIRL IN THE CROWD, THE (1934, Brit.) PR:A
GIRL IN THE FLAT, THE (1934, Brit.) PR:A
GIRL IN THE GLASS CAGE, THE (1929) PR:A
GIRL IN THE HEADLINES, THE (SEE: MODEL MUR-DER CASE, THE) (1963, Brit.)
GIRL IN THE KREMLIN, THE (1957) PR:A
GIRL IN THE LEATHER SUIT (SEE: HELL'S BELLES) (1969)
GIRL IN THE NEWS, THE (1941, Brit.) PR:A
GIRL IN THE NIGHT, THE (1931, Brit.) PR:A
GIRL IN THE PAINTING, THE (1948, Brit.) PR:A
GIRL IN THE PICTURE, THE (1956, Brit.) PR:A
GIRL IN THE PICTURE, THE (1985, Brit.) PR:C
GIRL IN THE RED VELVET SWING, THE (1955) PR:C
GIRL IN THE SHOW, THE (1929) PR:A
GIRL IN THE TAXI, THE (1937, Brit.) PR:A
GIRL IN THE WOODS (1958) PR:A
GIRL IN 313 (1940) PR:A
GIRL IN TROUBLE (1963) PR:C
GIRL IN WHITE, THE (1952) PR:A
GIRL IS MINE, THE (1950, Brit.) PR:A
GIRL LOVES BOY (1937) PR:A
GIRL MADNESS (SEE: BEAST OF YUCCA FLATS, THE) (1961)
GIRL MERCHANTS (SEE: SELLERS OF GIRLS) (1967, Fr.)
GIRL MISSING (1933) PR:A
GIRL MOST LIKELY, THE (1957) PR:AA
GIRL MUST LIVE, A (1941, Brit.) PR:A
GIRL NAMED TAMIKO, A (1962) PR:A
GIRL NEXT DOOR, THE (1953) PR:A
GIRL O' MY DREAMS (1935) PR:A
GIRL OF MY DREAMS (SEE: SWEETHEART OF SIGMA CHI) (1933)
GIRL OF THE GOLDEN WEST (1930) PR:A
GIRL OF THE GOLDEN WEST, THE (1938) PR:AA
GIRL OF THE LIMBERLOST (1934) PR:A
GIRL OF THE LIMBERLOST, THE (1945) PR:A
GIRL OF THE MOORS, THE (1961, W. Ger.) PR:C-O
GIRL OF THE MOUNTAINS (1958, Gr.) PR:C-O

GIRL OF THE NIGHT (1960) PR:C-O
GIRL OF THE OZARKS (1936) PR:A
GIRL OF THE PORT (1930) PR:A
GIRL OF THE RIO (1932) PR:A
GIRL OF THE YEAR (SEE: PETTY GIRL, THE) (1950)
GIRL ON A CHAIN GANG (1966) PR:O
GIRL ON A MOTORCYCLE, THE (1968, Fr./Brit.) PR:O
GIRL ON APPROVAL (1962, Brit.) PR:A
GIRL ON THE BARGE, THE (1929) PR:A
GIRL ON THE BOAT, THE (1962, Brit.) PR:A
GIRL ON THE BRIDGE, THE (1951) PR:A
GIRL ON THE CANAL, THE (1947, Brit.) PR:A
GIRL ON THE FRONT PAGE, THE (1936) PR:A
GIRL ON THE PIER, THE (1953, Brit.) PR:A
GIRL ON THE RUN (1961) PR:A
GIRL ON THE SPOT (1946) PR:A
GIRL OVERBOARD (1929) PR:A
GIRL OVERBOARD (1937) PR:A
GIRL RUSH (1944) PR:A
GIRL RUSH, THE (1955) PR:A
GIRL SAID NO, THE (1930) PR:A
GIRL SAID NO, THE (1937) PR:A
GIRL SMUGGLERS (1967) PR:O
GIRL STROKE BOY (1971, Brit.) PR:C
GIRL SWAPPERS, THE (SEE: TWO AND TWO MAKE SIX) (1962, Brit.)
GIRL, THE BODY, AND THE PILL, THE (1967) PR:O
GIRL THIEF, THE (1938, Brit.) PR:AA
GIRL TROUBLE (1942) PR:A
GIRL WAS YOUNG, THE (SEE: YOUNG AND INNO-CENT) (1937, Brit.)
GIRL WHO CAME BACK, THE (1935) PR:A
GIRL WHO COULDN'T QUITE, THE (1949, Brit.) PR:A
GIRL WHO COULDN'T SAY NO, THE (1969, It.) PR:A
GIRL WHO DARED, THE (1944) PR:A
GIRL WHO FORGOT, THE (1939, Brit.) PR:A
GIRL WHO HAD EVERYTHING, THE (1953) PR:A
GIRL WHO KNEW TOO MUCH, THE (1969) PR:O
GIRL WITH A PISTOL, THE (1968, It.) PR:A
GIRL WITH A SUITCASE (1961, It.) PR:A
GIRL WITH GREEN EYES (1964, Brit.) PR:A-C
GIRL WITH IDEAS, A (1937) PR:A
GIRL WITH THE GOLDEN EYES, THE (1962, Fr.) PR:C
GIRL WITH THE RED HAIR, THE (1983, Neth.) PR:A
GIRL WITH THREE CAMELS, THE (1968, Czech.) PR:A
GIRL WITHOUT A ROOM (1933) PR:A
GIRLFRIENDS (1978) PR:A-C
GIRLFRIENDS, THE (SEE: LES BICHES) (1968, Fr./It.)
GIRLS, THE (1972, Swed.) PR:O
GIRLS ABOUT TOWN (1931) PR:O
GIRLS AT SEA (1958, Brit.) PR:A
GIRLS CAN PLAY (1937) PR:A
GIRLS DEMAND EXCITEMENT (1931) PR:A
GIRLS DISAPPEAR (SEE: ROAD TO SHAME, THE) (1962, Fr.)
GIRLS' DORMITORY (1936) PR:A
GIRLS FROM THUNDER STRIP, THE (1966) PR:O
GIRLS! GIRLS! GIRLS! (1962) PR:A
GIRLS HE LEFT BEHIND, THE (SEE: GANG'S ALL HERE, THE) (1943)
GIRLS IN ACTION (SEE: OPERATION DAMES) (1959)
GIRLS IN ARMS (SEE: OPERATION BULLSHINE) (1963)
GIRLS IN CHAINS (1943) PR:A
GIRLS IN PRISON (1956) PR:C
GIRLS IN THE NIGHT (1953) PR:C
GIRLS IN THE STREET (1937, Brit.) PR:A
GIRLS IN UNIFORM (SEE: MAEDCHEN IN UNIFORM) (1931, Ger.)
GIRLS IN UNIFORM (SEE: MAEDCHEN IN UNIFORM) (1965, Fr./W. Ger.)
GIRLS JUST WANT TO HAVE FUN (1985) PR:C
GIRLS NEVER TELL (SEE: HER FIRST ROMANCE) (1951)
GIRLS NITE OUT (1984) PR:O
GIRLS OF LATIN QUARTER (1960, Brit.) PR:A
GIRLS OF PLEASURE ISLAND, THE (1953) PR:A
GIRLS OF SPIDER ISLAND (SEE: IT'S HOT IN PARA-DISE) (1959, W. Ger.)
GIRLS OF THE BIG HOUSE (1945) PR:A
GIRLS OF THE ROAD (1940) PR:C
GIRLS ON PROBATION (1938) PR:A
GIRLS ON THE BEACH, THE (1965) PR:A
GIRLS ON THE LOOSE (1958) PR:O
GIRLS PLEASE! (1934, Brit.) PR:A
GIRLS' SCHOOL (1938) PR:A
GIRLS' SCHOOL (1950) PR:A
GIRLS SCHOOL SCREAMERS (1986) PR:O
GIRLS' TOWN (1942) PR:A
GIRLS' TOWN (1959) PR:C
GIRLS UNDER TWENTY-ONE (1940) PR:A
GIRLS WILL BE BOYS (1934, Brit.) PR:A
GIRLY (SEE: MUMSY, NANNY, SONNY AND GIRLY) (1970, Brit.)
GIRO CITY (1982, Brit.) PR:C
GIT! (1965) PR:AA
GIT ALONG, LITTLE DOGIES (1937) PR:A
GIU LA TESTA (SEE: DUCK, YOU SUCKER!) (1972, It.)

GIULIETTA DEGLI SPIRITI (SEE: JULIET OF THE SPIRITS) (1965, Fr./It./W. Ger.)
GIULIO CESARE IL CONQUISTATORE DELLE GALLIE (SEE: CAESAR THE CONQUEROR) (1963, It.)
GIUSEPPE VENDUTO DAI FRATELLI (SEE: STORY OF JOSEPH AND HIS BRETHREN, THE) (1962, It.)
GIVE A DOG A BONE (1967, Brit.) PR:A
GIVE A GIRL A BREAK (1953) PR:A
GIVE AND TAKE (1929) PR:A
GIVE AND TAKE (SEE: SINGIN' IN THE CORN) (1946)
GIVE 'EM HELL, HARRY! (1975) PR:A
GIVE HER A RING (1936, Brit.) PR:A
GIVE HER THE MOON (1970, Fr./It.) PR:A
GIVE ME A SAILOR (1938) PR:A
GIVE ME MY CHANCE (1958, Fr.) PR:C
GIVE ME THE STARS (1944, Brit.) PR:A
GIVE ME YOUR HEART (1936) PR:A
GIVE MY REGARDS TO BROAD STREET (1984, Brit.) PR:A-C
GIVE MY REGARDS TO BROADWAY (1948) PR:A
GIVE OUT, SISTERS (1942) PR:A
GIVE US THE MOON (1944, Brit.) PR:A
GIVE US THIS DAY (SEE: SALT TO THE DEVIL) (1949, Brit.)
GIVE US THIS NIGHT (1936) PR:A
GIVE US WINGS (1940) PR:A
GIVEN WORD, THE (1964, Braz.) PR:A
GLAD RAG DOLL, THE (1929) PR:O
GLAD TIDINGS (1953, Brit.) PR:A
GLADIATOR, THE (1938) PR:AA
GLADIATOR OF ROME (1963, It.) PR:C
GLADIATORERNA (SEE: GLADIATORS, THE) (1971, Swed.)
GLADIATORS, THE (1970, Swed.) PR:C-O
GLADIATORS 7 (1964, Sp./It.) PR:O
GLAMOROUS NIGHT (1937, Brit.) PR:C
GLAMOUR (1931, Brit.) PR:A
GLAMOUR (1934) PR:C
GLAMOUR BOY (SEE: MILLIONAIRE PLAYBOY) (1940)
GLAMOUR BOY (1941) PR:AA
GLAMOUR FOR SALE (1940) PR:A
GLAMOUR GIRL (1938, Brit.) PR:A
GLAMOUR GIRL (1947) PR:A
GLASS ALIBI, THE (1946) PR:A
GLASS BOTTOM BOAT, THE (1966) PR:A
GLASS CAGE, THE (SEE: GLASS TOMB, THE) (1955, Brit.)
GLASS CAGE, THE (1964) PR:O
GLASS HOUSES (1972) PR:O
GLASS KEY, THE (1935) PR:C
GLASS KEY, THE (1942) PR:O
GLASS MENAGERIE, THE (1950) PR:A
GLASS MENAGERIE, THE (1987) PR:A
GLASS MOUNTAIN, THE (1950, Brit.) PR:A
GLASS OF WATER, A (1962, W. Ger.) PR:A
GLASS SLIPPER, THE (1955) PR:A
GLASS SPHINX, THE (1968, Egypt/It./Sp.) PR:A
GLASS TOMB, THE (1955, Brit.) PR:A
GLASS TOWER, THE (1959, W. Ger.) PR:A
GLASS WALL, THE (1953) PR:A
GLASS WEB, THE (1953) PR:A
GLEAMING THE CUBE (1989) PR:C
GLEN OR GLENDA (1953) PR:O
GLENN MILLER STORY, THE (1953) PR:AA
GLENROWAN AFFAIR, THE (1951, Aus.) PR:C
GLI INDIFFERENTI (SEE: TIME OF INDIFFERENCE) (1965, Fr./It.)
GLI INTOCCABILI (SEE: MACHINE GUN MC CAIN) (1970, It.)
GLI OCCHI, LA BOCCA (SEE: EYES, THE MOUTH, THE) (1982, Fr./It.)
GLI SCHIAVI PIU FORTI DEL MONDO (SEE: SEVEN SLAVES AGAINST THE WORLD) (1965, It.)
GLI UOMINI DAL PASSO PESANTE (SEE: TRAMPLERS, THE) (1966, It.)
GLIMPSE OF PARADISE, A (1934, Brit.) PR:A
GLITCH (1989) PR:O
GLITTERBALL, THE (1977, Brit.) PR:AA
GLOBAL AFFAIR, A (1964) PR:A
GLORIA (1980) PR:O
GLORIFYING THE AMERICAN GIRL (1930) PR:A
GLORIOUS SACRIFICE (SEE: GLORY TRAIL, THE) (1937)
GLORY (1955) PR:AA
GLORY (1989) PR:C
GLORY ALLEY (1952) PR:C
GLORY AT SEA (1952, Brit.) PR:A
GLORY BOY (1971) PR:O
GLORY BRIGADE, THE (1953) PR:C
GLORY GUYS, THE (1965) PR:C
GLORY OF FAITH, THE (1938, Fr.) PR:A
GLORY STOMPERS, THE (1967) PR:O
GLORY TRAIL, THE (1937) PR:A
GLOVE, THE (1980) PR:O
GLOWING AUTUMN (1981, Jap.) PR:A-C
GNAW: FOOD OF THE GODS II (1989, Can.) PR:O

GNOME-MOBILE, THE (1967) PR:AA
GO-BETWEEN, THE (1971, Brit.) PR:A-C
GO CHASE YOURSELF (1938) PR:A
GO FOR BROKE! (1951) PR:A
GO-GETTER, THE (1937) PR:A
GO-GO SET (SEE: GET YOURSELF A COLLEGE GIRL) (1964)
GO INTO YOUR DANCE (1935) PR:A
GO, JOHNNY, GO! (1959) PR:A
GO KART GO (1964, Brit.) PR:AA
GO, MAN, GO! (1954) PR:A
GO MASTERS, THE (1985, Jap./Chi.) PR:C
GO NAKED IN THE WORLD (1961) PR:O
GO TELL IT ON THE MOUNTAIN (1984) PR:A
GO TELL THE SPARTANS (1978) PR:O
GO TO BLAZES (1962, Brit.) PR:A
GO WEST (1940) PR:A
GO WEST, YOUNG LADY (1941) PR:A
GO WEST, YOUNG MAN (1936) PR:C
GOALIE'S ANXIETY AT THE PENALTY KICK, THE (1971, W. Ger.) PR:C
GOBEN NO TSUBAKI (SEE: SCARLET CAMELLIA, THE) (1965, Jap.)
GOBOTS: BATTLE OF THE ROCK LORDS (1986) PR:AA
GOBS AND GALS (1952) PR:A
GOD FORGIVES – I DON'T! (1969, It./Sp.) PR:O
GOD GAME, THE (SEE: MAGUS, THE) (1968, Brit.)
GOD GAVE HIM A DOG (SEE: BISCUIT EATER, THE) (1940)
GOD IS MY CO-PILOT (1945) PR:A
GOD IS MY PARTNER (1957) PR:A
GOD SPEAKS TODAY (SEE: SUPREME SECRET, THE) (1958, Brit.)
GOD TOLD ME TO (1976) PR:O
GODDESS, THE (1958) PR:C-O
GODDESS, THE (1962, India) PR:C
GODDESS OF LOVE, THE (1960, It./Fr.) PR:O
GODFATHER, THE (1972) PR:O
GODFATHER, PART II, THE (1974) PR:O
GODLESS GIRL, THE (1929) PR:C
GOD'S COUNTRY (1946) PR:A
GOD'S COUNTRY AND THE MAN (1931) PR:A
GOD'S COUNTRY AND THE MAN (1937) PR:A
GOD'S COUNTRY AND THE WOMAN (1937) PR:A
GOD'S GIFT TO WOMEN (1931) PR:A
GOD'S GUN (1977) PR:O
GOD'S LITTLE ACRE (1958) PR:O
GODS MUST BE CRAZY, THE (1984, Botswana) PR:C
GODSEND, THE (1980, Can.) PR:O
GODSON, THE (1972, It./Fr.) PR:C-O
GODSPELL (1973) PR:C
GODY MOLODYYE (SEE: TRAIN GOES TO KIEV, THE) (1961, USSR)
GODZILLA (SEE: GODZILLA, KING OF THE MONSTERS) (1956, Jap.)
GODZILLA, KING OF THE MONSTERS (1956, Jap.) PR:C
GODZILLA 1985 (1985, Jap.) PR:C
GODZILLA TAI MOTHRA (SEE: GODZILLA VS. THE THING) (1964, Jap.)
GODZILLA VERSUS MEGALON (1976, Jap.) PR:C
GODZILLA VERSUS THE COSMIC MONSTER (1974, Jap.) PR:C
GODZILLA VERSUS THE SEA MONSTER (1966, Jap.) PR:C
GODZILLA VERSUS THE SMOG MONSTER (1972, Jap.) PR:C
GODZILLA VERSUS THE THING (1964, Jap.) PR:C
GODZILLA'S REVENGE (1969, Jap.) PR:C
GOFORTH (SEE: BOOM!) (1968, US/Brit.)
GOG (1954) PR:A
GOHA (1958, Tunisia) PR:O
GOIN' COCONUTS (1978) PR:AA
GOIN' DOWN THE ROAD (1970, Can.) PR:O
GOIN' HOME (1976) PR:AA
GOIN' SOUTH (1978) PR:O
GOIN' TO TOWN (1935) PR:C
GOIN' TO TOWN (1944) PR:A
GOING AND COMING BACK (1985, Fr.) PR:O
GOING APE! (1981) PR:A
GOING APE (SEE: WHERE'S POPPA?) (1970)
GOING BERSERK (1983) PR:O
GOING GAY (SEE: KISS ME GOODBYE) (1933, Brit.)
GOING HIGHBROW (1935) PR:A
GOING HOLLYWOOD (1933) PR:A
GOING HOME (1971) PR:O
GOING HOME (1988, Brit./Can.) PR:C
GOING IN STYLE (1979) PR:C
GOING MY WAY (1944) PR:AA
GOING PLACES (1938) PR:A
GOING PLACES (1974, Fr.) PR:O
GOING STEADY (1958) PR:A
GOING STRAIGHT (1933, Brit.) PR:A
GOING TO TOWN (SEE: MA AND PA KETTLE GO TO TOWN) (1950)
GOING UNDERCOVER (1989, Brit.) PR:C
GOING WILD (1931) PR:A
GOJIRA NO MUSUKO (SEE: SON OF GODZILLA) (1967, Jap.)

GOJIRA TAI HEDORA (SEE: GODZILLA VERSUS THE SMOG MONSTER) (1972, Jap.)
GOJIRA TAI MEGARO (SEE: GODZILLA VERSUS MEGALON) (1976, Jap.)
GOJIRA TAI MEKAGOJIRA (SEE: GODZILLA VERSUS THE COSMIC MONSTER) (1974, Jap.)
GOJIRA TAI MOSUHA (SEE: GODZILLA VS. THE THING) (1964, Jap.)
GOJIRA TAI MOSURA (SEE: GODZILLA VERSUS THE THING) (1964, Jap.)
GOJIRO NO GYAKUSHYU (SEE: GIGANTIS) (1959, US/Jap.)
GOJUMAN-NIN NO ISAN (SEE: LEGACY OF THE 500,000, THE) (1964, Jap.)
GOKE, BODYSNATCHER FROM HELL (1968, Jap.) PR:O
GOLD (1932) PR:A
GOLD (1934, Ger.) PR:C
GOLD (1974, Brit.) PR:O
GOLD DIGGERS IN PARIS (1938) PR:A
GOLD DIGGERS OF BROADWAY (1929) PR:A
GOLD DIGGERS OF 1933 (1933) PR:A
GOLD DIGGERS OF 1935 (1935) PR:A
GOLD DIGGERS OF 1937 (1936) PR:A
GOLD DUST GERTIE (1931) PR:A
GOLD EXPRESS, THE (1955, Brit.) PR:A
GOLD FEVER (1952) PR:A
GOLD FOR THE CAESARS (1964, Fr./It.) PR:C
GOLD GUITAR, THE (1966) PR:A
GOLD IS WHERE YOU FIND IT (1938) PR:A
GOLD MINE IN THE SKY (1938) PR:A
GOLD OF NAPLES (1954, It.) PR:C-O
GOLD OF THE SEVEN SAINTS (1961) PR:A
GOLD RACKET, THE (1937) PR:A
GOLD RAIDERS, THE (1952) PR:A
GOLD RUSH MAISIE (1940) PR:A
GOLDBERGS, THE (1950) PR:A
GOLDEN APPLES OF THE SUN (1971, Can.) PR:O
GOLDEN ARROW, THE (1936) PR:A
GOLDEN ARROW, THE (SEE: GAY ADVENTURE, THE) (1953, Brit.)
GOLDEN ARROW, THE (1964, It.) PR:A
GOLDEN BLADE, THE (1953) PR:A
GOLDEN BOX, THE (1970) PR:O
GOLDEN BOY (1939) PR:A
GOLDEN BULLET (SEE: IMPASSE) (1969)
GOLDEN CAGE, THE (1933, Brit.) PR:A
GOLDEN CALF, THE (1930) PR:AA
GOLDEN CHILD, THE (1986) PR:C
GOLDEN COACH, THE (1952, Fr./It.) PR:A
GOLDEN DAWN (1930) PR:A
GOLDEN DEMON (1954, Jap.) PR:C
GOLDEN DISK (SEE: IN-BETWEEN AGE, THE) (1958, BRIT.)
GOLDEN EARRINGS (1947) PR:C
GOLDEN EIGHTIES (1986, Fr./Bel./Switz.) PR:A
GOLDEN EYE, THE (SEE: MYSTERY OF THE GOLDEN EYE, THE) (1948)
GOLDEN FLEECING, THE (1940) PR:A
GOLDEN GATE GIRL (1941) PR:C
GOLDEN GIRL (1951) PR:AA
GOLDEN GLOVES (SEE: EX-CHAMP) (1939)
GOLDEN GLOVES (1940) PR:A
GOLDEN GLOVES STORY, THE (1950) PR:A
GOLDEN GOOSE, THE (1966, E. Ger.) PR:AA
GOLDEN HARVEST (1933) PR:A
GOLDEN HAWK, THE (1952) PR:A
GOLDEN HEAD, THE (1965, Hung./US) PR:A
GOLDEN HEIST, THE (SEE: INSIDE OUT) (1975, Brit.)
GOLDEN HELMET (SEE: CASQUE D'OR) (1952)
GOLDEN HOOFS (1941) PR:A
GOLDEN HORDE, THE (1951) PR:A
GOLDEN HOUR, THE (SEE: POT O' GOLD) (1941)
GOLDEN IDOL, THE (1954) PR:A
GOLDEN IVORY (SEE: WHITE HUNTRESS) (1954)
GOLDEN LADY, THE (1979, Brit.) PR:O
GOLDEN LINK, THE (1954, Brit.) PR:A
GOLDEN MADONNA, THE (1949, Brit.) PR:A
GOLDEN MARIE (SEE: CASQUE D'OR) (1952, Fr.)
GOLDEN MASK, THE (1954, Brit.) PR:A
GOLDEN MISTRESS, THE (1954) PR:A
GOLDEN MOUNTAINS (1958, Den.) PR:A
GOLDEN NEEDLES (1974) PR:O
GOLDEN NYMPHS, THE (SEE: HONEYMOON OF HORROR) (1964)
GOLDEN PLAGUE, THE (1963, W. Ger.) PR:A
GOLDEN RABBIT, THE (1962, Brit.) PR:A
GOLDEN RENDEZVOUS (1977) PR:O
GOLDEN SALAMANDER (1950, Brit.) PR:A
GOLDEN SEAL, THE (1983) PR:AA
GOLDEN STALLION, THE (1949) PR:A
GOLDEN TRAIL, THE (SEE: RIDERS OF THE WHISTLING SKULL) (1937)
GOLDEN TRAIL, THE (1940) PR:A
GOLDEN VIRGIN (SEE: STORY OF ESTHER COSTELLO, THE) (1957, Brit.)
GOLDEN VOYAGE OF SINBAD, THE (1974, Brit.) PR:AA
GOLDEN WEST, THE (1932) PR:A

GOLDENGIRL (1979) PR:O
GOLDFINGER (1964, Brit.) PR:C-O
GOLDIE (1931) PR:A
GOLDIE GETS ALONG (1933) PR:A
GOLDSTEIN (1964) PR:O
GOLDTOWN GHOST RIDERS (1953) PR:A
GOLDWYN FOLLIES, THE (1938) PR:A
GOLEM, THE (1937, Czech./Fr.) PR:C
GOLEM (1980, Pol.) PR:C
GOLFO (SEE: GIRL OF THE MOUNTAINS) (1958, Gr.)
GOLGOTHA (1937, Fr.) PR:A
GOLIATH AGAINST THE GIANTS (1963, It./Sp.) PR:A
GOLIATH AND THE BARBARIANS (1960, It.) PR:A
GOLIATH AND THE DRAGON (1961, It./Fr.) PR:A
GOLIATH AND THE SINS OF BABYLON (1964, It.)
   PR:A
GOLIATH AND THE VAMPIRES (1964, It.) PR:C
GOLIATHON (1979, Hong Kong) PR:C
GOMAR — THE HUMAN GORILLA (SEE: NIGHT OF
   THE BLOODY APES) (1968, Mex.)
GONE ARE THE DAYS (1963) PR:A
GONE IN 60 SECONDS (1974) PR:C
GONE TO EARTH (SEE: WILD HEART, THE) (1950,
   Brit.)
GONE TO THE DOGS (1939, Aus.) PR:A
GONE WITH THE WIND (1939) PR:A
GONG SHOW MOVIE, THE (1980) PR:C
GONKS GO BEAT (1965, Brit.) PR:A
GOOD BAD GIRL, THE (1931) PR:A
GOOD BEGINNING, THE (1953, Brit.) PR:A
GOOD COMPANIONS, THE (1957, Brit.) PR:A
GOOD COMPANIONS, THE (1933, Brit.) PR:A
GOOD DAME (1934) PR:A
GOOD DAY FOR A HANGING (1958) PR:A
GOOD DAY FOR FIGHTING (SEE: CUSTER OF THE
   WEST) (1967)
GOOD DIE YOUNG, THE (1954, Brit.) PR:C
GOOD DISSONANCE LIKE A MAN, A (1977) PR:C
GOOD EARTH, THE (1937) PR:A
GOOD FAIRY, THE (1935) PR:A
GOOD FATHER, THE (1986, Brit.) PR:O
GOOD FELLOWS, THE (1943) PR:A
GOOD GIRLS GO TO PARIS (1939) PR:A
GOOD GUYS ALWAYS WIN, THE (SEE: OUTFIT, THE)
   (1973)
GOOD GUYS AND THE BAD GUYS, THE (1969) PR:A-
   C
GOOD GUYS WEAR BLACK (1978) PR:O
GOOD HUMOR MAN, THE (1950) PR:A
GOOD INTENTIONS (1930) PR:A
GOOD LUCK, MISS WYCKOFF (1979) PR:O
GOOD LUCK, MR. YATES (1943) PR:A
GOOD MARRIAGE, A (SEE: LE BEAU MARIAGE)
   (1982, Fr.)
GOOD MORNING (SEE: OHAYO) (1962, Jap.)
GOOD MORNING. . . AND GOODBYE (1967) PR:O
GOOD MORNING, BABYLON (1987, US/It./Fr.) PR:C-O
GOOD MORNING, BOYS (SEE: WHERE THERE'S A
   WILL) (1937, Brit.)
GOOD MORNING, DOCTOR (SEE: YOU BELONG TO
   ME) (1941)
GOOD MORNING, JUDGE (1943) PR:A
GOOD MORNING, MISS DOVE (1955) PR:A
GOOD MORNING, VIETNAM (1987) PR:O
GOOD MOTHER, THE (1988) PR:O
GOOD NEIGHBOR SAM (1964) PR:A-C
GOOD NEWS (1930) PR:A
GOOD NEWS (1947) PR:AA
GOOD OLD DAYS, THE (1939, Brit.) PR:A
GOOD OLD SCHOOLDAYS (SEE: THOSE WERE THE
   DAYS) (1940)
GOOD OLD SOAK, THE (1937) PR:A
GOOD SAM (1948) PR:A
GOOD SOLDIER SCHWEIK, THE (1963, W. Ger.) PR:C
GOOD SOUP, THE (SEE: LA BONNE SOUPE) (1964,
   Fr./It.)
GOOD SPORT (1931) PR:A
GOOD, THE BAD, AND THE UGLY, THE (1967, It./Sp.)
   PR:O
GOOD TIME GIRL (1950, Brit.) PR:O
GOOD TIMES (1967) PR:A
GOOD WIFE, THE (1986, Aus.) PR:C-O
GOODBYE AGAIN (1933) PR:A
GOODBYE AGAIN (1961, Fr.) PR:C
GOODBYE BROADWAY (1938) PR:A
GOODBYE BRUCE LEE: HIS LAST GAME OF DEATH
   (SEE: GAME OF DEATH, THE) (1976)
GOODBYE CHARLIE (1964) PR:C
GOODBYE, CHILDREN (SEE: AU REVOIR LES EN-
   FANTS) (1988)
GOODBYE COLUMBUS (1969) PR:O
GOODBYE EMMANUELLE (1980, Fr.) PR:O
GOODBYE FRANKLIN HIGH (1978) PR:A
GOODBYE GEMINI (1970, Brit.) PR:O
GOODBYE GIRL, THE (1977) PR:C
GOODBYE LOVE (1934) PR:A
GOODBYE MR. CHIPS (1939, Brit.) PR:AA
GOODBYE, MR. CHIPS (1969, US/Brit.) PR:A

GOODBYE, MOSCOW (1968, Jap.) PR:O
GOODBYE, MY FANCY (1951) PR:A
GOODBYE, MY LADY (1956) PR:AA
GOODBYE, NEW YORK (1985, Israel) PR:O
GOODBYE, NORMA JEAN (1976) PR:O
GOODBYE PEOPLE, THE (1984) PR:A-C
GOODBYE PORK PIE (1981, New Zealand) PR:C
GOODBYE TO THE HILL (SEE: PADDY) (1970, Ireland)
GOODNIGHT, LADIES AND GENTLEMEN (1977, It.)
   PR:C-O
GOODNIGHT SWEETHEART (1944) PR:A
GOODNIGHT VIENNA (SEE: MAGIC NIGHT) (1932,
   Brit.)
GOODWIN SANDS (SEE: LADY FROM THE SEA, THE)
   (1929, Brit.)
GOOFBALLS (1987) PR:C
GOONIES, THE (1985) PR:C
GOOSE AND THE GANDER, THE (1935) PR:A
GOOSE GIRL, THE (1967, W. Ger.) PR:C-O
GOOSE STEP (SEE: BEASTS OF BERLIN) (1939)
GOOSE STEPS OUT, THE (1942, Brit.) PR:A
GOR (1989) PR:C
GORATH (1964, Jap.) PR:C
GORBALS STORY, THE (1950, Brit.) PR:C
GORDEYEV FAMILY, THE (1961, USSR) PR:O
GORDON IL PIRATA NERO (SEE: RAGE OF THE BUC-
   CANEERS) (1962, It.)
GORDON'S WAR (1973) PR:O
GORGO (1961, Brit.) PR:C
GORGON, THE (1964, Brit.) PR:C-O
GORILLA, THE (1931) PR:A
GORILLA, THE (1939) PR:A
GORILLA (SEE: NABONGA) (1944)
GORILLA (1964, Swed.) PR:C
GORILLA AT LARGE (1954) PR:C
GORILLA GREETS YOU, THE (1958, Fr.) PR:C
GORILLA MAN (1942) PR:A
GORILLA SHIP, THE (1932) PR:A
GORILLAS IN THE MIST (1988) PR:C
GORKY PARK (1983) PR:O
GORP (1980) PR:O
GOSPEL ACCORDING TO ST. MATTHEW, THE (1964,
   Fr./It.) PR:A
GOSPEL ACCORDING TO VIC, THE (1986, Brit.) PR:C
GOSPEL ROAD, THE (1973) PR:A
GOSTI IZ GALA KSIJE (SEE: VISITORS FROM THE
   GALAXY) (1981, Yugo.)
GOT IT MADE (1974, Brit.) PR:C-O
GOTCHA! (1985) PR:O
GOTHIC (1987, Brit.) PR:O
GOTTERDAMMERUNG (SEE: DAMNED, THE) (1969,
   It./W. Ger.)
GOUPI MAINS ROUGES (SEE: IT HAPPENED AT THE
   INN) (1945, Fr.)
GOVERNMENT GIRL (1943) PR:A
GOYOKIN (1969, Jap.) PR:O
GRABBERS, THE (SEE: SCAVENGERS, THE) (1969)
GRACE MOORE STORY, THE (SEE: SO THIS IS LOVE)
   (1953)
GRACE QUIGLEY (SEE: ULTIMATE SOLUTION OF
   GRACE QUIGLEY, THE) (1984)
GRACIE ALLEN MURDER CASE, THE (1939) PR:A
GRADUATE, THE (1967) PR:A
GRADUATION DAY (1981) PR:O
GRAFT (1931) PR:C
GRAIL, THE (SEE: LANCELOT OF THE LAKE) (1975,
   Fr.)
GRAN AMORE DEL CONDE DRACULA (SEE:
   DRACULA'S GREAT LOVE) (1972, Sp.)
GRAN VARIETA (1955, It.) PR:A
GRANATOVYY BRASLET (SEE: GARNET BRACELET,
   THE) (1966, USSR)
GRAND CANARY (1934) PR:A
GRAND CANYON (1949) PR:A
GRAND CANYON TRAIL (1948) PR:A
GRAND CENTRAL MURDER (1942) PR:A
GRAND DUKE AND MR. PIMM (SEE: LOVE IS A
   BALL) (1963)
GRAND ESCAPADE, THE (1946, Brit.) PR:A
GRAND EXIT (1935) PR:A
GRAND FINALE (1936, Brit.) PR:A
GRAND HIGHWAY, THE (1988, Fr.) PR:O
GRAND HOTEL (1932) PR:A
GRAND ILLUSION (1937, Fr.) PR:A
GRAND JURY (1936) PR:A
GRAND JURY SECRETS (1939) PR:A
GRAND KHAN (SEE: MARCO POLO) (1962, Fr./It.)
GRAND MANEUVER, THE (1956, Fr.) PR:C
GRAND NATIONAL NIGHT (SEE: WICKED WIFE,
   THE) (1953, Brit.)
GRAND OLD GIRL (1935) PR:A
GRAND OLE OPRY (1940) PR:A
GRAND PARADE, THE (1930) PR:A
GRAND PRIX (1934, Brit.) PR:A
GRAND PRIX (1966) PR:O

GRAND SLAM (1933) PR:A
GRAND SLAM (1968, It./Sp./W. Ger.) PR:A-C
GRAND SUBSTITUTION, THE (1965, Hong Kong) PR:C
GRAND THEFT AUTO (1977) PR:C
GRANDAD RUDD (1935, Aus.) PR:A
GRANDMOTHER'S HOUSE (1989) PR:O
GRANDPA GOES TO TOWN (1940) PR:A
GRANDVIEW, U.S.A. (1984) PR:O
GRANNY GET YOUR GUN (1940) PR:A
GRAPES OF WRATH (1940) PR:A
GRASS EATER, THE (1961) PR:C
GRASS IS GREENER, THE (1960, Brit.) PR:A
GRASS IS SINGING, THE (1982, Brit./Swed.) PR:A
GRASS IS SINGING, THE (SEE: KILLING HEAT) (1982,
   Brit./Swed.)
GRASSHOPPER, THE (1970) PR:O
GRAVE OF THE VAMPIRE (1972) PR:O
GRAVE ROBBERS FROM OUTER SPACE (SEE: PLAN
   9 FROM OUTER SPACE) (1959)
GRAVESIDE STORY, THE (SEE: COMEDY OF HOR-
   RORS, THE) (1964)
GRAVEYARD OF HORROR (1971, Sp.) PR:O
GRAVEYARD SHIFT (1987) PR:C-O
GRAVEYARD TRAMPS (SEE: INVASION OF THE BEE
   GIRLS) (1973)
GRAVY TRAIN, THE (1974) PR:O
GRAY LADY DOWN (1978) PR:C
GRAYEAGLE (1977) PR:C
GRAZIE ZIA (SEE: THANK YOU, AUNT) (1967, It.)
GREASE (1978) PR:A
GREASE 2 (1982) PR:C-O
GREASED LIGHTNING (1977) PR:C
GREASER'S PALACE (1972) PR:C
GREAT ADVENTURE, THE (1955, Swed.) PR:AA
GREAT ADVENTURE, THE (1976, Sp./It.) PR:A
GREAT ALLIGATOR (1980, It.) PR:O
GREAT AMERICAN BROADCAST, THE (1941) PR:A
*GREAT AMERICAN BUGS BUNNY-ROAD RUNNER
   CHASE* (1979) PR:AA
GREAT AMERICAN PASTIME, THE (1956) PR:A
GREAT ARMORED CAR SWINDLE, THE (1964, Brit.)
   PR:A
GREAT AWAKENING, THE (SEE: NEW WINE) (1941)
GREAT BALLOON ADVENTURE, THE (SEE: OLLY
   OLLY OXEN FREE) (1978)
GREAT BALLS OF FIRE (1989) PR:C
GREAT BANK HOAX, THE (1977) PR:C
GREAT BANK ROBBERY, THE (1969) PR:A
GREAT BARRIER, THE (SEE: SILENT BARRIERS)
   (1937, Brit.)
GREAT BIG THING, A (1968, US/Can.) PR:C
GREAT BIG WORLD AND LITTLE CHILDREN, THE
   (1962, Pol.) PR:A
GREAT BRAIN, THE (1978) PR:AA
GREAT BRAIN MACHINE, THE (SEE: BRAIN MA-
   CHINE, THE) (1955, Brit.)
GREAT BRITISH TRAIN ROBBERY, THE (1967, W.
   Ger.) PR:A
GREAT CARUSO, THE (1951) PR:A
GREAT CATHERINE (1968, Brit.) PR:AA
GREAT CHICAGO CONSPIRACY CIRCUS, THE (SEE:
   CHICAGO '70) (1970)
GREAT CITIZEN, THE (1939, USSR) PR:A
GREAT COMMANDMENT, THE (1941) PR:A
GREAT DAN PATCH, THE (1949) PR:AA
GREAT DAWN (SEE: THEY WANTED PEACE) (1940,
   USSR)
GREAT DAWN, THE (1947, It.) PR:A
GREAT DAY (1945, Brit.) PR:A
GREAT DAY, THE (SEE: SPECIAL DAY, A) (1977)
GREAT DAY IN THE MORNING (1956) PR:A
GREAT DECISION, THE (SEE: MEN OF AMERICA)
   (1933)
GREAT DEFENDER, THE (1934, Brit.) PR:A
GREAT DIAMOND ROBBERY, THE (1953) PR:A
GREAT DICTATOR, THE (1940) PR:AA
GREAT DIVIDE, THE (1930) PR:A
GREAT DREAM, THE (SEE: EMBRACERS, THE) (1966)
GREAT ESCAPE, THE (1963) PR:A
GREAT EXPECTATIONS (1934) PR:A
GREAT EXPECTATIONS (1946, Brit.) PR:AA
GREAT EXPECTATIONS (1975, Brit.) PR:AA
GREAT FEED, THE (SEE: LA GRANDE BOUFFE) (1973,
   Fr./It.)
GREAT FLAMARION, THE (1945) PR:A-C
GREAT FLIRTATION, THE (1934) PR:A
GREAT GABBO, THE (1929) PR:C
GREAT GAMBINI, THE (1937) PR:A
GREAT GAME, THE (1930, Brit.) PR:A
GREAT GAME, THE (1953, Brit.) PR:A
GREAT GARRICK, THE (1937) PR:A
GREAT GATSBY, THE (1949) PR:A
GREAT GATSBY, THE (1974) PR:A
GREAT GAY ROAD, THE (1931, Brit.) PR:A
GREAT GENERATION, THE (1986, Hung.) PR:O
GREAT GEORGIA BANK HOAX (SEE: GREAT BANK
   HOAX) (1977)

GREAT GILBERT AND SULLIVAN, THE (1953, Brit.)
PR:A
GREAT GILDERSLEEVE, THE (1942) PR:A
GREAT GOD GOLD (1935) PR:A
GREAT GUNDOWN, THE (1977) PR:O
GREAT GUNFIGHTER, THE (SEE: GUNFIGHT AT
COMANCHE CREEK) (1964)
GREAT GUNS (1941) PR:AA
GREAT GUY (1936) PR:A
GREAT HOPE, THE (1954, It.) PR:C
GREAT HOSPITAL MYSTERY, THE (1937) PR:A
GREAT HOTEL MURDER, THE (1935) PR:A
GREAT IMPERSONATION, THE (1935) PR:A
GREAT IMPERSONATION, THE (1942) PR:A
GREAT IMPOSTOR, THE (1960) PR:A
GREAT JASPER, THE (1933) PR:A
GREAT JESSE JAMES RAID, THE (1953) PR:A
GREAT JEWEL ROBBER, THE (1950) PR:A
GREAT JOHN L., THE (1945) PR:A
GREAT LIE, THE (1941) PR:A
GREAT LOCOMOTIVE CHASE, THE (1956) PR:AA
GREAT LOVER, THE (1931) PR:A
GREAT LOVER, THE (1949) PR:A
GREAT MAC ARTHY, THE (1975, Aus.) PR:C-O
GREAT MAN, THE (1957) PR:A
GREAT MAN VOTES, THE (1939) PR:A
GREAT MANHUNT, THE (SEE: DOOLINS OF OKLA-
HOMA) (1949)
GREAT MANHUNT, THE (1951, Brit.) PR:A
GREAT MAN'S LADY, THE (1942) PR:A
GREAT MC GONAGALL, THE (1975, Brit.) PR:O
GREAT MC GINTY, THE (1940) PR:A
GREAT MEADOW, THE (1931) PR:A
GREAT MIKE, THE (1944) PR:A
GREAT MISSOURI RAID, THE (1950) PR:A
GREAT MR. HANDEL, THE (1942, Brit.) PR:A
GREAT MR. NOBODY, THE (1941) PR:A
GREAT MOMENT, THE (1944) PR:A
GREAT MOUSE DETECTIVE, THE (1986) PR:AA
GREAT MUPPET CAPER, THE (1981, Brit.) PR:AA
GREAT NORTHFIELD, MINNESOTA RAID, THE (1972)
PR:O
GREAT O'MALLEY, THE (1937) PR:A
GREAT OUTDOORS, THE (1988) PR:A-C
GREAT PLANE ROBBERY, THE (1940) PR:A
GREAT PLANE ROBBERY, THE (1950) PR:A
GREAT PONY RAID, THE (1968, Brit.) PR:AA
GREAT POWER, THE (1929) PR:A
GREAT PROFILE, THE (1940) PR:A
GREAT RACE, THE (1965) PR:A-C
GREAT RADIO MYSTERY, THE (SEE: TAKE THE
STAND) (1934)
GREAT RUPERT, THE (1950) PR:AA
GREAT ST. TRINIAN'S TRAIN ROBBERY, THE (1966,
Brit.) PR:AA
GREAT SANTINI, THE (1979) PR:C
GREAT SCHNOZZLE, THE (SEE: PALOOKA) (1934)
GREAT SCOUT AND CATHOUSE THURSDAY, THE
(1976) PR:O
GREAT SINNER, THE (1949) PR:A
GREAT SIOUX MASSACRE, THE (1965) PR:A
GREAT SIOUX UPRISING, THE (1953) PR:A
GREAT SMOKEY ROADBLOCK, THE (1978) PR:C
GREAT SPY CHASE, THE (1966, Fr.) PR:C
GREAT SPY MISSION, THE (SEE: OPERATION CROSS-
BOW) (1965, US/It.)
GREAT ST. LOUIS BANK ROBBERY, THE (1959) PR:C-
O
GREAT STAGECOACH ROBBERY (1945) PR:A
GREAT STUFF (1933, Brit.) PR:A
GREAT SWINDLE, THE (1941) PR:A
GREAT TEXAS DYNAMITE CHASE, THE (1976) PR:O
GREAT TRAIN ROBBERY, THE (1941) PR:A
GREAT TRAIN ROBBERY, THE (1979, Brit.) PR:A
GREAT VAN ROBBERY, THE (1963, Brit.) PR:O
GREAT VICTOR HERBERT, THE (1939) PR:AA
GREAT WALDO PEPPER, THE (1975) PR:C
GREAT WALL, THE (1965, Jap.) PR:O
GREAT WALL, A (1986) PR:A
GREAT WALL OF CHINA, THE (1970, Brit.) PR:C-O
GREAT WALTZ, THE (1938) PR:A
GREAT WALTZ, THE (1972) PR:AA
GREAT WAR, THE (1961, Fr./It.) PR:O
GREAT WHITE, THE (1982, It.) PR:O
GREAT WHITE HOPE, THE (1970) PR:C-O
GREAT YEARNING, THE (1930, Ger.) PR:A
GREAT ZIEGFELD, THE (1936) PR:A
GREATER LOVE, THE (SEE: RIDER OF THE PLAINS)
(1934)
GREATEST, THE (1977, US/Brit.) PR:C-O
GREATEST LOVE, THE (1954, It.) PR:C
GREATEST SHOW ON EARTH, THE (1952) PR:AA
GREATEST STORY EVER TOLD, THE (1965) PR:AA
GREED IN THE SUN (1965, Fr./It.) PR:O
GREED OF WILLIAM HART, THE (1948, Brit.) PR:C-O
GREEK STREET (SEE: LATIN LOVE) (1930, Brit.)
GREEK TYCOON, THE (1978) PR:O
GREEKS HAD A WORD FOR THEM (1932) PR:A

GREEN BERETS, THE (1968) PR:C
GREEN BUDDHA, THE (1954, Brit.) PR:A
GREEN CARNATION (SEE: MAN WITH THE GREEN
CARNATION, THE) (1960)
GREEN CARNATION, THE (SEE: GREEN BUDDHA,
THE) (1954, Brit.)
GREEN COCKATOO, THE (1947, Brit.) PR:A
GREEN DOLPHIN STREET (1947) PR:A-C
GREEN-EYED BLONDE, THE (1957) PR:C
GREEN EYES (1934) PR:A
GREEN FIELDS (1937) PR:A
GREEN FINGERS (1947, Brit.) PR:A
GREEN FIRE (1955) PR:C
GREEN FOR DANGER (1946, Brit.) PR:A
GREEN GLOVE, THE (1952) PR:A
GREEN GODDESS, THE (1930) PR:A
GREEN GRASS OF WYOMING (1948) PR:AA
GREEN GROW THE RUSHES (1951, Brit.) PR:A
GREEN HELL (1940) PR:A
GREEN HELMET, THE (1961, Brit.) PR:A
GREEN ICE (1981, Brit.) PR:C
GREEN LIGHT (1937) PR:A
GREEN MAN, THE (1957, Brit.) PR:A
GREEN MANSIONS (1959) PR:A
GREEN MARE, THE (1961, Fr./It.) PR:O
GREEN MONKEY (SEE: BLUE MONKEY) (1988)
GREEN PACK, THE (1934, Brit.) PR:C
GREEN PASTURES (1936) PR:AA
GREEN PROMISE, THE (1949) PR:A
GREEN ROOM, THE (1978, Fr.) PR:C-O
GREEN SCARF, THE (1954, Brit.) PR:A
GREEN SLIME, THE (1969, US/Jap.) PR:C
GREEN TREE, THE (1965, It.) PR:A
GREEN YEARS, THE (1946) PR:A
GREEN-EYED WOMAN (SEE: TAKE A LETTER, DAR-
LING) (1942)
GREENE MURDER CASE, THE (1929) PR:A
GREENGAGE SUMMER, THE (SEE: LOSS OF INNO-
CENCE) (1961, Brit.)
GREENWICH VILLAGE (1944) PR:A
GREENWICH VILLAGE STORY (1963) PR:C
GREENWOOD TREE, THE (SEE: UNDER THE GREEN-
WOOD TREE) (1930, Brit.)
GREGORY'S GIRL (1982, Brit.) PR:C
GREH (1962, Yugo./W. Ger.) PR:O
GREMLINS (1984) PR:O
GRENDEL GRENDEL GRENDEL (1981, Aus.) PR:AA
GREY FOX, THE (1983, Can.) PR:C
GREYFRIARS BOBBY (1961, Brit.) PR:AA
GREYHOUND LIMITED, THE (1929) PR:A
*GREYSTOKE: THE LEGEND OF TARZAN, LORD OF
THE APES* (1984, Brit.) PR:C
GRIBOUILLE (SEE: HEART OF PARIS) (1939, Fr.)
GRIDIRON FLASH (1935) PR:A
GRIEF STREET (1931) PR:A
GRIGSBY (SEE: LAST GRENADE, THE) (1970, Brit.)
GRIJPSTRA AND DE GIER (SEE: OUTSIDER IN AM-
STERDAM) (1983, Neth.)
GRIM REAPER, THE (1981, It.) PR:O
GRINGO (1963, It./Sp.) PR:O
GRIP OF THE STRANGLER (SEE: HAUNTED STRAN-
GLER, THE) (1958, Brit.)
GRISBI (1953, Fr.) PR:C
GRISSLY'S MILLIONS (1945) PR:A
GRISSOM GANG, THE (1971) PR:C-O
GRITOS EN LA NOCHE (SEE: AWFUL DR. ORLOFF,
THE) (1964, Fr./Sp.)
GRIZZLY (1976) PR:C
GROOM WORE SPURS, THE (1951) PR:A
GROOVE TUBE, THE (1974) PR:O
GROSS ANATOMY (1989) PR:C
GROUCH, THE (1961, Gr.) PR:A
GROUND ZERO (1973) PR:O
GROUND ZERO (1989, Aus.) PR:C
GROUNDS FOR MARRIAGE (1950) PR:A
GROUNDSTAR CONSPIRACY, THE (1972, Can.) PR:C
GROUP, THE (1966) PR:O
GROUPIE GIRL (SEE: I AM A GROUPIE) (1970, Brit.)
GROVE, THE (SEE: NAKED ZOO, THE) (1970)
GROWING PAINS (SEE: BAD MANNERS) (1984)
GROWN-UP CHILDREN (1963, USSR) PR:A
GRUESOME TWOSOME (1968) PR:O
GRUMPY (1930) PR:A
GRUNER FELDER (SEE: GREEN FIELDS) (1937)
GRUNT! THE WRESTLING MOVIE (1985) PR:O
GRUPPO DI FAMIGLIA IN UN INTERNO (SEE: CON-
VERSATION PIECE) (1976, Fr./It.)
GUADALAJARA (1943, Mex.) PR:A
GUADALCANAL DIARY (1943) PR:C
GUARD THAT GIRL (1935) PR:A
GUARDIAN OF HELL (1985, It.) PR:O
GUARDIAN OF THE WILDERNESS (1977) PR:AA
GUARDSMAN, THE (1931) PR:A
GUDRUN (SEE: SUDDENLY, A WOMAN!) (1963, Den.)
GUERRE PLANETARI (SEE: BATTLE OF THE
WORLDS) (1961, It.)
GUERRE SECRET (SEE: DIRTY GAME, THE) (1965,
Fr./It./W. Ger.)

GUERRILLA GIRL (1953) PR:C
GUESS WHAT!?! (SEE: GUESS WHAT WE LEARNED
IN SCHOOL TODAY?) (1970)
GUESS WHAT HAPPENED TO COUNT DRACULA
(1970) PR:O
GUESS WHAT WE LEARNED IN SCHOOL TODAY?
(1970) PR:O
GUESS WHO'S COMING TO DINNER (1967) PR:C
GUEST, THE (1963, Brit.) PR:C
GUEST, THE (1977, South Africa) PR:O
GUEST HOUSE, THE (SEE: IN OLD CHEYENNE) (1931)
GUEST IN THE HOUSE (1944) PR:A
GUEST OF HONOR (1934, Brit.) PR:A
GUEST WIFE (1945) PR:A
GUESTS ARE COMING (1965, Pol.) PR:A
GUEULE D'ANGE (SEE: PLEASURES AND VICES)
(1962, Fr.)
GUIDE, THE (1965, US/India) PR:A
GUIDE FOR THE MARRIED MAN, A (1967) PR:C
GUILIA E GUILIA (SEE: JULIA AND JULIA) (1988)
GUILT (1930, Brit.) PR:A
GUILT (1967, Swed.) PR:O
GUILT IS MY SHADOW (1950, Brit.) PR:O
GUILT IS NOT MINE (1968, It.) PR:A
GUILT OF JANET AMES, THE (1947) PR:A
GUILTY? (1930) PR:A
GUILTY, THE (1947) PR:C
GUILTY? (1956, Brit.) PR:C
GUILTY AS CHARGED (SEE: GUILTY AS HELL) (1932)
GUILTY AS HELL (1932) PR:A
GUILTY BYSTANDER (1950) PR:C
GUILTY GENERATION, THE (1931) PR:A
GUILTY HANDS (1931) PR:C
GUILTY MELODY (1936, Brit.) PR:A
GUILTY OF TREASON (1950) PR:C
GUILTY PARENTS (1934) PR:C
GUILTY TRAILS (1938) PR:A
GUINEA PIG, THE (SEE: OUTSIDER, THE) (1949, Brit.)
GUINGUETTE (1959, Fr.) PR:C
GULD OG GRONNE SKOVE (SEE: GOLDEN MOUN-
TAINS) (1958, Den.)
GULLIVER'S TRAVELS (1939) PR:AA
GULLIVER'S TRAVELS (1977, Brit./Bel.) PR:AA
GULLIVER'S TRAVELS BEYOND THE MOON (1966,
Jap.) PR:AA
GUMBALL RALLY, THE (1976) PR:A
GUMBO YA-YA (SEE: GIRLS! GIRLS! GIRLS!) (1962)
GUMSHOE (1972, Brit.) PR:C
GUN, THE (1978, It.) PR:O
GUN BATTLE AT MONTEREY (1957) PR:C
GUN BELT (1953) PR:A
GUN BROTHERS (1956) PR:A
GUN CODE (1940) PR:A
GUN CRAZY (1949) PR:O
GUN DUEL IN DURANGO (1957) PR:A
GUN FEVER (1958) PR:O
GUN FIGHT (1961) PR:C
GUN FOR A COWARD (1957) PR:O
GUN FURY (1953) PR:A
GUN GLORY (1957) PR:A
GUN HAND, THE (SEE: HE RIDES TALL) (1964)
GUN HAWK, THE (1963) PR:C
GUN JUSTICE (1934) PR:A
GUN LAW (1933) PR:A
GUN LAW (1938) PR:A
GUN LAW JUSTICE (1949) PR:A
GUN LORDS OF STIRRUP BASIN (1937) PR:A
GUN MAN FROM BODIE, THE (1941) PR:A
GUN MOLL (SEE: JIGSAW) (1949)
GUN PACKER (1938) PR:A
GUN PLAY (1936) PR:A
GUN RANGER, THE (1937) PR:A
GUN RIDERS, THE (1969) PR:O
GUN RUNNER (1949) PR:A
GUN RUNNER, THE (SEE: SANTIAGO) (1956)
GUN RUNNER (1969) PR:O
GUN RUNNERS, THE (1958) PR:A
GUN SMOKE (1931) PR:A
GUN SMOKE (1936) PR:A
GUN SMUGGLERS (1948) PR:A
GUN STREET (1962) PR:C
GUN TALK (1948) PR:A
GUN THAT WON THE WEST, THE (1955) PR:C
GUN THE MAN DOWN (1957) PR:C
GUN TOWN (1946) PR:A
GUNEY'S THE WALL (SEE: WALL, THE) (1983, Fr.)
GUNFIGHT, A (1971) PR:O
GUNFIGHT AT COMANCHE CREEK (1964) PR:A
GUNFIGHT AT DODGE CITY, THE (1959) PR:A
GUNFIGHT AT RED SANDS (SEE: GRINGO) (1963,
It./Sp.)
GUNFIGHT AT THE O.K. CORRAL (1957) PR:C
GUNFIGHT IN ABILENE (1967) PR:C
GUNFIGHTER, THE (1950) PR:C
GUNFIGHTERS (1947) PR:A
GUNFIGHTERS OF ABILENE (1960) PR:A
GUNFIGHTERS OF CASA GRANDE (1965, US/Sp.) PR:C
GUNFIRE (1950) PR:A

GUNFIRE AT INDIAN GAP (1957) PR:A
GUNG HO! (1943) PR:C
GUNG HO (1986) PR:C
GUNGA DIN (1939) PR:C
GUNMAN HAS ESCAPED, A (1948, Brit.) PR:C
GUNMAN'S CODE (1946) PR:A
GUNMAN'S WALK (1958) PR:C
GUNMEN FROM LAREDO (1959) PR:O
GUNMEN OF ABILENE (1950) PR:A
GUNMEN OF THE RIO GRANDE (1965, Fr./It./Sp.) PR:C
GUNN (1967) PR:C
GUNNING FOR JUSTICE (1948) PR:A
GUNPLAY (1951) PR:A
GUNPOINT! (SEE: AT GUNPOINT) (1955)
GUNPOINT (1966) PR:A
GUNPOWDER (1987, Brit.) PR:C
GUNRUNNER, THE (1989, Can.) PR:C
GUNRUNNERS, THE (SEE: GUN RUNNER) (1969)
GUNS (1980, Fr.) PR:O
GUNS A'BLAZING (SEE: LAW AND ORDER) (1932)
GUNS AND GUITARS (1936) PR:A
GUNS AND THE FURY, THE (1983) PR:O
GUNS AT BATASI (1964, Brit.) PR:C
GUNS FOR SAN SEBASTIAN (1968, US/Fr./Mex./It.) PR:O
GUNS, GIRLS AND GANGSTERS (1958) PR:C
GUNS IN THE AFTERNOON (SEE: RIDE THE HIGH COUNTRY) (1962)
GUNS IN THE DARK (1937) PR:A
GUNS IN THE HEATHER (1968, Brit.) PR:AA
GUNS OF A STRANGER (1973) PR:A
GUNS OF DARKNESS (1962, Brit.) PR:C
GUNS OF DIABLO (1964) PR:C
GUNS OF FORT PETTICOAT, THE (1957) PR:A
GUNS OF HATE (1948) PR:A
GUNS OF NAVARONE, THE (1961, US/Brit.) PR:C
GUNS OF THE BLACK WITCH (1961, Fr./It.) PR:C
GUNS OF THE LAW (1944) PR:A
GUNS OF THE MAGNIFICENT SEVEN (1969) PR:C
GUNS OF THE PECOS (1937) PR:A
GUNS OF THE TIMBERLAND (1960) PR:A
GUNS OF THE TREES (1964) PR:O
GUNS OF WRATH (SEE: GUNS OF HATE) (1948)
GUNS OF WYOMING (SEE: CATTLE KING) (1963)
GUNS, SIN AND BATHTUB GIN (SEE: LADY IN RED, THE) (1979)
GUNSIGHT RIDGE (1957) PR:A
GUNSLINGER (1956) PR:C
GUNSLINGERS (1950) PR:A
GUNSMOKE (1953) PR:A
GUNSMOKE IN TUCSON (1958) PR:A
GUNSMOKE MESA (1944) PR:A
GUNSMOKE RANCH (1937) PR:A
GUNSMOKE TRAIL (1938) PR:A
GURU, THE (1969, US/India) PR:C
GURU, THE MAD MONK (1971) PR:O
GUS (1976) PR:AA
GUSARSKAYA BALLADA (SEE: BALLAD OF A HUSSAR, THE) (1963)
GUTS IN THE SUN (SEE: CHECKERBOARD) (1959, Fr.)
GUTTER GIRLS (1964, Brit.) PR:O
GUV'NOR, THE (SEE: MISTER HOBO) (1936, Brit.)
GUY, A GAL, AND A PAL, A (1945) PR:A
GUY CALLED CAESAR, A (1962, Brit.) PR:A
GUY COULD CHANGE, A (1946) PR:A
GUY NAMED JOE, A (1944) PR:A
GUY WHO CAME BACK, THE (1951) PR:A
GUY WITH A GRIN (SEE: NO TIME FOR COMEDY) (1940)
GUYANA, CULT OF THE DAMNED (1980, Mex./Sp./Pan.) PR:O
GUYS AND DOLLS (1955) PR:A
GWENDOLINE (SEE: PERILS OF GWENDOLINE, THE) (1984, Fr.)
GYAKUTEN RYOKO (SEE: TOPSY-TURVY JOURNEY) (1970, Jap.)
GYCKLARNAS AFTON (SEE: NAKED NIGHT, THE) (1953, Swed.)
GYMKATA (1985) PR:O
GYPSY (1937, Brit.) PR:A
GYPSY (1962) PR:C
GYPSY AND THE GENTLEMAN, THE (1958, Brit.) PR:O
GYPSY COLT (1954) PR:AA
GYPSY FURY (1950, Fr.) PR:A
GYPSY GIRL (1966, Brit.) PR:C
GYPSY MELODY (1936, Brit.) PR:A
GYPSY MOTHS, THE (1969) PR:O
GYPSY WILDCAT (1944) PR:A

H

H-MAN, THE (1959, Jap.) PR:O
H.A.R.M. MACHINE, THE (SEE: AGENT FOR H.A.R.M.) (1966)
H.E.A.L.T.H. (SEE: HEALTH) (1980)
H.M. PULHAM, ESQ. (1941) PR:A
H.M.S. DEFIANT (SEE: DAMN THE DEFIANT!) (1962, Brit.)
H.O.T.S. (1979) PR:O

HA'PENNY BREEZE (1950, Brit.) PR:A
HABRICHA EL HASHEMESH (SEE: ESCAPE TO THE SUN) (1972, Fr./Israel/W. Ger.)
HADAKA NO SHIMA (SEE: ISLAND, THE) (1962, Jap.)
HADAKA NO TAISHO (SEE: NAKED GENERAL, THE) (1964, Jap.)
HADLEY'S REBELLION (1984) PR:C
HAGBARD AND SIGNE (1968, Den./Iceland/Swed.) PR:C-O
HAI CHIUSO UN'ALTRA VOLTA (SEE: RETURN OF SABATA) (1972, Fr./It./W. Ger.)
HAII. (1973) PR:O
HAIL AND FAREWELL (1936, Brit.) PR:A
HAIL, HERO! (1969) PR:C
HAIL MAFIA (1965, Fr./It.) PR:O
HAIL, MARY (1985, Fr./Switz./Brit.) PR:O
HAIL THE CONQUERING HERO (1944) PR:A
HAIL TO THE CHIEF (SEE: HAIL) (1972)
HAIL TO THE RANGERS (1943) PR:A
HAIR (1979) PR:C-O
HAIR OF THE DOG (1962, Brit.) PR:A
HAIRSPRAY (1988) PR:A-C
HAIRY APE, THE (1944) PR:A
HAKUCHI (SEE: IDIOT, THE) (1963, Jap.)
HAKUJA DEN (SEE: PANDA AND THE MAGIC SERPENT) (1961, Jap.)
HALCON Y LA PRESA, EL (SEE: BIG GUNDOWN, THE) (1968)
HALF A HERO (1953) PR:AA
HALF A SINNER (1934) PR:A
HALF A SINNER (1940) PR:A
HALF A SIXPENCE (1967, Brit.) PR:A
HALF ANGEL (1936) PR:C
HALF ANGEL (1951) PR:A
HALF-BREED, THE (1952) PR:A
HALF HUMAN (1955, Jap.) PR:C-O
HALF-MARRIAGE (1929) PR:A
HALF MOON STREET (1986) PR:O
HALF-NAKED TRUTH, THE (1932) PR:A
HALF PAST MIDNIGHT (1948) PR:A
HALF PINT, THE (1960) PR:AA
HALF SHOT AT SUNRISE (1930) PR:A
HALF-WAY HOUSE, THE (1945, Brit.) PR:C
HALF WAY TO HEAVEN (1929) PR:A
HALF WAY TO SHANGHAI (1942) PR:C
HALLELUJAH (1929) PR:A
HALLELUJAH, I'M A BUM (1933) PR:A
HALLELUJAH, I'M A THIEF (SEE: HALLELUJAH, I'M A BUM) (1933)
HALLELUJAH THE HILLS (1963) PR:C
HALLELUJAH TRAIL, THE (1965) PR:A
HALLIDAY BRAND, THE (1957) PR:C
HALLOWEEN (1978) PR:O
HALLOWEEN II (1981) PR:O
HALLOWEEN III: SEASON OF THE WITCH (1982) PR:O
HALLOWEEN IV: THE RETURN OF MICHAEL MYERS (1988) PR:O
HALLOWEEN 5: THE REVENGE OF MICHAEL MYERS (1989) PR:O
HALLS OF ANGER (1970) PR:O
HALLS OF MONTEZUMA (1951) PR:C
HALLUCINATION GENERATION (1966) PR:C
HALLUCINATORS, THE (SEE: NAKED ZOO, THE) (1970)
HAMBONE AND HILLIE (1984) PR:A
HAMBURGER HILL (1987) PR:O
HAMBURGER. . . THE MOTION PICTURE (1986) PR:O
HAMLET (1948, Brit.) PR:A
HAMLET (1962, W. Ger.) PR:A
HAMLET (1964) PR:A
HAMLET (1966, USSR) PR:C
HAMLET (1969, Brit.) PR:A
HAMLET (1976, Brit.) PR:O
HAMMER (1972) PR:O
HAMMER THE TOFF (1952, Brit.) PR:A
HAMMERHEAD (1968, Brit.) PR:C
HAMMERSMITH IS OUT (1972) PR:C
HAMMETT (1982) PR:C
HAMMOND MYSTERY, THE (SEE: UNDYING MONSTER, THE) (1942)
HAMNSTED (SEE: PORT OF CALL) (1948, Swed.)
HAMP (SEE: KING AND COUNTRY) (1964, Brit.)
HAMPSTER OF HAPPINESS (SEE: SECOND-HAND HEARTS) (1980)
HANA TO NAMIDA TO HONOO (SEE: PERFORMERS, THE) (1970, Jap.)
HAND, THE (1960, Brit.) PR:C
HAND, THE (1981) PR:O
HAND IN HAND (1960, Brit.) PR:AA
HAND IN THE TRAP, THE (1963, Arg./Sp.) PR:C
HAND OF DEATH (1962) PR:C
HAND OF NIGHT, THE (1968, Brit.) PR:C
HANDCUFFED (1929) PR:A
HANDCUFFS, LONDON (1955, Brit.) PR:A
HANDFUL OF CLOUDS, A (SEE: DOORWAY TO HELL) (1930)
HANDFUL OF DUST, A (1988, Brit.) PR:C
HANDFUL OF RICE (SEE: JUNGLE OF CHANG) (1951)

HANDGUN (SEE: DEEP IN THE HEART) (1983)
HANDLE WITH CARE (1932) PR:A
HANDLE WITH CARE (1935, Brit.) PR:A
HANDLE WITH CARE (1958) PR:A
HANDLE WITH CARE (1964) PR:A
HANDLE WITH CARE (SEE: CITIZENS BAND) (1977)
HANDS ACROSS THE BORDER (1943) PR:A
HANDS ACROSS THE TABLE (1935) PR:A
HANDS OF A STRANGER (1962) PR:C
HANDS OF DESTINY (1954, Brit.) PR:A
HANDS OF ORLAC, THE (SEE: MAD LOVE) (1935)
HANDS OF ORLAC, THE (1964, Brit./Fr.) PR:A
HANDS OF STEEL (1986, It.) PR:O
HANDS OF THE RIPPER (1971, Brit.) PR:O
HANDS OF THE STRANGLER (SEE: HANDS OF ORLAC) (1964, Brit./Fr.)
HANDSOME SERGE (SEE: LE BEAU SERGE) (1958, Fr.)
HANDY ANDY (1934) PR:A
HANG 'EM HIGH (1968) PR:C
HANGAR 18 (1980) PR:A
HANGED MAN'S FARM (SEE: LA FERME DU PENDU) (1948, Fr.)
HANGING TREE, THE (1959) PR:C
HANGMAN, THE (1959) PR:A
HANGMAN WAITS, THE (1947, Brit.) PR:C
HANGMAN'S KNOT (1952) PR:C
HANGMAN'S WHARF (1950, Brit.) PR:A
HANGMEN ALSO DIE! (1943) PR:C-O
HANGOVER (SEE: FEMALE JUNGLE, THE) (1955)
HANGOVER SQUARE (1945) PR:C
HANGUP (1974) PR:O
HANK WILLIAMS STORY, THE (SEE: YOUR CHEATIN' HEART) (1964)
HANK WILLIAMS: THE SHOW HE NEVER GAVE (1982, Can.) PR:C
HANKY-PANKY (1982) PR:A-C
HANNAH AND HER SISTERS (1986) PR:C
HANNAH K. (1983, Fr.) PR:C
HANNAH LEE (1953) PR:A
HANNA'S WAR (1988) PR:C-O
HANNIBAL (1960, It.) PR:A
HANNIBAL BROOKS (1969, Brit.) PR:C
HANNIE CALDER (1971, Brit.) PR:O
HANOI HANNA – QUEEN OF CHINA (SEE: CHELSEA GIRLS, THE) (1966)
HANOI HILTON, THE (1987) PR:O
HANOVER STREET (1979, Brit.) PR:C
HANS CHRISTIAN ANDERSEN (1952) PR:AA
HANSEL AND GRETEL (1954) PR:AA
HANSEL AND GRETEL (1965, W. Ger.) PR:AA
HANUSSEN (1989, Hung./W. Ger.) PR:A
HANY AZ ORA, VEKKER UR? (SEE: WHAT'S THE TIME, MR. CLOCK?) (1985, Hung.)
HAPPENING, THE (1967) PR:C
HAPPENING IN AFRICA (SEE: KAREN, THE LOVEMAKER) (1970)
HAPPIDROME (1943, Brit.) PR:A
HAPPIEST DAYS OF YOUR LIFE (1950, Brit.) PR:A
HAPPIEST MILLIONAIRE, THE (1967) PR:AA
HAPPILY EVER AFTER (SEE: MORE THAN A MIRACLE) (1967, Fr./It.)
HAPPINESS (SEE: LE BONHEUR) (1966, Fr.)
HAPPINESS AHEAD (1934) PR:A
HAPPINESS CAGE, THE (1972) PR:C
HAPPINESS C.O.D. (1935) PR:A
HAPPINESS OF THREE WOMEN, THE (1954, Brit.) PR:A
HAPPINESS OF US ALONE (1962, Jap.) PR:A
HAPPY (1934, Brit.) PR:A
HAPPY ALEXANDER (SEE: VERY HAPPY ALEXANDER) (1969, Fr.)
HAPPY ANNIVERSARY (1959) PR:C
HAPPY AS THE GRASS WAS GREEN (1973) PR:A
HAPPY BIRTHDAY, DAVY (1970) PR:O
HAPPY BIRTHDAY, GEMINI (1980) PR:O
HAPPY BIRTHDAY TO ME (1981, Can.) PR:O
HAPPY BIRTHDAY, WANDA JUNE (1971) PR:C
HAPPY DAYS (1930) PR:A
HAPPY DAYS ARE HERE AGAIN (1936, Brit.) PR:A
HAPPY DAYS REVUE (SEE: HAPPY DAYS ARE HERE AGAIN) (1936, Brit.)
HAPPY DEATHDAY (1969, Brit.) PR:C
HAPPY END (1968, Czech.) PR:C-O
HAPPY ENDING, THE (1931, Brit.) PR:A
HAPPY ENDING, THE (1969) PR:C
HAPPY EVER AFTER (1932, Ger./Brit.) PR:A
HAPPY EVER AFTER (SEE: TONIGHT'S THE NIGHT) (1954, Brit.)
HAPPY FAMILY, THE (SEE: MERRY FRINKS, THE) (1934)
HAPPY FAMILY, THE (1936, Brit.) PR:A
HAPPY FAMILY, THE (SEE: MR. LORD SAYS NO) (1952)
HAPPY GO LOVELY (1951, Brit.) PR:A
HAPPY GO LUCKY (SEE: HALLELUJAH, I'M A BUM) (1933)
HAPPY-GO-LUCKY (1937) PR:A
HAPPY GO LUCKY (1943) PR:AA

HAPPY GYPSIES (SEE: I EVEN MET HAPPY GYPSIES) (1968, Yugo.)
HAPPY HOOKER, THE (1975) PR:O
HAPPY HOOKER GOES HOLLYWOOD, THE (1980) PR:O
HAPPY HOOKER GOES TO WASHINGTON, THE (1977) PR:O
HAPPY HOUR (1987) PR:O
HAPPY IS THE BRIDE (1958, Brit.) PR:A
HAPPY LAND (1943) PR:A
HAPPY LANDING (SEE: FLYING HIGH) (1931)
HAPPY LANDING (1934) PR:A
HAPPY LANDING (1938) PR:A
HAPPY MOTHER'S DAY. . . LOVE, GEORGE (1973) PR:C
HAPPY NEW YEAR (1987) PR:C
HAPPY NEW YEAR (1973, Fr./It.) PR:C
HAPPY ROAD, THE (1957, US/Fr.) PR:A
HAPPY THIEVES, THE (1962) PR:C
HAPPY TIME, THE (1952) PR:AA
HAPPY TIMES (SEE: INSPECTOR GENERAL) (1949)
HAPPY YEARS, THE (1950) PR:A
HAR HAR DU DITT LIV (SEE: HERE'S YOUR LIFE) (1966, Swed.)
HARA-KIRI (SEE: BATTLE, THE) (1934, Fr.)
HARAKIRI (1963, Jap.) PR:O
HARASSED HERO, THE (1954, Brit.) PR:A
HARBOR LIGHT YOKOHAMA (1970, Jap.) PR:C-O
HARBOR LIGHTS (1963) PR:A
HARBOR OF MISSING MEN (1950) PR:A
HARD-BOILED CANARY (SEE: THERE'S MAGIC IN MUSIC) (1941)
HARD BOILED MAHONEY (1947) PR:A
HARD BUNCH, THE (SEE: HARD TRAIL) (1969)
HARD CHOICES (1984) PR:O
HARD CONTRACT (1969) PR:C
HARD COUNTRY (1981) PR:O
HARD DAY'S NIGHT, A (1964, Brit.) PR:A
HARD DRIVER (SEE: LAST AMERICAN HERO, THE) (1973)
HARD, FAST, AND BEAUTIFUL (1951) PR:A
HARD GUY (1941) PR:A
HARD HOMBRE (1931) PR:A
HARD KNOCKS (1980, Aus.) PR:O
HARD MAN, THE (1957) PR:A
HARD ON THE TRAIL (SEE: HARD TRAIL) (1969)
HARD PART BEGINS, THE (1973, Can.) PR:C
HARD RIDE, THE (1971) PR:C
HARD ROAD, THE (1970) PR:O
HARD ROCK HARRIGAN (1935) PR:A
HARD STEEL (1941, Brit.) PR:A
HARD TICKET TO HAWAII (1987) PR:O
HARD TIMES (1975) PR:A-C
HARD TIMES (1988, Portugal) PR:A
HARD TO GET (1929) PR:A
HARD TO GET (1938) PR:A
HARD TO HANDLE (1933) PR:A
HARD TO HANDLE (SEE: PAID TO DANCE) (1937)
HARD TO HOLD (1984) PR:A-C
HARD TRAIL (1969) PR:O
HARD TRAVELING (1985) PR:C
HARD WAY, THE (1942) PR:A-C
HARDBODIES (1984) PR:O
HARDBODIES 2 (1986) PR:O
HARDBOILED ROSE (1929) PR:A
HARDCASE AND FIST (1989) PR:C
HARDCORE (1979) PR:O
HARDER THEY COME, THE (1973, Jamaica) PR:C
HARDER THEY FALL, THE (1956) PR:O
HARDLY WORKING (1981) PR:A
HARDYS RIDE HIGH, THE (1939) PR:AA
HAREM (1985, Fr.) PR:O
HAREM BUNCH; OR WAR AND PIECE, THE (1969) PR:C-O
HAREM GIRL (1952) PR:A
HAREM HOLIDAY (SEE: HARUM SCARUM) (1965)
HARLEM GLOBETROTTERS, THE (1951) PR:A
HARLEM IS HEAVEN (1932) PR:A
HARLEM NIGHTS (1989) PR:O
HARLEM ON THE PRAIRIE (1938) PR:A
HARLEM RIDES THE RANGE (1939) PR:A
HARLEQUIN (1980, Aus.) PR:C-O
HARLOW (1965) PR:C
HARLOW (1965) PR:C
HARMON OF MICHIGAN (1941) PR:A
HARMONY AT HOME (1930) PR:A
HARMONY HEAVEN (1930, Brit.) PR:A
HARMONY LANE (1935) PR:A
HARMONY PARADE (SEE: PIGSKIN PARADE) (1936)
HARMONY ROW (1933, Aus.) PR:A
HARMONY TRAIL (SEE: WHITE STALLION) (1947)
HAROLD AND MAUDE (1971) PR:A-C
HAROLD ROBBINS' THE BETSY (SEE: BETSY, THE) (1978)
HAROLD TEEN (1934) PR:A
HARPER (1966) PR:C
HARPER VALLEY, P.T.A. (1978) PR:C
HARPOON (1948) PR:A
HARRAD EXPERIMENT, THE (1973) PR:O

HARRAD SUMMER, THE (1974) PR:O
HARRIET CRAIG (1950) PR:A-C
HARRIGAN'S KID (1943) PR:A
HARRY AND SON (1984) PR:C
HARRY AND THE HENDERSONS (1987) PR:A-C
HARRY AND TONTO (1974) PR:C
HARRY AND WALTER GO TO NEW YORK (1976) PR:C
HARRY BLACK AND THE TIGER (1958, Brit.) PR:C
HARRY FRIGG (SEE: SECRET WAR OF HARRY FRIGG, THE) (1968)
HARRY IN YOUR POCKET (1973) PR:C
HARRY TRACY—DESPERADO (1982, Can.) PR:C
HARRY'S WAR (1981) PR:C
HARUM SCARUM (1965) PR:A
HARVARD, HERE I COME (1942) PR:A
HARVEST (1939, Fr.) PR:O
HARVEST MELODY (1943) PR:A
HARVESTER, THE (1936) PR:A
HARVEY (1950) PR:A
HARVEY GIRLS, THE (1946) PR:AA
HARVEY MIDDLEMAN, FIREMAN (1965) PR:C
HAS ANYBODY SEEN MY GAL? (1952) PR:A
HASSAN, TERRORIST (1968, Algeria) PR:O
HASTY HEART, THE (1949, Brit.) PR:A
HAT CHECK GIRL (1932) PR:O
HAT CHECK HONEY (1944) PR:A
HAT, COAT AND GLOVE (1934) PR:A
HATARI! (1962) PR:A
HATCHET FOR A HONEYMOON (1969, Sp./It.) PR:O
HATCHET MAN, THE (1932) PR:C-O
HATCHET MURDERS, THE (SEE: DEEP RED) (1976, It.)
HATE FOR HATE (1967, It.) PR:A
HATE IN PARADISE (1938, Brit.) PR:A
HATE SHIP, THE (1930, Brit.) PR:A
HATE WITHIN (SEE: STARK FEAR) (1963)
HATFUL OF RAIN, A (1957) PR:C
HA'TIMHONI (SEE: DREAMER, THE) (1970, US/Israel)
HATRED (1941, Fr.) PR:A
HATS OFF (1937) PR:A
HATS OFF TO RHYTHM (SEE: EARL CARROLL SKETCHBOOK) (1946)
HATTER'S CASTLE (1948, Brit.) PR:C
HATTER'S GHOST, THE (1982, Fr.) PR:C
HAUNTED (1976) PR:O
HAUNTED AND THE HUNTED (SEE: DEMENTIA 13) (1963)
HAUNTED GOLD (1932) PR:A
HAUNTED HONEYMOON (SEE: BUSMAN'S HONEY-MOON) (1940, Brit.)
HAUNTED HONEYMOON (1986) PR:A
HAUNTED HOUSE, THE (1928) PR:A
HAUNTED HOUSE, THE (1940) PR:A
HAUNTED HOUSE OF HORROR (SEE: HORROR HOUSE) (1970, Brit.)
HAUNTED PALACE, THE (1963) PR:C-O
HAUNTED RANCH, THE (1943) PR:A
HAUNTED STRANGLER, THE (1958, Brit.) PR:O
HAUNTING, THE (1963, US/Brit.) PR:C-O
HAUNTING OF CASTLE MONTEGO (SEE: CASTLE OF EVIL) (1967)
HAUNTING OF HAMILTON HIGH, THE (SEE: HELLO MARY LOU: PROM NIGHT II) (1987)
HAUNTING OF JULIA, THE (1981, Brit./Can.) PR:O
HAUNTING OF M, THE (1979) PR:C
HAUNTS (1977) PR:O
HAUPTMANN VON KOEPENICK (SEE: CAPTAIN FROM KOEPENICK) (1933, Ger.)
HAUS DER TAUSEND FREUDEN (SEE: HOUSE OF 1,000 DOLLS) (1967, Sp./W. Ger.)
HAUS DES LEBENS (SEE: HOUSE OF LIFE) (1953, W. Ger.)
HAUTE INFIDELITE (SEE: HIGH INFIDELITY) (1965, Fr./It.)
HAVANA ROSE (1951) PR:A
HAVANA WIDOWS (1933) PR:A
HAVE A HEART (1934) PR:A
HAVE A NICE WEEKEND (1975) PR:O
HAVE ROCKET, WILL TRAVEL (1959) PR:A
HAVING A WILD WEEKEND (1965, Brit.) PR:A
HAVING WONDERFUL CRIME (1945) PR:A
HAVING WONDERFUL TIME (1938) PR:A
HAWAII (1966) PR:C
HAWAII BEACH BOY (SEE: BLUE HAWAII) (1961)
HAWAII CALLS (1938) PR:A
HAWAIIAN BUCKAROO (1938) PR:A
HAWAIIAN NIGHTS (SEE: DOWN TO THEIR LAST YACHT) (1934)
HAWAIIAN NIGHTS (1939) PR:A
HAWAIIANS, THE (1970) PR:C
HAWK, THE (SEE: RIDE HIM COWBOY) (1932)
HAWK OF POWDER RIVER, THE (1948) PR:A
HAWK OF WILD RIVER, THE (1952) PR:A
HAWK THE SLAYER (1980, Brit.) PR:A
HAWKS AND THE SPARROWS, THE (1967, It.) PR:C
HAWLEY'S OF HIGH STREET (1933, Brit.) PR:A
HAWMPS! (1976) PR:A
HAZARD (1948) PR:A
HAZEL'S PEOPLE (1978) PR:C

HAZING, THE (1978) PR:C
HE COULDN'T SAY NO (1938) PR:A
HE COULDN'T TAKE IT (1934) PR:A
HE FOUND A STAR (1941, Brit.) PR:A
HE GYMNE TAXIARCHIA (SEE: NAKED BRIGADE, THE) (1965, US/Gr.)
HE HIRED THE BOSS (1943) PR:A
HE KNEW WOMEN (1930) PR:A
HE KNOWS YOU'RE ALONE (1980) PR:O
HE LAUGHED LAST (1956) PR:A
HE LEARNED ABOUT WOMEN (1933) PR:A
HE LIVED TO KILL (SEE: NIGHT OF TERROR) (1933)
HE LOVED AN ACTRESS (1938, Brit.) PR:A
HE MARRIED HIS WIFE (1940) PR:A
HE OR SHE (SEE: GLEN OR GLENDA) (1953)
HE RAN ALL THE WAY (1951) PR:C
HE RIDES TALL (1964) PR:A
HE, SHE OR IT! (SEE: DOLL, THE) (1963, Fr.)
HE SNOOPS TO CONQUER (1944, Brit.) PR:A
HE STAYED FOR BREAKFAST (1940) PR:A
HE WALKED BY NIGHT (1948) PR:C
HE WAS HER MAN (1934) PR:A-C
HE WHO RIDES A TIGER (1966, Brit.) PR:A
HE WHO SHOOTS FIRST (1966, It.) PR:C
HEAD, THE (1961, W. Ger.) PR:O
HEAD (1968) PR:A
HEAD FOR THE DEVIL, A (SEE: HEAD, THE) (1969, W. Ger.)
HEAD FOR THE HILLS (SEE: SOD SISTERS) (1969)
HEAD OF A TYRANT (1960, Fr./It.) PR:C
HEAD OF THE FAMILY (1933, Brit.) PR:A
HEAD OF THE FAMILY, THE (1967, It./Fr.) PR:C
HEAD OFFICE (1936, Brit.) PR:A
HEAD OFFICE (1986) PR:C
HEAD ON (1971) PR:O
HEAD ON (1981, Can.) PR:O
HEAD OVER HEELS (SEE: CHILLY SCENES OF WINTER) (1979)
HEAD OVER HEELS IN LOVE (1937, Brit.) PR:A
HEAD THAT WOULDN'T DIE (SEE: BRAIN THAT WOULDN'T DIE, THE) (1959)
HEADIN' EAST (1937) PR:A
HEADIN' FOR BROADWAY (1980) PR:C
HEADIN' FOR GOD'S COUNTRY (1943) PR:A
HEADIN' FOR THE RIO GRANDE (1937) PR:A
HEADIN' FOR TROUBLE (1931) PR:A
HEADIN' NORTH (1930) PR:A
HEADING FOR HEAVEN (1947) PR:A
HEADLESS GHOST, THE (1959, Brit.) PR:A
HEADLEYS AT HOME, THE (1939) PR:A
HEADLINE (1943, Brit.) PR:A
HEADLINE CRASHER (1937) PR:A
HEADLINE HUNTERS (1955) PR:A
HEADLINE HUNTERS (1968, Brit.) PR:AA
HEADLINE SHOOTER (1933) PR:A
HEADLINE WOMAN, THE (1935) PR:A
HEADS UP (1930) PR:A
HEADS WE GO (SEE: CHARMING DECEIVER, THE) (1933, Brit.)
HEALER, THE (1935) PR:A
HEALTH (1980) PR:C-O
HEAR ME GOOD (1957) PR:A
HEARSE, THE (1980) PR:A
HEART AND SOUL (1950, It.) PR:A
HEART BEAT (1979) PR:O
HEART IS A LONELY HUNTER, THE (1968) PR:O
HEART LIKE A WHEEL (1983) PR:C
HEART OF A CHILD (1958, Brit.) PR:C
HEART OF A MAN, THE (1959, Brit.) PR:A
HEART OF A NATION, THE (1943, Fr.) PR:A
HEART OF ARIZONA (1938) PR:A
HEART OF DIXIE (1989) PR:C
HEART OF MIDNIGHT (1989) PR:O
HEART OF NEW YORK, THE (SEE: HALLELUJAH, I'M A BUM) (1933)
HEART OF NEW YORK, THE (1932) PR:A
HEART OF PARIS (1939, Fr.) PR:A
HEART OF THE GOLDEN WEST (1942) PR:A
HEART OF THE MATTER, THE (1954, Brit.) PR:A-C
HEART OF THE NORTH (1938) PR:A
HEART OF THE RIO GRANDE (1942) PR:A
HEART OF THE ROCKIES (1937) PR:A
HEART OF THE ROCKIES (1951) PR:A
HEART OF THE STAG (1984, New Zealand) PR:O
HEART OF THE WEST (1937) PR:A
HEART OF VIRGINIA (1948) PR:A
HEART PUNCH (1932) PR:A
HEART SONG (1933, Brit.) PR:A
HEART WITHIN, THE (1957, Brit.) PR:A
HEARTACHES (1947) PR:A
HEARTACHES (1981, Can.) PR:O
HEARTBEAT (1946) PR:A
HEARTBEEPS (1981) PR:A
HEARTBREAK (1931) PR:A
HEARTBREAK HOTEL (1988) PR:C
HEARTBREAK KID, THE (1972) PR:C-O
HEARTBREAK RIDGE (1986) PR:O
HEARTBREAKER (1983) PR:C

HEARTBREAKERS (1984) PR:C-O
HEARTBURN (1986) PR:C-O
HEARTLAND (1980) PR:A
HEART'S DESIRE (1937, Brit.) PR:A
HEARTS DIVIDED (1936) PR:A
HEARTS IN BONDAGE (1936) PR:A
HEARTS IN DIXIE (1929) PR:A
HEARTS IN EXILE (1929) PR:A
HEARTS IN REUNION (SEE: REUNION) (1936)
HEARTS OF FIRE (1987) PR:NR
HEARTS OF HUMANITY (1932) PR:A
HEARTS OF HUMANITY (1936, Brit.) PR:A
HEARTS OF THE WEST (1975) PR:A
HEAT (1970, Arg.) PR:O
HEAT (1987) PR:O
HEAT AND DUST (1983, Brit.) PR:C
HEAT AND SUNLIGHT (1988) PR:O
HEAT LIGHTNING (1934) PR:A
HEAT OF DESIRE (1981, Fr./Sp.) PR:O
HEAT OF MIDNIGHT (1967, Fr.) PR:O
HEAT OF THE SUMMER (1961, Fr.) PR:A
HEAT WAVE (1935, Brit.) PR:A
HEATHCLIFF: THE MOVIE (1986) PR:AA
HEATHERS (1989) PR:O
HEAT'S ON, THE (1943) PR:A-C
HEATWAVE (1954, Brit.) PR:A
HEATWAVE (1983, Aus.) PR:O
HEAVEN BOUND (SEE: BIG TIME OR BUST) (1934)
HEAVEN CAN WAIT (1943) PR:A
HEAVEN CAN WAIT (1978) PR:C
HEAVEN HELP US (1985) PR:O
HEAVEN IS ROUND THE CORNER (1944, Brit.) PR:A
HEAVEN KNOWS, MR. ALLISON (1957) PR:A
HEAVEN ON EARTH (1931) PR:A
HEAVEN ON EARTH (1960, It./US) PR:A
HEAVEN ONLY KNOWS (1947) PR:A
HEAVEN SENT (SEE: THANK HEAVEN FOR SMALL
   FAVORS) (1965, Fr.)
HEAVEN WITH A BARBED WIRE FENCE (1939) PR:A
HEAVEN WITH A GUN (1969) PR:C
HEAVENLY BODIES (1985) PR:O
HEAVENLY BODY, THE (1943) PR:A
HEAVENLY DAYS (1944) PR:A
HEAVENLY KID, THE (1985) PR:O
HEAVENLY PURSUITS (SEE: GOSPEL ACCORDING
   TO VIC, THE) (1986, Brit.)
HEAVENS ABOVE! (1963, Brit.) PR:AA
HEAVENS CALL, THE (SEE: SKY CALLS, THE) (1959,
   USSR)
HEAVEN'S GATE (1980) PR:O
HEAVY METAL (1981, Can.) PR:O
HEDDA (1975, Brit.) PR:A-C
HEIDI (1937) PR:AA
HEIDI AND PETER (1955, Switz.) PR:AA
HEIDI (1954, Switz.) PR:AA
HEIDI (1968, Aust.) PR:AA
HEIDI'S SONG (1982) PR:AA
HEIGHTS OF DANGER (1962, Brit.) PR:A
HEIMAT (1985, W. Ger.) PR:C-O
HEINZELMANNCHEN (SEE: SHOEMAKER AND THE
   ELVES, THE) (1967, W. Ger.)
HEIR TO TROUBLE (1936) PR:A
HEIRESS, THE (1949) PR:A
HEIRLOOM MYSTERY, THE (1936, Brit.) PR:A
HEIST, THE (1979, It.) PR:A
HEIST, THE (SEE: $ (DOLLARS)) (1971)
HELD FOR RANSOM (1938) PR:A
HELD IN TRUST (1949, Brit.) PR:A
HELDEN (SEE: ARMS AND THE MAN) (1962, W. Ger.)
HELDEN – HIMMEL UND HOLLE (SEE: CAVERN,
   THE) (1965, W. Ger.)
HELDINNEN (1962, W. Ger.) PR:A
HELDORADO (SEE: HELLDORADO) (1946)
HELEN MORGAN STORY, THE (1957) PR:A
HELEN OF TROY (1956, It.) PR:A
HELICOPTER SPIES, THE (1968) PR:A
HELL AND HIGH WATER (1933) PR:A
HELL AND HIGH WATER (1954) PR:A
HELL BELOW (1933) PR:A
HELL BELOW ZERO (1954, Brit.) PR:A
HELL BENT FOR 'FRISCO (1931) PR:A
HELL BENT FOR GLORY (SEE: LAFAYETTE ESCA-
   DRILLE) (1957)
HELL BENT FOR LEATHER (1960) PR:A
HELL BENT FOR LOVE (1934) PR:A
HELL BOATS (1970, Brit.) PR:A
HELL BOUND (1931) PR:A
HELL BOUND (1957) PR:A
HELL CANYON OUTLAWS (1957) PR:A
HELL CAT, THE (1934) PR:A
HELL COMES TO FROGTOWN (1988) PR:O
HELL DIVERS (1932) PR:A
HELL DRIVERS (1958, Brit.) PR:A
HELL FIRE AUSTIN (1932) PR:A
HELL HARBOR (1930) PR:A
HELL, HEAVEN OR HOBOKEN (1958, Brit.) PR:A
HELL HIGH (1989) PR:O
HELL IN KOREA (1956, Brit.) PR:C

HELL IN THE CITY (SEE: AND THE WILD, WILD
   WOMEN) (1961, It.)
HELL IN THE HEAVENS (1934) PR:A
HELL IN THE PACIFIC (1968) PR:O
HELL IS A CITY (1960, Brit.) PR:A
HELL IS EMPTY (1967, Brit./It.) PR:C
HELL IS FOR HEROES (1962) PR:C
HELL IS SOLD OUT (1951, Brit.) PR:A
HELL NIGHT (1981) PR:O
HELL ON DEVIL'S ISLAND (1957) PR:A
HELL ON EARTH (1934, Ger.) PR:A
HELL ON FRISCO BAY (1956) PR:C
HELL ON WHEELS (1967) PR:A
HELL RAIDERS (1968) PR:A-C
HELL RAIDERS OF THE DEEP (1954, It.) PR:A
HELL-SHIP MORGAN (1936) PR:A
HELL SHIP MUTINY (1957) PR:A
HELL SQUAD (1958) PR:A
HELL SQUAD (1986) PR:O
HELL TO ETERNITY (1960) PR:A
HELL TO MACAO (SEE: CORRUPT ONES, THE) (1967,
   Fr./It./W. Ger.)
HELL TOWN (SEE: BORN TO THE WEST) (1937)
HELL UP IN HARLEM (1973) PR:O
HELL WITH HEROES, THE (1968) PR:C
HELL'S HIGHWAY (SEE: VIOLENT ROAD) (1958)
HELLBENDERS, THE (1967, US/It./Sp.) PR:A
HELLBOUND: HELLRAISER II (1988, Brit.) PR:O
HELLCATS, THE (1968) PR:O
HELLCATS OF THE NAVY (1957) PR:A
HELLDORADO (1935) PR:A
HELLDORADO (1946) PR:A
HELLER IN PINK TIGHTS (1960) PR:C
HELLFIGHTERS (1968) PR:A
HELLFIRE (1949) PR:A
HELLFIRE CLUB, THE (1963, Brit.) PR:C
HELLGATE (1952) PR:A
HELLHOLE (1985) PR:O
HELLIONS, THE (1962, Brit.) PR:O
HELLO AGAIN (1987) PR:A-C
HELLO, ANNAPOLIS (1942) PR:A
HELLO BEAUTIFUL (SEE: POWERS GIRL, THE) (1942)
HELLO, DOLLY! (1969) PR:AA
HELLO DOWN THERE (1969) PR:A
HELLO, ELEPHANT (1954, It.) PR:A
HELLO, EVERYBODY (1933) PR:A
HELLO, FRISCO, HELLO (1943) PR:A
HELLO GOD (1951, US/It.) PR:A
HELLO – GOODBYE (1970) PR:O
HELLO LONDON (1958, Brit.) PR:A
HELLO MARY LOU, PROM NIGHT II (1987, Can.) PR:O
HELLO SISTER (1930) PR:A
HELLO SISTER! (1933) PR:C-O
HELLO SUCKER (1941) PR:A
HELLO SWEETHEART (1935, Brit.) PR:A
HELLO TROUBLE (1932) PR:A
HELLRAISER (1987, Brit.) PR:O
HELL'S ANGELS (1930) PR:C
HELL'S ANGELS ON WHEELS (1967) PR:O
HELL'S ANGELS '69 (1969) PR:O
HELL'S BELLES (1969) PR:O
HELL'S BLOODY DEVILS (1970) PR:O
HELL'S CARGO (1935, Brit.) PR:A
HELL'S CARGO (SEE: DANGEROUS CARGO) (1939)
HELL'S CHOSEN FEW (1968) PR:O
HELL'S CROSSROADS (1957) PR:A
HELL'S FIVE HOURS (1958) PR:A
HELL'S HALF ACRE (1954) PR:A
HELL'S HEADQUARTERS (1932) PR:A
HELL'S HEROES (1930) PR:A
HELL'S HIGHWAY (1932) PR:A
HELL'S HORIZON (1955) PR:A
HELL'S HOUSE (1932) PR:A
HELL'S ISLAND (1930) PR:A
HELL'S ISLAND (1955) PR:A
HELL'S KITCHEN (1939) PR:A
HELL'S OUTPOST (1955) PR:A
HELL'S PLAYGROUND (1967) PR:A
HELLZAPOPPIN' (1941) PR:A
HELP! (1965, Brit.) PR:A
HELP I'M INVISIBLE (1952, W. Ger.) PR:A
HELP YOURSELF (1932, Brit.) PR:A
HELTER SKELTER (1949, Brit.) PR:A
HEM HAYU ASAR (SEE: THEY WERE TEN) (1961, Is-
   rael)
HEMINGWAY'S ADVENTURES OF A YOUNG MAN
   (SEE: ADVENTURES OF A YOUNG MAN) (1962)
HENNESSY (1975, Brit.) PR:C
HENPECKED (SEE: BLONDIE IN SOCIETY) (1947)
HENRIETTE'S HOLIDAY (SEE: HOLIDAY FOR HENRI-
   ETTE) (1955, Fr.)
HENRY ALDRICH, BOY SCOUT (1944) PR:A
HENRY ALDRICH, EDITOR (1942) PR:A
HENRY ALDRICH FOR PRESIDENT (1941) PR:A
HENRY ALDRICH GETS GLAMOUR (1942) PR:A
HENRY ALDRICH HAUNTS A HOUSE (1943) PR:A
HENRY ALDRICH PLAYS CUPID (1944) PR:A
HENRY ALDRICH SWINGS IT (1943) PR:A

HENRY ALDRICH'S LITTLE SECRET (1944) PR:A
HENRY AND DIZZY (1942) PR:A
HENRY GOES ARIZONA (1939) PR:A
HENRY LIMPET (SEE: INCREDIBLE MR. LIMPET,
   THE) (1964)
HENRY STEPS OUT (1940, Brit.) PR:A
HENRY VIII (SEE: PRIVATE LIFE OF HENRY VIII,
   THE) (1933, Brit.)
HENRY VIII AND HIS SIX WIVES (1972, Brit.) PR:A
HENRY V (1944, Brit.) PR:A
HENRY V (1989, Brit.) PR:A
HENRY IV (1984, It.) PR:C
HENRY, THE RAINMAKER (1949) PR:A
HENTAI (1966, Jap.) PR:O
HER ADVENTUROUS NIGHT (1946) PR:A
HER ALIBI (1989) PR:C
HER BODYGUARD (1933) PR:A
HER CARDBOARD LOVER (1942) PR:A
HER ENLISTED MAN (SEE: RED SALUTE) (1935)
HER FAVORITE HUSBAND (SEE: TAMING OF DORO-
   THY, THE) (1950, Brit.)
HER FIRST AFFAIR (1947, Fr.) PR:A
HER FIRST AFFAIRE (1932, Brit.) PR:A
HER FIRST BEAU (1941) PR:A
HER FIRST MATE (1933) PR:A
HER FIRST ROMANCE (1940) PR:A
HER FIRST ROMANCE (1951) PR:A
HER FORGOTTEN PAST (1933) PR:A
HER HIGHNESS AND THE BELLBOY (1945) PR:A
HER HUSBAND LIES (1937) PR:A
HER HUSBAND'S AFFAIRS (1947) PR:A
HER HUSBAND'S SECRETARY (1937) PR:A
HER IMAGINARY LOVER (1933, Brit.) PR:A
HER JUNGLE LOVE (1938) PR:A
HER KIND OF MAN (1946) PR:A
HER LAST AFFAIRE (1935, Brit.) PR:A
HER LUCKY NIGHT (1945) PR:A
HER MAD NIGHT (1932) PR:A
HER MAJESTY LOVE (1931) PR:A
HER MAN (1930) PR:C
HER MAN GILBEY (1949, Brit.) PR:A
HER MASTER'S VOICE (1936) PR:A
HER NIGHT OUT (1932, Brit.) PR:A
HER PANELLED DOOR (1951, Brit.) PR:A
HER PRIMITIVE MAN (1944) PR:A
HER PRIVATE AFFAIR (1930) PR:A
HER PRIVATE LIFE (1929) PR:A
HER REPUTATION (1931, Brit.) PR:A
HER REPUTATION (SEE: BROADWAY BAD) (1933)
HER RESALE VALUE (1933) PR:A
HER SACRIFICE (SEE: BLIND DATE) (1934)
HER SISTER'S SECRET (1946) PR:A
HER SPLENDID FOLLY (1933) PR:A
HER STRANGE DESIRE (1931, Brit.) PR:A
HER TWELVE MEN (1954) PR:A
HER WEDDING NIGHT (1930) PR:A
HERBIE GOES BANANAS (1980) PR:AA
HERBIE GOES TO MONTE CARLO (1977) PR:AA
HERBIE RIDES AGAIN (1974) PR:AA
HERCULE CONTRE MOLOCH (SEE: CONQUEST OF
   MYCENE) (1963)
HERCULES (1959, It.) PR:C-O
HERCULES (1983) PR:A
HERCULES AGAINST THE MOON MEN (1965, Fr./It.)
   PR:A
HERCULES AGAINST THE SONS OF THE SUN (1964,
   Sp./It.) PR:A
HERCULES AND THE CAPTIVE WOMEN (1963, Fr./It.)
   PR:A
HERCULES AND THE HYDRA (SEE: LOVES OF
   HERCULES) (1960, Fr./It.)
HERCULES IN NEW YORK (1970) PR:A
HERCULES IN THE HAUNTED WORLD (1964, It.) PR:C
HERCULES' PILLS (1960, It.) PR:C
HERCULES, SAMSON & ULYSSES (1964, It.) PR:A
HERCULES II (1985) PR:C
HERCULES UNCHAINED (1960, It./Fr.) PR:A
HERCULES VS THE GIANT WARRIORS (1965, Fr./It.)
   PR:A
HERE COME THE CO-EDS (1945) PR:AA
HERE COME THE GIRLS (1953) PR:A
HERE COME THE HUGGETTS (1948, Brit.) PR:A
HERE COME THE JETS (1959) PR:A
HERE COME THE LITTLES (1985) PR:AA
HERE COME THE MARINES (1952) PR:A
HERE COME THE NELSONS (1952) PR:A
HERE COME THE TIGERS (1978) PR:C
HERE COME THE WAVES (1944) PR:A
HERE COMES A POLICEMAN (SEE: STRICTLY
   ILLEGAL) (1935, Brit.)
HERE COMES CARTER (1936) PR:A
HERE COMES COOKIE (1935) PR:A
HERE COMES ELMER (1943) PR:A
HERE COMES HAPPINESS (1941) PR:A
HERE COMES KELLY (1943) PR:A
HERE COMES MR. JORDAN (1941) PR:A
HERE COMES SANTA CLAUS (1984) PR:AA

HERE COMES THAT NASHVILLE SOUND (SEE: COUNTRY BOY) (1966)
HERE COMES THE BAND (1935) PR:A
HERE COMES THE GROOM (1934) PR:A
HERE COMES THE GROOM (1951) PR:A
HERE COMES THE NAVY (1934) PR:A
HERE COMES THE SUN (1945, Brit.) PR:A
HERE COMES TROUBLE (1936) PR:A
HERE COMES TROUBLE (1948) PR:A
HERE I AM A STRANGER (1939) PR:A
HERE IS A MAN (SEE: DEVIL AND DANIEL WEBSTER, THE) (1941)
HERE IS MY HEART (1934) PR:A
HERE LIES LOVE (SEE: SECOND WOMAN, THE) (1951)
HERE WE GO 'ROUND THE MULBERRY BUSH (1968, Brit.) PR:C
HERE WE GO AGAIN (1942) PR:AA
HERE'S FLASH CASEY (1937) PR:A
HERE'S GEORGE (1932, Brit.) PR:A
HERE'S THE KNIFE, DEAR; NOW USE IT (SEE: NIGHTMARE) (1963, Brit.)
HERE'S TO ROMANCE (1935) PR:A
HERE'S YOUR LIFE (1966, Swed.) PR:C-O
HERETIC (SEE: EXORCIST II: THE HERETIC) (1977)
HERITAGE (1935, Aus.) PR:A
HERITAGE OF THE DESERT (1933) PR:A
HERITAGE OF THE DESERT (1939) PR:A
HERKER VON LONDON, DER (SEE: MAD EXECUTIONERS, THE) (1965, W. Ger.)
HERO, THE (SEE: BLOOMFIELD) (1971, Brit./Israel)
HERO (1982, Brit.) PR:C
HERO AIN'T NOTHIN' BUT A SANDWICH, A (1977) PR:C-O
HERO AND THE TERROR (1988) PR:O
HERO AT LARGE (1980) PR:A
HERO FOR A DAY (1939) PR:A
HERO OF BABYLON (1963, It.) PR:A
HERO OF PINE RIDGE, THE (SEE: YODELIN' KID FROM PINE RIDGE) (1937)
HEROD THE GREAT (1960, It.) PR:C
HEROES, THE (SEE: INVINCIBLE SIX) (1970, US/Iran)
HEROES (1977) PR:A
HEROES ARE MADE (1944, USSR) PR:C-O
HEROES DIE YOUNG (1960) PR:C
HEROES FOR SALE (1933) PR:A
HEROES IN BLUE (1939) PR:A
HEROES OF TELEMARK, THE (1965, Brit.) PR:C
HEROES OF THE ALAMO (1938) PR:A
HEROES OF THE HILLS (1938) PR:A
HEROES OF THE RANGE (1936) PR:A
HEROES OF THE SADDLE (1940) PR:A
HEROES OF THE SEA (1941, USSR) PR:A
HEROIN GANG, THE (SEE: SOL MADRID) (1968)
HEROINA (1965) PR:C
HEROISM (SEE: EROICA) (1966, Pol.)
HERO'S ISLAND (1962) PR:A
HEROS SANS RETOUR (SEE: COMMANDO) (1964, Bel./It./Sp./W. Ger.)
HEROSTRATUS (1968, Brit.) PR:C
HERRIN DER WELT (SEE: MISTRESS OF THE WORLD) (1959, Fr./It./W. Ger.)
HERRSCHER OHNE KRONE (SEE: KING IN SHADOW) (1961, W. Ger.)
HERS TO HOLD (1943) PR:A
HERZBUBE (SEE: KING, QUEEN, KNAVE) (1972, US/W. Ger.)
HE'S A COCKEYED WONDER (1950) PR:A
HE'S MY GIRL (1987) PR:C
HE'S MY GUY (1943) PR:A
HESTER STREET (1975) PR:C
HETS (SEE: TORMENT) (1944, Swed.)
HEX (1973) PR:O
HEXEN BIS AUFS BLUT GEQUALT (SEE: MARK OF THE DEVIL) (1970, Brit./W. Ger.)
HEXEN GESCHANDET UND TODE GEQUALT (SEE: MARK OF THE DEVIL II) (1975, Brit./W. Ger.)
HEY BABE! (1984, Can.) PR:A
HEY BABU RIBA (1987, Yugo.) PR:C
HEY BOY! HEY GIRL! (1959) PR:A
HEY, GOOD LOOKIN' (1982) PR:O
HEY! HEY! U.S.A. (1938, Brit.) PR:A
HEY, LET'S TWIST! (1961) PR:A
HEY, ROOKIE (1944) PR:A
HEY, SAILOR! (SEE: HERE COMES THE NAVY) (1934)
HEY THERE, IT'S YOGI BEAR (1964) PR:AA
HI, BEAUTIFUL! (1944) PR:A
HI, BUDDY (1943) PR:A
HI-DE-HO (1947) PR:A
HI, DIDDLE DIDDLE (1943) PR:A
HI, GANG! (1941, Brit.) PR:A
HI, GAUCHO! (1936) PR:A
HI, GOOD-LOOKIN' (1944) PR:A
HI IN THE CELLAR (SEE: UP IN THE CELLAR) (1970)
HI-JACKED (1950) PR:A
HI-JACKERS, THE (1963, Brit.) PR:A
HI MO TSUKI MO (SEE: THROUGH DAYS AND MONTHS) (1969, Jap.)

HI, MOM! (1970) PR:O
HI, NEIGHBOR (1942) PR:A
HI, NELLIE! (1934) PR:A
HI NO TORI-2772 (SEE: SPACE FIREBIRD 2772) (1979, Jap.)
HI-RIDERS (1978) PR:O
HI 'YA, CHUM (1943) PR:A
HI' YA, SAILOR (1941) PR:A
HIAWATHA (1952) PR:AA
HICKEY AND BOGGS (1972) PR:C
HIDDEN, THE (1987) PR:O
HIDDEN DANGER (1949) PR:A
HIDDEN ENEMY (1940) PR:A
HIDDEN EYE, THE (1945) PR:A
HIDDEN FACE (SEE: JAIL BAIT) (1954)
HIDDEN FEAR (1957) PR:C
HIDDEN FORTRESS, THE (1958, Jap.) PR:C
HIDDEN GOLD (1933) PR:A
HIDDEN GOLD (1940) PR:A
HIDDEN GUNS (1956) PR:C
HIDDEN HAND, THE (1942) PR:C
HIDDEN HOMICIDE (1959, Brit.) PR:C
HIDDEN MENACE, THE (1940, Brit.) PR:A
HIDDEN POWER (1939) PR:A
HIDDEN ROOM, THE (1949, Brit.) PR:A
HIDDEN ROOM OF 1,000 HORRORS (SEE: TELL-TALE HEART, THE) (1962, Brit.)
HIDDEN SECRET (SEE: YANK IN INDO-CHINA, A) (1952)
HIDDEN VALLEY (1932) PR:A
HIDDEN VALLEY OUTLAWS (1944) PR:A
HIDE AND SEEK (1964, Brit.) PR:A
HIDE IN PLAIN SIGHT (1980) PR:C
HIDEAWAY (1937) PR:A
HIDEAWAY GIRL (1937) PR:A
HIDEAWAYS, THE (SEE: FROM THE MIXED-UP FILES OF MRS. BASIL E. FRANKWEILER) (1973)
HIDEOUS SUN DEMON, THE (1959) PR:C
HIDE-OUT, THE (1930) PR:A
HIDE-OUT (1934) PR:A
HIDEOUT (1948, Brit.) PR:C
HIDEOUT (1949) PR:A
HIDEOUT, THE (1956, Brit.) PR:C
HIDEOUT IN THE ALPS (1938, Brit.) PR:A
HIDING OUT (1987) PR:C
HIDING PLACE, THE (1975) PR:C-O
HIGASHI KARA KITA OTOKO (SEE: MAN FROM THE AST, THE) (1961, Jap.)
HIGASHI SHINAKAI (SEE: EAST CHINA SEA) (1969, Jap.)
HIGGINS FAMILY, THE (1938) PR:A
HIGH (1968, Can.) PR:O
HIGH AND DRY (1954, Brit.) PR:A
HIGH AND LOW (1963, Jap.) PR:C-O
HIGH AND THE MIGHTY, THE (1954) PR:A
HIGH ANXIETY (1977) PR:C
HIGH-BALLIN' (1978, US/Can.) PR:C
HIGH BARBAREE (1947) PR:A
HIGH BRIGHT SUN, THE (SEE: MC GUIRE, GO HOME!) (1965, Brit.)
HIGH COMMAND, THE (1938, Brit.) PR:A
HIGH COMMISSIONER, THE (1968, US/Brit.) PR:C-O
HIGH CONQUEST (1947) PR:A
HIGH COST OF LOVING, THE (1958) PR:A
HIGH COUNTRY, THE (1981, Can.) PR:A
HIGH EXPLOSIVE (1943) PR:A
HIGH FINANCE (1933, Brit.) PR:A
HIGH FLIGHT (1957, Brit.) PR:A
HIGH FLYERS (1937) PR:A
HIGH FURY (1947, Brit.) PR:A
HIGH GEAR (1933) PR:A
HIGH HAT (1937) PR:A
HIGH HEELS (SEE: DOCTEUR POPAUL) (1972, Fr.)
HIGH HELL (1958, Brit.) PR:C
HIGH HOPES (1988, Brit.) PR:C
HIGH INFIDELITY (1965, Fr./It.) PR:O
HIGH JINKS IN SOCIETY (1949, Brit.) PR:A
HIGH JUMP (1959, Brit.) PR:A
HIGH LONESOME (1950) PR:A
HIGH NOON (1952) PR:C
HIGH PLAINS DRIFTER (1973) PR:O
HIGH POWERED (1945) PR:A
HIGH-POWERED RIFLE, THE (1960) PR:A
HIGH PRESSURE (1932) PR:A
HIGH RISK (1981) PR:O
HIGH ROAD, THE (SEE: LADY OF SCANDAL, THE) (1930)
HIGH ROAD TO CHINA (1983) PR:C
HIGH ROLLING (1977, Aus.) PR:O
HIGH SCHOOL (1940) PR:A
HIGH SCHOOL BIG SHOT (1959) PR:C
HIGH SCHOOL CAESAR (1960) PR:C
HIGH SCHOOL CONFIDENTIAL! (1958) PR:O
HIGH SCHOOL GIRL (1935) PR:A
HIGH SCHOOL HELLCATS (1958) PR:O
HIGH SCHOOL HERO (1946) PR:A
HIGH SCHOOL HONEYMOON (SEE: TOO SOON TO LOVE) (1960)

HIGH SEAS (1929, Brit.) PR:A
HIGH SEASON (1988, Brit.) PR:C-O
HIGH SIERRA (1941) PR:C
HIGH SOCIETY (1932, Brit.) PR:A
HIGH SOCIETY (1955) PR:AA
HIGH SOCIETY (1956) PR:A
HIGH SOCIETY BLUES (1930) PR:A
HIGH SPEED (1932) PR:A
HIGH SPEED (1986, Fr.) PR:O
HIGH SPIRITS (1988, US/Brit.) PR:C
HIGH STAKES (1931) PR:A
HIGH STAKES (1989) PR:O
HIGH TENSION (1936) PR:A
HIGH TERRACE, THE (1957, Brit.) PR:A
HIGH TIDE (1947) PR:A
HIGH TIDE (1987, Aus.) PR:A-C
HIGH TIDE AT NOON (1957, Brit.) PR:A
HIGH TIME (1960) PR:A
HIGH TREASON (1929, Brit.) PR:A
HIGH TREASON (1937, Brit.) PR:A
HIGH TREASON (1951, Brit.) PR:A
HIGH VELOCITY (1977) PR:C
HIGH VENTURE (SEE: PASSAGE WEST) (1951)
HIGH VOLTAGE (1929) PR:A
HIGH WALL (1947) PR:A
HIGH, WIDE AND HANDSOME (1937) PR:A
HIGH WIND IN JAMAICA, A (1965, US/Brit.) PR:A
HIGH WINDOW, THE (SEE: BRASHER DOUBLOON, THE) (1947)
HIGH YELLOW (1965) PR:C-O
HIGHER AND HIGHER (1943) PR:A
HIGHEST BIDDER, THE (SEE: WOMAN HUNT, THE) (1975, US/Phil.)
HIGHLAND FLING (1936, Brit.) PR:A
HIGHLANDER (1986) PR:O
HIGHLY DANGEROUS (1950, Brit.) PR:A
HIGHPOINT (1984, Can.) PR:C
HIGHWAY DRAGNET (1954) PR:A
HIGHWAY PATROL (1938) PR:A
HIGHWAY PICKUP (1965, Fr./It.) PR:C
HIGHWAY 13 (1948) PR:A
HIGHWAY 301 (1950) PR:C
HIGHWAY TO BATTLE (1961, Brit.) PR:A
HIGHWAY TO FREEDOM (SEE: JOE SMITH, AMERICAN) (1942)
HIGHWAY TO HELL (SEE: RUNNING HOT) (1984)
HIGHWAY WEST (1941) PR:A
HIGHWAYMAN, THE (1951) PR:C
HIGHWAYMAN RIDES, THE (SEE: BILLY THE KID) (1930)
HIGHWAYS BY NIGHT (1942) PR:A
HIJACK (SEE: ACTION STATIONS) (1959, Brit.)
HIKEN (SEE: YOUNG SWORDSMAN) (1964, Jap.)
HIKEN YABURI (1969, Jap.) PR:C
HIKINIGE (SEE: MOMENT OF TERROR) (1969, Jap.)
HILDA CRANE (1956) PR:A
HILDUR AND THE MAGICIAN (1969) PR:AA
HILFE ICHE BIN UNSICHTBAR (SEE: HELP I'M INVISIBLE) (1952, W. Ger.)
HILL, THE (1965, Brit.) PR:O
HILL IN KOREA, A (SEE: HELL IN KOREA) (1956, Brit.)
HILL 24 DOESN'T ANSWER (1955, Israel) PR:A
HILLBILLY BLITZKRIEG (1942) PR:A
HILLBILLYS IN A HAUNTED HOUSE (1967) PR:A
HILLS HAVE EYES, THE (1978) PR:O
HILLS HAVE EYES II, THE (1985) PR:O
HILLS OF DONEGAL, THE (1947, Brit.) PR:A
HILLS OF HOME (1948) PR:AA
HILLS OF OKLAHOMA (1950) PR:A
HILLS OF OLD WYOMING (1937) PR:A
HILLS OF THE BRAVE (SEE: PALOMINO, THE) (1950)
HILLS OF UTAH (1951) PR:A
HILLS RUN RED, THE (1967, It.) PR:C
HIM (SEE: EL) (1952, Mex.)
HIMATSURI (1985, Jap.) PR:O
HIMMO, KING OF JERUSALEM (1988, Israel) PR:C-O
HINDENBURG, THE (1975) PR:C
HINDLE WAKES (1931, Brit.) PR:A
HINDLE WAKES (SEE: HOLIDAY WEEK) (1952, Brit.)
HINDU, THE (1953, Brit.) PR:AA
HING LOU MENG (SEE: DREAM OF THE RED CHAMBER, THE) (1966, Chi.)
HINOTORI (1980, Jap.) PR:O
HIPPODROME (1961, Aust./W. Ger.) PR:C-O
HIPPOLYT, THE LACKEY (1932, Hung.) PR:A
HIPS, HIPS, HOORAY (1934) PR:A
HIRED GUN, THE (1957) PR:A
HIRED GUN (SEE: LAST GUNFIGHTER, THE) (1961, Can.)
HIRED HAND, THE (1971) PR:A
HIRED KILLER, THE (1967, Fr./It.) PR:C
HIRED WIFE (1934) PR:A
HIRED WIFE (1940) PR:A
HIRELING, THE (1973, Brit.) PR:C
HIROSHIMA, MON AMOUR (1959, Fr./Jap.) PR:C-O
HIS AFFAIR (SEE: THIS IS MY AFFAIR) (1937)
HIS AND HERS (1961, Brit.) PR:A
HIS AND HIS (SEE: HONEYMOON HOTEL) (1964)

HIS BEST MAN (SEE: TIMES SQUARE PLAYBOY) (1936)
HIS BROTHER'S GHOST (1945) PR:A
HIS BROTHER'S KEEPER (1939, Brit.) PR:A-C
HIS BROTHER'S WIFE (1936) PR:A-C
HIS BUTLER'S SISTER (1943) PR:A
HIS CAPTIVE WOMAN (1929) PR:A
HIS DOUBLE LIFE (1933) PR:A
HIS EXCELLENCY (1952, Brit.) PR:A
HIS EXCITING NIGHT (1938) PR:A
HIS FAMILY TREE (1936) PR:A
HIS FIGHTING BLOOD (1935) PR:A
HIS FIRST COMMAND (1929) PR:A
HIS GIRL FRIDAY (1940) PR:C
HIS GLORIOUS NIGHT (1929) PR:C
HIS GRACE GIVES NOTICE (1933, Brit.) PR:A
HIS GREATEST GAMBLE (1934) PR:A
HIS, HERS AND THEIRS (SEE: YOURS, MINE AND OURS) (1968)
HIS KIND OF WOMAN (1951) PR:C-O
HIS LAST ADVENTURE (SEE: BATTLING BUCKA-ROO) (1932)
HIS LAST TWELVE HOURS (1953, It.) PR:A
HIS LORDSHIP (1932, Brit.) PR:A
HIS LORDSHIP (SEE: MAN OF AFFAIRS) (1937, Brit.)
HIS LORDSHIP GOES TO PRESS (1939, Brit.) PR:A
HIS LORDSHIP REGRETS (1938, Brit.) PR:A
HIS LUCKY DAY (1929) PR:A
HIS MAJESTY AND CO (1935, Brit.) PR:A
HIS MAJESTY BUNKER BEAN (SEE: BUNKER BEAN) (1936)
HIS MAJESTY, KING BALLYHOO (1931, Ger.) PR:A
HIS MAJESTY O'KEEFE (1953, Brit.) PR:A
HIS NIGHT OUT (1935) PR:A
HIS OTHER WOMAN (SEE: DESK SET) (1957)
HIS PRIVATE SECRETARY (1933) PR:A
HIS ROYAL HIGHNESS (1932, Aus.) PR:A
HIS WIFE'S HABIT (SEE: WOMEN AND BLOODY TERROR) (1970)
HIS WIFE'S MOTHER (1932, Brit.) PR:A
HIS WOMAN (1931) PR:A
HISTOIRE D'ADELE H (SEE: STORY OF ADELE H. THE) (1975, Fr.)
HISTOIRE D'AIMER (SEE: LOVE IS A FUNNY THING) (1970, Fr./It.)
HISTORY (1988, It.) PR:O
HISTORY IS MADE AT NIGHT (1937) PR:C
HISTORY OF MR. POLLY, THE (1949, Brit.) PR:A
HISTORY OF THE WORLD, PART 1 (1981) PR:C-O
HIT, THE (1985, Brit.) PR:O
HIT AND RUN (1957) PR:C
HIT AND RUN (1982) PR:C-O
HIT MAN (1972) PR:O
HIT ME AGAIN (SEE: SMARTY) (1934)
HIT PARADE, THE (1937) PR:A
HIT PARADE OF 1941 (1940) PR:A
HIT PARADE OF 1943 (1943) PR:A
HIT PARADE OF 1947 (1947) PR:A
HIT PARADE OF 1951 (1950) PR:A
HIT THE DECK (1930) PR:A
HIT THE DECK (1955) PR:AA
HIT THE HAY (1945) PR:A
HIT THE ICE (1943) PR:A
HIT THE ROAD (1941) PR:A
HIT THE SADDLE (1937) PR:A
HIT! (1973) PR:O
HITCH HIKE LADY (1936) PR:A
HITCH HIKE TO HEAVEN (1936) PR:A
HITCH-HIKER, THE (1953) PR:C-O
HITCH IN TIME, A (1978, Brit.) PR:AA
HITCHER, THE (1986) PR:O
HITCHHIKE TO HAPPINESS (1945) PR:A
HITCHHIKERS, THE (1972) PR:O
HITLER (1962) PR:C
HITLER – DEAD OR ALIVE (1942) PR:A
HITLER, EIN FILM AUS DEUTSCHLAND (SEE: OUR HITLER, A FILM FROM GERMANY) (1977, W. Ger.)
HITLER GANG, THE (1944) PR:A
HITLER: THE LAST TEN DAYS (1973, Brit./It.) PR:C
HITLER – BEAST OF BERLIN (SEE: BEASTS OF BERLIN) (1939)
HITLER'S CHILDREN (1942) PR:C
HITLER'S GOLD (SEE: INSIDE OUT) (1975, Brit.)
HITLER'S MADMAN (1943) PR:A
HITLER'S WOMEN (SEE: WOMEN IN BONDAGE) (1943)
HITMAN (SEE: AMERICAN COMMANDOES) (1986)
HITOKIRI (SEE: TENCHU!) (1970, Jap.)
HITTIN' THE TRAIL (1937) PR:A
HITTING A NEW HIGH (1937) PR:A
HITTING THE HEADLINES (SEE: YOKEL BOY) (1942)
HITTING THE JACKPOT (SEE: BLONDIE HITS THE JACKPOT) (1949)
HIUCH HA'GDI (SEE: SMILE OF THE LAMB, THE) (1986, Israel)
HI-YO SILVER (1940) PR:AA
HO (1968, Fr.) PR:O
HO FOVOS (SEE: FEAR, THE) (1967, Gr.)

HO GROUSOUZES (SEE: GROUCH, THE) (1961, Gr.)
HO ZESTOS MENAS AUGOUSTOS (SEE: HOT MONTH OF AUGUST, THE) (1969, Gr.)
HOA-BINH (1971, Fr.) PR:C-O
HOAX, THE (1972) PR:C
HOBSON'S CHOICE (1931, Brit.) PR:A
HOBSON'S CHOICE (1954, Brit.) PR:A
HOEDOWN (1950) PR:A
HOFFMAN (1970, Brit.) PR:A
HOG WILD (1980, Can.) PR:O
HOL VOLT, HOL NEM VOLT (SEE: HUNGARIAN FAIRY TALE, A) (1989, Hung.)
HOLCROFT COVENANT, THE (1985, Brit.) PR:O
HOLD BACK THE DAWN (1941) PR:A
HOLD BACK THE NIGHT (1956) PR:A
HOLD BACK TOMORROW (1955) PR:O
HOLD 'EM JAIL (1932) PR:A
HOLD 'EM NAVY! (1937) PR:A
HOLD 'EM YALE (1935) PR:A
HOLD EVERYTHING (1930) PR:AA
HOLD ME TIGHT (1933) PR:A
HOLD MY HAND (1938, Brit.) PR:A
HOLD ON! (1966) PR:A
HOLD THAT BABY! (1949) PR:A
HOLD THAT BLONDE (1945) PR:A
HOLD THAT CO-ED (1938) PR:A
HOLD THAT GHOST (1941) PR:AA
HOLD THAT GIRL (1934) PR:A
HOLD THAT GIRL (SEE: HOLD THAT CO-ED) (1938)
HOLD THAT HYPNOTIST (1957) PR:A
HOLD THAT KISS (1938) PR:A
HOLD THAT LINE (1952) PR:A
HOLD THAT WOMAN (1940) PR:A
HOLD THE PRESS (1933) PR:C
HOLD-UP A LA MILANAISE (SEE: FIASCO IN MILAN) (1963, Fr.)
HOLD YOUR MAN (1929) PR:C
HOLD YOUR MAN (1933) PR:C
HOLE IN THE HEAD, A (1959) PR:A
HOLE IN THE WALL, THE (1929) PR:A-C
HOLIDAY (1930) PR:A
HOLIDAY (1938) PR:A
HOLIDAY AFFAIR (1949) PR:A
HOLIDAY CAMP (1947, Brit.) PR:C
HOLIDAY FOR HENRIETTA (1955, Fr.) PR:A
HOLIDAY FOR LOVERS (1959) PR:A
HOLIDAY FOR SINNERS (1952) PR:C
HOLIDAY HOTEL (1978, Fr.) PR:C-O
HOLIDAY IN HAVANA (1949) PR:A
HOLIDAY IN MEXICO (1946) PR:A
HOLIDAY IN SPAIN (SEE: SCENT OF MYSTERY) (1960)
HOLIDAY INN (1942) PR:A
HOLIDAY RHYTHM (1950) PR:A
HOLIDAY WEEK (1952, Brit.) PR:A
HOLIDAY'S END (1937, Brit.) PR:A
HOLIDAYS WITH PAY (1948, Brit.) PR:A
HOLLENJAGD AUF HEISSE WARE (SEE: SECRET AGENT SUPER DRAGON) (1966, Fr./It./Monaco/W. Ger.)
HOLLOW TRIUMPH (1948) PR:A
HOLLY AND THE IVY, THE (1954, Brit.) PR:A
HOLLYWEIRD (SEE: FLICKS) (1987)
HOLLYWOOD AND VINE (1945) PR:AA
HOLLYWOOD BARN DANCE (1947) PR:A
HOLLYWOOD BOULEVARD (1936) PR:A
HOLLYWOOD BOULEVARD (1976) PR:O
HOLLYWOOD CANTEEN (1944) PR:A
HOLLYWOOD CAVALCADE (1939) PR:A
HOLLYWOOD CHAINSAW HOOKERS (1988) PR:O
HOLLYWOOD COWBOY (1937) PR:A
HOLLYWOOD COWBOY (SEE: HEARTS OF THE WEST) (1975)
HOLLYWOOD HARRY (1985) PR:O
HOLLYWOOD HIGH (1977) PR:O
HOLLYWOOD HIGH PART II (1984) PR:O
HOLLYWOOD HOODLUM (SEE: HOLLYWOOD MYSTERY) (1934)
HOLLYWOOD HOT TUBS (1984) PR:O
HOLLYWOOD HOTEL (1937) PR:AA
HOLLYWOOD KNIGHTS, THE (1980) PR:O
HOLLYWOOD MEAT CLEAVER MASSACRE, THE (SEE: MEAT CLEAVER MASSACRE, THE) (1977)
HOLLYWOOD MYSTERY (1934) PR:C
HOLLYWOOD OR BUST (1956) PR:A
HOLLYWOOD PARTY (1934) PR:AA
HOLLYWOOD ROUND-UP (1938) PR:A
HOLLYWOOD SHUFFLE (1987) PR:O
HOLLYWOOD SPEAKS (1932) PR:C-O
HOLLYWOOD STADIUM MYSTERY (1938) PR:A
HOLLYWOOD STORY (1951) PR:A
HOLLYWOOD STRANGLER, THE (SEE: DON'T ANSWER THE PHONE) (1980)
HOLLYWOOD THRILLMAKERS (SEE: MOVIE STUNTMEN) (1953)
HOLLYWOOD VICE SQUAD (1986) PR:O
HOLLYWOOD ZAP! (1986) PR:O
HOLOCAUST 2000 (SEE: CHOSEN, THE) (1978, Brit./It.)

HOLY INNOCENTS, THE (1984, Sp.) PR:O
HOLY MATRIMONY (1943) PR:A
HOLY MOUNTAIN, THE (1973, US/Mex.) PR:O
HOLY TERROR, A (1931) PR:A
HOLY TERROR, THE (1937) PR:A
HOLY TERROR (SEE: ALICE, SWEET ALICE) (1978)
HOMBRE (1967) PR:C
HOMBRE MIRANDO AL SUDESTE (SEE: MAN FACING SOUTHEAST) (1986, Arg.)
HOME AND AWAY (1956, Brit.) PR:A
HOME AND THE WORLD, THE (1984, India) PR:C
HOME AT SEVEN (SEE: MURDER ON MONDAY) (1952, Brit.)
HOME BEFORE DARK (1958) PR:C
HOME FOR TANYA, A (1961, USSR) PR:A
HOME FREE ALL (1984) PR:O
HOME FROM HOME (1939, Brit.) PR:A
HOME FROM THE HILL (1960) PR:O
HOME FRONT (SEE: MORGAN STEWART'S COMING HOME) (1987)
HOME IN INDIANA (1944) PR:AA
HOME IN OKLAHOMA (SEE: BIG SHOW, THE) (1937)
HOME IN OKLAHOMA (1946) PR:A
HOME IN WYOMIN' (1942) PR:A
HOME IS THE HERO (1959, Ireland) PR:C
HOME IS WHERE THE HART IS (1987, Can.) PR:C
HOME IS WHERE THE HEART IS (SEE: SQUARE DANCE) (1987)
HOME MOVIES (1979) PR:C
HOME OF THE BRAVE (1949) PR:C
HOME ON THE PRAIRIE (1939) PR:A
HOME ON THE RANGE (1935) PR:A
HOME ON THE RANGE (1946) PR:A
HOME, SWEET HOME (1933, Brit.) PR:A
HOME SWEET HOME (1945, Brit.) PR:A
HOME SWEET HOME (1981) PR:O
HOME SWEET HOMICIDE (1946) PR:AA
HOME TO DANGER (1951, Brit.) PR:A
HOME TOWN STORY (1951) PR:C
HOME TOWNERS, THE (1928) PR:A
HOMEBODIES (1974) PR:O
HOMEBOY (1989) PR:C
HOMECOMING (1948) PR:A
HOMECOMING, THE (1973) PR:C
HOMER (1970) PR:C
HOMESTEADERS, THE (1953) PR:A
HOMESTEADERS OF PARADISE VALLEY (1947) PR:A
HOMESTRETCH, THE (1947) PR:A
HOMETOWN U.S.A. (1979) PR:C
HOMETOWNERS (SEE: LADIES MUST LIVE) (1940)
HOMEWORK (1982) PR:O
HOMICIDAL (1961) PR:O
HOMICIDE (1949) PR:C
HOMICIDE BUREAU (1939) PR:O
HOMICIDE FOR THREE (1948) PR:C
HOMICIDE SQUAD, THE (1931) PR:A
HONDO (1953) PR:C
HONEY (1930) PR:A
HONEY, I SHRUNK THE KIDS (1989) PR:A
HONEY POT, THE (1967, US/Brit./It.) PR:A
HONEYBABY, HONEYBABY (1974) PR:C
HONEYCHILE (1951) PR:A
HONEYMOON (1947) PR:A
HONEYMOON ADVENTURE, A (SEE: FOOTSTEPS IN THE NIGHT) (1932, Brit.)
HONEYMOON AHEAD (1945) PR:A
HONEYMOON DEFERRED (1940) PR:A
HONEYMOON DEFERRED (1951, Brit.) PR:A
HONEYMOON FOR THREE (1935, Brit.) PR:A
HONEYMOON FOR THREE (1941) PR:A
HONEYMOON HOTEL (1946, Brit.) PR:A
HONEYMOON HOTEL (1964) PR:C
HONEYMOON IN BALI (1939) PR:A
HONEYMOON KILLERS, THE (1969) PR:O
HONEYMOON LANE (1931) PR:A
HONEYMOON LIMITED (1936) PR:A
HONEYMOON LODGE (1943) PR:A
HONEYMOON MACHINE, THE (1961) PR:A
HONEYMOON MERRY-GO-ROUND (1939, Brit.) PR:AA
HONEYMOON OF HORROR (1964) PR:O
HONEYMOON OF TERROR (1961) PR:O
HONEYMOON'S OVER, THE (1939) PR:C
HONEYSUCKLE ROSE (1980) PR:C
HONG GAOLIANG (SEE: RED SORGHUM) (1988, USSR)
HONG KONG (1951) PR:A
HONG KONG AFFAIR (1958) PR:A
HONG KONG CONFIDENTIAL (1958) PR:A
HONG KONG NIGHTS (1935) PR:A
HONKERS, THE (1972) PR:C
HONKON NO YORU (SEE: STAR OF HONG KONG) (1962, Jap.)
HONKY (1971) PR:O
HONKY TONK (1929) PR:A
HONKY TONK (1941) PR:C
HONKY TONK FREEWAY (1981) PR:C
HONKYTONK MAN (1982) PR:A-C
HONNO (SEE: LOST SEX) (1968, Jap.)

HONOLULU (1939) PR:A
HONOLULU LU (1941) PR:A
HONOLULU-TOKYO-HONG KONG (1963, Hong Kong/Jap.) PR:A
HONOR AMONG LOVERS (1931) PR:A
HONOR OF THE FAMILY (1931) PR:A
HONOR OF THE MOUNTED (1932) PR:A
HONOR OF THE PRESS (1932) PR:A
HONOR OF THE RANGE (1934) PR:A
HONOR OF THE WEST (1939) PR:A
HONORABLE MR. WONG, THE (SEE: HATCHET MAN, THE) (1932)
HONORE GOZE ORIN (SEE: BANISHED) (1978, Jap.)
HONOURABLE MURDER, AN (1959, Brit.) PR:C
HONOURS EASY (1935, Brit.) PR:A
HOODLUM, THE (1951) PR:C
HOODLUM EMPIRE (1952) PR:A
HOODLUM PRIEST, THE (1961) PR:C
HOODLUM SAINT, THE (1946) PR:A
HOODWINK (1981, Aus.) PR:C
HOOK, THE (1962) PR:C
HOOK, LINE AND SINKER (1930) PR:A
HOOK, LINE AND SINKER (1969) PR:A
HOOKED GENERATION, THE (1969) PR:O
HOOPER (1978) PR:A
HOOP-LA (1933) PR:C
HOORAY FOR LOVE (1935) PR:A
HOOSIER HOLIDAY (1943) PR:A
HOOSIER SCHOOLBOY (1937) PR:A
HOOSIER SCHOOLMASTER, THE (1935) PR:A
HOOSIERS (1986) PR:A-C
HOOTENANNY HOOT (1963) PR:A
HOOTS MON! (1939, Brit.) PR:A
HOPALONG CASSIDY (1935) PR:A
HOPALONG CASSIDY ENTERS (SEE: HOPALONG CASSIDY) (1935)
HOPALONG CASSIDY RETURNS (1936) PR:C
HOPALONG RIDES AGAIN (1937) PR:A
HOPE AND GLORY (1987, Brit.) PR:C
HOPE OF HIS SIDE (1935, Brit.) PR:A
HOPELESS ONES, THE (SEE: ROUND UP, THE) (1969, Hung.)
HOPPITY GOES TO TOWN (SEE: MR. BUG GOES TO TOWN) (1941)
HOPPY'S HOLIDAY (1947) PR:A
HOPPY SERVES A WRIT (1943) PR:A
HOPSCOTCH (1980) PR:C
HORI MA PANENKO (SEE: FIREMAN'S BALL, THE) (1967, Czech.)
HORIZONS WEST (1952) PR:A
HORIZONTAL LIEUTENANT, THE (1962) PR:A
HORLA, THE (SEE: DIARY OF A MADMAN) (1967)
HORN BLOWS AT MIDNIGHT, THE (1945) PR:AA
HORNET'S NEST, THE (1955, Brit.) PR:A
HORNET'S NEST (1970) PR:O
HOROKI (SEE: LONELY LANE) (1963, Jap.)
HOROSCOPE (1950, Yugo.) PR:O
HORRIBLE DR. HICHCOCK, THE (1964, It.) PR:O
HORRIBLE HOUSE ON THE HILL, THE (SEE: DEVIL TIMES FIVE) (1974)
HORRIBLE MILL WOMEN, THE (SEE: MILL OF THE STONE WOMEN) (1963, Fr./It.)
HORROR CASTLE (1956, It.) PR:O
HORROR CHAMBER OF DR. FAUSTUS, THE (1959, Fr./It.) PR:O
HORROR CREATURES OF THE PREHISTORIC PLANET (SEE: HORROR OF THE BLOOD MONSTERS) (1970, US/Phil.)
HORROR EXPRESS (1972, Brit./Sp.) PR:C
HORROR HIGH (1974) PR:O
HORROR HOSPITAL (1973, Brit.) PR:O
HORROR HOTEL (1960, Brit.) PR:C
HORROR HOTEL (SEE: EATEN ALIVE!) (1976)
HORROR HOUSE (1970, Brit.) PR:O
HORROR ISLAND (1941) PR:O
HORROR MANIACS (SEE: GREED OF WILLIAM HART, THE) (1948, Brit.)
HORROR OF DRACULA, THE (1958, Brit.) PR:O
HORROR OF FRANKENSTEIN, THE (1970, Brit.) PR:O
HORROR OF IT ALL, THE (1964, Brit.) PR:A
HORROR OF PARTY BEACH, THE (1964) PR:C
HORROR OF THE BLOOD MONSTERS (1970, US/Phil.) PR:O
HORROR OF THE STONE WOMEN (SEE: MILL OF THE STONE WOMEN) (1963, Fr./It.)
HORROR OF THE ZOMBIES (1974, Sp.) PR:C
HORROR ON SNAPE ISLAND (SEE: BEYOND THE FOG) (1981, Brit.)
HORROR PLANET (1982, Brit.) PR:O
HORROR SHOW, THE (1989) PR:O
HORROR STAR, THE (SEE: FRIGHTMATE) (1983)
HORROR Y SEXO (SEE: NIGHT OF THE BLOODY APES) (1968, Mex.)
HORRORS OF SPIDER ISLAND (SEE: IT'S HOT IN PARADISE) (1959, Yugo./W. Ger.)
HORRORS OF THE BLACK MUSEUM (1959, US/Brit.) PR:O

HORRORS OF THE BLACK ZOO (SEE: BLACK ZOO) (1963)
HORRORS OF THE RED PLANET (SEE: WIZARD OF MARS, THE) (1964)
HORSE, THE (1982, Turk.) PR:O
HORSE FEATHERS (1932) PR:A
HORSE IN THE GRAY FLANNEL SUIT, THE (1968) PR:AA
HORSE, MY HORSE (SEE: HORSE, THE) (1984, Turk.)
HORSE NAMED COMANCHE, A (SEE: TONKA) (1958)
HORSE OF PRIDE (1980, Fr.) PR:A
HORSE SOLDIERS, THE (1959) PR:C
HORSEMEN, THE (1971) PR:O
HORSEMEN OF THE SIERRAS (1950) PR:A
HORSEPLAY (1933) PR:A
HORSE'S MOUTH, THE (1953, Brit.) PR:A
HORSE'S MOUTH, THE (1958, Brit.) PR:A
HORSIE (SEE: QUEEN FOR A DAY) (1951)
HOSPITAL, THE (1971) PR:C
HOSPITAL MASSACRE (1982) PR:O
HOSTAGE, THE (1956, Brit.) PR:A
HOSTAGE, THE (1966) PR:A
HOSTAGE (1987) PR:C-O
HOSTAGE: DALLAS (SEE: GETTING EVEN) (1986)
HOSTAGES (1943) PR:A
HOSTILE COUNTRY (1950) PR:A
HOSTILE GUNS (1967) PR:A
HOSTILE WITNESS (1968, Brit.) PR:A
HOT AND COLD (SEE: WEEKEND AT BERNIE'S) (1989)
HOT AND DEADLY (1984) PR:O
HOT ANGEL, THE (1958) PR:C
HOT BLOOD (1956) PR:A
HOT BOX, THE (1972, US/Phil.) PR:O
HOT CAR GIRL (1958) PR:O
HOT CARGO (1946) PR:A
HOT CARS (1956) PR:A
HOT CHILD IN THE CITY (1987) PR:O
HOT CHILI (1986) PR:O
HOT CURVES (1930) PR:A
HOT DOG. . . THE MOVIE (1984) PR:O
HOT ENOUGH FOR JUNE (SEE: AGENT 8 3/4) (1963, Brit.)
HOT FOR PARIS (1930) PR:A
HOT FRUSTRATIONS (SEE: FRUSTRATIONS) (1967, Fr./It.)
HOT HEIRESS, THE (1931) PR:A
HOT HORSE (SEE: ONCE UPON A HORSE) (1958)
HOT HOURS (1963, Fr.) PR:O
HOT ICE (1952, Brit.) PR:A
HOT IN PARADISE (SEE: IT'S HOT IN PARADISE) (1959, Yugo./W. Ger.)
HOT LEAD (1951) PR:A
HOT LEAD AND COLD FEET (1978) PR:AA
HOT MILLIONS (1968, Brit.) PR:C
HOT MONEY (1936) PR:A
HOT MONEY GIRL (1962, Brit./W. Ger.) PR:C
HOT MONTH OF AUGUST, THE (1969, Gr.) PR:C
HOT MOVES (1984) PR:O
HOT NEWS (1936, Brit.) PR:A
HOT NEWS (1953) PR:A
HOT ONE, THE (SEE: CORVETTE SUMMER) (1978)
HOT PEARLS (SEE: BLONDE FROM SINGAPORE) (1941)
HOT PEPPER (1933) PR:A
HOT POTATO (1976) PR:O
HOT PURSUIT (1987) PR:C-O
HOT RESORT (1985) PR:O
HOT RHYTHM (1944) PR:A
HOT ROCK, THE (1972) PR:A-C
HOT ROD (1950) PR:A
HOT ROD GANG (1958) PR:A
HOT ROD GIRL (1956) PR:A
HOT ROD HULLABALOO (1966) PR:C
HOT ROD RUMBLE (1957) PR:C
HOT RODS TO HELL (1967) PR:C-O
HOT SATURDAY (1932) PR:A
HOT SEAT (SEE: CHAIR, THE) (1989)
HOT SHOT (1987) PR:A
HOT SHOTS (1956) PR:A
HOT SPELL (1958) PR:C-O
HOT SPOT (SEE: I WAKE UP SCREAMING) (1942)
HOT SPUR (1968) PR:O
HOT STEEL (1940) PR:A
HOT STUFF (1929) PR:A
HOT STUFF (1979) PR:C
HOT SUMMER NIGHT (1957) PR:A
HOT SUMMER WEEK (1973, Can.) PR:O
HOT TARGET (1985, New Zealand) PR:C-O
HOT TIMES (1974) PR:O
HOT TIP (1935) PR:A
HOT TO TROT (1988) PR:C
HOT TOMORROWS (1978) PR:C
HOT WATER (1937) PR:A
HOTEL (1967) PR:A
HOTEL BERLIN (1945) PR:A
HOTEL COLONIAL (1987, US/It.) PR:O
HOTEL CONTINENTAL (1932) PR:A

HOTEL FOR WOMEN (1939) PR:A
HOTEL HAYWIRE (1937) PR:A
HOTEL IMPERIAL (1939) PR:A
HOTEL NEW HAMPSHIRE, THE (1984) PR:C-O
HOTEL NEW YORK (1985) PR:O
HOTEL PARADISO (1966, US/Brit.) PR:C
HOTEL RESERVE (1946, Brit.) PR:A
HOTEL SAHARA (1951, Brit.) PR:A
HOTEL SPLENDIDE (1932, Brit.) PR:A
HOTEL VARIETY (1933) PR:A
HOTHEAD (1963) PR:C
HOTSPRINGS HOLIDAY (1970, Jap.) PR:A
HOTTENTOT, THE (1929) PR:A
HOUDINI (1953) PR:A
HOUGHLAND MURDER CASE, THE (SEE: MURDER BY TELEVISION) (1935)
HOUND-DOG MAN (1959) PR:A
HOUND OF THE BASKERVILLES, THE (1932, Brit.) PR:A
HOUND OF THE BASKERVILLES, THE (1939) PR:A
HOUND OF THE BASKERVILLES, THE (1959, Brit.) PR:C
HOUND OF THE BASKERVILLES, THE (1980, Brit.) PR:C
HOUND OF THE BASKERVILLES, THE (1983, Brit.) PR:C
HOUNDED (SEE: JOHNNY ALLEGRO) (1949)
HOUNDS. . . OF NOTRE DAME, THE (1980, Can.) PR:A
HOUNDS OF ZAROFF, THE (SEE: MOST DANGEROUS GAME, THE) (1932)
HOUR BEFORE THE DAWN, THE (1944) PR:A
HOUR OF DECISION (1957, Brit.) PR:A
HOUR OF GLORY (1949, Brit.) PR:A
HOUR OF THE ASSASSIN (1987) PR:O
HOUR OF THE GUN (1967) PR:C
HOUR OF THE STAR, THE (1986, Braz.) PR:O
HOUR OF THE WOLF, THE (1968, Swed.) PR:O
HOUR OF THIRTEEN, THE (1952, Brit.) PR:A
HOURS BETWEEN, THE (SEE: 24 HOURS) (1931)
HOURS OF LONELINESS (1930, Brit.) PR:C
HOURS OF LOVE, THE (1965, It.) PR:A
HOUSE (1986) PR:C-O
HOUSE ACROSS THE BAY, THE (1940) PR:A
HOUSE ACROSS THE LAKE, THE (SEE: HEATWAVE) (1954, Brit.)
HOUSE ACROSS THE STREET, THE (1949) PR:A
HOUSE BROKEN (1936, Brit.) PR:A
HOUSE BY THE CEMETERY, THE (1984, It.) PR:O
HOUSE BY THE LAKE, THE (1977, Can.) PR:O
HOUSE BY THE RIVER (1950) PR:C
HOUSE CALLS (1978) PR:C
HOUSE DIVIDED, A (1932) PR:C
HOUSE IN MARSH ROAD, THE (1959, Brit.) PR:A
HOUSE IN NIGHTMARE PARK, THE (SEE: CRAZY HOUSE) (1973, Brit.)
HOUSE IN THE SQUARE, THE (SEE: I'LL NEVER FORGET YOU) (1951, Brit.)
HOUSE IN THE WOODS, THE (1957, Brit.) PR:C
HOUSE IS NOT A HOME, A (1964) PR:O
HOUSE OF A THOUSAND CANDLES, THE (1936) PR:A
HOUSE OF BAMBOO (1955) PR:C
HOUSE OF BLACKMAIL (1953, Brit.) PR:C
HOUSE OF CARDS (SEE: DESIGNING WOMEN) (1934, Brit.)
HOUSE OF CARDS (1969) PR:C
HOUSE OF CONNELLY (SEE: CAROLINA) (1934)
HOUSE OF CRAZIES (SEE: ASYLUM) (1972, Brit.)
HOUSE OF DANGER (1934) PR:A
HOUSE OF DARK SHADOWS (1970) PR:C-O
HOUSE OF DARKNESS (1948, Brit.) PR:O
HOUSE OF DEATH (1932, USSR) PR:C
HOUSE OF DOOM (SEE: BLACK CAT, THE) (1934)
HOUSE OF DRACULA (1945) PR:A
HOUSE OF ERRORS (1942) PR:A
HOUSE OF EVIL (1968, US/Mex.) PR:O
HOUSE OF EXORCISM, THE (1976, It.) PR:O
HOUSE OF FATE, THE (SEE: MUSS 'EM UP) (1936)
HOUSE OF FEAR (SEE: LAST WARNING, THE) (1929)
HOUSE OF FEAR, THE (1939) PR:A
HOUSE OF FEAR, THE (1945) PR:A
HOUSE OF FRANKENSTEIN (1944) PR:A
HOUSE OF FREAKS (1973, It.) PR:O
HOUSE OF FRIGHT (1961, Brit.) PR:C
HOUSE OF GAMES (1987) PR:O
HOUSE OF GOD, THE (1984) PR:O
HOUSE OF GREED (1934, USSR) PR:A
HOUSE OF HORROR, THE (1929) PR:A
HOUSE OF HORRORS (1946) PR:C
HOUSE OF INSANE WOMEN (SEE: EXORCISM'S DAUGHTER) (1974, Sp.)
HOUSE OF INTRIGUE, THE (1959, It.) PR:A
HOUSE OF LIFE (1953, W. Ger.) PR:A
HOUSE OF MENACE (SEE: KING LADY) (1935)
HOUSE OF MORTAL SIN, THE (SEE: CONFESSIONAL) (1977, Brit.)
HOUSE OF MYSTERY (1934) PR:A
HOUSE OF MYSTERY (1941, Brit.) PR:A
HOUSE OF MYSTERY (SEE: NIGHT MONSTER) (1942)
HOUSE OF MYSTERY (1961, Brit.) PR:C
HOUSE OF NUMBERS (1957) PR:A

HOUSE OF 1,000 DOLLS (1967, Sp./W. Ger.) PR:O
HOUSE OF PLEASURE (SEE: LE PLAISIR) (1952, Fr.)
HOUSE OF PSYCHOTIC WOMEN, THE (1973, Sp.) PR:O
HOUSE OF RICORDI (1956, It./Fr.) PR:A
HOUSE OF ROTHSCHILD, THE (1934) PR:A
HOUSE OF SECRETS (1929) PR:O
HOUSE OF SECRETS, THE (1937) PR:A
HOUSE OF SECRETS (SEE: TRIPLE DECEPTION) (1956, Brit.)
HOUSE OF SETTLEMENT (SEE: MR. SOFT TOUCH) (1949)
HOUSE OF SEVEN CORPSES, THE (1974) PR:C-O
HOUSE OF SEVEN JOYS (SEE: WRECKING CREW, THE) (1969)
HOUSE OF STRANGE LOVES, THE (1969, Jap.) PR:C
HOUSE OF STRANGERS (1949) PR:C
HOUSE OF THE ARROW, THE (1930, Brit.) PR:A
HOUSE OF THE ARROW, THE (SEE: CASTLE OF CRIMES) (1940, Brit.)
HOUSE OF THE ARROW. THE (1953, Brit.) PR:A
HOUSE OF THE BLACK DEATH (1965) PR:O
HOUSE OF THE DAMNED (1963) PR:C
HOUSE OF THE DARK STAIRWAY (SEE: BLADE IN THE DARK, A) (1986, It.)
HOUSE OF THE LIVING DEAD (1973, South Africa) PR:C
HOUSE OF THE LONG SHADOWS (1983, Brit.) PR:O
HOUSE OF THE SEVEN GABLES, THE (1940) PR:A
HOUSE OF THE SEVEN HAWKS, THE (1959, Brit.) PR:A
HOUSE OF THE SPANIARD, THE (1936, Brit.) PR:A
HOUSE OF THE THREE GIRLS, THE (1961, Aust.) PR:A
HOUSE OF TRENT, THE (1933, Brit.) PR:A
HOUSE OF UNCLAIMED WOMEN (SEE: SCHOOL FOR UNCLAIMED GIRLS) (1973, Brit.)
HOUSE OF UNREST, THE (1931, Brit.) PR:A
HOUSE OF USHER (1960) PR:A
HOUSE OF WAX (1953) PR:C
HOUSE OF WHIPCORD (1974, Brit.) PR:O
HOUSE OF WOMEN (1962) PR:O
HOUSE ON CARROLL STREET, THE (1988) PR:C
HOUSE ON 56TH STREET, THE (1933) PR:C
HOUSE ON HAUNTED HILL (1958) PR:C
HOUSE ON 92ND STREET, THE (1945) PR:A
HOUSE ON SKULL MOUNTAIN, THE (1974) PR:C
HOUSE ON SORORITY ROW, THE (1983) PR:O
HOUSE ON TELEGRAPH HILL, THE (1951) PR:C
HOUSE ON THE EDGE OF THE PARK (1985, It.) PR:O
HOUSE ON THE FRONT LINE, THE (1963, USSR) PR:A
HOUSE ON THE SAND (1967) PR:C
HOUSE ON THE SQUARE, THE (SEE: I'LL NEVER FORGET YOU) (1951, Brit.)
HOUSE OPPOSITE, THE (1931, Brit.) PR:A
HOUSE THAT CRIED MURDER, THE (SEE: BRIDE, THE) (1973)
HOUSE THAT DRIPPED BLOOD, THE (1971, Brit.) PR:O
HOUSE THAT SCREAMED, THE (1970, Sp.) PR:O
HOUSE THAT VANISHED, THE (1974, Brit.) PR:O
HOUSE II: THE SECOND STORY (1987) PR:C-O
HOUSE WHERE DEATH LIVES, THE (1984) PR:O
HOUSE WHERE EVIL DWELLS, THE (1982) PR:O
HOUSE WITH AN ATTIC, THE (1964, USSR) PR:A
HOUSE WITHOUT WINDOWS (SEE: SEVEN ALONE) (1975)
HOUSEBOAT (1958) PR:A
HOUSEHOLDER, THE (1963, US/India) PR:A
HOUSEKEEPER, THE (1987, Can.) PR:C
HOUSEKEEPER'S DAUGHTER, THE (1939) PR:A
HOUSEKEEPING (1987) PR:A-C
HOUSEMASTER (1938, Brit.) PR:A
HOUSEWIFE (1934) PR:A
HOUSTON STORY, THE (1956) PR:A
HOVERBUG (1970, Brit.) PR:AA
HOW ABOUT US? (SEE: EPILOGUE) (1964, Den.)
HOW COME NOBODY'S ON OUR SIDE? (1975) PR:A
HOW DO I LOVE THEE? (1970) PR:C
HOW DO YOU DO? (1946) PR:A
HOW GREEN WAS MY VALLEY (1941) PR:A
HOW I GOT INTO COLLEGE (1989) PR:C
HOW I WON THE WAR (1967, Brit.) PR:C
HOW LOW CAN YOU FALL? (SEE: TILL MARRIAGE DO US PART) (1974, It.)
HOW MANY ROADS (SEE: LOST MAN, THE) (1969)
HOW NOT TO ROB A DEPARTMENT STORE (1965, Fr./It.)
HOW NOW, SWEET JESUS? (SEE: TO BE FREE) (1972)
HOW SWEET IT IS (1968) PR:C-O
HOW THE WEST WAS WON (1963) PR:AA
HOW TO BE VERY, VERY POPULAR (1955) PR:A
HOW TO BEAT THE HIGH COST OF LIVING (1980) PR:A
HOW TO COMMIT MARRIAGE (1969) PR:A
HOW TO FRAME A FIGG (1971) PR:AA
HOW TO GET AHEAD IN ADVERTISING (1989, Brit.) PR:C
HOW TO MAKE A MONSTER (1958) PR:C
HOW TO MAKE IT (SEE: TARGET: HARRY) (1969)
HOW TO MARRY A MILLIONAIRE (1953) PR:A
HOW TO MURDER A RICH UNCLE (1957, Brit.) PR:A
HOW TO MURDER YOUR WIFE (1965) PR:A

HOW TO ROB A BANK (SEE: NICE LITTLE BANK THAT SHOULD BE ROBBED, A) (1958)
HOW TO SAVE A MARRIAGE—AND RUIN YOUR LIFE (1968) PR:A
HOW TO SEDUCE A PLAYBOY (1968, Aust./Fr./It.) PR:C
HOW TO SEDUCE A WOMAN (1974) PR:O
HOW TO STEAL A DIAMOND IN FOUR EASY LESSONS (SEE: HOT ROCK, THE) (1972)
HOW TO STEAL A MILLION (1966) PR:A
HOW TO STUFF A WILD BIKINI (1965) PR:A
HOW TO SUCCEED IN BUSINESS WITHOUT REALLY TRYING (1967) PR:A
HOW WILLINGLY YOU SING (1975, Aus.) PR:A-C
HOWARD CASE, THE (1936, Brit.) PR:A
HOWARD THE DUCK (1986) PR:A-C
HOWARDS OF VIRGINIA, THE (1940) PR:A
HOWLING, THE (1981) PR:O
HOWLING TWO: YOUR SISTER IS A WEREWOLF (1985) PR:O
HOWLING III, THE (1987, Aus.) PR:C-O
HOWLING IV. . . THE ORIGINAL NIGHTMARE (1988, Brit.) PR:O
HOWLING 5: THE REBIRTH, THE (1989) PR:C
HOW'S ABOUT IT? (1943) PR:A
HOW'S CHANCES (SEE: DIPLOMATIC LOVER, THE) (1934, Brit.)
HOWZER (1973) PR:A
H.R. PUFNSTUF (SEE: PUFNSTUF) (1970)
HU-MAN (1975, Fr.) PR:C
HUCKLEBERRY FINN (1931) PR:AA
HUCKLEBERRY FINN (1939) PR:A
HUCKLEBERRY FINN (SEE: ADVENTURES OF HUCKLEBERRY FINN, THE) (1960)
HUCKLEBERRY FINN (1974) PR:AA
HUCKSTERS, THE (1947) PR:A
HUD (1963) PR:O
HUDDLE (1932) PR:A
HUDSON'S BAY (1940) PR:A
HUE AND CRY (1950, Brit.) PR:A
HUGGETTS ABROAD, THE (1949, Brit.) PR:A
HUGO THE HIPPO (1976, Hung./US) PR:AA
HUGS AND KISSES (1968, Swed.) PR:O
HUK (1956) PR:O
HULLABALOO (1940) PR:A
HULLABALOO OVER GEORGIE AND BONNIE'S PICTURES (1979, Brit.) PR:A
HUMAN BEAST, THE (SEE: LA BETE HUMAINE) (1938, Fr.)
HUMAN CARGO (1936) PR:A
HUMAN COMEDY, THE (1943) PR:A
HUMAN CONDITION, THE (1959, Jap.) PR:O
HUMAN DESIRE (1954) PR:C
HUMAN DUPLICATORS, THE (1965) PR:A
HUMAN EXPERIMENTS (1980) PR:O
HUMAN FACTOR, THE (1975, Brit.) PR:O
HUMAN FACTOR, THE (1979, Brit.) PR:C
HUMAN HIGHWAY (1982) PR:O
HUMAN INTEREST STORY, THE (SEE: BIG CARNIVAL, THE) (1951)
HUMAN JUNGLE, THE (1954) PR:A
HUMAN MONSTER, THE (1940, Brit.) PR:O
HUMAN SABOTAGE (SEE: MURDER IN THE BIG HOUSE) (1942)
HUMAN SIDE, THE (1934) PR:A
HUMAN TARGETS (1932) PR:A
HUMAN TORNADO, THE (1976) PR:O
HUMAN VAPOR, THE (1964, Jap.) PR:A
HUMANITY (1933) PR:A
HUMANOID, THE (1979, It.) PR:C
HUMANOIDS FROM THE DEEP (1980) PR:O
HUMONGOUS (1982, Can.) PR:O
HUMORESQUE (1946) PR:A-C
HUMPHREY TAKES A CHANCE (1950) PR:A
HUNCH, THE (1967, Brit.) PR:AA
HUNCHBACK OF NOTRE DAME, THE (1939) PR:A-C
HUNCHBACK OF NOTRE DAME, THE (1957, Fr.) PR:A-C
HUNCHBACK OF ROME, THE (1963, Fr./It.) PR:C
HUNCHBACK OF THE MORGUE, THE (1972, Sp.) PR:O
HUNDRA (1984, Sp.) PR:C
HUNDRED HOUR HUNT (1953, Brit.) PR:A
HUNDRED POUND WINDOW, THE (1943, Brit.) PR:A
HUNGARIAN FAIRY TALE, A (1989, Hung.) PR:A
HUNGER (1968, Den./Norway/Swed.) PR:O
HUNGER, THE (1983) PR:O
HUNGRY HILL (1947, Brit.) PR:C
HUNGRY WIVES (1973) PR:O
HUNK (1987) PR:C
HUNS, THE (1962, Fr./It.) PR:C
HUNT, THE (1967, Sp.) PR:O
HUNT THE MAN DOWN (1950) PR:A
HUNT TO KILL (SEE: WHITE BUFFALO, THE) (1977)
HUNTED, THE (1948) PR:A
HUNTED (SEE: STRANGER IN BETWEEN, THE) (1952, Brit.)
HUNTED, THE (SEE: TOUCH ME NOT) (1976, Brit.)
HUNTED IN HOLLAND (1961, Brit.) PR:AA
HUNTED MEN (1938) PR:A
HUNTER, THE (1980) PR:C

HUNTER OF THE APOCALYPSE (SEE: LAST HUNTER, THE) (1984, It.)
HUNTERS, THE (1958) PR:A-C
HUNTER'S BLOOD (1987) PR:O
HUNTERS OF THE GOLDEN COBRA, THE (1984, It.) PR:A
HUNTING IN SIBERIA (1962, USSR) PR:A
HUNTING PARTY, THE (1971, Brit.) PR:O
HURRICANE (1929) PR:A
HURRICANE, THE (1937) PR:A
HURRICANE, THE (SEE: VOICE OF THE HURRICANE) (1964)
HURRICANE (1979) PR:A
HURRICANE HORSEMAN (1931) PR:A
HURRICANE ISLAND (1951) PR:A
HURRICANE SMITH (1942) PR:A
HURRICANE SMITH (1952) PR:A
HURRY, CHARLIE, HURRY (1941) PR:A
HURRY SUNDOWN (1967) PR:O
HURRY UP OR I'LL BE 30 (1973) PR:C
HUSBANDS (1970) PR:C
HUSBAND'S HOLIDAY (1931) PR:A
HUSH-A-BYE MURDER (SEE: MY LOVER, MY SON) (1970, US/Brit.)
HUSH. . . HUSH, SWEET CHARLOTTE (1964) PR:O
HUSH MONEY (1931) PR:A
HUSTLE (1975) PR:O
HUSTLER, THE (1961) PR:C
HUSTLER SQUAD, THE (SEE: DOLL SQUAD, THE) (1974)
HUSTRUER, 2—TI AR ETTER (SEE: WIVES—TEN YEARS AFTER) (1985, Norway)
HYDE PARK CORNER (1935, Brit.) PR:A
HYPERBOLOID OF ENGINEER GARIN, THE (1965, USSR) PR:A
HYPNOSIS (1966, It./Sp./W. Ger.) PR:C-O
HYPNOTIC EYE, THE (1960) PR:O
HYPNOTIST, THE (SEE: SCOTLAND YARD DRAGNET) (1957, Brit.)
HYPNOTIZED (1933) PR:A
HYSTERIA (1965, Brit.) PR:O
HYSTERICAL (1983) PR:O

I

I ACCUSE (SEE: J'ACCUSE) (1939, Fr.)
I ACCUSE! (1958, Brit.) PR:A
I ACCUSE MY PARENTS (1945) PR:A
I ADORE YOU (1933, Brit.) PR:A
I AIM AT THE STARS (1960) PR:A
I AM A CAMERA (1955, Brit.) PR:A
I AM A CRIMINAL (1939) PR:A
I AM A FUGITIVE FROM A CHAIN GANG (1932) PR:O
I AM A GROUPIE (1970, Brit.) PR:O
I AM A THIEF (1935) PR:A
I AM CURIOUS GAY (SEE: HAPPY BIRTHDAY, DAVY) (1970)
I AM NOT AFRAID (1939) PR:A
I AM SUZANNE (1934) PR:A
I AM THE CHEESE (1983) PR:A
I AM THE LAW (1938) PR:A
I AND MY LOVERS (SEE: GALIA) (1966, Fr./It.)
I BASTARDI (SEE: SONS OF SATAN) (1969, Fr./It./W. Ger.)
I BECAME A CRIMINAL (1947, Brit.) PR:A
I BELIEVE IN YOU (1953, Brit.) PR:A
I BELIEVED IN YOU (1934) PR:A
I BOMBED PEARL HARBOR (1961, Jap.) PR:A
I BURY THE LIVING (1958) PR:A
I CALL FIRST (SEE: WHO'S THAT KNOCKING AT MY DOOR?) (1968)
I CAN GET IT FOR YOU WHOLESALE (1951) PR:A
I CAN'T ESCAPE (1934) PR:A
I CAN'T GIVE YOU ANYTHING BUT LOVE, BABY (1940) PR:A
I CAN'T. . . I CAN'T (SEE: WEDDING NIGHT) (1970, Ireland)
I CHANGED MY SEX (SEE: GLEN OR GLENDA) (1953)
I CHEATED THE LAW (1949) PR:A
I COLTELLI DEL VENDICATORE (SEE: KNIVES OF THE AVENGER) (1967, It.)
I COMPAGNI (SEE: ORGANIZER, THE) (1964, Fr./It./Yugo.)
I CONFESS (1953) PR:A
I CONQUER THE SEA (1936) PR:A
I CORPI PRESENTANO TRACCE DI VIOLENZA CARNALE (SEE: TORSO) (1974, It.)
I COSSACCHI (SEE: COSSACKS, THE) (1960, It.)
I COULD GO ON SINGING (1963, Brit.) PR:A
I COULD NEVER HAVE SEX WITH ANY MAN WHO HAS SO LITTLE REGARD FOR MY HUSBAND (1973) PR:O
I COVER BIG TOWN (1947) PR:A
I COVER CHINATOWN (1938) PR:A
I COVER THE UNDERWORLD (SEE: I COVER BIG TOWN) (1947)
I COVER THE UNDERWORLD (1955) PR:A
I COVER THE WAR (1937) PR:A
I COVER THE WATERFRONT (1933) PR:A

I CROSSED THE COLOR LINE (SEE: BLACK KLANS-
MAN, THE) (1966)
I DEAL IN DANGER (1966) PR:A
I DEMAND PAYMENT (1938) PR:A
I DIAVOLI DELLO SPAZIO (SEE: SNOW DEVILS, THE)
(1965, It.)
I DIDN'T DO IT (1945, Brit.) PR:A
I DIED A THOUSAND TIMES (1955) PR:A-C
I DISMEMBER MAMA (1974) PR:O
I DON'T CARE GIRL, THE (1952) PR:A
I DON'T WANT TO BE BORN (SEE: DEVIL WITHIN
HER, THE) (1976, Brit.)
I DOOD IT (1943) PR:A
I DREAM OF JEANIE (1952) PR:A
I DREAM TOO MUCH (1935) PR:A
I DRINK YOUR BLOOD (1971) PR:O
I EAT YOUR SKIN (1971)
I ESCAPED FROM DEVIL'S ISLAND (1973) PR:O
I ESCAPED FROM THE GESTAPO (1943) PR:A
I EVEN MET HAPPY GYPSIES (1968, Yugo.) PR:A
I FANTASTICI TRE SUPERMAN (SEE: FANTASTIC
THREE, THE) (1967, Fr./It./W. Ger./Yugo.)
I FIDANZATI (SEE: FIANCES, THE) (1964, It.)
I FOUND STELLA PARISH (1935) PR:A
I GIORNI DELL'IRA (SEE: DAY OF ANGER) (1970,
It./W. Ger.)
I GIRASOLI (SEE: SUNFLOWER) (1970, Fr./It.)
I GIVE MY HEART (SEE: LOVES OF MADAME DU-
BARRY, THE) (1938, Brit.)
I GIVE MY HEART (SEE: GIVE ME YOUR HEART)
(1936)
I GIVE MY LOVE (1934) PR:A
I HAD SEVEN DAUGHTERS (SEE: MY SEVEN LITTLE
SINS) (1956, Fr./It.)
I HATE BLONDES (1981, It.) PR:A
I HATE MY BODY (1975, Sp./Switz.) PR:A
I HATE YOUR GUTS! (SEE: INTRUDER, THE) (1962)
I HAVE LIVED (1933) PR:A
I HAVE SEVEN DAUGHTERS (SEE: MY SEVEN LIT-
TLE SINS) (1954, Fr./It.)
I, JANE DOE (1948) PR:A
I KILLED EINSTEIN, GENTLEMEN (1970, Czech.) PR:A
I KILLED GERONIMO (1950) PR:A
I KILLED THAT MAN (1942) PR:A
I KILLED THE COUNT (SEE: WHO IS GUILTY?) (1940,
Brit.)
I KILLED WILD BILL HICKOK (1956) PR:A
I KNOW WHERE I'M GOING (1947, Brit.) PR:A
I LED TWO LIVES (SEE: GLEN OR GLENDA) (1953)
I LIKE IT THAT WAY (1934) PR:A
I LIKE MONEY (1962, Brit.) PR:A
I LIKE YOUR NERVE (1931) PR:A
I LIVE FOR LOVE (1935) PR:A
I LIVE FOR YOU (SEE: I LIVE FOR LOVE) (1935)
I LIVE IN FEAR (1967, Jap.) PR:A
I LIVE IN GROSVENOR SQUARE (SEE: YANK IN LON-
DON, A) (1946, Brit.)
I LIVE MY LIFE (1935) PR:A
I LIVE ON DANGER (1942) PR:A
I LIVED WITH YOU (1933, Brit.) PR:A
I LOVE A BANDLEADER (1945) PR:A
I LOVE A MYSTERY (1945) PR:A
I LOVE A SOLDIER (1944) PR:A
I LOVE IN JERUSALEM (SEE: MY MARGO) (1967, Is-
rael)
I LOVE MELVIN (1953) PR:A
I LOVE MY WIFE (1970) PR:O
I LOVE N.Y. (1987) PR:C
I LOVE THAT MAN (1933) PR:A
I LOVE TROUBLE (1947) PR:A
I LOVE YOU (SEE: JE T'AIME) (1974, Can.)
I LOVE YOU AGAIN (1940) PR:A
I LOVE YOU, ALICE B. TOKLAS! (1968) PR:O
I LOVE YOU, I KILL YOU (1972, W. Ger.) PR:O
I LOVED A WOMAN (1933) PR:A
I LOVED YOU WEDNESDAY (1933) PR:A
I, MADMAN (1989) PR:C-O
I MARRIED A COMMUNIST (SEE: WOMAN ON PIER
13) (1950)
I MARRIED A DOCTOR (1936) PR:A
I MARRIED A MONSTER FROM OUTER SPACE (1958)
PR:O
I MARRIED A NAZI (SEE: MAN I MARRIED, THE)
(1940)
I MARRIED A SPY (1938, Brit.) PR:A
I MARRIED A WITCH (1942) PR:A
I MARRIED A WOMAN (1958) PR:A
I MARRIED AN ANGEL (1942) PR:A
I MARRIED TOO YOUNG (SEE: MARRIED TOO
YOUNG) (1962)
I, MAUREEN (1978, Can.) PR:A
I MET A MURDERER (1939, Brit.) PR:C-O
I MET HIM IN PARIS (1937) PR:A
I MET MY LOVE AGAIN (1938) PR:A
I MISS YOU, HUGS AND KISSES (1978, Can.) PR:C-O
I MISTERI DELLA GIUNGLA NERA (SEE: MYSTERY
OF THUG ISLAND, THE) (1966, It./W. Ger.)
I, MOBSTER (1959) PR:C-O

I, MONSTER (1971, Brit.) PR:C
I NEVER PROMISED YOU A ROSE GARDEN (1977) PR:O
I NEVER SANG FOR MY FATHER (1970) PR:A-C
I NUOVI BARBARI (SEE: NEW BARBARIANS, THE)
(1983, It.)
I NUOVI MOSTRI (SEE: VIVA ITALIA) (1978, It.)
I ONLY ARSKED! (1958, Brit.) PR:A
I OUGHT TO BE IN PICTURES (1982) PR:C
I PASSED FOR WHITE (1960) PR:A
I PHOTOGRAPHIA (SEE: PHOTOGRAPH, THE) (1987,
Gr.)
I PIANETI CONTRO DI NOI (SEE: PLANETS AGAINST
US, THE) (1961, It./Fr.)
I PROMISE TO PAY (1937) PR:A
I PROMISE TO PAY (SEE: PAYROLL) (1962, Brit.)
I REMEMBER MAMA (1948) PR:AA
I RING DOORBELLS (1946) PR:A
I SAILED TO TAHITI WITH AN ALL GIRL CREW
(1969) PR:A
I SAW WHAT YOU DID (1965) PR:C-O
I SEE A DARK STRANGER (SEE: ADVENTURESS,
THE) (1946, Brit.)
I SEE ICE (1938) PR:A
I SELL ANYTHING (1934) PR:A
I SENT A LETTER TO MY LOVE (1980, Fr.) PR:A
I SHALL RETURN (SEE: AMERICAN GUERRILLA IN
THE PHILIPPINES, AN) (1950)
I SHOT BILLY THE KID (1950) PR:A
I SHOT JESSE JAMES (1949) PR:A
I SOGNI NEL CASSETTO (SEE: DREAMS IN A
DRAWER) (1957, Fr./It.)
I SOVVERSIVO (SEE: SUBVERSIVES, THE) (1967, It.)
I SPIT ON YOUR GRAVE (1962, Fr.) PR:O
I SPIT ON YOUR GRAVE (1983) PR:O
I SPY (1933, Brit.) PR:A
I SPY, YOU SPY (SEE: BANG! BANG! YOU'RE DEAD)
(1966, Brit.)
I STAND ACCUSED (1938) PR:A
I STAND CONDEMNED (1936, Brit.) PR:A
I START COUNTING (1970, Brit.) PR:O
I STOLE A MILLION (1939) PR:A
I SURRENDER DEAR (1948) PR:A
I TAKE THIS OATH (1940) PR:A
I TAKE THIS WOMAN (1931) PR:A
I TAKE THIS WOMAN (1940) PR:A
I THANK A FOOL (1962, Brit.) PR:A-C
I THANK YOU (1941, Brit.) PR:A
I, THE JURY (1953) PR:C-O
I, THE JURY (1982) PR:O
I TITANI (SEE: MY SON, THE HERO) (1963, It./Fr.)
I, TOO, AM ONLY A WOMAN (1963, W. Ger.) PR:C
I TRE VOLTI (SEE: THREE FACES OF A WOMAN)
(1965, It.)
I TRE VOLTI DELLA PAURA (SEE: BLACK SABBATH)
(1963, It.)
I VAMPIRI (SEE: DEVIL'S COMMANDMENT, THE)
(1956, It.)
I VITELLONI (SEE: VITELLONI) (1953, It./Fr.)
I WAKE UP SCREAMING (1942) PR:A
I WALK ALONE (1948) PR:C
I WALK THE LINE (1970) PR:A
I WALKED WITH A ZOMBIE (1943) PR:C-O
I WANNA HOLD YOUR HAND (1978) PR:A
I WANT A DIVORCE (1940) PR:A
I WANT HER DEAD (SEE: W) (1974)
I WANT TO LIVE! (1958) PR:O
I WANT WHAT I WANT (1972, Brit.) PR:O
I WANT YOU (1951) PR:A
I WANTED WINGS (1941) PR:A
I WAS A CAPTIVE IN NAZI GERMANY (1936) PR:A
I WAS A COMMUNIST FOR THE F.B.I. (1951) PR:C
I WAS A CONVICT (1939) PR:A
I WAS A MALE WAR BRIDE (1949) PR:A
I WAS A PRISONER ON DEVIL'S ISLAND (1941) PR:A
I WAS A SHOPLIFTER (1950) PR:A
I WAS A SPY (1934, Brit.) PR:A
I WAS A TEENAGE FRANKENSTEIN (1958) PR:C-O
I WAS A TEENAGE T.V. TERRORIST (1987) PR:C
I WAS A TEENAGE WEREWOLF (1957) PR:C-O
I WAS A TEENAGE ZOMBIE (1987) PR:O
I WAS AN ADVENTURESS (1940) PR:A
I WAS AN AMERICAN SPY (1951) PR:A
I WAS FAITHLESS (SEE: CYNARA) (1932)
I WAS FRAMED (1942) PR:A
I WAS HAPPY HERE (SEE: TIME LOST AND TIME RE-
MEMBERED) (1966, Brit.)
I WAS MONTY'S DOUBLE (SEE: HELL, HEAVEN OR
HOBOKEN) (1958, Brit.)
I WILL. . . . I WILL. . . FOR NOW (1976) PR:C
I WONDER WHO'S KISSING HER NOW (1947) PR:A
I WOULDN'T BE IN YOUR SHOES (1948) PR:A
ICARUS XB-1 (SEE: VOYAGE TO THE END OF THE
UNIVERSE) (1963, Czech.)
ICE (1970) PR:O
ICE-CAPADES (1941) PR:A
ICE-CAPADES REVUE (1942) PR:A
ICE CASTLES (1978) PR:A

ICE COLD IN ALEX (SEE: DESERT ATTACK) (1958,
Brit.)
ICE FOLLIES OF 1939, THE (1939) PR:A
ICE HOUSE, THE (1969) PR:O
ICE PALACE (1960) PR:A-C
ICE PALACE, THE (1987, Norway) PR:C
ICE PIRATES, THE (1984) PR:A-C
ICE STATION ZEBRA (1968) PR:A
ICELAND (1942) PR:A
ICEMAN (1984) PR:A-C
ICEMAN COMETH, THE (1973) PR:C
ICH BIN AUCH NUR EINE FRAU (SEE: I, TOO, AM
ONLY A WOMAN) (1963, W. Ger.)
ICH LIEBE DICH TOETE DICH (SEE: I LOVE YOU, I
KILL YOU) (1972, W. Ger.)
ICH UND DIE KAISERIN (SEE: EMPRESS AND I, THE)
(1933, Ger.)
ICHABOD AND MR. TOAD (SEE: ADVENTURES OF
ICHABOD AND MR. TOAD, THE) (1949)
ICHIJOJI NO KETTO (SEE: SAMURAI (PART II)) (1967,
Jap.)
I'D CLIMB THE HIGHEST MOUNTAIN (1951) PR:A
I'D GIVE MY LIFE (1936) PR:A
I'D RATHER BE RICH (1964) PR:A
IDAGINE SU UN CITTADINO AL DI DOPRA DI OGNI
SOSPETTO (SEE: INVESTIGATION OF A CITIZEN
ABOVE SUSPICION) (1970, It.)
IDAHO (1943) PR:A
IDAHO KID, THE (1937) PR:A
IDAHO TRANSFER (1975) PR:C
IDEA GIRL (1946) PR:A
IDEAL HUSBAND, AN (1948, Brit.) PR:A
IDEAL LODGER, THE (1957, W. Ger.) PR:O
IDENTIFICATION MARKS: NONE (1969, Pol.) PR:A
IDENTIFICATION OF A WOMAN (1983, It.) PR:C-O
IDENTIKIT (SEE: DRIVER'S SEAT, THE) (1975, It.)
IDENTITY PARADE (SEE: LINEUP, THE) (1934)
IDENTITY UNKNOWN (1945) PR:A
IDENTITY UNKNOWN (1960, Brit.) PR:A
IDI I SMOTRI (SEE: COME AND SEE) (1986, USSR)
IDIOT, THE (1948, Fr.) PR:A
IDIOT, THE (1960, USSR) PR:A
IDIOT, THE (1963, Jap.) PR:C-O
IDIOT'S DELIGHT (1939) PR:A
IDLE RICH, THE (1929) PR:A
IDO ZERO DAISAKUSEN (SEE: LATITUDE ZERO)
(1970, US/Jap.)
IDOL, THE (1966, Brit.) PR:O
IDOL OF PARIS (1948, Brit.) PR:A
IDOL OF THE CROWDS (1937) PR:A
IDOL ON PARADE (1959, Brit.) PR:A
IDOLMAKER, THE (1980) PR:A-C
IDOLS IN THE DUST (SEE: SATURDAY'S HERO)
(1951)
IERI, OGGI E DOMANI (SEE: YESTERDAY, TODAY
AND TOMORROW) (1964, Fr./It.)
IF. . . (1968, Brit.) PR:O
IF A MAN ANSWERS (1962) PR:A
IF EVER I SEE YOU AGAIN (1978) PR:C
IF HE HOLLERS, LET HIM GO (1968) PR:O
IF I HAD A MILLION (1932) PR:A
IF I HAD MY WAY (1940) PR:A
IF I WERE BOSS (1938, Brit.) PR:A
IF I WERE FREE (1933) PR:A
IF I WERE KING (SEE: VAGABOND KING, THE) (1930)
IF I WERE KING (1938) PR:A
IF I WERE RICH (1936, Brit.) PR:A
IF I'M LUCKY (1946) PR:A
IF IT'S TUESDAY, THIS MUST BE BELGIUM (1969)
PR:A
IF PARIS WERE TOLD TO US (1956, Fr.) PR:A
IF THIS BE SIN (1950, Brit.) PR:A
IF WINTER COMES (1947) PR:A
IF YOU COULD ONLY COOK (1936) PR:A
IF YOU COULD SEE WHAT I HEAR (1982, Can.) PR:A
IF YOU FEEL LIKE SINGING (SEE: SUMMER STOCK)
(1950)
IF YOU KNEW SUSIE (1948) PR:A
IGOROTA, THE LEGEND OF THE TREE OF LIFE
(1970, Phil.) PR:O
IKARIE XB 1 (SEE: VOYAGE TO THE END OF THE
UNIVERSE) (1963, Czech.)
IKIMONO NO KIROUKU (SEE: I LIVE IN FEAR) (1967,
Jap.)
IKIRU (1952, Jap.) PR:A
IL BIDONE (SEE: SWINDLE, THE) (1962, Fr./It.)
IL BODONE (SEE: SWINDLE, THE) (1955, It.)
IL BUONO, IL BRUTTO, IL CATTIVO (SEE: GOOD,
THE BAD, AND THE UGLY, THE) (1967, It./Sp.)
IL CASO MORO (SEE: MORO AFFAIR, THE) (1987, It.)
IL CASTELLO DE MORTI VIVI (SEE: CASTLE OF THE
LIVING DEAD) (1964, Fr./It.)
IL CASTELLO IN SVEZIA (SEE: NUTTY, NAUGHTY
CHATEAU) (1964, Fr./It.)
IL COBRA (SEE: COBRA, THE) (1968, It./Sp.)
IL CONFORMISTA (SEE: CONFORMIST, THE) (1970,
It./Fr.)

IL CONTE DI MONTECRISTO (SEE: STORY OF THE COUNT OF MONTE CRISTO, THE) (1962, Fr./It.)
IL CRISTO PROIBITO (SEE: STRANGE DECEPTION) (1953, It.)
IL CROLLO DI ROMA (SEE: FALL OF ROME, THE) (1963, It.)
IL DESERTO ROSSO (SEE: RED DESERT) (1964, Fr./It.)
IL DESERTORE E I NOMADI (SEE: DESERTER AND THE NOMADS, THE) (1969, Czech./It.)
IL DESTINO (SEE: DESTINY) (1938, It.)
IL DIABOLICO DR. MABUSE (SEE: THOUSAND EYES OF DR. MABUSE, THE) (1960, Fr./It./W. Ger.)
IL DIARIO DI UNA CAMERIERA (SEE: DIARY OF A CHAMBERMAID) (1964, Fr./It.)
IL DIAVOLO BIANCO (SEE: WHITE DEVIL, THE) (1948, It.)
IL DIAVOLO IN CORPO (SEE: DEVIL IN THE FLESH) (1986, Fr./It.)
IL DISORDINE (SEE: DISORDER) (1964, Fr./It.)
IL DISPREZZO (SEE: CONTEMPT) (1963, It./Fr.)
IL FEDERALE (SEE: FASCIST, THE) (1965, It.)
IL FIUME DEL GRANDE CAIMANO (SEE: GREAT ALLIGATOR) (1980, It.)
IL GATTOPARDO (SEE: LEOPARD, THE) (1963, It.)
IL GENERALE DELLA ROVERE (SEE: GENERAL DELLA ROVERE) (1959, It./Fr.)
IL GIARDINO DEL FINZI-CONTINI (SEE: GARDEN OF THE FINZI-CONTINIS, THE) (1971, It./W. Ger.)
IL GIORNO DELLA CIVETTA (SEE: DAY OF THE OWL, THE) (1968, Fr./It.)
IL GIORNO E L'ORA (SEE: DAY AND THE HOUR, THE) (1963, Fr./It.)
IL GRIDO (1962, US/It.) PR:C
IL GRIDO DELLA TERRA (SEE: EARTH CRIES OUT) (1948, It.)
IL LAGO DI SANTANA (SEE: SHE BEAST, THE) (1966, Brit./It./Yugo.)
IL MAESTRO (SEE: TEACHER AND THE MIRACLE, THE) (1961, It./Sp.)
IL MAESTRO DI DON GIOVANNI (SEE: CROSSED SWORDS) (1954, US/It.)
IL MAGNIFICO CORNUTO (SEE: MAGNIFICENT CUCKOLD, THE) (1965, Fr./It.)
IL MARITO E MIO E L'AMAZZO QUANDO MI PARE (SEE: DROP DEAD, MY LOVE) (1968, It.)
IL MIO NOME E NESSUNO (SEE: MY NAME IS NOBODY) (1974, Fr./It./W. Ger.)
IL MIO NOME E SHANGHAI JOE (SEE: TO KILL OR TO DIE) (1973, It.)
IL MISTERO DEI TRE CONTINENTI (SEE: MISTRESS OF THE WORLD) (1959, Fr./It./W. Ger.)
IL MISTERO DELLA QUATTRO CORONA (SEE: TREASURE OF THE FOUR CROWNS) (1983, US/Sp.)
IL MITO (SEE: MYTH, THE) (1965, It.)
IL MONDO DI YOR (SEE: YOR, THE HUNTER FROM THE FUTURE) (1983, It.)
IL MONSTRO DELL ISOLA (SEE: MONSTER OF THE ISLAND) (1953, It.)
IL MONTAGNA DI DIO CANNIBALE (SEE: SLAVE OF THE CANNIBAL GOD) (1978, It.)
IL MOSTRO DI VENEZIA (SEE: EMBALMER, THE) (1966, It.)
IL MOSTRO E IN TAVOLA... BARONE FRANKENSTEIN (SEE: ANDY WARHOL'S FRANKENSTEIN) (1974, Fr./It.)
IL NATALE CHE QUASI NON FU (SEE: CHRISTMAS THAT ALMOST WASN'T, THE) (1966, It.)
IL NEMICO DI MIA MOGLIE (SEE: MY WIFE'S ENEMY) (1967, It.)
IL PASSATORE (SEE: BULLET FOR STEFANO) (1950, It.)
IL PICCOLO MARTIRE (SEE: LITTLE MARTYR, THE) (1947, It.)
IL PORTIERE DI NOTTE (SEE: NIGHT PORTER, THE) (1974, US/It.)
IL POZZO DELLE TRE VERITA (SEE: THREE FACES OF SIN) (1963, Fr./It.)
IL RE DEI FAISARI (SEE: COUNTERFEITERS OF PARIS, THE) (1962, Fr./It.)
IL ROSO SEGMO DELLA POLLIAS (SEE: HATCHET FOR A HONEYMOON) (1969, It./Sp.)
IL SAPORE DELLA VENDETTA (SEE: NARCO MEN, THE) (1971, It./Sp.)
IL SEGNO DI VENERA (SEE: SIGN OF VENUS) (1955, It.)
IL SEME DELL'UOMO (SEE: SEED OF MAN, THE) (1970, It.)
IL SEPOLCRO DEI RE (SEE: CLEOPATRA'S DAUGHTER) (1963, Fr./It.)
IL SIGILLO DE PECHINO (SEE: CORRUPT ONES, THE) (1967, Fr./It./W. Ger.)
IL SOGNO DI BUTTERFLY (SEE: DREAM OF BUTTERFLY, THE) (1941, It.)
IL SOLE SORGE ANCORA (SEE: OUTCRY) (1949, It.)
IL SORPASSO (SEE: EASY LIFE, THE) (1963, It.)
IL SUFFIT D'AIMER (SEE: BERNADETTE OF LOURDES) (1962, Fr.)

IL TESORO DI ROMMEL (SEE: ROMMEL'S TREASURE) (1962, It.)
IL VANGELO SECONDE MATTEO (SEE: GOSPEL ACCORDING TO ST. MATTHEW, THE) (1964, Fr./It.)
IL VI SITATORE (SEE: VISITOR, THE) (1980, US/It.)
I'LL BE SEEING YOU (1944) PR:A
I'LL BE YOUR SWEETHEART (1945, Brit.) PR:A
I'LL BE YOURS (1947) PR:A
I'LL CRY TOMORROW (1955) PR:A-C
I'LL FIX IT (1934) PR:A
I'LL GET BY (1950) PR:A
I'LL GET YOU (1953, Brit.) PR:A
I'LL GET YOU FOR THIS (SEE: LUCKY NICK CAIN) (1951)
I'LL GIVE A MILLION (1938) PR:A
I'LL GIVE MY LIFE (1959) PR:A
I'LL LOVE YOU ALWAYS (1935) PR:A
ILL MET BY MOONLIGHT (SEE: NIGHT AMBUSH) (1957, Brit.)
I'LL NEVER FORGET WHAT'S 'IS NAME (1967, Brit.) PR:AC
I'LL NEVER FORGET YOU (1951, Brit.) PR:A
I'LL REMEMBER APRIL (1945) PR:A
I'LL SAVE MY LOVE (SEE: TWO LOVES) (1961)
I'LL SEE YOU IN MY DREAMS (1951) PR:A
I'LL SELL MY LIFE (1941) PR:A
I'LL STICK TO YOU (1933, Brit.) PR:A
I'LL TAKE ROMANCE (1937) PR:A
I'LL TAKE SWEDEN (1965) PR:A
I'LL TELL THE WORLD (1934) PR:A
I'LL TELL THE WORLD (1945) PR:AA
I'LL TURN TO YOU (1946, Brit.) PR:A
I'LL WAIT FOR YOU (1941) PR:A
I'LL WALK BESIDE YOU (1943, Brit.) PR:A
ILLEGAL (1932, Brit.) PR:A
ILLEGAL (1955) PR:C
ILLEGAL DIVORCE, THE (SEE: SECOND-HAND WIFE) (1933)
ILLEGAL ENTRY (1949) PR:A
ILLEGAL RIGHTS (SEE: HAIL TO THE RANGERS) (1943)
ILLEGAL TRAFFIC (1938) PR:A
ILLEGALLY YOURS (1988) PR:A
ILLIAC PASSION, THE (1968) PR:O
ILLICIT (1931) PR:C
ILLICIT INTERLUDE (1951, Swed.) PR:O
ILLUMINATIONS (1976, Aus.) PR:O
ILLUSION (1929) PR:A
ILLUSION OF BLOOD (1966, Jap.) PR:O
ILLUSION TRAVELS BY STREETCAR, THE (1977, Mex.) PR:C
ILLUSIONIST, THE (1985, Neth.) PR:C
ILLUSTRATED MAN, THE (1969) PR:O
ILLUSTRIOUS ENERGY (1988, New Zealand) PR:C
ILS SONT NUS (SEE: WE ARE ALL NAKED) (1970, Can./Fr.)
ILYA MOUROMETZ (SEE: SWORD AND THE DRAGON, THE) (1960, USSR)
I'M A STRANGER (1952, Brit.) PR:A
I'M ALL RIGHT, JACK (1959, Brit.) PR:A
I'M AN EXPLOSIVE (1933, Brit.) PR:A
I'M CRAZY ABOUT YOU (SEE: TE QUIERO CON LOCURA) (1935)
I'M DANCING AS FAST AS I CAN (1982) PR:C-O
I'M FROM ARKANSAS (1944) PR:A
I'M FROM MISSOURI (1939) PR:A
I'M FROM THE CITY (1938) PR:A
I'M GOING TO GET YOU... ELLIOT BOY (1971, Can.) PR:O
I'M GONNA GIT YOU SUCKA (1988) PR:O
IM LAUF DER ZEIT (SEE: KINGS OF THE ROAD) (1976, W. Ger.)
I'M NO ANGEL (1933) PR:C
I'M NOBODY'S SWEETHEART NOW (1940) PR:A
IM STAHLNETZ DES DR. MABUSE (SEE: RETURN OF DR. MABUSE, THE) (1961, Fr./It./W. Ger.)
I'M STILL ALIVE (1940) PR:A
IMAGEMAKER, THE (1986) PR:C-O
IMAGEN LATENTE (SEE: LATENT IMAGE) (1988, Chile)
IMAGES (1972, Ireland) PR:C-O
IMAGINARY SWEETHEART (SEE: PROFESSIONAL SWEETHEART) (1933)
IMAGO (SEE: TO BE FREE) (1972)
IMERES TOU 36 (SEE: DAYS OF 36) (1972, Gr.)
IMITATION GENERAL (1958) PR:A
IMITATION OF LIFE (1934) PR:A
IMITATION OF LIFE (1959) PR:A
IMMEDIATE DISASTER (SEE: STRANGER FROM VENUS, THE) (1954, Brit.)
IMMEDIATE FAMILY (1989) PR:C
IMMORAL CHARGE (1962, Brit.) PR:A
IMMORAL MOMENT, THE (1967, Fr.) PR:C
IMMORTAL BACHELOR, THE (1980, It.) PR:O
IMMORTAL BATTALION, THE (1944, Brit.) PR:A
IMMORTAL GARRISON, THE (1957, USSR) PR:A
IMMORTAL GENTLEMAN (1935, Brit.) PR:A

IMMORTAL MONSTER (SEE: CALTIKI, THE IMMORTAL MONSTER) (1959, It.)
IMMORTAL SERGEANT, THE (1943) PR:A
IMMORTAL STORY, THE (1968, Fr.) PR:C
IMMORTAL VAGABOND (1931, Ger.) PR:A
IMPACT (1949) PR:A
IMPACT (1963, Brit.) PR:C
IMPASSE (1969) PR:O
IMPASSE DES VERTUS (SEE: LOVE AT NIGHT) (1961, Fr.)
IMPASSIVE FOOTMAN, THE (SEE: WOMAN IN CHAINS) (1932, Brit.)
IMPATIENT MAIDEN, THE (1932) PR:C
IMPATIENT YEARS, THE (1944) PR:A
IMPERFECT LADY, THE (SEE: PERFECT GENTLEMAN, THE) (1935)
IMPERFECT LADY, THE (1947) PR:A
IMPERIAL VENUS (1963, It./Fr.) PR:A
IMPERSONATOR, THE (1962, Brit.) PR:C
IMPORTANCE OF BEING EARNEST, THE (1952, Brit.) PR:A
IMPORTANT MAN, THE (1961, Mex.) PR:O
IMPORTANT WITNESS, THE (1933) PR:A
IMPOSSIBLE LOVER (SEE: HUDDLE) (1932)
IMPOSSIBLE OBJECT (1973, Fr.) PR:C-O
IMPOSSIBLE ON SATURDAY (1966, Fr./Israel) PR:A
IMPOSSIBLE YEARS, THE (1968) PR:A
IMPOSTER, THE (1944) PR:A
IMPOSTORS (1979) PR:O
"IMP"PROBABLE MR. WEE GEE, THE (1966) PR:A
IMPRESSIVE FOOTMAN, THE (SEE: WOMAN IN CHAINS) (1932, Brit.)
IMPROPER CHANNELS (1981, Can.) PR:C
IMPROPER DUCHESS, THE (1936, Brit.) PR:A
IMPULSE (1955, Brit.) PR:C
IMPULSE (1975) PR:O
IMPULSE (1984) PR:O
IN (SEE: HIGH) (1969, Can.)
IN A GLASS CAGE (1989, Sp.) PR:O
IN A LONELY PLACE (1950) PR:C
IN A MONASTERY GARDEN (1935, Brit.) PR:A
IN A SECRET GARDEN (SEE: OF LOVE AND DESIRE) (1963)
IN A YEAR OF THIRTEEN MOONS (1980, W. Ger.) PR:O
IN-BETWEEN AGE, THE (1958, Brit.) PR:A
IN CALIENTE (1935) PR:A
IN CASE OF ADVERSITY (SEE: LOVE IS MY PROFESSION) (1959, Fr.)
IN CELEBRATION (1975, Brit.) PR:O
IN COLD BLOOD (1967) PR:O
IN COUNTRY (1989) PR:C
IN DARKNESS WAITING (SEE: STRATEGY OF TERROR) (1969)
IN DE SCHADUW VAN DE OVERWINNING (SEE: SHADOW OF VICTORY) (1986, Neth.)
IN DER HOLLE IST NOCH PLATZ (SEE: THERE IS STILL ROOM IN HELL) (1963, W. Ger.)
IN EARLY ARIZONA (1938) PR:A
IN EINEM JAHR MIT 13 MONDEN (SEE: IN A YEAR OF THIRTEEN MOONS) (1980, W. Ger.)
IN ENEMY COUNTRY (1968) PR:A-C
IN FAST COMPANY (1946) PR:A
IN GAY MADRID (1930) PR:A
IN GOD WE TRUST (1980) PR:C-O
IN HARM'S WAY (1965) PR:A
IN HIS STEPS (1936) PR:A
IN-LAWS, THE (1979) PR:A
IN LIKE FLINT (1967) PR:A
IN LOVE AND WAR (1958) PR:A
IN LOVE WITH LIFE (1934) PR:A
IN MACARTHUR PARK (1977) PR:C-O
IN NAME DER MENSCHLICHKEIT (SEE: TRIAL, THE) (1948, Aust.)
IN NAME ONLY (1939) PR:A
IN NOME DEL PAPE RE (SEE: IN THE NAME OF THE POPE KING) (1978, It.)
IN OLD AMARILLO (1951) PR:A
IN OLD ARIZONA (1929) PR:A
IN OLD CALIENTE (1939) PR:A
IN OLD CALIFORNIA (1929) PR:A
IN OLD CALIFORNIA (1942) PR:A
IN OLD CHEYENNE (1931) PR:A
IN OLD CHEYENNE (1941) PR:A
IN OLD CHICAGO (1938) PR:A
IN OLD COLORADO (1941) PR:A
IN OLD KENTUCKY (1935) PR:A
IN OLD MEXICO (1938) PR:A
IN OLD MISSOURI (1940) PR:A
IN OLD MONTANA (1939) PR:A
IN OLD MONTEREY (1939) PR:A
IN OLD NEW MEXICO (1945) PR:AA
IN OLD OKLAHOMA (1943) PR:A
IN OLD SACRAMENTO (1946) PR:C
IN OLD SANTA FE (1935) PR:A
IN OUR TIME (1944) PR:C
IN PERSON (1935) PR:A
IN PIENO SOLE (SEE: PURPLE NOON) (1961, Fr./It.)
IN PRAISE OF OLDER WOMEN (1978, Can.) PR:O

IN ROSIE'S ROOM (SEE: ROSIE, THE RIVETER) (1944)
IN SAIGON, SOME MAY LIVE (SEE: SOME MAY LIVE) (1967, Brit.)
IN SEARCH OF ANNA (1978, Aus.) PR:O
IN SEARCH OF GREGORY (1970, Brit./It.) PR:O
IN SEARCH OF HISTORIC JESUS (1980) PR:AA
IN SEARCH OF THE CASTAWAYS (1962, Brit.) PR:AA
IN SOCIETY (1944) PR:AA
IN SPITE OF DANGER (1935) PR:A
IN STRANGE COMPANY (SEE: FIRST AID) (1931)
IN THE COOL OF THE DAY (1963) PR:C
IN THE COUNTRY (1967) PR:A
IN THE DAYS OF THE THUNDERING HERD (SEE: THUNDERING HERD, THE) (1934)
IN THE DEVIL'S GARDEN (SEE: ASSAULT) (1971, Brit.)
IN THE DOGHOUSE (1964, Brit.) PR:A
IN THE FALL OF '55 EDEN CRIED (SEE: EDEN CRIED) (1967)
IN THE FRENCH STYLE (1963, US/Fr.) PR:O
IN THE GOOD OLD SUMMERTIME (1949) PR:AA
IN THE HEADLINES (1929) PR:A
IN THE HEAT OF THE NIGHT (1967) PR:C
IN THE LINE OF DUTY (1931) PR:A
IN THE MEANTIME, DARLING (1944) PR:A
IN THE MONEY (1934) PR:A
IN THE MONEY (1958) PR:AA
IN THE MOOD (1987) PR:C
IN THE MOUTH OF THE WOLF (1988, Peru/Sp.) PR:O
IN THE NAME OF LIFE (1947, USSR) PR:O
IN THE NAME OF THE POPE KING (1978, It.) PR:O
IN THE NAVY (SEE: ABBOTT AND COSTELLO IN THE NAVY) (1941)
IN THE NEXT ROOM (1930) PR:A
IN THE NICK (1960, Brit.) PR:A
IN THE NIGHT (SEE: GANG'S ALL HERE) (1941)
IN THE SHADOW OF KILIMANJARO (1986, US/Brit./Kenya) PR:O
IN THE SOUP (1936, Brit.) PR:A
IN THE WAKE OF A STRANGER (1960, Brit.) PR:C
IN THE WAKE OF THE BOUNTY (1933, Aus.) PR:A
IN THE WHITE CITY (1983, Switz./Portugal) PR:C-O
IN THE WILD MOUNTAINS (1986, Chi.) PR:C
IN THE WOODS (SEE: RASHOMON) (1950, Jap.)
IN THE YEAR 2889 (1966) PR:C
IN THIS CORNER (1948) PR:A
IN THIS OUR LIFE (1942) PR:C-O
IN TROUBLE WITH EVE (1964, Brit.) PR:A
IN WALKED EVE (SEE: IN TROUBLE WITH EVE) (1964, Brit.)
IN WHICH WE SERVE (1942, Brit.) PR:A
INADMISSIBLE EVIDENCE (1968, Brit.) PR:C
INBREAKER, THE (1974, Can.) PR:O
INCENDIARY BLONDE (1945) PR:A
INCENSE FOR THE DAMNED (1970, Brit.) PR:O
INCHON (1981, US/S.K.) PR:O
INCIDENT (1948) PR:C
INCIDENT, THE (1967) PR:C
INCIDENT AT MIDNIGHT (1966, Brit.) PR:A
INCIDENT AT PHANTOM HILL (1966) PR:A
INCIDENT IN AN ALLEY (1962) PR:A
INCIDENT IN SHANGHAI (1937, Brit.) PR:A
INCORRIGIBLE (1980, Fr.) PR:C
INCREDIBLE INVASION, THE (1971, Mex./US) PR:C-O
INCREDIBLE JOURNEY, THE (1963) PR:AA
INCREDIBLE MELTING MAN, THE (1978) PR:O
INCREDIBLE MR. LIMPET, THE (1964) PR:AA
INCREDIBLE PETRIFIED WORLD, THE (1959) PR:A
INCREDIBLE PRAYING MANTIS, THE (SEE: DEADLY MANTIS, THE) (1957)
INCREDIBLE SARAH, THE (1976, Brit.) PR:C
INCREDIBLE SHRINKING MAN, THE (1957) PR:A
INCREDIBLE SHRINKING WOMAN, THE (1981) PR:C
INCREDIBLE TORTURE SHOW, THE (SEE: BLOOD-SUCKING FREAKS) (1982)
INCREDIBLE TWO-HEADED TRANSPLANT, THE (1971) PR:O
INCREDIBLY STRANGE CREATURES, THE (SEE: INCREDIBLY STRANGE CREATURES WHO STOPPED LIVING AND BECAME CRAZY MIXED-UP ZOMBIES, THE) (1965)
INCREDIBLY STRANGE CREATURES WHO STOPPED LIVING AND BECAME CRAZY MIXED-UP ZOMBIES, THE (1965) PR:O
INCUBUS (1966) PR:O
INCUBUS, THE (1982, Can.) PR:O
INDECENT (1962, W. Ger.) PR:O
INDECENT OBSESSION, AN (1985, Aus.) PR:C-O
INDEPENDENCE DAY (1976) PR:C-O
INDEPENDENCE DAY (1983) PR:O
INDESTRUCTIBLE MAN, THE (1956) PR:A
INDIAN AGENT (1948) PR:A
INDIAN FIGHTER, THE (1955) PR:C
INDIAN LOVE CALL (SEE: ROSE MARIE) (1936)
INDIAN PAINT (1965) PR:AA
INDIAN SCOUT (SEE: DAVY CROCKETT, INDIAN SCOUT) (1950)
INDIAN SUMMER (SEE: JUDGE STEPS OUT, THE) (1949)

INDIAN TERRITORY (1950) PR:A
INDIAN TOMB, THE (SEE: JOURNEY TO THE LOST CITY) (1959, Fr./It./W. Ger.)
INDIAN UPRISING (1951) PR:A
INDIANA JONES AND THE LAST CRUSADE (1989) PR:A-C
INDIANA JONES AND THE TEMPLE OF DOOM (1984) PR:C-O
INDIANAPOLIS SPEEDWAY (1939) PR:A
INDISCREET (1931) PR:C
INDISCREET (1958, Brit.) PR:A-C
INDISCRETION (SEE: CHRISTMAS IN CONNECTICUT) (1945)
INDISCRETION OF AN AMERICAN WIFE (1954, US/It.) PR:A-C
INDISCRETIONS OF EVE (1932, Brit.) PR:A
INFAMOUS (SEE: CHILDREN'S HOUR, THE) (1961)
INFERNAL IDOL (SEE: CRAZE) (1974, Brit.)
INFERNAL MACHINE (1933) PR:A
INFERNO (1953) PR:O
INFERNO (1980, It.) PR:O
INFERNO DEI MORTI-VIVENTI (SEE: ZOMBIE CREEPING FLESH) (1981, It./Sp.)
INFERNO IN DIRETTA (SEE: CUT AND RUN) (1986, It.)
INFORMATION KID (SEE: FAST COMPANIONS) (1932)
INFORMATION RECEIVED (1962, Brit.) PR:C
INFORMER, THE (1929, Brit.) PR:A
INFORMER, THE (1935) PR:A
INFORMERS, THE (SEE: UNDERWORLD INFORMERS) (1965, Brit.)
INFRA-MAN (1975, Hong Kong) PR:C
INFRA SUPERMAN, THE (SEE: INFRA-MAN) (1975, Hong Kong)
INGAGI (1931) PR:C
INGENJOR ANDREES LUFTFARD (SEE: FLIGHT OF THE EAGLE) (1982, Norway/Swed./W. Ger.)
INGLORIOUS BASTARDS (SEE: COUNTERFEIT COMMANDOS) (1978, It.)
INHERIT THE WIND (1960) PR:A
INHERITANCE, THE (1951, Brit.) PR:A
INHERITANCE, THE (1964, Jap.) PR:C
INHERITANCE, THE (1976, It.) PR:O
INHERITANCE IN PRETORIA (1936, Ger.) PR:C
INHERITORS, THE (1982, Aust.) PR:O
INITIATION, THE (1984) PR:O
INJUN FENDER (1973) PR:O
INJUSTICE (SEE: ROAD GANG) (1936)
INN FOR TROUBLE (1960, Brit.) PR:A
INN OF THE DAMNED (1974, Aus.) PR:O
INN OF THE FRIGHTENED PEOPLE (SEE: TERROR FROM UNDER THE HOUSE) (1971, Brit.)
INN OF THE SIXTH HAPPINESS, THE (1958, Brit.) PR:AA
INNER CIRCLE, THE (1946) PR:A
INNER SANCTUM (1948) PR:A
INNERSPACE (1987) PR:C
INNERVIEW, THE (1974) PR:O
INNOCENCE IS BLISS (SEE: MISS GRANT TAKES RICHMOND) (1949)
INNOCENCE UNPROTECTED (1971, Yugo.) PR:C
INNOCENT, THE (1976, It.) PR:O
INNOCENT, THE (1988, Fr.) PR:O
INNOCENT AFFAIR, AN (SEE: DON'T TRUST YOUR HUSBAND) (1948)
INNOCENT AND THE DAMNED (SEE: GIRLS' TOWN) (1959)
INNOCENT BYSTANDERS (1973, Brit.) PR:O
INNOCENT MAN, AN (1989) PR:C
INNOCENT MEETING (1959, Brit.) PR:C
INNOCENT SINNERS (1958, Brit.) PR:AA
INNOCENTS, THE (1961, US/Brit.) PR:C-O
INNOCENTS IN PARIS (1955, Brit.) PR:A
INNOCENTS OF CHICAGO, THE (SEE: WHY SAPS LEAVE HOME) (1932, Brit.)
INNOCENTS OF PARIS (1929) PR:A
INNOCENTS WITH DIRTY HANDS (SEE: DIRTY HANDS) (1976, Fr.)
INQUEST (1931, Brit.) PR:C
INQUEST (1939, Brit.) PR:C
INQUISITOR, THE (1982, Fr.) PR:C-O
INSECT, THE (SEE: INSECT WOMAN, THE) (1964, Jap.)
INSECT WOMAN, THE (1964, Jap.) PR:C
INSEL DER AMAZONEN (SEE: SEVEN DARING GIRLS) (1962, W. Ger.)
INSEMINOID (SEE: HORROR PLANET) (1982, Brit.)
INSIDE AMY (1975) PR:O
INSIDE DAISY CLOVER (1965) PR:O
INSIDE DETROIT (1955) PR:O
INSIDE INFORMATION (1934) PR:A
INSIDE INFORMATION (1939) PR:A
INSIDE INFORMATION (SEE: LONE PRAIRIE, THE) (1942)
INSIDE JOB (1946) PR:A
INSIDE LOOKING OUT (1977, Aus.) PR:C
INSIDE MOVES (1980) PR:C
INSIDE OUT (SEE: LIFE UPSIDE DOWN) (1964, Fr.)
INSIDE OUT (1975, Brit.) PR:C
INSIDE OUT (1986) PR:O

INSIDE STORY (1939) PR:A
INSIDE STORY, THE (1948) PR:A
INSIDE STRAIGHT (1951) PR:O
INSIDE THE LAW (1942) PR:A
INSIDE THE LINES (1930) PR:A
INSIDE THE MAFIA (1959) PR:O
INSIDE THE ROOM (1935, Brit.) PR:C
INSIDE THE WALLS OF FOLSOM PRISON (1951) PR:C
INSIDIOUS DR. FU MANCHU, THE (SEE: MYSTERIOUS DR. FU MANCHU) (1929)
INSIGNIFICANCE (1985, Brit.) PR:O
INSOMNIACS (1986, Arg.) PR:O
INSPECTOR, THE (SEE: LISA) (1961, Brit.)
INSPECTOR CALLS, AN (1954, Brit.) PR:O
INSPECTOR CLOUSEAU (1968, Brit.) PR:A
INSPECTOR GENERAL, THE (1937, Czech.) PR:A
INSPECTOR GENERAL, THE (1949) PR:AA
INSPECTOR HORNLEIGH (1939, Brit.) PR:A
INSPECTOR HORNLEIGH GOES TO IT (SEE: MAIL TRAIN) (1941, Brit.)
INSPECTOR HORNLEIGH ON HOLIDAY (1939, Brit.) PR:A
INSPECTOR MAIGRET (SEE: MAIGRET LAYS A TRAP) (1958, Fr.)
INSPIRATION (1931) PR:C
INSTANT JUSTICE (1986) PR:O
INSULT (1932, Brit.) PR:C
INSURANCE INVESTIGATOR (1951) PR:C
INTELLIGENCE MEN, THE (SEE: SPYLARKS) (1965, Brit.)
INTENT TO KILL (1958, Brit.) PR:A
INTERFERENCE (1928) PR:A
INTERIORS (1978) PR:C-O
INTERLUDE (SEE: INTERMEZZO) (1937, Swed.)
INTERLUDE (1957) PR:A
INTERLUDE (1968, Brit.) PR:C
INTERMEZZO (1937, Ger.) PR:A
INTERMEZZO (1937, Swed.) PR:A
INTERMEZZO: A LOVE STORY (1939) PR:A
INTERNATIONAL CRIME (1938) PR:A
INTERNATIONAL HOUSE (1933) PR:A
INTERNATIONAL LADY (1941) PR:A
INTERNATIONAL POLICE (SEE: PICKUP ALLEY) (1957, Brit.)
INTERNATIONAL SETTLEMENT (1938) PR:A
INTERNATIONAL SPY (SEE: SPY RING, THE) (1938)
INTERNATIONAL SQUADRON (1941) PR:A
INTERNATIONAL VELVET (1978, Brit.) PR:AA
INTERNECINE PROJECT, THE (1974, Brit.) PR:O
INTERNES CAN'T TAKE MONEY (1937) PR:A
INTERNS, THE (1962) PR:O
INTERPOL (SEE: PICKUP ALLEY) (1957, Brit.)
INTERRUPTED HONEYMOON, THE (1936, Brit.) PR:A
INTERRUPTED HONEYMOON, AN (SEE: HOMICIDE FOR THREE) (1948)
INTERRUPTED JOURNEY, THE (1949, Brit.) PR:A-C
INTERRUPTED MELODY (1955) PR:A
INTERVAL (1973, Mex./US) PR:C
INTERVISTA (1987, It.) PR:C
INTIMACY (1966) PR:O
INTIMATE LIGHTING (1969, Czech.) PR:A
INTIMATE POWER (1986, Can.) PR:C-O
INTIMATE RELATIONS (1937, Brit.) PR:A
INTIMATE RELATIONS (SEE: LES PARENTS TERRIBLES) (1948, Fr.)
INTIMATE RELATIONS (SEE: DISOBEDIENT) (1953, Brit.)
INTIMATE STRANGER, THE (SEE: FINGER OF GUILT) (1956, Brit.)
INTIMNI OSVETLENI (SEE: INTIMATE LIGHTING) (1969, Czech.)
INTO THE BLUE (SEE: MAN IN THE DINGHY, THE) (1950, Brit.)
INTO THE NIGHT (1985) PR:O
INTO THE STRAIGHT (1950, Aus.) PR:C
INTRAMUROS (SEE: WALLS OF HELL, THE) (1964, US/Phil.)
INTRIGUE (1947) PR:A
INTRIGUE IN PARIS (SEE: MISS V FROM MOSCOW) (1942)
INTRUDER, THE (1932) PR:A
INTRUDER, THE (1955, Brit.) PR:C
INTRUDER, THE (1962) PR:C
INTRUDER IN THE DUST (1949) PR:C-O
INVADER, THE (SEE: OLD SPANISH CUSTOM, AN) (1936, Brit.)
INVADERS, THE (1941, Brit.) PR:A
INVADERS FROM MARS (1953) PR:A
INVADERS FROM MARS (1986) PR:C
INVASION (1965, Brit.) PR:A
INVASION EARTH 2150 A.D. (SEE: DALEKS – INVASION EARTH 2150 A.D.) (1966, Brit.)
INVASION FORCE (SEE: HANGAR 18) (1980)
INVASION FROM THE MOON (SEE: MUTINY IN OUTER SPACE) (1965)
INVASION OF ASTRO-MONSTERS (SEE: MONSTER ZERO) (1970, Jap.)

INVASION OF THE ANIMAL PEOPLE (1962, US/Swed.)
PR:A
INVASION OF THE ASTROS (SEE: MONSTER ZERO)
(1970, Jap.)
INVASION OF THE BEE GIRLS (1973) PR:O
INVASION OF THE BLOOD FARMERS (1972) PR:O
INVASION OF THE BODY SNATCHERS (1956) PR:A
INVASION OF THE BODY SNATCHERS (1978) PR:C-O
INVASION OF THE BODY STEALERS (SEE: BODY
STEALERS, THE) (1969, Brit.)
INVASION OF THE FLYING SAUCERS (SEE: EARTH
VS. THE FLYING SAUCERS) (1956)
INVASION OF THE HELL CREATURES (SEE: INVA-
SION OF THE SAUCER MEN) (1957)
INVASION OF THE SAUCER MEN (1957) PR:C
INVASION OF THE STAR CREATURES (1962) PR:A
INVASION OF THE VAMPIRES, THE (1961, Mex.) PR:O
INVASION OF THE ZOMBIES (SEE: HORROR OF
PARTY BEACH, THE) (1964)
INVASION QUARTET (1961, Brit.) PR:A
INVASION 1700 (1965, Fr./It./Yugo.) PR:C
INVASION SINIESTRA (SEE: INCREDIBLE INVASION,
THE) (1971, US/Mex.)
INVASION U.S.A. (1952) PR:A
INVASION U.S.A. (1985) PR:O
INVESTIGATION (1979, Fr.) PR:O
INVESTIGATION OF A CITIZEN ABOVE SUSPICION
(1970, It.) PR:O
INVESTIGATION OF MURDER, AN (SEE: LAUGHING
POLICEMAN, THE) (1973)
INVINCIBLE GLADIATOR, THE (1963, It./Sp.) PR:C
INVINCIBLE SIX, THE (1970, US/Iran) PR:A
INVISIBLE AGENT (1942) PR:A
INVISIBLE AVENGER, THE (1958) PR:A
INVISIBLE BOY, THE (1957) PR:AA
INVISIBLE CREATURE, THE (SEE: HOUSE IN MARSH
ROAD, THE) (1959, Brit.)
INVISIBLE DR. MABUSE, THE (1965, W. Ger.) PR:C
INVISIBLE ENEMY (1938) PR:A
INVISIBLE GHOST, THE (1941) PR:C
INVISIBLE HORROR, THE (SEE: INVISIBLE DR.
MABUSE, THE) (1965, W. Ger.)
INVISIBLE INFORMER, THE (1946) PR:A
INVISIBLE INVADERS (1959) PR:C
INVISIBLE KID, THE (1988) PR:C
INVISIBLE KILLER, THE (1940) PR:A
INVISIBLE MAN, THE (1933) PR:C
INVISIBLE MAN, THE (1958, Mex.) PR:A
INVISIBLE MAN, THE (1963, W. Ger.) PR:A
INVISIBLE MAN RETURNS, THE (1940) PR:A
INVISIBLE MAN'S REVENGE (1944) PR:A
INVISIBLE MENACE, THE (1938) PR:A
INVISIBLE MESSAGE, THE (SEE: GUN PLAY) (1936)
INVISIBLE OPPONENT (1933, Ger.) PR:A
INVISIBLE POWER (SEE: WASHINGTON MERRY-GO-
ROUND) (1932)
INVISIBLE RAY, THE (1936) PR:C
INVISIBLE STRANGLER (1984) PR:C-O
INVISIBLE STRIPES (1940) PR:A
INVISIBLE WALL, THE (1947) PR:A
INVISIBLE WOMAN, THE (1941) PR:A
INVITATION (1952) PR:A
INVITATION, THE (1975, Fr./Switz.) PR:C-O
INVITATION AU VOYAGE (1982, Fr.) PR:O
INVITATION TO A GUNFIGHTER (1964) PR:C
INVITATION TO A HANGING (SEE: LAW OF THE
LAWLESS) (1964)
INVITATION TO HAPPINESS (1939) PR:A
INVITATION TO MURDER (1962, Brit.) PR:C
INVITATION TO THE DANCE (1956) PR:A
INVITATION TO THE WALTZ (1935, Brit.) PR:A
IO. . . TU. . . Y. . . ELLA (1933) PR:A
IPCRESS FILE, THE (1965, Brit.) PR:A-C
IPHIGENIA (1977, Gr.) PR:A
IPNOSI (SEE: HYPNOSIS) (1966, It./Sp./W. Ger.)
IRELAND'S BORDER LINE (1939, Ireland) PR:A
IRENE (1940) PR:A
IREZUMI (SPIRIT OF TATTOO) (1982, Jap.) PR:O
IRISH AND PROUD OF IT (1938, Ireland) PR:A
IRISH EYES ARE SMILING (1944) PR:A
IRISH FOR LUCK (1936, Brit.) PR:A
IRISH HEARTS (SEE: NORAH O'NEALE) (1934, Brit.)
IRISH IN US, THE (1935) PR:A
IRISH LUCK (1939) PR:A
IRISH WHISKEY REBELLION (1973) PR:C
IRISHMAN, THE (1978, Aus.) PR:A
IRMA LA DOUCE (1963) PR:C-O
IRO (SEE: SPOILS OF THE NIGHT) (1969, Jap.)
IRON ANGEL (1964) PR:A
IRON COLLAR, THE (SEE: SHOWDOWN) (1963)
IRON CURTAIN, THE (1948) PR:A
IRON DUKE, THE (1935, Brit.) PR:A
IRON EAGLE (1986) PR:C
IRON EAGLE II (1988) PR:C
IRON FIST (SEE: AWAKENING OF JIM BURKE) (1935)
IRON GLOVE, THE (1954) PR:A
IRON KISS, THE (SEE: NAKED KISS, THE) (1964)

IRON MAIDEN, THE (SEE: SWINGING MAIDEN, THE)
(1962, Brit.)
IRON MAJOR, THE (1943) PR:A
IRON MAN, THE (1931) PR:A
IRON MAN (1951) PR:C
IRON MASK, THE (1929) PR:A
IRON MASTER, THE (1933) PR:A
IRON MISTRESS, THE (1952) PR:C
IRON MOUNTAIN TRAIL (1953) PR:A
IRON PETTICOAT, THE (1956, Brit.) PR:A
IRON ROAD, THE (SEE: BUCKSKIN FRONTIER) (1943)
IRON SHERIFF, THE (1957) PR:A
IRON STAIR, THE (1933, Brit.) PR:A
IRON TRIANGLE, THE (1989) PR:O
IRONWEED (1987) PR:C-O
IROQUOIS TRAIL, THE (1950) PR:A
IRRECONCILABLE DIFFERENCES (1984) PR:A-C
IS EVERYBODY HAPPY? (1929) PR:A
IS EVERYBODY HAPPY? (1943) PR:A
IS MY FACE RED? (1932) PR:A
IS PARIS BURNING? (1966, US/Fr.) PR:A
IS-SLOTTET (SEE: ICE PALACE, THE) (1988, Norway)
IS THERE JUSTICE? (1931) PR:A
IS THIS TRIP REALLY NECESSARY? (1970) PR:O
IS YOUR HONEYMOON REALLY NECESSARY? (1953,
Brit.) PR:A
ISAAC LITTLEFEATHERS (1984, Can.) PR:C
ISABEL (1968, Can.) PR:O
ISADORA (1968, Brit.) PR:O
ISHTAR (1987) PR:A-C
ISLA DE LOS MUERTOS (SEE: SNAKE PEOPLE, THE)
(1968, US/Mex.)
ISLAND, THE (1962, Jap.) PR:C
ISLAND, THE (1980) PR:O
ISLAND AT THE TOP OF THE WORLD, THE (1974)
PR:AA
ISLAND CAPTIVES (1937) PR:A
ISLAND CLAWS (1981) PR:O
ISLAND ESCAPE (SEE: NO MAN IS AN ISLAND) (1962)
ISLAND IN THE SKY (1938) PR:A
ISLAND IN THE SKY (1953) PR:A
ISLAND IN THE SUN (1957) PR:C
ISLAND MAN (SEE: MEN OF IRELAND) (1938, Ireland)
ISLAND MONSTER, THE (SEE: MONSTER OF THE IS-
LAND) (1953, It.)
ISLAND OF ALLAH (1956) PR:A
ISLAND OF DESIRE (SEE: LOVE TRADER, THE) (1930)
ISLAND OF DESIRE (1952, Brit.) PR:C
ISLAND OF DR. MOREAU, THE (1977) PR:C
ISLAND OF DOOM (1933, USSR) PR:A
ISLAND OF DOOMED MEN (1940) PR:C
ISLAND OF LOST MEN (1939) PR:A
ISLAND OF LOST SOULS (1933) PR:C
ISLAND OF LOST WOMEN (1959) PR:A
ISLAND OF LOVE (1963) PR:A
ISLAND OF MONTE CRISTO (SEE: SWORD OF
VENUS) (1952)
ISLAND OF PROCIDA, THE (1952, It.) PR:C
ISLAND OF TERROR (1967, Brit.) PR:C
ISLAND OF THE BLUE DOLPHINS (1964) PR:AA
ISLAND OF THE BURNING DAMNED (1971, Brit.) PR:C
ISLAND OF THE DAMNED (1976, Sp.) PR:O
ISLAND OF THE DOOMED (1968, Sp./W. Ger.) PR:C
ISLAND OF THE FISHMEN, THE (SEE: SCREAMERS)
(1978, It.)
ISLAND RESCUE (1952, Brit.) PR:A
ISLAND WOMAN (SEE: ISLAND WOMEN) (1958)
ISLAND WOMEN (1958) PR:A
ISLANDS IN THE STREAM (1977) PR:C
ISLE OF DESTINY (1940) PR:A
ISLE OF ESCAPE (1930) PR:C
ISLE OF FORGOTTEN SINS (1943) PR:A
ISLE OF FURY (1936) PR:A
ISLE OF LOST SHIPS, THE (1929) PR:A
ISLE OF LOST WRANGLERS (SEE: 99 WOUNDS)
(1931)
ISLE OF MISSING MEN (1942) PR:A
ISLE OF SIN (1963, W. Ger.) PR:C-O
ISLE OF THE DEAD (1945) PR:C
ISLE OF THE SNAKE PEOPLE (SEE: SNAKE PEOPLE,
THE) (1968, US/Mex.)
ISN'T IT ROMANTIC? (1948) PR:A
ISN'T LIFE A BITCH? (SEE: LA CHIENNE) (1975, Fr.)
ISN'T LIFE WONDERFUL! (1953, Brit.) PR:A
ISTANBUL (1957) PR:A
ISTORIYA AS: KLYACHIMOL (SEE: ASYA'S HAPPI-
NESS) (1988, USSR)
IT! (1967, Brit.) PR:O
IT AIN'T EASY (1972) PR:C-O
IT AIN'T HAY (1943) PR:AA
IT ALL CAME TRUE (1940) PR:A-C
IT ALWAYS RAINS ON SUNDAY (1949, Brit.) PR:C
IT CAME FROM BENEATH THE SEA (1955) PR:A
IT CAME FROM OUTER SPACE (1953) PR:A
IT CAME WITHOUT WARNING (SEE: WITHOUT
WARNING) (1980)
IT CAN BE DONE (1929) PR:A
IT CAN'T LAST FOREVER (1937) PR:A

IT COMES UP LOVE (1943) PR:A
IT COMES UP MURDER (SEE: HONEY POT, THE)
(1967)
IT CONQUERED THE WORLD (1956) PR:A
IT COULD HAPPEN TO YOU (1937) PR:A
IT COULD HAPPEN TO YOU (1939) PR:A
IT COULDN'T HAPPEN HERE (1988, Brit.) PR:C-O
IT COULDN'T HAVE HAPPENED (SEE: IT COULDN'T
HAVE HAPPENED – BUT IT DID) (1936)
IT COULDN'T HAVE HAPPENED – BUT IT DID (1936)
PR:A
IT DON'T PAY TO BE AN HONEST CITIZEN (1985)
PR:O
IT FELL FROM THE FLAME BARRIER (SEE: FLAME
BARRIER) (1958)
IT FELL FROM THE SKY (1980) PR:C
IT GROWS ON TREES (1952) PR:A
IT HAD TO BE YOU (1947) PR:A
IT HAD TO HAPPEN (1936) PR:A
IT HAPPENED AT THE INN (1945, Fr.) PR:A
IT HAPPENED AT THE WORLD'S FAIR (1963) PR:A
IT HAPPENED HERE (1966, Brit.) PR:C
IT HAPPENED IN ATHENS (1962) PR:A
IT HAPPENED IN BROAD DAYLIGHT (1960, Switz./W.
Ger.) PR:A
IT HAPPENED IN BROOKLYN (1947) PR:A
IT HAPPENED IN CANADA (1962, Can.) PR:A
IT HAPPENED IN FLATBUSH (1942) PR:A
IT HAPPENED IN GIBRALTAR (1943, Fr.) PR:A
IT HAPPENED IN HOLLYWOOD (SEE: ANOTHER
FACE) (1935)
IT HAPPENED IN HOLLYWOOD (1937) PR:A
IT HAPPENED IN NEW YORK (1935) PR:A
IT HAPPENED IN PARIS (1935, Brit.) PR:A
IT HAPPENED IN PARIS (SEE: DESPERATE ADVEN-
TURE, A) (1938)
IT HAPPENED IN PARIS (SEE: LADY IN QUESTION,
THE) (1940)
IT HAPPENED IN PARIS (1953, Fr.) PR:A
IT HAPPENED IN ROME (1959, It.) PR:A
IT HAPPENED IN SOHO (1948, Brit.) PR:C
IT HAPPENED ON 5TH AVENUE (1947) PR:A
IT HAPPENED ONE NIGHT (1934) PR:A
IT HAPPENED ONE SUMMER (SEE: STATE FAIR)
(1945)
IT HAPPENED ONE SUNDAY (1944, Brit.) PR:A
IT HAPPENED OUT WEST (1937) PR:A
IT HAPPENED TO JANE (1959) PR:A
IT HAPPENED TO ONE MAN (1941, Brit.) PR:A
IT HAPPENED TOMORROW (1944) PR:A
IT HAPPENS EVERY SPRING (1949) PR:AA
IT HAPPENS EVERY THURSDAY (1953) PR:A
IT HURTS ONLY WHEN I LAUGH (SEE: ONLY WHEN I
LAUGH) (1981)
IT ISN'T DONE (1937, Aus.) PR:A
IT LIVES AGAIN (1978) PR:O
IT LIVES BY NIGHT (SEE: BAT PEOPLE, THE) (1974)
IT ONLY HAPPENS TO OTHERS (1971, Fr./It.) PR:C
IT ONLY TAKES 5 MINUTES (SEE: ROTTEN APPLE,
THE) (1963)
IT PAYS TO ADVERTISE (1931) PR:A
IT SEEMED LIKE A GOOD IDEA AT THE TIME (1975,
Can.) PR:O
IT SHOULD HAPPEN TO YOU (1954) PR:A
IT SHOULDN'T HAPPEN TO A DOG (1946) PR:A
IT SHOULDN'T HAPPEN TO A VET (SEE: ALL
THINGS BRIGHT AND BEAUTIFUL) (1979, Brit.)
IT STALKED THE OCEAN FLOOR (SEE: MONSTER
FROM THE OCEAN FLOOR, THE) (1954)
IT STARTED AT MIDNIGHT (SEE: SCHWEIK'S NEW
ADVENTURES) (1943, Brit.)
IT STARTED IN NAPLES (1960) PR:C
IT STARTED IN PARADISE (1952, Brit.) PR:A
IT STARTED IN THE ALPS (1966, Jap.) PR:A
IT STARTED WITH A KISS (1959) PR:C
IT STARTED WITH EVE (1941) PR:A
IT TAKES A THIEF (1960, Brit.) PR:C
IT TAKES ALL KINDS (1969, US/Aus.) PR:C
IT! THE TERROR FROM BEYOND SPACE (1958) PR:C
IT! THE VAMPIRE FROM BEYOND SPACE (SEE: IT!
THE TERROR FROM BEYOND SPACE) (1958)
IT WON'T RUB OFF, BABY! (SEE: SWEET LOVE, BIT-
TER) (1967)
ITALIAN CONNECTION, THE (1973, US/It./W. Ger.)
PR:O
ITALIAN JOB, THE (1969, Brit.) PR:A
ITALIAN MOUSE, THE (SEE: MAGIC WORLD OF
TOPO GIGIO, THE) (1961, It.)
ITALIAN SECRET SERVICE (1968, It.) PR:C
ITALIANI BRAVA GENTE (SEE: ITALIANO BRAVA
GENTE) (1965, It./USSR)
ITALIANO BRAVA GENTE (1965, It./USSR) PR:A
IT'S A BET (1935, Brit.) PR:A
IT'S A BIG COUNTRY (1951) PR:AA
IT'S A BIKINI WORLD (1967) PR:A
IT'S A BOY (1934, Brit.) PR:A
IT'S A COP (1934, Brit.) PR:A
IT'S A DATE (1940) PR:A

IT'S A DOG'S LIFE (SEE: BAR SINISTER) (1955)
IT'S A GIFT (1934) PR:AA
IT'S A GRAND LIFE (1953, Brit.) PR:A
IT'S A GRAND OLD WORLD (1937, Brit.) PR:A
IT'S A GREAT DAY (1956, Brit.) PR:A
IT'S A GREAT FEELING (1949) PR:A
IT'S A GREAT LIFE (1930) PR:A
IT'S A GREAT LIFE (1936) PR:A
IT'S A GREAT LIFE (1943) PR:AA
IT'S A JOKE, SON! (1947) PR:A
IT'S A KING (1933, Brit.) PR:A
IT'S A MAD, MAD, MAD, MAD WORLD (1963) PR:AA
IT'S A PLEASURE (1945) PR:A
IT'S A SMALL WORLD (1935) PR:A
IT'S A SMALL WORLD (1950) PR:A
IT'S A 2'6" ABOVE THE GROUND WORLD (1972, Brit.)
  PR:O
IT'S A WISE CHILD (1931) PR:A
IT'S A WONDERFUL DAY (1949, Brit.) PR:A
IT'S A WONDERFUL LIFE (1946) PR:AA
IT'S A WONDERFUL WORLD (1939) PR:A
IT'S A WONDERFUL WORLD (1956, Brit.) PR:A
IT'S ALIVE! (1968) PR:C
IT'S ALIVE (1974) PR:O
IT'S ALIVE II (SEE: IT LIVES AGAIN) (1978)
IT'S ALIVE III: ISLAND OF THE ALIVE (1988) PR:O
IT'S ALL HAPPENING (SEE: DREAM MAKER, THE)
  (1963, Brit.)
IT'S ALL OVER TOWN (1963, Brit.) PR:A
IT'S ALL YOURS (1937) PR:A
IT'S ALWAYS FAIR WEATHER (1955) PR:A
IT'S GREAT TO BE ALIVE (1933) PR:A
IT'S GREAT TO BE YOUNG (1946) PR:A
IT'S GREAT TO BE YOUNG (1956, Brit.) PR:A
IT'S HARD TO BE GOOD (1950, Brit.) PR:A
IT'S HOT IN HELL (SEE: MONKEY IN WINTER, A)
  (1962, Fr.)
IT'S HOT IN PARADISE (1959, Yugo./W. Ger.) PR:C
IT'S IN THE AIR (1935) PR:A
IT'S IN THE AIR (1940, Brit.) PR:A
IT'S IN THE BAG (1936, Brit.) PR:A
IT'S IN THE BAG (1943, Brit.) PR:A
IT'S IN THE BAG (1945) PR:A
IT'S IN THE BLOOD (1938, Brit.) PR:A
IT'S LOVE AGAIN (1936, Brit.) PR:A
IT'S LOVE I'M AFTER (1937) PR:A
IT'S MAGIC (SEE: ROMANCE ON THE HIGH SEAS)
  (1948)
IT'S MY LIFE (SEE: MY LIFE TO LIVE) (1962, Fr.)
IT'S MY TURN (1980) PR:C
IT'S NEVER TOO LATE (1958, Brit.) PR:A
IT'S NEVER TOO LATE (1977, Sp.) PR:O
IT'S NEVER TOO LATE TO MEND (1937, Brit.) PR:A
IT'S NOT CRICKET (1937, Brit.) PR:A
IT'S NOT CRICKET (1949, Brit.) PR:A
IT'S NOT THE SIZE THAT COUNTS (1979, Brit.) PR:O
IT'S ONLY MONEY (SEE: DOUBLE DYNAMITE) (1951)
IT'S ONLY MONEY (1962) PR:A
IT'S SAM SMALL AGAIN (SEE: SAM SMALL LEAVES
  TOWN) (1937, Brit.)
IT'S THAT MAN AGAIN (1943, Brit.) PR:A
IT'S TOUGH TO BE FAMOUS (1932) PR:A
IT'S TRAD, DAD! (SEE: RING-A-DING RHYTHM)
  (1962, Brit.)
IT'S TURNED OUT NICE AGAIN (SEE: TURNED OUT
  NICE AGAIN, Brit.)
IT'S WHAT'S HAPPENING (SEE: HAPPENING, THE)
  (1967)
IT'S YOU I WANT (1936, Brit.) PR:A
IVAN GROZNYI (SEE: IVAN THE TERRIBLE, PARTS I
  & II) (1945, USSR)
IVAN THE TERRIBLE, PARTS I & II (1945, USSR) PR:A
IVANHOE (1952, Brit.) PR:A
IVANOVO DETSTVO (SEE: MY NAME IS IVAN) (1962,
  USSR)
IVAN'S CHILDHOOD (SEE: MY NAME IS IVAN) (1962,
  USSR)
I'VE ALWAYS LOVED YOU (1946) PR:A
I'VE BEEN AROUND (1935) PR:A
I'VE GOT A HORSE (1938, Brit.) PR:A
I'VE GOT YOUR NUMBER (1934) PR:A
I'VE GOTTA HORSE (1965, Brit.) PR:A
I'VE LIVED BEFORE (1956) PR:A
IVORY-HANDLED GUN, THE (1935) PR:A
IVORY HUNTER (1952, Brit.) PR:A
IVORY HUNTERS, THE (SEE: IVORY HUNTER) (1952,
  Brit.)
IVY (1947) PR:A
IZBAVIT-ELJ (SEE: RAT SAVIOUR, THE) (1977, Yugo.)

JK

J-MEN FOREVER (1980) PR:C
J.D.'S REVENGE (1976) PR:O
J.R. (SEE: WHO'S THAT KNOCKING AT MY DOOR?)
  (1968)
J.W. COOP (1971) PR:A
JABBERWOCKY (1977, Brit.) PR:O
J'ACCUSE (1939, Fr.) PR:C-O

JACK AHOY! (1935, Brit.) PR:A
JACK AND THE BEANSTALK (1952) PR:AA
JACK AND THE BEANSTALK (1970) PR:AA
JACK FROST (1966, USSR) PR:AA
JACK KEROUAC'S AMERICA (SEE: KEROUAC) (1985)
JACK LONDON (1943) PR:A
JACK LONDON'S KLONDIKE FEVER (SEE: KLON-
  DIKE FEVER) (1980)
JACK MCCALL, DESPERADO (1953) PR:A
JACK OF ALL TRADES (SEE: TWO OF US, THE) (1938,
  Brit.)
JACK OF DIAMONDS, THE (1949, Brit.) PR:A
JACK OF DIAMONDS (1967, US/W. Ger.) PR:A
JACK SLADE (1953) PR:C
JACK THE GIANT KILLER (1962) PR:AA
JACK THE RIPPER (1959, Brit.) PR:O
JACKALS, THE (1967, South Africa) PR:A
JACKALS (SEE: AMERICAN JUSTICE) (1986)
JACKASS MAIL (1942) PR:A
JACKIE ROBINSON STORY, THE (1950) PR:AA
JACKNIFE (1989) PR:C
JACKO AND LISE (1979, Bel./Fr./Tahiti) PR:C
JACKPOT, THE (1950) PR:A
JACKPOT (1960, Brit.) PR:A
JACK'S BACK (1988) PR:O
JACK'S THE BOY (SEE: NIGHT AND DAY) (1933, Brit.)
JACK'S WIFE (SEE: HUNGRY WIVES) (1973)
JACKSON COUNTY JAIL (1976) PR:O
JACKTOWN (1962) PR:A
JACOB TWO-TWO MEETS THE HOODED FANG (1979,
  Can.) PR:AA
JACQUELINE (1956, Brit.) PR:A
JACQUELINE SUSANN'S ONCE IS NOT ENOUGH
  (SEE: ONCE IS NOT ENOUGH) (1975)
JACQUES AND NOVEMBER (1985, Can.) PR:C
JACQUES BREL IS ALIVE AND WELL AND LIVING IN
  PARIS (1975) PR:A
JADA, GOSCIE, JADA (SEE: GUESTS ARE COMING)
  (1965, Pol.)
JADE MASK, THE (1945) PR:A
JAGA WA HASHITTA (SEE: CREATURE CALLED
  MAN, THE) (1970, Jap.)
JAGGED EDGE (1985) PR:O
JAGUAR (1956) PR:A
JAGUAR (1980, Phil.) PR:C
JAGUAR LIVES! (1979) PR:C
JAIL BAIT (1954) PR:C
JAIL BAIT (1977, W. Ger.) PR:O
JAIL BUSTERS (1955) PR:AA
JAIL HOUSE BLUES (1942) PR:A
JAILBIRD ROCK (1988) PR:O
JAILBIRDS (SEE: PARDON US) (1931)
JAILBIRDS (1939, Brit.) PR:A
JAILBREAK (1936) PR:A
JAILBREAKERS, THE (1960) PR:A
JAILHOUSE ROCK (1957) PR:A
JAKE SPEED (1986) PR:A-C
JALNA (1935) PR:A
JALOPY (1953) PR:AA
JALSAGHAR (SEE: MUSIC ROOM, THE) (1963, India)
JAM SESSION (1944) PR:A
JAMAICA INN (1939, Brit.) PR:C
JAMAICA RUN (1953) PR:A
JAMBOREE (SEE: ROOKIES ON PARADE) (1941)
JAMBOREE (1944) PR:A
JAMBOREE (1957) PR:A
JAMES BROTHERS, THE (SEE: TRUE STORY OF
  JESSE JAMES, THE) (1957)
JAMES JOYCE'S WOMEN (1985) PR:O
JANE AUSTEN IN MANHATTAN (1980) PR:A
JANE EYRE (1935) PR:A
JANE EYRE (1944) PR:A
JANE EYRE (1971, Brit.) PR:A
JANE STEPS OUT (1938, Brit.) PR:A
JANIE (1944) PR:AA
JANIE GETS MARRIED (1946) PR:A
JANITOR, THE (SEE: EYEWITNESS) (1981)
JANUARY MAN, THE (1989) PR:C
JAPAN SINKS (SEE: TIDAL WAVE) (1975, US/Jap.)
JAPANESE WAR BRIDE (1952) PR:A
JASON AND THE ARGONAUTS (1963, Brit.) PR:AA
JASON LIVES: FRIDAY THE 13TH PART VI (SEE: FRI-
  DAY THE 13TH PART VII — THE NEW BLOOD) (1988)
JASSY (1948, Brit.) PR:A
JATSZANI KELL (SEE: LILY IN LOVE) (1985, US/Hung.)
JAVA HEAD (1935, Brit.) PR:C
JAVA SEAS (SEE: EAST OF JAVA) (1935)
J'AVAIS SEPT FILLES (SEE: MY SEVEN LITTLE SINS)
  (1956, Fr./It.)
JAWS (1975) PR:C-O
JAWS 2 (1978) PR:A
JAWS 3-D (1983) PR:C-O
JAWS OF DEATH, THE (SEE: MAKO: THE JAWS OF
  DEATH) (1976)
JAWS OF JUSTICE (1933) PR:A
JAWS OF SATAN (1980) PR:O
JAWS OF THE JUNGLE (1936) PR:C
JAWS: THE REVENGE (1987) PR:O

JAYHAWKERS, THE (1959) PR:A
JAZZ AGE, THE (1929) PR:A
JAZZ BOAT (1960, Brit.) PR:A
JAZZ CINDERELLA (1930) PR:A
JAZZ HEAVEN (1929) PR:A
JAZZ SINGER, THE (1927) PR:A
JAZZ SINGER, THE (1953) PR:A
JAZZ SINGER, THE (1980) PR:A
JAZZBAND FIVE, THE (1932, Ger.) PR:A
JAZZBOAT (SEE: JAZZ BOAT) (1960, Brit.)
JAZZMAN (1984, USSR) PR:C
JE T'AIME (1974, Can.) PR:C
JE T'AIME, JE T'AIME (1972, Fr./Swed.) PR:C
JE VOUS SALUE, MAFIA (SEE: HAIL MAFIA) (1985,
  Fr./It.)
JEALOUSY (1929) PR:C
JEALOUSY (1931, Brit.) PR:A
JEALOUSY (1934) PR:C
JEALOUSY (1945) PR:A
JEALOUSY (SEE: EMERGENCY WEDDING) (1950)
JEAN DE FLORETTE (1986, Fr.) PR:A
JEAN DE FLORETTE 2 (SEE: MANON OF THE
  SPRING) (1986, Fr.)
JEAN MARC OR CONJUGAL LIFE (SEE: ANATOMY
  OF A MARRIAGE (MY DAYS WITH JEAN-MARC
  AND MY NIGHTS WITH FRANCOISE)) (1964, Fr.)
JEANNE EAGELS (1957) PR:C
JEANNIE (SEE: GIRL IN DISTRESS) (1941, Brit.)
JEDDA, THE UNCIVILIZED (1956, Aus.) PR:A
JEDER FUR SICH UND GOTT GEGEN ALLE (SEE:
  EVERY MAN FOR HIMSELF AND GOD AGAINST
  ALL) (1975, W. Ger.)
JEEPERS CREEPERS (1939) PR:A
JEKYLL AND HYDE. . . TOGETHER AGAIN (1982) PR:O
JEKYLL'S INFERNO (SEE: HOUSE OF FRIGHT) (1961,
  Brit.)
JENATSCH (1987, Switz./Fr.) PR:C
JENIFER HALE (1937, Brit.) PR:A
JENNIE (1941) PR:A
JENNIE (SEE: PORTRAIT OF JENNIE) (1949)
JENNIE GERHARDT (1933) PR:A
JENNIE LESS HA UNA NUOVA PISTOLA (SEE: GUN-
  MEN OF THE RIO GRANDE) (1965, Fr./It./Sp.)
JENNIFER (1953) PR:A
JENNIFER (1978) PR:C-O
JENNIFER ON MY MIND (1971) PR:O
JENNIFER (THE SNAKE GODDESS) (SEE: JENNIFER)
  (1978)
JENNY (1969) PR:A
JENNY KISSED ME (1985, Aus.) PR:C
JENNY LAMOUR (1948, Fr.) PR:A
JENNY LIND (SEE: LADY'S MORALS, A) (1930)
JENSEITS DES RHEINS (SEE: TOMORROW IS MY
  TURN) (1962, Fr./It./W. Ger.)
JEOPARDY (1953) PR:A
JEREMIAH JOHNSON (1972) PR:C-O
JEREMY (1973) PR:A
JERICHO (SEE: DARK SANDS) (1938, Brit.)
JERK, THE (1979) PR:O
JERRICO, THE WONDER CLOWN (SEE: THREE RING
  CIRCUS) (1954)
JERUSALEM FILE, THE (1972, US/Israel) PR:C
JESSE AND LESTER, TWO BROTHERS IN A PLACE
  CALLED TRINITY (1972, It.) PR:A
JESSE JAMES (1939) PR:A
JESSE JAMES AT BAY (1941) PR:A
JESSE JAMES, JR. (1942) PR:A
JESSE JAMES MEETS FRANKENSTEIN'S DAUGHTER
  (1966) PR:A
JESSE JAMES VS. THE DALTONS (1954) PR:A
JESSE JAMES' WOMEN (1954) PR:A
JESSICA (1962, US/It./Fr.) PR:C
JESSICA (SEE: MISS JESSICA IS PREGNANT) (1970)
JESSIE'S GIRLS (1976) PR:O
JEST OF GOD, A (SEE: RACHEL, RACHEL) (1968)
JESTER, THE (1987, Portugal) PR:O
JESUS (1979) PR:A
JESUS CHRIST, SUPERSTAR (1973) PR:A
JESUS TRIP, THE (1971) PR:C
JET ATTACK (1958) PR:A
JET JOB (1952) PR:A
JET MEN OF THE AIR (SEE: AIR CADET) (1951)
JET OVER THE ATLANTIC (1960) PR:A
JET PILOT (1957) PR:C
JET SQUAD (SEE: JET ATTACK) (1958)
JET STORM (1959, Brit.) PR:A
JETLAG (1981, US/Sp.) PR:C
JETSTREAM (SEE: JET STORM) (1959, Brit.)
JEU DE MASSACRE (SEE: KILLING GAME, THE)
  (1968, Fr.)
JEUNE FILLE, UN SEUL AMOUR, UNE (SEE: MAGNIF-
  ICENT SINNER) (1963, Fr.)
JEUNES FILLES EN UNIFORME (SEE: MAEDCHEN IN
  UNIFORM) (1965, Fr./W. Ger.)
JEUX D'ADULTES (SEE: HEAD OF THE FAMILY)
  (1967, Fr./It.)
JEUX PRECOCES (SEE: LIPSTICK) (1965, Fr./It.)
JEW SUSS (SEE: POWER) (1934, Brit.)

JEWEL, THE (1933, Brit.) PR:A
JEWEL OF THE NILE, THE (1985) PR:C
JEWEL ROBBERY (1932) PR:A
JEWELS OF BRANDENBURG (1947) PR:A
JEZEBEL (1938) PR:A
JEZEBELLES, THE (SEE: SWITCHBLADE SISTERS) (1975)
JIG SAW (1965, Brit.) PR:A
JIGGS AND MAGGIE IN SOCIETY (1948) PR:AA
JIGGS AND MAGGIE OUT WEST (1950) PR:AA
JIGOKUHEN (SEE: PORTRAIT OF HELL) (1969, Jap.)
JIGOKUMEN (SEE: GATE OF HELL) (1953, Jap.)
JIGSAW (1949) PR:A
JIGSAW (SEE: JIG SAW) (1965)
JIGSAW (1968) PR:O
JIGSAW MAN, THE (1984, Brit.) PR:C
JIM HANVEY, DETECTIVE (1937) PR:A
JIM, THE WORLD'S GREATEST (1976) PR:A
JIM THORPE—ALL AMERICAN (1951) PR:A
JIMMY AND SALLY (1933) PR:A
JIMMY BOY (1935, Brit.) PR:A
JIMMY ORPHEUS (1966, W. Ger.) PR:C
JIMMY REARDON (SEE: NIGHT IN THE LIFE OF JIMMY REARDON, A) (1988)
JIMMY THE GENT (1934) PR:A
JIMMY THE KID (1982) PR:A
JIMMY VALENTINE (SEE: ALIAS JIMMY VALENTINE) (1928)
JINCHOGE (SEE: DAPHNE, THE) (1967, Jap.)
JINX MONEY (1948) PR:A
JINXED! (1982) PR:O
J'IRAI CRACHER SUR VOS TOMBES (SEE: I SPIT ON YOUR GRAVE) (1962, Fr.)
JITTERBUGS (1943) PR:AA
JIVARO (1954) PR:A
JIVE JUNCTION (1944) PR:A
JO JO DANCER, YOUR LIFE IS CALLING (1986) PR:C-O
JOAN AT THE STAKE (1954, It./Fr.) PR:A
JOAN BEDFORD IS MISSING (SEE: HOUSE OF HORRORS) (1946)
JOAN OF ARC (1948) PR:A
JOAN OF OZARK (1942) PR:A
JOAN OF PARIS (1942) PR:A
JOAN OF THE ANGELS (1962, Pol.) PR:O
JOANNA (1968, Brit.) PR:O
JOAQUIN MARRIETA (SEE: MURIETA) (1965, Sp.)
JOB LAZADASA (SEE: REVOLT OF JOB, THE) (1983, Hung./W. Ger.)
JOCK PETERSEN (SEE: PETERSEN) (1975, Aus.)
JOCKS (1987) PR:O
JOE (1970) PR:O
JOE AND ETHEL TURP CALL ON THE PRESIDENT (1939) PR:A
JOE BUTTERFLY (1957) PR:A
JOE DAKOTA (1957) PR:C
JOE, EL IMPLACABLE (SEE: NAVAJO JOE) (1967, It./Sp.)
JOE HILL (1971, Swed./US) PR:C
JOE KIDD (1972) PR:C
JOE LOUIS STORY, THE (1953) PR:A
JOE MACBETH (1955, Brit.) PR:C
JOE NAVIDAD (SEE: CHRISTMAS KID, THE) (1968, Sp.)
JOE PALOOKA (SEE: PALOOKA) (1934)
JOE PALOOKA, CHAMP (1946) PR:A
JOE PALOOKA IN FIGHTING MAD (SEE: FIGHTING MAD) (1948)
JOE PALOOKA IN HUMPHREY TAKES A CHANCE (SEE: HUMPHREY TAKES A CHANCE) (1950)
JOE PALOOKA IN THE BIG FIGHT (1949) PR:AA
JOE PALOOKA IN THE COUNTERPUNCH (1949) PR:AA
JOE PALOOKA IN THE SQUARED CIRCLE (1950) PR:A
JOE PALOOKA IN TRIPLE CROSS (1951) PR:AA
JOE PALOOKA IN WINNER TAKE ALL (1948) PR:AA
JOE PALOOKA MEETS HUMPHREY (1950) PR:AA
JOE PANTHER (1976) PR:AA
JOE SMITH, AMERICAN (1942) PR:A
JOE VALACHI: I SEGRETTI DI COSA NOSTRA (SEE: VALACHI PAPERS, THE) (1972, Fr./It.)
JOEY BOY (1965, Brit.) PR:O
JOHANSSON GETS SCOLDED (1945, Swed.) PR:A
JOHN AND JULIE (1957, Brit.) PR:AA
JOHN AND MARY (1969) PR:O
JOHN GOLDFARB, PLEASE COME HOME (1964) PR:A-C
JOHN HALIFAX—GENTLEMAN (1938, Brit.) PR:A
JOHN LOVES MARY (1949) PR:A
JOHN MEADE'S WOMAN (1937) PR:C
JOHN OF THE FAIR (1962, Brit.) PR:AA
JOHN PAUL JONES (1959) PR:A
JOHN WESLEY (1954, Brit.) PR:AA
JOHNNY ALLEGRO (1949) PR:A-C
JOHNNY ANGEL (1945) PR:A
JOHNNY APOLLO (1940) PR:A
JOHNNY BANCO (1969, Fr./It./W. Ger.) PR:O
JOHNNY BE GOOD (1988) PR:O
JOHNNY BELINDA (1948) PR:C
JOHNNY COME LATELY (1943) PR:A
JOHNNY COMES FLYING HOME (1946) PR:A

JOHNNY CONCHO (1956) PR:A
JOHNNY COOL (1963) PR:O
JOHNNY DANGEROUSLY (1984) PR:C
JOHNNY DARK (1954) PR:A
JOHNNY DOESN'T LIVE HERE ANY MORE (1944) PR:A
JOHNNY DOUGHBOY (1942) PR:AA
JOHNNY EAGER (1942) PR:C
JOHNNY FRENCHMAN (1946, Brit.) PR:A
JOHNNY GOT HIS GUN (1971) PR:O
JOHNNY GUITAR (1954) PR:C
JOHNNY HAMLET (1972, It.) PR:O
JOHNNY HANDSOME (1989) PR:O
JOHNNY HOLIDAY (1949) PR:A
JOHNNY IN THE CLOUDS (1945, Brit.) PR:A
JOHNNY NOBODY (1965, Brit.) PR:O
JOHNNY NORTH (SEE: KILLERS, THE) (1964)
JOHNNY O'CLOCK (1947) PR:A
JOHNNY ON THE RUN (1953, Brit.) PR:AA
JOHNNY ON THE SPOT (1954, Brit.) PR:A
JOHNNY ONE-EYE (1950) PR:A
JOHNNY ORO (SEE: RINGO AND HIS GOLDEN PISTOL) (1966, It.)
JOHNNY RENO (1966) PR:O
JOHNNY ROCCO (1958) PR:A
JOHNNY STEALS EUROPE (1932, Ger.) PR:A
JOHNNY STOOL PIGEON (1949) PR:C
JOHNNY THE GIANT KILLER (1953, Fr.) PR:AA
JOHNNY TIGER (1966) PR:A
JOHNNY TREMAIN (1957) PR:AA
JOHNNY TROUBLE (1957) PR:A
JOHNNY VAGABOND (SEE: JOHNNY COME LATELY) (1943)
JOHNNY VIK (1973) PR:C
JOHNNY, YOU'RE WANTED (1956, Brit.) PR:A
JOHNNY YUMA (1967, It.) PR:O
JOI-UCHI (SEE: REBELLION) (1967, Jap.)
JOIN THE MARINES (1937) PR:A
JOKE OF DESTINY LYING IN WAIT AROUND THE CORNER LIKE A STREET BANDIT, A (1983, It.) PR:C
JOKER, THE (1961, Fr.) PR:O
JOKER IS WILD, THE (1957) PR:C
JOKERS, THE (1967, Brit.) PR:A-C
JOKO, INVOCO DIO. . . E MOURI (SEE: VENGEANCE) (1968, It./W. Ger.)
JOLLY BAD FELLOW, A (1964, Brit.) PR:C
JOLLY OLD HIGGINS (SEE: EARL OF PUDDLESTONE) (1940)
JOLSON SINGS AGAIN (1949) PR:A
JOLSON STORY, THE (1946) PR:A
JONAH—WHO WILL BE 25 IN THE YEAR 2000 (1976, Switz.) PR:C
JONATHAN (1973, W. Ger.) PR:O
JONATHAN LIVINGSTON SEAGULL (1973) PR:A
JONES FAMILY IN HOLLYWOOD, THE (1939) PR:A
JONI (1980) PR:A
JONIKO (SEE: JONIKO AND THE KUSH TA KA) (1969)
JONIKO AND THE KUSH TA KA (1969) PR:AA
JONNY STIEHLT EUROPA (SEE: JOHNNY STEALS EUROPE) (1932, Ger.)
JORY (1972) PR:A
JOSEPH AND HIS BRETHREN (SEE: STORY OF JOSEPH AND HIS BRETHREN) (1962, It.)
JOSEPH ANDREWS (1977, Brit.) PR:O
JOSEPH DESA (SEE: RELUCTANT SAINT, THE) (1962, US/It.)
JOSEPH SOLD BY HIS BROTHERS (SEE: STORY OF JOSEPH AND HIS BRETHREN, THE) (1962, It.)
JOSEPHINE AND MEN (1955, Brit.) PR:A
JOSETTE (1938) PR:A
JOSHUA (1976) PR:O
JOSHUA THEN AND NOW (1985, Can.) PR:O
JOSSER IN THE ARMY (1932, Brit.) PR:A
JOSSER JOINS THE NAVY (1932, Brit.) PR:A
JOSSER ON THE FARM (1934, Brit.) PR:A
JOSSER ON THE RIVER (1932, Brit.) PR:A
JOTAI (SEE: VIXEN) (1970, Jap.)
JOUR DE FETE (1949, Fr.) PR:A
JOURNAL OF A CRIME (1934) PR:C
JOURNEY, THE (1959, US/Aust.) PR:A-C
JOURNEY AHEAD (1947, Brit.) PR:A
JOURNEY AMONG WOMEN (1977, Aus.) PR:O
JOURNEY (1971, Can.) PR:O
JOURNEY BACK TO OZ (1974) PR:AA
JOURNEY BENEATH THE DESERT (1967, Fr./It.) PR:A
JOURNEY, THE (1986, Switz./W. Ger.) PR:O
JOURNEY FOR MARGARET (1942) PR:AA
JOURNEY INTO DARKNESS (1968, Brit.) PR:A
JOURNEY INTO FEAR (1942) PR:A
JOURNEY INTO FEAR (1976, Can.) PR:O
JOURNEY INTO LIGHT (1951) PR:C
JOURNEY INTO MIDNIGHT (1968, Brit.) PR:A
JOURNEY INTO NOWHERE (1963, Brit.) PR:A
JOURNEY OF NATTY GANN, THE (1985) PR:C
JOURNEY THROUGH ROSEBUD (1972) PR:O
JOURNEY TO FREEDOM (1957) PR:A
JOURNEY TO ITALY (SEE: STRANGERS, THE) (1955, It.)

JOURNEY TO LOVE (1953, It.) PR:A
JOURNEY TO SHILOH (1968) PR:C
JOURNEY TO SPIRIT ISLAND (1988) PR:AA
JOURNEY TO THE BEGINNING OF TIME (1966, Czech.) PR:AA
JOURNEY TO THE CENTER OF THE EARTH (1959) PR:AA
JOURNEY TO THE CENTER OF TIME (1967) PR:A
JOURNEY TO THE FAR SIDE OF THE SUN (1969, Brit.) PR:A
JOURNEY TO THE LOST CITY (1959, Fr./It./W. Ger.) PR:A
JOURNEY TO THE SEVENTH PLANET (1962, US/Den.) PR:C
JOURNEY TOGETHER (1946, Brit.) PR:A
JOURNEY'S END (1930, US/Brit.) PR:C
JOURNEYS FROM BERLIN—1971 (1980) PR:O
JOVITA (1970, Pol.) PR:O
JOY (1983, Fr./Can.) PR:O
JOY HOUSE (1964, Fr.) PR:O
JOY IN THE MORNING (1965) PR:O
JOY OF LEARNING, THE (SEE: LE GAI SAVOIR) (1968, Fr.)
JOY OF LIVING (1938) PR:A
JOY OF SEX (1984) PR:O
JOY PARADE, THE (SEE: LIFE BEGINS IN COLLEGE) (1937)
JOY RIDE (1935, Brit.) PR:A
JOY RIDE (1958) PR:C
JOYRIDE (1977) PR:O
JOYSTICKS (1983) PR:O
JUAREZ (1939) PR:A
JUAREZ AND MAXIMILLIAN (SEE: MAD EMPRESS, THE) (1940)
JUBAL (1956) PR:C
JUBILEE (1978, Brit.) PR:O
JUBILEE TRAIL (1954) PR:A
JUBILEE WINDOW (1935, Brit.) PR:A
JUD (1971) PR:O
JUDAS CITY (SEE: SATAN'S BED) (1965)
JUDAS WAS A WOMAN (SEE: LA BETE HUMAINE) (1938, Fr.)
JUDEX (1966, Fr./It.) PR:C
JUDGE, THE (1949) PR:O
JUDGE AND THE ASSASSIN, THE (1979, Fr.) PR:C
JUDGE AND THE SINNER, THE (1964, W. Ger.) PR:C
JUDGE HARDY AND SON (1939) PR:AA
JUDGE HARDY'S CHILDREN (1938) PR:AA
JUDGE PRIEST (1934) PR:AA
JUDGE STEPS OUT, THE (1949) PR:A
JUDGEMENT IN STONE, A (SEE: HOUSEKEEPER, THE) (1987, Can.)
JUDGMENT AT NUREMBERG (1961) PR:C
JUDGMENT DEFERRED (1952, Brit.) PR:A
JUDGMENT IN BERLIN (1988) PR:A
JUDGMENT IN THE SUN (SEE: OUTRAGE, THE) (1964)
JUDITH (1965, US/Brit./Israel) PR:C-O
JUDO SAGA (1965, Jap.) PR:C
JUDO SHOWDOWN (1966, Jap.) PR:C
JUDY GOES TO TOWN (SEE: PUDDIN' HEAD) (1941)
JUDY'S LITTLE NO-NO (1969) PR:A
JUGGERNAUT (1937, Brit.) PR:O
JUGGERNAUT (1974, Brit.) PR:A-C
JUGGLER, THE (1953) PR:C-O
JUJIN YUKIOTOKO (SEE: HALF HUMAN) (1955, Jap.)
JUKE BOX JENNY (1942) PR:AA
JUKE BOX RACKET (1960) PR:A
JUKE BOX RHYTHM (1959) PR:A
JUKE GIRL (1942) PR:A
JULES AND JIM (1962, Fr.) PR:C-O
JULES VERNE'S ROCKET TO THE MOON (SEE: THOSE FANTASTIC FLYING FOOLS) (1967, Brit.)
JULIA (1977) PR:A-C
JULIA AND JULIA (1988, It.) PR:C-O
JULIA, DU BIST ZAUBER-HAFT (SEE: ADORABLE JULIA) (1964, Fr./Aust.)
JULIA MISBEHAVES (1948) PR:A
JULIA UND DIE GEISTER (SEE: JULIET OF THE SPIRITS) (1965, Fr./It./W. Ger.)
JULIE (1956) PR:A
JULIE DARLING (1982, Can./W. Ger.) PR:O
JULIE THE REDHEAD (1963, Fr.) PR:A
JULIET OF THE SPIRITS (1965, Fr./It./W. Ger.) PR:A-C
JULIETTA (1957, Fr.) PR:A
JULIETTE DES ESPRITS (SEE: JULIET OF THE SPIRITS) (1965, Fr./It./W. Ger.)
JULIUS CAESAR (1952) PR:A
JULIUS CAESAR (1953) PR:C
JULIUS CAESAR (1970, Brit.) PR:A
JULY PORK BELLIES (SEE: FOR PETE'S SAKE) (1977)
JUMBO (1962) PR:AA
JUMP (1971) PR:A
JUMP FOR GLORY (SEE: WHEN THIEF MEETS THIEF) (1937, Brit.)
JUMP INTO HELL (1955) PR:A
JUMPIN' JACK FLASH (1986) PR:O
JUMPING FOR JOY (1956, Brit.) PR:A
JUMPING JACKS (1952) PR:A

JUNCTION CITY (1952) PR:A
JUNE BRIDE (1948) PR:A
JUNE MOON (1931) PR:A
JUNGE LORD, DER (SEE: YOUNG LORD, THE) (1970)
JUNGE SCHRIE MORD, EIN (SEE: BOY CRIED MURDER, THE) (1966, Brit./W. Ger./Yugo.)
JUNGLE, THE (1952) PR:AA
JUNGLE ATTACK (SEE: CROSSWINDS) (1951)
JUNGLE BOOK (1942) PR:A
JUNGLE BOOK, THE (1967) PR:AA
JUNGLE BRIDE (1933) PR:A
JUNGLE CAPTIVE (1945) PR:A
JUNGLE FIGHTERS (SEE: LONG AND THE SHORT AND THE TALL, THE) (1961, Brit.)
JUNGLE FLIGHT (1947) PR:A
JUNGLE GENTS (1954) PR:AA
JUNGLE GODDESS (1948) PR:A
JUNGLE HEAT (1957) PR:A
JUNGLE ISLAND (SEE: WOLVES OF THE SEA) (1938)
JUNGLE JIM (1948) PR:AA
JUNGLE JIM IN THE FORBIDDEN LAND (1952) PR:AA
JUNGLE MAN (1941) PR:A
JUNGLE MAN-EATERS (1954) PR:AA
JUNGLE MANHUNT (1951) PR:AA
JUNGLE MOON MEN (1955) PR:AA
JUNGLE OF CHANG (1951) PR:A
JUNGLE PATROL (1948) PR:A
JUNGLE PRINCESS, THE (1936) PR:A
JUNGLE RAIDERS (1986, It.) PR:A-C
JUNGLE RAMPAGE (SEE: RAMPAGE) (1963)
JUNGLE SIREN (1942) PR:A
JUNGLE STREET (SEE: JUNGLE STREET GIRLS) (1963, Brit.)
JUNGLE STREET GIRLS (1963, Brit.) PR:A
JUNGLE TERROR (SEE: FIREBALL JUNGLE) (1968)
JUNGLE VIRGIN (SEE: JAWS OF THE JUNGLE) (1936)
JUNGLE WARRIORS (1984, US/Mex./W. Ger.) PR:O
JUNGLE WOMAN (1944) PR:A
JUNGLE WOMAN (SEE: NABONGA) (1944)
JUNINATTEN (SEE: NIGHT IN JUNE, A) (1940, Swed.)
JUNIOR ARMY (1943) PR:AA
JUNIOR BONNER (1972) PR:A-C
JUNIOR MISS (1945) PR:AA
JUNIOR PROM (1946) PR:AA
JUNKET 89 (1970, Brit.) PR:AA
JUNKMAN, THE (1982) PR:C-O
JUNO AND THE PAYCOCK (1930, Brit.) PR:A
JUPITER (1952, Fr.) PR:A
JUPITER'S DARLING (1955) PR:A
JUPITER'S THIGH (1980, Fr.) PR:C
JURY OF ONE (SEE: VERDICT, THE) (1974, Fr./It.)
JURY OF THE JUNGLE (SEE: FURY OF THE JUNGLE) (1934)
JURY'S EVIDENCE (1936, Brit.) PR:A
JURY'S SECRET, THE (1938) PR:A
JUST A BIG, SIMPLE GIRL (1949, Fr.) PR:A
JUST A GIGOLO (1931) PR:A
JUST A GIGOLO (1979, W. Ger.) PR:O
JUST ACROSS THE STREET (1952) PR:A
JUST ANOTHER DAY AT THE RACES (SEE: WIN, PLACE, OR STEAL) (1975)
JUST AROUND THE CORNER (1938) PR:AA
JUST BEFORE DAWN (1946) PR:A
JUST BEFORE DAWN (1980) PR:O
JUST BEFORE NIGHTFALL (1975, Fr./It.) PR:A-C
JUST BETWEEN FRIENDS (1986) PR:O
JUST FOR A SONG (1930, Brit.) PR:A
JUST FOR FUN (1963, Brit.) PR:AA
JUST FOR THE HELL OF IT (1968) PR:O
JUST FOR YOU (1952) PR:A
JUST GREAT (SEE: TOUT VA BIEN) (1973, Fr.)
JUST IMAGINE (1930) PR:A
JUST JOE (1960, Brit.) PR:A
JUST LIKE A WOMAN (1939, Brit.) PR:A
JUST LIKE A WOMAN (1967, Brit.) PR:C
JUST LIKE HEAVEN (1930) PR:A
JUST ME (1950, Fr.) PR:A
JUST MY LUCK (1933, Brit.) PR:A
JUST MY LUCK (1957, Brit.) PR:A
JUST OFF BROADWAY (1942) PR:A
JUST ONCE MORE (1963, Swed.) PR:O
JUST ONE MORE (SEE: JUST ONCE MORE) (1963, Swed.)
JUST ONE OF THE GUYS (1985) PR:C
JUST OUT OF REACH (1979, Aus.) PR:C
JUST SMITH (SEE: LEAVE IT TO SMITH) (1934)
JUST TELL ME WHAT YOU WANT (1980) PR:C
JUST THE WAY YOU ARE (1984) PR:C
JUST THIS ONCE (1952) PR:A
JUST TO BE LOVED (SEE: NEW LIFE STYLE, THE) (1970)
JUST WILLIAM (1939, Brit.) PR:AA
JUST WILLIAM'S LUCK (1948, Brit.) PR:A
JUST YOU AND ME, KID (1979) PR:C
JUSTE AVANT LA NUIT (SEE: JUST BEFORE NIGHTFALL) (1975, Fr./It.)
JUSTICE CAIN (SEE: CAIN'S WAY) (1970)
JUSTICE FOR SALE (SEE: NIGHT COURT) (1932)

JUSTICE OF THE RANGE (1935) PR:A
JUSTICE RIDES AGAIN (SEE: DESTRY RIDES AGAIN) (1932)
JUSTICE TAKES A HOLIDAY (1933) PR:A
JUSTINE (1969) PR:C
JUSTINE (1969, It./Sp.) PR:O
JUVENILE COURT (1938) PR:A
JUVENILE JUNGLE (1958) PR:A
JUVENTUD A LA IMTEMPERIE (SEE: UNSATISFIED, THE) (1964, Sp.)
K-9 (1989) PR:C
KADOYNG (1974, Brit.) PR:AA
KAGEMUSHA (1980, Jap.) PR:C
KAGI (SEE: ODD OBSESSION) (1959, Jap.)
KAIDAN (SEE: KWAIDAN) (1964, Jap.)
KAIJU DAISENSO (SEE: MONSTER ZERO) (1970, Jap.)
KAIJU SOSHINGEKI (SEE: DESTROY ALL MONSTERS) (1969, Jap.)
KAITEI GUNKA (SEE: ATRAGON) (1965, Jap.)
KAJA, UBIT CU TE (SEE: KAYA, I'LL KILL YOU) (1969, Jap.)
KAJIKKO (SEE: ANGRY ISLAND) (1960, Jap.)
KAKUSHI TORIDE NO SAN AKUNIN (SEE: HIDDEN FORTRESS, THE) (1958, Jap.)
KALEIDOSCOPE (1966, Brit.) PR:A-C
KAMATA KOSHINKYOKU (SEE: FALL GUY) (1985, Jap.)
KAMERADSCHAFT (1931, Ger.) PR:A-C
KAMIGAMI NO FUKAKI YOKUBO (SEE: KURAGEJIMA — LEGENDS FROM A SOUTHERN ISLAND) (1970, Jap.)
KAMIKAZE '89 (1982, W. Ger.) PR:O
KAMILLA (1984, Norway) PR:A-C
KAMOURASKA (1973, Can./Fr.) PR:O
KAMPF UM ROM (PART I) (SEE: FIGHT FOR ROME) (1969, Rum./W. Ger.)
KANAL (1957, Pol.) PR:C
KANCHENJUNGHA (1966, India) PR:A
KANDYLAND (1988) PR:O
KANGAROO (1952) PR:A
KANGAROO (1986, Aus.) PR:C
KANGAROO KID, THE (1950, Aus./US) PR:A
KANOJO (SEE: SHE AND HE) (1967, Jap.)
KANSAN, THE (1943) PR:A
KANSAS (1988) PR:C-O
KANSAS CITY BOMBER (1972) PR:O
KANSAS CITY CONFIDENTIAL (1952) PR:C-O
KANSAS CITY KITTY (1944) PR:A
KANSAS CITY PRINCESS (1934) PR:A
KANSAS CYCLONE (1941) PR:A
KANSAS PACIFIC (1953) PR:A
KANSAS RAIDERS (1950) PR:A
KANSAS TERRITORY (1952) PR:A
KANSAS TERRORS, THE (1939) PR:A
KAOS (1985, It.) PR:O
KAPHETZOU (SEE: FORTUNE TELLER, THE) (1961, Gr.)
KAPIT SA PALATIM (SEE: BAYAN KO) (1984, Fr./Phil.)
KAPITANLEUTENANT PRIEN — DER STIER VON SCAPA FLOW (SEE: U-47 LT. COMMANDER PRIEN) (1967, W. Ger.)
KAPO (1964, It./Fr./Yugo.) PR:O
KARAMAZOV (1931, Ger.) PR:C
KARAMI-AI (SEE: INHERITANCE, THE) (1964, Jap.)
KARATE KID, THE (1984) PR:A-C
KARATE KID PART II, THE (1986) PR:A-C
KARATE KID PART III, THE (1989) PR:A-C
KARATE KILLERS, THE (1967) PR:A
KARATE, THE HAND OF DEATH (1961) PR:C
KARE JOHN (SEE: DEAR JOHN) (1964, Swed.)
KAREN, THE LOVEMAKER (1970) PR:O
KARHOZAT (SEE: DAMNATION) (1988, Hung.)
KARMA (1933, Brit./India) PR:A
KARMA (1986, Switz.) PR:O
KATE PLUS TEN (1938, Brit.) PR:A
KATERINA IZMAILOVA (1969, USSR) PR:A
KATHLEEN (1938, Ireland) PR:A
KATHLEEN (1941) PR:AA
KATHLEEN MAVOURNEEN (1930) PR:A
KATHY O' (1958) PR:A
KATHY'S LOVE AFFAIR (SEE: COURTNEY AFFAIR, THE) (1947, Brit.)
KATIA (SEE: MAGNIFICENT SINNER) (1960, Fr.)
KATIE DID IT (1951) PR:A
KATINA (SEE: ICELAND) (1942)
KATOK I SKRIPKA (SEE: VIOLIN AND ROLLER) (1962, USSR)
KAVALER ZOLOTOI ZVEZDY (SEE: DREAM OF A COSSACK) (1982, USSR)
KAWAITA MIZUUMI (SEE: YOUTH IN FURY) (1961)
KAYA, I'LL KILL YOU (1969, Yugo./Fr.) PR:A
KAZABLAN (1974, Israel) PR:A
KAZAN (1949) PR:AA
KEELER AFFAIR, THE (SEE: CHRISTINE KEELER AFFAIR, THE) (1964, Brit.)
KEEP, THE (1983) PR:O
KEEP 'EM FLYING (1941) PR:AA
KEEP 'EM ROLLING (1934) PR:A

KEEP 'EM SLUGGING (1943) PR:AA
KEEP FIT (1937, Brit.) PR:A
KEEP HIM ALIVE (SEE: GREAT PLANE ROBBERY, THE) (1940)
KEEP IT CLEAN (1956, Brit.) PR:A
KEEP IT COOL (SEE: LET'S ROCK) (1958)
KEEP IT QUIET (1934, Brit.) PR:A
KEEP MY GRAVE OPEN (1980) PR:O
KEEP SMILING (1938) PR:A
KEEP SMILING (SEE: SMILING ALONG) (1938)
KEEP YOUR POWDER DRY (1945) PR:A
KEEP YOUR SEATS PLEASE (1936, Brit.) PR:A
KEEPER, THE (1976, Can.) PR:A
KEEPER OF THE BEES, THE (1935) PR:A
KEEPER OF THE BEES (1947) PR:A
KEEPER OF THE FLAME (1942) PR:A
KEEPERS OF YOUTH (1931, Brit.) PR:A
KEEPING COMPANY (1941) PR:A
KEK BALVANY (SEE: BLUE IDOL, THE) (1931, Hung.)
KELLY AND ME (1957) PR:AA
KELLY OF THE SECRET SERVICE (1936) PR:A
KELLY THE SECOND (1936) PR:A
KELLY'S HEROES (1970, US/Yugo.) PR:C-O
KEMPO SAMURAI (SEE: SAMURAI FROM NOWHERE) (1964)
KEMPY (SEE: WISE GIRLS) (1930)
KENNEL MURDER CASE, THE (1933) PR:A
KENNER (1969) PR:C
KENNY AND CO. (1976) PR:C
KENTUCKIAN, THE (1955) PR:A
KENTUCKY (1938) PR:AA
KENTUCKY BLUE STREAK (1935) PR:A
KENTUCKY FRIED MOVIE, THE (1977) PR:O
KENTUCKY JUBILEE (1951) PR:A
KENTUCKY KERNELS (1935) PR:A
KENTUCKY MINSTRELS (1934, Brit.) PR:A
KENTUCKY MOONSHINE (1938) PR:AA
KENTUCKY RIFLE (1956) PR:A
KEPT HUSBANDS (1931) PR:C
KEROUAC (1985) PR:O
KES (1970, Brit.) PR:C
KETTLE CREEK (SEE: MOUNTAIN JUSTICE) (1930)
KETTLES IN THE OZARKS, THE (1956) PR:AA
KETTLES ON OLD MACDONALD'S FARM, THE (1957) PR:AA
KETTO GENRYU JIMA (SEE: SAMURAI (PART III)) (1967, Jap.)
KEY, THE (1934) PR:A
KEY, THE (1958, Brit.) PR:O
KEY EXCHANGE (1985) PR:O
KEY LARGO (1948) PR:C
KEY MAN, THE (1957, Brit.) PR:A
KEY TO HARMONY (1935, Brit.) PR:A
KEY TO THE CITY (1950) PR:A
KEY WITNESS (1947) PR:C
KEY WITNESS (1960) PR:O
KEYHOLE, THE (1933) PR:A
KEYS OF THE KINGDOM, THE (1944) PR:A
KHARTOUM (1966, Brit.) PR:C
KHYBER PATROL (1954) PR:A
KIBITZER, THE (1929) PR:A
KICK IN (1931) PR:C
KICKBOXER (1989) PR:C
KICKING THE MOON AROUND (SEE: PLAYBOY, THE) (1942, Brit.)
KID BLUE (1973) PR:C
KID COLOSSUS, THE (SEE: ROOGIE'S BUMP) (1954)
KID COMES BACK, THE (1937) PR:A
KID COURAGEOUS (1935) PR:A
KID DYNAMITE (1943) PR:AA
KID FOR TWO FARTHINGS, A (1956, Brit.) PR:A
KID FROM AMARILLO, THE (1951) PR:A
KID FROM ARIZONA, THE (1931) PR:A
KID FROM BROKEN GUN, THE (1952) PR:A
KID FROM BROOKLYN, THE (1946) PR:AA
KID FROM CANADA, THE (1957, Brit.) PR:AA
KID FROM CLEVELAND, THE (1949) PR:A
KID FROM GOWER GULCH, THE (1949) PR:A
KID FROM KANSAS, THE (1941) PR:A
KID FROM KOKOMO, THE (1939) PR:A
KID FROM LEFT FIELD, THE (1953) PR:AA
KID FROM SANTA FE, THE (1940) PR:AA
KID FROM SPAIN, THE (1932) PR:AA
KID FROM TEXAS (1950) PR:C
KID FROM TEXAS, THE (1939) PR:AA
KID GALAHAD (1937) PR:A-C
KID GALAHAD (1962) PR:A
KID GLOVE KILLER (1942) PR:C
KID GLOVES (1929) PR:C
KID MILLIONS (1934) PR:AA
KID MONK BARONI (1952) PR:C
KID NIGHTINGALE (1939) PR:A
KID RANGER, THE (1936) PR:A
KID RIDES AGAIN, THE (1943) PR:A
KID RODELO (1966, US/Sp.) PR:C
KID SISTER, THE (1945) PR:A
KID VENGEANCE (1977) PR:C
KIDCO (1984) PR:C

KIDNAP OF MARY LOU, THE (SEE: ALMOST HUMAN) (1974)
KIDNAPPED (SEE: MISS FANE'S BABY IS STOLEN) (1934)
KIDNAPPED (1938) PR:AA
KIDNAPPED (1948) PR:AA
KIDNAPPED (1960) PR:AA
KIDNAPPED (1971, Brit.) PR:AA
KIDNAPPERS, THE (SEE: LITTLE KIDNAPPERS, THE) (1954, Brit.)
KIDNAPPERS, THE (1964, US/Phil.) PR:A
KIDNAPPING OF THE PRESIDENT, THE (1980, Can.) PR:O
KID'S LAST FIGHT, THE (SEE: LIFE OF JIMMY DOLAN, THE) (1933)
KID'S LAST RIDE, THE (1941) PR:A
KIEV COMEDY, A (1963, USSR) PR:C
KIKI (1931) PR:A
KIL 1 (SEE: SKIN GAME, THE) (1965, Brit.)
KILL (1968, Jap.) PR:C
KILL, THE (1968) PR:O
KILL (SEE: KILL! KILL! KILL!) (1972, Fr./Sp./It./W. Ger.)
KILL A DRAGON (1967) PR:O
KILL AND GO HIDE (SEE: CHILD, THE) (1977)
KILL AND KILL AGAIN (1981) PR:O
KILL BABY KILL (1966, It.) PR:O
KILL CASTRO (SEE: CUBA CROSSING) (1980)
KILL HER GENTLY (1958, Brit.) PR:O
KILL! KILL! KILL! (1972, Fr./It./Sp./W. Ger.) PR:O
KILL ME TOMORROW (1958, Brit.) PR:C
KILL OR BE KILLED (1950) PR:C
KILL OR BE KILLED (1967, It.) PR:C
KILL OR BE KILLED (1980) PR:C
KILL OR CURE (1962, Brit.) PR:C
KILL SQUAD (1982) PR:O
KILL THE UMPIRE (1950) PR:AA
KILL THEM ALL AND COME BACK ALONE (1970, It./Sp.) PR:O
KILL ZONE (1985) PR:O
KILLBOTS (SEE: CHOPPING MALL) (1986)
KILLER, THE (SEE: MYSTERY RANCH) (1932)
KILLER, THE (SEE: SACRED KNIVES OF VENGEANCE, THE) (1974, Hong Kong)
KILLER! (SEE: THIS MAN MUST DIE) (1970, Fr./It.)
KILLER APE (1953) PR:AA
KILLER AT LARGE (1936) PR:O
KILLER AT LARGE (1947) PR:O
KILLER BATS (SEE: DEVIL BAT, THE) (1941)
KILLER BEHIND THE MASK, THE (SEE: SAVAGE WEEKEND) (1983)
KILLER DILL (1947) PR:C
KILLER DINO (SEE: DINO) (1957)
KILLER ELITE, THE (1975) PR:O
KILLER FISH (1979, It./Braz.) PR:O
KILLER FORCE (1975, Ireland/Switz.) PR:O
KILLER GRIZZLY (SEE: GRIZZLY) (1976)
KILLER INSIDE ME, THE (1976) PR:O
KILLER IS LOOSE, THE (1956) PR:O
KILLER KLOWNS FROM OUTER SPACE (1988) PR:C-O
KILLER LEOPARD (1954) PR:A
KILLER MC COY (1947) PR:A
KILLER OF KILLERS (SEE: MECHANIC, THE) (1972)
KILLER ON A HORSE (SEE: WELCOME TO HARD TIMES) (1967)
KILLER ORPHAN (SEE: FRIDAY THE 13TH. . . THE ORPHAN) (1979)
KILLER PARTY (1986) PR:O
KILLER SHARK (1950) PR:A
KILLER SHREWS, THE (1959) PR:C
KILLER THAT STALKED NEW YORK, THE (1950) PR:O
KILLER WALKS, A (1952, Brit.) PR:A
KILLER WITH A LABEL (SEE: ONE TOO MANY) (1950)
KILLER WORKOUT (1987) PR:O
KILLERS, THE (1946) PR:C
KILLERS, THE (1964) PR:C-O
KILLERS, THE (1984) PR:O
KILLERS ARE CHALLENGED (SEE: SECRET AGENT FIREBALL) (1966, Fr./It.)
KILLER'S CAGE (SEE: CODE OF SILENCE) (1960)
KILLERS FROM SPACE (1954) PR:A
KILLER'S KISS (1955) PR:C
KILLERS OF KILIMANJARO (1960, Brit.) PR:A
KILLERS OF THE PRAIRIE (SEE: KING OF THE SIERRAS) (1938)
KILLERS OF THE WILD (1940) PR:AA
KILLERS THREE (1968) PR:O
KILLING, THE (1956) PR:C
KILLING AFFAIR, A (1985) PR:C
KILLING FIELDS, THE (1984, Brit.) PR:O
KILLING GAME, THE (1968, Fr.) PR:C
KILLING HEAT (1984) PR:O
KILLING HOUR, THE (1982) PR:O
KILLING KIND, THE (1973) PR:O
KILLING OF A CHINESE BOOKIE, THE (1976) PR:C
KILLING OF ANGEL STREET, THE (1983, Aus.) PR:A
KILLING URGE (SEE: JET STORM) (1959)
KILLPOINT (1984) PR:O
KILROY ON DECK (SEE: FRENCH LEAVE) (1948)

KILROY WAS HERE (1947) PR:AA
KIM (1950) PR:AA
KIMBERLEY JIM (1965, South Africa) PR:A
KIN FOLK (SEE: KINFOLK) (1970)
KIND HEARTS AND CORONETS (1949, Brit.) PR:A-C
KIND LADY (1935) PR:A
KIND LADY (1951) PR:O
KIND STEPMOTHER (1936, Hung.) PR:AA
KINDRED, THE (1987) PR:O
KINEMA NO TENCHI (SEE: FINAL TAKE: THE GOLDEN AGE OF MOVIES) (1986, Jap.)
KINFOLK (1970) PR:O
KING, THE (SEE: ROYAL AFFAIR, A) (1950, Fr.)
KING AND COUNTRY (1964, Brit.) PR:C
KING AND FOUR QUEENS, THE (1956) PR:A
KING AND HIS MOVIE, A (1986, Arg.) PR:C
KING AND I, THE (1956) PR:AA
KING AND THE CHORUS GIRL, THE (1937) PR:AA
KING ARTHUR WAS A GENTLEMAN (1942, Brit.) PR:A
KING BLANK (1983) PR:O
KING COBRA (SEE: JAWS OF SATAN) (1980)
KING CREOLE (1958) PR:O
KING DAVID (1985) PR:C
KING DINOSAUR (1955) PR:AA
KING FOR A NIGHT (1933) PR:C
KING IN NEW YORK, A (1957, Brit.) PR:A
KING IN SHADOW (1961, W. Ger.) PR:A
KING KELLY OF THE U.S.A. (1934) PR:A
KING KONG (1933) PR:A-C
KING KONG (1976) PR:C-O
KING KONG ESCAPES (1968, Jap.) PR:C
KING KONG LIVES (1986) PR:C
KING KONG VERSUS GODZILLA (1963, Jap.) PR:C
KING LEAR (1971, Brit./Den.) PR:O
KING LEAR (1988, US/Fr.) PR:A-C
KING MURDER, THE (1932) PR:O
KING, MURRAY (1969) PR:O
KING OEDIPUS (SEE: OEDIPUS REX) (1957, Can.)
KING OF AFRICA (SEE: ONE STEP TO HELL) (1969)
KING OF ALCATRAZ (1938) PR:C
KING OF BURLESQUE (1936) PR:A
KING OF CHINATOWN (1939) PR:O
KING OF COMEDY, THE (1983) PR:C
KING OF DODGE CITY (1941) PR:A
KING OF GAMBLERS (1937) PR:A
KING OF HEARTS (1936, Brit.) PR:AA
KING OF HEARTS (1967, Fr./It.) PR:C
KING OF HOCKEY (1936) PR:AA
KING OF KINGS (1961) PR:AA
KING OF MARVIN GARDENS, THE (1972) PR:C-O
KING OF PARIS, THE (1934, Brit.) PR:A
KING OF THE ARENA (1933) PR:A
KING OF THE BANDITS (1948) PR:A
KING OF THE BULLWHIP (1950) PR:C
KING OF THE CASTLE (1936, Brit.) PR:A
KING OF THE CORAL SEA (1956, Aus.) PR:C
KING OF THE COWBOYS (1943) PR:AA
KING OF THE DAMNED (1936, Brit.) PR:C
KING OF THE GAMBLERS (1948) PR:A
KING OF THE GRIZZLIES (1970, US/Can.) PR:AA
KING OF THE GYPSIES (1978) PR:O
KING OF THE ICE RINK (SEE: KING OF HOCKEY) (1936)
KING OF THE JUNGLE (1933) PR:A
KING OF THE JUNGLELAND (SEE: DARKEST AFRICA) (1936)
KING OF THE KHYBER RIFLES (SEE: BLACK WATCH, THE) (1929)
KING OF THE KHYBER RIFLES (1953) PR:A
KING OF THE LUMBERJACKS (1940) PR:A
KING OF THE MOUNTAIN (SEE: BEDTIME STORY) (1964)
KING OF THE MOUNTAIN (1981) PR:O
KING OF THE NEWSBOYS (1938) PR:A
KING OF THE PECOS (1936) PR:A
KING OF THE RITZ (1933, Brit.) PR:A
KING OF THE ROARING 20S – THE STORY OF ARNOLD ROTHSTEIN (1961) PR:C
KING OF THE ROYAL MOUNTED (1936) PR:A
KING OF THE SIERRAS (1938) PR:A
KING OF THE STALLIONS (1942) PR:A
KING OF THE STREETS (1986) PR:O
KING OF THE TURF (1939) PR:A
KING OF THE UNDERWORLD (1939) PR:A-C
KING OF THE UNDERWORLD (1952, Brit.) PR:A
KING OF THE WILD (SEE: KING OF THE WILD HORSES, THE) (1934)
KING OF THE WILD HORSES, THE (1934) PR:A
KING OF THE WILD HORSES (1947) PR:A
KING OF THE WILD STALLIONS (1959) PR:AA
KING OF THE ZOMBIES (1941) PR:O
KING, QUEEN, KNAVE (1972, US/W. Ger.) PR:O
KING RAT (1965) PR:O
KING RICHARD AND THE CRUSADERS (1954) PR:A
KING SOLOMON OF BROADWAY (1935) PR:A
KING SOLOMON'S MINES (1937, Brit.) PR:A
KING SOLOMON'S MINES (1950) PR:A

KING SOLOMON'S MINES (1985) PR:C
KING SOLOMON'S TREASURE (1978, Can.) PR:A
KING STEPS OUT, THE (1936) PR:A
KINGDOM OF THE SPIDERS (1977) PR:C
KINGFISH CAPER, THE (1976, South Africa) PR:A
KINGFISHER CAPER, THE (SEE: KINGFISH CAPER, THE) (1976, South Africa)
KINGS AND DESPERATE MEN (1984, Brit.) PR:C
KING'S CUP, THE (1933, Brit.) PR:A
KINGS GO FORTH AND GIANTS GO FIFTH (1958) PR:A
KING'S JESTER, THE (1947, It.) PR:O
KINGS OF THE ROAD (1976, W. Ger.) PR:C
KINGS OF THE SUN (1963) PR:O
KING'S PIRATE, THE (1967) PR:A
KING'S RHAPSODY (1955, Brit.) PR:A
KINGS ROW (1942) PR:C-O
KING'S THIEF, THE (1955) PR:A
KING'S VACATION, THE (1933) PR:A
KINGU KONGO NO GYAKUSHU (SEE: KING KONG ESCAPES) (1968, Jap.)
KINJITE: FORBIDDEN SUBJECTS (1989) PR:O
KIPPERBANG (1984, Brit.) PR:A-C
KIPPS (SEE: REMARKABLE MR. KIPPS, THE) (1942, Brit.)
KIRI NI MUSEBU YORU (SEE: HARBOR LIGHT YOKOHAMA) (1970, Jap.)
KIRLIAN WITNESS, THE (1978) PR:O
KIRU (SEE: KILL) (1968, Jap.)
KISENGA, MAN OF AFRICA (1952, Brit.) PR:C
KISMET (1930) PR:A
KISMET (1944) PR:A
KISMET (1955) PR:A
KISS, THE (1988) PR:C
KISS AND KILL (SEE: BLOOD OF FU MANCHU, THE) (1968, US/Brit./Sp./W. Ger.)
KISS AND MAKE UP (1934) PR:A
KISS AND TELL (1945) PR:A
KISS BEFORE DYING, A (1956) PR:A
KISS BEFORE THE MIRROR, THE (1933) PR:A
KISS FOR CORLISS, A (1949) PR:A
KISS FROM EDDIE, A (SEE: AROUSERS, THE) (1970)
KISS IN THE DARK, A (1949) PR:A
KISS ME (SEE: LOVE KISS, THE) (1930)
KISS ME AGAIN (1931) PR:A
KISS ME DEADLY (1955) PR:O
KISS ME GOODBYE (1935, Brit.) PR:A
KISS ME GOODBYE (1982) PR:C
KISS ME KATE (1953) PR:AA
KISS ME, SERGEANT (1930, Brit.) PR:A
KISS ME, STUPID (1964) PR:C
KISS MY BUTTERFLY (SEE: I LOVE YOU, ALICE B. TOKLAS!) (1968)
KISS OF DEATH (1947) PR:C-O
KISS OF EVIL (1963, Brit.) PR:C
KISS OF FIRE, THE (1940, Fr.) PR:A
KISS OF FIRE (1955) PR:A
KISS OF THE SPIDER WOMAN (1985, US/Braz.) PR:O
KISS OF THE TARANTULA (1975) PR:O
KISS OF THE VAMPIRE, THE (SEE: KISS OF EVIL) (1963, Brit.)
KISS THE BLOOD OFF MY HANDS (1948) PR:C-O
KISS THE BOYS GOODBYE (1941) PR:A
KISS THE BRIDE GOODBYE (1944, Brit.) PR:A
KISS THE GIRLS AND MAKE THEM DIE (1967, US/It.) PR:O
KISS THE OTHER SHEIK (1968, Fr./It.) PR:C
KISS THEM FOR ME (1957) PR:A
KISS TOMORROW GOODBYE (1950) PR:C-O
KISSES FOR BREAKFAST (1941) PR:A
KISSES FOR MY PRESIDENT (1964) PR:A
KISSES FOR THE PRESIDENT (SEE: KISSES FOR MY PRESIDENT) (1964)
KISSIN' COUSINS (1964) PR:A
KISSING BANDIT, THE (1948) PR:A
KISSING CUP'S RACE (1930, Brit.) PR:A
KIT CARSON (1940) PR:A
KITCHEN, THE (1961, Brit.) PR:A
KITTEN ON THE KEYS (SEE: DO YOU LOVE ME?) (1946)
KITTEN WITH A WHIP (1964) PR:C-O
KITTY (1929, Brit.) PR:A
KITTY (1945) PR:A
KITTY AND THE BAGMAN (1983, Aus.) PR:O
KITTY FOYLE (1940) PR:A-C
KLANSMAN, THE (1974) PR:C
KLASSENVERHALTNISSE (SEE: CLASS RELATIONS) (1986, W. Ger.)
KLAUN FERDINAND A RAKETA (SEE: ROCKET TO NOWHERE) (1962, Czech.)
KLEINE MELODIE AUS WIEN (SEE: LITTLE MELODY FROM VIENNA) (1948, Aust.)
KLEINES ZELT UND GROSSE LIEBE (SEE: TWO IN A SLEEPING BAG) (1964, W. Ger.)
KLONDIKE (1932) PR:A
KLONDIKE ANNIE (1936) PR:A-C
KLONDIKE FEVER (1980) PR:A
KLONDIKE FURY (1942) PR:A

KLONDIKE KATE (1944) PR:A

KLUTE (1971) PR:O

KNACK, THE (SEE: KNACK... AND HOW TO GET IT, THE) (1965, Brit.)

KNACK... AND HOW TO GET IT, THE (1965, Brit.) PR:C

KNAVE OF HEARTS (SEE: LOVERS, HAPPY LOVERS!) (1954, Brit./Fr.)

KNICKERBOCKER HOLIDAY (1944) PR:A

KNIFE IN THE BODY, THE (SEE: MURDER CLINIC, THE) (1967, Fr./It.)

KNIFE IN THE WATER (1962, Pol.) PR:O

KNIGHT IN LONDON, A (1930, Brit./Ger.) PR:A

KNIGHT OF THE PLAINS (1939) PR:A

KNIGHT WITHOUT ARMOR (1937, Brit.) PR:A

KNIGHTRIDERS (1981) PR:C

KNIGHTS FOR A DAY (1937, Brit.) PR:A

KNIGHTS OF THE BLACK CROSS (SEE: KNIGHTS OF THE TEUTONIC ORDER, THE) (1960, Pol.)

KNIGHTS OF THE CITY (1985) PR:O

KNIGHTS OF THE RANGE (1940) PR:A

KNIGHTS OF THE ROUND TABLE (1953) PR:A

KNIGHTS OF THE TEUTONIC ORDER, THE (1960, Pol.) PR:A

KNIVES OF THE AVENGER (1967, It.) PR:A

KNOCK (1955, Fr.) PR:A

KNOCK ON ANY DOOR (1949) PR:C

KNOCK ON WOOD (1954) PR:A

KNOCKOUT (1941) PR:A

KNOWING MEN (1930, Brit.) PR:A

KNUTE ROCKNE—ALL AMERICAN (1940) PR:AA

KOENIGSMARK (1935, Brit./Fr.) PR:A

KOGDA DEREVYA BYLI BOLSHIMI (SEE: WHEN THE TREES WERE TALL) (1965, USSR)

KOHAYAGAWA-KE NO AKI (SEE: EARLY AUTUMN) (1962, Jap.)

KOJIRO (1967, Jap.) PR:A

KOKKINA PHANARIA (SEE: RED LANTERNS, THE) (1965, Gr.)

KOKOSEI BANCHO (SEE: WAY OUT, WAY IN) (1970, Jap.)

KOKS I KULISSEN (SEE: LADIES ON THE ROCKS) (1985, Den.)

KOL MAMZER MELECH (SEE: EVERY BASTARD A KING) (1968, Israel)

KOLBERG (1945, Ger.) PR:O

KOLYBELNAYA (SEE: LULLABY) (1961, USSR)

KOMIKKU ZASSHI NANKA IRANI (SEE: COMIC MAGAZINE) (1986, Jap.)

KOMMANDO SINAI (SEE: SINAI COMMANDOS: THE STORY OF THE SIX DAY WAR) (1968, Israel/W. Ger.)

KONA COAST (1968) PR:C

KONBU FINZE (SEE: TERRORIZERS, THE) (1987, Taiwan)

KONEC SPRNA V HOTELU OZON (SEE: END OF AUGUST AT THE HOTEL OZONE, THE) (1967, Czech.)

KONGA (SEE: KONGA, THE WILD STALLION) (1939)

KONGA (1961, Brit.) PR:C

KONGA, THE WILD STALLION (1939) PR:AA

KONGI'S HARVEST (1971, US/Nigeria) PR:A

KONGO (1932) PR:O

KONJIKI YASHA (SEE: GOLDEN DEMON) (1954, Jap.)

KONSKA OPERA (SEE: LEMONADE JOE) (1966, Czech.)

KOREA PATROL (1951) PR:C

KORT AR SOMMAREN (SEE: SHORT IS THE SUMMER) (1968, Swed.)

KOSHOKU ICHIDAI ONNA (SEE: LIFE OF OHARU) (1952, Jap.)

KOSMITCHESKY REIS (SEE: SPACE SHIP, THE) (1935, USSR)

KOTCH (1971) PR:A-C

KOTO (SEE: TWIN SISTERS OF KYOTO) (1964, Jap.)

KOTO NO TAIYO (SEE: NO GREATER LOVE THAN THIS) (1969, Jap.)

KRADETSUT NA PRASKOVI (SEE: PEACH THIEF, THE) (1969)

KRAKATIT (1948, Czech.) PR:C

KRAKATOA, EAST OF JAVA (1969) PR:A

KRALJ PETROLEJA (SEE: RAMPAGE AT APACHE WELLS) (1966, Fr./It./Yugo./W. Ger.)

KRAMER VS. KRAMER (1979) PR:A

KRASNAYA PALATKA (SEE: RED TENT, THE) (1971, It./USSR)

KREMLIN LETTER, THE (1970) PR:C-O

KRIEG UND FRIEDEN (SEE: WAR AND PEACE) (1983, W. Ger.)

KRIEGSGERICHT (SEE: COURT MARTIAL) (1962, W. Ger.)

KRIVI PUT (SEE: CROOKED ROAD, THE) (1965, Brit./Yugo.)

KRONOS (1957) PR:A

KRONOS (SEE: CAPTAIN KRONOS: VAMPIRE HUNTER) (1974)

KRUEZER EMDEN (SEE: CRUISER EMDEN) (1932, Ger.)

KRULL (1983, Brit.) PR:A

KRUSH GROOVE (1985) PR:O

KRZYZACY (SEE: KNIGHTS OF THE TEUTONIC ORDER) (1960, Pol.)

KUMONOSUJO (SEE: THRONE OF BLOOD) (1957, Jap.)

KUNG FU MASTER (1989, Fr.) PR:O

KUNGSLEDEN (SEE: OBSESSION) (1968, Swed.)

KUNI LEMEL IN TEL AVIV (SEE: RABBI AND THE SHIKSE, THE) (1976, Israel)

KUNISADA CHUJI (SEE: GAMBLING SAMURAI, THE) (1966, Jap.)

KURAGEJIMA—LEGENDS FROM A SOUTHERN ISLAND (1970, Jap.) PR:O

KUREIZI OGON SAKUSEN (SEE: LAS VEGAS FREE-FOR-ALL) (1968, Jap.)

KUROBE NO TAIYO (SEE: TUNNEL TO THE SUN) (1968, Jap.)

KURONEKO (1968, Jap.) PR:O

KUTUZOV (SEE: 1812) (1944, USSR)

KUU ON VAARALLINEN (SEE: PRELUDE TO ECSTASY) (1963, Fin.)

KVARTERET KORPEN (SEE: RAVEN'S END) (1970)

KVINNODROM (SEE: DREAMS) (1955, Swed.)

KVINNORS VANTAN (SEE: SECRETS OF WOMEN) (1952, Swed.)

KWAIDAN (1964, Jap.) PR:O

KYOMO WARE OZORANI ARI (SEE: TIGER FLIGHT) (1965, Jap.)

KYONETSU NO KISETSU (SEE: WEIRD LOVE MAKERS, THE) (1963, Jap.)

KYUBI NO KITSUNE TO TOBIMARU (SEE: FOX WITH NINE TAILS, THE) (1969, Jap.)

KYUKETSUKI GOKEMIDORO (SEE: GOKE, THE BODYSNATCHER FROM HELL) (1968, Jap.)

L

FANGS OF THE LIVING DEAD (SEE: MALENKA, THE VAMPIRE) (1972, It./Sp.)

L-SHAPED ROOM, THE (1962, Brit.) PR:C

L'EBREO ERRANTE (SEE: WANDERING JEW, THE) (1948, It.)

L'EMPREINTE DU DIEU (SEE: TWO WOMEN) (1940, Fr.)

L'HOMME DU JOUR (SEE: MAN OF THE HOUR) (1940, Fr.)

L.A. STREETFIGHTERS (SEE: NINJA TURF) (1986)

LA BABY SITTER (1975, Fr./It./W. Ger.) PR:O

LA BAI DES ANGES (SEE: BAY OF ANGELS) (1964, Fr.)

LA BALANCE (1982, Fr.) PR:O

LA BAMBA (1987) PR:C

LA BANDA J&S CRONACA CRIMINALE DEL FAR WEST (SEE: SONNY AND JED) (1974, It.)

LA BANDERA (SEE: ESCAPE FROM YESTERDAY) (1939, Fr.)

LA BATAILLE DU RAIL (SEE: BATTLE OF THE RAILS) (1949, Fr.)

LA BEAUTE DU DIABLE (SEE: BEAUTY AND THE DEVIL) (1952, Fr.)

LA BELLA MUGNAIA (SEE: MILLER'S WIFE, THE) (1955, It.)

LA BELLE AMERICAINE (1961, Fr.) PR:A

LA BELLE CAPTIVE (SEE: BEAUTIFUL PRISONER, THE) (1983, Fr.)

LA BELLE EQUIPE (SEE: THEY WERE FIVE) (1936, Fr.)

LA BELLE ET LA BETE (SEE: BEAUTY AND THE BEAST) (1946, Fr.)

LA BELLE ET LE CAVALIER (SEE: MORE THAN A MIRACLE) (1967, Fr./It.)

LA BESTIA UCCIDE A SANGUE FREDDO (SEE: SLAUGHTER HOTEL) (1971, It.)

LA BETE HUMAINE (1938, Fr.) PR:A

LA BISBETICA DOMATA (SEE: TAMING OF THE SHREW, THE) (1967, US/It.)

LA BOCA DEL LOBO (SEE: IN THE MOUTH OF THE WOLF) (1988, Peru/Sp.)

LA BOHEME (1965, Switz.) PR:A

LA BONNE ANNEE (SEE: HAPPY NEW YEAR) (1973, Fr./It.)

LA BONNE SOUPE (1964, Fr./It.) PR:C

LA BOUM (1981, Fr.) PR:A

L.A. BOUNTY (1989) PR:O

LA CADUTA DEGLI DEI (SEE: DAMNED, THE) (1969, It./W. Ger.)

LA CAGE (1975, Fr.) PR:C

LA CAGE AUX FOLLES (1979, Fr./It.) PR:O

LA CAGE AUX FOLLES II (1980, It./Fr.) PR:C-O

LA CAGE AUX FOLLES 3: THE WEDDING (1985, Fr./It.) PR:C

LA CAMARA DEL TERROR (SEE: FEAR CHAMBER, THE) (1968, US/Mex.)

LA CASA CON LA SCALA NEL BUIO (SEE: BLADE IN THE DARK, A) (1986, It.)

LA CASA DE TERROR (SEE: FACE OF THE SCREAMING WEREWOLF) (1959, Mex.)

LA CASA DELL' EXORCISMO (SEE: HOUSE OF EXORCISM, THE) (1976, It.)

LA CASA NEL PARCO (SEE: HOUSE ON THE EDGE OF THE PARK) (1985, It.)

LA CASSE (SEE: BURGLARS, THE) (1972, It./Fr.)

LA CEREMONIA (SEE: CEREMONY, THE) (1963, US/Sp.)

LA CHAMBRE VERTE (SEE: GREEN ROOM, THE) (1978, Fr.)

LA CHASSE A L'HOMME (SEE: MALE HUNT) (1965, Fr./It.)

LA CHEVRE (1985, Fr.) PR:A

LA CHIENNE (1931, Fr.) PR:C-O

LA CHINOISE (1967, Fr.) PR:C-O

LA CICADA (SEE: CRICKET, THE) (1979, It.)

LA CIGARRA NO ES UN BICHO (SEE: GAMES MEN PLAY, THE) (1968, Arg.)

LA CINTURA DI CASTITA (SEE: CHASTITY BELT, THE) (1969, US/It.)

LA CIOCIARA (SEE: TWO WOMEN) (1960, Fr./It.)

LA CITTA PRIGIONIERA (SEE: CONQUERED CITY) (1966, It.)

LA CITTA SI DIFENDE (SEE: FOUR WAYS OUT) (1954, It.)

LA CIUDAD Y LOS PERROS (SEE: CITY AND THE DOGS, THE) (1987, Peru)

LA COLLECTIONNEUSE (1971, Fr.) PR:C-O

LA CONGA NIGHTS (1940) PR:A

LA CONGIUNTURA (SEE: ONE MILLION DOLLARS) (1965, It.)

LA COPLA DE LA DOLORES (SEE: DOLORES) (1949, Sp.)

LA CORTE DE FARAON (SEE: COURT OF THE PHARAOH, THE) (1985, Fr.)

LA CORTIGIANA DI BABILONIA (SEE: QUEEN OF BABYLON) (1956, It.)

LA CROIX DES VIVANTS (SEE: CROSS OF THE LIVING) (1963, Fr.)

LA CUCARACHA (1961, Mex.) PR:A

LA DALLE ARDENNE ALL' INFERNO (SEE: DIRTY HEROES) (1971, Fr./It./W. Ger.)

LA DAME DANS L'AUTO AVEC DES LUNETTES ET UN FUSIL (SEE: LADY IN THE CAR WITH GLASSES AND A GUN) (1970, US/Fr.)

LA DECADE PRODIGIEUSE (SEE: TEN DAYS' WONDER) (1972, Fr.)

LA DENTELLIERE (SEE: LACEMAKER, THE) (1977, Fr.)

LA DIAGONALE DU FOU (SEE: DANGEROUS MOVES) (1984, Switz.)

LA DIGA SUL PACIFICO (SEE: THIS ANGRY AGE) (1958, US/Fr./It.)

LA DOLCE VITA (1960, It./Fr.) PR:C

LA DONNA DEI FARAOINI (SEE: PHARAOHS' WOMAN, THE) (1961, It.)

LA DONNA DEL FIUME (SEE: WOMAN OF THE RIVER) (1954, Fr./It.)

LA DONNA DEL GIORNO (SEE: DOLL THAT TOOK THE TOWN, THE) (1965, It.)

LA ESTRELLA VACIA (SEE: EMPTY STAR, THE) (1962, Mex.)

LA FABULEUSE AVENTURE DE MARCO POLO (SEE: MARCO THE MAGNIFICENT) (1966, Afghanistan/Egypt/Fr./It./Yugo.)

LA FAMIGLIA (SEE: FAMILY, THE) (1987, It./Fr.)

LA FEMME D'A COTE (SEE: WOMAN NEXT DOOR, THE) (1981, Fr.)

LA FEMME AUX BOTTES ROUGES (SEE: WOMAN WITH RED BOOTS, THE) (1974, Fr./Sp.)

LA FEMME DE MON POTE (SEE: MY BEST FRIEND'S GIRL) (1983, Fr.)

LA FEMME DU BOULANGERS (SEE: BAKER'S WIFE, THE) (1938, Fr.)

LA FEMME ET LE PAUTIN (SEE: FEMALE, THE) (1960, Fr.)

LA FEMME INFIDELE (1969, Fr./It.) PR:C

LA FERME DU PENDU (1946, Fr.) PR:C

LA FETE A HENRIETTE (SEE: HOLIDAY FOR HENRIETTE) (1955, Fr.)

LA FEU FOLLET (SEE: FIRE WITHIN, THE) (1964, Fr./It.)

LA FIANCEE DU PIRATE (SEE: VERY CURIOUS GIRL, A) (1969, Fr.)

LA FIGLIA DELLO SCEICCO (SEE: DESERT WARRIOR) (1961, It./Sp.)

LA FILLE DE HAMBOURG (SEE: PORT OF DESIRE) (1960, Fr.)

LA FILLE DE MATA HARI (SEE: MATA HARI'S DAUGHTER) (1954, Fr./It.)

LA FILLE DE PUISATIER (SEE: WELL-DIGGERS DAUGHTER, THE) (1946, Fr.)

LA FILLE DU DIABLE (SEE: DEVIL'S DAUGHTER) (1949, Fr.)

LA FILLE SANS VOILE (SEE: GIRL IN THE BIKINI, THE) (1958, Fr.)

LA FIN DU JOUR (SEE: END OF A DAY, THE) (1939, Fr.)

LA FIN DU MONDE (SEE: END OF THE WORLD, THE) (1930, Fr.)

LA FLUTE A SIX SCHTROUMPFS (SEE: SMURFS AND THE MAGIC FLUTE, THE) (1984, Bel./Fr.)

LA FOLLE DES GRANDEURS (SEE: DELUSIONS OF GRANDEUR) (1971, Fr.)

LA FORTUNA DI ESSERE DONNA (SEE: LUCKY TO BE A WOMAN) (1955, It./Fr.)
LA FUGA (1966, It.) PR:O
LA GIORNATA BALORDA (SEE: FROM A ROMAN BALCONY) (1961, Fr./It.)
LA GRANDE BOUFFE (1973, Fr.) PR:C-O
LA GRANDE BOURGEOISE (1977, It.) PR:C
LA GRANDE CACCIA (SEE: EAST OF KILIMANJARO) (1959, Brit./It.)
LA GRANDE ILLUSION (SEE: GRAND ILLUSION) (1937, Fr.)
LA GRANDE SPERANZA (SEE: GREAT HOPE, THE) (1954, It.)
LA GRANDE VARROUILLE (SEE: DON'T LOOK NOW) (1969, Brit./Fr.)
LA GUERRE EST FINIE (1967, Fr./Swed.) PR:C-O
LA HABANERA (1937, Ger.) PR:A
L.A. HEAT (1989) PR:C
LA HIJA DE FRANKENSTEIN (SEE: SANTO CONTRA LA HIJA DE FRANKENSTEIN) (1971, Mex.)
LA HIJA DEL ENGANO (SEE: DAUGHTER OF DECEIT) (1977, Mex.)
LA HISTORIA OFICIAL (SEE: OFFICIAL STORY, THE) (1985, Arg.)
LA ILLUSION EN TRANVIA (SEE: ILLUSION TRAVELS BY STREETCAR, THE) (1977, Mex.)
LA ISLA DE LA PASION (SEE: PASSION ISLAND) (1943, Mex.)
LA ISLA DEL TESORO (SEE: TREASURE ISLAND) (1972, Brit./Fr./Sp./W. Ger.)
LA JOVEN (SEE: YOUNG ONE, THE) (1961, Mex.)
LA JUMENT VAPEUR (SEE: DIRTY DISHES) (1976, Fr.)
LA KERMESSE HEROIQUE (SEE: CARNIVAL IN FLANDERS) (1935, Fr.)
LA LAMA NEL CORPO (SEE: MURDER CLINIC, THE) (1967, Fr./It.)
LA LECTRICE (1989, Fr.) PR:O
LA LEGENDA DEL RUDIO MALESE (SEE: JUNGLE RAIDERS) (1986, It.)
LA LEGGE (SEE: WHERE THE HOT WIND BLOWS) (1958, Fr./It.)
LA LEI DEL DESEO (SEE: LAW OF DESIRE, THE) (1987, Sp.)
LA LEYENDA DE BANDIDO (SEE: LEGEND OF A BANDIT, THE) (1945, Mex.)
LA LINEA DEL CIELO (SEE: SKYLINE) (1983, Sp.)
LA LOI (SEE: WHERE THE HOT WIND BLOWS) (1958, Fr./It.)
LA LUMIERE D'EN FACE (SEE: LIGHT ACROSS THE STREET) (1957, Fr.)
LA LUNE DANS LE CANIVEAU (SEE: MOON IN THE GUTTER, THE) (1983, Fr./It.)
LA LUPA MANNURA (SEE: LEGEND OF THE WOLF WOMAN, THE) (1977, Sp.)
LA MALDICION DE A LLORONA (SEE: CURSE OF THE CRYING WOMAN, THE) (1969, Mex.)
LA MALDICION DE LA MOMIA AZTECA (SEE: CURSE OF THE AZTEC MUMMY, THE) (1965, Mex.)
LA MAMAM ET LA PUTAIN (SEE: MOTHER AND THE WHORE, THE) (1973, Fr.)
LA MANDARINE (SEE: SWEET DECEPTION) (1972, Fr.)
LA MANDRAGOLA (SEE: MANDRAGOLA) (1966, Fr./It.)
LA MARCA DEL MUERTO (SEE: CREATURE OF THE WALKING DEAD) (1960, Mex.)
LA MARIE DU PORT (1951, Fr.) PR:C
LA MARIEE ETAIT EN NOIR (SEE: BRIDE WORE BLACK, THE) (1968, Fr./It.)
LA MARSEILLAISE (1938, Fr.) PR:A
LA MATERNELLE (1933, Fr.) PR:A
LA MESSA E FINITA (SEE: MASS IS ENDED, THE) (1988, It.)
LA MOGLIE DEL PRETE (SEE: PRIEST'S WIFE, THE) (1971, Fr./It.)
LA MOMIA AZTECA CONTRA EL ROBOT HUMANO (SEE: AZTEC MUMMY, THE) (1957, Mex.)
LA MORT DE MARIO RICCI (SEE: DEATH OF MARIO RICCI, THE) (1985, Fr./Switz.)
LA MORT EN CE JARDIN (SEE: DEATH IN THE GARDEN) (1956, Fr./Mex.)
LA MORT EN DIRECT (SEE: DEATH WATCH) (1979, Fr./W. Ger.)
LA MORTADELLA (SEE: LADY LIBERTY) (1972, It.)
LA MORTE EN DIRECT (SEE: DEATH WATCH) (1980, Fr./W. Ger.)
LA MORTE RISALE A IERI SERA (SEE: DEATH TOOK PLACE LAST NIGHT) (1970, It./W. Ger.)
LA MORTE VESTITA DI DOLLARI (SEE: DOG EAT DOG) (1963, US/It./W. Ger.)
LA MORTE VIENE DALLA SPAZIO (SEE: DAY THE SKY EXPLODED, THE) (1958, Fr./It.)
LA MORTE — SAISON DES AMOURS (SEE: SEASON FOR LOVE, THE) (1963, Fr.)
LA MUERTA EN EST JARDIN (SEE: DEATH IN THE GARDEN) (1956, Mex.)
LA NAVE DE LOS MONSTRUOS (1959, Mex.) PR:C-O
LA NIPOTE DEL VAMPIRO (SEE: MALENKA, THE VAMPIRE) (1972, It./Sp.)

LA NOCHE DE LOS MIL GATOS (SEE: NIGHT OF A THOUSAND CATS) (1974, Mex.)
LA NOCHE DE WALPURGIS (SEE: WEREWOLF VS. THE VAMPIRE WOMAN, THE) (1970, Sp./W. Ger.)
LA NOCHE DELL TERROR CIEGO (SEE: BLIND DEAD) (1972, Sp.)
LA NOIA (SEE: EMPTY CANVAS, THE) (1964, Fr./It.)
LA NOTTE (1961, Fr./It.) PR:C-O
LA NOTTE BRAVA (1962, Fr./It.) PR:O
LA NOTTE CHE EVELYN USCA DALLA TOMBA (SEE: NIGHT EVELYN CAME OUT OF THE GRAVE, THE) (1973, It.)
LA NOTTE DELLE SPIE (SEE: NIGHT ENCOUNTER) (1959, Fr./It.)
LA NOTTI BIANCHE (SEE: WHITE NIGHTS) (1957, Fr./It.)
LA NUIT (SEE: NIGHT IS OURS) (1930, Fr.)
LA NUIT AMERICAINE (SEE: DAY FOR NIGHT) (1973, Fr.)
LA NUIT DE VARENNES (1982, Fr./It.) PR:O
LA NUIT DES ESPIONS (SEE: NIGHT ENCOUNTER) (1959, Fr./It.)
LA NUIT DES GENERAUX (SEE: NIGHT OF THE GENERALS, THE) (1966, Fr./Brit.)
LA ORGIA NOCTURNA DE LOS VAMPIROS (SEE: VAMPIRE'S NIGHT ORGY, THE) (1973, It./Sp.)
LA PALOMBIERE (SEE: BIRD WATCH, THE) (1983, Fr.)
LA PARISIENNE (1958, Fr./It.) PR:C-O
LA PART DE L'OMBRE (SEE: BLIND DESIRE) (1948, Fr.)
LA PASSANTE (1982, Fr./W. Ger.) PR:C
LA PASSION BEATRICE (SEE: BEATRICE) (1988)
LA PAURA (SEE: FEAR) (1954, It./W. Ger.)
LA PEAU DOUCE (SEE: SOFT SKIN, THE) (1964, Fr.)
LA PELICULA DEL REY (SEE: KING AND HIS MOVIE, A) (1986, Arg.)
LA PERMISSION (SEE: STORY OF A THREE DAY PASS, THE) (1968, Fr.)
LA PETIT SIRENE (1984, Fr.) PR:C
LA PETITE CAFE (SEE: PLAYBOY OF PARIS) (1930)
LA PIU BELLA SERATA DELLA MIA VITA (SEE: MOST WONDERFUL EVENING OF MY LIFE, THE) (1972, Fr./It.)
LA PLANETE SAUVAGE (SEE: FANTASTIC PLANET) (1973, Fr./Czech.)
LA POUPEE (SEE: DOLL, THE) (1962, Fr.)
LA PRISE DE POUVOIR PAR LOUIS XIV (SEE: RISE OF LOUIS XIV, THE) (1966, Fr.)
LA PRISONNIERE (1969, Fr./It.) PR:O
LA PROMISE DE L'AUBE (SEE: PROMISE AT DAWN) (1970, US/Fr.)
LA PROVINCIALE (SEE: GIRL FROM LORRAINE, THE) (1982, Fr.)
LA QUESTION (SEE: QUESTION, THE) (1977, Fr.)
LA RABIA (SEE: RAGE, THE) (1963, US/Mex.)
LA RAGAZZA CHE SAPEVA TROPPO (SEE: EVIL EYE) (1964, It.)
LA RAGAZZA DI LATTA (SEE: TIN GIRL, THE) (1970, It.)
LA REBELION DE LOS COLGADOS (SEE: REBELLION OF THE HANGED, THE) (1954, Mex.)
LA RECREATION (SEE: PLAYTIME) (1967, Fr.)
LA REGLE DU JEU (SEE: RULES OF THE GAME) (1939, Fr.)
LA RELIGIEUSE (SEE: NUN, THE) (1971, Fr.)
LA RESIDENCIA (SEE: HOUSE THAT SCREAMED, THE) (1970, Sp.)
LA RIVOLTA DEI GLADIATORI (SEE: WARRIOR AND THE SLAVE GIRL, THE) (1959, It.)
LA ROMANA (SEE: WOMAN OF ROME) (1956, It.)
LA RONDE (1950, Fr.) PR:O
LA ROSE ESCORCHEE (SEE: BLOOD ROSE, THE) (1970, Fr.)
LA ROUTE EST BELLE (SEE: ROAD IS FINE, THE) (1930, Fr.)
LA RUE DES AMOURS FACILES (SEE: RUN WITH THE DEVIL) (1963, Fr./It.)
LA SABINA (SEE: SABINA, THE) (1979. Sp./Swed.)
LA SAGA DE LOS DRACULA (SEE: SAGA OF DRACULA, THE) (1975, Sp.)
LA SCARLATINE (1983, Fr.) PR:C
LA SEGUA (1985, Costa Rica/Mex.) PR:O
LA SEPOLTA VIVA (SEE: BURIED ALIVE) (1951, It.)
LA SIGNORA SENZA CAMELIE (SEE: LADY WITHOUT CAMELLIAS, THE) (1981, It.)
LA SIRENE DU MISSISSIPPI (SEE: MISSISSIPPI MERMAID) (1970, Fr./It.)
LA SMANIA ANDOSSO (SEE: EYE OF THE NEEDLE, THE) (1965, Fr./It.)
LA SPINA DORSALE DEL DIAVOLO (SEE: DESERTER, THE) (1971, US/It./Yugo.)
LA STRADA (1954, It.) PR:A-C
LA STRADA PER FORT ALAMO (SEE: ROAD TO FORT ALAMO, THE) (1966, Fr./It.)
LA SYMPHONIE PASTORALE (SEE: SYMPHONIE PASTORALE) (1948, Fr.)
LA TATICHE DE ERCOLE (SEE: HERCULES) (1959, It.)

LA TENDA ROSSA (SEE: RED TENT, THE) (1971, It./USSR)
LA TERRA TREMA (1947, It.) PR:A
LA TERRAZA (SEE: TERRACE, THE) (1964, Arg.)
LA TRAVERSEE DE PARIS (SEE: FOUR BAGS FULL) (1956, Fr./It.)
LA TRAVIATA (1968, It.) PR:A
LA TRAVIATA (1982, It.) PR:A
LA TRUITE (SEE: TROUT, THE) (1982, Fr.)
LA VACANZA (SEE: VACATION, THE) (1971, It.)
LA VACCA E IL PRIGIONIERO (SEE: COW AND I, THE) (1961, Fr./It./W. Ger.)
LA VACHE ET LE PRISONNIER (SEE: COW AND I, THE) (1961, Fr./It./W. Ger.)
LA VALLEE DES PHARAOHS (SEE: CLEOPATRA'S DAUGHTER) (1963, Fr./It.)
LA VENGANZA DEL SEXO (SEE: CURIOUS DR. HUMPP) (1967, Arg.)
LA 25E HEURE (SEE: 25TH HOUR, THE) (1967, Fr./It./Yugo.)
LA VENTICINQUESIMA ORA (SEE: 25TH HOUR, THE) (1967, Fr./It./Yugo.)
LA VERGINE DE NORIMBERGA (SEE: HORROR CASTLE) (1956, It.)
LA VERGINE DI SAMOA (SEE: DRUMS OF TABU, THE) (1967, It./Sp.)
LA VIA LATTEA (SEE: MILKY WAY, THE) (1969, Fr./It.)
LA VIACCIA (1962, Fr./It.) PR:C-O
LA VICTOIRE EN CHANTANT (SEE: BLACK AND WHITE IN COLOR) (1976, Fr.)
LA VIE COMMENCE DEMAIN (SEE: LIFE BEGINS TOMORROW) (1952, Fr.)
LA VIE CONTINUE (1982, Fr.) PR:A
LA VIE DE CHATEAU (1967, Fr.) PR:A
LA VIE DEVANT SOI (SEE: MADAME ROSA) (1977, Fr.)
LA VIE EST UN ROMAN (SEE: LIFE IS A BED OF ROSES) (1984, Fr.)
LA VIE FACILE (SEE: EASY LIFE, THE) (1971, Fr.)
LA VIOLENZA E L'MORE (SEE: MYTH, THE) (1965, It.)
LA VISITA (1966, It./Fr.) PR:O
LA VOGLIA MATTA (SEE: CRAZY DESIRE) (1964, It.)
LA VOIE LACTEE (SEE: MILKY WAY, THE) (1969, Fr./It.)
LABBRA ROSSE (SEE: RED LIPS) (1964, Fr./It.)
LABURNUM GROVE (1936, Brit.) PR:A
LABYRINTH (SEE: REFLECTION OF FEAR, A) (1973)
LABYRINTH (1986) PR:AA
LACEMAKER, THE (1977, Fr.) PR:O
LACOMBE, LUCIEN (1974) PR:O
LAD, THE (1935, Brit.) PR:A
LAD: A DOG (1962) PR:AA
LAD FROM OUR TOWN (1941, USSR) PR:A
LADDIE (1935) PR:AA
LADDIE (1940) PR:AA
L'ADDITION (1984, Fr.) PR:O
LADIES AND GENTLEMEN, THE FABULOUS STAINS (1982) PR:O
LADIES CLUB, THE (1986) PR:O
LADIES COURAGEOUS (1944) PR:A
LADIES CRAVE EXCITEMENT (1935) PR:A
LADIES' DAY (1943) PR:A
LADIES IN DISTRESS (1938) PR:A
LADIES IN LOVE (1930) PR:A
LADIES IN LOVE (1936) PR:A
LADIES IN RETIREMENT (1941) PR:C
LADIES IN WASHINGTON (SEE: LADIES OF WASHINGTON) (1944)
LADIES LOVE BRUTES (1930) PR:A
LADIES LOVE DANGER (1935) PR:A
LADIES' MAN (1931) PR:C
LADIES' MAN (1947) PR:A
LADIES' MAN, THE (1961) PR:A
LADIES MUST LIVE (1940) PR:A
LADIES MUST LOVE (1933) PR:A
LADIES MUST PLAY (1930) PR:A
LADIES OF LEISURE (1930) PR:A-C
LADIES OF THE BIG HOUSE (1932) PR:A
LADIES OF THE CHORUS (1948) PR:A
LADIES OF THE JURY (1932) PR:A
LADIES OF THE LOTUS (1987, Can.) PR:O
LADIES OF THE MOB (SEE: HOUSE OF WOMEN) (1962)
LADIES OF THE PARK (1964, Fr.) PR:C
LADIES OF WASHINGTON (1944) PR:A
LADIES ON THE ROCKS (1985, Den.) PR:C-O
LADIES SHOULD LISTEN (1934) PR:A
LADIES THEY TALK ABOUT (1933) PR:A
LADIES WHO DO (1964, Brit.) PR:A
L'ADOLESCENT (SEE: ADOLESCENT, THE) (1978, Fr./W. Ger.)
LADRI DI BICICLETTE (SEE: BICYCLE THIEF, THE) (1949, It.)
LADY AND GENT (1932) PR:A
LADY AND THE BANDIT, THE (1951) PR:A
LADY AND THE DOCTOR, THE (SEE: LADY AND THE MONSTER, THE) (1944)
LADY AND THE MOB, THE (1939) PR:A
LADY AND THE MONSTER, THE (1944) PR:C

LADY AND THE OUTLAW, THE (SEE: BILLY TWO HATS) (1974)
LADY AND THE TRAMP (1955) PR:AA
LADY AT MIDNIGHT (1948) PR:A
LADY BE CAREFUL (1936) PR:A
LADY BE GAY (SEE: LAUGH IT OFF) (1939)
LADY BE GOOD (1941) PR:A
LADY BEHAVE (1937) PR:A
LADY BEWARE (SEE: THIRTEENTH GUEST, THE) (1932)
LADY BODYGUARD (1942) PR:A
LADY BY CHOICE (1934) PR:A
LADY CAROLINE LAMB (1972, US/Brit./It.) PR:A
LADY CHASER (1946) PR:A
LADY CHATTERLEY'S LOVER (1955, Fr.) PR:A
LADY CHATTERLEY'S LOVER (1981, Fr./Brit.) PR:O
LADY CONFESSES, THE (1945) PR:A
LADY CONSENTS, THE (1936) PR:A
LADY CRAVED EXCITEMENT, THE (1950, Brit.) PR:A
LADY DANCES, THE (SEE: MERRY WIDOW, THE) (1934)
LADY DOCTOR, THE (1963, Fr./It./Sp.) PR:C
LADY DRACULA, THE (1974) PR:O
LADY ESCAPES, THE (1937) PR:A
LADY EVE, THE (1941) PR:A
LADY FIGHTS BACK, THE (1937) PR:A
LADY FOR A DAY (1933) PR:A
LADY FOR A NIGHT (1941) PR:A
LADY FRANKENSTEIN (1971, It.) PR:O
LADY FROM BOSTON, THE (SEE: PARDON MY FRENCH) (1951, US/Fr.)
LADY FROM CHEYENNE, THE (1941) PR:A
LADY FROM CHUNGKING (1943) PR:A
LADY FROM LISBON (1942, Brit.) PR:A
LADY FROM LOUISIANA (1941) PR:A
LADY FROM NOWHERE (1936) PR:A
LADY FROM NOWHERE (1931) PR:A
LADY FROM SHANGHAI, THE (1948) PR:C
LADY FROM TEXAS, THE (1951) PR:A
LADY FROM THE SEA, THE (1929, Brit.) PR:A
LADY GAMBLES, THE (1949) PR:A
LADY GANGSTER (1942) PR:A
LADY GENERAL, THE (1965, Hong Kong) PR:A
LADY GODIVA (1955) PR:A
LADY GODIVA RIDES AGAIN (1955, Brit.) PR:A
LADY GREY (1980) PR:O
LADY HAMILTON (SEE: THAT HAMILTON WOMAN) (1941)
LADY HAMILTON (1969, It./Fr./W. Ger.) PR:O
LADY HAS PLANS, THE (1942) PR:A
LADY ICE (1973) PR:A-C
LADY IN A CAGE (1964) PR:O
LADY IN A JAM (1942) PR:A
LADY IN CEMENT (1968) PR:O
LADY IN DANGER (1934, Brit.) PR:A
LADY IN DISTRESS (1942, Brit.) PR:A
LADY IN QUESTION, THE (1940) PR:A
LADY IN RED, THE (1979) PR:O
LADY IN THE CAR WITH GLASSES AND A GUN, THE (1970, US/Fr.) PR:O
LADY IN THE DARK (1944) PR:A
LADY IN THE DEATH HOUSE (1944) PR:A
LADY IN THE FOG (SEE: SCOTLAND YARD INSPECTOR) (1952, Brit.)
LADY IN THE IRON MASK (1952) PR:A
LADY IN THE LAKE (1947) PR:A
LADY IN THE MORGUE, THE (1938) PR:A
LADY IN WHITE (1988) PR:C
LADY IS A SQUARE, THE (1959, Brit.) PR:A
LADY IS FICKLE, THE (1948, It.) PR:A
LADY IS WILLING, THE (1934, Brit.) PR:A
LADY IS WILLING, THE (1942) PR:A
LADY JANE (1986, Brit.) PR:C
LADY JANE GREY (1936, Brit.) PR:A
LADY KILLER (1933) PR:A
LADY KILLER OF ROME, THE (SEE: ASSASSIN, THE) (1965, Fr./It.)
LADY KILLERS, THE (SEE: LADYKILLERS, THE) (1956, Brit.)
LADY L (1965, Fr./It.) PR:C
LADY, LET'S DANCE (1944) PR:A
LADY LIBERTY (1972, It./Fr.) PR:C
LADY LIES, THE (1929) PR:A
LADY LUCK (1936) PR:A
LADY LUCK (1946) PR:A
LADY MISLAID, A (1958, Brit.) PR:A
LADY OBJECTS, THE (1938) PR:A
LADY OF BURLESQUE (1943) PR:C
LADY OF CHANCE, A (1928) PR:A
LADY OF DECEIT (SEE: BORN TO KILL) (1947)
LADY OF MONZA, THE (1970, It.) PR:O
LADY OF MYSTERY (SEE: CLOSE CALL FOR BOSTON BLACKIE, A) (1946)
LADY OF SCANDAL, THE (1930) PR:A
LADY OF SECRETS (1936) PR:A
LADY OF THE BOULEVARDS (SEE: NANA) (1934)
LADY OF THE CAMELIAS (1987, W. Ger.) PR:C

LADY OF THE PAVEMENTS (1929) PR:A
LADY OF THE ROSE (SEE: BRIDE OF THE REGIMENT) (1930)
LADY OF THE SHADOWS (SEE: TERROR, THE) (1963)
LADY OF THE TROPICS (1939) PR:C
LADY OF VENGEANCE (1957, Brit.) PR:A
LADY ON A TRAIN (1945) PR:A
LADY ON THE TRACKS, THE (1968, Czech.) PR:A
LADY OSCAR (1979, Fr./Jap.) PR:C
LADY PAYS OFF, THE (1951) PR:A
LADY POSSESSED (1952) PR:A
LADY REFUSES, THE (1931) PR:A
LADY REPORTER (SEE: BULLDOG EDITION) (1936)
LADY SAYS NO, THE (1951) PR:A
LADY SCARFACE (1941) PR:A
LADY SINGS THE BLUES (1972) PR:O
LADY, STAY DEAD (1982, Aus.) PR:O
LADY SURRENDERS, A (1930) PR:A
LADY SURRENDERS, A (1947, Brit.) PR:A
LADY TAKES A CHANCE, A (1943) PR:A
LADY TAKES A FLYER, THE (1958) PR:A
LADY TAKES A SAILOR, THE (1949) PR:A
LADY TO LOVE, A (1930) PR:A
LADY TUBBS (1935) PR:A
LADY VANISHES, THE (1938, Brit.) PR:A
LADY VANISHES, THE (1980, Brit.) PR:C
LADY WANTS MINK, THE (1953) PR:A
LADY WHO DARED, THE (1931) PR:A
LADY WINDERMERE'S FAN (SEE: FAN, THE) (1949)
LADY WITH A LAMP, THE (1951, Brit.) PR:A
LADY WITH A PAST (1932) PR:A
LADY WITH RED HAIR (1940) PR:A
LADY WITH THE DOG, THE (1962, USSR) PR:A
LADY WITHOUT CAMELLIAS, THE (1981, It.) PR:C-O
LADY WITHOUT PASSPORT, A (1950) PR:A
LADYBUG, LADYBUG (1963) PR:C
LADYHAWKE (1985) PR:C
LADYKILLERS, THE (1956, Brit.) PR:A-C
LADY'S FROM KENTUCKY, THE (1939) PR:A
LADY'S MORALS, A (1930) PR:A
LADY'S PROFESSION, A (1933) PR:A
LAFAYETTE (1963, Fr./It.) PR:AA
LAFAYETTE ESCADRILLE (1958) PR:A
L'AFRICAN (SEE: AFRICAN, THE) (1983, Fr.)
L'AGE D'OR (1930, Fr.) PR:C
LAILA (SEE: MAKE WAY FOR LILA) (1962, Swed./W. Ger.)
LAIR OF THE WHITE WORM, THE (1988, Brit.) PR:O
LAKE, THE (1970, Jap.) PR:O
LAKE OF DRACULA (1973, Jap.) PR:O
LAKE PLACID SERENADE (1944) PR:A
L'ALBERO DEGLI ZOCCOLI (SEE: TREE OF WOODEN CLOGS, THE) (1979, It.)
L'AMANT DE LADY CHATTERLEY (SEE: LADY CHATTERLEY'S LOVER) (1955, Fr.)
LAMBETH WALK, THE (1940, Brit.) PR:A
LAMENT OF THE PATH, THE (SEE: PATHER PANCHALI) (1955, India)
L'AMI DE MON AMIE (SEE: BOYFRIENDS AND GIRLFRIENDS) (1988, Fr.)
L'AMORE (SEE: WAYS OF LOVE) (1950, It.)
L'AMORE DIFFICILE (SEE: OF WAYWARD LOVE) (1964, It./W. Ger.)
L'AMOUR (1973) PR:O
L'AMOUR EN FUITE (SEE: LOVE ON THE RUN) (1979, Fr.)
L'AMOUR, L'APRES-MIDI (SEE: CHLOE IN THE AFTERNOON) (1972, Fr.)
L'AMOUR PAR TERRE (SEE: LOVE ON THE GROUND) (1984, Fr.)
LAMP, THE (SEE: OUTING, THE) (1987)
LAMP IN ASSASSIN MEWS (1962, Brit.) PR:A
LAMP STILL BURNS, THE (1943, Brit.) PR:A
L'ANATRA ALL'ARANCIA (SEE: DUCK IN ORANGE SAUCE) (1976, It.)
LANCASHIRE LUCK (1937, Brit.) PR:A
LANCELOT AND GUINEVERE (SEE: SWORD OF LANCELOT) (1963)
LANCELOT OF THE LAKE (1975, Fr.) PR:C
LANCER SPY (1937) PR:A
LAND AND THE LAW (SEE: BLACK MARKET RUSTLERS) (1943)
LAND BEFORE TIME, THE (1988) PR:AA
LAND BEYOND THE LAW (1937) PR:A
LAND OF DOOM (1986) PR:C
LAND OF FIGHTING MEN (1938) PR:A
LAND OF FURY (1955, Brit.) PR:A
LAND OF HUNTED MEN (1943) PR:A
LAND OF MISSING MEN, THE (1930) PR:A
LAND OF NO RETURN, THE (1981) PR:A
LAND OF OZ (SEE: WONDERFUL LAND OF OZ) (1969)
LAND OF THE LAWLESS (1947) PR:A
LAND OF THE MINOTAUR (1976, US/Gr.) PR:O
LAND OF THE OPEN RANGE (1941) PR:A
LAND OF THE OUTLAWS (1944) PR:A
LAND OF THE PHARAOHS (1955) PR:A-C
LAND OF THE SILVER FOX (1928) PR:AA
LAND OF THE SIX GUNS (1940) PR:A

LAND OF WANTED MEN (1932) PR:A
LAND RAIDERS (1970) PR:C
LAND THAT TIME FORGOT, THE (1975, Brit.) PR:A
LAND UNKNOWN, THE (1957) PR:A
LAND WE LOVE, THE (SEE: HERO'S ISLAND) (1962)
LAND WITHOUT MUSIC (SEE: FORBIDDEN MUSIC) (1936, Brit.)
LANDFALL (1953, Brit.) PR:A
LANDLORD, THE (1970) PR:C
LANDRU (1963, Fr./It.) PR:O
LANDRUSH (1946) PR:A
LANDSCAPE IN THE MIST (1988, Gr./Fr./It.) PR:C
LANDSCAPE SUICIDE (1986) PR:O
LANDSLIDE (1937, Brit.) PR:A
LANGTAN (SEE: NIGHT GAMES) (1966, Swed.)
L'ANNEE DERNIERE A MARIENBAD (SEE: LAST YEAR AT MARIENBAD) (1961, Fr./It.)
L'ANNEE DES MEDUSES (1984, Fr.) PR:O
LARAMIE (1949) PR:A
LARAMIE MOUNTAINS (1952) PR:A
LARAMIE TRAIL, THE (1944) PR:A
LARCENY (1948) PR:A-C
LARCENY IN HER HEART (1946) PR:A
LARCENY, INC. (1942) PR:A
LARCENY LANE (SEE: BLONDE CRAZY) (1931)
LARCENY ON THE AIR (1937) PR:A
LARCENY STREET (1941, Brit.) PR:A
LARCENY WITH MUSIC (1943) PR:A
LARGE ROPE, THE (1953, Brit.) PR:A
LARGE ROPE, THE (SEE: LONG ROPE) (1961)
L'ARGENT (1984, Fr./Switz.) PR:O
L'ARGENT DE POCHE (SEE: SMALL CHANGE) (1976, Fr.)
L'ARMA (SEE: GUN, THE) (1978, It.)
LAS CUATRO VERDADES (SEE: THREE FABLES OF LOVE) (1963, Fr./It./Sp.)
L'AS DES AS (SEE: ACE OF ACES) (1982, Fr./W. Ger.)
LAS LUCHADORAS CONTRA EL MEDICO RESINO (SEE: DOCTOR OF DOOM) (1962, Mex.)
LAS LUCHADORAS CONTRA LA MOMIA (SEE: WRESTLING WOMEN VS. THE AZTEC MUMMY) (1964, Mex.)
LAS RATAS NO DUERMEN DE NOCHE (1974, Sp./Fr.) PR:O
LAS VEGAS 500 MILLIONS (SEE: THEY CAME TO ROB LAS VEGAS) (1969, Fr./It./Sp./W. Ger.)
LAS VEGAS FREE-FOR-ALL (1968, Jap.) PR:C
LAS VEGAS HILLBILLYS (1966) PR:A
LAS VEGAS LADY (1976) PR:A
LAS VEGAS NIGHTS (1941) PR:A
LAS VEGAS SHAKEDOWN (1955) PR:A
LAS VEGAS STORY, THE (1952) PR:A
LAS VEGAS WEEKEND (1985) PR:O
LASCA OF THE RIO GRANDE (1931) PR:A
LASERBLAST (1978) PR:C
LASH, THE (1930) PR:A
LASH, THE (1934, Brit.) PR:C
LASH OF THE PENITENTES (SEE: PENITENTE MURDER CASE) (1937)
LASKY JEDNE PLAVOLASKY (SEE: LOVES OF A BLONDE) (1965, Czech.)
L'ASSASSIN HABITE AU 21 (SEE: MURDERER LIVES AT NUMBER 21, THE) (1947, Fr.)
LASSIE, COME HOME (1943) PR:AA
LASSIE FROM LANCASHIRE (1938, Brit.) PR:AA
LASSIE'S GREAT ADVENTURE (1963) PR:AA
LASSITER (1984, Brit.) PR:O
L'ASSOCIE (SEE: ASSOCIATE, THE) (1982, Fr./W. Ger.)
LAST ACT OF MARTIN WESTON, THE (1970, Can./Czech.) PR:C
LAST ADVENTURE, THE (1968, Fr./It.) PR:A
LAST ADVENTURERS, THE (1937, Brit.) PR:A
LAST AFFAIR, THE (1976) PR:O
LAST AMERICAN HERO, THE (1973) PR:C
LAST AMERICAN VIRGIN, THE (1982) PR:O
LAST ANGRY MAN, THE (1959) PR:A
LAST BANDIT, THE (1949) PR:A
LAST BARRICADE, THE (1938, Brit.) PR:C
LAST BATTLE, THE (SEE: LE DERNIER COMBAT) (1983, Fr.)
LAST BLITZKRIEG, THE (1958) PR:A
LAST BRIDGE, THE (1957, Aust.) PR:O
LAST CASTLE, THE (SEE: ECHOES OF A SUMMER) (1976)
LAST CHALLENGE, THE (1967) PR:A
LAST CHANCE, THE (1937, Brit.) PR:A
LAST CHANCE, THE (1945, Switz.) PR:A
LAST CHANCE FOR A BORN LOSER (SEE: STATELINE MOTEL) (1976, It.)
LAST CHASE, THE (1981) PR:A
LAST COMMAND, THE (SEE: PRISONER OF JAPAN) (1942)
LAST COMMAND, THE (1955) PR:A
LAST COUPON, THE (1932, Brit.) PR:A
LAST CROOKED MILE, THE (1946) PR:A
LAST CURTAIN, THE (1937, Brit.) PR:A
LAST DANCE, THE (1930) PR:A

LAST DAY OF THE WAR, THE (1969, US/It./Sp.) PR:A
LAST DAYS OF BOOT HILL (1947) PR:A
LAST DAYS OF DOLWYN, THE (1949, Brit.) PR:A
LAST DAYS OF MAN ON EARTH, THE (1975, Brit.) PR:O
LAST DAYS OF MUSSOLINI (1974, It.)
LAST DAYS OF PLANET EARTH (SEE: PROPHECIES
   OF NOSTRADAMUS) (1974, Jap.)
LAST DAYS OF POMPEII, THE (1935) PR:A
LAST DAYS OF POMPEII, THE (1960, It.) PR:A
LAST DAYS OF SODOM AND GOMORRAH, THE
   (SEE: SODOM AND GOMORRAH) (1962, US/Fr./It.)
LAST DETAIL, THE (1973) PR:O
LAST DRAGON, THE (1985) PR:C
LAST EMBRACE (1979) PR:O
LAST EMPEROR, THE (1987) PR:C
LAST ESCAPE, THE (1970, Brit.) PR:A
LAST EXPRESS, THE (1938) PR:A
LAST FIGHT, THE (1983) PR:O
LAST FLIGHT, THE (1931) PR:A
LAST FLIGHT OF NOAH'S ARK, THE (1980) PR:AA
LAST FOUR DAYS, THE (SEE: LAST DAYS OF MUS-
   SOLINI) (1974, It.)
LAST FRONTIER, THE (1955) PR:A
LAST FRONTIER UPRISING (1947) PR:A
LAST GAME, THE (1964, USSR) PR:C
LAST GANGSTER, THE (1937) PR:A
LAST GANGSTER, THE (SEE: ROGER TOUHY, GANG-
   STER!) (1944)
LAST GENTLEMAN, THE (1934, Egypt) PR:A
LAST GLORY OF TROY (SEE: AVENGER, THE) (1962,
   Fr./It.)
LAST GRAVE, THE (SEE: NAVAJO RUN) (1964)
LAST GREAT TREASURE, THE (SEE: MOTHER LODE)
   (1982)
LAST GRENADE, THE (1970, Brit.) PR:C
LAST GUNFIGHTER, THE (1961, Can.) PR:A
LAST GUNFIGHTER, THE (SEE: DEATH OF A GUN-
   FIGHTER) (1969)
LAST HARD MEN, THE (1976) PR:O
LAST HERO (SEE: LONELY ARE THE BRAVE) (1962)
LAST HILL, THE (1945, USSR) PR:A
LAST HOLIDAY (1950, Brit.) PR:A
LAST HORROR FILM, THE (1984) PR:O
LAST HORSEMAN, THE (1944) PR:A
LAST HOUR, THE (1930, Brit.) PR:A
LAST HOURS, THE (SEE: BIG FRAME, THE) (1953,
   Brit.)
LAST HOUSE ON DEAD END STREET (1977) PR:O
LAST HOUSE ON THE LEFT (1972) PR:O
LAST HOUSE ON THE LEFT, PART II (SEE: TWITCH
   OF THE DEATH NERVE) (1972, It.)
LAST HUNT, THE (1956) PR:C
LAST HUNTER, THE (1984, It.) PR:O
LAST HURRAH, THE (1958) PR:A
LAST JOURNEY, THE (1936, Brit.) PR:A
LAST LOAD, THE (1948, Brit.) PR:AA
LAST MAN, THE (1932) PR:A
LAST MAN, THE (1968, Fr.) PR:C
LAST MAN ON EARTH, THE (1964, US/It.) PR:O
LAST MAN TO HANG, THE (1956, Brit.) PR:C
LAST MARRIED COUPLE IN AMERICA, THE (1980) PR:O
LAST MERCENARY, THE (1969, It./Sp./W. Ger.) PR:C
LAST MESSAGE FROM SAIGON (SEE: OPERATION
   CIA) (1965)
LAST METRO, THE (1980, Fr.) PR:C-O
LAST MILE, THE (1932) PR:A
LAST MILE, THE (1959) PR:C
LAST MOMENT, THE (1954, Brit.) PR:A
LAST MOMENT, THE (1966) PR:C
LAST MOVIE, THE (1971) PR:O
LAST MUSKETEER, THE (1952) PR:A
LAST NIGHT AT THE ALAMO (1984) PR:O
LAST OF MRS. CHEYNEY, THE (1929) PR:A
LAST OF MRS. CHEYNEY, THE (1937) PR:A
LAST OF SHEILA, THE (1973) PR:C
LAST OF SUMMER (SEE: EARLY AUTUMN) (1962,
   Jap.)
LAST OF THE BADMEN (1957) PR:A
LAST OF THE BUCCANEERS (1950) PR:A
LAST OF THE CAVALRY, THE (SEE: ARMY GIRL)
   (1938)
LAST OF THE CLINTONS, THE (1935) PR:A
LAST OF THE COMANCHES (1952) PR:A
LAST OF THE COWBOYS, THE (SEE: GREAT
   SMOKEY ROADBLOCK, THE) (1978)
LAST OF THE DESPERADOES (1956) PR:A
LAST OF THE DUANES (1930) PR:A
LAST OF THE DUANES, THE (1941) PR:A
LAST OF THE FAST GUNS, THE (1958) PR:A
LAST OF THE KNUCKLEMEN, THE (1981, Aus.) PR:A
LAST OF THE LONE WOLF, THE (1930) PR:A
LAST OF THE MOHICANS, THE (1936) PR:A
LAST OF THE PAGANS (1936) PR:A
LAST OF THE PONY RIDERS (1953) PR:A
LAST OF THE RED HOT LOVERS (1972) PR:A
LAST OF THE REDMEN (1947) PR:AA
LAST OF THE REDSKINS (SEE: LAST OF THE RED-
   MEN) (1947)

LAST OF THE RENEGADES (1966, Fr./It./W. Ger./Yugo.)
   PR:A
LAST OF THE SECRET AGENTS?, THE (1966) PR:A
LAST OF THE VIKINGS, THE (1962, Fr./It.) PR:A
LAST OF THE WARRENS (1936) PR:A
LAST OF THE WILD HORSES (1948) PR:A
LAST OUTLAW, THE (1936) PR:A
LAST OUTPOST, THE (1935) PR:A
LAST OUTPOST, THE (1951) PR:A
LAST PAGE, THE (SEE: MAN BAIT) (1952, Brit.)
LAST PARADE, THE (1931) PR:A
LAST PERFORMANCE, THE (1929) PR:C
LAST PICTURE SHOW, THE (1971) PR:C-O
LAST PORNO FLICK, THE (1974) PR:O
LAST POSSE, THE (1953) PR:A
LAST POST, THE (1929, Brit.) PR:C
LAST REBEL, THE (1961, Mex.) PR:C
LAST REBEL, THE (1971) PR:C
LAST REMAKE OF BEAU GESTE, THE (1977) PR:C
LAST RESORT (1986) PR:O
LAST RHINO, THE (1961, Brit.) PR:AA
LAST RIDE, THE (1932) PR:A
LAST RIDE, THE (1944) PR:A
LAST RITES (1980) PR:O
LAST RITES (1988) PR:O
LAST ROSE OF SUMMER, THE (1937, Brit.) PR:A
LAST ROUND-UP, THE (1934) PR:A
LAST ROUND-UP, THE (1947) PR:AA
LAST RUN, THE (1971) PR:A
LAST SAFARI, THE (1967, Brit.) PR:A
LAST SHOT YOU HEAR, THE (1969, Brit.) PR:C
LAST STAGE, THE (SEE: LAST STOP, THE) (1949, Pol.)
LAST STAGECOACH WEST, THE (1957) PR:A
LAST STAND, THE (1938) PR:A
LAST STARFIGHTER, THE (1984) PR:C
LAST STOP, THE (1949, Pol.) PR:O
LAST STRAW, THE (1987, Can.) PR:O
LAST SUMMER (1969) PR:O
LAST SUNSET, THE (1961) PR:C-O
LAST TANGO IN PARIS (1973, Fr./It.) PR:O
LAST TEMPTATION OF CHRIST, THE (1988) PR:O
LAST TEN DAYS, THE (1956, W. Ger.) PR:A
LAST TIME I SAW ARCHIE, THE (1961) PR:A
LAST TIME I SAW PARIS, THE (1954) PR:A
LAST TOMAHAWK, THE (1965, It./Sp./W. Ger.) PR:A
LAST TOMB OF LIGEIA (SEE: TOMB OF LIGEIA,
   THE) (1965, Brit.)
LAST TRAIL, THE (1934) PR:A
LAST TRAIN FROM BOMBAY (1952) PR:A
LAST TRAIN FROM GUN HILL (1959) PR:C
LAST TRAIN FROM MADRID, THE (1937) PR:A
LAST TYCOON, THE (1976) PR:C
LAST UNICORN, THE (1982) PR:AA
LAST VALLEY, THE (1971, Brit.) PR:A
LAST VICTIM, THE (SEE: FORCED ENTRY) (1975)
LAST VOYAGE, THE (1960) PR:A
LAST WAGON, THE (1956) PR:C
LAST WALTZ, THE (1936, Brit.) PR:A
LAST WALTZ, THE (1962, Jap.) PR:C
LAST WAR, THE (1962, Jap.) PR:C
LAST WARNING, THE (1929) PR:A
LAST WARNING, THE (1938) PR:A
LAST WARRIOR, THE (SEE: FLAP) (1970)
LAST WARRIOR, THE (1989, Brit.) PR:C-O
LAST WAVE, THE (1978, Aus.) PR:A
LAST WILL OF DR. MABUSE, THE (SEE: TESTAMENT
   OF DR. MABUSE, THE) (1933, Ger.)
LAST WOMAN OF SHANG, THE (1964, Hong Kong)
   PR:A
LAST WOMAN ON EARTH, THE (1960) PR:A
LAST WORD, THE (1979) PR:A
LAST YEAR AT MARIENBAD (1961, Fr./It.) PR:C
L'ATALANTE (1934, Fr.) PR:C
LATE AT NIGHT (1946, Brit.) PR:A
LATE AUTUMN (1973, Jap.) PR:A
LATE EDWINA BLACK, THE (SEE: OBSESSED) (1951,
   Brit.)
LATE EXTRA (1935, Brit.) PR:A
LATE GEORGE APLEY, THE (1947) PR:A
LATE LIZ, THE (1971) PR:A
LATE SHOW, THE (1977) PR:A-C
LATE SUMMER BLUES (1988, Israel) PR:C
LATENT IMAGE (1988, Chile) PR:O
LATIN LOVE (1930, Brit.) PR:A
LATIN LOVERS (1953) PR:A
LATIN QUARTER (SEE: FRENZY) (1946, Brit.)
LATINO (1985) PR:C-O
LATITUDE ZERO (1970, US/Jap.) PR:AA
L'ATLANTIDE (SEE: JOURNEY BENEATH THE DES-
   ERT) (1967, Fr./It.)
L'ATTENTAT (SEE: FRENCH CONSPIRACY, THE)
   (1973, Fr.)
L'AUBERGE ROUGE (SEE: RED INN, THE) (1954, Fr.)
LAUGH AND GET RICH (1931) PR:A
LAUGH IT OFF (1939) PR:A
LAUGH IT OFF (1940, Brit.) PR:A
LAUGH PAGLIACCI (1948, It.) PR:A
LAUGH YOUR BLUES AWAY (1943) PR:A
LAUGHING ANNE (1954, Brit./US) PR:A

LAUGHING AT DANGER (1940) PR:A
LAUGHING AT LIFE (1933) PR:A
LAUGHING AT TROUBLE (1937) PR:A
LAUGHING BOY (1934) PR:A
LAUGHING IN THE SUNSHINE (1953, Brit./Swed.) PR:A
LAUGHING IRISH EYES (1936) PR:A
LAUGHING LADY, THE (1930) PR:A
LAUGHING LADY, THE (1950, Brit.) PR:A
LAUGHING POLICEMAN, THE (1973) PR:O
LAUGHING SINNERS (1931) PR:C
LAUGHTER (1930) PR:A-C
LAUGHTER IN HELL (1933) PR:A
LAUGHTER IN PARADISE (1951, Brit.) PR:AA
LAUGHTER IN THE AIR (SEE: MYRT AND MARGE)
   (1934)
LAUGHTERHOUSE (1984, Brit.) PR:C
LAURA (1944) PR:A
LAUTLOSE WAFFEN (SEE: DEFECTOR, THE) (1966,
   Fr./W. Ger.)
LAVENDER HILL MOB, THE (1951, Brit.) PR:A
L'AVEU (SEE: CONFESSION, THE) (1970, Fr.)
LAVIRINT SMRTI (SEE: FLAMING FRONTIER) (1968,
   Yugo./W. Ger.)
L'AVVENTURA (1959, It./Fr.) PR:A
L'AVVENTURIERO (SEE: ROVER, THE) (1967, It.)
LAW, THE (SEE: LAW AND ORDER) (1940)
LAW, THE (SEE: WHERE THE HOT WIND BLOWS)
   (1958, Fr./It.)
LAW AND DISORDER (1940, Brit.) PR:A
LAW AND DISORDER (1958, Brit.) PR:A
LAW AND DISORDER (1974) PR:O
LAW AND JAKE WADE, THE (1958) PR:A
LAW AND LAWLESS (1932) PR:A
LAW AND LEAD (1937) PR:A
LAW AND ORDER (1932) PR:A
LAW AND ORDER (SEE: FUGITIVE SHERIFF, THE)
   (1936)
LAW AND ORDER (SEE: FAST BULLETS) (1936)
LAW AND ORDER (1940) PR:A
LAW AND ORDER (1942) PR:A
LAW AND ORDER (1953) PR:A
LAW AND THE LADY, THE (1951) PR:A
LAW AND TOMBSTONE, THE (SEE: HOUR OF THE
   GUN) (1967)
LAW BEYOND THE RANGE (1935) PR:A
LAW COMES TO TEXAS, THE (1939) PR:A
LAW COMMANDS, THE (1938) PR:A
LAW FOR TOMBSTONE (1937) PR:A
LAW IN HER HANDS, THE (1936) PR:A
LAW IS THE LAW, THE (1959, Fr.) PR:A
LAW MEN (1944) PR:A
LAW OF DESIRE, THE (1987, Sp.) PR:O
LAW OF THE BADLANDS (1950) PR:A
LAW OF THE BARBARY COAST (1949) PR:A
LAW OF THE GOLDEN WEST (1949) PR:A
LAW OF THE JUNGLE (1942) PR:A
LAW OF THE LASH (1947) PR:A
LAW OF THE LAWLESS (1964) PR:A
LAW OF THE NORTH (1932) PR:AA
LAW OF THE NORTHWEST (1943) PR:A
LAW OF THE PAMPAS (1939) PR:A
LAW OF THE PANHANDLE (1950) PR:A
LAW OF THE PLAINS (1938) PR:A
LAW OF THE RANGE (1941) PR:A
LAW OF THE RANGER (1937) PR:A
LAW OF THE RIO GRANDE (1931) PR:A
LAW OF THE SADDLE (1944) PR:A
LAW OF THE SEA (1932) PR:A
LAW OF THE TEXAN (1938) PR:A
LAW OF THE TIMBER (1941) PR:A
LAW OF THE TONG (1931) PR:A
LAW OF THE TROPICS (1941) PR:A
LAW OF THE UNDERWORLD (1938) PR:A
LAW OF THE VALLEY (1944) PR:A
LAW OF THE WEST (1949) PR:A
LAW RIDES, THE (1936) PR:A
LAW RIDES AGAIN, THE (1943) PR:A
LAW RIDES WEST, THE (SEE: SANTA FE TRAIL, THE)
   (1930)
LAW VS. BILLY THE KID, THE (1954) PR:A
LAW WEST OF TOMBSTONE, THE (1938) PR:A
LAWFUL LARCENY (1930) PR:A
LAWLESS, THE (1950) PR:A-C
LAWLESS BORDER (1935) PR:A
LAWLESS BREED, THE (1946) PR:AA
LAWLESS BREED, THE (1952) PR:A
LAWLESS CLAN (SEE: LAWLESS BREED, THE) (1946)
LAWLESS CODE (1949) PR:A
LAWLESS COWBOYS (1952) PR:A
LAWLESS EIGHTIES, THE (1957) PR:C
LAWLESS EMPIRE (1946) PR:A
LAWLESS FRONTIER, THE (1935) PR:A
LAWLESS LAND (1937) PR:A
LAWLESS NINETIES, THE (1936) PR:A
LAWLESS PLAINSMEN (1942) PR:A
LAWLESS RANGE (1935) PR:A
LAWLESS RIDER, THE (1954) PR:A
LAWLESS RIDERS (1936) PR:A

LAWLESS STREET, A (1955) PR:A
LAWLESS VALLEY (1938) PR:A
LAWLESS WOMAN, THE (1931) PR:A
LAWMAN (1971) PR:C
LAWMAN IS BORN, A (1937) PR:A
LAWRENCE OF ARABIA (1962, Brit.) PR:C
LAWTON STORY, THE (1949) PR:A
LAWYER, THE (1969) PR:O
LAWYER MAN (1933) PR:A
LAWYER'S SECRET, THE (1931) PR:A
LAXDALE HALL (SEE: SCOTCH ON THE ROCKS)
    (1954, Brit.)
LAY THAT RIFLE DOWN (1955) PR:A
LAZY BONES (SEE: HALLELUJAH, I'M A BUM) (1933)
LAZY RIVER (1934) PR:A
LAZYBONES (1935, Brit.) PR:A
LE AMICHE (1962, It.) PR:C
LE AVVENTURE E GLI AMORI DI MIGUEL CERVAN-
    TES (SEE: YOUNG REBEL, THE) (1969, Fr./It./Sp.)
LE BAL (1983, Fr./It./Algeria) PR:A
LE BEAU MARIAGE (1982, Fr.) PR:C-O
LE BEAU SERGE (1958, Fr.) PR:C-Ô
LE BLE EN HERBE (SEE: GAME OF LOVE, THE) (1954)
LE BON PLAISIR (1984, Fr.) PR:A-C
LE BONHEUR (1966, Fr.) PR:C
LE BOUCHER (1971, Fr./It.) PR:O
LE CAPORAL EPINGLE (SEE: ELUSIVE CORPORAL,
    THE) (1962, Fr.)
LE CARROSSE D'OR (SEE: GOLDEN COACH, THE)
    (1952, Fr./It.)
LE CAVALEUR (PRACTICE MAKES PERFECT) (1979,
    Fr.) PR:C
LE CAVE SE REBIFFE (SEE: COUNTERFEITERS OF
    PARIS, THE) (1962, Fr./It.)
LE CERVEAU (SEE: BRAIN, THE) (1969, Fr./US)
LE CHALAND QUI PASSE (SEE: L'ATALANTE) (1947,
    Fr.)
LE CHARME DISCRET DE LA BOURGEOISIE (SEE:
    DISCREET CHARM OF THE BOURGEOISIE, THE)
    (1972, Fr.)
LE CHAT (SEE: CAT, THE) (1971, Fr.)
LE CHAT DANS LE SAC (SEE: CAT IN THE SACK,
    THE) (1967, Can.)
LE CHAT ET LA SOURIS (SEE: CAT AND MOUSE)
    (1975, Fr.)
LE CHEVAL D'ORGEUIL (SEE: HORSE OF PRIDE)
    (1980, Fr.)
LE CHOIX DES ARMES (SEE: CHOICE OF ARMS)
    (1981, Fr.)
LE CIEL EST A VOUS (1957, Fr.) PR:A
LE CLAN DES SICILIENS (SEE: SICILIAN CLAN, THE)
    (1970, Fr.)
LE CLOCHARD (SEE: MAGNIFICENT TRAMP, THE)
    (1962, Fr./It.)
LE COCU MAGNIFIQUE (SEE: MAGNIFICENT CUCK-
    OLD, THE) (1965, Fr./It.)
LE COMPLOT (SEE: TO KILL A PRIEST) (1989, Fr.)
LE COMTE DE MONTE CRISTO (SEE: STORY OF THE
    COUNT OF MONTE CRISTO, THE) (1962, Fr.)
LE CORBEAU (SEE: RAVEN, THE) (1948, Fr.)
LE CORNIAUD (SEE: SUCKER, THE) (1966, Fr./It.)
LE CRABE TAMBOUR (1977, Fr.) PR:O
LE CRIME DE M. LANGE (SEE: CRIME OF MON-
    SIEUR LANGE, THE) (1936, Fr.)
LE CULTE DE BEAUTE (SEE: ARTHUR) (1931, Fr.)
LE DANGER VIENT DE L'ESCAPE (SEE: DAY THE
    SKY EXPLODED, THE) (1958, Fr./It.)
LE DECLIN DE L'EMPIRE AMERICAIN (SEE: DE-
    CLINE OF THE AMERICAN EMPIRE, THE) (1986,
    Can.)
LE DEJEUNER SUR L'HERBE (SEE: PICNIC ON THE
    GRASS) (1959, Fr.)
LE DENIER MILLIARDAIRE (1934, Fr.) PR:A
LE DERNIER COMBAT (1983, Fr.) PR:O
LE DERNIER METRO (SEE: LAST METRO, THE)
    (1980, Fr.)
LE DESERT DES TARTARES (SEE: DESERT OF THE
    TARTARS, THE) (1976, Fr./It./Iran)
LE DESERT ROUGE (SEE: RED DESERT) (1964, Fr./It.)
LE DESORDRE (SEE: DISORDER) (1964, Fr./It.)
LE DIABLE AU CORPS (SEE: DEVIL IN THE FLESH,
    THE) (1947, Fr.)
LE DIABLE ET LAS DIX COMMANDEMENTS (SEE:
    DEVIL AND THE TEN COMMANDMENTS, THE)
    (1962, Fr./It.)
LE DIABLE PAR LA QUEUE (SEE: DEVIL BY THE
    TAIL, THE) (1969, Fr./It.)
LE DIABLE PROBABLEMENT (SEE: DEVIL PROBA-
    BLY, THE) (1977, Fr.)
LE DIABOLIQUE DOCTEUR MABUSE (SEE: THOU-
    SAND EYES OF DR. MABUSE, THE) (1960, Fr./It./W.
    Ger.)
LE DISTRAIT (SEE: DAYDREAMER, THE) (1975, Fr.)
LE DOLCI SIGNORE (SEE: ANYONE CAN PLAY)
    (1968, It.)
LE DRAME DE SHANGHAI (SEE: SHANGHAI
    DRAMA) (1945, Fr.)

LE DUE VITE DI MATTIA PASCAL (SEE: TWO LIVES
    OF MATTIA PASCAL, THE) (1985, Brit./Fr./Gr./It.)
LE FACTEUR S'EN VA-T-EN GUERRE (SEE: POST-
    MAN GOES TO WAR, THE) (1968, Fr.)
LE FANTOME DE LA LIBERTE (SEE: PHANTOM OF
    LIBERTY, THE) (1974, Fr.)
LE FARCEUR (SEE: JOKER, THE) (1961, Fr.)
LE FATE (SEE: QUEENS, THE) (1968, It./Fr.)
LE FEU DE PAILLE (SEE: FIRE IN THE STRAW) (1943,
    Fr.)
LE FRUIT DEFENDU (SEE: FORBIDDEN FRUIT) (1959,
    Fr.)
LE GAI SAVOIR (1968, Fr.) PR:A
LE GEANT A LA COUR DE KUBLAI KHAN (SEE: SAM-
    SON AND THE SEVEN MIRACLES OF THE
    WORLD) (1963, Fr./It.)
LE GENDARME ET LES EXTRATERRESTRES (1978,
    Fr.) PR:C
LE GENOU DE CLAIRE (SEE: CLAIRE'S KNEE) (1970,
    Fr.)
LE GENTLEMAN DE COCODY (SEE: MAN FROM
    COCODY) (1966, Fr./It.)
LE GORILLE A MORDU L'ARCHEVEQUE (SEE:
    DEADLY DECOYS, THE) (1962, Fr.)
LE GORILLE VOUS SALUE BIEN (SEE: GORILLA
    GREETS YOU, THE) (1958, Fr.)
LE GRAND BLEU (SEE: BIG BLUE, THE) (1988)
LE GRAND BLOND AVEC UNE CHAUSSURE NOIRE
    (SEE: TALL BLOND MAN WITH ONE BLACK SHOE,
    THE) (1972, Fr.)
LE GRAND CHEF (SEE: BIG CHIEF, THE) (1960, Fr.)
LE GRAND CHEMIN (SEE: GRAND HIGHWAY, THE)
    (1988)
LE GRAND JEU (SEE: FLESH AND THE WOMAN)
    (1954, Fr./It.)
LE JEUNE FOLLE (SEE: DESPERATE DECISION)
    (1954, Fr.)
LE JEUNE MARIE (1983, Fr.) PR:C
LE JOUER D'ECHECS (SEE: DEVIL IS AN EMPRESS,
    THE) (1939, Fr.)
LE JOUEUR (SEE: GAMBLER, THE) (1958, Fr.)
LE JOUR ET L'HEURE (SEE: DAY AND THE HOUR,
    THE) (1963, Fr./It.)
LE JOUR SE LEVE (SEE: DAYBREAK) (1939, Fr.)
LE JOURNAL D'UNE FEMME DE CHAMBRE (SEE:
    DIARY OF A CHAMBERMAID) (1964, Fr./It.)
LE JOURNAL D'UNE CURE DE CAMPAGNE (SEE:
    DIARY OF A COUNTRY PRIEST) (1950, Fr.)
LE JUGE ET L'ASSASSIN (SEE: JUDGE AND THE AS-
    SASSIN, THE) (1979, Fr.)
LE JUPON ROUGE (SEE: MANUELA'S LOVES) (1987,
    Fr.)
LE LEOPARD (1984, Fr.) PR:O
LE LIEU DU CRIME (SEE: SCENE OF THE CRIME)
    (1986, Fr.)
LE LIT A DEUX PLACES (SEE: DOUBLE BED, THE)
    (1965, Fr./It.)
LE LOCATAIRE (SEE: TENANT, THE) (1976, Fr.)
LE LONG DES TROTTOIRS (SEE: DIARY OF A BAD
    GIRL) (1958, Fr.)
LE MAGNIFIQUE (SEE: MAGNIFICENT ONE, THE)
    (1974, Fr./It.)
LE MAGNIFIQUE (SEE: MAGNIFICENT ONE, THE)
    (1973, Fr./It.)
LE MANS (1971) PR:A
LE MARIAGE DE FIGARO (SEE: MARRIAGE OF
    FIGARO, THE) (1963, Fr.)
LE MEPRIS (SEE: CONTEMPT) (1963, Fr.)
LE MERAVIGLIOSE AVVENTURE DI MARCO POLO
    (SEE: MARCO THE MAGNIFICENT) (1966, Afghani-
    stan/Egypt/It./Fr./Yugo.)
LE MERCENARIRE (SEE: SWORDSMAN OF SIENA,
    THE) (1962, Fr./It.)
LE MILLION (SEE: MILLION, THE) (1931, Fr.)
LE MIROIR A DEUX FACES (SEE: MIRROR HAS TWO
    FACES, THE) (1959, Fr.)
LE MONDAT (SEE: MANDABI) (1970, Fr./Senegal)
LE MONDE TREMBLERA (1939, Fr.) PR:A
LE MOUTON ENRAGE (SEE: FRENCH WAY, THE)
    (1975, Fr.)
LE MUR (SEE: WALL, THE) (1983, Fr.)
LE NOTTI BIANCHE (SEE: WHITE NIGHTS) (1957,
    Fr./It.)
LE ORE NUDE (SEE: NAKED HOURS, THE) (1964, It.)
LE PASSAGER DE LA PLUIE (SEE: RIDER ON THE
    RAIN) (1970, Fr./It.)
LE PASSE MURAILLE (SEE: MR. PEEK-A-BOO) (1951,
    Fr.)
LE PAYS BLEU (SEE: BLUE COUNTRY, THE) (1977, Fr.)
LE PERE TRANQUILLE (SEE: MR. ORCHID) (1948, Fr.)
LE PETIT AMOUR (SEE: KUNG FU MASTER) (1989,
    Fr.)
LE PETIT MONDE DE DON CAMILLO (SEE: LITTLE
    WORLD OF DON CAMILLO, THE) (1953, Fr./It.)
LE PETIT SOLDAT (1965, Fr.) PR:C
LE PETIT THEATRE DE JEAN RENOIR (1974, Fr.) PR:C
LE PILLOLE DE ERCOLE (SEE: HERCULES' PILLS)
    (1960, It.)

LE PISTONNE (SEE: MAN WITH CONNECTIONS,
    THE) (1970, Fr.)
LE PLAISIR (1952, Fr.) PR:C-O
LE POUVOIR DU MAL (SEE: POWER OF EVIL, THE)
    (1985, Fr./It.)
LE PUITS AUX TROIS VERITES (SEE: THREE FACES
    OF SIN) (1963, Fr./It.)
LE QUAI DES BRUMES (SEE: PORT OF SHADOWS)
    (1938, Fr.)
LE QUATTRO VERITA (SEE: THREE FABLES OF
    LOVE) (1963, Fr./It./Sp.)
LE RETOUR DU GRAND BLOND (SEE: RETURN OF
    THE TALL BLOND MAN WITH ONE BLACK SHOE,
    THE) (1974, Fr.)
LE ROI (SEE: ROYAL AFFAIR, A) (1950, Fr.)
LE ROI DE COEUR (SEE: KING OF HEARTS) (1967,
    Fr./It.)
LE ROMAN D'UN TRICHEUR (SEE: STORY OF A
    CHEAT, THE) (1938, Fr.)
LE ROSIER DE MADAME HUSSON (SEE: PRIZE, THE)
    (1952, Fr.)
LE ROUBLE A DEUX FACES (SEE: DAY THE HOTL-
    INE GOT HOT, THE) (1968, Fr./It.)
LE ROUGE AUX LEVRES (SEE: DAUGHTERS OF
    DARKNESS) (1971, Bel./Fr./It./W. Ger.)
LE ROUGE ET LA NOIR (SEE: RED AND THE BLACK,
    THE) (1954, Fr./It.)
LE ROUTE DE CORINTH (SEE: WHO'S GOT THE
    BLACK BOX?) (1970, Fr./Gr./It.)
LE SALAIRE DE LA PEUR (SEE: WAGES OF FEAR,
    THE) (1955, Fr./It.)
LE SAMOURAI (SEE: GODSON, THE) (1972, Fr./It.)
LE SANG D'UN POETE (SEE: BLOOD OF A POET,
    THE) (1930, Fr.)
LE SCANDALE (SEE: CHAMPAGNE MURDERS, THE)
    (1968, Fr.)
LE SERPENT (SEE: SERPENT, THE) (1973, Fr./It./W.
    Ger.)
LE SEX SHOP (1972, Fr.) PR:O
LE SILENCE EST D'OR (SEE: MAN ABOUT TOWN)
    (1947, Fr.)
LE SOEURS BRONTE (SEE: BRONTE SISTERS, THE)
    (1979, Fr.)
LE SOUFFLE AU COEUR (SEE: MURMUR OF THE
    HEART) (1971, Fr./It./W. Ger.)
LE SPECIALSTE (SEE: DROP THEM OR I'LL SHOOT)
    (1969, Fr./Sp./W. Ger.)
LE SUE ULTIME 12 ORE (SEE: HIS LAST TWELVE
    HOURS) (1953, It.)
LE TEMPS DES ASSASSINS (SEE: DEADLIER THAN
    THE MALE) (1957, Fr.)
LE TESTAMENT (SEE: VERDICT, THE) (1974, Fr./It.)
LE TESTAMENT D'ORPHEE (SEE: TESTAMENT OF
    ORPHEUS, THE) (1959, Fr.)
LE TESTAMENT DU DR. MABUSE (SEE: TESTAMENT
    OF DR. MABUSE, THE) (1933, Ger.)
LE THE AU HAREM D'ARCHIMEDE (SEE: TEA IN
    THE HAREM OF ARCHIMEDE) (1985, Fr.)
LE VENT D'EST (SEE: WIND FROM THE EAST) (1970,
    Fr./It./W. Ger.)
LE VICOMTE REGLE SES COMPTES (SEE: VIS-
    COUNT, THE) (1967, Fr./Sp./It./W. Ger.)
LE VIEIL HOMME ET L'ENFANT (SEE: TWO OF US,
    THE) (1967, Fr.)
LE VIOL (1968, Fr./Swed.) PR:O
LE VOILE BLEU (SEE: BLUE VEIL, THE) (1947, Fr.)
LE VOLEUR (SEE: THIEF OF PARIS, THE) (1967, Fr./It.)
LE VOYAGE EN AMERIQUE (SEE: VOYAGE TO
    AMERICA) (1952, Fr.)
LE VOYOU (SEE: CROOK, THE) (1971, Fr.)
LEAD LAW (SEE: CROOKED TRAIL) (1936)
LEADBELLY (1976) PR:C-O
LEADER OF THE PACK (SEE: UNHOLY ROLLERS)
    (1972)
LEADVILLE GUNSLINGER (1952) PR:A
LEAGUE OF FRIGHTENED MEN, THE (1937) PR:A
LEAGUE OF GENTLEMEN, THE (1961, Brit.) PR:A-C
LEAN ON ME (1989) PR:C
LEAP INTO THE VOID (1982, It.) PR:O
LEAP OF FAITH (1931, Brit.) PR:A
LEAP YEAR (1932, Brit.) PR:A
LEARN, BABY, LEARN (SEE: LEARNING TREE, THE)
    (1969)
LEARNING TREE, THE (1969) PR:O
LEASE OF LIFE (1954, Brit.) PR:A
LEATHER AND NYLON (1969, Fr./It.) PR:A-C
LEATHER BOYS, THE (1965, Brit.) PR:O
LEATHER BURNERS, THE (1943) PR:A
LEATHER GLOVES (1948) PR:A
LEATHER-PUSHERS, THE (1940) PR:A
LEATHER SAINT, THE (1956) PR:A
LEATHERNECK, THE (1929) PR:A
LEATHERNECKING (1930) PR:A
LEATHERNECKS HAVE LANDED, THE (1936) PR:A
LEAVE HER TO HEAVEN (1946) PR:O
LEAVE IT TO BLANCHE (1934, Brit.) PR:A
LEAVE IT TO BLONDIE (1945) PR:A
LEAVE IT TO HENRY (1949) PR:A

LEAVE IT TO ME (1933, Brit.) PR:A
LEAVE IT TO ME (1937, Brit.) PR:A
LEAVE IT TO SMITH (1934, Brit.) PR:A
LEAVE IT TO THE IRISH (1944) PR:A
LEAVE IT TO THE MARINES (1951) PR:A
LEAVENWORTH CASE, THE (1936) PR:A
LEBENSBORN (SEE: ORDERED TO LOVE) (1963, W. Ger.)
LEBENSZEICHEN (SEE: SIGNS OF LIFE) (1981, W. Ger.)
L'ECHE LLE BLANCHE (SEE: SECRET WORLD) (1969, Fr.)
L'ECLIPSE (SEE: ECLIPSE) (1962, Fr./It.)
L'ECLISSE (SEE: ECLIPSE) (1962, Fr./It.)
L'ECOLE BUISSONIERE (SEE: PASSION FOR LIFE) (1951, Fr.)
LEDA (SEE: WEB OF PASSION) (1961, Fr.)
LEECH WOMAN, THE (1960) PR:C
LEFT HAND OF GOD, THE (1955) PR:A
LEFT-HANDED GUN, THE (1958) PR:C
LEFT-HANDED LAW (1937) PR:A
LEFT-HANDED WOMAN, THE (1980, W. Ger.) PR:C-O
LEFT, RIGHT AND CENTRE (1959, Brit.) PR:A
LEFTOVER LADIES (1931) PR:A
LEGACY (1976) PR:O
LEGACY, THE (1979, Brit.) PR:O
LEGACY OF A SPY (SEE: DOUBLE MAN, THE) (1967, Brit.)
LEGACY OF BLOOD (1973) PR:O
LEGACY OF BLOOD (1978) PR:O
LEGACY OF MAGGIE WALSH (SEE: LEGACY, THE) (1979, Brit.)
LEGACY OF THE 500,000, THE (1964, Jap.) PR:A
LEGAL EAGLES (1986) PR:C
LEGAL LARCENY (SEE: SILVER CITY RAIDERS) (1943)
LEGEND (1985, Brit.) PR:A
LEGEND IN LEOTARDS (SEE: RETURN OF CAPTAIN INVINCIBLE, THE) (1983, Aus./US)
LEGEND OF A BANDIT, THE (1945, Mex.) PR:A
LEGEND OF BILLIE JEAN, THE (1985) PR:O
LEGEND OF BLOOD CASTLE (SEE: FEMALE BUTCHER, THE) (1972, It./Sp.)
LEGEND OF BLOOD MOUNTAIN, THE (1965) PR:O
LEGEND OF BOGGY CREEK, THE (1973) PR:A-C
LEGEND OF COUGAR CANYON (1974) PR:A
LEGEND OF FRENCHIE KING, THE (1971, Fr./It./Sp./Brit.) PR:C
LEGEND OF HELL HOUSE, THE (1973, Brit.) PR:C
LEGEND OF HILLBILLY JOHN, THE (SEE: WHO FEARS THE DEVIL) (1972)
LEGEND OF LOBO, THE (1962) PR:AA
LEGEND OF LYLAH CLARE, THE (1968) PR:A-C
LEGEND OF MUSASHI, THE (SEE: SAMURAI) (1954, Jap.)
LEGEND OF NIGGER CHARLEY, THE (1972) PR:C
LEGEND OF ROBIN HOOD, THE (SEE: CHALLENGE FOR ROBIN HOOD) (1968, Brit.)
LEGEND OF SPIDER FOREST, THE (1976, Brit.) PR:C
LEGEND OF SURAM FORTRESS, THE (1985, USSR) PR:C
LEGEND OF THE BAYOU (SEE: EATEN ALIVE!) (1976)
LEGEND OF THE LONE RANGER, THE (1981) PR:C
LEGEND OF THE LOST (1957, US/Panama/It.) PR:C
LEGEND OF THE SEA WOLF (SEE: WOLF LARSEN) (1974)
LEGEND OF THE SEVEN GOLDEN VAMPIRES, THE (SEE: DRACULA AND THE SEVEN GOLDEN VAMPIRES) (1974, Brit./Chi.)
LEGEND OF THE TREE OF LIFE (SEE: IGOROTA, THE LEGEND OF THE TREE OF LIFE) (1970)
LEGEND OF THE WOLF WOMAN, THE (1977, Sp.) PR:O
LEGEND OF TOM DOOLEY, THE (1959) PR:A
LEGEND OF WITCH HOLLOW (SEE: WITCHMAKER, THE) (1969)
LEGENDARY CURSE OF LEMORA (SEE: LADY DRACULA) (1973)
LEGION OF LOST FLYERS (1939) PR:A
LEGION OF MISSING MEN (1937) PR:A
LEGION OF TERROR (1936) PR:A
LEGION OF THE DOOMED (1958) PR:A
LEGION OF THE LAWLESS (1940) PR:A
LEGIONS OF THE NILE (1960, It.) PR:A
LEJONSOMMAR (SEE: VIBRATION) (1969, Swed.)
L'ELISIR D'AMORE (SEE: THIS WINE OF LOVE) (1948, It.)
LEMON DROP KID, THE (1934) PR:A
LEMON DROP KID, THE (1951) PR:A
LEMON GROVE KIDS MEET THE MONSTERS, THE (1966) PR:C
LEMONADE JOE (1966, Czech.) PR:A
LEMORA THE LADY DRACULA (SEE: LADY DRACULA) (1973)
L'EMPIRE DE LA NUIT (SEE: EMPIRE OF THE NIGHT, THE) (1963, Fr.)
LENA RIVERS (1932) PR:A
LEND ME YOUR EAR (SEE: LIVING GHOST, THE) (1942)
LEND ME YOUR HUSBAND (1935, Brit.) PR:A
LEND ME YOUR WIFE (1935, Brit.) PR:A

L'ENFANCE NUE (SEE: ME) (1970, Fr.)
L'ENFANT SAUVAGE (SEE: WILD CHILD, THE) (1970, Fr.)
L'ENIGMATIQUE MONSIEUR PARKES (1930) PR:A
LENIN V POLSHE (SEE: PORTRAIT OF LENIN) (1967, Pol./USSR)
L'ENNUI ET SA DIVERSION (SEE: EMPTY CANVAS, THE) (1964, Fr./It.)
LENNY (1974) PR:C-O
LEO AND LOREE (1980) PR:A
LEO THE LAST (1970, Brit.) PR:O
LEONARD PART 6 (1987) PR:A-C
LEONOR (1977, Fr./Sp./It.) PR:O
LEOPARD, THE (1963, It.) PR:A-C
LEOPARD IN THE SNOW (1979, Brit./Can.) PR:A
LEOPARD MAN, THE (1943) PR:O
LEPKE (1975, US/Israel) PR:O
LES ABYSSES (1964, Fr.) PR:O
LES AMANTS (SEE: LOVERS, THE) (1959, Fr.)
LES AMANTS DE TOLEDO (SEE: LOVERS OF TO-LEDO, THE) (1954, Fr./It./Sp.)
LES AMANTS DE VERONE (SEE: LOVERS OF VE-RONA) (1951, Fr.)
LES AMITIES PARTICULIERES (SEE: THIS SPECIAL FRIENDSHIP) (1967, Fr.)
LES ANGES DU PECHE (SEE: ANGELS OF THE STREETS) (1950, Fr.)
LES ANNEES LUMIERES (SEE: LIGHT YEARS AWAY) (1982, Fr./Switz.)
LES AVENTURES EXTRAORDINAIRES DE CERVAN-TES (SEE: YOUNG REBEL, THE) (1969, Fr./It./Sp.)
LES BAS FONDS (SEE: LOWER DEPTHS, THE) (1936, Fr.)
LES BELLES-DE-NUIT (1952, Fr.) PR:C
LES BICHES (1968, It./Fr.) PR:O
LES BONNES CAUSES (SEE: DON'T TEMPT THE DEVIL) (1964, Fr./It.)
LES CAMARADES (SEE: ORGANIZER, THE) (1964, Fr./It./Yugo.)
LES CAPRICES DE MARIE (SEE: GIVE HER THE MOON) (1970, Fr./It.)
LES CARABINIERS (1963, Fr./It.) PR:O
LES CHOSES DE LA VIE (SEE: THINGS OF LIFE, THE) (1970, Fr./It.)
LES CLANDESTINS (SEE: CLANDESTINE) (1948, Fr.)
LES COEURS VERTS (SEE: NAKED HEARTS) (1970, Fr.)
LES COMPERES (1983, Fr.) PR:A
LES CORROMPUS (SEE: CORRUPT ONES, THE) (1967, Fr./It./W. Ger.)
LES COUSINS (SEE: COUSINS, THE) (1959, Fr.)
LES CREATURES (1969, Fr./Swed.) PR:A
LES DAMES DE BOIS DE BOULOGNE (SEE: LADIES OF THE PARK) (1964, Fr.)
LES DEMOISELLES DE ROCHEFORT (SEE: YOUNG GIRLS OF ROCHEFORT, THE) (1967, Fr.)
LES DEMONS DE MINUIT (SEE: MIDNIGHT FOLLY) (1962, Fr.)
LES DERNIERES VACANCES (1947, Fr.) PR:A-C
LES DEUX ANGLAISES ET LE CONTINENT (SEE: TWO ENGLISH GIRLS) (1972, Fr.)
LES DIABOLIQUES (SEE: DIABOLIQUE) (1955, Fr.)
LES DIMANCHES DE VILLE D'AVRAY (SEE: SUN-DAYS AND CYBELE) (1962, Fr.)
LES DOIGTS CROISES (SEE: CATCH ME A SPY) (1971, Brit./Fr.)
LES ENFANTS DU PARADIS (SEE: CHILDREN OF PAR-ADISE) (1945, Fr.)
LES ENFANTS TERRIBLES (1950, Fr.) PR:A-C
LES ESPIONS (1957, Fr.) PR:A
LES FANTOMES DU CHAPELIER (SEE: HATTER'S GHOST, THE) (1982, Fr.)
LES FAVORIS DE LA LUNE (SEE: FAVORITES OF THE MOON) (1985, Fr./It.)
LES FELINS (SEE: JOY HOUSE) (1964, Fr.)
LES FLEURS DU SOLEIL (SEE: SUNFLOWER) (1970, Fr./It.)
LES GARCONS (SEE: LA NOTTE BRAVA) (1962, Fr./It.)
LES GAULOISES BLEUES (1969, Fr.) PR:A
LES GIRLS (1957) PR:A
LES GRANDES MANOEUVRES (SEE: GRAND MANUEVER, THE) (1956, Fr.)
LES GUERISSEURS (SEE: ADUEFUE) (1988, Fr./Ivory Coast)
LES HOMMES EN BLANC (SEE: DOCTORS, THE) (1956, Fr.)
LES HOMMES PREFERENT LES GROSSES (SEE: MEN PREFER FAT GIRLS) (1981, Fr.)
LES INCONNUS DANS LA MAISON (SEE: STRANG-ERS IN THE HOUSE) (1949, Fr.)
LES INNOCENTS (SEE: INNOCENT, THE) (1988, Fr.)
LES INNOCENTS AUX MAINS SALES (SEE: DIRTY HANDS) (1976, Fr./It./W. Ger.)
LES JEUX INTERDIT (SEE: FORBIDDEN GAMES) (1953, Fr.)
LES JEUX SONT FAITS (1947, Fr.) PR:A-C
LES LACHES VIVENT D'ESPOIR (SEE: MY BABY IS BLACK!) (1965, Fr.)

LES LETTRES DE MON MOULIN (SEE: LETTERS FROM MY WINDMILL) (1955, Fr.)
LES LIAISONS DANGEREUSES (1961, Fr./It.) PR:O
LES LIENS DE SANG (SEE: BLOOD RELATIVES) (1978, Fr./Can.)
LES LOUVES (SEE: DEMONIAQUE) (1958, Fr.)
LES MAINS D'ORLAC (SEE: HANDS OF ORLAC) (1964, Brit./Fr.)
LES MAINS SALES (1954, Fr.) PR:A-C
LES MAITRES DU TEMPS (1982, Fr./Switz./W. Ger.) PR:A
LES MAUDITS (SEE: DAMNED, THE) (1948, Fr.)
LES MISERABLES (1935) PR:A
LES MISERABLES (1936, Fr.) PR:A
LES MISERABLES (1952) PR:A
LES MISERABLES (1982) PR:A
LES MYSTERES D'ANGKOR (SEE: MISTRESS OF THE WORLD) (1959, Fr./It./W. Ger.)
LES NOCES DU SABLE (SEE: DAUGHTER OF THE SANDS) (1952, Fr.)
LES NUITS DE L'EVPOUVANTE (SEE: MURDER CLINIC, THE) (1967, Fr./It.)
LES NUITS DE LA PLEINE LUNE (SEE: FULL MOON IN PARIS) (1984, Fr.)
LES OGRESSES (SEE: QUEENS, THE) (1968, It./Fr.)
LES OISEAUX VONT MOURIR AU PERU (SEE: BIRDS COME TO PERU TO DIE) (1968, Fr.)
LES ORDRES (SEE: ORDERS, THE) (1977, Can.)
LES PARENTS TERRIBLES (1948, Fr.) PR:A
LES PATRES DU SORDRE (SEE: THANOS AND DESPINA) (1970, Fr./Gr.)
LES PEMPS DES AMANTS (SEE: PLACE FOR LOV-ERS, A) (1969, It./Fr.)
LES PERLES DES COURONNE (SEE: PEARLS OF THE CROWN) (1938, Fr.)
LES PETROLEUSES (SEE: LEGEND OF FRENCHIE KING, THE) (1971, Fr./It./Sp./Brit.)
LES PLOUFFE (1985, Can.) PR:C
LES PORTES DE LA NUIT (SEE: GATES OF THE NIGHT) (1950, Fr.)
LES PORTES TOURNANTES (SEE: REVOLVING DOORS, THE) (1988, Can./Fr.)
LES QUATRES CENTS COUPS (SEE: FOUR HUNDRED BLOWS, THE) (1959, Fr.)
LES QUATRES VERITES (SEE: THREE FABLES OF LOVE) (1963, Fr./It./Sp.)
LES RIPOUX (SEE: MY NEW PARTNER) (1984, Fr.)
LES SOMNAMBULES (SEE: MON ONCLE D'AMERIQUE) (1978, Fr.)
LES STANCES A SOPHIE (SEE: SOPHIE'S WAYS) (1970, Fr.)
LES TITANS (SEE: MY SON, THE HERO) (1963, It./Fr.)
LES TRICHEURS (SEE: CHEATERS, THE) (1961, Fr./It.)
LES TRIPES AU SOLEIL (SEE: CHECKERBOARD) (1969, Fr.)
LES TROIS COURONNES DU MATELOT (SEE: THREE CROWNS OF THE SAILOR) (1984, Fr.)
LES VACANCES DE MONSIEUR HULOT (SEE: MR. HULOT'S HOLIDAY) (1953, Fr.)
LES VALSEUSES (SEE: GOING PLACES) (1974, Fr.)
LES VISITEURS DU SOIR (SEE: DEVIL'S ENVOYS, THE) (1947, Fr.)
LES YEUX SANS VISAGE (SEE: HORROR CHAMBER OF DR. FAUSTUS, THE) (1959, Fr./It.)
LESBIAN TWINS (SEE: VIRGIN WITCH, THE) (1973, Brit.)
LESNAYA PESNYA (SEE: SONG OF THE FOREST) (1963, USSR)
L'ESPION (SEE: DEFECTOR, THE) (1966, Fr./W. Ger.)
LESS THAN ZERO (1987) PR:O
LESSON IN LOVE, A (1954, Swed.) PR:C
LEST WE FORGET (1934, Brit.) PR:C
LEST WE FORGET (SEE: HANGMEN ALSO DIE!) (1943)
LET 'EM HAVE IT (1935) PR:A
LET FREEDOM RING (1939) PR:A
LET GEORGE DO IT (1940, Brit.) PR:A
LET IT RIDE (1989) PR:C
LET JOY REIGN SUPREME (1977, Fr.) PR:C
LET ME EXPLAIN, DEAR (1932) PR:A
LET NO MAN WRITE MY EPITAPH (1960) PR:A
LET THE BALLOON GO (1977, Aus.) PR:A
LET THE PEOPLE LAUGH (SEE: SING AS YOU SWING) (1937, Brit.)
LET THE PEOPLE SING (1942, Brit.) PR:A
LET THEM LIVE! (1937) PR:A
LET US BE GAY (1930) PR:A
LET US LIVE (1939) PR:A
L'ETA DEL MALESSERE (SEE: LOVE PROBLEMS) (1970, It.)
L'ETE MEURTRIER (SEE: ONE DEADLY SUMMER) (1983, Fr.)
L'ETERNEL RETOUR (SEE: ETERNAL RETURN, THE) (1943, Fr.)
LETHAL OBSESSION (1988, W. Ger.) PR:O
LETHAL WEAPON (1987) PR:O
LETHAL WEAPON 2 (1989) PR:O
L'ETOILE DU NORD (1983, Fr.) PR:O

L'ETOILE DU SUD (SEE: SOUTHERN STAR) (1969, Brit./Fr.)
L'ETRANGER (SEE: STRANGER, THE) (1967, Algeria/Fr./It.)
LET'S BE FAMOUS (1939, Brit.) PR:A
LET'S BE HAPPY (1957, Brit.) PR:A
LET'S BE RITZY (1934) PR:A
LET'S DANCE (1950) PR:A
LET'S DO IT (SEE: JUDY'S LITTLE NO-NO) (1969)
LET'S DO IT AGAIN (1953) PR:A
LET'S DO IT AGAIN (1975) PR:A
LET'S FACE IT (1943) PR:A
LET'S FALL IN LOVE (1934) PR:A
LET'S GET HARRY (1987) PR:O
LET'S GET MARRIED (1937) PR:A
LET'S GET MARRIED (1960, Brit.) PR:A
LET'S GET TOUGH (1942) PR:A
LET'S GO COLLEGIATE (1941) PR:A
LET'S GO NATIVE (1930) PR:A
LET'S GO NAVY (1951) PR:A
LET'S GO PLACES (1930) PR:A
LET'S GO STEADY (1945) PR:A
LET'S GO, YOUNG GUY! (1967, Jap.) PR:A
LET'S HAVE A MURDER (SEE: STICK 'EM UP) (1950, Brit.)
LET'S HAVE FUN (SEE: LAUGH YOUR BLUES AWAY) (1943)
LET'S KILL UNCLE (1966) PR:C
LET'S LIVE A LITTLE (1948) PR:A
LET'S LIVE AGAIN (1948) PR:A
LET'S LIVE TONIGHT (1935) PR:A
LET'S LOVE AND LAUGH (SEE: BRIDEGROOM FOR TWO) (1932, Brit.)
LET'S MAKE A NIGHT OF IT (1937, Brit.) PR:A
LET'S MAKE A MILLION (1937) PR:A
LET'S MAKE IT LEGAL (1951) PR:A
LET'S MAKE LOVE (1960) PR:A
LET'S MAKE MUSIC (1940) PR:A
LET'S MAKE UP (1955, Brit.) PR:A
LET'S ROCK (1958) PR:A
LET'S SCARE JESSICA TO DEATH (1971) PR:C
LET'S SING AGAIN (1936) PR:A
LET'S TALK ABOUT WOMEN (1964, Fr./It.) PR:C
LET'S TALK IT OVER (1934) PR:A
LET'S TRY AGAIN (1934) PR:A
LETTER, THE (1929) PR:A
LETTER, THE (1940) PR:A
LETTER FOR EVIE, A (1945) PR:A
LETTER FROM A NOVICE (SEE: RITA) (1963, Fr./It.)
LETTER FROM AN UNKNOWN WOMAN (1948) PR:A
LETTER FROM KOREA (SEE: YANK IN KOREA, A) (1951)
LETTER OF INTRODUCTION (1938) PR:A
LETTER THAT WAS NEVER SENT, THE (1962, USSR) PR:A
LETTER TO BREZHNEV (1986, Brit.) PR:C-O
LETTER TO THREE WIVES, A (1948) PR:A
LETTERS FROM MY WINDMILL (1955, Fr.) PR:A
LETTING IN THE SUNSHINE (1933, Brit.) PR:A
LETTY LYNTON (1932) PR:A-C
LETYAT ZHURAVIT (SEE: CRANES ARE FLYING, THE) (1957, USSR)
L'EVANGILE SELON SAINT MATTHIEU (SEE: GOSPEL ACCORDING TO ST. MATTHEW, THE) (1964, Fr./It.)
LEVIATHAN (1961, Fr.) PR:O
LEVIATHAN (1989) PR:C
LEZIONE DI CHIMICA (SEE: SCHOOLGIRL DIARY) (1947, It.)
L'HOMME AU CERVEAU GREFFE (SEE: MAN WITH THE TRANSPLANTED BRAIN, THE) (1970, Fr./It./W. Ger.)
L'HOMME AU CHAPEAU ROND (SEE: ETERNAL HUSBAND, THE) (1946, Fr.)
L'HOMME BLESSE (1985, Fr.) PR:O
L'HOMME D'ISTAMBUL (SEE: THAT MAN IN ISTANBUL) (1966, Fr./It./Sp.)
L'HOMME DE RIO (SEE: THAT MAN FROM RIO) (1964, Fr./It.)
L'HOMME DU MINNESOTA (SEE: MINNESOTA CLAY) (1966, It./Fr./Sp.)
L'HOMME EN COLERE (SEE: ANGRY MAN, THE) (1979, Fr./Can.)
L'HOMME QUI AIMAT LES FEMMES (SEE: MAN WHO LOVED WOMEN, THE) (1977, Fr.)
L'HOMME QUI MENT (SEE: MAN WHO LIES, THE) (1970, Czech./Fr.)
L'HORLOGER DE SAINT-PAUL (SEE: CLOCKMAKER, THE) (1974, Fr.)
L'HOTEL DE LA PLAGE (SEE: HOLIDAY HOTEL) (1978, Fr.)
LIANG SHAN-PO YU CHU YING-TAI (SEE: LOVE ETERNE, THE) (1964)
LIANNA (1983) PR:O
LIARS, THE (1964, Fr.) PR:A
LIAR'S DICE (1980) PR:O
LIAR'S MOON (1982) PR:O
LIBEL (1959, Brit.) PR:A

LIBELED LADY (1936) PR:A
LIBERATION OF L.B. JONES, THE (1970) PR:O
LIBIDO (1973, Aus.) PR:O
LICENCE TO KILL (1989, Brit.) PR:C-O
LICENSE TO DRIVE (1988) PR:O
LICENSED TO KILL (SEE: SECOND BEST SECRET AGENT IN THE WHOLE WIDE WORLD, THE) (1965, Brit.)
L'IDIOT (SEE: IDIOT, THE) (1948, Fr.)
LIDO MYSTERY, THE (SEE: ENEMY AGENTS MEET ELLERY QUEEN) (1942)
LIE DETECTOR, THE (SEE: TRUTH ABOUT MURDER, THE) (1946)
LIEBESSPIELE (SEE: SKI FEVER) (1969)
LIES (1984, Brit.) PR:C
LIES MY FATHER TOLD ME (1975, Can.) PR:A
LIES MY FATHER TOLD ME (1960, Brit.) PR:A
LIEUTENANT DARING, RN (1935, Brit.) PR:A
I.T. ROBIN CRUSOE, U.S.N. (1966) PR:AA
LIEUTENANT WORE SKIRTS, THE (1956) PR:A
LIFE AFTER DARK (SEE: GIRLS IN THE NIGHT) (1953)
LIFE AND DEATH OF COLONEL BLIMP, THE (1945, Brit.) PR:A
LIFE AND LOVES OF BEETHOVEN, THE (1937, Fr.) PR:A
LIFE AND LOVES OF MOZART, THE (1959, W. Ger.) PR:C
LIFE AND TIMES OF CHESTER-ANGUS RAMSGOOD, THE (1971, Can.) PR:C
LIFE AND TIMES OF GRIZZLY ADAMS, THE (1974) PR:AA
LIFE AND TIMES OF JUDGE ROY BEAN, THE (1972) PR:C
LIFE AT STAKE, A (SEE: KEY MAN) (1957, Brit.)
LIFE AT THE TOP (1965, Brit.) PR:C
LIFE BEGINS (1932) PR:C
LIFE BEGINS ANEW (1938, Ger.) PR:A
LIFE BEGINS AT 8:30 (1942) PR:A
LIFE BEGINS AT 40 (1935) PR:AA
LIFE BEGINS AT 17 (1958) PR:C
LIFE BEGINS FOR ANDY HARDY (1941) PR:A
LIFE BEGINS IN COLLEGE (1937) PR:AA
LIFE BEGINS TOMORROW (1952, Fr.) PR:C
LIFE BEGINS WITH LOVE (1937) PR:A
LIFE DANCES ON, CHRISTINE (SEE: UN CARNET DE BAL) (1938, Fr.)
LIFE FOR RUTH (SEE: WALK IN THE SHADOW) (1966, Brit.)
LIFE GOES ON (1932, Brit.) PR:A-C
LIFE IN DANGER (1964, Brit.) PR:A
LIFE IN EMERGENCY WARD 10 (1959, Brit.) PR:C
LIFE IN HER HANDS (1951, Brit.) PR:C
LIFE IN THE BALANCE, A (1955) PR:O
LIFE IN THE RAW (1933) PR:A
LIFE IS A BED OF ROSES (1984, Fr.) PR:C
LIFE IS A CIRCUS (1962, Brit.) PR:A
LIFE LOVE DEATH (1969, Fr./It.) PR:O
LIFE, LOVES AND ADVENTURES OF OMAR KHAYYAM, THE (1957) PR:A
LIFE OF A COUNTRY DOCTOR (1961, Jap.) PR:A
LIFE OF BRIAN (SEE: MONTY PYTHON'S LIFE OF BRIAN) (1979, Brit.)
LIFE OF EMILE ZOLA, THE (1937) PR:AA
LIFE OF HER OWN, A (1950) PR:A-C
LIFE OF JIMMY DOLAN, THE (1933) PR:A
LIFE OF OHARU (1952, Jap.) PR:C
LIFE OF RILEY, THE (1949) PR:A
LIFE OF THE COUNTRY DOCTOR (SEE: LIFE OF A COUNTRY DOCTOR) (1963, Jap.)
LIFE OF THE PARTY, THE (1930) PR:A
LIFE OF THE PARTY, THE (1934, Brit.) PR:A
LIFE OF THE PARTY, THE (1937) PR:A
LIFE OF VERGIE WINTERS, THE (1934) PR:C
LIFE RETURNS (1939) PR:C
LIFE STUDY (1973) PR:O
LIFE UPSIDE DOWN (1965, Fr.) PR:C
LIFE WITH BLONDIE (1946) PR:AA
LIFE WITH FATHER (1947) PR:AA
LIFE WITH HENRY (1941) PR:AA
LIFE WITH THE LYONS (SEE: FAMILY AFFAIR) (1954, Brit.)
LIFEBOAT (1944) PR:A
LIFEFORCE (1985) PR:O
LIFEGUARD (1976) PR:C
LIFESPAN (1975, US/Brit./Neth.) PR:C
LIFT, THE (1965, Brit./Can.) PR:O
LIFT, THE (1983, Neth.) PR:C
LIGEIA (SEE: TOMB OF LIGEIA, THE) (1965)
LIGHT (SEE: LUMIERE) (1976, Fr.)
LIGHT ACROSS THE STREET, THE (1957, Fr.) PR:O
LIGHT AT THE EDGE OF THE WORLD, THE (1971, US/Sp./Lichtenstein) PR:O
LIGHT BLUE (SEE: BACHELOR OF HEARTS) (1958)
LIGHT FANTASTIC, THE (SEE: LOVE IS BETTER THAN EVER) (1952)
LIGHT FANTASTIC (1964) PR:A
LIGHT FINGERS (1929) PR:A
LIGHT FINGERS (1957, Brit.) PR:A

LIGHT IN THE FOREST, THE (1958) PR:AA
LIGHT IN THE PIAZZA (1962) PR:A
LIGHT OF DAY (1987) PR:C
LIGHT OF HEART, THE (SEE: LIFE BEGINS AT 8:30) (1942)
LIGHT OF WESTERN STARS, THE (1930) PR:A
LIGHT OF WESTERN STARS, THE (1940) PR:A
LIGHT THAT FAILED, THE (1939) PR:A
LIGHT TOUCH, THE (1951) PR:C
LIGHT TOUCH, THE (1955, Brit.) PR:A
LIGHT UP THE SKY (1960, Brit.) PR:A
LIGHT YEARS (1988, Fr.) PR:C
LIGHT YEARS AWAY (1982, Fr./Switz.) PR:C
LIGHTHORSEMEN, THE (1988, Aus.) PR:A-C
LIGHTHOUSE (1947) PR:A
LIGHTHOUSE KEEPER'S DAUGHTER, THE (SEE: GIRL IN THE BIKINI, THE) (1958, Fr.)
LIGHTNIN' (1930) PR:A
LIGHTNIN' BILL CARSON (1936) PR:A
LIGHTNIN' CRANDALL (1937) PR:A
LIGHTNIN' IN THE FOREST (1948) PR:C
LIGHTNING BOLT (1967, It./Sp.) PR:A
LIGHTNING CONDUCTOR (1938, Brit.) PR:A
LIGHTNING FLYER (1931) PR:A
LIGHTNING GUNS (1950) PR:A
LIGHTNING RAIDERS (1945) PR:A
LIGHTNING RANGE (1934) PR:A
LIGHTNING STRIKES TWICE (1935) PR:A
LIGHTNING STRIKES TWICE (1951) PR:C
LIGHTNING STRIKES WEST (1940) PR:A
LIGHTNING SWORDS OF DEATH (SEE: SHOGUN ASSASSIN) (1974, Jap.)
LIGHTNING—THE WHITE STALLION (1986) PR:A
LIGHTS AND SHADOWS (SEE: WOMAN RACKET, THE) (1930)
LIGHTS OF NEW YORK (1928) PR:A
LIGHTS OF OLD SANTA FE (1944) PR:A
LIGHTS OF VARIETY (SEE: VARIETY LIGHTS) (1965, It.)
LIGHTS OUT (SEE: BRIGHT VICTORY) (1951)
LIGHTSHIP, THE (1986) PR:C
LIKE A CROW ON A JUNE BUG (1972) PR:C
LIKE A TURTLE ON ITS BACK (1981, Fr.) PR:O
LIKE FATHER, LIKE SON (SEE: YOUNG SINNER, THE) (1965)
LIKE FATHER, LIKE SON (1987) PR:C
LIKELY LADS, THE (1976, Brit.) PR:A
LIKELY STORY, A (1947) PR:A
LI'L ABNER (1940) PR:AA
LI'L ABNER (1959) PR:AA
LILA (SEE: MAKE WAY FOR LILA) (1962, Swed./W. Ger.)
LILA (SEE: MANTIS IN LACE) (1968)
LILA—LOVE UNDER THE MIDNIGHT SUN (SEE: MAKE WAY FOR LILA) (1962, Swed./W. Ger.)
LILAC DOMINO, THE (1940, Brit.) PR:A
LILACS IN THE SPRING (SEE: LET'S MAKE UP) (1955, Brit.)
L'ILE DU BOUT DU MONDE (SEE: TEMPTATION) (1962, Fr.)
LILI (1953) PR:AA
LILI MARLEEN (1981, W. Ger.) PR:O
LILI MARLENE (SEE: LILLI MARLENE) (1951, Brit.)
LILIES OF THE FIELD (1930) PR:O
LILIES OF THE FIELD (1934, Brit.) PR:A
LILIES OF THE FIELD (1963) PR:A
LILIOM (1930) PR:C
LILIOM (1935, Fr.) PR:A
LILITH (1964) PR:C
LILLI MARLENE (1951, Brit.) PR:C
LILLIAN RUSSELL (1940) PR:A
LILLY TURNER (1933) PR:C
LILY CHRISTINE (1932, Brit.) PR:C
LILY IN LOVE (1985, US/Hung.) PR:C
LILY OF KILARNEY (SEE: BRIDE OF THE LAKE) (1934, Brit.)
LILY OF LAGUNA (1938, Brit.) PR:C
LILY OF LAGUNA (1938, Brit.) PR:C
LIMBO (SEE: REBEL ROUSERS) (1970)
LIMBO (1972) PR:O
LIMBO LINE, THE (1969, Brit.) PR:O
LIMEHOUSE BLUES (1934) PR:A-C
LIMELIGHT (SEE: BACKSTAGE) (1937, Brit.)
LIMELIGHT (1952) PR:A
LIMIT, THE (1972) PR:C
LIMIT UP (1989) PR:C
L'IMMORTELLE (1969, Fr./It./Turkey) PR:C
LIMONADOVY JOE (SEE: LEMONADE JOE) (1966, Czech.)
LIMPING MAN, THE (1931, Brit.) PR:A
LIMPING MAN, THE (1936, Brit.) PR:A
LIMPING MAN, THE (1953, Brit.) PR:A
L'IMPORTANT C'EST D'AIMER (SEE: MAIN THING IS TO LOVE, THE) (1975, Fr./It.)
LINCOLN CONSPIRACY, THE (1977) PR:A
LINDA (1960, Brit.) PR:A
LINDA BE GOOD (1947) PR:A
LINE (SEE: PASSIONATE DEMONS, THE) (1961, Norway)

LINE, THE (1982) PR:C
LINE ENGAGED (1935, Brit.) PR:A
LINE OF DUTY (SEE: INCIDENT IN AN ALLEY) (1962)
LINEUP, THE (1934) PR:A
LINEUP, THE (1958) PR:O
LINK (1986, Brit.) PR:O
LINKS OF JUSTICE (1958, Brit.) PR:A
L'INNOCENTE (SEE: INNOCENT, THE) (1976, It.)
L'INTRIGO (SEE: DARK PURPOSE) (1964, US/Fr./It.)
LIOLA (SEE: VERY HANDY MAN, A) (1966)
LION, THE (1962, Brit.) PR:A
LION AND THE HORSE, THE (1952) PR:A
LION AND THE LAMB, THE (1931) PR:A
LION AND THE MOUSE, THE (1928) PR:A
LION HAS WINGS, THE (1940, Brit.) PR:A
LION HUNTERS, THE (1951) PR:AA
LION IN THE STREETS, A (SEE: LION IS IN THE
    STREETS, A) (1953)
LION IN WINTER, THE (1968, Brit.) PR:A
LION IS IN THE STREETS, A (1953) PR:A
LION OF ST. MARK (1967, It.) PR:A
LION OF SPARTA (SEE: 300 SPARTANS, THE) (1962)
LION OF THE DESERT (1981, Libya/Brit.) PR:O
LIONHEART (1968, Brit.) PR:AA
LION'S DEN, THE (1936) PR:A
LIONS LOVE (1969) PR:O
LIPSTICK (1965, Fr./It.) PR:C-O
LIPSTICK (1976) PR:O
LIQUID SKY (1982) PR:O
LIQUIDATOR, THE (1966, Brit.) PR:C
LISA (1962, US/Brit.) PR:O
LISA AND THE DEVIL (SEE: HOUSE OF EXORCISM,
    THE) (1976, It.)
LISA, TOSCA OF ATHENS (1961, Gr.) PR:A
LISBON (1956) PR:O
LISBON STORY, THE (1946, Brit.) PR:A
LISETTE (1961) PR:C
L'ISOLA DEGLI UOMINI PESCE (SEE: SCREAMERS)
    (1978, It.)
LIST OF ADRIAN MESSENGER, THE (1963) PR:A
LISTEN, DARLING (1938) PR:AA
LISTEN, LET'S MAKE LOVE (1969, Fr./It.) PR:O
LISTEN TO ME (1989) PR:C
LISTEN TO THE CITY (1984, Can.) PR:O
LISZTOMANIA (1975, Brit.) PR:O
LITTLE ACCIDENT, THE (1930) PR:A
LITTLE ACCIDENT (1939) PR:A
LITTLE ADVENTURESS, THE (1938) PR:AA
LITTLE ANGEL (1961, Mex.) PR:A
LITTLE ARK, THE (1972) PR:AA
LITTLE AUSTRALIANS (1940, Aus.) PR:C
LITTLE BALLERINA, THE (1951, Brit.) PR:AA
LITTLE BIG HORN (1951) PR:C
LITTLE BIG MAN (1970) PR:C-O
LITTLE BIG SHOT (1935) PR:AA
LITTLE BIG SHOT (1952, Brit.) PR:A
LITTLE BIT OF BLUFF, A (1935, Brit.) PR:A
LITTLE BIT OF HEAVEN, A (1940) PR:AA
LITTLE BOY BLUE (1963, Mex.) PR:A
LITTLE BOY LOST (1953) PR:A
LITTLE CAESAR (1931) PR:C
LITTLE CIGARS (1973) PR:A
LITTLE COLONEL, THE (1935) PR:AA
LITTLE CONVICT, THE (1980, Aus.) PR:AA
LITTLE DAMOZEL, THE (1933, Brit.) PR:A
LITTLE DARLINGS (1980) PR:O
LITTLE DOLLY DAYDREAM (1938, Brit.) PR:AA
LITTLE DORRIT (1988, Brit.) PR:A
LITTLE DRAGONS, THE (1980) PR:A-C
LITTLE DRUMMER GIRL, THE (1984) PR:C-O
LITTLE EGYPT (1951) PR:A
LITTLE FAUSS AND BIG HALSY (1970) PR:O
LITTLE FLAMES (1985, It.) PR:A
LITTLE FOXES, THE (1941) PR:A-C
LITTLE FRIEND (1934, Brit.) PR:C
LITTLE FUGITIVE, THE (1953) PR:A
LITTLE GEL (SEE: KING OF HEARTS) (1936, Brit.)
LITTLE GIANT, THE (1933) PR:A
LITTLE GIANT (1946) PR:A
LITTLE GIRL WHO LIVES DOWN THE LANE, THE (1977,
    Can.) PR:O
LITTLE HUMPBACKED HORSE, THE (1962, USSR) PR:A
LITTLE HUT, THE (1957) PR:A
LITTLE IODINE (1946) PR:A
LITTLE JOE, THE WRANGLER (1942) PR:A
LITTLE JOHNNY JONES (1930) PR:A
LITTLE JUNGLE BOY (1969, Aus.) PR:A
LITTLE KIDNAPPERS, THE (1954, Brit.) PR:AA
LITTLE LAURA AND BIG JOHN (1973) PR:O
LITTLE LORD FAUNTLEROY (1936) PR:AA
LITTLE MALCOLM (1974, Brit.) PR:C
LITTLE MAN, WHAT NOW? (1934) PR:A
LITTLE MARTYR, THE (1947, It.) PR:A
LITTLE MELODY FROM VIENNA (1948, Aust.) PR:A
LITTLE MEN (1935) PR:A
LITTLE MEN (1940) PR:AA
LITTLE MERMAID, THE (1989) PR:AA
LITTLE MINISTER, THE (1934) PR:A

LITTLE MISS BIG (1946) PR:A
LITTLE MISS BROADWAY (1938) PR:A
LITTLE MISS BROADWAY (1947) PR:A
LITTLE MISS DEVIL (1951, Egypt) PR:A
LITTLE MISS MARKER (1934) PR:AA
LITTLE MISS MARKER (1980) PR:C
LITTLE MISS MOLLY (1940, Brit.) PR:A
LITTLE MISS NOBODY (1933, Brit.) PR:A
LITTLE MISS NOBODY (1936) PR:AA
LITTLE MISS ROUGHNECK (1938) PR:AA
LITTLE MISS SOMEBODY (1937, Brit.) PR:A
LITTLE MISS THOROUGHBRED (1938) PR:AA
LITTLE MISTER JIM (1946) PR:A
LITTLE MOTHER (1973, US/Yugo./W. Ger.) PR:O
LITTLE MURDERS (1971) PR:O
LITTLE NELLIE KELLY (1940) PR:A
LITTLE NIGHT MUSIC, A (1977, Aust./US/W. Ger.) PR:C
LITTLE NIKITA (1988) PR:A-C
LITTLE NUNS, THE (1965, It.) PR:A
LITTLE OF WHAT YOU FANCY, A (1968, Brit.) PR:A
LITTLE OLD NEW YORK (1940) PR:A
LITTLE ONES, THE (1965, Brit.) PR:AA
LITTLE ORPHAN ANNIE (1932) PR:AA
LITTLE ORPHAN ANNIE (1938) PR:A
LITTLE ORVIE (1940) PR:AA
LITTLE PAL (SEE: HEALER, THE) (1935)
LITTLE PRINCE, THE (1974, Brit.) PR:AA
LITTLE PRINCESS, THE (1939) PR:AA
LITTLE RED MONKEY (SEE: CASE OF THE RED
    MONKEY) (1954, Brit.)
LITTLE RED RIDING HOOD (1963, Mex.) PR:A
LITTLE RED RIDING HOOD AND HER FRIENDS
    (1964, Mex.) PR:A
LITTLE RED RIDING HOOD AND THE MONSTERS
    (1965, Mex.) PR:C
LITTLE RED SCHOOLHOUSE, THE (1936) PR:AA
LITTLE ROMANCE, A (1979, US/Fr.) PR:A
LITTLE SAVAGE, THE (1959) PR:A
LITTLE SEX, A (1982) PR:O
LITTLE SHEPHERD OF KINGDOM COME, THE (1961)
    PR:A
LITTLE SHOP OF HORRORS (1961) PR:C-O
LITTLE SHOP OF HORRORS (1986) PR:C
LITTLE SISTER (SEE: MARLOWE) (1969)
LITTLE SISTER, THE (1985) PR:O
LITTLE SOLDIER, THE (SEE: LE PETIT SOLDAT)
    (1965, Fr.)
LITTLE STRANGER (1934, Brit.) PR:A
LITTLE THEATER OF JEAN RENOIR, THE (SEE: LE
    PETIT THEATRE DE JEAN RENOIR) (1974, Fr./It./W.
    Ger.)
LITTLE THIEF, THE (1989, Fr.) PR:O
LITTLE TOKYO, U.S.A. (1942) PR:A
LITTLE TOUGH GUY (1938) PR:A
LITTLE TOUGH GUYS IN SOCIETY (1938) PR:A
LITTLE TREASURE (1985) PR:O
LITTLE VERA (1988, USSR) PR:O
LITTLE WILDCAT, THE (1928) PR:A
LITTLE WOMEN (1933) PR:AA
LITTLE WOMEN (1949) PR:AA
LITTLE WORLD OF DON CAMILLO, THE (1953, Fr./It.)
    PR:A
LITTLEST HOBO, THE (1958) PR:AA
LITTLEST HORSE THIEVES, THE (1977, Brit.) PR:AA
LITTLEST OUTLAW, THE (1955) PR:A
LITTLEST REBEL, THE (1935) PR:AA
LIVE A LITTLE, LOVE A LITTLE (1968) PR:A
LIVE A LITTLE, STEAL A LOT (SEE: MURF THE
    SURF) (1974)
LIVE AGAIN (1936, Brit.) PR:A
LIVE AND LET DIE (1973, Brit.) PR:C
LIVE FAST, DIE YOUNG (1958) PR:A
LIVE FOR LIFE (1967, Fr./It.) PR:A
LIVE IT UP (SEE: SING AND SWING) (1964, Brit.)
LIVE, LOVE AND LEARN (1937) PR:A
LIVE NOW – PAY LATER (1962, Brit.) PR:A
LIVE TO LOVE (SEE: DEVIL'S HAND, THE) (1961)
LIVE TODAY FOR TOMORROW (SEE: ACT OF MUR-
    DER, AN) (1948)
LIVE WIRE, THE (1937, Brit.) PR:A
LIVE WIRES (1946) PR:A
LIVE YOUR OWN WAY (1970, Jap.) PR:A
LIVELY SET, THE (1964) PR:A
LIVER EATERS, THE (SEE: SPIDER BABY) (1968)
LIVES OF A BENGAL LANCER, THE (1935) PR:A
LIVING (SEE: IKIRU) (1960, Jap.)
LIVING BETWEEN TWO WORLDS (1963) PR:A
LIVING COFFIN, THE (1965, Mex.) PR:C
LIVING CORPSE, THE (1940, Fr.) PR:A
LIVING DANGEROUSLY (1936, Brit.) PR:A
LIVING DANGEROUSLY (1988, Cuba) PR:C
LIVING DAYLIGHTS, THE (1987, Brit.) PR:C
LIVING DEAD, THE (1936, Brit.) PR:A
LIVING DEAD AT MANCHESTER MORGUE (SEE:
    DON'T OPEN THE WINDOW) (1974, It./Sp.)
LIVING FREE (1972, Brit.) PR:A
LIVING GHOST, THE (1942) PR:A
LIVING HEAD, THE (1969, Mex.) PR:O

LIVING IDOL, THE (1957) PR:C-O
LIVING IN A BIG WAY (1947) PR:A
LIVING IT UP (1954) PR:A
LIVING LEGEND (1980) PR:O
LIVING ON LOVE (1937) PR:A
LIVING ON TOKYO TIME (1987) PR:C
LIVING ON VELVET (1935) PR:A
LIVING VENUS (1961) PR:O
LIZA (1976, Fr./It.) PR:O
LIZZIE (1957) PR:C
LJUBAVNI SLUJAC ILI TRAGEDIJA SLUZBENICE
    P.T.T. (SEE: LOVE AFFAIR; OR THE CASE OF THE
    MISSING SWITCHBOARD OPERATOR) (1967, Yugo.)
LLANO KID, THE (1940) PR:A
LLEGARON LOS MARCIANOS (SEE: TWELVE-
    HANDED MEN OF MARS, THE) (1964, It./Sp.)
LLOYDS OF LONDON (1936) PR:A
LO CHIAMAVANO TRINITA (SEE: THEY CALL ME
    TRINITY) (1971, It.)
LO CHIAMAVANO TRINITA (SEE: THIRSTY DEAD,
    THE) (1975)
LO SCEICCO BIANCO (SEE: WHITE SHEIK, THE)
    (1952, Fr./It.)
LO SCEICCO ROSSO (SEE: RED SHEIK, THE) (1963, It.)
LO SCOPANE SCIENTIFICO (SEE: SCIENTIFIC CARD-
    PLAYER, THE) (1972, It.)
LO SPETTRO (SEE: GHOST, THE) (1965, It.)
LO STRANIERO (SEE: STRANGER, THE) (1967, Alge-
    ria/Fr./It.)
LO STRANO VIZIO DELLA SIGNORA WARDH (SEE:
    NEXT!) (1971, It./Sp.)
LOADED DICE (SEE: CROSS MY HEART) (1937, Brit.)
LOADED PISTOLS (1948) PR:A
LOAN SHARK (1952) PR:A
LOCAL BAD MAN (1932) PR:A
LOCAL BOY MAKES GOOD (1931) PR:A
LOCAL COLOR (1978) PR:O
LOCAL HERO (1983, Brit.) PR:A-C
LOCK UP (1989) PR:O
LOCK UP YOUR DAUGHTERS (1969, Brit.) PR:C-O
LOCK YOUR DOORS (SEE: APE MAN, THE) (1943)
LOCKED DOOR, THE (1929) PR:A
LOCKER 69 (1962, Brit.) PR:A
LOCKET, THE (1946) PR:C
LOCURA DE AMOR (SEE: MAD QUEEN, THE) (1950,
    Sp.)
LODGER, THE (SEE: PHANTOM FIEND, THE) (1935,
    Brit.)
LODGER, THE (1944) PR:C-O
L'OEIL DU MALIN (SEE: THIRD LOVER, THE) (1963,
    Fr./It.)
LOGAN'S RUN (1976) PR:A
L'OISEAU DE PARADIS (SEE: DRAGON SKY) (1964,
    Fr.)
LOLA (SEE: YOUNG BLOOD) (1932)
LOLA (1961, Fr./It.) PR:C
LOLA (1971, Brit./It.) PR:C-O
LOLA (1982, W. Ger.) PR:O
LOLA MONTES (1955, Fr./W. Ger.) PR:C
LOLA'S MISTAKE (SEE: THIS REBEL BREED) (1960)
LOLITA (1962, US/Brit.) PR:C-O
LOLLIPOP (1966, Braz.) PR:O
LOLLIPOP (SEE: FOREVER YOUNG, FOREVER FREE)
    (1976)
LOLLIPOP COVER, THE (1965) PR:A
LOLLY-MADONNA XXX (1973) PR:A
LONDON BELONGS TO ME (SEE: DULCIMER
    STREET) (1948, Brit.)
LONDON BLACKOUT MURDERS (1942) PR:A
LONDON BY NIGHT (1937) PR:A
LONDON CALLING (SEE: HELLO LONDON) (1958,
    Brit.)
LONDON MELODY (1930, Brit.) PR:A
LONDON MELODY (SEE: GIRL IN THE STREET)
    (1938, Brit.)
LONDON TOWN (SEE: MY HEART GOES CRAZY)
    (1953, Brit.)
LONDRA CHIAMA POLO NORD (SEE: HOUSE OF IN-
    TRIGUE, THE) (1959, It.)
LONE AVENGER, THE (1933) PR:A
LONE CLIMBER, THE (1950, Brit./Aust.) PR:AA
LONE COWBOY (1934) PR:A
LONE GUN, THE (1954) PR:A
LONE HAND (1953) PR:A
LONE HAND TEXAN, THE (1947) PR:A
LONE PRAIRIE, THE (1942) PR:A
LONE RANGER, THE (1955) PR:AA
LONE RANGER AND THE LOST CITY OF GOLD, THE
    (1958) PR:AA
LONE RIDER, THE (1930) PR:A
LONE RIDER AMBUSHED, THE (1941) PR:A
LONE RIDER AND THE BANDIT, THE (1942) PR:A
LONE RIDER CROSSES THE RIO, THE (1941) PR:A
LONE RIDER FIGHTS BACK, THE (1941) PR:A
LONE RIDER IN CHEYENNE, THE (1941) PR:A
LONE RIDER IN GHOST TOWN, THE (1941) PR:A
LONE STAR (1952) PR:A
LONE STAR LAW MEN (1942) PR:A

LONE STAR LAWMAN (SEE: TEXAS LAWMEN) (1951)
LONE STAR PIONEERS (1939) PR:A
LONE STAR RAIDERS (1940) PR:A
LONE STAR RANGER, THE (1930) PR:A
LONE STAR RANGER (1942) PR:A
LONE STAR TRAIL, THE (1943) PR:A
LONE STAR VIGILANTES, THE (1942) PR:A
LONE TEXAN (1959) PR:A
LONE TEXAS RANGER, THE (1945) PR:A
LONE TRAIL, THE (1932) PR:A
LONE TROUBADOR, THE (SEE: TWO-GUN TROUB-ADOR) (1939)
LONE WOLF AND HIS LADY, THE (1949) PR:A
LONE WOLF IN LONDON, THE (1947) PR:A
LONE WOLF IN MEXICO, THE (1947) PR:A
LONE WOLF IN PARIS, THE (1938) PR:A
LONE WOLF KEEPS A DATE, THE (1940) PR:A
LONE WOLF McQUADE (1983) PR:C-O
LONE WOLF MEETS A LADY, THE (1940) PR:A
LONE WOLF RETURNS, THE (1936) PR:A
LONE WOLF SPY HUNT, THE (1939) PR:A
LONE WOLF STRIKES, THE (1940) PR:A
LONE WOLF TAKES A CHANCE, THE (1941) PR:A
LONE WOLF'S DAUGHTER, THE (1929) PR:A
LONE WOLF'S DAUGHTER, THE (SEE: LONE WOLF SPY HUNT, THE) (1939)
LONELINESS OF THE LONG DISTANCE RUNNER, THE (1962, Brit.) PR:C-O
LONELY ARE THE BRAVE (1962) PR:C
LONELY GUY, THE (1984) PR:O
LONELY HEART BANDITS (SEE: LONELY HEARTS BANDITS) (1950)
LONELY HEARTS (1983, Aus.) PR:O
LONELY HEARTS BANDITS (1950) PR:A
LONELY HEARTS KILLER (SEE: HONEYMOON KILL-ERS, THE) (1969)
LONELY HEARTS KILLERS (SEE: HONEYMOON KILLERS, THE) (1969)
LONELY LADY, THE (SEE: STRANGERS, THE) (1955, It.)
LONELY LADY, THE (1983) PR:O
LONELY LANE (1963, Jap.) PR:O
LONELY MAN, THE (1957) PR:A
LONELY MAN, THE (SEE: GUN RIDERS, THE) (1969)
LONELY PASSION OF JUDITH HEARNE, THE (1988, Brit.) PR:O
LONELY ROAD, THE (SEE: SCOTLAND YARD COM-MANDS) (1937, Brit.)
LONELY STAGE (SEE: I COULD GO ON SINGING) (1963, Brit.)
LONELY TRAIL, THE (1936) PR:A
LONELY WIVES (1931) PR:A
LONELY WOMAN, THE (SEE: STRANGERS, THE) (1955, It.)
LONELYHEARTS (1958) PR:C
LONER, THE (SEE: RUCKUS) (1981)
LONERS, THE (1972) PR:O
LONESOME (1928) PR:A
LONESOME COWBOYS (1968) PR:O
LONESOME TRAIL, THE (1930) PR:A
LONESOME TRAIL, THE (1955) PR:A
LONG ABSENCE, THE (1962, Fr./It.) PR:A
LONG AGO, TOMORROW (1971, Brit.) PR:C
LONG AND THE SHORT AND THE TALL, THE (1961, Brit.) PR:A
LONG ARM, THE (SEE: THIRD KEY, THE) (1957, Brit.)
LONG CORRIDOR (SEE: SHOCK CORRIDOR) (1963)
LONG DARK HALL, THE (1951, Brit.) PR:A-C
LONG, DARK NIGHT, THE (SEE: PACK, THE) (1977)
LONG DAY'S DYING, THE (1968, Brit.) PR:C-O
LONG DAY'S JOURNEY INTO NIGHT (1962) PR:C
LONG DISTANCE (SEE: HOT MONEY GIRL) (1962, Brit./W. Ger.)
LONG DUEL, THE (1967, Brit.) PR:A
LONG GOOD FRIDAY, THE (1982, Brit.) PR:O
LONG GOODBYE, THE (1973) PR:O
LONG GRAY LINE, THE (1955) PR:A
LONG HAUL, THE (1957, Brit.) PR:A
LONG, HOT SUMMER, THE (1958) PR:A-C
LONG IS THE ROAD (1948, W. Ger.) PR:A
LONG JOHN SILVER (1954, Aus.) PR:A
LONG KNIFE, THE (1958, Brit.) PR:C
LONG, LONG TRAIL, THE (1929) PR:A
LONG, LONG TRAIL, THE (SEE: TEXAS TO BATAAN) (1942)
LONG, LONG TRAILER, THE (1954) PR:A
LONG LOST FATHER (1934) PR:A
LONG MEMORY, THE (1953, Brit.) PR:A
LONG NIGHT, THE (1947) PR:A
LONG NIGHT, THE (1976) PR:A
LONG RIDE, THE (SEE: BRADY'S ESCAPE) (1984, US/Hung.)
LONG RIDE FROM HELL, A (1970, It.) PR:O
LONG RIDE HOME, THE (SEE: TIME FOR KILLING, A) (1967)
LONG RIDERS, THE (1980) PR:O
LONG ROPE, THE (1961) PR:A
LONG SHADOW, THE (1961, Brit.) PR:A

LONG SHIPS, THE (1964, Brit./Yugo.) PR:C
LONG SHOT, THE (1939) PR:A
LONG SHOT (1981, Brit.) PR:C
LONG VOYAGE HOME, THE (1940) PR:A
LONG WAIT, THE (1954) PR:A
LONG WEEKEND (1978, Aus.) PR:C-O
LONGEST DAY, THE (1962) PR:A
LONGEST NIGHT, THE (1936) PR:A
LONGEST SPUR (SEE: HOT SPUR) (1968)
LONGEST YARD, THE (1974) PR:O
LONGHORN, THE (1951) PR:A
LONGING FOR LOVE (1966, Jap.) PR:O
LONGSHOT, THE (1986) PR:O
LONNIE (1963) PR:C
LOOK BACK IN ANGER (1959, Brit.) PR:C-O
LOOK BEFORE YOU LAUGH (SEE: MAKE MINE A MILLION) (1965)
LOOK BEFORE YOU LOVE (1948, Brit.) PR:A
LOOK DOWN AND DIE, MEN OF STEEL (SEE: STEEL) (1980)
LOOK FOR THE SILVER LINING (1949) PR:A
LOOK IN ANY WINDOW (1961) PR:O
LOOK OUT FOR LOVE (SEE: GIRLS IN THE STREET) (1938, Brit.)
LOOK OUT SISTER (1948) PR:A
LOOK UP AND LAUGH (1935, Brit.) PR:A
LOOK WHO'S LAUGHING (1941) PR:A
LOOK WHO'S TALKING (1989) PR:C
LOOKER (1981) PR:O
LOOKIN' GOOD (SEE: CORKY) (1972)
LOOKIN' TO GET OUT (1982) PR:O
LOOKING FOR DANGER (1957) PR:A
LOOKING FOR EILEEN (1987, Neth.) PR:O
LOOKING FOR LOVE (1964) PR:A
LOOKING FOR MR. GOODBAR (1977) PR:C-O
LOOKING FOR TROUBLE (SEE: TIP-OFF, THE) (1931)
LOOKING FOR TROUBLE (1934) PR:A
LOOKING FORWARD (1933) PR:A
LOOKING GLASS WAR, THE (1970, Brit.) PR:C
LOOKING ON THE BRIGHT SIDE (1932, Brit.) PR:A
LOOKING UP (1977) PR:C
LOOKS AND SMILES (1982, Brit.) PR:C
LOONIES ON BROADWAY (SEE: ZOMBIES ON BROADWAY) (1945)
LOOPHOLE (1954) PR:A
LOOPHOLE (1981, Brit.) PR:C
LOOSE ANKLES (1930) PR:A
LOOSE CONNECTIONS (1984, Brit.) PR:C
LOOSE ENDS (1930, Brit.) PR:A
LOOSE ENDS (1975) PR:C
LOOSE IN LONDON (1953) PR:A
LOOSE JOINTS (SEE: FLICKS) (1987)
LOOSE PLEASURES (SEE: TIGHT SKIRTS, LOOSE PLEASURES) (1966, Fr.)
LOOSE SCREWS (1985) PR:O
LOOSE SHOES (1980) PR:C
LOOT (1971, Brit.) PR:C
LOOTERS, THE (1955) PR:A
L'OPERA DE QUAT'SOUS (SEE: THREEPENNY OPERA, THE) (1931, US/Ger.)
LOPERJENTEN (SEE: KAMILLA) (1984, Norway)
LORD BABS (1932, Brit.) PR:A
LORD BYRON OF BROADWAY (1930) PR:A
LORD CAMBER'S LADIES (1932, Brit.) PR:A
LORD EDGEWARE DIES (1934, Brit.) PR:A
LORD JEFF (1938) PR:AA
LORD JIM (1965, Brit.) PR:A
LORD LOVE A DUCK (1966) PR:A
LORD MOUNTDRAGO (SEE: THREE CASES OF MUR-DER) (1955)
LORD OF THE FLIES (1963, Brit.) PR:A-C
LORD OF THE JUNGLE (1955) PR:A
LORD OF THE MANOR (1933, Brit.) PR:A
LORD OF THE RINGS, THE (1978) PR:A
LORD RICHARD IN THE PANTRY (1930, Brit.) PR:A
LORD SHANGO (1975) PR:O
LORDS OF DISCIPLINE, THE (1983) PR:O
LORDS OF FLATBUSH, THE (1974) PR:C
LORDS OF THE STREET, THE (SEE: ADUEFUE) (1988, Fr./Ivory Coast)
LORNA DOONE (1935, Brit.) PR:A
LORNA DOONE (1951) PR:A
L'ORRIBILE SEGRETO DEL DR. HICHCOCK (SEE: HORRIBLE DR. HICHCOCK, THE) (1964, It.)
LOS AMANTES DE VERONA (SEE: ROMEO AND JU-LIET) (1968, It./Sp.)
LOS AMANTES DEL DESIERTO (SEE: DESERT WAR-RIOR) (1961, It./Sp.)
LOS AMIGOS (SEE: DEAF SMITH AND JOHNNY EARS) (1973, It.)
LOS ASTRONAUTAS (1960, Mex.) PR:A
LOS AUTOMATAS DE LA MUERTE (1960, Mex.) PR:A
LOS ESPADACHINES DE LA REINA (SEE: QUEEN'S SWORDSMEN, THE) (1963, Mex.)
LOS INSOMNES (SEE: INSOMNIACS) (1986, Arg.)
LOS INVISIBLES (1961, Mex.) PR:A
LOS OJOS AZULES DE LA MUNECA ROTA (SEE: HOUSE OF PSYCHOTIC WOMEN, THE) (1973, Sp.)

LOS OLVIDADOS (1950, Mex.) PR:O
LOS PLATILLOS VOLADORES (1955, Mex.) PR:A
LOS SANTOS INOCENTES (SEE: HOLY INNOCENTS, THE) (1984, Sp.)
LOSER TAKE ALL (SEE: LEATHER GLOVES) (1948)
LOSER TAKES ALL (1956, Brit.) PR:A
LOSER, THE HERO, THE (1985, Taiwan) PR:A
LOSERS, THE (1968) PR:O
LOSERS, THE (1970) PR:O
LOSIN' IT (1983) PR:O
LOSING GAME, THE (SEE: PAY-OFF, THE) (1930)
LOSS OF FEELING (1935, USSR) PR:A
LOSS OF INNOCENCE (1961, Brit.) PR:C
LOST (SEE: TEARS FOR SIMON) (1957, Brit.)
LOST AND FOUND (1979) PR:A-C
LOST ANGEL (1944) PR:A
LOST ANGELS (1989) PR:C
LOST ATLANTIS (SEE: MISTRESS OF ATLANTIS, THE) (1932, Ger.)
LOST BATTALION (1961, US/Phil.) PR:A
LOST BOUNDARIES (1949) PR:A
LOST BOYS, THE (1987) PR:O
LOST CANYON (1943) PR:A
LOST CHORD, THE (1937, Brit.) PR:A
LOST COMMAND (1966) PR:A-C
LOST CONTINENT (1951) PR:A
LOST CONTINENT, THE (1968, Brit.) PR:A
LOST EMPIRE, THE (1985) PR:O
LOST FACE, THE (1965, Czech.) PR:C
LOST HAPPINESS (1948, It.) PR:A
LOST HONEYMOON (1947) PR:A
LOST HONOR OF KATHARINA BLUM, THE (1975, W. Ger.) PR:C
LOST HORIZON (1937) PR:A
LOST HORIZON (1973) PR:A
LOST ILLUSION, THE (SEE: FALLEN IDOL, THE) (1949, Brit.)
LOST IN A HAREM (1944) PR:A
LOST IN ALASKA (SEE: ABBOTT AND COSTELLO LOST IN ALASKA) (1952)
LOST IN AMERICA (1985) PR:O
LOST IN THE LEGION (1934, Brit.) PR:A
LOST IN THE STARS (1974) PR:A
LOST IN THE STRATOSPHERE (1935) PR:A
LOST JUNGLE, THE (1934) PR:A
LOST LADY, THE (SEE: SAFE IN HELL) (1931)
LOST LADY, A (1934) PR:A
LOST LAGOON (1958) PR:A
LOST, LONELY AND VICIOUS (1958) PR:O
LOST MAN, THE (1969) PR:C
LOST MEN (SEE: HOMICIDE SQUAD) (1931)
LOST MISSILE, THE (1958, US/Can.) PR:A
LOST MOMENT, THE (1947) PR:A
LOST ON THE WESTERN FRONT (1940, Brit.) PR:A
LOST ONE, THE (1951, W. Ger.) PR:C
LOST PATROL, THE (1934) PR:C
LOST PEOPLE, THE (1950, Brit.) PR:A
LOST RANCH (1937) PR:A
LOST SEX (1968, Jap.) PR:O
LOST SOULS (1961, It.) PR:O
LOST SQUADRON, THE (1932) PR:C
LOST STAGE VALLEY (SEE: STAGE TO TUCSON) (1950)
LOST TRAIL, THE (1945) PR:A
LOST TREASURE OF THE AMAZON (SEE: JIVARO) (1954)
LOST TRIBE, THE (1949) PR:A
LOST VOLCANO, THE (1950) PR:AA
LOST WEEKEND, THE (1945) PR:C-O
LOST WOMEN (SEE: MESA OF LOST WOMEN) (1952)
LOST WORLD, THE (1960) PR:A
LOST WORLD OF SINBAD, THE (1965, Jap.) PR:A
LOST ZEPPELIN, THE (1930) PR:A
LOTNA (1966, Pol.) PR:C
LOTTERY BRIDE, THE (1930) PR:A
LOTTERY LOVER (1935) PR:A
LOTUS LADY (1930) PR:A
LOUDEST WHISPER, THE (SEE: CHILDREN'S HOUR, THE) (1961)
LOUDSPEAKER, THE (1934) PR:A
LOUIE, THERE'S A CROWD DOWNSTAIRS (SEE: START THE REVOLUTION WITHOUT ME) (1970)
LOUISA (1950) PR:A
LOUISE (1940, Fr.) PR:A
LOUISIANA (1947) PR:A
LOUISIANA GAL (SEE: OLD LOUISIANA) (1938)
LOUISIANA HAYRIDE (1944) PR:A
LOUISIANA HUSSY (1960) PR:C
LOUISIANA PURCHASE (1941) PR:A
LOUISIANA TERRITORY (1953) PR:A
LOUISIANE (1984, Fr./Can.) PR:A-C
LOULOU (1980, Fr.) PR:O
L'OURS (SEE: BEAR, THE) (1963, Fr./It.)
LOVABLE AND SWEET (SEE: RUNAROUND, THE) (1931)
LOVABLE CHEAT, THE (1949) PR:A
LOVE A LA CARTE (1965, It.) PR:O
LOVE (1982, Can.) PR:C

LOVE (1972, Hung.) PR:C
LOVE AFFAIR (1932) PR:A
LOVE AFFAIR (1939) PR:A
LOVE AFFAIR OF THE DICTATOR, THE (SEE: DICTATOR, THE) (1935, Brit./Ger.)
LOVE AFFAIR; OR THE CASE OF THE MISSING SWITCHBOARD OPERATOR (1967, Yugo.) PR:O
LOVE AMONG THE MILLIONAIRES (1930) PR:A
LOVE AND ANARCHY (1973, It.) PR:O
LOVE AND BULLETS (1979, Brit.) PR:C
LOVE AND DEATH (1975) PR:A-C
LOVE AND HISSES (1937) PR:A
LOVE AND KISSES (1965) PR:A
LOVE AND LARCENY (1963, Fr./It.) PR:A
LOVE AND LEARN (1947) PR:A
LOVE AND MARRIAGE (1966, It.) PR:C
LOVE AND MONEY (1982) PR:O
LOVE AND PAIN AND THE WHOLE DAMN THING (1973) PR:C
LOVE AND THE FRENCHWOMAN (1961, Fr.) PR:C-O
LOVE AND THE MIDNIGHT AUTO SUPPLY (1978) PR:C-O
LOVE AT FIRST BITE (1979) PR:C
LOVE AT FIRST SIGHT (1930) PR:A
LOVE AT FIRST SIGHT (1977, Can.) PR:A
LOVE AT NIGHT (1961, Fr.) PR:C-O
LOVE AT SEA (1936, Brit.) PR:A
LOVE AT SECOND SIGHT (SEE: GIRL THIEF, THE) (1938, Brit.)
LOVE AT THE TOP (SEE: FRENCH WAY, THE) (1975, Fr.)
LOVE AT TWENTY (1963, Fr./It./Jap./Pol./W. Ger.) PR:C
LOVE BAN, THE (SEE: IT'S A 2'6" ABOVE THE GROUND WORLD) (1972, Brit.)
LOVE BEFORE BREAKFAST (1936) PR:A
LOVE BEGINS AT TWENTY (1936) PR:A
LOVE BIRDS (1934) PR:A
LOVE BLACKMAILER, THE (SEE: ADULTEROUS AFFAIR) (1966, Can.)
LOVE BOUND (1932) PR:A
LOVE BUG, THE (1968) PR:AA
LOVE BUTCHER, THE (1982) PR:O
LOVE CAGE, THE (SEE: JOY HOUSE) (1964, Fr.)
LOVE CHILD (1982) PR:O
LOVE CHILDREN (SEE: PSYCH-OUT) (1968)
LOVE COMES ALONG (1930) PR:A
LOVE CONTRACT, THE (1932, Brit.) PR:A
LOVE CRAZY (1941) PR:A
LOVE CYCLES (1969, Gr.) PR:C
LOVE DOCTOR, THE (1929) PR:A
LOVE ETERNAL (SEE: ETERNAL RETURN, THE) (1943, Fr.)
LOVE ETERNE, THE (1964, Hong Kong) PR:A
LOVE FACTORY, THE (SEE: WHITE, RED, YELLOW, AND PINK) (1966, It.)
LOVE FEAST, THE (1966, W. Ger.) PR:O
LOVE FINDS A WAY (SEE: ALIAS FRENCH GERTIE) (1930)
LOVE FINDS ANDY HARDY (1938) PR:AA
LOVE FROM A STRANGER (1937, Brit.) PR:C
LOVE FROM A STRANGER (1947) PR:A
LOVE GOD?, THE (1969) PR:A
LOVE HABIT, THE (1931, Brit.) PR:A
LOVE HAPPY (1949) PR:A
LOVE HAS MANY FACES (1965) PR:C
LOVE, HONOR AND BEHAVE (1938) PR:A
LOVE, HONOR AND GOODBYE (1945) PR:A
LOVE, HONOR, AND OH BABY! (1933) PR:A
LOVE, HONOR, AND OH, BABY (1940) PR:A
LOVE HUNGER (1965, Arg.) PR:O
LOVE IN A BUNGALOW (1937) PR:A
LOVE IN A FOUR LETTER WORLD (1970, Can.) PR:O
LOVE IN A GOLDFISH BOWL (1961) PR:A
LOVE IN A HOT CLIMATE (1958, Fr./Sp.) PR:A
LOVE IN A TAXI (1980) PR:A
LOVE IN BLOOM (1935) PR:A
LOVE IN COLD BLOOD (SEE: ICE HOUSE, THE) (1969)
LOVE IN EXILE (1936, Brit.) PR:A
LOVE IN 4 DIMENSIONS (1965, Fr./It.) PR:C
LOVE IN GERMANY, A (1984, Fr./W. Ger.) PR:O
LOVE IN LAS VEGAS (SEE: VIVA LAS VEGAS) (1964)
LOVE IN MOROCCO (1933, Brit./Fr.) PR:A
LOVE IN PAWN (1953, Brit.) PR:A
LOVE IN THE AFTERNOON (1957) PR:A
LOVE IN THE DESERT (1929) PR:A
LOVE IN THE ROUGH (1930) PR:A
LOVE IN WAITING (1948, Brit.) PR:A
LOVE-INS, THE (1967) PR:C
LOVE IS A BALL (1963) PR:A
LOVE IS A CAROUSEL (1970) PR:O
LOVE IS A DAY'S WORK (SEE: FROM A ROMAN BALCONY) (1961)
LOVE IS A DOG FROM HELL (1987, Bel.) PR:O
LOVE IS A FAT WOMAN (1988, Arg.) PR:O
LOVE IS A FUNNY THING (1970, Fr./It.) PR:C
LOVE IS A HEADACHE (1938) PR:A
LOVE IS A MANY-SPLENDORED THING (1955) PR:A

LOVE IS A RACKET (1932) PR:A
LOVE IS A SPLENDID ILLUSION (1970, Brit.) PR:O
LOVE IS A WEAPON (SEE: HELL'S ISLAND) (1955)
LOVE IS A WOMAN (1967, Brit.) PR:C
LOVE IS BETTER THAN EVER (1952) PR:A
LOVE IS LIKE THAT (SEE: JAZZ CINDERELLA) (1930)
LOVE IS LIKE THAT (1933) PR:A
LOVE IS MY PROFESSION (1959, Fr.) PR:O
LOVE IS NEWS (1937) PR:A
LOVE IS ON THE AIR (1937) PR:A
LOVE ISLAND (1952) PR:A
LOVE ITALIAN STYLE (SEE: LOVE, THE ITALIAN WAY) (1964, It.)
LOVE KISS, THE (1930) PR:A
LOVE LAUGHS AT ANDY HARDY (1946) PR:A
LOVE LETTERS (1945) PR:A
LOVE LETTERS (1983) PR:C
LOVE LETTERS OF A STAR (1936) PR:A
LOVE LIES (1931, Brit.) PR:A
LOVE, LIFE AND LAUGHTER (1934, Brit.) PR:A
LOVE, LIVE AND LAUGH (1929) PR:A
LOVE LOTTERY, THE (1954, Brit.) PR:A
LOVE MACHINE, THE (1971) PR:O
LOVE MADNESS (SEE: REEFER MADNESS) (1936)
LOVE MAKERS, THE (SEE: LA VIACCIA) (1962, Fr./It.)
LOVE MATCH, THE (1955, Brit.) PR:A
LOVE MATES (1967, Swed.) PR:A
LOVE MATES, THE (SEE: MADLY) (1970, Fr.)
LOVE ME DEADLY (1972) PR:O
LOVE ME FOREVER (1935) PR:A
LOVE ME OR LEAVE ME (1955) PR:A
LOVE ME TENDER (1956) PR:A
LOVE ME TONIGHT (1932) PR:A
LOVE MERCHANT, THE (1966) PR:O
LOVE MERCHANTS (SEE: LOVE MERCHANT, THE) (1966)
LOVE NEST, THE (1933, Brit.) PR:A
LOVE NEST (1951) PR:A
LOVE NOW. . . PAY LATER (1966) PR:O
LOVE NOW. . . PAY LATER (1966, It.) PR:C
LOVE OF THREE QUEENS (SEE: LOVES OF THREE QUEENS) (1953, It.)
LOVE ON A BET (1936) PR:A
LOVE ON A BUDGET (1938) PR:A
LOVE ON A PILLOW (1963, Fr./It.) PR:O
LOVE ON SKIS (1933, Brit.) PR:A
LOVE ON THE DOLE (1945, Brit.) PR:A
LOVE ON THE GROUND (1984, Fr.) PR:C
LOVE ON THE RIVIERA (1964, Fr./It.) PR:C
LOVE ON THE RUN (1936) PR:A
LOVE ON THE RUN (1979, Fr.) PR:A-C
LOVE ON THE SPOT (1932, Brit.) PR:A
LOVE ON TOAST (1937) PR:A
LOVE ON WHEELS (1932, Brit.) PR:A
LOVE PARADE, THE (1929) PR:A-C
LOVE PAST THIRTY (1934) PR:A
LOVE PLAY (SEE: PLAYTIME) (1967, Fr.)
LOVE PROBLEMS (1970, It.) PR:C
LOVE RACE, THE (1931, Brit.) PR:A
LOVE RACE (SEE: GIRL O' MY DREAMS) (1935)
LOVE RACKET, THE (1929) PR:A
LOVE REDEEMED (SEE: DRAGNET PATROL) (1932)
LOVE ROBOTS, THE (1965, Jap.) PR:O
LOVE ROOT, THE (SEE: MANDRAGOLA) (1966, Fr./It.)
LOVE SLAVES OF THE AMAZONS (1957) PR:A
LOVE, SOLDIERS AND WOMEN (SEE: DAUGHTERS OF DESTINY) (1953, Fr./It.)
LOVE SONGS (1984, Fr./Can.) PR:C
LOVE SPECIALIST, THE (1959, It.) PR:A
LOVE STARVED (SEE: YOUNG BRIDE) (1932)
LOVE STORM, THE (1931, Brit.) PR:A
LOVE STORY (SEE: LADY SURRENDERS, A) (1947, Brit.)
LOVE STORY (1949, Fr.) PR:C
LOVE STORY (1970) PR:A-C
LOVE STREAMS (1984) PR:C
LOVE— TAHITI STYLE (SEE: NUDE ODYSSEY) (1962, Fr./It.)
LOVE TAKES FLIGHT (1937) PR:A
LOVE TEST, THE (1935, Brit.) PR:A
LOVE THAT BRUTE (1950) PR:A
LOVE, THE ITALIAN WAY (1964, It.) PR:C
LOVE THY NEIGHBOR (1940) PR:A
LOVE TILL FIRST BLOOD (1985, Hung.) PR:C-O
LOVE TIME (1934) PR:A
LOVE TRADER, THE (1930) PR:A
LOVE TRAP, THE (1929) PR:A
LOVE UNDER FIRE (1937) PR:A
LOVE UNDER THE CRUCIFIX (1965, Jap.) PR:A
LOVE UP THE POLE (1936, Brit.) PR:A
LOVE WAGER, THE (1933, Brit.) PR:A
LOVE WALTZ, THE (1930, Ger.) PR:A
LOVE WITH THE PROPER STRANGER (1963) PR:C
LOVED ONE, THE (1965) PR:C
LOVELESS, THE (1982) PR:O
LOVELINES (1984) PR:O
LOVELY TO LOOK AT (SEE: THIN ICE) (1937)
LOVELY TO LOOK AT (1952) PR:A

LOVELY WAY TO DIE, A (1968) PR:C
LOVELY WAY TO GO, A (SEE: LOVELY WAY TO DIE, A) (1968)
LOVEMAKER, THE (SEE: MAIN STREET) (1956, Sp.)
LOVEMAKERS, THE (SEE: LA VIACCIA) (1962, Fr./It.)
LOVER BOY (SEE: LOVERS, HAPPY LOVERS!) (1954, Brit./Fr.)
LOVER COME BACK (1931) PR:A
LOVER COME BACK (1946) PR:A
LOVER COME BACK (1961) PR:A
LOVER FOR THE SUMMER, A (SEE: MISTRESS FOR THE SUMMER, A) (1964, Fr./It.)
LOVER, WIFE (SEE: WIFE MISTRESS) (1977, It.)
LOVERBOY (1989) PR:C
LOVERS, THE (1959, Fr.) PR:O
LOVERS, THE (1972, Brit.) PR:C
LOVERS AND LIARS (1981, It.) PR:O
LOVERS AND LOLLIPOPS (1956) PR:A
LOVERS AND LUGGERS (1938, Aus.) PR:A
LOVERS AND OTHER STRANGERS (1970) PR:C
LOVERS COURAGEOUS (1932) PR:A
LOVERS, HAPPY LOVERS! (1954, Brit./Fr.) PR:C
LOVERS IN LIMBO (SEE: NAME OF THE GAME IS KILL, THE) (1968)
LOVERS LIKE US (SEE: SAVAGE, THE) (1975, Fr.)
LOVERS MUST LEARN (SEE: ROME ADVENTURE) (1962)
LOVER'S NET (1957, Fr.) PR:C
LOVERS OF LISBON (SEE: LOVER'S NET) (1957, Fr.)
LOVERS OF MONTPARNASSE, THE (SEE: MODIGLIANI OF MONTPARNASSE) (1961, Fr./It.)
LOVERS OF TERUEL, THE (1962, Fr.) PR:A
LOVERS OF TOLEDO, THE (1954, Fr./Sp./It.) PR:A
LOVERS OF VERONA, THE (1951, Fr.) PR:A
LOVERS ON A TIGHTROPE (1962, Fr.) PR:A
LOVERS' ROCK (1966, Chi.) PR:A
LOVE'S A LUXURY (SEE: CARETAKER'S DAUGHTER, THE) (1952, Brit.)
LOVES AND TIMES OF SCARAMOUCHE, THE (1976, It.) PR:C
LOVES OF A BLONDE (1965, Czech.) PR:A
LOVES OF A DICTATOR (SEE: DICTATOR, THE) (1935, Brit./Ger.)
LOVES OF ARIANE, THE (SEE: ARIANE) (1931, Ger.)
LOVES OF CARMEN, THE (1948) PR:C
LOVES OF EDGAR ALLAN POE, THE (1942) PR:A
LOVES OF HERCULES, THE (1960, It./Fr.) PR:A
LOVES OF ISADORA, THE (SEE: ISADORA) (1968, Brit.)
LOVES OF JOANNA GODDEN, THE (1947, Brit.) PR:A
LOVES OF MADAME DU BARRY, THE (1938, Brit.) PR:A
LOVES OF ROBERT BURNS, THE (1930, Brit.) PR:A
LOVES OF SALAMMBO, THE (1962, Fr./It.) PR:A
LOVES OF THREE QUEENS, THE (1954, It./Fr.) PR:A
LOVE'S OLD SWEET SONG (1933, Brit.) PR:A
LOVESICK (1983) PR:C
LOVIN' MOLLY (1974) PR:O
LOVIN' THE LADIES (1930) PR:A
LOVING (1970) PR:C
LOVING COUPLES (1966, Swed.) PR:O
LOVING COUPLES (1980) PR:O
LOVING MEMORY (1970, Brit.) PR:O
LOVING YOU (1957) PR:A
LOW BLOW (1986) PR:O
LOWER DEPTHS, THE (1936, Fr.) PR:C
LOWER DEPTHS, THE (1957, Jap.) PR:C
LOYAL HEART (1946, Brit.) PR:AA
LOYALTIES (1934, Brit.) PR:A
LOYALTIES (1986, Brit./Can.) PR:O
LOYALTY OF LOVE (1937, It.) PR:A
LSD, I HATE YOU (SEE: MOVIE STAR, AMERICAN STYLE OR, LSD, I HATE YOU) (1966)
LUCAS (1986) PR:A
L'UCELLO DALLE PLUME DI CRISTALLO (SEE: BIRD WITH THE CRYSTAL PLUMMAGE, THE) (1969, It./W. Ger.)
LUCI DEL VARIETA (SEE: VARIETY LIGHTS) (1965, It.)
LUCIANO (1963, It.) PR:C
LUCIFER PROJECT, THE (SEE: BARRACUDA) (1978)
LUCK OF A SAILOR, THE (1934, Brit.) PR:A
LUCK OF GINGER COFFEY, THE (1964, US/Can.) PR:A-C
LUCK OF ROARING CAMP, THE (1937) PR:A
LUCK OF THE GAME (SEE: GRIDIRON FLASH) (1935)
LUCK OF THE IRISH, THE (1937, Ireland) PR:A
LUCK OF THE IRISH, THE (1948) PR:A
LUCK OF THE NAVY (SEE: NORTH SEA PATROL) (1939, Brit.)
LUCK OF THE TURF (1936, Brit.) PR:A
LUCKIEST GIRL IN THE WORLD, THE (1936) PR:A
LUCKIEST MAN IN THE WORLD, THE (1989) PR:A-C
LUCKY: SEE: BOY, A GIRL, AND A DOG, A) (1946)
LUCKY BOOTS (SEE: GUN PLAY) (1936)
LUCKY BOY (1929) PR:A
LUCKY BRIDE, THE (1948, USSR) PR:AA
LUCKY CISCO KID (1940) PR:A
LUCKY DAYS (1935, Brit.) PR:A

LUCKY DAYS (SEE: SING A JINGLE) (1943)
LUCKY DEVILS (1933) PR:A
LUCKY DEVILS (1941) PR:C
LUCKY DOG (1933) PR:AA
LUCKY GIRL (1932, Brit.) PR:A
LUCKY IN LOVE (1929) PR:A
LUCKY JADE (1937, Brit.) PR:A
LUCKY JIM (1957, Brit.) PR:C
LUCKY JORDAN (1942) PR:A
LUCKY LADIES (1932, Brit.) PR:A
LUCKY LADY (1975) PR:C-O
LUCKY LARRIGAN (1933) PR:A
LUCKY LEGS (1942) PR:A
LUCKY LOSER (1934, Brit.) PR:A
LUCKY LOSERS (1950) PR:C
LUCKY LUCIANO (SEE: RE: LUCKY LUCIANO) (1974, US/Fr./It.)
LUCKY LUKE (1971, Fr./Bel.) PR:A
LUCKY MASCOT, THE (1951, Brit.) PR:A
LUCKY ME (1954) PR:A
LUCKY NICK CAIN (1951, Brit.) PR:A
LUCKY NIGHT (1939) PR:A
LUCKY NUMBER, THE (1933, Brit.) PR:A
LUCKY PARTNERS (1940) PR:A
LUCKY RALSTON (SEE: LAW AND ORDER) (1940)
LUCKY STAR (1929) PR:A
LUCKY STAR, THE (1980, Can.) PR:A
LUCKY STIFF, THE (1949) PR:A
LUCKY SWEEP, A (1932, Brit.) PR:A
LUCKY TERROR (1936) PR:A
LUCKY TEXAN, THE (1934) PR:A
LUCKY 13 (SEE: RUNNING HOT) (1984)
LUCKY TO BE A WOMAN (1955, It.) PR:C-O
LUCKY TO ME (1939, Brit.) PR:AA
LUCRECE BORGIA (1953, It./Fr.) PR:O
LUCRETIA BORGIA (SEE: LUCRECE BORGIA) (1953, Fr./It.)
LUCREZIA BORGIA (1937, Fr.) PR:A
LUCY GALLANT (1955) PR:C
LUDWIG (1973, It./Fr./W. Ger.) PR:O
LUGGAGE OF THE GODS (1983) PR:C
LULLABY, THE (SEE: SIN OF MADELON CLAUDET, THE) (1931)
LULLABY (1961, USSR) PR:A
LULLABY OF BROADWAY, THE (1951) PR:A
L'ULTIMO UOMO DELLA TERRA (SEE: LAST MAN ON EARTH, THE) (1964, US/It.)
LULU (1962, Aust.) PR:O
LULU (1978) PR:O
LULU BELLE (1948) PR:A
LUM AND ABNER ABROAD (1956) PR:AA
L'UMANOIDE (SEE: HUMANOID, THE) (1979, It.)
LUMBERJACK (1944) PR:A
LUMIERE (1976, Fr.) PR:O
LUMIERE D'ETE (1943, Fr.) PR:C
LUMMOX (1930) PR:A
L'UN ET L'AUTRE (SEE: OTHER ONE, THE) (1967, Fr.)
LUNA (1979, It.) PR:O
LUNATICS, THE (1986, Hong Kong) PR:O
LUNCH HOUR (1962, Brit.) PR:C
LUNCH ON THE GRASS (SEE: PICNIC ON THE GRASS) (1959, Fr.)
LUNCH WAGON (1981) PR:O
LUNCH WAGON GIRLS (SEE: LUNCH WAGON) (1981)
L'UNE CHANTE L'AUTRE PAS (SEE: ONE SINGS, THE OTHER DOESN'T) (1977, Fr.)
LUNG-MEN K'O-CHAN (SEE: DRAGON INN) (1968, Chi.)
L'UOMO DALLE DUE OMBRE (SEE: COLD SWEAT) (1974, It./Fr.)
LUPE (1967) PR:O
LURE, THE (1933, Brit.) PR:A
LURE OF THE ISLANDS (1942) PR:A
LURE OF THE JUNGLE, THE (1970, Den.) PR:AA
LURE OF THE SWAMP (1957) PR:C
LURE OF THE WASTELAND (1939) PR:A
LURE OF THE WILDERNESS (1952) PR:C
LURED (1947) PR:A
LUST FOR A VAMPIRE (1971, Brit.) PR:O
LUST FOR EVIL (SEE: PURPLE NOON) (1961, Fr./It.)
LUST FOR GOLD (1949) PR:O
LUST FOR LIFE (1956) PR:C
LUST IN THE DUST (1985) PR:O
LUST OF EVIL (SEE: PURPLE NOON) (1961)
LUSTY BRAWLERS (SEE: THIS MAN CAN'T DIE) (1970)
LUSTY MEN, THE (1952) PR:C
LUTHER (1974) PR:C
LUTRING (SEE: WAKE UP AND DIE) (1967, Fr./It.)
LUV (1967) PR:A-C
LUXURY GIRLS (1953, It.) PR:C
LUXURY LINER (1933) PR:A
LUXURY LINER (1948) PR:A
LYCANTHROPUS (SEE: WEREWOLF IN A GIRL'S DORMITORY) (1961, Aust./It.)
LYDIA (1941) PR:A
LYDIA (1964, Can.) PR:O
LYDIA ATE THE APPLE (SEE: PARTINGS) (1962, Pol.)

LYDIA BAILEY (1952) PR:A
LYONS IN PARIS, THE (1955, Brit.) PR:A
LYONS MAIL, THE (1931, Brit.) PR:A
LYSISTRATA (SEE: DAUGHTERS OF DESTINY) (1953, Fr./It.)

M

M (1931, Ger.) PR:O
M (1951) PR:C
MA AND PA KETTLE (1949) PR:A
MA AND PA KETTLE AT HOME (1954) PR:A
MA AND PA KETTLE AT THE FAIR (1952) PR:A
MA AND PA KETTLE AT WAIKIKI (1955) PR:A
MA AND PA KETTLE BACK ON THE FARM (1951) PR:A
MA AND PA KETTLE GO TO PARIS (SEE: MA AND PA KETTLE ON VACATION) (1953)
MA AND PA KETTLE GO TO TOWN (1950) PR:A
MA AND PA KETTLE ON VACATION (1953) PR:A
MA BARKER'S KILLER BROOD (1960) PR:O
MA, HE'S MAKING EYES AT ME! (1940) PR:A
MA NUIT CHEZ MAUD (SEE: MY NIGHT AT MAUD'S) (1969, Fr.)
MA POMME (SEE: JUST ME) (1950, Fr.)
MAARAKAT ALGER (SEE: BATTLE OF ALGIERS, THE) (1966, Algeria/It.)
MAC AND ME (1988) PR:AA
MACABRA (SEE: DEMONOID) (1981)
MACABRE (1958) PR:C
MACAO (1952) PR:C
MACARIO (1961, Mex.) PR:AA
MACARONI (1985, It.) PR:C
MAC ARTHUR (1977) PR:A
MACARTHUR'S CHILDREN (1985, Jap.) PR:C-O
MACBETH (1948) PR:A
MACBETH (1963, US/Brit.) PR:A
MACBETH (1971, Brit.) PR:O
MACCHERONI (SEE: MACARONI) (1985, It.)
MACDONALD OF THE CANADIAN MOUNTIES (SEE: PONY SOLDIER) (1951)
MACHETE (1958) PR:A
MACHINE GUN KELLY (1958) PR:C-O
MACHINE GUN MAMA (1944) PR:A
MACHINE GUN MC CAIN (1970, It.) PR:O
MACHISMO—40 GRAVES FOR 40 GUNS (1970) PR:O
MACHO CALLAHAN (1970) PR:O
MACISTE AGAINST THE CZAR (SEE: ATLAS AGAINST THE CZAR) (1964, It.)
MACISTE ALLA CORTE DEL GRAN KHAN (SEE: SAMSON AND THE SEVEN MIRACLES OF THE WORLD) (1963, Fr./It.)
MACISTE CONTRO GLI UOMINI DELLA LUNA (SEE: HERCULES AGAINST THE MOON MEN) (1965, Fr./It.)
MACK, THE (1973) PR:O
MAC KENNA'S GOLD (1969) PR:C
MAC KINTOSH & T.J. (1975) PR:C-O
MAC KINTOSH MAN, THE (1973, Brit.) PR:C
MACOMBER AFFAIR, THE (1947) PR:C
MACON COUNTY LINE (1974) PR:O
MACUMBA LOVE (1960) PR:A
MACUSHLA (1937, Brit.) PR:A
MAD ABOUT MEN (1954, Brit.) PR:A
MAD ABOUT MONEY (SEE: HE LOVED AN ACTRESS) (1938, Brit.)
MAD ABOUT MUSIC (1938) PR:A
MAD ADVENTURES OF "RABBI" JACOB, THE (SEE: ADVENTURES OF RABBI JACOB, THE) (1973, Fr.)
MAD AT THE WORLD (1955) PR:C
MAD ATLANTIC, THE (1967, Jap.) PR:O
MAD BOMBER, THE (1973) PR:O
MAD CAGE, THE (SEE: LA CAGE AUX FOLLES) (1978, Fr./It.)
MAD DOCTOR, THE (1941) PR:A
MAD DOCTOR OF BLOOD ISLAND, THE (1969, Phil./US) PR:O
MAD DOCTOR OF MARKET STREET, THE (1942) PR:A
MAD DOG (SEE: MAD DOG MORGAN) (1976, Aus.)
MAD DOG COLL (1961) PR:C
MAD DOG MORGAN (1976, Aus.) PR:O
MAD EMPRESS, THE (1940) PR:A
MAD EXECUTIONERS, THE (1965, W. Ger.) PR:O
MAD GAME, THE (1933) PR:A
MAD GENIUS, THE (1931) PR:A-C
MAD GHOUL, THE (1943) PR:A
MAD HATTER, THE (SEE: BREAKFAST IN HOLLYWOOD) (1946)
MAD HATTERS, THE (1935, Brit.) PR:A
MAD HOLIDAY (1936) PR:A
MAD LITTLE ISLAND (1958, Brit.) PR:A
MAD LOVE (1935) PR:C
MAD, MAD MOVIE MAKERS, THE (SEE: LAST PORNO FLICK, THE) (1974)
MAD MAGAZINE PRESENTS UP THE ACADEMY (SEE: UP THE ACADEMY) (1980)
MAD MAGICIAN, THE (1954) PR:C
MAD MARTINDALES, THE (1942) PR:A

MAD MASQUERADE (SEE: WASHINGTON MASQUERADE) (1932)
MAD MAX (1979, Aus.) PR:O
MAD MAX BEYOND THUNDERDOME (1985, Aus.) PR:C-O
MAD MAX 2 (SEE: ROAD WARRIOR, THE) (1981)
MAD MISS MANTON, THE (1938) PR:A-C
MAD MONSTER, THE (1942) PR:A
MAD MONSTER PARTY (1967) PR:AA
MAD PARADE, THE (1931) PR:A
MAD QUEEN, THE (1950, Sp.) PR:A
MAD ROOM, THE (1969) PR:O
MAD TRAPPER OF THE YUKON (SEE: CHALLENGE TO BE FREE) (1976)
MAD WEDNESDAY (1950) PR:A
MAD YOUTH (1940) PR:A
MADALENA (1965, Gr.) PR:O
MADAME (1963, Fr./It./Sp.) PR:A-C
MADAME AKI (1963, Jap.) PR:O
MADAME BOVARY (1949) PR:A
MADAME BUTTERFLY (1932) PR:A
MADAME BUTTERFLY (1955, It./Jap.) PR:A
MADAME CURIE (1943) PR:AA
MADAME DE... (SEE: EARRINGS OF MADAME DE..., THE) (1953, Fr./It.)
MADAME DEATH (1968, Mex.) PR:O
MADAME DU BARRY (1934) PR:A
MADAME DU BARRY (1954, Fr./It.) PR:C
MADAME FRANKENSTEIN (SEE: LADY FRANKENSTEIN) (1971, It.)
MADAME GUILLOTINE (1931, Brit.) PR:A
MADAME JULIE (SEE: WOMAN BETWEEN, THE) (1931)
MADAME LOUISE (1951, Brit.) PR:A
MADAME PIMPERNEL (SEE: PARIS UNDERGROUND) (1945)
MADAME RACKETEER (1932) PR:A
MADAME ROSA (1977, Fr.) PR:O
MADAME SANS-GENE (SEE: MADAME) (1963, Fr./It./Sp.)
MADAME SATAN (1930) PR:A
MADAME SOUSATZKA (1988, Brit.) PR:A-C
MADAME SPY (1934) PR:A
MADAME SPY (1942) PR:A
MADAME WHITE SNAKE (1963, Hong Kong) PR:C
MADAME X (1929) PR:A
MADAME X (1937) PR:A
MADAME X (1966) PR:A
MADCAP (SEE: TAMING THE WILD) (1937)
MADCAP OF THE HOUSE (1950, Mex.) PR:A
MADCHEN FUR DIE MAMBO-BAR (SEE: $100 A NIGHT) (1968, W. Ger.)
MADCHEN IN UNIFORM (SEE: MAEDCHEN IN UNIFORM) (1965, Fr./W. Ger.)
MADDEST CAR IN THE WORLD, THE (1974, W. Ger.) PR:A-A
MADDEST STORY EVER TOLD, THE (SEE: SPIDER BABY) (1968)
MADE (1972, Brit.) PR:C
MADE FOR EACH OTHER (1939) PR:AA
MADE FOR EACH OTHER (1971) PR:C
MADE IN HEAVEN (1952, Brit.) PR:A
MADE IN HEAVEN (1987) PR:A
MADE IN ITALY (1967, Fr./It.) PR:C
MADE IN PARIS (1966) PR:A
MADE IN U.S.A. (1966, Fr.) PR:C
MADE IN USA (1989) PR:O
MADE ON BROADWAY (1933) PR:A
MADELEINE (1950, Brit.) PR:A
MADELEINE IS (1971, Can.) PR:O
MADEMOISELLE (1966, Fr./Brit.) PR:C
MADEMOISELLE DOCTEUR (SEE: UNDER SECRET ORDERS) (1943, Brit.)
MADEMOISELLE FIFI (1944) PR:A
MADEMOISELLE FRANCE (SEE: REUNION IN FRANCE) (1942)
MADHOUSE (1974, Brit.) PR:C
MADIGAN (1968) PR:C
MADIGAN'S MILLIONS (1970, It./Sp.) PR:A
MADISON AVENUE (1962) PR:A
MADISON SQUARE GARDEN (1932) PR:A
MADLY (1970, Fr.) PR:O
MADMAN (1982) PR:O
MADMAN OF LAB 4, THE (1967, Fr.) PR:A
MADMEN OF EUROPE (1940, Brit.) PR:A
MADMEN OF MANDORAS (SEE: THEY SAVED HITLER'S BRAIN) (1963)
MADNESS OF THE HEART (1949, Brit.) PR:A
MADONNA OF AVENUE A, THE (1929) PR:A
MADONNA OF THE DESERT (1948) PR:A
MADONNA OF THE SEVEN MOONS (1945, Brit.) PR:C
MADONNA OF THE STREETS (1930) PR:A
MADONNA'S SECRET, THE (1946) PR:A
MADRON (1970) PR:O
MADWOMAN OF CHAILLOT, THE (1969) PR:A
MAEDCHEN IN UNIFORM (1931, Ger.) PR:O
MAEDCHEN IN UNIFORM (1965, Fr./W. Ger.) PR:C
MAEVA (1961) PR:O

MAFIA (1969, Fr./It.) PR:C
MAFIA, THE (1972, Arg.) PR:C
MAFIA GIRLS, THE (1969) PR:C-O
MAFIOSO (1962, It.) PR:C
MAFU CAGE, THE (1978) PR:O
MAGGIE, THE (SEE: HIGH AND DRY) (1954, Brit.)
MAGIC (1978) PR:O
MAGIC BOW, THE (1947, Brit.) PR:A
MAGIC BOX, THE (1952, Brit.) PR:AA
MAGIC BOY (1960, Jap.) PR:A
MAGIC CARPET, THE (1951) PR:A
MAGIC CHRISTIAN, THE (1970, Brit.) PR:C-O
MAGIC CHRISTMAS TREE (1964) PR:A
MAGIC FACE, THE (1951, Aust.) PR:A
MAGIC FIRE (1956) PR:C
MAGIC FOUNTAIN, THE (1961) PR:A
MAGIC GARDEN, THE (SEE: PENNYWHISTLE
   BLUES, THE) (1952, South Africa)
MAGIC GARDEN OF STANLEY SWEETHART, THE
   (1970) PR:O
MAGIC NIGHT (1932, Brit.) PR:A
MAGIC OF LASSIE, THE (1978) PR:AA
MAGIC SPECTACLES (1961) PR:O
MAGIC SWORD, THE (1962) PR:A
MAGIC TOWN (1947) PR:AA
MAGIC VOYAGE OF SINBAD, THE (1962, USSR) PR:A
MAGIC WEAVER, THE (1965, USSR) PR:A
MAGIC WORLD OF TOPO GIGIO, THE (1961, It.) PR:A
MAGICAL SPECTACLES (SEE: MAGIC SPECTACLES)
   (1961)
MAGICIAN, THE (1958, Swed.) PR:C
MAGICIAN OF LUBLIN, THE (1979, Israel/W. Ger.) PR:C
MAGNET, THE (1950, Brit.) PR:A
MAGNETIC MONSTER, THE (1953) PR:C
MAGNIFICENT AMBERSONS, THE (1942) PR:A
MAGNIFICENT BANDITS, THE (1969, It./Sp.) PR:C
MAGNIFICENT BRUTE, THE (1936) PR:A
MAGNIFICENT CONCUBINE, THE (1964, Hong Kong)
   PR:A
MAGNIFICENT CUCKOLD, THE (1965, Fr./It.) PR:A
MAGNIFICENT DOLL (1946) PR:A
MAGNIFICENT DOPE, THE (1942) PR:A
MAGNIFICENT FRAUD, THE (1939) PR:A
MAGNIFICENT LIE, THE (1931) PR:A
MAGNIFICENT MATADOR, THE (1955) PR:A
MAGNIFICENT OBSESSION (1935) PR:A
MAGNIFICENT OBSESSION (1954) PR:A
MAGNIFICENT ONE, THE (1973, Fr./It.) PR:A
MAGNIFICENT OUTCAST (SEE: ALMOST A GENTLE-
   MAN) (1939)
MAGNIFICENT ROGUE, THE (1946) PR:A
MAGNIFICENT ROUGHNECKS (1956) PR:A
MAGNIFICENT SEVEN, THE (SEE: SEVEN SAMURAI,
   THE) (1954, Jap.)
MAGNIFICENT SEVEN, THE (1960) PR:C
MAGNIFICENT SEVEN DEADLY SINS, THE (1971,
   Brit.) PR:A-C
MAGNIFICENT SEVEN RIDE, THE (1972) PR:A
MAGNIFICENT SHOWMAN, THE (SEE: CIRCUS
   WORLD) (1964)
MAGNIFICENT SINNER (1960, Fr.) PR:A
MAGNIFICENT TRAMP, THE (1962, Fr./It.) PR:A
MAGNIFICENT TWO, THE (1967, Brit.) PR:A
MAGNIFICENT YANKEE, THE (1950) PR:AA
MAGNUM FORCE (1973) PR:C-O
MAGOICHI SAGA, THE (1970, Jap.) PR:C
MAGUS, THE (1968, Brit.) PR:C
MAHANAGAR (SEE: BIG CITY, THE) (1964, India)
MAHLER (1974, Brit.) PR:A-C
MAHOGANY (1975) PR:C
MAID AND THE MARTIAN, THE (SEE: PAJAMA
   PARTY) (1964)
MAID FOR MURDER (1963, Brit.) PR:A
MAID HAPPY (1933, Brit.) PR:A
MAID OF SALEM (1937) PR:A
MAID OF THE MOUNTAINS, THE (1932, Brit.) PR:A
MAID TO ORDER (1932) PR:A
MAID TO ORDER (1987) PR:C
MAIDEN, THE (1961, Fr.) PR:A
MAIDEN FOR A PRINCE, A (1967, Fr./It.) PR:A
MAIDS, THE (1975, Brit.) PR:C
MAID'S NIGHT OUT (1938) PR:A
MAIDSTONE (1970) PR:C
MAIGRET LAYS A TRAP (1958, Fr.) PR:C
MAIL ORDER BRIDE (1964) PR:A
MAIL TRAIN (1941, Brit.) PR:A
MAILBAG ROBBERY (1957, Brit.) PR:A-C
MAIN ATTRACTION, THE (1962, Brit.) PR:A
MAIN CHANCE, THE (1966, Brit.) PR:A
MAIN EVENT, THE (1938) PR:A
MAIN EVENT, THE (1979) PR:A-C
MAIN STREET (SEE: I MARRIED A DOCTOR) (1936)
MAIN STREET (1956, Sp.) PR:A
MAIN STREET AFTER DARK (1944) PR:A
MAIN STREET GIRL (SEE: PAROLED FROM THE BIG
   HOUSE) (1938)
MAIN STREET KID, THE (1947) PR:A
MAIN STREET LAWYER (1939) PR:A

MAIN STREET TO BROADWAY (1953) PR:A
MAIN THING IS TO LOVE, THE (1975, It./Fr.) PR:C
MAIS OU ET DONC ORNICAR (1979, Fr.) PR:C
MAISIE (1939) PR:A
MAISIE GETS HER MAN (1942) PR:A
MAISIE GOES TO RENO (1944) PR:A
MAISIE WAS A LADY (1941) PR:A
MAJDHAR (1984, Brit.) PR:C
MAJIN (1968, Jap.) PR:A
MAJOR AND THE MINOR, THE (1942) PR:A
MAJOR BARBARA (1941, Brit.) PR:A
MAJOR DUNDEE (1965) PR:C-O
MAJOR LEAGUE (1989) PR:O
MAJORITY OF ONE, A (1961) PR:A
MAKE A FACE (1971) PR:C
MAKE A MILLION (1935) PR:A
MAKE A WISH (1937) PR:A
MAKE AND BREAK (SEE: TELL ME LIES) (1968, Brit.)
MAKE BELIEVE BALLROOM (1949) PR:A
MAKE HASTE TO LIVE (1954) PR:A
MAKE IT THREE (1938, Brit.) PR:A
MAKE LIKE A THIEF (1966, US/Fin.) PR:A
MAKE ME A STAR (1932) PR:A
MAKE ME A WOMAN (SEE: SISTERS, THE) (1969, Gr.)
MAKE ME AN OFFER (1954, Brit.) PR:A
MAKE MINE A DOUBLE (1961, Brit.) PR:A
MAKE MINE A MILLION (1965, Brit.) PR:A
MAKE MINE MINK (1960, Brit.) PR:A
MAKE MINE MUSIC (1946) PR:AA
MAKE ROOM FOR TOMORROW (1979, Fr.) PR:O
MAKE-UP (1937, Brit.) PR:A
MAKE WAY FOR A LADY (1936) PR:A
MAKE WAY FOR LILA (1962, Swed./W. Ger.) PR:A
MAKE WAY FOR TOMORROW (1937) PR:A
MAKE YOUR OWN BED (1944) PR:A
MAKER OF MEN (1931) PR:A
MAKING IT (1971) PR:O
MAKING LOVE (1982) PR:O
MAKING MR. RIGHT (1987) PR:C-O
MAKING OF A LADY, THE (SEE: LADY HAMILTON)
   (1969, It./Fr./W. Ger.)
MAKING THE GRADE (1929) PR:A
MAKING THE GRADE (1984) PR:O
MAKING THE HEADLINES (1938) PR:A
MAKIOKA SISTERS, THE (1985, Jap.) PR:C-O
MAKO: THE JAWS OF DEATH (1976) PR:C
MAKUCHI (SEE: IDIOT, THE) (1963, Jap.)
MALA NOCHE (1989) PR:A
MALACHI'S COVE (1973, Brit.) PR:AA
MALAGA (SEE: FIRE OVER AFRICA) (1954, Brit.)
MALAGA (1960, Brit.) PR:A
MALANDRO (1986, Braz./Fr.) PR:C
MALATESTA'S CARNIVAL (1973) PR:O
MALAY NIGHTS (1933) PR:A
MALAYA (1950) PR:A
MALAYUNTA (SEE: BAD COMPANY) (1986, Arg.)
MALCOLM (1986, Aus.) PR:C
MALE AND FEMALE SINCE ADAM AND EVE (1961,
   Arg.) PR:A
MALE ANIMAL, THE (1942) PR:A
MALE COMPANION (1965, Fr./It.) PR:A
MALE HUNT (1965, Fr./It.) PR:A
MALE SERVICE (1966) PR:O
MALEFICES (SEE: WHERE THE TRUTH LIES) (1962,
   Fr.)
MALENKA, THE VAMPIRE (1972, Sp./It.) PR:O
MALENKAYA VERA (SEE: LITTLE VERA) (1989,
   USSR)
MALEVIL (1981, Fr./W. Ger.) PR:C
MALIBU (SEE: SEQUOIA) (1934)
MALIBU BEACH (1978) PR:C
MALIBU BIKINI SHOP, THE (1987) PR:O
MALIBU HIGH (1979) PR:O
MALICE (SEE: MALICIOUS) (1973, It.)
MALICIOUS (1973, It.) PR:O
MALIZIA (SEE: MALICIOUS) (1973, It.)
MALONE (1987) PR:O
MALOU (1981, W. Ger.) PR:C
MALPAS MYSTERY, THE (1967, Brit.) PR:A
MALPERTUIS (1972, Bel./Fr.) PR:C
MALTA STORY (1954, Brit.) PR:A-C
MALTESE BIPPY, THE (1969) PR:A
MALTESE FALCON, THE (1931) PR:A
MALTESE FALCON, THE (1941) PR:A
MAMA LOVES PAPA (1933) PR:A
MAMA LOVES PAPA (1945) PR:A
MAMA RUNS WILD (1938) PR:A
MAMA STEPS OUT (1937) PR:A
MAMBA (1930) PR:A
MAMBO (1955, It.) PR:C
MAME (1974) PR:A
MAMMA DRACULA (1980, Bel./Fr.) PR:O
MAMMA ROMA (1962, It.) PR:C
MAMMY (1930) PR:A
MAN, THE (1972) PR:A
MAN, A WOMAN, AND A BANK, A (1979, Can.) PR:C
MAN, A WOMAN AND A KILLER, A (1975) PR:O
MAN ABOUT THE HOUSE, A (1947, Brit.) PR:A

MAN ABOUT TOWN (1932) PR:A
MAN ABOUT TOWN (1939) PR:AA
MAN ABOUT TOWN (1947, Fr.) PR:A
MAN ACCUSED (1959, Brit.) PR:C
MAN AFRAID (1957) PR:A
MAN AGAINST MAN (1961, Jap.) PR:C
MAN AGAINST WOMAN (1932) PR:A
MAN ALIVE (1945) PR:A
MAN ALONE, A (1955) PR:A
MAN AND A WOMAN, A (1966, Fr.) PR:A-C
MAN AND A WOMAN: 20 YEARS LATER, A (1986, Fr.)
   PR:C
MAN AND BOY (1972) PR:A
MAN AND HIS MATE (SEE: ONE MILLION B.C.) (1940)
MAN AND THE BEAST, THE (1951, Arg.) PR:A
MAN AND THE MOMENT, THE (1929) PR:A
MAN AND THE MONSTER, THE (1958, Mex.) PR:A
MAN AT LARGE (1941) PR:A
MAN AT SIX (SEE: GABLES MYSTERY, THE) (1931,
   Brit.)
MAN AT THE CARLTON TOWER (1961, Brit.) PR:C
MAN AT THE TOP (1973, Brit.) PR:A
MAN BAIT (1952, Brit.) PR:A
MAN BEAST (1956) PR:A
MAN BEHIND THE GUN, THE (1952) PR:A
MAN BEHIND THE MASK, THE (1936, Brit.) PR:A
MAN BETRAYED, A (1937) PR:A
MAN BETRAYED, A (1941) PR:A
MAN BETWEEN, THE (1953, Brit.) PR:A
MAN CALLED ADAM, A (1966) PR:C
MAN CALLED BACK, THE (1932) PR:C
MAN CALLED DAGGER, A (1967) PR:A
MAN CALLED FLINTSTONE, THE (1966) PR:AA
MAN CALLED GANNON, A (1969) PR:A
MAN CALLED HORSE, A (1970) PR:O
MAN CALLED NOON, THE (1973, Brit.) PR:C
MAN CALLED PETER, A (1955) PR:AA
MAN CALLED SLEDGE, A (1971, It.) PR:O
MAN CALLED SULLIVAN, A (SEE: GREAT JOHN L.,
   THE) (1945)
MAN COULD GET KILLED, A (1966) PR:A
MAN CRAZY (1953) PR:A
MAN DETAINED (1961, Brit.) PR:C
MAN-EATER (SEE: SHARK!) (1970, US/Mex.)
MAN EATER OF HYDRA (SEE: ISLAND OF THE
   DOOMED) (1968, Sp./W. Ger.)
MAN-EATER OF KUMAON (1948) PR:A
MAN ESCAPED, A (1957, Fr.) PR:A
MAN FACING SOUTHEAST (1986, Arg.) PR:O
MAN FOLLOWING THE SUN (SEE: SANDU FOL-
   LOWS THE SUN) (1965, USSR)
MAN FOR ALL SEASONS, A (1966, Brit.) PR:A
MAN FRIDAY (1975, Brit.) PR:A-C
MAN FROM BITTER RIDGE, THE (1955) PR:A
MAN FROM BLACK HILLS, THE (1952) PR:A
MAN FROM BLANKLEY'S, THE (1930) PR:A
MAN FROM BUTTON WILLOW, THE (1965) PR:AA
MAN FROM CAIRO, THE (1953, It.) PR:A
MAN FROM CHEYENNE (1942) PR:A
MAN FROM CHICAGO, THE (1931, Brit.) PR:A
MAN FROM COCODY (1966, Fr/It.) PR:A
MAN FROM COLORADO, THE (1948) PR:A-C
MAN FROM C.O.T.T.O.N. (SEE: GONE ARE THE
   DAYS) (1963)
MAN FROM DAKOTA, THE (1940) PR:A
MAN FROM DEATH VALLEY, THE (1931) PR:A
MAN FROM DEL RIO (1956) PR:A
MAN FROM DOWN UNDER, THE (1943) PR:A-C
MAN FROM FRISCO (1944) PR:A
MAN FROM GALVESTON, THE (1964) PR:A
MAN FROM GOD'S COUNTRY (1958) PR:A
MAN FROM GUN TOWN, THE (1936) PR:A
MAN FROM HEADQUARTERS (1942) PR:A
MAN FROM HELL, THE (1934) PR:A
MAN FROM HELL'S EDGES (1932) PR:A
MAN FROM HONG KONG (1975) PR:O
MAN FROM LARAMIE, THE (1955) PR:C
MAN FROM MONTANA (1941) PR:A
MAN FROM MONTEREY, THE (1933) PR:A
MAN FROM MONTREAL, THE (1940) PR:A
MAN FROM MOROCCO, THE (1946, Brit.) PR:A
MAN FROM MUSIC MOUNTAIN (1938) PR:A
MAN FROM MUSIC MOUNTAIN (1943) PR:A
MAN FROM NEVADA, THE (SEE: NEVADAN, THE)
   (1950)
MAN FROM NEW MEXICO, THE (1932) PR:A
MAN FROM NOWHERE, THE (SEE: ARIZONA COLT)
   (1965, Fr./It./Sp.)
MAN FROM OKLAHOMA, THE (1945) PR:AA
MAN FROM O.R.G.Y., THE (1970) PR:O
MAN FROM PLANET X, THE (1951) PR:A
MAN FROM RAINBOW VALLEY, THE (1946) PR:A
MAN FROM SNOWY RIVER, THE (1983, Aus.) PR:C
MAN FROM SUNDOWN, THE (1939) PR:A
MAN FROM TANGIER (SEE: THUNDER OVER TANG-
   IER) (1957, Brit.)
MAN FROM TEXAS. THE (1939) PR:A
MAN FROM TEXAS, THE (1948) PR:A

MAN FROM THE ALAMO, THE (1953) PR:A
MAN FROM THE BIG CITY, THE (SEE: IT HAPPENED OUT WEST) (1937)
MAN FROM THE DINERS' CLUB, THE (1963) PR:A
MAN FROM THE EAST, THE (1961, Jap.) PR:A
MAN FROM THE EAST, A (1974, It./Fr.) PR:C-O
MAN FROM THE FIRST CENTURY, THE (1961, Czech.) PR:A
MAN FROM THE FOLIES BERGERE, THE (SEE: FOLIES BERGERE) (1935)
MAN FROM THE PAST, THE (SEE: MAN FROM THE FIRST CENTURY, THE) (1961, Czech.)
MAN FROM THE RIO GRANDE, THE (1943) PR:A
MAN FROM THUNDER RIVER, THE (1943) PR:A
MAN FROM TORONTO, THE (1933, Brit.) PR:A
MAN FROM TUMBLEWEEDS, THE (1940) PR:A
MAN FROM UTAH, THE (1934) PR:A
MAN FROM WYOMING, A (1930) PR:A
MAN FROM YESTERDAY, THE (1932) PR:A
MAN FROM YESTERDAY, THE (1949, Brit.) PR:O
MAN GOES THROUGH THE WALL, A (SEE: MAN WHO WALKED THROUGH THE WALL) (1964, W. Ger.)
MAN HE FOUND, THE (SEE: WHIP HAND, THE) (1951)
MAN HUNT (1933) PR:A
MAN HUNT (1936) PR:A
MAN HUNT (1941) PR:A
MAN HUNTER, THE (1930) PR:A
MAN HUNTERS OF THE CARIBBEAN (1938) PR:A
MAN I KILLED (SEE: BROKEN LULLABY) (1932)
MAN I LOVE, THE (1929) PR:A
MAN I LOVE, THE (1946) PR:A
MAN I MARRIED, THE (1940) PR:A
MAN I MARRY, THE (1936) PR:A
MAN I WANT, THE (1934, Brit.) PR:A
MAN IN A COCKED HAT (1959, Brit.) PR:A
MAN IN BLACK, THE (1950, Brit.) PR:C-O
MAN IN BLUE, THE (1937) PR:A
MAN IN GREY, THE (1943, Brit.) PR:A-C
MAN IN HALF-MOON STREET, THE (1944) PR:A
MAN IN HIDING (SEE: MAN-TRAP) (1961)
MAN IN LOVE, A (1987, Fr.) PR:O
MAN IN MOMMY'S BED, A (SEE: WITH SIX YOU GET EGGROLL) (1968)
MAN IN OUTER SPACE (SEE: MAN FROM THE FIRST CENTURY, THE) (1961, Czech.)
MAN IN POSSESSION, THE (1931) PR:A-C
MAN IN POSSESSION, THE (SEE: PERSONAL PROPERTY) (1937)
MAN IN THE ATTIC (1953) PR:C
MAN IN THE BACK SEAT, THE (1961, Brit.) PR:A
MAN IN THE DARK (1953) PR:A
MAN IN THE DARK (1963, Brit.) PR:A
MAN IN THE DINGHY, THE (1951, Brit.) PR:A
MAN IN THE GLASS BOOTH, THE (1975) PR:A
MAN IN THE GRAY FLANNEL SUIT, THE (1956) PR:A
MAN IN THE IRON MASK, THE (1939) PR:A
MAN IN THE MIDDLE (1964, US/Brit.) PR:A-C
MAN IN THE MIDDLE (SEE: 48 HOURS TO LIVE) (1960, Brit./Swed.)
MAN IN THE MIRROR, THE (1936, Brit.) PR:A
MAN IN THE MOON (1961, Brit.) PR:A
MAN IN THE MOONLIGHT MASK, THE (1958, Jap.) PR:A
MAN IN THE NET, THE (1959) PR:A
MAN IN THE ROAD, THE (1957, Brit.) PR:A
MAN IN THE SADDLE (1951) PR:A
MAN IN THE SHADOW (1957) PR:A
MAN IN THE SHADOW (SEE: VIOLENT STRANGER) (1957, Brit.)
MAN IN THE SKY (SEE: DECISION AGAINST TIME) (1957, Brit.)
MAN IN THE STEEL MASK, THE (SEE: WHO?) (1975, Brit./W. Ger.)
MAN IN THE STORM, THE (1969, Jap.) PR:A
MAN IN THE TRUNK, THE (1942) PR:A
MAN IN THE VAULT (1956) PR:A
MAN IN THE WATER, THE (1963) PR:A
MAN IN THE WHITE SUIT, THE (1952, Brit.) PR:A
MAN IN THE WILDERNESS (1971, US/Sp.) PR:O
MAN INSIDE, THE (1958, Brit.) PR:C
MAN IS ARMED, THE (1956) PR:A
MAN IS TEN FEET TALL, A (SEE: EDGE OF THE CITY) (1957)
MAN KILLER (SEE: PRIVATE DETECTIVE 62) (1933)
MAN-KILLER (SEE: OTHER LOVE, THE) (1947)
MAN LIKE EVA, A (1985, W. Ger.) PR:O
MAN MAD (SEE: NO PLACE TO LAND) (1958)
MAN MADE MONSTER (1941) PR:A
MAN MISSING (SEE: YOU HAVE TO RUN FAST) (1961)
MAN OF A THOUSAND FACES (1957) PR:A
MAN OF AFFAIRS (1937, Brit.) PR:A
MAN OF AFRICA (1956, Brit.) PR:A
MAN OF BRONZE (SEE: JIM THORPE – ALL AMERICAN) (1951)
MAN OF CONFLICT (1953) PR:A
MAN OF CONQUEST (1939) PR:A
MAN OF COURAGE (1943) PR:A

MAN OF EVIL (1948, Brit.) PR:A
MAN OF FLOWERS (1984, Aus.) PR:O
MAN OF IRON (1935) PR:A
MAN OF IRON (SEE: RAILROAD MAN, THE) (1965, It.)
MAN OF IRON (1981, Pol.) PR:C
MAN OF LA MANCHA (1972) PR:C
MAN OF MARBLE (1979, Pol.) PR:C-O
MAN OF MAYFAIR (1931, Brit.) PR:A
MAN OF MUSIC (1953, USSR) PR:A
MAN OF SENTIMENT, A (1933) PR:A
MAN OF THE FAMILY (SEE: TOP MAN) (1943)
MAN OF THE FOREST (1933) PR:A
MAN OF THE HOUR, THE (1940, Fr.) PR:A
MAN OF THE HOUR (SEE: COLONEL EFFINGHAM'S RAID) (1945)
MAN OF THE MOMENT (1935, Brit.) PR:A
MAN OF THE MOMENT (1955, Brit.) PR:A
MAN OF THE PEOPLE (1937) PR:A
MAN OF THE WEST (1958) PR:C-O
MAN OF THE WORLD (1931) PR:A
MAN OF TWO WORLDS (1934) PR:A
MAN OF VIOLENCE (1970, Brit.) PR:O
MAN ON A STRING (1960) PR:A
MAN ON A SWING (1974) PR:C
MAN ON A TIGHTROPE (1953) PR:A
MAN ON AMERICA'S CONSCIENCE, THE (SEE: TENNESSEE JOHNSON) (1942)
MAN ON FIRE (1957) PR:A
MAN ON FIRE (1987, It./Fr.) PR:O
MAN ON THE EIFFEL TOWER, THE (1949) PR:A
MAN ON THE FLYING TRAPEZE, THE (1935) PR:A
MAN ON THE PROWL (1957) PR:A
MAN ON THE RUN (1949, Brit.) PR:A
MAN ON THE RUN (SEE: KIDNAPPERS, THE) (1964, US/Phil.)
MAN OR GUN (1958) PR:A
MAN OUTSIDE, THE (1933, Brit.) PR:A
MAN OUTSIDE, THE (1968, Brit.) PR:A
MAN OUTSIDE (1988) PR:C
MAN-PROOF (1938) PR:A
MAN STOLEN (1934, Fr.) PR:A
MAN THEY COULD NOT HANG, THE (1939) PR:C
MAN THEY COULDN'T ARREST, THE (1933, Brit.) PR:A
MAN TO MAN (1931) PR:A
MAN TO REMEMBER, A (1938) PR:A
MAN TRAILER, THE (1934) PR:A
MAN-TRAP (1961) PR:A
MAN TROUBLE (1930) PR:A
MAN UNDER SUSPICION (1985, W. Ger.) PR:C
MAN UPSTAIRS, THE (1959, Brit.) PR:A
MAN WANTED (1932) PR:A
MAN WHO BROKE THE BANK AT MONTE CARLO, THE (1935) PR:A
MAN WHO CAME BACK, THE (1931) PR:C
MAN WHO CAME BACK, THE (SEE: SWAMP WATER) (1941)
MAN WHO CAME FOR COFFEE, THE (1970, It.) PR:O
MAN WHO CAME TO DINNER, THE (1942) PR:A
MAN WHO CHANGED HIS MIND (SEE: MAN WHO LIVED AGAIN, THE) (1936, Brit.)
MAN WHO CHANGED HIS NAME, THE (1934, Brit.) PR:A
MAN WHO CHEATED HIMSELF, THE (1951) PR:A
MAN WHO COULD CHEAT DEATH, THE (1959, Brit.) PR:C
MAN WHO COULD WORK MIRACLES, THE (1937, Brit.) PR:A
MAN WHO COULDN'T WALK, THE (1964, Brit.) PR:A
MAN WHO CRIED WOLF, THE (1937) PR:A
MAN WHO DARED, THE (1933) PR:AA
MAN WHO DARED, THE (1939) PR:A
MAN WHO DARED, THE (1946) PR:A
MAN WHO DIED TWICE, THE (1958) PR:A
MAN WHO ENVIED WOMEN, THE (1985) PR:C
MAN WHO FELL TO EARTH, THE (1976, Brit.) PR:C-O
MAN WHO FINALLY DIED, THE (1967, Brit.) PR:A
MAN WHO FOUND HIMSELF, THE (1937) PR:A
MAN WHO HAD POWER OVER WOMEN, THE (1970, Brit.) PR:C
MAN WHO HAUNTED HIMSELF, THE (1970, Brit.) PR:A
MAN WHO KILLED BILLY THE KID, THE (1967, Sp./It.) PR:A
MAN WHO KNEW TOO MUCH, THE (1935, Brit.) PR:C
MAN WHO KNEW TOO MUCH, THE (1956) PR:A
MAN WHO LAUGHS, THE (1966, It.) PR:O
MAN WHO LIES, THE (1970, Czech./Fr.) PR:C
MAN WHO LIKED FUNERALS, THE (1959, Brit.) PR:A
MAN WHO LIVED AGAIN, THE (1936, Brit.) PR:A
MAN WHO LIVED TWICE, THE (1936) PR:A
MAN WHO LOST HIMSELF, THE (1941) PR:A
MAN WHO LOST HIS WAY, THE (SEE: CROSSROADS) (1942)
MAN WHO LOVED CAT DANCING, THE (1973) PR:C-O
MAN WHO LOVED REDHEADS, THE (1955, Brit.) PR:A
MAN WHO LOVED WOMEN, THE (1977, Fr.) PR:O
MAN WHO LOVED WOMEN, THE (1983) PR:O
MAN WHO MADE DIAMONDS, THE (1937, Brit.) PR:A

MAN WHO NEVER WAS, THE (1956, Brit.) PR:A
MAN WHO PAWNED HIS SOUL, THE (SEE: UNKNOWN BLONDE) (1934)
MAN WHO PLAYED GOD, THE (1932) PR:A
MAN WHO RECLAIMED HIS HEAD, THE (1935) PR:A
MAN WHO RETURNED TO LIFE, THE (1942) PR:A
MAN WHO SHOT LIBERTY VALANCE, THE (1962) PR:A
MAN WHO STOLE THE SUN, THE (1980, Jap.) PR:C
MAN WHO TALKED TOO MUCH, THE (1940) PR:A
MAN WHO THOUGHT LIFE, THE (1969, Den.) PR:A
MAN WHO TURNED TO STONE, THE (1957) PR:C
MAN WHO UNDERSTOOD WOMEN, THE (1959) PR:A-C
MAN WHO WAGGED HIS TAIL, THE (1957, It./Sp.) PR:A
MAN WHO WALKED ALONE, THE (1945) PR:A
MAN WHO WALKED THROUGH THE WALL, THE (1964, W. Ger.) PR:A
MAN WHO WAS NOBODY, THE (1960, Brit.) PR:C
MAN WHO WAS SHERLOCK HOLMES, THE (1937, Ger.) PR:A
MAN WHO WASN'T THERE, THE (1983) PR:C
MAN WHO WATCHED TRAINS GO BY, THE (SEE: PARIS EXPRESS) (1953, Brit.)
MAN WHO WON, THE (1933, Brit.) PR:A
MAN WHO WOULD BE KING, THE (1975, Brit.) PR:A-C
MAN WHO WOULD NOT DIE, THE (1975) PR:C
MAN WHO WOULDN'T DIE, THE (1942) PR:A
MAN WHO WOULDN'T TALK, THE (1940) PR:A
MAN WHO WOULDN'T TALK, THE (1958, Brit.) PR:A
MAN WITH A CLOAK, THE (1951) PR:A
MAN WITH A GUN (1958) PR:C
MAN WITH A MILLION (1954, Brit.) PR:A
MAN WITH BOGART'S FACE, THE (1980) PR:A-C
MAN WITH CONNECTIONS, THE (1970, Fr.) PR:C
MAN WITH MY FACE, THE (1951) PR:A
MAN WITH NINE LIVES, THE (1940) PR:A
MAN WITH 100 FACES, THE (1938, Brit.) PR:A
MAN WITH ONE RED SHOE, THE (1985) PR:C
MAN WITH THE BALLOONS, THE (1968, It./Fr.) PR:A
MAN WITH THE DEADLY LENS, THE (SEE: WRONG IS RIGHT) (1982)
MAN WITH THE ELECTRIC VOICE, THE (SEE: FIFTEEN WIVES) (1934)
MAN WITH THE GOLDEN ARM, THE (1955) PR:O
MAN WITH THE GOLDEN GUN, THE (1974, Brit.) PR:A
MAN WITH THE GREEN CARNATION, THE (SEE: GREEN BUDDHA, THE) (1954, Brit.)
MAN WITH THE GREEN CARNATION, THE (1960, Brit.) PR:A
MAN WITH THE GUN (1955) PR:C
MAN WITH THE MAGNETIC EYES, THE (1945, Brit.) PR:C
MAN WITH THE SYNTHETIC BRAIN, THE (SEE: PSYCHO A GO-GO!) (1965)
MAN WITH THE TRANSPLANTED BRAIN, THE (1972, Fr./It./W. Ger.) PR:A
MAN WITH THE X-RAY EYES, THE (SEE: "X" – THE MAN WITH THE X-RAY EYES) (1963)
MAN WITH THE YELLOW EYES (SEE: PLANETS AGAINST US, THE) (1961, It./Fr.)
MAN WITH THIRTY SONS, THE (SEE: MAGNIFICENT YANKEE, THE) (1950)
MAN WITH TWO BRAINS, THE (1983) PR:O
MAN WITH TWO FACES, THE (1934) PR:A-C
MAN WITH TWO HEADS, THE (1972) PR:O
MAN WITH TWO LIVES, THE (1942) PR:A
MAN WITHIN, THE (SEE: SMUGGLERS, THE) (1948, Brit.)
MAN WITHOUT A BODY, THE (1957, Brit.) PR:A
MAN WITHOUT A FACE (SEE: WHO?) (1975, Brit./W. Ger.)
MAN WITHOUT A FACE, THE (1935, Brit.) PR:A
MAN WITHOUT A FACE (SEE: PYRO) (1964, US/Sp.)
MAN WITHOUT A FACE, THE (SEE: SHADOWMAN) (1975, Fr./It.)
MAN WITHOUT A GUN (SEE: MAN WITH THE GUN) (1955)
MAN WITHOUT A STAR (1955) PR:C
MAN, WOMAN AND CHILD (1983) PR:A
MANCHU EAGLE MURDER CAPER MYSTERY, THE (1975) PR:A
MANCHURIAN AVENGER (1985) PR:O
MANCHURIAN CANDIDATE, THE (1962) PR:C-O
MANDABI (1970, Fr./Senegal) PR:A
MANDALAY (1934) PR:A-C
MANDARIN MYSTERY, THE (1937) PR:A
MANDEN DER TAENKTE TING (SEE: MAN WHO THOUGHT LIFE, THE) (1969, Den.)
MANDINGO (1975) PR:O
MANDRAGOLA (1966, Fr./It.) PR:A
MANDY (SEE: CRASH OF SILENCE) (1952, Brit.)
MANFISH (1956) PR:A
MANGANINNIE (1982, Aus.) PR:A
MANGIATI VIVI (SEE: DOOMED TO DIE) (1985, It.)
MANGO TREE, THE (1981, Aus.) PR:O
MANHANDLED (1949) PR:A
MANHATTAN (1979) PR:C

MANHATTAN ANGEL (1948) PR:A
MANHATTAN BABY (1986, It.) PR:O
MANHATTAN COCKTAIL (1928) PR:A
MANHATTAN HEARTBEAT (1940) PR:A
MANHATTAN LOVE SONG (1934) PR:A
MANHATTAN MADNESS (SEE: ADVENTURE IN BLACKMAIL) (1943, Brit.)
MANHATTAN MELODRAMA (1934) PR:A
MANHATTAN MERRY-GO-ROUND (1937) PR:A
MANHATTAN MOON (1935) PR:A
MANHATTAN MUSIC BOX (SEE: MANHATTAN MERRY-GO-ROUND) (1937)
MANHATTAN PARADE (1931) PR:A
MANHATTAN PROJECT, THE (1986) PR:A
MANHATTAN SHAKEDOWN (1939) PR:A
MANHATTAN TOWER (1932) PR:A
MANHUNT (SEE: FROM HELL TO TEXAS) (1958)
MANHUNT (SEE: ITALIAN CONNECTION, THE) (1973, US/It./W. Ger.)
MANHUNT, THE (1986, It.) PR:O
MANHUNT IN THE JUNGLE (1958) PR:A
MANHUNTER (1986) PR:O
MANIA (1961, Brit.) PR:O
MANIAC (1934) PR:O
MANIAC (1963, Brit.) PR:C
MANIAC! (1977) PR:C
MANIAC (SEE: MANIAC MANSION) (1978, It.)
MANIAC (1980) PR:O
MANIAC COP (1988) PR:O
MANIAC MANSION (1978, It.) PR:O
MANIACS ARE LOOSE, THE (SEE: THRILL KILLERS, THE) (1965)
MANIACS ON WHEELS (1951, Brit.) PR:A
MANIFESTO (1988) PR:O
MANILA CALLING (1942) PR:A
MANINA (SEE: GIRL IN THE BIKINI, THE) (1958, Fr.)
MANIPULATOR, THE (SEE: EFFECTS) (1980)
MANITOU, THE (1978) PR:C
MANJI (SEE: PASSION) (1968, Jap.)
MANKILLERS (1987) PR:O
MANNEQUIN (1933, Brit.) PR:A
MANNEQUIN (1937) PR:A
MANNEQUIN (1987) PR:A-C
MANNER (SEE: MEN) (1985, W. Ger.)
MANNER MUSSEN SO SEIN (SEE: HIPPODROME) (1961, W. Ger.)
MANNISKOR MOTS OCH LJUV MUSIK UPPSTAR I HJARTAT (SEE: PEOPLE MEET AND SWEET MUSIC FILLS THE HEART) (1964, Den./Swed.)
MANNY'S ORPHANS (SEE: HERE COME THE TIGERS) (1978)
MANO DELLA STRANIERO (SEE: STRANGER'S HAND, THE) (1955, Brit.)
MANOLETE (1950, Sp.) PR:A
MANOLIS (1962, Brit.) PR:A
MANON (1950, Fr.) PR:A
MANON (1987, Venezuela) PR:O
MANON OF THE SPRING (1986, Fr.) PR:C
MANON 70 (1968, Fr.) PR:O
MANOS, THE HANDS OF FATE (1966) PR:C
MANPOWER (1941) PR:A
MAN'S AFFAIR, A (1949, Brit.) PR:A
MAN'S CASTLE, A (1933) PR:A
MAN'S COUNTRY (1938) PR:A
MAN'S FAVORITE SPORT (?) (1964) PR:A
MAN'S GAME, A (1934) PR:A
MAN'S HERITAGE (SEE: SPIRIT OF CULVER, THE) (1939)
MAN'S HOPE (1947, Sp.) PR:A
MAN'S LAND, A (1932) PR:A
MAN'S WORLD, A (1942) PR:A
MANSION OF THE DOOMED (1976) PR:O
MANSLAUGHTER (1930) PR:A
MANSTER, THE (1962, US/Jap.) PR:A
MANTIS IN LACE (1968) PR:O
MANTRAP, THE (1943) PR:A
MANTRAP (SEE: WOMAN IN HIDING) (1953, Brit.)
MANTRAP (SEE: MAN-TRAP) (1961)
MANUELA (SEE: STOWAWAY GIRL) (1957, Brit.)
MANUELA'S LOVES (1987, Fr.) PR:C-O
MANULESCU (1933, Ger.) PR:A
MANUSCRIPT FOUND IN SARAGOSSA (SEE: SARAGOSSA MANUSCRIPT, THE) (1972, Pol.)
MANY A SLIP (1931) PR:A
MANY HAPPY RETURNS (1934) PR:A
MANY RIVERS TO CROSS (1955) PR:A
MANY TANKS MR. ATKINS (1938, Brit.) PR:A
MANY WATERS (1931, Brit.) PR:A
MAOS SANGRENTAS (SEE: VIOLENT AND THE DAMNED, THE) (1962, Braz.)
MAPANTSULA (1989, South Africa/Brit./Aus.) PR:C
MARA MARU (1952) PR:A
MARA OF THE WILDERNESS (1966) PR:A
MARACAIBO (1958) PR:A
MARAT/SADE (SEE: PERSECUTION AND ASSASSINATION OF JEAN-PAUL MARAT AS PERFORMED BY THE INMATES OF THE ASYLUM OF CHARENTON

UNDER THE DIRECTION OF THE MARQUIS DE SADE) (1967, Brit.)
MARATHON MAN (1976) PR:O
MARAUDERS, THE (1947) PR:A
MARAUDERS, THE (1955) PR:A
MARAUDERS, THE (SEE: MERRILL'S MARAUDERS) (1962)
MARCH HARE, THE (1956, Brit.) PR:A
MARCH OF THE SPRING HARE (1969) PR:O
MARCH OF THE WOODEN SOLDIERS, THE (SEE: BABES IN TOYLAND) (1934)
MARCH ON PARIS 1914 – OF GENERALOBERST ALEXANDER VON KLUCK – AND HIS MEMORY OF JESSIE HOLLADAY (1977) PR:C
MARCH OR DIE (1977, Brit.) PR:C-O
MARCHA O MUERE (SEE: COMMANDO) (1964, Bel./It./Sp./W. Ger.)
MARCHANDES D'ILLUSIONS (SEE: NIGHTS OF SHAME) (1961, Fr.)
MARCHANDS DE FILLES (SEE: SELLERS OF GIRLS) (1967, Fr.)
MARCHING ALONG (SEE: STARS AND STRIPES FOREVER) (1952)
MARCIA O CREPA (SEE: COMMANDO) (1964, Bel./It./Sp./W. Ger.)
MARCO (1973) PR:A
MARCO POLO (1962, Fr./It.) PR:A
MARCO POLO JUNIOR (1973, Aus.) PR:A
MARCO THE MAGNIFICENT (1966, It./Fr./Yugo./Egypt/Afghanistan) PR:C
MARDI GRAS (1958) PR:A
MARDI GRAS MASSACRE (1978) PR:O
MARGEM, A (SEE: MARGIN, THE) (1969, Braz.)
MARGIE (1940) PR:A
MARGIE (1946) PR:AA
MARGIN, THE (1969, Braz.) PR:A
MARGIN FOR ERROR (1943) PR:A
MARIA CANDELARIA (SEE: PORTRAIT OF MARIA) (1946, Mex.)
MARIA CHAPDELAINE (SEE: NAKED HEART, THE) (1955, Brit.)
MARIA ELENA (SEE: SHE-DEVIL ISLAND) (1936, Mex.)
MARIA MARTEN (SEE: MURDER IN THE RED BARN) (1936, Brit.)
MARIA, THE WONDERFUL WEAVER (SEE: MAGIC WEAVER, THE) (1965, USSR)
MARIAGE A L'ITALIENNE (SEE: MARRIAGE, ITALIAN STYLE) (1964, Fr./It.)
MARIANNE (1929) PR:A
MARIANNE (SEE: MIRRORS) (1984)
MARIA'S LOVERS (1985) PR:O
MARIE (1985) PR:C
MARIE-ANN (1978, Can.) PR:A
MARIE ANTOINETTE (1938) PR:A
MARIE DES ILES (SEE: MARIE OF THE ISLES) (1960, Fr.)
MARIE GALANTE (1934) PR:A
MARIE OF THE ISLES (1960, Fr.) PR:A
MARIE WALEWSKA (SEE: CONQUEST) (1937)
MARIGOLD (1938, Brit.) PR:A
MARIGOLD MAN (1970) PR:C
MARIGOLDS IN AUGUST (1984, South Africa) PR:C
MARILYN (1953, Brit.) PR:O
MARINE BATTLEGROUND (1966, US/S.K.) PR:A
MARINE RAIDERS (1944) PR:A
MARINES ARE COMING, THE (1935) PR:A
MARINES ARE HERE, THE (1938) PR:A
MARINES COME THROUGH, THE (1943) PR:A
MARINES FLY HIGH, THE (1940) PR:A
MARINES, LET'S GO! (1961) PR:A
MARIUS (1931, Fr.) PR:C
MARIZINIA (1962, US/Braz.) PR:A
MARJORIE MORNINGSTAR (1958) PR:A-C
MARK, THE (1961, Brit.) PR:C
MARK IT PAID (1933) PR:A
MARK OF CAIN, THE (1948, Brit.) PR:A
MARK OF TERROR (SEE: DRUMS OF JEOPARDY) (1931)
MARK OF THE APACHE (SEE: TOMAHAWK TRAIL) (1957)
MARK OF THE AVENGER (SEE: MYSTERIOUS RIDER, THE) (1938)
MARK OF THE CLAW (SEE: DICK TRACY'S DILEMMA) (1947)
MARK OF THE DEVIL (1970, Brit./W. Ger.) PR:O
MARK OF THE DEVIL II (1975, Brit./W. Ger.) PR:O
MARK OF THE GORILLA (1950) PR:A
MARK OF THE HAWK, THE (1958) PR:A
MARK OF THE LASH (1948) PR:A
MARK OF THE PHOENIX (1958, Brit.) PR:C
MARK OF THE RENEGADE (1951) PR:A
MARK OF THE VAMPIRE (1935) PR:C
MARK OF THE VAMPIRE (SEE: VAMPIRE, THE) (1957)
MARK OF THE WHISTLER, THE (1944) PR:A
MARK OF THE WITCH (1970) PR:C
MARK OF ZORRO, THE (1940) PR:A

MARK TWAIN (SEE: ADVENTURES OF MARK TWAIN, THE) (1985)
MARKED BULLET, THE (SEE: PRAIRIE STRANGER) (1941)
MARKED FOR MURDER (1945) PR:A
MARKED GIRLS (1949, Fr.) PR:A
MARKED MAN, THE (SEE: MARK OF THE WHISTLER, THE) (1944)
MARKED MEN (1940) PR:A
MARKED ONE, THE (1963, Brit.) PR:A
MARKED TRAILS (1944) PR:A
MARKED WOMAN (1937) PR:C
MARKETA LAZAROVA (1968, Czech.) PR:O
MARKO POLO (SEE: MARCO THE MAGNIFICENT) (1966, Afghanistan/Egypt/Fr./It./Yugo.)
MARKOPOULOS PASSION, THE (SEE: ILLIAC PASSION, THE) (1968)
MARKSMAN, THE (1953) PR:C
MARLOWE (1969) PR:A
MARNIE (1964) PR:C
MAROC 7 (1967, Brit.) PR:A
MAROONED (1933, Brit.) PR:C
MAROONED (1969) PR:A
MARQUIS DE SADE: JUSTINE (SEE: JUSTINE) (1969, It./Sp.)
MARRIAGE, A (1983) PR:C
MARRIAGE BOND, THE (1932, Brit.) PR:A
MARRIAGE BY CONTRACT (1928) PR:A
MARRIAGE CAME TUMBLING DOWN, THE (1968, Fr.) PR:A
MARRIAGE FORBIDDEN (SEE: DAMAGED GOODS) (1937)
MARRIAGE-GO-ROUND, THE (1960) PR:A
MARRIAGE IN THE SHADOWS (1948, W. Ger.) PR:A
MARRIAGE IS A PRIVATE AFFAIR (1944) PR:A
MARRIAGE – ITALIAN STYLE (1964, Fr./It.) PR:O
MARRIAGE OF A YOUNG STOCKBROKER, THE (1971) PR:A
MARRIAGE OF BALZAMINOV, THE (1966, USSR) PR:A
MARRIAGE OF CONVENIENCE (SEE: HIRED WIFE) (1934)
MARRIAGE OF CONVENIENCE (1970, Brit.) PR:A
MARRIAGE OF CORBAL (SEE: PRISONER OF CORBAL) (1939, Brit.)
MARRIAGE OF FIGARO, THE (1963, Fr.) PR:A
MARRIAGE OF FIGARO, THE (1970, W. Ger.) PR:A
MARRIAGE OF MARIA BRAUN, THE (1979, W. Ger.) PR:O
MARRIAGE ON APPROVAL (1934) PR:A
MARRIAGE ON THE ROCKS (1965) PR:A-C
MARRIAGE PLAYGROUND, THE (1929) PR:A
MARRIAGE SYMPHONY (SEE: LET'S TRY AGAIN) (1934)
MARRIED AND IN LOVE (1940) PR:A
MARRIED BACHELOR (1941) PR:A
MARRIED BEFORE BREAKFAST (1937) PR:A
MARRIED BUT SINGLE (SEE: THIS THING CALLED LOVE) (1940)
MARRIED IN HASTE (SEE: CONSOLATION MARRIAGE) (1931)
MARRIED IN HASTE (SEE: MARRIAGE ON APPROVAL) (1934)
MARRIED IN HOLLYWOOD (1929) PR:A
MARRIED TO THE MOB (1988) PR:O
MARRIED TOO YOUNG (1962) PR:A
MARRIED WOMAN, THE (1964, Fr.) PR:C
MARRIED WOMAN NEEDS A HUSBAND, A (SEE: SENORA CASADA NECESSITA MARIDO) (1935)
MARRY ME (1932, Brit.) PR:A
MARRY ME! (1949, Brit.) PR:A
MARRY ME AGAIN (1953) PR:A
MARRY ME! MARRY ME! (1969, Fr.) PR:A
MARRY THE BOSS' DAUGHTER (1941) PR:A
MARRY THE GIRL (1935, Brit.) PR:A
MARRY THE GIRL (1937) PR:A
MARRYING KIND, THE (1952) PR:A
MARRYING WIDOWS (1934) PR:C
MARS INVADES PUERTO RICO (SEE: FRANKENSTEIN MEETS THE SPACE MONSTER) (1965)
MARS NEEDS WOMEN (1966) PR:A
MARSCHIER ODER KREIPER (SEE: COMMANDO) (1964, Bel./It./Sp./W. Ger.)
MARSEILLAISE (SEE: LA MARSEILLAISE) (1939, Fr.)
MARSEILLES CONTRACT, THE (SEE: DESTRUCTORS, THE) (1974, Brit.)
MARSHAL OF AMARILLO (1948) PR:A
MARSHAL OF CEDAR ROCK (1953) PR:A
MARSHAL OF CRIPPLE CREEK (1947) PR:A
MARSHAL OF GUNSMOKE (1944) PR:A
MARSHAL OF HELDORADO (1950) PR:A
MARSHAL OF LAREDO (1945) PR:A
MARSHAL OF MESA CITY, THE (1939) PR:A
MARSHAL OF RENO (1944) PR:A
MARSHAL'S DAUGHTER, THE (1953) PR:A
MARSHMALLOW MOON (SEE: AARON SLICK FROM PUNKIN CRICK) (1952)

MARSUPIALS: THE HOWLING III (SEE: HOWLING III, THE) (1987, Aus.)
MARTHA JELLNECK (1988, W. Ger.) PR:C
MARTIAN IN PARIS, A (1961, Fr.) PR:A
MARTIN (1978) PR:O
MARTIN LUTHER (1953, US/W. Ger.) PR:AA
MARTIN ROUMAGNAC (SEE: ROOM UPSTAIRS, THE) (1948, Fr.)
MARTIN'S DAY (1985, Can.) PR:C
MARTY (1955) PR:A
MARTYR, THE (1976, Israel/W. Ger.) PR:C
MARTYRS OF LOVE (1968, Czech.) PR:A
MARUSA NO ONNA (SEE: TAXING WOMAN, A) (1987, Jap.)
MARUSA NO ONNA II (SEE: TAXING WOMAN'S RETURN, A) (1988, Jap.)
MARVIN AND TIGE (1983) PR:C
MARX BROTHERS AT THE CIRCUS (SEE: AT THE CIRCUS) (1939)
MARX BROTHERS GO WEST (SEE: GO WEST) (1940)
MARY (SEE: MURDER) (1930, Brit.)
MARY BURNS, FUGITIVE (1935) PR:A
MARY HAD A LITTLE. . . (1961, Brit.) PR:C
MARY JANE'S PA (1935) PR:A
MARY LOU (1948) PR:A
MARY, MARY (1963) PR:A-C
MARY, MARY, BLOODY MARY (1975, US/Mex.) PR:O
MARY NAMES THE DAY (SEE: DR. KILDARE'S WEDDING DAY) (1941)
MARY OF SCOTLAND (1936) PR:A
MARY POPPINS (1964) PR:AA
MARY, QUEEN OF SCOTS (1971, Brit.) PR:A-C
MARY RYAN, DETECTIVE (1949) PR:A-C
MARY STEVENS, M.D. (1933) PR:A
MARYA-ISKUSNITSA (SEE: MAGIC WEAVER, THE) (1965, USSR)
MARYJANE (1968) PR:O
MARYLAND (1940) PR:A
MAS ALLA DE LAS MONTANAS (SEE: DESPERATE ONES, THE) (1968, US/Sp.)
MASCARA (1987, US/Bel./Neth./Fr.) PR:O
MASCULINE FEMININE (1966, Fr./Swed.) PR:C-O
*M*A*S*H* (1970) PR:C-O
MASK, THE (1961, US/Can.) PR:O
MASK (1985) PR:C
MASK OF DIIJON, THE (1946) PR:A-C
MASK OF DIMITRIOS, THE (1944) PR:A
MASK OF DUST (SEE: RACE FOR LIFE) (1954, Brit.)
MASK OF FU MANCHU, THE (1932) PR:C
MASK OF FURY (SEE: FIRST YANK INTO TOKYO) (1945)
MASK OF KOREA (1950, Fr.) PR:A
MASK OF THE AVENGER (1951) PR:A
MASK OF THE DRAGON (1951) PR:A
MASK OF THE HIMALAYAS (SEE: STORM OVER TIBET) (1952)
MASKED PIRATE, THE (SEE: PIRATES OF CAPRI, THE) (1949)
MASKED RAIDERS (1949) PR:A
MASKED RIDER, THE (1941) PR:A
MASKED STRANGER (SEE: DURANGO KID, THE) (1940)
MASKS (SEE: PERSONA) (1966, Swed.)
MASOCH (1980, It.) PR:O
MASON OF THE MOUNTED (1932) PR:A
MASQUE OF THE RED DEATH, THE (1964, US/Brit.) PR:C
MASQUERADE (1929) PR:A
MASQUERADE (1965, Brit.) PR:A
MASQUERADE (1988) PR:O
MASQUERADE IN MEXICO (1945) PR:A-C
MASQUERADER, THE (1933) PR:A
MASS APPEAL (1984) PR:A
MASS IS ENDED, THE (1988, It.) PR:C
MASSACRE (1934) PR:A
MASSACRE (1956) PR:A
MASSACRE AT CENTRAL HIGH (1976) PR:O
MASSACRE AT FORT HOLMAN (SEE: REASON TO LIVE, A REASON TO DIE, A) (1974, It./Fr./Sp./W. Ger.)
MASSACRE AT THE ROSEBUD (SEE: GREAT SIOUX MASSACRE, THE) (1965)
MASSACRE CANYON (1954) PR:A
MASSACRE HILL (1949, Brit.) PR:A
MASSACRE IN ROME (1973, It.) PR:C
MASSACRE RIVER (1949) PR:A
MASSIVE RETALIATION (1984) PR:O
MASTER AND MAN (1934, Brit.) PR:A
MASTER GUNFIGHTER, THE (1975) PR:C
MASTER MINDS (1949) PR:A
MASTER OF BALLANTRAE, THE (1953, US/Brit.) PR:A
MASTER OF BANKDAM (1947, Brit.) PR:A
MASTER OF HORROR (1965, Arg.) PR:C-O
MASTER OF LASSIE (SEE: HILLS OF HOME) (1948)
MASTER OF MEN (1933) PR:A
MASTER OF TERROR (SEE: 4D MAN) (1959)
MASTER OF THE ISLANDS (SEE: HAWAIIANS, THE) (1970)
MASTER OF THE WORLD (1935, Ger.) PR:A

MASTER OF THE WORLD (1961) PR:A
MASTER PLAN, THE (1955, Brit.) PR:A
MASTER RACE, THE (1944) PR:C
MASTER SPY (1964, Brit.) PR:A
MASTER SWORDSMAN (SEE: SAMURAI) (1954, Jap.)
MASTER TOUCH, THE (1974, It./W. Ger.) PR:C
MASTERBLASTER (1987) PR:C-O
MASTERMIND (1977) PR:A
MASTERS OF THE UNIVERSE (1987) PR:C-O
MASTERSON OF KANSAS (1954) PR:A
MASTERWORKS OF TERROR (SEE: MASTER OF HORROR) (1965, Arg.)
MATA HARI (1931) PR:A
MATA HARI (1965, Fr./It.) PR:C
MATA HARI (1985) PR:O
MATA HARI'S DAUGHTER (1954, Fr./It.) PR:A
MATALOS Y VUELVE (SEE: KILL THEM ALL AND COME BACK ALONE) (1970, It./Sp.)
MATCH KING, THE (1932) PR:C
MATCHLESS (1967, It.) PR:C
MATCHLESS (1974, Aus.) PR:O
MATCHMAKER, THE (1958) PR:A
MATCHMAKING OF ANNA, THE (1972, Gr.) PR:O
MATE DOMA IVA? (SEE: DO YOU KEEP A LION AT HOME?) (1966, Czech.)
MATEWAN (1987) PR:C
MATHIAS SANDORF (1963, Fr.) PR:A
MATILDA (1978) PR:A
MATINEE IDOL (1933, Brit.) PR:A
MATING GAME, THE (1959) PR:A
MATING OF MILLIE, THE (1948) PR:A
MATING OF THE SABINE WOMEN, THE (SEE: SHAME OF THE SABINE WOMEN, THE) (1962, Mex.)
MATING SEASON, THE (1951) PR:A
MATKA JOANNA OD ANIOLOW (SEE: JOAN OF THE ANGELS) (1962, Pol.)
MATRIMONIAL BED, THE (1930) PR:A
MATRIMONIO ALL'ITALIANA (SEE: MARRIAGE, ITALIAN STYLE) (1964, Fr./It.)
MATT RIKER (SEE: MUTANT HUNT) (1987)
MATTER OF CHOICE, A (1963, Brit.) PR:A
MATTER OF CONVICTION, A (SEE: YOUNG SAVAGES, THE) (1961)
MATTER OF DAYS, A (1969, Fr./Czech.) PR:O
MATTER OF INNOCENCE, A (1968, Brit.) PR:A
MATTER OF LIFE AND DEATH, A (SEE: STAIRWAY TO HEAVEN) (1946, Brit.)
MATTER OF MORALS, A (1961, US/Swed.) PR:O
MATTER OF MURDER, A (1949, Brit.) PR:A
MATTER OF RESISTANCE, A (SEE: LA VIE DE CHATEAU) (1966, Fr.)
MATTER OF TIME, A (1976, It./US) PR:A-C
MATTER OF WHO, A (1962, Brit.) PR:A
MAURICE (1987, Brit.) PR:O
MAURIE (1973) PR:A
MAUSOLEUM (1983) PR:O
MAUVAIS SANG (SEE: BAD BLOOD) (1987, Fr.)
MAVERICK, THE (1952) PR:A
MAVERICK QUEEN, THE (1956) PR:A
MAX DUGAN RETURNS (1983) PR:A
MAXIE (1985) PR:C
MAXIME (1962, Fr.) PR:A
MAXIMUM OVERDRIVE (1986) PR:O
MAXWELL ARCHER, DETECTIVE (1942, Brit.) PR:C
MAYA (1966) PR:A
MAYA (1982) PR:C
MAYBE BABY (SEE: FOR KEEPS) (1988)
MAYBE IT'S LOVE (1930) PR:A
MAYBE IT'S LOVE (1935) PR:A
MAYERLING (1936, Fr.) PR:C-O
MAYERLING (1968, Brit./Fr.) PR:C
MAYFAIR GIRL (1933, Brit.) PR:A
MAYFAIR MELODY (1937, Brit.) PR:A
MAYHEM (SEE: SCREAM, BABY, SCREAM) (1969)
MAYOR OF 44TH STREET, THE (1942) PR:A
MAYOR OF HELL, THE (1933) PR:C
MAYOR'S NEST, THE (1932, Brit.) PR:A
MAYOR'S NEST, THE (SEE: RETURN OF DANIEL BOONE, THE) (1941)
MAYTIME (1937) PR:A
MAYTIME IN MAYFAIR (1952, Brit.) PR:A
MAZE, THE (1953) PR:C
MAZEL TOV OU LE MARIAGE (SEE: MARRY ME! MARRY ME!) (1969, Fr.)
M'BLIMEY (1931, Brit.) PR:A
MC KLUSKY (SEE: WHITE LIGHTNING) (1973)
MC CABE AND MRS. MILLER (1971) PR:O
MC CONNELL STORY, THE (1955) PR:A
MC CORD (SEE: MINUTE TO PRAY, A SECOND TO DIE, A) (1968, US/It.)
MC CULLOCHS, THE (SEE: WILD MC CULLOCHS, THE) (1975)
MC FADDEN'S FLATS (1935) PR:A
MC GLUSKY THE SEA ROVER (SEE: HELL'S CARGO) (1935, Brit.)
MCGUFFIN, THE (1985, Brit.) PR:A-C
MC GUIRE, GO HOME! (1965, Brit.) PR:A
MC HALE'S NAVY (1964) PR:A

MC HALE'S NAVY JOINS THE AIR FORCE (1965) PR:A
MCKENNA OF THE MOUNTED (1932) PR:A
MC KENZIE BREAK, THE (1970, Brit.) PR:C
MC LINTOCK! (1963) PR:A
MC MASTERS, THE (1970) PR:O
MC Q (1974) PR:O
MC VICAR (1982, Brit.) PR:C
ME (1970, Fr.) PR:A
ME AND MARLBOROUGH (1935, Brit.) PR:A
ME AND MY BROTHER (1969) PR:O
ME AND MY GAL (1932) PR:A
ME AND MY PAL (1939, Brit.) PR:A
ME AND THE COLONEL (1958) PR:A
ME, NATALIE (1969) PR:C
MEACHOREI HASORAGIM (SEE: BEOND THE WALLS) (1985, Israel)
MEAL, THE (1975) PR:O
MEAN DOG BLUES (1978) PR:O
MEAN FRANK AND CRAZY TONY (1976, It.) PR:O
MEAN JOHNNY BARROWS (1976) PR:O
MEAN SEASON, THE (1985) PR:O
MEAN STREETS (1973) PR:O
MEANEST GAL IN TOWN, THE (1934) PR:A
MEANEST MAN IN THE WORLD, THE (1943) PR:A
MEANWHILE BACK AT THE RANCH (SEE: BALLAD OF JOSIE, THE) (1968)
MEANWHILE, FAR FROM THE FRONT (SEE: SECRET WAR OF HARRY FRIGG, THE) (1968)
MEAT CLEAVER MASSACRE (1977) PR:O
MEATBALLS (1979, Can.) PR:C
MEATBALLS PART II (1984) PR:C
MEATBALLS III (1987) PR:O
MECHANIC, THE (1972) PR:O
MED MORD I BAGAGET (SEE: NO TIME TO KILL) (1963, Brit./Swed./W. Ger.)
MEDAL FOR BENNY, A (1945) PR:A
MEDAL FOR THE GENERAL (SEE: GAY INTRUDERS, THE) (1949, Brit.)
MEDALS (SEE: SEVEN DAYS' LEAVE) (1930)
MEDEA (1971, It./Fr./W. Ger.) PR:O
MEDICINE MAN, THE (1930) PR:A
MEDICINE MAN, THE (1933, Brit.) PR:A
MEDICO OF PAINTED SPRINGS, THE (1941) PR:A
MEDIUM, THE (1951) PR:A
MEDIUM COOL (1969) PR:O
MEDJU JASTREBOVIMA (SEE: FRONTIER HELLCAT) (1966, Fr./It./Yugo./W. Ger.)
MEDUSA TOUCH, THE (1978, Brit./Fr.) PR:C
MEET BOSTON BLACKIE (1941) PR:A
MEET DANNY WILSON (1952) PR:A
MEET DR. CHRISTIAN (1939) PR:A
MEET JOHN DOE (1941) PR:A
MEET MAXWELL ARCHER (SEE: MAXWELL ARCHER, DETECTIVE) (1942, Brit.)
MEET ME AFTER THE SHOW (1951) PR:A
MEET ME AT DAWN (1947, Brit.) PR:A
MEET ME AT THE FAIR (1952) PR:A
MEET ME IN LAS VEGAS (1956) PR:A
MEET ME IN MOSCOW (1966, USSR) PR:A
MEET ME IN ST. LOUIS (1944) PR:AA
MEET ME ON BROADWAY (1946) PR:A
MEET ME TONIGHT (SEE: TONIGHT AT 8:30) (1953, Brit.)
MEET MISS BOBBY SOCKS (1944) PR:A
MEET MISS MARPLE (SEE: MURDER SHE SAID) (1961, Brit.)
MEET MR. CALLAGHAN (1954, Brit.) PR:A
MEET MR. LUCIFER (1953, Brit.) PR:A
MEET MR. MALCOLM (1954, Brit.) PR:A
MEET MR. PENNY (1938, Brit.) PR:A
MEET MY SISTER (1933, Brit.) PR:A
MEET NERO WOLFE (1936) PR:A
MEET SEXTON BLAKE (1944, Brit.) PR:A
MEET SIMON CHERRY (1949, Brit.) PR:A
MEET THE BARON (1933) PR:A
MEET THE BOY FRIEND (1937) PR:A
MEET THE CHUMP (1941) PR:A
MEET THE DUKE (1949, Brit.) PR:A
MEET THE GIRLS (1938) PR:A
MEET THE HOLLOWHEADS (1989) PR:O
MEET THE MAYOR (1938) PR:A
MEET THE MISSUS (1937) PR:A
MEET THE MISSUS (1940) PR:A
MEET THE MOB (1942) PR:A
MEET THE NAVY (1946, Brit.) PR:A
MEET THE NELSONS (SEE: HERE COME THE NELSONS) (1952)
MEET THE PEOPLE (1944) PR:A
MEET THE STEWARTS (1942) PR:A
MEET THE WIFE (1931) PR:A
MEET THE WILDCAT (1940) PR:A
MEET WHIPLASH WILLIE (SEE: FORTUNE COOKIE, THE) (1966)
MEETING AT MIDNIGHT (SEE: CHARLIE CHAN IN BLACK MAGIC) (1944)
MEETINGS WITH REMARKABLE MEN (1979, Brit.) PR:A
MEGAFORCE (1982) PR:C

MEGLIO VEDOVA (SEE: BETTER A WIDOW) (1969, Fr./It.)
MEIER (1987, W. Ger.) PR:O
MEIN KAMPF— MY CRIMES (1940, Brit.) PR:C
MELANIE (1982, Can.) PR:A
MELBA (1953, Brit.) PR:A
MELINDA (1972) PR:O
MELO (1988, Fr.) PR:A
MELODIE EN SOUS-SOL (SEE: ANY NUMBER CAN WIN) (1963, Fr.)
MELODY (1971, Brit.) PR:AA
MELODY AND MOONLIGHT (1940) PR:A
MELODY AND ROMANCE (1937, Brit.) PR:A
MELODY CLUB (1949, Brit.) PR:A
MELODY CRUISE (1933) PR:A
MELODY FOR THREE (1941) PR:A
MELODY FOR TWO (1937) PR:A
MELODY GIRL (SEE: SING, DANCE, PLENTY HOT) (1940)
MELODY IN GRAY (SEE: BANISHED) (1978, Jap.)
MELODY IN SPRING (1934) PR:A
MELODY IN THE DARK (1948, Brit.) PR:A
MELODY INN (SEE: RIDING HIGH) (1943)
MELODY LANE (1929) PR:A
MELODY LANE (1941) PR:A
MELODY LINGERS ON, THE (1935) PR:A
MELODY MAKER, THE (1933, Brit.) PR:A
MELODY MAKER (SEE: DING DONG WILLIAMS) (1946)
MELODY MAN (1930) PR:A
MELODY OF LIFE (SEE: SYMPHONY OF SIX MILLION) (1932)
MELODY OF LOVE (1928) PR:A
MELODY OF LOVE (1954, It.) PR:A
MELODY OF MY HEART (1936, Brit.) PR:A
MELODY OF THE PLAINS (1937) PR:A
MELODY OF YOUTH (SEE: THEY SHALL HAVE MUSIC) (1939)
MELODY PARADE (1943) PR:A
MELODY RANCH (1940) PR:A
MELODY TIME (1948) PR:AA
MELODY TRAIL (1935) PR:AA
MELTING POT, THE (SEE: BETTY CO-ED) (1946)
MELVIN AND HOWARD (1980) PR:O
MELVIN, SON OF ALVIN (1984, Aus.) PR:O
MEMBER OF THE JURY (1937, Brit.) PR:A
MEMBER OF THE WEDDING, THE (1952) PR:A
MEMED MY HAWK (1984, Brit.) PR:C
MEMENTO MEI (1963) PR:C
MEMOIRS (1984, Can.) PR:O
MEMOIRS OF A SURVIVOR (1981, Brit.) PR:C
MEMOIRS OF PRISON (1984, Braz.) PR:O
MEMORIAS DO CARCERE (SEE: MEMOIRS OF PRISON) (1984, Braz.)
MEMORIES OF ME (1988) PR:C
MEMORY EXPERT, THE (SEE: MAN ON THE FLYING TRAPEZE, THE) (1935)
MEMORY FOR TWO (SEE: I LOVE A BANDLEADER) (1945)
MEMORY OF US (1974) PR:A
MEN, THE (1950) PR:C
MEN (1985, W. Ger.) PR:O
MEN AGAINST THE SKY (1940) PR:A
MEN AGAINST THE SUN (1953, Brit.) PR:A
MEN ARE CHILDREN TWICE (1953, Brit.) PR:A
MEN ARE LIKE THAT (1930) PR:A
MEN ARE LIKE THAT (1931) PR:A
MEN ARE NOT GODS (1937, Brit.) PR:A-C
MEN ARE SUCH FOOLS (1933) PR:A
MEN ARE SUCH FOOLS (1938) PR:A
MEN BEHIND BARS (SEE: DUFFY OF SAN QUENTIN) (1954)
MEN CALL IT LOVE (1931) PR:C
MEN IN EXILE (1937) PR:A
MEN IN HER DIARY (1945) PR:A
MEN IN HER LIFE (1931) PR:A
MEN IN HER LIFE, THE (1941) PR:A
MEN IN WAR (1957) PR:A-C
MEN IN WHITE (1934) PR:A
MEN LIKE THESE (SEE: TRAPPED IN A SUBMARINE) (1931, Brit.)
MEN MUST FIGHT (1933) PR:A
MEN OF AMERICA (1933) PR:A
MEN OF BOYS TOWN (1941) PR:AA
MEN OF CHANCE (1932) PR:A
MEN OF DESTINY (SEE: MEN OF TEXAS) (1942)
MEN OF IRELAND (1938, Ireland) PR:A
MEN OF SAN QUENTIN (1942) PR:A
MEN OF SHERWOOD FOREST (1957, Brit.) PR:A
MEN OF STEEL (1932, Brit.) PR:A
MEN OF STEEL (SEE: BILL CRACKS DOWN) (1937)
MEN OF STEEL (SEE: STEEL) (1980)
MEN OF TEXAS (1942) PR:A
MEN OF THE DEEP (SEE: ROUGH, TOUGH, AND READY) (1945)
MEN OF THE FIGHTING LADY (1954) PR:A
MEN OF THE HOUR (1935) PR:A
MEN OF THE NIGHT (1934) PR:A

MEN OF THE NORTH (1930) PR:A
MEN OF THE PLAINS (1936) PR:A
MEN OF THE SEA (1938, USSR) PR:A
MEN OF THE SEA (1951, Brit.) PR:A
MEN OF THE SKY (1931) PR:A
MEN OF THE TENTH (SEE: RED, WHITE, AND BLACK, THE) (1970)
MEN OF THE TIMBERLAND (1941) PR:A
MEN OF TOMORROW (1935, Brit.) PR:A
MEN OF TWO WORLDS (SEE: KISENGA, MAN OF AFRICA) (1952, Brit.)
MEN OF YESTERDAY (1936, Brit.) PR:A
MEN ON CALL (1931) PR:A
MEN ON HER MIND (SEE: GIRL FROM TENTH AVENUE, THE) (1935)
MEN ON HER MIND (1944) PR:A
MEN PREFER FAT GIRLS (1981, Fr.) PR:C
MEN WITH WINGS (1938) PR:A
MEN WITHOUT HONOUR (1939, Brit.) PR:A
MEN WITHOUT LAW (1930) PR:A
MEN WITHOUT NAMES (1935) PR:A
MEN WITHOUT SOULS (1940) PR:A
MEN WITHOUT WOMEN (1930) PR:A
MEN WOMEN LOVE (SEE: SALVATION NELL) (1931)
MENACE, THE (1932) PR:A-C
MENACE (1934) PR:A
MENACE (SEE: WHEN LONDON SLEEPS) (1934, Brit.)
MENACE IN THE NIGHT (1958, Brit.) PR:A
MENNESKER MODES OG SOD MUSIK OPSTAR I HJERTET (SEE: PEOPLE MEET AND SWEET MUSIC FILLS THE HEART) (1964, Den./Swed.)
MEN'S CLUB, THE (1986) PR:C-O
MENS SAGFOR EREN SOVER (SEE: WHILE THE ATTORNEY IS ASLEEP) (1945, Den.)
MENSCHEN IM NETZ (SEE: UNWILLING AGENT) (1968, W. Ger.)
MEPHISTO (1981, Hung./W. Ger.) PR:O
MEPHISTO WALTZ, THE (1971) PR:C-O
MERCENARIES, THE (SEE: DARK OF THE SUN) (1968, Brit.)
MERCENARY, THE (1970, It./Sp.) PR:C
MERCENARY FIGHTERS (1988) PR:O
MERCHANT OF SLAVES (1949, It.) PR:C
MERCY ISLAND (1941) PR:A
MERCY PLANE (1940) PR:A
MERELY MARY ANN (1931) PR:A
MERELY MR. HAWKINS (1938, Brit.) PR:A
MERMAID, THE (1966, Hong Kong) PR:A
MERMAIDS OF TIBURON, THE (1962) PR:A-C
MERRILL'S MARAUDERS (1962) PR:C-O
MERRILY WE GO TO. . . (SEE: MERRILY WE GO TO HELL) (1932)
MERRILY WE GO TO HELL (1932) PR:A-C
MERRILY WE LIVE (1938) PR:A
MERRY ANDREW (1958) PR:AA
MERRY CHRISTMAS, MR. LAWRENCE (1983, Jap./Brit.) PR:O
MERRY COMES TO STAY (1937, Brit.) PR:A
MERRY COMES TO TOWN (SEE: MERRY COMES TO STAY) (1937, Brit.)
MERRY FRINKS, THE (1934) PR:A
MERRY-GO-ROUND (1948, Brit.) PR:A
MERRY-GO-ROUND OF 1938 (1937) PR:A
MERRY MONAHANS, THE (1944) PR:A
MERRY WIDOW, THE (1934) PR:A-C
MERRY WIDOW, THE (1952) PR:A
MERRY WIVES, THE (1940, Czech.) PR:C
MERRY WIVES OF RENO, THE (1934) PR:A
MERRY WIVES OF TOBIAS ROUKE, THE (1972, Can.) PR:A
MERRY WIVES OF WINDSOR, THE (1952, W. Ger.) PR:A
MERRY WIVES OF WINDSOR, THE (1966, Aust.) PR:A
MERTON OF THE MOVIES (1947) PR:A
MES FEMMES AMERICAINES (SEE: RUN FOR YOUR WIFE) (1966, Fr./It.)
MESA OF LOST WOMEN, THE (1956) PR:A
MESDAMES ET MESSIEURS (SEE: BIRDS, THE BEES, AND THE ITALIANS, THE) (1967, Fr./It.)
MESHTE NASTRESHU (SEE: DREAM COME TRUE, A) (1963, USSR)
MESQUITE BUCKAROO (1939) PR:A
MESSAGE, THE (SEE: MOHAMMAD, MESSENGER OF GOD) (1977)
MESSAGE FROM SPACE (1978, Jap.) PR:A
MESSAGE TO GARCIA, A (1936) PR:A
MESSALINE (1952, Fr./It.) PR:A
MESSENGER OF DEATH (1988) PR:C
MESSENGER OF PEACE (1950) PR:A
MESSIAH OF EVIL (SEE: DEAD PEOPLE) (1974)
METALSTORM: THE DESTRUCTION OF JARED-SYN (1983) PR:C
METAMORPHOSES (1978) PR:A
METEMPSYCO (SEE: TOMB OF TORTURE) (1966, It.)
METEOR (1979) PR:C
METEOR MONSTER (SEE: TEENAGE MONSTER) (1957)
METROPOLITAN (1935) PR:A

MEURTRE EN 45 TOURS (SEE: MURDER AT 45 RPM) (1965, Fr.)
MEXICALI KID, THE (1938) PR:A
MEXICALI ROSE (1929) PR:A
MEXICALI ROSE (1939) PR:A
MEXICAN, THE (SEE: HURRICANE HORSEMAN) (1931)
MEXICAN BUS RIDE (1951, Mex.) PR:A-C
MEXICAN HAYRIDE (1948) PR:A
MEXICAN MANHUNT (1953) PR:A
MEXICAN SPITFIRE (1939) PR:A
MEXICAN SPITFIRE AT SEA (1942) PR:A
MEXICAN SPITFIRE OUT WEST (1940) PR:A
MEXICAN SPITFIRE SEES A GHOST (1942) PR:A
MEXICAN SPITFIRE'S BABY (1941) PR:A
MEXICAN SPITFIRE'S BLESSED EVENT (1943) PR:A
MEXICAN SPITFIRE'S ELEPHANT (1942) PR:A
MEXICANA (1945) PR:A
MEXICO IN FLAMES (1982, USSR/Mex./It.) PR:O
MI MUJER ES DOCTOR (SEE: LADY DOCTOR, THE) (1963, Fr./It./Sp.)
MIAMI EXPOSE (1956) PR:A
MIAMI RENDEZVOUS (SEE: PASSION HOLIDAY) (1963)
MIAMI STORY, THE (1954) PR:A
MICHAEL AND MARY (1932, Brit.) PR:A
MICHAEL O'HALLORAN (1937) PR:A
MICHAEL O'HALLORAN (1948) PR:A
MICHAEL SHAYNE, PRIVATE DETECTIVE (1940) PR:A
MICHAEL STROGOFF (SEE: SOLDIER AND THE LADY, THE) (1937)
MICHAEL STROGOFF (1960, Fr./It./Yugo.) PR:A
MICHELLE (1970, Fr.) PR:C
MICHIGAN KID, THE (1947) PR:A
MICKEY (1948) PR:A
MICKEY ONE (1965) PR:C-O
MICKEY, THE KID (1939) PR:A
MICKI & MAUDE (1984) PR:C
MICROSCOPIA (SEE: FANTASTIC VOYAGE) (1966)
MICROWAVE MASSACRE (1983) PR:O
MID-DAY MISTRESS (1968) PR:O
MIDAREGUMO (SEE: TWO IN THE SHADOW) (1968, Jap.)
MIDARERU (SEE: YEARNING) (1964, Jap.)
MIDAS RUN (1969) PR:C
MIDAS TOUCH, THE (1940, Brit.) PR:A
MIDDLE AGE CRAZY (1980, Can.) PR:O
MIDDLE AGE SPREAD (1979, New Zealand) PR:O
MIDDLE COURSE, THE (1961, Brit.) PR:A
MIDDLE OF NOWHERE (SEE: WEBSTER BOY, THE) (1962, Brit.)
MIDDLE OF THE NIGHT (1959) PR:A-C
MIDDLE WATCH, THE (1930, Brit.) PR:A
MIDDLE WATCH, THE (1939, Brit.) PR:A
MIDDLETON FAMILY AT THE N.Y. WORLD'S FAIR (1939) PR:A
MIDNIGHT (1934) PR:A
MIDNIGHT (1939) PR:A
MIDNIGHT (1983) PR:O
MIDNIGHT ALIBI (1934) PR:A
MIDNIGHT ANGEL (1941) PR:A
MIDNIGHT AT MADAME TUSSAUD'S (SEE: MIDNIGHT AT THE WAX MUSEUM) (1936, Brit.)
MIDNIGHT AT THE WAX MUSEUM (1936, Brit.) PR:A
MIDNIGHT AUTO SUPPLY (SEE: LOVE AND MIDNIGHT AUTO SUPPLY) (1978)
MIDNIGHT CLUB (1933) PR:A
MIDNIGHT COP (1989, W. Ger.) PR:O
MIDNIGHT COURT (1937) PR:A
MIDNIGHT COWBOY (1969) PR:O
MIDNIGHT CROSSING (1988) PR:O
MIDNIGHT DADDIES (1929) PR:A
MIDNIGHT EPISODE (1951, Brit.) PR:A
MIDNIGHT EXPRESS (1978, Brit.) PR:O
MIDNIGHT FOLLY (1962, Fr.) PR:C
MIDNIGHT INTRUDER (1938) PR:A
MIDNIGHT LACE (1960) PR:C
MIDNIGHT LADY (1932) PR:A
MIDNIGHT LIMITED (1940) PR:A
MIDNIGHT MADNESS (1980) PR:C
MIDNIGHT MADONNA (1937) PR:A
MIDNIGHT MAN, THE (1974) PR:O
MIDNIGHT MARY (1933) PR:A-C
MIDNIGHT MEETING (1962, Fr.) PR:A
MIDNIGHT MELODY (SEE: MURDER IN THE MUSIC HALL) (1946)
MIDNIGHT MENACE (SEE: BOMBS OVER LONDON) (1937, Brit.)
MIDNIGHT MORALS (1932) PR:A
MIDNIGHT MYSTERY (1930) PR:A
MIDNIGHT PATROL, THE (1932) PR:A
MIDNIGHT PLEASURES (1975, It.) PR:O
MIDNIGHT RAIDERS (SEE: OKLAHOMA RAIDERS) (1944)
MIDNIGHT RUN (1988) PR:O
MIDNIGHT SPECIAL (1931) PR:A
MIDNIGHT STORY, THE (1957) PR:A
MIDNIGHT TAXI, THE (1928) PR:A

MIDNIGHT TAXI (1937) PR:A
MIDNIGHT WARNING, THE (1932) PR:A
MIDSHIPMAID GOB (1932, Brit.) PR:A
MIDSHIPMAN, THE (SEE: MIDSHIPMAN GOB) (1932, Brit.)
MIDSHIPMAN EASY (SEE: MEN OF THE SEA) (1951, Brit.)
MIDSHIPMAN JACK (1933) PR:A
MIDSTREAM (1929) PR:A
MIDSUMMER NIGHT'S DREAM, A (1935) PR:A
MIDSUMMER NIGHT'S DREAM, A (1961, Czech.) PR:AA
MIDSUMMER NIGHT'S DREAM, A (1966) PR:A
MIDSUMMER NIGHT'S DREAM, A (1969, Brit.) PR:A
MIDSUMMER NIGHT'S DREAM, A (1984, Brit./Sp.) PR:O
MIDSUMMER NIGHT'S SEX COMEDY, A (1982) PR:C-O
MIDWAY (1976) PR:A
MIDWIFE, THE (1961, Gr.) PR:A
MIGHT MAKES RIGHT (SEE: FOX AND HIS FRIENDS) (1975, W. Ger.)
MIGHTY, THE (1929) PR:A
MIGHTY BARNUM, THE (1934) PR:A
MIGHTY CRUSADERS, THE (1961, It.) PR:A
MIGHTY GORGA, THE (1969) PR:A
MIGHTY JOE YOUNG (1949) PR:A
MIGHTY JUNGLE, THE (1965, US/Mex.) PR:A
MIGHTY MCGURK, THE (1946) PR:A
MIGHTY MOUSE IN THE GREAT SPACE CHASE (1983) PR:AA
MIGHTY PEKING MAN, THE (SEE: GOLIATHAN) (1979, Hong Kong)
MIGHTY QUINN, THE (1989) PR:C-O
MIGHTY TREVE, THE (1937) PR:AA
MIGHTY TUNDRA, THE (SEE: TUNDRA) (1936)
MIGHTY URSUS (1962, It./Sp.) PR:A
MIGHTY WARRIOR, THE (SEE: TROJAN HORSE, THE) (1962, Fr./It.)
MIKADO, THE (1939, Brit.) PR:AA
MIKADO, THE (1967, Brit.) PR:AA
MIKAN NO TAIKYOKU (SEE: GO MASTERS, THE) (1985, Chi./Jap.)
MIKE'S MURDER (1984) PR:O
MIKEY AND NICKY (1976) PR:C-O
MIL GRITOS TIENE LA NOCHE (SEE: PIECES) (1983, Puerto Rico/Sp.)
MILAGRO BEANFIELD WAR, THE (1988) PR:C
MILCZACA GWIAZDA (SEE: FIRST SPACESHIP ON VENUS) (1962, E. Ger./Pol.)
MILDRED PIERCE (1945) PR:A
MILE A MINUTE (SEE: RIDERS OF THE SANTA FE) (1944)
MILE A MINUTE LOVE (1937) PR:A
MILES FROM HOME (1988) PR:C
MILESTONES (1975) PR:C
MILITARY ACADEMY (1940) PR:A
MILITARY ACADEMY WITH THAT TENTH AVENUE GANG (1950) PR:A
MILITARY POLICEMAN (SEE: OFF LIMITS) (1952)
MILITARY SECRET (1945, USSR) PR:A
MILKMAN, THE (1950) PR:A
MILKY WAY, THE (1936) PR:AA
MILKY WAY, THE (1969, Fr./It.) PR:C
MILL OF THE STONE WOMEN (1963, Fr./It.) PR:O
MILL ON THE FLOSS, THE (1939, Brit.) PR:A
MILLENNIUM (1989) PR:A
MILLER'S WIFE, THE (1955, It.) PR:O
MILLERSON CASE, THE (1947) PR:A
MILLIE (1931) PR:A
MILLIE'S DAUGHTER (1947) PR:A
MILLION, THE (1931, Fr.) PR:A
MILLION DOLLAR BABY (1935) PR:A
MILLION DOLLAR BABY (1941) PR:A
MILLION DOLLAR COLLAR, THE (1929) PR:A
MILLION DOLLAR KID (1944) PR:A
MILLION DOLLAR LEGS (1932) PR:A
MILLION DOLLAR LEGS (1939) PR:A
MILLION DOLLAR MANHUNT (1956, Brit.) PR:A
MILLION DOLLAR MERMAID (1952) PR:A
MILLION DOLLAR MYSTERY (1987) PR:A-C
MILLION DOLLAR PURSUIT (1951) PR:A
MILLION DOLLAR RANSOM (1934) PR:A
MILLION DOLLAR WEEKEND (1948) PR:A
MILLION EYES OF SU-MURU, THE (1967, Brit.) PR:A
MILLION POUND NOTE (SEE: MAN WITH A MILLION) (1954, Brit.)
MILLION TO ONE, A (1938) PR:A
MILLIONAIRE, THE (1931) PR:A
MILLIONAIRE FOR A DAY (SEE: LET'S BE RITZY) (1934)
MILLIONAIRE FOR CHRISTY, A (1951) PR:A
MILLIONAIRE KID (1936) PR:A
MILLIONAIRE MERRY-GO-ROUND (SEE: PLAYBOY, THE) (1942, Brit.)
MILLIONAIRE MERRY-GO-ROUND (SEE: PLAYBOY, THE) (1942, Brit.)
MILLIONAIRE PLAYBOY (SEE: PARK AVENUE LOGGER) (1937)

MILLIONAIRE PLAYBOY (1940) PR:A
MILLIONAIRES IN PRISON (1940) PR:A
MILLIONAIRESS, THE (1960, Brit.) PR:A
MILLIONS (1936, Brit.) PR:A
MILLIONS IN THE AIR (1935) PR:A
MILLIONS LIKE US (1943, Brit.) PR:A
MILLONAIRES D'UN JOUR (SEE: SIMPLE CASE OF MONEY, A) (1952, Fr.)
MILLS OF THE GODS (1935) PR:A
MILOSC DWUDZIESTOLATKOW (SEE: LOVE AT TWENTY) (1963, Fr./It./Jap./Pol./W. Ger.)
MILWR BYCHAN (SEE: BOY SOLDIER) (1987, Wales)
MIMI (1935, Brit.) PR:A
MIMI METALLURGICO FERITO NELL'ONORE (SEE: SEDUCTION OF MIMI, THE) (1972, It.)
MIN AND BILL (1930) PR:A
MIN VAN BALTHAZAR (SEE: AU HASARD, BALTHAZAR) (1970, Fr.)
MINAMI NO SHIMA NI YUKI GA FURA (SEE: SNOW IN THE SOUTH SEAS) (1963, Jap.)
MIND BENDERS, THE (1963, Brit.) PR:C-O
MIND OF MR. REEDER, THE (SEE: MYSTERIOUS MR. REEDER, THE) (1940, Brit.)
MIND OF MR. SOAMES, THE (1970, Brit.) PR:A
MIND READER, THE (1933) PR:A
MIND SNATCHERS, THE (SEE: HAPPINESS CAGE, THE) (1972)
MIND YOUR OWN BUSINESS (1937) PR:A
MINDWARP: AN INFINITY OF TERROR (SEE: GALAXY OF TERROR) (1981)
MINE OWN EXECUTIONER (1948, Brit.) PR:C-O
MINE WITH THE IRON DOOR, THE (1936) PR:A
MINESWEEPER (1943) PR:A
MINI-AFFAIR, THE (1968, Brit.) PR:A
MINI-SKIRT MOB, THE (1968) PR:O
MINI WEEKEND (SEE: TOMCAT, THE) (1968, Brit.)
MINISTRY OF FEAR (1945) PR:C
MINISTRY OF VENGEANCE (1989) PR:C
MINIVER STORY, THE (1950, Brit./US) PR:A
MINNESOTA CLAY (1966, It./Fr./Sp.) PR:C
MINNIE AND MOSKOWITZ (1971) PR:C
MINOTAUR, THE (1961, It.) PR:A
MINOTAUR (SEE: LAND OF THE MINOTAUR) (1976, Gr.)
MINOTAUR, WILD BEAST OF CRETE (SEE: MINOTAUR, THE) (1961, It.)
MINSTREL BOY, THE (1937, Brit.) PR:A
MINSTREL MAN (1944) PR:A
MINUTE TO PRAY, A SECOND TO DIE, A (1968, US/It.) PR:C
MINX, THE (1969) PR:O
MIO FIGILIO NERONE (SEE: NERO'S MISTRESS) (1962, Fr./It.)
MIO NOME E PECOS (SEE: MY NAME IS PECOS) (1966, It.)
MIR VKHODYASHCHEMU (SEE: PEACE TO HIM WHO ENTERS) (1963, USSR)
MIRACLE, THE (SEE: WAYS OF LOVE) (1950, It.)
MIRACLE, THE (1959) PR:A
MIRACLE CAN HAPPEN, A (SEE: ON OUR MERRY WAY) (1948)
MIRACLE IN HARLEM (1948) PR:A
MIRACLE IN MILAN (1951, It.) PR:A
MIRACLE IN SOHO (1957, Brit.) PR:A
MIRACLE IN THE RAIN (1956) PR:A
MIRACLE IN THE SAND (SEE: THREE GODFATHERS) (1936)
MIRACLE KID, THE (1942) PR:A
MIRACLE MAN, THE (1932) PR:A
MIRACLE MILE (1989) PR:C-O
MIRACLE OF FATIMA (SEE: MIRACLE OF OUR LADY OF FATIMA, THE) (1952)
MIRACLE OF LIFE (SEE: OUR DAILY BREAD) (1934)
MIRACLE OF MORGAN'S CREEK, THE (1944) PR:C
MIRACLE OF OUR LADY OF FATIMA, THE (1952) PR:A
MIRACLE OF SAN SEBASTIAN (SEE: GUNS FOR SAN SEBASTIAN) (1968, US/Fr./It./Mex.)
MIRACLE OF THE BELLS, THE (1948) PR:A
MIRACLE OF THE HILLS, THE (1959) PR:A
MIRACLE OF THE WHITE STALLIONS (1963) PR:AA
MIRACLE ON MAIN STREET, A (1940) PR:A
MIRACLE ON 34TH STREET (1947) PR:AA
MIRACLE WOMAN, THE (1931) PR:A-C
MIRACLE WORKER, THE (1962) PR:A
MIRACLES (1987) PR:C
MIRACLES DO HAPPEN (1938, Brit.) PR:A
MIRACLES FOR SALE (1939) PR:A
MIRACOLO A MILANO (SEE: MIRACLE IN MILAN) (1951, It.)
MIRACULOUS JOURNEY (1948) PR:A
MIRAGE (1965) PR:A-C
MIRAGE (1972, Peru) PR:C
MIRANDA (1949, Brit.) PR:A
MIRIAM (SEE: TRUMAN CAPOTE'S TRILOGY) (1969)
MIRROR CRACK'D, THE (1980, Brit.) PR:A-C
MIRROR HAS TWO FACES, THE (1959, Fr.) PR:A
MIRRORS (1984) PR:O

MIRTH AND MELODY (SEE: LET'S GO PLACES) (1930)
MISADVENTURES OF MERLIN JONES, THE (1964) PR:A
MISBEHAVING HUSBANDS (1941) PR:A
MISBEHAVING LADIES (1931) PR:A
MISCHIEF (1931, Brit.) PR:A
MISCHIEF (1969, Brit.) PR:A
MISCHIEF (1985) PR:O
MISFIT BRIGADE, THE (1988) PR:O
MISFITS, THE (1961) PR:C
MISHIMA (1985) PR:O
MISHPACHAT SIMCHON (SEE: SIMCHON FAMILY, THE) (1969, Israel)
MISLEADING LADY, THE (1932) PR:A
MISS ANNIE ROONEY (1942) PR:A
MISS FANE'S BABY IS STOLEN (1934) PR:A
MISS FIRECRACKER (1989) PR:C
MISS FIX-IT (SEE: KEEP SMILING) (1938)
MISS GRANT TAKES RICHMOND (1949) PR:A
MISS JESSICA IS PREGNANT (1970) PR:O
MISS JUDE (SEE: TRUTH ABOUT SPRING, THE) (1965, Brit.)
MISS LONDON LTD. (1943, Brit.) PR:A
MISS MARY (1986, Arg.) PR:O
MISS MINK OF 1949 (1949) PR:A
MISS MONA (1987, Fr.) PR:O
MISS MUERTE (SEE: DIABOLICAL DR. Z, THE) (1967, Fr./Sp.)
MISS PACIFIC FLEET (1935) PR:A
MISS PILGRIM'S PROGRESS (1950, Brit.) PR:A
MISS PINKERTON (1932) PR:A
MISS PRESIDENT (1935, Hung.) PR:A
MISS ROBIN CRUSOE (1954) PR:A
MISS ROBIN HOOD (1952, Brit.) PR:A
MISS SADIE THOMPSON (1953) PR:O
MISS SUSIE SLAGLE'S (1945) PR:A
MISS TATLOCK'S MILLIONS (1948) PR:A
MISS TULIP STAYS THE NIGHT (1955, Brit.) PR:A
MISS V FROM MOSCOW (1942) PR:A
MISSILE BASE AT TANIAK (1953) PR:A
MISSILE FROM HELL (1958, Brit.) PR:A
MISSILE TO THE MOON (1959) PR:A
MISSING (1982) PR:A-C
MISSING, BELIEVED MARRIED (1937, Brit.) PR:A
MISSING CORPSE, THE (1945) PR:A
MISSING DAUGHTERS (1939) PR:A
MISSING EVIDENCE (1939) PR:A
MISSING GIRLS (1936) PR:A
MISSING GUEST, THE (1938) PR:A
MISSING IN ACTION (1984) PR:O
MISSING IN ACTION 2—THE BEGINNING (1985) PR:O
MISSING JUROR, THE (1944) PR:A
MISSING LADY, THE (1946) PR:A
MISSING MILLION, THE (1942, Brit.) PR:A
MISSING NOTE, THE (1961, Brit.) PR:AA
MISSING PEOPLE, THE (1940, Brit.) PR:A
MISSING PERSONS (SEE: BUREAU OF MISSING PERSONS) (1933)
MISSING REMBRANDT, THE (1932, Brit.) PR:A
MISSING TEN DAYS (1941, Brit.) PR:A
MISSING WITNESS (SEE: LOVE'S OLD SWEET SONG) (1933, Brit.)
MISSING WITNESSES (1937) PR:A
MISSING WOMEN (1951) PR:A
MISSION, THE (1984, Brit.) PR:O
MISSION, THE (1986, Brit.) PR:C
MISSION BATANGAS (1968) PR:A
MISSION BLOODY MARY (1967, Fr./It./Sp.) PR:A
MISSION GALACTICA: THE CYLON ATTACK (1979) PR:A
MISSION KILL (1987) PR:C-O
MISSION MARS (1968) PR:A
MISSION OVER KOREA (1953) PR:A
MISSION STARDUST (1968, It./Sp./W. Ger.) PR:A
MISSION TO HELL (SEE: SAVAGE!) (1962)
MISSION TO HONG KONG (SEE: RED-DRAGON) (1967, US/It./W. Ger.)
MISSION TO MOSCOW (1943) PR:A
MISSIONARY, THE (1982, Brit.) PR:O
MISSISSIPPI (SEE: HEAVEN ON EARTH) (1931)
MISSISSIPPI (1935) PR:A
MISSISSIPPI BURNING (1988) PR:O
MISSISSIPPI GAMBLER, THE (1929) PR:A
MISSISSIPPI GAMBLER (1942) PR:A
MISSISSIPPI GAMBLER, THE (1953) PR:C
MISSISSIPPI MERMAID (1969, Fr./It.) PR:A
MISSISSIPPI RHYTHM (1949) PR:A
MISSISSIPPI SUMMER (1971) PR:C
MISSOURI BREAKS, THE (1976) PR:C-O
MISSOURI OUTLAW, A (1942) PR:A
MISSOURI TRAVELER, THE (1958) PR:A
MISSOURIANS, THE (1950) PR:A
MR. ACE (1946) PR:A
MR. AND MRS. NORTH (1941) PR:A
MR. AND MRS. SMITH (1941) PR:A
MISTER ANTONIO (1929) PR:A
MR. ARKADIN (1955, Brit./Fr./Sp.) PR:C

MR. ASHTON WAS INDISCREET (SEE: SENATOR WAS INDISCREET, THE) (1947)
MR. BELVEDERE RINGS THE BELL (1951) PR:A
MR. BELVEDERE GOES TO COLLEGE (1949) PR:A
MISTER BIG (1943) PR:A
MR. BILL THE CONQUEROR (SEE: MAN WHO WON, THE) (1933, Brit.)
MR. BILLION (1977) PR:A
MR. BLANDINGS BUILDS HIS DREAM HOUSE (1948) PR:A
MR. BOGGS STEPS OUT (1938) PR:A
MISTER BROWN (1972) PR:C
MR. BROWN COMES DOWN THE HILL (1966, Brit.) PR:A
MISTER BUDDWING (1966) PR:C
MR. BUG GOES TO TOWN (1941) PR:AA
MR. CELEBRITY (1942) PR:A
MR. CHEDWORTH STEPS OUT (1939, Aus.) PR:A
MR. CHUMP (1938) PR:A
MISTER CINDERELLA (1936) PR:A
MISTER CINDERS (1934, Brit.) PR:A
MR. COHEN TAKES A WALK (1936, Brit.) PR:A
MISTER CORY (1957) PR:A
MR. DEEDS GOES TO TOWN (1936) PR:A
MR. DENNING DRIVES NORTH (1953, Brit.) PR:A
MR. DISTRICT ATTORNEY (1941) PR:A
MR. DISTRICT ATTORNEY (1946) PR:A
MR. DISTRICT ATTORNEY IN THE CARTER CASE (SEE: CARTER CASE, THE) (1947)
MR. DODD TAKES THE AIR (1937) PR:A
MR. DOODLE KICKS OFF (1938) PR:A
MR. DRAKE'S DUCK (1951, Brit.) PR:A
MR. DREW (SEE: FOR THEM THAT TRESPASS) (1949, Brit.)
MR. DYNAMITE (1935) PR:A
MR. DYNAMITE (1941) PR:A
MISTER 880 (1950) PR:AA
MR. EMMANUEL (1945, Brit.) PR:A
MR. FAINTHEART (SEE: $10 RAISE) (1935)
MR. FORBUSH AND THE PENGUINS (SEE: CRY OF THE PENGUINS) (1971, Brit.)
MR. FOX OF VENICE (SEE: HONEY POT, THE) (1967, Brit.)
MISTER FREEDOM (1970, Fr.) PR:A
MR. GRIGGS RETURNS (SEE: COCKEYED MIRACLE, THE) (1946)
MR. H.C. ANDERSEN (1950, Brit.) PR:A
MR. HEX (1946) PR:A
MR. HOBBS TAKES A VACATION (1962) PR:AA
MISTER HOBO (1936, Brit.) PR:A
MR. HOT SHOT (SEE: FLAMINGO KID, THE) (1984)
MR. HULOT'S HOLIDAY (1953, Fr.) PR:AA
MR. IMPERIUM (1951) PR:A
MR. INNOCENT (SEE: HAPPENING, THE) (1967)
MR. INVISIBLE (SEE: MR. SUPERINVISIBLE) (1974, It./Sp./W. Ger.)
MR. JIM — AMERICAN, SOLDIER, AND GENTLEMAN (SEE: SERGEANT JIM) (1962, Yugo.)
MR. KLEIN (1976, Fr.) PR:C
MR. LEMON OF ORANGE (1931) PR:A
MR. LIMPET (SEE: INCREDIBLE MR. LIMPET, THE) (1964)
MR. LORD SAYS NO (1952, Brit.) PR:A
MR. LOVE (1986, Brit.) PR:A
MR. LUCKY (1943) PR:A
MR. MAGOO'S HOLIDAY FESTIVAL (1970) PR:AA
MR. MAJESTYK (1974) PR:C
MR. MOM (1983) PR:A-C
MISTER MOSES (1965, Brit.) PR:A
MR. MOTO AND THE PERSIAN OIL CASE (SEE: RETURN OF MR. MOTO, THE) (1965, Brit.)
MR. MOTO IN DANGER ISLAND (1939) PR:A
MR. MOTO TAKES A CHANCE (1938) PR:A
MR. MOTO TAKES A VACATION (1939) PR:A
MR. MOTO'S GAMBLE (1938) PR:A
MR. MOTO'S LAST WARNING (1939) PR:A
MR. MUGGS RIDES AGAIN (1945) PR:A
MR. MUGGS STEPS OUT (1943) PR:A
MR. MUSIC (1950) PR:A
MR. NORTH (1988) PR:A
MR. ORCHID (1948, Fr.) PR:A
MR. PATMAN (1980, Can.) PR:C
MR. PEABODY AND THE MERMAID (1948) PR:AA
MR. PEEK-A-BOO (1951, Fr.) PR:A
MR. PERRIN AND MR. TRAILL (1948, Brit.) PR:A
MR. POTTS GOES TO MOSCOW (1953, Brit.) PR:A
MR. QUILP (1975, Brit.) PR:A
MR. QUINCEY OF MONTE CARLO (1933, Brit.) PR:A
MR. RADISH AND MR. CARROT (SEE: TWILIGHT PATH) (1965, Jap.)
MR. RECKLESS (1948) PR:A
MR. REEDER IN ROOM 13 (SEE: MYSTERY OF ROOM 13) (1941, Brit.)
MR. RICCO (1975) PR:C
MISTER ROBERTS (1955) PR:A
MR. ROBINSON CRUSOE (1932) PR:A
MISTER ROCK AND ROLL (1957) PR:A
MR. SARDONICUS (1961) PR:C

MR. SATAN (1938, Brit.) PR:A
MR. SCOUTMASTER (1953) PR:A
MR. SEBASTIAN (SEE: SEBASTIAN) (1968, Brit.)
MR. SKEFFINGTON (1944) PR:C
MR. SKITCH (1933) PR:A
MR. SMITH CARRIES ON (1937, Brit.) PR:A
MR. SMITH GOES TO WASHINGTON (1939) PR:AA
MR. SOFT TOUCH (1949) PR:A
MR. STRINGFELLOW SAYS NO (1937, Brit.) PR:A
MR. SUPERINVISIBLE (1974, It./Sp./W. Ger.) PR:AA
MR. SYCAMORE (1975) PR:A
MISTER TEN PERCENT (1967, Brit.) PR:A
MR. TOPAZE (SEE: I LIKE MONEY) (1962, Brit.)
MR. UNIVERSE (1951) PR:A
MISTER V (SEE: PIMPERNEL SMITH) (1942, Brit.)
MR. WALKIE TALKIE (1952) PR:A
MR. WASHINGTON GOES TO TOWN (1941) PR:A
MR. WHAT'S-HIS-NAME (1935, Brit.) PR:A
MR. WINKLE GOES TO WAR (1944) PR:A
MR. WISE GUY (1942) PR:A
MR. WONG AT HEADQUARTERS (SEE: FATAL HOUR, THE) (1940)
MR. WONG, DETECTIVE (1938) PR:A
MR. WONG IN CHINATOWN (1939) PR:A
MISTER, YOU ARE A WIDOWER (SEE: SIR, YOU ARE A WIDOWER) (1971, Czech.)
MISTERIOS DEL ULTRATUMBA (SEE: BLACK PIT OF DOCTOR M) (1958, Mex.)
MISTERIOUS DE ULTRATUMBA (SEE: BLACK PIT OF DR. M) (1958, Mex.)
MISTRESS FOR THE SUMMER, A (1964, Fr./It.) PR:C
MISTRESS OF ATLANTIS, THE (1932, Ger.) PR:A
MISTRESS OF THE APES (1981) PR:O
MISTRESS OF THE WORLD (1959, It./Fr./W. Ger.) PR:A
MISTY (1961) PR:AA
MISUNDERSTOOD (1984) PR:C
MIT EVA DIE SUNDE AN (SEE: PLAYGIRLS AND THE BELLBOY, THE) (1962, Fr.)
MITCHELL (1975) PR:O
MITT LIV SOM HUND (SEE: MY LIFE AS A DOG) (1987, Swed.)
MITTEN INS HERZ (SEE: STRAIGHT THROUGH THE HEART) (1985, W. Ger.)
MIVTZA KAHIR (SEE: TRUNK TO CAIRO) (1966, Israel/W. Ger.)
MIX ME A PERSON (1962, Brit.) PR:C
MIXED BLOOD (1984) PR:O
MIXED COMPANY (1974) PR:C
MIXED DOUBLES (1933, Brit.) PR:A
MIYAMOTO MUSASHI (SEE: SAMURAI) (1954, Jap.)
M'LISS (1936) PR:A
MOB, THE (1951) PR:C-O
MOB TOWN (1941) PR:A
MOB WAR (1989) PR:O
MOBS INC (1956) PR:A
MOBY DICK (1956, Brit.) PR:C
MOBY DICK (1930) PR:A
MODEL AND THE MARRIAGE BROKER, THE (1951) PR:A
MODEL FOR MURDER (1960, Brit.) PR:A
MODEL MURDER CASE, THE (1964, Brit.) PR:A
MODEL SHOP, THE (1969) PR:C-O
MODEL WIFE (1941) PR:A
MODELS, INC. (1952) PR:C
MODERATO CANTABILE (1964, Fr./It.) PR:C
MODERN GIRLS (1986) PR:O
MODERN HERO, A (1934) PR:A
MODERN HERO, A (SEE: KNUTE ROCKNE-ALL AMERICAN) (1941)
MODERN LOVE (1929) PR:A
MODERN MADNESS (SEE: BIG NOISE, THE) (1936)
MODERN MARRIAGE, A (1950) PR:O
MODERN MIRACLE, THE (SEE: STORY OF ALEXANDER GRAHAM BELL, THE) (1939)
MODERN PROBLEMS (1981) PR:A-C
MODERN ROMANCE (1981) PR:C
MODERN TIMES (1936) PR:A
MODERNS, THE (1988) PR:O
MODESTY BLAISE (1966, Brit.) PR:A
MODIGLIANI OF MONTPARNASSE (1961, Fr./It.) PR:A
MOERU AKI (SEE: GLOWING AUTUMN) (1981, Jap.)
MOGAMBO (1953) PR:A
MOGLIAMANTE (SEE: WIFE MISTRESS) (1977, It.)
MOHAMMAD, MESSENGER OF GOD (1976, Lebanon/Brit.) PR:C-O
MOHAN JOSHI HAAZIR HO (1984, India) PR:A
MOHAWK (1956) PR:A
MOJAVE FIREBRAND (1944) PR:A
MOKEY (1942) PR:A
MOLCHANIYE DOKTORAIVENS (SEE: SILENCE OF DR. EVANS, THE) (1973, USSR)
MOLE, THE (SEE: EL TOPO) (1971, Mex.)
MOLE PEOPLE, THE (1956) PR:A
MOLESTER, THE (SEE: NEVER TAKE CANDY FROM A STRANGER) (1961, Brit.)
MOLLY (SEE: GOLDBERGS, THE) (1950)
MOLLY AND LAWLESS JOHN (1972) PR:A
MOLLY AND ME (1929) PR:A

MOLLY AND ME (1945) PR:A
MOLLY LOUVAIN (SEE: STRANGE LOVE OF MOLLY LOUVAIN, THE) (1932)
MOLLY MAGUIRES, THE (1970) PR:C-O
MOM AND DAD (1948) PR:O
MOMENT BY MOMENT (1978) PR:O
MOMENT OF DANGER (SEE: MALAGA) (1960, Brit.)
MOMENT OF INDISCRETION (1958, Brit.) PR:A
MOMENT OF TERROR (1969, Jap.) PR:C
MOMENT OF TRUTH (SEE: NEVER LET GO) (1960, Brit.)
MOMENT OF TRUTH, THE (1965, It./Sp.) PR:A
MOMENT TO MOMENT (1966) PR:A
MOMENTS (1974, Brit.) PR:O
MOMMAN, LITTLE JUNGLE BOY (SEE: LITTLE JUNGLE BOY) (1969, Aust.)
MOMMIE DEAREST (1981) PR:C-O
MON GOSSE DE PERE (SEE: PARISIAN, THE) (1931, Fr.)
MON ONCLE (SEE: MY UNCLE) (1958, Fr.)
MON ONCLE ANTOINE (SEE: MY UNCLE ANTOINE) (1971, Can.)
MON ONCLE D'AMERIQUE (1978, Fr.) PR:C
MON PREMIER AMOUR (SEE: MY FIRST LOVE) (1978, Fr.)
MONA KENT (SEE: SIN OF MONA KENT) (1961)
MONA LISA (1986, Brit.) PR:O
MONASTERY GARDEN (SEE: IN A MONASTERY GARDEN) (1935, Brit.)
MONDAY'S CHILD (1967, US/Arg.) PR:A-C
MONDO TRASHO (1970) PR:O
MONEY, THE (1975) PR:O
MONEY AND THE WOMAN (1940) PR:A
MONEY FOR JAM (SEE: IT AIN'T HAY) (1943)
MONEY FOR NOTHING (1932, Brit.) PR:A
MONEY FOR SPEED (1933, Brit.) PR:A
MONEY FROM HOME (1953) PR:A
MONEY ISN'T EVERYTHING (SEE: JEEPERS CREEPERS) (1939)
MONEY JUNGLE, THE (1968) PR:A
MONEY MAD (1934, Brit.) PR:A
MONEY MADNESS (1948) PR:A
MONEY MEANS NOTHING (1934) PR:A
MONEY MEANS NOTHING (1932, Brit.) PR:A
MONEY, MONEY, MONEY (SEE: COUNTERFEITERS OF PARIS, THE) (1962, Fr./It.)
MONEY MOVERS (1978, Aus.) PR:O
MONEY ON THE STREET (1930, Aust.) PR:A
MONEY ORDER, THE (SEE: MANDABI) (1970, Fr./Senegal)
MONEY PIT, THE (1986) PR:A-C
MONEY TALKS (1933, Brit.) PR:A
MONEY TO BURN (1940) PR:A
MONEY TRAP, THE (1966) PR:C
MONEY, WOMEN AND GUNS (1958) PR:A
MONGOLS, THE (1966, Fr./It.) PR:A
MONGREL (1982) PR:O
MONITORS, THE (1969) PR:C
MONKEY BUSINESS (1931) PR:A
MONKEY BUSINESS (1952) PR:A
MONKEY GRIP (1983, Aus.) PR:A
MONKEY HUSTLE, THE (1976) PR:C-O
MONKEY IN WINTER, A (1962, Fr.) PR:A
MONKEY ON MY BACK (1957) PR:C
MONKEY SHINES: AN EXPERIMENT IN FEAR (1988) PR:O
MONKEYS, GO HOME! (1967) PR:AA
MONKEY'S PAW, THE (1933) PR:C
MONKEY'S PAW, THE (1948, Brit.) PR:A
MONKEY'S UNCLE, THE (1965) PR:AA
MONOLITH MONSTERS, THE (1957) PR:A
MONSEIGNEUR (1950, Fr.) PR:A
MONSIEUR (1964, Fr.) PR:A
MONSIEUR BEAUCAIRE (1946) PR:A
MONSIEUR COGNAC (SEE: WILD AND WONDERFUL) (1964)
MONSIEUR FABRE (SEE: AMAZING MONSIEUR FABRE, THE) (1952, Fr.)
MONSIEUR HULOT'S HOLIDAY (SEE: MR. HULOT'S HOLIDAY) (1953, Fr.)
MONSIEUR RIPOIS (SEE: LOVERS, HAPPY LOVERS!) (1954, Brit./Fr.)
MONSIEUR VERDOUX (1947) PR:O
MONSIEUR VINCENT (1949, Fr.) PR:A
MONSIGNOR (1982) PR:O
MONSOON (1953) PR:C
MONSTER (1979) PR:O
MONSTER (SEE: HUMANOIDS FROM THE DEEP) (1980)
MONSTER A GO-GO (1965) PR:C
MONSTER AND THE GIRL, THE (1941) PR:C
MONSTER AND THE WOMAN, THE (SEE: FOUR-SIDED TRIANGLE) (1953, Brit.)
MONSTER BARAN, THE (SEE: VARAN THE UNBELIEVABLE) (1962, US/Jap.)
MONSTER CLUB, THE (1981, Brit.) PR:C
MONSTER DOG (1986) PR:O
MONSTER FROM THE GREEN HELL (1958) PR:A

MONSTER FROM THE OCEAN FLOOR, THE (1954) PR:A
MONSTER FROM THE SURF (SEE: BEACH GIRLS
  AND THE MONSTER, THE) (1965)
MONSTER IN THE CLOSET (1987) PR:A-C
MONSTER ISLAND (1981, Sp./US) PR:C
MONSTER MAKER, THE (1944) PR:C
MONSTER MAKER (SEE: MONSTER FROM THE
  OCEAN FLOOR, THE) (1954)
MONSTER MEETS THE GORILLA (SEE: BELA
  LUGOSI MEETS A BROOKLYN GORILLA) (1952)
MONSTER OF HIGHGATE PONDS, THE (1961, Brit.)
  PR:AA
MONSTER OF LONDON CITY, THE (1967, W. Ger.)
  PR:O
MONSTER OF PIEDRAS BLANCAS, THE (1959) PR:C
MONSTER OF TERROR (SEE: DIE, MONSTER, DIE!)
  (1965, US/Brit.)
MONSTER OF THE ISLAND (1953, It.) PR:A
MONSTER OF THE WAX MUSEUM (SEE: NIGHT-
  MARE IN WAX) (1969)
MONSTER ON THE CAMPUS (1958) PR:C
MONSTER SHARK (1986, It./Fr.) PR:O
MONSTER SHOW, THE (SEE: FREAKS) (1932)
MONSTER SQUAD, THE (1987) PR:A-C
MONSTER THAT CHALLENGED THE WORLD, THE
  (1957) PR:A
MONSTER WALKED, THE (SEE: MONSTER WALKS,
  THE) (1932)
MONSTER WALKS, THE (1932) PR:A
MONSTER WANGMAGWI (1967, S.K.) PR:A
MONSTER YONGKARI (SEE: YONGKARI MONSTER
  FROM THE DEEP) (1967, S.K.)
MONSTER ZERO (1970, Jap.) PR:A
MONSTERS ARE LOOSE (SEE: THRILL KILLERS,
  THE) (1965)
MONSTERS FROM THE MOON (SEE: ROBOT MON-
  STER) (1953)
MONSTERS FROM THE UNKNOWN PLANET (1975,
  Jap.) PR:A
MONSTERS INVADE EXPO '70 (SEE: GAMERA VER-
  SUS MONSTER K) (1970, Jap.)
MONSTROSITY (SEE: ATOMIC BRAIN, THE) (1964)
MONTANA (1950) PR:A
MONTANA BELLE (1952) PR:A
MONTANA DESPERADO (1951) PR:A
MONTANA JUSTICE (SEE: MAN FROM MONTANA)
  (1941)
MONTANA KID, THE (1931) PR:A
MONTANA MIKE (SEE: HEAVEN ONLY KNOWS)
  (1947)
MONTANA MOON (1930) PR:A
MONTANA TERRITORY (1952) PR:A
MONTE CARLO (1930) PR:AA
MONTE CARLO BABY (1953, Fr.) PR:A
MONTE CARLO MADNESS (SEE: BOMBARDMENT
  OF MONTE CARLO, THE) (1931, Ger.)
MONTE CARLO NIGHTS (1934) PR:A
MONTE CARLO OR BUST (SEE: THOSE DARING
  YOUNG MEN IN THEIR JAUNTY JALOPIES) (1969,
  Fr./Brit./It.)
MONTE CARLO STORY, THE (1957, It.) PR:A
MONTE CASSINO (1948, It.) PR:A
MONTE CRISTO'S REVENGE (SEE: RETURN OF
  MONTE CRISTO, THE) (1946)
MONTE WALSH (1970) PR:C
MONTENEGRO (1981, Brit./Swed.) PR:O
MONTENEGRO – OR PIGS AND PEARLS (SEE: MON-
  TENEGRO) (1981, Brit./Swed.)
MONTPARNASSE 19 (SEE: MODIGLIANI OF
  MONTPARNASSE) (1961, Fr./It.)
MONTREAL MAIN (1974, Can.) PR:A
MONTY PYTHON AND THE HOLY GRAIL (1975, Brit.)
  PR:O
MONTY PYTHON'S LIFE OF BRIAN (1979, Brit.) PR:O
MONTY PYTHON'S THE MEANING OF LIFE (1983, Brit.)
  PR:O
MOON AND SIXPENCE, THE (1942) PR:A
MOON IN SCORPIO (1987) PR:O
MOON IN THE GUTTER, THE (1983, Fr./It.) PR:O
MOON IS BLUE, THE (1953) PR:A-C
MOON IS DOWN, THE (1943) PR:C
MOON OVER BURMA (1940) PR:A
MOON OVER HER SHOULDER (1941) PR:A
MOON OVER LAS VEGAS (1944) PR:AA
MOON OVER MIAMI (1941) PR:A
MOON OVER PARADOR (1988) PR:C
MOON OVER THE ALLEY (1980, Brit.) PR:O
MOON PILOT (1962) PR:AA
MOON-SPINNERS, THE (1964, US/Brit.) PR:AA
MOON WALK (SEE: TICKLISH AFFAIR, A) (1963)
MOON ZERO TWO (1970, Brit.) PR:O
MOONBEAM MAN, THE (SEE: MAN IN THE MOON-
  LIGHT MASK, THE) (1958, Jap.)
MOONCHILD (1972) PR:O
MOONFIRE (1970) PR:O
MOONFLEET (1955) PR:A
MOONLIGHT AND CACTUS (1944) PR:A

MOONLIGHT AND MELODY (SEE: MOONLIGHT
  AND PRETZELS) (1933)
MOONLIGHT AND PRETZELS (1933) PR:A
MOONLIGHT IN HAVANA (1942) PR:A
MOONLIGHT IN HAWAII (1941) PR:A
MOONLIGHT IN VERMONT (1943) PR:A
MOONLIGHT MASQUERADE (1942) PR:A
MOONLIGHT MURDER (1936) PR:A
MOONLIGHT ON THE PRAIRIE (1936) PR:A
MOONLIGHT ON THE RANGE (1937) PR:A
MOONLIGHT RAID (SEE: CHALLENGE OF THE
  RANGE) (1949)
MOONLIGHT SONATA (1938, Brit.) PR:A
MOONLIGHTER, THE (1953) PR:A
MOONLIGHTING (1982, Brit.) PR:C
MOONLIGHTING WIVES (1966) PR:O
MOONRAKER, THE (1958, Brit.) PR:A
MOONRAKER (1979, Brit.) PR:A
MOONRISE (1948) PR:C
MOONRUNNERS (1975) PR:A
MOON'S OUR HOME, THE (1936) PR:A
MOONSHINE COUNTY EXPRESS (1977) PR:C
MOONSHINE MOUNTAIN (1964) PR:O
MOONSHINE WAR, THE (1970) PR:C
MOONSHINER'S WOMAN (1968) PR:O
MOONSHOT (SEE: COUNTDOWN) (1968)
MOONSTONE, THE (1934) PR:A
MOONSTRUCK (1987) PR:C
MOONTIDE (1942) PR:A
MOONWOLF (1966, Fin./W. Ger.) PR:A
MORALIST, THE (1964, It.) PR:A
MORALS FOR WOMEN (1931) PR:A
MORALS OF MARCUS, THE (1936, Brit.) PR:A
MORD UND TOTSCHLAG (SEE: DEGREE OF MUR-
  DER, A) (1969, W. Ger.)
MORDEI HA'OR (SEE: SANDS OF BEERSHEBA) (1966,
  US/Israel)
MORDER UNTER UNS (SEE: M) (1931, Ger.)
MORE (1969, Luxembourg) PR:O
MORE AMERICAN GRAFFITI (1979) PR:C
MORE DEAD THAN ALIVE (1968) PR:C
MORE DEADLY THAN THE MALE (1961, Brit.) PR:C
MORE THAN A MIRACLE (1967, Fr./It.) PR:O
MORE THAN A SECRETARY (1936) PR:A
MORE THE MERRIER, THE (1943) PR:A
MORGAN! (1966, Brit.) PR:C
MORGAN STEWART'S COMING HOME (1987) PR:A-C
MORGAN THE PIRATE (1961, Fr./It.) PR:A
MORITURI (1965) PR:C
MORNING AFTER, THE (1986) PR:C-O
MORNING CALL (SEE: STRANGE CASE OF DR. MAN-
  NING, THE) (1958, Brit.)
MORNING DEPARTURE (SEE: OPERATION DISAS-
  TER) (1951, Brit.)
MORNING GLORY (1933) PR:C
MORNING STAR (1962, USSR) PR:A
MORO AFFAIR, THE (1986, It.) PR:C-O
MORO WITCH DOCTOR (1964, US/Phil.) PR:C
MOROCCO (1930) PR:C
MORONS FROM OUTER SPACE (1985, Brit.) PR:C
MOROZKO (SEE: JACK FROST) (1966, USSR)
MORTADELLA (SEE: LADY LIBERTY) (1972, It.)
MORTAL STORM, THE (1940) PR:A
MORTE A VENEZIA (SEE: DEATH IN VENICE) (1971,
  It./Fr.)
MORTON OF THE MOUNTED (SEE: TIMBER TER-
  RORS) (1935)
MORTUARY (1983) PR:O
MOSCOW – CASSIOPEIA (1974, USSR) PR:A
MOSCOW DOES NOT BELIEVE IN TEARS (1979, USSR)
  PR:A
MOSCOW NIGHTS (SEE: I STAND CONDEMNED)
  (1935, Brit.)
MOSCOW ON THE HUDSON (1984) PR:C-O
MOSCOW SHANGHAI (1936, Ger.) PR:A
MOSES (1976, Brit./It.) PR:A
MOSES AND AARON (1975, Fr./It./W. Ger.) PR:C
MOSKAU SHANGHAI: DER WEG NACH SHANGHAI
  (SEE: MOSCOW SHANGHAI) (1936, Ger.)
MOSKVA – KASSIOPEIA (SEE: MOSCOW –
  CASSIOPEIA) (1974, USSR)
MOSKWA SLJESAM NJE JERIT (SEE: MOSCOW DOES
  NOT BELIEVE IN TEARS) (1979, USSR)
MOSQUITO COAST, THE (1986) PR:O
MOSQUITO SQUADRON (1970, Brit.) PR:A
MOSS ROSE (1947) PR:A
MOST BEAUTIFUL AGE, THE (1970, Czech.) PR:C
MOST DANGEROUS GAME, THE (1932) PR:C-O
MOST DANGEROUS MAN ALIVE (1961) PR:A
MOST DANGEROUS MAN IN THE WORLD, THE
  (SEE: CHAIRMAN, THE) (1969, Brit.)
MOST IMMORAL LADY, A (1929) PR:A
MOST PRECIOUS THING IN LIFE (1934) PR:A
MOST WANTED MAN, THE (1962, Fr./It.) PR:A
MOST WONDERFUL EVENING OF MY LIFE, THE
  (1972, Fr./It.) PR:A
MOSURA (SEE: MOTHRA) (1962, Jap.)
MOTEL (SEE: PINK MOTEL) (1983)

MOTEL HELL (1980) PR:O
MOTEL, THE OPERATOR (1940) PR:C
MOTEL VACANCY (SEE: TALKING WALLS) (1987)
MOTH, THE (1934) PR:A
MOTHER (SEE: UP YOUR TEDDY BEAR) (1970)
MOTHER (1952, Jap.) PR:A
MOTHER AND DAUGHTER (1965, USSR) PR:A
MOTHER AND SON (1931) PR:A
MOTHER AND THE WHORE, THE (1973, Fr.) PR:C
MOTHER CAREY'S CHICKENS (1938) PR:A
MOTHER DIDN'T TELL ME (1950) PR:A
MOTHER GOOSE A GO-GO (1966) PR:A
MOTHER IS A FRESHMAN (1949) PR:A
MOTHER JOAN OF THE ANGELS (SEE: JOAN OF THE
  ANGELS) (1962, Pol.)
MOTHER, JUGS & SPEED (1976) PR:O
MOTHER KNOWS BEST (1928) PR:A
MOTHER KNOWS BEST (SEE: MOTHER IS A FRESH-
  MAN) (1949)
MOTHER KUSTERS GOES TO HEAVEN (1976, W. Ger.)
  PR:C-O
MOTHER LODE (1982) PR:C
MOTHER OUGHT TO MARRY (SEE: SECOND TIME
  AROUND, THE) (1961)
MOTHER RILEY MEETS THE VAMPIRE (SEE: MY
  SON, THE VAMPIRE) (1952, Brit.)
MOTHER SIR (SEE: NAVY WIFE) (1956)
MOTHER SUPERIOR (SEE: TROUBLE WITH ANGELS,
  THE) (1966)
MOTHER WORE TIGHTS (1947) PR:A
MOTHER'S CRY (1930) PR:A
MOTHER'S BOY (1929) PR:A
MOTHER'S DAY (1980) PR:O
MOTHER'S MILLIONS (SEE: SHE-WOLF, THE) (1931)
MOTHERS OF TODAY (1939) PR:C
MOTHERS, FATHERS AND LOVERS (SEE: TOM) (1973)
MOTHRA (1962, Jap.) PR:A
MOTIVE FOR REVENGE (1935) PR:A
MOTIVE WAS JEALOUSY, THE (1970, It./Sp.) PR:C
MOTOR MADNESS (1937) PR:A
MOTOR PATROL (1950) PR:A
MOTOR PSYCHO (1965) PR:O
MOTORCYCLE GANG (1957) PR:C-O
MOUCHETTE (1970, Fr.) PR:C
MOULIN ROUGE (1934) PR:A
MOULIN ROUGE (1944, Fr.) PR:A
MOULIN ROUGE (1952, Brit.) PR:A-C
MOUNTAIN, THE (1935, Brit.) PR:A
MOUNTAIN, THE (1956) PR:A
MOUNTAIN DESPERADOES (SEE: LARAMIE MOUN-
  TAINS) (1952)
MOUNTAIN FAMILY ROBINSON (1979) PR:A
MOUNTAIN JUSTICE (1930) PR:A
MOUNTAIN JUSTICE (1937) PR:A
MOUNTAIN MAN (SEE: GUARDIAN OF THE WILDER-
  NESS) (1977)
MOUNTAIN MEN, THE (1980) PR:O
MOUNTAIN MOONLIGHT (1941) PR:A
MOUNTAIN MUSIC (1937) PR:A
MOUNTAIN OF CANNIBAL GODS (SEE: SLAVE OF
  THE CANNIBAL GOD) (1978, It.)
MOUNTAIN RHYTHM (1939) PR:A
MOUNTAIN RHYTHM (1942) PR:AA
MOUNTAIN ROAD, THE (1960) PR:A
MOUNTAINS O'MOURNE (1938, Brit.) PR:A
MOUNTAINTOP MOTEL MASSACRE (1986) PR:O
MOUNTED FURY (1931) PR:A
MOUNTED STRANGER, THE (1930) PR:A
MOURNING BECOMES ELECTRA (1947) PR:C
MOURNING SUIT, THE (1975, Can.) PR:C
MOUSE AND HIS CHILD, THE (1977) PR:A
MOUSE AND THE WOMAN, THE (1981, Brit.) PR:O
MOUSE ON THE MOON, THE (1963, Brit.) PR:AA
MOUSE THAT ROARED, THE (1959, Brit.) PR:AA
MOUTH TO MOUTH (1978, Aus.) PR:C
MOUTHPIECE, THE (1932) PR:A
MOVE (1970) PR:C
MOVE OVER, DARLING (1963) PR:A
MOVERS AND SHAKERS (1985) PR:C
MOVIE CRAZY (1932) PR:A
MOVIE HOUSE MASSACRE (1986) PR:O
MOVIE MOVIE (1978) PR:A-C
MOVIE STAR, AMERICAN STYLE, OR, LSD I HATE
  YOU! (1966) PR:C
MOVIE STRUCK (SEE: PICK A STAR) (1937)
MOVIE STUNTMEN (1953) PR:A
MOVIETONE FOLLIES OF 1929 (SEE: FOX
  MOVIETONE FOLLIES) (1929)
MOVIETONE FOLLIES OF 1930 (SEE: FOX
  MOVIETONE FOLLIES OF 1930) (1930)
MOVING (1988) PR:O
MOVING FINGER, THE (1963) PR:C
MOVING IN SOCIETY (SEE: MOUNTAIN MOON-
  LIGHT) (1941)
MOVING TARGET, THE (SEE: HARPER) (1966)
MOVING TARGETS (1987, Aus.) PR:C
MOVING VIOLATION (1976) PR:C
MOVING VIOLATIONS (1985) PR:O

MOZAMBIQUE (1966, Brit.) PR:A
MOZART (1940, Brit.) PR:A
MOZART (SEE: LIFE AND LOVES OF MOZART, THE) (1959, W. Ger.)
MOZART STORY, THE (1948, Aust.) PR:A
MRS. BROWN, YOU'VE GOT A LOVELY DAUGHTER (1968, Brit.) PR:A
MRS. DANE'S DEFENCE (1933, Brit.) PR:A
MRS. FITZHERBERT (1950, Brit.) PR:A
MRS. GIBBONS' BOYS (1962, Brit.) PR:A
MRS. LORING'S SECRET (SEE: IMPERFECT LADY, THE) (1947)
MRS. MIKE (1949) PR:A
MRS. MINIVER (1942) PR:A
MRS. O'MALLEY AND MR. MALONE (1950) PR:A
MRS. PARKINGTON (1944) PR:A
MRS. POLLIFAX — SPY (1971) PR:A
MRS. PYM OF SCOTLAND YARD (1939, Brit.) PR:A
MRS. SOFFEL (1984) PR:C
MRS. WARREN'S PROFESSION (1960, W. Ger.) PR:A
MRS. WIGGS OF THE CABBAGE PATCH (1934) PR:A
MRS. WIGGS OF THE CABBAGE PATCH (1942) PR:AA
MS. 45 (1981) PR:O
MUCEDNICI LASKY (SEE: MARTYRS OF LOVE) (1968, Czech.)
MUCH TOO SHY (1942, Brit.) PR:A
MUCHACHITA DE VALLADOLID (SEE: GIRL FROM VALLADOLID) (1958, Sp.)
MUD (SEE: STICK UP, THE) (1978, Brit.)
MUD HONEY (SEE: ROPE OF FLESH) (1965)
MUDDY RIVER (1982, Jap.) PR:A
MUDLARK, THE (1950, Brit.) PR:A
MUERTO 4-3-2-1-0 (SEE: MISSION STARDUST) (1969, It./Sp./W. Ger.)
MUG TOWN (1943) PR:A
MUGGER, THE (1958) PR:A
MUHOMATSU NO ISSHO (SEE: RICKSHAW MAN, THE) (1960, Jap.)
MULE TRAIN (1950) PR:A
MUMMY, THE (1932) PR:C-O
MUMMY, THE (1959, Brit.) PR:C
MUMMY'S BOYS (1936) PR:A
MUMMY'S CURSE, THE (1944) PR:A
MUMMY'S GHOST, THE (1944) PR:A
MUMMY'S HAND, THE (1940) PR:A
MUMMY'S SHROUD, THE (1967, Brit.) PR:C
MUMMY'S TOMB, THE (1942) PR:C
MUMSY, NANNY, SONNY, AND GIRLY (1970, Brit.) PR:O
MUMU (1961, USSR) PR:A
MUNCHIES (1987) PR:C
MUNECOS INFERNALES (SEE: CURSE OF THE DOLL PEOPLE) (1968, Mex.)
MUNKBROGREVEN (SEE: COUNT OF THE MONK'S BRIDGE, THE) (1934, Swed.)
MUNSTER, GO HOME (1966) PR:A
MUPPET MOVIE, THE (1979, Brit.) PR:AA
MUPPETS TAKE MANHATTAN, THE (1984) PR:AA
MURDER (1930, Brit.) PR:A
MURDER A LA MOD (1968) PR:C
MURDER AHOY (1964, Brit.) PR:A
MURDER AMONG FRIENDS (1941) PR:A
MURDER AT COVENT GARDEN (1932, Brit.) PR:A
MURDER AT DAWN (1932) PR:A
MURDER AT 45 RPM (1965, Fr.) PR:A
MURDER AT GLEN ATHOL (1936) PR:A
MURDER AT MALIBU BEACH (SEE: TRAP, THE) (1947)
MURDER AT MIDNIGHT (1931) PR:A
MURDER AT MONTE CARLO (1935, Brit.) PR:A
MURDER AT SITE THREE (1959, Brit.) PR:A
MURDER AT THE BASKERVILLES (1941, Brit.) PR:A
MURDER AT THE BURLESQUE (SEE: MYSTERY AT THE BURLESQUE) (1950, Brit.)
MURDER AT THE CABARET (1936, Brit.) PR:A
MURDER AT THE GALLOP (1963, Brit.) PR:A
MURDER AT THE INN (1934, Brit.) PR:A
MURDER AT THE VANITIES (1934) PR:A
MURDER AT THE WINDMILL (SEE: MYSTERY AT THE BURLESQUE) (1950, Brit.)
MURDER AT 3 A.M. (1953, Brit.) PR:A
MURDER BY AGREEMENT (SEE: JOURNEY INTO NOWHERE) (1963, Brit.)
MURDER BY AN ARISTOCRAT (1936) PR:A
MURDER BY CONTRACT (1958) PR:C
MURDER BY DEATH (1976) PR:C
MURDER BY DECREE (1979, Brit./Can.) PR:C
MURDER BY INVITATION (1941) PR:A
MURDER BY MAIL (SEE: SCHIZOID) (1980)
MURDER BY PHONE (SEE: BELLS) (1981, Can.)
MURDER BY PROXY (SEE: BLACKOUT) (1954, Brit.)
MURDER BY ROPE (1936, Brit.) PR:A
MURDER BY TELEVISION (1935) PR:A
MURDER BY THE CLOCK (1931) PR:A
MURDER CAN BE DEADLY (1963, Brit.) PR:A
MURDER CLINIC, THE (1967, It./Fr.) PR:C
MURDER CZECH STYLE (1968, Czech.) PR:A
MURDER FOR SALE (SEE: TEMPORARY WIDOW) (1930, Brit./Ger.)

MURDER GAME, THE (1966, Brit.) PR:A
MURDER GOES TO COLLEGE (1937) PR:A
MURDER, HE SAYS (1945) PR:A
MURDER IN EDEN (1962, Brit.) PR:A
MURDER IN GREENWICH VILLAGE (1937) PR:A
MURDER IN MISSISSIPPI (1965) PR:C
MURDER IN MOROCCO (SEE: SCREAM IN THE NIGHT) (1943)
MURDER IN REVERSE (1946, Brit.) PR:A-C
MURDER IN SOHO (SEE: MURDER IN THE NIGHT) (1940, Brit.)
MURDER IN THE AIR (1940) PR:A
MURDER IN THE BIG HOUSE (SEE: JAILBREAK) (1936)
MURDER IN THE BIG HOUSE (1942) PR:A
MURDER IN THE BLUE ROOM (1944) PR:A
MURDER IN THE CATHEDRAL (1952, Brit.) PR:A
MURDER IN THE CLOUDS (1934) PR:A
MURDER IN THE FAMILY (1938, Brit.) PR:A
MURDER IN THE FLEET (1935) PR:A
MURDER IN THE FOOTLIGHTS (SEE: TROJAN BROTHERS, THE) (1946, Brit.)
MURDER IN THE MUSEUM (1934) PR:C
MURDER IN THE MUSIC HALL (1946) PR:O
MURDER IN THE NIGHT (1940, Brit.) PR:O
MURDER IN THE PRIVATE CAR (1934) PR:A
MURDER IN THE RED BARN (1936, Brit.) PR:A
MURDER IN THORTON SQUARE (SEE: GASLIGHT) (1944)
MURDER IN TIMES SQUARE (1943) PR:O
MURDER IN TRINIDAD (1934) PR:O
MURDER, INC. (SEE: ENFORCER, THE) (1950)
MURDER, INC. (1960) PR:O
MURDER IS MY BEAT (1955) PR:O
MURDER IS MY BUSINESS (1946) PR:O
MURDER IS NEWS (1939) PR:O
MURDER MAN, THE (1935) PR:C
MURDER MISSISSIPPI (SEE: MURDER IN MISSISSIPPI) (1965)
MURDER MOST FOUL (1964, Brit.) PR:A
MURDER, MY SWEET (1945) PR:C-O
MURDER OF DR. HARRIGAN, THE (1936) PR:O
MURDER ON A BRIDLE PATH (1936) PR:A
MURDER ON A HONEYMOON (1935) PR:A
MURDER ON APPROVAL (1956, Brit.) PR:C
MURDER ON DIAMOND ROW (1937, Brit.) PR:C
MURDER ON MONDAY (1953, Brit.) PR:C
MURDER ON THE AIR (SEE: TWENTY QUESTIONS MURDER, THE) (1950, Brit.)
MURDER ON THE BLACKBOARD (1934) PR:A
MURDER ON THE BRIDGE (SEE: END OF THE GAME) (1976, It./W. Ger.)
MURDER ON THE CAMPUS (1934) PR:A
MURDER ON THE CAMPUS (1963, Brit.) PR:A
MURDER ON THE ORIENT EXPRESS (1974, Brit.) PR:C
MURDER ON THE ROOF (1930) PR:A
MURDER ON THE RUNAWAY TRAIN (SEE: MURDER IN THE PRIVATE CAR) (1934)
MURDER ON THE SECOND FLOOR (1932, Brit.) PR:A
MURDER ON THE SET (1936, Brit.) PR:A
MURDER ON THE WATERFRONT (1943) PR:A
MURDER ON THE YUKON (1940) PR:A
MURDER ONE (1988, Can.) PR:O
MURDER OVER NEW YORK (1940) PR:A
MURDER REPORTED (1958, Brit.) PR:C
MURDER RING, THE (SEE: ELLERY QUEEN AND THE MURDER RING) (1941)
MURDER SHE SAID (1961, Brit.) PR:A
MURDER SOCIETY, THE (SEE: MURDER CLINIC, THE) (1967, Fr./It.)
MURDER TOMORROW (1938, Brit.) PR:A
MURDER WILL OUT (1930) PR:A
MURDER WILL OUT (1939, Brit.) PR:A
MURDER WILL OUT (1953, Brit.) PR:A
MURDER WITH PICTURES (1936) PR:A
MURDER WITHOUT CRIME (1951, Brit.) PR:A
MURDER WITHOUT TEARS (1953) PR:A
MURDERER, THE (SEE: ENOUGH ROPE) (1966, Fr./It./W. Ger.)
MURDERER AMONG US (SEE: M) (1931, Ger.)
MURDERER DMITRI KARAMAZOV, THE (SEE: KARAMAZOV) (1931, Ger.)
MURDERER LIVES AT NUMBER 21, THE (1947, Fr.) PR:A
MURDERERS AMONG US (1948, W. Ger.) PR:O
MURDERERS ARE AMONGST US (SEE: MURDERERS AMONG US) (1948, W. Ger.)
MURDERERS' ROW (1966) PR:C
MURDERS IN THE RUE MORGUE (1932) PR:C
MURDERS IN THE RUE MORGUE (1971) PR:O
MURDERS IN THE ZOO (1933) PR:O
MURF THE SURF (1974) PR:C
MURIEL (1963, Fr./It.) PR:A
MURIEL, OU LE TEMPS D'UN RETOUR (SEE: MURIEL) (1963, Fr./It.)
MURIETA (1965, Sp.) PR:O
MURMUR OF THE HEART (1971, Fr./It./W. Ger.) PR:O
MURPHY'S LAW (1986) PR:O

MURPHY'S ROMANCE (1985) PR:C-O
MURPHY'S WAR (1971, Brit.) PR:C-O
MURRI AFFAIR, THE (SEE: LA GRANDE BOURGEOISE) (1977, It.)
MUSCLE BEACH PARTY (1964) PR:AA
MUSEUM MYSTERY (1937, Brit.) PR:A
MUSHROOM EATER, THE (1976, Mex.) PR:O
MUSIC AND MILLIONS (SEE: SUCH IS LIFE) (1936, Brit.)
MUSIC BOX (1989) PR:C
MUSIC BOX KID, THE (1960) PR:C
MUSIC FOR MADAME (1937) PR:A
MUSIC FOR MILLIONS (1944) PR:AA
MUSIC GOES 'ROUND, THE (1936) PR:A
MUSIC HALL (1934, Brit.) PR:A
MUSIC HALL PARADE (1939, Brit.) PR:A
MUSIC HATH CHARMS (1935, Brit.) PR:A
MUSIC IN MANHATTAN (1944) PR:A
MUSIC IN MY HEART (1940) PR:A
MUSIC IN THE AIR (1934) PR:A
MUSIC IS MAGIC (1935) PR:A
MUSIC LOVERS, THE (1971, Brit.) PR:O
MUSIC MACHINE, THE (1979, Brit.) PR:O
MUSIC MAKER, THE (1936, Brit.) PR:A
MUSIC MAN (1948) PR:AA
MUSIC MAN, THE (1962) PR:AA
MUSIC ROOM, THE (1963, India) PR:A
MUSICAL MUTINY (1970) PR:A
MUSIK I MORKER (SEE: NIGHT IS MY FUTURE) (1963, Swed.)
MUSS 'EM UP (1936) PR:A
MUSTANG (1959) PR:A
MUSTANG COUNTRY (1976) PR:A
MUTANT (SEE: FORBIDDEN WORLD) (1982)
MUTANT HUNT (1987) PR:O
MUTANT ON THE BOUNTY (1989) PR:C
MUTATIONS, THE (1974, Brit.) PR:O
MUTILATOR, THE (1985) PR:O
MUTINEERS, THE (1949) PR:A
MUTINEERS, THE (SEE: DAMN THE DEFIANT!) (1962, Brit.)
MUTINY (1952) PR:A
MUTINY AHEAD (1935) PR:A
MUTINY IN OUTER SPACE (SEE: SPACE MASTER X-7) (1958)
MUTINY IN OUTER SPACE (1965) PR:A
MUTINY IN THE ARCTIC (1941) PR:A
MUTINY IN THE BIG HOUSE (1939) PR:A
MUTINY OF THE ELSINORE, THE (1939, Brit.) PR:A
MUTINY ON THE BLACKHAWK (1939) PR:A
MUTINY ON THE BOUNTY (1935) PR:A
MUTINY ON THE BOUNTY (1962) PR:C-O
MUTINY ON THE SEAS (SEE: OUTSIDE THE 3-MILE LIMIT) (1940)
MUTINY, THE (SEE: WHITE SALVE SHIP) (1962, Fr./It.)
MUTTER KUSTERS FAHRT ZUM HIMMEL (SEE: MOTHER KUSTERS GOES TO HEAVEN) (1976, W. Ger.)
MY AIN FOLK (1944, Brit.) PR:A
MY AIN FOLK (1974, Brit.) PR:A
MY AMERICAN COUSIN (1985, Can.) PR:A-C
MY AMERICAN WIFE (1936) PR:A
MY APPLE (SEE: JUST ME) (1950, Fr.)
MY BABY IS BLACK! (1965, Fr.) PR:A
MY BEAUTIFUL LAUNDRETTE (1986, Brit.) PR:O
MY BEST FRIEND'S GIRL (1983, Fr.) PR:O
MY BEST GAL (1944) PR:A
MY BILL (1938) PR:A
MY BLUE HEAVEN (1950) PR:A
MY BLOOD RUNS COLD (1965) PR:O
MY BLOODY VALENTINE (1981, Can.) PR:O
MY BODY HUNGERS (1967) PR:O
MY BODYGUARD (1980) PR:A
MY BOYS ARE GOOD BOYS (1978) PR:A
MY BREAKFAST WITH BLASSIE (1983) PR:O
MY BRILLIANT CAREER (1980, Aus.) PR:O
MY BROTHER HAS BAD DREAMS (1977) PR:O
MY BROTHER JONATHAN (1949, Brit.) PR:A
MY BROTHER TALKS TO HORSES (1946) PR:AA
MY BROTHER, THE OUTLAW (1951) PR:A
MY BROTHER'S KEEPER (1949, Brit.) PR:A
MY BROTHER'S WEDDING (1983) PR:A
MY BUDDY (1944) PR:A
MY CHAUFFEUR (1986) PR:O
MY CHILDHOOD (1972, Brit.) PR:A
MY COUSIN RACHEL (1952) PR:A
MY DARK LADY (1987) PR:A
MY DARLING CLEMENTINE (1946) PR:A
MY DAUGHTER JOY (SEE: OPERATION X) (1951, Brit.)
MY DEAR MISS ALDRICH (1937) PR:A
MY DEAR SECRETARY (1948) PR:A-C
MY DEATH IS A MOCKERY (1952, Brit.) PR:C-O
MY DEMON LOVER (1987) PR:C
MY DINNER WITH ANDRE (1981) PR:A-C
MY DOG, BUDDY (1960) PR:C
MY DOG RUSTY (1948) PR:AA
MY DREAM IS YOURS (1949) PR:A

MY ENEMY, THE SEA (SEE: ALONE ON THE PACIFIC) (1964, Jap.)
MY FAIR LADY (1964) PR:AA
MY FATHER, MY MASTER (SEE: PADRE PADRONE) (1977, It.)
MY FATHER'S HOUSE (1947, Palestine) PR:A
MY FATHER'S MISTRESS (1970, Swed.) PR:C
MY FAVORITE BLONDE (1942) PR:A
MY FAVORITE BRUNETTE (1947) PR:A
MY FAVORITE SPY (1942) PR:A
MY FAVORITE SPY (1951) PR:A
MY FAVORITE WIFE (1940) PR:A
MY FAVORITE YEAR (1982) PR:C
MY FIRST LOVE (1978, Fr.) PR:O
MY FIRST WIFE (1985, Aus.) PR:O
MY FOOLISH HEART (1949) PR:A-C
MY FORBIDDEN PAST (1951) PR:C
MY FRIEND FLICKA (1943) PR:AA
MY FRIEND IRMA (1949) PR:A
MY FRIEND IRMA GOES WEST (1950) PR:A
MY FRIEND THE KING (1931, Brit.) PR:A
MY GAL LOVES MUSIC (1944) PR:A
MY GAL SAL (1942) PR:A
MY GEISHA (1962) PR:A
MY GIRL TISA (1948) PR:A
MY GUN IS QUICK (1957) PR:O
MY HANDS ARE CLAY (1948, Ireland) PR:A
MY HEART BELONGS TO DADDY (1942) PR:A
MY HEART GOES CRAZY (1953, Brit.) PR:A
MY HEART IS CALLING (1935, Brit.) PR:A
MY HERO (SEE: SOUTHERN YANKEE, A) (1948)
MY HOBO (1963, Jap.) PR:A
MY IRISH MOLLY (SEE: LITTLE MISS MOLLY) (1940, Brit.)
MY KIND OF TOWN (1984, Can.) PR:A
MY KINGDOM FOR A COOK (1943) PR:A
MY LAST DUCHESS (SEE: ARRIVEDERCI, BABY!) (1966, Brit.)
MY LEARNED FRIEND (1943, Brit.) PR:A
MY LEFT FOOT (1989, Ireland) PR:A
MY LIFE AS A DOG (1985, Swed.) PR:C
MY LIFE IS YOURS (SEE: PEOPLE VS. DR. KILDARE, THE) (1941)
MY LIFE TO LIVE (1962, Fr.) PR:A
MY LIFE WITH CAROLINE (1941) PR:A-C
MY LIPS BETRAY (1933) PR:A
MY LITTLE CHICKADEE (1940) PR:A
MY LITTLE PONY (1986) PR:AA
MY LOVE CAME BACK (1940) PR:A
MY LOVE FOR YOURS (SEE: HONEYMOON IN BALI) (1939)
MY LOVE LETTERS (SEE: LOVE LETTERS) (1983)
MY LOVER, MY SON (1970, Brit.) PR:O
MY LUCKY STAR (1933, Brit.) PR:A
MY LUCKY STAR (1938) PR:A
MY MAIN MAN FROM STONY ISLAND (SEE: STONY ISLAND) (1978)
MY MAN (1928) PR:A
MY MAN ADAM (1986) PR:O
MY MAN AND I (1952) PR:A
MY MAN GODFREY (1936) PR:A
MY MAN GODFREY (1957) PR:A
MY MARGO (1969, Israel) PR:C
MY MARRIAGE (1936) PR:A
MY MOTHER (1933) PR:A
MY NAME IS IVAN (1962, USSR) PR:O
MY NAME IS JOHN (SEE: WHO FEARS THE DEVIL) (1972)
MY NAME IS JULIA ROSS (1945) PR:A
MY NAME IS NOBODY (1974, It./Fr./W. Ger.) PR:O
MY NAME IS PECOS (1966, It.) PR:A
MY NEW PARTNER (1984, Fr.) PR:O
MY NIGHT AT MAUD'S (1969, Fr.) PR:A
MY NIGHT WITH MAUD (SEE: MY NIGHT AT MAUD'S) (1969, Fr.)
MY OLD DUCHESS (1933, Brit.) PR:A
MY OLD DUTCH (1934, Brit.) PR:A
MY OLD KENTUCKY HOME (1938) PR:A
MY OLD MAN'S PLACE (SEE: GLORY BOY) (1972)
MY OTHER HUSBAND (1983, Fr.) PR:C
MY OUTLAW BROTHER (SEE: MY BROTHER, THE OUTLAW) (1951)
MY OWN TRUE LOVE (1948) PR:A
MY PAL GUS (1952) PR:A
MY PAL, THE KING (1932) PR:A
MY PAL TRIGGER (1946) PR:AA
MY PAL, WOLF (1944) PR:A
MY PARTNER MR. DAVIS (SEE: MYSTERIOUS MR. DAVIS, THE) (1936, Brit.)
MY PAST (1931) PR:A
MY REPUTATION (1946) PR:A-C
MY SCIENCE PROJECT (1985) PR:C-O
MY SEVEN LITTLE SINS (1956, Fr./It.) PR:A
MY SIDE OF THE MOUNTAIN (1969) PR:AA
MY SIN (1931) PR:A-C
MY SISTER AND I (1948, Brit.) PR:C
MY SISTER EILEEN (1942) PR:AA
MY SISTER EILEEN (1955) PR:AA

MY SISTER, MY LOVE (SEE: MAFU CAGE, THE) (1978)
MY SIX CONVICTS (1952) PR:A-C
MY SIX LOVES (1963) PR:AA
MY SON ALONE (SEE: AMERICAN EMPIRE) (1942)
MY SON IS A CRIMINAL (1939) PR:A
MY SON IS GUILTY (1940) PR:C
MY SON, JOHN (1952) PR:C
MY SON, MY SON! (1940) PR:A
MY SON NERO (SEE: NERO'S MISTRESS) (1962, It.)
MY SON, THE HERO (1943) PR:A
MY SON, THE HERO (1963, It./Fr.) PR:A
MY SON, THE VAMPIRE (1952, Brit.) PR:A
MY SONG FOR YOU (1935, Brit.) PR:A
MY SONG GOES ROUND THE WORLD (1934, Brit.) PR:A
MY SOUL RUNS NAKED (SEE: RAT FINK) (1965)
MY STEPMOTHER IS AN ALIEN (1988) PR:C
MY SWEET LITTLE VILLAGE (1985, Czech.) PR:A
MY TEENAGE DAUGHTER (SEE: TEENAGE BAD GIRL) (1956, Brit.)
MY THIRD WIFE BY GEORGE (SEE: MY THIRD WIFE GEORGE) (1968)
MY THIRD WIFE GEORGE (1968) PR:A
MY TRUE STORY (1951) PR:A
MY TUTOR (1983) PR:O
MY TWO HUSBANDS (SEE: TOO MANY HUSBANDS) (1940)
MY UNCLE (1958, Fr.) PR:AA
MY UNCLE ANTOINE (1971, Can.) PR:C
MY UNCLE FROM AMERICA (SEE: MON ONCLE D'AMERIQUE) (1978, Fr.)
MY UNCLE, MR. HULOT (SEE: MY UNCLE) (1958, Fr.)
MY UNIVERSITY (SEE: UNIVERSITY OF LIFE) (1941, USSR)
MY WAY (1974, South Africa) PR:A
MY WAY HOME (1978, Brit.) PR:C
MY WEAKNESS (1933) PR:AA
MY WIDOW AND I (1950, It.) PR:C
MY WIFE'S BEST FRIEND (1952) PR:A
MY WIFE'S ENEMY (1967, It.) PR:A
MY WIFE'S FAMILY (1932, Brit.) PR:A
MY WIFE'S FAMILY (1941, Brit.) PR:A
MY WIFE'S FAMILY (1962, Brit.) PR:A
MY WIFE'S HUSBAND (1965, Fr./It.) PR:A
MY WIFE'S LODGER (1952, Brit.) PR:A
MY WIFE'S RELATIVES (1939) PR:AA
MY WILD IRISH ROSE (1947) PR:A
MY WOMAN (1933) PR:A
MY WORLD DIES SCREAMING (1958) PR:C
MYRT AND MARGE (1934) PR:A
MYSTERIANS, THE (1959, Jap.) PR:A
MYSTERIES (1979, Neth.) PR:C
MYSTERIOUS AVENGER, THE (1936) PR:A
MYSTERIOUS CROSSING (1937) PR:A-C
MYSTERIOUS DESPERADO, THE (1949) PR:A
MYSTERIOUS DR. FU MANCHU, THE (1929) PR:A
MYSTERIOUS DOCTOR, THE (1943) PR:C
MYSTERIOUS HOUSE OF DR. C., THE (1976) PR:A
MYSTERIOUS INTRUDER (1946) PR:A
MYSTERIOUS INVADER, THE (SEE: ASTOUNDING SHE-MONSTER, THE) (1958)
MYSTERIOUS ISLAND, THE (1929) PR:A
MYSTERIOUS ISLAND (1941, USSR) PR:A
MYSTERIOUS ISLAND (1961, US/Brit.) PR:AA
MYSTERIOUS ISLAND, THE (SEE: MYSTERIOUS IS-LAND OF CAPTAIN NEMO, THE) (1973, Fr./It./Sp./Cameroon)
MYSTERIOUS ISLAND OF CAPTAIN NEMO, THE (1973, Fr./It./Sp./Cameroon) PR:AA
MYSTERIOUS MISS X, THE (1939) PR:A
MYSTERIOUS MR. DAVIS, THE (1936, Brit.) PR:A
MYSTERIOUS MR. MOTO (1938) PR:A
MYSTERIOUS MR. MOTO OF DEVIL'S ISLAND (SEE: MYSTERIOUS MR. MOTO) (1938)
MYSTERIOUS MR. NICHOLSON, THE (1947, Brit.) PR:A
MYSTERIOUS MR. REEDER, THE (1940, Brit.) PR:A-C
MYSTERIOUS MR. VALENTINE, THE (1946) PR:A
MYSTERIOUS MR. WONG, THE (1935) PR:C
MYSTERIOUS RIDER, THE (1933) PR:A
MYSTERIOUS RIDER, THE (1938) PR:A
MYSTERIOUS RIDER, THE (1942) PR:A
MYSTERIOUS SATELLITE, THE (1956, Jap.) PR:A
MYSTERIOUS STRANGER, THE (SEE: WESTERN GOLD) (1937)
MYSTERIOUS STRANGER, THE (SEE: CODE OF THE LAWLESS) (1945)
MYSTERY AT MONTE CARLO (SEE: REVENGE AT MONTE CARLO) (1933)
MYSTERY AT THE BURLESQUE (1950, Brit.) PR:A
MYSTERY AT THE VILLA ROSE (1930, Brit.) PR:A
MYSTERY BROADCAST (1943) PR:A
MYSTERY HOUSE (1938) PR:A
MYSTERY IN MEXICO (1948) PR:A
MYSTERY JUNCTION (1951, Brit.) PR:A
MYSTERY LAKE (1953) PR:A
MYSTERY LINER (1934) PR:A

MYSTERY MAN, THE (1935) PR:A
MYSTERY MAN (1944) PR:A
MYSTERY MANSION (1984) PR:C
MYSTERY OF ALEXINA, THE (1985, Fr.) PR:O
MYSTERY OF DIAMOND ISLAND, THE (SEE: RIP ROARING RILEY) (1935)
MYSTERY OF EDWIN DROOD, THE (1935) PR:C
MYSTERY OF KASPAR HAUSER, THE (SEE: EVERY MAN FOR HIMSELF AND GOD AGAINST ALL) (1975, W. Ger.)
MYSTERY OF MARIE ROGET, THE (1942) PR:A
MYSTERY OF MR. WONG, THE (1939) PR:A
MYSTERY OF MR. X, THE (1934) PR:C
MYSTERY OF ROOM 13 (1941, Brit.) PR:A
MYSTERY OF THE BLACK JUNGLE (1955) PR:A
MYSTERY OF THE GOLDEN EYE, THE (1948) PR:A
MYSTERY OF THE HOODED HORSEMEN, THE (1937) PR:A
MYSTERY OF THE MARIE CELESTE (SEE: PHAN-TOM SHIP) (1937, Brit.)
MYSTERY OF THE PINK VILLA, THE (SEE: MYSTERY AT THE VILLA ROSE) (1930, Brit.)
MYSTERY OF THE 13TH GUEST, THE (1943) PR:A
MYSTERY OF THE WAX MUSEUM, THE (1933) PR:C
MYSTERY OF THE WENTWORTH CASTLE, THE (SEE: DOOMED TO DIE) (1940)
MYSTERY OF THE WHITE ROOM (1939) PR:A
MYSTERY OF THUG ISLAND, THE (1966, It./W. Ger.) PR:A
MYSTERY ON BIRD ISLAND (1954, Brit.) PR:AA
MYSTERY ON MONSTER ISLAND (SEE: MONSTER ISLAND) (1981, US/Sp.)
MYSTERY PLANE (1939) PR:A
MYSTERY RANCH (1932) PR:A
MYSTERY RANGE (1937) PR:A
MYSTERY SEA RAIDER (1940) PR:A
MYSTERY SHIP (1941) PR:A
MYSTERY STREET (1950) PR:C
MYSTERY SUBMARINE (1950) PR:A
MYSTERY SUBMARINE (1963, Brit.) PR:A
MYSTERY TRAIN (1931) PR:A
MYSTERY TRAIN (1989) PR:O
MYSTERY WOMAN (1935) PR:A
MYSTIC CIRCLE MURDER (1939) PR:A
MYSTIC HOUR, THE (1934) PR:A
MYSTIC PIZZA (1988) PR:O
MYSTIFIERS, THE (SEE: SYMPHONY FOR A MASSA-CRE) (1965, Fr./It.)
MYSTIQUE (1981) PR:O
MYTH, THE (1965, It.) PR:O

N

N.P. (1971, It.) PR:A
NA KOMETE (SEE: ON THE COMET) (1970, Czech.)
NA SEMI VETRAKH (SEE: HOUSE ON THE FRONT LINE, THE) (1963, USSR)
NABONGA (1944) PR:A
NACHTS, WENN DER TEUFEL KAM (SEE: DEVIL STRIKES AT NIGHT, THE) (1959, W. Ger.)
NACKT UNTER WOLFEN (SEE: NAKED AMONG THE WOLVES) (1967, W. Ger.)
NADA GANG, THE (1974, Fr./It.) PR:A
NADA MAS QUE UNA MUJER (1934) PR:A
NADIA (1984, US/Yugo.) PR:C
NADINE (1987) PR:C
NAGANA (1933) PR:A
NAGOOA (SEE: DRIFTING) (1983, Israel)
NAIL GUN MASSACRE (1988) PR:O
NAKED ALIBI (1954) PR:A
NAKED AMONG THE WOLVES (1967, E. Ger.) PR:C
NAKED AND THE DEAD, THE (1958) PR:O
NAKED ANGELS (1969) PR:O
NAKED APE, THE (1973) PR:C
NAKED AUTUMN (1963, Fr.) PR:A
NAKED BRIGADE, THE (1965, US/Gr.) PR:A
NAKED CAGE, THE (1986) PR:O
NAKED CHILDHOOD (SEE: ME) (1970, Fr.)
NAKED CITY, THE (1948) PR:C
NAKED DAWN, THE (1955) PR:A
NAKED EARTH, THE (1958, Brit.) PR:A
NAKED EDGE, THE (1961, US/Brit.) PR:A-C
NAKED EVIL (SEE: EXORCISM AT MIDNIGHT) (1966, Brit.)
NAKED FACE, THE (1984) PR:C
NAKED FLAME, THE (1970, Can.) PR:C
NAKED FURY (1959, Brit.) PR:C
NAKED FURY, THE (SEE: PLEASURE LOVERS, THE) (1964, Brit.)
NAKED GENERAL, THE (1964, Jap.) PR:A
NAKED GODDESS, THE (SEE: DEVIL'S HAND, THE) (1961)
NAKED GUN, THE (1956) PR:A
NAKED GUN, THE (1988) PR:C-O
NAKED HEART, THE (1955, Brit.) PR:A
NAKED HEARTS (1970, Fr.) PR:A
NAKED HILLS, THE (1956) PR:A
NAKED HOURS, THE (1964, It.) PR:C
NAKED IN THE SUN (1957) PR:C

NAKED ISLAND (SEE: ISLAND, THE) (1962, Jap.)
NAKED JUNGLE, THE (1953) PR:A-C
NAKED KISS, THE (1964) PR:O
NAKED MAJA, THE (1959, It./US) PR:A
NAKED NIGHT, THE (1953, Swed.) PR:O
NAKED PARADISE (1957) PR:A
NAKED PREY, THE (1966, US/South Africa) PR:O
NAKED RUNNER, THE (1967, Brit.) PR:A-C
NAKED SPUR, THE (1953) PR:A-C
NAKED SPUR (SEE: HOT SPUR) (1968)
NAKED STREET, THE (1955) PR:C
NAKED TEMPTRESS, THE (SEE: NAKED WITCH, THE) (1964)
NAKED TRUTH, THE (SEE: YOUR PAST IS SHOWING) (1958, Brit.)
NAKED UNDER LEATHER (SEE: GIRL ON A MOTORCYCLE) (1968, Brit./Fr.)
NAKED VENGEANCE (1986, US/Phil.) PR:O
NAKED WITCH, THE (1964) PR:C
NAKED WOMAN, THE (1950, Fr.) PR:A
NAKED WORLD OF HARRISON MARKS, THE (1967, Brit.) PR:O
NAKED YOUTH (1961, Jap.) PR:C-O
NAKED YOUTH (SEE: WILD YOUTH) (1961)
NAKED ZOO, THE (1970) PR:C
NAM ANGELS (SEE: LOSERS, THE) (1970)
NAME FOR EVIL, A (1970) PR:C-O
NAME OF THE GAME IS KILL, THE (1968) PR:C
NAME OF THE ROSE, THE (1986) PR:C-O
NAME THE WOMAN (1934) PR:A
NAMELESS (SEE: FRAULEIN DOKTOR) (1969, It./Yugo.)
NAMONAKU MAZUSHIKU UTSUKUSHIKU (SEE: HAPPINESS OF US ALONE) (1962, Jap.)
NAMU, THE KILLER WHALE (1966) PR:A
NANA (1934) PR:C
NANA (1957, Fr./It.) PR:A-C
NANA (1983, It.) PR:O
NANCY DREW AND THE HIDDEN STAIRCASE (1939) PR:AA
NANCY DREW – DETECTIVE (1938) PR:AA
NANCY DREW – REPORTER (1939) PR:AA
NANCY DREW, TROUBLE SHOOTER (1939) PR:AA
NANCY GOES TO RIO (1950) PR:A
NANCY STEELE IS MISSING (1937) PR:A
NANKAI NO DAIKAIJU (SEE: YOG – MONSTER FROM SPACE) (1970, Jap.)
NANKAI NO KAI KETTO (SEE: GODZILLA VERSUS THE SEA MONSTER) (1966, Jap.)
NANNY, THE (1965, Brit.) PR:O
NAPLO GYERMEKEIMNEK (SEE: DIARY FOR MY CHILDREN) (1984, Hung.)
NAPOLEON (1955, Fr.) PR:A
NAPOLEON AND SAMANTHA (1972) PR:AA
NARAYAMA-BUSHI-KO (SEE: BALLAD OF NARAYAMA) (1961, Jap.)
NARCO MEN, THE (1971, It./Sp.) PR:O
NARCOTICS STORY, THE (1958) PR:O
NARK, THE (SEE: LA BALANCE) (1982, Fr.)
NARROW CORNER, THE (1933) PR:C
NARROW MARGIN, THE (1952) PR:A
NARROWING CIRCLE, THE (1956, Brit.) PR:C
NASHVILLE (1975) PR:C-O
NASHVILLE GIRL (SEE: NEW GIRL IN TOWN) (1977)
NASHVILLE REBEL (1966) PR:A
NASILJE NA TRGU (SEE: SQUARE OF VIOLENCE) (1963, US/Yugo.)
NASTY HABITS (1976, Brit.) PR:C
NASTY RABBIT, THE (1964) PR:A
NATALKA POLTAVKA (SEE: GIRL FROM POLTAVKA) (1937)
NATCHEZ TRACE (1960) PR:C
NATE AND HAYES (1983, US/New Zealand) PR:C
NATHALIE (1958, Fr.) PR:A
NATHALIE, AGENT SECRET (1960, Fr.) PR:A
NATHALIE GRANGER (1972, Fr.) PR:C
NATHANIEL HAWTHORNE'S "TWICE TOLD TALES" (SEE: TWICE-TOLD TALES) (1963)
NATION AFLAME (1937) PR:A
NATIONAL BARN DANCE (1944) PR:A
NATIONAL HEALTH, OR NURSE NORTON'S AFFAIR, THE (1973, Brit.) PR:C
NATIONAL LAMPOON'S ANIMAL HOUSE (1978) PR:C
NATIONAL LAMPOON'S CHRISTMAS VACATION (1989) PR:C
NATIONAL LAMPOON'S CLASS REUNION (1982) PR:O
NATIONAL LAMPOON'S EUROPEAN VACATION (1985) PR:C
NATIONAL LAMPOON'S VACATION (1983) PR:C
NATIONAL VELVET (1944) PR:AA
NATIVE LAND (1942) PR:A
NATIVE SON (1951, US/Arg.) PR:C-O
NATIVE SON (1986) PR:C
NATSUKASHIKI FUE YA TAIKO (SEE: EYES, THE SEA AND A BALL) (1968, Jap.)
NATTLEK (SEE: NIGHT GAMES) (1966, Swed.)
NATTVARDSGASTERNA (SEE: WINTER LIGHT, THE) (1962, Swed.)

NATURAL, THE (1984) PR:C
NATURAL BORN SALESMAN (SEE: EARTHWORM TRACTORS) (1936)
NATURAL ENEMIES (1979) PR:O
NATURE'S MISTAKES (SEE: FREAKS) (1932)
NAUGHTY ARLETTE (1951, Brit.) PR:C-O
NAUGHTY BUT NICE (1939) PR:A
NAUGHTY CINDERELLA (1933, Brit.) PR:A
NAUGHTY FLIRT, THE (1931) PR:A
NAUGHTY MARIETTA (1935) PR:A
NAUGHTY NINETIES, THE (1945) PR:AA
NAVAJO (1952) PR:A
NAVAJO JOE (1967, It./Sp.) PR:C
NAVAJO KID, THE (1946) PR:A
NAVAJO RUN (1964) PR:C
NAVAJO TRAIL, THE (1945) PR:A
NAVAJO TRAIL RAIDERS (1949) PR:A
NAVAL ACADEMY (1941) PR:A
NAVIGATOR, THE (1989, Aus.) PR:A
NAVY BLUE AND GOLD (1937) PR:A
NAVY BLUES (1930) PR:A
NAVY BLUES (1937) PR:A
NAVY BLUES (1941) PR:A
NAVY BORN (1936) PR:A
NAVY BOUND (1951) PR:A
NAVY COMES THROUGH, THE (1942) PR:A
NAVY HEROES (1959, Brit.) PR:A
NAVY LARK, THE (1959, Brit.) PR:A
NAVY SECRETS (1939) PR:A
NAVY SPY (1937) PR:A
NAVY STEPS OUT, THE (SEE: GIRL, A GUY, AND A GOB, A) (1941)
NAVY VS. THE NIGHT MONSTERS, THE (1966) PR:C
NAVY WAY, THE (1944) PR:A
NAVY WIFE (1936) PR:A
NAVY WIFE (1956) PR:A
NAZARIN (1968, Mex.) PR:A
NAZI AGENT (1942) PR:A
NAZI SPY RING (SEE: DAWN EXPRESS, THE) (1942)
NE JOUEZ PAS AVEC LES MARTIENS (SEE: DON'T PLAY WITH MARTIANS) (1967, Fr.)
NEANDERTHAL MAN, THE (1953) PR:A
NEAPOLITAN CAROUSEL (1961, It.) PR:A
NEAR DARK (1987) PR:O
NEAR THE RAINBOW'S END (1930) PR:A
NEAR THE TRAIL'S END (1931) PR:A
NEARLY A NASTY ACCIDENT (1962, Brit.) PR:A
NEARLY EIGHTEEN (1943) PR:A
'NEATH BROOKLYN BRIDGE (1942) PR:A
'NEATH THE ARIZONA SKIES (1934) PR:A
NEBO ZOVYOT (SEE: BATTLE BEYOND THE SUN) (1963)
NEBRASKAN, THE (1953) PR:A
NECK AND NECK (1931) PR:A
NECO Z ALENKY (SEE: ALICE) (1988, Brit./Switz./W. Ger.)
NECROMANCER (1989) PR:O
NECROMANCY (1972) PR:C
NECROPHAGUS (SEE: GRAVEYARD OF HORROR) (1971, Sp.)
NECROPOLIS (1987) PR:O
NED KELLY (1970, Brit.) PR:C
NEFERTITE, REGINA DEL NILO (SEE: QUEEN OF THE NILE) (1964)
NEGATIVES (1968, Brit.) PR:C
NEHEZELETUEK (SEE: ROUND UP, THE) (1969, Hung.)
NEIGE (SEE: SNOW) (1982, Fr.)
NEIGHBORS (1981) PR:C-O
NEIGHBORS' WIVES (1933) PR:A
NEIL SIMON'S THE SLUGGER'S WIFE (SEE: SLUGGER'S WIFE, THE) (1985)
NEITHER BY DAY NOR BY NIGHT (1972, US/Israel) PR:A
NEITHER THE SEA NOR THE SAND (1974, Brit.) PR:A
NEJKRASNEJSI VEK (SEE: MOST BEAUTIFUL AGE, THE) (1970, Czech.)
NEL SEGNO (SEE: SIGN OF THE GLADIATOR) (1959, Fr./It./W. Ger.)
NELL GWYN (1935, Brit.) PR:A-C
NELLA CITTA L'INFERNO (SEE: AND THE WILD, WILD WOMEN) (1961, It.)
NELLA STRETTA M ORSA DEL RAGNO (SEE: WEB OF THE SPIDER) (1972, Fr./It./W. Ger.)
NELLY'S VERSION (1983, Brit.) PR:A
NELSON AFFAIR, THE (1973, Brit.) PR:C
NELSON TOUCH, THE (SEE: CORVETTE K-225) (1943)
NEMO (SEE: DREAM ONE) (1984, Brit./Fr.)
NEON MANIACS (1986) PR:O
NEON PALACE, THE (1970, Can.) PR:A
NEOTPRAVLENNOYE PISMO (SEE: LETTER THAT WAS NEVER SENT, THE) (1962, USSR)
NEPTUNE DISASTER, THE (SEE: NEPTUNE FACTOR, THE) (1973, Can.)
NEPTUNE FACTOR, THE (1973, Can.) PR:A
NEPTUNE'S DAUGHTER (1949) PR:A
NERO'S BIG WEEKEND (SEE: NERO'S MISTRESS) (1962, It.)
NERO'S MISTRESS (1962, It.) PR:C

NEST, THE (1980, Sp.) PR:A
NEST OF THE CUCKOO BIRDS, THE (1965) PR:C
NEST OF VIPERS (1979, It.) PR:O
NESTING (1981) PR:O
NET, THE (SEE: PROJECT M7) (1953, Brit.)
NETWORK (1976) PR:C
NEUNZIG MINUTEN NACH MITTER NACHT (SEE: TERROR AFTER MIDNIGHT) (1965)
NEUTRAL PORT (1941, Brit.) PR:A
NEUTRON CONTRA EL DR. CARONTE (1962, Mex.) PR:A
NEUTRON EL ENMASCARADO NEGRO (1962, Mex.) PR:A
NEVADA (1936) PR:A
NEVADA (1944) PR:A
NEVADA BADMEN (1951) PR:A
NEVADA CITY (1941) PR:A
NEVADA SMITH (1966) PR:C
NEVADAN, THE (1950) PR:A
NEVER A DULL MOMENT (1943) PR:A
NEVER A DULL MOMENT (1950) PR:A
NEVER A DULL MOMENT (1968) PR:A
NEVER BACK LOSERS (1967, Brit.) PR:A
NEVER CRY WOLF (1983) PR:C
NEVER FEAR (1950) PR:A
NEVER GIVE A SUCKER A BREAK (SEE: NUISANCE, THE) (1933)
NEVER GIVE A SUCKER AN EVEN BREAK (1941, US/Fr.) PR:A
NEVER GIVE AN INCH (SEE: SOMETIMES A GREAT NOTION) (1971)
NEVER LET GO (1960, Brit.) PR:C
NEVER LET ME GO (1953, US/Brit.) PR:A
NEVER LOOK BACK (1952, Brit.) PR:A
NEVER LOVE A STRANGER (1958) PR:A
NEVER MENTION MURDER (1964, Brit.) PR:A
NEVER NEVER LAND (1982) PR:A
NEVER ON SUNDAY (1960, Gr.) PR:O
NEVER PUT IT IN WRITING (1964) PR:A
NEVER SAY DIE (1939) PR:A
NEVER SAY DIE (SEE: DON'T SAY DIE) (1950, Brit.)
NEVER SAY GOODBYE (1946) PR:A
NEVER SAY GOODBYE (1956) PR:A
NEVER SAY NEVER AGAIN (1983, Brit.) PR:A
NEVER SO FEW (1959) PR:C
NEVER STEAL ANYTHING SMALL (1959) PR:C
NEVER STEAL ANYTHING WET (SEE: CATALINA CAPER) (1967)
NEVER TAKE CANDY FROM A STRANGER (1961, Brit.) PR:C-O
NEVER TAKE NO FOR AN ANSWER (1951, Brit./It.) PR:A
NEVER THE TWAIN SHALL MEET (1931) PR:A
NEVER TO LOVE (SEE: BILL OF DIVORCEMENT) (1940)
NEVER TOO LATE (1965) PR:A
NEVER TOO YOUNG TO DIE (1986) PR:O
NEVER TROUBLE TROUBLE (1931, Brit.) PR:A
NEVER TRUST A GAMBLER (1951) PR:A
NEVER WAVE AT A WAC (1952) PR:A
NEVERENDING STORY, THE (1984, W. Ger.) PR:C
NEVINOST BEZ ZASTITE (SEE: INNOCENCE UNPROTECTED) (1971, Yugo.)
NEW ADVENTURES OF DR. FU MANCHU, THE (SEE: RETURN OF DR. FU MANCHU) (1930)
NEW ADVENTURES OF DON JUAN (SEE: ADVENTURES OF DON JUAN) (1949)
NEW ADVENTURES OF GET-RICH-QUICK WALLINGFORD, THE (1931) PR:A
NEW ADVENTURES OF PIPPI LONGSTOCKING, THE (1988) PR:A
NEW ADVENTURES OF TARZAN, THE (1935) PR:A
NEW ADVENTURES OF THE BIONIC BOY, THE (SEE: DYNAMITE JOHNSON) (1978, Phil.)
NEW BARBARIANS, THE (1983, It.) PR:O
NEW CENTURIONS, THE (1972) PR:O
NEW EARTH, THE (1937, Jap./Ger.) PR:A
NEW FACE IN HELL (SEE: P.J.) (1968)
NEW FACES (1954) PR:A
NEW FACES OF 1937 (1937) PR:A
NEW FRONTIER, THE (1935) PR:A
NEW FRONTIER (1939) PR:A
NEW GIRL IN TOWN (1977) PR:C-O
NEW HORIZONS (1939, USSR) PR:A
NEW HOTEL, THE (1932, Brit.) PR:A-C
NEW HOUSE ON THE LEFT, THE (1978, Brit.) PR:O
NEW INTERNS, THE (1964) PR:C
NEW INVISIBLE MAN, THE (SEE: INVISIBLE MAN, THE) (1958, Mex.)
NEW KIDS, THE (1985) PR:O
NEW KIND OF LOVE, A (1963) PR:A-C
NEW LAND, THE (1973, Swed.) PR:A
NEW LEAF, A (1971) PR:C-O
NEW LIFE, A (1988) PR:C
NEW LIFE STYLE, THE (1970, W. Ger.) PR:O
NEW LOVE (1968, Chile) PR:O
NEW MEXICO (1951) PR:A
NEW MONSTERS, THE (SEE: VIVA ITALIA) (1978, It.)

NEW MOON (1930) PR:A
NEW MOON (1940) PR:A
NEW MORALS FOR OLD (1932) PR:A
NEW MOVIETONE FOLLIES OF 1930, THE (SEE: FOX MOVIETONE FOLLIES OF 1930) (1930)
NEW ONE-ARMED SWORDSMAN, THE (SEE: TRIPLE IRONS) (1973, Hong Kong)
NEW ORLEANS (1929) PR:A
NEW ORLEANS (1947) PR:A
NEW ORLEANS AFTER DARK (1958) PR:C
NEW ORLEANS UNCENSORED (1955) PR:A
NEW TEACHER, THE (1941, USSR) PR:A
NEW WINE (1941) PR:A
NEW YEAR'S DAY (1989) PR:C
NEW YEAR'S EVIL (1980) PR:O
NEW YORK (SEE: HALLELUJAH, I'M A BUM) (1933)
NEW YORK APPELLE SUPER DRAGON (SEE: SECRET AGENT SUPER DRAGON) (1966, Fr./It./Monaco/W. Ger.)
NEW YORK CONFIDENTIAL (1955) PR:C
NEW YORK, NEW YORK (1977) PR:C
NEW YORK NIGHTS (1929) PR:A
NEW YORK NIGHTS (1984) PR:O
NEW YORK STORIES (1989) PR:C-O
NEW YORK TOWN (1941) PR:A
NEW YORK'S FINEST (1988) PR:O
NEWCOMERS, THE (SEE: WILD COUNTRY, THE) (1971)
NEWLY RICH (1931) PR:AA
NEWMAN'S LAW (1974) PR:A
NEWS HOUNDS (1947) PR:A
NEWS IS MADE AT NIGHT (1939) PR:A
NEWSBOYS' HOME (1939) PR:A
NEWSFRONT (1979, Aus.) PR:C
NEXT! (1971, It./Sp.) PR:O
NEXT IN LINE (SEE: RIDERS OF THE NORTHLAND) (1943)
NEXT MAN, THE (1976) PR:O
NEXT OF KIN (1942, Brit.) PR:A
NEXT OF KIN (1983, Aus.) PR:O
NEXT OF KIN (1989) PR:O
NEXT ONE, THE (1982, US/Gr.) PR:C
NEXT STOP, GREENWICH VILLAGE (1976) PR:C
NEXT TIME I MARRY (1938) PR:A
NEXT TIME WE LOVE (1936) PR:A
NEXT TO NO TIME (1960, Brit.) PR:A
NEXT VOICE YOU HEAR, THE (1950) PR:AA
NGATI (1987, New Zealand) PR:A
NI-LO-HO NU-ERH (SEE: DAUGHTER OF THE NILE) (1988, Taiwan)
NIAGARA (1953) PR:C
NICE GIRL? (1941) PR:A
NICE GIRL LIKE ME, A (1969, Brit.) PR:C
NICE GIRLS DON'T EXPLODE (1987) PR:C
NICE LITTLE BANK THAT SHOULD BE ROBBED, A (1958) PR:A
NICE WOMAN (1932) PR:A
NICHOLAS AND ALEXANDRA (1971, Brit.) PR:C
NICHOLAS NICKLEBY (1947, Brit.) PR:A
NICHT VERSÖHNT ODER "ES HILFT NUR GEWALT, WO GEWALT HERRSCHT" (SEE: NOT RECONCILED, OR "ONLY VIOLENCE HELPS WHERE IT RULES") (1969)
NICK CARTER IN PRAGUE (SEE: ADELE HASN'T HAD HER SUPPER YET) (1978, Czech.)
NICK CARTER, MASTER DETECTIVE (1939) PR:A
NICKEL MOUNTAIN (1985) PR:C
NICKEL QUEEN, THE (1971, Aus.) PR:A
NICKEL RIDE, THE (1974) PR:C
NICKELODEON (1976) PR:C
NIEBO ZOWIET (SEE: SKY CALLS, THE) (1959, USSR)
NIGHT, THE (SEE: LA NOTTE) (1961, Fr./It.)
NIGHT AFFAIR (1961, Fr.) PR:A
NIGHT AFTER NIGHT (1932) PR:C
NIGHT AFTER NIGHT AFTER NIGHT (1970, Brit.) PR:C-O
NIGHT ALARM (1935) PR:A
NIGHT ALONE (1938, Brit.) PR:A
NIGHT AMBUSH (1958, Brit.) PR:A
NIGHT AND DAY (1933, Brit.) PR:A
NIGHT AND DAY (1946) PR:A
NIGHT AND THE CITY (1950, Brit.) PR:O
NIGHT ANGEL, THE (1931) PR:A
NIGHT ANGELS (1987, Braz.) PR:O
NIGHT AT EARL CARROLL'S, A (1940) PR:A
NIGHT AT THE OPERA, A (1935) PR:A
NIGHT AT THE RITZ, A (1935) PR:A
NIGHT BEAT (1932) PR:A
NIGHT BEAT (1948, Brit.) PR:A
NIGHT BEFORE CHRISTMAS, A (1963, USSR) PR:A
NIGHT BEFORE THE DIVORCE, THE (1942) PR:A
NIGHT BIRDS (1931, Brit.) PR:A
NIGHT BOAT TO DUBLIN (1946, Brit.) PR:A
NIGHT CALL NURSES (1974) PR:O
NIGHT CALLER, THE (SEE: BLOOD BEAST FROM OUTER SPACE) (1965, Brit.)
NIGHT CALLER FROM OUTER SPACE (SEE: BLOOD BEAST FROM OUTER SPACE) (1965, Brit.)

NIGHT CARGO (1936) PR:A
NIGHT CHILD (1975, Brit./It.) PR:O
NIGHT CLUB (SEE: GIGOLETTE) (1935)
NIGHT CLUB GIRL (1944) PR:A
NIGHT CLUB GIRL (SEE: GLAMOUR GIRL) (1947)
NIGHT CLUB HOSTESS (SEE: UNMARRIED) (1939)
NIGHT CLUB LADY, THE (1932) PR:A
NIGHT CLUB MURDER (SEE: ROMANCE IN RHYTHM) (1934, Brit.)
NIGHT CLUB QUEEN (1934, Brit.) PR:A
NIGHT CLUB SCANDAL (1937) PR:A
NIGHT COMES TOO SOON (1948, Brit.) PR:C
NIGHT COURT (1932) PR:A
NIGHT CRAWLERS, THE (SEE: NAVY VS. THE NIGHT MONSTERS, THE) (1966)
NIGHT CREATURE (1979) PR:A
NIGHT CREATURES (1962, Brit.) PR:A
NIGHT CROSSING (1982) PR:C
NIGHT DIGGER, THE (1971, Brit.) PR:O
NIGHT EDITOR (1946) PR:A
NIGHT ENCOUNTER (1959, Fr./It.) PR:A
NIGHT EVELYN CAME OUT OF THE GRAVE, THE (1973, It.) PR:O
NIGHT EXPRESS, THE (SEE: WESTERN LIMITED) (1932)
NIGHT FIGHTERS, THE (1960, Brit.) PR:A
NIGHT FLIGHT (1933) PR:A
NIGHT FLIGHT FROM MOSCOW (SEE: SERPENT, THE) (1973, Fr./It./W. Ger.)
NIGHT FLOWERS (1979) PR:O
NIGHT FOR CRIME, A (1942) PR:A
NIGHT FREIGHT (1955) PR:A
NIGHT FULL OF RAIN, A (SEE: END OF THE WORLD (IN OUR USUAL BED IN A NIGHT FULL OF RAIN), THE) (1978, It.)
NIGHT GAME (1989) PR:O
NIGHT GAMES (1966, Swed.) PR:O
NIGHT GAMES (1980) PR:O
NIGHT GOD SCREAMED, THE (1975) PR:O
NIGHT HAIR CHILD (1971, Brit.) PR:O
NIGHT HAS A THOUSAND EYES (1948) PR:C
NIGHT HAS EYES, THE (SEE: TERROR HOUSE) (1942, Brit.)
NIGHT HAWK, THE (1938) PR:A
NIGHT HEAVEN FELL, THE (1958, Fr.) PR:O
NIGHT HOLDS TERROR, THE (1955) PR:C
NIGHT HUNT (SEE: IF HE HOLLERS, LET HIM GO!) (1968)
NIGHT IN BANGKOK (1966, Jap.) PR:A
NIGHT IN CAIRO, A (SEE: BARBARIAN, THE) (1933)
NIGHT IN CASABLANCA, A (1946) PR:A
NIGHT IN HAVANA (SEE: BIG BOODLE, THE) (1957)
NIGHT IN HEAVEN, A (1983) PR:O
NIGHT IN HONG KONG, A (1961, Jap.) PR:A
NIGHT IN JUNE, A (1940, Swed.) PR:A
NIGHT IN MONTMARTE, A (1931, Brit.) PR:A
NIGHT IN NEW ORLEANS, A (1942) PR:A
NIGHT IN PARADISE, A (1946) PR:A
NIGHT IN THE LIFE OF JIMMY REARDON, A (1988) PR:O
NIGHT INTO MORNING (1951) PR:A
NIGHT INVADER, THE (1943, Brit.) PR:C
NIGHT IS ENDING, THE (SEE: PARIS AFTER DARK) (1943)
NIGHT IS MY FUTURE (1962, Swed.) PR:A
NIGHT IS OURS (1930, Fr.) PR:A
NIGHT IS THE PHANTOM (SEE: WHAT!) (1965, Fr./Brit./It.)
NIGHT IS YOUNG, THE (1935) PR:A
NIGHT IS YOUNG, THE (SEE: BAD BLOOD) (1987, Fr.)
NIGHT JOURNEY (1938, Brit.) PR:A
NIGHT KEY (1937) PR:A
NIGHT LEGS (SEE: FRIGHT) (1971, Brit.)
NIGHT LIFE IN RENO (1931) PR:A
NIGHT LIFE OF THE GODS (1935) PR:A
NIGHT LIKE THIS, A (1932, Brit.) PR:A
NIGHT MAIL (1935, Brit.) PR:C
NIGHT MAYOR, THE (1932) PR:A
NIGHT MONSTER (1942) PR:A
'NIGHT, MOTHER (1986) PR:C
NIGHT MOVES (1975) PR:C
NIGHT MUST FALL (1937) PR:O
NIGHT MUST FALL (1964, Brit.) PR:O
NIGHT MY NUMBER CAME UP, THE (1955, Brit.) PR:A-C
NIGHT NURSE (1931) PR:A-C
NIGHT OF A THOUSAND CATS (1974, Mex.) PR:O
NIGHT OF ADVENTURE, A (1944) PR:A
NIGHT OF ANUBIS (SEE: NIGHT OF THE LIVING DEAD) (1968)
NIGHT OF BLOODY HORROR (1969) PR:O
NIGHT OF DARK SHADOWS (1971) PR:C
NIGHT OF EVIL (1962) PR:C
NIGHT OF JANUARY 16TH, THE (1941) PR:A
NIGHT OF JUNE 13, THE (1932) PR:A
NIGHT OF LUST (1965, Fr.) PR:C
NIGHT OF MAGIC, A (1944, Brit.) PR:A
NIGHT OF MYSTERY (1937) PR:A

NIGHT OF NIGHTS, THE (1939) PR:A
NIGHT OF PASSION (SEE: DURING ONE NIGHT) (1962, Brit.)
NIGHT OF SAN LORENZO, THE (SEE: NIGHT OF THE SHOOTING STARS) (1982, It.)
NIGHT OF TERROR (1933) PR:A
NIGHT OF TERRORS (SEE: MURDER CLINIC, THE) (1967, Fr./It.)
NIGHT OF THE ASKARI (1976, South Africa/W. Ger.) PR:C
NIGHT OF THE BEAST (SEE: HOUSE OF THE BLACK DEATH) (1965)
NIGHT OF THE BLOOD BEAST (1958) PR:A
NIGHT OF THE BLOODY APES (1968, Mex.) PR:O
NIGHT OF THE CLAW (SEE: ISLAND CLAWS) (1980)
NIGHT OF THE COBRA WOMAN (1974, US/Phil.) PR:O
NIGHT OF THE COMET (1984) PR:C-O
NIGHT OF THE CREEPS (1986) PR:O
NIGHT OF THE DARK FULL MOON (SEE: SILENT NIGHT, BLOODY NIGHT) (1972)
NIGHT OF THE DEMON (SEE: CURSE OF THE DEMON) (1958, Brit.)
NIGHT OF THE DEMON, THE (SEE: TOUCH OF SATAN, THE) (1971)
NIGHT OF THE DEMONS (1989) PR:O
NIGHT OF THE EAGLE (SEE: BURN, WITCH, BURN!) (1962, Brit.)
NIGHT OF THE FLESH EATERS (SEE: NIGHT OF THE LIVING DEAD) (1968)
NIGHT OF THE FOLLOWING DAY, THE (1969) PR:O
NIGHT OF THE FULL MOON, THE (1954, Brit.) PR:C
NIGHT OF THE GARTER (1933, Brit.) PR:A
NIGHT OF THE GENERALS, THE (1967, Brit./Fr.) PR:O
NIGHT OF THE GHOULS (1959) PR:O
NIGHT OF THE GRIZZLY, THE (1966) PR:A
NIGHT OF THE HUNTER, THE (1955) PR:O
NIGHT OF THE IGUANA, THE (1964) PR:O
NIGHT OF THE JUGGLER (1980) PR:O
NIGHT OF THE LAUGHING DEAD (SEE: CRAZY HOUSE) (1973, Brit.)
NIGHT OF THE LEPUS (1972) PR:C
NIGHT OF THE LIVING DEAD (1968) PR:O
NIGHT OF THE PARTY, THE (1934, Brit.) PR:A
NIGHT OF THE PROWLER (1962, Brit.) PR:C
NIGHT OF THE PROWLER, THE (1979, Aus.) PR:O
NIGHT OF THE QUARTER MOON (1959) PR:C
NIGHT OF THE SEAGULL, THE (1970, Jap.) PR:C
NIGHT OF THE SHOOTING STARS, THE (1982, It.) PR:O
NIGHT OF THE SILICATES (SEE: ISLAND OF TERROR) (1967, Brit.)
NIGHT OF THE STRANGLER (1975) PR:O
NIGHT OF THE TIGER, THE (SEE: RIDE BEYOND VENGEANCE) (1966)
NIGHT OF THE WITCHES (1970) PR:O
NIGHT OF THE ZOMBIES (1981) PR:O
NIGHT OF THE ZOMBIES (1983, Sp./It.) PR:O
NIGHT PARADE (1929) PR:A
NIGHT PASSAGE (1957) PR:A
NIGHT PATROL (1984) PR:O
NIGHT PEOPLE (1954) PR:A
NIGHT PLANE FROM CHUNGKING (1942) PR:A
NIGHT PORTER, THE (1973, It./US) PR:O
NIGHT RAIDERS (1952) PR:A
NIGHT RIDE (1930) PR:A
NIGHT RIDE (1937, Brit.) PR:C
NIGHT RIDER, THE (1932) PR:A
NIGHT RIDERS, THE (1939) PR:A
NIGHT RIDERS OF MONTANA (1951) PR:A
NIGHT RUNNER, THE (1957) PR:A
NIGHT SCHOOL (1981) PR:O
NIGHT SHADOWS (1984) PR:O
NIGHT SHIFT (1982) PR:C
NIGHT SONG (1947) PR:A
NIGHT SPOT (1938) PR:A
NIGHT STAGE TO GALVESTON (1952) PR:A
NIGHT STALKER, THE (1987) PR:O
NIGHT THE LIGHTS WENT OUT IN GEORGIA, THE (1981) PR:C
NIGHT THE SUN CAME OUT, THE (SEE: WATERMELON MAN) (1970)
NIGHT THE WORLD EXPLODED, THE (1957) PR:A
NIGHT THEY KILLED RASPUTIN, THE (1962, Fr./It.) PR:C
NIGHT THEY RAIDED MINSKY'S, THE (1968) PR:C-O
NIGHT THEY ROBBED BIG BERTHA'S, THE (1975) PR:O
NIGHT TIDE (1963) PR:C
NIGHT TIME IN NEVADA (1948) PR:A
NIGHT TO REMEMBER, A (1942) PR:A
NIGHT TO REMEMBER, A (1958, Brit.) PR:A
NIGHT TRAIN (1940, Brit.) PR:A
NIGHT TRAIN (SEE: TRAIN RIDE TO HOLLYWOOD) (1975)
NIGHT TRAIN FOR INVERNESS (1960, Brit.) PR:C
NIGHT TRAIN TO MEMPHIS (1946) PR:A
NIGHT TRAIN TO MUNDO FINE (1966) PR:A
NIGHT TRAIN TO PARIS (1964, Brit.) PR:A
NIGHT UNTO NIGHT (1949) PR:A
NIGHT VISITOR, THE (1970, Swed./US) PR:C

NIGHT WAITRESS (1936) PR:A
NIGHT WALK (SEE: DEATHDREAM) (1972, Can.)
NIGHT WALKER, THE (1964) PR:C
NIGHT WARNING (SEE: BUTCHER BAKER (NIGHT-
MARE MAKER)) (1982)
NIGHT WAS OUR FRIEND (1951, Brit.) PR:C-O
NIGHT WATCH, THE (1964, Fr./It.) PR:A
NIGHT WATCH (1973, Brit.) PR:C
NIGHT WE DROPPED A CLANGER, THE (SEE: MAKE
MINE A DOUBLE) (1961, Brit.)
NIGHT WE GOT THE BIRD, THE (1961, Brit.) PR:C
NIGHT WIND (1948) PR:A
NIGHT WITHOUT PITY (1962, Brit.) PR:C
NIGHT WITHOUT SLEEP (1952) PR:C
NIGHT WITHOUT STARS (1953, Brit.) PR:A
NIGHT WON'T TALK, THE (1952, Brit.) PR:C
NIGHT WORK (1930) PR:A
NIGHT WORK (1939) PR:A
NIGHT WORLD (1932) PR:A
NIGHT ZOO (1988, Can.) PR:O
NIGHTBEAST (1982) PR:C-O
NIGHTCOMERS, THE (1971, Brit.) PR:C-O
NIGHTFALL (1956) PR:A
NIGHTFALL (1988) PR:C
NIGHTFLYERS (1987) PR:O
NIGHTFORCE (1987) PR:O
NIGHTHAWKS (1978, Brit.) PR:O
NIGHTHAWKS (1981) PR:O
NIGHTMARE (1942) PR:C
NIGHTMARE (1956) PR:C
NIGHTMARE (1963, Brit.) PR:O
NIGHTMARE (1981) PR:O
NIGHTMARE (SEE: CITY OF THE WALKING DEAD)
(1983, Sp./It.)
NIGHTMARE ALLEY (1947) PR:C-O
NIGHTMARE CASTLE (1966, It.) PR:C
NIGHTMARE CITY (SEE: CITY OF THE WALKING
DEAD) (1983, Sp./It.)
NIGHTMARE HONEYMOON (1973) PR:O
NIGHTMARE IN BLOOD (1978) PR:O
NIGHTMARE IN THE SUN (1964) PR:O
NIGHTMARE IN WAX (1969) PR:O
NIGHTMARE ISLAND (SEE: SLAYER, THE) (1982)
NIGHTMARE MAKER (SEE: BUTCHER BAKER
(NIGHTMARE MAKER)) (1982)
NIGHTMARE ON ELM STREET, A (1984) PR:O
*NIGHTMARE ON ELM STREET PART 2: FREDDY'S RE-
VENGE, A* (1985) PR:O
NIGHTMARE ON ELM STREET 3: DREAM WARRIORS, A
(1987) PR:O
*NIGHTMARE ON ELM STREET 4: THE DREAM MAS-
TER, A* (1988) PR:O
*NIGHTMARE ON ELM STREET 5: THE DREAM CHILD,
A* (1989) PR:O
NIGHTMARE WEEKEND (1986, Brit./US/Fr.) PR:O
NIGHTMARES (1983) PR:O
NIGHTMARE'S PASSENGERS (1986, Arg.) PR:O
NIGHTS IN A HAREM (SEE: SON OF SINBAD) (1955)
NIGHTS OF CABIRIA (1957, It.) PR:C
NIGHTS OF LUCRETIA BORGIA, THE (1960, It.) PR:A
NIGHTS OF PRAGUE, THE (1968, Czech.) PR:C
NIGHTS OF SHAME (1961, Fr.) PR:O
NIGHTS WHEN THE DEVIL CAME (SEE: DEVIL
STRIKES AT NIGHT, THE) (1959, W. Ger.)
NIGHTSONGS (1984) PR:C
NIGHTWARS (1988) PR:O
NIGHTWING (1979) PR:O
NIHON NO ICHIBAN NAGAI HI (SEE: EMPEROR AND
A GENERAL, THE) (1968, Jap.)
NIJINSKY (1980, Brit.) PR:C-O
NIJUSHI NO HITOMI (SEE: TWENTY-FOUR EYES)
(1954, Jap.)
NIKKI, WILD DOG OF THE NORTH (1961, US/Can.)
PR:AA
NIKUTAI NO GAKKO (SEE: SCHOOL FOR SEX) (1966,
Jap.)
NIKUTAI NO MON (SEE: GATE OF FLESH) (1964, Jap.)
9 1/2 WEEKS (1986) PR:O
NINE DAYS A QUEEN (SEE: LADY JANE GREY) (1936,
Brit.)
NINE DAYS OF ONE YEAR (1964, USSR) PR:O
9 DEATHS OF THE NINJA (1985) PR:O
NINE FORTY-FIVE (1934, Brit.) PR:A
NINE GIRLS (1944) PR:C
NINE HOURS TO RAMA (1963, US/Brit.) PR:C
NINE LIVES ARE NOT ENOUGH (1941) PR:A
NINE LIVES ARE NOT ENOUGH (SEE: NINE LIVES
ARE NOT ENOUGH) (1941)
NINE MEN (1943, Brit.) PR:A
9 MILES TO NOON (1963) PR:C
976-EVIL (1989) PR:O
9/30/55 (1977) PR:C
NINE TILL SIX (1932, Brit.) PR:A
NINE TO FIVE (1980) PR:C-O
1918 (1985) PR:C
1984 (1956, Brit.) PR:A-C
1984 (1984, Brit.) PR:O
1941 (1979) PR:C-O

1914 (1932, Ger.) PR:C
1900 (1976, It.) PR:C-O
1919 (1984, Brit.) PR:O
1990: THE BRONX WARRIORS (1983, It.) PR:C
1969 (1988) PR:C
90 DAYS (1986, Can.) PR:O
90 DEGREES IN THE SHADE (1966, Czech./Brit.) PR:O
99 AND 44/100% DEAD (1974) PR:C-O
99 RIVER STREET (1953) PR:C
99 WOUNDS (1931) PR:A
92 IN THE SHADE (1975, US/Brit.) PR:C
NINGEN NO JOKEN (SEE: HUMAN CONDITION, THE)
(1959, Jap.)
NINGEN NO JOKEN II (SEE: ROAD TO ETERNITY)
(1961, Jap.)
NINGEN NO JOKEN III (SEE: SOLDIER'S PRAYER, A)
(1970, Jap.)
NINJA III — THE DOMINATION (1984) PR:O
NINJA TURF (1986) PR:O
NINOTCHKA (1939) PR:A
NINTH CIRCLE, THE (1961, Yugo.) PR:O
NINTH CONFIGURATION, THE (1980) PR:O
NINTH GUEST, THE (1934) PR:A
NINTH HEART, THE (1980, Czech.) PR:A
NINTH SYMPHONY (SEE: FINAL CHORD, THE) (1936,
Ger.)
NIPPER, THE (SEE: BRAT, THE) (1930, Brit.)
NIPPON CHIUBOTSU (SEE: TIDAL WAVE) (1975,
US/Jap.)
NIPPON KONCHUKI (SEE: INSECT WOMAN, THE)
(1964, Jap.)
NIPPON NO ICHIBAN NAGAI HI (SEE: EMPEROR
AND A GENERAL, THE) (1968, Jap.)
NITWITS, THE (1935) PR:A
NIX ON DAMES (1929) PR:A
NO BLADE OF GRASS (1970, Brit.) PR:O
NO BRAKES (SEE: OH, YEAH!) (1929)
NO DEAD HEROES (1987) PR:O
NO DEADLY MACHINE (SEE: YOUNG DOCTORS,
THE) (1961)
NO DEFENSE (1929) PR:A
NO DEPOSIT, NO RETURN (1976) PR:AA
NO DOWN PAYMENT (1957) PR:C
NO DRUMS, NO BUGLES (1971) PR:A
NO ESCAPE (1934, Brit.) PR:C
NO ESCAPE (1936, Brit.) PR:C
NO ESCAPE (SEE: I ESCAPED FROM THE GESTAPO)
(1943)
NO ESCAPE (1953) PR:O
NO EXIT (1930, Brit.) PR:A
NO EXIT (1962, US/Arg.) PR:O
NO FUNNY BUSINESS (1934, Brit.) PR:A
NO GREATER GLORY (1934) PR:A
NO GREATER LOVE (SEE: ALOHA) (1931)
NO GREATER LOVE (1932) PR:A
NO GREATER LOVE (1944, USSR) PR:O
NO GREATER LOVE (SEE: HUMAN CONDITION,
THE) (1959, Jap.)
NO GREATER LOVE THAN THIS (1969, Jap.) PR:C
NO GREATER SIN (1941) PR:A
NO GREATER SIN (SEE: EIGHTEEN AND ANXIOUS)
(1957)
NO HABRA MAS PENAS NI OLVIDO (SEE: FUNNY,
DIRTY LITTLE WAR, A) (1983, Arg.)
NO HANDS ON THE CLOCK (1941) PR:A
NO HAUNT FOR A GENTLEMAN (1952, Brit.) PR:A
NO HIGHWAY (SEE: NO HIGHWAY IN THE SKY)
(1951, Brit.)
NO HIGHWAY IN THE SKY (1951, Brit.) PR:A
NO HOLDS BARRED (1952) PR:A
NO HOLDS BARRED (1989) PR:C
NO KIDDING (SEE: BEWARE OF CHILDREN) (1961,
Brit.)
NO KNIFE (SEE: FRISCO KID, THE) (1979)
NO LADY (1931, Brit.) PR:A
NO LEAVE, NO LOVE (1946) PR:A
NO LIMIT (1931) PR:A
NO LIMIT (1935, Brit.) PR:A
NO LIVING WITNESS (1932) PR:A
NO LONGER ALONE (1978) PR:C
NO LOVE FOR JOHNNIE (1961, Brit.) PR:O
NO LOVE FOR JUDY (1955, Brit.) PR:C
NO MAN IS AN ISLAND (1962) PR:C
NO MAN OF HER OWN (1933) PR:A
NO MAN OF HER OWN (1950) PR:A
NO MAN WALKS ALONE (SEE: BLACK LIKE ME)
(1964)
NO MAN'S LAND (SEE: HELL ON EARTH) (1934, Ger.)
NO MAN'S LAND (1964) PR:O
NO MAN'S LAND (1987) PR:O
NO MAN'S RANGE (1935) PR:A
NO MAN'S WOMAN (1955) PR:C
NO MARRIAGE TIES (1933) PR:A
NO MERCY (1986) PR:O
NO MERCY MAN, THE (1975) PR:O
NO MINOR VICES (1948) PR:A
NO MONKEY BUSINESS (1935, Brit.) PR:A
NO MORE EXCUSES (1968) PR:O

NO MORE LADIES (1935) PR:C
NO MORE ORCHIDS (1933) PR:A
NO MORE WOMEN (1934) PR:A
NO, MY DARLING DAUGHTER! (1964, Brit.) PR:A
NO NAME ON THE BULLET (1959) PR:A
NO, NO NANETTE (1930) PR:A
NO, NO NANETTE (1940) PR:A
NO ONE MAN (1932) PR:A
NO ORCHIDS FOR MISS BLANDISH (1948, Brit.) PR:O
NO OTHER WOMAN (1933) PR:A
NO PARKING (1938, Brit.) PR:A
NO PLACE FOR A LADY (1943) PR:A
NO PLACE FOR JENNIFER (1950, Brit.) PR:A
NO PLACE LIKE HOMICIDE (SEE: WHAT A CARVE
UP!) (1962, Brit.)
NO PLACE TO GO (1939) PR:A
NO PLACE TO HIDE (1956) PR:A
NO PLACE TO HIDE (1975) PR:C-O
NO PLACE TO LAND (1958) PR:A-C
NO QUESTIONS ASKED (1951) PR:A
NO RANSOM (1935) PR:A
NO RESTING PLACE (1952, Brit.) PR:A
NO RETREAT, NO SURRENDER (1986) PR:C
NO RETREAT, NO SURRENDER II (1989, Hong Kong)
PR:O
NO RETURN ADDRESS (1961) PR:A
NO ROAD BACK (1957, Brit.) PR:A
NO ROOM AT THE INN (1950, Brit.) PR:A
NO ROOM FOR THE GROOM (1952) PR:A
NO ROOM TO DIE (1969, It.) PR:O
NO ROSES FOR OSS 117 (1968, Fr.) PR:C
NO SAD SONGS FOR ME (1950) PR:A-C
NO SAFE HAVEN (1989) PR:C
NO SAFETY AHEAD (1959, Brit.) PR:C
NO SEX PLEASE — WE'RE BRITISH (1979, Brit.) PR:C
NO SLEEP TILL DAWN (SEE: BOMBERS B-52) (1957)
NO SMALL AFFAIR (1984) PR:O
NO SMOKING (1955, Brit.) PR:A
NO SURRENDER (1986, Brit.) PR:O
NO SURVIVORS, PLEASE (1963, W. Ger.) PR:C
NO TIME FOR BREAKFAST (1978, Fr.) PR:O
NO TIME FOR COMEDY (1940) PR:A
NO TIME FOR ECSTASY (1963, Fr.) PR:O
NO TIME FOR FLOWERS (1952) PR:A
NO TIME FOR LOVE (1943) PR:A
NO TIME FOR SERGEANTS (1958) PR:A
NO TIME FOR TEARS (SEE: PURPLE HEART DIARY)
(1951)
NO TIME FOR TEARS (1957, Brit.) PR:A
NO TIME TO BE YOUNG (1957) PR:O
NO TIME TO DIE (SEE: TANK FORCE) (1958, Brit.)
NO TIME TO KILL (1963, Brit./Swed./W. Ger.) PR:C
NO TIME TO MARRY (1938) PR:A
NO TOYS FOR CHRISTMAS (SEE: ONCE BEFORE I
DIE) (1967)
NO TRACE (1950, Brit.) PR:A
NO TREE IN THE STREET (1964, Brit.) PR:A
NO WAY BACK (1949, Brit.) PR:C
NO WAY BACK (1976) PR:O
NO WAY OUT (1950) PR:A
NO WAY OUT (1972, Fr./It.) PR:O
NO WAY OUT (1987) PR:O
NO WAY TO TREAT A LADY (1968) PR:C-O
NOAH'S ARK (1928) PR:A-C
NOB HILL (1945) PR:A
NOBI (SEE: FIRES ON THE PLAIN) (1959, Jap.)
NOBODY LIVES FOREVER (1946) PR:A
NOBODY LOVES A DRUNKEN INDIAN (SEE: FLAP)
(1970)
NOBODY RUNS FOREVER (SEE: HIGH COMMIS-
SIONER, THE) (1968, US/Brit.)
NOBODY WAVED GOODBYE (1965, Can.) PR:C
NOBODY'S BABY (1937) PR:A
NOBODY'S CHILDREN (1940) PR:AA
NOBODY'S DARLING (1943) PR:A
NOBODY'S FOOL (1936) PR:A
NOBODY'S FOOL (1986) PR:C
NOBODY'S PERFECT (1968) PR:A
NOBODY'S PERFEKT (1981) PR:C
NOBORIRYU TEKKAHADA (SEE: FRIENDLY KILLER,
THE) (1970)
NOCE IN GALILEE (SEE: WEDDING IN GALILEE)
(1988)
NOCTURNA (1979) PR:O
NOCTURNE (1946) PR:C
NODDY IN TOYLAND (1958, Brit.) PR:A
NOI TRE (SEE: WE THREE) (1985, It.)
NOIR ET BLANC (SEE: BLACK AND WHITE) (1986, Fr.)
NOISY NEIGHBORS (1929) PR:A
NOMADIC LIVES (1977) PR:C
NOMADS (1985) PR:O
NON SI SEVE PROFANARE OL SONNE DIE MORTE
(SEE: DON'T OPEN THE WINDOW) (1974, It./Sp.)
NON-STOP NEW YORK (1937, Brit.) PR:A
NON TIRATE IL DIAVOLO PER LA CODA (SEE: DEVIL
BY THE TAIL, THE) (1969, Fr./It.)
NONE BUT THE BRAVE (SEE: FOR THE LOVE OF
MIKE) (1960)

NONE BUT THE BRAVE (1963) PR:C
NONE BUT THE BRAVE (1965, US/Jap.) PR:O
NONE BUT THE LONELY HEART (1944) PR:A
NONE SHALL ESCAPE (1944) PR:A
NOOSE (SEE: SILK NOOSE, THE) (1950, Brit.)
NOOSE FOR A GUNMAN (1960) PR:A
NOOSE FOR A LADY (1953, Brit.) PR:A
NOOSE HANGS HIGH, THE (1948) PR:AA
NOR THE MOON BY NIGHT (SEE: ELEPHANT GUN)
   (1959, Brit.)
NORA INU (SEE: STRAY DOG) (1949, Jap.)
NORA PRENTISS (1947) PR:A
NORAH O'NEALE (1934, Brit.) PR:A
NORMA RAE (1979) PR:A-C
NORMAN CONQUEST (1953, Brit.) PR:A
NORMAN. . . IS THAT YOU? (1976) PR:C
NORMAN LOVES ROSE (1982, Aus.) PR:O
NORSEMAN, THE (1978) PR:C
NORTH AVENUE IRREGULARS, THE (1979) PR:A
NORTH BY NORTHWEST (1959) PR:A
NORTH DALLAS FORTY (1979) PR:C-O
NORTH FROM LONE STAR (1941) PR:A
NORTH OF NOME (1937) PR:A
NORTH OF SHANGHAI (1939) PR:A
NORTH OF THE GREAT DIVIDE (1950) PR:A
NORTH OF THE RIO GRANDE (1937) PR:A
NORTH OF THE YUKON (1939) PR:A
NORTH SEA HIJACK (SEE: FFOLKES) (1979, Brit.)
NORTH SEA PATROL (1939, Brit.) PR:A
NORTH SHORE (1987) PR:C
NORTH STAR, THE (1943) PR:A-C
NORTH STAR, THE (SEE: L'ETOILE DU NORD) (1981,
   Fr.)
NORTH TO ALASKA (1960) PR:A
NORTH TO THE KLONDIKE (1942) PR:A
NORTH WEST FRONTIER (SEE: FLAME OVER INDIA)
   (1960, Brit.)
NORTHERN FRONTIER (1935) PR:A
NORTHERN LIGHTS (1978) PR:A
NORTHERN PATROL (1953) PR:A
NORTHERN PURSUIT (1943) PR:A
NORTHFIELD CEMETERY MASSACRE, THE (SEE:
   NORTHVILLE CEMETERY MASSACRE, THE) (1976)
NORTHVILLE CEMETERY MASSACRE, THE (1976) PR:O
NORTHWEST MOUNTED POLICE (1940) PR:A
NORTHWEST OUTPOST (1947) PR:A
NORTHWEST PASSAGE (1940) PR:A-C
NORTHWEST RANGERS (1942) PR:A
NORTHWEST STAMPEDE (1948) PR:A
NORTHWEST TERRITORY (1952) PR:A
NORTHWEST TRAIL (1945) PR:A
NORWOOD (1970) PR:A
NOSFERATU, THE VAMPIRE (1979, Fr./W. Ger.) PR:C-O
NOSTALGHIA (1984, USSR/It.) PR:O
NOT A HOPE IN HELL (1960, Brit.) PR:A
NOT AGAINST THE FLESH (SEE: VAMPYR) (1932,
   Fr./Ger.)
NOT AS A STRANGER (1955) PR:A-C
NOT DAMAGED (1930) PR:C
NOT EXACTLY GENTLEMEN (SEE: THREE ROGUES)
   (1931)
NOT FOR HONOR AND GLORY (SEE: LOST COM-
   MAND) (1966)
NOT FOR PUBLICATION (1984) PR:C-O
NOT MINE TO LOVE (1969, Israel) PR:A
NOT NOW DARLING (1975, Brit.) PR:O
NOT OF THIS EARTH (1957) PR:A
NOT OF THIS EARTH (1988) PR:O
NOT ON YOUR LIFE (SEE: ISLAND OF LOVE) (1963)
NOT ON YOUR LIFE (1965, It./Sp.) PR:C-O
NOT QUITE DECENT (1929) PR:A
NOT QUITE JERUSALEM (1985, Brit.) PR:O
NOT RECONCILED, OR "ONLY VIOLENCE HELPS
   WHERE IT RULES" (1969, W. Ger.) PR:C
NOT SINCE CASANOVA (1988) PR:O
NOT SO DUMB (1930) PR:A
NOT SO DUSTY (1936, Brit.) PR:A
NOT SO DUSTY (1956, Brit.) PR:A
NOT SO QUIET ON THE WESTERN FRONT (1930,
   Brit.) PR:A
NOT WANTED (1949) PR:A
NOT WANTED ON VOYAGE (SEE: TREACHERY ON
   THE HIGH SEAS) (1939, Brit.)
NOT WANTED ON VOYAGE (1957, Brit.) PR:A
NOT WITH MY WIFE, YOU DON'T! (1966) PR:A
NOTEBOOKS OF MAJOR THOMPSON (SEE: FRENCH,
   THEY ARE A FUNNY RACE, THE) (1956, Fr.)
NOTHING BARRED (1961, Brit.) PR:A
NOTHING BUT A MAN (1964) PR:A
NOTHING BUT THE BEST (1964, Brit.) PR:C
NOTHING BUT THE NIGHT (1975, Brit.) PR:A
NOTHING BUT THE TRUTH (1929) PR:A
NOTHING BUT THE TRUTH (1941) PR:A
NOTHING BUT TROUBLE (1944) PR:AA
NOTHING IN COMMON (1986) PR:A-C
NOTHING LASTS FOREVER (1984) PR:C
NOTHING LIKE PUBLICITY (1936, Brit.) PR:A
NOTHING PERSONAL (1980, Can.) PR:A-C

NOTHING SACRED (1937) PR:A
NOTHING TO LOSE (SEE: TIME GENTLEMEN
   PLEASE!) (1953, Brit.)
NOTHING VENTURE (1948, Brit.) PR:AA
NOTORIOUS (1946) PR:A
NOTORIOUS AFFAIR, A (1930) PR:A
NOTORIOUS BUT NICE (1934) PR:A
NOTORIOUS CLEOPATRA, THE (1970) PR:O
NOTORIOUS GENTLEMAN, A (1935) PR:A
NOTORIOUS GENTLEMAN (1945, Brit.) PR:C
NOTORIOUS LANDLADY, THE (1962) PR:A-C
NOTORIOUS LONE WOLF, THE (1946) PR:A
NOTORIOUS MR. MONKS, THE (1958) PR:C
NOTORIOUS SOPHIE LANG, THE (1934) PR:A
NOTRE DAME DE PARIS (SEE: HUNCHBACK OF
   NOTRE DAME, THE) (1957, Fr.)
NOTTE EROTIQUE (SEE: NIGHT OF LUST) (1965, Fr.)
NOUS IRONS A MONTE CARLO (SEE: MONTE
   CARLO BABY) (1953, Fr.)
NOUS IRONS A PARIS (1949, Fr.) PR:A
NOUS MAIGRIRONS ENSEMBLE (SEE: WE'LL GROW
   THIN TOGETHER) (1979, Fr.)
NOUS SOMMES TOUS DES ASSASSINS (SEE: WE
   ARE ALL MURDERERS) (1957, Fr.)
NOVECENTO (SEE: 1900) (1976, It.)
NOVEL AFFAIR, A (1957, Brit.) PR:A
NOW ABOUT ALL THESE WOMEN (SEE: ALL THESE
   WOMEN) (1964, Swed.)
NOW AND FOREVER (1934) PR:A
NOW AND FOREVER (1956, Brit.) PR:A
NOW AND FOREVER (1983, Aus.) PR:O
NOW BARABBAS (SEE: NOW BARABBAS WAS A
   ROBBER) (1949, Brit.)
NOW BARABBAS WAS A ROBBER. . . (1949, Brit.) PR:A
NOW I LAY ME DOWN (SEE: RACHEL, RACHEL)
   (1958)
NOW I'LL TELL (1934) PR:A-C
NOW IT CAN BE TOLD (SEE: SECRET DOOR, THE)
   (1964)
NOW THAT APRIL'S HERE (1958, Can.) PR:A
NOW, VOYAGER (1942) PR:A-C
NOW YOU SEE HIM, NOW YOU DON'T (1972) PR:AA
NOWHERE TO GO (1959, Brit.) PR:A
NOWHERE TO HIDE (1987, Can.) PR:O
NOWHERE TO RUN (1989) PR:O
NOZ W WODZIE (SEE: KNIFE IN THE WATER) (1962,
   Pol.)
NUDE BOMB, THE (1980) PR:A
NUDE IN A WHITE CAR (1960, Fr.) PR:C
NUDE IN HIS POCKET (1962, Fr.) PR:A
NUDE ODYSSEY (1962, Fr./It.) PR:A
NUDE. . . SI MUORE (SEE: YOUNG, THE EVIL AND
   THE SAVAGE, THE) (1968, It.)
NUDES ON CREDIT (SEE: LOVE NOW. . . PAY LATER)
   (1966)
NUDES ON THE ROCKS (SEE: 50,000 YEARS BC (BE-
   FORE CLOTHING)) (1963)
NUISANCE, THE (1933) PR:A
NUITS DE FEU (SEE: LIVING CORPSE, THE) (1940, Fr.)
NUITS ROUGES (SEE: SHADOWMAN) (1974, Fr./It.)
NO. 96 (1974, Aus.) PR:C
NUMBER ONE (1969) PR:C
NUMBER ONE (1984, Brit.) PR:C
NUMBER ONE WITH A BULLET (1987) PR:C-O
NUMBER SEVENTEEN (1928, Brit./Ger.) PR:A
NUMBER SEVENTEEN (1932, Brit.) PR:A
NUMBER SIX (1962, Brit.) PR:A
NO. 13 DEMON STREET (SEE: DEVIL'S MESSENGER,
   THE) (1962, US/Swed.)
NUMBER TWO (1975, Fr.) PR:O
NUMBERED MEN (1930) PR:A
NUMERO DEUX (SEE: NUMBER TWO) (1975, Fr.)
NUN, THE (1971, Fr.) PR:C
NUN AND THE SERGEANT, THE (1962) PR:A
NUN AT THE CROSSROADS, A (1970, It./Sp.) PR:A
NUN OF MONZA, THE (SEE: LADY OF MONZA, THE)
   (1970)
NUN'S STORY, THE (1959) PR:A
NUNZIO (1978) PR:O
NUR TOTE ZEUGEN SCHWEIGEN (SEE: HYPNOSIS)
   (1966, It./Sp./W. Ger.)
NURSE EDITH CAVELL (1939) PR:A
NURSE FROM BROOKLYN (1938) PR:A
NURSE ON WHEELS (1964, Brit.) PR:O
NURSE SHERRI (1978) PR:O
NURSE WHO DISAPPEARED, THE (1939, Brit.)
   PR:A
NURSE'S SECRET, THE (1941) PR:A
NUT FARM, THE (1935) PR:A
NUTCRACKER (1982, Brit.) PR:O
NUTCRACKER FANTASY (1979) PR:AA
NUTCRACKER: THE MOTION PICTURE (1986) PR:AA
NUTS (1987) PR:C-O
NUTTY, NAUGHTY CHATEAU (1964, Fr./It.) PR:C
NUTTY PROFESSOR, THE (1963) PR:A
NVUIIRANDO NO WAKADAISHO (SEE: YOUNG GUY
   ON MT. COOK) (1969, Jap.)
NYBYGGARNA (SEE: NEW LAND, THE) (1973, Swed.)

NYUJIRANDO NO WAKADAISHO (SEE: YOUNG GUY
   ON MT. COOK) (1969)

O

O BOBO (SEE: JESTER, THE) (1987, Portugal)
O CANGACEIRO (SEE: MAGNIFICENT BANDITS,
   THE) (1969, It./Sp.)
O LUCKY MAN! (1973, Brit.) PR:O
O, MY DARLING CLEMENTINE (1943) PR:A
O PAGADOR DE PROMESSAS (SEE: GIVEN WORD,
   THE) (1964, Braz.)
O SLAVNOSTI A HOSTECH (SEE: REPORT ON THE
   PARTY AND THE GUESTS, A) (1968, Czech.)
O-GIN SAMA (SEE: LOVE UNDER THE CRUCIFIX)
   (1965, Jap.)
O. HENRY'S FULL HOUSE (1952) PR:AA
O.C. AND STIGGS (1987) PR:O
O.K. CONNERY (SEE: OPERATION KID BROTHER)
   (1967, It.)
O.M.H.S. (SEE: YOU'RE IN THE ARMY NOW) (1937,
   Brit.)
O.S.S. (1946) PR:C
OASIS, THE (1984) PR:O
OBCH OD NA KORZE (SEE: SHOP ON MAIN STREET,
   THE) (1965, Czech.)
OBERST REDL (SEE: COLONEL REDL) (1985,
   Aust./Hung./W. Ger.)
OBEY THE LAW (1933) PR:A
OBJECTIVE, BURMA! (1945) PR:C
OBJECTIVE 500 MILLION (1966, Fr.) PR:C
OBLIGING YOUNG LADY (1941) PR:A
OBLONG BOX, THE (1969, Brit.) PR:O
OBRAS MAESTRAS DEL TERROR (SEE: MASTER OF
   HORROR) (1965, Arg.)
OBSESSED (1951, Brit.) PR:C
OBSESSED (1988, Can.) PR:C
OBSESSION (SEE: HIDDEN ROOM, THE) (1949, Brit.)
OBSESSION (1954, Fr./It.) PR:C
OBSESSION (1968, Swed.) PR:C
OBSESSION (1976) PR:C
OBVIOUS SITUATION, AN (SEE: HOURS OF LONELI-
   NESS) (1930, Brit.)
OCCHI SENZA VOLTO (SEE: HORROR CHAMBER OF
   DR. FAUSTUS, THE) (1959, Fr./It.)
OCEAN BREAKERS (1949, Swed.) PR:A
OCEAN DRIVE WEEKEND (1986) PR:C
OCEAN'S ELEVEN (1960) PR:A
OCHAZUKE NO AJI (SEE: TEA AND RICE) (1964, Jap.)
OCI CIORNIE (SEE: DARK EYES) (1987, It.)
OCTAGON, THE (1980) PR:O
OCTAMAN (1971) PR:O
OCTOBER MAN, THE (1948, Brit.) PR:A
OCTOBER MOTH (1960, Brit.) PR:O
OCTOMAN (SEE: OCTAMAN) (1971)
OCTOPUSSY (1983, Brit.) PR:C
ODD ANGRY SHOT, THE (1979, Aus.) PR:C
ODD COUPLE, THE (1968) PR:O
ODD JOB, THE (1978, Brit.) PR:O
ODD JOBS (1986) PR:C-O
ODD MAN OUT (1947, Brit.) PR:C-O
ODD OBSESSION (1959, Jap.) PR:O
ODDO (1967) PR:O
ODDS AGAINST TOMORROW (1959) PR:C
ODE TO BILLY JOE (1976) PR:O
ODESSA FILE, THE (1974, Brit./W. Ger.) PR:C
ODETTE (1951, Brit.) PR:C
ODIO LE BIONDE (SEE: I HATE BLONDES) (1981, It.)
ODIO MI CUERPO (SEE: I HATE MY BODY) (1975,
   Sp./Switz.)
ODIO PER ODIO (SEE: HATE FOR HATE) (1967, It.)
ODISSEA NUDA (SEE: NUDE ODYSSEY) (1962, Fr./It.)
ODONGO (1956, Brit.) PR:A
ODYSSEY OF THE PACIFIC (1981, Can./Fr.) PR:AA
OEDIPUS REX (1957, Can.) PR:A
OEDIPUS THE KING (1968, Brit.) PR:C
OF BEDS AND BROADS (SEE: TALES OF PARIS)
   (1962, Fr./It.)
OF FLESH AND BLOOD (1964, Fr./It.) PR:C
OF HUMAN BONDAGE (1934) PR:C-O
OF HUMAN BONDAGE (1946) PR:C
OF HUMAN BONDAGE (1964, Brit.) PR:O
OF HUMAN HEARTS (1938) PR:A
OF LOVE AND DESIRE (1963) PR:O
OF MICE AND MEN (1939) PR:O
OF STARS AND MEN (1961) PR:AA
OF UNKNOWN ORIGIN (1983, Can.) PR:O
OF WAYWARD LOVE (1964, It./W. Ger.) PR:O
OFF BEAT (1986) PR:C
OFF LIMITS (1953) PR:A
OFF LIMITS (1988) PR:O
OFF THE BEATEN TRACK (SEE: BEHIND THE EIGHT
   BALL) (1942)
OFF THE DOLE (1935, Brit.) PR:A
OFF THE RECORD (1939) PR:A
OFF THE WALL (1977) PR:C
OFF THE WALL (1983) PR:O
OFF TO THE RACES (1937) PR:A
OFFBEAT (1961, Brit.) PR:A

OFFENDERS, THE (1980) PR:O
OFFENSE, THE (1973, Brit.) PR:O
OFFERING, THE (1966, Can.) PR:C
OFFERINGS (1989) PR:O
OFFICE GIRL, THE (1932, Brit.) PR:A
OFFICE GIRLS (1974, W. Ger.) PR:O
OFFICE PICNIC, THE (1974, Aus.) PR:C
OFFICE SCANDAL, THE (1929) PR:A
OFFICE WIFE, THE (1930) PR:A
OFFICER AND A GENTLEMAN, AN (1982) PR:O
OFFICER AND THE LADY, THE (1941) PR:A
OFFICER O'BRIEN (1930) PR:A
OFFICER 13 (1933) PR:A
OFFICER'S MESS, THE (1931, Brit.) PR:A
OFFICIAL STORY, THE (1985, Arg.) PR:O
OFFRET-SA CRIFICATIO (SEE: SACRIFICE) (1986,
   Fr./Swed.)
OFFSPRING, THE (1987) PR:O
O'FLYNN, THE (SEE: FIGHTING O'FLYNN, THE)
   (1949)
OGGI A ME DOMANI A TE? (SEE: TODAY IT'S ME. . .
   TOMORROW YOU?) (1968, It.)
OGNUNO PER SE (SEE: RUTHLESS FOUR, THE) (1969,
   It./W. Ger.)
OH, ALFIE (SEE: ALFIE DARLING) (1975, Brit.)
OH BOY! (1938, Brit.) PR:A
OH BROTHERHOOD (SEE: FRATERNITY ROW) (1977)
OH! CALCUTTA! (1972) PR:O
OH, CHARLIE (SEE: HOLD THAT GHOST) (1941)
OH DAD, POOR DAD, MAMA'S HUNG YOU IN THE
   CLOSET AND I'M FEELIN' SO SAD (1967) PR:C
OH DADDY! (1935, Brit.) PR:A
OH, DOCTOR (1937) PR:A
OH, DOCTOR (SEE: HIT THE ICE) (1943)
OH, FOR A MAN! (1930) PR:A
OH! FOR A MAN! (SEE: WILL SUCCESS SPOIL ROCK
   HUNTER?) (1957)
OH, GOD! (1977) PR:A-C
OH GOD! BOOK II (1980) PR:A-C
OH GOD! YOU DEVIL (1984) PR:A-C
OH, HEAVENLY DOG! (1980) PR:O
OH JOHNNY, HOW YOU CAN LOVE! (1940) PR:A
OH, MEN! OH, WOMEN! (1957) PR:A-C
OH, MR. PORTER! (1937, Brit.) PR:A
OH MY DARLING CLEMENTINE (SEE: O, MY DAR-
   LING CLEMENTINE) (1943)
OH NO DOCTOR! (1934, Brit.) PR:A
OH, ROSALINDA!! (1956, Brit.) PR:A
OH! SAILOR, BEHAVE! (1930) PR:AA
OH, SUSANNA (1937) PR:A
OH, SUSANNA (1951) PR:A
OH! THOSE MOST SECRET AGENTS (SEE: 00-2 MOST
   SECRET AGENTS) (1965, It.)
OH THOSE MOST SECRET AGENTS (SEE: 00-2 MOST
   SECRET AGENTS) (1965, It.)
OH WHAT A DUCHESS! (SEE: MY OLD DUCHESS)
   (1933, Brit.)
OH! WHAT A LOVELY WAR (1969, Brit.) PR:A-C
OH, WHAT A NIGHT (1935, Brit.) PR:A
OH, WHAT A NIGHT (1944) PR:A
OH, YEAH! (1929) PR:A
OH, YOU BEAUTIFUL DOLL (1949) PR:A
O'HARA'S WIFE (1983) PR:C
OHAYO (1962, Jap.) PR:A
OIL FOR THE LAMPS OF CHINA (1935) PR:A
OIL GIRLS, THE (SEE: LEGEND OF FRENCHIE KING,
   THE) (1971, Fr./It./Sp./Brit.)
OIL TOWN (SEE: LUCY GALLANT) (1955)
OKASAN (SEE: MOTHER) (1952, Jap.)
OKAY AMERICA (1932) PR:A
OKAY BILL (1971) PR:O
OKAY FOR SOUND (1937, Brit.) PR:A
OKEFENOKEE (1960) PR:O
OKINAWA (1952) PR:A
OKLAHOMA! (1955) PR:AA
OKLAHOMA ANNIE (1952) PR:A
OKLAHOMA BADLANDS (1948) PR:A
OKLAHOMA BLUES (1948) PR:A
OKLAHOMA CRUDE (1973) PR:O
OKLAHOMA CYCLONE (1930) PR:A
OKLAHOMA FRONTIER (1939) PR:A
OKLAHOMA JIM (1931) PR:A
OKLAHOMA JUSTICE (1951) PR:A
OKLAHOMA KID, THE (1939) PR:A
OKLAHOMA RAIDERS (1944) PR:A
OKLAHOMA RENEGADES (1940) PR:A
OKLAHOMA TERRITORY (1960) PR:A
OKLAHOMA TERROR (1939) PR:A
OKLAHOMA WOMAN, THE (1956) PR:C
OKLAHOMAN, THE (1957) PR:A
OLD ACQUAINTANCE (1943) PR:A-C
OLD BARN DANCE, THE (1938) PR:A
OLD BILL AND SON (1940, Brit.) PR:A
OLD BONES OF THE RIVER (1938, Brit.) PR:A
OLD BOYFRIENDS (1979) PR:O
OLD CHISHOLM TRAIL (1943) PR:A
OLD CORRAL, THE (SEE: SONG OF THE GRINGO)
   (1936)

OLD CORRAL, THE (1937) PR:A
OLD CURIOSITY SHOP, THE (1935, Brit.) PR:A
OLD CURIOSITY SHOP, THE (SEE: MR. QUILP) (1975,
   Brit.)
OLD DARK HOUSE, THE (1932) PR:A
OLD DARK HOUSE, THE (1963, US/Brit.) PR:A
OLD DRACULA (1975, Brit.) PR:C
OLD ENGLISH (1930) PR:A
OLD ENOUGH (1984) PR:C
OLD FAITHFUL (1935, Brit.) PR:A
OLD-FASHIONED GIRL, AN (1948) PR:A
OLD-FASHIONED WAY, THE (1934) PR:A
OLD FRONTIER, THE (1950) PR:A
OLD GREATHEART (SEE: WAY BACK HOME) (1932)
OLD GRINGO (1989) PR:C
OLD GROUCHY (SEE: GROUCH, THE) (1961, Gr.)
OLD HOMESTEAD, THE (1935) PR:A
OLD HOMESTEAD, THE (1942) PR:A
OLD HUTCH (1936) PR:A
OLD IRON (1938, Brit.) PR:A
OLD LOS ANGELES (1948) PR:A
OLD LOUISIANA (1938) PR:A
OLD MAC (1961, Brit.) PR:A
OLD MAID, THE (1939) PR:C
OLD MAN, THE (1932, Brit.) PR:A
OLD MAN AND THE BOY, THE (SEE: TWO OF US,
   THE) (1967, Fr.)
OLD MAN AND THE SEA, THE (1958) PR:A
OLD MAN RHYTHM (1935) PR:A
OLD MOTHER RILEY (1937, Brit.) PR:A
OLD MOTHER RILEY (1952, Brit.) PR:A
OLD MOTHER RILEY AT HOME (1945, Brit.) PR:A
OLD MOTHER RILEY CATCHES A QUISLING (SEE:
   OLD MOTHER RILEY IN PARIS) (1938, Brit.)
OLD MOTHER RILEY, DETECTIVE (1943, Brit.) PR:A
OLD MOTHER RILEY, HEADMISTRESS (1950, Brit.)
   PR:A
OLD MOTHER RILEY IN BUSINESS (1940, Brit.) PR:A
OLD MOTHER RILEY IN PARIS (1938, Brit.) PR:A
OLD MOTHER RILEY IN SOCIETY (1940, Brit.) PR:A
OLD MOTHER RILEY JOINS UP (1939, Brit.) PR:A
OLD MOTHER RILEY MEETS THE VAMPIRE (SEE:
   MY SON, THE VAMPIRE) (1952, Brit.)
OLD MOTHER RILEY MP (1939, Brit.) PR:A
OLD MOTHER RILEY OVERSEAS (1943, Brit.) PR:A
OLD MOTHER RILEY'S CIRCUS (1941, Brit.) PR:A
OLD MOTHER RILEY'S GHOSTS (1941, Brit.) PR:A
OLD MOTHER RILEY'S JUNGLE TREASURE (1951,
   Brit.) PR:A
OLD MOTHER RILEY'S NEW VENTURE (SEE: OLD
   MOTHER RILEY) (1952, Brit.)
OLD OKLAHOMA PLAINS (1952) PR:A
OLD OVERLAND TRAIL (1953) PR:A
OLD ROSES (1935, Brit.) PR:A
OLD SCHOOL TIE, THE (SEE: WE WENT TO COL-
   LEGE) (1936)
OLD SHATTERHAND (1968, Fr./It./W. Ger./Yugo.) PR:A
OLD SOLDIERS NEVER DIE (1931, Brit.) PR:A
OLD SPANISH CUSTOM, AN (1936, Brit.) PR:A
OLD SPANISH CUSTOMERS (1932, Brit.) PR:A
OLD SUREHAND, 1. TIEL (SEE: FLAMING FRONTIER)
   (1968, Yugo./W. Ger.)
OLD SWIMMIN' HOLE, THE (1941) PR:A
OLD TEXAS TRAIL, THE (1944) PR:A
OLD WEST, THE (1952) PR:A
OLD WYOMING TRAIL, THE (1937) PR:A
OLD YELLER (1957) PR:A
OLDEST CONFESSION, THE (SEE: HAPPY THIEVES,
   THE) (1962)
OLDEST PROFESSION, THE (1968, Fr./It./W. Ger.) PR:O
O'LEARY NIGHT (SEE: TONIGHT'S THE NIGHT)
   (1954, Brit.)
OLGA'S GIRLS (1964) PR:O
OLIVE TREES OF JUSTICE, THE (1967, Fr.) PR:A
OLIVER! (1968, Brit.) PR:AA
OLIVER & COMPANY (1988) PR:AA
OLIVER TWIST (1933) PR:A
OLIVER TWIST (1951, Brit.) PR:AA
OLIVER'S STORY (1978) PR:C
OLLY OLLY OXEN FREE (1978) PR:A
OLSEN'S BIG MOMENT (1934) PR:A
OLSEN'S NIGHT OUT (SEE: OLSEN'S BIG MOMENT)
   (1934)
OLTRAGGIO AL PUDORE (SEE: ALL THE OTHER
   GIRLS DO) (1966, Fr./It.)
OLTRE IL BENE E IL MALE (SEE: BEYOND GOOD
   AND EVIL) (1984, It./Fr./W. Ger.)
OLYMPIC HONEYMOON (SEE: HONEYMOON
   MERRY-GO-ROUND) (1939, Brit.)
OMAHA TRAIL, THE (1942) PR:A
O'MALLEY OF THE MOUNTED (1936) PR:A
OMAR KHAYYAM (SEE: LIFE, LOVES AND ADVEN-
   TURES OF OMAR KHAYYAM, THE) (1957)
OMAR MUKHTAR (SEE: LION OF THE DESERT)
   (1981, Brit./Libya)
OMBRE BIANCHE (SEE: SAVAGE INNOCENTS, THE)
   (1961)
OMEGA MAN, THE (1971) PR:C

OMEGA SYNDROME (1987) PR:O
OMEN, THE (1976) PR:O
OMICRON (1963, It.) PR:A
OMOO OMOO, THE SHARK GOD (1949) PR:A
ON A CLEAR DAY YOU CAN SEE FOREVER (1970)
   PR:AA
ON A VOLE LA CUISSE DE JUPITER (SEE: JUPITER'S
   THIGH) (1980, Fr.)
ON AGAIN – OFF AGAIN (1937) PR:A
ON AN ISLAND WITH YOU (1948) PR:A
ON ANY STREET (SEE: LA NOTTE BRAVA) (1962,
   Fr./It.)
ON APPROVAL (1930, Brit.) PR:A
ON APPROVAL (1944, Brit.) PR:A
ON BORROWED TIME (1939) PR:A
ON DANGEROUS GROUND (1951) PR:C
ON DRESS PARADE (SEE: DEAD END KIDS ON
   DRESS PARADE) (1939)
ON FRIDAY AT ELEVEN (SEE: WORLD IN MY
   POCKET, THE) (1962, Fr./It./W. Ger.)
ON GOLDEN POND (1981) PR:A-C
ON GUARD (SEE: OUTPOST OF THE MOUNTIES)
   (1939)
ON HER BED OF ROSES (1966) PR:C
ON HER MAJESTY'S SECRET SERVICE (1969, Brit.) PR:C
ON HIS OWN (1939, USSR) PR:A
ON MOONLIGHT BAY (1951) PR:AA
ON MY WAY TO THE CRUSADES I MET A GIRL WHO.
   . . (SEE: CHASTITY BELT, THE) (1969, US/It.)
ON OUR LITTLE PLACE (SEE: ON OUR SELECTION)
   (1930, Aus.)
ON OUR MERRY WAY (1948) PR:A
ON OUR SELECTION (1930, Aus.) PR:A
ON PROBATION (1935) PR:A
ON PROBATION (SEE: DADDY-O) (1959)
ON SECRET SERVICE (SEE: SECRET AGENT) (1933,
   Brit.)
ON SECRET SERVICE (SEE: TRAILIN' WEST) (1936)
ON SPECIAL DUTY (SEE: BULLETS FOR RUSTLERS)
   (1940)
ON STAGE EVERYBODY (1945) PR:A
ON SUCH A NIGHT (1937) PR:A
ON THE AIR (1934, Brit.) PR:A
ON THE AIR LIVE WITH CAPTAIN MIDNIGHT (1979)
   PR:C
ON THE AVENUE (1937) PR:AA
ON THE BEACH (1959) PR:O
ON THE BEAT (1962, Brit.) PR:A
ON THE BRINK (SEE: THESE ARE THE DAMNED)
   (1965, Brit.)
ON THE BUSES (1972, Brit.) PR:C
ON THE CARPET (SEE: LITTLE GIANT) (1946)
ON THE COMET (1970, Czech.) PR:A
ON THE DOUBLE (1961) PR:A
ON THE EDGE (1985) PR:O
ON THE FIDDLE (SEE: OPERATION SNAFU) (1965,
   Brit.)
ON THE GREAT WHITE TRAIL (1938) PR:A
ON THE ISLE OF SAMOA (1950) PR:A
ON THE LEVEL (1930) PR:A
ON THE LINE (1984, Sp.) PR:O
ON THE LOOSE (1951) PR:A
ON THE MAKE (SEE: DEVIL WITH WOMEN, A) (1930)
ON THE NICKEL (1980) PR:O
ON THE NIGHT OF THE FIRE (SEE: FUGITIVE, THE)
   (1940, Brit.)
ON THE OLD SPANISH TRAIL (1947) PR:A
ON THE RIGHT TRACK (1981) PR:C
ON THE RIVIERA (1951) PR:A
ON THE ROAD AGAIN (SEE: HONEYSUCKLE ROSE)
   (1980)
ON THE RUN (1958, Brit.) PR:A
ON THE RUN (1967, Brit.) PR:A
ON THE RUN (1969, Brit.) PR:A
ON THE RUN (1983, Aus.) PR:C
ON THE SPOT (1940) PR:A
ON THE STROKE OF NINE (SEE: MURDER ON THE
   CAMPUS) (1934)
ON THE SUNNY SIDE (1942) PR:AA
ON THE SUNNYSIDE (1936, Swed.) PR:A
ON THE THRESHOLD OF SPACE (1956) PR:A
ON THE TOWN (1949) PR:A
ON THE WATERFRONT (1954) PR:O
ON THE YARD (1978) PR:O
ON THEIR OWN (1940) PR:A
ON THIN ICE (1933, Brit.) PR:A
ON TOP OF OLD SMOKY (1953) PR:A
ON TOP OF THE WORLD (SEE: EVERYTHING OKAY)
   (1936, Brit.)
ON TRIAL (1928) PR:A
ON TRIAL (1939) PR:A
ON VALENTINE'S DAY (1986) PR:A-C
ON VELVET (1938, Brit.) PR:A
ON WINGS OF SONG (SEE: LOVE ME FOREVER)
   (1935)
ON WITH THE SHOW (1929) PR:A
ON YOUR BACK (1930) PR:A
ON YOUR TOES (1939) PR:A

ONCE (1974) PR:C
ONCE A CROOK (1941, Brit.) PR:A
ONCE A DOCTOR (1937) PR:A
ONCE A GENTLEMAN (1930) PR:A
ONCE A JOLLY SWAGMAN (SEE: MANIACS ON
 WHEELS) (1951, Brit.)
ONCE A LADY (1931) PR:A
ONCE A RAINY DAY (1968, Jap.) PR:A
ONCE A SINNER (1931) PR:A
ONCE A SINNER (1952, Brit.) PR:A
ONCE A THIEF (1935, Brit.) PR:A
ONCE A THIEF (1950) PR:A
ONCE A THIEF (SEE: HAPPY THIEVES, THE) (1962)
ONCE A THIEF (1965, US/Fr.) PR:C
ONCE BEFORE I DIE (1967, US/Phil.) PR:C
ONCE BITTEN (1985) PR:O
ONCE IN A BLUE MOON (1936) PR:A
ONCE IN A LIFETIME (1932) PR:A
ONCE IN A MILLION (SEE: WEEKEND MILLION-
 AIRE) (1937, Brit.)
ONCE IN A NEW MOON (1935, Brit.) PR:A
ONCE IN PARIS. . . (1978) PR:C
ONCE IS NOT ENOUGH (1975) PR:O
ONCE MORE, MY DARLING (1949) PR:A
ONCE MORE, WITH FEELING (1960, Brit.) PR:A-C
ONCE THERE WAS A GIRL (1945, USSR) PR:C
ONCE TO EVERY BACHELOR (1934) PR:A
ONCE TO EVERY WOMAN (1934) PR:A
ONCE UPON A COFFEE HOUSE (1965) PR:A
ONCE UPON A DREAM (1949, Brit.) PR:A
ONCE UPON A HONEYMOON (1942) PR:A
ONCE UPON A HORSE (1958) PR:A
ONCE UPON A SCOUNDREL (1973) PR:A
ONCE UPON A SUMMER (SEE: GIRL WITH GREEN
 EYES) (1964, Brit.)
ONCE UPON A THURSDAY (SEE: AFFAIRS OF MAR-
 THA) (1942)
ONCE UPON A TIME (1944) PR:A
ONCE UPON A TIME (SEE: MORE THAN A MIRACLE)
 (1967, Fr./It.)
ONCE UPON A TIME IN AMERICA (1984) PR:O
ONCE UPON A TIME IN THE WEST (1969, US/It.) PR:O
ONCE YOU KISS A STRANGER (1969) PR:O
ONDATA DI CALORE (SEE: DEAD OF SUMMER)
 (1970, It./Fr.)
ONE AGAINST SEVEN (SEE: COUNTER-ATTACK)
 (1945)
ONE AND ONLY, THE (1978) PR:C
*ONE AND ONLY GENUINE ORIGINAL FAMILY BAND,
 THE* (1968) PR:AA
ONE BIG AFFAIR (1952) PR:A
ONE BODY TOO MANY (1944) PR:A
ONE BORN EVERY MINUTE (SEE: FLIM-FLAM MAN,
 THE) (1967)
ONE BRIEF SUMMER (1971, Brit.) PR:A
ONE CRAZY SUMMER (1986) PR:C
ONE CROWDED NIGHT (1940) PR:A
ONE DANGEROUS NIGHT (1943) PR:A
ONE DARK NIGHT (1939) PR:A
ONE DARK NIGHT (1983) PR:A
ONE DAY IN THE LIFE OF IVAN DENISOVICH (1971,
 US/Brit./Norway) PR:A
ONE DEADLY SUMMER (1983, Fr.) PR:O
ONE DESIRE (1955) PR:AA
ONE DOWN TWO TO GO (1982) PR:O
ONE EMBARRASSING NIGHT (1930, Brit.) PR:A
1=2? (1975, Fr.) PR:C
ONE EXCITING ADVENTURE (1935) PR:A
ONE EXCITING NIGHT (1945) PR:A
ONE EXCITING NIGHT (SEE: YOU CAN'T DO WITH-
 OUT LOVE) (1946, Brit.)
ONE EXCITING WEEK (1946) PR:A
ONE-EYED JACKS (1961) PR:O
ONE-EYED SOLDIERS (1967, US/Brit./Yugo.) PR:C
ONE FAMILY (1930, Brit.) PR:A
ONE FATAL HOUR (SEE: FIVE STAR FINAL) (1931)
ONE FATAL HOUR (SEE: TWO AGAINST THE
 WORLD) (1936)
ONE FLEW OVER THE CUCKOO'S NEST (1975) PR:O
ONE FOOT IN HEAVEN (1941) PR:AA
ONE FOOT IN HELL (1960) PR:A
ONE FOR ALL (SEE: PRESIDENT'S MYSTERY, THE)
 (1936)
ONE FOR SORROW, TWO FOR JOY (SEE: SIGNS OF
 LIFE) (1989)
ONE FOR THE BOOKS (SEE: VOICE OF THE TURTLE,
 THE) (1947)
ONE FRIGHTENED NIGHT (1935) PR:A
ONE FROM THE HEART (1982) PR:O
ONE GIRL'S CONFESSION (1953) PR:C
ONE GOOD TURN (1936, Brit.) PR:A
ONE GOOD TURN (1955, Brit.) PR:A
ONE HEAVENLY NIGHT (1931) PR:A
ONE HORSE TOWN (SEE: SMALL TOWN GIRL) (1936)
ONE HOUR LATE (1935) PR:A
ONE HOUR TO DOOM'S DAY (SEE: CITY BENEATH
 THE SEA) (1953)
ONE HOUR TO LIVE (1939) PR:A

ONE HOUR WITH YOU (1932) PR:A-C
ONE HUNDRED AND ONE DALMATIANS (1961)
 PR:AA
$100 A NIGHT (1968, W. Ger.) PR:C
100 MEN AND A GIRL (1937) PR:AA
ONE HUNDRED PERCENT PURE (SEE: GIRL FROM
 MISSOURI, THE) (1934)
100 RIFLES (1969) PR:O
125 ROOMS OF COMFORT (1974, Can.) PR:O
ONE HYSTERICAL NIGHT (1930) PR:A
ONE IN A MILLION (1935) PR:A
ONE IN A MILLION (1936) PR:A
ONE IS A LONELY NUMBER (1972) PR:C
ONE IS GUILTY (1934) PR:A
ONE JUMP AHEAD (1955, Brit.) PR:A
ONE JUST MAN (1955, Brit.) PR:A
ONE LAST FLING (1949) PR:A
ONE LIFE (SEE: END OF DESIRE) (1962, Fr./It.)
ONE LITTLE INDIAN (1973) PR:AA
ONE LOOK AND LOVE BEGINS (SEE: EIN BLICK —
 UND DIE LIEBE BRICHT AUS) (1987, W. Ger.)
ONE MAD KISS (1930) PR:A
ONE MAGIC CHRISTMAS (1985) PR:AA
ONE MAN (1979, Can.) PR:C
ONE MAN JURY, THE (1978) PR:O
ONE-MAN JUSTICE (1937) PR:A
ONE-MAN LAW (1932) PR:A
ONE-MAN MUTINY (SEE: COURT-MARTIAL OF
 BILLY MITCHELL, THE) (1955)
ONE MAN'S JOURNEY (1933) PR:A
ONE MAN'S LAW (1940) PR:A
ONE MAN'S WAY (1964) PR:A
ONE MILE FROM HEAVEN (1937) PR:A
ONE MILLION B.C. (1940) PR:A-C
$1,000,000 DUCK (1971) PR:AA
$1,000,000 RACKET (1937) PR:A
ONE MILLION DOLLARS (1965, It.) PR:A
1,000,000 EYES OF SU-MURU (SEE: MILLION EYES
 OF SU-MURU, THE) (1967, Brit.)
ONE MILLION YEARS B.C. (1967, Brit.) PR:A
ONE MINUTE TO MIDNIGHT (1988) PR:NR
ONE MINUTE TO ZERO (1952) PR:A
ONE MORE SATURDAY NIGHT (1986) PR:C-O
ONE MORE SPRING (1935) PR:A
ONE MORE TIME (1970, US/Brit.) PR:A
ONE MORE TOMORROW (1946) PR:A
ONE MORE TRAIN TO ROB (1971) PR:A
ONE MYSTERIOUS NIGHT (1944) PR:A
ONE NEW YORK NIGHT (1935) PR:A
ONE NIGHT. . .A TRAIN (1968, Fr./Bel.) PR:C
ONE NIGHT AT SUSIE'S (1930) PR:A
ONE NIGHT IN LISBON (1941) PR:A
ONE NIGHT IN PARIS (1940, Brit.) PR:A
ONE NIGHT IN THE TROPICS (1940) PR:A
ONE NIGHT OF LOVE (1934) PR:A
ONE NIGHT ONLY (1986, Can.) PR:O
ONE NIGHT STAND (1976, Fr.) PR:O
ONE NIGHT WITH YOU (1948, Brit.) PR:A
ONE OF OUR AIRCRAFT IS MISSING (1942, Brit.) PR:A
ONE OF OUR DINOSAURS IS MISSING (1975, Brit.)
 PR:AA
ONE OF OUR SPIES IS MISSING (1966) PR:A
ONE OF THE MANY (SEE: HE COULDN'T TAKE IT)
 (1933)
ONE ON ONE (1977) PR:A
ONE-PIECE BATHING SUIT, THE (SEE: MILLION DOL-
 LAR MERMAID) (1952)
ONE PLUS ONE (1961, Can.) PR:C-O
ONE PLUS ONE (1969, Brit.) PR:O
ONE POTATO, TWO POTATO (1964) PR:C
ONE PRECIOUS YEAR (1933, Brit.) PR:A
ONE RAINY AFTERNOON (1936) PR:A
ONE ROMANTIC NIGHT (1930) PR:A
ONE SINGS, THE OTHER DOESN'T (1977, Fr.) PR:C-O
ONE SPY TOO MANY (1966) PR:A
ONE STEP TO HELL (1969, US/It./Sp.) PR:C
ONE STOLEN NIGHT (1929) PR:A
ONE SUMMER LOVE (1976) PR:C
ONE SUNDAY AFTERNOON (1933) PR:A
ONE SUNDAY AFTERNOON (1948) PR:A
ONE THAT GOT AWAY, THE (1958, Brit.) PR:A
ONE THIRD OF A NATION (1939) PR:A
1001 ARABIAN NIGHTS (1959) PR:AA
1,000 CONVICTS AND A WOMAN (1971, Brit.) PR:O
$1,000 A MINUTE (1935) PR:A
$1,000 A TOUCHDOWN (1939) PR:A
1,000 FEMALE SHAPES (SEE: 1,000 SHAPES OF A FE-
 MALE) (1963)
1,000 PLANE RAID, THE (1969) PR:A
1,000 SHAPES OF A FEMALE (1963) PR:A
ONE THRILLING NIGHT (1942) PR:A
ONE TOO MANY (1950) PR:A
ONE TOUCH OF VENUS (1948) PR:A
ONE-TRICK PONY (1980) PR:O
ONE, TWO, THREE (1961) PR:A
1 2 3 MONSTER EXPRESS (1977, Thai.) PR:C
ONE WAY OUT (SEE: CONVICTED) (1950)

ONE WAY OUT (1955, Brit.) PR:A
ONE WAY PASSAGE (1932) PR:A
ONE WAY PENDULUM (1965, Brit.) PR:A
ONE WAY STREET (1950) PR:A
ONE-WAY TICKET (1935) PR:A
ONE-WAY TICKET, A (1988, Dominican Republic) PR:C
ONE WAY TICKET TO HELL (1955) PR:A
ONE WAY TO LOVE (1946) PR:A
ONE WAY TRAIL, THE (1931) PR:A
ONE WAY WAHINI (1965) PR:C-O
ONE WILD NIGHT (1938) PR:A
ONE WILD OAT (1951, Brit.) PR:A
ONE WISH TOO MANY (1956, Brit.) PR:A
ONE WITH THE FUZZ, THE (SEE: SOME KIND OF
 NUT) (1969)
ONE WOMAN'S STORY (1949, Brit.) PR:A
ONE YEAR LATER (1933) PR:A
ONEICHAN MAKARI TORU (SEE: THREE DOLLS
 FROM HONG KONG) (1966, Jap.)
ONI NO SUMU YAKATA (SEE: DEVIL'S TEMPLE,
 THE) (1969, Jap.)
ONI SHLI NA VOSTOK (SEE: ITALIANO BRAVA
 GENTE) (1965, It./USSR)
ONIBABA (1965, Jap.) PR:C
ONIMASA (1983, Jap.) PR:O
ONION FIELD, THE (1979) PR:C-O
ONIONHEAD (1958) PR:A
ONKEL TOMS HUTTE (SEE: UNCLE TOM'S CABIN)
 (1969, Fr./It./W. Ger.)
ONLY A WOMAN (SEE: I, TOO, AM ONLY A WOMAN)
 (1963, W. Ger.)
ONLY ANGELS HAVE WINGS (1939) PR:A
ONLY EIGHT HOURS (SEE: SOCIETY DOCTOR) (1935)
ONLY GAME IN TOWN, THE (1970) PR:C
ONLY GIRL, THE (SEE: HEART SONG) (1933, Brit.)
ONLY GOD KNOWS (1974, Can.) PR:A
ONLY ONCE IN A LIFETIME (1979) PR:C
ONLY ONE NIGHT (1942, Swed.) PR:C
ONLY SAPS WORK (1930) PR:A
ONLY THE BEST (SEE: I CAN GET IT FOR YOU
 WHOLESALE) (1951)
ONLY THE BRAVE (1930) PR:A
ONLY THE FRENCH CAN (SEE: FRENCH CANCAN)
 (1955, Fr.)
ONLY THE VALIANT (1951) PR:A
ONLY THING YOU KNOW, THE (1971, Can.) PR:C
ONLY TWO CAN PLAY (1962, Brit.) PR:C
ONLY WAY, THE (1970, Panama/Den./US) PR:A
ONLY WAY HOME, THE (1972) PR:C
ONLY WHEN I LARF (1968, Brit.) PR:A
ONLY WHEN I LAUGH (1981) PR:O
ONLY YESTERDAY (1933) PR:C
ONNA GA KAIDAN O AGARUTOKI (SEE: WHEN A
 WOMAN ASCENDS THE STAIRS) (1963, Jap.)
ONNA GOROSHI ABURA JIGOKU (SEE: PRODIGAL
 SON, THE) (1964, Jap.)
ONNA NO MIZUUMI (SEE: LAKE, THE) (1970, Jap.)
ONNA NO NAKANI IRU TANIN (SEE: THIN LINE,
 THE) (1967, Jap.)
ONNA NO REKISHI (SEE: WOMAN'S LIFE, A) (1964,
 Jap.)
ONNA NO ZA (SEE: WISER AGE, THE) (1962, Jap.)
ONNA UKIYOBURO (SEE: HOUSE OF STRANGE
 LOVES, THE) (1969, Jap.)
ONORE E SACRIFICIO (SEE: DISHONORED) (1950, It.)
ONSEN GERIRA DAI SHOGEKI (SEE: HOTSPRINGS
 HOLIDAY) (1970, Jap.)
OOH, YOU ARE AWFUL (SEE: GET CHARLIE TULLY)
 (1972, Brit.)
OPEN ALL NIGHT (1934, Brit.) PR:O
OPEN CITY (1945, It.) PR:O
OPEN HOUSE (1987) PR:O
OPEN ROAD, THE (1940, Fr.) PR:A
OPEN SEASON (1974, US/Sp.) PR:O
OPEN SECRET (1948) PR:A
OPEN THE DOOR AND SEE ALL THE PEOPLE (1964)
 PR:A
OPENED BY MISTAKE (1940) PR:A
OPENING NIGHT (1977) PR:C
OPERACION GOLDMAN (SEE: LIGHTNING BOLT)
 (1967, Fr./It./Sp.)
OPERACION LOTO AZUL (SEE: MISSION BLOODY
 MARY) (1967, Fr./It./Sp.)
OPERATION AMSTERDAM (1960, Brit.) PR:A
OPERATION BIKINI (1963) PR:A
OPERATION BLUE BOOK (SEE: BAMBOO SAUCER,
 THE) (1968)
OPERATION BOTTLENECK (1961) PR:A
OPERATION BULLSHINE (1963, Brit.) PR:A
OPERATION CAMEL (1961, Den.) PR:A
OPERATION CIA (1965) PR:A
OPERATION CICERO (SEE: FIVE FINGERS) (1952)
OPERATION CONSPIRACY (1957, Brit.) PR:A
OPERATION CROSS EAGLES (1969, US/Yugo.) PR:A
OPERATION CROSSBOW (1965, Brit./It.) PR:A
OPERATION CUPID (1960, Brit.) PR:A
OPERATION DAMES (1959) PR:C
OPERATION DAYBREAK (1976, US/Brit./Czech.) PR:A

OPERATION DELILAH (1966, US/Sp.) PR:A
OPERATION DIAMOND (1948, Brit.)
OPERATION DIPLOMAT (1953, Brit.) PR:A
OPERATION DISASTER (1951, Brit.) PR:A
OPERATION EICHMANN (1961) PR:A
OPERATION ENEMY FORT (1964, Jap.) PR:A
OPERATION GANYMED (1977, W. Ger.) PR:C
OPERATION HAYLIFT (1950) PR:A
OPERATION KID BROTHER (1967, It.) PR:A
OPERATION LOTUS BLEU (SEE: MISSION BLOODY MARY) (1967, Fr./It./Sp.)
OPERATION LOVEBIRDS (1968, Den.) PR:A
OPERATION M (SEE: HELL'S BLOODY DEVILS) (1970)
OPERATION MAD BALL (1957) PR:A
OPERATION MANHUNT (1954) PR:A
OPERATION MASQUERADE (SEE: MASQUERADE) (1965, Brit.)
OPERATION MERMAID (SEE: BAY OF SAINT MICHEL) (1963, Brit.)
OPERATION MURDER (1957, Brit.) PR:A
OPERATION PACIFIC (1951) PR:A
OPERATION PETTICOAT (1959) PR:A
OPERATION ST. PETER'S (1968, It.) PR:A
OPERATION SAN GENNARO (SEE: TREASURE OF SAN GENNARO) (1968, Fr./It./W. Ger.)
OPERATION SECRET (1952) PR:A
OPERATION SNAFU (1965, Brit.) PR:A
OPERATION SNATCH (1962, Brit.) PR:A
OPERATION THIRD FORM (1966, Brit.) PR:AA
OPERATION THUNDERBOLT (1978, Israel) PR:C
OPERATION UNDER COVER (SEE: REPORT TO THE COMMISSIONER) (1975)
OPERATION WAR HEAD (SEE: OPERATION SNAFU) (1965, Brit.)
OPERATION X (1951, Brit.) PR:A-C
OPERATION X (1963, Jap.) PR:C
OPERATOR 13 (1934) PR:A
OPERAZIA GOLDMAN (SEE: LIGHTNING BOLT) (1965, It.)
OPERAZIONE CROSSBOW (SEE: OPERATION CROSS-BOW) (1965, US/It.)
OPERAZIONE PARADISO (SEE: KISS THE GIRLS AND MAKE THEM DIE) (1967, US/It.)
OPERAZIONE PAURA (SEE: KILL BABY KILL) (1966, It.)
OPERETTA (1949, W. Ger.) PR:A
OPHELIA (1964, Fr.) PR:C
OPIATE '67 (1967, Fr./It.) PR:C
OPPOSING FORCE (1987) PR:O
OPPOSITE SEX, THE (1956) PR:A
OPTIMIST, THE (SEE: BIG SHOT, THE) (1931)
OPTIMIST, THE (SEE: HALLELUJAH, I'M A BUM) (1933)
OPTIMISTIC TRAGEDY, THE (1964, USSR) PR:A
OPTIMISTICHESKAYA TRAGEDIYA (SEE: OPTIMISTIC TRAGEDY, THE) (1964, USSR)
OPTIMISTS, THE (1973, Brit.) PR:A
OPTIMISTS OF NINE ELMS, THE (SEE: OPTIMISTS, THE) (1973, Brit.)
OPTIONS (1989) PR:C
OR POUR LES CESARS (SEE: GOLD FOR THE CAESARS) (1964, Fr./It.)
ORACLE, THE (SEE: HORSE'S MOUTH, THE) (1953, Brit.)
ORAZIO E COURIAZI (SEE: DUEL OF CHAMPIONS) (1964, It./Sp.)
ORBITA MORTAL (SEE: MISSION STARDUST) (1968, It./Sp./W. Ger.)
ORCA (1977) PR:C
ORCHESTRA WIVES (1942) PR:A
ORCHIDS TO YOU (1935) PR:A
ORDEAL BY INNOCENCE (1984, Brit.) PR:C
ORDER OF DEATH (SEE: CORRUPT) (1984, It.)
ORDERED TO LOVE (1963, W. Ger.) PR:O
ORDERS, THE (1977, Can.) PR:C-O
ORDERS ARE ORDERS (1959, Brit.) PR:A
ORDERS IS ORDERS (1934, Brit.) PR:A
ORDERS TO KILL (1958, Brit.) PR:A
ORDET (1955, Den.) PR:A-C
ORDINARY PEOPLE (1980) PR:O
OREGON PASSAGE (1958) PR:A
OREGON TRAIL, THE (1936) PR:A
OREGON TRAIL (1945) PR:A
OREGON TRAIL, THE (1959) PR:A
OREGON TRAIL SCOUTS (1947) PR:A
ORFEU NEGRO (SEE: BLACK ORPHEUS) (1959, Fr./It./Braz.)
ORGANIZATION, THE (1971) PR:C
ORGANIZER, THE (1964, Fr./It./Yugo.) PR:A
ORGY OF BLOOD (SEE: BRIDES OF BLOOD) (1968, US/Phil.)
ORGY OF THE DEAD (1965) PR:O
ORGY OF THE GOLDEN NUDES (SEE: HONEYMOON OF HORROR) (1964)
ORIANE (1985, Fr./Venezuela) PR:O
ORIENT EXPRESS (1934) PR:A
ORIENTAL DREAM (SEE: KISMET) (1944)

ORIGINAL OLD MOTHER RILEY, THE (SEE: OLD MOTHER RILEY)
O'RILEY'S LUCK (SEE: ROSE BOWL) (1936)
ORLAK, THE HELL OF FRANKENSTEIN (1960, Mex.) PR:C-O
ORMENS VAG PA HALLEBERGET (SEE: SERPENT'S WAY) (1987, Swed.)
ORPHAN OF THE PECOS (1938) PR:A
ORPHAN OF THE RING (SEE: KID FROM KOKOMO, THE) (1939)
ORPHAN OF THE WILDERNESS (1937, Aus.) PR:A
ORPHANS (1987) PR:A-C
ORPHANS OF THE NORTH (1940) PR:AA
ORPHANS OF THE STREET (1939) PR:AA
ORPHEE (SEE: ORPHEUS) (1950, Fr.)
ORPHEUS (1950, Fr.) PR:A
ORU KAIJU DAISHINGEKI (SEE: GODZILLA'S REVENGE) (1969, Jap.)
OSA (1985) PR:O
OSAKA MONOGATARI (SEE: DAREDEVIL IN THE CASTLE) (1961, Jap.)
OSCAR, THE (1966) PR:A
OSCAR WILDE (1960, Brit.) PR:C
OSETROVNA (SEE: SIGN OF THE VIRGIN) (1969, Czech.)
O'SHAUGHNESSY'S BOY (1935) PR:A
OSMY DZIEM TYGODNIA (SEE: EIGHTH DAY OF THW WEEK, THE) (1959, W. Ger./Pol.)
OSOSHIKI (SEE: FUNERAL, THE) (1984, Jap.)
OSS 117 MINACCIA BANGKOK (SEE: SHADOW OF EVIL) (1967, Fr./It.)
OSS 117 — DOUBLE AGENT (SEE: NO ROSES FOR OSS 117) (1968, Fr.)
OSS 117 — MISSION FOR A KILLER (1966, Fr./It.) PR:C
OSSESSIONE (1942, It.) PR:C
OSTATNI ETAP (SEE: LAST STOP, THE) (1949, Pol.)
OSTERMAN WEEKEND, THE (1983) PR:C-O
OSTRE SLEDOVANE VLAKY (SEE: CLOSELY WATCHED TRAINS) (1966, Czech.)
OTAC NA SLUZBENOH PUTU (SEE: WHEN FATHER WAS AWAY ON BUSINES) (1985, Yugo.)
OTCHI TCHORNIA (SEE: DARK EYES) (1938, Fr.)
OTCHIY DOM (SEE: HOME FOR TANYA, A) (1961, USSR)
OTEL U POGIBSHCHEGO ALPINISTA (SEE: DEAD MOUNTAINEER HOTEL, THE) (1979, USSR)
OTELLO (1986, It.) PR:A-C
OTETS SOLDATA (SEE: FATHER OF A SOLDIER) (1966, USSR)
OTHELLO (1955, US/Fr./It.) PR:C
OTHELLO (1960, USSR) PR:A
OTHELLO (1965, Brit.) PR:A
OTHER, THE (1972) PR:O
OTHER LOVE, THE (1947) PR:A
OTHER MEN'S WOMEN (1931) PR:A-C
OTHER ONE, THE (1967, Fr.) PR:C
OTHER PEOPLE'S BUSINESS (SEE: WAY BACK HOME) (1932)
OTHER PEOPLE'S SINS (1931, Brit.) PR:A
OTHER SIDE OF BONNIE AND CLYDE, THE (1968) PR:O
OTHER SIDE OF MIDNIGHT, THE (1977) PR:O
OTHER SIDE OF PARADISE, THE (SEE: FOXTROT) (1977, Mex./Switz.)
OTHER SIDE OF THE MOUNTAIN, THE (1975) PR:A
OTHER SIDE OF THE MOUNTAIN — PART 2, THE (1978) PR:A
OTHER SIDE OF THE UNDERNEATH, THE (1972, Brit.) PR:O
OTHER TOMORROW, THE (1930) PR:A
OTHER WOMAN, THE (1931, Brit.) PR:A
OTHER WOMAN, THE (1954) PR:C-O
OTKLONENIE (SEE: DETOUR, THE) (1968, Bulgaria)
OTLEY (1969, Brit.) PR:C
OTOKO TAI OTOKO (SEE: MAN AGAINST MAN) (1961, Jap.)
OTOKOWA TSURAIYOO TORAIJIRO KOKORO NO TABIJI (SEE: TORA-SAN GOES TO VIENNA) (1986, Jap.)
OTRA HISTORIA DE AMOR (SEE: ANOTHER LOVE STORY) (1986, Arg.)
OTRA VUELTA DE TUERCA (SEE: TURN OF THE SCREW) (1985, Sp.)
OTROKI VO VSELENNOI (SEE: TEENAGERS IN SPACE) (1975, USSR)
OTTO E MEZZO (SEE: 8 1/2) (1963, It.)
OUANGA (1936, Brit.) PR:A
OUR BETTERS (1933) PR:C
OUR BLUSHING BRIDES (1930) PR:A
OUR DAILY BREAD (1934) PR:A
OUR DAILY BREAD (1950, W. Ger.) PR:A
OUR FATHER (1985, Sp.) PR:O
OUR FIGHTING NAVY (SEE: TORPEDOED!) (1939, Brit.)
OUR GIRL FRIDAY (SEE: ADVENTURES OF SADIE, THE) (1955, Brit.)

OUR HEARTS WERE GROWING UP (1946) PR:A
OUR HEARTS WERE YOUNG AND GAY (1944) PR:A
OUR HERITAGE (SEE: THIS ENGLAND) (1941, Brit.)
OUR HITLER, A FILM FROM GERMANY (1977, W. Ger.) PR:O
OUR LADY OF FATIMA (SEE: MIRACLE OF OUR LADY OF FATIMA, THE) (1952)
OUR LEADING CITIZEN (1939) PR:A
OUR LITTLE GIRL (1935) PR:AA
OUR MAN FLINT (1966) PR:A
OUR MAN IN HAVANA (1960, Brit.) PR:A
OUR MAN IN MARRAKESH (SEE: BANG! BANG!YOU'RE DEAD) (1966, Brit.)
OUR MAN IN MARRAKESH (SEE: THAT MAN GEORGE) (1967, Fr./It./Sp.)
OUR MISS BROOKS (1956) PR:AA
OUR MISS FRED (1972, Brit.) PR:C
OUR MODERN MAIDENS (1929) PR:A
OUR MOTHER'S HOUSE (1967, US/Brit.) PR:O
OUR NEIGHBORS — THE CARTERS (1939) PR:AA
OUR RELATIONS (1936) PR:AA
OUR SILENT LOVE (1969, Jap.) PR:A
OUR TIME (1974) PR:O
OUR TOWN (1940) PR:A
OUR VERY OWN (1950) PR:A
OUR VINES HAVE TENDER GRAPES (1945) PR:A
OUR WIFE (1941) PR:A
OUR WINNING SEASON (1978) PR:C
OURSELVES ALONE (SEE: RIVER OF UNREST) (1937, Brit.)
OUT (1982) PR:C-O
OUT ALL NIGHT (1933) PR:A
OUT CALIFORNIA WAY (1946) PR:A
OUT COLD (1989) PR:O
OUT OF AFRICA (1985) PR:C
OUT OF BOUNDS (1986) PR:O
OUT OF CONTROL (1985) PR:O
OUT OF IT (1969) PR:A
OUT OF MY WAY (SEE: STORY OF FAUSTA) (1988, Braz.)
OUT OF ORDER (1985, W. Ger.) PR:C
OUT OF ROSENHEIM (SEE: BAGDAD CAFE) (1987)
OUT OF SEASON (1975, Brit.) PR:C-O
OUT OF SIGHT (1966) PR:A
OUT OF SINGAPORE (1932) PR:C
OUT OF THE BLUE (1931, Brit.) PR:A
OUT OF THE BLUE (1947) PR:A
OUT OF THE BLUE (1982) PR:O
OUT OF THE CLOUDS (1957, Brit.) PR:A
OUT OF THE DARKNESS (SEE: TEENAGE CAVEMAN) (1958)
OUT OF THE DARKNESS (SEE: NIGHT CREATURE) (1979)
OUT OF THE DEPTHS (1946) PR:A
OUT OF THE FOG (1941) PR:C
OUT OF THE FOG (1962, Brit.) PR:A
OUT OF THE FRYING PAN (SEE: YOUNG AND WILLING) (1943)
OUT OF THE NIGHT (SEE: STRANGE ILLUSION) (1945)
OUT OF THE PAST (1933, Brit.) PR:A
OUT OF THE PAST (1947) PR:C
OUT OF THE SHADOW (SEE: MURDER ON THE CAMPUS) (1963, Brit.)
OUT OF THE STORM (1948) PR:A
OUT OF THE TIGER'S MOUTH (1962) PR:A
OUT OF THIS WORLD (1945) PR:A
OUT OF TOWNERS, THE (SEE: DEAR HEART) (1964)
OUT OF TOWNERS, THE (1970) PR:A
OUT WEST WITH THE HARDYS (1938) PR:AA
OUT WEST WITH THE PEPPERS (1940) PR:AA
OUTBACK (1971, Aus.) PR:O
OUTCAST, THE (1934, Brit.) PR:A
OUTCAST (1937) PR:A
OUTCAST, THE (SEE: MAN IN THE SADDLE) (1951)
OUTCAST, THE (1954) PR:A
OUTCAST LADY (1934) PR:A
OUTCAST OF BLACK MESA (1950) PR:A
OUTCAST OF THE ISLANDS (1952, Brit.) PR:A
OUTCASTS OF POKER FLAT, THE (1937) PR:A
OUTCASTS OF POKER FLAT, THE (1952) PR:A
OUTCASTS OF THE CITY (1958) PR:A
OUTCASTS OF THE TRAIL (1949) PR:A
OUTCRY (1949, It.) PR:C-O
OUTCRY, THE (SEE: IL GRIDO) (1962, US/It.)
OUTER GATE, THE (1937) PR:A
OUTER HEAT (SEE: ALIEN NATION) (1988)
OUTER TOUCH (SEE: SPACED OUT) (1981, Brit.)
OUTFIT, THE (1973) PR:C-O
OUTING, THE (1987) PR:O
OUTLAND (1981, Brit.) PR:O
OUTLAW, THE (1943) PR:O
OUTLAW AND THE LADY, THE (SEE: WACO) (1952)
OUTLAW BLUES (1977) PR:A
OUTLAW BRAND (1948) PR:A
OUTLAW COUNTRY (1949) PR:A
OUTLAW DEPUTY, THE (1935) PR:A
OUTLAW EXPRESS (1938) PR:A

OUTLAW GOLD (1950) PR:A
OUTLAW JOSEY WALES, THE (1976) PR:O
OUTLAW JUSTICE (1933) PR:A
OUTLAW MOTORCYCLES (1967) PR:O
OUTLAW OF THE PLAINS (1946) PR:A
OUTLAW STALLION, THE (1954) PR:A
OUTLAW TERRITORY (SEE: HANNAH LEE) (1953)
OUTLAW: THE SAGE OF GISLI (1982, Iceland) PR:C
OUTLAW TRAIL (1944) PR:A
OUTLAW TREASURE (1955) PR:A
OUTLAW WOMEN (1952) PR:A
OUTLAWED GUNS (1935) PR:A
OUTLAW'S DAUGHTER, THE (1954) PR:A
OUTLAWS IS COMING, THE (1965) PR:A
OUTLAWS OF PINE RIDGE (1942) PR:A
OUTLAWS OF SANTA FE (1944) PR:A
OUTLAWS OF SONORA (1938) PR:A
OUTLAWS OF STAMPEDE PASS (1943) PR:A
OUTLAWS OF TEXAS (1950) PR:A
OUTLAWS OF THE CHEROKEE TRAIL (1941) PR:A
OUTLAWS OF THE DESERT (1941) PR:A
OUTLAWS OF THE ORIENT (1937) PR:A
OUTLAWS OF THE PANHANDLE (1941) PR:A
OUTLAWS OF THE PRAIRIE (1938) PR:A
OUTLAWS OF THE RIO GRANDE (1941) PR:A
OUTLAWS OF THE ROCKIES (1945) PR:A
OUTLAWS OF THE WEST (SEE: CALL THE
   MESQUITEERS) (1938)
OUTLAW'S PARADISE (1939) PR:A
OUTLAW'S SON (1957) PR:A
OUTPOST IN MALAYA (1952, Brit.) PR:A
OUTPOST IN MOROCCO (1949) PR:A
OUTPOST OF HELL (1966, Jap.) PR:A
OUTPOST OF THE MOUNTIES (1939) PR:A
OUTRAGE (1950) PR:C
OUTRAGE, THE (1964) PR:C
OUTRAGEOUS! (1977, Can.) PR:O
OUTRAGEOUS FORTUNE (1987) PR:O
OUTRIDERS, THE (1950) PR:A
OUTSIDE IN (1972) PR:C
OUTSIDE MAN, THE (1973, US/Fr.) PR:C
OUTSIDE OF PARADISE (1938) PR:A
OUTSIDE THE LAW (1930) PR:A
OUTSIDE THE LAW (SEE: STRANGE CASE OF DR.
   MEADE, THE) (1939)
OUTSIDE THE LAW (SEE: CITADEL OF CRIME) (1941)
OUTSIDE THE LAW (1956) PR:A
OUTSIDE THE 3-MILE LIMIT (1940, Brit.) PR:A
OUTSIDE THE WALL (1950) PR:A
OUTSIDE THESE WALLS (1939) PR:A
OUTSIDER, THE (1933, Brit.) PR:A
OUTSIDER, THE (1940, Brit.) PR:A
OUTSIDER, THE (1949, Brit.) PR:A
OUTSIDER, THE (1962) PR:A-C
OUTSIDER, THE (1980) PR:O
OUTSIDER IN AMSTERDAM (1983, Neth.) PR:O
OUTSIDERS, THE (SEE: BAND OF OUTSIDERS) (1964,
   Fr.)
OUTSIDERS, THE (1983) PR:C
OUTSIDERS, THE (1987, Taiwan) PR:O
OUTWARD BOUND (1930) PR:C
OVER-EXPOSED (1956) PR:C
OVER GRENSEN (SEE: FELDMANN CASE, THE)
   (1987, Norway)
OVER MY DEAD BODY (1942) PR:A
OVER SHE GOES (1937, Brit.) PR:A
OVER THE BORDER (1950) PR:A
OVER THE BROOKLYN BRIDGE (1984) PR:O
OVER THE EDGE (1979) PR:O
OVER THE GARDEN WALL (1934, Brit.) PR:A
OVER THE GARDEN WALL (1950, Brit.) PR:A
OVER THE GOAL (1937) PR:A
OVER THE HILL (1931) PR:C
OVER THE MOON (1940, Brit.) PR:A
OVER THE ODDS (1961, Brit.) PR:A
OVER THE RIVER (SEE: ONE MORE RIVER) (1934)
OVER THE SUMMER (1986) PR:O
OVER THE TOP (1987) PR:C
OVER THE WALL (1938) PR:A
OVER 21 (1945) PR:C
OVER-UNDER, SIDEWAYS-DOWN (1977) PR:C
OVERBOARD (1987) PR:C
OVERCOAT, THE (1965, USSR) PR:O
OVERKILL (1987) PR:O
OVERLAND BOUND (1929) PR:A
OVERLAND EXPRESS, THE (1938) PR:A
OVERLAND MAIL (1939) PR:A
OVERLAND MAIL ROBBERY (1943) PR:A
OVERLAND PACIFIC (1954) PR:A
OVERLAND RIDERS (1946) PR:A
OVERLAND STAGE RAIDERS (1938) PR:A
OVERLAND STAGECOACH (1942) PR:A
OVERLAND TELEGRAPH (1951) PR:A
OVERLAND TRAIL (SEE: TRAIL RIDERS) (1942)
OVERLANDERS, THE (1946, Brit./Aus.) PR:C
OVERLORD (1975, Brit.) PR:O
OVERNIGHT (1933, Brit.) PR:C
OVERTURE TO GLORY (1940) PR:C

OVIRI (SEE: WOLF AT THE DOOR, THE) (1986,
   Den./Fr.)
OWD BOB (SEE: TO THE VICTOR) (1938, Brit.)
OWL AND THE PUSSYCAT, THE (1970) PR:C
OX-BOW INCIDENT, THE (1943) PR:C-O
OXFORD BLUES (1984) PR:O
OZ (SEE: 20TH CENTURY OZ) (1977, Aus.)

PQ

P.C. JOSSER (1931, Brit.) PR:A
P.J. (1968) PR:O
P.K. AND THE KID (1987) PR:A
P.O.W. THE ESCAPE (1986) PR:O
P.O.W., THE (1973) PR:C
PA SOLSIDAN (SEE: ON THE SUNNYSIDE) (1936,
   Swed.)
PACE THAT THRILLS, THE (1952) PR:C
PACIFIC ADVENTURE (1947, Aus.) PR:A
PACIFIC BLACKOUT (SEE: MIDNIGHT ANGEL) (1941)
PACIFIC DESTINY (1956, Brit.) PR:A
PACIFIC LINER (1939) PR:C
PACIFIC RENDEZVOUS (1942) PR:A
PACK, THE (1977) PR:O
PACK TRAIN (1953) PR:A
PACK UP YOUR TROUBLES (1932) PR:AA
PACK UP YOUR TROUBLES (1939) PR:AA
PACK UP YOUR TROUBLES (1940, Brit.) PR:A
PACKAGE, THE (1989) PR:C
PAD. . . AND HOW TO USE IT, THE (1966, Brit.) PR:O
PADDY (1970, Ireland) PR:O
PADDY O'DAY (1935) PR:A
PADDY, THE NEXT BEST THING (1933) PR:A
PADRE PADRONE (1977, It.) PR:C
PAGAN, THE (1929) PR:A-C
PAGAN HELLCAT (SEE: MAEVA) (1961)
PAGAN ISLAND (1961) PR:A
PAGAN LADY (1931) PR:A
PAGAN LOVE SONG (1950) PR:A
PAGE MISS GLORY (1935) PR:A
PAGLIACCI (SEE: CLOWN MUST LAUGH, A) (1936,
   Brit.)
PAI-SHE CHUAN (SEE: MADAME WHITE SNAKE)
   (1963, Hong Kong)
PAID (1930) PR:A
PAID IN ERROR (1938, Brit.) PR:A
PAID IN FULL (1950) PR:A
PAID TO DANCE (1937) PR:C
PAID TO KILL (1954, Brit.) PR:C
PAINT YOUR WAGON (1969) PR:C
PAINTED ANGEL, THE (1929) PR:A
PAINTED BOATS (SEE: GIRL ON THE CANAL, THE)
   (1947, Brit.)
PAINTED DESERT, THE (1931) PR:A
PAINTED DESERT, THE (1938) PR:A
PAINTED FACES (1929) PR:A
PAINTED HILLS, THE (1951) PR:AA
PAINTED SMILE, THE (SEE: MURDER CAN BE
   DEADLY) (1963, Brit.)
PAINTED TRAIL, THE (1938) PR:A
PAINTED VEIL, THE (1934) PR:A
PAINTED WOMAN (1932) PR:A
PAINTING THE CLOUDS WITH SUNSHINE (1951)
   PR:A
PAIR OF BRIEFS, A (1963, Brit.) PR:A
PAISA (SEE: PAISAN) (1946, It.)
PAISAN (1946, It.) PR:C
PAJAMA GAME, THE (1957) PR:A
PAJAMA PARTY (1964) PR:AA
PAJAMA PARTY IN THE HAUNTED HOUSE (SEE:
   GHOST IN THE INVISIBLE BIKINI, THE) (1966)
PAL FROM TEXAS, THE (1939) PR:A
PAL JOEY (1957) PR:C
PALACE OF NUDES (1961, Fr./It.) PR:C
PALE ARROW (SEE: PAWNEE) (1957)
PALE RIDER (1985) PR:O
PALEFACE, THE (1948) PR:A
PALLET ON THE FLOOR (1984, New Zealand) PR:O
PALM BEACH (1979, Aus.) PR:O
PALM BEACH STORY, THE (1942) PR:A
PALM SPRINGS (1936) PR:A
PALM SPRINGS AFFAIR (SEE: PALM SPRINGS) (1936)
PALM SPRINGS WEEKEND (1963) PR:C
PALMY DAYS (1931) PR:A
PALOMINO, THE (1950) PR:AA
PALOOKA (1934) PR:AA
PALS OF THE GOLDEN WEST (1952) PR:A
PALS OF THE PECOS (1941) PR:A
PALS OF THE RANGE (1935) PR:A
PALS OF THE SADDLE (1938) PR:A
PALS OF THE SILVER SAGE (1940) PR:A
PAMPA SALVAJE (SEE: SAVAGE PAMPAS) (1967,
   US/Sp./Arg.)
PAN-AMERICANA (1945) PR:A
PANAMA FLO (1932) PR:A
PANAMA HATTIE (1942) PR:A
PANAMA LADY (1939) PR:A
PANAMA PATROL (1939) PR:A
PANAMA SAL (1957) PR:A

PANAMINT'S BAD MAN (1938) PR:A
PANCHO VILLA (1975, Sp.) PR:C
PANCHO VILLA RETURNS (1950, Mex.) PR:A
PANDA AND THE MAGIC SERPENT (1961, Jap.) PR:A
PANDEMONIUM (1982) PR:C
PANDORA AND THE FLYING DUTCHMAN (1951,
   Brit.) PR:A-C
PANHANDLE (1948) PR:A
PANIC (SEE: PANIQUE) (1946, Fr.)
PANIC (1966, Brit.) PR:A
PANIC BUTTON (1964) PR:A
PANIC IN NEEDLE PARK, THE (1971) PR:O
PANIC IN THE CITY (1968) PR:O
PANIC IN THE PARLOUR (1957, Brit.) PR:A
PANIC IN THE STREETS (1950) PR:C
PANIC IN YEAR ZERO! (1962) PR:O
PANIC ON THE AIR (SEE: YOU MAY BE NEXT!) (1936)
PANIC ON THE TRANS-SIBERIAN TRAIN (SEE: HOR-
   ROR EXPRESS) (1974, Brit./Sp.)
PANIQUE (1947, Fr.) PR:C
PANNY Z WILKA (SEE: YOUNG GIRLS OF WILKO,
   THE) (1979, Fr./Pol.)
PANTHER ISLAND (SEE: BOMBA ON PANTHER IS-
   LAND) (1949)
PANTHER SQUAD (1986, Fr./Bel.) PR:A
PANTHER'S CLAW, THE (1942) PR:A
PANTHER'S MOON (SEE: SPY HUNT) (1950)
PAPA'S DELICATE CONDITION (1963) PR:A
PAPER BULLETS (1941) PR:A
PAPER CHASE, THE (1973) PR:A-C
PAPER GALLOWS (1950, Brit.) PR:A
PAPER LION (1968) PR:A
PAPER MOON (1973) PR:C
PAPER ORCHID (1949, Brit.) PR:C
PAPER TIGER (1975, Brit.) PR:A-C
PAPERBACK HERO (1973, Can.) PR:O
PAPERHOUSE (1989, Brit.) PR:C
PAPILLON (1973) PR:O
PAR LE FER ET PAR LE FEU (SEE: INVASION 1700)
   (1965, Fr./It./Yugo.)
PAR OU T'ES RENTRE? ON T'A PAS VUE SORTIR
   (1984, Fr./Tunisia) PR:A
PARACHUTE BATTALION (1941) PR:A
PARACHUTE JUMPER (1933) PR:A
PARACHUTE NURSE (1942) PR:A
PARADE D'AMOUR (SEE: LOVE PARADE, THE) (1929)
PARADE OF THE WEST (1930) PR:A
PARADES (1972) PR:O
PARADINE CASE, THE (1947) PR:A-C
PARADISE (1982) PR:O
PARADISE ALLEY (1962) PR:A
PARADISE ALLEY (1978) PR:O
PARADISE CANYON (1935) PR:A
PARADISE EXPRESS (1937) PR:A
PARADISE FOR THREE (1938) PR:A
PARADISE FOR TWO (SEE: GAIETY GIRLS, THE)
   (1938, Brit.)
PARADISE, HAWAIIAN STYLE (1966) PR:A
PARADISE ISLAND (1930) PR:A
PARADISE ISLE (1937) PR:A
PARADISE LAGOON (SEE: ADMIRABLE CRICHTON,
   THE) (1957, Brit.)
PARADISE MOTEL (1985) PR:O
PARADISE POUR TOUS (1982, Fr.) PR:C-O
PARADISE ROAD (SEE: BIG DADDY) (1969)
PARADISIO (1962, Brit.) PR:O
PARALLAX VIEW, THE (1974) PR:O
PARALLELS (1980, Can.) PR:A-C
PARANOIAC (1963, Brit.) PR:O
PARASITE (1982) PR:O
PARASITE MURDERS, THE (SEE: THEY CAME FROM
   WITHIN) (1976, Can.)
PARATROOP COMMAND (1959) PR:A
PARATROOPER (1954, Brit.) PR:A
PARBESZED (SEE: DIALOGUE) (1967, Hung.)
PARDNERS (1956) PR:A
PARDON MON AFFAIRE (1976, Fr.) PR:A-C
PARDON MY BRUSH (1964) PR:O
PARDON MY FRENCH (1951, US/Fr.) PR:A
PARDON MY GUN (1930) PR:A
PARDON MY GUN (1942) PR:A
PARDON MY PAST (1945) PR:A
PARDON MY RHYTHM (1944) PR:A
PARDON MY SARONG (1942) PR:AA
PARDON MY STRIPES (1942) PR:A
PARDON MY TRUNK (SEE: HELLO, ELEPHANT)
   (1954, It.)
PARDON OUR NERVE (1939) PR:A
PARDON US (1931) PR:AA
PARENT TRAP, THE (1961) PR:AA
PARENTHOOD (1989) PR:C
PARENTS (1989) PR:C
PARENTS ON TRIAL (1939) PR:A
PARIS (1929) PR:A
PARIS AFTER DARK (1943) PR:A
PARIS AU MOIS D'AOUT (SEE: PARIS IN THE
   MONTH OF AUGUST) (1968, Fr.)
PARIS BELONGS TO US (1962, Fr.) PR:A-C

PARIS BLUES (1961) PR:O
PARIS BOUND (1929) PR:A
PARIS BRULE-T-IL? (SEE: IS PARIS BURNING?) (1966, Fr.)
PARIS CALLING (1941) PR:A
PARIS DOES STRANGE THINGS (SEE: ELENA AND HER MEN) (1957, Fr./It.)
PARIS EROTIKA (SEE: PARIS OOH-LA-LA!) (1966, US/Fr.)
PARIS EXPRESS, THE (1952, Brit.) PR:A
PARIS FOLLIES OF 1956 (SEE: FRESH FROM PARIS) (1955)
PARIS HOLIDAY (1958) PR:A
PARIS HONEYMOON (1939) PR:A
PARIS IN SPRING (1935) PR:A
PARIS IN THE MONTH OF AUGUST (1968, Fr.) PR:A
PARIS INTERLUDE (1934) PR:A
PARIS IS OURS (SEE: PARIS BELONGS TO US) (1962, Fr.)
PARIS LOVE SONG (SEE: PARIS IN SPRING) (1935)
PARIS MODEL (1953) PR:A
PARIS NOUS APPARTIENT (SEE: PARIS BELONGS TO US) (1962, Fr.)
PARIS OOH-LA-LA! (1963, US/Fr.) PR:O
PARIS PICK-UP (1963, Fr./It.) PR:C
PARIS PLANE (1933, Brit.) PR:A
PARIS PLAYBOYS (1954) PR:A
PARIS, TEXAS (1984, Fr./W. Ger.) PR:C-O
PARIS UNDERGROUND (1945) PR:A
PARIS VU PAR (SEE: SIX IN PARIS) (1968, Fr.)
PARIS WAS MADE FOR LOVERS (SEE: TIME FOR LOVING, A) (1971, Brit.)
PARIS WHEN IT SIZZLES (1964) PR:A
PARISIAN, THE (1931, Fr.) PR:A
PARISIAN ROMANCE, A (1932) PR:A
PARISIENNE (SEE: LA PARISIENNE) (1958, Fr./It.)
PARK AVENUE LOGGER (1937) PR:A
PARK PLAZA 605 (SEE: NORMAN CONQUEST) (1953, Brit.)
PARK ROW (1952) PR:A
PARKING (1985, Fr.) PR:C
PARLIAMO DI DONNE (SEE: LET'S TALK ABOUT WOMEN) (1964, Fr./It.)
PARLOR, BEDROOM AND BATH (1931) PR:A
PARMI LES VAUTOURS (SEE: FRONTIER HELLCAT) (1966, Fr./It./W. Ger./Yugo.)
PARNELL (1937) PR:A-C
PAROLE (1936) PR:A
PAROLE FIXER (1940) PR:A
PAROLE GIRL (1933) PR:A
PAROLE, INC. (1949) PR:A
PAROLE RACKET (1937) PR:A
PAROLED FROM THE BIG HOUSE (1938) PR:A
PAROLED—TO DIE (1938) PR:A
PAROXISMUS (SEE: VENUS IN FURS) (1970, Brit./It./W. Ger.)
PARRISH (1961) PR:A
PARSIFAL (1983, Fr.) PR:A
PARSON AND THE OUTLAW, THE (1957) PR:A
PARSON OF PANAMINT, THE (1941) PR:A
PART TIME WIFE (1930) PR:A
PART-TIME WIFE (1961, Brit.) PR:A
PART 2, WALKING TALL (SEE: WALKING TALL, PART 2) (1975)
PARTING GLANCES (1986) PR:O
PARTINGS (1962, Pol.) PR:A
PARTIR REVENIR (SEE: GOING AND COMING BACK) (1985, Fr.)
PARTLY CONFIDENTIAL (SEE: THANKS FOR LISTENING) (1937)
PARTNER, THE (1966, Brit.) PR:A
PARTNERS (1932) PR:A
PARTNERS (1976, Can.) PR:C
PARTNERS (1982) PR:O
PARTNERS IN CRIME (1937) PR:A
PARTNERS IN FORTUNE (SEE: ROCKIN' IN THE ROCKIES) (1945)
PARTNERS IN TIME (1946) PR:A
PARTNERS OF THE PLAINS (1938) PR:A
PARTNERS OF THE SUNSET (1948) PR:A
PARTNERS OF THE TRAIL (1931) PR:A
PARTNERS OF THE TRAIL (1944) PR:A
PARTS: THE CLONUS HORROR (SEE: CLONUS HORROR, THE) (1979)
PARTY, THE (1968) PR:A
PARTY CAMP (1987) PR:O
PARTY CRASHERS, THE (1958) PR:A
PARTY GIRL (1930) PR:A
PARTY GIRL (1958) PR:C
PARTY GIRLS FOR THE CANDIDATE (SEE: CANDIDATE, THE) (1964)
PARTY HUSBAND (1931) PR:A
PARTY PARTY (1983, Brit.) PR:C
PARTY WIRE (1935) PR:A
PARTY'S OVER, THE (1966, Brit.) PR:O
PARTY'S OVER, THE (1934) PR:A
PAS DE MENTALITE (SEE: WORLD IN MY POCKET, THE) (1962, Fr./It./W. Ger.)

PAS DE ROSES POUR OSS 117 (SEE: NO ROSES FOR OSS 117) (1968, Fr.)
PAS QUESTION LE SEMEDI (SEE: IMPOSSIBLE ON SATURDAY) (1966, Fr./Israel)
PASAJEROS DE UNA PESADILLA (SEE: MIGHTMARE'S PASSENGERS) (1986, Arg.)
PASAZERKA (SEE: PASSENGER, THE) (1970, Pol.)
PASCALI'S ISLAND (1988, Brit.) PR:C-O
PASI SPRE LUNA (SEE: STEPS TO THE MOON) (1963, Rum.)
PASQUALINO SETTEBELLEZZE (SEE: SEVEN BEAUTIES) (1976, It.)
PASQUALINO: SEVEN BEAUTIES (SEE: SEVEN BEAUTIES) (1976, It.)
PASS THE AMMO (1988) PR:O
PASS TO ROMANCE (SEE: HI, BEAUTIFUL!) (1944)
PASSAGE, THE (1979, Brit.) PR:O
PASSAGE FROM HONG KONG (1941) PR:A
PASSAGE HOME (1955, Brit.) PR:A
PASSAGE OF LOVE (SEE: TIME LOST AND TIME REMEMBERED) (1966, Brit.)
PASSAGE TO INDIA, A (1984, Brit.) PR:C
PASSAGE TO MARSEILLE (1944) PR:A
PASSAGE WEST (1951) PR:A
PASSAGES FROM JAMES JOYCE'S FINNEGANS WAKE (SEE: FINNEGANS WAKE) (1965)
PASSENGER, THE (1970, Pol.) PR:O
PASSENGER, THE (1975, It.) PR:C
PASSENGER TO LONDON (1937, Brit.) PR:A
PASSING OF THE THIRD FLOOR BACK, THE (1936, Brit.) PR:A
PASSING SHADOWS (1934, Brit.) PR:A
PASSING SHOW, THE (SEE: HOTEL VARIETY) (1933)
PASSING STRANGER, THE (1954, Brit.) PR:A
PASSING THROUGH (1977) PR:O
PASSION (1954) PR:A
PASSION (1968, Jap.) PR:O
PASSION (1983, Fr./Switz.) PR:O
PASSION FLOWER (1930) PR:A
PASSION FOR LIFE (1951, Fr.) PR:A
PASSION HOLIDAY (1963) PR:O
PASSION IN THE SUN (1964) PR:O
PASSION ISLAND (1943, Mex.) PR:A
PASSION OF ANNA, THE (1969, Swed.) PR:C
PASSION OF LOVE (1982, It./Fr.) PR:O
PASSION OF SLOW FIRE, THE (1962, Fr.) PR:C
PASSION OF THE SUN (SEE: PASSION IN THE SUN) (1964)
PASSION PIT, THE (SEE: SCREAM OF THE BUTTERFLY) (1965)
PASSION PIT, THE (SEE: ICE HOUSE, THE) (1969)
PASSION STREET, U.S.A. (1964) PR:C
PASSIONATE DEMONS, THE (1962, Norway) PR:A
PASSIONATE FRIENDS, THE (SEE: ONE WOMAN'S STORY) (1949, Brit.)
PASSIONATE PLUMBER, THE (1932) PR:A
PASSIONATE SENTRY, THE (1952, Brit.) PR:C
PASSIONATE STRANGER, THE (SEE: NOVEL AFFAIR, A) (1957, Brit.)
PASSIONATE STRANGERS, THE (1968, Phil.) PR:C
PASSIONATE SUMMER (1959, Brit.) PR:A
PASSIONATE SUNDAY (SEE: DARK ODYSSEY) (1961)
PASSIONATE THIEF, THE (1961, It.) PR:A
PASSIONE D'AMORE (SEE: PASSION OF LOVE) (1982, It./Fr.)
PASSKEY TO DANGER (1946) PR:A
PASSOVER PLOT, THE (1976, Israel) PR:C
PASSPORT HUSBAND (1938) PR:A
PASSPORT TO ADVENTURE (SEE: PASSPORT TO DESTINY) (1944)
PASSPORT TO ALCATRAZ (1940) PR:A
PASSPORT TO CHINA (1961, Brit.) PR:A
PASSPORT TO DESTINY (1944) PR:A
PASSPORT TO HELL (1932) PR:A
PASSPORT TO HELL (SEE: PASSPORT TO ALCATRAZ) (1940)
PASSPORT TO OBLIVION (SEE: WHERE THE SPIES ARE) (1966, Brit.)
PASSPORT TO PIMLICO (1949, Brit.) PR:A
PASSPORT TO SHAME (SEE: ROOM 43) (1959, Brit.)
PASSPORT TO SUEZ (1943) PR:A
PASSPORT TO TREASON (1956, Brit.) PR:A
PASSWORD IS COURAGE, THE (1962, Brit.) PR:A
PAST OF MARY HOLMES, THE (1933) PR:A
PASTEUR (1936, Fr.) PR:A
PASTOR HALL (1940, Brit.) PR:A
PAT AND MIKE (1952) PR:A
PAT GARRETT AND BILLY THE KID (1973) PR:C
PATAKIN (1985, Cuba) PR:A
PATATE (SEE: FRIEND OF THE FAMILY) (1965, Fr./It.)
PATCH (SEE: DEATH OF A GUNFIGHTER) (1969)
PATCH OF BLUE, A (1965) PR:A
PATERNITY (1981) PR:C
PATH OF GLORY, THE (1934, Brit.) PR:A
PATHER PANCHALI (1955, India) PR:A
PATHFINDER, THE (1952) PR:A
PATHS OF GLORY (1957) PR:C
PATIENT IN ROOM 18, THE (1938) PR:A

PATIENT VANISHES, THE (1947, Brit.) PR:A
PATRICIA GETS HER MAN (1937, Brit.) PR:A
PATRICK (1979, Aus.) PR:O
PATRICK THE GREAT (1945) PR:A
PATRIOT (1928) PR:C
PATRIOT, THE (1986) PR:O
PATSY, THE (1964) PR:A
PATTERN FOR PLUNDER (SEE: BAY OF SAINT MICHEL) (1963, Brit.)
PATTERN OF EVIL (SEE: SATAN IN HIGH HEELS) (1962)
PATTERNS (1956) PR:A
PATTERNS OF POWER (SEE: PATTERNS) (1956)
PATTI ROCKS (1988) PR:O
PATTON (1970) PR:C
PATTY HEARST (1988) PR:O
PAUL AND MICHELLE (1974, Fr./Brit.) PR:O
PAUL TEMPLE RETURNS (1952, Brit.) PR:A
PAUL TEMPLE'S TRIUMPH (1951, Brit.) PR:A
PAULA (SEE: FRAMED) (1947)
PAULA (1952) PR:A
PAULINE A LA PLAGE (SEE: PAULINE AT THE BEACH) (1983, Fr.)
PAULINE AT THE BEACH (1983, Fr.) PR:O
PAURA NELLA CITTA DEI MORTI VIVENTI (SEE: GATES OF HELL, THE) (1983, US/It.)
PAVLOVA—A WOMAN FOR ALL TIME (1985, Brit./USSR) PR:A-C
PAW (SEE: LURE OF THE JUNGLE, THE) (1970, Den.)
PAWNBROKER, THE (1965) PR:C
PAWNEE (1957) PR:A
PAY BOX ADVENTURE (1936, Brit.) PR:A
PAY-OFF, THE (1930) PR:A
PAY OR DIE (1960) PR:C
PAY THE DEVIL (SEE: MAN IN THE SHADOW) (1957)
PAYDAY (1972) PR:O
PAYMENT DEFERRED (1932) PR:A
PAYMENT IN BLOOD (1968, It.) PR:O
PAYMENT ON DEMAND (1951) PR:A-C
PAYOFF, THE (1935) PR:A
PAYOFF, THE (1943) PR:A
PAYROLL (1962, Brit.) PR:A
PEACE FOR A GUNFIGHTER (1967) PR:C
PEACE KILLERS, THE (1971) PR:O
PEACE TO HIM WHO ENTERS (1963, USSR) PR:A
PEACEMAKER (SEE: AMBASSADOR, THE) (1984)
PEACEMAKER, THE (1956) PR:A
PEACH-O-RENO (1931) PR:A
PEACH THIEF, THE (1969, Bulgaria) PR:C
PEACOCK ALLEY (1930) PR:A
PEACOCK FEATHERS (SEE: OPEN THE DOOR AND SEE ALL THE PEOPLE) (1964)
PEARL, THE (1948, US/Mex.) PR:A
PEARL OF DEATH, THE (1944) PR:A
PEARL OF THE SOUTH PACIFIC (1955) PR:A
PEARL OF TLAYUCAN (1964, Mex.) PR:A
PEARLS BRING TEARS (1937, Brit.) PR:A
PEARLS OF THE CROWN (1938, Fr.) PR:A
PEAU D'ANE (SEE: DONKEY SKIN) (1975, Fr.)
PEAU DE BANANE (SEE: BANANA PEEL) (1965, Fr./It.)
PEAU D'ESPION (SEE: TO COMMIT A MURDER) (1970, Fr./It./W. Ger.)
PECCATORI IN BLUE-JEANS (SEE: CHEATERS, THE) (1961, Fr./It.)
PECK'S BAD BOY (1934) PR:AA
PECK'S BAD BOY WITH THE CIRCUS (1938) PR:AA
PECOS RIVER (1951) PR:A
PEDDLIN' IN SOCIETY (1949, It.) PR:A
PEDESTRIAN, THE (1974, W. Ger.) PR:C
PEE-WEE'S BIG ADVENTURE (1985) PR:A
PEEK-A-BOO (1954, Fr.) PR:O
PEEPER (1975) PR:A
PEEPING TOM (1960, Brit.) PR:O
PEER GYNT (1965) PR:A
PEG O' MY HEART (1933) PR:A
PEG OF OLD DRURY (1936, Brit.) PR:A
PEGGY (1950) PR:A
PEGGY SUE GOT MARRIED (1986) PR:C
PEKING BLONDE (SEE: BLONDE FROM PEKING, THE) (1968, Fr.)
PEKING EXPRESS (1951) PR:A
PEKING MEDALLION, THE (SEE: CORRUPT ONES, THE) (1967, Fr./It./W. Ger.)
PEKING OPERA BLUES (1986, Hong Kong) PR:C
PELLE THE CONQUEROR (1987, Swed./Den.) PR:NR
PENAL CODE, THE (1933) PR:A
PENALTY, THE (1941) PR:C
PENALTY OF FAME (SEE: OKAY AMERICA) (1932)
PENDULUM (1969) PR:A-C
PENELOPE (1966) PR:A
PENGUIN POOL MURDER (1932) PR:A
PENGUIN POOL MYSTERY, THE (SEE: PENGUIN POOL MURDER, THE) (1932)
PENITENT, THE (1988) PR:C-O
PENITENTE MURDER CASE, THE (1936) PR:O
PENITENTIARY (1938) PR:A
PENITENTIARY (1979) PR:O
PENITENTIARY II (1982) PR:O

PENITENTIARY III (1987) PR:O
PENN & TELLER GET KILLED (1989) PR:O
PENN OF PENNSYLVANIA (SEE: COURAGEOUS MR. PENN) (1941, Brit.)
PENNIES FROM HEAVEN (1936) PR:A
PENNIES FROM HEAVEN (1981) PR:C-O
PENNY PARADISE (1938, Brit.) PR:A
PENNY POINTS TO PARADISE (1951, Brit.) PR:A
PENNY POOL, THE (1937, Brit.) PR:A
PENNY PRINCESS (1953, Brit.) PR:A
PENNY SERENADE (1941) PR:A
PENNYWHISTLE BLUES, THE (1952, South Africa) PR:A
PENROD AND HIS TWIN BROTHER (1938) PR:AA
PENROD AND SAM (1931) PR:AA
PENROD AND SAM (1937) PR:AA
PENROD'S DOUBLE TROUBLE (1938) PR:AA
PENTHOUSE (1933) PR:A
PENTHOUSE, THE (1967, Brit.) PR:O
PENTHOUSE PARTY (1936) PR:A
PENTHOUSE RHYTHM (1945) PR:A
PEOPLE AGAINST O'HARA, THE (1951) PR:C
PEOPLE ARE FUNNY (1945) PR:A
PEOPLE MEET AND SWEET MUSIC FILLS THE HEART (1969, Den./Swed.) PR:O
PEOPLE NEXT DOOR, THE (1970) PR:O
PEOPLE THAT TIME FORGOT, THE (1977, Brit.) PR:AA
PEOPLE TOYS (SEE: DEVIL TIMES FIVE) (1974)
PEOPLE VS. DR. KILDARE, THE (1941) PR:A
PEOPLE WHO OWN THE DARK (1975, Sp.) PR:O
PEOPLE WILL TALK (1935) PR:A
PEOPLE WILL TALK (1951) PR:A-C
PEOPLE'S ENEMY, THE (1935) PR:A
PEPE (1960) PR:AA
PEPE LE MOKO (1937, Fr.) PR:C
PEPPER (1936) PR:AA
PEPPERMINT SODA (1979, Fr.) PR:C
PER ASPERA AD ASTRA (SEE: CHEREZ TERNII K SVEZDAM) (1981, USSR)
PER IL BENE E PER IL MALE (SEE: ANATOMY OF A MARRIAGE (MY DAYS WITH JEAN-MARC AND MY NIGHTS WITH FRANCOISE)) (1964, Fr./It.)
PER LE ANTICHE SCALE (SEE: DOWN THE ANCIENT STAIRCASE) (1975, It.)
PER MOTIVI DI GELOSIA (SEE: MOTIVE WAS JEAL-OUSY, THE) (1970, It./Sp.)
PER QUALCHE DOLLARO IN PIU (SEE: FOR A FEW DOLLARS MORE) (1964, It./Sp./W. Ger.)
PER UN PUGNO DI DOLLARI (SEE: FISTFUL OF DOL-LARS, A) (1964, It./Sp./W. Ger.)
PERCY (1971, Brit.) PR:O
PERCY'S PROGRESS (SEE: IT'S NOT THE SIZE THAT COUNTS) (1979, Brit.)
PERFECT (1985) PR:O
PERFECT ALIBI, THE (1931, Brit.) PR:A
PERFECT CLUE, THE (1935) PR:A
PERFECT COUPLE, A (1979) PR:A-C
PERFECT CRIME, THE (1928) PR:A-C
PERFECT CRIME, THE (SEE: ELLERY QUEEN AND THE PERFECT CRIME) (1941)
PERFECT CRIME, THE (1937, Brit.) PR:A
PERFECT FLAW, THE (1934, Brit.) PR:A
PERFECT FRIDAY (1970, Brit.) PR:C
PERFECT FURLOUGH, THE (1958) PR:A
PERFECT GENTLEMAN, THE (1935) PR:A
PERFECT LADY, THE (1931, Brit.) PR:A
PERFECT MARRIAGE, THE (1946) PR:A
PERFECT MATCH, THE (1987) PR:A
PERFECT MODEL, THE (1989) PR:C
PERFECT SET-UP, THE (SEE: ONCE YOU KISS A STRANGER) (1969)
PERFECT SNOB, THE (1941) PR:A
PERFECT SPECIMEN, THE (1937) PR:A
PERFECT STRANGERS (SEE: VACATION FROM MAR-RIAGE) (1945, Brit.)
PERFECT STRANGERS (1950) PR:A
PERFECT STRANGERS (1984) PR:C
PERFECT UNDERSTANDING (1933, Brit.) PR:A-C
PERFECT WEEKEND, A (SEE: ST. LOUIS KID, THE) (1934)
PERFECT WOMAN, THE (1950, Brit.) PR:A
PERFECTIONIST, THE (1952, Fr.) PR:A
PERFORMERS, THE (1970, Jap.) PR:C
PERIL (1985, Fr.) PR:O
PERIL FOR THE GUY (1956, Brit.) PR:A
PERILOUS HOLIDAY (1946) PR:A
PERILOUS JOURNEY, A (SEE: BAD BOY) (1939)
PERILOUS JOURNEY, A (1953) PR:A
PERILOUS WATERS (1948) PR:A
PERILS OF GWENDOLINE, THE (1984, Fr.) PR:O
PERILS OF PAULINE, THE (1947) PR:A
PERILS OF PAULINE, THE (1967) PR:A
PERILS OF P.K., THE (1986) PR:O
PERIOD OF ADJUSTMENT (1962) PR:A-C
PERMANENT RECORD (1988) PR:C
PERMANENT VACATION (1982) PR:C
PERMETTE? ROCCO PAPALEO (SEE: ROCCO PAPALEO) (1971, It./Fr.)

PERMETTE SIGNORA CHE AMI VOSTRA FIGLIA (SEE: CLARETTA AND BEN) (1983, It./Fr.)
PERMISSION TO KILL (1975, US/Aust.) PR:C
PERRY RHODAN-SOS AUS DEM WELTALLO (SEE: MISSION STARDUST) (1968, It./Sp./W. Ger.)
PERSECUTION (1974, Brit.) PR:C
PERSECUTION AND ASSASSINATION OF JEAN-PAUL MARAT AS PERFORMED BY THE INMATES OF THE ASYLUM OF CHARENTON UNDER THE DIREC-TION OF THE MARQUIS DE SADE, THE (1967, Brit.) PR:C
PERSECUTION OF HASTA VALENCIA (SEE: NARCO MEN, THE) (1971, It./Sp.)
PERSONA (1966, Swed.) PR:O
PERSONAL AFFAIR (1954, Brit.) PR:C
PERSONAL BEST (1982) PR:C-O
PERSONAL COLUMN (1939, Fr.) PR:C
PERSONAL COLUMN (SEE: LURED) (1946)
PERSONAL FOUL (1987) PR:A-C
PERSONAL HONOR (SEE: HELLO ANNAPOLIS) (1942)
PERSONAL MAID (1931) PR:A
PERSONAL MAID'S SECRET (1935) PR:A
PERSONAL PROPERTY (1937) PR:A
PERSONAL SECRETARY (1938) PR:A
PERSONAL SERVICES (1987, Brit.) PR:O
PERSONALITY (1930) PR:A
PERSONALITY KID, THE (1934) PR:A
PERSONALITY KID (1946) PR:AA
PERSONALS, THE (1982) PR:C
PERSONS IN HIDING (1939) PR:A-C
PERSONS UNKNOWN (SEE: BIG DEAL ON MADONNA STREET) (1958, It.)
PERSUADER, THE (1957) PR:A
PERVYY DEN MIRA (SEE: DAY THE WAR ENDED, THE) (1961, USSR)
PET SEMATARY (1989) PR:O
PETE KELLY'S BLUES (1955) PR:C
PETE 'N' TILLIE (1972) PR:A-C
PETER IBBETSON (1935) PR:A
PETER PAN (1953) PR:AA
PETER RABBIT AND TALES OF BEATRIX POTTER (1971, Brit.) PR:AA
PETER THE CRAZY (SEE: PIERROT LE FOU) (1965, Fr./It.)
PETERSEN (1974, Aus.) PR:C
PETERVILLE DIAMOND, THE (1942, Brit.) PR:A
PETE'S DRAGON (1977) PR:AA
PETEY WHEATSTRAW (1978) PR:O
PETIT CON (1985, Fr.) PR:C-O
PETRIFIED FOREST, THE (1936) PR:A
PETS (1974) PR:O
PETTICOAT FEVER (1936) PR:A
PETTICOAT LARCENY (1943) PR:A
PETTICOAT PIRATES (1961, Brit.) PR:A
PETTICOAT POLITICS (1941) PR:A
PETTICOATS AND BLUEJEANS (SEE: PARENT TRAP, THE) (1961)
PETTY GIRL, THE (1950) PR:A
PETULIA (1968, US/Brit.) PR:C
PEYTON PLACE (1957) PR:C
PHAEDRA (1962, US/Gr./Fr.) PR:C
PHANTASM (1979) PR:O
PHANTASM II (1988) PR:O
PHANTOM BROADCAST, THE (1933) PR:A
PHANTOM COWBOY, THE (1941) PR:A
PHANTOM EXPRESS, THE (1932) PR:A
PHANTOM FIEND, THE (1935, Brit.) PR:A
PHANTOM FIEND (SEE: RETURN OF DR. MABUSE, THE) (1961, Fr./It./W. Ger.)
PHANTOM FROM SPACE (1953) PR:A
PHANTOM FROM 10,000 LEAGUES, THE (1956) PR:A
PHANTOM GOLD (1938) PR:A
PHANTOM HORSEMAN, THE (SEE: BORDER OUT-LAWS) (1950)
PHANTOM IN THE HOUSE, THE (1929) PR:A
PHANTOM KILLER (1942) PR:A
PHANTOM LADY (1944) PR:C
PHANTOM LIGHT, THE (1935, Brit.) PR:C
PHANTOM OF CHINATOWN (1940) PR:A
PHANTOM OF CRESTWOOD, THE (1932) PR:A
PHANTOM OF 42ND STREET, THE (1945) PR:A
PHANTOM OF LIBERTY, THE (1974, Fr.) PR:O
PHANTOM OF PARIS, THE (1931) PR:A
PHANTOM OF PARIS (SEE: MYSTERY OF MARIE ROGET, THE) (1942)
PHANTOM OF SANTA FE, THE (1937) PR:A
PHANTOM OF SOHO, THE (1967, W. Ger.) PR:C
PHANTOM OF TERROR, THE (SEE: BIRD WITH THE CRYSTAL PLUMAGE, THE) (1969, It./W. Ger.)
PHANTOM OF THE AIR (SEE: PHANTOM BROAD-CAST, THE) (1933)
PHANTOM OF THE DESERT (1930) PR:A
PHANTOM OF THE JUNGLE (1955) PR:A
PHANTOM OF THE MALL: ERIC'S REVENGE (1989) PR:O
PHANTOM OF THE OPERA, THE (1929) PR:A
PHANTOM OF THE OPERA (1943) PR:A
PHANTOM OF THE OPERA, THE (1962, Brit.) PR:C-O

PHANTOM OF THE OPERA (1989) PR:O
PHANTOM OF THE PARADISE (1974) PR:C
PHANTOM OF THE PLAINS (1945) PR:A
PHANTOM OF THE RANGE, THE (1938) PR:A
PHANTOM OF THE RUE MORGUE (1954) PR:C
PHANTOM PATROL (1936) PR:A
PHANTOM PLAINSMEN, THE (1942) PR:A
PHANTOM PLANET, THE (1961) PR:A
PHANTOM PRESIDENT, THE (1932) PR:A
PHANTOM RAIDERS (1940) PR:A
PHANTOM RANCHER (1940) PR:A
PHANTOM RANGER (1938) PR:A
PHANTOM SHIP (1937, Brit.) PR:A
PHANTOM SPEAKS, THE (1945) PR:A
PHANTOM STAGE, THE (1939) PR:A
PHANTOM STAGECOACH, THE (1957) PR:A
PHANTOM STALLION, THE (1954) PR:A
PHANTOM STOCKMAN, THE (1953, Aus.) PR:A
PHANTOM STRIKES, THE (1939, Brit.) PR:A
PHANTOM SUBMARINE, THE (1941) PR:A
PHANTOM THIEF, THE (1946) PR:A
PHANTOM THUNDERBOLT, THE (1933) PR:A
PHANTOM TOLLBOOTH, THE (1970) PR:AA
PHANTOM VALLEY (1948) PR:A
PHAR LAP (1984, Aus.) PR:C
PHARAOH'S CURSE (1957) PR:A
PHARAOHS' WOMAN, THE (1961, It.) PR:A
PHASE IV (1974, Brit.) PR:A
PHENIX CITY STORY, THE (1955) PR:C
PHENOMENA (SEE: CREEPERS) (1985, It.)
PHFFFT! (1954) PR:A
PHILADELPHIA ATTRACTION, THE (1985, Hung.) PR:A
PHILADELPHIA EXPERIMENT, THE (1984) PR:C
PHILADELPHIA STORY, THE (1940) PR:A
PHILIP (SEE: RUN WILD, RUN FREE) (1969, Brit.)
PHILLY (SEE: PRIVATE LESSONS) (1981)
PHILO VANCE RETURNS (1947) PR:A
PHILO VANCE'S GAMBLE (1947) PR:A
PHILO VANCE'S SECRET MISSION (1947) PR:A
PHOBIA (1980, Can.) PR:O
PHOBIA (SEE: NESTING, THE) (1981)
PHOBIA (1988, Aus.) PR:O
PHOENIX, THE (SEE: WAR OF THE WIZARDS) (1983, Taiwan)
PHOENIX CITY STORY (SEE: PHENIX CITY STORY) (1955)
PHONE CALL FROM A STRANGER (1952) PR:A-C
PHONY AMERICAN, THE (1964, W. Ger.) PR:A
PHOTOGRAPH, THE (1987, Gr.) PR:C
PHYNX, THE (1970) PR:C
PHYSICAL EVIDENCE (1989) PR:C
PIAF—THE EARLY YEARS (1982, US/Fr.) PR:A-C
PICCADILLY (1932, Brit.) PR:A-C
PICCADILLY INCIDENT (1948, Brit.) PR:A
PICCADILLY JIM (1936) PR:A
PICCADILLY NIGHTS (1930, Brit.) PR:A
PICCADILLY THIRD STOP (1960, Brit.) PR:A
PICCOLI FUOCHI (SEE: LITTLE FLAMES) (1985, It.)
PICK A STAR (1937) PR:AA
PICK-UP (1933) PR:A
PICK-UP ARTIST, THE (1987) PR:A-C
PICK-UP SUMMER (1981, Can.) PR:O
PICKPOCKET (1963, Fr.) PR:A
PICKUP (1951) PR:A
PICKUP ALLEY (1957, Brit.) PR:A
PICKUP IN ROME (SEE: FROM A ROMAN BALCONY) (1961, Fr./It.)
PICKUP ON 101 (1972) PR:C
PICKUP ON SOUTH STREET (1953) PR:C
PICKWICK PAPERS, THE (1952, Brit.) PR:AA
PICNIC (1955) PR:A
PICNIC AT HANGING ROCK (1975, Aus.) PR:C-O
PICNIC ON THE GRASS (1959, Fr.) PR:C
PICTURE BRIDES (1934) PR:A
PICTURE MOMMY DEAD (1966) PR:O
PICTURE OF DORIAN GRAY, THE (1945) PR:C
PICTURE SHOW MAN, THE (1980, Aus.) PR:A
PICTURE SNATCHER (1933) PR:A-C
PICTURES (1982, New Zealand) PR:A-C
PIE IN THE SKY (1964) PR:A
PIECE OF THE ACTION, A (1977) PR:C
PIECES (1983, Sp./Puerto Rico) PR:O
PIECES OF DREAMS (1970) PR:C
PIED PIPER, THE (1942) PR:C
PIED PIPER, THE (SEE: CLOWN AND THE KIDS, THE) (1968, US/Bulgaria)
PIED PIPER, THE (1972, Brit.) PR:C
PIEGES (SEE: PERSONAL COLUMN) (1939, Fr.)
PIEL DE VERANO (SEE: SUMMERSKIN) (1962, Arg.)
PIER 5, HAVANA (1959) PR:A
PIER 13 (SEE: ME AND MY GAL) (1932)
PIER 13 (1940) PR:A
PIER 23 (1951) PR:A
PIERRE OF THE PLAINS (1942) PR:A
PIERROT LE FOU (1968, Fr./It.) PR:O
PIGEON THAT TOOK ROME, THE (1962) PR:C
PIGEONS (SEE: SIDELONG GLANCES OF A PIGEON KICKER) (1970, Brit.)

PIGS (1984, Ireland) PR:C
PIGS, THE (SEE: DADDY'S DEADLY DARLING) (1984)
PIGSKIN PARADE (1936) PR:A
PIKOVAYA DAMA (SEE: QUEEN OF SPADES) (1961, USSR)
PILGRIM, FAREWELL (1980) PR:C
PILGRIM LADY, THE (1947) PR:A
PILGRIMAGE (1933) PR:A-C
PILGRIMAGE (1972) PR:C
PILL, THE (SEE: GIRL, THE BODY, AND THE PILL, THE) (1967)
PILLAR OF FIRE, THE (1963, Israel) PR:A
PILLARS OF SOCIETY (1936, Ger.) PR:A
PILLARS OF THE SKY (1956) PR:A
PILLOW OF DEATH (1945) PR:A
PILLOW TALK (1959) PR:A
PILLOW TO POST (1945) PR:A
PILOT, THE (1979) PR:C
PILOT NO. 5 (1943) PR:A
PILOT X (SEE: DEATH IN THE SKY) (1937)
PIMPERNEL SMITH (1942, Brit.) PR:A
PIMPERNEL SVENSSON (1953, Swed.) PR:A
PIN (1989, Can.) PR:O
PIN UP GIRL (1944) PR:A
PINBALL PICK-UP (SEE: PICK-UP SUMMER) (1981, Can.)
PINBALL SUMMER (SEE: PICK-UP SUMMER) (1981, Can.)
PINK CADILLAC (1989) PR:C
PINK FLOYD—THE WALL (1982, Brit.) PR:O
PINK JUNGLE, THE (1968) PR:A
PINK MOTEL (1983) PR:O
PINK NIGHTS (1985) PR:A
PINK PANTHER, THE (1964) PR:A
PINK PANTHER STRIKES AGAIN, THE (1976, Brit.) PR:A
PINK STRING AND SEALING WAX (1950, Brit.) PR:A
PINKY (1949) PR:A
PINOCCHIO (1940) PR:AA
PINOCCHIO (1969, E. Ger.) PR:AA
PINOCCHIO AND THE EMPEROR OF THE NIGHT (1987) PR:AA
PINOCCHIO IN OUTER SPACE (1965, US/Bel.) PR:AA
PINTO BANDIT, THE (1944) PR:A
PINTO CANYON (1940) PR:AA
PINTO KID, THE (1941) PR:A
PINTO RUSTLERS (1937) PR:A
PIONEER BUILDERS (SEE: CONQUERORS, THE) (1932)
PIONEER DAYS (1940) PR:A
PIONEER, GO HOME (SEE: FOLLOW THAT DREAM) (1962)
PIONEER JUSTICE (1947) PR:A
PIONEER MARSHAL (1950) PR:A
PIONEER TRAIL (1938) PR:A
PIONEERS, THE (1941) PR:A
PIONEERS OF THE FRONTIER (1940) PR:A
PIONEERS OF THE WEST (1940) PR:A
PIPE DREAMS (1976) PR:C
PIPER, THE (SEE: CLOWN AND THE KIDS, THE) (1968, US/Bulgaria)
PIPER'S TUNE, THE (1962, Brit.) PR:AA
PIPPI IN THE SOUTH SEAS (1974, Swed./W. Ger.) PR:AA
PIPPI ON THE RUN (1977) PR:AA
PIRANHA (1978) PR:O
PIRAHANA II: FLYING KILLERS (SEE: PIRAHNA II: THE SPAWNING) (1981, Neth.)
PIRANHA II: THE SPAWNING (1981, Neth.) PR:O
PIRATE, THE (1948) PR:A
PIRATE AND THE SLAVE GIRL, THE (1961, Fr./It.) PR:A
PIRATE MOVIE, THE (1982, Aus.) PR:C
PIRATE OF THE BLACK HAWK, THE (1961, Fr./It.) PR:A
PIRATE SHIP (SEE: MUTINEERS, THE) (1949)
PIRATES (1986, Fr./Tunisia) PR:C
PIRATES OF BLOOD RIVER, THE (1962, Brit.) PR:A
PIRATES OF CAPRI, THE (1949) PR:A
PIRATES OF MONTEREY (1947) PR:A
PIRATES OF PENZANCE, THE (1983, Brit.) PR:A
PIRATES OF THE PRAIRIE (1942) PR:A
PIRATES OF THE SEVEN SEAS (1941, Brit.) PR:A
PIRATES OF THE SKIES (1939) PR:A
PIRATES OF TORTUGA (1961) PR:A
PIRATES OF TRIPOLI (1955) PR:A
PIRATES ON HORSEBACK (1941) PR:A
PISTOL FOR RINGO, A (1966, It./Sp.) PR:C
PISTOL HARVEST (1951) PR:A
PISTOL PACKIN' MAMA (1943) PR:A
PISTOLERO (SEE: LAST CHALLENGE, THE) (1967)
PIT, THE (SEE: FIVE MILLION YEARS TO EARTH) (1968, Brit.)
PIT AND THE PENDULUM, THE (1961) PR:C
PIT OF DARKNESS (1961, Brit.) PR:A
PIT STOP (1969) PR:O
PITFALL (1948) PR:C
PITTSBURGH (1942) PR:A
PITTSBURGH KID, THE (1941) PR:A
PIXOTE (1981, Braz.) PR:O
PIZZA TRIANGLE, THE (1970, It./Sp.) PR:O

PLACE CALLED GLORY, A (1966, Sp./W. Ger.) PR:C
PLACE FOR LOVERS, A (1969, It./Fr.) PR:C-O
PLACE IN THE SUN, A (1951) PR:C
PLACE OF ONE'S OWN, A (1945, Brit.) PR:A
PLACE OF WEEPING (1986, South Africa) PR:C-O
PLACE TO GO, A (1964, Brit.) PR:A
PLACES IN THE HEART (1984) PR:A-C
PLAGUE (1978, Can.) PR:C
PLAGUE DOGS, THE (1984, US/Brit.) PR:C-O
PLAGUE-M3: THE GEMINI STRAIN (SEE: PLAGUE) (1978, Can.)
PLAGUE OF THE ZOMBIES, THE (1966, Brit.) PR:C
PLAINSMAN, THE (1937) PR:C
PLAINSMAN, THE (SEE: RAIDERS, THE) (1964)
PLAINSMAN, THE (1966, Brit.) PR:C
PLAINSMAN AND THE LADY (1946) PR:A
PLAINSONG (1982) PR:C
PLAN 9 FROM OUTER SPACE (1959) PR:A
PLANES, TRAINS AND AUTOMOBILES (1987) PR:O
PLANET OF BLOOD (SEE: PLANET OF THE VAMPIRES) (1965, US/It./Sp.)
PLANET OF BLOOD (SEE: QUEEN OF BLOOD) (1966)
PLANET OF DINOSAURS (1978) PR:A
PLANET OF HORRORS (SEE: GALAXY OF TERROR) (1981)
PLANET OF STORMS (SEE: STORM PLANET) (1962, USSR)
PLANET OF THE APES (1968) PR:C
PLANET OF THE VAMPIRES (1965, US/It./Sp.) PR:C
PLANET ON THE PROWL (SEE: WAR BETWEEN THE PLANETS) (1971, It.)
PLANETA CIEGO (SEE: PEOPLE WHO OWN THE DARK) (1975, Sp.)
PLANETS AGAINST US, THE (1961, It./Fr.) PR:C
PLANK, THE (1967, Brit.) PR:A
PLANTER'S WIFE, THE (SEE: OUTPOST IN MALAYA) (1952, Brit.)
PLANTS ARE WATCHING US, THE (SEE: KIRLIAN WITNESS, THE) (1978)
PLASTIC DOME OF NORMA JEAN, THE (1966) PR:C
PLATINUM BLONDE (1931) PR:A
PLATINUM HIGH SCHOOL (1960) PR:A
PLATOON (1986) PR:O
PLATOON LEADER (1988) PR:O
PLAY DEAD (1981) PR:O
PLAY DEAD (1986) PR:O
PLAY DIRTY (1969, Brit.) PR:C
PLAY GIRL (1932) PR:A
PLAY GIRL (1940) PR:A
PLAY IT AGAIN, SAM (1972) PR:C
PLAY IT AS IT LAYS (1972) PR:O
PLAY IT COOL (1963, Brit.) PR:A
PLAY IT COOL (1970, Jap.) PR:C
PLAY MISTY FOR ME (1971) PR:O
PLAY UP THE BAND (1935, Brit.) PR:A
PLAYBACK (1962, Brit.) PR:A
PLAYBOY, THE (1942, Brit.) PR:AA
PLAYBOY OF PARIS (1930) PR:A
PLAYBOY OF THE WESTERN WORLD, THE (1963, Ireland) PR:C
PLAYERS (1979) PR:O
PLAYERS (SEE: CLUB, THE) (1980, Aus.)
PLAYGIRL (1954) PR:A
PLAYGIRL (SEE: THAT WOMAN) (1968, W. Ger.)
PLAYGIRL AFTER DARK (SEE: TOO HOT TO HANDLE) (1961, Brit.)
PLAYGIRL AND THE WAR MINISTER, THE (SEE: AMOROUS MR. PRAWN, THE) (1965, Brit.)
PLAYGIRL GANG (SEE: SWITCHBLADE SISTERS) (1975)
PLAYGIRL KILLER (SEE: DECOY FOR TERROR) (1970, Can.)
PLAYGIRLS AND THE BELLBOY, THE (1962, W. Ger.) PR:O
PLAYGIRLS AND THE VAMPIRE, THE (1964, It.) PR:O
PLAYGROUND, THE (1965) PR:O
PLAYING AROUND (1930) PR:A
PLAYING AWAY (1986, Brit.) PR:A-C
PLAYING FOR KEEPS (1986) PR:C
PLAYING THE GAME (SEE: TOUCHDOWN) (1931)
PLAYMATES (1941) PR:A
PLAYMATES (1969, Fr./It.) PR:O
PLAYTHING, THE (1929, Brit.) PR:A
PLAYTIME (1967, Fr.) PR:C
PLAYTIME (1973, Fr.) PR:AA
PLAZA SUITE (1971) PR:A-C
PLEASANTVILLE (1976) PR:A
PLEASE BELIEVE ME (1950) PR:A
PLEASE DON'T EAT THE DAISIES (1960) PR:A
PLEASE! MR. BALZAC (1957, Fr.) PR:C
PLEASE MURDER ME (1956) PR:A
PLEASE, NOT NOW! (1963, Fr./It.) PR:C
PLEASE SIR (1971, Brit.) PR:A
PLEASE STAND BY (1972) PR:C
PLEASE TEACHER (1937, Brit.) PR:A
PLEASE TURN OVER (1960, Brit.) PR:C
PLEASURE (1933) PR:A
PLEASURE CRAZED (1929) PR:A

PLEASURE CRUISE (1933) PR:A
PLEASURE GIRL (SEE: GIRL WITH A SUITCASE) (1961, Fr./It.)
PLEASURE GIRLS, THE (1966, Brit.) PR:C
PLEASURE LOVER (SEE: PLEASURE LOVERS, THE) (1964, Brit.)
PLEASURE LOVERS, THE (1964, Brit.) PR:C
PLEASURE OF HIS COMPANY, THE (1961) PR:A
PLEASURE PLANTATION (1970) PR:O
PLEASURE SEEKERS, THE (1964) PR:A
PLEASURES AND VICES (1962, Fr.) PR:C
PLEASURES OF THE FLESH, THE (1965, Jap.) PR:C
PLEDGEMASTERS, THE (1971) PR:O
PLEIN SOLEIL (SEE: PURPLE NOON) (1961, Fr./It.)
PLEIN SUD (SEE: HEAT OF DESIRE) (1981, Fr.)
PLENTY (1985) PR:O
PLEURE PAS LA BOUCHE PLEINE (SEE: DON'T CRY WITH YOUR MOUTH FULL) (1974, Fr.)
PLOT THICKENS, THE (SEE: HERE COMES COOKIE) (1935)
PLOT THICKENS, THE (1936) PR:A
PLOT TO KILL ROOSEVELT, THE (SEE: CONSPIRACY IN TEHERAN) (1948, Brit.)
PLOUGH AND THE STARS, THE (1936) PR:A
PLOUGHMAN'S LUNCH, THE (1984, Brit.) PR:O
PLUCK OF THE IRISH (SEE: GREAT GUY) (1936)
PLUCKED (1969, Fr./It.) PR:C-O
PLUMBER, THE (1980, Aus.) PR:C-O
PLUNDER (1931, Brit.) PR:A
PLUNDER OF THE SUN (1953) PR:A
PLUNDER ROAD (1957) PR:A
PLUNDERERS, THE (1948) PR:A
PLUNDERERS, THE (1960) PR:A
PLUNDERERS OF PAINTED FLATS (1959) PR:A
PLYMOUTH ADVENTURE (1952) PR:AA
POACHER'S DAUGHTER, THE (1958, Brit.) PR:A
POCATELLO KID (1932) PR:A
POCKET MONEY (1972) PR:A-C
POCKETFUL OF MIRACLES (1961) PR:AA
POCO (1977) PR:AA
POCOMANIA (1939) PR:C
POE'S TALES OF HORROR (SEE: TALES OF TERROR) (1962)
POET'S PUB (1949, Brit.) PR:A
POET'S SILENCE, THE (1987, W. Ger.) PR:C
POI TI SPOSERO (SEE: MALE COMPANION) (1965, Fr./It.)
POIL DE CAROTTE (1932, Fr.) PR:A
POINT BLANK (SEE: PRESSURE POINT) (1962)
POINT BLANK (1967) PR:O
POINT OF TERROR (1971) PR:O
POINTED HEELS (1930) PR:A
POINTING FINGER, THE (1934, Brit.) PR:A
POISON PEN (1941, Brit.) PR:A
POISONED DIAMOND, THE (1934, Brit.) PR:A
POITIN (1979, Ireland) PR:A
POKAYANIYE (SEE: REPENTANCE) (1987, USSR)
POLICE (1986, Fr.) PR:O
POLICE ACADEMY (1984) PR:O
POLICE ACADEMY 2: THEIR FIRST ASSIGNMENT (1985) PR:O
POLICE ACADEMY 3: BACK IN TRAINING (1986) PR:C-O
POLICE ACADEMY 4: CITIZENS ON PATROL (1987) PR:C
POLICE ACADEMY 5: ASSIGNMENT MIAMI BEACH (1988) PR:C
POLICE ACADEMY 6: CITY UNDER SIEGE (1989) PR:A-C
POLICE BULLETS (1942) PR:A
POLICE CALL (1933) PR:A
POLICE CAR 17 (1933) PR:A
POLICE CONNECTION: DETECTIVE GERONIMO (SEE: MAD BOMBER, THE) (1973)
POLICE COURT (SEE: FAME STREET) (1932)
POLICE DOG (1955, Brit.) PR:A
POLICE DOG STORY, THE (1961) PR:A
POLICE NURSE (1963) PR:A
POLICE PYTHON 357 (1976, Fr.) PR:C
POLICEMAN OF THE 16TH PRECINCT, THE (1963, Gr.) PR:A
POLICEWOMEN (1974) PR:O
POLITICAL ASYLUM (1975, Mex./Guat.) PR:A
POLITICAL PARTY, A (1933, Brit.) PR:A
POLITICS (1931) PR:A
POLLY FULTON (SEE: B.F.'S DAUGHTER) (1948)
POLLY OF THE CIRCUS (1932) PR:A
POLLYANNA (1960) PR:AA
POLO JOE (1936) PR:A
POLTERGEIST (1982) PR:C-O
POLTERGEIST II (1986) PR:O
POLTERGEIST III (1988) PR:C-O
POLYESTER (1981) PR:O
POM-POM GIRLS, THE (1976) PR:O
POMOCNIK (SEE: ASSISTANT, THE) (1982, Czech.)
PONCOMANIA (SEE: POCOMANIA) (1939)
PONTIUS PILATE (1967, Fr./It.) PR:A
PONY EXPRESS (1953) PR:A

PONY EXPRESS RIDER (1976) PR:A
PONY POST (1940) PR:A
PONY SOLDIER (1952) PR:A
POOKIE (SEE: STERILE CUCKOO, THE) (1969)
POOL OF LONDON (1951, Brit.) PR:A
POOR ALBERT AND LITTLE ANNIE (SEE: I DISMEM-
   BER MAMA) (1974)
POOR COW (1968, Brit.) PR:C
POOR LITTLE RICH GIRL (1936) PR:A
POOR OLD BILL (1931, Brit.) PR:A
POOR OUTLAWS, THE (SEE: ROUND UP, THE) (1969,
   Hung.)
POOR RICH, THE (1934) PR:A
POOR WHITE TRASH (SEE: BAYOU) (1957)
POOR WHITE TRASH II (SEE: SCUM OF THE EARTH)
   (1976)
POP ALWAYS PAYS (1940) PR:A
POPDOWN (1968, Brit.) PR:A
POPE JOAN (1972, Brit.) PR:C
POPE OF GREENWICH VILLAGE, THE (1984) PR:O
POPE ONDINE STORY, THE (SEE: CHELSEA GIRLS,
   THE) (1966)
POPEYE (1980) PR:A
POPI (1969) PR:A
POPIOL Y DIAMENT (SEE: ASHES AND DIAMONDS)
   (1958, Pol.)
POPPY (1936) PR:A
POPPY IS ALSO A FLOWER, THE (1966) PR:C
POPSY POP (1971, Fr.) PR:A
POR MIS PISTOLAS (1969, Mex.) PR:A
POR UN PUNADO DE DOLARES (SEE: FISTFUL OF
   DOLLARS, A) (1964, It./Sp./W. Ger.)
PORGY AND BESS (1959) PR:A-C
PORK CHOP HILL (1959) PR:C
PORKY'S (1982) PR:O
PORKY'S II: THE NEXT DAY (1983) PR:O
PORKY'S REVENGE (1985) PR:O
PORRIDGE (SEE: DOING TIME) (1979, Brit.)
PORT AFRIQUE (1956, Brit.) PR:A
PORT DES LILAS (SEE: GATES OF PARIS) (1958, Fr./It.)
PORT O' DREAMS (SEE: GIRL OVERBOARD) (1929)
PORT OF CALL (1948, Swed.) PR:C
PORT OF DESIRE (1960, Fr.) PR:C
PORT OF ESCAPE (1955, Brit.) PR:A
PORT OF 40 THIEVES, THE (1944) PR:A
PORT OF HATE (1939) PR:A
PORT OF HELL (1955) PR:A
PORT OF LOST DREAMS (1935) PR:A
PORT OF MISSING GIRLS (1938) PR:A
PORT OF NEW YORK (1949) PR:A
PORT OF SEVEN SEAS (1938) PR:A
PORT OF SHADOWS (1938, Fr.) PR:A
PORT OF SHAME (SEE: LOVER'S NET) (1957, Fr.)
PORT SAID (1948) PR:A
PORT SINISTER (1953) PR:A
PORTIA ON TRIAL (1937) PR:A
PORTLAND EXPOSE (1957) PR:A
PORTNOY'S COMPLAINT (1972) PR:O
PORTRAIT FROM LIFE (SEE: GIRL IN THE PAINTING,
   THE) (1948, Brit.)
PORTRAIT IN BLACK (1960) PR:A-C
PORTRAIT IN SMOKE (1957, Brit.) PR:O
PORTRAIT IN TERROR (1965) PR:O
PORTRAIT OF A MOBSTER (1961) PR:C
PORTRAIT OF A SINNER (1961, Brit.) PR:C
PORTRAIT OF A WOMAN (1946, Fr.) PR:A
PORTRAIT OF ALISON (SEE: POSTMARK FOR DAN-
   GER) (1956, Brit.)
PORTRAIT OF CHIEKO (1968, Jap.) PR:A
PORTRAIT OF CLARE (1951, Brit.) PR:A
PORTRAIT OF HELL (1969, Jap.) PR:A
PORTRAIT OF INNOCENCE (1948, Fr.) PR:A
PORTRAIT OF JENNIE (1949) PR:A
PORTRAIT OF LENIN (1967, Pol./USSR) PR:A
PORTRAIT OF MARIA (1946, Mex.) PR:C
PORTRAIT OF THE ARTIST AS A YOUNG MAN, A (1979,
   Ireland) PR:A
POSEIDON ADVENTURE, THE (1972) PR:A
POSITIONS (SEE: PUT UP OR SHUT UP) (1968, Arg.)
POSITIONS OF LOVE (SEE: PUT UP OR SHUT UP)
   (1968, Arg.)
POSITIVE I.D. (1986) PR:O
POSSE (1975) PR:C
POSSE FROM HELL (1961) PR:A
POSSESSED (1931) PR:A-C
POSSESSED (1947) PR:A-C
POSSESSION (1981, Fr./W. Ger.) PR:O
POSSESSION OF JOEL DELANEY, THE (1972) PR:O
POST OFFICE INVESTIGATOR (1949) PR:A
POSTAL INSPECTOR (1936) PR:A
POSTMAN ALWAYS RINGS TWICE, THE (1946) PR:O
POSTMAN ALWAYS RINGS TWICE, THE (1981) PR:O
POSTMAN DIDN'T RING, THE (1942) PR:A
POSTMAN GOES TO WAR, THE (1968, Fr.) PR:A
POSTMAN'S KNOCK (1966, Brit.) PR:A
POSTMARK FOR DANGER (1956, Brit.) PR:A
POT CARRIERS, THE (1962, Brit.) PR:A
POT LUCK (1936, Brit.) PR:A

POT O'GOLD (1941) PR:A
POTE TIN KYRIAKI (SEE: NEVER ON SUNDAY)
   (1960, Gr.)
POTIPHAR'S WIFE (SEE: HER STRANGE DESIRE)
   (1931, Brit.)
POTOMOK BELONGO BARSSA (SEE: DESCENDANT
   OF THE SNOW LEOPARD, THE) (1986, USSR)
POUND PUPPIES AND THE LEGEND OF BIG PAW
   (1988) PR:AA
POURQUOI PAS! (1979, Fr.) PR:C
POUVOIR INTIME (SEE: INTIMATE POWER) (1986,
   Can.)
POWDER RIVER (1953) PR:A
POWDER RIVER RUSTLERS (1949) PR:A
POWDER TOWN (1942) PR:A
POWDERSMOKE RANGE (1935) PR:A
POWER (1934, Brit.) PR:A
POWER, THE (1968) PR:A
POWER, THE (1984) PR:O
POWER (1986) PR:O
POWER AND GLORY (SEE: POWER AND THE GLORY,
   THE) (1933)
POWER AND THE GLORY, THE (1933) PR:A-C
POWER AND THE PRIZE, THE (1956) PR:A
POWER DIVE (1941) PR:A
POWER OF EVIL, THE (1985, Fr./It.) PR:O
POWER OF JUSTICE (SEE: BEYOND THE SACRA-
   MENTO) (1941)
POWER OF POSSESSION (SEE: LAWLESS EMPIRE)
   (1945)
POWER OF THE PRESS (1943) PR:A
POWER OF THE WHISTLER, THE (1945) PR:A
POWER PLAY (1978, Brit./Can.) PR:C
POWERFORCE (1983) PR:O
POWERS GIRL, THE (1942) PR:A
POZEGNANIA (SEE: PARTINGS) (1962, Pol.)
PRACTICALLY YOURS (1944) PR:A
PRAIRIE, THE (1948) PR:A
PRAIRIE BADMEN (1946) PR:A
PRAIRIE EXPRESS (1947) PR:A
PRAIRIE JUSTICE (1938) PR:A
PRAIRIE LAW (1940) PR:A
PRAIRIE MOON (1938) PR:A
PRAIRIE OUTLAWS (1948) PR:A
PRAIRIE PALS (1942) PR:A
PRAIRIE PIONEERS (1941) PR:A
PRAIRIE ROUNDUP (1951) PR:A
PRAIRIE RUSTLERS (1945) PR:A
PRAIRIE SCHOONERS (1940) PR:A
PRAIRIE STRANGER (1941) PR:A
PRAIRIE THUNDER (1937) PR:A
PRAISE MARX AND PASS THE AMMUNITION (1970,
   Brit.) PR:A
PRANCER (1989) PR:AA
PRATLDWANDI (SEE: ADVERSARY, THE) (1973, India)
PRAY FOR DEATH (1986) PR:O
PRAYER FOR THE DYING, A (1987, Brit.) PR:C-O
PRAYING MANTIS (1982, Brit.) PR:C
PRAZSKE NOCI (SEE: NIGHT OF PRAGUE, THE)
   (1968, Czech.)
PREACHERMAN (1971) PR:O
PRECINCT 45: LOS ANGELES POLICE (SEE: NEW
   CENTURIONS, THE) (1972)
PRECIOUS JEWELS (1969) PR:C
PREDATOR (1987) PR:O
PREHISTORIC PLANET WOMEN (SEE: WOMEN OF
   THE PREHISTORIC PLANET) (1966)
PREHISTORIC WOMEN (1950) PR:C
PREHISTORIC WOMEN (1967, Brit.) PR:O
PREHISTORIC WORLD (SEE: TEENAGE CAVEMAN)
   (1958)
PREJUDICE (1949) PR:A
PRELUDE TO ECSTASY (1963, Fin.) PR:C
PRELUDE TO FAME (1950, Brit.) PR:A
PREMATURE BURIAL, THE (1962) PR:C
PREMIER RENDEZVOUS (SEE: HER FIRST AFFAIR)
   (1947, Fr.)
PREMIERE (SEE: ONE NIGHT IN PARIS) (1940, Brit.)
PREMONITION, THE (1976) PR:C
PRENOM: CARMEN (SEE: FIRST NAME: CARMEN)
   (1984, Fr.)
PREPAREZ VOS MOUCHOIRS (SEE: GET OUT YOUR
   HANDKERCHIEFS) (1977, Bel./Fr.)
PREPPIES (1984) PR:O
PREPPIES (SEE: MAKING THE GRADE) (1984)
PRESCOTT KID, THE (1936) PR:A
PRESCRIPTION FOR ROMANCE (1937) PR:A
PRESENT ARMS (SEE: LEATHERNECKING) (1930)
PRESENTING LILY MARS (1943) PR:A
PRESIDENT VANISHES, THE (1934) PR:A
PRESIDENT'S ANALYST, THE (1967) PR:O
PRESIDENT'S LADY, THE (1953) PR:A-C
PRESIDENT'S MYSTERY, THE (1936) PR:A
PRESIDIO, THE (1988) PR:C-O
PRESS FOR TIME (1966, Brit.) PR:A
PRESSURE (1976, Brit.) PR:C
PRESSURE OF GUILT (1964, Jap.) PR:C
PRESSURE POINT (1962) PR:C

PRESTIGE (1932) PR:A
PRETENDER, THE (1947) PR:A
PRETTY BABY (1950) PR:A
PRETTY BABY (1978) PR:O
PRETTY BOY FLOYD (1960) PR:C-O
PRETTY BUT WICKED (1965, Braz.) PR:O
PRETTY IN PINK (1986) PR:C
PRETTY MAIDS ALL IN A ROW (1971) PR:O
PRETTY POISON (1968) PR:C-O
PRETTY POLLY (SEE: MATTER OF INNOCENCE, A)
   (1968, Brit.)
PRETTY SMART (1987) PR:O
PRETTYKILL (1987) PR:O
PREVIEW MURDER MYSTERY (1936) PR:A
PREY, THE (1984) PR:O
PRICE OF A SONG, THE (1935, Brit.) PR:A
PRICE OF FEAR, THE (1956) PR:A
PRICE OF FLESH, THE (1962, Fr.) PR:O
PRICE OF FOLLY, THE (1937, Brit.) PR:A
PRICE OF FREEDOM, THE (SEE: OPERATION DAY-
   BREAK) (1976)
PRICE OF POWER, THE (1969, It./Sp.) PR:C
PRICE OF SILENCE, THE (1960, Brit.) PR:A
PRICE OF THINGS, THE (1930, Brit.) PR:A
PRICE OF WISDOM, THE (1935, Brit.) PR:A
PRICK UP YOUR EARS (1987, Brit.) PR:O
PRIDE AND PREJUDICE (1940) PR:A
PRIDE AND THE PASSION, THE (1957) PR:C
PRIDE OF KENTUCKY (SEE: STORY OF SEABISCUIT,
   THE) (1949)
PRIDE OF MARYLAND (1951) PR:A
PRIDE OF ST. LOUIS, THE (1952) PR:AA
PRIDE OF THE ARMY (1942) PR:AA
PRIDE OF THE BLUE GRASS (1954) PR:A
PRIDE OF THE BLUEGRASS (1939) PR:AA
PRIDE OF THE BOWERY (1941) PR:A
PRIDE OF THE BOWERY, THE (SEE: MR. HEX) (1946)
PRIDE OF THE FORCE, THE (1933, Brit.) PR:A
PRIDE OF THE LEGION, THE (1932) PR:A
PRIDE OF THE MARINES (1936) PR:A
PRIDE OF THE MARINES (1945) PR:C
PRIDE OF THE NAVY (1939) PR:A
PRIDE OF THE PLAINS (1944) PR:A
PRIDE OF THE WEST (1938) PR:A
PRIDE OF THE YANKEES, THE (1942) PR:AA
PRIEST OF LOVE (1981, Brit.) PR:O
PRIEST OF ST. PAULI, THE (1970, W. Ger.) PR:C
PRIEST'S WIFE, THE (1971, It./Fr.) PR:O
PRIMA DELLA REVOLUTIONA (SEE: BEFORE THE
   REVOLUTION) (1964, It.)
PRIMAL SCREAM (1988) PR:O
PRIME CUT (1972) PR:O
PRIME MINISTER, THE (1941, Brit.) PR:A
PRIME OF MISS JEAN BRODIE, THE (1969, Brit.) PR:C
PRIME RISK (1985) PR:C
PRIME TIME, THE (1960) PR:A
PRIMITIVE LOVE (1966, It.) PR:O
PRIMITIVES, THE (1962, Brit.) PR:A
PRIMROSE PATH, THE (1934, Brit.) PR:A
PRIMROSE PATH (1940) PR:A
PRINCE AND THE PAUPER, THE (1937) PR:AA
PRINCE AND THE PAUPER, THE (1969) PR:AA
PRINCE AND THE PAUPER, THE (SEE: CROSSED
   SWORDS) (1978, Panama)
PRINCE AND THE SHOWGIRL, THE (1957, Brit.) PR:A
PRINCE JACK (1985) PR:A
PRINCE OF ARCADIA (1933, Brit.) PR:AA
PRINCE OF DARKNESS (1987) PR:O
PRINCE OF DIAMONDS (1930) PR:A
PRINCE OF FOXES (1949) PR:C
PRINCE OF PEACE, THE (1951) PR:AA
PRINCE OF PIRATES (1953) PR:A
PRINCE OF PLAYERS (1955) PR:C
PRINCE OF THE BLUE GRASS (SEE: PRIDE OF THE
   BLUE GRASS) (1954)
PRINCE OF THE CITY (1981) PR:O
PRINCE OF THE PLAINS (1949) PR:A
PRINCE OF THIEVES, THE (1948) PR:A
PRINCE VALIANT (1954) PR:AA
PRINCE WHO WAS A THIEF, THE (1951) PR:A
PRINCESS, THE (SEE: TIME IN THE SUN, A) (1970,
   Swed.)
PRINCESS ACADEMY, THE (1987, US/Yugo./Fr.) PR:C-O
PRINCESS AND THE MAGIC FROG, THE (1965) PR:AA
PRINCESS AND THE PIRATE, THE (1944) PR:A
PRINCESS AND THE PLUMBER, THE (1930) PR:A
PRINCESS BRIDE, THE (1987) PR:A-C
PRINCESS CHARMING (1935, Brit.) PR:A
PRINCESS COMES ACROSS, THE (1936) PR:A
PRINCESS OF THE NILE (1954) PR:AA
PRINCESS O'HARA (1935) PR:A
PRINCESS O'ROURKE (1943) PR:A
PRINCIPAL, THE (1987) PR:O
PRINSESSAN (SEE: TIME IN THE SUN, A) (1970, Swed.)
PRIORITIES ON PARADE (1942) PR:A
PRISM (1971) PR:C
PRISON (1988) PR:O
PRISON BREAK (1938) PR:A

PRISON BREAKER (1936, Brit.) PR:A
PRISON CAMP (SEE: FUGITIVE FROM A PRISON
   CAMP) (1940)
PRISON FARM (1938) PR:A
PRISON GIRL (1942) PR:A
PRISON NURSE (1938) PR:A
PRISON SHADOWS (1936) PR:A
PRISON SHIP (1945) PR:C
PRISON SHIP (SEE: STAR SLAMMER: THE ESCAPE)
   (1988)
PRISON TRAIN (1938) PR:A
PRISON WARDEN (1949) PR:A
PRISON WITHOUT BARS (1939, Brit.) PR:A
PRISONER, THE (1955, Brit.) PR:C
PRISONER OF CORBAL (1939, Brit.) PR:C
PRISONER OF JAPAN (1942) PR:A
PRISONER OF SECOND AVENUE, THE (1975) PR:A-C
PRISONER OF SHARK ISLAND, THE (1936) PR:A
PRISONER OF THE IRON MASK (1962, Fr./It.) PR:A
PRISONER OF THE SKULL (SEE: WHO?) (1975, Brit./W.
   Ger.)
PRISONER OF THE VOLGA (1960, Fr./It.) PR:C
PRISONER OF WAR (1954) PR:C
PRISONER OF ZENDA, THE (1937) PR:A
PRISONER OF ZENDA, THE (1952) PR:A
PRISONER OF ZENDA, THE (1979) PR:A
PRISONERS (1929) PR:A
PRISONERS IN PETTICOATS (1950) PR:A
PRISONERS OF THE CASBAH (1953) PR:A
PRIVATE ACCESS (1988, It.) PR:C-O
PRIVATE AFFAIRS (SEE: PUBLIC STENOGRAPHER)
   (1935)
PRIVATE AFFAIRS (1940) PR:A
PRIVATE AFFAIRS OF BEL AMI, THE (1947) PR:A
PRIVATE ANGELO (1949, Brit.) PR:A
PRIVATE BENJAMIN (1980) PR:O
PRIVATE BUCKAROO (1942) PR:A
PRIVATE COLLECTION (1972, Aus.) PR:O
PRIVATE DETECTIVE (1939) PR:A
PRIVATE DETECTIVE 62 (1933) PR:A
PRIVATE DUTY NURSES (1972) PR:O
PRIVATE ENTERPRISE, A (1975, Brit.) PR:A
PRIVATE EYES (1953) PR:A
PRIVATE EYES, THE (1980) PR:A
PRIVATE FILES OF J. EDGAR HOOVER, THE (1978)
   PR:C
PRIVATE FUNCTION, A (1985, Brit.) PR:O
PRIVATE HELL 36 (1954) PR:C
PRIVATE INFORMATION (1952, Brit.) PR:A
PRIVATE JONES (1933) PR:A
PRIVATE LESSONS (1981) PR:O
PRIVATE LIFE (SEE: VERY PRIVATE AFFAIR, A) (1962,
   Fr.)
PRIVATE LIFE OF DON JUAN, THE (1934, Brit.) PR:A
PRIVATE LIFE OF HENRY VIII, THE (1933, Brit.) PR:A-C
PRIVATE LIFE OF LOUIS XIV (1936, Ger.) PR:A
PRIVATE LIFE OF PAUL JOSEPH GOEBBELS, THE
   (SEE: ENEMY OF WOMEN) (1944)
PRIVATE LIFE OF SHERLOCK HOLMES, THE (1970,
   US/Brit.) PR:C
PRIVATE LIVES (1931) PR:A
PRIVATE LIVES OF ADAM AND EVE, THE (1961) PR:C
PRIVATE LIVES OF ELIZABETH AND ESSEX, THE
   (1939) PR:A
PRIVATE NAVY OF SGT. O'FARRELL, THE (1968) PR:A
PRIVATE NUMBER (1936) PR:A
PRIVATE NURSE (1941) PR:A
PRIVATE PARTS (1972) PR:O
PRIVATE POOLEY (1962, Brit./E. Ger./W. Ger.) PR:C
PRIVATE POTTER (1963, Brit.) PR:A-C
PRIVATE PROPERTY (1960) PR:O
PRIVATE RESORT (1985) PR:O
PRIVATE RIGHT, THE (1967, Brit.) PR:A
PRIVATE ROAD (1971, Brit.) PR:O
PRIVATE SCANDAL, A (1932) PR:A
PRIVATE SCANDAL (1934) PR:A
PRIVATE SCHOOL (1983) PR:O
PRIVATE SECRETARY, THE (1935, Brit.) PR:A
PRIVATE SHOW (1985, Phil.) PR:O
PRIVATE SNUFFY SMITH (SEE: SNUFFY SMITH,
   YARD BIRD) (1942)
PRIVATE WAR OF MAJOR BENSON, THE (1955) PR:A
PRIVATE WORE SKIRTS, THE (SEE: NEVER WAVE AT
   A WAC) (1952)
PRIVATE WORLDS (1935) PR:A-C
PRIVATE'S AFFAIR, A (1959) PR:A
PRIVATES ON PARADE (1984, Brit.) PR:O
PRIVATE'S PROGRESS (1956, Brit.) PR:A
PRIVATKLINIK PROF. LUND (SEE: DAS LETZTE
   GEHEIMNIS) (1959, W. Ger.)
PRIVILEGE (1967, Brit.) PR:A
PRIVILEGED (1982, Brit.) PR:C-O
PRIZE, THE (1952, Fr.) PR:A
PRIZE, THE (1963) PR:C
PRIZE FIGHTER, THE (1979) PR:C
PRIZE OF ARMS, A (1962, Brit.) PR:A
PRIZE OF GOLD, A (1955, Brit.) PR:A

PRIZED AS A MATE! (SEE: SPOILED ROTTEN) (1968,
   Gr.)
PRIZEFIGHTER AND THE LADY, THE (1933) PR:A
PRIZZI'S HONOR (1985) PR:O
PRO, THE (SEE: NUMBER ONE) (1969)
PROBATION (1932) PR:A
PROBLEM GIRLS (1953) PR:A
PROCES DE JEANNE D'ARC (SEE: TRIAL OF JOAN
   OF ARC) (1965, Fr.)
PRODIGAL, THE (1931) PR:A
PRODIGAL, THE (1955) PR:A-C
PRODIGAL, THE (1984) PR:A
PRODIGAL GUN (SEE: MINUTE TO PRAY, A SECOND
   TO DIE, A) (1968, US/It.)
PRODIGAL SON, THE (1935) PR:A
PRODIGAL SON, THE (1964, Jap.) PR:C
PRODUCERS, THE (1967) PR:O
PROFESSION: REPORTER (SEE: PASSENGER, THE)
   (1975, It.)
PROFESSIONAL BLONDE (SEE: BLONDE FROM PE-
   KING) (1969, Fr./It./W. Ger.)
PROFESSIONAL GUN, A (SEE: MERCENARY, THE)
   (1970, It./Sp.)
PROFESSIONAL SOLDIER (1936) PR:A
PROFESSIONAL SWEETHEART (1933) PR:A
PROFESSIONALS, THE (1960, Brit.) PR:A
PROFESSIONALS, THE (1966) PR:O
PROFESSOR BEWARE (1938) PR:A
PROFESSOR TIM (1957, Ireland) PR:A
PROFILE (1954, Brit.) PR:A
PROFILE OF TERROR, THE (SEE: SADIST, THE) (1963)
PROFUNDO ROSSO (SEE: DEEP RED) (1976, It.)
PROGRAMMED TO KILL (1987) PR:O
PROJECT: KILL (1976) PR:O
PROJECT MOONBASE (1953) PR:A
PROJECT M7 (1953, Brit.) PR:A
PROJECT X (1949) PR:A
PROJECT X (1968) PR:A
PROJECT X (1987) PR:A
PROJECTED MAN, THE (1967, Brit.) PR:A
PROJECTIONIST, THE (1970) PR:A-C
PROLOGUE (1970, Can.) PR:C
PROM NIGHT (1980) PR:O
PROMISE, THE (1969, Brit.) PR:A
PROMISE, THE (1979) PR:A-C
PROMISE AT DAWN (1970, US/Fr.) PR:A
PROMISE HER ANYTHING (SEE: PROMISES! PROM-
   ISES!) (1963)
PROMISE HER ANYTHING (1966, Brit.) PR:A
PROMISE OF A BED, A (SEE: THIS, THAT AND THE
   OTHER) (1970, Brit.)
PROMISED LAND (1988) PR:O
PROMISES IN THE DARK (1979) PR:C
PROMISES! PROMISES! (1963) PR:O
PROMOTER, THE (1952, Brit.) PR:A
PROPER TIME, THE (1959) PR:A
PROPERTY (1979) PR:A-C
PROPHECIES OF NOSTRADAMUS (1974, Jap.) PR:C
PROPHECY (1979) PR:C-O
PROSHCHAYTE (SEE: FAREWELL, DOVES) (1962,
   USSR)
PROSPERITY (1932) PR:A
PROSTITUTE (1980, Brit.) PR:O
PROSTITUTION (1965, Fr.) PR:C
PROTECTOR, THE (1985, Hong Kong/US) PR:O
PROTECTORS, THE (SEE: COMPANY OF KILLERS)
   (1970)
PROTECTORS, BOOK 1, THE (1981) PR:O
PROTOCOL (1984) PR:A-C
PROUD AND THE DAMNED, THE (1972) PR:C-O
PROUD AND THE PROFANE, THE (1956) PR:A-C
PROUD, DAMNED AND DEAD (SEE: PROUD AND
   THE DAMNED, THE) (1972)
PROUD ONES, THE (1956) PR:A
PROUD REBEL, THE (1958) PR:A
PROUD RIDER, THE (1971, Can.) PR:C
PROUD VALLEY, THE (1941, Brit.) PR:A
PROVIDENCE (1977, Fr./Switz.) PR:O
PROWL GIRLS (1968) PR:O
PROWLER, THE (1951) PR:C-O
PROWLER, THE (1981) PR:O
PRUDENCE AND THE PILL (1968, Brit.) PR:O
PRZYPADEK (SEE: BLIND CHANCE) (1987, Pol.)
PSYCH-OUT (1968) PR:O
PSYCHE 59 (1964, Brit.) PR:C
PSYCHIC, THE (1977, It.) PR:O
PSYCHIC KILLER (1975) PR:O
PSYCHIC LOVER, THE (SEE: SWEET SMELL OF
   LOVE) (1969, It./W. Ger.)
PSYCHO (1960) PR:O
PSYCHO II (1983) PR:O
PSYCHO III (1986) PR:O
PSYCHO A GO-GO! (1965) PR:O
PSYCHO-CIRCUS (1967, Brit.) PR:O
PSYCHO FROM TEXAS (1982) PR:O
PSYCHO KILLERS (SEE: MANIA) (1961, Brit.)
PSYCHOMANIA (1964) PR:O
PSYCHOMANIA (1974, Brit.) PR:O

PSYCHOPATH, THE (1966, Brit.) PR:O
PSYCHOPATH, THE (1973) PR:O
PSYCHOS IN LOVE (1987) PR:O
PSYCHOTRONIC MAN, THE (1980) PR:O
PSYCHOUT FOR MURDER (1971, Arg./It.) PR:O
PSYCOSISSIMO (1962, It.) PR:O
PT 109 (1963) PR:A
PT RAIDERS (SEE: SHIP THAT DIED OF SHAME, THE)
   (1956, Brit.)
P'TANG, YANG, KIPPERBANG (SEE: KIPPERBANG)
   (1984, Brit.)
PUBERTY BLUES (1983, Aus.) PR:O
PUBLIC AFFAIR, A (1962) PR:C
PUBLIC BE DAMNED (SEE: WORLD GONE MAD,
   THE) (1933)
PUBLIC BE HANGED (SEE: WORLD GONE MAD,
   THE) (1933)
PUBLIC COWBOY NO. 1 (1937) PR:A
PUBLIC DEB NO. 1 (1940) PR:C
PUBLIC DEFENDER, THE (1931) PR:A
PUBLIC ENEMIES (1941) PR:A
PUBLIC ENEMY, THE (1931) PR:O
PUBLIC ENEMY'S WIFE (1936) PR:A
PUBLIC EYE, THE (1972, Brit.) PR:A
PUBLIC HERO NO. 1 (1935) PR:A
PUBLIC LIFE OF HENRY THE NINTH, THE (1934, Brit.)
   PR:A
PUBLIC MENACE (1935) PR:C
PUBLIC NUISANCE NO. 1 (1936, Brit.) PR:A
PUBLIC OPINION (1935) PR:A
PUBLIC PIGEON NO. 1 (1957) PR:A
PUBLIC STENOGRAPHER (1935) PR:C
PUBLIC WEDDING (1937) PR:A
PUDDIN' HEAD (1941) PR:AA
PUFNSTUF (1970) PR:AA
PULGARCITO (SEE: TOM THUMB) (1967, Mex.)
PULP (1972, Brit.) PR:C
PULSE (1988) PR:C
PULSEBEAT (1986, Sp.) PR:O
PUMPKIN EATER, THE (1964, Brit.) PR:O
PUMPKINHEAD (1988) PR:O
PUNCH AND JUDY MAN, THE (1963, Brit.) PR:A
PUNCHLINE (1988) PR:C
PUNISHMENT PARK (1971) PR:O
PUO UNA MORTA RIVIVERE PER AMORE? (SEE:
   VENUS IN FURS) (1970, Brit./It./W. Ger.)
PUPPET ON A CHAIN (1971, Brit.) PR:O
PUPPETS OF FATE (SEE: WOLVES OF THE UNDER-
   WORLD) (1935, Brit.)
PURCHASE PRICE, THE (1932) PR:O
PURE HELL OF ST. TRINIAN'S, THE (1961, Brit.) PR:C
PURE S (1976, Aus.) PR:O
PURLIE VICTORIOUS (SEE: GONE ARE THE DAYS)
   (1963)
PROMISES IN THE DARK (1979) PR:C
PURPLE GANG, THE (1960) PR:O
PURPLE HAZE (1982) PR:O
PURPLE HEART, THE (1944) PR:C-O
PURPLE HEART DIARY (1951) PR:A
PURPLE HEARTS (1984) PR:C-O
PURPLE HILLS, THE (1961) PR:A
PURPLE MASK, THE (1955) PR:A
PURPLE NOON (1961, Fr./It.) PR:O
PURPLE PLAIN, THE (1954, Brit.) PR:A-C
PURPLE RAIN (1984) PR:O
PURPLE RIDERS, THE (SEE: PURPLE VIGILANTES,
   THE) (1938)
PURPLE ROSE OF CAIRO, THE (1985) PR:C
PURPLE TAXI, THE (1977, Fr./It./Ireland) PR:O
PURPLE V, THE (1943) PR:O
PURPLE VIGILANTES, THE (1938) PR:A
PURSE STRINGS (1933, Brit.) PR:A
PURSUED (1934) PR:A
PURSUED (1947) PR:C-O
PURSUERS, THE (1961, Brit.) PR:O
PURSUIT (1935) PR:A
PURSUIT (1975) PR:O
PURSUIT OF D.B. COOPER, THE (1981) PR:C
PURSUIT OF HAPPINESS, THE (1934) PR:C
PURSUIT OF HAPPINESS, THE (1971) PR:O
PURSUIT OF THE GRAF SPEE (1957, Brit.) PR:A
PURSUIT TO ALGIERS (1945) PR:A
PUSHER, THE (1960) PR:O
PUSHERS, THE (SEE: HOOKED GENERATION, THE)
   (1968)
PUSHOVER (1954) PR:A
PUSHOVER, THE (SEE: MYTH, THE) (1965, It.)
PUSS AND KRAM (SEE: HUGS AND KISSES) (1968,
   Swed.)
PUSS 'N' BOOTS (1964, Mex.) PR:AA
PUSS 'N' BOOTS (1967, W. Ger.) PR:AA
PUSS OCH KRAM (SEE: HUGS AND KISSES) (1968,
   Swed.)
PUSSYCAT ALLEY (1965, Brit.) PR:O
PUSSYCAT, PUSSYCAT, I LOVE YOU (1970) PR:O
PUT ON THE SPOT (1936) PR:A
PUT UP OR SHUT UP (1968, Arg.) PR:O
PUTNEY SWOPE (1969) PR:O
PUTTIN' ON THE RITZ (1930) PR:A

PUTYOVKA V ZHIZN (SEE: ROAD TO LIFE) (1932, USSR)
PUZZLE OF A DOWNFALL CHILD (1970) PR:O
PYGMALION (1938, Brit.) PR:A
PYGMY ISLAND (1950) PR:A
PYRO (1964, US/Sp.) PR:O
PYRO-THE THING WITHOUT A FACE (SEE: PYRO) (1964, US/Sp.)
PYX, THE (1973, Can.) PR:O
Q (1982) PR:O
Q PLANES (SEE: CLOUDS OVER EUROPE) (1939, Brit.)
Q-SHIPS (SEE: BLOCKADE) (1928, Brit.)
QUACKSER FORTUNE HAS A COUSIN IN THE BRONX (1970, Ireland) PR:A-C
QUADROON (1972) PR:O
QUADROPHENIA (1979, Brit.) PR:O
QUAI DE GRENELLE (SEE: DANGER IS A WOMAN) (1952, Fr.)
QUAI DES ORFEVRES (SEE: JENNY LAMOUR) (1948, Fr.)
QUALCOSA DI BIONDO (1985, It.) PR:O
QUALITY STREET (1937) PR:A
QUANDO DE DONNE AVEVANDO LA CODA (SEE: WHEN WOMEN HAD TAILS) (1970, It.)
QUANDO EL AMOR RIE (1933) PR:A
QUANTEZ (1957) PR:A
QUANTRILL'S RAIDERS (1958) PR:A
QUARE FELLOW, THE (1962, Ireland/Brit.) PR:C-O
QUARTERBACK, THE (1940) PR:A
QUARTET (1949, Brit.) PR:C
QUARTET (1981, Brit./Fr.) PR:C
QUARTIERE (1987, It.) PR:O
QUATERMASS AND THE PIT (SEE: FIVE MILLION YEARS TO EARTH) (1968, Brit.)
QUATERMASS CONCLUSION (1980, Brit.) PR:C
QUATERMASS EXPERIMENT, THE (SEE: CREEPING UNKNOWN, THE) (1956, Brit.)
QUATERMASS II (SEE: ENEMY FROM SPACE) (1957, Brit.)
QUATRO MOSCHE DI VELLUTO GRIS (SEE: FOUR FLIES ON GREY VELVET) (1972, Fr./It.)
QUE LA BETE MEURE (SEE: THIS MAN MUST DIE) (1970, Fr./It.)
QUE LA FETE COMMENCE (SEE: LET JOY REIGN SUPREME) (1977, Fr.)
QUEBEC (1951) PR:A
QUEEN BEE (1955) PR:C
QUEEN BEE (SEE: CONJUGAL BED, THE) (1963, Fr./It.)
QUEEN CHRISTINA (1933) PR:A
QUEEN FOR A DAY (1951) PR:A
QUEEN HIGH (1930) PR:A
QUEEN OF ATLANTIS (SEE: SIREN OF ATLANTIS) (1948)
QUEEN OF BABYLON, THE (1956, It.) PR:A
QUEEN OF BLOOD (1966) PR:O
QUEEN OF BROADWAY (1942) PR:A
QUEEN OF BROADWAY (SEE: KID DYNAMITE) (1943)
QUEEN OF BURLESQUE (1946) PR:C
QUEEN OF CLUBS (SEE: LOVE CYCLES) (1969, Gr.)
QUEEN OF CRIME (SEE: KATE PLUS TEN) (1938, Brit.)
QUEEN OF DESTINY (SEE: SIXTY GLORIOUS YEARS) (1938, Brit.)
QUEEN OF HEARTS (1936, Brit.) PR:A
QUEEN OF HEARTS (1989, Brit.) PR:C
QUEEN OF OUTER SPACE (1958) PR:A
QUEEN OF SHEBA (1953, It.) PR:C
QUEEN OF SPADES (1948, Brit.) PR:A-C
QUEEN OF SPADES (1961, USSR) PR:C
QUEEN OF SPIES (SEE: JOAN OF OZARK) (1942)
QUEEN OF THE AMAZONS (1947) PR:A
QUEEN OF THE CANNIBALS (SEE: DR. BUTCHER, M.D.) (1982, It.)
QUEEN OF THE GORILLAS (SEE: BRIDE AND THE BEAST, THE) (1958)
QUEEN OF THE MOB (1940) PR:C
QUEEN OF THE NIGHTCLUBS (1929) PR:A-C
QUEEN OF THE NILE (1964, It.) PR:C
QUEEN OF THE PIRATES (1961, It./W. Ger.) PR:C
QUEEN OF THE WEST (SEE: CATTLE QUEEN) (1951)
QUEEN OF THE YUKON (1940) PR:A
QUEENS, THE (1968, It./Fr.) PR:O
QUEEN'S AFFAIR, THE (SEE: RUNAWAY QUEEN, THE) (1935, Brit.)
QUEEN'S GUARDS, THE (1963, Brit.) PR:C
QUEEN'S HUSBAND, THE (SEE: ROYAL BED, THE) (1931)
QUEEN'S SWORDSMEN, THE (1963, Mex.) PR:AA
QUEER CARGO (SEE: PIRATES OF THE SEVEN SEAS) (1941, Brit.)
QUEI DISPERATI CHE PUZZANO DI SUDORE E DI MORTE (SEE: BULLET FOR SANDOVAL, A) (1970, It./Sp.)
QUEI TEMERARI SULLE LORO PAZZE, SCATENATE, SCALCINATE CARRIOLE (SEE: THOSE DARING YOUNG MEN IN THEIR JAUNTY JALOPIES) (1969, Fr./Brit./It.)
QUEIMADA (SEE: BURN!) (1969, Fr./It.)

QUELLA SPORCA STORIA DEL WEST (SEE: JOHNNY HAMLET) (1972, It.)
QUELLA VILLA ACCANTO AL CIMITERO (SEE: HOUSE BY THE CEMETERY, THE) (1984, It.)
QUELLI CHE NON MUOIONO (SEE: GUILT IS NOT MINE) (1968, It.)
QUELQUES JOURS PRES (SEE: MATTER OF DAYS, A) (1969, Fr./Czech.)
QUELQU'UN DERRIERE LA PORTE (SEE: SOMEONE BEHIND THE DOOR) (1971, Fr./Brit.)
QUEMADA! (SEE: BURN!) (1969, Fr./It.)
QUENTIN DURWARD (1955) PR:A
QUERELLE (1983, Fr./W. Ger.) PR:O
QUERY (1945, Brit.) PR:O
QUEST FOR FIRE (1982, Fr./Can.) PR:O
QUEST FOR LOVE (1971, Brit.) PR:C
QUESTI FANTASMI (SEE: GHOSTS, ITALIAN STYLE) (1969, Fr./It.)
QUESTION, THE (1977, Fr.) PR:O
QUESTION OF ADULTERY, A (1959, Brit.) PR:C
QUESTION OF SILENCE, A (1983, Neth.) PR:O
QUESTION OF SUSPENSE, A (1961, Brit.) PR:C
QUESTION 7 (1961, US/W. Ger.) PR:C
QUESTIONE DI PELLE (SEE: CHECKERBOARD) (1969, Fr.)
QUICK AND THE DEAD, THE (1963) PR:O
QUICK, BEFORE IT MELTS (1964) PR:A
QUICK GUN, THE (1964) PR:A
QUICK, LET'S GET MARRIED (1965) PR:C
QUICK MILLIONS (1931) PR:C
QUICK MILLIONS (1939) PR:A
QUICK MONEY (1938) PR:A
QUICK ON THE TRIGGER (1949) PR:A
QUICKSAND (1950) PR:C
QUICKSILVER (1986) PR:A-C
QUIEN SABE? (SEE: BULLET FOR THE GENERAL, A) (1968, It.)
QUIET AMERICAN, THE (1958) PR:A
QUIET COOL (1986) PR:O
QUIET DAY IN BELFAST, A (1974, Can.) PR:C
QUIET EARTH, THE (1985, New Zealand) PR:O
QUIET GUN, THE (1957) PR:A
QUIET MAN, THE (1952) PR:A
QUIET PLACE IN THE COUNTRY, A (1970, It./Fr.) PR:O
QUIET PLEASE (1938, Brit.) PR:A
QUIET PLEASE, MURDER (1942) PR:A
QUIET WEDDING (1941, Brit.) PR:A
QUIET WEEKEND (1948, Brit.) PR:A
QUIET WOMAN, THE (1951, Brit.) PR:A
QUILLER MEMORANDUM, THE (1966, US/Brit.) PR:C
QUILOMBO (1984, Braz.) PR:O
QUINCANNON, FRONTIER SCOUT (1956) PR:A
QUINTET (1979) PR:C-O
QUITTER, THE (SEE: QUITTERS, THE) (1934)
QUITTERS, THE (1934) PR:A
QUO VADIS (1951) PR:C
QUOI DE NEUF, PUSSYCAT? (SEE: WHAT'S NEW, PUSSYCAT?) (1965, US/Fr.)

R

R.O.T.O.R. (1988) PR:O
R.P.M. (1970) PR:C
RABBI AND THE SHIKSE, THE (1976, Israel) PR:A
RABBIT, RUN (1970) PR:O
RABBIT TEST (1978) PR:C-O
RABBIT TRAP, THE (1959) PR:A
RABBLE, THE (1965, Jap.) PR:A
RABID (1976, Can.) PR:O
RABID GRANNIES (1989) PR:O
RACCONTI D'ESTATE (SEE: LOVE ON THE RIVIERA) (1964, Fr./It.)
RACE FOR GLORY (1989) PR:C
RACE FOR LIFE, A (1955, Brit.) PR:A
RACE FOR THE YANKEE ZEPHYR (SEE: TREASURE OF THE YANKEE ZEPHYR) (1984)
RACE FOR YOUR LIFE, CHARLIE BROWN (1977) PR:AA
RACE GANG (SEE: GREEN COCKATOO, THE) (1947, Brit.)
RACE STREET (1948) PR:C
RACE WITH THE DEVIL (1975) PR:C
RACERS, THE (1955) PR:A
RACETRACK (1933) PR:A
RACHEL AND THE STRANGER (1948) PR:A
RACHEL CADE (SEE: SINS OF RACHEL CADE, THE) (1960)
RACHEL PAPERS, THE (1989, Brit.) PR:C
RACHEL, RACHEL (1968) PR:A-C
RACHEL RIVER (1989) PR:A
RACING BLOOD (1938) PR:A
RACING BLOOD (1954) PR:A
RACING FEVER (1964) PR:C
RACING LADY (1937) PR:A
RACING LUCK (SEE: RED HOT TIRES) (1935)
RACING LUCK (1948) PR:A
RACING ROMANCE (1937, Brit.) PR:A
RACING STRAIN, THE (1933) PR:A
RACING WITH THE MOON (1984) PR:C

RACING YOUTH (1932) PR:A
RACK, THE (1956) PR:A
RACKET, THE (1951) PR:C
RACKET BUSTERS (1938) PR:A
RACKET MAN, THE (1944) PR:A
RACKETEER, THE (1929) PR:A
RACKETEERS IN EXILE (1937) PR:A
RACKETEERS OF THE RANGE (1939) PR:A
RACKETY RAX (1932) PR:A
RACQUET (1979) PR:O
RAD (1986) PR:A-C
RADAN (SEE: RODAN) (1958, Jap.)
RADAR SECRET SERVICE (1950) PR:A
RADIO CAB MURDER (1954, Brit.) PR:A
RADIO CITY REVELS (1938) PR:A
RADIO DAYS (1987) PR:A-C
RADIO FOLLIES (1935, Brit.) PR:A
RADIO LOVER (1936, Brit.) PR:A
RADIO MURDER MYSTERY, THE (SEE: LOVE IS ON THE AIR) (1937)
RADIO ON (1980, Brit./W. Ger.) PR:C
RADIO PARADE OF 1935 (SEE: RADIO FOLLIES) (1935, Brit.)
RADIO PATROL (1932) PR:A
RADIO PIRATES (1935, Brit.) PR:A
RADIO REVELS OF 1942 (SEE: SWING IT SOLDIER) (1941)
RADIO STAR, THE (SEE: LOUDSPEAKER, THE) (1934)
RADIO STARS ON PARADE (1945) PR:A
RADIOACTIVE DREAMS (1986) PR:O
RADIOGRAFIA D'UN COLPO D'ORO (SEE: THEY CAME TO ROB LAS VEGAS) (1969, Fr./It./Sp./W. Ger.)
RADISHES AND CARROTS (SEE: TWILIGHT PATH) (1965, Jap.)
RADON (SEE: RODAN) (1958, Jap.)
RADON THE FLYING MONSTER (SEE: RODAN) (1958, Jap.)
RAFFERTY AND THE GOLD DUST TWINS (1975) PR:C-O
RAFFICA DI COLTELLI (SEE: KNIVES OF THE AVENGER) (1967, It.)
RAFFLES (1930) PR:A
RAFFLES (1939) PR:A
RAFTER ROMANCE (1934) PR:A
RAG DOLL (SEE: YOUNG, WILLING AND EAGER) (1962, Brit.)
RAGE, THE (1963, US/Mex.) PR:O
RAGE (1966, US/Mex.) PR:C
RAGE (1972) PR:C
RAGE (SEE: RABID) (1976, Can.)
RAGE AT DAWN (1955) PR:A
RAGE IN HEAVEN (1941) PR:C
RAGE OF HONOR (1987) PR:O
RAGE OF PARIS, THE (1938) PR:A
RAGE OF THE BUCCANEERS (1963, It.) PR:A
RAGE TO LIVE, A (1965) PR:C
RAGE WITHIN, THE (SEE: RAGE, THE) (1963, US/Mex.)
RAGGED ANGELS (SEE: THEY SHALL HAVE MUSIC) (1939)
RAGGEDY ANN AND ANDY (1977) PR:AA
RAGGEDY MAN (1981) PR:C
RAGING BULL (1980) PR:O
RAGING MOON, THE (SEE: LONG AGO, TOMORROW) (1971, Brit.)
RAGING TIDE, THE (1951) PR:A
RAGING WATERS (SEE: GREEN PROMISE, THE) (1949)
RAGMAN'S DAUGHTER, THE (1974, Brit.) PR:C
RAGS TO RICHES (1941) PR:A
RAGTIME (1981, US/Brit.) PR:C
RAGTIME COWBOY JOE (1940) PR:A
RAID, THE (1954) PR:A-C
RAID ON ROMMEL (1971) PR:C
RAIDERS, THE (1952) PR:A
RAIDERS, THE (1964) PR:A
RAIDERS FROM BENEATH THE SEA (1964) PR:A
RAIDERS OF LEYTE GULF, THE (1963, US/Phil.) PR:A
RAIDERS OF OLD CALIFORNIA (1957) PR:A
RAIDERS OF RED GAP (1944) PR:A
RAIDERS OF SAN JOAQUIN (1943) PR:A
RAIDERS OF SUNSET PASS (1943) PR:A
RAIDERS OF THE BORDER (1944) PR:A
RAIDERS OF THE DESERT (1941) PR:A
RAIDERS OF THE LOST ARK (1981) PR:C-O
RAIDERS OF THE RANGE (1942) PR:A
RAIDERS OF THE SEVEN SEAS (1953) PR:A
RAIDERS OF THE SOUTH (1947) PR:A
RAIDERS OF THE WEST (1942) PR:A
RAIDERS OF TOMAHAWK CREEK (1950) PR:A
RAILROAD MAN, THE (1965, It.) PR:A
RAILROAD WORKERS (1948, Swed.) PR:A
RAILROADED (1947) PR:C
RAILS INTO LARAMIE (1954) PR:A
RAILWAY CHILDREN, THE (1971, Brit.) PR:A
RAIN (1932) PR:C-O
RAIN FOR A DUSTY SUMMER (1971, US/Sp.) PR:C
RAIN MAN (1988) PR:C-O
RAIN OR SHINE (1930) PR:A
RAIN PEOPLE, THE (1969) PR:C-O

RAINBOW, THE (1944, USSR) PR:C
RAINBOW, THE (1989) PR:O
RAINBOW BOYS, THE (1973, Can.) PR:A
RAINBOW BRITE AND THE STAR STEALER (1985) PR:AA
RAINBOW ISLAND (1944) PR:A
RAINBOW JACKET, THE (1954, Brit.) PR:A
RAINBOW MAN (1929) PR:A
RAINBOW ON THE RIVER (1936) PR:A
RAINBOW OVER BROADWAY (1933) PR:A
RAINBOW OVER TEXAS (1946) PR:A
RAINBOW OVER THE RANGE (1940) PR:A
RAINBOW OVER THE ROCKIES (1947) PR:A
RAINBOW RANCH (1933) PR:A
RAINBOW 'ROUND MY SHOULDER (1952) PR:A
RAINBOW TRAIL (1932) PR:A
RAINBOW VALLEY (1935) PR:A
RAINBOW'S END (1935) PR:A
RAINMAKER, THE (1956) PR:A
RAINMAKERS, THE (1935) PR:A
RAINS CAME, THE (1939) PR:A
RAINS OF RANCHIPUR, THE (1955) PR:A
RAINTREE COUNTY (1957) PR:C
RAISE THE ROOF (1930, Brit.) PR:A
RAISE THE TITANIC (1980, Brit.) PR:A-C
RAISIN IN THE SUN, A (1961) PR:A
RAISING A RIOT (1957, Brit.) PR:A
RAISING ARIZONA (1987) PR:C
RAISING THE WIND (SEE: BIG RACE, THE) (1934)
RAISING THE WIND (SEE: ROOMMATES) (1962, Brit.)
RAKE'S PROGRESS, THE (SEE: NOTORIOUS GENTLE-
  MAN) (1945, Brit.)
RALLARE (SEE: RAILROAD WORKERS) (1948, Swed.)
RALLY 'ROUND THE FLAG, BOYS! (1958) PR:C
RAMBO: FIRST BLOOD, PART II (1985) PR:O
RAMBO III (1988) PR:O
RAMONA (1936) PR:A
RAMPAGE (1963) PR:A
RAMPAGE AT APACHE WELLS (1966, Fr./It./W.
  Ger./Yugo.) PR:A
RAMPANT AGE, THE (1930) PR:A
RAMPARTS WE WATCH, THE (1940) PR:A
RAMROD (1947) PR:A
RAMRODDER, THE (1969) PR:O
RAMSBOTTOM RIDES AGAIN (1956, Brit.) PR:A
RAN (1985, Jap./Fr.) PR:O
RANCHO DELUXE (1975) PR:C
RANCHO GRANDE (1938, Mex.) PR:A
RANCHO GRANDE (1940) PR:A
RANCHO NOTORIOUS (1952) PR:A
RANDOLPH FAMILY, THE (1945, Brit.) PR:A
RANDOM HARVEST (1942) PR:A
RANDY RIDES ALONE (1934) PR:A
RANDY STRIKES OIL (SEE: FIGHTING TEXANS)
  (1933)
RANGE BEYOND THE BLUE (1947) PR:A
RANGE BUSTERS, THE (1940) PR:A
RANGE DEFENDERS (1937) PR:A
RANGE FEUD, THE (1931) PR:A
RANGE JUSTICE (1949) PR:A
RANGE LAND (1949) PR:A
RANGE LAW (1931) PR:A
RANGE LAW (1944) PR:A
RANGE RENEGADES (1948) PR:A
RANGE WAR (1939) PR:A
RANGER AND THE LADY, THE (1940) PR:A
RANGER COURAGE (1937) PR:A
RANGER OF CHEROKEE STRIP (1949) PR:A
RANGER'S CODE, THE (1933) PR:A
RANGERS OF FORTUNE (1940) PR:AA
RANGERS RIDE, THE (1948) PR:A
RANGER'S ROUNDUP, THE (1938) PR:A
RANGERS STEP IN, THE (1937) PR:A
RANGERS TAKE OVER, THE (1942) PR:A
RANGLE RIVER (1939, Aus.) PR:A
RANGO (1931) PR:A
RANI RADOVI (SEE: EARLY WORKS) (1970, Yugo.)
RANSOM (1956) PR:A
RANSOM (SEE: TERRORISTS, THE) (1975, Brit.)
RANSOM (SEE: MANIAC!) (1977)
RAPE, THE (1965, Gr.) PR:O
RAPE, THE (SEE: LE VIOL) (1968, Fr./Swed.)
RAPE OF MALAYA (SEE: TOWN LIKE ALICE, A)
  (1956, Brit.)
RAPE OF THE SABINES, THE (SEE: SHAME OF THE
  SABINE WOMEN, THE) (1962, Mex.)
RAPE SQUAD (SEE: ACT OF VENGEANCE) (1974)
RAPPIN' (1985) PR:O
RAPTURE (1950, It.) PR:A
RAPTURE (1965, US/Fr.) PR:C
RAQ LO B'SHABBAT (SEE: IMPOSSIBLE ON SATUR-
  DAY) (1966, Fr./Israel)
RARE BREED, THE (1966) PR:A
RARE BREED (1984) PR:A
RASCAL (1969) PR:AA
RASCALS (1938) PR:A
RASHOMON (1950, Jap.) PR:A-C
RASPOUTINE (1954, Fr.) PR:C

RASPUTIN (SEE: RASPUTIN AND THE EMPRESS)
  (1932)
RASPUTIN (1932, Ger.) PR:A
RASPUTIN (1939, Fr.) PR:A
RASPUTIN (1981, USSR) PR:O
RASPUTIN AND THE EMPRESS (1932) PR:C
RASPUTIN – THE MAD MONK (SEE: RASPUTIN AND
  THE EMPRESS) (1932)
RASPUTIN – THE MAD MONK (1966, Brit.) PR:C
RAT, THE (1938, Brit.) PR:A
RAT (1960, Yugo.) PR:A
RAT FINK (1965) PR:C
RAT PFINK AND BOO BOO (1966) PR:A
RAT RACE, THE (1960) PR:A
RAT SAVIOUR, THE (1977, Yugo.) PR:A
RATATAPLAN (1979, It.) PR:A
RATBOY (1986) PR:C
RATIONING (1944) PR:A
RATON PASS (1951) PR:A
RATS, THE (1955, W. Ger.) PR:A
RATS ARE COMING! THE WEREWOLVES ARE HERE!,
  THE (1972) PR:O
RATS, THE (SEE: DEADLY EYES) (1982)
RATS OF TOBRUK (1951, Aus.) PR:A
RATTLE OF A SIMPLE MAN (1964, Brit.) PR:C
RATTLERS (1976) PR:C
RAUTHA SKIKKJAN (SEE: HAGBARD AND SIGNE)
  (1968, Den./Iceland/Swed.)
RAVAGER, THE (1970) PR:O
RAVAGERS, THE (1965, US/Phil.) PR:A
RAVAGERS, THE (1979) PR:A
RAVEN, THE (1935) PR:A
RAVEN, THE (1948, Fr.) PR:A
RAVEN, THE (1963) PR:C
RAVEN'S END (1970, Swed.) PR:A
RAVISHING IDIOT, A (1966, It./Fr.) PR:A
RAW COURAGE (1984) PR:O
RAW DEAL (1948) PR:A-C
RAW DEAL (1977, Aus.) PR:A
RAW DEAL (1986) PR:O
RAW EDGE (1956) PR:A
RAW FORCE (1982) PR:O
RAW MEAT (SEE: DEATHLINE) (1973, Brit.)
RAW TIMBER (1937) PR:A
RAW WEEKEND (1964) PR:O
RAW WIND IN EDEN (1958) PR:A
RAWHEAD REX (1987, Brit.) PR:O
RAWHIDE (1938) PR:A
RAWHIDE (1951) PR:A
RAWHIDE HALO, THE (SEE: SHOOT OUT AT BIG
  SAG) (1962)
RAWHIDE RANGERS (1941) PR:A
RAWHIDE TRAIL, THE (1958) PR:A
RAWHIDE YEARS, THE (1956) PR:A
RAYMIE (1960) PR:AA
RAZORBACK (1984, Aus.) PR:O
RAZOR'S EDGE, THE (1946) PR:A
RAZOR'S EDGE, THE (1984) PR:C-O
RE-ANIMATOR (1985) PR:O
RE: LUCKY LUCIANO (1974, US/Fr./It.) PR:O
RE-UNION (SEE: IN LOVE WITH LIFE) (1934)
REACH FOR GLORY (1963, Brit.) PR:A
REACH FOR THE SKY (1957, Brit.) PR:A
REACHING FOR THE MOON (1931) PR:A
REACHING FOR THE SUN (1941) PR:A
REACHING OUT (1983) PR:O
READY FOR LOVE (1934) PR:A
READY FOR THE PEOPLE (1964) PR:A
READY, WILLING AND ABLE (1937) PR:A
REAL BLOKE, A (1935, Brit.) PR:A
REAL GENIUS (1985) PR:C
REAL GLORY, THE (1939) PR:A
REAL GONE GIRLS, THE (SEE: MAN FROM O.R.G.Y.,
  THE) (1970)
REAL LIFE (1979) PR:C
REAL LIFE (1984, Brit.) PR:C
REALM OF FORTUNE, THE (1986, Mex.) PR:O
REAP THE WILD WIND (1942) PR:A
REAR WINDOW (1954) PR:C
REASON TO LIVE, A REASON TO DIE, A (1974,
  It./Fr./Sp./W. Ger.) PR:A
REASONABLE DOUBT (1936, Brit.) PR:A
REBECCA (1940) PR:C
REBECCA OF SUNNYBROOK FARM (1932) PR:A
REBECCA OF SUNNYBROOK FARM (1938) PR:AA
REBEL, THE (1933, Ger.) PR:A
REBEL, THE (SEE: CALL ME GENIUS) (1961, Brit.)
REBEL (1985, Aus.) PR:O
REBEL ANGEL (1962) PR:C
REBEL CITY (1953) PR:A
REBEL GLADIATORS, THE (1963, It.) PR:A
REBEL IN TOWN (1956) PR:A
REBEL LOVE (1986) PR:C-O
REBEL ROUSERS (1970) PR:O
REBEL SET, THE (1959) PR:A
REBEL SON, THE (1939, Brit.) PR:A
REBEL WITH A CAUSE (SEE: LONELINESS OF THE
  LONG DISTANCE RUNNER, THE) (1962, Brit.)

REBEL WITHOUT A CAUSE (1955) PR:C-O
REBELLION (1938) PR:A
REBELLION (1967, Jap.) PR:C
REBELLION OF THE HANGED, THE (1954, Mex.) PR:C
REBELLIOUS DAUGHTERS (1938) PR:A
REBELLIOUS ONE, THE (SEE: WILD SEED) (1965)
REBELS DIE YOUNG (SEE: TOO YOUNG, TOO IMMO-
  RAL!) (1962)
REBOUND (1931) PR:A
RECAPTURED LOVE (1930) PR:A
RECESS (1967) PR:A
RECKLESS (1935) PR:A
RECKLESS (1984) PR:O
RECKLESS AGE (1944) PR:A
RECKLESS AGE, THE (SEE: DRAGSTRIP RIOT) (1958)
RECKLESS HOUR, THE (1931) PR:A
RECKLESS LIVING (1931) PR:A
RECKLESS LIVING (1938) PR:A
RECKLESS MOMENT, THE (1949) PR:A-C
RECKLESS RANGER (1937) PR:A
RECKLESS ROADS (1935) PR:A
RECKONING, THE (1932) PR:A
RECKONING, THE (1971, Brit.) PR:C-O
RECOIL (1953) PR:A
RECOMMENDATION FOR MERCY (1975, Can.) PR:O
RECONSTRUCTION OF A CRIME (1970, Gr.) PR:A
RECORD CITY (1978) PR:A-C
RECORD 413 (1936, Fr.) PR:A
RECORD OF A LIVING BEING (SEE: I LIVE IN FEAR)
  (1967, Jap.)
RECRUITS (1986) PR:O
RED (1970, Can.) PR:C
RED AND THE BLACK, THE (1954, Fr./It.) PR:A
RED AND THE WHITE, THE (1969, Hung./USSR) PR:A
RED BADGE OF COURAGE, THE (1951) PR:C
RED BALL EXPRESS (1952) PR:A
RED BARON, THE (SEE: VON RICHTOFEN AND
  BROWN) (1970)
RED BEARD (1965, Jap.) PR:C-O
RED BERET, THE (SEE: PARATROOPER) (1954, Brit.)
RED BLOOD OF COURAGE (1935) PR:A
RED CANYON (1949) PR:A
RED CLOAK, THE (1961, It./Fr.) PR:A
RED DANUBE, THE (1949) PR:A
RED DAWN (1984) PR:O
RED DESERT (1949) PR:A
RED DESERT (1964, Fr./It.) PR:O
RED DRAGON, THE (1946) PR:A
RED-DRAGON (1967, US/It./W. Ger.) PR:A
RED DRESS, THE (1954, Brit.) PR:A
RED DUST (1932) PR:C
RED ENSIGN (SEE: STRIKE!) (1934, Brit.)
RED FORK RANGE (1931) PR:A
RED GARTERS (1954) PR:A
RED-HAIRED ALIBI, THE (1932) PR:A
RED HANGMAN, THE (SEE: BLOODY PIT OF HOR-
  ROR) (1965, US/It.)
RED HEAD, THE (SEE: POIL DE CAROTTE) (1932, Fr.)
RED HEAD (1934) PR:A
RED HEADED STRANGER (1987) PR:C-O
RED HEADED WOMAN (1932) PR:A
RED HEAT (1988) PR:O
RED HEAT (1988, US/W. Ger.) PR:O
RED, HOT AND BLUE (1949) PR:A
RED HOT RHYTHM (1930) PR:A
RED HOT SPEED (1929) PR:A
RED HOT TIRES (1935) PR:A
RED HOT WHEELS (SEE: TO PLEASE A LADY) (1950)
RED HOUSE, THE (1947) PR:A
RED INN, THE (1954, Fr.) PR:A
RED KISS (1985, Fr./W. Ger.) PR:O
RED LANTERNS, THE (1965, Gr.) PR:C
RED LIGHT (1949) PR:A-C
RED LIGHTS AHEAD (1937) PR:A
RED LINE 7000 (1965) PR:C
RED LION (1971, Jap.) PR:A
RED LIPS (1964, Fr./It.) PR:O
RED MANTLE, THE (SEE: HAGBARD AND SIGNE)
  (1968, Den./Iceland/Swed.)
RED MENACE, THE (1949) PR:A
RED MONARCH (1983, Brit.) PR:C
RED MORNING (1935) PR:A
RED MOUNTAIN (1951) PR:A-C
RED OCEAN (SEE: MONSTER SHARK) (1986, Fr./It.)
RED ON RED (SEE: SCARRED) (1984)
RED OVER RED (SEE: COME SPY WITH ME) (1967)
RED PLANET MARS (1952) PR:A
RED PONY, THE (1949) PR:AA
RED RIVER (1948) PR:A
RED RIVER RANGE (1938) PR:A
RED RIVER RENEGADES (1946) PR:A
RED RIVER ROBIN HOOD (1943) PR:A
RED RIVER SHORE (1953) PR:A
RED RIVER VALLEY (1936) PR:A
RED RIVER VALLEY (1941) PR:A
RED ROCK OUTLAW (1950) PR:A
RED ROPE, THE (1937) PR:A
RED RUNS THE RIVER (1963) PR:A

RED SALUTE (1935) PR:A
RED SCORPION (1989) PR:C-O
RED SHEIK, THE (1963, It.) PR:A
RED SHOES, THE (1948, Brit.) PR:A
RED SKIES OF MONTANA (1952) PR:A
RED SKY AT MORNING (1971) PR:C
RED SNOW (1952) PR:A
RED SONJA (1985) PR:C-O
RED SORGHUM (1988, Chi.) PR:O
RED STALLION, THE (1947) PR:A
RED STALLION IN THE ROCKIES (1949) PR:AA
RED SUN (1972, Fr./It./Sp.) PR:A
RED SUNDOWN (1956) PR:A
RED TENT, THE (1971, It./USSR) PR:A
RED TIDE, THE (SEE: BLOOD TIDE) (1982)
RED TOMAHAWK (1967) PR:A
RED WAGON (1936, Brit.) PR:A
RED, WHITE AND BLACK, THE (1970) PR:C
RED, WHITE, AND BUSTED (SEE: OUTSIDE IN) (1972)
REDEEMER, THE (1965, US/Sp.) PR:A
REDEEMER, THE (SEE: RAT SAVIOUR, THE) (1977, Yugo.)
REDEEMER, THE (1978) PR:O
REDEEMING SIN, THE (1929) PR:A
REDEMPTION (1930) PR:A
REDHEAD (1941) PR:A
REDHEAD AND THE COWBOY, THE (1950) PR:A
REDHEAD FROM MANHATTAN (1943) PR:A
REDHEAD FROM WYOMING, THE (1953) PR:A
REDHEADS ON PARADE (1935) PR:A
REDL EZREDES (SEE: COLONEL REDL) (1985, Aust./Hung./W. Ger.)
REDNECK (1975, It./Sp.) PR:O
REDS (1981) PR:C-O
REDUCING (1931) PR:A
REDWOOD FOREST TRAIL (1950) PR:A
REEFER MADNESS (1936) PR:C-O
REFLECTION OF FEAR, A (1973) PR:C
REFLECTIONS (1984, Brit.) PR:C
REFLECTIONS IN A GOLDEN EYE (1967) PR:O
REFORM GIRL (1933) PR:A
REFORM SCHOOL (1939) PR:A
REFORM SCHOOL GIRL (1957) PR:A
REFORM SCHOOL GIRLS (1986) PR:O
REFORMATORY (1938) PR:A
REFORMER AND THE REDHEAD, THE (1950) PR:A
REFUGE (1981) PR:O
REFUGEE, THE (SEE: THREE FACES WEST) (1940)
REGAIN (SEE: HARVEST) (1939, Fr.)
REGAL CAVALCADE (1935, Brit.) PR:A
REGISTERED NURSE (1934) PR:A
REG'LAR FELLERS (1941) PR:A
REHEARSAL FOR A CRIME (SEE: CRIMINAL LIFE OF ARCHIBALDO DE LA CRUZ, THE) (1955, Mex.)
REIGN OF TERROR (SEE: BLACK BOOK, THE) (1949, Brit.)
REINCARNATE, THE (1971, Can.) PR:C
REINCARNATION OF PETER PROUD, THE (1975) PR:C-O
REIVERS, THE (1969) PR:C
REKKA (SEE: ECSTACY OF YOUNG LOVE) (1936, Czech.)
REKOPIS ZNALEZIONY W SARAGOSSIE (SEE: SARAGOSSA MANUSCRIPT, THE) (1966, Pol.)
RELAZIONI PERICOLOSE (SEE: LES LIAISONS DAN-GEREUSES) (1961, Fr./It.)
RELENTLESS (1948) PR:A
RELENTLESS (1989) PR:O
RELIGIOUS RACKETEERS (SEE: MYSTIC CIRCLE MURDERS) (1939)
RELUCTANT ASTRONAUT, THE (1967) PR:A
RELUCTANT BRIDE (SEE: TWO GROOMS FOR A BRIDE) (1957)
RELUCTANT DEBUTANTE, THE (1958) PR:A
RELUCTANT DRAGON, THE (1941) PR:AA
RELUCTANT HEROES (1951, Brit.) PR:A
RELUCTANT SAINT, THE (1962, US/It.) PR:A
RELUCTANT WIDOW, THE (1951, Brit.) PR:A
REMAINS TO BE SEEN (1953) PR:A
REMANDO AL VIENTO (SEE: ROWING WITH THE WIND) (1988, Sp.)
REMARKABLE ANDREW, THE (1942) PR:A
REMARKABLE MR. KIPPS (1942, Brit.) PR:A
REMARKABLE MR. PENNYPACKER, THE (1959) PR:A
REMBETIKO (1985, Gr.) PR:C
REMBRANDT (1936, Brit.) PR:A
REMBRANDT LAUGHING (1989) PR:A
REMEDY FOR RICHES (1941) PR:A
REMEMBER? (1939) PR:A
REMEMBER LAST NIGHT? (1935) PR:A
REMEMBER MY NAME (1978) PR:O
REMEMBER PEARL HARBOR (1942) PR:A
REMEMBER THAT FACE (SEE: MOB, THE) (1951)
REMEMBER THE DAY (1941) PR:A
REMEMBER THE NIGHT (1940) PR:A
REMEMBER WHEN (SEE: RIDING HIGH) (1937, Brit.)
REMEMBRANCE (1982, Brit.) PR:C-O

REMO WILLIAMS: THE ADVENTURE BEGINS (1985) PR:C
REMORQUES (SEE: STORMY WATERS) (1946, Fr.)
REMOTE CONTROL (1930) PR:A
REMOTE CONTROL (1988) PR:C
REMOVALISTS, THE (1975, Aus.) PR:C
RENALDO AND CLARA (1978) PR:O
RENDEZ-VOUS (1932, Ger.) PR:A
RENDEZVOUS (1935) PR:A
RENDEZVOUS (SEE: DARLING, HOW COULD YOU!) (1951)
RENDEZVOUS (1985, Fr.) PR:O
RENDEZVOUS AT MIDNIGHT (1935) PR:A
RENDEZVOUS 24 (1946) PR:A
RENDEZVOUS WITH ANNIE (1946) PR:A
RENEGADE GIRL (1946) PR:A
RENEGADE GIRLS (1974) PR:O
RENEGADE POSSE (SEE: BULLET FOR A BADMAN) (1964)
RENEGADE RANGER, THE (1938) PR:A
RENEGADE TRAIL, THE (1939) PR:A
RENEGADES (1930) PR:A
RENEGADES (1946) PR:A
RENEGADES (1989) PR:O
RENEGADES OF SONORA (1948) PR:A
RENEGADES OF THE RIO GRANDE (1945) PR:A
RENEGADES OF THE SAGE (1949) PR:A
RENEGADES OF THE WEST (1932) PR:A
RENFREW OF THE ROYAL MOUNTED (1937) PR:A
RENFREW OF THE ROYAL MOUNTED ON THE GREAT WHITE TRAIL (SEE: ON THE GREAT WHITE TRAIL) (1938)
RENFREW ON THE GREAT WHITE TRAIL (SEE: ON THE GREAT WHITE TRAIL) (1938)
RENO (1930) PR:A
RENO (1939) PR:A
RENO AND THE DOC (1984, Can.) PR:O
RENT-A-COP (1988) PR:C
"RENT-A-GIRL" (1965) PR:O
RENT CONTROL (1981) PR:O
RENTADICK (1972, Brit.) PR:O
RENTED (SEE: "RENT-A-GIRL") (1965)
RENTED LIPS (1988) PR:C
REPEAT PERFORMANCE (1947) PR:A
REPENT AT LEISURE (1941) PR:A
REPENTANCE (1987, USSR) PR:C
REPLICA OF A CRIME (SEE: MANIAC MANSION) (1978, It.)
REPO (SEE: ZERO TO SIXTY) (1978)
REPO MAN (1984) PR:O
REPORT ON THE PARTY AND THE GUESTS, A (1968, Czech.) PR:A
REPORT TO THE COMMISSIONER (1975) PR:C
REPORTED MISSING (1937) PR:A
REPRIEVE (SEE: CONVICTS FOUR) (1962)
REPRIEVED (SEE: SING SING NIGHTS) (1935)
REPRISAL! (1956) PR:A
REPTILE, THE (1966, Brit.) PR:C
REPTILICUS (1962, US/Den.) PR:A
REPULSION (1965, Brit.) PR:O
REPUTATION (SEE: LADY WITH A PAST) (1932)
REQUIEM FOR A GUNFIGHTER (1965) PR:A
REQUIEM FOR A HEAVYWEIGHT (1962) PR:C
REQUIEM FOR A SECRET AGENT (1966, It.) PR:A
RESCUE, THE (1988) PR:A-C
RESCUE SQUAD (1935) PR:A
RESCUE SQUAD, THE (1963, Brit.) PR:A
RESCUERS, THE (1977) PR:AA
RESERVED FOR LADIES (1932, Brit.) PR:AA
REST IS SILENCE, THE (1960, W. Ger.) PR:C
RESTLESS (SEE: MAN-TRAP) (1961)
RESTLESS BREED, THE (1957) PR:A
RESTLESS NIGHT, THE (1964, W. Ger.) PR:C
RESTLESS ONES, THE (1965) PR:A
RESTLESS YEARS, THE (1958) PR:A
RESURRECTION (1931) PR:A
RESURRECTION (1963, USSR) PR:A
RESURRECTION (1980) PR:C
RESURRECTION OF ZACHARY WHEELER, THE (1971) PR:A
RESURRECTION SYNDICATE (SEE: NOTHING BUT THE NIGHT) (1972, Brit.)
RETALIATOR (SEE: PROGRAMMED TO KILL) (1987)
RETENEZ MOI... OU JE FAIS UN MALHEUR (SEE: TO CATCH A COP) (1984, Fr.)
RETREAT, HELL! (1952) PR:A
RETRIBUTION (1988) PR:O
RETRIEVERS, THE (SEE: HOT AND DEADLY) (1984)
RETURN, THE (1980) PR:C
RETURN (1986) PR:O
RETURN FROM THE ASHES (1965, US/Brit.) PR:A
RETURN FROM THE PAST (SEE: DR. TERROR'S GAL-LERY OF HORRORS) (1967)
RETURN FROM THE SEA (1954) PR:A
RETURN FROM WITCH MOUNTAIN (1978) PR:AA
RETURN OF A MAN CALLED HORSE, THE (1976) PR:C
RETURN OF A STRANGER (SEE: FACE BEHIND THE SCAR) (1940, Brit.)

RETURN OF A STRANGER (1962, Brit.) PR:C
RETURN OF BULLDOG DRUMMOND, THE (1934, Brit.) PR:A
RETURN OF CAPTAIN INVINCIBLE, THE (1983, Aus./US) PR:C
RETURN OF CAROL DEANE, THE (1938, Brit.) PR:A
RETURN OF CASEY JONES, THE (1933) PR:A
RETURN OF COUNT YORGA, THE (1971) PR:C
RETURN OF DANIEL BOONE, THE (1941) PR:A
RETURN OF DR. FU MANCHU, THE (1930) PR:A
RETURN OF DR. MABUSE, THE (1961, Fr./It./W. Ger.) PR:C
RETURN OF DOCTOR X, THE (1939) PR:C
RETURN OF DRACULA, THE (1958) PR:C
RETURN OF FRANK JAMES, THE (1940) PR:A
RETURN OF GODZILLA, THE (SEE: GIGANTIS) (1959, US/Jap.)
RETURN OF JACK SLADE, THE (1955) PR:A
RETURN OF JESSE JAMES, THE (1950) PR:A
RETURN OF JIMMY VALENTINE, THE (1936) PR:A
RETURN OF JOSEY WALES, THE (1987) PR:C
RETURN OF MARTIN GUERRE, THE (1982, Fr.) PR:C
RETURN OF MAXWELL SMART, THE (SEE: NUDE BOMB, THE) (1980)
RETURN OF MR. H, THE (SEE: THEY SAVED HITLER'S BRAIN) (1964)
RETURN OF MR. MOTO, THE (1965, Brit.) PR:A
RETURN OF MONTE CRISTO, THE (1946) PR:A
RETURN OF OCTOBER, THE (1948) PR:A
RETURN OF OLD MOTHER RILEY, THE (SEE: OLD MOTHER RILEY) (1937, Brit.)
RETURN OF PETER GRIMM, THE (1935) PR:A
RETURN OF RAFFLES, THE (1932, Brit.) PR:A
RETURN OF RIN TIN TIN, THE (1947) PR:AA
RETURN OF RINGO, THE (1966, It./Sp.) PR:A
RETURN OF SABATA (1972, It./Fr./W. Ger.) PR:C
RETURN OF SHE, THE (SEE: VENGEANCE OF SHE, THE) (1968, Brit.)
RETURN OF SHERLOCK HOLMES, THE (1929) PR:A
RETURN OF SOPHIE LANG, THE (1936) PR:A
RETURN OF SWAMP THING, THE (1989) PR:C
RETURN OF THE APE MAN (1944) PR:A
RETURN OF THE BADMEN (1948) PR:C
RETURN OF THE BLACK EAGLE (1949, It.) PR:A
RETURN OF THE BOOMERANG (SEE: ADAM'S WOMAN) (1972, Aus.)
RETURN OF THE CISCO KID, THE (1939) PR:A
RETURN OF THE CORSICAN BROTHERS (SEE: BAN-DITS OF CORSICA, THE) (1953)
RETURN OF THE DRAGON (1974, Chi.) PR:O
RETURN OF THE FLY (1959) PR:A
RETURN OF THE FROG, THE (1938, Brit.) PR:A
RETURN OF THE FRONTIERSMAN (1950) PR:A
RETURN OF THE JEDI (1983) PR:A-C
RETURN OF THE KILLER TOMATOES (1988) PR:NR
RETURN OF THE LASH (1947) PR:A
RETURN OF THE LIVING DEAD (SEE: DEAD PEO-PLE) (1974)
RETURN OF THE LIVING DEAD (1985) PR:O
RETURN OF THE LIVING DEAD PART II (1988) PR:O
RETURN OF THE PINK PANTHER, THE (1975, Brit.) PR:A-C
RETURN OF THE RANGERS, THE (1943) PR:A
RETURN OF THE RAT, THE (1929, Brit.) PR:A
RETURN OF THE SCARLET PIMPERNEL (1938, Brit.) PR:A
RETURN OF THE SECAUCUS SEVEN (1980) PR:O
RETURN OF THE SEVEN (1966, US/Sp.) PR:A
RETURN OF THE SOLDIER, THE (1983, Brit.) PR:C
RETURN OF THE TALL BLOND MAN WITH ONE BLACK SHOE, THE (1974, Fr.) PR:A-C
RETURN OF THE TERROR (1934) PR:C
RETURN OF THE TEXAN (1952) PR:A
RETURN OF THE VAMPIRE, THE (1944) PR:A
RETURN OF THE VIGILANTES, THE (SEE: VIGILAN-TES RETURN, THE) (1947)
RETURN OF THE WHISTLER, THE (1948) PR:A
RETURN OF WILD BILL, THE (1940) PR:A-C
RETURN OF WILDFIRE, THE (1948) PR:A
RETURN TO BOGGY CREEK (1977) PR:AA
RETURN TO CAMPUS (1975) PR:C
RETURN TO HORROR HIGH (1987) PR:O
RETURN TO MACON COUNTY (1975) PR:C-O
RETURN TO OZ (1985) PR:C
RETURN TO PARADISE (1953) PR:A
RETURN TO PEYTON PLACE (1961) PR:A
RETURN TO SALEM'S LOT, A (1988) PR:O
RETURN TO SENDER (1963, Brit.) PR:A
RETURN TO SNOWY RIVER: PART II (1988, Aus.) PR:A
RETURN TO THE HORRORS OF BLOOD ISLAND (SEE: BEAST OF BLOOD) (1970, US/Phil.)
RETURN TO TREASURE ISLAND (1954) PR:A
RETURN TO WARBOW (1958) PR:A
RETURN TO WATERLOO (1985, Brit.) PR:C
RETURN TO YESTERDAY (1940, Brit.) PR:A
RETURNING, THE (1983) PR:O
REUBEN, REUBEN (1983) PR:O
REUNION (1932, Brit.) PR:A

REUNION (1936) PR:A
REUNION IN FRANCE (1942) PR:A
REUNION IN RENO (1951) PR:A
REUNION IN VIENNA (1933) PR:A-C
REVEILLE-TOI ET MEURS (SEE: WAKE UP AND DIE) (1967, Fr./It.)
REVEILLE WITH BEVERLY (1943) PR:A
REVENGE (SEE: END OF THE TRAIL) (1936)
REVENGE (SEE: TERROR FROM UNDER THE HOUSE) (1971, Brit.)
REVENGE (SEE: BLOOD FEUD) (1979, It.)
REVENGE (1986) PR:O
REVENGE AT EL PASO (1968, It.) PR:A
REVENGE AT MONTE CARLO (1933) PR:A
REVENGE OF DRACULA (SEE: DRACULA – PRINCE OF DARKNESS) (1966, Brit.)
REVENGE OF FRANKENSTEIN, THE (1958, Brit.) PR:C
REVENGE OF GENERAL LING (SEE: WIFE OF GENERAL LING) (1938, Brit.)
REVENGE OF KING KONG, THE (SEE: KING KONG ESCAPES) (1968, Jap.)
REVENGE OF MILADY, THE (SEE: FOUR MUSKETEERS, THE) (1975)
REVENGE OF THE BLOOD BEAST, THE (SEE: SHE BEAST, THE) (1966, Brit./It./Yugo.)
REVENGE OF THE CHEERLEADERS (1976) PR:O
REVENGE OF THE CREATURE (1955) PR:A
REVENGE OF THE DEAD (SEE: NIGHT OF THE GHOULS) (1959)
REVENGE OF THE GLADIATORS (1965, It.) PR:A
REVENGE OF THE INNOCENTS (SEE: SOUTH BRONX HEROES) (1985)
REVENGE OF THE LIVING DEAD (SEE: MURDER CLINIC, THE) (1967, Fr./It.)
REVENGE OF THE NERDS (1984) PR:C-O
REVENGE OF THE NERDS II: NERDS IN PARADISE (1987) PR:C
REVENGE OF THE NINJA (1983) PR:A
REVENGE OF THE PINK PANTHER (1978) PR:A-C
REVENGE OF THE SCREAMING DEAD (SEE: DEAD PEOPLE) (1974)
REVENGE OF THE SHOGUN WOMEN (1982, Taiwan) PR:O
REVENGE OF THE TEENAGE VIXENS FROM OUTER SPACE, THE (1986) PR:C
REVENGE OF THE ZOMBIES (1943) PR:A
REVENGE OF UKENO-JO, THE (SEE: ACTOR'S REVENGE, AN) (1963, Jap.)
REVENGE RIDER, THE (1935) PR:A
REVENGERS, THE (1972, US/Mex.) PR:A-C
REVENUE AGENT (1950) PR:A
REVERSE BE MY LOT, THE (1938, Brit.) PR:A
REVOLT AT FORT LARAMIE (1957) PR:A
REVOLT IN THE BIG HOUSE (1958) PR:A
REVOLT OF JOB, THE (1983. Hung./W. Ger.) PR:O
REVOLT OF MAMIE STOVER, THE (1956) PR:A
REVOLT OF THE BOYARS. THE (SEE: IVAN THE TERRIBLE, PARTS I & II) (1945, USSR)
REVOLT OF THE MERCENARIES (1964, It./Sp.) PR:A
REVOLT OF THE SLAVES, THE (1961, It./Sp./W. Ger.) PR:C
REVOLT OF THE ZOMBIES (1936) PR:C
REVOLUTION (1985, Brit./Norway) PR:C
REVOLUTIONARY, THE (1970, Brit.) PR:A-C
REVOLUTIONS PER MINUTE (SEE: R.P.M.) (1970)
REVOLVER, THE (SEE: BLOOD IN THE STREETS) (1975, Fr./It.)
REVOLVING DOORS, THE (1988, Can./Fr.) PR:A
REWARD, THE (1965) PR:A
REY DE AFRICA (SEE: ONE STEP TO HELL) (1969, US/It./Sp.)
RHAPSODIE IN BLEI (SEE: HOT MONEY GIRL) (1962, Brit./W. Ger.)
RHAPSODY (1954) PR:A
RHAPSODY IN BLUE (1945) PR:AA
RHINESTONE (1984) PR:C
RHINO! (1964) PR:A
RHINOCEROS (1974) PR:A-C
RHODES (1936, Brit.) PR:A
RHODES OF AFRICA (SEE: RHODES) (1936, Brit.)
RHOSYN A RHITH (SEE: COMING UP ROSES) (1986, Brit.)
RHUBARB (1951) PR:A
RHYTHM HITS THE ICE (SEE: ICE-CAPADES REVUE) (1942)
RHYTHM IN THE AIR (1936, Brit.) PR:A
RHYTHM IN THE CLOUDS (1937) PR:A
RHYTHM INN (1951) PR:A
RHYTHM OF THE ISLANDS (1943) PR:A
RHYTHM OF THE RIO GRANDE (1940) PR:A
RHYTHM OF THE SADDLE (1938) PR:A
RHYTHM ON THE RANGE (1936) PR:A
RHYTHM ON THE RANGE (SEE: ROOTIN' TOOTIN' RHYTHM) (1937)
RHYTHM ON THE RIVER (SEE: FRESHMAN LOVE) (1936)
RHYTHM ON THE RIVER (1940) PR:A
RHYTHM PARADE (1943) PR:A

RHYTHM RACKETEER (1937, Brit.) PR:A
RHYTHM ROMANCE (SEE: SOME LIKE IT HOT) (1939)
RHYTHM SERENADE (1943, Brit.) PR:A
RICE GIRL (1963, Fr./It.) PR:C-O
RICH AND FAMOUS (1981) PR:O
RICH AND STRANGE (1932, Brit.) PR:C
RICH ARE ALWAYS WITH US, THE (1932) PR:A
RICH BRIDE, THE (SEE: COUNTRY BRIDE) (1938, USSR)
RICH, FULL LIFE, THE (SEE: CYNTHIA) (1947)
RICH KIDS (1979) PR:C
RICH MAN, POOR GIRL (1938) PR:A
RICH MAN'S FOLLY (1931) PR:A
RICH PEOPLE (1929) PR:A
RICH, YOUNG AND DEADLY (SEE: PLATINUM HIGH SCHOOL) (1960)
RICH, YOUNG AND PRETTY (1951) PR:A-C
RICHARD (1972) PR:C
RICHARD TAUBER STORY, THE (SEE: YOU ARE THE WORLD FOR ME) (1964, Aust.)
RICHARD III (1956, Brit.) PR:A-C
RICHARD'S THINGS (1981, Brit.) PR:O
RICHELIEU (SEE: CARDINAL RICHELIEU) (1935)
RICHES AND ROMANCE (SEE: ROMANCE AND RICHES) (1937, Brit.)
RICHEST GIRL IN THE WORLD, THE (1934) PR:A
RICHEST MAN IN THE WORLD, THE (SEE: SINS OF THE CHILDREN) (1930)
RICHEST MAN IN TOWN, THE (1941) PR:A
RICKSHAW MAN, THE (1960, Jap.) PR:C-O
RICKY 1 (1988) PR:NR
RICOCHET (1966, Brit.) PR:C
RICOCHET ROMANCE (1954) PR:AA
RIDDLE OF THE SANDS, THE (1984, Brit.) PR:C
RIDE A CROOKED MILE (1938) PR:C
RIDE A CROOKED TRAIL (1958) PR:A-C
RIDE A NORTHBOUND HORSE (1969) PR:AA
RIDE A VIOLENT MILE (1957) PR:C
RIDE A WILD PONY (1976, US/Aus.) PR:AA
RIDE BACK, THE (1957) PR:C
RIDE BEYOND VENGEANCE (1966) PR:O
RIDE CLEAR OF DIABLO (1954) PR:C
RIDE 'EM COWBOY (1936) PR:A
RIDE 'EM COWBOY (1942) PR:AA
RIDE 'EM COWGIRL (1939) PR:A
RIDE HIM, COWBOY (1932) PR:A
RIDE IN A PINK CAR (1974, Can.) PR:C-O
RIDE IN THE WHIRLWIND (1966) PR:C
RIDE, KELLY, RIDE (1941) PR:A
RIDE LONESOME (1959) PR:C
RIDE ON VAQUERO (1941) PR:A
RIDE OUT FOR REVENGE (1957) PR:C
RIDE, RANGER, RIDE (1936) PR:A
RIDE, RYDER, RIDE! (1949) PR:A
RIDE, TENDERFOOT, RIDE (1940) PR:A
RIDE THE HIGH COUNTRY (1962) PR:C
RIDE THE HIGH IRON (1956) PR:A
RIDE THE HIGH WIND (1967, South Africa) PR:A
RIDE THE MAN DOWN (1952) PR:C
RIDE THE PINK HORSE (1947) PR:C
RIDE THE WILD SURF (1964) PR:A
RIDE TO HANGMAN'S TREE, THE (1967) PR:A
RIDE, VAQUERO! (1953) PR:A
RIDER FROM TUCSON (1950) PR:A
RIDER IN THE NIGHT, THE (1968, South Africa) PR:C
RIDER OF DEATH VALLEY (1932) PR:A
RIDER OF THE LAW, THE (1935) PR:A
RIDER OF THE PLAINS (1931) PR:A
RIDER ON A DEAD HORSE (1962) PR:C
RIDER ON THE RAIN (1970, Fr./It.) PR:C
RIDERS FROM NOWHERE (1940) PR:A
RIDERS IN THE SKY (1949) PR:A
RIDERS OF BLACK MOUNTAIN (1941) PR:A
RIDERS OF BLACK RIVER (1939) PR:A
RIDERS OF DESTINY (1933) PR:A
RIDERS OF PASCO BASIN (1940) PR:A
RIDERS OF THE BADLANDS (1941) PR:A
RIDERS OF THE BLACK HILLS (1938) PR:A
RIDERS OF THE CACTUS (1931) PR:A
RIDERS OF THE DAWN (1937) PR:A
RIDERS OF THE DAWN (1945) PR:A
RIDERS OF THE DEADLINE (1943) PR:A
RIDERS OF THE DESERT (1932) PR:A
RIDERS OF THE DUSK (1949) PR:A
RIDERS OF THE FRONTIER (1939) PR:A
RIDERS OF THE GOLDEN GULCH (1932) PR:A
RIDERS OF THE NORTH (1931) PR:A
RIDERS OF THE NORTHLAND (1942) PR:A
RIDERS OF THE NORTHWEST MOUNTED (1943) PR:A
RIDERS OF THE PURPLE SAGE (1931) PR:A
RIDERS OF THE PURPLE SAGE (1941) PR:A
RIDERS OF THE RANGE (1949) PR:A
RIDERS OF THE RIO GRANDE (1943) PR:A
RIDERS OF THE ROCKIES (1937) PR:A
RIDERS OF THE SANTA FE (1944) PR:A
RIDERS OF THE STORM (1988, Brit.) PR:O
RIDERS OF THE TIMBERLINE (1941) PR:A
RIDERS OF THE WEST (1942) PR:A

RIDERS OF THE WHISTLING PINES (1949) PR:A
RIDERS OF THE WHISTLING SKULL (1937) PR:A-C
RIDERS OF VENGEANCE (SEE: RAIDERS, THE) (1952)
RIDERS TO THE STARS (1954) PR:A
RIDIN' DOWN THE CANYON (1942) PR:A
RIDIN' DOWN THE TRAIL (1947) PR:A
RIDIN' FOR JUSTICE (1932) PR:A
RIDIN' LAW (1930) PR:A
RIDIN' ON A RAINBOW (1941) PR:A
RIDIN' THE LONE TRAIL (1937) PR:A
RIDIN' THE OUTLAW TRAIL (1951) PR:A
RIDING AVENGER, THE (1936) PR:A
RIDING HIGH (1937, Brit.) PR:A
RIDING HIGH (1943) PR:A
RIDING HIGH (1950) PR:A
RIDING ON (1937) PR:A
RIDING ON AIR (1937) PR:AA
RIDING SHOTGUN (1954) PR:A
RIDING SPEED (1934) PR:A
RIDING TALL (SEE: SQUARES) (1972)
RIDING THE CHEROKEE TRAIL (1941) PR:A
RIDING THE SUNSET TRAIL (1941) PR:A
RIDING THE WIND (1942) PR:A
RIDING TORNADO, THE (1932) PR:A
RIDING WEST (1944) PR:A
RIFF RAFF GIRLS (1962, Fr./It.) PR:O
RIFFRAFF (1936) PR:A
RIFFRAFF (1947) PR:A
RIFIFFI A TOKYO (SEE: RIFIFI IN TOKYO) (1963, Fr.)
RIFIFI (1955, Fr.) PR:A-C
RIFIFI FOR GIRLS (SEE: RIFF RAFF GIRLS) (1962, Fr./It.)
RIFIFI FRA LE DONNE (SEE: RIFF RAFF GIRLS) (1962, Fr./It.)
RIFIFI IN PARIS (SEE: UPPER HAND, THE) (1967, Fr./It./W. Ger.)
RIFIFI IN TOKYO (1963, Fr./It.) PR:A-C
RIFIFI INTERNAZIONALE (SEE: UPPER HAND, THE) (1967, Fr./It./W. Ger.)
RIGHT AGE TO MARRY, THE (1935, Brit.) PR:A
RIGHT APPROACH, THE (1961) PR:A
RIGHT CROSS (1950) PR:A-C
RIGHT HAND OF THE DEVIL, THE (1963) PR:C
RIGHT MAN, THE (SEE: HER FIRST ROMANCE) (1940)
RIGHT OF WAY, THE (1931) PR:A
RIGHT STUFF, THE (1983) PR:A-C
RIGHT TO LIVE, THE (1933, Brit.) PR:A
RIGHT TO LIVE, THE (1935) PR:A
RIGHT TO LIVE, THE (SEE: FOREVER YOURS) (1945)
RIGHT TO LOVE, THE (1931) PR:C
RIGHT TO ROMANCE, THE (1933) PR:A-C
RIGHT TO THE HEART (1942) PR:A
RIGOLETTO (1949) PR:A
RIKKY AND PETE (1988, Aus.) PR:O
RIKUGUN HAYABUSA SENTOTAI (SEE: FALCON FIGHTERS, THE) (1970, Jap.)
RIM OF THE CANYON (1949) PR:A
RIMFIRE (1949) PR:A
RING, THE (1952) PR:A
RING-A-DING RHYTHM (1962, Brit.) PR:A
RING AROUND THE CLOCK (1953, It.) PR:A
RING AROUND THE MOON (1936) PR:A
RING OF BRIGHT WATER (1969, Brit.) PR:A
RING OF FEAR (1954) PR:A
RING OF FIRE (1961) PR:A-C
RING OF SPIES (1964, Brit.) PR:A
RING OF TERROR (1962) PR:A
RING OF TREASON (SEE: RING OF SPIES) (1964, Brit.)
RING UP THE CURTAIN (SEE: BROADWAY TO HOLLYWOOD) (1933)
RINGER, THE (1932, Brit.) PR:A
RINGER, THE (1953, Brit.) PR:A
RINGO AND HIS GOLDEN PISTOL (1966, It.) PR:A
RINGS ON HER FINGERS (1942) PR:A
RINGSIDE (1949) PR:A
RINGSIDE MAISIE (1941) PR:A
RIO (1939) PR:A
RIO ABAJO (SEE: ON THE LINE) (1984, Sp.)
RIO BRAVO (1959) PR:A
RIO CONCHOS (1964) PR:A
RIO GRANDE (1939) PR:A
RIO GRANDE (1950) PR:A
RIO GRANDE PATROL (1950) PR:A
RIO GRANDE RAIDERS (1946) PR:A
RIO GRANDE RANGER (1937) PR:A
RIO GRANDE ROMANCE (1936) PR:A
RIO LOBO (1970) PR:A
RIO RITA (1929) PR:A
RIO RITA (1942) PR:AA
RIO 70 (1970, US/Sp./W. Ger.) PR:C
RIO VENGENCE (SEE: MOTOR PSYCHO) (1965)
RIOT (1969) PR:O
RIOT AT LAUDERDALE (SEE: HELL'S PLAYGROUND) (1967)
RIOT IN CELL BLOCK 11 (1954) PR:C
RIOT IN JUVENILE PRISON (1959) PR:C
RIOT ON PIER 6 (SEE: NEW ORLEANS UNCENSORED) (1955)

RIOT ON SUNSET STRIP (1967) PR:C
RIOT SQUAD (1941) PR:A
RIP-OFF (1971, Can.) PR:O
RIP ROARIN' BUCKAROO (1936) PR:A
RIP ROARING RILEY (1935) PR:A
RIP TIDE (1934) PR:A
RIPPED-OFF (1971, It.) PR:C-O
RISATE DI GIOLA (SEE: PASSIONATE THIEF, THE)
   (1961, Fr.)
RISE AGAINST THE SWORD (1966, Jap.) PR:A
RISE AND FALL OF LEGS DIAMOND, THE (1960) PR:C
RISE AND RISE OF MICHAEL RIMMER, THE (1970,
   Brit.) PR:C
RISE AND SHINE (1941) PR:A
RISE OF CATHERINE THE GREAT (SEE: CATHERINE
   THE GREAT) (1934, Brit.)
RISE OF HELGA, THE (SEE: SUSAN LENOX – HER
   FALL AND RISE) (1931)
RISE OF LOUIS XIV, THE (1966, Fr.) PR:A
RISING DAMP (1980, Brit.) PR:C
RISING OF THE MOON, THE (1957, Ireland) PR:A
RISING TO FAME (SEE: SUSAN LENOX – HER FALL
   AND RISE) (1931)
RISK, THE (1961, Brit.) PR:A
RISKY BUSINESS (1939) PR:A
RISKY BUSINESS (1983) PR:O
RISO AMARO (SEE: BITTER RICE) (1950, It.)
RITA (1963, Fr./It.) PR:C
RITA, SUE AND BOB TOO! (1987, Brit.) PR:O
RITEN (SEE: RITUAL, THE) (1970, Swed.)
RITRATTO DI BORGHESIA IN NERO (SEE: NEST OF
   VIPERS) (1979, It.)
RITUAL, THE (1970, Swed.) PR:O
RITUALS (SEE: CREEPER, THE) (1978, Can.)
RITZ, THE (1976, Brit.) PR:C-O
RIVALEN DER MANEGE (SEE: BIMBO THE GREAT)
   (1961, W. Ger.)
RIVALS, THE (1963, Brit.) PR:A
RIVALS (1972) PR:O
RIVE GAUCHE (SEE: DIE MANNER UM LUCIE) (1931,
   Fr./Ger.)
RIVER, THE (1928) PR:A
RIVER, THE (1951) PR:A
RIVER, THE (1961, India) PR:A
RIVER, THE (1984) PR:A-C
RIVER BEAT (1954, Brit.) PR:A
RIVER CHANGES, THE (1956) PR:A
RIVER GANG (1945) PR:A
RIVER HOUSE GHOST, THE (1932, Brit.) PR:A
RIVER HOUSE MYSTERY, THE (1935, Brit.) PR:A
RIVER LADY (1948) PR:A
RIVER NIGER, THE (1976) PR:O
RIVER OF FOREVER (1967, Jap.) PR:A-C
RIVER OF MISSING MEN (SEE: TRAPPED BY G-MEN)
   (1937)
RIVER OF NO RETURN (1954) PR:A
RIVER OF POISON (SEE: SOUTH OF DEATH VALLEY)
   (1949)
RIVER OF ROMANCE (1929) PR:A
RIVER OF UNREST (1937, Brit.) PR:A
RIVER RAT, THE (1984) PR:A
RIVER WOLVES, THE (1934, Brit.) PR:A
RIVER WOMAN, THE (1928) PR:A
RIVERBOAT RHYTHM (1946) PR:A
RIVERRUN (1968) PR:O
RIVER'S EDGE, THE (1957) PR:C
RIVER'S EDGE (1987) PR:O
RIVER'S END (1931) PR:A
RIVER'S END (1940) PR:A
RIVERSIDE MURDER, THE (1935, Brit.) PR:A
ROAD, THE (SEE: LA STRADA) (1954, It.)
ROAD AGENT (1941) PR:A
ROAD AGENT (1952) PR:A
ROAD BACK, THE (1937) PR:A
ROAD BUILDER, THE (SEE: NIGHT DIGGER, THE)
   (1971, Brit.)
ROAD DEMON (1938) PR:A
ROAD GANG (1936) PR:C
ROAD GANGS, ADVENTURES IN THE CREEP ZONE
   (SEE: SPACEHUNTER: ADVENTURES IN THE FOR-
   BIDDEN ZONE) (1983)
ROAD HOME, THE (1947, USSR) PR:A
ROAD HOUSE (1934, Brit.) PR:A
ROAD HOUSE (1948) PR:C
ROAD HOUSE (1989) PR:O
ROAD HUSTLERS, THE (1968) PR:C
ROAD IS FINE, THE (1930, Fr.) PR:A
ROAD MOVIE (1974) PR:O
ROAD SHOW (SEE: CHASING RAINBOWS) (1930)
ROAD SHOW (1941) PR:A
ROAD TO ALCATRAZ (1945) PR:A
ROAD TO BALI (1952) PR:AA
ROAD TO DENVER, THE (1955) PR:A
ROAD TO ETERNITY (1962, Jap.) PR:O
ROAD TO FORT ALAMO, THE (1966, Fr./It.) PR:C
ROAD TO FORTUNE, THE (1930, Brit.) PR:A
ROAD TO FRISCO (SEE: THEY DRIVE BY NIGHT)
   (1940)

ROAD TO GLORY, THE (1936) PR:A-C
ROAD TO HAPPINESS (1942) PR:A
ROAD TO HONG KONG, THE (1962, US/Brit.) PR:AA
ROAD TO LIFE (1932, USSR) PR:A
ROAD TO MOROCCO (1942) PR:AA
ROAD TO PARADISE (1930) PR:A
ROAD TO RENO, THE (1931) PR:A
ROAD TO RENO, THE (1938) PR:A
ROAD TO RIO (1947) PR:AA
ROAD TO RUIN (1934) PR:O
ROAD TO SALINA (1971, Fr./It.) PR:O
ROAD TO SHAME, THE (1962, Fr.) PR:C-O
ROAD TO SINGAPORE (1931) PR:A
ROAD TO SINGAPORE (1940) PR:AA
ROAD TO THE BIG HOUSE (1947) PR:A
ROAD TO UTOPIA (1945) PR:A
ROAD TO ZANZIBAR (1941) PR:AA
ROAD TRIP (SEE: JOCKS) (1987)
ROAD WARRIOR, THE (1982, Aus.) PR:O
ROAD WEST, THE (SEE: THIS SAVAGE LAND) (1969)
ROADBLOCK (1951) PR:A
ROADGAMES (1981, Aus.) PR:O
ROADHOUSE GIRL (SEE: MARILYN) (1953, Brit.)
ROADHOUSE MURDER, THE (1932) PR:A
ROADHOUSE NIGHTS (1930) PR:A
ROADHOUSE 66 (1984) PR:C
ROADIE (1980) PR:A-C
ROADRACERS, THE (1959) PR:A
ROAMING COWBOY, THE (1937) PR:A
ROAMING LADY (1936) PR:A
ROAR (1981) PR:A
ROAR OF THE CROWD (1953) PR:A
ROAR OF THE DRAGON (1932) PR:A
ROAR OF THE PRESS (1941) PR:A
ROARIN' GUNS (1936) PR:A
ROARIN' LEAD (1937) PR:A
ROARING CITY (1951) PR:A
ROARING RANCH (1930) PR:A
ROARING ROADS (1935) PR:A
ROARING SIX GUNS (1937) PR:A
ROARING TIMBER (1937) PR:A
ROARING TIMBERS (SEE: COME AND GET IT) (1936)
ROARING TWENTIES, THE (1939) PR:C
ROARING WESTWARD (1949) PR:A
ROB ROY (SEE: ROB ROY, THE HIGHLAND ROGUE)
   (1954, Brit.)
ROB ROY, THE HIGHLAND ROGUE (1954, Brit.) PR:A
ROBBER SYMPHONY, THE (1937, Brit.) PR:A
ROBBERS OF THE RANGE (1941) PR:A
ROBBERS' ROOST (1933) PR:A
ROBBER'S ROOST (1955) PR:A
ROBBERY (1967, Brit.) PR:A-C
ROBBERY UNDER ARMS (1958, Brit.) PR:A
ROBBERY WITH VIOLENCE (1958, Brit.) PR:A
ROBBO (SEE: ROBIN AND THE SEVEN HOODS) (1964)
ROBBY (1968) PR:AA
ROBE, THE (1953) PR:A
ROBERTA (1935) PR:A
ROBIN AND MARIAN (1976, Brit.) PR:A-C
ROBIN AND THE SEVEN HOODS (1964) PR:A-C
ROBIN HOOD (SEE: ADVENTURES OF ROBIN HOOD,
   THE) (1938)
ROBIN HOOD (SEE: STORY OF ROBIN HOOD, THE)
   (1952)
ROBIN HOOD (1973) PR:AA
ROBIN HOOD OF EL DORADO, THE (1936) PR:C
ROBIN HOOD OF TEXAS (1947) PR:A
ROBIN HOOD OF THE PECOS (1941) PR:A
ROBIN HOOD OF THE RANGE (1943) PR:A
ROBINSON CRUSOE (SEE: ADVENTURES OF ROBIN-
   SON CRUSOE, THE) (1952, Mex.)
ROBINSON CRUSOE ON MARS (1964) PR:A
ROBINSON CRUSOE-LAND (SEE: UTOPIA) (1950,
   Fr./It.)
ROBINSON SOLL NICHT STERBEN (SEE: GIRL AND
   THE LEGEND, THE) (1969, W. Ger.)
ROBINSON'S GARDEN (1988, Jap.) PR:O
ROBO DE DIAMANTES (SEE: RUN LIKE A THIEF)
   (1968, Sp.)
ROBO NO ISHI (SEE: WAYSIDE PEBBLE, THE) (1960,
   Jap.)
ROBOCOP (1987) PR:O
ROBOT HOLOCAUST (1987) PR:O
ROBOT MONSTER (1953) PR:A
ROBOT VS. THE AZTEC MUMMY, THE (1965, Mex.) PR:O
ROCCO AND HIS BROTHERS (1961, Fr./It.) PR:C
ROCCO E I SUOI FRATELLI (SEE: ROCCO AND HIS
   BROTHERS) (1961, Fr./It.)
ROCCO PAPALEO (1971, It./Fr.) PR:O
ROCK-A-BYE BABY (1958) PR:A
ROCK ALL NIGHT (1957) PR:A
ROCK AROUND THE CLOCK (1956) PR:A
ROCK AROUND THE WORLD (1957, Brit.) PR:A
ROCK BABY, ROCK IT (1957) PR:A
ROCK ISLAND TRAIL (1950) PR:A
ROCK 'N' ROLL HIGH SCHOOL (1979) PR:C
ROCK 'N' ROLL NIGHTMARE (1987, Can.) PR:O

ROCK 'N' ROLL WRESTLING WOMEN VS. THE
   AZTEC MUMMY (SEE: WRESTLING WOMEN VS.
   THE AZTEC MUMMY) (1964, Mex.)
ROCK, PRETTY BABY (1956) PR:A
ROCK RIVER RENEGADES (1942) PR:A
ROCK, ROCK, ROCK (1956) PR:A
ROCK YOU SINNERS (1957, Brit.) PR:A
ROCKABILLY BABY (1957) PR:A
ROCKABYE (1932) PR:A
ROCKERS (1980) PR:O
ROCKET ATTACK, U.S.A. (1961) PR:A
ROCKET FROM CALABUCH, THE (SEE: CALABUCH)
   (1956, Sp./It.)
ROCKET GIBRALTAR (1988) PR:A
ROCKET MAN, THE (1954) PR:A
ROCKET SHIP (SEE: FLASH GORDON) (1936)
ROCKET TO NOWHERE (1962, Czech.) PR:AA
ROCKET TO THE MOON (SEE: CAT WOMEN OF THE
   MOON) (1954)
ROCKETS GALORE (SEE: MAD LITTLE ISLAND)
   (1958, Brit.)
ROCKETS IN THE DUNES (1960, Brit.) PR:AA
ROCKETSHIP X-M (1950) PR:A
ROCKIN' IN THE ROCKIES (1945) PR:A
ROCKIN' ROAD TRIP (1986) PR:C-O
ROCKING HORSE WINNER, THE (1950, Brit.) PR:C-O
ROCKS OF VALPRE, THE (SEE: HIGH TREASON)
   (1937, Brit.)
ROCKY (1948) PR:A
ROCKY (1976) PR:A-C
ROCKY II (1979) PR:A-C
ROCKY III (1982) PR:A-C
ROCKY IV (1985) PR:C
ROCKY HORROR PICTURE SHOW, THE (1975, Brit.)
   PR:O
ROCKY MOUNTAIN (1950) PR:A
ROCKY MOUNTAIN MYSTERY (1935) PR:A
ROCKY MOUNTAIN RANGERS (1940) PR:A
ROCKY RHODES (1934) PR:A
RODAN (1956, Jap.) PR:A
RODEO (1952) PR:A
RODEO KING AND THE SENORITA (1951) PR:A
RODEO RHYTHM (1941) PR:AA
RODNIK DLIA ZHAZHDUSHCHIKH (SEE: SPRING
   FOR THE THIRSTY, A) (1988, USSR)
ROGER TOUHY, GANGSTER! (1944) PR:A-C
ROGUE COP (1954) PR:C
ROGUE OF THE RANGE (1937) PR:A
ROGUE OF THE RIO GRANDE (1930) PR:A
ROGUE RIVER (1951) PR:A
ROGUE SONG, THE (1930) PR:A
ROGUE'S GALLERY (SEE: DEVIL'S TRAIL, THE)
   (1942)
ROGUES GALLERY (1945) PR:A
ROGUE'S MARCH (1952) PR:A
ROGUES OF SHERWOOD FOREST (1950) PR:A
ROGUES' REGIMENT (1948) PR:A
ROGUES' TAVERN, THE (1936) PR:A
ROGUE'S YARN (1956, Brit.) PR:A
ROLL ALONG, COWBOY (1938) PR:A
ROLL ON (SEE: LAWLESS PLAINSMEN) (1942)
ROLL ON TEXAS MOON (1946) PR:A
ROLL, THUNDER, ROLL! (1949) PR:A
ROLL, WAGONS, ROLL (1939) PR:A
ROLLER BLADE (1986) PR:O
ROLLER BOOGIE (1979) PR:C
ROLLERBALL (1975) PR:O
ROLLERCOASTER (1977) PR:C-O
ROLLIN' HOME TO TEXAS (1941) PR:A
ROLLIN' PLAINS (1938) PR:A
ROLLIN' WESTWARD (1939) PR:A
ROLLING CARAVANS (1938) PR:A
ROLLING DOWN THE GREAT DIVIDE (1942) PR:A
ROLLING HOME (1935, Brit.) PR:A
ROLLING IN MONEY (1934, Brit.) PR:A
ROLLING THUNDER (1977) PR:O
ROLLOVER (1981) PR:O
ROMA (1972, It./Fr.) PR:O
ROMA, CITTA APERTA (SEE: OPEN CITY) (1945, It.)
ROMA CONTRO ROMA (SEE: WAR OF THE ZOMBIES,
   THE) (1970, US/Jap.)
ROMA RIVUOLE CESARE (SEE: ROME WANTS AN-
   OTHER CAESAR) (1974, It.)
ROMAN HOLIDAY (1953) PR:A
ROMAN POLANSKI'S DIARY OF FORBIDDEN
   DREAMS (SEE: DIARY OF FORBIDDEN DREAMS)
   (1972, It./Fr./W. Ger.)
ROMAN SCANDALS (1933) PR:A-C
ROMAN SPRING OF MRS. STONE, THE (1961, US/Brit.)
   PR:C
ROMANCE (1930) PR:A
ROMANCE A LA CARTE (1938, Brit.) PR:A
ROMANCE AND RHYTHM (SEE: COWBOY FROM
   BROOKLYN) (1938)
ROMANCE AND RICHES (1937, Brit.) PR:A
ROMANCE DA EMPREGADA (SEE: STORY OF
   FAUSTA) (1988, Braz.)

ROMANCE FOR THREE (SEE: PARADISE FOR THREE) (1938)
ROMANCE IN FLANDERS, A (SEE: LOST ON THE WESTERN FRONT) (1940, Brit.)
ROMANCE IN MANHATTAN (1935) PR:A
ROMANCE IN RHYTHM (1934, Brit.) PR:C
ROMANCE IN THE DARK (1938) PR:A
ROMANCE IN THE RAIN (1934) PR:A
ROMANCE IS SACRED (SEE: KING AND THE CHORUS GIRL, THE) (1937)
ROMANCE OF A HORSE THIEF (1971) PR:A
ROMANCE OF ROSY RIDGE, THE (1947) PR:A
ROMANCE OF SEVILLE, A (1929, Brit.) PR:A
ROMANCE OF THE LIMBERLOST (1938) PR:A
ROMANCE OF THE REDWOODS (1939) PR:A
ROMANCE OF THE RIO GRANDE (1929) PR:A
ROMANCE OF THE RIO GRANDE (1941) PR:A
ROMANCE OF THE ROCKIES (1938) PR:A
ROMANCE OF THE WEST (1946) PR:A
ROMANCE ON THE BEACH (SEE: SIN ON THE BEACH) (1964, Fr.)
ROMANCE ON THE HIGH SEAS (1948) PR:A
ROMANCE ON THE RANGE (1942) PR:A
ROMANCE ON THE RUN (1938) PR:A
ROMANCE RIDES THE RANGE (1936) PR:A
ROMANCING THE STONE (1984) PR:C-O
ROMANOFF AND JULIET (1961) PR:A
ROMANTIC AGE, THE (SEE: SISTERS UNDER THE SKIN) (1934)
ROMANTIC AGE, THE (SEE: NAUGHTY ARLETTE) (1951, Brit.)
ROMANTIC COMEDY (1983) PR:A-C
ROMANTIC ENGLISHWOMAN, THE (1975, Brit./Fr.) PR:O
ROMANY LOVE (1931, Brit.) PR:A
ROME ADVENTURE (1962) PR:A
ROME EXPRESS (1933, Brit.) PR:A
ROME, OPEN CITY (SEE: OPEN CITY) (1945, It.)
ROME WANTS ANOTHER CAESAR (1974, It.) PR:A
ROMEO AND JULIET (1936) PR:C
ROMEO AND JULIET (1954, Brit.) PR:A
ROMEO AND JULIET (1955, USSR) PR:A
ROMEO AND JULIET (1966, Brit.) PR:A
ROMEO AND JULIET (1968, Brit./It.) PR:C
ROMEO AND JULIET (1968, It./Sp.) PR:A-C
ROMEO AND JULIET, 1971 — A GENTLE TALE OF SEX, VIOLENCE, CORRUPTION AND MURDER (SEE: WHAT BECAME OF JACK AND JILL?) (1972, Brit.)
ROMEO IN PYJAMAS (SEE: PARLOR, BEDROOM, AND BATH) (1931)
ROMEO, JULIET AND DARKNESS (SEE: SWEET LIGHT IN A DARK ROOM) (1966, Czech.)
ROMERO (1989) PR:O
ROMMEL-DESERT FOX (SEE: DESERT FOX, THE) (1951)
ROMMEL'S TREASURE (1962, It.) PR:A
ROMOLO E REMO (SEE: DUEL OF THE TITANS) (1963, It.)
ROOF, THE (1933, Brit.) PR:A
ROOF GARDEN, THE (SEE: TERRACE, THE) (1964, Arg.)
ROOFTOPS (1989) PR:C
ROOGIE'S BUMP (1954) PR:A
ROOK, THE (SEE: SOMETHING FOR EVERYONE) (1970)
ROOKERY NOOK (SEE: ONE EMBARRASSING NIGHT) (1930, Brit.)
ROOKIE, THE (1959) PR:A
ROOKIE COP, THE (1939) PR:A
ROOKIE FIREMAN (1950) PR:A
ROOKIES (SEE: BUCK PRIVATES) (1941)
ROOKIES COME HOME (SEE: BUCK PRIVATES COME HOME) (1947)
ROOKIES IN BURMA (1943) PR:A
ROOKIES ON PARADE (1941) PR:A
ROOM AT THE TOP (1959, Brit.) PR:O
ROOM FOR A STRANGER (SEE: ADULTEROUS AFFAIR) (1966, Can.)
ROOM FOR ONE MORE (1952) PR:AA
ROOM FOR TWO (1940, Brit.) PR:A
ROOM 43 (1959, Brit.) PR:A
ROOM IN THE HOUSE (1955, Brit.) PR:A
ROOM SERVICE (1938) PR:A
ROOM TO LET (1949, Brit.) PR:A
ROOM UPSTAIRS, THE (1948, Fr.) PR:C
ROOM WITH A VIEW, A (1986, Brit.) PR:C
ROOMATES (SEE: MARCH OF THE SPRING HARE) (1969)
ROOMMATES (1962, Brit.) PR:AA
ROOMMATES (1971) PR:O
ROOMMATES, THE (1973) PR:O
ROONEY (1958, Brit.) PR:A
ROOSTER COGBURN (1975) PR:A
ROOT OF ALL EVIL, THE (1947, Brit.) PR:A
ROOTIN' TOOTIN' RHYTHM (1937) PR:A
ROOTS OF HEAVEN, THE (1958) PR:C
ROPE (1948) PR:C-O
ROPE (SEE: ROPE OF FLESH) (1965)

ROPE OF FLESH (1965) PR:O
ROPE OF SAND (1949) PR:A
ROSALIE (1937) PR:A
ROSARY, THE (1931, Brit.) PR:O
ROSARY MURDERS, THE (1987) PR:O
ROSE, THE (1979) PR:O
ROSE BERND (SEE: SINS OF ROSE BERND, THE) (1959, W. Ger.)
ROSE BOWL (1936) PR:A
ROSE BOWL STORY, THE (1952) PR:A
ROSE FOR EVERYONE, A (1967, It.) PR:O
ROSE GARDEN, THE (1989, W. Ger./US) PR:C
ROSE MARIE (1936) PR:AA
ROSE MARIE (1954) PR:AA
ROSE OF CIMARRON (1952) PR:A
ROSE OF THE RANCHO (1936) PR:A
ROSE OF THE RIO GRANDE (SEE: GOD'S COUNTRY AND THE MAN) (1931)
ROSE OF THE RIO GRANDE (1938) PR:A
ROSE OF THE YUKON (1949) PR:A
ROSE OF TRALEE (1938, Ireland) PR:A
ROSE OF TRALEE (1942, Brit.) PR:A
ROSE OF WASHINGTON SQUARE (1939) PR:A
ROSE TATTOO, THE (1955) PR:C-O
ROSEANNA MC COY (1949) PR:AA
ROSEBUD (1975) PR:C
ROSEBUD BEACH HOTEL, THE (1984) PR:C-O
ROSELAND (1977) PR:C
ROSEMARY (1960, W. Ger.) PR:C
ROSEMARY'S BABY (1968) PR:O
ROSEMARY'S KILLER (SEE: PROWLER, THE) (1981)
ROSEN FUR DEN STAATSANWALT (SEE: ROSES FOR THE PROSECUTOR) (1961, W. Ger.)
ROSES ARE RED (1947) PR:A
ROSES FOR THE PROSECUTOR (1961, W. Ger.) PR:A
ROSIE! (1967) PR:A
ROSIE, THE RIVETER (1944) PR:A
ROSMUNDA E ALBOINO (SEE: SWORD OF THE CONQUEROR) (1962, It.)
ROSSINI (1948, It.) PR:A
ROSSITER CASE, THE (1950, Brit.) PR:A
ROTHSCHILD (1938, Fr.) PR:A
ROTTEN APPLE, THE (1963) PR:O
ROTTEN TO THE CORE (1965, Brit.) PR:C
ROTWEILER: DOGS OF HELL (1984) PR:O
ROUGE BAISER (SEE: RED KISS) (1985, Fr./W. Ger.)
ROUGE OF THE NORTH (1988, Taiwan) PR:C
ROUGH AND THE SMOOTH, THE (SEE: PORTRAIT OF A SINNER) (1961, Brit.)
ROUGH CUT (1980, Brit.) PR:C
ROUGH NIGHT IN JERICHO (1967) PR:O
ROUGH RIDERS OF CHEYENNE (1945) PR:A
ROUGH RIDERS OF DURANGO (1951) PR:A
ROUGH RIDERS' ROUNDUP (1939) PR:A
ROUGH RIDIN' RHYTHM (1937) PR:A
ROUGH RIDING RANGER (1935) PR:A
ROUGH RIDING ROMEO (SEE: FLAMING GUNS) (1933)
ROUGH ROMANCE (1930) PR:A
ROUGH SHOOT (SEE: SHOOT FIRST) (1953, Brit.)
ROUGH, TOUGH AND READY (1945) PR:A
ROUGH, TOUGH WEST, THE (1952) PR:A
ROUGH WATERS (1930) PR:AA
ROUGHLY SPEAKING (1945) PR:A
ROUGHSHOD (1949) PR:A
ROUND MIDNIGHT (1986, Fr./US) PR:C
ROUND TRIP (1967) PR:C
ROUND UP, THE (1969, Hung.) PR:O
ROUNDERS, THE (1965) PR:A-C
ROUNDTRIP (SEE: ROUND TRIP) (1967)
ROUNDUP, THE (1941) PR:A
ROUNDUP TIME IN TEXAS (1937) PR:A
ROUSTABOUT (1964) PR:A
ROVER, THE (1967, It.) PR:C
ROVIN' TUMBLEWEEDS (1939) PR:A
ROVING ROGUE, A (SEE: OUTLAWS OF THE ROCKIES) (1945)
ROWDYMAN, THE (1973, Can.) PR:C
ROWING WITH THE WIND (1988, Sp.) PR:C
ROXANNE (1987) PR:A-C
ROXIE HART (1942) PR:A
ROYAL AFFAIR, A (1950, Fr.) PR:A
ROYAL AFFAIRS IN VERSAILLES (1957, Fr.) PR:A
ROYAL AFRICAN RIFLES, THE (1953) PR:A
ROYAL BED, THE (1931) PR:A
ROYAL BOX, THE (1930) PR:A
ROYAL CAVALCADE (SEE: REGAL CAVALCADE) (1935, Brit.)
ROYAL DEMAND, A (1933, Brit.) PR:A
ROYAL DIVORCE, A (1938, Brit.) PR:A
ROYAL EAGLE (1936, Brit.) PR:A
ROYAL FAMILY OF BROADWAY, THE (1930) PR:A
ROYAL FLASH (1975, Brit.) PR:A-C
ROYAL FLUSH (SEE: TWO GUYS FROM MILWAUKEE) (1946)
ROYAL GAME, THE (SEE: BRAINWASHED) (1961, W. Ger.)

ROYAL HUNT OF THE SUN, THE (1969, Brit.) PR:A
ROYAL MOUNTED PATROL, THE (1941) PR:A
ROYAL ROMANCE, A (1930) PR:A
ROYAL SCANDAL, A (1945) PR:C-O
ROYAL TRACK, THE (SEE: OBSESSION) (1968, Swed.)
ROYAL WALTZ, THE (1936) PR:A
ROYAL WEDDING (1951) PR:A
ROZMARNE LETO (SEE: CAPRICIOUS SUMMER) (1968, Czech.)
RUBA AL PROSSIMO TUO (SEE: FINE PAIR, A) (1969, It.)
RUBBER GUN, THE (1977, Can.) PR:C
RUBBER RACKETEERS (1942) PR:A
RUBY (1971) PR:C
RUBY (1977) PR:O
RUBY GENTRY (1952) PR:C-O
RUBY VIRGIN, THE (SEE: HELL'S ISLAND) (1955)
RUCKUS (1981) PR:C
RUDE AWAKENING (1989) PR:O
RUDE BOY (1980, Brit.) PR:O
RUDYARD KIPLING'S JUNGLE BOOK (SEE: JUNGLE BOOK) (1942)
RUE CASES NEGRES (SEE: SUGAR CANE ALLEY) (1983, Fr.)
RUGGED O'RIORDANS, THE (1949, Aus.) PR:A
RUGGLES OF RED GAP (1935) PR:A
RULER OF THE WORLD (SEE: MASTER OF THE WORLD) (1935, Ger.)
RULERS OF THE SEA (1939) PR:A
RULES OF THE GAME, THE (1939, Fr.) PR:C
RULING CLASS, THE (1972, Brit.) PR:O
RULING VOICE, THE (1931) PR:A
RUMBA (1935) PR:A
RUMBLE FISH (1983) PR:O
RUMBLE ON THE DOCKS (1956) PR:A
RUMMELPLATZ DER LIEBE (SEE: CIRCUS OF LOVE) (1958, W. Ger.)
RUMPELSTILTSKIN (1965, W. Ger.) PR:A
RUMPELSTILTSKIN (1987) PR:AA
RUMPELSTILZCHEN (SEE: RUMPELSTILTSKIN) (1965, W. Ger.)
RUN ACROSS THE RIVER (1961) PR:A
RUN, ANGEL, RUN! (1969) PR:O
RUN FOR COVER (1955) PR:A-C
RUN FOR THE HILLS (1953) PR:A
RUN FOR THE ROSES (1978) PR:C
RUN FOR THE SUN (1956) PR:A
RUN FOR YOUR MONEY, A (1950, Brit.) PR:A
RUN FOR YOUR WIFE (1966, Fr./It.) PR:C
RUN HERO RUN (SEE: HELL WITH HEROS, THE) (1968)
RUN HOME SLOW (1965) PR:C
RUN LIKE A THIEF (SEE: MAKE LIKE A THIEF) (1966, US/Fin.)
RUN LIKE A THIEF (1968, Sp.) PR:C
RUN OF THE ARROW (1957) PR:C-O
RUN ON GOLD, A (SEE: MIDAS RUN) (1969)
RUN SHADOW RUN (SEE: COVER ME BABE) (1970)
RUN SILENT, RUN DEEP (1958) PR:A-C
RUN, STRANGER, RUN (SEE: HAPPY MOTHER'S DAY. . . LOVE, GEORGE) (1973)
RUN WILD, RUN FREE (1969, Brit.) PR:A
RUN WITH THE DEVIL (1963, Fr./It.) PR:A
RUN WITH THE WIND (1966, Brit.) PR:O
RUN, REBEL, RUN (SEE: WHERE'S JACK?) (1969, Brit.)
RUNAROUND, THE (1931) PR:A
RUNAROUND, THE (1946) PR:A
RUNAWAY, THE (1964, Brit.) PR:A
RUNAWAY (1984) PR:C-O
RUNAWAY BRIDE, THE (1930) PR:A
RUNAWAY BUS, THE (1954, Brit.) PR:A
RUNAWAY DAUGHTER (SEE: RED SALUTE) (1935)
RUNAWAY DAUGHTERS (1957) PR:A
RUNAWAY DAUGHTERS (SEE: PROWL GIRLS) (1968)
RUNAWAY GIRL (1966) PR:C
RUNAWAY LADIES (1935, Brit.) PR:A
RUNAWAY QUEEN, THE (1935, Brit.) PR:A
RUNAWAY RAILWAY (1965, Brit.) PR:AA
RUNAWAY TRAIN (1985) PR:O
RUNAWAYS, THE (SEE: SOUTH BRONX HEROES) (1985)
RUNNER STUMBLES, THE (1979) PR:C
RUNNERS (1983, Brit.) PR:A
RUNNING (1979, Can.) PR:C
RUNNING BRAVE (1983, Can.) PR:C
RUNNING HOT (1984) PR:O
RUNNING MAN, THE (1963, Brit.) PR:A-C
RUNNING MAN, THE (1987) PR:O
RUNNING ON EMPTY (1988) PR:C
RUNNING OUT OF LUCK (1986) PR:O
RUNNING SCARED (SEE: GHOST AND MR. CHICKEN, THE) (1966)
RUNNING SCARED (1972, Brit.) PR:C-O
RUNNING SCARED (1986) PR:C-O
RUNNING TARGET (1956) PR:A
RUNNING WILD (1955) PR:A
RUNNING WILD (1973) PR:AA
RUSH (1984, It.) PR:C-O

RUSSIAN ROULETTE (1975) PR:C
*RUSSIANS ARE COMING, THE RUSSIANS ARE COM-
ING, THE* (1966) PR:A
RUSSKIES (1987) PR:A
RUSTLERS (1949) PR:A
RUSTLER'S HIDEOUT (1944) PR:A
RUSTLERS OF DEVIL'S CANYON (1947) PR:A
RUSTLERS ON HORSEBACK (1950) PR:A
RUSTLERS' PARADISE (1935) PR:A
RUSTLERS' RHAPSODY (1985) PR:C
RUSTLERS' ROUNDUP (1933) PR:A
RUSTLER'S ROUNDUP (1946) PR:A
RUSTLER'S VALLEY (1937) PR:A
RUSTY LEADS THE WAY (1948) PR:A
RUSTY RIDES ALONE (1933) PR:A
RUSTY SAVES A LIFE (1949) PR:A
RUSTY'S BIRTHDAY (1949) PR:A
RUTHLESS (1948) PR:A
RUTHLESS FOUR, THE (1969, It./W. Ger.) PR:C
RUTHLESS PEOPLE (1986) PR:C-O
RUUSUJEN AIKA (SEE: TIME OF ROSES) (1970, Fin.)
RUY BLAS (1948, Fr.) PR:A
RX MURDER (1958, Brit.) PR:A
RYAN'S DAUGHTER (1970, Brit.) PR:O
RYDER, P.I. (1986) PR:C-O
RYMDINVASION I LAPPLAND (SEE: INVASION OF
THE ANIMAL PEOPLE) (1962, US/Swed.)
RYSOPIS (SEE: IDENTIFICATION MARKS: NONE)
(1969, Pol.)

S

S LYUBOV I NEZHNOST (SEE: WITH LOVE AND TEN-
DERNESS) (1978, Bulgaria)
S.O.B. (1981) PR:O
S.O.S. ICEBERG (1933) PR:A
S.O.S. TIDAL WAVE (1939) PR:A
S.T.A.B. (1976, Hong Kong/Thai.) PR:O
S.W.A.L.K. (SEE: MELODY) (1971, Brit.)
SAADIA (1953) PR:A
SABAKA (SEE: HINDU, THE) (1953)
SABALEROS (SEE: PUT UP OR SHUT UP) (1968, Arg.)
SABATA (1969, It.) PR:C
SABINA, THE (1979, Sp./Swed.) PR:O
SABOTAGE (SEE: WHEN LONDON SLEEPS) (1934,
Brit.)
SABOTAGE (1937, Brit.) PR:O
SABOTAGE (1939) PR:A
SABOTAGE AT SEA (1942, Brit.) PR:A
SABOTAGE SQUAD (1942) PR:A
SABOTEUR (1942) PR:A
SABOTEUR, CODE NAME MORITURI (SEE:
MORITURI) (1965)
SABRA (1970, Fr./It./Israel) PR:C
SABRE AND THE ARROW, THE (SEE: LAST OF THE
COMANCHES, THE) (1952)
SABRE JET (1953) PR:A
SABRINA (1954) PR:A
SABRINA FAIR (SEE: SABRINA) (1954)
SABU AND THE MAGIC RING (1957) PR:A
SACCO AND VANZETTI (1971, It./Fr.) PR:C
SACRED FLAME, THE (1929) PR:A
SACRED FLAME, THE (SEE: RIGHT TO LIVE, THE)
(1935)
SACRED GROUND (1984) PR:C
SACRED HEARTS (1984, Brit.) PR:A
SACRED KNIVES OF VENGEANCE, THE (1974, Hong
Kong) PR:O
SACRIFICE (1986, Fr./Swed.) PR:C
SACRIFICE D'HONNEUR (SEE: SCACRIFICE OF
HONOR) (1938, Fr.)
SACRIFICE OF HONOR (1938, Fr.) PR:A
SAD HORSE, THE (1959) PR:AA
SAD SACK, THE (1957) PR:A
SAD SACK, THE (SEE: ARMY GAME, THE) (1963, Fr.)
SADDLE BUSTER, THE (1932) PR:A
SADDLE LEGION (1951) PR:A
SADDLE MOUNTAIN ROUNDUP (1941) PR:A
SADDLE PALS (1947) PR:A
SADDLE THE WIND (1958) PR:A
SADDLE TRAMP (1950) PR:A
SADDLEMATES (1941) PR:A
SADIE MCKEE (1934) PR:A
SADIST, THE (1963) PR:A
SADKO (SEE: MAGIC VOYAGE OF SINBAD, THE)
(1962, USSR)
SAFARI (1940) PR:A
SAFARI (1956, Brit.) PR:A
SAFARI DRUMS (1953) PR:A
SAFARI 3000 (1982) PR:A-C
SAFE AFFAIR, A (1931, Brit.) PR:A
SAFE AT HOME! (1962) PR:A
SAFE IN HELL (1931) PR:C
SAFE PLACE, A (1971) PR:A
SAFECRACKER, THE (1958, Brit.) PR:A
SAFETY IN NUMBERS (1930) PR:A
SAFETY IN NUMBERS (1938) PR:A
SAFFO, VENERE DE LESBO (SEE: WARRIOR EM-
PRESS, THE) (1961, Fr./It.)

SAGA OF DEATH VALLEY (1939) PR:A
SAGA OF DRACULA, THE (1975, Sp.) PR:O
SAGA OF HEMP BROWN, THE (1958) PR:A
SAGA OF THE FLYING HOSTESS (SEE: GIRL GAME)
(1968, Braz./Fr./It.)
SAGA OF THE ROAD, THE (SEE: PATHER PANCHALI)
(1955, India)
SAGA OF THE VAGABONDS (1964, Jap.) PR:A
SAGA OF THE VIKING WOMEN AND THEIR VOYAGE
TO THE WATERS OF THE GREAT SEA SERPENT,
THE (1957) PR:A
SAGEBRUSH FAMILY TRAILS WEST, THE (1940) PR:A
SAGEBRUSH LAW (1943) PR:A
SAGEBRUSH POLITICS (1930) PR:A
SAGEBRUSH TRAIL (1934) PR:A
SAGEBRUSH TROUBADOR, THE (1935) PR:A
SAGINAW TRAIL (1953) PR:A
SAHARA (1943) PR:A
SAHARA (1984) PR:C
SAID O'REILLY TO MACNAB (SEE: SEZ O'REILLY TO
MACNAB) (1938, Brit.)
SAIGON (1948) PR:A
SAIGON (SEE: OFF LIMITS) (1988)
SAIKAKU ICHIDAI ONNA (SEE: LIFE OF OHARU)
(1964, Jap.)
SAIL A CROOKED SHIP (1961) PR:A
SAIL INTO DANGER (1957, Brit.) PR:A
SAILING ALONG (1938, Brit.) PR:A
SAILOR BE GOOD (1933) PR:A
SAILOR BEWARE (1951) PR:A
SAILOR BEWARE? (SEE: PANIC IN THE PARLOUR)
(1956, Brit.)
SAILOR FROM GIBRALTAR, THE (1967, Brit.) PR:O
SAILOR OF THE KING (1953, Brit.) PR:A
SAILOR TAKES A WIFE, THE (1946) PR:A
SAILOR WHO FELL FROM GRACE WITH THE SEA, THE
(1976, Brit.) PR:O
SAILORS DON'T CARE (1940, Brit.) PR:A
SAILOR'S HOLIDAY (1929) PR:A
SAILOR'S HOLIDAY (1944) PR:A
SAILOR'S LADY (1940) PR:A
SAILOR'S LUCK (1933) PR:A
SAILORS ON LEAVE (1941) PR:A
SAILOR'S RETURN, THE (1978, Brit.) PR:O
SAILORS THREE (SEE: THREE COCKEYED SAILORS)
(1940, Brit.)
ST. BENNY THE DIP (1951) PR:A
ST. ELMO'S FIRE (1985) PR:O
ST. GEORGE AND THE 7 CURSES (SEE: MAGIC
SWORD, THE) (1962)
ST. HELENS (1981) PR:A
SAINT IN LONDON, THE (1939, Brit.) PR:A
SAINT IN NEW YORK, THE (1938) PR:A
SAINT IN PALM SPRINGS, THE (1941) PR:A
ST. IVES (1976) PR:O
SAINT JACK (1979) PR:O
SAINT JOAN (1957, Brit.) PR:A-C
ST. LOUIS BLUES (1939) PR:A
ST. LOUIS BLUES (1958) PR:A
ST. LOUIS KID, THE (1934) PR:A
ST. MARTIN'S LANE (SEE: SIDEWALKS OF LONDON)
(1940, Brit.)
SAINT MEETS THE TIGER, THE (1943, Brit.) PR:A
SAINT STRIKES BACK, THE (1939) PR:A
SAINT TAKES OVER, THE (1940) PR:A
ST. VALENTINE'S DAY MASSACRE, THE (1967) PR:O
SAINTED SISTERS, THE (1948) PR:A
SAINTLY SINNERS (1962) PR:A
SAINTS AND SINNERS (1949, Brit.) PR:A
SAINT'S DOUBLE TROUBLE, THE (1940) PR:A
SAINT'S GIRL FRIDAY, THE (1954, Brit.) PR:A
SAINT'S RETURN, THE (SEE: SAINT'S GIRL FRIDAY,
THE) (1954, Brit.)
SAINT'S VACATION, THE (1941, Brit.) PR:A
SAL OF SINGAPORE (1929) PR:A
SALAAM BOMBAY! (1988, India) PR:O
SALAMANDER, THE (1983, US/It./Brit.) PR:O
SALAMMBO (SEE: LOVES OF SALAMMBO, THE)
(1962, Fr./It.)
SALARIO PARA MATAR (SEE: MERCENARY, THE)
(1970, It./Sp.)
SALERNO BEACHHEAD (SEE: WALK IN THE SUN, A)
(1945)
SALESLADY (1938) PR:A
SALLAH (1965, Israel) PR:C
SALLY (1929) PR:A
SALLY AND SAINT ANNE (1952) PR:A
SALLY BISHOP (1932, Brit.) PR:C
SALLY FIELDGOOD & CO. (1975, Can.) PR:C-O
SALLY IN OUR ALLEY (1931, Brit.) PR:A
SALLY, IRENE AND MARY (1938) PR:A
SALLY OF THE SUBWAY (1932) PR:C
SALLY'S HOUNDS (1968) PR:C
SALLY'S IRISH ROGUE (SEE: POACHER'S DAUGH-
TER, THE) (1958, Brit.)
SALOME (1953) PR:C
SALOME (1986, Fr./It.) PR:O
SALOME, WHERE SHE DANCED (1945) PR:C

SALOME'S LAST DANCE (1988, Brit.) PR:O
SALOMY JANE (SEE: WILD GIRL) (1932)
SALOON BAR (1940, Brit.) PR:C
SALSA (1988) PR:C
SALT & PEPPER (1968, US/Brit.) PR:C
SALT AND THE DEVIL (SEE: SALT TO THE DEVIL)
(1949, Brit.)
SALT LAKE RAIDERS (1950) PR:A
SALT OF THE EARTH (1954) PR:C
SALT TO THE DEVIL (1949, Brit.) PR:A
SALTO (1966, Pol.) PR:O
SALTO MORTALE (SEE: TRAPEZE) (1932, Ger.)
SALTY (1975) PR:A
SALTY O'ROURKE (1945) PR:A-C
SALUTE (1929) PR:A
SALUTE FOR THREE (1943) PR:A
SALUTE JOHN CITIZEN (1942, Brit.) PR:A
SALUTE THE TOFF (1952, Brit.) PR:A
SALUTE TO A REBEL (SEE: PATTON) (1970)
SALUTE TO COURAGE (SEE: NAZI AGENT) (1942)
SALUTE TO ROMANCE (SEE: ANNAPOLIS SALUTE)
(1937)
SALUTE TO THE MARINES (1943) PR:C
SALVADOR (1986, Brit.) PR:O
SALVAGE GANG, THE (1958, Brit.) PR:AA
SALVARE LA FACCIA (SEE: PSYCHOUT FOR MUR-
DER) (1971, Arg./It.)
SALVATION! (1987) PR:O
SALVATION NELL (1931) PR:A
SALVATORE GIULIANO (1966, It.) PR:O
SALZBURG CONNECTION, THE (1972) PR:C
SAM COOPER'S GOLD (SEE: RUTHLESS FOUR, THE)
(1969, It./W. Ger.)
SAM MARLOW, PRIVATE EYE (SEE: MAN WITH
BOGART'S FACE, THE) (1980)
SAM SMALL LEAVES TOWN (1937, Brit.) PR:A
SAM WHISKEY (1969) PR:C-O
SAMANTHA (SEE: NEW KIND OF LOVE, A) (1963)
SAMAR (1962) PR:C
SAMARITAN, THE (SEE: SOUL OF THE SLUMS) (1931)
SAME TIME, NEXT YEAR (1978) PR:A-C
SAME TO YOU (1987, Switz/W. Ger.) PR:O
SAMMY AND ROSIE GET LAID (1987, Brit.) PR:O
SAMMY GOING SOUTH (SEE: BOY TEN FEET TALL,
A) (1965, Brit.)
SAMMY STOPS THE WORLD (1978) PR:C
SAMPO (SEE: DAY THE EARTH FROZE, THE) (1959,
USSR/Fin.)
SAM'S SON (1984) PR:A-C
SAM'S SONG (1971) PR:O
SAMSON (1961, It.) PR:A
SAMSON AND DELILAH (1949) PR:C
SAMSON AND THE SEVEN MIRACLES OF THE
WORLD (1963, Fr./It.) PR:A
SAMSON AND THE SLAVE QUEEN (1963, It.) PR:A
SAMSON IN THE WAX MUSEUM (SEE: SANTO EN EL
MUSEO DE CERA) (1963, Mex.)
SAMSON VS. THE GIANT KING (SEE: ATLAS
AGAINST THE CZAR) (1964, It.)
SAMURAI (1945) PR:A-C
SAMURAI ASSASSIN (1965, Jap.) PR:O
SAMURAI (1954, Jap.) PR:O
SAMURAI BANNERS (SEE: UNDER THE BANNER OF
SAMURAI) (1964, Jap.)
SAMURAI (SEE: SAMURAI ASSASSIN) (1965, Jap.)
SAMURAI FROM NOWHERE (1964, Jap.) PR:C
SAMURAI (PART II) (1967, Jap.) PR:C-O
SAMURAI (PART III) (1967, Jap.) PR:C-O
SAMURAI PIRATE (SEE: LOST WORLD OF SINBAD,
THE) (1965, Jap.)
SAN ANTONE (1953) PR:C
SAN ANTONE AMBUSH (1949) PR:A
SAN ANTONIO (1945) PR:A-C
SAN ANTONIO KID, THE (1944) PR:A
SAN ANTONIO ROSE (1941) PR:A
SAN DEMETRIO, LONDON (1947, Brit.) PR:C
SAN DIEGO, I LOVE YOU (1944) PR:A
SAN FERNANDO VALLEY (1944) PR:A
SAN FERRY ANN (1965, Brit.) PR:A
SAN FRANCISCO (1936) PR:A
SAN FRANCISCO DOCKS (1941) PR:A
SAN FRANCISCO STORY, THE (1952) PR:A
SAN QUENTIN (1937) PR:C
SAN QUENTIN (1946) PR:A
SANCTUARY (1961) PR:O
SAND (1949) PR:A
SAND AND BLOOD (1989, Fr.) PR:O
SAND CASTLE, THE (1961) PR:AA
SAND PEBBLES, THE (1966) PR:C-O
SANDA TAI GAILAH (SEE: WAR OF THE GAR-
GANTUAS, THE) (1970, US/Jap.)
SANDAI KAIJU CHIKYU SAIDAI NO KESSEN (SEE:
GHIDRAH, THE THREE-HEADED MONSTER) (1965,
Jap.)
SANDERS (1963, Brit.) PR:A
SANDERS OF THE RIVER (1935, Brit.) PR:A-C
SANDFLOW (1937) PR:A
SANDOKAN THE GREAT (1964, Fr./It./Sp.) PR:A

SANDPIPER, THE (1965) PR:C-O
SANDPIT GENERALS, THE (SEE: WILD PACK, THE) (1972)
SANDRA (1966, It.) PR:O
SANDS OF BEERSHEBA (1966, US/Israel) PR:O
SANDS OF IWO JIMA (1949) PR:C
SANDS OF THE DESERT (1960, Brit.) PR:A
SANDS OF THE KALAHARI (1965, Brit.) PR:O
SANDU FOLLOWS THE SUN (1965, USSR) PR:AA
SANDWICH MAN, THE (1966, Brit.) PR:A
SANDY GETS HER MAN (1940) PR:AA
SANDY IS A LADY (1940) PR:AA
SANDY TAKES A BOW (SEE: UNEXPECTED FATHER) (1939)
SANDY THE SEAL (1969, Brit.) PR:AA
SANG ET LUMIERES (SEE: LOVE IN A HOT CLI-MATE) (1958)
SANGAREE (1953) PR:C
SANITORIUM (SEE: TRIO) (1950, Brit.)
SANJURO (1962, Jap.) PR:C
SANS MOBILE APPARENT (SEE: WITHOUT APPAR-ENT MOTIVE) (1972, Fr.)
SANS TAMBOUR NI TROMPETTE (SEE: DIE GANS VON SEDAN) (1962, Fr./W. Ger.)
SANS TOIT NI LOI (SEE: VAGABOND) (1985, Fr.)
SANSHO DAYU (SEE: SANSHO THE BAILIFF) (1954, Jap.)
SANSHO THE BAILIFF (1954, Jap.) PR:A
SANSONE (SEE: SAMSON) (1961, It.)
SANTA (1932, Mex.) PR:O
SANTA AND THE THREE BEARS (1970) PR:AA
SANTA CLAUS (1960, Mex.) PR:AA
SANTA CLAUS CONQUERS THE MARTIANS (1964) PR:C-O
SANTA CLAUS: THE MOVIE (1985) PR:A
SANTA FE (1951) PR:A
SANTA FE BOUND (1937) PR:A
SANTA FE MARSHAL (1940) PR:A
SANTA FE PASSAGE (1955) PR:O
SANTA FE SADDLEMATES (1945) PR:A
SANTA FE SATAN (SEE: CATCH MY SOUL) (1974)
SANTA FE SCOUTS (1943) PR:A
SANTA FE STAMPEDE (1938) PR:C
SANTA FE TRAIL, THE (1930) PR:A
SANTA FE TRAIL (1940) PR:C
SANTA FE UPRISING (1946) PR:A
SANTA'S CHRISTMAS CIRCUS (1966) PR:AA
SANTEE (1973) PR:O
SANTIAGO (1956) PR:A
SANTO AND THE BLUE DEMON VS. THE MONSTERS (SEE: SANTO Y BLUE DEMON CONTRA LOS MON-STROUS) (1968, Mex.)
SANTO CONTRA BLUE DEMON EN LA ATLANTIDA (1968, Mex.) PR:O
SANTO CONTRA EL CEREBRO DIABOLICO (1962, Mex.) PR:C
SANTO CONTRA EL DOCTOR MUERTE (1974, Sp./Mex.) PR:O
SANTO CONTRA LA HIJA DE FRANKENSTEIN (1971, Mex.) PR:O
SANTO CONTRA LA INVASION DE LOS MARCIANOS (1966, Mex.) PR:O
SANTO EN EL MUSEO DE CERA (1963, Mex.) PR:O
SANTO EN LA VENGANZA DE LAS MUJERES VAMPIRO (SEE: VENGEANCE OF THE VAMPIRE WOMEN, THE) (1969, Mex.)
SANTO VERSUS THE MARTIAN INVASION (SEE: SANTO CONTRA LA INVASION DE LOS MARCIA-NOS) (1966, Mex.)
SANTO Y BLUE DEMON CONTRA LOS MONSTRUOS (1968, Mex.) PR:O
SAP, THE (1929) PR:A
SAP FROM ABROAD, THE (SEE: SAP FROM SYRA-CUSE, THE) (1930)
SAP FROM SYRACUSE, THE (1930) PR:A
SAPHO (SEE: WARRIOR EMPRESS, THE) (1961, Fr./It.)
SAPPHIRE (1959, Brit.) PR:A
SAPS AT SEA (1940) PR:A
SARABA MOSUKUWA GURENTAI (SEE: GOODBYE MOSCOW) (1968, Jap.)
SARABAND (1949, Brit.) PR:A
SARABAND FOR DEAD LOVERS (SEE: SARABAND) (1949, Brit.)
SARACEN BLADE, THE (1954) PR:A
SARAGOSSA MANUSCRIPT, THE (1966, Pol.) PR:A
SARAH AND SON (1930) PR:A
SARATOGA (1937) PR:A
SARATOGA TRUNK (1945) PR:A-C
SARDINIA: RANSOM (1968, It.) PR:C
SARDONICUS (SEE: MR. SARDONICUS) (1961)
SARGE GOES TO COLLEGE (1947) PR:A
SARONG GIRL (1943) PR:A
SARUMBA (1950) PR:A
SASAKI KOJIRO (SEE: KOJIRO) (1967, Jap.)
SASAYASHI NO JOE (SEE: WHISPERING JOE) (1969, Jap.)
SASKATCHEWAN (1954) PR:A-C

SASOM I EN SPEGEL (SEE: THROUGH A GLASS DARKLY) (1961, Swed.)
SASQUATCH (1978) PR:A
SATAN BUG, THE (1965) PR:A
SATAN IN HIGH HEELS (1962) PR:O
SATAN MET A LADY (1936) PR:A
SATAN NEVER SLEEPS (1962) PR:C
SATANIC RITES OF DRACULA, THE (SEE: COUNT DRACULA AND HIS VAMPIRE BRIDE) (1978, Brit.)
SATAN'S BED (1965) PR:O
SATAN'S CHEERLEADERS (1977) PR:O
SATAN'S CLAW (SEE: BLOOD ON SATAN'S CLAW, THE) (1970, Brit.)
SATAN'S CRADLE (1949) PR:A
SATAN'S MISTRESS (1982) PR:O
SATAN'S SADISTS (1969) PR:O
SATAN'S SATELLITES (1958) PR:AA
SATAN'S SKIN (SEE: BLOOD ON SATAN'S CLAW, THE) (1970, Brit.)
SATAN'S SLAVE (1976, Brit.) PR:O
SATELLITE IN THE SKY (1956, Brit.) PR:A
SATELLITE OF BLOOD (SEE: FIRST MAN INTO SPACE) (1959, Brit.)
SATIN MUSHROOM, THE (1969) PR:C
SATIN VENGEANCE (SEE: NAKED VENGEANCE) (1986, US/Phil.)
SATISFACTION (1988) PR:C-O
SATURDAY ISLAND (SEE: ISLAND OF DESIRE) (1952, Brit.)
SATURDAY NIGHT AND SUNDAY MORNING (1961, Brit.) PR:O
SATURDAY NIGHT AT THE BATHS (1975) PR:O
SATURDAY NIGHT AT THE PALACE (1987. South Af-rica) PR:C
SATURDAY NIGHT FEVER (1977) PR:C-O
SATURDAY NIGHT IN APPLE VALLEY (1965) PR:C
SATURDAY NIGHT KID, THE (1929) PR:A
SATURDAY NIGHT OUT (1964, Brit.) PR:A
SATURDAY NIGHT REVUE (1937, Brit.) PR:A
SATURDAY THE 14TH (1981) PR:A
SATURDAY THE 14TH STRIKES BACK (1989) PR:A
SATURDAY'S CHILDREN (1929) PR:A
SATURDAY'S CHILDREN (1940) PR:A
SATURDAY'S HERO (1951) PR:A
SATURDAY'S HEROES (1937) PR:A
SATURDAY'S MILLIONS (1933) PR:A
SATURN 3 (1980) PR:C
SATYRICON (SEE: FELLINI SATYRICON) (1969, Fr./It.)
SAUL AND DAVID (1968, It./Sp.) PR:A
SAUTERELLE (SEE: FEMMINA) (1968, Fr./It./W. Ger.)
SAUVE QUI PEUT/LA VIE (SEE: EVERY MAN FOR HIMSELF) (1980, Fr.)
SAVAGE, THE (1953) PR:A
SAVAGE! (1962) PR:A
SAVAGE ABDUCTION (1975) PR:O
SAVAGE, THE (1975, Fr.) PR:C
SAVAGE AMERICAN, THE (SEE: TALISMAN, THE) (1966)
SAVAGE APOCALYPSE (SEE: CANNIBALS IN THE STREETS) (1982, It./Sp.)
SAVAGE BRIGADE (1948, Fr.) PR:A
SAVAGE DAWN (1984) PR:O
SAVAGE DRUMS (1951) PR:A
SAVAGE EYE, THE (1960) PR:C-O
SAVAGE FRONTIER (1953) PR:A
SAVAGE GIRL, THE (1932) PR:A
SAVAGE GOLD (1933) PR:C
SAVAGE GUNS, THE (1962, US/Sp.) PR:A
SAVAGE HARVEST (1981) PR:A
SAVAGE HORDE, THE (1950) PR:A
SAVAGE INNOCENTS, THE (1960, Fr./It./Brit.) PR:A
SAVAGE IS LOOSE, THE (1974) PR:O
SAVAGE ISLAND (1985, US/It./Sp.) PR:O
SAVAGE ISLANDS (SEE: NATE AND HAYES) (1983, US/New Zealand)
SAVAGE MESSIAH (1972, Brit.) PR:O
SAVAGE MUTINY (1953) PR:A
SAVAGE PAMPAS (1967, US/Sp./Arg.) PR:C
SAVAGE SAM (1963) PR:A
SAVAGE SEVEN, THE (1968) PR:O
SAVAGE SISTERS (1974) PR:O
SAVAGE STREETS (1984) PR:O
SAVAGE WEEKEND (1983) PR:O
SAVAGE WILD, THE (1970) PR:A
SAVAGE WILDERNESS (SEE: LAST FRONTIER, THE) (1955)
SAVAGES (1972) PR:O
SAVAGES FROM HELL (1968) PR:O
SAVANNAH SMILES (1983) PR:AA
SAVE A LITTLE SUNSHINE (1938, Brit.) PR:A
SAVE THE TIGER (1973) PR:C-O
SAVING GRACE (1986) PR:A
SAWDUST AND TINSEL (SEE: NAKED NIGHT, THE) (1953, Swed.)
SAXO (1988, Fr.) PR:O
SAXON CHARM, THE (1948) PR:A
SAY ANYTHING (1989) PR:A-C
SAY HELLO TO YESTERDAY (1971, Brit.) PR:C

SAY IT IN FRENCH (1938) PR:A
SAY IT WITH DIAMONDS (1935, Brit.) PR:A
SAY IT WITH FLOWERS (1934, Brit.) PR:A
SAY IT WITH MUSIC (1932, Brit.) PR:A
SAY IT WITH SONGS (1929) PR:A
SAY ONE FOR ME (1959) PR:C
SAY YES (1986) PR:O
SAYAT NOVA (SEE: COLOR OF POMEGRANATES, THE) (1980, USSR)
SAYONARA (1957) PR:C
SCALAWAG (1973, Yugo.) PR:A
SCALPEL (1976) PR:O
SCALPHUNTERS, THE (1968) PR:C-O
SCALPS (1983) PR:O
SCAMP, THE (SEE: STRANGE AFFECTION) (1957, Brit.)
SCANDAL (1929) PR:A
SCANDAL (1964, Jap.) PR:A
SCANDAL (1989, Brit.) PR:O
SCANDAL AT SCOURIE (1953) PR:A
SCANDAL FOR SALE (1932) PR:A
SCANDAL IN DENMARK (1970, Den.) PR:O
SCANDAL IN PARIS, A (1946) PR:A
SCANDAL IN SORRENTO (1957, It./Fr.) PR:O
SCANDAL INCORPORATED (1956) PR:A
SCANDAL SHEET (1931) PR:A
SCANDAL SHEET (1940) PR:A
SCANDAL SHEET (1931) PR:C
SCANDAL '64 (SEE: CHRISTINE KEELER AFFAIR, THE) (1964, Brit.)
SCANDAL STREET (1938) PR:A
SCANDALOUS (1984, Brit.) PR:C
SCANDALOUS ADVENTURES OF BURAIKAN, THE (1970, Jap.) PR:C
SCANDALS (SEE: GEORGE WHITE'S SCANDALS) (1934)
SCANDALS OF PARIS (1935, Brit.) PR:A
SCANNERS (1981, Can.) PR:O
SCAPEGOAT, THE (1959, Brit.) PR:A
SCAPPAMENTO APERTO (SEE: BACKFIRE) (1965, Fr.)
SCAR, THE (SEE: HOLLOW TRIUMPH) (1948)
SCARAB (1982, US/Sp.) PR:O
SCARAB MURDER CASE, THE (1936, Brit.) PR:A
SCARAMOUCHE (1952) PR:A
SCARAMOUCHE (SEE: ADVENTURES OF SCARA-MOUCHE, THE) (1964, Fr./It./Sp.)
SCARECROW (1973) PR:C-O
SCARECROW, THE (1982, New Zealand) PR:C
SCARECROW IN A GARDEN OF CUCUMBERS (1972) PR:C
SCARECROWS (1988) PR:O
SCARED STIFF (1945) PR:A
SCARED STIFF (1953) PR:A
SCARED TO DEATH (1947) PR:A
SCARED TO DEATH (1981) PR:O
SCAREHEADS (1931) PR:A
SCAREMAKER, THE (SEE: GIRLS NITE OUT) (1984)
SCARF, THE (1951) PR:A
SCARFACE (1932) PR:O
SCARFACE (1983) PR:O
SCARFACE MOB, THE (1962) PR:A
SCARLET ANGEL (1952) PR:A
SCARLET BLADE, THE (SEE: CRIMSON BLADE, THE) (1964, Brit.)
SCARLET BRAND, THE (1932) PR:A
SCARLET BUCCANEER, THE (SEE: SWASHBUCK-LER) (1976)
SCARLET CAMELLIA, THE (1965, Jap.) PR:C
SCARLET CLAW, THE (1944) PR:A
SCARLET CLUE, THE (1945) PR:A
SCARLET COAT, THE (1955) PR:A
SCARLET DAWN (1932) PR:A
SCARLET EMPRESS, THE (1934) PR:C
SCARLET HOUR, THE (1956) PR:A
SCARLET LETTER, THE (1934) PR:A
SCARLET PAGES (1930) PR:A
SCARLET PIMPERNEL, THE (1935, Brit.) PR:A
SCARLET RIVER (1933) PR:A
SCARLET SPEAR, THE (1954, Brit.) PR:A
SCARLET STREET (1945) PR:C
SCARLET THREAD (1951, Brit.) PR:A
SCARLET WEB, THE (1954, Brit.) PR:A
SCARLET WEEKEND, A (1932) PR:A
SCARRED (1984) PR:O
SCARS OF DRACULA, THE (1970, Brit.) PR:O
SCATTERBRAIN (1940) PR:A
SCATTERGOOD BAINES (1941) PR:A
SCATTERGOOD MEETS BROADWAY (1941) PR:A
SCATTERGOOD PULLS THE STRINGS (1941) PR:A
SCATTERGOOD RIDES HIGH (1942) PR:A
SCATTERGOOD SURVIVES A MURDER (1942) PR:A
SCAVENGER HUNT (1979) PR:C
SCAVENGERS, THE (1959, US/Phil.) PR:A
SCAVENGERS (1988) PR:C
SCAVENGERS, THE (1969) PR:O
SCENE OF THE CRIME (1949) PR:A
SCENE OF THE CRIME (1986, Fr.) PR:C-O
SCENES FROM A MARRIAGE (1973, Swed.) PR:C-O

SCENES FROM THE CLASS STRUGGLE IN BEVERLY HILLS (1989, Brit.) PR:O
SCENES FROM THE GOLDMINE (1988) PR:C
SCENIC ROUTE, THE (1978) PR:A
SCENT OF A WOMAN (1976, It.) PR:O
SCENT OF MYSTERY (1960) PR:A
SCHACHNOVELLE (SEE: THREE MOVES TO FREE-DOM) (1960, W. Ger.)
SCHATTEN UBER TIRAN – KOMMANDO SINAI (SEE: SINAI COMMANDOS: THE STORY OF THE SIX DAY WAR) (1968, Israel/W. Ger.)
SCHEHERAZADE (1965, Fr./It./Sp.) PR:A
SCHIZO (1977, Brit.) PR:O
SCHIZO (SEE: ALL WOMAN) (1958)
SCHIZOID (1980) PR:O
SCHLAGER-PARADE (1953, W. Ger.) PR:A
SCHLOCK (1973) PR:A
SCHLUSSAKKORD (SEE: FINAL CHORD, THE) (1936, Ger.)
SCHNEEWEISSCHEN UND ROSENROT (SEE: SNOW WHITE AND ROSE RED) (1966, W. Ger.)
SCHNEEWITTCHEN UND DIE SIEBEN ZWERGE (SEE: SNOW WHITE) (1965, W. Ger.)
SCHNOOK, THE (SEE: SWINGIN' ALONG) (1962)
SCHOOL DAZE (1988) PR:O
SCHOOL FOR BRIDES (1952, Brit.) PR:A
SCHOOL FOR DANGER (1947, Brit.) PR:A
SCHOOL FOR GIRLS (1935) PR:A
SCHOOL FOR HUSBANDS (1939, Brit.) PR:A
SCHOOL FOR RANDLE (1949, Brit.) PR:A
SCHOOL FOR SCANDAL, THE (1930, Brit.) PR:A
SCHOOL FOR SCOUNDRELS (1960, Brit.) PR:AA
SCHOOL FOR SECRETS (1946, Brit.) PR:A
SCHOOL FOR SEX (1966, Jap.) PR:O
SCHOOL FOR SEX (1969, Brit.) PR:O
SCHOOL FOR STARS (1935, Brit.) PR:A
SCHOOL FOR UNCLAIMED GIRLS (1973, Brit.) PR:O
SCHOOL FOR VIOLENCE (SEE: HIGH SCHOOL HELL-CATS) (1958)
SCHOOL OF LOVE (SEE: SCHOOL FOR SEX) (1966, Jap.)
SCHOOL SPIRIT (1985) PR:C-O
SCHOOLBOY PENITENTIARY (SEE: LITTLE RED SCHOOLHOUSE, THE) (1936)
SCHOOLGIRL DIARY (1947, It.) PR:A
SCHOOLMASTER, THE (SEE: HOOSIER SCHOOL-MASTER, THE) (1935)
SCHOONER GANG, THE (1937, Brit.) PR:A
SCHUSS IM MORGENGRAUEN (SEE: SHOT AT DAWN, A) (1934, Ger.)
SCHWARZE NYLONS-HEISSE NACHTE (SEE: INDE-CENT) (1962, W. Ger.)
SCHWEIK'S NEW ADVENTURES (1943, Brit.) PR:A
SCHWESTERN, ODER DIE BALANCE DES GLUECKS (SEE: SISTERS, OR THE BALANCE OF HAPPINESS) (1979, W. Ger.)
SCIENTIFIC CARDPLAYER, THE (1972, It.) PR:A
SCINTILLATING SIN (SEE: VIOLATED PARADISE) (1963, It./Jap.)
SCIPIO, THE AFRICAN (SEE: DEFEAT OF HANNIBAL, THE) (1937, It.)
SCIPIONE L'AFRICANO (SEE: DEFEAT OF HANNI-BAL, THE) (1937, It.)
SCIUSCIA (SEE: SHOESHINE) (1946, It.)
SCOBIE MALONE (1975, Aus.) PR:O
SCOOP, THE (SEE: HONOR OF THE PRESS) (1932)
SCOOP, THE (1934, Brit.) PR:A
SCORCHY (1976) PR:O
SCORING (1979) PR:O
SCORPIO (1973) PR:C
SCOTCH ON THE ROCKS (1954, Brit.) PR:A
SCOTLAND YARD (1930) PR:A
SCOTLAND YARD (1941) PR:A
SCOTLAND YARD COMMANDS (1937, Brit.) PR:A
SCOTLAND YARD DRAGNET (1957, Brit.) PR:A
SCOTLAND YARD HUNTS DR. MABUSE (1963, W. Ger.) PR:A
SCOTLAND YARD INSPECTOR (1952, Brit.) PR:A
SCOTLAND YARD INVESTIGATOR (1945) PR:A
SCOTLAND YARD MYSTERY, THE (SEE: LIVING DEAD, THE) (1936, Brit.)
SCOTT JOPLIN (1977) PR:C
SCOTT OF THE ANTARCTIC (1949, Brit.) PR:A
SCOUNDREL, THE (1935) PR:C
SCOUNDREL IN WHITE (SEE: DOCTEUR POPAUL) (1972, Fr.)
SCOUTS OF THE AIR (SEE: DANGER FLIGHT) (1939)
SCRAMBLE (1970, Brit.) PR:AA
SCRATCH HARRY (1969) PR:O
SCREAM (SEE: NIGHT GOD SCREAMED, THE) (1975)
SCREAM AND DIE (SEE: HOUSE THAT VANISHED, THE) (1974, Brit.)
SCREAM AND SCREAM AGAIN (1970, Brit.) PR:O
SCREAM, BABY, SCREAM (1969) PR:O
SCREAM, BLACULA, SCREAM! (1973) PR:O
SCREAM BLOODY MURDER (1972) PR:O
SCREAM FOR HELP (1984) PR:O
SCREAM FREE (SEE: FREE GRASS) (1969)

SCREAM IN THE DARK, A (1943) PR:A
SCREAM IN THE NIGHT (1943) PR:A
SCREAM OF FEAR (1961, Brit.) PR:C
SCREAM OF THE BUTTERFLY (1965) PR:O
SCREAMERS (1978, It.) PR:A
SCREAMING EAGLES (1956) PR:A
SCREAMING HEAD, THE (SEE: HEAD, THE) (1969, W. Ger.)
SCREAMING MIMI (1958) PR:O
SCREAMING SKULL, THE (1958) PR:A
SCREAMPLAY (1986) PR:O
SCREAMS OF A WINTER NIGHT (1979) PR:A
SCREAMTIME (1986, Brit.) PR:O
SCREEN TEST (1986) PR:O
SCREWBALL HOTEL (1989) PR:O
SCREWBALLS (1983) PR:O
SCROOGE (1935, Brit.) PR:AA
SCROOGE (SEE: CHRISTMAS CAROL, A) (1951, Brit.)
SCROOGE (1970, Brit.) PR:AA
SCROOGED (1988) PR:C
SCRUBBERS (1984, Brit.) PR:O
SCRUFFY (1938, Brit.) PR:AA
SCUDDA-HOO! SCUDDA-HAY! (1948) PR:A
SCUM (1979, Brit.) PR:O
SCUM OF THE EARTH! (1963) PR:O
SCUM OF THE EARTH (1976) PR:O
SCUSI, FACCIAMO L'AMORE? (SEE: LISTEN, LET'S MAKE LOVE) (1969, Fr./It.)
SE PERMETTETE, PARLIAMO DI DONNE (SEE: LET'S TALK ABOUT WOMEN) (1964, Fr./It.)
SE TUTTE LE DONNE DEL MONDO (SEE: KISS THE GIRLS AND MAKE THEM DIE) (1967, US/It.)
SEA BAT, THE (1930) PR:A
SEA CHASE, THE (1955) PR:A-C
SEA DEVILS (1931) PR:A
SEA DEVILS (1937) PR:A
SEA DEVILS (1953, Brit.) PR:A
SEA FURY (1929) PR:A
SEA FURY (1959, Brit.) PR:A
SEA GHOST, THE (1931) PR:A
SEA GOD, THE (1930) PR:A
SEA GULL, THE (1968, US/Brit.) PR:A-C
SEA GYPSIES, THE (1978) PR:AA
SEA HAWK, THE (1940) PR:A
SEA HORNET, THE (1951) PR:A
SEA LEGS (1930) PR:A
SEA NYMPHS (SEE: VIOLATED PARADISE) (1963, It./Jap.)
SEA OF GRASS, THE (1947) PR:A-C
SEA OF LOST SHIPS (1953) PR:A
SEA OF LOVE (1989) PR:O
SEA OF SAND (SEE: DESERT PATROL) (1962, Brit.)
SEA PIRATE, THE (1967, Fr./Sp./It.) PR:A
SEA SERPENT, THE (1937) PR:A
SEA SHALL NOT HAVE THEM, THE (1955, Brit.) PR:A-C
SEA SPOILERS, THE (1936) PR:A
SEA TIGER (1952) PR:A
SEA WALL, THE (SEE: THIS ANGRY AGE) (1958, US/Fr./It.)
SEA WIFE (1957, Brit.) PR:A
SEA WOLF, THE (1930) PR:A
SEA WOLF, THE (1941) PR:C
SEA WOLVES, THE (1981, Brit.) PR:A
SEA WYF AND BUSCUIT (SEE: SEA WIFE) (1957, Brit.)
SEABO (1978) PR:O
SEAFIGHTERS, THE (SEE: OPERATION BIKINI) (1963)
SEAGULLS OVER SORRENTO (SEE: CREST OF THE WAVE) (1954, Brit.)
SEALED CARGO (1951) PR:A
SEALED LIPS (SEE: AFTER TOMORROW) (1932)
SEALED LIPS (1941) PR:A
SEALED VERDICT (1948) PR:A
SEANCE ON A WET AFTERNOON (1964, Brit.) PR:C
SEARCH, THE (1948) PR:A
SEARCH AND DESTROY (1981) PR:C
SEARCH FOR BEAUTY (1934) PR:A
SEARCH FOR BRIDEY MURPHY, THE (1956) PR:A
SEARCH FOR DANGER (1949) PR:A
SEARCH FOR THE MOTHER LODE (SEE: MOTHER LODE) (1982)
SEARCH OF THE CASTAWAYS (SEE: IN SEARCH OF THE CASTAWAYS) (1967, US/Brit.)
SEARCHERS, THE (1956, Brit.) PR:AA
SEARCHING WIND, THE (1946) PR:A-C
SEAS BENEATH (1931) PR:A
SEASIDE SWINGERS (1965, Brit.) PR:AA
SEASON FOR LOVE, THE (1963, Fr.) PR:A-C
SEASON OF DREAMS (SEE: STACKING) (1987)
SEASON OF FEAR (1989) PR:O
SEASON OF PASSION (1961, Aus./Brit.) PR:C
SEASON OF THE WITCH (SEE: HUNGRY WIVES) (1973)
SEATED AT HIS RIGHT (1968, It.) PR:O
SEAWEED CHILDREN, THE (SEE: MALACHI'S COVE) (1973, Brit.)
SEBASTIAN (1968, Brit.) PR:A
SECOND BEST BED (1937, Brit.) PR:A

SECOND BEST SECRET AGENT IN THE WHOLE WIDE WORLD, THE (1965, Brit.) PR:A-C
SECOND BUREAU (1936, Fr.) PR:A
SECOND BUREAU (1937, Brit.) PR:A
SECOND CHANCE (1947) PR:A
SECOND CHANCE (1953) PR:A-C
SECOND CHANCES (SEE: PROBATION) (1932)
SECOND CHOICE (1930) PR:A
SECOND CHORUS (1940) PR:A
SECOND COMING, THE (SEE: DEAD PEOPLE) (1974)
SECOND COMING OF SUZANNE, THE (1974) PR:C
SECOND FACE, THE (1950) PR:A
SECOND FIDDLE (1939) PR:A
SECOND FIDDLE (1957, Brit.) PR:A
SECOND FIDDLE TO A STEEL GUITAR (1965) PR:A
SECOND FLOOR MYSTERY, THE (1930) PR:A
SECOND GREATEST SEX, THE (1955) PR:A
SECOND-HAND HEARTS (1981) PR:A-C
SECOND-HAND WIFE (1933) PR:A
SECOND HONEYMOON (1931) PR:A
SECOND HONEYMOON (1937) PR:A
SECOND HOUSE FROM THE LEFT (SEE: NEW HOUSE ON THE LEFT, THE) (1978, Brit.)
SECOND MATE, THE (1950, Brit.) PR:A
SECOND MR. BUSH, THE (1940, Brit.) PR:A
SECOND MRS. TANQUERAY, THE (1952, Brit.) PR:A
SECOND STORY MURDER, THE (SEE: SECOND FLOOR MYSTERY, THE) (1930)
SECOND THOUGHTS (SEE: CRIME OF PETER FRAME, THE) (1938, Brit.)
SECOND THOUGHTS (1983) PR:C
SECOND TIME AROUND, THE (1961) PR:A
SECOND TIME LUCKY (1984, Aus./New Zealand) PR:C
SECOND WIFE (1930) PR:A
SECOND WIFE (1936) PR:A
SECOND WIND (1976, Can.) PR:A
SECOND WIND, A (1978, Fr.) PR:C
SECOND WOMAN, THE (1951) PR:A-C
SECONDS (1966) PR:C
SECRET, THE (1955, Brit.) PR:A
SECRET, THE (1979, Hong Kong) PR:C-O
SECRET ADMIRER (1985) PR:C
SECRET AGENT (1933, Brit.) PR:A
SECRET AGENT (1936, Brit.) PR:C
SECRET AGENT FIREBALL (1965, Fr./It.) PR:A-C
SECRET AGENT OF JAPAN (1942) PR:A
SECRET AGENT SUPER DRAGON (1966, Fr./It./Monaco/W. Ger.) PR:A
SECRET BEYOND THE DOOR, THE (1948) PR:C
SECRET BRIDE, THE (1935) PR:A
SECRET BRIGADE, THE (1951, USSR) PR:A
SECRET CALL, THE (1931) PR:A
SECRET CAVE, THE (1953, Brit.) PR:A
SECRET CEREMONY (1968, Brit.) PR:O
SECRET COMMAND (1944) PR:A
SECRET DIARY OF SIGMUND FREUD, THE (1984) PR:O
SECRET DOCUMENT – VIENNA (1954, Fr.) PR:A
SECRET DOOR, THE (1964) PR:A
SECRET ENEMIES (1942) PR:A
SECRET ENEMY (SEE: ENEMY AGENT) (1940)
SECRET EVIDENCE (1941) PR:A
SECRET FILE: HOLLYWOOD (1962) PR:A-C
SECRET FLIGHT (SEE: SCHOOL FOR SECRETS) (1946, Brit.)
SECRET FOUR, THE (1940, Brit.) PR:A
SECRET FOUR, THE (SEE: KANSAS CITY CONFIDEN-TIAL) (1952)
SECRET FURY, THE (1950) PR:A
SECRET GARDEN, THE (1949) PR:AA
SECRET HEART, THE (1946) PR:C
SECRET HONOR (1984) PR:C
SECRET INTERLUDE (SEE: PRIVATE NUMBER) (1936)
SECRET INTERLUDE (SEE: VIEW FROM POMPEY'S HEAD, THE) (1955)
SECRET INVASION, THE (1964) PR:A
SECRET JOURNEY (SEE: AMONG HUMAN WOLVES) (1940, Brit.)
SECRET LIFE OF AN AMERICAN WIFE, THE (1968) PR:C-O
SECRET LIFE OF WALTER MITTY, THE (1947) PR:A
SECRET LIVES (SEE: I MARRIED A SPY) (1938)
SECRET MAN, THE (1958, Brit.) PR:A
SECRET MARK OF D'ARTAGNAN, THE (1963, Fr./It.) PR:A
SECRET MENACE (1931) PR:A
SECRET MISSION (1944, Brit.) PR:A
SECRET MISSION (1949, USSR) PR:A
SECRET MOTIVE (SEE: LONDON BLACKOUT MUR-DERS) (1942)
SECRET OF ANNA, THE (SEE: CRIA!) (1975, Sp.)
SECRET OF BLOOD ISLAND, THE (1965, Brit.) PR:A
SECRET OF CONVICT LAKE, THE (1951) PR:A
SECRET OF DEEP HARBOR (1961) PR:C
SECRET OF DR. ALUCARD, THE (SEE: TASTE OF BLOOD, A) (1967)
SECRET OF DR. KILDARE, THE (1939) PR:A

SECRET OF DORIAN GRAY, THE (SEE: DORIAN GRAY) (1970, It./Lichtenstein/W. Ger.)
SECRET OF G.32 (SEE: FLY BY NIGHT) (1942)
SECRET OF LINDA HAMILTON (SEE: SECRETS OF A SORORITY GIRL) (1946)
SECRET OF MADAME BLANCHE, THE (1933) PR:A
SECRET OF MAGIC ISLAND, THE (1964, Fr./It.) PR:AA
SECRET OF MONTE CRISTO, THE (1961, Brit.) PR:A
SECRET OF MY SUCCESS, THE (1965, Brit.) PR:A-C
SECRET OF MY SUCCESS, THE (1987) PR:O
SECRET OF NIKOLA TESLA, THE (1980, Yugo.) PR:A
SECRET OF NIMH, THE (1982) PR:AA
SECRET OF OUTER SPACE ISLAND (SEE: SECRET OF MAGIC ISLAND, THE) (1964, Fr./It.)
SECRET OF ST. IVES, THE (1949) PR:A
SECRET OF SANTA VITTORIA, THE (1969) PR:A
SECRET OF STAMBOUL, THE (1936, Brit.) PR:A
SECRET OF THE BLUE ROOM (1933) PR:A
SECRET OF THE CHATEAU (1935) PR:A
SECRET OF THE FOREST, THE (1955, Brit.) PR:AA
SECRET OF THE INCAS (1954) PR:A
SECRET OF THE LOCH, THE (1934, Brit.) PR:A
SECRET OF THE PURPLE REEF, THE (1960) PR:A
SECRET OF THE SACRED FOREST, THE (1970) PR:A
SECRET OF THE SWORD, THE (1985) PR:AA
SECRET OF THE TELEGIAN, THE (1961, Jap.) PR:A
SECRET OF THE WHISTLER, THE (1946) PR:A
SECRET OF TREASURE MOUNTAIN (1956) PR:A
SECRET PARTNER, THE (1961, Brit.) PR:A
SECRET PASSION, THE (SEE: FREUD) (1962)
SECRET PATROL (1936) PR:A
SECRET PEOPLE (1952, Brit.) PR:A
SECRET PLACE, THE (1958, Brit.) PR:A
SECRET PLACES (1984, Brit.) PR:C
SECRET SCROLLS (PART I) (1968, Jap.) PR:A-C
SECRET SCROLLS (PART II) (1968, Jap.) PR:A-C
SECRET SERVICE (1931) PR:A
SECRET SERVICE INVESTIGATOR (1948) PR:A
SECRET SERVICE OF THE AIR (1939) PR:A
SECRET SEVEN, THE (1940) PR:A
SECRET SEVEN, THE (1966, It./Sp.) PR:A
SECRET SINNERS (1933) PR:A
SECRET SIX, THE (1931) PR:C
SECRET STRANGER, THE (SEE: ROUGH RIDING RANGER) (1935)
SECRET TENT, THE (1956, Brit.) PR:A
SECRET VALLEY (1937) PR:A
SECRET VENTURE (1955, Brit.) PR:A
SECRET VOICE, THE (1936, Brit.) PR:A
SECRET WAR OF HARRY FRIGG, THE (1968) PR:A-C
SECRET WAR, THE (SEE: DIRTY GAME, THE) (1965, Fr./It./W. Ger.)
SECRET WAYS, THE (1961) PR:A-C
SECRET WEAPON, THE (SEE: SHERLOCK HOLMES AND THE SECRET WEAPON) (1942)
SECRET WITNESS, THE (1931) PR:A
SECRET WORLD (1969, Fr.) PR:C
SECRETS (1933) PR:A-C
SECRETS (SEE: SECRETS OF THE LONE WOLF) (1941)
SECRETS (1971) PR:O
SECRETS (1984, Brit.) PR:A-C
SECRETS D'ALCOVE (1954, Fr./It.) PR:C
SECRETS OF A CO-ED (1942) PR:A
SECRETS OF A MODEL (1940) PR:C
SECRETS OF A NURSE (1938) PR:A
SECRETS OF A SECRETARY (1931) PR:A
SECRETS OF A SORORITY GIRL (1946) PR:A
SECRETS OF A SOUL (SEE: CONFESSIONS OF AN OPIUM EATER) (1962)
SECRETS OF A WINDMILL GIRL (1966, Brit.) PR:O
SECRETS OF A WOMAN'S TEMPLE (1969, Jap.) PR:O
SECRETS OF AN ACTRESS (1938) PR:A-C
SECRETS OF CHINATOWN (1935) PR:A
SECRETS OF MONTE CARLO (1951) PR:A
SECRETS OF SCOTLAND YARD (1944) PR:A
SECRETS OF SEX (1970, Brit.) PR:O
SECRETS OF SIN (SEE: FALSE RAPTURE) (1941)
SECRETS OF THE CITY (SEE: CITY OF SECRETS) (1963, W. Ger.)
SECRETS OF THE FRENCH POLICE (1932) PR:A
SECRETS OF THE LONE WOLF (1941) PR:A
SECRETS OF THE MARIE CELESTE, THE (SEE: PHANTOM SHIP) (1937, Brit.)
SECRETS OF THE UNDERGROUND (1943) PR:A
SECRETS OF THE WASTELANDS (1941) PR:A
SECRETS OF WOMEN (1952, Swed.) PR:C
SECRETS OF WU SIN (1932) PR:A
SECRETS SECRETS (1985, It.) PR:O
SECURITY RISK (1954) PR:A
SEDDOK, L'EREDE DI SATANA (SEE: ATOM AGE VAMPIRE) (1963, It.)
SEDMI KONTINENT (SEE: SEVENTH CONTINENT, THE) (1968, Czech./Yugo.)
SEDMIKRASKY (SEE: DAISIES) (1967, Czech.)
SEDUCED AND ABANDONED (1964, Fr./It.) PR:C
SEDUCERS, THE (1962) PR:C
SEDUCTION, THE (1982) PR:O
SEDUCTION BY THE SEA (1967, Yugo./W. Ger.) PR:C

SEDUCTION OF JOE TYNAN, THE (1979) PR:C-O
SEDUCTION OF MIMI, THE (1972, It.) PR:O
SEDUCTION: THE CRUEL WOMAN (1989, W. Ger.) PR:O
SEDUCTRESS, THE (SEE: TEACHER, THE) (1974)
SEDUTO ALLA SUA DESTRA (SEE: SEATED AT HIS RIGHT) (1968, It.)
SEE AMERICA THIRST (1930) PR:A
SEE HERE, PRIVATE HARGROVE (1944) PR:A
SEE HOW THEY RUN (1955, Brit.) PR:A
SEE MY LAWYER (1945) PR:A
SEE NO EVIL (1971, Brit.) PR:C
SEE NO EVIL, HEAR NO EVIL (1989) PR:C-O
SEE YOU IN HELL, DARLING (SEE: AMERICAN DREAM, AN) (1966)
SEE YOU IN THE MORNING (1989) PR:C
SEED (1931) PR:A
SEED OF INNOCENCE (1980) PR:O
SEED OF MAN, THE (1970, It.) PR:C-O
SEED OF TERROR (SEE: GRAVE OF THE VAMPIRE) (1972)
SEEDS OF DESTRUCTION (1952) PR:A
SEEDS OF EVIL (1972) PR:O
SEEDS OF FREEDOM (1943, US/USSR) PR:A
SEEING IS BELIEVING (1934, Brit.) PR:A
SEEING IT THROUGH (SEE: MOTH, THE) (1934)
SEEKERS, THE (SEE: LAND OF FURY) (1955, Brit.)
SEEMS LIKE OLD TIMES (1980) PR:A-C
SEGRETI CHE SCOTTANO (SEE: DEAD RUN) (1969, Fr./It./W. Ger.)
SEGRETI SEGRETI (SEE: SECRETS SECRETS) (1985, It.)
SEI DONNE PER L'ASSASSINO (SEE: BLOOD AND BLACK LACE) (1965, Fr./It./W. Ger.)
SEI SEI VIVO (SEE: DJANGO KILL) (1967, It./Sp.)
SEISHUN MONOTOGARI (SEE: NAKED YOUTH) (1961, Jap.)
SEISHUN ZANKOKU MONOTOGARI (SEE: NAKED YOUTH) (1961, Jap.)
SEITE NOTE IN NERO (SEE: PSYCHIC, THE) (1979, It.)
SEIZURE (1974) PR:C
SEKAI DAISENSO (SEE: LAST WAR, THE) (1962, Jap.)
SEKKA TOMURAI ZASHI (SEE: IREZUMI (SPIRIT OF TATTOO)) (1982, Jap.)
SELF-MADE LADY (1932, Brit.) PR:A
SELF-PORTRAIT (1973, US/Chile) PR:O
SELL OUT, THE (1976, Brit./It.) PR:C
SELLERS OF GIRLS (1967, Fr.) PR:O
SELLOUT, THE (1951) PR:A
SEMBAZURU (SEE: THOUSAND CRANES) (1969, Jap.)
SEMI-TOUGH (1977) PR:C-O
SEMINOLE (1953) PR:C
SEMINOLE UPRISING (1955) PR:A
SEN NOCI SVATOJANSKE (SEE: MIDSUMMER NIGHT'S DREAM, A) (1961, Czech.)
SENATOR WAS INDISCREET, THE (1947) PR:A
SEND FOR PAUL TEMPLE (1946, Brit.) PR:A
SEND ME NO FLOWERS (1964) PR:A
SENDER, THE (1982, Brit.) PR:O
SENGOKU GUNTO-DEN (SEE: SAGA OF THE VAGABONDS) (1964, Jap.)
SENGOKU JIEITAI (SEE: TIME SLIP) (1981, Jap.)
SENGOKU YARO (SEE: WARRING CLANS) (1963, Jap.)
SENIOR PROM (1958) PR:A
SENIORS, THE (1978) PR:O
SENJO NI NAGARERU UTA (SEE: WE WILL REMEMBER) (1966, Jap.)
SENOR AMERICANO (1929) PR:A
SENORA CASADA NECESSITA MARIDO (1935) PR:A
SENORITA FROM THE WEST (1945) PR:A
SENSATION (1936, Brit.) PR:A
SENSATION (SEE: SEDUCERS, THE) (1970, It.)
SENSATION HUNTERS (1934) PR:A
SENSATION HUNTERS (1945) PR:A
SENSATIONS (SEE: SENSATIONS OF 1945) (1944)
SENSATIONS OF 1945 (1944) PR:A
SENSE OF FREEDOM, A (1985, Brit.) PR:C
SENSO (1968, It.) PR:A
SENSUALITA (1954, It.) PR:A
SENSUOUS VAMPIRES (SEE: VAMPIRE HOOKERS, THE) (1979, Phil.)
SENTENCE SUSPENDED (SEE: MILITARY ACADEMY WITH THAT TENTH AVENUE GANG) (1950)
SENTENCED FOR LIFE (1960, Brit.) PR:A
SENTENZA DI MORTE (SEE: DEATH SENTENCE) (1967, It.)
SENTIMENTAL BLOKE (1932, Aus.) PR:A
SENTIMENTAL JOURNEY (1946) PR:A
SENTIMIENTOS: MIRTA DE LINIERS A ESTAMBUL (1987, Arg.) PR:A
SENTINEL, THE (1977) PR:O
SENZA PIETA (SEE: WITHOUT PITY) (1949, It.)
SEPARATE BEDS (SEE: WHEELER DEALERS, THE) (1963)
SEPARATE PEACE, A (1972) PR:A
SEPARATE TABLES (1958) PR:A-C
SEPARATE VACATIONS (1986, Can.) PR:O
SEPARATE WAYS (1981) PR:O

SEPARATION (1968, Brit.) PR:A
SEPIA CINDERELLA (1947) PR:A
SEPPUKU (SEE: HARAKIRI) (1963, Jap.)
SEPT FOIS FEMME (SEE: WOMAN TIMES SEVEN) (1967, US/Fr./It.)
SEPT HOMMES EN OR (SEE: SEVEN GOLDEN MEN) (1969, Fr./It./Sp./W. Ger.)
SEPTEMBER (1987) PR:A
SEPTEMBER AFFAIR (1950) PR:A
SEPTEMBER STORM (1960) PR:A
SEPTEMBER 30, 1955 (SEE: 9/30/55) (1978)
SEQUESTRO DI PERSONA (SEE: SARDINIA: RANSOM) (1968, It.)
SEQUOIA (1934) PR:A
SERAFINO (1970, Fr./It.) PR:A
SERDTSE MATERI (SEE: SONS AND MOTHERS) (1967, USSR)
SERE CUALQUIER COSA PERO TE QUIERO (1986, Arg.) PR:C-O
SERENA (1962, Brit.) PR:A-C
SERENADE (1956) PR:A
SERENADE FOR TWO SPIES (1966, It./W. Ger.) PR:A
SERENADE OF THE WEST (SEE: GIT ALONG, LITTLE DOGIES) (1937)
SERENADE OF THE WEST (SEE: COWBOY SERENADE) (1942)
SERENITY (1962, Gr.) PR:A
SERGEANT, THE (1968) PR:O
SERGEANT BERRY (1938, Ger.) PR:A
SERGEANT DEADHEAD (1965) PR:A
SERGEANT DEADHEAD THE ASTRONAUT (SEE: SERGEANT DEADHEAD) (1965)
SERGEANT JIM (1962, Yugo.) PR:A
SERGEANT MADDEN (1939) PR:A
SERGEANT MIKE (1945) PR:A
SERGEANT MURPHY (1938) PR:A
SGT. PEPPER'S LONELY HEARTS CLUB BAND (1978) PR:A
SERGEANT RUTLEDGE (1960) PR:C
SERGEANT RYKER (1968) PR:A
SERGEANT STEINER (SEE: BREAKTHROUGH) (1978, W. Ger.)
SERGEANT WAS A LADY, THE (1961) PR:A
SERGEANT YORK (1941) PR:A
SERGEANTS 3 (1962) PR:A
SERIAL (1980) PR:O
SERIOUS CHARGE (SEE: IMMORAL CHARGE) (1962, Brit.)
SERPENT, THE (1973, Fr./It./W. Ger.) PR:A-C
SERPENT AND THE RAINBOW, THE (1988) PR:O
SERPENT ISLAND (1954) PR:A
SERPENT OF THE NILE (1953) PR:A
SERPENT'S EGG, THE (1977, US/W. Ger.) PR:O
SERPENTS OF THE PIRATE MOON, THE (1973) PR:O
SERPENT'S WAY, THE (1987, Swed.) PR:O
SERPICO (1973) PR:C-O
SERVANT, THE (1964, Brit.) PR:O
SERVANTS' ENTRANCE (1934) PR:A
SERVICE (SEE: LOOKING FORWARD) (1933)
SERVICE DE LUXE (1938) PR:A
SERVICE FOR LADIES (SEE: RESERVED FOR LADIES) (1932, Brit.)
SERYOZHA (SEE: SUMMER TO REMEMBER, A) (1961, USSR)
SESAME STREET PRESENTS: FOLLOW THE BIRD (1985) PR:AA
SESSION WITH THE COMMITTEE (SEE: COMMITTEE, THE) (1968, Brit.)
SET, THE (1970, Aus.) PR:O
SET-UP, THE (1949) PR:C
SET-UP, THE (1963, Brit.) PR:A
SETTE CONTRO LA MORTE (SEE: CAVERN, THE) (1965, It./W. Ger.)
SETTE DONNE PER I MAC GREGOR (SEE: UP THE MAC GREGORS) (1967, It./Sp.)
SETTE PISTOLE PER I MAC GREGOR (SEE: SEVEN GUNS FOR THE MAC GREGORS) (1968, It./Sp.)
SETTE UOMINI D'ORO (SEE: SEVEN GOLDEN MEN) (1969, Fr./It./Sp./W. Ger.)
SETTE VOLTE DONNA (SEE: WOMAN TIMES SEVEN) (1967, US/Fr./It.)
SETTE WINCHESTER PER UN MASSACRO (SEE: PAYMENT IN BLOOD) (1968, It.)
SETTLERS, THE (SEE: NEW LAND, THE) (1973, Swed.)
SEVEN (1979) PR:O
SEVEN AGAINST THE SUN (1968, South Africa) PR:A
SEVEN ALONE (1975) PR:AA
SEVEN ANGRY MEN (1955) PR:A
SEVEN BAD MEN (SEE: RAGE AT DAWN) (1955)
SEVEN BEAUTIES (1976, It.) PR:O
SEVEN BRAVE MEN (1936, USSR) PR:A
SEVEN BRIDES FOR SEVEN BROTHERS (1954) PR:AA
SEVEN BROTHERS MEET DRACULA, THE (SEE: DRACULA AND THE SEVEN GOLDEN VAMPIRES) (1974, Brit./Chi.)
SEVEN CAPITAL SINS (1962, Fr./It.) PR:O
SEVEN CITIES OF GOLD (1955) PR:A-C

SEVEN CITIES TO ATLANTIS (SEE: WARLORDS OF ATLANTIS) (1978, Brit.)
SEVEN DARING GIRLS (1962, W. Ger.) PR:A
SEVEN DAYS ASHORE (1944) PR:A
SEVEN DAYS IN MAY (1964) PR:C
SEVEN DAYS' LEAVE (1930) PR:A
SEVEN DAYS' LEAVE (1942) PR:A
SEVEN DAYS TO NOON (1950, Brit.) PR:C
SEVEN DEADLY SINS, THE (1953, Fr./It.) PR:A
SEVEN DIFFERENT WAYS (SEE: QUICK, LET'S GET MARRIED) (1965)
SEVEN DOORS TO DEATH (1944) PR:A
SEVEN DWARFS TO THE RESCUE, THE (1965, It.) PR:A
SEVEN FACES (1929) PR:A
SEVEN FACES OF DR. LAO (1964) PR:A
SEVEN FOOTPRINTS TO SATAN (1929) PR:C
SEVEN GOLDEN MEN (1969, Fr./It./Sp./W. Ger.) PR:A
SEVEN GRAVES FOR ROGAN (SEE: TIME TO DIE, A) (1983)
SEVEN GUNS FOR THE MAC GREGORS (1968, It./Sp.) PR:A
SEVEN GUNS TO MESA (1958) PR:A
SEVEN HILLS OF ROME, THE (1958, US/It.) PR:A
SEVEN HOURS TO JUDGEMENT (1988) PR:O
711 OCEAN DRIVE (1950) PR:C
SEVEN KEYS (1962, Brit.) PR:A
SEVEN KEYS TO BALDPATE (1930) PR:A
SEVEN KEYS TO BALDPATE (1935) PR:A
SEVEN KEYS TO BALDPATE (1947) PR:A
SEVEN LITTLE FOYS, THE (1955) PR:AA
SEVEN MEN FROM NOW (1956) PR:A
SEVEN MILES FROM ALCATRAZ (1942) PR:A
SEVEN MINUTES, THE (1971) PR:O
SEVEN MINUTES IN HEAVEN (1986) PR:C
SEVEN NIGHTS IN JAPAN (1976, Brit./Fr.) PR:C
SEVEN-PER-CENT SOLUTION, THE (1977, Brit.) PR:C
SEVEN REVENGES, THE (1967, It.) PR:C
SEVEN SAMURAI, THE (1954, Jap.) PR:C
SEVEN SEAS TO CALAIS (1963, It.) PR:A
SEVEN SECRETS OF SU-MARU, THE (SEE: RIO 70) (1970, US/Sp./W. Ger.)
SEVEN SINNERS (SEE: DOOMED CARGO) (1936, Brit.)
SEVEN SINNERS (1940) PR:A
SEVEN SISTERS (SEE: HOUSE ON SORORITY ROW, THE) (1983)
SEVEN SLAVES AGAINST THE WORLD (1965, It.) PR:A
SEVEN SWEETHEARTS (1942) PR:A
SEVEN TASKS OF ALI BABA, THE (1963, It.) PR:A
SEVEN THIEVES (1960) PR:A-C
SEVEN THUNDERS (SEE: BEASTS OF MARSEILLES, THE) (1959, Brit.)
7254 (1971) PR:O
SEVEN-UPS, THE (1973) PR:C
SEVEN WAVES AWAY (SEE: ABANDON SHIP!) (1957, Brit.)
SEVEN WAYS FROM SUNDOWN (1960) PR:A
SEVEN WERE SAVED (1947) PR:A
SEVEN WOMEN (1966) PR:C
SEVEN WOMEN FROM HELL (1961) PR:A
SEVEN YEAR ITCH, THE (1955) PR:A-C
SEVENTEEN (1940) PR:A
1776 (1972) PR:A
SEVENTH CAVALRY (1956) PR:A
7TH COMMANDMENT, THE (1961) PR:A
SEVENTH CONTINENT, THE (1968, Czech./Yugo.) PR:A
SEVENTH CROSS, THE (1944) PR:C
SEVENTH DAWN, THE (1964, US/Brit.) PR:A-C
SEVENTH HEAVEN (1937) PR:A-C
SEVENTH JUROR, THE (1964, Fr.) PR:A
SEVENTH SEAL, THE (1956, Swed.) PR:C
SEVENTH SIGN, THE (1988) PR:C
SEVENTH SIN, THE (1957) PR:A
SEVENTH SURVIVOR, THE (1941, Brit.) PR:A
SEVENTH VEIL, THE (1946, Brit.) PR:A-C
SEVENTH VICTIM, THE (1943) PR:A
SEVENTH VOYAGE OF SINBAD, THE (1958) PR:AA
SEVENTY DEADLY PILLS (1964, Brit.) PR:AA
77 PARK LANE (1931, Brit.) PR:A
70,000 WITNESSES (1932) PR:A
SEVERED HEAD, A (1971, Brit.) PR:O
SEX AGENT (SEE: THERE IS STILL ROOM IN HELL) (1963, W. Ger.)
SEX AND THE SINGLE GIRL (1964) PR:C
SEX AND THE TEENAGER (SEE: TO FIND A MAN) (1972)
SEX APPEAL (1986) PR:O
SEX AT NIGHT (SEE: LOVE AT NIGHT) (1961, Fr.)
SEX IS A WOMAN (SEE: LOVE IS A WOMAN) (1967, Brit.)
SEX KITTENS GO TO COLLEGE (1960) PR:A
SEX, LIES AND VIDEOTAPE (1989) PR:C
SEX O'CLOCK NEWS, THE (1986) PR:O
SEX RACKETEERS, THE (SEE: MAN OF VIOLENCE) (1970, Brit.)
SEXORCISTS, THE (SEE: TORMENTED, THE) (1978, It.)
SEXTETTE (1978) PR:C

SEXTON BLAKE AND THE BEARDED DOCTOR (1935, Brit.) PR:A
SEXTON BLAKE AND THE HOODED TERROR (1938, Brit.)
SEXTON BLAKE AND THE MADEMOISELLE (1935, Brit.) PR:A
SEXY GANG (SEE: MICHELLE) (1970, Fr.)
SEZ O'REILLY TO MACNAB (1938, Brit.) PR:A
SFIDA A RIO BRAVO (SEE: GUNMEN OF THE RIO GRANDE) (1965, Fr./It./Sp.)
SH! THE OCTOPUS (1937) PR:A
SHABBY TIGER, THE (SEE: MASQUERADE) (1965, Brit.)
SHACK OUT ON 101 (1955) PR:A
SHADES OF SILK (1979, Can.) PR:O
SHADEY (1987, Brit.) PR:C
SHADOW, THE (1936, Brit.) PR:A
SHADOW, THE (1937) PR:A
SHADOW AND THE MISSING LADY, THE (SEE: MISSING LADY, THE) (1946)
SHADOW BETWEEN, THE (1932, Brit.) PR:A
SHADOW IN THE SKY (1951) PR:A
SHADOW MAN (1953, Brit.) PR:A
SHADOW OF A DOUBT (1935) PR:A
SHADOW OF A DOUBT (1943) PR:C
SHADOW OF A MAN (1955, Brit.) PR:A-C
SHADOW OF A WOMAN (1946) PR:A
SHADOW OF CHIKARA (SEE: WISHBONE CUTTER) (1978)
SHADOW OF EVIL (1967, Fr./It.) PR:A
SHADOW OF FEAR (1956, Brit.) PR:A
SHADOW OF FEAR (1963, Brit.) PR:A
SHADOW OF MIKE EMERALD, THE (1935, Brit.) PR:A
SHADOW OF SUSPICION (1944) PR:A
SHADOW OF TERROR (1945) PR:A
SHADOW OF THE CAT, THE (1961, Brit.) PR:A
SHADOW OF THE EAGLE (1955, Brit.) PR:A
SHADOW OF THE HAWK (1976, Can.) PR:A
SHADOW OF THE LAW (1930) PR:A
SHADOW OF THE PAST (1950, Brit.) PR:A
SHADOW OF THE THIN MAN (1941) PR:A
SHADOW OF THE WEREWOLF (SEE: WEREWOLF VS. THE VAMPIRE WOMAN, THE) (1970, Sp./W. Ger.)
SHADOW OF VICTORY (1986, Neth.) PR:O
SHADOW ON THE WALL (1950) PR:A
SHADOW ON THE WINDOW, THE (1957) PR:A
SHADOW PLAY (1986) PR:O
SHADOW RANCH (1930) PR:A
SHADOW RETURNS, THE (1946) PR:A
SHADOW STRIKES, THE (1937) PR:A
SHADOW VALLEY (1947) PR:A
SHADOW VERSUS THE THOUSAND EYES OF DR. MABUSE, THE (SEE: THOUSAND EYES OF DR. MABUSE, THE) (1960, Fr./It./W. Ger.)
SHADOW WARRIOR, THE (SEE: KAGEMUSHA) (1980, Jap.)
SHADOWED (1946) PR:A
SHADOWED EYES (1939, Brit.) PR:A-C
SHADOWMAN (1974, Fr./It.) PR:A
SHADOWS (1931, Brit.) PR:A-C
SHADOWS (1960) PR:O
SHADOWS GROW LONGER, THE (1962, Switz./W. Ger.) PR:A
SHADOWS IN AN EMPTY ROOM (SEE: STRANGE SHADOWS IN AN EMPTY ROOM) (1977, Can./It.)
SHADOWS IN THE NIGHT (1944) PR:A
SHADOWS OF DEATH (1945) PR:A
SHADOWS OF FORGOTTEN ANCESTORS (1965, USSR) PR:A
SHADOWS OF SING SING (1934) PR:A
SHADOWS OF SINGAPORE (SEE: MALAY NIGHTS) (1933)
SHADOWS OF THE ORIENT (1937) PR:A
SHADOWS OF THE PEACOCK (SEE: ECHOES OF PARADISE) (1989, Aus.)
SHADOWS OF THE WEST (1949) PR:A
SHADOWS OF TOMBSTONE (1953) PR:A
SHADOWS ON THE SAGE (1942) PR:A
SHADOWS ON THE STAIRS (1941) PR:A
SHADOWS OVER CHINATOWN (1946) PR:A
SHADOWS OVER SHANGHAI (1938) PR:A
SHADOWS RUN BLACK (1986) PR:O
SHADY LADY, THE (1929) PR:A
SHADY LADY (1945) PR:A
SHAFT (1971) PR:O
SHAFT IN AFRICA (1973) PR:O
SHAFT'S BIG SCORE! (1972) PR:O
SHAG (1989, Brit.) PR:C
SHAGGY (1948) PR:AA
SHAGGY D.A., THE (1976) PR:AA
SHAGGY DOG, THE (1959) PR:AA
SHAKE HANDS WITH MURDER (1944) PR:A
SHAKE HANDS WITH THE DEVIL (1959, Ireland) PR:C
SHAKE, RATTLE, AND ROCK? (1957) PR:A
SHAKEDOWN, THE (1929) PR:A
SHAKEDOWN (SEE: BIG SHAKEDOWN, THE) (1934)
SHAKEDOWN (1936) PR:A
SHAKEDOWN (1950) PR:C

SHAKEDOWN, THE (1960, Brit.) PR:C
SHAKEDOWN (1988) PR:O
SHAKESPEARE WALLAH (1966, India) PR:A
SHAKIEST GUN IN THE WEST, THE (1968) PR:A
SHALAKO (1968, Brit.) PR:O
SHALL THE CHILDREN PAY? (SEE: WHAT PRICE INNOCENCE?) (1933)
SHALL WE DANCE (1937) PR:A
SHAME (SEE: INTRUDER, THE) (1962)
SHAME (1968, Swed.) PR:O
SHAME (1988, Aus.) PR:O
SHAME OF MARY BOYLE, THE (SEE: JUNO AND THE PAYCOCK) (1930, Brit.)
SHAME OF PATTY SMITH, THE (SEE: CASE OF PATTY SMITH, THE) (1962)
SHAME OF THE SABINE WOMEN, THE (1962, Mex.) PR:A
SHAME, SHAME, EVERYBODY KNOWS HER NAME (1969) PR:O
SHAMELESS OLD LADY, THE (1966, Fr.) PR:A
SHAMPOO (1975) PR:O
SHAMROCK HILL (1949) PR:AA
SHAMUS (1959, Brit.) PR:AA
SHAMUS (1973) PR:C
SHAN-KO LIEN (SEE: SHEPHERD GIRL, THE) (1965, Hong Kong)
SHANE (1953) PR:C
SHANGHAI (1935) PR:A
SHANGHAI CHEST, THE (1948) PR:A
SHANGHAI COBRA, THE (1945) PR:A
SHANGHAI DRAMA, THE (1945, Fr.) PR:A
SHANGHAI EXPRESS (1932) PR:O
SHANGHAI GESTURE, THE (1941) PR:C
SHANGHAI LADY (1929) PR:A
SHANGHAI MADNESS (1933) PR:A
SHANGHAI STORY, THE (1954) PR:A
SHANGHAI SURPRISE (1986, Brit.) PR:C
SHANGHAIED LOVE (1931) PR:A
SHANGRI-LA (1961) PR:O
SHANKS (1974) PR:A
SHANNONS OF BROADWAY, THE (1929) PR:A
SHANTY TRAMP (1967) PR:O
SHANTYTOWN (1943) PR:A
SHAPE OF THINGS TO COME, THE (1979, Can.) PR:A
SHARE OUT, THE (1966, Brit.) PR:A
SHARK! (1970, US/Mex.) PR:C
SHARK (SEE: GREAT WHITE, THE) (1982, It.)
SHARK GOD, THE (SEE: OMOO OMOO, THE SHARK GOD) (1949)
SHARK REEF (SEE: SHE GODS OF SHARK REEF) (1958)
SHARK RIVER (1953) PR:A
SHARK WOMAN, THE (1941) PR:A
SHARKFIGHTERS, THE (1956) PR:A
SHARK'S TREASURE (1975) PR:A
SHARKY'S MACHINE (1981) PR:O
SHARPSHOOTERS (1938) PR:A
SHATTER (SEE: CALL HIM MR. SHATTER) (1976, Brit./Hong Kong)
SHATTERHAND (SEE: OLD SHATTERHAND) (1968, Yugo./Fr./It./W. Ger.)
SHE (1935) PR:A
SHE (1965, Brit.) PR:A-C
SHE (1985, It.) PR:O
SHE ALWAYS GETS THEIR MAN (1962, Brit.) PR:A
SHE AND HE (1967, Jap.) PR:A
SHE AND HE (1969, It.) PR:O
SHE ASKED FOR IT (1937) PR:A
SHE BEAST, THE (1966, Brit./It./Yugo.) PR:C
SHE COULDN'T SAY NO (1930) PR:A
SHE COULDN'T SAY NO (1939, Brit.) PR:A
SHE COULDN'T SAY NO (1941) PR:A
SHE COULDN'T SAY NO (1954) PR:A
SHE COULDN'T TAKE IT (1935) PR:A
SHE-CREATURE, THE (1956) PR:A
SHE DANCES ALONE (1981, Aust./US) PR:A
SHE DEMONS (1958) PR:A
SHE DEVIL (1957) PR:A
SHE-DEVIL (1989) PR:A
SHE-DEVIL ISLAND (1936, Mex.) PR:A
SHE-DEVILS ON WHEELS (1968) PR:O
SHE DIDN'T SAY NO? (1962, Brit.) PR:A
SHE DONE HIM WRONG (1933) PR:C
SHE FREAK (1967) PR:O
SHE GETS HER MAN (1935) PR:A
SHE GETS HER MAN (1945) PR:A
SHE GODS OF SHARK REEF (1958) PR:A
SHE GOES TO WAR (1929) PR:A
SHE GOT HER MAN (SEE: MAISIE GETS HER MAN) (1942)
SHE GOT WHAT SHE WANTED (1930) PR:A
SHE HAD TO CHOOSE (1934) PR:A
SHE HAD TO EAT (1937) PR:A
SHE HAD TO SAY YES (1933) PR:A
SHE HAD TO SAY YES (SEE: SHE COULDN'T SAY NO) (1954)
SHE HAS WHAT IT TAKES (1943) PR:A
SHE KNEW ALL THE ANSWERS (1941) PR:A

SHE KNEW WHAT SHE WANTED (1936, Brit.) PR:A
SHE KNOWS Y'KNOW (1962, Brit.) PR:C
SHE LEARNED ABOUT SAILORS (1934) PR:A
SHE LET HIM CONTINUE (SEE: PRETTY POISON) (1968)
SHE LOVED A FIREMAN (1937) PR:A
SHE LOVES ME NOT (1934) PR:A
SHE MADE HER BED (1934) PR:A
SHE MAN, THE (1967) PR:C
SHE MARRIED A COP (1939) PR:A
SHE MARRIED AN ARTIST (1938) PR:A
SHE MARRIED HER BOSS (1935) PR:A
SHE MONSTER OF THE NIGHT (SEE: FRANKENSTEIN'S DAUGHTER) (1958)
SHE PLAYED WITH FIRE (1957, Brit.) PR:C
SHE SHALL HAVE MURDER (1950, Brit.) PR:A
SHE SHALL HAVE MUSIC (1935, Brit.) PR:A
SHE SHOULDA SAID NO (SEE: WILD WEED) (1949)
SHE STEPS OUT (SEE: HARMONY AT HOME) (1930)
SHE WANTED A MILLIONAIRE (1932) PR:A
SHE WAS A HIPPY VAMPIRE (SEE: WILD WORLD OF BATWOMAN, THE) (1966)
SHE WAS A LADY (1934) PR:A
SHE WAS ONLY A VILLAGE MAIDEN (1933, Brit.) PR:A
SHE WENT TO THE RACES (1945) PR:A
SHE WHO DARES (SEE: THREE RUSSIAN GIRLS) (1943)
SHE-WOLF, THE (1931) PR:A
SHE-WOLF, THE (1963, USSR) PR:A
SHE-WOLF OF LONDON (1946) PR:A
SHE WORE A YELLOW RIBBON (1949) PR:A
SHE WOULDN'T SAY YES (1945) PR:A
SHE WROTE THE BOOK (1946) PR:A
SHEBA BABY (1975) PR:C
SHED NO TEARS (1948) PR:A
SHEENA (1984) PR:C-O
SHEEPDOG OF THE HILLS (1941, Brit.) PR:A
SHEEPMAN, THE (1958) PR:A
SHEER MADNESS (1983, W. Ger.) PR:C
SHEHERAZADE (SEE: SCHEHERAZADE) (1965, Fr./It./Sp.)
SHEIK STEPS OUT, THE (1937) PR:A
SHEILA LEVINE IS DEAD AND LIVING IN NEW YORK (1975) PR:A-C
SHE'LL HAVE TO GO (SEE: MAID FOR MURDER) (1963, Brit.)
SHELL SHOCK (1964) PR:C
SHENANDOAH (1965) PR:C
SHENANIGANS (SEE: GREAT BANK HOAX, THE) (1977)
SHEP COMES HOME (1949) PR:AA
SHEPHERD GIRL, THE (1965, Hong Kong) PR:A
SHEPHERD OF THE HILLS, THE (1941) PR:A
SHEPHERD OF THE HILLS, THE (1964) PR:A
SHEPHERD OF THE OZARKS (1942) PR:A
SHEPPER-NEWFOUNDER, THE (SEE: PART TIME WIFE) (1930)
SHERIFF OF CIMARRON (1945) PR:A
SHERIFF OF FRACTURED JAW, THE (1958, Brit.) PR:A
SHERIFF OF LAS VEGAS (1944) PR:A
SHERIFF OF REDWOOD VALLEY (1946) PR:A
SHERIFF OF SAGE VALLEY (1942) PR:A
SHERIFF OF SUNDOWN (1944) PR:A
SHERIFF OF TOMBSTONE (1941) PR:A
SHERIFF OF WICHITA (1949) PR:A
SHERLOCK HOLMES (SEE: ADVENTURES OF SHERLOCK HOLMES, THE) (1939)
SHERLOCK HOLMES (1932) PR:A
SHERLOCK HOLMES AND THE DEADLY NECKLACE (1962, W. Ger.) PR:A
SHERLOCK HOLMES AND THE SCARLET CLAW (SEE: SCARLET CLAW, THE) (1944)
SHERLOCK HOLMES AND THE SECRET CODE (SEE: DRESSED TO KILL) (1946)
SHERLOCK HOLMES AND THE SECRET WEAPON (1942) PR:A
SHERLOCK HOLMES AND THE SPIDER WOMAN (1944) PR:A
SHERLOCK HOLMES AND THE VOICE OF TERROR (1942) PR:A
SHERLOCK HOLMES FACES DEATH (1943) PR:O
SHERLOCK HOLMES' FATAL HOUR (1931, Brit.) PR:A
SHERLOCK HOLMES GROSSTER FALL (SEE: STUDY IN TERROR, A) (1966, Brit./W. Ger.)
SHERLOCK HOLMES IN WASHINGTON (1943) PR:A
SHE'S A SOLDIER TOO (1944) PR:A
SHE'S A SWEETHEART (1944) PR:A
SHE'S BACK ON BROADWAY (1953) PR:A
SHE'S DANGEROUS (1937) PR:A
SHE'S FOR ME (1943) PR:A
SHE'S GOT EVERYTHING (1938) PR:A
SHE'S GOTTA HAVE IT (1986) PR:O
SHE'S HAVING A BABY (1988) PR:C-O
SHE'S IN THE ARMY (1942) PR:A
SHE'S MY LOVELY (SEE: GET HEP TO LOVE) (1942)
SHE'S MY WEAKNESS (1930) PR:A
SHE'S NO LADY (1937) PR:A
SHE'S OUT OF CONTROL (1989) PR:A

SHE'S WORKING HER WAY THROUGH COLLEGE (1952) PR:A
SHICHININ NO SAMURAI (SEE: SEVEN SAMURAI, THE) (1954, Jap.)
SHIELD FOR MURDER (1954) PR:A
SHIELD OF FAITH, THE (1956, Brit.) PR:A
SHILLINGBURY BLOWERS, THE (1980, Brit.) PR:A
SHIN NO SHIKOTEI (SEE: GREAT WALL, THE) (1965, Jap.)
SHINBONE ALLEY (1971) PR:A
SHINE ON, HARVEST MOON (1938) PR:A
SHINE ON, HARVEST MOON (1944) PR:A
SHINEL (SEE: OVERCOAT, THE) (1965, USSR)
SHINING, THE (1980, Brit.) PR:C-O
SHINING HOUR, THE (1938) PR:A-C
SHINING STAR (SEE: THAT'S THE WAY OF THE WORLD) (1975)
SHINING VICTORY (1941) PR:A
SHINJU TEN NO AMIJIMA (SEE: DOUBLE SUICIDE) (1969, Jap.)
SHINJUKU DOROBO NIKKI (SEE: DIARY OF A SHINJUKU BURGLAR) (1968, Jap.)
SHIP AHOY (1942) PR:A
SHIP CAFE (1935) PR:A
SHIP FROM SHANGHAI, THE (1930) PR:A
SHIP OF CONDEMNED WOMEN, THE (1963, It.) PR:A
SHIP OF FOOLS (1965) PR:C
SHIP OF WANTED MEN (1933) PR:A
SHIP OF ZOMBIES (SEE: HORROR OF THE ZOMBIES) (1974, Sp.)
SHIP THAT DIED OF SHAME, THE (1956, Brit.) PR:A
SHIP WAS LOADED, THE (SEE: CARRY ON ADMIRAL) (1957, Brit.)
SHIPBUILDERS, THE (1943, Brit.) PR:A
SHIPMATES (1931) PR:A
SHIPMATES FOREVER (1935) PR:A
SHIPMATES O' MINE (1936, Brit.) PR:A
SHIPS OF HATE (1931) PR:A
SHIPS WITH WINGS (1942, Brit.) PR:A
SHIPWRECK (SEE: SEA GYPSIES. THE) (1978)
SHIPYARD SALLY (1940, Brit.) PR:A
SHIRALEE, THE (1957, Brit.) PR:C
SHIRIKURAE MAGOICHI (SEE: MAGOICHI SAGA, THE) (1970, Jap.)
SHIRLEY THOMPSON VERSUS THE ALIENS (1968, Aus.) PR:O
SHIRLEY VALENTINE (1989, Brit.) PR:C
SHIRO TO KURO (SEE: PRESSURE OF GUILT) (1961, Jap.)
SHIVERS (SEE: THEY CAME FROM WITHIN) (1976, Can.)
SHIVERS (1984, Pol.) PR:C
SHLOSHA YAMIN VE' YELED (SEE: NOT MINE TO LOVE) (1969, Israel)
SHNEI KUNI LEMEL (SEE: FLYING MATCHMAKER, THE) (1970, Israel)
SHOCK (1934) PR:C
SHOCK (1946) PR:O
SHOCK (SEE: BEYOND THE DOOR II) (1979, It.)
SHOCK CORRIDOR (1963) PR:O
SHOCK TREATMENT (1964) PR:O
SHOCK TREATMENT (1973, Fr.) PR:O
SHOCK TREATMENT (1981) PR:O
SHOCK TROOPS (1968, It./Fr.) PR:O
SHOCK WAVES (1977) PR:O
SHOCKER (SEE: TOWN WITHOUT PITY) (1961, US/Switz./W. Ger.)
SHOCKER (1989) PR:O
SHOCKING MISS PILGRIM, THE (1947) PR:A
SHOCKPROOF (1949) PR:C
SHOEMAKER AND THE ELVES, THE (1967, W. Ger.) PR:AA
SHOES OF THE FISHERMAN, THE (1968) PR:A
SHOESHINE (1946, It.) PR:C
SHOGUN ASSASSIN (1974, Jap.) PR:O
SHOGUN ISLAND (SEE: RAW FORCE) (1982)
SHONEN SARUTOBI SASUKE (SEE: MAGIC BOY) (1961, Jap.)
SHOOT (1976, Can.) PR:O
SHOOT FIRST (1953, Brit.) PR:C-O
SHOOT FIRST, LAUGH LAST (1967, US/It./W. Ger.) PR:O
SHOOT FOR THE SUN (1986, Brit.) PR:C-O
SHOOT IT: BLACK, SHOOT IT: BLUE (1974) PR:O
SHOOT LOUD, LOUDER. . . I DON'T UNDERSTAND (1966, It.) PR:O
SHOOT OUT (1971) PR:C
SHOOT OUT AT BIG SAG (1962) PR:C
SHOOT-OUT AT MEDICINE BEND (1957) PR:A
SHOOT THE MOON (1982) PR:C-O
SHOOT THE PIANO PLAYER (1960, Fr.) PR:C
SHOOT THE WORKS (1934) PR:A
SHOOT TO KILL (1947) PR:C
SHOOT TO KILL (1961, Brit.) PR:A
SHOOT TO KILL (1988) PR:O
SHOOTIN' IRONS (SEE: WEST OF TEXAS) (1943)
SHOOTING, THE (1971) PR:O
SHOOTING HIGH (1940) PR:A

SHOOTING PARTY, THE (1985, Brit.) PR:O
SHOOTING STRAIGHT (1930) PR:A
SHOOTIST, THE (1976) PR:O
SHOOTOUT (SEE: SHOOT OUT) (1971)
SHOP ANGEL (1932) PR:C
SHOP AROUND THE CORNER, THE (1940) PR:A
SHOP AT SLY CORNER, THE (SEE: CODE OF SCOTLAND YARD) (1948, Brit.)
SHOP ON HIGH STREET, THE (SEE: SHOP ON MAIN STREET, THE) (1965, Czech.)
SHOP ON MAIN STREET, THE (1965, Czech.) PR:C-O
SHOPWORN (1932) PR:A
SHOPWORN ANGEL, THE (1928) PR:A
SHOPWORN ANGEL, THE (1938) PR:A
SHORT CIRCUIT (1986) PR:A-C
SHORT CIRCUIT 2 (1988) PR:A
SHORT CUT TO HELL (1957) PR:O
SHORT EYES (1977) PR:O
SHORT GRASS (1950) PR:C
SHORT IS THE SUMMER (1968, Swed.) PR:O
SHOT AT DAWN, A (1934, Ger.) PR:C
SHOT IN THE DARK, A (1933, Brit.) PR:A
SHOT IN THE DARK, A (1935) PR:C
SHOT IN THE DARK, A (1941) PR:C
SHOT IN THE DARK, A (1964, US/Brit.) PR:A-C
SHOTGUN (1955) PR:O
SHOTGUN PASS (1932) PR:A
SHOTGUN WEDDING, THE (1963) PR:A-C
SHOULD A DOCTOR TELL? (1931, Brit.) PR:C
SHOULD A GIRL MARRY? (1929) PR:A
SHOULD A GIRL MARRY? (1939) PR:A
SHOULD HUSBANDS WORK? (1939) PR:AA
SHOULD LADIES BEHAVE? (1933) PR:C-O
SHOUT, THE (1978, Brit.) PR:O
SHOUT AT THE DEVIL (1976, Brit.) PR:C
SHOW BOAT (1929) PR:A
SHOW BOAT (1936) PR:A
SHOW BOAT (1951) PR:A
SHOW BUSINESS (1944) PR:AA
SHOW FLAT (1936, Brit.) PR:A
SHOW FOLKS (1928) PR:A
SHOW GIRL (1928) PR:A
SHOW GOES ON, THE (1937, Brit.) PR:A
SHOW GOES ON, THE (1938, Brit.) PR:C
SHOW-OFF, THE (1934) PR:A
SHOW-OFF, THE (1946) PR:A
SHOW THEM NO MERCY (1935) PR:C
SHOWDOWN, THE (1940) PR:A
SHOWDOWN, THE (SEE: WEST OF ABILENE) (1940)
SHOWDOWN, THE (1950) PR:A
SHOWDOWN (1963) PR:A
SHOWDOWN (1973) PR:A
SHOWDOWN AT ABILENE (1956) PR:A
SHOWDOWN AT BOOT HILL (1958) PR:A
SHOWDOWN FOR ZATOICHI (1968, Jap.) PR:C-O
SHOWGIRL IN HOLLYWOOD (1930) PR:A
SHOWTIME (1948, Brit.) PR:A
SHRIEK IN THE NIGHT, A (1933) PR:A
SHRIEK OF THE MUTILATED (1974) PR:O
SHRIKE, THE (1955) PR:C
SHUBIN (SEE: SCANDAL) (1964, Jap.)
SHUT MY BIG MOUTH (1942) PR:AA
SHUTTERED ROOM, THE (1968, Brit.) PR:C-O
SHY PEOPLE (1988) PR:O
SI PARIS NOUS ETAIT CONTE (SEE: IF PARIS WERE TOLD TO US) (1956, Fr.)
SI VERSAILLES M'ETAIT CONTE (SEE: ROYAL AFFAIRS IN VERSAILLES) (1957, Fr.)
SIAMMO QUATTRO MARZIANI (SEE: TWELVE-HANDED MEN OF MARS, THE) (1964, It./Sp.)
SIAVASH IN PERSEPOLIS (1966, Iran) PR:C
SICILIAN, THE (1987) PR:O
SICILIAN CLAN, THE (1970, Fr.) PR:O
SICILIAN CONNECTION, THE (1977) PR:O
SICILIANS, THE (1964, Brit.) PR:A
SID AND NANCY (1986, Brit.) PR:O
SIDDHARTHA (1972) PR:C
SIDE SHOW (1931) PR:A
SIDE STREET (1929) PR:A
SIDE STREET (1950) PR:C
SIDE STREET ANGEL (1937, Brit.) PR:A
SIDE STREETS (1934) PR:A
SIDECAR RACERS (1975, Aus.) PR:A
SIDEHACKERS, THE (SEE: FIVE THE HARD WAY) (1969)
SIDELONG GLANCES OF A PIGEON KICKER, THE (1970) PR:O
SIDESHOW (1950) PR:C
SIDEWALK STORIES (1989) PR:C
SIDEWALKS OF LONDON (1940, Brit.) PR:AA
SIDEWALKS OF NEW YORK (1931) PR:AA
SIDEWINDER 1 (1977) PR:C
SIDNEY SHELDON'S BLOODLINE (SEE: BLOODLINE) (1979)
SIEGE (1983, Can.) PR:O
SIEGE AT RED RIVER, THE (1954) PR:C
SIEGE OF FORT BISMARK (1968, Jap.) PR:C-O

SIEGE OF HELL STREET, THE (SEE: SIEGE OF SID-NEY STREET, THE) (1960, Brit.)
SIEGE OF PINCHGUT (SEE: FOUR DESPERATE MEN) (1960, Aus.)
SIEGE OF SIDNEY STREET, THE (1960, Brit.) PR:O
SIEGE OF SYRACUSE (1962, Fr./It.) PR:C
SIEGE OF THE SAXONS (1963, Brit.) PR:A
SIERRA (1950) PR:A
SIERRA BARON (1958) PR:A
SIERRA DE TERUEL (SEE: MAN'S HOPE) (1947, Sp.)
SIERRA PASSAGE (1951) PR:A
SIERRA STRANGER (1957) PR:C
SIERRA SUE (1941) PR:A
SIESTA (1987) PR:NR
SIETE HOMBRES DE ORO (SEE: SEVEN GOLDEN MEN) (1966, Fr./It./Sp./W. Ger.)
SIGN OF AQUARIUS (1970) PR:O
SIGN OF FOUR, THE (1932, Brit.) PR:C
SIGN OF FOUR, THE (1983, Brit.) PR:C
SIGN OF THE CROSS (1932) PR:C-O
SIGN OF THE GLADIATOR (1959, Fr./It./W. Ger.) PR:C
SIGN OF THE PAGAN (1954) PR:C
SIGN OF THE RAM, THE (1948) PR:A
SIGN OF THE VIRGIN (1969, Czech.) PR:O
SIGN OF THE WOLF (1941) PR:AA
SIGN OF VENUS, THE (1955, It.) PR:C
SIGN OF ZORRO, THE (1960) PR:AA
SIGNAL 7 (1984) PR:O
SIGNALS— AN ADVENTURE IN SPACE (1970, E. Ger./Pol.) PR:A
SIGNE CHARLOTTE (SEE: SINCERELY CHARLOTTE) (1986, Fr.)
SIGNED JUDGEMENT (SEE: COWBOY FROM LONE-SOME RIVER) (1944)
SIGNORA SENZA CAMELIE (SEE: LADY WITHOUT CAMELLIAS) (1953, It.)
SIGNORE E SIGNORI (SEE: BIRDS, THE BEES, AND THE ITALIANS, THE) (1967, Fr./It.)
SIGNORE E SIGNORI, BUONANOTTE (SEE: GOOD-NIGHT, LADIES AND GENTLEMEN) (1977, It.)
SIGNPOST TO MURDER (1964) PR:O
SIGNS OF LIFE (1981, W. Ger.) PR:O
SIGNS OF LIFE (1989) PR:C
SILENCE (1931) PR:O
SILENCE, THE (1963, Swed.) PR:O
SILENCE (1974) PR:AA
SILENCE HAS NO WINGS (1971, Jap.) PR:A
SILENCE OF DEAN MAITLAND, THE (1934, Aus.) PR:C-O
SILENCE OF DR. EVANS, THE (1973, USSR) PR:C
SILENCE OF THE NORTH (1981, Can.) PR:C
SILENCERS, THE (1966) PR:O
SILENT ASSASSINS (1988) PR:O
SILENT BARRIERS (1937, Brit.) PR:A
SILENT BATTLE, THE (SEE: CONTINENTAL EX-PRESS) (1939, Brit.)
SILENT CALL, THE (1961) PR:A
SILENT CONFLICT (1948) PR:A
SILENT DEATH (SEE: VOODOO ISLAND) (1957)
SILENT DUST (1949, Brit.) PR:A
SILENT ENEMY, THE (1930) PR:A
SILENT ENEMY, THE (1959, Brit.) PR:C
SILENT FLUTE, THE (SEE: CIRCLE OF IRON) (1979)
SILENT INVASION, THE (1962, Brit.) PR:A
SILENT MADNESS (1984) PR:O
SILENT MOVIE (1976) PR:A-C
SILENT NIGHT, BLOODY NIGHT (1972) PR:O
SILENT NIGHT, DEADLY NIGHT (1984) PR:O
SILENT NIGHT, DEADLY NIGHT PART II (1987) PR:O
SILENT NIGHT, DEADLY NIGHT 3: BETTER WATCH OUT! (1989) PR:O
SILENT NIGHT, EVIL NIGHT (SEE: BLACK CHRIST-MAS) (1974, Can.)
SILENT ONE, THE (1984, New Zealand) PR:A
SILENT PARTNER (1944) PR:C
SILENT PARTNER, THE (1979, Can.) PR:C-O
SILENT PASSENGER, THE (1935, Brit.) PR:A
SILENT PLAYGROUND, THE (1964, Brit.) PR:C-O
SILENT RAGE (1982) PR:O
SILENT RAIDERS (1954) PR:C
SILENT RUNNING (1972) PR:C
SILENT SCREAM (1980) PR:O
SILENT STAR (SEE: FIRST SPACESHIP ON VENUS) (1960, Pol./W. Ger.)
SILENT STRANGER, THE (SEE: STEP DOWN TO TER-ROR) (1958)
SILENT VOICE, THE (SEE: MAN WHO PLAYED GOD, THE) (1932)
SILENT VOICE, THE (SEE: PAULA) (1952)
SILENT WITNESS, THE (1932) PR:C
SILENT WITNESS (SEE: SECRETS OF A CO-ED) (1942)
SILENT WITNESS, THE (1962) PR:O
SILHOUETTES (1982) PR:C
SILIP (1985, Phil.) PR:O
SILK (1986, Phil.) PR:O
SILK EXPRESS, THE (1933) PR:A
SILK HAT KID (1935) PR:A
SILK NOOSE, THE (1950, Brit.) PR:A

SILK STOCKINGS (1957) PR:A
SILKEN AFFAIR, THE (1957, Brit.) PR:A
SILKEN SKIN (SEE: SOFT SKIN, THE) (1964, Fr.)
SILKEN TRAP, THE (SEE: MONEY JUNGLE, THE) (1968)
SILKWOOD (1983) PR:C-O
SILLY BILLIES (1936) PR:A
SILVER BANDIT, THE (1950) PR:A
SILVER BEARS (1978, Brit.) PR:C
SILVER BLAZE (SEE: MURDER AT THE BASKER-VILLES) (1941, Brit.)
SILVER BULLET, THE (1942) PR:C
SILVER CANYON (1951) PR:A
SILVER CHAINS (SEE: KID FROM AMARILLO, THE) (1951)
SILVER CHALICE, THE (1954) PR:A
SILVER CITY (SEE: ALBUQUERQUE) (1948)
SILVER CITY (1951) PR:C
SILVER CITY (1985, Aus.) PR:C
SILVER CITY BONANZA (1951) PR:A
SILVER CITY KID (1944) PR:A
SILVER CITY RAIDERS (1943) PR:A
SILVER CORD, THE (1933) PR:A
SILVER DARLINGS, THE (1947, Brit.) PR:A
SILVER DEVIL (SEE: WILD HORSE) (1931)
SILVER DOLLAR (1932) PR:A
SILVER DREAM RACER (1982, Brit.) PR:C
SILVER DUST (1953, USSR) PR:C
SILVER FLEET, THE (1945, Brit.) PR:A
SILVER HORDE, THE (1930) PR:A
SILVER KEY, THE (SEE: GIRL IN THE CASE) (1944)
SILVER LINING, THE (1932) PR:A
SILVER LODE (1954) PR:A
SILVER ON THE SAGE (1939) PR:A
SILVER QUEEN (1942) PR:A
SILVER RAIDERS (1950) PR:A
SILVER RIVER (1948) PR:A
SILVER SKATES (1943) PR:A
SILVER SPOON, THE (1934, Brit.) PR:A
SILVER SPURS (1936) PR:A
SILVER SPURS (1943) PR:A
SILVER STALLION (1941) PR:A
SILVER STAR, THE (1955) PR:A
SILVER STREAK, THE (1935) PR:A
SILVER STREAK (1976) PR:C
SILVER TOP (1938, Brit.) PR:A
SILVER TRAIL, THE (1937) PR:A
SILVER TRAILS (1948) PR:A
SILVER WHIP, THE (1953) PR:A
SILVERADO (1985) PR:C
SIMBA (1955, Brit.) PR:O
SIMCHON FAMILY, THE (1969, Israel) PR:C
SIMON (1980) PR:A-C
SIMON AND LAURA (1956, Brit.) PR:C-O
SIMON, KING OF THE WITCHES (1971) PR:O
SIMPLE CASE OF MONEY, A (1952, Fr.) PR:A
SIMPLY TERRIFIC (1938, Brit.) PR:A
SIN, THE (SEE: GOOD LUCK MISS WYCOFF) (1979)
SIN FLOOD (SEE: WAY OF ALL MEN, THE) (1930)
SIN NOW. . . PAY LATER (SEE: LOVE NOW. . . PAY LATER) (1966, It.)
SIN OF HAROLD DIDDLEBOCK, THE (SEE: MAD WEDNESDAY) (1950)
SIN OF MADELON CLAUDET, THE (1931) PR:C
SIN OF MONA KENT, THE (1961) PR:O
SIN OF NORA MORAN (1933) PR:A
SIN ON THE BEACH (1964, Fr.) PR:O
SIN SHIP, THE (1931) PR:A
SIN TAKES A HOLIDAY (1930) PR:A
SIN TOWN (1942) PR:A
SIN YOU SINNERS (1963) PR:O
SINAI COMMANDOS: THE STORY OF THE SIX DAY WAR (1968, Israel/W. Ger.) PR:C
SINAIA (SEE: CLOUDS OVER ISRAEL) (1966, Israel)
SINBAD AND THE EYE OF THE TIGER (1977, US/Brit.) PR:A-A
SINBAD THE SAILOR (1947) PR:A
SINCE YOU WENT AWAY (1944) PR:A
SINCERELY CHARLOTTE (1986, Fr.) PR:C-O
SINCERELY YOURS (1955) PR:A
SINFONIA PER DUE SPIE (SEE: SERENADE FOR TWO SPIES) (1966, It./W. Ger.)
SINFONIA PER UN MASSACRO (SEE: SYMPHONY FOR A MASSACRE) (1965, Fr./It.)
SINFUL DAVEY (1969, Brit.) PR:O
SING A JINGLE (1943) PR:A
SING ALONG WITH ME (1952, Brit.) PR:A
SING AND BE HAPPY (1937) PR:A
SING AND LIKE IT (1934) PR:A
SING AND SWING (1964, Brit.) PR:C
SING ANOTHER CHORUS (1941) PR:A
SING AS WE GO (1934, Brit.) PR:A
SING AS YOU SWING (1937, Brit.) PR:A
SING, BABY, SING (1936) PR:A
SING, BOY, SING (1958) PR:C
SING, COWBOY, SING (1937) PR:A
SING, DANCE, PLENTY HOT (1940) PR:A
SING FOR YOUR SUPPER (1941) PR:AA

SING ME A LOVE SONG (SEE: MANHATTAN MOON) (1935)
SING ME A LOVE SONG (1936) PR:A
SING, NEIGHBOR, SING (1944) PR:A
SING SING NIGHTS (1935) PR:C
SING SINNER, SING (1933) PR:A
SING WHILE YOU DANCE (1946) PR:A
SING WHILE YOU'RE ABLE (1937) PR:A
SING YOU SINNERS (1938) PR:AA
SING YOUR WAY HOME (1945) PR:A
SING YOUR WORRIES AWAY (1942) PR:A
SINGAPORE (1947) PR:A
SINGAPORE, SINGAPORE (1969, Fr./It.) PR:C
SINGAPORE WOMAN (1941) PR:A
SINGER AND THE DANCER, THE (1977, Aus.) PR:C
SINGER FROM SEVILLE, THE (SEE: CALL OF THE FLESH) (1930)
SINGER NOT THE SONG, THE (1961, Brit.) PR:O
SINGIN' IN THE CORN (1946) PR:A
SINGIN' IN THE RAIN (1952) PR:A
SINGING BLACKSMITH (1938) PR:C
SINGING BUCKAROO, THE (1937) PR:AA
SINGING COP, THE (1938, Brit.) PR:A
SINGING COWBOY, THE (1936) PR:A
SINGING COWGIRL, THE (1939) PR:A
SINGING FOOL, THE (1928) PR:A
SINGING GUNS (1950) PR:A
SINGING HILL, THE (1941) PR:AA
SINGING IN THE DARK (1956) PR:A
SINGING KID, THE (1936) PR:A
SINGING MARINE, THE (1937) PR:A
SINGING MUSKETEER, THE (SEE: THREE MUSKE-TEERS, THE) (1939)
SINGING NUN, THE (1966) PR:A
SINGING OUTLAW (1937) PR:A
SINGING PRINCESS, THE (1967, It.) PR:A
SINGING SHERIFF, THE (1944) PR:A
SINGING TAXI DRIVER (1953, It.) PR:A
SINGING THROUGH (1935, Brit.) PR:A
SINGING VAGABOND, THE (1935) PR:A
SINGLE-HANDED (SEE: SAILOR OF THE KING) (1953, Brit.)
SINGLE-HANDED SANDERS (1932) PR:A
SINGLE ROOM FURNISHED (1968) PR:O
SINGLE SIN (1931) PR:A
SINGLETON'S PLUCK (SEE: LAUGHTERHOUSE) (1984, Brit.)
SINGOALLA (SEE: GYPSY FURY) (1953, Fr.)
SINISTER HANDS (1932) PR:A
SINISTER HOUSE (SEE: WHO KILLED "DOC" ROB-BIN?) (1948)
SINISTER JOURNEY (1948) PR:A
SINISTER MAN, THE (1965, Brit.) PR:C
SINISTER URGE, THE (1961) PR:O
SINK THE BISMARCK! (1960, Brit.) PR:A
SINNER TAKE ALL (1936) PR:C
SINNERS, THE (SEE: 5 SINNERS) (1961, W. Ger.)
SINNERS GO TO HELL (SEE: NO EXIT) (1962, US/Arg.)
SINNER'S HOLIDAY (1930) PR:A
SINNERS IN PARADISE (1938) PR:C
SINNERS IN THE SUN (1932) PR:C
SINS OF JEZEBEL (1953) PR:C
SINS OF LOLA MONTES, THE (SEE: LOLA MONTES) (1955, Fr./W. Ger.)
SINS OF MAN (1936) PR:A
SINS OF RACHEL CADE, THE (1960) PR:O
SINS OF ROSE BERND, THE (1959, W. Ger.) PR:O
SINS OF THE BORGIAS (SEE: LUCRECE BORGIA) (1953, Fr./It.)
SINS OF THE CHILDREN (1930) PR:A
SINS OF THE FATHERS (1928) PR:A
SINS OF THE FATHERS (1948, Can.) PR:C
SIN'S PAYDAY (1932) PR:A
SIOUX CITY SUE (1946) PR:A
SIR GAWAIN AND THE GREEN KNIGHT (SEE: GAWAIN AND THE GREEN KNIGHT) (1973, Brit.)
SIR HENRY AT RAWLINSON END (1980, Brit.) PR:O
SIR, YOU ARE A WIDOWER (1971, Czech.) PR:O
SIREN OF ATLANTIS (1948) PR:A
SIREN OF BAGHDAD (1953) PR:A
SIRENE DU MISSISSIPPI (SEE: MISSISSIPPI MER-MAID) (1969, Fr.)
SIROCCO (1951) PR:A
SIROCCO D'HIVER (SEE: WINTER WIND) (1970, Fr./Hung.)
SIS HOPKINS (1941) PR:A
SISSI (SEE: FOREVER MY LOVE) (1962, Aus.)
SISTER-IN-LAW, THE (1975) PR:O
SISTER KENNY (1946) PR:A
SISTER OF LOVE (SEE: BAR 51 — SISTER OF LOVE) (1986, Israel)
SISTER, SISTER (1988) PR:O
SISTER TO ASSIST'ER, A (1930, Brit.) PR:A
SISTER TO ASSIST'ER, A (1938, Brit.) PR:A
SISTER TO ASSIST'ER, A (1948, Brit.) PR:A
SISTERS (1930) PR:A
SISTERS, THE (1938) PR:A
SISTERS, THE (1969, Gr.) PR:C

SISTERS (1973) PR:O
SISTERS (SEE: SOME GIRLS) (1989)
SISTERS OF THE GION (1936, Jap.) PR:A-C
SISTERS, OR THE BALANCE OF HAPPINESS (1979, W. Ger.) PR:O
SISTERS UNDER THE SKIN (1934) PR:C
SIT TIGHT (1931) PR:A
SITTING BULL (1954) PR:C
SITTING DUCKS (1979) PR:C
SITTING ON THE MOON (1936) PR:A
SITTING PRETTY (1933) PR:A
SITTING PRETTY (1948) PR:AA
SITTING TARGET (1972, Brit.) PR:O
SITUATION HOPELESS – BUT NOT SERIOUS (1965) PR:A
SIX BLACK HORSES (1962) PR:A
SIX BRIDGES TO CROSS (1955) PR:A
SIX CYLINDER LOVE (1931) PR:A
SIX-DAY BIKE RIDER (1934) PR:A
SIX DAYS A WEEK (1966, Fr./It./Sp.) PR:O
SIX FEMMES POUR L'ASSASSIN (SEE: BLOOD AND BLACK LACE) (1965, Fr./It./W. Ger.)
SIX GUN GOLD (1941) PR:A
SIX-GUN GOSPEL (1943) PR:A
SIX-GUN LAW (1948) PR:AA
SIX GUN MAN (1946) PR:A
SIX-GUN RHYTHM (1939) PR:A
SIX GUN SERENADE (1947) PR:A
SIX HOURS TO LIVE (1932) PR:C
SIX IN PARIS (1968, Fr.) PR:C-O
SIX INCHES TALL (SEE: ATTACK OF THE PUPPET PEOPLE) (1958)
SIX LESSONS FROM MADAME LA ZONGA (1941) PR:A
SIX MEN, THE (1951, Brit.) PR:A
SIX OF A KIND (1934) PR:A
SIX PACK (1982) PR:C
SIX PACK ANNIE (1975) PR:O
SIX P.M. (1946, USSR) PR:A
6.5 SPECIAL (1958, Brit.) PR:A
SIX SHOOTIN' SHERIFF (1938) PR:A
633 SQUADRON (1964, US/Brit.) PR:C
6000 ENEMIES (1939) PR:C
SIX WEEKS (1982) PR:C
SIXTEEN (SEE: LIKE A CROW ON A JUNE BUG) (1972)
SIXTEEN CANDLES (1984) PR:A-C
SIXTEEN FATHOMS DEEP (1934) PR:A
SIXTEEN FATHOMS DEEP (1948) PR:A
SIXTH AND MAIN (1977) PR:C
SIXTH MAN, THE (SEE: OUTSIDER, THE) (1962)
SIXTH OF JUNE, THE (SEE: D-DAY, THE SIXTH OF JUNE) (1956)
'68 (1988) PR:O
SIXTY GLORIOUS YEARS (1938, Brit.) PR:A
SIZZLE BEACH, U.S.A. (1986) PR:O
SJECAS LI SE DOLLY BELL? (SEE: DO YOU REMEMBER DOLLY BELL?) (1986, Yugo.)
SKAMMEN (SEE: SHAME) (1968, Swed.)
SKATEBOARD (1978) PR:C
SKATETOWN, U.S.A. (1979) PR:A
SKATING-RINK AND THE VIOLIN, THE (SEE: VIOLIN AND ROLLER) (1962, USSR)
SKAZA O KONKE-GORBUNKE (SEE: LITTLE HUMP-BACKED HORSE, THE) (1962, USSR)
SKELETON COAST (1989) PR:O
SKELETON ON HORSEBACK (1940, Czech.) PR:C
SKI BATTALION (1938, USSR) PR:C
SKI BUM, THE (1971) PR:O
SKI FEVER (1969, US/Aust./Czech.) PR:C
SKI PARTY (1965) PR:A
SKI PATROL (1940) PR:A
SKI RAIDERS, THE (SEE: SNOW JOB) (1972)
SKI TROOP ATTACK (1960) PR:C
SKID KIDS (1953, Brit.) PR:AA
SKIDOO (1968) PR:C
SKIES ABOVE (SEE: SKY ABOVE HEAVEN) (1964, Fr./It.)
SKIMPY IN THE NAVY (1949, Brit.) PR:A
SKIN DEEP (1929) PR:C
SKIN DEEP (1978, New Zealand) PR:O
SKIN DEEP (1989) PR:O
SKIN GAME, THE (1931, Brit.) PR:C
SKIN GAME, THE (1965, Brit.) PR:O
SKIN GAME (1971) PR:C
SKINNER STEPS OUT (1929) PR:A
SKIP TRACER, THE (1979, Can.) PR:C
SKIPALONG ROSENBLOOM (1951) PR:A
SKIPPER (SEE: TODD KILLINGS, THE) (1971)
SKIPPER SURPRISED HIS WIFE, THE (1950) PR:A
SKIPPY (1931) PR:AA
SKIRTS AHOY! (1952) PR:A
SKULL, THE (1965, Brit.) PR:O
SKULL AND CROWN (1938) PR:AA
SKULLDUGGERY (1970) PR:C
SKUPLIJACI PERJA (SEE: I EVEN MET HAPPY GYPSIES) (1968, Yugo.)
SKY ABOVE HEAVEN (1964, Fr./It.) PR:C
SKY BANDITS, THE (1940) PR:A

SKY BANDITS (1986, Brit.) PR:A-C
SKY BEYOND HEAVEN (SEE: SKY ABOVE HEAVEN) (1964, Fr./It.)
SKY BIKE, THE (1967, Brit.) PR:AA
SKY BRIDE (1932) PR:A
SKY CALLS, THE (1959, USSR) PR:A
SKY COMMANDO (1953) PR:A
SKY DEVILS (1932) PR:A
SKY DRAGON (1949) PR:A
SKY FULL OF MOON (1952) PR:A
SKY GIANT (1938) PR:A
SKY HAWK, THE (1929) PR:A
SKY HIGH (1952) PR:A
SKY IS RED, THE (1952, It.) PR:O
SKY IS YOURS, THE (SEE: LE CIEL EST A VOUS) (1957, Fr.)
SKY LINER (1949) PR:A
SKY MURDER (1940) PR:A
SKY PARADE, THE (1936) PR:A
SKY PATROL (1939) PR:A
SKY PIRATE, THE (1970) PR:C
SKY RAIDERS (1931) PR:A
SKY RAIDERS, THE (1938, Brit.) PR:A
SKY RIDERS (1976, US/Gr.) PR:C
SKY SPIDER, THE (1931) PR:A
SKY TERROR (SEE: SKYJACKED) (1972)
SKY WEST AND CROOKED (SEE: GYPSY GIRL) (1966, Brit.)
SKYDIVERS, THE (1963) PR:C
SKYJACKED (1972) PR:A
SKYLARK (1941) PR:A
SKYLARKS (1936, Brit.) PR:A
SKYLINE (1931) PR:A
SKYLINE (1983, Sp.) PR:C
SKY'S THE LIMIT, THE (1937, Brit.) PR:A
SKY'S THE LIMIT, THE (1943) PR:A
SKYSCRAPER SOULS (1932) PR:A
SKYSCRAPER WILDERNESS (SEE: BIG CITY) (1937)
SKYWATCH (SEE: LIGHT UP THE SKIES) (1960, Brit.)
SKYWAY (1933) PR:A
SLA FORST, FREDE? (SEE: OPERATION LOVEBIRDS) (1968, Den.)
SLADE (SEE: JACK SLADE) (1953)
SLAMDANCE (1987, US/Brit.) PR:O
SLAMMER (SEE: SHORT EYES) (1977)
SLAMS, THE (1973) PR:O
SLANDER (1956) PR:A
SLANDER HOUSE (1938) PR:A
SLAP SHOT (1977) PR:O
SLAPSTICK OF ANOTHER KIND (1984) PR:A-C
SLASH DANCE (1989) PR:C
SLASHER, THE (1953, Brit.) PR:O
SLASHER, THE (1975) PR:O
SLATTERY'S HURRICANE (1949) PR:C
SLAUGHTER (1972) PR:O
SLAUGHTER HIGH (1987) PR:O
SLAUGHTER HOTEL (1971, It.) PR:O
SLAUGHTER IN SAN FRANCISCO (1981) PR:O
SLAUGHTER OF THE VAMPIRES, THE (SEE: CURSE OF THE BLOOD GHOULS) (1969, It.)
SLAUGHTER ON TENTH AVENUE (1957) PR:A-C
SLAUGHTER TRAIL (1951) PR:A
SLAUGHTERHOUSE (1988) PR:O
SLAUGHTERHOUSE-FIVE (1972) PR:O
SLAUGHTERHOUSE ROCK (1988) PR:O
SLAUGHTER'S BIG RIP-OFF (1973) PR:O
SLAVE, THE (1963, It.) PR:A
SLAVE GIRL (1947) PR:A
SLAVE GIRLS (SEE: PREHISTORIC WOMEN) (1967, Brit.)
SLAVE OF THE CANNIBAL GOD (1979, It.) PR:O
SLAVE SHIP (1937) PR:A
SLAVE, THE (SEE: FABLE, A) (1971)
SLAVERS (1977, W. Ger.) PR:O
SLAVES (1969) PR:O
SLAVES OF BABYLON (1953) PR:A
SLAVES OF NEW YORK (1989) PR:O
SLAYER, THE (1982) PR:O
SLAYGROUND (1984, Brit.) PR:O
SLEEP, MY LOVE (1948) PR:A
SLEEPAWAY CAMP (1983) PR:O
SLEEPAWAY CAMP 2: UNHAPPY CAMPERS (1988) PR:O
SLEEPAWAY CAMP 3: TEENAGE WASTELAND (1989) PR:O
SLEEPER (1973) PR:A-C
SLEEPERS EAST (1934) PR:A
SLEEPERS WEST (1941) PR:A
SLEEPING BEAUTY (1959) PR:AA
SLEEPING BEAUTY (1965, W. Ger.) PR:AA
SLEEPING BEAUTY, THE (1966, USSR) PR:AA
SLEEPING CAR (1933, Brit.) PR:A
SLEEPING CAR MURDER, THE (1966, Fr.) PR:C-O
SLEEPING CAR TO TRIESTE (1949, Brit.) PR:A
SLEEPING CARDINAL, THE (SEE: SHERLOCK HOLMES' FATAL HOUR) (1931, Brit.)
SLEEPING CITY, THE (1950) PR:C
SLEEPING DOGS (1977, New Zealand) PR:C
SLEEPING PARTNERS (1930, Brit.) PR:A

SLEEPING PARTNERS (SEE: CARNIVAL OF CRIME) (1964)
SLEEPING PARTNERS (SEE: CARNIVAL OF CRIME) (1964)
SLEEPING TIGER, THE (1954, Brit.) PR:C
SLEEPLESS NIGHTS (1933, Brit.) PR:A
SLEEPY LAGOON (1943) PR:A
SLEEPYTIME GAL (1942) PR:A
SLENDER THREAD, THE (1965) PR:C
SLEPOY MUZYKANT (SEE: SOUND OF LIFE, THE) (1962, USSR)
SLEUTH (1972, Brit.) PR:C-O
SLIGHT CASE OF LARCENY, A (1953) PR:A
SLIGHT CASE OF MURDER, A (1938) PR:A
SLIGHTLY DANGEROUS (1943) PR:A
SLIGHTLY FRENCH (1949) PR:A
SLIGHTLY HONORABLE (1940) PR:A
SLIGHTLY MARRIED (1933) PR:A
SLIGHTLY SCANDALOUS (1946) PR:A
SLIGHTLY SCARLET (1930) PR:A
SLIGHTLY SCARLET (1956) PR:C
SLIGHTLY TEMPTED (1940) PR:A
SLIGHTLY TERRIFIC (1944) PR:A
SLIM (1937) PR:A
SLIM CARTER (1957) PR:A
SLIME PEOPLE, THE (1963) PR:A
SLIPPER AND THE ROSE, THE (1976, Brit.) PR:AA
SLIPPER EPISODE, THE (1938, Fr.) PR:A
SLIPPING INTO DARKNESS (1989) PR:O
SLIPPY MCGEE (1948) PR:A
SLIPSTREAM (1974, Can.) PR:O
SLITHER (1973) PR:C
SLITHIS (1978) PR:C
SLOGAN (1970, Fr.) PR:C
SLOW DANCING IN THE BIG CITY (1978) PR:C
SLOW MOTION (SEE: EVERY MAN FOR HIMSELF) (1980, Fr.)
SLOW MOVES (1984) PR:O
SLOW RUN (1968) PR:O
SLUGGER'S WIFE, THE (1985) PR:C-O
SLUMBER PARTY '57 (1977) PR:O
SLUMBER PARTY IN A HAUNTED HOUSE (SEE: GHOST IN THE INVISIBLE BIKINI, THE) (1966)
SLUMBER PARTY MASSACRE, THE (1982) PR:O
SLUMBER PARTY MASSACRE II (1987) PR:O
SMALL BACK ROOM, THE (SEE: HOUR OF GLORY) (1949, Brit.)
SMALL CHANGE (1976, Fr.) PR:C
SMALL CIRCLE OF FRIENDS, A (1980) PR:O
SMALL HOTEL (1957, Brit.) PR:A
SMALL HOURS, THE (1962) PR:O
SMALL MAN, THE (1935, Brit.) PR:A
SMALL MIRACLE, THE (SEE: NEVER TAKE NO FOR AN ANSWER) (1951, Brit.)
SMALL TOWN BOY (1937) PR:A
SMALL TOWN DEB (1941) PR:A
SMALL TOWN GIRL (1936) PR:A
SMALL TOWN GIRL (1953) PR:A
SMALL TOWN IN TEXAS, A (1976) PR:C
SMALL TOWN LAWYER (SEE: MAIN STREET LAWYER) (1939)
SMALL TOWN STORY (1953, Brit.) PR:A
SMALL VOICE, THE (SEE: HIDEOUT) (1948, Brit.)
SMALL WORLD OF SAMMY LEE, THE (1963, Brit.) PR:C
SMALLEST SHOW ON EARTH, THE (1957) PR:A
SMART ALEC (1951, Brit.) PR:A
SMART ALECKS (1942) PR:A
SMART BLONDE (1937) PR:A
SMART GIRL (1935) PR:A
SMART GIRLS DON'T TALK (1948) PR:A
SMART GUY (1943) PR:A
SMART MONEY (1931) PR:A
SMART POLITICS (1948) PR:A
SMART WOMAN (1931) PR:A
SMART WOMAN (1948) PR:A
SMARTEST GIRL IN TOWN (1936) PR:A
SMARTY (1934) PR:A
SMASH AND GRAB (SEE: LARCENY STREET) (1941, Brit.)
SMASH PALACE (1982, New Zealand) PR:O
SMASH-UP, THE STORY OF A WOMAN (1947) PR:C
SMASHING BIRD I USED TO KNOW, THE (SEE: SCHOOL FOR UNCLAIMED GIRLS) (1973, Brit.)
SMASHING THE CRIME SYNDICATE (SEE: HELL'S BLOODY DEVILS) (1970)
SMASHING THE MONEY RING (1939) PR:A
SMASHING THE RACKETS (1938) PR:A
SMASHING THE SPY RING (1939) PR:A
SMASHING THROUGH (SEE: CHEYENNE CYCLONE, THE) (1932)
SMASHING TIME (1967, Brit.) PR:C
SMELL OF HONEY, THE (SEE: SMELL OF HONEY, A SWALLOW OF BRINE!, A) (1966)
SMELL OF HONEY, A SWALLOW OF BRINE!, A (1966) PR:O
SMILE (1975) PR:C-O
SMILE OF THE LAMB, THE (1986, Israel) PR:O

SMILE ORANGE (1976, Jamaica) PR:C
SMILES OF A SUMMER NIGHT (1955, Swed.) PR:A
SMILEY (1957, Brit.) PR:A
SMILEY GETS A GUN (1959, Brit.) PR:A
SMILIN' THROUGH (1932) PR:A
SMILIN' THROUGH (1941) PR:A
SMILING ALONG (1938, Brit.) PR:A
SMILING GHOST, THE (1941) PR:A
SMILING IRISH EYES (1929) PR:A
SMILING LIEUTENANT, THE (1931) PR:A-C
SMITH! (1969) PR:A
SMITH OF MINNESOTA (1942) PR:A
SMITHEREENS (1982) PR:O
SMITH'S WIVES (1935, Brit.) PR:A
SMITHY (1933, Brit.) PR:A
SMITHY (SEE: PACIFIC ADVENTURE) (1947, Aus.)
SMOKE IN THE WIND (1975) PR:C
SMOKE JUMPERS (SEE: RED SKIES OF MONTANA) (1952)
SMOKE SIGNAL (1955) PR:A
SMOKE TREE RANGE (1937) PR:A
SMOKESCREEN (1964, Brit.) PR:A
SMOKEY AND THE BANDIT (1977) PR:C-O
SMOKEY AND THE BANDIT II (1980) PR:C-O
SMOKEY AND THE BANDIT—PART 3 (1983) PR:C-O
SMOKEY BITES THE DUST (1981) PR:C
SMOKEY SMITH (1935) PR:A
SMOKING GUNS (1934) PR:A
SMOKY (1933) PR:A
SMOKY (1946) PR:A
SMOKY (1966) PR:A
SMOKY CANYON (1952) PR:A
SMOKY MOUNTAIN MELODY (1949) PR:A
SMOKY TRAILS (1939) PR:A
SMOOTH AS SILK (1946) PR:A
SMOOTH TALK (1985) PR:C-O
SMORGASBORD (1983) PR:C
SMUGGLED CARGO (1939) PR:A
SMUGGLERS, THE (1948, Brit.) PR:A
SMUGGLERS, THE (1969, Fr.) PR:C
SMUGGLERS' COVE (1948) PR:A
SMUGGLER'S GOLD (1951) PR:A
SMUGGLER'S ISLAND (1951) PR:A
SMULTRONSTALLET (SEE: WILD STRAWBERRIES) (1957, Swed.)
SMURFS AND THE MAGIC FLUTE, THE (1984, Bel./Fr.) PR:AA
SNAFU (1945) PR:A
SNAKE PEOPLE, THE (1968, US/Mex.) PR:O
SNAKE PIT, THE (1948) PR:C
SNAKE RIVER DESPERADOES (1951) PR:A
SNAKE WOMAN, THE (1961, Brit.) PR:C
SNAPSHOT (SEE: DAY AFTER HALLOWEEN, THE) (1981, Aus.)
SNIPER, THE (1952) PR:O
SNIPER'S RIDGE (1961) PR:A
SNO-LINE (1986) PR:O
SNOOPY, COME HOME (1972) PR:AA
SNORKEL, THE (1958, Brit.) PR:A
SNOUT, THE (SEE: UNDERWORLD INFORMERS) (1965, Brit.)
SNOW (1982, Fr.) PR:O
SNOW COUNTRY (1969, Jap.) PR:O
SNOW CREATURE, THE (1954) PR:A
SNOW DEVILS, THE (1965, It.) PR:A
SNOW DOG (1950) PR:AA
SNOW IN THE SOUTH SEAS (1963, Jap.) PR:C
SNOW JOB (1972) PR:A
SNOW QUEEN, THE (1959, USSR) PR:AA
SNOW TREASURE (1968) PR:A
SNOW WHITE (1965, W. Ger.) PR:AA
SNOW WHITE AND ROSE RED (1966, W. Ger.) PR:AA
SNOW WHITE AND THE SEVEN DWARFS (1937) PR:AA
SNOW WHITE AND THE THREE CLOWNS (SEE: SNOW WHITE AND THE THREE STOOGES) (1961)
SNOW WHITE AND THE THREE STOOGES (1961) PR:A
SNOWBALL (1960, Brit.) PR:A
SNOWBALL EXPRESS (1972) PR:AA
SNOWBOUND (1949, Brit.) PR:A
SNOWED UNDER (1936) PR:A
SNOWFIRE (1958) PR:AA
SNOWMAN (SEE: LAND OF NO RETURN, THE) (1981)
SNOWS OF KILIMANJARO, THE (1952) PR:C
SNUFFY SMITH (SEE: SNUFFY SMITH, YARD BIRD) (1942)
SNUFFY SMITH, YARD BIRD (1942) PR:A
SO BIG (1932) PR:A
SO BIG (1953) PR:A
SO BRIGHT THE FLAME (SEE: GIRL IN WHITE, THE) (1952)
SO DARK THE NIGHT (1946) PR:C
SO DEAR TO MY HEART (1949) PR:AA
SO ENDS OUR NIGHT (1941) PR:A
SO EVIL MY LOVE (1948, Brit.) PR:C
SO EVIL SO YOUNG (1961, Brit.) PR:A
SO FINE (1981) PR:C-O
SO GOES MY LOVE (1946) PR:A
SO LITTLE TIME (1953, Brit.) PR:A

SO LONG AT THE FAIR (1951, Brit.) PR:A
SO LONG, BLUE BOY (1973) PR:O
SO LONG LETTY (1929) PR:A
SO LONG PHILIPPINE (SEE: ADIEU PHILIPPINE) (1963, Fr.)
SO PROUDLY WE HAIL (1943) PR:A
SO RED THE ROSE (1935) PR:A
SO SAD ABOUT GLORIA (1973) PR:C-O
SO THIS IS AFRICA (1933) PR:A
SO THIS IS COLLEGE (1929) PR:A
SO THIS IS LONDON (1930) PR:A
SO THIS IS LONDON (1940, Brit.) PR:A
SO THIS IS LOVE (1953) PR:A
SO THIS IS NEW YORK (1948) PR:A
SO THIS IS PARIS (1954) PR:A
SO THIS IS WASHINGTON (1943) PR:A
SO THIS WAS PARIS (SEE: THIS WAS PARIS) (1942, Brit.)
SO WELL REMEMBERED (1947, Brit.) PR:A-C
SO YOU WON'T TALK? (1935, Brit.) PR:A
SO YOU WON'T TALK (1940) PR:A
SO YOUNG, SO BAD (1950) PR:A
SOAK THE RICH (1936) PR:A
SOAPBOX DERBY (1958, Brit.) PR:AA
SOB SISTER (1931) PR:A
SOCIAL ENEMY NO. 1 (SEE: NO GREATER SIN) (1941)
SOCIAL LION, THE (1930) PR:A
SOCIAL REGISTER, THE (1934) PR:A
SOCIETY DOCTOR (1935) PR:A
SOCIETY FEVER (1935) PR:A
SOCIETY GIRL (1932) PR:A
SOCIETY LAWYER (1939) PR:A
SOCIETY SMUGGLERS (1939) PR:A
SOD SISTERS (1969) PR:O
SODOM AND GOMORRAH (1962, US/Fr./It.) PR:C
SOFI (1967) PR:A
SOFIA (1948) PR:A
SOFIA (1987, Arg.) PR:O
SOFT BEDS AND HARD BATTLES (SEE: UNDERCOVERS HERO) (1975, Brit.)
SOFT BODY OF DEBORAH, THE (SEE: SWEET BODY OF DEBORAH, THE) (1969, It./Fr.)
SOFT SKIN, THE (1964, Fr.) PR:C-O
SOFT SKIN AND BLACK LACE (SEE: SOFT SKIN ON BLACK SILK) (1964, Fr./Sp.)
SOFT SKIN ON BLACK SILK (1964, Fr./Sp.) PR:O
SOFT WARM EXPERIENCE, A (SEE: SATIN MUSHROOM, THE) (1969)
SOGEKI (SEE: SUN ABOVE, DEATH BELOW) (1969, Jap.)
SOGGY BOTTOM U.S.A. (1982) PR:C
SOHO CONSPIRACY (1951, Brit.) PR:A
SOHO INCIDENT (SEE: SPIN A DARK WEB) (1956, Brit.)
SOL MADRID (1968) PR:C
SOLANGE DU DA BIST (SEE: AS LONG AS YOU'RE NEAR ME) (1956, W. Ger.)
SOLARBABIES (1986) PR:A-C
SOLARIS (1972, USSR) PR:C
SOLDATERKAMMERATER PA VAGT (SEE: OPERATION CAMEL) (1961, Den.)
SOLDIER, THE (1982) PR:O
SOLDIER AND THE LADY, THE (1937) PR:C
SOLDIER BLUE (1970) PR:O
SOLDIER IN LOVE (SEE: FANFAN THE TULIP) (1952, Fr.)
SOLDIER IN SKIRTS (SEE: TRIPLE ECHO) (1973, Brit.)
SOLDIER IN THE RAIN (1963) PR:C
SOLDIER OF FORTUNE (1955) PR:C
SOLDIER OF ORANGE (1977, Neth.) PR:O
SOLDIER, SAILOR (1944, Brit.) PR:A
SOLDIER'S PAY, A (SEE: SOLDIER'S PLAYTHING, A) (1931)
SOLDIERS, THE (SEE: LES CARABINIERS) (1963, Fr.)
SOLDIERS AND WOMEN (1930) PR:A
SOLDIERS OF FORTUNE (SEE: WAR CORRESPONDENT) (1932)
SOLDIERS OF PANCHO VILLA, THE (SEE: LA CUCARACHA) (1961, Mex.)
SOLDIERS OF THE KING (SEE: WOMAN IN COMMAND) (1934, Brit.)
SOLDIERS OF THE STORM (1933) PR:A
SOLDIER'S PLAYTHING, A (1931) PR:A
SOLDIER'S PRAYER, A (1970, Jap.) PR:C
SOLDIER'S REVENGE (1986) PR:C
SOLDIER'S STORY, A (1984) PR:C
SOLDIER'S TALE, THE (1964, Brit.) PR:A
SOLDIERS THREE (1951) PR:A
SOLDIERS 3 (SEE: SERGEANTS 3) (1962)
SOLE SURVIVOR (1984) PR:O
SOLEIL ROUGE (SEE: RED SUN) (1972, Fr./It./Sp.)
SOLID GOLD CADILLAC, THE (1956) PR:A
SOLIMANO IL CONQUISTATORE (SEE: SULEIMAN THE CONQUEROR) (1963, It.)
SOLITAIRE MAN, THE (1933) PR:A
SOLITARY CHILD, THE (1958, Brit.) PR:A
SOLNTSE SVETIT VSEM (SEE: SUN SHINES FOR ALL, THE) (1961, USSR)

SOLO (1970, Fr.) PR:O
SOLO (1978, New Zealand/Aus.) PR:O
SOLO CONTRO ROMA (SEE: ALONE AGAINST ROME) (1963, It.)
SOLO FOR SPARROW (1966, Brit.) PR:A
SOLOMON AND SHEBA (1959) PR:C
SOLOMON KING (1974) PR:O
SOLUTION BY PHONE (1954, Brit.) PR:A
SOMBRERO (1953) PR:A-C
SOMBRERO KID, THE (1942) PR:A
SOME BLONDES ARE DANGEROUS (1937) PR:A
SOME CALL IT LOVING (1973) PR:O
SOME CAME RUNNING (1959) PR:C
SOME DAY (1935, Brit.) PR:A
SOME GIRLS (1989) PR:C
SOME GIRLS DO (1969, Brit.) PR:C
SOME KIND OF A NUT (SEE: DOWN AMONG THE Z-MEN) (1959, Brit.)
SOME KIND OF A NUT (1969) PR:C
SOME KIND OF HERO (1982) PR:C
SOME KIND OF WONDERFUL (1987) PR:C
SOME LIKE IT COOL (1979, Aust./It./Fr./W. Ger.) PR:O
SOME LIKE IT HOT (1939) PR:A
SOME LIKE IT HOT (1959) PR:C
SOME MAY LIVE (1967, Brit.) PR:A
SOME OF MY BEST FRIENDS ARE. . . (1971) PR:O
SOME PEOPLE (1964, Brit.) PR:A
SOME WILL, SOME WON'T (1970, Brit.) PR:A
SOMEBODY ELSE'S CHILDREN (SEE: STEPCHILDREN) (1962, USSR)
SOMEBODY KILLED HER HUSBAND (1978) PR:A
SOMEBODY LOVES ME (1952) PR:A
SOMEBODY UP THERE LIKES ME (1956) PR:C
SOMEONE (1968) PR:O
SOMEONE AT THE DOOR (1936, Brit.) PR:A
SOMEONE AT THE DOOR (1950, Brit.) PR:A
SOMEONE BEHIND THE DOOR (1971, Fr./Brit.) PR:C
SOMEONE TO LOVE (1988) PR:O
SOMEONE TO REMEMBER (1943) PR:A
SOMEONE TO WATCH OVER ME (1987) PR:O
SOMETHING ALWAYS HAPPENS (1934, Brit.) PR:A
SOMETHING BIG (1971) PR:A
SOMETHING FOR EVERYONE (1970) PR:O
SOMETHING FOR THE BIRDS (1952) PR:A
SOMETHING FOR THE BOYS (1944) PR:A
SOMETHING IN THE CITY (1950, Brit.) PR:A
SOMETHING IN THE WIND (1947) PR:A
SOMETHING IS OUT THERE (SEE: DAY OF THE ANIMALS) (1977)
SOMETHING LIKE THE TRUTH (SEE: OFFENSE, THE) (1973, Brit.)
SOMETHING MONEY CAN'T BUY (1952, Brit.) PR:A
SOMETHING OF VALUE (1957) PR:O
SOMETHING SHORT OF PARADISE (1979) PR:C-O
SOMETHING SPECIAL! (1987) PR:C
SOMETHING TO HIDE (1972, Brit.) PR:C-O
SOMETHING TO LIVE FOR (1952) PR:A
SOMETHING TO SHOUT ABOUT (1943) PR:A
SOMETHING TO SING ABOUT (1937) PR:A
SOMETHING WAITS IN THE DARK (SEE: SCREAMERS) (1978, It.)
SOMETHING WEIRD (1967) PR:O
SOMETHING WICKED THIS WAY COMES (1983) PR:C
SOMETHING WILD (1961) PR:A
SOMETHING WILD (1986) PR:O
SOMETHING'S ROTTEN (1979, Can.) PR:C
SOMETIMES A GREAT NOTION (1971) PR:O
SOMETIMES GOOD (1934, Brit.) PR:A
SOMEWHERE I'LL FIND YOU (1942) PR:A
SOMEWHERE IN BERLIN (1949, E. Ger./W. Ger.) PR:A
SOMEWHERE IN CAMP (1942, Brit.) PR:A
SOMEWHERE IN CIVVIES (1943, Brit.) PR:A
SOMEWHERE IN ENGLAND (1940, Brit.) PR:A
SOMEWHERE IN FRANCE (1943, Brit.) PR:A
SOMEWHERE IN POLITICS (1949, Brit.) PR:A
SOMEWHERE IN SONORA (1933) PR:A
SOMEWHERE IN THE NIGHT (1946) PR:C
SOMEWHERE IN TIME (1980) PR:C
SOMEWHERE ON LEAVE (1942, Brit.) PR:A
SOMMARLEK (SEE: ILLICIT INTERLUDE) (1954, Swed.)
SOMMARNATTENS LEENDE (SEE: SMILES OF A SUMMER NIGHT) (1955, Swed.)
SOMOMA E GOMORRA (SEE: SODOM AND GOMORRAH) (1962, US/Fr./It.)
SON COMES HOME, A (1936) PR:A
SON-DAUGHTER, THE (1932) PR:A
SON OF A BADMAN (1949) PR:A
SON OF A GUNFIGHTER (1966, US/Sp.) PR:A
SON OF A SAILOR (1933) PR:A
SON OF A STRANGER (1957, Brit.) PR:O
SON OF ALI BABA (1952) PR:A
SON OF BELLE STARR (1953) PR:A
SON OF BILLY THE KID (1949) PR:A
SON OF BLOB (SEE: BEWARE! THE BLOB) (1972)
SON OF CAPTAIN BLOOD, THE (1964, US/It./Sp.) PR:A
SON OF DAVY CROCKETT, THE (1941) PR:A
SON OF DR. JEKYLL, THE (1951) PR:A

SON OF DRACULA (1943) PR:C
SON OF DRACULA (1974, Brit.) PR:C
SON OF FLUBBER (1963) PR:AA
SON OF FRANKENSTEIN (1939) PR:C
SON OF FURY (1942) PR:A
SON OF GOD'S COUNTRY (1948) PR:A
SON OF GODZILLA (1967, Jap.) PR:C
SON OF GREETINGS (SEE: HI, MOM!) (1970)
SON OF INDIA (1931) PR:A
SON OF INGAGI (1940) PR:A
SON OF KONG (1933) PR:A
SON OF LASSIE (1945) PR:AA
SON OF MINE (SEE: FAME STREET) (1932)
SON OF MONGOLIA (1936, USSR) PR:A
SON OF MONTE CRISTO, THE (1941) PR:A
SON OF OKLAHOMA (1932) PR:A
SON OF PALEFACE (1952) PR:A
SON OF ROARING DAN (1940) PR:A
SON OF ROBIN HOOD (1959, Brit.) PR:A
SON OF SAMSON (1962, Fr./It./Yugo.) PR:A
SON OF SINBAD (1955) PR:A
SON OF SPARTACUS (SEE: SLAVE, THE) (1963, It.)
SON OF THE BLOB (SEE: BEWARE! THE BLOB) (1972)
SON OF THE BORDER (1933) PR:A
SON OF THE GODS (1930) PR:A
SON OF THE NAVY (1940) PR:A
SON OF THE PLAINS (1931) PR:A
SON OF THE RED CORSAIR (1963, It.) PR:A
SON OF THE REGIMENT (1948, USSR) PR:A
SON OF THE RENEGADE (1953) PR:A
SONG AND DANCE MAN, THE (1936) PR:A
SONG AND THE SILENCE, THE (1969) PR:A
SONG AT EVENTIDE (1934, Brit.) PR:C
SONG FOR MISS JULIE, A (1945) PR:A
SONG FOR TOMORROW, A (1948, Brit.) PR:A
SONG FROM MY HEART, THE (1970, Jap.) PR:A
SONG IS BORN, A (1948) PR:A
SONG O' MY HEART (1930) PR:A
SONG OF ARIZONA (1946) PR:A
SONG OF BERNADETTE, THE (1943) PR:AA
SONG OF FREEDOM (1938, Brit.) PR:A
SONG OF IDAHO (1948) PR:A
SONG OF INDIA (1949) PR:A
SONG OF KENTUCKY (1929) PR:A
SONG OF LIFE, THE (1931, Ger.) PR:A
SONG OF LOVE, THE (1929) PR:A
SONG OF LOVE (1947) PR:A
SONG OF MEXICO (1945) PR:A
SONG OF MY HEART (1947) PR:A
SONG OF NEVADA (1944) PR:A
SONG OF NORWAY (1970) PR:A
SONG OF OLD WYOMING (1945) PR:A
SONG OF PARIS (SEE: BACHELOR IN PARIS) (1953,
   Brit.)
SONG OF RUSSIA (1943) PR:A
SONG OF SCHEHERAZADE (1947) PR:A
SONG OF SOHO (1930, Brit.) PR:A
SONG OF SONGS (1933) PR:A-C
SONG OF SURRENDER (1949) PR:A
SONG OF TEXAS (1943) PR:A
SONG OF THE BUCKAROO (1939) PR:A
SONG OF THE CABALLERO (1930) PR:A
SONG OF THE CITY (1937) PR:A
SONG OF THE DRIFTER (1948) PR:A
SONG OF THE EAGLE (1933) PR:A
SONG OF THE FLAME (1930) PR:A
SONG OF THE FOREST (1963, USSR) PR:A
SONG OF THE FORGE (1937, Brit.) PR:A
SONG OF THE GRINGO (1936) PR:A
SONG OF THE ISLANDS (1942) PR:A
SONG OF THE LOON (1970) PR:O
SONG OF THE OPEN ROAD (1944) PR:A
SONG OF THE PLOUGH (SEE: COUNTY FAIR) (1933,
   Brit.)
SONG OF THE ROAD (SEE: END OF THE ROAD, THE)
   (1936, Brit.)
SONG OF THE ROAD (1937, Brit.) PR:A
SONG OF THE ROAD, THE (SEE: PATHER PANCHALI)
   (1955, India)
SONG OF THE SADDLE (1936) PR:A
SONG OF THE SARONG (1945) PR:A
SONG OF THE SIERRAS (1946) PR:A
SONG OF THE SIERRAS (SEE: SPRINGTIME IN THE
   SIERRAS) (1947)
SONG OF THE SOUTH (1946) PR:AA
SONG OF THE THIN MAN (1947) PR:A
SONG OF THE TRAIL (1936) PR:A
SONG OF THE WASTELAND (1947) PR:A
SONG OF THE WEST (1930) PR:A
SONG OVER MOSCOW (1964, USSR) PR:A
SONG TO REMEMBER, A (1945) PR:A
SONG WITHOUT END (1960) PR:A
SONG YOU GAVE ME, THE (1934, Brit.) PR:A
SONGS AND BULLETS (1938) PR:A
SONGWRITER (1984) PR:C-O
SONNY AND JED (1974, It.) PR:O
SONNY BOY (1929) PR:A
SONORA STAGECOACH (1944) PR:A

SONS AND LOVERS (1960, Brit.) PR:C
SONS AND MOTHERS (1967, USSR) PR:A
SONS O' GUNS (1936) PR:A
SONS OF ADVENTURE (1948) PR:A
SONS OF GOOD EARTH (1967, Hong Kong) PR:A-C
SONS OF KATIE ELDER, THE (1965) PR:A
SONS OF MATTHEW (SEE: RUGGED O'RIORDANS,
   THE) (1949, Aus.)
SONS OF NEW MEXICO (1949) PR:A
SONS OF SATAN (1969, It./Fr./W. Ger.) PR:C
SONS OF STEEL (1935) PR:A
SONS OF THE DESERT (1933) PR:A
SONS OF THE LEGION (SEE: SONS OF THE DESERT)
   (1933)
SONS OF THE LEGION (1938) PR:A
SONS OF THE MUSKETEERS (SEE: AT SWORD'S
   POINT) (1951)
SONS OF THE PIONEERS (1942) PR:A
SONS OF THE SADDLE (1930) PR:A
SONS OF THE SEA (1939, Brit.) PR:A
SONS OF THE SEA (SEE: ATLANTIC FERRY) (1941,
   Brit.)
SOOKY (1931) PR:A
SOPHIE LANG (SEE: NOTORIOUS SOPHIE LANG,
   THE) (1934)
SOPHIE LANG GOES WEST (1937) PR:A
SOPHIE'S CHOICE (1982) PR:O
SOPHIE'S PLACE (1970, US/Brit.) PR:C
SOPHIE'S WAYS (1970, Fr.) PR:O
SOPHOMORE, THE (1929) PR:A
SORCERER (1977) PR:O
SORCERERS, THE (1967, Brit.) PR:C
SORCERESS (1983) PR:O
SORORITY GIRL (1957) PR:C
SORORITY HOUSE (1939) PR:A
SORORITY HOUSE MASSACRE (1986) PR:O
SORRELL AND SON (1934, Brit.) PR:A
SORROWFUL JONES (1949) PR:A
SORRY, WRONG NUMBER (1948) PR:C
SORRY YOU'VE BEEN TROUBLED (SEE: LIFE GOES
   ON) (1932, Brit.)
SORTILEGES (SEE: BELLMAN, THE) (1947, Fr.)
SORYU HIKEN (SEE: SECRET SCROLLS (PART II))
   (1968, Jap.)
SOS PACIFIC (1960, Brit.) PR:A
SO'S YOUR AUNT EMMA (SEE: MEET THE MOB)
   (1942)
SO'S YOUR UNCLE (1943) PR:A
SOTTO GLI OCCHI DELL'ASSASSINO (SEE: UNSANE)
   (1982, It.)
SOTTO IL SOLE DI ROMA (SEE: UNDER THE SUN OF
   ROME) (1949, It.)
SOTTO IL TALLONE (SEE: CLOPORTES) (1966, Fr./It.)
SOTTO. . . SOTTO (1984, It.) PR:O
SOUHVEZDI PANNY (SEE: SIGN OF THE VIRGIN)
   (1969. Czech.)
SOUL KISS (SEE: LADY'S MORALS, A) (1930)
SOUL MAN (1986) PR:C
SOUL OF A MONSTER, THE (1944) PR:A
SOUL OF NIGGER CHARLEY, THE (1973) PR:O
SOUL OF THE SLUMS (1931) PR:A
SOUL SOLDIERS (SEE: RED, WHITE, AND BLACK,
   THE) (1970)
SOULS AT SEA (1937) PR:A
SOULS FOR SABLES (SEE: LOVE BOUND) (1932)
SOULS FOR SALE (SEE: CONFESSIONS OF AN
   OPIUM EATER) (1962)
SOULS IN CONFLICT (1955, Brit.) PR:A
SOULS OF SIN (SEE: MALE AND FEMALE SINCE
   ADAM AND EVE) (1961, Arg.)
SOUND AND FURY (1988, Fr.) PR:O
SOUND AND THE FURY, THE (1959) PR:C-O
SOUND BARRIER, THE (SEE: BREAKING THE
   SOUND BARRIER) (1952)
SOUND FROM A MILLION YEARS AGO (SEE: SOUND
   OF HORROR) (1966, Sp.)
SOUND OF FURY, THE (1950) PR:C
SOUND OF HORROR (1966, Sp.) PR:C
SOUND OF LIFE, THE (1962, USSR) PR:A
SOUND OF MUSIC, THE (1965) PR:AA
SOUND OF TRUMPETS, THE (1963, It.) PR:A
SOUND OFF (1952) PR:A
SOUNDER (1972) PR:AA
SOUNDER, PART 2 (1976) PR:AA
SOUP FOR ONE (1982) PR:O
SOUP TO NUTS (1930) PR:A
SOUP TO NUTS (SEE: WAITRESS) (1982)
SOURDOUGH (1977) PR:AA
SOURSWEET (1988, Brit.) PR:C-O
SOUS LE SOLEIL DE SATAN (SEE: UNDER SATAN'S
   SUN) (1988)
SOUS LES TOITS DE PARIS (SEE: UNDER THE ROOFS
   OF PARIS) (1930, Fr.)
SOUTH (1988, Arg./Fr.) PR:O
SOUTH AMERICAN GEORGE (1941, Brit.) PR:A
SOUTH BRONX HEROES (1985) PR:O
SOUTH OF ALGIERS (SEE: GOLDEN MASK, THE)
   (1954, Brit.)

SOUTH OF ARIZONA (1938) PR:A
SOUTH OF CALIENTE (1951) PR:A
SOUTH OF DEATH VALLEY (1949) PR:A
SOUTH OF DIXIE (1944) PR:A
SOUTH OF PAGO PAGO (1940) PR:A
SOUTH OF PANAMA (1941) PR:A
SOUTH OF RIO (1949) PR:A
SOUTH OF ST. LOUIS (1949) PR:A
SOUTH OF SANTA FE (1932) PR:A
SOUTH OF SANTA FE (1942) PR:A
SOUTH OF SONORA (1930) PR:A
SOUTH OF SUEZ (1940) PR:A
SOUTH OF TAHITI (1941) PR:A
SOUTH OF THE BORDER (1939) PR:A
SOUTH OF THE RIO GRANDE (1932) PR:A
SOUTH OF THE RIO GRANDE (1945) PR:A
SOUTH PACIFIC (1958) PR:A
SOUTH PACIFIC TRAIL (1952) PR:A
SOUTH RIDING (1938, Brit.) PR:A
SOUTH SEA ROSE (1929) PR:A
SOUTH SEA SINNER (1950) PR:A
SOUTH SEA WOMAN (1953) PR:A
SOUTH SEAS FURY (SEE: HELL'S ISLAND) (1955)
SOUTH TO KARANGA (1940) PR:A
SOUTHERN COMFORT (1981) PR:O
SOUTHERN MAID, A (1933, Brit.) PR:A
SOUTHERN ROSES (1936, Brit.) PR:A
SOUTHERN STAR, THE (1969, Fr./Brit.) PR:C
SOUTHERN YANKEE, A (1948) PR:AA
SOUTHERNER, THE (SEE: PRODIGAL, THE) (1931)
SOUTHERNER, THE (1945) PR:A
SOUTHSIDE 1-1000 (1950) PR:A
SOUTHWARD HO! (1939) PR:A
SOUTHWEST PASSAGE (1954) PR:A
SOUTHWEST TO SONORA (SEE: APPALOOSA, THE)
   (1966)
SOYLENT GREEN (1973) PR:C
SPACE AMOEBA, THE (SEE: YOG – MONSTER FROM
   SPACE) (1970, Jap.)
SPACE CHILDREN, THE (1958) PR:A
SPACE CRUISER (1977, Jap.) PR:A
SPACE DEVILS, THE (SEE: SNOW DEVILS, THE)
   (1965, It.)
SPACE FIREBIRD 2772 (1979, Jap.) PR:A
SPACE HUNTER: ADVENTURES IN THE FORBIDDEN
   ZONE (SEE: SPACEHUNTER: ADVENTURES IN THE
   FORBIDDEN ZONE) (1983)
SPACE INVASION FROM LAPLAND (SEE: INVASION
   OF THE ANIMAL PEOPLE) (1962, US/Swed.)
SPACE MASTER X-7 (1958) PR:A
SPACE MEN (SEE: ASSIGNMENT OUTER SPACE)
   (1960, It.)
SPACE MEN APPEAR IN TOKYO (SEE: MYSTERIOUS
   SATELLITE, THE) (1956, Jap.)
SPACE MISSION OF THE LOST PLANET (SEE: HOR-
   ROR OF THE BLOOD MONSTERS) (1970, US/Phil.)
SPACE MONSTER (1965) PR:A
SPACE RAGE (1987) PR:O
SPACE RAIDERS (1983) PR:C
SPACE SHIP, THE (1935, USSR) PR:A
SPACE SOLDIERS (SEE: FLASH GORDON) (1936)
SPACE STATION X (SEE: MUTINY IN OUTER SPACE)
   (1965)
SPACE STATION X-14 (SEE: MUTINY IN OUTER
   SPACE) (1965)
SPACEBALLS (1987) PR:C
SPACECAMP (1986) PR:A
SPACED OUT (1981, Brit.) PR:O
SPACEFLIGHT IC-1 (1965, Brit.) PR:A
SPACEHUNTER: ADVENTURES IN THE FORBIDDEN
   ZONE (1983) PR:C
SPACEMAN AND KING ARTHUR, THE (SEE: UNIDEN-
   TIFIED FLYING ODDBALL, THE) (1979, Brit.)
SPACEMEN SATURDAY NIGHT (SEE: INVASION OF
   THE SAUCER MEN) (1957)
SPACESHIP (SEE: DAY MARS INVADED THE EARTH,
   THE) (1963)
SPACESHIP (SEE: CREATURE WASN'T NICE, THE)
   (1981)
SPACESHIP TO THE UNKNOWN (SEE: FLASH GOR-
   DON) (1936)
SPACESHIP TO VENUS (SEE: FIRST SPACESHIP ON
   VENUS) (1962, Pol./W. Ger.)
SPACEWAYS (1953, Brit.) PR:A
SPANIARD'S CURSE, THE (1958, Brit.) PR:A
SPANISH AFFAIR (1958, Sp.) PR:A
SPANISH CAPE MYSTERY (1935) PR:A
SPANISH EYES (1930, Brit.) PR:A
SPANISH FLY (1975, Brit.) PR:O
SPANISH GARDENER, THE (1957, Brit.) PR:A
SPANISH MAIN, THE (1945) PR:A
SPANISH SWORD, THE (1962, Brit.) PR:A
SPARA FORTE, PIU FORTE. . . NON CAPISCO (SEE:
   SHOOT LOUD, LOUDER. . . I DON'T UNDER-
   STAND) (1966, It.)
SPARE A COPPER (1940, Brit.) PR:A
SPARE THE ROD (1961, Brit.) PR:A
SPARKLE (1976) PR:C-O

SPARO! (SEE: DJANGO KILL) (1967, It./Sp.)
SPARROWS CAN'T SING (1963, Brit.) PR:A
SPARTACUS (1960) PR:C
SPASMS (1983, Can.) PR:O
SPATS TO SPURS (SEE: HENRY GOES ARIZONA) (1939)
SPAWN OF THE NORTH (1938) PR:A
SPAWN OF THE SLITHIS (SEE: SLITHIS) (1978)
SPEAK EASILY (1932) PR:A
SPEAKEASY (1929) PR:A
SPEAKING PARTS (1989, Can.) PR:O
SPECIAL AGENT (1935) PR:A-C
SPECIAL AGENT (1949) PR:A
SPECIAL AGENT K-7 (1937) PR:A
SPECIAL DAY, A (1977, It./Can.) PR:C
SPECIAL DELIVERY (1955, W. Ger.) PR:A
SPECIAL DELIVERY (1976) PR:C
SPECIAL EDITION (1938, Brit.) PR:A
SPECIAL EFFECTS (1984) PR:O
SPECIAL INSPECTOR (1939) PR:A
SPECIAL INVESTIGATOR (1936) PR:A
SPECIALIST, THE (1975) PR:O
SPECKLED BAND, THE (1931, Brit.) PR:A
SPECTER OF FREEDOM, THE (SEE: PHANTOM OF LIBERTY, THE) (1974, Fr.)
SPECTER OF THE ROSE (1946) PR:C
SPECTRE OF EDGAR ALLAN POE, THE (1974) PR:O
SPEED (1936) PR:A
SPEED BRENT WINS (SEE: BREED OF THE BORDER) (1933)
SPEED CRAZY (1959) PR:C
SPEED DEVILS (1935) PR:A
SPEED LIMIT 65 (SEE: LIMIT, THE) (1972)
SPEED LIMITED (1940) PR:A
SPEED LOVERS (1968) PR:A
SPEED MADNESS (1932) PR:A
SPEED REPORTER (SEE: SCAREHEADS) (1931)
SPEED REPORTER (1936) PR:A
SPEED TO BURN (1938) PR:A
SPEED TO SPARE (1937) PR:A
SPEED TO SPARE (1948) PR:A
SPEED WINGS (1934) PR:A
SPEED ZONE (1989) PR:C
SPEEDTRAP (1978) PR:A
SPEEDWAY (1968) PR:A
SPELL OF AMY NUGENT, THE (1945, Brit.) PR:A
SPELL OF THE HYPNOTIST (1956) PR:A
SPELLBINDER (1988) PR:NR
SPELLBINDER, THE (1939) PR:A
SPELLBOUND (SEE: SPELL OF AMY NUGENT, THE) (1941, Brit.)
SPELLBOUND (1945) PR:A-C
SPENCER'S MOUNTAIN (1963) PR:C
SPENDTHRIFT (1936) PR:A
SPESSART INN, THE (1961, W. Ger.) PR:A
SPETTERS (1980, Neth.) PR:O
SPHINX, THE (1933) PR:A
SPHINX (1981) PR:C
SPICE OF LIFE (1954, Fr.) PR:A
SPIDER, THE (1931) PR:A
SPIDER, THE (1940, Brit.) PR:A
SPIDER, THE (1945) PR:A
SPIDER, THE (1958) PR:A
SPIDER AND THE FLY, THE (1952, Brit.) PR:A
SPIDER BABY (1968) PR:O
SPIDER BABY, OR THE MADDEST STORY EVER TOLD (SEE: SPIDER BABY) (1968)
SPIDER WOMAN (SEE: SHERLOCK HOLMES AND THE SPIDER WOMAN) (1944)
SPIDER WOMAN STRIKES BACK, THE (1946) PR:A
SPIDER'S WEB, THE (1960, Brit.) PR:A
SPIDER'S WEB, THE (SEE: IT'S HOT IN PARADISE) (1959, Yugo./W. Ger.)
SPIELER, THE (1929) PR:A
SPIES A GO-GO (SEE: NASTY RABBIT, THE) (1964)
SPIES AT WORK (SEE: SABOTAGE) (1939)
SPIES LIKE US (1985) PR:C
SPIES OF THE AIR (1940, Brit.) PR:A
SPIES, THE (SEE: LES ESPIONS) (1957, Fr.)
SPIKE OF BENSONHURST (1988) PR:C
SPIKER (1986) PR:C-O
SPIKES GANG, THE (1974) PR:C
SPIN A DARK WEB (1956, Brit.) PR:A
SPIN OF A COIN (SEE: GEORGE RAFT STORY, THE) (1961)
SPINAL TAP (SEE: THIS IS SPINAL TAP) (1984)
SPINOUT (1966) PR:A
SPIONE UNTER SICHE (SEE: DIRTY GAME, THE) (1966, Fr./It./W. Ger.)
SPIRAL ROAD, THE (1962) PR:A
SPIRAL STAIRCASE, THE (1946) PR:C
SPIRAL STAIRCASE, THE (1975, Brit.) PR:C-O
SPIRIT AND THE FLESH, THE (1948, It.) PR:A
SPIRIT IS WILLING, THE (1967) PR:A
SPIRIT OF CULVER, THE (1939) PR:A
SPIRIT OF NOTRE DAME, THE (1931) PR:A
SPIRIT OF ST. LOUIS, THE (1957) PR:AA
SPIRIT OF STANFORD, THE (1942) PR:A

SPIRIT OF THE BEEHIVE, THE (1976, Sp.) PR:C
SPIRIT OF THE DEAD (SEE: ASPHYX, THE) (1972, Brit.)
SPIRIT OF THE PEOPLE (SEE: ABE LINCOLN IN ILLINOIS) (1940)
SPIRIT OF THE WEST (1932) PR:A
SPIRIT OF THE WIND (1979) PR:A
SPIRIT OF WEST POINT, THE (1947) PR:A
SPIRIT OF YOUTH (1937) PR:A
SPIRITISM (1965, Mex.) PR:C
SPIRITS OF THE DEAD (1969, Fr./It.) PR:O
SPIRITUALIST, THE (1948) PR:A
SPITFIRE (1934) PR:A
SPITFIRE (1943, Brit.) PR:A
SPLASH (1984) PR:A-C
SPLATTER UNIVERSITY (1984) PR:O
SPLENDID FELLOWS (1934, Aus.) PR:A
SPLENDOR (1935) PR:A
SPLENDOR IN THE GRASS (1961) PR:C
SPLINTERS (1929, Brit.) PR:A
SPLINTERS IN THE AIR (1937, Brit.) PR:A
SPLINTERS IN THE NAVY (1931, Brit.) PR:A
SPLIT, THE (SEE: MANSTER, THE) (1962, Jap.)
SPLIT, THE (1968) PR:O
SPLIT DECISIONS (1988) PR:O
SPLIT IMAGE (1982) PR:O
SPLIT SECOND (1953) PR:A
SPLITFACE (SEE: DICK TRACY) (1945)
SPLITTING UP (1981, Neth.) PR:C
SPLITZ (1984) PR:O
SPOILED ROTTEN (1968, Gr.) PR:C-O
SPOILERS, THE (1930) PR:A
SPOILERS, THE (1942) PR:A
SPOILERS, THE (1955) PR:C
SPOILERS OF THE FOREST (1957) PR:A
SPOILERS OF THE NORTH (1947) PR:A
SPOILERS OF THE PLAINS (1951) PR:A
SPOILERS OF THE RANGE (1939) PR:A
SPOILS OF THE NIGHT (1969, Jap.) PR:C-O
SPOOK BUSTERS (1946) PR:A
SPOOK CHASERS (1957) PR:A
SPOOK TOWN (1944) PR:A
SPOOK WHO SAT BY THE DOOR, THE (1973) PR:O
SPOOKS RUN WILD (1941) PR:A
SPOOKY MOVIE SHOW, THE (SEE: MASK, THE) (1961, US/Can.)
SPORT OF A NATION (SEE: ALL-AMERICAN, THE) (1932)
SPORT OF KINGS, THE (1931, Brit.) PR:A
SPORT OF KINGS (1947) PR:A
SPORT PARADE, THE (1932) PR:A
SPORTING BLOOD (1931) PR:A
SPORTING BLOOD (1940) PR:A
SPORTING CHANCE (1931) PR:A
SPORTING CHANCE, A (1945) PR:A
SPORTING CLUB, THE (1971) PR:O
SPORTING LIFE (SEE: NIGHT PARADE) (1929)
SPORTING LOVE (1936, Brit.) PR:A
SPORTING WIDOW, THE (SEE: MADAME RACKETEER) (1932)
SPOT (SEE: DOGPOUND SHUFFLE) (1975, Can.)
SPOT OF BOTHER, A (1938, Brit.) PR:A
SPOTLIGHT SCANDALS (1943) PR:A
SPOTS ON MY LEOPARD, THE (1974, South Africa) PR:A
SPREAD EAGLE (SEE: EAGLE AND THE HAWK, THE) (1950)
SPRING (1948, USSR) PR:A
SPRING AFFAIR (1960) PR:A
SPRING AND PORT WINE (1970, Brit.) PR:C-O
SPRING BREAK (1983) PR:O
SPRING FEVER (1983, Can.) PR:C
SPRING FOR THE THIRSTY, A (1988, USSR) PR:A-C
SPRING HANDICAP (1937, Brit.) PR:A
SPRING IN PARK LANE (1949, Brit.) PR:A
SPRING IN THE AIR (1934, Brit.) PR:A
SPRING IS HERE (1930) PR:A
SPRING MADNESS (1938) PR:A
SPRING MEETING (1941, Brit.) PR:A
SPRING NIGHT, SUMMER NIGHT (SEE: MISS JESSICA IS PREGNANT) (1970)
SPRING PARADE (1940) PR:A
SPRING REUNION (1957) PR:A
SPRING SHOWER (1932, Hung.) PR:A
SPRING SONG (SEE: SPRINGTIME) (1948, Brit.)
SPRING SYMPHONY (1983, W. Ger./E. Ger.) PR:A-C
SPRING TONIC (1935) PR:A
SPRINGFIELD RIFLE (1952) PR:A
SPRINGTIME (1948, Brit.) PR:A
SPRINGTIME FOR HENRY (1934) PR:A
SPRINGTIME IN THE ROCKIES (1937) PR:A
SPRINGTIME IN THE ROCKIES (1942) PR:A
SPRINGTIME IN THE SIERRAS (1947) PR:A
SPRINGTIME ON THE VOLGA (1961, USSR) PR:A
SPURS (1930) PR:A
SPUTNIK (1958, Fr.) PR:A
SPY BUSTERS (SEE: GUNS IN THE HEATHER) (1968, Brit.)

SPY CHASERS (1956) PR:A
SPY FOR A DAY (1939, Brit.) PR:A
SPY HUNT (1950) PR:A
SPY IN BLACK, THE (1939, Brit.) PR:A
SPY IN THE GREEN HAT, THE (1966) PR:A
SPY IN THE PANTRY (SEE: MISSING TEN DAYS) (1941, Brit.)
SPY IN THE SKY (1958) PR:A
SPY IN WHITE, THE (SEE: SECRET OF STAMBOUL, THE) (1936, Brit.)
SPY IN YOUR EYE (1966, It.) PR:A
SPY OF NAPOLEON (1939, Brit.) PR:A
SPY RING, THE (1938) PR:A
SPY 77 (SEE: SECRET AGENT) (1933, Brit.)
SPY SHIP (1942) PR:A
SPY 13 (SEE: OPERATION 13) (1934)
SPY TRAIN (1943) PR:A
SPY WHO CAME IN FROM THE COLD, THE (1965, Brit.) PR:A-C
SPY WHO LOVED ME, THE (1977, Brit.) PR:C
SPY WITH A COLD NOSE, THE (1966, Brit.) PR:A
SPY WITH MY FACE, THE (1966) PR:A
SPYASHCHAYA KRASAVITSA (SEE: SLEEPING BEAUTY, THE) (1966, USSR)
SPYLARKS (1965, Brit.) PR:A
*S*P*Y*S* (1974) PR:C
SQUAD CAR (1961) PR:A
SQUADRON LEADER X (1943, Brit.) PR:A
SQUADRON OF HONOR (1938) PR:A
SQUALL, THE (1929) PR:A
SQUAMISH FIVE, THE (1988, Can.) PR:C
SQUARE DANCE (1987) PR:C
SQUARE DANCE JUBILEE (1949) PR:A
SQUARE DANCE KATY (1950) PR:A
SQUARE JUNGLE, THE (1955) PR:A
SQUARE OF VIOLENCE (1963, US/Yugo.) PR:A
SQUARE PEG, THE (1958, Brit.) PR:A
SQUARE RING, THE (1955, Brit.) PR:A
SQUARE ROOT OF ZERO, THE (1964) PR:C
SQUARE SHOOTER, THE (SEE: SKIPALONG ROSENBLOOM) (1951)
SQUARE SHOULDERS (1929) PR:A
SQUARED CIRCLE, THE (SEE: JOE PALOOKA IN THE SQUARED CIRCLE) (1950)
SQUARES (1972) PR:A
SQUATTER'S DAUGHTER (1933, Aus.) PR:A
SQUAW MAN, THE (1931) PR:A
SQUEAKER, THE (1930, Brit.) PR:A
SQUEAKER, THE (SEE: MURDER ON DIAMOND ROW) (1937, Brit.)
SQUEALER, THE (1930) PR:A
SQUEEZE, THE (1977, Brit.) PR:O
SQUEEZE A FLOWER (1970, Aus.) PR:A
SQUEEZE, THE (1980, It.) PR:O
SQUEEZE, THE (1987) PR:O
SQUEEZE PLAY (1981) PR:O
SQUIBS (1935, Brit.) PR:A
SQUIRM (1976) PR:C
SQUIZZY TAYLOR (1984, Aus.) PR:O
SREDI DOBRYKH LYUDEY (SEE: MOTHER AND DAUGHTER) (1965, USSR)
SSSSNAKE (SEE: SSSSSSSS) (1973)
SSSSSSSS (1973) PR:C
STABLEMATES (1938) PR:A
STACEY! (1973) PR:O
STACEY AND HER GANGBUSTERS (SEE: STACEY!) (1973)
STACKING (1987) PR:A-C
STACY'S KNIGHTS (1983) PR:C
STADIUM MURDERS, THE (SEE: HOLLYWOOD STADIUM MYSTERY) (1938)
STAGE DOOR (1937) PR:A-C
STAGE DOOR CANTEEN (1943) PR:A
STAGE FRIGHT (1950, Brit.) PR:A-c
STAGE FROM BLUE RIVER (SEE: STAGE TO BLUE RIVER) (1951)
STAGE MOTHER (1933) PR:A
STAGE STRUCK (1936) PR:A
STAGE STRUCK (1948) PR:C
STAGE STRUCK (1958) PR:A-C
STAGE TO BLUE RIVER (1951) PR:A
STAGE TO CHINO (1940) PR:A
STAGE TO MESA CITY (1947) PR:A
STAGE TO THUNDER ROCK (1964) PR:A
STAGE TO TUCSON (1950) PR:A
STAGE WHISPERS (SEE: GRIEF STREET) (1931)
STAGECOACH (1939) PR:C
STAGECOACH (1966) PR:A-C
STAGECOACH BUCKAROO (1942) PR:A
STAGECOACH DAYS (1938) PR:A
STAGECOACH EXPRESS (1942) PR:A
STAGECOACH KID (1949) PR:A
STAGECOACH LINE (SEE: OLD TEXAS TRAIL, THE) (1944)
STAGECOACH OUTLAWS (1945) PR:A
STAGECOACH TO DANCERS' ROCK (1962) PR:A
STAGECOACH TO DENVER (1946) PR:A
STAGECOACH TO FURY (1956) PR:A

STAGECOACH TO HELL (SEE: STAGE TO THUNDER ROCK) (1964)
STAGECOACH TO MONTEREY (1944) PR:A
STAGECOACH WAR (1940) PR:A
STAIRCASE (1969, US/Brit./Fr.) PR:C-O
STAIRWAY TO HEAVEN (1946, Brit.) PR:A
STAKEOUT! (1962) PR:A
STAKEOUT (1987) PR:O
STAKEOUT ON DOPE STREET (1958) PR:C
STALAG 17 (1953) PR:C
STALKER (1982, USSR) PR:C
STALKING MOON, THE (1969) PR:A
STALLION CANYON (1949) PR:A
STALLION ROAD (1947) PR:A
STAMBOUL (1931, Brit.) PR:A
STAMBOUL QUEST (1934) PR:A
STAMMHEIM (1986, W. Ger.) PR:C
STAMPEDE (1936) PR:A
STAMPEDE (1949) PR:A
STAMPEDE (SEE: GUNS OF THE TIMBERLAND) (1960)
STAMPEDED (SEE: BIG LAND, THE) (1957)
STAND ALONE (1985) PR:O
STAND AND DELIVER (SEE: BOWERY BLITZKRIEG) (1941)
STAND AND DELIVER (1988) PR:A
STAND AT APACHE RIVER, THE (1953) PR:A
STAND BY FOR ACTION (1942) PR:A
STAND BY ME (1986) PR:C
STAND EASY (SEE: DOWN AMONG THE Z-MEN) (1959, Brit.)
STAND EASY (SEE: DOWN AMONG THE Z MEN) (1952)
STAND-IN (1937) PR:A
STAND-IN, THE (1985) PR:C-O
STAND UP AND BE COUNTED (1972) PR:C
STAND UP AND CHEER (1934) PR:A
STAND UP AND FIGHT (1939) PR:A-C
STAND UP VIRGIN SOLDIERS (1977, Brit.) PR:O
STANDING ROOM ONLY (1944) PR:A
STANLEY (1973) PR:O
STANLEY AND LIVINGSTONE (1939) PR:AA
STAR, THE (1953) PR:A
STAR! (1968) PR:A-C
STAR CHAMBER, THE (1983) PR:C-O
STAR CHILD (SEE: SPACE RAIDERS) (1983)
STAR CRASH (SEE: STARCRASH) (1979)
STAR CRYSTAL (1986) PR:O
STAR DUST (1940) PR:A
STAR 80 (1983) PR:O
STAR FELL FROM HEAVEN, A (1936, Brit.) PR:AA
STAR FOR A NIGHT (1936) PR:A
STAR IN THE DUST (1956) PR:A
STAR IN THE WEST (SEE: SECOND TIME AROUND, THE) (1961)
STAR INSPECTOR, THE (1980, USSR) PR:A
STAR IS BORN, A (1937) PR:C
STAR IS BORN, A (1954) PR:A-C
STAR IS BORN, A (1976) PR:C-O
STAR MAKER, THE (1939) PR:AA
STAR OF HONG KONG (1962, Jap.) PR:A
STAR OF INDIA (1956, Brit.) PR:A
STAR OF MIDNIGHT (1935) PR:A
STAR OF MY NIGHT (1954, Brit.) PR:C
STAR OF TEXAS (1953) PR:A
STAR OF THE CIRCUS (SEE: HIDDEN MENACE, THE) (1940, Brit.)
STAR PACKER, THE (1934) PR:A
STAR PILOT (1977, It.) PR:A
STAR REPORTER (1939) PR:A
STAR SAID NO, THE (SEE: CALLAWAY WENT THATA-WAY) (1951)
STAR SLAMMER: THE ESCAPE (1988) PR:O
STAR SPANGLED GIRL (1971) PR:A
STAR SPANGLED RHYTHM (1942) PR:A
STAR TREK: THE MOTION PICTURE (1979) PR:A
STAR TREK II: THE WRATH OF KHAN (1982) PR:A
STAR TREK III: THE SEARCH FOR SPOCK (1984) PR:A-C
STAR TREK IV: THE VOYAGE HOME (1986) PR:A-C
STAR TREK V: THE FINAL FRONTIER (1989) PR:A
STAR WARS (1977) PR:A-C
STAR WITNESS (1931) PR:A
STARCHASER: THE LEGEND OF ORIN (1985) PR:C
STARCRASH (1979) PR:C
STARDUST (SEE: HE LOVED AN ACTRESS) (1938, Brit.)
STARDUST (1974, Brit.) PR:O
STARDUST MEMORIES (1980) PR:C
STARDUST ON THE SAGE (1942) PR:A
STARFIGHTERS, THE (1964) PR:A
STARHOPS (1978) PR:O
STARK FEAR (1963) PR:C
STARK MAD (1929) PR:A
STARLIFT (1951) PR:A
STARLIGHT HOTEL (1987, New Zealand) PR:A
STARLIGHT OVER TEXAS (1938) PR:A
STARLIGHT SLAUGHTER (SEE: EATEN ALIVE!) (1976)

STARMAN (1984) PR:C
STARS AND BARS (1988) PR:C-O
STARS AND STRIPES FOREVER (1952) PR:AA
STARS ARE SINGING, THE (1953) PR:A
STARS IN MY CROWN (1950) PR:A
STARS IN YOUR BACKYARD (SEE: PARADISE ALLEY) (1962)
STARS IN YOUR EYES (1956, Brit.) PR:A
STARS LOOK DOWN, THE (1940, Brit.) PR:A-C
STARS ON PARADE (1944) PR:A
STARS OVER ARIZONA (1937) PR:A
STARS OVER BROADWAY (1935) PR:A
STARS OVER TEXAS (1946) PR:A
STARSHIP INVASIONS (1978, Can.) PR:AA
STARSTRUCK (1982, Aus.) PR:C
START CHEERING (1938) PR:A
START THE REVOLUTION WITHOUT ME (1970) PR:C-O
STARTING OVER (1979) PR:C-O
STASTNY KONEC (SEE: HAPPY END) (1968, Czech.)
STATE DEPARTMENT — FILE 649 (1949) PR:A
STATE FAIR (1933) PR:A
STATE FAIR (1945) PR:A
STATE FAIR (1962) PR:A
STATE OF SIEGE (1972, Fr./US/It./W. Ger.) PR:C
STATE OF THE UNION (1948) PR:A
STATE OF THINGS, THE (1982) PR:A
STATE PENITENTIARY (1950) PR:A
STATE POLICE (1938) PR:A
STATE POLICE (SEE: WHIRLWIND RAIDERS) (1948)
STATE SECRET (SEE: GREAT MANHUNT, THE) (1951, Brit.)
STATE STREET SADIE (1928) PR:C
STATE TROOPER (1933) PR:A
STATELESS (SEE: NO EXIT) (1962, US/Arg.)
STATELINE MOTEL (1976, It.) PR:A
STATE'S ATTORNEY (1932) PR:A
STATIC (1985) PR:C-O
STATION SIX-SAHARA (1964, Brit./W. Ger.) PR:C
STATION WEST (1948) PR:A
STATUE, THE (1971, Brit.) PR:O
STAVISKY (1974, Fr.) PR:C
STAY AS YOU ARE (1978, It./Sp.) PR:O
STAY AWAY, JOE (1968) PR:A
STAY HUNGRY (1976) PR:O
STAYING ALIVE (1983) PR:C
STAYING TOGETHER (1989) PR:C
STEADY COMPANY (1932) PR:A
STEAGLE, THE (1971) PR:O
STEALING HEAVEN (1989, Brit./Yugo.) PR:C
STEALING HOME (1988) PR:C
STEAMBOAT 'ROUND THE BEND (1935) PR:A
STEAMING (1985, Brit.) PR:O
STEEL (1980) PR:C
STEEL AGAINST THE SKY (1941) PR:A
STEEL ARENA (1973) PR:C
STEEL BAYONET, THE (1958, Brit.) PR:A
STEEL CAGE, THE (1954) PR:A
STEEL CLAW, THE (1961) PR:A
STEEL DAWN (1987) PR:C
STEEL FIST, THE (1952) PR:A
STEEL HELMET, THE (1951) PR:C
STEEL HIGHWAY, THE (SEE: OTHER MEN'S WOMEN) (1931)
STEEL JUNGLE, THE (1956) PR:A
STEEL KEY, THE (1953, Brit.) PR:A
STEEL LADY, THE (1953) PR:A
STEEL MAGNOLIAS (1989) PR:C
STEEL TOWN (1952) PR:A
STEEL TRAP, THE (1952) PR:A
STEELE JUSTICE (1987) PR:O
STEELYARD BLUES (1973) PR:C
STEFANIA (1968, Gr.) PR:O
STELLA (1950) PR:A
STELLA DALLAS (1937) PR:A
STELLA PARISH (SEE: I FOUND STELLA PARISH) (1935)
STELLA STAR (SEE: STARCRASH) (1979)
STEP BY STEP (1946) PR:A
STEP DOWN TO TERROR (1958) PR:A
STEP LIVELY (1944) PR:A
STEP LIVELY, JEEVES (1937) PR:A
STEPCHILD (1947) PR:A
STEPCHILDREN (1962, USSR) PR:A
STEPFATHER, THE (1987) PR:O
STEPFATHER 2: MAKE ROOM FOR DADDY (1989) PR:O
STEPFORD WIVES, THE (1975) PR:A-C
STEPHANIA (SEE: STEFANIA) (1968, Gr.)
STEPHEN KING'S SILVER BULLET (1985) PR:O
STEPMOTHER, THE (1974) PR:O
STEPPE, THE (1963, Fr./It.) PR:A
STEPPENWOLF (1974) PR:O
STEPPIN' IN SOCIETY (1945) PR:A
STEPPING INTO SOCIETY (SEE: DOUGHNUTS AND SOCIETY) (1936)
STEPPING SISTERS (1932) PR:A
STEPPING TOES (1938, Brit.) PR:A
STEPS TO THE MOON (1963, Rum.) PR:A
STEPTOE AND SON (1972, Brit.) PR:A-C

STEREO (1969, Can.) PR:O
STERILE CUCKOO, THE (1969) PR:C
STEVIE (1978, Brit.) PR:A
STEWARDESS SCHOOL (1986) PR:O
STICK (1985) PR:O
STICK 'EM UP (1950, Brit.) PR:A
STICK TO YOUR GUNS (1941) PR:A
STICK UP, THE (1978, Brit.) PR:A
STICKY FINGERS (1988) PR:C
STIGMA (1972) PR:O
STILETTO (1969) PR:O
STILL OF THE NIGHT (1982) PR:O
STILL ROOM IN HELL (SEE: THERE IS STILL ROOM IN HELL) (1963, W. Ger.)
STILL SMOKIN' (1983) PR:O
STING, THE (1973) PR:C
STING II, THE (1983) PR:C
STING OF DEATH (1966) PR:C
STINGAREE (1934) PR:A
STINGRAY (1978) PR:C
STIR (1980, Aus.) PR:O
STIR CRAZY (1980) PR:C-O
STITCH IN TIME, A (1967, Brit.) PR:A
STITCHES (1985) PR:O
STOCK CAR (1955, Brit.) PR:A
STOKER, THE (1932) PR:A
STOKER, THE (1935, Brit.) PR:A
STOLEN AIRLINER, THE (1962, Brit.) PR:AA
STOLEN ASSIGNMENT (1955, Brit.) PR:A
STOLEN DIRIGIBLE, THE (1966, Czech.) PR:AA
STOLEN FACE (1952, Brit.) PR:A
STOLEN HARMONY (1935) PR:A
STOLEN HEAVEN (1931) PR:A
STOLEN HEAVEN (1938) PR:A
STOLEN HOLIDAY (1937) PR:A
STOLEN HOURS (1963, Brit.) PR:A-C
STOLEN IDENTITY (1953) PR:A
STOLEN KISSES (1929) PR:A
STOLEN KISSES (1968, Fr.) PR:O
STOLEN LIFE (1939, Brit.) PR:A
STOLEN LIFE, A (1946) PR:A-C
STOLEN PLANS, THE (1962, Brit.) PR:AA
STOLEN SWEETS (1934) PR:A
STOLEN TIME (SEE: BLONDE BLACKMAILER) (1955, Brit.)
STOLEN WEALTH (SEE: BLAZING SIX SHOOTERS) (1940)
STONE (1974, Aus.) PR:O
STONE BOY, THE (1984) PR:C
STONE COLD DEAD (1980, Can.) PR:O
STONE KILLER, THE (1973) PR:O
STONE OF SILVER CREEK (1935) PR:A
STONY ISLAND (1978) PR:C
STOOGE, THE (1952) PR:A
STOOGEMANIA (1986) PR:A
STOOGES GO WEST (SEE: GOLD RAIDERS) (1952)
STOOLIE, THE (1972) PR:C
STOP, LOOK, AND LOVE (1939) PR:A
STOP ME BEFORE I KILL! (1961, Brit.) PR:C
STOP PRESS GIRL (1949, Brit.) PR:A
STOP THAT CAB (1951) PR:A
STOP THE WORLD — I WANT TO GET OFF (1966, Brit.) PR:A
STOP THE WORLD I WANT TO GET OFF (SEE: SAMMY STOPS THE WORLD) (1978)
STOP TRAIN 349 (1964, Fr./It./W. Ger.) PR:A
STOP, YOU'RE KILLING ME (1952) PR:A
STOPOVER FOREVER (1964, Brit.) PR:A
STOPOVER TOKYO (1957) PR:A
STORIA DI UNA DONNA (SEE: STORY OF A WOMAN) (1970, US/It.)
STORIA DI UNA MONACA DI CLAUSURA (SEE: DIARY OF A CLOISTERED NUN) (1973, Fr./It./W. Ger.)
STORIA SENZA PAROLE (SEE: STORY WITHOUT WORDS) (1981, It.)
STORIES FROM A FLYING TRUNK (1979, Brit.) PR:AA
STORK (1971, Aus.) PR:O
STORK BITES MAN (1947) PR:A
STORK CLUB, THE (1945) PR:A
STORK PAYS OFF, THE (1941) PR:A
STORK TALK (1964, Brit.) PR:O
STORM, THE (1930) PR:A
STORM (1989, Can.) PR:C
STORM, THE (1938) PR:A
STORM AT DAYBREAK (1933) PR:A
STORM BOY (1976, Aus.) PR:AA
STORM CENTER (1956) PR:A
STORM FEAR (1956) PR:A
STORM IN A TEACUP (1937, Brit.) PR:A
STORM IN A WATER GLASS (1931, Aust.) PR:A
STORM OVER AFRICA (SEE: ROYAL AFRICAN RIFLES, THE) (1953)
STORM OVER BENGAL (1938) PR:A
STORM OVER LISBON (1944) PR:A
STORM OVER THE ANDES (1935) PR:A
STORM OVER THE NILE (1955, Brit.) PR:A
STORM OVER THE PACIFIC (SEE: I BOMBED PEARL HARBOR) (1961, Jap.)

STORM OVER TIBET (1952) PR:A
STORM OVER WYOMING (1950) PR:A
STORM PLANET (1962, USSR) PR:A
STORM RIDER, THE (1957) PR:A
STORM WARNING (1950) PR:C-O
STORM WITHIN, THE (SEE: LES PARENTS TERRI-
   BLES) (1948, Fr.)
STORMBOUND (1951, It.) PR:A
STORMS OF AUGUST, THE (1988, Wales/Brit.) PR:C
STORMY (1935) PR:A
STORMY CROSSING (1958, Brit.) PR:A-C
STORMY MONDAY (1988, Brit.) PR:O
STORMY TRAILS (1936) PR:A
STORMY WATERS (1946, Fr.) PR:A
STORMY WEATHER (1935, Brit.) PR:A
STORMY WEATHER (1943) PR:A
STORMYYD AWST (SEE: STORMS OF AUGUST, THE)
   (1988, Brit./Wales)
STORY OF A CHEAT, THE (1938, Fr.) PR:O
STORY OF A CITIZEN ABOVE ALL SUSPICION (SEE:
   INVESTIGATION OF A CITIZEN ABOVE SUSPI-
   CION) (1970, It.)
STORY OF A DRAFT DODGER, THE (SEE: WIND-
   FLOWERS) (1968)
STORY OF A LOVE STORY (SEE: IMPOSSIBLE OB-
   JECT) (1973, Fr.)
STORY OF A TEENAGER (SEE: JIM, THE WORLD'S
   GREATEST) (1976)
STORY OF A THREE DAY PASS, THE (1968, Fr.) PR:O
STORY OF A WOMAN (1970, US/It.) PR:O
STORY OF ADELE H., THE (1975, Fr.) PR:C-O
STORY OF ALEXANDER GRAHAM BELL, THE (1939)
   PR:AA
STORY OF ARNOLD ROTHSTEIN (SEE: KING OF THE
   ROARING 20'S — THE STORY OF ARNOLD ROTHST-
   EIN) (1961)
STORY OF CINDERELLA, THE (SEE: SLIPPER AND
   THE ROSE, THE) (1976, Brit.)
STORY OF DAVID, A (1960, Brit.) PR:A
STORY OF DR. EHRLICH'S MAGIC BULLET, THE
   (SEE: DR. EHRLICH'S MAGIC BULLET) (1940)
STORY OF DR. WASSELL, THE (1944) PR:A-C
STORY OF ESTHER COSTELLO, THE (1957, Brit.) PR:C
STORY OF FAUSTA, THE (1988, Braz.) PR:C
STORY OF G.I. JOE, THE (1945) PR:A-C
STORY OF GILBERT AND SULLIVAN, THE (SEE:
   GREAT GILBERT AND SULLIVAN, THE) (1953, Brit.)
STORY OF JOSEPH AND HIS BRETHREN, THE (1962,
   It.) PR:A
STORY OF LOUIS PASTEUR, THE (1936) PR:AA
STORY OF MANKIND, THE (1957) PR:A
STORY OF MOLLY X, THE (1949) PR:A
STORY OF MONTE CRISTO, THE (SEE: STORY OF
   THE COUNT OF MONTE CRISTO, THE) (1962, Fr./It.)
STORY OF ROBIN HOOD, THE (1952, Brit.) PR:AA
STORY OF ROBIN HOOD AND HIS MERRIE MEN,
   THE (SEE: STORY OF ROBIN HOOD, THE) (1952,
   Brit.)
STORY OF RUTH, THE (1960) PR:A
STORY OF SEABISCUIT, THE (1949) PR:A
STORY OF SHIRLEY YORKE, THE (1948, Brit.) PR:A
STORY OF TEMPLE DRAKE, THE (1933) PR:O
STORY OF THE COUNT OF MONTE CRISTO, THE
   (1962, Fr./It.) PR:A
STORY OF THE CRUELTIES OF YOUTH, A (SEE:
   NAKED YOUTH) (1961, Jap.)
STORY OF THREE LOVES, THE (1953) PR:A
STORY OF VERNON AND IRENE CASTLE, THE (1939)
   PR:A
STORY OF VICKIE, THE (1958, Aust.) PR:A
STORY OF WILL ROGERS, THE (1952) PR:A
STORY OF WOMEN (1989, Fr.) PR:O
STORY ON PAGE ONE, THE (1959) PR:C
STORY WITHOUT A NAME (SEE: WITHOUT WARN-
   ING) (1952)
STORY WITHOUT WORDS (1981, It.) PR:A
STOWAWAY (1932) PR:A
STOWAWAY (1936) PR:AA
STOWAWAY GIRL (1957, Brit.) PR:A
STOWAWAY IN THE SKY (1962, Fr.) PR:AA
STRAIGHT FROM THE HEART (1935) PR:A
STRAIGHT FROM THE SHOULDER (1936) PR:A
STRAIGHT IS THE WAY (1934) PR:A
STRAIGHT ON TILL MORNING (1974, Brit.) PR:O
STRAIGHT, PLACE AND SHOW (1938) PR:A
STRAIGHT SHOOTER (1940) PR:A
STRAIGHT THROUGH THE HEART (1985, W. Ger.)
   PR:O
STRAIGHT TIME (1978) PR:O
STRAIGHT TO HEAVEN (1939) PR:A
STRAIGHT TO HELL (1987, Brit.) PR:O
STRAIGHT TO THE HEART (1988, Can./Switz.) PR:O
STRAIGHTAWAY (1934) PR:A
STRAIT-JACKET (1964) PR:O
STRAITJACKET (SEE: SHOCK CORRIDOR) (1963)
STRANDED (1935) PR:A
STRANDED (1965) PR:O
STRANDED (SEE: VALLEY OF MYSTERY) (1967)

STRANDED (1987) PR:A-C
STRANDED IN PARIS (SEE: ARTISTS AND MODELS
   ABROAD) (1938)
STRANGE ADVENTURE (1932) PR:A
STRANGE ADVENTURE, A (1956) PR:A
STRANGE ADVENTURES OF MR. SMITH, THE (1937,
   Brit.) PR:A
STRANGE AFFAIR (1944) PR:A
STRANGE AFFAIR, THE (1968, Brit.) PR:O
STRANGE AFFAIR OF UNCLE HARRY, THE (SEE:
   UNCLE HARRY) (1945)
STRANGE AFFECTION (1957, Brit.) PR:A
STRANGE ALIBI (1941) PR:A
STRANGE AWAKENING, THE (SEE: FEMALE
   FIENDS) (1958, Brit.)
STRANGE BARGAIN (1949) PR:A
STRANGE BEDFELLOWS (1965) PR:A-C
STRANGE BEHAVIOR (SEE: DEAD KIDS) (1981,
   Aus./New Zealand)
STRANGE BOARDERS (1938, Brit.) PR:A
STRANGE BREW (1983) PR:C
STRANGE CARGO (1929) PR:A
STRANGE CARGO (1936, Brit.) PR:A
STRANGE CARGO (1940) PR:C
STRANGE CASE OF CLARA DEANE, THE (1932) PR:A
STRANGE CASE OF DAVID GRAY, THE (SEE:
   VAMPYR) (1932, Fr./Ger.)
   PR:A
STRANGE CASE OF DR. MANNING, THE (1958, Brit.)
   PR:A
STRANGE CASE OF DR. MEADE, THE (1939) PR:A
STRANGE CASE OF DR. RX, THE (1942) PR:A
STRANGE CASE OF MADELINE (SEE: MADELEINE)
   (1950, Brit.)
STRANGE CASE OF THE MAN AND THE BEAST, THE
   (SEE: MAN AND BEAST, THE) (1951. Arg.)
STRANGE CONFESSION (SEE: IMPOSTER, THE)
   (1944)
STRANGE CONFESSION (1945) PR:A
STRANGE CONQUEST (1946) PR:A
STRANGE CONSPIRACY, THE (SEE: PRESIDENT VAN-
   ISHES, THE) (1934)
STRANGE DEATH OF ADOLF HITLER, THE (1943)
   PR:A
STRANGE DECEPTION (SEE: ACCUSED, THE) (1949)
STRANGE DECEPTION (1953, It.) PR:O
STRANGE DOOR, THE (1951) PR:A
STRANGE EVIDENCE (1933, Brit.) PR:A
STRANGE EXPERIMENT (1937, Brit.) PR:A
STRANGE FACES (1938) PR:A
STRANGE FASCINATION (1952) PR:A
STRANGE FETISHES, THE (1967) PR:O
STRANGE FETISHES OF THE GO-GO GIRLS (SEE:
   STRANGE FETISHES, THE) (1967)
STRANGE GAMBLE (1948) PR:A
STRANGE HOLIDAY (1945) PR:A
STRANGE HOLIDAY (1969, Aus.) PR:A
STRANGE ILLUSION (1945) PR:A
STRANGE IMPERSONATION (1946) PR:A
STRANGE INCIDENT (SEE: OX-BOW INCIDENT, THE)
   (1943)
STRANGE INTERLUDE (1932) PR:C
STRANGE INTERVAL (SEE: STRANGE INTERLUDE)
   (1932)
STRANGE INTRUDER (1956) PR:A
STRANGE INVADERS (1983) PR:O
STRANGE JOURNEY (1946) PR:A
STRANGE JOURNEY (SEE: FANTASTIC VOYAGE)
   (1966)
STRANGE JUSTICE (1932) PR:A
STRANGE LADY IN TOWN (1955) PR:A
STRANGE LAWS (SEE: CHEROKEE STRIP) (1937)
STRANGE LOVE OF MARTHA IVERS, THE (1946) PR:C
STRANGE LOVE OF MOLLY LOUVAIN, THE (1932)
   PR:A
STRANGE LOVERS (1963) PR:O
STRANGE MR. GREGORY, THE (1945) PR:A
STRANGE MRS. CRANE, THE (1948) PR:A
STRANGE ONE, THE (1957) PR:O
STRANGE ONES, THE (SEE: LES ENFANTS TERRI-
   BLES) (1950, Fr.)
STRANGE PEOPLE (1933) PR:A
STRANGE ROADS (SEE: EXPOSED) (1932)
STRANGE SHADOWS IN AN EMPTY ROOM (1977,
   Can./It.) PR:O
STRANGE TRIANGLE (1946) PR:A
STRANGE VENGEANCE OF ROSALIE, THE (1972)
   PR:C
STRANGE VOYAGE (1945) PR:A
STRANGE WIVES (1935) PR:A
STRANGE WOMAN, THE (1946) PR:C
STRANGE WORLD (1952) PR:A
STRANGE WORLD OF PLANET X, THE (SEE: COS-
   MIC MONSTERS) (1958, Brit.)
STRANGER, THE (SEE: STRANGER FROM TEXAS,
   THE) (1940)
STRANGER, THE (1946) PR:C
STRANGER, THE (SEE: INTRUDER, THE) (1962)
STRANGER, THE (1967, Algeria/Fr./It.) PR:C-O

STRANGER, THE (1987, US/Arg.) PR:O
STRANGER AT MY DOOR (1950, Brit.) PR:A
STRANGER AT MY DOOR (1956) PR:A
STRANGER CAME HOME, THE (SEE: UNHOLY FOUR,
   THE) (1954, Brit.)
STRANGER FROM ARIZONA, THE (1938) PR:A
STRANGER FROM PECOS, THE (1943) PR:A
STRANGER FROM TEXAS, THE (1940) PR:A
STRANGER FROM VENUS, THE (1954, Brit.) PR:A
STRANGER IN BETWEEN, THE (1952, Brit.) PR:A
STRANGER IN HOLLYWOOD (1968) PR:A-C
STRANGER IN MY ARMS (1959) PR:A
STRANGER IN THE HOUSE (SEE: COP-OUT) (1967,
   Brit.)
STRANGER IN THE HOUSE (SEE: BLACK CHRIST-
   MAS) (1974, Can.)
STRANGER IN TOWN (1932) PR:A
STRANGER IN TOWN, A (1943) PR:A
STRANGER IN TOWN (1957, Brit.) PR:A
STRANGER IN TOWN, A (1968, US/It.) PR:C
STRANGER IS WATCHING, A (1982) PR:O
STRANGER KNOCKS, A (1963, Den.) PR:C
STRANGER ON HORSEBACK (1955) PR:A
STRANGER ON THE PROWL (1953, It.) PR:A-C
STRANGER ON THE THIRD FLOOR (1940) PR:C
STRANGER RETURNS, THE (1968, US/It./Sp./W. Ger.)
   PR:A
STRANGER THAN LOVE (SEE: STRANGE LOVERS)
   (1963)
STRANGER THAN PARADISE (1984, US/W. Ger.) PR:O
STRANGER WALKED IN, A (SEE: LOVE FROM A
   STRANGER) (1947)
STRANGER WORE A GUN, THE (1953) PR:A
STRANGERS, THE (1955, It.) PR:A
STRANGERS (SEE: I NEVER SANG FOR MY FATHER)
   (1970)
STRANGERS ALL (1935) PR:A
STRANGERS CAME, THE (SEE: YOU CAN'T FOOL AN
   IRISHMAN) (1950, Ireland)
STRANGER'S GUNDOWN, THE (1974, It.) PR:C
STRANGER'S HAND, THE (1955, Brit.) PR:A
STRANGERS HONEYMOON (1937, Brit.) PR:A
STRANGERS IN LOVE (1932) PR:A
STRANGERS IN THE CITY (1962) PR:A
STRANGERS IN THE HOUSE (1949, Fr.) PR:C
STRANGERS IN THE NIGHT (1944) PR:A-C
STRANGERS KISS (1984) PR:C
STRANGERS MAY KISS (1931) PR:A
STRANGERS' MEETING (1957, Brit.) PR:A
STRANGERS OF THE EVENING (1932) PR:A
STRANGERS ON A HONEYMOON (SEE: STRANGERS
   HONEYMOON) (1937, Brit.)
STRANGERS ON A TRAIN (1951) PR:C-O
STRANGER'S RETURN, THE (1933) PR:A
STRANGERS WHEN WE MEET (1960) PR:C
STRANGEST CASE, THE (SEE: CRIME DOCTOR'S
   STRANGEST CASE) (1943)
STRANGLEHOLD (1931, Brit.) PR:A
STRANGLEHOLD (1962, Brit.) PR:A
STRANGLER, THE (1941, Brit.) PR:C
STRANGLER, THE (1964) PR:A
STRANGLER OF THE SWAMP (1945) PR:A
STRANGLER'S WEB (1966, Brit.) PR:A-C
STRANGLERS OF BOMBAY, THE (1960, Brit.) PR:C
STRATEGIC AIR COMMAND (1955) PR:A
STRATEGY OF TERROR (1969) PR:A
STRATTON STORY, THE (1949) PR:AA
STRAW DOGS (1971, Brit.) PR:O
STRAW MAN, THE (1953, Brit.) PR:A
STRAWBERRY BLONDE, THE (1941) PR:A
STRAWBERRY ROAN (1933) PR:A
STRAWBERRY ROAN (1945, Brit.) PR:A
STRAWBERRY ROAN, THE (1948) PR:A
STRAWBERRY STATEMENT, THE (1970) PR:C
STRAY DOG (1949, Jap.) PR:A-C
STREAMERS (1983) PR:O
STREAMLINE EXPRESS (1935) PR:A
STREET ANGEL (1928) PR:A
STREET BANDITS (1951) PR:A
STREET CORNER (1948) PR:C
STREET CORNER (SEE: BOTH SIDES OF THE LAW)
   (1953, Brit.)
STREET FIGHTER (1959) PR:A
STREET GANG (SEE: VIGILANTE) (1983)
STREET GIRL (1929) PR:A
STREET IS MY BEAT, THE (1966) PR:C
STREET JUSTICE (1989) PR:C
STREET MUSIC (1982) PR:A-C
STREET OF CHANCE (1930) PR:A
STREET OF CHANCE (1942) PR:A
STREET OF DARKNESS (1958) PR:A
STREET OF MEMORIES (1940) PR:A
STREET OF MISSING MEN (1939) PR:A
STREET OF MISSING WOMEN (SEE: CAFE HOSTESS)
   (1940)
STREET OF SHADOWS (SEE: SHADOW MAN) (1953,
   Brit.)

STREET OF SINNERS (1957) PR:A
STREET OF WOMEN (1932) PR:A
STREET PARTNER, THE (SEE: SECRET PARTNER, THE) (1961, Brit.)
STREET PEOPLE (1976, US/It.) PR:O
STREET SCENE (1931) PR:C
STREET SINGER, THE (1937, Brit.) PR:A
STREET SMART (1987) PR:O
STREET SONG (1935, Brit.) PR:A
STREET STORY (1988) PR:O
STREET TRASH (1987) PR:O
STREET WITH NO NAME, THE (1948) PR:C-O
STREETCAR NAMED DESIRE, A (1951) PR:C-O
STREETFIGHTER, THE (SEE: HARD TIMES) (1975)
STREETS OF FIRE (1984) PR:C
STREETS OF GHOST TOWN (1950) PR:A
STREETS OF GOLD (1986) PR:C
STREETS OF LAREDO (1949) PR:A-C
STREETS OF NEW YORK (1939) PR:A
STREETS OF SAN FRANCISCO (1949) PR:A
STREETS OF SIN (SEE: NOT WANTED) (1949)
STREETWALKIN' (1985) PR:O
STRICTLY CONFIDENTIAL (SEE: BROADWAY BILL) (1934)
STRICTLY CONFIDENTIAL (1959, Brit.) PR:A
STRICTLY DISHONORABLE (1931) PR:A-C
STRICTLY DISHONORABLE (1951) PR:A
STRICTLY DYNAMITE (1934) PR:A
STRICTLY FOR PLEASURE (SEE: PERFECT FUR-LOUGH, THE) (1958)
STRICTLY FOR THE BIRDS (1963, Brit.) PR:C
STRICTLY ILLEGAL (1935, Brit.) PR:A
STRICTLY IN THE GROOVE (1942) PR:A
STRICTLY MODERN (1930) PR:A
STRICTLY PERSONAL (1933) PR:A
STRICTLY UNCONVENTIONAL (1930) PR:A
STRIKE! (1934, Brit.) PR:A
STRIKE IT RICH (1933, Brit.) PR:A
STRIKE IT RICH (1948) PR:A
STRIKE ME DEADLY (SEE: CRAWLING HAND, THE) (1963)
STRIKE ME PINK (1936) PR:A
STRIKE UP THE BAND (1940) PR:AA
STRIKEBOUND (1984, Aus.) PR:C-O
STRIKERS, THE (SEE: ORGANIZER, THE) (1964, Fr./It./Yugo.)
STRIP, THE (1951) PR:C
STRIP POKER (SEE: BIG SWITCH, THE) (1970, Brit.)
STRIP-TEASE (SEE: SWEET SKIN) (1965, Fr./It.)
STRIP TEASE MURDER (1961, Brit.) PR:C-O
STRIPES (1981) PR:O
STRIPPED TO KILL (1987) PR:O
STRIPPED TO KILL II: LIVE GIRLS (1989) PR:O
STRIPPER, THE (1963) PR:O
STRIPPER (1986) PR:O
STRIPTEASE LADY (SEE: LADY OF BURLESQUE) (1943)
STROKER ACE (1983) PR:C
STROMBOLI (1949, It.) PR:C-O
STRONGER SEX, THE (1931, Brit.) PR:A
STRONGER THAN DESIRE (1939) PR:A
STRONGER THAN FEAR (SEE: EDGE OF DOOM) (1950)
STRONGER THAN THE SUN (1980, Brit.) PR:A
STRONGEST MAN IN THE WORLD, THE (1975) PR:A
STRONGHOLD (1952, Mex.) PR:A
STRONGROOM (1962, Brit.) PR:A
STRUGGLE, THE (1931) PR:A-C
STRYKER (1983, Phil.) PR:O
STUCK ON YOU (1983) PR:O
STUCKEY'S LAST STAND (1980) PR:C
STUD, THE (1979, Brit.) PR:O
STUDENT BODIES (1981) PR:O
STUDENT BODY, THE (1976) PR:O
STUDENT NURSES, THE (1970) PR:O
STUDENT PRINCE, THE (1954) PR:A
STUDENT TEACHERS, THE (1973) PR:O
STUDENT TOUR (1934) PR:A
STUDENT'S ROMANCE, THE (1936, Brit.) PR:A
STUDIO MURDER MYSTERY, THE (1929) PR:A
STUDIO ROMANCE (SEE: TALENT SCOUT) (1937)
STUDS LONIGAN (1960) PR:A
STUDY IN SCARLET, A (1933) PR:A
STUDY IN TERROR, A (1966, Brit./W. Ger.) PR:A
STUETZEN DER GESELLSCHAFT (SEE: PILLARS OF SOCIETY) (1936, Ger.)
STUFF, THE (1985) PR:C
STUNT MAN, THE (1980) PR:O
STUNT PILOT (1939) PR:A
STUNTS (1977) PR:C-O
STURM IM WASSERGLAS (SEE: STORM IN A WATER GLASS) (1931, Aust.)
STURME DER LEIDENSCHAFT (SEE: TEMPEST) (1932, Ger.)
SUB-A-DUB-DUB (SEE: HELLO DOWN THERE) (1969)
SUBIDA AL CIELO (SEE: MEXICAN BUS RIDE) (1951, Mex.)
SUBJECT WAS ROSES, THE (1968) PR:C

SUBMARINE ALERT (1943) PR:A
SUBMARINE BASE (1943) PR:A
SUBMARINE COMMAND (1951) PR:A
SUBMARINE D-1 (1937) PR:A
SUBMARINE PATROL (1938) PR:A
SUBMARINE RAIDER (1942) PR:A
SUBMARINE SEAHAWK (1959) PR:A
SUBMARINE X-1 (1969, Brit.) PR:A
SUBMARINE ZONE (SEE: ESCAPE TO GLORY) (1940)
SUBMERSION OF JAPAN, THE (SEE: TIDAL WAVE) (1975, US/Jap.)
SUBSTITUTION (1970) PR:O
SUBTERFUGE (1969, US/Brit.) PR:A
SUBTERRANEANS, THE (1960) PR:C
SUBURBAN WIVES (1973, Brit.) PR:O
SUBURBIA (1984) PR:O
SUBVERSIVES, THE (1967, It.) PR:C
SUBWAY (1985, Fr.) PR:C-O
SUBWAY EXPRESS (1931) PR:A
SUBWAY IN THE SKY (1959, Brit.) PR:C
SUBWAY RIDERS (1981) PR:O
SUCCESS (SEE: AMERICAN SUCCESS COMPANY, THE) (1979)
SUCCESS AT ANY PRICE (1934) PR:A
SUCCESS IS THE BEST REVENGE (1984, Brit.) PR:O
SUCCESSFUL CALAMITY, A (1932) PR:A
SUCCESSFUL FAILURE, A (1934) PR:A
SUCCESSFUL MAN, A (1987, Cuba) PR:O
SUCH A GORGEOUS KID LIKE ME (1973, Fr.) PR:O
SUCH GOOD FRIENDS (1971) PR:O
SUCH IS LIFE (1936, Brit.) PR:A
SUCH IS THE LAW (1930, Brit.) PR:A
SUCH MEN ARE DANGEROUS (1930) PR:A
SUCH MEN ARE DANGEROUS (SEE: RACERS, THE) (1955)
SUCH THINGS HAPPEN (SEE: LOVE IS A RACKET) (1932)
SUCH WOMEN ARE DANGEROUS (1934) PR:A
SUCKER, THE (1966, Fr./It.) PR:A
SUCKER MONEY (1933) PR:A
SUCKER. . . OR HOW TO BE GLAD WHEN YOU'VE BEEN HAD!, THE (SEE: SUCKER, THE) (1966, Fr./It.)
SUDAN (1945) PR:A-C
SUDDEN BILL DORN (1938) PR:A
SUDDEN DANGER (1955) PR:A
SUDDEN DEATH (1985) PR:O
SUDDEN FEAR (1952) PR:A-C
SUDDEN FURY (1975, Can.) PR:C
SUDDEN IMPACT (1983) PR:O
SUDDEN MONEY (1939) PR:A
SUDDEN TERROR (1970, Brit.) PR:A
SUDDENLY (1954) PR:C
SUDDENLY, A WOMAN! (1967, Den.) PR:O
SUDDENLY IT'S SPRING (1947) PR:A
SUDDENLY, LAST SUMMER (1959, Brit.) PR:O
SUED FOR LIBEL (1940) PR:A
SUENO DE NOCHE DE VERANO (SEE: MIDSUMMER NIGHT'S DREAM, A) (1984, Brit./Sp.)
SUEZ (1938) PR:A
SUGAR CANE ALLEY (1983, Fr.) PR:C
SUGAR HILL (1974) PR:C
SUGARBABY (1985, W. Ger.) PR:C-O
SUGARFOOT (1951) PR:A
SUGARLAND EXPRESS, THE (1974) PR:C
SUGATA SANSHIRO (SEE: JUDO SAGA) (1965, Jap.)
SUICIDE BATTALION (1958) PR:A
SUICIDE CLUB, THE (SEE: TROUBLE FOR TWO) (1936)
SUICIDE CLUB, THE (1988) PR:C
SUICIDE FLEET (1931) PR:A
SUICIDE LEGION (1940, Brit.) PR:C
SUICIDE MISSION (1956, Brit.) PR:C
SUICIDE RUN (SEE: TOO LATE THE HERO) (1970)
SUICIDE SQUADRON (1942, Brit.) PR:A
SUITABLE CASE FOR TREATMENT, A (SEE: MOR-GAN!) (1966, Brit.)
SUITOR, THE (1963, Fr.) PR:C
SULEIMAN THE CONQUEROR (1963, It.) PR:A
SULLIVANS, THE (1944) PR:A
SULLIVAN'S EMPIRE (1967) PR:A
SULLIVAN'S TRAVELS (1941) PR:C
SULT (SEE: HUNGER) (1968, Den./Norway/Swed.)
SULTAN'S DAUGHTER, THE (1943) PR:A
SUMMER (1986, Fr.) PR:O
SUMMER (1988, W. Ger.) PR:A
SUMMER AND SMOKE (1961) PR:C-O
SUMMER CAMP (1979) PR:O
SUMMER CAMP NIGHTMARE (1987) PR:C
SUMMER FIRES (SEE: MADEMOISELLE) (1966, Fr./Brit.)
SUMMER FLIGHT (SEE: STOLEN HOURS) (1963)
SUMMER HEAT (1987) PR:O
SUMMER HOLIDAY (1948) PR:AA
SUMMER HOLIDAY (1963, Brit.) PR:A
SUMMER INTERLUDE (SEE: ILLICIT INTERLUDE) (1951, Swed.)
SUMMER LIGHTNING (1933, Brit.) PR:A

SUMMER LIGHTNING (SEE: SCUDDA-HOO SCUDDA-HAY) (1948)
SUMMER LOVE (1958) PR:A
SUMMER LOVERS (1982) PR:O
SUMMER MADNESS (SEE: SUMMERTIME) (1955)
SUMMER MAGIC (1963) PR:AA
SUMMER OF '42 (1971) PR:O
SUMMER OF SECRETS (1976, Aus.) PR:O
SUMMER OF '64 (SEE: GIRLS ON THE BEACH) (1965)
SUMMER OF THE SEVENTEENTH DOLL (SEE: SEA-SON OF PASSION) (1960, Brit./Aus.)
SUMMER PLACE, A (1959) PR:C
SUMMER RENTAL (1985) PR:C
SUMMER RUN (1974) PR:A
SUMMER SCHOOL (1987) PR:C
SUMMER SCHOOL TEACHERS (1977) PR:O
SUMMER SOLDIERS (1972, Jap.) PR:C
SUMMER STOCK (1950) PR:A
SUMMER STORM (1944) PR:C
SUMMER STORY, A (1988, US/Brit.) PR:C-O
SUMMER TALES (SEE: LOVE ON THE RIVIERA) (1964, Fr./It.)
SUMMER TO REMEMBER, A (1961, USSR) PR:A
SUMMER WISHES, WINTER DREAMS (1973) PR:A
SUMMERDOG (1977) PR:AA
SUMMERFIELD (1977, Aus.) PR:O
SUMMERPLAY (SEE: ILLICIT INTERLUDE) (1954, Swed.)
SUMMER'S CHILDREN (1979, Can.) PR:O
SUMMERSKIN (1962, Arg.) PR:C
SUMMERSPELL (1983) PR:C
SUMMERTIME (1955) PR:A-C
SUMMERTIME KILLER (1973, Fr./It./Sp.) PR:C
SUMMERTREE (1971) PR:C
SUMMONS FOR MOHAN JOSHI (SEE: MOHAN JOSHI HAAZIR HO) (1984, India)
SUMURU (SEE: MILLION EYES OF SU-MURU, THE) (1967, Brit.)
SUMURU (SEE: RIO 70) (1970, US/Sp./W. Ger.)
SUN ABOVE, DEATH BELOW (1969, Jap.) PR:C
SUN ALSO RISES, THE (1957) PR:C
SUN ALWAYS RISES, THE (SEE: OUTCRY) (1949, It.)
SUN COMES UP, THE (1949) PR:AA
SUN DEMON, THE (SEE: HIDEOUS SUN DEMON, THE) (1959)
SUN IS UP, THE (SEE: BOY. . . A GIRL, A) (1969)
SUN NEVER SETS, THE (1939) PR:A
SUN SETS AT DAWN, THE (1950) PR:A
SUN SHINES, THE (1939, Hung.) PR:A
SUN SHINES BRIGHT, THE (1953) PR:A
SUN SHINES FOR ALL, THE (1961, USSR) PR:A
SUN SHINES FOR EVERYBODY, THE (SEE: SUN SHINES FOR ALL, THE) (1961, USSR)
SUN VALLEY CYCLONE (1946) PR:A
SUN VALLEY SERENADE (1941) PR:AA
SUNA NO KAORI (SEE: NIGHT OF THE SEAGULL, THE) (1970, Jap.)
SUNA NO ONNA (SEE: WOMAN IN THE DUNES) (1964, Jap.)
SUNBONNET SUE (1945) PR:A
SUNBURN (1979) PR:C
SUNDAY DINNER FOR A SOLDIER (1944) PR:A
SUNDAY IN AUGUST (1949, It.) PR:A
SUNDAY IN NEW YORK (1963) PR:C
SUNDAY IN THE COUNTRY (1975, Can.) PR:O
SUNDAY IN THE COUNTRY, A (1984, Fr.) PR:A
SUNDAY LOVERS (1980, It./Fr.) PR:O
SUNDAY PUNCH (1942) PR:A
SUNDAY TOO FAR AWAY (1975, Aus.) PR:C
SUNDAY, BLOODY SUNDAY (1971, Brit.) PR:O
SUNDAYS AND CYBELE (1962, Fr.) PR:C
SUNDOWN (1941) PR:C
SUNDOWN IN SANTA FE (1948) PR:A
SUNDOWN JIM (1942) PR:A
SUNDOWN KID, THE (1942) PR:A
SUNDOWN ON THE PRAIRIE (1939) PR:A
SUNDOWN RIDER, THE (1933) PR:AA
SUNDOWN RIDERS (1948) PR:A
SUNDOWN SAUNDERS (1937) PR:A
SUNDOWN TRAIL (1931) PR:A
SUNDOWN VALLEY (1944) PR:A
SUNDOWNERS, THE (1950) PR:A
SUNDOWNERS, THE (1960) PR:A
SUNFLOWER (1970, Fr./It.) PR:A
SUNNY (1930) PR:A
SUNNY (1941) PR:A
SUNNY SIDE OF THE STREET (1951) PR:A
SUNNY SIDE UP (1929) PR:A
SUNNY SKIES (1930) PR:A
SUNNYSIDE (1979) PR:O
SUNRISE AT CAMPOBELLO (1960) PR:A
SUNRISE TRAIL, THE (1931) PR:A
SUNSCORCHED (1966, Sp./W. Ger.) PR:O
SUNSET (1988) PR:C
SUNSET BOULEVARD (1950) PR:C-O
SUNSET COVE (1978) PR:O
SUNSET IN EL DORADO (1945) PR:A
SUNSET IN THE WEST (1950) PR:A

SUNSET IN VIENNA (SEE: SUICIDE LEGION) (1940, Brit.)
SUNSET IN WYOMING (1941) PR:A
SUNSET MURDER CASE (1941) PR:C
SUNSET OF A CLOWN (SEE: NAKED NIGHT, THE) (1953, Swed.)
SUNSET OF POWER (1936) PR:A
SUNSET ON THE DESERT (1942) PR:AA
SUNSET PASS (1933) PR:A
SUNSET PASS (1946) PR:A
SUNSET RANGE (1935) PR:A
SUNSET SERENADE (1942) PR:A
SUNSET STRIP (1985) PR:O
SUNSET TRAIL (1932) PR:A
SUNSET TRAIL (1938) PR:A
SUNSHINE AHEAD (1936, Brit.) PR:A
SUNSHINE BOYS, THE (1975) PR:A-C
SUNSHINE SUSIE (SEE: OFFICE GIRL, THE) (1932, Brit.)
SUNSTRUCK (1973, Aus.) PR:A
SUPER COPS, THE (1974) PR:O
SUPER DRAGON (SEE: SECRET AGENT SUPER DRAGON) (1966, Fr./It./Monaco/W. Ger.)
SUPER DUDE (SEE: HANGUP) (1974)
SUPER FUZZ (1981) PR:C
SUPER INFRAMAN, THE (SEE: INFRA-MAN) (1975, Hong Kong)
SUPER SLEUTH (1937) PR:A
SUPER SPOOK (1975) PR:O
SUPER VAN (1977) PR:C
SUPERARGO (1968, It./Sp.) PR:A
SUPERARGO VERSUS DIABOLICUS (1966, It./Sp.) PR:A
SUPERBEAST (1972) PR:O
SUPERBUG, SUPER AGENT (1976, W. Ger.) PR:AA
SUPERCHICK (1973) PR:O
SUPERDAD (1974) PR:A-A
SUPERFANTAGENIO (SEE: ALADDIN) (1987, It.)
SUPERFLY (1972) PR:O
SUPERFLY T.N.T. (1973) PR:O
SUPERGIRL (1984, Brit.) PR:C
SUPERMAN (1978) PR:AA
SUPERMAN II (1980, US/Brit.) PR:A
SUPERMAN III (1983) PR:A
SUPERMAN IV: THE QUEST FOR PEACE (1987) PR:C
SUPERMAN AND THE MOLE MEN (1951) PR:A
SUPERMAN AND THE STRANGE PEOPLE (SEE: SUPERMAN AND THE MOLE MEN) (1951)
SUPERNATURAL (1933) PR:A-C
SUPERNATURALS, THE (1987) PR:O
SUPERSNOOPER (SEE: SUPER FUZZ) (1981)
SUPERSONIC MAN (1979, Sp.) PR:A
SUPERSPEED (1935) PR:A
SUPERSTITION (1985) PR:O
SUPERZAN AND THE SPACE BOY (1972, Mex.) PR:AA
SUPPORT YOUR LOCAL GUNFIGHTER (1971) PR:A
SUPPORT YOUR LOCAL SHERIFF (1969) PR:A
SUPPOSE THEY GAVE A WAR AND NOBODY CAME? (1970) PR:A
SUPREME KID, THE (1976, Can.) PR:C
SUPREME SECRET, THE (1958, Brit.) PR:A
SUR (SEE: SOUTH) (1988, Arg./Fr.)
SUR LA ROUTE DE SALINA (SEE: ROAD TO SALINA) (1971, Fr./It.)
SURCOUF, LE DERNIER CORSAIRE (SEE: SEA PIRATE, THE) (1967, Fr./It./Sp.)
SURE THING, THE (1985) PR:C
SURF, THE (SEE: OCEAN BREAKERS) (1949, Swed.)
SURF NAZIS MUST DIE (1987) PR:C-O
SURF PARTY (1964) PR:A
SURF TERROR (SEE: BEACH GIRLS AND THE MONSTER, THE) (1965)
SURF II (1984) PR:O
SURFTIDE 77 (1962) PR:O
SURGEON'S KNIFE, THE (1957, Brit.) PR:C
SURPRISE PACKAGE (1960, Brit.) PR:C
SURPRISE PARTY (1985, Fr.) PR:C
SURRENDER (1931) PR:A
SURRENDER (1950) PR:A
SURRENDER (1987) PR:A-C
SURRENDER — HELL! (1959) PR:C
SURROGATE, THE (1984, Can.) PR:O
SURVIVAL (SEE: PANIC IN YEAR ZERO!) (1962)
SURVIVAL (SEE: GUIDE, THE) (1965, US/India)
SURVIVAL (1976) PR:O
SURVIVAL RUN (1980) PR:O
SURVIVE! (1977, Mex.) PR:O
SURVIVOR, THE (1980, Aus.) PR:C-O
SURVIVORS, THE (1983) PR:C-O
SUSAN AND GOD (1940) PR:A
SUSAN LENOX — HER FALL AND RISE (1931) PR:C
SUSAN SLADE (1961) PR:A
SUSAN SLEPT HERE (1954) PR:C
SUSANNA (SEE: SHEPHERD OF THE OZARKS) (1942)
SUSANNA PASS (1949) PR:A
SUSANNAH OF THE MOUNTIES (1939) PR:AA
SUSIE STEPS OUT (1946) PR:A
SUSPECT, THE (1944) PR:C

SUSPECT (SEE: RISK, THE) (1961, Brit.)
SUSPECT (1987) PR:O
SUSPECTED (SEE: TEXAS DYNAMO) (1950)
SUSPECTED ALIBI (SEE: SUSPENDED ALIBI) (1956, Brit.)
SUSPECTED PERSON (1943, Brit.) PR:A
SUSPENDED ALIBI (1957, Brit.) PR:A
SUSPENSE (1930, Brit.) PR:C
SUSPENSE (1946) PR:A-C
SUSPICION (1941) PR:A-C
SUSPIRIA (1977, It.) PR:O
SUSUZ YAZ (SEE: DRY SUMMER) (1967, Turk.)
SUZANNE (1980, Can.) PR:C
SUZY (1936) PR:C
SVALT (SEE: HUNGER) (1965, Den./Swed./Norway)
SVEGLIATI E UCCIDI (SEE: WAKE UP AND DIE) (1967, Fr./It.)
SVENGALI (1931) PR:A-C
SVENGALI (1955, Brit.) PR:C
SVIRACHUT (SEE: CLOWN AND THE KIDS, THE) (1968, US/Bulgaria)
SWALLOWS AND AMAZONS (1977, Brit.) PR:AA
SWAMP COUNTRY (1966) PR:O
SWAMP DIAMONDS (SEE: SWAMP WOMEN) (1956)
SWAMP FIRE (1946) PR:A
SWAMP THING (1982) PR:C
SWAMP WATER (1941) PR:A
SWAMP WOMAN (1941) PR:A
SWAMP WOMEN (1956) PR:A
SWAN, THE (1956) PR:A
SWAN LAKE, THE (1967) PR:AA
SWANEE RIVER (1939) PR:A-C
SWANN IN LOVE (1984, Fr./W. Ger.) PR:C-O
SWAP MEET (1979) PR:O
SWAP, THE (SEE: SAM'S SONG) (1971)
SWAPPERS, THE (1970, Brit.) PR:O
SWARM, THE (1978) PR:C
SWASHBUCKLER (1976) PR:O
SWASTIKA SAVAGES (SEE: HELL'S BLOODY DEVILS) (1970)
SWEATER GIRL (1942) PR:A
SWEDENHIELMS (1935, Swed.) PR:A
SWEDISH MISTRESS, THE (1964, Swed.) PR:O
SWEDISH WEDDING NIGHT (1965, Swed.) PR:C
SWEENEY (1977, Brit.) PR:O
SWEENEY TODD, THE DEMON BARBER OF FLEET STREET (SEE: DEMON BARBER OF FLEET STREET, THE) (1939, Brit.)
SWEENEY 2 (1978, Brit.) PR:O
SWEEPINGS (1933) PR:A
SWEEPSTAKE ANNIE (1935) PR:A
SWEEPSTAKE RACKETEERS (SEE: UNDERCOVER AGENT) (1939)
SWEEPSTAKES (1931) PR:A
SWEEPSTAKES WINNER (1939) PR:A
SWEET ADELINE (1935) PR:A
SWEET ALOES (SEE: GIVE ME YOUR HEART) (1936)
SWEET AND LOWDOWN (1944) PR:A
SWEET AND SOUR (1964, Fr./It.) PR:A
SWEET BEAT (1962, Brit.) PR:A
SWEET BIRD OF YOUTH (1962) PR:O
SWEET BODY, THE (SEE: SWEET BODY OF DEBORAH, THE) (1969, It./Fr.)
SWEET BODY OF DEBORAH, THE (1969, It./Fr.) PR:O
SWEET CHARITY (1969) PR:A
SWEET COUNTRY (1987) PR:O
SWEET CREEK COUNTY WAR, THE (1979) PR:A
SWEET DEVIL (1937, Brit.) PR:A
SWEET DIRTY TONY (SEE: CUBA CROSSING) (1980)
SWEET DREAMS (SEE: OKAY BILL) (1971)
SWEET DREAMS (1985) PR:C-O
SWEET ECSTASY (1962, Fr.) PR:C
SWEET GINGER BROWN (SEE: FLAMINGO KID, THE) (1984)
SWEET HEART'S DANCE (1988) PR:C-O
SWEET HUNTERS (1969, Panama) PR:C
SWEET INNISCARRA (1934, Brit.) PR:A
SWEET JESUS, PREACHER MAN (1973) PR:O
SWEET KILL (SEE: AROUSERS, THE) (1970)
SWEET KITTY BELLAIRS (1930) PR:A
SWEET LIBERTY (1986) PR:A-C
SWEET LIES (1989) PR:C
SWEET LIGHT IN A DARK ROOM (1966, Czech.) PR:A
SWEET LORRAINE (1987) PR:C
SWEET LOVE, BITTER (1967) PR:C
SWEET MAMA (1930) PR:A
SWEET MUSIC (1935) PR:A
SWEET NOVEMBER (1968) PR:A
SWEET REVENGE (SEE: DANDY, THE ALL AMERICAN GIRL) (1976)
SWEET REVENGE (1987) PR:O
SWEET RIDE, THE (1968) PR:C
SWEET ROSIE O'GRADY (1943) PR:A
SWEET SIXTEEN (1983) PR:O
SWEET SKIN (1965, Fr./It.) PR:O
SWEET SMELL OF LOVE (1966, It./W. Ger.) PR:A

SWEET SMELL OF SUCCESS (1957) PR:C-O
SWEET STEPMOTHER (SEE: KIND STEPMOTHER) (1936, Hung.)
SWEET SUBSTITUTE (1964, Can.) PR:C
SWEET SUGAR (1972) PR:O
SWEET SURRENDER (1935) PR:A
SWEET SUZY (1973) PR:O
SWEET TRASH (1970) PR:O
SWEET VIOLENCE (SEE: SWEET ECSTASY) (1962, Fr.)
SWEET WILLIAM (1980, Brit.) PR:O
SWEETHEART OF SIGMA CHI, THE (1933) PR:A
SWEETHEART OF SIGMA CHI (1946) PR:A
SWEETHEART OF THE CAMPUS (1941) PR:A
SWEETHEART OF THE FLEET (1942) PR:A
SWEETHEART OF THE NAVY (1937) PR:A
SWEETHEARTS (1938) PR:A
SWEETHEARTS AND WIVES (1930) PR:A
SWEETHEARTS OF THE U.S.A. (1944) PR:A
SWEETHEARTS ON PARADE (1930) PR:A
SWEETHEARTS ON PARADE (SEE: SWEETHEARTS OF THE U.S.A.) (1944)
SWEETHEARTS ON PARADE (1953) PR:A
SWEETIE (1929) PR:A
SWEETIE (1989, Aus.) PR:O
SWELL GUY (1946) PR:A
SWELL-HEAD (1935) PR:A
SWELLHEAD, THE (1930) PR:A
SWEPT AWAY. . . BY AN UNUSUAL DESTINY IN THE BLUE SEA OF AUGUST (1974, It.) PR:O
SWIFT VENGEANCE (SEE: ROOKIE COP, THE) (1939)
SWIFTY (1936) PR:A
SWIMMER, THE (1968) PR:C
SWIMMER, THE (1988, USSR) PR:A
SWINDLE, THE (1955, Fr./It.) PR:A
SWINDLERS, THE (SEE: WHITE TIE AND TAILS) (1946)
SWING AND SWAY (SEE: SWING IN THE SADDLE) (1944)
SWING FEVER (1943) PR:A
SWING HIGH (1930) PR:A
SWING HIGH (SEE: JIVE JUNCTION) (1944)
SWING HIGH, SWING LOW (1937) PR:A-C
SWING HOSTESS (1944) PR:A
SWING IN THE SADDLE (1944) PR:A
SWING IT BUDDY (SEE: SWING IT, PROFESSOR) (1937)
SWING IT, PROFESSOR (1937) PR:A
SWING IT SAILOR! (1937) PR:A
SWING IT SOLDIER (1941) PR:A
SWING OUT, SISTER (1945) PR:A
SWING OUT THE BLUES (1943) PR:A
SWING PARADE OF 1946 (1946) PR:A
SWING SHIFT (1984) PR:A-C
SWING SHIFT MAISIE (1943) PR:A
SWING, SISTER, SWING (1938) PR:A
SWING THAT CHEER (1938) PR:A
SWING TIME (1936) PR:AA
SWING YOUR LADY (1938) PR:A
SWING YOUR PARTNER (1943) PR:A
SWING, TEACHER, SWING (SEE: COLLEGE SWING) (1938)
SWINGER, THE (1966) PR:A
SWINGER'S PARADISE (1965, Brit.) PR:A
SWINGIN' AFFAIR, A (1963) PR:A
SWINGIN' ALONG (1962) PR:A
SWINGIN' SUMMER, A (1965) PR:A
SWINGIN' MAIDEN, THE (1962, Brit.) PR:A
SWINGIN' ON A RAINBOW (1945) PR:A
SWINGING BARMAIDS, THE (1976) PR:O
SWINGING FINK (SEE: RAT FINK) (1965)
SWINGING PEARL MYSTERY, THE (SEE: PLOT THICKENS, THE) (1936)
SWINGING SET (SEE: GET YOURSELF A COLLEGE GIRL) (1964)
SWINGING THE LEAD (1934, Brit.) PR:A
SWINGTIME JOHNNY (1944) PR:A
SWIRL OF GLORY (SEE: SUGARFOOT) (1951)
SWISS CONSPIRACY, THE (1976, US/W. Ger.) PR:C
SWISS FAMILY ROBINSON (1940) PR:AA
SWISS FAMILY ROBINSON (1960, Brit.) PR:AA
SWISS HONEYMOON (1947, Brit.) PR:A
SWISS MISS (1938) PR:AA
SWISS TOUR (SEE: FOUR DAYS LEAVE) (1950)
SWITCH, THE (1963, Brit.) PR:C
SWITCHBLADE SISTERS (1975) PR:O
SWITCHING CHANNELS (1988) PR:C
SWORD AND THE DRAGON, THE (1960, USSR) PR:A
SWORD AND THE ROSE, THE (1953, Brit.) PR:A
SWORD AND THE SORCERER, THE (1982) PR:O
SWORD IN THE DESERT (1949) PR:C
SWORD IN THE STONE, THE (1963) PR:AA
SWORD OF ALI BABA, THE (1965) PR:A
SWORD OF DOOM, THE (1966, Jap.) PR:C-O
SWORD OF EL CID, THE (1965, Sp./It.) PR:A
SWORD OF HEAVEN (1985) PR:O
SWORD OF HONOUR (1938, Brit.) PR:A
SWORD OF LANCELOT (1963, Brit.) PR:A
SWORD OF MONTE CRISTO, THE (1951) PR:A

SWORD OF SHERWOOD FOREST (1961, Brit.) PR:A
SWORD OF THE AVENGER (1948) PR:A
SWORD OF THE CONQUEROR (1962, It.) PR:C
SWORD OF THE VALIANT (1984, Brit.) PR:C
SWORD OF VENUS (1953) PR:A
SWORDKILL (1984) PR:C
SWORDS OF BLOOD (SEE: CARTOUCHE) (1962, Fr./It.)
SWORDSMAN, THE (1947) PR:A
SWORDSMAN OF SIENA, THE (1962, Fr./It.) PR:A
SWORN ENEMY (1936) PR:A
SYLVESTER (1985) PR:A
SYLVIA (1965) PR:O
SYLVIA (1985, New Zealand) PR:A-C
SYLVIA AND THE GHOST (SEE: SYLVIA AND THE
   PHANTOM) (1945, Fr.)
SYLVIA AND THE PHANTOM (1945, Fr.) PR:A
SYLVIA SCARLETT (1936) PR:A-C
SYLVIE AND THE PHANTOM (SEE: SYLVIA AND THE
   PHANTOM) (1945, Fr.)
SYMPATHY FOR THE DEVIL (SEE: ONE PLUS ONE)
   (1969, Brit.)
SYMPHONIE FANTASTIQUE (1947, Fr.) PR:A
SYMPHONIE PASTORALE (1948, Fr.) PR:C
SYMPHONY FOR A MASSACRE (1965, Fr./It.) PR:A
SYMPHONY IN TWO FLATS (1930, Brit.) PR:A
SYMPHONY OF LIFE (1949, USSR) PR:A
SYMPHONY OF LIVING (1935) PR:A
SYMPHONY OF LOVE (SEE: ECSTASY) (1933, Czech.)
SYMPHONY OF SIX MILLION (1932) PR:A
SYMPTOMS (1976, Brit.) PR:O
SYN MONGOLII (SEE: SON OF MONGOLIA) (1936,
   USSR)
SYNANON (1965) PR:C
SYNCOPATION (1929) PR:A
SYNCOPATION (1942) PR:A
SYNDICATE, THE (1968, Brit.) PR:A
SYSTEM, THE (1953) PR:A
SYSTEM, THE (SEE: GIRL GETTERS, THE) (1966, Brit.)
SYTTEN (SEE: ERIC SOYA'S "17") (1967, Den.)
SZAMARKOHOGES (SEE: WHOOPING COUGH) (1987,
   Hung.)
SZEGENYLEGENYEK (NEHEZELETUEK) (SEE:
   ROUND UP, THE) (1969, Hung.)
SZERELEM (SEE: LOVE) (1972, Hung.)
SZERELEM ELSO VERIG (SEE: LOVE TILL FIRST
   BLOOD) (1985, Hung.)

T

T.A.G.: THE ASSASSINATION GAME (1982) PR:C
T-BIRD GANG (1959) PR:C
T-MEN (1947) PR:C
T.P.A. (SEE: PRESIDENT'S ANALYST, THE) (1967)
T.R. BASKIN (1971) PR:C
TA CHI (SEE: LAST WOMEN OF SHANG) (1964, Jap.)
TABLE BAY (SEE: CODE 7, VICTIM 5!) (1964, Brit.)
TABLE FOR FIVE (1983) PR:C
TABU (SEE: DRUMS OF TABU, THE) (1967, It./Sp.)
TAFFIN (1988, US/Brit.) PR:C
TAFFY AND THE JUNGLE HUNTER (1965) PR:AA
TAGGART (1964) PR:C
TAHITI HONEY (1943) PR:A
TAHITI NIGHTS (1945) PR:A
TAHITIAN, THE (1956) PR:A
TAI-PAN (1986) PR:O
TAIHEIYO HITORIBOTCHI (SEE: ALONE ON THE PA-
   CIFIC) (1964, Jap.)
TAIHEIYO NO ARASHI (SEE: I BOMBED PEARL HAR-
   BOR) (1961, Jap.)
TAIL OF THE TIGER (1984, Aus.) PR:AA
TAIL SPIN (1939) PR:A
TAILOR MADE MAN, A (1931) PR:A
TAINSTVENNI OSTROV (SEE: MYSTERIOUS IS-
   LAND) (1941, USSR)
TAINTED MONEY (SEE: SHOW THEM NO MERCY)
   (1935)
TAIYO O NUSUNDA OTOKO (SEE: MAN WHO STOLE
   THE SUN, THE) (1980, Jap.)
TAJNA NIKOLE TESLE (SEE: SECRET OF NIKOLA
   TESLA, THE) (1980, Yugo.)
TAKE, THE (1974) PR:C
TAKE A CHANCE (1933) PR:A
TAKE A CHANCE (1937, Brit.) PR:A
TAKE A GIANT STEP (1959) PR:A
TAKE A GIRL LIKE YOU (1970, Brit.) PR:O
TAKE A HARD RIDE (1975, US/It.) PR:C
TAKE A LETTER, DARLING (1942) PR:A
TAKE A POWDER (1953, Brit.) PR:A
TAKE ALL OF ME (1978, It.) PR:O
TAKE CARE OF MY LITTLE GIRL (1951) PR:A
TAKE DOWN (1979) PR:C
TAKE HER BY SURPRISE (1967, Can.) PR:A
TAKE HER, SHE'S MINE (1963) PR:A
TAKE IT ALL (1966, Can.) PR:A
TAKE IT BIG (1944) PR:A
TAKE IT FROM ME (1937, Brit.) PR:A
TAKE IT OR LEAVE IT (1944) PR:A
TAKE ME AWAY, MY LOVE (1962, Gr.) PR:O
TAKE ME HIGH (1973, Brit.) PR:A

TAKE ME OUT TO THE BALL GAME (1949) PR:AA
TAKE ME OVER (1963, Brit.) PR:A
TAKE ME TO PARIS (1951, Brit.) PR:A
TAKE ME TO THE FAIR (SEE: IT HAPPENED AT THE
   WORLD'S FAIR) (1963)
TAKE ME TO TOWN (1953) PR:A
TAKE MY LIFE (1942) PR:A
TAKE MY LIFE (1948, Brit.) PR:A
TAKE MY TIP (1937, Brit.) PR:A
TAKE OFF THAT HAT (1938, Brit.) PR:A
TAKE ONE FALSE STEP (1949) PR:C
TAKE THE HEIR (1930) PR:AA
TAKE THE HIGH GROUND (1953) PR:A
TAKE THE MONEY AND RUN (1969) PR:C
TAKE THE STAGE (SEE: CURTAIN CALL AT CACTUS
   CREEK) (1950)
TAKE THE STAND (1934) PR:A
TAKE THIS JOB AND SHOVE IT (1981) PR:C-O
TAKEN BY SURPRISE (SEE: TAKE HER BY SUR-
   PRISE) (1967, Can.)
TAKERS, THE (SEE: MALAGA) (1962, Brit.)
TAKING OF PELHAM ONE, TWO, THREE, THE (1974)
   PR:O
TAKING OFF (1971) PR:O
TAKING SIDES (SEE: LIGHTNING GUNS) (1950)
TAKING TIGER MOUNTAIN (1983, US/Wales) PR:O
TALE OF FIVE CITIES, A (SEE: TALE OF FIVE
   WOMEN, A) (1951, Brit.)
TALE OF FIVE WOMEN, A (1951, Brit.) PR:A
TALE OF RUBY ROSE, THE (1987, Aus.) PR:C
TALE OF THE COCK (SEE: CHILDREN, THE) (1969)
TALE OF THREE WOMEN, A (1954, Brit.) PR:A
TALE OF TWO CITIES, A (1935) PR:A
TALE OF TWO CITIES, A (1958, Brit.) PR:A
TALENT SCOUT (1937) PR:A
TALES AFTER THE RAIN (SEE: UGETSU) (1953, Jap.)
TALES FROM THE CRYPT (1972, Brit.) PR:C
TALES FROM THE CRYPT PART II (SEE: VAULT OF
   HORROR) (1973, Brit.)
TALES OF A SALESMAN (1965) PR:C
TALES OF A TRAVELING SALESMAN (SEE: TALES
   OF A SALESMAN) (1965)
TALES OF BEATRIX POTTER (SEE: PETER RABBIT
   AND TALES OF BEATRIX POTTER) (1971, Brit.)
TALES OF HOFFMANN, THE (1951, Brit.) PR:A
TALES OF MANHATTAN (1942) PR:AA
TALES OF ORDINARY MADNESS (1983, It.) PR:O
TALES OF PARIS (1962, Fr./It.) PR:A
TALES OF ROBIN HOOD (1951) PR:A
TALES OF TERROR (1962) PR:C
TALES OF THE THIRD DIMENSION (1985) PR:O
TALES OF THE UNCANNY (1932, Ger.) PR:C
TALES THAT WITNESS MADNESS (1973, Brit.) PR:O
TALISMAN, THE (1966) PR:C
TALK ABOUT A LADY (1946) PR:A
TALK ABOUT A STRANGER (1952) PR:A
TALK ABOUT JACQUELINE (1942, Brit.) PR:A
TALK OF A MILLION (SEE: YOU CAN'T BEAT THE
   IRISH) (1952, Brit.)
TALK OF HOLLYWOOD, THE (1929) PR:A
TALK OF THE DEVIL (1937, Brit.) PR:A
TALK OF THE TOWN, THE (1942) PR:AA
TALK RADIO (1988) PR:O
TALKING BEAR, THE (SEE: BEAR, THE) (1963, Fr./It.)
TALKING FEET (1937, Brit.) PR:A
TALKING TO STRANGERS (1988) PR:O
TALKING WALLS (1987) PR:O
TALL BLOND MAN WITH ONE BLACK SHOE, THE
   (1972, Fr.) PR:C
TALL, DARK AND HANDSOME (1941) PR:A
TALL HEADLINES (SEE: FRIGHTENED BRIDE, THE)
   (1952, Brit.)
TALL IN THE SADDLE (1944) PR:A
TALL LIE, THE (SEE: FOR MEN ONLY) (1952)
TALL MAN RIDING (1955) PR:A
TALL MEN, THE (1955) PR:A
TALL STORY (1960) PR:C
TALL STRANGER, THE (1957) PR:A
TALL T, THE (1957) PR:A
TALL TARGET, THE (1951) PR:A
TALL TEXAN, THE (1953) PR:A
TALL TIMBER (SEE: BIG TIMBER) (1950)
TALL TIMBERS (1937, Aus.) PR:A
TALL TROUBLE, THE (SEE: HELL CANYON OUT-
   LAWS) (1957)
TALL WOMEN, THE (1967, Aust./It./Sp.) PR:A
TALVISOTA (1989, Fin.) PR:O
TAM-LIN (SEE: DEVIL'S WIDOW, THE) (1972)
TAMAHINE (1964, Brit.) PR:C
TAMANGO (1959, Fr.) PR:C
TAMARIND SEED, THE (1974, Brit.) PR:C
TAMING OF DOROTHY, THE (1950, Brit.) PR:A
TAMING OF THE SHREW, THE (1929) PR:A
TAMING OF THE SHREW, THE (1967, US/It.) PR:A-C
TAMING OF THE WEST, THE (1939) PR:A
TAMING SUTTON'S GAL (1957) PR:A
TAMING THE WILD (1937) PR:A
TAMMY (SEE: TAMMY AND THE BACHELOR) (1957)

TAMMY AND THE BACHELOR (1957) PR:A
TAMMY AND THE DOCTOR (1963) PR:A
TAMMY AND THE MILLIONAIRE (1967) PR:A
TAMMY, TELL ME TRUE (1961) PR:A
TAMPICO (1944) PR:A
TAMPOPO (1986, Jap.) PR:C-O
TANGA-TIKA (1953) PR:A
TANGANYIKA (1954) PR:A
TANGIER (1946) PR:A
TANGIER ASSIGNMENT (1954, Brit.) PR:A
TANGIER INCIDENT (1953) PR:A
TANGLED DESTINIES (1932) PR:A
TANGLED EVIDENCE (1934, Brit.) PR:A
TANGO (1936) PR:A
TANGO AND CASH (1989) PR:O
TANGO BAR (1935) PR:A
TANGO BAR (1989) PR:C
TANIN NO KAO (SEE: FACE OF ANOTHER, THE)
   (1967, Jap.)
TANK (1984) PR:C
TANK BATTALION (1958) PR:A
TANK COMMANDO (SEE: TANK COMMANDOS)
   (1959)
TANK COMMANDOS (1959) PR:A
TANK FORCE (1958, Brit.) PR:A
TANKS A MILLION (1941) PR:A
TANKS ARE COMING, THE (1951) PR:A
TANNED LEGS (1929) PR:A
TANTE ZITA (SEE: ZITA) (1968, Fr.)
TANYA'S ISLAND (1981, Can.) PR:O
TAP (1989) PR:C
TAP ROOTS (1948) PR:C
TAPEHEADS (1988) PR:O
TAPS (1981) PR:C
TARAN KOVA (SEE: BETRAYAL) (1939, Fr.)
TARANTULA (1955) PR:A
TARAS BULBA (1962) PR:A
TARAS FAMILY, THE (1946, USSR) PR:A
TARAWA BEACHHEAD (1958) PR:A
TARGET (1952) PR:A
TARGET (1985) PR:O
TARGET EARTH (1954) PR:A
TARGET FOR SCANDAL (SEE: WASHINGTON
   STORY) (1952)
TARGET: HARRY (1969) PR:C
TARGET HONG KONG (1952) PR:A
TARGET IN THE SUN (SEE: MAN WHO WOULD NOT
   DIE, THE) (1975)
TARGET UNKNOWN (1951) PR:A
TARGET ZERO (1955) PR:A
TARGETS (1968) PR:O
TARNISHED (1950) PR:A
TARNISHED ANGEL (1938) PR:A
TARNISHED ANGELS, THE (1957) PR:C
TARNISHED HEROES (1961, Brit.) PR:A
TARNISHED LADY (1931) PR:A
TAROT (1986, W. Ger.) PR:C
TARS AND SPARS (1946) PR:A
TARTARS, THE (1962, It./Yugo.) PR:A
TARTU (SEE: ADVENTURES OF TARTU) (1943, Brit.)
TARZAN AND HIS MATE (1934) PR:A-C
TARZAN AND THE AMAZONS (1945) PR:A
TARZAN AND THE GREAT RIVER (1967, US/Switz.)
   PR:A
TARZAN AND THE GREEN GODDESS (1938) PR:AA
TARZAN AND THE HUNTRESS (1947) PR:AA
TARZAN AND THE JUNGLE BOY (1968, US/Switz.)
   PR:AA
TARZAN AND THE JUNGLE QUEEN (SEE: TARZAN'S
   PERIL) (1951)
TARZAN AND THE LEOPARD WOMAN (1946) PR:AA
TARZAN AND THE LOST SAFARI (1957, Brit.) PR:AA
TARZAN AND THE MERMAIDS (1948) PR:AA
TARZAN AND THE SHE-DEVIL (1953) PR:AA
TARZAN AND THE SLAVE GIRL (1950) PR:AA
TARZAN AND THE VALLEY OF GOLD (1966,
   US/Switz.) PR:AA
TARZAN ESCAPES (1936) PR:A-C
TARZAN FINDS A SON (1939) PR:AA
TARZAN GOES TO INDIA (1962, US/Brit./Switz.) PR:AA
TARZAN NO. 22 (SEE: TARZAN AND THE JUNGLE
   BOY) (1968, US/Switz.)
TARZAN '65 (SEE: TARZAN AND THE VALLEY OF
   GOLD) (1966)
TARZAN '66 (SEE: TARZAN AND THE VALLEY OF
   GOLD) (1966)
TARZAN, THE APE MAN (1932) PR:AA
TARZAN, THE APE MAN (1959) PR:A
TARZAN, THE APE MAN (1981) PR:O
TARZAN THE FEARLESS (1933) PR:AA
TARZAN THE MAGNIFICENT (1960, Brit.) PR:A
TARZAN TRIUMPHS (1943) PR:A
TARZAN VERSUS I.B.M. (SEE: ALPHAVILLE, A
   STRANGE CASE OF LEMMY CAUTION) (1965, Fr./It.)
TARZANA, THE WILD GIRL (1970) PR:O
TARZANOVA SMRT (SEE: DEATH OF TARZAN, THE)
   (1968, Czech.)
TARZAN'S DEADLY SILENCE (1970) PR:AA

TARZAN'S DESERT MYSTERY (1943) PR:AA
TARZAN'S FIGHT FOR LIFE (1958) PR:AA
TARZAN'S GREATEST ADVENTURE (1959, Brit.)
　PR:AA
TARZAN'S HIDDEN JUNGLE (1955) PR:AA
TARZAN'S JUNGLE REBELLION (1970) PR:AA
TARZAN'S MAGIC FOUNTAIN (1949) PR:AA
TARZAN'S NEW YORK ADVENTURE (1942) PR:AA
TARZAN'S PERIL (1951) PR:A
TARZAN'S REVENGE (1938) PR:AA
TARZAN'S SAVAGE FURY (1952) PR:AA
TARZAN'S SECRET TREASURE (1941) PR:AA
TARZAN'S THREE CHALLENGES (1963) PR:AA
TASK FORCE (1949) PR:A
TASTE FOR WOMEN, A (1966, Fr./It.) PR:O
TASTE OF BLOOD, A (1967) PR:O
TASTE OF EXCITEMENT (1969, Brit.) PR:C
TASTE OF FEAR (SEE: SCREAM OF FEAR) (1961, Brit.)
TASTE OF FLESH, A (1967) PR:O
TASTE OF HELL, A (1973) PR:C
TASTE OF HONEY, A (1962, Brit.) PR:C
TASTE OF HOT LEAD, A (SEE: HOT LEAD) (1951)
TASTE OF MONEY, A (1960, Brit.) PR:A
TASTE OF SIN, A (1983) PR:O
TASTE THE BLOOD OF DRACULA (1970, Brit.) PR:O
TATSU (1962, Jap.) PR:C
TATTERED DRESS, THE (1957) PR:C
TATTOO (1981) PR:O
TATTOOED STRANGER, THE (1950) PR:O
TAVASZI ZAPOR (SEE: SPRING SHOWER) (1932, Hung.)
TAWNY PIPIT (1947, Brit.) PR:A
TAXI! (1932) PR:A
TAXI (1953) PR:A
TAXI DI NOTTE (SEE: SINGING TAXI DRIVER) (1953, It.)
TAXI DRIVER (1976) PR:O
TAXI FOR TOBRUK (1965, Fr./Sp./W. Ger.) PR:A
TAXI FOR TWO (1929, Brit.) PR:A
TAXI NACH TOBRUK (SEE: TAXI FOR TOBRUK) (1965, Fr.)
TAXI 13 (1928) PR:AA
TAXING WOMAN, A (1988, Jap.) PR:C-O
TAXING WOMAN'S RETURN, A (1988, Jap.) PR:C-O
TAZA, SON OF COCHISE (1954) PR:A
TE DEUM (SEE: CON MEN, THE) (1973, It./Sp.)
TE QUIERO CON LOCURA (1935) PR:A
TEA AND RICE (1964, Jap.) PR:A
TEA AND SYMPATHY (1956) PR:C-O
TEA FOR TWO (1950) PR:A
TEA IN THE HAREM OF ARCHIMEDE (1985, Fr.) PR:C-O
TEA LEAVES IN THE WIND (SEE: HATE IN PARA-DISE) (1938, Brit.)
TEACHER, THE (1974) PR:C
TEACHER AND THE MIRACLE, THE (1961, It./Sp.) PR:A
TEACHER'S PET (1958) PR:A
TEACHERS (1984) PR:C-O
TEAHOUSE OF THE AUGUST MOON, THE (1956) PR:AA
TEAR GAS SQUAD (1940) PR:A
TEARS FOR SIMON (1957, Brit.) PR:A
TEARS OF HAPPINESS (1974) PR:A
TECHNIQUE D'UN MEURTRE (SEE: HIRED KILLER, THE) (1967, Fr./It.)
TECKMAN MYSTERY, THE (1955, Brit.) PR:A
TECNICA DI UN OMICIDO (SEE: HIRED KILLER, THE) (1967, Fr./It.)
TEDDY BEAR, THE (SEE: MY FATHER'S MISTRESS) (1970, Swed.)
TEEN-AGE CRIME WAVE (1955) PR:C
TEEN-AGE STRANGLER (1967) PR:O
TEEN AGE TRAMP (SEE: THAT KIND OF GIRL) (1963, Brit.)
TEEN KANYA (SEE: TWO DAUGHTERS) (1961, India)
TEEN MOTHERS (SEE: SEED OF INNOCENCE) (1980)
TEEN WITCH (1989) PR:A
TEEN WOLF (1985) PR:A-C
TEEN WOLF TOO (1987) PR:A-C
TEENAGE BAD GIRL (1959, Brit.) PR:O
TEENAGE CAVEMAN (1958) PR:A
TEENAGE DELINQUENTS (SEE: NO TIME TO BE YOUNG) (1957)
TEENAGE DOLL (1957) PR:O
TEENAGE FRANKENSTEIN (SEE: I WAS A TEENAGE FRANKENSTEIN) (1958)
TEENAGE GANG DEBS (1966) PR:O
TEENAGE LOVERS (SEE: TOO SOON TO LOVE) (1960)
TEENAGE MILLIONAIRE (1961) PR:A
TEENAGE MONSTER (1958) PR:A
TEENAGE MOTHER (1967) PR:O
TEENAGE PSYCHO MEETS BLOODY MARY (SEE: IN-CREDIBLY STRANGE CREATURES WHO STOPPED LIVING AND BECAME CRAZY MIXED-UP ZOM-BIES, THE) (1965)
TEENAGE REBEL (1956) PR:A

TEENAGE THUNDER (1957) PR:A
TEENAGE ZOMBIES (1960) PR:C
TEENAGERS FROM OUTER SPACE (1959) PR:A
TEENAGERS IN SPACE (1975, USSR) PR:AA
TEHERAN (SEE: CONSPIRACY IN TEHERAN) (1948, Brit.)
TEL AVIV TAXI (1957, Israel) PR:A
TELEFON (1977) PR:C-O
TELEGIAN, THE (SEE: SECRET OF THE TELEGIAN) (1961, Jap.)
TELEGRAPH TRAIL, THE (1933) PR:A
TELEPHONE, THE (1988) PR:O
TELEPHONE OPERATOR (1938) PR:A
TELEVISION SPY (1939) PR:A
TELEVISION TALENT (1937, Brit.) PR:A
TELI SIROKKO (SEE: WINTER WIND) (1970, Fr./Hung.)
TELL ENGLAND (SEE: BATTLE OF GALLIPOLI) (1931, Brit.)
TELL IT TO A STAR (1945) PR:A
TELL IT TO THE JUDGE (1949) PR:A
TELL IT TO THE MARINES (SEE: HERE COME THE MARINES) (1952)
TELL ME A RIDDLE (1980) PR:A
TELL ME IN THE SUNLIGHT (1967) PR:C-O
TELL ME LIES (1968, Brit.) PR:O
TELL ME THAT YOU LOVE ME, JUNIE MOON (1970) PR:A-C
TELL NO TALES (1939) PR:A
TELL-TALE HEART, THE (SEE: BUCKET OF BLOOD) (1934, Brit.)
TELL-TALE HEART, THE (1962, Brit.) PR:O
TELL THEM WILLIE BOY IS HERE (1969) PR:C
TELL YOUR CHILDREN (SEE: REEFER MADNESS) (1936)
TEMPEST (1932, Ger.) PR:C
TEMPEST (1958, It./Yugo./Fr.) PR:C
TEMPEST (1982) PR:C-O
TEMPLE DRAKE (SEE: STORY OF TEMPLE DRAKE, THE) (1933)
TEMPLE TOWER (1930) PR:A
TEMPO DI MASSACRO (SEE: BRUTE AND THE BEAST, THE) (1968, It.)
TEMPORARY WIDOW, THE (1930, Ger./Brit.) PR:C
TEMPOS DIFICEIS (SEE: HARD TIMES) (1988, Portugal)
TEMPS DES LOUPS (SEE: TIME OF THE WOLVES) (1970, Fr.)
TEMPTATION (1935, Brit.) PR:A
TEMPTATION (1936) PR:A
TEMPTATION (1946) PR:A
TEMPTATION (1962, Fr.) PR:C
TEMPTATION HARBOR (1949, Brit.) PR:A
TEMPTER, THE (SEE: DEVIL IS A WOMAN, THE) (1975, Brit./It.)
TEMPTER, THE (1978, It.) PR:O
TEMPTRESS, THE (1949, Brit.) PR:A
TEMPTRESS AND THE MONK, THE (1963, Jap.) PR:C
10 (1979) PR:O
TEN CENTS A DANCE (1931) PR:A
TEN CENTS A DANCE (1945) PR:A
TEN COMMANDMENTS, THE (1956) PR:AA
TEN DAYS IN PARIS (SEE: MISSING TEN DAYS) (1941, Brit.)
TEN DAYS THAT SHOOK THE WORLD, THE (1977, Yugo./Czech.) PR:A-C
TEN DAYS TO TULARA (1958) PR:A
TEN DAYS' WONDER (1972, Fr.) PR:O
$10 RAISE (1935) PR:A
TEN GENTLEMEN FROM WEST POINT (1942) PR:A
TEN LAPS TO GO (1938) PR:A
TEN LITTLE INDIANS (1965, Brit.) PR:A
TEN LITTLE INDIANS (1975, It./Fr./Sp./W. Ger.) PR:C
TEN LITTLE NIGGERS (SEE: AND THEN THERE WERE NONE) (1945)
TEN MINUTE ALIBI (1935, Brit.) PR:A
TEN NIGHTS IN A BARROOM (1931) PR:A
10 RILLINGTON PLACE (1971, Brit.) PR:O
TEN SECONDS TO HELL (1959, Brit.) PR:A
TEN TALL MEN (1951, Brit.) PR:AA
10:30 P.M. SUMMER (1966, US/Sp.) PR:O
TEN THOUSAND BEDROOMS (1957) PR:A
10,000 DOLLARS BLOOD MONEY (1966, It.) PR:O
10 TO MIDNIGHT (1983) PR:O
10 VIOLENT WOMEN (1982) PR:O
TEN WANTED MEN (1955) PR:A-C
TEN WHO DARED (1960) PR:A
TENANT, THE (1976, Fr.) PR:O
TENCHU! (1970, Jap.) PR:O
TENDER COMRADE (1943) PR:A
TENDER FLESH (1976) PR:O
TENDER HEARTS (1955) PR:A
TENDER IS THE NIGHT (1961) PR:C
TENDER MERCIES (1983) PR:A-C
TENDER SCOUNDREL (1967, Fr./It.) PR:C
TENDER TRAP, THE (1955) PR:A
TENDER WARRIOR, THE (1971) PR:AA
TENDER YEARS, THE (1947) PR:A-C
TENDERFOOT, THE (1932) PR:A

TENDERFOOT GOES WEST, A (1937) PR:A
TENDERLOIN (1928) PR:A
TENDERLY (SEE: GIRL WHO COULDN'T SAY NO) (1969)
TENDRE POULET (SEE: DEAR DETECTIVE) (1978, Fr.)
TENDRE VOYOU (SEE: TENDER SCOUNDREL) (1967, Fr./It.)
TENDRES COUSINES (1980, Fr.) PR:O
TENEBRAE (SEE: UNSANE) (1982, It.)
TENGOKU TO-JIGOKU (SEE: HIGH AND LOW) (1963, Jap.)
TENNESSEE BEAT, THE (SEE: THAT TENNESSEE BEAT) (1966)
TENNESSEE CHAMP (1954) PR:A
TENNESSEE JOHNSON (1942) PR:A
TENNESSEE'S PARTNER (1955) PR:C
TENSION (1949) PR:O
TENSION AT TABLE ROCK (1956) PR:A
TENTACLES (1977, It.) PR:C
TENTH AVENUE ANGEL (1948) PR:A
TENTH AVENUE KID (1938) PR:A
TENTH MAN, THE (1937, Brit.) PR:A
TENTH VICTIM, THE (1965, Fr./It.) PR:O
TENTING TONIGHT ON THE OLD CAMP GROUND (1943) PR:A
TEOREMA (1969, It.) PR:O
TEQUILA SUNRISE (1988) PR:O
TERESA (1951) PR:A
TERM OF TRIAL (1962, Brit.) PR:C
TERMINAL CHOICE (1985, Can.) PR:O
TERMINAL ISLAND (1973) PR:O
TERMINAL MAN, THE (1974) PR:C
TERMINAL STATION (SEE: INDISCRETION OF AN AMERICAN WIFE) (1954, US/It.)
TERMINATOR, THE (1984) PR:O
TERMS OF ENDEARMENT (1983) PR:A-C
TERRA EM TRANSE (SEE: EARTH ENTRANCED) (1970, Braz.)
TERRACE, THE (1964, Arg.) PR:O
TERRIBLE BEAUTY, A (SEE: NIGHT FIGHTERS) (1960, Brit.)
TERRIFIED! (1963) PR:O
TERROR, THE (1928) PR:A
TERROR, THE (1941, Brit.) PR:A
TERROR, THE (1963) PR:C
TERROR (1979, Brit.) PR:O
TERROR ABOARD (1933) PR:A
TERROR AFTER MIDNIGHT (1965, W. Ger.) PR:C
TERROR AT BLACK FALLS (1962) PR:O
TERROR AT HALFDAY (SEE: MONSTER A GO-GO) (1965)
TERROR AT MIDNIGHT (1956) PR:A
TERROR BENEATH THE SEA (1966, Jap.) PR:C
TERROR BY NIGHT (SEE: SECRET WITNESS, THE) (1931)
TERROR BY NIGHT (1946) PR:A
TERROR CIRCUS (SEE: BARN OF THE NAKED DEAD) (1976)
TERROR-CREATURES FROM THE GRAVE (1967, US/It.) PR:O
TERROR EN EL ESPACIO (SEE: PLANET OF THE VAMPIRES) (1965, US/It./Sp.)
TERROR EYES (1981) PR:O
TERROR FACTOR, THE (SEE: SCARED TO DEATH) (1981)
TERROR FROM THE SUN (SEE: HIDEOUS SUN DEMON, THE) (1959)
TERROR FROM THE YEAR 5000 (1958) PR:A
TERROR FROM UNDER THE HOUSE (1971, Brit.) PR:C
TERROR HOUSE (1942, Brit.) PR:C
TERROR HOUSE (1972) PR:O
TERROR IN A TEXAS TOWN (1958) PR:A
TERROR IN THE CITY (SEE: PIE IN THE SKY) (1964)
TERROR IN THE FOREST (SEE: FOREST, THE) (1983)
TERROR IN THE HAUNTED HOUSE (SEE: MY WORLD DIES SCREAMING) (1958)
TERROR IN THE JUNGLE (1968) PR:A
TERROR IN THE MIDNIGHT SUN (SEE: INVASION OF THE ANIMAL PEOPLE) (1962, US/Swed.)
TERROR IN THE WAX MUSEUM (1973) PR:C
TERROR IS A MAN (1959, US/Phil.) PR:C
TERROR OF DR. CHANEY, THE (SEE: MANSION OF THE DOOMED) (1976)
TERROR OF DR. MABUSE, THE (1965, W. Ger.) PR:C
TERROR OF FRANKENSTEIN (SEE: VICTOR FRANKENSTEIN) (1975, Swed./Ireland)
TERROR OF GODZILLA (SEE: MONSTERS FROM THE UNKNOWN PLANET) (1975, Jap.)
TERROR OF SHEBA (SEE: PERSECUTION) (1974, Brit.)
TERROR OF THE BLACK MASK (1967, Fr./It.) PR:A
TERROR OF THE BLOODHUNTERS (1962) PR:A
TERROR OF THE HATCHET MEN (SEE: TERROR OF THE TONGS, THE) (1961, Brit.)
TERROR OF THE MAD DOCTOR, THE (SEE: TERROR OF DR. MABUSE, THE) (1965, W. Ger.)
TERROR OF THE TONGS, THE (1961, Brit.) PR:O
TERROR OF TINY TOWN, THE (1938) PR:A
TERROR ON A TRAIN (1953) PR:A

TERROR ON BLOOD ISLAND (SEE: BRIDES OF BLOOD) (1968, US/Phil.)
TERROR ON TIPTOE (1936, Brit.) PR:A
TERROR ON TOUR (1980) PR:O
TERROR SHIP (1954, Brit.) PR:A
TERROR STREET (1953, Brit.) PR:A
TERROR STRIKES, THE (SEE: WAR OF THE COLOSSAL BEAST) (1958)
TERROR TRAIL (1933) PR:A
TERROR TRAIN (1980, Can.) PR:O
TERROR WITHIN, THE (1989) PR:O
TERRORE NELLO SPAZIO (SEE: PLANET OF THE VAMPIRES) (1965, US/It./Sp.)
TERRORISTS, THE (1975, Brit.) PR:C
TERRORNAUTS, THE (1967, Brit.) PR:A
TERRORS ON HORSEBACK (1946) PR:A
TERRORVISION (1986) PR:O
TESEO CONTRO IL MINOTAURO (SEE: MINOTAUR, THE) (1961, It.)
TESHA (1929, Brit.) PR:A
TESS (1979, Fr./Brit.) PR:A-C
TESS OF THE STORM COUNTRY (1932) PR:A
TESS OF THE STORM COUNTRY (1961) PR:A
TEST OF LOVE (SEE: ANNIE'S COMING OUT) (1985, Aus.)
TEST OF PILOT PIRX, THE (1978, Pol./USSR) PR:C
TEST PILOT (1938) PR:A
TESTAMENT (1983) PR:A
TESTAMENT (1988, Brit.) PR:C
TESTAMENT OF DR. MABUSE, THE (SEE: TERROR OF DR. MABUSE, THE) (1965, W. Ger.)
TESTAMENT OF DR. MABUSE, THE (1933, Ger.) PR:C
TESTAMENT OF ORPHEUS, THE (1959, Fr.) PR:C
TESTIGO PARA UN CRIMEN (SEE: VIOLATED LOVE) (1966, Arg.)
TEUFEL IN SEIDE (SEE: DEVIL IN SILK) (1968, W. Ger.)
TEVYA (1939) PR:A
TEX (1982) PR:A
TEX RIDES WITH THE BOY SCOUTS (1937) PR:A
TEX TAKES A HOLIDAY (1932) PR:A
TEXAN, THE (1930) PR:A
TEXAN MEETS CALAMITY JANE, THE (1950) PR:A
TEXANS, THE (1938) PR:A
TEXANS NEVER CRY (1951) PR:A
TEXAS (1941) PR:A
TEXAS ACROSS THE RIVER (1966) PR:A
TEXAS BAD MAN (1932) PR:A
TEXAS BAD MAN (1953) PR:A
TEXAS, BROOKLYN AND HEAVEN (1948) PR:A
TEXAS BUDDIES (1932) PR:A
TEXAS CARNIVAL (1951) PR:A
TEXAS CHAIN SAW MASSACRE, THE (1974) PR:O
TEXAS CHAINSAW MASSACRE PART 2, THE (1986) PR:O
TEXAS CITY (1952) PR:A
TEXAS CYCLONE (1932) PR:A
TEXAS DESPERADOS (SEE: DRIFT FENCE) (1936)
TEXAS DYNAMO (1950) PR:A
TEXAS GUN FIGHTER (1932) PR:A
TEXAS KID, THE (1944) PR:A
TEXAS KID (SEE: TEXICAN, THE) (1966)
TEXAS KID, OUTLAW (SEE: KID FROM TEXAS, THE) (1950)
TEXAS LADY (1955) PR:A
TEXAS LAWMEN (1951) PR:A
TEXAS LIGHTNING (1981) PR:O
TEXAS MAN HUNT (1942) PR:A
TEXAS MARSHAL, THE (1941) PR:A
TEXAS MASQUERADE (1944) PR:A
TEXAS PIONEERS (1932) PR:A
TEXAS RANGER, THE (1931) PR:A
TEXAS RANGERS, THE (1936) PR:A
TEXAS RANGERS, THE (1951) PR:A
TEXAS RANGERS RIDE AGAIN (1940) PR:A
TEXAS ROAD AGENT (SEE: ROAD AGENT) (1941)
TEXAS ROSE (SEE: RETURN OF JACK SLADE, THE) (1955)
TEXAS SERENADE (SEE: OLD CORRAL, THE) (1937)
TEXAS STAGECOACH (1940) PR:A
TEXAS STAMPEDE (1939) PR:A
TEXAS TERROR (1935) PR:A
TEXAS TERRORS (1940) PR:A
TEXAS TO BATAAN (1942) PR:A
TEXAS TORNADO (1934) PR:A
TEXAS TRAIL (1937) PR:A
TEXAS WILDCATS (1939) PR:A
TEXICAN, THE (1966, US/Sp.) PR:A
THANK EVANS (1938, Brit.) PR:A
THANK GOD IT'S FRIDAY (1978) PR:C
THANK HEAVEN FOR SMALL FAVORS (1965, Fr.) PR:A
THANK YOU ALL VERY MUCH (1969, Brit.) PR:C
THANK YOU, AUNT (1969, It.) PR:O
THANK YOU, JEEVES (1936) PR:A
THANK YOU, MR. MOTO (1937) PR:A
THANK YOUR LUCKY STARS (1943) PR:A
THANK YOUR STARS (SEE: SHOOT THE WORKS) (1934)
THANKS A MILLION (1935) PR:A
THANKS FOR EVERYTHING (1938) PR:A

THANKS FOR LISTENING (1937) PR:A
THANKS FOR THE MEMORY (1938) PR:A
THANOS AND DESPINA (1970, Fr./Gr.) PR:C
THARK (1932, Brit.) PR:A
THAT BRENNAN GIRL (1946) PR:A
THAT CERTAIN AGE (1938) PR:A
THAT CERTAIN FEELING (1956) PR:A
THAT CERTAIN SOMETHING (1941, Aus.) PR:A
THAT CERTAIN WOMAN (1937) PR:A-C
THAT CHAMPIONSHIP SEASON (1982) PR:O
THAT COLD DAY IN THE PARK (1969, US/Can.) PR:O
THAT DANGEROUS AGE (SEE: IF THIS BE SIN) (1950, Brit.)
THAT DARN CAT (1965) PR:AA
THAT FORSYTE WOMAN (1949) PR:A-C
THAT FUNNY FEELING (1965) PR:C
THAT GANG OF MINE (1940) PR:A
THAT GIRL FROM BEVERLY HILLS (SEE: CORPSE OF BEVERLY HILLS, THE) (1965, W. Ger.)
THAT GIRL FROM COLLEGE (SEE: SORORITY HOUSE) (1939)
THAT GIRL FROM PARIS (1937) PR:A
THAT HAGEN GIRL (1947) PR:A-C
THAT HAMILTON WOMAN (1941) PR:A
THAT HOUSE IN THE OUTSKIRTS (1980, Sp.) PR:C-O
THAT I MAY LIVE (1937) PR:A
THAT KIND OF GIRL (SEE: MODELS, INC.) (1952)
THAT KIND OF GIRL (1963, Brit.) PR:O
THAT KIND OF WOMAN (1959) PR:C
THAT LADY (1955, Brit.) PR:C
THAT LADY IN ERMINE (1948) PR:A
THAT LUCKY TOUCH (1975, Brit.) PR:A-C
THAT MAD MR. JONES (SEE: FULLER BRUSH MAN, THE) (1948)
THAT MAN BOLT (1973) PR:O
THAT MAN FLINTSTONE (SEE: MAN CALLED FLINTSTONE, THE) (1966)
THAT MAN FROM RIO (1964, Fr./It.) PR:A
THAT MAN FROM TANGIER (1953) PR:A
THAT MAN GEORGE (1967, Fr./It./Sp.) PR:A-C
THAT MAN IN ISTANBUL (1966, It./Fr./Sp.) PR:A-C
THAT MAN MR. JONES (SEE: FULLER BRUSH MAN) (1949)
THAT MAN'S HERE AGAIN (1937) PR:A
THAT MIDNIGHT KISS (1949) PR:A
THAT NAVY SPIRIT (SEE: HOLD 'EM NAVY!) (1937)
THAT NAZTY NUISANCE (1943) PR:A
THAT NIGHT (1957) PR:A
THAT NIGHT IN LONDON (SEE: OVERNIGHT) (1933, Brit.)
THAT NIGHT IN RIO (1941) PR:A-C
THAT NIGHT WITH YOU (1945) PR:A
THAT OBSCURE OBJECT OF DESIRE (1977, Fr./Sp.) PR:O
THAT OTHER WOMAN (1942) PR:A
THAT RIVIERA TOUCH (1968, Brit.) PR:A
THAT SINKING FEELING (1979, Brit.) PR:A
THAT SPLENDID NOVEMBER (1971, It./Fr.) PR:C-O
THAT SUMMER (1979, Brit.) PR:A-C
THAT TENDER AGE (SEE: ADOLESCENTS, THE) (1967, Can.)
THAT TENDER TOUCH (1969) PR:O
THAT TENNESSEE BEAT (1966) PR:A
THAT THEY MAY LIVE (SEE: J'ACCUSE) (1939, Fr.)
THAT TOUCH OF MINK (1962) PR:C
THAT UNCERTAIN FEELING (1941) PR:A
THAT WAS THEN. . . THIS IS NOW (1985) PR:O
THAT WAY WITH WOMEN (1947) PR:A
THAT WOMAN (1968, W. Ger.) PR:C-O
THAT WOMAN OPPOSITE (SEE: CITY AFTER MIDNIGHT) (1957, Brit.)
THAT WONDERFUL URGE (1948) PR:A
THAT'LL BE THE DAY (1974, Brit.) PR:C
THAT'S A GOOD GIRL (1933, Brit.) PR:A
THAT'S GRATITUDE (1934) PR:A
THAT'S LIFE! (1986) PR:C
THAT'S MY BABY (1944) PR:A
THAT'S MY BOY (1932) PR:A
THAT'S MY BOY (1951) PR:A
THAT'S MY GAL (1947) PR:A
THAT'S MY MAN (1947) PR:A
THAT'S MY STORY (1937) PR:A
THAT'S MY UNCLE (1935, Brit.) PR:A
THAT'S MY WIFE (1933, Brit.) PR:A
THAT'S RIGHT – YOU'RE WRONG (1939) PR:A
THAT'S THE SPIRIT (1945) PR:A
THAT'S THE TICKET (1940, Brit.) PR:A
THAT'S THE WAY OF THE WORLD (1975) PR:C
THEATRE OF BLOOD (1973, Brit.) PR:O
THEATRE OF DEATH (1967, Brit.) PR:C-O
THEATRE ROYAL (SEE: ROYAL FAMILY OF BROADWAY, THE) (1930)
THEATRE ROYAL (1943, Brit.) PR:A
THEIR BIG MOMENT (1934) PR:A
THEIR NIGHT OUT (1933, Brit.) PR:A
THEIR OWN DESIRE (1929) PR:A
THEIR SECRET AFFAIR (SEE: TOP SECRET AFFAIR) (1957)

THELMA JORDAN (SEE: FILE ON THELMA JORDAN, THE) (1950)
THEM! (1954) PR:C
THEM NICE AMERICANS (1958, Brit.) PR:A
THEN THERE WERE THREE (1961) PR:A-C
THEODORA GOES WILD (1936) PR:A
THEOREM (SEE: TEOREMA) (1968, It.)
THERE AIN'T NO JUSTICE (1939, Brit.) PR:A
THERE GOES KELLY (1945) PR:A
THERE GOES MY GIRL (1937) PR:A
THERE GOES MY HEART (1938) PR:A
THERE GOES SUSIE (SEE: SCANDALS OF PARIS) (1935, Brit.)
THERE GOES THE BRIDE (1933, Brit.) PR:A
THERE GOES THE BRIDE (1980, Brit.) PR:C
THERE GOES THE GROOM (1937) PR:A
THERE IS ANOTHER SUN (SEE: WALL OF DEATH) (1951, Brit.)
THERE IS NO 13 (1977) PR:O
THERE IS STILL ROOM IN HELL (1963, W. Ger.) PR:C-O
THERE WAS A CROOKED MAN (1962, Brit.) PR:A
THERE WAS A CROOKED MAN (1970) PR:C
THERE WAS A YOUNG LADY (1953, Brit.) PR:A
THERE WAS A YOUNG MAN (1937, Brit.) PR:A
THERE WAS AN OLD COUPLE (1967, USSR) PR:A
THERE'S A GIRL IN MY HEART (1949) PR:A
THERE'S A GIRL IN MY SOUP (1970, Brit.) PR:C
THERE'S ALWAYS A THURSDAY (1957, Brit.) PR:A
THERE'S ALWAYS A WOMAN (1938) PR:A
THERE'S ALWAYS TOMORROW (1956) PR:A
THERE'S ALWAYS TOMORROW (1934)
THERE'S ALWAYS VANILLA (1972) PR:C
THERE'S MAGIC IN MUSIC (1941) PR:A
THERE'S NO BUSINESS LIKE SHOW BUSINESS (1954) PR:A
THERE'S NO PLACE BY SPACE (SEE: HOLD ON!) (1965)
THERE'S ONE BORN EVERY MINUTE (1942) PR:A
THERE'S SOMETHING ABOUT A SOLDIER (1943) PR:A
THERE'S SOMETHING FUNNY GOING ON (SEE: MAIDEN FOR A PRINCE, A) (1967, Fr./It.)
THERE'S THAT WOMAN AGAIN (1938) PR:AA
THERESE (1963, Fr.) PR:O
THERESE (1986, Fr.) PR:C
THERESE AND ISABELLE (1968, US/W. Ger.) PR:O
THERESE DESQUEYROUX (SEE: THERESE) (1963, Fr.)
THERESE RAQUIN (SEE: ADULTERESS, THE) (1959, Fr.)
THERESE UND ISABELL (SEE: THERESE AND ISABELLE) (1968, US/W. Ger.)
THESE ARE THE DAMNED (1965, Brit.) PR:C
THESE CHARMING PEOPLE (1931, Brit.) PR:A
THESE DANGEROUS YEARS (SEE: DANGEROUS YOUTH) (1958, Brit.)
THESE GLAMOUR GIRLS (1939) PR:A
THESE THIRTY YEARS (1934) PR:A
THESE THOUSAND HILLS (1959) PR:A
THESE THREE (1936) PR:C
THESE WILDER YEARS (1956) PR:C
THESEUS AGAINST THE MINOTAUR (SEE: MINOTAUR, THE) (1961, It.)
THEY ALL COME OUT (1939) PR:A
THEY ALL DIED LAUGHING (SEE: JOLLY BAD FELLOW, A) (1964, Brit.)
THEY ALL KISSED THE BRIDE (1942) PR:A-C
THEY ALL LAUGHED (1981) PR:A
THEY ARE GUILTY (SEE: ARE THESE OUR PARENTS?) (1944)
THEY ARE NOT ANGELS (1948, Fr.) PR:A
THEY ASKED FOR IT (1939) PR:A
THEY CALL HER ONE EYE (1974, Swed.) PR:O
THEY CALL IT SIN (1932) PR:A
THEY CALL ME BRUCE (1982) PR:C
THEY CALL ME MISTER TIBBS (1970) PR:C
THEY CALL ME ROBERT (1967, USSR) PR:A
THEY CALL ME TRINITY (1971, It.) PR:A
THEY CAME BY NIGHT (1940, Brit.) PR:A
THEY CAME FROM BEYOND SPACE (1967, Brit.) PR:A
THEY CAME FROM WITHIN (1976, Can.) PR:O
THEY CAME TO A CITY (1944, Brit.) PR:A
THEY CAME TO BLOW UP AMERICA (1943) PR:A
THEY CAME TO CORDURA (1959) PR:C
THEY CAME TO ROB LAS VEGAS (1969, Fr./It./Sp./W. Ger.) PR:O
THEY CAN'T HANG ME (1955, Brit.) PR:A
THEY DARE NOT LOVE (1941) PR:A
THEY DIDN'T KNOW (1936, Brit.) PR:A
THEY DIED WITH THEIR BOOTS ON (1942) PR:A
THEY DON'T WEAR PAJAMAS AT ROSIE'S (SEE: FIRST TIME, THE) (1969)
THEY DRIVE BY NIGHT (1938, Brit.) PR:C
THEY DRIVE BY NIGHT (1940) PR:A-C
THEY FLEW ALONE (SEE: WINGS AND THE WOMAN) (1942, Brit.)
THEY GAVE HIM A GUN (1937) PR:A
THEY GOT ME COVERED (1943) PR:A
THEY HAD TO SEE PARIS (1929) PR:A

THEY JUST HAD TO GET MARRIED (1933) PR:A
THEY KNEW MR. KNIGHT (1945, Brit.) PR:A
THEY KNEW WHAT THEY WANTED (1940) PR:C
THEY LEARNED ABOUT WOMEN (1930) PR:A
THEY LIVE (1988) PR:O
THEY LIVE BY NIGHT (1949) PR:C
THEY LIVE IN FEAR (1944) PR:A
THEY LOVE AS THEY PLEASE (SEE: GREENWICH VILLAGE STORY) (1963)
THEY LOVED LIFE (SEE: KANAL) (1957, Pol.)
THEY MADE HER A SPY (1939) PR:A
THEY MADE ME A CRIMINAL (1939) PR:A
THEY MADE ME A CRIMINAL (SEE: I BECAME A CRIMINAL) (1947)
THEY MADE ME A FUGITIVE (SEE: I BECAME A CRIMINAL) (1947, Brit.)
THEY MADE ME A KILLER (1946) PR:A
THEY MEET AGAIN (1941) PR:A
THEY MEET AT MIDNIGHT (SEE: PICCADILLY INCIDENT) (1948, Brit.)
THEY MET IN A TAXI (1936) PR:A
THEY MET IN ARGENTINA (1941) PR:A
THEY MET IN BOMBAY (1941) PR:A
THEY MET IN THE DARK (1945, Brit.) PR:A
THEY MET ON SKIS (1940, Fr.) PR:A
THEY MIGHT BE GIANTS (1971) PR:A
THEY NEVER COME BACK (1932) PR:A
THEY ONLY KILL THEIR MASTERS (1972) PR:C
THEY PASS THIS WAY (SEE: FOUR FACES WEST) (1948)
THEY RAID BY NIGHT (1942) PR:A
THEY RAN FOR THEIR LIVES (1968) PR:A
THEY RODE WEST (1954) PR:A
THEY SAVED HITLER'S BRAIN (1964) PR:C
THEY SHALL HAVE MUSIC (1939) PR:A
THEY SHOOT HORSES, DON'T THEY? (1969) PR:O
THEY STILL CALL ME BRUCE (1987) PR:A-C
THEY WANTED PEACE (1940, USSR) PR:A
THEY WANTED TO MARRY (1937) PR:A
THEY WENT THAT-A-WAY AND THAT-A-WAY (1978) PR:C
THEY WERE EXPENDABLE (1945) PR:A
THEY WERE FIVE (1938, Fr.) PR:A
THEY WERE NOT DIVIDED (1951, Brit.) PR:A
THEY WERE SISTERS (1945, Brit.) PR:A
THEY WERE SO YOUNG (1955) PR:A
THEY WERE TEN (1961, Israel) PR:A
THEY WHO DARE (1954, Brit.) PR:A
THEY WON'T BELIEVE ME (1947) PR:C
THEY WON'T FORGET (1937) PR:C
THEY'RE A WEIRD MOB (1966, Aus.) PR:A
THEY'RE COMING TO GET YOU (SEE: BLOOD OF FRANKENSTEIN) (1970)
THEY'RE OFF (SEE: STRAIGHT, PLACE AND SHOW) (1938)
THEY'RE PLAYING WITH FIRE (1984) PR:O
THIEF, THE (1952) PR:C
THIEF (1981) PR:O
THIEF OF BAGHDAD, THE (1940, Brit.) PR:AA
THIEF OF BAGHDAD, THE (1961, It./Fr.) PR:A
THIEF OF DAMASCUS (1952) PR:A
THIEF OF HEARTS (1984) PR:C-O
THIEF OF PARIS, THE (1967, Fr./It.) PR:A
THIEF OF VENICE, THE (1952) PR:A
THIEF WHO CAME TO DINNER, THE (1973) PR:A
THIEVES (1977) PR:A
THIEVES FALL OUT (1941) PR:A
THIEVES' HIGHWAY (1949) PR:C
THIEVES' HOLIDAY (SEE: SCANDAL IN PARIS) (1946)
THIEVES LIKE US (1974) PR:C
THIN AIR (SEE: BODY STEALERS, THE) (1969, Brit.)
THIN ICE (1937) PR:A
THIN LINE, THE (1967, Jap.) PR:C
THIN MAN, THE (1934) PR:A
THIN MAN GOES HOME, THE (1944) PR:A
THIN RED LINE, THE (1964) PR:O
THING, THE (1951) PR:C
THING, THE (1982) PR:O
THING FROM ANOTHER WORLD, THE (SEE: THING, THE) (1951)
THING THAT COULDN'T DIE, THE (1958) PR:C
THING WITH TWO HEADS, THE (1972) PR:C
THING WITHOUT A FACE, A (SEE: PYRO) (1964, US/Sp.)
THINGS ARE LOOKING UP (1934, Brit.) PR:A
THINGS ARE TOUGH ALL OVER (1982) PR:O
THINGS CHANGE (1988) PR:A
THINGS HAPPEN AT NIGHT (1948, Brit.) PR:A
THINGS OF LIFE, THE (1970, Fr./It./Switz.) PR:C
THINGS TO COME (1936) PR:C
THINK DIRTY (1970, Brit.) PR:O
THINK FAST, MR. MOTO (1937) PR:A
THIRD ALARM, THE (1930) PR:A
THIRD ALIBI, THE (1961, Brit.) PR:A
THIRD CLUE, THE (1934, Brit.) PR:A
THIRD DAY, THE (1965) PR:C
THIRD FINGER, LEFT HAND (1940) PR:A
THIRD KEY, THE (1957, Brit.) PR:A
THIRD LOVER, THE (1963, Fr./It.) PR:O

THIRD MAN, THE (1950, Brit.) PR:C
THIRD MAN ON THE MOUNTAIN (1959) PR:A
THIRD OF A MAN (1962) PR:C
THIRD PARTY RISK (SEE: DEADLY MANTIS, THE) (1957)
THIRD ROAD, THE (SEE: SEVENTH DAWN, THE) (1964, US/Brit.)
THIRD SECRET, THE (1964, Brit.) PR:C
THIRD STRING, THE (1932, Brit.) PR:A
THIRD TIME LUCKY (1931, Brit.) PR:A
THIRD TIME LUCKY (1950, Brit.) PR:A
THIRD VISITOR, THE (1951, Brit.) PR:A
THIRD VOICE, THE (1960) PR:O
THIRD WALKER, THE (1978, Can.) PR:C
THIRST (1979, Aus.) PR:O
THIRSTY DEAD, THE (1975) PR:O
THIRTEEN, THE (1937, USSR) PR:A
13 (SEE: EYE OF THE DEVIL, THE) (1967, Brit.)
13 EAST STREET (1952, Brit.) PR:A
13 FIGHTING MEN (1960) PR:C
THIRTEEN FRIGHTENED GIRLS (1963) PR:A
THIRTEEN GHOSTS (1960) PR:A
13 HOURS BY AIR (1936) PR:A
13 LEAD SOLDIERS (1948) PR:A
13 MEN AND A GUN (1938, Brit.) PR:A
13 NUNS (SEE: REVENGE OF THE SHOGUN WOMEN) (1982, Taiwan)
13 RUE MADELEINE (1946) PR:A-C
13 WEST STREET (1962) PR:O
THIRTEEN WOMEN (1932) PR:C
THIRTEENTH CANDLE, THE (1933, Brit.) PR:A
THIRTEENTH CHAIR, THE (1930) PR:A
THIRTEENTH CHAIR, THE (1937) PR:A
THIRTEENTH GUEST, THE (1932) PR:A
13TH HOUR, THE (1947) PR:A
13TH LETTER, THE (1951) PR:C
THIRTEENTH MAN, THE (1937) PR:A
— 30 — (1959) PR:A-C
THIRTY-DAY PRINCESS (1934) PR:A
THIRTY DAYS (SEE: SILVER LINING, THE) (1932)
30 FOOT BRIDE OF CANDY ROCK, THE (1959) PR:AA
30 IS A DANGEROUS AGE, CYNTHIA (1968, Brit.) PR:A-C
39 STEPS, THE (1935, Brit.) PR:A
39 STEPS, THE (1960, Brit.) PR:C
THIRTY NINE STEPS, THE (1978, Brit.) PR:C
THIRTY SECONDS OVER TOKYO (1944) PR:A
36 FILLETTE (1988, Fr.) PR:O
THIRTY-SIX HOURS (SEE: TERROR STREET) (1953, Brit.)
36 HOURS (1965) PR:C
36 HOURS TO KILL (1936) PR:A
THIS ABOVE ALL (1942) PR:A
THIS ACTING BUSINESS (1933, Brit.) PR:A
THIS ANGRY AGE (1958, US/It./Fr.) PR:C
THIS COULD BE THE NIGHT (1957) PR:AA
THIS DAY AND AGE (1933) PR:A
THIS EARTH IS MINE (1959) PR:O
THIS ENGLAND (1941, Brit.) PR:A
THIS GREEN HELL (1936, Brit.) PR:A
THIS GUN FOR HIRE (1942) PR:C-O
THIS HAPPY BREED (1944, Brit.) PR:A
THIS HAPPY FEELING (1958) PR:A
THIS IMMORAL AGE (SEE: SQUARE ROOT OF ZERO, THE) (1964)
THIS IS A HIJACK (1973) PR:C
THIS IS ELVIS (1982) PR:A
THIS IS HEAVEN (1929) PR:A
THIS IS MY AFFAIR (1937) PR:A
THIS IS MY LOVE (1954) PR:O
THIS IS MY STREET (1964, Brit.) PR:O
THIS IS NOT A TEST (1962) PR:A
THIS IS SPINAL TAP (1984) PR:C-O
THIS IS THE ARMY (1943) PR:AA
THIS IS THE LIFE (1933, Brit.) PR:A
THIS IS THE LIFE (1935) PR:A
THIS IS THE LIFE (1944) PR:A
THIS IS THE NIGHT (1932) PR:A
THIS ISLAND EARTH (1955) PR:A
THIS LAND IS MINE (1943) PR:A
THIS LOVE OF OURS (1945) PR:C
THIS MAD WORLD (1930) PR:C
THIS MADDING CROWD (1964, Jap.) PR:C
THIS MAN CAN'T DIE (1970, It.) PR:O
THIS MAN IN PARIS (1939, Brit.) PR:A
THIS MAN IS DANGEROUS (SEE: PATIENT VANISHES, THE) (1947, Brit.)
THIS MAN IS MINE (1934) PR:A
THIS MAN IS MINE (1946, Brit.) PR:A
THIS MAN IS NEWS (1939, Brit.) PR:A
THIS MAN MUST DIE (1970, Fr./It.) PR:O
THIS MAN REUTER (SEE: DISPATCH FROM REUTERS, A) (1940)
THIS MAN'S NAVY (1945) PR:AA
THIS MARRIAGE BUSINESS (1938) PR:A
THIS MODERN AGE (1931) PR:A-C
THIS OTHER EDEN (1959, Brit.) PR:A
THIS PROPERTY IS CONDEMNED (1966) PR:O

THIS REBEL AGE (SEE: BEAT GENERATION, THE) (1959)
THIS REBEL BREED (1960) PR:O
THIS RECKLESS AGE (1932) PR:A
THIS SAVAGE LAND (1969) PR:A
THIS SIDE OF HEAVEN (1934) PR:AA
THIS SIDE OF THE LAW (1950) PR:A
THIS SPECIAL FRIENDSHIP (1967, Fr.) PR:O
THIS SPORTING AGE (1932) PR:A
THIS SPORTING LIFE (1963, Brit.) PR:O
THIS STRANGE PASSION TORMENTS (SEE: EL) (1952, Mex.)
THIS STUFF'LL KILL YA! (1971) PR:O
THIS, THAT AND THE OTHER (1970, Brit.) PR:O
THIS THING CALLED LOVE (1929) PR:C
THIS THING CALLED LOVE (1940) PR:C
THIS TIME FOR KEEPS (1942) PR:A
THIS TIME FOR KEEPS (1947) PR:AA
THIS WAS A WOMAN (1949, Brit.) PR:O
THIS WAS PARIS (1942, Brit.) PR:C
THIS WAY PLEASE (1937) PR:AA
THIS WEEK OF GRACE (1933, Brit.) PR:A
THIS WINE OF LOVE (1948, It.) PR:AA
THIS WOMAN IS DANGEROUS (1952) PR:A-C
THIS WOMAN IS MINE (SEE: 18 MINUTES) (1935, Brit.)
THIS WOMAN IS MINE (1941) PR:A
THIS'LL MAKE YOU WHISTLE (1938, Brit.) PR:A
THISTLEDOWN (1938, Brit.) PR:A
THOMAS CROWN AFFAIR, THE (1968) PR:C
THOMASINE AND BUSHROD (1974) PR:O
THOROUGHBRED, THE (1930) PR:A
THOROUGHBRED (1932, Brit.) PR:A
THOROUGHBRED (1936, Aus.) PR:A
THOROUGHBRED (SEE: RUN FOR THE ROSES) (1978)
THOROUGHBREDS (1945) PR:AA
THOROUGHBREDS DON'T CRY (1937) PR:AA
THOROUGHLY MODERN MILLIE (1967) PR:A
THOSE CALLOWAYS (1964) PR:AA
THOSE DARING YOUNG MEN IN THEIR JAUNTY JALOPIES (1969, Fr./Brit./It.) PR:A
THOSE DIRTY DOGS (1974, US/It./Sp.) PR:C
THOSE ENDEARING YOUNG CHARMS (1945) PR:A
THOSE FANTASTIC FLYING FOOLS (1967, Brit.) PR:AA
THOSE HIGH GREY WALLS (1939) PR:C
THOSE KIDS FROM TOWN (1942, Brit.) PR:A
THOSE LIPS, THOSE EYES (1980) PR:O
THOSE MAGNIFICENT MEN IN THEIR FLYING MACHINES; OR HOW I FLEW FROM LONDON TO PARIS IN 25 HOURS AND 11 MINUTES (1965, Brit.) PR:A
THOSE PEOPLE NEXT DOOR (1952, Brit.) PR:A
THOSE REDHEADS FROM SEATTLE (1953) PR:AA
THOSE THREE FRENCH GIRLS (1930) PR:A
THOSE WE LOVE (1932) PR:C
THOSE WERE THE DAYS (1934, Brit.) PR:A
THOSE WERE THE DAYS (1940) PR:A
THOSE WERE THE HAPPY TIMES (SEE: STAR!) (1968)
THOSE WHO DANCE (1930) PR:A
THOSE WHO LOVE (1929, Brit.) PR:A
THOU SHALT NOT KILL (1939) PR:A
THOUSAND AND ONE NIGHTS, A (1945) PR:A
THOUSAND CLOWNS, A (1965) PR:A-C
THOUSAND CRANES (1969, Jap.) PR:O
THOUSAND EYES OF DR. MABUSE, THE (1960, Fr./It./W. Ger.) PR:O
THOUSAND PLANE RAID (SEE: 1,000 PLANE RAID) (1969)
THOUSANDS CHEER (1943) PR:A
THRASHIN' (1986) PR:A-C
THREADS (1932, Brit.) PR:A
THREAT, THE (1949) PR:O
THREAT, THE (1960) PR:O
THREE (1967, Yugo.) PR:C
THREE (1969, Brit.) PR:O
THREE AMIGOS (1986) PR:C
THREE BAD MEN IN THE HIDDEN FORTRESS (SEE: HIDDEN FORTRESS, THE) (1958, Jap.)
THREE BAD SISTERS (1956) PR:C
THREE BITES OF THE APPLE (1967) PR:A
THREE BLIND MICE (1938) PR:A
THREE BLONDES IN HIS LIFE (1961) PR:C
THREE BRAVE MEN (1957) PR:A
THREE BROADWAY GIRLS (SEE: GREEKS HAD A WORD FOR THEM) (1932)
THREE BROTHERS (SEE: SIDE STREET) (1929)
THREE BROTHERS (1981, It.) PR:C
THREE CABALLEROS, THE (1944) PR:AA
THREE CAME HOME (1950) PR:A
THREE CAME TO KILL (1960) PR:C
THREE CARD MONTE (1978, Can.) PR:C
THREE CASES OF MURDER (1955, Brit.) PR:A
THREE CHEERS FOR LOVE (1936) PR:A
THREE CHEERS FOR THE IRISH (1940) PR:A
THREE COCKEYED SAILORS (1940, Brit.) PR:A
THREE COINS IN THE FOUNTAIN (1954) PR:C
THREE COMRADES (1938) PR:A
THREE CORNERED FATE (1954, Brit.) PR:A
THREE-CORNERED MOON (1933) PR:A

THREE CRAZY LEGIONNAIRES, THE (SEE: THREE LEGIONNAIRES, THE) (1936)
THREE CROOKED MEN (1958, Brit.) PR:A
THREE CROWNS OF THE SAILOR (1984, Fr.) PR:O
THREE DARING DAUGHTERS (1948) PR:A
THREE DAYS AND A CHILD (SEE: NOT MINE TO LOVE) (1969, Israel)
THREE DAYS OF THE CONDOR (1975) PR:C-O
THREE DAYS OF VIKTOR TSCHERNIKOFF (1968, USSR) PR:C
THREE DESPERATE MEN (1951) PR:A
THREE DOLLS FROM HONG KONG (1966, Jap.) PR:C
THREE DOLLS GO TO HONG KONG (SEE: THREE DOLLS FROM HONG KONG) (1966, Jap.)
THREE FABLES OF LOVE (1963, Fr./It./Sp.) PR:C
THREE FACES EAST (1930) PR:A
THREE FACES OF A WOMAN (1965, It.) PR:C
THREE FACES OF EVE, THE (1957) PR:A-C
THREE FACES OF SIN (1963, Fr./It.) PR:O
THREE FACES WEST (1940) PR:A
3:15, THE MOMENT OF TRUTH (1986) PR:O
THREE FOR BEDROOM C (1952) PR:A
THREE FOR JAMIE DAWN (1956) PR:A
THREE FOR THE RACES (SEE: WIN, PLACE, OR STEAL) (1975)
THREE FOR THE ROAD (1987) PR:C
THREE FOR THE SHOW (1955) PR:A
THREE FUGITIVES (1989) PR:A-C
THREE GIRLS ABOUT TOWN (1941) PR:A
THREE GIRLS LOST (1931) PR:A
THREE GODFATHERS (1936) PR:A
THREE GODFATHERS, THE (1948) PR:A
THREE GUNS FOR TEXAS (1968) PR:A
THREE GUYS NAMED MIKE (1951) PR:A
THREE HATS FOR LISA (1965, Brit.) PR:A
THREE HEARTS FOR JULIA (1943) PR:A
THREE HOURS (1944, Fr.) PR:A
THREE HOURS TO KILL (1954) PR:A
365 NIGHTS IN HOLLYWOOD (1934) PR:A
300 SPARTANS, THE (1962) PR:A
300 YEAR WEEKEND (1971) PR:C
THREE HUSBANDS (1950) PR:A
THREE IN EDEN (SEE: ISLE OF FURY) (1936)
THREE IN ONE (1956, Aus.) PR:A
THREE IN THE ATTIC (1968) PR:O
THREE IN THE CELLAR (SEE: UP IN THE CELLAR) (1970)
THREE IN THE SADDLE (1945) PR:A
THREE INTO TWO WON'T GO (1969, Brit.) PR:O
3 IS A FAMILY (1944) PR:A
THREE KIDS AND A QUEEN (1935) PR:A
THREE LEGIONNAIRES, THE (1937) PR:A
THREE LITTLE GIRLS IN BLUE (1946) PR:A
THREE LITTLE SISTERS (1944) PR:A
THREE LITTLE WORDS (1950) PR:AA
THREE LIVE GHOSTS (1929) PR:A
THREE LIVE GHOSTS (1935) PR:A
THREE LIVES OF THOMASINA, THE (1963, US/Brit.) PR:AA
THREE LOVES HAS NANCY (1938) PR:A
THREE MARRIED MEN (1936) PR:A
THREE MAXIMS, THE (SEE: SHOW GOES ON, THE) (1938, Brit.)
THREE MEN AND A BABY (1987) PR:A-C
THREE MEN AND A CRADLE (1985, Fr.) PR:C
THREE MEN AND A GIRL (SEE: KENTUCKY MOON-SHINE) (1938)
THREE MEN AND A GIRL (SEE: GAY ADVENTURE, THE) (1949, Brit.)
THREE MEN FROM TEXAS (1940) PR:A
THREE MEN IN A BOAT (1933, Brit.) PR:A
THREE MEN IN A BOAT (1958, Brit.) PR:A
THREE MEN IN WHITE (1944) PR:A
THREE MEN ON A HORSE (1936) PR:A
THREE MEN TO DESTROY (1980, Fr.) PR:O
THREE MESQUITEERS, THE (1936) PR:A
THREE MOVES TO FREEDOM (1960, W. Ger.) PR:A
THREE MUSKETEERS, THE (1939) PR:A
THREE MUSKETEERS, THE (1948) PR:A
THREE MUSKETEERS, THE (1974, Brit.) PR:C
THREE NIGHTS OF LOVE (1969, It.) PR:O
THREE NUTS IN SEARCH OF A BOLT (1964) PR:O
THREE O'CLOCK HIGH (1987) PR:C
THREE OF A KIND (1936) PR:A
THREE ON A COUCH (1966) PR:A
THREE ON A HONEYMOON (1934) PR:A
THREE ON A MATCH (1932) PR:C
THREE ON A SPREE (1961, Brit.) PR:A
THREE ON A TICKET (1947) PR:A
THREE ON A WEEKEND (SEE: BANK HOLIDAY) (1938, Brit.)
THREE ON THE TRAIL (1936) PR:A
THREE OUTLAWS. THE (1956) PR:A
THREE PENNY OPERA (1963, Fr./W. Ger.) PR:A
THREE RASCALS IN THE HIDDEN FORTRESS (SEE: HIDDEN FORTRESS, THE) (1958, Jap.)
THREE RING CIRCUS (1954) PR:A
THREE ROGUES (1931) PR:A

THREE RUSSIAN GIRLS (1943) PR:A
THREE SAILORS AND A GIRL (1953) PR:A
THREE SECRETS (1950) PR:A
THREE SHADES OF LOVE (SEE: THIS REBEL BREED) (1960)
THREE SILENT MEN (1940, Brit.) PR:A
THREE SINNERS (SEE: THREE FACES OF SIN) (1963, Fr./It.)
THREE SISTERS, THE (1930) PR:A
THREE SISTERS, THE (1969, USSR) PR:C
THREE SISTERS (1974, Brit.) PR:C
THREE SISTERS, THE (1977) PR:A
THREE SMART GIRLS (1937) PR:AA
THREE SMART GIRLS GROW UP (1939) PR:A
THREE SONS (1939) PR:A
THREE SONS O'GUNS (1941) PR:A
THREE SPARE WIVES (1962, Brit.) PR:A
THREE STEPS IN THE DARK (1953, Brit.) PR:A
THREE STEPS NORTH (1951, US/It.) PR:A
THREE STEPS TO THE GALLOWS (SEE: WHITE FIRE) (1953, Brit.)
THREE STOOGES GO AROUND THE WORLD IN A DAZE, THE (1963) PR:AA
THREE STOOGES IN ORBIT, THE (1962) PR:AA
THREE STOOGES MEET HERCULES, THE (1962) PR:AA
THREE STOOGES MEET THE GUNSLINGER (SEE: OUTLAWS IS COMING, THE) (1965)
THREE STOOGES VS. THE WONDER WOMEN (1975, It./Chi.) PR:C
THREE STRANGERS (1946) PR:A-C
THREE STRIPES IN THE SUN (1955) PR:A
THREE SUNDAYS TO LIVE (1957, Brit.) PR:A
THREE TALES OF CHEKHOV (1961, USSR) PR:A
3:10 TO YUMA (1957) PR:O
THREE TEXAS STEERS (1939) PR:A
THREE THE HARD WAY (1974) PR:O
3,000 A.D. (SEE: CAPTIVE WOMEN) (1952)
THREE TO GO (1971, Aus.) PR:A-C
THREE TOUGH GUYS (1974, US/It.) PR:C
THREE VIOLENT PEOPLE (1956) PR:A
THREE WARRIORS (1977) PR:A
THREE-WAY SPLIT (1970) PR:O
THREE WEEKS OF LOVE (1965) PR:A
THREE WEIRD SISTERS, THE (1948, Brit.) PR:A
THREE WHO LOVED (1931) PR:A
THREE WISE FOOLS (1946) PR:A
THREE WISE GIRLS (1932) PR:A
THREE WISE GUYS, THE (1936) PR:A
THREE WITNESSES (1935, Brit.) PR:A
THREE WOMEN (1977) PR:C
THREE WORLDS OF GULLIVER, THE (1960, Brit.) PR:AA
THREE YOUNG TEXANS (1954) PR:A
THREEPENNY OPERA, THE (1931, US/Ger.) PR:O
THREE'S A CROWD (1945) PR:A
THREE'S COMPANY (1953, Brit.) PR:A
THREES, MENAGE A TROIS (1968) PR:O
THRESHOLD (1983, Can.) PR:C
THRILL HUNTER, THE (1933) PR:A
THRILL KILLERS, THE (1965) PR:O
THRILL OF A LIFETIME (1937) PR:A
THRILL OF A ROMANCE (1945) PR:A
THRILL OF BRAZIL, THE (1946) PR:A
THRILL OF IT ALL, THE (1963) PR:A
THRILL OF YOUTH (1932) PR:A
THRILL SEEKERS (SEE: GUTTER GIRLS) (1964, Brit.)
THRONE OF BLOOD (1957, Jap.) PR:O
THROUGH A GLASS DARKLY (1961, Swed.) PR:O
THROUGH DAYS AND MONTHS (1969, Jap.) PR:A-C
THROUGH HELL TO GLORY (SEE: JET ATTACK) (1958)
THROUGH THE LOOKING GLASS (SEE: VELVET VAMPIRE, THE) (1971)
THROUGH THE STORM (SEE: PRAIRIE SCHOONERS) (1940)
THROW MOMMA FROM THE TRAIN (1987) PR:C-O
THROWBACK, THE (1935) PR:A
THRU DIFFERENT EYES (1929) PR:A
THRU DIFFERENT EYES (1942) PR:A
THUMB TRIPPING (1972) PR:O
THUMBELINA (1970) PR:AA
THUMBS UP (1943) PR:A
THUNDER ACROSS THE PACIFIC (SEE: WILD BLUE YONDER, THE) (1951)
THUNDER AFLOAT (1939) PR:A
THUNDER ALLEY (1967) PR:C
THUNDER AND LIGHTNING (1977) PR:C
THUNDER AT THE BORDER (1966, Fr./It./W. Ger./Yugo.) PR:A
THUNDER BAY (1953) PR:A
THUNDER BELOW (1932) PR:A
THUNDER BIRDS (1942) PR:A
THUNDER IN CAROLINA (1960) PR:A
THUNDER IN DIXIE (1965) PR:A
THUNDER IN GOD'S COUNTRY (1951) PR:A
THUNDER IN THE BLOOD (1962, Fr.) PR:C
THUNDER IN THE CITY (1937, Brit.) PR:A

THUNDER IN THE DESERT (1938) PR:A
THUNDER IN THE DUST (SEE: SUNDOWNERS, THE) (1950)
THUNDER IN THE EAST (SEE: BATTLE, THE) (1934, Fr.)
THUNDER IN THE EAST (1953) PR:A
THUNDER IN THE NIGHT (1935) PR:A
THUNDER IN THE PINES (1949) PR:A
THUNDER IN THE SUN (1959) PR:A
THUNDER IN THE VALLEY (SEE: BOB, SON OF BATTLE) (1947)
THUNDER ISLAND (1963) PR:A-C
THUNDER MOUNTAIN (1935) PR:A
THUNDER MOUNTAIN (1947) PR:A
THUNDER MOUNTAIN (SEE: SHEPHERD OF THE HILLS, THE) (1964)
THUNDER OF DRUMS, A (1961) PR:A-C
THUNDER ON THE HILL (1951) PR:A
THUNDER ON THE TRAIL (SEE: THUNDERING TRAIL, THE) (1951)
THUNDER OVER ARIZONA (1956) PR:A
THUNDER OVER HAWAII (SEE: NAKED PARADISE) (1957)
THUNDER OVER SANGOLAND (1955) PR:A
THUNDER OVER TANGIER (1957, Brit.) PR:A
THUNDER OVER TEXAS (1934) PR:A
THUNDER OVER THE PLAINS (1953) PR:A
THUNDER OVER THE PRAIRIE (1941) PR:A
THUNDER PASS (SEE: THUNDER TRAIL) (1937)
THUNDER PASS (1954) PR:A
THUNDER RIVER FEUD (1942) PR:A
THUNDER ROAD (1958) PR:C
THUNDER ROCK (1944, Brit.) PR:A
THUNDER RUN (1986) PR:C
THUNDER TOWN (1946) PR:A
THUNDER TRAIL (1937) PR:A
THUNDER WARRIOR (1986, It.) PR:O
THUNDERBALL (1965, Brit.) PR:A-C
THUNDERBIRD 6 (1968, Brit.) PR:A
THUNDERBIRDS (1952) PR:A
THUNDERBIRDS ARE GO (1968, Brit.) PR:A
THUNDERBOLT (1929) PR:A
THUNDERBOLT (1936) PR:A-C
THUNDERBOLT AND LIGHTFOOT (1974) PR:O
THUNDERCLOUD (SEE: COLT .45) (1950)
THUNDERGAP OUTLAWS (SEE: BAD MEN OF THUNDER GAP) (1943)
THUNDERHEAD—SON OF FLICKA (1945) PR:AA
THUNDERHOOF (1948) PR:A
THUNDERING CARAVANS (1952) PR:A
THUNDERING FRONTIER (1940) PR:A
THUNDERING GUN SLINGERS (1944) PR:A
THUNDERING HERD, THE (1934) PR:A
THUNDERING HOOFS (1941) PR:A
THUNDERING JETS (1958) PR:A
THUNDERING TRAIL, THE (1951) PR:A
THUNDERING TRAILS (1943) PR:A
THUNDERING WEST, THE (1939) PR:A
THUNDERING WHEELS (SEE: THUNDER IN DIXIE) (1965)
THUNDERSTORM (1934, USSR) PR:A
THUNDERSTORM (1956) PR:A
THURSDAY THE 12TH (SEE: PANDEMONIUM) (1982)
THURSDAY'S CHILD (1943, Brit.) PR:A
THX 1138 (1971) PR:C
THY NEIGHBOR'S WIFE (1953) PR:C
TI-CUL TOUGAS (1977, Can.) PR:C
TIARA TAHITI (1962, Brit.) PR:A
. . . TICK. . . TICK. . . TICK. . . (1970) PR:A
TICKET (1987, S.K.) PR:O
TICKET OF LEAVE (1936, Brit.) PR:A
TICKET OF LEAVE MAN, THE (1937, Brit.) PR:A
TICKET TO CRIME (1934) PR:A
TICKET TO HEAVEN (1981) PR:C
TICKET TO PARADISE (1936) PR:A
TICKET TO PARADISE (1961, Brit.) PR:A
TICKET TO TOMAHAWK, A (1950) PR:A
TICKLE ME (1965) PR:A
TICKLED PINK (SEE: MAGIC SPECTACLES) (1961)
TICKLISH AFFAIR, A (1963) PR:A
TIDAL WAVE (SEE: S.O.S. TIDAL WAVE) (1939)
TIDAL WAVE (1975, US/Jap.) PR:A-C
TIEMPO DE MORIR (SEE: TIME TO DIE, A) (1983, Colombia/Cuba)
TIERRA BRUTAL (SEE: SAVAGE GUNS, THE) (1961, US/Sp.)
TIFFANY JONES (1976, Brit.) PR:O
TIGER AMONG US, THE (SEE: 13 WEST STREET) (1962)
TIGER AND THE FLAME, THE (1955, India) PR:A-C
TIGER AND THE PUSSYCAT, THE (1967, US/It.) PR:A-C
TIGER BAY (1933, Brit.) PR:A
TIGER BAY (1959, Brit.) PR:A
TIGER BY THE TAIL (SEE: CROSS-UP) (1958, Brit.)
TIGER BY THE TAIL (1970) PR:C
TIGER FANGS (1943) PR:A
TIGER FLIGHT (1965, Jap.) PR:A
TIGER GIRL (1955, USSR) PR:A

TIGER IN THE SKY (SEE: MC CONNELL STORY, THE) (1955)
TIGER IN THE SMOKE (1956, Brit.) PR:A
TIGER MAKES OUT, THE (1967) PR:A-C
TIGER MAN (SEE: LADY AND THE MONSTER, THE) (1944)
TIGER OF BENGAL (SEE: JOURNEY TO THE LOST CITY) (1959, Fr./It./W. Ger.)
TIGER OF THE SEVEN SEAS (1964, Fr./It.) PR:A
TIGER ROSE (1930) PR:A
TIGER SHARK (1932) PR:A-C
TIGER WALKS, A (1964, Brit.) PR:C
TIGER WARSAW (1988) PR:NR
TIGER WOMAN, THE (1945) PR:A
TIGER'S TALE, A (1988) PR:C-O
TIGHT LITTLE ISLAND (1949, Brit.) PR:A
TIGHT SHOES (1941) PR:A
TIGHT SKIRTS (SEE: TIGHT SKIRTS, LOOSE PLEASURES) (1966, Fr.)
TIGHT SKIRTS, LOOSE PLEASURES (1966, Fr.) PR:O
TIGHT SPOT (1955) PR:O
TIGHTROPE (1984) PR:C-O
TIJUANA STORY, THE (1957) PR:A
TIKI TIKI (1971, Can.) PR:AA
TIKO AND THE SHARK (1966, US/It./Fr.) PR:A
TIKOYO AND HIS SHARK (SEE: TIKO AND HIS SHARK) (1966, US/It./Fr.)
'TIL WE MEET AGAIN (1940) PR:A
TILL DEATH (1978) PR:C-O
TILL DEATH DO US PART (SEE: ALF 'N' FAMILY) (1968, Brit.)
TILL MARRIAGE DO US PART (1974, It.) PR:O
TILL THE CLOUDS ROLL BY (1946) PR:AA
TILL THE END OF TIME (1946) PR:A-C
TILL TOMORROW COMES (1962, Jap.) PR:C
TILL WE MEET AGAIN (1936) PR:A
TILL WE MEET AGAIN (1944) PR:A
TILLIE AND GUS (1933) PR:A
TILLIE THE TOILER (1941) PR:A
TILLY OF BLOOMSBURY (1931, Brit.) PR:A
TILLY OF BLOOMSBURY (1940, Brit.) PR:A
TILT (1979) PR:C
TIM (1981, Aus.) PR:C
TIM DRISCOLL'S DONKEY (1955, Brit.) PR:AA
TIMBER (1942) PR:A
TIMBER FURY (1950) PR:A
TIMBER QUEEN (1944) PR:A
TIMBER STAMPEDE (1939) PR:A
TIMBER TERRORS (1935) PR:A
TIMBER TRAIL, THE (1948) PR:A
TIMBER WAR (1936) PR:A
TIMBERJACK (1955) PR:A
TIMBUCTOO (1933, Brit.) PR:A
TIMBUKTU (1959) PR:A
TIME AFTER TIME (1979, Brit.) PR:O
TIME AFTER TIME (1985, Brit.) PR:A-C
TIME AND THE TOUCH, THE (1962) PR:C
TIME BANDITS (1981, Brit.) PR:A-C
TIME BOMB (SEE: TERROR ON A TRAIN) (1953)
TIME BOMB (1961, Fr./It.) PR:A
TIME FLIES (1944, Brit.) PR:A
TIME FOR ACTION (SEE: TIP ON A DEAD JOCKEY) (1957)
TIME FOR DYING, A (1971) PR:C
TIME FOR GIVING, A (SEE: GENERATION) (1969)
TIME FOR HEROS, A (SEE: HELL WITH HEROS, THE) (1968)
TIME FOR KILLING, A (1967) PR:A
TIME FOR LOVING (1971, Brit.) PR:A-C
TIME GENTLEMEN PLEASE! (1953, Brit.) PR:A
TIME IN THE SUN, A (1970, Swed.) PR:O
TIME IS MY ENEMY (1957, Brit.) PR:A
TIME LIMIT (1957) PR:C
TIME LOCK (1959, Brit.) PR:A
TIME LOST AND TIME REMEMBERED (1966, Brit.) PR:A
TIME MACHINE, THE (1960, Brit./US) PR:A
TIME OF DESIRE, THE (1957, Swed.) PR:O
TIME OF DESTINY, A (1988) PR:C
TIME OF HIS LIFE, THE (1955, Brit.) PR:A
TIME OF INDIFFERENCE (1965, Fr./It.) PR:A
TIME OF RETURN, THE (SEE: MURIEL) (1963, Fr./It.)
TIME OF ROSES (1970, Fin.) PR:C
TIME OF THE HEATHEN (1962) PR:C
TIME OF THE WOLVES (1970, Fr.) PR:O
TIME OF THEIR LIVES, THE (1946) PR:AA
TIME OF YOUR LIFE, THE (1948) PR:A-C
TIME OUT FOR LOVE (1963, It./Fr.) PR:A
TIME OUT FOR MURDER (1938) PR:A
TIME OUT FOR RHYTHM (1941) PR:A
TIME OUT FOR ROMANCE (1937) PR:A
TIME OUT OF MIND (1947) PR:A
TIME SLIP (1981, Jap.) PR:C
TIME, THE PLACE AND THE GIRL, THE (1929) PR:A
TIME, THE PLACE AND THE GIRL, THE (1946) PR:A
TIME TO DIE, A (1983) PR:O
TIME TO DIE, A (1985, Colombia/Cuba) PR:C
TIME TO KILL (1942) PR:A

TIME TO KILL, A (1955, Brit.) PR:A
TIME TO LOVE AND A TIME TO DIE, A (1958) PR:A-C
TIME TO REMEMBER (1962, Brit.) PR:A
TIME TO RUN, A (SEE: FEMALE BUNCH, THE) (1969)
TIME TO SING, A (1968) PR:A
TIME TRACKERS (1989) PR:A
TIME TRAP (SEE: TIME TRAVELERS, THE) (1964)
TIME TRAVELERS, THE (1964) PR:A
TIME WALKER (1982) PR:A
TIME WITHOUT PITY (1957, Brit.) PR:C
TIMERIDER (1983) PR:C
TIMES GONE BY (1953, It.) PR:C
TIMES SQUARE (1929) PR:A
TIMES SQUARE (1980) PR:O
TIMES SQUARE LADY (1935) PR:A
TIMES SQUARE PLAYBOY (1936) PR:A
TIMESLIP (SEE: ATOMIC MAN, THE) (1955, Brit.)
TIMETABLE (1956) PR:A
TIMOTHY'S QUEST (1936) PR:A
TIN DRUM, THE (1979, Fr./Yugo./Pol./W. Ger.) PR:O
TIN GIRL, THE (1970, It.) PR:A
TIN GODS (1932, Brit.) PR:A
TIN MAN (1983) PR:A
TIN MEN (1987) PR:C-O
TIN PAN ALLEY (1940) PR:A
TIN STAR, THE (1957) PR:A
TINDER BOX, THE (1968, E. Ger.) PR:AA
TINGLER, THE (1959) PR:C
TINI ZABUTYKH PREDKIV (SEE: SHADOWS OF FORGOTTEN ANCESTORS) (1965, USSR)
TINKER (1949, Brit.) PR:AA
TINTORERA. . . BLOODY WATERS (1977, Brit./Mex.) PR:O
TIOGA KID, THE (1948) PR:A
TIP-OFF, THE (1931) PR:A
TIP-OFF GIRLS (1938) PR:A
TIP ON A DEAD JOCKEY (1957) PR:A-C
TIRE AU FLANC (SEE: ARMY GAME, THE) (1963, Fr.)
TIREZ SUR LE PIANISTE (SEE: SHOOT THE PIANO PLAYER) (1960, Fr.)
'TIS PITY SHE'S A WHORE (1973, It.) PR:O
TISH (1942) PR:A
TITAN FIND (SEE: CREATURE) (1985)
TITANIC (1953) PR:A-C
TITFIELD THUNDERBOLT, THE (1953, Brit.) PR:A
TITLE SHOT (1982, Can.) PR:C
TLAYUCAN (SEE: PEARL OF TLAYUCAN) (1964, Mex.)
TNT JACKSON (1975) PR:O
TO ALL A GOODNIGHT (1980) PR:O
TO BE A CROOK (1967, Fr.) PR:A
TO BE A LADY (1934, Brit.) PR:A
TO BE A MAN (SEE: CRY OF BATTLE) (1963, US/Phil.)
TO BE FREE (1972) PR:O
TO BE OR NOT TO BE (1942) PR:A
TO BE OR NOT TO BE (1983) PR:C
TO BEAT THE BAND (1935) PR:A
TO BED OR NOT TO BED (SEE: DEVIL, THE) (1963, It.)
TO BEGIN AGAIN (1982, Sp.) PR:C
TO CATCH A COP (1984, Fr.) PR:A
TO CATCH A SPY (SEE: CATCH ME A SPY) (1971, Brit./Fr.)
TO CATCH A THIEF (1936, Brit.) PR:A
TO CATCH A THIEF (1955) PR:C
TO COMMIT A MURDER (1970, Fr./It./W. Ger.) PR:C
TO DENDRO POU PLIGONAME (SEE: TREE WE HURT, THE) (1987, Gr.)
TO DIE FOR (1989) PR:O
TO DOROTHY, A SON (SEE: CASH ON DELIVERY) (1956, Brit.)
TO EACH HIS OWN (1946) PR:A-C
TO ELVIS WITH LOVE (SEE: TOUCHED BY LOVE) (1980)
TO FIND A MAN (1972) PR:A
TO HAVE AND HAVE NOT (1944) PR:A-C
TO HAVE AND TO HOLD (1951, Brit.) PR:A
TO HAVE AND TO HOLD (1963, Brit.) PR:A
TO HELL AND BACK (1955) PR:A-C
TO KILL A CLOWN (1972) PR:C-O
TO KILL A DRAGON (SEE: THAT MAN BOLT) (1973)
TO KILL A MOCKINGBIRD (1962) PR:C
TO KILL A PRIEST (1989, Fr.) PR:O
TO KILL A STRANGER (1985) PR:O
TO KILL OR TO DIE (1973, It.) PR:C
TO LIVE (SEE: IKIRU) (1960, Jap.)
TO LIVE AND DIE IN L.A. (1985) PR:O
TO LIVE IN PEACE (1947, It.) PR:A
TO LOVE (1964, Swed.) PR:O
TO LOVE A VAMPIRE (SEE: LUST FOR A VAMPIRE) (1971, Brit.)
TO MARY – WITH LOVE (1936) PR:A
TO NEW SHOES (SEE: LIFE BEGINS ANEW) (1938, Ger.)
TO OBLIGE A LADY (1931, Brit.) PR:A
TO OUR LOVES (SEE: A NOS AMOURS) (1984, Fr.)
TO PARIS WITH LOVE (1955, Brit.) PR:A
TO PLEASE A LADY (1950) PR:A
TO PROXENIO TIS ANNAS (SEE: MATCHMAKING OF ANNA, THE) (1972, Gr.)

TO SIR, WITH LOVE (1967, Brit.) PR:A
TO THE DEVIL A DAUGHTER (1976, Brit./W. Ger.) PR:O
TO THE ENDS OF THE EARTH (1948) PR:A-C
TO THE LAST MAN (1933) PR:A
TO THE SHORES OF HELL (1966) PR:A
TO THE SHORES OF TRIPOLI (1942) PR:A
TO THE VICTOR (1938, Brit.) PR:A
TO THE VICTOR (1948) PR:A
TO TRAP A SPY (1966) PR:A
TO WHAT RED HELL (1929, Brit.) PR:A
TOAST OF NEW ORLEANS, THE (1950) PR:A
TOAST OF NEW YORK, THE (1937) PR:A
TOAST OF THE LEGION (SEE: KISS ME AGAIN) (1931)
TOAST TO LOVE (1951, Mex.) PR:A
TOBACCO ROAD (1941) PR:A
TOBENAI CHINMOKU (SEE: SILENCE HAS NO WINGS) (1971, Jap.)
TOBOR THE GREAT (1954) PR:AA
TOBRUK (1966) PR:A
TOBY MCTEAGUE (1986, Can.) PR:A
TOBY TYLER (1960) PR:AA
TODAY (1930) PR:A
TODAY I HANG (1942) PR:A
TODAY IT'S ME. . . TOMORROW YOU? (1968, It.) PR:C
TODAY WE LIVE (1933) PR:A
TODAY WE LIVE (SEE: DAY AND THE HOUR, THE) (1963, Fr./It.)
TODD KILLINGS, THE (1971) PR:O
TOGETHER (1956, Brit.) PR:A
TOGETHER AGAIN (1944) PR:A
TOGETHER BROTHERS (1974) PR:C
TOGETHER FOR DAYS (1972) PR:C
TOGETHER IN PARIS (SEE: PARIS WHEN IT SIZZLES) (1964)
TOGETHER WE LIVE (1935) PR:A
TOILERS OF THE SEA (1936, Brit.) PR:A
TOKYO AFTER DARK (1959) PR:A
TOKYO FILE 212 (1951) PR:A
TOKYO JOE (1949) PR:A
TOKYO POP (1988, Jap.) PR:O
TOKYO ROSE (1945) PR:A
TOKYO STORY (1972, Jap.) PR:A
TOKYO YAWA (SEE: DIPLOMAT'S MANSION, THE) (1961, Jap.)
TOL'ABLE DAVID (1930) PR:A
TOLL OF THE DESERT (1936) PR:A
TOLLER HECHT AUF KRUMMER TOUR (SEE: PHONY AMERICAN, THE) (1964, W. Ger.)
TOM (1973) PR:O
TOM BROWN OF CULVER (1932) PR:AA
TOM BROWN'S SCHOOL DAYS (1940) PR:AA
TOM BROWN'S SCHOOLDAYS (1951, Brit.) PR:AA
TOM, DICK AND HARRY (1941) PR:A
TOM HORN (1980) PR:O
TOM JONES (1963, Brit.) PR:O
TOM SAWYER (1930) PR:AA
TOM SAWYER (SEE: ADVENTURES OF TOM SAWYER, THE) (1938)
TOM SAWYER (1973) PR:AA
TOM SAWYER, DETECTIVE (1939) PR:A
TOM THUMB (1958, Brit./US) PR:AA
TOM THUMB (1967, Mex.) PR:A
TOMAHAWK (1951) PR:A
TOMAHAWK AND THE CROSS, THE (SEE: PILLARS OF THE SKY) (1956)
TOMAHAWK TRAIL, THE (SEE: IROQUOIS TRAIL, THE) (1950)
TOMAHAWK TRAIL (1957) PR:A
TOMB, THE (1986) PR:O
TOMB OF LIGEIA, THE (1965, Brit.) PR:C
TOMB OF THE CAT (SEE: TOMB OF LIGEIA, THE) (1965, Brit.)
TOMB OF THE LIVING DEAD (SEE: MAD DOCTOR OF BLOOD ISLAND, THE) (1969)
TOMB OF THE UNDEAD (1972) PR:O
TOMB OF TORTURE (1966, It.) PR:O
TOMBOY (1940) PR:A
TOMBOY (1985) PR:O
TOMBOY AND THE CHAMP (1961) PR:A
TOMBS OF HORROR (SEE: CASTLE OF BLOOD) (1964, Fr./It.)
TOMBS OF THE BLIND DEAD (SEE: BLIND DEAD) (1972, Sp.)
TOMBSTONE CANYON (1932) PR:A
TOMBSTONE TERROR (1935) PR:A
TOMBSTONE, THE TOWN TOO TOUGH TO DIE (1942) PR:A
TOMCAT, THE (1968, Brit.) PR:O
TOMMY (1975, Brit.) PR:C
TOMMY STEELE STORY, THE (SEE: ROCK AROUND THE WORLD) (1957, Brit.)
TOMMY THE TOREADOR (1960, Brit.) PR:A
TOMORROW (1972) PR:C
TOMORROW AND TOMORROW (1932) PR:A
TOMORROW AT MIDNIGHT (SEE: FOR LOVE OR MONEY) (1939)
TOMORROW AT SEVEN (1933) PR:A
TOMORROW AT TEN (1964, Brit.) PR:A

TOMORROW IS ANOTHER DAY (1951) PR:A
TOMORROW IS FOREVER (1946) PR:A
TOMORROW IS MY TURN (1962, Fr./It./W. Ger.) PR:C
TOMORROW NEVER COMES (1978, Brit./Can.) PR:O
TOMORROW THE WORLD (1944) PR:A
TOMORROW WE LIVE (1936, Brit.) PR:C
TOMORROW WE LIVE (1942) PR:A
TOMORROW WE LIVE (SEE: AT DAWN WE DIE) (1943, Brit.)
TOMORROW'S YOUTH (1935) PR:A
TONI (1934, Fr.) PR:C
TONIGHT A TOWN DIES (1961, Pol.) PR:C
TONIGHT AND EVERY NIGHT (1945) PR:A
TONIGHT AT 8:30 (1953, Brit.) PR:A
TONIGHT AT TWELVE (1929) PR:A
TONIGHT FOR SURE! (1962) PR:O
TONIGHT IS OURS (1933) PR:A
TONIGHT OR NEVER (1931) PR:A-C
TONIGHT THE SKIRTS FLY (1956, Fr.) PR:C
TONIGHT WE RAID CALAIS (1943) PR:A
TONIGHT WE SING (1953) PR:A
TONIGHT'S THE NIGHT (1932, Brit.) PR:A
TONIGHT'S THE NIGHT (1954, Brit.) PR:A
TONIO KROGER (1964, Fr./W. Ger.) PR:C
TONKA (1958) PR:AA
TONS OF MONEY (1931, Brit.) PR:A
TONS OF TROUBLE (1956, Brit.) PR:AA
TONTO BASIN OUTLAWS (1941) PR:A
TONY DRAWS A HORSE (1951, Brit.) PR:A-C
TONY ROME (1967) PR:C
TOO BAD SHE'S BAD (1954, It.) PR:C
TOO BUSY TO WORK (1932) PR:A
TOO BUSY TO WORK (1939) PR:A
TOO DANGEROUS TO LIVE (1939, Brit.) PR:A
TOO DANGEROUS TO LOVE (SEE: PERFECT STRANGERS) (1950)
TOO HOT TO HANDLE (1938) PR:A-C
TOO HOT TO HANDLE (1961, Brit.) PR:C
TOO LATE BLUES (1962) PR:C
TOO LATE FOR TEARS (1949) PR:O
TOO LATE THE HERO (1970) PR:C
TOO MANY BLONDES (1941) PR:A
TOO MANY CHEFS (SEE: WHO IS KILLING THE GREAT CHEFS OF EUROPE?) (1978, US/W. Ger.)
TOO MANY COOKS (1931) PR:A
TOO MANY CROOKS (1959, Brit.) PR:A
TOO MANY GIRLS (1940) PR:A
TOO MANY HUSBANDS (1938, Brit.) PR:AA
TOO MANY HUSBANDS (1940) PR:A
TOO MANY MILLIONS (1934, Brit.) PR:A
TOO MANY PARENTS (1936) PR:A
TOO MANY THIEVES (1968) PR:A
TOO MANY WINNERS (1947) PR:A
TOO MANY WIVES (1933, Brit.) PR:A
TOO MANY WIVES (1937) PR:A
TOO MANY WOMEN (SEE: GOD'S GIFT TO WOMEN) (1931)
TOO MANY WOMEN (1942) PR:A
TOO MUCH BEEF (1936) PR:A
TOO MUCH FOR ONE MAN (SEE: CLIMAX, THE) (1967, Fr./It.)
TOO MUCH HARMONY (1933) PR:A
TOO MUCH, TOO SOON (1958) PR:C
TOO SCARED TO SCREAM (1985) PR:O
TOO SOON TO LOVE (1960) PR:C
TOO TOUGH TO KILL (1935) PR:A
TOO YOUNG TO KISS (1951) PR:A
TOO YOUNG TO KNOW (1945) PR:A
TOO YOUNG TO LOVE (1960, Brit.) PR:C
TOO YOUNG TO MARRY (1931) PR:A
TOO YOUNG, TOO IMMORAL! (1962) PR:O
TOOLBOX MURDERS, THE (1978) PR:O
TOOMORROW (1970, Brit.) PR:A
TOOTSIE (1982) PR:C
TOP BANANA (1954) PR:A
TOP FLOOR GIRL (1959, Brit.) PR:A
TOP GUN (1955) PR:A-C
TOP GUN (1986) PR:A-C
TOP HAT (1935) PR:A
TOP JOB (SEE: GRAND SLAM) (1968, It./Sp./W. Ger.)
TOP MAN (1943) PR:A
TOP O' THE MORNING (1949) PR:A
TOP OF THE BILL (SEE: FANNY FOLEY HERSELF) (1931)
TOP OF THE FORM (1953, Brit.) PR:A
TOP OF THE HEAP (1972) PR:O
TOP OF THE TOWN (1937) PR:A
TOP OF THE WORLD (1955) PR:A
TOP SECRET (SEE: MR. POTTS GOES TO MOSCOW) (1953, Brit.)
TOP SECRET! (1984) PR:C
TOP SECRET AFFAIR (1957) PR:A
TOP SENSATION (SEE: SEDUCERS, THE) (1970, It.)
TOP SERGEANT (1942) PR:A
TOP SERGEANT MULLIGAN (1941) PR:A
TOP SPEED (1930) PR:A
TOPAZ (1969) PR:C
TOPAZE (1933) PR:C

TOPAZE (1935, Fr.) PR:A
TOPEKA (1953) PR:A
TOPEKA TERROR, THE (1945) PR:A
TOPKAPI (1964) PR:A-C
TOPPER (1937) PR:A
TOPPER RETURNS (1941) PR:A
TOPPER TAKES A TRIP (1939) PR:A
TOPS IS THE LIMIT (SEE: ANYTHING GOES) (1936)
TOPSY-TURVY JOURNEY (1970, Jap.) PR:A
TORA-SAN GOES TO VIENNA (1989, Jap.) PR:A
TORA-SAN PART 2 (1970, Jap.) PR:C
TORA! TORA! TORA! (1970, US/Jap.) PR:C
TORCH, THE (1950) PR:A
TORCH SINGER (1933) PR:A
TORCH SONG (1953) PR:A
TORCH SONG TRILOGY (1988) PR:O
TORCHLIGHT (1984) PR:O
TORCHY BLANE IN CHINATOWN (1938) PR:A
TORCHY BLANE IN PANAMA (1938) PR:A
TORCHY BLANE, THE ADVENTUROUS BLONDE (SEE: ADVENTUROUS BLONDE, THE) (1937)
TORCHY GETS HER MAN (1938) PR:A
TORCHY PLAYS WITH DYNAMITE (1939) PR:A
TORCHY RUNS FOR MAYOR (1939) PR:A
TORMENT (1944, Swed.) PR:A
TORMENT (SEE: PAPER GALLOWS) (1950, Brit.)
TORMENT (1986) PR:O
TORMENTED (1960) PR:C
TORMENTED, THE (1978, It.) PR:O
TORN CURTAIN (1966) PR:C
TORNADO (1943) PR:A
TORNADO RANGE (1948) PR:A
TORPEDO ALLEY (1953) PR:A
TORPEDO BAY (1964, It./Fr.) PR:C
TORPEDO BOAT (1942) PR:A
TORPEDO RUN (1958) PR:A-C
TORPEDO ZONE (SEE: GREAT HOPE, THE) (1954, It.)
TORPEDOED! (1939, Brit.) PR:C
TORRID ZONE (1940) PR:A
TORSO (1974, It.) PR:O
TORSO MURDER MYSTERY, THE (1940, Brit.) PR:C
TORTILLA FLAT (1942) PR:A
TORTURE CHAMBER OF DR. SADISM, THE (SEE: BLOOD DEMON, THE) (1967, W. Ger.)
TORTURE DUNGEON (1970) PR:O
TORTURE GARDEN (1968, Brit.) PR:O
TORTURE ME KISS ME (1970) PR:O
TORTURE SHIP (1939) PR:A
TOTO AND THE POACHERS (1958, Brit.) PR:AA
TOTO IN THE MOON (1957, It./Sp.) PR:A
TOTO NELIA LUNA (SEE: TOTO IN THE MOON) (1957, It./Sp.)
TOTO, VITTORIO E LA DOTTORESSA (SEE: LADY DOCTOR, THE) (1963, Fr./It./Sp.)
TOUCH, THE (1971, US/Swed.) PR:O
TOUCH AND GO (SEE: LIGHT TOUCH, THE) (1955, Brit.)
TOUCH AND GO (1980, Aus.) PR:C
TOUCH AND GO (1986) PR:C-O
TOUCH OF CLASS, A (1973, Brit.) PR:C
TOUCH OF DEATH (1962, Brit.) PR:A
TOUCH OF EVIL (1958) PR:C
TOUCH OF FLESH, THE (1960) PR:C
TOUCH OF HELL, A (SEE: IMMORAL CHARGE) (1962, Brit.)
TOUCH OF HER FLESH, THE (1967) PR:O
TOUCH OF HER LIFE, THE (SEE: TOUCH OF HER FLESH, THE) (1967)
TOUCH OF LARCENY, A (1960, Brit.) PR:A
TOUCH OF LOVE, A (SEE: THANK YOU ALL VERY MUCH) (1969, Brit.)
TOUCH OF SATAN, THE (1971) PR:O
TOUCH OF THE MOON, A (1936, Brit.) PR:A
TOUCH OF THE OTHER, A (1970, Brit.) PR:O
TOUCH OF THE SUN, A (1956, Brit.) PR:A
TOUCH WHITE, TOUCH BLACK (SEE: VIOLENT ONES, THE) (1967)
TOUCHDOWN (1931) PR:A
TOUCHDOWN, ARMY (1938) PR:A
TOUCHE PAS A LA FEMME BLANCHE (SEE: DON'T TOUCH WHITE WOMEN!) (1974, Fr.)
TOUCHED (1983) PR:C
TOUCHED BY LOVE (1980) PR:A
TOUGH AS THEY COME (1942) PR:A
TOUGH ASSIGNMENT (1949) PR:A
TOUGH ENOUGH (1983) PR:C
TOUGH GUY (1936) PR:A
TOUGH GUYS (1986) PR:C
TOUGH GUYS DON'T DANCE (1987) PR:O
TOUGH KID (1939) PR:A
TOUGH TO HANDLE (1937) PR:A
TOUGHER THAN LEATHER (1988) PR:O
TOUGHER THEY COME, THE (1950) PR:A
TOUGHEST GUN IN TOMBSTONE (1958) PR:A
TOUGHEST MAN ALIVE (1955) PR:A
TOUGHEST MAN IN ARIZONA (1952) PR:A

TOURBILLON DE PARIS (SEE: WHIRLWIND OF PARIS) (1946, Fr.)
TOURIST TRAP, THE (1979) PR:C
TOUT VA BIEN (1973, Fr.) PR:C
TOVARICH (1937) PR:AA
TOWARD THE UNKNOWN (1956) PR:A
TOWER OF EVIL (SEE: BEYOND THE FOG) (1981, Brit.)
TOWER OF LONDON (1939) PR:A
TOWER OF LONDON (1962) PR:A
TOWER OF TERROR, THE (1942, Brit.) PR:A
TOWER OF TERROR (SEE: ASSAULT) (1971, Brit.)
TOWERING INFERNO, THE (1974) PR:C
TOWING (1978) PR:C
TOWN CALLED BASTARD, A (SEE: TOWN CALLED HELL, A) (1971, Brit./Sp.)
TOWN CALLED HELL, A (1971, Brit./Sp.) PR:O
TOWN LIKE ALICE, A (1958, Brit.) PR:A
TOWN ON TRIAL (1957, Brit.) PR:C
TOWN TAMER (1965) PR:A
TOWN THAT CRIED TERROR, THE (SEE: MANIAC!) (1977)
TOWN THAT DREADED SUNDOWN, THE (1977) PR:O
TOWN WENT WILD, THE (1945) PR:A
TOWN WITHOUT PITY (1961, Switz./US/W. Ger.) PR:C-O
TOXI (1952, W. Ger.) PR:A
TOXIC AVENGER, THE (1985) PR:O
TOXIC AVENGER, PART II, THE (1989) PR:O
TOXIC AVENGER PART III, THE: THE LAST TEMPTATION OF TOXIE (1989) PR:O
TOY, THE (1982) PR:C
TOY GRABBERS, THE (SEE: UP YOUR TEDDY BEAR) (1970)
TOY SOLDIERS (1984) PR:O
TOY TIGER (1956) PR:AA
TOY WIFE, THE (1938) PR:A-C
TOYS ARE NOT FOR CHILDREN (1972) PR:O
TOYS IN THE ATTIC (1963) PR:A
TRACK OF THE CAT (1954) PR:C
TRACK OF THE MOONBEAST (1976) PR:C-O
TRACK OF THE VAMPIRE, (SEE: BLOOD BATH) (1966)
TRACK OF THUNDER (1967) PR:A
TRACK THE MAN DOWN (1956, Brit.) PR:A
TRACK 29 (1988, Brit.) PR:O
TRACKDOWN (1976) PR:O
TRACKS (1977) PR:O
TRADE WINDS (1938) PR:A
TRADER HORN (1931) PR:C
TRADER HORN (1973) PR:A
TRADER HORNEE (1970) PR:O
TRADING HEARTS (1988) PR:A-C
TRADING PLACES (1983) PR:C-O
TRAFFIC (1972, Fr.) PR:AA
TRAFFIC IN CRIME (1946) PR:A
TRAGEDY AT MIDNIGHT, A (1942) PR:A
TRAGEDY OF A RIDICULOUS MAN, THE (1982, It.) PR:A
TRAIL BEYOND, THE (1934) PR:A
TRAIL BLAZERS, THE (1940) PR:A
TRAIL DRIVE, THE (1934) PR:A
TRAIL DUST (1936) PR:A
TRAIL GUIDE (1952) PR:A
TRAIL OF KIT CARSON (1945) PR:A
TRAIL OF ROBIN HOOD (1950) PR:A
TRAIL OF TERROR (1935) PR:AA
TRAIL OF TERROR (1944) PR:A
TRAIL OF THE LONESOME PINE, THE (1936) PR:A-C
TRAIL OF THE PINK PANTHER, THE (1982, Brit.) PR:C
TRAIL OF THE SILVER SPURS (1941) PR:A
TRAIL OF THE VIGILANTES (1940) PR:A
TRAIL OF THE YUKON (1949) PR:A
TRAIL OF VENGEANCE (1937) PR:A
TRAIL RIDERS (1942) PR:AA
TRAIL STREET (1947) PR:A
TRAIL TO GUNSIGHT (1944) PR:AA
TRAIL TO SAN ANTONE (1947) PR:A
TRAIL TO VENGEANCE (1945) PR:A
TRAILIN' TROUBLE (1930) PR:A
TRAILIN' WEST (1936) PR:A
TRAILING DOUBLE TROUBLE (1940) PR:A
TRAILING THE KILLER (1932) PR:A
TRAILING TROUBLE (1937) PR:A
TRAIL'S END (1949) PR:A
TRAILS OF DANGER (1930) PR:A
TRAILS OF PERIL (SEE: TRAILS OF DANGER) (1930)
TRAILS OF THE WILD (1935) PR:A
TRAIN, THE (1965, Fr./It./US) PR:C
TRAIN GOES EAST, THE (1949, USSR) PR:A
TRAIN GOES TO KIEV, THE (1961, USSR) PR:A
TRAIN OF DREAMS (1987, Can.) PR:C-O
TRAIN OF EVENTS (1952, Brit.) PR:A
TRAIN OF TERROR (SEE: TERROR TRAIN) (1980, Can.)
TRAIN RIDE TO HOLLYWOOD (1975) PR:A
TRAIN ROBBERS, THE (1973) PR:A
TRAIN ROBBERY CONFIDENTIAL (1965, Braz.) PR:A
TRAIN TO ALCATRAZ (1948) PR:A
TRAIN TO TOMBSTONE (1950) PR:A

TRAIN 2419 (SEE: RETURN OF CASEY JONES) (1933)
TRAINED TO KILL (SEE: NO MERCY MAN, THE) (1975)
TRAINED TO KILL (SEE: WHITE DOG) (1982)
TRAITEMENT DE CHOC (SEE: SHOCK TREATMENT) (1973, Fr.)
TRAITOR, THE (1936) PR:A
TRAITOR SPY (SEE: TORSO MURDER MYSTERY, THE) (1940, Brit.)
TRAITOR WITHIN, THE (1942) PR:A
TRAITORS (1957, Jap.) PR:A
TRAITORS, THE (SEE: ACCURSED, THE) (1958, Brit.)
TRAITORS, THE (1963, Brit.) PR:A
TRAITOR'S GATE (1966, Brit./W. Ger.) PR:A
TRAMP, TRAMP, TRAMP (1942) PR:A
TRAMPLERS, THE (1966, It.) PR:C
TRANCERS (1985) PR:O
TRANS-EUROP-EXPRESS (1968, Fr.) PR:O
TRANSATLANTIC (1931) PR:A
TRANSATLANTIC (1961, Brit.) PR:A
TRANSATLANTIC MERRY-GO-ROUND (1934) PR:A
TRANSATLANTIC TROUBLE (SEE: TAKE IT FROM ME) (1937, Brit.)
TRANSATLANTIC TUNNEL (1935, Brit.) PR:A
TRANSCONTINENT EXPRESS (SEE: ROCK ISLAND TRAIL) (1950)
TRANSFORMERS: THE MOVIE, THE (1986) PR:A-C
TRANSGRESSION (1931) PR:A
TRANSIENT LADY (1935) PR:A
TRANSPORT FROM PARADISE (1962, Czech.) PR:A
TRANSPORT Z RAJE (SEE: TRANSPORT FROM PARA-DISE) (1962, Czech.)
TRANSVESTITE, THE (SEE: GLEN OR GLENDA) (1953)
TRANSYLVANIA 6-5000 (1985) PR:C
TRAP, THE (1947) PR:A
TRAP, THE (1959) PR:A
TRAP, THE (1967, Can./Brit.) PR:A
TRAP DOOR, THE (1980) PR:O
TRAPEZE (1932, Ger.) PR:A
TRAPEZE (1956) PR:A-C
TRAPP FAMILY, THE (1961, W. Ger.) PR:A
TRAPPED (1931) PR:A
TRAPPED (1937) PR:A
TRAPPED (1949) PR:A
TRAPPED BY BOSTON BLACKIE (1948) PR:A
TRAPPED BY G-MEN (1937) PR:A
TRAPPED BY TELEVISION (1936) PR:A
TRAPPED BY THE TERROR (1949, Brit.) PR:AA
TRAPPED BY WIRELESS (SEE: YOU MAY BE NEXT!) (1936)
TRAPPED IN A SUBMARINE (1931, Brit.) PR:A
TRAPPED IN TANGIERS (1960, It./Sp.) PR:A
TRAPPED IN THE SKY (1939) PR:A
TRAQUENARDS (SEE: EROTIQUE) (1969, Fr.)
TRAUM VON SCHONBRUNN (SEE: DREAM OF SCHONBRUNN, THE) (1933, Aust.)
TRAUMA (1962) PR:C
TRAUMSTADT (SEE: DREAM TOWN) (1973, W. Ger.)
TRAUMULUS (SEE: DREAMER, THE) (1936, Ger.)
TRAVELING EXECUTIONER, THE (1970) PR:O
TRAVELING HUSBANDS (1931) PR:O
TRAVELING LADY (SEE: BABY THE RAIN MUST FALL) (1965)
TRAVELING SALESLADY, THE (1935) PR:A
TRAVELING SALESWOMAN (1950) PR:A
TRAVELLER'S JOY (1951, Brit.) PR:A
TRAVELLING AVANT (1988, Fr.) PR:O
TRAVELLING NORTH (1988, Aus.) PR:C
TRAVELS WITH ANITA (SEE: LOVERS AND LIARS) (1981, It.)
TRAVELS WITH MY AUNT (1972) PR:C
TRAXX (1988) PR:O
TRE NOTTI D'AMORE (SEE: THREE NIGHTS OF LOVE) (1969, It.)
TRE NOTTI VIOLENTE (SEE: WEB OF VIOLENCE) (1966, It./Sp.)
TRE PASSI NEL DELIRIO (SEE: SPIRITS OF THE DEAD) (1968, Fr./It.)
TREACHERY ON THE HIGH SEAS (1939, Brit.) PR:A
TREACHERY RIDES THE RANGE (1936) PR:A
TREAD SOFTLY (1952, Brit.) PR:A
TREAD SOFTLY, STRANGER (1959, Brit.) PR:A
TREASON (SEE: OLD LOUISIANA) (1938)
TREASON (SEE: GUILTY OF TREASON) (1950)
TREASURE AT THE MILL (1957, Brit.) PR:AA
TREASURE HUNT (1952, Brit.) PR:A
TREASURE ISLAND (1934) PR:A
TREASURE ISLAND (1950, Brit.) PR:A-C
TREASURE ISLAND (1972, Brit./Sp./Fr./W. Ger.) PR:A
TREASURE OF FEAR (SEE: SCARED STIFF) (1945)
TREASURE OF JAMAICA REEF, THE (1976) PR:C
TREASURE OF KALIFA (SEE: STEEL LADY, THE) (1953)
TREASURE OF LOST CANYON, THE (1952) PR:A
TREASURE OF MAKUBA, THE (1967, US/Sp.) PR:A
TREASURE OF MATECUMBE (1976) PR:AA
TREASURE OF MONTE CRISTO (1949) PR:A

TREASURE OF MONTE CRISTO, THE (SEE: SECRET OF MONTE CRISTO, THE) (1961, Fr./It.)
TREASURE OF PANCHO VILLA, THE (1955) PR:A
TREASURE OF RUBY HILLS (1955) PR:A
TREASURE OF SAN GENNARO (1968, Fr./It./W. Ger.) PR:A
TREASURE OF SAN TERESA, THE (SEE: HOT MONEY GIRL) (1962, Brit./W. Ger.)
TREASURE OF SILVER LAKE (1965, Fr./It./W. Ger./Yugo.) PR:A
TREASURE OF THE AMAZON, THE (1985, Mex.) PR:O
TREASURE OF THE FOUR CROWNS (1983, Sp./US) PR:A
TREASURE OF THE GOLDEN CONDOR (1953) PR:A
TREASURE OF THE PIRANHA (SEE: KILLER FISH) (1979, It./Braz.)
TREASURE OF THE SIERRA MADRE, THE (1948) PR:C
TREASURE OF THE YANKEE ZEPHYR (1984) PR:A-C
TREAT EM' ROUGH (1942) PR:A
TREATMENT, THE (SEE: STOP ME BEFORE I KILL!) (1961, Brit.)
TRECHI MYNYDD Y TEIGR (SEE: TAKING TIGER MOUNTAIN) (1983, US/Wales)
TREE, THE (1969) PR:O
TREE GROWS IN BROOKLYN, A (1945) PR:C
TREE OF LIBERTY (SEE: HOWARDS OF VIRGINIA, THE) (1940)
TREE OF WOODEN CLOGS, THE (1979, It.) PR:A-C
TREE WE HURT, THE (1986, Gr.) PR:A
TREMENDOUSLY RICH MAN, A (1932, Ger.) PR:A
TRENCHCOAT (1983) PR:A
TRENT'S LAST CASE (1953, Brit.) PR:A
TRES NOCHES VIOLENTAS (SEE: WEB OF VIO-LENCE) (1966, It./Sp.)
TRESPASSER, THE (1929) PR:A
TRESPASSER, THE (SEE: NIGHT EDITOR) (1946)
TRESPASSER, THE (1947) PR:A
TRESPASSERS, THE (1976, Aus.) PR:O
TRI (SEE: THREE) (1967, Yugo.)
TRI SESTRY (SEE: THREE SISTERS, THE) (1969, USSR)
TRIAL, THE (1948, Aust.) PR:A
TRIAL (1955) PR:A
TRIAL, THE (1963, Fr./It./W. Ger.) PR:C
TRIAL AND ERROR (1962, Brit.) PR:A
TRIAL BY COMBAT (SEE: DIRTY KNIGHT'S WORK) (1976, Brit.)
TRIAL OF BILLY JACK, THE (1974) PR:C
TRIAL OF JOAN OF ARC (1965, Fr.) PR:C
TRIAL OF LEE HARVEY OSWALD, THE (1964) PR:A
TRIAL OF MADAME X, THE (1948, Brit.) PR:A
TRIAL OF MARY DUGAN, THE (1929) PR:C
TRIAL OF MARY DUGAN, THE (1941) PR:A
TRIAL OF PORTIA MERRIMAN, THE (SEE: PORTIA ON TRIAL) (1937)
TRIAL OF SERGEANT RUTLEDGE, THE (SEE: SER-GEANT RUTLEDGE) (1960)
TRIAL OF THE CATONSVILLE NINE, THE (1972) PR:A
TRIAL OF VIVIENNE WARE, THE (1932) PR:A
TRIAL WITHOUT JURY (1950) PR:A
TRIALS OF OSCAR WILDE, THE (SEE: MAN WITH THE GREEN CARNATION, THE) (1960, Brit.)
TRIANGLE ON SAFARI (SEE: WOMAN AND THE HUNTER, THE) (1957)
TRIBES (1970) PR:A
TRIBUTE (1980, Can.) PR:C
TRIBUTE TO A BADMAN (1956) PR:C
TRICET JEDNA VE STINU (SEE: 90 DEGREES IN THE SHADE) (1966, Czech./Brit.)
TRICK BABY (1973) PR:O
TRICK FOR TRICK (1933) PR:A
TRICK OR TREAT (1986) PR:O
TRICK OR TREATS (1982) PR:O
TRICKED (SEE: BANDITS OF EL DORADO) (1951)
TRICKED (SEE: BANDITS OF EL DORADO) (1981)
TRIGGER FINGERS (1939) PR:A
TRIGGER HAPPY (SEE: DEADLY COMPANIONS, THE) (1961)
TRIGGER, JR. (1950) PR:A
TRIGGER PALS (1939) PR:A
TRIGGER SMITH (1939) PR:A
TRIGGER TRAIL (1944) PR:A
TRIGGER TRICKS (1930) PR:A
TRIGGER TRIO, THE (1937) PR:A
TRILOGY (SEE: TRUMAN CAPOTE'S TRILOGY) (1969)
TRINITY IS STILL MY NAME (1971, It.) PR:A
TRIO (1950, Brit.) PR:A
TRIP, THE (1967) PR:O
TRIP, THE (SEE: CHELSEA GIRLS, THE) (1966)
TRIP, THE (SEE: VOYAGE, THE) (1974, It.)
TRIP TO AMERICA, A (SEE: VOYAGE TO AMERICA) (1952, Fr.)
TRIP TO BOUNTIFUL, THE (1985) PR:C
TRIP TO ITALY, A (SEE: STRANGERS, THE) (1955, It.)
TRIP TO PARIS, A (1938) PR:A
TRIP TO TERROR (SEE: IS THIS TRIP REALLY NECES-SARY?) (1970)
TRIP WITH ANITA, A (SEE: LOVERS AND LIARS) (1981, It.)

TRIPLE CROSS, THE (SEE: JOE PALOOKA IN TRIPLE CROSS) (1951)
TRIPLE CROSS (1967, Fr./Brit.) PR:C-O
TRIPLE DECEPTION (1956, Brit.) PR:A
TRIPLE ECHO, THE (1973, Brit.) PR:O
TRIPLE IRONS (1973, Hong Kong) PR:O
TRIPLE JUSTICE (1940) PR:A
TRIPLE THREAT (1948) PR:A
TRIPLE TROUBLE (SEE: KENTUCKY KERNELS) (1935)
TRIPLE TROUBLE (1950) PR:A
TRIPOLI (1950) PR:A
TRISTANA (1970, Sp./It./Fr.) PR:C
TRITIY TAYM (SEE: LAST GAME, THE) (1964, USSR)
TRIUMPH OF SHERLOCK HOLMES, THE (1935, Brit.) PR:A
TRIUMPH OF THE SPIRIT (1989) PR:C
TRIUMPHS OF A MAN CALLED HORSE (1983, US/Mex.) PR:O
TRO, HAB OG KARLIGHED (SEE: TWIST & SHOUT) (1984, Den.)
TROCADERO (1944) PR:A
TROG (1970, Brit.) PR:A
TROIKA (1969) PR:O
TROIS HOMMES A ABATTRE (SEE: THREE MEN TO DESTROY) (1980, Fr.)
TROIS VERITES (SEE: THREE FACES OF SIN) (1963, Fr./It.)
TROJAN BROTHERS, THE (1946, Brit.) PR:A
TROJAN HORSE, THE (1962, Fr./It.) PR:AA
TROJAN WAR, THE (SEE: TROJAN HORSE, THE) (1962, Fr./It.)
TROJAN WOMEN, THE (1971, Gr./US) PR:C
TROLL (1986) PR:C
TROLLENBERG TERROR, THE (SEE: CRAWLING EYE, THE) (1958, Brit.)
TROMBA, THE TIGER MAN (1952, W. Ger.) PR:C
TROMBONE FROM HEAVEN (SEE: FOLLOW THE BAND) (1943)
TRON (1982) PR:A
TROOP BEVERLY HILLS (1989) PR:A-C
TROOPER, THE (SEE: FIGHTING TROOPER, THE) (1935)
TROOPER HOOK (1957) PR:C
TROOPERS THREE (1930) PR:AA
TROOPSHIP (1938, Brit.) PR:C
TROPIC FURY (1939) PR:A
TROPIC HOLIDAY (1938) PR:A
TROPIC ZONE (1953) PR:A
TROPICAL HEAT WAVE (1952) PR:A
TROPICAL TROUBLE (1936, Brit.) PR:A
TROPICANA (SEE: HEAT'S ON, THE) (1943)
TROPICS (1969, It.) PR:O
TROTTIE TRUE (SEE: GAY LADY, THE) (1949, Brit.)
TROUBLE (1933, Brit.) PR:A
TROUBLE AHEAD (1936, Brit.) PR:A
TROUBLE ALONG THE WAY (1953) PR:O
TROUBLE AT MIDNIGHT (1937) PR:A
TROUBLE AT 16 (SEE: PLATINUM HIGH SCHOOL) (1960)
TROUBLE BREWING (1939, Brit.) PR:A
TROUBLE CHASER (SEE: LI'L ABNER) (1940)
TROUBLE-FETE (1964, Can.) PR:A
TROUBLE FOR TWO (1936) PR:A
TROUBLE IN MIND (1985) PR:O
TROUBLE IN MOROCCO (1937) PR:A
TROUBLE IN PANAMA (SEE: TORCHY BLANE IN PANAMA) (1938)
TROUBLE IN PARADISE (1932) PR:C
TROUBLE IN STORE (1955, Brit.) PR:A
TROUBLE IN SUNDOWN (1939) PR:A
TROUBLE IN TEXAS (1937) PR:A
TROUBLE IN THE AIR (1948, Brit.) PR:A
TROUBLE IN THE GLEN (1954, Brit.) PR:A
TROUBLE IN THE SKY (1961, Brit.) PR:C
TROUBLE MAKERS (1948) PR:AA
TROUBLE MAN (1972) PR:O
TROUBLE PREFERRED (1949) PR:A
TROUBLE WITH ANGELS, THE (1966) PR:AA
TROUBLE WITH DICK, THE (1987) PR:O
TROUBLE WITH EVE (SEE: IN TROUBLE WITH EVE) (1964, Brit.)
TROUBLE WITH GIRLS (AND HOW TO GET INTO IT), THE (1969) PR:A
TROUBLE WITH HARRY, THE (1955) PR:A-C
TROUBLE WITH WOMEN, THE (1947) PR:A
TROUBLED WATERS (1936, Brit.) PR:A
TROUBLEMAKER, THE (1964) PR:O
TROUBLES THROUGH BILLETS (SEE: BLONDIE FOR VICTORY) (1942)
TROUBLESOME DOUBLE, THE (1971, Brit.) PR:AA
TROUT, THE (1982, Fr.) PR:O
TRUANT, THE (SEE: PIE IN THE SKY) (1964)
TRUCK BUSTERS (1943) PR:A
TRUCK STOP WOMEN (1974) PR:O
TRUCK TURNER (1974) PR:O
TRUE AND THE FALSE, THE (1955, Swed.) PR:O
TRUE AS A TURTLE (1957, Brit.) PR:A

TRUE BELIEVER (1989) PR:O
TRUE BLOOD (1989) PR:C-O
TRUE CONFESSION (1937) PR:A
TRUE CONFESSIONS (1981) PR:O
TRUE GRIT (1969) PR:A
TRUE LOVE (1989) PR:O
TRUE STORIES (1986) PR:A
TRUE STORY OF A WAHINE (SEE: MAEVA) (1961)
TRUE STORY OF ESKIMO NELL, THE (1975, Aus.)
  PR:O
TRUE STORY OF JESSE JAMES, THE (1957) PR:A
TRUE STORY OF LYNN STUART, THE (1958) PR:A
TRUE TO LIFE (1943) PR:A
TRUE TO THE ARMY (1942) PR:AA
TRUE TO THE NAVY (1930) PR:A
TRUMAN CAPOTE'S TRILOGY (1969) PR:A
TRUMPET BLOWS, THE (1934) PR:A
TRUNK, THE (1961, Brit.) PR:C
TRUNK CRIME (SEE: DESIGN FOR MURDER) (1940,
  Brit.)
TRUNK MYSTERY, THE (SEE: ONE NEW YORK
  NIGHT) (1935)
TRUNK TO CAIRO (1966, Israel/W. Ger.) PR:C
TRUNKS OF MR. O.F., THE (1932, Ger.) PR:A
TRUST ME (1989) PR:A
TRUST THE NAVY (1935, Brit.) PR:A
TRUST YOUR WIFE (SEE: FALL GUY, THE) (1930)
TRUSTED OUTLAW, THE (1937) PR:A
TRUTH, THE (1961, Fr./It.) PR:O
TRUTH ABOUT MURDER, THE (1946) PR:A
TRUTH ABOUT SPRING, THE (1965, Brit.) PR:AA
TRUTH ABOUT WOMEN, THE (1958, Brit.) PR:A
TRUTH ABOUT YOUTH, THE (1930) PR:A
TRUTH IS STRANGER (SEE: WHEN LADIES MEET)
  (1933)
TRY AND FIND IT (SEE: HI, DIDDLE DIDDLE) (1943)
TRY AND GET ME (SEE: SOUND OF FURY, THE) (1950)
TRYGON FACTOR, THE (1969, Brit.) PR:C
TSAR'S BRIDE, THE (1966, USSR) PR:A
TSARSKAYA NEVESTA (SEE: TSAR'S BRIDE, THE)
  (1966, USSR)
TSUBAKI SANJURO (SEE: SANJURO) (1962, Jap.)
TU PERDONAS..YO NO (SEE: GOD FORGIVES—I
  DON'T) (1969, It./Sp.)
TU SERAS TERRIBLEMENT GENTILLE (SEE: YOU
  ONLY LIVE ONCE) (1969, Fr.)
TUCKER: THE MAN AND HIS DREAM (1988) PR:A
TUCSON (1949) PR:A
TUCSON RAIDERS (1944) PR:A
TUDOR ROSE (SEE: LADY JANE GREY) (1936, Brit.)
TUFF TURF (1985) PR:O
TUGBOAT ANNIE (1933) PR:A
TUGBOAT ANNIE SAILS AGAIN (1940) PR:AA
TULIPS (1981, Can.) PR:C
TULSA (1949) PR:A
TULSA KID, THE (1940) PR:A
TUMBLEDOWN RANCH IN ARIZONA (1941) PR:A
TUMBLEWEED (1953) PR:A
TUMBLEWEED TRAIL (1946) PR:A
TUMBLING TUMBLEWEEDS (1935) PR:AA
TUNA CLIPPER (1949) PR:A
TUNDRA (1936) PR:A
TUNES OF GLORY (1960, Brit.) PR:C
TUNNEL, THE (SEE: TRANSATLANTIC TUNNEL)
  (1935, Brit.)
TUNNEL OF LOVE, THE (1958) PR:C
TUNNEL TO THE SUN (1968, Jap.) PR:C
TUNNEL 28 (SEE: ESCAPE FROM EAST BERLIN)
  (1962, US/W. Ger.)
TUNNELVISION (1976) PR:O
TURK 182! (1985) PR:C
TURKEY SHOOT (SEE: ESCAPE 2000) (1983, Aus.)
TURKEY TIME (1933, Brit.) PR:A
TURKISH CUCUMBER, THE (1963, W. Ger.) PR:C
TURLIS ABENTEUER (SEE: PINOCCHIO) (1969, E. Ger.)
TURN BACK THE CLOCK (1933) PR:A
TURN OF THE SCREW (1985, Sp.) PR:O
TURN OF THE TIDE (1935, Brit.) PR:A
TURN OFF THE MOON (1937) PR:A
TURN ON TO LOVE (1969) PR:O
TURN THE KEY SOFTLY (1954, Brit.) PR:C
TURNABOUT (1940) PR:A
TURNED OUT NICE AGAIN (1941, Brit.) PR:A
TURNER & HOOCH (1989) PR:C
TURNERS OF PROSPECT ROAD, THE (1947, Brit.) PR:A
TURNING POINT, THE (1952) PR:C-O
TURNING POINT, THE (1977) PR:C
TURTLE DIARY (1985, Brit.) PR:C
TUSK (1980, Fr.) PR:A
TUTTE LE ALTRE RAGAZZE LO FANNO (SEE: ALL
  THE OTHER GIRLS DO) (1967, It.)
TUTTI A CASA (SEE: EVERYBODY GO HOME!) (1962,
  Fr./It.)
TUTTI FRUTTI (SEE: CATCH AS CATCH CAN) (1968,
  Fr./It.)
TUTTI PAZZI MENO IO (SEE: KING OF HEARTS)
  (1967, Fr./It.)
TUTTLES OF TAHITI, THE (1942) PR:A

TUXEDO JUNCTION (1941) PR:A
TVA LEVANDE OCH EN DOD (SEE: TWO LIVING,
  ONE DEAD) (1964, Brit./Swed.)
TWEENERS (SEE: TRADING HEARTS) (1988)
TWELFTH NIGHT (1956, USSR) PR:A
12 ANGRY MEN (1957) PR:A
TWELVE CHAIRS, THE (1970) PR:A-C
TWELVE CROWDED HOURS (1939) PR:A
TWELVE GOOD MEN (1936, Brit.) PR:A
TWELVE-HANDED MEN OF MARS, THE (1964, It./Sp.)
  PR:A
TWELVE HOURS TO KILL (1960) PR:A
TWELVE MILES OUT (SEE: SECOND WOMAN, THE)
  (1951)
12 MILLION DOLLAR BOY (SEE: DYNAMITE JOHN-
  SON) (1978, Phil.)
TWELVE O'CLOCK HIGH (1949) PR:C
TWELVE PLUS ONE (1970, Fr./It.) PR:A
TWELVE TO THE MOON (1960) PR:A
TWENTIETH CENTURY (1934) PR:A
20TH CENTURY OZ (1977, Aus.) PR:A
25TH HOUR, THE (1967, Fr./It./Yugo.) PR:C
24-HOUR LOVER (1970, W. Ger.) PR:O
24 HOURS (1931) PR:A
24 HOURS IN A WOMAN'S LIFE (1968, Fr./W. Ger.) PR:C
24 HOURS OF A WOMAN'S LIFE (SEE: AFFAIR IN
  MONTE CARLO) (1953, Brit.)
24 HOURS OF THE REBEL (SEE: 9/30/55) (1978)
24 HOURS TO KILL (1966, Brit.) PR:A
20 MILLION MILES TO EARTH (1957) PR:A
TWENTY MILLION SWEETHEARTS (1934) PR:A
20 MULE TEAM (1940) PR:A
29 OCACIA AVENUE (SEE: FACTS OF LOVE) (1949,
  Brit.)
TWENTY-ONE DAYS (SEE: TWENTY-ONE DAYS TO-
  GETHER) (1940, Brit.)
TWENTY-ONE DAYS TOGETHER (1940, Brit.) PR:A
TWENTY PLUS TWO (1961) PR:C-O
TWENTY QUESTIONS MURDER MYSTERY, THE
  (1950, Brit.) PR:A
27A (1974, Aus.) PR:O
27TH DAY, THE (1957) PR:A-C
20,000 EYES (1961) PR:C
20,000 LEAGUES UNDER THE SEA (1954) PR:A
20,000 MEN A YEAR (1939) PR:A
20,000 POUNDS KISS, THE (1964, Brit.) PR:C
20,000 YEARS IN SING SING (1933) PR:A
23 1/2 HOURS' LEAVE (1937) PR:A
23 PACES TO BAKER STREET (1956) PR:C
TWENTY-FOUR EYES (1954, Jap.) PR:A
TWICE A MAN (1964) PR:O
TWICE AROUND THE DAFFODILS (1962, Brit.) PR:A
TWICE BLESSED (1945) PR:A
TWICE BRANDED (1936, Brit.) PR:A
TWICE DEAD (1989) PR:C
TWICE IN A LIFETIME (1985) PR:O
TWICE UPON A TIME (1953, Brit.) PR:A
TWICE UPON A TIME (1983) PR:A
TWICE-TOLD TALES (1963) PR:C
TWILIGHT FOR THE GODS (1958) PR:A
TWILIGHT HOUR (1944, Brit.) PR:A
TWILIGHT IN THE SIERRAS (1950) PR:A
TWILIGHT OF HONOR (1963) PR:C
TWILIGHT OF THE DEAD (SEE: GATES OF HELL,
  THE) (1983, US/It.)
TWILIGHT ON THE PRAIRIE (1944) PR:A
TWILIGHT ON THE RIO GRANDE (1947) PR:A
TWILIGHT ON THE TRAIL (1941) PR:A
TWILIGHT PATH (1965, Jap.) PR:C
TWILIGHT PEOPLE (1972, Phil.) PR:O
TWILIGHT STORY, THE (1962, Jap.) PR:O
TWILIGHT TIME (1983, US/Yugo.) PR:C
TWILIGHT WOMEN (1952, Brit.) PR:C
TWILIGHT ZONE—THE MOVIE (1983) PR:C-O
TWILIGHT'S LAST GLEAMING (1977, US/W. Ger.) PR:O
TWIN BEDS (1929) PR:A
TWIN BEDS (1942) PR:A
TWIN FACES (1937, Brit.) PR:A
TWIN HUSBANDS (1934) PR:A
TWIN SISTERS OF KYOTO (1964, Jap.) PR:C
TWINKLE AND SHINE (SEE: IT HAPPENED TO JANE)
  (1959)
TWINKLE IN GOD'S EYE, THE (1955) PR:A
TWINKLE, TWINKLE, KILLER KANE (SEE: NINTH
  CONFIGURATION, THE) (1980)
TWINKY (SEE: LOLA) (1971, Brit.)
TWINS (1988) PR:A
TWINS OF EVIL (1971, Brit.) PR:O
TWIST, THE (1976, Fr.) PR:C-O
TWIST ALL NIGHT (1961) PR:A
TWIST & SHOUT (1984, Den.) PR:O
TWIST AROUND THE CLOCK (1961) PR:A
TWIST OF FATE (SEE: BEAUTIFUL STRANGER, THE)
  (1954, Brit.)
TWIST OF SAND, A (1968, Brit.) PR:A
TWISTED BRAIN (SEE: HORROR HIGH) (1974)
TWISTED LIVES (SEE: LIARS, THE) (1964, Fr.)
TWISTED NERVE (1969, Brit.) PR:O

TWISTED ROAD, THE (SEE: THEY LIVE BY NIGHT)
  (1949)
TWISTER (1989) PR:A-C
TWITCH OF THE DEATH NERVE (1973, It.) PR:O
TWO (1975) PR:O
TWO A PENNY (1968, Brit.) PR:A
TWO AGAINST THE WORLD (1932) PR:A
TWO AGAINST THE WORLD (1936) PR:A
TWO ALONE (1934) PR:A
TWO AND ONE TWO (1934) PR:A
TWO AND TWO MAKE SIX (1962, Brit.) PR:C
TWO ARE GUILTY (1964, Fr./It.) PR:C
TWO BLACK SHEEP (SEE: TWO SINNERS) (1935)
TWO BLONDES AND A REDHEAD (1947) PR:A
TWO BRIGHT BOYS (1939) PR:A
TWO COLONELS, THE (1963, It.) PR:A
TWO DAUGHTERS (1961, India) PR:A
TWO DOLLAR BETTOR (1951) PR:A
TWO ENEMIES (SEE: BEST OF ENEMIES, THE) (1962,
  Brit.)
TWO ENGLISH GIRLS (1972, Fr.) PR:O
TWO EYES, TWELVE HANDS (1958, India) PR:C
TWO-FACED WOMAN (1941) PR:A
TWO FACES OF DR. JEKYLL (SEE: HOUSE OF
  FRIGHT) (1961, Brit.)
TWO FISTED (1935) PR:A
TWO FISTED AGENT (SEE: BONANZA TOWN) (1951)
TWO-FISTED GENTLEMAN (1936) PR:A
TWO-FISTED JUSTICE (1931) PR:A
TWO-FISTED JUSTICE (1943) PR:A
TWO-FISTED LAW (1932) PR:AA
TWO-FISTED RANGERS (1940) PR:A
TWO-FISTED SHERIFF (1937) PR:A
TWO FLAGS WEST (1950) PR:A
TWO FOR DANGER (1940, Brit.) PR:A
TWO FOR THE ROAD (1967, Brit.) PR:C
TWO FOR THE SEESAW (1962) PR:C
TWO FOR TONIGHT (1935) PR:A
TWO GALS AND A GUY (1951) PR:A
TWO GENTLEMEN SHARING (1969, Brit.) PR:O
TWO GIRLS AND A SAILOR (1944) PR:A
TWO GIRLS ON BROADWAY (1940) PR:A
TWO GROOMS FOR A BRIDE (1957, Brit.) PR:A
TWO-GUN CUPID (SEE: BAD MAN, THE) (1941)
TWO-GUN JUSTICE (1938) PR:A
TWO-GUN LADY (1956) PR:A
TWO-GUN LAW (1937) PR:A
TWO GUN MAN, THE (1931) PR:A
TWO GUN SHERIFF (1941) PR:A
TWO-GUN TROUBADOR (1939) PR:A
TWO GUNS AND A BADGE (1954) PR:A
TWO GUYS FROM MILWAUKEE (1946) PR:A
TWO GUYS FROM TEXAS (1948) PR:A
TWO-HEADED SPY, THE (1959, Brit.) PR:C
TWO HEADS ON A PILLOW (1934) PR:A
TWO HEARTS IN HARMONY (1935, Brit.) PR:A
TWO HEARTS IN WALTZ TIME (1934, Brit.) PR:A
TWO HUNDRED MOTELS (1971, Brit.) PR:O
TWO IN A CROWD (1936) PR:A
TWO IN A MILLION (SEE: EAST OF FIFTH AVE.) (1933)
TWO IN A SLEEPING BAG (1964, W. Ger.) PR:C
TWO IN A TAXI (1941) PR:A
TWO IN REVOLT (1936) PR:AA
TWO IN THE DARK (1936) PR:A
TWO IN THE SHADOW (1968, Jap.) PR:C
TWO IS A HAPPY NUMBER (SEE: ONE IS A LONELY
  NUMBER) (1972)
TWO KINDS OF WOMEN (1932) PR:C
TWO KOUNEY LEMELS (1966, Israel) PR:A
TWO-LANE BLACKTOP (1971) PR:O
TWO LATINS FROM MANHATTAN (1941) PR:A
TWO LEFT FEET (1965, Brit.) PR:O
TWO LETTER ALIBI (1962, Brit.) PR:A
TWO LITTLE BEARS, THE (1961) PR:AA
TWO LIVES OF MATTIA PASCAL, THE (1985,
  It./Fr./Gr./Brit.) PR:O
TWO LIVING, ONE DEAD (1964, Brit./Swed.) PR:C
TWO LOST WORLDS (1950) PR:A
TWO LOVES (1961) PR:C
TWO-MAN SUBMARINE (1944) PR:A
TWO MEN AND A GIRL (SEE: HONEYMOON) (1947)
TWO MEN AND A MAID (1929) PR:A
TWO MEN IN TOWN (1973, Fr.) PR:O
TWO-MINUTE WARNING (1976) PR:O
TWO MINUTES' SILENCE (1934, Brit.) PR:A
TWO MINUTES TO PLAY (1937) PR:A
TWO MOON JUNCTION (1988) PR:O
TWO MRS. CARROLLS, THE (1947) PR:A-C
TWO MULES FOR SISTER SARA (1970, US/Mex.) PR:C
TWO NIGHTS WITH CLEOPATRA (1953, It.) PR:C
TWO O'CLOCK COURAGE (1945) PR:C
TWO OF A KIND (1951) PR:C
TWO OF A KIND (1983) PR:C
TWO OF US, THE (1938, Brit.) PR:A
TWO OF US, THE (1967, Fr.) PR:A
TWO ON A DOORSTEP (1936, Brit.) PR:A
TWO ON A GUILLOTINE (1965) PR:C

TWO ON THE TILES (SEE: SCHOOL FOR BRIDES) (1952, Brit.)
TWO OR THREE THINGS I KNOW ABOUT HER (1970, Fr.) PR:O
TWO PENNIES WORTH OF HOPE (1952, It.) PR:A
TWO PEOPLE (1973) PR:O
2 + 5 MISSIONE HYDRA (SEE: STAR PILOT) (1977, It.)
TWO ROADS (SEE: TEXAS STAGECOACH) (1940)
TWO RODE TOGETHER (1961) PR:C
TWO SECONDS (1932) PR:C
TWO SENORITAS FROM CHICAGO (1943) PR:A
TWO SINNERS (1935) PR:A
TWO SISTERS (1938) PR:A
TWO SISTERS FROM BOSTON (1946) PR:A
TWO SMART MEN (1940, Brit.) PR:A
TWO SMART PEOPLE (1946) PR:A
TWO SOLITUDES (1978, Can.) PR:A
TWO SUPER COPS (1978, It.) PR:C
TWO TEXAS KNIGHTS (SEE: TWO GUYS FROM TEXAS) (1948)
TWO THOROUGHBREDS (1939) PR:A
2001: A SPACE ODYSSEY (1968, US/Brit.) PR:A
TWO THOUSAND MANIACS (1964) PR:O
2010 (1984) PR:C
2020 TEXAS GLADIATORS (1985, It.) PR:O
2,000 WEEKS (1970, Aus.) PR:C
2,000 WOMEN (1944, Brit.) PR:A
2000 YEARS LATER (1969) PR:O
TWO TICKETS TO BROADWAY (1951) PR:A
TWO TICKETS TO LONDON (1943) PR:A
TWO TICKETS TO PARIS (1962) PR:A
TWO TIMES TWO (SEE: START THE REVOLUTION WITHOUT ME) (1970)
TWO TO TANGO (1989, US/Arg.) PR:O
TWO VOICES (1966) PR:C
TWO-WAY DRIFTER (SEE: DRIFTER) (1975)
TWO-WAY STRETCH (1961, Brit.) PR:A-C
TWO WEEKS IN ANOTHER TOWN (1962) PR:O
TWO WEEKS IN SEPTEMBER (1967, Fr./Brit.) PR:O
TWO WEEKS OFF (1929) PR:A
TWO WEEKS TO LIVE (1943) PR:A
TWO WEEKS WITH LOVE (1950) PR:A
TWO WHITE ARMS (SEE: WIVES BEWARE) (1933, Brit.)
TWO WHO DARED (1937, Brit.) PR:A
TWO WISE MAIDS (1937) PR:A
TWO WIVES AT ONE WEDDING (1961, Brit.) PR:A
TWO WOMEN (1940, Fr.) PR:A
TWO WOMEN (1960, It./Fr.) PR:C-O
TWO WORLDS (1930, Brit./Ger.) PR:A
TWO WORLDS OF CHARLY GORDON, THE (SEE: CHARLY) (1968)
TWO YANKS IN TRINIDAD (1942) PR:A
TWO YEARS BEFORE THE MAST (1946) PR:C
TWO YEARS HOLIDAY (SEE: STOLEN DIRIGIBLE, THE) (1966, Czech.)
TWO'S COMPANY (1939, Brit.) PR:A
TWONKY, THE (1953) PR:A
TYCOON (1947) PR:A
TYPHOON (1940) PR:A
TYPHOON TREASURE (1939, Aus.) PR:A
TYRANT OF SYRACUSE, THE (SEE: DAMON AND PYTHIAS) (1962, US/It.)
TYRANT OF THE SEA (1950) PR:A
TYSTNADEN (SEE: SILENCE, THE) (1964, Swed.)

UV

U-BOAT 29 (SEE: SPY IN BLACK, THE) (1939, Brit.)
U-BOAT PRISONER (1944) PR:A
U-47 LT. COMMANDER PRIEN (1967, W. Ger.) PR:A
U KRUTOGO YARA (SEE: SHE-WOLF, THE) (1963, USSR)
U-TURN (1973, Can.) PR:C
U.S.S. TEAKETTLE (SEE: YOU'RE IN THE NAVY NOW) (1951)
UCCELLACCI E UCCELLINI (SEE: HAWKS AND THE SPARROWS, THE) (1967, It.)
UCCIDERO UN UOMO (SEE: THIS MAN MUST DIE) (1970, Fr./It.)
UCCIDI O MUORI (SEE: KILL OR BE KILLED) (1967, It.)
UCHU KARA NO MESSEJI (SEE: MESSAGE FROM SPACE) (1978, Jap.)
UCHUDAI DOGORA (SEE: DOGORA THE SPACE MONSTER) (1964, Jap.)
UCHUJIN TOKYO NI ARAWARU (SEE: MYSTERIOUS SATELLITE, THE) (1956, Jap.)
UCHUSENKAN YAMATO (SEE: SPACE CRUISER) (1977, Jap.)
UFO (SEE: UNIDENTIFIED FLYING ODDBALL, THE) (1979, Brit.)
UFO: TARGET EARTH (1974) PR:A
UFORIA (1985) PR:C
UGETSU (1953, Jap.) PR:A
UGLY AMERICAN, THE (1963) PR:A-C
UGLY DACHSHUND, THE (1966) PR:AA
UGLY DUCKLING, THE (1959, Brit.) PR:A
UGLY ONES, THE (1968, It./Sp.) PR:O

UHF (1989) PR:C
UIT ELKAAR (SEE: SPLITTING UP) (1981, Neth.)
UKIGUSA (SEE: FLOATING WEEDS) (1959, Jap.)
ULISSE (SEE: ULYSSES) (1955, It.)
ULTIMATE SOLUTION OF GRACE QUIGLEY, THE (1984) PR:C
ULTIMATE THRILL, THE (1974) PR:A-C
ULTIMATE WARRIOR, THE (1975) PR:O
ULTIMATUM (1940, Fr.) PR:A
ULYSSES (1955, It.) PR:C
ULYSSES (1967, US/Brit.) PR:C
ULZANA'S RAID (1972) PR:O
UMBERTO D. (1952, It.) PR:C
UMBRELLA, THE (1933, Brit.) PR:A
UMBRELLA WOMAN, THE (SEE: GOOD WIFE, THE) (1986, Aus.)
UMBRELLAS OF CHERBOURG, THE (1964, Fr./W. Ger.) PR:A-C
UN AMI VIENDRA CE SOIR (SEE: FRIEND WILL COME TONIGHT, A) (1948, Fr.)
UN AMOUR DE POCHE (SEE: NUDE IN HIS POCKET) (1962, Fr.)
UN AMOUR DE SWANN (SEE: SWANN IN LOVE) (1984, Fr./W. Ger.)
UN AMOUR EN ALLEMAGNE (SEE: LOVE IN GERMANY, A) (1984, Fr./W. Ger.)
UN ANGEL PASO POR BROOKLYN (SEE: MAN WHO WAGGED HIS TAIL, THE) (1957, It./Sp.)
UN ANGELO E SCESO A BROOKLYN (SEE: MAN WHO WAGGED HIS TAIL, THE) (1957, It./Sp.)
UN AUTRE HOMME, UNE AUTRE CHANCE (SEE: ANOTHER MAN, ANOTHER CHANCE) (1977, US/Fr.)
UN BELLISSIMA NOVEMBRE (SEE: THAT SPLENDID NOVEMBER) (1971, Fr./It.)
UN CARNET DE BAL (1938, Fr.) PR:A
UN COIN TRANQUILLE A LA CAMPAGNE (SEE: QUIET PLACE IN THE COUNTRY, A) (1970, Fr./It.)
UN DETECTIVE (SEE: DETECTIVE BELLI) (1970, It.)
UN, DEUX, TROIS, QUATRE? (SEE: BLACK TIGHTS) (1962, Fr.)
UN DIMANCHE A LA CAMPAGNE (SEE: SUNDAY IN THE COUNTRY, A) (1984, Fr.)
UN DOLLARO PER 7 VIGLIACCHI (SEE: MADIGAN'S MILLIONS) (1970, It./Sp.)
UN ELEPHANT CA TROMPE ENORMEMENT (SEE: PARDON MON AFFAIRE) (1976, Fr.)
UN ESERCITO DI 5 UOMINI (SEE: FIVE MAN ARMY, THE) (1970, It.)
UN FILE (SEE: COP, A) (1973, Fr.)
UN GENIO, DUE COMPARI, UN POLLO (SEE: GENIUS, THE) (1976, Fr./It./W. Ger.)
UN GIORNO IN PRETURA (SEE: DAY IN COURT) (1965, It.)
UN GRAND AMOUR DE BEETHOVEN (SEE: LIFE AND LOVES OF BEETHOVEN, THE) (1937, Fr.)
UN GRAND PATRON (SEE: PERFECTIONIST, THE) (1952, It.)
UN HOMBRE DE EXITO (SEE: SUCCESSFUL MAN, A) (1987, Cuba)
UN HOMBRE VIOLENTE (1986, Mex.) PR:O
UN HOMME A DETRUIRE (SEE: STRANGERS ON THE PROWL) (1953, It.)
UN HOMME AMOUREUX (SEE: MAN IN LOVE, A) (1987, Fr.)
UN HOMME EST MORT (SEE: OUTSIDE MAN, THE) (1973, US/Fr.)
UN HOMME ET UNE FEMME (SEE: MAN AND A WOMAN, A) (1966, Fr.)
UN HOMME ET UNE FEMME: VINGT ANS DEJA (SEE: MAN AND A WOMAN: 20 YEARS LATER, A) (1986, Fr.)
UN MALEDETTO IMBROGLIO (SEE: FACTS OF THE MURDER, THE) (1965, It.)
UN PASAJE DE IDA (SEE: ONE-WAY TICKET, A) (1988, Dominican Republic)
UN SECOND SOUFFLE (SEE: SECOND WIND, A) (1978, Fr.)
UN SEUL AMOUR (SEE: MAGNIFICENT SINNER) (1963, Fr.)
UN SI JOLI VILLAGE (SEE: INVESTIGATION) (1979, Fr.)
UN SOIR DE RAFLE (SEE: DRAGNET NIGHT) (1931, Fr.)
UN TAXI MAUVE (SEE: PURPLE TAXI, THE) (1977, Fr./Ireland/It.)
UN TRANQUILLO POSTO DI CAMPAGNA (SEE: QUIET PLACE IN THE COUNTRY, A) (1970, Fr./It.)
UN UOMO DA RISPETTARE (SEE: MASTER TOUCH, THE) (1974, It./W. Ger.)
UN UOMO DALLA PELLE DURA (SEE: RIPPED-OFF) (1971, It.)
UN UOMO, UN CAVALLO, UNA PISTOLA (SEE: STRANGER RETURNS, THE) (1968, US/It./W. Ger.)
UN ZOO LA NUIT (SEE: NIGHT ZOO) (1987, Can.)
UNA BREVA VACANZA (SEE: BRIEF VACATION, A) (1975, It.)
UNA HACKA PARA LA LUNA DE MIEL (SEE: HATCHET FOR A HONEYMOON) (1969, It./Sp.)

UNA MOGLIE AMERICANA (SEE: RUN FOR YOUR WIFE) (1966, Fr./It.)
UNA MUJER SIN AMOR (SEE: WOMAN WITHOUT LOVE, A) (1951, Mex.)
UNA RAGIONE PER VIVERE E UNA PER MORIRE (SEE: REASON TO LIVE, A REASON TO DIE, A) (1974, It./Fr./Sp./W. Ger.)
UNA ROSA PER TUTTI (SEE: ROSE FOR EVERYONE, A) (1967, It.)
UNA SIGNORA DELL'OVEST (1942, It.) PR:A
UNAKRSNA VATRA (SEE: OPERATION CROSS EAGLES) (1969, US/Yugo.)
UNASHAMED (1932) PR:A
UNASHAMED (1938) PR:O
UNBEARABLE LIGHTNESS OF BEING, THE (1988) PR:O
UNCANNY, THE (1977, Brit./Can.) PR:C
UNCENSORED (1944, Brit.) PR:A
UNCERTAIN GLORY (1944) PR:A
UNCERTAIN LADY (1934) PR:A
UNCHAINED (1955) PR:A
UNCHAINED (SEE: ANGEL UNCHAINED) (1970)
UNCIVILISED (1937, Aus.) PR:A
UNCLE, THE (1966, Brit.) PR:A
UNCLE BUCK (1989) PR:A
UNCLE HARRY (1945) PR:C
UNCLE JOE SHANNON (1978) PR:C
UNCLE SCAM (1981) PR:O
UNCLE SILAS (SEE: INHERITANCE, THE) (1951, Brit.)
UNCLE TOM'S CABIN (1969, Fr./It./Yugo./W. Ger.) PR:C
UNCLE VANYA (1958) PR:A
UNCLE VANYA (1972, USSR) PR:A
UNCLE VANYA (1977, Brit.) PR:A
UNCOMMON THIEF, AN (1967, USSR) PR:A
UNCOMMON VALOR (1983) PR:O
UNCONQUERED (1947) PR:A
UNCONSCIOUS (SEE: FEAR) (1986)
UNCONVENTIONAL LINDA (SEE: HOLIDAY) (1938)
UND DEMMER RUFT DAS HERZ (SEE: MOONWOLF) (1966, Fin./W. Ger.)
UND MORGEN FAHRT IHR ZUR HOLIE (SEE: DIRTY HEROES) (1971, Fr./It./W. Ger.)
UNDEAD, THE (1957) PR:A
UNDEFEATED, THE (1969) PR:A
UNDER A CLOUD (1937, Brit.) PR:A
UNDER A TEXAS MOON (1930) PR:A
UNDER AGE (1941) PR:A-C
UNDER AGE (1964) PR:O
UNDER ARIZONA SKIES (1946) PR:A
UNDER CALIFORNIA SKIES (SEE: UNDER CALIFORNIA STARS) (1948)
UNDER CALIFORNIA STARS (1948) PR:A
UNDER CAPRICORN (1949, Brit.) PR:C
UNDER COLORADO SKIES (1947) PR:A
UNDER COVER (1987) PR:O
UNDER-COVER MAN (1932) PR:A
UNDER COVER OF NIGHT (1937) PR:A
UNDER COVER ROGUE (SEE: WHITE VOICES, THE) (1964, Fr./It.)
UNDER EIGHTEEN (1932) PR:A
UNDER FIESTA STARS (1941) PR:A
UNDER FIRE (1957) PR:A
UNDER FIRE (1983) PR:O
UNDER MEXICALI SKIES (SEE: UNDER MEXICALI STARS) (1950)
UNDER MEXICALI STARS (1950) PR:A
UNDER MILKWOOD (1973, Brit.) PR:C
UNDER MONTANA SKIES (1930) PR:A
UNDER MY SKIN (1950) PR:A
UNDER NEVADA SKIES (1946) PR:A
UNDER NEW MANAGEMENT (SEE: HONEYMOON HOTEL) (1946, Brit.)
UNDER PRESSURE (1935) PR:A
UNDER PROOF (1936, Brit.) PR:A
UNDER-PUP, THE (1939) PR:A
UNDER SATAN'S SUN (1988, Fr.) PR:C-O
UNDER SECRET ORDERS (1933) PR:A
UNDER SECRET ORDERS (1943, Brit.) PR:A-C
UNDER STRANGE FLAGS (1937) PR:A
UNDER SUSPICION (1931) PR:A
UNDER SUSPICION (1937) PR:A
UNDER TEN FLAGS (1960, US/It.) PR:C
UNDER TEXAS SKIES (1931) PR:A
UNDER TEXAS SKIES (1940) PR:A
UNDER THE BANNER OF SAMURAI (1969, Jap.) PR:C
UNDER THE BIG TOP (1938) PR:A
UNDER THE CHERRY MOON (1986) PR:O
UNDER THE CLOCK (SEE: CLOCK, THE) (1945)
UNDER THE GREENWOOD TREE (1930, Brit.) PR:A
UNDER THE GUN (1951) PR:A
UNDER THE GUN (1989) PR:O
UNDER THE PAMPAS MOON (1935) PR:A
UNDER THE RAINBOW (1981) PR:C
UNDER THE RED ROBE (1937, Brit.) PR:A
UNDER THE ROOFS OF PARIS (1930, Fr.) PR:A
UNDER THE SUN OF ROME (1949, It.) PR:A
UNDER THE TONTO RIM (1933) PR:A
UNDER THE TONTO RIM (1947) PR:A
UNDER THE VOLCANO (1984) PR:O

UNDER THE YUM-YUM TREE (1963) PR:C-O
UNDER TWO FLAGS (1936) PR:A-C
UNDER WESTERN SKIES (1945) PR:A
UNDER WESTERN STARS (1938) PR:A
UNDER YOUR HAT (1940, Brit.) PR:A
UNDER YOUR SPELL (1936) PR:A
UNDERCOVER (SEE: UNDERGROUND GUERRIL-
  LAS) (1944, Brit.)
UNDERCOVER AGENT (1939) PR:A
UNDERCOVER AGENT (1953, Brit.) PR:A
UNDERCOVER DOCTOR (1939) PR:A
UNDERCOVER GIRL (1950) PR:A
UNDERCOVER GIRL (1957, Brit.) PR:A
UNDERCOVER MAISIE (1947) PR:A
UNDERCOVER MAN (1936) PR:A
UNDERCOVER MAN (1942) PR:A
UNDERCOVER MAN, THE (1949) PR:C
UNDERCOVER WOMAN, THE (1946) PR:A
UNDERCOVERS HERO (1975, Brit.) PR:O
UNDERCURRENT (1946) PR:A-C
UNDERDOG, THE (1943) PR:A
UNDERGROUND (1941) PR:A
UNDERGROUND (1970, Brit.) PR:C
UNDERGROUND AGENT (1942) PR:A
UNDERGROUND GUERRILLAS (1944, Brit.) PR:A
UNDERGROUND RUSTLERS (1941) PR:A
UNDERGROUND U.S.A. (1980) PR:O
UNDERNEATH THE ARCHES (1937, Brit.) PR:A
UNDERSEA GIRL (1957) PR:A
UNDERSEA ODYSSEY, AN (SEE: NEPTUNE FACTOR,
  THE) (1973, Can.)
UNDERTOW (1930) PR:A
UNDERTOW (1949) PR:A
UNDERWATER! (1955) PR:C-O
UNDERWATER CITY, THE (1962) PR:A
UNDERWATER ODYSSEY, AN (SEE: NEPTURE FAC-
  TOR, THE) (1973, Can.)
UNDERWATER WARRIOR (1958) PR:A
UNDERWORLD (1937) PR:A-C
UNDERWORLD AFTER DARK (SEE: BIG TOWN
  AFTER DARK) (1947)
UNDERWORLD INFORMERS (1965, Brit.) PR:A
UNDERWORLD SCANDAL (SEE: BIG TOWN SCAN-
  DAL) (1948)
UNDERWORLD STORY, THE (SEE: WHIPPED, THE)
  (1950)
UNDERWORLD U.S.A. (1961) PR:C
UNDYING MONSTER, THE (1942) PR:A
UNE BAISER DE FEU (SEE: KISS OF FIRE) (1940, Fr.)
UNE BELLE FILLE COMME MOI (SEE: SUCH A GOR-
  GEOUS KID LIKE ME) (1973, Fr.)
UNE FEMME A SA FENTRE (SEE: WOMAN AT HER
  WINDOW, A) (1978, Fr./It./W. Ger.)
UNE FEMME DEUCE (SEE: GENTLE CREATURE, A)
  (1971, Fr.)
UNE FEMME EST UNE FEMME (SEE: WOMAN IS A
  WOMAN, A) (1961, Fr.)
UNE FEMME MARIEE (SEE: MARRIED WOMAN,
  THE) (1964, Fr.)
UNE GRANDE FILLE TONTE SIMPLE (SEE: JUST A
  BIG, SIMPLE GIRL) (1949, Fr.)
UNE HISTOIRE IMMORTELLE (SEE: IMMORTAL
  STORY, THE) (1968, Fr.)
UNE JEUNE FILLE (SEE: MAGNIFICENT SINNER)
  (1963, Fr.)
UNE MERE, UNE FILLE (SEE: ANNA) (1981, Fr./Hung.)
UNE PARISIENNE (SEE: LA PARISIENNE) (1958, Fr./It.)
UNE RAVISSANTE IDIOTE (SEE: RAVISHING IDIOT,
  A) (1966, Fr./It.)
UNEARTHLY, THE (1957) PR:O
UNEARTHLY STRANGER, THE (1964, Brit.) PR:A
UNEASY TERMS (1948, Brit.) PR:A
UNEASY VIRTUE (1931, Brit.) PR:A
UNEXPECTED FATHER (1939) PR:A
UNEXPECTED FATHER, THE (1932) PR:A
UNEXPECTED GUEST (1946) PR:A
UNEXPECTED UNCLE (1941) PR:A
UNFAITHFUL (1931) PR:A
UNFAITHFUL, THE (1947) PR:A
UNFAITHFUL WIFE, THE (SEE: LA FEMME IN-
  FIDELE) (1969, Fr./It.)
UNFAITHFULLY YOURS (1948) PR:A-C
UNFAITHFULLY YOURS (1984) PR:C
UNFAITHFULS, THE (1960, It.) PR:A
UNFINISHED BUSINESS (1941) PR:A
UNFINISHED BUSINESS (1985, Aus.) PR:O
UNFINISHED BUSINESS. . . (1987) PR:C-O
UNFINISHED DANCE, THE (1947) PR:A
UNFINISHED SYMPHONY, THE (1935, Aust./Brit.) PR:A
UNFORGIVEN, THE (1960) PR:C
UNGUARDED HOUR, THE (1936) PR:A
UNGUARDED MOMENT, THE (1956) PR:A
UNHEIMLICHE GESCHICHTEN (SEE: TALES OF THE
  UNCANNY) (1932, Ger.)
UNHINGED (1982) PR:O
UNHOLY, THE (1988) PR:O
UNHOLY DESIRE (1964, Jap.) PR:O

UNHOLY FOUR, THE (1954, Brit.) PR:A
UNHOLY FOUR, THE (1969, It.) PR:C
UNHOLY GARDEN, THE (1931) PR:A
UNHOLY LOVE (1932) PR:A
UNHOLY NIGHT, THE (1929) PR:A
UNHOLY PARTNERS (1941) PR:A
UNHOLY QUEST, THE (1934, Brit.) PR:A
UNHOLY ROLLERS (1972) PR:O
UNHOLY THREE, THE (1930) PR:C
UNHOLY WIFE, THE (1957) PR:A
UNIDENTIFIED FLYING ODDBALL, THE (1979, Brit.)
  PR:A
UNIFORM LOVERS (SEE: HOLD 'EM YALE) (1935)
UNINHIBITED, THE (1968, Fr./It./Sp.) PR:C
UNINVITED, THE (1944) PR:C
UNINVITED, THE (1988) PR:O
UNION CITY (1980) PR:A
UNION DEPOT (1932) PR:A
UNION PACIFIC (1939) PR:A
UNION STATION (1950) PR:C
UNIVERSAL SOLDIER (1971, Brit.) PR:C
UNIVERSITY OF LIFE (1941, USSR) PR:C
UNKILLABLES, THE (SEE: DARING GAME) (1968)
UNKISSED BRIDE, THE (SEE: MOTHER GOOSE A GO-
  GO) (1966)
UNKNOWN, THE (1946) PR:A
UNKNOWN BATTLE, THE (SEE: HEROES OF TELE-
  MARK) (1965, Brit.)
UNKNOWN BLONDE (1934) PR:A
UNKNOWN GUEST, THE (1943) PR:A
UNKNOWN ISLAND (1948) PR:A
UNKNOWN MAN, THE (1951) PR:C
UNKNOWN MAN OF SHANDIGOR, THE (1967, Switz.)
  PR:A
UNKNOWN RANGER, THE (1936) PR:A
UNKNOWN SATELLITE OVER TOKYO (SEE: MYSTE-
  RIOUS SATELLITE, THE) (1956, Jap.)
UNKNOWN TERROR, THE (1957) PR:A
UNKNOWN VALLEY (1933) PR:A
UNKNOWN WOMAN (1935) PR:A
UNKNOWN WORLD (1951) PR:A
UNMAN, WITTERING AND ZIGO (1971, Brit.) PR:C
UNMARRIED (1939) PR:A
UNMARRIED WOMAN, AN (1978) PR:C-O
UNMASKED (1929) PR:A
UNMASKED (1950) PR:A
UNO DEI TRE (SEE: TWO ARE GUILTY) (1964, Fr./It.)
UNORDNUNG UND FRUEHES LEID (SEE: DISORDER
  AND EARLY TORMENT) (1977, W. Ger.)
UNPUBLISHED STORY (1942, Brit.) PR:A
UNRECONCILED (SEE: NOT RECONCILED, OR
  "ONLY VIOLENCE HELPS WHERE IT RULES")
  (1969, W. Ger.)
UNREMARKABLE LIFE, AN (1989) PR:C
UNRUHIGE NACHT (SEE: RESTLESS NIGHT, THE)
  (1964, W. Ger.)
UNSANE (1982, It.) PR:O
UNSATISFIED, THE (1964, Sp.) PR:A
UNSEEN, THE (1945) PR:A
UNSEEN, THE (1981) PR:O
UNSEEN ENEMY (1942) PR:A
UNSEEN HEROES (SEE: MISSILE FROM HELL) (1960,
  Brit.)
UNSENT LETTER, THE (SEE: LETTER THAT WAS
  NEVER SENT, THE) (1962, USSR)
UNSER BOSS IST EINE DAME (SEE: TREASURE OF
  SAN GENNARO) (1968, Fr./It./W. Ger.)
UNSICHTBARE GEGNER (SEE: INVISIBLE OPPO-
  NENT) (1933, Ger.)
UNSINKABLE MOLLY BROWN, THE (1964) PR:A
UNSTOPPABLE MAN, THE (1961, Brit.) PR:A
UNSTRAP ME (1968) PR:O
UNSUITABLE JOB FOR A WOMAN, AN (1982, Brit.) PR:C-
  O
UNSUNG HEROES (SEE: WAR DOGS) (1942)
UNSUSPECTED, THE (1947) PR:A
UNTAMED (1929) PR:A-C
UNTAMED (1940) PR:A
UNTAMED (1955) PR:C-O
UNTAMED BREED, THE (1948) PR:A
UNTAMED FRONTIER (1952) PR:A
UNTAMED FURY (1947) PR:A
UNTAMED HEIRESS (1954) PR:A
UNTAMED MISTRESS (1960) PR:O
UNTAMED WEST, THE (SEE: FAR HORIZONS, THE)
  (1955)
UNTAMED WOMEN (1952) PR:A
UNTAMED YOUTH (1957) PR:A
UNTEL PERE ET FILS (SEE: HEART OF A NATION,
  THE) (1943, Fr.)
UNTER GEIERN (SEE: FRONTIER HELLCAT) (1966,
  Fr./It./Yugo./W. Ger.)
UNTIL SEPTEMBER (1984) PR:O
UNTIL THEY SAIL (1957) PR:C
UNTITLED (SEE: HEAD) (1968)
UNTOUCHABLES, THE (SEE: SCARFACE MOB, THE)
  (1962)
UNTOUCHABLES, THE (1987) PR:O

UNTOUCHED (1956) PR:A
UNVANQUISHED, THE (SEE: APARAJITO) (1959, India)
UNWED MOTHER (1958) PR:C-O
UNWELCOME STRANGER, THE (1935) PR:A
UNWELCOME VISITORS (SEE: LONE STAR PIO-
  NEERS) (1939)
UNWILLING AGENT (1968, W. Ger.) PR:A
UNWRITTEN CODE, THE (1944) PR:A
UNWRITTEN LAW, THE (1932) PR:A
UOMINI H (SEE: H-MAN, THE) (1959, Jap.)
UP FOR MURDER (1931) PR:A
UP FOR THE CUP (1931, Brit.) PR:A
UP FOR THE CUP (1950, Brit.) PR:A
UP FOR THE DERBY (1933, Brit.) PR:A
UP FRANKENSTEIN (SEE: ANDY WARHOL'S
  FRANKENSTEIN) (1974, Fr./It.)
UP FROM THE BEACH (1965) PR:A
UP FROM THE DEPTHS (1979, Phil.) PR:O
UP FRONT (1951) PR:A
UP GOES MAISIE (1946) PR:A
UP IN ARMS (1944) PR:AA
UP IN CENTRAL PARK (1948) PR:A
UP IN MABEL'S ROOM (1944) PR:A
UP IN SMOKE (1957) PR:A
UP IN SMOKE (1978) PR:O
UP IN THE AIR (1940) PR:A
UP IN THE AIR (1969, Brit.) PR:AA
UP IN THE CELLAR (1970) PR:C
UP IN THE WORLD (1957, Brit.) PR:A
UP JUMPED A SWAGMAN (1965, Brit.) PR:A
UP PERISCOPE (1959) PR:A
UP POMPEII (1971, Brit.) PR:O
UP POPS THE DEVIL (1931) PR:A
UP SHE GOES (SEE: UP GOES MAISIE) (1945)
UP THE ACADEMY (1980) PR:O
UP THE CHASTITY BELT (1971, Brit.) PR:O
UP THE CREEK (1958, Brit.) PR:A
UP THE CREEK (1984) PR:O
UP THE DOWN STAIRCASE (1967) PR:A-C
UP THE FRONT (1972, Brit.) PR:C
UP THE JUNCTION (1968, Brit.) PR:O
UP THE MAC GREGORS (1967, It./Sp.) PR:A
UP THE RIVER (1930) PR:A
UP THE RIVER (1938) PR:A
UP THE SANDBOX (1972) PR:C-O
UP TO HIS EARS (1966, Fr./It.) PR:C
UP TO HIS NECK (1954, Brit.) PR:A
UP TO THE NECK (1933, Brit.) PR:A
UP WITH THE LARK (1943, Brit.) PR:A
UP YOUR TEDDY BEAR (1970) PR:O
UPHILL ALL THE WAY (1986) PR:C
UPPER HAND, THE (1967, Fr./It./W. Ger.) PR:C
UPPER UNDERWORLD (SEE: RULING VOICE, THE)
  (1931)
UPPER WORLD (1934) PR:A
UPSTAIRS AND DOWNSTAIRS (1961, Brit.) PR:A
UPSTATE MURDERS, THE (SEE: SAVAGE WEEKEND)
  (1983)
UPTIGHT (1968) PR:O
UPTOWN NEW YORK (1932) PR:A
UPTOWN SATURDAY NIGHT (1974) PR:C
UPTURNED GLASS, THE (1947, Brit.) PR:A-C
URAMISTEN (SEE: PHILADELPHIA ATTRACTION,
  THE) (1985, Hung.)
URANIUM BOOM (1956) PR:A
URBAN COWBOY (1980) PR:C
URGE TO KILL (1960, Brit.) PR:C
URGENT CALL (SEE: AGAINST THE LAW) (1934)
URSUS (SEE: MIGHTY URSUS) (1962, It./Sp.)
URSUS, IL GLADIATORE RIBELLE (SEE: REBEL
  GLADIATORS, THE) (1963, It.)
USCHI DAI SENSO (SEE: BATTLE IN OUTER SPACE)
  (1960, Jap.)
USED CARS (1980) PR:O
UTAH (1945) PR:A
UTAH BLAINE (1957) PR:A
UTAH KID, THE (1930) PR:A
UTAH TRAIL (1938) PR:A
UTAH WAGON TRAIN (1951) PR:A
UTILITIES (1983, Can.) PR:C-O
UTLAGINN: GISLA SAGA SURSSONAR (SEE: OUT-
  LAW: THE SAGE OF GISLI) (1982, Iceland)
UTOPIA (1950, Fr./It.) PR:A
UTU (1984, New Zealand) PR:O
UTVANDRARNA (SEE: EMIGRANTS, THE) (1972,
  Swed.)
V1 (SEE: MISSILE FROM HELL) (1958, Brit.)
V.D. (1961) PR:O
V.I.P.s, THE (1963, Brit.) PR:C
VACATION, THE (1971, It.) PR:C
VACATION DAYS (1947) PR:A
VACATION FROM LOVE (1938) PR:A
VACATION FROM MARRIAGE (1945, Brit.) PR:A
VACATION IN RENO (1946) PR:A
VADO. . . L'AMMAZZO E TORNO (SEE: ANY GUN
  CAN PLAY) (1968, It./Sp.)
VAGABOND (1985, Fr.) PR:O
VAGABOND KING, THE (1930) PR:A

VAGABOND KING, THE (1956) PR:A
VAGABOND LADY (1935) PR:A
VAGABOND LOVER, THE (1929) PR:A
VAGABOND QUEEN, THE (1931, Brit.) PR:A
VAGABOND VIOLINIST (SEE: BROKEN MELODY, THE) (1934, Brit.)
VAGHE STELLE DELL'ORSA (SEE: SANDRA) (1966, It.)
VALACHI PAPERS, THE (1972, It./Fr.) PR:O
VALBORGSMASSOAFTON (SEE: WALPURGIS NIGHT) (1941, Swed.)
VALDEZ IS COMING (1971) PR:O
VALDEZ, THE HALFBREED (SEE: CHINO) (1976, Fr./It./Sp.)
VALENTINO (1951) PR:C
VALENTINO (1977, Brit.) PR:C-O
VALENTINO RETURNS (1989) PR:O
VALERI CHKALOV (SEE: WINGS OF VICTORY) (1941, USSR)
VALERIE (1957) PR:C
VALET GIRLS (1987) PR:O
VALFANGARE (SEE: WHALERS, THE) (1942, Swed.)
VALHALLA (1986, Den.) PR:AA
VALIANT, THE (1929) PR:A-C
VALIANT, THE (1962, Brit./It.) PR:A
VALIANT HOMBRE (1948) PR:A
VALIANT IS THE WORD FOR CARRIE (1936) PR:A-C
VALLEY GIRL (1983) PR:C
VALLEY OF DEATH, THE (SEE: TANK BATTALION) (1958)
VALLEY OF DECISION, THE (1945) PR:A
VALLEY OF FEAR (SEE: SHERLOCK HOLMES AND THE DEADLY NECKLACE) (1962, W. Ger.)
VALLEY OF FIRE (1951) PR:A
VALLEY OF FURY (SEE: CHIEF CRAZY HORSE) (1955)
VALLEY OF GWANGI, THE (1969) PR:A
VALLEY OF HUNTED MEN (1942) PR:A
VALLEY OF MYSTERY (1967) PR:A
VALLEY OF SONG (SEE: MEN ARE CHILDREN TWICE) (1953, Brit.)
VALLEY OF THE DOLLS (1967) PR:O
VALLEY OF THE DRAGONS (1961) PR:A
VALLEY OF THE EAGLES (1952, Brit.) PR:A
VALLEY OF THE GIANTS (1938) PR:A
VALLEY OF THE HEADHUNTERS (1953) PR:A
VALLEY OF THE KINGS (1954) PR:A-C
VALLEY OF THE LAWLESS (1936) PR:A
VALLEY OF THE REDWOODS (1960) PR:A
VALLEY OF THE SUN (1942) PR:A
VALLEY OF THE SWORDS (SEE: CASTILIAN, THE) (1963, US/Sp.)
VALLEY OF THE WHITE WOLVES (SEE: MARA OF THE WILDERNESS) (1966)
VALLEY OF THE ZOMBIES (1946) PR:C
VALMONT (1989) PR:O
VALS, THE (1985) PR:O
VALUE FOR MONEY (1957, Brit.) PR:A
VAMP (1986) PR:O
VAMPING (1984) PR:O
VAMPIRA (SEE: OLD DRACULA) (1975, Brit.)
VAMPIRE, THE (SEE: VAMPYR) (1932, Fr./Ger.)
VAMPIRE, THE (1957) PR:C
VAMPIRE, THE (1968, Mex.) PR:C
VAMPIRE AND THE BALLERINA, THE (1962, It.) PR:C
VAMPIRE AND THE ROBOT, THE (SEE: MY SON, THE VAMPIRE) (1952, Brit.)
VAMPIRE BAT, THE (1933) PR:C
VAMPIRE BEAST CRAVES BLOOD, THE (SEE: BLOOD BEAST TERROR, THE) (1969, Brit.)
VAMPIRE CIRCUS (1972, Brit.) PR:C-O
VAMPIRE GIRLS, THE (SEE: VAMPIRE, THE) (1968, Mex.)
VAMPIRE HOOKERS, THE (1979, Phil.) PR:O
VAMPIRE LOVERS, THE (1970, Brit.) PR:O
VAMPIRE MEN OF THE LOST PLANET (SEE: HORROR OF THE BLOOD MONSTERS) (1970, US/Phil.)
VAMPIRE OVER LONDON (SEE: MY SON, THE VAMPIRE) (1952, Brit.)
VAMPIRE PEOPLE, THE (SEE: BLOOD DRINKERS, THE) (1966, US/Phil.)
VAMPIRE PLAYGIRLS (SEE: DEVIL'S NIGHTMARE, THE) (1971, Bel./It.)
VAMPIRES (SEE: DEVIL'S COMMANDMENT, THE) (1956, It.)
VAMPIRES, THE (1969, Mex.) PR:O
VAMPIRE'S COFFIN, THE (1958, Mex.) PR:O
VAMPIRE'S GHOST, THE (1945) PR:C
VAMPIRES IN HAVANA (1985, Cuba) PR:C-O
VAMPIRE'S NIGHT ORGY, THE (1973, Sp./It.) PR:O
VAMPYR (1932, Fr./Ger.) PR:O
VAMPYRES, DAUGHTERS OF DRACULA (1977, Brit.) PR:O
VAN, THE (1977) PR:O
VAN NUYS BLVD. (1979) PR:O
VANDERGILT DIAMOND MYSTERY, THE (1936, Brit.) PR:A
VANESSA, HER LOVE STORY (1935) PR:A

VANISHING AMERICAN, THE (1955) PR:A
VANISHING FRONTIER, THE (1932) PR:A
VANISHING FRONTIER (SEE: BROKEN LAND, THE) (1962)
VANISHING OUTPOST, THE (1951) PR:A
VANISHING POINT (1971) PR:C
VANISHING VIRGINIAN, THE (1941) PR:A
VANISHING WESTERNER, THE (1950) PR:A
VANITY (1935) PR:A
VANITY FAIR (1932) PR:C
VANITY STREET (1932) PR:A
VANQUISHED, THE (1953) PR:A
VAR HERR LUGGAR JOHANSSON (SEE: JOHANSSON GETS SCOLDED) (1945, Swed.)
VARAN THE UNBELIEVABLE (1962, US/Jap.) PR:A
VARELSERNA (SEE: LES CREATURES) (1969, Fr./Swed.)
VARGTIMMEN (SEE: HOUR OF THE WOLF, THE) (1968, Swed.)
VARIETY (1935, Brit.) PR:A
VARIETY (1984) PR:O
VARIETY GIRL (1947) PR:AA
VARIETY HOUR (1937, Brit.) PR:A
VARIETY JUBILEE (1945, Brit.) PR:A
VARIETY LIGHTS (1965, It.) PR:A
VARIETY PARADE (1936, Brit.) PR:A
VARSITY (1928) PR:A
VARSITY SHOW (1937) PR:A
VASECTOMY: A DELICATE MATTER (1986) PR:O
VAULT OF HORROR, THE (1973, Brit.) PR:C-O
VAXDOCKAN (SEE: DOLL, THE) (1964, Swed.)
VECHERA NA KHUTORE BLIZ DIKANKI (SEE: NIGHT BEFORE CHRISTMAS, A) (1963, USSR)
VEIL, THE (SEE: HAUNTS) (1977)
VEILED WOMAN, THE (1929) PR:C
VEILS OF BAGDAD, THE (1953) PR:A
VELVET HOUSE (SEE: CRUCIBLE OF HORROR) (1971, Brit.)
VELVET TOUCH, THE (1948) PR:A
VELVET TRAP, THE (1966) PR:O
VELVET VAMPIRE, THE (1971) PR:O
VENDETTA (1950) PR:A
VENDETTA (SEE: MURIETA) (1965, Sp.)
VENDETTA (1986) PR:O
VENDETTA DELLA MASCHERA DI FERRO (SEE: PRISONER OF THE IRON MASK) (1962, Fr./It.)
VENDREDI 13 HEURES (SEE: WORLD IN MY POCKET, THE) (1962, Fr./It./W. Ger.)
VENERE IMPERIALE (SEE: IMPERIAL VENUS) (1963, Fr./It.)
VENETIAN AFFAIR, THE (1967) PR:C
VENETIAN BIRD (SEE: ASSASSIN, THE) (1953, Brit.)
VENETIAN NIGHTS (SEE: CARNIVAL) (1931, Brit.)
VENGA A PRENDERO IL CAFFE DA NOI (SEE: MAN WHO CAME FOR COFFEE, THE) (1970, It.)
VENGEANCE (1930) PR:A
VENGEANCE (SEE: VALLEY OF VENGEANCE) (1944)
VENGEANCE (SEE: TRAIL TO VENGEANCE) (1945)
VENGEANCE (1964) PR:A
VENGEANCE (SEE: BRAIN, THE) (1965, Brit./W. Ger.)
VENGEANCE (1968, It./W. Ger.) PR:C
VENGEANCE IS MINE (1948, Brit.) PR:A
VENGEANCE IS MINE (1969, It./Sp.) PR:A
VENGEANCE IS MINE (1980, Jap.) PR:O
VENGEANCE OF FU MANCHU, THE (1968, Brit./Hong Kong/Ireland/W. Ger.) PR:A
VENGEANCE OF GREGORY (SEE: FEUD OF THE WEST) (1936)
VENGEANCE OF SHE, THE (1968, Brit.) PR:A
VENGEANCE OF THE DEEP (1940, Aus.) PR:A
VENGEANCE OF THE VAMPIRE WOMEN, THE (1969, Mex.) PR:O
VENGEANCE VALLEY (1951) PR:A
VENOM (1968, Den./Swed.) PR:O
VENOM (SEE: LEGEND OF SPIDER FOREST, THE) (1976, Brit.)
VENOM (1982, Brit.) PR:O
VENTO DELL'EST (SEE: WIND FROM THE EAST) (1970, Fr./It./W. Ger.)
VENUS DER PIRATEN (SEE: QUEEN OF THE PIRATES) (1961, It./W. Ger.)
VENUS IN FURS (1970, It./Brit./W. Ger.) PR:O
VENUS MAKES TROUBLE (1937) PR:A
VENUSIAN, THE (SEE: STRANGER FROM VENUS, THE) (1954, Brit.)
VERA (1987, Braz.) PR:O
VERA CRUZ (1954) PR:C-O
VERBOTEN! (1959) PR:C
VERBRECHEN NACH SCHULSCHLUSS (SEE: YOUNG GO WILD, THE) (1962, W. Ger.)
VERDICT, THE (1946) PR:C
VERDICT, THE (1964, Brit.) PR:A
VERDICT, THE (1974, Fr./It.) PR:C
VERDICT, THE (1982) PR:C-O
VERDICT OF THE SEA (1932, Brit.) PR:A
VERFUHRUNG AM MEER (SEE: SEDUCTION BY THE SEA) (1967, Yugo./W. Ger.)

VERGELTUNG IN CATANO (SEE: SUNSCORCHED) (1966, Sp./It.)
VERGINITA (1953, It.) PR:A-C
VERKLUGENE MELODIE (SEE: DEAD MELODY) (1938, Ger.)
VERMILION DOOR (1969, Hong Kong) PR:A
VERNE MILLER (1988) PR:O
VERONA TRIAL, THE (1963, It.) PR:A
VERONIKA VOSS (1982, W. Ger.) PR:O
VERSPATUNG IN MARIENBORN (SEE: STOP TRAIN 349) (1964, Fr./It./W. Ger.)
VERTIGO (1958) PR:C
VERY BIG WITHDRAWAL, A (SEE: MAN, A WOMAN, AND A BANK, A) (1979, Can.)
VERY CLOSE QUARTERS (1986) PR:O
VERY CURIOUS GIRL, A (1969, Fr.) PR:O
VERY EDGE, THE (1963, Brit.) PR:C
VERY HANDY MAN, A (1966, Fr./It.) PR:C
VERY HAPPY ALEXANDER (1969, Fr.) PR:A
VERY HONORABLE GUY, A (1934) PR:A
VERY IDEA, THE (1929) PR:A
VERY IMPORTANT PERSON, A (SEE: COMING-OUT PARTY, A) (1962, Brit.)
VERY NATURAL THING, A (1974) PR:O
VERY PRIVATE AFFAIR, A (1962, Fr./It.) PR:C
VERY SPECIAL FAVOR, A (1965) PR:A
VERY THOUGHT OF YOU, THE (1944) PR:A
VERY YOUNG LADY, A (1941) PR:A
VESNICKO MA STREDISKOVA (SEE: MY SWEET LITTLE VILLAGE) (1985, Czech.)
VESSEL OF WRATH (SEE: BEACHCOMBER, THE) (1938, Brit.)
VET IN THE DOGHOUSE (SEE: IN THE DOGHOUSE) (1964, Brit.)
VETERAN, THE (SEE: DEATHDREAM) (1972, Can.)
VIA MARGUTTA (SEE: RUN WITH THE DEVIL) (1963, Fr./It.)
VIA PONY EXPRESS (1933) PR:A
VIAGGIO IN ITALIA (SEE: STRANGERS, THE) (1955, It.)
VIBRATION (1969, Swed.) PR:O
VICAR OF BRAY, THE (1937, Brit.) PR:A
VICE ACADEMY (1989) PR:C
VICE AND VIRTUE (1965, Fr./It.) PR:O
VICE DOLLS (1961, Fr.) PR:C
VICE GIRLS, LTD. (1964) PR:O
VICE RACKET (1937) PR:A
VICE RAID (1959) PR:C
VICE SQUAD, THE (1931) PR:A
VICE SQUAD (1953) PR:A
VICE SQUAD (1982) PR:O
VICE VERSA (1948, Brit.) PR:A
VICE VERSA (1988) PR:A-C
VICIOUS CIRCLE, THE (1948) PR:A
VICIOUS CIRCLE, THE (SEE: CIRCLE, THE) (1959, Brit.)
VICIOUS YEARS, THE (1950) PR:A
VICKI (1953) PR:C
VICOLI E DELITTI (SEE: CAMORRA) (1986, It.)
VICTIM (1961, Brit.) PR:C-O
VICTIM FIVE (SEE: CODE 7, VICTIM 5!) (1964, Brit.)
VICTIMS OF PERSECUTION (1933) PR:A
VICTIMS OF THE BEYOND (SEE: SUCKER MONEY) (1933)
VICTOR FRANKENSTEIN (1975, Swed./Ireland) PR:C
VICTORIA THE GREAT (1937, Brit.) PR:A
VICTORS, THE (1963, US/Brit.) PR:O
VICTOR/VICTORIA (1982, Brit.) PR:O
VICTORY (1940) PR:A-C
VICTORY (1981) PR:A-C
VIDEO DEAD (1987) PR:O
VIDEO MADNESS (SEE: JOYSTICKS) (1983)
VIDEODROME (1983, Can.) PR:O
VIENNA, CITY OF SONGS (1931, Ger.) PR:A
VIENNA WALTZES (1961, Aust.) PR:A
VIENNESE NIGHTS (1930) PR:A
VIEW FROM POMPEY'S HEAD, THE (1955) PR:C-O
VIEW FROM THE BRIDGE, A (1962, Fr./It.) PR:C
VIEW TO A KILL, A (1985, Brit.) PR:C
VIGIL (1984, New Zealand) PR:C
VIGIL IN THE NIGHT (1940) PR:C
VIGILANTE (1983) PR:O
VIGILANTE FORCE (1976) PR:C
VIGILANTE HIDEOUT (1950) PR:A
VIGILANTE TERROR (1953) PR:A
VIGILANTES OF BOOMTOWN (1947) PR:A
VIGILANTES OF DODGE CITY (1944) PR:AA
VIGILANTES RETURN, THE (1947) PR:A
VIGOUR OF YOUTH (SEE: SPIRIT OF NOTRE DAME, THE) (1931)
VIKING, THE (1931) PR:A
VIKING QUEEN, THE (1967, Brit.) PR:A
VIKING WOMEN AND THE SEA SERPENT (SEE: SAGA OF THE VIKING WOMEN AND THEIR VOYAGE TO THE WATERS OF THE GREAT SEA SERPENT, THE) (1957)
VIKINGS, THE (1958) PR:C
VILLA! (1958) PR:A

VILLA RIDES (1968) PR:O
VILLAGE, THE (1953, Brit./Switz.) PR:A
VILLAGE BARN DANCE (1940) PR:A
VILLAGE OF DAUGHTERS (1962, Brit.) PR:A
VILLAGE OF THE DAMNED (1960, Brit.) PR:C
VILLAGE OF THE GIANTS (1965) PR:A
VILLAGE SQUIRE, THE (1935, Brit.) PR:A
VILLAGE TALE (1935) PR:A
VILLAIN (1971, Brit.) PR:O
VILLAIN, THE (1979) PR:A
VILLAIN STILL PURSUED HER, THE (1940) PR:A
VILLE ETRANGERE (SEE: FOREIGN CITY, A) (1988, Fr.)
VILLE SANS PITTE (SEE: TOWN WITHOUT PITY) (1961, US/Switz./W. Ger.)
VILLIERS DIAMOND, THE (1938, Brit.) PR:A
VILNA LEGEND, A (1949, US/Pol.) PR:A
VINDICATOR (SEE: DESERT WARRIOR) (1985)
VINETU (SEE: APACHE GOLD) (1965, Fr./It./Yugo./W. Ger.)
VINETU II (SEE: LAST OF THE RENEGADES) (1966, Fr./It./Yugo./W. Ger.)
VINETU III (SEE: DESPERADO TRAIL, THE) (1967, W. Ger./Yugo.)
VINTAGE, THE (1957) PR:A
VINTAGE WINE (1935, Brit.) PR:A
VIOLATED (1953) PR:C
VIOLATED (1986) PR:O
VIOLATED LOVE (1966, Arg.) PR:C
VIOLATED PARADISE (1963, It./Jap.) PR:O
VIOLATORS, THE (1957) PR:A
VIOLENCE (1947) PR:A
VIOLENCE ET PASSION (SEE: CONVERSATION PIECE) (1976, Fr./It.)
VIOLENT AND THE DAMNED, THE (1962, Braz.) PR:C
VIOLENT ANGELS, THE (SEE: ANGELS DIE HARD!) (1970)
VIOLENT BREED, THE (1986, It.) PR:O
VIOLENT CITY (SEE: FAMILY, THE) (1974, Fr./It.)
VIOLENT ENEMY, THE (1969, Brit.) PR:A
VIOLENT FOUR, THE (1968, It.) PR:A
VIOLENT HOUR, THE (SEE: DIAL 1119) (1950)
VIOLENT JOURNEY (SEE: FOOL KILLER, THE) (1965)
VIOLENT LOVE (SEE: TAKE HER BY SURPRISE) (1967, Can.)
VIOLENT MEN, THE (1955) PR:A
VIOLENT MIDNIGHT (SEE: PSYCHOMANIA) (1964)
VIOLENT MOMENT (1966, Brit.) PR:C
VIOLENT ONES, THE (1967) PR:C
VIOLENT PLAYGROUND (1958, Brit.) PR:A
VIOLENT ROAD (1958) PR:A
VIOLENT SATURDAY (1955) PR:O
VIOLENT STRANGER (1957, Brit.) PR:A
VIOLENT STREETS (SEE: THIEF) (1981)
VIOLENT SUMMER (1961, Fr./It.) PR:C
VIOLENT WOMEN (1960) PR:O
VIOLENT YEARS, THE (1956) PR:C-O
VIOLENZA PER UNA MONACA (SEE: NUN AT THE CROSSROADS, A) (1970, It./Sp.)
VIOLETS ARE BLUE (1986) PR:C-O
VIOLETTE (1978, Fr.) PR:O
VIOLIN AND ROLLER (1962, USSR) PR:A
VIPER, THE (1938, Brit.) PR:A
VIRGIN AND THE GYPSY, THE (1970, Brit.) PR:O
VIRGIN AQUA SEX, THE (SEE: MERMAIDS OF TIBURON, THE) (1962)
VIRGIN COCOTTE, THE (SEE: COQUETTE) (1929)
VIRGIN FOR THE PRINCE, A (SEE: MAIDEN FOR A PRINCE, A) (1967, It.)
VIRGIN ISLAND (1960, Brit.) PR:C
VIRGIN PRESIDENT, THE (1968) PR:A
VIRGIN QUEEN, THE (1955) PR:A-C
VIRGIN QUEEN OF ST. FRANCIS HIGH, THE (1987, Can.) PR:A
VIRGIN SACRIFICE (1959) PR:C
VIRGIN SOLDIERS, THE (1970, Brit.) PR:O
VIRGIN SPRING, THE (1960, Swed.) PR:C
VIRGIN WITCH, THE (1973, Brit.) PR:O
VIRGINIA (1941) PR:A
VIRGINIA CITY (1940) PR:A
VIRGINIA JUDGE, THE (1935) PR:A
VIRGINIAN, THE (1929) PR:A
VIRGINIAN, THE (1946) PR:A-C
VIRGINIA'S HUSBAND (1934, Brit.) PR:AA
VIRIDIANA (1961, Mex./Sp.) PR:C-O
VIRTUE (1932) PR:C
VIRTUOUS HUSBAND, THE (1931) PR:A
VIRTUOUS SIN, THE (1930) PR:A
VIRTUOUS TRAMPS, THE (SEE: DEVIL'S BROTHER, THE) (1933)
VIRTUOUS WIFE, THE (SEE: MEN ARE LIKE THAT) (1931)
VIRUS (1980, Jap.) PR:C
VIRUS (SEE: CANNIBALS IN THE STREETS) (1982, It./Sp.)
VIRUS KNOWS NO MORALS, A (1986, W. Ger.) PR:O
VISA TO CANTON (SEE: PASSPORT TO CHINA) (1961, Brit.)

VISA U.S.A. (1987, Colombia/Cuba) PR:C
VISCOUNT, THE (1967, Fr./Sp./It./W. Ger.) PR:C
VISION QUEST (1985) PR:O
VISIT, THE (1964, Fr./It./US/W. Ger.) PR:C
VISIT TO A CHIEF'S SON (1974) PR:AA
VISIT TO A SMALL PLANET (1960) PR:A
VISITING HOURS (1982, Can.) PR:O
VISITOR, THE (1973, Can.) PR:C-O
VISITOR, THE (1980, US/It.) PR:O
VISITORS, THE (1972) PR:O
VISITORS FROM THE GALAXY (1981, Yugo.) PR:AA
VISKINGAR OCH ROP (SEE: CRIES AND WHISPERS) (1972, Swed.)
VISSZASZAMLALAS (SEE: COUNTDOWN) (1985, Hung.)
VITA PRIVATA (SEE: VERY PRIVATE AFFAIR, A) (1962, Fr./It.)
VITE PERDUTE (SEE: LOST SOULS) (1961, It.)
VITELLONI (1953, It./Fr.) PR:C
VIVA CISCO KID (1940) PR:A
VIVA ITALIA (1978, It.) PR:O
VIVA KNIEVEL! (1977) PR:A
VIVA LA MUERTE. . . TUA (SEE: DON'T TURN THE OTHER CHEEK) (1974, It./Sp./W. Ger.)
VIVA LAS VEGAS (SEE: MEET ME IN LAS VEGAS) (1956)
VIVA LAS VEGAS (1964) PR:A
VIVA MARIA (1965, Fr./It.) PR:C
VIVA VILLA! (1934) PR:A-C
VIVA ZAPATA! (1952) PR:C
VIVACIOUS LADY (1938) PR:A
VIVEMENT DIAMANCHE? (SEE: CONFIDENTIALLY YOURS!) (1983, Fr.)
VIVERE PER VIVERE (SEE: LIVE FOR LIFE) (1967, Fr./It.)
VIVIAMO OGGI (SEE: DAY AND THE HOUR, THE) (1963, Fr./It.)
VIVIR DESVIVIENDOSE (SEE: MOMENT OF TRUTH) (1965, It./Sp.)
VIVO PER LA TUA MORTE (SEE: LONG RIDE FROM HELL, A) (1970, It.)
VIVRE POUR VIVRE (SEE: LIVE FOR LIFE) (1967, Fr./It.)
VIVRE SA VIE (SEE: MY LIFE TO LIVE) (1962, Fr.)
VIXEN (1970, Jap.) PR:O
VIXENS, THE (1969) PR:O
VLCI BOUDA (SEE: WOLF'S HOLE) (1987, Czech.)
VOGUES OF 1938 (1937) PR:A
VOICE FROM THE GRAVE (SEE: SIN OF NORA MORAN) (1933)
VOICE IN THE MIRROR (1958) PR:A
VOICE IN THE NIGHT (1934) PR:A
VOICE IN THE NIGHT, A (1941, Brit.) PR:A
VOICE IN THE NIGHT (SEE: WANTED FOR MURDER) (1946, Brit.)
VOICE IN THE WIND (1944) PR:A
VOICE IN YOUR HEART, A (1952, It.) PR:C
VOICE OF BUGLE ANN, THE (1936) PR:A
VOICE OF MERRILL, THE (SEE: MURDER WILL OUT) (1953, Brit.)
VOICE OF TERROR (SEE: SHERLOCK HOLMES AND THE VOICE OF TERROR) (1942)
VOICE OF THE CITY (1929) PR:A
VOICE OF THE HURRICANE (1964) PR:A
VOICE OF THE TURTLE, THE (1947) PR:A
VOICE OF THE WHISTLER (1945) PR:C
VOICE WITHIN, THE (1945, Brit.) PR:A
VOICES (1973, Brit.) PR:O
VOICES (1979) PR:C
VOLCANO (1953, It.) PR:A
VOLCANO (SEE: KRAKATOA, EAST OF JAVA) (1969)
VOLOCHAYESKIYE DNI (SEE: DEFENSE OF VOLOTCHAYEVSK, THE) (1938, USSR)
VOLPONE (1947, Fr.) PR:A
VOLTAIRE (1933) PR:A
VOLUNTEERS (1985) PR:O
VOLVER A EMPEZAR (SEE: TO BEGIN AGAIN) (1982, Sp.)
VOM HIMMEL GEFALLEN (SEE: SPECIAL DELIVERY) (1955, W. Ger.)
VON RICHTHOFEN AND BROWN (1970) PR:C
VON RYAN'S EXPRESS (1965) PR:C
VOODOO BLOOD BATH (SEE: I EAT YOUR SKIN) (1971)
VOODOO GIRL (SEE: SUGAR HILL) (1974)
VOODOO HEARTBEAT (1972) PR:O
VOODOO ISLAND (1957) PR:A
VOODOO MAN (1944) PR:A
VOODOO TIGER (1952) PR:A
VOODOO WOMAN (1957) PR:A
VOR SONNENUNTERGANG (1961, W. Ger.) PR:A
VORTEX (SEE: DAY TIME ENDED, THE) (1980, Sp.)
VORTEX (1982) PR:O
VOSKRESENIYE (SEE: RESURRECTION) (1963, USSR)
VOTE FOR HUGGETT (1948, Brit.) PR:A
VOULEZ-VOUS DANSER AVEC MOI (SEE: COME DANCE WITH ME!) (1960, Fr.)

VOW, THE (1947, USSR) PR:A
VOYAGE, THE (1974, It.) PR:O
VOYAGE BEYOND THE SUN (SEE: SPACE MONSTER) (1965)
VOYAGE IN A BALLOON (SEE: STOWAWAY IN THE SKY) (1962, Fr.)
VOYAGE OF SILENCE (1968, Fr.) PR:A
VOYAGE OF THE DAMNED (1976, Brit.) PR:A-C
VOYAGE TO AMERICA (1952, Fr.) PR:A
VOYAGE TO PREHISTORY (SEE: JOURNEY TO THE BEGINNING OF TIME) (1966, Czech.)
VOYAGE TO THE BOTTOM OF THE SEA (1961) PR:A
VOYAGE TO THE END OF THE UNIVERSE (1963, Czech.) PR:A
VOYAGE TO THE PLANET OF PREHISTORIC WOMEN (1966) PR:A
VOYAGE TO THE PREHISTORIC PLANET (1965) PR:A
VOYNA I MIR (SEE: WAR AND PEACE) (1968, USSR)
VRAZDA PO CESKU (SEE: MURDER CZECH STYLE) (1968, Czech.)
VRAZDA PO NASEM (SEE: MURDER CZECH STYLE) (1968, Czech.)
VREDENS DAG (SEE: DAY OF WRATH) (1943, Den.)
VROEGER IS DOOD (SEE: BYGONES) (1988, Neth.)
VROODER'S HOOCH (SEE: CRAZY WORLD OF JULIUS VROODER, THE) (1974)
VU DU PONT (SEE: VIEW FROM THE BRIDGE, A) (1962, Fr./It.)
VULCAN AFFAIR, THE (SEE: TO TRAP A SPY) (1966)
VULCANO (SEE: VOLCANO) (1950, It.)
VULTURE, THE (1937, Brit.) PR:A
VULTURE, THE (1967, US/Brit./Can.) PR:C
VULTURES OF THE LAW (SEE: SON OF THE PLAINS) (1931)
VYNALEZ ZKAZY (SEE: FABULOUS WORLD OF JULES VERNE, THE) (1958, Czech.)
VZROSLYYE DETI (SEE: GROWN-UP CHILDREN) (1963, USSR)

W

W (1974) PR:C
"W" PLAN, THE (1931, Brit.) PR:A
W.C. FIELDS AND ME (1976) PR:C
W.I.A. (WOUNDED IN ACTION) (1966) PR:A
W.W. AND THE DIXIE DANCEKINGS (1975) PR:A
WABASH AVENUE (1950) PR:A
WAC FROM WALLA WALLA, THE (1952) PR:A
WACKIEST SHIP IN THE ARMY, THE (1961) PR:A
WACKIEST WAGON TRAIN IN THE WEST, THE (1976) PR:A
WACKO (1983) PR:C
WACKY WORLD OF DR. MORGUS, THE (1962) PR:A
WACKY WORLD OF MOTHER GOOSE, THE (1967) PR:AA
WACO (1952) PR:A
WACO (1966) PR:C
WAGA KOI WAGA UTA (SEE: SONG FROM MY HEART, THE) (1970, Jap.)
WAGES OF FEAR, THE (1955, Fr./It.) PR:O
WAGES OF FEAR (SEE: SORCERER) (1977)
WAGNER (1983, Brit./Hung./Aust.) PR:C-O
WAGON MASTER, THE (1929) PR:A
WAGON TEAM (1952) PR:A
WAGON TRACKS WEST (1943) PR:A
WAGON TRAIL (1935) PR:A
WAGON TRAIN (1940) PR:A
WAGON TRAIN (SEE: WAGON TEAM) (1952)
WAGON WHEELS (1934) PR:A
WAGON WHEELS WESTWARD (1946) PR:AA
WAGONMASTER (1950) PR:A
WAGONS ROLL AT NIGHT, THE (1941) PR:A
WAGONS WEST (1952) PR:A
WAGONS WESTWARD (1940) PR:A
WAHINE (SEE: MAEVA) (1961)
WAIKIKI WEDDING (1937) PR:A
WAIT FOR ME IN HEAVEN (1988, Sp.) PR:C
WAIT TILL THE SUN SHINES, NELLIE (1952) PR:A
WAIT UNTIL DARK (1967) PR:O
WAITING AT THE CHURCH (SEE: RUNAROUND, THE) (1931)
WAITING FOR CAROLINE (1969, Can.) PR:C
WAITING FOR THE BRIDE (SEE: RUNAROUND, THE) (1931)
WAITING FOR THE MOON (1987) PR:A
WAITING WOMEN (SEE: SECRETS OF WOMEN) (1952, Swed.)
WAITRESS (1982) PR:O
WAJAN (1938, Bali) PR:A
WAKAMBA! (1955) PR:AA
WAKAMONO TACHI (SEE: LIVE YOUR OWN WAY) (1970, Jap.)
WAKARE (SEE: FAREWELL, MY BELOVED) (1969, Jap.)
WAKARETE IKURU TOKI MO (SEE: ETERNITY OF LOVE) (1961, Jap.)
WAKE ISLAND (1942) PR:A
WAKE ME WHEN IT'S OVER (1960) PR:A
WAKE OF THE RED WITCH (1949) PR:A-C

WAKE UP AND DIE (1967, Fr./It.) PR:C
WAKE UP AND DREAM (1934) PR:A
WAKE UP AND DREAM (SEE: WHAT'S COOKIN'?) (1942)
WAKE UP AND DREAM (1946) PR:A
WAKE UP AND LIVE (1937) PR:AA
WAKE UP FAMOUS (1937, Brit.) PR:A
WALK A CROOKED MILE (1948) PR:A
WALK A CROOKED PATH (1969, Brit.) PR:O
WALK A TIGHTROPE (1964, US/Brit.) PR:A-C
WALK, DON'T RUN (1966) PR:A
WALK EAST ON BEACON (1952) PR:A
WALK IN THE SHADOW (1966, Brit.) PR:A
WALK IN THE SPRING RAIN, A (1970) PR:C
WALK IN THE SUN, A (1945) PR:C
WALK INTO HELL (1957, Aus.) PR:A
WALK LIKE A DRAGON (1960) PR:O
WALK LIKE A MAN (1987) PR:A-C
WALK ON THE MOON, A (1987) PR:O
WALK ON THE WILD SIDE (1962) PR:O
WALK PROUD (1979) PR:C
WALK SOFTLY, STRANGER (1950) PR:C
WALK TALL (1960) PR:A
WALK THE ANGRY BEACH (1961) PR:C
WALK THE DARK STREET (1956) PR:C
WALK THE PROUD LAND (1956) PR:A
WALK THE WALK (1970) PR:O
WALK WITH LOVE AND DEATH, A (1969) PR:C
WALKABOUT (1971, Aus./US) PR:C
WALKER (1987) PR:O
WALKING DEAD, THE (1936) PR:A
WALKING DOWN BROADWAY (SEE: HELLO SISTER!) (1933)
WALKING DOWN BROADWAY (1938) PR:A
WALKING HILLS, THE (1949) PR:A
WALKING MY BABY BACK HOME (1953) PR:A
WALKING ON AIR (1936) PR:A
WALKING ON AIR (1946, Brit.) PR:AA
WALKING ON WATER (SEE: STAND AND DELIVER) (1988)
WALKING STICK, THE (1970, Brit.) PR:C
WALKING TALL (1973) PR:O
WALKING TALL, PART II (1975) PR:O
WALKING TARGET, THE (1960) PR:C
WALKING THE EDGE (1985) PR:O
WALKOVER (1969, Pol.) PR:C
WALL, THE (SEE: PINK FLOYD—THE WALL) (1982, Brit.)
WALL, THE (1983, Fr.) PR:O
WALL-EYED NIPPON (1963, Jap.) PR:A
WALL FOR SAN SEBASTIAN (SEE: GUNS FOR SAN SEBASTIAN) (1968, US/Fr./It./Mex.)
WALL OF DEATH (1951, Brit.) PR:A
WALL OF NOISE (1963) PR:A
WALL STREET (1929) PR:A
WALL STREET (1987) PR:O
WALL STREET COWBOY (1939) PR:A
WALLABY JIM OF THE ISLANDS (1937) PR:A
WALLET, THE (1952, Brit.) PR:A
WALLFLOWER (1948) PR:A
WALLS CAME TUMBLING DOWN, THE (1946) PR:A
WALLS OF GOLD (1933) PR:C
WALLS OF HELL, THE (1964, US/Phil.) PR:A
WALLS OF JERICHO, THE (1948) PR:C
WALLS OF MALAPAGA, THE (1950, Fr./It.) PR:A
WALPURGIS NIGHT (1941, Swed.) PR:A-C
WALTZ ACROSS TEXAS (1982) PR:A-C
WALTZ OF THE TOREADORS (1962, Brit.) PR:A-C
WALTZ TIME (1933, Brit.) PR:A
WALTZ TIME (1946, Brit.) PR:A
WALTZES FROM VIENNA (SEE: STRAUSS'S GREAT WALTZ) (1934, Brit.)
WANDA (1971) PR:C
WANDA NEVADA (1979) PR:A-C
WANDER LOVE STORY (SEE: WANDERLOVE) (1970)
WANDERER, THE (1969, Fr.) PR:A
WANDERER OF THE WASTELAND (1935) PR:A
WANDERER OF THE WASTELAND (1945) PR:A
WANDERERS, THE (1979) PR:O
WANDERERS OF THE WEST (1941) PR:A
WANDERING JEW, THE (1933) PR:A
WANDERING JEW, THE (1935, Brit.) PR:A
WANDERING JEW, THE (1948, It.) PR:O
WANDERLOVE (1970) PR:O
WANDERLUST (SEE: MARY JANE'S PA) (1935)
WANNSEE CONFERENCE, THE (1987, Aust./W. Ger.) PR:A-C
WANT A RIDE LITTLE GIRL? (SEE: IMPULSE) (1975)
WANTED (SEE: HIGH VOLTAGE) (1929)
WANTED (SEE: POLICE CALL) (1933)
WANTED (1937, Brit.) PR:A
WANTED BY SCOTLAND YARD (1939, Brit.) PR:A
WANTED BY THE POLICE (1938) PR:A
WANTED: DEAD OR ALIVE (1987) PR:O
WANTED FOR MURDER (1946, Brit.) PR:C
WANTED! JANE TURNER (1936) PR:A
WANTED MEN (SEE: LAW OF THE RIO GRANDE) (1931)

WANTED WOMEN (SEE: JESSIE'S GIRLS) (1976)
WANTON CONTESSA, THE (SEE: SENSO) (1968, It.)
WAR (SEE: RAT) (1960, Yugo.)
WAR AGAINST MRS. HADLEY, THE (1942) PR:A
WAR AND LOVE (1985) PR:O
WAR AND PEACE (1956, It./US) PR:A-C
WAR AND PEACE (1968, USSR) PR:A-C
WAR AND PEACE (1983, W. Ger.) PR:C
WAR ARROW (1953) PR:A
WAR BETWEEN MEN AND WOMEN, THE (1972) PR:A-C
WAR BETWEEN THE PLANETS (1971, It.) PR:A
WAR BIRDS (1989) PR:C
WAR CORRESPONDENT (1932) PR:A
WAR CORRESPONDENT (SEE: STORY OF G.I. JOE, THE) (1945)
WAR DOGS (1942) PR:A
WAR DRUMS (1957) PR:A
WAR GAMES (SEE: SUPPOSE THEY GAVE A WAR AND NO ONE CAME?) (1970)
WAR GAMES (SEE: WARGAMES) (1983)
WAR GODS OF THE DEEP (SEE: CITY UNDER THE SEA) (1965, Brit.)
WAR HEAD (SEE: OPERATION SNAFU) (1965, Brit.)
WAR HERO, WAR MADNESS (SEE: WAR IS HELL) (1964)
WAR HUNT (1962) PR:C
WAR IS A RACKET (1934) PR:A-C
WAR IS HELL (1964) PR:A-C
WAR IS OVER, THE (SEE: LA GUERRE EST FINIE) (1967, Fr./Swed.)
WAR ITALIAN STYLE (1967, It.) PR:A
WAR LORD, THE (1965) PR:O
WAR LORD, THE (SEE: WEST OF SHANGHAI) (1937)
WAR LOVER, THE (1962, Brit.) PR:C-O
WAR MADNESS (SEE: WAR IS HELL) (1969)
WAR NURSE (1930) PR:A
WAR OF THE ALIENS (SEE: STARSHIP INVASIONS) (1978, Can.)
WAR OF THE BUTTONS (1963, Fr.) PR:A
WAR OF THE COLOSSAL BEAST (1958) PR:A
WAR OF THE GARGANTUAS, THE (1970, Jap.) PR:A
WAR OF THE MONSTERS (1972, Jap.) PR:A
WAR OF THE PLANETS (1977, Jap.) PR:A
WAR OF THE ROSES, THE (1989) PR:O
WAR OF THE SATELLITES (1958) PR:A
WAR OF THE WILDCATS (SEE: IN OLD OKLAHOMA) (1943)
WAR OF THE WIZARDS (1983, Taiwan) PR:C
WAR OF THE WORLDS, THE (1953) PR:C
WAR OF THE WORLDS—NEXT CENTURY, THE (1981, Pol.) PR:C
WAR OF THE ZOMBIES, THE (1965, It.) PR:C-O
WAR ON THE RANGE (1933) PR:A
WAR PAINT (1953) PR:A
WAR PARTY (1965) PR:A
WAR PARTY (1989) PR:A
WAR SHOCK (SEE: WOMAN'S DEVOTION, A) (1956)
WAR WAGON, THE (1967) PR:A
WAR ZONE (SEE: DEADLINE) (1987, Brit./Israel/W. Ger.)
WARD 13 (SEE: HOSPITAL MASSACRE) (1982)
WARDOGS (1987, Swed.) PR:O
WARE CASE, THE (1939, Brit.) PR:A
WARGAMES (1983) PR:A
WARKILL (1968, US/Phil.) PR:O
WARLOCK (1959) PR:C
WARLORD OF CRETE, THE (SEE: MINOTAUR, THE) (1961, It.)
WARLORDS OF ATLANTIS (1978, Brit.) PR:AA
WARLORDS OF THE DEEP (SEE: CITY UNDER THE SEA) (1965, Brit.)
WARLORDS OF THE 21ST CENTURY (SEE: BATTLETRUCK) (1982)
WARM BODY, THE (SEE: THUNDER IN THE BLOOD) (1962, Fr.)
WARM CORNER, A (1930, Brit.) PR:AA
WARM DECEMBER, A (1973, Brit.) PR:C
WARM IN THE BUD (1970) PR:A
WARM NIGHTS ON A SLOW MOVING TRAIN (1987, Aus.) PR:C
WARM-BLOODED SPY, THE (SEE: RAVISHING IDIOT, A) (1966, Fr./It.)
WARN LONDON! (1934, Brit.) PR:A
WARN THAT MAN (1943, Brit.) PR:A
WARNING FROM SPACE (SEE: MYSTERIOUS SATELLITE, THE) (1956, Jap.)
WARNING SHOT (1967) PR:A-C
WARNING SIGN (1985) PR:O
WARNING TO WANTONS, A (1949, Brit.) PR:A
WARPATH (1951) PR:A
WARREN CASE, THE (1934, Brit.) PR:A
WARRING CLANS (1963, Jap.) PR:C
WARRIOR AND THE SLAVE GIRL, THE (1959, It.) PR:A
WARRIOR AND THE SORCERESS, THE (1984) PR:O
WARRIOR EMPRESS, THE (1961, It./Fr.) PR:O
WARRIOR QUEEN (1987) PR:O
WARRIOR'S REST (SEE: LOVE ON A PILLOW) (1963, Fr./It.)

WARRIORS, THE (1955, Brit.) PR:A-C
WARRIORS, THE (SEE: KELLY'S HEROES) (1970)
WARRIORS, THE (1979) PR:O
WARRIORS FIVE (1962, Fr./It.) PR:A
WARRIOR'S HUSBAND, THE (1933) PR:C
WARRIORS OF THE WASTELAND (1984, It.) PR:O
WARRIORS OF THE WIND (1984, Jap.) PR:C
WARUI YATSU HODO YOKU NEMURU (SEE: BAD SLEEP WELL, THE) (1960, Jap.)
WARUM LAUFT HERR R AMOK? (SEE: WHY DOES HERR R. RUN AMOK?) (1977, W. Ger.)
WAS FRAUEN TRAUMEN (SEE: WHAT WOMEN DREAM) (1933, Ger.)
WASHINGTON B.C. (SEE: HAIL) (1973)
WASHINGTON BC (SEE: HAIL) (1973)
WASHINGTON COWBOY (SEE: ROVIN' TUMBLE-WEEDS) (1939)
WASHINGTON MASQUERADE (1932) PR:A
WASHINGTON MELODRAMA (1941) PR:A
WASHINGTON MERRY-GO-ROUND (1932) PR:A
WASHINGTON STORY (1952) PR:A
WASP WOMAN, THE (1959) PR:A
WASTREL, THE (1963, It.) PR:C
WASTRELS, THE (SEE: VITELLONI) (1953, Fr./It.)
WATASHI GA SUTETA ONNA (SEE: GIRL I ABANDONED, THE) (1970, Jap.)
WATCH BEVERLY (1932, Brit.) PR:A
WATCH IT, SAILOR! (1961, Brit.) PR:A
WATCH ON THE RHINE (1943) PR:A
WATCH THE BIRDIE (1950) PR:A
WATCH YOUR STERN (1961, Brit.) PR:A
WATCHED (1974) PR:O
WATCHER IN THE WOODS, THE (1980, Brit.) PR:C
WATCHERS (1988) PR:NR
WATCHMAKER OF LYON, THE (SEE: CLOCKMAKER, THE) (1974, Fr.)
WATER (1985, Brit.) PR:C-O
WATER AND SOAP (SEE: ACQUA E SAPONE) (1985, It.)
WATER BABIES, THE (1979, Brit.) PR:AA
WATER CYBORGS (SEE: TERROR BENEATH THE SEA) (1966)
WATER FOR CANITOGA (1939, Ger.) PR:A
WATER GYPSIES, THE (1932, Brit.) PR:A
WATER RUSTLERS (1939) PR:A
WATERFRONT (1939) PR:A
WATERFRONT (1944) PR:A
WATERFRONT (SEE: WATERFRONT WOMEN) (1952, Brit.)
WATERFRONT AT MIDNIGHT (1948) PR:A
WATERFRONT LADY (1935) PR:A
WATERFRONT WOMEN (1952, Brit.) PR:A
WATERHOLE #3 (1967) PR:C
WATERLOO (1970, It./USSR) PR:C
WATERLOO BRIDGE (1931) PR:C
WATERLOO BRIDGE (1940) PR:A
WATERLOO ROAD (1949, Brit.) PR:A
WATERMELON MAN (1970) PR:C
WATERSHIP DOWN (1978, Brit.) PR:C-O
WATTS MONSTER, THE (SEE: DR. BLACK, MR. HYDE) (1976)
WATUSI (1959) PR:A
WATUSI A GO-GO (SEE: GET YOURSELF A COLLEGE GIRL) (1964)
WAVE, A WAC AND A MARINE, A (1944) PR:A
WAVELENGTH (1983) PR:C
WAXWORK (1988) PR:O
WAY AHEAD, THE (SEE: IMMORTAL BATALLION, THE) (1944, Brit.)
WAY BACK HOME (1932) PR:A
WAY DOWN EAST (1935) PR:A
WAY DOWN SOUTH (1939) PR:A
WAY FOR A SAILOR (1930) PR:A
WAY OF A GAUCHO (1952) PR:A
WAY OF ALL FLESH, THE (1940) PR:A
WAY OF ALL MEN, THE (1930) PR:A
WAY OF LIFE, THE (SEE: THEY CALL IT SIN) (1932)
WAY OF LOST SOULS, THE (1930, Brit.) PR:A
WAY OF THE WEST, THE (1934) PR:A
WAY OF YOUTH, THE (1934, Brit.) PR:A
WAY OUT, THE (1955, Brit.) PR:A
WAY OUT (1966) PR:O
WAY OUT LOVE (SEE: TOUCH OF HER FLESH, THE) (1967)
WAY OUT, WAY IN (1970, Jap.) PR:O
WAY OUT WEST (1930) PR:A
WAY OUT WEST (1937) PR:AA
WAY TO LOVE, THE (1933) PR:A
WAY TO THE GOLD, THE (1957) PR:A
WAY TO THE STARS, THE (SEE: JOHNNY IN THE CLOUDS) (1945, Brit.)
WAY. . . WAY OUT (1966) PR:C-O
WAY WE LIVE, THE (1946, Brit.) PR:A
WAY WE LIVE NOW, THE (1970) PR:O
WAY WE WERE, THE (1973) PR:C
WAY WEST, THE (1967) PR:A
WAYLAID WOMEN (SEE: INDECENT) (1962, W. Ger.)
WAYNE MURDER CASE, THE (SEE: STRANGE ADVENTURE) (1932)

WAYS OF LOVE (1950, It./Fr.) PR:C-O
WAYSIDE PEBBLE, THE (1962, Jap.) PR:A
WAYWARD (1932) PR:A
WAYWARD BUS, THE (1957) PR:C
WAYWARD GIRL, THE (1957) PR:A
WE ARE ALL MURDERERS (1957, Fr.) PR:C
WE ARE ALL NAKED (1970, Can./Fr.) PR:O
WE ARE IN THE NAVY NOW (SEE: WE JOINED THE
   NAVY) (1962, Brit.)
WE ARE NOT ALONE (1939) PR:A-C
WE DIVE AT DAWN (1943, Brit.) PR:A
WE GO FAST (1941) PR:A
WE HAVE ONLY ONE LIFE (1963, Gr.) PR:A
WE HAVE OUR MOMENTS (1937) PR:A
WE HUMANS (SEE: YOUNG AMERICA) (1942)
WE JOINED THE NAVY (1962, Brit.) PR:A
WE LIVE AGAIN (1934) PR:C
WE NEED NO MONEY (SEE: HIS MAJESTY, KING
   BALLYHOO!) (1931, Ger.)
WE OF THE NEVER NEVER (1983, Aus.) PR:C
WE SHALL RETURN (1963) PR:A
WE SHALL SEE (1964, Brit.) PR:C
WE STILL KILL THE OLD WAY (1967, It.) PR:C
WE THE LIVING (1942, It.) PR:A
WE THINK THE WORLD OF YOU (1989, Brit.) PR:A-C
WE THREE (SEE: COMPROMISED) (1931)
WE THREE (1985, It.) PR:C
WE WANT TO LIVE ALONE (SEE: FATHER CAME
   TOO) (1964, Brit.)
WE WENT TO COLLEGE (1936) PR:A
WE WERE DANCING (1942) PR:A
WE WERE STRANGERS (1949) PR:C
WE WHO ARE ABOUT TO DIE (1937) PR:A
WE WHO ARE YOUNG (1940) PR:A-C
WE WILL REMEMBER (1966, Jap.) PR:A-C
WEAK AND THE WICKED, THE (1954, Brit.) PR:A
WEAKER SEX, THE (1949, Brit.) PR:A
WEAPON, THE (1957, Brit.) PR:C
WEARY RIVER (1929) PR:A
WEATHER IN THE STREETS, THE (1983, Brit.) PR:C
WEB, THE (1947) PR:A
WEB OF DANGER, THE (1947) PR:A
WEB OF EVIDENCE (1959, Brit.) PR:C
WEB OF FEAR (1966, Fr./Sp.) PR:C
WEB OF PASSION (1961, Fr.) PR:C
WEB OF SUSPICION (1959, Brit.) PR:A
WEB OF THE SPIDER (1972, It./Fr./W. Ger.) PR:O
WEB OF VIOLENCE (1966, It./Sp.) PR:C
WEBSTER BOY, THE (1962, Brit.) PR:A
WEDDING, A (1978) PR:C
WEDDING BELLS (SEE: ROYAL WEDDING) (1951)
WEDDING BREAKFAST (SEE: CATERED AFFAIR,
   THE) (1956)
WEDDING GROUP (SEE: WRATH OF JEALOUSY)
   (1936, Brit.)
WEDDING IN GALILEE (1988, Bel./Fr.) PR:O
WEDDING IN WHITE (1972, Can.) PR:O
WEDDING NIGHT (1970, Ireland) PR:O
WEDDING NIGHT, THE (1935) PR:A
WEDDING OF LILLI MARLENE, THE (1953, Brit.) PR:A
WEDDING PARTY, THE (1969) PR:O
WEDDING PRESENT (1936) PR:A
WEDDING PRESENT (SEE: TURKISH CUCUMBER,
   THE) (1963, W. Ger.)
WEDDING REHEARSAL (1932, Brit.) PR:A
WEDDING RINGS (1930) PR:A
WEDDINGS AND BABIES (1960) PR:A
WEDDINGS ARE WONDERFUL (1938, Brit.) PR:A
WEDNESDAY CHILDREN, THE (1973) PR:C
WEDNESDAY'S CHILD (1934) PR:A
WEDNESDAY'S CHILD (SEE: FAMILY LIFE) (1971,
   Brit.)
WEDNESDAY'S LUCK (1936, Brit.) PR:A
WEE GEORDIE (1956, Brit.) PR:A
WEE WILLIE WINKIE (1937) PR:AA
WEEDS (1987) PR:O
WEEK-END MADNESS (SEE: AUGUST WEEK-END)
   (1936, Brit.)
WEEK-END MARRIAGE (1932) PR:A
WEEK-ENDS ONLY (1932) PR:A
WEEKEND (1964, Den.) PR:C
WEEKEND (1968, Fr./It.) PR:O
WEEKEND A ZUYDCOOTE (SEE: WEEKEND AT
   DUNKIRK) (1966, Fr./It.)
WEEKEND AT BERNIE'S (1989) PR:O
WEEKEND AT DUNKIRK (1966, Fr./It.) PR:A
WEEK-END AT THE WALDORF (1945) PR:A
WEEKEND BABYSITTER (SEE: WEEKEND WITH THE
   BABYSITTER) (1970)
WEEKEND FOR THREE (1941) PR:A
WEEKEND IN HAVANA (1941) PR:A
WEEKEND LIVES (SEE: WEEK-END MARRIAGE)
   (1932)
WEEKEND MILLIONAIRE (1937, Brit.) PR:A
WEEKEND MURDERS, THE (1972, It.) PR:O
WEEKEND OF FEAR (1966) PR:C
WEEKEND OF SHADOWS (1978, Aus.) PR:C
WEEKEND PASS (1944) PR:A

WEEKEND PASS (1984) PR:O
WEEKEND WARRIORS (1986) PR:O
WEEKEND WITH FATHER (1951) PR:A
WEEKEND WITH LULU, A (1961, Brit.) PR:A
WEEKEND WITH THE BABYSITTER (1970) PR:O
WEEKEND WIVES (SEE: WEEKEND, ITALIAN
   STYLE) (1967, Fr./It./Sp.)
WEEKEND, ITALIAN STYLE (1967, Fr./It./Sp.) PR:A
WEIRD LOVE MAKERS, THE (1963, Jap.) PR:O
WEIRD ONES, THE (1962) PR:O
WEIRD SCIENCE (1985) PR:O
WEIRD WOMAN (1944) PR:A
WELCOME DANGER (1929) PR:A
WELCOME HOME (1935) PR:A
WELCOME HOME (SEE: SNAFU) (1945)
WELCOME HOME (1989) PR:C
WELCOME HOME, SOLDIER BOYS (1972) PR:O
WELCOME IN VIENNA (1988, Aust./W. Ger.) PR:O
WELCOME KOSTYA! (1965, USSR) PR:AA
WELCOME, MR. BEDDOES (SEE: MAN COULD GET
   KILLED, A) (1966)
WELCOME, MR. WASHINGTON (1944, Brit.) PR:A
WELCOME STRANGER (1947) PR:A
WELCOME STRANGER (SEE: ACROSS THE SIERRAS)
   (1941)
WELCOME TO ARROW BEACH (SEE: TENDER
   FLESH) (1976)
WELCOME TO BLOOD CITY (1977, Brit./Can.) PR:O
WELCOME TO 18 (1986) PR:O
WELCOME TO GERMANY (1988, W. Ger./Brit./Switz.)
   PR:C
WELCOME TO HARD TIMES (1967) PR:O
WELCOME TO L.A. (1976) PR:O
WELCOME TO THE CLUB (1971, Brit.) PR:O
WELL, THE (1951) PR:A
WELL-DIGGER'S DAUGHTER, THE (1946, Fr.) PR:C
WELL DONE, HENRY (1936, Brit.) PR:A
WELL-GROOMED BRIDE, THE (1946) PR:A
WE'LL GROW THIN TOGETHER (1979, Fr.) PR:C
WE'LL MEET AGAIN (1942, Brit.) PR:A
WE'LL SMILE AGAIN (1942, Brit.) PR:A
WELLS FARGO (1937) PR:A
WELLS FARGO GUNMASTER (1951) PR:A
WENT THE DAY WELL? (SEE: 48 HOURS) (1944, Brit.)
WE'RE GOING TO BE RICH (1938, Brit.) PR:A
WE'RE IN THE ARMY NOW (SEE: PACK UP YOUR
   TROUBLES) (1939)
WE'RE IN THE LEGION NOW (1937) PR:A
WE'RE IN THE MONEY (1935) PR:A
WE'RE NO ANGELS (1955) PR:A-C
WE'RE NO ANGELS (1989) PR:C
WE'RE NOT DRESSING (1934) PR:A
WE'RE NOT MARRIED (1952) PR:A
WE'RE ON THE JURY (1937) PR:A
WE'RE ONLY HUMAN (1936) PR:A
WE'RE RICH AGAIN (1934) PR:A
WEREWOLF, THE (1956) PR:C-O
WEREWOLF IN A GIRL'S DORMITORY (1961, It./Aust.)
   PR:C-O
WEREWOLF OF LONDON (1935) PR:C
WEREWOLF OF WASHINGTON (1973) PR:C
WEREWOLF VS. THE VAMPIRE WOMAN, THE (1970,
   Sp./W. Ger.) PR:O
WEREWOLVES ON WHEELS (1971) PR:O
WEST 11 (1963, Brit.) PR:C
WEST OF ABILENE (1940) PR:A
WEST OF BROADWAY (1931) PR:A
WEST OF CARSON CITY (1940) PR:A
WEST OF CHEYENNE (1931) PR:A
WEST OF CHEYENNE (1938) PR:A
WEST OF CIMARRON (1941) PR:A
WEST OF EL DORADO (1949) PR:A
WEST OF KERRY (SEE: MEN OF IRELAND) (1938, Ire-
   land)
WEST OF MONTANA (SEE: MAIL ORDER BRIDE)
   (1964)
WEST OF NEVADA (1936) PR:A
WEST OF PINTO BASIN (1940) PR:A
WEST OF RAINBOW'S END (1938) PR:A
WEST OF SHANGHAI (1937) PR:A
WEST OF SINGAPORE (1933) PR:A
WEST OF SONORA (1948) PR:A
WEST OF SUEZ (SEE: FIGHTING WILDCATS, THE)
   (1957, Brit.)
WEST OF TEXAS (1943) PR:A
WEST OF THE ALAMO (1946) PR:A
WEST OF THE BRAZOS (1950) PR:A
WEST OF THE DIVIDE (1934) PR:A
WEST OF THE GREAT DIVIDE (SEE: NORTH OF THE
   GREAT DIVIDE) (1950)
WEST OF THE LAW (1942) PR:A
WEST OF THE PECOS (1935) PR:A-C
WEST OF THE PECOS (1945) PR:A
WEST OF THE ROCKIES (1929) PR:A
WEST OF THE ROCKIES (1931) PR:A
WEST OF THE SANTA FE (1938) PR:A
WEST OF THE SUEZ (SEE: FIGHTING WILDCATS,
   THE) (1957, Brit.)

WEST OF TOMBSTONE (1942) PR:A
WEST OF WYOMING (1950) PR:A
WEST OF ZANZIBAR (1954, Brit.) PR:A
WEST POINT OF THE AIR (1935) PR:A
WEST POINT STORY, THE (1950) PR:A
WEST POINT WIDOW (1941) PR:A
WEST SIDE KID (1943) PR:A
WEST SIDE STORY (1961) PR:A-C
WEST TO GLORY (1947) PR:A
WESTBOUND (1959) PR:A
WESTBOUND LIMITED (1937) PR:A
WESTBOUND MAIL (1937) PR:A
WESTBOUND STAGE (1940) PR:A
WESTERN CARAVANS (1939) PR:A
WESTERN COURAGE (1935) PR:A
WESTERN CYCLONE (1943) PR:A
WESTERN FRONTIER (1935) PR:A
WESTERN GOLD (1937) PR:A
WESTERN HERITAGE (1948) PR:A
WESTERN JAMBOREE (1938) PR:A
WESTERN JUSTICE (1935) PR:A
WESTERN LIMITED (1932) PR:A
WESTERN MAIL (1942) PR:A
WESTERN PACIFIC AGENT (1950) PR:A
WESTERN RENEGADES (1949) PR:A
WESTERN TRAILS (1938) PR:A
WESTERN UNION (1941) PR:A
WESTERNER, THE (1936) PR:A
WESTERNER, THE (1940) PR:A
WESTLAND CASE, THE (1937) PR:A
WESTLER (SEE: EAST OF THE WALL) (1986, W. Ger.)
WESTMINSTER PASSION PLAY – BEHOLD THE
   MAN, THE (1951, Brit.) PR:A
WESTWARD BOUND (1931) PR:A
WESTWARD BOUND (1944) PR:A
WESTWARD DESPERADO (1961, Jap.) PR:C
WESTWARD HO (1936) PR:A
WESTWARD HO (1942) PR:A
WESTWARD HO, THE WAGONS! (1956) PR:A
WESTWARD PASSAGE (1932) PR:A
WESTWARD THE WOMEN (1951) PR:A
WESTWARD TRAIL, THE (1948) PR:A
WESTWORLD (1973) PR:C
WET PARADE, THE (1932) PR:C
WETBACKS (1956) PR:A
WETHERBY (1985, Brit.) PR:O
WE'VE NEVER BEEN LICKED (1943) PR:A
WHALE OF A TALE, A (1977) PR:AA
WHALERS, THE (1942, Swed.) PR:A
WHALES OF AUGUST, THE (1987) PR:A-C
WHARF ANGEL, THE (1934) PR:A
WHAT! (1965, Fr./Brit./It.) PR:O
WHAT? (SEE: DIARY OF FORBIDDEN DREAMS)
   (1972, It./Fr./W. Ger.)
WHAT A BLONDE (1945) PR:A
WHAT A CARRY ON! (1949, Brit.) PR:A
WHAT A CARVE UP! (1962, Brit.) PR:A
WHAT A CHASSIS! (SEE: LA BELLE AMERICAINE)
   (1961, Fr.)
WHAT A CRAZY WORLD (1963, Brit.) PR:A
WHAT A LIFE (1939) PR:A
WHAT A MAN (1930) PR:A
WHAT A MAN! (1937, Brit.) PR:A
WHAT A MAN (SEE: NEVER GIVE A SUCKER AN
   EVEN BREAK) (1941)
WHAT A MAN! (1944) PR:A
WHAT A NIGHT! (1931, Brit.) PR:A
WHAT A WAY TO GO! (1964) PR:A-C
WHAT A WHOPPER! (1961, Brit.) PR:A
WHAT A WIDOW! (1930) PR:A
WHAT A WOMAN (SEE: THERE'S THAT WOMAN
   AGAIN) (1939)
WHAT A WOMAN! (1943) PR:A
WHAT A WOMAN! (SEE: BEAUTIFUL CHEAT, THE)
   (1946)
WHAT AM I BID? (1967) PR:A
WHAT BECAME OF JACK AND JILL? (1972, Brit.) PR:C-
   O
WHAT CHANGED CHARLEY FARTHING? (1976,
   Brit./Sp.) PR:C
WHAT COMES AROUND (1986) PR:C
WHAT DID YOU DO IN THE WAR, DADDY? (1966)
   PR:A-C
WHAT DO WE DO NOW? (1945, Brit.) PR:A
WHAT EVER HAPPENED TO AUNT ALICE? (1969) PR:C
WHAT EVERY WOMAN KNOWS (1934) PR:A
WHAT EVERY WOMAN WANTS (1954, Brit.) PR:A
WHAT EVERY WOMAN WANTS (1962, Brit.) PR:A
WHAT HAPPENED THEN? (1934, Brit.) PR:A
WHAT HAPPENED TO HARKNESS (1934, Brit.) PR:AA
WHAT LOLA WANTS (SEE: DAMN YANKEES) (1958)
WHAT MEN WANT (1930) PR:A
WHAT NEXT, CORPORAL HARGROVE? (1945) PR:A
WHAT! NO BEER? (1933) PR:A
WHAT PRICE BEAUTY? (SEE: FALSE FACES) (1932)
WHAT PRICE CRIME? (1935) PR:A
WHAT PRICE DECENCY? (1933) PR:O
WHAT PRICE GLORY? (1952) PR:C

WHAT PRICE HOLLYWOOD? (1932) PR:C
WHAT PRICE INNOCENCE? (1933) PR:A
WHAT PRICE MELODY? (SEE: LORD BYRON OF BROADWAY) (1930)
WHAT PRICE VENGEANCE? (1937) PR:A
WHAT SHALL IT PROFIT (SEE: HARD STEEL) (1941, Brit.)
WHAT THE BUTLER SAW (1950, Brit.) PR:A
WHAT THE PEEPER SAW (SEE: NIGHT HAIR CHILD) (1971)
WHAT WAITS BELOW (1986) PR:C
WHAT WIVES DON'T WANT (SEE: VIRTUOUS HUSBAND) (1931)
WHAT WOMEN DREAM (1933, Ger.) PR:A
WHAT WOULD YOU DO, CHUMS? (1939, Brit.) PR:A
WHAT WOULD YOU SAY TO SOME SPINACH (1976, Czech.) PR:A
WHAT YOU TAKE FOR GRANTED (1984) PR:O
WHAT'S IN IT FOR HARRY? (SEE: TARGET: HARRY) (1969)
WHATEVER HAPPENED TO BABY JANE? (1962) PR:C
WHATEVER IT TAKES (1986) PR:O
WHAT'S BUZZIN COUSIN? (1943) PR:A
WHAT'S COOKIN'? (1942) PR:A
WHAT'S GOOD FOR THE GOOSE (1969, Brit.) PR:O
WHAT'S NEW, PUSSYCAT? (1965, US/Fr.) PR:C
WHAT'S NEXT? (1975, Brit.) PR:AA
WHAT'S SO BAD ABOUT FEELING GOOD? (1968) PR:A
WHAT'S THE MATTER WITH HELEN? (1971) PR:O
WHAT'S THE TIME, MR. CLOCK? (1985, Hung.) PR:A
WHAT'S UP, DOC? (1972) PR:AA
WHAT'S UP FRONT (1964) PR:C
WHAT'S UP, TIGER LILY? (1966) PR:C
WHAT'S YOUR RACKET? (1934) PR:A
WHEEL OF ASHES (1970, Fr.) PR:C
WHEEL OF FATE (1953, Brit.) PR:A
WHEEL OF FORTUNE (SEE: MAN BETRAYED, A) (1941)
WHEEL OF LIFE, THE (1929) PR:A
WHEELER DEALERS, THE (1963) PR:A
WHEELS OF DESTINY (1934) PR:A
WHEELS OF FIRE (SEE: DESERT WARRIOR) (1985)
WHEELS OF TERROR (SEE: MISFIT BRIGADE, THE) (1988)
WHEN A FELLER NEEDS A FRIEND (1932) PR:A
WHEN A GIRL'S BEAUTIFUL (1947) PR:A
WHEN A MAN RIDES ALONE (1933) PR:A
WHEN A MAN SEES RED (1934) PR:A
WHEN A MAN'S A MAN (1935) PR:A
WHEN A STRANGER CALLS (1979) PR:O
WHEN A WOMAN ASCENDS THE STAIRS (1963, Jap.) PR:C
WHEN ANGELS DON'T FLY (SEE: AWAKENING, THE) (1958, It.)
WHEN BLONDE MEETS BLONDE (SEE: ANYBODY'S BLONDE) (1931)
WHEN DINOSAURS RULED THE EARTH (1971, Brit.) PR:A
WHEN EIGHT BELLS TOLL (1971, Brit.) PR:C
WHEN FATHER WAS AWAY ON BUSINESS (1985, Yugo.) PR:O
WHEN G-MEN STEP IN (1938) PR:A
WHEN GANGLAND STRIKES (1956) PR:A
WHEN GIRLS LEAVE HOME (SEE: MISSING GIRLS) (1936)
WHEN HARRY MET SALLY. . . (1989) PR:C
WHEN HELL BROKE LOOSE (1958) PR:A
WHEN I GROW UP (1951) PR:AA
WHEN IN ROME (1952) PR:A
WHEN JOHNNY COMES MARCHING HOME (1943) PR:A
WHEN KNIGHTHOOD WAS IN FLOWER (SEE: SWORD AND THE ROSE, THE) (1953)
WHEN KNIGHTS WERE BOLD (1942, Brit.) PR:A
WHEN LADIES MEET (1933) PR:A
WHEN LADIES MEET (1941) PR:A-C
WHEN LONDON SLEEPS (1932, Brit.) PR:A
WHEN LONDON SLEEPS (1934, Brit.) PR:A
WHEN LOVE IS YOUNG (1937) PR:A
WHEN LOVERS MEET (SEE: LOVER COME BACK) (1946)
WHEN MEN ARE BEASTS (SEE: WOMEN IN THE NIGHT) (1948)
WHEN MY BABY SMILES AT ME (1948) PR:A-C
WHEN NATURE CALLS (1985) PR:O
WHEN STRANGERS MARRY (1933) PR:A
WHEN STRANGERS MARRY (1944) PR:C
WHEN STRANGERS MEET (1934) PR:A
WHEN THE BOUGH BREAKS (1947, Brit.) PR:A
WHEN THE BOYS MEET THE GIRLS (1965) PR:A
WHEN THE CLOCK STRIKES (1961) PR:A
WHEN THE DALTONS RODE (1940) PR:A
WHEN THE DEVIL WAS WELL (1937, Brit.) PR:A
WHEN THE DOOR OPENED (SEE: ESCAPE) (1940)
WHEN THE GIRLS MEET THE BOYS (SEE: GIRL CRAZY) (1943)
WHEN THE GIRLS TAKE OVER (1962) PR:C

WHEN THE LEGENDS DIE (1972) PR:C
WHEN THE LIGHTS GO ON AGAIN (1944) PR:A
WHEN THE RAVEN FLIES (1985, Iceland/Swed.) PR:O
WHEN THE REDSKINS RODE (1951) PR:A
WHEN THE TREES WERE TALL (1965, USSR) PR:A
WHEN THE WHALES CAME (1989, Brit.) PR:AA
WHEN THE WIND BLOWS (1988, Brit.) PR:C
WHEN THIEF MEETS THIEF (1937, Brit.) PR:A
WHEN TIME RAN OUT (1980) PR:C
WHEN TOMORROW COMES (1939) PR:A
WHEN TOMORROW DIES (1966, Can.) PR:C
WHEN WE ARE MARRIED (1943, Brit.) PR:A
WHEN WE LOOK BACK (SEE: FRISCO WATERFRONT) (1935)
WHEN WERE YOU BORN? (1938) PR:A
WHEN WILLIE COMES MARCHING HOME (1950) PR:A
WHEN WOMEN HAD TAILS (1970, It.) PR:O
WHEN WOMEN HAD TAILS (1970, It.) PR:O
WHEN WORLDS COLLIDE (1951) PR:A
WHEN YOU COME HOME (1947, Brit.) PR:A
WHEN YOU COMIN' BACK, RED RYDER? (1979) PR:O
WHEN YOU'RE IN LOVE (1937) PR:A
WHEN YOU'RE SMILING (1950) PR:A
WHEN YOUTH CONSPIRES (SEE: OLD SWIMMIN' HOLE, THE) (1941)
WHEN'S YOUR BIRTHDAY? (1937) PR:AA
WHERE ANGELS GO. . . TROUBLE FOLLOWS (1968) PR:C
WHERE ARE THE CHILDREN? (1986) PR:O
WHERE ARE YOUR CHILDREN? (1943) PR:A
WHERE DANGER LIVES (1950) PR:A
WHERE DID YOU GET THAT GIRL? (1941) PR:A
WHERE DO WE GO FROM HERE? (1945) PR:AA
WHERE DOES IT HURT? (1972) PR:C-O
WHERE EAGLES DARE (1968, Brit.) PR:C
WHERE HAS POOR MICKEY GONE? (1964. Brit.) PR:A
WHERE IS MY CHILD? (1937) PR:A
WHERE IS PARSIFAL? (1984, Brit.) PR:C
WHERE IS THIS LADY? (1932, Brit.) PR:A
WHERE IT'S AT (1969) PR:O
WHERE LOVE HAS GONE (1964) PR:C
WHERE NO VULTURES FLY (SEE: IVORY HUNTER) (1952, Brit.)
WHERE SINNERS MEET (1934) PR:A
WHERE THE BOYS ARE (1960) PR:A-C
WHERE THE BOYS ARE '84 (1984) PR:O
WHERE THE BUFFALO ROAM (1938) PR:A
WHERE THE BUFFALO ROAM (1980) PR:O
WHERE THE BULLETS FLY (1966, Brit.) PR:A
WHERE THE GREEN ANTS DREAM (1984, W. Ger.) PR:O
WHERE THE HOT WIND BLOWS (1958. Fr./It.) PR:O
WHERE THE LILIES BLOOM (1974) PR:A
WHERE THE RED FERN GROWS (1974) PR:A
WHERE THE RIVER BENDS (SEE: BEND OF THE RIVER) (1952)
WHERE THE RIVER RUNS BLACK (1986) PR:A
WHERE THE SIDEWALK ENDS (1950) PR:C
WHERE THE SPIES ARE (1965, Brit.) PR:A
WHERE THE TRUTH LIES (1962, Fr.) PR:A-C
WHERE THE WEST BEGINS (1938) PR:A
WHERE THERE'S A WILL (1936, Brit.) PR:A
WHERE THERE'S A WILL (1937, Brit.) PR:A
WHERE THERE'S A WILL (1955, Brit.) PR:A
WHERE THERE'S LIFE (1947) PR:A
WHERE TRAILS DIVIDE (1937) PR:A
WHERE WERE YOU WHEN THE LIGHTS WENT OUT? (1968) PR:A-C
WHERE'S CHARLEY? (1952, Brit.) PR:AA
WHERE'S GEORGE? (SEE: HOPE OF HIS SIDE) (1935, Brit.)
WHERE'S JACK? (1969, Brit.) PR:A
WHERE'S PICONE? (1984, It.) PR:O
WHERE'S POPPA? (1970) PR:C-O
WHERE'S SALLY? (1936, Brit.) PR:A
WHERE'S THAT FIRE? (1939, Brit.) PR:A
WHEREVER SHE GOES (1953, Aus.) PR:A
WHEREVER YOU ARE (1988, Brit./Pol./W. Ger.) PR:O
WHICH WAY IS UP? (1977) PR:O
WHICH WAY TO THE FRONT? (1970) PR:A
WHICH WILL YOU HAVE? (SEE: NOW BARABBAS WAS A ROBBER) (1949, Brit.)
WHIFFS (1975) PR:A
WHILE I LIVE (1947, Brit.) PR:A
WHILE LONDON SLEEPS (SEE: WHEN LONDON SLEEPS) (1934, Brit.)
WHILE NEW YORK SLEEPS (SEE: NOW I'LL TELL) (1934)
WHILE NEW YORK SLEEPS (1938) PR:A
WHILE PARENTS SLEEP (1935, Brit.) PR:A
WHILE PARIS SLEEPS (1932) PR:A
WHILE PLUCKING THE DAISIES (SEE: PLEASE! MR. BALZAC) (1957, Fr.)
WHILE THE ATTORNEY IS ASLEEP (1945, Den.) PR:A
WHILE THE CITY SLEEPS (1956) PR:C
WHILE THE PATIENT SLEPT (1935) PR:A
WHILE THE SUN SHINES (1950, Brit.) PR:A
WHIP HAND, THE (1951) PR:A
WHIPLASH (1948) PR:A

WHIPPED, THE (1950) PR:A
WHIP'S WOMEN (1968) PR:O
WHIPSAW (1936) PR:A
WHIRLPOOL (1934) PR:A
WHIRLPOOL (1949) PR:A
WHIRLPOOL (1959, Brit.) PR:A
WHIRLPOOL OF FLESH (SEE: WHIRLPOOL OF WOMAN) (1966, Jap.)
WHIRLPOOL OF WOMAN (1966, Jap.) PR:O
WHIRLWIND (1951) PR:A
WHIRLWIND (1968, Jap.) PR:C
WHIRLWIND HORSEMAN (1938) PR:A
WHIRLWIND OF PARIS (1946, Fr.) PR:A
WHIRLWIND RAIDERS (1948) PR:A
WHISKY GALORE (SEE: TIGHT LITTLE ISLAND) (1949, Brit.)
WHISPERERS, THE (1967, Brit.) PR:C
WHISPERING CITY (1947, Can.) PR:A
WHISPERING DEATH (SEE: NIGHT OF THE ASKARI) (1976, South Africa/W. Ger.)
WHISPERING ENEMIES (1939) PR:A
WHISPERING FOOTSTEPS (1943) PR:A
WHISPERING GHOSTS (1942) PR:A
WHISPERING JOE (1969, Jap.) PR:O
WHISPERING SKULL, THE (1944) PR:A
WHISPERING SMITH (1948) PR:A
WHISPERING SMITH HITS LONDON (SEE: WHISPERING SMITH VERSUS SCOTLAND YARD) (1952, Brit.)
WHISPERING SMITH SPEAKS (1935) PR:A
WHISPERING SMITH VERSUS SCOTLAND YARD (1952, Brit.) PR:A
WHISPERING TONGUES (1934, Brit.) PR:A
WHISPERING WINDS (1929) PR:A
WHISTLE AT EATON FALLS (1951) PR:A
WHISTLE BLOWER, THE (1987, Brit.) PR:A
WHISTLE DOWN THE WIND (1961, Brit.) PR:A
WHISTLE STOP (1946) PR:A-C
WHISTLER, THE (1944) PR:A
WHISTLIN' DAN (1932) PR:A
WHISTLING BULLETS (1937) PR:A
WHISTLING HILLS (1951) PR:A
WHISTLING IN BROOKLYN (1943) PR:A
WHISTLING IN DIXIE (1942) PR:A
WHISTLING IN THE DARK (1933) PR:A
WHISTLING IN THE DARK (1941) PR:A
WHITE ANGEL, THE (1936) PR:A
WHITE BANNERS (1938) PR:A
WHITE BONDAGE (1937) PR:A
WHITE BUFFALO, THE (1977) PR:C-O
WHITE CAPTIVE (SEE: WHITE SAVAGE) (1943)
WHITE CARGO (1930, Brit.) PR:C
WHITE CARGO (1942) PR:C
WHITE CHRISTMAS (1954) PR:AA
WHITE CLIFFS OF DOVER, THE (1944) PR:A-C
WHITE COCKATOO, THE (1935) PR:A
WHITE CORRIDORS (1952, Brit.) PR:A
WHITE CRADLE INN (SEE: HIGH FURY) (1947, Brit.)
WHITE DAWN, THE (1974) PR:O
WHITE DEATH (1936, Aus.) PR:A
WHITE DEMON, THE (1932, Ger.) PR:C
WHITE DEVIL, THE (1948, It.) PR:C
WHITE DOG (1982) PR:O
WHITE EAGLE (1932) PR:A
WHITE ELEPHANT (1984, Brit.) PR:C
WHITE ENSIGN (1934, Brit.) PR:A
WHITE FACE (1933, Brit.) PR:A
WHITE FANG (1936) PR:A
WHITE FEATHER (1955) PR:A
WHITE FIRE (1953, Brit.) PR:A
WHITE GHOST (1988) PR:C
WHITE GODDESS (1953) PR:A
WHITE GORILLA (1947) PR:A
WHITE HEAT (1934) PR:O
WHITE HEAT (1949) PR:C
WHITE HORSE INN, THE (1959, W. Ger.) PR:A
WHITE HUNTER (1936) PR:A
WHITE HUNTER (1965) PR:A
WHITE HUNTRESS (1957, Brit.) PR:A
WHITE LEGION, THE (1936) PR:A
WHITE LIES (1935) PR:A
WHITE LIGHTNIN' ROAD (1967) PR:A
WHITE LIGHTNING (1953) PR:A
WHITE LIGHTNING (1973) PR:C
WHITE LILAC (1935, Brit.) PR:A
WHITE LINE, THE (1952, It.) PR:C
WHITE LINE FEVER (1975, Can.) PR:C
WHITE MAN, THE (SEE: SQUAW MAN, THE) (1931)
WHITE MISCHIEF (1988, Brit.) PR:O
WHITE NIGHTS (1961, It./Fr.) PR:O
WHITE NIGHTS (1985) PR:C
WHITE OF THE EYE (1988, Brit.) PR:O
WHITE ORCHID, THE (1954) PR:A
WHITE PARADE, THE (1934) PR:A
WHITE PONGO (1945) PR:AA
WHITE RAT (1972) PR:O
WHITE, RED, YELLOW, AND PINK (1966, It.) PR:C-O
WHITE ROSE OF HONG KONG (1965, Jap.) PR:O
WHITE SAVAGE (SEE: SOUTH OF TAHITI) (1941)

WHITE SAVAGE (1943) PR:A
WHITE SHADOWS IN THE SOUTH SEAS (1928) PR:A
WHITE SHEIK, THE (1952, Fr./It.) PR:C
WHITE SHOULDERS (1931) PR:A
WHITE SICKNESS, THE (SEE: SKELETON ON HORSE-
   BACK) (1940, Czech.)
WHITE SISTER, THE (1933) PR:A
WHITE SISTER (1973, It./Sp./Fr.) PR:O
WHITE SLAVE (1986, It.) PR:O
WHITE SLAVE SHIP (1962, Fr./It.) PR:C
WHITE SQUAW, THE (1956) PR:A
WHITE STALLION (1947) PR:A
WHITE TIE AND TAILS (1946) PR:A
WHITE TOWER, THE (1950) PR:A
WHITE TRAP, THE (1959, Brit.) PR:C
WHITE TRASH ON MOONSHINE MOUNTAIN (SEE:
   MOONSHINE MOUNTAIN) (1964)
WHITE UNICORN, THE (SEE: BAD SISTER) (1947,
   Brit.)
WHITE VOICES, THE (1964, Fr./It.) PR:O
WHITE WARRIOR, THE (1961, It./Yugo.) PR:C
WHITE WATER SUMMER (1987) PR:C
WHITE WITCH DOCTOR (1953) PR:A
WHITE WOMAN (1933) PR:C
WHITE ZOMBIE (1932) PR:O
WHO? (1975, Brit./W. Ger.) PR:C
WHO CAN KILL A CHILD (SEE: ISLAND OF THE
   DAMNED) (1976, Sp.)
WHO DARES WIN (SEE: FINAL OPTION, THE) (1983,
   Brit.)
WHO DONE IT? (1942) PR:A
WHO DONE IT? (1956, Brit.) PR:C
WHO FEARS THE DEVIL (1972) PR:A
WHO FRAMED ROGER RABBIT (1988) PR:A
WHO GOES NEXT? (1938, Brit.) PR:C
WHO GOES THERE? (SEE: PASSIONATE SENTRY,
   THE) (1952, Brit.)
WHO HAS SEEN THE WIND (1980, Can.) PR:A
WHO IS GUILTY? (1940, Brit.) PR:A
WHO IS HARRY KELLERMAN AND WHY IS HE SAY-
   ING THOSE TERRIBLE THINGS ABOUT ME? (1971)
   PR:C
WHO IS HOPE SCHUYLER? (1942) PR:A
WHO IS KILLING THE GREAT CHEFS OF EUROPE?
   (1978, US/W. Ger.) PR:C
WHO IS KILLING THE STUNTMEN? (SEE: STUNTS)
   (1977)
WHO KILLED AUNT MAGGIE? (1940) PR:A
WHO KILLED "DOC" ROBBIN? (1948) PR:AA
WHO KILLED FEN MARKHAM? (1937, Brit.) PR:A
WHO KILLED GAIL PRESTON? (1938) PR:A
WHO KILLED JESSIE? (1965, Czech.) PR:C
WHO KILLED JOHN SAVAGE? (1937, Brit.) PR:A
WHO KILLED MARY WHAT'SER NAME? (1971) PR:O
WHO KILLED TEDDY BEAR? (1965) PR:O
WHO KILLED THE CAT? (1966, Brit.) PR:A-C
WHO KILLED VAN LOON? (1984, Brit.) PR:A
WHO RIDES WITH KANE? (SEE: YOUNG BILLY
   YOUNG) (1969)
WHO SAYS I CAN'T RIDE A RAINBOW? (1971) PR:AA
WHO SLEW AUNTIE ROO? (1971, US/Brit.) PR:O
WHO STOLE MY WHEELS? (SEE: TOWING) (1978)
WHO WANTS TO KILL JESSIE? (SEE: WHO KILLED
   JESSIE?) (1965, Czech.)
WHO WAS MADDOX? (1964, Brit.) PR:A
WHO WAS THAT LADY? (1960) PR:A
WHO WOULD KILL A CHILD (SEE: ISLAND OF THE
   DAMNED) (1976, Sp.)
WHOEVER SLEW AUNTIE ROO? (SEE: WHO SLEW
   AUNTIE ROO?) (1971, US/Brit.)
WHOLE SHOOTIN' MATCH, THE (1979) PR:C
WHOLE TOWN'S TALKING, THE (1935) PR:A
WHOLE TRUTH, THE (1958, Brit.) PR:A
WHO'LL STOP THE RAIN? (1978) PR:C
WHOLLY MOSES (1980) PR:C
WHOM THE GODS DESTROY (1934) PR:A
WHOM THE GODS LOVE (SEE: MOZART) (1940, Brit.)
WHOOPEE (1930) PR:AA
WHOOPEE BOYS, THE (1986) PR:O
WHOOPING COUGH (1987, Hung.) PR:O
WHO'S AFRAID OF VIRGINIA WOOLF? (1966) PR:O
WHO'S BEEN SLEEPING IN MY BED? (1963) PR:C
WHO'S GOT THE ACTION? (1962) PR:A
WHO'S GOT THE BLACK BOX? (1970, Fr./Gr./It.) PR:O
WHO'S HARRY CRUMB? (1989) PR:C
WHO'S MINDING THE MINT? (1967) PR:A
WHO'S MINDING THE STORE? (1963) PR:A
WHO'S THAT GIRL (1987) PR:A
WHO'S THAT KNOCKING AT MY DOOR? (1968) PR:O
WHO'S YOUR FATHER? (1935, Brit.) PR:A
WHO'S YOUR LADY FRIEND? (1937, Brit.) PR:A
WHOSE LIFE IS IT ANYWAY? (1981) PR:C-O
WHY ANNA? (SEE: DIARY OF A SCHIZOPHRENIC
   GIRL) (1970, It.)
WHY BOTHER TO KNOCK (1964, Brit.) PR:O
WHY BRING THAT UP? (1929) PR:A
WHY CHANGE YOUR HUSBAND? (SEE: GOLD DUST
   GERTIE) (1931)

WHY DOES HERR R. RUN AMOK? (1977, W. Ger.) PR:O
WHY GIRLS LEAVE HOME (1945) PR:C
WHY LEAVE HOME? (1929) PR:A
WHY MUST I DIE? (1960) PR:C
WHY NOT? (SEE: POURQUOI PAS) (1979, Fr.)
WHY PICK ON ME? (1937, Brit.) PR:A
WHY ROCK THE BOAT? (1974, Can.) PR:O
WHY RUSSIANS ARE REVOLTING (1970) PR:O
WHY SAILORS LEAVE HOME (1930, Brit.) PR:A
WHY SAPS LEAVE HOME (1932, Brit.) PR:A
WHY SHOOT THE TEACHER (1977, Can.) PR:C
WHY SPY? (SEE: MAN CALLED DAGGER, A) (1968)
WHY WOULD ANYONE WANT TO KILL A NICE GIRL
   LIKE YOU? (SEE: TASTE OF EXCITEMENT) (1969,
   Brit.)
WHY WOULD I LIE? (1980) PR:C
WICHITA (1955) PR:A
WICKED (1931) PR:A
WICKED AS THEY COME (SEE: PORTRAIT IN
   SMOKE) (1957, Brit.)
WICKED DIE SLOW, THE (1968) PR:O
WICKED DREAMS OF PAULA SCHULTZ, THE (1968)
   PR:C
WICKED GO TO HELL, THE (1961, Fr.) PR:O
WICKED LADY, THE (1946, Brit.) PR:A
WICKED LADY, THE (1983, Brit.) PR:O
WICKED STEPMOTHER (1989) PR:A
WICKED, WICKED (1973) PR:O
WICKED WIFE (1955, Brit.) PR:O
WICKED WOMAN, A (1934) PR:C
WICKED WOMAN (1953) PR:O
WICKER MAN, THE (1974, Brit.) PR:O
WICKHAM MYSTERY, THE (1931, Brit.) PR:A
WIDE BOY (1952, Brit.) PR:A
WIDE OPEN (1930) PR:A
WIDE OPEN FACES (1938) PR:A
WIDE OPEN TOWN (1941) PR:A
WIDOW AND THE GIGOLO, THE (SEE: ROMAN
   SPRING OF MRS. STONE, THE) (1961)
WIDOW FROM CHICAGO, THE (1930) PR:A-C
WIDOW FROM MONTE CARLO, THE (1936) PR:A
WIDOW IN SCARLET (1932) PR:A
WIDOW IS WILLING, THE (SEE: VIOLENT SUMMER)
   (1961, Fr./It.)
WIDOW'S MIGHT (1934, Brit.) PR:A
WIDOWS' NEST (1977, US/Sp.) PR:O
WIELKA WIELKSZA NAJWIELKSZA (SEE: GREAT
   BIG WORLD AND LITTLE CHILDREN, THE) (1962,
   Pol.)
WIEN, DU STADT DER LIEDER (SEE: VIENNA, CITY
   OF SONGS) (1931, Ger.)
WIEN TANZT (SEE: VIENNA WALTZES) (1961, Aust.)
WIFE, DOCTOR AND NURSE (1937) PR:A
WIFE, HUSBAND AND FRIEND (1939) PR:A
WIFE OF GENERAL LING (1938, Brit.) PR:A
WIFE OF MONTE CRISTO, THE (1946) PR:A
WIFE OR TWO, A (1935, Brit.) PR:A
WIFE SWAPPERS, THE (SEE: SWAPPERS, THE) (1970,
   Brit.)
WIFE TAKES A FLYER, THE (1942) PR:A
WIFE VS. SECRETARY (1936) PR:A
WIFE WANTED (1946) PR:A
WIFE-MISTRESS (1977, It.) PR:O
WIFE'S FAMILY, THE (SEE: MY WIFE'S FAMILY)
   (1932, Brit.)
WILBY CONSPIRACY, THE (1975, Brit.) PR:C
WILD AFFAIR, THE (1966, Brit.) PR:O
WILD AND THE INNOCENT, THE (1959) PR:C
WILD AND THE SWEET, THE (SEE: LOVIN' MOLLY)
   (1974)
WILD AND THE WILLING, THE (SEE: YOUNG AND
   WILLING) (1962, Brit.)
WILD AND WILLING (SEE: RAT FINK) (1965)
WILD AND WONDERFUL (1964) PR:A
WILD AND WOOLLY (1937) PR:A
WILD ANGELS, THE (1966) PR:O
WILD ARCTIC (SEE: SAVAGE WILD, THE) (1970)
WILD BEAUTY (1946) PR:A
WILD BILL HICKOK RIDES (1942) PR:A
WILD BLUE YONDER, THE (1952) PR:A
WILD BOY (1934, Brit.) PR:A
WILD BOYS OF THE ROAD (1933) PR:A-C
WILD BRIAN KENT (1936) PR:A
WILD BUNCH, THE (1969) PR:O
WILD CARGO (SEE: WHITE SLAVE SHIP) (1952, Fr./It.)
WILD CHILD, THE (1970, Fr.) PR:C-O
WILD COMPANY (1930) PR:A
WILD COUNTRY (1947) PR:A
WILD COUNTRY, THE (1971) PR:AA
WILD DAKOTAS, THE (1956) PR:A
WILD DUCK, THE (1977, Aust./W. Ger.) PR:A
WILD DUCK, THE (1983, Aus.) PR:C
WILD EYE, THE (1968, It.) PR:O
WILD FOR KICKS (SEE: BEAT GIRL) (1962, Brit.)
WILD, FREE AND HUNGRY (1970) PR:C
WILD FRONTIER, THE (1947) PR:A
WILD GAME (SEE: JAIL BAIT) (1977, W. Ger.)
WILD GEESE, THE (1978, Brit.) PR:O

WILD GEESE II (1985, Brit.) PR:O
WILD GEESE CALLING (1941) PR:A-C
WILD GIRL (1932) PR:A
WILD GOLD (1934) PR:A
WILD GUITAR (1962) PR:A
WILD GYPSIES (1969) PR:O
WILD HARVEST (1947) PR:A
WILD HARVEST (1962) PR:O
WILD HEART, THE (1952, Brit.) PR:C
WILD HERITAGE (1958) PR:A
WILD HORSE (1931) PR:A
WILD HORSE AMBUSH (1952) PR:A
WILD HORSE CANYON (1939) PR:A
WILD HORSE HANK (1979, Can.) PR:A
WILD HORSE MESA (1932) PR:A
WILD HORSE MESA (1947) PR:A
WILD HORSE PHANTOM (1944) PR:A
WILD HORSE RODEO (1938) PR:A
WILD HORSE ROUND-UP (1937) PR:A
WILD HORSE RUSTLERS (1943) PR:A
WILD HORSE STAMPEDE (1943) PR:A
WILD HORSE VALLEY (1940) PR:A
WILD HORSES (1984, New Zealand) PR:C
WILD IN THE COUNTRY (1961) PR:A
WILD IN THE SKY (SEE: BLACK JACK) (1973)
WILD IN THE STREETS (1968) PR:C
WILD INNOCENCE (1937, Aus.) PR:A
WILD IS MY LOVE (1963) PR:O
WILD IS THE WIND (1957) PR:A
WILD JUNGLE CAPTIVE (SEE: JUNGLE CAPTIVE)
   (1945)
WILD LIFE, THE (1984) PR:C-O
WILD LOVE-MAKERS (SEE: WEIRD LOVE MAKERS,
   THE) (1963, Jap.)
WILD MAN OF BORNEO, THE (1941) PR:A
WILD MC CULLOCHS, THE (1975) PR:O
WILD MONEY (1937) PR:A
WILD MUSTANG (1935) PR:A
WILD 90 (1968) PR:O
WILD NORTH, THE (1952) PR:A
WILD ON THE BEACH (1965) PR:A
WILD ONE, THE (1953) PR:C
WILD ONES ON WHEELS (1967) PR:C-O
WILD PACK, THE (1972) PR:O
WILD PAIR, THE (1987) PR:O
WILD PARTY, THE (1929) PR:A
WILD PARTY, THE (1956) PR:C-O
WILD PARTY, THE (1975) PR:O
WILD RACERS, THE (1968) PR:A-C
WILD REBELS, THE (1967) PR:O
WILD RIDE, THE (1960) PR:C
WILD RIDERS (1971) PR:O
WILD RIVER (1960) PR:A-C
WILD ROVERS (1971) PR:C-O
WILD SCENE, THE (1970) PR:O
WILD SEASON (1968, South Africa) PR:A
WILD SEED (1965) PR:A
WILD SIDE, THE (SEE: SUBURBIA) (1984)
WILD STALLION (1952) PR:A
WILD STRAWBERRIES (1957, Swed.) PR:O
WILD THING (1987, US/Can.) PR:C-O
WILD WEED (1949) PR:A-C
WILD WEST (1946) PR:A
WILD WEST WHOOPEE (1931) PR:A
WILD WESTERNERS, THE (1962) PR:A
WILD WHEELS (1969) PR:O
WILD, WILD PLANET, THE (1967, It.) PR:A-C
WILD, WILD WINTER (1966) PR:A
WILD, WILD WOMEN, THE (SEE: AND THE WILD,
   WILD WOMEN) (1961, It.)
WILD WOMEN OF WONGO, THE (1959) PR:C
WILD WORLD OF BATWOMAN, THE (1966) PR:C
WILD YOUTH (1961) PR:C
WILDCAT (1942) PR:A
WILDCAT (SEE: GREAT SCOUT AND CATHOUSE
   THURSDAY, THE) (1976)
WILDCAT BUS (1940) PR:A
WILDCAT OF TUCSON (1941) PR:A
WILDCAT TROOPER (1936) PR:A
WILDCATS (1986) PR:C-O
WILDCATS OF ST. TRINIAN'S, THE (1980, Brit.) PR:A
WILDCATTER, THE (1937) PR:A
WILDE SEISON (SEE: WILD SEASON) (1968, South Af-
   rica)
WILDERNESS FAMILY, PART 2 (SEE: FURTHER AD-
   VENTURES OF THE WILDERNESS FAMILY — PART
   TWO) (1978)
WILDERNESS MAIL (1935) PR:A
WILDFIRE (1945) PR:A
WILDROSE (1985) PR:C
WILDWECHSEL (SEE: JAIL BAIT) (1977, W. Ger.)
WILL ANY GENTLEMAN? (1955, Brit.) PR:A
WILL JAMES' SAND (SEE: SAND) (1949)
WILL PENNY (1968) PR:A-C
WILL SUCCESS SPOIL ROCK HUNTER? (1957) PR:A-C
WILL TOMORROW EVER COME (SEE: THAT'S MY
   MAN) (1947)
WILLARD (1971) PR:O

WILLIAM COMES TO TOWN (1948, Brit.) PR:A
WILLIAM FOX MOVIETONE FOLLIES OF 1929 (SEE:
    FOX MOVIETONE FOLLIES) (1929)
WILLIE AND JOE BACK AT THE FRONT (SEE: BACK
    AT THE FRONT) (1952)
WILLIE AND PHIL (1980) PR:O
WILLIE DYNAMITE (1973) PR:O
WILLOW (1988) PR:AA
WILLS AND BURKE (1985, Aus.) PR:C
WILLY (1963, US/W. Ger.) PR:A
WILLY MCBEAN AND HIS MAGIC MACHINE (1965,
    US/Jap.) PR:AA
WILLY MILLY (SEE: SOMETHING SPECIAL!) (1987)
WILLY WONKA AND THE CHOCOLATE FACTORY
    (1971) PR:A
WILSON (1944) PR:A
WIN, PLACE AND SHOW (SEE: CRAZY OVER
    HORSES) (1951)
WIN, PLACE, OR STEAL (1975) PR:A
WINCHESTER '73 (1950) PR:C
WIND, THE (1928) PR:C
WIND, THE (1987) PR:O
WIND ACROSS THE EVERGLADES (1958) PR:C
WIND AND THE LION, THE (1975) PR:C
WIND BLOWETH WHERE IT LISTETH, THE (SEE:
    MAN ESCAPED, A) (1957, FR.)
WIND CANNOT READ, THE (1958, Brit.) PR:A
WIND FROM THE EAST (1970, Fr./It./W. Ger.) PR:C
WIND OF CHANGE, THE (1961, Brit.) PR:A
WINDBAG THE SAILOR (1937, Brit.) PR:A
WINDFALL (1935, Brit.) PR:A
WINDFALL (1955, Brit.) PR:A
WINDFLOWERS (1968) PR:C
WINDJAMMER, THE (1931, Brit.) PR:A
WINDJAMMER (1937) PR:A
WINDMILL, THE (1937, Brit.) PR:A
WINDOM'S WAY (1958, Brit.) PR:A-C
WINDOW, THE (1949) PR:C
WINDOW IN LONDON, A (SEE: LADY IN DISTRESS)
    (1942, Brit.)
WINDOW TO THE SKY, A (SEE: OTHER SIDE OF THE
    MOUNTAIN, THE) (1975)
WINDOWS (1980) PR:O
WINDOWS OF TIME, THE (1969, Hung.) PR:A
WINDS OF THE WASTELAND (1936) PR:A
WINDSPLITTER, THE (1971) PR:C
WINDWALKER (1980) PR:A
WINDY CITY (1984) PR:C
WINE AND THE MUSIC, THE (SEE: PIECES OF
    DREAMS) (1970)
WINE, WOMEN AND HORSES (1937) PR:A
WINE, WOMEN, AND SONG (1934) PR:A
WING AND A PRAYER (1944) PR:A
WINGED DEVILS (SEE: ABOVE THE CLOUDS) (1934)
WINGED SERPENT (SEE: STARSHIP INVASIONS)
    (1978, Can.)
WINGED SERPENT, THE (SEE: Q) (1982)
WINGED VICTORY (1944) PR:A
WINGS AND THE WOMAN (1942, Brit.) PR:A
WINGS FOR THE EAGLE (1942) PR:A
WINGS IN THE DARK (1935) PR:A
WINGS OF ADVENTURE (1930) PR:A
WINGS OF CHANCE (1961, Can.) PR:A
WINGS OF DANGER (SEE: DEAD ON COURSE) (1952,
    Brit.)
WINGS OF DESIRE (1987, Fr./W. Ger.) PR:C
WINGS OF EAGLES, THE (1957) PR:A
WINGS OF MYSTERY (1963, Brit.) PR:AA
WINGS OF THE HAWK (1953) PR:A
WINGS OF THE MORNING (1937, Brit.) PR:A
WINGS OF THE NAVY (1939) PR:A
WINGS OF VICTORY (1941, USSR) PR:A
WINGS OVER AFRICA (1939) PR:A
WINGS OVER HONOLULU (1937) PR:A
WINGS OVER THE PACIFIC (1943) PR:A
WINGS OVER WYOMING (SEE: HOLLYWOOD COW-
    BOY) (1937)
WINK OF AN EYE (1958) PR:A
WINNER, THE (SEE: PIT STOP) (1969)
WINNER TAKE ALL (1932) PR:A
WINNER TAKE ALL (1939) PR:A
WINNER TAKE ALL (SEE: JOE PALOOKA IN WINNER
    TAKE ALL) (1948)
WINNERS, THE (SEE: MY WAY) (1974, South Africa)
WINNER'S CIRCLE, THE (1948) PR:A
WINNERS TAKE ALL (1988, Brit.) PR:A-C
WINNETOU, PART I (SEE: APACHE GOLD) (1965,
    Fr./It./W. Ger./Yugo.)
WINNETOU, PART II (SEE: LAST OF THE RENE-
    GADES) (1966, Fr./It./W. Ger./Yugo.)
WINNETOU, PART III (SEE: DESPERADO TRAIL,
    THE) (1967, Fr./It./Yugo./W. Ger.)
WINNETOU UND SEIN FREUND (SEE: THUNDER AT
    THE BORDER) (1966, Fr./It./Yugo./W. Ger.)
WINNING (1969) PR:A-C
WINNING OF THE WEST (1953) PR:A
WINNING POSITION (SEE: NOBODY'S PERFECT)
    (1968)

WINNING TEAM, THE (1952) PR:A
WINNING TICKET, THE (1935) PR:A
WINNING WAY, THE (SEE: ALL-AMERICAN, THE)
    (1953)
WINSLOW BOY, THE (1950, Brit.) PR:A
WINSTANLEY (1979, Brit.) PR:C
WINSTON AFFAIR, THE (SEE: MAN IN THE MIDDLE)
    (1964, US/Brit.)
WINTER A-GO-GO (1965) PR:A
WINTER CARNIVAL (1939) PR:A
WINTER FLIGHT (1984, Brit.) PR:C
WINTER KEPT US WARM (1968, Can.) PR:C
WINTER KILLS (1979) PR:O
WINTER LIGHT, THE (1962, Swed.) PR:C
WINTER MEETING (1948) PR:A
WINTER OF OUR DREAMS (1982, Aus.) PR:O
WINTER PEOPLE (1989) PR:C
WINTER RATES (SEE: OUT OF SEASON) (1975, Brit.)
WINTER WAR, THE (SEE: TALVISOTA) (1989, Fin.)
WINTER WIND (1970, Fr./Hung.) PR:C
WINTER WONDERLAND (1947) PR:A
WINTERHAWK (1976) PR:C
WINTER'S TALE, THE (1968, Brit.) PR:A
WINTERSET (1936) PR:A-C
WINTERTIME (1943) PR:A
WIR BRAUCHEN KEIN GELD (SEE: HIS MAJESTY,
    KING BALLYHOO!) (1931, Ger.)
WIRED (1989) PR:C
WIRED TO KILL (1986) PR:O
WIRETAPPERS (1956) PR:A
WISDOM (1986) PR:O
WISE BLOOD (1979, US/W. Ger.) PR:O
WISE GIRL (1937) PR:A
WISE GIRLS (1930) PR:A
WISE GUYS (1937, Brit.) PR:A
WISE GUYS (1969, Fr./It.) PR:A
WISE GUYS (1986) PR:C-O
WISER AGE, THE (1962, Jap.) PR:C
WISER SEX, THE (1932) PR:A
WISH YOU WERE HERE (1987, Brit.) PR:C-O
WISHBONE, THE (1933, Brit.) PR:A
WISHBONE CUTTER (1978) PR:C
WISHING MACHINE (1971, Czech./Fr.) PR:AA
WISTFUL WIDOW, THE (SEE: WISTFUL WIDOW OF
    WAGON GAP, THE) (1947)
WISTFUL WIDOW OF WAGON GAP, THE (1947) PR:A
WITCH, THE (1969, It.) PR:C
WITCH BENEATH THE SEA, THE (SEE: MARIZINIA)
    (1962, US/Braz.)
WITCH DOCTOR (SEE: KISENGA, MAN OF AFRICA)
    (1952, Brit.)
WITCH WITHOUT A BROOM, A (1967, US/Sp.) PR:C
WITCH, THE (SEE: SUPERSTITION) (1985)
WITCHBOARD (1987) PR:O
WITCHCRAFT (1964, Brit.) PR:A
WITCHES, THE (SEE: DEVIL'S OWN, THE) (1967, Brit.)
WITCHES, THE (1969, Fr./It.) PR:C
WITCHES CURSE, THE (SEE: WITCH'S CURSE, THE)
    (1963, It.)
WITCHES OF EASTWICK, THE (1987) PR:O
WITCHES — VIOLATED AND TORTURED TO DEATH
    (SEE: MARK OF THE DEVIL II) (1975, Brit./W. Ger.)
WITCHFINDER GENERAL (SEE: CONQUEROR
    WORM, THE) (1968, Brit.)
WITCHFIRE (1986) PR:O
WITCHING, THE (SEE: NECROMANCY) (1972)
WITCHING HOUR, THE (1934) PR:A
WITCHMAKER, THE (1969) PR:O
WITCH'S CURSE, THE (1963, It.) PR:A
WITCH'S MIRROR, THE (1960, Mex.) PR:C
WITH A SMILE (1939, Fr.) PR:A
WITH A SONG IN MY HEART (1952) PR:A
WITH FIRE AND SWORD (SEE: INVASION 1700)
    (1965, Fr./It./Yugo.)
WITH GUNILLA MONDAY EVENING AND TUESDAY
    (SEE: GUILT) (1967, Swed.)
WITH JOYOUS HEART (SEE: TWO WEEKS IN SEP-
    TEMBER) (1967, Fr./Brit.)
WITH LOVE AND KISSES (1937) PR:A
WITH LOVE AND TENDERNESS (1978, Bulgaria) PR:A
WITH SIX YOU GET EGGROLL (1968) PR:A
WITHIN THE LAW (SEE: PAID) (1930)
WITHIN THE LAW (1939) PR:A
WITHIN THESE WALLS (1945) PR:A
WITHNAIL AND I (1987, Brit.) PR:O
WITHOUT A CLUE (1988, Brit.) PR:A-C
WITHOUT A HOME (1939, Pol.) PR:A
WITHOUT A TRACE (SEE: WITNESS, THE) (1982,
    Hung.)
WITHOUT A TRACE (1983) PR:A
WITHOUT APPARENT MOTIVE (1972, Fr.) PR:O
WITHOUT CHILDREN (SEE: PENTHOUSE PARTY)
    (1936)
WITHOUT EACH OTHER (1962) PR:A
WITHOUT HONOR (1949) PR:A
WITHOUT HONORS (1932) PR:A
WITHOUT LOVE (1945) PR:A
WITHOUT ORDERS (1936) PR:A

WITHOUT PITY (1949, It.) PR:C
WITHOUT REGRET (1935) PR:A
WITHOUT RESERVATIONS (1946) PR:A
WITHOUT RISK (SEE: PECOS RIVER) (1951)
WITHOUT WARNING (1952) PR:C
WITHOUT WARNING (1980) PR:O
WITHOUT YOU (1934, Brit.) PR:A
WITNESS, THE (1959, Brit.) PR:AA
WITNESS, THE (1982, Hung.) PR:C
WITNESS (1985) PR:C-O
WITNESS CHAIR, THE (1936) PR:A
WITNESS FOR THE PROSECUTION (1957) PR:A
WITNESS IN THE DARK (1959, Brit.) PR:A
WITNESS OUT OF HELL (1967, Yugo./W. Ger.) PR:O
WITNESS TO MURDER (1954) PR:C
WITNESS VANISHES, THE (1939) PR:A
WIT'S END (SEE: G.I. EXECUTIONER, THE) (1985)
WIVES AND LOVERS (1963) PR:A
WIVES BEWARE (1933, Brit.) PR:A
WIVES NEVER KNOW (1936) PR:A
WIVES — TEN YEARS AFTER (1985, Norway) PR:O
WIVES UNDER SUSPICION (1938) PR:A
WIZ, THE (1978) PR:C
WIZARD, THE (1989) PR:A
WIZARD OF BAGHDAD, THE (1960) PR:A
WIZARD OF GORE, THE (1970) PR:O
WIZARD OF LONELINESS, THE (1988) PR:C
WIZARD OF MARS, THE (1964) PR:A
WIZARD OF OZ, THE (1939) PR:AA
WIZARDS (1977) PR:C
WIZARDS OF THE LOST KINGDOM (1985, US/Arg.)
    PR:A
WO DIE GRUNEN AMEISEN TRAUMEN (SEE:
    WHERE THE GREEN ANTS DREAM) (1984, W. Ger.)
WOJNA SWAITOW — NASTEPNE STULECIE (SEE:
    WAR OF THE WORLDS — NEXT CENTURY, THE)
    (1981, Pol.)
WOLF AT THE DOOR, THE (1986, Fr./Den.) PR:C-O
WOLF CALL (1939) PR:A
WOLF DOG (1958, Can.) PR:AA
WOLF HUNTERS, THE (1949) PR:A
WOLF LARSEN (1958) PR:A
WOLF LARSEN (1978, It.) PR:A
WOLF MAN, THE (1941) PR:C
WOLF OF NEW YORK (1940) PR:A
WOLF OF WALL STREET, THE (1929) PR:C
WOLF SONG (1929) PR:A-C
WOLF'S CLOTHING (1936, Brit.) PR:A
WOLF'S HOLE (1986, Czech.) PR:C
WOLFEN (1981) PR:O
WOLFMAN (1979) PR:O
WOLFPACK (SEE: MC KENZIE BREAK, THE) (1970,
    Brit.)
WOLFPEN PRINCIPLE, THE (1974, Can.) PR:AA
WOLVES (1930, Brit.) PR:A
WOLVES OF THE RANGE (1943) PR:A
WOLVES OF THE SEA (1938) PR:A
WOLVES OF THE UNDERWORLD (1935, Brit.) PR:A
WOMAN ACCUSED, THE (1933) PR:A-C
WOMAN AGAINST THE WORLD (1938) PR:A
WOMAN AGAINST WOMAN (1938) PR:A
WOMAN ALONE, A (SEE: TWO WHO DARED) (1937,
    Brit.)
WOMAN AND THE HUNTER, THE (1957) PR:A
WOMAN AND THE PUPPET, THE (SEE: FEMALE,
    THE) (1960, Fr.)
WOMAN AT HER WINDOW, A (1978, Fr./It./W. Ger.)
    PR:O
WOMAN BETWEEN, THE (1931) PR:C
WOMAN BETWEEN, THE (SEE: WOMAN DECIDES,
    THE) (1932, Brit.)
WOMAN BETWEEN, THE (SEE: WOMAN I LOVE,
    THE) (1937)
WOMAN CHASES MAN (1937) PR:A
WOMAN COMMANDS, A (1932) PR:A
WOMAN DECIDES, THE (1932, Brit.) PR:A
WOMAN DESTROYED, A (SEE: SMASH-UP, THE
    STORY OF A WOMAN) (1947)
WOMAN DOCTOR (1939) PR:A
WOMAN EATER, THE (1959, Brit.) PR:C
WOMAN FLAMBEE, A (SEE: WOMAN IN FLAMES, A)
    (1983, W. Ger.)
WOMAN FOR CHARLEY, A (SEE: COCKEYED COW-
    BOYS OF CALICO COUNTY) (1970)
WOMAN FOR JOE, THE (1955, Brit.) PR:A
WOMAN FROM HEADQUARTERS (1950) PR:A
WOMAN FROM MONTE CARLO, THE (1932) PR:A
WOMAN FROM TANGIER, THE (1948) PR:A
WOMAN HATER (1949, Brit.) PR:A
WOMAN HE SCORNED, THE (SEE: WAY OF LOST
    SOULS, THE) (1930, Brit.)
WOMAN HUNGRY (1931) PR:C
WOMAN HUNT (1962) PR:C
WOMAN HUNT, THE (1975, US/Phil.) PR:O
WOMAN I LOVE, THE (1937) PR:A
WOMAN I STOLE, THE (1933) PR:A
WOMAN IN A DRESSING GOWN (1957, Brit.) PR:A

WOMAN IN BONDAGE (SEE: WOMAN IN CHAINS) (1932, Brit.)
WOMAN IN BROWN (SEE: VICIOUS CIRCLE, THE) (1948)
WOMAN IN CHAINS (1932, Brit.) PR:A
WOMAN IN COMMAND, THE (1934, Brit.) PR:A
WOMAN IN DISTRESS (1937) PR:A
WOMAN IN FLAMES, A (1983, W. Ger.) PR:O
WOMAN IN GREEN, THE (1945) PR:C
WOMAN IN HER THIRTIES, A (SEE: SIDE STREETS) (1934)
WOMAN IN HIDING (1949) PR:A-C
WOMAN IN HIDING (1953, Brit.) PR:A
WOMAN IN HIS HOUSE, THE (SEE: ANIMAL KINGDOM, THE) (1932)
WOMAN IN QUESTION, THE (SEE: FIVE ANGLES ON MURDER) (1950, Brit.)
WOMAN IN RED, THE (1935) PR:A
WOMAN IN RED, THE (1984) PR:C
WOMAN IN ROOM 13, THE (1932) PR:A
WOMAN IN THE CASE (SEE: HEADLINE WOMAN, THE) (1935)
WOMAN IN THE CASE, THE (SEE: ALLOTMENT WIVES) (1945)
WOMAN IN THE DARK (1934) PR:A
WOMAN IN THE DARK (1952) PR:A
WOMAN IN THE DUNES (1964, Jap.) PR:O
WOMAN IN THE HALL, THE (1949, Brit.) PR:A
WOMAN IN THE WINDOW, THE (1945) PR:C
WOMAN IN WHITE, THE (1948) PR:C
WOMAN INSIDE, THE (1981) PR:O
WOMAN IS A WOMAN, A (1961, Fr./It.) PR:A
WOMAN IS THE JUDGE, A (1939) PR:A
WOMAN NEXT DOOR, THE (1981, Fr.) PR:O
WOMAN OBSESSED (1959) PR:A-C
WOMAN OBSESSED, A (1989) PR:O
WOMAN OF ANTWERP (SEE: DEDEE) (1949, Fr.)
WOMAN OF DARKNESS (1968, Swed.) PR:O
WOMAN OF DISTINCTION, A (1950) PR:A
WOMAN OF DOLWYN (SEE: LAST DAYS OF DOLWYN, THE) (1949, Brit.)
WOMAN OF EXPERIENCE, A (1931) PR:A
WOMAN OF MYSTERY, A (1957, Brit.) PR:A
WOMAN OF ROME (1956, It.) PR:O
WOMAN OF SIN (1961, Fr.) PR:A
WOMAN OF STRAW (1964, Brit.) PR:C
WOMAN OF SUMMER (SEE: STRIPPER, THE) (1963)
WOMAN OF THE DUNES (SEE: WOMAN IN THE DUNES) (1964, Jap.)
WOMAN OF THE NORTH COUNTRY (1952) PR:A
WOMAN OF THE RIVER (1954, Fr./It.) PR:O
WOMAN OF THE TOWN, THE (1944) PR:A
WOMAN OF THE WORLD, A (SEE: OUTCAST LADY) (1934)
WOMAN OF THE YEAR (1942) PR:AA
WOMAN ON FIRE, A (1970, It.) PR:O
WOMAN ON PIER 13, THE (1950) PR:A
WOMAN ON THE BEACH, THE (1947) PR:A
WOMAN ON THE RUN (1950) PR:A
WOMAN POSSESSED, A (1958, Brit.) PR:A
WOMAN RACKET, THE (1930) PR:A
WOMAN REBELS, A (1936) PR:A-C
WOMAN TAMER (SEE: SHE COULDN'T TAKE IT) (1935)
WOMAN THEY ALMOST LYNCHED, THE (1953) PR:A
WOMAN TIMES SEVEN (1967, US/Fr./It.) PR:C-O
WOMAN TO WOMAN (1929, Brit.) PR:A
WOMAN TO WOMAN (1946, Brit.) PR:A
WOMAN TRAP (1929) PR:A
WOMAN TRAP (1936) PR:A
WOMAN UNAFRAID (1934) PR:A
WOMAN UNDER THE INFLUENCE, A (1974) PR:C
WOMAN WHO CAME BACK (1945) PR:A
WOMAN WHO WOULDN'T DIE, THE (1965, Brit.) PR:A
WOMAN-WISE (1937) PR:A
WOMAN WITH A WHIP (SEE: FORTY GUNS) (1957)
WOMAN WITH NO NAME, THE (SEE: HER PANELLED DOOR) (1951, Brit.)
WOMAN WITH RED BOOTS, THE (1977, Fr./Sp.) PR:O
WOMAN WITHOUT A FACE (SEE: MISTER BUDDWING) (1966)
WOMAN WITHOUT CAMELLIAS, THE (SEE: LADY WITHOUT CAMELIAS) (1953, It.)
WOMAN WITHOUT LOVE, A (1951, Mex.) PR:C
WOMANHOOD (1934, Brit.) PR:A
WOMANLIGHT (1979, Fr./It./W. Ger.) PR:C
WOMAN'S ANGLE, THE (1954, Brit.) PR:A
WOMAN'S DEVOTION, A (1956) PR:A
WOMAN'S FACE, A (1939, Swed.) PR:A
WOMAN'S FACE, A (1941) PR:A-C
WOMAN'S LIFE, A (1964, Jap.) PR:A
WOMAN'S PLACE, A (SEE: WISER AGE, THE) (1962, Jap.)
WOMAN'S REVENGE, A (SEE: MAN FROM SUNDOWN, THE) (1939)
WOMAN'S SECRET, A (1949) PR:A
WOMAN'S TEMPTATION, A (1959, Brit.) PR:A

WOMAN'S VENGEANCE, A (SEE: MAN FROM SUNDOWN, THE) (1939)
WOMAN'S VENGEANCE, A (1947) PR:A
WOMAN'S WORLD (1954) PR:A-C
WOMBLING FREE (1977, Brit.) PR:AA
WOMEN, THE (1939) PR:C
WOMEN, THE (SEE: VIXENS, THE) (1969)
WOMEN AND BLOODY TERROR (1970) PR:O
WOMEN AND WAR (1965, Fr.) PR:C
WOMEN ARE LIKE THAT (1938) PR:A
WOMEN ARE TROUBLE (1936) PR:A
WOMEN AREN'T ANGELS (1942, Brit.) PR:A
WOMEN EVERYWHERE (1930) PR:A
WOMEN GO ON FOREVER (1931) PR:A
WOMEN IN BONDAGE (1943) PR:A
WOMEN IN CELL BLOCK 7 (1977, It./US) PR:O
WOMEN IN HIS LIFE, THE (1934) PR:A
WOMEN IN LIMBO (SEE: LIMBO) (1972)
WOMEN IN LOVE (1969, Brit.) PR:O
WOMEN IN PRISON (SEE: LADIES THEY TALK ABOUT) (1933)
WOMEN IN PRISON (1938) PR:A
WOMEN IN PRISON (1957, Jap.) PR:O
WOMEN IN THE NIGHT (1948) PR:A
WOMEN IN THE WIND (1939) PR:A
WOMEN IN WAR (1940) PR:A
WOMEN IN WAR (SEE: WOMEN AND WAR) (1965, Fr.)
WOMEN LOVE ONCE (1931) PR:A
WOMEN MEN MARRY (1931) PR:A
WOMEN MEN MARRY, THE (1937) PR:A
WOMEN MUST DRESS (1935) PR:A
WOMEN OF ALL NATIONS (1931) PR:A-C
WOMEN OF DESIRE (1968) PR:O
WOMEN OF GLAMOUR (1937) PR:A
WOMEN OF NAZI GERMANY (SEE: HITLER) (1962)
WOMEN OF PITCAIRN ISLAND, THE (1957) PR:A
WOMEN OF THE PREHISTORIC PLANET (1966) PR:A
WOMEN OF TWILIGHT (SEE: TWILIGHT WOMEN) (1952, Brit.)
WOMEN ON THE VERGE OF A NERVOUS BREAKDOWN (1988, Sp.) PR:C
WOMEN THEY TALK ABOUT (1928) PR:A
WOMEN WHO PLAY (1932, Brit.) PR:A
WOMEN WITHOUT MEN (SEE: BLONDE BAIT) (1956, US/Brit.)
WOMEN WITHOUT NAMES (1940) PR:A
WOMEN WON'T TELL (1933) PR:A
WOMEN'S PRISON (1955) PR:A-C
WOMEN'S PRISON MASSACRE (1986, It./Fr.) PR:O
WON TON TON, THE DOG WHO SAVED HOLLYWOOD (1976) PR:A
WONDER BAR (1934) PR:A
WONDER BOY (1951, Brit./Aust.) PR:A
WONDER CHILD (SEE: WONDER BOY) (1951, Brit./Aust.)
WONDER MAN (1945) PR:AA
WONDER OF WOMEN (1929) PR:A
WONDER PLANE (SEE: MERCY PLANE) (1940)
WONDER WOMEN (1973, Phil.) PR:C
WONDERFUL COUNTRY, THE (1959) PR:A
WONDERFUL DAY (SEE: I'VE GOTTA HORSE) (1965, Brit.)
WONDERFUL LAND OF OZ, THE (1969) PR:AA
WONDERFUL LIFE (SEE: SWINGER'S PARADISE) (1965, Brit.)
WONDERFUL STORY, THE (1932, Brit.) PR:A
WONDERFUL THINGS! (1958, Brit.) PR:A
WONDERFUL TO BE YOUNG! (1962, Brit.) PR:A
WONDERFUL WORLD OF THE BROTHERS GRIMM, THE (1962) PR:A-C
WONDERFUL YEARS, THE (SEE: RESTLESS YEARS, THE) (1958)
WONDERLAND (1988, Brit.) PR:O
WONDERS OF ALADDIN, THE (1961, Fr./It.) PR:AA
WONDERWALL (1969, Brit.) PR:O
WOODEN CROSSES (SEE: ROAD TO GLORY) (1936)
WOODEN HORSE, THE (1951, Brit.) PR:A
WOORUZHYON I OCHEN OPASEN (SEE: ARMED AND DANGEROUS) (1977, USSR)
WORD, THE (SEE: ORDET) (1955, Den.)
WORDS AND MUSIC (1929) PR:A
WORDS AND MUSIC (1948) PR:A
WORK IS A FOUR LETTER WORD (1968, Brit.) PR:C
WORKING GIRL (1988) PR:O
WORKING GIRLS (1931) PR:A
WORKING GIRLS, THE (1973) PR:O
WORKING GIRLS (1986) PR:O
WORKING MAN, THE (1933) PR:A
WORKING WIVES (SEE: WEEK-END MARRIAGE) (1932)
WORLD ACCORDING TO GARP, THE (1982) PR:C-O
WORLD ACCUSES, THE (1935) PR:A
WORLD AND HIS WIFE, THE (SEE: STATE OF THE UNION) (1948)
WORLD AND THE FLESH, THE (1932) PR:A
WORLD APART, A (1988, Brit.) PR:C-O
WORLD CHANGES, THE (1933) PR:A
WORLD FOR RANSOM (1954) PR:C-O

WORLD GONE MAD, THE (1933) PR:A
WORLD GONE WILD (1988) PR:O
WORLD IN HIS ARMS, THE (1952) PR:A-C
WORLD IN MY CORNER (1956) PR:A
WORLD IN MY POCKET, THE (1962, Fr./It./W. Ger.) PR:A
WORLD IS FULL OF MARRIED MEN, THE (1980, Brit.) PR:O
WORLD IS JUST A 'B' MOVIE, THE (1971) PR:O
WORLD MOVES ON, THE (1934) PR:A
WORLD OF APU, THE (1959, India) PR:A
WORLD OF HANS CHRISTIAN ANDERSEN, THE (1971, Jap.) PR:AA
WORLD OF HENRY ORIENT, THE (1964) PR:C
WORLD OF SPACE, THE (SEE: BATTLE IN OUTER SPACE) (1960, Jap.)
WORLD OF SUZIE WONG, THE (1960, Brit.) PR:O
WORLD OF YOR, THE (SEE: YOR, THE HUNTER FROM THE FUTURE) (1983, It.)
WORLD OWES ME A LIVING, THE (1944, Brit.) PR:A
WORLD PREMIERE (1941) PR:A
WORLD TEN TIMES OVER, THE (SEE: PUSSYCAT ALLEY) (1965, Brit.)
WORLD, THE FLESH, AND THE DEVIL, THE (1932, Brit.) PR:A
WORLD, THE FLESH, AND THE DEVIL, THE (1959) PR:A
WORLD WAS HIS JURY, THE (1958) PR:A
WORLD WITHOUT A MASK, THE (1934, Ger.) PR:A
WORLD WITHOUT END (1956) PR:A
WORLDLY GOODS (1930) PR:A
WORLDS APART (1980, US/Israel) PR:C
WORLD'S GREATEST ATHLETE, THE (1973) PR:AA
WORLD'S GREATEST LOVER, THE (1977) PR:A-C
WORLD'S GREATEST SINNER, THE (1962) PR:O
WORLD'S GREATEST SWINDLES (SEE: BEAUTIFUL SWINDLERS) (1967, Fr./It./Jap./Neth.)
WORLDS OF GULLIVER, THE (SEE: THREE WORLDS OF GULLIVER, THE) (1960, Brit.)
WORM EATERS, THE (1981) PR:O
WORM'S EYE VIEW (1951, Brit.) PR:A
WORST WOMAN IN PARIS (1933) PR:A
WORTH WINNING (1989) PR:O
WORTHY DECEIVER (SEE: BIG BLUFF, THE) (1933)
WOULD-BE GENTLEMAN, THE (1960, Fr.) PR:A
WOULD YOU BELIEVE IT! (1930, Brit.) PR:AA
WOZZECK (1962, E. Ger.) PR:A
WRAITH, THE (1986) PR:C
WRANGLER'S ROOST (1941) PR:A
WRATH OF GOD, THE (1972) PR:C-O
WRATH OF JEALOUSY (1936, Brit.) PR:A
WRECK OF THE MARY DEARE, THE (1959) PR:A
WRECKER, THE (1933) PR:A
WRECKERS, THE (SEE: FURY AT SMUGGLER'S BAY) (1963, Brit.)
WRECKING CREW (1942) PR:A
WRECKING CREW, THE (1968) PR:C
WRECKING YARD, THE (SEE: ROTTEN APPLE, THE) (1963)
WRESTLER, THE (1974) PR:C
WRESTLING WOMEN VS. THE AZTEC MUMMY, THE (1964, Mex.) PR:A
WRITTEN LAW, THE (1931, Brit.) PR:A
WRITTEN ON THE SAND (SEE: PLAY DIRTY) (1969, Brit.)
WRITTEN ON THE WIND (1956) PR:C
WRONG ARM OF THE LAW, THE (1963, Brit.) PR:A
WRONG BOX, THE (1966, Brit.) PR:A
WRONG DAMN FILM, THE (1975) PR:C-O
WRONG GUYS, THE (1988) PR:O
WRONG IS RIGHT (1982) PR:O
WRONG KIND OF GIRL, THE (SEE: BUS STOP) (1956)
WRONG MAN, THE (1956) PR:A
WRONG MOVE (1975, W. Ger.) PR:C-O
WRONG NUMBER (1959, Brit.) PR:A
WRONG ROAD, THE (1937) PR:A
WRONGLY ACCUSED (SEE: BAD MEN OF THE HILLS) (1942)
WU-HOU (SEE: EMPRESS WU) (1965, Hong Kong)
WUSA (1970) PR:C
WUTHERING HEIGHTS (1939) PR:C
WUTHERING HEIGHTS (1970, Brit.) PR:A
WUTHERING HEIGHTS (1953, Mex.) PR:C
WYLIE (SEE: EYE OF THE CAT) (1969)
WYOMING (1940) PR:A
WYOMING (1947) PR:A
WYOMING BANDIT, THE (1949) PR:A
WYOMING KID, THE (SEE: CHEYENNE) (1947)
WYOMING MAIL (1950) PR:A
WYOMING OUTLAW (1939) PR:A
WYOMING RENEGADES (1955) PR:A
WYOMING WILDCAT (1941) PR:A
WYROK SMIERCI (SEE: DEATH SENTENCE) (1986, Pol.)

XYZ

X (SEE: "X" — THE MAN WITH THE X-RAY EYES) (1963)

X-15 (1961) PR:A
X FROM OUTER SPACE, THE (SEE: GIRARA) (1967, Jap.)
X MARKS THE SPOT (1931) PR:A
X MARKS THE SPOT (1942) PR:A
X-RAY (SEE: HOSPITAL MASSACRE) (1982)
"X" –THE MAN WITH THE X-RAY EYES (1963) PR:C
X THE UNKNOWN (1957, Brit.) PR:A-C
X Y & ZEE (1972, Brit.) PR:O
XANADU (1980) PR:C
XICA (1982, Braz.) PR:O
XICA DA SILVA (SEE: XICA) (1982, Braz.)
XOCHIMILCO (SEE: PORTRAIT OF MARIA) (1946, Mex.)
XTRO (1983, Brit.) PR:O
XYZ MURDERS, THE (SEE: CRIMEWAVE) (1985)
. . . Y EL DEMONIO CREO A LOS HOMBRES (SEE: HEAT) (1970, Arg.)
YA KUPIL PAPU (SEE: DIMKA) (1964, USSR)
YA SHAGAYU PO MOSKVE (SEE: MEET ME IN MOSCOW) (1966, USSR)
YAABA (1989, Burkina Faso) PR:A
YABU NO NAKA NO KURONEKO (SEE: KURONEKO) (1968, Jap.)
YABUNIRAMI NIPPON (SEE: WALL-EYED NIPPON) (1963, Jap.)
YAGYU BUGEICHO (SEE: SECRET SCROLLS (PART I)) (1968, Jap.)
YAKUZA, THE (1975, US/Jap.) PR:O
YAMANEKO SAKUSEN (SEE: OPERATION ENEMY FORT) (1964, Jap.)
YAMBAO (SEE: YOUNG AND EVIL) (1957, Mex.)
YANCO (1964, Mex.) PR:A
YANG KWEI FEI (SEE: MAGNIFICENT CONCUBINE, THE) (1964, Hong Kong)
YANGTSE INCIDENT (SEE: BATTLE HELL) (1956, Brit.)
YANK AT ETON, A (1942) PR:A
YANK AT OXFORD, A (1938, Brit.) PR:A
YANK IN DUTCH, A (SEE: WIFE TAKES A FLYER, THE) (1942)
YANK IN ERMINE, A (1955, Brit.) PR:A
YANK IN INDO-CHINA, A (1952) PR:A
YANK IN KOREA, A (1951) PR:A
YANK IN LIBYA, A (1942) PR:A
YANK IN LONDON, A (1946, Brit.) PR:A
YANK IN THE R.A.F., A (1941) PR:A
YANK IN VIET-NAM, A (1964) PR:A
YANK ON THE BURMA ROAD, A (1942) PR:A
YANKEE AT KING ARTHUR'S COURT, THE (SEE: CONNECTICUT YANKEE, A) (1931)
YANKEE BUCCANEER (1952) PR:A
YANKEE DON (1931) PR:A
YANKEE DOODLE DANDY (1942) PR:AA
YANKEE FAKIR (1947) PR:A
YANKEE IN KING ARTHUR'S COURT, A (SEE: CONNECTICUT YANKEE IN KING ARTHUR'S COURT, A) (1949)
YANKEE PASHA (1954) PR:A
YANKS (1979, Brit.) PR:C-O
YANKS AHOY (1943) PR:A
YANKS ARE COMING, THE (1942) PR:A
YAQUI DRUMS (1956) PR:AA
YASEMIN (1988, W. Ger.) PR:C
YASHA (1985, Jap.) PR:O
YATO KAZE NO NAKA O HASHIRU (SEE: BANDITS ON THE WIND) (1962, Jap.)
YAWARA SEMPU DOTO NO TAIKETSU (SEE: JUDO SHOWDOWN) (1966, Jap.)
YE SHAN (SEE: IN THE WILD MOUNTAINS) (1986, Chi.)
YEAR MY VOICE BROKE, THE (1988, Aus.) PR:C
YEAR OF AWAKENING, THE (1986, Sp.) PR:O
YEAR OF LIVING DANGEROUSLY, THE (1982, Aus.) PR:C
YEAR OF THE CRICKET (SEE: KENNER) (1969)
YEAR OF THE DRAGON (1985) PR:O
YEAR OF THE HORSE, THE (1966) PR:AA
YEAR OF THE HORSE (SEE: HORSE IN THE GRAY FLANNEL SUIT, THE) (1968)
YEAR OF THE TIGER, THE (SEE: YANK IN VIET-NAM, A) (1964)
YEAR OF THE YAHOO (1971) PR:O
YEAR ONE (1974, It.) PR:A
YEAR 2889 (SEE: IN THE YEAR 2889) (1966)
YEARLING, THE (1946) PR:AA
YEARNING (1964, Jap.) PR:C
YEARS BETWEEN, THE (1947, Brit.) PR:A
YEARS WITHOUT DAYS (SEE: CASTLE ON THE HUDSON) (1940)
YEELEN (SEE: BRIGHTNESS) (1988, Mali)
YELLOW BALLOON, THE (1953, Brit.) PR:A
YELLOW CAB MAN, THE (1950) PR:A
YELLOW CANARY, THE (1944, Brit.) PR:A
YELLOW CANARY, THE (1963) PR:A
YELLOW CARGO (1936) PR:A
YELLOW DOG (1973, Brit.) PR:A-C
YELLOW DUST (1936) PR:A
YELLOW EARTH (1986, Chi.) PR:A

YELLOW FIN (1951) PR:A
YELLOW GOLLIWOG, THE (SEE: GUTTER GIRLS) (1964, Brit.)
YELLOW HAIR AND THE FORTRESS OF GOLD (1984, US/Sp.) PR:O
YELLOW HAT, THE (1966, Brit.) PR:A
YELLOW JACK (1938) PR:A
YELLOW MASK, THE (1930, Brit.) PR:A
YELLOW MOUNTAIN, THE (1954) PR:A
YELLOW PASSPORT, THE (SEE: YELLOW TICKET, THE) (1931)
YELLOW ROBE, THE (1954, Brit.) PR:A
YELLOW ROLLS-ROYCE, THE (1965, Brit.) PR:C
YELLOW ROSE OF TEXAS, THE (1944) PR:A
YELLOW SANDS (1938, Brit.) PR:A
YELLOW SKY (1948) PR:A
YELLOW SLIPPERS, THE (1965, Pol.) PR:A
YELLOW STOCKINGS (1930, Brit.) PR:AA
YELLOW SUBMARINE (1968, Brit.) PR:A
YELLOW TEDDYBEARS, THE (SEE: GUTTER GIRLS) (1964, Brit.)
YELLOW TICKET, THE (1931) PR:A
YELLOW TOMAHAWK, THE (1954) PR:A
YELLOWBEARD (1983) PR:C-O
YELLOWNECK (1955) PR:A
YELLOWSTONE (1936) PR:A
YELLOWSTONE KELLY (1959) PR:A
YENTL (1983) PR:C
YES, GIORGIO (1982) PR:C
YES, MADAM? (1938, Brit.) PR:A
YES, MR. BROWN (1933, Brit.) PR:A
YES, MY DARLING DAUGHTER (1939) PR:A
YES SIR, MR. BONES (1951) PR:A
YES SIR, THAT'S MY BABY (1949) PR:A
YESTERDAY (1980, Can.) PR:C
YESTERDAY, TODAY, AND TOMORROW (1963, It./Fr.) PR:O
YESTERDAY'S ENEMY (1959, Brit.) PR:O
YESTERDAY'S HERO (SEE: HOOSIER SCHOOLBOY) (1937)
YESTERDAY'S HERO (1979, Brit.) PR:C-O
YESTERDAY'S HEROES (1940) PR:A
YETI (1977, It.) PR:A
YEVO ZOVUT ROBERT (SEE: THEY CALL ME ROBERT) (1967, USSR)
YIDDLE WITH HIS FIDDLE (1937, Pol.) PR:A
YIELD TO THE NIGHT (SEE: BLONDE SINNER) (1956)
YINGXIONG BENSE (SEE: BETTER TOMORROW, A) (1987, Hong Kong)
YNGSJOMORDET (SEE: WOMAN OF DARKNESS) (1968, Swed.)
YO YO (1967, Fr.) PR:A
YODELIN' KID FROM PINE RIDGE (1937) PR:A
YOG –MONSTER FROM SPACE (1970, Jap.) PR:A
YOIDORE TENSHI (SEE: DRUNKEN ANGEL) (1948, Jap.)
YOJIMBO (1961, Jap.) PR:O
YOKEL BOY (1942) PR:A
YOL (1981, Turk.) PR:O
YOLANDA AND THE THIEF (1945) PR:A
YOLANTA (1964, USSR) PR:A
YONGKARI MONSTER FROM THE DEEP (1967, S.K.) PR:A
YOR, THE HUNTER FROM THE FUTURE (1983, It.) PR:A
YOSAKOI JOURNEY (1970, Jap.) PR:C
YOSAKOI RYOKO (SEE: YOSAKOI JOURNEY) (1970, Jap.)
YOSEI GORASU (SEE: GORATH) (1964, Jap.)
YOSIE GORATH (SEE: GORATH) (1964, Jap.)
YOTSUYA KAIDAN (SEE: ILLUSION OF BLOOD) (1966, Jap.)
YOU AND ME (1938) PR:A-C
YOU ARE THE WORLD FOR ME (1964, Aust.) PR:A
YOU BELONG TO ME (1934) PR:A
YOU BELONG TO ME (1941) PR:A
YOU BELONG TO MY HEART (SEE: MR. IMPERIUM) (1951)
YOU BETTER WATCH OUT (1980) PR:O
YOU CAME ALONG (1945) PR:A
YOU CAME TOO LATE (1962, Gr.) PR:A
YOU CAN'T BEAT LOVE (1937) PR:A
YOU CAN'T BEAT THE IRISH (1952, Brit.) PR:A
YOU CAN'T BEAT THE LAW (SEE: SMART GUY) (1943)
YOU CAN'T BUY EVERYTHING (1934) PR:A
YOU CAN'T BUY LUCK (1937) PR:A
YOU CAN'T CHEAT AN HONEST MAN (1939) PR:A
YOU CAN'T DO THAT TO ME (SEE: MAISIE GOES TO RENO) (1944)
YOU CAN'T DO WITHOUT LOVE (1946, Brit.) PR:A
YOU CAN'T ESCAPE (1955, Brit.) PR:A
YOU CAN'T ESCAPE FOREVER (1942) PR:A
YOU CAN'T FOOL AN IRISHMAN (1950, Ireland) PR:A
YOU CAN'T FOOL YOUR WIFE (1940) PR:A
YOU CAN'T GET AWAY WITH MURDER (1939) PR:A-C
YOU CAN'T HAVE EVERYTHING (1937) PR:A
YOU CAN'T HAVE EVERYTHING (SEE: CACTUS IN THE SNOW) (1972)

YOU CAN'T HURRY LOVE (1988) PR:O
YOU CAN'T RATION LOVE (1944) PR:A
YOU CAN'T RUN AWAY FROM IT (1956) PR:A
YOU CAN'T RUN FAR (SEE: WHEN THE CLOCK STRIKES) (1961)
YOU CAN'T SEE 'ROUND CORNERS (1969, Aus.) PR:A
YOU CAN'T SLEEP HERE (SEE: I WAS A MALE WAR BRIDE) (1949)
YOU CAN'T STEAL LOVE (SEE: MURF THE SURF) (1974)
YOU CAN'T TAKE IT WITH YOU (1938) PR:A
YOU CAN'T TAKE MONEY (SEE: INTERNES CAN'T TAKE MONEY) (1937)
YOU CAN'T WIN 'EM ALL (SEE: ONCE YOU KISS A STRANGER) (1969)
YOU CAN'T WIN 'EM ALL (1970, Brit.) PR:C
YOU DON'T NEED PAJAMAS AT ROSIE'S (SEE: FIRST TIME, THE) (1969)
YOU FOR ME (1952) PR:A
YOU GOTTA STAY HAPPY (1948) PR:A
YOU HAVE TO RUN FAST (1961) PR:A
YOU JUST KILL ME (SEE: ARRIVEDERCI, BABY!) (1966, Brit.)
YOU KNOW WHAT SAILORS ARE (1954, Brit.) PR:A
YOU LIGHT UP MY LIFE (1977) PR:C
YOU LIVE AND LEARN (1937, Brit.) PR:A
YOU LUCKY PEOPLE (1955, Brit.) PR:A
YOU MADE ME LOVE YOU (1934, Brit.) PR:A
YOU MAY BE NEXT! (1936) PR:A
YOU MUST BE JOKING! (1965, Brit.) PR:A
YOU MUST GET MARRIED (1936, Brit.) PR:A
YOU NEVER CAN TELL (1951) PR:A
YOU NEVER KNOW (SEE: YOU NEVER CAN TELL) (1951)
YOU ONLY LIVE ONCE (1937) PR:C
YOU ONLY LIVE ONCE (1969, Fr.) PR:A
YOU ONLY LIVE TWICE (1967, Brit.) PR:C
YOU PAY YOUR MONEY (1957, Brit.) PR:A
YOU SAID A MOUTHFUL (1932) PR:A
YOU WERE MEANT FOR ME (1948) PR:A
YOU WERE NEVER LOVELIER (1942) PR:A
YOU WILL REMEMBER (1941, Brit.) PR:A
YOU'D BE SURPRISED! (1930, Brit.) PR:A
YOU'LL FIND OUT (1940) PR:A
YOU'LL LIKE MY MOTHER (1972) PR:C
YOU'LL NEVER GET RICH (1941) PR:A
YOUNG AMERICA (1932) PR:AA
YOUNG AMERICA (1942) PR:A
YOUNG AND BEAUTIFUL (1934) PR:A
YOUNG AND DANGEROUS (1957) PR:A
YOUNG AND EAGER (SEE: CLAUDELLE INGLISH) (1961)
YOUNG AND EVIL (1957, Mex.) PR:C
YOUNG AND IMMORAL, THE (SEE: SINISTER URGE, THE) (1961)
YOUNG AND INNOCENT (1938, Brit.) PR:A
YOUNG AND THE BRAVE, THE (1963) PR:A
YOUNG AND THE COOL, THE (SEE: TWIST ALL NIGHT) (1961)
YOUNG AND THE DAMNED, THE (SEE: LOS OLVIDADOS) (1950, Mex.)
YOUNG AND THE GUILTY, THE (1958, Brit.) PR:A
YOUNG AND THE IMMORAL, THE (SEE: SINISTER URGE, THE) (1961)
YOUNG AND THE PASSIONATE, THE (SEE: VITELLONI) (1953, It./Fr.)
YOUNG AND WILD (1958) PR:A
YOUNG AND WILLING (1943) PR:A
YOUNG AND WILLING (1962, Brit.) PR:C
YOUNG ANIMALS, THE (SEE: BORN WILD) (1968)
YOUNG APHRODITES (1966, Gr.) PR:C
YOUNG AS YOU FEEL (1931) PR:A
YOUNG AS YOU FEEL (1940) PR:AA
YOUNG AT HEART (1955) PR:A
YOUNG BESS (1953) PR:A
YOUNG BILL HICKOK (1940) PR:A
YOUNG BILLY YOUNG (1969) PR:A
YOUNG BLOOD (1932) PR:A
YOUNG BRIDE (1932) PR:C
YOUNG BUFFALO BILL (1940) PR:AA
YOUNG CAPTIVES, THE (1959) PR:C
YOUNG CASSIDY (1965, US/Brit.) PR:C
YOUNG COMPOSER'S ODYSSEY, A (1986, USSR) PR:O
YOUNG CYCLE GIRLS, THE (1979) PR:O
YOUNG DANIEL BOONE (1950) PR:AA
YOUNG DESIRE (1930) PR:C
YOUNG DILLINGER (1965) PR:O
YOUNG DR. KILDARE (1938) PR:A
YOUNG DOCTORS, THE (1961) PR:A-C
YOUNG DOCTORS IN LOVE (1982) PR:O
YOUNG DONOVAN'S KID (1931) PR:A
YOUNG DON'T CRY, THE (1957) PR:C
YOUNG DRACULA (SEE: SON OF DRACULA) (1974, Brit.)
YOUNG DYNAMITE (1937) PR:A
YOUNG EAGLES (1930) PR:AA
YOUNG EINSTEIN (1989, Aus.) PR:AA
YOUNG FRANKENSTEIN (1974) PR:C

YOUNG FUGITIVES (1938) PR:A
YOUNG FURY (1965) PR:C
YOUNG GIANTS (1983) PR:A
YOUNG GIRLS OF ROCHEFORT, THE (1967, Fr.) PR:A
YOUNG GIRLS OF WILKO, THE (1979, Pol./Fr.) PR:C
YOUNG GO WILD, THE (1962, W. Ger.) PR:C
YOUNG GRADUATES, THE (1971) PR:O
YOUNG GUNS, THE (1956) PR:A-C
YOUNG GUNS (1988) PR:O
YOUNG GUNS OF TEXAS (1963) PR:C
YOUNG GUY GRADUATES (1969, Jap.) PR:C
YOUNG GUY ON MT. COOK (1969, Jap.) PR:A
YOUNG HELLIONS (SEE: HIGH SCHOOL CONFIDENTIAL!) (1958)
YOUNG HUSBANDS (1958, It./Fr.) PR:A
YOUNG IDEAS (1943) PR:A
YOUNG IN HEART, THE (1938) PR:A
YOUNG INVADERS (SEE: DARBY'S RANGERS) (1958)
YOUNG JESSE JAMES (1960) PR:C
YOUNG LAND, THE (1959) PR:A
YOUNG LIONS, THE (1958) PR:C
YOUNG LORD, THE (1970, W. Ger.) PR:A
YOUNG LOVERS, THE (SEE: NEVER FEAR) (1950)
YOUNG LOVERS, THE (SEE: CHANCE MEETING) (1954, Brit.)
YOUNG LOVERS, THE (1964) PR:C-O
YOUNG MAN OF MANHATTAN (1930) PR:A
YOUNG MAN OF MUSIC (SEE: YOUNG MAN WITH A HORN) (1950)
YOUNG MAN WITH A HORN (1950) PR:C
YOUNG MAN WITH IDEAS (1952) PR:A
YOUNG MAN'S FANCY (1943, Brit.) PR:A
YOUNG MR. LINCOLN (1939) PR:A
YOUNG MR. PITT, THE (1942, Brit.) PR:A
YOUNG MONK, THE (1978, W. Ger.) PR:O
YOUNG NOWHERES (1929) PR:A
YOUNG NURSES, THE (1973) PR:O
YOUNG NURSES IN LOVE (1989) PR:O
YOUNG ONE, THE (1961, Mex.) PR:O
YOUNG ONES, THE (SEE: WONDERFUL TO BE YOUNG!) (1962, Brit.)
YOUNG PAUL BARONI (SEE: KID MONK BARONI) (1952)
YOUNG PEOPLE (1940) PR:AA
YOUNG PHILADELPHIANS, THE (1959) PR:C
YOUNG RACERS, THE (1963) PR:C
YOUNG REBEL, THE (1969, Fr./It./Sp.) PR:C
YOUNG REBELS, THE (SEE: TEENAGE DOLL) (1957)
YOUNG RUNAWAYS, THE (1968) PR:O
YOUNG SAVAGES, THE (1961) PR:C
YOUNG SCARFACE (SEE: BRIGHTON ROCK) (1947, Brit.)
YOUNG SHERLOCK HOLMES (1985) PR:C
YOUNG SINNER, THE (1965) PR:C
YOUNG SINNERS (1931) PR:A
YOUNG STRANGER, THE (1957) PR:C
YOUNG SWINGERS, THE (1963) PR:AA
YOUNG SWORDSMAN (1964, Jap.) PR:C
YOUNG, THE EVIL AND THE SAVAGE, THE (1968, It.) PR:O
YOUNG TOM EDISON (1940) PR:AA
YOUNG TORLESS (1968, Fr./W. Ger.) PR:C
YOUNG WARRIORS, THE (1967) PR:C
YOUNG WARRIORS (1983) PR:O
YOUNG WIDOW (1946) PR:A
YOUNG, WILLING AND EAGER (1962, Brit.) PR:C
YOUNG WINSTON (1972, Brit.) PR:A-C
YOUNG WIVES' TALE (1954, Brit.) PR:A
YOUNG WOODLEY (1930, Brit.) PR:C
YOUNG WORLD, A (1966, Fr./It.) PR:C
YOUNGBLOOD (1978) PR:O
YOUNGBLOOD (1986) PR:O
YOUNGBLOOD HAWKE (1964) PR:O
YOUNGER BROTHERS, THE (1949) PR:A
YOUNGER GENERATION, THE (1929) PR:A
YOUNGEST PROFESSION, THE (1943) PR:A
YOUNGEST SPY, THE (SEE: MY NAME IS IVAN) (1962, USSR)
YOUR CHEATIN' HEART (1964) PR:A
YOUR MONEY OR YOUR WIFE (1965, Brit.) PR:A
YOUR PAST IS SHOWING (1958, Brit.) PR:A
YOUR RED WAGON (SEE: THEY LIVE BY NIGHT) (1949)
YOUR SHADOW IS MINE (1963, Fr./It.) PR:O
YOUR TEETH IN MY NECK (SEE: FEARLESS VAMPIRE KILLERS, OR PARDON ME BUT YOUR TEETH ARE IN MY NECK) (1967, US/Brit.)
YOUR THREE MINUTES ARE UP (1973) PR:O
YOUR TURN, DARLING (1963, Fr.) PR:C
YOUR UNCLE DUDLEY (1935) PR:A
YOUR WITNESS (SEE: EYE WITNESS) (1950, Brit.)
YOU'RE A BIG BOY NOW (1966) PR:C
YOU'RE A LUCKY FELLOW, MR. SMITH (1943) PR:A
YOU'RE A SWEETHEART (1937) PR:A
YOU'RE DEAD RIGHT (SEE: ARRIVEDERCI, BABY!) (1966, Brit.)
YOU'RE IN THE ARMY NOW (1937, Brit.) PR:A
YOU'RE IN THE ARMY NOW (1941) PR:A

YOU'RE IN THE NAVY NOW (1951) PR:A
YOU'RE MY EVERYTHING (1949) PR:A
YOU'RE NEVER TOO YOUNG (1955) PR:A
YOU'RE NOT SO TOUGH (1940) PR:A
YOU'RE ONLY YOUNG ONCE (1938) PR:A
YOU'RE ONLY YOUNG TWICE (1952, Brit.) PR:A
YOU'RE OUT OF LUCK (1941) PR:A
YOU'RE TELLING ME (1934) PR:A
YOU'RE TELLING ME (1942) PR:A
YOU'RE THE DOCTOR (1938, Brit.) PR:A
YOU'RE THE ONE (1941) PR:A
YOURS FOR THE ASKING (1936) PR:A
YOURS, MINE AND OURS (1968) PR:AA
YOUTH AFLAME (1945) PR:A
YOUTH AND HIS AMULET, THE (1963, Jap.) PR:C
YOUTH IN FURY (1961, Jap.) PR:O
YOUTH ON PARADE (1942) PR:AA
YOUTH ON PAROLE (1937) PR:A
YOUTH ON TRIAL (1945) PR:A
YOUTH RUNS WILD (1944) PR:C
YOUTH TAKES A FLING (1938) PR:AA
YOUTH TAKES A HAND (SEE: BEHIND PRISON WALLS) (1943)
YOUTH WILL BE SERVED (1940) PR:A
YOUTHFUL FOLLY (1934, Brit.) PR:A
YOU'VE GOT TO BE SMART (1967) PR:A
YOU'VE GOT TO WALK IT LIKE YOU TALK IT OR YOU'LL LOSE THAT BEAT (1971) PR:O
YR ALCOHOLIG LION (1984, Brit.) PR:O
YUKIGUMI (SEE: SNOW COUNTRY) (1969, Jap.)
YUKON FLIGHT (1940) PR:A
YUKON GOLD (1952) PR:A
YUKON MANHUNT (1951) PR:A
YUKON VENGEANCE (1954) PR:A
YUSHA NOMI (SEE: NONE BUT THE BRAVE) (1965)
YUSHU HEIYA (SEE: MADAME AKI) (1963, Jap.)
Z (1969, Fr./Algeria) PR:C-O
Z.P.G. (1972) PR:C
ZA DVUNMYA ZAYTSAMI (SEE: KIEV COMEDY, A) (1963, USSR)
ZABIL JSEM EINSTEINA, PANOVE (SEE: I KILLED EINSTEIN, GENTLEMEN) (1970, Czech.)
ZABRISKIE POINT (1970) PR:O
ZABUDNITE NA MOZARTA (SEE: FORGET MOZART!) (1985, Czech./W. Ger.)
ZACHARIAH (1971) PR:C
ZAMBA (1949) PR:A
ZAMBA THE GORILLA (SEE: ZAMBA) (1949)
ZANDY'S BRIDE (1974) PR:A
ZANZIBAR (1940) PR:A
ZAPOROZHETZ ZA DUNAYEM (SEE: COSSACKS IN EXILE) (1939, USSR)
ZAPPA (1984, Den.) PR:O
ZAPPED! (1982) PR:O
ZARAK (1956, Brit.) PR:C
ZARDOZ (1974, Brit.) PR:O
ZARTE HAUT IN SCHWARZER SEIDE (SEE: DANIELLA BY NIGHT) (1962, Fr./W. Ger.)
ZATO ICHI CHIKEMURI KAIDO (SEE: ZATOICHI CHALLENGED) (1970, Jap.)
ZATO ICHI KENKATABI (SEE: ZATOICHI) (1968, Jap.)
ZATO ICHI TO YONJINBO (SEE: ZATOICHI MEETS YOJIMBO) (1970, Jap.)
ZATOICHI (1968, Jap.) PR:A
ZATOICHI CHALLENGED (1970, Jap.) PR:A
ZATOICHI JOGKUTABI (SEE: SHOWDOWN FOR ZATOICHI) (1968, Jap.)
ZATOICHI MEETS YOJIMBO (1970, Jap.) PR:C
ZATOICHI'S CONSPIRACY (1974, Jap.) PR:A
ZAZA (1939) PR:C
ZAZIE (1961, Fr.) PR:A
ZAZIE DANS LE METRO (SEE: ZAZIE) (1961, Fr.)
ZBEHOVIA A PUTNICI (SEE: DESERTER AND THE NOMADS, THE) (1969, Czech./It.)
ZEBRA IN THE KITCHEN (1965) PR:AA
ZED & TWO NOUGHTS, A (1985, Brit./Neth.) PR:O
ZEE & CO. (SEE: X Y & ZEE) (1972, Brit.)
ZELIG (1983) PR:A
ZELLY AND ME (1988) PR:A
ZENOBIA (1939) PR:A
ZEPPELIN (1971, Brit.) PR:A
ZERO BOYS, THE (1987) PR:C-O
ZERO HOUR (SEE: ROAD TO GLORY) (1936)
ZERO HOUR, THE (1939) PR:C
ZERO HOUR! (1957) PR:A
ZERO IN THE UNIVERSE (1966) PR:O
ZERO POPULATION GROWTH (SEE: Z.P.G.) (1972)
ZERO TO SIXTY (1978) PR:C
00-2 MOST SECRET AGENTS (1965, It.) PR:A
ZHENITBA BALZAMINOVA (SEE: MARRIAGE OF BALZAMINOV, THE) (1966, USSR)
ZHILI-BYLI STARIK SO STARUKHOY (SEE: THERE WAS AN OLD COUPLE) (1967, USSR)
ZIEGFELD FOLLIES (1946) PR:AA
ZIEGFELD GIRL (1941) PR:A
ZIG-ZAG (1975, Fr./It.) PR:O
ZIGZAG (1970) PR:C
ZINA (1985, Brit.) PR:C

ZIS BOOM BAH (1941) PR:A
ZITA (1968, Fr.) PR:O
ZOEKEN NAAR EILEEN (SEE: LOOKING FOR EILEEN) (1987, Neth.)
ZOKU MIYAMOTO MUSHASHI (SEE: SAMURAI (PART II)) (1967, Jap.)
ZOKU NINGEN NO JOKEN (SEE: ROAD TO ETERNITY) (1961, Jap.)
ZOKU OTOKOWA TSURAIYO (SEE: TORA-SAN PART 2) (1970, Jap.)
ZOLTAN, HOUND OF DRACULA (SEE: DRACULA'S DOG) (1978)
ZOMBIE (SEE: I EAT YOUR SKIN) (1971)
ZOMBIE (1980, It.) PR:O
ZOMBIE CREEPING FLESH (1981, It./Sp.) PR:O
ZOMBIES OF MORA TAU (1957) PR:O
ZOMBIES OF SUGAR HILL (SEE: SUGAR HILL) (1974)
ZOMBIES OF THE STRATOSPHERE (SEE: SATAN'S SATELLITES) (1958)
ZOMBIES ON BROADWAY (1945) PR:A
ZONE TROOPERS (1986) PR:A
ZONING (1986, W. Ger.) PR:O
ZONTAR, THE THING FROM VENUS (1966) PR:A
ZOO BABY (1957, Brit.) PR:AA
ZOO GANG, THE (1985) PR:C
ZOO IN BUDAPEST (1933) PR:A
ZOOT SUIT (1981) PR:O
ZORBA THE GREEK (1964, US/Gr.) PR:A
ZORRO CONTRO MACISTE (SEE: SAMSON AND THE SLAVE QUEEN) (1963, It.)
ZORRO, THE GAY BLADE (1981) PR:A-C
ZOTZ! (1962) PR:A
ZTRACENA TVAR (SEE: LOST MAN, THE) (1969)
ZU NEUEN UFERN (SEE: LIFE BEGINS ANEW) (1938, Ger.)
ZUCKERBABY (SEE: SUGARBABY) (1985, W. Ger.)
ZULU (1964, Brit.) PR:C
ZULU DAWN (1980, Brit.) PR:C-O
ZVEROLOVY (SEE: HUNTING IN SIBERIA) (1962, USSR)
ZVONYAT, OTKROYTE DVER (SEE: GIRL AND THE BUGLER, THE) (1967, USSR)
ZVYODY I SOLDATY (SEE: RED AND THE WHITE, THE) (1969, Hung./USSR)
ZVYOZDNYI INSPECTOR (SEE: STAR INSPECTOR, THE) (1980, USSR)
ZWEI WELTEN (SEE: TWO WORLDS) (1930, Brit./Ger.)

Indices

FILMS BY GENRE

Listed below are all films included in this volume by genre. Films which can be classified by more than one genre are listed under each of the genres to which they are suited.

Action

ADVENTURES OF FORD FAIRLANE, THE
AMERICAN EAGLE
ANGEL TOWN
ANOTHER 48 HRS.
BACK TO BACK
BIG BAD JOHN
BLIND FURY
BLOOD OF HEROES
CAGED IN PARADISO
CIRCUITRY MAN
CLASS OF 1999
DARKMAN
DEAD AIM
DEATH WARRANT
DELTA FORCE 2
DEMONSTONE
DIE HARD 2
DOWNTOWN
FLASHBACK
FULL FATHOM FIVE
HEART CONDITION
HIT LIST
I COME IN PEACE
KINDERGARTEN COP
LAST OF THE FINEST, THE
LORD OF THE FLIES
MARKED FOR DEATH
NAVY SEALS
NIGHT OF THE SHARKS
PEACEMAKER
PREDATOR 2
PRIMARY TARGET
REAL BULLETS
RED SURF
RETURN OF SUPERFLY, THE
RIVERBEND
ROBOCOP 2
ROOKIE, THE
SAVAGE BEACH
SKINHEADS – THE SECOND COMING
   OF HATE
TEENAGE MUTANT NINJA TURTLES
TOTAL RECALL

Adventure

ANDY COLBY'S INCREDIBLY AWE-
   SOME ADVENTURE
BASHU, THE LITTLE STRANGER
DAMNED RIVER
DICK TRACY
HIGH DESERT KILL
JOE VERSUS THE VOLCANO
LIONHEART
LORD OF THE FLIES
MOUNTAINS OF THE MOON
PATHFINDER
REVENGE
RIVER OF DEATH
SLIPSTREAM
STAR QUEST: BEYOND THE RISING
   MOON
SURVIVAL QUEST
TUSKS
WHITE HUNTER, BLACK HEART

Animated

DUCKTALES: THE MOVIE – TREASURE
   OF THE LOST LAMP
HAPPILY EVER AFTER
JETSONS: THE MOVIE
NUTCRACKER PRINCE, THE
RESCUERS DOWN UNDER, THE
TWILIGHT OF THE COCKROACHES

Biography

IMPROMPTU
VINCENT AND THEO

Children's

ADVENTURES OF MILO AND OTIS, THE
ANDY COLBY'S INCREDIBLY AWE-
   SOME ADVENTURE
BASHU, THE LITTLE STRANGER
DUCKTALES: THE MOVIE – TREASURE
   OF THE LOST LAMP
HAPPILY EVER AFTER
JETSONS: THE MOVIE
NUTCRACKER PRINCE, THE
RESCUERS DOWN UNDER, THE

Comedy

ADVENTURES OF FORD FAIRLANE, THE
AIR AMERICA
ALICE
ALLIGATOR EYES
ALMOST AN ANGEL
AMERICAN BOYFRIENDS
ANIMAL BEHAVIOR
ANOTHER 48 HRS.
ARACHNOPHOBIA
BACK TO THE FUTURE PART III
BAIL JUMPER
BETSY'S WEDDING
BIG DIS, THE
BIRD ON A WIRE
BLADES
BLIND FURY
BLOOD SALVAGE
BONFIRE OF THE VANITIES
CADILLAC MAN
CINEMA PARADISO
COLD FEET
COUPE DE VILLE
CRAZY PEOPLE
CRY-BABY
DADDY'S DYIN'. . . WHO'S GOT THE
   WILL?
DICK TRACY
DR. CALIGARI
DON'T TELL HER IT'S ME
DOWN THE DRAIN
DOWNTOWN
ELLIOT FAUMAN, PH.D.
ERNEST GOES TO JAIL
FAR OUT MAN
FEUD, THE
FLASHBACK
FRANKENHOOKER
FRESHMAN, THE
FUNLAND
FUNNY ABOUT LOVE
GHOST DAD
GODS MUST BE CRAZY II, THE
GREEN CARD

GREMLINS 2 THE NEW BATCH
GUMSHOE KID, THE
HAPPY TOGETHER
HEART CONDITION
HOLLYWOOD HOT TUBS II: EDUCAT-
   ING CRYSTAL
HOME ALONE
HONEYMOON ACADEMY
HOUSE PARTY
HYPERSPACE
I LOVE YOU TO DEATH
ICICLE THIEF, THE
IN THE SPIRIT
JOE VERSUS THE VOLCANO
KINDERGARTEN COP
LABYRINTH OF PASSION
LASER MAN, THE
LEMON SISTERS, THE
LIFE IS A LONG QUIET RIVER
LIFE IS CHEAP. . . BUT TOILET PAPER IS
   EXPENSIVE
LONELY WOMAN SEEKS LIFE COMPAN-
   ION
LOOK WHO'S TALKING TOO
LOOSE CANNONS
LOVE AT LARGE
MADHOUSE
MAMA, THERE'S A MAN IN YOUR BED
MARTIANS GO HOME!
MAY FOOLS
ME AND HIM
MEN AT WORK
MERMAIDS
METROPOLITAN
MISADVENTURES OF MR. WILT, THE
MO' BETTER BLUES
MODERN LOVE
MONSTER HIGH
MY BLUE HEAVEN
MY 20TH CENTURY
NOBODY'S PERFECT
NUNS ON THE RUN
OPPORTUNITY KNOCKS
PERFECT MURDER, THE
PLOT AGAINST HARRY, THE
POSTCARDS FROM THE EDGE
PRETTY WOMAN
PROBLEM CHILD
QUICK CHANGE
REPOSSESSED
ROOKIE, THE
ROSALIE GOES SHOPPING
SHOCK TO THE SYSTEM, A
SHORT TIME
SHRIMP ON THE BARBIE, THE
SIBLING RIVALRY
SKI PATROL
SPACED INVADERS
STRIKE IT RICH
STUFF STEPHANIE IN THE INCINERA-
   TOR
TAKING CARE OF BUSINESS
TALES FROM THE DARKSIDE: THE
   MOVIE
TALL GUY, THE
TAX SEASON
TEXASVILLE
THREE MEN AND A LITTLE LADY
TIE ME UP! TIE ME DOWN!

TOO BEAUTIFUL FOR YOU
TREMORS
TUNE IN TOMORROW
UNBELIEVABLE TRUTH, THE
UNDER THE BOARDWALK
VAMPIRE'S KISS
WEDDING BAND
WELCOME HOME, ROXY CARMICHAEL
WHERE THE HEART IS
WHITE PALACE
WHY ME?
WILD AT HEART
WILDEST DREAMS
WITHOUT YOU, I'M NOTHING

Crime

AFTER DARK, MY SWEET
ANOTHER 48 HRS.
DOWN THE DRAIN
GODFATHER PART III, THE
GOODFELLAS
GRIFTERS, THE
HENRY: PORTRAIT OF A SERIAL KILLER
INTERNAL AFFAIRS
KILL ME AGAIN
KILL-OFF, THE
KING OF NEW YORK
KRAYS, THE
MIAMI BLUES
MILLER'S CROSSING
MY BLUE HEAVEN
PRESUMED INNOCENT
Q&A
QUICK CHANGE
RED SURF
STATE OF GRACE
TWISTED JUSTICE
TWO JAKES, THE

Dance

FORBIDDEN DANCE, THE

Docu-drama

MAN INSIDE, THE

Drama

ALLIGATOR EYES
AMERICAN BOYFRIENDS
AVALON
AWAKENINGS
BACKSTREET DREAMS
BELLY OF AN ARCHITECT, THE
BLACK RAIN
BLOOD RED
BODY CHEMISTRY
BYE BYE BLUES
CADILLAC MAN
C'EST LA VIE
CHATTAHOOCHEE
CHICAGO JOE AND THE SHOWGIRL
CINEMA PARADISO
COOK, THE THIEF, HIS WIFE & HER
    LOVER, THE
COUPE DE VILLE
CYRANO DE BERGERAC
DADDY'S DYIN'. . . WHO'S GOT THE
    WILL?
EVERYBODY WINS
FACE OF THE ENEMY
FIELD, THE
FLAME IN MY HEART, A
FOOLS OF FORTUNE
FORCED MARCH
FREEZE – DIE – COME TO LIFE
GOODFELLAS
HAMLET

HANDMAID'S TALE, THE
HAVANA
HENRY AND JUNE
HOMER & EDDIE
HOW TO MAKE LOVE TO A NEGRO
    WITHOUT GETTING TIRED
IMPORTED BRIDEGROOM, THE
INTERROGATION, THE
JESUS OF MONTREAL
JEZEBEL'S KISS
LAMBADA
LANDSCAPE IN THE MIST
LAST EXIT TO BROOKLYN
L'ETAT SAUVAGE
LIFE AND NOTHING BUT
LONGTIME COMPANION
MEN DON'T LEAVE
MEN IN LOVE
MR. AND MRS. BRIDGE
MO' BETTER BLUES
MY 20TH CENTURY
NASTY GIRL, THE
POSTCARDS FROM THE EDGE
PUMP UP THE VOLUME
Q&A
RAGGEDY RAWNEY, THE
REINCARNATION OF GOLDEN LOTUS,
    THE
REVENGE
REVERSAL OF FORTUNE
SHADOW OF THE RAVEN
SHELTERING SKY, THE
SHOCK TO THE SYSTEM, A
SHORT TIME
STANLEY AND IRIS
STELLA
STRAPLESS
SUMMER VACATION: 1999
TAXI BLUES
TEXASVILLE
TIME OF THE GYPSIES
TO SLEEP WITH ANGER
TORN APART
TORRENTS OF SPRING
TOUCH OF A STRANGER
TWISTED OBSESSION
UNBELIEVABLE TRUTH, THE
VERONICO CRUZ
VITAL SIGNS
WHERE THE HEART IS
WHITE GIRL, THE
WHITE HUNTER, BLACK HEART
WHITE PALACE
WILD AT HEART
WILD ORCHID

Fantasy

ALICE
ANDY COLBY'S INCREDIBLY AWE-
    SOME ADVENTURE
DREAMS
EDWARD SCISSORHANDS
GHOST
GHOST DAD
LORDS OF MAGICK, THE
MR. DESTINY
MONSTER HIGH
ROUGE
TEENAGE MUTANT NINJA TURTLES
WILDEST DREAMS
WITCHES, THE

Historical

COME SEE THE PARADISE
HEAVEN AND EARTH
MAHABHARATA, THE

MOUNTAINS OF THE MOON
MY UNCLE'S LEGACY
SHADOW OF THE RAVEN

Horror

ARACHNOPHOBIA
BASKETCASE 2
BLADES
BLOOD RELATIONS
BLOOD SALVAGE
BRAIN DEAD
BURNDOWN
CHILD'S PLAY 2
DEAD PIT
DEF BY TEMPTATION
DEMON WIND
DEMONSTONE
DISTURBANCE, THE
DR. CALIGARI
EXORCIST III, THE
FIRST POWER, THE
FLATLINERS
FRANKENHOOKER
FRANKENSTEIN UNBOUND
FRIGHT HOUSE
GRAVEYARD SHIFT
GREMLINS 2 THE NEW BATCH
GRIM PRAIRIE TALES
GUARDIAN, THE
HAUNTING OF MORELLA, THE
HENRY: PORTRAIT OF A SERIAL KILLER
INHERITOR
JACOB'S LADDER
LEATHERFACE: THE TEXAS CHAINSAW
    MASSACRE III
MASQUE OF THE RED DEATH
MISERY
MR. FROST
MONSTER HIGH
NIGHT ANGEL
NIGHT OF THE LIVING DEAD
NIGHTBREED
PREDATOR 2
PRIMAL RAGE
REPOSSESSED
SANTA SANGRE
SHADOWZONE
SLEEPING CAR, THE
SONNY BOY
SPONTANEOUS COMBUSTION
STEEL AND LACE
STUFF STEPHANIE IN THE INCINERA-
    TOR
TALES FROM THE DARKSIDE: THE
    MOVIE
TREMORS
TWO EVIL EYES
VAMPIRE'S KISS

Musical

CRY-BABY
GRAFFITI BRIDGE
LAMBADA
MACK THE KNIFE

Mystery

BAD INFLUENCE
BEDROOM EYES II
EVERYBODY WINS
MURDER BY NUMBERS
PERFECT MURDER, THE
PRESUMED INNOCENT
STUFF STEPHANIE IN THE INCINERA-
    TOR
TEN LITTLE INDIANS

Political

FORCE OF CIRCUMSTANCE
GAME, THE
HIDDEN AGENDA
INTERROGATION, THE
RIVERBEND
SHOW OF FORCE, A

Prison

CAGED FURY
CAGED IN PARADISO

Romance

ANIMAL BEHAVIOR
BIRD ON A WIRE
BYE BYE BLUES
COME SEE THE PARADISE
CYRANO DE BERGERAC
DON'T TELL HER IT'S ME
EAT A BOWL OF TEA
EDWARD SCISSORHANDS
FUNNY ABOUT LOVE
GHOST
GREEN CARD
HAPPY TOGETHER
IMPROMPTU
LONELY WOMAN SEEKS LIFE COMPAN-
    ION
LOVE AT LARGE
MAGDALENE
MERMAIDS
MODERN LOVE
PRETTY WOMAN
ROUGE
RUSSIA HOUSE, THE
STRIKE IT RICH
THREE MEN AND A LITTLE LADY
TIE ME UP! TIE ME DOWN!
TORN APART
TORRENTS OF SPRING
TUNE IN TOMORROW
WHITE PALACE
WILD AT HEART

Science Fiction

AFTERSHOCK
ALIENATOR
BACK TO THE FUTURE PART III
BLOOD OF HEROES
CIRCUITRY MAN
CLASS OF 1999
DARK SIDE OF THE MOON
DARKMAN
FRANKENSTEIN UNBOUND
HARDWARE
HIGH DESERT KILL
HYPERSPACE
I COME IN PEACE
JETSONS: THE MOVIE
MARTIANS GO HOME!
PEACEMAKER
ROBOCOP 2
ROBOT JOX
SHADOWZONE
SLIPSTREAM
SPACED INVADERS
STAR QUEST: BEYOND THE RISING
    MOON
STEEL AND LACE
STREET ASYLUM
TIME GUARDIAN, THE
TIME TROOPERS
TOTAL RECALL

Sports

DAYS OF THUNDER

OPPONENT, THE
ROCKY V
SIDE OUT

Spy

HONEYMOON ACADEMY
RUSSIA HOUSE, THE

Thriller

BACK TO BACK
BAD INFLUENCE
BEDROOM EYES II
BIRD ON A WIRE
BLUE STEEL
DEAD AIM
DESPERATE HOURS
FALSE IDENTITY
FORCE OF CIRCUMSTANCE
FOURTH WAR, THE
HIDDEN AGENDA
HIT LIST
HOSTILE TAKEOVER
HOT SPOT, THE
HUNT FOR RED OCTOBER, THE
IMPULSE
INNOCENT VICTIM
INTERNAL AFFAIRS
ISTANBUL, KEEP YOUR EYES OPEN
KILL ME AGAIN
LAST OF THE FINEST, THE
LIFE IS CHEAP. . . BUT TOILET PAPER IS
    EXPENSIVE
LISA
MONSIEUR HIRE
NARROW MARGIN
NIGHT EYES
NIGHT VISITOR
OVER EXPOSED
PACIFIC HEIGHTS
PAINT IT BLACK
REINCARNATION OF GOLDEN LOTUS,
    THE
SANTA SANGRE
STREETS
TWISTED JUSTICE

War

AIR AMERICA
DOG TAGS
FIRE BIRDS
FOURTH WAR, THE
MEMPHIS BELLE

FILMS BY PARENTAL RECOMMENDATION (PR)

Listed below are all films reviewed in this volume by parental recommendation (PR). The recommendations indicate:

AA – good for children; A – acceptable for children; C – cautionary, some scenes may be objectionable for children; O – objectionable for children.

AA

ADVENTURES OF MILO AND OTIS, THE
AMERICAN BOYFRIENDS
BASHU, THE LITTLE STRANGER
DUCKTALES: THE MOVIE – TREASURE
    OF THE LOST LAMP
GODS MUST BE CRAZY II, THE
JETSONS: THE MOVIE
NUTCRACKER PRINCE, THE
SPACED INVADERS

A

ALMOST AN ANGEL
ANIMAL BEHAVIOR
AVALON
AWAKENINGS
BACK TO THE FUTURE PART III
BYE BYE BLUES
COURAGE MOUNTAIN
CYRANO DE BERGERAC
DAYS OF THUNDER
DREAMS
ERNEST GOES TO JAIL
FEUD, THE
FORCE OF CIRCUMSTANCE
FULL FATHOM FIVE
GHOST DAD
HAMLET
HAPPILY EVER AFTER
HYPERSPACE
ICICLE THIEF, THE
JOE VERSUS THE VOLCANO
LIONHEART
LONELY WOMAN SEEKS LIFE COMPAN-
    ION
MACK THE KNIFE
MAGDALENE
MAHABHARATA, THE
MAMA, THERE'S A MAN IN YOUR BED
MARTIANS GO HOME!
MEN DON'T LEAVE
MR. AND MRS. BRIDGE
MY 20TH CENTURY
PERFECT MURDER, THE
TEENAGE MUTANT NINJA TURTLES
THREE MEN AND A LITTLE LADY
TO SLEEP WITH ANGER
VERONICO CRUZ
WITCHES, THE

A-C

ALICE
DICK TRACY
KINDERGARTEN COP
MR. DESTINY
NUNS ON THE RUN
OPPORTUNITY KNOCKS
PLOT AGAINST HARRY, THE
RESCUERS DOWN UNDER, THE
ROBOT JOX
TUNE IN TOMORROW
WEDDING BAND

C

AIR AMERICA
ALIENATOR
ALLIGATOR EYES
AMERICAN EAGLE
ANDY COLBY'S INCREDIBLY AWE-
    SOME ADVENTURE
ARACHNOPHOBIA
BACKSTREET DREAMS
BASKETCASE 2
BEDROOM EYES II
BETSY'S WEDDING
BIG BAD JOHN
BIRD ON A WIRE
BLADES
BLIND FURY
BLOOD OF HEROES
BLOOD RED
BRAIN DEAD
BURNDOWN
CADILLAC MAN
C'EST LA VIE
CINEMA PARADISO
CIRCUITRY MAN
COLD FEET
COUPE DE VILLE
CRAZY PEOPLE
DADDY'S DYIN'...WHO'S GOT THE
    WILL?
DANCES WITH WOLVES
DARK SIDE OF THE MOON
DEF BY TEMPTATION
DELTA FORCE 2
DON'T TELL HER IT'S ME
DOWNTOWN
EAT A BOWL OF TEA
EDWARD SCISSORHANDS
ELLIOT FAUMAN, PH.D.
EXORCIST III, THE
FACE OF THE ENEMY
FALSE IDENTITY
FIELD, THE
FIRE BIRDS
FLASHBACK
FLATLINERS
FOOLS OF FORTUNE
FORBIDDEN DANCE, THE
FORCED MARCH
FOURTH WAR, THE
FRANKENSTEIN UNBOUND
FREEZE – DIE – COME TO LIFE
FRESHMAN, THE
FUNNY ABOUT LOVE
GAME, THE
GHOST
GODFATHER PART III, THE
GRAFFITI BRIDGE
GRAVEYARD SHIFT
GREEN CARD
GREMLINS 2 THE NEW BATCH
GRIM PRAIRIE TALES
HAPPY TOGETHER
HAVANA
HEAVEN AND EARTH

HIDDEN AGENDA
HOME ALONE
HONEYMOON ACADEMY
HUNT FOR RED OCTOBER, THE
I COME IN PEACE
IMPORTED BRIDEGROOM, THE
IMPROMPTU
IN THE SPIRIT
INNOCENT VICTIM
ISTANBUL, KEEP YOUR EYES OPEN
KILL-OFF, THE
KING OF NEW YORK
KRAYS, THE
LAMBADA
LEMON SISTERS, THE
LIFE IS A LONG QUIET RIVER
LISA
LOOK WHO'S TALKING TOO
LORDS OF MAGICK, THE
LOVE AT LARGE
MADHOUSE
MAN INSIDE, THE
MEMPHIS BELLE
MEN AT WORK
MERMAIDS
METROPOLITAN
MIAMI BLUES
MILLER'S CROSSING
MODERN LOVE
MOUNTAINS OF THE MOON
MURDER BY NUMBERS
MY BLUE HEAVEN
MY UNCLE'S LEGACY
NARROW MARGIN
NAVY SEALS
NIGHT OF THE LIVING DEAD
NIGHT OF THE SHARKS
OPPONENT, THE
PACIFIC HEIGHTS
PATHFINDER
POSTCARDS FROM THE EDGE
PRESUMED INNOCENT
PRIMARY TARGET
QUICK CHANGE
QUIGLEY DOWN UNDER
RAGGEDY RAWNEY, THE
REAL BULLETS
REVERSAL OF FORTUNE
ROCKY V
ROUGE
RUSSIA HOUSE, THE
SHADOW OF THE RAVEN
SHORT TIME
SHOW OF FORCE, A
SHRIMP ON THE BARBIE, THE
SIBLING RIVALRY
SIDE OUT
SKI PATROL
SLEEPING CAR, THE
SLIPSTREAM
STANLEY AND IRIS
STAR QUEST: BEYOND THE RISING
    MOON
STELLA

STRAPLESS
STRIKE IT RICH
STUFF STEPHANIE IN THE INCINERA-
   TOR
TAKING CARE OF BUSINESS
TALL GUY, THE
TAX SEASON
TAXI BLUES
TEN LITTLE INDIANS
TEXASVILLE
TIME GUARDIAN, THE
TIME OF THE GYPSIES
TORN APART
TORRENTS OF SPRING
TOUCH OF A STRANGER
TREMORS
TWO EVIL EYES
TWO JAKES, THE
UNDER THE BOARDWALK
VAMPIRE'S KISS
VITAL SIGNS
WELCOME HOME, ROXY CARMICHAEL
WHERE THE HEART IS
WHITE GIRL, THE
WHITE HUNTER, BLACK HEART
WHY ME?
YOUNG GUNS II

C-O

COME SEE THE PARADISE
FAR OUT MAN
FIRST POWER, THE
HOMER & EDDIE
HOUSE PARTY
HOW TO MAKE LOVE TO A NEGRO
   WITHOUT GETTING TIRED
LEATHERFACE: THE TEXAS CHAINSAW
   MASSACRE III
MASQUE OF THE RED DEATH
ROOKIE, THE
ROSALIE GOES SHOPPING

O

ADVENTURES OF FORD FAIRLANE, THE
AFTER DARK, MY SWEET
AFTERSHOCK
ANGEL TOWN
ANOTHER 48 HRS.
BACK TO BACK
BAD INFLUENCE
BAIL JUMPER
BELLY OF AN ARCHITECT, THE
BIG DIS, THE
BLACK RAIN
BLOOD RELATIONS
BLOOD SALVAGE
BLUE STEEL
BODY CHEMISTRY
BONFIRE OF THE VANITIES
CAGED FURY
CAGED IN PARADISO
CHATTAHOOCHEE
CHICAGO JOE AND THE SHOWGIRL
CHILD'S PLAY 2
CLASS OF 1999
COOK, THE THIEF, HIS WIFE & HER
   LOVER, THE
CRY-BABY
DAMNED RIVER
DARKMAN
DEAD AIM
DEAD PIT
DEATH WARRANT
DEMON WIND
DEMONSTONE
DESPERATE HOURS

DIE HARD 2
DISTURBANCE, THE
DR. CALIGARI
DOG TAGS
DOWN THE DRAIN
EVERYBODY WINS
FLAME IN MY HEART, A
FRANKENHOOKER
FRIGHT HOUSE
FUNLAND
GOODFELLAS
GRIFTERS, THE
GUARDIAN, THE
GUMSHOE KID, THE
HANDMAID'S TALE, THE
HARD TO KILL
HARDWARE
HAUNTING OF MORELLA, THE
HEART CONDITION
HENRY AND JUNE
HENRY: PORTRAIT OF A SERIAL KILLER
HIGH DESERT KILL
HIT LIST
HOLLYWOOD HOT TUBS II: EDUCAT-
   ING CRYSTAL
HOSTILE TAKEOVER
HOT SPOT, THE
I LOVE YOU TO DEATH
IMPULSE
INHERITOR
INTERNAL AFFAIRS
INTERROGATION, THE
JACOB'S LADDER
JESUS OF MONTREAL
JEZEBEL'S KISS
KILL ME AGAIN
LABYRINTH OF PASSION
LANDSCAPE IN THE MIST
LASER MAN, THE
LAST EXIT TO BROOKLYN
LAST OF THE FINEST, THE
L'ETAT SAUVAGE
LIFE AND NOTHING BUT
LIFE IS CHEAP...BUT TOILET PAPER IS
   EXPENSIVE
LONGTIME COMPANION
LOOSE CANNONS
LORD OF THE FLIES
MARKED FOR DEATH
MAY FOOLS
ME AND HIM
MEN IN LOVE
MISADVENTURES OF MR. WILT, THE
MISERY
MR. FROST
MO' BETTER BLUES
MONSIEUR HIRE
MONSTER HIGH
NASTY GIRL, THE
NIGHT ANGEL
NIGHT EYES
NIGHT VISITOR
NIGHTBREED
NOBODY'S PERFECT
OVER EXPOSED
PAINT IT BLACK
PEACEMAKER
PREDATOR 2
PRETTY WOMAN
PRIMAL RAGE
PROBLEM CHILD
PUMP UP THE VOLUME
Q&A
RED SURF
REINCARNATION OF GOLDEN LOTUS,
   THE

REPOSSESSED
RETURN OF SUPERFLY, THE
REVENGE
RIVER OF DEATH
RIVERBEND
ROBOCOP 2
SANTA SANGRE
SAVAGE BEACH
SHADOWZONE
SHELTERING SKY, THE
SHOCK TO THE SYSTEM, A
SKINHEADS – THE SECOND COMING
   OF HATE
SONNY BOY
SPONTANEOUS COMBUSTION
STATE OF GRACE
STEEL AND LACE
STREET ASYLUM
STREETS
SUMMER VACATION: 1999
SURVIVAL QUEST
TALES FROM THE DARKSIDE: THE
   MOVIE
TIE ME UP! TIE ME DOWN!
TIME TROOPERS
TOO BEAUTIFUL FOR YOU
TOTAL RECALL
TUSKS
TWILIGHT OF THE COCKROACHES
TWISTED JUSTICE
TWISTED OBSESSION
UNBELIEVABLE TRUTH, THE
VINCENT AND THEO
WHITE PALACE
WILD AT HEART
WILD ORCHID
WILDEST DREAMS
WITHOUT YOU, I'M NOTHING

NAME INDEX

This index comprises a filmography for all the individuals listed in the cast and credits sections of the movie reviews in this volume. Names are arranged alphabetically by function as follows:

Actors
Animators
Art Directors
Choreographers
Cinematographers
Costumes
Directors
Editors
Makeup
Music Composers

Music Directors
Producers
Production Designers
Screenplay Authors
Set Designers
Source Authors
Special Effects
Stunts
Technical Advisers

ACTORS

Aalda, Mariann
PRETTY WOMAN

Aarn, Kimberleigh
QUICK CHANGE
PRESUMED INNOCENT
BONFIRE OF THE VANITIES

Aaron, Caroline
ALICE
EDWARD SCISSORHANDS

Aarron, Bob
STANLEY AND IRIS

Abas-Ross, Pamela
LOVE AT LARGE

Abascal, Paul
DIE HARD 2
PREDATOR 2

Abassi, Elizabeth
JACOB'S LADDER

Abbott, Philip
FIRST POWER, THE

Abernathy, Donzaleigh
GHOST DAD

Abernathy, Louisa
TAKING CARE OF BUSINESS

Ablack, Patrice
RETURN OF SUPERFLY, THE

Abraham, Ezra
NAVY SEALS

Abraham, F. Murray
SLIPSTREAM
BONFIRE OF THE VANITIES

Abril, Victoria
TIE ME UP! TIE ME DOWN!

Acerno, Paul
IMPULSE

Ackland, Joss
HUNT FOR RED OCTOBER, THE

Ackroyd, David
I COME IN PEACE

Adams, Ed
YOUNG GUNS II

Adams, Jane
VITAL SIGNS

Adams, Lynne
BLOOD RELATIONS

Adelman, Jesse
AVALON

Adler, Don
COME SEE THE PARADISE

Adonis, Frank
GOODFELLAS

Adzovic, Ljubica
TIME OF THE GYPSIES

Afravian, Adnan
BASHU, THE LITTLE STRANGER

Agostini, Diane
GODFATHER PART III, THE

Agren, Janet
NIGHT OF THE SHARKS
MAGDALENE

Agutter, Jenny
CHILD'S PLAY 2

Ahmad, Waheedah
AWAKENINGS

Aiello, Danny
JACOB'S LADDER

Aiello, Danny III
LOOSE CANNONS
MILLER'S CROSSING

Aiello, Rick
DOWNTOWN

Aintsey, Norman
RIVER OF DEATH

Airlie, Andrew
FRESHMAN, THE

Akashi, Mayuko
DREAMS

Akin, Charlotte
PROBLEM CHILD

Akin, Philip
STELLA

Akune, Shuko
COME SEE THE PARADISE

Alafouzos, S.
LANDSCAPE IN THE MIST

Alaimo, Marc
TOTAL RECALL

Alaimo, Michael
GUMSHOE KID, THE

Alaskey, Joe
SPACED INVADERS

Albanese, Frank
GOODFELLAS

Albano, Bea
EDWARD SCISSORHANDS

Albers, Stephanie
WITHOUT YOU, I'M NOTHING

Albert, Laura
DR. CALIGARI

Alberty, Edward
BACK TO BACK

Albright, Carol
DR. CALIGARI

Alcazar, Angel
LABYRINTH OF PASSION

Alda, Alan
BETSY'S WEDDING

Alderman, Doreen
BODY CHEMISTRY

Alderson, John
YOUNG GUNS II

Aldridge, Kitty
SLIPSTREAM

Aldridge, Leah
HOUSE PARTY

Aleandro, Norma
VITAL SIGNS

Alessandro, Anthony
GOODFELLAS
JACOB'S LADDER

Alexander, Alexis
YOUNG GUNS II

Alexander, Anthony
ROOKIE, THE

Alexander, Carmen J.
EDWARD SCISSORHANDS

Alexander, Dick
MADHOUSE

Alexander, Erica
MAHABHARATA, THE

Alexander, Jason
PRETTY WOMAN
WHITE PALACE
JACOB'S LADDER

Alexander, Kirk
TIME GUARDIAN, THE

Alexander, Max
HONEYMOON ACADEMY

Alexander, Tom
FORBIDDEN DANCE, THE

Alexander, Wayne
SPACED INVADERS

Alfano, Erasmus C.
GOODFELLAS

Alfaro, Manny
GOODFELLAS

Alford, Brenda
AVALON

Alice, Mary
TO SLEEP WITH ANGER

AWAKENINGS
BONFIRE OF THE VANITIES

Aliff, Lisa
DAMNED RIVER

Allain, Aurorah
ADVENTURES OF FORD FAIRLANE, THE

Allam, Roger
MISADVENTURES OF MR. WILT, THE

Alldredge, Michael
ROBOT JOX

Alleff, Tony
COOK, THE THIEF, HIS WIFE & HER
LOVER, THE

Allegret, Catherine
MR. FROST

Allegrucci, Scott
FEUD, THE

Allen, Barbara
ME AND HIM

Allen, Eugene
HOUSE PARTY

Allen, Ginger Lynn
YOUNG GUNS II

Allen, Karen
ANIMAL BEHAVIOR

Allen, Keith
CHICAGO JOE AND THE SHOWGIRL

Allen, Nancy
ROBOCOP 2

Allen, Pricilla
TOTAL RECALL

Allen, Rae
FAR OUT MAN

Allen, Rosalind
THREE MEN AND A LITTLE LADY

Allen, Sammy Lee
ALMOST AN ANGEL

Allen, Seth
ROOKIE, THE

Allen, Tommy
COME SEE THE PARADISE

Allen, Tony
SLIPSTREAM

Allen, Tyrees
RIVERBEND

Alley, Kirstie
MADHOUSE
SIBLING RIVALRY
LOOK WHO'S TALKING TOO

Allman, Jim
SKI PATROL

Allred, Anna Marie
PROBLEM CHILD

Allyn, Bethany Jaye
KINDERGARTEN COP

Almeida, Diane
ADVENTURES OF FORD FAIRLANE, THE

Almgren, Susan
HOW TO MAKE LOVE TO A NEGRO WITH-
OUT GETTING TIRED

Almodovar, Agustin
LABYRINTH OF PASSION

Almodovar, Pedro
LABYRINTH OF PASSION

Alonso, Maria Conchita
VAMPIRE'S KISS
PREDATOR 2

Alston, Mark
SKI PATROL

Alston, Peggy
EXORCIST III, THE

Alt, James
SKI PATROL

Altamura, John
WILDEST DREAMS

Alterman, Monique Nichole
LEMON SISTERS, THE

Althoff, Ron
AFTERSHOCK

Altman, Bob
GOODFELLAS

Alvarado, Trini
STELLA

Alvarez, Abraham
PREDATOR 2

Amabile, Vincent
LORD OF THE FLIES

Amada, Masou
DREAMS

Amador, Andrew
FIRST POWER, THE
TAKING CARE OF BUSINESS

Amato, Jezabelle
IMPROMPTU

Ambriz, Domingo
YOUNG GUNS II

Amick, Madchen
DON'T TELL HER IT'S ME

Amick, Ryan Paul
EXORCIST III, THE

Amis, Suzy
WHERE THE HEART IS

Ammon, Jack
SHORT TIME

Amos, John
DIE HARD 2

Anaclerio, Marinella
TORRENTS OF SPRING

Anagnos, Billy
LOOSE CANNONS

Ancona, Joey
MILLER'S CROSSING

Anderly, Adam
PROBLEM CHILD

Andersen, Isa
NIGHT ANGEL

Anderson, Aida
PACIFIC HEIGHTS

Anderson, Arthur
GREEN CARD

Anderson, Brian James
DESPERATE HOURS

Anderson, Doyle
EDWARD SCISSORHANDS

Anderson, J.J.
SPACED INVADERS

Anderson, Kathleen
FORCE OF CIRCUMSTANCE

Anderson, McKee
NIGHT OF THE LIVING DEAD

Anderson, Mamie Louis
MO' BETTER BLUES

Anderson, Raymond L.
MR. DESTINY

Anderson, Robert A.
PROBLEM CHILD

Anderson, Sam
I COME IN PEACE

Anderson, Scheryll
LEMON SISTERS, THE

Anderson, Scott
AMERICAN BOYFRIENDS

Anderson, Shane
DISTURBANCE, THE

Anderson-Gunter, Jeffrey
MARKED FOR DEATH

Andorai, Peter
MY 20TH CENTURY

Andreeff, Starr
STREETS

Andreozzi, Jack
HIT LIST

Andreson, Dion
HAVANA

Andrews, David
GRAVEYARD SHIFT

Andrews, Jason
LAST EXIT TO BROOKLYN

Andrews, Patricia
FRESHMAN, THE

Andzhaparidze, Georgi
RUSSIA HOUSE, THE

Anemone
TWISTED OBSESSION

Angel, Vanessa
KING OF NEW YORK

Angeloff, Serge
MAY FOOLS

Angeloni, Ramon
LAST OF THE FINEST, THE

Angelyne
HOMER & EDDIE

Anglim, Philip
MAN INSIDE, THE

Angotti, Nick
DIE HARD 2

Anholt, Christien
HAMLET

Anjelico, James
MURDER BY NUMBERS

Anker Ousdal, Sverre
ISTANBUL, KEEP YOUR EYES OPEN

Ankers, Robert
LORDS OF MAGICK, THE

Annesley, Imogen
STRAPLESS

Anspach, Susan
BLOOD RED
BACK TO BACK

Anthony, Paul
HOUSE PARTY

Anthony, Reed
PRETTY WOMAN

Antico, Pete
HUNT FOR RED OCTOBER, THE
IMPULSE

Antin, Robin
WITHOUT YOU, I'M NOTHING

Antin, Steve
WITHOUT YOU, I'M NOTHING
SURVIVAL QUEST

Antuofermo, Vito
GOODFELLAS
GODFATHER PART III, THE

Anzell, Hy
PACIFIC HEIGHTS

Anzumonyin, Eric
RUSSIA HOUSE, THE

Aoki, Margaret
SKI PATROL

Aota, Hideto
DREAMS

Apartella, Raul
CHATTAHOOCHEE

Apisa, Robert
HEART CONDITION
FORBIDDEN DANCE, THE

Appel, Peter
EVERYBODY WINS
DAYS OF THUNDER
PRESUMED INNOCENT

Applebaum, Bill
HEART CONDITION
PRETTY WOMAN

Appleby, Diane
AMERICAN EAGLE

Appleby, Shiri
I LOVE YOU TO DEATH

Applegate, Christina
STREETS

Applegate, Fred
SPACED INVADERS

Aprea, John
SAVAGE BEACH

Aprea, Nicole
SAVAGE BEACH

Aquilino, Frank
GOODFELLAS

Aquilon, Raymond
MR. FROST

Aragon, Frank
ANGEL TOWN

Aragon, Jesse
STREET ASYLUM

Arana, Tomas
HUNT FOR RED OCTOBER, THE

Arango, Jose Rafel
Q&A

Arcand, Denys
JESUS OF MONTREAL

Archard, Bernard
HIDDEN AGENDA

Archer, Anne
LOVE AT LARGE
NARROW MARGIN

Archerd, Selma
TAKING CARE OF BUSINESS

Arden, Drake
FRESHMAN, THE

Arenal, Alina
YOUNG GUNS II

Arenberg, Lee
CLASS OF 1999

Aresco, Joey
PRIMARY TARGET

Argenziano, Carmen
FIRST POWER, THE

Argo, Victor
QUICK CHANGE
KING OF NEW YORK

Arias, Imanol
LABYRINTH OF PASSION

Arkin, Alan
COUPE DE VILLE
HAVANA
EDWARD SCISSORHANDS

Arlen, Elizabeth
FIRST POWER, THE

Armand, Merete
WITCHES, THE

Armour, Annabel
MEN DON'T LEAVE

Armstrong, Alun
WHITE HUNTER, BLACK HEART

Armstrong, Herb
LOOSE CANNONS

Armstrong, R.G.
DICK TRACY

Armstrong, Valorie
PRETTY WOMAN

Armstrong, Vaughn
HIGH DESERT KILL

Armus, Sidney
POSTCARDS FROM THE EDGE

Arnett, Michael
WHITE PALACE

Arnold, Madison
PRESUMED INNOCENT

Arnold, Richard Mark
CADILLAC MAN

Arnold, Tracy
HENRY: PORTRAIT OF A SERIAL KILLER

Arnott, David
ADVENTURES OF FORD FAIRLANE, THE

Arntson, Bruce
ERNEST GOES TO JAIL

Aronson, Ethan
MADHOUSE

Aronson, Judie
SLEEPING CAR, THE

Aronson, Steve
CRY-BABY
AVALON

Arquette, Alexis
LAST EXIT TO BROOKLYN

Arters, Deborah
ME AND HIM

Arton, Joseph
STRIKE IT RICH

Arutt, Cheryl
PRIMAL RAGE

Asano, Atsuko
HEAVEN AND EARTH

Ashbrook, Dana
GHOST DAD

Ashby, Linden
NIGHT ANGEL

Ashley, Elizabeth
VAMPIRE'S KISS

Ashton, Dyrk
NIGHT OF THE LIVING DEAD

Ashton-Griffiths, Roger
MOUNTAINS OF THE MOON
CHICAGO JOE AND THE SHOWGIRL

Asiba, Asiba
MOUNTAINS OF THE MOON

Asis, Stan
LOVE AT LARGE

Askew, Luke
BACK TO BACK

Askin, Tony
BAIL JUMPER

Asner, Edward
HAPPILY EVER AFTER

Aso, Cynthia
COME SEE THE PARADISE

Asparagus, Fred
HAVANA

Asquith, Conrad
WHITE HUNTER, BLACK HEART

Assa, Rene
POSTCARDS FROM THE EDGE

Assam, Rene
WHY ME?

Assante, Armand
Q&A
ANIMAL BEHAVIOR

Astin, John
GREMLINS 2 THE NEW BATCH

Astin, Sean
MEMPHIS BELLE

Astor, Philip
STELLA

Ateah, Scott
AMERICAN EAGLE

Ateba, Samuel
HENRY AND JUNE

Atha, Mark
MURDER BY NUMBERS

Atherton, William
DIE HARD 2
GRIM PRAIRIE TALES

Atkine, Feodor
HENRY AND JUNE

Atkinson, Anthony "Wink"
HEART CONDITION

Atkinson, Michael
AMERICAN EAGLE

Atkinson, Rowan
TALL GUY, THE
WITCHES, THE

Attie, Paulette
LEMON SISTERS, THE

Attili, Antonella
CINEMA PARADISO

Atzen, Catherine
METROPOLITAN

Auberghen, Stephane
TOO BEAUTIFUL FOR YOU

Auberjonois, Rene
FEUD, THE

Aubert, Yves
STRIKE IT RICH
CYRANO DE BERGERAC

Auder, Alexandra
BAIL JUMPER

Auer, Tony
TAKING CARE OF BUSINESS

Auguardi, Matteo
ICICLE THIEF, THE

August, Alan
FLASHBACK

Aussedat, Pierre
CYRANO DE BERGERAC

Austin, Julia
TWISTED JUSTICE

Austin, Linda
PACIFIC HEIGHTS

Auteuil, Daniel
MAMA, THERE'S A MAN IN YOUR BED

Avellana, Jose Mari
DEMONSTONE

Avery, Brian
UNDER THE BOARDWALK

Avery, Margaret
RIVERBEND

RETURN OF SUPERFLY, THE

Avery, Rick
LOOK WHO'S TALKING TOO

Avidon, Sarajane
OPPORTUNITY KNOCKS

Avila, Christine
VITAL SIGNS

Avildsen, Chris
ROCKY V

Avildsen, Jonathan
ROCKY V

Aviles, Rick
GHOST
GODFATHER PART III, THE
GREEN CARD

Aviva, Rachel
LEMON SISTERS, THE
AVALON

Axelrod, Robert
LORDS OF MAGICK, THE

Ayers, Sam
QUICK CHANGE

Ayers, Stephen Michael
DAYS OF THUNDER

Aykroyd, Dan
LOOSE CANNONS

Ayler, Ethel
TO SLEEP WITH ANGER

Ayr, Michael
LISA

Ayvasian, Leslie
ME AND HIM

Azaria, Hank
PRETTY WOMAN

Azema, Sabine
LIFE AND NOTHING BUT

Azulai, Hanna
TORN APART

Azuma, Shizuko
DREAMS

B'Tiste, Iilana
FLATLINERS

Baaron
L'ETAT SAUVAGE

Babatunde, Obba
MIAMI BLUES

Babbitt, Bob
ERNEST GOES TO JAIL

Babcock, Barbara
HAPPY TOGETHER

Bacall, Lauren
INNOCENT VICTIM
MISERY

Bacarella, Mike
OPPORTUNITY KNOCKS

Bach, Judy
AVALON

Bachelier, Peter
L'ETAT SAUVAGE

Bachmann, Conrad
TREMORS

Bachmann, Hans
STAR QUEST: BEYOND THE RISING MOON

Backer, Brian
STEEL AND LACE

Bacon, Billy
VITAL SIGNS

Bacon, Kevin
TREMORS
FLATLINERS

Bacri, Jean-Pierre
C'EST LA VIE

Badalucco, Michael
MILLER'S CROSSING

Baer, Parley
ALMOST AN ANGEL

Baffico, James A.
ME AND HIM

Bah, Aissatou
MAMA, THERE'S A MAN IN YOUR BED

Bah, Mamadou
MAMA, THERE'S A MAN IN YOUR BED

Bahner, Blake
CAGED FURY

Bahr, Lilo
FOURTH WAR, THE

Bailey, Charles
ROBOCOP 2

Bailey, Cynthia
WITHOUT YOU, I'M NOTHING

Bailey, Fred
PRIMARY TARGET
DEMONSTONE

Bailey, Kathleen
NIGHT VISITOR

Bailey, Mark
UNBELIEVABLE TRUTH, THE

Baily, Shane
CHATTAHOOCHEE

Bain, Barbara
SKINHEADS – THE SECOND COMING OF
HATE

Bain, Conrad
POSTCARDS FROM THE EDGE

Bain, Cynthia
SPONTANEOUS COMBUSTION

Baird, Yogi
ROBOCOP 2

Baisho, Mitsuko
DREAMS

Bakaba, Sidiki
L'ETAT SAUVAGE

Baker, Becky Ann
JACOB'S LADDER
COME SEE THE PARADISE

Baker, Blanche
HANDMAID'S TALE, THE

Baker, Carroll
KINDERGARTEN COP

Baker, Connie
ME AND HIM

Baker, Kai
AMERICAN EAGLE

Baker, Kathy
EDWARD SCISSORHANDS
MR. FROST

Baker, Mickey
LIFE AND NOTHING BUT

Baker, Ray
HEART CONDITION
TOTAL RECALL

Baker, Scott
WILDEST DREAMS

Baker, Shaun
HOUSE PARTY

Baker, Tere L.
GODFATHER PART III, THE

Bakula, Scott
SIBLING RIVALRY

Balaban, Bob
ALICE

Balaski, Belinda
GREMLINS 2 THE NEW BATCH

Balasko, Josiane
TOO BEAUTIFUL FOR YOU

Baldwin, Adam
PREDATOR 2

Baldwin, Alec
MIAMI BLUES
HUNT FOR RED OCTOBER, THE
ALICE

Baldwin, Judith
PRETTY WOMAN

Baldwin, Karen Elise
NIGHT EYES

Baldwin, Ken
DIE HARD 2

Baldwin, Stephen
LAST EXIT TO BROOKLYN

Baldwin, William
INTERNAL AFFAIRS
FLATLINERS

Bale, Andy
DARKMAN

Balen, Airen
YOUNG GUNS II

Balgobin, Jennifer
DR. CALIGARI

Balint, Eszter
BAIL JUMPER

Ball, Earl Poole
TEXASVILLE

Ballard, Kaye
MODERN LOVE

Ballard, Michael
RIVERBEND

Ballo, Nick
ROOKIE, THE

Ballou, Mark
PUMP UP THE VOLUME

Balsam, Martin
TWO EVIL EYES

Balsamo, Vito
GOODFELLAS

Baltz, Kirk
DANCES WITH WOLVES

Bambushek, Vyacheslav
FREEZE – DIE – COME TO LIFE

Bamman, Gerry
DESPERATE HOURS
HOME ALONE

Bancroft, Bradford
DAMNED RIVER

Banderas, Antonio
LABYRINTH OF PASSION
TIE ME UP! TIE ME DOWN!

Banko, Jennifer
LEATHERFACE: THE TEXAS CHAINSAW
MASSACRE III

Banks, Jonathan
HONEYMOON ACADEMY

Bannen, Ian
GHOST DAD

Bannister, Reggie
SURVIVAL QUEST

Bannon, Jack
DEATH WARRANT

Baranski, Christine
REVERSAL OF FORTUNE

Baratelli, Joseph
DR. CALIGARI

Barathy, Richie
CAGED FURY

Barbe, Michel
BIRD ON A WIRE

Barbeau, Adrienne
TWO EVIL EYES

Barbee, Carol
DIE HARD 2

Barber, Gillian
SHORT TIME

Barber, Kevin
CHATTAHOOCHEE

Barbera, Norman
GOODFELLAS

Barberini, Urbano
TORRENTS OF SPRING

Barbin, Jean-Damien
CYRANO DE BERGERAC

Barbosa, Daniela
GOODFELLAS

Bardeaux, Michelle
AMERICAN BOYFRIENDS

Barden, Alice
PACIFIC HEIGHTS

Bardol, Daniel
PRETTY WOMAN

Bareham, Adam
MISADVENTURES OF MR. WILT, THE

Barlow, Timothy
TALL GUY, THE

Barnes, Chris
TAKING CARE OF BUSINESS

Barnes, Kristin Nicole
FIRE BIRDS

Barneson, H. Bradley
BODY CHEMISTRY

Barnett, Greg
HEART CONDITION

Baron, Cherie
EXORCIST III, THE

Barr, Andrew
LOVE AT LARGE

Barr, Douglas
SPACED INVADERS

Barr, Roseanne
LOOK WHO'S TALKING TOO

Barranco, Maria
TIE ME UP! TIE ME DOWN!

Barrault, Marie-Christine
L'ETAT SAUVAGE

Barrese, Katherine
JEZEBEL'S KISS

Barrett, Amy Louis
ALICE

Barrett, Andrew Lee
KILL-OFF, THE

Barrett, Elisabeth
TAKING CARE OF BUSINESS

Barrier, Maurice
LIFE AND NOTHING BUT

Barritt, Ian
MISADVENTURES OF MR. WILT, THE

Barron, Doug
BLUE STEEL
MR. DESTINY
JACOB'S LADDER

Barros, Enrique Chao
HAVANA

Barrows, Diana
ADVENTURES OF FORD FAIRLANE, THE

Barrymore, Deborah
LIONHEART

Bartel, Paul
FAR OUT MAN
GREMLINS 2 THE NEW BATCH

Bartenieff, George
LASER MAN, THE

Bartlett, Lisbeth
ME AND HIM

Bartlett, Robin
POSTCARDS FROM THE EDGE
ALICE

Barto, Dominic
DOWN THE DRAIN

Barty, Billy
RESCUERS DOWN UNDER, THE

Bass, Bobby
HEART CONDITION

Bass, Don Wayne
CHATTAHOOCHEE

Bass, Kenneth
DESPERATE HOURS

Bass, Suzi
CHATTAHOOCHEE

Basse, Alexandre
MAMA, THERE'S A MAN IN YOUR BED

Bassey, Jennifer
BONFIRE OF THE VANITIES

Bassham, Cynthia
FLATLINERS

Bastow, Jack
SHORT TIME

Bataille, Julie
C'EST LA VIE

Bates, Alan
MR. FROST
HAMLET

Bates, Frank
RIVERBEND

Bates, Jeanne
DIE HARD 2

Bates, Kathy
MEN DON'T LEAVE
DICK TRACY
WHITE PALACE
MISERY

Bates, Lavelle
TEXASVILLE

Bates, Mychael
PRETTY WOMAN

Bates, Paul
CRAZY PEOPLE
BONFIRE OF THE VANITIES

Bath, Iris
GUARDIAN, THE

Batten, Paul
SHORT TIME

Battiste, Arienne
I COME IN PEACE

Bauer, Amber
COLD FEET

Bauer, Belinda
ROBOCOP 2

Baumer, Ian
KINDERGARTEN COP

Baumgartner, Monika
NASTY GIRL, THE

Bautista, Marilyn
DEMONSTONE

Baxley, Barbara
SHOCK TO THE SYSTEM, A
EXORCIST III, THE

Baxley, Gary
I COME IN PEACE

Baxley, Kristin
I COME IN PEACE

Baxter-Birney, Meredith
JEZEBEL'S KISS

Bay, Frances
ARACHNOPHOBIA

Bayarri, Anthony
HAVANA

Baye, Nathalie
C'EST LA VIE
MAN INSIDE, THE

Beach, Michael
INTERNAL AFFAIRS

Beall, Sandra
STATE OF GRACE

Beals, Jennifer
VAMPIRE'S KISS

Bean, Sean
FIELD, THE

Bean, Steve
VITAL SIGNS

Beano
CAGED FURY
TAX SEASON

Beard, Cody
PROBLEM CHILD

Bearde, Roger
PACIFIC HEIGHTS

Beasley, Peggy
CHATTAHOOCHEE

Beatty, Ned
CHATTAHOOCHEE
BIG BAD JOHN
REPOSSESSED

Beatty, Warren
DICK TRACY

Beaumont, Carolina
GAME, THE

Beaver, Terry
DEAD AIM
FUNLAND

Becalick, David
NUNS ON THE RUN

Bechtel, Joan
DEAD PIT

Beckel, Graham
WELCOME HOME, ROXY CARMICHAEL

Becker, Gerry
MEN DON'T LEAVE
HOME ALONE

Beckman, Henry
I LOVE YOU TO DEATH

Bedelia, Bonnie
DIE HARD 2
PRESUMED INNOCENT

Beecher, Robert
DICK TRACY

Beecroft, David
SHADOWZONE

Beesley, Terence
STRIKE IT RICH

Behrens, Sam
MURDER BY NUMBERS

Beint, Michael
NUNS ON THE RUN

Belack, Doris
OPPORTUNITY KNOCKS

Belafonte, Shari
MURDER BY NUMBERS

Belcher, Patricia
FLATLINERS

Belgrey, Thomas
FRIGHT HOUSE

Bell, Aran
NUNS ON THE RUN

Bell, Chuck
LORD OF THE FLIES

Bell, Dan
IMPULSE
DARKMAN

Bell, John
STELLA

Bell, Marjorie
HAMLET

Bell, Marshall
TOTAL RECALL
DICK TRACY
AIR AMERICA

Bell, Maureen
HIDDEN AGENDA

Bell, Mindy Suzanne
OPPORTUNITY KNOCKS

Bell, Simon
TALL GUY, THE

Bell, Tobin
LOOSE CANNONS
FALSE IDENTITY
GOODFELLAS

Bell, Tom
KRAYS, THE

Bellamy, Ralph
PRETTY WOMAN

Bellante, Francesco Paolo
GODFATHER PART III, THE

Bellantoni, Natino
NARROW MARGIN

Bellman, Harvey
EDWARD SCISSORHANDS

Bello, Teodorina
PRESUMED INNOCENT

Bello, Teodorino
QUICK CHANGE

Beltzman, Mark
HOME ALONE

Belushi, James
HOMER & EDDIE
TAKING CARE OF BUSINESS
MR. DESTINY

Belzer, Richard
BONFIRE OF THE VANITIES

Bemis, Cliff
MODERN LOVE

Ben-Victor, Paul
ROOKIE, THE

Benben, Brian
I COME IN PEACE

Benden, Vlado
HUNT FOR RED OCTOBER, THE

Bendorf, Sherry
DEMON WIND

Benedict, Jay
RUSSIA HOUSE, THE

Benedict, Paul
FRESHMAN, THE
SIBLING RIVALRY

Benfield, John
HIDDEN AGENDA

Beni, Alphonse
L'ETAT SAUVAGE

Bening, Annette
POSTCARDS FROM THE EDGE
GRIFTERS, THE

Benko, Michael George
HUNT FOR RED OCTOBER, THE

Bennes, John
FEUD, THE

Bennett, Caroline
METROPOLITAN

Bennett, Geoffrey
SKI PATROL

Bennett, Jamie
KRAYS, THE

Bennett, Jason
KRAYS, THE

Bennett, Jill
SHELTERING SKY, THE

Bennett, Joanna
GOODFELLAS

Bennett, John Michael
PRESUMED INNOCENT

Bennett, Jolie
ME AND HIM

Bennett, Mac
ERNEST GOES TO JAIL

Bennett, Nigel
NARROW MARGIN

Bennett, Robert J.
DIE HARD 2

Benninghofen, Jeff
FUNLAND

Benson, Lyric
MODERN LOVE

Benson, Robby
MODERN LOVE

Benson, Sue
REAL BULLETS

Bentley, John
BONFIRE OF THE VANITIES

Benton, Jerome
GRAFFITI BRIDGE

Benton, Lee
DOWN THE DRAIN

Benureau, Didier
TOO BEAUTIFUL FOR YOU
C'EST LA VIE

Benya, Jonathan
CRY-BABY

Benyair, Orly
FRIGHT HOUSE

Bercovici, Luca
ANDY COLBY'S INCREDIBLY AWESOME
ADVENTURE
PACIFIC HEIGHTS

Berdahl, Sky
MR. DESTINY

Berenger, Tom
LOVE AT LARGE
FIELD, THE

Berenson, Marisa
WHITE HUNTER, BLACK HEART

Beresford, Susan
TALL GUY, THE

Berezin, Tanya
AWAKENINGS

Bergen, Polly
CRY-BABY

Berger, Aaron
MADHOUSE

Berger, Alan
DIE HARD 2

Berger, Gregg
SPACED INVADERS

Berger, Helmut
GODFATHER PART III, THE

Bergin, Patrick
MOUNTAINS OF THE MOON

Bergman, Anna
AVALON

Bergman, Boris
MR. FROST

Bergman, Jeff
GREMLINS 2 THE NEW BATCH

Bergman, Mary
ME AND HIM

Bergschneider, Conrad
STANLEY AND IRIS

Berkeley, Xander
LAST OF THE FINEST, THE
GUARDIAN, THE
SHORT TIME
GUMSHOE KID, THE
ROOKIE, THE

Berkheimer, Hank
BLADES

Berkoff, Steven
KRAYS, THE

Berlant, Jordan
NIGHT OF THE LIVING DEAD

Berleand, Francois
MAY FOOLS

Berlin, Jeannie
IN THE SPIRIT

Berlinger, Warren
TEN LITTLE INDIANS

Berman, Lester
WILD ORCHID

Berman, Shelley
ELLIOT FAUMAN, PH.D.

Bern, Mina
AVALON

Bernard, Eric
MARKED FOR DEATH
CYRANO DE BERGERAC

Bernard, Jason
PAINT IT BLACK

Bernard, Jay
MADHOUSE

Bernardini, Ida
GODFATHER PART III, THE

Bernhard, Sandra
WITHOUT YOU, I'M NOTHING

Bernsen, Collin
MR. DESTINY

Bernsen, Corbin
DEAD AIM

Bernstein, Al
ROCKY V

Bernstein, Alisa
AVALON

Berry, Richard
C'EST LA VIE

Berry, Stephanie
JACOB'S LADDER

Berry, Walter
NIGHT OF THE LIVING DEAD

Berryman, Michael
AFTERSHOCK

Bershad, James
STREET ASYLUM

Berthelot, Jean-Yves
FLAME IN MY HEART, A

Berthy, Claude
IMPROMPTU

Bertie, Diego
FULL FATHOM FIVE

Bertin, Roland
CYRANO DE BERGERAC

Bertram, Elisabeth
NASTY GIRL, THE

Besch, Bibi
TREMORS
BETSY'S WEDDING

Bessieres, Louis
HENRY AND JUNE

Betti, Laura
COURAGE MOUNTAIN

Beuth, Robert Alan
GRAVEYARD SHIFT

Beyer, Troy
WHITE GIRL, THE

Biana
FLAME IN MY HEART, A

Bianchi, Susannah
QUICK CHANGE

Bibby, C.K.
CHATTAHOOCHEE

Bibic, Vladimir
GREMLINS 2 THE NEW BATCH

Biehn, Michael
NAVY SEALS

Biel, Dick
GAME, THE

Big Crow, Maretta
DANCES WITH WOLVES

Big Eagle, Clayton
DANCES WITH WOLVES

Bihler, Urs
MAHABHARATA, THE

Bilas, Jay
I COME IN PEACE

Bilchick, Nadia
BURNDOWN

Bilginer, Haluk
LIONHEART

Billingsley, John
I LOVE YOU TO DEATH

Billy, George H.
HUNT FOR RED OCTOBER, THE

Bilsing, Sherry
DIE HARD 2

Binns, James
ROCKY V

Binzel, DeLynn
PREDATOR 2

Birchard, Paul
MEMPHIS BELLE

Bird, Billie
HOME ALONE

Bird, Ron
DESPERATE HOURS

Birdsong, Lori
BLOOD SALVAGE
HIGH DESERT KILL

Birkin, David
IMPROMPTU

Biro, Frank
GHOST DAD

Bishop, Anthony
QUICK CHANGE

Bishop, Joey
BETSY'S WEDDING

Bishop, Kelly
ME AND HIM

Bisset, Jacqueline
WILD ORCHID

Bizeau, Roberta
HOW TO MAKE LOVE TO A NEGRO WITH-
OUT GETTING TIRED

Bjork, Tracy
PRETTY WOMAN

Black, Karen
HOMER & EDDIE
TWISTED JUSTICE
OVER EXPOSED
NIGHT ANGEL

Black, Lewis
JACOB'S LADDER

Black, Mikey
GOODFELLAS

Black, Roger
FEUD, THE

Blackburn, Greta
UNDER THE BOARDWALK

Blackburn, Michael
STANLEY AND IRIS

Blackburn, Richard
STANLEY AND IRIS

Blackwood, Garry
GOODFELLAS

Blades, Ruben
MO' BETTER BLUES
TWO JAKES, THE
LEMON SISTERS, THE
PREDATOR 2

Blaguer, Asuncion
TWISTED OBSESSION

Blair, Linda
BEDROOM EYES II
REPOSSESSED

Blair, Nicky
GODFATHER PART III, THE
ROCKY V

Blaisdell, Deborah
WILDEST DREAMS

Blake, Geoffrey
MEN AT WORK

Blake, Joel
GOODFELLAS

Blakley, Ronee
MURDER BY NUMBERS

Blanc, Dominique
MAY FOOLS

Blanc, Mel
JETSONS: THE MOVIE

Blanc, Michel
STRIKE IT RICH
MONSIEUR HIRE

Blanchard, Danielle
YOUNG GUNS II

Blanche, Roland
TOO BEAUTIFUL FOR YOU

Bland, Rita
DICK TRACY
ADVENTURES OF FORD FAIRLANE, THE

Blasco, Daniel Anibal
WILD ORCHID

Bledsoe, Will
DARK SIDE OF THE MOON

Blethyn, Brenda
WITCHES, THE

Blicker, Jason
AMERICAN BOYFRIENDS

Blind, Anne-Marja
PATHFINDER

Bloch, Bernard
HIDDEN AGENDA

Bloch, David
MONSTER HIGH

Bloch, Scotty
SHOCK TO THE SYSTEM, A
BONFIRE OF THE VANITIES

Block, Larry
BETSY'S WEDDING

Block, Oliver
AWAKENINGS

Blocker, Dirk
LOVE AT LARGE

Blois, Adolfo
VERONICO CRUZ

Blommaert, Susan J.
EDWARD SCISSORHANDS

Blong, Jeni
CRY-BABY

Bloodworth, Robert
HYPERSPACE

Bloom, Gaetan
HENRY AND JUNE

Blossom, Roberts
HOME ALONE

Blount, Lisa
BLIND FURY

Blue, Michael
TAKING CARE OF BUSINESS

Blum, Kevin
AVALON

Blumberger, Erika
ROSALIE GOES SHOPPING

Blumenfeld, Alan
DARK SIDE OF THE MOON

Blunt, Gabrielle
MISADVENTURES OF MR. WILT, THE

Bluteau, Lothaire
JESUS OF MONTREAL

Bluto, John
ANDY COLBY'S INCREDIBLY AWESOME
ADVENTURE

Bly, John
FRIGHT HOUSE

Blyleven, Bert
TAKING CARE OF BUSINESS

Boalo, Tammy
EDWARD SCISSORHANDS

Bobby, Anne
NIGHTBREED

Boccio, Michael
GODFATHER PART III, THE

Bochner, Hart
MR. DESTINY

Boder, Lada
DICK TRACY

Boegel, Jessica
LOVE AT LARGE

Boen, Earl
MARKED FOR DEATH

Boggs, Bill
LEMON SISTERS, THE

Boggs, Gail
GHOST

Bohm, Katharina
MAGDALENE

Bohringer, Richard
COOK, THE THIEF, HIS WIFE & HER
LOVER, THE

Boidron, Emmanuelle
C'EST LA VIE

Boidron, Maxime
C'EST LA VIE

Bolender, Bill
ROBOCOP 2

Boles, Steve
COUPE DE VILLE

Bolger, John
LOOSE CANNONS

Bolkan, Edna
REVENGE

Bollen, Paul
DIE HARD 2

Bolling, Angie
TEXASVILLE

Bologna, Joseph
COUPE DE VILLE

Bologna, Michael
FUNLAND

Bon Jovi, Jon
YOUNG GUNS II

Bonange, Anne-Marie
MAY FOOLS

Bond, Cynthia
DEF BY TEMPTATION

Bond, James III
DEF BY TEMPTATION

Bond, Paula
CAGED IN PARADISO

Bond, Steve
MAGDALENE

Bongfeldt, Katherine
TEXASVILLE

Bonham Carter, Helena
HAMLET

Bonnaire, Sandrine
MONSIEUR HIRE

Bonnelly, Giovanna
HAVANA

Bonner, Tony
QUIGLEY DOWN UNDER

Bonnet, Adrienne
LIFE AND NOTHING BUT

Bono, Joseph
GOODFELLAS

Bono, Sonny
UNDER THE BOARDWALK

Bontempo, Pietro
TORRENTS OF SPRING

Boone, Mark Jr.
FORCE OF CIRCUMSTANCE

Boorman, Charlie
MR. FROST

Boothby, Victoria
GREEN CARD

Boretski, Peter
NUTCRACKER PRINCE, THE

Borges, Ernesto D. Jr.
MEN DON'T LEAVE

Borgese, Paul
FRIGHT HOUSE

Borgese, Sal
NIGHT OF THE SHARKS

Borgnine, Ernest
OPPONENT, THE

Bories, Marcel
MAY FOOLS

Borras, Louise
HUNT FOR RED OCTOBER, THE

Boryea, Jay
ROOKIE, THE

Bosco, Philip
BLUE STEEL
QUICK CHANGE

Boswall, Jonanthan
THREE MEN AND A LITTLE LADY

Botinis, P.
LANDSCAPE IN THE MIST

Bottomley, Caitlin Marie
MERMAIDS

Bottoms, Timothy
ISTANBUL, KEEP YOUR EYES OPEN
TEXASVILLE

Boucher, Mary
STEEL AND LACE

Bouquet, Carole
TOO BEAUTIFUL FOR YOU

Bourgeois, Robert
WHITE PALACE

Bourne, Douglas
MO' BETTER BLUES

Bourne, Lindsay
NARROW MARGIN

Bourque, Joe
COLD FEET

Bouton, Joy
YOUNG GUNS II

Bouyouklakis, Vassilis
LANDSCAPE IN THE MIST

Bovasso, Julie
BETSY'S WEDDING

Bowe, David
WEDDING BAND
ADVENTURES OF FORD FAIRLANE, THE
AIR AMERICA

Bowen, Dennis
LISA

Bowen, Erick
GODS MUST BE CRAZY II, THE

Bowen, James E. Jr.
AFTER DARK, MY SWEET

Bowen, Michael
GODFATHER PART III, THE

Bower, Tom
DIE HARD 2

Bowers, Wendy
MISERY

Bowman, Margaret
HOT SPOT, THE

Boyar, Sully
BETSY'S WEDDING
LEMON SISTERS, THE

Boyd, Chuck
PREDATOR 2

Boyd, Guy
LAST OF THE FINEST, THE
PACIFIC HEIGHTS

Boyd, Niven
CHICAGO JOE AND THE SHOWGIRL

Boyer, Bonnie
ADVENTURES OF FORD FAIRLANE, THE

Boyer, Chance
ARACHNOPHOBIA

Boyer, Myriam
TOO BEAUTIFUL FOR YOU

Boyle Slout, Marte
TAKING CARE OF BUSINESS

Boyle, Lara-Flynn
ROOKIE, THE

Bozman, Ron
MIAMI BLUES

Bracco, Lorraine
GOODFELLAS

Bradford, Jesse
PRESUMED INNOCENT

Bradford, Richard
INTERNAL AFFAIRS

Bradley, Brian
MURDER BY NUMBERS

Bradley, Doug
NIGHTBREED

Bradley, Joanne
LEMON SISTERS, THE

Bradley, Remone
KINDERGARTEN COP

Bradley, Spencer
GOODFELLAS

Bradshaw, Bill
OPPORTUNITY KNOCKS

Brady, Mike
UNBELIEVABLE TRUTH, THE

Braga, Sonia
ROOKIE, THE

Braha, Herb
CHILD'S PLAY 2

Branca, Jim "Bonk"
TAX SEASON

Brand, Larry
OVER EXPOSED

Brandauer, Klaus Maria
RUSSIA HOUSE, THE

Brando, Marlon
FRESHMAN, THE

Brandon, Clark
FUNLAND

Brandy
ARACHNOPHOBIA

Brannon, Sandi
DEAD AIM

Bransfield, Marjorie
TAKING CARE OF BUSINESS

Brantley, Betsy
I COME IN PEACE
HAVANA

Braque, Katrina
BONFIRE OF THE VANITIES

Brasington, John
CHATTAHOOCHEE

Brasseur, Claude
L'ETAT SAUVAGE

Bratcher, Joe
TAKING CARE OF BUSINESS

Braun, Bob
DIE HARD 2

Braun, Eddie
MEN AT WORK

Brauner, Asher
AMERICAN EAGLE

Braverman, Bart
HOLLYWOOD HOT TUBS II: EDUCATING
    CRYSTAL

Braverman, Marvin
PRETTY WOMAN

Brazeau, Jay
SHORT TIME

Breen, Patrick
NOBODY'S PERFECT

Breevelt, Arnie
COOK, THE THIEF, HIS WIFE & HER
    LOVER, THE

Brennan, Eileen
STELLA
WHITE PALACE
TEXASVILLE

Brens, Gustavo
Q&A

Brens, Martin E.
Q&A

Bresk, Carl
DARKMAN

Brett, Delia
AMERICAN BOYFRIENDS

Brewis, Peter
TALL GUY, THE

Breyette, William R.
I LOVE YOU TO DEATH

Brian, Mildred
BACK TO BACK

Bridges, Beau
DADDY'S DYIN'. . . WHO'S GOT THE WILL?

Bridges, Jeff
TEXASVILLE
COLD FEET

Bridges, Lloyd
JOE VERSUS THE VOLCANO

Bridges, Lynda
ALICE

Bridges, Verda
HOUSE PARTY

Brigden, Stephen
HIDDEN AGENDA

Bright, Richard
GODFATHER PART III, THE

Brighton, Barbra
FORBIDDEN DANCE, THE

Brill, Steven
POSTCARDS FROM THE EDGE
EDWARD SCISSORHANDS

Brimble, Nick
FRANKENSTEIN UNBOUND

Brine, Adrian
VINCENT AND THEO

Bringelson, Mark
MADHOUSE
FIRST POWER, THE

Brinkman, Bo
BAIL JUMPER

Briscoe, Donna
DEAD AIM

Briscoe, Jimmy
SPACED INVADERS

Brittan, Diana
DEAD AIM

Brizard, Philippe
L'ETAT SAUVAGE

Broadhurst, Kent
SHOCK TO THE SYSTEM, A

Brocas, Bernard
MAY FOOLS

Brochet, Anne
CYRANO DE BERGERAC

Brocksmith, Roy
TOTAL RECALL
ARACHNOPHOBIA

Broderick, Beth
BONFIRE OF THE VANITIES

Broderick, Matthew
FRESHMAN, THE

Bronner, Fritz
TAX SEASON

Bronson, Nicky
LEMON SISTERS, THE

Bronw, Einstein
MARKED FOR DEATH

Brook, Claudio
REVENGE

Brook, Jayne
KINDERGARTEN COP

Brook, Roger
BACK TO BACK

Brooks, Annabel
WITCHES, THE

Brooks, Cindy
STEEL AND LACE

Brooks, Francis
MADHOUSE

Brooks, Hildy
LISA
WHITE PALACE

Brooks, Jeff
BONFIRE OF THE VANITIES

Brooks, Laurelle
PRETTY WOMAN

Brooks, Mel
LOOK WHO'S TALKING TOO

Brooks, Richard
TO SLEEP WITH ANGER

Brooks, Ron
LEATHERFACE: THE TEXAS CHAINSAW
    MASSACRE III

Brookshire, F. Drucilla
CHATTAHOOCHEE

Brophy, Brian
SKINHEADS – THE SECOND COMING OF
    HATE

Broquedis, Stephane
MAY FOOLS

Broughton, Grace
WITHOUT YOU, I'M NOTHING

Broussard, Phillip
CRY-BABY

Broussard, Rebecca
TWO JAKES, THE

Browder, Ben
MEMPHIS BELLE

Brown, Andre Rosey
TAKING CARE OF BUSINESS

Brown, Barnaby
INNOCENT VICTIM

Brown, Blair
STRAPLESS

Brown, Bob
MEN AT WORK

Brown, Clancy
BLUE STEEL

Brown, Curtis
GAME, THE

Brown, Dwier
GUARDIAN, THE

Brown, Jim
TWISTED JUSTICE

Brown, Leon Addison
MO' BETTER BLUES

Brown, Matthew Rangi
DESPERATE HOURS

Brown, Michael
EDWARD SCISSORHANDS

Brown, Peter
DEMONSTONE

Brown, Ralph
IMPROMPTU

Brown, Richard Burton
MEN DON'T LEAVE

Brown, Roger Aaron
DOWNTOWN
ROBOCOP 2

Brown, Thomas Wilson
WELCOME HOME, ROXY CARMICHAEL

Brown, Todd Cameron
BACK TO THE FUTURE PART III

Brown, Willy
GODFATHER PART III, THE

Brozovic, Nick
COOK, THE THIEF, HIS WIFE & HER
    LOVER, THE

Brubaker, Tony
I COME IN PEACE

Bruce, Colin
CHICAGO JOE AND THE SHOWGIRL

Bruce, Georges
IMPROMPTU

Bruhanski, Alex
BIRD ON A WIRE
LOOK WHO'S TALKING TOO

Brull, Pamela
GUARDIAN, THE

Brunelle, Tom
MISERY

Bruni-Tedeschi, Valeria
C'EST LA VIE

Brunner, Jim
SAVAGE BEACH

Bruzan, Edward
HOME ALONE

Bryan, Kenneth Jensen
FLASHBACK

Bryant, Adam
AWAKENINGS

Bryant, Fred
TALL GUY, THE

Bryant, Paul Carlton
VITAL SIGNS

Brynolfsson, Renir
SHADOW OF THE RAVEN, THE

Bucarelly, Miguel
HAVANA

Buchanan, Yvette
NIGHT EYES

Buck, George
COME SEE THE PARADISE

Buckingham, Robert
HUNT FOR RED OCTOBER, THE

Buda, Crystal
ANIMAL BEHAVIOR

Buechler, John Carl
SLEEPING CAR, THE

Buffalo Child
DANCES WITH WOLVES

Buffer, Michael
ROCKY V

Buffinton, Bryan
MR. DESTINY

Bujold, Genevieve
FALSE IDENTITY

Buljo, Ellen Anne
PATHFINDER

Buljo, Henrik H.
PATHFINDER

Bulleit, Jim
CADILLAC MAN

Buller, Guy
FOURTH WAR, THE

Bullock, Earl
DIE HARD 2

Bullock, Gary
CHATTAHOOCHEE
ROBOCOP 2

Bulos, Yusef
AWAKENINGS

Bumiller, William
OVER EXPOSED

Bumstead, J.P.
PACIFIC HEIGHTS
HOLLYWOOD HOT TUBS II: EDUCATING
CRYSTAL

Bundy, Brooke
NIGHT VISITOR
SURVIVAL QUEST

Bunnage, Avis
KRAYS, THE

Bunster, Julian
STRAPLESS

Bunuel, Jean-Louis
HENRY AND JUNE

Burch, Tracey
MARKED FOR DEATH

Burchett, Iris R.
COLD FEET

Burden, Suzanne
STRAPLESS

Burden-Williams, Linda
CLASS OF 1999

Burdette, Nicole
GOODFELLAS

Burgess, James
EXORCIST III, THE

Burgin, Angus
LORD OF THE FLIES

Burke, Brian
STATE OF GRACE

Burke, Judith
BONFIRE OF THE VANITIES

Burke, Maggie
LEMON SISTERS, THE

Burke, Robert
UNBELIEVABLE TRUTH, THE

Burke, Tom
LISA

Burkholder, Scott
STEEL AND LACE

Burkley, Dennis
LAMBADA

Burks, Stephen
NIGHT EYES

Burlinson, Tom
TIME GUARDIAN, THE

Burns, Bobby
MEN AT WORK

Burns, Jere
HIT LIST

Burns, Linda
AWAKENINGS

Burns, Loy
MADHOUSE

Burns, Nora
JACOB'S LADDER

Burns, Susan
KINDERGARTEN COP

Burns, Traber
CHATTAHOOCHEE

Burr, Minda
PRETTY WOMAN

Burroughs, Bonnie
HARD TO KILL

Burrows, Darren E.
CRY-BABY
CLASS OF 1999

Burstyn, Igor
FOURTH WAR, THE

Burton, Chad
IN THE SPIRIT

Burton, Jordan
PROBLEM CHILD

Burton, Tony
ROCKY V

Burton, William H.
DANCES WITH WOLVES

Buscemi, Steve
TALES FROM THE DARKSIDE: THE MOVIE
FORCE OF CIRCUMSTANCE
MILLER'S CROSSING
KING OF NEW YORK

Busey, Gary
PREDATOR 2

Bush, Barbara
ERNEST GOES TO JAIL
PACIFIC HEIGHTS

Bush, Grand L.
FIRST POWER, THE
EXORCIST III, THE

Bustamante, Mark
YOUNG GUNS II

Busto, Bill
KILL-OFF, THE

Butkus, Dick
GREMLINS 2 THE NEW BATCH

Butler, Bill
ROSALIE GOES SHOPPING

Butler, Daniel
ERNEST GOES TO JAIL

Butler, David
NIGHT OF THE LIVING DEAD

Butler, Paul
TO SLEEP WITH ANGER
ROOKIE, THE

Butler, Vera
DR. CALIGARI

Butler, William
LEATHERFACE: THE TEXAS CHAINSAW
MASSACRE III
NIGHT OF THE LIVING DEAD

Buttram, Pat
BACK TO THE FUTURE PART III

Buxton, Sarah
PRIMAL RAGE

Buza, George
STELLA

Byers, Michael
POSTCARDS FROM THE EDGE

Byrd, Tom
YOUNG GUNS II

Byrd-Nethery, Miriam
LEATHERFACE: THE TEXAS CHAINSAW
MASSACRE III

Byrde, Edye
BONFIRE OF THE VANITIES

Byrge, Bill
ERNEST GOES TO JAIL

Byrne, Gabriel
LIONHEART
MILLER'S CROSSING

Byrnes, Burke
LAST OF THE FINEST, THE
AFTER DARK, MY SWEET
AIR AMERICA
TAKING CARE OF BUSINESS

C., Tony
TAX SEASON

Caan, James
DICK TRACY
MISERY

Caceres, Juanita
VERONICO CRUZ

Cade, John
DIE HARD 2

Cadou, Catherine
DREAMS

Cady, Bob
MONSTER HIGH

Cael, Jordan
QUICK CHANGE

Caesar, Harry
BIRD ON A WIRE

Caffrey, Stephen
LONGTIME COMPANION

Cage, Nicolas
FIRE BIRDS
VAMPIRE'S KISS
WILD AT HEART

Cagen, Don
OPPORTUNITY KNOCKS

Cagen, Rebecca
OPPORTUNITY KNOCKS

Cagle, Thom
PRESUMED INNOCENT

Cahill, John J.
ROCKY V

Cahn, Art
I LOVE YOU TO DEATH

Cain, Paul
ROCKY V

Caine, Michael
SHOCK TO THE SYSTEM, A
MR. DESTINY

Caine, Sari
MR. DESTINY

Calabria, Paul A.
IMPULSE

Calabro, Karin
  PRETTY WOMAN

Calandrino, Michael
  GOODFELLAS

Calderon, Antonio M.
  MEN DON'T LEAVE

Calderon, Paul
  Q&A
  KING OF NEW YORK

Caldicot, Richard
  MOUNTAINS OF THE MOON

Cale, David
  MEN DON'T LEAVE

Calendrillo, Joel
  GOODFELLAS

Caligiuri, Thomas John
  BETSY'S WEDDING

Call, Brandon
  BLIND FURY
  ADVENTURES OF FORD FAIRLANE, THE

Call, R.D.
  YOUNG GUNS II
  STATE OF GRACE

Callahan, Kara
  BLADES

Callaway, Thomas
  WHY ME?

Callender, L. Peter
  BLUE STEEL

Calles, Raul
  VERONICO CRUZ

Callow, Simon
  POSTCARDS FROM THE EDGE
  MR. AND MRS. BRIDGE

Calon, Jean-Claude
  LIFE AND NOTHING BUT

Calvin, Jeffrey
  LOVE AT LARGE

Calvin, John
  PRIMARY TARGET

Camero, Juan Jose
  VERONICO CRUZ

Cameron, Dean
  MEN AT WORK

Cameron, Hope
  IN THE SPIRIT

Cameron, John
  DARKMAN

Cameron, William
  NIGHT OF THE LIVING DEAD

Camilletti, Rob
  MADHOUSE

Camp, Cecile
  CYRANO DE BERGERAC

Camp, Hamilton
  DICK TRACY

Campanella, Frank
  PRETTY WOMAN
  BLOOD RED
  DICK TRACY

Campanella, Joseph
  BODY CHEMISTRY
  DOWN THE DRAIN

Campbell, Amelia
  EXORCIST III, THE

Campbell, Bruce
  DARKMAN

Campbell, C. Justin
  REAL BULLETS

Campbell, Colin
  NUNS ON THE RUN

Campbell, David
  TWISTED JUSTICE

Campbell, Graeme
  HOSTILE TAKEOVER

Campbell, J. Kenneth
  LAST OF THE FINEST, THE

Campbell, Jason
  FLASHBACK

Campbell, Jerry
  CHATTAHOOCHEE

Campbell, Joanne
  NUNS ON THE RUN

Campbell, Julia
  OPPORTUNITY KNOCKS

Campbell, Kenneth Hudson
  HOME ALONE

Campbell, Kevin
  WHITE GIRL, THE
  CHATTAHOOCHEE

Campbell, Patrick
  FAR OUT MAN

Campbell, Ron
  FOURTH WAR, THE

Campbell, Tevin
  GRAFFITI BRIDGE

Campbell, Tisha
  HOUSE PARTY
  ANOTHER 48 HRS.

Campbell, Tricia L.
  COME SEE THE PARADISE

Campitelli, Tom
  I COME IN PEACE

Camroux, Ken
  BIRD ON A WIRE

Camuti, Thomas E.
  GOODFELLAS

Canaberal, Bernard
  PRIMARY TARGET

Canada, Ron
  DOWNTOWN
  LAST OF THE FINEST, THE

Candido, Nino
  I COME IN PEACE

Candy, John
  HOME ALONE
  RESCUERS DOWN UNDER, THE

Canfield, Gene
  GOODFELLAS

Cann, John
  PREDATOR 2

Cannavale, Enzo
  CINEMA PARADISO

Canova, Larry
  TAX SEASON

Canovas, Anne
  VINCENT AND THEO

Cantafora, Antonio
  TORRENTS OF SPRING

Cantarini, Louis
  TEENAGE MUTANT NINJA TURTLES

Capetta, Joe
  MEN IN LOVE

Caplan, Twink
  NIGHT ANGEL
  LOOK WHO'S TALKING TOO

Capman, Daniel
  WILDEST DREAMS

Capodice, John
  BLUE STEEL
  Q&A
  GREMLINS 2 THE NEW BATCH
  JACOB'S LADDER

Capone, Vinnie
  CADILLAC MAN

Cappelman, Joola
  TALL GUY, THE

Cappuccino, Frank
  ROCKY V

Capri, Danny
  TOUCH OF A STRANGER

Capshaw, Kate
  LOVE AT LARGE

Cara, Irene
  HAPPILY EVER AFTER
  CAGED IN PARADISO

Carberry, Joseph
  PRESUMED INNOCENT

Cardille, Bill "Chilly Billy"
  NIGHT OF THE LIVING DEAD

Cardinal, Tantoo
  DANCES WITH WOLVES

Cardriche, Jaime
  HOUSE PARTY

Carette, Bruno
  MAY FOOLS

Carey, Harry Jr.
  BACK TO THE FUTURE PART III
  EXORCIST III, THE

Carey, Richenda
  STRIKE IT RICH

Carhart, Timothy
  HUNT FOR RED OCTOBER, THE

Cariaga, Marvelee
  DICK TRACY

Caridi, Carmine
  HAVANA
  GODFATHER PART III, THE

Carlin, Thomas A.
  JACOB'S LADDER

Carlisle, Steve
  SONNY BOY

Carlson, Erika
  TOTAL RECALL

Carlton, Hope Marie
  SAVAGE BEACH

Carlton, Mark
  TOTAL RECALL
  NAVY SEALS

Carlton, Sue
  TWO JAKES, THE

Carmen, Julie
  PAINT IT BLACK

Carnelutti, Francesco
  BELLY OF AN ARCHITECT, THE

Carnevali, Ida
  WHERE THE HEART IS

Carolan, Chris
  AWAKENINGS

Caron, Francois
  LIFE AND NOTHING BUT

Caron, Leslie
  COURAGE MOUNTAIN

Carpenter, David
  COME SEE THE PARADISE

Carr, Cathy "K.C."
  WHITE PALACE

Carr, Monica
BETSY'S WEDDING

Carr, Paul
NIGHT EYES

Carradine, David
BIRD ON A WIRE
SONNY BOY

Carradine, Keith
DADDY'S DYIN'... WHO'S GOT THE WILL?
COLD FEET

Carrasco, Carlos
RETURN OF SUPERFLY, THE

Carre, Isabelle
MAMA, THERE'S A MAN IN YOUR BED

Carrie, Kenny Scott
FORBIDDEN DANCE, THE

Carrier, Corey
MEN DON'T LEAVE
AFTER DARK, MY SWEET

Carrier, Tim
NIGHT OF THE LIVING DEAD

Carrillo, Elpidia
PREDATOR 2

Carrington, Debbie Lee
SPACED INVADERS
TOTAL RECALL

Carrington, Dwayne
FLASHBACK

Carroll, Corkey
UNDER THE BOARDWALK

Carroll, Helena
ROCKY V

Carroll, Larry
LAST OF THE FINEST, THE

Carson, Jackie
EDWARD SCISSORHANDS

Carson, John David
PRETTY WOMAN

Carter, Finn
TREMORS

Carter, Jack
CAGED FURY

Carter, Jim
WITCHES, THE

Carter, Mitch
FIRST POWER, THE

Carter, T.K.
SKI PATROL

Cartwright, Varonica
FALSE IDENTITY

Caruso, David
KING OF NEW YORK

Carver, Mary
ARACHNOPHOBIA

Carvey, Dana
OPPORTUNITY KNOCKS

Cascio, Salvatore
CINEMA PARADISO

Case, Catherine
DR. CALIGARI

Case, Justin
HAMLET

Case, Shaun Lee
COLD FEET

Casella, Martin
ROBOCOP 2

Caserta, Clem
GOODFELLAS

Casey, Bernie
ANOTHER 48 HRS.

Casey, Colleen
PRIMARY TARGET

Casini, Stefania
BELLY OF AN ARCHITECT, THE

Caspari, Cheri
PRETTY WOMAN

Casperson, Jack
FLASHBACK

Cassagne, Michel
LIFE AND NOTHING BUT

Cassaro, Nancy Ellen
GOODFELLAS

Cassavetes, Nick
BACKSTREET DREAMS

Cassel, Jean-Pierre
VINCENT AND THEO
MR. FROST

Cassel, Seymour
DICK TRACY

Cassidy, Joanna
WHERE THE HEART IS

Cassidy, Patrick
LONGTIME COMPANION

Castelo, Mel
STREETS

Castillo, Randy
ADVENTURES OF FORD FAIRLANE, THE

Castle, Martina
HOLLYWOOD HOT TUBS II: EDUCATING
CRYSTAL

Catamas, Scott
MEN IN LOVE

Cates, Phoebe
I LOVE YOU TO DEATH
GREMLINS 2 THE NEW BATCH

Cathey, Reg E.
LOOSE CANNONS
QUICK CHANGE

Catlett, Lloyd
TEXASVILLE

Caton, Juliette
COURAGE MOUNTAIN

Cattand, Gabriel
LIFE AND NOTHING BUT

Cattrall, Kim
HONEYMOON ACADEMY
BONFIRE OF THE VANITIES

Cavanaugh, Michael
FULL FATHOM FIVE

Cavazo, Carlos
ADVENTURES OF FORD FAIRLANE, THE

Cave, Robert
KINDERGARTEN COP

Cazenove, Christopher
THREE MEN AND A LITTLE LADY

Ceccaldi, Daniel
TWISTED OBSESSION

Cecchini, Mimi
CADILLAC MAN

Celia
L'ETAT SAUVAGE

Celozzi, Nick
MARKED FOR DEATH

Cembrowicz, Wlad
MURDER BY NUMBERS

Cenal, Alina
FAR OUT MAN

Ceresne, Ken
DISTURBANCE, THE

Cernugel, Frank R.
HOME ALONE

Cerullo, Al
BLUE STEEL

Cervantes, Carlos
FAR OUT MAN
MARKED FOR DEATH

Cerveris, Michael
STEEL AND LACE

Chacko, Lori
DR. CALIGARI

Chalem, Denise
TOO BEAUTIFUL FOR YOU

Chaliapin, Feodor Jr.
STANLEY AND IRIS

Chambers, Carol
DEAD AIM

Chambers, Lossen
BIRD ON A WIRE

Chambers, Marie
STREET ASYLUM
BONFIRE OF THE VANITIES

Chambers, Steve
DANCES WITH WOLVES

Chambers, Ty
TEXASVILLE

Champion, Jean
LIFE AND NOTHING BUT

Champion, Michael
TOTAL RECALL

Champion, Mike
FALSE IDENTITY

Chan, John K.
LIFE IS CHEAP... BUT TOILET PAPER IS
EXPENSIVE

Chan, Kim
CADILLAC MAN
ALICE

Chance, James
KINDERGARTEN COP

Chandel, Dina
ROSALIE GOES SHOPPING

Chandler, Freddi
STATE OF GRACE

Chanel, Tally
HOLLYWOOD HOT TUBS II: EDUCATING
CRYSTAL

Chaney, Frances
PAINT IT BLACK

Chang, David
LASER MAN, THE

Chang, Lia
FRANKENHOOKER

Chang, Sari
KING OF NEW YORK

Channing, Carol
HAPPILY EVER AFTER

Chapman, Alex
PREDATOR 2

Chapman, Michael
QUICK CHANGE

Charbonneau, Patricia
BRAIN DEAD

Charles, Greg
MEMPHIS BELLE

Charnota, Anthony
ROOKIE, THE

Chase, Channing
BONFIRE OF THE VANITIES

Chase, Maraya
BEDROOM EYES II

Chau, Kai-Bong
LIFE IS CHEAP. . . BUT TOILET PAPER IS EXPENSIVE

Chau, Mrs. Kai-Bong
LIFE IS CHEAP. . . BUT TOILET PAPER IS EXPENSIVE

Chaumeau, Andre
IMPROMPTU

Chauvin, Lilyan
PREDATOR 2

Chavez, Ingrid
GRAFFITI BRIDGE

Chaykin, Maury
WHERE THE HEART IS
MR. DESTINY
DANCES WITH WOLVES

Cheli, Bob "Rocky"
DIE HARD 2

Chen, Eric
SAVAGE BEACH

Chen, Joan
BLOOD OF HEROES

Chen, Lily
ROBOCOP 2

Chen, Philip
MARKED FOR DEATH

Cheng, Diane
ALICE

Chenier, Ron
TAKING CARE OF BUSINESS

Cher
MERMAIDS

Cheston, Cynthia
SKINHEADS – THE SECOND COMING OF HATE

Cheung, George
ROBOCOP 2

Cheung, Leslie
ROUGE

Chevalier, Catherine
NIGHTBREED

Chi, Leung Man
ROUGE

Chi, Mato
WILD ORCHID

Chianese, Dominick
Q&A

Chickering, Victoria
METROPOLITAN

Chieffet, Alexis
EXORCIST III, THE

Chieffo, Michael
I LOVE YOU TO DEATH

Chien, Yu
LIFE IS CHEAP. . . BUT TOILET PAPER IS EXPENSIVE

Chiles, Linden
FORBIDDEN DANCE, THE

Chin, Clint
GREEN CARD

Chin, Joey
KING OF NEW YORK

Chin, Susan
I LOVE YOU TO DEATH

Ching, Evelyn
LOVE AT LARGE

Chiquette, Charles
LAST OF THE FINEST, THE

Chisolm, Beirne
SKI PATROL

Chiswick, Geoffrey
MISADVENTURES OF MR. WILT, THE

Chivurenga, Boniface
DAMNED RIVER

Chizmadia, Steve
I COME IN PEACE

Cho, Emily
GREEN CARD

Chong, Paris
FAR OUT MAN

Chong, Rae Dawn
FAR OUT MAN
TALES FROM THE DARKSIDE: THE MOVIE

Chong, Robbi
FAR OUT MAN

Chong, Shelby
FAR OUT MAN

Chong, Tommy
FAR OUT MAN

Christiansen, Harvey
TEXASVILLE

Christie, Julie
FOOLS OF FORTUNE

Christopher, Dennis
CIRCUITRY MAN

Christopher, June
MISERY

Christopher, Paul
ADVENTURES OF FORD FAIRLANE, THE

Christopher, Thom
ANDY COLBY'S INCREDIBLY AWESOME ADVENTURE

Christy, George
PREDATOR 2

Chrosniak, Suzanne
EDWARD SCISSORHANDS

Chrysis, International
Q&A

Chu, Emily
ROUGE

Chuma, Boy Mathias
WHITE HUNTER, BLACK HEART

Chung, Lam
LIFE IS CHEAP. . . BUT TOILET PAPER IS EXPENSIVE

Ciarcia, Johnny Cha Cha
GOODFELLAS

Ciauri, Jerry
Q&A

Cicale, Peter
GOODFELLAS

Cicchetti, Mike
SHOCK TO THE SYSTEM, A

Cicchini, Robert
GODFATHER PART III, THE

Cienfuegos, Alfredo
REVENGE

Cieslak, Ryszard
MAHABHARATA, THE

Ciges, Luis
LABYRINTH OF PASSION

Cimarosa, Tano
CINEMA PARADISO

Cimino, Leo
FRESHMAN, THE

Cimino, Leonard
Q&A

Citriniti, Michael
GOODFELLAS

Citron, Jaqueline Alexandra
TAKING CARE OF BUSINESS

Citron, Kristen Amber
TAKING CARE OF BUSINESS

Citti, Franco
GODFATHER PART III, THE

Civita, Diane
HEART CONDITION

Claflin, Ned
DICK TRACY

Claire, Imogen
MISADVENTURES OF MR. WILT, THE

Clanton, Rony
DEF BY TEMPTATION
RETURN OF SUPERFLY, THE

Clark, Andrew
EDWARD SCISSORHANDS

Clark, Damon
GAME, THE

Clark, Gary
EDWARD SCISSORHANDS

Clark, John
LORDS OF MAGICK, THE

Clark, John P.
ROCKY V

Clark, Lynda
FEUD, THE

Clark, Lynn
DEMON WIND

Clark, Matt
BACK TO THE FUTURE PART III

Clark, Michael
COOK, THE THIEF, HIS WIFE & HER LOVER, THE

Clark, O. Laron
BONFIRE OF THE VANITIES

Clark, Pete
COLD FEET

Clark, Sharon
LISA

Clark, Stephanie
WITHOUT YOU, I'M NOTHING

Clark, William
BONFIRE OF THE VANITIES

Clarke, Joanna
COURAGE MOUNTAIN

Clarke, Margi
STRIKE IT RICH

Clarke, Michael Francis
DIE HARD 2

Clarke, Robert
ALIENATOR

Clarkson, Lana
HAUNTING OF MORELLA, THE

Clarkson, Patricia
TUNE IN TOMORROW

Clash, Kevin
TEENAGE MUTANT NINJA TURTLES

Claussen, Joy
BONFIRE OF THE VANITIES

Clay, Andrew Dice
ADVENTURES OF FORD FAIRLANE, THE

Clay, Nicholas
LIONHEART

Clayton, Edward
MISADVENTURES OF MR. WILT, THE

Cleator, Molly
KINDERGARTEN COP

Clemenson, Christian
BAD INFLUENCE

Clement, Marc
CHATTAHOOCHEE

Clements, Carol
ME AND HIM

Clements, Edward
METROPOLITAN

Clements, Shawn
SHORT TIME

Clennon, David
DOWNTOWN

Clevenger, Billy
DICK TRACY

Cliff, Jimmy
MARKED FOR DEATH

Clifford, Wendy
TUSKS

Clifton, Margaret
STRIKE IT RICH

Clinton, George
HOUSE PARTY
GRAFFITI BRIDGE

Clipper, Patricia
LAST OF THE FINEST, THE

Clive, Teagen
ALIENATOR

Clooney, George
RED SURF

Close, Del
OPPORTUNITY KNOCKS

Close, Glenn
REVERSAL OF FORTUNE
HAMLET

Cloud, David
LEATHERFACE: THE TEXAS CHAINSAW
MASSACRE III

Clunes, Martin
RUSSIA HOUSE, THE

Cluzet, Francois
TOO BEAUTIFUL FOR YOU

Clyde, Jeremy
MISADVENTURES OF MR. WILT, THE

Coan, T.J.
BONFIRE OF THE VANITIES

Cobb, Julie
LISA

Cobb, Kathryn
CHATTAHOOCHEE

Cobb, Randall "Tex"
BLIND FURY
ERNEST GOES TO JAIL

Coburn, David
SLEEPING CAR, THE

Coburn, James
YOUNG GUNS II

Coburn, James Jr.
TUSKS

Cochran, Mimi
I COME IN PEACE

Coduri, Camille
STRAPLESS
NUNS ON THE RUN

Coe, John A.
EXORCIST III, THE

Coffey, Scott
WILD AT HEART

Coffin, Barbara
CLASS OF 1999

Coffin, Frederick
HARD TO KILL

Coghill, Nikki
TIME GUARDIAN, THE

Cohen, Eva
AVALON

Cohen, Gilles
MAMA, THERE'S A MAN IN YOUR BED

Cohen, J.J.
BACK TO THE FUTURE PART III

Cohen, James
NIGHT EYES

Cohen, Jedediah
HOME ALONE

Cohen, Scott
JACOB'S LADDER

Cointepas, Odile
LIFE AND NOTHING BUT

Colaizzi, Robert
FIRST POWER, THE

Colby, Ronald L.
IMPULSE

Cole, Debra
HOT SPOT, THE

Cole, Victor
HOME ALONE

Coleman, Clifford C.
ROCKY V

Coleman, Dabney
WHERE THE HEART IS
SHORT TIME

Coleman, Erick
GAME, THE

Coleman, Mel
MADHOUSE

Colesberry, Robert F.
COME SEE THE PARADISE

Colet, Noel
DEMONSTONE

Coletta, Frank
STATE OF GRACE

Colicchio, Victor
Q&A
GOODFELLAS

Colin, Margaret
MARTIANS GO HOME!

Colisimo, Sandy
FRANKENHOOKER

Colitti, Rik
SHOCK TO THE SYSTEM, A

Collazo, Jose
Q&A

Collin, Anthony
STRIKE IT RICH

Collins, Bill
CHATTAHOOCHEE

Collins, Ruth
WILDEST DREAMS

Collins, Stephen
STELLA

Collins, William Hugh
CADILLAC MAN

Colon, Oscar
RETURN OF SUPERFLY, THE

Colton, Jacque Lynn
GREMLINS 2 THE NEW BATCH

Coltrane, Robbie
NUNS ON THE RUN

Colvin, Norm
RIVERBEND

Comart, Jean-Paul
LIFE AND NOTHING BUT

Combeau, Muriel
MAMA, THERE'S A MAN IN YOUR BED

Compan, Gilberto
REVENGE

Compton, Gary
ROCKY V

Conaway, Jeff
SLEEPING CAR, THE

Conder, Robert
SKI PATROL

Condor, Robert
DESPERATE HOURS

Conforti, Gino
GUMSHOE KID, THE

Conforti, Tony
GOODFELLAS

Connelly, Christopher
NIGHT OF THE SHARKS

Connelly, Jennifer
HOT SPOT, THE

Connery, Sean
HUNT FOR RED OCTOBER, THE
RUSSIA HOUSE, THE

Connick, Harry Jr.
MEMPHIS BELLE

Connolly, Kevin
ROCKY V

Connolly, Nora
WITCHES, THE

Connor, Tracy
HOME ALONE

Connors, Chuck
SKINHEADS – THE SECOND COMING OF
HATE
HIGH DESERT KILL

Connorton, Alice
METROPOLITAN

Conrad, Jim
ERNEST GOES TO JAIL

Conroy, Jenny
FIELD, THE

Conroy, Otakuye
DANCES WITH WOLVES

Considine, John
COUPE DE VILLE

Conte, Daniel P.
GOODFELLAS

Contessa, Mike
GOODFELLAS

Contreras, Victor
LAST OF THE FINEST, THE

Converse, Frank
EVERYBODY WINS

Coogan, Keith
UNDER THE BOARDWALK

Cook, Gregory
RETURN OF SUPERFLY, THE

Cook, Ron
COOK, THE THIEF, HIS WIFE & HER
LOVER, THE

Cooke, Christopher
UNBELIEVABLE TRUTH, THE

Cooke, Wendy
GRIM PRAIRIE TALES

Cooper, Barry
TAX SEASON

Cooper, Garry
MOUNTAINS OF THE MOON

Cooper, Gary
STAR QUEST: BEYOND THE RISING MOON

Cooper, Terence
SHRIMP ON THE BARBIE, THE

Copeland, Joan
LASER MAN, THE

Copleston, Geoffrey
BELLY OF AN ARCHITECT, THE

Copley, Teri
DOWN THE DRAIN

Coppola, Sam
BLUE STEEL
JACOB'S LADDER

Coppola, Sofia
GODFATHER PART III, THE

Corbellini, Vanni
BELLY OF AN ARCHITECT, THE

Corbin, Barry
SHORT TIME
GHOST DAD
HOT SPOT, THE

Cord, Alex
STREET ASYLUM

Cord, Erik
LOOSE CANNONS
TOTAL RECALL
ROBOCOP 2

Cordina, Jean-Louis
TOO BEAUTIFUL FOR YOU

Corello, Nick
MARKED FOR DEATH

Corff, Tracy
BURNDOWN

Corkum, Clark
SKINHEADS – THE SECOND COMING OF
HATE

Corley, Pat
MR. DESTINY

Corman, Catherine
FRANKENSTEIN UNBOUND

Corman, Maddie
ADVENTURES OF FORD FAIRLANE, THE

Cormier, Denise
MERMAIDS

Cornfeld, Stuart
DARKMAN

Cornwell, Charlotte
KRAYS, THE
WHITE HUNTER, BLACK HEART
RUSSIA HOUSE, THE

Corraface, Georges
MAHABHARATA, THE
IMPROMPTU

Corral, Benny
TOTAL RECALL

Correia, David
LOOSE CANNONS

Corri, Nick
PREDATOR 2

Corrigan, Kevin
MEN DON'T LEAVE
EXORCIST III, THE
GOODFELLAS

Corsair, Bill
PRESUMED INNOCENT
RETURN OF SUPERFLY, THE

Corsair, Janis
PRESUMED INNOCENT
GOODFELLAS

Corso, Gregory
GODFATHER PART III, THE

Cort, Bill
NAVY SEALS

Cort, Bud
BRAIN DEAD

Cortez, Katherine
STANLEY AND IRIS

Cortez, Stacey
I COME IN PEACE

Corti, Jesse
REVENGE

Cortino, Anthony
ALICE

Corvell, Tom
LORDS OF MAGICK, THE

Cosby, Bill
GHOST DAD

Costa, Lella
ICICLE THIEF, THE

Costa, Peter
LEMON SISTERS, THE

Costanza, Frank P.
DANCES WITH WOLVES

Costanzo, Robert
TOTAL RECALL
DICK TRACY
DIE HARD 2

Costello, Don
GODFATHER PART III, THE

Costello, Saasha
STATE OF GRACE

Costelloe, John
LAST EXIT TO BROOKLYN
DIE HARD 2

Coster, Nicolas
BETSY'S WEDDING

Costner, Annie
DANCES WITH WOLVES

Costner, Kevin
REVENGE
DANCES WITH WOLVES

Cothran, John Jr.
OPPORTUNITY KNOCKS

Cotton, James
AFTER DARK, MY SWEET

Coupal, Nathalie
HOW TO MAKE LOVE TO A NEGRO WITH-
OUT GETTING TIRED

Cousins, Brian
LONGTIME COMPANION

Cousins, Christian
KINDERGARTEN COP

Cousins, Joseph
KINDERGARTEN COP

Couvelard, Karine
HENRY AND JUNE

Covarrubias, Robert
GHOST DAD

Cowan, Greta
IMPORTED BRIDEGROOM, THE

Cowles, Matthew
STELLA

Cowley, John
FIELD, THE

Cowper, Nicola
LIONHEART

Cox, Brian
HIDDEN AGENDA

Cox, Courteney
MR. DESTINY

Cox, Ronny
LOOSE CANNONS
MARTIANS GO HOME!
TOTAL RECALL

Cox, Tony
SPACED INVADERS

Coyote, Peter
MAN INSIDE, THE

Cozart, Cylk
FIRE BIRDS

Craddock, Derrell
RIVERBEND

Craig, Donald
WHITE GIRL, THE

Craven, Matt
BLUE STEEL
CHATTAHOOCHEE
JACOB'S LADDER

Cravens, Rutherford
ROBOCOP 2

Crawford, Eve
STELLA

Crawford, Terry
TIME GUARDIAN, THE

Crawley, Charles
NIGHT OF THE LIVING DEAD

Crayton, Gloria
POSTCARDS FROM THE EDGE

Crear, Johnny
BONFIRE OF THE VANITIES

Creighton, Frank
METROPOLITAN

Crenna, Richard Anthony
PREDATOR 2

Crenshaw, Randy
ADVENTURES OF FORD FAIRLANE, THE

Crichlow, Brenda
SHORT TIME

Crick, Ed
KINDERGARTEN COP

Croasdale, Bill
MOUNTAINS OF THE MOON

Crofton, Andrew
EDWARD SCISSORHANDS

Crombie, Peter
DESPERATE HOURS

Cromer, Arnold
MO' BETTER BLUES

Cronenberg, David
NIGHTBREED

Cronin, Jeanette
SHRIMP ON THE BARBIE, THE

Cronin, Patrick
ROCKY V

Cronin, Sarah
FIELD, THE

Crosbie, Craig
MOUNTAINS OF THE MOON
NUNS ON THE RUN
RUSSIA HOUSE, THE

Crosby, Lucinda Sue
PRETTY WOMAN

Crosby, Mary
BODY CHEMISTRY

Cross, Harley
STANLEY AND IRIS

Cross, Marcia
BAD INFLUENCE

Crouse, Lindsay
DESPERATE HOURS

Crowder, Boots
COUPE DE VILLE

Crowley, David
IMPULSE

Crowley, Mermot
MISADVENTURES OF MR. WILT, THE

Cruise, Tom
DAYS OF THUNDER

Crumrine, Carol
EDWARD SCISSORHANDS

Cruz, Raymond
GREMLINS 2 THE NEW BATCH

Cryer, Cindy
FACE OF THE ENEMY

Cuddy, Jim
POSTCARDS FROM THE EDGE

Cudney, Roger
TOTAL RECALL

Cuka, Frances
MOUNTAINS OF THE MOON

Culbreth, Ron
FUNLAND

Culclasure, James "Fred"
CHATTAHOOCHEE

Culerier, Christiane
CYRANO DE BERGERAC

Culkin, Kieran
HOME ALONE

Culkin, Macaulay
JACOB'S LADDER
HOME ALONE

Cullen, Kerrie
MARKED FOR DEATH

Culley, Karen
HOT SPOT, THE

Cullum, Bill
MEMPHIS BELLE

Culp, Jason
SKINHEADS – THE SECOND COMING OF
HATE

Culp, Joseph
CAGED IN PARADISO

Cumbuka, Ji-Tu
CAGED IN PARADISO

Cummings, Jo B.
BACK TO THE FUTURE PART III

Cummins, Eli
PROBLEM CHILD

Cummins, Greg
CAGED FURY

Cummins, Ron
NARROW MARGIN

Cumpsty, Michael
STATE OF GRACE

Cundey, Dean
BACK TO THE FUTURE PART III

Cunningham, Dennis
STUFF STEPHANIE IN THE INCINERATOR

Cunningham, Michael
DIE HARD 2
STATE OF GRACE

Currie, Gordon
AMERICAN BOYFRIENDS

Curry, Bill W.
DANCES WITH WOLVES

Curry, Christopher
DESPERATE HOURS
RETURN OF SUPERFLY, THE

Curry, Russell
IMPULSE

Curry, Tim
HUNT FOR RED OCTOBER. THE

Curtin, Catherine
INHERITOR

Curtin, R.L.
DANCES WITH WOLVES

Curtis, Jamie Lee
BLUE STEEL

Curtis, Keene
LAMBADA

Curtis, Kenny
CRY-BABY

Cusack, Dick
CRAZY PEOPLE

Cusack, Joan
MEN DON'T LEAVE
MY BLUE HEAVEN

Cusack, John
GRIFTERS, THE

Cusack, Niamii
FOOLS OF FORTUNE

Cussiter, Daniel
DESPERATE HOURS

Cuticchio, Mimmo
GODFATHER PART III, THE

Cutter, Lise
HAVANA

Cybulski, Artur
HUNT FOR RED OCTOBER, THE

Cyler, Catherine
MR. FROST

Cypher, Jon
SPONTANEOUS COMBUSTION

Cyr, Miriam
HOW TO MAKE LOVE TO A NEGRO WITH-
OUT GETTING TIRED

Czvetko, Sandor
MY 20TH CENTURY

Czyzewska, Elzbieta
CADILLAC MAN

D'Ambrosio, Franc
GODFATHER PART III, THE

D'Ambrosio, Vito
BONFIRE OF THE VANITIES

d'Andrea, Oswald
LIFE AND NOTHING BUT

D'Angelo, Beverly
DADDY'S DYIN'. . . WHO'S GOT THE WILL?
PACIFIC HEIGHTS

D'Angelo, Victoria
HIDDEN AGENDA

D'Onofrio, Joseph
TEENAGE MUTANT NINJA TURTLES
GOODFELLAS

D'Onofrio, Vincent Phillip
BLOOD OF HEROES

D-Zire
HOUSE PARTY

D., Phinnaes
BACK TO THE FUTURE PART III

Da Silva, Antonio Mario
WILD ORCHID

Dabson, Jesse
ALIENATOR

Dafoe, Willem
CRY-BABY
WILD AT HEART

Dagory, Jean-Michel
IMPROMPTU

Dahlgren, Tom
IMPULSE

Daiana, Campeanu
HOME ALONE

Dair, John
CHICAGO JOE AND THE SHOWGIRL

Dal Ponte, Baldo
TAKING CARE OF BUSINESS

Dale, Badgett
LORD OF THE FLIES

Dale, James
ADVENTURES OF FORD FAIRLANE, THE

Dale, Janet
CHICAGO JOE AND THE SHOWGIRL

Dale, Troy
RIVERBEND

Daley, Ken
SURVIVAL QUEST

Dallas, Paul
OPPORTUNITY KNOCKS

Dallesandro, Joe
CRY-BABY

Daltrey, Roger
MACK THE KNIFE

Dame, Willian
STUFF STEPHANIE IN THE INCINERATOR

Damiano, James D.
GODFATHER PART III, THE

Damon, Gabriel
ROBOCOP 2

Danddridge, Gregg
WILD AT HEART

Daniel, Elisa
DANCES WITH WOLVES

Daniel, Sean
DARKMAN

Danielle, Kathryn
BONFIRE OF THE VANITIES

Danielli, Isa
CINEMA PARADISO

Daniels, Buddy
FAR OUT MAN
DOWN THE DRAIN
TAKING CARE OF BUSINESS

Daniels, Gray
GREMLINS 2 THE NEW BATCH

Daniels, Jeff
ARACHNOPHOBIA
WELCOME HOME, ROXY CARMICHAEL

Daniels, Ryan
FRIGHT HOUSE

Danika, Dayna
HOLLYWOOD HOT TUBS II: EDUCATING
CRYSTAL

Danker, Eli
IMPULSE

Danley, J. Mark
LEMON SISTERS, THE

Danner, Blythe
MR. AND MRS. BRIDGE
ALICE

Danner, Renaud
MAY FOOLS

Danns, David
WHITE HUNTER, BLACK HEART

Dano, Royal
SPACED INVADERS

Danon, Leslie
MARKED FOR DEATH

Danson, Ted
THREE MEN AND A LITTLE LADY

Danziger, Maia
LAST EXIT TO BROOKLYN

Dapolito, Lisa
GOODFELLAS

Darbo, Patrika
SPACED INVADERS
GREMLINS 2 THE NEW BATCH
DADDY'S DYIN'. . . WHO'S GOT THE WILL?
GHOST DAD

Darling, Toni
BLUE STEEL

Darlow, David
MILLER'S CROSSING

Darmohray, Kurt
FOURTH WAR, THE

Darnell, Vicki
FRANKENHOOKER

Darrow, Danny
Q&A

Darrow, Henry
LAST OF THE FINEST, THE

Darrow, Tony
GOODFELLAS

Darton, Marlon
MADHOUSE

Daughtry, Herbert
MO' BETTER BLUES

Davi, Robert
PEACEMAKER
PREDATOR 2

David, Cilfford
EXORCIST III, THE

David, Eleanor
SLIPSTREAM
WHITE HUNTER, BLACK HEART

David, Keith
MEN AT WORK
MARKED FOR DEATH

Davids, Goliath
RIVER OF DEATH

Davidson, Foziah
RIVER OF DEATH

Davidson, John
EDWARD SCISSORHANDS

Davidson, Lawrence
STRIKE IT RICH

Davies, Glynis
STELLA

Davies, Jackson
BIRD ON A WIRE

Davies, James
WILDEST DREAMS

Davies, John S.
PROBLEM CHILD

Davies, Lane
FUNLAND

Davies, Lori "Chacko"
MONSTER HIGH

Davin, Danny
IN THE SPIRIT

Davis, Brad
ROSALIE GOES SHOPPING

Davis, Bud
CHATTAHOOCHEE

Davis, Carole
SHRIMP ON THE BARBIE, THE

Davis, Daniel
HUNT FOR RED OCTOBER, THE
HAVANA

Davis, Debbie
LORDS OF MAGICK, THE

Davis, Don S.
LOOK WHO'S TALKING TOO

Davis, Duane
SKINHEADS – THE SECOND COMING OF
HATE

Davis, Geena
QUICK CHANGE

Davis, Gregg Todd
OPPONENT, THE

Davis, Hope
FLATLINERS
HOME ALONE

Davis, John
ERNEST GOES TO JAIL

Davis, Judy
ALICE
IMPROMPTU

Davis, Ossie
JOE VERSUS THE VOLCANO

Davis, Reggie
CRY-BABY

Davis, Roy Milton
BONFIRE OF THE VANITIES

Davis, Sammi
LIONHEART

Davis, Tom
FEUD, THE

Davis, Tracy
STAR QUEST: BEYOND THE RISING MOON

Davis, Vince
PROBLEM CHILD

Davis, Warren
FRESHMAN, THE

Davison, Bruce
LONGTIME COMPANION
STEEL AND LACE

Davydov, Anatoly
HUNT FOR RED OCTOBER, THE
BONFIRE OF THE VANITIES

Day, Morris
ADVENTURES OF FORD FAIRLANE, THE
GRAFFITI BRIDGE

Day, Patrick
HOLLYWOOD HOT TUBS II: EDUCATING
CRYSTAL

De Acutis, William
CHATTAHOOCHEE

De Baer, Jean
FUNNY ABOUT LOVE

de Bankole, Issach
HOW TO MAKE LOVE TO A NEGRO WITH-
OUT GETTING TIRED

de Banzie, Lois
ARACHNOPHOBIA

De Broux, Lee
YOUNG GUNS II

De Franco, Carmen
HAVANA

de Gall, Alexandre
HENRY AND JUNE

De Hart, Wayne
ROBOCOP 2

De Icaza, Luis
REVENGE

De Jager, Owen
BURNDOWN

De Jesus, Wanda
DOWNTOWN
ROBOCOP 2

de la Brosse, Simon
STRIKE IT RICH

De La Tour, Frances
STRIKE IT RICH

de Lancie, John
TAKING CARE OF BUSINESS

de Medeiros, Maria
HENRY AND JUNE

De Niro, Robert
STANLEY AND IRIS
GOODFELLAS
AWAKENINGS

De Nuys, Crispin
RIVER OF DEATH

De Oni, Christofer
REVENGE

De Palma, Brian
BONFIRE OF THE VANITIES

De Palma, Rossy
TIE ME UP! TIE ME DOWN!

de Penguern, Artus
HENRY AND JUNE

De Prume, Cathryn
NAVY SEALS

De Rose, Chris
AFTERSHOCK

De Sapio, Francesca
TORRENTS OF SPRING
BLOOD RED

De Young, Cliff
FLASHBACK

DeAcutis, William
ME AND HIM
MEN DON'T LEAVE

Deacy, Ed
GOODFELLAS

Deadrick, Rock
MARKED FOR DEATH

Dean, Jimmy
BIG BAD JOHN

DeAngelis, Richard
MEN DON'T LEAVE

Dear, H. Clay
GOODFELLAS

Dear, William
DARKMAN

Dearie, Kevin
MILLER'S CROSSING

Deayton, Angus
TALL GUY, THE

Deconcini, Karen
MADHOUSE

Decosterd, Kutira
MEN IN LOVE

Dee, Catherine
STUFF STEPHANIE IN THE INCINERATOR

Dee, Ruby
LOVE AT LARGE

Dees, Rick
JETSONS: THE MOVIE

Deeth, James
POSTCARDS FROM THE EDGE

DeFuria, Rick
PRESUMED INNOCENT

DeFusco, Ed
DIE HARD 2

DeGarnier, Ian Marshall
IMPROMPTU

Dehart, Wayne
I COME IN PEACE

Del Piero, Terese
ARACHNOPHOBIA

Del Rey, Pilar
FORBIDDEN DANCE, THE

Del Rio, Michael Philip
BLUE STEEL

Del Rosario, Monsour
DEMONSTONE

Delalande, Anatole
CYRANO DE BERGERAC

Delesandro, James
LAST OF THE FINEST, THE

Delgado, Guillermo
VERONICO CRUZ

Delgado, Kim
KINDERGARTEN COP

Delgado, Miguel
FLATLINERS

Deliso, Debra
DR. CALIGARI

Dellinger, Dana
NIGHT EYES

Delmonte, Richard
MARKED FOR DEATH

Delora, Jennifer
BEDROOM EYES II
FRIGHT HOUSE
FRANKENHOOKER

DeLuise, Dom
LOOSE CANNONS
HAPPILY EVER AFTER

DeMauro, Nick
DOWN THE DRAIN

DeMita, John
STEEL AND LACE

Dempsey, Jerome
TUNE IN TOMORROW

Dempsey, Patrick
COUPE DE VILLE
HAPPY TOGETHER

Denizon, Jean-Paul
MAHABHARATA, THE

Dennehy, Brian
LAST OF THE FINEST, THE
BELLY OF AN ARCHITECT, THE
PRESUMED INNOCENT

Dennehy, Kathleen
LAST OF THE FINEST, THE

Denney, David
ROSALIE GOES SHOPPING

Dennis, Danny
GREEN CARD

Dennis, Ellin
EDWARD SCISSORHANDS

Dennis, Winston
NUNS ON THE RUN

Dennison, Sabrina
SANTA SANGRE

Denos, John
PEACEMAKER

DePalma, Renee
MEN IN LOVE

Depardieu, Gerard
TOO BEAUTIFUL FOR YOU

CYRANO DE BERGERAC
GREEN CARD

Depatie, Beth
LEATHERFACE: THE TEXAS CHAINSAW
MASSACRE III

Deplanche, Philippe
LIFE AND NOTHING BUT

Depp, Johnny
CRY-BABY
EDWARD SCISSORHANDS

Deren, Bobby
EXORCIST III, THE

Derlon, Alexis
C'EST LA VIE

Dern, Bruce
AFTER DARK, MY SWEET

Dern, Laura
WILD AT HEART

Dernier, Lydie
BLOOD RELATIONS

DeRoy, Jamie
GOODFELLAS

Derwin, Jordan
CADILLAC MAN

DeSalvo, Anne
TAKING CARE OF BUSINESS

DeSantis, Stanley
VITAL SIGNS
TAKING CARE OF BUSINESS

DeSanto, Daniel
FRESHMAN, THE

DeSoto, Rosana
FACE OF THE ENEMY

DeSouza, Indrani
WITHOUT YOU, I'M NOTHING

Despotovich, Nada
FIRST POWER, THE

Deutsch, Patti
JETSONS: THE MOVIE

Devane, William
VITAL SIGNS

Devaney, Richie
MR. DESTINY

DeVaul, Ken
EDWARD SCISSORHANDS

Devereux, Clarke
HOME ALONE

Devereux, Monica
HOME ALONE

DeVille, Rhe
QUICK CHANGE

Devin, Lee
BLADES

Devine, Loretta
STANLEY AND IRIS

DeVito, Dominque
GOODFELLAS

DeVito, Karla
MODERN LOVE

Devlin, J.G.
RAGGEDY RAWNEY, THE

Devon, Tony
LEMON SISTERS, THE

Di Elsi, Frank
PACIFIC HEIGHTS

di Pinto, Nicolo
CINEMA PARADISO

Diamond, Barry
HOUSE PARTY

Diamond, Jessica Z.
POSTCARDS FROM THE EDGE

Diamond, Keith
AWAKENINGS

Diamond, Reed Edward
MEMPHIS BELLE

Diaz, John
PACIFIC HEIGHTS

Dibb, Andrew
GODS MUST BE CRAZY II, THE

DiBenedetto, John
GOODFELLAS

DiBenedetto, Tony
MARKED FOR DEATH

DiCenzo, George
FACE OF THE ENEMY
EXORCIST III, THE

DiCicco, Jessica
GODFATHER PART III, THE

Dickerson, George
AFTER DARK, MY SWEET
DEATH WARRANT

Dickinson, Amanda
INNOCENT VICTIM

Dickman, Robert
LOOSE CANNONS

Dickson, Damon
GRAFFITI BRIDGE

Dickson, Neil
LIONHEART

Dickson, Wendy
FRESHMAN, THE

DiCocco, Paul A. Jr.
TWO JAKES, THE
COME SEE THE PARADISE

Diedrich, Claus
FOURTH WAR, THE

Diehl, John
MADHOUSE
DARK SIDE OF THE MOON

Dierkop, Charles
BLOOD RED

Dietl, Richard "Bo"
GOODFELLAS

DiGiandomenico, Joe
WITHOUT YOU, I'M NOTHING

DiGregorio, Ben
COME SEE THE PARADISE

DiLeo, Frank
GOODFELLAS

Dill, David
Q&A

Dillan, Stephan
HAMLET

Diller, Phyllis
HAPPILY EVER AFTER
NUTCRACKER PRINCE, THE

Dillon, Brendan Jr.
LORDS OF MAGICK, THE

Dillon, Melinda
SPONTANEOUS COMBUSTION

Dillon, Mia
SHOCK TO THE SYSTEM, A

Dillon, Tedd
STELLA

DiLorenzo, Edward
ADVENTURES OF FORD FAIRLANE, THE

Dimiglio, Gerard
STRIKE IT RICH

Dimopoulos, Steven
LOOK WHO'S TALKING TOO

Dingle, Jane
STELLA

Dioguardi, Richard
GOODFELLAS

Dion, Daniel
FRESHMAN, THE

Dioume, Mamadou
MAHABHARATA, THE

Diskin, Ben
KINDERGARTEN COP

Diskin, Phil
HOLLYWOOD HOT TUBS II: EDUCATING
CRYSTAL

Disson, Jerry
DISTURBANCE, THE

Divoff, Andrew
HUNT FOR RED OCTOBER, THE
ANOTHER 48 HRS.
GRAVEYARD SHIFT

Dix, Lewis Jr.
FAR OUT MAN

Dixon, Eddie
WILD AT HEART

Dixon, Oliver
BONFIRE OF THE VANITIES

Do Carmo, Antonio Agusto
WILD ORCHID

Dobrin, Marilyn
CADILLAC MAN

Dobson, Peter
LAST EXIT TO BROOKLYN

Dobtcheff, Vernon
HAMLET

Doby, Kathryn
HANDMAID'S TALE, THE

Dodds, John
FOURTH WAR, THE

Dodds, K.K.
FLATLINERS

Dodge, Frederick
DEAD PIT

Dodson, Mark
GREMLINS 2 THE NEW BATCH

Doe, John
WITHOUT YOU, I'M NOTHING

Doenas, Gigi
DOG TAGS

Doerkson, Gordon
SHORT TIME

Doherty, Matt
HOME ALONE

Dokken, Don
FAR OUT MAN

Dolan, Susan
SKI PATROL

Dollarhide, April Dawn
CAGED FURY

Dolo, Akonio
L'ETAT SAUVAGE

Domange, Francois
LIFE AND NOTHING BUT

Domani, Sal
LEMON SISTERS, THE

Dombasle, Arielle
TWISTED OBSESSION

Dombo, Kathy
EDWARD SCISSORHANDS

Domeier, Richard
DIE HARD 2

Dominguez, Kevin
MONSTER HIGH

Donahue, Elinor
PRETTY WOMAN

Donahue, Fifi
FRESHMAN, THE

Donahue, Troy
CRY-BABY

Donai, Danial
DIE HARD 2

Donaldson, B.J.
JACOB'S LADDER

Donaldson, Kim
WILD ORCHID

Donaldson, Norma
HOUSE PARTY

Donat, Richard
AMERICAN BOYFRIENDS

Donatone, Mario
GODFATHER PART III, THE

Donnelly, Donal
GODFATHER PART III, THE

Donnelly, Jesse J.
MR. DESTINY

Donohue, Kourtney
LEMON SISTERS, THE

Donovan, Bazil
POSTCARDS FROM THE EDGE

Donovan, Erin
MACK THE KNIFE

Donovan, Tate
MEMPHIS BELLE

Dooley, Paul
FLASHBACK

Doolittle, John
ROBOCOP 2

DoQui, Robert
ROBOCOP 2

Doran, Jess
STREET ASYLUM

Dorff, Thomas
BLUE STEEL

Dornya, Marya
QUICK CHANGE

Dorsey, Kevin
WITHOUT YOU, I'M NOTHING

Dorson, Gloria
TOTAL RECALL

Dos Santos, Joao Carlos
WILD ORCHID

Dos Santos, Solange Dantas
WILD ORCHID

Dossett, John
LONGTIME COMPANION

Dottorini, Christian
TORRENTS OF SPRING

Douglas, Illeana
GOODFELLAS

Douglas, James
MR. DESTINY

Doukoure, Cheik
L'ETAT SAUVAGE

Dourif, Brad
SPONTANEOUS COMBUSTION
EXORCIST III, THE
GRIM PRAIRIE TALES
GRAVEYARD SHIFT
CHILD'S PLAY 2

HIDDEN AGENDA
SONNY BOY

Douville, Roland
EDWARD SCISSORHANDS

Dowd, Ann
GREEN CARD

Dowell, Raye
MO' BETTER BLUES

Dowling, Rachel
FIELD, THE

Downey, Morton Jr.
PREDATOR 2

Downey, Robert Jr.
AIR AMERICA

Downie, Penny
LIONHEART

Doyle, Barclay
TEXASVILLE

Doyle, Kathleen
FEUD, THE

Draber, Etienne
MAY FOOLS

Drago, Billy
DELTA FORCE 2

Drago, Joseph
GODFATHER PART III, THE

Drake, Larry
DARKMAN

Drake-Massey, Bebe
HOUSE PARTY

Draxton, Mark
HUNT FOR RED OCTOBER, THE

Drescher, Chester
CADILLAC MAN

Drescher, Fran
WEDDING BAND
CADILLAC MAN

Drescher, James
BLUE STEEL

Dreyfuss, Randy
ELLIOT FAUMAN, PH.D.

Dreyfuss, Richard
POSTCARDS FROM THE EDGE

Drinkx, Dave
MILLER'S CROSSING

Driscoll, Robin
TALL GUY, THE

Drotar, Dena
NIGHT EYES

Droz, Anthony
DIE HARD 2

Drukarova, Dinara
FREEZE—DIE—COME TO LIFE

Drummond, Alice
AWAKENINGS

Drury, Ken
MISADVENTURES OF MR. WILT, THE

Dubac, Robert
ROOKIE, THE

Dubois, Ja'net
HEART CONDITION

Dubois, Jean-Pol
LIFE AND NOTHING BUT

Dubost, Paulette
MAY FOOLS

Duchaussoy, Michel
MAY FOOLS
LIFE AND NOTHING BUT

Duchene, Kate
TALL GUY, THE

Duckworth, Dortha
STANLEY AND IRIS

Ducommun, Rick
HUNT FOR RED OCTOBER, THE
GREMLINS 2 THE NEW BATCH

Duda, John Joseph
FLATLINERS

Dudas, Vernon
WHITE PALACE

Dudgeon, Neil
FOOLS OF FORTUNE

Dudikoff, Michael
RIVER OF DEATH

Duerloo, Michael
WHITE GIRL, THE

Dufay, Eric
LIFE AND NOTHING BUT

Duff-Griffin, William
BETSY'S WEDDING

Duffee, Kirk
BYE BYE BLUES

Duffek, Patty
SAVAGE BEACH

Duffy, Conor
DANCES WITH WOLVES

Duffy, Dave
HAMLET

Duffy, Thomas F.
STATE OF GRACE

Duffy, William
TWO JAKES, THE

Dugan, Dennis
PROBLEM CHILD

Dugan, Tom
LISA
MARKED FOR DEATH
KINDERGARTEN COP

Duhe, A.J.
OPPONENT, THE

Dujmovic, Davor
TIME OF THE GYPSIES

Dukakis, Olympia
IN THE SPIRIT
LOOK WHO'S TALKING TOO

Duke, Bill
BIRD ON A WIRE

Duke, O.L.
WHITE GIRL, THE
RETURN OF SUPERFLY, THE

Dukes, David
HANDMAID'S TALE, THE

Dumas, Alain
CYRANO DE BERGERAC

Dumaurier, Francois
GREEN CARD

Dunagan, Deanna
MEN DON'T LEAVE

Dunard, David
CAGED IN PARADISO
GUMSHOE KID, THE

Dunaway, Faye
HANDMAID'S TALE, THE

Dunk, Jim
MISADVENTURES OF MR. WILT, THE

Dunkley, Anne
WHITE HUNTER, BLACK HEART

Dunlop, Vic
MARTIANS GO HOME!

Dunn, Kevin
BLUE STEEL
MARKED FOR DEATH
BONFIRE OF THE VANITIES

Dunn, Nora
MIAMI BLUES

Dunne, Griffin
ME AND HIM

Dunne, James Patrick
PRETTY WOMAN

Dunphy, Jerry
IMPULSE

Dunsmore, Rosemary
TOTAL RECALL

Dunst, Kirsten
BONFIRE OF THE VANITIES

Dunsworth, Loren
AMERICAN BOYFRIENDS

DuRand, Le Chance
AWAKENINGS

Durang, Christopher
SHOCK TO THE SYSTEM, A
IN THE SPIRIT

Durbin, John
DR. CALIGARI

Durkin, Fr. John
EXORCIST III, THE

Durkin, Patrick
LIONHEART

Durning, Charles
DICK TRACY

Durven, Richard
FOURTH WAR, THE

Dury, Ian
COOK, THE THIEF, HIS WIFE & HER
LOVER, THE
RAGGEDY RAWNEY, THE

Dusay, Debra
LOVE AT LARGE

Duse, Vittorio
GODFATHER PART III, THE

Dutch, Debbie
HAUNTING OF MORELLA, THE

Dutronc, Jaques
L'ETAT SAUVAGE

Dutton, Charles
Q&A

Duvall, Robert
HANDMAID'S TALE, THE
SHOW OF FORCE, A
DAYS OF THUNDER

Dworsky, Frank
MADHOUSE

Dwyer, David
FEUD, THE
CHATTAHOOCHEE
ROBOCOP 2
EXORCIST III, THE

Dye, Cameron
MEN AT WORK

Dye, Dale
FOURTH WAR, THE
FIRE BIRDS

Dykiel, Bozena
INTERROGATION, THE

Dyrek, Francois
LIFE AND NOTHING BUT

Dysart, Richard
BACK TO THE FUTURE PART III

Dyson, Kym
HIDDEN AGENDA

Dzundza, George
IMPULSE
WHITE HUNTER, BLACK HEART

E., Shelia
ADVENTURES OF FORD FAIRLANE, THE

Earley, Mark
COME SEE THE PARADISE

Easler, Michael
CHATTAHOOCHEE

Eastwood, Clint
WHITE HUNTER, BLACK HEART
ROOKIE, THE

Eastwood, Jayne
STELLA
HOSTILE TAKEOVER

Eaton, Marion
PAINT IT BLACK

Ebersole, Christine
GHOST DAD

Ebersole, Drew
CRY-BABY

Echeverria, Sol
VAMPIRE'S KISS

Eckmuller, Ossi
NASTY GIRL, THE

Eckstut, Bruce
PRETTY WOMAN

Ecoffey, Jean-Philippe
HENRY AND JUNE

Edaki, Mika
DREAMS

Edaki, Shigeru
DREAMS

Edelman, Gregg
GREEN CARD

Edelman, Rorey
DEAD PIT

Edelstein, Michael David
AVALON

Edernac, Pierre
HENRY AND JUNE

Edgcomb, James
IMPULSE

Edison, Dave
STEEL AND LACE

Edmiston, Walker
DICK TRACY

Edmondson, Michael Mark
PREDATOR 2

Edward, Jack
MADHOUSE

Edwards, Anthony
DOWNTOWN

Edwards, Brenda
COOK, THE THIEF, HIS WIFE & HER
LOVER, THE

Edwards, Bryant
GHOST DAD

Edwards, Jennifer
OVER EXPOSED

Edwards, Keith
MEMPHIS BELLE
RUSSIA HOUSE, THE

Edwards, Lance
PEACEMAKER

Edwards, Marnie
FRESHMAN, THE

Edwards, Vince
ANDY COLBY'S INCREDIBLY AWESOME
ADVENTURE

GUMSHOE KID, THE

Edwards, Whit
MR. DESTINY

Efroni, Yehuda
TEN LITTLE INDIANS

Egan, Aeryk
MADHOUSE
FLATLINERS

Egawa, Miyuki
DREAMS

Eggert, Nicole
HAUNTING OF MORELLA, THE

Egi, Stan
COME SEE THE PARADISE

Egurrola, Julieta
REVENGE

Ehlers, Jerome
QUIGLEY DOWN UNDER

Eichhorn, Lisa
GRIM PRAIRIE TALES

Eichhorst, Adam
MR. DESTINY

Eide, Elsie
WITCHES, THE

Eiding, Paul
MADHOUSE

Eigeman, Christopher
METROPOLITAN

Eiland, Michael
YOUNG GUNS II

Eiros
GODS MUST BE CRAZY II, THE

Eisenberg, Ned
AIR AMERICA

Eisenstein, Dan
PUMP UP THE VOLUME

Ekins, Buddy
PACIFIC HEIGHTS

El Razzac, Abdul Salaam
PRETTY WOMAN
DEATH WARRANT

Elam, Jack
BIG BAD JOHN

Elder, Gordon
LORD OF THE FLIES

Eldred, Stig
DICK TRACY

Elias, Cyrus
MAGDALENE

Elias, Rico
AWAKENINGS

Eliot, Drew
Q&A

Elise, Christine
CHILD'S PLAY 2

Elizondo, Everado
LORD OF THE FLIES

Elizondo, Hector
PRETTY WOMAN
TAKING CARE OF BUSINESS

Ellaraino
HOUSE PARTY
VITAL SIGNS

Elledge, Justin
PROBLEM CHILD

Elliott, Bob
QUICK CHANGE

Elliott, Chris
HYPERSPACE

Elliott, Robert
LOOSE CANNONS

Elliott, Sam
SIBLING RIVALRY

Elliott, Shawn
IMPULSE

Elliott, Stephen
TAKING CARE OF BUSINESS

Elliott, Steven
NIGHT OF THE SHARKS

Ellis, Berle
NIGHT OF THE LIVING DEAD

Ellis, Chenoa
LAST OF THE FINEST, THE

Ellis, Chris
DAYS OF THUNDER

Ellis, Hywel Williams
COOK, THE THIEF, HIS WIFE & HER
LOVER, THE

Ellis, John
STAR QUEST: BEYOND THE RISING MOON

Ellis, T.C.
GRAFFITI BRIDGE

Ellis, Tony
GOODFELLAS

Elm, Steve
MEMPHIS BELLE

Elrod, J. McRee
SHORT TIME

Elsner, Hannelore
TIME TROOPERS

Elso, Pascal
LIFE AND NOTHING BUT

Elterman, Eric
PROBLEM CHILD

Elwes, Cary
DAYS OF THUNDER

Emil, Michael
IN THE SPIRIT

Emizawa, Jumi
COME SEE THE PARADISE

Emling, Ward
PROBLEM CHILD

Endeveri, John
MARKED FOR DEATH

Endo, Emi
COME SEE THE PARADISE

Endo, Mugita
DREAMS

Endre, Lena
ISTANBUL, KEEP YOUR EYES OPEN

Eng, Sandra
TAKING CARE OF BUSINESS

England, Hal
BONFIRE OF THE VANITIES

English, Doug
BIG BAD JOHN

English, Rose
WITCHES, THE

Englund, Adam
TEXASVILLE

Englund, Robert
ADVENTURES OF FORD FAIRLANE, THE

Enoki, Takai
HEAVEN AND EARTH

Enomoto, Masaaki
DREAMS

Epper, Daniel
EXORCIST III, THE

Epper, Tony
DICK TRACY

Eppolito, Louis
GOODFELLAS
STATE OF GRACE
PREDATOR 2

Eric, James
FEUD, THE

Ericson, John
PRIMARY TARGET

Eriksen, Gordon
BIG DIS, THE

Eriksen, Kaj-Erik
SHORT TIME

Erland, Cynthia
RIVER OF DEATH

Erlich, Peter
DOG TAGS

Ermey, R. Lee
DEMONSTONE

Ermolayev, Vadim
FREEZE – DIE – COME TO LIFE

Erwin, Bill
HOME ALONE

Escargot, Maurice
HENRY AND JUNE

Escovedo, Juan Jose
ADVENTURES OF FORD FAIRLANE, THE

Escovedo, Peter Michael
ADVENTURES OF FORD FAIRLANE, THE

Escovedo, Zina
ADVENTURES OF FORD FAIRLANE, THE

Espinoza, Salvador R.
DR. CALIGARI

Esposito, Giancarlo
MO' BETTER BLUES
KING OF NEW YORK

Estabrook, Christine
PRESUMED INNOCENT

Esterman, Laura
ME AND HIM
AWAKENINGS

Estevez, Emilio
YOUNG GUNS II
MEN AT WORK

Estrada, Erik
TWISTED JUSTICE
CAGED FURY
SHOW OF FORCE, A

Etaix, Pierre
HENRY AND JUNE

Eusterman, Jim
SPACED INVADERS

Evangelatos, Grigoris
LANDSCAPE IN THE MIST

Evangelisti, Noel
PACIFIC HEIGHTS

Evans, Al
RIVERBEND

Evans, Art
DOWNTOWN
DIE HARD 2

Evans, Bentley
HOUSE PARTY

Evans, Bob
DESPERATE HOURS

Evans, Dannel
BACK TO THE FUTURE PART III

Evans, Gwyllum
AWAKENINGS

Evans, John
RIVERBEND

Evans, Roy
HAMLET

Evans, Troy
MEN AT WORK

Evans, Victor Romero
MARKED FOR DEATH

Everbeck, RC
PRETTY WOMAN

Everett, Mara
DEAD PIT

Everett, Sangoma
LIFE AND NOTHING BUT

Everett, Tom
LEATHERFACE: THE TEXAS CHAINSAW
MASSACRE III
DIE HARD 2
DANCES WITH WOLVES

Everhard, Nancy
DEMONSTONE

Evers, Bruce
MR. DESTINY

Evers, Jason
BASKETCASE 2

Eves, Victoria
STAR QUEST: BEYOND THE RISING MOON

Ewen, Lesley
BIRD ON A WIRE
NARROW MARGIN
LOOK WHO'S TALKING TOO

Ewing, Patrick
EXORCIST III, THE

Eyre, Peter
MOUNTAINS OF THE MOON

Ezaki, Yumi
DREAMS

Faber, Ron
NAVY SEALS

Fabian, Ava
WELCOME HOME, ROXY CARMICHAEL

Fabiani, Joel
TUNE IN TOMORROW

Fadlallah, Nehme
NAVY SEALS

Fagerbakke, Bill
LOOSE CANNONS

Fahey, Jeff
LAST OF THE FINEST, THE
IMPULSE
WHITE HUNTER, BLACK HEART

Fain, Peter
GOODFELLAS

Fair, William
FIRST POWER, THE

Fairbank, Christopher
WHITE HUNTER, BLACK HEART
HAMLET

Fairchild, Max
BLOOD OF HEROES

Fairley, Michelle
HIDDEN AGENDA

Faison, Frankie R.
BETSY'S WEDDING

Falco, Edie
UNBELIEVABLE TRUTH, THE

Falk, Peter
IN THE SPIRIT
TUNE IN TOMORROW

Falle, Assane
L'ETAT SAUVAGE

Fan, Nigel
NUNS ON THE RUN

Fantoni, Sergio
BELLY OF AN ARCHITECT, THE

Farago, Joe
ROOKIE, THE

Faraizl, Adam
ROBOCOP 2

Faraj, Said
DARKMAN

Faraldo, Daniel
FULL FATHOM FIVE

Fares, Debra
TAX SEASON

Fargas, Antonio
NIGHT OF THE SHARKS

Fargo, Francine
LEMON SISTERS, THE

Farid, Zaid
MEN DON'T LEAVE

Farina, Carolyn
METROPOLITAN

Farley, Teresa Yvon
WHITE GIRL, THE

Farnon, Shannon
FORBIDDEN DANCE, THE

Farnsworth, Richard
TWO JAKES, THE
HAVANA
MISERY

Farre, Jean-Paul
TOO BEAUTIFUL FOR YOU

Farrington, Hugh
CAGED FURY

Farrow, Dylan O'Sullivan
ALICE

Farrow, Mia
ALICE

Farugia, Lena
GODS MUST BE CRAZY II, THE

Farwell, Jonathan
HAUNTING OF MORELLA, THE

Fassler, Ron
GREMLINS 2 THE NEW BATCH

Faure, Philippe
TOO BEAUTIFUL FOR YOU

Fava, Claudio G.
ICICLE THIEF, THE

Fava, Tina
FAR OUT MAN

Fearon, Gerry
HIDDEN AGENDA

Fearon, Sarah
REVERSAL OF FORTUNE

Fehr, Dorothy
LOOK WHO'S TALKING TOO

Feig, Paul
SKI PATROL

Feitelson, Ben
STRIKE IT RICH

Feldbusch, Walter
YOUNG GUNS II

Felden, Renee
TIME TROOPERS

Feldman, Corey
TEENAGE MUTANT NINJA TURTLES

Feldman, Ed
GREEN CARD

Feldstein, Don
PRETTY WOMAN

Felix the Cat
HEART CONDITION

Felix, Nicole
CYRANO DE BERGERAC

Feller, Howard
AWAKENINGS

Fenmore, Tanya
LISA

Fenn, Sherilyn
WILD AT HEART
BACKSTREET DREAMS

Fenton, Sarah-Jane
TALL GUY, THE

Fenwick, Perry
RAGGEDY RAWNEY, THE

Ferency, Adam
INTERROGATION, THE

Ferguson, Jesse Lawrence
DARKMAN

Ferguson, Larry
HUNT FOR RED OCTOBER, THE

Ferguson, Sherry
EDWARD SCISSORHANDS

Fernandez, Alexis
DESPERATE HOURS

Fernandez, Esteban
MILLER'S CROSSING

Fernandez, Evelina
FLATLINERS
POSTCARDS FROM THE EDGE

Fernandez, George
MILLER'S CROSSING

Fernandez-Muro, Marta
LABYRINTH OF PASSION

Ferran, Catherine
CYRANO DE BERGERAC

Ferrara, Charles
MILLER'S CROSSING

Ferrara, Frank
SHOCK TO A SYSTEM, A

Ferrara, Peter
FAR OUT MAN

Ferre, Francesca
MAGDALENE

Ferrell, Conchata
EDWARD SCISSORHANDS

Ferrell, Tyra
EXORCIST III, THE

Ferrer, Miguel
REVENGE
GUARDIAN, THE

Ferris, Barbara
KRAYS, THE

Fertal, Andy
BLADES

Feuer, Debra
NIGHT ANGEL

Fidandis, Philip
STAR QUEST: BEYOND THE RISING MOON

Field, Allison
PRESUMED INNOCENT

Field, Susan
TALL GUY, THE

Field, Todd
BACK TO BACK
FULL FATHOM FIVE

Fields, Christopher
JACOB'S LADDER

Fields, Edith
HOUSE PARTY
THREE MEN AND A LITTLE LADY

Fields, Tony
BACKSTREET DREAMS

Fierro, Frank Jr.
YOUNG GUNS II

Figg, Robert
LAST OF THE FINEST, THE

Figueroa, Anaysha
MO' BETTER BLUES

Filippo, Lou
ROCKY V

Fine, B.
HOUSE PARTY

Fine, Ben
STATE OF GRACE

Fineman, Karen
VITAL SIGNS

Fink, John
FLATLINERS
BONFIRE OF THE VANITIES

Finkel, Fyvush
Q&A

Finley, Greg
HOLLYWOOD HOT TUBS II: EDUCATING
CRYSTAL

Finn, John
LOOSE CANNONS
SHOCK TO THE SYSTEM, A
DESPERATE HOURS

Finn, Lila
ROBOCOP 2

Finnegan, John
LAST OF THE FINEST, THE
COME SEE THE PARADISE

Finnegan, Tom
DICK TRACY
DIE HARD 2
PREDATOR 2

Finnerman, Katie
NIGHT OF THE LIVING DEAD

Finney, Albert
MILLER'S CROSSING

Fiorentini, Al
STRIKE IT RICH

Fiorini, Marco
DOWN THE DRAIN

Firbank, Ann
STRAPLESS
LIONHEART

Firfer, Richard J.
HOME ALONE

Firios, Yannis
LANDSCAPE IN THE MIST

Firth, Peter
HUNT FOR RED OCTOBER, THE
BURNDOWN
INNOCENT VICTIM
RESCUERS DOWN UNDER, THE

Fischer, Bruce
GRIM PRAIRIE TALES

Fischer, John Louis
JACOB'S LADDER

Fischer, Takayo
PACIFIC HEIGHTS

Fischman, Aaron
GUARDIAN, THE

Fischman, Josh
GUARDIAN, THE

Fish, Nancy
EXORCIST III, THE

Fishburne, Larry
KING OF NEW YORK

Fisher, Carrie
TIME GUARDIAN, THE
SIBLING RIVALRY

Fisher, Frances
WELCOME HOME, ROXY CARMICHAEL

Fisher, Jasen
WITCHES, THE

Fisher, Tom
HUNT FOR RED OCTOBER, THE

Fisher, William
YOUNG GUNS II

Fistell, Shane
AWAKENINGS

Fitzgerald, Helen
NUNS ON THE RUN

Fitzgerald, Michael
TALL GUY, THE

Fitzgerald, Wilbur
CHATTAHOOCHEE

Fitzgibbon, Kitty
TEENAGE MUTANT NINJA TURTLES

Fitzhugh, Lisa
ROSALIE GOES SHOPPING

Fitzhugh, Lori
ROSALIE GOES SHOPPING

Fitzpatrick, Michael
NAVY SEALS
RUSSIA HOUSE, THE

Fitzsimmons, David
CHATTAHOOCHEE

Flack, John
WHITE PALACE

Flaherty, Lanny
MILLER'S CROSSING

Flaherty, Maureen
SHADOWZONE

Flanagan, Frances
WHERE THE HEART IS

Flanagan, Walter
BONFIRE OF THE VANITIES

Flanders, Ed
EXORCIST III, THE

Flannagan, Harley
BLUE STEEL

Flannagan, Markus
BLUE STEEL

Flavin, Jennifer
ROCKY V

Flavin, Julie
ROCKY V

Flavin, Tricia
ROCKY V

Flavor Flav
MO' BETTER BLUES

Flea
BACK TO THE FUTURE PART III

Fleetwood, Susan
KRAYS, THE

Fleischer, Charles
DICK TRACY

Fleming, Cliff
DARKMAN

Fleming, Juanita
RETURN OF SUPERFLY, THE

Fleming, Kathy
EDWARD SCISSORHANDS

Fleming, Nick
CRY-BABY

Flender, Gary
DESPERATE HOURS

Fletcher, Dexter
RAGGEDY RAWNEY, THE
TWISTED OBSESSION
LIONHEART

Fletcher, Leno
BACK TO THE FUTURE PART III

Fletcher, Louise
BLUE STEEL
SHADOWZONE

Fletcher, Piers
TALL GUY, THE

Flint, Matthew
PACIFIC HEIGHTS

Flowers, Kim
ME AND HIM
ME AND HIM
NOBODY'S PERFECT

Flynn, Barbara
QUICK CHANGE

Flynn, Darcy
WITCHES, THE

Flynn, Frederick
SHADOWZONE

Flynn, Mary Sue
UNBELIEVABLE TRUTH, THE

Flynn, Michael
DESPERATE HOURS

Flynn, Patrick
AVALON

Fogel, Joel S.
LEMON SISTERS, THE

Foley, Hank
METROPOLITAN

Foley, Tom Sean
NAVY SEALS

Folk, Alexander
HOUSE PARTY

Follows, Megan
NUTCRACKER PRINCE, THE

Fonda, Bridget
STRAPLESS
FRANKENSTEIN UNBOUND
GODFATHER PART III, THE

Fonda, Jane
STANLEY AND IRIS

Fong, Allen
LIFE IS CHEAP. . . BUT TOILET PAPER IS EX-
PENSIVE

Fong, Darryl
ME AND HIM

Fontaine, Brooke
GHOST DAD

Fontana, Randy
DEAD PIT

Foody, Ralph
HOME ALONE

Foote, Horton Jr.
BLOOD RED

Foraker, Lois
EXORCIST III, THE

Foray, June
DUCKTALES: THE MOVIE – TREASURE OF
THE LOST LAMP

Ford, Bette
MARKED FOR DEATH

Ford, Buck
ERNEST GOES TO JAIL

Ford, Harrison
PRESUMED INNOCENT

Ford, Kenny Jr
GHOST DAD

Ford, Maria
HAUNTING OF MORELLA, THE

Ford, Tommy A.
Q&A

Foree, Ken
LEATHERFACE: THE TEXAS CHAINSAW
MASSACRE III
WITHOUT YOU, I'M NOTHING
DOWN THE DRAIN
TAKING CARE OF BUSINESS

Forgo, Elisabeth
MR. FROST

Forleo, Steve
GOODFELLAS

Forman, David
TEENAGE MUTANT NINJA TURTLES
NUNS ON THE RUN

Forrest, Frederic
TWO JAKES, THE

Forristal, Susan
INTERNAL AFFAIRS
TWO JAKES, THE
POSTCARDS FROM THE EDGE
BONFIRE OF THE VANITIES

Forster, Robert
PEACEMAKER

Forsyth, Tony
TALL GUY, THE

Forsythe, William
TORRENTS OF SPRING
DICK TRACY

Fortell, Albert
TIME TROOPERS

Fortune, Nadio
STRIKE IT RICH

Foss, Shirlene
DEAD AIM
FUNLAND

Foster, Meg
BLIND FURY
JEZEBEL'S KISS

Foster, Stacie
NIGHT OF THE LIVING DEAD

Foster, Steffen Gregory
DEAD PIT
DIE HARD 2

Foti, Raymond E.
GHOST DAD

Foucheux, Rick
STAR QUEST: BEYOND THE RISING MOON

Fowler, Harry
CHICAGO JOE AND THE SHOWGIRL

Fox, Bernard
RESCUERS DOWN UNDER, THE

Fox, Damita Jo
REAL BULLETS

Fox, Glenn
BACK TO THE FUTURE PART III

Fox, James
RUSSIA HOUSE, THE

Fox, Jorjan
KILL-OFF, THE

Fox, Lesley
GODS MUST BE CRAZY II, THE

Fox, Michael
SKINHEADS – THE SECOND COMING OF
HATE

Fox, Michael J.
BACK TO THE FUTURE PART III

Franciosa, Anthony
BACKSTREET DREAMS

Francis, Staci
BONFIRE OF THE VANITIES

Francisa, Lia
BLOOD OF HEROES

Frank, Diana
MONSTER HIGH

Frank, Marilyn Dodds
FLATLINERS

Frank, Tony
YOUNG GUNS II
RIVERBEND

Frankel, Scott
POSTCARDS FROM THE EDGE

Frankenheimer, Kristi
CHATTAHOOCHEE

Franklin, Brouke
WILDEST DREAMS

Franklin, John
ANDY COLBY'S INCREDIBLY AWESOME
ADVENTURE

Franklin-Robbins, John
LIONHEART

Franz, Dennis
DIE HARD 2

Fraser, Alex
COOK, THE THIEF, HIS WIFE & HER
LOVER, THE

Fraser, Alison
ME AND HIM

Fraser, Brent
CLASS OF 1999
WILD AT HEART
JEZEBEL'S KISS

Fraser, Liz
CHICAGO JOE AND THE SHOWGIRL

Fratellini, Annie
HENRY AND JUNE

Fratkin, Stuart
UNDER THE BOARDWALK

Frazer, Alison Jane
MURDER BY NUMBERS

Frazier, Cliff
HOUSE PARTY

Frazier, Randy
RETURN OF SUPERFLY, THE

Frazier, Ron
PRESUMED INNOCENT

Frechette, Peter
PAINT IT BLACK

Frederick, Randall
MONSTER HIGH

Fredman, Beatrice
OPPORTUNITY KNOCKS

Freeman, Bob
RUSSIA HOUSE, THE

Freeman, J.E.
WILD AT HEART
MILLER'S CROSSING

Freeman, Jonathan
SHOCK TO THE SYSTEM, A

Freeman, Kathleen
GREMLINS 2 THE NEW BATCH

Freeman, Morgan
BONFIRE OF THE VANITIES

Freeman, Myles
WHITE HUNTER, BLACK HEART

Freeman, Scott
PACIFIC HEIGHTS

Freilino, Brian
GODFATHER PART III, THE

French, Arthur
LOOSE CANNONS

French, Howard
I COME IN PEACE
COME SEE THE PARADISE

French, Lachlen
SKI PATROL

French, Mark
POSTCARDS FROM THE EDGE

French, Michael
PRETTY WOMAN

French, Susan
FLATLINERS

Frerot, Alain
LIFE AND NOTHING BUT

Frewer, Matt
SHORT TIME

Fricker, Brenda
FIELD, THE

Fridjhon, Anthony
AMERICAN EAGLE

Friels, Colin
DARKMAN

Fritsche, Mark David
DEMON WIND

Fromager, Alain
MAMA, THERE'S A MAN IN YOUR BED

Fromin, Troy
MONSTER HIGH

Frossard, Jerome
LIFE AND NOTHING BUT

Frye, Virgil
HOT SPOT, THE

Fuchs, Leo
AVALON

Fudge, Alan
EDWARD SCISSORHANDS

Fuhrer, David
MONSTER HIGH

Fujii, Harumi
DREAMS

Fujinaka, Mariko
COME SEE THE PARADISE

Fujioka, John
PAINT IT BLACK

Fujita, Kenji
DREAMS

Fulford, Christopher
MOUNTAINS OF THE MOON

Fuller, David J.
DANCES WITH WOLVES

Fuller, Kurt
BONFIRE OF THE VANITIES

Fuller, Tex
NUNS ON THE RUN

Funk, Greg
NIGHT OF THE LIVING DEAD

Furlan, Rate
BELLY OF AN ARCHITECT, THE

Furness, Deborra-Lee
LAST OF THE FINEST, THE

Furrh, Chris
LORD OF THE FLIES

Fusco, John
YOUNG GUNS II

G'Vera, Ivan
HUNT FOR RED OCTOBER, THE

Gabai, Richard
DEMON WIND

Gabay, Claudine
CYRANO DE BERGERAC

Gabor, Eva
RESCUERS DOWN UNDER, THE

Gabor, Zsa Zsa
HAPPILY EVER AFTER

Gabriel, John
RETURN OF SUPERFLY, THE

Gabriel, Tedra
NIGHT ANGEL

Gadler, Steve
MR. FROST

Gaffney, Mo
STATE OF GRACE

Gagnon, Norman
STAR QUEST: BEYOND THE RISING MOON

Gaines, Rosie
GRAFFITI BRIDGE

Gains, Courtney
MEMPHIS BELLE

Gajos, Janusz
INTERROGATION, THE

Gale, David
FIRST POWER, THE

Gale, Gregory A.
FOURTH WAR, THE

Gale, Vincent
BYE BYE BLUES

Galeota, James
LOOK WHO'S TALKING TOO

Galinsky, Garry
FOURTH WAR, THE

Gallagher, Gina
ALICE
EDWARD SCISSORHANDS

Gallagher, Peter
TUNE IN TOMORROW

Gallauner, Barbara
NASTY GIRL, THE

Galligan, Zach
GREMLINS 2 THE NEW BATCH

Gallin, Scott
OPPONENT, THE

Gallin, Tim
STATE OF GRACE

Gallion, Jalaine
EDWARD SCISSORHANDS

Gallivan, Megan
STELLA
UNDER THE BOARDWALK

Gallo, Ernesto
GREEN CARD

Gallo, Paula
GOODFELLAS

Gallo, Vinnie
GOODFELLAS

Gallo, William
PRETTY WOMAN

Galloway, Jane
POSTCARDS FROM THE EDGE

Gallup, Michael
DICK TRACY

Galomb, Tal
OPPORTUNITY KNOCKS

Galt, John William
ROSALIE GOES SHOPPING
PROBLEM CHILD

Galvane, Candace
LORDS OF MAGICK, THE

Gambina, James
ROCKY V

Gamble, Val
HOUSE PARTY

Gamboa, Joonee
PRIMARY TARGET
DEMONSTONE

Gambon, Michael
COOK, THE THIEF, HIS WIFE & HER
LOVER, THE

Gammon, James
REVENGE
COUPE DE VILLE
I LOVE YOU TO DEATH

Gandhi, Prabha
WHERE THE HEART IS

Gangemi, Paula Lee
STUFF STEPHANIE IN THE INCINERATOR

Ganger, Ben
NIGHT ANGEL

Ganios, Tony
DIE HARD 2

Ganster, Alex
HAVANA

Gant, Richard
FRESHMAN, THE
ROCKY V

Gantt, Leland
PRESUMED INNOCENT

Ganz, Bruno
STRAPLESS

Ganz, George
GHOST DAD

Garber, Jon
BIRD ON A WIRE

Garcia, Andy
INTERNAL AFFAIRS
SHOW OF FORCE, A
GODFATHER PART III, THE

Garcia, Bernie Ben
SKI PATROL

Garcia, Carlotta
YOUNG GUNS II

Garcia, Gilbert
DIE HARD 2

Garcini, Salvador
REVENGE

Gardner, Jerry
YOUNG GUNS II

Gardner, Jessica
DIE HARD 2

Gardner, Jimmy
MOUNTAINS OF THE MOON

Gardner, Llew
HIDDEN AGENDA

Garfield, Allen
NIGHT VISITOR
DICK TRACY

Garfield, Julie
STANLEY AND IRIS
GOODFELLAS

Garg, Medha
KINDERGARTEN COP

Garlin, Carole
DISTURBANCE, THE

Garnett, Gale
MR. AND MRS. BRIDGE

Garr, Michael
NASTY GIRL, THE

Garr, Teri
SHORT TIME

Garrett, Austin
GHOST DAD

Garrett, Hank
STEEL AND LACE

Garrick, Barbara
POSTCARDS FROM THE EDGE

Garrison, John
SKI PATROL

Garrison, Miranda
MACK THE KNIFE
FORBIDDEN DANCE, THE

Garrison, Rob
HOLLYWOOD HOT TUBS II: EDUCATING
CRYSTAL

Garson, Willie
ADVENTURES OF FORD FAIRLANE, THE

Gartenkraut, David
ISTANBUL, KEEP YOUR EYES OPEN

Garver, John
MR. DESTINY

Gary, Ann Pearl
JACOB'S LADDER

Gary, Linda
HAPPILY EVER AFTER

Gaspar, Titina
VERONICO CRUZ

Gass, Kyle
JACOB'S LADDER

Gasser, Wolfgang
TIME TROOPERS

Gatsby, Jill
CLASS OF 1999

Gaughan, Michael
EDWARD SCISSORHANDS

Gaul, Patricia
THREE MEN AND A LITTLE LADY

Gaup, Aliu
PATHFINDER

Gaup, Mikkel
PATHFINDER

Gaup, Sara Marit
PATHFINDER

Gauthier, Marie-Josee
HOW TO MAKE LOVE TO A NEGRO WITH-
OUT GETTING TIRED

Gauthier, Mark
LORDS OF MAGICK, THE

Gautier, Jean-Yves
LIFE AND NOTHING BUT

Gautier, Martine
MAY FOOLS

Gavas, Cassandra
DEAD AIM

Gavin, James W.
LAST OF THE FINEST, THE

Gavor, Radu
HUNT FOR RED OCTOBER, THE

Gaynor, Ruby
GOODFELLAS

Gaynor, Violet
GOODFELLAS

Gazarian, John
REAL BULLETS

Gazarov, Sergei
TAXI BLUES

Gaznick, Tony
BACK TO BACK

Geary, Anthony
HIGH DESERT KILL

Geary, Tim
COOK, THE THIEF, HIS WIFE & HER
LOVER, THE

Geer, Faith
BLUE STEEL

Geeves, Peter
NUNS ON THE RUN

Geldhart, Ed
ROSALIE GOES SHOPPING
ROBOCOP 2

Gelin, Daniel
LIFE IS A LONG QUIET RIVER
MR. FROST

Gelke, Becky
BLUE STEEL

Gelman, Jacob
GUARDIAN, THE

Gelt, Grant
AVALON
MARKED FOR DEATH

Gemma, Julian
OPPONENT, THE

Genaro, Tony
TREMORS

Genebach, Michael
STAR QUEST: BEYOND THE RISING MOON

Genet, Michael
PRESUMED INNOCENT

Genevie, Michael
MR. DESTINY

Gentry, Minnie
DEF BY TEMPTATION

Geoffrion, Lisa
DISTURBANCE, THE

George, John
DISTURBANCE, THE

George, Libby
FEUD, THE

George, T.M. Nelson
EVERYBODY WINS

Georgouli, Aliki
LANDSCAPE IN THE MIST

Gerachty, Billy
MISADVENTURES OF MR. WILT, THE

Geraci, Ben
ROCKY V

Gerard, Danny
DESPERATE HOURS

Gerber, Joan
DUCKTALES: THE MOVIE – TREASURE OF
THE LOST LAMP

Gerber, Kathy
EXORCIST III, THE

Gerchen, Bob
STELLA

Gerdes, Heather Lea
LOOK WHO'S TALKING TOO

Gere, Richard
INTERNAL AFFAIRS
PRETTY WOMAN

German, Felix
HAVANA

German, Greg
CHILD'S PLAY 2

Gero, Edward
DIE HARD 2

Geronimo
WILD ORCHID

Gersak, Savina
SONNY BOY

Gertz, Geha
DEAD PIT

Gertz, Jami
DON'T TELL HER IT'S ME
SIBLING RIVALRY

Gerulaitis, Vitas
NOBODY'S PERFECT

Getty, Balthazar
LORD OF THE FLIES
YOUNG GUNS II

Getz, John
INTERNAL AFFAIRS
MEN AT WORK

Giamatti, Marcus
MR. AND MRS. BRIDGE

Giambalvo, Louis
BONFIRE OF THE VANITIES

Giannini, Giancarlo
BLOOD RED

Giardina, Joe
BEDROOM EYES II

Gibb, Cynthia
DEATH WARRANT

Gibbons, Leeza
ROBOCOP 2

Gibbs, Nigel
PUMP UP THE VOLUME

Gibson, David
HAVANA

Gibson, Henry
GREMLINS 2 THE NEW BATCH
NIGHT VISITOR
TUNE IN TOMORROW

Gibson, Mel
BIRD ON A WIRE
AIR AMERICA
HAMLET

Gidley, Pam
LAST OF THE FINEST, THE

Gielgud, John
STRIKE IT RICH

Giggenbach, Robert
NASTY GIRL, THE

Gil, Jorge
TAX SEASON

Gilbert, Arlette
LIFE AND NOTHING BUT

Gilbert, Ed
RESCUERS DOWN UNDER, THE

Gilbert-Hall, Richard
BONFIRE OF THE VANITIES

Gilden, Ken
TOTAL RECALL

Giles, Nancy
ME AND HIM

Gill, Jack
STANLEY AND IRIS

Gillespie, Emer
COOK, THE THIEF, HIS WIFE & HER
LOVER, THE

Gillett, Debra
WITCHES, THE

Gilliam, Burton
BACK TO THE FUTURE PART III

Gilliam, Elizabeth
COME SEE THE PARADISE

Gillies, Isabel
METROPOLITAN

Gillies, Linda
METROPOLITAN

Gillin, Hugh
BACK TO THE FUTURE PART III

Gillis, Paulina
WHERE THE HEART IS

Gillis, Philip A.
DARKMAN

Gilpin, Jack
QUICK CHANGE

Gimenez, Thierry
LIFE AND NOTHING BUT

Ginsberg, Lawrence
AMERICAN EAGLE

Ginty, Robert
MADHOUSE

Ginzberg, Matus
FOURTH WAR, THE

Gioco, Joseph P.
GOODFELLAS

Giordani, Rocky
AFTER DARK, MY SWEET

Giosa, Sue
FIRST POWER, THE

Giovane, Bob
ROCKY V

Girard, Philippe
CYRANO DE BERGERAC

Girard, Remy
JESUS OF MONTREAL

Girardeau, Frank
BLUE STEEL
STATE OF GRACE

Giraud, Bernadette
VINCENT AND THEO

Giraud, Roland
MR. FROST

Gish, Annabeth
COUPE DE VILLE

Giuntoli, Neil
MEMPHIS BELLE

Glanzman, Ray
KINDERGARTEN COP

Glaudini, Robert
HOMER & EDDIE

Gleason, Mary Pat
VITAL SIGNS

Gleason, Paul
MIAMI BLUES

Gledhill, Karen
CHICAGO JOE AND THE SHOWGIRL

Gleeson, Brendan
FIELD, THE

Gleeson, Patrick
FLATLINERS

Gleeson, Redmond
YOUNG GUNS II

Gleizer, Michele
LIFE AND NOTHING BUT

Glen, Iain
MOUNTAINS OF THE MOON

FOOLS OF FORTUNE

Glenn, Eric
ROBOCOP 2

Glenn, Scott
HUNT FOR RED OCTOBER, THE

Gloster, Jim
CHATTAHOOCHEE

Glover, Crispin
WHERE THE HEART IS
WILD AT HEART

Glover, Danny
TO SLEEP WITH ANGER
PREDATOR 2

Glover, John
GREMLINS 2 THE NEW BATCH
ROBOCOP 2

Glover, Julian
TUSKS

Glover, Kara
ME AND HIM

Gluckstein, Peter
MISADVENTURES OF MR. WILT, THE

Glynn, Carlin
BLOOD RED

Glynn, Carrie
AMERICAN EAGLE

Gochnauer, Danny
DEAD PIT

Godbout, Roger Romero
MARKED FOR DEATH

Goddard, Wayne
LIONHEART

Goethals, Angela
HOME ALONE

Goetzman, Gary
MIAMI BLUES

Goff, Carla
PRESUMED INNOCENT

Goker, Zeki
ISTANBUL, KEEP YOUR EYES OPEN

Gokul
FIRST POWER, THE

Gold, Russel
MACK THE KNIFE

Goldberg, Kelly
CRY-BABY

Goldberg, Whoopi
HOMER & EDDIE
GHOST

Goldblum, Jeff
TALL GUY, THE
TWISTED OBSESSION
MR. FROST

Golden, Dan
ALIENATOR

Goldenberg, Ira
IMPORTED BRIDEGROOM, THE

Goldin, Ricky Paull
LAMBADA

Goldman, Robert
DANCES WITH WOLVES

Goldschmidt, Miriam
MAHABHARATA, THE

Goldsmith, Jerry
GREMLINS 2 THE NEW BATCH

Goldsmith, Merwin
CADILLAC MAN

Goldstein, Mark
ADVENTURES OF FORD FAIRLANE, THE

Goldwyn, Tony
GHOST

Golino, Valeria
TORRENTS OF SPRING

Golio, Rocky
OPPONENT, THE

Gollas, Ellen
TOTAL RECALL

Gollnick, Amy
MERMAIDS

Golonka, Arlene
GUMSHOE KID, THE

Golub, Bob
GOODFELLAS

Gomez, Mateo
DELTA FORCE 2

Gomez, Nicholas Sean
YOUNG GUNS II

Gomez, Rita
GUARDIAN, THE

Goncalves, Milton
WILD ORCHID

Goncalves, Oscar
BIRD ON A WIRE

Gonin, Amelie
CYRANO DE BERGERAC

Gonzales, Anna Maria
VERONICO CRUZ

Gonzales, German
FULL FATHOM FIVE

Gonzalez, Adriano
HAVANA

Gonzalez, Gonzo
FLATLINERS

Gonzalez, Joseph
FRANKENHOOKER

Gonzalez-Gonzalez, Pedro
DOWN THE DRAIN

Goodchild, Sophie
COOK, THE THIEF, HIS WIFE & HER
LOVER, THE

Goode, Brad
SKI PATROL

Goode, Jack Jr.
DICK TRACY

Goodfriend, Lynda
PRETTY WOMAN

Gooding, Barbara
BONFIRE OF THE VANITIES

Gooding, Omar
GHOST DAD

Goodman, John
STELLA
ARACHNOPHOBIA

Goodman, Ron J.
FIRST POWER, THE

Goodrow, Gary
QUICK CHANGE

Goodspeed, Miriam
EDWARD SCISSORHANDS

Goodwin, John
TREMORS

Goody, Bob
COOK, THE THIEF, HIS WIFE & HER
LOVER, THE

Goomas, Deborah
FLATLINERS

Goossen, Gregory
LOOSE CANNONS

Gordon, Adam
BURNDOWN

Gordon, Dexter
AWAKENINGS

Gordon, Don
EXORCIST III, THE

Gordon, Eve
AVALON

Gordon, Leo V.
ALIENATOR

Gordon, Meredith
GHOST DAD

Gordon, Wendy
IMPULSE

Gordy, Alison
JACOB'S LADDER

Gorg, Galyn
ROBOCOP 2

Gorham, Mel
AWAKENINGS

Goring, Marius
STRIKE IT RICH

Gorman, Lynne
NUTCRACKER PRINCE, THE

Gormick, Jarrod Scott
ME AND HIM

Goss, Christopher Allen
MARKED FOR DEATH

Gossett, Cyndi James
GHOST DAD

Goto, Masato
DREAMS

Goto, Takuya
HEAVEN AND EARTH

Gottfried, Gilbert
ADVENTURES OF FORD FAIRLANE, THE
PROBLEM CHILD
LOOK WHO'S TALKING TOO

Gough, Michael
STRAPLESS

Gould, Brewster
HAUNTING OF MORELLA, THE

Gould, Elliott
NIGHT VISITOR
LEMON SISTERS, THE

Gould, Robert
LOVE AT LARGE

Goz, Harry
DEAD AIM

Graas, John Christian
KINDERGARTEN COP

Grace, David
NIGHT OF THE LIVING DEAD

Grace, Mark
TAKING CARE OF BUSINESS

Grace, Wayne
HOMER & EDDIE
DANCES WITH WOLVES

Gracen, Elizabeth
LISA
MARKED FOR DEATH

Gracie, Sally
OPPORTUNITY KNOCKS

Grady, Ed
CHATTAHOOCHEE

Graf, Allan
FLASHBACK
COME SEE THE PARADISE

Graff, Ralph
KILL-OFF, THE

Graff, Todd
OPPORTUNITY KNOCKS

Gragnani, Stefano
BELLY OF AN ARCHITECT, THE

Graham, Gary
ROBOT JOX

Graham, Gerrit
MARTIANS GO HOME!
CHILD'S PLAY 2

Graham, Heather
I LOVE YOU TO DEATH

Graham, Holter
CRY-BABY

Graham, Julie
NUNS ON THE RUN

Graham, Nikki
LOOK WHO'S TALKING TOO

Grahn, Neil
FOURTH WAR, THE

Grand, Dale
QUICK CHANGE

Granotier, Sylvie
MAN INSIDE, THE

Grant, Beth
FLATLINERS
DON'T TELL HER IT'S ME
CHILD'S PLAY 2

Grant, David Marshall
AIR AMERICA

Grant, Faye
INTERNAL AFFAIRS

Grant, Hugh
IMPROMPTU

Grant, Jana
TAX SEASON

Grant, Micah
HIGH DESERT KILL

Grant, Richard E.
MOUNTAINS OF THE MOON
HENRY AND JUNE

Grant, Rodney A.
DANCES WITH WOLVES

Grant, Salim
GHOST DAD

Granville, Alan
BURNDOWN

Gravel, Robert
CHATTAHOOCHEE

Graves, Kristy
ALICE

Graves, Ruthanna
RETURN OF SUPERFLY, THE

Gray, Bo
YOUNG GUNS II

Gray, Charles
STELLA

Gray, Kathleen
POSTCARDS FROM THE EDGE

Grazer, Corki
PROBLEM CHILD

Graziano, Michaelangelo
GOODFELLAS

Greatbatch, Paul
OPPORTUNITY KNOCKS

Green, Dennis
JACOB'S LADDER

Green, Dianne L.
EDWARD SCISSORHANDS

Green, Fanni
BONFIRE OF THE VANITIES

Green, John-Martin
JACOB'S LADDER

Green, Rhetta
STREETS

Green, Russell
EDWARD SCISSORHANDS

Green, Seth
PUMP UP THE VOLUME

Greenberg, Marti
EDWARD SCISSORHANDS

Greenberg, Stacey Renee
JEZEBEL'S KISS

Greene, Daniel
OPPONENT, THE

Greene, Ellen
ME AND HIM
PUMP UP THE VOLUME

Greene, Gary
PRETTY WOMAN

Greene, Graham
DANCES WITH WOLVES

Greene, Michael
KILL ME AGAIN
LORD OF THE FLIES

Greenquist, Brad
LOOSE CANNONS

Greenway, Andy
BLOOD SALVAGE

Greenwood, Bruce
WILD ORCHID

Greenwood, Rosamud
WITCHES, THE

Greer, Dabbs
PACIFIC HEIGHTS

Greeson, Timothy
DISTURBANCE, THE

Gregg, Bradley
MADHOUSE
CLASS OF 1999

Gregory, Andre
BONFIRE OF THE VANITIES

Gregory, Constantin
RUSSIA HOUSE, THE

Gregory, Michael
TOTAL RECALL

Greist, Kim
WHY ME?

Grenier, Zach
SHOCK TO THE SYSTEM, A

Gressieux, Stephen
STRIKE IT RICH

Grey, Rhonda
MONSTER HIGH

Grier, David Alan
ME AND HIM
LOOSE CANNONS

Grier, Pam
CLASS OF 1999

Gries, Jonathan
KILL ME AGAIN

Grifasi, Joe
FEUD, THE
PRESUMED INNOCENT

Griffin, Elizabeth A.
QUICK CHANGE

Griffin, Eric
RETURN OF SUPERFLY, THE

Griffin, Michael
SONNY BOY

Griffis, William
MR. DESTINY

Griffith, Melanie
IN THE SPIRIT
PACIFIC HEIGHTS
BONFIRE OF THE VANITIES

Griffith, Tracy
FIRST POWER, THE

Griffiths, Dan
CRY-BABY

Griffiths, Roger Ashton
COOK, THE THIEF, HIS WIFE & HER
LOVER, THE

Grissom Hardin, Dorothy L.
CHATTAHOOCHEE

Grodin, Charles
TAKING CARE OF BUSINESS

Grody, Kathryn
QUICK CHANGE
LEMON SISTERS, THE

Groh, David
RETURN OF SUPERFLY, THE

Gross, Arye
COUPE DE VILLE

Gross, Edan
COUPE DE VILLE
LISA
CHILD'S PLAY 2

Gross, Loretta
KILL-OFF, THE

Gross, Michael
TREMORS

Grossberg, Bruce
GAME, THE

Grote, Vernon
PROBLEM CHILD

Gruault, Isabelle
CYRANO DE BERGERAC

Gruen, Barbara
JACOB'S LADDER

Gruner, Olivier
ANGEL TOWN

Guastaferro, Stacey
MEN DON'T LEAVE

Guastaferro, Vincent
STATE OF GRACE

Guerard, Margaux
GOODFELLAS

Guerra, Blanca
SANTA SANGRE

Guerra, Pepito
HAVANA

Guertchikoff, Louba
LIFE AND NOTHING BUT

Guiard, Isabelle
IMPROMPTU

Guideau, Donald
YOUNG GUNS II

Guidera, Anthony
GODFATHER PART III, THE

Guido, Michael
HOME ALONE

Guilfoyle, Paul
CADILLAC MAN

Guillaume, Michael
NASTY GIRL, THE

Guillaume, Robert
DEATH WARRANT

Guilliard, Leontine
HEART CONDITION

Guiot, Fernand
IMPROMPTU

Gullotta, Leo
CINEMA PARADISO

Guma, Howie
TAKING CARE OF BUSINESS

Gumeny, Peter
Q&A

Gunning, Charles
MILLER'S CROSSING

Gunnlaugsdottir, Tinna
SHADOW OF THE RAVEN, THE

Gunther, Ulrich
MAGDALENE

Gurk, Lily
MEN IN LOVE

Gutstein, Ken
POSTCARDS FROM THE EDGE

Guttenberg, Steve
DON'T TELL HER IT'S ME
THREE MEN AND A LITTLE LADY

Gutteridge, Lucy
TUSKS

Guttman, Ronald
HUNT FOR RED OCTOBER, THE
AVALON
GREEN CARD

Guttorm, Ingvald
PATHFINDER

Guwaza, David
TUSKS

Guzman, Luis
Q&A

Gwaltney, Jack
VITAL SIGNS

Gwynne, Michael C.
LAST OF THE FINEST, THE

Gyse, Alisa
ME AND HIM

Haas, Charlie
GREMLINS 2 THE NEW BATCH

Haase, Cathy
KILL-OFF, THE

Haase, Heather
GREMLINS 2 THE NEW BATCH

Haber, Joey
FRIGHT HOUSE

Hackett, John
TWO JAKES, THE

Hackman, Gene
LOOSE CANNONS
POSTCARDS FROM THE EDGE
NARROW MARGIN

Haddad, Anna
BLADES

Haddon, Laurence
CAGED IN PARADISO

Haddrick, Ron
QUIGLEY DOWN UNDER

Hagen, Daniel
BONFIRE OF THE VANITIES

Hagen, Ross
ALIENATOR

Hagen, Uta
REVERSAL OF FORTUNE

Hagerty, Julie
REVERSAL OF FORTUNE

Hagerty, Michael G.
AFTER DARK, MY SWEET
DICK TRACY

Haggerty, Dan
INHERITOR

Haggerty, Fred
NUNS ON THE RUN

Haggerty, Sean
CLASS OF 1999

Hagler, Nik
I COME IN PEACE

Hahn, Archie
GREMLINS 2 THE NEW BATCH

Hahn, Archie III
MISERY

Haid, Charles
NIGHTBREED

Haideman, Tim
GUMSHOE KID, THE

Haiduk, Stacy
STEEL AND LACE

Haig, James
BIG DIS, THE

Haig, Kevin
BIG DIS, THE

Haig, Sid
FORBIDDEN DANCE, THE

Haines, Sean
MONSTER HIGH

Haining, Alice
SHOCK TO THE SYSTEM, A

Hajduk, Joseph
GHOST DAD

Hale, Elvi
INNOCENT VICTIM

Haley, R.M.
EVERYBODY WINS
POSTCARDS FROM THE EDGE

Hall, Angela
MO' BETTER BLUES

Hall, Anthony Michael
EDWARD SCISSORHANDS

Hall, Brad
GUARDIAN, THE

Hall, Carrie
DARKMAN

Hall, Darlene J.
TAKING CARE OF BUSINESS

Hall, Darwin
MADHOUSE

Hall, E. Pat
CHATTAHOOCHEE

Hall, Harriet
HIT LIST

Hall, Jennifer
NUNS ON THE RUN

Hall, Randy
NAVY SEALS

Hall, Vondi Curtis
DIE HARD 2

Halley, Russell
GOODFELLAS

Halligan, Tim
QUICK CHANGE

Halphie, Michael
NAVY SEALS

Halsey, Brett
GODFATHER PART III, THE

Halsted, Christopher
HAUNTING OF MORELLA, THE

Hamada, Akira
HEAVEN AND EARTH

Hamada, Kiyo
SKI PATROL

Hamel, Veronica
TAKING CARE OF BUSINESS

Hamill, Mark
SLIPSTREAM

Hamill, Pete
KING OF NEW YORK

Hamilton, George
GODFATHER PART III, THE

Hamilton, Jane
BEDROOM EYES II
WILDEST DREAMS

Hamilton, John
NIGHT OF THE LIVING DEAD

Hamilton, Linda
MR. DESTINY

Hamilton, Neil
TALL GUY, THE

Hamler, Brad
JACOB'S LADDER

Hamlin, Joey Joe
YOUNG GUNS II

Hamlin, Phyllis
HEART CONDITION

Hamm, James
LORD OF THE FLIES

Hammer, Ben
CRAZY PEOPLE
SURVIVAL QUEST

Hammil, John
YOUNG GUNS II
KINDERGARTEN COP

Hammond, John
ADVENTURES OF FORD FAIRLANE, THE

Hampton, Adrienne
LOOSE CANNONS

Hampton, Garland
PROBLEM CHILD

Hampton, James
PUMP UP THE VOLUME

Hancock, John
DEAD AIM
BONFIRE OF THE VANITIES
WHY ME?

Hancock, Sheila
THREE MEN AND A LITTLE LADY

Hancock, Stephen
CHICAGO JOE AND THE SHOWGIRL

Handwerger, Jeb
GREEN CARD

Handy, James
ARACHNOPHOBIA

Hanft, Helen
BETSY'S WEDDING

Hanis, Ray
PACIFIC HEIGHTS

Hanis, Raymond
FLATLINERS

Hankin, Larry
PRETTY WOMAN
HOME ALONE

Hanks, Tom
JOE VERSUS THE VOLCANO
BONFIRE OF THE VANITIES

Hannah, Bob
CHATTAHOOCHEE

Hannah, Daryl
CRAZY PEOPLE

Hannah, Don
WHITE GIRL, THE

Hannah, Page
GREMLINS 2 THE NEW BATCH

Hanner, Carter
. DANCES WITH WOLVES

Hansen, Lisa M.
FAR OUT MAN

Hansen, Michael
HOME ALONE

Hansen, Nina
EXORCIST III, THE

Hansley, Adam
SPACED INVADERS

Hansome, Rhonda
PRETTY WOMAN

Hanson, Nicole
SLEEPING CAR, THE

Hara, Satoshi
DREAMS

Harada, Mieko
DREAMS

Harada, Yuko
DREAMS

Harden, Marcia Gay
MILLER'S CROSSING

Hardesty, Kevin
HAPPY TOGETHER

Hardie, Kate
KRAYS, THE
INNOCENT VICTIM

Hardin, Jerry
HOT SPOT, THE
PACIFIC HEIGHTS

Hardin, Melora
LAMBADA

Hardison, Kadeem
DEF BY TEMPTATION

Hardjito, Hapsarif
MAHABHARATA, THE

Hardman, Cederick
HOUSE PARTY

Hardwick, Mark
MEN DON'T LEAVE

Hardy, John
HOME ALONE

Hare, Doris
NUNS ON THE RUN

Hare, Joe
STRAPLESS

Hare, Will
GRIM PRAIRIE TALES

Harewood, Dorian
PACIFIC HEIGHTS

Hargray, Dwayne
DIE HARD 2

Harimoto, Dale
MARKED FOR DEATH

Harlander, Willy
ROSALIE GOES SHOPPING

Harlmann, Didier
LIFE AND NOTHING BUT

Harper, Gloria
AWAKENINGS

Harper, Tess
DADDY'S DYIN'... WHO'S GOT THE WILL?

Harragin, Serena
WITCHES, THE

Harrah, Randy
OPPORTUNITY KNOCKS

Harrell, James
HOT SPOT, THE

Harrell, Jim
RIVERBEND

Harrell, Michele
TAKING CARE OF BUSINESS

Harrigan, Bobby
QUICK CHANGE

Harrington, Claudia
VITAL SIGNS

Harris, Baxter
MERMAIDS

Harris, Burtt
Q&A

Harris, Danielle
MARKED FOR DEATH

Harris, Deidre
HEART CONDITION

Harris, Donna
WILDEST DREAMS

Harris, Ed
STATE OF GRACE

Harris, Fox
ALIENATOR
DR. CALIGARI

Harris, Gail
HAUNTING OF MORELLA, THE

Harris, Glenn Walker Jr.
WILD AT HEART

Harris, Jack David
MILLER'S CROSSING

Harris, Jonathan
HAPPILY EVER AFTER

Harris, Julius
DARKMAN

Harris, Lara
FOURTH WAR, THE
BLOOD RED

Harris, Randy
HOUSE PARTY

Harris, Richard
MACK THE KNIFE
FIELD, THE

Harris, Robin
HOUSE PARTY
MO' BETTER BLUES

Harrison, Jim
COLD FEET

Harrison, Maxine
RETURN OF SUPERFLY, THE

Harry, Deborah
TALES FROM THE DARKSIDE: THE MOVIE

Harshbarger, Lance
WHITE PALACE

Harston, Wendelin
FLASHBACK

Hart, Eric
SKI PATROL

Hart, Linda
STELLA

Hart, Tina
KINDERGARTEN COP

Harte-Browne, Harry
STREET ASYLUM

Hartigan, Ben
HUNT FOR RED OCTOBER, THE

Hartman, Don
FEUD, THE

Hartman, Phil
QUICK CHANGE

Hartz, April
DR. CALIGARI

Harvey, Don
DIE HARD 2

Harvey, Robert
YOUNG GUNS II
ROOKIE, THE

Harwood, Stewart
MOUNTAINS OF THE MOON
NUNS ON THE RUN
MISADVENTURES OF MR. WILT, THE

Hasegawa, Makoto
DREAMS

Hasimovic, Husnija
TIME OF THE GYPSIES

Haskell, Peter
CHILD'S PLAY 2

Haskell, Robert
TEENAGE MUTANT NINJA TURTLES

Hasse, Liz
HENRY AND JUNE

Hassett, James
OPPORTUNITY KNOCKS

Hata, Megumi
DREAMS

Hateley, John
ROBOCOP 2

Hatfield, Mert
EVERYBODY WINS
FEUD, THE

Hauer, Rutger
BLOOD OF HEROES
BLIND FURY

Haufrecht, Robert
DOG TAGS

Haugk, Charlie
PREDATOR 2

Hauser, Wings
BEDROOM EYES II
STREET ASYLUM

Haveland, Harlon
KRAYS, THE

Haveland, Sam
KRAYS, THE

Havey, Allan
INTERNAL AFFAIRS

Hawke, Charlie
VITAL SIGNS
ADVENTURES OF FORD FAIRLANE, THE

Hawker, John
LISA
HOT SPOT, THE

Hawkes, John
ROSALIE GOES SHOPPING

Hawkins, Cecil
EDWARD SCISSORHANDS

Hawkins, Linda
MO' BETTER BLUES

Hawksley, Brian
WITCHES, THE

Hawn, Goldie
BIRD ON A WIRE

Hawthorne, Denys
RUSSIA HOUSE, THE

Hawtrey, Nicholas
IMPROMPTU

Hayami, Noriko
DREAMS

Hayashi, Marc
LASER MAN, THE

Hayashi, Yoko
DREAMS

Hayden, Ashley
BURNDOWN

Hayden, John Patrick
RETURN OF SUPERFLY, THE

Hayden, Ted
GHOST DAD

Hayes, Edward
GOODFELLAS

Haygarth, Tony
INNOCENT VICTIM

Hayman, Barton
BONFIRE OF THE VANITIES

Haynes, Cody
HOT SPOT, THE

Haynes, George
HOT SPOT, THE

Haynes, Jayne
AWAKENINGS

Haynes, Tiger
AWAKENINGS

Haynie, Jim
MEN DON'T LEAVE
I COME IN PEACE

Hays, Kent
DANCES WITH WOLVES

Hays, Robert
HONEYMOON ACADEMY

Haysbert, Dennis
NAVY SEALS

Haywood, Chris
QUIGLEY DOWN UNDER

Haze, Stan
HOUSE PARTY

Headly, Glenne
DICK TRACY

Heald, Anthony
POSTCARDS FROM THE EDGE

Healy, David
UNBELIEVABLE TRUTH, THE

Healy, Peter
TIME GUARDIAN, THE

Healy, Tim
BIRD ON A WIRE

Heard, John
AWAKENINGS
HOME ALONE

Hearst, Debra
MISADVENTURES OF MR. WILT, THE

Hearst, Patricia
CRY-BABY

Heath, Mary Jane
EDWARD SCISSORHANDS

Heatherton, Joey
CRY-BABY

Heavener, David
TWISTED JUSTICE

Hecht, Harold Jr.
FOURTH WAR, THE

Heck, Gene
SHORT TIME

Heckerling, Louis
LOOK WHO'S TALKING TOO

Hedaya, Dan
JOE VERSUS THE VOLCANO
PACIFIC HEIGHTS
TUNE IN TOMORROW

Hedren, Tippi
PACIFIC HEIGHTS

Heffner, Nettie
DEAD PIT

Heiler, Frank
HENRY AND JUNE

Heinemann, Joe
COME SEE THE PARADISE

Helland, Roy
POSTCARDS FROM THE EDGE

Heller, Gedren
NUNS ON THE RUN

Helmkamp, Charlotte
FRANKENHOOKER

Hemingway, Winston
TEENAGE MUTANT NINJA TURTLES

Hemmings, Nolan
MAHABHARATA, THE

Hendrickson, Terri
HAVANA

Henfrey, Janet
COOK, THE THIEF, HIS WIFE & HER
LOVER, THE

Hengstler, Dee
DICK TRACY

Henley, Kaleb
BACK TO THE FUTURE PART III

Hennes, Peter
OPPORTUNITY KNOCKS

Henning, Ted
DEAD AIM

Henning-Beyrhammer, Irmgard
NASTY GIRL, THE

Hennings, Sam
NIGHT ANGEL

Henriksen, Lance
HIT LIST
SURVIVAL QUEST

Henry, Alexi
ALICE

Henry, Beverley
SHORT TIME

Henry, Buck
TUNE IN TOMORROW

Henry, David
RUSSIA HOUSE, THE

Henry, Justine L.
SPACED INVADERS

Hensley, Sonia
RETURN OF SUPERFLY, THE

Henson, Betty Lou
KINDERGARTEN COP

Henson-Phillips, Veronica
NIGHT EYES

Herbert, Ellen
PLOT AGAINST HARRY, THE

Herbert, Sylvie
IMPROMPTU

Herlin, Jacques
TORRENTS OF SPRING

Herman, Dr. Berry
GUARDIAN, THE

Herman, Jimmy
DANCES WITH WOLVES

Herman, Paul
CADILLAC MAN
QUICK CHANGE
GOODFELLAS

Hernandez, Monica
REVENGE

Hernandez, Richard
DESPERATE HOURS

Hernandez, Samuel
FIRE BIRDS

Herring, Laura
FORBIDDEN DANCE, THE

Herring, Raquel
OPPONENT, THE

Herry-Leclerc, Jeanne
MAY FOOLS

Hershey, Barbara
TUNE IN TOMORROW

Hertford, Whitby
TAKING CARE OF BUSINESS

Hertzberg, Paul
FAR OUT MAN

Hesler, Christian
BLOOD SALVAGE

Heslov, Grant
VITAL SIGNS

Hess, Linda Hess
EDWARD SCISSORHANDS

Heston, Charlton
ALMOST AN ANGEL

Hewetson, Nicholas
NUNS ON THE RUN

Hewett, Christine
STRIKE IT RICH

Hewitt, Jery
MILLER'S CROSSING

Hewlett, David
WHERE THE HEART IS

Hewson, Thomas
GOODFELLAS

Heyman, Barton
QUICK CHANGE
AWAKENINGS

Hickey, Tom
NUNS ON THE RUN

Hickey, William
TALES FROM THE DARKSIDE: THE MOVIE
MY BLUE HEAVEN
MAGDALENE

Hicks, Barbara
MISADVENTURES OF MR. WILT, THE

Hicks, Chuck
DICK TRACY

Hicks, Danny
DARKMAN

Hicks, David
SHADOWZONE

Hicks, Kevin
BLOOD RELATIONS

Hicks, Lenny
TAKING CARE OF BUSINESS

Hiegel, Catherine
LIFE IS A LONG QUIET RIVER

Higashimura, Motoyuki
DREAMS

Higelin, Ken
MAHABHARATA, THE

Highlands, Delbert
FLASHBACK

Hightower, Donald
MONSTER HIGH

Hild, James
STAR QUEST: BEYOND THE RISING MOON

Hildebrand, Dan
NUNS ON THE RUN
MISADVENTURES OF MR. WILT, THE

Hill, Amy
GHOST DAD

Hill, Bernard
MOUNTAINS OF THE MOON

Hill, Dana
JETSONS: THE MOVIE

Hill, Dave
RAGGEDY RAWNEY, THE

Hill, Eddita
MR. DESTINY

Hill, Rodney
HOUSE PARTY

Hill, Roy
REAL BULLETS

Hill, Steven
WHITE PALACE

Hiller, Bernard
AVALON

Hillman, Rachel
LEMON SISTERS, THE

Hillwood, Amanda
DIE HARD 2

Hilton, Chris
DOG TAGS

Hinchcliffe, Debbee
LOOSE CANNONS

Hinckley, Tommy
MEN AT WORK

Hindle, Dawne
AVALON

Hinds, Ciaran
COOK, THE THIEF, HIS WIFE & HER
LOVER, THE

Hines, Desi Arnez III
HOUSE PARTY

Hingle, Pat
GRIFTERS, THE

Hinkley, Brent
JACOB'S LADDER

Hinson, Don
TAX SEASON

Hirano, Asako
DREAMS

Ho, Rocky
LIFE IS CHEAP... BUT TOILET PAPER IS
EXPENSIVE

Ho, Wai Ching
CADILLAC MAN

Hoag, Judith
TEENAGE MUTANT NINJA TURTLES
CADILLAC MAN

Hoak, Clare
MASQUE OF THE RED DEATH

Hochman, Stanley R.
ROCKY V

Hock, Peter
GOODFELLAS

Hodge, Kate
LEATHERFACE: THE TEXAS CHAINSAW
MASSACRE III

Hodge, Mike
BLUE STEEL
BONFIRE OF THE VANITIES

Hodgkins, Al
MERMAIDS

Hodoruk, Nina
LEMON SISTERS, THE

Hodson, Ed
PACIFIC HEIGHTS

Hoffman, Avi
IMPORTED BRIDEGROOM, THE

Hoffman, Basil
LAMBADA

Hoffman, Bridget
DARKMAN

Hoffman, Dominic
SURVIVAL QUEST

Hoffman, Dustin
DICK TRACY

Hoffman, Leila
WITCHES, THE

Hoffman, Thurn
IN THE SPIRIT

Hogan, Hulk
GREMLINS 2 THE NEW BATCH

Hogan, Michael
STELLA

Hogan, Paul
ALMOST AN ANGEL

Hogan, Susan
NARROW MARGIN

Hoge, Alicia
SHOCK TO THE SYSTEM, A

Hogue, Jeffrey C.
ALIENATOR

Holden, Marjean
DR. CALIGARI

Holder, Roy
MACK THE KNIFE

Holland, Agnieszka
INTERROGATION, THE

Holland, Antony
NARROW MARGIN

Hollis, Gary
KINDERGARTEN COP

Holly, Lauren
ADVENTURES OF FORD FAIRLANE, THE

Holm, Ian
HAMLET

Holmes, William
SPACED INVADERS

Holt, Patrick
STRIKE IT RICH

Holy, Marvin
DANCES WITH WOLVES

Holyfield, Evander
BLOOD SALVAGE

Honda, Gene
OPPORTUNITY KNOCKS

Hong, Dong Ji
MACK THE KNIFE

Hong, James
CAGED FURY
TAX SEASON
TWO JAKES, THE
SHADOWZONE

Hongthai, Sinjai
AIR AMERICA

Honigman, Richard
GODFATHER PART III, THE

Honma, Ayako
DREAMS

Hooks, Jan
FUNLAND

Hootkins, William
HARDWARE

Hoover, Christian
STELLA

Hoover, Elva Mai
STELLA

Hope, Leslie
MEN AT WORK

Hope, Margot
DOWN THE DRAIN

Hopkins, Anthony
DESPERATE HOURS

Hopkins, Bo
BIG BAD JOHN

Hopkins, Telma
VITAL SIGNS

Hopper, Dennis
FLASHBACK
CHATTAHOOCHEE
BLOOD RED

Hopper, Robert
LORDS OF MAGICK, THE

Hopson, Lew
INTERNAL AFFAIRS

Hopwood, Lynna
SKINHEADS — THE SECOND COMING OF
HATE

Horan, Gerard
CHICAGO JOE AND THE SHOWGIRL

Horino, Tad
COME SEE THE PARADISE

Horn, Lew
DICK TRACY

Horrocks, Jane
WITCHES, THE
MEMPHIS BELLE

Horruzey, Paul
STANLEY AND IRIS

Horsford, Anna Maria
PRESUMED INNOCENT

Horton, Michael
HAPPILY EVER AFTER

Horton, Peter
SIDE OUT

Hosaka, Sanae
COME SEE THE PARADISE

Hosea, Robert
MURDER BY NUMBERS

Hoshi, Shizuko
COME SEE THE PARADISE

Hosking, Craig
VITAL SIGNS
DARKMAN

Hoskins, Bob
HEART CONDITION
RAGGEDY RAWNEY, THE
MERMAIDS

Hotton, Donald
DANCES WITH WOLVES

Hounson, Djimon
WITHOUT YOU, I'M NOTHING

Houston-Jones, Ishmael
BAIL JUMPER

Howard, Alan
STRAPLESS
COOK, THE THIEF, HIS WIFE & HER
LOVER, THE

Howard, Arliss
MEN DON'T LEAVE

Howard, Barbara
WHITE PALACE

Howard, Jeff
UNBELIEVABLE TRUTH, THE

Howard, K. Theodore
FAR OUT MAN

Howard, Kevin
I COME IN PEACE

Howard, Sherman
I COME IN PEACE

Howe, Adrienne
FRESHMAN, THE

Howell, C. Thomas
SIDE OUT
FAR OUT MAN

Howell, Hoke
ALIENATOR

Howell, Jimmy
TEXASVILLE

Howell, Linda
TOTAL RECALL

Howze, Zakee L.
MO' BETTER BLUES

Hubatsek, Andrew
BLUE STEEL

Huckabee, Cooper
NIGHT EYES

Hudlin, Reginald
HOUSE PARTY

Hudlin, Warrington
HOUSE PARTY

Hudson, Gary
NIGHT ANGEL

Hudson, Jim
DIE HARD 2

Hudson, Toni
LEATHERFACE: THE TEXAS CHAINSAW
MASSACRE III

Huertes, Christina
AWAKENINGS

Hues, Matthias
AFTERSHOCK
I COME IN PEACE

Huff, Tom
HEART CONDITION

Huffman, Felicity
REVERSAL OF FORTUNE

Huffman, Linus
MARKED FOR DEATH

Hughes, Kathleen
REVENGE

Hughes, Miko
KINDERGARTEN COP

Hughes, Whitey
CHATTAHOOCHEE

Hugot, Marceline
ALICE

Huguel, Sylvie
HENRY AND JUNE

Hui, Cinda
LIFE IS CHEAP. . . BUT TOILET PAPER IS EX-
PENSIVE

Humann, Helena
PROBLEM CHILD

Hummel, Hermann
NASTY GIRL, THE

Hundley, Dylan
METROPOLITAN

Hunt, Linda
KINDERGARTEN COP

Hunt, Neil
THREE MEN AND A LITTLE LADY

Hunt, W.M.
BONFIRE OF THE VANITIES

Hunter, Heather
FRANKENHOOKER

Hunter, Holly
ANIMAL BEHAVIOR

Hunter, Kim
TWO EVIL EYES

Hunter, R. Darrell
PRETTY WOMAN

Huri, Machram
TORN APART

Hurley, Melissa
THREE MEN AND A LITTLE LADY

Hurst, Ellen
RUSSIA HOUSE, THE

Hurst, Gordon
TEXASVILLE

Hurt, John
FRANKENSTEIN UNBOUND
FIELD, THE

Hurt, William
I LOVE YOU TO DEATH
ALICE

Husmann, Andrew
MONSTER HIGH

Hussein, Adam
NAVY SEALS

Hussey, John
BURNDOWN

Huston, Anjelica
WITCHES, THE
GRIFTERS, THE

Hutchence, Michael
FRANKENSTEIN UNBOUND

Hutchings, Geoffrey
WHITE HUNTER, BLACK HEART

Hutchinson, Mike
ERNEST GOES TO JAIL

Hutter, Mark
OPPORTUNITY KNOCKS

Hutton, Timothy
TORRENTS OF SPRING
Q&A

Hyatt, Ron Jeremy
CAGED FURY
LORDS OF MAGICK, THE

Hyatt, Su
TEXASVILLE

Hyde, Michael
AWAKENINGS

Hyde-White, Alex
LOOSE CANNONS
PRETTY WOMAN

Hynes, Kevin
NIGHT EYES

Hyser, Joyce
WEDDING BAND

Hytner, Stephen
SKI PATROL

Iandoli, Dean
MONSTER HIGH

Iannicelli, Ray
BONFIRE OF THE VANITIES

Ibu, Masuto
HEAVEN AND EARTH

Ichihara, Etsuko
BLACK RAIN

Ichihashi, Machiko
DREAMS

Ickes, John
BACK TO THE FUTURE PART III

Idle, Eric
NUNS ON THE RUN

Igawa, Hisashi
DREAMS

Igawa, Togo
MISADVENTURES OF MR. WILT, THE

Iida, Eiji
DREAMS

Ikaida, Aya
DREAMS

Ikariya, Chosuke
DREAMS

Ikeguchi, Takumaro
COME SEE THE PARADISE

Ikejiri, Ron
STAR QUEST: BEYOND THE RISING MOON

Ikeya, Mika
DREAMS

Ilku, David
BLUE STEEL

Imai, Yoshimi
COME SEE THE PARADISE

Imamura, Koichi
DREAMS

Imamura, Lenny
COME SEE THE PARADISE

Imperio, Liz
DICK TRACY

Imperioli, Michael
GOODFELLAS

Inaba, Akitoku
DREAMS

Inal, Engin
ISTANBUL, KEEP YOUR EYES OPEN

Incerto, Carlo
MEN IN LOVE

Indelicato, Santo
GODFATHER PART III, THE

Ingle, John
ROBOCOP 2

Ingold, Larry
BACK TO THE FUTURE PART III

Ingoldsby, Joe
FRESHMAN, THE

Ingram, Jay
LOOSE CANNONS

Innes, Alexandra
HOW TO MAKE LOVE TO A NEGRO WITH-
OUT GETTING TIRED

Innocent, Harold
TALL GUY, THE

Insana, Tino
WEDDING BAND

Inscoe, Joe
TEENAGE MUTANT NINJA TURTLES

Ireland, Kathy
MR. DESTINY

Ireson, Richard
CHICAGO JOE AND THE SHOWGIRL

Irinaga, Fred
COME SEE THE PARADISE

Irizarry, Gloria
Q&A
JACOB'S LADDER

Irons, Jeremy
REVERSAL OF FORTUNE

Ironside, Michael
HOSTILE TAKEOVER
TOTAL RECALL

Irving, Amy
SHOW OF FORCE, A

Irwin, Bill
MY BLUE HEAVEN

Irwin, Tom
MEN DON'T LEAVE

Irwin, Wynn
DIE HARD 2

Isaacs, Jason
TALL GUY, THE

Isabella
MO' BETTER BLUES

Isaki, Mitsunori
DREAMS

Isami, Shizuka
DREAMS

Iselin, Jason
FLASHBACK

Isenstein, Mindy Loren
AVALON

Ishida, Jim
PREDATOR 2

Ishida, Keisuke
BLACK RAIN

Ishida, Taro
HEAVEN AND EARTH

Ishikawa, Kou
DREAMS

Ishimoto, Dale
COME SEE THE PARADISE

Ishiwa, Yuko
DREAMS

Ishizuka, Kumiko
DREAMS

Isler, Seth
VITAL SIGNS
PACIFIC HEIGHTS

Isobe, Shinko
COME SEE THE PARADISE

Israel, Al
MARKED FOR DEATH

Israel, Mollie
LOOK WHO'S TALKING TOO

Israel, Neal
LOOK WHO'S TALKING TOO

Issa, Zam Zam
MOUNTAINS OF THE MOON

Ital Joe, Prince
MARKED FOR DEATH

Itier, Jean-Christophe
MAMA, THERE'S A MAN IN YOUR BED

Ito, Binpachi
HEAVEN AND EARTH

Ito, Takashi
DREAMS

Ito, Tetsuya
DREAMS

Ito, Toshiya
DREAMS

Ivanov, Ivan
HUNT FOR RED OCTOBER, THE

Ivens, Terri
MARKED FOR DEATH

Ivey, Dana
POSTCARDS FROM THE EDGE

Ivey, Judith
EVERYBODY WINS

Ivie, Connie
QUICK CHANGE

Iwamoto, Richard
COME SEE THE PARADISE

Iwanaga, Yasuyuki
DREAMS

Izumi, Wasuke
DREAMS

J., Myra
HOUSE PARTY
FAR OUT MAN

J.J.
TAKING CARE OF BUSINESS

Jaber, Corrine
MAHABHARATA, THE

Jablonsky, Bernardo
WILD ORCHID

Jackos, George
NAVY SEALS

Jacksina, Judy
AWAKENINGS

Jackson, Anne
FUNNY ABOUT LOVE

Jackson, Deejay
SHORT TIME

Jackson, Donald
BLADES

Jackson, Ernestine
BONFIRE OF THE VANITIES

Jackson, Ernie
FOURTH WAR, THE

Jackson, Freddie
DEF BY TEMPTATION
KING OF NEW YORK

Jackson, Jim Jim
KINDERGARTEN COP

Jackson, Mary
EXORCIST III, THE

Jackson, Roger
CHATTAHOOCHEE

Jackson, Sam
RETURN OF SUPERFLY, THE

Jackson, Samuel L.
SHOCK TO THE SYSTEM, A
DEF BY TEMPTATION
BETSY'S WEDDING
MO' BETTER BLUES
EXORCIST III, THE
GOODFELLAS

Jackson, Tyrone
SHOCK TO THE SYSTEM, A

Jackson, Victoria
I LOVE YOU TO DEATH

Jacob, Catherine
LIFE IS A LONG QUIET RIVER

Jacob, Joel
DISTURBANCE, THE

Jacobi, Lou
AVALON

Jacobs, Brian
LORD OF THE FLIES

Jacobs, Dan
FUNLAND

Jacobs, Mark Evan
GOODFELLAS

Jacobs, Martin
WHITE HUNTER, BLACK HEART

Jacobs, Michael
DEAD PIT

Jacobs, Ted
IMPORTED BRIDEGROOM, THE

Jacobson, Dean
COUPE DE VILLE

Jacobson, Jake
DEMON WIND

Jacoby, Bobby
TREMORS

Jacoby, Dale
DIE HARD 2

Jacques, Yves
JESUS OF MONTREAL

Jaeckel, Richard
DELTA FORCE 2

Jaffrey, Madhur
PERFECT MURDER, THE

Jaffrey, Sakin
PERFECT MURDER, THE

Jaiia
MEN IN LOVE

Jaimsie, Mairtin
FIELD, THE

James, Anne
FLATLINERS

James, Brion
ANOTHER 48 HRS.
STREET ASYLUM

James, Clifton
BONFIRE OF THE VANITIES

James, Denise E.
HUNT FOR RED OCTOBER, THE

James, Diana
PREDATOR 2

James, Geraldine
TALL GUY, THE

James, Jackie
FRIGHT HOUSE

James, Jeff
FORBIDDEN DANCE, THE

James, Jesse
MEN DON'T LEAVE

James, Steve
RIVERBEND

Jamrog, Joe
BLUE STEEL

Janczar, Christopher
TORRENTS OF SPRING
HUNT FOR RED OCTOBER, THE

Janda, Krystyna
INTERROGATION, THE

Janeyrand, Gilles
LIFE AND NOTHING BUT

Janic, Davor
MY UNCLE'S LEGACY

Janis, Conrad
SONNY BOY

Jankowski, Oleg
MY 20TH CENTURY

Jaquin, Caroline
MAMA, THERE'S A MAN IN YOUR BED

Jarrel, Andy
HOMER & EDDIE

Jarres, Jill
PUMP UP THE VOLUME

Jarrett, Cody
ADVENTURES OF FORD FAIRLANE, THE

Jarrett, Paul
BIRD ON A WIRE
SHORT TIME

Jarvis, Graham
MISERY

Jarvis, Robert Lee
LAST OF THE FINEST, THE

Jason, Harvey
AIR AMERICA

Jason, Peter
ARACHNOPHOBIA
MARKED FOR DEATH

Jawdokimov, Alexei
RUSSIA HOUSE, THE

Jay, Julie
STREETS

Jaynes, Leiland
TEXASVILLE

Jazede, Franck
CYRANO DE BERGERAC

Jeffries, Adam
GHOST DAD

Jeffries, Chuck
AFTERSHOCK

Jeffries, Todd
FIRST POWER, THE

Jemison, Kimble
LAST OF THE FINEST, THE

Jenesky, George
DEATH WARRANT

Jenkins, Julian
BELLY OF AN ARCHITECT, THE

Jenkins, Ken
AIR AMERICA

Jenkins, Rebecca
BYE BYE BLUES

Jenkins, Richard
BLUE STEEL

Jenkins, Sam
BONFIRE OF THE VANITIES

Jenkins, Timothy
BONFIRE OF THE VANITIES

Jennings, Brent
ANOTHER 48 HRS.

Jennings, Dominque
DIE HARD 2

Jensen, John
COME SEE THE PARADISE

Jequier, Marblum
L'ETAT SAUVAGE

Jessup, Cortland
ME AND HIM

Jesus, Carlinhos
WILD ORCHID

Jeter, Michael
MILLER'S CROSSING

Jewel, Jimmy
KRAYS, THE

Jhin, Philip
PROBLEM CHILD

Jodorowsky, Adan
SANTA SANGRE

Jodorowsky, Axel
SANTA SANGRE

Johann, Cameron
LAST EXIT TO BROOKLYN

Johansen, David
TALES FROM THE DARKSIDE: THE MOVIE

John, Abineri
GODFATHER PART III, THE

Johns, Tracy Camilla
MO' BETTER BLUES

Johnskareng, Amund
PATHFINDER

Johnson, A.J.
HOUSE PARTY

Johnson, Anne-Marie
ROBOT JOX

Johnson, Anthony
HOUSE PARTY

Johnson, Arte
TAX SEASON

Johnson, Ben
BACK TO BACK

Johnson, Cage S.
FLATLINERS

Johnson, Connie
ADVENTURES OF FORD FAIRLANE, THE

Johnson, Dasanea
HEART CONDITION

Johnson, Deborah Lee
QUICK CHANGE

Johnson, Don
HOT SPOT, THE

Johnson, Douglas
GHOST DAD

Johnson, Francis
TALL GUY, THE

Johnson, Heather
BIG DIS, THE

Johnson, Jadili
SKINHEADS – THE SECOND COMING OF
HATE

Johnson, Jason
SKI PATROL

Johnson, Jill
WILDEST DREAMS
TAKING CARE OF BUSINESS

Johnson, Johnnie
HEART CONDITION

Johnson, Johquache
HEART CONDITION

Johnson, Kate
HOME ALONE

Johnson, Kenny
FORBIDDEN DANCE, THE

Johnson, Kent H.
ROCKY V

Johnson, Kirk
GRAFFITI BRIDGE

Johnson, Lorna Raver
OPPORTUNITY KNOCKS

Johnson, Mel Jr.
TOTAL RECALL
MURDER BY NUMBERS

Johnson, Patrick
SPACED INVADERS

Johnson, Rynel
RETURN OF SUPERFLY, THE

Johnson, Shauntae
HEART CONDITION

Johnson, Tamasin Scarlet
MERMAIDS

Johnson, Toni Ann
RETURN OF SUPERFLY, THE

Johnston, Alexander
I COME IN PEACE

Johnston, Aratha
BIG DIS, THE

Johnston, Bobby
DEMON WIND

Johnston, John D. III
LAST OF THE FINEST, THE

Johnston, Michelle
OPPORTUNITY KNOCKS
DICK TRACY

Joliff, Lisa
RETURN OF SUPERFLY, THE

Jolly, Helen
MILLER'S CROSSING

Jones, Duane
FRIGHT HOUSE

Jones, Alyson
GOODFELLAS

Jones, Doug
NIGHT ANGEL

Jones, Eddie
STANLEY AND IRIS
CADILLAC MAN

Jones, Freddie
WILD AT HEART

Jones, Gary
POSTCARDS FROM THE EDGE

Jones, Griff Rhys
MISADVENTURES OF MR. WILT, THE

Jones, Harry
CHICAGO JOE AND THE SHOWGIRL

Jones, Henry
DICK TRACY
ARACHNOPHOBIA
GRIFTERS, THE

Jones, James Earl
HUNT FOR RED OCTOBER, THE
GRIM PRAIRIE TALES

Jones, Jay Arlen
VITAL SIGNS

Jones, Jeffrey
HUNT FOR RED OCTOBER, THE

Jones, Jill
GRAFFITI BRIDGE

Jones, John Christopher
DESPERATE HOURS
AWAKENINGS

Jones, Judy
PROBLEM CHILD

Jones, Kim
MONSTER HIGH

Jones, Kit
FRIGHT HOUSE
FRIGHT HOUSE

Jones, L.Q.
RIVER OF DEATH

Jones, Laurie
IN THE SPIRIT

Jones, Melody
PROBLEM CHILD

Jones, Michael Steve
ARACHNOPHOBIA

Jones, Mickey
TOTAL RECALL

Jones, O-Lan
PACIFIC HEIGHTS
EDWARD SCISSORHANDS

Jones, Pearl
TEXASVILLE

Jones, Rick
KINDERGARTEN COP

Jones, Robbie
CRY-BABY

Jones, Russell
MERMAIDS

Jones, Simon
GREEN CARD

Jones, Tommy Lee
FIRE BIRDS

Joost, Sixto
YOUNG GUNS II

Jordan, Leslie
SKI PATROL

Jordan, Richard
HUNT FOR RED OCTOBER, THE

Jordan, Tom
FIELD, THE

Joseph, Jackie
GREMLINS 2 THE NEW BATCH

Joseph, Michael A.
Q&A

Joseph, Ron
NAVY SEALS

Joshua, Larry
QUICK CHANGE
DANCES WITH WOLVES

Joshua, Pineniece
MOUNTAINS OF THE MOON

Josselyn, Randy
ANDY COLBY'S INCREDIBLY AWESOME
ADVENTURE

Joubert, Claire
HENRY AND JUNE

Joy, Thomas
AVALON

Joyce, Walker
BONFIRE OF THE VANITIES

Joyner, Kay
LOOSE CANNONS

Joyner, Michelle
I LOVE YOU TO DEATH
GRIM PRAIRIE TALES

Judge, Doug
BIRD ON A WIRE

Judy, Angela
STAR QUEST: BEYOND THE RISING MOON

Julia, Raul
MACK THE KNIFE
PRESUMED INNOCENT
HAVANA
FRANKENSTEIN UNBOUND
ROOKIE, THE

Julian, Janet
TAKING CARE OF BUSINESS
KING OF NEW YORK

Julien, Jett
FRIGHT HOUSE

Juma, Leonard
MOUNTAINS OF THE MOON

Jung, Nathan
DARKMAN

Junior, Mark Boone
DIE HARD 2

Junkin, John
CHICAGO JOE AND THE SHOWGIRL

Jurasik, Peter
PROBLEM CHILD

Jury, Liz
FLASHBACK

Juskiewenski, Denise
MAY FOOLS

Jutkevich, Paul
RUSSIA HOUSE, THE

Kabler, Roger
ALLIGATOR EYES

Kabouche, Aziz
FLAME IN MY HEART, A

Kachpur, Vladimir
TAXI BLUES

Kadi, Charlotte
LIFE AND NOTHING BUT

Kadi, Nicholas
NAVY SEALS

Kado, Miki
DREAMS

Kadowaki, Saburo
DREAMS

Kagan, Diane
MR. AND MRS. BRIDGE
JACOB'S LADDER

Kagan, Elaine
IMPULSE
GOODFELLAS

Kagen, David
BODY CHEMISTRY

Kageyama, Rodney
PRETTY WOMAN

Kahan, Steve
PREDATOR 2

Kahlenberg, Charles
FIRE BIRDS

Kahler, Thom
BACK TO BACK

Kahn, Madeline
BETSY'S WEDDING

Kahn, Michael Alan
ADVENTURES OF FORD FAIRLANE, THE

Kairys, Ted
YOUNG GUNS II

Kaitan, Elizabeth
UNDER THE BOARDWALK

Kajimoto, Yasuhiro
DREAMS

Kalember, Patricia
JACOB'S LADDER

Kamal, Jon Rashad
BONFIRE OF THE VANITIES

Kamberidis, D.
LANDSCAPE IN THE MIST

Kamekona, Danny
PROBLEM CHILD
ROBOT JOX
COME SEE THE PARADISE

Kamel, Stanley
MURDER BY NUMBERS

Kamimura, Mayumi
DREAMS

Kaminsky, Kathleen
WILD ORCHID

Kaminsky, Steven
WILD ORCHID

Kanar, Beth
PREDATOR 2

Kanda, Koji
DREAMS

Kane, Carol
FLASHBACK
MY BLUE HEAVEN
LEMON SISTERS, THE

Kaner, Jaz
ADVENTURES OF FORD FAIRLANE, THE

Kanska, Joanna
TALL GUY, THE

Kapfhamer, Jack W.
EDWARD SCISSORHANDS

Kaplan, Lou
MODERN LOVE

Kaplan, Marvin
WILD AT HEART

Kaposi, Sandor
MACK THE KNIFE

Karaki, Al
AMERICAN EAGLE

Karamsumarau, Setsuko
TWILIGHT OF THE COCKROACHES

Karas, Barry
IMPORTED BRIDEGROOM, THE

Karasek, Valerie
PREDATOR 2

Karen, James
VITAL SIGNS

Karen, Zara
TAX SEASON

Karina, Pia
REVENGE

Karpanny, Tom
TIME GUARDIAN, THE

Karr, Patti
TAX SEASON

Karr, Sarah Rose
KINDERGARTEN COP

Kasdan, Jon
I LOVE YOU TO DEATH

Kase, Koichi
DREAMS

Kasem, Jean
ELLIOT FAUMAN, PH.D.

Kashka
PREDATOR 2

Kastner, Stella
DEMON WIND

Katarina, Anna
BLOOD OF HEROES

Katims, David
FIRST POWER, THE

Katims, Robert
PRESUMED INNOCENT

Katlin, Bruce
BLADES

Kato, Douglas
COME SEE THE PARADISE

Kato, Shigeo
DREAMS

Katrivanos, Kyr.
LANDSCAPE IN THE MIST

Katsumoto, Ken
COME SEE THE PARADISE

Katt, William
WEDDING BAND

Katz, David
DIE HARD 2

Katz, Marlene
ARACHNOPHOBIA

Katzen, Becky
GHOST DAD

Katzman, Lon
NARROW MARGIN

Kauders, Sylvia
PREDATOR 2

Kaufman, Lloyd
ROCKY V

Kavana, Ron
HIDDEN AGENDA

Kavanaugh, Patrick
HIDDEN AGENDA

Kavner, Julie
ALICE
AWAKENINGS

Kawada, Michiko
DREAMS

Kawaguchi, Setsuko
DREAMS

Kawai, Ryoko
DREAMS

Kawana, Miyako
DREAMS

Kawanabe, Eiichi Edward
PROBLEM CHILD

Kay, Diane
ANDY COLBY'S INCREDIBLY AWESOME
ADVENTURE

Kay, Nadine
GOODFELLAS

Kaye, Debra
AMERICAN EAGLE

Kaye, Lila
NUNS ON THE RUN

Kazama, Morio
HEAVEN AND EARTH

Kazamatsuri, Yuki
HEAVEN AND EARTH

Kazan, Sandra
PLOT AGAINST HARRY, THE

Kazan, Vangelis
LANDSCAPE IN THE MIST

Keach, Stacy
CLASS OF 1999
FALSE IDENTITY

Keach, Stacy Sr.
PRETTY WOMAN

Kean, Greg
AIR AMERICA

Keanan, Staci
LISA

Keane, Eamon
FIELD, THE

Keane, James
DICK TRACY

Keating, Charles
AWAKENINGS

Keaton, Diane
LEMON SISTERS, THE
GODFATHER PART III, THE

Keaton, Michael
PACIFIC HEIGHTS

Keays-Byrne, Hugh
BLOOD OF HEROES

Kee, Lee Sau
EAT A BOWL OF TEA

Keegan, John
HIDDEN AGENDA

Keelor, Greg
POSTCARDS FROM THE EDGE

Keenan, Harvey
PRETTY WOMAN

Keener, Catharine
SURVIVAL QUEST

Keenleyside, Eric
STELLA

Keevil, Harriet
TALL GUY, THE

Kehler, Jack
I LOVE YOU TO DEATH

Kehoe, Jack
DICK TRACY
YOUNG GUNS II

Keitel, Harvey
TWO JAKES, THE

TWO EVIL EYES

Keith, David
TWO JAKES, THE

Keith, Hardy
WITHOUT YOU, I'M NOTHING

Keith, Leticia
LOVE AT LARGE

Keithley, Georgia
LOOK WHO'S TALKING TOO

Kellerman, Sally
HAPPILY EVER AFTER

Kelley, Sheila
WHERE THE HEART IS

Kellogg, Mary Ann
ME AND HIM

Kelly, David Patrick
ADVENTURES OF FORD FAIRLANE, THE
WILD AT HEART

Kelly, Ellen
KILL-OFF, THE

Kelly, Hugh
HAVANA

Kelly, Peter
TALL GUY, THE

Kelly, Sheila
LAST OF THE FINEST, THE

Kelly, Susannah
LAST OF THE FINEST, THE

Kelly, Tom
FOURTH WAR, THE

Kelman, Allen
FEUD, THE

Kemp, Gary
KRAYS, THE

Kemp, Heidi
GREMLINS 2 THE NEW BATCH

Kemp, Martin
KRAYS, THE

Kemp, Tom
MERMAIDS

Kempe, Will
METROPOLITAN

Kempf, Heidi
BLUE STEEL

Kendall, Chrissie
MACK THE KNIFE

Kendrick, Henry
BACK TO BACK

Kendrick, Tommy G.
WILD AT HEART

Kenia
VITAL SIGNS

Kenin, Alexa
ANIMAL BEHAVIOR

Kenmegne, Lazare
L'ETAT SAUVAGE

Kennedy, George
BRAIN DEAD

Kennedy, Holly
JACOB'S LADDER

Kennedy, Michael Stanton
FEUD, THE

Kennedy, Mimi
PUMP UP THE VOLUME

Kennedy, T.J.
RIVERBEND

Kennerly, David Hume
GODFATHER PART III, THE

Kenny, Laura
LOVE AT LARGE

Kensei, Ken
CADILLAC MAN

Kensit, Patsy
CHICAGO JOE AND THE SHOWGIRL

Kent, Allan
PRETTY WOMAN

Kent, Enid
VITAL SIGNS

Kent, Steven
BACK TO BACK

Kenworthy, Mary Lou
ROOKIE, THE

Keosian, Jessie
GREEN CARD

Kern, Dan
TAKING CARE OF BUSINESS

Kerwin, Nicola
STUFF STEPHANIE IN THE INCINERATOR

Kery, Gyula
MY 20TH CENTURY

Kerzner, D.J.
MONSTER HIGH

Kesting, Hans
VINCENT AND THEO

Kestner, Bryan
FIRE BIRDS

Keyes, Irwin
DOWN THE DRAIN

Keyser, Wayne
STAR QUEST: BEYOND THE RISING MOON

Khan, Amjad
PERFECT MURDER, THE

Khoshrowshahi, Celal
ISTANBUL, KEEP YOUR EYES OPEN

Kid Creole & The Coconuts
FORBIDDEN DANCE, THE

Kida, Michio
DREAMS

Kidman, Nicole
DAYS OF THUNDER

Kidnie, James
BIRD ON A WIRE

Kietel, Stella
GOODFELLAS

Kiger, Robby
WELCOME HOME, ROXY CARMICHAEL

Kihira, Yoshle
DREAMS

Kihlberg, Emma
ISTANBUL, KEEP YOUR EYES OPEN

Killmeyer, Lynne
FEUD, THE

Kilmer, Val
KILL ME AGAIN

Kilpatrick, Patrick
CLASS OF 1999
DEATH WARRANT

Kim, Leigh C.
VITAL SIGNS

Kim, Miki
PRIMARY TARGET

Kimberlain, Sandrine
CYRANO DE BERGERAC

Kimberley, Stephen
LOVE AT LARGE

Kimble, Bill
BLADES

Kimmel, Mike
PAINT IT BLACK

Kimmins, Kenneth
STELLA

Kimura, Sakae
DREAMS

King, Alan
BONFIRE OF THE VANITIES

King, Caroline Junko
COME SEE THE PARADISE

King, Erik
CADILLAC MAN

King, Jerome
GAME, THE

King, Larry
EXORCIST III, THE

Kingi, Henri
FAR OUT MAN

Kingi, Henry
PREDATOR 2

Kingkade, Howard
MR. DESTINY

Kingsley, Ben
SLIPSTREAM

Kingston, Alex
COOK, THE THIEF, HIS WIFE & HER
LOVER, THE

Kinkade, Chris
I COME IN PEACE

Kinkel, Dean
I COME IN PEACE

Kinlaw, Chuck
EXORCIST III, THE

Kinney, Kathy
STANLEY AND IRIS
ARACHNOPHOBIA

Kinney, Michael
TAKING CARE OF BUSINESS

Kinsey, Lance
WEDDING BAND
HONEYMOON ACADEMY

Kinski, Nastassja
TORRENTS OF SPRING
MAGDALENE

Kirby, Bruno
FRESHMAN, THE

Kirby, Michael
WHERE THE HEART IS

Kirby, Roget W.
METROPOLITAN

Kirk, Keith
RIVERBEND

Kirk, Neil
AVALON

Kirk, Shelley
POSTCARDS FROM THE EDGE

Kirkland, Sally
REVENGE
PAINT IT BLACK
TWO EVIL EYES
COLD FEET

Kirkland, Terence
FAR OUT MAN

Kirtzman, Jesse
GOODFELLAS

Kiser, Terry
SIDE OUT

Kishida, Kyoko
HEAVEN AND EARTH

Kissoon, Jeffrey
MAHABHARATA, THE

Kitaen, Eilizabeth
AFTERSHOCK

Kitamura, Kazuo
BLACK RAIN

Kitchen, Michael
FOOLS OF FORTUNE
RUSSIA HOUSE, THE

Kivett, Howard
FEUD, THE

Klar, Gary
CHATTAHOOCHEE
QUICK CHANGE

Klar, Gary H.
CADILLAC MAN

Klasek, Carol D.
EDWARD SCISSORHANDS

Klastorin, Michael
BACK TO THE FUTURE PART III

Klein, Barbara Ann
NIGHT EYES

Klein, Bill
EDWARD SCISSORHANDS

Klein, Elizabeth Ann
EVERYBODY WINS

Klein, Jeff
I LOVE YOU TO DEATH

Klein, Robert
TALES FROM THE DARKSIDE: THE MOVIE

Klein, Timothy D.
STATE OF GRACE

Klenck, Margaret
LOOSE CANNONS

Kline, Colby
PROBLEM CHILD

Kline, Gerald M.
RETURN OF SUPERFLY, THE

Kline, Kevin
I LOVE YOU TO DEATH

Kneeland, Elizabeth
MADHOUSE

Knell, David
TOTAL RECALL

Knepper, Robert
YOUNG GUNS II

Knight, William
NAVY SEALS

Knotts, Kathryn
TAX SEASON

Knower, Rosemary
MEN DON'T LEAVE

Knox, Mickey
FRANKENSTEIN UNBOUND
GODFATHER PART III, THE

Knupffer, Peter
RUSSIA HOUSE, THE

Kobayashi, Kaoru
TWILIGHT OF THE COCKROACHES

Kobayashi, Sayuri
DREAMS

Kober, Jeff
FIRST POWER, THE

Kodisch, George
Q&A

Kohne, Bill
SKINHEADS – THE SECOND COMING OF
HATE

Koide, Teri Eiko
COME SEE THE PARADISE

Koizumi, Ariane
KING OF NEW YORK

Kojima, Yuka
DREAMS

Kolb, Joseph
PROBLEM CHILD

Koliakanova, Natalia
TAXI BLUES

Kolovos, Vassilis
LANDSCAPE IN THE MIST

Komarek, Heidi
ICICLE THIEF, THE

Kondrashoff, Kim
BIRD ON A WIRE
SHORT TIME

Kong, Gary
LIFE IS CHEAP. . . BUT TOILET PAPER IS
EXPENSIVE

Konig, Tex
FRESHMAN, THE

Kono, Casey
SAVAGE BEACH

Konrad, Tim
BACK TO THE FUTURE PART III

Kontomitras, Jeanette
MILLER'S CROSSING

Koonce, B.J.
CHATTAHOOCHEE

Koop, C. Everett
EXORCIST III, THE

Kopache, Thomas
LOOSE CANNONS

Kope, Henry
FOURTH WAR, THE

Kopperman, Maryann
WHITE PALACE

Kopyc, Frank
TOTAL RECALL

Korda, Alexia
TORRENTS OF SPRING

Korduner, Yefim
FOURTH WAR, THE

Koromzay, Alix
KINDERGARTEN COP

Koronszi, Endre
MY 20TH CENTURY

Korosa, Eddie
MEN DON'T LEAVE
HOME ALONE

Korsmo, Charlie
MEN DON'T LEAVE
DICK TRACY

Koslo, Paul
LOOSE CANNONS
ROBOT JOX

Koss, Dwight
SHORT TIME

Koss, Jamie
WHITE HUNTER, BLACK HEART

Kostmayer, John
I LOVE YOU TO DEATH

Kostmayer, Samantha
I LOVE YOU TO DEATH

Kosugi, Sho
BLIND FURY

Kotamanidou, Eva
LANDSCAPE IN THE MIST

Koteas, Elias
TEENAGE MUTANT NINJA TURTLES
BLOOD RED

DESPERATE HOURS
ALMOST AN ANGEL
LOOK WHO'S TALKING TOO

Kotero, Apollonia
BACK TO BACK

Kottenbrook, Carol
SURVIVAL QUEST

Kotto, Maka
HOW TO MAKE LOVE TO A NEGRO WITHOUT GETTING TIRED

Kouros, N.
LANDSCAPE IN THE MIST

Kouyate, Sotigui
MAHABHARATA, THE

Kovacic, Chuck
ANDY COLBY'S INCREDIBLY AWESOME ADVENTURE

Kovacs, Agnes
MY 20TH CENTURY

Kovacs, Danny
PACIFIC HEIGHTS

Kovacs, Eszter
MY 20TH CENTURY

Kovan, Gregg
DIE HARD 2

Kovell, Kenton
HUNT FOR RED OCTOBER, THE

Kovner, Pete
MERMAIDS

Kovner-Zaks, Debra
AWAKENINGS

Kowanko, Peter
CAGED IN PARADISO

Kozak, Harley Jane
SIDE OUT
ARACHNOPHOBIA

Kozak, Jon
STELLA

Kozlowski, Linda
ALMOST AN ANGEL

Kraft, Armin
MAGDALENE

Kraft, Kendal
NIGHT OF THE LIVING DEAD

Kraus, Courtney
ROSALIE GOES SHOPPING

Kraus, Stephan
YOUNG GUNS II

Krauss, Michael
AVALON

Krawford, Gary
WHERE THE HEART IS

Kreppel, Paul
JETSONS: THE MOVIE

Krieger, Ed
CHILD'S PLAY 2

Kristensen, John S.
PATHFINDER

Kronwell, Karen
MADHOUSE

Krum, Dorie
TAX SEASON

Krupa, Olek
MILLER'S CROSSING

Krupinkski, Renny
MOUNTAINS OF THE MOON

Krutonog, Boris
HUNT FOR RED OCTOBER, THE

Kubozono, Junichi
DREAMS

Kuehne, Rod
BACK TO THE FUTURE PART III

Kuleyz, Kathy
TUSKS

Kuniholm, Mai-Lis
ARACHNOPHOBIA

Kupchenko, Irina
LONELY WOMAN SEEKS LIFE COMPANION

Kurian, Joseph
MAHABHARATA, THE

Kurlander, Tom
FLATLINERS
YOUNG GUNS II
KINDERGARTEN COP

Kurtiz, Tuncel
MAHABHARATA, THE

Kurtz, Swoosie
STANLEY AND IRIS
SHOCK TO THE SYSTEM, A

Kusatsu, Clyde
BIRD ON A WIRE

Kwong, Peter
ANGEL TOWN

Kwouk, Burt
AIR AMERICA

Kyle, George
HEART CONDITION

L'Ecuyer, Isabelle
HOW TO MAKE LOVE TO A NEGRO WITHOUT GETTING TIRED

La Salle, Eriq
JACOB'S LADDER

Labini, Caterina Sylos
ICICLE THIEF, THE

LaBrosse, Robert
MILLER'S CROSSING

Lacey, Chuck
TAX SEASON

Ladd, Cheryl
LISA

Ladd, Diane
WILD AT HEART

Laezza, Luigi
GODFATHER PART III, THE

LaFayette, John
FULL FATHOM FIVE

LaFleur, Art
DEATH WARRANT

Laglois, Herve
MR. FROST

LaGuardia, Michael
TOTAL RECALL

Lahaie, Brigitte
HENRY AND JUNE

Lahr, John
CHICAGO JOE AND THE SHOWGIRL

Lahti, Christine
FUNNY ABOUT LOVE

Lake, Ricki
CRY-BABY
LAST EXIT TO BROOKLYN

Lala
ADVENTURES OF FORD FAIRLANE, THE
PUMP UP THE VOLUME

Lala, Joe
HAVANA

Lalande, Francois
IMPROMPTU

Lally, James
ME AND HIM

BONFIRE OF THE VANITIES

Lamb, Charles
TALL GUY, THE

Lamb, Charlie
ERNEST GOES TO JAIL

Lamb, Peadar
FIELD, THE

Lambert, Christopher
WHY ME?

Lambert, Gay
BURNDOWN

Lambton, Anna
WITCHES, THE

Lamon-Anderson, Ariana
LOVE AT LARGE

Lamos, Mark
LONGTIME COMPANION

Lampert, Zohra
STANLEY AND IRIS
EXORCIST III, THE

Lampman, Hugh
PROBLEM CHILD

LaMura, Mark
RUSSIA HOUSE, THE

Lan, Law
EAT A BOWL OF TEA

Lancaster, James
DIE HARD 2

Lancaster, Stuart
EDWARD SCISSORHANDS

Land, Paul
WILD ORCHID

Landau, Darlene
REAL BULLETS

Landau, Martin
REAL BULLETS
PAINT IT BLACK

Lander, David L.
FUNLAND
STEEL AND LACE

Landey, Clayton
HEART CONDITION
FIRST POWER, THE
PUMP UP THE VOLUME

Landi, Sal
BACK TO BACK

Landis, John
SPONTANEOUS COMBUSTION
DARKMAN

Landis, Monte
HEART CONDITION

Lando, Joe
I LOVE YOU TO DEATH

Landon, Hal Jr.
PACIFIC HEIGHTS

Lane, Diane
VITAL SIGNS

Lane, Nathan
LEMON SISTERS, THE

Lang, Ben
PLOT AGAINST HARRY, THE

Lang, Doreen
ALMOST AN ANGEL

Lang, Elizabeth
MADHOUSE

Lang, Perry
JACOB'S LADDER

Lang, Stephen
LAST EXIT TO BROOKLYN

Lange, Hope
TUNE IN TOMORROW

Lange, Jessica
MEN DON'T LEAVE

Langerak, Thierry
TORRENTS OF SPRING

Langevin, Terrence
STELLA

Langham, Wallace
VITAL SIGNS

Langlet, Daniel
LIFE AND NOTHING BUT

Langrick, Margaret
AMERICAN BOYFRIENDS

Langton, Diane
COOK, THE THIEF, HIS WIFE & HER
LOVER, THE

Langton, Jeff
DIE HARD 2

Langton-Lloyd, Robert
MAHABHARATA, THE

Lanoil, Bruce
SPACED INVADERS

Lantry, Helene
IMPORTED BRIDEGROOM, THE

Lanyer, Charles
FIRE BIRDS
DIE HARD 2

LaPaglia, Anthony
BETSY'S WEDDING

LaPensee, Francine
DEMON WIND

LaPlaca, Alison
MADHOUSE

Large, Norman
PRETTY WOMAN

Larkin, Bryan
JACOB'S LADDER
EDWARD SCISSORHANDS

Larroquette, John
MADHOUSE
TUNE IN TOMORROW

Larsen, Annabelle
ALLIGATOR EYES

Larson, Darrell
DEAD AIM
MEN AT WORK

Larson, Eric
DEMON WIND

LaRue, Eva
HEART CONDITION

LaRue, Roger
ROOKIE, THE

LaSardo, Robert
ME AND HIM

Laser, Dieter
MAN INSIDE, THE

Lasser, Louise
FRANKENHOOKER
MODERN LOVE

Lassick, Sydney
SONNY BOY

Latinopoulos, Dede
FLATLINERS

Laudicina, Dino
GOODFELLAS

Laudiere, Herve
MR. FROST

Laurance, Matthew
SIBLING RIVALRY

Laurenson, James
MAN INSIDE, THE

Laurie, Hugh
STRAPLESS

Lavachielli, John
MEN AT WORK

Lavarre, Louis
CYRANO DE BERGERAC

Lavell, Bradley
MEMPHIS BELLE

Lavi, Amos
TORN APART

Law, John Phillip
ALIENATOR

Law, Phyllida
INNOCENT VICTIM

Law, Steven
MACK THE KNIFE

Lawford, Christopher
IMPULSE
RUSSIA HOUSE, THE

Lawler, Charles
CHATTAHOOCHEE

Lawrence, Lee
ADVENTURES OF FORD FAIRLANE, THE

Lawrence, Marc
BLOOD RED

Lawrence, Martin
HOUSE PARTY

Lawrence, Matthew
TALES FROM THE DARKSIDE: THE MOVIE

Lawrence, Scott
FIRST POWER, THE

Lawson, Charles
MISADVENTURES OF MR. WILT, THE

Lawson, Cheryl
DEAD PIT

Layne, Randi
FUNLAND

Lazarus, Jerry
HONEYMOON ACADEMY

Le Brock, Kelley
HARD TO KILL

Le Duke, Harrison
FIRE BIRDS

Le Master, Garth
FIRE BIRDS

Le Tallec, Rozenn
MAY FOOLS

Leachman, Cloris
TEXASVILLE

Leader Charge, Doris
DANCES WITH WOLVES

Leader Charge, Richard
DANCES WITH WOLVES

Leamy, Harry John
MARKED FOR DEATH

Leatham, Bradley
DESPERATE HOURS

Leatherbury, Sheridan
POSTCARDS FROM THE EDGE

Leavy, Donna Lynn
VITAL SIGNS

Lebarbe, Flavien
TOO BEAUTIFUL FOR YOU

Lebby, Fannie Belle
WHITE PALACE

LeBell, Gene
LOOSE CANNONS

Lebert, Jean-Christophe
LIFE AND NOTHING BUT

Lebherz, Louis P.
BONFIRE OF THE VANITIES

Leboulanger, Stephanie
HENRY AND JUNE

Lechter, Mary
AVALON

Leder, Bryan
METROPOLITAN

Lee Chasing His Horse, Nathan
DANCES WITH WOLVES

Lee, Bill
MO' BETTER BLUES

Lee, Christopher
GREMLINS 2 THE NEW BATCH
HONEYMOON ACADEMY

Lee, George Earl
FEUD, THE

Lee, Joie
BAIL JUMPER
MO' BETTER BLUES

Lee, Kevin
GHOST DAD

Lee, Paul L.Q.
CADILLAC MAN

Lee, Sheryl
WILD AT HEART

Lee, Spike
MO' BETTER BLUES

Lee, Stephen
ROBOCOP 2

Lee, William
LOVE AT LARGE

Leegant, Dan
ERNEST GOES TO JAIL

Leek, Tiiu
FIRST POWER, THE

LeFevre, Adam
BONFIRE OF THE VANITIES

LeFleur, Art
AIR AMERICA

Lefranc, Candice
C'EST LA VIE

Legere, Phoebe
KING OF NEW YORK

Leggett, Doris
BONFIRE OF THE VANITIES

Leguizamo, John
REVENGE
DIE HARD 2

Lehnert, Herbert
NASTY GIRL, THE

Lehre, Cindy
ADVENTURES OF FORD FAIRLANE, THE

Lehrman, Hal
Q&A

Leigh, Carrie
BLOOD RELATIONS

Leigh, Jennifer Jason
MIAMI BLUES
LAST EXIT TO BROOKLYN

Leiner, Greg
BLADES

Lekas, Christopher James
AVALON

Leland-St. John, Sharmagne
DICK TRACY

LeMaster, Garth
PEACEMAKER

Lemercier, Valerie
MAY FOOLS

Lemmons, Kasi
VAMPIRE'S KISS

Lemon, Ben
DIE HARD 2

Lemus, Luis
I COME IN PEACE

Lena, Roberta
CINEMA PARADISO

Lende, Howard
WHERE THE HEART IS

Leng, Deborah
SLIPSTREAM

Lennie, Elizabeth
STELLA

Lenz, Kay
STREETS

Leon, Loles
TIE ME UP! TIE ME DOWN!

Leonard, Lu
WITHOUT YOU, I'M NOTHING
SHADOWZONE
CIRCUITRY MAN

Leonard, Robert Sean
MR. AND MRS. BRIDGE

Leonardi, Marco
CINEMA PARADISO

Leone, Maria
BIRD ON A WIRE

Leone, Marianne
GOODFELLAS

Leong, Al
SAVAGE BEACH

Leong, Albert
I COME IN PEACE

Leong, Page
ANOTHER 48 HRS.

Leong, Susan
SLIPSTREAM

Lepage, Robert
JESUS OF MONTREAL

LePriol, Alison
CAGED FURY

Lerer, Joe
TAKING CARE OF BUSINESS

Lerer, Shifra
AVALON

Lerner, Ken
HIT LIST
ROBOCOP 2
EXORCIST III, THE

Leroux, Maxime
MAMA, THERE'S A MAN IN YOUR BED
MR. FROST

LeRoy, Zoaunne
FLATLINERS

LeSache, Claude
STRIKE IT RICH

Lesco, Kenneth
DARK SIDE OF THE MOON

Leskin, Boris
CADILLAC MAN

Leslie, Jean
PLOT AGAINST HARRY, THE

Lessner, Josh
AVALON

Lester, Noble Lee
BONFIRE OF THE VANITIES

Letherer, Lauren
DIE HARD 2

Letizia, Jodi
ROCKY V

Letladi, Patrick
MOUNTAINS OF THE MOON

Letner, Ken
TAX SEASON

Leung, Tony Ka-Fei
LASER MAN, THE

Levasseur, Aline
BYE BYE BLUES

Levi, Nili
FLATLINERS

Levin, Matt
MARKED FOR DEATH

Levin, Rachel
WHITE PALACE

Levin, Zolly
MILLER'S CROSSING

Levine, Bunny
CADILLAC MAN

Levine, Ted
LOVE AT LARGE

Levinson, Brian
PREDATOR 2

Levinson, Herb
AVALON

Levitin, Nicholas
BONFIRE OF THE VANITIES

Levroney, Angie
CRY-BABY

Levy, Salvadore
HAVANA

Lew, James
AFTERSHOCK
SAVAGE BEACH

Lewis, Al
FRIGHT HOUSE

Lewis, Brittney
SKI PATROL
DESPERATE HOURS

Lewis, David
MONSTER HIGH

Lewis, Gayle
GOODFELLAS

Lewis, Ira
LOOSE CANNONS

Libby, Brian
FIRST POWER, THE

Libertini, Richard
ANIMAL BEHAVIOR
DUCKTALES: THE MOVIE – TREASURE OF
THE LOST LAMP
LEMON SISTERS, THE
AWAKENINGS
BONFIRE OF THE VANITIES

Liddy, G. Gordon
STREET ASYLUM

Lieber, Paul
STEEL AND LACE

Lieh, Lo
LIFE IS CHEAP. . . BUT TOILET PAPER IS EX-
PENSIVE

Liew, Wan Thye
TIME GUARDIAN, THE

Lillo-Thieman, Connie
DIE HARD 2

Lilly, Sarah
GREMLINS 2 THE NEW BATCH

Limerick, Alison
MOUNTAINS OF THE MOON

Lin, Ben
CADILLAC MAN
LEMON SISTERS, THE

Lin, Traci
CLASS OF 1999
SURVIVAL QUEST

Lincoln, Abbey
MO' BETTER BLUES

Lind, Robert M.
MONSTER HIGH

Lind, Traci
HANDMAID'S TALE, THE

Lindfors, Viveca
EXORCIST III, THE

Lindo, Delroy
BLOOD OF HEROES
MOUNTAINS OF THE MOON

Lindon, Vincent
C'EST LA VIE

Lindsay, Ian
TALL GUY, THE

Lindsay, Robert
STRIKE IT RICH

Line, Helga
LABYRINTH OF PASSION

Linero, Jeannie
GODFATHER PART III, THE

Linkman, Wolfgang
REAL BULLETS

Linn-Baker, Mark
ME AND HIM

Lioni, Sal
CADILLAC MAN

Liotta, Ray
GOODFELLAS

Lip, Tony
GOODFELLAS

Lipman, David
BONFIRE OF THE VANITIES

Lipscomb, Dennis
FIRST POWER, THE

Lipton, Robert
DIE HARD 2

Lisi, Gaetano
GOODFELLAS

Lisi, Joe
COME SEE THE PARADISE

Lister, Moira
TEN LITTLE INDIANS

Lithgow, John
MEMPHIS BELLE

Little, Cleavon
MURDER BY NUMBERS

Little, Ivan
HIDDEN AGENDA

Little, Jack
SHORT TIME

Little, Michelle
LAST OF THE FINEST, THE

Lively, Ernie
AIR AMERICA

Livingstone, Annie
WITHOUT YOU, I'M NOTHING

Livingstone, Joshua
OPPORTUNITY KNOCKS

Livingstone, Sidney
MISADVENTURES OF MR. WILT, THE

Lleras, Anibal
Q&A

Lloyd, Christopher
BACK TO THE FUTURE PART III
DUCKTALES: THE MOVIE – TREASURE OF
THE LOST LAMP
WHY ME?

Lloyd, Emily
CHICAGO JOE AND THE SHOWGIRL

Lloyd, Emily Ann
KINDERGARTEN COP

Lloyd, Patrick
REAL BULLETS

Lloyd, Tricia
EDWARD SCISSORHANDS

Lobo, Luiz
WILD ORCHID

Loc, Tone
ADVENTURES OF FORD FAIRLANE, THE

Locane, Amy
CRY-BABY

Lock, Kate
RUSSIA HOUSE, THE

Locke, Nancy
PRETTY WOMAN

Lockhart, Anne
BIG BAD JOHN

Lockhart, Calvin
WILD AT HEART
PREDATOR 2

Locklin, Loryn
TAKING CARE OF BUSINESS

Lockwood, Vera
FRESHMAN, THE

Lockyer, Thomas
TALL GUY, THE

Locy, Ellen
PROBLEM CHILD

Loder, Kurt
ADVENTURES OF FORD FAIRLANE, THE

Loffredo, Philippe
TOO BEAUTIFUL FOR YOU

Loftin, J.K.
BETSY'S WEDDING

Lofton, Janet
WHITE PALACE

Logan, Bellina
BLUE STEEL
WILD AT HEART
JACOB'S LADDER

Logan, Gary
COOK, THE THIEF, HIS WIFE & HER
LOVER, THE

Logan, George
HOUSE PARTY

Logan, Maurine
BLOOD RED

Logan, Pat
NIGHT OF THE LIVING DEAD

Logan, Ricky Dean
BACK TO THE FUTURE PART III

Loggia, Robert
OPPORTUNITY KNOCKS

LoGiudice, Gaetano
GOODFELLAS

Logothetis, Ilias
LANDSCAPE IN THE MIST

Logsdon, Kent
OPPORTUNITY KNOCKS

Lom, Herbert
TEN LITTLE INDIANS
RIVER OF DEATH

Lombardi, Chris
COUPE DE VILLE

Lombardo, Coleby
ROOKIE, THE

London, Lisa
SAVAGE BEACH

Lone Hill, Jason R.
DANCES WITH WOLVES

Lonergan, Kate
TALL GUY, THE

Long, David
AVALON

Long, Jodi
EXORCIST III, THE

Long, Shelley
DON'T TELL HER IT'S ME

Longo, Tony
MR. DESTINY

Lookwhy, Douglas
AMERICAN EAGLE

Lopez, George
SKI PATROL

Lopez, Perry
TWO JAKES, THE

Lopez, Sal
DOWN THE DRAIN

Loran, Marion
LIFE AND NOTHING BUT

Lords, Traci
CRY-BABY

Loren, Eric
MEMPHIS BELLE

Lorentz, Eric
FLASHBACK

Lorenz, James
LAST EXIT TO BROOKLYN

Loring, Richard
GODS MUST BE CRAZY II, THE

Lorinz, James
FRANKENHOOKER

Lottimer, Eb
STREETS

Lotz, Jack
RETURN OF SUPERFLY, THE

Lou, Bowlegged
HOUSE PARTY

Loughlin, Terry
COUPE DE VILLE
MR. DESTINY

Louis, Justin
STELLA

Louiso, Todd
STELLA

Loustau, Christian
CYRANO DE BERGERAC

Love, Gary
KRAYS, THE

Love, Patti
KRAYS, THE

Lovitz, Jon
MR. DESTINY

Low, Chuck
GOODFELLAS

Low, Roger
HAMLET

Lowe, Chad
NOBODY'S PERFECT

Lowe, Patrick
PRIMAL RAGE

Lowe, Rob
BAD INFLUENCE

Lowe, Susan
CRY-BABY

Lowell, Carey
ME AND HIM
GUARDIAN, THE

Lowenthal, Mark
HEART CONDITION
POSTCARDS FROM THE EDGE
I COME IN PEACE

Lowery, Martin
DIE HARD 2

Lowman, Kristen
PROBLEM CHILD

Lowry, Thomas
GOODFELLAS

Loy, Joe
CHATTAHOOCHEE

Lozoff, Joshua Bo
TEENAGE MUTANT NINJA TURTLES
FEUD, THE

Lucas, Eric
CRY-BABY

Lucci, Fran
COME SEE THE PARADISE

Lucia, Charles
GUMSHOE KID, THE

Lucia, Chip
PRIMARY TARGET

Lucien, Michelle
QUICK CHANGE

Ludlow, Kathryn
COURAGE MOUNTAIN

Ludwig, Karen
STANLEY AND IRIS

Lujan, Bob
VAMPIRE'S KISS

Lujan, Robert
FIRE BIRDS

Lukaszewicz, Olgiard
INTERROGATION, THE

Luke, Keye
GREMLINS 2 THE NEW BATCH
ALICE

Lulu
MEN IN LOVE

Lumbly, Carl
TO SLEEP WITH ANGER
PACIFIC HEIGHTS

Lumet, Jenny
Q&A

Lumley, Coleman
LOOK WHO'S TALKING TOO

Lumsden, Norman
WHITE HUNTER, BLACK HEART

Lund, Caroline
DON'T TELL HER IT'S ME

Lund, Jordan
ADVENTURES OF FORD FAIRLANE, THE
ROOKIE, THE

Lund, Sally
DON'T TELL HER IT'S ME

Lundgren, Dolph
I COME IN PEACE

Lundquist, Steve
SLEEPING CAR, THE

Lundy, Jessica
MADHOUSE

Lunsford, Charles
STAR QUEST: BEYOND THE RISING MOON

Lurie, Evan
FORCE OF CIRCUMSTANCE

Lurie, John
WILD AT HEART

Lustig, Aaron
DARKMAN
EDWARD SCISSORHANDS

Lustig, William
DARKMAN

Lykins, Ray
COUPE DE VILLE

Lyle, Andrew
METROPOLITAN

Lyle, Laurel
STANLEY AND IRIS

Lyles, A.C.
HUNT FOR RED OCTOBER, THE

Lyman, Will
HOSTILE TAKEOVER

Lynch, Alfred
KRAYS, THE

Lynch, Edward
EXORCIST III, THE

Lynch, Heather
MR. DESTINY

Lynch, John
METROPOLITAN
HARDWARE

Lynch, Kelly
DESPERATE HOURS

Lynch, Richard
FORBIDDEN DANCE, THE
AFTERSHOCK

Lynch, Skipp
BLUE STEEL
QUICK CHANGE

Lynn, Jonathan
THREE MEN AND A LITTLE LADY

Lynne, Amy
GUMSHOE KID, THE

Lyonnet, Louis
LIFE AND NOTHING BUT

Lyons, Robert F.
AMERICAN EAGLE

Ma, Tzi
ROBOCOP 2

Mabray, Stuart
CHILD'S PLAY 2

McAleer, Des
HIDDEN AGENDA

McAllister, Jim
HIDDEN AGENDA

McArthur, Steve
BACK TO THE FUTURE PART III

Macat, Sandra
HOME ALONE

Macaulay, Marc
EDWARD SCISSORHANDS

McBeath, Tom
NARROW MARGIN

McCabe, Michael
CAGED IN PARADISO
BURNDOWN

McCabe, Ruth
FIELD, THE

McCafferty, Frankie
FOOLS OF FORTUNE

McCall, Andrea
PROBLEM CHILD

McCall, Mitzi
WHITE PALACE

McCallum, David
HAUNTING OF MORELLA, THE

McCalman, Macon
COLD FEET

McCann, Brian
HIDDEN AGENDA

McCann, Chuck
DUCKTALES: THE MOVIE – TREASURE OF
THE LOST LAMP

McCansh, Constance Barnes
LOOK WHO'S TALKING TOO

McCarthy, Frank
DOWNTOWN

McCarthy, Jeff
ROBOCOP 2

McCarthy, Julia
MISADVENTURES OF MR. WILT, THE

McCarthy, Julianna
FIRST POWER, THE

McCarthy, Kendall
HEART CONDITION

McCarthy, Kevin
SLEEPING CAR, THE

McCarthy, Neil
TEN LITTLE INDIANS

McCarthy, Nobu
PACIFIC HEIGHTS

McCarthy, Sheila
DIE HARD 2
PACIFIC HEIGHTS

McCaughan, Charles
IMPULSE

McCharen, David
TEENAGE MUTANT NINJA TURTLES

McClain, Saundra
MR. AND MRS. BRIDGE

McClanahan, Rue
MODERN LOVE

McClarnon, Kevin
LOOSE CANNONS

McCleery, Michael
IMPULSE

McClendon, Ernestine
HOMER & EDDIE

McClory, Sean T.
FOOLS OF FORTUNE

McClure, Marc
BACK TO THE FUTURE PART III
GRIM PRAIRIE TALES

McClure, Molly
DADDY'S DYIN'. . . WHO'S GOT THE WILL?

McClure, Paula
FIRST POWER, THE
TOTAL RECALL

McClure, Rob
STELLA

McColpin, John
COME SEE THE PARADISE

Maccone, Ronald
GOODFELLAS

McConnachie, Brian
QUICK CHANGE

McConnell, John
MILLER'S CROSSING

McConnohie, Michael
TEENAGE MUTANT NINJA TURTLES

McCord, Kent
PREDATOR 2

McCourt, Malachy
MR. AND MRS. BRIDGE
BONFIRE OF THE VANITIES
GREEN CARD
FIELD, THE

McCraken, Mark
OPPONENT, THE

McCready, Ed
DICK TRACY

McCreary, Ben
KINDERGARTEN COP

McCuller, Arnold
WITHOUT YOU, I'M NOTHING

McCulloch, Allen
ALLIGATOR EYES

McCullough, Rohan
STRAPLESS

McCune, Judson
LORD OF THE FLIES

McCutcheon, Bill
MR. DESTINY
TUNE IN TOMORROW

McDaniel, F. Douglas
CHATTAHOOCHEE

McDermott, Dylan
HARDWARE

McDermott, Kevin
COME SEE THE PARADISE

McDermottroe, Conor
QUIGLEY DOWN UNDER

MacDonald, Ann-Marie
WHERE THE HEART IS

MacDonald, Bill
FOURTH WAR, THE

MacDonald, Braden
LORD OF THE FLIES

MacDonald, Daniel
PACIFIC HEIGHTS

McDonald, Edward
GOODFELLAS

McDonald, Frank
FIELD, THE

McDonald, Mac
MEMPHIS BELLE
RUSSIA HOUSE, THE

MacDonald, Michael
NUTCRACKER PRINCE, THE

McDonald, Nancy
BONFIRE OF THE VANITIES

MacDonald, Wendy
DARK SIDE OF THE MOON

McDonnell, John
HIDDEN AGENDA

McDonnell, Mary
DANCES WITH WOLVES

McDonough, Ann
MEN DON'T LEAVE

McDonough, Mary
FUNLAND

McDonough, Neal
DARKMAN

McDormand, Frances
CHATTAHOOCHEE
DARKMAN

HIDDEN AGENDA

McDougal, Martin
MEMPHIS BELLE

MacDowell, Andie
GREEN CARD

McDowell, Jay
NIGHT OF THE LIVING DEAD

McDowell, Malcolm
HAPPILY EVER AFTER
JEZEBEL'S KISS

McDowell, Malcom
CLASS OF 1999

McElduff, Ellen
DESPERATE HOURS

McElhinney, Ian
HIDDEN AGENDA

McElroy, Thomas
OPPORTUNITY KNOCKS

McElvain, Richard
MERMAIDS

McEnery, John
KRAYS, THE
HAMLET

McEntire, Reba
TREMORS

McEwen, Kirk
CRY-BABY

McFadden, Catherine
FOOLS OF FORTUNE

McFadden, Davenia
QUICK CHANGE

McFadden, Gates
HUNT FOR RED OCTOBER, THE
TAKING CARE OF BUSINESS

McFadden, Reggie
JACOB'S LADDER

McGann, Paul
INNOCENT VICTIM

McGarvin, Dick
DIE HARD 2

McGee, Fran
GOODFELLAS

McGee, Pennington
OPPORTUNITY KNOCKS

McGee, Vonetta
TO SLEEP WITH ANGER

McGhee, Bill
RIVERBEND

McGill, Everett
JEZEBEL'S KISS

McGinley, Sean
FIELD, THE

McGivern, Geoffrey
MISADVENTURES OF MR. WILT, THE

McGovern, Barry
JOE VERSUS THE VOLCANO

McGovern, Don Charles
DIE HARD 2

McGovern, Elizabeth
HANDMAID'S TALE, THE
SHOCK TO THE SYSTEM, A
TUNE IN TOMORROW

McGovern, Terence
DUCKTALES: THE MOVIE – TREASURE OF
THE LOST LAMP

McGowen, Anthony
AWAKENINGS

McGrath, Matt
DESPERATE HOURS

MacGregor, Chris S.
LOOSE CANNONS

MacGregor, Jeff
HEART CONDITION

McGregor, Richard
HOUSE PARTY

McGroarty, Pat
AFTERSHOCK

McGuane, Tom
COLD FEET

McGuire, Bryan Michael
ELLIOT FAUMAN, PH.D.

McGuire, Kim
CRY-BABY

McGuire, Lisa
INHERITOR

Machado, Mario
ROBOCOP 2

McHarry, Neil
STUFF STEPHANIE IN THE INCINERATOR

Machlis, Neil
POSTCARDS FROM THE EDGE

Macht, Stephen
GRAVEYARD SHIFT

MacHugh, Doug
COME SEE THE PARADISE

McIlwaine, Mandy
HIDDEN AGENDA

McIntire, James
CLASS OF 1999
GHOST DAD

MacIntosh, Joan E.
AWAKENINGS

MacIntyre, David
COME SEE THE PARADISE

Macintyre, Gandhi
BLOOD OF HEROES

McIntyre, Lucile
HANDMAID'S TALE, THE

McIntyre, Marvin J.
BACK TO THE FUTURE PART III

McIssac, Paul
GOODFELLAS

Mack, Michael
STAR QUEST: BEYOND THE RISING MOON

Mackay, John
STATE OF GRACE
ALLIGATOR EYES

McKay, Warner
BACK TO BACK

McKean, Michael
FLASHBACK

McKee, Gina
MISADVENTURES OF MR. WILT, THE

McKee, Michelle
FLATLINERS

McKenzie, Matt
ROOKIE, THE

McKeon, Philip
RED SURF

Mackey, Cynthia
ROBOCOP 2

McKinney, Bill
BACK TO THE FUTURE PART III

McKinney, Greg
NAVY SEALS

MacKintosh, Steven
MEMPHIS BELLE

MacLachlan, Kyle
DON'T TELL HER IT'S ME

McLain, Mary
ALLIGATOR EYES

MacLaine, Shirley
POSTCARDS FROM THE EDGE

MacLane, Gretchen
ME AND HIM

McLaren, Conrad
GREEN CARD

McLarnon, Fergus
MISADVENTURES OF MR. WILT, THE

McLarty, Ron
FEUD, THE

McLaughlin, Cliff
IMPULSE

McLaughlin, John Patrick
JACOB'S LADDER

McLaughlin-Gray, Jack
OPPORTUNITY KNOCKS

McLaurin, David
ADVENTURES OF FORD FAIRLANE, THE

McLean, Dwayne
STELLA

McLean, Hilda
MILLER'S CROSSING

McLennan, Chuck
MEN DON'T LEAVE

McLoughlin, Bina
FIELD, THE

McMahon, John
EDWARD SCISSORHANDS

McManus, Don
BONFIRE OF THE VANITIES

McManus, Mike
FUNLAND

McMartin, John
SHOCK TO THE SYSTEM, A

McMullen, Donna
FLASHBACK

McMurtrey, Joan
WELCOME HOME, ROXY CARMICHAEL

McNab, Michael
FIRST POWER, THE
TAKING CARE OF BUSINESS

McNair, Heather
MADHOUSE

McNally, Terrence E.
TAKING CARE OF BUSINESS

McNamara, Brian
ARACHNOPHOBIA

McNamara, J. Patrick
FIRST POWER, THE

McNamara, William
STELLA
TEXASVILLE

Macnee, Patrick
MASQUE OF THE RED DEATH

McNeice, Ian
RUSSIA HOUSE, THE

McNeill, Kent
FOURTH WAR, THE

MacNeill, Peter
STELLA

McNulty, Kevin
BIRD ON A WIRE
SHORT TIME
NARROW MARGIN

McPeters, Brad
BACK TO THE FUTURE PART III

MacPherson, Elle
ALICE

McPherson, Julie
MONSTER HIGH

MacPherson, Walt
EXORCIST III, THE

McQueen, Armelia
GHOST

McQueens, James
ROBOCOP 2

McQuillun, Gail
RIVER OF DEATH

McTiernan, John Sr.
HUNT FOR RED OCTOBER, THE

McWilliams, Caroline
MERMAIDS

Macy, Bill
SIBLING RIVALRY

Madden, Patricia
MERMAIDS

Madden, Tommy
SPACED INVADERS

Madonna
DICK TRACY

Madsen, Harry
Q&A

Madsen, Michael
KILL ME AGAIN
BLOOD RED

Madsen, Virginia
HOT SPOT, THE

Mager, Jad
REVERSAL OF FORTUNE

Maggio, Pupella
CINEMA PARADISO

Maggio, Tony
BAD INFLUENCE

Magimel, Benoit
LIFE IS A LONG QUIET RIVER

Magnuson, Ann
LOVE AT LARGE

Magri, Jade
COURAGE MOUNTAIN

Maguelon, Pierre
CYRANO DE BERGERAC

Maguire, Michael
COOK, THE THIEF, HIS WIFE & HER
LOVER, THE

Maguire, Oliver
HIDDEN AGENDA

Maher, Toni
MEN IN LOVE

Mahler, Bruce
FUNLAND

Mahmud-Bey, Shiek
BONFIRE OF THE VANITIES

Mahon, Michael C.
QUICK CHANGE

Mahoney, John
RUSSIA HOUSE, THE

Mailer, Stephen
CRY-BABY

Maille, Maite
HENRY AND JUNE

Maitland, Marne
BELLY OF AN ARCHITECT, THE

Majonga, Godfrey
TUSKS

Major, Boris
FORCE OF CIRCUMSTANCE

Maki, Hiroko
DREAMS

Maki, Yoshiko
DREAMS

Mako
TAKING CARE OF BUSINESS
PACIFIC HEIGHTS

Maldonado, Frank
CRY-BABY
QUICK CHANGE

Malet, Arthur
DICK TRACY

Malina, Judith
AWAKENINGS

Malinger, Ross
KINDERGARTEN COP

Malkin, Sam
STELLA
SHORT TIME
BLOOD RELATIONS

Malkovich, John
SHELTERING SKY, THE

Mallory, Troy
AMERICAN BOYFRIENDS

Malloy, Matt
UNBELIEVABLE TRUTH, THE

Malone, Patrick
BONFIRE OF THE VANITIES

Maloney, Michael
HAMLET

Malpas, George
MOUNTAINS OF THE MOON

Malte-Cruz, Rey
DEMONSTONE

Maltin, Leonard
GREMLINS 2 THE NEW BATCH

Malunga, Norman
WHITE HUNTER, BLACK HEART

Maly, Xavier
TORRENTS OF SPRING

Mamonov, Piotr
TAXI BLUES

Mamouni, Samir
REAL BULLETS

Man, Alex
ROUGE

Man, Sin Lap
REINCARNATION OF GOLDEN LOTUS, THE

Man, Wu Kin
LIFE IS CHEAP. . . BUT TOILET PAPER IS EX-
PENSIVE

Manca, John
GOODFELLAS

Mance, Sabrina
FORBIDDEN DANCE, THE

Mancini, Al
LOOSE CANNONS
FAR OUT MAN
MILLER'S CROSSING

Mancini, Ray "Boom Boom"
BACKSTREET DREAMS

Mandel, Howie
GREMLINS 2 THE NEW BATCH

Mane, Doura
L'ETAT SAUVAGE

Mangiantini, Joseph
COLD FEET

Mangiardi, Robert
ADVENTURES OF FORD FAIRLANE, THE

Mangs, Sune
SHADOW OF THE RAVEN, THE

Manheim, Camryn
BONFIRE OF THE VANITIES

Manker, Paulus
MY 20TH CENTURY

Mankuma, Blu
BIRD ON A WIRE
RUSSIA HOUSE, THE

Mann, Richard Steven
OPPORTUNITY KNOCKS

Mann, Wesley
CHATTAHOOCHEE

Mannen, Monique
ADVENTURES OF FORD FAIRLANE, THE

Manning, Mark
MADHOUSE

Manoff, Dinah
WELCOME HOME, ROXY CARMICHAEL

Mansbach, Lynn
HOME ALONE

Mansy, Deborah Anne
HIGH DESERT KILL

Mantegna, Joe
ALICE
GODFATHER PART III, THE

Mantell, Joe
TWO JAKES, THE

Mantle, Clive
MACK THE KNIFE
WHITE HUNTER, BLACK HEART

Mantle, Doreen
MOUNTAINS OF THE MOON

Maples, Marla
FUNLAND

Mapp, Jim
HOMER & EDDIE

Mappin, Jefferson
FRESHMAN, THE

Mara, Mary
BLUE STEEL

Marais, Drummond
AMERICAN EAGLE

Marbury, Robert
CRY-BABY

March, Zachary
KINDERGARTEN COP

Marchant, Stephen
TALL GUY, THE

Marchisio, Justin
MERMAIDS

Marco, Bonita
HAVANA

Marcon, Andre
FLAME IN MY HEART, A

Marcus, Richard
TREMORS

Mardirosian, Tom
BETSY'S WEDDING
PRESUMED INNOCENT

Margiotta, Katherine
ROCKY V

Margolin, Stuart
BYE BYE BLUES

Margolis, Ilona
FLATLINERS

Margolis, Mark
DELTA FORCE 2

Margolyes, Miriam
 I LOVE YOU TO DEATH
 PACIFIC HEIGHTS

Margot, Sandra
 SLEEPING CAR, THE

Margulies, David
 FUNNY ABOUT LOVE

Marich, Allison
 TEXASVILLE

Marie, Francois
 CYRANO DE BERGERAC

Marie, Jeanne
 WILDEST DREAMS

Marie, Lisa
 ALICE

Mariette, Mykel
 CHATTAHOOCHEE

Marin, Cheech
 FAR OUT MAN
 SHRIMP ON THE BARBIE, THE

Marinan, Terry
 BACK TO BACK

Marinaro, Ed
 DEAD AIM

Mariner, Peter
 RUSSIA HOUSE, THE

Marion, Madeleine
 CYRANO DE BERGERAC

Markell, Jodie
 ME AND HIM

Markland, Ted
 ANOTHER 48 HRS.

Marlowe, Branden
 FRIGHT HOUSE

Marlowe, Lisa
 STREET ASYLUM

Marlowe, Stephen
 STRIKE IT RICH

Maronna, Michael C.
 HOME ALONE

Marot, Irene
 NUNS ON THE RUN

Marotta, Rick
 ADVENTURES OF FORD FAIRLANE, THE

Marques, Juana
 TOO BEAUTIFUL FOR YOU

Marrick, David
 STRIKE IT RICH

Marriott, David
 MONSTER HIGH

Marsalis, Branford
 MO' BETTER BLUES

Marsh, Matthew
 MOUNTAINS OF THE MOON

Marshall, David Anthony
 ANOTHER 48 HRS.

Marshall, E.G.
 TWO EVIL EYES

Marshall, Kathi
 PRETTY WOMAN

Marshall, Ken
 GODS MUST BE CRAZY II, THE
 BURNDOWN

Marshall, Mike
 MR. FROST

Marshall, Robert
 POSTCARDS FROM THE EDGE

Marshall, Scott A.
 PRETTY WOMAN

Marshall, William J.
 BLUE STEEL

Marta, Lynn
 FIRST POWER, THE

Marta, Lynne
 THREE MEN AND A LITTLE LADY

Martel, Andria
 MARKED FOR DEATH

Martell, Leon
 DOWN THE DRAIN

Martin, Aaron
 BLOOD OF HEROES

Martin, Christopher
 HOUSE PARTY

Martin, George
 AWAKENINGS

Martin, Helen
 NIGHT ANGEL

Martin, John Benjamin
 FLATLINERS

Martin, Joshua
 PROBLEM CHILD

Martin, Meade
 ROCKY V

Martin, Mel
 WHITE HUNTER, BLACK HEART

Martin, Melissa
 PROBLEM CHILD

Martin, Nan
 ANIMAL BEHAVIOR

Martin, Richard
 TOO BEAUTIFUL FOR YOU

Martin, Steve
 MY BLUE HEAVEN

Martinez, Jerry
 IMPULSE

Martinez, Joaquin
 REVENGE

Martinez, Kenneth J.
 HEART CONDITION

Martinez, Leo
 PRIMARY TARGET

Martino, Al
 GODFATHER PART III, THE

Maruoka, Frank
 PACIFIC HEIGHTS

Marx, Alan
 HYPERSPACE

Marx, Brett
 UNDER THE BOARDWALK

Marxuach, A.M.
 JACOB'S LADDER

Marzan, Rick
 HEART CONDITION

Marzello, Vincent
 WITCHES, THE

Masa, Tony
 CADILLAC MAN

Masamune, Tohoru
 PACIFIC HEIGHTS

Maschmeyer, Kyle
 FOURTH WAR, THE

Masdongar, Clement
 MAHABHARATA, THE

Mase, Marino
 BELLY OF AN ARCHITECT, THE
 GODFATHER PART III, THE

Mashita, Nelson
 DARKMAN

Maskel, Haile
 MARKED FOR DEATH

Mason, Cynthia
 BONFIRE OF THE VANITIES

Mason, Hilary
 ROBOT JOX

Mason, Marsha
 STELLA

Mason, Tom
 MEN DON'T LEAVE

Mason, Yvonne Denise
 CHATTAHOOCHEE

Massey, Anna
 MOUNTAINS OF THE MOON
 TALL GUY, THE
 IMPROMPTU

Massieu, Patrick
 LIFE AND NOTHING BUT

Masten, Gordon
 STANLEY AND IRIS

Masterson, Alexandra
 BLOOD RED

Masterson, Mary Stuart
 FUNNY ABOUT LOVE

Mastrantonio, Mary Elizabeth
 FOOLS OF FORTUNE

Mastrogiacomo, Gina
 GOODFELLAS

Masuda, Tokuju
 DREAMS

Masur, Richard
 FLASHBACK

Matanky, Gary
 POSTCARDS FROM THE EDGE

Materas, Krystle
 KINDERGARTEN COP

Materas, Tiffany
 KINDERGARTEN COP

Mathe, Gabor
 MY 20TH CENTURY

Mathers, Jerry
 DOWN THE DRAIN

Mathews, Jon
 ANIMAL BEHAVIOR

Mathews, Tony
 MISADVENTURES OF MR. WILT, THE

Mathis, Carmen A.
 CADILLAC MAN

Mathis, Samantha
 PUMP UP THE VOLUME

Matsumura, Yuko
 DREAMS

Matthews, Brian
 LORD OF THE FLIES

Matthews, Dakin
 GHOST DAD

Mattia, Gina
 GOODFELLAS

Mattocks, John C.P.
 STRIKE IT RICH

Matuszak, John
 DOWN THE DRAIN

Maude-Roxby, Roddy
 WHITE HUNTER, BLACK HEART

Maund, Sue
 COOK, THE THIEF, HIS WIFE & HER
 LOVER, THE

Maury, Charlotte
 LIFE AND NOTHING BUT

Maury, Marc
HENRY AND JUNE

Maury-Lascoux, Erika
HENRY AND JUNE

Max
CADILLAC MAN

Max, Ron
OPPORTUNITY KNOCKS

May, Elaine
IN THE SPIRIT

Mayeno, Ken Y.
COME SEE THE PARADISE

Mayer, Pauline
COOK, THE THIEF, HIS WIFE & HER
  LOVER, THE

Mayfield, Julie
PROBLEM CHILD

Mayfield, Katherine
UNBELIEVABLE TRUTH, THE

Mayne, Ferdy
MAGDALENE

Mayron, Gale
FEUD, THE

Mayron, Melanie
MY BLUE HEAVEN

Mazar, Debi
GOODFELLAS

Mazey, Nina
DISTURBANCE, THE

Mazur, Arnold
RETURN OF SUPERFLY, THE

Mazur, Heather
NIGHT OF THE LIVING DEAD

Mazurki, Mike
DICK TRACY

Mazzella, Vincent Joseph Jr.
AFTER DARK, MY SWEET
DIE HARD 2

Mazzello, Joseph
PRESUMED INNOCENT

Mazzocco, John
COME SEE THE PARADISE

Mbandu, Konga
MOUNTAINS OF THE MOON

Mdleleni, Fikile
MOUNTAINS OF THE MOON

Mead, Nicolas
STRIKE IT RICH

Meade, Julia
PRESUMED INNOCENT

Meadows, Jayne
MURDER BY NUMBERS

Meadows, Stephen
NIGHT EYES

Meaney, Colm
DICK TRACY
DIE HARD 2
COME SEE THE PARADISE

Meara, Anne
AWAKENINGS

Mears, DeAnn
PRESUMED INNOCENT

Mechoso, Julio Oscar
INTERNAL AFFAIRS

Medak, Kate Suzanne
LOVE AT LARGE

Medak, Susan
LOVE AT LARGE

Medeiros, Lucila Carvalho
WILD ORCHID

Medeiros, Michael
ROBOCOP 2

Medina, Ben
PRIMARY TARGET

Medina, Crispin
DEMONSTONE

Medina, James
HAVANA

Meek, Jeffrey
HEART CONDITION

Meisle, Kathryn
BASKETCASE 2

Meisner, Gunter
MAGDALENE

Melainey, John
MISADVENTURES OF MR. WILT, THE

Meldrum, Wendel
WHY ME?

Mele, Nicholas
IMPULSE

Melennec, Patrice
MR. FROST

Melhuse, Peder
IMPULSE

Mell, Randle
QUICK CHANGE

Melleney, Victor
BURNDOWN
RIVER OF DEATH
TUSKS

Mellis, Louis
NUNS ON THE RUN

Melocchi, Vince
CHILD'S PLAY 2

Meltzer, Albert S.
ROCKY V

Meltzer, Ileane
LOVE AT LARGE

Mende, Lisa
GREMLINS 2 THE NEW BATCH

Mendelsohn, Ben
QUIGLEY DOWN UNDER

Mendelsohn, Robert L.
COLD FEET

Mendenhall, David
STREETS

Mendez, Ned
HAMLET

Mendoza, Diana
HOUSE PARTY

Menese, John P.
TAKING CARE OF BUSINESS

Meninger, Frederique
LIFE AND NOTHING BUT

Menuez, Stephanie
GREMLINS 2 THE NEW BATCH

Menyuk, Eric
GHOST DAD

Menzano, John
ADVENTURES OF FORD FAIRLANE, THE

Mercado, Hector
DELTA FORCE 2

Mercer, Crystal
FUNLAND

Mercer, Ernestine
SLEEPING CAR, THE
JEZEBEL'S KISS

Merck, Wallace
CHATTAHOOCHEE
ROBOCOP 2

Meredith, Angela
TALL GUY, THE

Meredith, Burgess
STATE OF GRACE
ROCKY V

Merediz, Olga
Q&A

Merkerson, S. Epatha
LOOSE CANNONS
NAVY SEALS
JACOB'S LADDER

Merle, Stesha
MEN DON'T LEAVE

Merner, George
NUTCRACKER PRINCE, THE

Merrill, Norman
GHOST DAD

Merrill, Peter
TIME GUARDIAN, THE

Merritt, George
BONFIRE OF THE VANITIES

Meshack, Charles
FORBIDDEN DANCE, THE
CHILD'S PLAY 2

Messick, Don
JETSONS: THE MOVIE

Metcalf, Laurie
INTERNAL AFFAIRS
PACIFIC HEIGHTS

Metcalfe, Robert
BIRD ON A WIRE

Metzler, Jim
CIRCUITRY MAN

Meurer, Eileen
EDWARD SCISSORHANDS

Meyer, Carla
RESCUERS DOWN UNDER, THE

Meyera, Dennis
FRIGHT HOUSE

Meyers, Kim
WHITE PALACE

Meyers, Lawrence Steven
DICK TRACY

Mezick, Shyree
COME SEE THE PARADISE

Mezieres, Myriam
FLAME IN MY HEART, A

Mezzogiorno, Vittorio
MAHABHARATA, THE

Mhike, Johnny Choil
FIELD, THE

Mhuire, Aine Ni
FIELD, THE

Miao, Cora
EAT A BOWL OF TEA
LIFE IS CHEAP. . . BUT TOILET PAPER IS EX-
PENSIVE

Michael, Brad
MEN DON'T LEAVE

Michael, Ralph
LIONHEART

Michael-Standing, David
BACK TO BACK

Michaels, Chad
MONSTER HIGH

Michaels, Marie
GOODFELLAS

Michaels, Peter
FIRE BIRDS

Michaels, Robin
FRIGHT HOUSE

Michaels, Roxanna
CAGED FURY

Michalski, Jeff
PRETTY WOMAN

Michlin, Barry
BONFIRE OF THE VANITIES

Mickins, Beverly
STEEL AND LACE

Midler, Bette
STELLA

Migenes, Julia
MACK THE KNIFE
KRAYS, THE

Mihailoff, R.A.
LEATHERFACE: THE TEXAS CHAINSAW
MASSACRE III

Mikasa, Michael
SAVAGE BEACH

Miki, Norihei
BLACK RAIN

Milazzo, Joe
LEMON SISTERS, THE

Miley, Peggy
ALICE

Milian, Thomas
HAVANA

Milian, Tomas
REVENGE

Military, Frank
EVERYBODY WINS
LAST EXIT TO BROOKLYN

Milk, Andy
STUFF STEPHANIE IN THE INCINERATOR

Millais, Hugh
CHICAGO JOE AND THE SHOWGIRL

Millar, Gregory
WHY ME?

Miller, Annette
IMPORTED BRIDEGROOM, THE

Miller, Barry
LOVE AT LARGE

Miller, Belal
HOUSE PARTY

Miller, Dennis
MADHOUSE

Miller, Dick
UNDER THE BOARDWALK
GREMLINS 2 THE NEW BATCH

Miller, Dutch
LOOSE CANNONS

Miller, Harvey
AWAKENINGS

Miller, Jason
EXORCIST III, THE

Miller, Joshua
CLASS OF 1999
DEATH WARRANT

Miller, Judith
STAR QUEST: BEYOND THE RISING MOON

Miller, Larry
PRETTY WOMAN

Miller, Mark Jeffrey
TEENAGE MUTANT NINJA TURTLES

Miller, Neil
LEMON SISTERS, THE

Miller, Penelope Ann
DOWNTOWN
FRESHMAN, THE

KINDERGARTEN COP
AWAKENINGS

Miller, Peter
MEN DON'T LEAVE

Milligan, Tuck
RUSSIA HOUSE, THE

Millington, J.H.
FRESHMAN, THE

Million, Cindy
DISTURBANCE, THE

Mills, Edith
HOT SPOT, THE

Mills, Jed
OPPORTUNITY KNOCKS

Mills, Michael John
BACK TO THE FUTURE PART III

Milmeister, Jared
FLATLINERS

Milner, Megan
LOOK WHO'S TALKING TOO

Milo, Jean-Roger
LIFE AND NOTHING BUT

Milsom, Annette
IMPROMPTU

Min, Cheng Kwan
LIFE IS CHEAP. . . BUT TOILET PAPER IS
EXPENSIVE

Minailo, Michelle
SKI PATROL

Minault, Kent
SPACED INVADERS

Miner, Jan
MERMAIDS

Miner, Rachel
ALICE

Ming, Lau Siu
EAT A BOWL OF TEA

Minjares, Joe
LAST OF THE FINEST, THE

Minnick, Dani
SLEEPING CAR, THE

Minns, Byron Keith
JACOB'S LADDER

Minor, Willie
PROBLEM CHILD
I COME IN PEACE

Minter, Kelly Jo
HOUSE PARTY

Minter, Kristen
HOME ALONE

Minton, Faith
SKI PATROL

Miou-Miou
MAY FOOLS

Miranda, Carlos
HAVANA
GODFATHER PART III, THE

Miranda, Rogerio
GODFATHER PART III, THE

Miranda, Ron
PROBLEM CHILD

Miro, Jennifer
DR. CALIGARI

Mirren, Helen
COOK, THE THIEF, HIS WIFE & HER
LOVER, THE

Misawa, Goh
COME SEE THE PARADISE

Misery the Pig
MISERY

Mitchel, Ryan
QUICK CHANGE

Mitchell, Brian
GHOST DAD

Mitchell, Darryl
HOUSE PARTY

Mitchell, Derek
FRESHMAN, THE

Mitchell, Donna
ROOKIE, THE

Mitchell, Eric
FORCE OF CIRCUMSTANCE

Mitchell, Gene
SKINHEADS – THE SECOND COMING OF
HATE
FORBIDDEN DANCE, THE

Mitchell, James A.
DANCES WITH WOLVES

Mitchell, Patrick
CRY-BABY

Mitchell, Susan
Q&A

Mitchum, Christopher
AFTERSHOCK

Mitler, Matt
BASKETCASE 2

Mitzman, Marcia
BONFIRE OF THE VANITIES

Mixon, Paul B.
BETSY'S WEDDING

Miya, Masatoshi
DREAMS

Miyajima, Eri
SUMMER VACATION: 1999

Miyasaka, Hiroshi
DREAMS

Miyata, Yumiko
DREAMS

Miyazawa, Rika
DREAMS

Mizel, Alicia
LOOK WHO'S TALKING TOO

Mizuhara, Rie
SUMMER VACATION: 1999

Mobley, Shepler
PROBLEM CHILD

Mochida, Masayo
DREAMS

Mockingbird, Tequila
DR. CALIGARI

Modine, Matthew
LEMON SISTERS, THE
MEMPHIS BELLE
PACIFIC HEIGHTS

Moe, Elaine
MADHOUSE

Moffat, Donald
BONFIRE OF THE VANITIES

Moffett, D.W.
LISA
PACIFIC HEIGHTS

Moffett, Shannon
MEN DON'T LEAVE

Monaghan, Marjorie
BONFIRE OF THE VANITIES

Monarque, Steve
UNDER THE BOARDWALK

Moncibais, S. "Monty"
PROBLEM CHILD

Monclova, Rene
HAVANA

Moncure, Lisa
LISA

Monero, Mark
MISADVENTURES OF MR. WILT, THE

Mongezi, Leslie
DAMNED RIVER

Monica, Kathleen
ADVENTURES OF FORD FAIRLANE, THE

Monich, Tim
CHATTAHOOCHEE

Monju, Justin
BLOOD OF HEROES

Monk, Roger
KRAYS, THE

Monnet, Gabriel
CYRANO DE BERGERAC

Mono, Joseph
L'ETAT SAUVAGE

Monroe, Paul
FAR OUT MAN

Monroe, Steve
KILL-OFF, THE

Mons, Maurice
LIFE IS A LONG QUIET RIVER

Montalbo, J.D.
QUICK CHANGE

Montanio, Wayne
MARKED FOR DEATH

Montano, Felix
WITHOUT YOU, I'M NOTHING

Montez, Paul-Felix
FRANKENHOOKER
STATE OF GRACE

Montgomery, Michael
ERNEST GOES TO JAIL

Montgomery, Paul
AWAKENINGS

Monty, Mike
DOG TAGS

Moon, Philip
SHOCK TO THE SYSTEM, A
CADILLAC MAN

Moor, Bill
CADILLAC MAN

Moore, Demi
GHOST

Moore, Dudley
CRAZY PEOPLE
ADVENTURES OF MILO AND OTIS, THE

Moore, Edwina
THREE MEN AND A LITTLE LADY

Moore, Jeanie
AFTER DARK, MY SWEET

Moore, John Rixey
TUSKS

Moore, Julianne
TALES FROM THE DARKSIDE: THE MOVIE

Moore, Laurens
CHATTAHOOCHEE

Moore, Lenny
OPPONENT, THE

Moore, Lorraine
BONFIRE OF THE VANITIES

Moore, Maggie
DARKMAN

Moore, Mary
CHATTAHOOCHEE

Moore, Melba
DEF BY TEMPTATION

Moore, Melissa
REPOSSESSED

Moore, Muriel
FUNLAND

Moore, Norma
PROBLEM CHILD

Moore, Patience
SHOCK TO THE SYSTEM, A
ALICE
PREDATOR 2

Moore, Sheila
BYE BYE BLUES

Moore, Terry
AMERICAN BOYFRIENDS

Mooring, Jeff
FIRST POWER, THE

Moorman, Clem
LOOSE CANNONS

Morales, Gonzalo
VERONICO CRUZ

Moran, Dan
ME AND HIM

Moran, Grant
MADHOUSE

Moran, Michael P.
STATE OF GRACE

Moran, Nancy
FLATLINERS

Moran, Rob
NAVY SEALS

Moranis, Rick
MY BLUE HEAVEN

Morant, Angela
CHICAGO JOE AND THE SHOWGIRL

More, Camilla
DARK SIDE OF THE MOON

Morelli, Tony
SHORT TIME

Moreno, Belita
MEN DON'T LEAVE

Moreno, Rene L.
MADHOUSE
YOUNG GUNS II

Moreno, Ruben
FORBIDDEN DANCE, THE

Moreno, Simone
WILD ORCHID

Morgan, Robert
NUNS ON THE RUN

Morgan, Stafford
DIE HARD 2

Morgan, Tommy
TAKING CARE OF BUSINESS

Morgenstern, Stephanie
NUTCRACKER PRINCE, THE

Mori, Jeanne
LAST OF THE FINEST, THE
VITAL SIGNS
GHOST DAD
ROOKIE, THE

Moriarty, Cathy
BURNDOWN
KINDERGARTEN COP

Moriarty, Michael
FULL FATHOM FIVE

Morier-Genoud, Philippe
CYRANO DE BERGERAC

Morim, Michael
TORN APART

Morin, Elizabeth
SHOCK TO THE SYSTEM, A

Morley, Robert
ISTANBUL, KEEP YOUR EYES OPEN

Moroff, Mike
ANGEL TOWN

Morris, Alex
RIVERBEND
I COME IN PEACE

Morris, Anita
MARTIANS GO HOME!

Morris, Barbara
AVALON

Morris, Haviland
SHOCK TO THE SYSTEM, A
GREMLINS 2 THE NEW BATCH

Morris, Jane
MEN DON'T LEAVE

Morris, Jeff
TWO JAKES, THE

Morris, Jizelle
GHOST DAD

Morris, Virginia
BONFIRE OF THE VANITIES

Morrison, Holly
LOVE AT LARGE

Morrison, Rudy F.
LAST OF THE FINEST, THE

Morrison, Tommy "Duke"
ROCKY V

Morrow, Britt
NUNS ON THE RUN

Morse, David
DESPERATE HOURS

Mortensen, Viggo
LEATHERFACE: THE TEXAS CHAINSAW
MASSACRE III
YOUNG GUNS II

Mortfee, Jane
AMERICAN BOYFRIENDS

Morton, Gary
POSTCARDS FROM THE EDGE

Morton, Mickey
DOWN THE DRAIN

Moschitta, John Jr.
DICK TRACY

Moseley, Bill
FIRST POWER, THE

Mosere, Christine
AVALON

Moses, Senta
HOME ALONE

Mosley, Bill
NIGHT OF THE LIVING DEAD

Mosley, Roger E.
HEART CONDITION

Mosley, Tony
GRAFFITI BRIDGE

Moss, Carol
MERMAIDS

Moss, Kathi
ME AND HIM

Moss, Ron
PREDATOR 2

Mostel, Josh
ANIMAL BEHAVIOR

Mott, Zachary
NIGHT OF THE LIVING DEAD

Mougey, Paul
GOODFELLAS

Mounicou, Louis Charles III
MILLER'S CROSSING

Mourouzi, Nadia
LANDSCAPE IN THE MIST

Mouton, Benjamin
FLATLINERS

Moya, Angela
FORBIDDEN DANCE, THE

Mpepela, Shimane
GODS MUST BE CRAZY II, THE

Mr. Bill
FAR OUT MAN

Mucary, Charles
NIGHT OF THE SHARKS

Mueller, Julia
UNBELIEVABLE TRUTH, THE

Mueller, Myke
ERNEST GOES TO JAIL

Mueller-Stahl, Armin
AVALON

Muhammed, Norta
MOUNTAINS OF THE MOON

Mui, Anita
ROUGE

Mukogawa, Marian
COME SEE THE PARADISE

Mulholland, Declan
TALL GUY, THE

Mulholland, Gordon
RIVER OF DEATH

Mull, Martin
SKI PATROL
FAR OUT MAN

Mullally, Richard
GOODFELLAS

Mullen, Patty
FRANKENHOOKER

Muller, Hans-Reinhard
NASTY GIRL, THE

Mulligan, Terry David
LOOK WHO'S TALKING TOO

Mullinix, Ken
DISTURBANCE, THE

Mullis, John
COOK, THE THIEF, HIS WIFE & HER
LOVER, THE

Mullner, Wolfgang
TIME TROOPERS

Mulot, Christian
GREEN CARD

Mulroney, Dermot
LONGTIME COMPANION
SURVIVAL QUEST

Mulroney, Kieran
HEART CONDITION

Mumford, Dean
LOOSE CANNONS

Munafo, Tony
ROCKY V

Munday, Mary
GHOST DAD

Mundi, Coati
MO' BETTER BLUES

Munro, Janet
LOOK WHO'S TALKING TOO

Murakoshi, Suzen
QUICK CHANGE

Murcelo, Karmin
REVENGE

Murney, Christopher
LOOSE CANNONS
LAST EXIT TO BROOKLYN

Murota, Hideo
HEAVEN AND EARTH

Murphy, Cathy
MEMPHIS BELLE

Murphy, Charles Q.
MO' BETTER BLUES

Murphy, Chris
JACOB'S LADDER

Murphy, Eddie
ANOTHER 48 HRS.

Murphy, Edward D.
GOODFELLAS

Murphy, Greg
LOVE AT LARGE

Murphy, Justin
MARKED FOR DEATH

Murphy, M.R.
STUFF STEPHANIE IN THE INCINERATOR

Murphy, Michael P.
GAME, THE

Murray, Bill
QUICK CHANGE

Murray, Paul
FAR OUT MAN

Murray, Sean
HAMLET

Murrell, Gene
FUNLAND

Muser, Wolf
CAGED IN PARADISO

Myerovich, Alvin
AVALON

Myers Davidson, Maggy
PACIFIC HEIGHTS

Myers, Bruce
MAHABHARATA, THE
HENRY AND JUNE

Myers, Kenny
BACK TO THE FUTURE PART III

Myles, Albert J.
ROCKY V

Myracle, Wilma
WHITE PALACE

N!Xau
GODS MUST BE CRAZY II, THE

N'Gom, Abdoulaye
GREEN CARD

Naakkarat, Meesak
AIR AMERICA

Nader, Laura
EDWARD SCISSORHANDS

Nadies
GODS MUST BE CRAZY II, THE

Nadler, Marty
PRETTY WOMAN

Naff, Lycia
TOTAL RECALL

Nagasawa, Ryo
DREAMS

Nagatani, Goichi
DREAMS

Nagorsky, Nicole
KINDERGARTEN COP

Nahan, Stu
TAKING CARE OF BUSINESS
ROCKY V

Nahra, Nancy Ann
SKI PATROL

Naito, Katsumi
DREAMS

Najee
DEF BY TEMPTATION

Najera, Rick
RED SURF

Nakajima, Shu
DREAMS

Nakanishi, Kazue
DREAMS

Nakano, Miyuki
SUMMER VACATION: 1999

Nakano, Naomi
COME SEE THE PARADISE

Nakano, Toshihiko
DREAMS

Nakasako, Spencer
LIFE IS CHEAP. . . BUT TOILET PAPER IS
EXPENSIVE

Nakayama, Teruko
DREAMS

Nanao, Reiko
DREAMS

Nance, Consuela
ADVENTURES OF FORD FAIRLANE, THE

Nance, Jack
WILD AT HEART
HOT SPOT, THE

Nannerello, George
CHATTAHOOCHEE

Nano, Agnese
CINEMA PARADISO

Nantatanti, Natta
AIR AMERICA

Napier, Charles
MIAMI BLUES
HIT LIST
ERNEST GOES TO JAIL

Nardo, Lo
GOODFELLAS

Naruse, Masataka
HEAVEN AND EARTH

Nascar, Dolores
LORDS OF MAGICK, THE

Natali, Jerome
TWISTED OBSESSION

Nathenson, Zoe
RAGGEDY RAWNEY, THE

Natori, Yukimasa
DREAMS

Natsuki, Junpei
DREAMS

Natsuyagi, Isao
HEAVEN AND EARTH

Naughton, David
SLEEPING CAR, THE
OVER EXPOSED
STEEL AND LACE

Nayber, Laurie
ALICE

Nazarov, Pavel
FREEZE – DIE – COME TO LIFE

Neal, Billie
JACOB'S LADDER

Neal, Lucia
THREE MEN AND A LITTLE LADY

Neale, Leslie
GREMLINS 2 THE NEW BATCH

Needles, David Paul
YOUNG GUNS II

Neeson, Liam
DARKMAN

Negishi, Toshie
DREAMS

Negret, Francois
MR. FROST

Neil, Vince
ADVENTURES OF FORD FAIRLANE, THE

Neill, Brian
Q&A

Neill, Sam
HUNT FOR RED OCTOBER, THE

Neilson, Catherine
WHITE HUNTER, BLACK HEART

Neilson, Scott
CRY-BABY

Neiman, Leroy
ROCKY V

Nelson, Bill
CADILLAC MAN

Nelson, Craig T.
ME AND HIM

Nelson, Danny
BLOOD SALVAGE

Nelson, David
CRY-BABY

Nelson, Jerry
ROBOCOP 2

Nelson, Judd
FAR OUT MAN

Nelson, Lloyd
PRETTY WOMAN
ROOKIE, THE

Nelson, Novella
BONFIRE OF THE VANITIES
GREEN CARD

Nelson, Peter
DIE HARD 2

Nelson, Robert
KINDERGARTEN COP

Nelson, Ruth
AWAKENINGS

Nelson, Shawn
GREMLINS 2 THE NEW BATCH

Nemacheck, Lisa Mene
GHOST DAD

Nemeth, Chris
GUARDIAN, THE

Nemeth, Craig
GUARDIAN, THE

Nemo, Henry
PLOT AGAINST HARRY, THE

Nero, Franco
DIE HARD 2
MAGDALENE

Neube, Moses
DAMNED RIVER

Neube, Mtcheso
DAMNED RIVER

Neuberger, Jan
EXORCIST III, THE

Neukirch, Rob
VITAL SIGNS

Neustadt, Ted
PRESUMED INNOCENT

Neuwirth, Bebe
GREEN CARD

Nevirs, Michele
GREEN CARD

Newcomb, Richard L.
PRESUMED INNOCENT

Newhart, Bob
RESCUERS DOWN UNDER, THE

Newholy, Raymond
DANCES WITH WOLVES

Newington, Joey
BACK TO THE FUTURE PART III

Newlin, Joan
VITAL SIGNS

Newman, Abby
PROBLEM CHILD

Newman, Frederick
ME AND HIM

Newman, Paul
MR. AND MRS. BRIDGE

Newman, William
CHATTAHOOCHEE

Newmark, Charles
LORD OF THE FLIES

Newton, Wayne
ADVENTURES OF FORD FAIRLANE, THE

Neyland, Spencer
KILL-OFF, THE

Nez, Redwing Ted
DANCES WITH WOLVES

Nezer, Chr.
LANDSCAPE IN THE MIST

Ng'Ong'A, Wilson
MOUNTAINS OF THE MOON

Ngai, Bonnie
LIFE IS CHEAP. . . BUT TOILET PAPER IS EX-
PENSIVE

Ngema, Bheki Tonto
MOUNTAINS OF THE MOON

Ngong, Marina M'boa
MAMA, THERE'S A MAN IN YOUR BED

Nhlapo, Rocks
MOUNTAINS OF THE MOON

Niblack, Nicole
FLATLINERS

Nichetti, Maurizio
ICICLE THIEF, THE

Nicholas, Angela
WILDEST DREAMS

Nicholas, Denise
GHOST DAD

Nichols, Jeff
STELLA

Nichols, Taylor
METROPOLITAN

Nicholson, Jack
TWO JAKES, THE

Nici, Anthony J.
AWAKENINGS

Nicolson, Dave
TOTAL RECALL

Niebel, Greg
FORBIDDEN DANCE, THE

Niekrug, Barry
DOWN THE DRAIN
BONFIRE OF THE VANITIES

Nielsen, Karen
FRIGHT HOUSE

Nielsen, Leslie
REPOSSESSED

Nielsen, Paul
STUFF STEPHANIE IN THE INCINERATOR

Nieman, Ray
TAX SEASON

Nieves, Ralph
BLUE STEEL

Nighy, Bill
MACK THE KNIFE

Nikiforov, Gina
RUSSIA HOUSE, THE

Nikiforov, Vladek
RUSSIA HOUSE, THE

Nikitin, Nikolai
RUSSIA HOUSE, THE

Nikko, Matt
CADILLAC MAN

Nipar, Yvette
SKI PATROL

Nishi, Hatsue
DREAMS

Nishino, Akemi
COME SEE THE PARADISE

Nishio, Chika
DREAMS

Niven, David Jr.
LISA

Njiru, Esther
MOUNTAINS OF THE MOON

Nocerino, Anthony
TOUCH OF A STRANGER

Nogulich, Natalia
GUARDIAN, THE
POSTCARDS FROM THE EDGE

Noiret, Philippe
CINEMA PARADISO
LIFE AND NOTHING BUT

Nolan, Maura
MEN IN LOVE

Nolan, Tom
LAST OF THE FINEST, THE
PRETTY WOMAN
LISA
TAKING CARE OF BUSINESS
PACIFIC HEIGHTS

Nolte, Nick
EVERYBODY WINS
Q&A
ANOTHER 48 HRS.

Nomura, Hironobu
HEAVEN AND EARTH

Noon, Frank
SKINHEADS – THE SECOND COMING OF
HATE
GUARDIAN, THE
DARKMAN

Noonan, Tom
ROBOCOP 2

Nordmann, Jean-Gabriel
FLAME IN MY HEART, A

Nordra, Greta
WITCHES, THE

Norikoff, Lawrence
FRIGHT HOUSE

Norman, John
RIVERBEND

Norman, Zack
CADILLAC MAN

Normington, John
MISADVENTURES OF MR. WILT, THE

Norris, Chuck
DELTA FORCE 2

Norris, Dean
GREMLINS 2 THE NEW BATCH
TOTAL RECALL
DESPERATE HOURS

Norris, Rufus
DEMON WIND

North, Alan
CRAZY PEOPLE

North, Robert
BLADES

North, Robert D.
MEN DON'T LEAVE

Northover, Mark
MACK THE KNIFE
HARDWARE

Norton, Alex
WHITE HUNTER, BLACK HEART

Norton, Jim
HIDDEN AGENDA

Norum, John
FAR OUT MAN

Nossek, Ralph
MOUNTAINS OF THE MOON
CHICAGO JOE AND THE SHOWGIRL

Novakovic, Tomislav
AWAKENINGS

Novello, Don
GODFATHER PART III, THE

Novogrudsky, Boris
FOURTH WAR, THE

Nowell, David
SKI PATROL

Nozaki, Kaitaro
HEAVEN AND EARTH

Nthodi, Reuben
AMERICAN EAGLE

Nunez, Miguel
SHADOWZONE

Nunn, Bill
CADILLAC MAN
DEF BY TEMPTATION
MO' BETTER BLUES

Nussbaum, Mike
DESPERATE HOURS

Nygren, Carrie
KING OF NEW YORK

O'Brien, Gary
STRAPLESS

O'Brien, Glenn
FORCE OF CIRCUMSTANCE

O'Brien, Tom
FLASHBACK

O'Connell, Deirdre
STATE OF GRACE

O'Connell, Elinore
FLATLINERS

O'Connell, John
PROBLEM CHILD

O'Connor, Kevin J.
LOVE AT LARGE

O'Donnell, Chris
MEN DON'T LEAVE

O'Donnell, Michael Donovan
DICK TRACY

O'Donovan, Noel
FIELD, THE

O'Grady, Gail
NOBODY'S PERFECT

O'Hanlon, George
JETSONS: THE MOVIE

O'Hara, Brad
LONGTIME COMPANION

O'Hara, Catherine
DICK TRACY
BETSY'S WEDDING
HOME ALONE

O'Herlihy, Daniel
ROBOCOP 2

O'Leary, Jer
FIELD, THE

O'Malley, Bingo
TWO EVIL EYES

O'Malley, Jason
BACKSTREET DREAMS

O'Malley, Marie
RETURN OF SUPERFLY, THE

O'Meara, Evan
JACOB'S LADDER

O'Neal, Cynthia
Q&A

O'Neal, Pat
DIE HARD 2

O'Neal, Patrick
Q&A
ALICE

O'Neil, F.J.
HUNT FOR RED OCTOBER, THE

O'Neill, Barry
SPACED INVADERS

O'Neill, Dick
LOOSE CANNONS

O'Neill, Ed
ADVENTURES OF FORD FAIRLANE, THE
SIBLING RIVALRY

O'Neill, Remy
FORBIDDEN DANCE, THE
HOLLYWOOD HOT TUBS II: EDUCATING
CRYSTAL

O'Quinn, Terrance
BLIND FURY

O'Reilly, Cyril
NAVY SEALS

O'Ross, Ed
ANOTHER 48 HRS.
DICK TRACY

O'Shea, Daniel
STATE OF GRACE

O'Shea, Milo
OPPORTUNITY KNOCKS

O'Sullivan, Barney
NARROW MARGIN

O'Sullivan, Sean
KILL-OFF, THE

O'Toole, Peter
NUTCRACKER PRINCE, THE

O'Toole, Annette
LOVE AT LARGE

O'Toole, Matt
MARKED FOR DEATH

Obata, Toshishiro
TEENAGE MUTANT NINJA TURTLES

Obayashi, Takeshi
HEAVEN AND EARTH

Oberbeck, William
WHITE PALACE

Obregon, Rodrigo
SAVAGE BEACH

Ocampo, Juan Carlos
VERONICO CRUZ

Ocham, Martin
MOUNTAINS OF THE MOON

Ochs, Meegan Lee
LOVE AT LARGE

Odajima, Takashi
DREAMS

Odent, Christophe
LIFE AND NOTHING BUT

Odo, Chris
GREEN CARD

Odums, Lynda
FLATLINERS

Ogata, Robert
SAVAGE BEACH

Ogier, Quentin
CYRANO DE BERGERAC

Oguri, Sachiko
DREAMS

Ohama, Natsuko
FLATLINERS

Oida, Yoshi
MAHABHARATA, THE

Okamoto, Maiko
DREAMS

Okello, Martin
MOUNTAINS OF THE MOON

Oki, Ryujiro
DREAMS

Okita, Hiroyuki
HEAVEN AND EARTH

Okrzesik, Robert
HOME ALONE

Okumura, Tadashi
DREAMS

Okuno, Hiroko
DREAMS

Olafsson, Egil
SHADOW OF THE RAVEN, THE

Olaguivel, Rene
VERONICO CRUZ

Oldman, Gary
CHATTAHOOCHEE
STATE OF GRACE

Olin, Lena
HAVANA

Oliu, Ingrid
FLATLINERS

Oliver, Jason
CLASS OF 1999

Oliver, Michael
PROBLEM CHILD

Oliver, Prudence
COOK, THE THIEF, HIS WIFE & HER
LOVER, THE

Oliveri, Robert
EDWARD SCISSORHANDS

Olivier, Deanna
AFTERSHOCK

Olsen, Alfa-Betty
QUICK CHANGE

Olsen, Gary
COOK, THE THIEF, HIS WIFE & HER
LOVER, THE

Olsen, Svein Birger
PATHFINDER

Olson, Jeff
DESPERATE HOURS

Olson, Phil
EDWARD SCISSORHANDS

Ondevilla, Jericho
DOG TAGS

Ones, Arvid
WITCHES, THE

Ono, Mayumi
DREAMS

Onofre, Antonio
WILD ORCHID

Onofre, Marco
WILD ORCHID

Onorati, Peter
FIRE BIRDS
GOODFELLAS
POSTCARDS FROM THE EDGE

Onsongo, Paul
MOUNTAINS OF THE MOON

Ontkean, Michael
BYE BYE BLUES
POSTCARDS FROM THE EDGE

Oppenheimer, Michael
OPPORTUNITY KNOCKS

Orbach, Jerry
LAST EXIT TO BROOKLYN

Orcier, Sylvie
TOO BEAUTIFUL FOR YOU

Orlandi, Felice
ANOTHER 48 HRS.

Orlandini, Hal
BURNDOWN

Ornstein, Fred
COUPE DE VILLE

Oropeza, Luis
PACIFIC HEIGHTS

Orrison, George
ROOKIE, THE

Ortega, Karyne
DICK TRACY

Ortelli, Dyana
ALIENATOR

Ortlieb, Jim
FLATLINERS
HOME ALONE

Oscar, Billy
HEART CONDITION

Osowski, Pam
FORCE OF CIRCUMSTANCE

Osterhage, Jeff
MASQUE OF THE RED DEATH
BIG BAD JOHN

Ostuni, Thomas
FRIGHT HOUSE

Ota, Mon
DREAMS

Otakara, Tomoko
SUMMER VACATION: 1999

Otaki, Hideji
HEAVEN AND EARTH

Otieno, Michael
MOUNTAINS OF THE MOON

Otis, Carre
WILD ORCHID

Otnes, Ola
WITCHES, THE

Otowa, Kumeko
DREAMS

Ott, Dennis
SKINHEADS – THE SECOND COMING OF
HATE

Ottavino, John
PRESUMED INNOCENT
STATE OF GRACE

Otto, Deborah
MADHOUSE

Otto, Russell
INHERITOR

Otway, John
STRIKE IT RICH

Overall, Park
KINDERGARTEN COP

Owens, Christopher
NUTCRACKER PRINCE, THE

Owens, Elizabeth
BONFIRE OF THE VANITIES

Oxenberg, Catherine
OVER EXPOSED

Ozawa, Shoichi
BLACK RAIN

Ozdogru, Nuvit
ISTANBUL, KEEP YOUR EYES OPEN

Ozeki, Masam
DREAMS

Pace, Ralph
CHATTAHOOCHEE

Pace, William
BLADES

Pachis, Stratos
LANDSCAPE IN THE MIST

Pacino, Al
DICK TRACY
GODFATHER PART III, THE

Pack, Roger Lloyd
COOK, THE THIEF, HIS WIFE & HER
LOVER, THE
MISADVENTURES OF MR. WILT, THE

Pacula, Joanna
MARKED FOR DEATH

Padovani, Paola
OPPONENT, THE

Pagano, Karrie
COOK, THE THIEF, HIS WIFE & HER
LOVER, THE

Page, Justin
KINDERGARTEN COP

Page, Kevin
I COME IN PEACE

Pagowski, Filip
FORCE OF CIRCUMSTANCE

Paige, Anthony T.
QUICK CHANGE

Paine, Heidi
WILDEST DREAMS

Pais, Josh
TEENAGE MUTANT NINJA TURTLES

Pak, Tae
TEENAGE MUTANT NINJA TURTLES

Palaiologou, Tania
LANDSCAPE IN THE MIST

Palatin, Suzy
HENRY AND JUNE

Palatsidis, T.
LANDSCAPE IN THE MIST

Paley, Petronia
WHITE GIRL, THE

Palffy, David
FOURTH WAR, THE

Palmer, Kathleen Murphy
BONFIRE OF THE VANITIES

Palmer, Peter
EDWARD SCISSORHANDS

Panagopoulou, Vasia
LANDSCAPE IN THE MIST

Panczak, Hans Georg
TIME TROOPERS

Panebianco, Richard
CADILLAC MAN

Panichpan, Purin
AIR AMERICA

Pankin, Stuart
ARACHNOPHOBIA

Pantages, Tony
SHORT TIME

Pantaleo, Peter
HOME ALONE

Pantoliano, Joe
DOWNTOWN
LAST OF THE FINEST, THE
SHORT TIME
BACKSTREET DREAMS

Panych, Morris
LOOK WHO'S TALKING TOO

Papajohn, Michael
PREDATOR 2

Papazafiropoulou, N.
LANDSCAPE IN THE MIST

Pappageorge, Demetrios
EXORCIST III, THE

Pappas, Iris
YOUNG GUNS II

Pappas, John
TREMORS

Parenti, Rose
SPACED INVADERS

Pares, Cesar
KILL-OFF, THE

Paris, Julie
PRETTY WOMAN

Parisi, James
EVERYBODY WINS

Park, Gry
ADVENTURES OF FORD FAIRLANE, THE

Park, Hili
ADVENTURES OF FORD FAIRLANE, THE

Park, Steve
QUICK CHANGE

Parker, Bill
BACK TO BACK

Parker, Corey
WHITE PALACE

Parker, Ellen
DESPERATE HOURS

Parker, F. William
PACIFIC HEIGHTS

Parker, Gary
CHICAGO JOE AND THE SHOWGIRL
DESPERATE HOURS

Parker, Holt
YOUNG GUNS II

Parker, Jarrett
LORDS OF MAGICK, THE

Parker, Mary-Louise
LONGTIME COMPANION

Parker, Michael J.
PACIFIC HEIGHTS

Parker, Nathaniel
HAMLET

Parker, Noelle
LOOK WHO'S TALKING TOO

Parker, Norman
BONFIRE OF THE VANITIES

Parker, Oliver
NUNS ON THE RUN

Parker, Sachi
WELCOME HOME, ROXY CARMICHAEL

Parker, Sunshine
TREMORS
LOVE AT LARGE

Parks, Bert
FRESHMAN, THE

Parks, Michael
CAGED FURY

Parks, Van Dyke
TWO JAKES, THE

Parrott, Jerry E.
DIE HARD 2

Parry, David
DR. CALIGARI

Parsily, Susan
ROCKY V

Parsons, Estelle
DICK TRACY
LEMON SISTERS, THE

Parsons, Nancy
LOOSE CANNONS
HOMER & EDDIE

Parsons, Willy
GUARDIAN, THE

Partington, David
FIRST POWER, THE

Pascal, Lucien
CYRANO DE BERGERAC

Pasdar, Adrian
VITAL SIGNS
TORN APART

Pasquale, Janet
BETSY'S WEDDING

Pastor, Julian
REVENGE

Pastore, Vinny
GOODFELLAS
AWAKENINGS

Pastorelli, Robert
DANCES WITH WOLVES

Pastukhov, Nikolair
RUSSIA HOUSE, THE

Pataki, Michael
HOLLYWOOD HOT TUBS II: EDUCATING
CRYSTAL
ROCKY V

Patarot, Helene
MAHABHARATA, THE

Pater, Jacques
CYRANO DE BERGERAC

Paterson, Bill
WITCHES, THE

Paterson, Florence
BIRD ON A WIRE

Pathakshah, Ratna
PERFECT MURDER, THE

Patinkin, Mandy
DICK TRACY
IMPROMPTU

Paton, Angela
FLATLINERS

Patric, Jason
AFTER DARK, MY SWEET
FRANKENSTEIN UNBOUND

Patrick, Kristy Lynne
PROBLEM CHILD

Patrick, Randal
DEAD AIM
FUNLAND

Patrick, Robert
DIE HARD 2

Patterson, Jay
TEENAGE MUTANT NINJA TURTLES

Patterson, Robert
NUNS ON THE RUN
HIDDEN AGENDA

Patterson, William
PACIFIC HEIGHTS

Patton, Will
EVERYBODY WINS
SHOCK TO THE SYSTEM, A

Pauchon, Herve
CYRANO DE BERGERAC

Paul, Adrian
MASQUE OF THE RED DEATH

Paul, Georgie
LAST OF THE FINEST, THE

Paul, Richard Joseph
UNDER THE BOARDWALK
QUICK CHANGE

Paulin, Scott
PUMP UP THE VOLUME
GRIM PRAIRIE TALES

Pavani, Federico
OPPONENT, THE

Pavao, Seacia
MERMAIDS

Paxton, Bill
LAST OF THE FINEST, THE
BRAIN DEAD
SLIPSTREAM
NAVY SEALS
BACK TO BACK
PREDATOR 2

Paymer, David
CRAZY PEOPLE

Payne, Eric
RETURN OF SUPERFLY, THE

Payne, Julie
MISERY

Paysinger, Sherri
BONFIRE OF THE VANITIES

Payton-Wright, Pamela
FRESHMAN, THE

Peabody, Dossy
MERMAIDS

Peacock, Trevor
HAMLET

Pearce, Mary Vivian
CRY-BABY

Pearcey, Kristin
ADVENTURES OF FORD FAIRLANE, THE

Pearlman, Stephen
GREEN CARD

Pearson Rose, Robin
GHOST DAD

Pease, Patsy
ANDY COLBY'S INCREDIBLY AWESOME
ADVENTURE

Peck, Anthony
HUNT FOR RED OCTOBER, THE

Peck, Bob
LORD OF THE FLIES
SLIPSTREAM

Peck, Cecilia
TORN APART

Peck, J. Eddie
LAMBADA

Peldon, Ashley
STELLA
LEMON SISTERS, THE

Pellegrino, Frank
GOODFELLAS

Pelletier, Gilles
JESUS OF MONTREAL

Pena, Elizabeth
BLUE STEEL
JACOB'S LADDER

Pena, Frank
DISTURBANCE, THE

Pendleton, Austin
MR. AND MRS. BRIDGE

Penhall, Bruce
SAVAGE BEACH

Penix, Dr. Jack
MADHOUSE

Penn, Sean
STATE OF GRACE

Penner, Jonathan
WHITE PALACE

Pennock, Christopher
CAGED IN PARADISO

Pentangelo, Joe
QUICK CHANGE

Pentz, Robert
LOOSE CANNONS

Pereira, Marcelo Mandonca
WILD ORCHID

Peretz, Susan
LOOSE CANNONS

Perez, Alain
CYRANO DE BERGERAC

Perez, Junior
Q&A

Perez, Michael
SHOCK TO THE SYSTEM, A

Perez, Vincent
CYRANO DE BERGERAC

Pering, Kay
TEXASVILLE

Perion, Leo
HOME ALONE

Perkins, Elizabeth
LOVE AT LARGE
AVALON

Perkins, Jo
ROBOCOP 2

Perkins, Merle
MERMAIDS

Perman, Miles A.
AVALON

Perri, Paul
DELTA FORCE 2

Perrier, Jean-Francois
VINCENT AND THEO

Perrin, Jacques
CINEMA PARADISO

Perron, Fred
SHORT TIME

Perrone, Marc
LIFE AND NOTHING BUT

Perrot, Francois
LIFE AND NOTHING BUT

Perry, Blayne
METROPOLITAN

Perry, Felton
ROBOCOP 2

Perry, Jaime
JACOB'S LADDER

Perry, Linda
EDWARD SCISSORHANDS

Perry, William R.
PREDATOR 2

Pershing, Steve
DIE HARD 2

Persky, Lisa Jane
LAST OF THE FINEST, THE
VITAL SIGNS

Pesch, Jeanne Savarino
GODFATHER PART III, THE

Pesci, Joe
BETSY'S WEDDING
GOODFELLAS
HOME ALONE

Pescia, Lisa
BODY CHEMISTRY

Pesta, Alice
FOURTH WAR, THE

Peter, Jens
WILD ORCHID

Peters, Bernadette
ALICE
IMPROMPTU

Peters, Elisebeth
ROCKY V

Petersen, William
YOUNG GUNS II

Peterson, Ed
MADHOUSE

Peterson, Robyn
PRETTY WOMAN

Petrucelli, Rick
SHOCK TO THE SYSTEM, A

Petty, Lori
CADILLAC MAN

Pfeiffer, Dedee
RED SURF

Pfeiffer, Lori
ADVENTURES OF FORD FAIRLANE, THE

Pfeiffer, Michelle
RUSSIA HOUSE, THE

Phalen, Robert
IMPULSE

Phelan, Mark
COLD FEET

Phelps, Brian
ROCKY V

Phetoe, David
TUSKS

Philbin, John
MARTIANS GO HOME!

Phillips, Barry
DR. CALIGARI

Phillips, Betty
SHORT TIME

Phillips, Ethan
GREEN CARD

Phillips, Leslie
MOUNTAINS OF THE MOON

Phillips, Lou Diamond
FIRST POWER, THE
SHOW OF FORCE, A
YOUNG GUNS II

Phillips, Neville
MISADVENTURES OF MR. WILT, THE

Phillips, Sarah
HAMLET

Phoenix, River
I LOVE YOU TO DEATH

Pianviti, Beppe
GODFATHER PART III, THE

Picard, Don
MILLER'S CROSSING

Picard, Mary Louise
CAGED IN PARADISO

Picardo, Robert
GREMLINS 2 THE NEW BATCH
TOTAL RECALL

Piccioni, Anna
TORRENTS OF SPRING

Piccoli, Michel
L'ETAT SAUVAGE
MAY FOOLS

Pickens, Jimmy
ROBOCOP 2

Picone, Vito
GOODFELLAS

Piening, Laura
LORDS OF MAGICK, THE

Pierce, Tony
DANCES WITH WOLVES

Pieroni, Donna
EDWARD SCISSORHANDS

Pierre, Reggie
OPPONENT, THE

Pierrot, Frederic
LIFE AND NOTHING BUT

Pierson, Tye
RETURN OF SUPERFLY, THE

Pietropinto, Angela
GOODFELLAS

Pigg, Alexandra
STRAPLESS
CHICAGO JOE AND THE SHOWGIRL

Pignet, Christine
LIFE IS A LONG QUIET RIVER

Pilch, Murray
WILDEST DREAMS

Pillars, Jeffrey
MR. DESTINY

Pillsbury, Drew
LISA

Pinkard, Craig
MARKED FOR DEATH

Pinvidic, Margot
RUSSIA HOUSE, THE

Piper, Lara
ANDY COLBY'S INCREDIBLY AWESOME
ADVENTURE

Pipoly, Danuel
LORD OF THE FLIES

Pisano, Franco
WILD ORCHID

Pistilli, Carl
PREDATOR 2

Pitillo, Maria
WHITE PALACE

Pitt, Chris
LIONHEART

Piven, Jeremy
WHITE PALACE
GRIFTERS, THE

Plana, Tony
HAVANA
ROOKIE, THE
WHY ME?

Platt, Oliver
FLATLINERS
POSTCARDS FROM THE EDGE

Plaza, Begonia
DELTA FORCE 2

Pleasence, Donald
TEN LITTLE INDIANS
RIVER OF DEATH

Plimpton, George
BONFIRE OF THE VANITIES

Plimpton, Martha
STANLEY AND IRIS

Plowright, Joan
I LOVE YOU TO DEATH
AVALON

Plowright, Louise
MACK THE KNIFE

Plum, Paula
MERMAIDS

Plummer, Amanda
JOE VERSUS THE VOLCANO

Plummer, Christopher
WHERE THE HEART IS

Plunket, Robert
WHITE PALACE

Pniewski, Michael
HOUSE PARTY

Podhora, Roman
FOURTH WAR, THE

Poe, Edgar Allan IV
OPPONENT, THE

Poe, Harlan Cary
CADILLAC MAN

Pogue, Ken
WHERE THE HEART IS

Poindexter, Larry
NIGHT EYES

Poitier, Pamela
GHOST DAD

Poitrenaud, Jacques
MAMA, THERE'S A MAN IN YOUR BED

Polak, Margrit
TORN APART

Pole, Edward Tudor
WHITE HUNTER, BLACK HEART

Polemeni, Anthony
GOODFELLAS

Polet, Philippe
MR. FROST

Polis, Joel
ROOKIE, THE

Polito, Jon
FRESHMAN, THE
MILLER'S CROSSING

Polizos, Vic
GRAVEYARD SHIFT

Pollack, Bernie
HAVANA

Pollack, Leonard
PAINT IT BLACK

Pollak, Cheryl
PUMP UP THE VOLUME

Pollak, Kevin
AVALON

Pollard, Michael J.
NIGHT VISITOR

DICK TRACY
I COME IN PEACE
WHY ME?

Ponziani, Antonella
TORRENTS OF SPRING

Pop, Iggy
CRY-BABY
HARDWARE

Pope, Tony
SPACED INVADERS

Popova, Yelena
FREEZE – DIE – COME TO LIFE

Popovich, Reed
HUNT FOR RED OCTOBER, THE

Poppel, Marc
DAMNED RIVER

Poppick, Eric
PROBLEM CHILD

Porsanger, Sverre
PATHFINDER

Port, Debra
EXORCIST III, THE

Porter, Alisan
STELLA
I LOVE YOU TO DEATH

Portnow, Richard
CHATTAHOOCHEE
HAVANA
KINDERGARTEN COP

Posey, Matthew
I COME IN PEACE

Poslof, Jim
REAL BULLETS

Postlewaite, Pete
HAMLET

Potter, Charlie
WITCHES, THE

Potter, Jerry
BIG BAD JOHN
MISERY

Potter, Madeleine
TWO EVIL EYES

Pottinger, Alan
REVERSAL OF FORTUNE

Potts, Annie
TEXASVILLE

Potts, Stephen
LIFE AND NOTHING BUT

Pounder, C.C.H.
POSTCARDS FROM THE EDGE

Poundstone, Paula
HYPERSPACE

Pountney, Charles
INNOCENT VICTIM

Powell, Clifton
HOUSE PARTY

Power, Robin
GRAFFITI BRIDGE

Powers, Alexandra
SONNY BOY

Powers, Anthony
CADILLAC MAN
GOODFELLAS

Powers, Tany Taylor
LEMON SISTERS, THE

Pownall, Leon
BYE BYE BLUES

Poynter, David
I COME IN PEACE

Prebble, Simon
INNOCENT VICTIM

Prentice, Jacki
INHERITOR

Prentiss, Robert
I COME IN PEACE

Presley, Priscilla
ADVENTURES OF FORD FAIRLANE, THE

Press, Barry M.
CLASS OF 1999

Presson, Jason
GREMLINS 2 THE NEW BATCH

Preston, J.A.
FIRE BIRDS
NARROW MARGIN

Preston, William
EXORCIST III, THE

Prica, Alma
MY UNCLE'S LEGACY

Price, Bobby
FLASHBACK

Price, Marianne
STRIKE IT RICH

Price, Tim
BIRD ON A WIRE

Price, Victoria
EDWARD SCISSORHANDS

Price, Vincent
EDWARD SCISSORHANDS

Prickett, Leslie A.
BACK TO THE FUTURE PART III

Priest, Christopher
MISADVENTURES OF MR. WILT. THE

Priest, Martin
PLOT AGAINST HARRY, THE

Prieur, Benjamin
MAY FOOLS

Prieur, Nicolas
MAY FOOLS

Primus, Barry
TORN APART

Prince
GRAFFITI BRIDGE

Prince, William
SPONTANEOUS COMBUSTION
STEEL AND LACE

Pringle, Bryan
THREE MEN AND A LITTLE LADY

Pringle, Danny
LOOK WHO'S TALKING TOO

Priscopie, Sorin Serebe
IMPULSE

Privat, Gilles
MAMA, THERE'S A MAN IN YOUR BED

Prochnow, Jurgen
FOURTH WAR, THE
MAN INSIDE, THE

Prodan, Andrea
BELLY OF AN ARCHITECT, THE

Prophet, Melissa
GOODFELLAS

Prosky, Robert
LOOSE CANNONS
GREMLINS 2 THE NEW BATCH
FUNNY ABOUT LOVE
GREEN CARD

Proudstar, Jon
MADHOUSE

Provenza, Paul
SURVIVAL QUEST

Pruitt, John
NAVY SEALS

Pryor, Liz
GREMLINS 2 THE NEW BATCH

Pryor, Nicholas
BRAIN DEAD
PACIFIC HEIGHTS

Pugh, Willard
ROBOCOP 2

Pugsley, Don
GUMSHOE KID, THE
CHILD'S PLAY 2

Pulice, Tim
PACIFIC HEIGHTS

Pulliam, Darcy
THREE MEN AND A LITTLE LADY

Pullman, Bill
BRAIN DEAD
COLD FEET
SIBLING RIVALRY

Purcell, Beverly
CAGED IN PARADISO

Purchase, Bruce
LIONHEART

Purdee, Nathan
RETURN OF SUPERFLY, THE

Puscas, Jessica
ANDY COLBY'S INCREDIBLY AWESOME
ADVENTURE

Putch, John
MEN AT WORK

Pyper-Ferguson, John
BIRD ON A WIRE

Pythian, John
NUNS ON THE RUN

Quadros, Stephen
DR. CALIGARI

Quadros, Steven
DEMON WIND

Quaid, Dennis
POSTCARDS FROM THE EDGE
COME SEE THE PARADISE

Quaid, Randy
MARTIANS GO HOME!
DAYS OF THUNDER
QUICK CHANGE
TEXASVILLE

Quarry, Robert
ALIENATOR

Quarshie, Hugh
NIGHTBREED

Quattrochi, James
GOODFELLAS

Quayle, Anthony
MAGDALENE

Queensbury, Ann
MISADVENTURES OF MR. WILT, THE

Quick, Diana
MISADVENTURES OF MR. WILT, THE

Quick, Jim E.
CHATTAHOOCHEE

Quigley, Gerry
STANLEY AND IRIS

Quigley, May
GREMLINS 2 THE NEW BATCH

Quigley, Michelle
OPPORTUNITY KNOCKS

Quilter, David
MISADVENTURES OF MR. WILT, THE

Quinlan, Shannon
HOT SPOT, THE

Quinn, Aidan
HANDMAID'S TALE, THE
LEMON SISTERS, THE
AVALON

Quinn, Anthony
REVENGE

Quinn, Ava Eileen
AVALON

Quinn, Charlie
BLADES

Quinn, Daniel
IMPULSE

Quinn, Dayna
REAL BULLETS

Quinn, Geraldine
FRESHMAN, THE

Quinn, J.C.
DAYS OF THUNDER

Quinn, Paul
AVALON

Quinten, Christpher
ROBOCOP 2

Quintero, Joe
JACOB'S LADDER

Quisenberry, Laura
FRIGHT HOUSE

Rabal, Francisco
TIE ME UP! TIE ME DOWN!

Rabasa, Ruben
OPPONENT, THE

Rabett, Catherine
FRANKENSTEIN UNBOUND

Rabinowitz, Max
AWAKENINGS

Rachins, Alan
HEART CONDITION

Rad, Shawnee
LOVE AT LARGE

Radcliffe, Brittany
HOME ALONE

Radcliffe, Porscha
HOME ALONE

Radjune, Rosa
REVENGE

Radonich, Robert
I LOVE YOU TO DEATH

Raffaelli, Bruno
LIFE AND NOTHING BUT

Rafferty, Roy
TIME GUARDIAN, THE

Rager, Jayne
STELLA

Rahr, Jennifer
SKI PATROL

Raia, Omi
WILD ORCHID

Raimi, Sam
MILLER'S CROSSING

Raimi, Theodore
DARKMAN

Rainey, Saffron
COOK, THE THIEF, HIS WIFE & HER
LOVER, THE

Rainone, John
PROBLEM CHILD

Raiter, Frank
Q&A

Rakow, Peter
KINDERGARTEN COP

Ralls, Lee
EDWARD SCISSORHANDS

Ralph, Michael
MARKED FOR DEATH

Ralph, Sheryl Lee
TO SLEEP WITH ANGER

Rammel, James A.
BACK TO THE FUTURE PART III

Ramon, Franck
CYRANO DE BERGERAC

Ramos, Doreen
NARROW MARGIN

Ramos, Luis
RETURN OF SUPERFLY, THE

Ramos, Oscar
BIRD ON A WIRE

Ramsey, Anne
HOMER & EDDIE

Ramsey, Remak
MR. AND MRS. BRIDGE

Rand, Corey
PREDATOR 2

Randal, Jason
PRETTY WOMAN

Randall, Pete
ROOKIE, THE

Randall, Tony
GREMLINS 2 THE NEW BATCH

Randazzon, Steve
AWAKENINGS

Randle, Theresa
HEART CONDITION
GUARDIAN, THE
KING OF NEW YORK

Randolph, John
SIBLING RIVALRY

Randolph, Randy
CHATTAHOOCHEE

Randolph, Ty
CAGED FURY

Rangel, Maria
IMPULSE
FULL FATHOM FIVE

Rankin, Jill
CHATTAHOOCHEE

Ransom, Tim
VITAL SIGNS

Rapley, John
WHITE HUNTER, BLACK HEART

Rapoport, Audrey
I LOVE YOU TO DEATH

Rascal
SKI PATROL

Rasche, David
WEDDING BAND

Rashed, Nimer
IMPROMPTU

Raskin, Jessica
CRY-BABY

Ratliff, Garette Patrick
ARACHNOPHOBIA

Rattee, Paul
RUSSIA HOUSE, THE

Rattray, Devin
HOME ALONE

Rattray, Heather
BASKETCASE 2

Rawlins, Adrian
MOUNTAINS OF THE MOON

Ray, Aldo
BLOOD RED

Raye, Bill
MILLER'S CROSSING

Rayl, Missy
MONSTER HIGH

Raymond, Bill
ME AND HIM
QUICK CHANGE

Raymond, Charles
FIRST POWER, THE

Raymond, Jack
STRIKE IT RICH
RUSSIA HOUSE, THE

Rayner, Martin
PROBLEM CHILD

Read, Michaele D.
TIME GUARDIAN, THE

Ready, Carol A.
ROCKY V

Reardon, Lindsey
RIVER OF DEATH

Reardon, Lyndsey
BURNDOWN

Reaves, Amber
KINDERGARTEN COP

Reaves, Tiffany
KINDERGARTEN COP

Rebhorn, James
DESPERATE HOURS

Reconti, Paco
GODFATHER PART III, THE

Redbow, Chief Buddy
YOUNG GUNS II

Redfield, Dennis
PROBLEM CHILD

Redford, Ian
THREE MEN AND A LITTLE LADY

Redford, Robert
HAVANA

Redglare, Rockets
IN THE SPIRIT
FORCE OF CIRCUMSTANCE

Redpath, Ralph
LOOSE CANNONS

Redwine, Symone
PROBLEM CHILD

Reed, B.J.
STANLEY AND IRIS

Reed, Jeffrey
PREDATOR 2

Reed, Kesha
FLATLINERS

Reed, Pamela
CHATTAHOOCHEE
CADILLAC MAN
KINDERGARTEN COP

Reed, Penelope Jane
FAR OUT MAN

Rees, Lanny
CLASS OF 1999

Rees, Roger
MOUNTAINS OF THE MOON

Reese, Pat
NIGHT OF THE LIVING DEAD

Reese, Roxanne
WITHOUT YOU, I'M NOTHING

Reeves, Keanu
I LOVE YOU TO DEATH
TUNE IN TOMORROW

Reevis, Steve
DANCES WITH WOLVES

Regent, Benoit
FLAME IN MY HEART, A

Reger, John Patrick
OVER EXPOSED

Register, Meg
BACKSTREET DREAMS

Reichardt, Kelly
UNBELIEVABLE TRUTH, THE

Reid, Christopher
HOUSE PARTY

Reid, Kate
BYE BYE BLUES

Reid, Michael Earl
ME AND HIM

Reid, Tim
FOURTH WAR, THE

Reilly, J.D.
ADVENTURES OF FORD FAIRLANE, THE

Reilly, John C.
DAYS OF THUNDER
STATE OF GRACE

Reilly, Luke
BYE BYE BLUES

Reiner, Richard
FUNLAND

Reiner, Rob
POSTCARDS FROM THE EDGE

Reiner, Tracy
MASQUE OF THE RED DEATH
PRETTY WOMAN

Reinhardt, Ray
HUNT FOR RED OCTOBER, THE
GUARDIAN, THE

Reinhold, Judge
ROSALIE GOES SHOPPING
DADDY'S DYIN'. . . WHO'S GOT THE WILL?

Reis, Terrence
AMERICAN EAGLE

Reiser, Paul
CRAZY PEOPLE

Reitman, Jason
KINDERGARTEN COP

Relph, Emma
WITCHES, THE

Remar, James
TALES FROM THE DARKSIDE: THE MOVIE

Remotti, Remo
GODFATHER PART III, THE

Remsberg, Calvin
PRETTY WOMAN

Remsen, Bert
DADDY'S DYIN'. . . WHO'S GOT THE WILL?
DICK TRACY
PEACEMAKER
JEZEBEL'S KISS

Renteria, Joe
MARKED FOR DEATH

Repo Martell, Liisa
AMERICAN BOYFRIENDS

Restivo, Steve
PRETTY WOMAN

Reusenko, Sergei
RUSSIA HOUSE, THE

Revill, Clive
MACK THE KNIFE

Rey, Antonia
JACOB'S LADDER

Rey, Reynaldo
FAR OUT MAN

Reyes, Julian
DIE HARD 2
PREDATOR 2

Reyes, Lico
PROBLEM CHILD

Reyes, Richard
ROBOCOP 2

Reyes, Rina
DEMONSTONE

Reynal, Madeleine
DR. CALIGARI

Reynolds, Burt
MODERN LOVE

Reynolds, Colin
MONSTER HIGH

Reynolds, Harriet
STRIKE IT RICH

Reynolds, James Ellis
JACOB'S LADDER

Rhames, Ving
JACOB'S LADDER

Rhine, Bert
FIRE BIRDS

Rhodes, Andrew
NARROW MARGIN

Rhys, Paul
VINCENT AND THEO

Rhys-Davies, John
TUSKS

Ribalta, Jose Nino
OPPONENT, THE

Ribeiro, Yomiko
WILD ORCHID

Ribiero, Joe
AMERICAN EAGLE

Ricci, Christina
MERMAIDS

Rice, Brett
EDWARD SCISSORHANDS

Rice, John
FORBIDDEN DANCE, THE
INHERITOR

Rice, Warren
ARACHNOPHOBIA

Rich, Allan
BETSY'S WEDDING

Richard, Firmine
MAMA, THERE'S A MAN IN YOUR BED

Richard, Junior
HIT LIST

Richards, Ariana
TREMORS

Richards, Arianna
SPACED INVADERS

Richards, Arleigh
JACOB'S LADDER

Richards, Beah
HOMER & EDDIE

Richards, Charles David
PREDATOR 2
THREE MEN AND A LITTLE LADY

Richards, Michael
PROBLEM CHILD

Richardson, Jay
ALIENATOR

Richardson, Lee
Q&A
EXORCIST III, THE

Richardson, Miranda
TWISTED OBSESSION

Richardson, Natasha
HANDMAID'S TALE, THE

Richardson, Sy
MEN AT WORK
STREET ASYLUM

Richardson, Vicki
FRIGHT HOUSE

Richmond, Branscombe
HARD TO KILL

Richmond, Deon
MO' BETTER BLUES

Richwood, Patrick
STREETS
PRETTY WOMAN

Rickman, Alan
QUIGLEY DOWN UNDER

Riddle, Hal
SPACED INVADERS

Riegert, Peter
SHOCK TO THE SYSTEM, A

Rifkin, Richard
LORDS OF MAGICK, THE

Riley, Timothy G.
FLASHBACK

Rimoux, Alain
CYRANO DE BERGERAC

Ringwald, Molly
STRIKE IT RICH
BETSY'S WEDDING

Rionda, Sasha
TOTAL RECALL

Rios, Javier
Q&A

Rippy, Leon
LOOSE CANNONS
YOUNG GUNS II
HOT SPOT, THE

Riser, Ronn
HOUSE PARTY

Rist, Robbie
TEENAGE MUTANT NINJA TURTLES

Ritter, John
PROBLEM CHILD

Rivera, Geraldo
BONFIRE OF THE VANITIES

Rivera, Rene
ME AND HIM

Rivers, Leslie
GUMSHOE KID, THE

Rivers, Lisa
BIG DIS, THE

Rivers, Victor
HAVANA

Rizzo, Federico
ICICLE THIEF, THE

Roa, Anabelle
PRIMARY TARGET

Roach, Frank R.
HEART CONDITION

Roach, Jennifer
LOOSE CANNONS

Roat, Richard
MURDER BY NUMBERS

Robards, Jason Jr.
QUICK CHANGE

Robbin, Catherine
STELLA

Robbins, Jane Marla
ARACHNOPHOBIA
ROCKY V

Robbins, Lisa
STREET ASYLUM

Robbins, Rex
STELLA

Robbins, Tim
CADILLAC MAN
JACOB'S LADDER

Robert, Jeffrey
STRIKE IT RICH

Roberts, Cindy
ROCKY V

Roberts, Conrad
GREEN CARD

Roberts, Douglas
POSTCARDS FROM THE EDGE

Roberts, Eric
BLOOD RED

Roberts, Jay Jr.
AFTERSHOCK

Roberts, Jessica
JACOB'S LADDER

Roberts, Julia
PRETTY WOMAN
BLOOD RED
FLATLINERS

Roberts, Russell J.
SHORT TIME

Roberts, Tanya
NIGHT EYES

Roberts, William
NAVY SEALS

Roberts, Wink
SKI PATROL

Robertson, William Preston
MILLER'S CROSSING

Robertson, Anthony
DR. CALIGARI

Robertson, Chris
CHATTAHOOCHEE

Robertson, R.J.
HAUNTING OF MORELLA, THE

Robertson, Rachel
MACK THE KNIFE

Robertson, Tim
TIME GUARDIAN, THE

Robillard, Kim
COME SEE THE PARADISE

Robins, Laila
WELCOME HOME, ROXY CARMICHAEL

Robinson, Alexia
TOTAL RECALL

Robinson, Claudia
PAINT IT BLACK

Robinson, Doug
VITAL SIGNS

Robinson, Hank
TAKING CARE OF BUSINESS

Robinson, Matthew
MEN AT WORK

Robinson, Scot Anthony
MO' BETTER BLUES

Robledo, Rafael H.
DARKMAN

Robson, Wayne
BYE BYE BLUES
RESCUERS DOWN UNDER, THE

Robutti, Enzo
GODFATHER PART III, THE

Rochelle, Bob
REAL BULLETS

Rock, Kevin
RETURN OF SUPERFLY, THE

Rockas, Anjelique
WITCHES, THE

Rockenbaugh, Zane
LORD OF THE FLIES

Rocket, Charles
HONEYMOON ACADEMY
DANCES WITH WOLVES

Rockwell, Sam
TEENAGE MUTANT NINJA TURTLES
LAST EXIT TO BROOKLYN

Rodgers, Anton
IMPROMPTU

Rodgers, David Stuart
WITHOUT YOU, I'M NOTHING

Rodgers, T.
TAKING CARE OF BUSINESS

Rodriguez, David Jose
HAVANA

Rodriguez, Franklin
HAVANA

Rodriguez, Marco
ROOKIE, THE

Rodriguez, Valente
IMPULSE

Rodriquez, Rod
Q&A

Rodriquez, Trini
REVENGE

Roe, Matt
CHILD'S PLAY 2

Roeves, Maurice
HIDDEN AGENDA

Rogers, Edward III
Q&A

Rogers, Gary D.
COLD FEET

Rogers, John
TEENAGE MUTANT NINJA TURTLES

Rogers, Mimi
DESPERATE HOURS

Rogers, Tristan
RESCUERS DOWN UNDER, THE

Rogerson, Bob
MERMAIDS

Rogerson, Iain
MACK THE KNIFE

Rohl, Michelle
SKI PATROL

Roitblat, Bob
LISA

Roizman, Owen
HAVANA

Rojo, Daniel
REVENGE

Rolf, Frederick
Q&A

Rolston, Mark
IMPULSE
ROBOCOP 2
SURVIVAL QUEST

Roma
KINDERGARTEN COP

Romano, Andy
PUMP UP THE VOLUME

PAINT IT BLACK

Romano, Tony
I LOVE YOU TO DEATH

Romantowska, Anna
INTERROGATION, THE

Ronzal, Ken
LORDS OF MAGICK, THE

Rooker, Michael
HENRY: PORTRAIT OF A SERIAL KILLER
DAYS OF THUNDER

Rooney, Carl
MILLER'S CROSSING

Root, Stephen
STANLEY AND IRIS
KINDERGARTEN COP

Roper-Knight, Courtney
LIONHEART

Rosa, Ricky
PRESUMED INNOCENT

Rosado, Raul
HAVANA

Rosales, Thomas Jr.
IMPULSE

Rosales, Tommy
ROBOCOP 2

Rosario, Willie
STELLA

Rosborough, Patty
JACOB'S LADDER

Rose, Deborah
SKI PATROL

Rose, Emily A.
LEMON SISTERS, THE

Rose, J. Harden
METROPOLITAN

Rose, Nicky
GREMLINS 2 THE NEW BATCH

Rose, Roger
SKI PATROL

Roselius, John
STATE OF GRACE

Rosen, Marissa
KINDERGARTEN COP

Rosenberg, Alan
IMPULSE

Rosenblum, Joseph
WHITE PALACE

Rosencrantz, Zachary
HARD TO KILL

Rosenfeld, Moishe
AVALON

Rosengren, Clive
TAX SEASON

Ross, Annie
BASKETCASE 2
PUMP UP THE VOLUME

Ross, Hugh
NIGHTBREED

Ross, Jason
LAST OF THE FINEST, THE

Ross, Justin
QUICK CHANGE

Ross, Mark
OPPORTUNITY KNOCKS

Ross, Monty
MO' BETTER BLUES

Ross, Neil
GREMLINS 2 THE NEW BATCH
DICK TRACY

Ross, Ramsay
FULL FATHOM FIVE

Ross, Richard Lee
GAME, THE

Ross, Sandi
WHERE THE HEART IS

Ross, Shane
PRETTY WOMAN

Ross, Willie
STRIKE IT RICH
COOK, THE THIEF, HIS WIFE & HER
LOVER, THE

Ross-Azikiwe, Jason
DIE HARD 2

Rosselli, Vincent
INHERITOR

Rossellini, Isabella
WILD AT HEART

Rossi, Leo
HIT LIST

Rossi, Luke
I LOVE YOU TO DEATH

Rossovich, Rick
NAVY SEALS
PAINT IT BLACK

Rossummoen, Sverre
WITCHES, THE

Rotblatt, Janet
GUMSHOE KID, THE

Roth, Cecilia
LABYRINTH OF PASSION

Roth, George
RUSSIA HOUSE, THE

Roth, Joseph
DIE HARD 2

Roth, Tim
COOK, THE THIEF, HIS WIFE & HER
LOVER, THE
VINCENT AND THEO

Roundtree, Richard
NIGHT VISITOR

Rourke, Mickey
WILD ORCHID
DESPERATE HOURS

Rouse, Hugh
BURNDOWN

Roussillon, Baptiste
CYRANO DE BERGERAC

Rowan, Edward
Q&A

Rowe, Douglas
IMPULSE

Rowe, Hansford
FIRST POWER, THE
BONFIRE OF THE VANITIES

Rowe, Micah
LAST OF THE FINEST, THE

Rowe, Robert
DESPERATE HOURS

Roxas, Manny
PRIMARY TARGET

Roy, Christian
CYRANO DE BERGERAC

Roy, Edward
FRESHMAN, THE

Roy, Rob
SHORT TIME

Rozen, Robert
NARROW MARGIN

Rubens, Jeff
MONSTER HIGH

Rubenstein, Phil
ROBOCOP 2

Rubes, Jan
COURAGE MOUNTAIN
BLOOD RELATIONS

Rubin, Lisa
MADHOUSE

Rubin, Rick
MEN DON'T LEAVE

Rubinek, Frania
AVALON

Rubinek, Israel
AVALON

Rubinek, Saul
BONFIRE OF THE VANITIES

Rubinow, John
DIE HARD 2

Rubio, Jorge Pascual
REVENGE

Ruby, Mauricio
REVENGE

Ruck, Alan
YOUNG GUNS II

Rucker, Bo
PRESUMED INNOCENT

Rucki, Anne
FLAME IN MY HEART, A

Rudder, David
WILD ORCHID

Rudin, Stuart
QUICK CHANGE

Rudnick, Barbara
TIME TROOPERS

Rudoy, Joshua
FLATLINERS

Ruehl, Mercedes
CRAZY PEOPLE

Ruff, Kerry
TAX SEASON

Ruffin, Don
IMPULSE

Ruiz, Alex
Q&A

Ruiz, Mia
DEMON WIND

Rule, Gary
LORD OF THE FLIES

Runacre, Jenny
WITCHES, THE

Runnels, Tameka
KINDERGARTEN COP

Running Fox, Joseph
BLOOD RED

Ruprecht, David
TAKING CARE OF BUSINESS

Ruscio, Al
BLOOD RED
GODFATHER PART III, THE

Ruscio, Elizabeth
DESPERATE HOURS
JEZEBEL'S KISS

Rush, Peter
COOK, THE THIEF, HIS WIFE & HER
LOVER, THE

Ruspoli, Dado
GODFATHER PART III, THE

Russell, Barbara E.
NARROW MARGIN

Russell, Bing
DICK TRACY

Russell, Karen
DICK TRACY
HAVANA

Russell, Ken
RUSSIA HOUSE, THE

Russell, Kimberly
GHOST DAD

Russell, Paul
COOK, THE THIEF, HIS WIFE & HER
LOVER, THE

Russell, Sebastian
WITHOUT YOU, I'M NOTHING

Russell, Theresa
IMPULSE

Russell, William
KILL-OFF, THE

Russo, Daniel
LIFE AND NOTHING BUT

Russo, Gianni
FRESHMAN, THE

Russo, Jonathon
INHERITOR

Russo, Michele
GODFATHER PART III, THE

Russo, Mike
DEAD AIM

Russo, Rene
MR. DESTINY

Ruth, Rebecca
TOTAL RECALL

Rutherford, Nicolas
PACIFIC HEIGHTS

Rutherford, Peter
MACK THE KNIFE

Rutherford, Richard Lee
STAR QUEST: BEYOND THE RISING MOON

Rutledge-Parisi, Allison
METROPOLITAN

Ruttan, Susan
FUNNY ABOUT LOVE

Ryall, David
MISADVENTURES OF MR. WILT, THE
RUSSIA HOUSE, THE

Ryan, Frank P.
GREMLINS 2 THE NEW BATCH

Ryan, Jim
HOME ALONE

Ryan, John P.
CLASS OF 1999
DELTA FORCE 2

Ryan, Meg
JOE VERSUS THE VOLCANO

Ryan, Ron
QUICK CHANGE

Ryan, Stephanie
FRANKENHOOKER

Ryan, Thomas
MURDER BY NUMBERS

Ryazanova, Raisa
RUSSIA HOUSE, THE

Rydall, Derek
NIGHT VISITOR

Rydell, Christopher
UNDER THE BOARDWALK
SIDE OUT

Rydell, Mark
HAVANA

Ryder, Michael Allen
SURVIVAL QUEST

Ryder, Winona
WELCOME HOME, ROXY CARMICHAEL
MERMAIDS
EDWARD SCISSORHANDS

Ryen, Adam
CHILD'S PLAY 2
RESCUERS DOWN UNDER, THE

Ryhs, Paul
LIONHEART

Ryu, Chishu
DREAMS

Ryusaki, Bill M.
COME SEE THE PARADISE

Saachiko
GREMLINS 2 THE NEW BATCH
COME SEE THE PARADISE

Sabatini, Rick
STAR QUEST: BEYOND THE RISING MOON

Sabel, Valeria
GODFATHER PART III, THE

Sabela, Simon
GODS MUST BE CRAZY II, THE

Sacchi, Robert
FUNLAND
DIE HARD 2

Sacco, John
ME AND HIM

Sacco, Lawrence
GOODFELLAS

Sacha, Orlando
FULL FATHOM FIVE

Sacilotto, Massimo
ICICLE THIEF, THE

Sacks, Benjamin
C'EST LA VIE

Sadanaga, Satoshi
HEAVEN AND EARTH

Sadler, Martin
TALL GUY, THE

Sadler, William
HARD TO KILL
DIE HARD 2
HOT SPOT, THE

Sadza, Sekai
TUSKS

Safonova, Elena
TAXI BLUES

Sagal, Elizabeth
SKINHEADS – THE SECOND COMING OF
    HATE

Sage, Bill
UNBELIEVABLE TRUTH, THE

Sagebrecht, Marianne
ROSALIE GOES SHOPPING

Sagnier, Ludivine
CYRANO DE BERGERAC

Sahagun, Elana
MARKED FOR DEATH

Sahagun, Elena
CAGED FURY

Said, Fatima
MOUNTAINS OF THE MOON

St. George, Clement
LORDS OF MAGICK, THE

St. James, Judy
STUFF STEPHANIE IN THE INCINERATOR

Saint James, Lou
VITAL SIGNS

St. John, Marco
STATE OF GRACE

St. Peter, Renee
LORDS OF MAGICK, THE

Saint, Jan
JACOB'S LADDER

Saint-Macary, Hubert
MAY FOOLS

Sainte-Marie, Diane
GREMLINS 2 THE NEW BATCH

Saito, James
TEENAGE MUTANT NINJA TURTLES

Sakabe, Osamu
MR. DESTINY

Sakai, Megumi
DREAMS

Sakai, Sachio
DREAMS

Sakata, Shoichiro
DREAMS

Sakurai, Masaru
DREAMS

Saldana, Theresa
ANGEL TOWN

Salgado, Leo
VERONICO CRUZ

Sali, Elvira
TIME OF THE GYPSIES

Salinger, Diane
ALICE

Salkey, Jason
MEMPHIS BELLE
RUSSIA HOUSE, THE

Salomao, Marina
WILD ORCHID

Salort, Michael
GREMLINS 2 THE NEW BATCH

Salter, Henry
TIME GUARDIAN, THE

Salviat, Catherine
MAMA, THERE'S A MAN IN YOUR BED

Samms, Emma
SHRIMP ON THE BARBIE, THE

Sampaio, Gilmar
WILD ORCHID

Sampson, Robert
DARK SIDE OF THE MOON
ROBOT JOX

San Giacomo, Laura
PRETTY WOMAN
VITAL SIGNS
QUIGLEY DOWN UNDER

Sanchez, Juan
WHERE THE HEART IS

Sanchez, Paul
NAVY SEALS

Sander, Casey
SPACED INVADERS
PREDATOR 2

Sanders, Alvin
SHORT TIME

Sanders, Damon
TIME GUARDIAN, THE

Sanders, Henry G.
MAN INSIDE, THE

Sanders, Jay O.
MR. DESTINY

Sanders, Peppi
MADHOUSE

Sanderson, William
DEAD AIM

Sandlund, Debra
MURDER BY NUMBERS

Sandoval, Miguel
GUMSHOE KID, THE

Sandre, Bel
MURDER BY NUMBERS

Sands, Julian
ARACHNOPHOBIA
IMPROMPTU

Sands, Peggy F.
FAR OUT MAN

Sanet, Brian
CADILLAC MAN

Sangare, Bakary
MAHABHARATA, THE

Santiago, Edgar
DEMONSTONE

Santiago, Elliot
QUICK CHANGE

Santiago, Socorro
SHOCK TO THE SYSTEM, A

Santos, Joe
REVENGE

Santos, Karen A.
STUFF STEPHANIE IN THE INCINERATOR

Sanvido, Guy
STANLEY AND IRIS

Sarabhar, Mallika
MAHABHARATA, THE

Sarandon, Chris
FORCED MARCH

Sarandon, Susan
WHITE PALACE

Sarchielli, Massimo
TORRENTS OF SPRING

Sargent, Dick
MURDER BY NUMBERS

Sartain, Gailard
LOVE AT LARGE
ERNEST GOES TO JAIL
GRIFTERS, THE

Sartor, Anya
WILD ORCHID

Sartor, Fabio
BELLY OF AN ARCHITECT, THE

Sasaki, Makio
COME SEE THE PARADISE

Sasaki, Masaaki
DREAMS

Sasso, Dick
MEN DON'T LEAVE

Satake, Nagamitsu
DREAMS

Sato, Toshio
CADILLAC MAN

Sauer, Gary
UNBELIEVABLE TRUTH, THE

Saul, Christopher
MISADVENTURES OF MR. WILT, THE

Sauls, Dwight
OPPONENT, THE

Saunders, Enid
SHORT TIME

Saunders, J. Jay
HOUSE PARTY

Savage, John
GODFATHER PART III, THE

Savage, Nick
IMPULSE

Savan, Glenn
WHITE PALACE

Savant, Doug
RED SURF
PAINT IT BLACK

Savident, John
MOUNTAINS OF THE MOON
IMPROMPTU

Saviola, Camille
BETSY'S WEDDING

Savoy, Suzanne
I COME IN PEACE

Sawalha, Nadim
LIONHEART

Sawayama, Yuji
DREAMS

Sawtelle, Kym
DEMON WIND

Sawyer, Connie
BONFIRE OF THE VANITIES

Sax, Gary
HEART CONDITION

Saxon, Edward
MIAMI BLUES

Saxon, John
AFTERSHOCK
BLOOD SALVAGE

Saylor, Stephen
BLOOD RELATIONS

Scacchi, Greta
PRESUMED INNOCENT

Scaife, Sara Jane
FIELD, THE

Scandiuzzi, Gian-Carlo
BONFIRE OF THE VANITIES

Scanlan, John
GREEN CARD

Scannell, Kevin
DON'T TELL HER IT'S ME

Scarpa, Renato
ICICLE THIEF, THE

Schacht, Sam
SHOCK TO THE SYSTEM, A

Schack, Kevin
METROPOLITAN

Schaefer, Todd
NOBODY'S PERFECT

Schapova, Elena
TORRENTS OF SPRING

Scharffenberg, Svein
PATHFINDER

Schecter, Al
TAX SEASON

Scheider, Roy
FOURTH WAR, THE
RUSSIA HOUSE, THE

Scheine, Raynor
GHOST DAD

Schell, Maurice
Q&A

Schell, Maximilian
FRESHMAN, THE

Schell, Ronnie
JETSONS: THE MOVIE

Schiavelli, Vincent
HOMER & EDDIE
GHOST
COLD FEET

Schiff, Richard
YOUNG GUNS II

Schmidt, Folkert
I COME IN PEACE

Schnabel, Stefan
GREEN CARD

Schnauder, John Jr.
MILLER'S CROSSING

Schneider, Carol
BLUE STEEL
JACOB'S LADDER

Schneider, Dan
HAPPY TOGETHER

Schneider, Jana
ME AND HIM

Schoeffling, Michael
LONGTIME COMPANION
MERMAIDS

Schofield, David
INNOCENT VICTIM

Scholl, George
FOURTH WAR, THE

Schoppert, Bill
LORD OF THE FLIES

Schott, Bob
AFTERSHOCK

Schramm, David
SHOCK TO THE SYSTEM, A

Schreiber, Joel S.
METROPOLITAN

Schuck, John
DICK TRACY

Schull, Richard B.
TUNE IN TOMORROW

Schultes, Willi
NASTY GIRL, THE

Schultze, Paul
UNBELIEVABLE TRUTH, THE

Schulze, Christina
MURDER BY NUMBERS

Schumann, Katja
ALICE

Schwab, Lana
REPOSSESSED

Schwartz, Andrei
MY 20TH CENTURY

Schwartz, Theo
ARACHNOPHOBIA

Schwarzenegger, Arnold
TOTAL RECALL
KINDERGARTEN COP

Schwickert, Vincent
MEN IN LOVE

Sciore, Jean-Claude
HOME ALONE

Sciorra, Anabella
INTERNAL AFFAIRS
REVERSAL OF FORTUNE

Sciorra, Annabella
CADILLAC MAN

Scofield, Paul
HAMLET

Scoggins, Tracy
GUMSHOE KID, THE

Scollay, Fred J.
STANLEY AND IRIS

Scorpio, Jay
ARACHNOPHOBIA

Scorsese, Martin
DREAMS

Scorsese, Catherine
GOODFELLAS
GODFATHER PART III, THE

Scorsese, Charles
GOODFELLAS

Scott, Barry
ERNEST GOES TO JAIL

Scott, Campbell
LONGTIME COMPANION
SHELTERING SKY, THE

Scott, Cedric
GHOST DAD

Scott, Donovan
BACK TO THE FUTURE PART III

Scott, George C.
EXORCIST III, THE
RESCUERS DOWN UNDER, THE

Scott, Judith
OPPORTUNITY KNOCKS

Scott, Kimberly
DOWNTOWN
FLATLINERS

Scott, Rande
DIE HARD 2

Scott, Timothy
CHATTAHOOCHEE

Scott, Victoria
BLADES

Scrivano, Enrica Maria
BELLY OF AN ARCHITECT, THE

Scudiero, Andrew
GOODFELLAS

Scultz, Albert
WHERE THE HEART IS

Seacer, Levi Jr.
GRAFFITI BRIDGE

Seacombe, Louise
LIONHEART

Seagal, Steven
HARD TO KILL
MARKED FOR DEATH

Seagrove, Jenny
GUARDIAN, THE

Seal, Elizabeth
MACK THE KNIFE

Seale, Douglas
MR. DESTINY
RESCUERS DOWN UNDER, THE

Sears, Ian
COOK, THE THIEF, HIS WIFE & HER
LOVER, THE

Sears, Teresa
NUTCRACKER PRINCE, THE

Sederholm, David
HUNT FOR RED OCTOBER, THE

Sedgwick, Kyra
MR. AND MRS. BRIDGE

Sedgwick, Robert
TALES FROM THE DARKSIDE: THE MOVIE
TUNE IN TOMORROW

Seely, Tim
STRIKE IT RICH

Segal, Josh
COUPE DE VILLE

Segall, Pamela
ADVENTURES OF FORD FAIRLANE, THE

Segda, Dorotha
MY 20TH CENTURY

Seibel, Mary
MEN DON'T LEAVE

Seide, Stuart
IMPROMPTU

Seidner, Justin
ROBOCOP 2

Seigal, Harvey
WILDEST DREAMS

Seils, Adam
FLASHBACK

Seitz, John
FORCED MARCH
PRESUMED INNOCENT

Seka
MEN DON'T LEAVE

Seki, Dann
SAVAGE BEACH

Selby, Hubert Jr.
LAST EXIT TO BROOKLYN

Selby, Shirley Anne
NUNS ON THE RUN

Self, Doug
MEN IN LOVE

Selleck, Tom
QUIGLEY DOWN UNDER
THREE MEN AND A LITTLE LADY

Seltzer, Robert
ROCKY V

Sena, Rudy
YOUNG GUNS II

Seneca, Joe
MO' BETTER BLUES

Seremba, George
WHERE THE HEART IS

Sereys, Jaques
L'ETAT SAUVAGE

Serna, Assumpta
WILD ORCHID

Serna, Pepe
POSTCARDS FROM THE EDGE
ROOKIE, THE

Serra, Raymond
TEENAGE MUTANT NINJA TURTLES

Serrano, Julieta
TIE ME UP! TIE ME DOWN!

Serre, Henri
MR. FROST

Serreau, Nicolas
MAMA, THERE'S A MAN IN YOUR BED

Serret, John
STRIKE IT RICH

Serrone, Christopher
GOODFELLAS

Seth, Roshan
MOUNTAINS OF THE MOON

Severance, Joan
BIRD ON A WIRE

Seweryn, Andrzej
MAHABHARATA, THE

Shabba-Doo
LAMBADA

Shaffer, Paul
LOOK WHO'S TALKING TOO

Shafran, Philip
LOOSE CANNONS

Shah, Naseeruddin
PERFECT MURDER, THE

Shait, Brian
AVALON

Shalhoub, Tony
QUICK CHANGE

Shallo, Karen
ME AND HIM

Shane, Michael
SAVAGE BEACH

Shannon, James
BLUE STEEL

Shannon, Jamie
STELLA

Shannon, Tara
FUNNY ABOUT LOVE

Sharp, Thom
TAKING CARE OF BUSINESS

Sharp, Thom J.
REPOSSESSED

Shatner, Melanie
FIRST POWER, THE

Shauffler, Florence
PROBLEM CHILD

Shaver, Helen
INNOCENT VICTIM

Shaw, Dianne B.
WHITE GIRL, THE
HOME ALONE

Shaw, Fiona
MOUNTAINS OF THE MOON
THREE MEN AND A LITTLE LADY

Shaw, Vanessa
GAME, THE

Shawn, Eric
GREMLINS 2 THE NEW BATCH

Shawn, Erick
GAME, THE

Shea, Robert
LORD OF THE FLIES

Sheedy, Ally
BETSY'S WEDDING

Sheehan, Michael
ROCKY V

Sheehy, Joan
FIELD, THE

Sheeler, Sandra
ADVENTURES OF FORD FAIRLANE, THE

Sheen, Charlie
COURAGE MOUNTAIN
NAVY SEALS
MEN AT WORK
ROOKIE, THE

Sheffer, Craig
NIGHTBREED

Sheldon, Don
COUPE DE VILLE

Sheldon, Joe
EDWARD SCISSORHANDS

Shellabarger, Jill
OPPORTUNITY KNOCKS

Shellen, Stephen
DAMNED RIVER

Shellhammer, Albert
NIGHT OF THE LIVING DEAD

Shelly, Adrienne
UNBELIEVABLE TRUTH, THE

Shenk, Samantha
AVALON

Shepard, Hilary
PEACEMAKER

Shepard, Jewel
HOLLYWOOD HOT TUBS II: EDUCATING
CRYSTAL

Shepherd, Cybill
TEXASVILLE

ALICE

Shepherd, John
HUNT FOR RED OCTOBER, THE

Shepherd, Suzanne
GOODFELLAS
JACOB'S LADDER

Sheppard, Delia
ADVENTURES OF FORD FAIRLANE, THE
ROCKY V

Sheppard, W. Morgan
WILD AT HEART

Sheptekita, Valery
LONELY WOMAN SEEKS LIFE COMPANION

Sher, Brian
AVALON

Sheridan, Jamey
STANLEY AND IRIS
QUICK CHANGE

Sheridan, Jo
MR. FROST

Sherman, Don
ROCKY V

Sherman, Patty
AVALON

Sherrill, David
ROOKIE, THE

Sherwood, Anthony
HOSTILE TAKEOVER

Sheybal, Vladek
STRIKE IT RICH

Shibuya, Mitsuru
DREAMS

Shields, Brooke
BACKSTREET DREAMS

Shigemizu, Naoto
DREAMS

Shimizu, Keenan
CADILLAC MAN

Shimoda, Shaun
PROBLEM CHILD

Shimono, Sab
PRESUMED INNOCENT
COME SEE THE PARADISE

Shimura, Yukie
DREAMS

Shimuzu, Keenan
COME SEE THE PARADISE

Shipley, Sandra
MERMAIDS

Shirahama, Kenzo
DREAMS

Shire, Talia
GODFATHER PART III, THE
ROCKY V

Shirley, Adrian
TIME GUARDIAN, THE

Shirley, Clinton Austin
ROBOCOP 2

Shively, Debby
MARKED FOR DEATH

Shockley, William
ADVENTURES OF FORD FAIRLANE, THE
STREET ASYLUM

Shook, Reid "Pete"
COUPE DE VILLE

Shore, Pauly
WEDDING BAND

Shorty, Guitar
FAR OUT MAN

Shoshan, Illana
FIRE BIRDS

Shower, Kathy
BEDROOM EYES II

Shrider, Kay
FEUD, THE

Shropshire, Anne
GREEN CARD

Shub, Vivienne
CRY-BABY

Shue, Elisabeth
BACK TO THE FUTURE PART III

Shulman, Constance
MEN DON'T LEAVE

Shulman, Rick
ERNEST GOES TO JAIL

Sibanda, Maita
DAMNED RIVER

Sidirov, Vladimir
RUSSIA HOUSE, THE

Siegel, Harvey
BEDROOM EYES II

Siegl, Dietrich
TIME TROOPERS

Signer, Gordon
FOURTH WAR, THE

Signorelli, Tom
DICK TRACY

Sikking, James B.
NARROW MARGIN

Silberstein, Doug
FRESHMAN, THE

Siler, Rick
GAME, THE

Siller, Morag
MEMPHIS BELLE

Silva, Billy
LOVE AT LARGE

Silva, Henry
DICK TRACY

Silver, Norm
FLASHBACK

Silver, Ron
BLUE STEEL
REVERSAL OF FORTUNE

Silveri, Ivano
NIGHT OF THE SHARKS

Silverman, Julie
HEART CONDITION

Silverstein, Mark
YOUNG GUNS II

Silvestri, Larry
BLUE STEEL
GOODFELLAS

Sim, Matthew
LIONHEART

Simek, Vasek
HAVANA
GREEN CARD

Simmons, Dion
JACOB'S LADDER

Simmons, Gene
RED SURF

Simmons, Kenneth
CADILLAC MAN

Simms, Jane
QUICK CHANGE

Simon, Sylvie
TOO BEAUTIFUL FOR YOU

Simotes, Tony
PACIFIC HEIGHTS

Simpson, Don
DAYS OF THUNDER
YOUNG GUNS II

Simpson, Lee
NUNS ON THE RUN

Simpson, Michael
LAST OF THE FINEST, THE

Simpson, Perry
CHATTAHOOCHEE

Simpson, Richard
NUNS ON THE RUN

Sims, Ellen
WITHOUT YOU, I'M NOTHING

Sims, Jackson
KILL-OFF, THE

Sims, Warwick
NIGHT EYES

Sinclair, Baby Simon
HAMLET

Sinclair, Pamela
HAMLET

Singer, Hal
TAXI BLUES

Singer, Marc
BODY CHEMISTRY
HIGH DESERT KILL

Singer, Raymond
CHILD'S PLAY 2

Singh, Mano
REVERSAL OF FORTUNE

Singleton, Penny
JETSONS: THE MOVIE

Sinitzyn, Herman
HUNT FOR RED OCTOBER, THE

Siragusa, Peter
HOME ALONE

Sirico, Tony
GOODFELLAS

Sirotin, Pavel
RUSSIA HOUSE, THE

Sissons, Kimber
ADVENTURES OF FORD FAIRLANE, THE

Sisti, Michelan
TEENAGE MUTANT NINJA TURTLES

Sisto, Rocco
ME AND HIM

Siverio, Manny
QUICK CHANGE

Sivero, Frank
GOODFELLAS

Sivod, Doug
RIVERBEND

Siyolwe, Wabei
NUNS ON THE RUN

Sizemore, Tom
BLUE STEEL

Skarsgard, Stellan
HUNT FOR RED OCTOBER, THE
PERFECT MURDER, THE

Skeffrey, Christopher
MO' BETTER BLUES

Skerritt, Tom
ROOKIE, THE

Skiadaressis, T.
LANDSCAPE IN THE MIST

Skie, Shawn
LORD OF THE FLIES

Skinner, Kisha
JACOB'S LADDER

Skinner, Margo
QUICK CHANGE

Skipper, Pat
DEMONSTONE
PREDATOR 2

Skolimowski, Jerzy
TORRENTS OF SPRING

Skulason, Helgi
PATHFINDER

Skybell, Steven
EVERYBODY WINS

Skyhawk, Sonny
YOUNG GUNS II

Skyler, Tristine
CADILLAC MAN

Slack, Ben
COME SEE THE PARADISE

Slate, Jeremy
DEAD PIT

Slater, Christian
TALES FROM THE DARKSIDE: THE MOVIE
YOUNG GUNS II
PUMP UP THE VOLUME

Slater, Helen
HAPPY TOGETHER

Slattery, Mike
DAYS OF THUNDER

Sleete, Gina
TEXASVILLE

Sloan, Chuck
TOTAL RECALL

Sloan, Doug
PRIMAL RAGE

Slotky, Anna
HOME ALONE

Slyker, Rob
TAX SEASON

Small, Neva
LASER MAN, THE

Small, Ralph
WHERE THE HEART IS

Smallwood, Tucker
PRESUMED INNOCENT

Smart, Sam
MISADVENTURES OF MR. WILT, THE

Smeltzer, Susan
MONSTER HIGH

Smerczak, Ron
BURNDOWN
AMERICAN EAGLE

Smillie, Bill
DIE HARD 2

Smirnov, Fyodor
RUSSIA HOUSE, THE

Smith, Amanda
FRESHMAN, THE

Smith, B.A. "Smitty"
NARROW MARGIN

Smith, Brandon
ROBOCOP 2
I COME IN PEACE

Smith, Bubba
GREMLINS 2 THE NEW BATCH

Smith, Buck
AWAKENINGS

Smith, Charles Martin
HOT SPOT, THE

Smith, Don Oscar
HUNT FOR RED OCTOBER, THE

Smith, Duncan
NAVY SEALS

Smith, Earl
MADHOUSE

Smith, Elmer
. ROCKY V

Smith, Freida
MADHOUSE

Smith, Garry
PROBLEM CHILD

Smith, Janet Savarino
GODFATHER PART III, THE

Smith, Karl Anthony
IMPULSE

Smith, Kate
HIDDEN AGENDA

Smith, Kelly Shaye
OPPONENT, THE

Smith, Kurtwood
QUICK CHANGE

Smith, Lane
AIR AMERICA

Smith, Liz
COOK, THE THIEF, HIS WIFE & HER
LOVER, THE

Smith, Lois
GREEN CARD

Smith, Margaret
GOODFELLAS

Smith, Mel
MISADVENTURES OF MR. WILT, THE

Smith, Paul
CAGED FURY

Smith, Paul L.
TEN LITTLE INDIANS
SONNY BOY

Smith, Roger Guenver
KING OF NEW YORK

Smith, Shawnee
DESPERATE HOURS

Smith, Sukie
WITCHES, THE

Smith, Toukie
ME AND HIM

Smith, Virginia
HOME ALONE

Smith, William "Smitty"
ADVENTURES OF FORD FAIRLANE, THE

Smith, Wonderful
TO SLEEP WITH ANGER

Smitrovich, Bill
CRAZY PEOPLE

Smits, Jimmy
VITAL SIGNS

Smolka, Ken
DIE HARD 2

Smook, Jan
EXORCIST III, THE

Smoot-Hyde, Michelle
SKI PATROL

Sneed, Floyd
FAR OUT MAN

Snegoff, Gregory
MISERY

Snell, Terrie
HOME ALONE

Snipes, Jelani Asar
MO' BETTER BLUES

Snipes, Wesley
MO' BETTER BLUES
KING OF NEW YORK

Snow, David
LORDS OF MAGICK, THE

Snyder, Bonnie
GUARDIAN, THE

Snyder, Romy
TEXASVILLE

Sobel, Barry
MARTIANS GO HOME!

Sobestanovich, John
MO' BETTER BLUES

Soibelman, Ed
FOURTH WAR, THE

Solchik, Richard
Q&A

Soldano, Nina
NIGHT OF THE SHARKS

Soler, Symon
DEMONSTONE

Soles, P.J.
ALIENATOR

Solet, Ira
IMPORTED BRIDEGROOM, THE

Solovei, Elena
LONELY WOMAN SEEKS LIFE COMPANION

Sommer, Josef
FORCED MARCH

Song, Magie
DR. CALIGARI

Sorel, Ted
BASKETCASE 2

Sorenson, Bob
MADHOUSE

Sorvino, Paul
DICK TRACY
GOODFELLAS

Soto, Richard
FIRE BIRDS

Soussan, Phil
ADVENTURES OF FORD FAIRLANE, THE

Soutendijk, Renee
FORCED MARCH

Souther, J.D.
POSTCARDS FROM THE EDGE

Southerland, Boots
YOUNG GUNS II

Souza, Laurie
VITAL SIGNS

Spacey, Kevin
SHOW OF FORCE, A
HENRY AND JUNE

Spadaro, Claudio
BELLY OF AN ARCHITECT, THE

Spader, James
BAD INFLUENCE
WHITE PALACE

Spalding, B.J.
BAIL JUMPER

Spall, Timothy
WHITE HUNTER, BLACK HEART
SHELTERING SKY, THE

Sparke, Jackie
DISTURBANCE, THE

Sparks, Don
ANDY COLBY'S INCREDIBLY AWESOME
ADVENTURE

Sparrow, Monica
BIG DIS, THE

Spataro, Joe
RETURN OF SUPERFLY, THE

Spear, Mark
MONSTER HIGH

Spears, Michael
DANCES WITH WOLVES

Specht, Lisa
FIRST POWER, THE

Speed, Lucy
IMPROMPTU

Speelman, Luana
DEAD PIT

Speir, Dona
SAVAGE BEACH

Spence, Bruce
SHRIMP ON THE BARBIE, THE

Spence, Judson
FIRE BIRDS

Spencer, John
PRESUMED INNOCENT
GREEN CARD

Spencer, Skip
CRY-BABY

Spencer, Steve
FLASHBACK

Spensley, Christopher
CAGED IN PARADISO

Sperber, Wendie Jo
BACK TO THE FUTURE PART III

Spicer, James
EDWARD SCISSORHANDS

Spiegel, Scott
DARKMAN

Spielberg, David
ALICE

Spinetti, Victor
KRAYS, THE

Spira, Serge
TORRENTS OF SPRING

Spitzley, Nathaniel
ARACHNOPHOBIA

Spivak, Gary
FOURTH WAR, THE

Spradling, Charlie
WILD AT HEART

Spriggs, Elizabeth
IMPROMPTU

Spring, Barnaby
INHERITOR

Springsteen, Pamela
GUMSHOE KID, THE .

Squibb, June
ALICE

Stabenau, Erik
MEN AT WORK

Stack, Patricia
LAST OF THE FINEST, THE

Stack, Robert
JOE VERSUS THE VOLCANO

Stacy, Chris
MR. DESTINY

Stafford, Baird
DOG TAGS

Stahl, Andrew
ERNEST GOES TO JAIL
MR. DESTINY

Stahl, Lisa
HEART CONDITION

Stahly-Vishwanadan, Antonin
MAHABHARATA, THE

Stainback, Sheila
SHOCK TO THE SYSTEM, A

Staines, George
HIDDEN AGENDA

Staley, James
PACIFIC HEIGHTS

Stallone, Frank
TEN LITTLE INDIANS

Stallone, Sage
ROCKY V

Stallone, Sylvester
ROCKY V

Standing, Michael
AFTERSHOCK

Stang, Arnold
GHOST DAD

Stanton, Barry
LIONHEART

Stanton, Dan
GREMLINS 2 THE NEW BATCH

Stanton, Don
GREMLINS 2 THE NEW BATCH

Stanton, Harry Dean
FOURTH WAR, THE
WILD AT HEART

Staples, Mavis
GRAFFITI BRIDGE

Stapleton, Nicola
COURAGE MOUNTAIN

Stapley, Diane
NUTCRACKER PRINCE, THE

Staquet, Georges
LIFE AND NOTHING BUT

Starke, Anthony
REPOSSESSED

Starr, Beau
GOODFELLAS

Starr, Emerald
MEN IN LOVE

Starr, Mike
BLUE STEEL
SHOCK TO THE SYSTEM, A
GOODFELLAS
MILLER'S CROSSING

Starr, Monte
MILLER'S CROSSING

Starwalt, David
PREDATOR 2

Stathopoulou, Toula
LANDSCAPE IN THE MIST

Statler, Alex
PRETTY WOMAN

Staunton, Kim
SHOCK TO THE SYSTEM, A

Staup, Jacqueline
MAY FOOLS

Stavin, Mary
OPPONENT, THE

Steadman, Alison
MISADVENTURES OF MR. WILT, THE

Steagall, Red
BIG BAD JOHN

Steele, William Paul
MERMAIDS

Steenburgen, Mary
BACK TO THE FUTURE PART III

Steer, Libert
MARKED FOR DEATH

Stefka, Kurt James
ADVENTURES OF FORD FAIRLANE, THE

Stein, Irv
AVALON

Stein, June
Q&A

Stein, Margy
MONSTER HIGH

Steinberg, Robert
DIE HARD 2

Steiner, John
NIGHT OF THE SHARKS

Steinsland, Kirstin
WITCHES, THE

Stemple, Kyra
PEACEMAKER

Stenborg, Helen
BONFIRE OF THE VANITIES

Stenke, Claudia
REAL BULLETS

Stephen, Daniel
INHERITOR

Stephens, R. David
FIRST POWER, THE

Stephens, Robert
BONFIRE OF THE VANITIES

Stepkin, David
CADILLAC MAN

Stern, Daniel
COUPE DE VILLE
MY BLUE HEAVEN
HOME ALONE

Sternhagen, Frances
SIBLING RIVALRY
MISERY

Steuer, Monica
TOTAL RECALL

Steuter, Kimberly
MADHOUSE

Stevan, Robyn
BYE BYE BLUES

Stevens, Andrew
DOWN THE DRAIN
NIGHT EYES
TUSKS

Stevens, Fisher
REVERSAL OF FORTUNE

Stevens, Stella
DOWN THE DRAIN

Stevenson, Bill
SLEEPING CAR, THE
CHILD'S PLAY 2

Stevenson, Holly
BLADES

Stewart, Catherine
STATE OF GRACE

Stewart, Charlotte
TREMORS

Stewart, Ewan
COOK, THE THIEF, HIS WIFE & HER
LOVER, THE

Stewart, Megan
FLATLINERS

Stickney, Timothy
WHERE THE HEART IS
RETURN OF SUPERFLY, THE

Stidder, Ted
NARROW MARGIN

Still, Dana
NARROW MARGIN

Stiller, Ben
STELLA

Stillkrauth, Fred
NASTY GIRL, THE

Stinton, Colin
RUSSIA HOUSE, THE

Stitzel, Douglas
PRETTY WOMAN

Stock, Alan
STREETS

Stockwell, Dean
TIME GUARDIAN, THE

Stockwell, Guy
SANTA SANGRE

Stoddard, Malcolm
INNOCENT VICTIM

Stoddard, Ray
DICK TRACY

Stokie, Mike
JACOB'S LADDER

Stoklos, Randy
SIDE OUT

Stole, Mink
CRY-BABY

Stoler, Shirley
MIAMI BLUES
FRANKENHOOKER

Stoleru, Josiane
CYRANO DE BERGERAC

Stolow, Henry
LAST OF THE FINEST, THE

Stoltz, Eric
LIONHEART
MEMPHIS BELLE

Stolze, Lena
NASTY GIRL, THE

Stone, Danton
CRAZY PEOPLE

Stone, Dawn
FUNLAND

Stone, Jordan
WHITE PALACE

Stone, Sharon
TOTAL RECALL

Stoneham, Ben
COOK, THE THIEF, HIS WIFE & HER
LOVER, THE

Stoppelwerth, Josh
PROBLEM CHILD

Stormare, Peter
AWAKENINGS

Stout, Bud
YOUNG GUNS II

Stowe, Madeleine
REVENGE
TWO JAKES, THE

Strasser, Michael
LAST OF THE FINEST, THE

Strathairn, David
FEUD, THE
MEMPHIS BELLE

Stratton, David
FRESHMAN, THE

Strausbaugh, Ken
TOTAL RECALL

Strauss, Tatiana
NUNS ON THE RUN

Streep, Meryl
POSTCARDS FROM THE EDGE

Street, Elliott
FUNLAND

Strickland, Amzie
PRETTY WOMAN
BIG BAD JOHN

Strickland, Robert Ashiya Ganta
MARKED FOR DEATH

Stritch, Elaine
CADILLAC MAN

Stromberg, Larry
BLADES

Strong, Dennis
WHERE THE HEART IS

Stroud, Don
TWISTED JUSTICE
DOWN THE DRAIN

Stroyeva, Elena
RUSSIA HOUSE, THE

Strydom, Hans
GODS MUST BE CRAZY II, THE

Strzkowski, Henry
PRIMARY TARGET

Stuart, Blanche Irwin
JACOB'S LADDER

Stuart, Jason
KINDERGARTEN COP

Stuart, Patrick D.
PRETTY WOMAN

Studd, Big John
CAGED IN PARADISO

Studi, Wes
DANCES WITH WOLVES

Stunden, James A.
SKINHEADS – THE SECOND COMING OF
HATE

Sturgis, William
QUICK CHANGE

Stutchbury, Jessica
FORCE OF CIRCUMSTANCE

Suarez, Miguel Angel
HAVANA

Sudana, Tapa
MAHABHARATA, THE

Sudo, Masayuki
HEAVEN AND EARTH

Sugata, Haruka
DREAMS

Sullivan, George
DESPERATE HOURS

Sullivan, Michael-Vaughn
ALICE

Sullivan, Sean Gregory
SKI PATROL
CLASS OF 1999
BACK TO THE FUTURE PART III

Sullivan, Shawna
MERMAIDS

Sullivan, Tommy
STATE OF GRACE

Sullivan, William Bell
HUNT FOR RED OCTOBER, THE

Summers, Bunny
SKINHEADS – THE SECOND COMING OF
HATE
TAX SEASON

Summers, Neil
DICK TRACY

Summersett, Roy
SAVAGE BEACH

Sundin, Michel
LIONHEART

Sundstrom, Florence
PACIFIC HEIGHTS

Sung, Kimi
HOUSE PARTY

Sung, Richard Lee
TAX SEASON

Sunseri, Jack
DEAD PIT

Suriano, Philip
GOODFELLAS

Surman, John
CHICAGO JOE AND THE SHOWGIRL

Susmeier, Richard
NASTY GIRL, THE

Sussman, Lorne
LOOK WHO'S TALKING TOO

Sutherland, Kiefer
FLASHBACK
CHICAGO JOE AND THE SHOWGIRL
FLATLINERS
YOUNG GUNS II
NUTCRACKER PRINCE, THE

Sutton, Robert
ALMOST AN ANGEL

Suwanapa, Chanarong
AIR AMERICA

Suydam, Red
FEUD, THE

Suzan, Leslie
TAKING CARE OF BUSINESS

Suzman, Janet
NUNS ON THE RUN

Suzuki, Mie
DREAMS

Svenson, Bo
ANDY COLBY'S INCREDIBLY AWESOME
ADVENTURE
PRIMAL RAGE

Sverre, Johan
WITCHES, THE

Swanepoel, Lourens
GODS MUST BE CRAZY II, THE

Swann, Dale
GREMLINS 2 THE NEW BATCH

Swanson, Brenda
STEEL AND LACE

Swanson, Gary
GUARDIAN, THE
BLOOD RED

Swanson, Jeff
GREMLINS 2 THE NEW BATCH

Swartz, Deborah
MADHOUSE

Swayze, Patrick
GHOST

Sweda, Wendell
QUICK CHANGE

Swedberg, Heidi
KINDERGARTEN COP

Sweeney, D.B.
MEMPHIS BELLE

Sweeney, Julia
GREMLINS 2 THE NEW BATCH

Sweet, Becky
GHOST DAD

Sweet, Vonte
WITHOUT YOU, I'M NOTHING
PREDATOR 2

Swift, Rod
COUPE DE VILLE

Swope, Hayes
ROCKY V

Sylvester, Harold
HIT LIST

Sylvia, Marie
SHOCK TO THE SYSTEM, A

Symons, David
SHORT TIME

Synder, Arlen Dean
MARKED FOR DEATH

Szulc, Karina
MAGDALENE

Tabakin, Ralph
AVALON

Tablian, Vic
NAVY SEALS

Tabrizi, Alexander
DOWN THE DRAIN

Tabrizi-Zadeh, Mahmoud
MAHABHARATA, THE

Tacon, Gary
LOOSE CANNONS
AWAKENINGS

Tadesse, Myriam
MAHABHARATA, THE

Taft, Andrew
LORD OF THE FLIES

Taft, Edward
LORD OF THE FLIES

Taggart, Rita
COUPE DE VILLE

Taggert, Jimmy Medina
CLASS OF 1999

Taglang, Tom
TAKING CARE OF BUSINESS

Tai, Ling
MISADVENTURES OF MR. WILT, THE

Tail, John
DANCES WITH WOLVES

Taimak
WHITE GIRL, THE

Takahashi, Ayaka
DREAMS

Takahashi, Umiko
DREAMS

Takeda, Hideharu
DREAMS

Takei, Nori
DREAMS

Takemura, Ken
DREAMS

Takenouchi, Keiki
DREAMS

Takeshita, Wat
PACIFIC HEIGHTS

Talbot, Godfrey
STRIKE IT RICH

Tallman, Patricia
NIGHT OF THE LIVING DEAD

Tamblyn, Russ
AFTERSHOCK

Tambor, Jeffrey
LISA

Tamburo, Frank
AVALON

Tamburrelli, Karla
DIE HARD 2

Tamura, Hiroto
DREAMS

Tanaka, Toru
TAX SEASON
DARKMAN

Tanaka, Yoshiko
BLACK RAIN

Tandy, Mark
STRIKE IT RICH

Taner, Merden
ISTANBUL, KEEP YOUR EYES OPEN

Tang, Gary
NUNS ON THE RUN

Tanksley, Ronnie
FAR OUT MAN

Tanl
MEN DON'T LEAVE

Tanney, Michael David
GREEN CARD

Tanzini, Philip
MARKED FOR DEATH

Tapia, Faviola Elenka
SANTA SANGRE

Tarantina, Brian
JACOB'S LADDER

Tarrant, Gage
ROBOCOP 2

Tarrau, Segundo
HAVANA

Tarsia, Frank
GODFATHER PART III, THE

Tarver, Milt
TOTAL RECALL

Tashiro, Akira
DREAMS

Taslimi, Susan
BASHU, THE LITTLE STRANGER

Tate, Misato
DREAMS

Tate, Nick
STEEL AND LACE

Tate, Vanessa
RIVERBEND

Tati, Sambou
MAMA, THERE'S A MAN IN YOUR BED

Taylor, Adam
YOUNG GUNS II

Taylor, Billy
ALICE

Taylor, Bobby
FAR OUT MAN

Taylor, Buck
BIG BAD JOHN

Taylor, Carole
SKI PATROL

Taylor, Chad
TAX SEASON

Taylor, Dub
BACK TO THE FUTURE PART III

Taylor, Holland
ALICE

Taylor, Jacques
PLOT AGAINST HARRY, THE

Taylor, James A.
MEN IN LOVE

Taylor, Kimberly
BEDROOM EYES II
FRANKENHOOKER

Taylor, Kirk
RETURN OF SUPERFLY, THE
BONFIRE OF THE VANITIES

Taylor, Larry
BURNDOWN

Taylor, Mark L.
ARACHNOPHOBIA

Taylor, Renee
WHITE PALACE

Taylor, Rip
DUCKTALES: THE MOVIE – TREASURE OF
THE LOST LAMP

Taylor, Roberta
WITCHES, THE

Taylor, Ron
HEART CONDITION

Taylor, Russi
JETSONS: THE MOVIE
DUCKTALES: THE MOVIE – TREASURE OF
THE LOST LAMP
RESCUERS DOWN UNDER, THE

Taylor, Wally
PEACEMAKER

Taylor-Block, Haley
TOUCH OF A STRANGER

Taylor-Young, Leigh
HONEYMOON ACADEMY

Teague, Marshall
FIRE BIRDS

Teigen, Trenton
GHOST DAD

Telfer, Robert Frank
ARACHNOPHOBIA

Tembi
TUSKS

Templeman, Simon
RUSSIA HOUSE, THE

Tengende, Oliver
TUSKS

Tennant, Victoria
HANDMAID'S TALE, THE

Tennon, Julius
RIVERBEND

Tepper, Leonard
AWAKENINGS

Ter Steege, Johanna
VINCENT AND THEO

Terada, Machiko
DREAMS

Terao, Akira
DREAMS

Terashita, Jill
WHY ME?

Terhune, Bob
LOVE AT LARGE

Terlesky, John
DAMNED RIVER

Termine, Ergidio
NIGHT OF THE SHARKS

Terrell, John Canada
DEF BY TEMPTATION
ELLIOT FAUMAN, PH.D.
MO' BETTER BLUES
RETURN OF SUPERFLY, THE

Terris, Malcolm
CHICAGO JOE AND THE SHOWGIRL

Tery, Sandor
MY 20TH CENTURY

Terzo, Nino
CINEMA PARADISO

Tess
SKI PATROL

Testa, Mary
STANLEY AND IRIS

Teuber, Andreas
IMPORTED BRIDEGROOM, THE

Tewson, Josephine
MISADVENTURES OF MR. WILT, THE

Thaler, Karin
NASTY GIRL, THE

Thatcher, Kirk
SPACED INVADERS
GREMLINS 2 THE NEW BATCH

Therasse, Bruno
LIFE AND NOTHING BUT

Thiel, James
HOMER & EDDIE

Thiel, Jeffrey
HOMER & EDDIE

Thigpen, Lynne
IMPULSE

Thmer, Udo
NASTY GIRL, THE

Thomas, G. Valmont
I LOVE YOU TO DEATH

Thomas, Hugh
TALL GUY, THE

Thomas, Leonard
MO' BETTER BLUES
RETURN OF SUPERFLY, THE

Thomas, Leonard Lee
KING OF NEW YORK

Thomas, Marlo
IN THE SPIRIT

Thomas, Raymond
MO' BETTER BLUES

Thomas, Raymond Anthony
JACOB'S LADDER

Thomas, Tabetha
EDWARD SCISSORHANDS

Thomas, Tressa
FLATLINERS

Thomas, Vanessa
ALICE

Thomerson, Tim
AIR AMERICA

Thompson, Deborah
FLATLINERS

Thompson, Elizabeth
METROPOLITAN

Thompson, Emma
TALL GUY, THE
IMPROMPTU

Thompson, Fred Dalton
HUNT FOR RED OCTOBER, THE
DAYS OF THUNDER
DIE HARD 2

Thompson, Kevin
SPACED INVADERS

Thompson, Kim
TALL GUY, THE

Thompson, Lea
BACK TO THE FUTURE PART III

Thompson, Linda
ROBOCOP 2

Thompson, Mark
ROCKY V

Thompson, Martin
MR. DESTINY

Thompson, Matt
VITAL SIGNS

Thompson, Nick
DANCES WITH WOLVES

Thomsen, Kevin
BEDROOM EYES II

Thomson, Davidson
JACOB'S LADDER

Thomson, Rosalyn
EDWARD SCISSORHANDS

Thon, Tom
UNBELIEVABLE TRUTH, THE

Thorn, Frankie
LISA

Thornberg, Lee
ADVENTURES OF FORD FAIRLANE, THE

Thorne, Tracy
EXORCIST III, THE

Thorne-Smith, Courtney
SIDE OUT

Thornhill, David
AVALON

Thornton, James
DESPERATE HOURS

Thornton, Tina
METROPOLITAN

Thorp, Sarah Maur
TEN LITTLE INDIANS
RIVER OF DEATH

Thorpe, Paul
WITHOUT YOU, I'M NOTHING

Thorsen, Sven-Ole
HUNT FOR RED OCTOBER, THE

Threet, Ken
RETURN OF SUPERFLY, THE

Threlfall, David
RUSSIA HOUSE, THE

Throb, Hart
MADHOUSE

Thuillier, Luc
MONSIEUR HIRE

Thurman, Uma
WHERE THE HEART IS
HENRY AND JUNE

Thurston, Robert
BIRD ON A WIRE

Ticotin, Rachel
TOTAL RECALL

Tidof, Max
MAGDALENE

Tiefen, David
HOLLYWOOD HOT TUBS II: EDUCATING
CRYSTAL

Tiemele, Jean-Baptiste
L'ETAT SAUVAGE

Tierney, Lawrence
WHY ME?

Tiffany
JETSONS: THE MOVIE

Tiffe, Angelo
IMPULSE
VITAL SIGNS

Tighe, Kevin
ANOTHER 48 HRS.

Tilden, Leif
TEENAGE MUTANT NINJA TURTLES

Till, Paul
LOVE AT LARGE

Tilley, Don
COUPE DE VILLE

Tillman, Henry D.
ROCKY V

Tilly, Meg
TWO JAKES, THE

Timbrook, Corby
SKI PATROL

Timm, Charles
GAME, THE

Timson, David
RUSSIA HOUSE, THE

Tinio, Rolando
DEMONSTONE

Tippit, Wayne
MADHOUSE

Tirard, Ann
WITCHES, THE

Tirelli, Jaime
STATE OF GRACE

Titus, Libby
AWAKENINGS

Tixou, Thelma
SANTA SANGRE

Toback, James
ALICE

Tobey, Kenneth
GREMLINS 2 THE NEW BATCH

Tobolowsky, Stephen
BIRD ON A WIRE
FUNNY ABOUT LOVE
WELCOME HOME, ROXY CARMICHAEL

Tocha, Paolo
PREDATOR 2

Tochi, Brian
TEENAGE MUTANT NINJA TURTLES

Todd, Ryan
SPACED INVADERS

Todd, Tony
NIGHT OF THE LIVING DEAD

Todisco, Mario
CADILLAC MAN
BETSY'S WEDDING
MILLER'S CROSSING

Todorovic, Bora
TIME OF THE GYPSIES

Tofel, Thomas
DIE HARD 2

Togo, Haruko
DREAMS

Tokita, Fujio
DREAMS

Tokuhashi, Tatsunori
DREAMS

Tolan, Michael
PRESUMED INNOCENT

Tolbe, Joe
MEN IN LOVE

Tolbert, Berlinda
GOODFELLAS

Toler, Ray
HOME ALONE

Tolkan, James
OPPORTUNITY KNOCKS
BACK TO THE FUTURE PART III
DICK TRACY

Tom, Lauren
BLUE STEEL
CADILLAC MAN

Tomassini, Ferdinando
NIGHT OF THE SHARKS

Tomelty, Frances
FIELD, THE

Tomita, Tamlyn
COME SEE THE PARADISE

Tomlins, Jason
POSTCARDS FROM THE EDGE

Tomlinson, Michael
JACOB'S LADDER

Tomoi, Tatsuhiko
HEAVEN AND EARTH

Tomomori, Shogo
DREAMS

Tonomura, Shin
DREAMS

Toner, Thomas
MILLER'S CROSSING

Tonomura, Shin
DREAMS

Torchio, Deborah
FLATLINERS

Toriki, Kento
DREAMS

Torn, Rip
HIT LIST
COLD FEET

Tornabene, Salvatore H.
MILLER'S CROSSING

Torpe, Brian
BIRD ON A WIRE

Torre, Joe
TAKING CARE OF BUSINESS

Torrei, Gabriele
GODFATHER PART III, THE

Torrens, Pip
MOUNTAINS OF THE MOON

Torres, Silvia Gomez
WILD ORCHID

Torta, Carlina
ICICLE THIEF, THE

Tortora, Oz
FIRST POWER, THE

Totino, Frank
LOOK WHO'S TALKING TOO

Towles, Tom
MEN DON'T LEAVE
HENRY: PORTRAIT OF A SERIAL KILLER
NIGHT OF THE LIVING DEAD

Towner, William
BLADES

Townsend, Betsey
MERMAIDS

Townsend, Tonya Natalie
WITHOUT YOU, I'M NOTHING

Towstik, Mike
KILL-OFF, THE

Toy, Patty
HOLLYWOOD HOT TUBS II: EDUCATING
CRYSTAL

Toya, Gigi
COME SEE THE PARADISE

Trabaud, Pierre
LIFE AND NOTHING BUT

Trailer, Rex
MERMAIDS

Trainor, Mary Ellen
FIRE BIRDS

Tramod, Yani
AIR AMERICA

Tran, Kady
STREETS

Trapnell, Jon
STAR QUEST: BEYOND THE RISING MOON

Trapp, Robin
LOOK WHO'S TALKING TOO

Travis, Nancy
INTERNAL AFFAIRS
LOOSE CANNONS
AIR AMERICA
THREE MEN AND A LITTLE LADY

Travis, Stacey
HARDWARE

Travolta, John
LOOK WHO'S TALKING TOO

Treas, Terri
FRANKENSTEIN UNBOUND

Trejo, Al
PROBLEM CHILD

Trejo, Danny
MARKED FOR DEATH

Tremblay, Johanne-Marie
JESUS OF MONTREAL

Tretout, Alain
MAMA, THERE'S A MAN IN YOUR BED

Trevino, Frank V.
LAST OF THE FINEST, THE

Trew, Rafton
RETURN OF SUPERFLY, THE

Triboulet, Pierre
CYRANO DE BERGERAC

Trieste, Leopoldo
CINEMA PARADISO

Trinidad, Arsenio "Sonny"
DARKMAN

Triska, Jan
LOOSE CANNONS

Tritter, Wes
BIRD ON A WIRE
SHORT TIME

Trivett, Christina
FRESHMAN, THE

Trocha, Frank
COME SEE THE PARADISE

Tronc, Nicolas
LIFE AND NOTHING BUT

Troobnick, Gene
IMPORTED BRIDEGROOM, THE

Troum, Kenn
TEENAGE MUTANT NINJA TURTLES

Troy, Phillip
FIRE BIRDS

Trpkova, Sinolicka
TIME OF THE GYPSIES

Trujillo, Albert
YOUNG GUNS II

Truro, Victor
SHOCK TO THE SYSTEM, A
PRESUMED INNOCENT

Tsang, Eric
REINCARNATION OF GOLDEN LOTUS, THE

Tshabalala, Treasure
GODS MUST BE CRAZY II, THE

Tsiang Chi Wai, Eric
EAT A BOWL OF TEA

Tsturvan, Yegueshe
RUSSIA HOUSE, THE

Tsugawa, Masahiko
HEAVEN AND EARTH

Tsurutani, Brady
COME SEE THE PARADISE

Tsuwako, Mitsuji
DREAMS

Tubert, Marc
POSTCARDS FROM THE EDGE

Tucci, Stanley
FEUD, THE
QUICK CHANGE

Tucek, Sarabeth
FLATLINERS

Tuerk, Lauren
BODY CHEMISTRY

Tulasne, Patricia
HOW TO MAKE LOVE TO A NEGRO WITH-
OUT GETTING TIRED

Tullis, Dan Jr.
FIRST POWER, THE

Tunstall, Peter
GODS MUST BE CRAZY II, THE

Turkel, Joe
DARK SIDE OF THE MOON

Turley, Myra
VITAL SIGNS

Turner, Bonnie
FUNLAND

Turner, Ross
UNBELIEVABLE TRUTH, THE

Turney, Michael
TEENAGE MUTANT NINJA TURTLES

Turnipseed, Sheldon
MO' BETTER BLUES

Turturro, John
MO' BETTER BLUES
STATE OF GRACE
MILLER'S CROSSING

Turturro, Nicholas
MO' BETTER BLUES

Turuoka, Yasushige
DREAMS

Tweed, Shannon
TWISTED JUSTICE
NIGHT VISITOR

Twiggy
ISTANBUL, KEEP YOUR EYES OPEN

Tyler, Cary
DARKMAN

Tyler, Ian
NAVY SEALS

Tynan, Will
TWO JAKES, THE

Tyree, Robert
CRY-BABY

Tyrrell, Susan
CRY-BABY

Tyson, Richard
KINDERGARTEN COP

Tzortzoglou, Stratos
LANDSCAPE IN THE MIST

Tzudiker, Bob
TOTAL RECALL

U'kset, Umban
L'ETAT SAUVAGE

Uceda, Luis
VERONICO CRUZ

Uchan, Philippe
LIFE AND NOTHING BUT

Uchida, Christine
ME AND HIM

Uddin, Najma
WHERE THE HEART IS

Udenio, Fabiana
ROBOCOP 2

Ullman, Tracey
I LOVE YOU TO DEATH
HAPPILY EVER AFTER

Ullrick, Sharon
TEXASVILLE

Underwood, David
FLASHBACK

Underwood, Jay
GUMSHOE KID, THE

Unger, Joe
LEATHERFACE: THE TEXAS CHAINSAW
MASSACRE III

Upchurch, William
YOUNG GUNS II

Urbano, Maryann
LASER MAN, THE

Urman, Haley
KINDERGARTEN COP

Urquidez, Benny "The Jet"
DOWN THE DRAIN

Ussani, Riccardo
BELLY OF AN ARCHITECT, THE

Utazawa, Torauemon
DREAMS

Utley, Byron
AWAKENINGS

Utroska, Alex
PROBLEM CHILD

Utsi, Inger
PATHFINDER

Utsi, Nils
PATHFINDER

Utt, Kenneth
MIAMI BLUES

Uttamayodhin, Wasan
AIR AMERICA

Uys, Stephen
METROPOLITAN

Vaccaro, Brenda
TEN LITTLE INDIANS

Vahanian, Gregory
FIRE BIRDS

Vale, Jerry
GOODFELLAS

Valencia, Vance
DIE HARD 2

Valentin, Anthony
GOODFELLAS

Valentino, Tony
ANGEL TOWN

Valkeapaa, Nils-Aslek
PATHFINDER

Valli, Frankie
MODERN LOVE

Vallier, Vincent
VINCENT AND THEO

Vallone, Raf
GODFATHER PART III, THE

Van Damme, Jean-Claude
DEATH WARRANT

Van de Ven, Monique
PAINT IT BLACK
MAN INSIDE, THE

Van Der Woude, Teresa
NIGHT VISITOR

Van Dyke, Dick
DICK TRACY

Van Hentenryck, Kevin
BASKETCASE 2

Van Londersele, Kelli
FLASHBACK

Van Niekerk, Louis
DAMNED RIVER

Van Patten, James
TWISTED JUSTICE

Van Pletzen, Pierre
GODS MUST BE CRAZY II, THE

Van Riesen, Wendy
BIRD ON A WIRE

Van Santen, Patricia
FAR OUT MAN

Van Sickle, Jan
FLASHBACK

Vance, Courtney B.
HUNT FOR RED OCTOBER, THE

Vance, Ladd
ADVENTURES OF FORD FAIRLANE, THE

Vanderberry, Rob
FEUD, THE

Vanderpyl, Jean
JETSONS: THE MOVIE

Vanstone, Richard
WHITE HUNTER, BLACK HEART

Varelli, Alfredo
BELLY OF AN ARCHITECT, THE

Vargas, Angel
QUICK CHANGE

Varney, Jim
ERNEST GOES TO JAIL

Varon, Miriam
IMPORTED BRIDEGROOM, THE

Varon, Susan
GOODFELLAS

Varouchas, A.
LANDSCAPE IN THE MIST

Vasquez, Daniel
HAVANA

Vasquez, Nelson
BONFIRE OF THE VANITIES

Vasquez, Roberta
STREET ASYLUM
ROOKIE, THE

Vassallo, Rita
GHOST DAD

Vaughan, Peter
MOUNTAINS OF THE MOON

Vaughn, Ned
HUNT FOR RED OCTOBER, THE
BIG BAD JOHN

Vaughn, Ralph Pruitt
BLOOD SALVAGE

Vaughn, Reggie
STAR QUEST: BEYOND THE RISING MOON

Vaughn, Robert
NOBODY'S PERFECT
RIVER OF DEATH

Vaughn, Steven L.
THREE MEN AND A LITTLE LADY

Vaur, Georges
MAY FOOLS

Vawter, Ron
INTERNAL AFFAIRS

Vazquez, Bob
ROCKY V

Vegas, Ray
LAST OF THE FINEST, THE

Vela, Rosie
TWO JAKES, THE

Velez, Sharon
HAVANA

Veljohnson, Reginald
DIE HARD 2

Veluma
WILD ORCHID

Veneto, Tony
HUNT FOR RED OCTOBER, THE

Vennema, John
PRESUMED INNOCENT

Vennera, Chick
NIGHT EYES

Venov, Gennady
RUSSIA HOUSE, THE

Vento, Robert
GODFATHER PART III, THE

Ventura, Mildred I.
HAVANA

Venture, Richard
NAVY SEALS

Vera, Axel
WITHOUT YOU, I'M NOTHING

Vera, Luis
CAGED IN PARADISO

Verbois, Jack
I COME IN PEACE

Verdon, Gwen
ALICE

Verea, John
POSTCARDS FROM THE EDGE

Vergne, Benoit
CYRANO DE BERGERAC

Verica, Tom
DIE HARD 2

Verlor, Catherine
LIFE AND NOTHING BUT

Vernier, Pierre
MAMA, THERE'S A MAN IN YOUR BED

Vernon, Glen
SPACED INVADERS

Vernon, John
HOSTILE TAKEOVER

Vernon, Kate
HOSTILE TAKEOVER

Vernon, Philippa
BURNDOWN

Verreos, Rita
MARKED FOR DEATH

Vertinskaya, Marianna
LONELY WOMAN SEEKS LIFE COMPANION

Vidov, Oleg
WILD ORCHID

Viezzi, John
BACKSTREET DREAMS

Viezzi, Joseph
BACKSTREET DREAMS

Vignal, Pascale
LIFE AND NOTHING BUT

Vigoda, Abe
JOE VERSUS THE VOLCANO

Villa, Edmund E.
ADVENTURES OF FORD FAIRLANE, THE

Villella, Michael
WILD ORCHID

Villiers, James
MOUNTAINS OF THE MOON

Vimol, Chet
AIR AMERICA

Vince, Pruitt Taylor
JACOB'S LADDER
COME SEE THE PARADISE

Vincent, Alex
CHILD'S PLAY 2

Vincent, Annie
HENRY AND JUNE

Vincent, Frank
GOODFELLAS

Vincent, Helene
LIFE IS A LONG QUIET RIVER

Vincent, Ian
MOUNTAINS OF THE MOON

Vincent, Jan-Michael
HIT LIST
ALIENATOR
DEMONSTONE

Vincent, Louise
MR. FROST

Vincent, Lucia
QUICK CHANGE

Vincent, Phil
STUFF STEPHANIE IN THE INCINERATOR

Vincente, Fiona
IMPROMPTU

Vinovich, Steve
AWAKENINGS

Vint, Jesse
I COME IN PEACE

Vinton, Robbie
GOODFELLAS

Viterelli, Joe
STATE OF GRACE

Vito, Sonny
Q&A

Vivino, Floyd
CRAZY PEOPLE

Vlasis, Denise
WITHOUT YOU, I'M NOTHING

Vogel, Jack
DEMON WIND

Vogler, Rudiger
L'ETAT SAUVAGE

Volter, Philippe
CYRANO DE BERGERAC

Volty, Estuardo M.
WITHOUT YOU, I'M NOTHING

Von Erich, Kerry
PROBLEM CHILD

Von Franckenstein, Clement
HAUNTING OF MORELLA, THE

Von Leer, Hunter
UNDER THE BOARDWALK

Von Sydow, Max
AWAKENINGS

Von Zerneck, Danielle
UNDER THE BOARDWALK

Vorgan, Gigo
VITAL SIGNS

Vorshim, Alfredo
HAVANA

Voss, Philip
MOUNTAINS OF THE MOON

Voth, Tom
METROPOLITAN

Vouyoukas, Th.
LANDSCAPE IN THE MIST

Voyagis, Yorgo
COURAGE MOUNTAIN

Vraa, Sanna
FLATLINERS

Vrba, Joseph
FOURTH WAR, THE

Vu-An, Eric
SHELTERING SKY, THE

Wade, Douglas
RETURN OF SUPERFLY, THE

Wadowski, Kevin
MADHOUSE

Wagner, Brian
KINDERGARTEN COP

Wagner, Michael Dan
TREMORS

Wagner, Tom
AFTER DARK, MY SWEET

Wahl, Joanna
GAME, THE

Wai, Lo
LIFE IS CHEAP. . . BUT TOILET PAPER IS
EXPENSIVE

Waidzulis, Vince
HOME ALONE

Waites, Thomas G.
STATE OF GRACE

Waits, Tom
COLD FEET

Walcott, Noel L. III
MARKED FOR DEATH

Wald, Amy
KINDERGARTEN COP

Waldocks, Moshe
IMPORTED BRIDEGROOM, THE

Waldon, John
TALL GUY, THE

Walken, Christopher
KING OF NEW YORK

Walker, Allysun
BIG DIS, THE

Walker, Chris
BLUE STEEL

Walker, Francine
NUNS ON THE RUN

Walker, Jack David
GUARDIAN, THE

Walker, Johnny
HEART CONDITION

Walker, Linwood
RIVERBEND

Walker, Liza
TWISTED OBSESSION

Walker, Pierre
L'ETAT SAUVAGE

Walker, Tammy
AVALON

Wall, Max
STRIKE IT RICH

Wallace, Basil
MARKED FOR DEATH

Wallace, Craig
CRY-BABY

Wallace, George
POSTCARDS FROM THE EDGE

Wallace, Jack
STATE OF GRACE

Wallace, Julie T.
MACK THE KNIFE

Wallach, Eli
TWO JAKES, THE
GODFATHER PART III, THE

Wallach, Katherine
GOODFELLAS

Walle, Aina
MR. FROST

Walle, Knut
PATHFINDER

Wallem, Linda
ALICE

Walls, Ashley
LEMON SISTERS, THE

Walls, Lauren
LEMON SISTERS, THE

Walls, Melissa
LEMON SISTERS, THE

Walls, Napoleon
AFTER DARK, MY SWEET

Walsh, Dylan
WHERE THE HEART IS
BETSY'S WEDDING

Walsh, Fiona
ARACHNOPHOBIA

Walsh, J.T.
CRAZY PEOPLE
NARROW MARGIN
GRIFTERS, THE
RUSSIA HOUSE, THE
WHY ME?

Walsh, M. Emmet
CHATTAHOOCHEE
NARROW MARGIN

Walsh, Robert
CRY-BABY

Walsh, Sidney
THREE MEN AND A LITTLE LADY

Walston, Ray
SKI PATROL
BLOOD RELATIONS
BLOOD SALVAGE

Walter, Harriet
MAY FOOLS

Walter, Luke
GOODFELLAS

Walter, Perla
VITAL SIGNS

Walter, Tracey
HOMER & EDDIE
UNDER THE BOARDWALK
YOUNG GUNS II
TWO JAKES, THE
PACIFIC HEIGHTS

Walters, Julie
MACK THE KNIFE

Walters, Patricia
COOK, THE THIEF, HIS WIFE & HER
LOVER, THE

Waltman, Michael
MADHOUSE

Wan, Chan Kim
LIFE IS CHEAP. . . BUT TOILET PAPER IS
EXPENSIVE

Wanamaker, Zoe
RAGGEDY RAWNEY, THE

Wandachristine
MEN DON'T LEAVE

Wandt, Adam
GOODFELLAS

Wang, Peter
LASER MAN, THE

Ward, Donald Lardner
METROPOLITAN

Ward, Fred
TREMORS
MIAMI BLUES
HENRY AND JUNE

Ward, Jim
QUICK CHANGE

Ward, Joanne
BURNDOWN

Ward, John D.
TEENAGE MUTANT NINJA TURTLES

Ward, Rachel
AFTER DARK, MY SWEET

Ward, Roger
QUIGLEY DOWN UNDER

Ward, Stan
ROCKY V

Ward, Wally
UNDER THE BOARDWALK

Ward-Freeman, Cassandra
TEENAGE MUTANT NINJA TURTLES

Warden, Jack
EVERYBODY WINS
PROBLEM CHILD

Warhit, Douglas
LOOK WHO'S TALKING TOO

Warner, David
HOSTILE TAKEOVER
MAGDALENE

Warner, Julie
FLATLINERS

Warner, Rick
FEUD, THE

Warnick, Allan
TWO JAKES, THE

Warren, Brian
FOURTH WAR, THE

Warren, Kimelly Anne
SHORT TIME

Warren, Lauri
TWISTED JUSTICE

Warren, Steve
MEN IN LOVE

Warring, James
OPPONENT, THE

Warwick, Richard
WHITE HUNTER, BLACK HEART
HAMLET

Wasa, Maxine
SAVAGE BEACH

Washburn, Don
ANDY COLBY'S INCREDIBLY AWESOME
ADVENTURE

Washburn, Rick
DEAD AIM

Washington, Denzel
HEART CONDITION
MO' BETTER BLUES

Washington, Lou D.
HOUSE PARTY

Washington, Ludie C.
WITHOUT YOU, I'M NOTHING

Wasman, David
CLASS OF 1999

Wasserman, Allan
ADVENTURES OF FORD FAIRLANE, THE

Wasserman, Jerry
SHORT TIME

Wasserman, Mona
NUTCRACKER PRINCE, THE

Wasserman, Wayne
CAGED IN PARADISO

Watanabe, Gedde
GREMLINS 2 THE NEW BATCH

Watanabe, Mai
DREAMS

Watanabe, Tetsu
DREAMS

Watase, Tsunehiko
HEAVEN AND EARTH

Waterman, Felicity
DIE HARD 2

Waters, Claire
GAME, THE

Waters, Jan
LIONHEART

Waters, John
HOMER & EDDIE

Waters, Oren
WITHOUT YOU, I'M NOTHING

Watson, John M. Sr.
OPPORTUNITY KNOCKS

Watson, Mike
BACK TO THE FUTURE PART III

Watson, Miles
PRESUMED INNOCENT

Watson, Mitch
PRIMAL RAGE

Watson, Woody
ROBOCOP 2
I COME IN PEACE

Watters, Sandra V.
MEN DON'T LEAVE

Wattley, Danny
BIRD ON A WIRE

Watts, Jeff "Tain"
MO' BETTER BLUES

Wayans, Damon
LOOK WHO'S TALKING TOO

Wayton, Gary
LORDS OF MAGICK, THE

Weatherly, Shawn
SHADOWZONE

Weaver, Miko
GRAFFITI BRIDGE

Weaver, Rose
VITAL SIGNS

Webb, Chloe
HEART CONDITION
BELLY OF AN ARCHITECT, THE

Webb, Julius Clifton
LEMON SISTERS, THE

Webb, Kim
CRY-BABY

Webb, Mitch
MEMPHIS BELLE

Weber, Jacques
CYRANO DE BERGERAC

Webster, Marc
RETURN OF SUPERFLY, THE

Wedgeworth, Ann
GREEN CARD

Weigel, Teri
MARKED FOR DEATH
SAVAGE BEACH
PREDATOR 2

Weikinger, Ralf
MAGDALENE

Weil, Sean
EVERYBODY WINS

Wein, Dean
HEART CONDITION

Weinberg, David
RETURN OF SUPERFLY, THE

Weinberg, Sylvia
AVALON

Weiner, Michael
COUPE DE VILLE

Weiner, Thelma
AVALON

Weinstein, David
LORD OF THE FLIES

Weinstein, Nicole
LEMON SISTERS, THE

Weinstein, Seth
MONSTER HIGH

Weinstock, Murray
LEMON SISTERS, THE

Weir, Graham
BURNDOWN

Weiseman, Bob
POSTCARDS FROM THE EDGE

Weisman, Robin
THREE MEN AND A LITTLE LADY

Weiss, Adam Jason
OPPORTUNITY KNOCKS

Weiss, Gordon Joseph
AWAKENINGS

Weiss, Jeff
MR. DESTINY

Weissman, Jeffrey
BACK TO THE FUTURE PART III

Weist, Lucinda
PREDATOR 2

Welch, Jackie
ERNEST GOES TO JAIL

Welden, Michael
HUNT FOR RED OCTOBER, THE

Welker, Frank
GREMLINS 2 THE NEW BATCH
HAPPILY EVER AFTER
RESCUERS DOWN UNDER, THE

Weller, Michael
ROBOCOP 2

Weller, Peter
ROBOCOP 2

Weller, Robb
NIGHT EYES

Welles, Vernon
AMERICAN EAGLE

Wellins, Cori
ARACHNOPHOBIA

Welliver, Titus
NAVY SEALS

Wells, Reginald
BLUE STEEL

Wells, Terry
LORD OF THE FLIES

Wells, Tico
RETURN OF SUPERFLY, THE

Wells, Vernon
SHRIMP ON THE BARBIE, THE
CIRCUITRY MAN

Welsh, John
FAR OUT MAN

Welsh, Kenneth
FRESHMAN, THE

Welsh, Margaret
MR. AND MRS. BRIDGE

Welty, Roger
AIR AMERICA

Welzer, Irving
GOODFELLAS

Wendl, Alan J.
CRY-BABY

Wenner, Martin
RUSSIA HOUSE, THE

Werhenberg, Andy
FUNLAND

Werhenberg, Marisu
DEAD AIM
FUNLAND

Weselis, Danny
DIE HARD 2

West, Hot Tub Johnny
ADVENTURES OF FORD FAIRLANE, THE

Westerman, Floyd Red Crow
DANCES WITH WOLVES

Westfall, Rita-Jo
ME AND HIM

Wexel, Shane
EXORCIST III, THE

Weyers, Marius
HAPPY TOGETHER

Whaley, Frank
FRESHMAN, THE

Whalley, Andrew
WHITE HUNTER, BLACK HEART

Whalley-Kilmer, Joanne
KILL ME AGAIN
NAVY SEALS

Wharton, Richard
MEN DON'T LEAVE

Whatu, Anne
MONSTER HIGH

Wheeler, Ed
PRESUMED INNOCENT

Wheeler, Ira
QUICK CHANGE
NAVY SEALS
ALICE

Wheeler, Melanie
ERNEST GOES TO JAIL

Wheeler-Nicholson, Dana
CIRCUITRY MAN

Whelan, Jeremy
BLADES

Whelan, Robert
MOUNTAINS OF THE MOON

Whitaker, Dwayne
LEATHERFACE: THE TEXAS CHAINSAW
MASSACRE III

Whitaker, Forest
DOWNTOWN

Whitaker, Steve
GUMSHOE KID, THE

Whitcraft, Elizabeth
GOODFELLAS

White Bull, Ryan
DANCES WITH WOLVES

White Plume, Percy
DANCES WITH WOLVES

White, James
RIVER OF DEATH

White, John-Paul
KRAYS, THE

White, Kelsy
COME SEE THE PARADISE

White, Lillias
ME AND HIM

White, Michael
KRAYS, THE

White, Ron
STELLA

White, Sebastian
I COME IN PEACE

White, Stanley
MARKED FOR DEATH
DESPERATE HOURS

White, Steve
ADVENTURES OF FORD FAIRLANE, THE
MO' BETTER BLUES

White, Welker
SHOCK TO THE SYSTEM, A
GOODFELLAS

Whitehead, Robert
AMERICAN EAGLE

Whitelaw, Billie
KRAYS, THE

Whitfield, Lynn
DEAD AIM

Whitford, Bradley
VITAL SIGNS
PRESUMED INNOCENT
YOUNG GUNS II
AWAKENINGS

Whitlock, Isiah Jr.
GREMLINS 2 THE NEW BATCH
GOODFELLAS

Whitman, Kari
MEN AT WORK

Whitman, Parker
TOTAL RECALL

Whitman, Stuart
HEAVEN AND EARTH

Whitney, Ann
HOME ALONE

Whittley, John
BURNDOWN

Whitworth, Hollister
WILD ORCHID

Whyte, Laura
BLOOD SALVAGE

Wick, Claudia
AFTERSHOCK

Wickes, Mary
POSTCARDS FROM THE EDGE

Wickman, Karl
DARKMAN

Wicks, Victoria
STRIKE IT RICH

Wiener, Jeff
WITHOUT YOU, I'M NOTHING

Wiest, Dianne
EDWARD SCISSORHANDS

Wiggins, Barry
HOUSE PARTY

Wiggins, Carol M.
MO' BETTER BLUES

Wijngaarden, Jip
VINCENT AND THEO

Wilbee, Codie Lucas
NARROW MARGIN

Wilborn, Carlton
WITHOUT YOU, I'M NOTHING

Wilbur, George P.
LOOSE CANNONS
COME SEE THE PARADISE

Wilburn, Lise
DESPERATE HOURS

Wilder, Alan
HOME ALONE

Wilder, Gene
FUNNY ABOUT LOVE

Wilder, Glen
FAR OUT MAN

Wildman, John
AMERICAN BOYFRIENDS

Wildsmith, Dawn
ALIENATOR

Wiles, Michael Shamus
LEATHERFACE: THE TEXAS CHAINSAW
MASSACRE III

Wiley, Richard
ALIENATOR

Wilhoite, Kathleen
EVERYBODY WINS
BAD INFLUENCE

Wilkening, Catherine
JESUS OF MONTREAL

Wilkey, Jim
DICK TRACY

Wilkof, Lee
CHATTAHOOCHEE

Wilks, Darrell
SHOCK TO THE SYSTEM, A

Willhite, Denisa
MONSTER HIGH

William, Sam
BURNDOWN

Williams, Afram Bill
FLATLINERS

Williams, Alva
JACOB'S LADDER

Williams, Billy
GAME, THE

Williams, Billy "Sly"
PREDATOR 2

Williams, Chino
HOUSE PARTY

Williams, Cynda
MO' BETTER BLUES

Williams, Dick Anthony
MO' BETTER BLUES
EDWARD SCISSORHANDS

Williams, Don
MISADVENTURES OF MR. WILT, THE

Williams, Elizabeth
PRESUMED INNOCENT

Williams, Gerard G.
PREDATOR 2

Williams, Glenn III
MO' BETTER BLUES

Williams, Hal
ROOKIE, THE

Williams, John
GOODFELLAS

Williams, John Anthony
STATE OF GRACE

Williams, Justin
ME AND HIM

Williams, Kimberli
WITHOUT YOU, I'M NOTHING

Williams, Lloyd T.
PRETTY WOMAN

Williams, Michael
ROCKY V

Williams, Philip
WHERE THE HEART IS

Williams, Robin
CADILLAC MAN
AWAKENINGS

Williams, Roosevelt
HOT SPOT, THE

Williams, Sam
TUSKS

Williams, Sherry
WHITE GIRL, THE

Williams, Spice
HOLLYWOOD HOT TUBS II: EDUCATING
CRYSTAL

Williams, Steven Lloyd
FORBIDDEN DANCE, THE

Williams, Tamara
ELLIOT FAUMAN, PH.D.

Williams, Terrence
MO' BETTER BLUES

Williams, Tonya Lee
SPACED INVADERS

Williams, Treat
NIGHT OF THE SHARKS

Williamson, Ermal
BONFIRE OF THE VANITIES

Williamson, Matt
ALICE

Williamson, Mykel T.
FIRST POWER, THE

Williamson, Nicol
EXORCIST III, THE

Williamson, Scott
FIRE BIRDS

Williard, Carol
PRETTY WOMAN

Willingham, Noble
BLIND FURY

Willis, Bruce
DIE HARD 2
BONFIRE OF THE VANITIES
LOOK WHO'S TALKING TOO

Willis, David Sr.
DIE HARD 2

Willis, Jack
PROBLEM CHILD
I COME IN PEACE

Willis, Johnny
I LOVE YOU TO DEATH

Willoughby, Pat
MADHOUSE

Wills, Sherrie
EXORCIST III, THE

Wilmot, David
FIELD, THE

Wilmot, Ronan
FIELD, THE

Wilms, Andre
MONSIEUR HIRE
LIFE IS A LONG QUIET RIVER

Wilson, Andy
COOK, THE THIEF, HIS WIFE & HER
LOVER, THE

Wilson, David Lloyd
PACIFIC HEIGHTS

Wilson, Donna
DAYS OF THUNDER

Wilson, Jodie
MEMPHIS BELLE

Wilson, Lambert
BELLY OF AN ARCHITECT, THE

Wilson, Mary Louise
EVERYBODY WINS
GREEN CARD

Wilson, Michael
LOVE AT LARGE

Wilson, Rita
BONFIRE OF THE VANITIES

Wilson, Scott
YOUNG GUNS II
EXORCIST III, THE

Wilson, Thomas F.
BACK TO THE FUTURE PART III

Wilson, Zoey
HANDMAID'S TALE, THE

Wimmer, Brian
UNDER THE BOARDWALK

Windbush, Troy
BONFIRE OF THE VANITIES

Windom, William
DEAD AIM
FUNLAND

Windsor, Romy
BIG BAD JOHN

Wine, Landon
CLASS OF 1999

Winfield, Paul
PRESUMED INNOCENT

Winger, Debra
EVERYBODY WINS
SHELTERING SKY, THE

Winkler, Bill
PRESUMED INNOCENT

Winkler, Margo
GOODFELLAS

Winklis, Jeff
SPACED INVADERS

Winling, Jean-Marie
CYRANO DE BERGERAC

Winslow, Michael
FAR OUT MAN

Winston, Adina
BONFIRE OF THE VANITIES

Winston, George
HUNT FOR RED OCTOBER, THE

Winston, Leslie
FUNLAND

Winter, Alex
ROSALIE GOES SHOPPING

Winters, Anthony
GREMLINS 2 THE NEW BATCH

Winters, Shelley
TOUCH OF A STRANGER

Winters, Time
GREMLINS 2 THE NEW BATCH

Winters, Vicki
VITAL SIGNS

Wise, Michael
FIRST POWER, THE

Wise, William
BLUE STEEL

Wiseman, Jeffrey
HOME ALONE

Wiseman, Michael
PREDATOR 2

Witherspoon, John
HOUSE PARTY

Witker, Kristi
GREMLINS 2 THE NEW BATCH

Woessner, Hank
DEATH WARRANT

Wohl, David
PRESUMED INNOCENT

Wohrman, Bill
OPPONENT, THE

Wolf, Hillary
HOME ALONE

Wolf, Kelly
GRAVEYARD SHIFT

Wolf, Rita
SLIPSTREAM

Wolfchild, Sheldon
DANCES WITH WOLVES

Wolfe, Ian
DICK TRACY

Wolfe, Twila
WHITE GIRL, THE

Wolinki, Hawk
MEN AT WORK

Wolk, Emil
TALL GUY, THE

Wolston, Dianne
REAL BULLETS

Wong, Anthony
KINDERGARTEN COP

Wong, B.D.
FRESHMAN, THE

Wong, Everett
THREE MEN AND A LITTLE LADY

Wong, Joi
REINCARNATION OF GOLDEN LOTUS, THE

Wong, Russell
EAT A BOWL OF TEA

Wong, Victor
TREMORS
EAT A BOWL OF TEA
LIFE IS CHEAP. . . BUT TOILET PAPER IS
EXPENSIVE

Wonge, Darryl M. Jr.
MO' BETTER BLUES

Wood, Clive
DOG TAGS

Wood, Elijah
AVALON

Wood, John Lisbon
DARKMAN

Wood, Tom
AVALON

Woodard, Charlaine
ME AND HIM

Woodard, Jimmy
GRAVEYARD SHIFT

Woodeson, Nicholas
RUSSIA HOUSE, THE

Woodnut, John
MACK THE KNIFE

Woodruff, Anthony
TALL GUY, THE

Woodruff, Kim
DISTURBANCE, THE

Woodruff, Rod
MOUNTAINS OF THE MOON

Woods, Barbara Alyn
CIRCUITRY MAN

Woods, Connie
FORBIDDEN DANCE, THE

Woods, Lauren K.
ROCKY V

Woods, Maxine
PLOT AGAINST HARRY, THE

Woods, Richard
MILLER'S CROSSING

Woods, Terry
HIDDEN AGENDA

Woodside, Julie
AFTERSHOCK

Woodson, William
BONFIRE OF THE VANITIES

Woodward, Joanne
MR. AND MRS. BRIDGE

Woodward, Meredith Bain
SHORT TIME

Wooldridge, Susan
BYE BYE BLUES

Woolf, Alain
RIVER OF DEATH

Woolf, Ian
COME SEE THE PARADISE

Woollard, Emma
WHERE THE HEART IS

Woolsey, Brent
FOURTH WAR, THE

Woolsey, Jacqueline
PRETTY WOMAN

Worden, Hank
ALMOST AN ANGEL

Woronov, Mary
DICK TRACY

Worth, Nicholas
DARKMAN

Woyt, Jim
KILL-OFF, THE

Wozniak, Daniel
RUSSIA HOUSE, THE

Wozniak, Theresa
MEN DON'T LEAVE

Wray, Peter
BLADES

Wren, Clare
STEEL AND LACE

Wright, Amy
DADDY'S DYIN'. . . WHO'S GOT THE WILL?

Wright, Beccy
MISADVENTURES OF MR. WILT, THE

Wright, Jeffrey
PRESUMED INNOCENT

Wright, Jenny
SHOCK TO THE SYSTEM, A
YOUNG GUNS II

Wright, Joey
LAST OF THE FINEST, THE

Wright, Larry
GREEN CARD

Wright, Mary Catherine
HEART CONDITION
AWAKENINGS

Wright, Richard "Dub"
ROCKY V

Wright, Robin
STATE OF GRACE

Wright, Samuel E.
ME AND HIM

Wright, Steven J.
SHORT TIME

Wright, Timothy D.
EVERYBODY WINS

Wright, Tom
FORCE OF CIRCUMSTANCE
MARKED FOR DEATH

Wu, Ping
HUNT FOR RED OCTOBER, THE

Wuhr, Ludwig
NASTY GIRL, THE

Wuhrer, Kari
ADVENTURES OF FORD FAIRLANE, THE

Wyatt, J.D.
BONFIRE OF THE VANITIES

Wyatt, Sharon
CLASS OF 1999

Wylie, Adam
CHILD'S PLAY 2
KINDERGARTEN COP

Wyman, Brad
MEN AT WORK

Wynands, Danny
PACIFIC HEIGHTS

Wynn, Darlene
HAVANA

Wynn, Kristin
FIRE BIRDS

Wynne, Christopher
BACK TO THE FUTURE PART III

Xavier, Celia
NIGHT ANGEL

Xuereb, Emmanuel
BONFIRE OF THE VANITIES

Yablans, Mickey
FIRE BIRDS

Yamabe, Chika
DREAMS

Yamada, Akisato
DREAMS
HEAVEN AND EARTH

Yamakawa, Nana
DREAMS

Yamamoto, Ronald
COME SEE THE PARADISE

Yamamoto, Sakiko
DREAMS

Yamanaka, Yasuhito
DREAMS

Yamashita, Tessho
DREAMS

Yannatos, Michalis
LANDSCAPE IN THE MIST

Yasbeck, Amy
PRETTY WOMAN
PROBLEM CHILD

Yasuda, Doug
CRAZY PEOPLE

Yatsko, Sasha
RUSSIA HOUSE, THE

Yayama, Osamu
DREAMS
HEAVEN AND EARTH

Yeager, Biff
GUMSHOE KID, THE
EDWARD SCISSORHANDS

Yeager, Ed
PROBLEM CHILD

Yeh, Sally
LASER MAN, THE

Yen, Lam Chun
REINCARNATION OF GOLDEN LOTUS, THE

Yeo, Leslie
BYE BYE BLUES

Yochimi, Sumimaro
DREAMS

Yoda, Masumi
DREAMS

Yoffe, Beatrice
AVALON

Yohnka, Merritt
REAL BULLETS

Yong, Su
STRIKE IT RICH

Yordanoff, Wladimir
VINCENT AND THEO

York, John J.
STEEL AND LACE

York, Kathleen
FLASHBACK
I LOVE YOU TO DEATH
COLD FEET

York, Michael
COME SEE THE PARADISE

York, Nora
ME AND HIM

York, Roy
HAMLET

York, Tyler
ME AND HIM

Yorra, Seth
IMPORTED BRIDEGROOM, THE

Yoshida, Harunobu
COME SEE THE PARADISE

Yoshioka, Sayuri
DREAMS

Yoshizawa, Tomomi
DREAMS

Young, Alan
DUCKTALES: THE MOVIE – TREASURE OF
THE LOST LAMP

Young, Burt
BLOOD RED
LAST EXIT TO BROOKLYN
BETSY'S WEDDING
BACKSTREET DREAMS
ROCKY V

Young, Charles W.
DARKMAN

Young, David Allen
LAST OF THE FINEST, THE

Young, Debra
LORDS OF MAGICK, THE

Young, Dey
PRETTY WOMAN

Young, Henry
MONSTER HIGH

Young, Howie
YOUNG GUNS II

Young, Jordan
AVALON

Young, Neil
LOVE AT LARGE

Young, Paula
MONSTER HIGH

Young, Sean
FIRE BIRDS

Young, Wycliffe
CAGED IN PARADISO

Youngman, Henny
GOODFELLAS

Yu, Ju
TEENAGE MUTANT NINJA TURTLES

Yue, Ozzie
NUNS ON THE RUN

Yuen, Galen
STREET ASYLUM

Yui, Masayuki
DREAMS

Yule, Ian
RIVER OF DEATH

Yulin, Harris
NARROW MARGIN

Yun, Lang
PAINT IT BLACK

Yunker, Peter
SHORT TIME

Yustman, Odette
KINDERGARTEN COP

Zabou
C'EST LA VIE

Zabriskie, Grace
WILD AT HEART
CHILD'S PLAY 2

Zackerian, Ruth
LORDS OF MAGICK, THE

Zada, Ramy
TWO EVIL EYES

Zadok, Arnon
TORN APART

Zaitchenko, Piotr
TAXI BLUES

Zaizen, Naomi
HEAVEN AND EARTH

Zal, Roxana
UNDER THE BOARDWALK

Zale, Dan
BIRD ON A WIRE

Zalkind, Robert
AVALON

Zaloom, Joe
SHOCK TO THE SYSTEM, A

Zamperla, Rinaldo
NIGHT OF THE SHARKS

Zand, Michael
MADHOUSE

Zane, Billy
MEMPHIS BELLE

Zane, Lisa
BAD INFLUENCE

Zane, Lora
MEN DON'T LEAVE

Zanini, Marcel
LIFE AND NOTHING BUT

Zappa, Ahmet
PUMP UP THE VOLUME

Zavala, Jimmy
ADVENTURES OF FORD FAIRLANE, THE

Zbruyev, Alexander
LONELY WOMAN SEEKS LIFE COMPANION

Zehentmayr, Patricia
ROSALIE GOES SHOPPING

Zeitsman, Elzabe
RIVER OF DEATH

Zeke, Michalis
LANDSCAPE IN THE MIST

Zemarel, James A.
AVALON

Zentz, Martin
LORD OF THE FLIES

Zepeda, Gerardo
REVENGE

Zerna, Gene
DR. CALIGARI

Zette
LAST EXIT TO BROOKLYN

Zetterling, Mai
WITCHES, THE
HIDDEN AGENDA

Zezima, Michael
WILDEST DREAMS

Zimmerman, Patric
JETSONS: THE MOVIE

Zingler, Jay
BACK TO BACK

Zinner, Peter
HUNT FOR RED OCTOBER, THE

Ziskie, Daniel
VITAL SIGNS

Zoloto, Steven
OPPORTUNITY KNOCKS

Zozzora, Carmine
PREDATOR 2

Zuber, Marc
NAVY SEALS

Zucha, Jessica
PROBLEM CHILD

Zuckerman, Alexander
EXORCIST III, THE

Zuelke, Mark
ADVENTURES OF FORD FAIRLANE, THE

Zulcoski, Dan Charles
HOME ALONE

Zully, Stewart J.
BONFIRE OF THE VANITIES

Zunetov, Vladimir
RUSSIA HOUSE, THE

Zushi, Yoshitaka
DREAMS

Zwerin, Mike
LIFE AND NOTHING BUT

Zylberman, Noam
NUTCRACKER PRINCE, THE

ANIMATORS

Aquino, Ruben A.
RESCUERS DOWN UNDER, THE

Available Light Ltd.
MR. DESTINY

Brizzi, Gaetan
DUCKTALES: THE MOVIE – TREASURE OF
THE LOST LAMP

Brizzi, Paul
DUCKTALES: THE MOVIE – TREASURE OF
THE LOST LAMP

Burks, Jeff
TOTAL RECALL

Canfield, Charlie
HUNT FOR RED OCTOBER, THE

Chiodo Brothers Productions
DARKMAN

Cutler, David
RESCUERS DOWN UNDER, THE

DeRosa, Anthony
RESCUERS DOWN UNDER, THE

Dierdorff, Christopher
HUNT FOR RED OCTOBER, THE

Edmonds, Russ
RESCUERS DOWN UNDER, THE

Friday, Jammie
DARKMAN

Gombert, Ed
RESCUERS DOWN UNDER, THE

Gonzales, Allen
ERNEST GOES TO JAIL
DICK TRACY

Henn, Mark
RESCUERS DOWN UNDER, THE

Johnson, Jay
I COME IN PEACE

Jones, Chuck
GREMLINS 2 THE NEW BATCH

Kean, Katherine
MR. DESTINY

Keane, Glen
RESCUERS DOWN UNDER, THE

Keene, Lisa
RESCUERS DOWN UNDER, THE

Kensington Falls Animation
NIGHT OF THE LIVING DEAD

Kurogane, Hiroshi
TWILIGHT OF THE COCKROACHES

Kutchaver, Kevin
DARKMAN

Marjoribanks, Duncan
RESCUERS DOWN UNDER, THE

Meyers, Pat
HUNT FOR RED OCTOBER, THE

Moreau, Harry
CHILD'S PLAY 2

Pallant, Clive
DUCKTALES: THE MOVIE – TREASURE OF
THE LOST LAMP

Patterson, Ray
JETSONS: THE MOVIE

Perpetual Motion Pictures
SPACED INVADERS

Ranieri, Nik
RESCUERS DOWN UNDER, THE

Recinos, Sanuel
DICK TRACY

Rodric, Mattias Marcos
DUCKTALES: THE MOVIE – TREASURE OF
THE LOST LAMP

Swenson, Eric
HUNT FOR RED OCTOBER, THE

Takahashi, Wes
BACK TO THE FUTURE PART III

Tippett, Phil
ROBOCOP 2

Van Vliet, John T.
MR. DESTINY

Woodcock, Vincent
DUCKTALES: THE MOVIE – TREASURE OF
THE LOST LAMP

Zielinski, Kathy
RESCUERS DOWN UNDER, THE

ART DIRECTORS

Abrahamson, Doug
SKINHEADS – THE SECOND COMING OF
HATE

Adams, Kevin
WITHOUT YOU, I'M NOTHING

Ahmad, Maher
GOODFELLAS

Alexander, Scott
SPACED INVADERS

Allen, John
FACE OF THE ENEMY

Ammon, Ruth
LONGTIME COMPANION

Anderson, Cletus
TWO EVIL EYES

Aranzamendez, Sammy
DEMONSTONE

Baron, Alan
JEZEBEL'S KISS

Barr, Ginni
DOWN THE DRAIN

Beal, Charley
EVERYBODY WINS

Berger, Richard
MY BLUE HEAVEN

Berto, Max
MR. FROST

Bertolino, Frank
FORBIDDEN DANCE, THE

Bingham, Michael
PROBLEM CHILD

Blaxland, Andrew
TIME GUARDIAN, THE

Brandenburg, Rosemary
WELCOME HOME, ROXY CARMICHAEL

Brisbin, David
ANIMAL BEHAVIOR

Buchanan, Mike
STRIKE IT RICH

Buckley, Gae
REPOSSESSED

Bulajic, Bora
HOSTILE TAKEOVER

Burian-Mohr, Christopher
ARACHNOPHOBIA

Burkhart, James
MARKED FOR DEATH

Candido, Nino
I COME IN PEACE

Canes, George
TEN LITTLE INDIANS

Cavedon, Jane
WILD ORCHID

Cavers, Clinton
NUNS ON THE RUN

Chang, Jennifer
LORD OF THE FLIES

Cisek, Tony
ELLIOT FAUMAN, PH.D.

Combs, William S.
BAD INFLUENCE

Conway, Jeremy
JACOB'S LADDER

Cortese, Tom
MARTIANS GO HOME!

Crone, Bruce
SIDE OUT

Cruse, William
HUNT FOR RED OCTOBER, THE

Cutler, Bernie
GHOST DAD

Dagort, Phil
DARKMAN

Daoudal, Gerard
IMPROMPTU

de Chauvigny, Emmanuel
MAHABHARATA, THE

Deluxe, Dolores
CRY-BABY

Densmore, Brian
CAGED IN PARADISO
AFTERSHOCK
BACK TO BACK

Dobbie, Scott
BYE BYE BLUES

Dorme, Norman
WITCHES, THE

Douret, Dominique
VINCENT AND THEO

Duffield, Tom
EDWARD SCISSORHANDS

Dultz, Jim
FLATLINERS

Durrell, William J. Jr.
LOOSE CANNONS

Durrell, William Jr.
ROCKY V

Edwards, Vaughn
NAVY SEALS

Ellis, John
STAR QUEST: BEYOND THE RISING MOON

Farentello, Nick
DISTURBANCE, THE

Feng, James
NIGHT OF THE LIVING DEAD

Fenton-Wells, Carol
DAMNED RIVER

Fernandez, Benjamin
DAYS OF THUNDER

Flood, Frank Hallinan
FIELD, THE

Fowler, Maurice
MOUNTAINS OF THE MOON

Fowlie, Michael
BURNDOWN

Frank, Jeremie
RETURN OF SUPERFLY, THE

Fraser, Eric
SHORT TIME

Frick, John
HOT SPOT, THE

Frigerio, Ezio
CYRANO DE BERGERAC

Fujiwara, Kazuhiko
HEAVEN AND EARTH

Galvin, Timothy
STATE OF GRACE

Gavric, Vlastimir
MAGDALENE

Ginn, Jeffrey
STELLA

Ginsburg, Gershon
PACIFIC HEIGHTS

Glon, Georges
HENRY AND JUNE

Goldstein, Robert
EXORCIST III, THE

Gomez, Raul
MAHABHARATA, THE

Gracie, Ian
QUIGLEY DOWN UNDER

Granada, Jose Rodriguez
TOTAL RECALL

Groom, Bill
AWAKENINGS

Grusd, John
HAPPILY EVER AFTER

Guerra, Bob
PRESUMED INNOCENT

Haack, Mark
LAST EXIT TO BROOKLYN

Haas, Nathan
FUNNY ABOUT LOVE

Haber, David M.
PRETTY WOMAN
THREE MEN AND A LITTLE LADY

Hamilton, Gina
BLOOD RELATIONS

Hammond, Mark
WILDEST DREAMS

Hardwicke, Catherine
MR. DESTINY

Hardy, Kenneth A.
AFTER DARK, MY SWEET

Harrington, John Mark
MEN DON'T LEAVE

Harris, Henry
INNOCENT VICTIM

Harvin, Nancy
MODERN LOVE

Hausman, Shawn
STATE OF GRACE

Hole, Fred
MOUNTAINS OF THE MOON
AVALON

Holland, Richard
CHICAGO JOE AND THE SHOWGIRL

Hopkins, Speed
QUICK CHANGE
ALICE

Horowitz, Ben
AMERICAN EAGLE

Hubbard, Geoff
LAST OF THE FINEST, THE
PREDATOR 2

Hudolin, Richard
BIRD ON A WIRE

Hunt, Maurice
RESCUERS DOWN UNDER, THE

Hutman, Jon
I LOVE YOU TO DEATH

Ichida, Kiichi
TWILIGHT OF THE COCKROACHES

Inagaki, Hisao
BLACK RAIN

Jacobson, Jaqueline
IN THE SPIRIT

Johnson, Marc Henry
DEF BY TEMPTATION

Johnson, P. Michael
HOMER & EDDIE

Johnston, Tucker
PEACEMAKER

Kaplan, Corey
UNDER THE BOARDWALK
COLD FEET

Karapiperis, Mikes
LANDSCAPE IN THE MIST

Karatzas, Steve
LOVE AT LARGE

Kaufman, Susan
WHERE THE HEART IS

Keywan, Alicia
STANLEY AND IRIS
FRESHMAN, THE

King, John
MEMPHIS BELLE

Klawonn, Patricia
MEN AT WORK
DESPERATE HOURS

Koo, Collete
LIFE IS CHEAP. . . BUT TOILET PAPER IS
EXPENSIVE

Kuhn, Beth
Q&A

Lamont, Michael
HAMLET

Lauderbaugh, Lindah
ALIENATOR

Le Tenoux, Johan
STREETS

Lee, Robert E.
DEATH WARRANT

Levchenko, Alexei
LONELY WOMAN SEEKS LIFE COMPANION

Levy, Angela
GRIM PRAIRIE TALES

Lewinsohn, Yeda
WILD ORCHID

Licursi, Jack
HOLLYWOOD HOT TUBS II: EDUCATING
CRYSTAL

Ling, Tang Wei
REINCARNATION OF GOLDEN LOTUS, THE

Lucky, Joe
GREMLINS 2 THE NEW BATCH

McAterr, James
WHERE THE HEART IS

McCrow, William
INHERITOR

McDonald, Leslie
MILLER'S CROSSING
GRIFTERS, THE

Maltese, Dan
VITAL SIGNS

Man, Lee King
REINCARNATION OF GOLDEN LOTUS, THE

Mandel, Howard
PLOT AGAINST HARRY, THE

Mann, Louis
HARD TO KILL

Mansbridge, Mark
MISERY

Marchione, Luigi
MAGDALENE

Marcotte, Pam
ROBOCOP 2

Marcotte, Pamela
HIT LIST

Marty, Jack
RIVERBEND

Maskovich, Donald
TREMORS
CHILD'S PLAY 2

Mays, Richard
KINDERGARTEN COP

Melton, Gregory
HANDMAID'S TALE, THE

Mercier, Gilbert
BRAIN DEAD

Meyer, Alexandre
WILD ORCHID

Meyers, Troy
MASQUE OF THE RED DEATH

Michelson, Harold
DICK TRACY

Miller, Bruce
GUARDIAN, THE

Miller, David B.
FAR OUT MAN

Mingate, Don
TUSKS

Moehrle, Peter
NUTCRACKER PRINCE, THE

Mooney, Kim
NARROW MARGIN

Moore, Andrew
BETSY'S WEDDING

Munro, Christa
YOUNG GUNS II

Murakami, James J.
COUPE DE VILLE

Muraki, Yoshiro
DREAMS

Myers, Troy
TO SLEEP WITH ANGER

Myhre, John
WELCOME HOME, ROXY CARMICHAEL

Naert, Didier
MAN INSIDE, THE

Nicdao, Mon
DOG TAGS

Nielsen, Seven L.
SKI PATROL

Nowak, Christopher
GREEN CARD

Orbom, Eric
STANLEY AND IRIS
NARROW MARGIN

Padvovan, Federico
OPPONENT, THE

Phelps, Nigel
HIDDEN AGENDA

Pickrell, Gregory
DOWNTOWN

Pope, Leslie A.
OPPORTUNITY KNOCKS

Raes, Tony
TIME GUARDIAN, THE

Ragland, Mark
ERNEST GOES TO JAIL

Reading, Tony
AIR AMERICA
WHITE HUNTER, BLACK HEART

Richardson, Edward
AVALON

Richardson, George
HAVANA

Richardson, Susan
HOUSE PARTY

Rideout, Ransom
DEAD PIT

Roberts, Rick
FOURTH WAR, THE

Robinson, Cliff
LIONHEART

Roelfs, Jan
VINCENT AND THEO

Rosewarne, John
RIVER OF DEATH

Ruben, Vola
MEN IN LOVE

Ruscio, Nina
WELCOME HOME, ROXY CARMICHAEL

Russell, Peter
CHICAGO JOE AND THE SHOWGIRL

Rutt, Todd
BEDROOM EYES II

St. John Blakey, Ella
BODY CHEMISTRY

Sainz, Jorge
REVENGE

Sakash, Evelyn
MERMAIDS

Saklad, Steve
MERMAIDS

Sakuragi, Akira
DREAMS

Sanders, Andrew
SHELTERING SKY, THE

Sanders, Tom
REVENGE

Schreiber, Richard
TWO JAKES, THE

Scott, Trey
FALSE IDENTITY

Seymour, Sharon
PACIFIC HEIGHTS

Shaffer, Henry
EXORCIST III, THE

Shaw, Robert K. Jr.
SHOCK TO THE SYSTEM, A

Sheehan, Janna
DARK SIDE OF THE MOON

Silva, Karen
DUCKTALES: THE MOVIE – TREASURE OF
    THE LOST LAMP

Simpson, C.J.
MADHOUSE

Sissman, Rob
BLOOD SALVAGE

Skinner, Dian
TWISTED JUSTICE

Skinner, William L.
DANCES WITH WOLVES

Spence, Steve
AIR AMERICA

Stephens, Pam E.
MO' BETTER BLUES

Stern, Kandy
POSTCARDS FROM THE EDGE

Stevens, John Wright
WHITE PALACE

Stewart-Richardson, Alison
INNOCENT VICTIM

Stone, Malcolm
SLIPSTREAM

Stone McShirley, Marjorie
BACK TO THE FUTURE PART III

Sullivan, Michael
HOT SPOT, THE

Tagliaferro, Pat
FIRST POWER, THE
FIRE BIRDS

Tagliaferro, Patrick
CHATTAHOOCHEE

Tandy, Jeff
ALLIGATOR EYES

Tankus, Zeev
DOWN THE DRAIN

Tavoularis, Alex
GODFATHER PART III, THE

Teegarden, Jim
BACK TO THE FUTURE PART III

Thevenet, Pierre-Louis
TWISTED OBSESSION

Thomas, Michael
WEDDING BAND

Tocci, James
TOTAL RECALL

Tomkins, Alan
MEMPHIS BELLE

Van, Ben
VINCENT AND THEO

Vedovelli, Luciana
BELLY OF AN ARCHITECT, THE

Verreaux, Ed
ROOKIE, THE

Wagener, Christiaan
DIE HARD 2
ADVENTURES OF FORD FAIRLANE, THE

Wager, Dianne
HUNT FOR RED OCTOBER, THE

Webster, Dan
HOME ALONE

Welden, James Terry
FLASHBACK

Wilcox, Richard
LOOK WHO'S TALKING TOO

Williams, Ed
NAVY SEALS

Willitt, John
COME SEE THE PARADISE

Willson, David
NARROW MARGIN

Wing, Chan Yiu
REINCARNATION OF GOLDEN LOTUS, THE

Wissner, Gary
TEENAGE MUTANT NINJA TURTLES

Wolverton, Lynn
DEAD AIM

Woodbridge, Patricia
CADILLAC MAN

Woodruff, Donald
HUNT FOR RED OCTOBER, THE

Yamaguchi, Shu
SUMMER VACATION: 1999

Yedekar, Ram
PERFECT MURDER, THE

Yeung, Yuen Ching
REINCARNATION OF GOLDEN LOTUS, THE

Yip, Timmy
EAT A BOWL OF TEA

Yu, Ricky
PRIMARY TARGET

Yurkevich, Valeri
TAXI BLUES

Ziemer, Stephanie
KING OF NEW YORK

CHOREOGRAPHERS

Adkins, Jeff J.
SKI PATROL

Allain, Aurorah
ADVENTURES OF FORD FAIRLANE, THE

Allen, Barbara
ME AND HIM

Aoyagi, Robert
SAVAGE BEACH

Armitage, Karole
WITHOUT YOU, I'M NOTHING

Augins, Charles
TALL GUY, THE

Birch, Pat
STELLA

Bocchino, Chrissy
MADHOUSE

Calhoun, Jeffrey
HAPPY TOGETHER

Campbell, Tisha
HOUSE PARTY

Chavez, Felix
FORBIDDEN DANCE, THE

DeVito, Joanne
NIGHT ANGEL

Eastside, Lori
CRY-BABY

Erlbaum, Nathalie
HENRY AND JUNE

Fazan, Eleanor
MOUNTAINS OF THE MOON

Florentine, Isaac
DOWN THE DRAIN

Fournier, Jean-Pierre
HEAVEN AND EARTH

Garrison, Miranda
FORBIDDEN DANCE, THE

Gursman, Dorian
MARKED FOR DEATH

Hata, Michiyo
DREAMS

Heyes, Warren
CHICAGO JOE AND THE SHOWGIRL

Hornaday, Jeffrey
OPPORTUNITY KNOCKS
DICK TRACY

Jeffries, Brad
BACK TO THE FUTURE PART III

Johnson, A.J.
HOUSE PARTY

Johnson, Pat
TEENAGE MUTANT NINJA TURTLES

Kid 'N Play
HOUSE PARTY

Kuze, Hiroshi
HEAVEN AND EARTH

Mann, Anita
LEMON SISTERS, THE

Murphy, Richard
WHERE THE HEART IS

Paterson, Vincent
HAVANA

Phillips, Arlene
WHITE HUNTER, BLACK HEART

Sacks, Quinny
TUNE IN TOMORROW

Sallid, Otis
GRAFFITI BRIDGE

Seagal, Steven
HARD TO KILL

Shabba-Doo
LAMBADA

Steinberg, Morleigh
WILD ORCHID

Tadloch, Tad
I LOVE YOU TO DEATH

Taylor-Corbett, Lynne
MY BLUE HEAVEN

Thorslund, Linda
AMERICAN BOYFRIENDS

Toguri, David
MACK THE KNIFE
MEMPHIS BELLE

Van Laast, Anthony
LIONHEART

CINEMATOGRAPHERS

Ahlberg, Mac
ROBOT JOX

Albert, Arthur
HEART CONDITION

Alcaine, Jose Luis
TIE ME UP! TIE ME DOWN!
TWISTED OBSESSION

Alonzo, John A.
INTERNAL AFFAIRS
GUARDIAN, THE
NAVY SEALS

Alsobrook, Russ T.
DARK SIDE OF THE MOON

Andersen, Erling Thurmann
ISTANBUL, KEEP YOUR EYES OPEN

Aronovitch, Ricardo
MAN INSIDE, THE

Arvanitis, Giorgos
LANDSCAPE IN THE MIST

Atherton, Howard
MERMAIDS

Auroux, Bernard
FALSE IDENTITY

Bailey, John
MY BLUE HEAVEN

Baker, Ian
RUSSIA HOUSE, THE

Baldwin, Robert M.
BASKETCASE 2
FRANKENHOOKER

Ballhaus, Michael
GOODFELLAS
POSTCARDS FROM THE EDGE

Bartkowiak, Andrzej
Q&A

Battistoni, Mario
ICICLE THIEF, THE

Bazelli, Bojan
KING OF NEW YORK

Bergamini, Giovanni
NIGHT OF THE SHARKS

Berrie, John
HOW TO MAKE LOVE TO A NEGRO WITH-
OUT GETTING TIRED

Berta, Renato
MAY FOOLS

Beymer, John
FEUD, THE

Biddle, Adrian
TALL GUY, THE

Blake, Ian
EVERYBODY WINS

Bogner, Ludek
HOSTILE TAKEOVER

Boyd, Russell
ALMOST AN ANGEL

Brenguier, Dominique
MR. FROST

Brewster, Mike
TEENAGE MUTANT NINJA TURTLES

Brylyakov, Vladimir
FREEZE – DIE – COME TO LIFE

Burgess, Don
UNDER THE BOARDWALK
BLIND FURY

Burnside, Bruce
LORDS OF MAGICK, THE

Burton, Geoff
TIME GUARDIAN, THE

Butler, Bill
GRAFFITI BRIDGE

Byrne, Bobby
LEMON SISTERS, THE

Cabrera, John
HONEYMOON ACADEMY

Callaway, Thomas
DEMON WIND

Callaway, Thomas L.
STEEL AND LACE

Caramico, Bob
REAL BULLETS

Carpenter, Russell
DEATH WARRANT

Carter, James L.
LEATHERFACE: THE TEXAS CHAINSAW
MASSACRE III
SPACED INVADERS
BACK TO BACK

Chapman, Michael
QUICK CHANGE
KINDERGARTEN COP

Chivers, Steven
HARDWARE

Climati, Antonio
PRIMAL RAGE

Collins, Marty
DEAD PIT

Collister, Peter Lyons
PROBLEM CHILD

Connor, John
SHORT TIME

Conroy, Jack
FIELD, THE

Cook, Philip
STAR QUEST: BEYOND THE RISING MOON

Crockett, Todd
ALLIGATOR EYES

Cronenweth, Jordan
STATE OF GRACE

Cundey, Dean
BACK TO THE FUTURE PART III

Czapsky, Stefan
FLASHBACK
LAST EXIT TO BROOKLYN
VAMPIRE'S KISS
CHILD'S PLAY 2
EDWARD SCISSORHANDS

Daviau, Allen
AVALON

Davis, Elliot
LOVE AT LARGE

Davis, John
DEAD AIM

de Almeida, Acacio
FLAME IN MY HEART, A

De Bont, Jan
HUNT FOR RED OCTOBER, THE
FLATLINERS

de Keyzer, Bruno
LIFE AND NOTHING BUT
IMPROMPTU

Deakins, Roger
MOUNTAINS OF THE MOON
AIR AMERICA

Decca, Anghel
RETURN OF SUPERFLY, THE

Del Ruth, Thomas
LOOK WHO'S TALKING TOO

Deming, Peter
HOUSE PARTY
MARTIANS GO HOME!
WHY ME?

DeRoche, Axel
NASTY GIRL, THE

Desatoff, Paul
STREET ASYLUM

Di Palma, Carlo
ALICE

Dickerson, Ernest
LASER MAN, THE
DEF BY TEMPTATION
FRIGHT HOUSE
MO' BETTER BLUES

Draper, Robert
TALES FROM THE DARKSIDE: THE MOVIE

Dufaux, Guy
JESUS OF MONTREAL

Duggan, Bryan
COLD FEET

Dunn, Andrew
STRAPLESS
CHATTAHOOCHEE

Eggby, David
BLOOD OF HEROES
QUIGLEY DOWN UNDER

Elliott, Paul
DADDY'S DYIN'. . . WHO'S GOT THE WILL?
WELCOME HOME, ROXY CARMICHAEL

Elmes, Frederick
WILD AT HEART

Elswit, Robert
BAD INFLUENCE

Evstigneev, Denis
TAXI BLUES

Feeny, Gerry
VERONICO CRUZ

Fernandes, Joao
DELTA FORCE 2

Fernandez, Angel L.
LABYRINTH OF PASSION

Ferragut, Jean-Noel
MAMA, THERE'S A MAN IN YOUR BED

Ferrando, Giancarlo
OPPONENT, THE

Filac, Vilko
TIME OF THE GYPSIES

Fischer, Gerry
FOURTH WAR, THE

Fisher, Gerry
EXORCIST III, THE

Fraker, William A.
FRESHMAN, THE

Friedman, Joseph
INHERITOR

Fuhrer, Martin
LORD OF THE FLIES

Fujii, Hideo
ADVENTURES OF MILO AND OTIS, THE

Fujimoto, Tak
MIAMI BLUES

Fuller, Herb
STUFF STEPHANIE IN THE INCINERATOR

Garcia, Ron
SIDE OUT

Gardiner, Greg
FAR OUT MAN

Garfath, Michael
NUNS ON THE RUN

Genkins, Harvey
GUMSHOE KID, THE

Gibson, Paul
GAME, THE

Giurato, Blasco
CINEMA PARADISO

Glennon, James
SHOW OF FORCE, A

Goldblatt, Stephen
JOE VERSUS THE VOLCANO

Goldsmith, Paul
SHOCK TO THE SYSTEM, A

Goldstein, Eric
MONSTER HIGH

Gracia, Angel
DISTURBANCE, THE

Graver, Gary
ALIENATOR
REAL BULLETS

Green, Jack N.
WHITE HUNTER, BLACK HEART
ROOKIE, THE

Greenberg, Adam
GHOST
THREE MEN AND A LITTLE LADY

Gribble, David
CADILLAC MAN

Grossman, Karen
SHADOWZONE

Grumman, Francis
MURDER BY NUMBERS

Gruszynski, Alexander
TREMORS

Hammer, Victor
ROCKY V

Harrison, Harvey
WITCHES, THE

Hayes, Bob
REAL BULLETS

Hayman, James
BLADES

Heffron, Brian
IMPORTED BRIDEGROOM, THE

Heinl, Bernd
ROSALIE GOES SHOPPING

Hochstatter, Zoran
HAUNTING OF MORELLA, THE
FORCE OF CIRCUMSTANCE

Hora, John
GREMLINS 2 THE NEW BATCH

Hue, David
TWISTED JUSTICE

Hugo, Michel
HIGH DESERT KILL

Hyams, Peter
NARROW MARGIN

Imi, Tony
FIRE BIRDS

Indergand, Peter
FACE OF THE ENEMY

Insley, David
CRY-BABY

Irwin, Mark
CLASS OF 1999

ROBOCOP 2
PAINT IT BLACK
I COME IN PEACE

Isaacks, Levie
SPONTANEOUS COMBUSTION

Jannelli, Tony
LONGTIME COMPANION

Jansen, Peter
NIGHT VISITOR

Jewett, Thomas
PEACEMAKER

Kahm, Marsha
MEN IN LOVE

Karp, Michael
BLOOD SALVAGE

Karpick, Avi
RIVER OF DEATH

Katz, Stephen M.
BACKSTREET DREAMS

Kawamata, Takashi
BLACK RAIN

Kemper, Victor J.
CRAZY PEOPLE

Kimball, Jeffrey
REVENGE
JACOB'S LADDER

Kline, Richard H.
DOWNTOWN

Koltai, Lajos
HOMER & EDDIE
WHITE PALACE

Kurita, Toyomichi
BLOOD RED

Lamkin, Ken
BIG BAD JOHN
RIVERBEND

Lanci, Gui Feppe
C'EST LA VIE

Langley, Norman
MISADVENTURES OF MR. WILT, THE

Lassally, Walter
PERFECT MURDER, THE

Laszlo, Andrew
GHOST DAD

Lavis, Arthur
TEN LITTLE INDIANS

Le Blanc, John
ANGEL TOWN

Lebegue, Pascal
LIFE IS A LONG QUIET RIVER

Lemmo, James
HIT LIST

Lenoir, Denis
MONSIEUR HIRE

Leonetti, Matthew F.
HARD TO KILL
ANOTHER 48 HRS.

Lepine, Jean
VINCENT AND THEO

Levy, Peter
PREDATOR 2

Lewis, David
SLEEPING CAR, THE
NIGHT ANGEL

Lewiston, Denis
MADHOUSE

Lhomme, Pierre
L'ETAT SAUVAGE
CYRANO DE BERGERAC

Lieberman, Charlie
HENRY: PORTRAIT OF A SERIAL KILLER

Lind, Kevan
DEMONSTONE

Lindley, John
VITAL SIGNS

Lloyd, Walt
TO SLEEP WITH ANGER
PUMP UP THE VOLUME

Loof, Claus
NOBODY'S PERFECT

Lubtchansky, William
MAHABHARATA, THE

Luther, Igor
HANDMAID'S TALE, THE

McAlpine, Donald
STANLEY AND IRIS

Macat, Julio
HOME ALONE

McCallum, John
DOG TAGS

McKinney, Austin
PRIMARY TARGET

McMillan, Kenneth
INNOCENT VICTIM

Maeda, Yonezo
HEAVEN AND EARTH

Magierski, Tomasz
BAIL JUMPER

Malekzadeh, Firooz
BASHU, THE LITTLE STRANGER

Margulies, Michael
REPOSSESSED

Mark, Ivan
FORCED MARCH

Markowitz, Barry
TORN APART

Mathe, Tibor
MY 20TH CENTURY

Mathers, James
DOWN THE DRAIN
NIGHT EYES

Michelson, Paul
BURNDOWN

Mills, Alec
LIONHEART

Milo, Areni
HOLLYWOOD HOT TUBS II: EDUCATING
CRYSTAL

Milsome, Doug
DESPERATE HOURS

Minski, Janusz
GRIM PRAIRIE TALES

Minsky, Charles
PRETTY WOMAN

Misumi, Kenji
TWILIGHT OF THE COCKROACHES

Mokri, Amir
EAT A BOWL OF TEA
BLUE STEEL
PACIFIC HEIGHTS

Mokri, Amir M.
LIFE IS CHEAP. . . BUT TOILET PAPER IS
EXPENSIVE

Morita, Rhett
BLOOD RELATIONS

Morris, Reginald H.
LOOSE CANNONS

Murphy, Fred
FUNNY ABOUT LOVE

Nannunzi, Daniele
SANTA SANGRE

Nannuzzi, Armando
MAGDALENE
FRANKENSTEIN UNBOUND

Negrin, Michael
TOUCH OF A STRANGER

Nepomniaschy, Alex
LISA

O'Brien, John
BIG DIS, THE

Okada, Daryn
SURVIVAL QUEST

Ondricek, Miroslav
AWAKENINGS

Pantzer, Jerry
TUSKS

Papamichael, Phedon
STREETS
BODY CHEMISTRY

Paynter, Robert
STRIKE IT RICH

Pei, Edward
MASQUE OF THE RED DEATH

Pennella, Joe
HAPPY TOGETHER

Petrycki, Jacek
INTERROGATION, THE

Piazzoli, Roberto D'Ettorre
LAMBADA
SONNY BOY

Pierce-Roberts, Tony
MR. AND MRS. BRIDGE

Pike, Kelvin
BETSY'S WEDDING

Plummer, Mark
AFTER DARK, MY SWEET

Polak, Hanus
TIME TROOPERS

Pope, Bill
DARKMAN

Poster, Steven
OPPORTUNITY KNOCKS
ROCKY V

Primes, Robert
BIRD ON A WIRE

Prinzi, Frank
NIGHT OF THE LIVING DEAD

Quinlan, Dick
IN THE SPIRIT

Quinn, Declan
KILL-OFF, THE

Ragalyi, Elemer
MACK THE KNIFE

Reniers, Peter
TWO EVIL EYES

Revene (Agfa Gevaert Color), Larry
BEDROOM EYES II

Revene, Larry
WILDEST DREAMS

Revine, Larry
FRIGHT HOUSE

Reynolds, Brian
JEZEBEL'S KISS

Reynolds, Buster
GODS MUST BE CRAZY II, THE

Roizman, Owen
I LOVE YOU TO DEATH
HAVANA

Roland, Erich
ELLIOT FAUMAN, PH.D.

Rosenthal, James
CAGED IN PARADISO

Rousselot, Philippe
TOO BEAUTIFUL FOR YOU
HENRY AND JUNE

Ruiz-Anchia, Juan
LAST OF THE FINEST, THE

Russell, Ward
DAYS OF THUNDER

Saito, Takao
DREAMS

Salomon, Mikael
ARACHNOPHOBIA

Sarin, Vic
BYE BYE BLUES

Schmidt, Ronn
BRAIN DEAD

Schwartzman, John
RED SURF

Sebaldt, Christian
WEDDING BAND

Semler, Dean
IMPULSE
YOUNG GUNS II
DANCES WITH WOLVES

Seresin, Michael
COME SEE THE PARADISE

Shing, Ma Chor
REINCARNATION OF GOLDEN LOTUS, THE

Simpson, Geoffrey
GREEN CARD

Smoot, Reed
DON'T TELL HER IT'S ME

Sobocinski, Witold
TORRENTS OF SPRING

Sonnenfeld, Barry
MILLER'S CROSSING
MISERY

Southon, Mike
CHICAGO JOE AND THE SHOWGIRL

Spellvin, David
ANIMAL BEHAVIOR

Spencer, Brenton
AMERICAN BOYFRIENDS

Sperling, David
OVER EXPOSED
ANDY COLBY'S INCREDIBLY AWESOME
ADVENTURE

Spiller, Michael
UNBELIEVABLE TRUTH, THE

Spinotti, Dante
TORRENTS OF SPRING

Stapleton, Oliver
GRIFTERS, THE

Steiger, Ueli
HOT SPOT, THE

Stein, Peter
ERNEST GOES TO JAIL
GRAVEYARD SHIFT

Stephens, John
SKI PATROL

Stevens, Robert
TUNE IN TOMORROW

Stewart, Rod
AMERICAN EAGLE

Steyn, Jacques
KILL ME AGAIN
COURAGE MOUNTAIN

Storaro, Vittorio
  DICK TRACY
  SHELTERING SKY, THE

Stringer, R. Michael
  FORBIDDEN DANCE, THE

Suhrstedt, Tim
  MEN AT WORK

Surtees, Bruce
  MEN DON'T LEAVE

Suschitzky, Peter
  WHERE THE HEART IS

Takama, Kenji
  SUMMER VACATION: 1999

Tattersall, Gale
  WILD ORCHID

Thomas, John
  METROPOLITAN

Thompson, Jamie
  CIRCUITRY MAN

Thomson, Alex
  KRAYS, THE
  MR. DESTINY

Thurmann-Andersen, Erling
  PATHFINDER

Tickner, Clive
  HIDDEN AGENDA

Tidy, Frank
  RAGGEDY RAWNEY, THE
  SLIPSTREAM

Tirl, George
  DAMNED RIVER

Tomita, Shinji
  ADVENTURES OF MILO AND OTIS, THE

Tovoli, Luciano
  REVERSAL OF FORTUNE

Trutkovsky, Vasily
  LONELY WOMAN SEEKS LIFE COMPANION

Tufty, Christpher G.
  MODERN LOVE

Ueda, Masahuro
  DREAMS

Vacano, Jost
  TOTAL RECALL

Van de Sande, Theo
  FIRST POWER, THE

Van Der Kloot, William
  FUNLAND

Vidgeon, Robin
  NIGHTBREED

Vierny, Sacha
  COOK, THE THIEF, HIS WIFE & HER
    LOVER, THE
  BELLY OF AN ARCHITECT, THE

Villalobos, Reynaldo
  COUPE DE VILLE
  SIBLING RIVALRY

von Jansky, Ladi
  DR. CALIGARI

Von Sternberg, Nicholas
  SKINHEADS – THE SECOND COMING OF
    HATE

von Sternberg, Nicholas
  TEXASVILLE

Vuorinen, Esa
  SHADOW OF THE RAVEN, THE

Waite, Ric
  MARKED FOR DEATH

Walsh, David M.
  TAKING CARE OF BUSINESS

Watkin, David
  MEMPHIS BELLE
  HAMLET

Weindler, Helge
  ME AND HIM

Wexler, Howard
  SAVAGE BEACH
  STEEL AND LACE

Wiatrak, Kenneth
  CAGED FURY

Wilcots, Joseph M.
  WHITE GIRL, THE

Williams, Billy
  STELLA

Willis, Gordon
  PRESUMED INNOCENT
  GODFATHER PART III, THE

Wood, Oliver
  DIE HARD 2
  ADVENTURES OF FORD FAIRLANE, THE

Woster, Eric
  FAR OUT MAN

Yacker, Fawn
  MEN IN LOVE

Yacoe, Joseph
  WITHOUT YOU, I'M NOTHING

Young, Robert
  PLOT AGAINST HARRY, THE

Ziegler, Fred
  HAPPILY EVER AFTER

Zielinski, Jerzy
  FOOLS OF FORTUNE

Zsigmond, Vilmos
  TWO JAKES, THE
  BONFIRE OF THE VANITIES

COSTUMES

Abbot, Michael
  PUMP UP THE VOLUME

Acheson, James
  SHELTERING SKY, THE

Ackerman, Kevin
  TWISTED JUSTICE

Aguilar, Maria
  STEEL AND LACE

Albright, Irene
  VAMPIRE'S KISS

Aldredge, Theoni V.
  STANLEY AND IRIS

Allen, Marit
  EAT A BOWL OF TEA
  WITCHES, THE
  MERMAIDS

American Costume
  GRIM PRAIRIE TALES

Amos, Dorothy
  STREET ASYLUM

Ander, Hedwig
  ISTANBUL, KEEP YOUR EYES OPEN

Anderson, Barbara
  TWO EVIL EYES
  NIGHT OF THE LIVING DEAD

Arseni, Anatasia
  LANDSCAPE IN THE MIST

Atwood, Colleen
  HANDMAID'S TALE, THE
  JOE VERSUS THE VOLCANO
  EDWARD SCISSORHANDS

Aulisi, Joseph G.
  MY BLUE HEAVEN

Austin, Michael
  BLOOD RELATIONS

Bafaloukas, Eugenie
  ME AND HIM

Ballard, Leslie
  CLASS OF 1999

Bansmer, Dennis Michael
  FAR OUT MAN

Barry, Shawn
  ERNEST GOES TO JAIL

Bartley, Gail
  FRIGHT HOUSE

Beavan, Jenny
  MOUNTAINS OF THE MOON
  IMPROMPTU

Becker, Susan
  MEN DON'T LEAVE
  DAYS OF THUNDER
  LEMON SISTERS, THE

Beckett, Angee
  SKI PATROL

Bergin, Joan
  FIELD, THE

Bergstrom, Cindy
  UNDER THE BOARDWALK

Berman, Claudia
  FRIGHT HOUSE

Bernay, Lynn
  HIGH DESERT KILL

Bertram, Susan
  FORBIDDEN DANCE, THE

Bloomfield, John
  MACK THE KNIFE

Bordone, Beatrice
  CINEMA PARADISO

Bowen, John
  LORDS OF MAGICK, THE

Boxer, John
  PRESUMED INNOCENT

Brenick, Linda
  FUNLAND

Bright, John
  MOUNTAINS OF THE MOON

Bronson-Howard, Aude
  REVENGE
  STATE OF GRACE

Brown, Winnie D.
  GHOST DAD

Bushnell, Scott
  VINCENT AND THEO

Campbell, Dee
  AMERICAN EAGLE

Cannon, Poppy
  DAMNED RIVER

Canonero, Milena
  DICK TRACY
  REVERSAL OF FORTUNE
  GODFATHER PART III, THE

Capone, Clifford
  LOOSE CANNONS

Caracciolo, Fabrizio
  MAGDALENE

Carnahan, Julie
  AFTERSHOCK

Carter, Ruth E.
  MO' BETTER BLUES

Castro, Eduardo
  BIRD ON A WIRE

Cecchi, Nana
  LIONHEART

Cibula, Nan
OPPORTUNITY KNOCKS

Cleator, Pippa
MAHABHARATA, THE

Cohen, Ellis
FIRE BIRDS

Conner, Jill
ALIENATOR

Cook, Catherine
SLIPSTREAM

Cook, Helen
STAR QUEST: BEYOND THE RISING MOON

D'Arcy, Tim
FIRST POWER, THE
REPOSSESSED

Dalay, Lino
PRIMARY TARGET

Dare, Daphne
HIDDEN AGENDA

de Nesle, Yvonne Sassinot
HENRY AND JUNE

DeCaro, Charles
DESPERATE HOURS

Di Palma, Valentina
OPPONENT, THE

Dover, Kady
DELTA FORCE 2

Dover, Katherine
BLIND FURY

Dover, Katherine Kady
HOMER & EDDIE

Dunn, John
SHOCK TO THE SYSTEM, A

Dunn, Sheri
ELLIOT FAUMAN, PH.D.

Edell Phillips, Erica
TOTAL RECALL

Evans, Harold
HOUSE PARTY

Everton, Deborah
VITAL SIGNS

Fedoruk, Sharon
BLOOD RELATIONS

Feldman, Shari
LISA

Ferrin, Ingrid
LOVE AT LARGE

Ferry, Alice
ALMOST AN ANGEL

Figueroa, Tolita
SANTA SANGRE

Finkelman, Wayne
BIRD ON A WIRE
TWO JAKES, THE
QUIGLEY DOWN UNDER

Finn, Mali
WELCOME HOME, ROXY CARMICHAEL

Fionn
STREETS

Flynt, Cynthia
AWAKENINGS

Fonteray, Jacques
L'ETAT SAUVAGE

Fort, Mary Jane
METROPOLITAN

Frank, Ivette
TWISTED OBSESSION

Frogley, Louise
HEART CONDITION
THREE MEN AND A LITTLE LADY

Gaultier, Jean-Paul
COOK, THE THIEF, HIS WIFE & HER
LOVER, THE

Gearon, Ida
TALES FROM THE DARKSIDE: THE MOVIE
RETURN OF SUPERFLY, THE

Gibbons, Carla
SURVIVAL QUEST

Gower-Grudzinski, Elizabeth
HIT LIST

Greenwood, Jane
MR. DESTINY

Gresham, Gloria
AVALON
KINDERGARTEN COP
MISERY

Grossman, Jennifer
AMERICAN BOYFRIENDS

Gutierrez, James
FAR OUT MAN

Gyarmathy, Agnes
MY 20TH CENTURY

Handwork, Nancy
STAR QUEST: BEYOND THE RISING MOON

Hays, Sania M.
MASQUE OF THE RED DEATH

Hays, Sanja Milkovic
SPACED INVADERS

Heiman, Betsy
TUNE IN TOMORROW

Hemming, Lindy
KRAYS, THE

Hester, D. Jean
BLOOD SALVAGE

Hicklin, Walter
LONGTIME COMPANION

Highfill, J. Allen
MEN DON'T LEAVE

Hiscox, Maureen
BYE BYE BLUES

Holmestrand, Marit Sofie
PATHFINDER

Hopper, Deborah
IMPULSE
ROOKIE, THE

Horatio, Helen
GRAFFITI BRIDGE

Hornung, Richard
MILLER'S CROSSING

Hunter, Joan
LEATHERFACE: THE TEXAS CHAINSAW
MASSACRE III

Hurley, Jay
HOME ALONE

Inglehart, Barbara
DARK SIDE OF THE MOON

Jensen, Sandra Araya
BODY CHEMISTRY

Jenson, Lisa
WHITE PALACE

Johnston, Joanna
BACK TO THE FUTURE PART III

Johnston, Renee
NIGHT ANGEL

Jorry, Corinne
L'ETAT SAUVAGE

Keller, Thomas Lee
GOODFELLAS

Kelly, Bridget
PACIFIC HEIGHTS

Kennedy, Eileen
FLASHBACK
PROBLEM CHILD

Kerrigan, Daryl
KILL-OFF, THE

Kidd, Barbara
INNOCENT VICTIM

Klesert, Iris
STUFF STEPHANIE IN THE INCINERATOR

Kochergina, Tatyana
FREEZE – DIE – COME TO LIFE

Kramer, Gini
BACK TO BACK

Kramer, Virginia
SHADOWZONE

La Gorce Kramer, Deborah
CADILLAC MAN

Lapidus, Jim
MADHOUSE

Leamon, Ron
FEUD, THE

Lee, Raymond
WITHOUT YOU, I'M NOTHING

Lewis, Keith
MEN AT WORK

Lewis, Robin
MONSTER HIGH
MODERN LOVE

Loman, Brad
NAVY SEALS

Lucas Lawler, Janet
RIVERBEND

Luef, Evelyn
TIME TROOPERS

Lyman, Dana
EXORCIST III, THE

Lynch, Sharon
TOUCH OF A STRANGER

McCrow, Donna
INHERITOR

Maginnis, Molly
LOOK WHO'S TALKING TOO
COME SEE THE PARADISE

Major, Ross
QUIGLEY DOWN UNDER

Makovsky, Judianna
REVERSAL OF FORTUNE

Malin, Mary
BETSY'S WEDDING

Martinez, Ronni
PRIMARY TARGET

Matheson, Linda
WHERE THE HEART IS

Matthews, Marilyn
TAKING CARE OF BUSINESS
GREEN CARD

Meltzer, Ileane
WILD ORCHID

Mermande-Cerf, Michele
TOO BEAUTIFUL FOR YOU

Millenotti, Maurizio
BELLY OF AN ARCHITECT, THE

Milliant, Natalya
FREEZE – DIE – COME TO LIFE

Mirojnick, Ellen
NARROW MARGIN
JACOB'S LADDER

Mollo, John
AIR AMERICA
WHITE HUNTER, BLACK HEART

Monico, Francoise
L'ETAT SAUVAGE

Moorcroft, Judy
FOOLS OF FORTUNE

Moore, Dan
ANOTHER 48 HRS.

Moreau, Jacqueline
LIFE AND NOTHING BUT

Morley, Ruth
GHOST

Myers, Ruth
BLOOD RED
RUSSIA HOUSE, THE

Nguyen, Ha
NIGHT EYES

Nierhaus, Brigitte
MAN INSIDE, THE

Nonkin, Elizabeth Warner
ROSALIE GOES SHOPPING

Norris, Patricia
WILD AT HEART

Norton, Rosanna
GREMLINS 2 THE NEW BATCH
ROBOCOP 2

O'Donnell, Susan
GOODFELLAS

Oditz, Carol
LAST EXIT TO BROOKLYN

Olaguivel, Rene
VERONICO CRUZ

Paredes, Daniel
DOWNTOWN

Parsons, Jennifer L.
ARACHNOPHOBIA

Partridge, Lily
PLOT AGAINST HARRY, THE

Partridge, Wendy
HEAVEN AND EARTH

Patch, Karen
CHATTAHOOCHEE

Perrot, Monique
MAMA, THERE'S A MAN IN YOUR BED

Phillips, Arianne
BAIL JUMPER

Pia Angelini, Maria
ICICLE THIEF, THE

Pistek, Theodor
TORRENTS OF SPRING
RAGGEDY RAWNEY, THE

Pollack, Bernie
HAVANA

Pollack, Leonard
PAINT IT BLACK

Porro, Joseph
DEATH WARRANT
I COME IN PEACE

Preston, Grania
DARKMAN

Ramsey, Carol
MR. AND MRS. BRIDGE
KING OF NEW YORK

Rand, Tom
STRIKE IT RICH

Reichardt, Kelly
UNBELIEVABLE TRUTH, THE

Reichek, Robyn
MARTIANS GO HOME!

Reimers, Nadine
ANDY COLBY'S INCREDIBLY AWESOME
ADVENTURE

Riggs, Rita
TEXASVILLE

Ringwood, Bob
CHICAGO JOE AND THE SHOWGIRL

Robbins, Carrie
IN THE SPIRIT

Robinson, Jane
MEMPHIS BELLE

Rodgers, Aggie Guerard
I LOVE YOU TO DEATH

Roth, Ann
EVERYBODY WINS
Q&A
POSTCARDS FROM THE EDGE
PACIFIC HEIGHTS

Rowton, Jan
DEMON WIND

Ruskin, Judy
YOUNG GUNS II

Russal, Varcra
RETURN OF SUPERFLY, THE

Ryan, Christopher
SHORT TIME

Sacks, Renee Alaina
GUARDIAN, THE

Schjolberg, Eva
PATHFINDER

Scott, Deborah
COUPE DE VILLE

Scott, Elisabeth
BACKSTREET DREAMS

Shannon-Burnett, Gaye
TO SLEEP WITH ANGER

Shearon, Jim
GRAFFITI BRIDGE

Shissler, Richard
BLUE STEEL

Simmons, Denise
TALL GUY, THE

Simmons, Paul
WHITE GIRL, THE

Skaist, Pamela
CHILD'S PLAY 2

Smith, Robyn
RIVER OF DEATH
TUSKS

Smith, Van
CRY-BABY

Soprani, Luciano
WILD ORCHID

Spisak, Neil
Q&A

Squarciapino, Franca
CYRANO DE BERGERAC

Stein, Linda
DOWN THE DRAIN

Stewart, Marlene
WILD ORCHID

Stolz, Mary Kay
HOT SPOT, THE

Stranan, Monique
BIRD ON A WIRE

Summers, Ray
FOURTH WAR, THE

Taieb, Catherine
BRAIN DEAD

Talsky, Ron
GUMSHOE KID, THE

Tandy, Jeff
ALLIGATOR EYES

Tashiro, Yoko
HEAVEN AND EARTH

Taucher, Rozanne
WEDDING BAND

Tolsky, Ron
GRIM PRAIRIE TALES

Traywick, Kay
STUFF STEPHANIE IN THE INCINERATOR

Truthmann, Ute
NASTY GIRL, THE

Turnbull, Jean
TIME GUARDIAN, THE

Turner, Sally
PERFECT MURDER, THE

Tyson, James
HUNT FOR RED OCTOBER, THE

Ulsamer, Sibylle
TORRENTS OF SPRING

Van Runkle, Theadora
STELLA

Van Soest Chubb, Isabella
MARKED FOR DEATH

Vance-Straker, Marilyn
LAST OF THE FINEST, THE
PRETTY WOMAN
DIE HARD 2
ADVENTURES OF FORD FAIRLANE, THE
PREDATOR 2

Vasquez, Sylvia
FACE OF THE ENEMY
GRIM PRAIRIE TALES

Villiers, Dianna
TEN LITTLE INDIANS

Vogt, Mary
CRAZY PEOPLE

Wada, Emi
DREAMS

Wallach, Jeffrey
BEDROOM EYES II
WILDEST DREAMS

Waller, Liz
MISADVENTURES OF MR. WILT, THE

Warner Nankin, Elizabeth
DADDY'S DYIN'... WHO'S GOT THE WILL?

Watkinson, Doreen
LORD OF THE FLIES

Weis, Barbara
LASER MAN, THE

Weiss, Julie
FRESHMAN, THE

Williams-Sayadian, Belinda
DR. CALIGARI

Wilson, Alonzo
TEENAGE MUTANT NINJA TURTLES

Wolsky, Albert
FUNNY ABOUT LOVE

Wood, Carol
DON'T TELL HER IT'S ME
COLD FEET

Wood, Durinda
SIBLING RIVALRY

Wright, Glenn
ROOKIE, THE

Yarmo, Leslie
SKINHEADS — THE SECOND COMING OF
HATE

Yelland, Susan
NUNS ON THE RUN

Zakowska, Donna
QUICK CHANGE

Zamparelli, Elsa
DANCES WITH WOLVES

Zbroniec, Ewa
MURDER BY NUMBERS

DIRECTORS

Abrahams, Jim
WELCOME HOME, ROXY CARMICHAEL

Adlon, Percy
ROSALIE GOES SHOPPING

Alda, Alan
BETSY'S WEDDING

Allen, James
BURNDOWN

Allen, Woody
ALICE

Almodovar, Pedro
LABYRINTH OF PASSION
TIE ME UP! TIE ME DOWN!

Altman, Robert
VINCENT AND THEO

Amiel, Jon
TUNE IN TOMORROW

Amurri, Franco
FLASHBACK

Angelopoulos, Theo
LANDSCAPE IN THE MIST

Anthony, Len
FRIGHT HOUSE

Arcand, Denys
JESUS OF MONTREAL

Ardolino, Emile
THREE MEN AND A LITTLE LADY

Arehn, Mats
ISTANBUL, KEEP YOUR EYES OPEN

Argento, Dario
TWO EVIL EYES

Armitage, George
MIAMI BLUES

Avildsen, John G.
ROCKY V

Badham, John
BIRD ON A WIRE

Barbera, Joseph
JETSONS: THE MOVIE

Barker, Clive
NIGHTBREED

Barreto, Bruno
SHOW OF FORCE, A

Barron, Steve
TEENAGE MUTANT NINJA TURTLES

Baxley, Craig R.
I COME IN PEACE

Bear, Liza
FORCE OF CIRCUMSTANCE

Beatty, Warren
DICK TRACY

Beizai, Bahram
BASHU, THE LITTLE STRANGER

Benjamin, Richard
DOWNTOWN
MERMAIDS

Benoit, Jacques W.
HOW TO MAKE LOVE TO A NEGRO WITH-
OUT GETTING TIRED

Benson, Robby
MODERN LOVE

Berger, Pamela
IMPORTED BRIDEGROOM, THE

Bergman, Andrew
FRESHMAN, THE

Bertolucci, Bernardo
SHELTERING SKY, THE

Bierman, Robert
VAMPIRE'S KISS

Bigelow, Kathryn
BLUE STEEL

Bill, Tony
CRAZY PEOPLE

Birkinshaw, Alan
TEN LITTLE INDIANS

Blatty, William Peter
EXORCIST III, THE

Blier, Bertrand
TOO BEAUTIFUL FOR YOU

Bogdanovich, Peter
TEXASVILLE

Bond, James III
DEF BY TEMPTATION

Boorman, John
WHERE THE HEART IS

Boos, H. Gordon
RED SURF

Boskovich, John
WITHOUT YOU, I'M NOTHING

Bowen, Jenny
ANIMAL BEHAVIOR

Brand, Larry
MASQUE OF THE RED DEATH
OVER EXPOSED

Brickman, Paul
MEN DON'T LEAVE

Brock, Deborah
ANDY COLBY'S INCREDIBLY AWESOME
ADVENTURE

Brook, Peter
MAHABHARATA, THE

Brown, Curtis
GAME, THE

Brown, Greggory
STREET ASYLUM

Brown, Tony
WHITE GIRL, THE

Bugajski, Ryszard
INTERROGATION, THE

Burnett, Charles
TO SLEEP WITH ANGER

Burr, Jeff
LEATHERFACE: THE TEXAS CHAINSAW
MASSACRE III

Burton, Tim
EDWARD SCISSORHANDS

Butoy, Hendel
RESCUERS DOWN UNDER, THE

Campbell, Graeme
BLOOD RELATIONS

Cardone, J.S.
SHADOWZONE

Carroll, Robert Martin
SONNY BOY

Carver, Steve
RIVER OF DEATH

Caton-Jones, Michael
MEMPHIS BELLE

Champion, Gregg
SHORT TIME

Chatiliez, Etienne
LIFE IS A LONG QUIET RIVER

Cherry, John
ERNEST GOES TO JAIL

Chong, Tommy
FAR OUT MAN

Chopra, Joyce
LEMON SISTERS, THE

Cimino, Michael
DESPERATE HOURS

Clark, Bob
LOOSE CANNONS

Clark, Greydon
SKINHEADS – THE SECOND COMING OF
HATE
FORBIDDEN DANCE, THE

Coe, Wayne
GRIM PRAIRIE TALES

Coen, Joel
MILLER'S CROSSING

Columbus, Chris
HOME ALONE

Cook, Philip
STAR QUEST: BEYOND THE RISING MOON

Coppola, Francis Ford
GODFATHER PART III, THE

Corman, Roger
FRANKENSTEIN UNBOUND

Cornell, John
ALMOST AN ANGEL

Correll, Richard
SKI PATROL

Coscarelli, Don
SURVIVAL QUEST

Costner, Kevin
DANCES WITH WOLVES

Crowther, John
DAMNED RIVER

Curtis, Douglas
SLEEPING CAR, THE

D'Elia, Bill
FEUD, THE

Dahl, John
KILL ME AGAIN

Damski, Mel
HAPPY TOGETHER

Dante, Joe
GREMLINS 2 THE NEW BATCH

De Palma, Brian
BONFIRE OF THE VANITIES

Donaldson, Roger
CADILLAC MAN

Dornhelm, Robert
COLD FEET

Dorrie, Doris
ME AND HIM

Dugan, Dennis
PROBLEM CHILD

Durham, Todd
HYPERSPACE

Eastwood, Clint
WHITE HUNTER, BLACK HEART
ROOKIE, THE

Edel, Uli
LAST EXIT TO BROOKLYN

Egleson, Jan
SHOCK TO THE SYSTEM, A

Enyedi, Ildiko
MY 20TH CENTURY

Eriksen, Gordon
BIG DIS, THE

Erman, John
STELLA

Estevez, Emilio
MEN AT WORK

Faber, Christian
BAIL JUMPER

Falk, Harry
HIGH DESERT KILL

Farino, Ernest
STEEL AND LACE

Feldman, John
ALLIGATOR EYES

Ferrara, Abel
KING OF NEW YORK

Figgis, Michael
INTERNAL AFFAIRS

Firstenberg, Sam
RIVERBEND

Fisher, Jack
TORN APART

Fisk, Jack
DADDY'S DYIN'. . . WHO'S GOT THE WILL?

Foley, James
AFTER DARK, MY SWEET

Foster, Giles
INNOCENT VICTIM

Frankenheimer, John
FOURTH WAR, THE

Franklin, Carl
FULL FATHOM FIVE

Franklin, Howard
QUICK CHANGE

Frears, Stephen
GRIFTERS, THE

Friedkin, William
GUARDIAN, THE

Gabriel, Michael
RESCUERS DOWN UNDER, THE

Gaup, Nils
PATHFINDER

Gilbert, Brad
TOUCH OF A STRANGER

Girod, Francis
L'ETAT SAUVAGE

Golan, Menahem
MACK THE KNIFE

Gordon, Stuart
ROBOT JOX

Grazer, Brian
KINDERGARTEN COP

Green, David
FIRE BIRDS

Greenaway, Peter
COOK, THE THIEF, HIS WIFE & HER
LOVER, THE
BELLY OF AN ARCHITECT, THE

Greenwald, Maggie
KILL-OFF, THE

Guest, Cliff
DISTURBANCE, THE

Gunnlaugsson, Hrafn
SHADOW OF THE RAVEN, THE

Hai, Zafir
PERFECT MURDER, THE

Hanna, William
JETSONS: THE MOVIE

Hannant, Brian
TIME GUARDIAN, THE

Hanson, Curtis
BAD INFLUENCE

Hare, David
STRAPLESS

Harlin, Renny
DIE HARD 2
ADVENTURES OF FORD FAIRLANE, THE

Harris, Frank
AFTERSHOCK

Harrison, John
TALES FROM THE DARKSIDE: THE MOVIE

Hartley, Hal
UNBELIEVABLE TRUTH, THE

Hata, Masanori
ADVENTURES OF MILO AND OTIS, THE

Hathcock, Bob
DUCKTALES: THE MOVIE – TREASURE OF
THE LOST LAMP

Hawkins Moore, Tara
TUSKS

Heavener, David
TWISTED JUSTICE

Heckerling, Amy
LOOK WHO'S TALKING TOO

Henderson, Clark
PRIMARY TARGET

Henenlotter, Frank
BASKETCASE 2
FRANKENHOOKER

Hill, Walter
ANOTHER 48 HRS.

Hiller, Arthur
TAKING CARE OF BUSINESS

Hitzig, Rupert
NIGHT VISITOR
BACKSTREET DREAMS

Hook, Harry
LORD OF THE FLIES

Hooper, Tobe
SPONTANEOUS COMBUSTION

Hopkins, Stephen
PREDATOR 2

Hopper, Dennis
HOT SPOT, THE

Hoskins, Bob
RAGGEDY RAWNEY, THE

Howley, John
HAPPILY EVER AFTER

Hudlin, Reginald
HOUSE PARTY

Huestis, Marc
MEN IN LOVE

Hughes, Robert C.
DOWN THE DRAIN

Hunter, Tim
PAINT IT BLACK

Hyams, Peter
NARROW MARGIN

Ildari, Hassan
FACE OF THE ENEMY

Imamura, Shohei
BLACK RAIN

Israelson, Peter
SIDE OUT

Ivory, James
MR. AND MRS. BRIDGE

Jackson, Mick
CHATTAHOOCHEE

Joanou, Phil
STATE OF GRACE

Jodorowsky, Alejandro
SANTA SANGRE

Johnson, Patrick Read
SPACED INVADERS

Johnston, Tucker
BLOOD SALVAGE

Kadokawa, Haruki
HEAVEN AND EARTH

Kaneko, Shusuke
SUMMER VACATION: 1999

Kanevski, Vitaly
FREEZE – DIE – COME TO LIFE

Karson, Eric
ANGEL TOWN

Kasdan, Lawrence
I LOVE YOU TO DEATH

Kaufman, Philip
HENRY AND JUNE

Kaylor, Robert
NOBODY'S PERFECT

Keach, James
FALSE IDENTITY

Keith, Harvey
JEZEBEL'S KISS

Kendal-Savegar, Brian
INHERITOR

Kennedy, Burt
BIG BAD JOHN

Kershner, Irvin
ROBOCOP 2

Kiersh, Fritz
UNDER THE BOARDWALK

Kincade, John
BACK TO BACK

King, Rick
FORCED MARCH

King, Zalman
WILD ORCHID

Klass, Ric
ELLIOT FAUMAN, PH.D.

Konchalovsky, Andrei
HOMER & EDDIE

Krishtofovich, Viacheslav
LONELY WOMAN SEEKS LIFE COMPANION

Kurosawa, Akira
DREAMS

Kurys, Diane
C'EST LA VIE

Kusturica, Emir
TIME OF THE GYPSIES

Kwan, Stanley
ROUGE

Lafia, John
CHILD'S PLAY 2

Lapine, James
IMPROMPTU

Law, Clara
REINCARNATION OF GOLDEN LOTUS, THE

Law, Tom
TAX SEASON

Leconte, Patrice
MONSIEUR HIRE

Leder, Paul
MURDER BY NUMBERS

Lee, Spike
MO' BETTER BLUES

Leitch, Christopher
COURAGE MOUNTAIN

Leonard, Brett
DEAD PIT

Lester, Mark L.
CLASS OF 1999

Levinson, Barry
AVALON

Lindsay, Lance
REAL BULLETS

Lisberger, Steven
SLIPSTREAM

Little, Dwight H.
MARKED FOR DEATH

Loach, Kenneth
HIDDEN AGENDA

Locke, Sondra
IMPULSE

Logan, Bob
REPOSSESSED

Lounguine, Pavel
TAXI BLUES

Lovy, Steven
CIRCUITRY MAN

Lumet, Sidney
Q&A

Lustig, William
HIT LIST

Lynch, David
WILD AT HEART

Lyne, Adrian
JACOB'S LADDER

Lynn, Jonathan
NUNS ON THE RUN

Mackenzie, John
LAST OF THE FINEST, THE

McNaughton, John
HENRY: PORTRAIT OF A SERIAL KILLER

McTiernan, John
HUNT FOR RED OCTOBER, THE

Malle, Louis
MAY FOOLS

Malmuth, Bruce
HARD TO KILL

Mandoki, Luis
WHITE PALACE

Manduke, Joseph
GUMSHOE KID, THE

Marsh, David
LORDS OF MAGICK, THE

Marshall, Frank
ARACHNOPHOBIA

Marshall, Garry
PRETTY WOMAN

Marshall, Penny
AWAKENINGS

Martino, Sergio
OPPONENT, THE

Masterson, Peter
BLOOD RED

Medak, Peter
KRAYS, THE

Mihalka, George
HOSTILE TAKEOVER

Milling, Bill
CAGED FURY

Moore, Charles Philip
DEMON WIND

Mowbray, Malcolm
DON'T TELL HER IT'S ME

Moyle, Allan
PUMP UP THE VOLUME

Mundhra, Jag
NIGHT EYES

Murphy, Geoff
YOUNG GUNS II

Murray, Bill
QUICK CHANGE

Nakasako, Spencer
LIFE IS CHEAP. . . BUT TOILET PAPER IS
EXPENSIVE

Nardo, Don
STUFF STEPHANIE IN THE INCINERATOR

Neiman, L.E.
TIME TROOPERS

Nichetti, Maurizio
ICICLE THIEF, THE

Nichols, Mike
POSTCARDS FROM THE EDGE

Nicholson, Jack
TWO JAKES, THE

Nimoy, Leonard
FUNNY ABOUT LOVE

Norris, Aaron
DELTA FORCE 2

Noyce, Phillip
BLIND FURY

O'Brien, John
BIG DIS, THE

O'Connor, Pat
FOOLS OF FORTUNE

Odell, David
MARTIANS GO HOME!

Orr, James
MR. DESTINY

Othenin-Girard, Dominique
NIGHT ANGEL

Pakula, Alan J.
PRESUMED INNOCENT

Papic, Krsto
MY UNCLE'S LEGACY

Parker, Alan
COME SEE THE PARADISE

Parriott, James D.
HEART CONDITION

Peoples, David
BLOOD OF HEROES

Pereira, Miguel
VERONICO CRUZ

Peterson, Kristine
BODY CHEMISTRY

Petrie, Donald
OPPORTUNITY KNOCKS

Poe, Rudiger
MONSTER HIGH

Poitier, Sidney
GHOST DAD

Pollack, Sydney
HAVANA

Prince
GRAFFITI BRIDGE

Prowse, Andrew J.
DEMONSTONE

Quintano, Gene
HONEYMOON ACADEMY
WHY ME?

Rafelson, Bob
MOUNTAINS OF THE MOON

Raich, Ken
HOLLYWOOD HOT TUBS II: EDUCATING
CRYSTAL

Raimi, Sam
DARKMAN

Rambaldi, Vittoria
PRIMAL RAGE

Rappeneau, Jean-Paul
CYRANO DE BERGERAC

Raskov, Daniel
WEDDING BAND

Rasmussen, Kjehl
ANIMAL BEHAVIOR

Ray, Fred Olen
ALIENATOR

Reiner, Carl
SIBLING RIVALRY

Reiner, Rob
MISERY

Reisz, Karel
EVERYBODY WINS

Reitman, Ivan
KINDERGARTEN COP

Rene, Norman
LONGTIME COMPANION

Resnikoff, Robert
FIRST POWER, THE

Richmond, Anthony
NIGHT OF THE SHARKS

Ritt, Martin
STANLEY AND IRIS

Roeg, Nicolas
WITCHES, THE

Roemer, Michael
PLOT AGAINST HARRY, THE

Romero, George
TWO EVIL EYES

Rondinella, Thomas R.
BLADES

Ropelewski, Tom
MADHOUSE

Rose, Bernard
CHICAGO JOE AND THE SHOWGIRL

Ross, Herbert
MY BLUE HEAVEN

Roth, Bobby
MAN INSIDE, THE

Roth, Joe
COUPE DE VILLE

Ruben, Katt Shea
STREETS

Rudolph, Alan
LOVE AT LARGE

Samann, Peter
TIME TROOPERS

Sarafian, Deran
DEATH WARRANT

Savini, Tom
NIGHT OF THE LIVING DEAD

Sayadian, Stephen
DR. CALIGARI

Scavolini, Romano
DOG TAGS

Schaffner, Franklin J.
LIONHEART

Schepisi, Fred
RUSSIA HOUSE, THE

Schibli, Paul
NUTCRACKER PRINCE, THE

Schlesinger, John
PACIFIC HEIGHTS

Schlondorff, Volker
HANDMAID'S TALE, THE

Schroeder, Barbet
REVERSAL OF FORTUNE

Schroeder, Michael
DAMNED RIVER

Schumacher, Joel
FLATLINERS

Scorsese, Martin
GOODFELLAS

Scott, James
STRIKE IT RICH

Scott, Tony
REVENGE
DAYS OF THUNDER

Seacat, Sandra
IN THE SPIRIT

Serreau, Coline
MAMA, THERE'S A MAN IN YOUR BED

Setbon, Philippe
MR. FROST

Shanley, John Patrick
JOE VERSUS THE VOLCANO

Sheridan, Jim
FIELD, THE

Sherman, Gary
LISA

Shore, Sig
RETURN OF SUPERFLY, THE

Sidaris, Andy
SAVAGE BEACH

Silberg, Joel
LAMBADA

Silver, Marisa
VITAL SIGNS

Simon, Adam
BRAIN DEAD

Simpson, Michael A.
FUNLAND

Singleton, Ralph S.
GRAVEYARD SHIFT

Skolimowski, Jerzy
TORRENTS OF SPRING

Smawley, Robert J.
AMERICAN EAGLE

Smith, Mel
TALL GUY, THE

Smithee, Allen
SHRIMP ON THE BARBIE, THE

Snyder, Mike
CAGED IN PARADISO

Spottiswoode, Roger
AIR AMERICA

Stanley, Richard
HARDWARE

Stillman, Whit
METROPOLITAN

Tanner, Alain
FLAME IN MY HEART, A

Tavernier, Bertrand
LIFE AND NOTHING BUT

Teague, Lewis
NAVY SEALS

Tenney, Kevin S.
PEACEMAKER

Teuber, Monica
MAGDALENE

Tornatore, Giuseppe
CINEMA PARADISO

Trueba, Fernando
TWISTED OBSESSION

Tuchner, Michael
MISADVENTURES OF MR. WILT, THE

Underwood, Ron
TREMORS

Uys, Jamie
GODS MUST BE CRAZY II, THE

Van Der Kloot, William
DEAD AIM

Verhoeven, Michael
NASTY GIRL, THE

Verhoeven, Paul
TOTAL RECALL

Vincent, Chuck
BEDROOM EYES II
WILDEST DREAMS

Wang, Peter
LASER MAN, THE

Wang, Wayne
EAT A BOWL OF TEA
LIFE IS CHEAP. . . BUT TOILET PAPER IS EX-
PENSIVE

Waters, John
CRY-BABY

Webster, D.J.
DARK SIDE OF THE MOON

Weir, Peter
GREEN CARD

Wheeler, Anne
BYE BYE BLUES

Wilson, Sandy
AMERICAN BOYFRIENDS

Wincer, Simon
QUIGLEY DOWN UNDER

Wynorski, Jim
HAUNTING OF MORELLA, THE

Yoshida, Hiroaki
TWILIGHT OF THE COCKROACHES

Zeffirelli, Franco
HAMLET

Zemeckis, Robert
BACK TO THE FUTURE PART III

Zucker, Jerry
GHOST

EDITORS

Alabiso, Eugenio
OPPONENT, THE

Albert, Ross
LISA

Allen, Dede
HENRY AND JUNE

Amicucci, Gianfranco
NIGHT OF THE SHARKS

Amix, Tim
ANDY COLBY'S INCREDIBLY AWESOME
ADVENTURE

Andersen, Niels Pagh
PATHFINDER

Anderson, William
SHOCK TO THE SYSTEM, A
ROBOCOP 2
GREEN CARD

Anthony, Len
FRIGHT HOUSE

Aron, Donn
ANOTHER 48 HRS.

Audsley, Mick
GRIFTERS, THE

Avildsen, John G.
ROCKY V

Baird, Stuart
DIE HARD 2

Ball, Lori
ROBOT JOX

Barthelmes, Raimund
ME AND HIM

Barton, John A.
DEATH WARRANT

Bassett, Craig
MEN AT WORK

Bauer, Mary
FRANKENSTEIN UNBOUND

Bear, Liza
FORCE OF CIRCUMSTANCE

Beason, Eric
KILL ME AGAIN

Begley, Damian
FRIGHT HOUSE

Beizai, Bahram
BASHU, THE LITTLE STRANGER

Berger, Peter
FUNNY ABOUT LOVE

Beyda, Kent
GREMLINS 2 THE NEW BATCH

Blesam, Alan
WHY ME?

Bloecher, Michael
FIRST POWER, THE

Bloom, John
EVERYBODY WINS
AIR AMERICA

Blunden, Chris
MISADVENTURES OF MR. WILT, THE

Boisson, Noelle
CYRANO DE BERGERAC

Bonanni, Mauro
SANTA SANGRE

Bornstein, Ken
RIVER OF DEATH

Boyle, Peter
TUNE IN TOMORROW

Bradsell, Michael
FOOLS OF FORTUNE

Brady, Jerry
NIGHT ANGEL

Bretherton, David
LIONHEART

Bricmont, Wendy
PUMP UP THE VOLUME

Brody, Ron
TIME TROOPERS

Brown, O. Nicholas
TREMORS
HAPPY TOGETHER
MARKED FOR DEATH

Brown, Robert
VITAL SIGNS
FLATLINERS

Brown, Toby
FACE OF THE ENEMY

Bruce, James
BAIL JUMPER

Buba, Pat
TWO EVIL EYES

Buckley, Norman
FIRE BIRDS

Buff, Conrad
SIDE OUT

Cambas, Jacqueline
DOWNTOWN
MERMAIDS

Campbell, M. Kathryn
MARTIANS GO HOME!

Candib, Richard
EAT A BOWL OF TEA

Carr, Adrian
QUIGLEY DOWN UNDER

Cassidy, Jay
FRANKENSTEIN UNBOUND

Castro, Emmanuelle
MAY FOOLS

Chadwick, Warren
MONSTER HIGH

Chambers, Brian
DOWNTOWN

Chew, Richard
MEN DON'T LEAVE

Chiate, Debra
LOOK WHO'S TALKING TOO

Christopher, Frank
MEN IN LOVE

Chulack, Fred
SHRIMP ON THE BARBIE, THE

Churgin, Lisa
LOVE AT LARGE

Cirincione, Richard
Q&A

Clark, Jim
MEMPHIS BELLE

Clark, Travis
SKINHEADS – THE SECOND COMING OF
HATE

Clayton, Curtiss
PAINT IT BLACK

Coates, Anne V.
I LOVE YOU TO DEATH

Cohen, Betty
SLEEPING CAR, THE

Coispeau, Francois
VINCENT AND THEO

Cole, Stan
LOOSE CANNONS
HOSTILE TAKEOVER

Conrad, Scott
CLASS OF 1999

Conte, Mark
DAMNED RIVER

Cook, Philip
STAR QUEST: BEYOND THE RISING MOON

Coscarelli, Don
SURVIVAL QUEST

Cowan, Larry C.
JETSONS: THE MOVIE

Cox, Joel
WHITE HUNTER, BLACK HEART
ROOKIE, THE

Crafford, Ian
WHERE THE HEART IS

Cristiani, Gabriella
SHELTERING SKY, THE

Cutry, Claudio
SONNY BOY

D'Amico, Cesare
TORRENTS OF SPRING

Dalattre, Chantal
LIFE IS A LONG QUIET RIVER

Davalos, James
BEDROOM EYES II
WILDEST DREAMS

Davies, Carmel
ANOTHER 48 HRS.

Davies, Freeman
ANOTHER 48 HRS.

Davis, Battle
AWAKENINGS

de la Bouillerie, Hubert C.
HONEYMOON ACADEMY

Dedieu, Isabelle
JESUS OF MONTREAL

Dixon, Humphrey
MR. AND MRS. BRIDGE

Dolan, Dennis
RED SURF

Dubensky, Tom
NIGHT OF THE LIVING DEAD

Duffner, J. Patrick
FIELD, THE

Duncin, Dan
PEACEMAKER

Dunham, Duwayne
WILD AT HEART

Duthie, Michael J.
DELTA FORCE 2

Edwards, Robert
FORBIDDEN DANCE, THE

Ellis, Michael
IMPROMPTU

Engelbrecht, Renee
GODS MUST BE CRAZY II, THE

Erickson, Glenn
NIGHT VISITOR

Eriksen, Gordon
BIG DIS, THE

Estrin, Robert
INTERNAL AFFAIRS

Everett, Gimel
DEAD PIT

Fairservice, Don
CHATTAHOOCHEE

Fallick, Mort
JEZEBEL'S KISS

Feeny, Gerry
VERONICO CRUZ

Ferretti, Robert A.
DIE HARD 2

Fields, Richard
TEXASVILLE

Finfer, David
HEART CONDITION

Fingado, Diane
HAUNTING OF MORELLA, THE

Flaum, Seth
GUARDIAN, THE

Foley, Pat
JETSONS: THE MOVIE

Francis-Bruce, Richard
BLOOD OF HEROES
CADILLAC MAN

Frank, Peter C.
SHOCK TO THE SYSTEM, A

Frazen, Nancy
FALSE IDENTITY

Freeman Ross, Jacquie
BLOOD SALVAGE

Freeman, Jeff
REPOSSESSED

Freeman-Fox, Lois
AIR AMERICA

Frias, Carmen
TWISTED OBSESSION

Fruchtman, Lisa
GODFATHER PART III, THE

Fuller, Brad
IN THE SPIRIT

Gall, Joe
HAPPILY EVER AFTER

Garvey, Michael
TORN APART

Gaster, Nicolas
MAHABHARATA, THE

Gaven, Seth
SPACED INVADERS

Ghaffari, Earl
GRIM PRAIRIE TALES

Gilberti, Nina
BODY CHEMISTRY

Glass, Edward H.
LEMON SISTERS, THE

Goldblatt, Mark
NIGHTBREED
PREDATOR 2

Goldenberg, William
TOUCH OF A STRANGER

Goldman, Mia
CRAZY PEOPLE

Gordon, Robert
NOBODY'S PERFECT
BACKSTREET DREAMS

Gosnell, Raja
HOME ALONE

Goursaud, Anne
TWO JAKES, THE

Green, Bruce
YOUNG GUNS II
WELCOME HOME, ROXY CARMICHAEL

Greenberg, Jerry
AWAKENINGS

Greene, Danford B.
VITAL SIGNS

Gross, Daniel
UNDER THE BOARDWALK
SPACED INVADERS

Gross, Jim
GRAVEYARD SHIFT

Grossman, Marc
WILD ORCHID

Grunewaldt, Luce
MAN INSIDE, THE

Guido, Elisabeth
TAXI BLUES

Hache, Joelle
MONSIEUR HIRE

Haight, Michael
SAVAGE BEACH

Haines, Richard
GUMSHOE KID, THE
LIONHEART

Hall, Ivan
GODS MUST BE CRAZY II, THE

Halsey, Richard
JOE VERSUS THE VOLCANO
EDWARD SCISSORHANDS

Hambing, Gerry
COME SEE THE PARADISE

Hampton, Janice
CRY-BABY

Hanley, Daniel
PROBLEM CHILD

Hartley, Hal
UNBELIEVABLE TRUTH, THE

Hartzell, Duane
ANGEL TOWN

Harvey, Marshall
DON'T TELL HER IT'S ME

Hathaway, Kurt
PUMP UP THE VOLUME

Healey, Leslie
BURNDOWN

Heard, Howard
AFTERSHOCK

Heim, Alan
QUICK CHANGE

Helfrich, Mark
I COME IN PEACE

Hennings, Barbara
NASTY GIRL, THE

Herbert, Judith
ELLIOT FAUMAN, PH.D.

Herring, Pembroke
GHOST DAD

Hill, Michael
PROBLEM CHILD

Hillgrove, Vivien
HENRY AND JUNE

Hindkers, Heiko
ROSALIE GOES SHOPPING

Hirsch, Paul
COUPE DE VILLE

Hoggan, Michael
HOLLYWOOD HOT TUBS II: EDUCATING
CRYSTAL

Holzman, Allan
SLEEPING CAR, THE

Honess, Peter
RUSSIA HOUSE, THE

Hook, Harry
LORD OF THE FLIES

Horn, Karen
FULL FATHOM FIVE

Huggins, Jere
AWAKENINGS

Hunt, Peter
DESPERATE HOURS

Jablow, Michael
MADHOUSE

Jaffe, Gib
MODERN LOVE

Jakubowicz, Alain
MACK THE KNIFE

Jimenez, Frank
KILL ME AGAIN

Johnson, Bill
FEUD, THE

Jones, Alan
RAGGEDY RAWNEY, THE

Jones, Robert C.
HEAVEN AND EARTH

Kahn, Michael
ARACHNOPHOBIA

Kahn, Sheldon
KINDERGARTEN COP

Keeley, Ric
PUMP UP THE VOLUME

Kelly, Michael
RESCUERS DOWN UNDER, THE

Keramidas, Harry
BACK TO THE FUTURE PART III

Kern, David
HIT LIST
SPONTANEOUS COMBUSTION

King, Charles
DUCKTALES: THE MOVIE – TREASURE OF
THE LOST LAMP

Klotz, Georges
PLOT AGAINST HARRY, THE

Knue, Michael N.
ROCKY V

Koehler, Bonnie
BAD INFLUENCE

Koller, Ingrid
TIME TROOPERS

Kornilova, Galina
FREEZE – DIE – COME TO LIFE

Kostenko, Andrzej
TORRENTS OF SPRING

Kwei, James Y.
KILL-OFF, THE

Lawson, Tony
WITCHES, THE

Lebenzon, Chris
REVENGE
DAYS OF THUNDER

Leder, Paul
MURDER BY NUMBERS

Lee-Thompson, Peter
EXORCIST III, THE

Leighton, Robert
MISERY

Leonard, Brett
DEAD PIT

Levin, Sidney
STANLEY AND IRIS

Lewis, Terry
PLOT AGAINST HARRY, THE

Linder, Stu
AVALON

Link, John F.
HARD TO KILL

Littleton, Carol
WHITE PALACE

Lloyd, David H.
NIGHT EYES

Lottman, Evan
FORCED MARCH
PRESUMED INNOCENT

Lovejoy, Ray
MR. FROST

Lovitt, Bert
PREDATOR 2

Ludwig, Jerrold L.
STELLA

McDermott, Debra
COLD FEET

Maciejko, Katarzyna
INTERROGATION, THE

McKay, Craig
MIAMI BLUES

McLaughlin, G. Gregg
DEATH WARRANT

McMahon, Michael
BLOOD RELATIONS

Maganini, Elena
HENRY: PORTRAIT OF A SERIAL KILLER

Malkin, Barry
FRESHMAN, THE
GODFATHER PART III, THE

Mallinson, Matthew
CAGED FURY

Malouf-Cundy, Pamela
WITHOUT YOU, I'M NOTHING

Manton, Marcus
LAMBADA
RIVERBEND

Marden, Richard
NIGHTBREED
HAMLET

Maris, Peter
BACK TO BACK

Mark, Stephen
MASQUE OF THE RED DEATH
STREETS

Marks, Richard
DICK TRACY

Marnier, Edward
STRAPLESS

Marsh, David
LORDS OF MAGICK, THE

Martin, David
NUNS ON THE RUN
INNOCENT VICTIM

Mazur, Lara
AMERICAN BOYFRIENDS

Merlin, Claudine
TOO BEAUTIFUL FOR YOU

Meshelski, Thomas
SHADOWZONE

Meulen, Kert Vander
STREET ASYLUM

Michaels, Kevin
BACK TO BACK

Miller, Harry B. III
TALES FROM THE DARKSIDE: THE MOVIE

Miller, Michael R.
LEMON SISTERS, THE
MILLER'S CROSSING
MR. DESTINY

Minami, Tome
DREAMS

Mitchell, James
NARROW MARGIN

Molin, Bud
SIBLING RIVALRY

Moore, Terry W.
JETSONS: THE MOVIE

Mora, Mario
CINEMA PARADISO

Morgan, Glenn A.
WILD ORCHID

Morgan, Randy Jon
GRAVEYARD SHIFT

Morris, Jonathan
HIDDEN AGENDA

Morriss, Frank
BIRD ON A WIRE
SHORT TIME

Morse, Susan E.
ALICE

Mullen, John
RETURN OF SUPERFLY, THE

Murch, Walter
GHOST
GODFATHER PART III, THE

Myers, Stephen
FAR OUT MAN

Napoli, James
STUFF STEPHANIE IN THE INCINERATOR

Nedd, Priscilla
PRETTY WOMAN

Nervig, Sandy
LIFE IS CHEAP. . . BUT TOILET PAPER IS
EXPENSIVE

Newton, Angus
VAMPIRE'S KISS

Nicolaou, Ted
ROBOT JOX

Noble, Thom
MOUNTAINS OF THE MOON

Nunes, Gilberto Costa
FAR OUT MAN

O'Brien, John
BIG DIS, THE

O'Connor, Dennis
FIRE BIRDS

O'Connor, John
DARK SIDE OF THE MOON

O'Hara, Brian
TUSKS

O'Meara, C. Timothy
FLASHBACK

O'Steen, Sam
POSTCARDS FROM THE EDGE

Oblath, Carol
BRAIN DEAD

Okayasu, Hajime
BLACK RAIN

Olivati, Rita
ICICLE THIEF, THE

Osada, Chizuko
ADVENTURES OF MILO AND OTIS, THE

Pankow, Bill
BONFIRE OF THE VANITIES

Patch, Jeffrey C.
HAPPILY EVER AFTER

Percy, Lee
BLUE STEEL
REVERSAL OF FORTUNE

Peroni, Geraldine
VINCENT AND THEO

Phifer Mate, Wende
HOT SPOT, THE

Polakow, Michael
BETSY'S WEDDING

Poll, Jon
FIRE BIRDS

Pollard, Sam
MO' BETTER BLUES

Pollock, Nicholas
DOG TAGS

Prowse, Andrew J.
TIME GUARDIAN, THE

Przygodda, Peter
LAST EXIT TO BROOKLYN

Psenny, Armand
LIFE AND NOTHING BUT

Puett, Dallas
BIRD ON A WIRE

Rae, Dan
TALL GUY, THE
CHICAGO JOE AND THE SHOWGIRL

Ramsay, Todd
EXORCIST III, THE

Rand, Patrick
OVER EXPOSED

Rawlings, Terry
SLIPSTREAM

Rawlins, David
COLD FEET

Ray, David
HANDMAID'S TALE, THE
BONFIRE OF THE VANITIES

Redman, Anthony
KING OF NEW YORK

Renault, Catherine
MAMA, THERE'S A MAN IN YOUR BED

Reynolds, William
TAKING CARE OF BUSINESS

Richardson, Henry
HOMER & EDDIE
SHOW OF FORCE, A

Richardson, Nancy
TO SLEEP WITH ANGER

Rigo, Maria
MY 20TH CENTURY

Rogers, Cynthia
ALLIGATOR EYES

Roland-Levy, J.P.
FORCE OF CIRCUMSTANCE

Rolf, Tom
JACOB'S LADDER

Rondinella, Thomas R.
BLADES

Ross, Rebecca
GRAFFITI BRIDGE

Ross, Sharyn L.
ERNEST GOES TO JAIL

Roth, Chris
ALIENATOR
DEMON WIND
STEEL AND LACE

Roth, Fred
REAL BULLETS

Rothman, Marion
OPPORTUNITY KNOCKS

Rotter, Stephen A.
MY BLUE HEAVEN

Roy, Dominique
HOW TO MAKE LOVE TO A NEGRO WITH-
OUT GETTING TIRED

Ruscio, Michael
DOWN THE DRAIN

Salcedo, Jose
LABYRINTH OF PASSION
TIE ME UP! TIE ME DOWN!

Samuelson, Thomas
ISTANBUL, KEEP YOUR EYES OPEN

Sanderson, Chris
LIFE IS CHEAP. . . BUT TOILET PAPER IS
EXPENSIVE

Scharf, William S.
HENRY AND JUNE

Schmidt, Arthur
BACK TO THE FUTURE PART III

Schoonmaker, Thelma
GOODFELLAS

Schorer, Gregory
TWISTED JUSTICE

Schwalm, Thomas
STRIKE IT RICH

Shaw, Jonathan
KILL ME AGAIN

Shaw, Penelope
TEN LITTLE INDIANS

Shugrue, Robert F.
FOURTH WAR, THE

Simmons, David
BLIND FURY

Simpson, Claire
STATE OF GRACE

Smith, Bud
DARKMAN

Smith, Howard
AFTER DARK, MY SWEET

Smith, Scott
DARKMAN

Steiner, G. Martin
DR. CALIGARI

Steinkamp, Fredric
HAVANA

Steinkamp, William
HAVANA

Stevenson, Michael A.
THREE MEN AND A LITTLE LADY

Stiven, David
DARKMAN
ALMOST AN ANGEL

Summer, Amy
IMPORTED BRIDEGROOM, THE

Sumner, Amy
INHERITOR

Suziki, Akira
HEAVEN AND EARTH

Tarnate, Marc
PRIMARY TARGET

Tate, Christopher
BYE BYE BLUES

Tellefsen, Chris
METROPOLITAN

Tent, Kevin
BASKETCASE 2
FRANKENHOOKER

Teschner, Peter
DARK SIDE OF THE MOON

Thaler, Jonas
WEDDING BAND
CIRCUITRY MAN

Thibault, Michael
DEMONSTONE

Thornton, Randy
BLOOD RED

Tomita, Isao
SUMMER VACATION: 1999

Travis, Neil
DANCES WITH WOLVES

Trigg, Derek
HARDWARE

Tronick, Michael
ADVENTURES OF FORD FAIRLANE, THE

Tsiotsias, Nicholas
DISTURBANCE, THE

Tsitsopoulos, Yannis
LANDSCAPE IN THE MIST

Uhler, Laurent
FLAME IN MY HEART, A

Urioste, Frank J.
TOTAL RECALL

Van Der Kloot, William
DEAD AIM
FUNLAND

Vigna, Tony
WHITE GIRL, THE

Virkler, Dennis
HUNT FOR RED OCTOBER, THE

Walker, Graham
LAST OF THE FINEST, THE

Wallace, Scott
SKI PATROL

Walsh, Martin
COURAGE MOUNTAIN
KRAYS, THE

Warner, Mark
PACIFIC HEIGHTS

Warschilka, Edward
CHILD'S PLAY 2

Warschilka, Edward Jr.
DADDY'S DYIN'... WHO'S GOT THE WILL?

Watson, Earl
HOUSE PARTY
FORBIDDEN DANCE, THE

Weber, Billy
DAYS OF THUNDER

Weinbren, Grahame
LASER MAN, THE

Weintraub, Joseph
ANIMAL BEHAVIOR
LEMON SISTERS, THE

Weiss, Chuck
AMERICAN EAGLE

Wenning, Katherine
LONGTIME COMPANION

Wheeler, John W.
IMPULSE
BIG BAD JOHN

Whittemore, Gloria
GAME, THE

Wilcots, Joseph M.
WHITE GIRL, THE

Williams, Wade
FUNLAND

Wilson, John
COOK, THE THIEF, HIS WIFE & HER
LOVER, THE
BELLY OF AN ARCHITECT, THE

Winding, Genevieve
L'ETAT SAUVAGE

Wright, John
HUNT FOR RED OCTOBER, THE

Yu, Hamilton
REINCARNATION OF GOLDEN LOTUS, THE

Yu, Li-Shin
DEF BY TEMPTATION

Zafosnik, Silvana
MAGDALENE

Zimmerman, Don
NAVY SEALS

Zucchero, Joseph
PRIMARY TARGET

MAKEUP

Adams, Cindy F.
NIGHT EYES

Aimi, Tameyuki
DREAMS

Allsopp, Christine
MACK THE KNIFE

Alpa, Medy
DOG TAGS

Anderson, Barry
DISTURBANCE, THE

Anderson, Lance
DEMON WIND

Andrews, Todd
MADHOUSE

Anoff, Matiki
MO' BETTER BLUES

Arrington, Richard
TAKING CARE OF BUSINESS

Arrollo, Bob
MARKED FOR DEATH

Arrollo, Gandhi Bob
CHATTAHOOCHEE

Aspock, Cordula
NASTY GIRL, THE

Austin, Teresa
NIGHT ANGEL

Austin, Teresa M.
GUARDIAN, THE

Balasz, Charles
FLASHBACK

Balazs, Charles
HOT SPOT, THE
MR. DESTINY

Banchelli, Guiseppe
TORRENTS OF SPRING

Barr, Cynthia
LOVE AT LARGE

Bartels, Annie
TEN LITTLE INDIANS

Bell, Suzanne
I COME IN PEACE

Benoit, Suzanne
STANLEY AND IRIS
STELLA

Bergman, Bridget
PAINT IT BLACK

Berkeley, Craig
TOTAL RECALL

Berns, Mel Jr.
LAST OF THE FINEST, THE

Beveridge, Christine
MOUNTAINS OF THE MOON
WITCHES, THE

Bihr, Kathryn
ME AND HIM
SHOCK TO THE SYSTEM, A
LAST EXIT TO BROOKLYN

Blair, Richard
STELLA

Blake, John
PEACEMAKER

Boost, Jenny
KRAYS, THE

Bowring, Felicity
AFTER DARK, MY SWEET

Boyle, Alan
CHICAGO JOE AND THE SHOWGIRL

Brickman, June Rudley
ERNEST GOES TO JAIL

Bruins, Rose
GODS MUST BE CRAZY II, THE

Buchman, Irving
AVALON

Buchner, Fern
PRESUMED INNOCENT

Burke (nose), Michele
CYRANO DE BERGERAC

Burwell, Lois
AIR AMERICA

Cabral, Susan
VITAL SIGNS

Caglione, John Jr.
THREE MEN AND A LITTLE LADY

Calvet, Camille
FIRST POWER, THE

Carrisosa, Frank
REVENGE
DANCES WITH WOLVES

Chadwick, N. Christine
ROSALIE GOES SHOPPING

Chapuis, Francoise
MAY FOOLS

Chase, Ken
KINDERGARTEN COP

Chin, Judy
UNBELIEVABLE TRUTH, THE

Christiani, Debbie
RIVER OF DEATH

Clark, Ron
I COME IN PEACE

Collini, Carol
MURDER BY NUMBERS

Cooper, Sandy
BIRD ON A WIRE

Coppard, Yvonne
LIONHEART

Corridoni, Franco
BELLY OF AN ARCHITECT, THE

Cozart, Stephanie R.
GHOST DAD

Craft, Nina
LORDS OF MAGICK, THE

Cranzano, Joe
Q&A

Crystal, Tracy
DAMNED RIVER

D'Iorio, Jeanne
RIVERBEND

Dancose, Jayne
SHORT TIME

Dawe, Bibi
ISTANBUL, KEEP YOUR EYES OPEN

Dawn, Jeff
KINDERGARTEN COP

Dawn, Jefferson
TOTAL RECALL

Dawn, Wes
HUNT FOR RED OCTOBER, THE

de Luca, Josee
MAHABHARATA, THE

Dean, Richard
JACOB'S LADDER

Deaton, Aileen
SLIPSTREAM

Deruelle, Michel
MAMA, THERE'S A MAN IN YOUR BED

Didden, Sjoerd
COOK, THE THIEF, HIS WIFE & HER
LOVER, THE

Drexler, Doug
THREE MEN AND A LITTLE LADY

Dudman, Nick
FRANKENSTEIN UNBOUND

Eagan, Lynne
NAVY SEALS

Eddo, Scott
ADVENTURES OF FORD FAIRLANE, THE

Eddo, Scott H.
DIE HARD 2
PREDATOR 2

Elliott, John
MISERY

Elliott, Margaret
MISERY

Engelen, Paul
WHITE HUNTER, BLACK HEART
SHELTERING SKY, THE

Engelman, Leonard
EVERYBODY WINS

Erden, Zubeyde
ISTANBUL, KEEP YOUR EYES OPEN

Eychenne, Jean-Pierre
CYRANO DE BERGERAC

Fava, Alberto
DESPERATE HOURS

Fava, Stefano
OPPONENT, THE

Fisher, Louise
HIDDEN AGENDA

Flowers, Sher
GUMSHOE KID, THE

Flying Fabrizi Sisters, The
TREMORS

Fox, Shelley
ALIENATOR

Freeman, Beverly
TIME GUARDIAN, THE

Fullerton, Carl
GOODFELLAS

Gebbia, Paul
AVALON

Gerard, Cedric
IMPROMPTU

Gerhardt, Pat
NARROW MARGIN

Germain, Michael
GREMLINS 2 THE NEW BATCH

Goodwin, Jeff
TEENAGE MUTANT NINJA TURTLES
BETSY'S WEDDING

Green, Patricia
FRESHMAN, THE

Gulko, Ralph
ROOKIE, THE

Hancock, Michael
IMPULSE
FIRE BIRDS
ROOKIE, THE

Haney, Kevin
DICK TRACY

Hay, Pat
NUNS ON THE RUN
LIONHEART

Hay, Paul
STRIKE IT RICH

Haymore, June
LISA

Helland, J. Roy
POSTCARDS FROM THE EDGE

Henderson, Donna Lou
FAR OUT MAN

Henriques, Ed
EVERYBODY WINS

Herman, Ilona
AWAKENINGS

Hills, Joan
MEMPHIS BELLE

Hjorth, Par
PATHFINDER

Hoi, Yam Chan
EAT A BOWL OF TEA

Hughes, Melanie
HIGH DESERT KILL

Hutchinson, Bruce
VITAL SIGNS

Ilson, Sharon
GREEN CARD

Image Animation
NIGHTBREED

Jacobs, Rodger
OPPORTUNITY KNOCKS

James, Kathrine
MILLER'S CROSSING

Jarbyn, Siw
PATHFINDER

Josefczyk, Jeanne
NIGHT OF THE LIVING DEAD

Kail, James R.
HUNT FOR RED OCTOBER, THE

Kay, Melanie
SURVIVAL QUEST

Kurtzman Nicotero & Berger EFX Group
LEATHERFACE: THE TEXAS CHAINSAW
MASSACRE III

Laden, Bob
STATE OF GRACE

Lambert, Elizabeth
COUPE DE VILLE

Landau, Harriett
FUNLAND

Larsen, Deborah
DARKMAN
CHILD'S PLAY 2

Lavau, Joel
TOO BEAUTIFUL FOR YOU
MAY FOOLS

Lavergne, Didier
HENRY AND JUNE

Lazzara, Louis
FOURTH WAR, THE

Levin, Angela
STREET ASYLUM

Liddiard, Gary
HAVANA

Loverde, Lorelei
STEEL AND LACE

Lucas, Tom
GODFATHER PART III, THE

Lunsford, Charles
STAR QUEST: BEYOND THE RISING MOON

McCarron, Bob
BLOOD OF HEROES

McCoy, James L.
ARACHNOPHOBIA

McIntosh, Todd
LOOK WHO'S TALKING TOO

Magallon, Al
FOURTH WAR, THE

Manderson, Tommie
FIELD, THE

Marini, Lamberto
SANTA SANGRE

Marsalis, Nancie
EAT A BOWL OF TEA

Matenus, Lauren
BLADES

Matonis, Lauren
RETURN OF SUPERFLY, THE

Mayer, Susan
MEN DON'T LEAVE

Maynor, Monica
ALIENATOR

Mazur, Bernadette
CADILLAC MAN
AWAKENINGS

Meerman, Sara
COOK, THE THIEF, HIS WIFE & HER
LOVER, THE

Mills, Bob
MEN DON'T LEAVE
STELLA
PRETTY WOMAN

Mills, Michael
BACK TO THE FUTURE PART III
PREDATOR 2

Mills, Robert James
DESPERATE HOURS

Minns, Cheri
DICK TRACY

Montagna, Peter
QUICK CHANGE

Montesanto-Medcalf, Cheri
ROBOCOP 2

Monzani, Sarah
LORD OF THE FLIES

Muller, Eric
L'ETAT SAUVAGE
LIFE AND NOTHING BUT

Myers, Kenny
BACK TO THE FUTURE PART III
HOME ALONE

Neill, Ve
FLATLINERS

Noe, Alfonso
WITHOUT YOU, I'M NOTHING

Norin, John M.
LAST OF THE FINEST, THE

Nye, Ben Jr.
I LOVE YOU TO DEATH

O'Reilly, Valli
PACIFIC HEIGHTS

Oropeza, Ester
REVENGE

Ortiz, Hiram
WILD ORCHID

Page, Barbara
SKI PATROL

Parker, Daniel
TALL GUY, THE

Phillips, Kim
HOME ALONE

Plez, Dominique
IMPROMPTU

Puzon, Violy
DEMONSTONE

Quashnick, David
ARACHNOPHOBIA

Rantscheff, Berndt
HENRY: PORTRAIT OF A SERIAL KILLER

Rosenast, Erica
BAIL JUMPER

Ross, Morag
TALL GUY, THE
MISADVENTURES OF MR. WILT, THE

Russier, Jean-Luc
IMPROMPTU

Sander, Helga
NASTY GIRL, THE

Sanders, Suzanne
LEATHERFACE: THE TEXAS CHAINSAW
MASSACRE III

SPACED INVADERS

Sano, Norio
DREAMS

Scott, Mickey
STANLEY AND IRIS

Sforza, Fabrizio
GODFATHER PART III, THE

Shircore, Jenny
INNOCENT VICTIM

Short, Sheri
FIRST POWER, THE
DR. CALIGARI

Simons, Jef
MARKED FOR DEATH

Smarz, Nena
PROBLEM CHILD

Smith, Van
CRY-BABY

Solomon, Margaret
NARROW MARGIN

Specter, Ron
WHITE PALACE

Stanhope, Paul
EXORCIST III, THE

Surrich, Jane
TIME GUARDIAN, THE

Tamura, Shigeo
HEAVEN AND EARTH

Taylor, Anne
BURNDOWN
TUSKS

Ternes, Ed
DESPERATE HOURS

Thomas, Michael R.
LOOSE CANNONS

Thompson, Laini
HOUSE PARTY

Trani, Maurizio
CINEMA PARADISO

Trimble, Toni
BLUE STEEL
SHOCK TO THE SYSTEM, A

Ueda, Shoshichiro
DREAMS

Van Phue, Jeanne
YOUNG GUNS II
MEN AT WORK

Vandale, Kathleen
ANDY COLBY'S INCREDIBLY AWESOME
ADVENTURE

Vassel, Marie-France
GREEN CARD

Wada, Ed
SURVIVAL QUEST

Wanzell, Steven
BACK TO BACK

Weisinger, Allen
GOODFELLAS

Weiss, Robin
TOTAL RECALL

Westmore, Kevin
PREDATOR 2

Westmore, Michael
BLOOD OF HEROES
ROCKY V

Wong, Ellen
REVENGE

Zoller, Debbie
FIRST POWER, THE

MUSIC COMPOSERS

Adler, Mark
EAT A BOWL OF TEA

Alder, Mark
LIFE IS CHEAP. . . BUT TOILET PAPER IS EX-
PENSIVE

Alonso, Tom
TUSKS

Arnow, Peter
TORN APART

Arntson, Bruce
ERNEST GOES TO JAIL

Artemyev, Eduard
HOMER & EDDIE

Bach, J.S.
FLAME IN MY HEART, A

Badalamenti, Angelo
WILD AT HEART

Bahler, Tom
COLD FEET

Band, Richard
SHADOWZONE

Banevich, Sergei
FREEZE – DIE – COME TO LIFE

Banks, Brian
INTERNAL AFFAIRS
GRAVEYARD SHIFT

Barry, John
DANCES WITH WOLVES

Bartley, David
STAR QUEST: BEYOND THE RISING MOON

Becker, Frank W.
HAPPILY EVER AFTER

Bernstein, Elmer
SLIPSTREAM
GRIFTERS, THE
FIELD, THE

Bicat, Nick
STRAPLESS

Bilderbeck, Ken
LORDS OF MAGICK, THE

Bishop, Michael
TIME TROOPERS

Bjerkestrand, Kjetil
PATHFINDER

Blades, Ruben
Q&A

Blondheim, George
BYE BYE BLUES

Boddicker, Michael
ADVENTURES OF MILO AND OTIS, THE

Bodine, Bill
HOLLYWOOD HOT TUBS II: EDUCATING
CRYSTAL

Boekelheide, Todd
BLOOD OF HEROES

Bongiovi, Tony
FRIGHT HOUSE

Boswell, Simon
SANTA SANGRE
HARDWARE

Branca, Glenn
BELLY OF AN ARCHITECT, THE

Bregovic, Goran
TIME OF THE GYPSIES

Brewis, Peter
TALL GUY, THE

Britten, Tony
BURNDOWN

Brothers Kendall, The
UNBELIEVABLE TRUTH, THE

Broughton, Bruce
BETSY'S WEDDING
NARROW MARGIN
RESCUERS DOWN UNDER, THE

Brown, Jimmy Lee
WHITE GIRL, THE

Bryans, Billy
HOSTILE TAKEOVER

Burke, Chris
FRIGHT HOUSE

Burwell, Carter
MILLER'S CROSSING

Chang, Gary
SHOCK TO THE SYSTEM, A
DEATH WARRANT

Chattaway, Jay
FAR OUT MAN

Chekassine, Vladimir
TAXI BLUES

Chemirani, Djamchid
MAHABHARATA, THE

Chopin, Frederic
IMPROMPTU

Cipriani, Stelvio
NIGHT OF THE SHARKS

Cirino, Chuck
ALIENATOR
HAUNTING OF MORELLA, THE

Clinton, George S.
TEN LITTLE INDIANS

Colcord, Ray
SLEEPING CAR, THE

Coleman, Jim
UNBELIEVABLE TRUTH, THE

Colombier, Michel
IMPULSE

Conti, Bill
FOURTH WAR, THE
BACKSTREET DREAMS
ROCKY V

Copeland, Stewart
FIRST POWER, THE
TAKING CARE OF BUSINESS
MEN AT WORK
HIDDEN AGENDA

Coppola, Carmine
BLOOD RED
GODFATHER PART III, THE

Cordio, Claudio Mario
SONNY BOY

Cox, Rick
BACK TO BACK

d'Andrea, Oswald
LIFE AND NOTHING BUT

Dancz, Steve
GRIM PRAIRIE TALES

Danna, Mychael
BLOOD RELATIONS

Daring, Mason
LASER MAN, THE

Davies, Phil
DARK SIDE OF THE MOON

Davis, Aaron
STREETS
HOSTILE TAKEOVER

Davis, Carl
FRANKENSTEIN UNBOUND

De Sica, Manuel
ICICLE THIEF, THE

DeBelles, Greg
LAMBADA

Debney, John
JETSONS: THE MOVIE

Delerue, Georges
JOE VERSUS THE VOLCANO
SHOW OF FORCE, A

Delia, Joe
CAGED FURY
KING OF NEW YORK

DeVorzon, Barry
EXORCIST III, THE

Dibango, Manu
HOW TO MAKE LOVE TO A NEGRO WITH-
OUT GETTING TIRED

Doldinger, Klaus
ME AND HIM

Donaggio, Pino
TWO EVIL EYES

Dr. Cranium and the Big Dis Crew
BIG DIS, THE

Du Prez, John
TEENAGE MUTANT NINJA TURTLES

Dudley, Anne
MISADVENTURES OF MR. WILT, THE

Duhamel, Antoine
TWISTED OBSESSION

Dunayer, Marty
FRIGHT HOUSE

Eddolls, Brian
FEUD, THE

Edelman, Randy
QUICK CHANGE
KINDERGARTEN COP
COME SEE THE PARADISE

Eidelman, Cliff
CRAZY PEOPLE
ANIMAL BEHAVIOR
MAGDALENE

Elfman, Danny
NIGHTBREED
DICK TRACY
DARKMAN
EDWARD SCISSORHANDS

Elliott, Jack
SIBLING RIVALRY

Erguner, Kudsi
MAHABHARATA, THE

Fenton, George
WHITE PALACE
MEMPHIS BELLE

Fiedel, Brad
BLUE STEEL

Figgis, Michael
INTERNAL AFFAIRS

Finch, Atticus
INHERITOR

Fisher, Morgan
TWILIGHT OF THE COCKROACHES

Folk, Robert
HAPPY TOGETHER
HONEYMOON ACADEMY

Forman, Mitchel
JEZEBEL'S KISS

Fox, Charles
GODS MUST BE CRAZY II, THE
REPOSSESSED

Frank, David Michael
HARD TO KILL

Frewer, Terry
AMERICAN BOYFRIENDS

Froom, Mitchell
DR. CALIGARI

Fuller, Parmer
NIGHT VISITOR

Gerut, Rosalie
IMPORTED BRIDEGROOM, THE

Glasser, Richard
NIGHT EYES

Goga, Jack Alan
TOUCH OF A STRANGER

Goldberg, Barry
FLASHBACK
FALSE IDENTITY

Goldenberg, Simon
WILD ORCHID

Goldsmith, Jerry
GREMLINS 2 THE NEW BATCH
TOTAL RECALL
LIONHEART
RUSSIA HOUSE, THE

Goodman, Miles
OPPORTUNITY KNOCKS
VITAL SIGNS
PROBLEM CHILD
FUNNY ABOUT LOVE

Gore, Michael
DON'T TELL HER IT'S ME

Governor, Mark
MASQUE OF THE RED DEATH
OVER EXPOSED

Grappelli, Stephane
MAY FOOLS

Gross, Charles
AIR AMERICA

Grusin, Dave
HAVANA
BONFIRE OF THE VANITIES

Hammer, Jan
I COME IN PEACE

Harrison, John
TALES FROM THE DARKSIDE: THE MOVIE

Hartley, Richard
INNOCENT VICTIM

Herrnstadt, Georg
TIME TROOPERS

Hertung, Mike
NASTY GIRL, THE

Hidden Faces
NUNS ON THE RUN

Hodian, John
BLADES

Hoenig, Michael
LAST OF THE FINEST, THE
CLASS OF 1999

Holland, Deborah
CIRCUITRY MAN

Horner, James
I LOVE YOU TO DEATH
ANOTHER 48 HRS.
ANDY COLBY'S INCREDIBLY AWESOME
ADVENTURE

Horowitz, Richard
SHELTERING SKY, THE

Horunzhy, Vladmir
FORBIDDEN DANCE, THE

Howard, James Newton
COUPE DE VILLE
PRETTY WOMAN
FLATLINERS
MARKED FOR DEATH
THREE MEN AND A LITTLE LADY

Hues, Jack
GUARDIAN, THE

Hunter, Steve
WEDDING BAND

Hyman, Dick
LEMON SISTERS, THE

Ikebe, Shinichiro
DREAMS

Isham, Mark
EVERYBODY WINS
LOVE AT LARGE
REVERSAL OF FORTUNE

Jacob, Joel
DISTURBANCE, THE

Jankel, Chaz
TALES FROM THE DARKSIDE: THE MOVIE

Jarre, Maurice
AFTER DARK, MY SWEET
GHOST
JACOB'S LADDER
ALMOST AN ANGEL

Jones, Ron
REAL BULLETS

Jones, Trevor
BAD INFLUENCE
ARACHNOPHOBIA

Kamen, Michael
RAGGEDY RAWNEY, THE
DIE HARD 2
KRAYS, THE

Kaproff, Dana
HIGH DESERT KILL

Karaindrou, Eleni
LANDSCAPE IN THE MIST

Kawczynski, Gerard
LIFE IS A LONG QUIET RIVER

Keane, John
CHATTAHOOCHEE

Kev Ses & Harry B.
BIG DIS, THE

Khrapachev, Vadim
LONELY WOMAN SEEKS LIFE COMPANION

Kitay, David
UNDER THE BOARDWALK
LOOK WHO'S TALKING TOO

Klingler, Kevin
CAGED IN PARADISO
AFTERSHOCK

Knieper, Jurgen
PAINT IT BLACK

Knopfler, Mark
LAST EXIT TO BROOKLYN

Komuro, Tetsuya
HEAVEN AND EARTH

Krizman, Rick
DOWN THE DRAIN

Laferriere, Yves
JESUS OF MONTREAL

Laurence, Paul
DEF BY TEMPTATION

Ledin, Tomas
ISTANBUL, KEEP YOUR EYES OPEN

Lee, Bill
MO' BETTER BLUES

Leonard, Patrick
HEART CONDITION

Lerios, Cory
NIGHT ANGEL

Levay, Sylvester
COURAGE MOUNTAIN
NAVY SEALS

Levine, Steven
MR. FROST

Lewin, Frank
PLOT AGAINST HARRY, THE

Liszt, Franz
IMPROMPTU

Lo, Richard
REINCARNATION OF GOLDEN LOTUS, THE

Lombardo, John
HOLLYWOOD HOT TUBS II: EDUCATING
CRYSTAL

Loomis, Paul
RIVERBEND

Lorber, Jeff
SIDE OUT

Lurie, Evan
KILL-OFF, THE

Lyons, Richard
MONSTER HIGH

McCollough, Paul
NIGHT OF THE LIVING DEAD

MacCormack, Geoff
WILD ORCHID

McHugh, David
DADDY'S DYIN'... WHO'S GOT THE WILL?

Mader, M.
FORCE OF CIRCUMSTANCE

Mamet, Bob
CAGED IN PARADISO
AFTERSHOCK

Mancini, Henry
GHOST DAD

Mansfield, David
DESPERATE HOURS

Manson, Bevan
IMPORTED BRIDEGROOM, THE

Manzie, Jim
LEATHERFACE: THE TEXAS CHAINSAW
MASSACRE III
TALES FROM THE DARKSIDE: THE MOVIE

Mar, Jeff
PRIMARY TARGET

Marcel, Leonard
STREET ASYLUM

Marinelli, Anthony
INTERNAL AFFAIRS
GRAVEYARD SHIFT

Marsalis, Wynton
TUNE IN TOMORROW

Martin, George Porter
WHITE GIRL, THE

Martin, Peter
WHERE THE HEART IS

Massari, John
STEEL AND LACE

Matson, Sasha
RED SURF
RIVER OF DEATH

Matz, Peter
GUMSHOE KID, THE

Mayfield, Curtis
RETURN OF SUPERFLY, THE

Mennonna, Joey
WILDEST DREAMS

Menzer, Kim
MAHABHARATA, THE

Mertens, Wim
BELLY OF AN ARCHITECT, THE

Michelini, Luciano
OPPONENT, THE

Miller, Bruce
SKI PATROL

Miller, Marcus
HOUSE PARTY

Monfaredzadeh, Esfandiar
FACE OF THE ENEMY

Morricone, Andrea
CINEMA PARADISO

Morricone, Ennio
CINEMA PARADISO
TIE ME UP! TIE ME DOWN!
STATE OF GRACE
HAMLET

Morris, John
STELLA

Muller, Marius
PATHFINDER

Myers, Stanley
TORRENTS OF SPRING
WITCHES, THE

Myrow, Fred
SURVIVAL QUEST

Nakamura, Yuriko
SUMMER VACATION: 1999

Newborn, Ira
SHORT TIME
MY BLUE HEAVEN

Newman, David
MADHOUSE
FIRE BIRDS
FRESHMAN, THE
DUCKTALES: THE MOVIE – TREASURE OF
THE LOST LAMP
MR. DESTINY

Newman, Randy
AVALON
AWAKENINGS

Newman, Thomas
MEN DON'T LEAVE
WELCOME HOME, ROXY CARMICHAEL

Niehaus, Lennie
WHITE HUNTER, BLACK HEART
ROOKIE, THE

Nitzsche, Jack
REVENGE
LAST OF THE FINEST, THE
HOT SPOT, THE
MERMAIDS

Nyman, Michael
COOK, THE THIEF, HIS WIFE & HER
LOVER, THE
MONSIEUR HIRE

Oliverio, James
DEAD AIM
FUNLAND

Olvis, William
KILL ME AGAIN

Parks, Van Dyke
TWO JAKES, THE

Peake, Don
MODERN LOVE

Petit, Jean-Claude
CYRANO DE BERGERAC

Pettit, Paul
DISTURBANCE, THE

Philip, Hans-Erik
SHADOW OF THE RAVEN, THE

Plumeri, Terry
ANGEL TOWN
BODY CHEMISTRY

Poledouris, Basil
HUNT FOR RED OCTOBER, THE
QUIGLEY DOWN UNDER

WHY ME?

Prince
GRAFFITI BRIDGE

Randles, Robert
NOBODY'S PERFECT

Redbone, Leon
EVERYBODY WINS

Reese, Jerome
MAMA, THERE'S A MAN IN YOUR BED

Regal, Donald James
MEN IN LOVE

Regan, Pat
LEATHERFACE: THE TEXAS CHAINSAW
MASSACRE III
TALES FROM THE DARKSIDE: THE MOVIE

Renzetti, Joe
BASKETCASE 2
LISA
FRANKENHOOKER

Resetarits, Willi
TIME TROOPERS

Revell, Graeme
SPONTANEOUS COMBUSTION
CHILD'S PLAY 2

Robbins, Richard
PERFECT MURDER, THE
BAIL JUMPER
MR. AND MRS. BRIDGE

Robins, Teddy
REINCARNATION OF GOLDEN LOTUS, THE

Robinson, J. Peter
BLIND FURY
CADILLAC MAN

Rosenman, Leonard
ROBOCOP 2

Rota, Nino
GODFATHER PART III, THE

Rotter, Peter Francis
BRAIN DEAD

Rubinstein, Donald A.
TALES FROM THE DARKSIDE: THE MOVIE

Rushen, Patrice
WITHOUT YOU, I'M NOTHING

Russo, David
SPACED INVADERS

Ryder, Mark
DARK SIDE OF THE MOON

Sakamoto, Ryuichi
HANDMAID'S TALE, THE
SHELTERING SKY, THE

Sarde, Philippe
LORD OF THE FLIES
C'EST LA VIE

Schloter, Elmar
NASTY GIRL, THE

Schroder, Robert
AMERICAN EAGLE

Schubert, Franz
TOO BEAUTIFUL FOR YOU

Schyman, Gary
HIT LIST

Scott, John
DOG TAGS

Shaiman, Marc
MISERY

Shelstad, Kirby
ERNEST GOES TO JAIL

Shore, Howard
QUICK CHANGE

Silver, Sheila
ALLIGATOR EYES

Silvestri, Alan
DOWNTOWN
BACK TO THE FUTURE PART III
YOUNG GUNS II
PREDATOR 2

Simon, Carly
POSTCARDS FROM THE EDGE

Slider, Dan
SKINHEADS — THE SECOND COMING OF HATE

Small, Michael
MOUNTAINS OF THE MOON

Stemple, James Wesley
DAMNED RIVER

Stewart, George
LORDS OF MAGICK, THE

Stockdale, Gary
DEMONSTONE
SAVAGE BEACH

Stone, Christopher L.
SURVIVAL QUEST

Summers, Bob
MURDER BY NUMBERS

Suozzo, Mark
METROPOLITAN

Sutherland, Ken
BIG BAD JOHN

Tabrizi-Zadeh, Mahmoud
MAHABHARATA, THE

Takemitsu, Toru
BLACK RAIN

Talgorn, Frederic
DELTA FORCE 2
ROBOT JOX

Tangerine Dream
MAN INSIDE, THE

Taylor, Stephen James
TO SLEEP WITH ANGER

Teetsel, Fredric Nesign
HAUNTING OF MORELLA, THE

Telson, Bob
ROSALIE GOES SHOPPING

Temple, Tim
BLOOD SALVAGE

Torres, Jaime
VERONICO CRUZ

Towns, Colin
VAMPIRE'S KISS

Trefousse, Roger
ELLIOT FAUMAN, PH.D.

Troost, Ernest
TREMORS
ANDY COLBY'S INCREDIBLY AWESOME ADVENTURE

Tsuchitori, Toshi
MAHABHARATA, THE

Valkeapaa, Nils-Aslak
PATHFINDER

Vidovszky, Laszlo
MY 20TH CENTURY

Walker, Shirley
CHICAGO JOE AND THE SHOWGIRL

Wallenstein, Bruce
DEMON WIND

Weill, Kurt
MACK THE KNIFE

Wild Blue Yonder
UNBELIEVABLE TRUTH, THE

Williams, John
STANLEY AND IRIS
PRESUMED INNOCENT

HOME ALONE

Williams, Patrick
CRY-BABY
IN THE SPIRIT

Wilson, Julia
GAME, THE

Yared, Gabriel
VINCENT AND THEO

Yello
NUNS ON THE RUN
ADVENTURES OF FORD FAIRLANE, THE

Zavod, Allan
MARTIANS GO HOME!
TIME GUARDIAN, THE

Zaza, Paul
LOOSE CANNONS

Zimmer, Hans
BIRD ON A WIRE
DAYS OF THUNDER
CHICAGO JOE AND THE SHOWGIRL
FOOLS OF FORTUNE
PACIFIC HEIGHTS
GREEN CARD

MUSIC DIRECTORS

Afterman, Peter
FIRE BIRDS

Ames, Morgan
WITHOUT YOU, I'M NOTHING

Barry, John
DANCES WITH WOLVES

Bedell, Steve
FALSE IDENTITY

Bogner, Jonathan Scott
MEN AT WORK

Brott, Boris
NUTCRACKER PRINCE, THE

Butler, Gerry
CHICAGO JOE AND THE SHOWGIRL

Carr, Budd
BEDROOM EYES II
TO SLEEP WITH ANGER

Chackler, David
HOMER & EDDIE

Collins, Audrey
FIELD, THE

Coppola, Carmine
GODFATHER PART III, THE

Crowe, Maureen
LOOK WHO'S TALKING TOO

Dilbeck, Michael
NAVY SEALS

Eidelman, Cliff
CRAZY PEOPLE
MAGDALENE

Feldman, Sam
AMERICAN BOYFRIENDS

Fitzpatrick, Frank
NUNS ON THE RUN

Franzetti, Carlos
Q&A

Freegard, Nicole
PUMP UP THE VOLUME

Goodman, Harlan
FRESHMAN, THE

Hoenig, Michael
HOT SPOT, THE

Isgro, Joe
IMPULSE

Jansen, Pierre
L'ETAT SAUVAGE

Kamen, Michael
DIE HARD 2

Kaplan, Seth
CLASS OF 1999

Kaufman, Philip
HENRY AND JUNE

Kaufman, Rose
HENRY AND JUNE

Krost, Jackie
FORBIDDEN DANCE, THE

LaMont, Joe
FORBIDDEN DANCE, THE

Lee, Bill
MO' BETTER BLUES

Levine, Barry
FAR OUT MAN

McNaughton, Robert
HENRY: PORTRAIT OF A SERIAL KILLER

Mancuso, Becky
OPPORTUNITY KNOCKS
CRY-BABY
AIR AMERICA

Marcus, Tony
PRIMARY TARGET

Mason, Allan
AVALON

Morricone, Ennio
STATE OF GRACE

Nyman, Michael
COOK, THE THIEF, HIS WIFE & HER LOVER, THE

Paich, Marty
THREE MEN AND A LITTLE LADY

Palmer, Christopher
WITCHES, THE

Pangikas, Chris
NIGHT OF THE LIVING DEAD

Power, Derek
CLASS OF 1999
SHORT TIME

Prince
GRAFFITI BRIDGE

Rabinowitz, Harry
LORD OF THE FLIES

Rosenman, Leonard
ROBOCOP 2

Rudolph, Dick
FLATLINERS

Russo, David
SPACED INVADERS

Seltzer, Dov
MACK THE KNIFE

Sexton, Tim
OPPORTUNITY KNOCKS
CRY-BABY
AIR AMERICA

Shaffer, Paul
LEMON SISTERS, THE

Shore, Howard
POSTCARDS FROM THE EDGE

Sill, Joel
COUPE DE VILLE

Splet, Alan
HENRY AND JUNE

Strauss, John
IMPROMPTU

Tobin, George
JETSONS: THE MOVIE

Troost, Ernest
TREMORS

Vollack, Lia
LONGTIME COMPANION

Walker, Shirley
BIRD ON A WIRE
PACIFIC HEIGHTS
CHILD'S PLAY 2

Williams, Ray
EVERYBODY WINS
SHELTERING SKY, THE

Worth, Jody Taylor
FLASHBACK

PRODUCERS

Adam, Alain
DOG TAGS

Adelson, Gary
HARD TO KILL

Adlon, Eleonore
ROSALIE GOES SHOPPING

Adlon, Percy
ROSALIE GOES SHOPPING

Albert, Richard L.
FORBIDDEN DANCE, THE

Almodovar, Agustin
TIE ME UP! TIE ME DOWN!

Amritraj, Amrok
NIGHT EYES

Anciano, Dominic
KRAYS, THE

Angelopoulos, Theo
LANDSCAPE IN THE MIST

Anthony, Len
FRIGHT HOUSE

Anthony, Tony
WILD ORCHID
HONEYMOON ACADEMY

Arcady, Alexander
C'EST LA VIE

Argento, Claudio
SANTA SANGRE

Argento, Dario
TWO EVIL EYES

Assonitis, Ovidio G.
SONNY BOY

Atkins, Dick
FORCED MARCH

Augustyn, Joe
NIGHT ANGEL

Avnet, Jon
MEN DON'T LEAVE
FUNNY ABOUT LOVE

Badalato, William
FIRE BIRDS

Band, Albert
ROBOT JOX

Band, Charles
ROBOT JOX

Barad, Tom
CRAZY PEOPLE

Barbera, Joseph
JETSONS: THE MOVIE

Bear, Liza
FORCE OF CIRCUMSTANCE

Beatty, Warren
DICK TRACY

Bennett, Michael
DEMON WIND

Benson, Robby
MODERN LOVE

Berger, Pamela
IMPORTED BRIDEGROOM, THE

Bernard, Judd
BLOOD RED

Bernt, Eric
MONSTER HIGH

Bevan, Tim
TALL GUY, THE
CHICAGO JOE AND THE SHOWGIRL

Bieber, Rick
FLATLINERS

Black, Todd
SHORT TIME

Blackwell, Gregory S.
UNDER THE BOARDWALK

Blocker, David
LOVE AT LARGE

Boeken, Ludi
VINCENT AND THEO

Bogdanovich, Peter
TEXASVILLE

Bond, James III
DEF BY TEMPTATION

Boorman, John
WHERE THE HEART IS

Borde, Mark
HOLLYWOOD HOT TUBS II: EDUCATING
CRYSTAL

Borman, Moritz
HOMER & EDDIE

Branco, Paulo
FLAME IN MY HEART, A

Braunstein, George G.
DON'T TELL HER IT'S ME

Bregman, Martin
BETSY'S WEDDING

Brezner, Larry
COUPE DE VILLE

Brown, Curtis
GAME, THE

Bruckheimer, Jerry
DAYS OF THUNDER

Burdis, Ray
KRAYS, THE

Burke, Ann
HOW TO MAKE LOVE TO A NEGRO WITH-
OUT GETTING TIRED

Burton, Tim
EDWARD SCISSORHANDS

Byrnes, Thomas S.
TO SLEEP WITH ANGER

Cady, James
HOMER & EDDIE

Callender, Colin
BELLY OF AN ARCHITECT, THE

Calley, John
POSTCARDS FROM THE EDGE

Camp, Alida
BODY CHEMISTRY

Cannady, James
WHITE GIRL, THE

Canton, Neil
BACK TO THE FUTURE PART III

Carcassonne, Philippe
MAMA, THERE'S A MAN IN YOUR BED
MONSIEUR HIRE

Casey, Patricia
BLOOD RED

Catamas, Scott
MEN IN LOVE

Cerasuola, Ron
DISTURBANCE, THE

Chan, David
TEENAGE MUTANT NINJA TURTLES

Charnin, Steven H.
UNDER THE BOARDWALK

Chartoff, Robert
ROCKY V

Chase, Stanley
MACK THE KNIFE

Chohan, Wahid
PERFECT MURDER, THE

Chubb, Caldecot
TO SLEEP WITH ANGER

Cimino, Michael
DESPERATE HOURS

Cingolani, Luigi
SPACED INVADERS

Clark, Greydon
SKINHEADS – THE SECOND COMING OF
HATE

Cleitman, Rene
MONSIEUR HIRE
LIFE AND NOTHING BUT
CYRANO DE BERGERAC

Clendenen, Randolph
ANIMAL BEHAVIOR

Coen, Ethan
MILLER'S CROSSING

Cohen, Rob
BIRD ON A WIRE

Colesberry, Robert F.
COME SEE THE PARADISE

Coppola, Francis Ford
GODFATHER PART III, THE

Corman, Julie
BRAIN DEAD

Corman, Roger
MASQUE OF THE RED DEATH
HAUNTING OF MORELLA, THE
OVER EXPOSED

Cornell, John
ALMOST AN ANGEL

Cort, Robert W.
THREE MEN AND A LITTLE LADY

Costner, Kevin
DANCES WITH WOLVES

Crawford, Wayne
PEACEMAKER

Cristaldi, Franco
CINEMA PARADISO

Cruickshank, Jim
MR. DESTINY

Curtis, Douglas
SLEEPING CAR, THE

D'Elia, Bill
FEUD, THE

Damon, Mark
WILD ORCHID

David, Pierre
INTERNAL AFFAIRS

Davis, John A.
LAST OF THE FINEST, THE
PREDATOR 2

Davis, Thomas Jr.
TAX SEASON

Davison, Jon
ROBOCOP 2

Dawson, Kim
TEENAGE MUTANT NINJA TURTLES

De Palma, Brian
BONFIRE OF THE VANITIES

DeCoteau, David
STEEL AND LACE

Dedmond, Lisa
HENRY: PORTRAIT OF A SERIAL KILLER

DeHaven, Carter
EXORCIST III, THE

DeLaurentiis, Dino
DESPERATE HOURS

Demme, Jonathan
MIAMI BLUES

Denure, Steven
AMERICAN BOYFRIENDS

Diaz, Philippe
MAN INSIDE, THE

DiNovi, Denise
EDWARD SCISSORHANDS

DiSalle, Mark
DEATH WARRANT

Dixon, Leslie
MADHOUSE

Donaldson, Roger
CADILLAC MAN

Donohue, Walter
BELLY OF AN ARCHITECT, THE

Douglas, Michael
FLATLINERS

Dowd, Ned
STATE OF GRACE

Drewno, Tadeuz
INTERROGATION, THE

Dunn, William J.
GRAVEYARD SHIFT

Dunne, Griffin
WHITE PALACE

Dyson, Lovell
HAMLET

Eastman, Brian
MISADVENTURES OF MR. WILT, THE

Easton, Graham
STRIKE IT RICH

Eastwood, Clint
WHITE HUNTER, BLACK HEART

Efraim, R. Ben
SHRIMP ON THE BARBIE, THE

Eichinger, Bernd
ME AND HIM
LAST EXIT TO BROOKLYN

Ellis, John
STAR QUEST: BEYOND THE RISING MOON

Elwes, Cassian
MEN AT WORK
COLD FEET

Engelman, Robert
LEATHERFACE: THE TEXAS CHAINSAW
MASSACRE III

Ephraim, Lionel
AMERICAN EAGLE

Eriksen, Gordon
BIG DIS, THE

Evans, Robert
TWO JAKES, THE

Everett, Gimel
DEAD PIT

Faber, Christian
BAIL JUMPER

Feigen, Brenda
NAVY SEALS

Feitshans, Buzz
TOTAL RECALL

Feldman, John
ALLIGATOR EYES

Fellner, Eric
HIDDEN AGENDA

Fiedler, John
TUNE IN TOMORROW

Field, Ted
THREE MEN AND A LITTLE LADY

Fields, Simon
TEENAGE MUTANT NINJA TURTLES

Finkelman Cox, Penney
WELCOME HOME, ROXY CARMICHAEL

Finnegan, John P.
BLADES

Finnell, Michael
GREMLINS 2 THE NEW BATCH

Fischer, Marc S.
FORBIDDEN DANCE, THE

Fischer, Martin J.
BLOOD SALVAGE

Fisher, Danny
TORN APART

Flak, George
HOSTILE TAKEOVER

Forstater, Mark
PAINT IT BLACK

Foster, Gary
SIDE OUT

Frappier, Roger
JESUS OF MONTREAL

Fredericks, Ed
BURNDOWN

Frederickson, Gray
GODFATHER PART III, THE

Fredriksz, Winnie
LIFE IS CHEAP. . . BUT TOILET PAPER IS
EXPENSIVE

Gale, Bob
BACK TO THE FUTURE PART III

Galin, Mitchell
TALES FROM THE DARKSIDE: THE MOVIE

Gallagher, Bob
CAGED FURY

Gassot, Charles
LIFE IS A LONG QUIET RIVER

Gazarian, John
REAL BULLETS

Geoffray, Jeff
NIGHT ANGEL

Gernert, Walter D.
STREET ASYLUM

Gillis, Kevin
NUTCRACKER PRINCE, THE

Ginnane, Antony I.
DEMONSTONE

Globus, Yoram
DELTA FORCE 2

Glotzer, Liz
SIBLING RIVALRY

Goetzman, Gary
MIAMI BLUES

Goldfine, Phillip B.
SKI PATROL

Goldwyn, Samuel Jr.
STELLA

Golin, Steve
KILL ME AGAIN

DADDY'S DYIN'. . . WHO'S GOT THE WILL?
WILD AT HEART

Gomez, Andres Vicente
TWISTED OBSESSION

Gontier, Jean
GREEN CARD

Gordon, Charles
DIE HARD 2

Gordon, Lawrence
ANOTHER 48 HRS.
DIE HARD 2
PREDATOR 2

Gordon, Mark R.
OPPORTUNITY KNOCKS

Grais, Michael
MARKED FOR DEATH

Gray, Bob
LOOK WHO'S TALKING TOO

Greenbaum, Brian
METROPOLITAN

Greenhut, Robert
QUICK CHANGE
ALICE

Greisman, Alan
LOOSE CANNONS

Grodnik, Daniel
BLIND FURY

Gueramian, Behrouz
FACE OF THE ENEMY

Guest, Cliff
DISTURBANCE, THE

Gundersen, Hakon
TOUCH OF A STRANGER

Hadar, Ronnie
DOWN THE DRAIN

Hahn, Richard
GRIM PRAIRIE TALES

Hamady, Ron
DON'T TELL HER IT'S ME

Hanna, William
JETSONS: THE MOVIE

Hansen, Lisa M.
FAR OUT MAN

Harris, Burtt
Q&A

Harris, Robert
GRIFTERS, THE

Hartley, Hal
UNBELIEVABLE TRUTH, THE

Harvey, Rupert
PUMP UP THE VOLUME

Hathcock, Bob
DUCKTALES: THE MOVIE – TREASURE OF
THE LOST LAMP

Heavener, David
TWISTED JUSTICE

Heidusehka, Veit
TIME TROOPERS

Henderson, Duncan
GREEN CARD

Henshaw, Jere
HAPPY TOGETHER

Hertzberg, Paul
HIT LIST

Hida, Mitsuhisa
SUMMER VACATION: 1999

Hogue, Jeffrey C.
ALIENATOR

Hool, Lance
DAMNED RIVER

Horovitz, Jed
ANDY COLBY'S INCREDIBLY AWESOME
ADVENTURE

Hudlin, Warrington
HOUSE PARTY

Hughes, John
HOME ALONE

Hunt, Paul
DEMON WIND

Ievins, Edgar
BASKETCASE 2
FRANKENHOOKER

Iino, Hisa
BLACK RAIN

Inoue, Mike Y.
DREAMS

Insana, Tino
WEDDING BAND

Irby, Beverly
IN THE SPIRIT

Jacobsen, John M.
PATHFINDER

Johnson, Mark
AVALON

Jones, Dalu
DOG TAGS

Jones, Keith C.
TUSKS

Jones, Steven A.
HENRY: PORTRAIT OF A SERIAL KILLER

Kakutani, Masaru
ADVENTURES OF MILO AND OTIS, THE

Kane, Mary
KING OF NEW YORK

Karmitz, Marin
TAXI BLUES

Karson, Eric
ANGEL TOWN

Kasander, Kees
COOK, THE THIEF, HIS WIFE & HER
LOVER, THE

Kaufman, Peter
HENRY AND JUNE

Kazanjian, Howard
ROOKIE, THE

Kelly, Joe
LEMON SISTERS, THE

Kennedy, Kathleen
ARACHNOPHOBIA

Kerner, Jordan
FUNNY ABOUT LOVE

Kidney, Ric
AFTER DARK, MY SWEET

Kimmel, Anne
PAINT IT BLACK

Kirschner, David
CHILD'S PLAY 2

Kivett, Carole
FEUD, THE

Klass, Ric
ELLIOT FAUMAN, PH.D.

Klune, Donald C.
MADHOUSE

Korzen, Benni
NOBODY'S PERFECT

Kottenbrook, Carol
SHADOWZONE

Krane, Jonathan D.
WITHOUT YOU, I'M NOTHING
LOOK WHO'S TALKING TOO

Krevoy, Brad
BACK TO BACK

Kropenin, Peter
ISTANBUL, KEEP YOUR EYES OPEN

Kurosawa, Hisao
DREAMS

Kurtz, Gary
SLIPSTREAM

Kurys, Diane
C'EST LA VIE

Lagettie, Robert
TIME GUARDIAN, THE

Lane, Andrew
PEACEMAKER

Lange, Henry
HOW TO MAKE LOVE TO A NEGRO WITH-
OUT GETTING TIRED

Lasker, Lawrence
AWAKENINGS

Leder, Paul
MURDER BY NUMBERS

Lee, Spike
MO' BETTER BLUES

Lencina, Julio
VERONICO CRUZ

Lerner, Avi
RIVER OF DEATH

Lester, David
SIBLING RIVALRY

Lester, Mark L.
CLASS OF 1999

Levinson, Barry
AVALON

Lewis, Paul
HOT SPOT, THE

Liimatainen, Arvi
BYE BYE BLUES

Lindsay, Lance
REAL BULLETS

Llosa, Luis
FULL FATHOM FIVE

Lloyd, Lauren
MERMAIDS

Lobell, Mike
FRESHMAN, THE

Loughery, David
FLASHBACK

Lowry, Hunt
REVENGE

Lurie, Jeffrey
I LOVE YOU TO DEATH

Lynch Brown, Elizabeth
FACE OF THE ENEMY

McAree, Roy
AFTERSHOCK

McCallum, Rick
STRAPLESS

McCormick, Patrick
SHOCK TO THE SYSTEM, A

McLaglen, Mary
COLD FEET

Madden, David
FIRST POWER, THE

Maddock, Brent
TREMORS

Maguire, Charles H.
DOWNTOWN

Mancuso, Frank Jr.
INTERNAL AFFAIRS

Manduke, Joseph
GUMSHOE KID, THE

Manzotti, Achille
TWO EVIL EYES

Maronati, Mario
ICICLE THIEF, THE

Marsh, David
LORDS OF MAGICK, THE

Marshall, Alan
JACOB'S LADDER

Martinelli, Gabriella
NIGHTBREED

Maslansky, Paul
RUSSIA HOUSE, THE

Matheson, Tim
BLIND FURY

Meledandri, Christopher
OPPORTUNITY KNOCKS

Melnick, Daniel
MOUNTAINS OF THE MOON
AIR AMERICA

Menkin, Jerry
TORN APART

Menocki, Sasha
VERONICO CRUZ

Merchant, Ismail
MR. AND MRS. BRIDGE

Milchan, Arnon
PRETTY WOMAN
Q&A

Miller, Don
SIBLING RIVALRY

Milling, Bill
CAGED FURY

Milloy, Ross
LORD OF THE FLIES

Moler, Ron
I LOVE YOU TO DEATH

Montgomery, Monty
DADDY'S DYIN'. . . WHO'S GOT THE WILL?
WILD AT HEART

Morgan, Andre
IMPULSE

Mulvehill, Charles
GODFATHER PART III, THE

Murray, Bill
QUICK CHANGE

Nardo, Don
STUFF STEPHANIE IN THE INCINERATOR

Narita, Naoya
SUMMER VACATION: 1999

Neiman, L.E.
TIME TROOPERS

Nelson, Terry
GHOST DAD

Neufeld, Mace
HUNT FOR RED OCTOBER, THE

Nichols, Mike
POSTCARDS FROM THE EDGE

Nicita, Wallis
MERMAIDS

Nicolaides, Steve
MISERY

O'Brien, John
BIG DIS, THE

O'Malley, Jason
BACKSTREET DREAMS

O'Toole, Stanley
LIONHEART
QUIGLEY DOWN UNDER

Oestreicher, Christine
STRIKE IT RICH

Ogata, Satoru
ADVENTURES OF MILO AND OTIS, THE

Ogris, Knut
TIME TROOPERS

Okada, Yutaka
HEAVEN AND EARTH

Oken, Stuart
IMPROMPTU

Orr, James
MR. DESTINY

Ostrow, Randy
STATE OF GRACE

Owensby, Earl
HYPERSPACE

Painten, James
GRIFTERS, THE

Palmer, Patrick
MERMAIDS

Pariser, Michael D.
MARTIANS GO HOME!

Parkes, Walter
AWAKENINGS

Pasic, Mirza
TIME OF THE GYPSIES

Pearce, Christopher
DELTA FORCE 2

Pearson, Noel
FIELD, THE

Perlman, Laurie
VITAL SIGNS

Perry, Steve
ADVENTURES OF FORD FAIRLANE, THE

Phillips, Randy
GRAFFITI BRIDGE

Piel, Jean-Louis
MAMA, THERE'S A MAN IN YOUR BED

Pilcher, Lydia Dean
KILL-OFF, THE

Pollack, Sydney
PRESUMED INNOCENT
HAVANA

Pressman, Edward R.
BLUE STEEL
REVERSAL OF FORTUNE

Prevost, Albert
LIFE AND NOTHING BUT

Propper, Michel
MAHABHARATA, THE

Puttnam, David
MEMPHIS BELLE

Quezada, Roberto
SURVIVAL QUEST

Radclyffe, Sarah
FOOLS OF FORTUNE

Raich, Ken
HOLLYWOOD HOT TUBS II: EDUCATING
CRYSTAL

Rasmussen, Kjehl
ANIMAL BEHAVIOR

Rauch, Michael
BLUE STEEL

Redlin, Robert
AFTER DARK, MY SWEET

Reich, Steven
CIRCUITRY MAN

Reiner, Rob
MISERY

Reitman, Ivan
KINDERGARTEN COP

Reuther, Steven
PRETTY WOMAN

Richard, Jef
HIT LIST

Rizzoli, Angello
TORRENTS OF SPRING

Robbins, Lance H.
BACKSTREET DREAMS

Robertson, Joseph F.
DR. CALIGARI

Robins, Teddy
REINCARNATION OF GOLDEN LOTUS, THE

Robinson, Amy
WHITE PALACE

Rocca, Catherine
FACE OF THE ENEMY

Roemer, Michael
PLOT AGAINST HARRY, THE

Rogers, Jim
SPONTANEOUS COMBUSTION

Roos, Fred
GODFATHER PART III, THE

Rose, Alexandra
QUIGLEY DOWN UNDER

Rosenberg, Mark
WHITE PALACE
PRESUMED INNOCENT

Ross, Herbert
MY BLUE HEAVEN

Roth, Richard
HAVANA

Rotholz, Ron
STATE OF GRACE

Roven, Charles
BLOOD OF HEROES
CADILLAC MAN

Ruben, Andy
STREETS

Rubin, Stanley
REVENGE

Rubinstein, Richard P.
TALES FROM THE DARKSIDE: THE MOVIE

Ruddy, Albert S.
IMPULSE

Rudin, Scott
PACIFIC HEIGHTS

Russo, John A.
NIGHT OF THE LIVING DEAD

Sackheim, William
PACIFIC HEIGHTS

Sadler, Richard
HOW TO MAKE LOVE TO A NEGRO WITH-
OUT GETTING TIRED

Sanders, Ken C.
BLOOD SALVAGE

Scheffer, Eric F.
JEZEBEL'S KISS

Scheimer, Lou
HAPPILY EVER AFTER

Scheinman, Andrew
MISERY

Schepisi, Fred
RUSSIA HOUSE, THE

Schiff, Paul
COUPE DE VILLE
YOUNG GUNS II

Schlossberg, Julian
IN THE SPIRIT

Schmidt, Wolf
FOURTH WAR, THE

Schneider, Harold
TWO JAKES, THE

Schouweiler, John
WEDDING BAND
CIRCUITRY MAN
STEEL AND LACE

Schumacher, Thomas C.
RESCUERS DOWN UNDER, THE

Schwab, Aaron
CHATTAHOOCHEE

Schwab, Faye
CHATTAHOOCHEE

Schwartz, Teri
JOE VERSUS THE VOLCANO

Schwenker, Ken
ALLIGATOR EYES

Scorsese, Martin
GRIFTERS, THE

Scott, Ann
INNOCENT VICTIM

Scott, Darin
TO SLEEP WITH ANGER

Seagal, Steven
MARKED FOR DEATH

Sellar, Joanne
HARDWARE

Sellers, Arlene
STANLEY AND IRIS

Senftleben, Michael
NASTY GIRL, THE

Seydoux, Michel
CYRANO DE BERGERAC

Shah, Ash R.
ANGEL TOWN

Shavick, James
FALSE IDENTITY

Shepherd, Peter
LAMBADA
SONNY BOY

Sherkow, Daniel A.
IMPROMPTU

Shils, Barry
VAMPIRE'S KISS

Shire, Talia
LIONHEART

Shivas, Mark
WITCHES, THE

Shore, Sig
RETURN OF SUPERFLY, THE

Shusett, Ronald
TOTAL RECALL

Sidaris, Arlene
SAVAGE BEACH

Siebert, Steven
ROOKIE, THE

Sighvatsson, Joni
WILD AT HEART

Sighvatsson, Sigurjon
KILL ME AGAIN
DADDY'S DYIN'. . . WHO'S GOT THE WILL?

Silver, Alain
NIGHT VISITOR

Silver, Joel
DIE HARD 2
ADVENTURES OF FORD FAIRLANE, THE
PREDATOR 2

Simon, Joel
HARD TO KILL

Simonds, Robert
PROBLEM CHILD

Simpson, Don
DAYS OF THUNDER

Simpson, Michael A.
DEAD AIM
FUNLAND

Singleton, Ralph S.
GRAVEYARD SHIFT

Smith, G. Warren
HIGH DESERT KILL

Smith, Irby
YOUNG GUNS II

Spelling, Aaron
LOOSE CANNONS

Spikings, Barry
TEXASVILLE

Stabler, Steven
BACK TO BACK

Steagall, Red
BIG BAD JOHN

Steloff, Robert
TIME TROOPERS

Stern, Sandy
PUMP UP THE VOLUME

Sternberg, Tom
EAT A BOWL OF TEA

Stewart, Colin
BURNDOWN

Stiefel, Arnold
GRAFFITI BRIDGE

Stiliadis, Nicolas
BLOOD RELATIONS

Stillman, Whit
METROPOLITAN

Stone Guttfreund, Andre
TOUCH OF A STRANGER

Stone, Oliver
BLUE STEEL
REVERSAL OF FORTUNE

Stott, Jeffrey
MISERY

Streiner, Russ
NIGHT OF THE LIVING DEAD

Stroller, Louis A.
BETSY'S WEDDING

Strong, John
SHOW OF FORCE, A

Sumayao, Isabel
PRIMARY TARGET

Summers, Cathlen
VITAL SIGNS

Sylbert, Anthea
MY BLUE HEAVEN

Taga, Hidenori
TWILIGHT OF THE COCKROACHES

Talalay, Rachel
CRY-BABY

Tapert, Robert
DARKMAN

Tarasova, Valentina
FREEZE – DIE – COME TO LIFE

Tarlov, Mark
TUNE IN TOMORROW

Taylor, Geoffrey
TAKING CARE OF BUSINESS

Thomas, Jeremy
EVERYBODY WINS
SHELTERING SKY, THE

Thomas, John G.
CAGED IN PARADISO

Tisch, Steve
HEART CONDITION
BAD INFLUENCE

Todman, Bill Jr.
HARD TO KILL

Tornberg, Ralph
MURDER BY NUMBERS

Towers, Harry Alan
TEN LITTLE INDIANS
RIVER OF DEATH

Troskie, Boet
GODS MUST BE CRAZY II, THE

Trybits, Paul
HARDWARE

Ujlaki, Stephen
COURAGE MOUNTAIN

Valdes, David
ROOKIE, THE

Van Der Kloot, William
DEAD AIM
FUNLAND

Vance, Samuel
RIVERBEND

Vance, Valerie
RIVERBEND

Vane, Richard
ARACHNOPHOBIA

Verhoeven, Michael
NASTY GIRL, THE

Vicisuno, Fulvio
NIGHT OF THE SHARKS

Victor, Mark
MARKED FOR DEATH

Vincent, Chuck
BEDROOM EYES II
WILDEST DREAMS

Wachs, Robert D.
ANOTHER 48 HRS.

Wallace, Josephine
BAIL JUMPER

Walley, Keith
DARK SIDE OF THE MOON

Wang, Peter
LASER MAN, THE

Warfield, David W.
KILL ME AGAIN

Webster, Cheryl
INHERITOR

Webster, Christopher
INHERITOR

Weinman, Richard C.
RED SURF

Weinstein, Lisa
GHOST

Weir, Peter
GREEN CARD

Weis, Bob
RAGGEDY RAWNEY, THE

Weiss, Bruce
UNBELIEVABLE TRUTH, THE

Wentworth, Peter
METROPOLITAN

West, Donald L.
SKI PATROL

Wheeler, Anne
BYE BYE BLUES

White, Michael
NUNS ON THE RUN

Wilkinson, Norman
TIME GUARDIAN, THE

Williams, Bernard
NAVY SEALS

Williams, Stacy
ERNEST GOES TO JAIL

Wilson, Danny
HANDMAID'S TALE, THE

Wilson, Jim
DANCES WITH WOLVES

Wilson, S.S.
TREMORS

Wilson, Sandy
AMERICAN BOYFRIENDS

Winitsky, Alex
STANLEY AND IRIS

Winkler, Irwin
GOODFELLAS
ROCKY V

Wisdom, Anthony
RETURN OF SUPERFLY, THE

Wizan, Joe
GUARDIAN, THE

Wizan, Steven
REPOSSESSED

Wlodkowski, Stan
LONGTIME COMPANION

Worth, Marvin
FLASHBACK

Wyler, Catherine
MEMPHIS BELLE

Wyman, Dan
DEAD PIT

Yablans, Frank
LISA

Yoshida, Hiroaki
TWILIGHT OF THE COCKROACHES

Young, Jeff
I COME IN PEACE

Young, Robert
PLOT AGAINST HARRY, THE

Zarrin, Ali Reza
BASHU, THE LITTLE STRANGER

Zimbert, Jonathan A.
NARROW MARGIN

Zitwer, Barbara
VAMPIRE'S KISS

PRODUCTION DESIGNERS

Adam, Ken
FRESHMAN, THE

Aguiar, Kiki
VERONICO CRUZ

Ahmad, Maher
MIAMI BLUES

Aichele, Ken
NIGHT ANGEL

Ako, Yuda
DOWN THE DRAIN

Almodovar, Pedro
LABYRINTH OF PASSION

Altman, Stephen
VINCENT AND THEO

Ammon, Ruth
TALES FROM THE DARKSIDE: THE MOVIE

Anderson, Cletus
NIGHT OF THE LIVING DEAD

Appel, Lynn Ruth
BAIL JUMPER

August, Chris
ERNEST GOES TO JAIL

Austin, Leo
MISADVENTURES OF MR. WILT, THE

Austin, Shay
REPOSSESSED

Barrett, Penny
TO SLEEP WITH ANGER

Beecroft, Jeffrey
DANCES WITH WOLVES

Benedict, Robert
SLEEPING CAR, THE

Bennett, Joseph
HARDWARE

Bertalan, Tivadar
MACK THE KNIFE

Bissell, James
ARACHNOPHOBIA

Blackie, John
BYE BYE BLUES

Bolander, Bruce
PUMP UP THE VOLUME

Bolton, Michael
SHORT TIME

Bourne, Mel
REVERSAL OF FORTUNE

Brenner, Albert
PRETTY WOMAN

Bronzi, Francesco
TORRENTS OF SPRING

Bumstead, Henry
GHOST DAD
ALMOST AN ANGEL

Burbank, Lynda
RED SURF

Cain, Syd
TUSKS

Cameron, Allan
AIR AMERICA

Cammer, Judy
ROOKIE, THE

Capra, Bernt
COLD FEET

Carrington, David
DEF BY TEMPTATION

Carter, Rick
BACK TO THE FUTURE PART III

Cassidy, William J.
SHOW OF FORCE, A
ROCKY V

Cavedon, Suzanne
ME AND HIM

Chapman, David
OPPORTUNITY KNOCKS

Clay, Jim
TUNE IN TOMORROW

Cohen, Lester
LASER MAN, THE

Comtois, Guy J.
NAVY SEALS

Conti, Carlos
WILD ORCHID

Conway, Frank
FIELD, THE

Copeland, Carl E.
MODERN LOVE

Corbett, Toby
BLUE STEEL

Cornford, Bill
LAMBADA

Cost, Thomas
HOLLYWOOD HOT TUBS II: EDUCATING
CRYSTAL

Costello, George
PROBLEM CHILD
BACKSTREET DREAMS

Craig, Stuart
MEMPHIS BELLE

Crampton, Hazel
AMERICAN EAGLE

Cresciman, Vincent
FLASHBACK

Crisanti, Andrea
CINEMA PARADISO

Cristante, Ivo
TREMORS
CHILD'S PLAY 2

Cummings, Howard
SHOCK TO THE SYSTEM, A

Danielsen, Dins
MEN AT WORK

Day, Don
FORBIDDEN DANCE, THE
MARTIANS GO HOME!
BACK TO BACK
DEMON WIND
SHADOWZONE

DeCarlo, Pierluca
FACE OF THE ENEMY

Dilley, Leslie
EXORCIST III, THE

Egede-Nissen, Harald
PATHFINDER

Elliott, William A.
IMPULSE

Fernandez, Benjamin
REVENGE

Ferretti, Dante
HAMLET

Fonseca, Gregg
GUARDIAN, THE

Foreman, Ron
BAD INFLUENCE

Fowlie, Michael
BURNDOWN

Fox, Robert
STREET ASYLUM

Francois, Guy-Claude
LIFE AND NOTHING BUT
HENRY AND JUNE

Franklin, Robert
OVER EXPOSED

Freed, Reuben
LOOK WHO'S TALKING TOO

Furst, Anton
AWAKENINGS

Garcia, Esther
TIE ME UP! TIE ME DOWN!

Garrity, Joseph T.
FIRST POWER, THE
CHATTAHOOCHEE
FIRE BIRDS

Garwood, Norman
MISERY

Gassner, Dennis
MILLER'S CROSSING

Gerona, Carla
UNBELIEVABLE TRUTH, THE

Gmuer, Al
JETSONS: THE MOVIE

Grafka, Batia
GUMSHOE KID, THE

Graham, Angelo
COUPE DE VILLE

Graysmark, John
WHITE HUNTER, BLACK HEART

Grocker, Woody
WHY ME?

Gropman, David
MR. AND MRS. BRIDGE

Hadder, Jimmy
SAVAGE BEACH

Hadfield, Veronica
NAVY SEALS

Hall, Roger
STRAPLESS

Hallowell, Todd
VITAL SIGNS

Hardie, Steve
NIGHTBREED

Hardwicke, Catherine
MARTIANS GO HOME!
BRAIN DEAD

Harrison, Philip
BIRD ON A WIRE

Hicks, Grant
TALL GUY, THE

Hinds, Marcia
HAPPY TOGETHER

Hobbs, Christopher
STRIKE IT RICH

Holland, Simon
NUNS ON THE RUN

Holzberg, Roger
HIGH DESERT KILL

Hulsey, James
STELLA

Hutman, Jon
TAKING CARE OF BUSINESS

Jackson, Gemma
CHICAGO JOE AND THE SHOWGIRL

Jamison, Peter
ROBOCOP 2

Javnoss, Andrew
LONGTIME COMPANION

Jenkins, George
PRESUMED INNOCENT

Johnson, Eric
ISTANBUL, KEEP YOUR EYES OPEN

Johnson, Martin
HIDDEN AGENDA

Jones, Bryan
HOUSE PARTY

Jorgenson, Walter
GAME, THE

Kalinowski, Waldemar
INTERNAL AFFAIRS

Kieser, Marina
FACE OF THE ENEMY

Kilvert, Lilly
I LOVE YOU TO DEATH

King, Robb Wilson
HARD TO KILL
COURAGE MOUNTAIN

Kirkland, Geoffrey
COME SEE THE PARADISE

Kraner, Doug
STATE OF GRACE

Labas, Zoltan
MY 20TH CENTURY

Lagola, Charles
FEUD, THE

Larkin, Peter
EVERYBODY WINS

Lee, Virginia
STREETS

Legler, Steven
LOVE AT LARGE
PAINT IT BLACK

Leigh, Dan
MADHOUSE

Leonard, Jamie
LORD OF THE FLIES
FOOLS OF FORTUNE

Leonard, Phillip M.
I COME IN PEACE

Levesque, Michel
HOMER & EDDIE

Liddle, George
TIME GUARDIAN, THE

Ling, Barbara
MEN DON'T LEAVE

Lloyd, John J.
CRAZY PEOPLE

Lomino, Dan
SIDE OUT

Loquasto, Santo
ALICE

Lorenzini, Vance
GRAFFITI BRIDGE

Lorick, Gigi
MONSTER HIGH

Lovy, Robert
CIRCUITRY MAN

Luna, Alejandro
SANTA SANGRE

McAlpine, Andrew
SLIPSTREAM

McCabe, Brian
NIGHT EYES

McDonald, Leslie
GRIFTERS, THE

MacDonald, Richard
RUSSIA HOUSE, THE

Major, Ross
QUIGLEY DOWN UNDER

Manzer, Alan
FOURTH WAR, THE

Marcotte, Pamela
HIT LIST

Marsh, Terence
HUNT FOR RED OCTOBER, THE
HAVANA

Martin, Blair
STEEL AND LACE

Matolin, Jiri
RAGGEDY RAWNEY, THE

Meighan, John
HOSTILE TAKEOVER

Meurisse, Theobald
TOO BEAUTIFUL FOR YOU

Minch, Michelle
KILL ME AGAIN
DADDY'S DYIN'... WHO'S GOT THE WILL?
DARK SIDE OF THE MOON

Molli, Mario
SONNY BOY

Moore, John Jay
BETSY'S WEDDING

Morgan, Skip
DUCKTALES: THE MOVIE – TREASURE OF
THE LOST LAMP

Morris, Brian
JACOB'S LADDER

Murton, Peter
BLIND FURY

Musky, Jane
GHOST

Muto, John
HEART CONDITION
HOME ALONE

Natalucci, Giovanni
ROBOT JOX

Nemec, Joseph C. III
ANOTHER 48 HRS.

Nicdao, Art
DOG TAGS

Noorani, Sartaj
PERFECT MURDER, THE

Norris, Patricia
WILD AT HEART

Nourafchan, Tori
WEDDING BAND

Nowak, Christopher
VAMPIRE'S KISS

Obolensky, Chloe
MAHABHARATA, THE

Oppewall, Jeannine
ANIMAL BEHAVIOR

Oppewall, Jeannine Claudia
WHITE PALACE
SIBLING RIVALRY

Orpen, Roger
TEN LITTLE INDIANS

Owens, Brent
WHITE GIRL, THE

Papamichael, Phedon
TEXASVILLE

Parrondo, Gil
LIONHEART

Patki, Kiran
PERFECT MURDER, THE

Paul, Victoria
DESPERATE HOURS

Paull, Lawrence G.
LAST OF THE FINEST, THE
PREDATOR 2

Pearl, Linda
DON'T TELL HER IT'S ME

Peranio, Vincent
CRY-BABY

Pickwoad, Michael
KRAYS, THE

Plaa, Michelle
MAMA, THERE'S A MAN IN YOUR BED

Popp, Hubert
NASTY GIRL, THE

Poreda, John
STAR QUEST: BEYOND THE RISING MOON

Pottle, Harry
LOOSE CANNONS

Quaranta, Gianni
MAGDALENE

Railton, Jeremy
TWO JAKES, THE

Rajk, Laszlo
FORCED MARCH

Randall, Gary
HAUNTING OF MORELLA, THE
BODY CHEMISTRY

Rennekamp, Mike
LORDS OF MAGICK, THE

Reynolds, Norman
MOUNTAINS OF THE MOON
AVALON

Roelfs, Jan
COOK, THE THIEF, HIS WIFE & HER
LOVER, THE

Rosen, Charles
DOWNTOWN
MY BLUE HEAVEN

Rosenberg, Philip
Q&A

Roth, Dena
WELCOME HOME, ROXY CARMICHAEL

Rothschild, Jon
NIGHT VISITOR

Rubeo, Bruno
BLOOD RED

Rudolf, Gene
CADILLAC MAN
YOUNG GUNS II

Rupnik, Kevin
WITHOUT YOU, I'M NOTHING

Ryan, Kevin
FALSE IDENTITY

Sandell, William
TOTAL RECALL

Sanders, Andrew
WITCHES, THE

Sawyer, Richard
TWO JAKES, THE

Sayadian, Stephen
DR. CALIGARI

Scarfiotti, Ferdinando
SHELTERING SKY, THE

Schiller, Joel
STANLEY AND IRIS
NARROW MARGIN

Schmidt, Phillip
AMERICAN BOYFRIENDS

Schnell, Curtis
DEATH WARRANT

Seely, Martha
IMPORTED BRIDEGROOM, THE

Seguin, Francois
JESUS OF MONTREAL

Ser, Randy
DARKMAN

Seymour, Michael
REVENGE
MR. DESTINY

Shaffer, Henry
ELLIOT FAUMAN, PH.D.

Shepard, Maxine
UNDER THE BOARDWALK

Sherman, Richard
TOUCH OF A STRANGER

Siegal, Andrew
SURVIVAL QUEST

Silvestri, Gianni
SHELTERING SKY, THE

Sissman, Rob
PEACEMAKER
BLOOD SALVAGE

Smith, Adrian
INNOCENT VICTIM

Smith, Michael C.
IN THE SPIRIT

Sosnowski, Janusz
INTERROGATION, THE

Spencer, James
GREMLINS 2 THE NEW BATCH

Spier, Carol
WHERE THE HEART IS

Spisak, Neil
PACIFIC HEIGHTS

Stites, Wendy
GREEN CARD

Stoddart, John
BLOOD OF HEROES

Storer, Stephen
FUNNY ABOUT LOVE

Strawn, Mick
LEATHERFACE: THE TEXAS CHAINSAW
MASSACRE III

Svec, J.C.
BLADES

Sylbert, Richard
DICK TRACY
BONFIRE OF THE VANITIES

Tavoularis, Alex
KING OF NEW YORK

Tavoularis, Dean
GODFATHER PART III, THE

Thomas, Wynn
MO' BETTER BLUES

Tokuda, Hiroshi
HEAVEN AND EARTH

Tovaglieri, Enrico
FRANKENSTEIN UNBOUND

Tremblay, Tony
SPACED INVADERS

Vallone, John
DIE HARD 2
ADVENTURES OF FORD FAIRLANE, THE

Van Os, Ben
COOK, THE THIEF, HIS WIFE & HER
LOVER, THE

Van Ryker, Patricia
LISA

Von Brandenstein, Patrizia
LEMON SISTERS, THE
POSTCARDS FROM THE EDGE
STATE OF GRACE

Walsh, Tom
HANDMAID'S TALE, THE

Weiler, Fred
SKI PATROL

Welch, Bo
JOE VERSUS THE VOLCANO
EDWARD SCISSORHANDS

White, Cary
HOT SPOT, THE

Wilheim, Ladislav
DELTA FORCE 2

Wilson King, Robb
MARKED FOR DEATH

Wissner, Gary
GRAVEYARD SHIFT

Woodbridge, Pamela
KILL-OFF, THE

Wurtzel, Stuart
MERMAIDS
THREE MEN AND A LITTLE LADY

Zanetti, Eugenio
FLATLINERS

Zea, Kristi
GOODFELLAS

Ziembicki, Bob
EAT A BOWL OF TEA

Zierhut, Anthony
GRIM PRAIRIE TALES

SCREENPLAY AUTHORS

Abrams, Jeffrey
TAKING CARE OF BUSINESS

Adlon, Eleonore
ROSALIE GOES SHOPPING

Adlon, Percy
ROSALIE GOES SHOPPING

Alda, Alan
BETSY'S WEDDING

Alderton, Philip
FACE OF THE ENEMY

Alexander, Scott
SPACED INVADERS
PROBLEM CHILD

Allen, Jim
HIDDEN AGENDA

Allen, Woody
ALICE

Almodovar, Pedro
LABYRINTH OF PASSION
TIE ME UP! TIE ME DOWN!

Angelopoulos, Theo
LANDSCAPE IN THE MIST

Anthony, Len
FRIGHT HOUSE

Arcand, Denys
JESUS OF MONTREAL

Arehn, Mats
ISTANBUL, KEEP YOUR EYES OPEN

Argento, Claudio
SANTA SANGRE

Argento, Dario
TWO EVIL EYES

Armitage, George
MIAMI BLUES
LAST OF THE FINEST, THE

Arnott, David
ADVENTURES OF FORD FAIRLANE, THE

Atkins, Dick
FORCED MARCH

Augustyn, Joe
NIGHT ANGEL

Bachmann, Hans
TIME TROOPERS

Bailey, Frederick
DEMONSTONE

Bailey, Sandra K.
FALSE IDENTITY

Bardack, Victor
GUMSHOE KID, THE

Bardosh, Charles K.
FORCED MARCH

Barker, Clive
NIGHTBREED

Barnes, Joslyn
TOUCH OF A STRANGER

Barr, Jackson
BODY CHEMISTRY

Barwick, Anthony
BURNDOWN

Baxter, John
TIME GUARDIAN, THE

Bean, Henry
INTERNAL AFFAIRS

Bear, Liza
FORCE OF CIRCUMSTANCE

Beaumont, Charles
BRAIN DEAD

Becket, James
TIME TROOPERS

Beizai, Bahram
BASHU, THE LITTLE STRANGER

Benedek, Barbara
MEN DON'T LEAVE

Benson, Robby
MODERN LOVE

Berger, Pamela
IMPORTED BRIDEGROOM, THE

Bergman, Andrew
FRESHMAN, THE

Berlin, Jeannie
IN THE SPIRIT

Bernhard, Sandra
WITHOUT YOU, I'M NOTHING

Bernstein, Nat
OPPORTUNITY KNOCKS

Berry, Joseph
BIG BAD JOHN

Berry, Michael
SHORT TIME

Bertolucci, Bernardo
SHELTERING SKY, THE

Bigelow, Kathryn
BLUE STEEL

Binder, Mike
COUPE DE VILLE

Bird, Sarah
DON'T TELL HER IT'S ME

Blake, Michael
DANCES WITH WOLVES

Blatty, William Peter
EXORCIST III, THE

Blier, Bertrand
TOO BEAUTIFUL FOR YOU

Block, Joel
NOBODY'S PERFECT

Blumenthal, John
SHORT TIME

Bogdanovich, Peter
TEXASVILLE

Bonaccorso, Arcangelo
TORRENTS OF SPRING

Bond, James III
DEF BY TEMPTATION

Boorman, John
WHERE THE HEART IS

Boorman, Telsche
WHERE THE HEART IS

Booth, Robert Brodie
OPPONENT, THE

Boskovich, John
WITHOUT YOU, I'M NOTHING

Boyd, William
TUNE IN TOMORROW

Brand, Larry
MASQUE OF THE RED DEATH
OVER EXPOSED

Brauner, Asher
AMERICAN EAGLE

Bridges, James
WHITE HUNTER, BLACK HEART

Brock, Deborah
ANDY COLBY'S INCREDIBLY AWESOME
ADVENTURE

Brook, Peter
MAHABHARATA, THE

Brosnan, Peter
HIT LIST

Brown, Curtis
GAME, THE

Brown, Tony
WHITE GIRL, THE

Bugajski, Ryszard
INTERROGATION, THE

Burnett, Alan
DUCKTALES: THE MOVIE – TREASURE OF
THE LOST LAMP

Burnett, Charles
TO SLEEP WITH ANGER

Burton, Tim
EDWARD SCISSORHANDS

Cappe, James
ADVENTURES OF FORD FAIRLANE, THE

Cardone, J.S.
SHADOWZONE

Carner, Charles Robert
BLIND FURY

Carpi, Tito
NIGHT OF THE SHARKS

Carriere, Jean-Claude
MAY FOOLS
MAHABHARATA, THE
CYRANO DE BERGERAC

Cash, Jim
DICK TRACY

Catamas, Scott
MEN IN LOVE

Chapman, Leigh
IMPULSE

Chatiliez, Etienne
LIFE IS A LONG QUIET RIVER

Chong, Tommy
FAR OUT MAN

Ciccoritti, Gerard
BEDROOM EYES II

Cirillo, Patrick
HOMER & EDDIE

Citrano, Tom
NIGHT EYES

Clark, Bob
LOOSE CANNONS

Clark, Greydon
SKINHEADS – THE SECOND COMING OF
HATE

Clark, Karen
LISA

Coe, Wayne
GRIM PRAIRIE TALES

Coen, Ethan
MILLER'S CROSSING

Coen, Joel
MILLER'S CROSSING

Cohen, Charlie
ERNEST GOES TO JAIL

Conchon, Georges
L'ETAT SAUVAGE

Cook, Philip
STAR QUEST: BEYOND THE RISING MOON

Cook, Tom S.
HIGH DESERT KILL

Coppola, Francis Ford
GODFATHER PART III, THE

Corman, Roger
FRANKENSTEIN UNBOUND

Coscarelli, Don
SURVIVAL QUEST

Cosmos, Jean
LIFE AND NOTHING BUT

Cox, Jim
RESCUERS DOWN UNDER, THE

Cristofer, Michael
BONFIRE OF THE VANITIES

Cruickshank, Jim
MR. DESTINY

Cunningham, Jere
LAST OF THE FINEST, THE

Cupano, Maria Perrone
OPPONENT, THE

Curtis, Richard
TALL GUY, THE

Cutler, Ron
BLOOD RED

D'Elia, Bill
FEUD, THE

Dahl, John
KILL ME AGAIN

Davis, Bart
FULL FATHOM FIVE

De Marco, John
IMPULSE

de Souza, Steven E.
DIE HARD 2

De Wilde, Nicole
RAGGEDY RAWNEY, THE

Deutsch, Andrew
RIVER OF DEATH

DeVore, Christopher
HAMLET

Dewolf, Patrick
MONSIEUR HIRE

Doherty, Christopher
ROSALIE GOES SHOPPING

Dorrie, Doris
ME AND HIM

Dougherty, Joseph
STEEL AND LACE

Durham, Todd
HYPERSPACE

Dymek, Janusz
INTERROGATION, THE

Edison, Dave
STEEL AND LACE

Edwards, Paul F.
FIRE BIRDS

Ehlman, Byrd
TIME TROOPERS

Enyedi, Ildiko
MY 20TH CENTURY

Ephron, Nora
MY BLUE HEAVEN

Epps, Jack Jr.
DICK TRACY

Eriksen, Gordon
BIG DIS, THE

Eskow, John
AIR AMERICA

Esposito, John
GRAVEYARD SHIFT

Estevez, Emilio
MEN AT WORK

Estienne, Marie-Helene
MAHABHARATA, THE

Everett, Gimel
DEAD PIT

Faber, Christian
BAIL JUMPER

Fasano, John
ANOTHER 48 HRS.

Feeney, F.X.
FRANKENSTEIN UNBOUND

Feldman, John
ALLIGATOR EYES

Ferguson, Larry
HUNT FOR RED OCTOBER, THE

Ferrini, Franco
TWO EVIL EYES

Filardi, Peter
FLATLINERS

Fire, Richard
HENRY: PORTRAIT OF A SERIAL KILLER

Fisher, Carrie
POSTCARDS FROM THE EDGE

Fiskin, Jeffrey
REVENGE

Foley, James
AFTER DARK, MY SWEET

Frank, Harriet Jr.
STANLEY AND IRIS

Frankel, David
FUNNY ABOUT LOVE

Franklin, Howard
QUICK CHANGE

Friedkin, William
GUARDIAN, THE

Friedman, Brent V.
HOLLYWOOD HOT TUBS II: EDUCATING
CRYSTAL

Friedman, Ken
CADILLAC MAN

Fusco, John
YOUNG GUNS II

Gale, Bob
BACK TO THE FUTURE PART III

Garson, Paul
ALIENATOR

Gaup, Nils
PATHFINDER

Gazarian, John
REAL BULLETS

Getchell, Robert
STELLA

Gholson, Craig
FORCE OF CIRCUMSTANCE

Gilbert, Brad
TOUCH OF A STRANGER

Gilbert, Michael A.
HOSTILE TAKEOVER

Girod, Francis
L'ETAT SAUVAGE

Goff, John
HIT LIST

Golan, Menahem
MACK THE KNIFE

Goldberg, Howard
SPONTANEOUS COMBUSTION

Goldhirsh, Martha
SIBLING RIVALRY

Goldin, Daniel
DARKMAN

Goldin, Joshua
DARKMAN

Goldman, Gary
TOTAL RECALL
NAVY SEALS

Goldman, William
MISERY

Goyer, David S.
DEATH WARRANT

Grais, Michael
MARKED FOR DEATH

Green, Walon
ROBOCOP 2

Greenaway, Peter
COOK, THE THIEF, HIS WIFE & HER
LOVER, THE
BELLY OF AN ARCHITECT, THE

Greenburg, Dan
GUARDIAN, THE

Greenwald, Maggie
KILL-OFF, THE

Gross, Larry
ANOTHER 48 HRS.

Guerra, Tonino
LANDSCAPE IN THE MIST

Gunnlaugsson, Hrafn
SHADOW OF THE RAVEN, THE

Haas, Charlie
MARTIANS GO HOME!
GREMLINS 2 THE NEW BATCH

Hadar, Moshe
DOWN THE DRAIN

Hai, Zafar
PERFECT MURDER, THE

Haldeman, Joe
ROBOT JOX

Haney, Daryl
MASQUE OF THE RED DEATH

Hannant, Brian
TIME GUARDIAN, THE

Hare, David
STRAPLESS

Harrigan, James
FRIGHT HOUSE

Harris, Tim
PAINT IT BLACK

Harris, Timothy
KINDERGARTEN COP

Harrison, Jim
REVENGE
COLD FEET

Harrison, William
MOUNTAINS OF THE MOON

Hartley, Hal
UNBELIEVABLE TRUTH, THE

Hawkins Moore, Tara
TUSKS

Hayes, Carey
DARK SIDE OF THE MOON

Hayes, Chad
DARK SIDE OF THE MOON

Hayes, Joseph
DESPERATE HOURS

Heavener, David
TWISTED JUSTICE

Heckerling, Amy
LOOK WHO'S TALKING TOO

Henderson, Clark
PRIMARY TARGET

Henenlotter, Frank
BASKETCASE 2
FRANKENHOOKER

Herbeck, Bobby
TEENAGE MUTANT NINJA TURTLES

Hicks, James
CHATTAHOOCHEE

Hill, John
QUIGLEY DOWN UNDER

Hirsch, Sherman
LORDS OF MAGICK, THE

Hirst, Michael
FOOLS OF FORTUNE

Hoffman, E.T.A.
NUTCRACKER PRINCE, THE

Hogan, Paul
ALMOST AN ANGEL

Hooper, Tobe
SPONTANEOUS COMBUSTION

Hopkins, Karen Leigh
WELCOME HOME, ROXY CARMICHAEL

Horovitz, Jed
ANDY COLBY'S INCREDIBLY AWESOME
ADVENTURE

Horrall, Craig
WILDEST DREAMS

Hoskins, Bob
RAGGEDY RAWNEY, THE

House, Ron
SHRIMP ON THE BARBIE, THE

Hudlin, Reginald
HOUSE PARTY

Hughes, John
HOME ALONE

Hunsicker, Jackson
TEN LITTLE INDIANS

Hyams, Peter
NARROW MARGIN

Imamura, Shohei
BLACK RAIN

Insana, Tino
WEDDING BAND

Ishido, Toshiro
BLACK RAIN

Israel, Neal
LOOK WHO'S TALKING TOO

Jakoby, Don
ARACHNOPHOBIA

Jodorowsky, Alejandro
SANTA SANGRE

Johnson, Bayard
DAMNED RIVER

Johnson, Patrick Read
SPACED INVADERS

Johnston, Tucker
BLOOD SALVAGE

Jones, Evan
SHOW OF FORCE, A

Jones, Laurie
IN THE SPIRIT

Jones, Peter
STUFF STEPHANIE IN THE INCINERATOR

Josten, Walter
NIGHT ANGEL

Joyner, C. Courtney
CLASS OF 1999

Juncker, Michael
ME AND HIM

Kadokawa, Haruki
HEAVEN AND EARTH

Kamata, Toshio
HEAVEN AND EARTH

Kanevski, Vitaly
FREEZE – DIE – COME TO LIFE

Karaszewski, Larry
PROBLEM CHILD

Katlin, Mitchel
OPPORTUNITY KNOCKS

Kaufman, Philip
HENRY AND JUNE

Kaufman, Rose
HENRY AND JUNE

Kayden, Tony
SLIPSTREAM

Kazan, Nicholas
REVERSAL OF FORTUNE

Keating, H.R.F.
PERFECT MURDER, THE

Keith, Harvey
JEZEBEL'S KISS

Kennedy, Burt
WHITE HUNTER, BLACK HEART

Kernochan, Sarah
IMPROMPTU

Ketron, Larry
VITAL SIGNS

King, Robert
UNDER THE BOARDWALK

King, Zalman
WILD ORCHID

Kirkpatrick, Harry
PRIMAL RAGE

Kirkpatrick, Karey
RESCUERS DOWN UNDER, THE

Kishida, Rio
SUMMER VACATION: 1999

Klass, Ric
ELLIOT FAUMAN, PH.D.

Klavan, Andrew
SHOCK TO THE SYSTEM, A

Knop, Patricia Louisianna
WILD ORCHID

Koepp, David
BAD INFLUENCE

Konner, Lawrence
DESPERATE HOURS

Korzen, Annie
NOBODY'S PERFECT

Kostmayer, John
I LOVE YOU TO DEATH

Kristal, Marc
TORN APART

Kurosawa, Akira
DREAMS

Kurys, Diane
C'EST LA VIE

Kusturica, Emir
TIME OF THE GYPSIES

Laferriere, Dany
HOW TO MAKE LOVE TO A NEGRO WITH-
OUT GETTING TIRED

Langen, Todd W.
TEENAGE MUTANT NINJA TURTLES

Langsdon, Roy
FORBIDDEN DANCE, THE
MONSTER HIGH

Lawton, J.F.
PRETTY WOMAN

Lazarus, Jerry
HONEYMOON ACADEMY

Le Henry, Alain
C'EST LA VIE

Leconte, Patrice
MONSIEUR HIRE

Leder, Paul
MURDER BY NUMBERS

Lee, Spike
MO' BETTER BLUES

Leight, Warren D.
ME AND HIM

Leonard, Brett
DEAD PIT

Leoni, Roberto
SANTA SANGRE

Lerner, Eric
BIRD ON A WIRE

Levinson, Barry
AVALON

Lindsay, Lance
REAL BULLETS

Lisberger, Steven
SLIPSTREAM

Logan, Bob
REPOSSESSED

London, Robby
HAPPILY EVER AFTER

Loughery, David
FLASHBACK

Lounguine, Pavel
TAXI BLUES

Lovy, Robert
CIRCUITRY MAN

Lovy, Steven
CIRCUITRY MAN

Lucas, Craig
LONGTIME COMPANION

Lumet, Sidney
Q&A

Lynch, Brad
MR. FROST

Lynch, David
WILD AT HEART

Lynn, Jonathan
NUNS ON THE RUN

Maas, Leonard Jr.
I COME IN PEACE

McDowell, Michael
TALES FROM THE DARKSIDE: THE MOVIE

McGuane, Tom
COLD FEET

McIntyre, Dennis
STATE OF GRACE

McKay, Steven
HARD TO KILL

McNaughton, John
HENRY: PORTRAIT OF A SERIAL KILLER

Maddock, Brent
TREMORS
GHOST DAD

Malle, Louis
MAY FOOLS

Mancini, Don
CHILD'S PLAY 2

Markowitz, Mitch
CRAZY PEOPLE

Marks, Dennis
JETSONS: THE MOVIE

Marsh, David
LORDS OF MAGICK, THE

Marshall, Andrew
MISADVENTURES OF MR. WILT, THE

Martin, Robert
FRANKENHOOKER

Martino, Sergio
OPPONENT, THE

Mass, Leonard Jr.
WHY ME?

Matheson, Richard
LOOSE CANNONS

Matheson, Richard Christian
LOOSE CANNONS

Matji, Manolo
TWISTED OBSESSION

Mauldin, Nat
DOWNTOWN

Mazursky, Jill
TAKING CARE OF BUSINESS

Merezhko, Viktor
LONELY WOMAN SEEKS LIFE COMPANION

Merrick, Monte
MEMPHIS BELLE

Meyjes, Menno
LIONHEART

Mezieres, Myriam
FLAME IN MY HEART, A

Mihic, Gordan
TIME OF THE GYPSIES

Miller, Arthur
EVERYBODY WINS

Miller, Frank
ROBOCOP 2

Milling, Bill
CAGED FURY

Minion, Joseph
VAMPIRE'S KISS

Mitchell, Julian
VINCENT AND THEO

Mitchell, Steven Long
SKI PATROL

Monti, Mauro
ICICLE THIEF, THE

Moore, Charles Philip
DEMON WIND

Moran, Martha
HAPPILY EVER AFTER

Morris, Grant
SHRIMP ON THE BARBIE, THE

Moyle, Allan
PUMP UP THE VOLUME

Muller, Eduardo Leiva
VERONICO CRUZ

Nakano, Desmond
LAST EXIT TO BROOKLYN

Nakasako, Spencer
LIFE IS CHEAP. . . BUT TOILET PAPER IS EX-
PENSIVE

Nardo, Don
STUFF STEPHANIE IN THE INCINERATOR

Nevius, Craig J.
HAPPY TOGETHER

Nichetti, Maurizio
ICICLE THIEF, THE

Nilsson, Bo Sigvard
ISTANBUL, KEEP YOUR EYES OPEN

O'Bannon, Dan
TOTAL RECALL

O'Brien, John
BIG DIS, THE

O'Hara, Gerry
TEN LITTLE INDIANS

O'Malley, Jason
BACKSTREET DREAMS

O'Neill, Greg
SLEEPING CAR, THE

Orr, James
MR. DESTINY

Outten, Richard
LIONHEART

Pace, William R.
BLADES

Pak-wah, Li
ROUGE

Pakula, Alan J.
PRESUMED INNOCENT

Papic, Krsto
MY UNCLE'S LEGACY

Parker, Alan
COME SEE THE PARADISE

Parriott, James D.
HEART CONDITION

Peoples, David
BLOOD OF HEROES

Peploe, Mark
SHELTERING SKY, THE

Pereira, Miguel
VERONICO CRUZ

Peters, Charlie
THREE MEN AND A LITTLE LADY

Peters, Stephen
FOURTH WAR, THE

Pfarrer, Chuck
NAVY SEALS
DARKMAN

Phillips, David
DEMONSTONE

Pierson, Frank
PRESUMED INNOCENT

Pikser, Jeremy
LEMON SISTERS, THE

Pileggi, Nicholas
GOODFELLAS

Pinter, Harold
HANDMAID'S TALE, THE

Platt, John
FORBIDDEN DANCE, THE
MONSTER HIGH

Pogue, Charles
SLIPSTREAM

Powers, John
STREET ASYLUM

Prawer Jhabvala, Ruth
MR. AND MRS. BRIDGE

Prince
GRAFFITI BRIDGE

Puzo, Mario
GODFATHER PART III, THE

Pyne, Daniel
PACIFIC HEIGHTS

Quentin, Florence
LIFE IS A LONG QUIET RIVER

Quintano, Gene
HONEYMOON ACADEMY

Rabe, David
STATE OF GRACE

Radford, Laura
DISTURBANCE, THE

Rafelson, Bob
MOUNTAINS OF THE MOON

Raimi, Ivan
DARKMAN

Raimi, Sam
DARKMAN

Ranft, Joe
RESCUERS DOWN UNDER, THE

Rappeneau, Jean-Paul
CYRANO DE BERGERAC

Rascoe, Judith
EAT A BOWL OF TEA
HAVANA

Ravetch, Irving
STANLEY AND IRIS

Rayfiel, David
HAVANA

Red, Eric
BLUE STEEL

Redlin, Robert
AFTER DARK, MY SWEET

Reese, Chris
GHOST DAD

Renan, Sheldon
LAMBADA

Renwick, David
MISADVENTURES OF MR. WILT, THE

Reskin, David
SKINHEADS – THE SECOND COMING OF
HATE

Resnikoff, Robert
FIRST POWER, THE

Reynolds, Lee
DELTA FORCE 2

Reynolds, Rebecca
OVER EXPOSED

Rhys-Davies, John
TUSKS

Rice, Susan
ANIMAL BEHAVIOR

Richardson, Doug
DIE HARD 2

Ridley, Philip
KRAYS, THE

Robert, Vincent
RED SURF

Roberts, June
MERMAIDS

Robertson, R.J.
HAUNTING OF MORELLA, THE

Roemer, Michael
PLOT AGAINST HARRY, THE

Romero, George
TALES FROM THE DARKSIDE: THE MOVIE
TWO EVIL EYES
NIGHT OF THE LIVING DEAD

Rondinella, Thomas R.
BLADES

Ropelewski, Tom
MADHOUSE

Rosenthal, Mark
DESPERATE HOURS

Ross, Kenneth
FOURTH WAR, THE

Roth, Bobby
MAN INSIDE, THE

Ruben, Andy
STREETS

Ruben, Katt Shea
STREETS

Rubin, Bruce Joel
GHOST
JACOB'S LADDER

Rudolph, Alan
LOVE AT LARGE

Rush, Richard
AIR AMERICA

Sadler, Richard
HOW TO MAKE LOVE TO A NEGRO WITH-
OUT GETTING TIRED

St. John, Nicholas
KING OF NEW YORK

Salem, Murray
KINDERGARTEN COP

Saltzman, Mark
ADVENTURES OF MILO AND OTIS, THE

Samuelson, Thomas
ISTANBUL, KEEP YOUR EYES OPEN

Sanders, Ken C.
BLOOD SALVAGE

Sargent, Alvin
WHITE PALACE

Sayadian, Stephen
DR. CALIGARI

Saylor, Stephen
BLOOD RELATIONS

Scavolini, Romano
DOG TAGS

Scavolini, Sauro
OPPONENT, THE

Schiff, Sara
LORD OF THE FLIES

Schow, David J.
LEATHERFACE: THE TEXAS CHAINSAW
MASSACRE III

Scorsese, Martin
GOODFELLAS

Scott, Allan
WITCHES, THE

Scott, James
STRIKE IT RICH

Seltzer, David
BIRD ON A WIRE

Serreau, Coline
MAMA, THERE'S A MAN IN YOUR BED

Setbon, Philippe
MR. FROST

Shanley, John Patrick
JOE VERSUS THE VOLCANO

Shearman, Alan
SHRIMP ON THE BARBIE, THE

Sheridan, Jim
FIELD, THE

Sherman, Gary
LISA

Shores, Del
DADDY'S DYIN'. . . WHO'S GOT THE WILL?

Shusett, Ronald
TOTAL RECALL

Sidaris, Andy
SAVAGE BEACH

Silberg, Joel
LAMBADA

Simon, Adam
BRAIN DEAD

Simpson, Byron
RESCUERS DOWN UNDER, THE

Simpson, Edward
RIVER OF DEATH

Simpson, Michael A.
DEAD AIM
FUNLAND

Skolimowski, Jerzy
TORRENTS OF SPRING

Skrow, George Frances
BACK TO BACK

Spiegel, Scott
ROOKIE, THE

Stahl, Jerry
DR. CALIGARI

Stallone, Sylvester
ROCKY V

Standing, Michael
AFTERSHOCK

Stanley, Richard
HARDWARE

Starr, Emerald
MEN IN LOVE

Steinberg, Norman
FUNNY ABOUT LOVE

Stevens, Andrew
NIGHT EYES

Stewart, Colin
BURNDOWN

Stewart, Donald
HUNT FOR RED OCTOBER, THE

Stillman, Whit
METROPOLITAN

Stoppard, Tom
RUSSIA HOUSE, THE

Strick, Wesley
ARACHNOPHOBIA

Strong, John
SHOW OF FORCE, A

Stuart, Jeb
VITAL SIGNS
ANOTHER 48 HRS.

Tally, Ted
WHITE PALACE

Tanner, Alain
FLAME IN MY HEART, A

Tavernier, Bertrand
LIFE AND NOTHING BUT

Tenney, Kevin S.
PEACEMAKER

Teuber, Monica
MAGDALENE

Thiel, Nick
FIRE BIRDS

Thomas, James E.
PREDATOR 2

Thomas, John C.
PREDATOR 2

Thompson, Caroline
EDWARD SCISSORHANDS

Thoreau, David
SIDE OUT

Thyne, Michele
CAGED IN PARADISO

Tornatore, Giuseppe
CINEMA PARADISO

Towne, Robert
DAYS OF THUNDER
TWO JAKES, THE

Trayne, John
DEMONSTONE

Trueba, Fernando
TWISTED OBSESSION

Turner, Bonnie
FUNLAND

Turner, Terry
FUNLAND

Tydor, Jonathan
I COME IN PEACE

Tyson, Nona
HOT SPOT, THE

Uricola, Robert
FEUD, THE

Uys, Jamie
GODS MUST BE CRAZY II, THE

Valtinos, Thanassis
LANDSCAPE IN THE MIST

Van Sickle, Craig W.
SKI PATROL

Vance, Samuel
RIVERBEND

Venosta, Louis
BIRD ON A WIRE

Verhoeven, Michael
NASTY GIRL, THE

Victor, Mark
MARKED FOR DEATH

Viertel, Peter
WHITE HUNTER, BLACK HEART

Visovich, Randal
NIGHT VISITOR

Volk, Stephen
GUARDIAN, THE

Wager, James
TIME TROOPERS

Wah, Lee Pik
REINCARNATION OF GOLDEN LOTUS, THE

Wallace, Josephine
BAIL JUMPER

Wang, Peter
LASER MAN, THE

Warfield, David W.
KILL ME AGAIN

Warren, S.N.
ANGEL TOWN

Waters, Daniel
ADVENTURES OF FORD FAIRLANE, THE

Waters, John
CRY-BABY

Watson, Patricia
NUTCRACKER PRINCE, THE

Weaver, Julian
INHERITOR

Webb, Weaver
COURAGE MOUNTAIN

Weingrod, Herschel
PAINT IT BLACK
KINDERGARTEN COP

Weir, Peter
GREEN CARD

Westlake, Donald E.
GRIFTERS, THE
WHY ME?

Wheeler, Anne
BYE BYE BLUES

Whiffler, Graham
SONNY BOY

Williams, Charles
HOT SPOT, THE

Williams, Gordon
INNOCENT VICTIM

Wilson, Julia
GAME, THE

Wilson, S.S.
TREMORS
GHOST DAD

Wilson, Sandy
AMERICAN BOYFRIENDS

Wisdom, Anthony
RETURN OF SUPERFLY, THE

Wright, Thomas Lee
LAST OF THE FINEST, THE

Yakin, Boaz
ROOKIE, THE

Yallop, David
CHICAGO JOE AND THE SHOWGIRL

Yoshida, Hiroaki
TWILIGHT OF THE COCKROACHES

Yoshihara, Isao
HEAVEN AND EARTH

Zaillian, Steve
AWAKENINGS

Zeffirelli, Franco
HAMLET

Zoller, Stephen
HOSTILE TAKEOVER

SET DESIGNERS

Alberti, Henry
DICK TRACY

Anderson, John
GREEN CARD

Arnold, William
MEN DON'T LEAVE

Barela, Rance
CHILD'S PLAY 2

Barr, Ginni
DARKMAN

Bayliss, Jim
MY BLUE HEAVEN

Bentley, Carol
DIE HARD 2

Berger, John
GREMLINS 2 THE NEW BATCH
ROOKIE, THE

Bernard, Andy
YOUNG GUNS II

Blackie, Janice
FOURTH WAR, THE

Bloom, Les
STANLEY AND IRIS
GOODFELLAS

Bode, Susan
QUICK CHANGE
ALICE

Boxer, Daniel
TEXASVILLE

Bradshaw, Robb
SURVIVAL QUEST

Breen, Charles
ADVENTURES OF FORD FAIRLANE, THE

Breen, Charles William
TAKING CARE OF BUSINESS

Brink, Gary
Q&A

Brolly, Barry W.
LOOK WHO'S TALKING TOO

Bruza, Scott
SURVIVAL QUEST

Buckley-Ayrea, Theresa
BLOOD RELATIONS

Burdick, Sarah
GUARDIAN, THE

Burns, Keith
VITAL SIGNS

Butler, Chris A.
POSTCARDS FROM THE EDGE

Carter, Fred
AIR AMERICA

Cartwright, John
GHOST DAD

Caziot, Jean-Jacques
L'ETAT SAUVAGE

Chang, Miguel
TOTAL RECALL

Cloudia
SIDE OUT

Combs, Debra
TREMORS

Combs, Will
MEN AT WORK

Conklin, Kate
LONGTIME COMPANION

Cordwell, Harry
MOUNTAINS OF THE MOON

Cramer, Lia
CHICAGO JOE AND THE SHOWGIRL

Cunningham, Lee
REPOSSESSED

Danielson, Chava
SPACED INVADERS

De Guzman, Mar
PRIMARY TARGET

de Vos, Constance
COOK, THE THIEF, HIS WIFE & HER
LOVER, THE

Dean, Lisa
EAT A BOWL OF TEA
DANCES WITH WOLVES

DeScenna, Linda
AVALON

Desideri, Giorgio
BELLY OF AN ARCHITECT, THE

Design, Joi
GODS MUST BE CRAZY II, THE

DeTitta, George
STATE OF GRACE

DeTitta, George Jr.
AWAKENINGS

Diers, Don
GUMSHOE KID, THE

Dolan, Kathleen
JACOB'S LADDER

Durden, Ginnie
SHADOWZONE

Dwyer, John
ROCKY V

Eagan, Beverli
BACK TO THE FUTURE PART III

Echeverria, Carlos
TOTAL RECALL

Eckel, Timothy J.
LOOSE CANNONS

Edelson, Rob
RIVERBEND

Erickson, Jim
COME SEE THE PARADISE

Eschelbach, Susan
DADDY'S DYIN'...WHO'S GOT THE WILL?

Eschelbach, Susan Mina
LOVE AT LARGE

Fabus, Mark
ADVENTURES OF FORD FAIRLANE, THE

Fellman, Florence
INTERNAL AFFAIRS

Fettis, Gary
GODFATHER PART III, THE

Fischer, Lisa
ANIMAL BEHAVIOR
WHITE PALACE
SIBLING RIVALRY

Flanegin, Molly
HOUSE PARTY

Fletcher-Trujillo, Karen
HOME ALONE

Fontaine, Pierre
LIFE AND NOTHING BUT

Fosser, Bill
HOME ALONE

Franco, Robert J.
SHOCK TO THE SYSTEM, A

Francois, Thierry
HENRY AND JUNE

Frank, Erzibet
NIGHT EYES

Fraser, Anita
TEN LITTLE INDIANS

Fumagalli, Franco
GODFATHER PART III, THE

Gelarden, James A.
WELCOME HOME, ROXY CARMICHAEL

Giladjian, Ian
MEMPHIS BELLE

Giorgetti, Nello
TORRENTS OF SPRING

Glass, Ted
MO' BETTER BLUES
GREEN CARD

Goddard, Dick
ALMOST AN ANGEL

Goldsmith, Margaret
AFTER DARK, MY SWEET

Gordon, Antoinette
THREE MEN AND A LITTLE LADY

Gray, Connie
ERNEST GOES TO JAIL

Griffith, Clay A.
PACIFIC HEIGHTS

Guidery, Wendy
FIRST POWER, THE

Guillaume, Dankert
RIVER OF DEATH

Haertling, Leonardo
WILD ORCHID

Hajdu, Miklos
MACK THE KNIFE

Hall, Jerry
TEENAGE MUTANT NINJA TURTLES

Hamamura, Koichi
DREAMS

Harris, Ann
EDWARD SCISSORHANDS

Hedinger, Steve
MISADVENTURES OF MR. WILT, THE

Heinrichs, Rick
EDWARD SCISSORHANDS

Hill, Derek
OPPORTUNITY KNOCKS

Hobbs, Christopher
STRIKE IT RICH

Holcombe, Robert
MURDER BY NUMBERS

Homsy, Stephen
FLATLINERS

Howitt, Peter
WHITE HUNTER, BLACK HEART

Hoyt, Dale Alan
STAR QUEST: BEYOND THE RISING MOON

Huston, Richard G.
WELCOME HOME, ROXY CARMICHAEL

Irwin, Colin
ROBOCOP 2

Ivey, Don
COUPE DE VILLE

Joffe, Carol
PRESUMED INNOCENT

Johnston, Martha
BACK TO THE FUTURE PART III

Kahn, Barbara
BETSY'S WEDDING

Kanter, Deborah
MERMAIDS

Karatzas, Steven
PAINT IT BLACK

Kaufman, Susan
BLUE STEEL

Kirkpatrick, T.K.
FAR OUT MAN

Klinker, Nigel
BACK TO BACK

Lee, Celeste
CHATTAHOOCHEE

Lee, Steven A.
SKI PATROL

Legori, Ada
ICICLE THIEF, THE

Leonard, Phillip M.
I COME IN PEACE

Lewis, Garrett
PRETTY WOMAN

Lindblom, Tom
DESPERATE HOURS

Lombard, Ron
FALSE IDENTITY

LoSchiavo, Francesca
HAMLET

MacAvin, Josie
LIONHEART
FIELD, THE

McCann, Chris
SKINHEADS – THE SECOND COMING OF HATE

McCulley, Anne D.
KINDERGARTEN COP

MacKenzie, Kim
NARROW MARGIN

McKenzie, Paul
DIE HARD 2

McKernin, Kathleen
MILLER'S CROSSING
MR. DESTINY

McSherry, Rose Marie
BIRD ON A WIRE

Maddy, Robert
MY BLUE HEAVEN

Mann, Louis
PREDATOR 2

Manzer, Alan
PREDATOR 2

Margetson, Gwendolyn
SHORT TIME

Martin, Fergus
DEMONSTONE

Mays, Richard
PREDATOR 2

Messina, Philip
MERMAIDS

Michaels, Mickey S.
HUNT FOR RED OCTOBER, THE

Michettoni, Ennio
FRANKENSTEIN UNBOUND

Miller, Erin
AMERICAN EAGLE

Montoya, Joanie
HIGH DESERT KILL

Morales, Leslie
BAD INFLUENCE

Mowat, Douglas A.
WITHOUT YOU, I'M NOTHING

Munoz, Lucie
WEDDING BAND

Murakami, James J.
DICK TRACY

Navarro, Nick
DIE HARD 2
MY BLUE HEAVEN

Newman, Lisa
BACK TO THE FUTURE PART III

Nichols, Virginia
CRY-BABY

Nickelberry, Nancy
BACK TO THE FUTURE PART III

Niehus, Vicki
TIME GUARDIAN, THE

Orbom, Eric
DICK TRACY
DIE HARD 2
ADVENTURES OF FORD FAIRLANE, THE

Overlock, Chester III
CRY-BABY

Pacelli, Joseph G.
BACK TO THE FUTURE PART III

Paltrinieri, Stefano
MAGDALENE

Papalia, Greg
GREMLINS 2 THE NEW BATCH

Parker, Cee
BODY CHEMISTRY

Pascale, Jan
HANDMAID'S TALE, THE

Patton, Nancy
LISA

Pitrel, Alain
IMPROMPTU

Pizzini, Denise
PROBLEM CHILD

Rau, Gretchen
ME AND HIM

Rea, Bill
FIRST POWER, THE
FIRE BIRDS

Remacle, Don
DOWNTOWN

Rodarte, Cecilia
FLASHBACK

Rollins, Leslie
MADHOUSE

Rosemarin, Hilton
EVERYBODY WINS

Roth, Sonja
KING OF NEW YORK

Rowland, Cricket
I LOVE YOU TO DEATH

St. Clair, Nick
TUSKS

Salas, Adolph
IMPULSE

Sallis, Crispian
REVENGE

Scaife, Hugh
EXORCIST III, THE

Scheuer, Abigail
STREETS

Schutt, Debra
NAVY SEALS
DON'T TELL HER IT'S ME

Scoppa, Justin Jr.
CADILLAC MAN

Scoppitici, Gina
UNDER THE BOARDWALK

Seirton, Michael
NUNS ON THE RUN
HAVANA

Serdena, Gene
MARTIANS GO HOME!
BRAIN DEAD

Shewchuk, Steve
STANLEY AND IRIS
STELLA

Shutt, Debra
PACIFIC HEIGHTS

Sim, Gordon
FRESHMAN, THE

Simpson, Rick
DICK TRACY

Siore, Pierre
VINCENT AND THEO

Snyder, Charlotte
RETURN OF SUPERFLY, THE

Snyder, Dawn
GREMLINS 2 THE NEW BATCH
ROOKIE, THE

Solorio, Fernando
REVENGE

Sonski, Paul
BACK TO THE FUTURE PART III
FLATLINERS
EDWARD SCISSORHANDS

Starks, Shirley
FORBIDDEN DANCE, THE
GRIM PRAIRIE TALES

Stehle, Jean-Marc
MAMA, THERE'S A MAN IN YOUR BED

Stensel, Carl J.
ARACHNOPHOBIA

Stollman, Sarah
UNBELIEVABLE TRUTH, THE

Stone, Malcolm
NAVY SEALS

Stonestreet, Brian J.
NIGHT OF THE LIVING DEAD

Suhayda, George
DARKMAN

Tarsnane, Robin
WITCHES, THE

Taucher, Rozanne
ANDY COLBY'S INCREDIBLY AWESOME
ADVENTURE

Thornton, Sally
PREDATOR 2

Thorton, Sally
DIE HARD 2

Trentini, Marco
TOTAL RECALL

Tropp, Stan
MISERY

Wakefield, Simon
RUSSIA HOUSE, THE

Walker, John Thomas
LAST OF THE FINEST, THE

Warga, Michael
HIT LIST

Webb, Bill
WHITE GIRL, THE

Webster, Christopher
TIME GUARDIAN, THE

Weibel, Patrick
MR. FROST

Weinman, Dave
QUICK CHANGE

Wolverten, Lynn
FUNLAND

Wong, Gilbert
MARKED FOR DEATH

Wunderlich, Jerry
TWO JAKES, THE

SOURCE AUTHORS

Aldiss, Brian
FRANKENSTEIN UNBOUND

Angelopoulos, Theo
LANDSCAPE IN THE MIST

Anthony, Len
FRIGHT HOUSE

Arnott, David
ADVENTURES OF FORD FAIRLANE, THE

Atwood, Margaret
HANDMAID'S TALE, THE

Barker, Clive
NIGHTBREED

Bauer, Bill
SLIPSTREAM

Beaumont, Charles
BRAIN DEAD

Benjamin, David
DISTURBANCE, THE

Berger, Thomas
FEUD, THE

Bird, Sarah
DON'T TELL HER IT'S ME

Blake, Michael
DANCES WITH WOLVES

Blatty, William Peter
EXORCIST III, THE

Boos, H. Gordon
RED SURF

Bowles, Paul
SHELTERING SKY, THE

Braughton, Fred
ANOTHER 48 HRS.

Brecht, Bertolt
MACK THE KNIFE

Brett, Simon
SHOCK TO THE SYSTEM, A

Brogger, Fred
COURAGE MOUNTAIN

Brogger, Mark
COURAGE MOUNTAIN

Brown, Curtis
GAME, THE

Brown, Frederc
MARTIANS GO HOME!

Brown, Greggory
STREET ASYLUM

Bruner, James
DELTA FORCE 2

Burton, Richard
MOUNTAINS OF THE MOON

Cahan, Abraham
IMPORTED BRIDEGROOM, THE

Cappe, James
ADVENTURES OF FORD FAIRLANE, THE

Cerasuola, Ron
DISTURBANCE, THE

Christie, Agatha
TEN LITTLE INDIANS

Chu, Louis
EAT A BOWL OF TEA

Clancy, Tom
HUNT FOR RED OCTOBER, THE

Collins, Stuart
BURNDOWN

Columbus, Chris
GREMLINS 2 THE NEW BATCH

Connell, Evan S.
MR. AND MRS. BRIDGE

Cronley, Jay
QUICK CHANGE

Cruise, Tom
DAYS OF THUNDER

Cunningham, Jere
LAST OF THE FINEST, THE

Dahl, Roald
WITCHES, THE

Dann, Patty
MERMAIDS

Davis, Brad
FULL FATHOM FIVE

De Marco, John
IMPULSE

Dershowitz, Alan
REVERSAL OF FORTUNE

Dick, Phillip K.
TOTAL RECALL

Doyle, Arthur Conan
TALES FROM THE DARKSIDE: THE MOVIE

Dye, Dale
FIRE BIRDS

Eastman, Kevin
TEENAGE MUTANT NINJA TURTLES

Faber, Christian
BAIL JUMPER

Fenton, Earl
NARROW MARGIN

Finnegan, John P.
BLADES

Fisher, Carrie
POSTCARDS FROM THE EDGE

Fusco, John
YOUNG GUNS II

Gale, Bob
BACK TO THE FUTURE PART III

Gamble, Brian
RED SURF

Gifford, Barry
WILD AT HEART

Gilbert, Michael A.
HOSTILE TAKEOVER

Golan, Menahem
DELTA FORCE 2

Golding, William
LORD OF THE FLIES

Goldman, Joseph
FORBIDDEN DANCE, THE

Goldsmith, Martin
NARROW MARGIN

Gordon, Stuart
ROBOT JOX

Gould, Chester
DICK TRACY

Greenburg, Dan
GUARDIAN, THE

Greene, Bob
FUNNY ABOUT LOVE

Greene, Graham
STRIKE IT RICH

Harrison, Jim
REVENGE

Harrison, William
MOUNTAINS OF THE MOON

Hata, Masanori
ADVENTURES OF MILO AND OTIS, THE

Hayes, Joseph
DESPERATE HOURS

Hendel, Kim
LEATHERFACE: THE TEXAS CHAINSAW
MASSACRE III

Herbeck, Bobby
TEENAGE MUTANT NINJA TURTLES

Hoffs, Jason
RED SURF

Hooper, Tobe
LEATHERFACE: THE TEXAS CHAINSAW
MASSACRE III
SPONTANEOUS COMBUSTION

Ibuse, Masuji
BLACK RAIN

Ildari, Hassan
FACE OF THE ENEMY

Irmas, Matthew
UNDER THE BOARDWALK

Jakoby, Don
ARACHNOPHOBIA

Jodorowsky, Alejandro
SANTA SANGRE

Kaionji, Chogoro
HEAVEN AND EARTH

Keane, John B.
FIELD, THE

Keating, H.R.F.
PERFECT MURDER, THE

Kendal-Savegar, Brian
INHERITOR

Ketron, Larry
VITAL SIGNS

King, Robert
UNDER THE BOARDWALK

King, Stephen
TALES FROM THE DARKSIDE: THE MOVIE
GRAVEYARD SHIFT
MISERY

Laferriere, Dany
HOW TO MAKE LOVE TO A NEGRO WITH-
OUT GETTING TIRED

Laird, Peter
TEENAGE MUTANT NINJA TURTLES

le Carre, John
RUSSIA HOUSE, THE

Leonard, Jack
NARROW MARGIN

Lerner, Eric
BIRD ON A WIRE

Lester, Mark L.
CLASS OF 1999

Llosa, Mario Vargas
TUNE IN TOMORROW

McDowell, Michael
TALES FROM THE DARKSIDE: THE MOVIE

MacLean, Alistair
RIVER OF DEATH

McMurtry, Larry
TEXASVILLE

Maddock, Brent
TREMORS
GHOST DAD

Mancini, Don
CHILD'S PLAY 2

Martino, Luciano
OPPONENT, THE

Meyjes, Menno
LIONHEART

Miller, Frank
ROBOCOP 2

Miner, Michael
ROBOCOP 2

Mitchell, Steven Long
SKI PATROL

Mizrahi, Moshe
MEN DON'T LEAVE

Moravia, Alberto
ME AND HIM

Nelson, Anne
SHOW OF FORCE, A

Neumeier, Edward
ROBOCOP 2

Nin, Anais
HENRY AND JUNE

O'Bannon, Dan
TOTAL RECALL

Peters, Stephen
FOURTH WAR, THE

Pileggi, Nicholas
GOODFELLAS

Poe, Edgar Allan
MASQUE OF THE RED DEATH
HAUNTING OF MORELLA, THE

Poe, Edgar Allen
TWO EVIL EYES

Povill, Jon
TOTAL RECALL

Prouty, Olive Higgins
STELLA

Quintano, Gene
HONEYMOON ACADEMY

Raimi, Sam
DARKMAN

Ramos, Fortunato
VERONICO CRUZ

Rascoe, Judith
HAVANA

Rattan, Aubrey K.
HIT LIST

Rendell, Ruth
INNOCENT VICTIM

Ricci, Tonino
NIGHT OF THE SHARKS

Robbins, Christopher
AIR AMERICA

Robert, Vincent
RED SURF

Roberts, Wink
SKI PATROL

Romero, George
NIGHT OF THE LIVING DEAD

Rostand, Edmond
CYRANO DE BERGERAC

Russo, John A.
NIGHT OF THE LIVING DEAD

Sacks, Oliver
AWAKENINGS

Salem, Murray
KINDERGARTEN COP

Savan, Glenn
WHITE PALACE

Selby, Hubert Hubert |L Selby |S Jr.
LAST EXIT TO BROOKLYN

Shakespeare, William
HAMLET

Sharpe, Tom
MISADVENTURES OF MR. WILT, THE

Shores, Del
DADDY'S DYIN'. . . WHO'S GOT THE WILL?

Shusett, Ronald
TOTAL RECALL

Silberg, Joel
LAMBADA

Simenon, Georges
MONSIEUR HIRE

Skrow, George Frances
BACK TO BACK

Smith, Franklin
BACK TO BACK

Speke, John Hanning
MOUNTAINS OF THE MOON

Stoudemire, Paul E.
BACK TO BACK

Swensson, John K.
FIRE BIRDS

Thompson, Jim
AFTER DARK, MY SWEET
GRIFTERS, THE
KILL-OFF, THE

Thorpe, Roderick
DIE HARD 2

Torres, Edwin
Q&A

Towne, Robert
DAYS OF THUNDER

Trevor, William
FOOLS OF FORTUNE

Turgenev, Ivan
TORRENTS OF SPRING

Turow, Scott
PRESUMED INNOCENT

Tyner, Step
FIRE BIRDS

Underwood, Ron
TREMORS

Van Sickle, Craig W.
SKI PATROL

Venosta, Louis
BIRD ON A WIRE

Viertel, Peter
WHITE HUNTER, BLACK HEART

Vincent, Chuck
WILDEST DREAMS

Wager, Walter
DIE HARD 2

Wallraff, Gunter
MAN INSIDE, THE

Weill, Kurt
MACK THE KNIFE

Weiner, Rex
ADVENTURES OF FORD FAIRLANE, THE

Westlake, Donald E.
WHY ME?

Willeford, Charles
MIAMI BLUES

Williams, Al
ARACHNOPHOBIA

Williams, Charles
HOT SPOT, THE

Wilson, S.S.
TREMORS
GHOST DAD

Wismar, C.B.
BIG BAD JOHN

Wolfe, Tom
BONFIRE OF THE VANITIES

Zeldis, Chayym
TORN APART

Zemeckis, Robert
BACK TO THE FUTURE PART III

SPECIAL EFFECTS

Agostini, Renato
SHELTERING SKY, THE

Allard, Eric
CLASS OF 1999

Anderson, David
YOUNG GUNS II

Anderson, Larz
PAINT IT BLACK

Anderson, Max W.
SLEEPING CAR, THE

Apogee Productions
GHOST DAD
MR. DESTINY
CHILD'S PLAY 2

Apone, Allan A.
DESPERATE HOURS

Arbogast, Roy
LOOSE CANNONS
I LOVE YOU TO DEATH

Art and Magic
DARK SIDE OF THE MOON

Baker, Rick
GREMLINS 2 THE NEW BATCH

Balsmeyer, Randall
SHOCK TO THE SYSTEM, A

Barkan, Sam
OPPORTUNITY KNOCKS

Bartalos, Gabe
BASKETCASE 2
FRANKENHOOKER

Bellissimo, Thomas L.
FAR OUT MAN

Benevides, Rob
DEF BY TEMPTATION

Benjamin, Al
LOOK WHO'S TALKING TOO

Bennett, Jack
PROBLEM CHILD

Bentley, Gary
SAVAGE BEACH

Biggs, Christopher
DARK SIDE OF THE MOON

Bivins, Ray
MR. DESTINY

Blake, John
MARKED FOR DEATH

Booth, Nigel
WITCHES, THE

Bottin, Rob
TOTAL RECALL
ROBOCOP 2

Bradley, Stewart
HEAVEN AND EARTH

Brevig, Eric
TOTAL RECALL

Brink, Connie
STANLEY AND IRIS
CADILLAC MAN
GOODFELLAS
JACOB'S LADDER

Brooks, Stephen
SPONTANEOUS COMBUSTION

Brumberger, Tom
MO' BETTER BLUES

Buechler, John Carl
SLEEPING CAR, THE

Buena Vista Visual Effects Group
DICK TRACY

Burdette, Grant
FOURTH WAR, THE

Burman, Thomas R.
AVALON

Burman, Tom
DIE HARD 2

Burrell, Everett
NIGHT OF THE LIVING DEAD

C5, Inc.
PRESUMED INNOCENT

Caban, Wilfred
BLADES

Caban, Willy
RETURN OF SUPERFLY, THE

Caglione, John Jr.
DICK TRACY

Cannom, Greg
EXORCIST III, THE

Carter, John
PEACEMAKER

Cavanaugh, Lawrence James
GODFATHER PART III, THE

Cecile, Hayley
SAVAGE BEACH

Ceglia, Frank
LOVE AT LARGE
SPACED INVADERS

Chandler Group, The
GHOST DAD

Chapman, Mack
WHITE PALACE

Chesney, Peter
YOUNG GUNS II
MILLER'S CROSSING

Chesney, Peter M.
PACIFIC HEIGHTS

Chris Walas, Inc.
LOOK WHO'S TALKING TOO

Conchonnet, Serge
DUCKTALES: THE MOVIE – TREASURE OF
THE LOST LAMP

Conway, Richard
MEMPHIS BELLE

Cook, Philip
STAR QUEST: BEYOND THE RISING MOON

Cory, Phil
GUARDIAN, THE
FLATLINERS
MISERY

Cramer, Fred
AFTERSHOCK

Criswell and Johnson Effects
SPACED INVADERS

Cutler, Rory
SHORT TIME

Dabdoub, John-Peter
LORD OF THE FLIES

David Allen Productions
ROBOT JOX

de Groote, Tony
TEN LITTLE INDIANS

Del Gino, Mike
IMPULSE

Dewey, Steven
JACOB'S LADDER

Dias, Errol
LORD OF THE FLIES

Diaz, Ken
DR. CALIGARI
AFTER DARK, MY SWEET

Die-Aktion
DEMONSTONE

Digaetano, Joe III
ROCKY V

DiGaetano, Joey
TEENAGE MUTANT NINJA TURTLES

Dion, Dennis
FLASHBACK
HOT SPOT, THE

DiSarro, Al
DIE HARD 2

Dolson, Mark
ALLIGATOR EYES

Domeyer, David
MONSTER HIGH
WILD AT HEART

Donen, Peter
MR. DESTINY

Dreiband-Burman, Bari
DIE HARD 2
AVALON

Drexler, Doug
DICK TRACY

Drury, Marcus
CAGED IN PARADISO

Dunn, Warren
LORD OF THE FLIES

Duran, Jesus
REVENGE

Edge, Frank
LORD OF THE FLIES

Edlund, Richard
GHOST

Egget, John D.
PEACEMAKER

Evans, John
NUNS ON THE RUN
WHITE HUNTER, BLACK HEART

Faggard, Jack
HIGH DESERT KILL

Faggard, Steve
HIGH DESERT KILL

Fante, John
DARK SIDE OF THE MOON

Faria, Guy
LISA

Farrar, Scott
BACK TO THE FUTURE PART III

Ferrari, Giorgio
LORD OF THE FLIES

Field, Roy
WHITE HUNTER, BLACK HEART

Fields, Roy
AIR AMERICA

Fisher, Thomas L.
TOTAL RECALL
DESPERATE HOURS

FourWard Productions
DARKMAN

Frazee, Logan
LORD OF THE FLIES

Frazee, Terry
LORD OF THE FLIES

Frazier, John
ROOKIE, THE

French, Edward
FIRST POWER, THE

Fullmer, Randy
RESCUERS DOWN UNDER, THE

FXSMITH Inc.
JACOB'S LADDER

Galich, Steve
BACK TO BACK

Gardner, Tony
DARKMAN
I COME IN PEACE

Gaspar, Chuck
ADVENTURES OF FORD FAIRLANE, THE

Gibbs, George
AIR AMERICA

Goetz, Bryan
MONSTER HIGH

Graham, Doug
STELLA

Gray, John E.
MEN DON'T LEAVE

Griswold, Al
STATE OF GRACE

Hall, Allen L.
AVALON

Hamlin, Larry
DARKMAN
I COME IN PEACE

Harris, David
MOUNTAINS OF THE MOON

Heller, Bruce
HAPPILY EVER AFTER

Helmer, Richard O.
CHATTAHOOCHEE
GHOST DAD

Huggins, Richard C.
MR. DESTINY

Hull, Greg
COUPE DE VILLE
BETSY'S WEDDING

Hynek, Joel
PREDATOR 2

Illusion Arts
FRANKENSTEIN UNBOUND

Image Animation
HARDWARE

Image Engineering
YOUNG GUNS II
MILLER'S CROSSING
PACIFIC HEIGHTS
CHILD'S PLAY 2

Industrial Light & Magic
JOE VERSUS THE VOLCANO
DIE HARD 2
GHOST
DREAMS

Introvision Systems International
DARKMAN

Jackson, Jeff
WITHOUT YOU, I'M NOTHING

Jim Henson's Creature Shop
WITCHES, THE

Johnson, Bill
BLOOD SALVAGE

Johnson, Brian
SLIPSTREAM

Johnson, Steve
NIGHT ANGEL

Jones, Starr
DEMONSTONE

K.N.B. EFX Group
TALES FROM THE DARKSIDE: THE MOVIE
NIGHT ANGEL

Kelsey, Dave
ALMOST AN ANGEL

Kirshoff, Steve
BLUE STEEL
CRY-BABY

KNB EFX Group
MISERY

Knoll, John
SPACED INVADERS

Knott, Robbie
DANCES WITH WOLVES

Kuran, Peter
ROBOCOP 2

Laas, Johan
TEN LITTLE INDIANS

Lantieri, Michael
BACK TO THE FUTURE PART III

Lazara, Louis
WILD AT HEART

Levy, Jerome
MAMA, THERE'S A MAN IN YOUR BED

Lombardi, Steve
SAVAGE BEACH

Macaluso, Jerry
STEEL AND LACE

McCarthy, Kevin
DOWN THE DRAIN

McHugh, Tim
ERNEST GOES TO JAIL

McTaggert, Albert
LORD OF THE FLIES

Make Up & Effects Labs, Inc.
DESPERATE HOURS

Malematsha, Rubin
TEN LITTLE INDIANS

Marsh, David
LORDS OF MAGICK, THE

Martin, Dale
MARKED FOR DEATH

Martin, Dale L.
LAST OF THE FINEST, THE

Martinez, Ed
DEAD PIT

Mason, Andrew
TIME GUARDIAN, THE

Mbuyawzwe, Wilson
TEN LITTLE INDIANS

Meinardus, Michael
LORD OF THE FLIES

Metz, Hans
FLATLINERS

Miller, Andy
LORD OF THE FLIES

Miller, David B.
WILD AT HEART

Mirage Effects
TIME GUARDIAN, THE

Mungle, Matthew
GUARDIAN, THE
MONSTER HIGH
NAVY SEALS

Musikwerks
JACOB'S LADDER

Nelson, Clovis
LORD OF THE FLIES

Newton, Tom
MO' BETTER BLUES

Norrington, Steve
WITCHES, THE

Parks, Stan
NARROW MARGIN

Paumgartten, Edu
WILD ORCHID

Pearce, Michael A.
INHERITOR

Pepiot, Ken
PREDATOR 2

Perpetual Motion Pictures, Inc.
SHADOWZONE

Pieri, Gilbert
IMPROMPTU

Pioneer FX, Inc.
SKI PATROL

Polycom
CAGED IN PARADISO

Purcell, Bill
EXORCIST III, THE
HOME ALONE

Quinlivan, Joe
RIVER OF DEATH

R/Greenburg Associates
GHOST DAD

Ralston, Ken
BACK TO THE FUTURE PART III

Rambaldi, Carlo
PRIMAL RAGE

Ratliff, Richard
IMPULSE
TAKING CARE OF BUSINESS
THREE MEN AND A LITTLE LADY

Ricci, Paolo
NIGHT OF THE SHARKS

Rnyrim, Roy
STEEL AND LACE

Roberts, Gary
DISTURBANCE, THE

St. James, Howard
MONSTER HIGH

Savini, Tom
TWO EVIL EYES

Schirmer, William H.
ERNEST GOES TO JAIL

Sherman, Aaron
KRAYS, THE

Sherman, Maralyn
KRAYS, THE

Shostrum, Mark
SHADOWZONE

Shouse, Tom
LORDS OF MAGICK, THE

Sindicich, Thomas F.
MEN AT WORK

Smith, Dick
TALES FROM THE DARKSIDE: THE MOVIE

Smith, Gordon J.
JACOB'S LADDER

Special Effects Shop
PEACEMAKER

Special Effects Unlimited
MONSTER HIGH

Special Effects, Unlimited
TEENAGE MUTANT NINJA TURTLES

Spectacular Effects Intl.
DEAD AIM

Squires, Scott
HUNT FOR RED OCTOBER, THE

Stears, John
NAVY SEALS

Steinheimer, R. Bruce
GODFATHER PART III, THE

Stephenson, John
WITCHES, THE

Stratton, Rick
CLASS OF 1999

Streett, J.D.
PACIFIC HEIGHTS

Sweeney, Matt
ARACHNOPHOBIA

Tagliaferro, Pat
FIRE BIRDS

Terribili, Elio
MAGDALENE

Thomas, John
BIRD ON A WIRE

Tifunovich, Neil
FRESHMAN, THE

Tiller, Bob
PEACEMAKER

Traynor, William
STATE OF GRACE

Trifunovich, Neil
STANLEY AND IRIS

Van Zeebroeck, Bruno
I COME IN PEACE

VCE, Inc
ROBOCOP 2

Vendetta Effects
HIDDEN AGENDA

Vickers, Roland
LORD OF THE FLIES

Vogel, Matt
KING OF NEW YORK
NIGHT OF THE LIVING DEAD

Vulich, John
NIGHT OF THE LIVING DEAD

Walas, Chris
ARACHNOPHOBIA

Warren, Gene Jr.
TREMORS

Washburn, Rick
RETURN OF SUPERFLY, THE

Wenger, Cliff
MADHOUSE

White, Michael
LIONHEART

Whiz-Bang Effects
SPACED INVADERS

Winston, Stan
EDWARD SCISSORHANDS
PREDATOR 2

Wood, Michael
EDWARD SCISSORHANDS

XFX Group
NIGHT ANGEL

Yagher, Kevin
CHILD'S PLAY 2

Zink, Gary
PRETTY WOMAN

STUNTS

Aiello, Danny III
LEMON SISTERS, THE

Armstrong, Vic
TOTAL RECALL
AIR AMERICA

Ateah, Scott
AMERICAN EAGLE

Avery, Rick
PRETTY WOMAN
LOOK WHO'S TALKING TOO

Baxley, Paul
CLASS OF 1999
EXORCIST III, THE

Baxley, Paul R. Jr.
I COME IN PEACE

Bedgood, Kevin
STAR QUEST: BEYOND THE RISING MOON

Borden, Chuck
STEEL AND LACE

Bovee, Brad
MADHOUSE

Bradford, Andy
INNOCENT VICTIM

Bragg, Bobby
ALIENATOR

Braun, Eddie
HOLLYWOOD HOT TUBS II: EDUCATING CRYSTAL

Burton, Billy
DICK TRACY
DESPERATE HOURS

Connoly, Paul
DAMNED RIVER

Cox, Monty
MR. DESTINY

Cudney, Cliff
CADILLAC MAN

Davis, B.J.
PEACEMAKER
BACKSTREET DREAMS

Davis, Bud
CHATTAHOOCHEE
NAVY SEALS
MEN AT WORK

Davis, Gary
PREDATOR 2

Delaney, Leon
FAR OUT MAN

Diamond, Peter
LIONHEART

Dixon, Shane
NIGHT ANGEL

Donno, Eddy
HOT SPOT, THE

Dowdall, Jim
TALL GUY, THE

Doyle, Chris
DARKMAN

Dunne, Joe
TAKING CARE OF BUSINESS

Ellis, David
EVERYBODY WINS
LAST OF THE FINEST, THE
IMPULSE
FRESHMAN, THE
MISERY

Erickson, Bill
FLATLINERS

Fantasia, Franco
TORRENTS OF SPRING

Ferguson, Bill
LOOK WHO'S TALKING TOO

Ferrandini, Dean
DELTA FORCE 2

Ferrara, Frank
SHOCK TO THE SYSTEM, A
BETSY'S WEDDING
QUICK CHANGE

Foxworth, Bobby
PACIFIC HEIGHTS

Frantz, Tom
TAX SEASON

Gatlin, Jerry
LORD OF THE FLIES

Gilbert, Mickey
COUPE DE VILLE
PROBLEM CHILD
YOUNG GUNS II

Gill, Jack
STANLEY AND IRIS
STELLA

Grace, Martin
NUNS ON THE RUN
PATHFINDER

Graf, Allan
FOURTH WAR, THE

Hancock, Dick
ROBOCOP 2

Hewitt, Don
BETSY'S WEDDING

Hewitt, Jery
BLUE STEEL
CRY-BABY
LEMON SISTERS, THE
STATE OF GRACE

MILLER'S CROSSING

Hice, Fred
IMPULSE

Hice, Freddie
HOME ALONE

Hodder, Kane
LEATHERFACE: THE TEXAS CHAINSAW
MASSACRE III

Hooker, Buddy Joe
HARD TO KILL
GUARDIAN, THE
GODFATHER PART III, THE

Howell, Norman L.
DANCES WITH WOLVES

Hymes, Gary
WHITE PALACE

Jefferson, Tony
SKI PATROL

Jensen, Gary
TREMORS
UNDER THE BOARDWALK

Johnson, Pat
TEENAGE MUTANT NINJA TURTLES

Joint, Alf
MOUNTAINS OF THE MOON

Kahan, Andy
KILL-OFF, THE

Kramer, Joel
TOTAL RECALL
AVALON
KINDERGARTEN COP

Lane, Paul M.
SHADOWZONE

LeFevour, Rick
MEN DON'T LEAVE

Leonard, Terry
DOWNTOWN
REVENGE
ROOKIE, THE

Luraschi, Mario
IMPROMPTU

McGauhgy, Mike
GREMLINS 2 THE NEW BATCH

McKay, Cole
BACK TO BACK

Madalone, Dennis
FIRE BIRDS

Mark, Solly
DOWN THE DRAIN

Marx, Solly
CAGED FURY

Milne, Gareth
MISADVENTURES OF MR. WILT, THE
CHICAGO JOE AND THE SHOWGIRL
INNOCENT VICTIM

Mite, Ellie A.
DOWN THE DRAIN

Mizen, Ike
WHITE PALACE

Moio, John
FIRST POWER, THE

Nay, A.J.
AFTER DARK, MY SWEET
PAINT IT BLACK

Neilson, Phil
KING OF NEW YORK
NIGHT OF THE LIVING DEAD

Nelson, Phil
JACOB'S LADDER

Norris, Guy
BLOOD OF HEROES

QUIGLEY DOWN UNDER

Oliney, Alan
GHOST DAD

Olley, Chris
TEN LITTLE INDIANS

Orrison, George
WHITE HUNTER, BLACK HEART

Orsatti, Ernie
OPPORTUNITY KNOCKS

Palmisano, Conrad E.
SHORT TIME
MARKED FOR DEATH

Parrish, Lane
SKI PATROL

Petit, Alain
HONEYMOON ACADEMY

Picerni, Charles
DIE HARD 2
ADVENTURES OF FORD FAIRLANE, THE

Picerni, Charles Jr.
HUNT FOR RED OCTOBER, THE
VITAL SIGNS

Pinter, Tamas
MACK THE KNIFE

Popick, Jeff
TAX SEASON

Rampe, J. Suzanne
SHADOWZONE

Randall, Glenn Jr.
LOOSE CANNONS

Razatos, Spiro
HIT LIST
SPACED INVADERS
GUMSHOE KID, THE

Reynolds, Buster
GODS MUST BE CRAZY II, THE

Ricci, Brian
MERMAIDS

Richman, Sandy
LEMON SISTERS, THE

Rodgers, Mic
BIRD ON A WIRE

Ruiters, Reo
TUSKS

Russo, Michael
GOODFELLAS

St. Paul, Stuart
KRAYS, THE

Scott, Ben
LISA

Scott, John
HEAVEN AND EARTH

Scott, Walter
BACK TO THE FUTURE PART III

Simon, Gunter
DOWN THE DRAIN

Smith, Eddie
HOUSE PARTY

Spicer, Jerry
WHITE PALACE

Statham, Pat
DEMONSTONE

Stevens, Warren
TWISTED JUSTICE

Stewart, John
SURVIVAL QUEST

Thomas, Betty
BIRD ON A WIRE

Walker, Greg
LOVE AT LARGE

Ward, Jeff
MO' BETTER BLUES

Warlock, Dick
CHILD'S PLAY 2

Waters, Chuck
ERNEST GOES TO JAIL
ARACHNOPHOBIA

Wayton, Gary
LORDS OF MAGICK, THE

Whinery, Webster
WILD ORCHID

Wilder, Glenn
NARROW MARGIN

Williamette, John
TAX SEASON

Woolsey, Brent
FOURTH WAR, THE
HEAVEN AND EARTH

TECHNICAL ADVISERS

Atterbury, Malcolm Jr.
GHOST DAD

Bihum, Oksana
DESPERATE HOURS

Birge, Ray
DESPERATE HOURS

Blanchard, Terence
MO' BETTER BLUES

Bristow, Vivian
TUSKS

Chalko, Christopher G.
FIRE BIRDS

Dye, Capt. Dale
FOURTH WAR, THE

Dye, Dale
JACOB'S LADDER

Fleming, Michael Max
MO' BETTER BLUES

Fordes, William N.
PRESUMED INNOCENT

Fraser, Steve
NAVY SEALS

Freeman, Roger
MEMPHIS BELLE

Garcia, Tommy
MEMPHIS BELLE

Giss, Harvey
DESPERATE HOURS

Harbrecht, Tom
NAVY SEALS

Harrison, Donald
MO' BETTER BLUES

Hendrick, Rick
DAYS OF THUNDER

Jessee, Dan
NAVY SEALS

Jordan, William C.
LAST OF THE FINEST, THE

Klein, Linda
VITAL SIGNS

Kray, Charlie
KRAYS, THE

Kristensen, Chuck
ARACHNOPHOBIA

Kutcher, Steven
ARACHNOPHOBIA

Leslie, Frank
NAVY SEALS

Lindsay, Christopher
NAVY SEALS

Manca, John
GOODFELLAS

Mata, Manny
MARKED FOR DEATH

Mills, Gerald
JETSONS: THE MOVIE

Murray, Fr. George
EXORCIST III, THE

Musacchia, Rocco
FRESHMAN, THE

Ojala, Arvo
BACK TO THE FUTURE PART III

Orriss, Bruce
MEMPHIS BELLE

Parrott, Jerry
DIE HARD 2

Peterson, Arnold
ARACHNOPHOBIA

Pfarrer, Chuck
NAVY SEALS

Pomposello, J.P.
PACIFIC HEIGHTS

Quisenberry, Clara
I LOVE YOU TO DEATH

Sacks, Greg
DAYS OF THUNDER

Sherman, Michael T.
HUNT FOR RED OCTOBER, THE

Smith, Duncan
NAVY SEALS

Steffanich, Mark
NAVY SEALS

Sullivan, Tommy
STATE OF GRACE

White, Stanley
DESPERATE HOURS

Woulard, Keith
NAVY SEALS

REVIEW ATTRIBUTION

Films reviewed in this volume are listed below by the author of the review.

Cassady, Charles
AFTERSHOCK
ANDY COLBY'S INCREDIBLY AWESOME
  ADVENTURE
BACK TO BACK
BIG BAD JOHN
BLOOD RELATIONS
DAMNED RIVER
DEMON WIND
DEMONSTONE
DISTURBANCE, THE
DOWN THE DRAIN
FUNLAND
GUMSHOE KID, THE
HOLLYWOOD HOT TUBS II: EDUCATING
  CRYSTAL
INHERITOR
INNOCENT VICTIM
ISTANBUL, KEEP YOUR EYES OPEN
LIONHEART
LORDS OF MAGICK, THE
MONSTER HIGH
NIGHT EYES
PAINT IT BLACK
RIVERBEND
SAVAGE BEACH
SHADOWZONE
STAR QUEST: BEYOND THE RISING MOON
STREET ASYLUM
SURVIVAL QUEST
TAX SEASON
TIME GUARDIAN, THE
TIME TROOPERS
TUSKS
WILDEST DREAMS

Charity, Tom
COOK, THE THIEF, HIS WIFE & HER
  LOVER, THE
MISADVENTURES OF MR. WILT, THE
TALL GUY, THE

Cramer, Barbara
ARACHNOPHOBIA
BYE BYE BLUES
CYRANO DE BERGERAC
HAMLET
HARDWARE
ICICLE THIEF, THE
LIFE IS A LONG QUIET RIVER
MR. AND MRS. BRIDGE
TAXI BLUES

Curran, Daniel
LAMBADA

Digilio, Nick
ADVENTURES OF FORD FAIRLANE, THE
ALICE
BAD INFLUENCE
BLUE STEEL
CHILD'S PLAY 2
CLASS OF 1999
DICK TRACY
DIE HARD 2
EDWARD SCISSORHANDS
FAR OUT MAN
FIRST POWER, THE
FOURTH WAR, THE
GREEN CARD
HENRY: PORTRAIT OF A SERIAL KILLER
HOME ALONE
HOMER & EDDIE
HOUSE PARTY
JACOB'S LADDER
LAST OF THE FINEST, THE
LOOSE CANNONS
MADHOUSE
MASQUE OF THE RED DEATH
MR. DESTINY

MR. FROST
MO' BETTER BLUES
PREDATOR 2
Q&A
QUIGLEY DOWN UNDER
ROBOT JOX
ROOKIE, THE
SKI PATROL
SPONTANEOUS COMBUSTION
STANLEY AND IRIS
STRIKE IT RICH
TOTAL RECALL
TUNE IN TOMORROW
WILD AT HEART
WITCHES, THE

Downey, Mike
LAST EXIT TO BROOKLYN
ROSALIE GOES SHOPPING

Garcia, Maria
DOG TAGS

Goldman, David
CADILLAC MAN
COUPE DE VILLE
CRAZY PEOPLE
LONGTIME COMPANION
MY BLUE HEAVEN

Goldman, David
QUICK CHANGE

Graham, J. Patrick
REVENGE

Graham, Pat
CINEMA PARADISO

Green, Douglas
BLIND FURY
DADDY'S DYIN'. . . WHO'S GOT THE WILL?
FORBIDDEN DANCE, THE
GHOST DAD
GRAFFITI BRIDGE
MARKED FOR DEATH
SIDE OUT

Hinckley, Tom
AIR AMERICA
ANGEL TOWN
ANOTHER 48 HRS.
AVALON
AWAKENINGS
BACK TO THE FUTURE PART III
BASHU, THE LITTLE STRANGER
BIRD ON A WIRE
BONFIRE OF THE VANITIES
CHATTAHOOCHEE
CIRCUITRY MAN
COURAGE MOUNTAIN
DANCES WITH WOLVES
DARKMAN
DELTA FORCE 2
DESPERATE HOURS
DON'T TELL HER IT'S ME
DOWNTOWN
DREAMS
EVERYBODY WINS
FACE OF THE ENEMY
FALSE IDENTITY
FIRE BIRDS
FLASHBACK
FORCED MARCH
FRANKENHOOKER
FRESHMAN, THE
GHOST
GODFATHER PART III, THE
GOODFELLAS
GREMLINS 2 THE NEW BATCH
GUARDIAN, THE
HAPPY TOGETHER

HARD TO KILL
HEART CONDITION
HENRY AND JUNE
HUNT FOR RED OCTOBER, THE
HYPERSPACE
I LOVE YOU TO DEATH
INTERNAL AFFAIRS
KILL ME AGAIN
KINDERGARTEN COP
LEMON SISTERS, THE
LISA
LONELY WOMAN SEEKS LIFE COMPANION
LOVE AT LARGE
MAHABHARATA, THE
MAN INSIDE, THE
MEN DON'T LEAVE
MISERY
MODERN LOVE
MOUNTAINS OF THE MOON
NARROW MARGIN
NIGHTBREED
NOBODY'S PERFECT
PACIFIC HEIGHTS
PERFECT MURDER, THE
POSTCARDS FROM THE EDGE
PRESUMED INNOCENT
PRETTY WOMAN
PROBLEM CHILD
RAGGEDY RAWNEY, THE
RED SURF
REINCARNATION OF GOLDEN LOTUS, THE
REPOSSESSED
RESCUERS DOWN UNDER, THE
REVERSAL OF FORTUNE
ROBOCOP 2
ROUGE
RUSSIA HOUSE, THE
SANTA SANGRE
SHADOW OF THE RAVEN
SHOCK TO THE SYSTEM, A
SHORT TIME
SHRIMP ON THE BARBIE, THE
SONNY BOY
STEEL AND LACE
STRAPLESS
STREETS
TAKING CARE OF BUSINESS
TALES FROM THE DARKSIDE: THE MOVIE
TEXASVILLE
TIME OF THE GYPSIES
TO SLEEP WITH ANGER
TORRENTS OF SPRING
TOUCH OF A STRANGER
TREMORS
TWILIGHT OF THE COCKROACHES
TWISTED JUSTICE
TWISTED OBSESSION
TWO JAKES, THE
WELCOME HOME, ROXY CARMICHAEL
WHITE HUNTER, BLACK HEART
WHITE PALACE
WILD ORCHID
YOUNG GUNS II

Ingram, Bruce
ANIMAL BEHAVIOR
BLOOD SALVAGE
BODY CHEMISTRY
GODS MUST BE CRAZY II, THE
NIGHT ANGEL
NUNS ON THE RUN
OVER EXPOSED
PEACEMAKER
WEDDING BAND

Leahy, William
HAVANA

Leonard, Kyle
BEDROOM EYES II
ERNEST GOES TO JAIL
FULL FATHOM FIVE
HAPPILY EVER AFTER
HAUNTING OF MORELLA, THE
HONEYMOON ACADEMY
SPACED INVADERS

McDonagh, Maitland
BIG DIS, THE
BLOOD OF HEROES
BRAIN DEAD
DAYS OF THUNDER
DEF BY TEMPTATION
DR. CALIGARI
EXORCIST III, THE
FEUD, THE
FIELD, THE
FLATLINERS
FORCE OF CIRCUMSTANCE
FRANKENSTEIN UNBOUND
GAME, THE
GRAVEYARD SHIFT
GRIM PRAIRIE TALES
HOT SPOT, THE
HOW TO MAKE LOVE TO A NEGRO WITH-
   OUT GETTING TIRED
I COME IN PEACE
KILL-OFF, THE
KING OF NEW YORK
KRAYS, THE
LABYRINTH OF PASSION
LEATHERFACE: THE TEXAS CHAINSAW
   MASSACRE III
LIFE IS CHEAP. . . BUT TOILET PAPER IS
   EXPENSIVE
MARTIANS GO HOME!
MIAMI BLUES
MILLER'S CROSSING
NIGHT OF THE LIVING DEAD
TEENAGE MUTANT NINJA TURTLES
TWO EVIL EYES
VAMPIRE'S KISS
WHITE GIRL, THE

Mueller, Jenny
VERONICO CRUZ

Munroe, Dale
ALMOST AN ANGEL
BETSY'S WEDDING
COME SEE THE PARADISE
FUNNY ABOUT LOVE
JETSONS: THE MOVIE
JOE VERSUS THE VOLCANO
LOOK WHO'S TALKING TOO
MEMPHIS BELLE

MEN AT WORK
MERMAIDS
NUTCRACKER PRINCE, THE
ROCKY V
THREE MEN AND A LITTLE LADY

Nickelberg, Diane
BASKETCASE 2

Noh, David
AFTER DARK, MY SWEET
BAIL JUMPER
BLACK RAIN
C'EST LA VIE
CHICAGO JOE AND THE SHOWGIRL
CRY-BABY
FLAME IN MY HEART, A
FOOLS OF FORTUNE
GRIFTERS, THE
LANDSCAPE IN THE MIST
L'ETAT SAUVAGE
MACK THE KNIFE
MAMA, THERE'S A MAN IN YOUR BED
MAY FOOLS
METROPOLITAN
NASTY GIRL, THE
PATHFINDER
PUMP UP THE VOLUME
STELLA
TIE ME UP! TIE ME DOWN!
VINCENT AND THEO
WITHOUT YOU, I'M NOTHING

Pardi, Bob
ALLIGATOR EYES
AMERICAN BOYFRIENDS
AMERICAN EAGLE
BLADES
BLOOD RED
BURNDOWN
CAGED FURY
CAGED IN PARADISO
COLD FEET
DARK SIDE OF THE MOON
DEAD AIM
DEAD PIT
EAT A BOWL OF TEA
FRIGHT HOUSE
HANDMAID'S TALE, THE
HEAVEN AND EARTH
HIDDEN AGENDA
HIGH DESERT KILL
HIT LIST
HOSTILE TAKEOVER
IN THE SPIRIT
INTERROGATION, THE
JEZEBEL'S KISS
LIFE AND NOTHING BUT

LORD OF THE FLIES
MAGDALENE
ME AND HIM
MONSIEUR HIRE
MURDER BY NUMBERS
MY 20TH CENTURY
NIGHT OF THE SHARKS
NIGHT VISITOR
OPPONENT, THE
PRIMAL RAGE
PRIMARY TARGET
REAL BULLETS
RETURN OF SUPERFLY, THE
RIVER OF DEATH
SHELTERING SKY, THE
SIBLING RIVALRY
SKINHEADS – THE SECOND COMING OF
   HATE
SLEEPING CAR, THE
SLIPSTREAM
STUFF STEPHANIE IN THE INCINERATOR
TEN LITTLE INDIANS
TOO BEAUTIFUL FOR YOU
TORN APART
UNBELIEVABLE TRUTH, THE
UNDER THE BOARDWALK
WHY ME?

Pride, Ray
SHOW OF FORCE, A
STATE OF GRACE

Schackman, Daniel
FREEZE – DIE – COME TO LIFE
IMPORTED BRIDEGROOM, THE
JESUS OF MONTREAL
MEN IN LOVE
SUMMER VACATION: 1999

Stewart, Linda
ADVENTURES OF MILO AND OTIS, THE
ALIENATOR
BACKSTREET DREAMS
DEATH WARRANT
ELLIOT FAUMAN, PH.D.
IMPULSE
NAVY SEALS
OPPORTUNITY KNOCKS
PLOT AGAINST HARRY, THE
VITAL SIGNS
WHERE THE HEART IS

Swanson, Annie Gerson
IMPROMPTU

Wallenfeldt, Jeffrey
BELLY OF AN ARCHITECT, THE

... about BASELINE

BASELINE is the world's leading supplier of information to the film and television industries and a pioneer in electronic publishing techniques. BASELINE information spans what's happening *now* in the film and television industry, as well as details of past projects, and a library of industry-related news. This information is available worldwide via the online system, by phone, in print, and through audiotex and fax services.

BASELINE was founded in 1983 by James Monaco, author of numerous books about film and television including the classic text, HOW TO READ A FILM, and the widely-read AMERICAN FILM NOW.

The BASELINE network currently stretches from Hong Kong to Abu Dhabi, and from Melbourne to Reykajavik (with members in 20 countries on all continents except Antartica) and is just as easy to use in Europe, Australia, and Japan as it is in the U.S. BASELINE members include executives and assistants at all the major studios and television networks; major production companies, agencies, and suppliers; a large number of journalists; film commissions and institutions, government organizations, ad agencies, advertisers, publishers, and many others.

The online BASELINE services cover: • industry professionals (comprehensive credits, contact information, directories, biographies, company rosters, corporate players); • film and television credits, grosses, and demographics); • industry news (*The Hollywood Reporter*, news wires, *Entertainment Litigation Reporter*, *Moving Pictures International*, and stories from our own sources); and much more including calendars, awards, release schedules, customized research, and even electronic mail!

The BASELINE research department provides customized research reports and analysis, as well as regular reports about projects in development and production, box office grosses, the television season, and topics of general media interest. Research is available to BASELINE members and non-members alike.

The *Hotline* service is designed to answer quick questions over the phone– just dial 1.800.CHAPLIN.

Dial 1.900.230.FILM for the *Hollywood Connection*, BASELINE's audiotex service that tracks daily industry news, film openings, video releases, audience reactions to major film openings, and domestic box office grosses — all for $1. per minute.

BASELINE also owns New York Zoetrope, a sixteen-year-old traditional book publishing company which is a recognized specialist in film and television titles.